American Foreign Policy Current Documents 1982

Department of State
Washington
1985

References:

Bevans	Treaties and Other International Agreements of the United States of America 1776–1949, compiled under the direction of Charles I. Bevans
P.L.	Public Law of the United States
Stat.	United States Statutes at Large
TIAS	Treaties and Other International Acts Series, issued singly in pamphlets by the Department of State
UNTS	United Nations Treaty Series
U.S.C.	United States Code
UST	United States Treaties and Other International Agreements (volumes published on a calendar-year basis beginning as of January 1, 1950)

Department of State Publication 9415

Department and Foreign Service Series 398

Bureau of Public Affairs

Office of the Historian

For sale by the Superintendent of Documents, U.S. Government Printing Office
Washington, D.C. 20402

Preface

This volume continues the Department of State series begun in 1950 with the publication of *A Decade of American Foreign Policy: Basic Documents, 1941–1949* (Senate Document 123, 81st Congress, 1st Session) and the subsequent publication in 1957 of *American Foreign Policy, 1950–1955: Basic Documents* (Department of State Publication 6446). Annual volumes entitled *American Foreign Policy: Current Documents* were issued for the years 1956–1967. After an interruption, the series was resumed in 1983 with the publication of *American Foreign Policy: Basic Documents, 1977–1980.* Two volumes to fill in the 1968–1976 time period are being planned for future publication. In late 1984 the Department revived the annual volumes with the publication of *American Foreign Policy: Current Documents, 1981.*

The volumes in this series present the principal public foreign policy messages, addresses, statements, interviews, press briefings and conferences, and congressional testimony by the executive branch of the U.S. Government. Their main focus is the contemporary public expression of U.S. foreign policy. Internal working documents relating to the policymaking process, press guidances, and telegraphic messages between Washington and posts abroad are not included in this volume unless they were released to the press and public at the time. Many documents in the present volume have already been published in other official publications. Others, including several background briefings, are printed here for the first time. Some documents issued by other governments or by international organizations or containing statements by foreign leaders have been included because they had a major impact on the formulation of the policies of the United States.

This volume covers all major foreign policy subjects and geographical areas. Comprehensive treatment of all issues in depth within the limitations of a single volume is not possible, but a careful effort has been made to select the most important documents on the major issues. Extracts from long documents were printed to provide the most important portions while saving space for the publication of other documents. The editors have consistently tried to balance the need for full documentation of the major crisis areas in U.S. foreign relations with less extensive coverage of a wide range of less critical but still significant issues.

The present volume is organized chronologically by functional and geographical subject in 15 chapters. The table of contents immediately precedes a complete list of documents; a list of persons and a list of abbreviations follow the list of documents. There is also an index by document number.

A microfiche supplement to this volume is scheduled for subsequent publication. It will consist of several important series of background documents, such as the Department of State numbered press releases and the transcripts of the Department of State daily press briefings. Neither the printed volume nor the supplement contains cross references to the other publication. Nevertheless, the microfiche supplement complements the printed volume in at least two ways. First, the series reproduced in it contain the full texts of many documents published as extracts in the printed volume. Second, it reproduces many important documents which relate to the compilations in the printed volume but could not be included there because of space limitations.

The preparation of this volume involved a systematic review of all major documentary sources. Documentary collections were identified and gathered from the Offices of the President's Press Secretary and the Vice President's Press Secretary; the Department of State Office of Press Relations as well as numerous other offices and bureaus of the Department; the Historical Office of the Office of the Secretary of Defense, and the Offices of the Joint Chiefs of Staff, Public Affairs, and International Security Policy of the Department of Defense; the External Program Department of the International Monetary Fund; the Offices of Public Affairs of the Agency for International Development, Arms Control and Disarmament Agency, International Communications Agency (renamed U.S. Information Agency in 1982), and the Departments of Agriculture, Commerce, and the Treasury; and the staffs of the various foreign affairs committees of the Congress.

Where a variety of source texts for a given document was available, the editors have selected the most primary version. Thus White House press releases are used as source texts rather than the texts subsequently published later in the *Weekly Compilation of Presidential Documents* or the *Public Papers of the Presidents of the United States.* Similarly, Department of State press releases, statements, or speeches in typescript are used as the source texts instead of the same versions printed later in the Department of State *Bulletin* or other publications. The accuracy of these later published versions is not in question, but there are occasionally minor differences, particularly when documents are condensed by the omission of long introductory or concluding remarks which do not relate directly to the subject. An exception to this practice is the congressional hearings; in such cases the printed hearing served as the source text. No attempt was made to obtain the transcripts of these hearings in typescript except in a few instances where the hearings were public but were not published.

Except for silent editing of obvious spelling errors, the manuscript versions used as source texts in the present volume have not been altered. All but the most perfunctory remarks at the beginning or end of documents ("good evening," "thank you," for example) are included. The names of briefers and of members of the press who might inadvertently have been included in the transcript of a background briefing have been deleted to preserve the anonymity of the participants; such deletions are denoted by an indication of ellipsis of three periods. If more than the brief opening or concluding remarks or the names of participants in background briefings are omitted, the document is called an "extract." The omitted portions are identified by ellipses of three periods in cases involving less than one paragraph; omissions of an entire paragraph or more are denoted by ellipses of seven points. Except for background briefings, which required formal clearance by the appropriate executive agencies, the omissions are solely matters of editorial judgment to exclude unrelated documentation and to conserve space.

The first footnote to each document indicates the source text used; if it is an unpublished text, this footnote also indicates where it has been printed. In the case of public speeches and statements, this footnote also indicates whether it is the text as actually delivered, if this information is known.

Annotation in the form of editorial notes has been used on occasion to introduce a new issue or to summarize a document (such as a special report or publication) or group of documents which could not be printed because of space limitations. These notes are designed to identify the events and to help the interested reader locate the documents. Footnotes have been used to explain references in the text and to provide cross—references to other documents or footnotes in the volume or in previous volumes in the series. The purpose of such annotation is to be helpful and informative while remaining simple and nondistracting. The editors have not attempted in footnotes to go into great detail or explain possible implications of a reference. Vague and merely allusive references in the text are not footnoted. Unpublished sources are not normally cited; but if important information derived from an unpublished, unclassified source is provided in a footnote, the source of the information is given.

Because of the multiplicity of files of unpublished sources searched for these volumes, some explanation of their citation in source footnotes is required. Department of State daily press briefings and numbered press releases, White House press releases, and the public statements of the Secretary of Defense, which are compiled in the Historical Office in the Office of the Secretary of Defense, are cited in the source notes because they are preserved intact as a series and later deposited in bound volumes or on microfiche in selected libraries. Unpublished documents are generally identified only by agency of origin, such as Department of Defense files, Department of the Treasury files, or Department of State files. More specific permanent file provenance designations are generally not possible for most contemporary documents. Where the Office of the Historian has obtained copies of documents for inclusion in these volumes is not germane to their permanent archival preservation. The editors therefore have not routinely included such information in the source annotations. The discovery of useful documents from a variety of sources within the U.S. Government only reemphasizes the role of this series of volumes in the systematic collection and publication of many important public documents which might otherwise be retrieved later only with difficulty.

This volume was prepared under the overall planning and direction of David S. Patterson. Paul Claussen, David W. Mabon, Nina J. Noring, Charles S. Sampson, Stanley

Shaloff, and Louis J. Smith supervised the compilation of the various portions. Mr. Patterson oversaw the steps leading to the publication of the volume. Nancy L. Golden provided research support. The compilers of each part were as follows: Chapter 1, Principles and Objectives of American Foreign Policy, Mr. Smith; Chapter 2, Organization and Conduct of American Foreign Policy, Harriet D. Schwar; Chapters 3 and 4, National Security Policy and Arms Control, Mr. Patterson; Chapter 5, Foreign Economic Policy, Sherrill B. Wells, William F. Sanford, Jr., and Margaret F. Gourlay; Chapters 6 and 9, United Nations and Developments in International Law, and International Information, Educational Exchange, and Cultural Affairs Programs, Suzanne E. Coffman; Chapter 7, Oceans and International Environmental and Scientific Affairs, Ms. Coffman and Ms. Gourlay; Chapter 8, Refugees, Human Rights, and Terrorism, Ms. Coffman and Ms. Wells; Chapter 10, Europe and Canada, David M. Baehler, Ronald D. Landa, James E. Miller, and Ms. Wells; Chapter 11, Middle East, Evan Duncan; Chapter 12, South Asia, Edward C. Keefer and Mr. Smith; Chapter 13, East Asia and the Pacific, Ms. Schwar, and Messrs. Keefer and Smith; Chapter 14, Africa, Bret D. Bellamy; and Chapter 15, Latin America, David S. Painter and Evans Gerakas.

Althea W. Robinson of the Publishing Services Division (Paul M. Washington, Chief) performed the technical editing under the supervision of Margie R. Wilber and Rita M. Baker. The index was compiled by CDB Enterprises.

WILLIAM Z. SLANY
The Historian
Office of the Historian
Bureau of Public Affairs

Contents

List of Documents

Page

CHAPTER 1. GENERAL PRINCIPLES AND OBJECTIVES OF AMERICAN FOREIGN POLICY

CHAPTER 2. THE ORGANIZATION AND CONDUCT OF AMERICAN FOREIGN POLICY

CHAPTER 3. NATIONAL SECURITY POLICY

CHAPTER 4. ARMS CONTROL

CHAPTER 5. FOREIGN ECONOMIC POLICY

A. GENERAL ECONOMIC POLICY

B. TRADE AND COMMERCIAL POLICY

C. FINANCIAL AND MONETARY POLICY

D. ENERGY POLICY

E. FOREIGN ASSISTANCE AND THIRD WORLD ISSUES

Page

F. INTERNATIONAL ECONOMIC SUMMIT CONFERENCES

CHAPTER 6. UNITED NATIONS: DEVELOPMENTS IN INTERNATIONAL LAW

CHAPTER 7. OCEANS AND INTERNATIONAL ENVIRONMENTAL AND SCIENTIFIC AFFAIRS

A. GENERAL

B. LAW OF THE SEA

CHAPTER 8. REFUGEES, HUMAN RIGHTS, TERRORISM

A. HUMAN RIGHTS

B. CAMPAIGN FOR DEMOCRACY

C. REFUGEES

D. TERRORISM

E. NARCOTICS

CHAPTER 9. INTERNATIONAL INFORMATION, EDUCATIONAL EXCHANGE, AND CULTURAL AFFAIRS PROGRAMS

CHAPTER 10. EUROPE AND CANADA

A. GENERAL POLICIES

B. REGIONAL ORGANIZATIONS

C. UNITED KINGDOM

D. WEST GERMANY

E. FRANCE

F. PORTUGAL

G. SPAIN

H. ITALY

I. VATICAN

J. GREECE

K. CYPRUS

L. TURKEY

M. SOVIET UNION AND EASTERN EUROPE

Page

N. CANADA

CHAPTER 11. THE MIDDLE EAST

A. REGIONAL DEVELOPMENTS AND GENERAL POLICIES

B. THE ARAB-ISRAELI DISPUTE

C. EGYPT

D. IRAN AND IRAQ

E. ISRAEL

F. JORDAN

G. LEBANON

H. LIBYA

I. MOROCCO

J. SAUDI ARABIA

K. TUNISIA

CHAPTER 12. SOUTH ASIA

A. REGIONAL POLICIES AND DEVELOPMENTS

Page

B. AFGHANISTAN

C. BANGLADESH

D. INDIA

Page

E. PAKISTAN

CHAPTER 13. EAST ASIA

A. REGIONAL POLICIES AND DEVELOPMENTS

1. General Statements of U.S. Policy in Asia

2. The ANZUS Pact

3. The Southwest Pacific

Page

C. BURMA

D. CHINA

E. INDONESIA

F. JAPAN

G. KAMPUCHEA

H. KOREA

I. NEW ZEALAND

J. PHILIPPINES

K. SINGAPORE

L. THAILAND

M. VIETNAM

CHAPTER 14. AFRICA

A. GENERAL POLICY

B. SOUTHERN AFRICA

C. ZAMBIA AND ZIMBABWE

Page

D. ZAIRE

E. WEST AFRICA: CAMEROON, GHANA, LIBERIA, NIGERIA, AND SENEGAL

F. THE HORN OF AFRICA

C. MEXICO, CENTRAL AMERICA, THE CARIBBEAN

D. SOUTH AMERICA

Brazil

Chile

Colombia

List of Abbreviations

ABM	anti-ballistic missile
ACLU	American Civil Liberties Union
ADA	Americans for Democratic Action
ADB	African Development Bank
ADF	Asian Development Fund
AEI	American Enterprise Institute
AEWC	Alaska Eskimo Whaling Commission
AFDF	African Development Fund
AFL–CIO	American Federation of Labor–Congress of Industrial Organizations
AID	Agency for International Development
AIFLD	American Institute for Free Labor Development
ANC	African National Congress
ANGTS	Alaska Natural Gas Transportation System
ANZUS	Australia, New Zealand, United States
APC	armored personnel carrier
ASAT	anti-satellite
ASEAN	Association of Southeast Asian Nations
ASPTR	Soviet Salvage, Rescue, and Underwater Technical Services Group
AWACS	airborne warning and control system
AZAP	Agence Zaire Presse
BA	budget authority
BANEX	Banco de Exportaciones (Export Bank) (Costa Rica)
BCP	Burmese Communist Party
BMD	ballistic missile defense
BPP	Border Patrol Police (Thailand)
CADA	Concerted Action for Development in Africa
CADC	Central American Democratic Community
CAP	common agricultural policy
CARE	Cooperative for American Relief Everywhere
CARICOM	Caribbean Common Market
CAS	Committee on Assurance of Supply
CBI	Caribbean Basin Initiative
CBU	cluster bomb unit
CCC	Commodity Credit Corporation
CCD	Conference of the Committee on Disarmament
CCDAC	Central Committee for Drug Abuse Control
CCE	Central Elections Commission (El Salvador)
CD	Committee on Disarmament
CDA	Cooperation for Development in Africa
CDE	Conference on Disarmament in Europe
CFF	compensatory financing facility
CFR	Code of Federal Regulations
CIA	Central Intelligence Agency
CIEE	Council on International Educational Exchange
CIF	Chinese Irregular Forces
CIME	Committee on International Investments and Multinational Enterprises (Organization for Economic Cooperation and Development)
CIP	commodity import program
CITES	Convention on International Trade in Endangered Species of Wild Flora and Fauna
CMIRB	Canadian Committee on Megaprojects, Industrial and Regional Benefits
CMMS	congressionally mandated mobility study
COCOM	Coordinating Committee for East-West Trade Policy
COE	Council of Europe
COGLA	Canada Oil and Gas Lands Administration
COMECON	Council for Mutual Economic Assistance
COPPAL	International Conference of Political Parties
CP	Consejo Permanente (Permanent Council) (Organization of American States)
CRS	Catholic Relief Services

CSCE	Conference on Security and Cooperation in Europe
CTB	comprehensive test ban
CTBT	Comprehensive Test Ban Treaty
DA	development assistance
DAC	Development Advisory Council
DEA	Drug Enforcement Administration
DIA	Defense Intelligence Agency
DK	Democratic Kampuchea
DMZ	demilitarized zone
DOD	Department of Defense
DOE	Department of Energy
DPRK	Democratic People's Republic of Korea
DSARC	Defense Systems Acquisition Review Council
DTEC	Department of Technical and Economic Cooperation (Thailand)
EC–10	The ten member countries of the European Communities
ECK	Emergency Communications Key
ECOWAS	Economic Community of West African States
EEC	European Economic Community
EFF	extended fund facility
ELN	Ejército de Liberación Nacional (National Liberation Army) (Colombia)
EMS	European Monetary System
EROS	Earth Resources Observation System
ESA	Energy Security Act (Canada)
ESA	European Space Agency
ESF	Economic Support Fund
ESF	Exchange Stabilization Fund
EURATOM	European Atomic Energy Community
EXIM	Export-Import Bank
FAA	Federal Aviation Administration
FAO	Food and Agriculture Organization (United Nations)
FARC	Fuerzas Armadas Revolucionarias de Colombia (Revolutionary Armed Forces of Colombia)
FBI	Federal Bureau of Investigation
FBIS	Foreign Broadcast Information Service
FDR	Frente Democrático Revolucionario (Democratic Revolutionary Front) (El Salvador)
FINATA	El Salvador agrarian reform institution
FIRA	Foreign Investment Review Agency (Canada)
FMLN	[Frente] Farabundo Martí de la Liberación Nacional (Farabundo Martí National Liberation [Front]) (El Salvador)
FMS	foreign military sales
FOB	free on board
FRELIMO	Frente de Libertação de Moçambique (Front for the Liberation of Mozambique)
FRG	Federal Republic of Germany
FSO	Fund for Special Operations
FT	*Financial Times* (London)
FY	fiscal year
G–77	Group of 77 developing nations
GAB	general arrangements to borrow
GATT	General Agreement on Tariffs and Trade
GCI	general capital increase
GE	General Electric Company
GLCM	ground-launched cruise missile
GmbH	Gesellschaft mit beschränkter Haftung (company with limited liability)
GNP	gross national product
GOES	Government of El Salvador
GOI	Government of Indonesia

GOJ	Government of Japan
GOP	Government of Pakistan
GOT	Government of Turkey
GOZ	Government of Zimbabwe
GPRA	Government of the People's Republic of Angola
GSA	General Services Administration
GSP	generalized system of preferences
HCR	United Nations High Commissioner for Refugees
HE	Her/His Excellency
HEU	highly enriched uranium
HR	House (of Representatives) Resolution
HMG	Her Majesty's Government (United Kingdom)
IAEA	International Atomic Energy Agency
IOC	initial operating capability
IBM	International Business Machines Corporation
IBRD	International Bank for Reconstruction and Development (World Bank)
ICA	International Communications Agency
ICBM	intercontinental ballistic missile
ICC	Interstate Commerce Commission
ICK	International Conference on Kampuchea
ICM	Intergovernmental Committee for Migration
ICRC	International Committee of the Red Cross
IDA	International Development Association
IDB	Inter-American Development Bank
IDCA	International Development Cooperation Agency
IDF	Israeli Defense Forces
IEA	International Energy Agency
IEEPA	International Emergency Economic Powers Act
IEP	International Energy Program
IESC	International Executive Service Corps
IFC	International Finance Corporation
IG	interagency group
IGGI	Intergovernmental Group on Indonesia
IIE	Institute of International Education
ILO	International Labor Organization
IMET	International Military Education and Training Program
IMF	International Monetary Fund
INA	Immigration and Naturalization Act
INC	International Narcotics Control
INF	intermediate-range nuclear forces
INM	Bureau of International Narcotics Matters, Department of State
INS	Immigration and Naturalization Service
ITA	International Tin Agreement
ITC	International Tin Council
ITU	International Telecommunications Union
IWC	International Whaling Commission
IUCN	International Union for Conservation of Nature and Natural Resources
JACC	Joint Agricultural Consultative Committee (United States–Nigeria)
JCS	Joint Chiefs of Staff
JMC	Joint Military Commission
KGB	Komitet Gosudarstvennyi Bezopastnosti (Committee for State Security) (Soviet Union)
KL	kiloton
KPNLF	Khmer People's National Liberation Front
LADE	Lineas Aereas del Estado (State Airlines) (Argentina)
LAF	Lebanese Armed Forces
LANDSAT	land remote sensing satellite system

LDC	less developed country
LIBOR	London Interbank Offered Rate
LOS	Law of the Sea
M–19	Colombian guerrilla group
MAC	Military Airlift Command
MAP	military assistance program
MAU	Marine amphibious unit
MBFR	mutual and balanced force reduction
MDB	Multilateral Development Banks
MDN	Movimiento Democrático Nicaragüense
MFA	Multifiber Agreement
MFN	most favored nation
MFO	multinational force and observers/multilateral force observers (Sinai)
MIA	missing in action
MIR	Movimiento de Izquierda Revolucionaria (Movement of the Revolutionary Left) (Chile)
MIRV	multiple independently targetable reentry vehicle
MLLA	Mineral Land Leasing Act
MNF	multinational force
MNR	Movimiento Nacional Revolucionario (National Revolutionary Movement) (El Salvador)
MPLA	Movimiento Popular de Libertação de Angola (Popular Movement for the Liberation of Angola)
MPS	multiple protective shelter
MTN	multilateral trade negotiations
MX	missile experimental
NASA	National Aeronautics and Space Administration
NATO	North Atlantic Treaty Organization
NBC	National Broadcasting Company
NCPAC	National Conservative Political Action Committee
ND	North Dakota
NDU	National Defense University
NEA	Bureau of Near Eastern and South Asian Affairs, Department of State
NEP	National Energy Program (Canada)
NNA	neutral/nonaligned
NNPA	Nuclear Non-Proliferation Act
NOAA	National Oceanic and Atmospheric Administration
NORAD	North American Aerospace Defense Command
NPD	Nationaldemokratische Partei Deutschlands (National Democratic Party of Germany) (Federal Republic of Germany)
NPG	Nuclear Planning Group (North Atlantic Treaty Organization)
NPT	Non-Proliferation Treaty
NRC	Nuclear Regulatory Commission
NSC	National Security Council
NSDD	National Security Decision Directive
NWFP	Northwest Frontier Province (Pakistan)
OAS	Organization of American States
OAU	Organization of African Unity
ODA	official development assistance
ODP	orderly departure program
OEA	Organización de los Estados Americanos (Organization of American States)
OECD	Organization for Economic Cooperation and Development
OES	Bureau of Oceans and International Environmental and Scientific Affairs, Department of State
OLP	Office of Ocean Law and Policy, Bureau of Oceans and International Environmental and Scientific Affairs, Department of State
ONCB	Office of Narcotics Control Board (Thailand)
OPEC	Organization of the Petroleum Exporting Countries
OPIC	Overseas Private Investment Corporation

ORDEN	Organización Democrática Nacionalista (Nationalist Democratic Organization) (El Salvador)
PA	Bureau of Public Affairs, Department of State
PAC	Pan Africanist Congress
PACAMS	Panama Canal military schools
PCB	polychlorinated biphenyl
PDASD	Principal Deputy Assistant Secretary of Defense
PDRY	People's Democratic Republic of Yemen
PIP	Petroleum Incentives Program (Canada)
PKF	peacekeeping force
PKO	peacekeeping operations
PL	public law
PLO	Palestine Liberation Organization
PNE	peaceful nuclear explosion
POLISARIO	[Frente] Popular para la Liberación de Saguia el-Hamra y Río de Oro (Popular Front for the Liberation of the Saguia el Hamra and the Río de Oro) (Western Sahara)
POW	prisoner of war
PR	proportional representation
PR	public relations
PRC	People's Republic of China
PRG	People's Revolutionary Government (Grenada)
PRI	Partido Revolucionario Institucional (Institutional Revolutionary Party) (Mexico)
PUNE	peaceful uses of nuclear energy
PVO	private voluntary organization
R&D	research and development
RADM	Rear Admiral
RDJTF	Rapid Deployment Joint Task Force
RERTR	Reduced Enrichment (uranium) for Research and Test Reactors
ROK	Republic of Korea
RTG	Royal Thai Government
SA	Société Anonyme
SADCC	Southern African Development Cooperation Council
SALT	strategic arms limitation talks
SAM	surface-to-air missile
SCG	Special Consultative Group (North Atlantic Treaty Organization)
SDR	special drawing rights
SEC	Supply Executive Committee
SFRC	Senate Foreign Relations Committee
SIG	senior interagency group
SIG–DP	Senior Interagency Group–Defense Policy
SIG–FP	Senior Interagency Group–Foreign Policy
SIG–I	Senior Interagency Group–Intelligence
SLBM	submarine-launched ballistic missile
SpA	Società per Azioni
SPR	strategic petroleum reserve
SRUB	Socialist Republic of the Union of Burma
SRV	Socialist Republic of Vietnam
START	strategic arms reduction talks
STS	space transportation system
SUA	Shan United Army
SWAPO	South West Africa People's Organization
SWAT	special weapons and tactics (police)
TASS	Telegraphnoye Agentstvo Sovyetskovo Soyuza (Telegraph Agency of the Soviet Union)
TASTEX	Tokai Advanced Safeguards Technology Exercise
TDP	trade and development program
TIAS	Treaties and Other International Acts Series
TOA	total obligational authority

TRA	Taiwan Relations Act
TTBT	Threshold Test Ban Treaty
UAE	United Arab Emirates
UCS	Union Comunal Salvadoreña (Salvadoran Campesinos Union)
UDN	Unión Democrática Nacionalista (National Democratic Union) (El Salvador)
UK	United Kingdom
UN	United Nations
UNCITRAL	United Nations Commission on International Trade Law
UNCTAD	United Nations Conference on Technology and Development
UNDP	United Nations Development Program
UNEP	United Nations Environmental Program
UNESCO	United Nations Educational, Scientific and Cultural Organization
UNFDAC	United Nations Fund for Drug Abuse Control
UNFICYP	United Nations Peacekeeping Force on Cyprus
UNGA	United Nations General Assembly
UNHCR	United Nations High Commissioner for Refugees
UNICEF	United Nations Children's Fund
UNIFIL	United Nations Interim Force in Lebanon
UNISPACE	United Nations Conference on the Exploration and Peaceful Uses of Outer Space
UNITA	Unitão Nacional para a Independência Total de Angola (National Union for the Total Independence of Angola)
UNITAS	United International Antisubmarine Warfare
UNSC	United Nations Security Council
UNSCR	United Nations Security Council Resolution
UNRWA	United Nations Relief and Works Agency for Palestine Refugees in the Near East
UNTAG	United Nations Transition Assistance Group
UPD	Unión de Partidos Democráticos (Union of Democratic Parties) (El Salvador)
USA	United States of America
USC	United States Code
USDA	United States Department of Agriculture
USG	United States Government
USIA	United States Information Agency
USICA	United States International Communications Agency
USSR	Union of Soviet Socialist Republics
USTR	United States Trade Representative
USUN	United States Mission to the United Nations
VOA	Voice of America
WIPO	World Intellectual Property Organization
YPF	Yacimientos Petroliferos Fiscales (State Oil Fields) (Argentina)
ZAPU	Zimbabwe African People's Union

List of Names

Abrams, Elliott, Assistant Secretary of State for Human Rights and Humanitarian Affairs
Addabbo, Rep. Joseph P. (D–N.Y.)
Adelman, Kenneth L., Deputy Representative to the United Nations
Alhegelan, Faisal, Saudi Arabian Ambassador to the United States
Allen, Gen. Lew, Jr., Chief of Staff, U.S. Air Force, to June 30, 1982
Allen, Richard V., Assistant to the President for National Security Affairs to January 4, 1982
Ali, Gen. Kamal Hassan, Egyptian Deputy Prime Minister and Foreign Minister
Andrei, Stefan, Romanian Foreign Minister
Andropov, Yuri Vladimirovich, Secretary of the Communist Party of the Soviet Union to November 12, 1982; thereafter General Secretary of the Communist Party of the Soviet Union
Arafat, Yasir, Chairman, Palestine Liberation Organization
Arens, Moshe, Israeli Ambassador to the United States from November 16, 1982
Armstrong, Sen. William (R–Col.)
Asencio, Diego C., Assistant Secretary of State for Consular Affairs
Assad, Hafiz al, President of Syria
Baker, Sen. Howard H., Jr. (R–Tenn.)
Baker, James A., III, Chief of Staff and Assistant to the President
Baldrige, Malcolm, Secretary of Commerce
Balsemão, Francisco Pinto, Prime Minister of Portugal
Barnes, Harry G., Jr., Ambassador to India
Barnes, Rep. Michael D. (D–Md.)
Begin, Menachem, Prime Minister of Israel
Belaúnde Terry, Fernando, President of Peru
Betancur Cuartas, Belisario, President of Colombia from August 1982
Biden, Sen. Joseph R., Jr. (D–Del.)
Bingham, Rep. Jonathan B. (D–N.Y.)
Bishop, James K., Deputy Assistant Secretary of State for African Affairs
Bishop, Maurice, Prime Minister of Grenada
Biya, Paul, Prime Minister of Cameroon to November 6, 1982; thereafter President of Cameroon
Block, John R., Secretary of Agriculture
Boland, Rep. Edward (D–Mass.)
Bonker, Rep. Don L. (D–Wash.)
Boschwitz, Sen. Rudy (R–Minn.)
Bosworth, Stephen W., Principal Deputy Assistant Secretary of State for Inter-American Affairs
Botha, Pieter Willem, Prime Minister of South Africa
Botha, Roelof F. (Pik), South African Foreign Minister
Bouabid, Maati, Prime Minister of Morocco
Boucetta, Mohammad, Moroccan Foreign Minister
Bourguiba, Habib, President of Tunisia
Boutros, Fuad, Lebanese Deputy Prime Minister and Foreign Minister
Boyatt, Thomas D., Ambassador to Colombia
Brezhnev, Leonid I., General Secretary, Central Committee of the Communist Party of the Soviet Union, to November 10, 1982
Brock, William E., III, U.S. Trade Representative
Broomfield, Rep. William S. (R–Mich.)
Buckley, James L., Under Secretary of State for Security Assistance, Science and Technology to May 9, 1982
Burns, Arthur F., Ambassador to West Germany
Burt, Richard R., Director, Bureau of Politico-Military Affairs, Department of State, to May 9, 1982; thereafter Assistant Secretary of State for European Affairs-Designate
Bush, George, Vice President of the United States
Byrd, Sen. Robert C. (D–W.Va.)
Calvo Sotelo y Bustelo, Leopoldo, Prime Minister of Spain to October 28, 1982
Carlucci, Frank C., Deputy Secretary of Defense to December 31, 1982
Carney, Rep. William (R–N.Y.)
Carrington, Lord Peter, British Foreign Secretary to April 5, 1982
Carstens, Karl, President of West Germany
Casey, William J., Director of Central Intelligence
Castañeda de la Rosa, Jorge, Mexican Foreign Minister

Castro Ruz, Fidel, Prime Minister of Cuba
Catto, Henry E., Jr., Assistant Secretary of Defense (Public Affairs)
Ceausescu, Nicolae, President of Romania
Chávez Mena, Fidel, El Salvadoran Foreign Minister
Cheysson, Claude, French Foreign Minister
Choo Young Bock, South Korean Defense Minister
Chun Doo Hwan, President of South Korea
Clark, William P., Deputy Secretary of State to February 9, 1982; thereafter Assistant to the President for National Security Affairs
Clausen, Alden W., President of the World Bank
Cohen, Sen. William S. (R–Me.)
Constable, Peter D., Deputy Assistant Secretary of State for Near Eastern and South Asian Affairs to October 8, 1982; thereafter Ambassador to Zaire
Conte, Rep. Silvio O. (R–Mass.)
Costa-Méndez, Nicanor, Argentine Foreign Minister to June 27, 1982
Cranston, Sen. Alan (D–Cal.)
Crocker, Chester A., Assistant Secretary of State for African Affairs
Crockett, Rep. George W., Jr. (D–Mich.)

D'Amato, Sen. Alfonse M. (R–N.Y.)
D'Escoto, Miguel, Nicaraguan Foreign Minister
Dam, Kenneth W., Deputy Secretary of State from September 23, 1982
Deaver, Michael K., Deputy Chief of Staff and Assistant to the President
Deng Xiaoping, Vice Chairman, Chinese Communist Party
Denton, Sen. Jeremiah (R–Ala.)
DiCarlo, Dominick L., Assistant Secretary of State for International Narcotics Matters
Dillon, Robert S., Ambassador to Lebanon
Diouf, Abdou, President of Senegal
Dixon, Rep. Julian C. (R–Cal.)
Dobrynin, Anatoliy, Soviet Ambassador to the United States
Dodd, Sen. Christopher J. (D–Conn.)
Douglas, H. Eugene, Department of State Coordinator for Refugee Affairs
Dragan, Zvone, Vice President of Yugoslavia
Draper, Morris, Deputy Assistant Secretary of State for Near Eastern and South Asian Affairs and Chief U.S Negotiator for the Middle East
Duarte, José Napoleon, President of El Salvador to April 29, 1982

Eagleburger, Lawrence S., Assistant Secretary of State for European Affairs to February 12, 1982; thereafter Under Secretary of State for Political Affairs
Ekwueme, Alex I., Vice President of Nigeria
Enders, Thomas O., Assistant Secretary of State for Inter-American Affairs
Enrile, Juan Ponce, Philippine Defense Minister
Ershad, Lt. Gen. Hussein Mohammed, Martial law leader of Bangladesh from March 24, 1982
Espriella, Ricardo de la, President of Panama
Essebsi, Beji Caid, Tunisian Foreign Minister
Evren, Gen. Kenan, Chairman, National Security Council, and Head of State of Turkey

Fairbanks, Richard M., III, Assistant Secretary of State for Congressional Relations to January 26, 1982; thereafter Special Middle East Peace Negotiator
Fascell, Rep. Dante B. (D–Fla.)
Fenwick, Rep. Millicent (R–N.J.)
Figueiredo, Joao Baptista de Oliveira, President of Brazil
Findley, Rep. Paul (R–Ill.)
Fischer, Dean E., Department of State Spokesman and Assistant Secretary of State for Public Affairs to August 19, 1982
Fraser, Malcolm, Prime Minister of Australia

Gabriel, Gen. Charles A., Chief of Staff, U.S. Air Force, from July 1, 1982
Galbraith, Evan, Ambassador to France
Galtieri, Lt. Gen. Leopoldo F., President of Argentina to June 17, 1982
Gandhi, Indira, Prime Minister of India
García Merino, Gen. Jośe Guillermo, El Salvadoran Minister of Defense and Public Security

Garza, Rep. E. (Kika) de la (D–Tex.)
Gejdenson, Rep. Samuel (D–Conn.)
Gemayal, Amin, President of Lebanon from September 23, 1982
Gemayal, Bashir, President of Lebanon to September 15, 1982
Genscher, Hans-Dietrich, West German Vice Chancellor and Foreign Minister
Gershman, Carl S., Representative in the Third Committee of the United Nations General Assembly
Ghorbal, Ashraf A., Egyptian Ambassador to the United States
Glenn, Sen. John H., Jr. (D–O.)
Goldwater, Sen. Barry (R–Ariz.)
Gonzalez Marques, Felipe, Prime Minister of Spain from October 28, 1982
Goodling, Rep. William F. (R–Pa.)
Gorsuch, Ann McGill, Administrator, Environmental Protection Agency
Goukouni, Oueddi, President of Chad to June 19, 1982
Gray, Rep. William H., III (D–Pa.)
Gromyko, Andrei A., Soviet Foreign Minister

Habib, Philip C., Special Representative of the President to the Middle East
Habre, Hissene, President of Chad from October 21, 1982
Haferkamp, Wilhelm, Vice President, Commission of the European Communities
Haig, Alexander M., Jr., Secretary of State to July 5, 1982
Hamilton, Rep. Lee H. (D–Ind.)
Hartling, Poul, U.N. High Commissioner for Refugees
Hartman, Arthur, Ambassador to the Soviet Union
Hassan II, King of Morocco
Hatfield, Sen. Mark O. (R–Ore.)
Hayakawa, Sen. Samuel I. (R–Cal.)
Helms, Sen. Jesse (R–N.C.)
Henderson, Sir Nicholas, British Ambassador to the United States to June 25, 1982
Herrera Campíns, Luis, President of Venezuela
Hewitt, Warren E., Representative to the U.N. Human Rights Commission
Hill, A. Alan, Chairman, Council on Environmental Quality
Hinton, Deane, R., Ambassador to El Salvador
Holdridge, John H., Assistant Secretary of State for East Asian and Pacific Affairs to December 10, 1982; thereafter Ambassador to Indonesia
Hollai, Imré, President of the U.N. General Assembly from September 21, 1982
Hollings, Sen. Ernest W. (D–S.C.)
Hormats, Robert D., Assistant Secretary of State for Economic and Business Affairs to August 25, 1982
Houphouët-Boigny, Félix, President of the Ivory Coast
Howe, Rear Adm. Jonathan T., Director, Bureau of Politico-Military Affairs, Department of State, from May 10, 1982
Hu Yaobang, Chairman Communist Party of the People's Republic of China
Huang Hua, Chinese Vice Premier and Foreign Minister
Hughes, John, Department of State Spokesman and Assistant Secretary of State for Public Affairs from August 22, 1982
Hughes, Rep. William (D–N.J.)
Hunt, Leamon R., Director-General of the Multinational Force and Observers (Middle East)
Hussein ibn Talal, King of Jordan
Hussein, Saddam, President of Iraq

Ibrahimi, Ahmed Taleb, Algerian Foreign Minister
Iklé, Fred, Under Secretary of Defense for Policy
Illueca, Jorge E., Panamanian Foreign Minister
Inouye, Sen. Daniel K. (D–Hawaii)

Jackson, Sen. Henry M. (D–Wash.)
Jaruzelski, Gen. Wojciech, Prime Minister of Poland, Polish Defense Minister, and First Secretary, Central Committee, Polish United Workers' Party
Jepsen, Sen. Roger W. (R–Iowa)
Johnston, Ernest B. Jr., Deputy Assistant Secretary of State for Economic and Business Affairs
Johnston, Sen. J. Bennett (D–La.)

Jones, Gen. David C., USAF, Chairman, Joint Chiefs of Staff to June 18, 1982
Jorge, Paulo T., Angolan Foreign Minister
Jouejati, Rafic, Syrian Ambassador to the United States
Juan Carlos I, King of Spain

Kampelman, Max M., Chairman, U.S. Delegation to the Conference on Security and Co-operation in Europe
Kassebaum, Sen. Nancy L. (R–Kans.)
Kassem, Marwan, Jordanian Foreign Minister
Kaunda, Kenneth D., President of Zambia
Kemp, Rep. Jack (R–N.Y.)
Kennedy, Sen. Edward M. (D–Mass.)
Kennedy, Richard T., Under Secretary of State for Management to December 14, 1982; thereafter Ambassador-at-Large and Special Adviser to the Secretary of State on Nonproliferation and Nuclear Energy
Khaddam, Abdel Halim, Syrian Deputy Prime Minister and Foreign Minister
Khien Samphon, Vice President of Democratic Kampuchea
Khoman, Thanat, Thai Foreign Minister
Khomeini, (Ayatollah) Ruhollah Mussavi, Leader of Iran
Kirkpatrick, Jeane J., Representative to the United Nations
Klibi, Chedli, Secretary General of the Arab League
Kohl, Helmut, Chancellor, Federal Republic of Germany from October 1, 1982
Kyprianou, Spiros, President of Cyprus

LaFalce, Rep. John J. (D–N.Y.)
Lagomarsino, Rep. Robert J. (R–Cal.)
Lantos, Rep. Tom (D–Cal.)
Laxalt, Sen. Paul (R–Nev.)
Leach, Rep. Jim (R–Iowa)
Le Kuan Yew, Prime Minister of the Republic of Singapore
Leland, Marc E., Assistant Secretary of the Treasury (International Affairs)
Levin, Sen. Carl (D–Mich.)
Levitsky, Melvyn, Deputy Assistant Secretary of State for Human Rights and Humanitarian Affairs
Lewis, Samuel L., Ambassador to Israel
Lichenstein, Charles M., Alternate Representative to the United Nations for Special Political Affairs
Ling Qing, Chinese Representative to the United Nations
Livingston, Rep. Robert L. (R–La.)
Lodwick, Seeley G., Under Secretary of Agriculture for International Affairs and Commodity Programs
Long, Rep. Clarence D. (D–Md.)
López-Portillo, José, President of Mexico
Luce, Gordon C., Alternate Representative to the United Nations
Lugar, Sen. Richard G. (R–Ind.)
Luns, Joseph, Secretary General, North Atlantic Treaty Organization
Lyman, Princeton, Deputy Assistant Secretary of State for African Affairs
Lyng, Richard E., Deputy Secretary of Agriculture

MacDonald, David R., Deputy U.S. Trade Representative
MacEachen, Allan J., Canadian Deputy Prime Minister and Finance Minister to September 10, 1982; thereafter Canadian Deputy Prime Minister and Secretary of State for External Affairs
MacGuigan, Mark, Canadian Secretary of State for External Affairs to September 10, 1982; thereafter Canadian Justice Minister and Attorney General
Magaña Borja, Alvaro Alfredo, Provisional President of El Salvador from May 1982
Malone, James L., Special Representative for the Law of the Sea Conferences and Assistant Secretary of State for Oceans and International Environmental and Scientific Affairs
Mansfield, Michael J., Ambassador to Japan
Marcos, Ferdinand E., President of the Philippines
Markey, Rep. Edward J. (D–Mass.)
Mathias, Sen. Charles McC., Jr. (R–Md.)
Matsunaga, Sen. Spark (D–Hawaii)

Mauroy, Pierre, Prime Minister of France
Mazzoli, Rep. Romano L. (D–Ky.)
McCloskey, Paul N., Jr. (R–Cal.)
McFarlane, Robert C., Special Envoy to the Middle East and Counselor of the Department of State to April 4, 1982; thereafter Deputy Assistant to the President for National Security Affairs
McKinney, Rep. Stewart B. (R–Conn.)
McNamar, Robert T., Deputy Secretary of the Treasury
McPherson, M. Peter, Administrator, Agency for International Development
Meese, Edwin, III, Counselor to the President
Middendorf, J. William, II, Representative to the Organization of American States
Mitterrand, Francois, President of France
Moi, Daniel T. arap, President of Kenya
Monge, Luis Alberto, President of Costa Rica
Moore, Powell A., Assistant Secretary of State for Congressional Relations
Moynihan, Sen. Daniel Patrick (D–N.Y.)
Mubarek, Mohamed Hosni, President of Egypt
Mugabe, Robert, Prime Minister of Zimbabwe
Muldoon, Robert D., Prime Minister of New Zealand
Murtha, Rep. John (D–Pa.)
Mzali, Mohamed, Prime Minister of Tunisia

Nakasone, Yasuhiro, Prime Minister of Japan
Newell, Gregory J., Assistant Secretary of State for International Organization Affairs from May 28, 1982
Nguyen Co Thach, Vietnamese Foreign Minister
Niles, Thomas M.T., Deputy Assistant Secretary for European Affairs
Nimeiri, Gaafar Mohamed, President of Sudan
Nitze, Paul H., Head, U.S. Delegation to the Intermediate Range Nuclear Forces Negotiations
Nott, John, British Defense Secretary
Nujoma, Sam, President of South West Africa People's Organization
Nunn, Sen. Sam (D–Ga.)
Nyerere, Julius K., President of Tanzania

O'Neill, Rep. Thomas P., Jr. (D–Mass.)
Ortega Saavedra, Daniel, Coordinator of the Government of National Reconstruction of Nicaragua

Packwood, Sen. Bob (R–Ore.)
Papandreou, Andreas, Prime Minister of Greece
Parsons, Sir Anthony, British Representative to the United Nations
Patterson, Rep. Jerry M. (D–Cal.)
Pell, Sen. Claiborne (D–R.I.)
Percy, Sen. Charles H. (R–Ill.)
Pérez de Cuéllar, Javier, United Nations Secretary-General
Pertini, Alessandro, President of Italy
Platt, Nicholas, Acting Assistant Secretary of the State for International Organization Affairs to May 28, 1982; thereafter Ambassador to Zambia from July 22, 1982
Pol Pot, Chairman of the Supreme Commission of the National Army and Commander in Chief of Kampuchea
Pressler, Sen. Larry (R–S.D.)
Pym, Francis, British Foreign Secretary from April 5, 1982

Qadhafi, Col. Muammar al-, Chief of State of Libya
Quainton, Anthony C.E., Ambassador to Nicaragua from March 26, 1982
Quijano, Raul A., Argentine Representative to the Organization of American States

Rawlings, Jerry John, Chairman, Provisional National Defense Council of Ghana
Reagan, Ronald, President of the United States
Regan, Donald T., Secretary of the Treasury
Reuss, Rep. Henry S. (D–Wisc.)
Richmond, Rep. Frederick W. (D–N.Y.)
Ríos Montt, José Efrain, Brig. Gen., President of Guatemala from April 1982

Roca, Eduardo A., Argentine Representative to the United Nations
Rodino, Rep. Peter W., Jr. (D–N.J.)
Romberg, Alan D., Department of State Deputy Spokesman
Romulo, Carlos P., Philippine Foreign Minister
Ros, Enrique, Argentine Under Secretary for Foreign Affairs
Rosenthal, Rep. Benjamin S. (D–N.Y.)
Rostow, Eugene V., Director, Arms Control and Disarmament Agency
Rowny, Edward L., Special Representative for Arms Control and Disarmament Negotiations
Ruddy, Frank S., Assistant Administrator for Africa, Agency for International Development

Sakurauchi, Yoshio, Japanese Foreign Minister
Samin, Heng, Chairman of the State Council, Kampuchea
Santos, José Eduardo dos, President of Angola
Sarbanes, Sen. Paul S. (D–Md.)
Sattar, Abdus, President of Bangladesh to March 23, 1982
Saud, Abdallah ibn Abd al-Aziz Al, Crown Prince and Deputy Prime Minister of Saudi Arabia from June 13, 1982
Saud, Fahd ibn Abd al-Aziz Al, King of Saudi Arabia from June 13, 1982
Saud, Khalid ibn Abd al-Aziz Al, King and Prime Minister of Saudi Arabia to June 13, 1982
Saud, Sultan ibn Abd al-Aziz Al, Saudi Arabian Minister of Defense and Aviation
Sayre, Robert M., Director, Office for Combatting Terrorism, Department of State
Schmidt, Helmut, Chancellor of West Germany to October 1, 1982
Schneider, David T., Deputy Assistant Secretary of State for Near Eastern and South Asian Affairs
Schweiker, Richard S., Secretary of Health and Human Services
Seaga, Edward, Prime Minister of Jamaica
Shagari, Alhaji Shehu, President of Nigeria
Shamanski, Rep. Robert N. (D–Ohio)
Shamir, Yitzhak, Israeli Foreign Minister
Sharon, Ariel, Israeli Defense Minister
Shoesmith, Thomas P., Deputy Assistant Secretary of State for East Asian and Pacific Affairs
Shultz, George P., Secretary of State from July 16, 1982
Siad Barre, Mohammad, President of Somalia
Simpson, Sen. Alan K. (R–Wyo.)
Smith, William French, Attorney General
Soeharto, President of Indonesia
Solarz, Rep. Stephen J. (D–N.Y.)
Spadolini, Giovanni, President of Italy until November 13, 1982
Speakes, Larry M., Principal Deputy Press Secretary to the President
Sprinkel, Beryl W., Under Secretary of the Treasury for Monetary Affairs
Stennis, Sen. John C. (D–Miss.)
Stevens, Sen. Ted (R–Alaska)
Stoessel, Walter J., Jr., Under Secretary of State for Political Affairs to February 11, 1982; then Deputy Secretary of State to September 22, 1982
Stratton, Rep. Samuel S. (D–N.Y.)
Studds, Rep. Gerry E. (D–Mass.)
Suazo Cordova, Roberto, President of Honduras
Suzuki, Zenko, Prime Minister of Japan to November 1982

Takacs, Esteban A., Argentine Ambassador to the United States
Thatcher, Margaret, Prime Minister of the United Kingdom
Thorn, Gaston, President of the Commission, European Communities
Thurmond, Sen. Strom (R–S.C.)
Tinsulanon, Gen. Prem, Prime Minister of Thailand
Toure, Ahmed Sekou, President of Guinea
Tower, Sen. John G. (R–Tex.)
Trudeau, Pierre Elliott, Prime Minister of Canada
Tsongas, Sen. Paul E. (D–Mass.)
Tueni, Ghassan, Lebanese Representative to the United Nations
Turbay Ayala, Julio Cesar, President of Colombia to August 7, 1982

Türkmen, Ilter, Turkish Foreign Minister
Turnage, Maj. Gen. Thomas K., Director, Selective Service System

Ülüsü, Adm. Bulend, Prime Minister of Turkey
Ustinov, Dmitriy Fedorovich, Soviet Defense Minister

Valdéz Otero, Estanislao, Uruguayan Foreign Minister to September 1982
Veliotes, Nicholas A., Assistant Secretary of State for Near Eastern and South Asian Affairs
Vessey, Gen. John W., Jr., USA, Chairman, Joint Chiefs of Staff from June 18, 1982
Vine, Richard D., Director, Bureau for Refugee Affairs, Department of State
Volcker, Paul A., Chairman, Federal Reserve Board

Wallen, Alex, Chairman, Export Credit Group, Organization for Economic Cooperation and Development
Wallis, W. Allen, Under Secretary of State for Economic Affairs from September 23, 1982
Wallop, Sen. Malcolm (R–Wyo.)
Walters, Vernon A., Ambassador-at-Large
Warner, Sen. John W. (R–Va.)
Weinberger, Caspar W., Secretary of Defense
Wendt, E. Allan, Deputy Assistant Secretary of State for International Energy Policy, Bureau of Economic and Business Affairs
West, Francis J., Jr., Assistant Secretary of Defense (International Security Affairs)
Wick, Charles Z., Director, U.S. Information Agency
Winn, Rep. Larry (R–Kans.)
Wisner, Frank G., Deputy Assistant Secretary of State for African Affairs
Wolfowitz, Paul D., Director, Policy Planning Staff, Department of State
Wolpe, Rep. Howard E. (D–Mich.)

Zablocki, Rep. Clement J. (D–Wisc.)
Zhao Ziyang, Prime Minister of China
Zia-ul-Haq, Gen. Mohammad, President of Pakistan

Chapter 1. General Principles and Objectives of American Foreign Policy

Document 1

Address by President Reagan Before a Joint Session of Congress, January 26, 1982 (Extract)[1]

The State of the Union

. . . .

So far, I've concentrated largely, now, on domestic matters. To view the state of the Union in perspective, we must not ignore the rest of the world. There isn't time tonight for a lengthy treatment of social—or foreign policy, I should say—a subject I intend to address in detail in the near future. A few words, however, are in order on the progress we've made over the past year reestablishing respect for our nation around the globe and some of the challenges and goals that we will approach in the year ahead.

At Ottawa and Cancun,[2] I met with leaders of the major industrial powers and developing nations. Now, some of those I met with were a little surprised that I didn't apologize for America's wealth. Instead, I spoke of the strength of the free marketplace system and how that system could help them realize their aspirations for economic development and political freedom. I believe lasting friendships were made and the foundation was laid for future cooperation.

In the Caribbean Basin, we are developing a program of aid, trade and investment incentives to promote self-sustaining growth and a better, more secure life for our neighbors to the south. Toward those who would export terrorism and subversion in the Caribbean and elsewhere, especially Cuba and Libya, we will act with firmness.

Our foreign policy is a policy of strength, fairness and balance. By restoring America's military credibility, by pursuing peace at the negotiating table wherever both sides are willing to sit down in good faith, and by beginning or regaining the respect of America's allies and adversaries alike, we have strengthened our country's position as a force for peace and progress in the world.

When action is called for, we are taking it. Our sanctions against the military dictatorship that has attempted to crush human rights in Poland—and against the Soviet regime behind that military dictatorship—clearly demonstrated to the world that America will not conduct "business as usual" with the forces of oppression. (Applause.)

If the events in Poland continue to deteriorate, further measures will follow. Let me also note that private American groups have taken the lead in making January 30th a day of solidarity with the people of Poland. So, too, the European Parliament has called for March 21st to be an international day of support for Afghanistan. Well, I urge all peace-loving peoples to join together on those days, to raise their voices, to speak and pray for freedom.

Meanwhile, we are working for reduction of arms and military activities. As I announced in my address to the Nation last November 18th,[3] we have proposed to the Soviet Union a far-reaching agenda for mutual reduction of military forces and have already initiated negotiations with them in Geneva on intermediate range nuclear forces.

In those talks it is essential that we negotiate from a position of strength. There must be a real incentive for the Soviets to take these talks seriously. This requires that we rebuild our defenses.

In the last decade, while we sought the moderation of Soviet power through a

---

[1] Source: White House Press Release, January 26, 1982, Office of the Press Secretary to the President; also printed in *Weekly Compilation of Presidential Documents*, February 1, 1982, pp. 81–83. For the full text, see *ibid.*, pp. 76–83. The President spoke at 9 p.m. in the House Chamber at the Capitol. The address was broadcast nationwide on radio and television.

[2] For documents on the economic summit conferences held at Ottawa, Canada, July 19–21, 1981, and Cancun, Mexico, October 22–23, 1981, see *American Foreign Policy: Current Documents, 1981*, Chapter 5, Part F.

[3] For the text of President Reagan's address on November 18, 1981, before the National Press Club in Washington, see *ibid.*, document 60.

process of restraint and accommodation, the Soviets engaged in an unrelenting buildup of their military forces.

The protection of our national security has required that we undertake a substantial program to enhance our military forces.

We have not neglected to strengthen our traditional alliances in Europe and Asia, or to develop key relationships with our partners in the Middle East and other countries.

Building a more peaceful world requires a sound strategy and the national resolve to back it up. When radical forces threaten our friends, when economic misfortune creates conditions of instability, when strategically vital parts of the world fall under the shadow of Soviet power, our response can make the difference between peaceful change or disorder and violence. That is why we have laid such stress not only on our own defense, but on our vital foreign assistance program. Your recent passage of the foreign assistance act sent a signal to the world that America will not shrink from making the investments necessary for both peace and security. Our foreign policy must be rooted in realism, not naivete or self-delusion.

A recognition of what the Soviet empire is about is the starting point. Winston Churchill, in negotiating with the Soviets, observed that they respect only strength and resolve in their dealings with other nations.

That is why we have moved to reconstruct our national defenses. We intend to keep the peace—we will also keep our freedom. (Applause.)

We have made pledges of a new frankness in our public statements and worldwide broadcasts. In the face of a climate of falsehood and misinformation, we have promised the world a season of truth—the truth of our great civilized ideas: individual liberty, representative government, the rule of law under God.

We have never needed walls or mine fields or barbwire to keep our people in. Nor do we declare martial law to keep our people from voting for the kind of government they want.

Yes, we have our problems; yes, we are in a time of recession. And it's true, there is no quick fix, as I said, to instantly end the tragic pain of unemployment. But we will end it—the process has already begun and we'll see its effect as the year goes on.

We speak with pride and admiration of that little band of Americans who overcame insuperable odds to set this nation on course 200 years ago. But our glory didn't end with them. Americans ever since have emulated their deeds.

We don't have to turn to our history books for heroes. They are all around us. One who sits among you here tonight epitomized that heroism at the end of the longest imprisonment ever inflicted on men of our armed forces. Who will ever forget that night when we waited for television to bring us the scene of that first plane landing at Clark Field in the Philippines—bringing our POW'S home. The plane door opened and Jeremiah Denton came slowly down the ramp. He caught sight of our flag, saluted it, and said, "God bless America," and then thanked us for bringing him home. (Applause.)

Just 2 weeks ago, in the midst of a terrible tragedy on the Potomac, we saw again the spirit of American heroism at its finest—the heroism of dedicated rescue workers saving crash victims from icy waters. And we saw the heroism of one of our young government employees, Lenny Skutnik, who, when he saw a woman lose her grip on the helicopter line, dived into the water and dragged her to safety. (Applause.)

And then there are countless quiet, everyday heroes of American life—parents who sacrifice long and hard so their children will know a better life than they've known; church and civic volunteers who help to feed, clothe, nurse and teach the needy; millions who have made our nation, and our nation's destiny so very special—unsung heroes who may not have realized their own dreams themselves but then who reinvest those dreams in their children.

Don't let anyone tell you that America's best days are behind her—that the American spirit has been vanquished. We've seen it triumph too often in our lives to stop believing in it now. (Applause.)

One hundred and twenty years ago, the greatest of all our Presidents delivered his second state of the Union message in this chamber. "We cannot escape history," Abraham Lincoln warned. "We of this Congress and this administration will be remembered in spite of ourselves." The "trial through which we pass will light us down in honor or dishonor to the latest generation."

That President and that Congress did not fail the American people. Together they weathered the storm and preserved the Union.

Let it be said of us that we, too, did not fail; that we, too, worked together to bring America through difficult times. Let us so conduct ourselves that two centuries from now, another Congress and another President, meeting in this chamber as we are meeting, will speak of us with pride, saying that we met the test and preserved for them in their day the sacred flame of liberty—this last, best hope of man on Earth.

God bless you. Thank you. (Applause.)

Document 2

Address by the Secretary of Defense (Weinberger) Before the Council on Foreign Relations, New York, April 20, 1982[4]

U.S. Defense Policy

Ladies and Gentlemen, I am delighted to be back at the Council on Foreign Relations tonight, and to have the opportunity of talking with such a distinguished group of Americans.

As some of you may know, the Reagan administration has been accused of having no clear defense policy or military strategy. Some accuse us of merely throwing money at Defense with no clear idea of what we are trying to accomplish. Others accuse us of provoking an arms race with the Soviet Union; an arms race without reason, carried upwards by its own momentum. Still others believe that by restoring America's military strength in peacetime, we are edging closer to war.

My purpose in speaking to you tonight is to lay these misconceptions to rest, and to sketch the fundamental points of our defense policy.

This administration, like others before it, has recognized the need for maintaining armed forces in peacetime, not as a precursor to war but as a guarantor of peace. We seek only to ensure that we and our allies can pursue our goals in peace; free from intimidation, coercion and aggression. To do so we and our allies must be able to deter aggression by maintaining the capability to respond to any aggression launched against us at the lowest possible level of violence.

But for deterrence to be successful it must be credible. For our deterrent to be credible, especially in times of crisis, we must be perceived to have both the military capability and the national will to meet and defeat aggression.

Our basic national objectives and goals have remained constant during the postwar period. Broadly speaking, we seek to survive as a nation, to be free to pursue our way of life, to preserve the democratic community of nations, and to live in a stable and peaceful world. In the postwar period the primary challenge to our successful pursuit of these goals has been from the Soviet Union. For the past 30 years, rapidly growing Soviet conventional and nuclear forces have provided the major threats to our own survival and that of our allies. Soviet global expansion has posed the major obstacle to world peace and stability.

Although our national objectives have remained constant for the last 30 years, the most likely threat to them has evolved over time. Successive administrations and Congresses have developed somewhat different defense policies and military strategies to deal with this evolving threat. While most Presidents have built upon the policies of their predecessors, President Reagan had two unenviable but vital tasks. First, he had to reassure our friends that America was indeed going to be a strong, constant, reliable ally. Second, he had to let our opponents know, in unmistakable terms, that we were going to regain the military strength necessary to deter attacks upon us. Both assurances had to be given after a decade or more of neglect of our armed forces, and after the Carter years of indecision, vacillation, and weakness.

The centerpiece of our national security policy in the post-war period has been the defense of Western Europe. With Soviet expansion into Eastern Europe immediately after the war, the United States and its North Atlantic Allies formed a collective defense. Although we and our allies deployed a significant number of conventional forces in Western Europe in the 1950s, the Soviet conventional forces heavily outweighed NATO's in most key areas. NATO's ultimate deterrent against attack by the superior conventional forces of the Warsaw Pact was the threat of retaliation by superior American nuclear forces. Soviet conventional superiority was checkmated by American nuclear superiority.

That Soviet conventional power was obtained by subordinating everything that ap-

---

[4] Source: *Public Statements of Secretary of Defense Weinberger,* 1982.

peals to men and women in the West, and indeed elsewhere, to the acquisition of military might.

Simultaneously, despite an economy that ekes out a standard of living none of us would accept, the Soviets began a single-minded, intense effort to match and then exceed our nuclear strength.

As Soviet nuclear power grew throughout the 1960s, NATO adopted a policy of flexible response. We and our NATO allies placed increasing emphasis on initial conventional defense, backed up by willingness to resort to nuclear escalation should conventional defenses fail.

By the end of the 1970s, American nuclear superiority had vanished and the Soviet momentum, made up of ceaseless efforts to improve the accuracy, yield, range and variety of their nuclear weapons, carried them to the "margin of superiority" which the President correctly stated they now possess. In the 1980s, we began, hesitantly, to strengthen our NATO conventional forces and urged our allies to do likewise. But by this time, many in the United States and elsewhere began to realize that something was very wrong indeed, not just with our European deterrent, but with our entire force posture.

As a result of a decade of declining defense budgets, some induced by the vain hope that the era of "détente" would lead the Soviets to reduce their massive military buildup; and the Vietnam War, which cost us untold billions but weakened us in every way instead of giving us any added military strength, our conventional forces in Western Europe and northeast Asia had become increasingly out of balance with the Soviets. The strategic nuclear balance was beginning to tip to the Soviet's advantage, eroding the deterrent value of our strategic nuclear forces. The Soviet deployment of a new generation of intermediate range missiles aimed at Europe eroded the deterrent value of our theater nuclear forces. In the midst of all this, President Carter announced his decision to prevent any outside force from gaining control of the Persian Gulf region,[5] but he neither sought nor was given the resources to implement that decision fully. Finally, the introduction of Soviet military presence and proxy forces into many regions of the world threatened to outflank the defenses of our allies.

When this administration took office we examined whether our military resources were capable of protecting our vital objectives. Although nuclear deterrence, collective defense in Europe and northeast Asia, and defense of other vital interests such as in southwest Asia were still valid, indeed vital, objectives, we found that we lacked the requisite military capability for adequate deterrence or defense of these objectives.

We have to take a more realistic view, both of the military threat confronting us and of our capabilities. We could not agree with those ideologues of détente, who—contrary to all evidence—persisted in the illusion that the United States was driving the arms race, and that we would persuade the Soviets into restraint by kindly conversations and cultural or trade exchanges.

We modified our defense policy to fit today's realities, and to make it less dangerous, and more flexible, so that we could cope with a threatening and uncertain future. For example, we abandoned reliance on the dangerous fallacy of a "short war"—that any conventional war would necessarily be short because the aggressor would retreat or the war would quickly escalate to the nuclear level. Also, we adopted a safer policy for responding to warnings—recognizing that warnings are likely to be ambiguous, and that we cannot count on an all-or-none signal telling us when we must prepare to deter an imminent attack.

Apart from rectifying such deficiencies in strategy, we had to face the fact that our military capabilities fell short. There were two reasons for this. Our military capability had declined seriously throughout the 1970s, just as the 20-year Soviet defense buildup was bringing them greatly improved military capabilities. This worsening trend had now resulted in a margin of superiority in many categories of Soviet strategic nuclear, theater nuclear, and conventional forces. In addition, the Soviet Union had also acquired sufficient reserves for a prolonged conventional war.

Therefore, we are requesting a 5-year major increase in defense spending to restore the U.S-Soviet military balance. At the same time, we are encouraging our allies to increase their contribution to our common defense, and we are also increasing our

---

[5] In his state of the Union address on January 23, 1980, President Carter stated that "an attempt by any outside force to gain control of the Persian Gulf region will be regarded as an assault on the vital interests of the United States of America, and such an assault will be repelled by any means necessary, including military force." For the text of President Carter's address, see *American Foreign Policy: Basic Documents, 1977–1980,* pp. 53–57.

economic and security assistance programs so that our friends can improve their own security. A network of alliances and strengthened friends is one of the best ways of providing a forward defense for ourselves, and for our friends.

In addition to our formal alliances in Europe and Asia, we have a number of other interests and commitments throughout the world which we will continue to protect. For example, the increasing economic interdependence of the world over the past decade has made our access to foreign markets and vital natural resources more critical than ever. Because growing Soviet naval power could threaten our control of the sealanes that link us with our allies, we must strengthen our maritime capability. Because Soviet military power has acquired a global reach, we need mobile and flexible forces, particularly to prevent Soviet conquest of the oil fields and other major targets in the Mideast. Also, we must not permit our strongest deployment of forces, in the European central front, to become a "Maginot Line" that the enemy could outflank.

In the Western Hemisphere, the Soviet attempt to expand its influence in the Caribbean Basin by lending direct and indirect support to totalitarian movements in Central America is another threat to our interests. Our strategy is to provide a security assistance program to help our neighbors in their self-defense efforts and a Caribbean Basin economic program to encourage their national development. Improved defense capabilities and economic growth in the nations of Central America are equally essential if we are to prevent the internal instability the Soviets and their proxies are currently exploiting. We cannot have economic growth, social reform, democratic development, or even civil rights, if totalitarian terrorists of either the far right or the far left are free to attack civilian populations.

A companion threat in the Western Hemisphere is Cuba's ability to project air and naval forces to interfere with our resupply of NATO if a war in Europe should break out. Since 70 percent of our European-bound reinforcements must pass through the Caribbean, we need improved maritime strength there too, to guarantee their safe passage. We must also find ways to curb the growth of the Soviet military presence in Cuba.

In the postwar era the Soviet Union has become the leading, indeed the only, imperialist power on Earth, and as such has been a major obstacle to world peace and stability. Its continued occupation of Eastern Europe, its intimidation of Poland, expansion over the years in Cuba, Vietnam, the Congo, and many other parts of Africa, Korea, Afghanistan, South Yemen, Ethiopia, and Angola—to name only a few—have shown that the Soviet Union has constantly sought to expand its influence.

Emboldened by America's post-Vietnam paralysis and its own increased military capabilities, the Soviet Union has pushed its traditional policy of global expansionism to a new dimension in recent years and has emerged as a mature global power. It now has the power and reach to challenge our interests almost anywhere in the world. Soviet efforts in the Third World have increased in scope, pace, and aggressiveness. Soviet naval combatants and long range military reconnaissance aircraft routinely patrol around the globe from bases strategically located astride major trade routes and choke points. Soviet proxies are now involved in Central America, supported by Soviet military assistance. And, as recent events in Poland demonstrate, the Soviet Union is willing to use the threat of overwhelming military intervention to achieve its political objectives.

To deal with this new dimension of Soviet threat we must be prepared to halt and seek to reverse the geographic expansion of Soviet control and military presence particularly when it threatens a vital interest or further erodes the geostrategic position of the United States and its allies.

The Soviet Union is increasingly acquiring the forces for global operations and must be deterred with flexible and mobile forces. A conventional conflict beginning in southwest Asia, the Far East or other areas could now have global implications. Our strategy is to deter Soviet aggression by the prospect of a collective military response at whatever level of conflict is required.

If armed aggression should occur, naturally, our defensive actions will seek to end the conflict as quickly as possible, at the point of aggression. But if a conventional war should be forced upon us, the United States and allied forces may also have to launch counteroffensives elsewhere to restore the peace and protect our freedom. The United States may take military actions that threaten Soviet vulnerabilities critical to their prosecution of the war, should that prove necessary to restore the peace.

The point is not that we wish to fight everywhere. In fact we wish to fight nowhere. But if we are to realize that wish, we must be in a position to respond to aggression effectively where our vital interests are threatened. Our budget requests emphasize increased mobility for our forces and repair of our deficient force structure.

The loss of clear superiority means we must take strategy more seriously then ever. Today we must respond to the challenges thrust upon us by Soviet conventional forces that outnumber us, and by Soviet strategic forces that have acquired a margin of superiority over us. To ignore those facts, or to decline to discuss them is to court greater danger than we now face.

To those who say we are trying to do too much, we must ask, what should we give up?

Should we give up defense of the Central Front in Europe?

Should we give up the Caribbean?

Should we give up any attempt to defend the oil fields, so vital to Europe and Japan?

Should we give up our defense of northeast Asia?

Should we give up any other vital interests?

For history tells us, and recent history at that, that if a nation with enormous military power and a historically aggressive policy of adding to its bases and its influence throughout the world, knows that it will meet no opposition in a particular crisis—if it knows in short that there is a vacuum, it will rush in to fill that vacuum, and another vital area will be lost to the West.

A credible deterrent cannot be reinforced by good plans alone, it must be backed up by tangible military capabilities. For years we have heard about a "hollow Army," and we have heard about airplanes that cannot fly and ships that cannot sail. The American people will no longer accept a mere facade of security by deploying forces that are not combat ready, that lack necessary equipment and training, and are not backed up by an adequate mobilization potential.

One of our highest priorities is to improve the combat readiness of our military. We sought more spare parts, training, and operations and maintenance in the FY 1981 and FY 1982 budgets, and we will continue to do so. In addition, we found manpower shortages in several categories. Skilled military personnel were leaving the military for higher paying jobs in the civilian economy. To retain this pool of skilled manpower we asked for and were granted increases in military pay and reenlistment bonuses and benefits. Now the All-Volunteer Force is working extremely well. We quite literally cannot accept all who apply; and their educational level is much higher than that of those applying two years ago. Also, many more experienced and trained enlisted personnel and officers are staying in the Service, and that is a most welcome change.

We next must be able to increase the sustainability of our forces in order to balance the Soviets' ability to endure a prolonged conventional conflict. Our budgets request monies for replacement equipment, spare parts, ammunition, fuel, and other consumables as well as upgraded equipment for the Guard and Reserves. Those improvements, and our efforts to rehabilitate the industrial base, send a clear signal to the Soviets that they cannot start a conflict in the hopes of outlasting the United States.

While our funding for readiness and sustainability contributes to the improvement of our forces today, we must also invest in the future. We need to modernize our military equipment so it can deter and if necessary defend against the new generations of Soviet intermediate range nuclear and conventional weapons.

To enhance our theater deterrent, we will deploy ground launched cruise missiles and Pershing II missiles in Europe. Of course if the Soviets accept President Reagan's proposal,[6] now under negotiation at Geneva, we would not have to deploy these weapons.

To counterbalance the increasing sophistication of Soviet conventional forces, we have a program to modernize the equipment of our ground and air combat forces. These new weapons, particularly the M–1 tank, the Bradley infantry fighting vehicle and the new generation of fighter aircraft, offer the optimum combination of firepower and maneuverability required on the modern battlefield. We cannot do less in the face of the quantitative advantages and the continuing qualitative improvements in Soviet weapons.

Now it is true that the tanks and the infantry fighting vehicle took far too long to

---

[6] President Reagan's "zero option" proposal, which was outlined in his address on November 18, 1981, cited in footnote 3, *supra*, indicated that the United States was prepared to cancel the deployment in Western Europe of Pershing II and ground launch missiles scheduled for 1983 if the Soviet Union would dismantle the SS–20, SS–4, and SS–5 missiles deployed in Eastern Europe.

develop and they are extraordinarily costly. We believe we have initiated management and contract improvements which will prevent these delays and unplanned cost additions in the future; but in the meantime we cannot simply throw out 20 years of tank development and start over. We need a modern tank too much right now to do that.

The Navy will also benefit from our modernization efforts. To repair the erosion of our conventional maritime strength we have designed a program which will increase the offensive striking power of the fleet, improve day-to-day fleet readiness and sustainability, strengthen our antisubmarine and anti-air defense, and modernize our existing naval forces. In short we seek naval strength sufficient to enable us to get where we need to be, when we have to be there.

By making major increases in the number of fleet ships and aircraft, we will provide protection for our maritime trade and supply convoys to Europe and Asia, as well as improve the mobility needed for our rapid deployment forces.

To provide the measure of mobility required for conventional flexibility, we have requested additional air and sealift capabilities. The largest single increase in this year's defense budget is for airlift. We also plan to increase our fleet of refueling aircraft to sustain our airlift over longer distances.

Since we cannot halt Soviet global expansion by ourselves, this administration also seeks to revitalize our military alliances and encourage our allies to contribute more to our collective defense. Finally, we seek to provide assistance to our friends and neighbors so that they can better defend themselves and in so doing, greatly help us.

I have purposely stressed our conventional forces, since 85 percent of our budget is devoted to nonnuclear forces. Although of late our nuclear forces have received much attention in public debate, they constitute only 15 percent of our defense budget. Contrary to what some have mistakenly alleged, we do not seek to restore U.S. nuclear superiority. Consistent with our defense policy, we have taken steps to deemphasize our reliance on nuclear weapons, steps such as not locking ourselves into a "short war" posture and strengthening the flexibility and mobility of our conventional forces. We must not allow the Soviets to think they could force us to choose between initiating nuclear war or accepting the loss of vital interests.

The only way to prevent nuclear war is to make sure that no aggressor will ever think he could profit from initiating a nuclear attack; in short to make sure nuclear war could not be won. We would prefer significantly lower nuclear force levels and we are developing a program to press for genuine and verifiable arms reduction. Contrary to popular impressions, we have not, over the years, increased the number of our nuclear weapons. In fact, we have fewer nuclear warheads today than we had in 1967—not a handful fewer but thousands fewer.

The Soviets have, however, done just the opposite. They have vastly increased their raw number of warheads. But in the final analysis it is not the number of warheads alone that counts. What matters is deterrent capability, involving such factors as survivability of deterrent forces and communications systems, accuracy and yield—in short whether we could respond effectively after a Soviet first strike.

That is why the President is so right when he says a simple freeze now would leave the Soviets ahead in strategic capability. Under these circumstances the essence of deterrence would be lost. They have designed their nuclear forces in such a way that they can be interpreted only as offensive, not just as deterrent forces. We also see disturbing evidence, such as their development of a refiring capability and major expenditures for civil defense shelters, that they think they can win a nuclear war—and that is a very dangerous development.

We are modernizing our strategic forces to ensure that they are survivable. This is the purpose of the President's program for Strategic Nuclear Forces. In particular, we are making our terrestrial and space-based communications, warning, and intelligence collection systems less vulnerable to the blast and pulse radiation of nuclear detonations by shielding them and building redundant systems.

Unfortunately we must modernize and strengthen all three legs of the Triad of deterrence at the same time. We have 25-year-old bombers, 20-year-old missiles, and submarine missiles that are neither as accurate nor as able to destroy hardened Soviet targets as they should be. We want to gain deterrent stability; we are not seeking merely to accumulate more destructive power. In fact, as previously announced, we have decided to dismantle some large missiles—the old Titans—because they are no longer a reliable, survivable second strike weapon.

Only by creating a credible deterrent will we have the strength necessary to achieve genuine arms reduction and to diminish the likelihood of conflict at all levels of violence. But, genuine and verifiable major arms reductions is indeed the only sure road to reducing risks while keeping the peace. Negotiations to secure these reductions can succeed only if we enter them with strength. The Soviets must perceive they have something to gain from such negotiations.

The restoration and upgrading of our military forces is an expensive and lengthy process. So are our programs of economic and security assistance. They are particularly difficult in this economy and given the sacrifices other programs are asked to make. But it is essential that we follow this long, hard road with resolution, determination and consistency.

If I had to state the essence of the administration's defense policy in a single sentence, it would be this: we seek to deter Soviet aggression against the United States and its allies by maintaining the capability to respond effectively at the lowest possible level of violence. This is, if you will, a common theme from which all else flows:

—traditional concepts such as flexible response;

—collective security to ensure allied solidarity in providing for a common defense;

—the emphasis of the Reagan administration on improvements in conventional forces, readiness and sustainability;

—a program greatly to enhance the mobility of our forces so that they can be brought to bear even when our vital interests are threatened at places distant from our shores;

—and finally, modernization of our strategic forces to reverse dangerous and destabilizing vulnerabilities that have developed over many years of neglect.

The burdens placed upon us in implementing this first principle have grown as the Soviets, subordinating all else, have poured a staggering portion of their national wealth into the massing of military power. As the Soviets have developed their capacity to project power abroad, the number of our friends and allies vulnerable to Soviet aggression has grown. And of necessity, not because of our choice, our requirements have grown accordingly. Our objective—this first principle—is no more ambitious today than it was in years past. But the cost of meeting it—the cost of countering the expansion of Soviet military power—must inevitably reflect the magnitude of the Soviet effort.

But we clearly have the resources and the greatest incentive of all—for it is nothing more or less than our survival as a nation, and the survival of freedom. So if we have the national will and the great strength of our past, I am convinced that the future is bright with hope and promise—provided only that we keep faith in ourselves. If we take full advantage of the great assets of the Free World, if we do not prop up the Soviet economy by mistaken subsidies and transfers, if we prudently exploit the weaknesses of the obsolescent Soviet empire, the people now living in the Soviet Union shall eventually live with us in peace in a world with vastly fewer arms and vastly greater hope.

Document 3

Address by the Secretary of State (Haig) Before the Annual Meeting of the United States Chamber of Commerce, Washington, April 27, 1982[7]

American Power and American Purpose

A French philosopher captured the experience of the twentieth century when he wrote that "a modern man—and this is what makes him modern—lives with many contraries." Modern science has enlightened us about ourselves and the universe as never before. It has also given us an unprecedented capacity for self-destruction. Modern technology has offered mankind a life of comfort and prosperity unknown to previous generations. But the same industrial processes harnessed to aggression have been used twice to plunge the world into the abyss of war.

The American people have participated to the full in these changes. We have known depression and prosperity, the ordeal of war and the tranquility of peace. Long ago, Alexis de Tocqueville wrote that a "perpetual stir" prevailed in our society. Perhaps as Americans we were unusually well-suited to thrive in a century of "contraries," for our

[7] Source: Department of State Press Release 147, April 27, 1982; also printed in Department of State *Bulletin*, June 1982, pp. 40–44.

experiences have dulled neither our enthusiasm nor our desire for quick results.

Observers have questioned, however, whether this "perpetual stir" makes for sound international relations. Americans do not like to believe that problems are intractable or that achievements can only be very modest, despite the effort. It has been argued that the resulting national impatience makes American foreign policy a series of cycles, of strenuous engagements followed by disillusioned withdrawals.

In this century, we have lived through two major such periods of impatience in foreign affairs. For 20 years after the First World War, we pretended to be immune from the suffering of an interdependent world. The cost to other nations and to ourselves was enormous. Determined to avoid this mistake again, we threw ourselves eagerly after the Second World War into the creation of a new international order. As Dean Acheson described it, the task was "to create half a world, a free half . . . without blowing the whole to pieces in the process."

The successful application of American power to this purpose created the basic security framework within which we and our allies have prospered. Western Europe and Japan have recovered their economic health and political stability. A multitude of independent countries, free to pursue their own development, have emerged from the Western colonial empires, and the U.S.-Soviet rivalry had led neither to war nor to the yielding of essential Western interests.

American resources, American perseverance and American wisdom provided the crucial underpinning of this international order. But our involvement in Southeast Asia and the denigration of executive authority in the Watergate scandal raised questions about our will and leadership. American foreign policy appeared beset by uncertainty, doubt, and division.

As a consequence, the United States found it difficult to deal with the complex international situation that has emerged over the past decade. The economic growth of Western Europe and Japan, the Sino-Soviet conflict, and the transfer of wealth to the oil producers have softened the sharp edges of American and Soviet dominance over the postwar world. The global military balance, however, is still the province of the superpowers.

Today it has become essential for the United States and its allies to deal with the new realities. Three trends in particular raise crucial questions about the prospects for Western security—and international peace—for the remainder of the century.

—First, lagging Western strength. The United States has gradually lost many of the military advantages over the Soviet Union that once provided a margin of safety for the West—in some cases by choice, in others through neglect and error. Meanwhile, the Western alliance has suffered increasing political and economic strain. The cooperative impulse still exists but it would be severely strained by another decade of relative military decline or sterile economic rivalry.

—Second, the increasing interdependence of the West and the developing countries, many of which adopt a strident public stance against Western interests and ideals. The Third World has emerged in all of its diversity, with its fragile unity already fragmented by regional conflict and global rivalry. At the same time, many developing nations are threatened by the increasing strain of sudden social, political, and economic change.

—Third, the emergence of the Soviet Union as a global military power, increasingly bold in the use of its might to promote violence, notably in areas of strategic significance to the West. This trend has developed even as the Communist bloc, once the instrument of Soviet purposes, has been shaken by the Sino-Soviet schism and growing internal problems. Chronic economic failure has eroded the appeal of Marxist-Leninist ideology.

Let us ask ourselves, as others are surely asking about us, whether we can change these trends.

—Can we increase our strength and improve our collaboration with our allies?

—Can the West and the developing countries find common interests?

—Can we create a more constructive relationship with the Soviet Union marked by greater Soviet restraint?

I believe that we can do these things. We can safeguard the legacy of Western values and achievements. And we can go beyond the postwar vision of half a world free toward a whole world of greater liberty, more peaceful change, and increasing economic progress.

The American people have emerged from their recent experiences convinced anew that there is no substitute for American leadership if we are to live in a world hospitable to our society and our values. In the 1980's, this new American consensus for a more vigorous defense of our interests demands a new balance in the style of our foreign policy. If we forsake ideals to manipulate interests, then America's sense of right will be offended. If we forsake power in order to pursue pieties, then America's sense of reality will be challenged.

A balanced American foreign policy, sustained by this consensus, will enable America to lead once again. But we must understand the complexities of our time if we are to move with the sureness and sensitivity that befits our historic responsibilities. There are opportunities to act, to navigate the sea of troubles to a safer and calmer water.

First, our relationship with our allies. We cannot pretend to lead unless we rally to our side those societies that share our values. The foundation of American foreign policy throughout the postwar era has been our partnership with the Atlantic Alliance and Japan. Sheltered by common security arrangements, and nourished by democratic values, we and our allies have created the most prosperous societies known to mankind. These historic achievements are the product of our joint labors, our sense of unity, and our strength.

We must recognize, however, that the trends of the past decade have contributed to a rising sense of frustration between the United States and its partners. U.S.-European relations, in particular, have been distressed by the convergence of several events:

—The loss of American strategic superiority and questions about the role of nuclear weapons in NATO strategy.

—Increasing European political and economic stakes in détente and East–West trade, despite aggressive Soviet actions in Afghanistan, Poland, and elsewhere.

—The recent record of low growth and high inflation among the industrial democracies leading to pressure for protectionist measures.

Angered by what they see as European reluctance to face the Soviet challenge, some Americans have been tempted to argue for withdrawal of American forces. Others, disturbed by persistent economic problems, have thought to retaliate by erecting protectionist barriers.

Those who advocate such actions ignore Churchill's admonition that "the only thing worse than fighting with allies is fighting without them." Not a single problem in the Atlantic relationship—diplomatic, military, or economic—can be resolved by unilateral American action. Let us ask ourselves—on both sides of the Atlantic—some fundamental questions. Does our alliance strengthen our security or weaken it? Do our ties increase our prosperity or diminish it? Do we improve the prospects for democracy and freedom in the world by working together or by going our separate ways?

The answer to these questions today is the same as that given over three decades ago by the generation whose lives were blighted by world war. The Atlantic Alliance is the foundation of our security. It is still the basic building block of a more peaceful and prosperous world, and its breakdown would make disaster for the industrial democracies inevitable.

These are the stakes—and our opportunity—for the eighties. Either the alliance goes forward together toward greater cooperation or the prospects of all its members will be darkened. But if we are to advance, it is high time that our dialogue proceeded on the basis of fact, especially the fact of who is doing what to sustain the common defense.

Arguments over burden sharing are second nature to any large alliance of sovereign nations. The current transatlantic exchanges, however, must be put in historical perspective. Americans should not forget that our NATO Allies substantially increased their defense spending over the past decade, while the United States was reducing its defense effort. Nor should we ignore that the European members of NATO supply a high percentage of the air, ground, and naval forces that constitute the conventional portion of deterrence in Europe. Even worldwide, the contributions of NATO Allies and Japan are an important and growing component of defense.

This is not to underestimate the very serious problems we face. We all need to do more together. But our joint concern for the common defense, rather than finger-pointing, should dominate the dialogue.

In the days ahead, as we and our allies discuss outstanding issues, the United States must exert not only strong but coherent leadership. The allies must know where we are going if we expect them to go with us. Their policies, especially in dealing with the Soviet Union, reflect not only differing perspectives of Soviet actions but also a tendency to hedge their bets against American swings between détente and confrontation.

The allies, for their part, must develop a broader vision and a sense of responsibility consonant with their interests and strength. They cannot expect the United States to carry the same share of the burden when our respective capabilities have changed and their own desire for influence has grown.

Much of our agenda will be dominated by the search for more constructive relations with the East. This search, arms control, and the military balance are all interrelated, not independent and sometimes competing objectives. It is essential that we carry out NATO's two-track decision of 1979,[8] to go forward with the modernization of intermediate-range nuclear systems while simultaneously pursuing arms control negotiations with the Soviet Union designed to limit these systems.

For too long, we have pretended that a relaxation of tensions in Europe would be immune to Soviet attempts to change the balance of power. For too long, we have imagined that the arms control process, in and of itself, could preserve that balance. Deterrence in the eighties will require painful sacrifices by every member of the alliance, but if we fail to pay the price now, we shall have neither a lasting improvement of relations with the East nor a meaningful reduction of arms.

Our collective economic well-being also demands sacrifices from each nation. We cannot afford a repetition of those unresolved quarrels that so damaged the international economic system in the 1930's. In this area, as in others, if we do not progress together we shall each suffer separately.

Finally, we should be conscious of our historic responsibilities as free societies in a world where individual liberty is too often suppressed. There is a tendency in the West to use a double standard in our judgment of international behavior. The advocates of freedom and democracy are subjected to a supercritical standard while the advocates of totalitarianism are given the benefit of the doubt. How much energy is spent criticizing and impugning the democratic revolution while rationalizing and forgiving the assaults of its enemies. Let us be clear about the consequences of this attitude. An alliance divided in its moral purposes and corroded by distrust of its own motivations cannot long endure.

A stronger, more cooperative alliance is an objective surely within our reach. Over the past 30 years, we have grappled successfully with numerous political, economic, military, and moral problems. Our cooperative institutions still exist. But it is time for the United States and its allies to grasp the nettles that obstruct the future.

Let me turn now to another major area where we have a great opportunity for change: our relations with the developing nations. It is one of the ironies of our age that as nations have become more powerful their destinies have grown more interdependent. Together, we and the leaders of the developing countries have an opportunity to make sure that this interdependence is a source of mutual benefit, founded on the solid ground of common interest. The consequences of failure to cooperate would be disastrous for both America and the Third World. But such cooperation must be based on the diverse realities of the present, not the slogans of the past.

The so-called "Third World" includes the oil-rich OPEC nations, the miracle growth rate Singapores, numerous countries utterly impoverished, and many that fit no category. Neither the fading memory of the struggle against imperialism nor the anti-Western tinge of many Third World pronouncements can suppress numerous differences in interests and perspectives. Beneath the surface, new opportunities for economic and political cooperation with the West are being seized by individual Third World states in ever more practical ways.

Such a situation calls for sensitivity and sophistication on our part if we are to expand our links with developing countries. We hold all sovereign states responsible for what they say and do. But we also must recognize the complex equations of economic and political survival in developing nations. Neither we nor they can afford ideological stereotypes in cases where they do not fit.

Another dimension of the Third World's diversity is violent conflict. Ethnic rivalries

---

[8] The "two-track" decision was taken by the NATO Foreign Ministers meeting in council at Brussels in December 1979. The first track called for the deployment of long-range theater nuclear forces in Europe. The second track was the determination to pursue simultaneously arms reduction negotiations with the Soviet Union. The text of the final communiqué, issued by the NATO Council on December 14, 1979, is printed in *American Foreign Policy: Basic Documents, 1977–1980*, pp. 496–499.

and territorial divisions, themselves potent sources of trouble, are being exploited by the Soviets and their allies. The United States, working with our Western and regional partners, can do much to help resolve such conflicts. But we should not succumb to the illusion that quick fixes are ready to hand.

The illusion of the quick fix is especially irrelevant to the vast economic crisis and tremendous economic potential that characterize so many of the developing nations. Both we and the nations of the Third World have learned that progress cannot simply be imported. Ultimately the productive forces of each society will make the difference between success and failure.

The leaders of the developing countries are therefore challenged today to deal with economic crises in the midst of economic potential by different and more pragmatic methods. The domestic economy, the international economic system, and political purposes must be brought into greater harmony. In part, this means that many leaders wedded to particular ideologies will have to recognize that their prescriptions are suffocating the chances for self-reliance and broad-based growth. But we in the developed world should also realize that growing economic insecurity is hardly conducive to either political stability or the fostering of democratic institutions.

The realities of diversity, conflict, and great potential are bringing about a crucial shift in the attitudes of many Third World nations. Their leaders face excruciating choices. Marxist-Leninist ideology has often been the locomotive that brought them to power but it has not become an engine for progress. The challenges of economic and social change cannot be overcome perpetually by the resort to archaic slogans and brutal coercion.

As a consequence, many countries with direct experience of the Soviet embrace are quietly attempting to broaden their relations, to encourage foreign investment, and to reduce dependence on a patron who has little to offer but the tools and techniques of violence. There is growing awareness among erstwhile skeptics in the developing world that it is the West which holds the best hope of negotiating—and the most incentive to negotiate—peaceful solutions to regional conflicts.

Such a convergence of interests offers a unique opportunity to create more constructive and beneficial ties between the West and the developing countries. If we do not seize this opportunity, today's leaders in the search for better relations with the West could well become tomorrow's victims in a more poisonous atmosphere of recrimination, economic slide, and armed conflict. Only our adversaries would be the beneficiaries.

Finally, our country faces an historic opportunity in dealing with the Soviet Union. The necessity to grasp the "contraries" and complexities of our era, even as we seek to pursue our purposes, is nowhere more critical than in relations between the two superpowers. This is nothing less than a challenge to our national survival—to the values that make life worth living as well as our physical existence.

The politics of the late twentieth century are still dominated by the struggle between two philosophies of justice and national power. In the name of a utopian ideal, Soviet totalitarianism imposes a single social model not only on its own people but on an expanding empire. In contrast, the forces of democracy seek to build national and international institutions based on diversity, individual choice, and peaceful change. The competition between these two approaches will continue.

This rivalry, however, is constrained by another central fact of our time—nuclear weapons. Total victory by military means has become a formula for mutual catastrophe. Even the use of conventional force risks unpredictable consequences.

Our enduring challenge is, therefore, to develop and to sustain a relationship with the Soviet Union which recognizes that the competition will proceed, but constrains the use or threat of force. We can develop a lasting framework for this relationship if we avoid the extremes that have distorted American foreign policy over the postwar period:

—First, that expressions of American good will and readiness to negotiate could somehow substitute for American strength and would move U.S.-Soviet relations from competition to cooperation.

—Second, that a posture of confrontation, a refusal to negotiate would somehow lead to capitulation by the other superpower.

We are living today with the consequences of this imbalanced approach, in particular, the legacy of a decade when negotiations often seemed to be a substitute for strength. Dominated by the psychology of Vietnam and rising domestic resistance to military programs, we fell into the easy belief that negotiations were not only an alternative to the balance of power but were also proof, in and of themselves, of an expanding community of interests with the USSR. Too few noticed and understood that détente did not alter Soviet priorities. Even as the West sought a reduction in tensions, the Soviet Union expanded its military forces.

The result of America's wishful thinking and profound national introspection has been swift and sure. Moscow has acted forcibly to expand its dominions. In Vietnam, in Kampuchea, in southern Africa and Ethiopia, in Afghanistan, and now in Central America, we have reaped the grim harvest of self-delusion.

As we rebuild our strength and seek once more to convince the Soviet Union that restraint is in our mutual interest, we must not allow ourselves the error of another extreme. We cannot claim that we are too weak to negotiate and at the same time insist that we are strong enough for a policy of all-out confrontation. Nothing is gained by appearing to fear diplomatic discussions—neither leverage over the Soviets, nor the respect and confidence of our allies. We can no more solve our problems by avoiding the negotiating table, than by resting our hopes upon it alone.

An American approach to the Soviet Union that balances strength and negotiations offers the best hope of significant accomplishment. We must place our policy in the context of important changes that are taking place in the world and in the Soviet empire that may make Moscow more amenable to the virtues of restraint. The Soviet attempt to change the balance of power has produced a backlash of increasing international resistance. The American people have shown that they will not accept military inferiority. Moscow has earned the fear and enmity of many nonaligned states through aggression in Afghanistan and support for Vietnam's subjugation of Kampuchea.

This backlash comes when Soviet prospects have dimmed. Moscow's allies are in deep economic trouble and the Soviet growth rate itself is declining. Agricultural shortfalls persist. Above all, as Poland has shown, the Soviet model and Soviet ideology are increasingly rejected by the workers themselves.

Over the decade of the 1980's, as the Soviet Union experiences a transition in leadership, it is likely to face greater economic difficulties and growing international isolation—a marked change from an era of unusual stability and expansion. This reality will contrast even more sharply than before with Moscow's carefully cultivated image of a progressive and peace-loving regime. The Soviet people themselves cannot remain entirely unaffected by the calls for peace and disarmament so avidly aimed by the Kremlin at the West. As a consequence, the Soviet leaders may find it increasingly difficult to sustain the status quo at home while exporting a failed ideology abroad.

During this sensitive and dangerous period of changing superpower relationships, the United States must make clear to the Soviet Union that there are penalties for aggression and incentives for restraint. We cannot conduct business as usual in the face of Soviet adventurism in Afghanistan or Soviet-instigated repression in Poland. But we have also held out the prospect of significant help for Poland if the reform process is renewed. And we are prepared to show Soviet leaders that international moderation can help them face painful domestic dilemmas through broader relations with the United States and other Western countries.

We must also create new realities in the military balance and in regions of crisis to encourage the Soviet Union to accept the need for moderation in its own interest. This is the objective of our new defense programs and of our diplomatic initiatives in areas such as southern Africa, the Middle East, and the Caribbean. Meanwhile, we will continue to probe Soviet willingness to engage in negotiations geared to achieve concrete results, recognizing that progress in all of these areas and arms control is inevitably affected by Soviet conduct and the climate of East–West relations.

An essential part of our strategy is to continue to differentiate among Communist countries themselves. This is a long-standing American policy that encourages autonomy and diversity. It responds not only to a natural sense of national independence but also the evolution of political pluralism.

Finally, just as the Soviet Union gives active support to Marxist-Leninist forces in the West and the South, we must give vigorous support to democratic forces wherever they are located—including countries which are now Communist. We should not hesitate to promote our own values, knowing that the freedom and dignity of man are the ideals that motivate the quest for social justice. A free press, free trade unions, free political parties, freedom to travel, and freedom to create are the ingredients of the democratic revolution of the future, not the status quo of a failed past. We want the competition of democracy and communism to be conducted in peaceful and political terms but we will provide other means if the Soviet Union insists upon violent methods of struggle. There must be a single standard.

In sum, the facts do not support the belief that there can be an early, sudden, or dramatic reconciliation of Soviet and American interests. The competition will continue. But we can make the Soviets more cautious by our action, and as a new generation of Soviet leaders emerges, we can signal the benefits of greater restraint. A balanced and persistent American policy, cognizant of both Soviet strengths and weaknesses, can gradually reduce the dangers inherent in the struggle between the two superpowers.

As the end of the twentieth century approaches, let us ask ourselves about the direction of events. Over the past decade, have we moved closer to our goal of a freer and more peaceful world? Unfortunately, many would answer no. Do we have the means, the will, and the skill to shape one? Surely the answer is yes.

To reach our goal is not only a matter of arms, though we need them. It is not only a matter of interests to defend, though defend them we must. And it cannot only be a matter of one framework or another, though our power must be disciplined. The most brilliant conception counts for little without the persistence to pursue it.

Ultimately, a foreign policy is the test of a nation's character. Today, the test of our character is whether we care enough about the values that make life worth living, the inner beliefs that have sustained Western civilization. Over the centuries, a certain idea of man has taken hold in our societies. The right of the individual, the responsibility of government to the governed, and the rule of law have distinguished our way of life. These ideals are the true source of our strength and the true source of the weakness of our adversaries.

A society where men are not free to speak their minds, where the dignity of the worker is denied, where the community's effort is poured into the weapons of war, is both unnatural and repugnant. In contrast, free expression by the one or by the many keeps our governments flexible and alert. Words, thoughts, and votes are the foundation of consent, not the police power of the state. And the resources reluctantly devoted to defense are subjected rightly to the most stringent examination and justification.

These ideals are by no means ours alone. They have universal appeal. Our material achievements are admired and emulated. But the power of Western science and technology comes from the power of ideas. The people of the world hunger for our ideas even as they seek the benefits of our machines. Yet if we do not care for our own values, we cannot expect others to respect them—or to respect us.

History teaches us that progress is not inevitable. Liberty and democracy have often been denied and peoples have been forcibly regimented to the dictates of mistaken philosophies. But if we have learned anything from this troubled century, it is, as Churchill declared, that only the swift gathering of forces to confront military and moral aggression can preserve the peace. Such a swift gathering of forces will enable us to create a whole world, a free world, without blowing it to pieces in the process. American power must be bent to this purpose.

Document 4

Address by President Reagan to the British Parliament, London, June 8, 1982[9]

Promoting Democracy and Peace

My Lord Chancellor, Mr. Speaker: The journey of which this visit forms a part is a long one. Already it has taken me to two great cities of the West, Rome and Paris, and to the economic summit at Versailles. And there, once again, our sister democra-

---

[9] Source: *Weekly Compilation of Presidential Documents*, June 14, 1982, pp. 764–770. The President spoke at 12:14 p.m. in the Royal Gallery at the Palace of Westminster. The President's visit to London was the third stop on a European trip which began in Paris on June 4, where an economic summit conference was held at Versailles on June 5 and 6, and Rome on June 7. For documentation dealing with the President's trip, which also took him to Bonn and Berlin, see Chapter 4; Chapter 5, Part F; and Chapter 10, Parts D and H.

cies have proved that even in a time of severe economic strain, free peoples can work together freely and voluntarily to address problems as serious as inflation, unemployment, trade, and economic development in a spirit of cooperation and solidarity.

Other milestones lie ahead. Later this week, in Germany, we and our NATO allies will discuss measures for our joint defense and America's latest initiatives for a more peaceful, secure world through arms reductions.

Each stop of this trip is important, but among them all, this moment occupies a special place in my heart and in the hearts of my countrymen—a moment of kinship and homecoming in these hallowed halls.

Speaking for all Americans, I want to say how very much at home we feel in your house. Every American would, because this is, as we have been so eloquently told, one of democracy's shrines. Here the rights of free people and the processes of representation have been debated and refined.

It has been said that an institution is the lengthening shadow of a man. This institution is the lengthening shadow of all the men and women who have sat here and all those who have voted to send representatives here.

This is my second visit to Great Britain as President of the United States. My first opportunity to stand on British soil occurred almost a year and a half ago when your Prime Minister graciously hosted a diplomatic dinner at the British Embassy in Washington. Mrs. Thatcher said then that she hoped I was not distressed to find staring down at me from the grand staircase a portrait of His Royal Majesty King George III. She suggested it was best to let bygones be bygones, and in view of our two countries' remarkable friendship in succeeding years, she added that most Englishmen today would agree with Thomas Jefferson that "a little rebellion now and then is a very good thing." [*Laughter*][10]

Well, from here I will go to Bonn and then Berlin, where there stands a grim symbol of power untamed. The Berlin Wall, that dreadful gray gash across the city, is in its third decade. It is the fitting signature of the regime that built it.

And a few hundred kilometers behind the Berlin Wall, there is another symbol. In the center of Warsaw, there is a sign that notes the distances to two capitals. In one direction it points toward Moscow. In the other it points toward Brussels, headquarters of Western Europe's tangible unity. The marker says that the distances from Warsaw to Moscow and Warsaw to Brussels are equal. The sign makes this point: Poland is not East or West. Poland is at the center of European civilization. It has contributed mightily to that civilization. It is doing so today by being magnificently unreconciled to oppression.

Poland's struggle to be Poland and to secure the basic rights we often take for granted demonstrates why we dare not take those rights for granted. Gladstone, defending the Reform Bill of 1866, declared, "You cannot fight against the future. Time is on our side." It was easier to believe in the march of democracy in Gladstone's day—in that high noon of Victorian optimism.

We're approaching the end of a bloody century plagued by a terrible political invention—totalitarianism. Optimism comes less easily today, not because democracy is less vigorous, but because democracy's enemies have refined their instruments of repression. Yet optimism is in order, because day by day democracy is proving itself to be a not-at-all-fragile flower. From Stettin on the Baltic to Varna on the Black Sea, the regimes planted by totalitarianism have had more than 30 years to establish their legitimacy. But none—not one regime—has yet been able to risk free elections. Regimes planted by bayonets do not take root.

The strength of the Solidarity movement in Poland demonstrates the truth told in an underground joke in the Soviet Union. It is that the Soviet Union would remain a one-party nation even if an opposition party were permitted, because everyone would join the opposition party. [*Laughter*]

America's time as a player on the stage of world history has been brief. I think understanding this fact has always made you patient with your younger cousins—well, not always patient. I do recall that on one occasion, Sir Winston Churchill said in exasperation about one of our most distinguished diplomats: "He is the only case I know of a bull who carries his china shop with him." [*Laughter*]

But witty as Sir Winston was, he also had that special attribute of great statesmen—the gift of vision, the willingness to see the future based on the experience of the past. It is this sense of history, this understanding

---

[10] All brackets appear in the source text.

of the past that I want to talk with you about today, for it is in remembering what we share of the past that our two nations can make common cause for the future.

We have not inherited an easy world. If developments like the Industrial Revolution, which began here in England, and the gifts of science and technology have made life much easier for us, they have also made it more dangerous. There are threats now to our freedom, indeed to our very existence, that other generations could never even have imagined.

There is first the threat of global war. No President, no Congress, no Prime Minister, no Parliament can spend a day entirely free of this threat. And I don't have to tell you that in today's world the existence of nuclear weapons could mean, if not the extinction of mankind, then surely the end of civilization as we know it. That's why negotiations on intermediate-range nuclear forces now underway in Europe and the START talks—Strategic Arms Reduction Talks—which will begin later this month, are not just critical to American or Western policy; they are critical to mankind. Our commitment to early success in these negotiations is firm and unshakable, and our purpose is clear: reducing the risk of war by reducing the means of waging war on both sides.

At the same time there is a threat posed to human freedom by the enormous power of the modern state. History teaches the dangers of government that overreaches—political control taking precedence over free economic growth, secret police, mindless bureaucracy, all combining to stifle individual excellence and personal freedom.

Now, I'm aware that among us here and throughout Europe there is legitimate disagreement over the extent to which the public sector should play a role in a nation's economy and life. But on one point all of us are united—our abhorrence of dictatorship in all its forms, but most particularly totalitarianism and the terrible inhumanities it has caused in our time—the great purge, Auschwitz and Dachau, the Gulag, and Cambodia.

Historians looking back at our time will note the consistent restraint and peaceful intentions of the West. They will note that it was the democracies who refused to use the threat of their nuclear monopoly in the forties and early fifties for territorial or imperial gain. Had that nuclear monopoly been in the hands of the Communist world, the map of Europe—indeed, the world—would look very different today. And certainly they will note it was not the democracies that invaded Afghanistan or suppressed Polish Solidarity or used chemical and toxin warfare in Afghanistan and Southeast Asia.

If history teaches anything it teaches self-delusion in the face of unpleasant facts is folly. We see around us today the marks of our terrible dilemma—predictions of doomsday, antinuclear demonstrations, an arms race in which the West must, for its own protection, be an unwilling participant. At the same time we see totalitarian forces in the world who seek subversion and conflict around the globe to further their barbarous assault on the human spirit. What, then, is our course? Must civilization perish in a hail of fiery atoms? Must freedom wither in a quiet, deadening accommodation with totalitarian evil?

Sir Winston Churchill refused to accept the inevitability of war or even that it was imminent. He said, "I do not believe that Soviet Russia desires war. What they desire is the fruits of war and the indefinite expansion of their power and doctrines. But what we have to consider here today while time remains is the permanent prevention of war and the establishment of conditions of freedom and democracy as rapidly as possible in all countries."

Well, this is precisely our mission today: to preserve freedom as well as peace. It may not be easy to see; but I believe we live now at a turning point.

In an ironic sense Karl Marx was right. We are witnessing today a great revolutionary crisis, a crisis where the demands of the economic order are conflicting directly with those of the political order. But the crisis is happening not in the free, non-Marxist West, but in the home of Marxist-Leninism, the Soviet Union. It is the Soviet Union that runs against the tide of history by denying human freedom and human dignity to its citizens. It also is in deep economic difficulty. The rate of growth in the national product has been steadily declining since the fifties and is less than half of what it was then.

The dimensions of this failure are astounding: A country which employs one-fifth of its population in agriculture is unable to feed its own people. Were it not for the private sector, the tiny private sector tolerated in Soviet agriculture, the country might be on the brink of famine. These private plots occupy a bare 3 percent of the arable land but account for nearly one-quarter of Soviet farm output and nearly one-third of meat products and vegetables. Overcentralized, with little or no incentives, year after year the Soviet system pours its best resource into the making of instruments of destruction. The constant shrinkage of economic growth combined with the growth of military production is putting a heavy strain on the Soviet people. What we see here is a political structure that no longer corresponds to its economic base, a society where productive forces are hampered by political ones.

The decay of the Soviet experiment should come as no surprise to us. Wherever the comparisons have been made between free and closed societies—West Germany and East Germany, Austria and Czechoslovakia, Malaysia and Vietnam—it is the democratic countries that are prosperous and responsive to the needs of their people. And one of the simple but overwhelming facts of our time is this: Of all the millions of refugees we've seen in the modern world, their flight is always away from, not toward the Communist world. Today on the NATO line, our military forces face east to prevent a possible invasion. On the other side of the line, the Soviet forces also face east to prevent their people from leaving.

The hard evidence of totalitarian rule has caused in mankind an uprising of the intellect and will. Whether it is the growth of the new schools of economics in America or England or the appearance of the so-called new philosophers in France, there is one unifying thread running through the intellectual work of these groups—rejection of the arbitrary power of the state, the refusal to subordinate the rights of the individual to the superstate, the realization that collectivism stifles all the best human impulses.

Since the exodus from Egypt, historians have written of those who sacrificed and struggled for freedom—the stand at Thermopylae, the revolt of Spartacus, the storming of the Bastille, the Warsaw uprising in World War II. More recently we've seen evidence of this same human impulse in one of the developing nations in Central America. For months and months the world news media covered the fighting in El Salvador. Day after day we were treated to stories and film slanted toward the brave freedom-fighters battling oppressive government forces in behalf of the silent, suffering people of that tortured country.

And then one day those silent, suffering people were offered a chance to vote, to choose the kind of government they wanted. Suddenly the freedom-fighters in the hills were exposed for what they really are—Cuban-backed guerrillas who want power for themselves, and their backers, not democracy for the people. They threatened death to any who voted, and destroyed hundreds of buses and trucks to keep the people from getting to the polling places. But on election day, the people of El Salvador, an unprecedented 1.4 million of them, braved ambush and gunfire, and trudged for miles to vote for freedom.

They stood for hours in the hot sun waiting for their turn to vote. Members of our Congress who went there as observers told me of a women who was wounded by rifle fire on the way to the polls, who refused to leave the line to have her wound treated until after she had voted. A grandmother, who had been told by the guerrillas she would be killed when she returned from the polls, and she told the guerrillas, "You can kill me, you can kill my family, kill my neighbors, but you can't kill us all." The real freedom-fighters of El Salvador turned out to be the people of that country—the young, the old, the in-between.

Strange, but in my own country there's been little if any news coverage of that war since the election. Now, perhaps they'll say it's—well, because there are newer struggles now.

On distant islands in the South Atlantic young men are fighting for Britain. And, yes, voices have been raised protesting their sacrifice for lumps of rock and earth so far away. But those young men aren't fighting for mere real estate. They fight for a cause—for the belief that armed aggression must not be allowed to succeed, and the people must participate in the decisions of government—[*applause*]—the decisions of government under the rule of law. If there had been firmer support for that principle some 45 years ago, perhaps our generation wouldn't have suffered the bloodletting of World War II.

In the Middle East now the guns sound once more, this time in Lebanon, a country that for too long has had to endure the tragedy of civil war, terrorism, and foreign intervention and occupation. The fighting in Lebanon on the part of all parties must stop, and Israel should bring its forces home. But this is not enough. We must all work to stamp out the scourge of terrorism that in the Middle East makes war an ever-present threat.

But beyond the troublespots lies a deeper, more positive pattern. Around the world today, the democratic revolution is gathering new strength. In India a critical test has been passed with the peaceful change of governing political parties. In Africa, Nigeria is moving in remarkable and unmistakable ways to build and strengthen its democratic institutions. In the Caribbean and Central America, 16 of 24 countries have freely elected governments. And in the United Nations, 8 of the 10 developing nations which have joined that body in the past 5 years are democracies.

In the Communist world as well, man's instinctive desire for freedom and self-determination surfaces again and again. To be sure, there are grim reminders of how brutally the police state attempts to snuff out this quest for self-rule—1953 in East Germany, 1956 in Hungary, 1968 in Czechoslovakia, 1981 in Poland. But the struggle continues in Poland. And we know that there are even those who strive and suffer for freedom within the confines of the Soviet Union itself. How we conduct ourselves here in the Western democracies will determine whether this trend continues.

No, democracy is not a fragile flower. Still it needs cultivating. If the rest of this century is to witness the gradual growth of freedom and democratic ideals, we must take actions to assist the campaign for democracy.

Some argue that we should encourage democratic change in right-wing dictatorships, but not in Communist regimes. Well, to accept this preposterous notion—as some well-meaning people have—is to invite the argument that once countries achieve a nuclear capability, they should be allowed an undisturbed reign of terror over their own citizens. We reject this course.

As for the Soviet view, Chairman Brezhnev repeatedly has stressed that the competition of ideas and systems must continue and that this is entirely consistent with relaxation of tensions and peace.

Well, we ask only that these systems begin by living up to their own constitutions, abiding by their own laws, and complying with the international obligations they have undertaken. We ask only for a process, a direction, a basic code of decency, not for an instant transformation.

We cannot ignore the fact that even without our encouragement there has been and will continue to be repeated explosions against repression and dictatorships. The Soviet Union itself is not immune to this reality. Any system is inherently unstable that has no peaceful means to legitimize its leaders. In such cases, the very repressiveness of the state ultimately drives people to resist it, if necessary, by force.

While we must be cautious about forcing the pace of change, we must not hesitate to declare our ultimate objectives and to take concrete actions to move toward them. We must be staunch in our conviction that freedom is not the sole prerogative of a lucky few, but the inalienable and universal right of all human beings. So states the United Nations Universal Declaration of Human Rights, which, among other things, guarantees free elections.

The objective I propose is quite simple to state: to foster the infrastructure of democracy, the system of a free press, unions, political parties, universities, which allows a people to choose their own way to develop their own culture, to reconcile their own differences through peaceful means.

This is not cultural imperialism, it is providing the means for genuine self-determination and protection for diversity. Democracy already flourishes in countries with very different cultures and historical experiences. It would be cultural condescension, or worse, to say that any people prefer dictatorship to democracy. Who would voluntarily choose not to have the right to vote, decide to purchase government propaganda handouts instead of independent newspapers, prefer government to worker-controlled unions, opt for land to be owned by the state instead of those who till it, want government repression of religious liberty, a single political party instead of a free choice, a rigid cultural orthodoxy instead of democratic tolerance and diversity?

Since 1917 the Soviet Union has given covert political training and assistance to Marxist-Leninists in many countries. Of course, it also has promoted the use of violence and subversion by these same forces. Over the past several decades, West European and other Social Democrats, Christian Democrats, and leaders have offered open assistance to fraternal, political, and social institutions to bring about peaceful and democratic progress. Appropriately, for a vigorous new democracy, the Federal Republic of Germany's political foundations have become a major force in this effort.

We in America now intend to take additional steps, as many of our allies have already done, toward realizing this same goal. The chairmen and other leaders of the national Republican and Democratic Party organizations are initiating a study with the bipartisan American political foundation to determine how the United States can best contribute as a nation to the global campaign for democracy now gathering force. They will have the cooperation of congressional leaders of both parties, along with representatives of business, labor, and other major institutions in our society. I look forward to receiving their recommendations and to working with these institutions and the Congress in the common task of strengthening democracy throughout the world.

It is time that we committed ourselves as a nation—in both the public and private sectors—to assisting democratic development.

We plan to consult with leaders of other nations as well. There is a proposal before the Council of Europe to invite parliamentarians from democratic countries to a meeting next year in Strasbourg. That prestigious gathering could consider ways to help democratic political movements.

This November in Washington there will take place an international meeting on free elections. And next spring there will be a conference of world authorities on constitutionalism and self-government hosted by the Chief Justice of the United States. Authorities from a number of developing and developed countries—judges, philosophers, and politicians with practical experience—have agreed to explore how to turn principle into practice and further the rule of law.

At the same time, we invite the Soviet Union to consider with us how the competition of ideas and values—which it is committed to support—can be conducted on a peaceful and reciprocal basis. For example, I am prepared to offer President Brezhnev an opportunity to speak to the American people on our television if he will allow me the same opportunity with the Soviet people. We also suggest that panels of our newsmen periodically appear on each other's television to discuss major events.

Now, I don't wish to sound overly optimistic, yet the Soviet Union is not immune from the reality of what is going on in the world. It has happened in the past—a small ruling elite either mistakenly attempts to ease domestic unrest through greater repression and foreign adventure, or it chooses a wiser course. It begins to allow its people a voice in their own destiny. Even if this latter process is not realized soon, I believe the renewed strength of the democratic movement, complemented by a global campaign for freedom, will strengthen the prospects for arms control and a world at peace.

I have discussed on other occasions, including my address on May 9th,[11] the elements of Western policies toward the Soviet Union to safeguard our interests and protect the peace. What I am describing now is a plan and a hope for the long term—the march of freedom and democracy which will leave Marxism-Leninism on the ash-heap of history as it has left other tyrannies which stifle the freedom and muzzle the self-expression of the people. And that's why we must continue our efforts to strengthen NATO even as we move forward with our Zero-Option initiative in the negotiations on intermediate-range forces and our proposal for a one-third reduction in strategic ballistic missile warheads.

Our military strength is a prerequisite to peace, but let it be clear we maintain this strength in the hope it will never be used, for the ultimate determinant in the struggle that's now going on in the world will not be bombs and rockets, but a test of wills and ideas, a trial of spiritual resolve, the values we hold, the beliefs we cherish, the ideals to which we are dedicated.

The British people know that, given strong leadership, time and a little bit of hope, the forces of good ultimately rally and triumph over evil. Here among you is the cradle of self-government, the Mother of Parliaments. Here is the enduring greatness of the British contribution to mankind, the great civilized ideas: individual liberty, representative government, and the rule of law under God.

I've often wondered about the shyness of some of us in the West about standing for these ideals that have done so much to ease the plight of man and the hardships of our imperfect world. This reluctance to use those vast resources at our command reminds me of the elderly lady whose home was bombed in the Blitz. As the rescuers moved about, they found a bottle of brandy she'd stored behind the staircase, which was all that was left standing. And since she was barely conscious, one of the workers pulled the cork to give her a taste of it. She came around immediately and said, "Here now—there now, put it back. That's for emergencies." [*Laughter*]

---

[11] For the text of President Reagan's address on May 9 at Eureka College on arms control and the future of East–West relations, see document 44.

Well, the emergency is upon us. Let us be shy no longer. Let us go to our strength. Let us offer hope. Let us tell the world that a new age is not only possible but probable.

During the dark days of the Second World War, when this island was incandescent with courage, Winston Churchill exclaimed about Britain's adversaries, "What kind of a people do they think we are?" Well, Britain's adversaries found out what extraordinary people the British are. But all the democracies paid a terrible price for allowing the dictators to underestimate us. We dare not make that mistake again. So, let us ask ourselves, "What kind of people do we think we are?" And let us answer, "Free people, worthy of freedom and determined not only to remain so but to help others gain their freedom as well."

Sir Winston led his people to great victory in war and then lost an election just as the fruits of victory were about to be enjoyed. But he left office honorably, and, as it turned out, temporarily, knowing that the liberty of his people was more important than the fate of any single leader. History recalls his greatness in ways no dictator will ever know. And he left us a message of hope for the future, as timely now as when he first uttered it, as opposition leader in the Commons nearly 27 years ago, when he said, "When we look back on all the perils through which we have passed and at the mighty foes that we have laid low and all the dark and deadly designs that we have frustrated, why should we fear for our future? We have," he said, "come safely through the worst."

Well, the task I've set forth will long outlive our own generation. But together, we too have come through the worst. Let us now begin a major effort to secure the best—a crusade for freedom that will engage the faith and fortitude of the next generation. For the sake of peace and justice, let us move toward a world in which all people are at last free to determine their own destiny.

Thank you.

Document 5

Statement by the Secretary of State-Designate (Shultz) Before the Senate Foreign Relations Committee, July 13, 1982 (Extract)[12]

The U.S. Role in World Affairs

. . . .

Mr. Chairman,[13] for those of us who have spent the better part of our lives watching America's deepening involvement in the world around us, it is easy to forget that the United States has throughout most of its history only episodically been concerned with foreign affairs. The world of 40 or so years ago seems almost nostalgically simple in comparison to the complexities we confront today.

In the decades that have passed, scores of new nations, many with frustrated aspirations, have achieved independence. The international economy is no longer managed from a few world capitals but has developed into a global network of mutually dependent partners. Extensive trade in goods and services, the international flow of critical raw materials, the emergence of new technologies, and the revolution in communications have created a world in which no nation is immune from the influence of the international economy.

Forty years ago we could not even glimpse the enormous dangers of nuclear weapons or the complexities we would face today in our efforts to control them. And 40 years ago few could foresee that the collapse of the old order would bring with it the spread of increasingly sophisticated military arms to new and contending nations, so that today regional conflicts carry with them the constant threat of escalation.

---

[12] Source: *Nomination of George P. Shultz: Hearings Before the Committee on Foreign Relations, United States Senate, Ninety-seventh Congress, Second Session* (Washington, 1982), pp. 8–10. Secretary Haig submitted his resignation to President Reagan on June 25, 1982. President Reagan accepted the resignation with "profound regret". For the exchange of letters between Haig and Reagan on June 25, see document 14. Secretary Shultz was confirmed by the Senate on July 15 and sworn in as the 60th Secretary of State on July 16. For the full text of Shultz's testimony before the Senate Foreign Relations Committee on July 13 and 14, including extensive questioning by committee members, see *Nomination of George P. Shultz*, pp. 1–216.

[13] Senator Charles H. Percy.

General Douglas MacArthur saw these broad interrelationships and put the point succinctly and eloquently as long ago as 1951: "The issues are global and so interlocked that to consider the problems of one sector oblivious to those of another is but to court disaster for the whole."

Today most Americans recognize that the nature and strength of our diplomacy and our strategic posture are linked to and heavily dependent on our performance at home. Our economy, despite current rough water, is fundamentally strong and will strengthen further as economic policies now in place and in prospect take hold. A strong and productive America makes us a strong trading partner and a resourceful ally, giving to our friends a confidence that strengthens their will to resist those who would deprive us of our freedoms.

Today most Americans are uncomfortable with the fact that we spend so much of our substance on defense, and rightly so, and yet most Americans also recognize that we must deal with reality as we find it, and that reality in its simplest terms is an uncertain world in which peace and security can be assured only if we have the strength and will to preserve them.

We have passed through a decade during which the Soviet Union expanded its military capability at a steady and rapid rate while we stood still. President Reagan has given us the leadership to turn that situation around, and just in time.

The past decade taught us once again an important lesson about United States-Soviet relations. In brief, it is that diminished American strength and resolve are an open invitation for Soviet expansion into areas of critical interest to the West and provide no incentive for moderation in the Soviet military buildup. Thus it is critical to the overall success of our foreign policy that we persevere in the restoration of our strength; but it is also true that the willingness to negotiate from that strength is a fundamental element of strength itself.

The President has put forward arms control proposals in the strategic theater and conventional arms areas that are genuinely bold and that will, if accepted, reduce the burdens and the dangers of armaments. Let no one doubt the seriousness of our purpose, but let no one believe that we will seek agreement for its own sake without a balanced and constructive outcome.

We recognize that an approach to the Soviet Union limited to the military dimension will not satisfy the American people. Our efforts in the area of arms reduction are inevitably linked to restraint in many dimensions of Soviet behavior, and as we enter a potentially critical period of transition in Soviet leadership, we must also make it clear that we are prepared to establish mutually beneficial and safer relationships on the basis of reciprocity.

Today most Americans recognize that a steady and coherent involvement by the United States in the affairs of the world is a necessary condition for peace and prosperity. Over and over again since the close of the World War, the United States has been the global power to whom others have turned for help, whether it be to assist in the process of economic development or in finding peaceful solutions to conflicts.

Our help continues, as in President Reagan's Caribbean Basin Initiative, an example of America's commitment to a more prosperous world. I would say, Mr. Chairman, this is a commitment on which we must deliver. It must be an example as well of the key role in economic development of private markets and private enterprise.

As the President said in his address in Cancun:

> "History demonstrates that time and again, in place after place, economic growth and human progress make their greatest strides in countries that encourage economic freedom. Individual farmers, laborers, owners, traders, and managers—they are the heart and soul of development. Trust them. Because whenever they are allowed to create and build, whenever they are given a personal stake in deciding economic policies and benefitting from their success, then societies become more dynamic, prosperous, progressive, and free."[14]

In our international endeavors we are strengthened by a structure of alliances that is of central importance. Ours is not a hegemonic world but a diverse and pluralistic one, reflecting the complexity of the free, independent, and democratic societies with which we are associated.

Just as we expect others to work in partnership with us, so we must conduct ourselves as a responsible partner. Frictions and differences are inevitable among allies,

---

[14] For the text of President Reagan's address at Cancun, Mexico, on October 22, 1981, see *American Foreign Policy: Current Documents, 1981,* document 89.

and we can never assume complacently that they will automatically disappear. Tolerance of the needs and perspectives of others [is essential]. So is candid recognition of our difficulties and challenges.

Above all, there has to be a commitment to the common values and interests on which the truly unique multilateral institutions of the last three and a half decades have been based. Our commitment is firm, as President Reagan made clear during his recent European trip. I am confident that the same is true of our allies.

Mr. Chairman, if we are strong, we buttress our allies and friends and leave our adversaries in no doubt about the consequences of aggression. If we provide assistance to help others to be strong, our own strength can be husbanded and brought to bear more effectively. If we are confident, we give confidence to those who seek to resolve disputes peacefully. If we are engaged, we give hope to those who otherwise would have no hope. If we live by our ideals, we can argue their merit to others with confidence and conviction.

. . . .

Document 6

Address by the Secretary of Defense (Weinberger) Before the American Bar Association, San Francisco, August 11, 1982[15]

National Security Consensus

. . . .

One of the greatest challenges in defending a free society rests in our democratic principles which require a consensus to be formed in favor of a strong defense, if we are to have one, and for that consensus continually to be maintained. This task has never been easy in open democratic societies. From the earliest days of our republic we have loved peace, and been suspicious of things military. Within six months of the end of the Revolutionary War, the Continental Congress, believing that "standing armies in time of peace are inconsistent with principles of republican Government" and "are dangerous to the liberties of a free people," disbanded the remnant of the Continental Army, reducing the number of troops from 700 regulars to 25 privates to guard the stores at Fort Pitt and 55 to guard the stores at West Point. No officer was permitted to remain in service above the rank of Captain.

Later, during the debates on the Constitution, a clause was offered that would have prohibited our new armed forces from exceeding 3,000 men. Washington said he would support the proposal if the author would accept an amendment that prohibited any invading army from exceeding 2,000.

Today the Reagan administration is striving to maintain a consensus for national security. This consensus has three important and mutually supportive tenets:

First—we will sustain adequate levels of defense strength and this requires time and money;

Second—we will honor commitments to our allies; and

Finally—we will pursue effective arms reduction agreements.

Because each of these tenets is important, I would like to discuss them in some detail.

I. First, the Reagan administration is committed to regaining and then maintaining a level of defense strength sufficient to deter any attack on us. In times of severe budgetary constraints, this is a painful commitment which has often produced conflict. Walter Lippmann once wrote, "In my youth, we all assumed that the money spent on battleships would be better spent on schoolhouses." This is a sympathetic theme and one that is reinforced by the paradox that if we, in the defense of our country, completely succeed in what we are doing, we will never have to use any of these weapons we must acquire.

The resources devoted to defense, if spent for other things, could accomplish considerable public good. But we must not forget that "the most important social service a government can do for its people is to keep them alive and free." This is an obligation we have been dangerously close to neglecting.

---

[15] Source: *Public Statements of Secretary of Defense Weinberger*, 1982. Brief introductory remarks by Weinberger have been omitted.

Apart from the Vietnam era, U.S. Defense spending, in constant dollars, remained virtually unchanged from the mid-1950's through the end of the 1970's. Moreover, relative to GNP, our defense effort dropped dramatically, declining from 8.3 percent of GNP in 1960 to 4.9 percent in 1979. The share of defense activity in the Federal budget also shrank by nearly one-half, falling from over 55 percent in 1960 to less than 25 percent in 1979. In the post-Vietnam era, we overlooked critically needed modernization requirements and permitted decay in the readiness of our forces. At the same time, the Soviet Union was greatly increasing expenditures for defense. As a result, we found ourselves in 1980 in a considerably weaker position than we had been in any period since World War II.

Eighteen months ago, the Reagan administration began its program to rebuild American defenses, and already we have made significant progress. This progress is reflected both in improved management of resources, and in increased resources.

We have made and continue to make major improvements in the Defense procurement system. A major achievement in this regard has been the introduction of multiyear planning and contracting for 18 major weapon systems. We have also improved our procedures to stop cost growth through more realistic budgeting and improved management. We have completely revamped the Pentagon planning, programming and budgeting system emphasizing long-term strategic planning, paper work reduction and full participation by the top civilian and uniformed leaders in the Pentagon.

In 18 months we have been able to influence three defense budgets and achieve much-needed enhancements including:

—Improved recruiting and retention, resulting in a force that is more fully manned with high caliber men and women. (Indeed the All Volunteer Force is now working so well that we are literally turning down a number of volunteers for whom we no longer have any spaces.)

—Substantially increased Air Force and Navy flying hours, improving air crew training and experience.

—Increased procurement of much needed combat equipment and ammunition to correct previous neglect of modernization and sustainability.

Nevertheless, we have only begun if we are to be able to meet our commitments to our allies, and to deter Soviet aggression. To those who contend that we cannot fund adequate levels of defense because funds are needed elsewhere, I can only reply that they are making the wrong calculations. Expenditures for defense cannot be determined by what is left over from other programs—rather, they must be measured against the threat we actually face. And that threat is very real today, and it is a growing threat. James Madison said: "The means of security can only be regulated by the means and the danger of attack . . . . If one nation maintains constantly a disciplined army, ready for the service of ambition or revenge, it obliges the most pacific nations, who may be within the reach of its enterprises, to take corresponding precautions."

II. The second way we can protect the nation is by honoring commitments to our allies. This is also an idea with a checkered history. From Washington's warning against entangling alliances, to modern proposals advocating withdrawal of our troops from Europe, our nation has possessed a strong strain of isolationism. But the period in which this isolationism could be supported by the natural barriers of our geography has long since passed. No longer can we delude ourselves that commitments to our allies spring only from an altruistic desire to preserve their freedom. In fact—defense of their freedom is simply the forward defense of our own freedom.

In 1935, Philip Jessup speculated "It may not be many years before it is alleged that the air frontiers of the United States are on the far sides of the Atlantic and Pacific Oceans." Mr. Jessup lived to see his prophecy fulfilled. It is clear that we could not survive for long in the world if Europe had been overrun.

Despite this reality, there are some today who are critical of our commitment to our allies, particularly those who seek a lessening of this administration's deep commitment to NATO. NATO, as one of the most successful alliances in world history, has assured Europe the longest period of peace in modern history. Its vitality has been reinforced recently by the entry of Spain. Because it has been so effective, it has been a cardinal point of Soviet strategy to try to destroy the alliance. There is also a temptation to take NATO's benefits for granted, and for some to wonder if the alliance is worth the effort. This leads to talk of inequitable burdensharing, particularly during periods of budgetary strain.

We cannot let such strains obscure the very real contributions of our allies to their own defense and to the defense of other nations. During the 1970's, our decade of neglect, many of our allies made significant contributions to shore up our weakened position. In recent years, within the NATO region, there have been many promising developments which show our allies' continual commitment. One example is host nation support, which enhances burdensharing within the alliance and enables more efficient use of U.S. forces. Other efforts are needed. Indeed we all must do more. But most of all we must keep NATO strong and united.

In recognition of the importance of other regions, particularly southwest Asia, to the economic well-being of the West, NATO is addressing out-of-area issues. We are working with our NATO allies on overflight rights, en route access, and support, in the event it should become necessary to our own security, and that of the West, to project our power to the Middle East, or elsewhere. The recent Falklands War shows how vital it is to be ready for unexpected contingencies, as well as the more likely crises.

It should be noted also that our allies in Europe have provided valuable assistance by agreeing to participate in the Sinai and other peacekeeping operations. The willingness of Great Britain, France, Italy, Norway, and the Netherlands to help maintain peace in the historically volatile Middle East represents a major contribution to the collective security of the West itself.

Despite our full commitment to our allies we must occasionally advocate positions that trouble them. We have encouraged our allies to increase their expenditures for Defense as we increase our own. This is never a popular request but it is a necessary one. Similarly, we have done all we can to avoid adding directly to the Soviets' already vast offensive military strength. This conviction is reflected in our policies toward technology transfers, the proposed Soviet pipeline to Western Europe, and credits. Necessarily some of these policies worry some of our allies.

III. The final tenet of our security consensus is the pursuit of effective arms reduction agreements. Early in the administration, we decided that the very best way to achieve lasting peace with the Soviets would be to persuade them to agree to major, verifiable arms reductions, down to equality on both sides at vastly lower levels than we now have.

The United States has put forward a comprehensive arms reduction program which includes the elimination of land-based intermediate range missiles, a one-third reduction in strategic ballistic missile warheads, a substantial reduction in NATO and Warsaw Pact ground and air forces, and new safeguards to reduce the risk of accidental war. However, we have not pursued this process blindly; we have established four essential criteria by which we will evalute any arms reduction proposals:

—*First,* we insist on significant reductions. We are committed to reducing the number and destructive potential of weapons, not just freezing them at high levels or authorizing even higher levels, as we did in previous SALT agreements.

—*Second,* we seek equality and will accept nothing less. We want agreements that will lead to mutual reductions down to equal levels of effective forces on both sides. We believe that this equality is absolutely necessary if we are to provide our country with adequate security. In measuring this equality, we will focus on the destructive power of weapons—not just on such considerations as numbers of launchers. A launcher by itself has no destructive power, yet that was the measure used in SALT II[16]and it was of course agreed to, indeed proposed by, the Soviets because it enabled them to continue, as they are to this very hour, to acquire more, heavier, and more accurate lethal weapons.

—*Third,* we will insist on verifiability. The United States will draft carefully the provisions of arms control agreements and insist on measures to ensure compliance by both sides. I am sure you can appreciate the absolute necessity of this requirement.

Indeed we have very good evidence that the Soviet Union has broken their "no first use of chemical weapons" agreement.[17]Moreover, certain Soviet tests have been of sufficient magnitude to raise serious questions about compliance with the

---

[16] The SALT II Treaty was signed in Vienna by President Carter and Soviet Chairman Brezhnev on June 18, 1979. U.S. Senate ratification of0 the treaty was indefinitely postponed after the Soviet invasion of Afghanistan on December 27, 1979. For the text of the treaty, see Department of State *Bulletin,* July 1979, pp. 23–47.

[17] The reference presumably is to the Protocol for the Prohibition of the Use in War of Asphyxiating, Poisonous or Other Gases, and of Bacteriological Methods of Warfare, signed by the Soviet Union and several other nations in Geneva in 1925 and entered into force in 1928. For text, see United States Arms Control and Disarmament Agency, *Arms Control and Disarmament Agreements* (Washington, 1982), pp. 14–18.

150-kiloton limit of the Threshold Test Ban Treaty.[18] These two points indicate the need for improved verification procedures. In this connection it is significant that we have always offered full on-site verification, and we still do.

We are yet a long way from Grenville Clark's utopia[19] where there is world peace through world law. In the world in which we presently live, arms reduction agreements provide no security without agreement on adequate and effective verification.

—*Finally*, we will insist that arms control agreements genuinely enhance United States and allied security. We must not accept cosmetic agreements that lull the public into a false sense of security. As lawyers we know that, while it may be easier to reach an agreement for a client if difficult issues are ignored or purposely blurred, in the long run, we have done our client no service. We will not fall into this trap. We do not seek arms agreements for agreements' sake, but rather to enhance our national security, and reduce the risk of nuclear war. Some feel that if we enter into negotiations, the end result must be an agreement, even if it is not a good agreement for us. I am afraid some of that reasoning permeated the SALT negotiations.

The prospect of nuclear war is of course thoroughly and totally abhorrent to all of us. The spector of carnage, death, and destruction which such a war or indeed any war would produce is indeed terrifying. Our shared fear of nuclear war has motivated some to advocate proposals which, while well-meaning, pose a serious threat to our ability to negotiate effective arms control agreements. These include the "nuclear freeze" and "no first use" proposals.

Advocates of a nuclear freeze believe arms control negotiations would more likely be successful if we declared in advance of the successful completion of these negotiations a willingness to freeze our nuclear capabilities at present levels. This approach has several dangers. First, it places no concurrent restraints on the Soviet Union which is almost daily improving and increasing its nuclear capabilities.

You may recall the brief mention I made at the beginning of the debate that occurred prior to the ratification of the Constitution. Some individuals argued that the Federal Constitution should contain a restraint against standing armies in time of peace. I quoted Washington's fears. James Madison's contribution to the debate was this: "If the Federal Constitution could chain the ambition or set bounds to the exertions of all other nations, then indeed might it prudently chain the discretion of its own government and set bounds to the exertions for its own safety."

This same fallacy is present in the various freeze proposals. They could well place restraints on the strength of the United States, freezing us into a position of permanent inferiority to the Soviets, without limiting the expansion of the Soviet strength.

But there is another danger of the freeze proposal, as well, that is that by weakening our resolve to strengthen our nuclear defense, advocates of the freeze would virtually destroy our ability to negotiate genuine arms reductions. As lawyers we know that our ability to negotiate a settlement before trial is dependent on the strength of our case and the willingness of our clients to go to trial if necessary. How many of us would voluntarily announce our intentions not to engage in discovery, or prepare for trial with the expectation that by thus restraining ourselves we could secure a better settlement? The notion is preposterous. Though discovery and trial preparation are time-consuming and expensive, we would be guilty of the grossest malpractice if we did not continue to prepare vigorously for trial, even though we may hope and even expect that a fair settlement is possible.

By the same token, we must continue to show our resolve to modernize our nuclear capability, even though we of course earnestly hope to negotiate major and effective arms reduction agreements. Only by maintaining our strength can we produce the pressure necessary to get the Soviets to agree to advantageous arms reduction agreements.

Furthermore, only by continuing to modernize our capabilities, while seeking fair arms reduction agreements, will we be adequately safeguarded, if negotiations should not be successful. Nuclear deterrence may be an unpopular notion, but

---

[18] The Threshold Test Ban Treaty was signed in Moscow on July 3, 1974, by President Nixon and Chairman Brezhnev. The treaty prohibited nuclear weapons test explosions of yields exceeding 150 kilotons. The treaty was submitted to the U.S. Senate for ratification in July 1976, but it has not been acted upon. For the text of the treaty, see *ibid.* pp. 167–170.

[19] The reference is to the proposals sketched by Grenville Clark and Louis B. Sohn in *World Peace Through World Law* (Cambridge, Mass., 1958).

there is no refuting the fact that it has worked. And just think for the moment of the alternatives—a military strength too weak to deter. It is no good uttering the banal cliché that each superpower has enough to blow each other up. We must do a more thorough analysis than that, and when we do, we see that the Soviets have greatly increased the accuracy, and the yield of their missiles, and their ability to withstand retaliatory strikes—while we have not. We have had enough deterrent strength in the past—enough to prevent nuclear war and also to prevent conventional war between the superpowers. We cannot abandon this crucial element of our security until it has been replaced by effective and verifiable arms reduction agreements, and the margin for error here is exceedingly small.

"No first use" proposals pose a different threat to our security by removing an important element necessary to deter the Soviet Union from use of their tremendous conventional capability. I already have alluded to the astonishing growth of the Soviets' conventional capability which far exceeds their requirements for defense and indeed represents enormous offensive potential. Those calling for a declaration of "No first use of Nuclear Weapons" by the United States have forgotten that we already have a no first use policy involving all our weapons—conventional or nuclear. Our weapons are intended for defense alone and we will not employ them unless necessary to preserve our peace and security. But to declare a policy of no first use of nuclear weapons is an open invitation to the Soviet Union to use their conventional strength to threaten us and our allies. Remember, that while the destructive power of nuclear weapons is awesome, conventional weapons also have the capacity to intimidate and to destroy all that we value. Until we negotiate real arms reduction agreements and are confident of our ability to provide a creditable conventional deterrent, we must not limit our ability to provide a flexible response to aggression.

These, then, are the important elements of a strong defense which the Reagan administration seeks to maintain: adequate rearmament in time (and it does require many years, and it is very expensive); firm commitment to our allies; and vigorous pursuit of effective arms reduction. Each of these elements is mutually supportive. We must maintain adequate levels of defense expenditures for several years to enable us to meet our commitments to our allies, and to provide incentives for arms reduction.

Our commitments to our allies enhance the effective use of our own resources and provide additional incentives for arms reduction.

Meaningful, verifiable arms reductions can lead to major reductions in defense expenditures and also enhance our ability to meet commitments to our allies.

Although each element of this Triad is important, each is in some measure subject to attack by those who do not understand the full extent of our security needs.

Of course, I respect the right of others to criticize these broad defense concepts and, in that way, attempt to dissolve the national consensus needed to sustain them. I am determined, however, that this minority will not be the only voice heard. I think it vital to speak for the security of my client, the Government and the people of the United States, and their freedoms. We know of no better or other way to protect them.

I urge you too as members of the bar and leaders in your community to join the debate. Alexis de Toqueville argued in the early days of our country that our democratic values would make us lovers of peace and thus perhaps unwilling to follow the difficult paths that will enable us to keep the peace and our freedom. He was correct—we are lovers of peace—and we must use this love of peace to do all the hard things that must be done if we are to preserve both the peace and the freedoms we properly value so highly. Peace alone is not enough.

Nothing can be more important than that we do everything we must and that we do it in time.

For, the future of all that we have and all we hold most dear turns upon whether we are willing and able now to call up again the efforts, the resources, and the skills that gave us this land and our freedoms.

Document 7

Address by Vice President Bush Before the National Convention of the American Legion, Chicago, August 26, 1982 (Extract)[20]

The U.S. Commitment to Freedom and Peace

. . . .

When President Reagan and I took the oath of office, we in the United States had witnessed great changes throughout the world in the previous 4 years.

Our predecessors proposed nuclear arms reductions. But when the Soviets said "Nyet," they backed off—and gave us SALT II which was rejected by the democratically controlled Senate.

In Central America, we stood by while Marxists overran Nicaragua—only 300 miles from the Panama Canal.

In the Middle East, South Yemen, a Soviet client, supported aggression against North Yemen—a Russian power play on the fringes of Saudi Arabia.

In Iran, the Shah—whom Carter had just toasted as our strongest ally in the region—was toppled by a coalition of radicals and bigots. Our Embassy was attacked, and our diplomats and Marines were kidnapped and brutalized.

Then finally, the Soviets invaded Afghanistan. And why not? What had the previous administration done to make them think twice? For nearly 3 years, the Carter administration had spoken softly and carried a little stick. So the Soviet tanks rolled.

And here at home we watched the deterioration of our armed forces and the reduction and demoralization of the Central Intelligence Agency.

If Americans were confused by all of this, they must have been even more confused by some of our foreign policy pronouncements.

We were told in 1977 by our Ambassador to the United Nations that Cuban troops in Africa were a stabilizing force. He later informed us that Ayatollah Khomeini might someday be viewed as a Saint. And our own President, after watching the Russians invade Afghanistan, told the American people that he had learned more about the Russians in the previous week than he had in his entire life. Well, the Russian revolution occurred in 1917; Jimmy Carter was born in 1924 and the invasion of Afghanistan occurred in 1979. I call that pretty slow learning.

In the face of the Soviet military buildup—the greatest in the history of mankind—our leaders in Washington cancelled the B–1 bomber, eliminated the neutron bomb and presided over the dismantlement of the U.S. Navy.

During the decade of the seventies, defense spending in the United States, in constant dollars, decreased by 28 percent. It fell from 8 percent of the gross national product in 1960 to 5.3 percent in 1980. The United States Navy which once could launch a thousand ships, as we entered the seventies, was reduced to just slightly more than 500 vessels in 1980.

While the previous administration, supported by Congress, cut into the meat, muscle and bone of our forces, the Soviet Union embarked upon a military buildup which today takes 12 to 14 percent of its gross national product. Even today, by some estimates, the Soviets are outspending us militarily by 50 percent and within the last decade their investment in weapon systems, military construction, research and development has been about $350 billion greater than our own.

Two years ago during the Presidential campaign, President Reagan told the American people that, if elected, he would take the steps necessary to restore America's margin of safety. He has tried to fulfill that pledge and he is doing so with your help. Every man and woman in this room understands that the price of liberty and the price of peace are not cheap. But despite the costs, we have no greater commitment to our country, to our children and to those generations of Americans yet to come, than to preserve our freedom and promote peace in the world.

We have embarked upon a defense program that will restore our military strength. We have revived the B–1 bomber and the neutron warhead. By protecting the identity of those who serve overseas, we are strengthening rather than tearing down the CIA. This is one administration that is

---

[20] Source: Press Release, August 26, 1982, Office of the Press Secretary to the Vice President. Introductory remarks relating to developments in the Middle East, and to the role of the American Legion in U.S. society have been omitted.

proud of the men and women who serve in uniform, and we are proud of the men and women who serve in the vital intelligence community. We are thankful for their service and we do not apologize for their decent and dedicated service to our country.

During the 20 months that we have been in office, I believe there is a new perception of the United States throughout the world. In Central America we stood up for our friends in Salvador as they were threatened by communist subversives attempting to destroy all hope for the democratic process. The Salvadoran people went to the polls in record numbers despite vicious threats by the Marxists. Fear and intimidation were stared down by 800,000 men and women who had the courage to choose freedom over tyranny.

Last year the people of Poland, following the leadership of Lech Walesa and his Solidarity union, made their wish to live in a free society known to the world. Those aspirations of freedom were crushed by the military regime on orders from the Kremlin. Poland's Communist leaders were given two choices by the Soviets: crush the solidarity movement or we will do it for you.

What transpired is known to all the world. But the martial law, the imprisonment of thousands, the exile of Lech Walesa, have been forgotten by too many people. But the President of the United States has not forgotten.

He told the Soviets if they didn't let up he would impose economic sanctions, and he did. When the repression continued, he took further sanctions. And just recently he prohibited American firms and their subsidiaries from providing highly sophisticated equipment to the Soviet Union for the construction of their gas pipeline—reminding the world once again that the neck of Poland's people remains firmly under the boot of repression.

Since that decision, we have heard a lot of protests from our European allies. We have taken a lot of criticism from editorial writers, columnists, public officials, and others. Well, ladies and gentlemen, I'm sorry. The United States is the leader of the free world and under this administration we are beginning once again to act like it. We don't accept the argument that our pipeline sanctions are unfair, that the Soviets can buy the equipment elsewhere, that we are only hurting American businesses. I don't believe any of that.

The absence of American equipment will delay the construction of that pipeline and the delivery of gas to Western Europe. And frankly, I don't believe that any American business should tie its future to leaders in the Kremlin—men who have no regard for the human rights of their own people, much less the people of Poland.

There are times to trade with the Soviets, but as the President has said, it should be on our terms, not on theirs. If the Soviets really want free and full trade with the United States, then let repression be lifted from Poland, let the Polish Government negotiate with Solidarity and let Lech Walesa walk as a free man.

I believe it would be wise for the Soviet leaders, in looking at Poland today, to remember the words of Daniel Webster who wrote, "Repression is the seed of revolution."

Instead they remember the words of their old mentor, that old fox himself, Lenin, who once said, "It is true that liberty is precious—so precious that it must be rationed."

Well, we have differences with the Soviet Union. Many of them are major and some of our differences in terms of freedom and human rights will never be resolved as long as the Soviet Union pursues its present political policies. But despite our differences, it is essential that we sit with the Soviets to discuss and negotiate solutions to the present circumstances that threaten peace.

Today, many Americans are expressing their concern regarding the risk of nuclear war. They are asking what their government is doing to reduce that risk and how we can best limit the cost of competition in nuclear arms.

Some have turned to seemingly attractive proposals, such as a unilateral nuclear weapons freeze, in the hope that this will increase security and make the world a safer place.

I think it is fair to ask, what has the United States done to make this world a safer place? The answer is this: the proposals laid down by this administration, designed to reduce the level of nuclear terror, are the most revolutionary and far-reaching since 1946.

I would like to remind the American people that the United States, under this President and other previous Presidents, has nothing to apologize for in its efforts to reduce nuclear armaments throughout the world. Since the end of World War II we have been the leader in advancing meaningful arms control proposals.

It was in 1946 when the United States, the only nuclear power in the world, advanced the Baruch Plan[21] at the United Nations. It called for control of nuclear weapons and nuclear energy by an international authority. To this initiative, the Soviets gave us an answer that all Americans would soon understand—nyet.

In 1955, President Eisenhower advanced a plan known as "Open skies."[22]Under his proposal, the United States and the Soviet Union would have exchanged blue prints of military establishments and provide for aerial reconnaissance. The Soviet response? Nyet.

It wasn't until 1963 that the Limited Test Ban Treaty,[23] proposed by President Kennedy, ended nuclear weapons testing in the atmosphere, in space or under water by participating nations.

In 1970, the treaty on the nonproliferation of nuclear weapons[24] was agreed to. The United States today remains deeply committed to the objectives of this treaty which include efforts to prevent the spread of nuclear weapons and to provide and maintain international safeguards on civil nuclear activities.

In the early seventies, the United States and Soviet Union, at the urging of the Nixon administration, reached an agreement that provided ceilings in some categories of weapons built by the two superpowers.[25]

Well, this President isn't interested in freezing nuclear weapons at the ceilings that are in effect today. He wants to greatly reduce both nuclear and conventional forces. Over a 7-month period in 1981 and 1982 President Reagan proposed the following:

"The elimination of land-based intermediate-range missiles;

"A one-third reduction in strategic ballistic warheads;

"A substantial reduction in NATO and Warsaw Pact ground and air forces; and

"New safeguards to reduce the risk of accidental war."

These proposals are both equitable and militarily important. They call for the verification of nuclear reductions—a measure that is in the best interest of both nations. Included in the President's proposals are offers to cancel deployment of the Pershing II ballistic missiles and ground-launched cruise missiles. In return we asked the Soviets to eliminate their SS–20, SS–4, and SS–5 missiles. This is an offer to eliminate the weapons systems which create the greatest concern to both sides. There are no other proposals as comprehensive as these, and I know of no other proposals that deserve more the full support of the American people. I hope the American Legion will support us in achieving these goals which seek to make this a safer world.

The simple solution of negotiating a freeze at current levels would be harmful to our security and that of our allies. It would undercut prospects for an effective nuclear arms reduction agreement with the Soviet Union.

The freeze would prevent us from taking the necessary steps to modernize our strategic force and it would reward the Soviets for its massive arms buildup for the past decade. By locking us into a position of military disadvantage, a freeze would undermine our attempt at the Strategic Arms Reduction Talks in Geneva by removing the Soviet incentive to negotiate seriously about reductions in nuclear arsenals.

I am sure many of you remember the great battle in the U.S. Senate in the early seventies regarding the construction of an antiballistic missile system. We had attempted to negotiate an ABM treaty with the Soviets, but their obstinance was no less than it was in 1946. It wash only after the Senate voted to provide the funding to build the ABM that the Soviet Union entered into meaningful negotiations. An

---

[21] Bernard Baruch, U.S. representative to the U.N. Atomic Energy Commission, presented a comprehensive plan for the international control of atomic energy in 1946. For documentation on the evolution of the Baruch plan, see *Foreign Relations of the United States,* 1946, Volume I, pp. 712–1109.

[22] President Eisenhower advanced the "Open Skies" proposal at the Geneva Conference on July 21, 1955. For the text of his statement on disarmament, see *Public Papers of the Presidents of the United States: Dwight D. Eisenhower,* 1955 (Washington, 1959), pp. 713–716.

[23] Signed in Moscow on August 5, 1963, and entered into force on October 10, 1963. (14 UST 1313)

[24] The Treaty on the Non-Proliferation of Nuclear Weapons was signed on July 1, 1968, and entered into force on March 5, 1970. (21 UST 483)

[25] For the text of the interim agreement between the United States and the Soviet Union on the Limitation of Strategic Offensive Arms, signed in Moscow on May 26, 1972, and entered into force on October 3, 1972, see 23 UST 3462.

ABM treaty was reached and ratified by the Senate in 1972.[26]

There is a lesson in that for us all. It is a lesson that I wish those who protest for a nuclear freeze would learn.

The United States is an honorable and decent nation. We have done more to advance the cause of freedom, to advance the cause of human rights, to make the world a safer and more prosperous place for all mankind than any nation in history.

I hope that those who want to freeze nuclear weapons recognize the good that our country has accomplished. I hope they will take the time to learn what we have done in the past to stop the nuclear arms race.

The next time a million people show up in New York City to rally for a nuclear freeze, I just hope that some of those slogans, some of those chants, some of those plaques, contain messages directed at the Soviet Union—a nation that has so many nuclear warheads aimed at the United States and at the Western democracy of Europe.

In all of this, the Soviets have worked hard to promote the nuclear freeze movement in Europe. At the same time they have continued their relentless buildup of both strategic and conventional forces. Shakespeare once said, "The devil can cite scripture for his purpose."

So can the Soviets.

Again, I appeal to you, as we strive to reduce nuclear weapons, to join with us and to give us your support in this the most important foreign policy initiative of the administration. It is important not only for the United States, but for free men and women everywhere.

As we journey down this difficult road we must keep upmost in our mind what it is we in the United States are trying to protect. One of America's great heroes, and a man who led many of you in battle during World War II, Omar Bradley, summed it up so eloquently when he said: "Freedom—no word was ever spoken that has held out greater hope, demanded greater sacrifice, needed more to be nurtured, blessed more the giver, damned more the destroyer, or come closer to be God's will on Earth. May America ever be its protector."

Thank you very much.

[26] The treaty on the Limitation of Anti-Ballistic Missile Systems was signed in Moscow on May 26, 1972, and entered into force on October 3, 1972. (23 UST 3435)

Document 8

Address by the Secretary of State (Shultz) Before the U.N. General Assembly, September 30, 1982[27]*0*

U.S. Foreign Policy: Realism and Progress

Mr. President, Mr. Secretary General, distinguished delegates, ladies and gentlemen: I begin by paying tribute to our new Secretary-General, who has brought great distinction to the office during his brief tenure. Dag Hammarskjold once told the General Assembly that whichever word one chooses, "independence, impartiality, objectivity—they all describe essential aspects of what, without exception, must be in the attitude of the Secretary-General." Javier Perez de Cuellar, a man of the Third World and, I am proud to note, of the New World as well, has already demonstrated his strict adherence to this most exacting standard. In so doing, he has earned the esteem of my Government and the gratitude of all who believe in the purposes of the Charter.

I congratulate, as well, Mr. Hollai of Hungary upon his election as President of the 37th Session of the General Assembly.

As I stand before you today I cannot help but reflect on my relation to this city and to this hall. I was born about 4 miles from here. I was reared and educated not far away, just across the Hudson River. And I took a tour through this building just after it opened in 1952 marveling at the reality of a temple erected in the hope, at least, of abolishing war.

When I took that tour back in the early fifties, there was great public interest in what was called "the Meditation Room." I understand the room is still here. But in the years since then, this institution has become more famous for talk than meditation. This hall has heard great ideas eloquently expressed. It has also heard doubletalk, platitudes, and ringing protestations of innocence—all too often aimed at camouflaging outrageous and inhuman acts.

But we must not ridicule words. I believe that the greatest advance in human history

[27] Source: Department of State Press Release 303, October 1, 1982; also printed in Department of State *Bulletin*, November 1982, pp. 1–9.

was not the wheel, the use of electricity, or the internal combustion engine. Indispensable to progress as these have been, our most remarkable achievement was the slow, clumsy but triumphant creation of language. It is words that released our ancestors from the prison of the solitary. Words gave us the means to transmit to our children and the future the crowning jewel of human existence: knowledge. The Code of Hammurabi, the Bible, the Analects of Confucius, the teachings of The Buddha, the Koran, the insights of Shakespeare, the creed of Mahatma Gandhi or Martin Luther King—all these were arrangements of words.

Is it not profoundly revealing that the first victims of tyrants are—words? No people better know the meaning of freedom than those who have been arrested or beaten or imprisoned or exiled because of what they said. A single man speaking out—a Lech Walesa for example—is more dangerous than an armored division.

All of us here, whether we arrived after a short 1-hour flight as I did, or came from the other side of the globe as many of you did, enter this auditorium for one main purpose—to talk about what our governments see as the problems ahead and how they should be solved. On one point at least we can all agree—the problems are many and difficult. I shall not try, in the minutes allotted me, to deal with each—or even most—of those issues in detail.

Instead, I want to give you some sense of the principles and general approach the United States will take toward our common problems.

Americans are, by history and by inclination, a practical and pragmatic people—yet a people with a vision. It is the vision—usually simple and sometimes naive—that has so often led us to dare and to achieve. President Reagan's approach to foreign policy is grounded squarely on standards drawn from the pragmatic American experience. As de Tocqueville pointed out, "To achieve its objective, America relies on personal interest, and gives full reign to the strength and reason of the individual." That is as true now as when it was said 150 years ago. Our principal instrument, now as then, is freedom. Our adversaries are the oppressors, the totalitarians, the tacticians of fear and pressure.

On this foundation, President Reagan's ideas and the structure of his foreign policy are so straightforward that those of us enmeshed in day-to-day details may easily lose sight of them. The President never does; he consistently brings us back to fundamentals. Today I will talk about those fundamentals. They consist of four ideas that guide our actions:

—we will start from realism;

—we will act from strength, both in power and purpose;

—we will stress the indispensable need to generate consent, build agreements, and negotiate on key issues; and

—we will conduct ourselves in the belief that progress is possible, even though the road to achievement is long and hard.

I. REALITY

If we are to change the world we must first understand it. We must face reality—with all its anguish and all its opportunities. Our era needs those who, as Pericles said, have the clearest vision of what is before them, glory and danger alike, and notwithstanding go out to meet it.

Reality is not an illusion nor a sleight of hand, though many would have us believe otherwise. The enormous, grinding machinery of Soviet propaganda daily seeks to distort reality, to bend truth for its own purposes. Our world is occupied by far too many governments which seek to conceal truth from their own people. They wish to imprison reality by controlling what can be read or spoken or heard. They would have us believe that black is white and up is down.

Much of present day reality is unpleasant. To describe conditions as we see them, as I do today, and as President Reagan has over the course of his Presidency, is not to seek confrontation. Far from it. Our purpose is to avoid misunderstanding and to create the necessary preconditions for change. And so, when we see aggression, we will call it aggression. When we see subversion, we will call it subversion. When we see repression, we will call it repression.

—Events in Poland, for example, cannot be ignored or explained away. The Polish people want to be their own master. Years of systematic tyranny could not repress this desire. And neither will martial law. But in Poland today, truth must hide in corners.

—Nor can we simply turn our heads and look the other way as Soviet divisions brutalize an entire population in Afghanistan. The resistance of the Afghan people is a valiant saga of our times. We demean that valor if we do not recognize its source.

—And Soviet surrogates intervene in many countries, creating a new era of colonialism at the moment in history when peoples around the globe had lifted that burden from their backs.

Nor will we shy away from speaking of other problems affecting the free and developing worlds.

—Much of the developing world is threatened by a crisis of confidence in financial institutions and the stultifying effects of state controlled economies.

—The naturally vibrant economies of many Western nations, and trade between the world's major trading partners, are threatened by recession and rising protectionism.

—And the great alliances that shore up world stability and growth—our hemispheric partnership, NATO, and the Western and Japanese industrial democracies, are challenged by new as well as chronic strains.

Finally, the shadow of war still darkens the future of us all.

—There is no ultimate safety in a nuclear balance of terror constantly contested. There is no peace of mind at a time when increasing numbers of nations appear willing to launch their armies into battles for causes which seem local but have ramifications for regional and even global harmony.

The list of troubles is long; the danger of despair great. But there is another side to the present reality; it is a reality of hope. We are living in a fantastic time of opportunity.

Historians in the future will surely marvel over the accomplishments achieved by human beings in the last half of this century. We have expanded the frontiers of thought—in science, in biology, in engineering, in painting and music and mathematics, in technology and architecture—far beyond the point anyone could have dared predict, much less hoped for. We know much today about the oceans and forests and the geological strata that lock in the story of our past. We know more about a baby—or the brain—than was accumulated in ten millenia before our time. We are learning to produce food for all of us; we are no longer helpless before the threat of disease; we explore our universe as a matter of course. We are confronting the nature of Nature herself. The opportunities are grand. This, too, is a clear reality.

Thus realism shows us a world deeply troubled, yet with reason for hope. There is one necessary condition: the only way we can enhance and amplify the human potential is by preserving, defending, and extending those most precious of conditions—freedom and peace.

II. STRENGTH

America's yearning for peace does not lead us to be hesitant in developing our strength or in using it when necessary. Indeed, clarity about the magnitude of the problems we face leads inevitably to a realistic appreciation of the importance of American strength. The strength of the free world imposes restraint, invites accommodation, and reassures those who would share in the creative work that is the wonderful consequence of liberty.

Strength means military forces to ensure that no other nation can threaten us, our interests, or our friends. But when I speak of strength I do not mean military power alone. To Americans, strength derives as well from a solid economic base and social vitality at home and with our partners. And, most fundamentally, the true wellspring of strength lies in America's moral commitment.

The bulwark of America's strength is military power for peace.

The American people have never accepted weakness, or hesitancy, or abdication. We will not put our destiny into the hands of the ruthless. Americans today are emphatically united on the necessity of a strong defense. This year's defense budget will ensure that the United States will help its friends and allies defend themselves—to make sure that peace is seen clearly by all to be the only feasible course in world affairs.

Along with military readiness and capability must come the willingness to employ it in the cause of peace, justice, and security. Today in Beirut the United States Marines—together with our allies, Italy and France—are helping the Lebanese Government and armed forces assure the safety of the peoples of that tormented capital. Our marines represent an extension of American power not for war but to secure the peace. They are there to speed the moment when all foreign forces depart from Lebanon. There must be early agreement on a timetable for the full application of Lebanon's independence, sovereignty, and territorial integrity. Lebanon deserves the world's help—to secure peace, and to rebuild a thriving society.

America will continue to use its strength with prudence, firmness and balance. We intend to command the respect of adversaries and to deserve the confidence of allies and partners.

The engine of America's strength is a sound economy.

In a time of recession, industrialized and less developed nations alike are bedeviled by excessive inflation, restricted markets, unused capacity, stagnating trade, growing pressure for protectionism—and the most potent enemy of expansion: pervasive uncertainty.

The United States with its vast human and scientific resources can survive an era of economic strife and decay. But our moral commitment and our self-interest require us to use our technological and productive abilities to build lasting prosperity at home and to contribute to a sound economic situation abroad.

President Reagan has instituted a bold program to get the American economy moving. Our rate of inflation is down markedly, and we will keep it down. This will add stability to the value of the dollar, and give greater confidence to international financial markets.

The recent drop in U.S. interest rates will stimulate new investments within and beyond our shores. Conservation through market pricing of energy has reduced United States demand for world energy supplies. We are putting the recession behind us. A growing and open American economy will provide new markets for goods and services produced elsewhere, and new opportunities for foreign investment. Just as we have a stake in worldwide recovery, others will prosper as our recovery develops.

For wider prosperity to take hold, we must cooperatively attend these international issues:

—The lure of protectionist trade policies must be resisted—whether in the form of overt import restrictions and export subsidies, or by more subtle domestic programs. These can only distort world trade and impair growth everywhere. Let us determine to make the November ministerial meeting of the GATT a time to stem these protectionist pressures and reinvigorate positive efforts for a more open trading system.[28]

—The implications of the external debt of many nations must be understood. Immediate debt problems are manageable if we use good sense and avoid destabilizing actions. But the magnitude of external debt will almost inevitably reduce resources available for future lending for development purposes. Economic adjustment is imperative. The IMF can provide critical help and guidance in any country's efforts to smooth the adjustment process. The new borrowing arrangement proposed by the United States can be crucial to this effort.

—And the necessity of reducing government interference in the market must be recognized. Every nation has the right to organize society as its inhabitants wish, but economic facts cannot be ignored. Those facts clearly demonstrate that the world's command economies have failed abysmally to meet the needs of their peoples. The newly prosperous industrialized nations are those with the most free and open markets.

The bedrock of our strength is our moral and spiritual character.

The sources of true strength lie deeper than economic or military power—in the dedication of a free people which knows its responsibility. America's institutions are those of freedom accessible to every person and of government as the accountable servant of the people. Equal opportunity, due process of law, open trial by jury, freedom of belief, speech and assembly—our Bill of Rights, our guarantees of liberty and limited government were hammered out in centuries of ordeal. Because we care about these human values for ourselves, so must we then be concerned, and legitimately so, with abuses of freedom, justice, and humanitarian principles beyond our borders. This is why we will speak and act for prisoners of conscience, against terrorism, and against the brutal silencing of the Soviet Helsinki Watch Committee. This is why we are anxious to participate in periodic reviews of the human rights performance of ourselves as well as others. We welcome scrutiny of our own system. We are not perfect and we know it, but we have nothing to hide.

Our belief in liberty guides our policies here in the United Nations as elsewhere. Therefore in this forum the United States will continue to insist upon fairness, balance, and truth. We take the debate on human rights seriously. We insist upon honesty in the use of language; we will point out inconsistencies, double standards, and lies. We will not compromise our commitment to truth.

---

[28] Documentation on the GATT ministerial meeting from November 24 to 29, 1982, at Geneva is in Chapter 5, Part B.

III. READINESS TO SOLVE PROBLEMS

The world has work to do for the realists, the pragmatists, and the free. With a clear understanding of the troubled circumstances of the hour, and with a strengthened ability to act, we need as well the vision to see beyond the immediate present.

All of us here represent nations which must understand and accept the imperative of fair engagement on the issues before us and, beyond that, of common effort toward shared goals. Whether we are seeking to bring peace to regional conflict or a resolution of commercial differences, the time of imposed solutions has passed. Conquest, pressure, acquiescence under duress were common in decades not long past—but not today. Not everybody who wants his concerns addressed will find us automatically receptive. But when negotiations are in order America is prepared to go to work on the global agenda, and to do so in a way that all may emerge better off and more secure than before.

We manage our problems more intelligently, and with greater mutual understanding, when we can bring ourselves to recognize them as expressions of mankind's basic dilemma. We are seldom confronted with simple issues of right and wrong, between good and evil. Only those who do not bear the direct burden of responsibility for decision and action can indulge themselves in the denial of that reality. The task of statesmanship is to mediate between two—or several—causes, each of which often has a legitimate claim.

It is on this foundation that the United States stands ready to try to solve the problems of our time—to overcome chaos, deprivation, and the heightened dangers of an era in which ideas and cultures too often tend to clash and technologies threaten to outpace our institutions of control.

We are engaged in negotiations and efforts to find answers to issues affecting every part of the globe and every aspect of our lives upon it. Let me take up just two of these with you.

The agony of the Middle East now exceeds the ability of news bulletins or speeches to express; it is a searing wound on our consciousness. The region is in constant ferment. Unrest flares into violence, terror, insurrection, and civil strife. War follows war. It is clear to everyone in this hall that international peace, security, and cooperative progress cannot be truly achieved until this terrible regional conflict is settled.

All of us have witnessed in the past several months a graphic reminder of the need for practical peace negotiations in the Middle East. Of the nations in the world which need and deserve peace, Israel surely holds a preeminent place. Of the peoples of the world who need and deserve a place with which they can truly identify, the Palestinian claim is undeniable.

But Israel can only have permanent peace in a context in which the Palestinian people also realize their legitimate rights. Similarly, the Palestinian people will be able to achieve their legitimate rights only in a context which gives to Israel what it so clearly has a right to demand—to exist, and to exist in peace and security.

This most complex of international conflicts cannot be resolved by force: neither the might of armies nor the violence of terrorists can succeed in imposing the will of the strong upon the weak. Nor can it be settled simply by the rhetoric of even the most carefully worded document. It can only be resolved through the give and take of direct negotiations leading to the establishment of practical arrangements on the ground.

In other words, it can only be resolved through hard work. For those who believe that there is no contradiction between permanent peace for Israel and the legitimate rights of the Palestinian people—and for those who believe that both are essential for peace and that neither can be achieved without the other—the task can truly be a labor of love.

On September 1, President Reagan challenged the parties to the Arab-Israeli conflict to make a fresh start on the road to peace in the Middle East.[29] The Camp David agreements, resting squarely on United Nations Security Council Resolution 242,[30] with its formula of peace for territory, remain available to those who would accept the challenge to make this journey with us. The road will not be easy, but in his statement President Reagan made a number of proposals which, for those who are willing to join the effort, make the journey safer and easier.

I call on all concerned to accept President Reagan's challenge and hasten the realization of true peace in the Middle East.

---

[29] For the text of the address broadcast by President Reagan to the Nation on September 1, see document 318.

[30] For the text of U.N. Security Council Resolution 242, adopted on November 22, 1967, see *American Foreign Policy: Current Documents, 1967* (Washington, 1969), pp. 616–617.

In addition to the imperative need to resolve regional problems, there is an equally significant global imperative: to halt, and reverse, the global arms buildup. As an American, I am aware that arms control and disarmament are a special responsibility of the world's most powerful nations, the United States and the Soviet Union. And as an American, I can report that we are fulfilling our responsibility to seek to limit and reduce conventional and nuclear arms to the lowest possible levels.

With this goal in mind, President Reagan has initiated a comprehensive program for negotiated arms reductions. In Central Europe, the most heavily armed region on this planet, the Western allies are seeking substantial reductions in NATO and Warsaw Pact troops to equal levels. To achieve this goal, we have recently introduced a new proposal designed to revitalize the talks in Vienna on mutual and balanced reductions in military manpower.[31]

In the area of strategic arms, the United States has also taken the initiative by calling for a one-third reduction in the number of nuclear warheads that American and Soviet ballistic missiles can deliver.[32] And in the talks in Geneva on intermediate-range nuclear forces, the United States has gone even further, by asking the Soviet Union to agree to a bold proposal for eliminating an entire category of weapons from the arsenals of the two sides.

But as important as these negotiations are, the problem of arms control cannot be left to the two superpowers. The threat of nuclear proliferation extends to every region in the world and demands the attention and energy of every government. This is not solely, or even primarily, a concern of the superpowers. The nonnuclear countries will not be safer if nuclear intimidation is added to already deadly regional conflicts. The developing nations will not be more prosperous if scarce resources and scientific talent are diverted to nuclear weapons and delivery systems.

Unfortunately, as the task becomes more important it also becomes more difficult. Greater quantities of dangerous materials are produced and new suppliers emerge who lack a clear commitment to nonproliferation. But the technology that helped to create the problems can supply answers as well. Vigorous action to strengthen the barriers to aggression and to resolve disputes peacefully can remove the insecurities that are the root of the problem. The United States, for its part, will work to tighten export controls; to promote broader acceptance of safeguards; to urge meaningful actions when agreements are violated; and to strengthen the International Atomic Energy Agency. As our action last week in Vienna should make clear,[33]we will not accept attempts to politicize—and therefore emasculate—such vital institutions.

IV. PROGRESS

Perhaps the most common phrase spoken by the American people in our more than two centuries of national life has been "you can't stop progress." Our people have always been imbued with the conviction that the future of a free people would be good. America continues to offer that vision to the world. With that vision, and with the freedom to act creatively, there is nothing that people of good will need fear.

I am not here to assert, however, that the way is easy, or quick, or that the future is bound to be bright. There is a poem by Carl Sandburg in which a traveler asks the Sphinx to speak and reveal the distilled wisdom of all the ages. The Sphinx does speak. Its words are: "Don't expect too much."

That is good counsel for all of us here. It does not mean that great accomplishments are beyond our reach. We can help shape more constructive international relations and give our children a better chance at life. It does mean, however, that risk, pain, expense, and above all endurance are needed to bring those achievements into our grasp.

We must recognize the complex and vexing character of this world. We should not indulge ourselves in fantasies of perfection or unfulfillable plans, or solutions gained by pressure. It is the responsibility of leaders not to feed the growing appetite for easy promises and grand assurances. The plain truth is this: we face the prospect

---

[31] For a summary of this U.S. proposal, see the transcript of ACDA Director Rostow's press conference on July 8, 1982, document 185.

[32] Reference is to President Reagan's proposal in his commencement address at Eureka College on May 9, 1982. For text, see document 44.

[33] On September 24, the U.S. delegation withdrew from the 26th General Conference of the International Atomic Energy Agency in Vienna after the organization voted to exclude Israel from participation. For information on this development, see documents 101 and 102.

of all too few decisive or dramatic breakthroughs; we face the necessity of dedicating our energies and creativity to a protracted struggle toward eventual success.

That is the approach of my country—because we see not only the necessity, but the possibility, of making important progress on a broad front. For example:

—Despite deep seated differences between us and the Soviet Union, negotiators of both sides are now at work in a serious, businesslike effort at arms control.

—President Reagan has issued an important call for an international conference on military expenditure.[34] The achievement of a common system for accounting and reporting is the prerequisite for subsequent agreement to limit or curtail defense budgets.

—The Caribbean Basin Initiative establishes the crucial bond between economic development and economic freedom. It can be a model for fair and productive cooperation between economies vastly different in size and character.

—And the diplomatic way is open to build stability and progress in southern Africa through independence for Namibia under internationally acceptable terms.

Realism and a readiness to work long and hard for fair and freely agreed solutions—that is our recipe for optimism. That is the message and the offer which my government brings to you today.

Mr. President, Mr. Secretary-General, Delegates, friends. I began my remarks here today with an informal personal word. Let me end in the same spirit.

We must be determined and confident. We must be prepared for trouble, but always optimistic. In this way the vast bounties produced by the human mind and imagination can be shared by all the races and nations we represent here in this hall.

A predecessor of mine as Secretary of State, whose portrait hangs in my office, conveyed the essence of America's approach to the world's dangers and dilemmas. He said we would act with "a stout heart and a clear conscience, and never despair."

That is what John Quincy Adams said nearly a century and a half ago. I give you my personal pledge today that we will continue in that spirit, with that determination, and with that confidence in the future.

Document 9

Address by the President's Assistant for National Security Affairs (Clark) Before the City Club and Chamber of Commerce, San Diego, October 29, 1982[35]

Framework for Peace

It is a special honor for me to join you today. I'll attempt to provide a status report on the President's efforts to restore U.S. leadership in the resolution of the many difficult issues facing us in international affairs. To set the stage for that, it is useful to recall the agenda before us when the President entered office and to recall the climate in which we had to operate.

As you know, the decade of the 1970s was not a happy one—as measured by U.S. fortunes in international politics. This reality was the consequence of many factors. The political legacy of the Vietnam war included, among other things, a serious questioning of the reliability of the United States as an ally. A separate and unrelated factor was the dramatic and very visible expansion of Soviet military power. This military ascendancy was accompanied by an increased Soviet willingness to take risks in its efforts to expand its influence beyond its borders. Starting with their sponsorship of Cuban activities in Angola and proceeding more visibly in their subversive efforts in Ethiopia and South Yemen, the Soviets became ever more bold in the absence of any apparent U.S. opposition. This trend of reticence, and uncertainty on our part, called into question our sense of purpose and resolve among our friends in Europe and elsewhere.

Another important factor was a substantial increase in our reliance, and that of our allies, on overseas resources for fueling our economies. The effect of this and other events at home—with no apparent answers on our part—led us to the brink of econom-

---

[34] President Reagan proposed an international conference on military expenditures in his address to the U.N. General Assembly Special Session on Disarmament on June 17, 1982. For text, see document 51.

[35] Source: Department of State *Bulletin*, December 1982, pp. 33–35.

ic catastrophe. These events and trends led the United States to be viewed from abroad—by the Soviet Union as well as our friends—as a nation in decline. We were seen as unreliable and, basically, as unable to solve problems, either our own or theirs.

The challenge facing President Reagan at the outset of his administration was to rally the Western world by demonstrating that the United States could once more lead in the resolution of these problems and play a positive role in international affairs.

Faced with this agenda, the President charted his course toward basic objectives which individually and collectively were designed to restore a measure of stability and peace within the international community and to foster economic growth and development among nations. There were compelling domestic reasons for devoting foremost attention to restoring economic stability here at home. Clearly, our economy and the American people were at a breaking point with interest rates above 20% and double-digit inflation. But it is equally true that no nation can deserve the respect of others in the resolution of problems if it cannot solve its own. It is also true, that the commanding position of the dollar and the diversity and reach of U.S. industry are essential to sustain recovery internationally.

For all of these reasons, the President set to work to put our own house in order. It is gratifying today to note evidence that we have clearly turned the corner. Who would have thought, 20 months ago, that interest rates would drop 50% and that inflation would drop by an even greater percentage? That is progress and, as the President has said, there is more in store if we only stay the course.

The second essential task to keeping the peace was to restore the foundation of strength which underwrites the concept of deterrence. For a number of reasons, the United States had allowed its investment in defense to decline steadily in real terms throughout the decade of the 1970's. We had not designed a new strategic missile since the late 1960's; our newest B–52 was built more than 20 years ago. Conversely, the average age of Soviet systems is less than 5 years.

This decline took place at a time when the Soviet Union was accelerating the most dramatic expansion of military power in the history of mankind. The U.S.S.R. passed the United States in terms of defense spending in 1971; in the course of that decade, their military investment exceeded ours by over $200 billion.

This dramatic expansion of Soviet power was translated into political effect by the very apparent increase in Soviet willingness to take risks, such as those in adventures I have already mentioned in developing countries from Africa to Afghanistan.

As a result of the President's initiatives, the program of rebuilding is now well launched, and if we will show the resolve to sustain it in years ahead, there is every promise that effective deterrence will endure and that peace can be preserved for our own and future generations.

The next important goal, in the President's judgment, was the reestablishment of a firm basis for U.S.-Soviet relations. In the course of his first year in office, the President made clear to Soviet leadership that he is willing to work seriously with them toward resolution of the full range of international problems on the basis of reciprocity and restraint. At the same time, he has made it equally clear that we will not stand mute in the face of Soviet-inspired repression, subversion, or direct aggression whether it takes place in Poland, Central America, or Afghanistan. It is in this area that the President has drawn criticism for his actions—specifically on sanctions imposed following the Soviet-inspired crackdown in Poland. To the President, those events before last Christmas provided contemporary confirmation that the Soviet Union has not altered its commitment to extend its false revolution, wherever possible, beyond its borders. That choice is obviously theirs to make; but there is another way—should they wish to take it. The opportunity for enjoying the benefits of free trade and peaceful discourse within the international community is clearly an option they could effect.

For as long as the Soviet Union continues to deprive its people and to divert its resources into a massive military buildup, the United States—at a minimum—will not contribute to that process by providing the technology, hardware, or credits to make the Soviet tasks easier. In this commitment, we believe it is reasonable to expect the support of other nations which share our values and our principles.

In the nuclear age—and particularly after a decade of such astonishing Soviet expansion of its arsenal—it remains the leading priority of every American President to prevent conflict and to seek to reduce the level of nuclear armament. The same concern is being expressed today by growing numbers of Americans. This emerging public interest in the control of nuclear weapons is an extremely healthy and welcome phenomenon. It can serve to enlighten the American people on the basic concepts and systems which determine the stability or instability of peace in the nuclear age. However, throughout the past 37 years, the subject of strategic nuclear weapons has been shrouded in secrecy, jargon, and rather arcane concepts which most people would find difficult to understand. The result has been that on the most important public policy issue of their generation, the American people have been uninformed. Thus, for that reason alone, the current debate represents a very useful exercise.

Let me digress for a moment to give you a couple of examples of the kind of misinformation that has clouded public attitudes on this subject. If I were to ask you whether the United States today possesses more or less explosive power (megatonnage) than it did 20 years ago, I am sure most of you would respond that we have more. The truth is that today's level is less than half that which existed during the Kennedy administration. Similarly, if I were to ask whether we have more—or fewer—warheads than we had 10 years ago, I am sure most would respond that we must have more. The truth, however, is that in the course of the past decade, we have reduced the number in our arsenal by about one-third.

But my point is not to belabor statistics. The President believes that regardless of the level, it remains too high and that we must do everything we can to reduce it. It is toward this objective that the President directed the development of sound, equitable arms control positions with which to seek to engage the Soviet Union in a serious program of reductions. That directive was to serve two purposes: first, to deal with strategic weapons and, second, effect reductions of intermediate-range weapons such as the Soviet SS–20 which threaten our friends in Europe and elsewhere.

With regard to intermediate-range weapons, the President has proposed to the Soviet Union that if they will agree to dismantle all of their land-based missiles, now numbering more than 300 globally, we will forego deployment of corresponding systems to counter. In other words, we propose a zero-zero balance. Our negotiators are now engaged in Geneva with their Soviet counterparts in an effort to persuade them of the benefits of this outcome, not only for their security but for all mankind. We hope that before long they will see the wisdom in this proposal.

With respect to strategic or intercontinental weapons, the President has proposed dramatic reductions to equal numbers on both sides—approximately a one-third reduction in the number of ballistic missile warheads and a reduction in deployed ballistic missile launchers to one-half of the current U.S. level. Here again, our negotiators are hard at work in Geneva seeking to reach Soviet agreement on this proposal.

It is in the context of these negotiations that it is worthwhile to consider a proposal that has been made both by President Brezhnev and by large numbers of well-meaning people in this country. They have urged that we adopt an immediate freeze on the production, testing, and deployment of nuclear weapons. The very simplicity of the freeze proposal has made it attractive, especially by those who are put off by the perceived complexity of the issue. But it takes little more than common sense to identify the flaws in such an approach.

For example, if you were asked if you would support a unilateral freeze, I am sure most of you would say no. But if we could not verify Soviet compliance with a bilateral freeze agreement, it would effectively constitute a unilateral freeze agreement. How could we be sure that the Soviet Union was abiding by a freeze proposal? Frankly, our experience in this area is not encouraging, and, as a consequence, it behooves us not to take for granted Soviet good faith where the margin for error is very small indeed.

Apart from the question of verification, it is also reasonable to ask whether it is sensible to freeze in place an imbalance which has resulted from a decade of Soviet building and U.S. decline. Here again, it is instructive to consider the existing imbalance in the category of intermediate-range forces. I mentioned earlier that the Soviet Union now possesses more than 300 SS–20 missiles which can reach all of Western Europe and many other parts of the world. Neither the United States—nor any of our allies—possesses any corresponding land-based system which can reach the Soviet Union. An imbalance of 300–0, which grows to 600–0 when the other Soviet INF land-based missiles are included, is neither fair nor does it contribute to stable peace. It is for this reason that we are in negotiations in Geneva in an effort to persuade the Soviets to dismantle those systems.

And this leads me to my third point. What would be the effect of a freeze on our hopes for progress in these arms control talks? To answer this I need only to ask you to put yourself in the place of the Soviet Union. If you are in a position where the balance is in your favor in a 600–0 ballgame and the other side agreed to freeze that imbalance, what possible incentive would you have for continuing to negotiate or play ball at all?

In short, because an immediate or instant freeze presents extremely problematical verification questions, because it would freeze a substantial imbalance in place, and because it would remove incentives for the Soviet Union to negotiate reductions, a freeze would not contribute to effective arms control. And it is for this reason that the President has proposed that we first reduce nuclear weapons to equal levels before adopting a freeze.

President Reagan is deeply convinced that with persistence and seriousness of purpose we can reach agreements which truly reduce the size of the nuclear arsenals on both sides. He is reinforced in this conviction by the record of negotiations which have taken place thus far, and with your support he will continue to pursue them to a sucessful conclusion.

The fifth objective of this administration in foreign affairs is to establish a new basis for conducting our relations with the developing countries of the world. The President's approach relies heavily on the energy of the private sector. It is most graphically represented in the program known as the Caribbean Basin initiative. Under this program, the President has blended a combination of trade, aid, and incentives for investment into a carefully balanced arrangement to facilitate the self-help effort of the people of the Caribbean region. We hope during the special session of the Congress—commencing next month—to achieve enactment of the trade and tax provisions of this program, providing incentives for U.S. businesses to invest in the Caribbean area. Through this process, together with modest amounts of aid and improved access to overseas markets, we believe we can give hope to the people of this area who have lived for so long in despair, experiencing worsening conditions of trade with no change in sight.

The sixth goal of President Reagan's foreign policy—and perhaps its centerpiece—concerns our responsibility as a peacemaker. Since the earliest days of his administration, the President has directed that a maximum effort be devoted to lending U.S. prestige and resources to the resolution of disputes throughout the world. Most recently we have devoted extremely intense efforts to furthering the peace process in southern Africa and in the Middle East.

For longer than any of us can remember, the people of the Middle East have lived from war to war with no apparent prospect for any alternative future. Because it is our moral obligation and because of our important interests in the area, the President has focused his personal attention on the history of this dispute and all of its complexities. The results of his analysis were reflected in his remarks to the American people on September 1. In a nutshell, the President was asking a very simple question to each of the three forces in the region.

To Israel, which in 34 years has experienced five wars, he asked: How is your security best assured? Is it by maintaining control over territory with the virtually certain expectation of war every few years, or is your security not better assured by reaching a political accommodation with your neighbors?

To the Palestine Liberation Organization, which has experienced devastating defeat three times in the past 12 years, the President asked: Is armed struggle truly the best way to establish Palestinian identity?

And more generally to the Arab States of the area, he asked: Has confrontation with Israel for the past generation truly served your interest?

The President believes deeply that we face an historic opportunity which must not be missed. In his exchanges thus far since September 1, we have received encouraging signs from many quarters. He is hopeful that in the weeks ahead we will succeed in reopening talks for establishing transitional arrangements in the West Bank and Gaza district through such a process which must involve the participation of other Arab countries. The peoples of this area can bring to an end this dark chapter of their history and look forward to a new era of development and prosperity. The President has pledged his best efforts to make this dream come true.

In some parts of the world, the word "peace" is lightly said, because peace in those parts is a reality—a reality more or less taken for granted. In the Middle East, the word "peace" is weighty, almost palpable, because the reality seems so out of reach. We in the United States need to remind ourselves of the importance of shaping a perfect peace that may be only a goal, if in seeking that goal we are able to keep or improve on the peace we have.

I wish now to speak briefly on a related matter. In a speech 2 days ago, Mr. Leonid Brezhnev addressed the top Soviet military command.[36] He spoke of the Soviet Union's dedication to a peace threatened by American "adventurism." We perceive the purpose of his speech was to reassure the Soviet military establishment that it continues to retain its favored place in Soviet society. His remarks about improved Soviet-China relations were meant to create an impression of improving international relations. All of this was predictable.

But to represent the Soviet Union as the advocate of a meaningful peace threatened by the United States is hardly convincing. If the Soviet Union continues year after year to pour some 15% of its gross national product, two-and-one-half times our own, into its military establishment, it is not because it faces external threat but because it needs this kind of a force to keep its own population under control, to intimidate its neighbors, and to support imperial adventures in far-away Africa, Central America, and Southeast Asia.

Although Mr. Brezhnev is not running for office, he is nevertheless a politician, and his appeal to nationalism and militarism must be interpreted in these terms. But how can we take seriously unfounded accusations clearly designed as nothing but an excuse for intensifying still further the Soviet Union's already enormous military buildup?

The U.S. record is clear. It did not use its nuclear power when it enjoyed a nuclear monopoly. It has offered, time and again, meaningful proposals of arms limitations and reductions. It has scrupulously adhered to the terms of treaties and accords. It has—without reciprocity from Moscow—reduced its military budget for years. Our current military effort has—as its principal purpose—assurance of a credible deterrent in the face of prodigious military advances the Soviet Union has made during the years of U.S. self-restraint. We make no apologies for our role in the pursuit of peace, which we continue to pursue.

---

36 For the complete text of Brezhnev's speech to a conference of Soviet army and navy leaders at the Kremlin on October 27, 1982, see *Current Digest of the Soviet Press*, 34 (November 24, 1982), pp. 1–3.

Chapter 2. The Organization and Conduct of American Foreign Policy

Document 10

Statement by the President's Deputy Press Secretary (Speakes), January 4, 1982[1]

The Expanded Role of the President's Newly Appointed National Security Adviser

The President today accepted with deep regret the resignation of Richard V. Allen as Assistant to the President for National Security Affairs.[2]

In his place, the President named William P. Clark, currently Deputy Secretary of State, to become his new national security adviser.

In a private meeting this afternoon, the President told Mr. Allen that he greatly appreciated the service that he had performed for him over the past year and in earlier years. In the President's view, Mr. Allen has made an outstanding contribution to the construction and development of a strong national security policy for the Nation.

The President also reported to Mr. Allen his pleasure that both the investigation by the Justice Department and a recently completed study by the White House Counsel's office had revealed no wrongdoing on Mr. Allen's part.

At the same time, both Mr. Allen and he agreed that in view of the controversy of recent weeks, it would be better for all concerned to seek a change in responsibilities. Toward that end, the President asked Mr. Allen to serve as his consultant for an indefinite period to assist in the organization of the President's Foreign Intelligence Advisory Board.

Mr. Clark brings to his new post at the White House a distinguished record of service in California and, more recently, at the State Department.

In consultation with the members of the National Security Council, Mr. Clark in his new role will be responsible for the development, coordination and implementation of national security policy, as approved by the President. In addition, he will be responsible for providing staff support and for administering the National Security Council. As Assistant to the President for National Security Affairs, Mr. Clark will have a direct reporting relationship to the President.

This expanded role for the Assistant to the President for National Security Affairs, as announced today, will implement recommendations made to the President by the Counselor to the President, Edwin Meese III, following a review of the national security process.

Document 11

Statement Issued by President Reagan, January 12, 1982[3]

Presidential Directive on National Security Council Structure

I. National Security Council

The National Security Council (NSC) shall be the principal forum for considera-

---

[1] Source: White House Press Release, January 4, 1982, Office of the Press Secretary to the President; printed also in *Weekly Compilation of Presidential Documents,* January 11, 1982, p. 3.

[2] For the text of the exchange of letters between President Reagan and Allen concerning the latter's resignation, see *ibid.*, pp. 3–4.

[3] Source: White House Press Release, Januray 12, 1982, Office of the Press Secretary to the President; also printed in *Weekly Compilation of Presidential Documents,* January 18, 1982, pp. 21–24. The directive was National Security Decision Directive Number 2 (NSDD–2). William P. Clark, Assistant to the President for National Security Affairs, announced on January 12 that the President had that day approved three National Security Directives: this one, the one *infra,* and one rescinding 32 directives from the Carter administration.

tion of national security policy issues requiring Presidential decision.

The functions and responsibilities of the NSC shall be as set forth in the National Security Act of 1947,[4] as amended.

The NSC shall meet regularly. Those heads of Departments and Agencies who are not regular members shall participate as appropriate, when matters affecting their Departments or Agencies are considered.

The Assistant to the President for National Security Affairs, in consultation with the regular members of the NSC, shall be responsible for developing, coordinating and implementing national security policy as approved by me. He shall determine and publish the agenda of NSC meetings. He shall ensure that the necessary papers are prepared and—except in unusual circumstances—distributed in advance to Council members. He shall staff and administer the National Security Council.

Decision documents shall be prepared by the Assistant to the President for National Security Affairs, and disseminated by him after approval by the President.

II. NSC Responsibilities of the Secretary of State

The Secretary of State is my principal foreign policy advisor. As such, he is responsible for the formulation of foreign policy and for the execution of approved policy.

I have assigned to the Secretary of State authority and responsibility, to the extent permitted by law, for the overall direction, coordination, and supervision of the interdepartmental activities incident to foreign policy formulation, and the activities of Executive Departments and Agencies of the United States overseas. Such activities do not include those of United States military forces operating in the field under the command of a United States area military commander, and such other military activities as I elect, as Commander-in-Chief, to conduct exclusively through military or other channels. Activities that are internal to the execution and administration of the approved programs of a single Department or Agency and which are not of such nature as to affect significantly the overall U.S. overseas program in a country or region are not considered to be activities covered within the meaning of this Directive.

The Secretary of State is responsible for preparation of those papers addressing matters affecting the foreign policy and foreign relations of the United States for consideration by the NSC.

III. NSC Responsibilities of the Secretary of Defense

The Secretary of Defense is my principal defense policy advisor. As such, he is responsible for the formulation of general defense policy, policy related to all matters of direct and primary concern to the Department of Defense, and for the execution of approved policy. The Joint Chiefs of Staff are the principal military advisors to me, the Secretary of Defense, and the NSC.

I have assigned to the Secretary of Defense authority and responsibility, to the extent permitted by law, for the overall direction, coordination, and supervision of the interdepartmental activities incident to defense policy formulation.

The Secretary of Defense is responsible for preparation of those papers addressing matters affecting the defense policy of the United States for consideration by the NSC.

IV. NSC Responsibilities of the Director of Central Intelligence

The Director of Central Intelligence is my principal advisor on intelligence matters. As such, he is responsible for the formulation of intelligence activities, policy, and proposals, as set forth in relevant Executive Orders. I have assigned to the Director of Central Intelligence authority and responsibility, to the extent permitted by law and Executive Order, for the overall direction, coordination, and supervision of the interdepartmental activities incident to intelligence matters.

The Director of Central Intelligence is responsible for the preparation of those papers addressing matters affecting the intelligence activities, policy, and proposals of the United States for consideration by the NSC.

V. Interagency Groups

To assist the NSC at large and its individual members in fulfilling their responsibilities, interagency groups are established as described herein. The focus of these interagency groups is to establish policy objectives, develop policy options, make ap-

[4] P.L. 253, approved July 26, 1947; 61 Stat. 495.

propriate recommendations, consider the implications of agency programs for foreign policy or overall national security policy, and undertake such other activities as may be assigned by the NSC.

A. THE SENIOR INTERAGENCY GROUP—FOREIGN POLICY (SIG–FP)

To advise and assist the NSC in exercising its authority and discharging its responsibility for foreign policy and foreign affairs matters, the SIG–FP is established. The SIG–FP shall be composed of the Director of Central Intelligence; the Assistant to the President for National Security Affairs; the Deputy Secretary of State (Chairman); the Deputy Secretary of Defense or Under Secretary of Defense for Policy; and the Chairman, Joint Chiefs of Staff. Representatives of other Departments and Agencies with responsibility for specific matters to be considered will attend on invitation by the Chairman.

When meeting to consider arms control matters, the Group will be augmented by the Director, Arms Control and Disarmament Agency.

The SIG–FP will:

1. Ensure that important foreign policy issues requiring interagency attention receive full, prompt, and systematic consideration;

2. Deal with interdepartmental matters raised by any member or referred to it by subordinate interagency groups, or, if such matters require higher-level consideration, report them to the Secretary of State for decision or referral to the NSC;

3. Assure a proper selectivity of the foreign policy/foreign affairs areas and issues to which the United States applies its efforts;

4. Monitor the execution of approved policies and decisions; and

5. Evaluate the adequacy and effectiveness of interdepartmental overseas programs and activities.

A permanent secretariat, composed of personnel of the State Department augmented as necessary by personnel provided in response to the Chairman's request by the Departments and Agencies represented on the SIG–FP, shall be established.

B. THE SENIOR INTERAGENCY GROUP—DEFENSE POLICY (SIG–DP)

To advise and assist the NSC in exercising its authority and discharging its responsibility for defense policy and defense matters, the SIG–DP is established. The SIG–DP shall consist of the Director of Central Intelligence; the Assistant to the President for National Security Affairs; the Deputy or an Under Secretary of State; the Deputy Secretary of Defense (Chairman); and the Chairman, Joint Chiefs of Staff. Representatives of other Departments and Agencies with responsibility for specific matters to be considered will attend on invitation by the Chairman.

The SIG–DP will:

1. Ensure that important defense policy issues requiring interagency attention receive full, prompt, and systematic consideration;

2. Deal with interdepartmental matters raised by any member or referred to it by subordinate interagency groups, or if such matters require higher-level consideration, report them to the Secretary of Defense for decision or referral to the NSC; and

3. Monitor the execution of approved policies and decisions.

A permanent secretariat, composed of personnel of the Department of Defense augmented as necessary by personnel provided in response to the Chairman's request by the Departments and Agencies represented on the SIG–DP, shall be established.

C. THE SENIOR INTERAGENCY GROUP—INTELLIGENCE (SIG–I)

To advise and assist the NSC in exercising its authority and discharging its responsibility for intelligence policy and intelligence matters, the SIG–I is established. The SIG–I shall consist of Director of Central Intelligence (Chairman); the Assistant to the President for National Security Affairs; the Deputy Secretary of State; the Deputy Secretary of Defense; and the Chairman, Joint Chiefs of Staff. Representatives of other Departments and Agencies will attend on invitation by the Chairman when such Departments and agencies have a direct interest in intelligence activities under consideration.

When meeting to consider sensitive intelligence collection activities referred by the Director of Central Intelligence, the membership of the Group shall be augmented, as necessary, by the head of each organization within the Intelligence Community directly involved in the activity in question. When meeting to consider counterintelligence activities, the Group shall be augmented by the Director, Federal Bureau of Investigation, and the Director, National Security Agency.

The SIG–I will:

1. Establish requirements and priorities for national foreign intelligence;

2. Review such National Foreign Intelligence Program and budget proposals and other matters as are referred to it by the Director of Central Intelligence;

3. Review proposals for sensitive foreign intelligence collection operations referred by the Director of Central Intelligence;

Develop standards and doctrine for the counterintelligence activities of the United States; resolve interagency differences concerning the implementation of counterintelligence policy; and develop and monitor guidelines, consistent with applicable law and Executive orders, for the maintenance of central counterintelligence records;

5. Consider and approve any counterintelligence activity referred to the Group by the head of any organization in the Intelligence Community;

6. Submit to the NSC an overall annual assessment of the relative threat to United States interests from intelligence and security services of foreign powers and from international terrorist activities; including an assessment of the effectiveness of the United States counterintelligence activities;

7. Conduct an annual review of ongoing sensitive national foreign intelligence collection operations and sensitive counterintelligence activities and report thereon to the NSC; and

8. Carry out such additional coordination review and approval of intelligence activities as the President may direct.

A permanent secretariat, composed of personnel of the Central Intelligence Agency augmented as necessary by personnel provided in response to the Chairman's request by the Departments and Agencies represented on the SIG–I, shall be established.

D. REGIONAL AND FUNCTIONAL INTERAGENCY GROUPS

To assist the SIG–FP, Interagency Groups (IGs) shall be established by the Secretary of State for each geographic region corresponding to the jurisdiction of the geographic bureaus in the Department of State, for Political-Military Affairs, and for International Economic Affairs. Each IG shall be comprised of the Director of Central Intelligence; the Assistant to the President for National Security Affairs; the Chairman, Joint Chiefs of Staff; the appropriate Assistant Secretary of State (Chairman); and a designated representative of the Secretary of Defense. Representatives of other Departments and Agencies with responsibility for specific matters to be considered will attend on invitation by the Chairman. The IG for International Economic Affairs will, in addition to the above membership, include representatives of the Secretary of Treasury, the Secretary of Commerce, and the U.S. Trade Representative.

IGs for arms control matters will, in addition to the above membership, include a representative of the Director, Arms Control and Disarmament Agency. Arms control IGs will be chaired by the representative of the Secretary of State or the representative of the Director, Arms Control and Disarmament Agency, in accordance with guidelines to be provided by the SIG–FP.

To assist the SIG–DP, IGs shall be established by the Secretary of Defense corresponding to the functional areas within the Department of Defense. Each IG shall be comprised of the appropriate Under or Assistant Secretary of Defense (Chairman); a representative of the Secretary of State; the Director of Central Intelligence; the Assistant to the President for National Security Affairs; and the Chairman, Joint Chiefs of Staff. Representatives of other Departments and Agencies will attend on invitation by the Chairman.

Under and Assistant Secretaries, in their capacities as Chairmen of the IGs, will assure the adequacy of United States policy in the areas of their responsibility and of the plans, programs, resources, and performance for implementing that policy. They will be responsible for the conduct of interagency policy studies within the areas of their responsibility for consideration by the SIG.

The Regional IGs also shall prepare contingency plans pertaining to potential crises in their respective areas of responsibility. Contingency planning will be conducted in coordination with the Chairman of the Political-Military IG, with the exception of the military response option for employment of forces in potential crises, which will remain within the purview of the Department of

Defense and will be developed by the Joint Chiefs of Staff.

To deal with specific contingencies, the IGs will establish full-time working groups, which will provide support to the crisis management operations of the NSC. These groups will reflect the institutional membership of the parent body, together with such additional members as may be required to respond to the contingency with the full weight of available expertise.

To assist the SIG–I, IGs shall be established by the Director of Central Intelligence. The IG for Counterintelligence shall consist of representatives of the Secretary of State; Secretary of Defense; the Director of Central Intelligence; the Director, Federal Bureau of Investigation; the Assistant to the President for National Security Affairs; Chairman, Joint Chiefs of Staff; the Director, National Security Agency; and a representative of the head of any other Intelligence Community organization directly involved in the activities under discussion. The IG for Counterintelligence will be under the chairmanship of the representative of the Director of Central Intelligence or the Director, Federal Bureau of Investigation, in accordance with guidelines to be provided by the SIG–I.

The operational responsibility or authority of a Secretary or other Agency head over personnel from the Department or Agency concerned serving on IGs—including the authority to give necessary guidance to the representatives in the performance of IG duties—is not limited by this Directive.

Document 12

Statement Issued by President Reagan, January 12, 1982[5]

Protection of Classified National Security Council and Intelligence Information

Unauthorized disclosure of classified information under the jurisdiction of the National Security Council and of classified intelligence reports is a problem of major proportions within the U.S. Government. The Constitution of the United States provides for the protection of individual rights and liberties, including freedom of speech and freedom of the press, but it also requires that government functions be discharged efficiently and effectively, especially where the national security is involved. As President of the United States, I am responsible for honoring both Constitutional requirements, and I intend to do so in a balanced and careful manner. I do not believe, however, that the Constitution entitles government employees, entrusted with confidential information critical to the functioning and effectiveness of the government, to disclose such information with impunity. Yet this is precisely the situation we have. It must not be allowed to continue.

To this end, I hereby establish and direct implementation of the following policies.

Contacts with the Media

All contacts with any element of the news media in which classified National Security Council matters or classified intelligence information are discussed will require the advance approval of a senior official. An administrative memorandum will be prepared as soon as possible after the contact, recording the subjects discussed and all information provided to the media representatives.

Access

The unauthorized disclosure of classified National Security Council information, documents, and deliberations requires further control to limit access and to ensure an accurate record of those who have had access. The number of officials with access to documents relating to NSC matters will be kept to the minimum essential to the orderly conduct of the government's business.

Investigations

The government's lack of success in identifying the sources of unauthorized disclosure of classified National Security Council information and documents of classified intelligence information must be remedied and appropriate disciplinary measures taken. Henceforth, in the event of unauthorized disclosure of such information, government employees who have had access to that information will be subject to investigation, to include the use of all legal methods.

---

[5] Source: White House Press Release, January 12, 1982, Office of the Press Secretary to the President; also printed in *Weekly Compilation of Presidential Documents,* January 18, 1982, pp. 24–25. The directive was National Security Decision Directive Number 19 (NSDD–19).

Applicability and Implementation

The provisions of this directive shall be effective immediately and shall apply to all employees of, and elements within agencies participating in the National Security Council system, including the Executive Office of the President. The Assistant to the President for National Security Affairs is directed to establish the detailed procedures to implement policies.[6]

Document 13

Executive Order 12356, Issued by President Reagan, April 2, 1982 (Extracts)[7]

National Security Information

This Order prescribes a uniform system for classifying, declassifying, and safeguarding national security information. It recognizes that it is essential that the public be informed concerning the activities of its Government, but that the interests of the United States and its citizens require that certain information concerning the national defense and foreign relations be protected against unauthorized disclosure. Information may not be classified under this Order unless its disclosure reasonably could be expected to cause damage to the national security.

NOW, by the authority vested in me as President by the Constitution and laws of the United States of America, it is hereby ordered as follows:

PART 1

Original Classification

Section 1.1 *Classification Levels.*

(a) National security information (hereinafter "classified information") shall be classified at one of the following three levels:

(1) "Top Secret" shall be applied to information, the unauthorized disclosure of which reasonably could be expected to cause exceptionally grave damage to the national security.

(2) "Secret" shall be applied to information, the unauthorized disclosure of which reasonably could be expected to cause serious damage to the national security.

(3) "Confidential" shall be applied to information, the unauthorized disclosure of which reasonably could be expected to cause damage to the national security.

(b) Except as otherwise provided by statute, no other terms shall be used to identify classified information.

(c) If there is reasonable doubt about the need to classify information, it shall be safeguarded as if it were classified pending a determination by an original classification authority, who shall make this determination within thirty (30) days. If there is reasonable doubt about the appropriate level of classification, it shall be safeguarded at the higher level of classification pending a determination by an original classification authority, who shall make this determination within thirty (30) days.

. . . .

Sec. 1.3 *Classification Categories.*

(a) Information shall be considered for classification if it concerns:

(1) military plans, weapons, or operations;

(2) the vulnerabilities or capabilities of systems, installations, projects, or plans relating to the national security;

(3) foreign government information;

(4) intelligence activities (including special activities), or intelligence sources or methods;

(5) foreign relations or foreign activities of the United States;

(6) scientific, technological, or economic matters relating to the national security;

---

[6] For a memorandum of February 2, 1982, by Clark, see *Weekly Compilation of Presidential Documents*, February 8, 1982, pp. 105–106.

[7] Source: White House Press Release, April 2, 1982, Office of the Press Secretary to the President; also printed in *Weekly Compilation of Presidential Documents*, April 5, 1982, pp. 423, 424–426, 431. For the full text, see *ibid.*, pp. 422–431, or *Federal Register*, April 6, 1982, pp. 14874–14884. For the text of the implementing directive prepared by the Information Security Oversight Office and approved by the National Security Council on June 22, 1982, see *ibid.*, June 25, 1982, pp. 27836–27842. Executive Order 12356 superseded Executive Order 12065 of June 28, 1978, extracts of which are printed in *American Foreign Policy: Basic Documents, 1977–1980*, pp. 96–97.

(7) United States Government programs for safeguarding nuclear materials or facilities;

(8) cryptology;

(9) a confidential source; or

(10) other categories of information that are related to the national security and that require protection against unauthorized disclosure as determined by the President or by agency heads or other officials who have been delegated original classification authority by the President. Any determination made under this subsection shall be reported promptly to the Director of the Information Security Oversight Office.

(b) Information that is determined to concern one or more of the categories in Section 1.3(a) shall be classified when an original classification authority also determines that its unauthorized disclosure, either by itself or in the context of other information, reasonably could be expected to cause damage to the national security.

(c) Unauthorized disclosure of foreign government information, the identity of a confidential foreign source, or intelligence sources or methods is presumed to cause damage to the national security.

(d) Information classified in accordance with Section 1.3 shall not be declassified automatically as a result of any unofficial publication or inadvertent or unauthorized disclosure in the United States or abroad of identical or similar information.

Sec. 1.4 *Duration of Classification.*

(a) Information shall be classified as long as required by national security considerations. When it can be determined, a specific date or event for declassification shall be set by the original classification authority at the time the information is originally classified.

(b) Automatic declassification determinations under predecessor orders shall remain valid unless the classification is extended by an authorized official of the originating agency. These extensions may be by individual documents or categories of information. The agency shall be responsible for notifying holders of the information of such extensions.

(c) Information classified under predecessor orders and marked for declassification review shall remain classified until reviewed for declassification under the provisions of this Order.

. . . .

Sec. 1.6 *Limitations on Classification.*

(a) In no case shall information be classified in order to conceal violations of law, inefficiency, or administrative error; to prevent embarrassment to a person, organization, or agency; to restrain competition; or to prevent or delay the release of information that does not require protection in the interest of national security.

(b) Basic scientific research information not clearly related to the national security may not be classified.

(c) The President or an agency head or official designated under Sections 1.2 (a)(2), 1.2 (b)(1), or 1.2 (c)(1) may reclassify information previously declassified and disclosed if it is determined in writing that (1) the information requires protection in the interest of national security; and (2) the information may reasonably be recovered. These reclassification actions shall be reported promptly to the Director of the Information Security Oversight Office.

(d) Information may be classified or reclassified after an agency has received a request for it under the Freedom of Information Act (5 U.S.C. 552) or the Privacy Act of 1974 (5 U.S.C. 552a), or the mandatory review provisions of this Order (Section 3.4) if such classification meets the requirements of this Order and is accomplished personally and on a document-by-document basis by the agency head, the deputy agency head, the senior agency official designated under Section 5.3(a)(1), or an official with original Top Secret classification authority.

. . . .

PART 3

Declassification and Downgrading

Sec. 3.1 *Declassification Authority.*

(a) Information shall be declassified or downgraded as soon as national security considerations permit. Agencies shall coordinate their review of classified information with other agencies that have a direct interest in the subject matter. Information that continues to meet the classification requirements prescribed by Section 1.3 despite the passage of time will continue to be protected in accordance with this Order.

. . . .

Ronald Reagan

Document 14

Exchange of Letters Between President Reagan and the Secretary of State (Haig), June 25, 1982[8]

Resignation of Secretary of State Alexander Haig

June 25, 1982

DEAR AL: It is with the most profound regret that I accept your letter of resignation. Almost forty years ago you committed yourself to the service of your country. Since that time your career has been marked by a succession of assignments demanding the highest level of personal sacrifice, courage and leadership. As a soldier and statesman facing challenges of enormous complexity and danger, you have established a standard of excellence and achievement seldom equalled in our history. On each occasion you have reflected a quality of wisdom which has been critical to the resolution of the most anguishing problems we have faced during the past generation—the conclusion of the Vietnam war, the transfer of executive authority at a time of national trauma and most recently, advancing the cause of peace among nations.

The Nation is deeply in your debt. As you leave I want you to know of my deep personal appreciation, and in behalf of the American people I express my gratitude and respect. You have been kind enough to offer your continued counsel and you may be confident that I will call upon you in the years ahead. Nancy joins me in extending our warmest personal wishes to you and Pat.

Sincerely,

RONALD REAGAN

[8] Source: White House Press Release, June 25, 1982, Office of the Press Secretary to the President; printed also in *Weekly Compilation of Presidential Documents*, June 28, 1982, pp. 841–842. The President announced at 3:04 p.m. that he had accepted Haig's resignation, that he planned to nominate George P. Shultz, who had earlier served as Secretary of Labor and Secretary of the Treasury, to succeed Haig, and that Shultz had accepted; for the text of the President's remarks, see *ibid.*, p. 841.

DEAR MR. PRESIDENT: Your accession to office on January 20, 1981, brought an opportunity for a new and forward looking foreign policy resting on the cornerstones of strength and compassion. I believe that we shared a view of America's role in the world as the leader of free men and an inspiration for all. We agreed that consistency, clarity and steadiness of purpose were essential to success. It was in this spirit that I undertook to serve you as Secretary of State.

In recent months, it has become clear to me that the foreign policy on which we embarked together was shifting from that careful course which we had laid out. Under these circumstances, I feel it necessary to request that you accept my resignation. I shall always treasure the confidence which you reposed in me. It has been a great honor to serve in your Administration, and I wish you every success in the future.

Sincerely,

ALEXANDER M. HAIG, JR.

Document 15

Testimony by the Secretary of State-Designate (Shultz) Before the Senate Foreign Relations Committee, July 13, 1982 (Extract)[9]

"It is the President's Policy . . . . He Is the Boss"

. . . .

SENATOR BIDEN . . . . Mr. Secretary, you are here—and I call you Mr. Secretary not because you have been confirmed yet but because you have been Secretary at least on two other occasions, and I expect on a third—you are here because there is a problem. You are not here in the normal course of events, although it has become normal in the last two administrations to see a Secretary of State leave in midstream.

[9] Source: *Nomination of George P. Shultz: Hearings Before the Committee on Foreign Relations, United States Senate, Ninety-seventh Congress, Second Session* (Washington, 1982), pp. 27–28. For an extract from Secretary-designate Shultz's statement before the Committee, see document 5.

And as you know as well as any of us on this committee through your worldwide travels and close relationships with the various world leaders—and I am not merely referring to the Middle East; I am referring to Europe, Germany, Great Britain—that is an extremely worrisome aspect of American foreign policy to our friends and foes alike.

So you are here because we have a problem. And your job is going to be to solve the problem, not merely to be the Secretary of State, which is an awesome responsibility.

To an outsider looking into an administration as I am, it seems as though in order to solve that problem, one of two things has to happen: Either there has to be a structural reorganization within this administration which has little foreign policy organization—and I say that about the last administration, too, although this is like Carter revisited from the right—you have the National Security Adviser bounced out after less than a year, a very strong figure, strong personality; you have the No. 1 person in the Cabinet bounced out in less than 2 years in an administration; the two chief foreign policy spokespersons of this administration, the only two with acknowledged expertise in the area of foreign policy prior to assuming the office, gone.

And now we have a man of your caliber. And I do not say that lightly. I think you are, of all the people who have been submitted in the four Presidential terms that I have been through as a U.S. Senator, you are at least as qualified intellectually, politically, morally, and every other way as any man who has ever sat before any of our committees.

But to get to the specific question. It is either a structural problem or a serious personality problem. And you in a newly published book criticize the overreliance on "the exact organizational form of the coordination mechanism for shaping policy. What counts more than the structure of the coordinating mechanisms are the personal qualities of the key officials and their ability to work together."

You go on to say, "The White House has many of the attributes of a royal court. Access to the President can easily become an end in itself. Intrigue can too easily replace analysis in policy formulation and execution."

Simply put, Mr. Secretary, how are you going to solve the problem for America? How are you going to solve the problem for this administration of having one person, one voice, one policy in foreign policy? Can you do the job, and how are you going to do it?

Mr. Shultz. I think it is basically extremely simple. The foreign policy we talk about is the President's foreign policy. My job is to help him formulate his foreign policy, along with others, and to take a major part, both in the formulation and in the effort to execute that policy, and maintain a consistency of it. But it is simple in that it is the President's policy. We are all in the administration, fundamentally working for him. He is the boss.

So I think it is a very simple proposition. There are procedures set out, and there is a National Security Directive that states the responsibilities of the Secretaries of Defense and State and the National Security Advisers and other Cabinet officials.[10] And I have that—I am sure you have it—that lays it out very clearly.

But I personally still agree with what I wrote, and which you read, that in the end you have a group of people there and they have to develop a good, solid, respectful working relationship. And that is always the way I have gone about it in other jobs that I have had in government and the university and companies, and that is the way I intend to go about it here.

. . . .

Document 16

Public Law 97–241, Approved August 24, 1982 (Extract)[11]

The Foreign Missions Act

TITLE II—FOREIGN MISSIONS

Short Title

Sec. 201. This title may be cited as the "Foreign Missions Act".

---

[10] See document 11.

[11] Source: 96 Stat. 282. Title II of P.L. 97–241 constituted the Foreign Missions Act. Title I constituted the Department of State Authorization Act, Fiscal Years 1982 and 1983; 96 Stat. 273. Title III, which constituted the United States Information Agency Authorization Act, Fiscal Years 1982 and 1983, redesignated the International Communication Agency as the United States Information Agency; 96 Stat. 291.

REGULATION OF FOREIGN MISSIONS

Sec. 202. (a) The State Department Basic Authorities Act of 1956[12] is amended by striking out "That the Secretary" in the first section and inserting in lieu thereof the following:

"TITLE I—BASIC AUTHORITIES GENERALLY

"Section 1. The Secretary".

(b) That Act is further amended by adding at the end thereof the following:

"TITLE II—AUTHORITIES RELATING TO THE REGULATION OF FOREIGN MISSIONS

"DECLARATION OF FINDINGS AND POLICY

"Sec. 201.(a) The Congress finds that the operation in the United States of foreign missions and public international organizations and the official missions to such organizations, including the permissible scope of their activities and the location and size of their facilities, is a proper subject for the exercise of Federal jurisdiction.

"(b) The Congress declares that it is the policy of the United States to support the secure and efficient operation of United States missions abroad, to facilitate the secure and efficient operation in the United States of foreign missions and public international organizations and the official missions to such organizations, and to assist in obtaining appropriate benefits, privileges, and immunities for those missions and organizations and to require their observance of corresponding obligations in accordance with international law.

"(c) The treatment to be accorded to a foreign mission in the United States shall be determined by the Secretary after due consideration of the benefits, privileges, and immunities provided to missions of the United States in the country or territory represented by that foreign mission.

"DEFINITIONS

"Sec. 202.(a) For purposes of this title—

"(1) 'benefit' (with respect to a foreign mission) means any acquisition, or authorization for an acquisition, in the United States by or for a foreign mission, including the acquisition of—

"(A) real property by purchase, lease, exchange, construction, or otherwise,

"(B) public services, including services relating to customs, importation, and utilities, and the processing of applications or requests relating to public services,

"(C) supplies, maintenance, and transportation,

"(D) locally engaged staff on a temporary or regular basis,

"(E) travel and related services, and

"(F) protective services,

and includes such other benefits as the Secretary may designate;

"(2) 'chancery' means the principal offices of a foreign mission used for diplomatic or related purposes, and annexes to such offices (including ancillary offices and support facilities), and includes the site and any building on such site which is used for such purposes;

"(3) 'Director' means the Director of the Office of Foreign Missions established pursuant to section 203(a);

"(4) 'foreign mission' means any official mission to the United States involving diplomatic, consular, or other governmental activities of—

"(A) a foreign government, or

"(B) an organization (other than an international organization, as defined in section 209(b) of this title)[13] representing a territory or political entity which has been granted diplomatic or other official privileges and immunities under the laws of the United States,

including any real property of such a mission and including the personnel of such a mission;

"(5) 'real property' includes any right, title, or interest in or to, or the beneficial use of, any real property in the United States, including any office or other building;

[12] P.L. 84–885, approved August 1, 1956; 70 Stat. 890.

[13] Section 209 provided that the Secretary could apply any provision of Title II to an international organization to the same extent that it was applicable with respect to a foreign mission if he determined that such application was necessary to carry out the policy set forth in section 201(b) and to further the objectives set forth in section 204(b).

"(6) 'Secretary' means the Secretary of State;

"(7) 'sending State' means the foreign government, territory, or political entity represented by a foreign mission; and

"(8) 'United States' means, when used in a geographic sense, the several States, the District of Columbia, the Commonwealth of Puerto Rico, and the territories and possessions of the United States.

"(b) Determinations with respect to the meaning and applicability of the terms used in subsection (a) shall be committed to the discretion of the Secretary.

"OFFICE OF FOREIGN MISSIONS

"Sec. 203.(a) The Secretary shall establish an Office of Foreign Missions as an office within the Department of State. The Office shall be headed by a Director, appointed by the Secretary, who shall perform his or her functions under the supervision and direction of the Secretary. The Secretary may delegate this authority for supervision and direction of the Director only to the Deputy Secretary of State or an Under Secretary of State.

"(b) The Secretary may authorize the Director to—

"(1) assist agencies of Federal, State, and municipal government with regard to ascertaining and according benefits, privileges, and immunities to which a foreign mission may be entitled;

"(2) provide or assist in the provision of benefits for or on behalf of a foreign mission in accordance with section 204; and

"(3) perform such other functions as the Secretary may determine necessary in furtherance of the policy of this title.

"PROVISION OF BENEFITS

"Sec. 204.(a) Upon the request of a foreign mission, benefits may be provided to or for that foreign mission by or through the Director on such terms and conditions as the Secretary may approve.

"(b) If the Secretary determines that such action is reasonably necessary on the basis of reciprocity or otherwise—

"(1) to facilitate relations between the United States and a sending State,

"(2) to protect the interests of the United States,

"(3) to adjust for costs and procedures of obtaining benefits for missions of the United States abroad, or

"(4) to assist in resolving a dispute affecting United States interests and involving a foreign mission or sending State,

then the Secretary may require a foreign mission (A) to obtain benefits from or through the Director on such terms and conditions as the Secretary may approve, or (B) to comply with such terms and conditions as the Secretary may determine as a condition to the execution or performance in the United States of any contract or other agreement, the acquisition, retention, or use of any real property, or the application for or acceptance of any benefit (including any benefit from or authorized by any Federal, State, or municipal governmental authority, or any entity providing public services).

"(c) Terms and conditions established by the Secretary under this section may include—

"(1) a requirement to pay to the Director a surcharge or fee, and

"(2) a waiver by a foreign mission (or any assignee of or person deriving rights from a foreign mission) of any recourse against any governmental authority, any entity providing public services, any employee or agent of such an authority or entity, or any other person, in connection with any action determined by the Secretary to be undertaken in furtherance of this title.

"(d) For purposes of effectuating a waiver of recourse which is required under this section, the Secretary may designate the Director or any other officer of the Department of State as the agent of a foreign mission (or of any assignee of or person deriving rights from a foreign mission). Any such waiver by an officer so designated shall for all purposes (including any court or administrative proceeding) be deemed to be a waiver by the foreign mission (or the assignee of or other person deriving rights from a foreign mission).

"(e) Nothing in this section shall be deemed to preclude or limit in any way the authority of the United States Secret Service to provide protective services pursuant to section 202 of title 3, United States Code, or section 3056 of title 18, United States Code, at a level commensurate with protective requirements as determined by the United States Secret Service."

. . . .

Chapter 3. National Security Policy

Document 17

Transcript of a White House Press Briefing, January 4, 1982 (Extracts)[1]

Restructuring of the Position of the President's National Security Adviser

. . . .

Q. Mr. Clark, when you first went up to the Senate and had your first confirmation hearings there was a lot of criticism about your knowledge of foreign policy affairs.[2] Do you feel in yourself that you are now fully equipped to handle the job of National Security Adviser?

MR. CLARK. Well, it is certainly not my judgment. It is, of course, the judgment of the President who has made that decision.

Q. Mr. Clark, what is your understanding of Ed Meese's role in the provision of or development of foreign policy in the National Security Council?

MR. CLARK. That, as you describe it, has really not been Mr. Meese's role and so, his basic role of acting as Counselor to the President will continue, both in the domestic and foreign policy fields.

Q. What is your understanding—

Q. What is that role in the policy field then, as you see it?

MR. CLARK. Basically to act as Counselor to the President and at any time that the foreign policy or national security issues should roll up against or lag over into domestic policy then Mr. Meese would have a further position of Counselor to the President to resolve any conflict between the domestic and foreign sides.

Q. Herein, Director, will you be reporting to Mr. Meese in any fashion, or will you report only directly to the President?

MR. CLARK. No, as the President has directed, I report directly to the President on a daily basis, or more often, as the issues of the day might require.

. . . .

Q. What we are trying to get at in questioning—has Meese's power in the foreign policy field in the White house been mentioned at all in terms of your elevation and the—more power given to this role now?

MR. CLARK. It is not a matter of anyone having any power. It is a matter of duty as directed by the President and I believe the statement, in that regard, speaks for itself.[3]

Q. No, it doesn't.

. . . .

Q. How is this definition of the job of National Security Adviser different from the job as it was originally perceived back in January—last January?

MR. CLARK. Again, the statement speaks for itself. The Assistant to the President for National Security Affairs reports directly to the President and acts at the President's direction in the developing, the coordinating, implementing, of national security affairs.

Q. How is that different? We were told that the job is going to be constituted differently and I am trying to understand how it differs.

---

[1] Source: White House Press Release, January 4, 1982, Office of the Press Secretary to the President. William P. Clark conducted the briefing in the Briefing Room of the White House beginning at 5:40 p.m.

[2] The reference is to the confirmation hearings of Clark for the position of Deputy Secretary of State on February 2 and 3, 1981. See *Nomination of Justice William Patrick Clark: Hearings Before the Committee on Foreign Relations, United States Senate, Ninety-seventh Congress, First Session* (Washington, 1981).

[3] Reference is to the statement, made earlier that day by Larry Speakes, Deputy Press Secretary to the President, that President Reagan had accepted with regret the resignation of Richard V. Allen as Assistant to the President for National Security Affairs and had named in his place William P. Clark as his new National Security Adviser.

MR. CLARK. As you are aware, my predecessor in this position did report through Mr. Meese to the President.

Q. Would you consider now that there is a Big Four rather than a Big Three? Do you consider yourself at the level of adviser as Meese, Baker, and Deaver?

MR. CLARK. No, there is no such consideration.

Q. Will you be attending the same morning meeting that now Baker, Meese, and Deaver have with the President?

MR. CLARK. I doubt that, for the reason that I am not going to be involved in the housekeeping matters of the White House. My province is at the direction and only at the direction of the President, involving myself in the national security affairs side.

Q. Mr. Clark, when the President came in a year ago, he consciously downgraded the concept and the role of the National Security Assistant. He said he didn't like the Kissinger model or the Brzezinski model. He wanted something a little more appropriate. Now the role has been upgraded again to something closer to that old role model. Doesn't that suggest that the experiment, if you want to call it that, has failed?

MR. CLARK. That's your characterization. I don't think the President was experimenting. Yes, sir.

Q. If I may ask you, what will you be doing concerning the briefing of the President? Will you see him every morning? Will there be morning briefings? Will anyone else sit in with you in those briefings?

MR. CLARK. I will be briefing the President daily. And, as I say, beyond, as issues may require as to who will be present, that is yet to be determined.

Q. Follow on that?

MR. CLARK. All right. Go ahead.

Q. Will Ed Meese be sitting in on those daily briefings of the President with you?

MR. CLARK. I would hope so. I've been working with Ed Meese now for about 16 years and certainly whether he's there or not he'll know what occurs in that meeting, as will Secretary Haig, Secretary Weinberger and other Cabinet members on the basis of involvement and need to know. Yes, sir.

. . . .

Q. What's your understanding of why this job has been restructured? If it's not a field experiment, what is it? Why is it being—

MR. CLARK. I think it shows the flexibility that must exist in the executive branch of government. Certainly—particularly in the first year of any administration, there are many changes in structure and I think in prior administrations far more changes in both structure and personnel than has been the case in this administration. That's part of the system. And thank goodness it is.

Q. Well, what improvements do you see, Mr. Clark? There's been a traditional rivalry between the head of the National Security Council staff and the State Department, even though you've had experience at the State Department, I guess history would teach that it's likely to happen again. How do you plan to handle that? Have you given any thought to that?

MR. CLARK. Yes, I have. The conflict of which you speak is inherent in the system, again, it's healthy, the give-and-take system of ideas that must exist in a democracy. And you refer, of course, to the transition from number two position in the State Department to White House, I now must view the area of national security from a presidential perspective rather than from the State Department perspective and I hope that that experience of the prior vantage spot will assist in the arriving at the teamwork that we all know must exist among the CIA, Department of Defense, and the State Department.

Q. Do you plan to speak out much in public as an enunciator of administration policy?

MR. CLARK. No, I'm quite certain the President made clear and has not changed his position from January, at which time he designated Secretary Haig as the formulator and the enunciator of foreign policy and foreign affairs.

Q. What changes will we see in national security operations here once you take over? Will there be more focus, more coordination? How would you describe the way you approach this job?

MR. CLARK. It's premature. As this unfolds, I'd prefer discussing procedures, the structure in its evolution rather than today. The appointment has just occurred.

Q. How many changes do you expect to see on the National Security Council staff now that you've taken over—

MR. CLARK. I have no plans at the moment regarding personnel and as has been stated, the President has directed that I shall do that subject to his approval on an ongoing basis and, again, it's premature to go into that.

. . . .

Q. Mr. Clark, when I asked you why this job was being restructured you said, "Well, it often happens." But, why? What were the reasons for making this change, for upgrading this job—

MR. CLARK. It's not just a matter of upgrading the job. Over the past 11 months, there have been many recommendations, the latest a summation presented to the President by Mr. Meese, recommendations from many people, including Mr. Allen, who helped develop some of the ideas that have led to the restructuring.

So it has not been a sudden process. It has been an evolutionary process over the last 11 months—recommendations from Cabinet members, staffs, and there will no doubt be other changes as we progress.

. . . .

Q. Since you said that you had been aware of the rivalry between State and the NSC and you have given thought to it, were there any preconditions that you put before you would accept the job that you had to discuss with the President to make you able to function better?

MR. CLARK. No preconditions. I spoke with the President at his request some three weeks ago as did other members of the Cabinet at the President's request for suggestions in this area. Many of them have gone into the report that Mr. Meese has submitted to the President.

Q. Did you speak with Mr. Meese also?

MR. CLARK. No, not on the occasion I just spoke of, no.

Q. Did you speak to him either before or afterwards—before his report went in—

MR. CLARK. Yes.

Q. —on the need to upgrade the job?

MR. CLARK. Well, it has not been done in the context of upgrading, I feel that perhaps we are spending a little bit too much time on that term. That would be a value judgment that I think has come into the mix and I think is a part of it. But it is much broader than an upgrading. It takes into consideration the needs of the primary agencies involved in national security affairs and that restructuring, I think, will speak for itself as it develops over the next several days.

. . . .

Document 18

Transcript of a White House Press Briefing, January 7, 1982 (Extract)[4]

Continuation of Standby Draft Registration

MR. MEESE. I'll read the statement that was issued by the President[5] and then with me, of course, is Cap Weinberger, the Secretary of Defense, who will be happy to answer any questions—particularly in the area of manpower, generally, and Tom Turnage, the Director of the Selective Service System, will be happy to answer any technical questions on Selective Service. The statement issued by the President reads as follows:

> "Last July, I established a presidential Military Manpower Task Force chaired by Defense Secretary Weinberger.[6] One of the mandates of the task force was to examine the cases for and against continued military draft registration as well as to review other issues affecting military manpower.
>
> "I have now received the report of the task force and the recommendations of its members.[7] On the basis of their find-

---

[4] Source: White House Press Release, January 7, 1982, Office of the Press Secretary to the President: Edwin Meese conducted the briefing in which Secretary of Defense Weinberger and Major General Thomas K. Turnage, Director of the Selective Service System, also participated. The briefing was held in the Briefing Room of the White House beginning at 4:33 p.m.

[5] The statement, quoted below in the source text, is also printed in *Weekly Compilation of Presidential Documents*, January 11, 1982, p. 8.

[6] For the text of the President's announcement on July 8, 1981, of the establishment of a Military Manpower Task Force, chaired by Secretary of Defense Weinberger, see *Public Papers of the Presidents of the United States: Ronald Reagan*, 1981 (Washington, 1982), p. 610.

[7] This report, which was transmitted to President Reagan in December 1981, has not been printed.

ings, I have decided to continue registration. Make no mistake: The continuation of peacetime registration does not foreshadow a return to the draft. I remain firm in my convictions stated in 1980 that only in the most severe national emergency does the government have a claim to the mandatory service of its young people. No such emergency now exists and registration is in no way a proxy for conscription.

"However, we live in a dangerous world. In the event of a future threat to national safety, registration could save the United States as much as 6 weeks in mobilizing emergency manpower.

"This administration remains steadfast in its commitment to an all-volunteer defense force. In 1981, we demonstrated that in a healthy just society, men and women will serve their country freely when given the proper encouragement, incentives, and respect.

"All services met their recruiting goals. Test scores improved dramatically and recruits included the highest proportion of high school graduates ever. Just as volunteer warriors won American independence more than two centuries ago, they stand as proud guardians of our freedom today.

"I know that this generation of young Americans shares the sense of patriotism and responsibility that past generations have always shown. All that the action I have taken today requires is that young men when they reach their 18th birthday provide their name, address, and Social Security number to the Selective Service or at any U.S. post office.

"Late registrations are being accepted and I have instructed the Department of Justice to make provision for a grace period for late registrants."

That is the end of the statement. We'll be glad collectively to take questions.

Q. Is there a time period for this decision? I mean is it into perpetuity?

MR. MEESE. You mean as far as the late registration?

Q. No, for the extension.

MR. MEESE. Oh, as far as the draft registration encompassed in this statement will continue until such time as the President should see fit to end it or unless it is otherwise ended by, for example, an act of Congress.

Q. To what extent do events in Poland play a part in this decision?

MR. MEESE. I think anything that is done is always done in the context of the times but that was not a major consideration. The major consideration as stated by the President was the new information which was different from what he had a year ago and that is the amount of time that would be saved by mobilization. The task force—

Q. The Polish crisis was not a major consideration?

MR. MEESE. The major consideration was the task force finding that contrary to the information that had been given out, I guess it was in early 1980?

DIRECTOR TURNAGE. Yes, sir.

MR. MEESE. And at which time it was estimated that this would only save a short period of days—something like 5 to 7 days. Information that—that report was repudiated by the Selective Service System itself and new information which was made available to the task force and by the task force to the President indicates that as much as 6 to 7 weeks could now be saved.

Q. Didn't Jimmy Carter say that it was going to save a matter of weeks when he announced it?[8]

MR. MEESE. I believe in 1980—I don't know what he said. I wasn't here at that time but I—

Q. He did say it was a matter of weeks. So, what's the difference?

MR. MEESE. In 1980, a report was issued by the Selective Service System indicating that the number of days would be somewhere under 10 days.

SECRETARY WEINBERGER. Five to seven—

Q. I know but President Reagan was opposed to the policy as enunciated by Jimmy Carter who said it would save several weeks and he seems to be making the exact arguments that President Carter made and yet he was so adamantly against this in the campaign.

MR. MEESE. At the time he was—at the time the President made his statements about registration, to my knowledge, they were only during 1980 and it was based

[8] On February 13 and 15, 1980, President Carter remarked that registration would save "90 to 100 days" in a time of mobilization. See *Public Papers of the Presidents of the United States: Jimmy Carter*, 1980, vol. I, pp. 312, 330.

upon that information which was at odds with what may have been said. I don't know exactly—

Q. What made him change his mind philosophically on the question of registration?

MR. MEESE. There is no philosophical change. It's a practical change as far as—the philosophical position that the President has always taken is opposition to a draft in peacetime in the absence of a national emergency. This is a tactical matter relating to whether or not you save mobilization time, and it is clear now that you do.

Q. Mr. Meese, there are estimated to be 800,000 youths who have not registered. Are you going to prosecute? What are you going to do?

MR. MEESE. We're not in the business of trying to prosecute people who—the Selective Service System is interested in registering people. We believe that most of these people, now that the issue has been clarified by the President—and that is one of the reasons for making it clear what his position is—and any uncertainty has been removed, that most of these people, if not all of them, will register.

Q. You said that it is not a philosophical change and yet in a letter that the President wrote in the summer of 1980 didn't he say that draft registration destroys the very values that our society is commited to defend?

MR. MEESE. He was talking primarily about the draft, and I believe in that same letter he talked about the fact that it would not save any time, that the information available then was that it would not save any time. That situation has changed.

Q. Mr. Meese, those that do not comply, despite your confidence, will this administration seek to prosecute them?

MR. MEESE. I think under the law they have to be prosecuted, yes.

Q. Do you know what the grace period is yet?

MR. MEESE. The grace period will be developed by the Department of Justice and I am not sure but I would anticipate that it would be something in the nature of 30 to 60 days, a reasonable period.

Q. May I ask Secretary Weinberger a question?

Despite the fact that the Polish crisis was not a major consideration in the President's decision, as Mr. Meese has explained, if he had not extended draft registration would that not have sort of confused the Russians about our intentions?

SECRETARY WEINBERGER. That is pretty hypothetical because we don't know what would confuse them or what would not. But I think the simple fact of the matter is that the President felt that anything that would save 6 to 7 weeks in the event that mobilization is needed, and that that requires such a very small amount of effort, so to speak, on the registrant's part, and is in no way connected with conscription or draft, were the motivating factors.

Q. Can you provide us with a copy of the report that explains why it is going to save so much more time than what we previously thought?

SECRETARY WEINBERGER. The Selective Service has examined that and I don't know what the classification—or whether it has been classified—that particular report. But there is no doubt in my mind, having read that, and also on the basis of the other information we have, that we would save a very substantial amount of time if the registration forms are on file in the event—which we hope will never occur—that we will have to use them.

Q. Was that your key motivation in urging the President to extend the draft registration? Or did you have anything else in your—

SECRETARY WEINBERGER. Well, the President made the decision. The President had before him the report of the Manpower Commission and other factors and I would hesitate to say what was the key factor in the President's mind in making the decision.

Q. Well, what was in your mind?

SECRETARY WEINBERGER. What was in my mind was my recommendation to the President, which as I have said so many times before, I don't really discuss, because those—

Q. Why not? This is a very important—

SECRETARY WEINBERGER. Because these are recommendations that are designed for him that he requests and that—I have always treated them as I used to in the days when I was earning a living as an attorney, when I made a recommendation to a client, it was privileged material, and I consider it the same way.

Q. You are implying that there are other factors that you thought were really important.

SECRETARY WEINBERGER. I think it is very important that in the event—the President said that it is a troubled world in which we live—and in the event that anything should be needed, then I think anything as simple as this, which saves 6 to 7 weeks, is a very vital—

Q. I don't understand what your reluctance to say on the record is—

SECRETARY WEINBERGER. I am sorry?

Q. I don't understand why you are so reluctant to say on the record, which some officials are saying on background, and that is that the Polish crisis and the desire not to send the Russians a wrong signal did play a part in this.

SECRETARY WEINBERGER. The President has indicated in his statement, which speaks for itself, that it is a dangerous world, and in the event of future threat to national safety, registration could save the United States as much as 6 weeks, and I don't see any need to elaborate on that because it is very clear and to my mind a very correct and easily understood statement.

Q. Is the Task Force contradicting the earlier finding by the Selective Service?

SECRETARY WEINBERGER. Is it the Task Force that is contradicting—No, it is the Selective Service System as presently constituted—

Q. They are contradicting themselves?

SECRETARY WEINBERGER. They aren't contradicting themselves. The Selective Service System is under new management and they have reexamined the entire situation and have found that those previous figures were just plain wrong, as I understand it.

Q. Which previous figures? I am confused about—

SECRETARY WEINBERGER. There were some figures in the President's letter in 1980, when he was campaigning, that said that the registration would only save somewhere between 5 and 7 days.

Q. Where did he get those figures?

SECRETARY WEINBERGER. From the Selective Service as it was constituted in 1980. Those have been reexamined and have been found to be quite wrong and that as much as 6 to 7 weeks would be saved.

. . . .

Document 19

Statement by the Secretary of Defense (Weinberger) Before the Senate Armed Services Committee, February 2, 1982[9]

Proposed Defense Budget for Fiscal Year 1983

[SECRETARY WEINBERGER.] I am going, Mr. Chairman, to go through, briefly, portions of this statement.[10] I will ask that it all be placed in the record; then, of course, when the embargo is lifted,[11] I assume it can be part of the public record.

CHAIRMAN TOWER. All unclassified material will be made a part of the hearing record.

[For the report of Secretary of Defense Caspar W. Weinberger to the Congress on the fiscal year 1983 budget, fiscal year 1984 authorization request and fiscal year 1983–87 defense programs, as of January 31, 1982, see p. 116.][12]

SECRETARY WEINBERGER. I am going to talk about three fundamental requirements:

First, I want to mention briefly the changes in defense policy that we have instituted. I don't want to spend too much time on that.

Second, I want to address the level of defense spending that our security requires and how we apportion these resources.

Third, I want to inform the committee if I can about our efforts to obtain the very best value for every defense dollar we spend through management improvement, savings and eliminating waste.

I agree with Senator Stennis,[13] it is going to be a very important part of the whole

---

[9] Source: *Department Defense Authorization for Appropriations for Fiscal Year 1983: Hearings Before the Committee on Armed Services, United States Senate, Ninety-seventh Congress, Second Session* (Washington, 1982), Part I, pp. 7–14.

[10] The reference is to Weinberger's prepared statement, *ibid.*, Part I, pp. 14–19.

[11] In his opening statement, Senator Tower remarked that because this hearing preceded the official release of the budget for fiscal year 1983 on February 8, 1982, all the information presented in that day's (February 2) hearing would be embargoed until February 8. *Ibid.*, Part I, p. 6.

[12] Brackets in the source text.

[13] In his opening statement, Senator Stennis said that he wanted to get an early start on the authorization and appropriation bills and wanted to guide them through this committee rather than resort to a continuing resolution. *Ibid.*, Part I, p. 6.

presentation during the course of the year, so we do want to emphasize it because it is one of the things that we consider most seriously in the Department.

First, briefly, on defense policy. Our policy, I think, is best described or defined as the means to the ends, the means that we can use within the resources that we have available, that the Congress makes available, to secure the ends; and, of course, that is to deter war. That is the ultimate goal toward which we are all working.

As the level of resources we devoted to defense became inadequate, so was our intellectual approach taken over by events. Our defense policy was not only obsolete because of new threats to security, but also it has been, in a sense, discredited by its failure to recognize and cope with the deterioration in the global military situation as far as we are concerned.

The adoption of new ideas, reforming defense policy, all of that, is certainly something we want very much to do. Reform cannot be—and I think most of the people who have been talking about reforms in a general way do not advocate that reform be—a substitute for unfortunately vastly increased defense efforts in spending, which is essential in view of both the nature of the threat and the fact that we have not kept up with it in the past decade.

Part of the need for reform in strategic thinking is precisely the realization that we do have to devote more resources to defense and, if we are not to be inflationary, this has to come from reductions in other total government spending. It is a very difficult policy, but a policy, I think which is essential that we continue to pursue. We remain committed to defensive use of military strength. Our objective remains to deter aggression and respond to it if deterrence fails, and not to initiate warfare.

It has been fundamental and part of our strategy for a long time and will continue to be. We have to face realistically the implications of this stand and that is, that since we will not strike first, we have to be prepared to react after the enemy has seized the first initiative and react so strongly that counterattacks of ours will inflict a high cost on the enemy.

We have to do three things right away, and I mentioned them generally in the confirmation hearings a year ago[14] and in later testimony throughout the year.

We have to make more realistic the manner in which our forces respond to warning. We have to increase substantially our readiness, our ability to utilize the forces that we have, and we have to enhance our preparations for mobilization. We need to repair the national capacity to expand defense production as well as bringing our own forces into action rapidly should we have to do so.

We need, of course, all the warning we can get, all of the unambiguous warning, and we need also to be sure that we get the warning in time, that we make the decision to respond, and that we have the means to respond. Our forces must be prepared to respond. Sometimes the warnings indicated are highly ambiguous. We have had some of those during the course of the year. The planning for that kind of response can be done at comparatively small cost.

I have initiated special efforts in NATO to speed up the planning for ambiguous warnings. It is one of the few things about which there is general and immediate agreement. Planning is cost-free but the backup is not. Timely and energetic response to warnings will not help us much unless our military forces are continuously maintained in a high state of readiness. That is why it has such an enormously important priority in the work we are trying to do.

The prolonged stringency in our defense budget in the past has led to underfunding in the things that determine readiness of our Armed Forces. Adequate manning, training, maintenance, supplies, spare parts, fuel, ammunition—all of these rather unglamorous and vital things—have been underfunded and the efforts for improved readiness and sustainability are necessary to enable us to respond to attack or ambiguous threat of attack. That is stressed because of the high importance, and high priority, we attach to them.

As the Secretary of Defense, I can't confine my attention to the long-term recovery of our military strength, even though that is an enormously important part of it. We have to be able to respond to things that might occur right now, and that crisis may come at any time. Therefore, improvements in readiness are essential for a defensive strategy, having both the advantage and the imperative. These improvements in readiness also will be realized very soon.

This has inspired some of our decisions on activation and reactivation of weapon systems. Reactivation of battleships, with

---

[14] *Nomination of Casper W. Weinberger to Be Secretary of Defense: Hearing Before the Committee on Armed Services, United States Senate, Ninety-seventh Congress First Session* (Washington, 1981).

updated electronics and so on, is a controversial matter, but we urge your approval along with employment of cruise missiles on attack submarines. These are quick ways to get more naval power at sea at far less cost than building new ships.

Preparation of large-scale military mobilization must complement our improved readiness. We would be complacent to assume we can readily call on American industry today to accomplish rapid expansion in defense production, so we have taken various steps to try to improve that.

Improvement in the acquisition process and multiyear procurement will help strengthen industry and give them more confidence in our long-term willingness to make the effort and sacrifice that is required in regaining our military strength.

We need steady acquisition programs. We cannot look at these problems in 1-year slices or between rather narrow, 12-month boundaries. To get the best value in terms of both cost and surge capability, we need steady acquisition programs in which everyone can have confidence that they will continue regardless of what other events may be taking place.

Another thing in defense policy is the increased recognition that our conventional forces must be designed for a wider range of contingencies. It is our aim to direct the improvement of our forces so as to create a better balance in meeting various threats. For many years it has been our policy to let investment and planning for conventional forces be determined primarily by requirements for fighting a war centered in Europe without weakening our resolve.

We must recognize that in recent years the Soviet Union has been increasing its ability to exploit instability and project military power in many other areas such as the Persian Gulf and the Caribbean. For the Persian Gulf region our strategy is based on the prospect of using U.S. forces, against other forces with far greater economic strength than we have in reserve, to insure continued access to the oilfields. This, coupled with the prospect of our carrying the war to other areas, is the most effective deterrent.

First, we have to have the capability to deploy enormous forces to hold and interdict and blunt the Soviet attack. That is, of course, the basis for the proposal to improve the Rapid Deployment Force that we make in this budget. Second, the strategy recognizes that we should have options for fighting on other fronts.

Our growing maritime capability will serve these options.

Third, we must recognize the complementary development of allied and friendly forces and facilities.

If we are alone, we will deal with the Soviet threat at very much greater cost. Our security assistance to many of these countries is much smaller today than in the past, yet it is more important to the United States today.

The President has sought to strengthen our security assistance to allied and friendly nations. Some of these we will be discussing tomorrow when President Mubarak is here.[15]

Some of the essential forces and facilities are owned by our own allies and by friends who cannot fund the desired force improvements on their own. I know Secretary Haig and I can count on support of members of this committee for our security assistance program because it is such a vital part of our whole defense posture.

The fallacy, we believe, in recent defense policy regarding conventional warfare has been the short war assumption, the idea that in planning strategy we can rely on the fact that conventional war will be of short duration. Unfortunately, commonsense and past experience tell us otherwise.

We have instituted changes to correct this fallacy. We believe deterrence would be weakened if the enemy were misled to believe that he could outlast us in conventional war. We have tried to improve our stability and strengthen our capability for defense production and, of course, we have concentrated additional efforts on trying to improve our whole conventional war capability.

The nuclear strategy I have left until this point, because while we do not regard nuclear strength as a substitute for conventional strength, and we do not seek nuclear superiority for the United States, we will make every necessary effort to prevent the Soviet Union from acquiring a superiority that they might mistakenly and tragically feel leads them to believe that a first strike of theirs could ever succeed.

We spend about 85 percent of our total budget on nonnuclear forces and that accurately reflects our priorities. This adminis-

---

[15] For documentation on Mubarak's visit, February 2–5, 1982, see Chapter 11, Part D.

tration must cope with the severe inadequacies it inherited in the realm of strategic and theater nuclear capabilities. We are faced with the necessity of modernizing and strengthening all three parts of the Triad at once, and that has begun.

We had full briefings last fall on the President's program for modernization of nuclear forces.[16] It is not only proceeding as planned but also we are actually exploring the possibility for accelerating delivery time of some of the most important strategic weapon systems. Nevertheless, we will stay within the roughly 14 percent of the total resources during the coming 6 years that will be necessary to put the new strategic nuclear force in place.

President Reagan's strategic force modernization program takes a long-term view and it is essential because these arms take such a long time to acquire and are part of our forces for many years.

We also have to take a longer term view of our overall military competition with the Soviet Union.

President Reagan's initiatives on transfer of technology and East–West trade and on terrorist or Soviet penetration in Africa and South America are part of the larger strategy, and so are his initiatives on arms control. We don't expect quick results but we know if we have the support of the Congress we can strengthen defense and improve other instruments: The long-term prospects I feel confident are bright.

Now, Mr. Chairman, very briefly on the specific budgetary questions, our budget must take account of the nature and size of the Soviet threat. We recognize full well that there are other threats, but only the Soviet Union has the power to inflict millions of casualties on our population. Only the Soviet Union has massive and modern conventional and nuclear forces deployed directly confronting our friends and allies in Europe and Asia and, of course, ourselves, with their intercontinental weapons. Only the Soviet Union has the forces and the geographic proximity to threaten the free world source of oil, and it is quite clear they are embarked on a sustained effort to supply arms to totalitarian forces in various parts of the world. They are willing to use their force directly, as in Afghanistan, or to intimidate and coerce from the outside, as in the case of Poland or to use client states, as in the case of the Caribbean.

Measured by that threat, we believe our proposed defense budget is fully justified and by no means extravagant, since the projected real growth of Soviet military investment is likely to exceed ours for many years to come. If we cut back our defense budget after only one year spent in regaining our strength, that gap will widen, resulting in intolerable deterioration of our security. It would also send all of the wrong signals all around the world to our friends as well as our adversaries.

If Congress approves our defense budget, I believe the danger to our security can indeed be brought under control.

We are requesting $258 billion in total obligational authority for fiscal year 1983. We estimate that will result in outlays of $215.9 billion if we actually achieve all the savings that we plan.

Our decision to fund fully the weapon systems that we are proposing, especially two additional aircraft carriers, and our decision to fund fully our multiyear procurement, accounts for the very large TOA and for 20 percent of the increase over the 1982 budget. If Congress approves the fiscal year 1983 request, we anticipate a lower rate of growth of total obligational authority for fiscal 1984.

In designing the 1983 budget we gave first priority, for these reasons I mentioned, to improving readiness of our forces. Flying hours of the Air Force pilots, which dipped as low as 13 hours a month in 1978, will again be increased, rising to 17 per month in 1982 and to 18.5 per month in 1983.

Our next priority is to improve sustainability of our forces, at the moment, some of our forward-deployed units have only a week's supply of key munitions over that provided in 1981 and 1982 and approved by the Congress. This situation will soon begin to improve, but our efforts must continue in 1983 and beyond.

Apart from the crucial program for the modernization of strategic nuclear forces, the most significant force expansion centers on the Navy, particularly those components that have offensive missions. By the end of fiscal 1982 our battle force will total 514 ships; 475 of those are general-purpose ships. By the end of this decade the deployable battle force will exceed 600 ships.

For fiscal 1983 our request includes 18 new ships, 6 conversions and 1 acquisition.

---

[16] For the text of the briefings by President Reagan and Weinberger on October 2, 1981, on the administration's proposals for strategic weapons systems, see *American Foreign Policy: Current Documents, 1981,* documents 45 and 46.

The 5-year plan totals 133 new construction ships, 10 conversions and 6 acquisitions.

Our objective for mobility over the next 5 years is to develop the capability to deploy the Rapid Deployment Force to Southwest Asia or indeed to other areas in 4 to 6 weeks, and subsequently to reinforce NATO with 6 Army divisions to bring up to strength of 10 divisions, 60 Air Force tactical fighter squadrons in 10 days.

Our program to do this contains additions to each component of airlift, prepositioning, and sealift.

After careful consideration of all the alternatives, Mr. Chairman, and this is one of the things we spent a great deal of time on this fall, we have decided to procure 50 new C–5 aircraft to be supplied by Lockheed on a fixed-price contract, and contract for 44 additional McDonnell Douglas KC–10 cargo tanker aircraft. We chose those because we needed to increase capability as rapidly as possible. This is the alternative that does this in the most effective way.

The C–5's and KC–10's are available at favorable, comparative prices, even to the C–17. The new C–5 is the result of lessons learned from the old C–5A's. The KC–10 can be used as a tanker or cargo aircraft. We will restructure the Civil Reserve Air Fleet enhancement program.

To complement this airlift in meeting early deployment objectives, we are continuing plans to preposition six Army division sets of equipment, one set for the brigade-sized Marine Force and to preposition selected items of Air Force equipment at bases in Europe and Southwest Asia.

We will also continue programs to store war reserves of material for our forces in Europe and Southwest Asia and in the Western Pacific.

To meet subsequent objectives that cannot be met sooner by ships in the commercial fleet, we plan to strengthen the Department's surge sealift capability and are requesting funds for this purpose to complete conversion of the SL–7's and to expand the Ready Reserve Fleet.

We are significantly enhancing Army and Navy capability for offloading cargo in austere or difficult ports.

We plan a fairly large growth of both Air Force and Navy tactical air forces. Fighter forces will grow from 36 notional [?] wings at the end of 1982 to 40 wings at the end of 1985, 26 Active and 14 Reserve.

At the same time we plan to increase our Navy active carrier wings from 12 to 14 by the end of 1987.

Our emphasis in developing more flexible and mobile forces does not mean we are neglecting our ground forces. We will maintain an overall U.S. ground force structure of 28 divisions, 16 Active and 8 Reserve Army divisions, and 3 Active and 1 Reserve Marine divisions.

We plan to make major progress in modernization. We hope to procure 776 of the new M–1 tanks in fiscal 1983, increasing the production rate from 30 to 60, and then going on up to 90 by mid-1985. A lot of that, I think, will depend on the successor to the Chrysler tank plant, now under negotiation.

We will also buy 600 of the Bradley fighting vehicles and 258 light armored vehicles.

I would like to close, Mr. Chairman, with just a word, again as I mentioned at the beginning, about the deep awareness we have of the compelling need to manage our resources with the maximum of efficiency.

We have instituted programs, which received first priority and precedence, in order to cut out all waste, find savings and eliminate any sort of mismanagement.

Deputy Secretary Carlucci, who has been the spearhead in this area, has done a magnificent job, his usual magnificent job. He will testify next week in greater detail on this vital program after the budget has been formally released and when I will be away.[17]

Our current funding policies result in specific 5-year savings in economies and budget authority of $41.4 billion when compared with the funding which has been required to follow the previous administration's policy.

In fiscal year 1987, if that year is included, the figure grows to $51.5 billion. We will be looking for even larger savings in the years to come.

Fiscal year 1983 defense outlays have already been reduced by more than $5 billion, based on new economies and efficiencies.

Constraints on effective further savings must be properly understood. Ninety-three cents of every defense outlay dollar is com-

---

[17] Carlucci's testimony on February 8 is in *Department of Defense Authorization for Appropriations for Fiscal Year 1983*, Part I, pp. 529–624.

mitted at the beginning of the year to cover prior-year programs for just the minimal operations of the Department.

This leaves 7 cents of each defense outlay dollar for spending for new programs.

Short-run outlay cuts in the budget imperil long-term goals. Because of defense spend-out patterns, to get $1 billion in outlay reductions requires program authority almost four times as large. This can cause disruption and reflects on the readiness function. When we hear a lot of very casual, and I have to say quite uninformed, talk about how we can cut another $10 billion in outlays without hurting defense, I have to say that simply demonstrates the lack of familiarity of the speaker.

The task before us really is too big and must be done much too quickly for any one country. We have one of our greatest tasks and challenges to integrate our plans and policies more completely with our allies for a common defense strong enough to insure freedom to all.

We must not do anything less than our fair share because some of our allies may not seem to do so. Nor should we abandon our effort to convince them that they should all do their fair share; nor should we abandon them.

I will sum up by saying we have to do two major things:

We have to bring to a halt further expansion and consolidation of the Soviet military empire, even though that expansion proceeds through indirect rather than direct military intervention; and our strategy must see to it that the productivity and the technological creativity of a free society are not exploited or handed over to the Soviets in order to make good the chronic deficiencies of their system under the false banner of trade.

Military strategy must be the servant of national policy, the policy that is the ultimate trustee of the Nation's interests.

It would not be fair, nor would I want to conclude without expressing the very deep appreciation I feel for the members of this committee who have unstintingly supported the Defense Department in the past year and in the face sometimes of very difficult countervailing positions. I appreciate very much this opportunity for the hearing, Mr. Chairman.

Document 20

Statement by the Chairman of the Joint Chiefs of Staff (Jones) Before the Senate Armed Services Committee, February 2, 1982[18]

Proposed Reforms in the Organization of the Joint Chiefs of Staff

Mr. Chairman and members of the committee, I look forward to starting my eighth and last year of posture hearings. From that side of the table it may not seem a long time but from this side it certainly does.

When I finish my term this summer, I will have been a member of the Joint Chiefs longer than anybody in history. During that time period I will have worked for four Secretaries of Defense, four Presidents, worked with four Secretaries of State and now I am working with my fifth National Security Adviser.

I mention this not to point out that I am the ultimate survivor in the national security business but that it does give me a somewhat unique perspective.

I started my military career in the 1940's. I am retiring in the 1980's. I see those as the two turbulent decades. The 1950's and 1960's and 1970's—when you look back on those you will see them as relatively stable compared to the 1940's and 1980's.

There is a great deal we have to do. We need to improve our defense posture. We look forward to testifying on the budget in specifics. We need more than the defense resources; we need the proper organization within the military to develop the strategy and the planning, particularly a good warfighting capability. In my judgment, we do not have that organization today. I have a much different perspective after nearly 4 years on the Joint Chiefs as Chairman than when I was a Service chief with a responsibility for fighting for the resources for my individual Service.

We have made progress in jointness. We have broadened our joint exercises in the last few years to include mobilization. In 1978 we ran an exercise which was the first mobilization exercise of any magnitude

[18] Source: *Department of Defense Authorization for Appropriations for Fiscal Year 1983*, Part I, pp. 20–22.

since World War II. We have formed the Joint Deployment Agency, where now we can integrate the efforts of the air-and sealift and move the forces of the four Services fairly rapidly.

We are integrating, at the recommendation of the Joint Chiefs of Staff, the land and sea transportation organizations. We are working on better integration of command and control—we now pay more attention to the problem of command and control, but we have a long way to go.

We have formed a Rapid Deployment Joint Task Force that has had a lot of growing pains. One thing we are accomplishing in that RDJTF—which is to become a unified command—is that it is the first headquarters at the operational level that in peacetime is involved with the forces of all four Services and will fight those forces at an operational level in time of war.

A lot of the problems that have not been resolved in the past—that is the four Services not working together on a day-to-day basis—can be solved through the RDJTF. So I am glad that there are growing pains and controversy because we are addressing some issues that have not been addressed for a long time.

The military Services by tradition and heritage properly have a role in recruiting people and training them in weapon system design and acquisition, logistics and so forth. To fight, we depend on all Services and we need better integration of the efforts of all Services so that we get a synergistic effect, the sum being greater than the individual parts.

The system we have now is remarkably resistant to change. It developed in a patchwork fashion during World War II and has had only limited changes in the 35 years since the National Security Act of 1947.[19]

In my judgment, the system is fraught with problems. This committee fully understands that committees can serve a useful purpose—there are many advantages of operating committees. But committees are notoriously poor at trying to run things. We have some unique factors relating to committees in the Pentagon—the Joint Chiefs of Staff "Committee" and the committees that work for us—that make things even more difficult.

First, arising out of World War II was the tremendous pressure for unanimity in joint committee action. It is written in the statute that if the Joint Chiefs of Staff cannot agree unanimously on an issue, we have to pass that information on to the Secretary of Defense. Therefore, there is great pressure on trying to accommodate differing views and great reluctance on having split views in the system. We do have a split on issues from time to time.

Second, we have five layers of committees with the Service staffs involved at every level of action, each with a de facto veto because of the great pressure for unanimity. Understandably there is great institutional pressure on the individual Service members of these committees. This committee understands pressures and constituencies. When a constituency believes that their Service is not getting a fair share of the budget, there is great pressure on the Service members working the joint problem, including the Service chiefs.

Finally, there is also very little incentive to be in the joint business—very little preparation for service on the Joint Staff or any other joint positions, and very few rewards.

In the decades that we have had the joint system, with all the senior people assigned as Director of the Joint Staff or head of directorates such as operations or plans, there has been only one person in history—General Earle Wheeler—who ever went on to be a Service chief or Chairman after serving in one of the senior positions on the Joint Staff.

I have been a participant in, or a very close observer of, the joint system for well over 20 years. The problem is clearly not people; it is the basic system. I am advocating changes. I am not advocating a general staff. I am not advocating unification of Services to where we would all end up wearing the same uniform.

I would retain many of the strengths of having the individual Services. But what I would do is strengthen the role of my successor—strengthen the role of the Chairman in many ways. I would also limit Service staff involvement in the joint process to one of providing input rather than holding this de facto veto of the system. I would insist that the Service chiefs get their advice on joint issues from joint people. It should come from people of the four Services—a joint operation.

I would give commanders-in-chief in the field, who are the ones we hold responsible for fighting the wars, greater say. They have a limited role today. The Secretary has been

---

[19] P.L. 80–253; 61 Stat. 495.

very helpful in having the commanders-in-chief appear before the Defense Resources Board. I would continue in that direction.

I would also enhance the preparation for and service on the Joint Staff and other joint positions—make them much more attractive assignments.

I intend in my last few months in office, Mr. Chairman, to work with my colleagues on the Joint Chiefs of Staff on some of the things the Joint Chiefs could implement on their own authority. I have already discussed it with the chiefs, and I have had a working group addressing the issue.

I intend also to work with the Secretary of Defense and the President and to propose some specific legislative action arising out of this study effort. This is going to be a difficult matter, but I think it is the most important defense issue that we will face in the years ahead.

Thank you, Mr. Chairman and gentlemen, for your attention.

Document 21

Budget Message to the Congress by President Reagan, February 8, 1982 (Extract)[20]

Defense Budget for Fiscal Year 1983

. . . .

Our 1983 budget plan continues the effort begun last year to strengthen our military posture in four primary areas: strategic forces, combat readiness, force mobility, and general purpose forces.

A thorough 8-month review of U.S. strategic forces and objectives preceded my decision this past October to strengthen our strategic forces.[21] The review found that the relative imbalance with the Soviet Union will be at its worst in the mid-1980's and hence needs to be addressed quickly. It also concluded that the multiple protective structure basing proposal for MX did not provide long-term survivability since the Soviets could counter it (at about the same cost) by simply deploying more warheads.

In addition, our review pointed to serious deficiencies in force survivability, endurance, and the capability to exercise command and control during nuclear war. Current communications and warning systems were found to be vulnerable to severe disruption from an attack of very modest scale.

The 1983 budget funds programs to correct these deficiencies. The 1983 strategic program of $23.1 billion, an increase of $6.9 billion over 1982, provides for both near-term improvements and longer-term programs. These initiatives include:

Early deployment of cruise missiles on existing bombers and attack submarines.

Acquisition of a new bomber (the B–1B) and development of advanced technology (Stealth) bomber for deployment in the 1990's to provide a continued capability to penetrate Soviet defenses.

Development and procurement of a new, larger, and more accurate landbased missile, the MX.

Continued deployment of Trident ballistic missile submarines to strengthen the sea-based leg of our strategic deterrent.

Longer-term programs include: development of a survivable deployment plan for the MX missile, development of a new submarine-launched ballistic missile, continued improvements in the survivability of warning and communications systems, and improvements in strategic defenses against both bomber and missile attacks.

The 1983 budget provides $114.3 billion in operations and military personnel costs, an increase of over $13 billion from the 1982 level to improve the combat readiness of our forces.

Today a major conflict involving the United States could occur without adequate time to upgrade U.S. force readiness. Our concerns with military readiness reflect both the long lead time required to procure sophisticated equipment (both parts and finished equipment) and past failures to provide adequate peacetime support for combat units. We cannot wait for a period

---

[20] Source: *Weekly Compilation of Presidential Documents*, February 15, 1982, pp. 139–141. For the full text of the President's message, see *ibid.*, pp. 129–142.

[21] Regarding the Reagan administration's proposals for strategic weapons systems, see the briefings by President Reagan and Secretary of Defense Weinberger, October 2, 1981, in *American Foreign Policy: Current Documents, 1981*, documents 45 and 46.

of rising tensions before bringing forces up to combat readiness.

My program will continue to bolster combat readiness by increasing training, operating rates, and equipment support. There will be increased aircraft flying hours and supply inventories. In addition, backlogs of combat equipment and real property awaiting maintenance will be reduced. Also, the 1983 budget will provide levels of military compensation that will improve the readiness and capability of the All-Volunteer Force.

Current U.S. mobility forces cannot move the required combat or combat support units fast enough to counter effectively military aggression in Europe, Korea or in the Southwest Asia/Persian Gulf region. For example, at present only a small light combat force could be moved rapidly to the Southwest Asia region. Major mobility shortages include wide-body military cargo aircraft; fast logistics ships; and prepositioned ships and associated support equipment. Elimination of these shortages is an essential first step toward improving U.S. military capability during the first 30 days after the beginning of a crisis.

The 1983 budget provides $4.4 billion for:

Initial procurement of a fleet of improved C–5 cargo aircraft, and additional KC–10A tanker/cargo aircraft that will double our wide-bodied military airlift capability by the 1990's.

Continued upgrading of existing C–5A aircraft to extend their effectiveness beyond the year 2000.

Conversion of four additional fast logistic ships that will provide the capability to move heavy combat forces rapidly.

Chartering a fleet of supply ships that can be stationed with equipment and supplies in Southwest Asia to reduce the time required for deployment of heavy forces.

In the last decade, the Soviet Union introduced large quantities of highly capable, new-generation tactical equipment including combat ships, tanks and aircraft, which must be countered by modernized U.S. forces. Also, the traditional U.S. superiority in system quality has been considerably narrowed, making Soviet quantitative advantages more serious. The Soviet military force buildup has increased the risk that they may rely on military power to support their foreign policy goals. For the U.S. to maintain, in concert with our allies, sufficient conventional forces to deter potential aggression, our forces must be provided with adequate numbers of new, modern tactical equipment.

My 1983 budget includes $106.2 billion for general purpose forces (including both operations and investment), an $18 billion increase over 1982. A key initiative is an expanded shipbuilding program. The United States, dependent on open seas for commerce and military resupply, must have the naval capability to maintain control of vital sea lanes. While our naval forces have declined from the mid-1960's, the Soviets have in existence or under construction eight new classes of submarines and eight new classes of major surface warships, including nuclear-powered cruisers and new aircraft carriers.

The budget provides an $18.6 billion shipbuilding program including full funding for two nuclear-powered aircraft carriers, to be constructed during 1983–87. Other ships included in my 1983 program are three large cruisers equipped with an advanced air defense system; two nuclear-powered attack submarines; two frigates for convoy protection and four mine countermeasure ships to improve fleet capability to operate in mined waters. My longer term objective is to increase the deployable battle force from 513 ships in 1982 to over 600 by the end of the decade.

In addition, the budget provides for increased production of ground and tactical air force weapons. Production rates will be increased for a variety of new systems such as the M–1 Abrams tank, light armored vehicles, and the AV–8B Marine Corps attack aircraft.

All of this will be done with a major reform of the acquisition process and vastly improved management of defense operations, which will save $51 billion by 1987. In a continuing fight against fraud, waste, and inefficiency, the Secretary of Defense has appointed an Assistant for Review and Oversight and a Council on Integrity and Management Improvement.

. . . .

Document 22

Transcript of a Department of State Press Briefing, February 27, 1982[22]

Security Assistance Programs for Fiscal Year 1983

Senior Official. I will be glad to take your questions. Whether I will answer them or not is something else.

Anyway, I appreciate this chance to brief you on the foreign assistance budget that we will be submitting to the Congress next week. And to rescue me from very tough and technical questions, I have two authorities there in the corner.

By way of preliminaries, I would like to state that the figures that we have requested, or will be requesting of the Congress, reflect a new budgetary process that we have put into effect this year, one that attempts to get better integration and better focus on the programs for which we are responsible. Essential to the process has been the definition of a limited number of key security and economic foreign policy objectives. Then we have used those objectives as a test against which to measure specific proposals.

In other words, what we have is not a collection of individual country requests in individual accounts, but rather requests in which we have carefully balanced political, economic, and security imperatives in the particular countries and areas in which we have been concentrating.

The briefing today is focused on security assistance versus development assistance because the 2-year authorization bill which was adopted last December by the Congress—that was the Foreign Assistance Bill[23]—covered Fiscal Years 1982 and 1983, and whereas generally speaking the levels for 1983 in the area of development assistance were satisfactory, we will need to ask for more in security assistance.

This was anticipated in the committee report,[24] which specifically noted that the Congress had gone forward into 1983 without having had the benefit of the administration's input, and the committee report also anticipated that we would be coming in with further requests.

This, of course, we have had to do because the globe simply doesn't stand still, and we have met continuing and increasing pressures in critical areas of the world which require us to maintain and, in some instances, to increase our efforts to enable key friends and allies to adequately defend themselves and to maintain viable economies.

For example, we still have a tinderbox in the Middle East. The peace process is going forward. We still have our problems and concerns in the Persian Gulf, the need for access to the Indian Ocean. The Vietnamese are still in Kampuchea, better armed than ever, posing direct threats to Thailand and Malaysia. And, of course, we are all familiar with what is happening in the Caribbean and the kind of potential pressures and dangers that have to be addressed in that area so close to home.

So in order to meet these and other needs, we are seeking a net increase of $1.67 billion for our Security Assistance Programs in 1983. This is an increase, of course, over that which has already been authorized.

The net budget increase will amount to $992 million, reflecting the fact that our foreign military sales guarantees are off-budget items.

The increases are all keyed to a limited number of specific programs dealing primarily with the Middle East. Southwest Asia, North Africa, and the Caribbean Basin, and some attention to Southeast Asia.

With these increases, FY 1983 authorization requests will look as follows:

Eighty-seven percent of the $3.4 billion in FMS guaranteed financing requests will

---

[22] Source: Department of State files. This background briefing was conducted by a senior official.

[23] The reference is to the International Security and Development Cooperation Act of 1981, approved on December 29, 1981. (P.L. 97–113; 95 Stat. 1519) For the text of President Reagan's statement on signing this bill into law, see *American Foreign Policy: Current Documents, 1981*, document 48.

[24] The reference presumably is to the conference report of the House of Representatives and Senate, which noted that the President had not yet made his budgetary requests for fiscal year 1983 and that the Congress would give full consideration to any additional recommendations by the executive branch. See *International Security and Development Cooperation Act of 1981*, Report of the Committee of Conference, Ninety-seventh Congress, First Session, H.R. Report No. 97–413, p. 56.

go to seven countries: Egypt, Israel, Turkey, Greece, Spain, Korea, and Pakistan.

The economic support funds and the concessional financing for military sales—of the $3.6 billion we are requesting for these programs, 78 percent will go to just six countries: Egypt, Israel, Sudan, Pakistan, Turkey, and El Salvador.

The question to be asked is, if we fail to secure these requested increases, what will be the impact on programs that are of critical importance to the United States?

We see the impact as follows: For example, if we do not get the requested funds, we would not be able to provide sufficient FMS guaranteed financing to initiate the Pakistan program, which was discussed with the Congress last year, to initiate it at the agreed levels, or to provide the increases that are required for the Israeli and Egyptian military programs, or to provide the necessary support to conclude our base negotiations in Spain.

If we don't get our requests, we would not have the concessionality—not be able to offer the concessionality that is absolutely essential to implement a critical military equipment program for Egypt, Sudan, Turkey, Thailand, Morocco, Tunisia, and Portugal.

If our economic support fund levels are not increased, we simply won't be able to follow through with the Caribbean Basin initiatives announced the other day by the President[25] nor will we be able to provide Turkey with the economic support that is particularly critical at this stage of their economic recovery.

In sum, increased sums being requested for Fiscal 1983 are vitally needed to maintain our ability to provide military equipment and training on affordable terms to keep countries of strategic importance to the United States, to insure that we have continued basing and access rights in important areas, and to provide the economic support required to assure stability in areas, again of vital importance to the United States.

A failure to go forward, on the other hand, would prove a very short-time term economy, because we are, through these programs, filling important security gaps around the globe which otherwise would have to be planned for through the use of our own forces, which in turn would mean a significant increase in defense spending.

I think that completes my introductory remarks.

Q. Do you have a breakdown for the individual countries?

A. We can't give you that breakdown at this time—something known as "congressional courtesy."

Q. When will that be available?

A. Tuesday or Wednesday?[26]

VOICE. Possibly Tuesday.

SENIOR OFFICIAL. Possibly Tuesday.

Q. I am just a little confused. Probably the others know this, but do you say that this request supplements funds already approved?

A. For the first time, last December, the Congress decided to adopt an authorization bill that covered two fiscal years instead of just one. They had been focusing on 1982, and then during those tense final weeks, they decided to go for 2 years, and, in effect, did a lot of straightlining. This did not give us the opportunity to come in with a specific program.

Q. Can you give us some help in terms of how these figures compare with amounts already approved, and how the total would compare as an increase over the Fiscal 1982 figures?

A. Yes. Let's see—that is the one sheet I don't have. Do you have that? Would you give those figures?

SECOND OFFICIAL. 1982 figures for foreign military sales credits direct were $800 million, and for 1983 they are $1,789 million.

The grant military assistance appropriation figure was $176.5 million. The 1983 request is $107.5 million. A difference of $69 million. I might add that includes a reimbursement to the Department of Defense of $20 million.

That is going down. The grant military assistance is going down. However, there is an increase in the foreign military sales credits.

On the Foreign Military Sales Guaranteed Program, I believe the figure in 1982 was $3,083.5 million, and that figure in FY 1983 is $3,928.8 million.

---

25 The reference is to President Reagan's address on the Caribbean Basin Initiative to the Organization of American States on February 24, 1982. For text, see document 675.

26 March 2 and 3, 1982.

The Economic Support Fund Program, the 1982 figure is $2,564 million, and in FY 1983 it is $2,886 million.

Q. Does this include the amounts that you are now sending up, or you will be sending up next week?

A. That is correct, and were in the President's budget that was transmitted several weeks ago.[27]

The peacekeeping operations—the program in 1982 was $151 million. This included the appropriations plus some additional funds that were transferred into that account to finance a peacekeeping operation in Chad. That will decrease in Fiscal Year 1983 to $43.5 million, the difference being that in 1982 we had the initial start-up costs for the Sinai Multilateral National Force and Observers, and the second year costs of that are considerably less.

In the International Military Education and Training Program, in 1982, the program was $38.4 million, and in 1983 it will be $53.7 million.

Q. What about the difference between the 1983 that was authorized by the Congress and the 1983 as you now see it?

A. May I just say something in the outset, in terms of words of art, we have used, proposed, what are called direct credits or concessional credits, concessional terms.

Last year the Congress decided to try to achieve the same objectives by a cocktail [*sic*] of absolute grants, of grants, versus the guarantees at standard commercial rates. So please don't be confused by some shifts in terminology.

Second Official. The difference—Congress has already authorized for Fiscal Year 1983 in guaranteed loans $3,269.5 million. The administration request is $3,928.8 million.

Q. The first one is $3,269 million?

A. That is correct. In direct credits, that is, U.S. Government credits, and Congress has already authorized $800 million on which repayment would be forgiven. We are requesting—and Congress provided no direct credits—already has authorized no direct credits. They would be simply concessional loans. And for 1983, for a combination of the two, that is, concessional loans and loans on which repayment would be forgiven, the administration is asking for $1,739 million.

In military assistance grants, Congress has already authorized $238.5 [million?]. Our request for an authorization is only $87.5 million. We do not need authorization for the full $107.5 million that we are requesting be appropriated because of a technical difference in the repayment to the Department of Defense for funds drawn down under a specific section of law in 1982.

International Military Education and Training, from $42 million to $53.7 million.

Economic support fund, $2,723.5 million to $2,886 million.

Peacekeeping operations, the Congress authorized $19 million, and we are requesting $43.5 million.

Q. So that comes to the total that Mr. . . .[28] talked about of a difference of $1.67 billion between—that is what that adds up to, doesn't it?

A. The net increase, yes, if our computer is correct.

Q. Sir, if you could just clarify this for me again. I am not quite sure I follow you, but what happened was that the Congress authorized a certain level of money for two years worth of programs.

A. That is right.

Q. And the administration is suggesting that these be increased by—what is it—$1.67 billion?

A. That is right. For 1983.

Q. For 1983, yes. What exactly is your reasoning for needing the additional money? I mean, you said that there are a certain number of foreign policy objectives that this money would go toward. What exactly is the reason for needing more money now than Congress authorized?

Senior Official. Don't forget we are talking about economic as well as military support. The President's speech on the Caribbean underscored a whole bunch of reasons for increases.

In preparing the 1983 budget, we keyed in significant increases in economic support for the Caribbean Basin, for example. This is ignored by straightlining 1982 figures.

Also, we have had discussions with Israel and Egypt that require additional financing to maintain or improve their military postures.

---

[27] See *supra*.

[28] All ellipses appear in the source text.

We have the phasing in of a brand new program in Pakistan.

We have the base negotiations going on with Spain today which would anticipate updating the levels established 5½ years ago in various categories of military assistance.

That kind of situation has occurred. In other words, the world goes on.

Q. One follow-up question? Is it possible to give just a percentage figure for how much of an increase this is, just a thumbnail, how much more are you asking over what the base is?

A. Well, you have the figures, if you can compute them. I have some figures that are not really relevant to your question, because it reflects increases over what we had requested in 1982, or requests of 1983, in which the overall increase would be about 25 percent. But, again, keep in mind that much of the increase that we have requested of about $860 million is off-budget.

Q. Is it correct, sir, the wire services are reporting that the increases include for the first time since funds were cut off some years ago, some kind of security assistance for Argentina, Chile, and Guatemala?

A. There will be allocations. Whether or not those allocations will be utilized will depend on the human rights and other considerations at the time specific requests are made.

Q. That is the first time that they were requested since then, is that right, the allocations themselves?

A. The allocations for Chile and Argentina are new, because legislation enacted last year made it possible for the President to certify—or make certain certifications as requested by the law dealing with human rights issues.

In the case of Guatemala, nothing needs to be done. But I just want to emphasize that an actual decision by the administration to make requests will be guided very heavily on those considerations.

Q. But is there an allocation for Guatemala in there?

A. There is an allocation, but I underscore that "allocation" is meaningless except in the context of conditions that would have to be met.

The problem is that otherwise you have to wait a year or a year and a half in order to respond, unless you anticipate possibilities.

That is one of the problems of this budget process, you have to look forward about a year and a half.

Q. Could you explain one other thing? Mr. . . . talked about the $800 million in direct U.S. Government credits that have been authorized in 1983 [*1982?*] previously for 1983.

Are those all of forgiven type loans, or is that forgiven plus concession?

A. Virtually, all.

Q. All forgiven?

A. Yes.

Q. And the new 1983 figure is up to $1,739. That includes a combination of forgiven plus concession.

A. That is right.

Q. A concessional just means better terms, is that it?

A. Yes. It means, for example, 3 percent versus 18 percent, which is a considerable gap. Of course, it is variable, but it is an attempt to be able to price equipment within the range of the capacity of a country to acquire.

Incidentally, I have a slight correction here.

The percentage increase in our total program over the amount already authorized for 1983 is 23 percent, and that includes the guarantees.

Q. Which are off-budget. Is it off-budget?

A. The 23 percent is the total request, of which—well, we have $1,067 million, total increase of which about $670,000 is guaranteed—add three more zeroes to that last number.

Q. This is all security assistance, though, not developmental assistance.

A. No. We did not cover developmental assistance because all you need to do is to read what was adopted. But, yes, we are going to have some, but totally insignificant in numbers. We are going to have some changes that were requested, some modifications.

Q. So development assistance that was authorized by the Congress is basically intact.

A. Basically I think we may be requesting another $50 or $60 million. Is that a correct figure?

VOICE. About $95 [million?].

A. About $95 million additional development assistance.

Q. Do these figures include all the money for anticipating helping El Salvador with for military purposes at this point?

A. Yes.

Q. So the contingency money being asked for Guatemala, is it on an IMET in the case of Guatemala?

A. Let me have my memory refreshed? I think it is.

Q. It is all IMET?

A. All IMET.

Q. The same for Argentina and Chile?

A. Yes.

Q. All three?

A. Yes.

Q. Since you are not going into detail, sir, you may not be able to handle this, but I would like to make sure I am not confused.

I have got about $160 million figure here for El Salvador, which I thought was purely economic aid, an economic aid program, with the $61 [million?] or whatever it is, additional for military assistance for 1983. And I had assumed that the $160 [million?] was only economic aid, but something you just said led me to believe that perhaps it was not.

Can you help me on that, although you are not going to get into details.

A. I am afraid I am not going to get country specific. It is one of these things that the presentation, the first formal public presentation, ought to be made to the Congress. And as a good reporter, you are zeroing in on that of special interests.

Q. I am afraid I am wrong.

Q. One final question for the record, it looks like this 23 percent increase is the largest increase of any ongoing program, including DOD.

How do you justify that in times of economic problems here at home? What are you going to say to people on the Hill?

A. A couple of things. Number one, that this is an increase over what the Congress authorized, which was well short of what we requested. So, it doesn't change that dramatic world view, if you will.

Number two, the fact is that in several areas of critical importance to the United States, the world has gotten more dangerous, and unfortunately we cannot subordinate our ability to counter those dangers by enabling countries of importance to us to better cope to achieve stability because of the constraints that we face budgetarily at home.

Thirdly,—or fourthly, I have lost count—per dollar spent, this is very efficient money, because to fail to move forward invites far larger problems to develop, and would also require significantly larger defense spending over a period.

When I talked at the outset about the budget process, we have gone over the figures time and again, consulting all the relevant players, seeking as low levels as possible, because of our total consciousness of these constraints in the Congress, and therefore, we feel very confident that we can justify each of our requests.

Q. thank you, very much.

Document 23

Editorial Note

On March 23, 1982, the Department of Defense released the declassified executive summary of the Townes Panel Report. This report was the result of an intensive study by a panel of 11 nongovernmental experts headed by Charles Townes, professor of physics at the University of California, Berkeley, which Secretary of Defense Weinberger had appointed on March 16, 1981, to study the basing mode for the MX missile system and make recommendations to the President and the Secretary of Defense. For the announcement of the appointment of the panel, see *New York Times*, March 17, 1981, page B14.

The Townes Panel completed its study in July 1981, but the executive summary was not declassified and released until March 1982. The report itself is still classified.

According to the Department of Defense press release accompanying the text of the executive summary, "There is a close correspondence between the conclusions and recommendations of the Townes Panel and the Administration's plan for modernization of our strategic forces which was announced by the President on October 2, 1981." Specifically, the Townes Panel Report emphasized command, control, and communications as the strategic area which "most urgently needs improvement," cited "highly vulnerable" ICBM silos in the near future, criticized the Multiple Protective Shelters proposal, recommended deployment "of a larger, more accurate SLBM on the Trident force," continued development of the MX missile, investigation of other basing modes, development of the concept of keeping ICBM's on continuous airborne patrol, expansion of the current BMD research and development effort, research on small missile basing, and full deployment of the Global Positioning System to improve the accuracy of sea and airborne mobile missile systems. Finally, a significant majority of the panel recommended "a commitment now to deploy 100 M-X missiles in 100 land-based shelters . . . with the further option, if required later, of rapidly deploying additional shelters for deceptive basing of the M-X missile." This recommendation would provide both a "hedge" and "augmentation" to present United States strategic forces. (Department of Defense Press Release 128–82, March 23, 1982)

This press release also briefly compared these panel recommendations with the President's strategic modernization program announced on October 2, 1981. For the texts of two press briefings announcing the features of this program, see *American Foreign Policy: Current Documents, 1981*, documents 45 and 46.

The executive summary of the Townes Panel Report is also printed in *Hearings on Military Posture and H.R. 5968 [H.R. 6030]*, Part 2, pages 181–183. Townes testified before the House Armed Services Committee in closed session on February 25, 1982. Much of his testimony was subsequently declassified and printed *ibid.*, Part 2, pages 175–202.

Document 24

Testimony by the Under Secretary of State for Security Assistance, Science and Technology (Buckley) Before a Subcommittee of the House Foreign Affairs Committee, April 1, 1982 (Extracts)[29]

The Administration's Foreign Assistance Program for Fiscal Year 1983

Believe it or not, Mr. Chairman and members of the committee, I am pleased to be here today, because I want to take advantage of this opportunity to talk about a budget that I believe to be both prudent and to meet the minimum needs of the security of this country.

The administration is mindful of and grateful for the efforts of this committee in passing a 2-year authorization bill last year. But as the committee report recognized, the authorizations for 1983 were made without the benefit of the administration's views, and it anticipated that the administration would be submitting requests for additional funds in due course.

We wish we could stay within the amounts you have already authorized, but we have no responsible choice but to present the additional levels of security assistance the administration is asking for fiscal year 1983. They reflect the hard necessity of responding effectively to events occurring outside our borders which have the most direct impact on our ultimate safety and well-being.

You are familiar with the events that have occurred in the past year. We have seen more and more countries undergoing pressure from the Soviets and their stand-ins. Afghanistan has been taken. The bid for greater freedom has been crushed in Poland. Vietnamese troops continue to occupy Kampuchea. And in Africa and in the Caribbean Basin, Cuban troops or Cuban-supported forces pose a direct threat to our most vital interest.

---

[29] Source: *Foreign Assistance Legislation for Fiscal Year 1983: Hearings Before the Subcommittee on International Security and Scientific Affairs of the Committee on Foreign Affairs, House of Representatives, Ninety-seventh Congress, Second Session* (Washington, 1982), Part 2, pp. 2–7, 41–42, 55–56. Buckley's prepared statement is *ibid.*, pp. 8–27.

Weakness attracts the predator. Hence, we have seen a shift in the global challenge from the industrialized states of Europe and Asia to the less developed nations of Asia, the Middle East, Africa, and closer to home in the Caribbean.

To meet these urgent challenges abroad and to minimize the costs to taxpayers at home, this administration has adopted a fundamentally new approach in arriving at our security assistance program for the new fiscal year. We have explicitly defined our Nation's vital foreign policy objectives and painstakingly allocated all foreign assistance resources against our priority goals.

As many of you can appreciate, this has necessarily prolonged the process and delayed the submission of some congressional presentation materials. However, we believe the resulting program contains the minimum required resources to:

One, promote peaceful solutions to regional rivalries;

Two, assure U.S. access to critical military facilities and basic raw materials;

Three, confront growing military threats from and subversive efforts by the Soviets and their proxies; and

Four, reduce the economic and social degradation that breeds domestic violence and invites external intervention.

The details of our fiscal 1983 request are set forth in the Department's booklet, "International Security and Economic Cooperation Program, Fiscal Year 1983,"[30] which has been made available to the Congress. What I would now like to do is review briefly the major foreign policy objectives described in that booklet and explain why the requested security assistance is necessary to the attainment of these goals. I will also summarize the few changes to the legislation which we will see.

Over 53 percent of the entire fiscal year 1983 security assistance program will be directed in support of our Middle East objectives; namely the search for a just and lasting peace and the urgent requirement that friends in the region be secure against external threats. These objectives are mutually reinforcing.

The security and economic health of Egypt and Israel are a requisite for further broadening of the peace of the Middle East. U.S. assistance programs tangibly reflect our support and help give these nations the confidence to continue on the path toward peace begun at Camp David.

Our assistance to Israel and Egypt, along with our aid to Jordan, Lebanon, and the regional programs, provides a security and economic base essential to ultimate stability and peace within the region.

The President is allocating 19 percent of the program; namely $1.6 billion, in support of our interests in Europe. The strategic importance to NATO of Europe's southern flank has been dramatically underlined by events this past year. With neighboring regions facing a growing challenge, our efforts to assist Greece, Turkey, Spain, and Portugal have assumed increasing importance.

Helping these nations through our security assistance programs is an important contribution to our common defense, not only against threats to Europe but against challenges to our own interests beyond the geographic bounds of the alliance. Turkey, for example, lies at the intersection of our NATO, Middle East, and Persian Gulf security concerns. Spain and Portugal, the other major security assistance recipients, are important not only to our NATO defenses, but to our capabilities to project military forces from the United States to Africa and on to the Middle East.

Ten percent of the fiscal year 1983 security assistance program is directed to insuring our continued access to Southwest Asia and the Persian Gulf, and to their critically important resources. Almost all nations in the area stretching from Pakistan in the east to Morocco in the west face serious economic problems and potential subversion or regional threats.

Our proposal for military modernization and economic assistance will help Pakistan to deter attacks from Afghanistan and facilitate the economic development essential to internal stability. Sudan, Morocco, and Tunisia all face, to one degree or another, threats of subversion or aggression emanating from Libya. All are important not only to our strategy for the security of the Persian Gulf, but potentially to the prospects for peace in the Middle East as well.

Our plan for restoring stability and improving economic prospects in the Caribbean Basin will require $433 million in security assistance for 1983. You are all thoroughly familiar with the approach that has been

---

[30] Reference is to *International Security and Economic Cooperation Program FY 1983*, Department of State Special Report No. 99, March 1982.

adopted by the administration in this regard. I would only point out that the amounts allocated for military assistance represent just 16 percent of our total program for the Caribbean Basin.

Requests in support of our important Pacific interests represent a modest fraction, only 6 percent, but nevertheless a vital part of our fiscal year 1983 security assistance program. This region is of major political, strategic, and economic importance to the United States. We have significant treaty relationships with Japan, Korea, the Philippines, Thailand, and our ANZUS partners. U.S. trade with the area now surpasses that with Western Europe.

We have in Northeast Asia a strong and economically vital South Korea that is able to deter its northern neighbor from military adventures. The Soviet-supported 200,000-man army remains in Kampuchea and threatens Thailand's security. The Philippines provide the United States with essential military facilities, and Indonesia and Malaysia straddle important sealanes.

To help secure our interests in the Indian Ocean, we are helping Kenya and Somalia achieve economic self-reliance and improved defense capabilities. In turn, both nations provide U.S. forces with access to facilities, thus [adding?] significantly to our ability to sustain a credible deterrent posture in the region.

Our proposed $177 million security assistance program for southern Africa is designed to advance the peaceful establishment of an independent Namibia, to help insure continued Western access to key strategic minerals, and to support the development process from Zaire to the Cape. We must fulfill our undertaking to assist the economic development of the frontline states of southern Africa, whose participation is essential to the stability of a region rich in minerals and essential to our economic well-being.

In west Africa, modest levels of security assistance are essential to maintaining economic and political resilience and to discouraging further Libyan attempts to exploit the financial difficulties faced by several nations.

To support these essential goals, the President is requesting and is committed to defending a total $8.7 billion security assistance program for fiscal year 1983. Of this, $4.8 billion requires budget authority. The balance of $3.9 billion is in the form of off-budget FMS guarantees.

The foreign policy objectives I have just outlined are those we strive to attain with these resources. As never before, the President's program has been carefully structured to address only our most critical needs.

We again seek authority to provide concessional assistance to key countries in order to make it possible for them to purchase defense equipment and services that we believe it is in our interest for them to have. We are asking this because we believe that concessional rates provide us with maximum flexibility in meeting the specific needs of our security assistance recipients. In contrast with grants over the longer term, they also lower the net cost to the U.S. taxpayer.

Let me now summarize the modifications we will seek in current legislation. Seven of them involve minor changes that will enhance the effectiveness of our security assistance programs. In addition, we seek new authority to establish an antiterrorism law enforcement assistance program, which my colleague Ambassador Robert Sayre will describe to you.[31]

The proposed revisions to the law are:

One, an emergency peacekeeping drawdown authority for the President in the amount of $10 million in commodities and services, if he determines that unforeseen circumstances have developed which necessitate immediate assistance.

Two, elimination of certain prohibitions on foreign assistance to the People's Republic of China, ending the discriminatory treatment of that country based on its past association with the Soviet bloc.

Three, a clarification to permit full cost recovery of all additional expenses incurred in carrying out administrative functions under the Arms Export Control Act.[32]

Four, exemption from the present 15-day notification to the Congress on reprograming funds up to $50,000 for IMET and international narcotics control programs.

Five, provision for a one to one exchange of U.S. and foreign military students at professional military schools.

Six, allowance of funds collected for administrative surcharges to be used for representation purposes.

---

[31] Robert M. Sayre's statement is in *Foreign Assistance Legislation for Fiscal Year 1983*, Part 2, pp. 28–30; his prepared statement is *ibid.*, pp. 30–40.

[32] P.L. 94–329; 90 Stat. 729; this law has been amended several times since its enactment in 1976.

And finally, seven, an allowance for the executive branch to sell Government-furnished equipment to U.S. firms acting as prime contractors for foreign governments or international organizations for incorporation into end items.

I assure you, gentlemen, that in this most difficult year the President would not be asking for additional security assistance if he were not absolutely convinced that these resources were essential to enhance the prospects for peace and protect essential American interests around the globe. Without them, the President would be forced to decide which objectives of our foreign policy to pursue and which to abandon or neglect.

For example, he would be forced to face such damaging choices as scaling back our Spanish bases in order to finance our Caribbean initiative, or of shifting resources away from Turkey to address our needs in Sudan, Kenya, and Somalia, or abandoning our undertakings and initiatives in such important areas as southern Africa and Southeast Asia in order to meet our commitments in the Middle East.

Unless we are willing to make these investments for peace and security today, we will risk far greater costs to both our safety and national treasure tomorrow.

Thank you.

. . . .

Chairman Zablocki. . . . We appreciate your statements, gentlemen. They naturally pose some very serious questions.

As I said in my opening statement,[33] Mr. Secretary, it is bad enough to ask for an additional $1 billion plus, but you have certain amendments to the legislation which I do not think will enhance its passage, but will cause more questions and make it more difficult.

For example, the seven provisions that you described very briefly raise some serious questions as to whether they are absolutely necessary. But we will develop those later.

My first question is this: As you know, last year, in order to enhance the possibility of approval of the bill and addressing the problem of the budget process, this committee suggested a modification of the administration request and proposed a formula for direct credits, which represented a significant increase over the previous year's administration.

I thought we had impressed upon the administration that if it wants anything in terms of a supplemental, it had better come along with the same type of formula. Now here you come with all direct credits for the additional amount, with total disregard for the last year's legislation. In your statement you noted that there were some guaranteed loans, but are they in FMS?

Mr. Buckley. Guaranteed loans, yes, in FMS.

Chairman Zablocki. What percentage is direct credits and what percentage is guaranteed loans?

Mr. Buckley. Our guaranteed loans are $3.9 billion. Our direct credits are $1.7 billion.

Chairman Zablocki. It is my understanding that the administration is requesting $1.7 billion in direct credits.

Mr. Buckley. Of which $950 million are grants, in recognition of a portion of the argument advanced by the Congress last year, in that some countries are so overburdened that we might as well recognize that fact. $500 million for Israel, $400 million for Egypt, $50 million for the Sudan.

The balance would be at low interest rates, which we believe, as I stated in my text, gives us much greater flexibility. But ultimately these countries can pay back. And so if you stretch out beyond this year and next year, there will be a net return to the Federal Government. So the net cost to the taxpayers would be lower.

Our other concern, frankly, Mr. Chairman, is we are talking about grants, and in grants to countries other than the potential basket cases, if you will. You are placing a burden on the countries that is very difficult. The actual concessionality through the formula that you referred to and that we received fell far short of what we felt was needed if we were, for example, to make it possible for a Kenya and a Thailand and so on to acquire the equipment they need.

It is for this reason that we once again advanced what we believe to be the better approach in the longer term, even though it requires a higher outlay figure. The economic impact is not going to be different between shifting from the grant and increasing the guarantees to offset the direct credits.

---

[33] For Zablocki's opening statement, see *Foreign Assistance Legislation for Fiscal Year 1983*, Part 2, pp. 1–2.

As I say, if you look at the welfare of the taxpayer down over the next 10 or 15 years, the taxpayers will be better off under our proposal.

. . . .

MR. BINGHAM. . . . Mr. Secretary, the chairman in his opening statement pointed to the fact that this year, this fiscal year, our arms sales will approach a figure of $20 billion, which, it was pointed out, is double the year before. Does this bother you at all? Should we be putting any kind of restraint on our arms sales policy?

MR. BUCKLEY. Actually, what you have here is an anomalous situation that is reflected directly in the length of the AWACS debate. Over a period of years we have been going at about $15 billion or $16 billion. I believe in 1980 it was $16 billion. We have projected for 1981–82 about $15 or $16 billion for the same level of sales.

What happened last year, we actually sold $8.5 billion. Then the AWACS package extended into fiscal 1982 and distorted the figure there, that plus a one-time sale to Korea. So we have not $20 billion in 1982, but closer to $25 billion. But if you take the 2 years together, the average is about $16 billion. As we look through to 1983, we seem at about the same range.

MR. BINGHAM. The previous administration indicated that while they may not have been very successful at it, they were trying to put restraints on arms sales. Does this administration take the same view, that it wants to restrain arms sales to the extent that it is practical or feasible to do so?

MR. BUCKLEY. I think we spelled out in great detail in the policy issued in June of last year that there are a number of criteria which are anything but open-handed.[34] We do not intend to destabilize an existing region. We want to make sure that it meets an actual defense need. We want to make sure that the system does not overtax the ability of the country to absorb, and so forth.

Nevertheless, because we are willing to deal with arms transfers as an instrument of foreign policy, whereas the Carter administration found it had to make constant exceptions to its own policy, the impression has gone abroad that we are wanting to spew these weapons all over the landscape.

But we scrutinize each request with a tremendous amount of care and do apply the criteria, the set of criteria. But I think the actual experience of 2 years under this administration proves that in fact this is restraint.

. . . .

Document 25

Address by the Secretary of State (Haig) Before the Center for Strategic and International Studies, Georgetown University, April 6, 1982[35]

Peace and Deterrence

It is a melancholy fact of the modern age that man has conceived a means capable of his own destruction. For 37 years mankind has had to live with the terrible burden of nuclear weapons. From the dawn of the nuclear age, these weapons have been the source of grave concern to our peoples, and the focus of continuous public debate. Every successive President of the United States has shared these concerns. Every administration has had to engage itself in this debate.

It is right that each succeeding generation should question anew the manner in which its leaders exercise such awesome responsibilities. It is right that each new administration should have to confront the awful dilemmas posed by the possession of nuclear weapons. It is right that our nuclear strategy should be exposed to continuous examination.

In debating these issues, we should not allow the complexity of the problems and the gravity of the stakes to blind us to the common ground upon which we all stand. No one has ever advocated nuclear war. No responsible voice has ever sought to minimize its horrors.

---

[34] Reference presumably is to the announcement of a Presidential directive on conventional arms transfer policy issued on July 9, 1981, not June 1981. For text, see *American Foreign Policy: Current Documents, 1981,* document 34.

[35] Source: Department of State Press Release 117, August 6, 1982; printed also in Department of State *Bulletin,* May 1982, pp. 31–34. The source text is the text as prepared for delivery.

On the contrary, from the earliest days of the post war era, America's leaders have recognized the only nuclear strategy consistent with our values and our survival—our physical existence, and what makes life worth living—is the strategy of deterrence. The massive destructive power of these weapons precludes their serving any lesser purpose. The catastrophic consequences of another world war—with or without nuclear weapons—make deterrence of conflict our highest objective, and our only rational military strategy in the modern age.

Thus, since the close of World War II American and Western strategy has assigned a single function to nuclear weapons: the prevention of war, and the preservation of peace. At the heart of this deterrence strategy is the requirement that the risk of engaging in war must be made to outweigh any possible benefits of aggression. The cost of aggression must not be confined to the victims of aggression.

This strategy of deterrence has won the consistent approval of the Western peoples. It has enjoyed the bipartisan support of the American Congress. It has secured the unanimous endorsement of every successive allied government.

Deterrence has been supported because deterrence works. Nuclear deterrence and collective defense have preserved peace in Europe, the crucible of two global wars in this century. Clearly neither improvement in the nature of man, nor strengthening of the international order have made war less frequent or less brutal. Millions have died since 1945 in over 130 international and civil wars. Yet nuclear deterrence has prevented a conflict between the two superpowers, a conflict which even without nuclear weapons would be the most destructive in mankind's history.

The simple possession of nuclear weapons does not guarantee deterrence. Throughout history societies have risked their total destruction if the prize of victory was sufficiently great, or the consequences of submission sufficiently grave. War, and in particular nuclear war, can be deterred, but only if we are able to deny an aggressor military advantage from his action, and thus ensure his awareness that he cannot prevail in any conflict with us. Deterrence, in short, requires the maintenance of a secure military balance, one which cannot be overturned through surprise attack, or sudden technological breakthrough. The quality and credibility of deterrence must be measured against these criteria. Successive administrations have understood this fact and stressed the importance of an overall balance. This administration can do no less.

The strategy of deterrence, in its essentials, has endured. But the requirements for maintaining a secure capability to deter in all circumstances have evolved. In the early days of unquestioned American nuclear superiority the task of posing an unacceptable risk to an aggressor was not difficult. The threat of massive retaliation was fully credible as long as the Soviet Union could not respond in kind. As the Soviet Union's nuclear arsenal grew, however, this threat began to lose credibility.

To sustain the credibility of Western deterrence, the concept of flexible response was elaborated, and formally adopted by the United States and its NATO partners in 1967.[36] Henceforth, it was agreed that NATO would meet aggression initially at whatever level it was launched, while preserving the flexibility to escalate the conflict, if necessary, to secure the cessation of aggression and the withdrawal of the aggressor. The purpose of this strategy is not just to conduct conflict successfully if it is forced upon us, but more importantly to prevent the outbreak of conflict in the first place.

Flexible response is not premised upon the view that nuclear war can be controlled. Every successive allied and American government has been convinced that a nuclear war, once initiated, could escape such control. They have therefore agreed upon a strategy which retains the deterrent effect of a possible nuclear response, without making such a step in any sense automatic.

The alliance based its implementation of flexible response upon a spectrum of forces, each of which plays an indispensable role in assuring the credibility of a Western strategy of deterrence. At one end of the spectrum are America's strategic forces, our heavy bombers, intercontinental missiles, and ballistic missile submarines. Since NATO's inception, these forces have been the ultimate guarantee of Western security, a role which they will retain in the future.

At the other end of the spectrum are the alliance's conventional forces, including U.S. troops in Europe. These forces must be strong enough to defeat all but the most

---

[36] For the text of the NATO announcement of "flexible response," see *American Foreign Policy: Current Documents, 1967* (Washington, 1969), p. 321.

massive and persistent conventional aggression. They must be resistant and durable enough to give political leaders time to measure the gravity of the threat, to confront the inherently daunting prospects of nuclear escalation, and to seek through diplomacy the cessation of conflict and restoration of any lost Western territory. The vital role which conventional forces play in deterrence is too often neglected, particularly by those most vocal in their concern over reliance upon nuclear weapons. A strengthened conventional posture both strengthens the deterrent effect of nuclear forces, and reduces the prospect of their ever being used.

Linking together strategic and conventional forces are theater nuclear forces, that is NATO's nuclear systems based in Europe. These systems are concrete evidence of the nature of the American commitment. They are a concrete manifestation of NATO's willingness to resort to nuclear weapons if necessary to preserve the freedom and independence of its members. Further, the presence of nuclear weapons in Europe ensures the Soviet Union will never believe that it can divide the United States from its allies, or wage a limited war with limited risks against any NATO member.

The strategy of flexible response and the forces that sustain its credibility reflect more than simply the prevailing military balance. Western strategy also reflects the political and geographical reality of an alliance of 15 independent nations, the most powerful of which is separated from all but one of the others by 4,000 miles of ocean.

Deterrence is consequently more than a military strategy. It is the essential political bargain which binds together the Western coalition. Twice in this century, America has been unable to remain aloof from European conflict, but unable to intervene in time to prevent the devastation of Western Europe. Neither we nor our allies can afford to see this pattern repeated a third time. We have, therefore, chosen a strategy which engages American power in the defense of Europe, and gives substance to the principle that the security of the alliance is indivisible.

During the past decade the Soviet Union has mounted a sustained buildup across the range of its nuclear forces designed to undermine the credibility of this alliance strategy. Soviet modernization efforts have far outstripped those of the West. The development and deployment of Soviet intercontinental ballistic missiles now pose a serious and increasing threat to a large part of our land-based ICBM force. A new generation of Soviet intermediate range missiles are targeted upon our European allies.

In the last 10 years, the Soviets introduced an unprecedented array of new strategic and intermediate range systems into their arsenals including the SS–17, SS–18, and SS–19 ICBM's, the Backfire bomber, the Typhoon submarine and several new types of submarine-launched missiles, and the SS–20 intermediate range missile. In contrast, during this same period, the United States exercised restraint, introducing only the Trident missile and submarine, and the slower air breathing cruise missile.

In order to deal with the resulting imbalances, President Reagan has adopted a defense posture and recommended programs to the U.S. Congress designed to maintain deterrence, rectify the imbalances, and thereby support the Western strategy I have outlined.

His bold strategic modernization program, announced last October, is designed to ensure the maintenance of a secure and reliable capability to deny an adversary advantage from any form of aggression, even a surprise attack.

The President's decision, in his first weeks in office, to go ahead with the production and deployment of the Pershing II and ground launched cruise missiles, in accordance with NATO's decision of December 1979,[37] represents an effort to reinforce the linkage between our strategic forces in the United States, and NATO's conventional and nuclear forces in Europe. A response to the massive buildup of Soviet SS–20's targeted on Western Europe, this NATO decision was taken to ensure that the USSR will never launch aggression in the belief that its own territory can remain immune from attack, or that European security can ever be decoupled from that of the United States.

The improvements we are making in our conventional forces—in their readiness, mobility, training, and equipment—are designed to ensure the kind of tough and resilient conventional capability required by the strategy of flexible response.

It is important to recognize the interrelationship of these three types of forces. The

---

[37] Reference is to the communiqués issued by the special meeting of the NATO Foreign and Defense Ministers, December 12, 1979, and the meeting of the NATO Foreign Ministers, December 14, 1979. For texts, see *American Foreign Policy: Basic Documents, 1977–1980,* pp. 494–499.

requirements in each category are dependent upon the scale of the others. Their functions are similarly linked. The Soviet Union understands this. That is why they have consistently proposed a pledge against the first use of nuclear weapons, an idea which has achieved some resonance here in the West.

NATO has consistently rejected such Soviet proposals, which are tantamount to making Europe safe for conventional aggression. If the West were to allow Moscow the freedom to choose the level of conflict which most suited it, and to leave entirely to Soviet discretion the nature and timing of any escalation, we would be forced to maintain conventional forces at least at the level of those of the Soviet Union and its Warsaw Pact allies.

Those in the West who advocate the adoption of a "no-first-use" policy[38] seldom go on to propose that the United States reintroduce the draft, triple the size of its armed forces, and put its economy on wartime footing. Yet in the absence of such steps, a pledge of no first use effectively leaves the West nothing with which to counterbalance the Soviet conventional advantages and geopolitical position in Europe.

Neither do Western proponents of a "no-first-use" policy acknowledge the consequences for the Western alliance of an American decision not to pose and accept the risk of nuclear war in the defense of Europe. A "no-first-use" policy would be the end of flexible response, and thus of the very credibility of the Western strategy of deterrence. In adopting such a stance, the United States would be limiting its commitment to Europe. But the alliance cannot function as a limited liability corporation. It can only survive as a partnership, to which all are equally and fully committed—shared benefits, shared burdens, shared risks.

Another concept which has recently attracted interest is that of a freeze on nuclear weapons. While being sensitive to the concerns underlying this proposal, we have had to underscore the flaws in such an approach. A freeze at current levels would perpetuate an unstable and unequal military balance. It would reward a decade of unilateral Soviet buildup, and penalize the United States for a decade of unilateral restraint. As President Reagan stressed last week,[39] such a freeze would remove all Soviet incentive to engage in meaningful arms control designed to cut armaments, and reduce the risk of war.

Much of the argumentation for a nuclear freeze revolves around the question of how much is enough. Each side possesses thousands of deliverable nuclear weapons. Does it then really make any difference who is ahead? The question itself is misleading, as it assumes that deterrence is simply a matter of numbers of weapons, or numbers of casualties which could be inflicted. It is not.

Let us remember, first and foremost, that we are trying to deter the Soviet Union, not ourselves. The dynamic nature of the Soviet nuclear buildup demonstrates that the Soviet leaders do not believe in the concept of "sufficiency." They are not likely to be deterred by a force based upon it.

Let us also recall that nuclear deterrence must work not just in times of peace, and moments of calm. Deterrence faces its true test at the time of maximum tension, even in the midst of actual conflict. In such extreme circumstances, when the stakes on the table may already be immense, when Soviet leaders may feel the very existence of their regime is threatened, who can say whether or not they would run massive risks if they believed that in the end the Soviet state would prevail.

Deterrence thus does not rest on a static comparison of the number or size of nuclear weapons. Rather, deterrence depends upon our capability, even after suffering a massive nuclear blow, to prevent an aggressor from securing a military advantage, and prevailing in a conflict. Only if we maintain such a capability can we deter such a blow. Deterrence, in consequence, rests upon a military balance measured not in warhead numbers, but in a complex interaction of capabilities and vulnerabilities.

The state of the military balance, and its impact upon the deterrent value of American forces cast a shadow over every significant geopolitical decision. It affects on a day-to-day basis the conduct of American diplomacy. It influences the management of international crises, and the terms upon which they are resolved.

The search for national interest and national security is a principal preoccupation

---

[38] See, for example, McGeorge Bundy, George F. Kennan, Robert S. McNamara, and Gerard Smith, "Nuclear Weapons and the Atlantic Alliance," *Foreign Affairs*, LX (Spring, 1982), pp. 753–768.

[39] Reference presumably is to statements on nuclear arms reductions made by President Reagan at his press conference, March 31. For text of the press conference, see *Weekly Compilation of Presidential Documents*, April 5, 1982, pp. 410–417.

of the leaders of every nation on the globe. Their decisions and their foreign policies are profoundly affected by their perception of the military balance between the United States and the Soviet Union, and the consequent capacity of either to help provide for their security or to threaten it.

More important still, perceptions of the military balance also affect the psychological attitude of both American and Soviet leaders, as they respond to events around the globe. For the foreseeable future the relationship between the United States and the Soviet Union will be one in which our differences outnumber points of convergence. Our objective must be to restrain this competition, to keep it below the level of force, while protecting our interests and those of our allies. Our ability to secure these objectives will be crucially influenced by the state of the strategic balance. Every judgment we make, and every judgment the Soviet leadership makes, will be shaded by it.

Thus the Soviet leadership, in calculating the risks of subversion or aggression, of acquiring new clients or propping up faltering proxies, must carefully evaluate the possibilities and prospects for an effective American response. Soviet calculations must encompass not only American capabilities to influence regional developments, but American willingness to face the prospect of U.S.-Soviet confrontation, and consequent escalation. American leaders, for their part, must go through comparable calculations in reacting to regional conflicts, responding to Soviet adventurism, and seeking to resolve international crises in a manner consistent with U.S. interests.

Put simply, our own vulnerability to nuclear blackmail, as well as the susceptibility of our friends to political intimidation, depends upon our ability and willingness to cope credibly with any Soviet threat. A strong and credible strategic posture enhances stability by reducing for the Soviets the temptations toward adventurism, at the same time that it strengthens our hand in responding to Soviet political-military threats.

In no area of diplomacy does the military balance have greater effect than in arms control. Arms control can reinforce deterrence, and stabilize a military balance at lower levels of risk and effort. Arms control cannot, however, either provide or restore a balance we are unwilling to maintain through our defense efforts.

Just as the only justifiable nuclear strategy is one of deterrence, so the overriding objective for arms control is reducing the risk of war. The essential purpose of arms control is not to save money, although it may do so. Its purpose is not to generate good feelings, or improve international relationships, although it may have that effect as well. Arms control's central purpose must be to reinforce the military balance, upon which deterrence depends, at reduced levels of weapons and risk.

On November 18, President Reagan laid out the framework for a comprehensive program of arms control designed to serve these objectives.[40] He committed the United States to seek major reductions in nuclear and conventional forces, leading to equal agreed limits on both sides. Last week he reviewed the steps we have taken:

—In Geneva we have put forth detailed proposals designed to limit intermediate range nuclear forces, and to eliminate entirely the missiles of greatest concern to each side. This proposal has won the strong and unified support of our allies.

—In Vienna, we are negotiating, alongside our allies, on reductions in conventional force levels in Europe. These negotiations have gone on without real progress for over 8 years. Because we are now facing diplomatic atrophy, we must urgently consider how to revitalize East–West discussions of conventional force reductions, and stimulate progress in these talks.

—Our highest priority, in the past several months, has been completing preparations for negotiations with the Soviet Union on strategic arms. Here too we will be proposing major reductions to verifiable, equal agreed levels. Here too we will be presenting detailed proposals when negotiations open.

The prospects for progress in each of these areas of arms control depend upon support of the President's defense programs. This imperative has been caricatured as a policy of building up arms in order to reduce them. This is simply not true. As President Reagan's proposals for intermediate range missiles make clear, we hope that we never have to deploy those systems. But we must demonstrate a willingness to maintain the balance through force deployments if we are to have any prospect of reducing and stabilizing it through arms control.

---

[40] For text of the President's speech, November 18, 1981, see *American Foreign Policy: Current Documents, 1981*, document 60.

Negotiations in the early 1970's, on a treaty limiting anti-ballistic missile systems provide an historic example. At the time, the Soviets had already built a system of ballistic missile defenses around Moscow. The United States had deployed no such system. Arms control offered the only means of closing off an otherwise attractive and expensive new avenue for arms competition. Yet it was not until the American administration sought and secured congressional support for an American ABM program that the Soviets began to negotiate seriously. The result was the 1972 treaty limiting anti-ballistic missile systems,[41] which remains in force today.

This same pattern was repeated more recently with intermediate range missiles. For years the Soviets had sought limits on U.S. nuclear forces in Europe, but refused to consider any limits upon their nuclear forces targeted upon Europe. Only after NATO took its decision of December 1979 to deploy U.S. Pershing II and ground launched cruise missiles did the USSR agree to put its SS–20 missiles on the negotiating table.

In the area of strategic arms, as well, there is little prospect the Soviet Union will ever agree to equal limits at lower levels unless first persuaded that the United States is otherwise determined to maintain equality at higher levels. It is, for instance, unrealistic to believe that the Soviet Union will agree to reduce the most threatening element of its force structure, its heavy, multiwarheaded intercontinental missiles, unless it is persuaded that otherwise the United States will respond by deploying comparable systems itself.

For many opposed to reliance on nuclear weapons—even for defense or deterrence—the issue is a moral one. For those who first elaborated the strategy of deterrence, and for those who seek to maintain its effect, this issue is also preeminently moral. A familiar argument is that, in a nuclear age, we must choose between our values and our existence. If nuclear weapons offer the only deterrent to nuclear blackmail, some would argue we should submit, rather than pose the risk of nuclear conflict. This choice, however, is a false one. By maintaining the military balance and sustaining deterrence, we protect the essential values of Western civilization—democratic government, personal liberty, and religious freedom—and preserve the peace. In failing to maintain deterrence, we would risk our freedoms, while actually increasing the likelihood of also suffering nuclear devastation.

As human beings and free men and women, we must reject this false alternative, and avoid the extremes of nuclear catastrophe and nuclear blackmail. In the nuclear age, the only choice consistent with survival and civilization is deterrence.

An eminent theologian once described our age as one in which "the highest possibilities are inextricably intermingled with the most dire perils." The scientific and technological advances so vital to our civilization also make possible its destruction. This reality cannot be wished away.

Americans have always been conscious of the dilemmas posed by the nuclear weapon. From the moment that science unleashed the atom, our instinct and policy has been to control it. Those who direct America's defense policies today share completely the desire of people everywhere to end the nuclear arms race and to begin to achieve substantial reductions in nuclear armament.

Confronted by the dire perils of such weapons, America has responded in a manner that best preserves both security and peace, that protects our society and our values and that offers hope without illusion. The strategy of deterrence has kept the peace for over 30 years. It has provided the basis for arms control efforts. And it offers the best chance to control and to reduce the dangers we face.

Deterrence is not automatic. It cannot be had on the cheap. Our ability to sustain it depends upon our ability to maintain the military balance now being threatened by the Soviet buildup. If we are to reinforce deterrence through arms control and arms reduction, we must convince the Soviets that their efforts to undermine the deterrent effect of our forces will not succeed.

The control and reduction of nuclear weapons, based on deterrence, is the only effective intellectual, political, and moral response to nuclear weapons. The stakes are too great and the consequences of error too catastrophic to exchange deterrence for a leap into the unknown. The incentives for real arms control exist and we have both the means and the duty to apply them.

Let us be clear about our objectives in the nuclear era. We seek to reduce the risk of war and to establish a stable military balance at lower levels of risk and effort. By

[41] For text, see 23 UST 3435.

doing so today, we may be able to build a sense of mutual confidence and cooperation, offering the basis for even more ambitious steps tomorrow. But above all, we shall be pursuing the "highest possibility" for peace.

Document 26

Transcript of a Press Conference by the Secretary of Defense (Weinberger), Cheyenne, Wyoming, May 15, 1982 (Extracts)[42]

Basing Mode Options for the MX Missile; the Defense Budget

Q. Did the tour of FE Warren Air Force Base today in any way influence your decision on the basing mode of the MX missile?

A. No, I don't think anything that we weren't basically aware of. It is considered, as everybody knows, one of the possible areas, one of the areas which have [*has*] been considered very carefully in the event we should go to either a temporary interim basing in existing silos or somewhat similar form of basing. But the final decision hasn't been made, and of course, that will depend on the congressional funding and on a number of technical factors that we're still examining very carefully. We think it's very important to get the MX in the ground as soon as it comes off the production line because it is the new, heavier, more modern missile with a greater accuracy and greater yield. And it is essential, I think, that entering into arms reduction talks that the Soviets know that we have a very strong, accurate missile that will add to the deterrent.

Q. Mr. Secretary, what's your feeling of the Dense Pack option?

A. It is one of the ones that's being very substantially recommended by a number of scientific people, people connected with our research and engineering; they say that it has the capability of being somewhat more easily defended if we should go to a BMD method and it has certain technical advantages. We are looking at all of these just as carefully as we can. We are looking at a number of other options. What we want is the most survivable system that we can have so that when we enter the strategic arms reductions talks, why the Soviets will know that we have something that is a very strong deterrent that will be very much to their advantage to have us give up.

Q. Would Dense Packing be feasible?

A. Yes, the soil conditions are considered to be very good. There's a natural hardening to the sites here. It's not the only site but it is certainly one of the ones that has been reported to be under favorable consideration.

Q. For Dense Pack?

A. For indeed the Dense Pack or being put into existing silos. There hasn't been any final decision on where that will go.

Q. What is your opinion of Senator Wallop's laser defense?[43]

A. I think it's a very promising system and one that we find a great deal of hope in. I was briefed on various elements of it at the Pentagon a couple of days ago—yesterday as a matter of fact—and it offers a lot of promise. The technology is considered to be some years away but we're investing, at Senator Wallop's initiative, a large amount into research because, of course, if you can stop the Soviet missiles before they get into the atmosphere that is by far the very best—offers the most hope to everybody. I personally am very interested in that kind of technology and I'm delighted the Senator has converted a great many of his colleagues in the Congress to support careful study and full examination of it. It offers a great deal of hope. I'd wish we could get it tomorrow. It's considered to be some years off. I think it's next best to my favorite method which is the method in which we would take the Soviet missiles as they come out of their silos and have a boomerang effect. He hasn't developed that yet.

. . . .

Q. Do you have a timetable on the MX decision?

A. Well, the Congress said last year that we had to have a permanent decision re-

---

[42] Source: *Public Statements of Secretary of Defense Weinberger*, 1982. Secretary Weinberger visited Wyoming and Colorado on May 15, among other things, to tour Air Force installations.

[43] Reference presumably is to the amendment to the Department of Defense authorization bill calling for research on a laser defense system, which Senator Wallop introduced in the Senate and the Senate approved on May 13. See *Congressional Record*, May 13, 1982, pp. S5092–S5097.

ported to them by next June.[44] This year the Senate which adopted our authorization bill said that we should have our permanent decision by December.[45] We have preferred and have recommended that we be allowed to do interim basing—getting the MX into existing silos and then spending some more time trying to find out what is the most survivable, protectable permanent basing mode. We will, of course, honor the congressional request and if it should be the final decision of both Houses that we make our recommendation by December, we will try to do that. We don't feel it gives us quite enough time to give the study the importance this matter warrants. It's one of the three parts of the strategic triad of deterrence. We want it to be as survivable as possible. The reason the President cancelled out the MPS system of the previous administration was because he felt it was not survivable and while we know that our interim suggestion is indeed just that, an interim suggestion, we would want it to be the most survivable permanent basing that we could find. We are looking at three or four quite promising, different options. But the close spaced basing is one of those and we are trying our best to meet the time table that Congress has set.

Q. President Reagan suggested that the Navy should have a large aircraft carrier fleet—with what happened in the Falklands to the two ships that were sunk by relatively inexpensive weapons compared to what they sunk, is this causing you any change in your thought?

A. Well, everybody has known that one of the things that you have to do with capital ships of any size is protect them in both an air cover and with air-to-surface missiles and/or with ships equipped with missiles—protect them against that. We do have plans with our aircraft carriers and the Senate has approved the authorization of two of the large carriers and I'm glad that they did because by doing that you can save a billion dollars in the acquisition of these carriers. We have plans in the battle groups, that they will be part of, to protect against heavier attack. We have the new AEGIS class cruisers which are particularly designed for this purpose, and of course, the large carriers can furnish their own air cover. The small carrier is not really able to do that. Large carriers have the ability to not only deliver a very substantial amount of attacking power if it should be needed but they also have the ability to protect themselves. The principal lesson from the Falklands sort of confirms what's known that you do have to take steps to cover these ships in one way or another.

Q. Some military people are saying that, for instance, a sub commander said that an aircraft carrier is an easy target, that he's never had any trouble hitting one and that the whole Soviet system is set up to hit those ships.

A. The Soviets have a very strong submarine force and we have very strong antisubmarine measures. I think you will find that many people within the Service (inaudible) to their own particular expressions.

Q. So, in other words, it hasn't changed your thinking?

A. No. We think that the large carriers give a flexibility to the defense that is vitally needed. We think we may very well have to operate in areas far from the shores of the United States and we feel we have to be prepared to do that and a large carrier is simply a floating airfield and it does have to be protected just the way an airfield has to be protected. It does have also an ability to deliver a very substantial power and we believe it is an essential addition to the fleet. And, as I say, we haven't changed our plans for requesting authorization of two more and by voting authorization of two, and Senator Wallop's taken a lead in a lot of these matters, you do have an ability to save a great deal of money, a billion dollars literally if you acquire two separately in spite the long—Also, you get them sooner, which if you accept the hypothesis that you need them is very desirable—we get them 22 months sooner and a billion dollars less cost by doing authorization of two. The outlays for that will be very small this year. It is a large expense but rearming America is a very expensive responsibility.

Q. Some observers would say that Reagan's budget proposals, probably the biggest point of compromise among Congress is going to have to be in defense. What would be your response to that?

A. Well, there have been a lot of assumptions that defense spending was going

---

[44] A provision in the Department of Defense Appropriations Act, 1982, P.L. 97–114, approved on December 29, 1981, required the Secretary of Defense to recommend to Congress a permanent basing mode for the MX missile no later than July 1, 1983; for text, see 95 Stat. 1577.

[45] The Defense authorization bill, which passed the Senate on May 14, 1982, set a December 1, 1982, deadline for the Department of Defense recommendation on a permanent basing mode for the MX missile.

to be cut very drastically this year. Actually, the Senate in an all-night session voted very nearly all the President had requested, within a very small amount considering the size of the budget. No one should possibly or can possibly deny the fact that it's an immense amount of money but it's the price we pay for neglect of the last few years and neglect during years when the Soviets were increasing their strength enormously. It's the only way that we can be assured that we can come out of strategic arms or any kind of arms reduction talks with any sort of effective result. Also, if those talks should fail, it's the only way we can be assured that we can maintain the deterrence that has kept the peace between the super powers since the end of World War II.

So there is a lot of talk about how Defense has to be cut but I think the more the Congress examines the proposals we made and the budget that we submitted, the more support it has gained. The House Committee has already voted an even larger amount than the Senate did—House Armed Services Committee—and that bill will be debated on the floor of the House very shortly. We think the need is there. We don't think anything has happened to change the need. We think the Soviet threat is every bit as strong as it was last year, if not stronger, and it's just as vital for us to increase our defensive strength as it was last year. The real problem is that it's not only a very expensive job but it's a long job. It takes a good 5 to 6 years of steady, resolute effort and I agree that with a liberal democratic society that's a hard thing to sustain because defense spending is not very popular. But, as someone said, it's the only social program that permits all the other social programs to exist. We think it is vital that we keep on with this very difficult, very expensive, basically kind of disagreeable job most people find it. Nothing more or less than the preservation of our freedom is at stake. Also, it's the only way, I think, we can get genuine arms reduction.

PRESS. Thank you, Mr. Secretary.

Document 27

Address by the Secretary of Defense (Weinberger) Before the Massachusetts Medical Society, Boston, May 19, 1982[46]

"Deterrence Has Stood the Test of Time and Usefulness Beyond Reproach"

I greatly appreciate and am honored by your invitation to give the Shattuck lecture this year. The generosity and public-spiritedness of Dr. George Cheyne Shattuck, the benefactor of these lectures, and the distinguished speakers who have kept this tradition since 1890, make this invitation an unusual honor.

I would like to talk today about a matter which concerns all of us equally. That is the threat of nuclear war which all of us, to our dismay, have lived with now for some 34 years. This is a most disagreeable and difficult subject, but I am deeply concerned because some Americans are expressing doubts that our President and his administration share their abhorrence for war and in particular nuclear war. This is a terrible misconception made even worse by various grim prognoses of the destruction nuclear weapons would wreak and by the pictures we see on television of old nuclear tests.

We have seen enough images of war lately and indeed many of us have seen far too much of war itself in our lifetimes. I would, therefore, prefer to offer, here, an image of peace even though I offer it in an undeniably turbulent world, at a most dangerous period of our history.

In the early part of Homer's *Iliad* Hector finds his wife, Andromache, with their child Astyanax on the walls above Troy. The little boy, frightened by his father's armor and helmet, cries out. Hector removes his helmet and the two parents laugh as the son recognizes the father. Hector then lifts Astyanax in his arms, jostles him in the air over his head, and the family shares a moment of peace.

This is a picture of life as we want it, not the terrible carnage churning below on the

---

[46] Source: *Public Statements of Secretary of Defense Weinberger*, 1982; printed also in the Department of Defense publication, *Defense 82*, August 1982, pp. 3–7.

plains of Troy, not even the glory of great soldiers which the *Iliad* also celebrates. The contrast intended by Homer between these scenes of war and peace is as vivid as the choice which every generation has had to face.

We choose peace, but not because we are Democrats or Republicans. We want peace because we are Americans and a civilized people. We reject war as a deliberate instrument of foreign policy because it is repugnant to our national morality. War prevents people from leading the kinds of lives which this country was fashioned to protect and to enhance. As civilized people, we reject war because it kills and maims soldiers and civilians alike and undermines the fabric of life.

But nuclear war is even more horrible than war in any other form. Its destructive power has been described at length in popular journals recently. The images are sufficiently horrible that the temptation is strong to turn our backs on the whole subject. But, grim as they are, those matters have to be thought about and dealt with. It is part of my job to do that, and to know not only what we are faced with, but how we may best prevent such a catastrophe from happening.

Physicians, it seems to me, must adopt a similar attitude to their work. A physician who deals with the sick every day sees many unpleasant things: cancer, heart disease, disorders of the nervous system, the patient's pain, and his family's anguish. The answer to these is manifestly not to walk away. It is not to throw up one's hands in dismay and respond with sentiment and emotion alone. That will save no one's life. What is required is a mixture of the compassion we all feel for the sick, plus the most objective and informed judgment about a course of action, followed by an equally steady hand in restoring the patient's health and easing his pain.

Those of us who are charged with the responsibility for the health and strength of this nation's defense are in a somewhat parallel position. The prospect of nuclear war is ghastly in the extreme. But we cannot allow the dread with which we look upon it to obscure our judgment on how to prevent it. Obviously, this too would not save lives.

To the extent of *our* powers we must, using all the judgment and technical skills and latest knowledge available, arrive at an objective, rational policy which will accomplish what we all want. Of course, we take, as our starting point, that which everyone agrees to: that nuclear war is so terrible that it must not be allowed to happen. This, however, is not a policy. It is a national objective which all of us share, very much like the compassion one feels for the sick.

Our policy to prevent war since the age of nuclear weapons began has been one of deterrence. Our strategic nuclear weapons are only retaliatory. Their purpose is to provide us with a credible retaliatory capability in the event we are struck first. The idea on which this is based is quite simple: to make the cost of fighting a nuclear war much higher than any possible benefit. This policy has been approved, through the political processes of the democratic nations it protects, since at least 1950. Most important, it works. It has worked in the face of major international tensions involving the great powers and it has worked in the face of war itself.

But while the idea of deterrence has stood the test of time and usefulness beyond reproach, the things we must do to maintain that deterrence have changed substantially as the Soviets' quest for nuclear superiority grew to fruition.

In the fifties the requirements of deterrence were minimal. Our overwhelming nuclear superiority both in weapons and the means of their delivery made moot the question of whether an adversary would be deterred by unacceptable costs, if he attacked first. It also gave us the ability to deter conventional attacks on our allies. By the mid-sixties, however, the Soviets' nuclear force had grown greatly in strength. They had also achieved a major edge in conventional weapons in Europe. To discourage the prospect of conflict there NATO decided that it would meet and answer force at whatever level it might be initiated, while retaining the option to use even greater force as the most effective preventative against aggression in the first place. It is important to remember here that the retention of this option is absolutely consistent with our original view of the purpose of our nuclear weapons; that is, to deter aggression and to prevent other nuclear weapons being used against us or our allies. In simple language, we do not start fights—in Europe or anywhere.

We see disturbing evidence, such as the Soviets' development of refiring capability and major expenditures for civil defense shelters, that they think they can fight and win a nuclear war. We do not share this perception; we know nuclear war is unwinnable. But we do not feel we can successfully deter attack from an adversary such as the USSR, if we relieve them of the necessity of all defensive planning. To do so would erode our deterrent by announcing that under no circumstances would we ever use our weapons first.

Recently it has been argued that we should adopt a policy of "no first use" of nuclear force in the defense of Europe.[47] While this sounds plausible enough, it lessens the effectiveness of deterrence. We must remember that NATO has effectively prevented Soviet aggression. In no small part, this is because our policy makes clear to the Soviets the tremendous risks to them of aggression. Also, a "no first use" policy might imply that the first use of *conventional* force *is* somehow acceptable. We reject this entirely. And we do so because our policy is to deter not to encourage the first use of force against us. The point is that we oppose the use of forces and arms as a means for anyone to secure his objectives. We have recently made that clear in our position in the conflict between the United Kingdom and Argentina in the South Atlantic. Force of arms is not the way to resolve international disputes.

I wish I could tell you that the Soviets shared this view. Unfortunately, history and all the facts we know about stand in the way of such a policy by them. For the past 21 years, the Soviets have concentrated tremendous efforts and resources on achieving a clear superiority in nuclear forces. The result has been the addition to their arsenal of new weapons systems such as the SS–17, SS–18, and SS-19 ICBM's, the backfire bomber, the typhoon submarine, several new types of cruise missiles, and the SS–20 intermediate range missile. These efforts dwarf our own. In fact since 1970, they have out-invested us by about $400 billion in military armaments.

No less important is the fact that the Soviets do regard their nuclear forces as a means of coercion. Well over two-thirds of their nuclear force sits in land-based ICBM's—weapons whose speed, destructive power, and above all, accuracy give those who possess them the capability to aim with assurance at the military targets in the United States in a first strike. By contrast, our own strategic weapons are apportioned among our submarines, land-based ICBM's, and bombers. The Soviets' clear advantage in land-based ICBM's gives them the ability to destroy segments of our relatively smaller and unfortunately less effective land-based missile force. We do not intend to match them missile for missile in land-based ICBM's. Our system of deterrence requires simply that we must be able to inflict damage so unacceptable that no one would attack us. This does not mean, however, that we can allow any part of our Triad to become vulnerable. Our ongoing ability to maintain deterrence rests on the continued accuracy, power, communications structure, and survivability of all our nuclear forces. The point is that while the number of weapons is important, it is less so than the combination of capabilities, forces, and their survivability along with the national resolve and will, essential to convince an aggressor that he could not hope to gain from attacking first.

Let me try to restate this, because it is over this question of how much destructive power is "enough" that the public debate often bogs down.

Suppose that a particular community were struck by an unforeseen disaster, say the collision of two passenger trains or a large tornado or an earthquake. No physician could possibly predict the receiving hospital's ability to handle this emergency by merely determining the number of beds. That variable, is, of course, important, but less so than the combination of the knowledge, preparedness, and training of the staff; their ability to sustain such an effort over an extended period; the actual matériel on hand to meet the emergency—drugs, i.v. solution, operating room supplies, transportation to the medical facility, and of course the number and skills of the doctors available.

It is clear that these measures will never prevent or deter an accident from taking place, so the medical analogy is limited. But the analogy is *good* inasmuch as it shows that deterrence also cannot be measured accurately by a single variable.

What then has deterrence done? Again, I must stress that it has worked and is working today. There have been 37 years of peace in Europe. Despite the threat of the Soviet Army, despite the threat of the Soviets' nuclear weapons, Western Europe has prospered. Its political freedoms have flourished, and its social institutions have grown stronger. Indeed, there has not been an equal period of uninterrupted peace on the European continent since the Roman

---

[47] See, for example, McGeorge Bundy, George F. Kennan, Robert S. McNamara, and Gerard Smith, "Nuclear Weapons and the Atlantic Alliance," *Foreign Affairs*, LX (Spring, 1982), pp. 753–768.

Empire fell. At the risk of stating the obvious, the United States and the rest of the world have also avoided the scourge of nuclear fire. Deterrence, thus, is and remains our best immediate hope of keeping peace.

However, it is not enough to assume that deterrence can be maintained simply by doing what we have done in the past. For the unavoidable fact is that even though the world remains at nuclear peace and nuclear threats do not appear on the horizon, still we do not feel safe. Many worry about the sophistication of modern delivery systems. Others fear the results of continuing to compete with the Soviets on this barren plain. Still more are alarmed at the destructive capability within the great powers' arsenals.

We are worried about all these matters too. That is why we are absolutely serious about the arms reduction negotiations currently underway in Geneva, and the President's new strategic arms reductions plans. But again, as with the policy of deterrence, the right approach to this process can only be one based on rational, prudent, and statesmanlike determination of ends and means.

The one thing we must not expect from arms reductions negotiations is the kind of world that existed before nuclear weapons were tested. The forbidden fruit has been tasted and in this case, the fruit is not the weapons, but the knowledge of them. As much as we would like to, we cannot erase that knowledge. Setting our sights on that object would be utterly unrealistic. The proper aim of arms reduction therefore should be *first* to reduce the probability of war. If possible it should also aim to reduce the costs of maintaining deterrence and should reduce the possibilities of war through misinterpretation or misunderstanding.

The proposal, to freeze current levels of nuclear weapons, was born partly at least of deeply felt convictions which this administration shares. A freeze, however, would not reduce the probability of war. It would go against the first and foremost aim of arms control because it would lock the United States and our allies into a position of permanent military disadvantage. And that disadvantage or imbalance, if you will, erodes deterrence which we believe has kept the peace. For if one side improves its forces, either by dint of its own efforts or through the other's inactivity, then the temptation will grow strong for the Soviet Union to use its superior systems, or, at a minimum to contemplate achieving dominion by the threat of nuclear war—nuclear blackmail it is called. It is an understatement that we must not allow either of these things to happen under any circumstances.

For similar reasons a freeze would chill any hopes we have of convincing the Soviets to agree to any meaningful arms reductions. If a freeze went into effect now, the advantage the Soviets currently enjoy would be irreversibly sealed and stamped with the official imprimatur of an international agreement. Why, then, would they wish to change—that is—to lower their forces together with us? Granting them but a thread of rationality, or even a normal supply, if we froze an imbalance in their favor, I cannot see that the Soviets would have the slightest incentive to achieve the major and bilateral reductions we must have if we are to lessen the danger now existing.

It is exactly those bilateral reductions which President Reagan's arms reduction proposals aim to achieve. In the past few months our highest priority has been to lay the groundwork for the strategic arms negotiations with the Soviet Union. The President has now proposed major reductions in strategic arms to verifiable, equal, and agreed levels. We are also continuing our negotiations to reduce the intermediate range nuclear weapons that threaten Europe and Asia. In Geneva we have put forward detailed proposals designed to limit those intermediate range nuclear forces and to eliminate entirely the missiles of greatest concern to each side. This approach, which has won the strong support of our allies, would go far towards lowering the threshold of risk which the Europeans feel so acutely today.

These proposals are not bargaining chips or ploys. Let all who doubt this know that President Reagan's greatest wish is for peace. I have heard him say more times than I can recall that if he could leave no other legacy, it would be that of having improved the prospects for peace. A meaningful reduction in nuclear arms would be a welcome first step in the arms control process, and an historic step towards the peace which lowered tensions nurture. No one should doubt that this is what drives our efforts. No one should doubt that this is what we are pledged to—in hope, in word, and in deed.

I wish that I could end this presentation by assuring you that our hopes and good faith could accomplish all that we want. But that I cannot do in all good conscience. Instead I must tell you what I see as the truth about our situation and not what I am sure all of us would prefer to hear: and that is that there is no easy road to peace, just as there is [no] easy road to anything really worthwhile. There is no miracle drug which will keep us and our allies safe and free while the nuclear threat is excised.

In the short term we must remember that as health is not just the absence of sickness, neither is peace just the absence of war. Health requires care to insure that it will continue, that disease will not occur. One needs the right diet, exercise, personal habits, and so on. So it is with peace. It cannot stand by itself. It needs care to insure its continuance. A nation must conduct its own business, maintain its strength, and aided by alliances be prepared to resist those for whom peace is not the first priority. Peace without these steps will not be peace for long. Thus we dare not permit our abhorrence of war to keep us from the work which our love of peace demands.

We cannot blink in the face of our worst fears. The Soviets are aware that their buildup is frightening. I think it safe to say that one of the chief effects which it was designed to create is the natural horror which all feel who are willing to face that buildup with realism. We cannot, though, and we must not, let this apprehension unstring us. If we fail in the short term to reestablish the balance, the danger will surely increase. "If you make yourself into a sheep, you'll find a wolf nearby" says the Russian proverb. We don't want to be wolves or sheep. We just want to live in peace with freedom and that means we must be able to deter any attack on us or our allies.

But if our immediate goal is to avoid war, our long term goal is to reduce its probability. Here, too, in the area of arms control we have seen the frustrating paradox that the road to peace is marked with the preparations for war. But there is no other rational solution. Who, for instance, can believe that the Soviets would ever consent to reduce their forces if they thought that we lacked the national will or reserve to maintain a balance in the first place?

Thus we must draw deeply upon our national patience and fortitude in the future if we are to accomplish what all of us really agree we must do: Protecting and strengthening the peace. For negotiations cannot succeed without patience—peace cannot succeed without fortitude.

I began with a story in the *Iliad.* There is, it seems to me, another metaphor in Astyanax's reaction to his helmeted father. And that is that the young and maybe even the not so young sometimes fail to recognize what it is that protects them. We are too old and, I hope, too wise to respond by crying out at the sight of our protectors. And we are too young to surrender our hopes in despair or our principles in fear.

The *Iliad* is the first book of great literature in a long tradition which reaches to us across the ages. It is a book about war but it questions war and it questions politics and it questions life. This questioning is one of the noblest traits of our civilization and it is one enshrined at Harvard under the rubric of "healthy skepticism". Others call it freedom. We owe it to our ancestors and to those who will come after, to do all within our power so that this civilization is preserved—and preserved in peace with freedom.

Thank you.

Document 28

Address by the President's Assistant for National Security Affairs (Clark) Before the Center for Strategic and International Studies, Georgetown University, May 21, 1982 (Extract)[48]

National Security Strategy

. . . .

I would begin by saying that the pace of national security affairs has seldom been faster than during the past one year and a half. The initial release of our strategic arms reduction proposals, the present crisis over the Falkland Islands, the upcoming summits in Versailles and Bonn, are but the latest in a series of scheduled and unscheduled events that have seized the attention of the national security community.

We have seen the return of the Sinai to Egypt and the regular launches and recovery of the Space Shuttle Enterprise. We

[48] Source: White House Press Release, May 21, 1982, Office of the Press Secretary to the President. Clark's brief introductory and concluding remarks are omitted.

have witnessed, in grief, the brutal murder of Anwar Sadat, General Dozier's kidnapping in Europe, war in the Middle East, and attempted guerrilla insurrections in the Caribbean.

We have begun intermediate range nuclear force negotiations in Geneva, participated in the Ottawa and Cancun summits, and met with 76 heads of state or government. I'm speaking now that the President has personally met 76 heads of state—unprecedented, I might add, in this period of time.

We have watched democracy at work in El Salvador and Jamaica. We have seen tyranny in Afghanistan and in Poland. It is a complex, interdependent world with opportunities often disguised, as the President has said, as challenges.

The pace is not likely to relent and in the rush of events it is easy to lose sight of the forest, given the trees we deal with are as ambulatory as Macbeth's Birnam Wood.

For these reasons, in early February of this year—February 5, to be exact—the President directed a review of our national security strategy. At that time our strategy was a collection of departmental policies which had been developed during the administration's first year in office. The President wanted to review the results of that first year with decisions often being made at the departmental level, to see where we were, to make sure our various policies were consistent, and to set the course for the future.

In particular, he wanted to make sure that any discussions we had with the leadership of Congress on reductions in our defense budget, any discussions with the leadership of the Soviet Union regarding arms reductions, were based both on a well-thought-through and integrated strategy for preserving our national security.

The President's involvement in this study is a good example of how he involves himself in national security affairs. As a former governor, President Reagan's past experience more clearly lies, as I think you would agree, in economic and domestic policy areas. But a lifetime of interest in and concern for, and debate of, national security issues, has built a framework of philosophy which Ronald Reagan articulated to the American people, and which they endorsed, a year and a half ago.

The conversion of that philosophy to policy has been one of the President's major efforts since January. He views national security as his most compelling responsibility. He has come to treat it accordingly.

In the past 4 months about a third of the President's office time—as I'm so often reminded by Mike Deaver as we attempt to schedule another appointment—has been devoted to national security work—more than any other area or endeavor. He has already signed 35 National Security Directives, 19 of them this year; a pace that compares favorably with his predecessors.

There have been 57 meetings of the National Security Council during this administration, nearly one a week. The President has personally chaired each and every one of them. Few Presidents—certainly none in peacetime—have paid as much attention to national security problems or issues.

In this particular security review that we discuss today, as I mentioned, the decision or directive having been issued this morning, the President played an extraordinarily active role. He progressively reviewed, and he commented, on all nine interagency draft segments as they were prepared. Sometimes we returned to the drawing board. Sometimes our fuzzy language was sharpened by the Presidential—first-person singular.

The NSC staff led the effort in its role as the broker of those ideas coming from the interagency efforts and beyond [. Those] such as Don Regan, Jeane Kirkpatrick, Mac Baldrige, participated as well, even though not within the formal NSC process, when issues pertaining to their areas arose.

And certainly Secretary Weinberger's 1982 defense policy provided an excellent foundation for the military portion of this study. The senior leadership at Defense, State, CIA, as I mentioned, were totally involved. JCS met 12 times, consider the various parts of their portion of the study. When it was done, the study and decision, as they must be, were the President's.

Now that the work is done or at least the first major portion and we're at a plateau here today. We have come to several conclusions, I believe, seven.

First, the purpose of our strategy should be to preserve our institutions of freedom and democracy—to protect our citizens, to promote their economic well-being, and to foster an international orderliness supportive of these institutions and these principles.

Second, we're confident that the policies of our first year have been internally consistent and that they do lay the groundwork for a strategy that will protect the security of the United States.

Third conclusion, a successful strategy must have diplomatic, political, economic, informational components built on a foundation of military strength.

Fourthly, our strategy must be forward looking and active. We must offer hope. As the President said last year at Notre Dame,[49] collectivism and the subordination of the individual to the state is now perceived around the world as a bizzare and evil episode of history whose last pages are even now being written. We have something better to offer—namely freedom. To secure the America we all want and the global stability and prosperity we all seek, we cannot sit back and hope that somehow it all will happen. We must believe in what we're doing and that requires initiative, patience, persistence. We find we must be prepared to respond vigorously to opportunities as they arise and to create opportunities where they have not existed before. We must be steadfast in those efforts.

The fifth conclusion, ours must be a coalition strategy. We, together with our friends, our allies, must pull together. And that effort will certainly be evidenced as we mentioned a moment ago, the President proceeds on the third of June to Versailles, Rome, London, Bonn, Berlin, and New York.

There's no other way, we must achieve an even closer linkage with regional allies and friends. Next month's NATO summit is a case in point, of course. There may be a vocal minority questioning the basic assumptions of the Atlantic Alliance. It's not the first time, nor will it be the last. But when President Reagan and other NATO leaders meet in Bonn, there should be a strong reaffirmation of Alliance unity, vitality, and resolve. A strong, unified NATO remains indispensable for the protection of all of our Western interests.

The differences among NATO members involve shaping NATO, not whether there should be an Alliance. At Bonn, we will witness fundamental agreement on the need to strengthen our deterrent posture. We will see a balanced approach to arms control, and NATO remains dedicated to the common task of preserving democracy.

Sixth, the economic component of our strategy is particularly important. We must promote a well-functioning international economic system with minimal distortion to trade and broadly agreed rules for resolving differences.

The summits at Ottawa and Cancun played a positive role in the search for a cooperative strategy for economic growth. The Caribbean Basin Initiative is a further contribution, offering a constructive, long-term commitment to countries in our hemisphere. Next month's Versailles summit will be another step. We anticipate an atmosphere of realism at Versailles. We hope it will inspire new thinking while deflating outworn concepts. We must also force our principal adversary, the Soviet Union, to bear the brunt of its economic shortcomings.

The seventh and final conclusion, the maintenance of peace, requires a strong, flexible, and responsive military. The rebuilding of our nation's defenses is now our urgent task.

For obvious reasons, I cannot discuss the defense portion of our review in the detail that I did to select members of Congress this morning[50] or perhaps in the detail that you might desire. I will try, however, to provide the highlights where I can, some degree of specificity.

Our interests are global and they conflict with those of the Soviet Union, a state which pursues worldwide policies, most unfriendly to our own. The Soviet Union maintains the most heavily armed military establishment in history and possesses the capability to project its military forces far beyond its own borders. It's a given [fact] that, of course, we have vital interests around the world, including maritime sea lanes of communication. The hard fact is that the military power of the Soviet Union is now able to threaten these vital interests as never before. The Soviet Union also complements its direct military capabilities with proxy forces and surrogates with extensive arms sales and grants by manipulation of terrorist and subversive organizations, and through support to a number of

[49] For the text of President Reagan's commencement address at the University of Notre Dame, May 17, 1981, see *Public Papers of the Presidents of the United States: Ronald Reagan,* 1981 (Washington, 1982), pp. 431–435.

[50] Clark testified that morning in executive joint session before the Senate and House Armed Services Committees and the Senate and House Defense Appropriations Subcommittees.

insurgencies and separatist movements—providing arms, advice, military training, and political backing.

Our military forces and those of our allies must protect our common interests in our increasingly turbulent environment. We must be prepared to deter attack and to defeat such attack when deterrence fails.

In this regard, the modernization of our strategic nuclear forces will receive first priority in our efforts to rebuild the military capabilities of the United States. Nuclear deterrence can only be achieved if our strategic nuclear posture makes Soviet assessment of the risks of war, under any contingency, so great as to remove any incentive for initiating attack.

The decisions reached on strategic nuclear forces, which the President announced last fall, remain the foundation of our policy. The highest priority was to be accorded to survivable strategic communications systems.

In addition, we plan to modernize the manned bomber force, increase the accuracy and payload of our submarine launched ballistic missiles, add sea launched cruise missiles, improve strategic defenses, and deploy a new larger, more accurate land based ballistic missile.

The latter decision was reaffirmed by the President last Monday.[51] He views the production of a modern ICBM, with the earliest possible introduction into the operational force, as absolutely essential.

The President provided some guidance to the Department of Defense on priorities he wished accorded to various basing and defense schemes, but he essentially asked Defense for their recommendation on a permanent basing mode by early fall so that he could comply with congressional desires for an administration position, well before the end of this year.

At the same time, the President made it clear that until a more survivable basing mode has been selected, funded, cleared for construction, he wishes to retain the option of deploying a limited number of MX and Minuteman silos as an integral part of the overall MX program.

The silo basing option provides a hedge against unforeseen technical developments and program changes. It is a clear incentive to the Soviets to negotiate arms reductions, and even in silos, MX gains in survivability as all three legs of the strategic triad are modernized.

The MX program, the President has said, is too important to allow the risk of technical, environmental, or arms control debates to delay introduction of the missile into force.

While the failure to strengthen our nuclear deterrent could be disastrous, recent history makes clear that conventional deterrence is now more important than ever. Current overseas deployments will be maintained to provide a capability for timely and flexible response to contingencies and to demonstrate resolve to honor our commitments. Ground, naval, and air forces will remain deployed in Europe, in the western Pacific, in Southwest Asia, and elsewhere as appropriate. In this hemisphere, naval forces will maintain a presence in the North Atlantic, the Caribbean Basin, the Mediterranean, the western Pacific, and in the Indian Ocean. Forward-deployed forces will be postured to facilitate rapid response. Intermittent overseas developments from the United States will be made as necessary.

Now, our strategic reserve of U.S.-based forces, both active and reserve components, will be maintained at a high state of readiness and will be periodically exercised. Last year's Bright Star exercise in the Middle East, last month's Ocean Venture 82 in the Caribbean provided a valuable experience for those forces. They also demonstrated a multinational, multiforce capability to defend our interests and those of our friends worldwide. Our need to swiftly reinforce worldwide means that improvements in our strategic mobility and in our reserve structure are terribly important.

Although the most prominent threat to our vital interests worldwide is the Soviet Union, our interests can also be put in jeopary by actions of other states, other groups. In contingencies not involving the Soviet Union, we hope to rely on friendly regional states to provide military force.

Should the threat exceed our capabilities within regional states, we must be prepared within the framework of our constitutional processes to commit U.S. forces to assist our allies. This, of course, does not mean that we must push ourselves into areas where we are neither wanted nor desired or needed. What it does mean is that we cannot reject in advance any options we might need to protect those same vital interests. To do so is to invite aggression, undermine

[51] The reference is apparently to President Reagan's approval of a National Security Council Directive on Monday, May 17.

our credibility and place at risk all global objectives.

Now, this highlights the importance of security assistance. By this term we mean military sales, grant assistance, international military education and training, economic support funds and peacekeeping operations. If we do not assist our allies and friends in meeting their legitimate defense requirements, then their ability to cope with conflict goes down and the pressure for eventual U.S. involvement goes up. Yet today security assistance is not doing the job it should, as discovered by these same studies.

Resources are inadequate, often of the wrong kind. During the 1950's, the security assistance budget ranged from 5 to 10 percent of the defense budget. But today, it's about 1.5 percent. While it is not necessary to return to the post-war levels that rearmed and secured Western Europe, some steady growth in security assistance can be our most cost-effective investment. Again, found by our studies.

The annual budget cycle constrains long-range planning. Countries participating in our security assistance program and procurement officers at the Defense Department both need to plan ahead. Procurement lead times limit the responsiveness of the overall program. And, finally, legislative restrictions reduce the ability of our government to react appropriately to emergency conditions.

An effective security assistance program, again, is a critical element in meeting our security objectives abroad. At times recently, [we] have had difficulty explaining that on the Hill. Thus, it is a real compliment to our own force struction. Security assistance can help deter conflict, can increase the ability of our friends and allies to defend themselves without the commitment of our own combat forces. Effective programs can establish a degree of compatibility between U.S. forces and the forces of recipient countries so we can work together in combat if necessary. Not only does security assistance offer a cost-effective way of enhancing our security worldwide but it also strengthens our economy in general and our defense production base in particular. In short, a little assistance buys a lot of security.

For these reasons, we are planning a priority effort to improve the effectiveness, the responsiveness of this vital component of our national security strategy. We will be looking at ways of reducing lead times. We will take a hard look at existing legislation [concerning?] future resources. Programs require predictability. This points toward more extensive use of multiyear commitments and a larger capitalization of the special defense acquisition fund.

In sum, security assistance needs fixing and we have a plan to fix it.

No one should mistake the main goal of American global strategy. The goal, of course, as the President has said over and again, is peace.

We have devoted too large a portion of our national resources and emotion over the past 40 years to the alleviation of want, hunger, suffering, and distress throughout the world, to want anything but peace in every corner of the planet. And those who slander the United States with charges of warmongering can barely paper over their own guilty consciences in this very regard.

In particular, the record of the Soviet Union in armed suppression of popular movements since 1945 is unparalleled among modern nations. To maintain peace with freedom, therefore, we are forced, reluctantly, to plan carefully for the possibility that our adversaries may prove unwilling to keep that peace. And when we turn to a strategy for our military forces, we enter the world of assumptions, scenarios, and hypothetical projections. It would be our strategy to employ military force to achieve specific political objectives quickly on terms favorable to the United States and our allies.

We need a better, more detailed strategy in order to buy the right equipment, develop forces, and lay detailed plans. This strategy must provide flexibility and yet allow preplanning. In trying to solve this problem we have looked at such strategy as a planning continuum over the last 4 months. At the lower end of the spectrum our guidance emphasizes the integration of economic aid and security assistance, foreign military training, and supplementary support capability.

At the higher end our strategy guidance takes into account the global military capabilities of the Soviet Union and the interrelationship of strategic theaters. We recognize that in spite of our efforts to preserve peace, any conflict with the Soviet Union could expand to global dimension.

Thus, global planning is a necessity. This does not mean that we must have the capability to successfully engage Soviet forces simultaneously on all fronts. We can't, simply can't. What it does mean is that we must procure balanced forces and establish priorities for sequential operations to insure that military power would be applied in the most effective way on a priority basis.

It is in the interest of the United States to limit the scope of any conflict. The capability for counteroffensives on other fronts is an essential element of our strategy, but it is not a substitute for adequate military capability to defend our vital interests in the area in which they are threatened.

On the other hand, the decision to expand a conflict may well not be ours to make. Therefore, U.S. forces must be capable of responding to a major attack with unmistakable global implications early on in any conflict.

The President has established priorities in the way our forces would be used in combat, in terms of geography, in terms of force development. We must ask, what do we fix first?

We have tried to analyze the risks we face. We cannot fix them all at once, in part because things take time, and in part because the Soviet military advantage results from a whole decade of investment and top priority. There is not enough money available to eliminate the risks we face overnight.

What we have tried to do is analyze those risks, put first things first, and develop how we will conduct ourselves if worst comes to worst.

On the other hand, we want to hope for the best, and we want to offer that hope to others, our allies, our friends, the Third World, and especially to the citizens of the Soviet Union.

It is our fondest hope that with an active yet prudent national security policy, we might one day convince the leadership of the Soviet Union to turn their attention inward, to seek the legitimacy that only comes from the consent of the governed, and thus to address the hopes and the dreams of their own people.

. . . .

Document 29

Address by the Secretary of Defense (Weinberger) Before the Foreign Policy Association, New York, May 21, 1982[52]

Reagan Administration's Offensive to Stop Soviet Acquisition of Western Technology for Military Purposes

I appreciate the opportunity to speak to this very distinguished group. I greatly admire the diversity of the Foreign Policy Association and its commitment to stimulating constructive and informed citizen participation in world affairs. I am honored to be asked to address such a group.

Today I plan to talk about the large-scale drain of Western technological expertise to the Soviet Union which has taken place over the past decade or so. I believe that the continuation of this trend could have extremely dangerous consequences for the free world.

Today's sophisticated science and industrial technologies are the foundation on which a great deal of a modern nation's economic strength is built. Especially significant is the vital role science and technology play in strengthening a nation's military potential to deter war, or if necessary, to win it.

The Soviets' efforts to take advantage of Western hardware prove that they grasp this quite firmly. Soviet leaders have learned they can obtain Western technology through both legal and illegal channels. Under the guise of purchases for benign, civilian objectives, the Soviets have obtained a wide range of equipment critical to their military program. Where they have failed to get what they want openly, they have resorted to a well-coordinated illegal acquisition program. Using agents, co-opting citizens, taking advantage of unsuspecting businessmen, moving goods through neutral and Third World countries, they are gaining access to Western technology on an unprecedented and alarming scale.

[52] Source: *Public Statements of Secretary of Defense Weinberger*, 1982. The source text is his address as prepared for delivery at the Waldorf Astoria Hotel.

Until now, the West has failed to respond to this challenge. Our export requirements were too loose. Our enforcement program was lax. Too many loopholes in the international control system persisted. Clear cut violations of international export laws were forgiven and forgotten.

Frequently, violators, when caught, were either not punished or got off with modest fines.

The result is that the Soviet raid on our technology base not only continued—it increased. In short, we have been selling them the rope—to hang us.

Let me describe for you how all this occurred, how the Soviets profited as a result, and what the administration is doing about it.

We would do well to recall that only a decade ago—at the height of detente—it was fashionable to believe the Soviet Union would shift its emphasis from military pursuits to improving the material well-being of its citizens. Many felt that what was needed was simply the right encouragement. It was hoped that then the Soviets would cut back their buildup and concentrate on producing consumer goods greatly desired by their people. So, export controls were given a low priority. Export promotion was encouraged.

Sophisticated goods and equipment were sold with winks and nods from free world countries. Indeed, it is a sad fact the United States actually requested and received more exceptions to the international control list than any other participating Western nation. It is even more grim to note, in retrospect, that many of the exceptions granted to the United States under the international control program contributed *directly* to Soviet military modernization.

Today, we can see the result of the laissez-faire attitude of the last decade in the size and technological capability of the Soviet armed forces. The Soviets have introduced new generations of smart weapons. They have dramatically improved their airlift capability and made their nuclear weapons more accurate and deadly. They have enhanced their command and control with better computers and communications.

Let me give some specific examples of what the Soviets have been able to achieve this way. Their strategic weapons program has benefited substantially from the acquisition of Western technology. The striking similarities between the US Minuteman silo and the Soviet SS–13 silo very likely resulted from acquisition of U.S. documents. The Soviets' ballistic missile systems, in particular, have over the past decade demonstrated qualitative improvements that probably would not have been achieved without Western acquisitions of ballistic missile guidance and control technology. The most striking example of this is the marked improvement in accuracy of the latest generation of Soviet ICBM's—an improvement which, given the level of relevant Soviet technologies a decade ago, appears almost certainly to have been speeded by the acquisition of Western technology. Their improved accuracy has been achieved through the exploitation and development of good-quality guidance components—such as gyroscopes and accelerometers. The quality of these instruments, in turn, depends to a considerable degree on the quality of the small, precision, high-speed bearings used.

Through the 1950's and into the 1960's, the Soviet precision bearing industry lagged significantly behind that of the West. However, through legal trade purchases in the 1970's, the Soviet Union acquired U.S. precision grinding machines for the production of small, high-precision bearings. Similar grinding machines, having lower production-rate capabilities, were available from several foreign countries. Only a few of these machines, either U.S. or foreign, would have been sufficient to supply Soviet missile designers with all the quality bearings they needed. These purchases gave the Soviets the capability to manufacture precision bearings in large volume sooner than would have been likely through indigenous development. The Soviets probably could have used indigenous grinding machines and produced the required quality of bearings over a long period by having an abnormally high rejection rate.

The IL–76 also is used by the Soviets as the platform for their new AWACS (Airborne Warning and Control System), which is expected to be operational in the mid-1980's. This system will provide the Soviets with a major improvement in attacking low-flying missiles and bombers. The Soviet AWACS is strikingly similar in many ways to the U.S. AWACS, and is a major improvement over their old system.

In the maintenance area, two huge floating drydocks purchased from the West for civilian use by the Soviets have been diverted to military use. Drydocks are critical for both routine and fast repair of ships damaged in warfare. In 1978, when the Soviets took possession of one of the drydocks, they diverted it to the Pacific Naval Fleet. The other was sent to the Northern Fleet in 1981.

These drydocks are so large that they can carry several naval ships. Most importantly, they are the only drydock facilities in either of the two major Soviet fleet areas—Northern or Pacific—capable of serving the new Kiev-class V/STOL aircraft carriers. Soviet advanced submarines carrying ballistic missiles, Soviet Kiev aircraft carriers, and Soviet destroyers were among the first ships repaired in the drydocks.

Western equipment and technology have also played a very important, if not crucial, role in the advancement of Soviet microelectronic production capabilities. This advancement comes as a result of over 10 years of successful acquisitions—through illegal, including clandestine, means—of hundreds of pieces of Western microelectronic equipment worth hundreds of millions of dollars to equip their military related manufacturing facilities. These acquisitions have permitted the Soviets to build systematically a modern microelectronics industry which will be the critical basis for enhancing the sophistication of future Soviet military systems for decades. The acquired equipment and know-how, if combined, could meet 100 percent of the Soviets' high-quality microelectronic needs for military purposes, or 50 percent of all their microelectronic needs. To give particular examples, this easily gained advance in microelectronics will allow the Soviets to develop on-board fire control computers for their jet fighters, advanced signal processing equipment for their radars, and highly sophisticated missiles of all kinds. In the past few weeks the world has had a clear demonstration of how terribly accurate and terribly lethal recent developments in missile guidance have made this particular weapon.

Most of these technologies transfers have occurred because of gaps in the international control system. That control system is centered around a voluntary organization called the "coordinating committee" or COCOM. Under COCOM control critical goods were legally exported to the Soviet Union.

But, even more alarming, these legal acquisitions have been supported by even more far reaching illegal acquisitions. For example, only this past summer, millions of dollars worth of high grade electronic polysilicon were diverted to the Soviet Union to fill military needs.

Illegal acquisitions are taking place across a wide front. To give just one example, the Soviet Union illegally acquired IBM 360 and 370 main frame computers from the West. Their objective was to use the IBM computer as the base design of their own RYAD computer series. The copy was nearly exact, and for a very good reason. They wanted a machine which would work with future generations of Western equipment, as they planned to update the system on a regular basis. It is interesting to note the Soviet RYAD computer series operates with the same software and peripheral equipment as the IBM. In addition, the RYAD computer uses the same repair manual as the IBM. The RYAD is an extremely valuable tool because it has a high capacity to perform the complex computations which are necessary to design all sorts of modern weapons systems. There is no doubt that the Soviets are using this equipment for that purpose at this very moment.

The Soviets support the illegal acquisition drive through controlled "front" corporations, by co-opting businessmen and factory workers; through bribery and shady deals. They use diplomatic pouches and other devices to move technical literature and small pieces of equipment freely to the Soviet Union.

They also maintain an intelligence system keyed strongly on emerging technologies of high military value.

One part of this collection system is devoted to exploiting Western technical literature, including technical information published by our own government.

They are taking advantage of the gaps in our export control system and the vulnerability of the West to easy exploitation. They are using our free institutions and our open system against us.

And, because our national defense system has not modernized fast enough, the Soviets are exploiting many civilian technological breakthroughs yet to be fully used to upgrade our own military hardware.

It is here we face the greatest danger. While we have committed ourselves to rebuilding our national defenses, it is going to take us time to do so. It is essential, while we improve our own defense, that we close down Soviet access to the technology they want for their military buildup. Selling them our valuable technology upon which we have historically based much of our security is short-sightedness raised to the level of a crime. What could be more foolish than to seek near-term gain in exchange for long-term disaster? What could be more foolish than to raise our costs of defense by giving the Soviets our own technology?

At stake is our ability to maintain the balance of power and protect the peace.

The Reagan administration is moving on a broad front to protect Western technology and blunt the Soviet acquisition effort.

—The administration is implementing a new program of domestic export controls designed to safeguard American technology from compromise. This effort is keyed on defense priority industries.

We are seeking to prevent critical manufacturing know-how from reaching the Soviet Union where it can be used to support their military industrial base, and, thus, their international ambitions. Our focus is on products which would contribute to Soviet military production capabilities.

—Last July President Reagan, at the Ottawa Summit, called for a high level meeting of the Coordinating Committee or COCOM.[53] Such a meeting, the first in 25 years, took place in January in Paris.[54] He urged more resources for enforcement.

Diplomatic efforts are now underway to continue and expand this effort to revitalize the COCOM system.

—Our administration is acting to strengthen enforcement of our export laws. This program includes greater inspection of cartons, crates and parcels leaving this country, a higher level intelligence effort, and implementation of a better tracking and coordination system. We have also stepped up our cooperative efforts to enforce the international embargo.

—We have begun high level consultations with the North Atlantic Treaty Organization in order to identify technologies important to the NATO collective security effort.

—Within the Defense Department we have improved our internal review effort to identify sensitive technologies. In addition, we are taking steps to safeguard important scientific and technical documents and research programs.

—The Reagan administration has also initiated discussions with neutral and nonaligned countries in order to establish effective ground rules protecting American and NATO technology transferred to those countries. We think considerable progress can be achieved in these discussions without disturbing normal and healthy trade relations.

All of these actions are designed to protect our national defense system and to safeguard our peace and freedom. But to succeed we must have the understanding and cooperation of the public.

Western manufacturers and industry associations need to understand better that there is indeed a serious threat to our technology—that we are the target of a coordinated effort by the Soviet Union and Warsaw Pact to acquire products, equipment and know-how which their incentiveless, state-run economy has not—and cannot—easily produce. To sum up, we cannot allow this outflow of our important equipment and research to go on unchallenged. The Soviets, through their own efforts and our neglect, have been encouraged to rely on the West for help in building the very military behemoth which threatens us all. The technological advances which they have been able to achieve at relatively low cost can only complicate the task of deterring future conflict—which is after all the chief purpose of our armed forces.

With the help of business and industry we *can* stop the Soviets from achieving technological superiority at our expense. For those of us who are not actively involved in defending America, that is the very least we can do to strengthen our nation.

Thank you.

---

[53] Documentation on the Ottawa Economic Summit Conference, July 19–21, 1981, is in *American Foreign Policy: Current Documents, 1981,* Chapter 5, Part F.

[54] The COCOM meeting took place in Paris, January 19–20, 1982.

Document 30

Transcript of an Interview With the Secretary of Defense (Weinberger), June 20, 1982 (Extract)[55]

"We Don't Think a Nuclear War Can Be Won"

. . . .

MR. BRINKLEY. I'd like first to ask you about what Secretary Haig was saying yesterday afternoon.[56]

A. Yes.

MR. BRINKLEY. He said, while Gromyko was at the United Nations speaking for the Soviet Union and making a great heart-warming speech[57]—I am taking a few liberties here—about disarmament and peace, they were at the same time testing a number of new weapons in a very large testing display. And he said this belied their words. Do you agree with that, and if you do, what does that mean?

A. Oh, yes, there's no question about it. It was an unprecedented display. They were not so much new weapons as other missiles that they have—intercontinental, immediate [*intermediate?*] range, submarine launch, anti-satellite. I don't know what it means. It may be that they are trying to send a signal, in effect reinforcing his point, that no matter what they say, they still have this growing and immense arsenal of strength and it underlines all of our points that we have been making, that much as we regret it, there is no way we can maintain a credible deterrent without modernizing our forces.

I know that sounds like a paradox to a lot of people, but I'd hate to try it the other way and let ours continue to be neglected while they move ahead.

MR. BRINKLEY. Well, if the signal is, as I understand you, if the signal is that they are going to build arms whatever they say, whatever they do at a bargaining table, whatever they say at the United Nations, why bother with all this?

A. With all what, the disarmament talks?

MR. BRINKLEY. Disarmament negotiations.

A. Well, there is always the hope that some rationality will take hold and they will see the wisdom of the President's proposals, both on intermediate range, where he has proposed reducing down to zero, and on intercontinental, as well as conventional forces. It is vital that we keep up the effort. When you give up, you are moving appreciably closer to war, and that we should certainly not do.

MR. WILL. Mr. Secretary, the sequence that Secretary Haig described was a five-step one. It began with an anti-satellite move, which would be the first step, perhaps, in a nuclear war, to blind the United States, and went through the launching of ground-based and sea-based missiles, intermediate missiles, and wound up with the firing of an ABM to block a retaliatory strike coming in. In other words, this looked to some people like a scenario for fighting a nuclear war. Is that the construction you put on it?

A. Well, I've said for a long time—yes, I agree with you—and I've said for a long time that the Soviets are now, by a number of pieces of evidence—and this is just another in that long chain—displaying the fact that they believe a nuclear war can be fought, can be won. And that's one of the things that we think is so dangerous. We don't think a nuclear war can be won, and our policy is based entirely on trying to acquire the necessary strength to keep our deterrent credible.

MR. WILL. Some people thought they heard in the Gromyko speech—leaving aside the no-first-use pledge in Europe by Brezhnev[58]—they thought they heard the outlines of a strategic nuclear deal. Did you detect that in that speech?

A. No, I didn't, and I don't know that he had checked with the Ministry of Defense over there because it didn't sound—the sequence of events that you have correctly described—didn't sound as if there had

---

[55] Source: *Public Statements of Secretary of Defense Weinberger,* 1982. Secretary Weinberger was interviewed in Washington on the ABC television program, "This Week With David Brinkley," by David Brinkley and Sam Donaldson of ABC News, and George Will, ABC consultant.

[56] For the text of Secretary Haig's press conference, June 19, see document 269.

[57] For a translation of extracts from Gromyko's speech, June 15, see *New York Times,* June 16, 1982, p. A20. For the full text, see U.N. document A/S-12/PV.12.

[58] The reference is to Brezhnev's statement, which Gromyko read during his speech to the U.N. Second Session on Disarmament on June 15. For text of the statement, see *New York Times,* June 16, 1982, p. A20.

been anything remotely resembling that. It sounded, in the whole way it took place, it looked as if it was to be a clear demonstration to the world that they were bringing their forces of all kinds—command and control, communications, and this kind of unprecedented exercise—to the point where they could show the world they plan to use some of this immense arsenal they have been accumulating at rapidly increasing rates for 21 years.

MR. DONALDSON. Well, if we don't think a nuclear war can be won, why are you studying plans to fight a protracted nuclear war?

A. Well, I'm glad you asked that question, because—

MR. DONALDSON. I'm glad I did, too.

SECRETARY WEINBERGER.—we are not studying plans—

MR. BRINKLEY. Because you've got an answer all ready.

SECRETARY WEINBERGER.—to fight—we are not studying—well, the story[59] was so wrong and has caused so much trouble that I am glad to have an opportunity to clear it up. We're not studying plans to fight a protracted nuclear war. What we are trying to do is to make sure, through modernization and improvement of our weapons, that we have an enduring survivability of our weapons so that we can indeed meet and deal with, and have the capability to deal with, a protracted nuclear war fought by the Soviets against us. And that's one of the dangers that are wrenching a few—

MR. DONALDSON. Wait a moment.

A. —That's one of the dangers of wrenching a few sentences out of context.

MR. DONALDSON. But it takes two to fight.

A. Well, if you—

MR. DONALDSON. We're not going to fight a protracted nuclear war but the Soviets might against us?

A. No, no. We are not going to launch a protracted nuclear war. We don't believe a nuclear war can be won, but we are certainly not going to sit by quietly and do nothing while they develop the capability to fight, and as they believe, apparently, to win what they call a protracted nuclear war. And the whole word "protracted" here is wrenched out of the context of the statement. The statement was never published in full. It is a sensitive statement. It was leaked or somebody stole it or something, but one way or another, the impression has been given that we are sitting down and saying, we will now plan to fight a protracted nuclear war.

What we're trying to do is develop an enduring sustainability of our forces, which we don't have sufficiently now, so that it would be very apparent to the Soviets that their plan for fighting a protracted nuclear war will be useless and should be discarded. And that is a very great difference.

If you only have the capability to fight a very short time, if you can only use your weapons once and they are then wiped out, then you have a hairtrigger situation in which every, every intendment is that you have to use yours immediately, and you put a hairtrigger on the most dangerous kind of all wars.

What we are trying our best to do is to acquire the capability that will demonstrate to them and deter them from making any kind of attack on us.

MR. DONALDSON. I am belaboring the point but let me try one more time. Why not say to the Soviets, don't even think about fighting a protracted nuclear war because it can't happen. We will destroy you in a massive series of exchanges. Instead, you seem to be saying, don't try to think about fighting a protracted nuclear war because we have plans to be able to fight one also?

A. To counter anything that you might do. And there is the most peculiar syndrome around in which we are criticized for the use of the term "prevail," and—

MR. DONALDSON. I didn't criticize you for it.

A. Well, others have, and they say that you shouldn't think about a protracted nuclear war because that is part of this philosophy of trying to prevail in any sort of contest. And I would say to you, you are—

MR. DONALDSON. But you said you can't win.

A. I'd say to you that we are planning to prevail if we are attacked. We are not planning to sit by meekly and say it can't be won so we aren't going to plan to do it. You show me a Secretary of Defense who is not planning to prevail and I'll show you a Secretary of Defense—

MR. DONALDSON. You say you can't win—

---

59 Reference is an article in the *New York Times*, May 30, 1982, pp. I1, I12, which extensively summarized and quoted in part a Department of Defense classified study, "Fiscal Year 1984–1988 Defense Guidance."

A. —and I'll show you a Secretary of Defense who ought to be impeached.

MR. DONALDSON. We can't win a nuclear war but we can prevail?

A. I don't think a nuclear war is winnable and that's why we think we're—

MR. DONALDSON. But we can prevail?

A. —we're trying to acquire the capacity that will demonstrate that it cannot be won and therefore deter it. and that's exactly what we've been doing from the very beginning.

. . . .

Document 31

Statement Issued by the White House, July 4, 1982[60]

National Space Policy

The President announced today a national space policy that will set the direction of U.S. efforts in space for the next decade. The policy is the result of an interagency review requested by the President in August 1981. The 10-month review included a comprehensive analysis of all segments of the national space program. The primary objective of the review was to provide a workable policy framework for an aggressive, farsighted space program that is consistent with the administration's national goals.

As a result, the President's Directive[61] reaffirms the national commitment to the exploration and use of space in support of our national well-being, and establishes the basic goals of United States space policy which are to:

—strengthen the security of the United States;

—maintain United States space leadership;

—obtain economic and scientific benefits through the exploitation of space;

—expand United States private sector investment and involvement in civil space and space related activities;

—promote international cooperative activities in the national interest; and

—cooperate with other nations in maintaining the freedom of space for activities which enhance the security and welfare of mankind.

The principles underlying the conduct of the United States space program, as outlined in the Directive are:

—The United States is committed to the exploration and use of space by all nations for peaceful purposes and for the benefit of mankind. "Peaceful purposes" allow activities in pursuit of national security goals.

—The United States rejects any claims to sovereignty by any nation over space or over celestial bodies, or any portion thereof, and rejects any limitations on the fundamental right to acquire data from space.

—The United States considers the space systems of any nation to be national property with the right of passage through and operation in space without interference. Purposeful interference with space systems shall be viewed as an infringement upon sovereign rights.

—The United States encourages domestic commercial exploitation of space capabilities, technology, and systems for national economic benefit. These activities must be consistent with national security concerns, treaties, and international agreements.

—The United States will conduct international cooperative space-related activities that achieve scientific, political, economic, or national security benefits for the nation.

—The United States space program will be comprised of two separate, distinct and strongly interacting programs—national security and civil. Close coordination, cooperation, and information exchange will be maintained among these programs to avoid unnecessary duplication.

—The United States Space Transportation System (STS) is the primary space launch system for both national security and civil government missions. STS capabilities and capacities shall be developed to meet appropriate national needs and shall be available to authorized users—domestic and foreign, commercial and governmental.

—The United States will pursue activities in space in support of its right of self-defense.

---

[60] Source: White House Press Release, July 4, 1982, Office of the Press Secretary to the President; printed also in *Weekly Compilation of Presidential Documents,* July 12, 1982, pp. 872–876.

[61] Reference is to Presidential Directive NSC–42, National Space Policy.

—The United States will continue to study space arms control options. The United States will consider verifiable and equitable arms control measures that would ban or otherwise limit testing and deployment of specific weapons system, should those measures be compatible with United States national security.

Space Transportation System

The Directive states that the Space Shuttle is to be a major factor in the future evolution of United States space programs, and that it will foster further cooperative roles between the national security and civil programs to insure efficient and effective use of national resources. The Space Transportation System (STS) is composed of the Space Shuttle, associated upper stages, and related facilities. The Directive establishes the following policies governing the development and operation of the Space Transportation System:

—The STS is a vital element of the United States space program, and is the primary space launch system for both United States national security and civil government missions. The STS will be afforded the degree of survivability and security protection required for a critical national space resource. The first priority of the STS program is to make the system fully operational and cost-effective in providing routine access to space.

—The United States is fully committed to maintaining world leadership in space transportation with a STS capacity sufficient to meet appropriate national needs. The STS program requires sustained commitments by each affected department or agency. The United States will continue to develop the STS through the National Aeronautics and Space Administration (NASA) in cooperation with the Department of Defense (DOD). Enhancement of STS operational capability, upper stages, and methods of deploying and retrieving payloads should be pursued, as national requirements are defined.

—United States Government spacecraft should be designed to take advantage of the unique capabilities of the STS. The completion of transition to the Shuttle should occur as expeditiously as practical.

—NASA will assure the Shuttle's utility to the civil users. In coordination with NASA, the DOD will assure the Shuttle's utility to national defense and integrate national security missions into the Shuttle system. Launch priority will be provided for national security missions.

—Expendable launch vehicle operations shall be continued by the United States Government until the capabilities of the STS are sufficient to meet its needs and obligations. Unique national security considerations may dictate developing special purpose launch capabilities.

—For the near term, the STS will continue to be managed and operated in an institutional arrangement consistent with the current NASA/DOD Memoranda of Understanding.[62] Responsibility will remain in NASA for operational control of the STS for civil missions and in the DOD for operational control of the STS for national security missions. Mission management is the responsibility of the mission agency. As the STS operations mature, the flexibility to transition to a different institutional structure will be maintained.

—Major changes to STS program capabilities will require Presidential approval.

The Civil Space Program

In accordance with the provisions of the National Aeronautics and Space Act,[63] the Directive states that the civil space program shall be conducted:

—to expand knowledge of the Earth, its environment, the solar system and the universe;

—to develop and promote selected civil applications of space technology;

—to preserve the United States leadership in critical aspects of space science, applications, and technology; and

—to further United States domestic and foreign policy objectives.

The Directive states the following policies which shall govern the conduct of the civil space program:

—United States Government programs shall continue a balanced strategy of research, development, operations, and exploration for science, applications and technology. The key objectives of these programs are to: (1) preserve the United States preeminence in critical space activities to enable continued exploitation and explora-

[62] Reference is to NASA/DOD Memorandum of Understanding on Basic Reimbursements, March 1977, and Memorandum of Understanding on Management and Operations, January 1977, updated March 1980.

[63] For the text of P.L. 85-568, approved on July 29, 1958, see 72 Stat. 426, and subsequent amendments.

tion of space; (2) conduct research and experimentation to expand understanding of: (a) astrophysical phenomena and the origin and evolution of the universe through long-lived astrophysical observation; (b) the Earth, its environment, its dynamic relation with the Sun; (c) the origin and evolution of the solar system through solar, planetary, and lunar sciences and exploration; and (d) the space environment and technology to advance knowledge in the biological sciences; (3) continue to explore the requirements, operational concepts, and technology associated with permanent space facilities; (4) conduct appropriate research and experimentation in advanced technology and systems to provide a basis for future civil applications.

—The United States Government will provide a climate conducive to expanded private sector investment and involvement in space activities, with due regard to public safety and national security. These space activities will be authorized and supervised or regulated by the government to the extent required by treaty and national security.

—The United States will continue cooperation with other nations in international space activities by conducting joint scientific and research programs, consistent with technology transfer policy, that yield sufficient benefits to the United States, and will support the public, nondiscriminatory direct readout of data from Federal civil systems to foreign ground stations and the provision of data to foreign users under specified conditions.

—The Department of Commerce, as manager of Federal operational space remote sensing systems, will: (1) aggregate Federal needs for these systems to be met by either the private sector or the Federal government; (2) identify needed research and development objectives for these systems; and (3) in coordination with other departments or agencies, provide regulation of private sector operation of these systems.

The National Security Space Program

The Directive states that the United States will conduct those activities in space that it deems necessary to its national security. National security space programs shall support such functions as command and control, communications, navigation, environmental monitoring, warning, surveillance, and space defense. The Directive states the following policies which shall govern the conduct of the national security program:

—Survivability and endurance of space systems, including all system elements, will be pursued commensurate with the planned use in crisis and conflict, with the threat, and with the availability of other assets to perform the mission. Deficiencies will be identified and eliminated, and an aggressive, long-term program will be undertaken to provide more-assured survivability and endurance.

—The United States will proceed with development of an anti-satellite (ASAT) capability, with operational deployment as a goal. The primary purposes of a United States ASAT capability are to deter threats to space systems of the United States and its allies and, within such limits imposed by international law, to deny any adversary the use of space-based systems that provide support to hostile military forces.

—The United States will develop and maintain an integrated attack warning, notification, verification, and contingency reaction capability which can effectively detect and react to threats to United States space systems.

—Security, including dissemination of data, shall be conducted in accordance with Executive orders and applicable directives for protection of national security information and commensurate with both the missions performed and the security measures necessary to protect related space activities.

Inter-Program Responsibilities

The Directive contains the following guidance applicable to and binding upon the United States national security and civil space programs:

—The national security and civil space programs will be closely coordinated and will emphasize technology sharing within necessary security constraints. Technology transfer issues will be resolved within the framework of directives, executive orders, and laws.

—Civil Earth-imaging from space will be permitted under controls when the requirements are justified and assessed in relation to civil benefits, national security, and foreign policy. These controls will be periodically reviewed to determine if the constraints should be revised.

—The United States Government will maintain and coordinate separate national security and civil operational space systems when differing needs of the programs dictate.

Policy Implementation

The Directive states that normal interagency coordinating mechanisms will be employed to the maximum extent possible to implement the policies enunciated. A Senior Interagency Group (SIG) on space is established by the Directive to provide a forum to all Federal agencies for their policy views, to review and advise on proposed changes to national space policy, and to provide for orderly and rapid referral of space policy issues to the President for decisions as necessary. The SIG (Space) will be chaired by the Assistant to the President for National Security Affairs and will include the Deputy Secretary of Defense, Deputy Secretary of State, Deputy Secretary of Commerce, Director of Central Intelligence, Chairman of the Joint Chiefs of Staff, Director of the Arms Control and Disarmament Agency, and the Administrator of the National Aeronautics and Space Administration. Representatives of the Office of Management and Budget and the Office of Science and Technology Policy will be included as observers. Other agencies or departments will participate based on the subjects to be addressed.

Background

In August 1981, the President directed a National Security Council review of space policy. The direction indicated that the President's Science Adviser, Dr. George Keyworth, in coordination with other affected agencies, should examine whether new directions in national space policy were warranted. An interagency working group was formed to conduct the study effort and Dr. Victor H. Reis, an Assistant Director of the Office of Science and Technology Policy, was designated as Chairman. The group addressed the following fundamental issues: (1) launch vehicle needs; (2) adequacy of existing space policy to ensure continued satisfaction of United States civil and national security program needs; (3) Shuttle organizational responsibilities and capabilities; and, (4) potential legislation for space policy. The reports on the various issues formed the basis of the policy decisions outlined here. The following agencies and departments participated: State, Defense, Commerce, Director of Central Intelligence, Joint Chiefs of Staff, Arms Control and Disarmament Agency and the National Aeronautics and Space Administration, as well as, the National Security Council Staff and the Office of Management and Budget.

Document 32

Letter From President Reagan to the Speaker of the House of Representatives (O'Neill), July 16, 1982[64]

Procurement of Aircraft for Airlift Program

DEAR MR. SPEAKER: One of my primary goals in restoring our defenses is to improve our capability to deploy forces rapidly to defend United States interests. Our airlift program as outlined in the FY 83 budget will reduce the critical mobility shortfall.

The Congressionally Mandated Mobility Study (CMMS)[65] recommended we increase our air cargo capability by about 25 million ton-miles per day, including at least 10 million ton-miles per day in "outsize" cargo capacity to accommodate critical combat equipment that will not fit on any existing aircraft except the C–5. It is of paramount importance that, when needed, outsize equipment arrive in a timely manner and in a usable configuration. Reassembly of critical components at a forward staging area, as required using commercial aircraft, would limit our combat capability. Moreover, procuring commercial carriers would also require the expenditure of additional funds for modifications that would still not yield the needed outsize cargo capability.

Our proposed airlift program currently before the Congress includes four related components. First, we intend to buy 50 additional C–5 aircraft to reduce quickly the

---

[64] White House Press Release, July 19, 1982, Office of the Press Secretary to the President; printed also in *Weekly Compilation of Presidential Documents*, July 26, 1982, p. 917. The letter was also sent to leaders of the House of Representatives and the Senate, who are not more specifically identified. President Reagan also sent another letter to the leaders of the House of Representatives, July 16, urging them "to send a clear signal of strong U.S. resolve to the Soviets by fully authorizing and appropriating the funds I have requested for the M-X, especially those funds needed to begin production of the M-X this year." For text, see *ibid.*, pp. 916–917.

[65] The reference is to the Department of Defense study, *The Congressionally-Mandated Mobility Study*, dated April 30, 1981. A provision of the Department of Defense Authorization Act, 1981, P.L. 96–342, approved on September 8, 1980, required the Secretary of Defense to conduct such a study to determine overall U.S. military mobility requirements for the decade of the 1980's. For the text of this provision, see 94 Stat. 1080.

critical shortfall in outsize capacity. Second, we will increase our air refueling/cargo capability by procurement of 44 KC–10 aircraft. Third, we will expand the Civil Reserve Air Fleet Enhancement Program, under which domestically owned carriers can be used in time of need. Finally, we plan to use available FY 81 funds in the C–X program to continue research and development on the C–17, thereby preserving the option of developing the C–17 for procurement in the late 1980s to provide outsize capability and be a potential replacement for C–130 and C–141 aircraft. We believe this combination of actions is required to develop the aircraft capability we urgently require.

In summary, I hope you will agree that the Department of Defense should not be required to substitute commercial aircraft that do not meet our needs. There are no savings if what we buy will not do the job that needs to be done. Therefore, I urge you to reject the commercial aircraft proposal and support our airlift budget as submitted.

Sincerely,
RONALD REAGAN

Document 33

Transcript of a Press Briefing by the Secretary of Defense (Weinberger), October 18, 1982 (Extracts)[66]

Military Manpower Task Force Report

MR. SPEAKES. The fact sheet[67] is being passed out at this time. The Secretary and Ed Meese have just completed a meeting with the President in which they presented the Manpower Task Force Report to the President and they will be available to brief along with others.

Q. Do you have some paper, Larry?

MR. SPEAKES. It's coming right there.

Q. It's coming to you, Ralph.

SECRETARY WEINBERGER. Ladies and gentlemen, we just presented the Task Force Military Manpower Report to the President and advised him that the report had concluded that we have basically accomplished the task he set for us to examine the military manpower situation and reported to him that they are—the military services are fully meeting their recruiting objectives under the All-Volunteer Armed Force Program—recruiting highly qualified and very patriotic young men who compare very favorably with the youth population of the Nation as a whole with respect to education and other qualifications.

The thing is really summed up best by the quotation from General Kroesen on page five of the summary. He says, "Our greatest strength is the overall caliber of the American soldier." And he said, again, continuing the quotation, "I've been in the Army 40 years and this is the best peacetime force I've ever seen." And that's General Frederick Kroesen who is the Commander of the United States Army forces in Europe.

We note that there will be an increased requirement for manpower from a diminishing pool of people in the age group in the next few years and this will require, of course, that the all-volunteer system be supported adequately by various compensation and educational benefits. And we are convinced that if that does take place, as we believe it should, that then the all-volunteer program will be able to meet the needs of the military services out into the future and we see no reason, whatever, for any draft.

Ed, do you want to add anything—

MR. MEESE. No.

Q. Mr. Secretary, how much is the increased pay and bonus program going to cost you throughout the 1980's?

SECRETARY WEINBERGER. I don't think I ought to specifically identify it. It's included in all of our budget projections. We have included a payraise of an amount that is necessary to keep up with inflation. And as you know, the budget for 1983 requested an 8 percent increase and in keeping with

---

[66] Source: White House Press Release, October 18, 1982, Office of the Press Secretary to the President. Edwin Meese, Major General Thomas K. Turnage, Director of the Selective Service System, and Dr. Lawrence J. Korb, Assistant Secretary of Defense (Manpower, Reserve Affairs, and Logistics), also participated in the briefing which took place in the Briefing Room of the White House beginning at 1:48 p.m. Regarding the creation of the Military Manpower Task Force, see footnote 6 above.

[67] Reference is to the executive summary of the Military Manpower Task Force Report, which was also printed in *Military Manpower Task Force: A Report to the President on the Status and Prospects of the All Volunteer Force* (Washington, 1983), Ch. 1.

the governmentwide program, there will be a 4 percent increase voted. But we believe that necessary educational and other benefits that are required are those that are included in the budget projections.

Q. If you're meeting your goals so well, as you say you're doing, are you going to rethink the continuing draft registration and the expense that—

SECRETARY WEINBERGER. No, it isn't a draft registration. We don't have a draft. The registration program is totally separate and it should continue because it will save us about 48 days in the event we should ever have to go to mobilization. But it is not registration for a draft. It is a registration program designed to enable us to move more quickly if we should have to.

Q. Mr. Secretary?

SECRETARY WEINBERGER. Yes.

Q. Do you see the possibility of—as the economic situation recovers—maybe fewer men wanting to go in and you may have to increase your intake of women?

SECRETARY WEINBERGER. These would not be related. We would be delighted to take more women and we are taking the women who apply. We do not turn down any. We don't believe that the improved economic conditions will have a significantly adverse effect on military recruiting because we're getting quite a few people now, a very good cross section of people from areas in the country where there is high employment. And while, unquestionably, the recession has something to do with the numbers that are coming in, I don't think it is a sole factor, by any means.

Q. Is there any relationship between this report or this study and that study of women in the army?

SECRETARY WEINBERGER. No, that's a study that is proceeding independently and basically concludes that there are a large number of positions that are performed equally well by women as by men and that we want to continue very much with the active recruiting of women for all of the military services.

Q. Mr. Secretary, you say the recession is a factor?

SECRETARY WEINBERGER. It's a factor.

Q. How big of a factor?

SECRETARY WEINBERGER. It's a little hard to measure. The recession is a factor. The improved compensation is a factor. The thing that I think is the biggest factor is the fact, as the President has very well said, that it's an honor to wear the uniform again[68] and that there's been quite a change in the country with respect to the way in which the military profession is viewed. We see that in increased ROTC applications. We see it in increased reserve enlistments. We see it in a number of ways. And, personally, it's one of the things I find most gratifying.

Q. Do you find that a bigger factor than the recession—

SECRETARY WEINBERGER. It's awfully hard to measure but I would certainly think that that is a larger factor than the recession primarily based on the fact that people are coming into the armed services from all over the country even areas where obviously they could get jobs of a different type. And so I don't think the recession is by any means a major factor in it, but certainly it is a factor. No question about that.

. . . .

Q. Mr. Meese or Secretary Weinberger, we haven't had time to go through all this. But now that you have done this assessment of our Task Force, would you tell us how our personnel, how you find they match up to the Soviets right now, both as far as quality and—

SECRETARY WEINBERGER. Well, I think—there wasn't any examination of that subject in this report. This was simply looking to the questions of whether or not we would be able to acquire the necessary people that we need to keep the Armed Services, military—Uniformed Services filled with a volunteer system and what were some of the problems incidental to that.

But I can certainly give you a personal opinion that man for man I'm delighted with the quality of our people and if the next question is would I exchange them with the Soviets, the answer is clearly, no.

. . . .

Q. Mr. Secretary, have you ascertained the cost difference between an all-volunteer course and a draft—

---

68 In remarks to members of Ohio veterans organizations in Columbus, Ohio, on October 4, 1982, for example, President Reagan said, "one thing that's made me particularly happy—more and more young Americans are proud again to wear their country's uniform." (*Weekly Compilation of Presidential Documents,* October 11, 1982, p. 1258)

SECRETARY WEINBERGER. I haven't got it in any way specifically or with the exactitude I'd like to present it to you. But it's my strong feeling that it would be vastly more expensive to go with the draft, unless you were willing to have something, I think, is not possible and that is a two-tier pay structure.

I don't see how you could draft a group of people and pay them vastly less than the regular forces are getting. And if you did not do that, if you paid the same scale, you would have two things happening. You would have a much larger number of people coming in, which would cost a great deal more. Or you would have so many exceptions and exceptions that the social fabric would be strained to the breaking point. And I just don't think that you're going to save any money by a draft. I know there's a popular idea that you save a lot of money with a draft. But it's my strong feeling that it would cost more in all ways, both fiscally as well as all the other ways.

Q. Sir, do you have enough doctors and nurses and dentists and pharmacists now? And are you giving some thought to asking Congress to give you standby authority to draft these—

SECRETARY WEINBERGER. No, we are not asking for standby draft authority, and my strong impression is we are getting sufficient numbers of all of those specialities. Dr. Korb may want to add something at that point.

DR. KORB. On this particular point, we're fine in the active force. What we're talking about now is the purpose of mobilization. There have been discussions about whether, in terms of—times of mobilization you ought to have standby authority, particularly to draft women professionals—health professionals, but that's just at the discussion stage.

Q. Mr. Secretary, how do you respond to the criticism that there have been an inordinate number of black people in the Army and that that creates a problem of having a certain race fighting for the rest of the country?

SECRETARY WEINBERGER. It is not a—it is a matter which is addressed on page 3 of the Executive Summary—

Q. Right.

SECRETARY WEINBERGER.—but it is not a matter which I find anything but the greatest pride in. The simple fact of the matter is that in every other line of endeavor, if these percentages of black participation were reported, people would be delighted. And I feel that this is an all-volunteer situation. It's a situation in which the—everybody is making up his own mind, and I think it reflects primarily the basic patriotism of the black volunteers. This is something they want to do. There's no coercion here at all. And the percentages are not that much out of line—22 percent black as opposed to 12 percent in the country doesn't seem to me to be anything that should cause anything except, again, congratulations to the black groups who are volunteering. They are making excellent soldiers and they—as they always have throughout our entire history of our country, and I think it's just a very fine tribute to their patriotism. I don't think it's a problem.

Q. Will the Reagan administration agree to another pay cap in the military next year?

SECRETARY WEINBERGER. I have no idea. That would depend on the economic conditions at the time.

Q. Mr. Secretary, what is the percentage now of registrants? Has that increased—

SECRETARY WEINBERGER. Ninety-four percent complies. And General Turnage is right here and is—that's Selective Service, that is, of course, in charge of that.

We have some suggestions within the report for ways in which the last 6 percent can be encouraged to register.

Q. Mr. Secretary, is the Air Force and the Navy keeping up so that they'll have airplanes and ships in case we need them?

SECRETARY WEINBERGER. Yes. At the moment we have a very happy condition to report on the personnel side. We are getting all the volunteers for all the positions that we can enlist under the amounts appropriated by Congress, and we actually have waiting lists in several of the recruiting offices, for all services.

Q. Mr. Secretary, you say there's a great wave of patriotism and people are once again happy to don the uniform of the United States. Are you getting a lot of college students and professional people just giving up and going in?

SECRETARY WEINBERGER. It's spread right across the board. The ROTC applications, as has been said, are higher than they've been for a long time. And the basic educational qualifications as measured by the high school diploma graduates and all is far higher. I don't have the precise percentages, but it's almost twice as much. And in every way, quality and quantity, we're very happy with what's occurring.

Q. Mr. Secretary, this section on black content of the force—

Q. Mr. Secretary, did you meet with—

SECRETARY WEINBERGER. I'm sorry.

Q. This section, in what I have—

SECRETARY WEINBERGER. Yes.

Q. —black content of the force—

SECRETARY WEINBERGER. Yes.

Q. —does that refer to West Germany and their request that the United States not assign a black[69]—

SECRETARY WEINBERGER. That has never been a request which has ever come to me, and if it ever had, it would be rejected totally out of hand. I've seen reports that such requests have been made, but there have been none of that kind made and I suspect that's just some sort of a story. There have been no official requests of that kind come in. If it did, it would be rejected without the slightest consideration. We are, as I say, extremely proud of the numbers who are volunteering and I don't think it's—not only I don't think it's a problem; I think it's a very great tribute.

. . . .

Q. Thank you.

I believe you used the phrase that "it is now an honor to wear the uniform again."

SECRETARY WEINBERGER. Yes.

Q. When was it not?

SECRETARY WEINBERGER. Well, I saw a great many things that disturbed me very much in the years immediately after the end of the Vietnam conflict. I saw American soliders coming home from Vietnam picketed and booed in San Francisco, an experience I hope never to have again. And I saw a great many people on college campuses in those years and college administrators and faculties insisting that ROTC programs not be a part of their curriculum, and things of that kind. And I think that that feeling has, to a very considerable extent, changed. And I think that is an extremely healthy thing and I think it is one of the things that is reflected in the very happy personnel situation that we have now.

Q. Mr. Secretary, one of the things Army, Air Force, and Navy personnel experts say is that pay comparability is really the key to keeping good people in the services.

SECRETARY WEINBERGER. It is certainly an important factor, without any question. And nobody joins the military services to make any money, but it is totally unfair to have them be penalized by doing so. And it is vital that we keep these compensation packages comparable and fair, and that they take into account inflation and all those other matters, because this is a very special kind of employment with all of the risks that are too obvious to talk about. So, yes, that is an important factor.

Q. I really had not gotten to my question.

SECRETARY WEINBERGER. I'm sorry.

Q. This year you went along with a cut in the projected increase, from 8 percent to 4 percent, and the apparent trade-off was some hardware items in the Defense Department budget. Would you do so again?

SECRETARY WEINBERGER. I think the assumption is unwarranted. I think that we had a general governmental policy with respect to pay increases and we certainly followed and went along with that general governmental policy because after all we are part of the general government. But they weren't a trade-off for anything. It was a factor that was imposed on the government as a whole because of economic conditions. We have submitted our recommendations for the 1984 budget and in keeping with longstanding rules we don't discuss those and the President will make up his mind about those and they will then become the President's budget, which will be supported.

Q. Is there a pay increase included in the FY 1984 budget?

SECRETARY WEINBERGER. There is a proposal for keeping the pay constant, yes.

Q. Approximately how many of the universities in the United States that abolished or banned ROTC units have brought them back?

69 Reference is to a newspaper report that a top Department of Defense official, speaking off the record to a scholarly conference, said that European allies, mainly West Germany, were quietly urging the United States to limit the number of blacks assigned to European bases. For this report, see *New York Times*, June 6, 1982, p. I21.

SECRETARY WEINBERGER. I really wouldn't know. We could get—look up—

Q. Would you say it is a substantial number?

SECRETARY WEINBERGER. There are quite a few, I think.

DR. KORB. More than two-thirds have tried to come back. We're in the happy position of, we can't take them all back because of the limitations on the scholarships. We get for each ROTC scholarship six qualified applicants. So right now we are in the excellent position of being able to be very selective in that area. But as universities apply we try to accommodate them, but we do have a backlog right now.

Q. How about the services academies? Is there an enormous increase in applicants?

DR. KORB. It's about 10 qualified applicants for each place at the service academies, and there are three qualified applicants for each place in officer candidate school or officer training school.

. . . .

Document 34

Letter From President Reagan to Members of the Congress, November 22, 1982[70]

"I Have Decided to Emplace 100 MX Missiles . . . in Superhard Silos in a Closely-spaced Basing Mode"

For many years, U.S. strategic forces have helped protect our Nation and the Free World by providing a capable and effective deterrent. Maintenance of these forces has historically enjoyed broad bipartisan support.

In recent years, our deterrent has become increasingly vulnerable in the face of a relentless Soviet military buildup. As part of our program to modernize the U.S. deterrent, I asked last year that you support improving the capability and survivability of the land-based component of our strategic forces by authorizing development and deployment of the MX intercontinental ballistic missile. I also agreed earlier this year to provide you with a permanent basing decision by December 1.[71]

In response to this requirement, the Department of Defense forwarded to me a series of basing options, with associated analyses of technical, environmental, arms control, and other factors. I have also received the counsel of my senior advisers, former Presidents and Administration officials, and Members of Congress. After careful study, I have decided to emplace 100 MX missiles, now known as "Peacekeeper," in superhard silos in a closely-spaced basing mode at Francis E. Warren Air Force Base near Cheyenne, Wyoming. Given Congressional support, these missiles will have an initial operational capability late in 1986. I am prepared also to consider deception and possibly ballistic missile defense, which are options if the Soviet Union continues its military buildup.

We all hope, however, that the Soviets will join us in seeking meaningful progress in arms control negotiations. This MX decision supports and complements the U.S. approach to arms control. While the U.S. must and will improve its forces to maintain a credible deterrent, we remain fully committed to our standing proposals for significant reductions in both sides' nuclear arsenals. We seek to reduce ballistic missiles by about one-half and ballistic missile warheads by about one-third.

Under separate cover, I am sending you a copy of my full statement on the decision outlined above.[72] I ask that you keep an open mind on this complex and important question and permit the Administration to make its case for the decision. We are prepared to respond, at your convenience, to formal and informal requests for additional information that you may desire. I look forward to receiving your counsel and assistance as we work toward our common

---

70 Source: White House Press Release, November 22, 1982, Office of the Press Secretary to the President; printed also in *Weekly Compilation of Presidential Documents,* November 29, 1982, p. 1515.

71 In his letter to leaders of the House of Representatives, July 16, President Reagan promised to propose a final basing mode for the MX by December. For text, see July 26, 1982, pp. 916–917.

72 For the text of President Reagan's statement explaining his decision on closely spaced basing for the MX missile, November 22, see *ibid.*, November 29, 1982, pp. 1513–1515.

goal of improving the security of our Nation.

Sincerely,
Ronald Reagan

Document 35

Transcript of a Press Conference by the Secretary of Defense (Weinberger), November 22, 1982[73]

Explication and Defense of the Closely Spaced Basing Mode for the MX Missile

PRINCIPAL DEPUTY ASSISTANT SECRETARY OF DEFENSE BEN WELLES. Ladies and gentlemen, Secretary Weinberger will now be making a statement, after which, if there is time, he will be available for some questions and answers. We're going to try and hold it to half an hour. Thank you.

SECRETARY WEINBERGER. We've had two or three major problems that we've been seeking all the time with the deployment of the MX because we've been convinced that it is necessary to modernize and strengthen and keep this leg of the triad. We have no doubt that with the technology that the Soviets have taken from us, one or the other, that they have the accuracy now to make very, very vulnerable the existing Minuteman system and it is necessary for us to develop a system that can be survivable and continuous with the retaliatory capability that can maintain deterrence that has preserved the peace of the world for about 37 years now.

We, therefore, have had the problem of trying to deploy against Soviet missiles that are very accurate, they're using our technology, have high yields and all the rest, to deploy the new more accurate heavy yield missile of the MX in a way that would be survivable. We also want to do it in a way that complies fully with our strategic arms control and arms reduction objectives and we believe that we have found that solution, but it has not been easy. We have, first of all, this problem of the accuracy of the Soviet missiles; we've had certain restraints placed on us by the Congress with respect to deploying in existing silos. We had two or three methods that the Congress made very clear we could not consider and were not to consider, and we had a December 1st deadline given us by Congress.

The close spaced basing that the President has chosen[74] seems now to comply with all of the requests of the Congress. It does give us survivability by pulling the silos closer together and making it therefore essential for the Soviets to change their existing systems and to do that within the time in which we could build this and deploy this system. So we believe that they are not going to be able to do that. We believe this will give us several years in varying conditions out into the—at least the mid-1990's before they will be able to change their system sufficiently to enable them to have any kind of confidence in making an attack on it.

The essence of deterrence is not that we have to use this system. The essence of deterrence is that it survives a first strike by the Soviets and that we have the retaliatory capability to inflict on them such damage that they would not make that first strike. That is the essence of deterrence. It has, as I say, preserved the peace of the world all of this time and it is vital that we continue it. It is not possible for us to give up the ICBM system or the ground based leg of the triad. We need the redundancy and the safety that is provided by both—having all three systems—the ground based systems, the submarines with the more accurate missiles which the President's program will provide for us and the new airplane, that can penetrate the Soviet greatly strengthened air defenses which the President's program last year will provide for us.

That is the only way in which we can maintain deterrence. It is the only way also in which the arms control, arms reduction objectives of the President can be maintained. Without the certain knowledge by the Soviets that we possess the will, the resolution, the capability, the resources to continue strengthening and modernizing our systems, they would have no incentive whatever to make reductions in their very strong systems. And so it is for this reason that the President has chosen this method, a method which can provide us the surviva-

---

[73] Source: *Public Statements of Secretary of Defense Weinberger*, 1982. The press conference was held at the Pentagon beginning at 3:30 p.m.

[74] See footnote 72 above.

bility and the strength and the capabilities of maintaining deterrence.

Not that we believe it will have to be used; not that we ever want to use it. The whole point of getting it is to make sure that we do not have to use it and to make sure that the Soviets are willing to make the reductions that are essential to carry out the only real way of preserving the peace. And that is deterrence and arms reduction, the two go together.

Q. Can you sell this to a Congress which is already on the record, some members of Congress, as saying we already have the votes to beat it? You have a tremendous fight ahead of you.

A. Well, they're doing some predictions. And I don't do any predictions. There is, I think, enough recognition in the Congress of the importance of maintaining a strategic deterrent and doing it by means of a triad. This is the only way we can have a strengthened, survivable system that will meet what the Soviets now have. I just very much hope that there will be sufficient understanding of these matters in the Congress, and I don't do any predictions as to what the Congress will do.

Q. Mr. Secretary, over the past weeks a number of critics have spoken up and said some very specific things about the unknown strikes, high radiations, simultaneous warheads. Are you convinced that you have answered each of those?

A. Yes, we are. We understand a lot of these objections. We understand that there are a lot of things the Soviets could do ultimately to try to counter this system. We also think we'll know about those things in time, and that we in turn have counters for it. So that this system will remain survivable. The Minuteman system has remained survivable now for in excess of 25 years. And it has been one of the key factors in helping preserve the peace of the world. We are convinced that this system can be, and will be, survivable for at least that length of time. There are various things the Soviets can start to do. There are things that when they start to do them, we will in turn have counters to that.

Q. Mr. Secretary, can you address what you can do to prevent them from pinning down your missiles—sequential attacks?

A. The pinning down that they might be able to attempt would, first of all, involve very large resources on their part and very major changes in the kinds of resources they now have. While they are getting ready to try to do that, and while we would know they were trying to get ready to do that, we would have the ability through various methods of launch and other methods of countering that particular ability to try to pin down. There have been talks about Earth penetrators—that they would get the missiles that would not explode in the air, would come down into the Earth. There are ways of countering that. In fact, comparatively simple ways of countering that. It's called a rockpile.

Q. Mr. Secretary, can I just read your article 4, sentence 1 of the pending SALT II treaty, which I know your administration has opposed but said it would not violate if the Russians didn't exceed the limit. It says "Each party undertakes not to start construction of additional fixed ICBM launchers."[75] My question is: if this is not a violation of that pending SALT II language, and if the Russians interpret it as being a violation regardless of your explanation, do you intend to go ahead anyhow with Dense Pack?

A. Well, that's very hypothetical, but I don't think there's any way in which they can claim successfully that this is a violation of the SALT II treaty. It's perfectly possible that they can claim that anything we did would be a violation of the language of that treaty. Bear in mind, that treaty is something that they were very eager to have signed, and that did enable and does enable them to make all of the expansions and enlargements they are talking about. But the silo, in which the MX in these superhardened canisters would be deployed, is not a new launcher. The silo cannot launch the missile. So we don't believe there is any violation of the agreement at all, and yes, we are determined to go ahead with it.

Q. Mr. Secretary, this MX missile has been with us for many, many years now. This is the latest of about three dozen different approaches to basing the MX in a survivable way. You, yourself, at one point seemed to favor putting them in big airplanes that flew around endlessly. The technology and the theories involved here have never been tested using weapons. Fratricide is theory, but not much else. The American people, it seems to us, are going to have to make a great leap of faith in order to accept what you propose in this Dense Pack.

---

[75] For the full text of the SALT II treaty between the United States and the Soviet Union, signed on June 18, 1979, see Department of State *Bulletin*, July 1979, pp. 23–47.

A. I hope the American people will be assisted in that leap by the facts. The facts are that we have not had three or four dozen proposals. There have been innumerable suggestions that have been made by a very large number of people—most of them not connected with any of the associations or organizations that would have to build, deploy, and operate the MX. These proposals—a lot of them—have been examined very carefully. But we're only talking really about two different kinds of permanent basing modes that have been proposed, and I think it's a good question and I think it's very important that they have a chance to set that before the people.

The MPS system was proposed by previous administrations and was rejected by this administration. We asked that as an interim basis, as an interim period while we had an opportunity to study more thoroughly this proposal, several other proposals, we put these in hardened, existing Minuteman silos, and the Congress said no. We then proposed the system that is before you today as a permanent basing mode. So there really have been two proposals, two actual proposals made. There have been all kinds of suggestions, you're absolutely right, far more than three dozen. But suggestions, that flowed in from all over, are, of course, important and some can be quite helpful. But this has not been a situation in which everybody veered back and forth and went all over, and there's never been the slightest doubt about the need for this kind of missile and that whole program has proceeded through several administrations and is still proceeding and is on time, but the important thing is where to base it. There was one proposal the President rejected, there is this new proposal which the President proposes.

Q. Mr. Secretary, nonetheless last year when you came out with your first MX announcement, although you had an interim basing scheme you also said here are the three most promising long term schemes that we're going to study[76] and you listed them and this was not among them. How come in a year, suddenly this is the final. Congress says we don't want interim basing, give us a final plan, and a year ago this wasn't even in the top three.

A. I have to disagree with you. This was in—anyone who read the first Townes report[77] would see that there was a great deal of emphasis and stress based upon the idea of examining the problems of fratricide and taking advantage of that phenomenon. The suggestion was very strong that we do that and there were a number of ways in which the idea was, before the various groups studying this and the Air Force and in our department, of how that could be done, and one of them was indeed deep underground basing. And we did study it and the reason it was rejected is that we could not get it on-line until 1995.

Q. First of all, the Townes report has never been released. We'd all be happy to read it if you would care to release it, but secondly, the documents, the statements you put out, all your testimony to Congress, the President's own statement in the White House listed three most promising options. The airplane, the BMD, and the underground basing. This was not one of those three and so I'm wondering how it has risen so fast in the last year.

A. Again, it hasn't risen all that fast. The airplane was specifically forbidden by the Congress to be considered.[78] Deep underground basing was considered but it would take too long to bring it on line. We want to get this on line as soon as we can and the missile itself has an initial operation capability of 1986 and we're still on time for that and I hope the various fundings necessary to keep us on time will be voted. But the protection of the BMD was the other method that you cited, and this is far more easily and far more effectively protected by BMD than the Minuteman system or any of the other things that we have. By putting it into an area of that general size and scale compared with this enormous spread, and that was only one of three for the Minuteman, you have a much more survivable, much more protectable system by BMD.

When you couple that with the admonition in the first Townes report to examine carefully the phenomenon of fratricide, why as I say, it was quite clear that things were

[76] In his press briefing on October 2, 1981, Secretary Weinberger said that the Reagan administration was studying three basing modes for the MX: continuous airborne patrol, deep underground basing, and more effective ballistic missile defense. See *American Foreign Policy: Current Documents, 1981*, document 46.

[77] Regarding the Townes Panel Report, see the editorial note, document 23.

[78] In its report on the Department of Defense authorization bill in May 1982, the House Armed Services Committee voted to delete the funds requested to study the continuous airborne patrol option. See *Department of Defense Authorization Act, 1983*, Report of the Committee on Armed Services, House of Representatives, Ninety-seventh Congress, Second Session, Report No. 97–482 (Washington, 1982), pp. 25–26.

pointing in this direction. I understand that because of the classified nature of the Townes report, and there's a great [deal?] about this phenomenon of fratricide, the destruction of the incoming Soviet missiles; the fact that they would have to change quite completely their present deployed method that led to the feeling that this was the kind of system that the President should recommend.

Q. Mr. Secretary, if the deterrence should fail and the Russians actually should fire some of these bombs as is the premise of your system, how many Americans would be killed?

A. Oh, I'm not going to get into any hypotheticals of that kind at all. What we have before us is a method of deterring that attack and it is a method of preserving the conditions which have given us that kind of peace all these years, and that's exactly the purpose of this. That is the way we think we can, and together with arms reduction, the only way we think we can preserve the peace.

Q. Mr. Secretary, 14 months ago you had asked in your recommendations that a final basing mode be made in 1984. Congress rushed it up and said December 1st of this year.

A. That's correct.

Q. To what extent has that had an impact on your final decision? Would you have wanted to spend that year or year and a half to come up with a different plan?

A. Well, I think that it's fair to say that in this field you want all the time you can have to study things. We need to study as carefully as we can a wide variety of options. I think the congressional mandate certainly focused our attention on completing the process sooner than might have been the case otherwise. The more time you have the better it is in the sense that there are a lot of things that you want to examine. We have done those things on an accelerated schedule in order to comply with that time demand of Congress.

We never wanted to do anything that would delay the IOC of the missile or our ability to deploy it in 1986, and essentially what Congress said was, we want a final basing mode recommendation from the President by December 1, 1982, and here it is.

Q. That some nuclear experts say this system is not survivable, that the Russians could take it out now with what they have without expending a great deal of their resources, and that you're spending billions of dollars for a few hours more of survivability and that eventually you will have to go to an antiballistic—

A. We obviously disagree with those statements. I understand they've been made and they will obviously continue to be made. You have to bear in mind there are a lot of people who don't want to deploy the missile at all. They don't want it built. They don't want it deployed. I understand that perfectly well and respect that viewpoint, but it is inaccurate to say that this does not give us any additional survivability. It does give us survivability well into the 1990's, and it forces the Soviets to divert their efforts to develop counters to it, and that was one of the problems with other systems. They had the counters already built and they just had to add a bit to it. But this system does force them to change and develop, devote a lot of resources to trying to counter it. It does give us the survivability, and if we do decide on the basis of learning that they are developing these counters, that it is necessary for us to do additional things to the system in order to add to the survivability, yes, then we do put in ballistic missile defense, either of the kind we have now which is very effective or as the President mentions, more improved and different types of BMD on which we're going to devote substantial amounts of resources to the research, then that will take us well into 2000. So you buy a very great deal with this, you buy really a continued effective deterrence and you buy the opportunity to secure major arms reductions which is one of the critically important factors of the whole thing.

Q. Mr. Secretary, do you also disagree with the concerns of Dr. Townes that maybe you will not be able to reach the hardened schedule that you laid out? Or that the Soviets might not develop a counter to this system—

A. Dr. Townes quite properly, and in response to specific requests from us, outlined the problems that are involved in this whole system. As has been made, I think, imminently clear, there is no system that is 100 percent guaranteed invulnerable and perfect. I tried to mention in the opening some of the reasons for that and the principal one is what we've given the Soviets in the way of technology.

But as Dr. DeLauer and others mentioned earlier,[79] you have no new technolo-

[79] Reference is to briefings which preceded this press conference by Weinberger.

gy involved in this. It's a question of additional reinforcing steel, and additional concrete and all of those things that we do know about. So yes, Dr. Townes is quite right. He pointed out some of the problems and some of the concerns, and the undeniable fact that no, this degree of hardness hasn't been achieved, but he didn't say it couldn't be achieved, and we have high confidence that it can be. We have one of the leading authorities on hardening in Chicago who has told us that yes, this is possible. Dr. Townes also indicated the uncertainty as to when the Soviets would respond, and there is no doubt about that. Nobody knows how or how quickly they will respond. We do know that we have counters as they begin to respond that can preserve the survivability of this type of system for several more years.

Q. Mr. Secretary, in talking about the Russians having to change their deployment and that you can meet them, you're talking about offense. What about defense? This must be a threat to thousands, MX warheads must be a threat to their land-based missiles. What are they doing about that threat?

A. Well, to be perfectly frank about it, they've already done it. That's why we need the MX. They have hardened. They have very hardened targets now. They have—

Q. You say it's a counterforce weapon then?

A. I don't think it's going to be very profitable to get into a lot of titles for this thing. What it is, it's designed to preserve the peace in the sense that it is designed to give us an effective deterrent, a deterrent for this ground-based leg of the triad which we feel we have to regain. We know the vulnerability of the Minutemen. We know that a first strike of the Soviets could take out in excess of 90 percent of that Minuteman system as it [is?] now deployed, and we know that it is absolutely essential to do something to preserve the effective deterrence that is given by that leg of the triad. We know the Soviets have hardened their silos and their targets. We know that they have added a very effective air defense. We know that whether anybody thinks it's effective or not, they're spending billions of dollars and more rubles on civil defense, and we think that that is all indicative of the fact that they believe that they are developing things that can render our deterrent far less effective.

Q. Mr. Secretary, if you received hard, confirmed information that a Soviet first strike had been launched and was on its way moments away from landing, would you recommend to the President that the missiles not be launched, that they be allowed to be destroyed or—

A. As most of you know, I'm willing to discuss almost anything but one of the things I'm not willing to discuss is the employment of nuclear weapons or launch policies. Those remain classified and we do not discuss that.

Q. What is your fall-back position, Mr. Secretary, if Congress does to CSB what you did to the MPS?

A. Well, we would certainly hope that the American public would not want the Congress to deny us the opportunity to maintain an effective deterrent and keep the peace. We believe this is the best way of accomplishing both of those.

PRESS. Thank you.

Document 36

Transcript of an Interview With the Secretary of Defense (Weinberger), December 8, 1982 (Extract)[80]

House of Representatives Defeat of Production Funds for the MX

MR. MORTON DEAN. The big defeat of the MX yesterday[81] was a big defeat for President Reagan, who has gone all out for the program, twisting arms and turning on the charm—it didn't work. What happens now, well, let's put that question to the Secretary of Defense, Caspar Weinberger, who is in Washington with Bill Lynch. How about it, Mr. Weinberger, what happens now?

SECRETARY WEINBERGER. Well, it was a setback, there is no question about that.

---

[80] Source: *Public Statements of Secretary of Defense Weinberger*, 1982. Secretary Weinberger was interviewed in Washington on the CBS television program, "Morning News," by Morton Dean and Bill Lynch of CBS News.

[81] On December 7, the House of Representatives, by a vote of 245 to 176, approved an amendment introduced by Representative Joseph P. Addabbo, which eliminated $988 million for start-up production for the MX in the defense appropriation bill for fiscal year 1983.

One thing that seems to have been overlooked in all the discussions so far is the fact that the same House that voted not to go ahead with the actual production of the missile and took out $980 million yesterday, also left in the bill a little over $2⅛ billion for the MX for continued development, continued research work, research on the basing mode, and those things. So, it isn't really a total repudiation of the missile itself. But it clearly is a setback; it's a very unwise, unfortunate vote, because it will almost inevitably insert some delays in the program in which we think delay is very very dangerous. You have to bear in mind what the Soviets have, an interesting statement from Ustinov yesterday in which he said that they will go ahead and start working out some kind of a response to the MX.[82] The problem is they deployed that response to the MX 3 years ago and they are now working on the next one. So we have a lot to do and we have to do it rapidly.

MR. LYNCH. Mr. Secretary, do you read this vote as a repudiation of the controversial Dense Pack basing mode or perhaps more as a sign that the Congress won't stand for higher defense spending?

A. No, I think it's a desire to vote no on some of the expenditures that are required for defense. I think there is a lot, as Mr. Addabbo said, there is a lot of feeling that the November vote had to be reflected in a vote in the House, some feeling that the defense expenditures have been high and everybody would like to have them lowered. The problem is you can't construct your defense budget on the basis of what seems to be fair to other departments or amounts that you would like to reduce. You have to do it on the basis of the threat. And some way we have not yet been able to convey to the American people or to the Congress, the really serious nature, the growing nature, the peril, I think, is not too strong a word to use in describing the Soviet advances, the Soviet arms, the buildup, the rapidity of that buildup, and what it portends for America and the Free World.

Q. Well, from a legislative strategy point of view, what is your next step? Do you think that you can win in the lame duck Senate?

A. We don't know whether we can win or not, it's a question really of whether freedom or peace wins. The point is that we will certainly make a major effort to make sure that some of the production money is restored so that we don't lose time. What isn't realized in these things is that clearly there is a desire to have the missile, at least based on the amount left in for research and development on the missile. What isn't realized is that all this vote did yesterday is make it a great deal more expensive and build in delays that are very dangerous. So the vote really is not going to accomplish what I think some of the members wanted which is to spend less on defense, it's actually going to cause us to spend more on defense because, when you delay production, although you go ahead with all the other items, you just automatically make things more costly.

MR. DEAN. Mr. Secretary, does this mean that you are going to go back to the drawing boards? Could we expect President Reagan to come up with another type of basing plan?

A. This wasn't a vote on the basing plan at all.

Q. Well, in a sense maybe it was.

A. Well, it may have been, but bear in mind what other votes had been on the basing plan. The President proposed last October, a year ago, that we should put the missiles, the production of which he currently urged, go forward into hardened existing Minuteman silos. The Congress said no, we don't want you to spend any money on that. They also went farther and said we've heard some reports you might want to put in an airborne deployment, in some kind of a new airplane and we don't want you to spend a nickle on that. And so we respected both of those. So we have proposed the most survivable basing mode that is available under the congressional restraints.

Q. Are you going to stay with that?

A. This vote yesterday was only on the production, it had nothing to do with basing mode.

Q. But are you going to stay with that basing plan?

A. Well, it is within the constraints that have been imposed by the Congress. It is the most survivable. It is the thing that gives us the essence of deterrence, the ability to withstand a Soviet first strike and have a retaliatory force that they'd find unac-

---

[82] In an interview in *Pravda* on December 7, Soviet Defense Minister Dmitri Ustinov said, among other things, that if the United States deployed its new MX missile, the Soviet Union would deploy a powerful new intercontinental missile of its own. (*Current Digest of the Soviet Press*, January 5, 1983, pp. 7–8)

ceptably high. And, yes, we'll stay with it unless the Congress says, no, you can't do that one either and then we'll have to go back and see what else we can find.

. . . .

Document 37

Transcript of an Interview With the Chairman of the Joint Chiefs of Staff (Vessey), December 10, 1982[83]

Position of the Joint Chiefs of Staff on the Dense Pack Basing Mode for the MX Missile

DAVID HARTMAN. . . . on Wednesday the MX seemed to run into some more trouble when General Vessey, who's Chairman of the Joint Chiefs of Staff, told a Senate Committee that a majority of the military chiefs opposed what is called the Dense Pack plan for the MX.[84] Well, this morning it is being reported that all five members of the Joint Chiefs have put aside their earlier reservations and decided to support the MX plan.[85] General Vessey is here with us this morning, here in Washington, and of course Steve is joining us. Good morning, General Vessey, nice to have you with us this morning.

GENERAL VESSEY. Good morning.

Q. Wednesday, as I just said, you testified that three of the five Generals, the top leaders, were against this Dense Pack. This morning, as I just said, we read that all the Generals say, "OK, we'll go along with Mr. President." What's going on here, General? People in this country must be this morning saying, "What is going on?"

A. First, let me clarify what I did testify to. I said that all of the Joint Chiefs agreed that we needed the MX as part of our deterrent force. That there were some differences on the basing mode and all agreed to support the President's decision to implement the closely spaced basing method. That's what I testified to the Congress on Wednesday.

Q. But this morning, however, we got a big flap; here we've got the President now coming out and saying that everybody is with me, you've got the Senate sitting over there waiting to vote. I mean, what effect is this going to have on the Senate vote? I mean, are you looking at a situation here where you're not going to get essentially this missile?

A. I think that we'll get the missile, we need the missile, it's very important that we deter the Soviets and that missile is an important part of this strategic force modernization program.

Q. So you think that you're going to get it, you don't think it's going to affect the vote in the Senate to the negative side?

A. Well—a great deal of confusion certainly isn't going to help the Senate vote, but I hope that clarifying this issue, and I believe it was clarified at the Senate hearing, it is simply how it was reported—

STEVE BELL. Let me try to clarify it a little further. You're saying that three of the Joint Chiefs, as I understand it, preferred a different system or weren't ready to make a decision, but then said they would go along with the President, is that it?

A. Let me make it clear, the Joint Chiefs weren't voting on the closely spaced basing system; they all had an opportunity to give their views to the Secretary of Defense and the President. They did that. Two, including myself, unanimously recommended that the President go ahead with the closely spaced basing system. All three of the others were concerned about technical uncertainties with the closely spaced basing system and two recommended that the President consider going ahead with something very similar to what the Congress told him he couldn't do, which was putting it in Minuteman holes. Now they all explained

---

[83] Source: Department of Defense files. General Vessey was interviewed in Washington on the ABC television program, "Good Morning America," by David Hartman and Steve Bell of ABC News.

[84] Regarding this statement by General Vessey before the Senate Armed Services Committee on Wednesday, December 8, see *The MX Missile and Associated Basing Decision: Hearing Before the Committee on Armed Services, United States Senate, Ninety-seventh Congress, Second Session* (Washington, 1983), p. 49.

[85] On December 9, President Reagan, in response to a reporter's question, remarked, ". . . the same Joint Chiefs—well, one or two at most—had different ideas that they thought might be better with all the confusing things. They did agree that if this was the method I chose, they would be in support of it." (*Weekly Compilation of Presidential Documents,* December 13, 1982, p. 1592)

their views to the President; I explained the views to the President, but they know what I explained. The Secretary of Defense explained why he was making his decision and they all agreed to support the President in implementing the decision. This was before the President made the decision.

Q. The President keeps talking about sending a signal to the Russians. But isn't it true that his MX plan is not as tough and big a plan as Jimmy Carter had nor is the Dense Pack as sure a protective system as the Carter plan?

A. Well, there's debate on the latter. I think the important thing is that deterrence of war is the object of the exercise. We're not trying to build a force that threatens the Russians, we want to make it very clear that the Russians can't obtain their own war objectives, and the MX and the closely spaced basing contributes greatly to that objective.

Q. How concerned are you about the Soviet perception over the last 3 or 4 days of this public debate?

A. Well, I think the newspaper headlines yesterday, I think it was, said that the Soviets are pleased with the MX defeat, ought to give you some clue as to how we ought to proceed from here. If the Soviets are pleased with what's happening to our strategic forces I'm concerned.

Q. General, when you get into a controversial system like this, can a Chief of Staff really say—I just—even after the President makes his decision or the Secretary of Defense makes a decision, could he possibly still object or go public with it, or is this something we almost have to line up?

A. Well, certainly he could continue to object. But the President is in fact the Commander-in-Chief, and we swear an oath to obey the orders of the Commander-in-Chief. As you started to say, the important part of this thing is that the Chiefs agreed the missile is needed. That's important. It needs to be based somewhere.

MR. HARTMAN. We are out of time, General Vessey, thank you for joining us this morning.

Document 38

Statement by President Reagan, December 17, 1982[86]

Senate Action on the MX Missile Program; Announcement of a Bipartisan Commission to Study Basing Options

The action taken early this morning by the Senate with regard to the MX missile program is both welcome and wise.[87] It expresses solid understanding and support for the need to modernize the land-based leg of the Triad. As the Senate recognizes, it is only through this Triad approach that we can hope to preserve an effective deterrent and go forward with negotiations toward real arms reductions.

Beyond that, the Senate was also expressing some rather serious concerns which I take very much to heart. Foremost among these was uncertainty with respect to the approach for basing the missile. This concern is reasonable, since the survivability of this system must be assured and an effective basing plan plays the central role. This extremely complex problem deserves very careful and deliberate consideration, and I am pleased that this will be allowed to take place early in the new Congress.

Between now and the time the final decision must be taken next spring, it is essential that every Member of Congress and, indeed, as many as possible of the American people gain a full appreciation of alternative solutions to this problem. Toward that end I pledge to the Congress and to all

---

[86] Source: *Weekly Compilation of Presidential Documents,* December 20, 1982, pp. 1634–1635.

[87] On December 17, the Senate passed a continuing resolution containing a compromise on the MX missile worked out between President Reagan and Republican and Democratic Senators on December 14. The compromise provided that funding for production of the MX missile would be retained but would be fenced. Removing the fence would be contingent on the President resubmitting a certification of his selection of basing modes together with information on alternative basing modes. Then both Houses of Congress within 45 days of the certification, would approve the basing mode selected by the President or any alternative basing mode they might select. For the remarks by President Reagan and congressional leaders on this compromise, December 14, see *ibid.*, pp. 1621–1623.

Americans the most exhaustive, renewed analysis possible of every apparent option. To assist in this effort, I am today announcing my intention to appoint a bipartisan commission, comprised of senior officials from previous administrations as well as technical experts.[88] I will ask the members to work with the Department of Defense and join together in a bipartisan effort to forge a consensus as to the plan which will best assure the national security interests of our country in the years ahead.

The contributions of this panel of distinguished Americans will be extremely important. In addition, I pledge to the Congress the fullest possible coordination of the work of this commission with Senators and Members. It is essential that if we are to reach our common goals within the time required by last night's vote, the Congress play a central role in shaping this, the most important strategic modernization decision of the post-war period. Again, I would like to express my appreciation for the responsible position taken by the Senate and ask that this wisdom be reflected in the House, as together we join in this important undertaking.

Document 39

Statement by President Reagan, December 21, 1982 (Extract)[89]

Administration Reservations to Continuing Appropriations Resolution for the Remainder of Fiscal Year 1983

. . . .

Unfortunately, this resolution also contains a number of provisions about which I have serious reservations. For example, the bill fails to provide specific funds for production of the Peacekeeper missile.[90] While I am disappointed in the congressional action on this vital strategic forces program, the language of the conference report[91] does enable us to keep to our schedule for initial deployment in 1986 once the Congress approves a permanent basing decision. Between now and this spring, I will work closely with members of Congress to address their concerns and to assure the fullest possible examination of alternative courses of action. Let there be no doubt that the United States remains strongly committed to the pursuit of both effective deterrence and meaningful arms control.

A similar problem is the failure of the resolution to provide full production funding for the Pershing II missile. We are developing this missile along with the ground-launched cruise missile in order to meet an Allied request for land-based systems in Europe that would help maintain deterrence. We intend to meet the scheduled deployment of these missiles in December 1983. We remain steadfast in our determination to meet these Alliance commitments.

The allocation of the funds contained in the continuing resolution for foreign assistance is also a concern. First, it cuts total budget authority for foreign aid, excluding the Export-Import Bank, by $571 million. Second, within that total it distributes limited resources unwisely and inequitably. As a consequence of these changes in this resolution, $800 million in foreign assistance requested for many deserving countries has been denied in order to further increase aid to a nation already receiving 28 percent of our total foreign aid in addition to a $300 million credit increase I proposed this fiscal year.

. . . .

---

88 On January 3, 1983, President Reagan announced the establishment of an 11-member Commission on Strategic Forces, chaired by Brent Scowcroft, former National Security Adviser to President Ford. (*Ibid.*, January 10, 1983, pp. 3–4)

89 Source: White House Press Release, December 21, 1983, Office of the Press Secretary to the President; printed also in *Weekly Compilation of Presidential Documents*, December 27, 1982, pp. 1652–1653. The President made this statement on signing into law H.J. Res. 631, Continuing Appropriations for Fiscal Year 1983, P.L. 97–377; for text, see 96 Stat. 1830.

90 The conference committee rejected funding for production of the MX missile, which the Senate had passed on December 17 as part of a compromise with the President. For that compromise, see footnote 87, *supra*. Instead, it retained the House version which eliminated $988 million for production of the MX missile, and Congress passed this version on December 20. Regarding the House version, see footnote 81 to document 36.

91 See *Making Further Continuing Appropriations and Providing for Productive Employment for the Fiscal Year Ending September 30, 1983*, Ninety-seventh Congress, Second Session, House Report No. 97–980, December 20, 1982 (Washington, 1982), pp. 17–20.

Document 40

Transcript of a Press Conference by the Secretary of Defense (Weinberger), December 30, 1982 (Extracts)[92]

Review of Defense Programs for Fiscal Years 1982 and 1983

PDASD/PA BENJAMIN WELLES. The Secretary will have an opening statement which you may already have. If not, we have it available. We will try to hold this to exactly a half hour.

SECRETARY WEINBERGER. Good morning, ladies and gentlemen. President Reagan took office 2 years ago with a legacy and a commitment. His legacy was a military balance that was undermined by a decade's neglect of our military forces and an enormous buildup of Soviet conventional and nuclear power, and his commitment was to rebuild our defenses, and preserve the peace by pursuing the twin policies of deterrence and genuine arms reduction.

In March of 1981 we submitted a 5-year Defense budget[93] proposing a $116 billion increase in outlays over the previous administration's defense plans for fiscal years 1982–1986. It was an increase that must be measured against the urgency of accomplishing these two crucial goals at the same time. We needed to restore our military readiness as quickly as we could and we needed to modernize our strategic and conventional forces so that we will be able to deter threats arising in the future.

Now despite these pressing needs, we did not exempt the Defense budget in the administration from the searching examination that was given to all spending plans. In the past 2 years we have already cut back some of our defense plans as our contribution to the government-wide effort to reduce deficits. In September of 1981 the President proposed a $20 billion reduction in the 5-year defense outlay program.[94] In his FY 1983 budget, because of our progress in reducing inflation, he proposed a further reduction of $14 billion. In May 1982 he agreed to a further 1983 reduction of $7 billion.[95] These cuts total $41 billion and that's more than one-third of the increase that President Reagan had added.

I do not believe that we can cut more from our defense programs for the next years without risk to our national security. We are doing everything possible to ensure that the defense dollar is spent wisely:

—We continue to examine the budget closely to eliminate all unnecessary programs and redundancies. With 1983's budget we have canceled over 48 of the marginal programs, and reduced many others.

—Management initiatives we have already introduced, such as multi-year procurement, increased competition, and honest budgeting for inflation and we believe these will save the taxpayer over $18 billion by 1987.

—We are also cracking down on waste, fraud, and abuse by reforming our whole audit system and auditors have identified over $2.3 billion in further potential savings.

So it will take time, as well as realistic budgets, to repair the nation's defenses. But I think we're already seeing some good results and this 2-year period is a good time to review some of those very briefly.

—Production of the B–1 long range bomber is ahead of schedule and well under planned costs, as of now; the first of the new Trident submarines has joined the fleet, the second, the *Michigan*, soon will complete her sea trials and join the fleet; and improvements are under way to reduce the vulnerability of our command and control system. The MX R&D funding that was approved by the Congress and the procedures adopted for the release of additional funds can enable us, if final approval is received this year, to keep our planned IOC.

—Our military readiness has improved substantially. The number of active units that are fully or substantially combat ready has increased by 32 percent since January 1981. Training time for all units time has increased, and spare parts and maintenance

---

[92] Source: *Public Statements of Secretary of Defense Weinberger*, 1982. The press conference took place at the Pentagon beginning at 10 a.m.

[93] For a summary of the Department of Defense budget for fiscal years 1982–1986, see *New York Times*, March 5, 1981, p. A1.

[94] Regarding the Reagan administration's proposals in September 1981 for reductions in the defense budget, see *American Foreign Policy: Current Documents, 1981*, documents 42–44.

[95] Reference is to an agreement reached on May 5, 1982, between President Reagan and the Senate Budget Committee for a reduction of about $6 billion in the 1983 fiscal year defense budget, which was later increased to $7 billion.

backlogs are being reduced and, in some cases, they have been completely eliminated.

The All-Volunteer Force is one of our happiest stories, that made a dramatic turnaround in 1981; was even more successful in 1982. Last year all three Services met and exceeded their recruiting quotas for the first time since 1976. The percentage of recruits with high school diplomas is now 86 percent, up 18 percentage points from 1980. Reenlistment rates are the highest they have been since 1964.

And I would just like to add that in all of the posts that I've had the privilege of visiting the morale has been one of the happiest features of those trips—the morale I think is very high and we've had reports from three of our major Commanders that have just confirmed that saying—that in all cases they are finding morale at the highest rate that they've seen in their entire years of service in the military. Sometimes that goes back 40 years which was the Commandant of the Marine Corps report.

During the past 2 years we've made significant progress toward meeting the goals of improved readiness and long-term force modernization, at the same time controlling costs. We believe that during the next 2 years, with our program truly underway, we will see far more progress. It was particularly gratifying that the Congress, which just adjourned, enacted 96 percent of the outlays requested by the President for defense. Included in the remaining 4 percent, was a 4 percent pay cap for military and civilians, currency fluctuation adjustments, and repricing of fuel due to lower fuel costs. Shortly, the President's 1984 defense request will go to Congress, we hope it will receive at least the same support we received in 1983. To falter now would be to undo our present gains and endanger our future security.

Q. Mr. Secretary, you have stated in here that the 5-year defense program outlays have been reduced to merely $75 billion more than President Carter's. I wonder if you could ask your staff to give us some backup documentation to that contention? And then I would like to ask you a question, inasmuch as you have asserted here—

A. Do you want specifics? Because the dollars are the—

Q. I would like the figures on how you arrived at it, yes.

A. —Well, the President asked for $116 billion additions in March of 1981. And the various reductions outlined in my statements and the reductions that he accepted rather reluctantly from the Congress, totaled $41 billion. So that is the difference as of now between what was originally requested and what is now requested for the 5-year period.

Q. Do you have the figures to illustrate that point?

A. Oh, yes.

Q. No, sir, you said that this was urgent, the $116 billion was an urgent matter. Are you receding closer to the Carter program than you expected? And what does this portend?

A. Well, there are two factors that have come into it: One is that we have been able to reduce inflation far below what a lot of the people in Congress and the country felt we could do when we put in our original request. And we have repriced some of the items to reflect that reduced inflation factor which we prudently put into the budget at the beginning. We have also managed to make substantial reductions in the operations of the department, and we have, as I said, canceled some 48 programs and we have all of those listed here for those of you who would like to see them.

We are still doing the things that we think are essential to do. There is no question whatever but that we could do more. We don't know exactly how much time we have but we think it is essential to regain the strength that we need to maintain deterrence. That's essentially what we're trying to do, what we believe we have been doing.

Q. Mr. Secretary, in saying that the nation's security cannot afford further reductions, are you really talking to David Stockman or are you talking to the Congress here?

A. No, I'm giving—

Q. And how close do you expect to get to the projected $257 billion level for fiscal'83 ['*84*?]

A. Well, we are making up the budget right now, and of course, until the President has sent it to the Congress as you know from long experience there is nothing I can say about totals. What we are trying to do is to deal with these priorities that we have, increasing readiness, increasing our modernization and general strengthening that we have to do, both conventional and strategic forces. We're doing that, I think, at a rate that is consistent with the recovery in time, we hope it will be, and nobody knows what that time will be, of our deterrence strength.

We think that strength was seriously eroded in the past. We think it has to be regained as quickly as possible. And I think the program results that we have had the first 2 years and the programs we will be proposing for the next 2 years will accomplish that.

Q. If I could follow that up and just ask you if in this budget process your views on the necessity for these levels of spending are totally shared by the people responsible for the overall budget; Stockman and—

A. Well, the person responsible for the budget is the President. The programs that have been submitted and the modifications of those programs have been entirely with the knowledge, consent, approval, and at the specific direction of the President. Our future programs and activities will obviously be carried on in the same way.

Q. Mr. Secretary, I would like to ask you a two-part question about the management of the defense budget and the building. A minute ago in answering a previous question you said "we have also managed to make substantial reductions in the operation of the department." I assume you mean in the cost of the operation of the department. Your statement and all previous statements tend to talk about $18 billion and you're claiming $51 billion in management savings out 5 years, 6 years, but I've never seen a figure in which you actually can list and document already saved money in the first 2 years, that you can show that operation would have cost X but, because you changed some way of doing business, it has actually cost a certain amount less. I wonder if we could have a piece of paper that would lay that out?

A. We would be glad to do that. The cancellation of programs is one thing. You cancel a lot of programs—48 programs were canceled. Several were reduced. The original MPS program was canceled and that was close to—a little over $40 billion.

Q. But you have to net that out against whatever—program you were—

A. That's right. And the new proposal was $26 [billion]. So you can get any one of a range of numbers. The multi-year procurement has saved a great deal. It does require that you put more money in the first year in order to get the efficient rates of production. But the specific figures that I used in the statement refer to some of the audit savings, some of the ways of doing business.

Q. What I'm asking about is actually netted savings from the fiscal years you have already been through, not projections of what you hope or reform of doing business will be.

A. Well, we have of course made projections because we are operating here on 5-year plans and we have to do that. When you are talking about savings that have been made in say the first year of operations, what you are talking about really is an amalgam of things.

We came in and we felt it necessary to request about, as I recall it, about a $20 billion increase in the two budgets that we had before us: the unenacted 1981 and the Carter-proposed 1982. A large part of that was pay increases because of what we felt was an extremely low rate of pay over the years. It turned out to be a 14.3 percent pay increase over those years. Those were some of the things we increased.

We decreased many of the things that it proposed by canceling programs. We have audit savings that we've identified at $2.6 billion, things of that kind. If you would like a full list—

Q. I'd just like to see it. And can I ask you one more point here? You talk about canceling marginal programs and spending these dollars wisely. I would just like to ask you a version of a question the President was asked a month or so ago.[96] He named three weapons: the M–1 tank, the F–18, and the Maverick missile. According to your last report, those will cost $66 billion yet they are three of a number of weapons which have failed the specifications set for them by the military and at the same time way overshot the price target which the military promised Congress they would come in at.

A. Let me take them up one by one.

Q. Why are you not canceling those weapons?

A. Well, we're not canceling the M–1 tank because the M–1 tank, it certainly is incorrect to say that it has failed to meet its specifications. The M–1 tank—

[96] For this question on problems in the administration's weapons procurement programs asked at President Reagan's press conference on November 11, 1982, and the President's response, see *Weekly Compilation of Presidential Documents*, November 15, 1982, p. 1463.

Q. It's incorrect to say that, Mr. Secretary. Excuse me. The specifications were sent out by the Army, they were published, they are in congressional testimony, they are in internal Army tests; the tank does not meet them.

A. Well, the tank has had a number of tests. Bear in mind the tank has been in development 20 years, which I have criticized before as being indefensible and quite outrageous. The tank, as it is now being delivered, meets the specifications that the Army requires at this point. The tank is a far greater improvement over anything that we have been able to field. And it gives us finally, and it will when it is fully delivered, the capability of dealing with Soviet tanks, which have frankly been ahead of the tanks that we have been able to field up until the M–1.

So the M–1 tank is necessary. It was a very long time in development. Canceling it would have left us without any kind of tank that was close to the Soviet capabilities in their current tank and their projected ones, and it would have meant a number of additional years in developing a whole new one. So clearly, having sunk that amount of money and time into a tank that is now performing the way the Army feels it should perform would have been very unwise.

As far as the F–18 is concerned, again, a very long amount of time had been spent in the development of that. The overruns that had occurred, over those years of development. The F–18 meets all of its requirements except one, and that is in the attack mode—it has not attained the 575 nautical mile range if it's fully armed. There are a number of ways of dealing with that: you can put on more fuel tanks, you can arm it somewhat less heavily. The countries that have ordered it—Australia, Canada—are quite content with it. And since the publication of the test data, Spain has indicated an intention to order it.

It's a plane which the Marine Corps urgently needs, which the Navy wants and it will perform the functions that are required. There certainly needs to have—it needs to be examined and have various things discussed as to whether or not it can meet this range. You have to consider, whether that range, that 575 nautical-mile range is absolutely essential. Obviously, we would rather it would have—

Q. It seems to be you thought it was or it you wouldn't have said it and you wouldn't have held a conference—

A. As you say, obviously we'd rather it would meet that, but the failure to meet that in a first test is not a decisive or a final thing.

Q. That was its final test, not its first test. Final operational evaluation before the DSARC after 7 years of development.

A. After 7 years of development but it was not a final test with any of the modifications that are now being discussed that can enable it to reach that range.

Q. Is it range or radius?

A. It's the attack radius.

Q. Radius not the range?

A. Yes.

Q. Have you signed off on that plane yet?

A. No, we have not finished with the consideration of that plane, and there are a number of things that we want to think about it. But canceling a program in which that number of years and that amount of money has been sunk is not a very wise decision. There is always a decision when you come in—as I've said many times before—you're the prisoner of a lot of decisions that have been made many years ago. Both of these have been in development for a long time and both of them are necessary additions.

The fact that they may not have been developed as well as we would have liked over those years, the fact that there may be things that we now have to do to modify them to get them into condition are facts that we faced. But the tank is performing extremely well and I talked to many of the soldiers to whom it's been delivered and they are frankly delighted with it and delighted also with the contrast between what they have had before.

So to cancel the M–1 tank at this point would have set us back literally another at least 7 years and left us in a situation of tank inferiority that I don't think was responsible to be in.

Q. Mr. Secretary, the Maverick?

A. The Maverick?

Q. Yes.

A. Well, again, you have a situation in which you have had much higher costs than anybody would have liked built up over the past. You have a necessary addition to the forces and you have a situation in which we are trying through modifications and improvements to make it the kind of addition that we urgently need. It was not a program that I felt should be canceled based on all the factors that I have mentioned. Now, we have here 48 that we did cancel because of a whole raft of reasons. Some of those were right on the margin. Some of them had gone a long time, too. But some of them did not seem to offer the prospect of being able to deliver the kinds of things we needed consistent with our priorities.

Q. Mr. Secretary, you seem to be fairly well pleased with what Congress did to your 1983 budget.

A. Reasonably well, yes, sir.

. . . .

Q. Mr. Secretary, did you have any disappointments this year? It sounds like it's a pretty good year.

A. Well, we have a lot of things that we would have preferred gone somewhat the other way. Certainly the MX was not killed and any program that has $2.5 billion appropriated for it is not really dead. We are worried about the delay. But again, as I indicated in the statement, the procedures are there for bringing the fence down that can enable us to meet the IOC for that program and I think it's very important that we do.

. . . .

Q. Mr. Secretary, in the last several weeks there have been a number of reports about potential Soviet, new Soviet missiles that are under development[97] that apparently the administration feels may or may not be a violation of the unratified SALT agreement. Can you give us some perspective? Are the Soviets doing something that you honestly are concerned about that may be a violation? What's happening?

A. In general terms, they are doing what we knew and have talked about and have warned about for a long time, and that is they are continually developing new and improved weapons of all kinds. They have various competing design bureaus for submarines and missiles, for tanks, and they are in a continuous process of increasing and adding to modernizing, strengthening all of their weapons. And that certainly is true of missiles.

I said perhaps too many times that they have deployed the fifth generation of missiles and already have the sixth on the drawing boards. What we are not receiving reports of are various tests of these new generations of missiles; some solid fuel propellant, some different kinds of ICBM's. As you know, the SS–20 is an extremely effective intermediate range weapon. But it's a continuous process and there is nothing new or startling about it. Whether these violate the unratified SALT Treaty or not, we don't have at this point enough information that I can share with you to say.

Q. Mr. Secretary, you are suspicious that they are getting very close to that line, are you not?

A. Let me say about SALT II that it has not inhibited in any way the Soviet development or deployment of all that they have now, which is frankly one of the reasons that I am not happy with and opposed SALT II and opposed it for many years, right off since we first heard about it—about its terms. I don't know, and I would not go beyond that at this point. I don't know whether any of these new missiles that they are testing would violate its terms or not.

Q. Mr. Secretary, there is a briefing that's been prepared by an analyst in the Department of Program Analysis and Evaluation which suggests that 5-year plans have historically been underestimated due to a variety of factors, changes in the configuration of a system, perhaps optimism about learning curves and unanticipated purchases of spares and other factors.[98] And the suggestion in this presentation is that this is a deeply entrenched problem which will afflict your 5-year plan also. Have you heard this presentation? Do you intend to hear this presentation? If you've heard it, can you comment on it?

A. Oh, I'm familiar with it, yes. I'm also familiar with the statements made by the

[97] In response to a report in the *Washington Post,* December 4, 1982, p. A3, Department of State Acting Spokesman Alan Romberg read a statement at the Department of State Daily Press Briefing on December 6, which said in part: "It is our general practice not to comment on the substance of confidential, diplomatic exchanges. But I can confirm the Soviet Union recently did inform the United States it had tested a new type of ICBM. And in doing so, the Soviets told us that this is their one new type ICBM permitted by the unratified SALT II Agreement." (Office of Press Relations, Department of State)

[98] Reference is to a report prepared by Franklin C. Spinney, analyst in the Office of Program Analysis and Evaluation, Department of Defense, which was summarized in *Wall Street Journal,* December 7, 1982, p. 3.

superior officer of the person who worked on that report and he pointed out quite correctly that this was a historical review and that the comments made related to the past, not the present, and pointed up some lessons which we hope and believe we have learned.

Q. Does this mean you have heard the presentation yourself?

A. I have been advised and am generally familiar with its terms, yes.

. . . .

Chapter 4. Arms Control

Document 41

Transcript of an Interview With the Secretary of State (Haig), March 5, 1982 (Extracts)[1]

Controlling Factors in the Preparation of the U.S. Position for the START Talks

. . . .

MR. OSTER. Mr. Secretary, I think we're all going to want to get back to Central America and the Caribbean Basin,[2] but I'd like to see if I could ask you to bring us up-to-date on what is happening on the arms talks, particularly the START talks. When we last left them, everyone had anticipated that we might get a date announced when you met with Mr. Gromyko in Geneva.[3] Because of Poland, that was not possible. And we were looking for what was last described as your looking for an improvement in the overall East–West situation, not directly involving Poland, but arms control, a role in it. I wonder if you can tell me when you anticipate that we will get started with the START talks, and if you have seen anything in the Soviet behavior that gives you hope that you will get these things started in short order?

SECRETARY HAIG. First, with respect to the U.S. position, which will be a controlling factor, we are, as I said on the Hill this week,[4] weeks rather than months away from the completion of our work. Some tend to complain about the length of time it has taken; but I know of no thread of the President's policy that is more important to him personally than to succeed in the arms control area in order to achieve substantial reductions. He has been dedicated to the proposition that we could not risk again the development of a draft agreement that would not elicit the necessary consensus here at home for its ratification. Therefore, we have been in a very detailed, methodical, interdepartmental exercise of trying to avoid either anomalies or deficiencies in our approach which could contribute to failure.

On the question of precise timing, I think the President is assessing the international situation very carefully day by day as well as the progress we are making in our interdepartmental efforts to finalize for a going-in position, and I just don't want to make any predictions.

MR. OSTER. Is it likely there is something you want to happen before he goes to Europe to the economic summit that you want to be able to say that the talks will begin before June 4, at least announce they will begin at some time after that?

SECRETARY HAIG. It depends on a number of uncertainties, and I don't want to prejudge that.

MR. OSTER. On that interdepartmental effort, Gene Rostow told us the first time on background, and then later he decided to make it public,[5] that the administration was within about 2 or 3 weeks of coming up with a new formulation for measuring strategic weapons; and rather than using exclusively launchers as the Carter administration had done, that what was under consideration was some formulation that would take into account explosive power of Soviet and U.S. nuclear weapons, perhaps in megatons, perhaps throw-weight—this sort of thing has been mentioned by others before. I wonder if you can tell me where that formulation stands now and how you stand on it?

SECRETARY HAIG. Well, there are a number of factors that must go into the meas-

---

[1] Source: Department of State files. Secretary Haig was questioned during a luncheon interview by Henry Trewitt of the *Baltimore Sun*, Patrick R. Oster of the *Chicago Sun-Times*, and James McCartney of Knight-Ridder Newspapers.

[2] Documentation on the Caribbean Basin Initiative is in Chapter 15, Part C.

[3] Regarding the Haig–Gromyko meeting in Geneva, January 26, see document 252.

[4] In testimony before the House Foreign Affairs Committee, March 2, Secretary Haig remarked that the preparatory work was "a matter of weeks, not months before it is concluded. . . ." See *East–West Relations—U.S. Security Assistance: Hearing Before the Committee on Foreign Affairs, House of Representatives, Ninety-seventh Congress, Second Session* (Washington, 1982), p. 12.

[5] Not further identified.

urement equation: warheads, missiles, growth potential in numbers of warheads; the yield, the throw-weight—the best mix and proportionality of mix—are still under review. There is a weight factor. Weight for various criteria is still under review.

MR. OSTER. Do you agree with Mr. Rostow's time frame where he said a week ago that [it will be?] 2 weeks from now until the administration is agreed to what it wants to do in the way of a new measurement formula?

SECRETARY HAIG. Well, I say that figure is right in the ballpark. I don't mean by that that it will necessarily happen that way; but I think that that is a very sound estimate.

MR. MCCARTNEY. May I ask a question about that? There was a story in the *New York Times* last Sunday that had some figures about the number of nuclear warheads, new nuclear warheads the administration planned to build, and the figure was about 17,000 above the present level.[6] Is that an accurate figure?

SECRETARY HAIG. I haven't seen the arithmetic on that, in a specific way. I think we know what we're building, and we know that it is urgently needed to close the gap which is increasing. If we don't close it, it will result in substantial Soviet superiority.

MR. MCCARTNEY. Not in warheads, certainly, as you're aware.

SECRETARY HAIG. Potentially as well in warheads—potentially.

[Inaudible]

MR. MCCARTNEY. Well, is our objective equality in warheads with the Soviets or to get ahead of them?

SECRETARY HAIG. No.

MR. OSTER. You're talking about the projections that they might jump ahead of us by about 1985. How can you do it?

SECRETARY HAIG. Well, it gets into the question of throw-weight and fractionalization and the potential for greater fractionalization—the huge thrust capacities of the –18's and –19's.

MR. OSTER. What I find fascinating is we're thinking of a new formulation or something that basically says we can't do another Vladivostok.[7] It's what we do on verification. A number of people in the administration have said that we are approaching the limits of the use of national technical means to verify even launchers because of the increasing mobile nuclear missiles by the Soviets. What you get into, of course, is the possibility that we might need on-site inspection and I think Mr. Rostow, in congressional hearings last November,[8] even raised the specter that we might ask for television monitors in Soviet manufacturing facilities, which seems, given the past Soviet track record on those sort of verification measures, a very unrealistic picture of what we might do.

And I'm wondering if you agree that this is going to be something that, No. 1, is necessary, and, No. 2, we really realistically have a chance of achieving from the Soviets?

SECRETARY HAIG. Well, I think verification is a very key aspect of the kind of mutual confidence that partners to negotiations must have in whatever agreement emerges.

It becomes especially important as we begin to see worrisome indications of it in less than strict adherence to international understanding by the Soviet Union since it's a question of yellow rain.

On the other hand, any rigid formulas for accomplishing acceptable confidence should await a very careful analysis of the final going-in position of the United States, and the kind of verification measures that are necessary to provide that confidence. But I don't think we enter into that and I don't think the President enters into any preconceived notions other than to be absolutely sure that any reasonable—even a worst-case analysis—is dealt with effectively.

MR. OSTER. Well, the reason why I bring that up is that there is, obviously, if you decide that you need verification of the nature that is unacceptable to the Soviets, what you wind up with is no arms control because you obviously are not going to accept an agreement you can't verify; and then what you wind up with is an arms race.

SECRETARY HAIG. Well, I mean you can build those theoretical boobytraps in al-

---

[6] See *New York Times*, February 28, 1982, pp. I1, I17.

[7] Reference is to the U.S.-Soviet agreement on a framework for offensive strategic arms reached at Vladivostok in November 1974. For the text of the joint statement and communiqué, see *Documents on Disarmament*, 1974 (Washington, 1976), pp. 746–750.

[8] See Rostow's statement in *Review of Administration Initiatives on Strategic, Theater, and Conventional Arms Control: Briefing of the Subcommittee on International Security and Scientific Affairs of the Committee on Foreign Affairs, House of Representatives, Ninety-seventh Congress, First Session* (Washington, 1982), p. 9.

most any process which is dynamic and is as complex as this one, and I think it's dangerous to do that.

But the simple answer to your question is: What is worse—an arms race, or an agreement in which no one has any confidence and is not going to stop the arms race in any event, and which will not be ratified, approved and binding on the parties?

And that answer that I'm giving you shouldn't be a value judgment on the issue rather than the broad observations I just gave you.

. . . .

MR. MCCARTNEY. Well now, then the critical question—at least to me: If you go back to the beginnings of these talks with the Russians and the numbers are escalated on both sides dramatically—and they keep going up; everybody is trying to get themselves in a better negotiating position, and so we can all kill each other many times more than when the talks started—how do you stop that?

SECRETARY HAIG. I think that's the precise question that the President feels so strongly about. He wants substantial reductions.

One of the great criticisms of SALT II was that while it accomplished some limitations in a number of areas of the weapons growth, it also provided freeways for future growth.

Then you get into the philosophy of how to go about the problem. In some instances, a very persuasive case can be made to seek such comprehensive limitations that that danger does not ensue. For others it says: there's much compelling logic to suggest that given the complexity of that task, it's better to at least get limitation in certain areas and then in turn try to deal with the others as confidence is built. Who knows?

Document 42

Transcript of the Department of State Daily Press Briefing, March 11, 1982 (Extract)[9]

Administration Reaction to the Nuclear Weapons Freeze Movement

MR. BURT. . . . As Dean said, I would like to make a brief statement on the nuclear freeze resolution which was introduced in the Senate yesterday.[10]

The President and his entire administration share the concern felt throughout the world over the danger that nuclear weapons pose for mankind. That is why in his speech of November 18th[11] the President proposed a far-reaching arms control program for seeking equitable and verifiable agreements which will not just freeze current nuclear and conventional forces but actually significantly reduce them.

In Geneva, the United States is now negotiating with the Soviet Union on the basis of the President's bold proposal of November 18th, which calls for the elimination of the Soviet nuclear systems, most threatening Europe, in exchange for cancellation of scheduled NATO deployments of comparable intermediate-range land-based nuclear missiles.

While we understand the spirit that motivates the freeze effort, the administration cannot support the freeze itself. A number of compelling facts argue against a freeze. It would freeze the United States

---

[9] Source: Office of Press Relations, Department of State. Richard R. Burt, Director, Bureau of Politico-Military Affairs, Department of State, conducted this portion of the briefing which began at 12:35 p.m. He was introduced by Dean Fischer, Department of State Spokesman. Burt's opening statement was also printed in Department of State *Bulletin*, May 1982. p. 42.

[10] Reference is to Senate Joint Resolution 163, introduced by Senator Kennedy, Senator Hatfield, and other Senators on March 10, which called for immediate negotiations with the Soviet Union on a mutual and verifiable freeze on the testing, production, and further deployment of nuclear weapons. For text, see *Nuclear Arms Reduction Proposals: Hearings Before the Committee on Foreign Relations, United States Senate, Ninety-seventh Congress, Second Session* (Washington, 1982), pp. 4–5.

[11] For the text of President Reagan's speech on arms control, November 18, 1981, see *American Foreign Policy: Current Documents, 1981*, document 60.

into a position of military disadvantage and dangerous vulnerability.

Soviet defense investments have far outpaced ours over the last decade. While we exercise substantial restraint, the Soviets' across-the-board modernization efforts have produced new weapons, including new generations of intercontinental ballistic missiles directly threatening our nuclear deterrent.

In Europe, Soviet deployments of new intermediate-range missiles have given the Soviet Union an overwhelming advantage over the West in this category of weapons.

As I noted, we want verifiable agreements that go beyond freezes to produce real reductions. The freeze proposal, which we don't believe is verifiable, nor, of course, would it reduce weapons, is not only bad defense but as Secretary of State Haig said yesterday,[12] it is also bad arms control.

The President needs the strategic modernization program if we are to have a credible chance to negotiate a good strategic arms reductions agreement with the Soviet Union. The freeze would, of course, kill the modernization program and with it our chances for achieving the reductions that we all seek.

Finally, as I have noted, we have embarked on a very important negotiation on intermediate-range nuclear weapons with the Soviet Union in Geneva. Thus, the United States and the NATO Alliance must have the flexibility to continue with the two-track approach that NATO agreed to in 1979.[13]

The freeze proposal would concede to the Soviet Union its present advantage in intermediate-range nuclear missiles and thus eliminate any Soviet incentive to reach a fair and balanced agreement that would reduce nuclear weapons in Europe.

I will be happy to respond to any questions you might have.

Q. Was there any consultation with Senator Kennedy and others who sponsored this prior to their doing it?

A. I do know that Senator Kennedy, as Secretary of State Haig said yesterday, was in touch with the Secretary of State prior to his introduction of the proposal yesterday.

Q. But not before that?

A. As far as I know, no.

Q. How do you account, then, for—I mean, you've made the point here several times that such a freeze would put the United States at a considerable disadvantage. How do you account for intelligent senators putting forward a proposal that would—

A. What I account for is the fact that the people who support the freeze share our desire to reduce the threat of nuclear war and to reduce existing nuclear stockpiles. I think we don't disagree at all with that objective.

In fact, President Reagan has strongly supported that objective not only in rhetoric but in practice. Our proposal in Geneva is designed to go beyond a freeze. It's designed to reduce to zero the most threatening weapons deployed against Europe today.

So our disagreement is not one of strategy or objectives; it's really one of tactics—what's the most effective way to stop or curb the nuclear weapons competition.

Q. Mr. Burt, a member of the Soviet delegation, diplomatic delegation here recently told me that we are really not serious there in Geneva, that various proposals have been put forward that we have not picked up on and that it was his view and of his colleagues that our position was that the Pershings were so much better than their various SS weapons that—that's what we're going after—superiority.

A. I would just say several things. Right now, in Europe, the Soviets have anywhere from a 3-to-1 to a 6-to-1 advantage in nuclear weapons. The Soviets right now have 288 SS–20 missiles. Each one of those missiles have three warheads targeted against, or could be used against targets in Europe. We have zero long-range land-base missiles. And to argue that somehow the Pershing would be more superior—first of all, I have to take into account the SS–20 is undergoing deployment right now, the Pershing isn't undergoing deployment.

The Pershing is a single warhead missile; the SS–20 has three warheads. So you just

---

[12] Secretary Haig made this statement in testimony before a subcommittee of the Senate Appropriations Committee, March 10. See *Foreign Assistance and Related Programs Appropriations for Fiscal Year 1983: Hearings Before a Subcommittee of the Committee on Appropriations, United States Senate, Ninety-seventh Congress, Second Session* (Washington, 1983), Part I, p. 64.

[13] Reference is to the communiqués issued by the special meeting of the NATO Foreign and Defense Ministers, December 12, 1979, and the meeting of the NATO Foreign Ministers, December 14, 1979. For texts, see *American Foreign Policy: Basic Documents, 1977–1980*, pp. 494–499.

simply cannot argue that there is anything approaching a balance in this category of weapons.

Secondly, as for being serious, we are completely serious. I would simply ask you, what side has laid down a treaty in Geneva? A treaty that we would be willing to sign very quickly if the Soviets would agree to it? That's, I think, a demonstration of how serious we are.

Q. One point. When John and I and some of us were over in Europe late last year, we were told that site preparations for the installation for the Pershings had begun.

A. That's precisely our point. If we want to negotiate freezes or real reductions, we have to give the Soviets incentives to negotiate.

Let me give you a little history here. After the Alliance, in December 1979, agreed to the so-called two-track decision, both to seek an arms control agreement and to deploy these new systems, the Soviets dragged their heels for almost a year before entering into negotiations because they believed that they could scuttle or derail that two-track decision.

It is only the unity of the Atlantic Alliance in moving ahead with these deployments that gives the Soviets the incentives to negotiate seriously, and that's the problem with this freeze proposal. The freeze proposal is essentially the Brezhnev proposal in Geneva.[14] They would like very much to freeze the current inequality in nuclear systems in Europe, and that's unacceptable.

Q. How do you account for the fact that somebody like former Vice President Mondale, who is certainly privy to practically all of the information that you have, has endorsed this?

A. I can't account for it. All I can simply say is that we share the objectives of Vice President Mondale and others to limit and curtail nuclear weapons competition. As I said before, we disagree on what is the most effective way to do it.

Q. Can you tell us, are you making any real progress at Geneva and, if so, how?

A. I think it's fair to say that we are because, as I said, we have gone now to great trouble to detail our proposal. The Soviets are asking us questions, detailed questions about our proposal. We are explaining it to them, and certainly that is the first step that has to take place in any negotiation. The two sides have to understand each other's position, and that process is underway.

It is just simply too soon to say whether this progress will result in an agreement in the near future. It's important now, I think, that the two sides understand each other's position, and explain those positions. That understanding is a prerequisite to further progress.

Q. Have the Soviets in Geneva gone beyond what they have said publicly about the one-third cutbacks and two-third cutbacks and freezes? Have they made any proposals in Geneva that you consider constructive?

A. They have made several different proposals. They have made most of those proposals in public. Basically, their proposals so far are designed to allow them to continue to maintain their superiority in SS–20's and other intermediate-range missiles and would deny the United States the ability to deploy any offsetting systems.

That's the theme of all their proposals. They are still trying to derail the decision taken in 1979 by the Alliance.

Q. How would this freeze proposal affect your preparations for the START talks?

A. Most importantly, Bernie, it would affect it by denying us the leverage we think we need to accomplish real reductions in arms control.

One of the principal problems with the SALT II Treaty[15] was that it would have provided for a substantial buildup of Soviet strategic capabilities through 1985. We want a reduction. And experience has demonstrated to us that the Soviets must have incentives to agree to reductions.

I'll just give you another historical example. Our ability to complete the ABM Treaty in 1972,[16] I think, was closely linked to the fact that the United States was moving ahead with its own ABM program. The Soviets thus concluded that it was in their interest, given the U.S. program, to reach an agreement.

We think the President's strategic modernization program is indispensable to

[14] The so-called Brezhnev proposal was the Soviet proposal for a qualitative and quantitative freeze on both sides' medium-range weapons in Europe during the arms control talks.

[15] For the text of the SALT II treaty (1979), see Department of State *Bulletin*, July 1979, pp. 23–47.

[16] For text, see 23 UST 3435.

achieving real reductions at the START negotiations.

Q. Do you think this freeze proposal stems from general frustration not only among Democrats but among large sectors of the public about the lack of progress, both at Geneva, and the lack of any start to the START talks?

A. No. I think that's too shortsighted. I think there is frustration. I don't think it's frustration directed against the Reagan administration in its arms control policies because, as I pointed out, the President, in his November 18th speech, I think, outlined one of the most ambitious and farsighted arms control agenda in many, many years.

What I think it reflects is a broader frustration with the continuing nuclear competition. A competition that we know has been going on for decades. We share that frustration, and this is one reason why we are taking new bold approaches to the problem of curbing arms.

Q. Can you tell us anything more today about the timetable for opening the START talks?

A. I don't want to say this, because others have addressed it, other than to simply say we are completing our analytical work so that we will be ready to negotiate sometime soon.

Q. Rick, paraphrasing one of your statements there, are you now saying that on the entire strategic picture, worldwide, that the United States is now, today, in a state of nuclear inferiority?

A. I did not say that. I did say that we felt that in certain important areas we are in a position of military disadvantage. And I would particularly focus it in two areas where we are concerned. One is land-based intercontinental ballistic missiles where the Soviet Union is achieving the capability to destroy a large fraction of our land-base missile force and the balance, and more realistically, more precisely the imbalance in intermediate-range nuclear capabilities where the Soviet Union continues to deploy SS–20 missiles at the rate of about one new missile every 5 days and the United States and its Allies, of course, have not yet begun to deploy any new offsetting systems.

Q. Are the START talks dependent to any degree upon progress in Geneva now?

A. No, we don't want to link the two. They are analytically linked in that we have said that any limits on any intermediate-range systems would, at some stage, be linked, or should be linked to strategic arms control, but we certainly do not want to let progress in the Geneva talks be driven by what we do at START.

Q. What happened about Poland? The Secretary made it quite clear in Geneva that there would not be a start to START until the situation changed considerably.[17]

A. That's not exactly what he said, John. What he said was events like Poland threaten to erode the political confidence that is necessary to proceed with effective arms control.

We are watching the situation in Poland carefully, and that will be one factor that we will want to analyze in looking at the question of initiating the START process. And I don't want to say anything beyond that.

Q. He went beyond simply saying that the environment would have to change. He linked it directly to changes inside Poland.

A. I don't want to argue about it.

. . . .

Document 43

Transcript of an Interview With Senator Edward M. Kennedy, April 18, 1982 (Extracts)[18]

"We Should Put in Place Now a Freeze That Would Be Negotiated, That Would Be Verifiable . . . , and Then Move Towards . . . Serious Reductions in the Nuclear Arms Stockpile"

MR. KALB. Our guest today on "Meet the Press" is Senator Edward Kennedy, Demo-

[17] Regarding Secretary Haig's remarks in Geneva, January 26, on the relationship between the situation in Poland and the beginning of the START negotiations, see document 252.

[18] Source: NBC News. Senator Kennedy was interviewed in Washington on the NBC television program, "Meet the Press," by Marvin Kalb and John Dancy of NBC News, David Broder of the *Washington Post*, and John Mashek of *U.S. News and World Report.*

crat of Massachusetts. Now in his 20th year in the U.S. Senate, he is the senior Democrat on the Labor and Human Resources Committee. Senator Kennedy is cosponsor of a controversial resolution calling for a global freeze on U.S. and Soviet nuclear arsenals.[19]

Senator, as you know, today begins a kind of nationwide, week-long seminar pointing out to the American people the dangers of nuclear war,[20] and perhaps in anticipation of that, President Reagan said yesterday, "To those who protest against nuclear war, I can only say I'm with you."[21] Do you take the President at his word?

SENATOR KENNEDY. Well, I've never questioned the motivation of the President of the United States, nor, really, any public official, although I do take strong issues with the policies of this administration in the area of the nuclear arms race. Basically, I don't believe that there is an arms control policy. There's an arms policy, there's a military policy, there's a national security policy, but there's not an arms control policy.

MR. KALB. What are the basic issues, the differences on issues, between you and the President on this?

SENATOR KENNEDY. Well, the basic difference between the administration and Senator Warner and Senator Jackson[22] and myself and Senator Hatfield is this: We believe that the United States, having 9,000 nuclear warheads, the Soviet Union 7,000, that each of us have [*has*] the capability to destroy each other. Effectively, what we have is substantial equivalency. And since we have substantial equivalency with the Soviet Union, we should put in place now a freeze that would be negotiated, that would be verifiable by the United States, as well as the Soviet Union, and then move toward the longer kind of negotiation, toward serious reductions in the nuclear arms stockpile of both nations.

The administration believes that we have to build more now, so that we can reduce later. That doesn't make any common sense, I don't think it makes any arms control sense, and it is what I have stated to be basically voodoo arms control.

MR. KALB. Senator, do you feel that this issue, which is certainly a popular one, will be important in the elections in 1982 and perhaps in 1984, as well?

SENATOR KENNEDY. Well, very definitely, it will be an issue. There's a grassroots movement across this country that feels very strongly about it, and there are a number of leaders in the Congress of the United States, Congressman Markey, Congressman Conti [*Conte*], Congressman Bingham, the other over 160 members of the—members of Congress, as well as Senators—Senator Hatfield and myself feel strongly about this.

It will be an issue. Hopefully, it's not a partisan issue, because I don't think the issue of survivability on this planet is a partisan issue, but they are going to hold the representatives accountable to their positions on this issue.

. . . .

MR. BRODER. Senator, what gets frozen in a freeze? Specifically, if this goes into effect, do we fire our weapons specialists, the people who design airplanes and submarines, the teams that are working on Cruise missiles and the Stealth bomber? Do the Russians have to fire their comparable specialists?

SENATOR KENNEDY. Well, basically, what we are talking about is putting into place a freeze now in all strategic nuclear weapons. Also, it would include tactical nuclear weapons. It covers all testing, production, and deployment. I believe that the best possibility for verification exists now in verifying the existing systems, rather than building and then moving to a freeze, as the President suggests, and trying to verify more complicated nuclear systems.

MR. BRODER. Do we fire the kind of people that I mentioned in the question?

SENATOR KENNEDY. I don't think it's a question of firing those individuals. I suppose the real question is the verification.

---

19 Regarding this resolution, see footnote 10 above.

20 Reference is to Ground Zero Week, April 18–24, nonpartisan national campaign to educate the public on the dangers of nuclear war. For the primer published in connection with this movement, see *Nuclear War: What's In It For You?* (New York, 1982), attributed to "Ground Zero" but actually written by Roger and Earl Molander.

21 The quotation is from President Reagan's radio address to the nation, April 17. For text, see *Weekly Compilation of Presidential Documents*, April 26, 1982, pp. 503–504.

22 For the text of Senate Joint Resolution 177 introduced by Senators Jackson, Warner, and many other Senators on March 30, which called for a long term (rather than immediate) nuclear weapons freeze at equal and sharply reduced levels, see *Nuclear Arms Reduction Proposals*, pp. 8–10.

This freeze is offered not because we like the Russians, nor because we trust the Russians, nor because we approve of their policies in different parts of the world. We offer this proposal because we believe that it's in the national security interest of the United States, and because we also believe that the Soviet Union will act in its national security interests, as they did at the time when we saw them sign the Test Ban Treaty, or the ABM Treaty, or even the early Assault [*SALT*] Agreements.[23] And so we believe that we ought to challenge the Soviet Union to do so.

The question about who's going to be employed or who's not going to be employed is not the issue.

MR. BRODER. Many of the defense specialists with whom I've talked say the test of the political honesty of a freeze advocate is this question: Does he know and will he tell the American people that the cost of maintaining a conventional, nonnuclear deterrent in Europe and around the world is going to be higher than the cost of a nuclear deterrent. Do you accept that?

SENATOR KENNEDY. I have no hesitancy whatsoever in saying that we have to increase our conventional force. I support a basic increase of 5 percent in real growth, and I would think that we would have to do a review or a study in terms of conventional force, as they exist around the world, but I have no hesitancy about that.

MR. KALB. Mr. Mashek?

SENATOR KENNEDY. They also ought to point out that the best estimate under our freeze is that we'll save $100 billion over the period of the next 5 years. We expend about $37 billion in strategic arms. If we're able to freeze, we save $100 billion in 5 years. If we're able to make further progress in the area of strategic weapons, we'll see further savings, and hopefully, Mr. Broder, that we will create the kind of climate and atmosphere where we can see a real reduction in the conventional force. That would certainly be a hope as well, once this process begins.

. . . .

MR. DANCY. Senator, if I could go back to the nuclear freeze for just a moment, one of the central questions, as you say, and a question which has been pretty much glossed over in talking about this is verification. How are you going to make sure the Soviets aren't cheating on a freeze?

SENATOR KENNEDY. Well, the same way that we were going to have some verification with regard to SALT II and that we currently have verification of the—now the agreements that have been placed between the Soviet Union and the United States in the past.

Let me point this—make this point. The administration accepts the concept of freeze, since they have indicated that they would support the Warner–Jackson proposal, which is build now, reduce and then freeze, so they accept the concept that they will be able to verify in a more complicated situation than we have at the present time.

MR. DANCY. But, Senator—

SENATOR KENNEDY. And the arms control experts that I have talked to and who have appeared before congressional committees say that the easiest aspect for verification is the existing system, easier than it would be in SALT II, and certainly easier than moving towards much more sophisticated weapons, as the Reagan administration would want to move to.

MR. DANCY. But, Senator, isn't verification going to depend on getting somebody on site to inspect, and not simply depending on satellite pictures and seismic monitor—

SENATOR KENNEDY. It would with regard—not with regards to testing and deployment, but it would with regards to production.

Now, I sat through negotiations that were taking place under the previous administration in Geneva on the comprehensive test ban, and during those negotiations, the issue of on-site inspection was not a block with the Soviet Union. They had agreed in principle to on-site inspection.

Now, I agree that that would have to be something that would be negotiated, but I do think that the lesson that we found from the negotiation at the comprehensive test ban is at least some indication that it may very well be possible.

MR. DANCY. But, Senator, doesn't that ask the Soviets not only to open up their society, but to open up their military to a degree which would be absolutely unprecedented?

---

[23] For the text of the Test Ban Treaty (1963), see 14 UST 1313; for the Anti-ballistic Missile Treaty (1972), see 23 UST 3435; for the SALT I Treaty (1972), see 23 UST 3462.

SENATOR KENNEDY. Well, the question is—there's no question with regards to production as one of the most complicated aspects. There's no question on that. That would have to be the result of hard negotiation. But the alternative—the alternative is an unlimited piling of nuclear weapon upon nuclear weapon, which every child would understand, as you build the building blocks, we'd see the falling of these weapons systems and the possibility of nuclear annihilation and destruction.

And I refuse to believe—I refuse to believe that we cannot work out some procedure or process which can reduce that possibility.

MR. DANCY. In other words, you believe the Soviets would agree to on-site inspection?

SENATOR KENNEDY. I think we ought to challenge them. I can't give you an answer on this program. What I can say is that the Soviets agreed in principle to the on-site inspection for comprehensive test ban.

I do believe that you put your finger on one of the difficult questions and challenges that will always be there at a time when we're going to verify any freeze—that suggested by the administration, or suggested by Senators Jackson and Warner, or suggested by ourselves—on the issue of production, but I think we ought to challenge the Soviet Union to try and work out a process and procedure for doing that. And I refuse to be put in a position, until we have tried to work that out as a result of negotiation, to step back from our proposal.

. . . .

Document 44

Commencement Address by President Reagan at Eureka College, Eureka, Illinois, May 9, 1982 (Extract)[24]

A Five-Point Program for Peace With the Soviet Union

. . . .

Graduation Day is called "Commencement" and properly so because it is both a recognition of completion and a beginning. And I would like, seriously, to talk to you about this new phase—the society in which you're now going to take your place as full-time participants. You're no longer observers. You will be called upon to make decisions and express your views on global events because those events will affect your lives.

I've spoken of similarities, and the 1980's like the 1930's may be one of those—a crucial juncture in history that will determine the direction of the future.

In about a month I will meet in Europe with the leaders of nations who are our closest friends and allies. At Versailles, leaders of the industrial powers of the world will seek better ways to meet today's economic challenges. In Bonn, I will join my colleagues from the Atlantic Alliance nations to renew those ties which have been the foundation of Western, free-world defense for 37 years. There will also be meetings in Rome and London.

Now, these meetings are significant for a simple but very important reason. Our own nation's fate is directly linked to that of our sister democracies in Western Europe. The values for which America and all democratic nations stand represent the culmination of Western culture. Andrei Sakharov, the distinguished Nobel Laureate and courageous Soviet human rights advocate, has written in a message smuggled to freedom, "I believe in Western man. I have faith in his mind which is practical and efficient and, at the same time, aspires to great goals. I have faith in his good intentions and in his decisiveness."

This glorious tradition requires a partnership to preserve and protect it. Only as partners can we hope to achieve the goal of a peaceful community of nations. Only as partners can we defend the values of democracy and human dignity that we hold so dear.

There is a single, major issue in our partnership which will underlie the discussions that I will have with the European leaders: The future of Western relations with the Soviet Union. How should we deal with the Soviet Union in the years ahead? What frame-work should guide our conduct and our policies toward it? And what can we realistically expect from a world power of

---

[24] Source: White House Press Release, May 9, 1982, Office of the Press Secretary to the President; printed also in *Weekly Compilation of Presidential Documents*, May 17, 1982, pp. 599–604.

such deep fears, hostilities, and external ambitions?

I believe the unity of the West is the foundation for any successful relationship with the East. Without Western unity, we'll squander our energies in bickering while the Soviets continue as they please. With unity, we have the strength to moderate Soviet behavior. We've done so in the past and we can do so again.

Our challenge is to establish a framework in which sound East–West relations will endure. I'm optimistic that we can build a more constructive relationship with the Soviet Union. To do so, however, we must understand the nature of the Soviet system and the lessons of the past.

The Soviet Union is a huge empire ruled by an elite that holds all power and all privilege. They hold it tightly because, as we've seen in Poland, they fear what might happen if even the smallest amount of control slips from their grasp. They fear the infectiousness of even a little freedom and because of this in many ways their system has failed. The Soviet empire is faltering because it is rigid—centralized control has destroyed incentives for innovation, efficiency and individual achievement. Spiritually, there is a sense of malaise and resentment.

But in the midst of social and economic problems, the Soviet dictatorship has forged the largest armed force in the world. It has done so by preempting the human needs of its people, and, in the end, this course will undermine the foundations of the Soviet system. Harry Truman was right when he said of the Soviets that, "When you try to conquer other people or extend yourself over vast areas you cannot win in the long run."

Yet Soviet aggressiveness has grown as Soviet military power has increased. To compensate, we must learn from the lessons of the past. When the West has stood unified and firm, the Soviet Union has taken heed. For 35 years Western Europe has lived free despite the shadow of Soviet military might. Through unity, you'll remember from your modern history courses, the West secured the withdrawal of occupation forces from Austria and the recognition of its rights in Berlin.

Other Western policies have not been successful. East–West trade was expanded in the hope of providing incentives for Soviet restraint, but the Soviets exploited the benefits of trade without moderating their behavior. Despite a decade of ambitious arms control efforts, the Soviet buildup continues. And despite its signature of the Helsinki agreements on human rights, the Soviet Union has not relaxed its hold on its own people or those of Western[25] Europe.

During the 1970's some of us forgot the warning of President Kennedy who said that the Soviets "have offered to trade us an apple for an orchard. We don't do that in this country." But we came perilously close to doing just that.

If East–West relations in the détente era in Europe have yielded disappointment, détente outside of Europe has yielded a severe disillusionment for those who expected a moderation of Soviet behavior. The Soviet Union continues to support Vietnam in its occupation of Kampuchea and its massive military presence in Laos. It is engaged in a war of aggression against Afghanistan. Soviet proxy forces have brought instability and conflict to Africa and Central America.

We are now approaching an extremely important phase in East–West relations as the current Soviet leadership is succeeded by a new generation. Both the current and the new Soviet leadership should realize aggressive policies will meet a firm Western response. On the other hand, a Soviet leadership devoted to improving its people's lives, rather than expanding its armed conquests, will find a sympathetic partner in the West. The West will respond with expanded trade and other forms of cooperation. But all of this depends on Soviet actions. Standing in the Athenian marketplace 2,000 years ago, Demosthenes said: "What sane man would let another man's words rather than his deeds proclaim who is at peace and who is at war with him?"

Peace is not the absence of conflict, but the ability to cope with conflict by peaceful means. I believe we can cope. I believe that the West can fashion a realistic, durable policy that will protect our interests and keep the peace, not just for this generation, but for your children and your grandchildren. (Applause)

I believe such a policy consists of five points: military balance, economic security, regional stability, arms reductions, and dialogue. Now, these are the means by which we can seek peace with the Soviet Union in the years ahead. Today, I want to set this

---

[25] Eastern. [Footnote correction in the source text.]

five-point program to guide the future of our East–West relations, set it out for all to hear and see.

First, a sound East–West military balance is absolutely essential. Last week NATO published a comprehensive comparison of its forces with those of the Warsaw Pact.[26] Its message is clear: During the past decade, the Soviet Union has built up its forces across the board. During that same period, the defense expenditures of the United States declined in real terms. The United States has already undertaken steps to recover from that decade of neglect. And I should add that the expenditures of our European allies have increased slowly but steadily, something we often fail to recognize here at home.

The second point on which we must reach consensus with our allies deals with economic security. Consultations are under way among Western nations on the transfer of militarily significant technology and the extension of financial credits to the East as well as on the question of energy dependence on the East, that energy dependence of Europe. We recognize that some of our allies' economic requirements are distinct from our own. But the Soviets must not have access to Western technology with military applications, and we must not subsidize the Soviet economy. The Soviet Union must make the difficult choices brought on by its military budgets and economic shortcomings.

The third element is regional stability with peaceful change. Last year in a speech in Philadelphia and in the summit meetings at Cancun,[27] I outlined the basic American plan to assist the developing world. These principles for economic development remain the foundation of our approach. They represent no threat to the Soviet Union. Yet in many areas of the developing world we find that Soviet arms and Soviet-supported troops are attempting to destabilize societies and extend Moscow's influence.

High on our agenda must be progress toward peace in Afghanistan. The United States is prepared to engage in a serious effort to negotiate an end to the conflict caused by the Soviet invasion of that country. We are ready to cooperate in an international effort to resolve this problem, to secure a full Soviet withdrawal from Afghanistan, and to ensure self-determination for the Afghan people.

In southern Africa, working closely with our Western allies and the African states, we've made real progress toward independence for Namibia. These negotiations, if successful, will result in peaceful and secure conditions throughout southern Africa. The simultaneous withdrawal of Cuban forces from Angola is essential to achieving Namibian independence, as well as creating long-range prospects for peace in the region.

Central America also has become a dangerous point of tension in East–West relations. The Soviet Union cannot escape responsibility for the violence and suffering in the region caused by its support for Cuban activities in Central America and its accelerated transfer of advanced military equipment to Cuba.

However, it was in Western Europe—or Eastern Europe, I should say—that the hopes of the 1970's were greatest, and it is there that they have been the most bitterly disappointed. There was hope that the people of Poland could develop a freer society. But the Soviet Union has refused to allow the people of Poland to decide their own fate, just as it refused to allow the people of Hungary to decide theirs in 1956, or the people of Czechoslovakia in 1968.

If martial law in Poland is lifted, if all the political prisoners are released, and if a dialogue is restored with the Solidarity Union, the United States is prepared to join in a program of economic support. Water cannons and clubs against the Polish people are hardly the kind of dialogue that gives us hope. It is up to the Soviets and their client regimes to show good faith by concrete actions.

The fourth point is arms reduction. I know that this weighs heavily on many of your minds. In our 1931 Prism, we quoted Carl Sandburg, who in his own beautiful way quoted the Mother Prairie, saying, "Have you seen a red sunset drip over one of my cornfields, the shore of night stars, the wave lines of dawn up a wheat valley?" What an idyllic scene that paints in our minds—and what a nightmarish prospect that a huge mushroom cloud might someday destroy such beauty. My duty as President is to ensure that the ultimate nightmare never occurs, that the prairies

---

[26] Reference is to the NATO publication, *NATO and the Warsaw Pact: Force Comparisons* (1982), which was reprinted under the same title by the Government Printing Office in 1983.

[27] For the text of President Reagan's speech in Philadelphia, October 15, 1981, see *American Foreign Policy: Current Documents, 1981*, document 16. For documentation on the Cancun summit, October 22–23, 1981, see *ibid.*, Chapter 5, Part F.

and the cities and the people who inhabit them remain free and untouched by nuclear conflict.

I wish more than anything there were a simple policy that would eliminate that nuclear danger. But there are only difficult policy choices through which we can achieve a stable nuclear balance at the lowest possible level.

I do not doubt that the Soviet people, and, yes, the Soviet leaders, have an overriding interest in preventing the use of nuclear weapons. The Soviet Union, within the memory of its leaders, has known the devastation of total conventional war and knows that nuclear war would be even more calamitous. Yet, so far, the Soviet Union has used arms control negotiations primarily as an instrument to restrict U.S. defense programs and, in conjunction with their own arms buildup, a means to enhance Soviet power and prestige.

Unfortunately, for some time suspicions have grown that the Soviet Union has not been living up to its obligations under existing arms control treaties. There is conclusive evidence the Soviet Union has provided toxins to the Laotians and Vietnamese for use against defenseless villagers in Southeast Asia. And the Soviets themselves are employing chemical weapons on the freedom fighters in Afghanistan.

We must establish firm criteria for arms control in the 1980's if we're to secure genuine and lasting restraint on Soviet military programs throughout arms control. We must seek agreements which are verifiable, equitable, and militarily significant. Agreements that provide only the appearance of arms control breed dangerous illusions.

Last November, I committed the United States to seek significant reductions on nuclear and conventional forces. In Geneva, we have since proposed limits on U.S. and Soviet intermediate-range missiles, including the complete elimination of the most threatening systems on both sides.

In Vienna, we're negotiating, together with our allies, for reductions of conventional forces in Europe. In the 40-nation Committee on Disarmament, the United Nations[28] seeks a total ban on all chemical weapons.

Since the first days of my administration, we've been working on our approach to the crucial issue of strategic arms and the control and negotiations for control of those arms with the Soviet Union. The study and analysis required has been complex and difficult. It had to be undertaken deliberately, thoroughly, and correctly. We've laid a solid basis for these negotiations. We're consulting with congressional leaders and with our allies, and we are now ready to proceed.

The main threat to peace posed by nuclear weapons today is the growing instability of the nuclear balance. This is due to the increasingly destructive potential of the massive Soviet buildup in its ballistic missile force.

Therefore, our goal is to enhance deterrence and achieve stability through significant reductions in the most destabilizing nuclear systems, ballistic missiles, and especially the giant intercontinental ballistic missiles, while maintaining a nuclear capability sufficient to deter conflict, to underwrite our national security and to meet our commitment to allies and friends.

For the immediate future, I'm asking my START—and START really means, we've given up on SALT, START means, "Strategic Arms Reduction Talks,"—negotiating team to propose to their Soviet counterparts a practical, phased reduction plan. The focus of our efforts will be to reduce significantly the most destabilizing systems, the ballistic missiles, the number of warheads they carry, and their overall destructive potential.

At the first phase, or the end of the first phase of START, I expect ballistic missile warheads, the most serious threat we face, to be reduced to equal levels, equal ceilings, at least a third below the current levels. To enhance stability, I would ask that no more than half of those warheads be land-based. I hope that these warhead reductions as well as significant reductions in missiles themselves could be achieved as rapidly as possible.

In a second phase, we'll seek to achieve an equal ceiling on other elements of our strategic nuclear forces including limits on the ballistic missile throw-weight at less than current American levels. In both phases, we shall insist on verification procedures to ensure compliance with the agreement.

This, I might say, will be the twentieth time that we have sought such negotiations with the Soviet Union since World War II.

The monumental task of reducing and reshaping our strategic forces to enhance

---

[28] United States. [Footnote correction in the source text.]

stability will take many years of concentrated effort. But I believe that it will be possible to reduce the risks of war by removing the instabilities that now exist and by dismantling the nuclear menace. (Applause)

I have written to President Brezhnev and directed Secretary Haig to approach the Soviet Government concerning the initiation of formal negotiations on the reduction of strategic nuclear arms, START, at the earliest opportunity. We hope negotiations will begin by the end of June.

We will negotiate seriously, in good faith, and carefully consider all proposals made by the Soviet Union. If they approach these negotiations in the same spirit, I'm confident that together we can achieve an agreement of enduring value that reduces the number of nuclear weapons, halts the growth in strategic forces and opens the way to even more far-reaching steps in the future. (Applause)

I hope the Commencement today will also mark the commencement of a new era, in both senses of the word a new start toward a more peaceful and secure world.

The fifth and final point I propose for East–West relations is dialogue. I've always believed that people's problems can be solved when people talk to each other instead of about each other. And I've already expressed my own desire to meet with President Brezhnev in New York next month.[29] If this can't be done, I'd hope we could arrange a future meeting where positive results can be anticipated. And when we sit down, I'll tell President Brezhnev that the United States is ready to build a new understanding based upon the principles I've outlined today. I'll tell him that his government and his people have nothing to fear from the United States. The free nations living at peace in the world community can vouch for the fact that we seek only harmony. And I'll ask President Brezhnev why our two nations can't practice mutual restraint. Why can't our peoples enjoy the benefits that would flow from real cooperation? Why can't we reduce the number of horrendous weapons?

Perhaps I should also speak to him of this school and these graduates who are leaving it today—of your hopes for the future, of your deep desire for peace, and yet your strong commitment to defend your values if threatened. Perhaps if he someday could attend such a ceremony as this, he'd better understand America. In the only system he knows, you would be here by the decision of government and on this day the government representatives would be here telling most, if not all of you, where you were going to report to work tomorrow.

But as we go to Europe for the talks and as we proceed in the important challenges facing this country, I want you to know that I will be thinking of you and of Eureka and what you represent. In one of my yearbooks, I remember reading that, "The work of the prairie is to be the soil for the growth of a strong western culture." I believe Eureka is fulfilling that work. You, the members of the 1982 graduating class, are this year's harvest.

I spoke of the difference between our two countries. I try to follow the humor of the Russian people. We don't hear much about the Russian people. We hear about the Russian leaders. But you can learn a lot because they do have a sense of humor and you can learn from the jokes they're telling. And one of the most recent jokes I found kind of—well, personally interesting. Maybe you [*it*] might—tell you something about your country. The joke they tell is that an American and a Russian were arguing about the differences between our two countries. And the American said, "Look. In my country I can walk into the Oval Office, I can hit the desk with my fist, and say, 'President Reagan, I don't like the way you're governing the United States.'" And the Russian said, "I can do that." The American said, "What?" He says, "I can walk into the Kremlin, into Brezhnev's office. I can pound Brezhnev's desk and I can say, 'Mr. President, I don't like the way Ronald Reagan is governing the United States.'" (Laughter) (Applause)

Eureka as an institution and you as individuals are sustaining the best of Western man's ideals. As a fellow graduate and in the office I hold, I'll do my best to uphold these same ideals. To the Class of'82, congratulations and God bless you.

---

[29] During a question-and-answer session with reporters on April 5, 1982, President Reagan said he would like to meet with Brezhnev at the United Nations in New York in June. For text of his remarks, see *Weekly Compilation of Presidential Documents*, April 12, 1982, p. 443.

Document 45

Testimony by the Secretary of State (Haig) Before the Senate Foreign Relations Committee, May 11, 1982 (Extracts)[30]

U.S. Position on the START Talks

SECRETARY HAIG. Thank you, Mr. Chairman,[31] and distinguished members of the committee.

The timing of these hearings could not be better. We are about to enter a new phase of strategic arms control. On Sunday, the President announced his desire to open strategic arms reduction talks by the end of June.[32] We have proposed to the Soviets that the talks take place in Geneva, and I hope we will be in a position to announce a specific date sometime in the next several weeks.

The decision to begin negotiations on strategic arms reductions is a crucial element in the President's comprehensive policy framework for arms control. In November, we launched America into an entirely new area of arms control, that involving intermediate range nuclear forces. More recently, we have begun to participate in efforts within the 40-member Committee on Disarmament to elaborate a total ban on chemical weapons. We are also engaged in discussions in that forum on nuclear testing. In Vienna, negotiations on reductions in conventional forces in Europe are also underway. In the coming months, we will renew our efforts to make progress there.

Each of these negotiations is important in its own right. Together, they present an opportunity to strengthen deterrence and to reduce the risk of war at all levels. But it is important to remember that arms control is a means to an end, and not an end in itself.

Our objective is to sustain our national security in a changing international environment, and in the face of an expanding Soviet force. Arms control can play a very important part in strengthening our security and restraining the growth of Soviet power through mutually beneficial agreements, but arms control can succeed in this task only if it is coordinated in a strategy that employs the other diplomatic, political, and economic assets at our disposal.

This means, among other things, that we must demonstrate our will and capacity to maintain the military balance. It means that we should consult closely with our allies, and it also means that we should seek balanced, equal and verifiable agreements that reduce the risk of war by reinforcing deterrence.

Our preparations for START have reflected these considerations. The President's proposals have also benefited from the lessons of a decade of American experience with the SALT process. Ironically, the strategic arms competition so troubling to us all reached new heights during the very period when the SALT negotiations seemed so promising.

We therefore developed eight criteria with which to judge alternative approaches to strategic arms control, and these have guided our recent decisions on START:

First, a START agreement must permit the United States to develop and possess sufficient military capability to deter the Soviet Union and to execute the U.S. national military strategy, taking into account the military capability that would be allowed the Soviet Union under such an agreement.

Second, an agreement must be based on the principle of equality. Nothing less than equality is acceptable in the provisions of any future strategic arms limitation agreement for military and political reasons.

Third, a START agreement must promote strategic stability by reducing the vulnerability of U.S. strategic forces.

Fourth, there must be effective verification with the necessary counting rules, collateral constraints, and cooperative measures.

Fifth, an agreement must lead to substantial reductions. We took as a given that whatever unit of account was adopted should lend itself to substantial reductions below current levels of forces, and that reductions should be to equal ceilings.

Sixth, we must be able to explain our objectives and proposals in clear and simple terms to insure that our START approach would enjoy broad public support.

---

[30] Source: *Nuclear Arms Reduction Proposals: Hearings Before the Committee on Foreign Relations, United States Senate, Ninety-seventh Congress, Second Session* (Washington 1982), pp. 111–116, 124–127, 143.

[31] Senator Charles H. Percy.

[32] Reference is to President Reagan's commencement address at Eureka College, *supra*.

Seventh, our approach had to take into account those matters of particular concern to our allies, including the ability of the United States to maintain a credible deterrent, the relationship of the START approach to the INF negotiations and the likelihood of success.

Eighth and finally, we needed to devise a sustainable position which could provide a framework for detailed negotiations and the basis for eventual agreement, even in the face of initial Soviet resistance. This meant the position needed to be demonstrably fair, mutually beneficial, and realistic.

Based upon these criteria, the President has set a new, more demanding goal for strategic arms negotiations. Our objective is to achieve significant reductions in the most destabilizing nuclear systems, especially intercontinental ballistic missiles, thereby strengthening deterrence and stability both for ourselves and for our allies and friends.

To achieve this objective, we will propose to the Soviets in Geneva a practical plan for phased reductions of strategic weapons. This plan is designed to reduce the risk of war by securing agreed steps which will enhance the stability of the balance. Such a goal can be achieved best by negotiating significant reductions in the most destabilizing weapons possessed by both sides—their numbers, their warheads, their overall destructive potential. This will be the primary focus of U.S. efforts.

In Geneva, the United States will propose that, at the end of the first stage of START reductions, ballistic missile warheads be reduced to equal levels at least one-third below current numbers. The United States will propose that, to further enhance stability, no more than one-half these warheads be deployed on land-based missiles. We wish to see those warhead reductions, as well as significant reductions in deployed missiles, achieved just as quickly as possible.

The conclusion of such an agreement would provide the best possible basis for negotiations, leading to a second phase agreement imposing equal ceilings on other elements of United States and Soviet strategic nuclear forces, including equal limits on ballistic missile throw-weight at less than current U.S. levels. In both phases, we will naturally insist on verification procedures to insure compliance with the agreement.

As President Reagan has noted, these proposals represent a very serious and ambitious undertaking. The sheer physical task of reducing United States and Soviet strategic forces and reshaping them to enhance stability will undoubtedly take years of concentrated effort. We believe, however, that the United States and the Soviet Union together can remove the instabilities that now exist, and reduce significantly nuclear forces on both sides.

Our ability to achieve these ambitious goals depends, in large measure, on the Soviets' willingness to negotiate seriously and in good faith. How seriously they will negotiate depends, in turn, on their view of how the military and political environment will look without an agreement.

If we fail to adopt the President's military modernization program, we will reduce not the nuclear danger, but instead the chances of reaching an arms control agreement on strategic forces. A demonstrated willingness to maintain the balance, through unilateral efforts if necessary, is as indispensable to the success of our efforts at strategic arms reductions as INF modernization is to the success of the ongoing talks in Geneva. More than any other single defense or political initiative, the President's strategic modernization program and the Congress support for the modernization program will make or break our attempt to negotiate a reasonable arms control agreement.

The need to maintain the Soviet incentive to negotiate reductions in destabilizing options would also be undercut by endorsement of many of the nuclear freeze proposals now before us.[33] Most proposals would freeze the existing instabilities and perpetuate existing Soviet advantages. They would eliminate the incentives for the Soviets to negotiate toward the even lower levels of nuclear weapons that we can achieve. We want to go beyond a freeze. We want to do better. We believe we can achieve real reductions and thus lessen the risk of war.

We all understand and share the anxiety that motivates those who support the freeze. We all agree that we must not miss this opportunity to make a major step toward meaningful arms control and significant reductions. We are concerned, however, that a freeze on nuclear weapons could frustrate our attempts to achieve stability and balance in this critical area.

The discussions and debates on nuclear policy in the Congress and the country at

---

[33] These Senate proposals, 12 in all, were printed in *Nuclear Arms Reduction Proposals*, pp. 4–28.

large reflect both public concern and our capacity as a Democracy to discuss the great issues of today. They have helped to focus American attention on the difficult task ahead of us. We particularly support the objectives set by Senators Warner, Jackson, and others for significant reductions in the number of weapons.[34] We hope, however, that this debate will not culminate in fresh battle lines between divided factions, but rather a new national consensus in support of the President's proposal for a fair, realistic, and truly beneficial strategic arms agreement.

We feel confident that a better understanding of the needs of deterrence, the state of the military balance and the possibilities for arms control will result in strong support for the initiatives we have taken to modernize our forces and to reduce the burden of arms and the risk of war through negotiation. Such support will be crucial in convincing the Soviets that we are determined to compete and, at the same time, that we are eager to reach a meaningful agreement. The incentives for real arms control exist. We have both the means and the duty to supply them.

As we embark on this vital enterprise, now is the time to rally behind the President's proposals. Thank you, Mr. Chairman. THE CHAIRMAN. Thank you very much, Mr. Secretary. . . . First, I would like to ask you for your reactions, beyond news reports now in *Pravda* and so forth, as to the Soviets' response. They were given several days' advance notice as to what the sense of the President's message would be. What indications do we have that the Soviets will be ready to start SALT negotiations by the end of June as proposed by the President? And what response can you give us that they have given to you as to their reactions to the proposals?

SECRETARY HAIG. Well, Mr. Chairman. I think it is too early to say what the official Soviet response may be. It is unfortunate that some of the observations made by certain American sources that were critical were immediately picked up in TASS.

THE CHAIRMAN. And reported in *Pravda*. SECRETARY HAIG. I think this is unfortunate. On the other hand, we have maintained a dialog on this subject over the months. I think, on balance, the Soviet leadership will welcome the resumption of these arms control talks at the strategic level. I have discussed it with Ambassador Dobrynin and anticipate fixing the date in the next several weeks.

We have recommended or proposed Geneva as the site for these talks. I think it is very clear that the unit of measure that has been put forth by the President for the numbers of warheads and missiles is, in general, compatible with the previous work that we had done under SALT II and earlier arms control discussions; and therefore, will be in general welcomed by the Soviet Union.

THE CHAIRMAN. Would you outline for us, with respect to the President's proposals, whether any onsite inspection would be necessary or would any means beyond national technical surveillance means be required? Under SALT I and SALT II, national surveillance was adequate. Under the proposal of the President, what additional requirements would be necessary to make the resulting treaty verifiable?

SECRETARY HAIG. I think, Senator, it is a bit too early to tell. We are talking about being absolutely sure, with respect to the units of measure that we have fixed for phase I and subsequently for phase II, that adequate verification can be assured.

As you know, under SALT II there were considerable concerns in the verification area, and especially in certain technical aspects such as telemetry. I know that Senator Glenn had strong reservations about that. We want to be absolutely sure that there is mutual confidence on both sides that the obligations that are incurred in the negotiations can, in fact, be verified with confidence.

So it is still somewhat too soon to say what kind of verification will be required. As you know, we did not and have not fixed our verification requirements for the INF talks, believing that it was far better to get on with the talks and to consider, as these talks develop, the best methodology which will probably go beyond purely national means.

THE CHAIRMAN. For more than a year I have been waiting for the administration's reaction to the request I made that they give us their recommendation with respect to whether the Senate should take up and ratify the Threshold Test Ban Treaty signed by President Nixon and the Peaceful Nuclear Explosions Treaty signed by President Ford.[35] We, in the committee, have

[34] Regarding the Jackson–Warner resolution, see footnote 22 to document 43.

[35] For the text of the Threshold Test Ban Treaty (1974), see Department of State *Bulletin*, July 29, 1974, pp. 217–218; for the text of the Peaceful Nuclear Explosions Treaty (1976), see *ibid.*, June 28, 1976, pp. 802–812.

been waiting for that recommendation for a year now.

The latter, the Peaceful Nuclear Explosions Treaty, contains unprecedented provisions for onsite inspection, a point of agreement which could be very useful in the upcoming START negotiations, particularly if you are going to count warheads.

In August of this year, I turned over to the administration a letter I received from former President Ford, strongly supporting ratification of both treaties. General Seignious, recently of the Arms Control Agency, came out just last week urging ratification.

Why is it taking the administration so long to make up its mind as to whether or not it is going to recommend ratification of two treaties that were signed years ago by two former Presidents?

SECRETARY HAIG. Mr. Chairman, as I think you are aware, we are heavily engaged now in the 40-nation ad hoc discussions in Geneva dealing with the subject, not just of chemical weapons as I mentioned in my talk, but more importantly, in the comprehensive test ban area. In principle, as you know, we support a comprehensive test ban as a long-term goal. There are a host of complex issues, especially those related to verification, involved in all of these treaties you touched upon, as well as in a comprehensive test ban treaty.

We are currently engaged in discussions in the Geneva Committee on Disarmament, focusing specifically on the verification question. Now, the consequences of those deliberations in Geneva will set the framework for our approach to the other related treaties that former President Ford endorsed and you have touched upon here. But until this process has been completed, I think it would be both risky and premature to comment, because we must have an international consensus on the vital subject of verification.

THE CHAIRMAN. But one of those treaties takes us a step much farther than the Soviets have even been willing to go before. They were fully negotiated. The Arms Control Agency was in being at the time. Some of the same people are on board, I suppose.

I know in the Carter administration the word we got back was that President Carter simply preferred his own treaty and had no interest in ratifying a treaty from previous Presidents. But in this case, it is two Republican Presidents. It does seem to carry us forward there, not any great shakes. I will admit that. One hundred fifty kilotons is a pretty big explosion. But still, if we had had it with China, it would have covered two-thirds of their explosions. It would be of some use and certainly, the onsite inspection would be, too.

Can we get from the administration a date by which it would say yes or no as to whether we can consider it, because I do not see it as possible to ratify with a two-thirds vote unless the administration says yes. It is the indecision that is affecting the situation.

SECRETARY HAIG. I do not want to suggest indecision. I want to suggest the need to refine the critical area of verification. Verification has always been the hangup on these lesser test ban agreements and on a comprehensive test ban. Therefore, it is vitally important that these things be clarified, and these involve not just the concerns, incidentally, of the United States and Soviet Union in this area. They involve very important concerns to other nuclear powers who have testing requirements of their own, such as Great Britain and France, for example.

I can assure you that there are concerns in those capitals with respect to the verification topic. I worked in the area of the treaties to which you are referring and I am very familiar with what was accomplished and what is still rather worrisome under those agreements.

What we are trying to do is eliminate all uncertainties and doubts and establish a good framework for verification in which the United States, the Soviet Union, and other nuclear powers can have mutual confidence.

THE CHAIRMAN. Well, I have confidence. As you know, I have been pushing very hard to get started on START. I am very satisfied now that we have the date set. The ball is in their court; it is up to them to respond.

I still think that to show the seriousness of our intention, we ought really to look at these two treaties that do move us forward. We are going to know more about verification and we will have in place verification data and materials if we get these implemented.

If that is the only thing hanging us up, I would hope we could make a quick decision on that and I would look forward to that, just as we have made a decision on the other one now. Thank you.

. . . .

SENATOR GLENN. . . . Would you run through some of the numbers for us, about the first stage, and what would happen in this reduction, the application of the one-third below current numbers and no more than half on land-based missiles? Does this leave aircraft out of this equation?

SECRETARY HAIG. Aircraft were not included in the President's statement, because we wanted a simple, understandable, conceptual approach which could be grasped not only by the Soviet Union but by the public at large. It does not mean, Senator, that we have not provided for aircraft, and indeed aircraft will be included in the American proposal at equitable levels.

SENATOR GLENN. Do the proposals you make here fit with the President's speeches? I read it in the press, about 850, and 5,000 warheads. They do not match up, the way I figure it out.

SECRETARY HAIG. I would prefer not to get into numbers in public session, because it begins to cheapen the approach that we are taking, which should be discussed at the table.

SENATOR GLENN. Well, there is one set of figures coming out in your statement here this morning, if we follow it through, or at least as I read it—and I am asking a question, I am not making a conclusion—as I read the President's statement on launchers and so on, and all that business, it does not come out the same at all. Is that correct?

SECRETARY HAIG. I think we know precisely what we are talking about. I do not know what you mean.

SENATOR GLENN. How about running through the numbers for me on these things, if you could, please? I do not understand what would happen. Let me ask this question first. We would make these reductions in warheads, and we would actually be destroying warheads, and the Soviets would be destroying warheads before we have any agreement at all on megatonnages or throw-weights. Is that correct?

SECRETARY HAIG. We would seek reductions in warheads and launchers.

SENATOR GLENN. That is the first phase.

SECRETARY HAIG. In the first phase. That would have the indirect consequence, I must tell you, Senator, of substantial reductions in throw-weight, although that would not be a measure of count.

SENATOR GLENN. OK. Let's say the first phase is agreed to. The Soviets agree and we agree. They accept your proposal, and we start pulling equipment down and they start pulling equipment down. We start destroying warheads, and they start destroying warheads. We still would have the megatonnage and throw-weight imbalances still in place.

SECRETARY HAIG. No, Senator. The actual consequences of the one-third reduction we are speaking of would have a substantial impact because of the land-based provisions. Only half the remaining missiles would be land-based. That means the Soviets are going to have to reduce a substantial number of their ICBM's, and the United States on its part, because we have the bulk of our forces in sea-based systems, will have to reduce a substantial number of sea-based systems. The consequence will be throw-weight reductions.

SENATOR GLENN. Do you envision now that the first phase could go into effect without the second phase being agreed to?

SECRETARY HAIG. Yes.

SENATOR GLENN. Well, then, I repeat, this will make a huge imbalance on megatonnage. If they stick with the SS–18's, for instance, and the megatonnage they throw, the capability that they have, it seems to me we stand a good chance of being put into a greater imbalance than we are correcting.

SECRETARY HAIG. Senator, it is precisely the opposite.

SENATOR GLENN. Well, you explain to me with numbers how that would not occur, because the numbers do not work out the way I plot them here.

SECRETARY HAIG. I can assure you they work out very well, and they involve precisely what we say, a 30-percent reduction in warheads, a one-third reduction in warheads.

SENATOR GLENN. But they would keep the SS–18. There is no doubt about that.

SECRETARY HAIG. And only half of the residual force would be land-based.

SENATOR GLENN. But they would keep their SS–18's. There is no doubt about that, right?

SECRETARY HAIG. That is a choice they will have to make in light of the reduction options that are open to them in land-based systems. Clearly, that is the most desirable system to retain. But under any set of reductions available to them, substantial reductions in throw-weight would result.

SENATOR GLENN. Would you run through the numbers as to how we do not wind up with an even greater megatonnage and throw-weight disadvantage than we have now?

SECRETARY HAIG. Well, clearly, in a public hearing, I am trying to avoid precisely what you are suggesting, but I would be very happy to explain it in a secure environment, and I think in a very convincing way, Senator, beyond a shadow of a doubt.

SENATOR GLENN. But all of these numbers are being made public, and I think the public has to understand these figures some time.

SECRETARY HAIG. There has been speculation in public, but we have not made them public.

SENATOR GLENN. Senator Pell asked in one of his questions about giving us the details of this. You will give us the details to all of these questions in private session. Is that correct?

SECRETARY HAIG. If you would like them, I am available to do that, but I think it is very important that we not indulge in public negotiations with the Soviet Union. I can assure you that the proposal that the President has put forward does not create the consequences your question suggested. Rather, precisely the opposite, and dramatically different than anything SALT II even visualized.

SENATOR GLENN. I certainly am willing to be convinced. Mr. Chairman, I think we absolutely have to get into that, because without that kind of understanding of why we do not wind up with a greater megatonnage throw-weight disadvantage than we have now, we have to get into the figures. Otherwise, the whole thing does not make any sense at all.

SECRETARY HAIG. Senator, your arithmetic is pretty good. We say we will reduce by one-third, and then only half of the residual force can be land-based. We are talking about very substantial reductions in the ICBM force of the Soviet Union, just as we are talking about our heavy suit, which is in sea-based systems, and substantial reductions there. Now, if they choose to keep their SS–18's and do away with other systems, then the amount of attrition is going to be all the more substantial to them.

SENATOR GLENN. If they keep their SS–18's, you said, the attrition will be more substantial?

SECRETARY HAIG. Yes, they would have to give up everything else.

SENATOR GLENN. Why would that be? I do not understand it.

SECRETARY HAIG. Because they would have to give up everything else. It is just that simple. We do have finite figures.

SENATOR GLENN. My time is up, and I am over now, but I must say this. Their throw-weight and megatonnage capacity would go up proportionally to the number of SS–18's they keep. It would have to.

SECRETARY HAIG. That is all right. They are going to have to get rid of other systems to get down to the totals.

SENATOR GLENN. But we do not have any megatonnage or throw-weight as part of the first phase. We would be reducing warheads. They would be reducing warheads. But the percent of megatonnage and throw-weight capacity would be going steadily up compared to ours.

SECRETARY HAIG. Let me assure you, Senator, that, indirectly, the consequences on throw-weight are substantial.

SENATOR GLENN. I hope so.

SECRETARY HAIG. I can assure you.

THE CHAIRMAN. Thank you, Senator Glenn.

. . . .

SENATOR GLENN. One further clarification. I understood you to say that the counts we are talking about here would only be on deployed missiles. In other words, they or we could stockpile as many as we wanted in any way, shape or form and those would not count in the agreements we are making; is that correct?

SECRETARY HAIG. No, that is really not quite it. The answer to the question was that the 30 percent or one-third reduction uses deployed warheads as a unit of measure.

THE CHAIRMAN. Thank you, Senator Glenn.

SENATOR GLENN. Just a minute, Mr. Chairman. This is a very vital point, it seems to me.

SECRETARY HAIG. Sure, you cannot verify the others.

SENATOR GLENN. Are we talking about the total inventory that the Soviets have and we have or are we not talking about the total inventory?

SECRETARY HAIG. Well, clearly one of the understandings that we have to deal with in negotiations of this kind is to have your assurances that we are not doing one another in by digging holes and putting vast resources there. That is one of the questions of verification that is so sensitive. In terms of our unit of measure for a negotiated solution, however, we are talking about deployed warheads with the assumption that there isn't any—

SENATOR GLENN. But we didn't get into the units of measure. That was something I wanted to get into in the next round. That is a whole different area, whether we are going to start a new unit of measure. We are talking in this particular thing you are proposing of warheads. That is a unit of measure.

SECRETARY HAIG. Warheads and launchers.

SENATOR GLENN. But the warheads we are talking about this morning are only deployed, then.

SECRETARY HAIG. Deployed for purposes of our counting, now, not for purposes of mutual understanding on our relative balances. You clearly cannot have that kind of situation.

SENATOR GLENN. That is the reason I would like to make them part of whatever we are agreeing to. I don't want to buy a pig in a poke, thinking we are buying one limitation or one reduction and meanwhile there isn't any real reduction to it, it is just counting one little part of what they could do or we could do.

Which way is it?

SECRETARY HAIG. You are really talking about breakout and putting curbs on breakout, et cetera.

SENATOR GLENN. I sure am, exactly, and I don't know that I got an answer exactly yet.

SECRETARY HAIG. You will get one.

THE CHAIRMAN. Thank you very much.

. . . .

Document 46

Prepared Statement by the Under Secretary of State for Management (Kennedy) Before a Subcommittee of the Senate Governmental Affairs Committee, May 13, 1982[36]

Reagan Administration's Policy on Nuclear Nonproliferation

Mr. Chairman: Thank you for the opportunity to appear before this committee to discuss certain aspects of U.S. policy to prevent the spread of nuclear explosives. Your letter of invitation[37] identified a number of questions in which the committee has expressed interest such as the management of our nonproliferation policy, the advisability of establishing legal controls on certain kinds of activities by U.S. companies or their licensees, and, finally, the administration's actions in response to Senate Resolution 179.[38]

I will, of course, address each of these in my statement. But I also thought I could profitably use this hearing to describe for you the key elements of this administration's nonproliferation policy.

From the beginning of the nuclear age, all administrations have been firmly committed to the goal of preventing the spread of nuclear explosives. While detailed policy approaches have varied, the last eight Presidents have recognized the critical relationship between nonproliferation and U.S. security interests. That recognition is at the core of President Reagan's policy.

---

[36] Source: *U.S. Policy on Export of Helium-3 and Other Nuclear Materials and Technology: Hearing Before the Subcommittee on Energy, Nuclear Proliferation, and Government Processes of the Committee on Governmental Affairs, United States Senate. Ninety-seventh Congress, Second Session* (Washington, 1982), pp. 36–56. Kennedy was appointed U.S. Representative to the International Atomic Energy Agency in July 1981. In the following month the Under Secretary of State for Management was given responsibility for overseeing the formulation and execution of Department of State policy on nuclear nonproliferation and its coordination with other agencies.

[37] The letter by Senator Percy, chairman of the subcommittee, has not been printed, but the nature of some of its contents is provided in Kennedy's prepared statement below.

[38] Reference is to Senate Resolution 179, which the Senate, without dissenting vote, passed on July 17, 1981. It called on the President to implement a series of important initiatives to strengthen the international nonproliferation regime.

Equally basic to our nonproliferation policy, and to the nonproliferation regime itself, is this administration's conviction that nuclear energy, in the United States and around the world, has a vital role to play over the next decades in providing environmentally safe and economically efficient power for home and industry. This conviction is shared by many other nations, from the EURATOM countries and Japan to developing countries like South Korea and Mexico. All see reliance on nuclear power as helping them meet an important part of their energy needs.

Consistent with our nonproliferation objectives, we are seeking ways to enable our nuclear industry to participate vigorously in these developments. As President Reagan observed in his July 16 statement,[39] "The United States will cooperate with other nations in the peaceful uses of nuclear energy . . . . To carry out these policies, I am instructing the Secretary of State, working with the other responsible agencies, to give priority attention to efforts . . . to reestablish a leadership role for the United States in international nuclear affairs." Unless we play such a leadership role we may be less able to achieve the nonproliferation goals we all share.

At the same time, with more and more nations embarking on civilian nuclear power programs, it is essential that the United States and other countries adopt policies that insure that the legitimate development of nuclear power is not accompanied by the spread of nuclear explosives. We will not compromise our nonproliferation principles in pursuit of commercial gain, and will continue to ask the same from others.

In matters of nonproliferation, just as in every other aspect of foreign policy, concrete distinctions sometimes have to be made among the various countries of the world. President Reagan has stated that the United States will not inhibit civil reprocessing and breeder development in countries with advanced nuclear programs where it is not a proliferation risk. This is a realistic recognition that Japan and the EURATOM countries believe that such advanced fuel cycle activities are needed for their energy security. However, we also recognize that plutonium and highly enriched uranium are dangerous materials whose use must be carefully controlled and safeguarded. To acknowledge that in certain cases, use of plutonium is seen to be a sensible energy course, is not to encourage reprocessing or advanced fuel cycle activities where they are not warranted as a coherent part of an advanced nuclear program.

Moreover, we believe that greater realism and flexibility in the exercise of U.S. consent rights is related to the degree to which other suppliers will be prepared to cooperate with us on important nonproliferation initiatives, such as improving export controls, making export policies more uniform, and improving IAEA safeguards. And by working together with Japan and EURATOM, we can best minimize the risks inherent in the presence and use of separated plutonium, whether in the area of physical security, of improved safeguards, or avoidance of unnecessary national stockpiling. And we will continue to make our concerns known on this subject, and to work with other nations to solve the difficult technical problems that exist.

The administration also is committed to making it more difficult for countries to acquire the technical capability to build nuclear explosives. As President Reagan stated in his July 16th policy statement, the United States will seek to inhibit the spread of sensitive technology, facilities, and material, particularly where the danger of proliferation demands. But such measures can only buy time. We must use such time wisely to reduce the motivations that may lead countries to seek a nuclear explosive capability. Steps need to be taken to alleviate the military and political insecurity of such countries. Ways also must be found to reduce mutual suspicion of neighboring countries, whether by encouraging adherence to the Treaty of Tlatelolco,[40] adherence to the Non-Proliferation Treaty,[41] or acceptance of full scope safeguards. Initiatives to improve regional and global stability are called for as well.

Efforts to strengthen IAEA safeguards are another essential element of our nonproliferation policy. Safeguards do not deal with all aspects of proliferation risk. Their purpose is to detect, and by the risk of such

---

[39] For the text of President Reagan's statement on U.S. nonproliferation policy, July 16, 1981, see *American Foreign Policy: Current Documents, 1981*, document 57.

[40] For the text of the Treaty for the Prohibition of Nuclear Weapons in Latin America, or Treaty of Tlatelolco, signed in 1967 and entered into force in 1968, see *Documents on Disarmament*, 1967 (Washington, 1968), pp. 69–83.

[41] For the text of the Nuclear Non-Proliferation Treaty (1970), see 21 UST 483.

detection, deter diversion, not prevent it. But it is critical that they do that defined task effectively. While the technical effectiveness of IAEA safeguards has improved steadily over the recent past, it still is more uneven than we wish. We are working both bilaterally in cooperation with the IAEA Secretariat and multilaterally through a number of special projects to improve IAEA safeguards. Several of these efforts focus on the particular problem of safeguarding sensitive nuclear facilities.

For example, we are working closely with the IAEA to improve the quality and capabilities of its inspectorate. Through courses given at U.S. laboratories and by U.S. experts who go to Vienna solely for this purpose, IAEA inspectors are continuously trained in new techniques and methods designed to enhance the effective and timely application of IAEA safeguards. This effort has so impressed the IAEA that they formed first a training unit, and then a training section to train systematically new inspectors and to keep veteran inspectors up to date. We plan to continue and even modestly expand our training efforts, hopefully in conjunction with other interested IAEA member states.

Similarly, in the area of safeguards instrumentation we have developed, explicitly for IAEA use over the past 5 years, 20 types of equipment for verification of nuclear material. Some of the equipment is in routine use and much of it is in great demand by the inspectorate. We are considering ways to join with other countries in helping the IAEA acquire and deploy this newly developed equipment. This should lead in the next few years to a significant increase in IAEA capabilities in measurement of uranium and plutonium by nondestructive techniques.

Further, through our program of technical assistance to IAEA safeguards, 213 mutually agreed projects have been completed since its inception in 1977, and another 50 are currently underway at a total cost of $27 million.

The executive branch and NRC also actively recruit personnel to serve in Vienna as inspectors. We are currently examining ways of improving our procedures for recruitment to assure that only the highest quality personnel are recommended to the IAEA. And we are encouraging other IAEA member states to do the same.

We strongly believe that the IAEA is a special organization within the UN family. In its safeguards role, it provides a unique service upon which all member states depend and around which nearly all nuclear commerce is organized. Preservation of the Agency's effectiveness and credibility is an essential part of U.S. nonproliferation efforts and the Agency must be supported and improved. The President made that clear in his statement of July 16, 1981. The administration has supported, therefore, modest real growth in the IAEA's budget, especially as it relates to safeguards. Coupled with modifications in IAEA recruitment procedures, this growth makes it possible for the IAEA to come closer to meeting its inspection goals.

Considerable concern has been raised recently about the technical task of safeguarding sensitive enrichment and reprocessing facilities. We recognize the problem, and are taking steps in cooperation with other countries to deal with it.

The United States is currently engaged in a multinational exercise to define effective safeguards approaches for gas centrifuge enrichment plants. In addition to the United States, Australia, Japan, the Urenco Governments, (UK, FRG, Netherlands), and the safeguards inspectorates of EURATOM, and the IAEA participate in this project, called the Hexapartite Safeguards project. All six countries now have, or plan to have, gas centrifuge enrichment facilities under IAEA safeguards. Much progress has been made. We expect that a recommendation for a preferred safeguards approach which should be adequate to the task will be made to the IAEA late this year.

We also are continuing our work on reprocessing plant safeguards. The Tokai Advanced Safeguards Technology Exercise (TASTEX) was successfully concluded about 1 year ago. Since then instruments and techniques developed through TASTEX are gaining acceptance internationally. Work on safeguards techniques also is being conducted at the Barnwell facility. We are continuing our efforts to have the new techniques and equipment incorporated into IAEA safeguards approaches for reprocessing facilities. Continued work and cooperation on the part of interested countries and the IAEA will be needed to develop successfully adequate safeguards techniques and equipment for the larger reprocessing plants now in the planning stage.

I would like now to address the specific issues raised in the chairman's April 14th letter inviting my testimony.

The first dealt with the management of our nonproliferation policy and the impact that certain personnel and organizational changes might have on its effectiveness. In my view, we have a very able team of people handling our nonproliferation policy, not only in the Department of State, but also in other parts of the executive branch including the National Security Council, the Arms Control and Disarmament Agency, the Department of Energy, and the Department of Defense. All are hard-working, dedicated professionals who are strongly committed to the objective of halting the spread of nuclear explosives.

The lead responsibility within the U.S. Government for managing our nonproliferation efforts rests with the Assistant Secretary of State for Oceans and International Environmental and Scientific Affairs (OES). The present OES Assistant Secretary, James L. Malone, has been asked by the President and Secretary Haig to devote full time to matters relating to the Law of the Sea and U.S. oceans policy. Mr. Malone, who has served since March 1981 as the President's Special Representative for Law of the Sea, has been nominated as Ambassador-at-Large to perform these responsibilities. Mr. Malone has been and continues to be responsible for the law of the sea, oceans policy, nuclear nonproliferation, and other subjects falling within the purview of the OES Bureau. He has done an excellent job in this capacity. The heavy demands related to oceans policy, now more than ever, simply make it good management sense to assign someone full-time to that job. Candidates are now being evaluated to succeed Mr. Malone as Assistant Secretary.

Each of the Under Secretaries of State has been asked by the Secretary to provide general policy guidance and oversight for certain specific areas of the Department's many activities. In addition to my general management area of responsibilities, the Secretary has asked also that I provide the broad policy guidance and oversight on his behalf over nonproliferation and safeguards matters. In that same connection, I serve as the United States representative to the International Atomic Energy Agency. I want to emphasize, however, that day-to-day supervision rests, as I indicated, with the Assistant Secretary for Oceans, and International Environmental and Scientific Affairs, and under him the Deputy Assistant Secretary of State for Nuclear Energy Affairs. In my policy guidance role, I maintain close and regular contact with the Deputy Secretary of Energy and the Director of the Arms Control and Disarmament Agency. Messrs. Davis, Rostow, and I work closely together in assuring a coherent and consistent policy thrust across the executive branch.

Other agencies also play an important part and have been extremely helpful in defining our overall policy as well as in bringing their expertise to bear on its detailed implementation. The Department of Energy has a particularly crucial part to play in providing technical assistance to our negotiations and in exercising primary responsibility in handling exports of nuclear technology and in processing subsequent arrangements including such important areas as reprocessing and plutonium use. The Department of Energy also plays a key role in providing technical expertise and assistance in the development and extension of effective safeguard systems equipment. Whatever the future role of DOE, I am assured that the important functions which that Department now exercises in the nonproliferation area will continue to be carried out in an effective way.

The Arms Control and Disarmament Agency (ACDA) plays an equally important part in our nonproliferation efforts. The initial development, of our policy as well as its further implementation, was closely coordinated with ACDA. On a day-to-day basis, the staff in ACDA provides critical expertise on issues ranging from improving IAEA safeguards to export issues related to sensitive countries. The ACDA staff also has been of great importance in efforts to upgrade the existing nuclear suppliers' trigger lists, and senior policy makers in ACDA participate on a regular basis across the whole range of nonproliferation issues.

The Department of Defense participates fully in interagency deliberations on export licensing and subsequent arrangements, and is involved in major nonproliferation policy development. This is in keeping with the strong emphasis of this administration on nonproliferation as an element of our national security policy.

The chairman also requested the administration's views on whether new legislation is needed to control the activities of U.S. companies in their dealings with certain countries of proliferation concern. I believe you have in mind two specific cases, one involving South Africa, the other Pakistan.

U.S. companies did assist in arranging for the fueling of South Africa's Koeberg reactors, acting as brokers for sellers of surplus enriched uranium in Europe and the South African buyers. The fuel then was provided to a French firm for fabrication under a longstanding contract. No U.S.-origin material, equipment, or technology was involved. Any company, abroad or in the United States, could provide such a service and such activity would not trigger supplier controls as would, for example, the export of fuel from one's own territory.

I do not believe that legislation, either prohibiting brokerage functions or requiring special authorization to engage in such activities, is likely to prove very practical for several reasons. First, brokerage is so very common in the international uranium market that it would be nearly impossible to control this kind of activity in the absence of widespread cooperation among all countries involved in the nuclear trade. However, it is highly unlikely that other governments would be prepared to regulate brokering. Second, brokering natural and enriched uranium takes place so frequently and so quickly that any effort to control these activities would only overload the bureaucracy and divert its attention and resources from more critical matters. Third, imposing special controls on firms dealing in brokering would unnecessarily hamper the smooth functioning of the international market, impose needless delays and costs on U.S. utilities and their foreign counterparts, and undermine countries' confidence in the security of international nuclear supply. This could in turn set back our efforts to restore the U.S. position as a reliable partner in international nuclear trade. Thus, we would regard attempts at controlling these types of activity to be impractical and possibly damaging to our overall interest and we prefer to rely on diplomacy and other methods as more appropriate and far more likely to be effective.

The second case referred to by the chairman's letter concerns rumored negotiations between Pakistan and a foreign licensee of a U.S. company for the purchase of nuclear power reactor technology. First, let me say that we are not aware that any such negotiations have occurred. The letter states that such a transfer would constitute an "end run" of our nonproliferation policy. In this area of activities by foreign licensees of U.S. firms, however, we are not without legal tools.

Section 57 of the Atomic Energy Act[42] provides authority for the control of nuclear technology exports by U.S. companies and for control over any retransfer of such technology by their licensees or other recipients of the technology. Current regulations on this subject are contained in Part 810 of title 10 of the Code of Federal Regulations. Exports of sensitive nuclear technology are subject to stringent controls under sections 123, 127, and 128 of the Atomic Energy Act, and under the Nuclear Suppliers Guidelines.[43] Activities not involving technology sensitive from the point of view of proliferation are generally authorized for the free world. Any activity by a foreign licensee or other entity of a U.S. company of sensitive nuclear technology would require specific government approval. The export of reactor technology by a U.S. firm to a foreign licensee, which is specifically mentioned in your letter, is authorized to all but certain embargoed destinations—generally COCOM countries. In the latter case, specific authorization again is needed, before such nonsensitive technology can be exported.

We understand your concern that this general authorization might permit the export of reactor technology to a country of significant proliferation risk. We are working with the Department of Energy which administers these regulations to determine whether changes are warranted, e.g., a change in the list of countries generally authorized to receive U.S. reactor technology. However, in thinking about possible changes, it is important not to overlook the complexity of this matter.

Based on our longstanding general authorization for free world countries, companies in the United States have entered licensing arrangements with foreign firms. Reactor technology is now widely available in public literature worldwide. The impacts of any changes in the general authorization on U.S. firms and their subsidiaries, and whether significant nonproliferation benefits can be expected, must be reviewed before a decision is made whether or not to change the regulations. We also have to avoid creating new uncertainty abroad and are perceived as once again changing the rules of the game retroactively.

The DOE regulations can be changed by the executive branch, without the need for new legislation, and the general authoriza-

[42] Section 57b of the Atomic Energy Act of 1954 was amended by the Nuclear Non-Proliferation Act of 1978, P.L. 95–242, approved on March 10, 1978; for text of the amended section, see 92 Stat. 126.

[43] The Nuclear Suppliers Guidelines were developed in the mid-1970's by several exporting nations of nuclear technology to define the conditions under which nuclear technology could be exported to other nations. In 1978 these guidelines, agreed to by at least 15 nations, were published as IAEA document INFCIRC/254.

tion can be revoked for particular countries or in particular cases. Finally, there also are more informal ways to make known our views in cases in which there may be an adverse nonproliferation impact of a given vendor's actions or those of its licensee.

Let me now turn more broadly to the administration's position on whether the Nuclear Non-Proliferation Act[44] should be amended at the present time. I raise this partly because of the amendments to the NNPA that have recently been introduced in the House.

The White House Fact Sheet released on July 16, 1981, accompanying the President's statement, called for a review of the laws, regulations, and procedures in the nonproliferation area to determine whether changes should be sought. Such a review was conducted and a number of possible areas for modification in the law were identified in an interagency discussion paper. But subsequently, a consensus was reached to postpone consideration of changes to the law for the time being and the administration decided not to submit proposed legislation to change the NNPA.

In recent years there have been a number of major changes in U.S. law and policy—an enrichment contracting moratorium, President Ford's policy statements, President Carter's policy statements, and the NNPA. A further set of changes at this time, or even starting the legislative process on such changes, would create a high degree of uncertainty both at home and abroad about the future content of U.S. nonproliferation law, procedures, and policy. Once we open the Nuclear Non-Proliferation Act in all its complexity to amendments, it is not clear what the outcome would be. Such uncertainty could so undermine the U.S. role in international nuclear commerce that we would be unable to achieve our nonproliferation objectives. It also would hinder our efforts to reforge cooperative ties with the other major suppliers and to enhance nuclear rules of trade.

The administration shares the Act's basic principles and is guided by them. Moreover, like us, foreign governments have come to understand the procedures that have been created and the system is beginning to function more and more efficiently. For all of these reasons it seems prudent not to seek changes of the law at this time.

Your letter also asked what steps the administration has taken to carry out the suggestions expressed in Senate Resolution 179 of July 1981. Among the various steps this resolution proposes is that the United States, in cooperation with other suppliers, tighten restrictions on nuclear trade by a) placing a moratorium on transfers of sensitive technology to areas of considerable nonproliferation concern such as the Middle East and South Asia; b) limiting the size of research reactors and eliminating the use of highly enriched uranium in such reactors; c) extending the list of nuclear equipment and components whose exports should be made only subject to safeguards; d) making nuclear exports conditional upon the acceptance of full-scope safeguards by recipient states; and e) imposing established sanctions in the event of a safeguards violation.

The President's statement of July 16, 1981, stated that the United States would continue to inhibit the transfer of sensitive nuclear equipment, materials, and technology, particularly where the danger of proliferation demands. We have made clear to other countries our concerns about the export of sensitive technologies such as enrichment and reprocessing, and we know of no plans by other nuclear suppliers to export such technologies to such volatile areas as the Middle East or South Asia. Other exporting states share our concerns about these two regions and are exercising great caution and restraint in their nuclear trade with these areas.

We also have taken the initiative in reducing or eliminating the need for highly enriched uranium in research reactor programs. The United States has had a program in effect for several years aimed at developing fuels for and making the necessary technical conversions to reduce the enrichment level of fuel in research reactors. This is called the Reduced Enrichment for Research and Test Reactors (RERTR) program. Other nations have been strong and indeed enthusiastic supporters of this program. However, our objectives cannot be achieved through threats or precipitate actions such as cutting off exports of HEU. Instead, a sound technical program of development and demonstration is needed to convince other countries of the technical feasibility, safety, and licensability of reduced enrichment fuels along with the obvious nonproliferation benefits of converting to these fuels. If we continue to pursue this approach in the spirit of cooperation and assistance, I am confident that we will succeed in our efforts to reduce significantly or virtually eliminate the use of HEU in research reactors around the world.

---

[44] P.L. 95–242; for text, see 92 Stat. 120.

We have been working very closely with the principal supplier states to assure that nuclear trade is subject to effective conditions and controls. We have deliberately avoided highly visible steps such as a formal reconvening of the London Suppliers Group, since we do not believe that this would contribute to our shared objective of further strengthening nuclear export controls. The London Suppliers Group has been characterized by developing countries as an effort by a cartel of advanced nuclear states to set unilaterally the rules of international nuclear trade, depriving developing countries of needed nuclear technology, preserving the advanced countries' monopoly on such technology, and relegating the developing countries to a position of technological inferiority. Although such charges are groundless, other supplier states are particularly sensitive about avoiding any steps which could be construed as a concerted action on the part of the principal exporting states. By contrast, quiet diplomacy and bilateral discussion are a more effective means of strengthening nonproliferation controls on nuclear exports.

In particular, a so-called trigger list was established by parties to the Treaty on the Non-Proliferation of Nuclear Explosives (NPT) in order to carry out their obligations under Article III of the treaty. The London Suppliers Guidelines established an expanded trigger list to include exports of sensitive nuclear technology. These lists have been generally effective in assuring that significant nuclear exports are not being made to unsafeguarded programs. However, many items on the list are quite general and there is a need to clarify and make more precise what particular equipment belongs on these lists. Moreover, certain dual use items which do not fall on any list should be subject to export controls to assure that they only go to safeguarded nuclear facilities. We have taken important initiatives on both these fronts.

Another area in which we have taken action is promoting more widespread acceptance of full-scope safeguards. The Nuclear Non-Proliferation Act requires that non-nuclear-weapons states have all their peaceful nuclear facilities under IAEA safeguards as a condition of U.S. nuclear exports. In addition, the President's nonproliferation message of last July stated that we would continue to urge other suppliers to require full-scope safeguards as a condition of any significant new supply. Though several other nuclear exporters are reluctant to adopt a full-scope safeguards requirement for their exports until all nuclear suppliers do the same, we have been stressing the importance of full-scope safeguards to the nonproliferation regime. This is a difficult and challenging area; but we are hopeful of progress and will continue to use our diplomatic resources to gain wider acceptance of this critical nonproliferation norm.

Finally, President Reagan's July 16th nonproliferation statement made clear that "the United States will view a material violation of (the Treaty of Tlatelolco or the NPT) or an international safeguards agreement as having profound consequences for international order and United States bilateral relations, and also view any nuclear explosion by a non-nuclear-weapons state with grave concern." It is not feasible or desirable, however, to establish in the abstract a precise and complete set of sanctions which the United States and other countries would impose in the event of a violation. Common sense suggests that the U.S. response would have to be tailored to our particular relationship with the country in question. Nevertheless, it is important that we and others make clear that our bilateral relations would be adversely affected in the event of such proliferation actions. We have done so and will continue to do so.

Thus, consistent with Senate Resolution 179, this administration clearly has taken the initiative on a number of fronts to strengthen the international nonproliferation regime. This sometimes is overlooked because little publicity has been given to these efforts. But we believe that the quiet diplomatic steps and measured technical approach we have taken have the best chance of improving nuclear export controls, expanding safeguards coverage, and winning widespread acceptance for reduced enrichment fuels. And these steps are but part of the overall nonproliferation effort I described earlier.

Senate Resolution 179 also called for a prompt reevaluation of world nuclear energy policy, culminating in a conference to agree upon ways both to reduce security concerns and strengthen the nonproliferation regime. The United States is involved in a number of international gatherings addressing questions of this nature. One is the Committee on Assurance of Supply (CAS) which is taking place under the auspices of the IAEA. The United States is an active participant in this effort which has been established to define ways to improve security of nuclear supply while assuring that international nuclear trade is fully consistent with the need to prevent the spread of nuclear weapons. In addition, a conference on the Peaceful Uses of Nuclear Energy (PUNE) is now being planned for August of 1983. Two preparatory conferences have already been held to lay the groundwork for the plenary meeting next year. The agenda for this conference is likely to be a wide-ranging one. While meetings such as these can produce positive results, they also carry certain risks and we must be alert to assure that they do not result in any weakening of international nonproliferation norms. For that reason the United States intends to participate actively and constructively in conferences like PUNE.

In his July 16, 1981, nonproliferation policy statement, President Reagan emphasized that "further proliferation would pose a severe threat to international peace, regional and global stability, and the security interests of the United States and other countries." President Reagan then reaffirmed this administration's commitment to the longstanding bipartisan goal of preventing the spread of nuclear explosives to other countries, a goal also shared by the vast majority of the world's nations.

To realize this goal, we have been pursuing many of the specific recommendations contained in Senate Resolution 179. Thus, this administration's fundamental commitment to the underlying goal of nuclear nonproliferation and to strengthening the global nonproliferation regime is clear; its readiness to work to that end is attested to by actions, many of which I have described today.

But if we are to realize our shared nonproliferation goals, we also need, Mr. Chairman, to restore and nurture that basic spirit of bipartisan cooperation to which President Reagan referred. Rather than engaging in contentious dispute, the executive branch and the Congress must work together. To that end, I reaffirm our readiness to consult closely with you on the critical issues and choices that lie ahead.

Cooperation also is needed between the branches of government and the nuclear industry. We in the executive branch and you in the Congress need to take account of the legitimate concerns of the nuclear industry as well as to make use of its readiness to contribute to realizing our common nonproliferation goals, particularly in strengthening safeguards. But for its part the nuclear industry must work, as does this administration, within the spirit as well as the letter of existing nuclear legislation.

Above all, a spirit of restored cooperation in the nuclear realm is required with other countries. A unilateral approach which too readily overlooks the particular energy needs, security perspectives, and domestic political requirements of other countries makes our common task more difficult. We cannot dictate to other countries; we must convince them of the desirability and benefits of cooperating with us to ensure that the peaceful use of nuclear energy does not lead to further nuclear explosives proliferation. For here too, failure to work together can only lead to a broader failure of our nonproliferation policies

Thank you, Mr. Chairman, and I welcome the committee's questions.

Document 47

Transcript of a Press Conference by President Reagan, May 13, 1982 (Extracts)[45]

Elaboration of the U.S. Proposal for START

THE PRESIDENT. Good evening. I have a statement to read. Four times in my life, I have seen America plunged into war—twice as part of tragic global conflicts that cost the lives of millions. Living through that experience has convinced me that America's highest mission is to stand as a leader among the free nations in the cause of peace. And that's why, hand-in-hand with our efforts to restore a credible national defense, my administration has been actively working for a reduction in nuclear and conventional forces that can help free the world from the threat of destruction.

In Geneva, the United States is now negotiating with the Soviet Union on a proposal I set forward last fall to reduce

---

[45] Source: White House Press Release, May 13, 1982, Office of the Press Secretary to the President; printed also in *Weekly Compilation of Presidential Documents*, May 17, 1982, pp. 634–635, 635–636, 639–640. For the complete text of the press conference, see *ibid.*, pp. 634–642. The press conference took place in the East Room of the White House beginning at 8 p.m. and was broadcast live on nationwide radio and television.

drastically the level of nuclear armament in Europe. In Vienna, we and our NATO allies are negotiating with the Warsaw Pact over ways to reduce conventional forces in Europe.

Last Sunday, I proposed a far-reaching approach to nuclear arms control—a phased reduction in strategic weapons beginning with those that are most dangerous and destabilizing—the warheads on ballistic missiles and especially those on intercontinental ballistic missiles.[46]

Today the United States and the Soviet Union each have about 7,500 nuclear warheads poised on missiles that can reach their targets in a matter of minutes. In the first phase of negotiations, we want to focus on lessening this imminent threat. We seek to reduce the number of ballistic missile warheads to about 5,000—one-third less than today's levels; limit the number of warheads on land-based missiles to half that number and cut the total number of all ballistic missiles to an equal level—about one-half that of the current U.S. level.

In the second phase, we'll seek reductions to equal levels of throw-weight—a critical indicator of overall destructive potential of missiles. To be acceptable, a new arms agreement with the Soviets must be balanced, equal, and verifiable. And most important, it must increase stability and the prospects of peace.

I have already written President Brezhnev and instructed Secretary Haig to approach the Soviet Government so that we can begin formal negotiations on the reduction of strategic nuclear arms—the START talks, at the earliest opportunity. And we hope that these negotiations can begin by the end of June and hope to hear from President Brezhnev in the near future.

Reaching an agreement with the Soviets will not be short or easy work. We know that from the past. But I believe that the Soviet people and their leaders understand the importance of preventing war. And I believe that a firm, forthright American position on arms reductions can bring us closer to a settlement.

Tonight, I want to renew my pledge to the American people and to the people of the world that the United States will do everything we can to bring such an agreement about.

. . . .

Q. And if wiping out the nuclear threat is so important to the world, why do you choose to ignore 7 long years of negotiations in which two Republican Presidents played a part? I speak of SALT II; we abide by the terms the Soviet Union does. Why not push for a ratification of that treaty as a first step and then go on to START? After all, a bird in hand.

THE PRESIDENT. Because, Helen, this bird isn't a very friendly bird. I remind you that a Democratic-controlled Senate refused to ratify it. And the reason for refusing to ratify, I think, is something we can't—

Q.—Republican Senate now.

THE PRESIDENT. But we can't ignore that. The reason why it was refused ratification, SALT stands for strategic arms limitation. And the limitation in that agreement would allow, in the life of the treaty, for the Soviet Union to just about double [their?] present nuclear capability. It would—it would allow—and does allow us—to increase ours. In other words, it simply legitimizes an arms race.

Now, the parts that we're observing of that have to do with the monitoring of each other's weaponry, and so both sides are doing that. What we're striving for is to reduce the power, the number, and particularly those destabilizing missiles that can be touched off by the push of a button—to reduce the number of those. And—it—there just is no—there's no ratio between that and—and what SALT was attempting to do. I think SALT was the wrong course to follow.

Q. Mr. President, you may know that former Secretary of State Henry Kissinger said yesterday that your approach might take far longer than the 7 years it took to require—to negotiate SALT II.[47] What sort of time frame do you anticipate it would take to negotiate these limits on warheads?

THE PRESIDENT. Well, I don't know that there—that you could project a time frame on that, when you look back at the history all the way back to the end of World War II with the Soviet Union on the negotiations. But I do think there is one thing present now that was not present before, and that is the determination of the United States to rebuild its national defenses. And the very fact that we have shown the will and are going forward on the rebuilding program is

---

[46] Reference is to President Reagan's commencement address at Eureka College, Sunday, May 9. For text, see document 44.

[47] Kissinger made this point in a speech given in The Hague, Netherlands, May 12. (*New York Times,* May 13, 1982. p. A17)

something that I think offers an inducement to the Soviet Union to come to that table and legitimately negotiate with us.

In the past several years, those negotiations took place with them having a superiority over us and us actually unilaterally disarming. Every time someone wanted a little more money for another program, they took it away from defense. That isn't true anymore.

. . . .

Q. Mr. President, in your arms proposals, you focus on a central intercontinental missile system to the two sides. If the Soviets were to come back and say they wanted to talk about bombers, about cruise missiles, about other weapon systems, would you be willing to include those, or are those excluded?

THE PRESIDENT. No, nothing is excluded. But one of the reasons for going at the ballistic missile—that is the one that is the most destabilizing. That one is the one that is the most frightening to most people. And let me just give you a little reasoning on that—of my own on that score.

That is the missile sitting there in its silo in which there could be the possibility of miscalculation. That is the one that people know that once that button is pushed, there is no defense; there is no recall. And it's a matter of minutes and the missiles reach the other country.

Those that are carried in bombers, those that are carried in ships of one kind or another, or submersibles, you are dealing there with a conventional type of weapon or instrument, and those instruments can be intercepted. They can be recalled if there has been a miscalculation. And so they don't have the same—I think—psychological effect that the presence of those other ones that, once launched, that's it, they're on their way and there's no preventing, no stopping them.

Q. Mr. President, there are many arms specialists, however, who say that the multiplication of cruise missiles in particular, those can be put on land, can be put on sea ships, submarines and so forth, also have that same effect, you can't call them back once they are launched. They have very short flight time, and there will be thousands of them.

THE PRESIDENT. They have a much longer flight time, actually, a matter of hours. They're not the speed of the ballistic missiles that go up into space and come back down again. But, this doesn't mean that we ignore anything. As I said, we're negotiating now on conventional weapons.

But I think you start with first things first. You can't bite it all off in one bite. And so our decision was to start with the most destabilizing and the most destructive.

Document 48

Transcript of the Department of State Daily Press Briefing, June 9, 1982 (Extract)[48]

A New U.S. Policy on Nuclear Reprocessing

. . . .

Q. Could you confirm the AP story which was carried by the *Washington Post* this morning on new U.S. policy on nuclear reprocessing?[49]

A. On nuclear reprocessing?

Q. Yes.

A. You will recall that the Presidential policy statement on nuclear cooperation and nonproliferation of July 16, 1981[50] directed the Secretary of State, in cooperation with other responsible agencies, to give priority attention to efforts to reduce proliferation risks, to enhance the international nonproliferation regime and, consistent with U.S. security interests, to reestablish a leadership role for the United States in international nuclear affairs. Under this mandate, one of the follow-on reviews has

---

[48] Source: Office of Press Relations, Department of State. The briefing was conducted by Department of State Acting Spokesman Alan Romberg beginning at 12:57 p.m.

[49] Reference is to an Associated Press story in the *Washington Post*, June 9, 1982, p. A3, which quoted administration sources as saying that President Reagan had approved a new policy giving other nations more control over the reprocessing of plutonium from nuclear fuel supplied by the United States.

[50] For the text of President Reagan's statement on nonproliferation and peaceful nuclear cooperation policy, July 16, 1981, see *American Foreign Policy: Current Documents, 1981*, document 57.

focused on approaches for a more predictable policy for exercising U.S. rights to approve reprocessing and use of plutonium subject to U.S. control under our peaceful nuclear cooperation agreements.

That review has now been completed, and the President has decided that in certain cases the United States will offer to work out predictable, programmatic arrangements for reprocessing and plutonium use for civilian power and research needs, in the context of seeking new or amended agreements as required by law. These agreements would involve only countries with effective commitments to nonproliferation, where there are advanced nuclear power programs, and where such activities do not constitute a proliferation risk and are under effective safeguards and controls.

U.S. approvals will be given only if U.S. statutory criteria are met, and will be valid only as long as these criteria and other conditions in the agreements continue to apply.

It should be noted that the United States has been approving reprocessing requests on an ad hoc, case-by-case basis under existing agreements for many years. What the President has not [*now*] approved is a new approach to granting longterm approvals in certain cases for the life of specific, carefully defined programs, as long as the conditions I have described are met.

. . . .

Document 49

Transcript of an Interview With the Secretary of Defense (Weinberger), June 12, 1982 (Extract)[51]

"To Freeze the Way It Is Now Would Be Very Dangerous"

CHARLAYNE HUNTER-GAULT. The issues of the arms race are of major concern to the Reagan administration's Secretary of Defense, Caspar Weinberger.

I spoke with him at the Pentagon in Washington about our nuclear strategy and I asked him whether today's rally[52] would have an impact on administration policy.

SECRETARY OF DEFENSE CASPAR WEINBERGER. Well, I think the impact that any visible segment of public opinion has—obviously public opinion in the final analysis is the only thing that counts in a democratic government, or should count.

But as far as whether or not a rally of that kind will make everybody suddenly change policies or not, I think clearly the answer is no. The policies have to be constructed and conducted on the way that seems best to the people who are the temporary guardians or trustees of these positions. And public opinion is expressed in elections.

The fact that a very large number of people turn out for a particular event is certainly something that people notice, but I don't think that anybody rushes back and says we have to change our policy, or Mr. President, you should make a different speech or something because there's been a rally. I don't think it goes that way at all.

On the other hand, I think it has to be pointed out that there is nobody that I know of in the United States, whether they turn out for a rally or not, who favors a nuclear war. Everybody that I know is against it, specifically including myself.

HUNTER-GAULT. But the rally is just one step in an otherwise larger and broader nuclear freeze movement. Are they wrong?

SECRETARY WEINBERGER. Yes. I think they're wrong. If they want a freeze, the situation the way it is now, I think that would be very wrong, very dangerous, would go against—work against the very things that the people were rallying for. Because I think if you freeze an unequal situation in this very delicate, dangerous business, you will erode the credibility of our deterrent and encourage the Soviets to feel that they could prevail either in a nuclear war or in a nuclear—an attempted nuclear blackmail. And I think that would be a very dangerous thing.

To freeze the way it is now would be very dangerous. To reduce sharply so that we achieve parity at much lower levels, as the

---

[51] Source: Department of Defense files. Secretary Weinberger was interviewed by Charlayne Hunter-Gault on the PBS program, "Call to Disarm."

[52] Reference is to a large anti-nuclear rally held that same day in New York City.

President has called for, in my mind, is clearly the way to avoid nuclear war.

HUNTER-GAULT. But there are those in the movement who are arms experts, former defense personnel, and so on, who say that we have enough deterrent capability. In fact, they say that we have nuclear power to wipe out Moscow, Leningrad, and at least 12 million Russians. Are they wrong? Isn't that enough?

SECRETARY WEINBERGER. You have to look at more than the numbers of raw warheads. You have to look at the strength of the Soviet target, the nature of the Soviet defenses, the accuracy of the Soviet missiles, their yield, the hardening of our targets, which is practically nothing. And all of those factors. And you have to ask yourself, put yourself in the situation and in the position of some of the people working on and planning the operation of the Soviet rocket nuclear forces. And you have to conclude, I think, that they have achieved, as the President has said, a definite edge, and that we have to embark upon the strategic strengthening program that he has called for.

And a freeze freezes into permanence, that kind, because once you have a freeze you'll never get a real disarmament, you'll never get anything below that. The Soviets would have no incentive whatever to agree to a reduction in arms if the freeze is obtained with the edge that they have now frozen into position. That's why we're against the freeze.

. . . .

Document 50

Statement Issued by the Department of State, June 17, 1982[53]

U.S. Rejection of the Soviet Proposal for the Non-First Use of Nuclear Weapons

Q. Is the Soviet non-first-use proposal new, or is it a reiteration of their older lines?

A. The Soviet Union's unilateral "pledge" of non-first use of nuclear weapons has surfaced for the first time. But it is based on a long history of similar non-first-use propaganda initiatives going back for years. Such Soviet proposals are appeals to emotions—not effective means to reduce the threat of nuclear war. A simple pledge of non-first use gives no assurance that an aggressor would not resort to the first use of nuclear weapons during conflict or crisis. Even if one could rely on such a pledge, its acceptance would, as Secretary Haig has said,[54] be tantamount to making Europe safe for conventional aggression.

Document 51

Address by President Reagan Before the U.N. Second Special Session on Disarmament, June 17, 1982[55]

The U.S. Agenda for Comprehensive Arms Control

Mr. Secretary-General, Mr. President, distinguished delegates, ladies and gentlemen, I speak today as both a citizen of the United States and of the world. I come with the heartfelt wishes of my people for peace, bearing honest proposals and looking for genuine progress.

Dag Hammarskjold said 24 years ago this month, "We meet in a time of peace, which is no peace."[56] His words are as true today

---

53 Source: Office of Press Relations, Department of State; posted statement. The statement was posted in response to a question asked at the Department of State Daily Press Briefing, June 16, concerning Gromyko's speech to the United Nations on June 15, in which he pledged Soviet no-first use of nuclear weapons.

54 Reference presumably is to Secretary Haig's speech before the Center for Strategic and International Studies, Georgetown University, April 6. For text, see document 25.

55 Source: White House Press Release, June 17, 1982, Office of the Press Secretary to the President; printed also in *Weekly Compilation of Presidential Documents*, June 21, 1982, pp. 807–812. President Reagan spoke in the General Assembly Hall beginning at 11:02 a.m.

56 Quotation is from Hammarskjold's speech at Cambridge, England, on June 5, 1958. For text, see *Public Papers of the Secretaries-General of the United Nations: Dag Hammarskjold, 1958–1960*, eds. Andrew W. Cordier and Wilder Foote (New York, 1974), vol. IV, pp. 90–95.

as they were then. More than 100 disputes have disturbed the peace among nations since World War II and today the threat of nuclear disaster hangs over the lives of all our people. The Bible tells us that there will be a time for peace, but so far this century mankind has failed to find it.

The United Nations is dedicated to world peace, and its Charter clearly prohibits the international use of force, yet the tide of belligerence continues to rise. The Charter's influence has weakened even in the 4 years since the first special session on disarmament. We must not only condemn aggression, we must enforce the dictates of our Charter and resume the struggle for peace.

The record of history is clear; citizens of the United States resort to force reluctantly and only when they must. Our foreign policy, as President Eisenhower once said, "is not difficult to state. We are for peace first, last, and always for very simple reasons. We know that only in a peaceful atmosphere, a peace with justice, one in which we can be confident, can America prosper as we have known prosperity in the past," he said.[57]

He said to those who challenge the truth of those words let me point out at the end of World War II, we were the only undamaged industrial power in the world. Our military supremacy was unquestioned. We had harnessed the atom, and had the ability to unleash its destructive force anywhere in the world. In short, we could have achieved world domination, but that was contrary to the character of our people. Instead we wrote a new chapter in the history of mankind. We used our power and wealth to rebuild the war-ravaged economies of the world both East and West, including those nations who had been our enemies. We took the initiative in creating such international institutions as this United Nations where leaders of good will could come together to build bridges for peace and prosperity.

America has no territorial ambitions. We occupy no countries, and we have built no walls to lock our people in. Our commitment to self-determination, freedom, and peace is the very soul of America. That commitment is as strong today as it ever was.

The United States has fought four wars in my lifetime. In each, we struggled to defend freedom and democracy. We were never the aggressors. America's strength, and yes, her military power, have been a force for peace, not conquest; for democracy, not despotism; for freedom, not tyranny.

Watching, as I have, succeeding generations of American youth bleed their lives onto far-flung battlefields to protect our ideals and secure the rule of law, I have known how important it is to deter conflict. But since coming to the Presidency, the enormity of the responsibility of this office has made my commitment even deeper. I believe that responsibility is shared by all of us here today.

On our recent trip to Europe,[58] my wife, Nancy, told me of a bronze statue, 22 feet high, that she saw on a cliff on the coast of France. The beach at the base of that cliff is called Saint Laurent, but countless American family Bibles have written it in on the flyleaf and know it as Omaha Beach. The pastoral quiet of that French countryside is in marked contrast to the bloody violence that took place there on a June day 38 years ago when the Allies stormed the Continent. At the end of just one day of battle, 10,500 Americans were wounded, missing or killed in what became known as the Normandy Landing.

The statue atop that cliff is called "The Spirit of American Youth Rising From the Waves." Its image of sacrifice is almost too powerful to describe.

The pain of war is still vivid in our national memory. It sends me to this special session of the United Nations eager to comply with the plea of Pope Paul VI when he spoke in this chamber nearly 17 years ago. "If you want to be brothers," His Holiness said, "let the arms fall from your hands."[59] Well, we Americans yearn to let them go. But we need more than mere words, more than empty promises before we can proceed. We look around the world and see rampant conflict and aggression. There are many sources of this conflict—expansionist ambitions, local rivalries, the striving to obtain justice and security. We must all work to resolve such discords by peaceful means and to prevent them from escalation.

In the nuclear era, the major powers bear a special responsibility to ease these sources

---

[57] Not further identified.

[58] President Reagan visited the United Kingdom, France, Italy, the Vatican, and Germany, June 2–11. Documentation on the trip is in Chapter 5, Part F, and Chapter 10.

[59] Quotation is from Pope Paul VI's speech to the U.N. General Assembly, October 4, 1965; for text, see *American Foreign Policy: Current Documents, 1965* (Washington, 1968), pp. 130–134.

of conflict and to refrain from aggression. And that's why we're so deeply concerned by Soviet conduct. Since World War II, the record of tyranny has included Soviet violation of the Yalta agreements leading to domination of Eastern Europe, symbolized by the Berlin Wall—a grim, gray monument to repression that I visited just a week ago. It includes the takeovers of Czechoslovakia, Hungary, and Afghanistan; and the ruthless repression of the proud people of Poland.

Soviet-sponsored guerrillas and terrorists are at work in Central and South America, in Africa, the Middle East, in the Caribbean and in Europe, violating human rights and unnerving the world with violence. Communist atrocities in Southeast Asia, Afghanistan and elsewhere continue to shock the free world as refugees escape to tell of their horror.

The decade of so-called détente witnessed the most massive Soviet buildup of military power in history. They increased their defense spending by 40 percent while American defense actually declined in the same real terms. Soviet aggression and support for violence around the world have eroded the confidence needed for arms negotiations.

While we exercised unilateral restraint they forged ahead and today possess nuclear and conventional forces far in excess of an adequate deterrent capability.

Soviet oppression is not limited to the countries they invade. At the very time the Soviet Union is trying to manipulate the peace movement in the West, it is stifling a budding peace movement at home. In Moscow, banners are scuttled, buttons are snatched, and demonstrators are arrested when even a few people dare to speak about their fears.

Eleanor Roosevelt, one of our first ambassadors to this body, reminded us that the high-sounding words of tyrants stand in bleak contradiction to their deeds. "Their promises", she said, "are in deep contrast to their performances."

My country learned a bitter lesson in this century: the scourge of tyranny cannot be stopped with words alone. So we have embarked on an effort to renew our strength that had fallen dangerously low. We refuse to become weaker while potential adversaries remain committed to their imperialist adventures.

My people have sent me here today to speak for them as citizens of the world, which they truly are, for we Americans are drawn from every nationality represented in this chamber today. We understand that men and women of every race and creed can and must work together for peace. We stand ready to take the next steps down the road of cooperation through verifiable arms reduction. Agreements on arms control and disarmament can be useful in reinforcing peace; but they're not magic. We should not confuse the signing of agreements with the solving of problems. Simply collecting agreements will not bring peace. Agreements genuinely reinforce peace only when they are kept. Otherwise we're building a paper castle that will be blown away by the winds of war. Let me repeat, we need deeds, not words, to convince us of Soviet sincerity, should they choose to join us on this path.

Since the end of World War II, the United States has been the leader in serious disarmament and arms control proposals. In 1946, in what became known as the Baruch Plan, the United States submitted a proposal for control of nuclear weapons and nuclear energy by an international authority. The Soviets rejected this plan. In 1955, President Eisenhower made his "Open Skies" proposal, under which the United States and the Soviet Union would have exchanged blueprints of military establishments and provided for aerial reconnaissance.[60] The Soviets rejected this plan. In 1963, the Limited Test Ban Treaty came into force. This treaty ended nuclear weapons testing in the atmosphere, outer space, or under water by participating nations. In 1970, the Treaty on the Non-Proliferation of Nuclear Weapons took effect.[61] The United States played a major role in this key effort to prevent the spread of nuclear explosives and to provide for international safeguards on civil nuclear activities.

My country remains deeply committed to those objectives today, and to strengthening the nonproliferation framework. This is essential to international security. In the early 1970's, again at United States urging, agreements were reached between the United States and the U.S.S.R. providing for ceilings on some categories of weapons. They could have been more meaningful if

[60] For the text of President Eisenhower's open skies proposal, which he revealed at the Geneva Conference, July 21, 1955, see *Public Papers of the Presidents of the United States: Dwight D. Eisenhower, 1955* (Washington, 1959), pp. 713–716.

[61] For text, see 21 UST 483.

Soviet actions had shown restraint and commitment to stability at lower levels of force.

The United Nations designated the 1970's as the First Disarmament Decade. But good intentions were not enough. In reality that 10 year period included an unprecedented buildup in military weapons and the flaring of aggression and use of force in almost every region of the world. We are now in the Second Disarmament Decade. The task at hand is to assure civilized behavior among nations, to unite behind an agenda of peace.

Over the past 7 months, the United States has put forward a broad-based, comprehensive series of proposals to reduce the risk of war: we have proposed four major points as an agenda for peace: elimination of land-based, intermediate-range missiles, a one-third reduction in strategic, ballistic missile warheads, a substantial reduction in NATO and Warsaw Pact ground and air forces, and new safeguards to reduce the risk of accidental war.[62]

We urge the Soviet Union today to join with us in this quest. We must act not for ourselves alone, but for all mankind. On November 18th of last year, I announced United States objectives in arms control agreements. They must be equitable and militarily significant. They must stabilize forces at lower levels, and they must be verifiable.

The United States and its allies have made specific, reasonable, and equitable proposals. In February, our negotiating team in Geneva offered the Soviet Union a draft treaty on intermediate-range nuclear forces. We offered to cancel deployment of our Pershing II ballistic missiles and ground-launched cruise missiles in exchange for Soviet elimination of the SS–20, SS–4, and SS–5 missiles. This proposal would eliminate with one stroke those systems about which both sides have expressed the greatest concern.

The United States is also looking forward to beginning negotiations on strategic arms reductions with the Soviet Union in less than 2 weeks. We will work hard to make these talks an opportunity for real progress in our quest for peace.

On May 9, I announced a phased approach to the reduction of strategic arms. In a first phase, the number of ballistic missile warheads on each side would be reduced to about 5,000. No more than half the remaining warheads would be on land-based missiles. All ballistic missiles would be reduced to an equal level at about one-half the current United States number.

In the second phase, we would reduce each side's overall destructive power to equal levels, including a mutual ceiling on ballistic missile throw-weight below the current U.S. level. We are also prepared to discuss other elements of the strategic balance.

Before I returned from Europe last week, I met in Bonn with the leaders of the North Atlantic Treaty Organization. We agreed to introduce a major new Western initiative for the Vienna negotiations on Mutual Balanced Force Reductions.[63] Our approach calls for common collective ceilings for both NATO and the Warsaw Treaty Organization. After 7 years, there would be a total of 700,000 ground forces and 900,000 ground and air force personnel combined. It also includes a package of associated measures to encourage cooperation and verify compliance.

We urge the Soviet Union and members of the Warsaw Pact to view our Western proposal as a means to reach agreement in Vienna after nine long years of inconclusive talks. We also urge them to implement the 1975 Helsinki agreement on security and cooperation in Europe.[64]

Let me stress that for agreements to work, both sides must be able to verify compliance. The building of mutual confidence in compliance can only be achieved through greater openness. I encourage the Special Session on Disarmament to endorse the importance of these principles in arms control agreements.

I have instructed our representatives at the 40-nation Committee on Disarmament to renew emphasis on verification and compliance. Based on a U.S. proposal, a committee has been formed to examine these issues as they relate to restrictions on nuclear testing. We are also pressing the need for effective verification provisions in agreements banning chemical weapons.

The use of chemical and biological weapons has long been viewed with revulsion by

[62] President Reagan's initiative on reducing the risk of accidental war was made in his speech in Berlin, June 11; for text, see document 184.

[63] See the statement issued by the North Atlantic Council, June 10, document 182.

[64] For the text of the final act of the multilateral Conference on Security and Cooperation in Europe, concluded in Helsinki on August 1, 1975, see Department of State *Bulletin*, September 1, 1975, pp. 323–350.

civilized nations. No peacemaking institution can ignore the use of those dread weapons and still live up to its mission. The need for a truly effective and verifiable chemical weapons agreement has been highlighted by recent events. The Soviet Union and their allies are violating the Geneva Protocol of 1925,[65] related rules of international law and the 1972 Biological Weapons Convention. There is conclusive evidence that the Soviet Government has provided toxins for use in Laos and Kampuchea, and are themselves using chemical weapons against freedom fighters in Afghanistan.

We have repeatedly protested to the Soviet Government, as well as to the Governments of Laos and Vietnam, their use of chemical and toxin weapons. We call upon them now to grant full and free access to their countries or to territories they control so that United Nations experts can conduct an effective, independent investigation to verify cessation of these horrors.

Evidence of noncompliance with existing arms control agreements underscores the need to approach negotiation of any new agreements with care. The democracies of the West are open societies. Information on our defenses is available to our citizens, our elected officials and the world. We do not hesitate to inform potential adversaries of our military forces and ask in return for the same information concerning theirs.

The amount and type of military spending by a country is important for the world to know, as a measure of its intentions, and the threat that country may pose to its neighbors. The Soviet Union and other closed societies go to extraordinary lengths to hide their true military spending not only from other nations, but from their own people. This practice contributes to distrust and fear about their intentions.

Today, the United States proposes an international conference on military expenditures to build on the work of this body in developing a common system for accounting and reporting. We urge the Soviet Union, in particular, to join this effort in good faith, to revise the universally discredited official figures it publishes, and to join with us in giving the world a true account of the resources we allocate to our armed forces.

[65] The United States deposited its ratification of the 1925 Protocol for the Prohibition of the Use in War of Asphyxiating, Poisonous or Other Gases, and of Bacteriological Methods of Warfare in 1975. For text of the Protocol, see 26 UST 571.

Last Friday in Berlin, I said that I would leave no stone unturned in the effort to reinforce peace and lessen the risk of war. It's been clear to me steps should be taken to improve mutual communication, confidence, and lessen the likelihood of misinterpretation.

I have, therefore, directed the exploration of ways to increase understanding and communication between the United States and the Soviet Union in times of peace and of crisis. We will approach the Soviet Union with proposals for reciprocal exchanges in such areas as advance notification of major strategic exercises that otherwise might be misinterpreted; advance notification of ICBM launches within, as well as beyond, national boundaries; and an expanded exchange of strategic forces data.

While substantial information on U.S. activities and forces in these areas already is provided, I believe that jointly and regularly sharing information would represent a qualitative improvement in the strategic nuclear environment and would help reduce the chance of misunderstandings. I call upon the Soviet Union to join the United States in exploring these possibilities to build confidence and I ask for your support of our efforts.

One of the major items before this conference is the development of a comprehensive program of disarmament. We support the effort to chart a course of realistic and effective measures in the quest for peace.

I have come to this hall to call for international recommitment to the basic tenet of the United Nations Charter—that all members practice tolerance and live together in peace as good neighbors under the rule of law, forsaking armed force as a means of settling disputes between nations. America urges you to support the agenda for peace that I have outlined today. We ask you to reinforce the bilateral and multilateral arms control negotiations between members of NATO and the Warsaw Pact and to rededicate yourselves to maintaining international peace and security, and removing threats to peace.

We, who have signed the U.N. Charter, have pledged to refrain from the threat or use of force against the territory or independence of any state. In these times when more and more lawless acts are going unpunished—as some members of this very body show a growing disregard for the U.N. Charter—the peace-loving nations of the world must condemn aggression and pledge again to act in a way that is worthy of the ideals that we have endorsed. Let us finally make the Charter live.

In late spring, 37 years ago, representatives of 50 nations gathered on the other side of this continent, in the San Francisco Opera House. The league of Nations had crumbled and World War II still raged. But those men and nations were determined to find peace. The result was this Charter for peace that is the framework of the United Nations.

President Harry Truman spoke of the revival of an old faith.[66] He said the everlasting moral force of justice prompting that United Nations Conference—such a force remains strong in America and in other countries where speech is free and citizens have the right to gather and make their opinions known.

And President Truman said, "If we should pay merely lip service to inspiring ideals, and later do violence to simple justice, we would draw down upon us the bitter wrath of generations yet unborn." Those words of Harry Truman have special meaning for us today as we live with the potential to destroy civilization.

"We must learn to live together in peace," he said. "We must build a new world—a far better world."

What a better world it would be if the guns were silent, if neighbor no longer encroached on neighbor, and all peoples were free to reap the rewards of their toil, and determine their own destiny and system of government, whatever their choice.

During my recent audience with His Holiness Pope John Paul II, I gave him the pledge of the American people to do everything possible for peace and arms reduction.[67] The American people believe forging real and lasting peace to be their sacred trust. Let us never forget that such a peace would be a terrible hoax if the world were no longer blessed with freedom and respect for human rights.

"The United Nations," Hammarskjold said, "was born out of the cataclysms of war. It should justify the sacrifices of all those who have died for freedom and justice. It is our duty to the past." Hammarskjold said, "And it is our duty to the future so to serve both our nations and the world."

As both patriots of our nations and the hope of all the world, let those of us assembled here in the name of peace deepen our understandings, renew our commitment to the rule of law, and take new and bolder steps to calm an uneasy world. Can any delegate here deny that in so doing he would be doing what the people, the rank and file of his own country—or her own country—want him or her to do?

Isn't it time for us to really represent the deepest most heartfelt yearnings of all of our people? Let no nation abuse this common longing to be free of fear. We must not manipulate our people by playing upon their nightmares. We must serve mankind through genuine disarmament. With God's help we can secure life and freedom for generations to come.

Thank you very much. (Applause)

Document 52

Prepared Statement by the Director of the Bureau of Politico-Military Affairs, Department of State (Howe), Before a Subcommittee of the House Foreign Affairs Committee, July 13, 1982[68]

Chemical Weapons: Arms Control and Deterrence

MR. CHAIRMAN AND MEMBERS OF THE COMMITTEE: I am pleased to have the opportunity to appear before you this morning to address foreign policy and arms control aspects of chemical weapons.

The policy of the United States in this area is clear. Our goal remains to stop the current use of chemical weapons in Afghanistan and Southeast Asia and to obtain a complete and verifiable ban on the development, production and stockpiling of them.

---

[66] For the text of President Truman's address to the United Nations Conference in San Francisco, April 25, 1945, which includes the quotations below, see *Public Papers of the Presidents of the United States: Harry S. Truman,* 1945 (Washington, 1961), pp. 20–23.

[67] For President Reagan's statement at the Vatican, June 7, see document 236.

[68] Source: *Foreign Policy and Arms Control Implications of Chemical Weapons: Hearings Before the Subcommittees on International Security and Scientific Affairs and on Asian and Pacific Affairs of the Committee on Foreign Affairs, House of Representatives, Ninety-seventh Congress, Second Session* (Washington, 1982), pp. 147–154. Howe testified before the Subcommittee on International Security and Scientific Affairs.

The Geneva Protocol of 1925, to which the United States is a party, prohibits the use in war of asphyxiating, poisonous, or other gases, and of biological methods of warfare. Unfortunately, the agreement bans only the use of chemical weapons, and not their possession. It is, furthermore, essentially a ban only on first use since most of the important military powers, including the United States and Soviet Union, have reserved the right to retaliate in kind to an enemy's use of chemical weapons. Our eventual objective is the achievement of a new multilateral treaty which bans chemical weapons altogether and requires effective verification and compliance.

Achievement of such a treaty would be a significant milestone for mankind. But it will not be easy.

The critical obstacle to forward movement has been Soviet intransigence on verification and compliance issues. Any effective chemical weapons agreement must ensure the destruction of chemical stocks, and must contain adequate monitoring provisions so that no party clandestinely retains or produces chemical weapons. Recent Soviet violations have underlined the absolute necessity for effective verification and monitoring of any chemical weapons agreement.

As a means of moving the process forward, we have shifted our effort from bilateral U.S.-Soviet negotiations to the Committee on Disarmament. The bilateral negotiations, begun in 1977, lapsed in deadlock in mid-1980. The Soviet Union was unwilling to accept reasonable provisions for verifying the destruction of existing stocks of chemical weapons and disposition of their places of manufacture. In addition the Soviets were not prepared to agree to effective procedures for assuring continued compliance.

For these reasons, we are focusing our current efforts in Geneva. It is the role of the Committee on Disarmament to develop multilateral arms control agreements. The United States is an active participant in ongoing efforts there towards elaborating a comprehensive agreement banning chemical weapons.

We have conducted this arms control effort against a background of unilateral restraint. Since 1969, we have not manufactured any lethal or incapacitating chemical weapons. Successive U.S. administrations have repeatedly assured that we will never initiate chemical warfare.

However, our restraint has not been matched by the Soviet Union. During this same 13-year period the Soviets have continued to strengthen their military chemical warfare capability. This Soviet buildup extends well beyond reasonable deterrence requirements.

This threat to our security has recently been brought into sharper focus by the actual use of chemical weapons in Afghanistan and chemical and toxin weapons in Southeast Asia. Compelling evidence was presented to Congress on March 22 and May 13 of this year.[69] That evidence continues to accumulate. We are analyzing indications that these attacks are continuing unabated, despite international efforts to stop them.

Such attacks are illegal. The use of chemical weapons is a violation of the 1925 Geneva Protocol and related rules of international law. Possession alone of toxin weapons is a violation of the 1972 Biological Weapons Convention. President Reagan specifically called attention to such violations in his address to the Second Special Session of the United Nations devoted to disarmament on June 17.

Unfortunately, our numerous démarches to the Soviets have been rebuffed. Despite overwhelming evidence, the Soviets continue to deny these illegal acts are taking place. A paper of rebuttal, attributed to experts from the USSR Academy of Sciences, the USSR Ministry of Health, and other Soviet organizations, which was submitted to the United Nations on May 21, has been described in a recent issue of *Science* magazine, an independent nongovernmental scientific publication, as containing "extravagant conjectures."[70]

Despite this discouraging background, we remain actively interested in achieving our goal of a universal and comprehensive chemical weapons ban. We intend, in the upcoming session of the Committee on Disarmament in July, to explore fully all areas of the Soviet proposal recently submitted to the U.N. Special Session on Disarmament. Preliminary analysis of this pro-

---

[69] Reference presumably is to the Department of State study, *Chemical Warfare in Southeast Asia and Afghanistan,* Special Report No. 98, March 22, 1982; for extracts, see documents 440 and 477. The May 13 evidence presented to Congress has not been further identified.

[70] Reference is to an editorial by Eliot Marshall, "The Soviet Elephant Grass Theory," *Science,* July 2, 1982, p. 32, which reviewed the Soviet 19-page study, "Chemical and Bacteriological (Biological) Weapons." (U.N. document A/37/233) The Soviet study was a critique of the Department of State study referred to in footnote 69, *supra.*

posal indicates that most of it is not new. However, it contains a few elements of potential interest. The significance of these new elements is not clear. However, it would be premature to conclude that there had been a breakthrough. Frankly, we have not resumed the bilateral discussions because there is little prospect for productive negotiations under existing circumstances. Should the Soviets demonstrate a willingness to accept genuinely effective verification and compliance arrangements, and should they demonstrate a willingness to abide by existing international obligations on chemical, biological, and toxin weapons, the prospects for serious bilateral work would be enhanced.

Mr. Chairman, all executive agencies of this administration concerned with national security, as well as previous Congresses, have concluded that we can no longer forego modernization of our chemical warfare deterrent, which is a modest one measured against Soviet capabilities. Our national security policy must address the realities of the world we live in. Our military forces must have the capability to deter threats to ourselves and our allies. This requires maintaining adequate U.S. stocks. It also requires improvement of protective and defensive measures against chemical attack, which is the primary emphasis of our program.

The report to Congress on the U.S. chemical warfare deterrence program submitted by DOD in March of this year[71] presents our situation in detail. The difficult decision to modernize our chemical weapons capability was undertaken only with reluctance after long and painstaking examination of our obsolete and deteriorating assets. The Congress, which actually moved ahead of the executive branch in encouraging modernization of our chemical deterrent, continues to review each step of this program carefully.

The United States has kept its allies fully informed of its program and of its decisions, over the past several years, to begin modernization of U.S. chemical warfare capabilities. In March of last year we informed our allies of the administration's decision to seek funding for the facility at Pine Bluff. In February of this year, we informed our allies of our decision to seek funding for production. We believe it is inappropriate to ask allies to share responsibility for a U.S. national security decision, and have not done so. No allied government has expressed opposition to these steps or otherwise commented on the substance of the decision to seek funds for production. For many years, it has been agreed NATO doctrine that an effective chemical warfare retaliatory capability is an essential part of the continuum of deterrence. We have informed our allies, as we have informed the Congress, that there has been no decision on forward deployment of binary chemical weapons and none is currently under consideration. Our allies have been assured we will consult fully with any other nation involved prior to making such a decision. Since it will be several years before production begins and several years thereafter before stockpiles are accumulated, no consideration of deployment elsewhere is likely for some time to come. Our allies understand and accept that we have no plans at this time to deploy any binary chemical munitions in any foreign country.

Our allies, like ourselves, are committed to seeking through arms control a complete ban on the production and stockpiling of chemical weapons. Together we are pressing for progress toward such an agreement in the Committee on Disarmament in Geneva. They also recognize that the principal hurdle to be overcome is that of verification and the need to assure effective compliance.

We are well aware that chemical weapons are an emotional issue, in allied countries as well as our own. But as leader of the free world, the United States has a particular obligation to demonstrate resolve in maintaining the peace. One can debate whether possession of a particular weapon will deter the use of similar weapons by others, and one can debate what types and levels of arms should be maintained. But debate about chemical warfare has yet to identify a deterrent that does not include a chemical weapons component, without posing the additional risks of undesirable escalation or unacceptable accommodation. The history of World War II bears witness to the effectiveness of chemical weapons as a component of such a deterrent. According to postwar testimony by enemy officials, allied possession of chemical weapons effectively deterred the Axis Powers from using their chemical weapons, though they had accumulated large stocks.

In sum, we seek to achieve through negotiations a verifiable ban on all chemical weapons. Until success is achieved, we must

[71] Reference is to Report to Congress on the United States Chemical Warfare Deterrence Program, March 1982.

reduce or eliminate Soviet incentives to use chemical weapons against us or our allies. This can be done by modernizing and maintaining an adequate chemical warfare deterrent posture. Our chemical weapons modernization actions do not represent a decision to place greater emphasis upon chemical warfare. Nor do we plan to match Soviet capabilities. Our objective is to have the safest, smallest level of chemical munitions which provides us the deterrent we need.

Document 53

Transcript of a White House Press Briefing, July 20, 1982[72]

Administration's Position on the Threshold Test Ban, Peaceful Nuclear Explosions, and Comprehensive Test Ban Treaties

SENIOR ADMINISTRATION OFFICIAL. The issue of nuclear testing has been under review within the administration as part of a broad-based review of arms control policies and initiatives. The administration and previous administrations have been devoted to the long-term goal of concluding a comprehensive test ban and, indeed, this remains the administration's goal. The administration believes that a comprehensive test ban should be considered in the context of broad, deep, and verifiable arms reductions, expanded confidence-building measures and improved verification capabilities that would justify confidence in Soviet compliance with a comprehensive test ban.

In the context of that broad rubric of arms control goals, we are proceeding, as you know, on a number of courses. We are in Geneva working toward deproductions in the START negotiations and in INF. We are in Vienna and have been for a long time negotiating for meaningful reductions in conventional arms. In other multinational foray, as you're familiar with I believe, we've been trying to make progress in securing Soviet agreement to confidence-building measures that reduce the risk of war and the chances of misinterpretation.

I should also [say] aside, I think, that there has been established, and is underway today, a working group in Geneva within the context of the CCD working upon verification issues in particular related, of course, to nuclear testing.

We think that a comprehensive ban on nuclear testing must remain a component of this administration's long-term arms control objectives, but there are problems to be overcome and these deal essentially with verification. My experience has been that the Soviets simply have not or have refused to accept measures that would assure effective verification.

When you deal specifically with the area of nuclear testing limitations, this administration is determined to make progress on this front. We're going to press forward and seek ways in which we can correct verification problems that have been associated with the Threshold Test Ban and with the Peaceful Nuclear Explosions Treaties.

At present, we cannot effectively verify the TTB and the PNE treaties.

Q. How about putting that in English? What's a TTB?

Q. Can you spell out those—

SENIOR ADMINISTRATION OFFICIAL. The Threshold Test Ban Treaty and the Peaceful Nuclear Explosions Treaties.

The United States and the Soviet Union in 1976 agreed that we would not test, either of us, in excess of 150 kilotons. The United States, for its part, has complied with that agreement. However, on several occasions, seismic signals from the Soviet Union have been of a sufficient magnitude to call into question Soviet compliance with the threshold of 150 kt., kilotons, and it's because of the uncertainties in our yield estimation process that the United States cannot prove beyond any reasonable doubt that the Soviets have violated the Threshold Test Ban Treaty.

The Soviets have always asserted, when challenged on this point, that they have not violated the agreement. But this underscores the problem. And that is uncertainty, and the requirement to remove this uncertainty to the maximum extent feasible by improved verification procedures.

---

72 Source: Office of the Press Secretary to the President. The briefing was conducted on background by two senior administration officials in the Briefing Room of the White House beginning at 1:59 p.m.

Our security, in the President's judgment, requires that we do not agree to an unverifiable treaty. We cannot have a repetition of our experience with the unverifiable biological weapons convention. And we cannot have a repetition of the yellow rain episode. Therefore, we are committed to securing improved verification arrangements for the TTBT and the Peaceful Nuclear Explosions Treaties.

Our objective is to seek Soviet agreement to negotiate improved verification procedures which would make the Threshold Test Ban Treaty and the PNE Treaty adequate for submission for ratification. And we will pursue that goal determinedly.

In addition, as we mentioned, we are, also, discussing verification measures on a multilateral basis in Geneva in a special working group established earlier this year in the Committee on Disarmament.

At this time, I, and my colleague, would welcome your questions.

Q. You are verifying the *New York Times* story?[73]

SENIOR ADMINISTRATION OFFICIAL. No; I would not go on every line and statement in the story.

Q. What do you object to?

SENIOR ADMINISTRATION OFFICIAL. Basically, I would rather take the positive cast and say just here—

Q. You came here to discuss the *New York Times* story. You did not come to make an announcement to this country of what you had done.

SENIOR ADMINISTRATION OFFICIAL. We came here to say what we intend to do. And that is what I have said.

Q. What you are telling us is you are going to try to renegotiate the Threshold Test Ban Treaty. You are going to try to renegotiate the PNE. And, while you are going to try to do something on the Comprehensive Test Ban, you have these problems with verification with it, also. Is that not the sum of what you are saying?

SENIOR ADMINISTRATION OFFICIAL. I think renegotiation is too broad an expression for what we intend here. What we are trying to do is to strengthen the verification provisions of both of those.

Q. Are you telling us that you are going to negotiate verification separately, before you negotiate future testing? You are not going to negotiate the Comprehensive Test Ban Treaty. And you are going to work on verifications first. Is that correct?

SENIOR ADMINISTRATION OFFICIAL. What we are saying is that there is a TTBT. There is a Threshold Test Ban Treaty in existence now. It was signed in 1974. It has not been ratified at this time by either the Soviets or by ourselves. As my colleague said, since 1976, we have been complying with this 150-kiloton threshold limit on testing. As we have looked again at whether we should ratify or not, the decision that he is referring to has to do with the fact that we do not feel that the verification provisions which are in the protocol to this treaty—which is part of the treaty, but it is separate; it is the protocol—we do not feel that those are adequate to give us confidence that we can verify this 150-kiloton ban within the limits that we feel we need to. For that reason, we are looking at the verification measures associated with the protocol to the TTBT Treaty.

Q. Sir, if you say you are trying to strengthen the ratification provisions in a treaty or treaties which have not yet been ratified by the Senate, are you not saying you are going to try to negotiate the treaties, or at least the protocols?

SENIOR ADMINISTRATION OFFICIAL. (No audible response.)

Q. Well, how do you strengthen verification without further negotiations with the Soviets on changes in the treaties?

Q. If there will be further negotiations, is that not renegotiating?

SENIOR ADMINISTRATION OFFICIAL. I do not mean to mislead. Earlier, I took the "renegotiation" to apply, broadly, to all of the provisions of the treaty. No; that is not true, the verification portions as they are contained in the protocols of the treaties.

Q. So you are going to try to renegotiate the protocols?

SENIOR ADMINISTRATION OFFICIAL. That is correct. These are not, however, essential changes to the treaties themselves. The treaty talks about the limit. And there are

[73] Reference is to the story in the *New York Times*, July 20, 1982, pp. A1, A4, which reported that President Reagan approved a National Security Council decision on June 19 that the United States would not resume negotiations with the Soviet Union and the United Kingdom on a comprehensive ban on nuclear testing. The decision was reportedly made because of the doubts of some members of the verifiability of a comprehensive ban and a need to continue testing new nuclear weapons.

certain basic provisions. The verification provisions in the TTBT are rather rudimentary. And we are saying we need to strengthen those.

Now, we do not know if the Soviet Union will want to do this.

SENIOR ADMINISTRATION OFFICIAL. No, we don't know if the Soviet Union will want to do this. All this has to be developed and proposed in the future.

Q. —saying that ratification is on hold until you get this verification worked out to your satisfaction?

SENIOR ADMINISTRATION OFFICIAL. That's right, yes.

Q. Are you not going to abide—

SENIOR ADMINISTRATION OFFICIAL. In the back there, please?

Q. What does this do to compliance? The United States would say it'd been complying since 1976. Are you now saying that you feel free to not comply because you can't verify the Soviets? What's the position on—

SENIOR ADMINISTRATION OFFICIAL. No, we don't—would not alter our policies toward continued compliance with—

Q. Would either of you explain what you have to do physically to get the verification that you want to get? Do you have to walk around on the ground in Russia or what physically has to be done?

SENIOR ADMINISTRATION OFFICIAL. Those specific details—whether you have to walk around the ground, it really depends on what limit of verification you're willing—what degree of uncertainty you're willing to live with. And those issues as to how much we can do without having to have on-site inspection, for example, have yet to be determined. We have to consider that in further work on verification. We have done some. But much more needs to be done and a decision has to be made by the President as to what specific verification policy we will have.

Q. Are you willing to live with "uncertainty" as you put it on this? You said it depends on what degree of uncertainty you're willing to live with. Are you willing to live with uncertainty? And insofar as treaties, has the Soviet Union shown a great inclination to live by many treaties, indeed, hardly any or what? I mean, all this uncertainty is a little bit rough when it deals with missiles and so forth, isn't it?

SENIOR ADMINISTRATION OFFICIAL. In this particular area where a nuclear explosion can have an explosive value which you may measure rather imprecisely, that is, your results may be orders of magnitude different depending upon variables which you cannot control here by the means currently being used. And what we're saying is that we're trying to substantially reduce the uncertainty which exists today.

Q. How can you—

SENIOR ADMINISTRATION OFFICIAL. And you can never be entirely, precisely certain.

Q. —except on-site, as I understand it. Isn't that the only way—

SENIOR ADMINISTRATION OFFICIAL. Even there—

Q. —you can get verification that's sure—on-site?

SENIOR ADMINISTRATION OFFICIAL. Not necessarily, no.

Q. Can I ask a couple of questions—

Q.—continue to abide by the terms?

SENIOR ADMINISTRATION OFFICIAL. That's right.

Q. Does this apply only to underground testing? It does not apply to any of the past treaties on the atmosphere?

SENIOR ADMINISTRATION OFFICIAL. No, it doesn't.

SENIOR ADMINISTRATION OFFICIAL. Those are all unaffected.

Q. Would you address the CTBT because really you haven't addressed that. You've told us about these other two. The *Times* story today said a decision had been made yesterday not to resume negotiations on the CTBT. Is that correct and you reaffirmed your interest in it but are you going to negotiate—

SENIOR ADMINISTRATION OFFICIAL. We think that the first thing that has to be done is to get to what we have and let's make that workable and effective and that is to strengthen the verification provisions of the TTBT and the PNE. . . .

Q. Are you going to put this aside until you get what you want on these other two treaties which is, in effect, saying you're going to postpone or you're going to put off negotiating a CTBT until you get the threshold and the PNE—

SENIOR ADMINISTRATION OFFICIAL. That's fair in general terms. The administration remains committed to the CTB as a goal but—

Q. Committed but you don't plan to do anything in the near-term about it—

SENIOR ADMINISTRATION OFFICIAL. It depends how well we do on the TTBT and the PNE and as well right now, we are in Geneva and will continue to participate and [*in*] verification working-group analyses that are related to CTB.

Q. Has the Soviet Union—

SENIOR ADMINISTRATION OFFICIAL. So, it's really not quite right to say that we will not remain engaged on related matters because we are and we will remain so.

Q. Has the Soviet Union given any indication that it's willing to look in any productive sense at those verification provisions?

SENIOR ADMINISTRATION OFFICIAL. We haven't had an exchange with them on that subject yet.

Q. Is it fair to say that—

SENIOR ADMINISTRATION OFFICIAL. I want to go to . . . just a minute.

Q. The 1980 Republican platform which I believe you had a hand in drafting and which Candidate Reagan and President Reagan strongly supported, pledges an end to what was called the Carter administration coverup of Soviet violations of the SALT I and II Treaties. When would you anticipate the administration is going to end the Carter coverup of these treaty violations?

SENIOR ADMINISTRATION OFFICIAL. Which treaty violations are you referring to?

Q. The Republican Party platform said that the Carter administration covered up Soviet violations of SALT I and II and that the present administration would end this coverup and expose these Soviet violations of those two treaties.

SENIOR ADMINISTRATION OFFICIAL. Well, I'm not prepared today to comment or give you a record sheet on what the Soviets may or may not have done with regard to SALT I and SALT II. In general, the Soviets have complied with their interpretation of SALT I and, to a large extent, to SALT II. I don't think we want to get into that today.

Q. Why not? I'd love to get into it.

SENIOR ADMINISTRATION OFFICIAL. These treaties have some verification problems that have been pointed out in the past and our verification in this regard is primarily with national, technical means.

Q. But in the judgment of either of you, has the Soviet Union violated either the SALT I or the SALT II Treaty?

SENIOR ADMINISTRATION OFFICIAL. I think we have made very clear and we continue to, ... Our briefings take place on the Hill by the community and the compliance community within the government here and the record of our carrying to the Soviet Union and the SEC in Geneva our attitude toward apparent violations of any of the 1970's agreements is quite a long history. And the position of this administration is firmly and unequivocally that, whenever there is an apparent violation, that we will make clear in emphatic terms our attitude about it, carry it to the SEC and try to get it resolved there.

Q. But you speak about it in the future tense, "whenever there is one". My question is, in your opinion, have the Soviets violated either the SALT I or SALT II Treaties which the Republican Party platform said they had?

SENIOR ADMINISTRATION OFFICIAL. If we hadn't had concerns about it, we wouldn't have raised the issues that we have on countless times and so, to your question of have they ever, if we hadn't felt that they had, we wouldn't have raised it. We did.

Q. Why don't you say, "Yes, they have"?

SENIOR ADMINISTRATION OFFICIAL. I said we did.

Q. May I ask you—You hinted—

Q. I thought he said he didn't want to talk about it. Why not just say, "Yes, they have violated frequently." In fact, it is a rarity when the Soviet Union keeps a treaty. Why not just come out and say it like the Republican platform did? I don't understand this evasion.

Q. Should we write when we go back that you are saying that the Soviets have not lived up to the treaty on the kilotons underground testing? Do you have proof of that?

SENIOR ADMINISTRATION OFFICIAL. What I said was that on several occasions the information that we were able to obtain surely did call into question whether or not the Soviet Union's test had been within the 150 KT limit and that uncertainty is what makes it essential that you get better verification.

Q. Did we question—

SENIOR ADMINISTRATION OFFICIAL. On each occasion we have questioned, yes.

Q. We protested?

SENIOR ADMINISTRATION OFFICIAL. Yes. Yes, several times.

Q. Were any of them recent? Like last month?

Q. Can you give us any kind of timetable on that? The last time that happened?

Q. This year?

SENIOR ADMINISTRATION OFFICIAL. This year.

Q. This year, this administration. Well, was there not one about a month ago?

SENIOR ADMINISTRATION OFFICIAL. No.

Q. The Chinese—

SENIOR ADMINISTRATION OFFICIAL. Yes.

Q. Apparently there's pretty broad bipartisan support for these two treaties on the Hill and you guys got some letters from both Democrats and Republicans urging you to go forward with these treaties. Do they have—are the people on the Hill that are behind these, unaware of these uncertainties you talk about or why are you deciding to go back when they've urged you to get them ratified?

SENIOR ADMINISTRATION OFFICIAL. I'm glad you put it that way because, frankly, I would kind of cast what we're saying here in a positive sense. I guess that's my job, but I mean it. I was at the Senate Armed Services Committee when we considered the SALT II Treaty and it was unquestionable that verification was a real concern.

Q. I'm not talking about—

SENIOR ADMINISTRATION OFFICIAL. Well, that's important, however. We are not about to go up with a treaty in which we feel strongly, on which we feel strongly, that we know cannot fail because there are real concerns on the Hill about verification. So, it's with the intent of getting an agreement that we can ratify, that we're going to get verification procedures incorporated into it that will not make it vulnerable to that criticism when it's submitted.

Q. I'm sorry if I'm still a little bit foggy. Can you explain to me again in real basic terms how it is that you're not stopping the discussions on the CBT? I was under the impression for a couple of minutes from some of the questioning that you were working on these other things and you were going to hold that in abeyance for a while. You're saying that's not so? I'm not following you.

SENIOR ADMINISTRATION OFFICIAL. I am glad that you mentioned that again. I think I did give that impression and, as I said, we are involved today in discussions in Geneva in the working group on verification and compliance that are related to the CTB and we are going to remain so. So if I created the impression that that is a total full stop, that isn't.

Q. You made the impression by saying you were going to go ahead with the other two treaties first. Now isn't that precisely what you said? Are you going to go ahead with the CTBT—I mean with the threshold and the PNE first, and therefore that is the implication.

SENIOR ADMINISTRATION OFFICIAL. I don't mean to mislead you. Yes, our priority is on TTBT and PNE, but we are not discontinuing all efforts full-stop. We are going to continue these efforts in Geneva which are related to the CTB.

Q. On verification?

SENIOR ADMINISTRATION OFFICIAL. That is right.

Q. What about the trilateral efforts—not the efforts in Geneva, but trilaterally?

SENIOR ADMINISTRATION OFFICIAL. They are stopped right now.

SENIOR ADMINISTRATION OFFICIAL. Since 1980—for a long time.

Q. Do you have any intention to resume those negotiations?

SENIOR ADMINISTRATION OFFICIAL. Because it remains our long-term goal—I mean, I think that is clear. But we have no—we think the near-term ought to focus upon these other matters.

SENIOR ADMINISTRATION OFFICIAL. They were not stopped by this administration. I think you should keep that in mind.

THE PRESS. Thank you.

Document 54

Transcript of a Press Briefing by Representatives William S. Broomfield, William Carney, and Samuel S. Stratton, August 4, 1982 (Extract)[74]

"We Are Proposing in Our Amendment . . . a Freeze, But a Freeze at Equal and Substantially Reduced Levels"

CONGRESSMAN BROOMFIELD. Thank you very much. The purpose of the meeting this morning with the President dealt, obviously, with the nuclear reduction amendment that we'll be sponsoring tomorrow.[75] We went into detail and we had about 15 members of Congress.

The President is deeply concerned that the proposal that we'll be offering, the so-called Broomfield–Carney–Stratton amendment, pass. He expressed the concern that a straight freeze, which has been recommended by the Committee of Foreign Affairs, would undercut the negotiation process in Geneva.

And last night I received a call from General Rowny verifying his deep concern that if the substitute which we're offering is not passed, it will certainly hamper the negotiations presently going on.

General Rowny assured me that the negotiations are dead serious and are moving ahead and hopefully that this resolution will endorse the START talks that got started on June 29th.

Bill or Sam, would you like to add to that and then we'll ask—

CONGRESSMAN CARNEY. I think the most significant thing is, as was brought out, and I certainly concur with the fact that if the Zablocki–Bingham resolution[76] were to be successful, it would certainly be a vote of no confidence to the administration and to the administration's efforts to go forward with the START talks and the INF talks in Geneva.

It would then, I think, bring about a situation where the Soviet Union would be more than glad to sit across the table from our negotiators and be there in, what you might want to say, less than good faith because they would have had their position negotiated for by the members of the United States Congress.

And I would hope that those members who attended the press conference—not the press conference, but the meeting today with the President and Secretary of State and negotiating teams and the Commanding General of the Joint Chiefs of Staff, General Vessey, would appreciate that so we can go to Geneva with both conferences continuing with a vote of confidence from the House of Representatives and the Senate of the United States and, therefore, from the people of the United States.

We are proposing in our amendment, which would be a substitute to the Zablocki amendment, a freeze, but a freeze at equal and substantially-reduced levels. And we believe we should negotiate to those levels before we freeze. And I would hope, again, that our colleagues had a clear understanding of it. Certainly, I believe it's a case of misunderstanding to a great extent with the United States public. If they had an opportunity to sit in with the President and with the group of advisors that were there today, I'm sure that each and every American sitting in there would support their efforts that are now taking part, now going on in Geneva.

Q. Congressman, why is that? What did you learn in there that we don't know that makes you so certain that the President's way is the only way to go?

---

[74] Source: White House Press Release, August 4, 1982, Office of the Press Secretary to the President. The briefing was conducted in the Briefing Room of the White House beginning at 11:03 a.m.

[75] The Broomfield–Carney–Stratton amendment to House Joint Resolution 521 called for "an equitable and verifiable agreement which freezes strategic nuclear forces at equal and substantially reduced levels." (*Washington Post,* August 6, 1982, p. A10)

[76] On June 23, the House Foreign Affairs Committee, by a vote of 26 to 4 (28 to 8, counting absentees who were permitted to record their votes by July 12), reported out favorably House Joint Resolution 521 (often called the Zablocki–Bingham amendment), which called for a mutual and verifiable freeze on the testing, production, and further deployment of nuclear weapons followed by reductions in nuclear weapons and nuclear delivery systems, and also prompt U.S. approval of the SALT II agreement provided adequate verification capabilities were maintained. For the committee vote and text of the resolution, see *Strategic Arms Control and U.S. National Security Policy: Hearings and Markup Before the Committee on Foreign Affairs and Its Subcommittee on International Security and Scientific Affairs, House of Representatives, Ninety-seventh Congress, Second Session* (Washington, 1982), pp. 241–243, 253–255.

Congressman Carney. Well, one of the things I think that we learned is that there's a great deal of sincerity from the President in his efforts to go forward to actually reduce our stockpiles as well as the stockpiles of the Soviet Union.

I think that's something that has not been touched upon and many people do not believe that our government would have a willingness to reduce our current levels.

He made it perfectly clear to us that he would go forward and do precisely that if the Soviet Union did that in good faith.

I think also we look at some of the problems that we're faced with. We talk about verification. Well, out of necessity, it would take perhaps 2, 3, 4 years, maybe, to negotiate a verifiable treaty at a freeze level right now.

Why not go forward and negotiate [not] at the levels that we're at now but at reduced levels? Reduced levels that are equal.

And the President made his case to the members of Congress today about the fact that he strongly believes, as well as I do, that the Soviet Union enjoys an advantage at this particular point.

Q. Stratton, you have a—

Congressman Broomfield. Let me make one other observation, if I may, Sam. I had received this letter from General Rowny on August the 7th [*2d?*], which he indicated, "as the negotiator responsible to the President," I'm quoting from his letter, "the Congress and the American people, it is my considered judgment that a congressional resolution calling for an immediate freeze would make it exceedingly difficult to achieve reduction which would lessen the risk of nuclear war. The resolution passed by House Foreign Affairs Committee on June 23d, would greatly hinder my efforts to negotiate substantial reduction," and, finally, in the last paragraph, he says, "your resolution"—referring to the Broomfield, Carney, Stratton—"will show the Soviet Union that the Congress is behind President Reagan's effort to accomplish substantial arms reduction." I think that is the important point.

Q. Mr. Stratton, do you have the votes here?

Congressman Stratton. we have not counted all the noses. But I think we will have the votes when we finally get to the vote, which will, presumably, occur on Thursday[77] rather than Wednesday as expected. I joined with Mr. Broomfield and Mr. Carney in supporting this as the Democratic member, because I am old fashioned enough to believe that politics ought to stop at the water's edge. And in defense and foreign policy, we ought to have a bipartisan policy. That is what we had in the Democratic administrations of Roosevelt and Truman and Kennedy. And it is only latter years that we have had—as this resolution which prompted our alternate—a sharp division between the two parties in both defense and foreign policy.

I think the fact of the matter is that the Kennedy–Hatfield–Zablocki resolution is defective for two reasons. First of all, because any of us that have had an intimate contact with defense know that, if we freeze at the present time, we will freeze in a position of inferiority ourselves. There is no question about that. All you have to do is to see the intelligence to know—and see the pictures—what the Soviet is up to.

The other point is that we already have negotiations underway now, started by the President of the United States. And the Constitution provides that the President of the United States shall be in charge of foreign policy. He got the negotiations started. What the Zablocki resolution does is, in effect, to direct the President to undertake some other negotiations than the ones that are going on. And I think not only would the Zablocki negotiations be harmful to the process that is underway, but the current negotiations are the ones that are seeking—as has already been indicated—substantial reductions and to reestablish, in nuclear weaponry, a balance. And I think that is the only way to go.

Q. Mr. Stratton, did anyone in the meeting argue against the President?

Congressman Stratton. No; there were several people who expressed that they came into the meeting as undecided. Two very important members expressed those doubts, three of them, as a matter of fact. The President responded. Others of us responded, Secretary Weinberger and Mr. Rostow. And, while I cannot guarantee it, it looks as though they have seen the light.

I pointed out to the President, by the way, that I thought our group, which is just

---

77 The Broomfield–Carney–Stratton amendment to House Joint Resolution 521 was approved by the House of Representatives on Thursday, August 5, by a vote of 204 to 202. The House then voted to pass the amended resolution by a 273-to-125 vote.

a small group, is, nevertheless, making substantial headway, because we have an editorial in the morning *Washington Post*,[78] which is not always supportive of the White House, which suggests that the freeze is already obsolete. What it is trying to do is too ambitious, with the verification procedures at hand. And we ought to get on with real negotiations, which are the ones that are underway. I think that is a very encouraging move for the President and for us.

Q. Who were the three that were undecided?

CONGRESSMAN STRATTON. I am not sure that I ought to identify them. I would be invading their privacy, I think.

Q. Were they Democrats?

CONGRESSMAN STRATTON. No; one of them was a Republican.

. . . .

Document 55

Address by the Director of the Arms Control and Disarmament Agency (Rostow) Before the Los Angeles World Affairs Council, Los Angeles, September 10, 1982[79]

Nuclear Arms Control and the Future of U.S.-Soviet Relations

My assignment is to contemplate the future of the Soviet-American relationship in the perspective of arms control—more particularly, in the perspective of our bilateral negotiations about nuclear weapons. To recall Dr. Johnson, nuclear arms control is one of those subjects which concentrate the mind. It is of special value in revealing the several realities of the Soviet-American relationship and the way in which they interact.

In attempting to carry out my assignment, I thought it would be useful to review the state of our nuclear arms negotiations with the Soviet Union—to report on where we are, and to peer through the glass darkly at the road ahead. As you know, two parallel Soviet-American negotiations are going on in Geneva. One deals primarily with Soviet intermediate-range nuclear weapons, those capable of being launched from the Soviet Union against targets in Western Europe, Japan, China, and the Middle East; the other deals with the intercontinental nuclear weapons on both sides. The talks on intermediate-range weapons, called the INF talks, began in November 1981, and are being conducted for us by Ambassador Paul H. Nitze. The START talks on nuclear weapons of intercontinental range began in June 1982 under Ambassador Edward L. Rowny.

We have agreed with the Soviet representatives that the details of the INF and START negotiations be kept confidential. But we have also made it clear to them that the Government of the United States has the duty to keep our people fully informed about the broad principles which govern our approach to the negotiations and the way in which they are developing. I have prepared my talk with full respect for these rules.

The INF and START talks are inextricably linked, for reasons both of security and of technology. The security reason for that linkage is so obvious that it is often taken to be self-evident and left unexplained. But the nuclear balance has been changing, and we can no longer take our traditional positions on these matters for granted. The political consequences of the changing nuclear balance should be faced head-on.

Looking back at the cycles of turbulence and stability since 1945, we have all come to realize, I think, that while the possibility of nuclear war can never be altogether excluded, especially in the case of countries governed by irrational political leaders, the principal significance of nuclear weapons is political. The political radiation of nuclear arsenals can be significant either for defense or for aggression—as a defensive deterrent, on the one hand, or as an aggressive instrument of political coercion, on the other. It is thus apparent that the INF and START talks involved the most fundamental issue of our foreign policy, the credibility of our security guaranties. Those guaranties all turn ultimately on the deterrent power of the American nuclear umbrella. The pressures of the Soviet race for nuclear supremacy during the last 10 years have intensified doubts about the continued effectiveness of the American nuclear deter-

---

[78] See *Washington Post*, August 4, 1982, p. A18.

[79] Source: *Current Policy* No. 425, September 10, 1982, Bureau of Public Affairs, Department of State.

rent—the rock on which the renaissance of the West since 1945 was built and the foundation for its security. Uncertainties on this basic point could lead to fatal miscalculations. A most important goal of our foreign policy as a whole, and thus of our arms control policy, is to restore full confidence in those guaranties on the part of friend and adversary alike.

The expansionist nature of Soviet foreign policy and the recent changes in the Soviet-American military balance—particularly with regard to nuclear weapons—directly challenge the major premise of modern American foreign policy. That premise is distilled from the harsh experience of two world wars which strong allied diplomacy could easily have prevented. It has been accepted by every President since 1945, and spelled out in long series of treaties, joint resolutions of the Congress, and other national commitments. Its essence is that the United States can no longer live in neutral isolation but must protect its interest in the world balance of power by preventing Soviet domination of Western Europe, Asia, or the Middle East at a minimum. The Concert of Europe which protected that American security interest for a century before 1914 does not exist. We can no longer take shelter behind the British fleet. If the job is to be done, we must take the lead in organizing the coalitions to do it. To recall the language of the North Atlantic Treaty under which NATO is established, and which is expressed in other security arrangements as well, an attack on these vital areas must also be considered an attack on the United States. In contemplating the future, every nation must take this permanent and immutable geopolitical interest of the United States fully into account.

Outside the government, Americans who write and speak about foreign policy may forget this ultimate truth and flirt nostalgically with the isolationist ideas of the 19th century. Occasionally the government of the day may do so for a time, under the pressure of events. But those who bear the responsibility of government cannot enjoy the luxury of escapism. The world should understand that the instincts for self-preservation of a politically mature people will always dominate American foreign policy in the end. As President Reagan has made clear, the United States will not retreat to "Fortress America" but will defend its alliances and interests throughout the world. What is at stake in the INF and START talks is nothing less than our capacity to carry out that policy through deterrence based on alliance solidarity: that is, through peaceful means and not by war.

The technical reason why the INF and START talks must be viewed together is equally simple. It is that intermediate-and intercontinental-range nuclear weapons do not constitute separate categories: Soviet weapons capable of hitting New York or Chicago could also be fired at London or Tokyo. There is, therefore, no way to evaluate the INF balance except in the START context. We cannot allow the whipsaw threat of Soviet INF and strategic forces to separate us from our allies and keep us from defending the security interests of the nation.

The United States is, therefore, closely coordinating the INF and START talks, which are based on the same analysis. Through these talks in tandem, we are trying to achieve the same goal—a radical reduction of the Soviet and American nuclear arsenals in a manner conducive to stability.

Before we can consider how the INF and START talks are progressing, we must agree on the criteria to be applied in judging their utility. To that end, let me briefly recall the analysis from which our negotiating position is derived and the implications of the goal we are trying to achieve. President Reagan is determined to take full advantage of our arms control experience during the 1970's. That effort has required a reexamination of the role of nuclear weapons and the arms control doctrines of the United States and the Soviet Union.

How should we define what we are seeking through the INF and START talks? The place to begin, we concluded more than a year ago, is to take a fresh look at the nuclear weapon itself. We have been living with it since 1945. The early assumption that the nuclear weapon was a magic force for peace has long since faded away. Even when we had a monopoly of nuclear weapons, and then great nuclear superiority, we had to use conventional forces—and those alone—to counter a long cycle of aggression by the Soviets and their surrogates. Save in a few important situations of extreme tension, we found the doctrine of "massive retaliation" to be an empty threat.

Since the late 1950's, at least, the primary strategic goal of the Soviet program of expansion has been to achieve world dominance by separating Western Europe from the United States and Canada. To achieve this goal, the Soviet Union has been and is seeking to outflank Europe from the north and the south, thus bringing the entire Eurasian land mass under Soviet control and, on that basis, taking over Africa and the Middle East. That done, the Soviet leaders believe, Japan and the other nations of the Pacific basin would accept Soviet suzerainty as inevitable; the peoples of Europe would lose hope; and the United States would be isolated, with no choice but to aquiesce in Soviet hegemony. All our experience in our bilateral nuclear arms talks with the Soviet Union is consistent with this hypothesis. Soviet strategy in SALT I and SALT II seems to be dominated by two ideas: to divide the United States from its allies and to prevent the modernization of the American Armed Forces. These are the main Soviet themes in the negotiation as they are the main themes of Soviet arms control propaganda.

Since the end of the Second World War, the United States and its allies have never stopped trying to persuade the Soviet Union that this course was the classic road to disaster. Nor have they flagged in their efforts to convince the leaders of the Soviet Union that a constructive alternative was always available—the alternative of genuine East–West cooperation, based on respect by each side for the legitimate security interests of the other and for the rules of the U.N. Charter against aggression. To this end, with varying degrees of success, the allies sought to contain Soviet expansion and proposed a long series of agreements designed to induce the Soviet Union to pursue its ambitions in world politics only by peaceful means. Among these proposals, those addressed to the nuclear menace have been of quite particular significance.

From the beginning of the nuclear age nearly 40 years ago, the American people and their government have been convinced—and rightly convinced—that nuclear weapons are revolutionizing both warfare and world politics and that extraordinary steps are required to protect civilization from the unthinkable disaster of nuclear war. Conventional war has profoundly damaged the fabric of civilization during this turbulent century. The consequences of nuclear war would be immeasurably worse.

The United States made its first proposal to eliminate the nuclear threat in 1946, when we had a monopoly of nuclear arms and nuclear technology. In the Baruch Plan[80] we offered to put the whole of nuclear science under international control. Looking back, it is obvious that the Soviet refusal even to consider that offer was one of the most destructive turning points in the history of the cold war.

The offer of the Baruch Plan does not stand alone. During the 1950's, President Eisenhower proposed the "open skies" plan, which has had far-reaching influence even though it was not formally accepted. The first major step in the control of nuclear arms was achieved in 1963 in the Limited Test Ban Treaty. The Nuclear Nonproliferation Treaty followed in 1968.

Beyond these agreements, there are treaties barring weapons of mass destruction from the Antarctic and from outer space and the cycle of agreements which are our primary concern today—the Soviet-American SALT agreements and the INF and START negotiations. SALT I comprised two agreements, the Interim Agreement limiting offensive strategic weapons, which expired in 1977, and the ABM Treaty, which severely restricts systems for intercepting and destroying ballistic missiles. The ABM Treaty is of indefinite duration. SALT I and SALT II disappointed the claims made for them and the expectations they generated. Against the background of the Soviet nuclear buildup under the SALT I Interim Agreement, SALT II would have sanctioned continued increases in Soviet nuclear capabilities to threaten world stability.

What is the moral of this cycle of experience for the policies President Reagan has proposed in the INF and START talks? First, we are more convinced than ever that the efforts of the United States since 1946 to eliminate the possibility of nuclear war were wise and necessary. They should be intensified, not relaxed or abandoned. Second, it is obvious that no impregnable wall can be erected between nuclear and conventional war. A nuclear stalemate will not be worth having if it is treated simply as a license for conventional wars of all against all.

In order to eliminate nuclear war, the nations must also eliminate conventional war: that is, the struggle to save mankind from nuclear catastrophe must be conceived as part of a wider struggle to estab-

[80] For the text of the comprehensive plan for the international control of atomic energy which Bernard Baruch, U.S. Representative to the U.N. Atomic Energy Commission, presented to the U.N. Atomic Energy Commission in 1946, see Department of State *Bulletin*, December 15, 1946, pp. 1090–1091.

lish world public order itself. The issue is not colonialism, or capitalism, or communism, or democracy, or the so-called arms race. It is aggression. The motives for aggression are irrelevant. And the arms race is the symptom and consequence, not the cause, of the breakdown in world public order. We live in a small, interdependent, and dangerous world. In that world, our world with its ominous nuclear dimension, aggression should be inadmissible, and peace should be indivisible.

As President Reagan has said, we can no longer tolerate a "double standard" with regard to Soviet aggression or aggression by any other power. Both we and the Soviet Union must obey the same rules with regard to the international use of force—the rules to which we both agreed when we signed the U.N. Charter. Unless these neutral and universal principles are generally and impartially enforced, they will cease to have any influence on the behavior of states. In President Reagan's phrase, the nations must not merely condemn aggression; they must prevent it and enforce the rules against it.

I now turn to the specific problems of INF and START negotiations. A year ago a consensus emerged within the administration on certain key propositions as the foundation for our negotiating approach in the two negotiations. The first and most important was that we should discard the premise that the United States and the Soviet Union shared the same view of nuclear weapons and the same goal for nuclear arms control negotiations. Ten years ago most Americans took that hypothesis for granted. Today it cannot be entertained at all. Officials used to assure us that the Soviet Union was only interested in equality, recognition as a great power, and a place in the sun and that when it achieved parity with the United States it would stop enlarging its armed forces. No one can say that after what happened during the 1970's.

For the United States, the only acceptable use for nuclear arms is in defense of our supreme national interests and those of our allies against the use of nuclear weapons and other forms of aggression. Our nuclear arsenal is defensive in character, and its mission is to deter aggression by presenting a visible and credible capacity to retaliate.

It is now obvious that the Soviet Union marches to a different drummer. While we in the West have been primarily concerned with deterring both conventional and nuclear attacks, Soviet doctrine and forces emphasize the ability to fight and win a nuclear war. Of course, the Soviet Government would prefer to have the fruits of military victory without having to wage war. To achieve that end, it believes, the nuclear superiority it is trying so hard to attain would be a political force of overpowering influence—the ultimate instrument of coercion and intimidation. The function of Soviet military superiority is to paralyze the American nuclear deterrent by threatening to overwhelm it, and thus make Soviet aggression with conventional forces possible. More than 75% of the Soviet strategic nuclear force consists of intercontinental ballistic missiles (ICBM's)—swift, accurate, and extremely destructive first-strike weapons which could destroy missiles deployed in hardened silos. Less than one-third of the American force consists of ICBM's. In addition, the Soviet Union has an intermediate-range ballistic missile force which, as yet, has no American counterpart. The Soviets currently have deployed at least 324 SS–20 launchers, 265 SS–4's, and 15 SS–5's. They have 1,232 warheads in all. With one refire missile per launcher, these intermediate-range missiles may have over 2,000 nuclear warheads, almost all of which can reach West European targets. The balance, all deployed on mobile SS–20 launchers, are now targeted from eastern Siberia. Given the transportability and range of the SS–20, all of these could be moved within reach of Europe. The United States has no weapons at all in this class. Partially to counter this threat, our Pershing II intermediate-range ballistic missile and ground-based cruise missile are in development and are scheduled for modest deployment in Europe late in 1983.

The Soviet lead in ground-based intermediate-range and intercontinental ballistic missiles is one of the most serious foreign policy problems we face. This advantage gives the Soviet Union the potential to destroy all of Europe or Japan and many targets in other parts of the world at a time when a preemptive first strike with its intercontinental ballistic missiles could in theory also destroy all our ICBM force, that portion of our submarines that are in port, and those of our bombers that are at their bases.

The combination of these doomsday possibilities is a recipe for nuclear coercion that could split our alliances and leave us isolated in the Western Hemisphere. Henry Kissinger deepened Western anxiety about the nuclear imbalance a few years ago with his celebrated comment that great powers do not commit suicide on behalf of their allies.[81] Former President Nixon has now made nuclear anxiety in this sense more acute. In an article in the *New York Times* on August 19, 1982,[82] he says:

"The Soviet Union's achievement of superiority in land-based nuclear missiles has made our nuclear strength no longer a credible deterrent against Moscow's creeping expansionism, in Africa, Asia, Latin America and the Middle East. We will not again be able to use the threat of that power as President Kennedy did in the Cuban missile crisis in 1962, when we had a 15-to-1 advantage, or even as I was able to do during the Arab-Israeli war in 1973, when our advantage was far less but still formidable. Even if we restore the balance of those nuclear forces, we will not fully restore their deterrent effect for such purposes. A threat of mutual suicide is simply not credible."

Political anxieties about the American nuclear umbrella would exist even if Dr. Kissinger and President Nixon had not spoken. They are what Chancellor Schmidt has called "subliminal" emanations of the Soviet nuclear arsenal and the state of the Soviet-American nuclear balance. They are there because we allowed the nuclear balance to deteriorate during the 1970's. We shall have to live with the consequences of that mistake until the balance is restored by some combination of American force modernization and arms control agreements.

The fears generated by the changing nuclear balance are manifest in many forms—in the antinuclear demonstrations and other movements for unilateral disarmament, isolationism, and accommodation, on the one hand, and for nuclear proliferation, on the other. If these movements prevail, here, in Europe, and in Asia, we shall wake up one day soon in a different world.

In the light of these considerations, President Reagan decided to make the removal of the destabilizing Soviet advantage in ground-based ballistic missiles the first goal of our nuclear arms control effort and the first aspect of the problem for us to take up with the Soviet Union. We were slightly ahead of the Soviet Union in the number of warheads on deployed ICBM's in 1972.

In 1982 the Soviets have a lead in this crucial area of approximately three to one. It follows that they have the theoretical capacity to execute a preemptive first strike by destroying our ICBM's and other nuclear forces with a fraction of their forces, holding the rest in an ominous reserve which could paralyze our remaining strategic forces. When the Soviet intermediate-range ballistic missiles are counted, the Soviet advantage in this category becomes even higher. Until this Soviet advantage in nuclear forces is eliminated, it will not be possible to achieve political stability.

The *New York Times* put the issue well in an editorial entitled "How Much Is Enough?" on April 11, 1982. The task of arms control diplomacy, the *Times* said, is to allow the United States to maintain deterrence "which has kept the industrial world at peace for the longest stretch in history" and "to forbid the weapons which defy deterrence . . . . That done, the arms race can subside. Unless it is done, there will never be enough."

This view of the matter is the basis for our approach to the INF and START talks. What we are seeking in these talks is to establish nuclear stability at equal and much lower levels of force—a posture on each side which would permit us to deter both nuclear war and other forms of aggression against our supreme interests. Such a policy would deny the Soviet Union the capacity for nuclear blackmail based on its present superiority in ground-based intermediate-range and intercontinental ballistic missiles.

The U.S. position in these talks was explained by President Reagan in his speech of November 18, 1981. During the first round of the INF talks beginning in November 1981, the U.S. delegation laid out the broad principles underlying the U.S. approach, defined the elements of an agreement which would take into account the legitimate interests of the two sides, and in February 1982 presented the text of a draft treaty which would implement those elements. The Soviet side elaborated somewhat on the positions that had been set forth by Chairman Brezhnev before the negotiations had begun and offered its criticism of the U.S. position. Mr. Brezhnev's plan has two elements: A moratorium for the duration of the negotiations and a program of reductions based on the assumption that both sides are now equal in intermediate-range missiles. The Soviets have proposed a limit of 300 "systems" for each side by 1990.

During the second round, beginning in May, the Soviet delegation presented a

---

81 Kissinger's comment has not been further identified.

82 See *New York Times*, August 19, 1982, p. A27.

draft text of an agreement which would embody the Soviet position. The United States offered its criticisms of the Soviet position and a full analysis of the issues between the sides.

As the third round of the INF negotiations is scheduled to begin at the end of this month, it is appropriate to review some of the major issues as they have emerged. You will remember that in 1976 the Soviet Union began the deployment of a new mobile and MIRVed intermediate-range missile system—the SS–20—as a replacement for the older fixed single-warhead systems on which it had relied for many years. The SS–20's are highly accurate; can strike all important targets in Europe, even from locations in the middle of Siberia; and have a short time of flight. They represent a threat different in kind, not just in degree, from the systems they have been replacing.

In 1979 the NATO nations unanimously agreed that it was necessary to counter this threat unless it was withdrawn. It was decided that the United States should move to deploy in Europe two somewhat comparable systems, the Pershing II ballistic missile and the BGM–109G ground-launched cruise missile and simultaneously seek negotiations with the Soviet Union for the limitation of comparable systems on both sides.[83] On November 18, 1981, President Reagan proposed that both the United States and the U.S.S.R. entirely forego such systems—the zero/zero solution.

The Soviet Union has not yet gone beyond its position that the INF talks are exclusively concerned with stability in the European theater. The United States insists that the INF problem is global and that the cause of world peace would not be advanced by exporting the Soviet INF nuclear advantage to Asia.

The Soviet Union also continues to claim that the United States and the Soviet Union have approximately the same number of intermediate-range nuclear weapons in the European theater and, therefore, that the NATO decision to deploy 572 Pershing II and ground-based cruise missiles in Europe is "provocative" and "destabilizing." The Soviet claim rests on two untenable propositions—first, that the British and French nuclear forces must be counted with the American forces and, second, that American bombers, submarine-launched missiles, and cruise missiles should be treated as equivalent to the Soviet SS–20. The Soviet calculations go beyond even these errors. In order to demonstrate the supposed equality of the two INF forces in Europe, the Soviet Union must count all American weapons as relevant—including American dual-purpose aircraft, as well as FB–111's, all of which are located in the United States—and also exclude many categories of the Soviet arsenal.

The principal issue between the sides centers on the treatment to be accorded the SS–20's and comparable missiles on the Soviet side, and the Pershing II and BGM–109G on the United States side. Whereas the United States draft treaty would ban them on both sides, the Soviet treaty would eliminate them only on the U.S. side; the Soviet side would be permitted to have up to 300 launchers for such missiles in the European portion of the Soviet Union and an unlimited number in the far-eastern portion of the Soviet Union.

In addition to this wholly one-sided treatment proposed by the Soviets as to the central issues, their proposed treaty would have other unequal effects. The Warsaw Pact has some 7,000 nuclear-capable aircraft in Europe, of which some 2,500 are assigned to nuclear combat roles. NATO has approximately one-third of the latter number; almost all U.S. nuclear-capable planes located in Europe are dual capable. The U.S. contribution to the conventional defense of Europe is almost wholly dependent on such dual-capable planes. Yet, the Soviet draft treaty would have the effect of forcing the almost total withdrawal from Europe of such U.S. dual-capable aircraft, while not affecting most Soviet dual-capable aircraft.

This effect results in part from the Soviet proposal that U.K. and French nuclear-capable systems be included under the aggregate ceiling limiting U.S. and Soviet intermediate-range missiles and aircraft. This proposal is both technically flawed and inequitable in principle. First, most of these U.K. and French forces are not, in fact, intermediate-range (or what the Soviets call medium-range); they are SLBM forces identical with Soviet and U.S. SLBM forces. Most of the remainder are nuclear-capable aircraft. The Soviet predominance in intermediate-range, nuclear-capable systems in Europe is so great that there would be no justification for compensation to the Soviet

---

[83] For the texts of the communiqués issued following the special meeting of the NATO Foreign and Defense Ministers on December 12, 1979, and the meeting of the NATO Foreign Ministers on December 14, 1979, which formally endorsed these decisions, see *American Foreign Policy: Basic Documents, 1977–1980*, pp. 494–499.

Union for British and French nuclear forces even if they were under NATO command.

Beyond this technical flaw, the claim of the Soviet Union for nuclear forces equal to or superior to those of all other nations combined would be unjustified. It is a demand for absolute security for one country, which is tantamount to absolute insecurity for all other countries. In short, it is a Soviet demand for hegemony. This will never be acceptable to the United States.

This Soviet demand is inappropriate in another way as well. The INF negotiations are bilateral negotiations between the United States and the U.S.S.R.; neither the United Kingdom nor France has authorized either the United States or the Soviet Union to negotiate on their behalf. On the contrary, they have stated their refusal to have their forces limited or compensated for in negotiations between us. From their standpoint, their nuclear forces are strategic; they represent their last line of defense in a potentially threatened position.

There are a number of other important issues separating the two sides. Much progress, however, has been achieved by the two delegations in sorting out what is important to each side and illuminating the way to possible solutions. A serious atmosphere has evolved in the INF talks. It is clear that a potentiality exists for accommodating the analytic concepts used by both sides. What is not yet clear is whether the Soviet Union is willing to accept agreement based exclusively on the principle of deterrence.

The first 2-month round of the START negotiations has now been completed. They are, of course, at an earlier stage than the INF talks, but the atmosphere is correspondingly serious and business-like.

The U.S. position was outlined in President Reagan's speech at Eureka College on May 9, 1982. Its essential idea is that of equal ceilings at much lower levels of force—ceilings that would strengthen deterrence and promote stability by significantly reducing the Soviet lead in ICBM's. Coupled with the dismantling of the Soviet intermediate-range ballistic missiles proposed in the INF talks, such a result would enable us to maintain an overall level of strategic nuclear capability sufficient to deter conflict, safeguard our national security, and meet our commitments to allies and friends.

To achieve this goal, the President announced a practical, phased approach to the negotiation, like the procedure being used in the INF talks. It is based on the principle that the two arsenals should be equal both in the number of weapons and in their destructive capacity. "The focus of our efforts," the President said, "will be to reduce significantly the most destabilizing systems—ballistic missiles, the number of warheads they carry, and their overall destructive potential."

While no aspect of the problem is excluded from consideration and the United States will negotiate in good faith on any topics the Soviets wish to raise, the United States proposes that the first topic to be considered in the negotiations should be the reduction of ballistic missile warheads to equal levels at least one-third below current numbers. Both ground-based and submarine-launched ballistic missiles are included in this proposal. No more than half these warheads would be deployed on land-based missiles. This provision alone should achieve substantial reductions in missile throw-weight. Our proposal calls for these warhead reductions, as well as significant reductions in the number of deployed missiles, to be achieved as quickly as possible.

In a second phase, closely linked to the first, we will seek equal ceilings on other elements of U.S. and Soviet strategic forces, including equal limits on ballistic missile throw-weight at less than current U.S. levels.

In both START and INF, the United States has made it clear that verification measures capable of assuring compliance are indispensable. For those provisions that cannot be monitored effectively by national technical means of verification, we will be proposing cooperative measures, data exchanges, and collateral constraints that should provide the necessary confidence in compliance. The Soviet Union has indicated that it will be prepared where necessary to consider cooperative measures going beyond national technical means. This is an encouraging sign. Without satisfactory verification provisions, meaningful agreements will be impossible to achieve.

The Soviet Union has attacked our START proposals as unfair, on the ground that they call for unequal reductions—indeed, that they call for "unilateral Soviet disarmament." It is hardly obvious why this is the case. Each side now has approximately 7,500 ballistic missile warheads. Under the American proposal, each side would have to reduce to no more than 5,000, of which no more than 2,500 could be on

ICBM's. True, the Soviet Union would have to dismantle more ICBM warheads than we would in order to comply with the ICBM sublimit, while we might have to dismantle more submarine-based missiles. But that is the point. There is nothing inequitable about an equal ceiling which strengthens deterrence and stability. It is discouraging that this feature of the American proposal was not mentioned in a recent article in the *Los Angeles Times* by General Starodubov, a senior member of the Soviet START delegation.[84] By omitting any reference to SLBM's, General Starodubov gives the reader an incomplete version of the American position.

If the INF and START talks are successful, the huge Soviet advantage in ground-based ballistic missiles will be eliminated. These alone are the weapons which "defy deterrence." If the Soviet Union accepts nuclear arms control agreements based on the principle of "deterrence only," which is the heart of our negotiating position, a Soviet first strike would be impossible without expending most of the Soviet force. Given such a change in the balance of the two forces, we could hope to protect our ICBM force effectively. Then—but only then—nuclear tension would diminish.

There is another aspect of our START negotiating position which deserves emphasis. As President Reagan's speech at Eureka College makes clear, the American approach to START is directed in the first instance at the most destabilizing weapons and proposes a new unit of account as the basis for a treaty dealing with them and all other intercontinental nuclear weapons. That unit of account, replacing the "deployed launchers" used in SALT I and SALT II, would compare the Soviet and American forces both in the number of weapons on each side and their destructive capacity. The measure of destructive capacity we propose is that of throw-weight—the maximum weight of weapons a missile can propel. What we are seeking is an equal throw-weight limit for each side at levels below the present American level. This goal would require a greater reduction on the Soviet side than on the American side. But the Soviet Union can hardly claim a right to preserve an advantage which could only be used for intimidation or aggression. Nor is there anything inequitable in the idea of unequal reductions to achieve equality. The United States made larger reductions than any other power under the Washington Naval Treaty of 1922.

If we yield in the end and wearily settle for INF and START agreements which allow the Soviet Union to preserve its overwhelming advantage in ballistic missiles, we should find ourselves confronting former President Nixon's bleak prognosis. Such an outcome would legitimize the superiority in intermediate-range and intercontinental ground-based ballistic missiles that the Soviet Union has achieved under SALT and authorize it to consolidate and improve that advantage. On that basis, the Soviet leaders would be justified in continuing to believe that they could translate their nuclear edge over the United States into political and diplomatic hegemony.

This would be a most dangerous illusion—the kind of illusion from which major wars have arisen in the past. President Reagan's approach to INF and START calls on the Soviet Union to join us in recognizing that the quest for hegemony is the greatest possible threat to the peace and that real nuclear parity between the Soviet Union and the United States—parity, that is, in deterrent capacity—is the most feasible foundation for a joint program to establish world political stability based on the rule of law.

The state of world politics does not justify the apocalyptic gloom of those who believe that resisting Soviet expansionism would be suicidal and, therefore, counsel an American retreat to isolation and submission. The Soviet drive for unlimited power faces insuperable obstacles. It confronts deep-seated economic and social problems at home and the ineradicable hostility of the nations it is seeking to rule abroad. It has suffered major defeats in peripheral campaigns, especially in the Middle East. And what Mr. Brezhnev has called "the crisis" in Poland is one of supreme importance to the future of the Soviet Union. Even the magnitude of its nuclear arsenal cannot protect the Soviet Union from the deeply rooted yearnings for freedom shared by people everywhere. Finally, and most important of all, the Soviet Union, like every other country, must accept the implacable logic of the nuclear weapon. As Khruschev once said, the nuclear weapon does not respect the difference between socialism and capitalism.

Foreign policy is not a mathematical exercise like chess. Like every other human enterprise, it must take account of the un-

[84] Reference is to the article by General Victor Starodubov in *Los Angeles Times*, July 23, 1982, II, p. 7.

foreseen. Chance, heroism, passion, and faith have greater influence in human affairs than the grim calculus of the nuclear equation.

The ultimate issue of Soviet-American relations since 1917 is defined in the nuclear arms talks with chilling clarity. It is whether the Soviet Union is a state like the others, willing to live as a member of the society of nations and to abide by its rules or, on the other hand, whether the Soviet Union will persist in the suicidal view that its mission is to lead a crusade to spread the "True Faith" by the sword. When the issue is raised with Soviet diplomats or professors, they say, "You are asking us to change a foreign policy rooted in the nature of our society and state." To that claim, the only possible answer is, "Not at all. So far as we are concerned, you can preach the gospel of communism as much as you like. But the rest of the world cannot tolerate the use of aggression to achieve it."

If the leaders of the Soviet Union are as rational and cautious as they are supposed to be, they should want a period of peace and stability in their relationship with the West. On the whole, I think they will. Like all his modern predecessors, President Reagan has made it clear to the Soviet leaders that he would welcome such a change and cooperate fully in making it a reality.

Document 56

Testimony by the Director of the Arms Control and Disarmament Agency (Rostow) Before a Subcommittee of the Senate Foreign Relations Committee, September 20, 1982 (Extracts)[85]

Complex Problems Inhibiting the Development of a Comprehensive U.S. Policy on Arms Control in Outer Space

. . . .

I turn now to recent international discussions of space arms control and what we have learned of its difficulty.

In 1978–79, as you said, Mr. Chairman,[86] the United States and the Soviet Union engaged in bilateral negotiations on anti-satellite weapons limitations. The talks covered both limits on actions against satellites and limits on capabilities for attacking satellites. They took place in Helsinki in June 1978, in Bern in January–February 1979, and in Vienna in April–June 1979.

During the first round of negotiations, the two sides outlined their general concerns, and during the second and third rounds some progress was made in examining and clarifying the key issues. However, important areas of disagreement emerged, both with regard to limits on actions against satellites and with regard to limits on ASAT capabilities.

I do not wish to belabor those differences here. I would note that there were important verification questions raised which must be resolved if ASAT arms control is to make progress, and I will return to these questions in a few minutes.

In addition, as you will recall, the international environment deteriorated toward the end of 1979. The Soviet invasion of Afghanistan was especially important in this connection.

Arms control measures for outer space have been a topic of discussion in the United Nations and in sessions of the Committee on Disarmament [CD][87] this year. The United States supported resolution 36/97C,[88] introduced by U.S. allies at the U.N. General Assembly last fall, which requested the CD to consider the question of negotiating further arms control measures in outer space.

In the summer of 1981, the Soviet Union sent to the U.N. a draft treaty that would ban the stationing of weapons in outer space. A U.N. resolution sponsored by the Soviet Union and its allies, calling for CD negotiations on such a treaty, also passed the General Assembly.[89] The Soviet draft

---

[85] Source: *Arms Control and the Militarization of Space: Hearing Before the Subcommittee on Arms Control, Oceans, International Operations and Environment of the Committee on Foreign Relations, United States Senate, Ninety-seventh Congress, Second Session* (Washington, 1982), pp. 10–15.

[86] For the opening statement of Senator Pressler, chairman of the subcommittee, see *Arms Control and the Militarization of Space*, pp. 1, 6–7.

[87] All bracketed notes appear in the source text.

[88] The United States voted for U.N. General Assembly Resolution 36/97C, Prevention of an Arms Race in Outer Space, which was approved on December 9, 1981, by a vote of 129–0–13.

[89] Reference is to U.N. General Assembly Res-

treaty neither defined a "weapon" nor seriously addressed questions of verification. In the 1982 spring and summer sessions, the United States participated in CD discussions on the highly complex, technical issues of space arms control.

We are deeply concerned about the wide-ranging scope of Soviet military activities in space—in particular the continuing Soviet deployment, development and testing of weapons for intercepting and destroying satellites, and the threat posed by Soviet satellites to our own military forces. Soviet development of ASAT weapons puts at risk not only U.S. satellites vital to national security but also the satellites of all nations which have been launched and are used for commercial, scientific, and other civil purposes.

This past June, at nearly the same time that Soviet Foreign Minister Gromyko was speaking before the U.N. about banning weapons from outer space,[90] the Soviet Union was conducting another in a continuing series of tests of its ASAT weapon,[91] which we have considered operational for more than a decade.

Finally, in connection with the U.N. and CD discussions, I should emphasize some of the broad problem areas we see. Military and arms control issues in outer space are complex; they present difficult obstacles to international negotiations, as you and I agree, Mr. Chairman. Furthermore, arms control in space is inseparable from broader arms control issues, and must be considered in that context. President Reagan continues to give serious attention to the prospects for space arms control that could contribute to U.S. national security. However, there are obstacles to progress in such areas as assuring effective verification, minimizing so-called residual ASAT capabilities, and countering the space components of threats to U.S. forces.

Some of these issues are technical ones for which we are seeking technical solutions. Such solutions are essential to any responsible and effective approach to space arms control.

The first question to be addressed in evaluating the wisdom of limits on space weapons in general and ASAT weapons in particular is whether the United States can afford to give up acquiring an ASAT weapon of its own. Two issues are important here. The first is the threat posed by present and prospective Soviet satellites to our military forces. There are a number of Soviet satellites that can be used to direct Soviet military forces against United States and allied forces. Any space weapon limitations which limit the threat to U.S. satellites will necessarily protect threatening Soviet satellites as well. Therefore, when we consider arms control limits on ASAT weapons, we must weigh how we are to balance two national security concerns, the need to preserve our own satellites versus the need to protect U.S. forces from threatening Soviet satellites. Dr. DeLauer will review these technologies in detail.[92]

A further complication is that a ban on ASAT's could not completely banish the threat. Some inherent ASAT capabilities or potential would remain in other weapon systems and space programs. This residual ASAT threat must also weigh in our evaluation.

The second important issue with regard to the U.S. acquisition of an ASAT weapon of its own is the deterrent effect such a system would have in contrast to the asymmetrical situation that confronts us at present. The Soviets have been conducting space tests of their ASAT interceptor for over a decade and are judged to have an operational ASAT system. The United States, on the other hand, has not yet conducted tests of the ASAT interceptor it is developing.

Any interruption in the U.S. program at this time would leave the Soviets with both a ready ASAT capability and a considerable body of ASAT test experience from more than a decade of testing. Additionally, the threat to our national security from advances in Soviet space programs will grow. Finally, the knowledge that the United States is making steady progress toward an operational ASAT of its own could be an important inducement for the Soviet Union to explore constructive limits on space weapons.

The second set of problems we face in evaluating the wisdom of negotiating limits for ASAT and outer space weapons is that of verification.

---

olution 36/99, adopted by a vote of 123–0–21 (with the United States abstaining), which endorsed a Soviet draft treaty (U.N. document A/36/192) on the Prohibition of the Stationing of Weapons of Any Kind in Outer Space.

[90] For the text of Gromyko's speech at the United Nations, June 15, see U.N. document A/S–12/PV.12.

[91] See Secretary Haig's revelations at his press conference, June 19, document 269.

[92] For DeLauer's testimony, see *Arms Control and the Militarization of Space*, pp. 23–44.

Effective verification is central in all arms control; it is important in space arms control for several particular reasons. Satellites which serve U.S. national security purposes are relatively few in number and yet in many instances they are vital and their tasks cannot readily be taken over by other systems. A variety of weapons could potentially be used for ASAT attacks, including some weapons such as certain ABM interceptor missiles that are permitted under other arms control accords.

If the Soviet Union should succeed in destroying even a small number of vital American satellites, while its own remain immune from attack, it might hope to secure an important military advantage in some cases. In these circumstances, even a few acts of cheating to acquire or retain a modest ASAT capability could have significant national security implications.

We would thus, under a complete ASAT ban, have to insure both that the existing Soviet ASAT system was dismantled and could not be readily reassembled and that no other Soviet systems could effectively perform this mission. There are, in addition, other verification problems. Without effective verification, an ASAT ban would simply not be in the U.S. interest.

ACDA and other agencies are studying possibilities for cooperative measures that could supplement national technical means to provide effective verification of space arms control agreements. However, the problem remains an extremely difficult one, and I cannot report any breakthroughs at this date.

These are enormously complex issues, involving not only evaluation of existing space and weapons technology but also the anticipation of future developments; space technology is evolving at a rapid rate, and these advances bring with them implications for the use of space, space weapons, and of course space arms control. We know that future developments may be important for our security, and yet our vision of the future is unavoidably clouded.

I mentioned, Mr. Chairman, in my opening remarks that outer space was an inseparable element of our broader security concerns.[93] Space arms control, too, is inextricably linked to our broader arms control initiatives. The President has now made a series of arms control proposals to the Soviet Union, on strategic and intermediate range nuclear missiles and on conventional forces in Europe. The outcome of these negotiations will have a profound effect upon our security concerns and upon our defense forces and requirements. Satellites serve the needs of both arms control verification and of defense. Hence, the demands we will place upon our satellites, and the risks we would be willing to accept under space arms control limitations, must be influenced by the course of these other negotiations.

I remarked in a speech I made last week in Los Angeles[94] summing up where we stand in the INF talks in Geneva that a serious atmosphere has evolved in those talks, and that we have come far enough to make it obvious that the analytical concepts used by both sides can be reconciled, but I said that what is not yet clear is whether the Soviet Union is willing to consider an agreement in the INF talks based entirely on the principle of deterrence. That is the fundamental issue that is being explored there and will be explored in the START [Strategic Arms Reduction Talks] negotiations and the MBFR talks, and it is critical to the possibility of space arms control as well.

The issues I have briefly discussed here today have been and are being actively and carefully reviewed by the administration. One of the products of that review was the President's recent far-reaching decision on national space policy.[95] He said that the administration will continue to study space arms control options and will consider verifiable and equitable space arms control measures that would ban or otherwise limit testing and deployment of specific weapons, should those measures be compatible with U.S. national security.

We are vigorously pursuing these issues, Mr. Chairman, with studies such as those on cooperative measures I cited above. I cannot predict we shall surmount the obstacles to meaningful space arms control, but should we see a potential for verifiable space arms control measures that enhance the U.S. security we are ready to take appropriate initiatives.

Thank you.

. . . .

SENATOR PRESSLER. . . . Recently some of the developments in this area were pub-

---

[93] See *ibid.*, pp. 7–8.

[94] *Supra.*

[95] See document 31.

lished in a Jack Anderson column[96] based upon research I have conducted. My research points out some of the accelerated steps that are occurring on both the Russian and the United States side. For the United States, this is a very expensive undertaking. The U.S. Air Force created a Space Command on September 1 of this year. The U.S. ASAT is said to be approaching flight test, and once deployed in the second half of the 1980's it will leapfrog the operational Soviet killer satellites, but it may be answered by the Soviets with a more advanced piece of technology.

On July 4 of this year, President Reagan announced that the United States was adopting a new national space policy. Among other things, this policy calls for the development and deployment of an operational ASAT capability, and the most recent space shuttle flight marked the first time that this vehicle was used to transport a military payload. Plans call for allocating one-third of the shuttle's payload for military missions. The budget of the Air Force's Space Command, colocated at Colorado Springs with the North American Air Defense Command, will increase from $2.9 billion in fiscal year 1982 to $4 billion in fiscal year 1983. The Space Command will coordinate all U.S. military space programs and it will operate the U.S. ASAT.

DOD is currently spending about $300 million a year on laser research. This could help pave the way for a space-based laser weapon in the next decade or beyond.

I am sure you are aware of all of these things, but the point is, we are getting into this space race at a very fast rate, are we not? It seems that if this pattern continues, we will be spending just an enormous number of billions of dollars on space weapons. I understand the Soviets did offer a new space treaty at the U.N. last year. Was it at the U.N. that they proposed this?

MR. ROSTOW. Yes, sir.

SENATOR PRESSLER. The Soviets have floated a proposed treaty.

MR. ROSTOW. Yes, sir, I referred to that.

SENATOR PRESSLER. What is your response to that?

MR. ROSTOW. Well, it presents certain problems immediately. It was proposed in August 1981, and the proposal was to ban the deployment in outer space of weapons of any kind, but one of the difficulties was that there was no definition of weapons offered, and the provisions with respect to verification were very sketchy. Our response to that treaty proposal is part of the general response to the potentialities for arms control in space to which I referred in my prepared statement.

That is, we are eagerly looking at these potentialities. We completely agree with you and others about the potential cost of any competition in the field of weapons for outer space. The United States has been very slow in responding to the Soviet initiative, in developing weapons for outer space. I remember we were conscious of that risk in the late sixties, when I was here in the State Department, and our response to the Soviet proposal of August 1981, is part of our continuing active study of the possibilities of this field, to try to determine what our policy should be.

SENATOR PRESSLER. Are we going to respond by making a counter offering? The Soviets have offered a draft space weapons treaty. If we are not satisfied with it, do we have a draft space weapons treaty that we are prepared to offer or have offered?

MR. ROSTOW. No, we have not offered any such treaty. We have not reached any conclusion in our study. I said at the very end of my prepared statement, should we see a potential for verifiable space arms control measures that enhance our security, we are ready and I should say eager to take appropriate initiatives.

SENATOR PRESSLER. Why don't we have a draft treaty? Why doesn't the U.S. Government have a proposal? The Soviets are outmaneuvering us here, they have a proposal. If we are serious about negotiating this, as you say we are, why don't we have a proposed draft treaty?

MR. ROSTOW. Because of the difficulties of the problem, because of the problem of preparation. As I told you and this committee when I was up for confirmation back in June 1981,[97] I am opposed to and the administration is opposed to moving forward into negotiations unless we have a solid footing for those negotiations. That is the gist of the advice we got from Lord Carrington a year or so ago that I mentioned in my opening statement.

---

[96] See *Washington Post,* August 31, 1982, p. B13.

[97] For the text of Rostow's statement at his confirmation hearings on June 22, 1981, see *American Foreign Policy: Current Documents, 1981,* document 54.

I think it is right. I do not think we should try to use negotiations as a way for working out our policy. I think we should work out our policy first, and sometimes, as in this case, it is an extraordinarily difficult task.

Senator Pressler. Yes. Well, both sides, both the Soviets and the United States are launching into this expensive race, and yet we say that we are not yet ready to start talking. I think we should both have some talks in this area, and I believe we should have a proposal of our own. Indeed, I know it is difficult to draft a proposed treaty before talks, but how do we get this process started when we do not have talks and we do not have a proposed treaty? How do we start negotiating in this area?

Mr. Rostow. But we have had talks.

Senator Pressler. But they have been cut off, have they not?

Mr. Rostow. They have sort of faded away in any event.

Senator Pressler. Were they not shut off? Did they fade away or were they deliberately shut off?

Mr. Rostow. Well, I was not part of the administration in 1979, so I cannot report on that.

Senator Pressler. But they faded away.

Mr. Rostow. But they faded away in the atmosphere of late 1979. The fundamental position of the administration is that while we are working hard on this subject, we are not yet ready to resume those talks, and certainly not yet ready to negotiate. We are trying to assess and evaluate all aspects of this complex problem. After all, there are many dimensions of the space problem that are defensive and constructive, even though they are military. For example, the use of satellites for surveillance. They come out of President Eisenhower's open skies proposal. They helped to overcome the traditional and historic reluctance of the Soviet Union to allow inspections and free visits and so on, and they are absolutely indispensable to many aspects of our military as well as our civil programs these days.

So that to determine, to try to isolate outer space from the military sphere, to try to end all competition in the area of space has been our yearning and our posture, but exactly how to do it beyond the prohibitions already enacted in the Outer Space Treaty and the Limited Test Ban Treaty[98] is a very daunting challenge.

Senator Pressler. I have one more question, and then I am going to yield to Senator Percy, who has another subject that he wants to raise.[99] But first, let me say that with the increasing use of satellites for communication, we are growing dependent on stability in outer space. I also serve on the Communications Subcommittee of the Commerce Committee. In another 10 years, we could be transmitting most of our communications, news and weather, via satellites. We are increasingly depending on satellites for agricultural information. Those are peaceful uses, of course, but if another country had the capability to destroy or disrupt our space systems, we would be in a position where we would be very vulnerable from a point of view of national defense as well as of agriculture and other areas that are related. This is why this is increasingly important.

What about linking space talks and the START talks?

Mr. Rostow. My first reaction to your suggestion, Mr. Chairman, is that the problems in the START talks are already complicated enough. I think the Outer Space Treaty already prohibits weapons of mass destruction of any kind to be stationed in outer space, so that the specific subject of the START talks, the intercontinental ballistic missiles and other nuclear weapons, the so-called aggressive nuclear weapons, are already covered so far as outer space is concerned, at least with respect to the emplacement of such weapons there.

The other aspects of the space problems are extremely important, potentially very important but we are not yet clear, as I said, what our policy should be.

. . . .

---

[98] For the texts of the Test Ban Treaty (1963) and the Outer Space Treaty (1967), see respectively 14 UST 1313 and 18 UST 2410.

[99] Reference is to Senator Percy's expression of growing impatience at the administration's delay in proceeding with ratification of the Threshold Test Ban and the Peaceful Nuclear Explosion Treaties, following improvements in verification arrangements. For his exchange with Rostow on this issue, see *Arms Control and the Militarization of Space*, pp. 15–19. For another exchange between the two at an earlier hearing, May 13, on the same issue, see *Nuclear Arms Reduction Proposals*, pp. 380–382.

Document 57

Transcript of a Press Conference by the Secretary of Defense (Weinberger), October 28, 1982 (Extracts)[1]

"We Think . . . a Nuclear Freeze Will Weaken the Deterrent Forces That We Have to Rely on to Prevent War"

Good morning, ladies and gentlemen. Welcome to the second annual general press conference. (Laughter)

I want to make a short statement about the freeze resolutions. Next week the voters in eight States will be asked to vote on resolutions calling for the negotiation of immediate bilateral U.S.-Soviet halt to the testing, production and deployment of nuclear weapons. The proponents believe that this will be a step to reduce the risk of war, and increase the prospects of nuclear arms reduction agreements. We think it'll be just exactly the opposite. We think the truth is that a nuclear freeze will weaken the deterrent forces that we have to rely on to prevent war. And we think it would make it far more difficult to negotiate anything like a substantive nuclear arms reduction with the Soviet Union.

The problem is that our strategic deterrent forces—the Minuteman ICBM, the B–52 bombers, and the Poseidon submarines—are largely the product of a building program of the 1960's. In the 1970's, when we were interested and tried urgently through a number of times—détente, and arms control, arms limitation negotiations—to get a better relationship, we reduced our strategic program substantially. In effect, we did freeze our force levels at that time and in return the Soviet Union increased its nuclear programs dramatically. It developed and deployed, in large numbers, two whole new generations of ICBM's; they've now deployed the fifth generation and [are] working on the sixth. We are still on the third. The most recent of their ICBM's have the capability of destroying our Minuteman force as it now exists.

From 1966 to 1982, we did not build a single new ballistic missile submarine. In the same period, the Soviets built 60 such submarines. The result of this pattern and restraint is that over three-quarters of our warheads are carried on launchers that are 15 years old or even older, and 75 percent—three-quarters of the Soviet warheads are on launchers that are 5 years old or less, and so if we froze today, as a result of Soviet deployments and our own inactivity, a significant percentage of our strategic retaliatory forces would remain vulnerable.

The Soviet Union under a freeze would keep their new, powerful, survivable, very accurate and threatening ICBM force; we would be prevented from modernizing our aging and vulnerable ICBM force. The Soviets could continue to improve their sophisticated air defenses—which are already the largest in the world—and we could not replace our B–52 bombers which are now over a quarter century old.

In Europe, the Soviets could keep their SS–20 missiles which threaten NATO from within; we would be prevented from fulfilling our commitment to NATO to build or deploy a countering system. We could not deploy our submarine modernizations that we feel are so essential. The net result would be that we would weaken our deterrent forces, we would undercut our ability to continue to deter successfully.

So if we freeze today, the Soviet Union would have no incentive whatever to negotiate any reductions, and indeed, they would wholly exploit the many aspects of the freeze which are indeed unverifiable. Negotiating a freeze would distract us from our real task—which is to negotiate a substantial reduction.

. . . .

Q. Mr. Secretary, do you believe that the nuclear freeze movements are being exploited by people who would weaken America?

A. I think the principal thing to worry about in the nuclear freeze movements is the impression that would be gained by some people at home and some people abroad that this meant that America no longer had the will and the resolution or the ability to regain a sufficient deterrent strength. The problems with the freeze are all the ones I've just outlined. There's a common misconception that both sides can destroy each other and everybody has the same number of warheads and all that. And that totally overlooks the effectiveness of

---

[1] Source: *Public Statements of Secretary of Defense Weinberger,* 1982. The press conference was held at the Pentagon.

the deterrent which is the only way you can really measure these.

The effectiveness of our deterrent has been eroding because of the modernization that the Soviets have put into their system and the fact that we have not. We now have systems that are too vulnerable to first strikes by the Soviets and it is essential that we rebuild them as quickly as we can and that's why a freeze would be so dangerous. I don't discuss motives at all. All I'm worried about are the results.

Q. Mr. Secretary, quite apart from technical issues of the age of these weapon systems or political questions, the Catholic bishops in this country have drafted a proposed pastoral letter[2] which declares that nuclear weapons at their very core, the possession of them is just downright immoral. While the bishops say that a certain amount of deterrence has to be tolerated for the time being, they say that new strategic systems just are sinful. Do you accept that?

A. Well, the bishops have sent me and I'm sure to many other people copies of that draft, and it is a draft. They've asked for comments and we are pleased with that, with the opportunity to make comments on that, and we would want to point out many of the points I've made this morning, that we think freezing at this point is something that will increase the danger of war. The moral aspects of it should be examined from that point of view. We also, of course, have in mind that His Holiness, the Pope, at the United Nations, a message delivered there for him indicated that deterrence is a moral policy.[3]

. . . .

Q. Regardless of the logic or the motivation behind the nuclear freeze movement, it is growing. There are not only the Roman Catholic bishops but the Lutheran and Episcopal bishops have written pastoral letters[4] asking people, virtually asking them to vote or support a freeze. The Congress, supporters of Congress, think they are going to win that. What would your strategy be if that does indeed come to pass?

A. You have to read some of these freeze resolutions. They're all extremely ambiguous. And if you read them as lawyers do, and I used to be a lawyer years ago when I was earning a living, why you find that they are subject to a wide number of interpretations. They nearly all call for an immediate cessation of production, testing, development of any nuclear weapon. They then call for an immediate entry into negotiations to bring about substantially lower levels that will be fully and completely verifiable.

Now those are interesting resolutions, but are they capable of fulfillment? We think that if you froze immediately with this kind of a problem here of modernization and loss of effectiveness of deterrence, that you would have no inducement whatever to the Soviets to go to the negotiating table or to stay there; no inducement whatever to reduce their weapons. They wouldn't have to. They would have much more modern, much more recent systems up against older systems that aren't hardened and all of that problem. I haven't even mentioned command and control and communications which is the first item on the President's strategic rearmament program. And you have the problem of verification and the Soviets have never permitted on-site verification, and the verification of a total freeze can only be carried out if you have an opportunity to have at the very least on-site or very thorough in-country verification, and they've never permitted that. It says a good deal about the difference between the two societies. We've always offered that and they've never permitted it.

So you've got people expressing in a freeze movement things that everybody feels. I don't know anybody who wants a nuclear war. I don't know anybody who wants a war of any kind. The idea that by passing a resolution of that kind you have advanced the cause of peace is the thing that we're trying to demonstrate and urge, really has exactly the opposite because it drives people away from the negotiating table. It removes any incentives for the

---

[2] Reference is to the second draft of the Catholic bishops' pastoral letter, entitled "The Challenge of Peace: God's Promise and Our Response," which was released to the public on October 25 and was published by the documentary service of the Catholic News Service, *Origins*, October 28, 1982, pp. 305–328.

[3] For Pope John Paul II's message to the U.N. Special Session on Disarmament, which was read by Cardinal Casaroli on June 11, 1982, see U.N. document A/S-12/PV.8.

[4] In a 2,000-word pastoral letter of guidance released on September 15 at the end of the church's House of Bishops convention, the bishops of the Episcopal Church called the arms race a "strange insanity" that corrupted the world and threatened to destroy it. (*Washington Post*, September 16, 1982, p. A27) The Lutheran Church was then seriously considering merging with the Episcopal Church.

Soviets to continue negotiations or certainly to reduce any of this very modern armament.

Q. Are you saying that you would try to get around it administratively?

A. No. No. No. It isn't a question of getting around anything. The California freeze asks the President of the United States—asks the Governor of California to write a letter to the President of the United States. Nobody is going to try to get around that. The Governor of California has written letters to the President of the United States in the past. You don't have to get around anything. It's the perception, the way in which the effect of a passage of a resolution of this kind would be portrayed, the way it would be conveyed abroad, the impression that would be given abroad to our allies that we were no longer very strong or resolute to our opponents, that it was perfectly all right to go on with this kind of a buildup because America wasn't going to do anything about it. Those are the things we're worried about. It isn't a question of getting around anything or arguing about them. They are quite ambiguous resolutions.

Q. You have not answered my questions.

A. Oh?

Q. What will you do if indeed the Congress does adopt a resolution, the one including the verification?

A. I don't know. The one including the verification simply says that we should go to the conference table and negotiate arms reductions which we're doing, and asks for verification, which we're doing. I would suspect we would continue doing in Geneva the path that we're following. We would have to. I would also suspect that if the California resolution passes, the Governor would write the letter and the President would read it.

Q. To follow up on that, Mr. Secretary, do you have any reason to believe that there are any Catholic, Lutheran, or Episcopal servicemen who would have less dedication to their civic duty in the armed services than the formula enunciated on September 12, 1960, by candidate John F. Kennedy?[5] And I have a followup to this.

A. The first answer then is, no, I have no reason to believe that.

Q. Do you feel that there is any indication that you know of that Catholic servicemen will be more obedient to the bishops on nuclear bombs than contraceptives? (Laughter)

A. I have no way of knowing anything about either of those aspects. (Laughter)

. . . .

Document 58

Statement Read by the Department of State Spokesman (Hughes), November 3, 1982[6]

Department of State's Reaction to Nuclear Freeze Referenda in the Elections

We view the results of the freeze referenda[7] as a strong expression of American concern about arms control and an expression of a variety of other concerns, including recognition of the Soviet military buildup of the 1970's. The administration shares those concerns, and we have undertaken a positive program of arms reduction initiatives as well as a modernization program to ensure the continuing strength and effectiveness of our nuclear deterrent.

To the extent that these referenda are an expression of the American people's concern and desire to achieve progress on arms control, we welcome the vote. However, the referenda did not give the American people a real choice between negotiating a freeze

---

[5] In an address to the Greater Houston Ministerial Association, September 12, 1960, Senator Kennedy said, " . . . if the time should ever come—I do not concede any conflict to be even remotely possible—when my office would require me to either violate my conscience or violate the national interest, then I would resign the office; and I would hope any conscientious public servant would do the same." (*New York Times*, September 13, 1960, pp. 1, 22)

[6] Source: Office of Press Relations, Department of State. The statement was read at the Department of State Daily Press Briefing beginning at 12:10 p.m.

[7] In the elections, November 2, freeze resolutions won in 25 out of 28 jurisdictions, including 8 States, where they appeared on the ballots.

or negotiating reductions. We believe the American people want reductions and effective verification. In fact, most of the referenda call for reductions.

We will continue to work toward that objective with vigor and determination, and we believe these efforts deserve the support of all Americans.

We are now negotiating with the Soviet Union on our proposals for major reductions of nuclear and conventional forces to equal levels with effective verification. We must give these negotiations an opportunity to succeed.

The resolutions are advisory in nature, and although we share the sentiment which has given rise to these votes, we do not believe that a freeze at current levels is an effective or sound approach to arms control.

Many aspects of a freeze on testing, production and deployment could not now be effectively verified. Verification measures would, in fact, require extensive prior negotiation, and even then, several aspects of the proposed freeze might not be effectively verifiable.

Although a freeze appears simple, because of its broad coverage, it would require extensive and lengthy negotiations on its terms. This would divert us from the task of seeking reductions.

A freeze at current levels would undercut our efforts to negotiate arms reductions because it would lock in existing Soviet military advantages, while preventing us from carrying out modernization necessary to insure that our nuclear deterrent forces are survivable, effective and credible. It would greatly reduce Soviet incentives to discuss seriously the proposals for cuts in nuclear arsenals that we have proposed in the START and the INF negotiations.

Document 59

Address by President Reagan, November 22, 1982[8]

"I intend to Search for Peace Along Two Parallel Paths: Deterrents and Arms Reductions . . . the Only Paths That Offer Any Real Hope for an Enduring Peace"

Good evening. The week before last was an especially moving one here in Washington. The Vietnam veterans finally came home once and for all to America's heart. They were welcomed with tears, with pride and with a monument to their great sacrifice. Many of their names, like those of our Republic's greatest citizens, are now engraved in stone in this city that belongs to all of us. On behalf of the nation, let me again thank the Vietnam veterans from the bottom of my heart for their courageous service to America.

Seeing those moving scenes, I know mothers of a new generation must have worried about their children and about peace. And that's what I would like to talk to you about tonight—the future of our children in a world where peace is made uneasy by the presence of nuclear weapons.

A year ago, I said the time was right to move forward on arms control. I outlined several proposals and said nothing would have a higher priority in this administration. Now, a year later, I want to report on those proposals and on other efforts we're making to ensure the safety of our children's future.

The prevention of conflict and the reduction of weapons are the most important public issues of our time. Yet, on no other issue are there more misconceptions and misunderstandings. You, the American people, deserve an explanation from your government on what our policy is on these

---

[8] Source: White House Press Release, November 22, 1982, Office of the Press Secretary to the President; printed also in *Weekly Compilation of Presidential Documents*, November 29, 1982, pp. 1516–1521. President Reagan spoke from the Oval Office in the White House beginning at 8 p.m. His address was broadcast live on nationwide radio and television.

issues. Too often, the experts have been content to discuss grandiose strategies among themselves, and cloud the public debate in technicalities no one can understand. The result is that many Americans have become frightened and, let me say, fear of the unknown is entirely understandable. Unfortunately, much of the information emerging in this debate bears little semblance to the facts.

To begin, let's go back to what the world was like at the end of World War II. The United States was the only undamaged industrial power in the world. Our military power was at its peak, and we alone had the atomic weapon. But we didn't use this wealth and this power to bully. We used it to rebuild. We raised up the war-ravaged economies, including the economies of those who had fought against us. At first, the peace of the world was unthreatened, because we alone were left with any real power, and we were using it for the good of our fellow man. Any potential enemy was deterred from aggression because the cost would have far outweighed the gain.

As the Soviets' power grew, we still managed to maintain the peace.

The United States had established a system of alliances with NATO as the centerpiece. In addition, we grew even more respected as a world leader with a strong economy and deeply-held moral values.

With our commitment to help shape a better world, the United States also pursued, and always pursued every diplomatic channel for peace. And for at least 30 years after World War II, the United States still continued to possess a large military advantage over the Soviet Union. Our strength deterred, that is, prevented, aggression against us.

This nation's military objective has always been to maintain peace by preventing war. This is neither a Democratic nor a Republican policy. It's supported by our allies. And most important of all, it's worked for nearly 40 years.

What do we mean when we speak of "nuclear deterrents"? Certainly, we don't want such weapons for their own sake. We don't desire excessive forces or what some people have called "overkill." Basically, it's a matter of others knowing that starting a conflict would be more costly to them than anything they might hope to gain.

And, yes, it is sadly ironic that in these modern times, it still takes weapons to prevent war. I wish it did not.

We desire peace. But peace is a goal, not a policy. Lasting peace is what we hope for at the end of our journey. It doesn't describe the steps we must take nor the paths we should follow to reach that goal.

I intend to search for peace along two parallel paths: deterrents and arms reductions. I believe these are the only paths that offer any real hope for an enduring peace.

And let me say I believe that if we follow prudent policies, the risk of nuclear conflict will be reduced.

Certainly the United States will never use its forces except in response to attack.

Through the years, Soviet leaders have also expressed a sober view of nuclear war. And if we maintain a strong deterrent, they are exceedingly unlikely to launch an attack.

Now, while the policy of deterrents has stood the test of time, the things we must do in order to maintain deterrents have changed. You often hear that the United States and the Soviet Union are in an arms race. Well, the truth is that while the Soviet Union has raced, we have not. As you can see from this blue U.S. line [see "Defense Spending"][9] in constant dollars, our defense spending in the 1960's went up because of Vietnam. And then it went downward through much of the 1970's.

And now follow the red line, which is Soviet spending. It's gone up and up and up. In spite of a stagnating Soviet economy, Soviet leaders invest 12 to 14 percent of their country's gross national product in military spending. Two to three times the level we invest.

I might add that the defense share of our United States Federal budget has gone way down, too. Watch the blue line again [see "Defense Share of Federal Budget"].[10] In 1962, when John Kennedy was President, 46 percent, almost half of the Federal budget, went to our national defense. In recent years, about one-quarter of our budget has gone to defense, while the share for social programs has nearly doubled. And most of our defense budget is spent on people, not weapons.

The combination of the Soviets spending more and the United States spending pro-

---

[9] See the accompanying chart, reproduced from *Current Policy* No. 435, November 22, 1982, Bureau of Public Affairs, Department of State, p. 2.

[10] See the accompanying chart, reproduced from *ibid.*

DEFENSE SPENDING

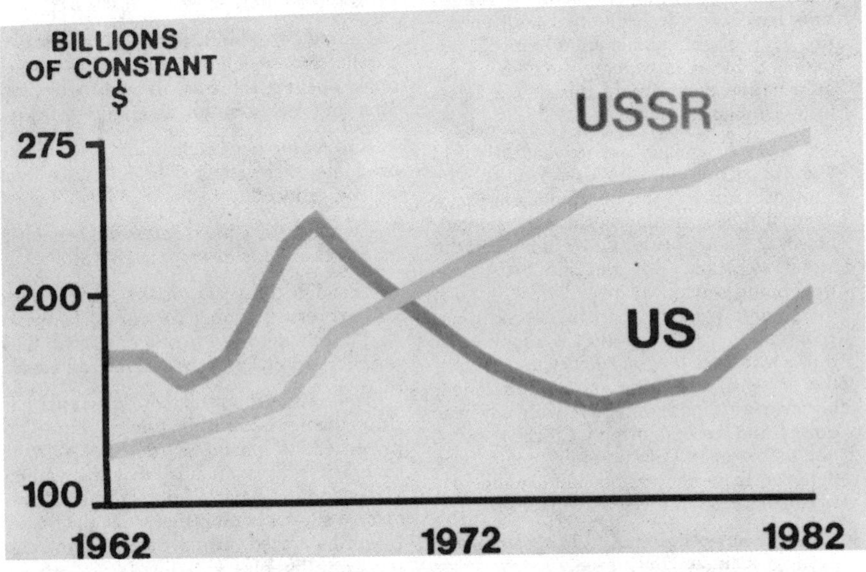

DEFENSE SHARE OF FEDERAL BUDGET

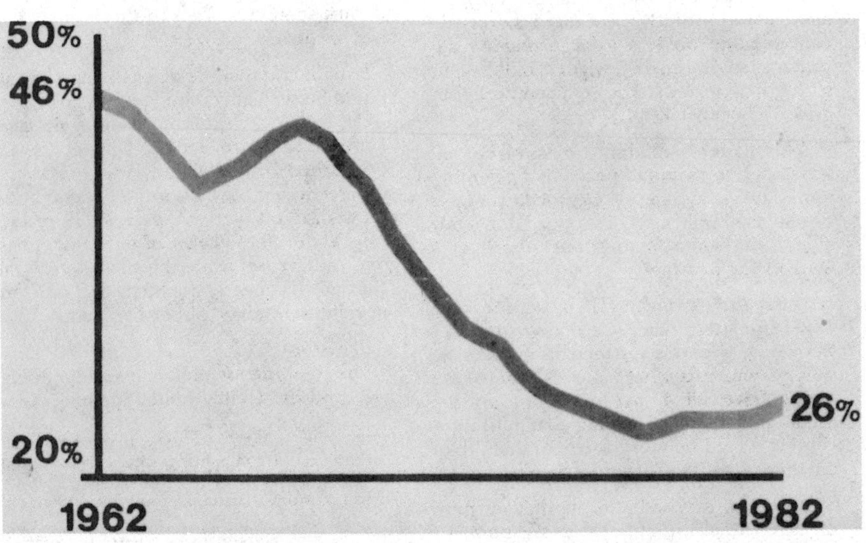

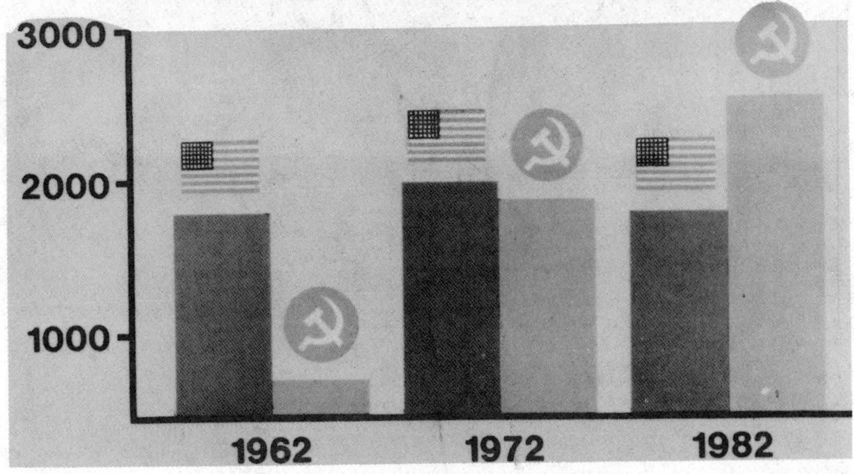
STRATEGIC
MISSILES AND BOMBERS
3000
2000
1000
1962
1972
1982

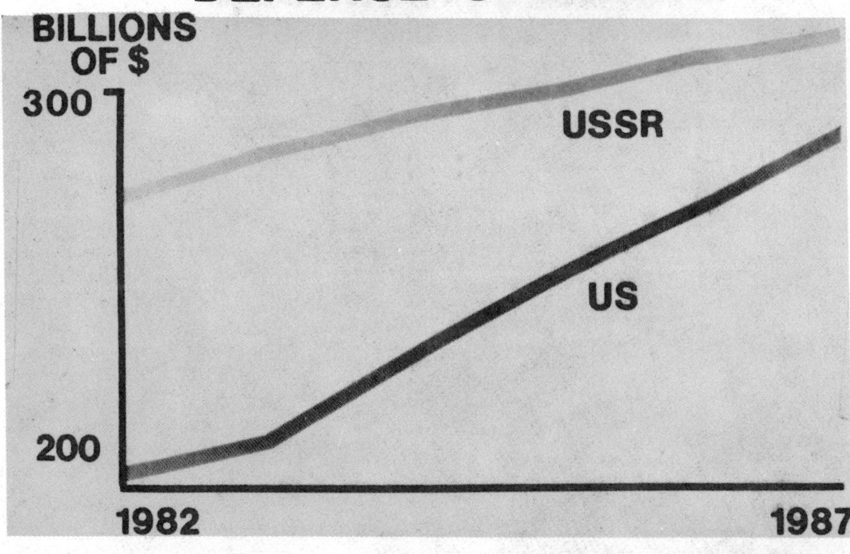
PROJECTED
DEFENSE SPENDING
BILLIONS
OF $
300
USSR
US
200
1982
1987

MISSILE WARHEADS
INTERMEDIATE RANGE•LAND BASED

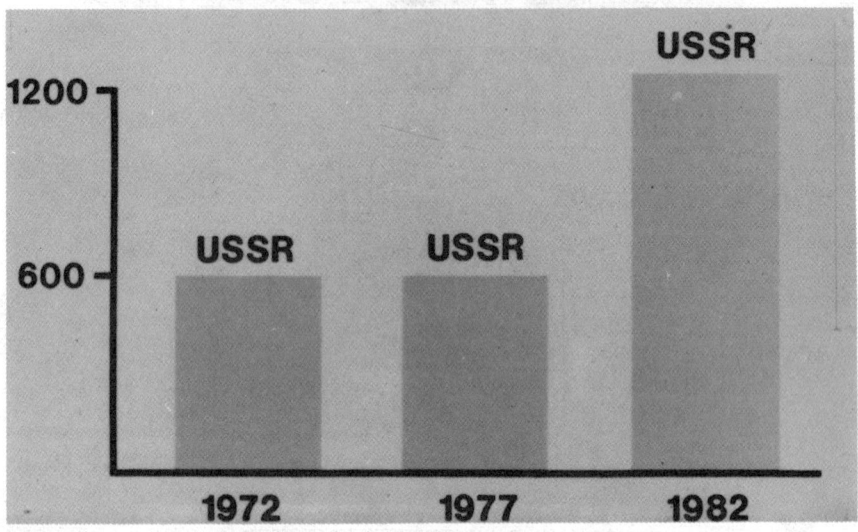

STRATEGIC BALLISTIC MISSILES

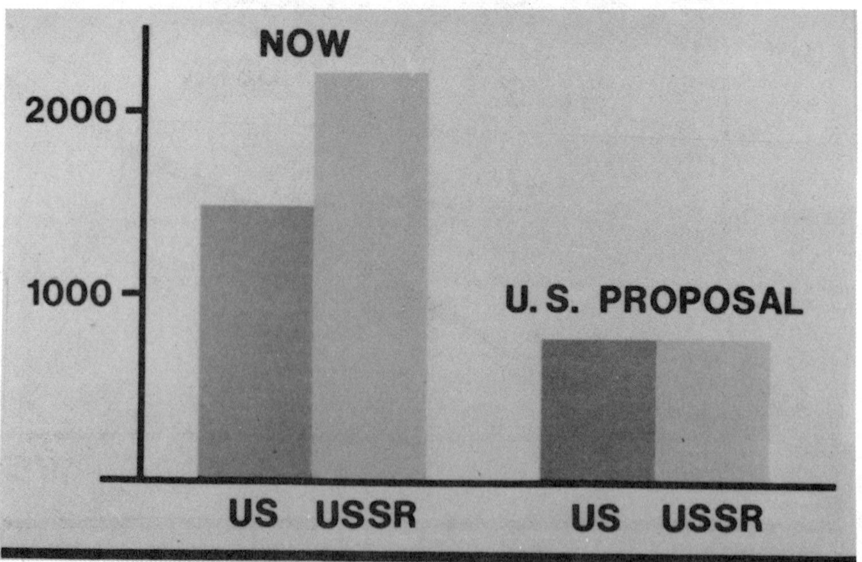

portionately less changed the military balance, and weakened our deterrent.

Today, in virtually every measure of military power, the Soviet Union enjoys a decided advantage. This chart [see "Strategic Missiles and Bombers"][11] shows the changes in the total number of intercontinental missiles and bombers. You will see that in 1962 and in 1972, the United States forces remained about the same—even dropping some by 1982. But take a look now at the Soviet side. In 1962, at the time of the Cuban Missile Crisis, the Soviets could not compare with us in terms of strength. In 1972, when we signed the SALT I Treaty, we were nearly equal. But in 1982—well, that red, Soviet bar stretching above the blue, American bar tells the story.

I could show you chart after chart where there is a great deal of red and a much lesser amount of U.S. blue. For example, the Soviet Union has deployed a third more, land-based intercontinental ballistic missiles than we have. Believe it or not, we froze our number in 1965, and have deployed no additional missiles since then. The Soviet Union put to sea 60 new ballistic missile submarines in the last 15 years. Until last year, we had not commissioned one in that same period. The Soviet Union has built over 200 modern backfire bombers, and is building 30 more a year. For 20 years, the United States has deployed no new strategic bombers. Many of our B–52 bombers are now older than the pilots who fly them.

The Soviet Union now has 600 of the missiles considered most threatening by both sides—the intermediate-range missiles based on land. We have none. The United States withdrew its intermediate-range land-based missiles from Europe almost 20 years ago.

The world has, also, witnessed unprecedented growth in the area of Soviet conventional forces. The Soviets far exceed us in the number of tanks, artillery pieces, aircraft, and ships they produce every year. What is more, when I arrived in this office, I learned that in our own forces we had planes that could not fly and ships that could not leave port mainly for lack of spare parts and crew members.

The Soviet military buildup must not be ignored. We have recognized the problem. And, together with our allies, we have begun to correct the imbalance. Look at this chart [see "Projected Defense Spending"][12] of projected, real defense spending for the next several years. Here is the Soviet line. Let us assume the Soviets rate of spending remains at the level they have followed since the 1960's. The blue line is the United States. If my defense proposals are passed, it will still take 5 years before we come close to the Soviet level. Yet, the modernization of our strategic and conventional forces will assure that deterrence works and peace prevails.

Our deployed nuclear forces were built before the age of microcircuits. It is not right to ask our young men and women in uniform to maintain and operate such antiques. Many have already given their lives in missile explosions and aircraft accidents caused by the old age of their equipment. We must replace and modernize our forces. And that is why I decided to proceed with the production and deployment of the new ICBM known as the MX. Three earlier Presidents worked to develop this missile.

Based on the best advice that I could get I concluded that the MX is the right missile at the right time. On the other hand, when I arrived in office I felt the proposal on where and how to base the missile simply cost too much in terms of money and the impact on our citizens' lives. I have concluded, however, it is absolutely essential that we proceed to produce this missile and that we base it in a series of closely based silos at Warren Air Force Base near Cheyenne, Wyoming. This plan requires only half as many missiles as the earlier plan and will fit in an area of only 20 square miles. It is the product of around-the-clock research that has been underway since I directed a search for a better, cheaper way.

I urge the Members of Congress who must pass this plan to listen and examine the facts before they come to their conclusion. Some may question what modernizing our military has to do with peace. Well, as I explained earlier, a secure force keeps others from threatening us and that keeps the peace. Just as important, it also increases the prospects of reaching significant arms reductions with the Soviets, and that is what we really want.

The United States wants deep cuts in the world's arsenal of weapons, but unless we demonstrate the will to rebuild our strength and restore the military balance, the Sovi-

[11] See the accompanying chart, reproduced from *ibid.*, p. 5.

[12] See the accompanying chart, reproduced from *ibid.*, p. 4.

ets, since they are so far ahead, have little incentive to negotiate with us. Let me repeat that point because it goes to the heart of our policies. Unless we demonstrate the will to rebuild our strength, the Soviets have little incentive to negotiate. If we had not begun to modernize, the Soviet negotiators would know we had nothing to bargain with except talk. They would know that we were bluffing without a good hand because they know what cards we hold just as we know what is in their hand.

You may recall that in 1969 the Soviets did not want to negotiate a treaty banning anti-ballistic missiles. It was only after our Senate narrowly voted to fund an anti-ballistic missile program that the Soviets agreed to negotiate. We then reached an agreement. We also know that one-sided arms control does not work. We have tried time and time again to set an example by cutting our own forces in the hope that the Soviets would do likewise. The result has always been that they keep building.

I believe that our strategy for peace will succeed. Never before has the United States proposed such a comprehensive program of nuclear arms control. Never in our history have we engaged in so many negotiations with the Soviets to reduce nuclear arms and to find a stable peace. What we are saying to them is this: We will modernize our military in order to keep the balance for peace, but wouldn't it be better if we both simply reduced our arsenals to a much lower level?

Let me begin with the negotiations on the intermediate-range nuclear forces that are currently underway in Geneva. As I said earlier, the most threatening of these forces are the land-based missiles which the Soviet Union now has aimed at Europe, the Middle East, and Asia.

This chart [see "Missile Warheads"][13] shows the number of warheads on these Soviet missiles. In 1972 there were 600. The United States was at zero. In 1977 there were 600. The United States was still at zero. Then the Soviets began deploying powerful new missiles with three warheads and a reach of thousands of miles—the SS-20. Since then the bar has gone through the roof—the Soviets have added a missile with three warheads every week. Still you see no United States blue on the chart. Although the Soviet leaders earlier this year declared they had frozen deployment of this dangerous missile, they have in fact continued deployment.

Last year, on November 18th, I proposed the total, global elimination of all these missiles. I proposed that the United States would deploy no comparable missiles which are scheduled for late 1983 if the Soviet Union would dismantle theirs. We would follow agreement on the land-based missiles with limits on other intermediate-range systems.

The European governments strongly support our initiative. The Soviet Union has thus far shown little inclination to take this major step to zero levels. Yet I believe and I am hoping that, as the talks proceed and as we approach the scheduled placement to our new systems in Europe, the Soviet leaders will see the benefits of such a far-reaching agreement.

This summer we also began negotiations on Strategic Arms Reductions, the proposal we call START. Here we're talking about intercontinental missiles—the weapons with a longer range than the intermediate range ones I was just discussing. We are negotiating on the basis of deep reductions. I proposed in May that we cut the number of warheads on these missiles to an equal number, roughly one-third below current levels. I also proposed that we cut the number of missiles themselves to an equal number, about half the current U.S. level. Our proposals would eliminate some 4,700 warheads and some 2,250 missiles. I think that would be quite a service to mankind.

This chart [see "Strategic Ballistic Missiles"][14] shows the current level of United States ballistic missiles, both land and sea-based. This is the Soviet level. We intend to convince the Soviets it would be in their own best interest to reduce these missiles. Look at the reduced numbers both sides would have under our proposal—quite a dramatic change. We also seek to reduce the total destructive power of these missiles and other elements of United States and Soviet strategic forces.

In 1977, when the last administration proposed more limited reductions, the Soviet Union refused even to discuss them. This time their reaction has been quite different. Their opening position is a serious one, and even though it doesn't meet our objective of deep reductions, there's no question we're heading in the right direction. One reason for this change is clear. The Soviet Union knows that we are now serious about our own strategic programs

[13] See the accompanying chart, reproduced from *ibid.*, p. 5.

[14] See the accompanying chart, reproduced from *ibid.*, p. 3.

and that they must be prepared to negotiate in earnest.

We also have other important arms control efforts underway. In the talks in Vienna on Mutual and Balanced Force Reductions, we've proposed cuts in military personnel to a far lower and equal level. And in the 40-nation Committee on Disarmament in Geneva, we're working to develop effective limitations on nuclear testing and chemical weapons. The whole world remains outraged by the Soviets' and their allies' use of biological and chemical weapons against defenseless people in Afghanistan, Cambodia, and Laos. This experience makes ironclad verification all the more essential for arms control.

There is, of course, much more that needs to be done. In an age when intercontinental missiles can span half the globe in less than half an hour, it's crucial that Soviet and American leaders have a clear understanding of each other's capabilities and intentions.

Last June in Berlin,[15] and again at the United Nations Special Session on Disarmament, I vowed that the United States would make every effort to reduce the risks of accident and misunderstanding and thus to strengthen mutual confidence between the United States and the Soviet Union. Since then, we've been actively studying detailed measures to implement this Berlin initiative.

Today I would like to announce some of the measures which I have proposed in a special letter just sent to the Soviet leadership and which I have instructed our ambassadors in Geneva to discuss with their Soviet counterparts. They include but also go beyond some of the suggestions I made in Berlin.

The first of these measures involves advance notification of all United States and Soviet test launches of intercontinental ballistic missiles. We will also seek Soviet agreement on notification of all sea-launched ballistic missiles as well as intermediate range land-based ballistic missiles of the type we're currently negotiating. This would remove surprise and uncertainty at the sudden appearance of such missiles on the warning screens of the two countries.

In another area of potential misunderstanding, we propose to the Soviets that we provide each other with advance notification of our major military exercises. Here again, our objective is to reduce the surprise and uncertainty surrounding otherwise sudden moves by either side.

These sorts of measures are designed to deal with the immediate issues of miscalculation in time of crisis. But there are deeper, longer-term problems as well. In order to clear away some of the mutual ignorance and suspicion between our two countries, I will propose that we both engage in a broad-ranging exchange of basic data about our nuclear forces. I am instructing our ambassadors at the negotiations on both strategic and intermediate forces to seek Soviet agreement on an expanded exchange of information. The more one side knows about what the other side is doing, the less room there is for surprise and miscalculation.

Probably everyone had heard of the so-called Hotline,[16] which enables me to communicate directly with the Soviet leadership in the event of a crisis. The existing Hotline is dependable and rapid—with both ground and satellite links. But because it's so important, I've also directed that we carefully examine any possible improvements to the existing Hotline system.

Now, although we've begun negotiations on these many proposals, this doesn't mean we've exhausted all the initiatives that could help to reduce the risk of accidental conflict. We'll leave no opportunity unexplored, and we'll consult closely with Senators Nunn, Jackson, and Warner, and other Members of the Congress who have made important suggestions in this field.

We are also making strenuous efforts to prevent the spread of nuclear weapons to additional countries. It would be tragic if we succeeded in reducing existing arsenals only to have new threats emerge in other areas of the world.

Earlier I spoke of America's contributions to peace following World War II, of all we did to promote peace and prosperity for our fellow man. Well, we're still those same people. We still seek peace above all else.

I want to remind our own citizens and those around the world of this tradition of American good will because I am concerned about the effects the nuclear fear is having on our people. The most upsetting

[15] See document 184.

[16] Reference is to the agreement for the establishment of a direct communications link, or "Hot Line," between the United States and Soviet Union in 1963; this link was improved in 1971. For texts of the two agreements, see, respectively, 14 UST 1313 and 22 UST 1598.

letters I receive are from schoolchildren who write to me as a class assignment. It's evident they've discussed the most nightmarish aspects of a nuclear holocaust in their classrooms. Their letters are often full of terror. Well, this should not be so.

The philosopher, Spinoza, said, "Peace is a virtue, a state of mind, a disposition for benevolence, confidence, justice." Well, those are the qualities we want our children to inherit, not fear. They must grow up confident if they're to meet the challenges of tomorrow as we will meet the challenges of today.

I began these remarks speaking of our children. I want to close on the same theme. Our children should not grow up frightened. They should not fear the future. We're working to make it peaceful and free. I believe their future can be the brightest, most exciting of any generation. We must reassure them and let them know that their parents and the leaders of this world are seeking, above all else, to keep them safe and at peace. I consider this to be a sacred trust.

My fellow Americans, on this Thanksgiving, when we have so much to be grateful for, let us give special thanks for our peace, our freedom and our good people.

I've always believed that this land was set aside in an uncommon way, that a divine plan placed this great continent between the oceans to be found by a people from every corner of the Earth who had a special love of faith, freedom, and peace.

Let us reaffirm America's destiny of goodness and good will. Let us work for peace; and as we do, let us remember the lines of the famous old hymn "Oh, God of Love, Oh, King of Peace, make wars throughout the world to cease."

Thank you. Good night and God bless you.

Document 60

Transcript of the Department of State Daily Press Briefing, November 26, 1982 (Extract)[17]

Relationship Between the MX Missile and the SALT Agreements

. . . .

Q. Do you have any comment on the Soviet response to the President's speech the other night,[18] saying in effect that the MX proposal as laid out is a violation of the SALT agreements?

A. Yes. First, the closely-spaced based system, which is a name for the system, does not involve fixed launches as set forth in SALT.

The launcher for the MX missile in the system will be a canister, specifically designed to be capable of being transported from one vertical shelter to another.

The vertical shelter, although fixed, is not a launcher. The transportable canister itself contains essentially all the equipment needed to launch the missile. Such a transportable launch canister is not considered to be a fixed launcher for SALT purposes.

We believe that this system clearly does not undercut the SALT agreements in any respect: the system is readily verifiable, it is a limited deployment which will not impede carrying out substantial reductions in strategic arms, and it fits well within the existing and proposed arms control structure.

It need not produce an increase in the number of ICBM's or ICBM warheads. This deployment can be accommodated under the reduced ceilings we have proposed in START. It is in no way contradictory to the object and purpose of the SALT agreements or with the purpose of the specific provisions of those agreements concerning fixed launchers.

---

17 Source: Office of Press Relations, Department of State. The press briefing was conducted by Department of State Spokesman John Hughes beginning at 12:27 p.m.

18 For the President's speech, see *supra.* The Soviet response was a statement published in *Pravda* on November 25; for a translated text, see *Current Digest of the Soviet Press,* December 22, 1982, pp. 7–9.

It is our policy that we will take no action which would undercut existing arms control agreements, so long as the Soviets show equal restraint. Deployment of this system is fully consistent with this policy.

Q. Can we have a copy of that, please?

A. Sure.

Q. Can I ask a couple of questions? Launchers under the SALT agreement that I've read are not restricted to fixed launchers. Mobile launchers would be included in the count as well.

A. This is not a mobile system.

Q. How is it not a silo, then, if it in fact acts like a silo, looks like a—

A. The canister goes in the silo, but the canister can be transported.

Q. What I'm saying is, why doesn't it come under the count of silos which has an overall ceiling?

A. Because it's not fixed.

Q. What I'm saying is that the silo ceiling also includes mobile launchers.

A. You're going a little bit beyond my expertise, and I'll have to do a little homework on that.

Q. Could you get an answer to that last question?[19]

A. All right. Fine.

Q. John, along that same line, in the administration's announced plans, they only plan to build 100 silos, and apparently have 100 MX missiles in those silos. There isn't any provision to move them any place, if you wanted to move them.

Does that suggest that the administration actually plans to dig more holes than it's publicly announced at this point?

A. No. I wouldn't project the future, but all we're saying is that those are not confined to those silos, but we're not talking about additional SAM's.

Q. John, are we saying that the canister can serve as the launch mechanism free of the silo, can be fired from above ground out of the canister without benefit of the silo's protection?

A. No. I don't think we're saying that.[20]

Q. It requires the silo, does it not?

A. I think it requires the silo.

Q. Then how does this fly?

A. What we're talking about are these particular silos, and this particular number.

Q. Let me put it the other way, then: The United States would have no objection if the Soviets were to go into such a canister system?

A. I'd have to do a little research on that.

Q. We'd welcome it. (Laughter)

. . . .

Document 61

Statement Issued by the Department of State, December 10, 1982[21]

Deployment of a Closely Spaced Basing MX System With Ballistic Missile Defense Would Not Violate the Anti-Ballistic Missile Treaty

Q. According to the 1974 Protocol to the ABM Treaty,[22] would the deployment of an ABM system around the MX site in Wyoming be a violation of that treaty?

---

[19] Regarding the question of whether mobile launchers would be included in the count of silos which have an overall ceiling under the SALT agreements, the Office of Press Relations, Department of State, posted the following response on November 29: "The MX would, of course, be counted under applicable SALT II numerical limitations. The relevant numerical limits which affect MX are no more than 10 warheads on a new type of ICBM, 1,200 launchers of MIRVed ballistic missiles, and 820 launchers of MIRVed ICBM's. The MX missile will not carry more than ten warheads. The deployment of MX would not prevent us from meeting such limits since older systems could be retired."

[20] The transportable canister itself contains essentially all the equipment needed to launch the missile. [Footnote in the source text.]

[21] Source: Office of Press Relations, Department of State; posted statement. The statement was posted in response to a question taken at the Department of State Daily Press Briefing on December 10 beginning at 12:28 p.m.

[22] For the text of the ABM Treaty (1972), see 23 UST 3435; for text of the 1974 Protocol to this treaty, see 27 UST 1645.

A. The M-X/CSB[23]—without BMD[24]—is an effective means of guaranteeing U.S. retaliatory capability in the event of a Soviet attack on our strategic forces. Should the Soviets be successful in developing technologies that are potentially threatening to CSB, there are a number of options which would be compatible with the system which could counter those threats. BMD is one of these options. Should we choose to employ BMD in the future in response to a new Soviet threat, we believe ballistic missile defense of CSB can be deployed within the provisions of the ABM Treaty.

The Protocol to the ABM Treaty defines the conditions under which the single BMD site permitted each side could be relocated from an ICBM field to the national capital. It does not prohibit relocation of a BMD site from one ICBM deployment area to another. The Protocol requires only that we dismantle the existing BMD site prior to relocation.

Document 62

Transcript of a White House Press Briefing, December 10, 1982 (Extract)[25]

Progress Report on the START Negotiations

. . . .

AMBASSADOR ROWNY. . . . I just met with the President who read my final assessment on the second of SALT—START—(Laughter)

Q. —ad lib—

AMBASSADOR ROWNY. And he asked me a few questions about the report and I reinforced a few of the points in my assessment. We talked about the conduct of negotiations. I told him that they continued to be serious and businesslike. And we continue to lay out our position. And then we talked some about the MX, of course, and I told him how—(Laughter)—important—it comes as no great suprise to you (Laughter)—I told him that the core of our proposal, really, is based on having very significant reductions. When we come to these much lower levels, we can't be left with inferior systems, down at these lower levels. And the entire START proposal, which is the most comprehensive and the deepest cut proposal that's ever been presented, calls for these deep reductions and is based on the assumption that we would have a modernized triad.

And if we don't have a modernized triad, then we have to reappraise our situation and see just what we have. On the other hand, I told him that I was confident that Congress would accept this notion and, therefore, we were proceeding full steam ahead and would work to bring home an equitable and a verifiable agreement.

Q. When do you think you'll have a START agreement?

AMBASSADOR ROWNY. When do we think we'll have a START agreement? That's hard to say? I—

Q. Within this administration?

AMBASSADOR ROWNY. Oh, I hope so. Certainly hope so.

Q. How close are you?

AMBASSADOR ROWNY. Well, that's hard to say. We—you know, when you make progress on a complex thing like this, you make progress on all the details that you lay out and we've made a lot of progress with a small "p". As far as the conceptual progress and coming to any real agreement, I can't say that—

Q. You all have any indication of the new Soviet leadership or the way they'll go?

AMBASSADOR ROWNY. The only indication we have of the new Soviet leadership is that they didn't miss a step, they didn't miss a beat. They continued in Geneva to negotiate on the same ground rules and the same guidelines and in the same manner. And, so, there's no indication of any change.

Q. Are you saying that you've reached agreement on some small details but on the overall, central issues, you haven't. Is that what—

AMBASSADOR ROWNY. I think that's a fair statement.

---

[23] Closely spaced basing. [Footnote in the source text.]

[24] Ballistic missile defense. [Footnote in the source text.]

[25] Source: White House Press Release, December 10, 1982, Office of the Press Secretary to the President. The briefing was conducted by Edward L. Rowny, Special Representative for Arms Control and Disarmament Negotiations, in the Briefing Room of the White House beginning at 2:21 p.m.

Q. So, there really hasn't been much progress?

AMBASSADOR ROWNY. There's been a lot of progress because there's a lot of details to lay out and there's a lot of things to discuss. This—

Q. Are those procedural?

AMBASSADOR ROWNY. No, no. They're not procedural. No. You come in with a new proposal as we did and you have a certain amount of—a great deal of departure from SALT—and you talk about missiles and their warheads and throw-weight, whereas in the old days we talked about launchers. These are—these have to be laid out. You have to define what you're talking about. You have to explain them in detail. You have to tell about the verification of these things. So, all of this is enormously complex and takes a lot of time. And—

Q. When do the negotiations resume, Mr. Ambassador?

AMBASSADOR ROWNY. The 2d of February.

Q. What do the Soviets think of the way we're handling the MX? Are they laughing at us? The President proposes it. Congress votes it down.

AMBASSADOR ROWNY. Well, I read the papers, as you do and—

Q. But you also meet with their negotiators. You must have some feel for, you know, what they think of how we're handling the MX.

AMBASSADOR ROWNY. We—see the President made his announcement on the 22d of November,[26] so I guess we were in session, what, another 10 days after that. And they reacted to it. And they said that—well, let me tell you what they said publicly back in Moscow. They said that, you know, that this is not in accord with the agreements. And we said, it is in accord with the existing agreements. And we're not undercutting existing agreements.

The reason I'm being somewhat careful here. I have asked Karpov[27] to take a confidentiality pledge on what we do at the negotiations itself and he's agreed, so I don't want to violate the confidentiality agreement.

But I want to talk to you about what's in the public domain and what—

Q. Just to follow that up, the President this morning noted that the Soviets think that Congress has done a wonderful thing and the President has said that if the Soviets are that pleased, we ought to be concerned.[28] You don't seem to be echoing the President's thought at all. I mean, I expected you to come out here and say the Soviets are just thrilled with what's going on, laughing with joy. You're not giving us that indication at all. Is that right?

AMBASSADOR ROWNY. No, you're putting—(laughter)—words into my mouth. I'm not saying that, but I'm not saying that they talked to me about singing with joy and so forth. I'm saying that they do watch our press very carefully. They watch our Congress very carefully. They were rather stunned at the 204 to 202 vote on the freeze.[29] And they said, "We didn't expect it to go that way." "We expected a victory," they said. So those are terms that they used. They do watch our Congress very carefully and I'm sure that they're watching this debate very carefully.

Q. Well, Mr. Ambassador, let me ask you: How damaging would it be for the START negotiations if MX is defeated?

AMBASSADOR ROWNY. Very, very damaging. Our proposal is based on a modernized triad and it's based on deep reduction and it's based, as I said, on the assumption that what we have left is not an old system, but a modern system. They have built new systems and built them at a rather rapid rate. And they have many of them.

Our system, as you know, the Minuteman, is over 15 years old. Now, of course, we have improved the warheads, so that it hasn't stood entirely still. But in terms of the overall measures such as throw-weight—You see, the Soviets' smallest, so-called light missile is three times as big as a Minuteman. Their 17's and their 19's are three times as big and as powerful. And their SS–18 is six times as powerful.

Q. What about it's accuracy?

AMBASSADOR ROWNY. As accurate. They have caught up in accuracy, so that—

Q. So, in layman's terms—

---

[26] Reference is to President Reagan's announcement of the closely spaced basing mode for the MX, November 22. See document 34 and footnote 72 to that document.

[27] Viktor Karpov, Soviet Ambassador to the START talks.

[28] Reference is to President Reagan's question-and-answer session with reporters beginning at 11:56 a.m., December 10. For text, see *Weekly Compilation of Presidential Documents*, December 13, 1982, pp. 1602–1605.

[29] See footnote 77 to document 54.

AMBASSADOR ROWNY. So that, in accuracy, they have caught up so—

Q. In layman's terms, without talking about triads and throw-weights—and I understand that's difficult because that's what you live—

AMBASSADOR ROWNY. Yes.

Q. —could you explain again the impact of a defeat on MX for these negotiations?

AMBASSADOR ROWNY. The impact on negotiating would be very serious because we have said that what we have to do is to restore stability in the situation and that there's a great instability in the situation because of the huge advance that they've made in weapons, particularly their ICBM's. And their ICBM's, intercontinental ballistic missiles, as you know, are the most accurate, most powerful, the ones that are under positive control, the ones you can communicate with, the ones that have the short flight time and the ones that are the most vulnerable. You put all that together and they have huge advantages in this important leg of the triad. And they've put ours at risk. We want to come down drastically in the numbers of weapons. When we come down to these lower numbers we can't be left with inferior types of systems and they have the better systems.

Q. Are you saying they'll never be negotiable?

AMBASSADOR ROWNY. What do you mean never?

Q. The whole—You say you want to have all this intact when you finally have an accord.

AMBASSADOR ROWNY. No, no. Our plan is based on the negotiability of this agreement, but the negotiability of this agreement is based on the assumption and we built this agreement on the assumption we'd have the MX and the D–5, for example.

Q. Should the Senate—

Q. As bargaining chips or is it—

AMBASSADOR ROWNY. Not as bargaining chips. I don't deal in bargaining chips.

Q. As the reality.

AMBASSADOR ROWNY. As a reality.

Q. Well, what are you trying to eliminate?

AMBASSADOR ROWNY. Am I trying to eliminate? Trying to limit—

Q. Everything else that's gone by the board?

AMBASSADOR ROWNY. We're trying to reduce the number of nuclear weapons drastically.

Q. Mr. Ambassador, what about the converse? What if we build the MX missile, what keeps the Soviet Union from saying, "Okay, you've built a new missile, a new accurate missile. Its throw-weight is whatever. We're going to outdo that and we're going to build an even better missile than you're building"?

AMBASSADOR ROWNY. The answer to that is very simple. You've already done it. You see, 3 years ago they have built better missiles—

Q. But they could do it again. To keep the margin, if they felt like they wanted to keep the margin, what prevents them from doing it? Could they do it if they wanted to?

AMBASSADOR ROWNY. We're both saying we will not undercut SALT II agreements, you see. So they're permitted one new missile which they've already tested.[30] Now we are saying we're going to deploy [a] new [one]. So they've already jumped the gun on the new one.

Q. But, in terms of the Soviet Union, they're saying we're violating SALT already.

AMBASSADOR ROWNY. No, they haven't.

Q. Well, by our basing system, by our silos.[31]

AMBASSADOR ROWNY. Oh, oh.

Q. They're saying those are—

AMBASSADOR ROWNY. Yes. That is a different issue. I mean, that is a different issue. And that, as you would expect, is a good debating point on their part, because it is awfully hard for a layman or anyone to understand the difference between a new-fix silo and a canister launcher. The technicians know the difference, and the people that deal in it.

Q. But you are saying there is no reason for the Soviet Union to continue to build a missile if we have another new missile—for them to escalate, and build another new missile.

AMBASSADOR ROWNY. Well, you know—where do they want to stop? If they have

---

30 Regarding the Soviet testing of a new type of missile, see footnote 97 to document 40.

31 See *supra.*

three times as many already—ICBM, and they have four times the throw-weight, yes; this new missile that they have tested will give them another increment. But they are already so far ahead of us. So what is the—

Q. It just seems to me that you are saying that we are building this new missile so that we can negotiate down.

AMBASSADOR ROWNY. I am saying that we are building the new missile so that, when we come down to these new, lower levels, they are not left with powerful weapons, and we are left with puny ones.

Q. Mr. Ambassador, are you saying that, if Congress turns down the MX, the President should go back and reevaluate his whole START proposal?

AMBASSADOR ROWNY. In the first place, I do not expect the Congress to turn it down. I think the Congress, one, understands the situation a little bit.

Q. The House has already turned it down.[32]

AMBASSADOR ROWNY. I know. A turn down certainly could occur. But I think that this thing has to be looked at and examined as to what we are doing. And I think that, once that is done, I think and I am confident that the Senate, that is going to move on this next, will look at this thing quite carefully. And then, you know, you see what happens.

Q. Would you answer his question?

Q. Are you saying that, if Congress turns down the MX, he should reevaluate your whole proposal?

AMBASSADOR ROWNY. Yes. I think, if Congress turns down the MX, we will have to reevaluate the proposal.

What I am saying, in effect, in the first instance is that it undercuts me considerably if the Congress turns down our position, because it shows the Soviets that we are not serious about what we are talking about. And that is protecting ICBM's and having a survivable force.

We are telling them that their ICBM's, now, can take out 95 percent of our force. And we have told them that we are going to have a portion of this force of our[s] survivable so they cannot take it out. Now, if we tell them we are not going to do that, they just wait and see what they can get. And they try to drive a different agreement. And I am, personally, not going to accept an agreement which undermines the security of the United States.

So we need it for security. And we need it for negotiating leverage.

Q. Do you think, to sell it now at this stage, that the President ought to withdraw the basing mode proposal, and make it more palatable?

AMBASSADOR ROWNY. No. Why?

Q. That seems to be the big stumbling block.

AMBASSADOR ROWNY. Again, I think that the President has made a decision on a number of options that have been presented to him. And he has made this decision based on good advice from his Secretary of Defense, from scientists—that this is a good proposal. And it is consistent with existing SALT agreements. It does not undercut those. So, therefore, I do not see why he would change.

Q. Some Generals think it is hairbrained.

Q. Mr. Ambassador, there is some talk about a compromise under which the production money would be voted, but there might be delay in the actual expenditure of it until there is further debate about the basing question.

Has there been any talk about that in your conversations with people within the administration, first? And secondly, how would that impact on the negotiations if you have that kind of compromise? Would that really undercut you?

AMBASSADOR ROWNY. No. The only discussions that I have had and I have heard is that the House vote was not really on the basing mode—that the House vote was on the production, and that the MX was not originally questioned. It was the basing mode that was in question. And really, it was the basing mode that was not really in question. So the production money was then withdrawn on the MX itself, which, kind of, contradicted this earlier estimate.

So, A, you need an MX, because you need an improved system—one to replace an aging system and one which is not nearly as good as the one that you now have developed, not nearly as good as the ones the Soviets have.

B, when you have it you should protect it because you don't want to place the new system—the new weapon under the same

---

32 See footnote 81 to document 36.

situation as the old one where it could also be taken out in a first strike. So the two go hand-in-hand. You have your improved system and you have a measured response. You have 100 of these MX's in a survivable way.

Q. If you would answer my question, sir, is there any talk about a compromise in terms of fencing on the expenditure of production money?

AMBASSADOR ROWNY. Not that I am party to. Not that I know about.

Q. Sir, what are the criticisms of your MX—

Q. Is it true that this will give us a first-strike capability and then the Soviets will be worried and they will go on—

AMBASSADOR ROWNY. No, that is not true. It is not true because—

Q. You deny that?

AMBASSADOR ROWNY. Yes. We have carefully constructed our proposals as well as our modernization programs so that we will not build a first-strike system. As I say, this is a modest improvement. It is a measured response and it does not give us a first-strike capability. If I had chart and chalk so that I could show you that you would need a lot more if you really wanted to have a first-strike capability.

Q. The President has characterized the Soviet offer as a serious one—the 1,800 level. Is there any prospect for a compromise between the 850 you proposed and the 1,500 that they have offered?

AMBASSADOR ROWNY. You see that compromise between 850 and 1,800 is really a comparison between unlike things. You see, we have said 850 deployed ballistic missiles. They have said 1,800 launchers. Now they have missiles and they also throw aircraft in. But they don't tell us how many warheads will be on those 1,800 and they have not revealed the details, so you don't really know what they are talking about.

Q. What I am really asking, sir, is there some prospect that the President's 850 will be increased in order to accommodate the Soviets?

AMBASSADOR ROWNY. I have not—

Q. You are not going to go back with any instructions on that?

AMBASSADOR ROWNY. No, no, and I don't anticipate any. In other words, the President's proposal is based on one which is as deep as he thinks the Soviets will accept—in other words, it has got to be negotiable—and the proposal has a great deal in it for them as well as for us.

Q. But you don't have any flexibility [in] what are you negotiating? It is sort of a take-it-or-leave-it attitude.

AMBASSADOR ROWNY. No, we are—we have lots of things to talk about and lots of systems and details to talk about.

Q. But the 850 is not a negotiable—

AMBASSADOR ROWNY. I have no instructions to change that, and it certainly is premature to talk about it when you don't know what their 1,800 number is all about.

Q. I would like to pursue this—what you said a little bit earlier about if Congress turns down the MX we will have to reevaluate the START proposals. I assume you mean by that reevaluate them downward so that we would have smaller reductions called for than the President now calls for.

AMBASSADOR ROWNY. I don't know. That is one of the outcomes. In other words, to answer your question positively, yes, we are able to go down that far because we assume that we would then have a modernized system of what is left. And if you cannot have a modernized system with what is left then you have got to reappraise, and you may not be able to go down this far.

Q. So you are warning Congress that the net effect of the defeat for the MX would be less ambitious START talks?

AMBASSADOR ROWNY. Oh, very much so. Very much so. In other words, one of the beauties of our position is that it does call for significant reductions—the most significant reductions ever proposed. And if you don't have modernized systems at the end—and they do—then you cannot go down as far to these equal levels. Equal numbers will exist but the quality will be different.

Q. Mr. Ambassador, if the Senate votes the same way as the House on the MX, will that just make the negotiations that you are participating in null and void?

AMBASSADOR ROWNY. It won't make it null and void but it is going to handcuff me—it is going to handicap me, and then we have got to see where we go from there. It is going to make it extremely difficult and we won't be able to get the ambitious kind of a program—ambitious kind of reductions, ambitious kind of arms control that we're looking for.

Q. Are you going to be talking to some Senators yourself?

AMBASSADOR ROWNY. Yes.

Q. Why do you think you were brought in to meet with the President today when you're not going back to Geneva until February?

AMBASSADOR ROWNY. He just read my report. I just submitted the report the other day and this is—done before. This is normal. A couple days after he gets my report, he reads it, talks to me, and then he talks to me again—once or twice.

Q. Do you feel that the Soviets violated the SALT II agreement by the test of their new ICBM without notification?

AMBASSADOR ROWNY. No, under the SALT II accord and SALT II is not an agreement but as long as people are abiding by that—they are allowed one new type. So, they have used up their—

Q. The test—

AMBASSADOR ROWNY. The test—they have used up their one new type.

Q. Weren't they supposed to provide advanced notification of a test of an ICBM which they did not do?

AMBASSADOR ROWNY. No, the advanced notification is something we're trying to get in the future under these confidence-building measures that we're—let me say in this respect that—

Q. In SALT II there are provisions for advanced notification?

AMBASSADOR ROWNY. No, no, there are [*is*] advanced notification of launches of test. And this wasn't a launch of a test. This is a launch of an ICBM. This was a test. They did notify us when they tested this new system.

Q. We were told 48 hours after the—

Q. Within 48 hours—

AMBASSADOR ROWNY. Within 48—

Q. After—

AMBASSADOR ROWNY. Yes, and that's the—under the present agreement what they're allowed.

Q. If you negotiate without having an MX, you said that you would—couldn't bring down the levels as drastically.

AMBASSADOR ROWNY. Yes.

Q. But would you do that and still preserve the security of the United States?

AMBASSADOR ROWNY. You'd have to look at the rest of your modernization program and see just how you preserve the security of the United States. These two go hand-in-hand. You have a modernization program and then with that you have an arms reduction program. If one part of this is cut out, then you see what the other two can do or see what else you can do. You have to reappraise the situation. But in any event, you take care—I'm sure the President is going to take care of the security of the United States in whatever proposal goes forward.

THE PRESS. Thank you.

Chapter 5. Foreign Economic Policy

A. General Economic Policy

Document 63

Statement by the Secretary of the Treasury (Regan) Before the Organization for Economic Cooperation and Development Council Meeting, Paris, May 10, 1982[1]

Economic Revitalization: The Key to a Sustained Recovery

Thank you, Mr. Chairman. I would like to express my pleasure at being able to meet here with the OECD Ministers for the first time, and having the opportunity to discuss with you the major challenges facing us.

That these challenges are serious indeed is a point I need not belabor. Many of us face record unemployment rates, weak economies, persistent though declining inflationary pressures, and high interest rates. We have industrial sectors that are no longer competitive in today's markets—but the recent OECD growth slowdown has been more widespread than in just our weakest sectors. It extends throughout our economies. Our citizens, disturbed at their growing economic difficulties, are demanding a solution to these problems.

Let me assure you that we in the United States are as acutely aware of these problems as any of you. The OECD is forecasting that there will be between 25 and 30 million workers unemployed this year in the OECD area—in the United States there are already over 10 million unemployed. Many key American businesses are in serious financial difficulty—in some cases, virtually entire industries like automobiles, construction, and the thrift industry. Political pressures for immediate action are at least as strong in the United States as in any other country represented here. Regrettably, in the United States, as in Europe, much of this political pressure finds its way into growing calls for protectionism, to shelter jobs from foreign competition.

As strong as the desire is to find a quick way out of our present situation, the fact is none of us has done so. To be sure, each of us could probably come up with a quick solution that might temporarily ease our pain. But before long, we would be back in an even worse mess.

An analogy comes to mind—how to get out of quicksand. The temptation, of course, is to try to struggle out immediately.

But this is a sure-fire way to sink deeper into the quicksand. The only way to get out of the mire is through well-thought-out, sure, and steady movements. It may take time, patience, and strength, but it is the only way to get out and stay out.

We must approach our economic problems with the same common sense and long-term outlook. Quick and dirty fixes—no matter how tempting—would only force us deeper into the economic quagmire in which we now find ourselves. We must have the courage to stay with policies that will provide for lasting, stable growth and a permanent departure from the stagflation of the last decade. It will not be easy, but we really have no other choice.

The key to a sustainable economic recovery is stable and noninflationary macroeconomic policy, formed with a long-term horizon—not juggled to fit each month's changing statistics and circumstances. In a stable and noninflationary environment, market signals can guide economic activity into efficient channels, so that today's resources are not squandered but rather are used to lay the basis for rapid growth of productivity in future years.

The process of economic revitalization must start with a credible commitment to noninflationary policy. Our people remember past inflationary policy excesses and premature government efforts to spur growth. They are skeptical that we have mended our ways. That skepticism translates into persisting expectations about in-

[1] Source: Department of the Treasury files. For additional information on this meeting, see *infra*.

flation, which distort consumption and savings behavior, and are built into wage demands and interest-rate levels.

A major impediment to the establishment and maintenance of long-term policies to reduce inflation and stimulate growth is the lingering presumption that there is a lasting trade-off between inflation and unemployment. But the experience of many nations over the past decade shows that there is no such trade-off. The sacrifice of sound long-term policies in efforts to support domestic employment in the short run has led in the end only to more inflation and more unemployment. Inflation and real economic growth are ultimately incompatible.

For any of our countries, policy for economic revitalization must focus on three crucial areas: monetary discipline, budgetary discipline, and greater reliance on market forces. A credible long-term program of monetary restraint is a prerequisite for price stability. Recent experience in the United States bears witness to the difficulty of reestablishing credibility in monetary policy once it has been lost—and to the extreme sensitivity of market and public psychology to any hint that the commitment to monetary restraint might be weakening. Recent U.S. experience also demonstrates the gains from monetary restraint. Our inflation rate has declined from a peak of nearly 13½ percent in 1979 to under 9 percent last year, and has dropped below 3½ percent in the early months of this year. This is no small achievement.

Budgetary discipline must operate on both sides of the government accounts. Expenditure restraint is needed to control what has until now been a steady rise in the share of economic output absorbed by government rather than the private sector. Restraint in taxation is crucial as well, to avoid unnecessary burdens on the private sector and distortions to private activity. Taxation which falls too heavily on production, work, and capital formation destroys incentives and jeopardizes future investment and productivity performance.

Finally, market forces must be given rein to adapt our economies to a changing economic environment, both domestically and externally. Government action to protect existing industries, firms, and jobs when they cannot survive in the face of competitive forces is a source of considerable internal rigidity. Over time, the potential adjustment burden facing sheltered industrial and financial sectors grows even larger. This growing loss of competitiveness exacerbates political pressures for protectionist measures to keep imports out of domestic markets. And protection in one country inevitably leads to pressure for retaliation by its trading partners.

Allowing market forces to prevail also means reducing government regulation. The web of regulations and artificial restraints which encircles our economies has sapped their strength and destroyed part of their vitality. Just as Jonathan Swift's Gulliver was rendered helpless by a myriad of tiny strings, so our inherently strong economies have been hampered by a myriad of government regulations. If we are to restore lasting growth, we must remove these impediments and allow the market forces which have been the key to Western economic development to reassert themselves.

Diverging economic policies and performance are a major source of the current international economic problems. Such problems become particularly acute when some nations are willing to tolerate high inflation while others are following policies to achieve price stability. Those with inflationary policies must face the exchange rate and balance-of-payments consequences of that choice. To the extent they are unwilling to accept those consequences, they are led to respond with capital controls, import restrictions, and exchange market intervention—efforts to deal with the manifestations of basic problems rather than the problems themselves. Distortions to international trade and capital flows grow, as do pressures on other nations to adopt accommodative policies.

Trade distortions, protectionist pressures, and exchange market fluctuations can all be negative consequences of diverging economic policies and performance. All of these are symptoms of underlying problems in economic policy: of inflationary policies and of a need for structural adjustment. Continuation of bad economic policy cannot help the situation. Neither can government intervention in markets to disguise the symptoms of incorrect policies. Exchange market intervention, for instance, will not succeed for any length of time in keeping exchange rates from moving in the face of powerful market forces. The only answer is to correct the policies themselves.

We are now trying in the United States to follow the sort of long-term approach I have outlined. I do not claim that recent U.S. economic performance is a model of success. But our policies are already producing results in some important respects, and we are convinced they will succeed.

Pulling out of the quicksand of stagflation is not a painless process that can be accomplished overnight. The immediate cost of the transition to firm ground is real, and is substantially increased when the effort to implement longer term policies is half-hearted. In the United States, the burden of the transition is dramatically visible in interest-rate levels. As I mentioned earlier, we have had major successes in our fight against inflation: inflation, as measured by the increase in consumer prices, was running at only a 1 percent annual rate in first quarter of 1982—and prices actually *fell* in March, the latest month for which data are available. However, our government budget deficit is likely to be bigger than we would wish, and we have had a difficult time reaching a slow and steady monetary growth path. Extended periods of overly-rapid money growth have alternated with periods of tightness or absolute decline. Our long-term trend in the rate of money growth is clearly downward, but variability of money growth is taking its toll. Both problems, fiscal and monetary, are having an impact on interest rates. We do not intend for either to persist much longer.

Our administration is in total agreement with the Federal Reserve on the goals for monetary policy—and we support fully the Fed's stated intention of attaining a smooth, slow monetary growth path.

On the budget front, we agree with the universal view that the deficit is too large. While the record shows no clear connection between budget deficits and interest rate behavior, there is concern that the deficit will consume resources which would otherwise be invested. Incentives for saving provided by the President's program, as well as the reduction in our inflation rate, will assure that ample funds are available to finance the deficit. However, because the uncertainty surrounding this issue is contributing substantially to risk premiums being added to U.S. interest rates, we are working with the Congress to forge a budget plan that will place the United States on a course of deficit reduction.

U.S. interest rates are well off their peaks of last summer. In terms of major reductions in inflation; in terms of the downward trend in the growth rate of the money supply and our efforts to reduce volatility in money growth; and in terms of the progress now being made toward a satisfactory budget settlement: the stage is being set for significant further reductions in rates in the coming months.

My colleagues will be speaking later in this meeting on the remaining agenda topics, but I want to note briefly two items of utmost concern to me: international investment and export credits.

Foreign investment is beneficial to all our economies. Like domestic investment, it introduces new technology, creates employment, and improves productivity. We are deeply concerned over the proliferation of national policy measures which distort international investment flows, and hope that this meeting will result in a Ministerial commitment to avoid such measures.

A further positive outcome would be Ministerial endorsement of an intensified work program within the OECD, leading to improved OECD instruments in the investment area, and to endorsement of a work program on trade-related investment problems at the November GATT Ministerial.[2]

As you know, important negotiations on export credit terms were held in Paris last week. Those talks resulted in a proposal by the chairman for a compromise package that now is under consideration in our capitals.[3] This compromise does not meet fully the requirements of the United States, but we are prepared to accept it in a cooperative spirit. We urge other governments to do the same promptly, so that we can continue our progress on this most critical issue and thus prevent the collapse of discipline and order in the export credit practices of the OECD countries.

In the context of our recent economic difficulties, we face strong political pressures. We would all like to solve our problems quickly and cleanly. Since no quick and easy solutions are available, our citizens sometimes tend to despair, or to turn outward to vent their frustrations.

---

[2] Regarding the General Agreement on Tariffs and Trade (GATT) Ministerial Meeting, November 24–29, 1982, see document 76.

[3] At the OECD talks on export credit terms held in Paris, May 6–7, 1982, Alex Wallen of Sweden, Chairman of the Export Credit Group of the OECD, proposed a compromise between the United States and the Export Credit Group (EC) regarding minimum interest rates and other conditions affecting official export credit. Known as the Wallen Compromise, this consensus arrangement on export credits was accepted, and, with a few modifications, led to the New International Arrangement on Export Credits which was adopted by the OECD on July 1, 1982. (Department of the Treasury Press Release 858, July 1, 1982)

I believe that while there is no quick and easy solution, we have it within our power to return our economies to a healthy state. What is required is a noninflationary and stable approach to economic policy, predicated on monetary discipline, budget discipline, and noninterference with market forces. We must set our sights on a long term planning horizon and not let passing events stampede us into bad decisions.

And in particular, we must deal with the *causes* of our present economic difficulties—reversing inflationary and undisciplined policies our countries have pursued in the past, and allowing structural adjustment to take place. Hiding the symptoms of these problems through government intervention is *not* the answer. Sound economic policy *is*.

Document 64

Communiqué Issued by the Council of the Organization for Economic Cooperation and Development at the Ministerial Level, Paris, May 11, 1982[4]

Cooperation to Surmount Economic Problems and Assure a Sustainable Recovery

1. The Council of the Organisation for Economic Co-operation and Development met at Ministerial Level on 10th–11th May to strengthen co-operation among their countries, in both surmounting current economic problems and assuring a sustainable recovery of non-inflationary economic growth and employment throughout the interdependent world economy in the 1980s. Ministers reviewed the work done on the trade issues of the 1980s, reaffirmed their commitment to combat all forms of protectionism and gave guidance for the Organisation's future work. They expressed determination that renewed economic growth must be broadly shared and that the co-operation with developing nations must be pursued actively.

2. The meeting was chaired by the Right Honorable R.D. Muldoon, Prime Minister and Minister of Finance of New Zealand. The Vice-Chairmen were Mr. E. Rekola, Minister for Foreign Trade of Finland, and Messrs. J. Delors, Minister of Economy and Finance, and C. Cheysson, Minister for External Relations of France.

3. Ministers agreed that the short-term prospect is for moderate expansion of economic activity in the OECD area, including perhaps a recovery in employment next year, but not one sufficient to lead to an early reduction in current high levels of unemployment. In many countries, unemployment is being exacerbated by continuing high inflows into the labour market. Progress has been made by individual Member countries in creating the conditions for sustained non-inflationary growth, but this has been uneven.

4. The reduction in inflation should help to encourage a recovery in real demand and output, but continued high interest rates, budget deficits and market rigidities are constraining factors. Ministers stressed the need to ensure stronger growth and lower unemployment over the coming years. They are convinced that this can be achieved if all Member countries, in accordance with their varying room for manoeuvre and within the framework of a common strategy, can successfully overcome their internal problems along the lines set out below, taking proper account of international interdependence and constraints.

5. Ministers agreed to carry forward the broad strategy they have been following since the second oil shock, and emphasized in particular that:

—there is a pressing need to reduce unemployment, but this objective cannot be achieved on a sustainable basis unless continued successful efforts are made to reduce inflation;

—sustained non-inflationary growth cannot be achieved unless there is more productive investment, better productivity, and technological progress; an increase in investment requires both sufficient profitability and a favourable prospect for an increase in production;

—maintenance of an open trading system, improvements in the functioning of markets, and positive structural adjustment are essential.

6. Ministers agreed that within this broad strategy individual countries need to set their economic policies in accordance with the varying nature and severity of the

---

[4] Source: OECD Press Release A(82)25, May 11, 1982.

structural and other impediments to growth faced by their economies. Ministers further stressed that close economic interdependence obliges all countries to pay careful attention to the external consequences of domestic policies. Convergent medium-term policies to establish non-inflationary growth are required.

IMPEDIMENTS TO BETTER PERFORMANCE

7. Ministers addressed the major structural and other impediments to a better performance and the appropriate range of policies to remedy them, stressing the need to continue to keep such problems and policies under close review. They recognised that failure to undertake such policies would lead to continuing slow growth, which itself undermines economic performance. It also increases the risk of protectionism. Slow growth involves not only insufficient productive investment but also the human costs of unemployment, including the erosion of skills and incentives to work, and the lack of work experience by unemployed youth.

The Inflation Constraint

8. Ministers agreed that although some countries have been successful in lowering underlying inflation, it nevertheless remains a serious problem. Where inflation or inflationary expectations are deeply entrenched, very high priority must continue to be placed on policies to bring inflation down.

Labour Costs, Profits and Employment

9. In a number of countries labour cost inflexibility and a squeeze on profitability have harmed employment. Low profitability and low rates of production have contributed to weak investment. High labour costs have encouraged capital-intensive investment even under conditions of high unemployment. Ministers agreed that while policies to address these problems were difficult to forge, there is a premium on them so as to speed required adjustment, and the reduction of high unemployment.

10. In some cases, wage settlements have reflected heightened emphasis on employment security, and the reduction of costs. Ministers welcomed such innovative approaches. They emphasized that greater realism emerging in the collective bargaining process would foster and sustain the recovery of output and employment. Such efforts might be facilitated by strengthening the dialogue between social partners. Ministers stressed the need for effective policies designed to moderate statutory employment costs, to enhance productivity, and to encourage innovation in the organisation of work. In this connection, Ministers welcomed the report from Mr. J.M. den Uyl[5] of the Netherlands who presided over the March 1982 meeting of the OECD Manpower and Social Affairs Committee at Ministerial Level.

Public Expenditure and Taxes

11. Ministers agreed that in many countries the growth in social security transfers has strained budgets, the increase in tax burdens has been too great, and at the same time public investment has been squeezed. These structural problems of budget control must continue to be tackled directly, independent of the desired overall budget deficit stance. They took the view that in general, when tax changes were enacted, these should remove distortions which discourage savings, employment and investment.

Public Sector Deficits

12. Public sector deficits are currently at historically high levels in most Member countries. Their reduction is a continuing policy objective. Ministers noted that weak activity and current high interest rates are factors adding to public sector deficits, but structural elements are also important in most countries. Ministers concluded that where public sector deficits are large relative to structural medium-term objectives, deficit reduction should not be postponed. Where underlying inflation has been significantly reduced, yet domestic demand is weak, the fiscal stance should be assessed with due regard to its likely impact on economic activity without jeopardising medium-term objectives.

High Interest Rates and International Tensions

13. Contrary to previous experience interest rates have remained high relative to inflation, thereby adding a new factor to public sector deficits and restraining demand in the private sector. Ministers recognised the variety of reasons for currently high interest rates noting, in particular, the impact of large budget deficits and uncertainty about the future course of fiscal and monetary policies. A durable reduction in

[5] The reference is to the "Report by the Chairman: Manpower and Social Affairs Committee," *Documentation for Meeting of Council at Ministerial Level on 10th and 11th May, 1982*, OECD Document C(82)51 Annex, April 8, 1982.

interest rates ultimately rests on a durable reduction in inflation and inflationary expectations. Ministers recognised the importance and results of anti-inflationary policies in the United States because of the key role of its economy and the dollar in the world economy. Many felt that more action should be taken now to reduce future budget deficits considerably, in order to ease the pressure on interest rates and savings flows.

14. Ministers recognised the importance of a smoother working of the exchange rate adjustment mechanism. Ministers agreed that under present circumstances improved co-operation with regard to convergence of economic policies to reduce excessive exchange rate fluctuations, such as have occurred in recent years, is necessary. Ministers noted, among the complexity of factors affecting exchange rates, the international transmission of high interest rates stemming from the desire to avoid currency depreciation and its unwelcome consequences. Ministers took the view that the economic performance of the OECD as a whole would benefit, and current international trade tensions be lessened, if interest rates came down, and if opportunities for trade, capital flows and investment were increased.

Policies for Changing Oil Situation

15. Ministers welcomed the contribution that energy conservation and progress in switching away from oil have made towards the continued fall in oil demand. They were aware of the risk of complacency and noted the continuing need for policies directed towards progress in achieving greater fuel efficiency and a more balanced energy mix.

16. Ministers agreed that particular attention should be paid to energy pricing including the need for oil prices to consumers to reflect expected longer-term world market price trends.

Positive Adjustment Policies

17. The major changes taking place in the world economy—adjustment to past energy price increases, impact of new technologies, increasing role of the developing countries—call for continuing structural change in the industrialised countries. While this is often painful under present adverse conditions, it is essential for growth and the preservation of mutually beneficial trading relations in the world economy.

18. Ministers welcomed the work done in the Organisation over the past three years on policies to facilitate structural change, and the Final Report of the Special Group of the Economic Policy Committee on Positive Adjustment Policies.[6] Underlining the importance they attach to this subject, they adopted the Statement annexed to this Communiqué and instructed the Organisation to continue to take positive adjustment policies into account in its ongoing work.

Current Trade Problems

19. Ministers reiterated their full commitment, as expressed in the Declaration on trade policy of June 1980,[7] to the open and multilateral trade system. They are fully aware of the contribution that a further expansion of world trade can make to higher employment, improved productivity and rising income worldwide. They also noted that renewed non-inflationary growth would stimulate production and employment and thereby lessen protectionist pressures. The resumption of such growth could, however, be frustrated by a proliferation of trade restrictions and domestic policy measures having similar effects.

20. As a follow-up to the Declaration referred to above, Ministers reviewed developments in the trade policy field over the past year. Despite present economic difficulties, the international trading system has held up reasonably well. Ministers noted with concern, however, a further extension of protectionist pressures and trade measures, many of which are not governed by multilateral rules and disciplines, as well as the increase in bilateral tensions and disputes which affect the climate of trade relations. They recognised the dangers which these trends pose for the future of the system.

21. Ministers therefore agreed on the need for further joint efforts to resist protectionist pressures, and to resolve urgent

---

[6] The reference is to the "Final Report of the Special Group of the Economic Policy Committee on Positive Adjustment Policies: Summary and Conclusions," OECD Document CPE/PAP(82)2(1st Revision), April 16, 1982.

[7] The reference is to the "Declaration on Trade Policy," adopted by the governments of the OECD on June 4, 1980, contained in Annex 1 to the OECD Communiqué issued in Paris, June 4, 1980. (OECD Press Release A(80)37)

short-term problems within the framework of the open and multilateral trading system. They are determined to maintain the credibility of this system at the present difficult juncture, and to work together with their trading partners on the longer-term issues which need to be tackled over the coming decade.

Safeguard Action

22. Ministers underlined the need for full application of international rules and disciplines. They also agreed on the importance of finding an early solution to the safeguard issue in the GATT framework.

Export Financing

23. Ministers welcomed the progress made on the issue of export credits towards the end of last year. They nevertheless regretted that it had not been possible for Participants to reach definite decisions on further improvements in the Arrangement at their meeting of 6th and 7th May. They noted however the initiative taken by the Chairman in presenting a set of measures which, taken as a whole, are intended to constitute a constructive compromise.[8] They stressed the importance they attribute to the Arrangement and agreed that all necessary efforts should be made to preserve and strengthen this instrument of international economic co-operation. Ministers also recognised the need to avoid any risk of distortion of trade and aid in the use of financing instruments which associate export credits with aid to developing countries and noted that particular attention was at present being given to this problem in the Organisation.

Trade in the 1980s

24. Ministers welcomed the intensive work done by the Organisation on the trade issues of the 1980s as requested at their last meeting. This had enabled them to identify and discuss a number of likely key trends in the world trading system over the next decade. It should provide a valuable stimulus to strengthen international co-operation in the Organisation and elsewhere on trade and trade-related issues in response to the important changes taking place in the world economy.

Growing Interdependence and the Increasing Importance of Capital Movements

25. The key features of the past two decades—the rising share of trade in economic activity, the rapid growth of financial interdependence, and the internationalisation of business—are likely to continue. Ministers recognise that this means that their economies are going to be more and more strongly influenced by developments in other countries.

26. The 1980s are likely to see the further evolution of an international monetary system which is characterised by large-scale capital movements and more flexible exchange rates, both strongly influenced by national macro-economic policies. Ministers noted that, should trade problems arise through excessive fluctuations in exchange rates, these can best be solved through improved co-operation regarding convergence of economic policies. In the light of this and the current trade problems described in paragraph 19, they requested the Secretary-General to examne ways of strengthening the existing work of the Organisation on the relation between macroeconomic policies and trade policies.

27. Growing interdependence also means that each country's actions not only in the field of trade policy but also in such fields as industrial, manpower, social, regional, agricultural and fisheries policies, will increasingly impact on the interests of its trading partners. Ministers therefore agreed:

—to make full use of the existing arrangements for consultation in the Organisation on measures taken by one Member country which may have important adverse effects on the trading interests of others.

—to request the Secretary-General to propose ways in which the effectiveness of the work of the Organisation on the restructuring of those industrial sectors facing particular structural difficulties can be strengthened, so as to ensure more transparency and a return to the normal play of market forces in a reasonable time.

—that there is a need for better information on the costs and benefits of trade and trade-related measures not only for those directly affected but also for society as a whole in terms of inflation, employment, income and growth.

28. Ministers recognised the growing importance of international investment flows for economic growth and agreed that efforts should be made to strengthen international co-operation on investment issues,

---

[8] Regarding the compromise arrangement on export credits proposed by the Chairman of the Export Credit Group of the OECD at the May 6–7, 1982 Ministerial meeting. see footnote 3 above.

building upon the existing agreements to which Member countries have subscribed. Particular attention should be given, in this regard, to measures affecting international investments that can have implications for trade flows in a balanced way which takes into account the interests and preoccupations of both investing and host countries.

29. Ministers recognised that, with the reduction of trade barriers and the growing internationalisation of business activities, there is an increasing likelihood that private restrictive business practice arrangements in one country may adversely affect the interests of its trading partners. They noted that the coverage of the present international arrangements for dealing with issues which arise at the frontier between competition and trade policies should be studied further by the competent bodies of the Organisation with a view to strengthening international co-operation in these matters.

New Trading Partners

30. The rapid growth of new markets and the emergence of new competitors is expected to continue in the 1980s; perhaps one-half of the increase in OECD exports will be to non-Member countries, compared with only one-quarter before 1973. Ministers are convinced that this will be an important dynamic factor in the world economy, leading to new opportunities for mutually beneficial trade relations between industrialised and developing countries.

Rapid Technological Change

31. The development of new technologies can and should play a key role in revitalising the world economy and enhancing the comparative advantage of the industrialised countries in capital and skill-intensive activities. There are varying degrees of government involvement in this area. Ministers agreed that an examination should be made of the specific problems which may arise in trade in high technology products and, where such problems are identified, of possible solutions. The Ministers also agreed that a study should be made of ways to facilitate the flow of technologies across national frontiers in order to promote economic growth and employment.

Services

32. International transactions in services of all kinds have been growing rapidly and now amount to about one-third of world trade in goods. Ministers agreed that this will continue to be another important dynamic factor in world trade in coming years. They therefore decided to encourage the competent Committees to progress as soon as possible in their analytical and fact-finding work on the complex issues involved so as to be able, in the light of the results, to begin examining ways of removing unjustified impediments to international trade in services and of improving international co-operation in this area.

Agriculture

33. Ministers welcomed the report "Study of Problems of Agricultural Trade"[9] prepared by the Organisation and endorsed its conclusions. They recognised that agricultural trade is affected by general economic developments and by domestic agricultural policies pursued by all countries which do not always take into account their international consequences. Ministers agreed that agricultural trade should be more fully integrated within the open and multilateral trading system. They recognised the specific characteristics of agriculture and the various objectives pursued by agricultural policies. Ministers agreed that the desirable adjustments in domestic policies can best take place if such moves are planned and co-ordinated within a concerted multilateral approach aimed at achieving a gradual reduction in protection and a liberalisation of trade, in which a balance should be maintained as between countries and commodities. They decided that the Organisation should study the various possible ways in which the above aims could be achieved as a contribution to progress in strengthening co-operation on agricultural trade issues and as a contribution to the development of practical multilateral and other solutions.

The GATT Ministerial Meeting

34. Ministers heard a statement by Mr. Arthur Dunkel, Director-General of the GATT,[10] on the preparation for a meeting

---

[9] The reference is to the 198-page "Study on Problems of Agricultural Trade," OECD Document AGR(82)4, February 26, 1982.

[10] The General Agreement on Tariffs and Trade (GATT) is a multilateral trade treaty negotiated and signed at Geneva, Switzerland, October 30, 1947, which entered into force for the United States on January 1, 1948. (4 Bevans 639) In addition to establishing a set of principles governing international trade, GATT has sponsored seven multilateral trade negotiations (MTN), the most recent of which were the Tokyo Round negotiations conducted in Geneva from 1973 to April 1979. For President Carter's June 19, 1979, announcement of the completion of the agreement signed April 12, 1979, which reduced tariffs and established new codes of conduct regarding nontariff barriers to trade, see *American Foreign Policy: Basic Documents, 1977–1980*, pp. 252–253.

of the GATT at Ministerial level in November. Realising the importance for the multilateral trading system of constructive and forward-looking decisions at that meeting in the interest of all participants, they expressed the determination of their governments to participate fully and constructively in this meeting and its preparation. Ministers noted the relevance of the issues they had discussed for that meeting.

Economic Relations With Non-Member Countries

ECONOMIC RELATIONS WITH DEVELOPING COUNTRIES

35. Ministers reviewed economic relations with developing countries which are characterised by increasing interdependence and diversity. They noted that the prevailing adverse world economic environment has created significant pressures on the developing countries, including increased debt problems. While the most important determinants of development are the developing countries' own efforts and policies, they emphasized the continuing commitment of their governments to co-operate with the developing countries in support of accelerated economic and social development. Ministers noted the progress made over the last year on international development co-operation both bilaterally and in multilateral fora while acknowledging generally that much further work needed to be done. They stressed the importance of implementing aid, trade, investment and finance policies in a comprehensive and co-ordinated manner in order to support the developing countries in their own efforts to strengthen their economic and social resilience.

The Dialogue

36. Noting the summary of the Co-Chairman of the Cancun Summit held last October,[11] Ministers confirmed the desirability of supporting at the United Nations, with a sense of urgency, a consensus to launch Global Negotiations on a basis to be mutually agreed and in circumstances offering the prospect of meaningful progress. They noted the recent proposals on launching the Global Negotiations which are currently under consideration in the United Nations[12] and agreed upon the importance of vigorous efforts to reach a consensus, including the basis for a mutually satisfactory definition of the central role of the Conference and respect for the competence of the specialised fora. Without prejudice to these efforts, Ministers also declared their determination to carry forward policy-oriented consultations as well as negotiations and co-operation on particular issues with developing countries both in the appropriate international fora and bilaterally in order to achieve new progress and positive results. In this connection, they noted in particular the forthcoming meetings of the GATT at Ministerial level and UNCTAD VI,[13] in which they intend to participate actively and constructively.

Trade and Investment Co-operation

37. For both developing and developed countries, trade like non-inflationary growth plays a central role in the complex of interdependent relationships between export earnings, use of international capital, debt servicing and borrowing capacity. It is clear that economic growth should allow a harmonious development of international trade in particular for developing countries. Ministers noted the growing role of developing countries in international trade and investment. They agreed that it would be important to facilitate the fuller participation of these countries in the open and multilateral trading system, with its shared rights and responsibilities, in order to provide a sound basis for their progressive integration into the world market economy. They foresaw a need for the improvement of arrangements for the discussion and resolution of international economic problems of special relevance to developing countries. They are ready to discuss with developing countries how this process can be advanced in the appropriate international fora.

Aid

---

[11] For the text of the statement issued by the Cochairmen of the International Meeting on Co-operation and Development, Cancun, Mexico, October 22–23, 1981, see *Ibid.: Current Documents, 1981,* document 91.

[12] In December 1979, the Group of 77 (G–77) nations proposed launching negotiations between rich and poor nations on issues involving international economic cooperation for development. The possibility of global negotiations under the sponsorship of the United Nations was authorized by U.N. General Assembly Resolution 34/138 which was passed on December 14, 1979. The original proposal has been revised several times, but the recent proposals referenced here refer to the March 31, 1982, draft resolution circulated informally by the G–77.

[13] The sixth U.N. Conference on Trade and Development (UNCTAD VI) was held from June 6 to 30, 1983, in Belgrade, Yugoslavia.

38. Ministers expressed the determination of their governments to maintain and, to the best of their ability, to increase the volume of aid to developing countries with a view to realising their commitments to the international aid objectives. They stressed the importance also of efforts to improve the quality and effectiveness of aid and also to facilitate flows of other financial resources to developing countries. In this connection, they underlined the essential role of the multilateral development institutions; they agreed on their need for continued substantial financial resources and encouraged increased co-ordination of multilateral and bilateral aid programmes. Ministers welcomed the increased importance being attached to the development of human resources in developing countries.

39. Ministers stressed the urgent character of the problems of developing countries, in particular the most disadvantaged among them, aggravated by present world economic conditions. They agreed that increased and better-adapted aid is necessary to assist notably the poorer countries in their development efforts and policies. They welcomed the constructive outcome of the United Nations Conference on the Least Developed Countries held in Paris in September 1981[14] and expressed their willingness to co-operate towards the implementation of the substantial new programme of action of that conference.

Food

40. The high priority and urgency of agricultural development and food production in developing countries is now accepted on all sides. Ministers welcomed and encouraged the new efforts being made to intensify international concertation and co-operation in this area, in particular initiatives for increased and better co-ordinated financial and technical assistance from developed countries in support of the formulation and implementation of comprehensive food strategies by developing countries. They recognised that this will require the commitment of sustained effort and resources by developed and developing countries.

Commodities

41. Ministers expressed their determination to continue their efforts to promote international co-operation in the commodity field. They reaffirmed their support for the Common Fund[15] and its objectives, urging that greater efforts be made by both developed and developing countries to bring the Agreement into operation as soon as possible. They also reaffirmed their support for further efforts to conclude commodity agreements where appropriate, taking due account of the specific characteristics of particular commodities.

Energy

42. Ministers agreed upon the importance of maintaining the impetus of energy development by strengthening and better co-ordinating bilateral and multilateral technical and financial assistance. They further recognised the need for identifying appropriate ways for example in the World Bank to organise and encourage additional public and private financial resources for this sector.

43. Ministers agreed on the importance of sustained and effective implementation of the Programme of Action adopted by the United Nations Conference on New and Renewable Sources of Energy in Nairobi,[16] which had established a constructive basis for improved co-operation with developing countries.

---

[14] In June 1979 UNCTAD V adopted a comprehensive resolution on the problems of the least developed countries which recommended convening a U.N. Conference on the Least Developed Countries to adopt the Substantial New Program of Action for the 1980's to aid the development of these countries. In its Resolution 34/203, adopted on December 19, 1979, the U.N. General Assembly endorsed the UNCTAD resolution, and the conference was held from September 1 to 14, 1981, in Paris. At the conference, the OECD countries modified the program of action to balance domestic and international measures including highlighting the importance of domestic economic policy measures and of agriculture, energy, and population sectors in the development of the least developed countries. The United States supported the modified Substantial New Program of Action embodied in U.N. General Assembly Resolution 36/194 adopted on December 17, 1981.

[15] The idea of a Common Fund or integrated program for commodities was proposed by the Group of 77 in 1978 with the guidance of the UNCTAD Secretariat. The purpose of the Fund was to help stabilize commodity earnings in the less developed countries by financing their buffer stock (commodities) for price stabilization purposes. The proposed $750 million Fund has not yet been established because while some countries have ratified the proposal, many, including the United States, have not.

[16] For the text of the Program of Action adopted by the U.N. Conference on New and Renewable Sources of Energy held in Nairobi, Kenya, August 10–21, 1981, see Department of State *Bulletin*, January 1982, pp. 66–78. Documentation on this conference is in *American Foreign Policy: Current Documents, 1981*, Chapter 5, Part D.

EAST–WEST ECONOMIC RELATIONS

44. Ministers recognised the value of the different aspects of the work of the Organisation on East–West economic relations, and agreed that their interrelations should be considered further within the Organisation.

ANNEX

STATEMENT ON POSITIVE ADJUSTMENT POLICIES

1. Faced with sluggish growth, abnormally high unemployment and widespread inflation, and recognising the interrelationship between economic growth and structural adjustment, the OECD Council at Ministerial Level approved in June 1978 "Some General Orientations for a Progressive Shift to More Positive Adjustment Policies".[17] In a situation of continuing unsatisfactory economic performance, the need for governments to pursue, in addition to appropriate macro-economic management, conscious policies for positive adjustment has lost none of its urgency. Ministers welcome therefore the results of the work of the Organisation which was commissioned in 1979 to investigate the adjustment process in market economies and to further inquire into the "Orientations" as a guide for policy-makers.

2. The Final Report on Positive Adjustment Policies[18] shows that there is either a virtuous circle of macro-economic stability and micro-economic flexibility or a vicious circle of instability and rigidity. An economy with the necessary flexibility to respond promptly to change can be kept more easily on a macro-economic equilibrium path. Conversely, stability in macro-economic developments assists micro-economic flexibility, because individuals can be more confident in their medium-term outlook, so that they can more easily adjust to new circumstances. To permit structural change at the maximum speed, which is politically feasible and socially acceptable, would greatly contribute to establishing the preconditions for increased economic growth, high employment, lower inflation and improved international trade relations.

3. Positive adjustment in an uncertain world economic environment calls not only for difficult judgements between the conflicting requirements of predictability and flexibility in macro-economic policies, but also for consistency between macro-and micro-economic policies. The achievement of macro-economic policies is jeopardised if governments allow industrial, regional, manpower and other micro-economic policies to contribute at the same time to conserving inefficient economic structures, thus undermining the market forces on which the success of macro-economic policy greatly depends. It is also essential that micro-economic policies should be consistent between themselves.

4. Ministers reaffirm the "General Orientations for a Progressive Shift to More Positive Adjustment Policies" and urge their effective implementation. They attach greatest importance to the following points:

—As time goes on, there is likely to be a deterioration in the trade-off between the short-term benefits and the longer run costs of measures to preserve existing inefficient structures. Defensive policies should therefore be subject to strict criteria.

—Wherever governments find it necessary to intervene to assist structurally weak industries, support should be temporary and should, wherever possible, be reduced progressively according to a prearranged timetable. Such action, if it is to succeed in bringing about adjustment, should be integrally linked to the implementation of plans to phase out obsolete capacity and re-establish financially viable entities.

—Innovation is crucial for future growth and positive adjustment. Governments also have a vital role to play, in promoting competitiveness and in providing a climate favourable to innovation, capital formation, investment, risk taking and skill acquisition.

—There are arguments for direct government support to develop new technologies. However, if this is directed to promoting promising new industrial activities, such intervention should be limited to particular cases and circumstances where governments are likely to perform better than the market.

—Broader political and social objectives such as national security, income distribution or environmental quality should be sought through policies which are consist-

[17] Reference is to the OECD report entitled "Some General Orientations for a Progressive Shift to More Positive Adjustment Policies," approved at the OECD Ministerial meeting, June 14–15, 1978, which is OECD Document C (78) 96 (Final), Annex II.

[18] Reference is to "The Final Report on Positive Adjustment Policies, Summary and Conclusions," OECD Document CPE/PAP(82)2(1st Revision), April 16, 1982.

ent with the functioning of the market economy or at least interfere as little as possible with flexible adjustment. Consideration of self-sufficiency should not be misused to justify measures of excessive protection and support.

—It is essential for positive adjustment that labour mobility and income formation should keep in close accordance with demand and supply conditions. Manpower policies—including training programmes—should therefore put renewed emphasis on measures designed to improve the basic conditions of labour-market adjustment.

—Job creation programmes should be targeted more directly to benefit clearly defined disadvantaged groups that encounter structural unemployment problems. Where measures are implemented to subsidise employment, they should not have the effect of locking labour into declining activities.

—The dividing line between domestic and international policies has become increasingly blurred. There is a risk that domestic policy distorts international competition, thereby shifting adjustment burdens and unemployment problems to other countries. It is therefore essential that the direct and indirect international implications of interventions in national markets should always be taken into account. Domestic adjustment should be sought by a policy design which minimises the negative side effects on other countries.

5. Ministers particularly underline that the maintenance of an open multilateral trading system is crucial to achieving the objectives of positive adjustment. They feel that the effective implementation of the GATT rules is of great significance in this context. In particular, they recognise the importance of the GATT codes resulting from the last Multilateral Trade Negotiations which are expressly aimed at averting also new, potential sources of trade friction.

6. Whenever governments intervene in national or international markets, transparency in the design and style of intervention facilitates an assessment of probable benefits and costs of policy. Transparency can thereby make an important contribution to positive adjustment.

7. As the issues of structural change will remain on the agenda during the 1980s, Ministers attach great importance to the Organisation's pursuit of the various aspects of positive adjustment policies in its further work.

Document 65

Address by the Secretary of the Treasury (Regan) Before the Development Committee of the International Bank for Reconstruction and Development and the International Monetary Fund, May 13, 1982[19]

A Positive and Responsive Approach to Economic Development

When the Development Committee met last September in Washington, I urged my fellow Ministers to join us in adopting a practical philosophy toward economic growth and development.[20] At that time, I called for a "positive and responsible" approach: *positive*—in the pursuit of economically sound policies to foster efficiency, productivity, and real income; and *responsible*—built on realistic policies which, though difficult or unpopular, would reinvigorate the international economy over the longer run. I stressed the role of open markets for trade, investment, and capital flows, and the overriding urgency of curtailing inflation. And I called for adoption of fundamentally sound domestic economic policies, letting market forces work to restore lasting growth. All of these, I explained, were basic to our approach for sustaining growth and development in developing countries.

Since then, we have enlarged on this "positive and responsible" approach to development in frank discussions with you and your colleagues—most prominently, in President Reagan's statements at last year's Cancun summit.[21] And since then, we have vigorously carried out our approach. We have taken specific steps to implement it—on the domestic front, as I reported yesterday to the Interim Committee; and internationally through an array of market-based, practical initiatives. Let me give some examples.

President Reagan's Caribbean Basin Initiative[22] is one which integrates the tools of

---

[19] Source: Department of the Treasury files.

[20] The reference is to Regan's remarks to the Development Committee on September 30, 1981.

[21] For the texts of President Reagan's statements made at the International Meeting on Cooperation and Development, Cancun, Mexico, October 22–23, 1981, see *American Foreign Policy: Current Documents, 1981,* documents 89 and 90.

[22] For the text of President Reagan's speech of

trade, commercial financial flows, direct private investment, and some official economic assistance. It will strengthen markets, foster sound policies, and bolster development in that region.

In agricultural development—a key sector in our approach—we have moved quickly to follow up President Reagan's commitment at Cancun to send expert advisory task forces to help address domestic policy issues in food and agricultural development, for those countries requesting our assistance. The first task forces have already gone to Peru and Egypt; six more are planned before the end of September.

In the important areas of trade and investment, we are renewing our commitment to trade liberalization and an open international trading system, in active preparations for November's GATT Ministerial session. We have, by the way, made special efforts to bring developing countries into that preparatory work, and into the ministerial conference itself, where we expect to make specific proposals of interest to them. Domestically, we are committed to seeking legislation to continue the Generalized System of Preferences[23] beyond its expiration in 1985, providing duty-free treatment to many imports from developing countries; and we have ended temporary import controls on footwear.

Clearly, there is wide support for improving the private investment climate in developing countries and for obtaining more private participation in development projects. We need to explore every avenue for enlarging this vital flow of capital to market-oriented developing economies.

In our own case, the U.S. Overseas Private Investment Corporation (OPIC), under renewed legislation, will now seek to expand its support for direct private investment in the middle-income developing countries. Our Agency for International Development will play an increasing role, with the establishment of its Bureau for Private Enterprise, in supporting economic policies and programs to help indigenous private sectors flourish in developing countries; it has already sent mutually agreed investment reconnaissance missions to several developing countries committed to a revitalized private sector.

We have encouraged work on investment ground rules in the OECD; supported the launching of an IFC study on investment incentives and performance requirements, which follows up on recommendations of a task force of this committee; have endorsed the World Bank's exploration of the concept of an investment insurance facility; and will press for progress on trade-related investment issues at the GATT Ministerial.

These efforts, and many others, represent our sincere and total commitment to assisting developing countries to achieve development goals in *practical* ways. It is a diverse approach, one which consciously mobilizes a range of forces that can feed accelerated and sustainable economic growth.

This "positive and responsible" approach also has special implications for the way in which we should regard the international financial, trade, and development organizations. These institutions are unique. They are designed, qualified, and committed to provide high-quality assistance and impartial guidance vital to developing countries in their growth efforts. The institutions were never expected to fulfill all needs of every country—yet their *collective* framework for meeting new problems and overcoming obstacles has already fostered unparalleled postwar progress in development. This collective framework now needs more comprehensive and creative use.

Much of the priority work of these international financial, trade, and development institutions centers on different—and valid—ways of tackling the same basic problems. At times, however, programs proceed within the confines of particular institutions, without an appreciation of complementary, sometimes similar, activities elsewhere, or of the totality of resources that can be brought to bear.

There are, of course, important exceptions. The International Monetary Fund and World Bank, for example, have achieved a major plateau of cooperation and coordinated programs with the IMF Extended Fund Facility and the IBRD Structural Adjustment Lending Program. The result can be more constructive country programs, consistent efforts, and an avoidance of wasteful duplication. Other possibilities for collective effort are likely to

---

February 24, 1982, where he outlined his Caribbean Basin Initiative to further economic development and foster free trade in that region, see document 675.

[23] The Generalized System of Preferences (GSP) is a system approved by GATT in 1971 authorizing developed countries to give preferential tariff treatment to developing countries; this system effectively waives the most-favored-nation principle.

be found in the work now underway, in many institutions, on investment. We need to make the elements of this work mutually reinforcing, not overlapping or conflicting.

I believe this theme of closer working relationships among the multilateral institutions has much to commend it. A more comprehensive, mutually reinforcing approach to solving development problems and achieving economic goals *can* be realized—even while each institution addresses those substantive issues it is best qualified and mandated to handle.

Turning to the specific items before the Committee today, I will cast my remarks in terms of our "positive and responsible" approach to development issues of the 1980's. Before concluding, I will also share, for future consideration, some thoughts on further opportunities for mutually reinforcing, multi-institutional development efforts.

Regarding IDA: While our administration was successful last year in obtaining legislative authorization to meet our full IDA VI obligations, budgetary realities dictated a stretchout in the timing of that contribution—with some regrettable delays in funding development efforts.[24] We appreciate the efforts by many to smooth out the process by finding supplementary funds, but the point needs to be made: we must, increasingly, concentrate IDA's limited financial resources on the neediest countries, first of all. And, as we concluded in our recent assessment of U.S. participation in the Multilateral Development Banks, the need for a better allocation of soft lending funds goes hand in hand with a more systematic policy of "maturation" of borrowers toward less concessional financing.

Regarding IBRD lending: We believe that the World Bank is adequately capitalized to support an expanding lending program. The impact can be magnified by mobilizing and catalyzing private, and other official, financial resources; by making operating adjustments to cover the Bank's lending costs; and by using its resources more selectively in particular countries and sectors.

Increasingly, the World Bank lending program must be regarded as fostering a transition process, for the more advanced borrowing countries, into nonconcessional and private financial markets. To this end, there should be expanded cofinancing and more effective implementation of the Bank's graduation policy, along the lines recently endorsed by its Executive Board.

For these and other reasons, including financial prudence, we cannot support the "permanent" expansion in the IBRD lending program which would result from accelerating use of the General Capital Increase (GCI).

Regarding energy lending: Here in particular, the role for the World Bank and regional banks as catalysts and mobilizers of private resources can be carried much further. We share the Bank's objective of expanding developing countries' energy production—but that goal is not one that can be accomplished primarily through official financing. Rates of return for much energy investment are sufficiently high to attract the necessary private resources. MDB policy advice and technical assistance can facilitate that process.

Regarding the final report of the task force on nonconcessional flows:[25] An assessment of the role and prospects for nonconcessional flows in developing countries is central to this committee's responsibilities. The task force's report, its conclusions, and its recommendations deserve our strong support—especially those confirming the soundness of the international financial system as an intermediary of capital surpluses to deficit countries, and those calling for the exploration of measures to enhance cofinancing between all MDB's and private lenders. In that light, we believe the Committee should, as recommended, periodically review developments in this field, including progress on implementing the task force's cofinancing recommendations.

In the areas of debt management and cofinancing covered by the task force, we

---

[24] The International Development Association (IDA), established in 1960 as an affiliate of the World Bank, provides low interest loan assistance to low income developing countries. In order to replenish its capital base, IDA has met regularly with its membership to secure additional lendable funds. IDA VI marked the sixth round of such replenishment negotiations which were completed in December 1979. The schedule of U.S. payments to IDA VI has been delayed by Congress, but other donors agreed to make additional contributions to cover the U.S. delay. The United States will complete its IDA VI payments by August 1985.

[25] Reference is to "Non-concessional Flows to Developing Countries," *Report of the Task Force on Non-concessional Flows to the Joint Ministerial Committee of the Boards of Governors of the Bank and the Fund on the Transfer of Real Resources to Developing Countries (Development Committee)*, May 1982. Nonconcessional flows are ordinary loans to governments at regular market interest rates.

see real possibilities for the idea of mutually reinforcing, multi-institutional efforts to which I referred a few moments ago.

On *debt*, while there can be no substitute for effective economic adjustment to achieve long-term, sustainable economic growth, many developing countries will experience balance-of-payments strains in the near term. Some have encountered difficulties in maintaining their external creditworthiness. Thus, we have recently been encouraging the Bank and Fund to expand their help to members seeking to improve their capabilities in macroeconomic management, including debt management, as an element of their adjustment efforts. Recent experience with expanded IMF assistance, and with the Bank's new structural adjustment lending activities, suggests that greater economic adjustment in some countries may have been impeded by insufficient technical and managerial expertise in these areas. Our impression is that many members would welcome more assistance in improving their fiscal, monetary, foreign exchange, and debt management.

We suggest that the Boards of the Bank and Fund continue to consider favorably ways of responding more effectively to requests for assistance in these areas—and, where appropriate, to anticipate such requests. In many cases, the appropriate response might include technical assistance in the form of training or outside consultants. In other cases, more frequent Fund staff missions and expansion of resident missions, which would provide a more continuous source of assistance, may be called for.

Finally, on *cofinancing*, the task force recommended that Multilateral Development Banks consult with the IFC on wider use of its cofinancing techniques. We would endorse—and broaden—this helpful idea to urge that the MDB's consult with the IFC on the full range of methods to promote economic development through growth of the private sector. The IFC has been particularly effective in leveraging its resources: for every dollar of project cost, the IFC resources account for less than 25 cents, with nearly half that amount then replaced by private financial institutions via syndications. I hope you can see why our administration has been especially enthusiastic about the IFC and the potential it demonstrates for a broad, cost-effective developmental impact by the MDB's.

Regarding the follow-up on the Bank's Sub-Saharan African Action Program: The urgent need to marshal and coordinate all the forces producing economic growth is most apparent in the sub-Saharan region. This area holds the largest number of the poorest developing countries. As I said last September, their bleak economic prospects *must* be softened, and ultimately reversed.

The Bank deserves high praise for its efforts to focus worldwide attention on the pressing difficulties, and to chart a future course, with its report and "agenda for action." The recent meeting it organized with African Governors of the World Bank and IMF at Dakar has special significance for future possibilities.[26]

We note that the African Governors emphasized external factors which have adversely affected their growth—thus, I am encouraged, in that connection, that I could report to the Interim Committee the significant progress we have made in the critical task of reducing inflation and restoring economic stability. The African Governors also acknowledged the need "to make efficient use of available resources" and the need for "adjustment and for a constant readaptation of development policies." While they justifiably saw those areas as the responsibilities of each sovereign country, I believe they also recognized the significance that appropriate domestic policies must have for the possibility of increased *external* assistance.

Most important, the Governors suggested a "wider dialogue" between Africa and the international community, with the help of the World Bank—a suggestion we wholeheartedly endorse. We appreciate the Bank's stated readiness to form additional consultative groups for this purpose. Country-specific dialogues and consultative groups could do much to build support for the objectives of individual countries' economic programs—while also promoting a more efficient, mutually reinforcing provision of development assistance by all donors, bilateral and multilateral.

Regarding the new task force on concessional flows: Our decision to participate in this new venture reflects our hope that its work can be constructive, balanced, and realistic—with a proper regard not only for the *sources* of concessional assistance, but also for achieving their effective and efficient *use*. We applaud the selection of Professor Lewis[27] to lead this work, which we

---

[26] The meeting of World Bank and International Monetary Fund officials with African Governors took place in Dakar, Senegal, March 1–3, 1982.

[27] Reference is to John P. Lewis, professor of

hope can become another example of the "positive and responsible" approach, in action.

Mr. Chairman,[28] I would like to touch briefly on three other areas, not on our agenda but of prime importance to development. Each of these has important possibilities for the mutually reinforcing, multi-institutional coordination of efforts I have been speaking of.

First, *trade liberalization:* Here we have a positive objective where more attention to related activities of the IMF, IBRD, and the GATT could produce benefits for all. The upcoming GATT Ministerial offers an appropriate opportunity to begin a major step forward. Even now, however, a fuller information flow from the Bank and Fund to the GATT contracting parties on those lending programs which use trade elements to promote economic adjustment would be useful. This would both strengthen awareness of the need for trade liberalization in broader economic growth and development, and more effectively alert trade officials and institutions to positive measures they would want to encourage.

Second, *foreign investment:* Much work is underway to improve the environment for economic, market-oriented investment, especially in developing countries, without creating distortions and political frictions. At a minimum, we and the international institutions need to keep each other apprised of this work and, as I have mentioned, be alert to opportunities for mutual reinforcement. At the same time, the IBRD, IFC, and Regional Development Banks could usefully step up their valuable technical assistance and policy advice on improving the policy framework for investment in member countries.

Third, *developing country capital markets:* The creation and strengthening of developing countries' own capital markets form a vital part of a sustainable growth process and, of course, helps to foster a healthy private sector. Appropriate policies and institutions, particularly equity institutions, are needed to mobilize intermediate domestic saving for productive investment; but this process can be frustrated unintentionally by a myriad of domestic laws and regulations. International financial institutions, particularly the IFC, have already been providing helpful technical and legal assistance—and funding as well—to overcome these burdens and establish appropriate investment "infrastructures." But we believe that activities in this area need more priority. We would hope that the IFC, IBRD, and Regional Banks can work, in concert, to provide it.

Mr. Chairman, I have sought to illustrate the many ways open to us for pursuing a "positive and responsible" approach to development. Existing international institutions possess a wealth of talent; and while differences are inevitable on specific approaches, and on the relative importance of specific issues, this must not immobilize us. There are substantial areas where progress can be made. This is not the time for posturing and debating, but rather a time to act—to dedicate ourselves to revitalization of our individual economies, and of the world economy. My government is committed to these goals.

---

economics at Princeton University and chairman of the task force on concessional flows set up by the Development Committee of the IBRD/IMF. Concessional flows are grants or loans to governments on concessional or very good terms, e.g., without interest or at very low interest rates.

[28] Manuel Ulloa Elias, Prime Minister and Minister of Economy, Finance, and Commerce of Peru.

Document 66

Address by the Secretary of the Treasury (Regan) Before the Annual Meeting of the Boards of Governors of the International Monetary Fund and the World Bank Group, Toronto, September 6, 1982[29]

The Need to Further Mutual Cooperation

I am happy to be here today, enjoying the hospitality of a neighbor with whom we share the world's longest unfortified border. I am delighted to be with you and to

[29] Source: International Monetary Fund, *Summary Proceedings of the Thirty-seventh Annual Meeting of the Board of Governors, September 6–9, 1982* (Washington [1983]), pp. 46–52. The 37th Annual Meeting of the Board of Governors of the International Monetary Fund was held jointly with the Boards of Governors of the World Bank Group in Toronto, Canada, September 6–9, 1982. The World Bank Group comprises the International Bank for Reconstruction and Development, the International Development Association, and the International Finance Corporation. Secretary Regan was the Governor of the Fund and the Bank for the United States.

join in welcoming three new members to this meeting—Antigua and Barbuda, Belize, and Hungary.

Last year, President Reagan met with this group in Washington and said: "We need to recognize our progress and talk about it more . . .[30] with one another. This in no way denies the immense problems we face. But without some sense of what we have achieved . . . we will succumb to defeatism or surrender to ill-advised solutions. . . [31]

During the past year, there have been major economic achievements, both in my country and in the international arena, and we would do well to recognize them. But first let me put these accomplishments in perspective.

At these meetings last year in Washington, at Helsinki,[32] and again at the economic summit in Versailles,[33] we were told that the U.S. budget deficit and high interest rates were the major economic problems for every other country in the world. In recognition of widespread concern and uncertainty in financial markets over the projected size of future U.S. budget deficits, we acted. In an atmosphere made difficult by domestic economic and political pressures—and despite our own unwavering commitment to incentive-oriented tax rate reductions—we asked the Congress to reduce budget deficits over the next three years by $380 billion, including the $99 billion in revenue increases which just passed the Congress. Although there are complaints about inadequate U.S. control of government expenditures, we have cut $270 billion from nondefense expenditures since taking office, in addition to the $280 billion in further cuts we are now asking for. President Reagan is personally committed to seeing these cuts through.

We are already seeing tangible results from our economic program. We have been predicting a decline in interest rates. This prediction met with entrenched skepticism, both at home and abroad. But the fact is that interest rates have been dropping for some time now. And while they are still much higher than we would like, they are far, far below their peaks.

The 3-month treasury bill rate, which peaked at 16.7 per cent at the beginning of 1981, is now at 8.6 per cent. The prime rate was over 20 per cent then. Today it is 13½ per cent. The federal funds rate has moved in the same period from 15 per cent to 9 per cent. These are major declines. With continued progress on inflation, we should see more in the months ahead.

The decline in long-term rates has lagged behind short-term rates. Historically, this has been the pattern, and the transition we are presently moving through is no exception. However, even long-term rates have now started downward.

In our first budget, we anticipated that the rate of consumer price increase in the United States would drop from the double-digit rates prevailing before we took office to about 8⅓ per cent this year and a little over 6 per cent in 1983.

Our critics, back then, scoffed at such projections. But in fact we have done even better. Consumer price inflation in the first half of this year ran at a 5.1 per cent annual rate, and we expect it to be only a bit higher than that for the year as a whole. Wage increases in the United States have averaged only about 6 per cent in the first 6 months of 1982. Wholesale prices are up only 2.5 per cent in the same period, and one of our major automobile manufacturers has increased prices for the 1983 models by a mere 1.9 per cent—a clear indication of weakened price pressures.

At last year's annual meeting, President Reagan said that ". . . each of our societies has a destiny to pursue. We have chosen ours in light of our experience, our strength, and our faith."

The theme of the United States under the Reagan administration is by now very familiar to you: we have faith in the market mechanism. Economic decisionmaking through private market activity simply produces more efficient results than decisions imposed by governments. And experience has demonstrated time and again that this is the case, both domestically and internationally.

In the United States, we have worked to put in place an economic program that embodies this approach. We have set our goals high—but they are attainable goals.

---

[30] All ellipses appear in the source text.

[31] For the text of President Reagan's address before the opening session of the Annual Meeting of the Boards of Governors of the International Monetary Fund and the World Bank Group, September 29, 1981, see *American Foreign Policy: Current Documents, 1981,* document 65.

[32] The meetings of the Interim Committee and the Development Committee of the IBRD and the IMF were held in Helsinki, Finland, May 12–14, 1981.

[33] For documentation on the economic summit meeting held at Versailles, June 4–6, 1982, see Part F.

The declines in interest rates and inflation that I have mentioned are welcome. But they provide only the first inkling of the real benefits that the U.S. and world economies will realize from the President's economic program.

The stage has been set for a strong recovery that is becoming more probable and more imminent with each passing day. Our index of leading indicators for July rose 1.3 per cent—the fourth consecutive monthly increase. The turnaround in U.S. real GNP, which began with modestly positive growth in the second quarter, will give us stronger growth later this year, before settling back into a sustained recovery with growth in the 4 per cent range.

While countries differ greatly in culture, traditions, and present economic circumstances, we believe that there is a broad blueprint for sound economic policy which is applicable to all. A stable and noninflationary macroeconomic policy, formulated with a long-term planning horizon and implemented steadfastly despite short-run pressures, is necessary for sustainable economic growth.

This type of macroeconomic policy must in our view be reinforced by a free-market orientation. When we allow market forces continually to adapt our economies to changing economic circumstances, adjustment is less abrupt. Governments can sometimes delay adjustment for a short time by using subsidies, protectionist measures, and capital controls—but sooner or later the adjustment has to be made.

These, then, are the components of our approach to both domestic and international economic issues: an emphasis on noninflationary, market-oriented domestic economic policies and on effective international cooperation. This is the philosophical framework that shapes our attitude toward the Fund and the Bank.

The Fund continues to be the key institution of the international monetary system. In the current environment the only acceptable approach is the one the Fund is taking—an approach designed to foster economic and balance of payments adjustment.

The types of problems our nations face have not changed in character. They still include excessive inflation, high unemployment, substantial payments imbalances, and the daily burden of poverty and hunger. But in the past 12 months there has been fundamental improvement on a number of fronts.

First and foremost, there has been broad—although not universal—improvement in the areas of inflation and payments imbalances. But we have only to look about us, or to listen to our citizens, to know that we still have a long way to go. A lasting world economic recovery, with significant reductions in unemployment, is now within our reach. But it will require continued diligence and perseverance to attain. From a worldwide perspective, the fires of inflation, while not as white-hot as they were a year or two ago, are still uncomfortably warm. In some countries, they continue to rage virtually unchecked.

Second, the experience of the past few months underscores the basic strength and resilience of the international financial system. The system is sound. It has coped with some difficult liquidity and debt problems, and I am confident that it will do so in the future.

At the same time, it is clear that the rapid growth of international debt has placed strains on the world banking system. Ironically, many current problems stem from government policies designed to stimulate rapid growth but which—because of their excesses and reliance on controls—have produced little or no growth and have greatly damaged economic performance in all respects.

All too often, governments have tried to follow overly ambitious national economic plans that exceed the real and financial resources of their nations. Confronted with the gap between aspirations and resources, the temptation is great to spend beyond one's means—a problem not unheard of in Washington. There are pressures for massive government deficit spending and temptations to monetize budget deficits, thus fueling inflation. And there are heavy pressures to borrow excessively abroad—to the point that a nation loses access to foreign credit markets altogether.

The results are inevitable: too little growth, too much inflation, too much debt. Confidence in the borrower's economy becomes shaken and money flees to other countries and to other currencies.

The lessons here for all of us—creditors and debtors—are plain. The international financial system is tough and resilient, but its resources are not inexhaustible. Societies cannot grow faster than their resources will allow. Attempts to promote unrealistic growth rates lead only to inflation.

The real solution to the problems we all face is to be found through a series of courageous and concerted steps toward adjustment.

As President Clausen said this morning: ". . . sustained growth in the developing countries inevitably depends on their own sound domestic policies. . . ."[34] The same applies to all.

Without sound national economic policies, both domestic and international resources—real and financial—are misallocated, and economic and social disruptions can only increase. With sound policies, the basis is laid for reconciling the necessary prudence in lending by the private sector with the need for continued financing during the period of adjustment.

Reluctance to tackle difficult economic decisions, coupled with recent sluggishness of the world economy, has made it all the more difficult to resist the political pressures for protectionism. But one of the lessons of history is that protectionism does not pay. Free-flowing trade and investment are part of the engine that drives economic growth.

For this reason it is essential that we maintain forward momentum on trade liberalization, rather than slipping back into politically motivated protectionism. While liberalization of international trade and investment, in itself, is no panacea for our economic difficulties, it is an essential component of any sustainable long-run recovery. We have been working hard to keep up momentum for such liberalization, and that will be the central focus of our efforts at this fall's GATT ministerial meetings.

As the major international monetary institution, the IMF has a central role to play in promoting greater discipline in national economies. One obvious way it can accomplish this is through its surveillance activities.

In this context, I am pleased to note that, with the assistance of the Managing Director,[35] we have begun the process of enhanced international economic and monetary cooperation that was agreed upon at the Versailles summit. We are hopeful that this effort will make an important contribution to greater convergence and stability in the policies of the major trading nations, and thereby to greater exchange market stability.

Another important area of the Fund's adjustment-related activities is its role in extending conditional balance of payments financing. For the Fund to have an effective role, this financing must remain temporary; and it must be directed toward support of sound adjustment programs.

The United States has urged that IMF support be directed to cases of genuine need, in order to conserve scarce financial resources; and that great care be given to the design and implementation of IMF-supported programs, to maximize the IMF's contribution to effective adjustment. We are pleased with progress in both of these areas: the Fund's current financial position is strong, as is its reputation for supporting sound economic programs on the part of its borrowers.

For the future, we must assure that the Fund maintains the capacity to respond to genuine needs for temporary financing and to cope with situations that place strains on the system as a whole. The increase in IMF quotas now under discussion in the Fund must be adequate to meet temporary balance of payments financing requirements under normal circumstances. We believe also that consideration should be given to establishment of an additional permanent borrowing arrangement, which would be available to the IMF on a contingency basis for use in extraordinary circumstances.

The United States is prepared to work closely with others in elaborating and considering this suggestion and believes that basic decisions both on it and on the quota review itself should be a realistic aim for next spring's meeting of the Interim Committee.

A year ago, when I first addressed this body, I urged a return to the types of economic policies that gave the world such an excellent record on growth and development during the first decades after World War II—market-oriented policies to mobilize private economic activity.

The events of the intervening year have served to remind us that, while such policies will lead us to lasting economic recovery and vigorous growth, the process is not quick. Nor is it easy. We are making solid progress toward reducing inflationary pressures and restoring the basis for growth—but much more remains to be done.

The International Monetary Fund and the World Bank continue to embody sound

---

[34] For the text of President A.W. Clausen's speech, see International Bank for Reconstruction and Development, International Finance Corporation, and International Development Association, *1982 Annual Meetings of the Boards of Governors: Summary Proceedings* (Washington, 1983), pp. 12–27.

[35] J. de Larosière, Managing Director of the International Monetary Fund.

principles. They continue to make very important contributions to world economic progress. The United States remains an energetic supporter of both the Fund and the Bank. It is clear, I am sure, that this administration holds fast to certain principles and to certain policies. At the same time, I hope it is evident that dialogue and cooperation are also bywords of this administration. We listen. We discuss. And thus we all have a continuing opportunity to learn from one another.

Thirty-eight years ago at Bretton Woods, another American Treasury Secretary, Henry Morgenthau, said: "We can accomplish our task only if we approach it not as bargainers but as partners—not as rivals but as men who recognize that their common welfare depends on . . . mutual trust and joint endeavor."[36] And with that view still in mind, we look forward to effective cooperation with these institutions and their members in the future.

B. Trade and Commercial Policy

Document 67

Statement by the Secretary of Commerce (Baldrige) Before the Joint Economic Committee of Congress, February 10, 1982[1]

The Importance of Expanding U.S. Trade

I am pleased to appear here before the Joint Economic Committee with Ambassador Brock to discuss U.S. trade policy.[2] I will comment on the world trade situation and the increasing pressures for turning to trade protectionism. I will also focus on the issues of U.S. competitiveness, especially in high-technology fields; East–West trade; and Commerce trade promotion programs.

The world trade situation has been aggravated by the severe, worldwide economic recession. International trade is being subjected to new stresses, which threaten the extensive liberalization of trade that has taken place since World War II. Already there has been a dramatic slowing in merchandise trade among the nations of the world. Last year, for the first time in three decades, the trade of the free world declined in real terms.

Historically, in times of recession, strong pressures develop for protectionism and the restriction of trade. To bolster their economies, many of our trading partners are resorting to new or expanded protectionist measures to limit imports and to expand exports through government-backed export incentives. These include trade-related performance requirements and restricted import levels.

Added to these difficulties are continuing distortions in trade resulting from past restraints, such as the use of nontariff barriers by some of our major trading partners. There is no question that the United States is demonstrating a greater commitment to a fair and open trading system than any major country in the world. How long we can continue to sustain this traditional role is getting to be an increasing question if other countries pursue their self-interests to our detriment.

U.S. trade data, market share figures—particularly for manufactured exports—and long-term indicators of industrial competitiveness show that our economy is falling behind our major competitors. Due to lower U.S. investment in plant and equipment and a smaller share of R. & D. spending than our competitors, productivity growth in the United States has been unable to offset a larger portion of wage increases as it has in other countries.

The bright spot in U.S. competitive performance and trade is trade in high-technology products. Since 1975 we have had a cumulative surplus of $128 billion in high-tech trade, compared to the cumulative surplus of $148 billion deficit in overall merchandise trade. In the last 2 years our surplus in the high-technology area has exceeded $60 billion.

But, if we look into the future we face a very broad challenge of other countries in

---

36 For the text of Henry Morgenthau's address to the plenary session of the U.N. Monetary and Financial Conference at Bretton Woods, New Hampshire, July 1, 1944, see *United Nations Monetary and Financial Conference, Bretton Woods, New Hampshire, July 1–22, 1944, Final Act and Related Documents,* Department of State Publication 2187 (Washington, 1944), pp. 3–6.

1 Source: *The 1982 Economic Report of the President: Hearings Before the Joint Economic Committee, Congress of the United States, Ninety-seventh Congress, Second Session* (Washington, 1982), Part 2, pp. 241–244.

2 For the text of the statement of William E. Brock, U.S. Trade Representative, see *infra.*

the high-technology area, including foreign government subsidized research and development and export support programs.

The implications of this trend indicate that we urgently support our high-technology industries and what must be done to maintain their preeminence.

Because of the importance of high-technology trade, in December the Cabinet Council on Commerce and Trade authorized a study on the competitive position of U.S. high-technology industries.

The efforts of this administration to solve the problems of the high-technology sector are being taken within the framework of our overall policy of free trade. The world system of free trade demands that all nations follow common principles of fairness. And fairness in the trading relations among nations includes the concept of reciprocal treatment. Let me assure you reciprocity does not mean protectionism in this sense. It means the demand for equivalent access to the markets of our trading partners.

Let me move, if I may, to East–West trade. This administration took office with the clear determination to protect vital U.S. and free world interests in the management of our commercial relations with Communist nations. We have placed the highest priority on the need to establish a consistent and predictable policy which will take into account the security, foreign policy, and economic conditions which exist today. As an element of that effort, we streamlined the export license processing system. We had a 2,000-case backlog when I took office. It is down to practically zero now.

This administration has made clear from the beginning that our approach to trade with the Soviet Union must be consistent with our political and security objectives. We are prepared to continue and expand our trade in nonstrategic areas if the Soviets act responsibly and with restraint in the international arena.

In December, martial law was declared in Poland; the repressive role of the Soviet Union in this situation called for a firm response. We, therefore, have imposed selected economic sanctions against the Soviet Union and Poland.[3]

At the same time we have sought to limit adverse effects on U.S. business and jobs that result from this action. Our business community has been generally understanding of our need to impose sanctions; our allies agreed not to undercut our actions by providing alternate sources. We view this as a commitment to restrain their companies which otherwise might take commercial advantage of this situation.

In the area of strategic militarily relevant dual-use technologies and equipment, we and our allies have begun improving the system of multilateral strategic controls that govern Western exports to the Soviet Union. We now have a political commitment within Cocom which provides the foundation for refocusing and strengthening international control efforts toward critical technologies and equipment. We also look toward streamlining and strengthening the rules and procedures which guide our joint efforts and a more coordinated and aggressive control enforcement effort.

Finally, this administration has moved ahead vigorously to normalize our trade ties with the People's Republic of China. In July 1981, the President announced a new and more liberal export policy toward the PRC.[4] This new policy is consistent with our mutual security and economic interests and increasingly friendly relations with the PRC.

Expanding exports remains a key component of the administration's economic recovery program. Export expansion means increased U.S. jobs, higher profits for U.S. business and a stronger national economy. The Department of Commerce has implemented a number of programs in pursuit of that goal, and others are being developed. Management changes and realinements have resulted in a leaner, more efficient organization, able to do more with less.

Major emphasis has been put on "reaching out" to involve more businesses, particularly small and medium-size ones, in exporting. At the same time increased cooperation with State and local governments and private sector organizations have broad-

---

[3] For the text of President Reagan's statement of December 29, 1981, in which he announced U.S. sanctions against the Soviet Union, see *American Foreign Policy: Current Documents, 1981*, document 270. For the text of President Reagan's statement of June 18, 1982, extending those sanctions, see document 160.

[4] For the text of Secretary of State Haig's press conference in Beijing, China, June 16, 1981, in which he announced that trade with the People's Republic of China would be expanded, see *American Foreign Policy: Current Documents, 1981*, document 493. On July 8, 1981, the Department of Commerce announced a Presidential decision to substantially liberalize controls on dual-use exports to China. (Department of Commerce Press Release, July 8, 1981)

ened the base of support for this export activity.

By encouraging the private sector to take a larger part in export assistance activity, we are focusing Government resources on areas where they can really make a difference. With the passage of the Export Trading Company Act,[5] which we hope the Congress will bring about this session, our business community will then have access to the kinds of assistance so effectively used by most of our major competitors.

One recent example of our new market promotion efforts was our highly successful high-level U.S. Trade and Investment Mission to Africa, which visited the Ivory Coast, Nigeria, Cameroon, and Morocco. Agriculture Secretary John Block and I led a group of 25 corporate executives of U.S. companies in agribusiness, agricultural commodities, construction, mining, and telecommunications fields.[6] Other Government participants included the Chairman of the Export-Import Bank, the President of OPIC, AID's Assistant Administrator for Private Enterprise and State Department officials.

The African governments and the local business communities warmly received us. In less than 2 weeks our business members submitted proposals and signed feasibility study agreements and contracts worth more than $170 million. They developed numerous other business and investment leads which they plan to pursue. We feel that this mission was an unqualified success for American business and our quality products and technology.

If I may, Representative Richmond, I would like to include for the record a copy of the letter that all 25 of these businessmen signed, to the President of the United States, on their return.[7]

Representative Richmond Without objection, Mr. Secretary.

Secretary Baldrige Let me close by emphasizing the importance to the U.S. economy of expanding U.S. trade opportunities. To do this we must continue to work for an open and fair trade system; to maintain and expand our competitive support position especially in high-technology exports; and to pursue trade policies that are consistent with U.S. security, political interests, and economic needs. We have the products, the technology, and the resources to be the strongest trading country; and with will and dedication to the job at hand, we will continue these strengths into the future. Thank you very much, Congressmen. [The addendum to Secretary Baldrige's statement,[8] together with the letter referred to, follows:]

Document 68

Statement by the U.S. Trade Representative (Brock) Before the Joint Economic Committee of Congress, February 10, 1982[9]

The Need to Preserve and Strengthen an Open Trading System

I want to express my delight at being back before this committee, on which I served—very pleasant, productive years.[10] I happen to believe this is far and away the most important joint committee that the Congress has, and I appreciate your interest in this subject.

When I came on my first visit about a year ago,[11] I mentioned two priorities—first, that we had to act quickly and decisively to restore our own domestic economic health in order to be competitive. I think we laid down the foundation for that recovery with the action taken by the Congress last year.

Second, I suggested the need to preserve and strengthen the open and fair-trading system we have been constructing for 35 years, on which our prosperity depends.

---

[5] For the text of the Export Trading Company Act (P.L. 97–290), approved October 8, 1982, see 96 Stat. 1233.

[6] Regarding the U.S. Trade and Investment Mission to Africa, January 9–16, 1982, see document 597.

[7] For the text of this letter of January 30, 1982, to President Reagan, see *The 1982 Economic Report of the President,* Part 2, pp. 253–258.

[8] For the text of the addendum entitled, "Update of the U.S. Foreign Trade Developments Full Year 1981," see *ibid.,* Part 2, pp. 245–252. Bracketed note appears in the source text.

[9] Source: *The 1982 Economic Report of the President,* Part 2, pp. 259–262.

[10] Brock, as a Republican Representative from Tennessee, served as a member of the Joint Economic Committee, 1967–1970.

[11] For the text of Brock's testimony before the Joint Economic Committee, February 24, 1981, see *The 1981 Economic Report of the President: Hearings Before the Joint Economic Committee, Congress of the United States, Ninety-seventh Congress, First Session* (Washington, 1981), Part 3, pp. 55–96.

The contribution of exports to domestic employment, agricultural production, corporate profits, and a strong currency require us to pursue further the reciprocal trade liberalization. Protectionism can only hurt us. It will damage American opportunities for strong export sectors. It will not provide revitalization of our presently weak sectors. I think those conclusions are no less true 1 year later.

The challenge of preserving and stengthening the system is perhaps even more critical today. There are an awful lot of factors, both positive and negative, weighing on the world trading system. We are building some momentum to tackle some of the most restrictive practices still affecting world trade, particularly in the area of agricultural services and investment. But on the other hand, the failure of past efforts to open some foreign markets for U.S. exports is causing increasing frustration in the Congress and in the administration.

It is my own belief that the trade pressures generated currently are more intense than at any time certainly since the early 1970's. The causes of that frustration are very real.

The United States has the most open market in the world. The opening of our market, however, has been predicated on the expectation that similar opportunities would be created for U.S. exports abroad. Our legitimate expectations, however, have not been fulfilled.

Worse still, protectionism seems to actually be on the increase in too many areas abroad, while in Japan we do have, as the chairman has stated, an unequal trading relationship.[12]

U.S. producers who are competitive everywhere else around the world have made little headway in penetrating the Japanese market. But it isn't just U.S. producers, by the way. It's any other producer. Small countries, large countries all have the same access difficulty.

The Japanese economy continues to expand. This expansion, however, is based on increasing Japanese exports, while domestic demand for imports stagnate.

Our deficit, which appeared in 1981, is in the area of $16 billion on an FOB basis, well in excess of $19 billion on a delivered basis, and may and probably will be worse in this year.

Japan, on the other hand, will run a surplus in its merchandise trade of about $21 billion in 1981, as much as $35 billion in 1982. Additionally, the surplus in Japan's current account is expected to triple this year, from $5.5 billion to $17 billion.

The announcements of Minister Abe about the reduction of many import barriers is encouraging.[13] However, these measures were rather narrow in focus, and therefore we are reserving judgment until we see what comprehensive actions are finally taken.

While our trade problems with Europe are probably less extensive, they may prove more difficult to deal with. Agriculture, steel, textiles, and export subsidies are areas of longstanding differences between ourselves and the community.

The next 2 years will be a crucial time for the world trading system. We face a major challenge in facing serious deterioration in the world trading system, while at the same time obtaining fair access to foreign markets for U.S. exports.

In the next several months a series of meetings will help us to achieve our goals. The meeting of the GATT Ministers, the Ministerial Meeting of the GATT, November of this year[14] is fundamentally important. It will provide us with an opportunity to solidify our efforts for free and more reciprocal trade.

Ministerial will help us focus full attention on the urgency of resolving the immediate problems facing us and of committing ourselves to addressing the longer term major trade issues of the 1980's like services and investment.

It's not intended to lead immediately to a major new round of multilateral trade negotiations in the near future. I'm not sure that any of the participants are ready for that yet.

But we do hope and I think have the right to insist on an international agree-

---

[12] For the opening statement of Representative Richmond, who served as Chairman of the Joint Economic Committee for this session, see *The 1982 Economic Report of the President,* Part 2, pp. 234–235.

[13] For discussion of the announcements made by Japan's Minister of Trade and Industry, Shintaro Abe, on January 16 and 21, 1982, that Japan would reduce many of its import barriers, see *New York Times,* January 17, 1982, p. 1, and January 22, 1982, IV, p. 10.

[14] Regarding the GATT Ministerial Meeting, November 24–29, 1982, see document 76.

ment on a work program on longer term trade issues during the Ministerial, as well as an international commitment to see that this program is carried out.

We will, likewise, be meeting with our major trade partners to review the implementation of the codes and the agreements which were established as a result of the Tokyo round.[15]

These provide a major opportunity for reducing some of the most damaging nontariff restrictions against U.S. exports in areas such as product standards, customs valuation, subsidization, and product definition. These codes, however, are no more effective than the extent to which they are implemented.

The success of this evolutionary process will be a critical factor in determining the fairness of the trading system of the 1980's. So, we're going to be an active and aggressive participant in defending U.S. rights.

The administration will continue its strict enforcement of U.S. law and international agreements relating to international trade. Specifically, our antidumping, countervailing duty and similar structures are designed to neutralize or eliminate trade-distortive practices which injure U.S. industry and agriculture.

We will continue to insist that our trading partners live up to the spirit and the letter of international trade agreements and that they recognize that trade is a two-way street. Accordingly, we will make full use of all available channels under the GATT for assuring compliance.

In addition to multilateral initiatives, we will continue to take up our trade grievances with individual countries in bilateral consultations. Through those consultations we will seek fully reciprocal market access, which is the best guarantee for the future of an open world trading system.

Some people have interpreted the recent emphasis on reciprocal market access [as] a movement of the United States away from the open market system. Nothing could be further from the truth. Reciprocity for the United States means resisting entrenched and mounting protectionism abroad and nudging our trading partners forward to a level of market openness more similar to our own.

Improving U.S. economic performance and U.S. export competitiveness and access to foreign markets are top priorities of this administration, not restricting foreign imports.

Accordingly, exports need to become even more of a national priority than they are today. We have moved in a decade from 9 percent of our production of goods exported to 20 percent in the past year; $240 billion worth of goods were exported, and that figure will have to move even higher if we are to reduce the trade deficit which has exceeded $24 billion in each of the last 5 years.

In meeting this challenge, we not only promote our trading interests but make a solid contribution to the restoration of the health and vitality of our national economy.

This administration strongly stated its policy of free and open trade based on mutually acceptable trading relations and rules in its statement of U.S. trade policy, our white paper of last summer.[16] I will reiterate that principle and policy today.

But we make no contribution to the achievement of this goal by ignoring attacks upon open trade by others. No nation can hope to sustain public support for a policy unless its people sense that there is equity for them in the application of that policy.

Thus, the 1980's will require the United States to pursue vigorously more equitable trade relations between nations. Such an effort, if undertaken with resolve and fortitude, can only strengthen our world trading structure in the GATT.

Of course, we need to insist upon full implementation of the Tokyo round, but we also need a renewed and revitalized trading system that is designed to deal with new barriers and problems as they arise through changing global economics and before they undermine past negotiating achievements.

During this past year, we have made a strong beginning toward such a goal, both domestically and internationally. As we respond to trade's message of change by adopting forward-looking economic poli-

[15] Regarding the Tokyo Round, see footnote 10 to document 64.

[16] For the text of Brock's white paper on U.S. trade policy, which he presented as a prepared statement to the Senate Subcommittees on International Trade and International Finance and Monetary Policy on July 8, 1981, see *Oversight of U.S. Trade Policy: Joint Hearings Before the Subcommittee on International Trade of the Committee on Finance and the Subcommittee on International Finance and Monetary Policy of the Committee on Banking, Housing, and Urban Affairs, United States Senate, Ninety-seventh Congress, First Session, July 8 and 9, 1981* (Washington, 1981), pp. 21–25.

cies, which also preserve and improve upon the system we have labored to create, I look forward to full and extensive cooperation with the members of this committee and with the Congress.

I thank you for your interest in the subject and the opportunity to be with you.

Document 69

Address by the Deputy Secretary of Agriculture (Lyng) Before the Iowa State Trade Conference, Ames, Iowa, May 20, 1982[17]

U.S. Efforts to Expand Agricultural Exports

Thank you for inviting me to join you today. It is certainly appropriate that here in Iowa, the nation's number one farm export state, you should have a conference like this, a conference which can play a vital role in exploring new ideas we can use to boost U.S. agricultural exports and put some vigor back into the farm economy. When Sentor Roger Jepson invited and urged me to participate here, I accepted immediately, both because of my high respect for him and because farm exports are so important, not only here in Iowa, but throughout the entire nation.

All of us at the U.S. Department of Agriculture, from Secretary of Agriculture John Block on down, are totally aware of the need for us to do everything we possibly can to maintain and expand exports. Let me start out by giving you an update on the work we've already done at USDA to promote exports and discuss a few of the new ideas we've been looking at recently. What we will hope to get from you and the other speakers here today is other views on that work and those ideas. In particular, I am eager to hear from representatives of the private sector because it's this administration's view that closer cooperation between private industry and government is the absolute key to realistic and workable ideas that can foster growth, not only in agricultural exports, but in the entire economy.

So what have we done for exports at USDA and what are some of the new ideas we have been looking at?

Let me take a few minutes to give you a broad overview of the actions we've already taken to boost exports. Many of these have focused on trade policy and access to foreign markets.

—First there was the removal of the embargo on agricultural sales to the USSR.[18] That embargo clearly hurt producers, especially here in Iowa, more than it hurt the Soviet Union. We'll be meeting with the Russians in Paris again in a few days about the current grain agreement.[19] It's a routine meeting, but the first with the Soviets since the Polish crisis. We are talking again. Since the embargo was lifted, the Soviets have purchased nearly 15 million tons of U.S. grain.

—Next we began a new series of market promotion efforts, including the dispatch of high-level sales teams to 14 developing countries with good growth potential in Africa, Latin America, and Asia.

—We've had a series of meetings with the Japanese to get them to liberalize their import quotas which still cover 25 agricultural items.[20] And we've made a concerted effort to get the EC to abandon its unfair trade policies.[21]

—The import restrictions and export subsidies—which have hurt our sales of wheat and other commodities. The sugar, pasta, poultry, and canned fruits and raisin industries have brought Section 301[22] com-

---

[17] Source: Department of Agriculture, *Major News Releases and Speeches,* May 14–21, 1982, pp. 11–15.

[18] For the text of President Reagan's announcement ending the embargo on agricultural sales to the Soviet Union, April 24, 1981, see *American Foreign Policy: Current Documents, 1981,* document 232.

[19] Regarding the second semiannual session of regular grain consultations between the United States and the Soviet Union held in Paris, May 21–22, 1982, see document 266. The existing 7-year U.S.-Soviet grain agreement signed on October 20, 1975, provided for the purchase by the Soviet Union of 6 to 8 million tons of U.S. grain yearly. For the text of the agreement, see 26 UST 2971.

[20] For documentation on meetings with the Japanese on liberalizing trade and other matters, see Chapter 13, Part F.

[21] Regarding U.S. efforts to persuade the European Community to abandon its trade practices which discriminate against the United States, see Brock's February 11, 1982, statement to the Subcommittee on International Trade of the Senate Finance Committee, document 173.

[22] Section 301 of the Trade Act of 1974 (P.L. 93–618) permits the President to take retaliatory action against a foreign government and allows domestic interests to bring to the government's attention the fact that foreign practices are adversely affecting U.S. interests; for the text of this section, see 88 Stat. 2041. When the Trade Act of 1974 was amended to become the Trade Agreements Act of 1979 (P.L. 96–39), Section 301 was augmented to include a list of procedures and actions the President was permitted to take; for the text, see 93 Stat. 295.

plaints against EC trade practices in the past year, adding their weight to the earlier protests by the citrus and flour industries.

—We've had new cooperator activities in China and West Africa and new agricultural trade offices in Beijing, Tunis, and Lagos. We are looking forward to the opening of new cooperators' offices in Beijing by the American Soybean Association, U.S. Feed Grains Council, and U.S. Wheat Associates.

—I think there has been more effective use of export credit, including the maximum possible use of an authorization of $2.5 billion for CCC credit guarantees and more careful targeting of both commodities and destinations to ensure maximum effect.

—There's been new impetus to work with the agriculture departments of the various states, including a major international food show in Atlanta next spring. We hope to see this show bring $100 million more in annual export sales of processed food products.

—President Reagan took a major step on March 22[23] to restore importer confidence in the United States as a reliable supplier. Reliability has been an important concern for a number of our overseas customers. In a speech to agricultural editors, the President pledged there would be no return to the stop and go export policies of the past several years.

He said flatly that no export restrictions will ever be imposed because of rising domestic prices, and he repeated his pledge that the only way a farm export embargo would be imposed would be in the context of a broader embargo mandated by an extreme foreign policy situation.

"Farm exports," the President said, "will not be used as an instrument of foreign policy except in extreme situations and as a part of a broader embargo. Agricultural products are fungible; that is, they are easily interchanged for the same commodity from other nations. For this reason, the embargo of 1980 was almost totally ineffective, yet it caused great economic hardship to U.S. agriculture. We will not repeat such an action."

Thus President Reagan became the first American President to flatly eliminate the possibility of any embargo for economic purposes. He went as far as any president safely could go in rejecting the embargo as a political instrument.

—We met with the other major wheat exporters in Ottawa last month.[24] We pointed out that the United States has taken decisive steps to reduce production to help prevent a further decline in commodity prices. We urged the other exporters to take parallel action, including the elimination of export subsidies.

—We also made it clear that other measures will be needed if our competitors take advantage of our actions to increase their production and exports.

These are some of the steps we have taken to build agricultural sales overseas. At the same time, the Congress has shown more interest in and more support for agricultural trade than at any time in my memory. For example:

—The Agriculture and Food Act of 1981[25] contains authority for export subsidies, if necessary, to counter unfair trade practices of other countries and it established an as yet unfunded export credit revolving fund to stimulate export sales.

—The Senate and the House have passed resolutions protesting the European Community's proposal to impose a tariff quota on imports of corn gluten feed.

—Members of the Congress have met with officials of both the EC and Japan to urge an end to their unfair trade practices.

That is a brief and incomplete overview of some positive steps we have taken on the export front. As I suggested earlier, we are open and responsive to any and all ideas on how to do the export assistance job better. We are actively promoting some of the new ideas you've heard about to expand overseas sales and we are looking into the feasibility of a number of others.

Secretary Block and the administration have been strong backers of the export trading company legislation pending on the Hill right now.[26] The virtue of export trad-

[23] For the text of President Reagan's address to representatives of agricultural publications and organizations, March 22, 1982, see *Weekly Compilation of Presidential Documents*, March 29, 1982, pp. 357–361.

[24] Under Secretary of Agriculture Seeley G. Lodwick headed the U.S. delegation at the meeting of representatives of the major wheat exporting countries held in Ottawa, Canada, April 22–23, 1982.

[25] For the text of the Agriculture and Food Act of 1981 (P.L. 97–98), approved December 22, 1981, see 95 Stat. 1213.

[26] For the text of the Export Trading Company Act (P.L. 97–290), approved October 8, 1982, see 96 Stat. 1233.

ing companies is that they can help us compete more effectively with countries like Japan and South Korea whose commercial and banking activities are more closely fused than ours.

In agriculture, we feel export trading companies can help supplement sales of bulk commodities with more exports of value-added products like processed foods. Sales of value-added products have been running $12 to $13 billion a year and there is definitely potential for more. Sales of these products not only help the farmer who provides the raw materials, they also create other jobs. If we add even $1 billion to these sales, we can generate 31,000 new jobs.

One of the ideas that has been a topic of discussion lately in the export field is bartering. Bartering by the Soviet Union, Argentina and Iran, and Thailand's use of bartering in its rice trade have brought this idea to the fore recently.

Since last March, we have been cooperating with several other government agencies in exploring the merits of bartering CCC stocks for petroleum and strategic and critical materials. At this time, a viable barter program of this type does not look too promising. We will continue to explore every barter opportunity, but also would encourage private sector initative in this area. Perhaps some good, old fashioned "Yankee trading" can be of value in the expansion of barter in our agricultural foreign trade.

We are also exploring new ideas in the credit area. The USDA realizes our competitors, particularly the EC, can offer very attractive credit arrangements for buyers.

While relatively new, GSM–102 credit guarantees[27] have proven themselves to be an effective tool in finding new markets for our farm products and maintaining our market share in the face of stiff competition. Thus far in fiscal 1982, these credit guarantees have been extended to importers in 21 countries for purchases of about $2 billion in U.S. agriculutral commodities.

We are assessing the potential benefits of additional export incentive programs against the likely cost to the taxpayer.

Financing exports is a critical area where we need to explore new possibilities, but we also need new ideas on improving the way we ship U.S. farm products. How well we service our customer's transportation needs is often every bit as important as financing.

The USDA's Office of Transportation has a number of ongoing projects aimed at improving the shipping of our agricultural exports—including improved containers for transporting cattle, fresh vegetables, and other farm products. An idea that has received considerable attention recently involves new methods for shipping grain from inland points like Iowa to Mexico.

One method would be to put loaded rail cars on barges and float them to Vera Cruz and Tampico and re-rail the cars there for movement to other Mexico destinations.

Another innovation would be to place barges loaded with grain on the decks of oceangoing barges for offloading at Mexican seaports.

Both ideas have considerable merit because they would reduce costs and allow delivery at shallow draft ports. An additional benefit is that they would help shippers avoid the railcar congestion at the Texas border. These kinds of ideas will help us keep U.S. grain competitive in both Mexico and Central America.

There are no instant solutions to the problems we face in agricultural exporting today. No massive and expensive federal program will ensure us of stronger exports. But there are a host of smaller and more practical steps we can take to build our overseas sales.

I've mentioned only a few of the things we have been doing and exploring at USDA. I am looking forward to discussing them with you and hearing about other steps we can take in the drive to boost overseas sales. It's only by sharing and testing out new ideas that farmers, agribusiness and the government can make the choices that spell success.

Thank you.

---

27 Reference is to the short-term credit guarantee program for agricultural exports operated by the Commodity Credit Corporation through the Office of the General Sales Manager (GSM).

Document 70

Statement by the Deputy Under Secretary of Agriculture for International Affairs and Commodity Programs (Tracy) Before the House Foreign Affairs Committee and the House Agriculture Committee, August 11, 1982[28]

Economic Problems Facing American Agriculture

Mr. Chairman,[29] we appreciate the opportunity to take part in this joint meeting—to discuss with you the economic problems faced by American agriculture. Farmers represent a small minority of Americans who continue to produce abundantly and efficiently for all of our people—but without gaining the prosperity they deserve.

This is the third consecutive year of depressed farm prices and incomes. Agricultural prices in the first half of 1982 were about 5 percent below those of the first half of 1981, although generally higher than prices at the end of last year. Prices received by farmers will likely continue to rise, but at a very slow rate.

With farm operating costs rising much more rapidly, the relationship between prices received and prices paid will decline this year for the third year in a row. This puts farm income in a continued squeeze, with a reduction in farm cash flow and an increase in borrowing. As a result, we may see a further decline in net cash income in 1982.

High interest rates are a factor in depressed farm prices, along with lagging general economic conditions in the United States and elsewhere, and record farm production last year.

So there are a number of factors working against farmers in 1982. Some of these—inflation and high interest rates—are being addressed by the President's economic program, which will benefit agriculture as well as the rest of the economy. In the shorter term, however, increased attention is being directed toward the problems facing agricultural exports.

U.S. agricultural exports in fiscal 1982 are officially forecast at around $42 billion, down 4 percent from last year's record of $43.8 billion. Our agricultural trade balance was a positive $25 billion. Although export volumes are likely to continue to rise—to a record 168 million tons—lower prices will result in a sharp reversal of the upward trend in export values that has been evident for more than a decade. This would have been the first time in more than a decade that we would have had less than a new record in our export value for agricultural products.

There are a number of reasons for this.

One is that the world economy, being slow, has softened demand in many countries, and particularly for animal products, and particularly for feed grains that go into those products.

At the same time, large crops here and in other countries have made world markets much more competitive. The strong dollar is also a factor, making U.S. exports more expensive in terms of other world currencies.

There are global forces, natural and economic, that will change in time. In interest rates and inflation, substantial progress has already been made. We know that we will not have world surpluses every year. We know that the world economy and world demand will not always be depressed. Farmers, more than most sectors of the economy, understand and accept the ups and downs of production and demand.

Farmers also understand, however, that some of our trade problems are not inevitable and inexorable—to be endured like a long spell of bad weather. Some are man-made, the product of unfair and mistaken policies of governments, ours as well as others. As such, these problems should be subject to remedy. American farmers are increasingly impatient with those trade limitations that artificially limit this country's ability to compete in foreign markets.

The objective of our agricultural trade policy is, of course, to defend and promote U.S. agricultural interests in the international market. Although we do have interests as an importer of certain commodities, such as coffee and bananas, because of the immense productive capacity of U.S. agriculture, our primary interest is in improving the climate for U.S. agricultural exports.

One of the ways in which the Government promotes agricultural exports is

---

[28] Source: *Review of Agricultural Trade Issues: Joint Hearing Before the Committee on Foreign Affairs and the Committee on Agriculture, House of Representatives, Ninety-seventh Congress, Second Session* (Washington, 1982), pp. 4–9.

[29] E. (Kika) de la Garza.

through market development programs overseas, that I know you are very familiar with and interested in, Mr. Chairman.

Direct export promotion stimulates interest in U.S. products, brings together exports with potential buyers, and assists them to understand the local market, including import regulations and practices. CCC credit guarantees, Public Law 480,[30] and the market development cooperator program are all proven export promotion tools.

The success of these direct market development efforts depends in large measure on whether that competition is fair. You have to have access to that market in order to be able to put into it.

Thus, a second aspect of our agricultural trade policy is market defense through bilateral efforts to maintain and increase access for U.S. agricultural products.

Japan and the European Community are both excellent markets for U.S. farm products, but both also pose significant problems for us.

Japan is our closet friend in Asia and the largest single market for U.S. farm exports, with sales of $6.6 billion in 1981—largest single-country market. However, we have been very disappointed at the lack of momentum on the Japanese side in liberalizing trade in agriculture.

Japan maintains quotas on 22 agricultural commodity groups. The beef and citrus quotas, if eliminated, would likely result in the greatest absolute increase in U.S. dollar sales to Japan. These quotas are ones that are subject to agreements negotiated during the Tokyo round, which provide for the annual expansion of citrus and beef imports until March 31, 1984.

Until these agreements expire, we are unable to challenge the GATT consistency of these particular quotas. The Japanese are committed, however, to entering into discussions with the United States midway through the life of the agreements regarding the liberalization of the quotas after March 31, 1984. We expect to begin these discussions with the Japanese in October, 6 months ahead of schedule.

I would like to point out that Japan's consumers would also benefit from a prompt change to a more open agricultural market. Japanese consumers spend about 23 percent of their disposable income on food—compared to 14 percent in the United States—and, at upward of $15 per pound, those expenditures do not include much beef. Japan is an extreme case, but the benefits to the consumers and economies of all countries from open markets are enormous.

Although we have a large surplus in agricultural trade with the European Community, $6.5 billion in 1981, European Community policy poses serious problems for U.S. agriculture. The European Community's common agricultural policy protects domestic producers through a variable levy system, encourages surplus production with very high support prices, and exports its surpluses with the aid of substantial subsidies.

About half of our agricultural exports to the European Community are soybeans and feedgrain substitutes—products exempt from the variable levy system.

A key element of our agricultural trade policy is to defend the duty-free status of these products, which comes under frequent challenges from European Community grain interests. Most recently, through the combined efforts of the administration and the Congress, we were able to persuade the European Community to hold off on a Commission request for a mandate to negotiate with us to limit corn gluten feed sales, and we certainly thank the Congress for their input into that.

In addition to defending our access to the European Community market, we are also challenging the European Community's export subsidy practices.

We have taken five subsidy cases to the GATT in carrying out this commitment. They are wheat flour, pasta, canned fruit and raisins, poultry, and sugar. In the case of poultry, we have also requested consultations with Brazil. Three of the cases are before panels at the present time. Wheat flour is the one closest to resolution with a panel finding expected in late September.

We are anxiously awaiting the panel decision in the wheat flour case because of the precedent it will set with regard to interpretations of the GATT subsidies code.[31]

---

[30] Reference is to the Agricultural Trade Development and Assistance Act of 1954, P.L. 480, approved July 10, 1954, which provides for the donation or sale at reduced prices of U.S. agricultural surpluses to friendly governments; for the text, see 68 Stat. 454.

[31] The reference is to the GATT Subsidies Code, one of the agreements signed at the Tokyo Round in 1979 which established new rules on subsidies behavior for signatory nations. For the text of the General Agreement on Tariffs and Trade: Interpretation and Application of Articles VI, XVI and XXIII, signed at Geneva April 12, 1979, and entered into force January 1, 1980, see 31 UST 513.

We are hopeful that at long last discipline can be exacted on the use of export subsidies through the vehicle of the code. Discipline was what our negotiators felt we got when the code was negotiated.

This brings me to the third aspect of our agricultural trade policy—an improvement of the multilateral trade system for agricultural products.

We want other nations to recognize that agricultural trade rules can and should be brought more in line with the rules governing industrial trade. We will seek a consensus on this issue at the upcoming GATT Ministerial meeting this fall, the first since 1973.

We are going to press hard to get a better deal for our farmers by creating an improved environment for agricultural trade. We recognize that this will be a difficult and lengthy process, given the temptations of protectionism when economies are depressed.

I would like to discuss some specific legislative proposals related to agricultural exports, but I would like to talk to a subject of great interest to the Congress, the United States-Soviet Grain Agreement.[32]

As you know, on July 30, the President announced his decision to explore with the Soviet Union the possibility of a one-year extension of the current grain agreement, through September 30, 1983.[33]

This decision takes account of the desire of the U.S. farm community for an assured minimum level of grain sales to the Soviet Union at a time of serious economic hardship in the U.S. farm sector. In announcing the decision, the President emphasized that U.S. farmers will continue to have a fair opportunity to export to the U.S.S.R.

At the same time, by proposing a simple extension of the agreement, the President did not compromise the sanctions he imposed against the Soviet Union last December,[34] which included postponing negotiations on a new long-term grain agreement. Thus, the President's decision on the grain agreement struck a balance between agricultural and foreign policy considerations.

The administration was asked to discuss certain pending legislative proposals, and I will do so in the context of the agricultural trade policy I have just outlined. One concept, embodied in several different bills, is "contract sanctity"; that is, restrictions on export controls on agricultural products covered by existing contracts.[35] These proposals are related to concerns about the reliability of the United States as a supplier.

The President has stated that he would not force the cancellation of any agricultural commodity contracts except in extreme situations and as part of a broader embargo.[36] Moreover, the President has stated that his offer to extend the U.S.–U.S.S.R. Grain Agreement for another year includes a commitment to the sanctity of contracts on those quantities specified in the agreement.

In issuing these statements, this administration has gone further than any previous administration in guaranteeing that the U.S. farmer will not be singled out to pay the price of pursuing this Nation's foreign policy and national security objectives.

For the administration to make commitments beyond those already made or to acquiesce in legislative mandates embodied in the "contract sanctity" bills currently pending in Congress, would be to surrender the President's flexibility of action in matters vital to this Nation's security.

Therefore, this administration must oppose any legislative restrictions on export controls on agricultural products covered by existing contracts beyond those found in current law.

The administration was also asked to comment on legislation which would subsidize agricultural exports and/or provide interest assistance to export credits through a buy down of interest rates by 4 to 5 percentage points. The administration

[32] Regarding the U.S.-Soviet Grain Agreement signed October 20, 1975, see footnote 19 above.

[33] For the text of President Reagan's announcement, July 30, 1982, of his willingness to explore the possibility of extending the grain agreement with the Soviet Union, see *Weekly Compilation of Presidential Documents,* August 2, 1982, pp. 975–976.

[34] For the text of President Reagan's statement of December 29, 1981, announcing U.S. sanctions against the Soviet Union, see *American Foreign Policy: Current Documents, 1981,* document 270.

[35] One of the "contract sanctity" bills before the 97th session of Congress was Senate Resolution 496, proposed by Senator Larry Pressler, which expressed the sense of the Senate that the United States should extend an export sales contract sanctity guarantee to the Soviet Union from November 30, 1982, to November 30, 1983. This resolution did not pass.

[36] Reference is to President Reagan's address to representatives of agricultural publications and organizations, March 22, 1982; see footnote 23 above.

shares the several objectives of this legislation, specifically: increasing U.S. agricultural exports; and alleviating the adverse impact of foreign export subsidies on U.S. agricultural trade.

In its efforts to meet the above objectives, the administration has taken the following steps: increased the level of annual funding for Commodity Credit Corporation export credit guarantees by 40 percent over the levels under the previous administration, from $2 billion a year to $2.8 billion a year; and increased the market development cooperator budget in the Foreign Agricultural Service by $1.2 million in 1983.

The new proposals before the committee raise a number of important considerations on both sides of the issue.

An export subsidy or a credit buy down could be used in such a way as to leverage a substantial increase in export shipments. It could be used to encourage developing countries to build their own reserve stocks. It could be used to counter competitor export subsidies. It could be used to increase agricultural exports at a time when American agriculture sorely needs expanded markets.

However, this subsidy could be matched by competitors, thus rendering the program ineffective. It could preempt our GATT cases and undermine our efforts to improve the multilateral disciplines on agricultural trade. It could increase the possibility of an agricultural trade and credit war.

We understand that you recognize the complexity of this issue. In addition to the steps described above which the administration is taking to expand agricultural exports, we are also carefully considering the pros and cons of subsidies.

If the administration decides to take such further steps as proposed here, we can do so under existing law. Therefore, we oppose any legislation that would mandate export subsidies or export credit buy downs. We do have that authority currently and are opposed to legislation which would mandate us to do something where we have existing authority.

Document 71

Address by the Secretary of Agriculture (Block) Before a European Forum on Trilateral Issues Among Industrialized Nations, Alpbach, Austria, September 2, 1982[37]

U.S. Agriculture As Part of a Global System

I appreciate the opportunity to take part in this distinguished forum. There could not be a more timely or important subject for discussion in 1982 than relations between the so-called "Tripartite" group of nations.[38]

With our nations accounting for over half of the world's gross product, the manner in which we pursue our economic relations is important to every other country in the world. It directly affects all aspects of economic policy within each of our own countries, including those having to do with agricultural production and trade.

One of the striking developments of the past 10 years is the degree to which food and agricultural issues have moved onto the central agenda of national governments and their international organizations. I first observed this as a farmer. I see it even more plainly now as a member of President Reagan's Cabinet.

A few years ago, the tendency was for each of our countries to view domestic agricultural policy as something which concerned only a limited domestic sector. We did not closely relate it to monetary or fiscal policy and certainly not to international policy. This has changed.

In my country, at least, it is clear that policy makers outside agriculture have come to recognize the importance of agriculture to monetary and fiscal policy. They have come to recognize that agricultural policy also impinges on our international relations and that, in turn, international politics affect our domestic agricultural policy. Too much so, we sometimes think.

A number of developments have brought this about, including:

---

[37] Source: Department of Agriculture, *Major News Releases and Speeches*, August 27–September 3, 1982, pp. 7–10.

[38] The reference is to the European Community, Japan, and the United States. It was not a formal group but was the theme of this forum.

—An enormous increase in the volume of international trade relative to nations' gross national products.

—The resulting growth in interdependency as nations became more dependent on access to reliable markets and reliable supplies and more sensitive to any threat of restraint.

—Enormous advances in our ability to communicate with each other and to transport people and products between countries.

—The emergence of a rapidly growing world market for processed products, now larger in international sales than the more traditional market for bulk products.

—The changing role of monetary exchange rates and the effects of this development on international trade in farm products.

All in all, we have had to learn that international developments affect our agriculture. We have had to learn that we cannot pursue domestic agricultural policy as if the rest of the world does not exist. We have to recognize that our own agriculture is interdependent with the economies of other nations.

The farmers of my country understand that principle quite well. It wasn't always so. Twenty years ago—even 10 years ago—we in agriculture had much less appreciation for the importance of international trade to the day-to-day business of American farming. Foreign markets were likely to be thought of as outlets for surplus commodities in time of U.S. overproduction. Or they were thought of in terms of world relief—to Europe at the end of World War II, for example, and to India during the drought years of the 1960's.

But then came the 1970's with the return of the Soviet Union to Western agricultural trade, the rapid growth of consumer demand around the world—the U.S. embargoes and partial embargoes in 1973, 1974, and 1975—the world food scare in 1974—and finally the U.S. embargo against shipments to the Soviets.[39] That action, in the first week of 1980, capped off an extraordinary decade in agricultural trade, leaving many of us to think that now we had seen everything.

[39] For the text of President Carter's address to the Nation, January 4, 1980, in which he announced the embargo on the sale of grain to the Soviet Union, see *American Foreign Policy: Basic Documents, 1977–1980*, pp. 812–814.

Events of the past decade in agricultural trade have made it clear to American farmers that they are indeed part of a global system. They know that foreign buyers now provide a market for 65 percent of their wheat production, 55 percent of their soybeans, 35 percent of their coarse grains, and large percentages of other crops. They know that, in a real sense, the world begins at their front gate.

This understanding, I believe, is at the root of much of the frustration that American farmers feel with respect to the agricultures of other countries. They feel they are producing for the world, adjusting production upward when the world needs more and accepting the burden of lower prices and surplus management in time of world overproduction.

American farmers also feel that farmers in certain other major trading countries do not fully share these adjustment burdens and are not functioning as part of the world system. More important, they are concerned that this pattern may be growing—that the agricultures of other nations are trying to build and maintain walls that will make it increasingly unnecessary for them to function as a part of the world system.

This is not an occasion to find fault. Every nation has problems dealing with protectionist interests at home, especially in times of overproduction and underconsumption. History has shown us that the protectionism is likely to be more prominent and more destructive in periods of economic distress such as the world is now experiencing.

These protectionist pressures occur in the United States just as they do in other countries. For example, we are not pleased with how the domestic dairy programs created huge surpluses in our country, with attendant large budget outlays and restrictions on imports. The administration of President Reagan is making every effort to correct that situation, and it will be corrected.

But for the most part, American farmers see themselves, realistically I believe, as part of a global system, sharing the world's problems and adjusting to its needs.

In the early 1970's, when the world grain supplies fell off sharply in the face of crop shortfalls in a number of countries, U.S. agriculture was called on to take up most of the slack in world production. Between 1971 and 1975, annual U.S. grain exports rose from 44 million tons to 85 million tons.

Meanwhile, an export tax in the European Community enabled the Community to keep its grain at home.

Now the situation is reversed. With world grain supplies at record highs, the EC's import levies permit the Community to continue producing at high levels and exporting at subsidized low prices. With the United States carrying out an acreage reduction program in an effort to hold down supplies, the EC has announced higher internal prices that can only encourage large production within Europe.

The immediate costs of these inequities to American agriculture are severe. We pay in lower farm prices and higher government budget outlays. But this concerns us less than does the prospect that European agriculture will withdraw further from the world system—isolating itself further within walls of border protection—denying the responsibility to share in world price and supply adjustments.

If this should occur, it would be a denial of the world leadership that Europe has shared with the United States in trade and economic advancement. It would be a tragedy if, at a time when nations are becoming more interdependent and their agricultural policies more integral to overall objectives, Europeans should find themselves pulled away from the world by agricultural isolationism.

We have seen that nations cannot afford to administer domestic agricultural policies as if other nations did not exist, as if agriculture were not a global system essential to a global economy. We are concerned about national policies that refuse to recognize the global system essential to a global nature of agriculture. We ask ourselves where the world will be in 10 years if we fail now to address the points I have raised here.

The world cannot afford policies that foster agricultural isolationism. Realism calls for policies that treat agriculture as a global system.

Document 72

Statement by the Deputy Secretary of the Treasury (McNamar) Before a Subcommittee of the House Ways and Means Committee, September 21, 1982[40]

Opposition to Local Content Legislation

MR. MCNAMAR. I am here today representing Secretary Regan, who is unfortunately out of town. He wanted to come because of his interest in opposing this legislation. We welcome the opportunity to present the Treasury Department's views on what we regard as the single most troubling piece of trade legislation to be considered in the last quarter century.

The proposed bill to impose local content requirements on automobile sales in the United States, although admittedly well intended when it was introduced in an effort to preserve jobs in the hard-hit automobile industry, H.R. 5133[41] would have profound negative implications for our own economy, international trading system and ultimately the people it would be intended to help, the average working men and women in America.

The administration strongly opposes local content legislation in any form whatsoever. In general, such legislation is a giant step away from the open market economy that would benefit us all and which was reaffirmed at the Versailles summit this summer.[42] It would transfer income from U.S. consumers and exporters to auto workers and parts producers. It would mortgage the future of the automobile industry and prevent the adjustment necessary to have a

---

[40] Source: *Fair Practices in Automotive Products Act: Hearings Before the Subcommittee on Trade of the Committee On Ways and Means, House of Representatives, Ninety-seventh Congress, Second Session* (Washington, 1982), pp. 44–47.

[41] The reference is to H.R. 5133, the "Fair Practices in Automotive Products Act," a measure to establish domestic content requirements for motor vehicles sold in the United States which was introduced by Representative Richard L. Ottinger on December 8, 1981. The proposed legislation would require all companies with annual sales in the United States of over 100,000 vehicles to locate some production in this country, hire some workers, and buy their parts in the United States. This bill passed the House of Representatives but not the Senate during the Ninety-seventh Congress.

[42] For documentation on the Versailles Economic Summit, June 4–6, 1982, see Part F.

viable automobile industry in this country. It would jeopardize jobs in the export sector, is a violation of U.S. international obligations on an unprecedented scale, threatens the unraveling of the international trading system, and could prevent a worldwide economic recovery.

Today, however, I would like to concentrate my remarks on my deep concern about the adverse implications of this legislation for the U.S. economy. I am sure that we all share the same vision of what the U.S. economy should be. It should be efficient, prosperous and able to adjust to changing economic circumstances. We must ask ourselves does this legislation contribute to this type of an economy. The answer is clearly "no."

Local content legislation is permanent protection for industries that are unable to compete for whatever reasons. The basic principle of local content is that U.S. inputs must be used whether or not they are competive.

If U.S. inputs are competitive, the legislation is unnecessary. If they are not competitive, we will be protecting and rewarding inefficiency and forcing U.S. auto consumers to pay the cost, that is, it is a hidden inflationary tax that is regressive because it falls mostly on those who must purchase cars. There would be no incentive to keep U.S. costs down. In fact, the higher U.S. costs, the easier it is to meet the local content requirement, a perverse effect.

Application of this principle to the economy as a whole would do most to bring about an unproductive, inflationary, inefficient economy. It is for those reasons that the administration is opposed to the principle of local content. This administration's opposition based on principle will not be sacrificed for the short-term political gain that some would seek.

The U.S. auto industry is currently engaged in a massive effort to shake off the legacy of its previous isolation from foreign competition. It is seeking to improve productivity, to become more innovative and efficient, and to offer consumers once again the kinds of autos they demand. Local content legislation can only thwart those efforts at a cost to the rest of the economy.

Let me elaborate. Local content legislation is an especially pernicious form of protectionism. It flies in the face of adjustment to international competition. It seeks to repeal the economic laws of competitive advantage. By offering long-term protection with no incentives for efficiency, it promotes a perpetually inefficient industry that can ultimately only be protected at a cost to the rest of the economy. Ambassador Brock mentioned the Australian experience.[43]

This is not merely a theoretical objection to local content legislation. Of the 22 OECD member countries, only Greece, Turkey, Spain, and Australia impose local content requirements. As a group, these countries are not noted for the efficiency of their automobile industries.

Indeed, the Australian experience has led to a high-cost inefficient industry which has led to calls by consumer groups for trade liberalization. Australian automobile production and employment have continued to fall despite the estimated $1 billion per year cost to Australian consumers.

Recently the stringent parts and labor requirements contained in the original bill, H.R. 5133, were modified in an effort to make local content less onerous. The result was the bill which we are considering today. This legislation broadens the concept of local content from parts and labor to include items such as taxes, advertising, overhead, and variable profits.

According to our analysis, this legislation now has the paradoxical effect of tying the hands of U.S. auto manufacturers with high levels of local content while apparently permitting numerous smaller foreign manufacturers to nip at their heels free of similar restrictions.

Because of their high volume of sales, U.S. manufacturers would have to meet local content requirements of 90 percent. In return, they would be protected from any one foreign manufacturer getting a large share of the U.S. market without meeting similar requirements. They would not, however, be protected from imports. Under the broad definition of local content, many manufacturers may be able to sell as many as 400,000 cars annually apiece without substantial increases in purchases of U.S. parts or investment in U.S. production facilities.

The impact on the U.S. auto industry would be substantial. At a time when the industry is beginning to make the necessary adjustments, this bill would preclude it from competitive worldwide sourcing, while leaving the industry vulnerable to imports

---

[43] For Brock's statement, see *Fair Practices in Automotive Products Act*, pp. 21–38.

from many foreign manufacturers with smaller U.S. sales which would not suffer the inefficiencies prompted by local content requirements.

I would point out that the impact of the worldwide sourcing would be particularly adverse on the Chrysler Corp., where this Congress has had a Chrysler loan guarantee program administered by the Treasury Department for some time.

The problem with this local content legislation, however, is not that it is unfair to the U.S. industry and too soft on imports. Rather, the problem is with the concept of local content itself. Adopting ineffective local content legislation now only opens the door to stricter local content requirements later, with enormous future costs.

Again, let me emphasize that although today we are discussing one form of local content bill, H.R. 5133, the administration's opposition is not limited just to this bill. There are no fixes that will make the concept of local content legislation acceptable to this administration.

There are additional costs to the economy besides the inefficiency inherent in local content legislation. Implicit in local content legislation is acceptance of the principle that it is acceptable public policy to require transfer payments from the rest of the economy to a particular sector, in this instance auto workers and parts producers. Indeed, this bill could be labeled an income redistribution bill designed to have the average American's income taxed and redistributed to automobile industry workers and managers.

I would ask the committee the question. Why not such a bill for lumber industry employees and savings and loan employees? Aren't they equally deserving?

Although difficult to estimate, U.S. consumers can expect to pay more for automobiles as a result of reduced foreign competition and a more inefficient domestic industry. U.S. exporters, generally our most efficient industries, can also expect to suffer. If other countries retaliate by restricting imports of U.S. agricultural products or export-dependent industrial goods, or if they mimic U.S. content requirement for their products, U.S. exports will pay the price of protection for the auto industry at home.

As auto exporting countries earn less income from their auto exports to the United States, their ability to purchase U.S. goods will also be diminished. Such countries may also purposefully choose to purchase non-U.S. products whenever they can as a form of retaliation. The potential risk to our exporting industries is substantial and must not be ignored—especially at a time when U.S. industries are clamoring for increased government assistance to exports.

The nature and extent of any jobs gain in the auto industry from this legislation is questionable. There is, however, no question that the legislation itself may jeopardize jobs in other parts of the economy. It would also cost the economy in terms of higher prices for consumers and jobs lost in the import-handling sector and through the closing of imported auto dealerships.

Clearly, the burden on the rest of the economy from such legislation is too high.

The United States cannot afford the luxury of passing legislation which inevitably promotes a noncompetitive industry which would act as a drag on the entire economy. The economic law of competitive advantage will still exist. This legislation won't change it. Rather, we must adopt policies to promote industries which are competitive domestically and worldwide, which contribute to sustained noninflationary growth. We cannot afford to foster industries which thwart these goals and must be supported at a high cost to the rest of the economy.

Indeed, the current dispute between the United States and the European Community over steel imports into the United States simply reflects the consequences of European Community policies to maintain their inefficient producers.

Once instituted, these types of protectionist policies substitute political judgments for economic realities. How would the Congress stop? How many industries can we protect this way and still claim we have a free economy?

Trade restrictions are not the answer to our fundamental economic problems. A better answer lies in the broader macroeconomic policies this administration has been pursuing to create the environment in which U.S. industries can again become healthy, vigorous and competitive. As you know, the cornerstones of this policy are:

Relief from excessive regulation; the reduction of inflation; tax measures to stimulate investment and savings; and reducing government spending.

These policies, designed to permit the efficiency of the market to operate, will assist U.S. industries such as the auto industry to regain that competitive edge, and at the same time, will insure that the rest of the economy and the world does not suffer the drag of industries that are avoiding the pains of adjustment because of protective legislation.

Document 73

Address by the Under Secretary of State for Economic Affairs (Wallis) before the Business Council, Hot Springs, Virginia, October 9, 1982[44]

Our Stake in the Trading System

Problems in the international economic arena today challenge even an economic giant like the United States. This morning, I will reflect with you on a subject which already has occupied a great deal of my time in the 2 months that I have been back in Washington, namely the state of the world trading system. If George Shultz had been able to be with us this weekend, in all probability he would have chosen the same topic.

It would be carrying coals to Newcastle to warn this group that the system of international trade that we have built up so laboriously over the past 35 years is in jeopardy. Yet I am convinced that all of us underestimate both the threat itself and the consequences that would follow disintegration of that system.

Let me cover quickly several aspects of the threat to the trading system. First, I will review the postwar evolution of trade, culminating with the situation today—warts and all. Second, I will yield to an unreformed and unrepentant academic's temptation to argue briefly the case for maintaning the momentum of trade liberalization. Finally, I will mention some things that we in the government are doing, with particular attention to the meeting at the end of November of the trade ministers of the 87 countries that have signed the General Agreement on Tariffs and Trade, usually referred to as GATT.[45] I hope to learn from you how we can best revive the vigorous support for free trade which, throughout the 50's and 60's, put us in the forefront of trade liberalization.

First, then, a brief history of the system we now know. At the end of the Second World War, the United States represented an overwhelming percentage of world trade. Virtually all the countries in the world—the United State included—severely restricted imports through a variety of barriers. The most visible of these barriers were high tariffs, averaging nearly 40 percent. (A tariff, incidentally, was once defined as a device to protect benevolent producers against greedy consumers.)

In the capital-short and war-torn economies of Europe and Japan, trade restrictions were supplemented by a network of foreign exchange controls. Although the postwar economies were immeasurably poorer than they are today, and were indeed shattered, we negotiated the GATT to provide "rules of the game" for a trading system which would be as predictable, stable, and open as possible.

Establishing the GATT reflected understanding of a basic fact first taught in 1776 by Adam Smith, that an economy based on free markets generates enough prosperity and efficiency to overcome temporary problems of adjustment. GATT provided a framework for negotiating mutual reductions in tariffs. It sought also to reduce nontariff barriers. The Agreement anticipated that there would be violation, or charges of violations, of its rules, so it set up a mechanism for settling disputes and differences. It also allowed certain departures from free trade, since even those governments most devoted to free trade must yield occasionally to mercantilist tendencies. Some people argue that the exceptions have become more numerous and more important than the rules. Others hold, to the contrary, that it was only the provision of some flexibility in applying the rules that made possile the degree of adherence to GATT and free trade principles which we have experienced.

Be that as it may, I believe that this system has worked well—not, perhaps, as well as its most ardent architects hoped, but certainly well enough to bring about a clear reduction in trade barriers and a dramatic increase in trade, accompanied by nearly four decades of sustained growth in world prosperity.

Nevertheless, it was apparent by the 1970's that significant barriers to trade remained, and that the continuing vitality of

---

[44] Source: Department of State files.

[45] See footnote 10 to document 64.

the system would depend on its ability to tackle these. The so-called Tokyo Round of GATT negotiations in the 70's cut average tariffs of industrialized countries to a fraction of their immediate postwar levels. They also made the first systematic attack on nontariff barriers. They made a start, but nontariff barriers to trade not only are still with us but probably are growing. These nontariff barriers are more insidious than the simple tariffs of the past. They threaten to undo the good work of the past 35 years.

Protectionist pressures in the major trading countries today are the most severe that they have been since the Second World War. Europe's response to the highest unemployment in 40 years includes a variety of devices for controlling access to its own market and for penetrating other markets. One hears, for example, of agreements which accord the Japanese auto industry only small percentages of European markets. The European Community subsidizes agricultural exports heavily. The GATT does not outlaw export subsidies on primary agricultural products, but the scale on which the European Community indulges in export subsidies and the impact on traditional U.S. markets for such commodities as grains, flour, and chickens have put intense pressure on the trading system—and, it is important to note, have put intense pressure on the largest group of supporters of free trade in the United States, namely farmers.

In Japan, traditional barriers to the internationalization of markets remain strong, and a complex network of regulations, procedures, and habits complicates access to that important market. Polls taken in Japan reveal that the Japanese themselves believe that they are the most protectionist country in the world. Japan's recent liberalizations have been small steps in the right direction, but progress in improving access to the Japanese market will continue to be slow. One bright spot was Prime Minister Suzuki's statement last May urging Japanese business and consumers to change their traditional negative attitude toward imports.[46] Years of export-led nationalistic trade policy will not be erased overnight, however, and the spectacle of restricted Japanese markets side-by-side with booming Japanese exports intensifies protectionist pressures elsewhere.

Most underdeveloped countries have relatively high trade barriers, including high tariffs and persistently overvalued exchange rates. Steep oil bills, declining commodity prices, high interest rates, and balance-of-payments pressures have led them to raise these barriers further. They do so despite the recognition by many that isolation from international competition will only make it more difficult to acquire the international markets needed to become self-sustaining. Developed countries, on the other hand, impose some of their strictest trade barriers against exactly those products that the poorer countries are best able to produce. Textiles, clothing, footwear, and numerous agricultural products are examples. Just recently, our Ambassador to Thailand[47] told me an instructive story. The United States, he said, has encouraged the Thais to cultivate coffee instead of poppies. Now the Thais find that they cannot market the coffee because of the rules of the International Coffee Agreement.[48]

What about us? For years, we have prided ourselves on our open market and on our efforts to get a general consensus in favor of free trade. Today, however, we face stronger pressures to "protect" various sectors of our economy than we have seen for many years. There is no issue to which I have personally devoted more attention in the short time I have been in Washington. I have testified against the "local content" legislation[49] pending in the House. I have been to ever so many meetings on how to deal with the extensive protectionist actions abroad that help fuel our domestic protectionists. Last week a highly respected and influential "free trade" Congressman told me categorically that any piece of protectionist legislation that reaches the floor of the House will pass. That is understandable, but nevertheless it is a grave threat to our economic welfare.

We in the United States are far from faultless. The extension of the "manufacturing clause" a few months ago over the President's veto is a case in point.[50] The

[46] Regarding Prime Minister Suzuki's statement of May 28, 1982, see footnote 22 to document 511.

[47] John Gunther Dean.

[48] For the text of the International Coffee Agreement, signed at London December 3, 1975, and entered into force for the United States, August 1, 1977, see 28 UST 6401.

[49] For the text of Wallis' testimony before the Subcommittee on Trade of the House Ways and Means Committee, September 30, 1982, on H.R. 5133, see *The Fair Practices in Automotive Products Act*, pp. 636–642.

[50] The reference is to the decision by Congress of July 13, 1982, to override President Reagan's veto to enact legislation which extended until 1986 the manufacturing clause in U.S. copyright law, requiring that books and periodicals in English by U.S. authors be printed and bound in the United States to receive full copyright protection; for the text of P.L. 97–215, the copyright law amendment, see 96 Stat. 178.

same can be said of the increased tariff on ethyl alcohol which was enacted a couple of years ago in violation of our GATT obligations.[51] We have welcomed Japanese restraints on auto exports. In agriculture, we now impose quotas on beef and sugar. While we have thus far stayed away from using another weapon which threatens the integrity of the trading system—export subsidies—the pressures to do just that are enormous. Congress recently ordered that $175 to $190 million be spent for what it called "export promotion" in agriculture.[52] In each of these cases, and others as well, it is easy to argue that the measures we instituted had ample provocation. But their cumulative effect is to damage ourselves. To get even with someone who has shot us in the foot, we shoot ourselves in the other foot.

Before we let ourselves be pulled down into this vicious whirlpool, we should review our economics and our history. The Smoot-Hawley tariff of 1930[53] was our most recent experience with a dramatic increase in the level of protection against imports. It provided for average *ad valorem* duties on dutiable imports of 53 percent, and it covered a wide range of imports. Retaliatory tariff increases followed throughout the world. The drastic reduction in world trade that followed was undoubtedly a major cause, not merely a result, of the Great Depression of the 1930's.

I do not want to exaggerate the parallels between 1982 and 1930. Both our domestic and our international economic systems now have many features which would brake so devastating a spiral. World trade did, however, fall in real terms last year, and an accelerated tendency to protectionism would result in further declines. The adverse impact on our economy would surely be substantial. It is no exaggeration to say that the system is teetering on the brink.

Declines in world trade would be far more damaging to our economy now than would have been the case 20 or 30 years ago. It is estimated that over 5 million American workers are dependent on foreign trade for their livelihood. According to one recent study, some 80 percent of all new manufacturing jobs created in the late 1970's were linked to exports. One American farm acre in three now produces for export. In Rochester, my home for the past 20 years, where an exceptionally high proportion of industrial production is exported, I have seen bumper stickers saying "Buy a Foreign Car—Protect your Export Job."

We cannot afford to ignore the impact on American jobs and consumers of the retaliation against American exports that will occur if we adopt protectionist measures. Clearly, we must defend our investors, our workers, and our consumers, but in choosing our defenses we must look carefully at all their effects, including unintended and delayed effects. Restrictions on imports in the short run may make it easier for American producers of goods that compete with imports; but, in the long run, they raise costs and divert resources from the more productive sectors of our economy.

All is not gloom-and-doom in our international trade. Far from it. We have maintained our share of industrialized countries' exports for the past 10 years. Although we have a large trade deficit with Japan, we have a large trade surplus with Europe. Our agricultural trade surplus continues to be substantial. Exports of services have soared during the last 10 years, offsetting the deficits in our trade balance. Our economic adjustments during the next 10 years are likely to lead to a significant expansion in the area referred to loosely as "high technology", an area in which we continue to lead the world. In your own businesses, you know that constant vigilance is necessary to remain competitive, either at home or abroad. The United States cannot be complacent and compete; we cannot simply do what we have always done, or even what we did last year.

In Washington, we are now preparing for a meeting of the trade ministers of the GATT countries[54]—the first since the Tokyo meeting in 1973 which initiated the latest Multilateral Trade Negotiations. This year's meeting is not intended to launch a new round of trade negotiations, and we do

---

[51] Subtitle G of the Omnibus Reconciliation Act of 1980 (P.L. 96-499), approved December 5, 1980, increased until 1993 the duties on certain imports of ethyl alcohol; for the text, see 94 Stat. 2599.

[52] Subtitle D of the Omnibus Budget Reconciliation Act of 1982 (P.L. 97-253), approved September 8, 1982, mandated that the Secretary of Agriculture spend $175 to $190 million in fiscal years 1983-1985 on export promotion in agriculture; for the text, see 96 Stat. 763.

[53] The Smoot-Hawley Tariff Act (P.L. 71-361), approved June 17, 1930, set the tariff rate at an average of 52.8 percent on the value of dutiable imports; for the text, see 46 Stat. 590.

[54] For information on the GATT Ministerial Meeting, November 24-29, 1982, see document 76.

not expect flashy short-term results. But we do see it as an extremely important endeavor, in which we expect all participants to think carefully about their stakes in the trading system and how they can strengthen it.

We hope for at least three important results from the GATT meeting:

—First, we believe it important that there be a firm resolute recommitment to the principles of free trade.

—Second, we expect that some unfinished business not resolved during the Tokyo Round will move forward.

—Third, and most important, we hope that work programs will be established in key areas where the trade problems of the future will lie. We have put forward proposals for working groups on trade in services, on trade-related investment issues, and on the problems of trade in high technology goods, and on agricultural export subsidies. With 87 nations participating in the meetings, inevitably some of them have different concerns from our own, and the end result will reflect negotiations and compromises on what GATT as a whole is able to tackle now.

Establishing these working groups would by no means be the non-event that it may seem at first blush. It is important that these emerging areas—some of my international colleagues have characterized them as "futuristic"—be looked at against a long time horizon. The Tokyo Round took 2 years to prepare and 6 to complete. While the negotiations on the nontariff barrier codes were breaking new ground, they took place in the context of a reasonably well understood relationship to the GATT articles. Rules for services and trade-related restrictions on investments are novel, and will require some fundamental consensus-building. Many countries, including our own, have to resolve new jurisdictional issues before any negotiations can begin in earnest, and some countries have reservations as to whether these issues are really the province of GATT. We believe it important to get these issues on the agenda now, and to get them taken seriously. We are also examining the possibility of setting a date now for a followup meeting of ministers, perhaps in a year and a half or so, to act on the results of the working groups.

None of this will be dramatic, but if it can be achieved it will be the kind of step-by-step advance from which lasting progress results.

Seven years ago I had the pleasure of addressing the Business Council on the topic "What Can We Do About It?" I said "About what? About the tide in public affairs that is moving in the wrong direction, and moving in the wrong direction at a rapid and accelerating pace." I was talking then about domestic policy. Today, in talking about international trade I will conclude by turning the tables and asking you, what can you do about it?

Document 74

Address by President Reagan, October 15, 1982[55]

Willingness to Sell Additional Grain to the Soviet Union

My fellow Americans, I am sorry for the delay in this broadcast due to technical difficulties. I am speaking to you from the White House over a special hook-up with radio stations across the farm belt.

I would like to discuss with you for a few moments the plans our administration has to meet important agricultural challenges we face together. I'm talking about increasing American farm exports, restoring our reputation as reliable suppliers, and regaining our world market share.

Before I do, may I just take a moment to congratulate you. Once again, you're making something look easy that would be considered a miracle almost anywhere else in the world. Farmers all over America are harvesting record crops. You know, I've always thought that when we Americans get up in the morning, when we see bacon, eggs, toast, and milk on our breakfast table, we should give thanks that our farmers are survivors. You are the real miracle workers of the modern world—keepers of an incredible system based on faith, freedom,

---

[55] Source: White House Press Release, October 15, 1982, Office of the Press Secretary to the President; printed also in *Weekly Compilation of Presidential Documents*, October 18, 1982, pp. 1317–1319. The President spoke at 9:30 a.m. from the Oval Office. The address was broadcast live and relayed to Station WHO in Des Moines, Iowa, and was available for coverage by a number of other agricultural networks.

hard work, productivity, and profit—a system that feeds us and sustains millions of the world's hungry.

Too often, people forget a basic fact of life. All those good things we enjoy come from the ache in your backs and your willingness to shoulder great personal risks. Right now, another fact of life in America's heartland is that things haven't been very good down on the farm. You, who produce the food and fiber essential to life itself, are carrying tremendous burdens—sometimes impossible burdens. U.S. agriculture is in the grip of a prolonged economic recession that began in 1980. The record inflation and interest rates of the late 1970's and that mistaken Soviet grain embargo laid the seeds for a very different bitter kind of harvest—a vicious cost-price squeeze and lost markets. Together, they eroded confidence and destroyed too many dreams for prosperity.

I believe this government's proper role, indeed its only role, is to act as friend, partner, and promoter of American farmers and their products. I want, with all my heart, to see your burdens lifted, to see farmers who have given so much to America receive the rewards they deserve.

As Dwight Eisenhower once said, "Without a prosperous agriculture, there is no prosperity in America." From the moment we arrived in Washington, we've been working to solve those long-neglected problems that were dragging America down. Like any small businessman, a farmer lives or dies on his ability to sustain an adequate cash flow. And when that cash flow is reduced to a trickle by high inflation and high interest rates, a farmer sometimes has no option but to shut down his operation.

Add to all this your bumper crops and we understand why the cost-price squeeze is so bad and threatens the survival of agriculture, America's bedrock industry.[56] It's been tough, slow work and, as I told the nation Wednesday night, we still have a long way to go.

But we're beginning to make real progress on four of the five most serious problems we inherited. We are bringing down spending, bringing down inflation, bringing down interest rates and reducing your taxes.

[56] For the text of the President's address to the Nation on October 13, see *ibid.*, October 18, 1982, pp. 1305–1310.

You know, one of the parts of our tax program that I'm most proud of addresses a special problem for farmers. We don't think widows and children should lose what generations of love and toil created just to pay Uncle Sam a tax, so we took action to correct that. We increased the estate tax exemption to $600,000 by 1987 and we eliminated altogether the estate tax for a surviving spouse. I hope all of these steps are beginning to bring some relief on your cost side of the equation.

As for prices, well, there are really only two ways to increase farmers' income—sell more or produce less. Now, I'm not one who believes you should be cursed by your own success. The philosophy of this administration is to help farmers to succeed in the marketplace, not depend on the U.S. Treasury. Deciding how much to produce and how much to sell is best left to you. We, in turn, will make every effort to remove the barriers to the exporting of your products.

So that brings me back to what I mentioned at the outset—our initiatives to increase exports, restore our reputation as a reliable supplier and regain our market share.

As you know, our administration moved early on to end that grain embargo which had hurt farmers so badly. Before the Soviet embargo, American farmers were supplying about 70 percent of Soviet needs. After the embargo, our market share dropped to less than 25 percent. Other nations had quickly moved in to fill the gap left by the embargo so that our farmers and our farmers almost alone bore the brunt of the embargo.

This year, we've fought our way back to 35 percent of the Soviet market. We're on our way back up. We can and we will do better there and around the world. Nothing is more crucial to the long-term health of agriculture than restoring this nation's reputation as a reliable supplier of agricultural products around the world.

During the past 20 months, we've pursued an agricultural export policy making three things plain. No restrictions will be imposed on farm exports because of rising domestic prices. No farm exports will be singled out as an instrument of foreign policy except in extreme situations and then only as part of a broad embargo supported by our trading partners. And world markets must be freed of trade barriers and unfair trade practices.

On that last point we've mounted a united front—the Departments of Agriculture,

State, Treasury, Commerce and the U.S. Trade Representative—to speak out and act against the unfair trade practices of our competitors abroad. We're committed to more open agricultural markets in all countries and we're challenging others in negotiations, particularly our friends in Europe and Japan, to fully match this commitment.

It's imperative that all of us work together to reduce the growing tide of protectionism and export subsidies overseas. If other countries can't understand an even-handed approach is in everybody's best interest, if they're not willing to play by the rules of the game, then let there be no mistake: We must and we will counter with strong measures of our own to permit American farmers to realize the benefits of their extraordinary productivity.

Now, in spite of my strong commitment, I know there is still concern in the farm community that we've not given sufficient assurance of delivery of our farm exports. I can understand farmers' skepticism. You've been burned so often in the past. But our new agricultural export policy means exactly what it says. We will honor our word.

Today I am directing Secretary of Agriculture Block to take two additional steps. Two weeks from now U.S. representatives will meet with the Soviets in Vienna for talks concerning additional grain purchases beyond the 8 million metric tons stipulated in Article I of the existing U.S.–U.S.S.R. grain agreement.[57] I am instructing the Secretary to make available a total of 23 million metric tons for purchase during the October 1, 1982–September 30, 1983 time period.

Second, the Secretary of Agriculture will extend to the additional purchases the same assurances of reliable delivery that the 8 million metric tons are afforded under Article II of the agreement, if the U.S.S.R. will contract for the additional tonnage during the month of November and provided that it is shipped within 180 days from the date of the contract. These same assurances, of course, also apply to soybean and other agricultural exports. We have a large crop. We need commitments to move that crop and strengthen markets. Now, of course, we can't guarantee the Soviets will make these purchases, but we know they're shopping and they still have large needs.

We want to demonstrate that actions speak louder than words and we're taking tangible actions to restore this market. Year in, year out, there is no better, more reliable producer of food anywhere than the United States of America.

Now, some will say that by offering to sell the Soviets more grain we are sending a weak signal. That's wrong. We're asking the Soviets to give us cash on the line for the food they buy. We're not providing them with any subsidies or pumping any Western currencies into Soviet pockets.

It's always seemed ironic to me that many people who are so quick to sacrifice the interest of farmers in an effort to seem tough are unwilling to do the real things we need to send a signal of national will and strength.

During the last decade we had two grain embargoes. But during those same years we were also reducing our commitment to a strong national defense, while the Soviets were undertaking the most massive military buildup in history. We're not making that mistake in 1982. We have our priorities straight.

I wish I could tell you today that we've turned everything around for American farmers. I can't. I can only say that we're doing everything we can as rapidly as we can to make things right.

Thank you for keeping up the struggle. Thank you for your strength, your vision, and your faith. I know we can return prosperity to our heartland and to America. God has blessed us with a strong spirit and rich soil. With His help and yours we can make America once again the source of all the dreams and opportunities she was placed on this good earth to provide. Thanks for listening and God bless you.

Document 75

Address by President Reagan, Camp David, Maryland, November 20, 1982[58]

The Importance of Free and Fair Trade to the World Economy

I have talked to you on a number of occasions about the economic problems

[57] For the text of the October 20, 1975 agreement, see 26 UST 2971.

[58] Source: White House Press Release, November 20, 1982, Office of the Press Secretary to the President; printed also in *Weekly Compilation of Presidential Documents*, November 29, 1982, pp. 1511–1512. The President spoke on nationwide radio at 12:06 p.m.

and opportunities our nation faces. Well, as you have probably heard on news reports, America's problems are not unique. Other nations face very severe economic difficulties. In fact, both developed and developing countries alike have been in the grip of the longest worldwide recession in post-war history. And that is bad news for all of us. When other countries do not grow, they buy less from us. And we see fewer jobs created at home. When we do not grow, we buy less from them, which weakens their economies and, of course, their ability to buy from us. It is a vicious cycle.

You can understand the danger of worldwide recession when you realize how much is at stake. Exports account for over five million jobs in the United States. Two out of every five acres planted by American farmers produce crops for exports. But because of their recessions, other countries are buying fewer American farm products than last year. Our farmers are hurting. And they are just one group.

So we are trying to turn this situation around. We are reminding the world that, yes, we all have serious problems. But our economic system based on individual freedom, private initiative, and free trade has produced more human progress than any other in history. It is in all of our interests to preserve it, protect it, and strengthen it. We are reminding our trading partners that preserving individual freedom and restoring prosperity also requires free and fair trade in the marketplace.

The United States took the lead after World War II in creating an international trading and financial system that limited governments' ability to disrupt free trade across borders. We did this because history had taught us an important lesson. Free trade serves the cause of economic progress. And it serves the cause of world peace. When governments get too involved in trade, economic costs increase and political disputes multiply. Peace is threatened. In the 1930's, the world experienced an ugly specter—protectionism and trade wars and, eventually, real wars and unprecedented suffering and loss of life.

There are some who seem to believe that we should run up the American flag in defense of our markets. They would embrace protectionism again, and insulate our markets from world competition. Well, the last time the United States tried that, there was enormous economic distress in the world. World trade fell by 60 percent. And young Americans soon followed the American flag into World War II.

I am old enough and, hopefully, wise enough not to forget the lessons of those unhappy years. The world must never live through such a nightmare again. We are in the same boat with our trading partners. If one partner shoots a hole in the boat, does it make sense for the other one to shoot another hole in the boat? Some say, yes—and call that getting tough. Well, I call it stupid. But we shouldn't be shooting holes. We should be working together to plug them up. We must strengthen the boat of free markets and fair trade so it can lead the world to economic recovery and greater political stability.

And here's how we're working to do that: We insist on sound domestic policies at home that bring down inflation. And we look to others for no less in their economies. The International Monetary Fund, the institution that deals with world financial issues, seeks to encourage its member countries to follow sound domestic policies and avoid government restrictions on international trade and investment to foster economic development and raise their people's standard of living.

We remind other countries that as the United States helps to lead the world out of this recession, they will benefit as we buy more goods from them. This will enable them to grow and buy more goods from us. And that will mean more jobs all around. That is the way of free markets and free trade. We must resist protectionism because it can only lead to fewer jobs for them and fewer jobs for us.

In just four days, the trade ministers of virtually all the free world countries will meet in Geneva, Switzerland.[59] They will seek ways to surmount challenges to the integrity of our international economic system. We were instrumental in convening this international meeting because we believe strongly that our trading system is at a crossroads. Either free world countries go forward and sustain the drive toward more open markets or they risk sliding back toward the mistakes of the 1930's and succumbing to the evils of more and more government intervention. And this is really no choice at all.

The United States will reject protectionist and defeatist proposals. Instead, we will set new goals and lay out a program for limiting government intervention in world markets. We will lead with a clear sense of our own commercial interests and a quiet

---

[59] See the communique, *infra*.

determination to defend these interests. We will take actions at home and abroad which enhance the ability of U.S. industries to compete in international trade.

Let no one misunderstand us. We're generous and farsighted in our goals and we intend to use our full power to achieve these goals. We seek to plug the holes in the boat of free markets and free trade and get it moving again in the direction of prosperity. And no one should mistake our determination to use our full power and influence to prevent others from destroying the boat and sinking us all.

That's how the United States is working in the world on behalf of freedom, economic prosperity and peace.

I'll be back again next week. Thanks for listening. God bless you.

Document 76

Communiqué Issued by the Ministers of the General Agreement on Tariffs and Trade Member Governments, Geneva, November 29, 1982[60]

GATT Ministers Pledge Further Liberalization and Expansion of Trade

The Ministerial-level meeting of GATT member governments ended early on 29 November with adoption by consensus of a joint declaration. The full text of the declaration is given below.

Ministerial Declaration

1. The Contracting Parties to the General Agreement on Tariffs and Trade have met at Ministerial level on 24–29 November 1982. They recognize that the multilateral trading system, of which the General Agreement is the legal foundation, is seriously endangered. In the current crisis of the world economy, to which the lack of convergence in national economic policies has contributed, protectionist pressures on governments have multiplied, disregard of GATT disciplines has increased and certain shortcomings in the functioning of the GATT system have been accentuated. Conscious of the role of the GATT system in furthering economic well-being and an unprecedented expansion of world trade, and convinced of the lasting validity of the basic principles and objectives of the General Agreement in a world of increasing economic interdependence, the Contracting Parties are resolved to overcome these threats to the system.

2. The deep and prolonged crisis of the world economy has severely depressed levels of production and trade. In many countries growth rates are low or negative; there is growing unemployment and a climate of uncertainty, exacerbated by persistent inflation, high rates of interest and volatile exchange rates, which seriously inhibit investment and structural adjustment and intensify protectionist pressures. Many countries, and particularly developing countries, now face critical difficulties created by the combination of uncertain and limited access to export markets, declining external demand, a sharp fall in commodity prices and the high cost of borrowing. The import capacity of developing countries, which is essential to their economic growth and development, is being impaired and is no longer serving as a dynamic factor sustaining the exports of the developed world. Acute problems of debt servicing threaten the stability of the financial system.

3. In the field of trade, the responses of governments to the challenges of the crisis have too often been inadequate and inward-looking. Import restrictions have increased and a growing proportion of them have for various reasons been applied outside GATT disciplines, thus undermining the multilateral trading system. Trade patterns have also been adversely affected by certain forms of economic assistance for production and exports and by some restrictive trade measures applied for non-economic purposes. In the depressed economic circumstances these measures, together with continuing pressures for further protective action, have contributed to further delays in necessary structural adjustment, increased economic uncertainty and discouraged productive investment.

4. The results of the Tokyo Round, including in particular the implementation on schedule of the tariff reductions, have provided some impetus to the functioning of the trading system. However, despite the strength and resilience which it has shown, the stresses on the system, which are re-

---

[60] Source: Press Release Issued by the General Agreement on Tariffs and Trade, document GATT/1328, Geneva, November 29, 1982.

flected in the growing number and intensity of disputes between contracting parties, many of which remain unresolved, have made more pronounced certain shortcomings in its functioning. Existing strains have been aggravated by differences of perception regarding the balance of rights and obligations under the GATT, the way in which these rights and obligations have been implemented and the extent to which the interests of different contracting parties have been met by the GATT. There are also concerns over the manner in which rights are being pursued as well as the manner in which obligations are being fulfilled. Disagreements persist over the interpretation of some important provisions and over their application. Disciplines governing the restriction of trade through safeguard measures are inadequate; there is widespread dissatisfaction with the application of GATT rules and the degree of liberalization in relation to agricultural trade, even though such trade has continued to expand; trade in textiles and clothing continues to be treated under an Arrangement which is a major derogation from the General Agreement—a matter of critical importance to developing countries in particular. Such differences and imbalances are particularly detrimental to the stability of the international trading system when they concern access to the markets of major trading countries or when, through the use of export subsidies, competition among major suppliers is distorted.

5. The Contracting Parties recognize that the interdependence of national economies means that no country can solve its trade problems in isolation and also that solutions would be greatly facilitated by parallel efforts in the financial and monetary fields. In this light, they commit themselves to reduce trade frictions, overcome protectionist pressures, avoid using export subsidies inconsistent with Article XVI of the GATT[61] and promote the liberalization and expansion of trade. They are therefore determined to create, through concerted action, a renewed consensus in support of the GATT system, so as to restore and reinforce confidence in its capacity to provide a stable and predictable trading environment and respond to new challenges.

6. The Contracting Parties have accordingly decided:

—to reaffirm their commitment to abide by their GATT obligations and to support and improve the GATT trading system, so that it may contribute vigorously to the further liberalization and expansion of trade based on mutual commitment, mutual advantage and overall reciprocity, and the most-favoured-nation clause;

—to preserve, in the operation and functioning of GATT instruments, the unity and consistency of the GATT system; and

—to ensure that GATT provides a continuing forum for negotiation and consultation, in which an appropriate balance of rights and obligations can be assured for all contracting parties and the rules and procedures of the system are effectively and fairly applied, on the basis of agreed interpretations, for the economic development and benefit of all.

7. In drawing up the work programme and priorities for the 1980's, the contracting parties undertake, individually and jointly:

(i) to make determined efforts to ensure that trade policies and measures are consistent with GATT principles and rules and to resist protectionist pressures in the formulation and implementation of national trade policy and in proposing legislation; and also to refrain from taking or maintaining any measures inconsistent with GATT and to make determined efforts to avoid measures which would limit or distort international trade;

(ii) to give fullest consideration, in the application of measures falling within the GATT framework, and in the general exercise of their GATT rights, to the trading interests of other contracting parties and the shared objective of trade liberalization and expansion;

(iii) to abstain from taking restrictive trade measures, for reasons of a non-economic character, not consistent with the General Agreement;

(iv)(a) to ensure the effective implementation of GATT rules and provisions and specifically those concerning the developing countries, thereby furthering the dynamic role of developing countries in international trade;

(b) to ensure special treatment for the least-developed countries, in the context of differential and more favourable treatment

---

[61] For the text of Article XVI on subsidies of the General Agreement on Tariffs and Trade signed October 30, 1947, at Geneva and entered into force, January 1, 1948, see 4 Bevans 639; for the text of the Interpretation and Application of Articles VI, XVI, and XXIII, signed at Geneva, April 12, 1979, and entered into force, January 1, 1980, see 31 UST 513.

for developing countries, in order to ameliorate the grave economic situation of these countries;

(v) to bring agriculture more fully into the multilateral trading system by improving the effectiveness of GATT rules, provisions and disciplines and through their common interpretation; to seek to improve terms of access to markets; and to bring export competition under greater discipline. To this end a major two-year work programme shall be undertaken.

(vi) to bring into effect expeditiously a comprehensive understanding on safeguards to be based on the principles of the General Agreement;

(vii) to ensure increased transparency of trade measures and the effective resolution of disputes through improvements in the operation of the pertinent procedures, supported by a determination to comply with rulings and respect recommendations;

(viii) to examine ways and means of, and to pursue measures aimed at, liberalizing trade in textiles and clothing, including the eventual application of the General Agreement, after the expiry of the 1981 Protocol extending the Arrangement Regarding International Trade in Textiles,[62] it being understood that in the interim the parties to the Arrangement shall adhere strictly to its rules;

(ix) to give continuing consideration to changes in the trading environment so as to ensure that the GATT is responsive to these changes.

Safeguards

The Contracting Parties decide:

1. That, having regard to the objectives and disciplines of the General Agreement, there is need for an improved and more efficient safeguard system which provides for greater predictability and clarity and also greater security and equity for both importing and exporting countries, so as to preserve the results of trade liberalization and avoid the proliferation of restrictive measures; and

2. That to this end, effect should be given to a comprehensive understanding to be based on the principles of the General Agreement which would contain, *inter alia*, the following elements:

(i) Transparency;

(ii) Coverage;

(iii) Objective criteria for action including the concept of serious injury or threat thereof;

(iv) Temporary nature, degressivity and structural adjustment;

(v) Compensation and retaliation; and

(vi) Notification, consultation, multilateral surveillance and dispute settlement with particular reference to the role and functions of the Safeguards Committee.

3. That such an understanding should be drawn up by the Council for adoption by the Contracting Parties not later than their 1983 Session.

GATT Rules and Activities Relating to Developing Countries

The Contracting Parties:

1. Instruct the Committee on Trade and Development bearing in mind particularly the special responsibility of the developed contracting parties in this regard, to consult on a regular basis with contracting parties individually or collectively, as appropriate to examine how individual contracting parties have responded to the requirements of Part IV.[63]

2. Urge contracting parties to implement more effectively Part IV and the Decision of 28 November 1979 regarding "differential and more favourable treatment, reciprocity and fuller participation of developing countries";[64]

3. Urge contracting parties to work towards further improvement of GSP or MFN treatment for products of particular export interest to least-developed countries, and the elimination or reduction of non-tariff measures affecting such products;

4. Agree to strengthen the technical cooperation programme of GATT;

---

[62] Reference is to the GATT Protocol extending the arrangement of December 20, 1973, regarding international trade in textiles, which was signed at Geneva, December 22, 1981, and entered into force, January 1, 1982. (TIAS 10323)

[63] For the text of the Protocol Amending the General Agreement on Tariffs and Trade To Introduce a Part IV on Trade and Development, which was signed at Geneva, February 8, 1965, and entered into force, June 27, 1966, see 17 UST 1977.

[64] For the text of the Decision of November 28, 1979, see *GATT: Basic Instruments and Selected Documents* (BISD), 26 Supplement, p. 203.

5. Instruct the Committee on Trade and Development to carry out an examination of the prospects for increasing trade between developed and developing countries and the possibilities in GATT for facilitating this objective;

To this effect, the Contracting Parties are also taking the decisions annexed and decide to review the action taken in these areas at their 1984 Session.

Dispute Settlement Procedures

The Contracting Parties:

Agree that the Understanding on Notification, Consultation, Surveillance and Dispute Settlement negotiated during the Tokyo Round (hereinafter referred to as the "Understanding")[65] provides the essential framework of procedures for the settlement of disputes among contracting parties and that no major change is required in this framework, but that there is scope for more effective use of the existing mechanism and for specific improvements in procedures to this end;

And agree further that:

(i) With reference to paragraph 8 of the Understanding, if a dispute is not resolved through consultations, any party to a dispute may, with the agreement of the other party, seek the good offices of the Director-General or of an individual or group of persons nominated by the Director-General. This conciliatory process would be carried out expeditiously, and the Director-General would inform the Council of the outcome of the conciliatory process. Conciliation proceedings, and in particular positions taken by the parties to the dispute during conciliation, shall be confidential, and without prejudice to the rights of either party in any further proceedings under Article XXIII:2. It would remain open at any time during any conciliatory process for either party to the dispute to refer the matter to the Contracting Parties.

(ii) In order to ensure more effective compliance with the provisions of paragraphs 11 and 12 of the Understanding, the Director-General shall inform the Council of any case in which it has not been found possible to meet the time limits for the establishment of a panel.

(iii) With reference to paragraph 13 of the Understanding, contracting parties will co-operate effectively with the Director-General in making suitably qualified experts available to serve on panels. Where experts are not drawn from Geneva, any expenses, including travel and subsistence allowance, shall be met from the GATT budget.

(iv) The secretariat of GATT has the responsibility of assisting the panel, especially on the legal, historical and procedural aspects of the matters dealt with.

(v) The terms of reference of a panel should be formulated so as to permit a clear finding with respect to any contravention of GATT provisions and/or on the question of nullification and impairment of benefits. In terms of paragraph 16 of the Understanding, and after reviewing the facts of the case, the applicability of GATT provisions and the arguments advanced, the panel should come to such a finding. Where a finding establishing a contravention of GATT provisions or nullification and impairment is made, the panel should make such suggestions as appropriate for dealing with the matter as would assist the Contracting Parties in making recommendations to the contracting parties which they consider to be concerned, or give a ruling on the matter, as appropriate.

(vi) Panels would aim to deliver their findings without undue delay, as provided in paragraph 20 of the Understanding. If a complete report cannot be made within the period foreseen in that paragraph, panels would be expected to so advise the Council and the report should be submitted as soon as possible thereafter.

(vii) Reports of panels should be given prompt consideration by the Contracting Parties. Where a decision on the findings contained in a report calls for a ruling or recommendation by the Council, the Council may allow the contracting party concerned a reasonable specified time to indicate what action it proposes to take with a view to a satisfactory settlement of the matter, before making any recommendation or ruling on the basis of the report.

(viii) The recommendation or ruling made by the Contracting Parties shall be aimed at achieving a satisfactory settlement of the matter in accordance with GATT obligations. In furtherance of the provisions of paragraph 22 of the Understanding

---

[65] For the text of the section entitled "Institutions, consultation and dispute settlement," Articles 13 and 14, of the Agreement on Technical Barriers to Trade, which was signed at Geneva, April 12, 1979, and entered in force, January 1, 1980, see 31 UST 405.

the Council shall periodically review the action taken pursuant to such recommendations. The contracting party to which such a recommendation has been addressed, shall report within a reasonable specified period on action taken or on its reasons for not implementing the recommendation or ruling by the Contracting Parties. The contracting party bringing the case may also ask the Contracting Parties to make suitable efforts with a view to finding an appropriate solution as provided in paragraph 22 of the Understanding.

(ix) The further action taken by the Contracting Parties in the above circumstances might include a recommendation for compensatory adjustment with respect to other products or authorization for the suspension of such concessions or other obligations as foreseen in Article XXIII:2, as the Contracting Parties may determine to be appropriate in the circumstances.

(x) The Parties to a dispute would fully participate in the consideration of the matter by the Contracting Parties under paragraph (vii) above, including the consideration of any rulings or recommendations the Contracting Parties might make pursuant to Article XXIII:2 of the General Agreement, and their views would be fully recorded. They would likewise participate and have their views recorded in the considerations of the further actions provided for under paragraphs (viii) and (ix) above. The Contracting Parties reaffirmed that consensus will continue to be the traditional method of resolving disputes; however, they agreed that obstruction in the process of dispute settlement shall be avoided.[66] It is understood that decisions in this process cannot add to or diminish the rights and obligations provided in the General Agreement.

Trade in Agriculture

With the purpose of accelerating the achievement of the objectives of the General Agreement, including Part IV, and recognizing that there is an urgent need to find lasting solutions to the problems of trade in agricultural products, the Contracting Parties decide:

1. That the following matters be examined, in the light of the objectives, principles and relevant provisions of the General Agreement and also taking into account the effects of national agricultural policies, with the purpose of making appropriate recommendations. The examination shall cover all measures affecting trade, market access and competition and supply in agricultural products, including subsidies and other forms of assistance.

(i) Trade measures affecting market access and supplies, with a view to achieving greater liberalization in the trade of agricultural products, with respect to tariffs and non-tariff measures, on a basis of overall reciprocity and mutual advantage under the General Agreement.

(ii) The operation of the General Agreement as regards subsidies affecting agriculture, especially export subsidies, with a view to examining its effectiveness, in the light of actual experience, in promoting the objectives of the General Agreement and avoiding subsidization seriously prejudicial to the trade or interests of contracting parties. Other forms of export assistance will be included in this examination.

(iii) Trade measures affecting agriculture maintained under exceptions or derogations without prejudice to the rights of contracting parties under the General Agreement.

2. That in carrying out the tasks enumerated above, full account shall be taken of the need for a balance of rights and obligations under the GATT, and of the special needs of developing countries in the light of the GATT provisions providing for differential and more favourable treatment for such contracting parties. Full account shall also be taken of specific characteristics and problems in agriculture, of the scope for improving the operation of GATT rules, provisions and disciplines and agreed interpretations of its provisions.

3. That for the purpose of carrying out this work, an improved and unified system of notifications shall be introduced so as to ensure full transparency.

4. That a Committee on Trade in Agriculture shall be established, open to all contracting parties, for the purpose of carrying out the tasks enumerated above and of making recommendations with a view to achieving greater liberalization in the trade of agricultural products. The Committee will report periodically on the results achieved and make appropriate recommendations to the Council and the Contracting Parties for consideration not later than their 1984 Session.

[66] This does not prejudice the provisions on decision making in the General Agreement. [Footnote in the source text.]

Tropical Products

The Contracting Parties decide to carry out, on the basis of the work programme pursued by the Committee on Trade and Development, consultations and appropriate negotiations aimed at further liberalization of trade in tropical products, including in their processed and semi-processed forms, and to review the progress achieved in eliminating or reducing existing obstacles to trade in tropical products at their 1984 Session.

Quantitative Restrictions and Other Non-Tariff Measures

The Contracting Parties decide:

1. To review, in a group created for the purpose, existing quantitative restrictions and other non-tariff measures, the grounds on which these are maintained, and their conformity with the provisions of the General Agreement, so as to achieve the elimination of quantitative restrictions which are not in conformity with the General Agreement or their being brought into conformity with the General Agreement, and also to achieve progress in liberalizing other quantitative restrictions and non-tariff measures, adequate attention being given to the need for action on quantitative restrictions and other measures affecting products of particular export interest to developing countries; and

2. That the group should make progress reports to the Council and that its complete report containing its findings and conclusions should be available for consideration by the Contracting Parties at their 1984 Session.

Tariffs

The Contracting Parties decide:

1. That prompt attention should be given to the problem of escalation of tariffs on products with increased processing with a view to effective action towards the elimination or reduction of such escalation where it inhibits international trade, taking into account the concerns relating to exports of developing countries; and agree

2. That wide acceptance of a common system for classifying products for tariff and statistical purposes would facilitate world trade and therefore recommend prompt action towards the introduction of such a system. They take note of the ongoing work to this end in the Customs Co-operation Council. They further agree that, if such a system is introduced, the general level of benefits provided by GATT concessions must be maintained, that existing concessions should normally remain unchanged and that any negotiations that may prove necessary should be initiated promptly so as to avoid any undue delay in the implementation of a system. They also agree that technical support shall be provided by the GATT secretariat to developing contracting parties in order to fully assist their participation in such a process.

MTN Agreements and Arrangements[67]

The Contracting Parties decide to review the operation of the MTN Agreements and Arrangements, taking into account reports from the Committees or Councils concerned, with a view to determining what action if any is called for, in terms of their decision of November 1979. The Contracting Parties further agree that, for this purpose, the review should focus on the adequacy and effectiveness of these Agreements and Arrangements and the obstacles to the acceptance of these Agreements and Arrangements by interested parties.

Structural Adjustment and Trade Policy

The Contracting Parties decide to continue the work on structural adjustment and trade policy in order to focus on the interaction between structural adjustment and the fulfillment of the objectives of the General Agreement, and to review the results of this work at their 1983 Session.

Trade in Counterfeit Goods

The Contracting Parties instruct the Council to examine the question of counterfeit goods with a view to determining the appropriateness of joint action in the GATT framework on the trade aspects of commercial counterfeiting and, if such joint action is found to be appropriate, the modalities for such action, having full regard to the competence of other international organizations. For the purposes of such examination, the Contracting Parties request the Director-General to hold consultations with the Director-General of WIPO in order to clarify the legal and institutional aspects involved.

---

[67] Regarding the multinational trade negotiations (MTN), see footnote 10 to document 64.

Export of Domestically Prohibited Goods

The Contracting Parties decide that contracting parties shall, to the maximum extent feasible, notify GATT of any goods produced and exported by them but banned by their national authorities for sale on their domestic markets on grounds of human health and safety. At their 1984 Session, the Contracting Parties will consider in the light of experience gained with this notification procedure, the need for study of problems relevant to the GATT in relation to exports of domestically prohibited goods and of any action that may be appropriate to deal with such problems.

Export Credits for Capital Goods

The Contracting Parties:

1. Are aware that official export credit provisions on capital goods which apply to developing countries may pose problems for the expansion of imports into these countries consistent with their trade and development needs;

2. Therefore recommend that contracting parties, members of those international arrangements concerning official export credit matters, when reviewing or revising their various international undertakings, give special attention to relevant credit provisions, including specific terms and conditions, in order to facilitate the expansion of developing countries' imports of capital goods consistent with their trade and development needs; and

3. Request the Director-General of the GATT to consult with the contracting parties concerned and report to the 39th Session.

Textiles and Clothing

The Contracting Parties decide:

1. To carry out on a priority basis a study of:

(i) the importance of textiles and clothing in world trade and particularly for the trade prospects of developing countries;

(ii) the impact on economic activity and prospects of countries participating in textiles trade, of the existing systems of restraints and restrictions relating to textiles and clothing, principally the MFA;

(iii) consequences for economic and trade prospects in these countries of a phasing out on the basis of the provisions of the General Agreement, or of the continued maintenance, of the restraints and restrictions applied under the existing textile and clothing regimes, principally the MFA; and

2. To examine expeditiously, taking into account the results of such a study, modalities of further trade liberalization in textiles and clothing including the possibilities for bringing about the full application of GATT provisions to this sector of trade.

3. This work should be completed for consideration by the Contracting Parties at their 1984 Session.

Problems of Trade in Certain Natural Resource Products

The Contracting Parties decide:

1. That problems relating to trade in the following natural resource products including in their semi-processed and processed forms, falling under the competence of the General Agreement relating to tariffs, non-tariff measures and other factors affecting trade, should be examined with a view to recommending possible solutions:

(a) Non-ferrous metals and minerals

(b) Forestry products

(c) Fish and fisheries products

2. That for this purpose the Council should decide, for each of these three items, the terms of reference, time frame and procedures.

Exchange Rate Fluctuations and Their Effect on Trade

The Contracting Parties decide:

To request the Director-General to consult the Managing Director of the International Monetary Fund on the possibility of a study of the effects of erratic fluctuations in exchange rates on international trade, to report to the Council on the results of these consultations and to forward any such study to the Council so that it may consider any implications for the General Agreement.

Dual Pricing and Rules of Origin

The Contracting Parties decide:

To request the Council to make arrangements for studies of dual-pricing practices and rules of origin; and

To consider what further action may be necessary with regard to these matters when the results of these studies are available.

Services

The Contracting Parties decide:

1. To recommend to each contracting party with an interest in services of different types to undertake, as far as it is able, national examination of the issues in this sector.

2. To invite contracting parties to exchange information on such matters among themselves, *inter alia* through international organizations such as GATT. The compilation and distribution of such information should be based on as uniform a format as possible.

3. To review the results of these examinations, along with the information and comments provided by relevant international organizations, at their 1984 Session and to consider whether any multilateral action in these matters is appropriate and desirable.

ANNEX

GATT Rules and Activities Relating to Developing Countries

The Contracting Parties:

1. Decide, in order to improve the review and surveillance procedures in regard to the implementation of Part IV, that:

(a) the Committee on Trade and Development, bearing in mind particularly the special responsibility of the developed contracting parties in this regard, shall adopt a programme of consultations with contracting parties individually or collectively, as appropriate, to examine how individual contracting parties have responded to the requirements of Part IV;

(b) each such consultation shall be based on information supplied by the contracting party or parties in question and additional factual material prepared by the secretariat;

(c) the Committee on Trade and Development shall also examine other aspects of existing procedures for reviewing the implementation of Part IV and for dealing with problems relating to the application of its provisions, and prepare guidelines for their improvement.

2. Invite the Committee on Trade and Development to review the operation of the Enabling Clause[68] as provided for in its paragraph 9, with a view to its more effective implementation, *inter alia,* with respect to objectivity and transparency of modifications to GSP schemes and the operation of consultative provisions relating to differential and more favourable treatment for developing countries;

3. Invite contracting parties to pursue action as follows towards facilitating trade of least-developed countries and reducing tariff and non-tariff obstacles to their exports:

(a) further improve GSP or m.f.n. treatment for products of particular export interest to least-developed countries, with the objective of providing fullest possible duty-free access to such products;

(b) use, upon request and where feasible, of more flexible requirements for rules of origin for products of particular export interest to least-developed countries;

(c) eliminate or reduce non-tariff measures affecting products of particular export interest to least-developed countries;

(d) facilitate the participation of least-developed countries in MTN Agreements and Arrangements;

(e) strengthen the technical assistance facilities of the GATT secretariat targeted to the special requirements of least-developed countries;

(f) strengthen trade promotion activities, through the ITC and other initiatives, such as by encouraging the establishment of import promotion offices in importing countries;

(g) give more emphasis to the discussion and examination of policy issues of interest to least-developed countries in the context of further efforts to liberalize trade.

4. Decide to strengthen the Technical Co-operation programme of the GATT with a view to facilitating the more effective participation of developing countries in the GATT trading system:

---

[68] For the text of the Enabling Clause entitled "Differential and More Favorable Treatment Reciprocity and Fuller Participation of Developing Countries," one of the agreements relating to the Framework for the Conduct of International Trade, adopted by the contracting parties to the GATT in their decision of November 28, 1979, see *GATT: Basic Instruments and Selected Documents* (BISD), 26 Supplement, p. 203.

(a) by responding to increasing requests for seminars and other technical assistance activities;

(b) by permitting increased participation in the GATT Commercial Policy Courses, and the inclusion in the training programme of a regular course in the Spanish language;

(c) by encouraging, in the context of this programmé, appropriate contributions from individual contracting parties.

5. Invite contracting parties individually to grant new voluntary contributions or provide other forms of assistance to the ITC.

C. Financial and Monetary Policy

Document 77

Address by the Under Secretary of the Treasury for Monetary Affairs (Sprinkel) Before the American Stock Exchange Conference, "U.S. Perspectives," October 20, 1982[1]

International Monetary Issues: The U.S. Approach

I would like to begin by telling you that I am honored to have been asked to speak to you this afternoon. It is a pleasure to address such a distinguished group, and to be part of such an interesting and timely program.

These are difficult times for the world economy, and this government faces a number of difficult international monetary issues. But while the exact forms in which these issues have arisen are often new, the underlying problems are familiar ones—ones the United States has coped with in the past.

To the degree that past U.S. policies were unsuccessful in resolving such issues, we hope we have learned a few lessons. To the degree we succeeded in weathering similar situations in the past, we can draw comfort. Thus, while recognizing the seriousness of the current strains on the banking system associated with the large debt burdens of sovereign borrowers, it is reassuring to remember that the international monetary system has proven flexible enough to cope with very difficult situations in the past. With a responsible approach on the part of all participants, we should be able to cope with this one as well.

The Reagan administration's market-oriented approach to international monetary issues has entailed some notable departures from previous U.S. policies, and has occasionally differed from the current policies of some of our allies. Making such a major change is difficult in many ways—it requires determination to put it into effect, credibility to make it work, and a receptive and cooperative attitude on the part of our allies to avoid misunderstandings over our methods and goals.

None of this can occur overnight. We have been working for some time to put across our point of view—our belief in limiting government interference with market decisions, and in stable and predictable economic policies. While differences remain, our approach is now better understood and more favorably received abroad. And we are confident that momentum will continue to move in our direction.

The market-oriented approach to economic issues already has a successful track record. During the first two decades after World War II, the United States was a leader in the liberalization of the international trade and payments system which underlay a dramatic world economic recovery. Our strong domestic economic performance and open capital markets made the United States a reliable world financial center, and the U.S. dollar the key international currency. By the mid-1970's, however, the United States had become a source of instability—particularly due to its deteriorating growth and inflation performance. Of course, some of this deterioration in U.S. performance came in response to the oil shocks, which we experienced in common with every other oil-importing nation. But the main cause of our disappointing record was the weakness of our domestic economic policy relative to that of other major countries.

Macroeconomic policy in the United States had turned increasingly to fine-tun-

---

[1] Source: Department of the Treasury files. The conference was held in Washington.

ing with a short-term policy horizon. In that environment, economic efficiency was put far down the list of priorities, and the ultimate results were a substantial worsening in U.S. productivity performance, and an inflationary bias in wage and price formation. The U.S. inflation rate developed a distinct upward trend, and as a result interest rates kept ratcheting upward to new historical highs.

Our current domestic economic program was designed to reverse this process. And in fact, while much remains to be done, we have had major success in our effort to put the country back on a sustainable noninflationary growth path.

Our domestic and foreign critics used to be most skeptical about our ability to get inflation and interest rates down from the stratospheric levels they had reached by the time this administration took office. I think it would be accurate to say that most financial market participants shared this skepticism to some extent, and for perfectly good reasons. Too many lenders have gotten "burned" in the past by believing government promises that inflation would be brought under control, only to see inflation and interest rates shoot up again to new highs soon afterward. This left them skeptical that inflation would ever be brought under lasting control, and unwilling to risk much on the good intentions of this, or any other, administration.

Fortunately, our good intentions have now been matched by perseverance and demonstrated performance. Consumer price inflation has been running at only a 5.1 percent annual rate so far this year, and we fully expect that we can sustain this type of performance next year as well. Short-term interest rates have come dramatically off their peaks, and long-term rates are now following them down as the longer-run inflation expectations of borrowers and lenders adjust to the reality of our commitment and our achievement.

I have no intention of ignoring the cost that has been paid for this reduction in inflation and interest rates. An unemployment rate of over 10 percent is a high price to pay no matter how you look at it—in terms of lost jobs, lost output, and hardship to families and businesses all over the country. In order to get inflation down, we had to slow the growth of the money supply. Lower money growth automatically led to weaker real economic activity during the transition from an environment of high inflation expectations and inflationary economic behavior, to one of price stability. Some temporary restriction of economic growth was inevitable, given the pervasiveness of inflation and the strength of expectations. We believe, however, that the resulting economic slowdown has been made both longer and more severe than necessary, as a result of the abruptness of the initial monetary slowdown, the volatility of money growth, and the difficulties we have had in getting a sound budget through the Congress.

Now, as we begin to count up the cost of getting inflation under control, we would do well to bear in mind why we did this. We must remember the overwhelming urgency which the American people, as well as our foreign allies, attached to getting the U.S. inflation rate down only 2 years ago. We had all seen the stagflationary consequences of the previous economic policies. The savings rate was dropping, investment was lagging, productivity growth was slowing, and the unemployment rate was trending upward. There came to be a widespread recognition of the danger chronic inflation poses to the American economy, and widespread consensus that controlling inflation would be worth the cost and should be our number one priority. The cost has been high—higher than necessary—but the benefits have also been significant and will grow over time. Having already paid the price, it would be a disgrace for us to retreat, and be forced to retake the already captured ground again in the future.

However, some observers now advocate just that—a policy of faster money growth in order to spur the economic recovery. In reply, I can only point again to the high price that has been paid to get the degree of price stability we have today. Were we to reopen the floodgates to inflation, the credibility of anti-inflation policy would be irreparably damaged and the cost of ever getting inflation under control again would make our recent experience seem pale in comparison.

As we have learned by experience, any short-term boost to real economic activity from overexpansion of the money supply would be based on speculative borrowing and lending, inflationary spending patterns, and declining investment and savings ratios. Such a stimulus could hardly be sustainable; rather, it would soon lead us right back into the stagflation trap from which the American people elected us to extricate them. Why make the same mistake all over again?

Our success in bringing inflation and interest rates down is yielding significant benefits in the international arena. The direct benefits are clear—lower dollar borrowing costs for all borrowers in international financial markets, including hard-pressed LDC borrowers, and removal of one source of upward pressure on domestic interest rates in other countries. Both are helping to strengthen world economic prospects.

Falling U.S. interest rates are yielding an important indirect benefit as well. As our interest rates have dropped in recent months, foreign interest rates have not come down nearly as much. At the same time, the U.S. dollar has remained very strong on exchange markets despite the movement of interest rate differentials against dollar assets. These events reinforce a message we have been trying to put across for some time. While high U.S. interest rates have had some negative impacts on other countries and have contributed to an already-difficult world situation, the problems of each of our economies are primarily a result of our respective domestic structural problems, economic policies, and economic performance. We regret the additional problems the transition process in the United States has caused our allies, and have been doing all we can to make our way quickly through this period of economic adjustment. But we have felt all along that each of our governments would be better served by looking for answers within, rather than outside, its own economy.

This having been said, I would like to underscore the tremendous importance we attach to effective international economic cooperation. While sound domestic policies are crucial, none of our economies can go it alone. We are very aware of the opinions and aspirations of our allies, and try to take every available opportunity to consult with them and arrive at common understandings. This obviously does not mean that we go into discussions intending to sell U.S. interests short—but that we are willing to work with our allies to find mutually acceptable solutions to our economic problems.

We carry out this commitment every day in a number of ways: through candid exchange of new ideas and points of view, through timely notifications of policy changes or upcoming economic events which impact on one another's policies, and through a thorough, quiet, and reasoned airing of any misunderstandings or differences. We are fully aware that the demands of international cooperation sometimes require a country to forego its immediate self-interest in pursuit of fundamental common goals. We are receptive to approaches which focus on lasting solutions to fundamental problems. Effective international economic cooperation should not be limited to short-run crisis management and muddling through day-to-day in a haphazard manner.

At the Versailles Summit,[2] the leaders of the Summit nations took what I hope will be a historic step in this direction, when they agreed to our proposal for an enhanced process of international economic cooperation.[3] This agreement represents a reaffirmation of the consensus achieved in 1975 at the first economic summit at Rambouillet[4]—a consensus which led directly to the Second Amendment of the IMF Articles of Agreement,[5] the legal basis for the present international monetary system.

The spirit of Rambouillet was that exchange market stability can stem only from stability in fundamental underlying economic policies and performance. Countries which have relatively weak economic policies and poor inflation performance simply cannot avoid persistent depreciation of their currencies, relative to countries with stronger economies. And as long as market participants are uncertain about the future direction of policies and performance in key countries, exchange rate volatility is likely to be a fact of life. Only when all are moving toward more stable, noninflationary economic policies can we expect more stability in exchange markets.

The IMF built on the Rambouillet consensus to develop a broad system of "sur-

---

[2] For documentation on the Versailles Economic Summit, June 4–6, 1982, see Part F.

[3] At the Versailles Economic Summit, the leaders agreed to the U.S. proposal to establish a "multilateral surveillance group," consisting of representatives of the summit nations, to help ensure that internal domestic policies were compatible with international economic growth. Meeting regularly, the "group", together with the Director of the International Monetary Fund, would review such items as budget deficits, money supply, interest rates, and general financial developments in the major industrial nations in order to encourage the convergence of national policies over a 2-to 3-year period which would enhance international currency stability and economic growth.

[4] The first economic summit was held at the Chateau de Rambouillet near Paris, France, November 15–17, 1975.

[5] For the text of the Second Amendment of the Articles of Agreement of the International Monetary Fund, which was approved by the IMF Board of Governors on April 30, 1976, and entered into force on April 1, 1978, see 29 UST 2203.

veillance" over its members' exchange rate policies and the economic policies which underlie them. To carry out this surveillance, the IMF conducts frank and confidential annual evaluations of national policies by its Executive Board and staff. While there is nothing inherent in the process which *forces* members to change their policies in response, it is generally felt that surveillance has had some impact.

The Versailles Summit cooperation agreement centers on periodic meetings of the Finance Ministers and Central Bank Governors of the five countries whose currencies make up the SDR—meetings which are aimed at achieving greater convergence in economic policies over the medium term. The first meeting among Ministers to begin implementing this agreement was held over Labor Day weekend in Toronto,[6] and we believe it was a success in the sense that all participants approached it seriously. I don't want to oversell the process—it is essentially still a consultative mechanism with a medium-term focus, and not intended to produce dramatic or immediate action. But I do expect that it will contribute to sounder and more informed economic policies in the participating countries.

I suppose if my name is associated with any issue in the international area, it is U.S. exchange market policy. At the time this administration took office, the U.S. Government was engaged in a policy of frequent large-scale intervention in exchange markets. Over the last 6 months of the previous administration the United States purchased nearly $8 billion equivalent in foreign currencies, and another $600 million was purchased in the early weeks of the Reagan administration.

At that point, we called "time out" to review our intervention policy. As a result of that review, we instituted our current policy of minimal intervention—intervening only if necessary to counter serious disorder in exchange markets. The underlying *rationale* for U.S. intervention operations remains the same as [it] had been over the entire floating exchange rate period—we stand ready to intervene in fulfillment of our commitment under Article IV of the IMF Articles of Agreement,[7] to counter disorderly market conditions. But our *implementation* of that policy has changed significantly.

This change generated controversy abroad, especially in the early stages. With their currencies weakening against the dollar, some of our economic partners asked us to reconsider and join them in large-scale intervention to support their currencies. An even more widespread argument was based on concerns about exchange rate volatility. It was suggested that a more activist U.S. approach to intervention would reduce the size and rapidity of short-term exchange rate movements.

Our response has been that we cannot ignore the lessons we drew from past intervention experience. Intervention can have an occasional role in dealing with serious episodes of market disorder. But our reading of recent history suggests that a more active intervention policy—one aimed at fixing or managing exchange rate levels—is unlikely to succeed.

We recognize there are still some differences of opinion as to the effectiveness of intervention. For that reason, we proposed at the summit that there be a thorough international study of the impacts of exchange market intervention in the past. This study is now underway, under the auspices of a group of experts from national governments. They are tasked with reviewing the evidence and collective experience on the negative and positive impacts of intervention, and producing a report for the Ministers. Their report is not intended to dictate or to prescribe what the future intervention policies of participating countries should be—rather, it is meant as an input to continuing discussion of this topic at policy level.

In the last 2 months, newspapers have been full of gloom and doom about prospects for the international banking system. A great deal has been written and said about the possibility of widespread loan defaults triggering a collapse of the banking system. There have clearly been significant strains, and there is room for concern, but I think many commentaries vastly overstate the danger. We are not in a crisis, nor do we believe a crisis is imminent. The banking system is resilient, and able to cope with such challenges.

While the Mexican situation is not yet resolved, the rapid and effective response of both private and official lenders demonstrates the capability of the financial system to deal with very difficult situations. More generally, borrowing countries are showing

---

6 The first meeting of the "multilateral surveillance group" was held in Toronto, Ontario, September 4–6, 1982.

7 Article IV of the IMF Articles of Agreement outlines "Obligations Regarding Exchange Arrangements."

a greater willingness to take adjustment measures. Assuming, as I do, that we will pass successfully through all our present difficulties, there is a valuable lesson to be learned. In order to maintain their creditworthiness, borrowers are going to have to make sure they pay greater attention to balance of payments adjustment in the future, and run more disciplined economic policies. Lenders, by exercising greater caution and prudence in their lending decisions, will help make sure they do so.

At the same time, I believe it is a positive thing that lenders have become more aware of the dangers of succumbing to the "herd instinct" which tends to cause overoptimistic lending in good times, and overly-rapid retrenchment when times are rough. Responsible self-interest suggests that lenders would do well to exercise normal prudence in their lending decisions at all times, and make sure that their rewards are an accurate reflection of the risks they take.

Somehow, early in this administration, there came to be a public belief that we "disapproved of" the International Monetary Fund. Nothing could be further from the truth. It is true that we spent considerable time and effort investigating ways in which the IMF could be more effective. But our reason for doing so stemmed from our basic conviction that it is an essential and successful component of the international monetary system.

The Fund's consultative mechanisms and surveillance activities have a major influence on the evolution and functioning of the system, and on the formation of members' economic policies. And the Fund also takes a more immediate part in the international adjustment process, by providing temporary balance of payments financing assistance conditioned on the borrowers' implementation of policies to correct their domestic and external imbalances.

In view of the large balance of payments financing needs faced by many countries, and of the many strains on the financial system, IMF resources will have to be expanded. However, an overly large quota increase would put the Fund under pressure to weaken its conditionality, and threaten to turn the IMF from a monetary institution into a development bank—and potentially into an engine of world inflation. The United States is supporting an *adequate* IMF quota increase in [the] current round of negotiations: an increase that would enable the Fund to meet the temporary balance of payments financing needs of its members under normal circumstances. We agreed in Toronto that these negotiations should be accelerated, and that we should try to reach decisions on the size and distribution of this quota increase by next spring's Interim Committee meeting.

In addition, as a complement to the quota increase, we have raised the idea of a new permanent borrowing arrangement in the IMF, designed to provide the Fund with a standby line of credit to deal with extraordinary circumstances which might seriously threaten the international monetary system. There has been some suspicion that we might be using this proposal as a diversionary tactic to delay or reduce the prospective quota increase. Because of this, I want to make very clear that this idea is for a facility which, if adopted, would be additional to and not a substitute for an adequate quota increase. Administered by the IMF, the borrowing arrangement would be available on a contingency basis and could be drawn upon by the IMF to finance access by members to Fund resources under extraordinary circumstances. The idea is being discussed further and will be considered by IMF members in the coming months, in conjunction with the quota discussions.

We also see an important continuing role for the multilateral development banks, such as the World Bank group. With some modifications in their procedures, the banks can expand their role as catalysts for the mobilization of the private sector resources which are essential to growth and development. In late February, we released a thorough report on U.S. participation in the MDB's which stressed the directions in which we think their activities should be guided. Our suggestions are aimed at enhancing both the catalytic role of the MDB's and their ability to provide sound economic policy advice.

The key elements of our proposals are straightforward. We want the MDB's to place greater emphasis on market forces—on the importance of appropriate pricing structures and incentives. We are asking the banks to make greater resort to cofinancing and other ways of stimulating increased private foreign investment in developing countries. And we will be working to ensure that scarce concessional loan funds are reserved for the poorest of the developing countries, while more creditworthy borrowers are graduated to "harder" lending.

In the meanwhile, as the MDB's are considering these and other ways of making more effective use of their resources, we will continue our own priority efforts to fulfill the previously-negotiated international understandings on funding for the MDB's.

The importance of sound economic policies to economic growth and development, and the rationale for this administration's policies toward the MDB's, are amply demonstrated in a recently-published review of foreign aid and development, written by Professor Raymond Mikesell under a contract from the Treasury and State Departments and the Agency for International Development.[8] Mikesell's review investigates major issues relating to official foreign aid policy and the effectiveness of foreign aid, and arrives at a number of specific conclusions about how best to target and use concessional aid resources.

The full text makes interesting reading, but for this purpose the recommendations could be summarized in a few sentences. First, donors should reserve and target scarce aid resources for those countries which need it the most and can use it most effectively. Second, recipients should use aid in ways that contribute to broad-based economic growth, and which complement private sector activity rather than replacing it. The aim on both sides should be to establish the preconditions for self-sustainable growth.

More broadly, the review indicates that the major lesson to be derived from existing studies of countries in the process of development is that the government policies which are most closely associated with successful development are those which allow the incentives of the free market to work, and which are conducive to the expansion of exports and to inflows of private capital. Within a sound policy environment, foreign aid can make a major contribution to economic development. There are undoubtedly cases in which aid has been of little value in promoting growth, and even cases in which it was counterproductive. But more generally there is ample evidence that aid, provided under proper conditions and used effectively, can be a powerful stimulant to development and to the establishment of the preconditions for self-sustainable growth.

Just as the current international monetary problems have a familiar ring to them, so does our policy response. Our emphasis on a coherent, predictable, market-oriented economic policy is not a new idea. Certainly we are not the first to recognize how crucial private enterprise is to economic growth and development.

What distinguishes Reagan administration policies is not their novel content, but rather the consistency and determination with which we are applying our basic economic philosophy. The resulting policies have sometimes differed considerably from those of previous administrations, and on occasion those departures have been viewed with skepticism and alarm.

This administration has worked hard since entering office, not only to put its policies in place but also to convince others of their validity. We considered it important to make clear that we expect no overnight miracles, but instead have designed our policies for consistently good economic performance over the long haul. Opinions and philosophies differ, but I hope that both our consistent and logical underlying approach, and the strengthening economic performance of the U.S. economy, are going a long way to convince the skeptical.

Document 78

Prepared Statement by the Secretary of the Treasury (Regan) Before the House Banking, Finance and Urban Affairs Committee, December 21, 1982[9]

International Debt and International Monetary Fund Resources

Mr. Chairman and members of the committee: I am pleased to meet with you today to discuss the international debt situation and current negotiations on an increase in the resources of the International Monetary Fund. The world faces extremely difficult economic and financial problems, essentially without precedent in the postwar period. Mismanagement of these problems would have serious adverse effects on the United States economy—on our recovery

---

[8] Reference is to Raymond F. Mikesell, *The Economics of Foreign Aid and Self-Sustaining Development* (Boulder, Colorado, 1983).

[9] Source: *International Financial Markets and Related Matters: Hearing Before the Committee on Banking, Finance and Urban Affairs, House of Representatives, Ninety-seventh Congress, Second Session* (Washington, 1983), pp. 23–50.

and on our ability to create needed new jobs. Orderly resolution will minimize the potential risks for our citizens. I would like to review the situation, the broad strategy for dealing with current problems and, given the critical role for the IMF in this approach, the status of international discussions on increasing IMF resources. Answers to the specific questions in your letter of invitation are appended to my statement.

International Financial Developments

The present troubled state of the world economy has its roots in emerging inflation pressures in the late 1960's, the twin oil shocks of the 1970's and policy responses that attempted to avoid adjustment to new economic realities.

The appropriate economic response to emerging problems and the oil price increases was monetary and fiscal restraint to counter inflationary pressure, and for real adjustment and resource reallocation to reflect new competitive conditions and the reduced real consumption possibilities implied by the large transfer of income and wealth to OPEC. Instead, many governments tried to maintain real incomes at levels prevailing prior to the price increases and preserve employment in uncompetitive industries by transfers. Reluctance to pay for these transfers and subsidies by increased taxation led to debt-financed increases in government outlays, with monetization of the resulting deficits producing faster monetary growth in turn. The results were higher inflation, slower real growth, and rising government sector deficits relative to GNP (primarily from enlarged transfer payments). In addition—and of central importance in today's debt situation—oil importing countries experienced unprecedented current account deficits and external borrowing requirements.

Most of the needed current account financing was provided through private markets, largely by commercial banks. Commercial banks served as the risk-taking intermediaries between OPEC and borrowing countries. The growth of lending was considerably larger, and the financing smoother, than many observers had thought possible; but the corollary has been the rapid growth of international debt.

In addition, the liquidity provided by the growth of international lending tended to postpone adjustment of domestic economies and helped maintain consumption at inflated levels. Continued borrowing and postponement of adjustment was encouraged by the belief on the part of debtors that inflation would erode their debt burden.

The increase in international lending—both private and official—was heavily concentrated on the non-OPEC developing countries. By the end of 1981, total non-OPEC LDC debt was about $500 billion—5 times the level of their debt in 1973. Net new borrowing by these countries from banks in the major industrialized countries reached a cyclical low of $11 billion in 1977, rose to $22 billion in 1978 (of which $13 billion went to Latin America) and $42 billion in 1981 (of which $33 billion went to Latin America). By June 1982, the stock of debt owed to the private Western banks by non-OPEC developing countries totaled around $265 billion, of which $168 billion was owed by countries in Latin America.

In recent months, financial markets have begun to recognize that the inflationary environment of the 1970's is changing fundamentally. Markets are beginning to believe that the world economy is in a disinflationary period that will continue for some time. Inflation expectations are undergoing dramatic change. Lenders are reevaluating loan portfolios that were established under quite different expectations about future inflation. Levels of debt previously expected to decline in real terms—and therefore to remain manageable relative to growing nominal export receipts under conditions of high inflation—are now seen to be high in real terms and large in the face of weak export prices and slow world economic growth. Interest rates—though down recently in nominal terms—are seen to be high and more burdensome in real terms because of lower expected inflation. On the other hand, the strong possibility that real interest rates will eventually be reduced is a positive factor in the outlook.

The reevaluation that is going on is an inevitable result of the collision between ongoing inflationary behavior and monetary policy that no longer provides sufficient money to finance continued high inflation. In general, national monetary authorities are demonstrating that anti-inflationary policies will not be reversed at the first signs of slow growth or higher unemployment. The world economy is in the midst of an unavoidable adjustment period which will continue until inflationary expectations abate and the public's behavior ceases to be based on the presumption that inflation will persist into the future as it has in the past.

In this atmosphere of shifting expectations, the overall tone in bank lending is cautious. The problems with major sovereign and corporate borrowers did not develop overnight. Many of them were foreseen in 1981, but did not reach the stage of individual liquidity or solvency crises until this year. Previously strong and well-known private companies in North America and Europe now require debt restructuring and rationalization. Major sovereign borrowers, beginning with Argentina, then Mexico and Brazil have faced liquidity problems and foreign exchange shortages; and a host of other countries—including Yugoslavia, Poland, Zaire, the Sudan—also have problems servicing debt. Internationally, rescheduling has become a growth industry.

Accordingly, banks are taking a harder look at lending, country exposure and transfer risk, and the strength of the other banks they deal with. They are increasing their loan loss provisions, and expect to be involved in debt restructurings with many of their sovereign borrowers.

The major international banks tend to view the basic LDC debt problem as one of liquidity rather than solvency. They see the key causes to be faulty domestic policies and the weak performance of the world economy. Most would assume there is a negligible risk of permanent default by major sovereign borrowers, and that corrective domestic policies, coupled with world economic recovery, will restore credit-worthiness of the LDC's over the longer term. The major uncertainties are in the delays in reestablishment of confidence and credit-worthiness, and questions about the adequacy and continued availability of new credits from the banking community to provide support as adjustments take place.

With the decline in inflation and interest rates, and the establishment of economic adjustment programs in key borrowing countries, the rate of increase in demand for new bank lending is not expected to be as high as in previous years. But some net new lending will be required. The essence of the problem is to assure that conditions are established that will reconcile the necessary prudence in lending with the need for continued financing while these adjustments take effect.

United States Interests

The world economy has become highly—and often uncomfortably—interdependent since World War II, with a strong growth in international trade and an extraordinary increase in international financing. International trade was the single most dynamic part of the world economy in the decade of the 1970's. Our own stake in the health of the world economy has grown rapidly as well. U.S. exports in the latter part of the decade grew twice as fast as the growth of world trade. Merchandise exports as a share of U.S. gross national product doubled between 1970 and 1979 and now account for 8 percent of U.S. GNP. By the end of the decade, exports accounted for one in three acres of U.S. agricultural production—or roughly 40 percent of our total agricultural production. One out of every eight jobs in the manufacturing sector produced for export; and nearly 20 percent of our total production of goods was exported. Imports have also risen rapidly, to the point that something like 20 percent of our consumption is supplied by imports, and imports form an integral part of the U.S. production process.

In the financial area, U.S.-owned banks account for about one-third of total international bank lending to final borrowers. International bank claims outstanding, after eliminating double counting from interbank transactions, total about $1 trillion, while U.S. banks' claims on foreign borrowers were around $349 billion as of mid-1982. Most U.S. bank lending involves customers in the developed country area, but about one-fourth goes to Latin America. These figures are indicative of the share of risk borne by U.S. banks, and are roughly proportional to the U.S. share of GNP in the OECD area.

The links between trade and banking are obvious. Moreover, U.S. banks' ability to finance domestic activity clearly benefits from a sound, profitable international lending business.

Mr. Chairman, as this discussion has indicated, the United States economy is strongly tied to developments abroad. We have very solid self-interests in assuring that the debt and financial situation is smoothly handled. In order to identify specific U.S. interests, I would like to discuss briefly a hypothetical case where the United States and major foreign governments follow a "hands-off" approach to debt problems, effectively allowing them to follow their course without official support.

From what we've seen in the last few months, private lenders have become extremely hesitant to extend new loans to LDC's saddled with sizeable debts. Private lenders are holding back until the borrowers—encouraged by the IMF—undertake new domestic policies aimed at reducing borrowing needs. For the sake of discussion, a "hands-off" attitude by the United States and others would most likely result in a cessation of new private lending to LDC's in general. What would that mean for the borrowers, for the world economy, for the United States, and for our citizens.

LDC borrowers received about $45 billion in new bank loans in 1981. We expect this year they will borrow something like $20–25 billion. Next year, if lenders pulled back sharply in the absence of any interest or action on the part of the major industrial countries, this lending could decline toward zero. Assuming that there is some new private lending next year, say $5–10 billion, LDC's would face a decline of $35–40 billion in loans over the 1981–83 period. Trade and current account deficits would have to be reduced accordingly to match the new lower level of external financing.

What would such a reduction in lending to LDC's imply for the world as a whole? First, the adjustment would come largely against industrial countries. As a consequence of unavoidable cuts in LDC imports, industrial country exports would be directly reduced by $35–40 billion. This would represent a direct loss of 0.3 to 0.5 percent of GNP in the industrial countries; secondary effects could double that loss to some 0.6 to 1.0 percent of their GNP. At the early stage of global recovery we're likely to be in next year, a drop of this magnitude from lost exports could abort the gradual rebuilding of consumer and investor confidence needed for a sustained recovery.

For the United States, the effects would be broadly similar. Growth would be about 1 percent less than we're expecting, and our trade deficit would grow very rapidly due to the loss of $12 billion or so in exports to LDC's. Lost jobs in vital export sectors would compound our recovery efforts.

The American citizen has the right to ask why he and his government need to be concerned with debt problems abroad. With high unemployment at home, why should we be assisting other countries, rather than, say, reducing taxes or increasing spending domestically? Why should he care what happens to the international financial system?

One way to look at this question is to ask what the implications are for workers in Providence, Pascoag or Woonsocket if foreign borrowers do not receive sufficient assistance to adjust in an orderly way. What if they are late in making interest payments to banks, or can't pay principal, and loans become nonperforming or are written off as a loss?

If interest payments are more than 90 days late, the banks stop accruing them on their books, they suffer reduced profits and bear the costs of continued funding of the loan. Provisions may have to be made for loss, and as loans are actually written off, the capital of the bank is reduced.

This in turn reduces the banks' capital/asset ratio, which forces banks to curtail lending to individual borrowers and lowers the overall total they can lend. The reduction in the amounts banks can lend will impact on the economy. So will the banks' reduced ability to make investments, which in everyday language includes the purchase of municipal bonds which help to finance the operations of the communities where individual Americans work and live. Reduced ability to lend could also raise interest rates.

I want to make very clear, Mr. Chairman, that we are not talking here just about the big money center banks and the multinational corportions. Well over 1,500 U.S. banks, or more than 10 percent of the total number of U.S. banks, have loaned money to Latin America alone. They range in size from over $100 billion in assets to about $100 million. Those banks are located in virtually every state, in virtually every congressional district, and in virtually every community of any size in the country. Those loans, among other things, financed exports, exports that resulted in jobs, housing, and investment being maintained or created throughout the United States.

If the foreign borrowers are not able to service those loans, not only will U.S. banks not be able to continue lending abroad, they will have to severely curtail their lending in the United States. Let me illustrate this point as graphically as I can. A sound, well-run U.S. bank of $10 billion in assets—not all that large today—might have capital of $600 million. It is required by the regulators to maintain the ratio of at least $6 in capital to every $100 in assets. What happens if 10 percent, or $60 million, of its capital is eroded through foreign loan losses? It must contract its lending by $1 billion. Now realistically, the regulators will not force it to contract immediately, but they will force it to restrict its growth until its capital can be rebuilt.

The net result in either event is $1 billion in loans that can't be made in that community—20,000 home mortgages at $50,000 each that can't be financed, or 10,000 lines of credit to local businesses at $100,000 each that can't be extended.

And of course, this reduction in lending also will have negative effects on financing of exports, imports, domestic investment, and production in individual cities and States around the United States, be it in shipping, tourist facilities, farming, or manufacturing. The impact will not only be on the banks—it will negatively affect the individual as well as the economic system as a whole. Higher unemployment and a reduction in economic activity, with all they entail for city, state and Federal budgets would be a further result. None of this is in the interest of the U.S. citizen.

The answer to the question why the United States should participate in efforts to manage and resolve current international financial problems is that our efforts are primarily in defense of the average American and his own economic interests. The purpose is to protect his job and his income. If the United States is to prosper, if unemployment is to be reduced and new jobs created, if the strength of the companies we work for and in which our pension funds and insurance companies invest is to be maintained, it is vitally important that our large and growing customers overseas should remain healthy and, when in economic difficulty, be helped to adjust and recover.

U.S. Strategy and the Role of the IMF

U.S. strategy to deal with current strains on the international financial system contains five key elements. If these operate as they should, there is no need for a potential crisis to be unmanageable. Indeed, there is good probability for a steady and sustained, albeit gradual, improvement, both in the basic, underlying situation as well as in the reestablishment of confidence.

These key elements are not new, nor are they hastily constructed palliatives. Rather, they go to the foundations of the international monetary and financial system.

First, the crux of any lasting effort to remedy the debt problems of less-developed countries must be orderly, but effective, domestic adjustment efforts by each country concerned. The necessary adjustments will vary from country to country since the causes of a country's external payments difficulties usually differ between countries. But experience shows that some combination of the following is likely to be found in a country experiencing debt problems: uncontrolled government expenditures, large fiscal deficits, inflationary money growth, inefficient state enterprises, subsidized or protected private enterprises, distorted prices, rigid exchange rates, and interest rate restrictions which discourage private savings and contribute to a misallocation of investment expenditures.

Not surprisingly, the economic adjustments necessary to restore a country's foreign borrowing capacity are also necessary to restore the conditions for stable and strong domestic economic growth. However, I do not want to underestimate the short-run economic and political difficulties of making the necessary adjustments.

The second key element is readiness to provide official financing on a transitional basis where that is needed to permit orderly adjustment to take place. The international institution best able to provide official support within the context of domestic economic adjustment is the IMF. In this connection, the IMF plays a number of key roles. The staff of the IMF works closely with member governments in order to help identify the causes of their economic problems and to identify the appropriate economic policy adjustments. The IMF also stands ready to provide temporary financial support to those countries willing and able to undertake the necessary economic policy measures to get out of their external financial problems. The IMF cannot force a member country to adopt an economic program. However, when committing its resources, the IMF has a special responsibility to assure itself that the economic adjustment program a country is following will restore domestic and external health, and that the economic adjustment program will lead to fewer restrictions on international trade and financial transactions.

Other forms of official financing can also provide increased direct assistance that can make a significant remedial contribution to troubled LDC debtors, as well as serving the commercial and financial interests of the lending country.

However, neither IMF nor other official credit, in themselves, will be sufficient to provide the required finance and liquidity to support the adjustment necessary to redress the economy of a major industrializing debtor country. Additional liquidity and trade finance must be forthcoming.

Thus, a third key element is commercial bank financing. The role of the commercial banks overshadows that of all other lenders combined. At the end of 1981, total non-OPEC LDC debt totaled about $500 billion, of which $255 billion (51 percent) was to private banks. During the first half of 1982, the proportion of debt to the commercial banking system increased further.

In the second half of 1982, U.S. regional and some foreign banks have sought to limit or reduce exposure. To the extent they are successful, they place a greater and disproportionate strain on the resources of the larger banks and official lenders that are committed to the international financial system, and on the borrowing countries, already faced with a severe adjustment burden. This increases the risk of precipitate, restrictive, and potentially politically destabilizing adjustment, rather than a more gradual, albeit still painful, process that we consider essential.

A cessation of commercial bank lending is not in the interest of the lending banks themselves. In some cases, it could push weak, but otherwise still viable, borrowers into a rescheduling. All those commercial banking institutions—large and small—that have played a part in the international lending that enabled LDC borrowers to run up debt, some of it nonproductive and non-foreign exchange earning, must be aware of the dangers should they attempt to reduce exposure during the adjustment process that is underway.

Thus continued—though reduced—flows of new financing by the banks are a necessary component of the overall financing package required to support orderly economic adjustment.

A fourth element is the official will and capacity to act in potential emergencies. As demonstrated in some recent cases, in limited instances when the stability of the system is at stake, there may be a need for immediate and sufficient *ad hoc* liquidity support which can be made available to countries while they negotiate with the IMF, formulate adjustment programs, work out orderly financing programs with their creditors, and begin the process of program implementation.

Central banks, working cooperatively among themselves and with the Bank for International Settlements, at times supplemented by U.S. Treasury resources, can provide short-term financial assistance, under appropriate conditions and with adequate assurance of repayment, until the borrower can work out an IMF adjustment program.

Let me mention the role of the Treasury's Exchange Stabilization Fund in the context of the current international economic situation. The ESF was established in 1934, to enable the Treasury to act when necessary to stabilize international exchange markets. The ESF has been used many times over the years, both to finance U.S. operations in the exchange markets and to provide short-term financing to other countries. Its provisions have been modified by the Congress from time to time to reflect the evolution of the international monetary system, including recognition of the shift to floating exchange rates and the central role of the IMF in providing official balance of payments financing.

In the present context, a need for short-term liquidity support has arisen where commercial banks have become concerned about their exposure in key borrowing countries and have acted to precipitously curtail lending. The immediate consequence is to make the borrowers' financing problems worse. For the longer-term, the economic adjustments undertaken in connection with an IMF program will strengthen the countries' ability to service debt, and such adjustment programs are a major factor in restoring banks' confidence and willingness to continue lending. But there is inevitably a lag between the time major liquidity problems arise, domestic programs are formulated, agreement is reached with the IMF, and implementation begins. It is during this period that uncertainty and risk of disruptive actions are perhaps greatest.

The ESF—in conjunction with the Federal Reserve and the monetary authorities of other major countries—is available to play a supporting role during this critical period, to help maintain stability while medium-term adjustment and financing programs are developed and put in place. These credit operations by the ESF are short-term in nature, well-secured, interest-earning and supportive of the IMF's central role, and are an entirely appropriate U.S. contribution to maintenance of international financial stability.

By their nature, these are short-term *ad hoc* solutions, but the major Central Banks and Finance Ministries must be capable of providing the necessary "bridge" finance needed in these situations. I think there is room for review of whether our data and mechanisms for identifying emerging problem cases are adequate and whether our arrangements for providing emergency financing work as smoothly as they should or could. I have raised these questions during a recent meeting of the Finance Ministers and Central Bank Governors of major countries, and we will be doing more work in this area.

The fifth key element is a set of economic policies in the major industrialized countries that will produce economic growth and a counter to the risks of inward-looking protectionism. What is currently missing in the world economy is business and consumer confidence. Investment spending is being postponed as capacity utilization remains low, and gloom and doom predictions about the global economy become commonplace. This lack of confidence spreads to consumers who, fearing the possibility of unemployment, postpone consumption in favor of rebuilding savings. At the current juncture, many economic players have adopted a "wait and see" approach—a decision which collectively can lead to an immobilized world economy.

The world economy is fundamentally poised for a sustained recovery: inflation rates in most major countries have receded; nominal interest rates have fallen sharply; inventory rundowns are largely complete. But most international observers do not foresee the source of growth that will reignite investment and consumption decisions.

Solid, observable U.S. recovery is one critical ingredient missing for world economic expansion. A second ingredient to establishing credible growth in the industrial economies is in the hands of European and Japanese policy officials. What the United States, Europe, and Japan can do to help promote credible growth in their domestic economies will be of major importance to each other and to the developing countries, whose current adjustment problems can be eased by an expansion of exports to the industrialized economies.

There are dangers in the current situation that must be borne in mind. Governments may succumb too quickly to political pressures to stimulate their economies further via excessive monetary or fiscal expansion. A major shift at this stage could place upward pressure on interest rates, discourage the downward movement in real interest rates critical to investment-led growth, and suggest a return to the stop-go policies of the seventies. If such an expansion were attempted via increased government spending, it would reverse important gains in reducing the involvement of governments in domestic economies.

In addition, rising protectionist pressures in the United States and elsewhere pose a real threat to global recovery. Signs already exist that other governments are turning to protectionist trade measures in an attempt to preserve jobs in noncompetitive industries and to reduce imports and/or increase exports; there is a real danger of spreading protectionist measures over the next year. Far too quickly, governments could react to trade measures by imposing their own restrictions, in a futile attempt to offset the efforts of other countries' trade policies.

The only solution is a strong endorsement of antiprotectionist policies. As the world's largest trader, the United States carries a major responsibility to lead the world away from a possible trade war. The clearest and strongest signal for other countries would be for the United States to renounce protectionist pressures at home and to preserve its essentially free trade policies.

The IMF's Role and Resources

The IMF was founded to promote a sound financial framework for the world economy and is at the center of international efforts to deal with current economic and financial problems. The resources of the IMF are available to provide temporary balance-of-payments financing in support of the efforts of members to implement the sound economic adjustment programs needed to restore their external positions to a sustainable basis. The economic policy conditions associated with use of IMF resources are designed to ensure that the adjustments are internationally responsible and effective and to assure repayment to the IMF over the medium term.

The IMF is a unique institution, and differs fundamentally from the multilateral development banks or other foreign aid agencies. There is no set class or group of lenders or borrowers in the IMF, no concept of "donor" or "recipient." Each member is obligated to provide its currency to the IMF to finance drawings by other countries facing balance-of-payments needs; and each country in turn has a right to draw upon the IMF in case of balance-of-payments need. The U.S. subscription to IMF resources has been used many times over the years. In turn the United States has drawn upon IMF resources frequently, most recently in 1978, for a total equivalent to about $6.5 billion, the second largest use of the entire membership.

The reemergence of large balance-of-payments financing needs and growing debt problems has led to a sharp resurgence in requests for IMF financing. Since 1980, the use of IMF credit has doubled and the amount of outstanding drawings on the IMF now totals about $18 billion. Some 33 countries, nearly a quarter of the membership, now have IMF programs in place.

Any assessment of the adequacy of IMF resources over the medium term is bound to be imprecise. The demand for IMF financing depends importantly on members' balance-of-payments financing needs, the availability of alternative sources of funds, and the willingness and ability of members to implement IMF policy conditions. Moreover, the amount of resources effectively available to the IMF to finance drawings at any time—the "liquidity" of the IMF—depends not only on the size of quotas and borrowing arrangements, but also on the composition of the IMF's currency holdings, whether the issuers of those currencies are in a strong enough position to allow their currencies to be used to provide credit to others, and the likelihood that liquid claims on the IMF will be utilized. All of these factors, and thus the ability of the IMF to meet official financing needs, are subject to rapid change.

Subject to this caveat, we estimate that the IMF at present has on the order of $33 billion in resources effectively available for lending, including $19 billion in usable currency and SDR holdings and $14 billion in existing credit lines. A portion of these funds, about $10 billion, is already committed under existing IMF programs. Thus, only about $23 billion at most is available for commitment to new programs, and even this amount is uncertain for the reasons I just mentioned. Some $14 billion is virtually certain to be committed in the near future, including commitments for major programs in Mexico, Argentina, and Brazil. Given the scope of today's financing problems, requests for IMF programs by many more countries must be anticipated over the next year, and it is quite possible that the IMF's ability to commit resources to adjustment programs could be exhausted during the course of 1983.

It is therefore clear that the IMF's liquidity position will be under serious strain in the near future. Although the IMF has sufficient resources to meet immediate cash needs, since actual drawings are phased and tied to performance under agreed programs, there is very little margin of safety. In particular, the Fund's ability to continue to commit financing, and permit its current holdings to be drawn down to low levels, depends importantly on assurances that further resources will be forthcoming soon.

The IMF must have adequate resources if it is to effectively fulfill its responsibilities for maintaining the sound financial system essential for U.S. and global economic recovery. The discussions that are currently underway have been focusing on two main elements of the IMF's resources:

—An increase in quotas, the IMF's traditional permanent resource base; and

—At U.S. initiative, establishment of a special borrowing arrangement, to be available for use by the IMF in situations posing a serious threat to the international monetary system.

The adequacy of IMF quotas is reviewed periodically in relation to the growth of international transactions, the size of payments imbalances and financing needs, and world economic prospects. The objective of such reviews is to ensure that the IMF has sufficient resources to meet the official financing needs of members in normal circumstances. The last increase in IMF quotas became effective in 1980, following several years of negotiations and legislative consideration, and raised quotas by about 50 percent to the equivalent of about $67 billion. During the present review, which began in 1981, the United States has been seeking an increase that should be sufficient to meet demands for IMF resources under normal circumstances over the next few years. Some countries have advocated very major increases—a doubling or in some cases even a tripling—which we consider excessive and unrealistic.

In addition to meeting normal requirements for official balance-of-payments financing, the IMF also serves as the financial backstop for the system. It must have, and be seen to have, the means to deal with the extraordinary financing demands that do arise from time to time. Consequently, the United States proposed earlier this year that consideration be given to creation of contingency borrowing arrangements to supplement quotas, which could be called upon by the IMF in case of need to deal with very serious balance-of-payments financing needs that threaten the stability of the system. We believe that such arrangements would have important attractions.

—Since credit lines would be established only with countries with relatively strong reserve and balance-of-payments positions, they could be expected to provide more effectively usable resources than a quota increase of comparable size. Consequently, such credit lines would be a more effective and efficient means of strengthening the IMF's ability to deal with extraordinary financial difficulties than a comparable increase in quotas.

—Second, by demonstrating that the IMF is positioned to deal with severe threats, such borrowing arrangements could provide the confidence to the private markets that is needed to ensure that capital continues to flow, thus reducing the risk that problems of one country will affect others.

—Finally, creditors under the arrangement would have an important voice in decisions on its activation and thus would be assured that the financing would be used only in cases of systemic need and in support of effective adjustment efforts by borrowing countries.

Our discussions with other countries in the past several months have indicated very considerable interest in this concept, and specifically in adapting and expanding the IMF's existing General Arrangements to Borrow for this purpose.

Where We Stand Today

The committee is well aware of the major country cases that have hit the headlines in recent months, particularly the Latin American cases of Mexico, Argentina, and Brazil and some countries in Eastern Europe. Together, the three Latin American countries have external debts outstanding totaling some $195 billion, of which about $137 billion represents debts to commercial banks in the industrial countries. The debt of these three countries alone represents some 40 percent of the total estimated for all of the developing country area. Clearly, major financing and debt servicing problems in these countries mean major potential problems for the international financial system as a whole, with adverse consequences for the United States and prospects for recovery. By the same token, progress toward resolution of problems in these three cases can provide both an example and a basis for confidence that the problems confronting the system as a whole can be managed. Let me describe briefly the recent events in each of these three countries.

Mexico was confronted with an extreme liquidity bind over the summer, and requested immediate liquidity support from the United States while it initiated discussions with other countries, with its commercial banks on a restructuring of its debts, and with the International Monetary Fund on development of a comprehensive economic adjustment program. The United States responded positively, first through activation of the existing Federal Reserve swap line with Mexico; by arranging for the advance payment, on commercial terms, for increased oil deliveries for the Strategic Petroleum Reserve; and, a few days later, by joining other industrial countries under the aegis of the Bank for International Settlements in arrangements to provide $1.85 billion in short-term credit to Mexico.

Mexico has now completed its negotiations with the IMF and has announced a series of strong adjustment measures at home. The economic adjustment program Mexico has formulated will be presented to the IMF Executive Board for formal approval on December 23. Mexico is also nearing completion of discussions with commercial banks on a program to restructure its public sector debt maturities coming due through the end of 1984, and to provide some $5 billion—tied to continued performance under its IMF program—in net new commercial bank financing in 1983.

Argentina's financing problems began to emerge around the time of the Falklands conflict, which drained the country's foreign exchange holdings and caused serious complications for domestic economic management. With the end to the Falklands conflict and steps toward normalization of its international financial relations, Argentina also initiated discussions with the commercial banks and with the IMF on an adjustment program. As in the Mexican case, both of these discussions are now nearing completion. Argentina and the IMF Management have completed negotiations on an IMF adjustment program; this will be brought to the Executive Board for action shortly. Argentina is also in the final stages of discussions with the commercial banks on a package involving debt restructuring, short-term bridge financing and provision of net new commercial bank financing totaling $1.5 billion in 1983, again dependent on compliance with the terms of the IMF program.

Finally, Brazil's difficulties in obtaining needed financing in the markets have received considerable press attention in recent days. As Brazil's liquidity problems began to emerge, the United States has extended short-term liquidity support to help provide breathing space while Brazil formulated an economic adjustment program and initiated negotiations with the IMF. It has just been announced that Brazil and the IMF have reached agreement on a program, and we expect that this will be brought to the Executive Board early next year. Brazil has also initiated discussions with the commercial banks on its financing requirements and plans for next year.

In sum, very substantial progress has been made in each of these cases in developing a cooperative and constructive approach to acute financing problems of significance to the international financial system as a whole. The countries concerned have acted responsibly and courageously to develop, with the help of the IMF, difficult but necessary economic adjustment programs. Collectively, these programs are intended to reduce these countries' current account deficits and net financing requirements from an estimated $22 billion in 1982 to $12 billion in 1983, with further reductions planned for 1984. The United States and other monetary authorities have provided short-term liquidity assistance where necessary to permit longer-range financing and adjustment programs to be worked out. The IMF has been the central actor in each case, in developing the specifics of the adjustment programs of the country concerned, and will be charged both with monitoring the implementation of those programs and providing transitional financial support as the programs take hold. And, of crucial importance, the commercial banks are demonstrating their preparedness to provide continued new financing as these countries work to reduce their deficits and external financing requirements in a deliberate, nondisruptive way.

The demands that are being placed on the IMF's financial resources by these and other countries are unprecedented. It is critically important that we move promptly toward agreement on an expansion of the IMF's resources, so that it can make commitments during the course of the next year in the firm knowledge that its resources will be increased in the reasonably near future.

The negotiations—negotiations, I might add, involving some 146 member countries—are proceeding reasonably well. Although there are still differences of view, substantial in some cases, the parameters of the negotiation have become fairly clear: the bulk of IMF member countries now appear to support a quota increase in the range of 40 to 60 percent, to a new level of SDR 85 to SDR 100 billion, and an expansion of the General Arrangements to Borrow to a total in the range of SDR 15 to 20 billion. In dollar terms, these ranges amount to about $93–110 billion for total new quotas and about $17–22 billion for the expanded GAB. The exact size of these arrangements, and the shares of U.S. participation in each, remain to be negotiated. Whatever the amounts finally agreed, it is important to emphasize that U.S. participation will not affect net U.S. budget outlays or the Federal deficit.

Detailed discussions on these and related questions are being held in the IMF Executive Board this week. We are hopeful that on the basis of these discussions and consultations with other countries, it will be possible to aim for completion of the negotiations early next year, after which we would promptly submit specific legislative proposals for your consideration.

Conclusion

In conclusion, Mr. Chairman, the world is faced with extraordinarily difficult but manageable international financial problems. But they will not manage themselves. It is crucially important to U.S. economic interests—to U.S. economic activity, jobs, production, and investment—that those problems be dealt with in a constructive and orderly way, and the United States cannot escape playing a leading role in that effort. An effective strategy is in place, and welcome progress is being made. The strategy will not succeed unattended. The IMF is a central element of the solution, and it is essential that we and others act to assure that it has adequate resources to perform that central role.

I appreciate this opportunity to consult with your Committee as we conduct the negotiations on IMF resources, and hope that we will be able to have specific legislative proposals for your consideration shortly. This Committee will, of course, have a decisive role in the disposition of this legislation, and I urge your strong support now for our negotiating approach and later for the legislation we will submit to you.

D. Energy Policy

Document 79

Statement by the Assistant Secretary of State for Economic and Business Affairs (Hormats) Before a Subcommittee of the Senate Energy and Natural Resources Committee, March 25, 1982[1]

The Strategic Petroleum Reserve

Mr. Chairman,[2] it has been only 10 months since I last appeared before this subcommittee and appealed for continued support of the strategic petroleum reserve, which I believe—and I think we both share this view—to be fundamental to the energy security of the United States.

In the following months, under your leadership, Congress worked with the administration to establish a new mechanism for funding accelerated SPR oil acquisitions. Purchases have proceeded at a record pace. We have added about 110 million barrels to the reserve in this short period of time.

During the same period the world oil market has softened, bringing with it a risk of complacency and leading some to conclude that the two oil crises of the 1970's cannot be repeated. However, the lesson of the 1970's is that supply interruptions can occur with great suddenness and that a tranquil market one day can be highly disrupted the next.

We cannot assume that a supply crisis will not recur, because if our assumption is wrong and we are ill-prepared, our economy and the world economy will suffer severe harm.

And so my primary message remains today the same as it was 10 months ago: That it is essential that we take advantage of the continuing surplus in oil supplies being offered for sale to fill the SPR as fast as permanent storage becomes available. In this respect, I agree with you, Mr. Chairman and Senator Melcher, that this is a particularly auspicious time for buying because of the weakness in the market.

Let me now address more broadly our international energy policy. A central theme of that policy is the need to reduce the extent to which an interruption of energy imports, particularly oil, could threaten the security and the welfare of the American people. At the same time international energy policy formulation must take into consideration a variety of external problems and interests.

I would offer two quick examples. First, U.S. national security is intertwined with the security of our allies in Western Europe and the Pacific Basin. This is also true of our energy security. To the extent that our allies face harm from an oil supply disruption, they may find themselves compelled to take such actions as engaging in a rush to acquire scarce oil supplies where only the oil exporters would be the winners. And some may be under heavy pressure to make political deals to secure needed energy supplies, thus weakening our diplomatic efforts.

Second, if the basis of cooperation is laid ahead of time, assistance from these countries might enable the United States to cope with an oil supply crisis more effectively than would be possible relying solely on domestic resources.

It was consideration of factors such as these that led the United States to become a signatory to the agreement on an International Energy Program[3] and to make participation in the International Energy Agency a central element of U.S. International Energy Policy.

As you know, Mr. Chairman, the IEA is unique in providing a forum for consultations on energy matters with most of Western Europe, Canada, Japan, Australia, and New Zealand. These consultations focus on assuring that the efforts of individual members to reduce the threat of oil trade disrup-

---

[1] Source: *Current Condition of the Strategic Petroleum Reserve: Hearings Before the Subcommittee On Energy and Mineral Resources of the Committee on Energy and Natural Resources, United States Senate, Ninety-seventh Congress, Second Session* (Washington, 1982), pp. 188–192.

[2] Senator John W. Warner.

[3] For the text of the Agreement on an International Energy Program, signed at Paris, November 18, 1974, and entered into force definitively, January 19, 1976, see 27 UST 1685. This agreement was signed by Austria, Belgium, Canada, Denmark, the Federal Republic of Germany, Ireland, Italy, Japan, Luxembourg, the Netherlands, Spain, Sweden, Switzerland, Turkey, Great Britain, and the United States. Article I of this Agreement states that the participating countries shall implement the International Energy Program through the International Energy Agency created by this Agreement.

tions are mutually reinforcing and that we can collectively avoid oil being used as an instrument of political pressure.

The bond which holds the IEA together is the mutual commitment contained in the IEP that member countries will work in concert in responding to oil supply crises. The IEP established an organizational framework for such responses. Our strategic petroleum reserve has a very important role to play within this framework of cooperation with our IEA partners.

The major policy problem in an oil supply crisis is how to balance demand for oil with available supplies. Solutions can and will vary from economy to economy. Each national government will insist on resolving through its own political processes the problem of apportioning the burdens of this adjustment process among its own citizens.

The IEP recognizes this fact of international life. In defining the obligations of its members, it does not speak of the specific measures they must adopt to correct internal oil supply disequilibria. Rather it seeks only to develop the general principle that its members have an obligation to one another, as interdependent members of a closely-knit international economic community, to prepare for oil supply crises in a way that will permit them to avoid as much as possible making unfair demands on their neighbors in a crisis and to be of some assistance to those neighbors should one or more of them, through no fault of their own, be stricken more severely by the crisis than the rest of the group.

As you know, Mr. Chairman, the IEP treats the second part of this obligation by outlining in substantial detail the structure and operating procedures of an emergency international oil sharing system designed to assure that no member country is subjected to disproportionate hardship by an oil crisis.

By contrast, the IEP treats the first part of the IEA membership obligation in a much more summary way, its only specific requirement being that each country maintain a minimum level of reserve oil stocks to be available for drawdown in a crisis. Each government is left to flesh out the details of its domestic preparedness strategy consistent with its own political requirements.

For purposes of this hearing, our primary concern is with the IEA oil stockpiling requirement. The IEP provides that "each member country shall maintain reserves sufficient to sustain consumption for at least 90 days with no net oil imports."

These reserves may be held by whatever entity or entities, public or private, the individual government chooses, and may include crude oil and petroleum products in whatever proportions the government deems appropriate. Should the IEA emergency system be activated member countries would be expected to begin to release for domestic consumption those stocks held under the 90-day requirement.

The IEP imposes no requirement for export of national stocks under any circumstances, nor does it impose any obligations on the use of any national stocks held in excess of the 90-day requirement.

The U.S. Government attaches great importance to the IEA oil stockpiling requirement. Even with the best of intentions and the most elaborate of international sharing systems, we and our allies will not be able to support one another or take steps to maintain order in the international oil market if we are caught without adequate reserves in a major supply interruption, and price increases and other forms of demand inhibition have to bear the entire burden of restoring balance between oil demand and supply.

By contrast, if IEA countries, together, maintain a sufficiently high level of reserve stocks, the immediate threat which a supply disruption could pose to member-country security and to market stability would diminish significantly.

We, therefore, monitor very closely the stock levels, not only of the United States, but also of our IEA partners. The IEA Secretariat distributes monthly reports on this subject, and stock levels are discussed regularly in meetings of the IEA Governing Board and its working groups.

In general we are pleased with IEA stockpiling efforts. With the exception of two or three of the poorer members, all IEA countries hold stocks at or above the required minimum. As a group, IEA countries, at the end of 1981, held stocks equivalent to 169 days of 1981 imports; 8 of the 19 member countries, who are net importers of oil, held in excess of 150 days of stocks. Taking into account both the SPR and privately held stocks, the United States was one of the IEA leaders, with 246 days of 1981 imports.

In addition, our IEA partners have agreed to begin to raise the minimum stock requirement. At the IEA Governing Board meeting last December, we reached an informal consensus to try not to let national stocks fall below the equivalent of 90 days of 1980, instead of "preceding year," net imports, except where oil consumption has declined because of clearly established long-term structural changes.

This should lead to stock levels higher than those which would exist if the preceding year formula were retained because consumption has fallen in most countries since 1980.

The European Community countries have followed up on that decision by revising the Community stocking requirement to 90 days of 1980 consumption. At a time when recession and unrealistically high oil prices have reduced oil consumption and imports to a level below recent long-term trends, we regard these steps as a reassuring sign of the strength of our IEA partners' commitment to maintaining high levels of oil stocks.

I would also make special note of the stockpiling efforts of Germany and Japan. Germany, with its heavy oil import dependence, has had an oil stockpiling program since 1965. Today stocks held by the German Government, by a special quasi-public corporation and by private companies amount to about 150 days of 1981 imports.

Japan, also heavily reliant on oil imports, while slower in establishing a substantial stockpiling program, has now raised its stocks above the 90-day minimum and has begun development of a Government-owned strategic stockpile. This reserve currently holds over 65 million barrels of oil or about 17 days of Japanese imports.

Plans call for its expansion to about 190 million barrels by 1988. We welcome these efforts, although we are urging Japan to consider measures for accelerating its reserve accumultaion rates.

At the same time, we believe that there is room for improvement in the IEA oil stockpiling effort. Here, we believe the performance of the United States in the creation of the strategic petroleum reserve sets a good example. As Bill Vaughan described for you in some detail last week,[4] the United States has taken advantage of recent slack market conditions to expand rapidly the SPR.

It has been suggested that U.S. stock statistics overstate the U.S. reserve position by failing to identify clearly the sizable volume of oil reserves which are required to allow the U.S. refining and transportation system to operate smoothly and which, therefore, are not actually available for use in a crisis.

It is certainly true that a substantial portion of private stocks are available for emergency use, but no one is certain precisely how much. The benefit of SPR oil is that it is unambiguously available for crisis use. It now amounts to more than 40 days of 1980 oil imports.

We will continue to press our IEA partners to redouble their stockpiling efforts. As we have pointed out repeatedly to them, both bilaterally and in the IEA, the rationale for a 750-million-barrel SPR in the United States also argues for them to maintain stockpiles in excess of the 90-day level.

With economic downturn and budget deficits now a common phenomenon among IEA countries, their response thus far has been somewhat reserved. We are hopeful that the recent drop in crude oil prices will give new impetus to IEA oil stockpiling efforts.

In sum, Mr. Chairman, the SPR is essential to our own energy security and we must continue to fill the reserve as fast as permanent storage becomes available. That is fundamentally in our national interest. Beyond that, there is general agreement in the IEA that oil stockpiling is basic to our cooperative strategy for responding to oil crises. We are confident that, as we continue to fill the SPR, more and more of our IEA partners will also find means to expand their participation in stockpiling efforts.

I thank you, Mr. Chairman. I would be delighted to answer any questions.

. . . .

---

[4] For the text of the testimony by William A. Vaughan, Assistant Secretary for Environmental Protection, Safety and Emergency Preparedness, Department of Energy, before this subcommittee on March 16, 1982, see *Current Condition of the Strategic Petroleum Reserve*, pp. 1–34.

Document 80

Address by the Deputy Assistant Secretary of State for International Energy Policy, Bureau of Economic and Business Affairs (Wendt), Before the Oxford Energy Seminar, Oxford, United Kingdom, September 9, 1982[5]

U.S. Energy Strategies

Almost 2 years after the election of President Reagan, I think most observers are aware that the United States has adopted a more market-oriented approach to energy policy. Even now, however, I fear there is inadequate appreciation of the degree of our commitment to reducing U.S. Government involvement in energy decisionmaking. Our program is comprehensive. We have joined the community of countries who have decontrolled oil prices; we have foresworn imposition of domestic allocation and price controls in future supply crises; and we have scaled down spending on synfuels development. Decontrol of natural gas prices remains a high priority.

Let me make clear, however, that we recognize the need for some exceptions to this "hands-off" approach. Energy supply today is too important to the security of a nation and the welfare of its populace to be left exclusively to the marketplace. Government must assume at least partial responsibility for stockpiling emergency oil supplies. Pipelines—oil, natural gas, and coal—require some regulation. Long-term research and development in nuclear energy and synthetic fuels merit some support. We must take steps to protect our citizens from the external diseconomies—harm to the environment, health and safety hazards—of energy production and use.

That being said, I would suggest that we, government officials and analysts alike, have in recent years carried the conviction that "the government must do something" rather farther than is justified.

In our view, it is time to refocus world attention on the ability of market forces to locate supplies of energy and deliver them to consumers. We can take our lead from the operation of the international oil market in the past few years. In 1975, fresh from the oil market disruption of 1973–74, the subject of commodity producer cartels was a topical item for debate among energy and economic analysts. Many observers were convinced that conditions existed in the international oil market—highly inelastic demand, producers able and willing to coordinate their actions and to sacrifice short-term in favor of long-term profits—which obstructed normal market forces and permitted the operation of an international producer cartel.

Recent events have demonstrated the limitations of this notion. Perhaps the oil market is not so different from others after all. In particular, we see that there are definite limits to the range of prices over which demand and supply remain highly inelastic. The members of OPEC, encouraged by their earlier successes, overplayed their hand in 1978–79. Consumers decided that, with oil at $35 a barrel and OPEC threatening further price increases, it was worth the expense to insulate their houses, buy more gasoline-efficient automobiles, convert their machinery to coal or natural gas, and develop their own oil resources. Demand for oil has plummeted, and there is evidence that this trend continues. Demand for OPEC oil has dropped by more than one-third. All of a sudden, we have a buyer's market for oil again, and prospects are for continuing decline in the real price of oil for some time to come.

I draw one major conclusion from this series of events. It is in the interest of all of us, producers and consumers alike, to show greater respect for the strength of traditional market forces. Price increases provoke decreases in demand and increases in supply in the oil market as in any other; they are just a little slow in coming.

We in the consuming countries have sustained some investment losses over the past year as oil price projections have been revised steadily downward. Boom in oil exploration and drilling has turned to bust. One after another of our synthetic fuel development projects has shut down. I suspect we will not be so quick in the future to act on predictions based on extrapolations from oil price increases.

The plight of most oil-producing countries, however, is even worse. Ambitious development plans are being scaled down. Country balance-of-payments difficulties are growing. The members of OPEC are bickering and underselling one another. Perhaps they will find it in their interest to exercise a little more restraint in seeking to push up prices the next time the oil market tightens.

[5] Source: *Current Policy* No. 423, September 9, 1982, Bureau of Public Affairs, Department of State.

Having affirmed my confidence in the role of market forces in the oil market, I would also explore briefly the costs of government intervention in that market. The United States, like many other consuming countries, controlled the price and the domestic allocation of oil throughout most of the past decade. There is general agreement that this program, however well-intentioned, was a failure. In part, the failure of allocation may have been due to problems peculiar to the United States. I have in mind particularly the size and complexity of the U.S. oil market. Given the enormous number of players in this market, attempting to allocate oil among them equitably through administrative fiat over an extended period of time became a bureaucratic nightmare. Were the U.S. economy no larger than the economies of some of its neighbors, the inefficiency of this process might not have been so serious. Certainly the experience of some of the smaller oil-importing countries with allocation has not been so disappointing as ours.

Price control, on the other hand, is likely to prove pernicious under almost any circumstances. Simple economics suggest that, provided there is any competition at all in the supply of oil, placing a ceiling on the price at which it will be sold institutionalizes disequilibrium between demand and supply. Controls inevitably generate all kinds of efforts at circumvention which in turn lead to additional controls. Countries that prevent full pass-through to the consumer of the cost of imported oil see those oil imports diverted to other, more remunerative markets. Countries with domestic production can obtain short-term benefit by isolating themselves from the international economy and imposing controls only on domestic production. In the longer term, however, they must accept that investment in exploration and development will shift to projects in other countries where there are no such limits on profits and that their valuable domestic production will stagnate.

Domestic allocation and price controls do not serve our longer term domestic and national security interests. Neither, I submit, does intervention in international oil trade. The comments I have heard from consuming country government officials show little sign of conviction that government-to-government oil purchase contracts or efforts to influence foreign company oil allocation during oil supply interruptions have significantly enhanced these countries' energy security.

I have tried to explain the reasons why the Reagan Administration is predisposed against intervention in the energy market place. I do not wish, however, to leave the impression that we will refuse to act under all circumstances. Rather, we expect advocates of government action to demonstrate convincingly that the benefits of such action outweigh the inevitable costs.

I noted at the beginning of my remarks a few examples of government action we consider justified. I would now like to explore in greater detail one of those areas in which I am involved at the Department of State. This is the area of energy security, particularly its international aspects.

In today's interdependent world, virtually all countries rely to an increasing extent on foreign sources not only for food and raw materials but also in many instances for energy. Reliance on foreign sources offers welfare gains but also increases the importing country's sense of vulnerability. Where the commodity in question is one so fundamental to economic activity as energy, every government has taken steps to reduce that vulnerability, although sometimes only after a dramatic and painful demonstration of the extent of that vulnerability.

The U.S. Government is no exception. We define energy security in terms of reducing vulnerability to oil import interruptions, although concern about the potential for interruptions in the supply of natural gas, not only to the United States but to our allies, is spreading.

What is the Reagan Administration's energy security program? I would identify five interrelated elements.

First, I state it once more, we will rely to the maximum extent possible on market forces to solve problems. In a country of 225 million people, centralization of economic decisionmaking is bound to create inefficiencies and inequities. One of President Reagan's first acts in office was to eliminate oil allocation and price controls in the United States. Although the operation of market forces in the natural gas market is constrained somewhat by infrastructure rigidities, I would expect the administration to press vigorously next year for accelerated decontrol of natural gas prices. Permitting producers and consumers to exercise their own ingenuity and market preferences in responding to supply interruptions may seem painful in the short term, but we believe it will substantially reduce medium and longer term damage to economic welfare.

The second element of our energy security program is oil stockpiling. For military, political, and economic reasons, we cannot afford to "run out" of this indispensable commodity, no matter how remote the possibility may seem. Ideally, oil consumers would stockpile oil products for themselves. But we recognize the limits of such behavior and the advantages of some centralized stockpiling. So, just as we stockpile other essential commodities for use in emergencies, we have created a federally funded Strategic Petroleum Reserve (SPR).

The administration is filling this reserve rapidly and it has just reached 270 million barrels, triple the level of 2 years ago. This quantity represents almost 20 percent of total primary oil stocks in the United States and almost 70 days of current U.S. oil imports. Current plans call for filling the reserve to 750 million barrels—roughly 190 days of current imports—by 1990. The cost of this stockpiling program is obviously enormous. But we think the potential benefits—reducing harmful effects of future oil supply interruptions—are substantially larger.

The third element of our energy security program is cooperation with other energy-importing countries. We attach importance to this cooperation for two reasons. First, we recognize that the actions of other consuming countries in a supply crisis will affect us. Second, we recognize that energy security is related to military security, and that, to be reliable, the mutual security guarantees we have exchanged with other countries must include an energy component.

The focus of this effort is, of course, the 21-member International Energy Agency (IEA) and, in particular, its oil crisis response system. This system provides for a variety of actions in response to serious oil supply interruptions. One is drawdown of reserve oil stocks—in anticipation of which the system requires member countries to stockpile oil equivalent to 90 days of imports. Another is the oil allocation scheme, which seeks to assure that no member country suffers disproportionately from a shortfall in oil supplies. To the extent that a member country finds itself unable to obtain a fair share of oil supplies during a supply interruption, the other members of the IEA are committed to make oil available to that country so as to rectify the imbalance.

In our view, the oil stockpiling and stock drawdown requirements are the most important components of the emergency system. We will only succeed in avoiding the harmful effects of an oil supply crisis if we have alternative supplies of oil to draw on. We believe it important to cooperate with other consuming countries in the accumulation and drawdown of oil stockpiles. The IEA provides a forum for such cooperation. We would like to see our allies join us in accumulating stockpiles substantially above the 90-day level. I note with satisfaction movement in this direction on the part of a number of our IEA partners.

Most IEA members believe that the IEA oil allocation system, if ever activated, would be cumbersome to operate. We would, therefore, expect the IEA to seek to rely in the first instance on market forces, supplemented perhaps by more informal government actions, to allocate oil in supply crises, and to activate the formal system only if such efforts fail. At the same time, the United States remains fully committed to the IEA emergency system, including its allocation components. Cooperation with our IEA partners will be important in mitigating damage from oil supply crises, and the IEA allocation system provides the guarantee of mutual assistance upon which such cooperation must be based.

While I am on the subject of international cooperation, I should say a word about U.S. policy concerning the Soviet natural gas pipeline, to which our opposition is well known. The press has carried detailed reports on recent developments, and you all know the background. I will simply note that, from the energy policy standpoint, which is what interests us here, we believe development of the indigenous energy resources of the OECD community of nations offers the best prospect for assuring security of supply.

This leads me to the fourth major element of the U.S. energy security program, which I will call the long-term element. Here I have in mind efforts to reduce dependence upon imports of energy from insecure sources and thus vulnerability to any individual interruptions. Obviously, where such longer term efforts are required, we can rely on the free market to take most of the initiative. However, there are cases where the market response to improving economic incentives for production and conservation has not been as dynamic as it might have been.

The U.S. Government can be of some assistance in promoting development and use of new energy sources. For example, we are participating actively in the IEA's so-called long-term cooperation program.

Under this program, we exchange information with our partner governments concerning long-term energy policy options and development activities, including research and development. In addition, we are looking at ways the U.S. Government can encourage development of neglected energy resources in developing countries. We believe commercial interests will develop larger energy resources without official encouragement other than a receptive investment climate. But smaller projects that could contribute significantly to satisfying developing country internal requirements are less likely to attract foreign private investment. We, therefore, are supporting through our bilateral assistance program projects designed: (1) to improve energy planning and management, particularly in public utilities, (2) to adapt and develop alternate energy technologies, and (3) to encourage the development of traditional fuels, most notably fuelwood. Bilateral funding for these programs totaled well over $100 million in 1982 and should continue at similar levels in 1983.

We also support the efforts of the multinational development banks, most notably the World Bank. In 1978 World Bank energy lending constituted 15 percent of its total lending or slightly over $1 billion. By 1982 that proportion increased to 25 percent and totaled over $3 billion. We are encouraging the Bank to concentrate its special talents in areas that offer the greatest promise of success: where coparticipation will give Bank involvement an important multiplier effect; in strengthening management skills of recipient governments; and in pre-exploration projects that assist countries to inventory their resources and collect data.

With respect to alternative fuels, we are seeking to correct the longstanding patterns of neglect of coal. Abundant supplies of coal are available from a number of secure sources. By sponsoring coal conferences, coal delegations to foreign countries, discussions and studies of coal in the IEA, and other similar activities, the U.S. Government has reinforced the efforts of private companies to demonstrate to energy users that coal is indeed a viable, attractive fuel. We are also continuing to contribute in a variety of ways to the development of other alternative energies—for example, synthetics and nuclear—where uncertainty or cost may slow development by the private sector. The U.S. administration is contributing funding to projects with long-term payoffs, leaving short-term payoff investments to the private sector.

The fifth and final element of our energy security program is the pursuit of an international environment conducive to stability of world oil trade—as well as to other trade and to economic development in general. I have in mind primarily our efforts to promote peace in the Middle East. It is one of the world's great tragedies that the enormous human and natural resources of this region continue to be dissipated in internecine struggle. As President Reagan has made clear, he considers resolution of these conflicts, to the extent the United States can contribute to their resolution, one of his premier foreign policy objectives. Success in this effort, perhaps more than any other action, will strengthen the energy security of the entire world.

I conclude my remarks with a glance at the future. Whether the various players like it or not, longer term market forces have begun to assert themselves, and will influence heavily energy market developments over the next several years. The trend toward conservation and increased energy efficiency in response to the 1978–79 price increases still has some distance to run, assuring softness in energy demand for some time. Growing fuel substitution capability has produced an increase in the short-term elasticity of demand for any individual fuel. Development of oil deposits in non-OPEC countries has increased supply-side competition in world oil trade. Economic development projects in many oil-producing countries have absorbed the bulk of their oil revenue and reduced their room for maneuver in attempting to control supply and price in world oil trade.

I see no reason why producers and consumers alike should not welcome this assertion of market forces. It should bring greater stability and transparency to the international oil market, thus benefiting all of us with large investments riding on the accuracy of oil market projections. A vigorous, well-functioning market should assure adequate supplies at prices fair to consumers and remunerative to producers.

With this future in prospect, I would urge that government policymakers consider returning energy policy to its rightful place—as a subset of economic policy. The emergence of energy policy as an independent discipline has had the positive effect of focusing attention on the importance of energy to economic life and on the consequent need for attention to energy problems. But it has also given rise to excesses. Traditional economic forces are not the only ones affecting the world energy outlook, but increasingly they are the most important ones. Let us mold our energy policies accordingly.

Document 81

Message From President Reagan to the Congress, December 1, 1982[6]

Strategic Petroleum Reserve

This is to advise the Congress that pursuant to Section 160(c)(1)(B) of the Energy Policy and Conservation Act (Public Law 94–163)[7] as amended by Section 4(a) of the Energy Emergency Preparedness Act of 1982 (Public Law 97–229),[8] I find it would not be in the national interest to fill the Strategic Petroleum Reserve at the rate of 300,000 barrels per day during Fiscal Year 1983.

When my administration took office 22 months ago, one of my first actions was to direct a rapid acceleration of the pace of oil acquisition for the Strategic Petroleum Reserve. As a result, the fill rate during Fiscal Year 1981 averaged over 290 thousand barrels per day. The fill rate for Fiscal Year 1982 averaged 215 thousand barrels per day. This contrasts sharply with the average fill rate of less than 77 thousand barrels per day achieved during the four years of the prior administration. Of the 288 million barrels now in the Strategic Petroleum Reserve, 178 million barrels, or 61 percent, were added during my administration.

This administration has also entered into long-term purchase commitments that will give greater assurance of maintaining our fill rate objectives over the coming year while lowering the cost of building the reserve.

Another major policy action instituted at the start of this administration—immediate decontrol of the domestic oil market—has also contributed greatly to our energy security by reducing oil imports and stimulating domestic production. In the 22 months of my administration, oil imports have declined dramatically. Our dependence on imports from OPEC sources is now only 51 percent of the 1980 level.

As a result of rapidly implementing these policy actions to enhance our energy security, the oil on hand today in the Strategic Petroleum Reserve would provide 130 days of complete replacement for OPEC imports in the event of an embargo. That is nearly six times the level of protection our nation averaged in 1980.

The commitment of this administration to building and maintaining an adequate Strategic Petroleum Reserve is clearly demonstrated by the record of accomplishment. But we are equally committed to carrying out this program in the most efficient, cost-effective manner. The fill rate at which we plan to operate during 1983 reflects a careful balance between these two objectives. To operate at the 300,000 barrel per day rate would require extensive use of temporary storage facilities, which would significantly increase the cost of the program for very limited incremental benefit.

I must also note that increasing our fill rate objective to 300,000 barrels per day in Fiscal Year 1983 would force additional expenditures of over $1 billion. In the current economic climate, I believe that this additional expenditure would be harmful to growth and job creation because of the increased Treasury borrowing it would necessitate. Compliance with the increased fill rate would thus be inappropriate due to economic conditions affecting the general welfare.

---

[6] Source: *Weekly Compilation of Presidential Documents,* December 13, 1982, pp. 1554–1555.

[7] Enacted December 22, 1975; for text, see 89 Stat. 871.

[8] Enacted August 3, 1982; for text, see 96 Stat. 248.

E. Foreign Assistance and Third World Issues

Document 82

Address by the Deputy Secretary of the Treasury (McNamar) Before the World Bank Group Conference, January 7, 1982[1]

The Role of the World Bank Group in Third World Development

Thank you for the opportunity to participate in this conference on the future role of the World Bank Group.

The World Bank Group is an integral component in the Reagan administration's overall approach to international economic development. However, the Bank will be severely tested in the near future to adapt its operations to the new economic realities both in capital markets and its Part One countries.[2]

The Bank has already demonstrated its flexibility in adapting its program to different recipient needs from 1946 until today.

During the 1945–1960 period, the Bank's efforts were focused on post-war reconstruction, with development emphasis picking up sharply later in the period.

1960–1970 saw the emergence of the "Third World" and the Bank's efforts were exclusively in developing countries and largely in infrastructure projects; IDA was founded during this period.

Despite major international economic disruptions, the period 1970–1980 saw a growth and reorientation of multilateral aid toward aiding the rural poor; the 1974 and 1979 oil-shocks moved the private banking sector into a major role as the providers of developing country external finance, while official finance became increasingly constrained toward the end of this period.

As for the 1980's, where do we go from here? I would like to share some of our thoughts with you today.

From an economic perspective there are some important facts that influence the United States view of the economic development process:

For oil importing developing countries domestic capital still provides the bedrock for most economic growth: foreign capital finances only one-seventh of their total investment;

Official development aid provides only about four percent of all external capital flows of non-oil developing countries;

Gross exports are the largest source of external capital providing about 83 percent of the total.

These figures show that to focus solely on official development aid, as occurs in many discussions of development, is analytically inadequate.

Aid is important for many of the poorest countries with limited exports and little access to funds on commercial terms. However, resisting protectionism and ensuring access to markets is of far more importance for the developing countries as a group. These issues should receive much more prominence in the consideration of economic development.

In external capital flows, the United States is an important partner in the developing countries' economic growth process. On the export side:

The United States is the largest market for LDC exports. In 1979, for example, the United States obtained a larger share (23 percent) of its imports from non-oil developing countries than any other industrialized country.

The U.S. market buys over 50 percent of all non-OPEC developing country exports of manufactured goods to developed countries.

---

[1] Source: Department of the Treasury files; printed also in *The Future Role of the World Bank*, edited by Edward R. Fried, and Henry D. Owen, The Brookings Institution (Washington, 1982), pp. 38–46. The World Bank Group, sponsored by the Brookings Institution, Washington, consists of the International Bank for Reconstruction and Development (World Bank), the International Development Association, and the International Finance Corporation, international institutions which provide financial and technical assistance to developing countries.

[2] Reference is to donor countries of the IDA. Part One members pay all subscriptions and supplementary resources provided to the IDA in convertible currencies which may be freely used by the IDA in its operations. The Part One countries are listed in the annual reports of the World Bank.

To put the importance of the U.S. market in perspective, all developing countries' earnings from exports to the United States are double the amount of foreign aid from the industrialized countries.

A strong U.S. economy means growing export markets for LDC's. Therefore, the greatest contribution the United States can make to developing countries is to have sustained noninflationary growth in its own economy.

With respect to financial flows:

U.S. banks are important intermediaries for financial resources, with approximately 40 percent of developing country loans from commercial banks being owed to U.S. banks or their branches and affiliates.

Another way noninflationary growth in the United States helps the developing world is in its impact on interest rates and debt service. Because much of the debt owed by developing countries is at floating rates, each one percentage point decline in interest rates will result in about a $1 billion reduction in developing country debt service.

—The immediate benefits of a 6 point drop in interest rates would be virtually equal to U.S. ODA.

—In fact, the fall in LIBOR to date from last spring's high rate of around 19–1/2 percent has eased developing country debt service by $5 billion—or approximately two-thirds of recent U.S. ODA.

Finally, the United States remains the largest contributor of official development assistance.

Funds derived from export earnings and from reduced debt service help to avoid what can be called the development dilemma—the existing paradox in aid programs.

Increased aid increases developed country budget deficits at a time when their deficits are already considered to be too large. Similarly, measures to increase liquidity such as SDR allocations increase international liquidity at a time liquidity is already excessive. The tendency has been to monetize these larger deficits, which along with this increased SDR liquidity, increases inflation and therefore interest rates. The higher interest rates increase the debt service burden on the LDC's and so on.

The result is to worsen conditions in developing country export markets. In effect, at some point the short-term "fix" may be self-defeating in the long run.

Of course, the contribution of sustained noninflationary growth in the United States also allows us to provide security assistance and a military umbrella ensuring the peace and stability which is a necessary environment to provide development. Indeed, those who criticize the United States for our "low" contribution to ODA should recognize the security umbrella we provide for development.

To those who suggest the United States has been "disgraceful" in its support of the multilateral institutions, I point out two facts:

If our aid has dropped 90 percent from the high water mark of the Marshall Plan days, our GNP as a part of the world GNP has dropped from 42 percent in 1950 to 21 percent in 1980.

And, the United States was the strongest supporter of the World Bank and IMF at the recent Cancun Summit.[3]

Reagan administration is second to none in its support of MDB's.

In order to address the current development dilemma, then, the United States must achieve sustained noninflationary growth which in turn can provide increased export earnings and reduced debt service for the developing countries.

In view of these statistical realities, a major focus of development policy must be the generation of non-aid capital flows. Within this context, there is a development capital continuum in which it is useful to view the World Bank and the development effort.

The poorest developing countries receive the most concessional aid through IDA, for example, with little nonconcessional financing.

As they reach progressive stages of "maturation", they become blend countries receiving IBRD financing.

Cofinancing with private sources gradually becomes a greater component of their external flows. Such cofinancing can occur with the development banks' regular lending as well as with the International Finance Corporation (IFC).

Finally, at the graduation stage, official lending which by then is a very small com-

[3] Reference is to the International Meeting on Cooperation and Development, held in Cancun, Mexico, October 22–23, 1981; for Reagan's statements at that conference, see *American Foreign Policy: Current Documents, 1981*, documents 89 and 90.

ponent ceases entirely. Indeed, such countries can become providers of capital for the development efforts of others.

In our view, World Bank Group lending should be seen in this continuum and judged against its ability to assist borrowers in moving through it.

Everyone must recognize the political environment in which we operate, the limited prospects for new or expanded aid initiatives, and the congressional difficulties involved in keeping aid at current levels.

In this context, we consider congressional authorization of IDA VI[4] at the negotiated levels a major victory for the Reagan administration. (Indeed, we have also gotten the Congress to pass the first Foreign Assistance Appropriations since 1978.)[5]

We eagerly await the specifics on the promised Bank initiative regarding repackaging IDA.

In considering a possible next IDA proposal, the new criteria must be economically sound, giving recognition to the economic and other factors previously mentioned. The new proposal must be responsive to criticisms or critics, or refute them with convincing analysis: not hollow rhetoric.

The key issues which must be faced in any proposed IDA are:

Length of maturities, including possible acceleration of repayment schedules;

Fees and rates charged;

Conditionality; and

Relationship to blend lending.

We cannot expect larger and larger replenishments for concessional financing. The political and economic realities will not permit it.

The Reagan administration will not make popular, convenient commitments that we know we can't get through the Congress. And we won't make commitments our successors will find difficult or impossible to get through the Congress. Although it is appealing in the short term, it would be disingenuous to create false expectations.

The maturation of the blend countries solely into the IBRD solely must be pursued substantially and consistently. "Traditional" treatment of particular countries must be re-thought in light of current realities—e.g., if a country can devote scarce resources to wasteful domestic programs, can it really be viewed as a major contender for concessional lending?

With regard to IBRD hard lending, I might briefly mention our pleasure that the General Capital Increase (GCI) authorization legislation has been signed by the President, as has the appropriation for the first U.S. subscription of $109.7 million in paid-in capital and the accompanying callable capital.[6]

We would like to see all blend countries that are in satisfactory balance of payment positions to be moved rapidly into only Bank lending.

With this greater dependence upon the IBRD, however, I must note with concern the Bank's past practice of making fixed rate commitments.

We await with interest the coming Bank analysis of floating rates and variable terms, which have become common in other financial institutions.

We would like to emphasize, however, the importance of thoroughly analyzing and understanding the problem. We don't want a solution in the energy affiliate mode. Bluntly put, this was an area that the private sector can and will adequately serve. The energy affiliate would have simply substituted less expensive public development capital for available private capital. Indeed, the Bank is meeting the challenge through expanded energy lending, within its budgetary limitations, which we support.

In considering new lending initiatives, the Bank should give greater weight to the appropriate policy response by recipients and the catalytic effect on non-Bank resource flows.

This brings me to a most important and potentially large segment of the continuum: private cofinancing with the multilateral development banks.

This role of catalyzing private financial flows is specifically stated in Article I of the World Bank's charter.

---

[4] Appropriations for the sixth replenishment of the International Development Association (IDA VI) through fiscal year 1984 were incorporated in the Omnibus Reconciliation Act of 1981 (P.L. 97–35), enacted August 13, 1981; for text, see 95 Stat. 357.

[5] Reference is to the International Security and Development Cooperation Act of 1981 (P.L. 97–113), enacted December 29, 1981; for text, see 95 Stat. 1519.

[6] The authorizing legislation was provided for in the Omnibus Budget Reconciliation Act of 1981; see footnote 4 above.

Article I calls for the Bank:

"To promote private foreign investment by means of guarantees or participations in loans and other investments made by private investors."[7]

The view that the MDB's must become more active financial catalysts for private capital flows in the years ahead is shared by Tom Clausen who stated in his inaugural speech to the Fund/Bank meetings last Fall that:

"The private sector particularly represents an immense potential source of investment capital . . . [8] (and) we will seek to increase substantially the level of private cofinancing in the next several years."[9]

Substantial progress to involve the private commercial banks in the activities of the MDB's began under Bob McNamara's presiding[10] and is continuing.

The MDB's have instituted active programs to involve commercial banks in greater cofinancing.

In 1976, the World Bank could count only 5 projects out of 73 which were cofinanced with private as opposed to public institutions, accounting for $272 million from the private sector.

In 1981, 18 of 79 cofinanced projects involved commercial banks with the amount of private cofinancing reaching $1.7 billion.

By way of perspective, this $1.7 billion exceeded the total lending of the Asian Development Bank and came close to matching the lending volume of the Inter-American Development Bank in their most recent fiscal years.

In other words, right now private cofinancing is a major and growing source of development assistance. We applaud this trend and hope to see it continue.

What can we expect in the future? Given the compelling logic and budgetary pressures toward growth of private cofinancing, it seems almost inevitable that this activity will expand rapidly.

In 1980 private cofinancing was involved in 21 of the Bank's 140 development projects financed during that year, amounting to about 15 percent of the projects and 20 cents of every dollar lent.

The World Bank hopes to see the number of private cofinancing operations reach 50 per year in the next 1 or 2 years or nearly one project in three.

The Bank also believes it is realistic to think in terms of a ratio as high as two out of three projects involving private sector cofinancing in 5 years time.

This expansion is not inevitable, however. Wanting it to happen won't make it happen. At least three things should take place if we are actually to fulfill the potential that is there.

Cofinancing must be more actively marketed by the MDB's.

The cofinancing package must be made more attractive to the private banks.

Regulatory concerns must be addressed.

This must primarily be a responsibility of the multilateral development banks' management.

The number of commercial banks involved in this activity must be expanded.

—To date, 36 U.S. commercial banks have participated in World Bank cofinanced projects. This is nearly one-third of all banks worldwide that have participated, but the total must be substantially increased.

In order to expand private cofinancing the cofinancing package may have to be made more attractive. Any or all of the following may prove necessary:

Project information will need to be shared throughout the life of the project not just in the beginning.

MDB/borrower dialogue must include cofinancing as a priority item.

For example, why shouldn't those countries approaching the IBRD graduation threshold be expected to have an increasingly larger percentage of their borrowings represented by cofinancing?

—The World Bank will shortly issue a Board paper on revisions in its graduation policy.[11]

---

[7] For the text of the Articles of Agreement of the International Bank for Reconstruction and Development, see *United States Monetary and Financial Conference, Bretton Woods, New Hampshire, July 1–22, 1944, Final Act and Related Documents*, Department of State Publication 2187 (Washington, 1944), pp. 68–95.

[8] All ellipses appear in the source text.

[9] For the text of the speech, see "Annual Address by A. W. Clausen," *1981 Annual Proceedings of the Boards of Governors: Summary Proceedings, Washington, D.C., September 29–October 2, 1981* (Washington, 1981), pp. 15–26.

[10] Robert S. McNamara was President of the World Bank from April 1, 1968, to June 30, 1981.

[11] For a discussion of the new graduation policy, see "World Bank's Graduation Policy Reaffirmed," *Finance and Development*, Vol. 19, No. 2, pp. 2–3.

—We hope the Bank will strongly consider making the role of cofinancing more explicit in its delineation of graduation and maturation stages.

The cross default clause[12] may have to be made mandatory. Perhaps some of you will share your thoughts on this issue in the question and answer period.

New cofinancing instruments and techniques may be necessary.

—The Bank is considering a scheme whereby certain new loans could contain two parts: an "A" loan funded exclusively by the IBRD, and a "B" loan normally funded by private lenders at market terms, but structured so it could include IBRD funds as well.

—The Bank is also considering taking a position in the "B" loan to provide added security and stretch maturities.

—And we also believe the International Finance Corporation (IFC) with its proven private sector track record can be helpful to the Bank in these efforts.

Of course the existing bank regulatory environment is of considerable importance in this whole area of private cofinancing.

You are all aware of the 10 percent of capital limit on a commercial bank's lending to a single borrower as stipulated by Federal Law 12 USC 84. How this 10 percent limit is [*as*] interpreted by the Comptroller of the Currency has implications for the growth of cofinancing.

I have just asked the new Comptroller of the Currency to re-examine the present interpretation when it comes to cofinanced loans with a multilateral development bank.

Legislative change may also be appropriate and will be considered.

Foreign bank supervisory bodies also appear to be taking a new look at their treatment of cofinanced loans.

In this regard the Bank of England has recently modified its views on MDB cofinanced loans.

In the future the Bank of England will adopt the view that: "the inclusion of more cofinancing loans in a bank's asset portfolio could well lead to a perception on the part of supervisors that the bank had *lowered the overall risk eiement in its lending* . . . and such a development would influence their assessment of the extent to which the bank could prudently expand its lending further."

I would also note the recognition by the Amsterdam–Rotterdam Bank of a separate evaluation for loans cofinancing with offical development institutions, wholly outside the country ceilings ordinarily used by the Bank.

—The lesser credit risk through the increased security in respect to political uncertainties and the quality of projects was used to justify this action.

—Those bankers who complain about the spreads on cofinanced loans being too thin would do well to take a lesson from their Dutch colleagues, especially since it is very consistent with modern portfolio theory. In fact, we believe the financial markets do work, and since there is less risk on an MDB cofinanced loan, the spreads may be appropriately smaller.

—Moreover, if loans cofinanced with the World Bank and other multilaterals are much less subject to rescheduling or default than other commercial bank loans, supervisory evaluations should reflect this. We intend to ask the relevant regulators in the United States to consider this action.

Another important vehicle for cofinancing is the World Bank's International Finance Corporation. Last year, for example, of the IFC's $180 million of equity and loan commitments, nearly half were backed through IFC syndications involving over 50 financial institutions.

In looking to the Bank to increase its catalytic role and leveraging its financial resources, I would like to raise the possibility of a larger relative role for the IFC. As some of you know, the United States has been talking with the IFC informally and has some ideas on the future directions it could move. Among these are:

The IFC should concentrate its activities more directly on those areas of its comparative advantage;

It should undertake projects where it has the greatest economic/development impact; and

It should seek ways to increase its type of financial activities either on its own or in concert with other international institutions.

There are four specific areas where IFC possesses substantial comparative advantage.

---

[12] Cross default clauses are contractual clauses that apply in cases where two loans are made to the same entity, and in the event there is a default on one loan, the other loan may or may not automatically be canceled, depending on whether it is mandatory or optional.

First, the development of capital markets, primarily through technical assistance, is an essential IFC activity which could be expanded.

The IFC has the singular capability to fashion impressive financing packages which result in tremendous financial leverage for a given IFC dollar.

Traditionally, its lending and equity programs have focused on private sector market-oriented industrial activity which should be viewed as an increased area of specialization.

The IFC is in a unique position to assist LDC's in developing more efficient industrial policies which are indispensable to stimulating private flows.

Finally, while it is too early to determine whether the IFC or the Bank will be the lead institution, I would like to at this point endorse in principle the investment insurance scheme mentioned by President Clausen. We look forward to seeing the specific proposal at a later time.

Finally, our development continuum leads us, naturally, to graduation from the Bank. Greater movement of countries through the development continuum cycle must of necessity involve an increased graduation effort.

As private flows increase, whether through cofinancing or other forms, our scarce aid resources should be focused increasingly on the most deserving. The winners in the competition for limited funds must be the poorest in income terms and those which promise—and deliver—the best performance.

In our view, there is no virtue in providing Bank funds to countries that do not need aid—all present and future loans should be audited in this light.

Of course, the ultimate goal is for countries to become self-sufficient and independent so that they do not need external capital. Indeed, a number of early borrowers from the Bank have achieved that status.

As you know, our MDB policy assessment[13]—the basis for much of what I've said—is nearly completed. We feel the assessment provides a sound analytical basis and justification for continued strong U.S. endorsement and support for all the MDB's, including the World Bank Group.

The Bank Group has been a critical means for effective policy reform in the developing world. In the future, it will increase its crucial role as a catalyst for private flows.

As the Bank changes, the United States will enthusiastically participate in its evolutionary process of building a consensus for new directions. It is important that the World Bank—as well as other international financial institutions—be protected against disruptive change which would shake the confidence of private investors. As President Reagan said at the last Bank/Fund Annual Meeting:

> "We strongly support the World Bank. And because of our strong support, we feel a special responsibility to provide constructive suggestions to make it more effective. We believe these suggestions will permit it to generate increased funds for development and to support the efforts developing countries are making to strengthen their economies."[14]

Take the ideas I've presented today in that spirit. The Reagan administration strongly supports the World Bank, and will continue to do so given the leadership and policy changes we can foresee in its future.

Thank you.

Document 83

Prepared Statement by the Acting Director, International Development Cooperation Agency, and Administrator, Agency for International Development (McPherson), Before the House Foreign Affairs Committee, February 24, 1982[15]

The Need to Promote Private Sector Involvement in Developing Countries

Mr. Chairman and members of the committee, I am honored to be here today as

---

[13] For the text of the assessment, see U.S. Department of the Treasury, *United States Participation in the Multilateral Development Banks in the 1980s* (Washington, February 1982).

[14] For the text of the September 29, 1981, address, see *American Foreign Policy: Current Documents, 1981*, document 65.

[15] Source: *Role of Private Sector in Development*

Acting Director of I.D.C.A. and as Administrator of A.I.D. to discuss "A.I.D./I.D.C.A. Policies and Programs for Private Sector Involvement in Development Abroad." This year will be important for the implementation for [*of*] all aspects of our foreign economic assistance program.

In his October speech to the World Affairs Council in Philadelphia,[16] President Reagan emphasized the importance of economic freedom to national development and human progress. He spoke of freedom to make decisions without overpowering governmental intervention, freedom to sell a product in the world market, and freedom of access to capital, as well as to the expertise and skills needed to produce goods and services. The exercise of these freedoms is as important for nations in the process of development as for the industrial nations. This belief underlies our private sector programs.

I would like to take this opportunity to lay out for the committee the general policy framework within which A.I.D. is working. The principal goals set forth in the Foreign Assistance Act[17] provide the point of departure for our planning:

(1) the alleviation of the worst physical manifestations of poverty among the world's poor majority;

(2) the promotion of conditions enabling developing countries to achieve self-sustaining growth with equitable distribution of benefits;

(3) the encouragement of development processes in which individual civil and economic rights are respected and enhanced; and

(4) the integration of the developing countries into an open and equitable international economic system.

Furthermore, Section 601 of the Act explicitly encourages free enterprise and private participation in "achieving rising levels of production standards of living essential to economic progress and development." It continues: "(I)t is declared to be the policy of the United States to encourage the efforts of other countries to increase the flow of international trade, to foster private initiative and competition . . . [18] and to encourage the contribution of United States enterprise toward the economic strength of less developed friendly countries, through private trade and investment abroad . . . ."

In looking at the experience of A.I.D. as well as other donors in attempting to meet these goals, it is clear that certain major constraints work to reduce the effectiveness of external economic assistance:

(1) Government policies in less developed countries (LDCs) which inhibit the operation of free markets, discourage private investment, inhibit resource mobilization, and allocate resources inefficiently. These policies tend to exclude access by the poor to productive resources and employment;

(2) LDC policies which make less than best use of limited government resources in such areas as industry, agriculture, irrigation, health, population, and education;

(3) Weak human and institutional capacity necessary to complement public and private investment;

(4) A lack of capability to develop and spread new, appropriate technologies that will both increase employment and raise the productivity and incomes of workers and farmers; and

(5) Limited private sector activity.

Consequently, I have established a basic A.I.D. policy framework[19] to ensure that A.I.D. projects are selected and designed so as to address these constraints. Appropriate programs are those which encourage policy reform, improve institutional capacity and upgrade human resources in LDCs, develop and spread new technologies, and increase the vitality of the private sector.

A.I.D.'s agencywide private sector thrust is intended to increase the benefits of development through economic growth, employment, and income generation. Indigenous private enterprises responding to profitable opportunities produce jobs, foreign exchange and a managerial and technical skill base. These byproducts of profitmaking en-

---

Abroad: Hearings Before the Committee on Foreign Affairs, House of Representatives, Ninety-seventh Congress, Second Session (Washington, 1982), pp. 7–21.

16 Reagan addressed the World Affairs Council in Philadelphia, October 15, 1981; for text, see *American Foreign Policy: Current Documents, 1981*, document 16.

17 Reference is to the Foreign Assistance Act of 1961 (P.L. 87–195), as amended, enacted September 4, 1961; for text, see 75 Stat. 424, and subsequent amendments.

18 All ellipses appear in the source text.

19 Details of the policy framework are embodied in Agency for International Development Policy Paper, *Private Enterprise Development*, (Washington, May 1982).

terprises are essential to meeting the needs of the poor majority in developing countries.

The mixed economies of most underdeveloped countries today recognize the inability of the public sector to carry out adequately necessary development activities. More and more, multilateral institutions such as the World Bank recognize that increased entrepreneurial participation in development is required, utilizing business people whose management skills, willingness to take risks, profit motivations, and free-market attitudes make them prime movers in stimulating economic development.

The key goal of A.I.D.'s private sector emphasis is to create an environment of economic opportunity conducive to the development of indigenous private sectors. In such an environment, people can work to improve their standard of living. More specifically, such an environment affords the opportunity for hungry people to produce and utilize more food, the opportunity for better health and nutrition, the opportunity to achieve better housing and schools and the opportunity for employment, earnings and savings. This requires, in many cases, a change to sounder economic policies within LDCs.

We agree with those individuals, such as Professor P. T. Bauer[20] of the London School of Economics, who argue that donor nations "should favor governments which, within their human and financial resources, try to perform the indispensable tasks of government, but who refrain from closely detailed control of the economy—briefly, governments who govern rather than plan. This emphasis would promote liberal economic systems, minimize coercion, reduce political tensions and favor material progress."

In looking at how we can achieve the goals set for us by the Congress in the Foreign Assistance Act, it is clear that the Agency has, in the recent past, tended to view government institutions as the primary instrument for achieving these goals. In doing so, A.I.D. has tended to deemphasize activities which use the private sector as an instrument for development. It has not appreciated that the objectives of our development efforts would be served best by revitalizing the market economy in less developed countries. In the developing world, the governments which have adopted and sustained the policies and business environment which encourage private initiative at home, private investment from abroad, and competitive pricing policies, are those which have enjoyed relatively high rates of economic growth, investment, employment and savings in spite of worldwide recession.

The development history of the past two decades also shows that those LDCs which have grown the fastest have followed market-oriented policies which encourage the growth of private enterprise, with the public sector playing a complementary, supportive role. It is the examples of the economic successes in Taiwan, Brazil, Singapore, and others plus the experience of our own country, which have led us to emphasize private sector programs.

After a thorough examination of pertinent development issues, the tools at hand, and direction from the Administration and the Congress we have translated our indigenous private sector development goal into the following objectives:

1. In association with host country and U.S. private investors, to assist in financing the establishment, improvement and expansion of productive, developmentally desirable private enterprises in priority sectors in developing countries;

2. To promote investment opportunities in developing countries by bringing together U.S. and host country capital and experienced management, thereby transferring technical, managerial and marketing expertise from the United States to the developing countries;

3. To stimulate and help create conditions conducive to the flow of U.S. and host country private capital into productive investment in developing countries.

Based upon A.I.D. experience, and observation of other entities committed to similar objectives, A.I.D.'s Regional and Central Bureaus as well as our new Bureau for Private Enterprise will undertake the following activities in carrying out these objectives:

—Facilitate or undertake private sector project identification, development, promotion, packaging, and financing;

—Help to establish, finance, and improve privately owned development finance companies and other financial institutions which will provide the capital and know-how for the development of the private sector in developing countries;

[20] Professor Bauer had recently explained his ideas in *Equality, the Third World and Economic Delusion* (Cambridge, Mass., 1981).

—Make investments, in forms appropriate to the situation, in individual productive private enterprises in developing countries;

—Encourage the growth of capital markets in the development countries;

—Provide counsel to host countries on how to create a climate conducive to the growth of private investment;

—Create in the capital-exporting countries interest in portfolio investments in enterprises located in the developing countries;

—Help to establish training institutions and programs, both managerial and technical, to support private sector development and linkages between the United States and LDC private sectors.

We intend to utilize our necessarily limited resources to attract investments from others, whether private U.S., public U.S., multilateral institution, or local private sector, to meet private sector investment and development needs in the LDCs. At the same time we are mindful of the fact that we are responsible for the appropriate use of taxpayer funds. We do not intend to permit private businesses to shift all or even the largest share of their entrepreneurial risk to the U.S. Government.

A.I.D.'s private sector initiative cuts across all bureaus in the Agency. The bulk of the funding of A.I.D.'s private sector activities will be provided through the normal programming process under our bilateral country programs. Our field missions will identify and justify private sector projects in the same manner as they do now for activities in other sectors. These projects will be formulated within the policy framework which will be issued shortly by the Agency, and which will conform to the principles set forth in this statement. We will take special care to ensure that, during project design, these projects will be developed within the new policy framework.

More specifically, in Latin America and the Caribbean region, we have in place or propose programs in 11 countries that: stimulate employment opportunities in the rural private sector, develop agribusiness capability, foster basic skills training, stimulate small business development, and create rural cooperative enterprises.

In the Africa region, we propose programs that span 7 countries. These programs include a farm implements manufacturing project, a livestock program for small business and an agricultural marketing development program.

In Asia we have programs to: install credit systems for farmers and other rural entrepreneurs, mobilize the private sector to help develop a national energy technology center and increase employment income and production by the private sector. In the Near East region we have a program to install credit systems for small businesses.

Our efforts are not limited to regional bureaus. A.I.D.'s Science and Technology Bureau for example, is working to develop the commercial seed industry; supply the appropriate technology for a multitude of private initiatives; and encourage small rural enterprise development. Also, because agriculture frequently constitutes the bulk of private sector activity in many lesser developed countries, many of the S&T Bureau's activities will have a private sector impact as well. Increased agricultural production by small farmers will improve the living standards of the poor majority.

We believe that this new agencywide initiative will be highly complementary to those of other internationally concerned agencies. With respect to the Overseas Private Investment Corporation (O.P.I.C.), the fit is particulary good. O.P.I.C.'s investment promotion tools complement the various debt instruments which the Agency will use. And A.I.D.'s overseas presence can serve not only A.I.D.'s needs with respect to this program, but also O.P.I.C.'s needs to a greater extent than at present.

The Agency's private sector program also fits well with the programs of the World Bank and its affiliate, the International Finance Corporation (I.F.C.). U.S. involvement with the latter can be expected to be more active than in the past through our common interest in developing indigenous private enterprises. At the same time, we anticipate that A.I.D.'s efforts will focus on some sectors which recently have received a relatively small percentage of I.F.C.'s resources (e.g. agribusiness), and, of course, A.I.D. will be concentrating on establishing links with the U.S. private sector.

Finally, the Trade and Development Program (T.D.P.) plays a unique role in fostering the development of middle income countries while promoting trade opportunities for the United States. T.D.P.'s focus is on the U.S. private sector and its export opportunities in the developing world which complements A.I.D.'s efforts to promote local private sector development. T.D.P. assistance helps give the developing countries access to U.S. technology, goods and services which they badly need. In return, the United States receives the revenue from the sale of such technology, goods and services.

T.D.P. plans to use its funds increasingly at the critical stage in the planning process of a development project; this is where U.S. firms, competing with foreign firms are in the final stages of the feasibility study selection process for large-scale projects. Experience has shown conclusively that the follow on construction and equipment supply contracts can be influenced as to source country by the feasibility study design specifications.

T.D.P. is also concentrating on the coal and alternate energy sectors. Developing nations desperately need to move away from oil-base energy sources to other sources of energy. T.D.P. is very active in marrying the needs of the developing nations with U.S. technology and the U.S. firms which can supply this technology. Moreover, by helping a nation to convert its power base from oil to energy sources such as coal—as T.D.P. is now doing in Jamaica—we also help open export markets for U.S. coal. T.D.P. is also looking for opportunities to diversify our sources of such key strategic resources as cobalt in such a way that new sources are developed with the involvement of U.S. firms.

I would now like to discuss briefly our new Private Enterprise Bureau.

With past A.I.D. experience as a guide, the Private Enterprise Bureau is designing programs capitalizing on the financial, technological and management expertise of the United States and existing indigenous private sectors, and multilateral and host country institutions. We are seeking ways to make A.I.D.'s funds more effective with private investment in selected LDCs.

The Bureau will spearhead the Agency's efforts in drafting innovative ways to create the policy environment for and promote the development of strong, growth-oriented private sectors. I have just signed the Bureau's policy statement, a "charter" for the Bureau's activities over the next several years.[21]

The Bureau for Private Enterprise is being staffed with experts from the private sector as well as career A.I.D. officers. We have initially targeted our efforts on ten LDCs currently served by A.I.D. programs. They are:

Costa Rica
Jamaica
Kenya
Ivory Coast
Zimbabwe
Egypt
Indonesia
Pakistan
Sri Lanka
Thailand

These countries were selected for several reasons, including: host government support for private sector development; strategic importance to the United States; attractiveness as a long-term trading partner; potential for private sector development; and presence of an existing A.I.D. program.

To date we have sent investment reconnaissance missions to Sri Lanka, Indonesia, Kenya, Thailand, and have had several trips by various experts to Jamaica. These teams are performing three main functions. First, they are examining the investment climate and host-country policies, and on request, consulting closely with the governments on possible policy reforms. In effect, they are identifying constraints which discourage private investment, and proposing ways for dealing with or eliminating them. Second, they are examining host-country financial institutions to ascertain whether the "infrastructure" is sufficient for private-sector development. Third, they are selling investment opportunities with a high development impact for local firms where possible with the U.S. private sector.

The teams consist of specialists from the private sector accompanied by an A.I.D. official. The specialists come from fields of high priority to the host country, such as agribusiness, technology transfer in manufacturing, industrial development strategies, and financial institutions. We also have had specialists in production operations, the energy (natural gas) industry, management training, capital markets, and foreign investment laws. A complete list of the people who have participated in these missions is appended to this testimony.[22]

In the five countries already visited, numerous potential projects have been identified. Some of the more promising ones which will be the subject of further analysis include:

---

21 For the text of the Bureau policy statement, see Agency for International Development Policy Paper, *Bureau for Private Enterprise Policy Paper* (Washington, May 1982).

22 For the list, see *Role of Private Sector in Development Abroad,* pp. 22–23.

Kenya

—seed production business

—line of credit for agribusiness projects through a commercial bank

—management training

Jamaica

—venture capital firm

Indonesia

—venture capital firm to serve small and medium size private enterprises

—agribusiness projects

—management training

Sri Lanka

—agribusiness projects

—financial intermediaries to serve small and medium size enterprises

Thailand

—capitalization of a private financial institution to provide credit to agribusiness activities

—management training

It should be emphasized that these projects require detailed analysis and negotiation prior to making any decision on their financing. We are well underway on several of these projects.

To develop and implement these and other projects, the Private Enterprise Bureau has been allocated approximately $26 million for FY'82 and a similar amount is requested for FY'83. Of these funds, $5.0 million each year will be used to support International Executive Service Corps (I.E.S.C.) programs with a particular emphasis on the Caribbean Basin and Central America. Also, from the program budgets allocated to the A.I.D. Missions in the ten target countries, funds totalling approximately $100 million in FY'82–'83 have been earmarked for additional private sector projects.

We will focus our efforts on the support and development of indigenous firms and institutions in targeted sectors and countries. This requires the promotion of LDC policy changes to ensure an environment conducive to private sector development. Also, specialized management training programs will be designed as required.

To the extent possible, we will capitalize on the financial, technological and management expertise of the U.S. and indigenous private sectors, multilateral institutions and Agency resources where appropriate. It may be some time before the long-term economic benefits of our new approach are evident. But it has already generated enthusiasm at home and abroad and we are confident that it has a central place in sound development planning.

Document 84

Statement by the Secretary of State (Haig) Before a Subcommittee of the House Appropriations Committee, March 4, 1982[23]

The Objectives of Foreign Economic and Security Assistance

It is always for me a pleasure to appear before the House Appropriations Subcommittee on Foreign Operations to present the Administration's proposed fiscal year 1983 foreign assistance program.

Over a year ago, in my first testimony here as Secretary of State,[24] I committed myself to developing a close working relationship with you, Mr. Chairman,[25] and all Committee members so that we could move together to strengthen our nation's international position. While we have not always agreed on specific issues, I believe we have developed a constructive relationship. Your wise advice has always been most appreciated.

Together, we have made an important beginning as we seek to reinvigorate American leadership abroad. For the first time in three years, the Congress has enacted foreign assistance appropriation legislation,[26]

---

[23] Source: *Foreign Assistance and Related Programs Appropriations for 1983: Hearings Before a Subcommittee of the Committee on Appropriations, House of Representatives, Ninety-seventh Congress, Second Session* (Washington, 1982), Part I, pp. 83–86. Haig made this statement before the Subcommittee on Foreign Operations and Related Agencies

[24] Apparent reference to Haig's appearance before the Subcommittee on April 28, 1981; for his testimony, see *Foreign Assistance and Related Programs Appropriations for 1982: Hearings Before a Subcommittee of the Committee on Appropriations, House of Representatives, Ninety-seventh Congress, First Session* (Washington, 1981), Part II, pp. 87–158.

[25] Representative Clarence D. Long.

[26] Regarding this legislation, see footnote 5 to document 82.

giving substance to President Reagan's declaration that "America will not shrink from making the investments necessary for both peace and security."[27]

But, we cannot stop here, Mr. Chairman. We must build on the progress we have made. The competition we face is far too serious, and our own requirements too great to rest now. A first-rate American foreign policy simply cannot be run on second-rate resources.

The task of statecraft is to master events, not simply to react to them. In this complex age of interdependence, American diplomacy requires broad and flexible assets to deal with a variety of situations. Foreign economic and security assistance is a critical element in giving us such flexibility.

For too long, foreign aid has been misunderstood and underrated, dismissed as naive idealism or ineffective philanthropy. Whatever the accuracy of such views in the past, they cannot be sustained today. We are requesting foreign assistance to serve compelling national security, foreign policy and economic needs.

Today, I would like to explain the President's request for an increase of $1.4 billion in security and economic aid in fiscal year 1983.[28] With your permission, I would like also to submit for the record a short but comprehensive report that details the major elements of our fiscal year 1983 foreign assistance proposals.[29] 0

As you know, the President has already asked for a supplemental appropriation in fiscal year 1982 of $350 million to meet our economic assistance commitments under the Caribbean Basin initiative, and an additional $60 million in security assistance for this same area.[30]

Let me be more specific about the risks to American national interests that would be the consequence of inadequate foreign assistance.

We would not be able to help reduce the economic misery in the Caribbean Basin that encourages domestic violence and external intervention.

We would risk critical setbacks to our peacekeeping efforts in the Middle East and southern Africa.

We might lose military facilities essential to the defense of Western interests in distant but vital regions of the world. Our access agreements to Kenya, Somalia, Oman and others help us to sustain a U.S. presence all along the vital oil routes to the Middle East.

We would court the danger of further deterioration in the military capabilities and economies of key allies, such as Turkey.

We might encourage the subversive efforts by Soviet and Soviet proxy forces. Our assistance is vitally important to countries friendly to the West, such as Pakistan, Sudan, Yemen, Morocco, Tunisia, Somalia, and Oman, all of which are under growing pressure from the Soviets or client states of the Soviet Union.

We risk damage to important markets and commercial ties. Today, more than one-quarter of our agricultural and manufactured exports goes to the developing world.

Finally, we might weaken valuable multilateral financial institutions which have contributed to economic growth and must continue their vital role in economic development.

The President's program of foreign assistance is not only a safeguard against all these dangers, but an integral element of the President's foreign policy. It is absolutely necessary if our strategies are to succeed in achieving their objectives.

For example, our policy in the Middle East pursues two goals: the search for a just and lasting peace, and the urgent requirement that our friends in the region be secure against threats from the outside and from Soviet surrogates and radical forces within the region. These goals reinforce each other.

No peace is possible unless local countries are secure from outside coercion, and security will not be achieved if we fail to address the underlying sources of conflict and instability.

Our foreign assistance serves both of these goals. It seeks to advance the welfare

---

[27] Reference is to President Reagan's remarks on foreign assistance in his January 26, 1982 State of the Union Address; for text, see *Weekly Compilation of Presidential Documents*, February 1, 1982, pp. 76–83.

[28] The President transmitted his budget request to Congress on February 8, 1982; for text, see *Budget of the United States Government, Fiscal Year 1983* (Washington, 1982).

[29] Reference is to *International Security and Economic Cooperation Program FY 1983*, Department of State Special Report No. 99, March 1982.

[30] The President's request was eventually passed by Congress as the Supplemental Appropriations Act (P.L. 97–257), enacted September 10, 1982; for text, see 96 Stat. 819. For documentation on the Caribbean Basin Initiative, see Chapter 15, Part C.

of the populations and the economic health of their countries to promote economic and political stability throughout the region. The security and economic health of Israel and Egypt give these nations the confidence to continue the path towards peace begun at Camp David.

Similarly, our policy in southwest Asia seeks to ensure Western access to oil from the Persian Gulf. Almost all the countries in the area stretching from Pakistan to Morocco are economically troubled. In addition, they face potential subversion or regional threats, in many cases supported by the Soviets or their proxies.

Our 5-year program of military modernization and economic assistance[31] will help Pakistan to meet the Soviet threat from Afghanistan and facilitate the development essential to internal stability. Our assistance helps Sudan, Morocco, and Tunisia to face threats of subversion or aggression emanating from Libya.

In the eastern Mediterranean, we seek to strengthen our relations with two major allies, Greece and Turkey, to buttress NATO's vital southeastern flank, and to facilitate the search for a solution to the Cyprus problem.

Our assistance is required for a strong Turkey, which lies at a key geo-political crossroad, the intersection of our NATO, southwest Asia, and Middle East interests. Both security and economic stability are essential to maintain the momentum toward restoration of democratic institutions in Turkey. Security assistance also helps a democratic Greece fulfill its NATO responsibility.

In the Caribbean, the President's policy seeks to provide both economic help that the nations of the region need to overcome legacies of poverty and injustice and the security assistance needed to prevent Castro from exploiting these conditions to establish new totalitarian regimes.

We must provide the resources needed until increased investment, a strengthened private sector, and expanded export markets enable these countries to achieve economic self-sufficiency. The amounts for security assistance are modest, equaling just over $100 million out of a total aid request of $675 million for the entire Basin area.

El Salvador, where insurgents seek to prevent elections and destroy the economy, would be the largest single recipient of both security and economic assistance. Jamaica will continue to need substantial assistance in order to restore the vitality of its shattered private sector.

Our support for Costa Rica's rapidly deteriorating economy will help that country to carry out fundamental economic reforms and to preserve the longest democratic tradition in Central America. In Honduras, another move toward democracy faces the dangerous combination of a quickening economic decline and a political-military crisis upon its borders.

To assure the most effective use of our scarce resources, the President has realigned foreign assistance allocations with careful attention to priorities. The promotion of a truly lasting economic growth remains one of our key objectives. Our program recognizes that assistance alone will not guarantee economic development. Growth also requires proper economic incentives, national commitment, and a reliance on the creativity and resourcefulness of the individual.

The program also responds to the pressing needs of key strategic nations for increased economic support and concessional military sales. Such nations must receive help in order to bolster their defense against outside subversion and to prevent economic crises at the same time.

Our new focus on essential strategic and development objectives should not obscure our pride in the continuing American commitment to traditional humanitarian objectives. We remain a major source of assistance to refugees in Africa, Pakistan, Southeast Asia and the Middle East.

We direct the bulk of our development and food aid to the world's poorest nations. These countries, with limited access to private capital markets, depend on concessional assistance to support their development efforts. To meet these needs, President Reagan committed the United States at Cancun to maintaining assistance levels to these nations.[32]

Mr. Chairman, I recognize that approval of foreign assistance at this time of austerity will be very difficult. But we shall pay a greater price later if we do not act now. America's most essential interests are under attack. The President firmly believes that the resources he has requested are crucial

31 For a breakdown of projected spending for 5 fiscal years, see *Budget of the United States Government, Fiscal Year 1983*.

32 Regarding President Reagan's statements at Cancun, Mexico, see footnote 3 to document 82.

to defense of these interests and to the promotion of a more peaceful and secure world. Our nation's security tomorrow requires that we make an investment in foreign assistance today.

Document 85

Prepared Statement by the Secretary of the Treasury (Regan) Before a Subcommittee of the Senate Appropriations Committee, May 4, 1982[33]

Funding Objectives for the Multilateral Development Banks

Mr. Chairman, and members of the committee, I welcome this opportunity to appear before you to discuss the administration's fiscal year 1983 budget proposals for the multilateral development banks.

As you know, last year's foreign assistance appropriations bill[34]was the first enacted in 3 years. The administration attached considerable importance to this legislation and we recognize and very much appreciate the constructive role played by you, Mr. Chairman, and by the members of this committee, throughout the process leading up to its enactment. We also value highly the frank and informative bipartisan dialogue we established with members and staff of the Congress during the preparation of our recently released report assessing future U.S. participation in the MDBs.[35]

For fiscal year 1983, the administration proposes $1,537 million in budget authority and $2,361 million under program limitations for subscriptions and contributions to the MDBs.

I would like to assure you that this proposal has been carefully scrutinized to fully reflect the administration's firm commitment to fiscal responsibility.

For the *International Bank for Reconstruction and Development* (IBRD), we propose $109,720,549 in budget authority and $1,353,220,096 under program limitations for the second of six installments toward the U.S. share of the 1981 General Capital Increase (GCI).

To subscribe to the U.S. share of the 1981 "companion" increase, we propose $30,158,750 under program limitations. This increase is designed to prevent dilution of member voting power by providing each member with 250 additional votes. The increase has no paid-in component and requires no budget authority.

To complete the U.S. subscription to the 1977 Selective Capital Increase, we propose $16,321,004 in budget authority and $146,897,067 under program limitations.

The total request for the IBRD is $126,041,533 in budget authority and $1,530,275,913 under program limitations.

For the *International Development Association* (IDA), the administration is proposing a third installment of our contribution to the sixth replenishment in the amount of $945,000,000. This level of funding is consistent with the ceiling placed on fiscal year 1983 appropriations for IDA in the Omnibus Budget Reconciliation Act of 1981.[36] The proposed level is also a reduction of $945 million from the amount originally envisioned by the administration in March 1981 and entails a significant reduction in the IDA lending program.

For the *Inter-American Development Bank* (IDB), we propose $62,423,437 in budget authority for paid-in capital and $828,137,742 under program limitations for callable capital to complete our subscription to the fifth replenishment.

For the *Fund for Special Operations* (FSO), we propose $175,000,000 for the fourth installment to the current replenishment and $46,677,000 for the unfunded portion of the previous replenishment—a total of $221,677,000.

For the *Asian Development Bank* (ADB), we propose $248,097 in budget authority and $2,243,811 under program limitations to complete the U.S. subscription to the most recent capital increase.

---

[33] Source: *Foreign Assistance and Related Programs Appropriations for Fiscal Year 1983: Hearings Before a Subcommittee of the Committee on Appropriations, United States Senate, Ninety-seventh Congress, Second Session* (Washington, 1983), Part 1, pp. 689–701. Secretary Regan prepared his statement for the Subcommittee on Foreign Operations.

[34] Regarding this legislation, see footnote 5 to document 82.

[35] Reference is to Department of the Treasury, *U.S. Participation in the Multilateral Development Banks in the 1980s* (Washington, July 1982).

[36] Regarding this act, see footnote 4 to document 82.

For the *Asian Development Fund* (ADF), we propose $111,250,000 for the fourth installment to the current replenishment and $20,384,478 for the unfunded portion of the previous replenishment, a total of $131,634,478.

For the *African Development Fund* (AFDF), we propose $50,000,000 for the first of three installments for the new replenishment. The administration will propose legislation in the coming weeks to authorize a U.S. contribution of $150,000,000 over the three years of this replenishment,[37] which totals a little more than $1 billion. While the proposed U.S. contribution over 3 years is 20 percent higher than the $125 million negotiated in 1978 for the previous 3-year replenishment, it is likely to represent a decline in real terms.

The total request represents an increase of $275.3 million in budget authority and $20.7 million under program limitations over the fiscal year 1982 appropriation.

With regard to the increase in MDB funding we are requesting, I would like to stress three points:

With the sole exception of the $50 million proposed for the African Development Fund, the FY 1983 request is based on international arrangements negotiated by the previous administration. President Reagan has stressed the importance of the United States living up to these arrangements. The U.S. contribution to the African Development Fund reflects our commitment to continue to support multilateral efforts to assist in the development of the world's poorest region.

The main reason for the increase over the FY 1982 appropriations is the proposed addition of $245 million for IDA—an increase which is directly traceable to this administration's decision to reduce contributions in the early part of the sixth replenishment and to make up the amounts later in the replenishment and to appropriations ceilings established by the Congress.

In the longer term, the trend of U.S. contributions is clearly down. By FY 1985, when the replenishments will have been largely negotiated by this administration, we plan total appropriation request levels of about $1.2 billion annually and accompanying amounts for callable capital subscriptions.

This will entail a significant reduction in real terms in U.S. contributions to new soft loan window replenishments.

Since becoming Secretary, I have met regularly with my counterparts from key industrial countries. Our common long-term goal is to build and maintain an international economic system that is open, growing, and characterized by increased efficiency and output. We hope and expect that such a system will encourage the development of democratic, pluralistic and free market societies. The MDBs represent one of the most visible and concrete examples of allied cooperation towards this end—not just cooperation for cooperation's sake, but because these institutions serve our common interests.

As you know, the Treasury Department has over the past year conducted an assessment designed to establish the necessary framework for future U.S. participation in the MDBs and to outline policy goals to be pursued. This was the most thorough U.S. examination of the institutions since they were established.

The administration is convinced that continued U.S. participation in the MDBs is justified by a fundamental national interest in a more stable and secure world, which we believe can be best achieved in an open, market-oriented international system. To the extent that the MDBs encourage the participation of developing countries in that international system on a permanent and self-sustaining basis, the MDBs can serve to advance important U.S. economic, strategic, and humanitarian interests.

Our conclusions underscore the role the MDBs can play as catalysts in the international economic system and as providers of sound economic advice.

We can see an example of the catalytic role the MDBs can play close to home and in strong support of U.S. foreign policy goals. The World Bank and Inter-American Development Bank chair consultative groups for the Caribbean and Central America, respectively, which will complement the President's Caribbean Basin Initiative.[38] In addition to providing a forum for donor coordination, the MDBs are also expected to provide development assistance in the range of $700 to $800 million annually to the region.

The fundamental decision in our assessment is to continue U.S. leadership in these

---

[37] On December 21, 1982, President Reagan signed into law a continuing appropriations bill providing $50 million for the African Development Fund. (P.L. 97–377; 96 Stat. 1831)

[38] For documentation on the Caribbean Basin Initiative, see Chapter 15, Part C.

programs and is based on our conclusion that U.S. foreign policy interests can be well-served by the MDBs. Cost sharing and financial leveraging mean that the MDBs can provide significant resources at a relatively small direct budgetary cost to the U.S. Government.

In the *Caribbean Basin*, the MDBs provided $234.3 million to Costa Rica, El Salvador, and Jamaica in 1981, while U.S. bilateral economic and military assistance was $165.9 million.

The region adjacent to the *Persian Gulf* is of critical importance to U.S. interests. In 1981, seven key countries—Kenya, Pakistan, Mauritius, Seychelles, Somalia, Sudan, and Oman—received $345.4 million from U.S. bilateral programs. The MDBs more than matched that amount with $700.5 million.

The United States maintains *basing arrangements* in Kenya, Oman, Somalia, Thailand, and the Philippines. These five countries accounted for a total of $1,456.6 million in MDB lending in 1981. Our total bilateral program provided $396 million to these same countries.

In seven countries of strategic importance to the United States in *Africa*—Botswana, Djibouti, Liberia, Sudan, Tunisia, Zambia, and Zimbabwe—U.S. bilateral economic and military assistance programs provided $247 million in 1981, while the MDBs provided $426.1 million in the same year.

For all 27 countries in the table I have attached to my statement,[39] *all* U.S. *bilateral* economic and military assistance programs provided $5.6 billion in 1981. If the MDB graduates, Israel, Oman, and Spain, are omitted, the bilateral total is $3.3 billion. The MDBs provided $3.8 billion to these countries.

The point that these statistics establish is that the MDBs—where the United States provides a fraction of the resources—are important complements to our bilateral assistance program.

We are also convinced that the MDBs can use their resources more effectively. To this end, U.S. support for the MDBs will be designed to encourage:

—adherence to free and open markets,

—emphasis on the private sector as a vehicle for growth,

—minimal government involvement, and

—assistance to the needy countries who demonstrate an ability to make good use of available resources by adopting appropriate domestic economic policies.

With regard to specific recommendations for improving MDB effectiveness, we will seek three primary goals.

(1) The first is to have MDB lending programs increasingly emphasize attention to market signals and incentives, to private sector development, and to greater financial participation by commercial banks, private investors and other sources of private financing. A critically important goal of the MDBs in the future will be to encourage the private sector to invest its own capital and expertise in sound projects. It is in this role, as a catalytic agent in the enhancement of entrepreneurship, investment capital and production, that the MDBs can make a particularly significant contribution to economic development.

—The International Finance Corporation knows the private sector and understands how to attract outside investors. We will be working closely with the IFC and other governments to develop additional ways to strengthen the private sector role in programs of the World Bank Group and the regional MDBs.

—At the request of Venezuela, the IDB is working with the United States and other interested members to fashion a program targeted on the private sector.

—The administration has encouraged the MDBs to extend project cofinancing with private financial institutions. We believe there are opportunities for U.S. financial corporations in the cofinancing field, and we are currently examining whether some U.S. regulations may unreasonably limit possibilties in this area.

(2) A second goal is more selectivity and policy conditionality in MDB operations, in effect linking MDB lending to a recipient's pursuit of appropriate micro and macro economic policies. Financing for countries pursuing ineffective policies should be curtailed, and, if circumstances dictate, terminated. The importance of efficient loan allocations is underscored by the fact that our assessment found indications that past MDB emphasis on lending targets had eroded MDB effectiveness in encouraging sound economic policies.

(3) A third goal is to encourage the MDBs to adopt effective policies to "gradu-

---

39 Reference is to "Comparison of Bilateral and MDB Assistance to Countries of Importance to the U.S.", which is appended to this document.

ate" countries from the hard loan windows, when these countries have advanced to the point that they can rely fully on private capital flows. Similarly, countries that have achieved a requisite level of creditworthiness should "mature" from the soft loan windows and borrow from the hard loan windows as rapidly as their debt servicing capacity permits.

By pursuing more selectivity in lending within a framework of effective graduation and maturation policies, we can ensure that scarce resources are concentrated on those countries which can best employ them and which are in the greatest need. And we can obtain more cost-effective development financing from the MDBs, while limiting budgetary outlays.

We are convinced that these policies which the United States is pursuing in the MDBs constitute a sound foundation from which economic development can be most efficiently promoted. I am also hopeful that they form an excellent basis for strong bipartisan congressional support for U.S. participation in these important institutions.

In the past, U.S. relations with the MDBs and other donors have frequently been clouded by uncertainties regarding U.S. implementation of internationally negotiated arrangements. It is important that U.S. efforts to improve the effectiveness of MDB operations not be undermined by such uncertainties. This underscores the importance of consultations between the executive and legislative branches on funding arrangements prior to and during the course of international negotiations, as well as prompt Congressional consideration of the U.S. contributions and subscriptions which follow from such international negotiations.

During the course of this year, the administration will be negotiating replenishments for the hard and soft loan windows of the Inter-American Development Bank and the Asian Development Bank. We plan to participate fully in these replenishments, but we will insist on realism and restraint in future lending programs. Before this administration enters into any understandings there will be thorough consultations with members of this committee and other interested members.

—The negotiations for an FSO replenishment have recently begun. We would expect to phase down the FSO, in light of the relatively high income levels which exist in Latin America.

—In replenishment negotiations for the Asian Development Bank and for the Inter-American Development Bank, we are suggesting the elimination of paid-in capital which would reduce the budgetary cost of U.S. participation in the MDBs.

Reduced levels of paid-in capital would have the effect of bringing MDB lending interest rates closer to market levels and of shifting the program cost from non-borrowing shareholders to borrowers, since interest-free paid-in capital would be replaced by borrowing from capital markets to support lending programs.

Our analysis indicates that the impact on the financial integrity of the MDBs would be minimal and would be offset by relatively modest increases in financial charges.

The Congress would retain full control over callable capital subscriptions to the MDBs. No U.S. subscriptions to callable capital could be made without approval by the Congress in authorizing and appropriations legislation. Callable capital subscriptions could only be made to the extent that the Congress provides for program limitations in appropriations acts.

However, other donors have reacted negatively to the idea of eliminating all paid-in capital. Some members of Congress also have reservations, and we are prepared to consider the views of others on this issue.

Some have asked how can we maintain sufficient influence to implement our policies when we are limiting our contributions to the MDBs.

The United States remains the largest contributor to the MDBs, and our leadership position ensures that our views will be given serious consideration. We believe our recommendations are sound and that they reflect not only our national interests, but the common interests of the democratic, largely free market oriented countries, who provide the major share of resources to these institutions. We are committed to pursuing actively recommendations in our assessment and to continuing to be a reliable financial supporter of the MDBs.

These factors provide solid foundations for anticipating continued strong U.S. influence in these institutions.

At the same time, there will obviously be difficulties in carrying out all our policy objectives because of the multilateral character of the institutions. The views and policy objectives of other countries must clearly be considered. We have, however,

Comparison of Bilateral and MDB Assistance to countries of Importance to the United States[42]
($ million)

	1981 MDB Lending[43]			FY 1981 U.S. Economic Military Assistance[44]
	Hard	**Soft**	**Total**	
Africa				
Botswana	17.0	15.8	32.8	16.5
Djibouti	—	—	—	5.2
Kenya	83.0	58.0	141.0	55.3
Liberia	5.0	4.0	9.0	33.0
Mauritius	30.0	—	30.0	4.9
Seychelles	—	8.6	8.6	1.2
Somalia	—	18.8	18.8	67.5
Sudan	—	90.1	90.1	137.2
Tunisia	152.6	—	152.6	—
Zambia	26.0	8.6	34.6	30.1
Zimbabwe	92.0	15.0	107.0	25.0
Asia				
Pakistan	55.0	357.0	412.0	53.0
Philippines	733.5	15.0	748.5	167.2
Thailand	533.3	15.0	548.3	79.7
Latin America				
Costa Rica	40.0	18.2	58.2	8.8
El Salvador	1.0	42.4	43.4	94.9
Jamaica	132.7	—	132.7	62.2
Near East				
Cyprus	14.0	—	14.0	24.0
Jordan	46.0	—	46.0	72.2
Lebanon	—	—	—	24.4
Oman	—	—	—	26.3
Turkey	722.0	—	722.0	451.6
Egypt	89.0	197.6	286.6	1739.6
Israel	—	—	—	2185.0
Europe				
Poland	—	—	—	—
Portugal	120.0	—	120.0	88.8
Spain	—	—	—	133.2
Total	2892.1	864.1	3756.2	5586.8

U.S. Treasury
February 24, 1982

generally been encouraged by the international reaction to our report. While there have been significant expressions of disappointment at the proposed reduction in U.S. contributions to the soft loan windows, members and MDB management have emphasized their willingness to work with us to improve MDB effectiveness. We are thus optimistic that we can, over time and with the cooperation of our partners, bring about many of the changes that we have recommended. And, in fact, we can already see some progress, especially in the World Bank.

—In December, the Congress mandated that the administration undertake negotiations to reduce the share of IDA credits provided to any given country.[40] The World Bank has firmly indicated to India the need to shift its borrowing from the IDA to the IBRD. We expect that in the World Bank fiscal year 1982, India's traditional 40 percent share of IDA will decline to about 34 percent and forsee a continuing decline in subsequent years.

—In the Asian Development Bank we have proposed—and other donors have supported our position—that relatively creditworthy countries, such as Thailand, Philippines, Indonesia, and Papua-New Guinea, cease to borrow from the bank's soft window, the Asian Development Fund. This position has generally been adopted, and the last ADF loans for these countries are being processed this year.

—In January, the World Bank Executive Directors reviewed the IBRD graduation policy and accepted new, more specific procedures for limiting and eventually phasing out lending to higher income countries.[41] While we welcomed these steps, we would prefer a lower trigger point than the proposed $2,650 per capita income level and are continuing to explore this issue with other executive directors and Bank management.

—The United States has worked hard in the IDB to encourage minimum standards for realistic user charges in power and transport projects. These user charges will be designed to cover operating and capital costs of these services.

The fiscal year 1983 budget proposals are a crucial element in our comprehensive long-term program to improve MDB effectiveness over the remainder of the decade. We believe that our request achieves the proper balance among our international and domestic requirements and fully reflects the real budgetary constraints upon the United States Government. At the same time it safeguards our considerable interests in the developing world and in the Banks.

Enactment of the legislation will affirm U.S. determination to exercise responsible economic and political leadership. It will also demonstrate the seriousness of our commitment to work to induce those changes in MDB policies which we have concluded are necessary to improve the effectiveness of these institutions. I hope we can count on your support.

Document 86

Statement by the Under Secretary of Agriculture for International Affairs and Commodity Programs (Lodwick) Before the 82d Session of the Food and Agricultural Organization of the United Nations, Rome, November 21, 1982[45]

U.S. International Food Assistance and the U.N. Food and Agricultural Organization

Mr. Director General, my fellow delegates and friends. It is both an honor and a

[40] The provision governing the U.S. contribution to the IDA was embodied in the Foreign Assistance and Related Appropriations Act, 1982 (P.L. 97–121), enacted December 29, 1981; for text, see 95 Stat. 1647.

[41] Regarding the World Bank's graduation policy, see footnote 11 to document 82.

[42] The countries are those which received an allocation of Economic Support Funds in fiscal year 1982. [Footnote in the source text.]

[43] The lending levels include commitments of the International Bank for Reconstruction and Development and the International Development Association in World Bank fiscal year 1981, and commitments from the Inter-American Development Bank (and its Fund for Special Operations), the Asian Development Bank and Fund and the African Development Fund during calendar year 1981. [Footnote in the source text.]

[44] USAID 1982 Congressional Presentation. [Footnote in the source text.]

[45] Source: U.S. Department of Agriculture *Major News Releases and Speeches*, November 19–November 26, 1982, pp. 1–6.

pleasure to address such a distinguished audience of world agricultural leaders. In working with officials from other countries and FAO, I have often been troubled by the fact that we rarely have a chance to meet face to face. Instead we try to resolve important agricultural issues by shuttling messages back and forth over distances of thousands of miles. This makes it difficult for us to appreciate each other's needs and goals. A meeting like this can overcome that problem and allow us to share our thoughts in a more personal way.

It has been nearly four decades since 44 nations met in Hot Springs, Virginia, to lay the groundwork for the Food and Agricultural Organization[46] we know today. And it seems appropriate for us to take stock of our efforts so far and our aspirations for the future. When this organization first met in Quebec in 1945,[47] suffering from famine and malnutrition were widespread—not only in the poorer nations of the world but also in the industrialized nations decimated by war. Since then, we have seen nations once critically dependent on food aid break through the barriers to self-reliance; we have seen agricultural trade revive to reach record levels; we have seen agriculture transformed by research and technology so we can now realistically aspire to end hunger and malnutrition in every part of the world.

Much progress has been made and a great deal of it can be attributed to the untiring efforts of FAO. You and your predecessors are to be commended for the vision and determination you have brought to this organization's programs. But there is still much work to do. The reports we have heard here on the food situation in Africa only highlight the need for even more progress.

Some of the issues we face here today are similar to those we faced when FAO was founded. All the purposes of FAO remain the same: improving nutrition and the standards of living in member nations, fostering rural development and making the production and distribution of food more efficient. But the dimensions and complexities of the problems have changed.

Hunger and malnutrition still afflict many nations, but now we are also confronted with other problems that complicate our task. Inflation has eaten into the budgets of our governments and of international organizations, a dangerous drift toward protectionism is undermining agricultural trade and development and a worldwide recession has reduced earnings for all and threatens our efforts to strengthen agriculture in the developing world.

I would like to share the views of the United States on these issues with you and offer some ideas on how we can work together to address them. In doing so, I will touch briefly on the United States' assistance to developing nations, our domestic and international agricultural policies, world food security, and FAO's programs and budget.

The productivity of U.S. farmers has given the United States unparalleled agricultural abundance. But we have not enjoyed our abundance with little regard for the rest of the world. We have always recognized the obligation to share our agricultural productivity with those who are less fortunate.

Since 1954, the United States has carried out the world's largest bilateral food aid program under Public Law 480.[48] Begun by President Eisenhower, the program is now aptly called "Food for Peace." Food aid through this program has already topped $40 billion, more than the aid given by all other donor nations combined. In addition to this ongoing program, the Reagan administration began a new initiative just last month. We are now making U.S. Government stocks of butter, cheese and nonfat dry milk available for donation to other governments and public and private organizations that work to assist needy people in other nations.[49]

But our bilateral programs are only part of the picture. We have also given strong support to multinational organizations like

[46] Reference is to the U.N. Conference on Food and Agriculture which convened at Hot Springs, Virginia, May 18, 1943, to discuss the postwar food and agricultural situation and establish an international institution to deal with world production and distribution of food.

[47] The Food and Agricultural Organization was established on October 16, 1945, when its Constitution was signed in Quebec.

[48] Reference is to the Agricultural Trade Development and Assistance Act of 1954 (P.L. 83–480), enacted July 10, 1954; for text, see 68 Stat. 454, and subsequent amendments.

[49] Secretary of Agriculture John R. Block announced on October 8, 1982, that the USDA would make dairy surpluses available for food assistance, under Section 416 of the Agriculture Act of 1949. (Department of Agriculture *Major News Releases and Speeches*, October 8–October 15, 1982, p. 5)

the World Food Program and UNICEF and to voluntary organizations.

As evidence of this, Secretary Block announced a record pledge to the World Food Program in October in honor of FAO's commemoration of World Food Day.[50] This pledge of $250 million for 1983–84 represents a substantial increase of 14 percent over our pledge for 1981–82. It further demonstrates our confidence in the World Food Program and its leadership.

Our domestic agricultural policy continues to emphasize production within a free market economy. But low crop prices and reduced demand for U.S. exports have necessitated an acreage reduction program aimed at raising the prices our farmers receive for major commodities. With record stocks already on hand, the issue becomes insuring the long-term productivity of U.S. agriculture by acting to support prices.

We must see to it that agriculture is profitable in the United States if U.S. farmers are to help meet the world's growing demand for food in the decades ahead.

The United States has placed high priority on agricultural research and we are promoting new measures to preserve our soil and water resources. USDA has worked both bilaterally and with international organizations like FAO to share the benefits of U.S. agricultural research and technical expertise. The Department now has technical assistance projects in 76 countries and some 239 cooperative international research projects.

Working with FAO and AID, USDA has provided training for over 70,000 agriculturalists from developing countries. And we now have scientific and technical exchanges with more than 30 developing and developed nations to share knowledge and experience in agriculture.

Our domestic research and conservation efforts will help guarantee our continued role as the largest supplier of food for world markets. At the same time, we stand ready to share our know-how with other nations to help them improve their productivity and protect their agricultural resources.

U.S. domestic agricultural production and policies are inextricably linked to international trade. Farmers in the United States now export about half of their soybean production, two-thirds of their wheat, and one-third of their corn. The situation is similar for a number of other commodities. The simple fact is that U.S. farmers must export because they now depend on overseas sales for a fourth of their income.

The United States is aggressively pursuing international trade policies in agriculture that will be in the long-run interests of all nations—developed and developing. One step taken recently should be of particular benefit to developing countries. It is a new blended credit program announced by Secretary Block.[51]

This program is directed primarily at helping developing countries to purchase more of the agricultural products they need by lowering interest costs. The program will eventually make $1.5 billion available to lower these costs, and should increase the ability of developing nations to buy U.S. food for current use or for building their reserves.

We are also working on the broader goal of liberalizing world trade in agriculture. I will be taking part in the GATT ministerials in Geneva later this week.[52] The United States has taken the position that agricultural trade must fall under the same GATT rules that govern trade in manufactured products. Export subsidies and trade barriers must become the exception and not the rule in international agricultural trade. They should be a last resort, used only when absolutely necessary.

The developing nations share our concern about how the routine use of export subsidies and trade barriers disrupts world agricultural trade and lessens the incentives for production.

We believe that more liberalized trade in agricultural commodities is essential both for world food security and to the economic well-being of developing nations. Certainly the United States has a vested interest in removing barriers to world trade. But we are not the only ones who can profit from freer trade in agriculture. And we do not view agricultural trade as a one-way street. The United States is the single largest mar-

[50] Block pledged the U.S. contribution October 15, 1982, in commemoration of World Food Day, October 16, 1982. (*Ibid.*, p. 21)

[51] On October 20, 1982, Block announced a program of interest-free direct government support credits to be blended with government guaranteed private credits to be used as loans to developing countries at below market rates. (*Ibid.*, October 29–November 12, 1982, pp. 18–19)

[52] The GATT Ministerial Meeting was held in Geneva, November 24–29, 1982; for the text of the resulting communiqué, see document 76.

ket for the agricultural exports of the developing countries in spite of our large domestic production.

Freer agricultural trade is essential to world food security, because without it we cannot encourage farmers to produce at a level to meet the world's food needs. The United States has already done more than its share to contribute to world food security. We are firmly committed to FAO's plan of action on world food security. The United States' grain reserves, now at the highest level in history, assure availability for our food aid commitments as well as our regular commercial customers.

But the U.S. stocks of grains for 1982/83 are in our opinion excessive and are far too high a percentage of the world's cereals stocks. Most of the other large grain producing and exporting countries have taken little, if any, action to build stocks during this period of excessive supplies.

Concrete action by these countries is warranted in view of their statements of support for FAO's plan of action for food security.

The United States strongly urges other governments to develop and maintain their own national grain reserve programs. We are making funds available through the U.S. Agency for International Development to help enhance food security in the developing countries. I would like to take a few moments to comment on some of FAO's ongoing programs.

The director general should be commended for the follow-up activities in support of the program of action adopted at the World Conference on Agrarian Reform and Rural Development.[53] As the nations involved work with FAO on this program, we urge them to maximize the role of the private sector in both rural development and improving the distribution of food and agricultural products.

As President Reagan noted at Cancun last year,[54] the tremendous potential of private enterprise has often been overlooked in development programs. Once private enterprise has been drawn into the picture, it remains a valuable resource.

President Reagan's offer to send agricultural task forces to help other nations with agricultural development fully reflects the U.S. emphasis on food and agriculture in its development efforts. Presidential Agricultural Task Forces from the United States have already visited Peru, Thailand, Honduras, Venezuela, and Liberia.

In another bilateral development program, the United States has begun to move quickly to distribute the special and additional funds Congress has approved for our Caribbean Basin Initiative.[55] A $350 million package of assistance has already been largely distributed and we expect Congress to take up the trade aspects of the program soon.

FAO has continued to do an excellent job of collecting and disseminating worldwide data on food and agriculture and maintaining an early warning system. The United States finds these activities particularly helpful in its own economic analyses of world agricultural conditions.

We are also pleased by FAO's activities in animal and plant pest control and its collaboration with other international agencies in Africa and Latin America in this effort. We welcome the greater emphasis FAO has given to more effective management of forest resources and hope to see the role forestry plays in FAO's programs expand even further in the future.

There is a growing appreciation of the vital role that forest conservation plays in agricultural development, particularly in the tropical countries. Better forest management will not only improve agricultural production, it can create jobs, build fuelwood supplies and help contain the spread of serious erosion. The World Food Program has made a significant contribution in the forestry area with its work on reforestation in developing countries.

There can be no question of the United States' continuing support for the essential programs being carried out by FAO. But at the same time the present economic crisis in the industrialized countries has begun to limit the resources available for many worthwhile tasks. The United States has made substantial cuts in domestic programs in an effort to rebuild its economy on a firmer, noninflationary base. We do not want to see another spiral of inflation. Inflated dollars would simply buy less of what the American people need at home and only devalue the funds we contribute to international activities.

[53] The World Conference on Agrarian Reform and Rural Development was held in Rome, July 12–20, 1979.

[54] Regarding President Reagan's statements at Cancun, Mexico, see footnote 3 to document 82.

[55] For documentation regarding the Caribbean Basin Initiative, see Chapter 15, Part C.

We agree with Director General Saouma that FAO must also work hard to control expenditures and see that its funds are well spent. He recently raised this issue at the FAO Regional Conferences for Latin America and Africa.[56] And we appreciate the steps he has already taken. All of us must work together to help FAO focus its resources on high priority areas and control administrative costs so its work will continue to be as effective as possible.

Great strides have been made in agricultural development in many nations—India, Pakistan, Brazil, the Philippines, Niger—to name only a few. Much of the credit for this can be taken by FAO. But there is much more to do before we can lay claim to winning the battle against hunger and malnutrition. If we are ever to make that claim, we must wage the battle together. We must appreciate each other's strengths and limitations. In that way, the progress we have made so far can be carried on and we can set a course for even greater achievements in the future.

F. International Economic Summit Conferences

Document 87

Statement by the Assistant Secretary of State for Economic and Business Affairs (Hormats) Before the Joint Economic Committee of Congress, May 27, 1982[1]

The Versailles Summit as Both a Challenge and an Opportunity

Thank you, Mr. Chairman.[2]

First of all, I would like to say that in calling this series of hearings, you have undertaken what I believe to be a very constructive and useful inquiry. I gather that over the last several days, you have looked at a number of aspects, both short term and long term, of U.S. international economic policy.

I would like to take the opportunity here to discuss the approach that the administration is taking to the question of Versailles, and then I would be delighted, of course, to answer any questions you have on the issues that you are going to cover today, which relate to the developing countries.

Before discussing the detailed issues for consideration at the Versailles summit, I would like to review a bit of the history of economic summits, to put them in a broader context.

French President Giscard D'Estaing called for a meeting of heads of state of the major industrialized countries in 1975.[3] It's useful to recall the situation of the international economy in the immediately preceding period. During the 5 years from 1970 to 1975, the world economy experienced:

The trauma of Vietnam, which strained traditionally close political relations between the United States and Western Europe;

Abandonment of the Bretton Woods parity system and great uncertainty about new arrangements;

Highly unstable commodity prices, in which food and raw material prices soared to record heights;

Quadrupling of energy prices, which not only strained the productive structure of industrialized countries, but created massive imbalances in global payments;

Major pressures on the international trading system, resulting from these imbalances and efforts of countries to offset them; and

Serious doubt as to the capability of the international financial system to cope with the requisite recycling of OPEC surpluses.

In sum, the international economic system was battered. There was widespread questioning of international institutions and of the ability of the major western countries to restore order.

It was in this setting that the first summit was held. Its objectives were to reassure the

---

[56] The FAO Regional Conference for Latin America was held in Managua, August 30–September 10, 1982; the one for Africa was held in Algiers, September 22–October 2, 1982.

[1] Source: *Versailles Summit and the World Economy: High Interest Rates and Protectionism: Hearings Before the Joint Economic Committee, Congress of the United States, Ninety-seventh Congress, Second Session* (Washington, 1982), pp. 228–231.

[2] Henry S. Reuss.

[3] The first international economic summit was held at the Chateau de Rambouillet near Paris, France, November 15–17, 1975.

peoples of the West that their leaders could successfully grapple with the severe problems facing the world economy. It stressed the value of consultation and common effort in dealing with these problems.

It was not a new international decision-making body, but rather was designed to reinforce international institutions, a commitment to close cooperation, and the need to avoid attempts by companies to solve problems at one another's expense.

In the intervening years, summits have strengthened common efforts in several areas:

Resisting protectionist pressures;

Reducing dependence on oil imports;

Supporting constructive relations with developing nations; and

Setting a firm anti-inflationary course after the 1979 oil shock.

Despite progress in several areas, serious problems remain. At Versailles, the legacy of inflation from the 1970's will still be a major consideration. In the United States, in Europe, and in Canada, unemployment is at record levels for the postwar period. The inability of young people to find their first job continues to disillusion an entire generation.

In the international economy, there is widespread questioning of the fairness and adequacy of the trade and investment rules, and doubt has been raised whether the trading system, which over the past three decades has increased trading opportunities and led to the most rapid growth in world trade ever experienced, can effectively serve the needs of the decades ahead.

The currently soft energy market threatens to make us complacent and to cause us to let down our guard. It distracts us from the still-urgent need to assure energy supplies necessary for our security and adequate for a full recovery.

This is a complex and difficult situation. There is no quick or easy solution. Both here and abroad, many are tempted to turn inward to try to solve their problems by:

Increased protection or subsidies;

Erratic changes in policy which may have short-term benefits but long-term costs;

Concentrating on the faults of others, rather than applying their efforts to needed domestic actions, such as increasing productive investment and the capacity of economies to adjust to new competitive challenges and opportunities;

Avoiding or circumventing international institutions, rather than making efforts to strengthen and improve them.

Following World War II, the United States and its major Western partners recognized that economic recovery in Europe and Japan, and the future prosperity of the West, required close cooperation to build an international economic system which increased opportunities for trade and investment. Each recognized that its own economic growth, while depending first and foremost on sound domestic policies, also required a well-functioning international economy.

The IMF, World Bank, GATT, European Community, and OECD stand as living monuments to the wisdom and leadership of Marshall, Monnet, Acheson, Spaak, and others. They permitted and brought about a steadily opening international economy, which gave an enormous boost to trade and in turn, to jobs in the United States and in other nations. The prosperity of the postwar period owes much to these institutions, which too frequently we tend today to take for granted.

Today, however, there are pressures in this country and in others to disengage from a system which sometimes seems cumbersome, unresponsive, or unfair, and to adopt a more introspective international posture.

Let's face it. There are serious problems before our economies, individually and collectively. We as a nation must address these forthrightly, by strengthening our domestic economy, by actively pursuing our interests internationally, and by insuring a common multilateral effort to improve those institutions on which, despite their problems, we still depend, and in which we still have a vital interest.

Our prosperity depends on our willingness and ability to defend America's interest in and within a well-functioning world economy.

There are those in this country, as in others, who counsel disengagement from the institutions and rules which make up the world economy. They tend to forget the tragic lessons of the interwar period. But there are others who, I believe, remain in the majority and most countries, who recognize that, while we have high unemployment and inflation today, a breakdown in the international economic system and a move to protectionism would seriously worsen both of these problems.

I profoundly share that view.

But while urging a rejection of pressures for unilateral solutions, and in order to remain credible in doing so, we must correct the problems which give rise to them. To this end, the leadership of the United States is essential.

We remain the world's major economy and the political and security leader of the West. But, unlike the period immediately following World War II, we share economic influence with other countries, and our ability to play a constructive role depends on our ability to insure a partnership of shared responsibility with other major economies.

That is what the Versailles summit is all about. It's a historic opportunity to identify areas for common action to strengthen the world economy, both in the interest of our own nations and that of the many other nations who look to us for responsible leadership.

I will mention but two of the areas in which we hope to make progress in Versailles.

First, on macroeconomic and international monetary policies, we will work to reinforce international consultations among the major economies. Through greater consultation, each country can frame its policies in a way which leads toward sustained, noninflationary economic growth in the medium term.

In the declaration of the first summit at Rambouillet,[4] the major countries accepted a particular responsibility for the stability of the international monetary system.

Questions have, from time to time, been raised whether other countries are sufficiently sensitive to, or knowledgeable of, one another's concerns on problems of domestic economic policy, and how greater economic stability in the financial markets can be achieved. More frequent and more intense consultations can enable nations to encourage one another toward sound economic policies, and to understand better the impact of each of these policies on the other.

Second, on trade, we are desperately close to undoing the multilateral trading system. That system is at a crossroads; either we improve it and strengthen its capacity to resolve problems, or risk its deterioration.

The benefits of an open trading system have been demonstrated over the years, but for it to continue, our citizens must have confidence that it is working fairly and effectively.

There are important areas which are not adequately addressed by the GATT rules. The ministerial meeting of the GATT this fall is an historic opportunity to address the trade issues of the 1980's.[5] We will seek at Versailles not only a strong endorsement of the value of the multilateral trading system, but also a commitment to make concrete progress at the GATT Ministerial, to begin the effort to strengthen the GATT and to insure that its rules cover new areas, such as services, high technology, and trade related investment issues.

I will conclude my introductory remarks here, Mr. Chairman, but look forward to a wide ranging discussion based on your and your colleagues' questions.

Thank you very much.

Document 88

Statement by the Secretary of the Treasury (Regan) at a Press Briefing, June 1, 1982 (Extract)[6]

Issues and Objectives at Versailles

. . . .

There will be about seven main topics for discussion at the economic summit at Versailles. First an obvious one is the macroeconomic policies and monetary policies of each of the nations with primary reference to that of the United States. Our

[4] For the text of the declaration issued at the first economic summit at Rambouillet, November 17, 1975, see Department of State *Bulletin*, December 8, 1975, pp. 805–807.

[5] For documentation on the GATT Ministerial Meeting held in Geneva, November 24–29, 1982, see Part B.

[6] Source: White House Press Release, June 1, 1982, Office of the Press Secretary to the President. This briefing was given jointly with Secretary of State Alexander M. Haig, Jr., in the Old Executive Office Building at 12:36 p.m.

economy is in a recession, our unemployment rate is high, and our interest rates are even higher.

The effect of these on the other nations at the summit will be the subject of much discussion. We will be indicating that we are not happy with our interest rates, our unemployment record. We are quite happy with our inflation record, and you will recall that at Ottawa in July of last year[7] that was the main topic—the inflation rate in the United States. It no longer is.

We will be trying to get more cooperation among our countries toward greater economic stability and a convergence of our economic policies, probably with reference to the IMF. That is, where the IMF now has an annual consultation with each nation regarding its own monetary policies, perhaps this should be done within some type of framework of a collective review of particularly the industrialized nations as to whether they are all, to use an old metaphor, pulling in harness, or whether there is one that is going one way and all the others going another way.

From the point of view of the world's economy the next most important subject is trade. There we again will be advocating more reliance on free and open markets. We will be advocating less in the way of subsidies for exports by the summit nations and less in their domestic programs of protectionism for their own industries to the detriment of others.

Obviously each of us differs in this respect but we will be advocating that we work mainly within the GATT in order to achieve these objectives. I might add there that probably what we—there are three items of trade that have been at least overlooked or not as often mentioned. Most people when they think in terms of trade think in terms of manufactured products moving between countries. We are going to stress there also the huge dependence in the United States on services where 70 percent of our employment is in the services industry and more and more of our trade is in the services area, which is giving us primarily our balance-of-payments surplus.

Agriculture—another important topic as far as trade is concerned and high technology. We will come back to high technology in a minute.

Now, the other issues, which Al will no doubt answer more fully later involve East–West issues regarding measures that should go along the line of what the recent meeting of the OECD[8] came up with, which is with regard to export credits to the Soviet Union, and somehow or other to resolve that problem to our mutual satisfaction of how to go about getting a handle on this problem.

We will be plugging for more help in the way of getting some dialogue started for rules on investment among nations. There are rules for international trade in the GATT. There are rules for monetary behavior in the IMF. There are no rules for investment in countries, both industrialized countries as well as the developing countries. And it certainly is a subject that needs treatment. I have only to look at the various rules of many of the people at the summit regarding investment in their own country by foreigners to realize the extent of what we're talking about. We don't expect any concrete results here except to get the process started leading some toward these generalized rules.

The—we'll also be talking there in terms of North–South relationships. As you know both at Ottawa and Cancun[9] we were discussing global negotiations. And we, again, will be discussing how we can get that process started. The G–77 has made certain recommendations.[10] Their recommendations will be discussed and, in particular, the United States views on the protection of

[7] For documentation on the Ottawa Economic Summit, July 19–21, 1981, see *American Foreign Policy: Current Documents, 1981*, Chapter 5, Part F.

[8] Regarding the OECD Ministerial Meeting held in Paris, May 10–11, 1982, see document 64.

[9] For documentation on the International Meeting on Cooperation and Development, Cancun, Mexico, October 22–23, 1981, see *American Foreign Policy: Current Documents, 1981*, Chapter 5, Part F.

[10] Group of 77 or G–77 refers to a group of developing nations which organized to set forth a program of action prior to the first meeting of the U.N. Conference on Trade and Development in 1964. The group, now expanded to an estimated 121 nations, operates as a developing country caucus on economic matters in the United Nations. In December 1979 the G–77 nations proposed that global negotiations on international economic cooperation for development, or large-scale multilateral meetings of rich and poor nations, be launched. The possibility of global negotiations under the sponsorship of the United Nations was authorized by U.N. General Assembly Resolution 34/138, which was passed on December 14, 1979. The original proposal has been revised several times, but the recommendations referenced here refer to the March 31, 1982 draft resolution circulated informally by the G–77 which was discussed at the Versailles Economic Summit.

the already existing institutions, such as the World Bank, the International Monetary Fund, the GATT itself, and many other institutions, and the necessity for protecting them during any such discussions and what would follow from the discussions.

And, finally, a main topic will be the subject of technology itself. This is something that President Mitterrand will put forth right at the outset of the summit; something that he wishes to push forward for because he thinks that this is the future, both from an employment point of view as well as from a better life type of view; what we can do with such things as biogenetics, improve communications with electronic data processing and other types of high tech area. This is apart from its application to defense or its application as far as nuclear [matters?] is concerned. Because there are many ways that technology can be used. So, obviously, a subject of great discussion.

I think that what we will be coming out of the summit with is a better feeling about how to cooperate in these areas with each other, and, of course, obviously the communiqué will make reference to the ways in which we intend to have that cooperation exhibited and what we intended to do about these topics between now and the next summit.

. . . .

Document 89

Transcript of an Interview With President Reagan, June 1, 1982 (Extract)[11]

The Exchange Market Intervention and East–West Credit Issue

Q. Thank you, Mr. President. Let's speak before the Versailles summit. The President of my country, Francois Mitterrand, among other European leaders, would like to reach a better harmony between the dollar, the Japanese yen and the European money. Do you foresee a possible compromise about this question?

The President. I don't know that it's so much a compromise as I believe that what is necessary to have a stable exchange is to have more stable economies for all of us. And I hope that out of our talks we can find ways to approach the problems that face all of us economically in such a way as to be going more in the same direction.

Here, we, in our own country, have undertaken to curb inflation and have had, I think, a remarkable success in that for the last three months it has been running at less than 1 percent rate here. And for the last 6 months, only 2.8 percent.

The exchange—the idea—we're opposed, as you know, to government intervention on an ongoing basis in exchange rates in our floating exchange. We would like to see a study made of the history, recent history of government intervention and what its record has been.

At the same time, we will support intervention for extreme disruptions and dislocations in the exchange rate. But above all, again, I repeat, I think that achieving a stable economy for all of our countries is the best insurance that we will have a stable rate of exchange.

Q. Mr. President, I remember that last year in Ottawa, you were promising, you were predicting that the U.S. interest rates would have decreased in 6 months. Are you going to do the same statement this year in Versailles?

The President. I think I could safely say that because, while at that time we had not yet put our economic program in place, we got the most of what we were asking from our Congress. And the interest rates did come down. They are down about 25 percent, but that's not nearly enough. When we stated in office, this administration stated we inherited interest rates that were the highest they had been in our country in more than 100 years. We did come down, as I say, about 25 percent, but with the increase in unemployment, they have stayed much too high. I am hoping that the Congress will be more forthcoming with regard to the new budget than they were last week because I believe that, when we get another budget of the kind we had last year that shows continued reductions in the rate of

---

[11] Source: White House Press Release, June 1, 1982, Office of the Press Secretary to the President; printed also in *Weekly Compilation of Presidential Documents*, June 7, 1982, pp. 733–738. The interview began at 3:20 p.m. in the library of the White House. Interviewing the President were Gerard Saint-Paul of French Television I, Sergio Telmon of Italian Television-RAI, Martin Bell of BBC Television, and Hans-Dieter Kronzucher of West German Television-ZDF.

increase in government spending here, we will see another drop in the interest rates before the end of the year.

Q. Mr. President, there hasn't been an economic summit, I think, which didn't end with a ringing declaration against protectionism and we expect that to happen now, although protectionism seems to be creeping onwards. I wonder if, whether on this issue as on others, it's going to make all that much difference whether you go to Versailles or whether you don't.

THE PRESIDENT. I'm going to Versailles, but that will be a very important subject and I am going to try hard and I'm sure that others will, too, to point out the fallacy of protectionism. What the world really needs today is a greater extension of free trade, removing the obstacles to that free trade and this is also very important with regard to the developing nations, the lesser developed nations that all of us have met with regard to helping as we met at Cancun.

One of the things that they need is to know that there is an open market for their product, whether it be agricultural produce or whether it be something manufactured. And I am going to strive hard to preach the sermon that protectionism actually ends up in a restraint of trade and open trade means more jobs for all our people.

Q. East–West trade, Mr. President, is an important prospect of European economy. It is said that you want to curb this trade. Especially, you want to refrain the Allies of providing the Soviet Union with extra-cheap credit for their economy. Could you elaborate on that?

THE PRESIDENT. Yes, I could. It's not a case of wanting a permanent quarantine of the Soviet Union or anything of that kind. But we have all discussed and have taken various actions because of our opposition to what the Soviet Union is doing in Poland, Afghanistan, its military buildup to the point that it hangs over all of us as something of a threat.

The Soviet Union is having its economic problems, too. And I just believe that now is a time not to continue subsidizing them with cheap credit so they can continue their military buildup. But is it time to approach them and point out that there is a different way? But none of the countries of the Western World represent a threat to the Soviet Union, none of us have any desire to be aggressive where they're concerned. But maybe we could through restraining credit and refusing any longer to subsidize their military buildup, that we could persuade them to come closer to becoming a member of the family of nations, Europe, and here, and in Asia, that want peace and want a trade relationship worldwide.

And so, what I will be proposing is not some return to the Cold War as such, but a temporary period of restraint while we show them what we have to offer, on the other hand, if they will give up their expansionist policies and their obvious militarism.

Q. You couldn't convince the European Allies of refraining from building the Trans-Siberian Pipeline.[12] How will you convince the allies of this program?

THE PRESIDENT. The reasons given for our not being able to convince them, at least given by our allies, was that these were contracts that in many instances had already been put in place before the present administration's leaders were in office. And so they felt bound by contract to go along with this.

I think the credit is a different matter, and again, I say, it doesn't make much sense to be forced into programs of costly arms buildup on our side simply to meet a threat that comes from one place and one alone, the Soviet Union, which, in the recent years of detente, during what was supposed to be a detente, was going forward with the greatest military buildup in the history of man. And maybe we need to get their attention.

. . . . . .

---

12 For documentation on President Reagan's opposition to the construction of the Trans-Siberian Pipeline and his extension of export sanctions against the Soviet Union on June 18, 1982, see Chapter 10, Part A.

Document 90

Transcript of a Press Briefing by the Secretary of the Treasury (Regan), Versailles, France, June 5, 1982[13]

Issues Raised at the First Plenary Session of the Versailles Economic Summit: Technology and International Monetary Policy

SECRETARY REGAN. Well, as you know, we had the first session this morning. It opened a little before 10 a.m. The main subject for the first part, lasting through the coffee break and until about 12:30 p.m., was the subject of research, technology, employment, growth.

Each of the Heads of State spoke in regard to this. President Mitterrand led off the discussion and then later passed out copies of his paper on the subject.[14]

The U. S. position was, as expressed by President Reagan, that we welcomed this initiative on the part of President Mitterrand, we agreed to—that there should be a working party that should further study the subject of technology and how to improve it.

The President cautioned, though, that this should be mainly in the private sector rather than in the public sector, pointing out that most of the innovations over the past half century or more have been in the private sector of the United States rather than through government. He gave out some figures to the effect that we have—or are spending in the United States about $80 billion on research and development, half of which is coming from the private sector. Of the $40-odd million that's in the public sector government spending, $5.5 billion of that is pure research, has nothing to do with applied research.

He also pointed out that a Presidential study in this area that was reported to President Roosevelt, Franklin, in the early 1930's, as to what would be the great innovation in research and development over the next 25 years, failed to mention such things as television, plastics, space technology, jet planes, organ transplants, laser beams, "and even," he said, "such a common item," and he held up his ballpoint pen, "as a ballpoint pen."[15]

So he said, "There's no way we can predict what will be happening over the next 25 years with any degree of clarity as to what the inventions will be."

He also said that we should not fear technology because a lot of people, a lot of nations do fear that there will be higher unemployment as a result of newly-introduced technology. And he used the homely illustration of the dial telephone, stating that when the dial telephone first came in, it was thought that all of the female telephone operators would be thrown out of work.

Well, he went on to say that today more than ever, there are more women employed in the United States than at any other time. And were women still on the dial—still manning the telephones, it would take every woman in the United States to man the telephone system of the United States, if, indeed, that were possible.

So, he said, we shouldn't fear the results of technology but rather should welcome it. He said that it would promote growth and that it would promote more employment.

Why don't I pause here now to—oh, as far as President Reagan is concerned, also, let me get to a second point, after the subject of technology had been pretty well exhausted, the summit turned to the subject of macroeconomics.

President Mitterrand asked Chancellor Schmidt to lead off. Schmidt said he didn't know how he got to be a Sherpa for macroeconomics, but, nevertheless, he went ahead and described his ideas of where the nations of the world stood at the current moment from an economic point of view.

Most of these facts are well known about high unemployment in most of the nations

---

[13] Source: White House Press Release, June 5, 1982, Office of the Press Secretary to the President. This briefing took place at L'Orangerie Press Center at 1:05 p.m.

[14] For the text of the "Report by Mr. Francois Mitterrand, President of the French Republic, at the summit of the industrialized countries," given at Versailles, Saturday, June 5, 1982, see *Summit of the Industrialized Countries, Versailles, June 4th, 5th, and 6th, 1982,* Ministère des Relations Exterieures, Direction des Services D'Information et de Presse (Paris, 1982), pp. 1–14.

[15] Reference is to a 338-page report entitled *Technology Trends and National Policy* (Washington, 1937) by the National Resources Committee under the chairmanship of the Secretary of the Interior Harold Ickes in 1937.

involved in the summit, about the fact that we simultaneously have high rates of interest and a recession, which is something very unusual.

He pointed out that the real rates of interest, particularly in the United States, were the highest they've ever been. He thought that this was something that all of us should work on. He said he wasn't pointing the finger at the United States, but all nations would have to get their domestic policies into effect, that there were too many transfer payments. Deficits are running too high. There's much too much public borrowing.

President Reagan then gave his intervention and in the course of it described our economy. Again, most of these facts are known to you. I'll tick them off rather quickly.

The fact that we do have high unemployment but he pointed out that the figures we received yesterday, that unemployment as a percentage is up from 9.4 to 9.5 at the same time indicated that over a million new job seekers were in the marketplace. Of that number, 800,000 had found employment and at the current moment, we were employing over 100 million Americans. That's the greatest number of employed Americans in our history.

He also stated that our high rates of interest were psychological in his judgment, that inflation was down. He gave the figures on inflation—a little over 6 percent for 12 months around—a little over 2 percent for 6 months, less than 1 percent for the last 3 months. In fact, 1 month of deflation. He said that that indicated to him that interest rates would come down as soon as the fear of those who are loaning money that we could have continually high federal deficits—those fears were allayed. And he thought that could be done by a budget process that would end in the near future with federal deficits showing that they would be down over the next 3 months—over the next 3 years with a balanced budget in sight. And at that point, there was an adjournment for luncheon. So, I'll pause here and take questions as long as I can before I have to leave.

Q. Sir, the Italian Government has just put out this statement saying that they would consider unacceptable any proposal for any mechanisms that would exclude Italy or could be limited to five countries only to the question of intervening in the exchanges markets.

You have been quoted as favorable as such a mechanism that is limited to five countries. Was this quotation correct? Are you in favor of this—does this proposal exist?

SECRETARY REGAN. I cannot answer with any degree of precision exactly what the quote says because I have not seen the quote nor am I aware of it. Let me tell you what went on. This was a subject that was discussed at the finance ministers' dinner last night. No conclusions were drawn. We are to look at a text of a statement that will describe this process at luncheon. It's the first item on our agenda.

As far as the United States is concerned, we have pointed out that we are for a study of whether or not intervention is worthwhile. The President said in his remarks this morning to the heads of state that our own studies made earlier in 1981 did not prove the value of intervention. Yet, he would be willing to have such a study.

We've also said that besides studying intervention, we also need close cooperation among the economies of the leading nations. Now, in no way have I ever said that I want Italy eliminated from any consideration in intervention. No way. There has been discussion in the finance ministers as to whether or not the so-called "SDR"[16] currencies which come under the IMF should be the practical aspects of the study. The five SDR currencies that make up the unit of the SDR are the franc, the D-mark,—the French franc, the D-mark, the yen, the pound sterling and the dollar. It does not include the lire. But that does not mean that Italy would not participate in the study.

So, there has been no judgment rendered on Italy and you can quote me to that effect.

Q. Mr. Secretary—

SECRETARY REGAN. Yes.

Q. A question on substance, if you please.

SECRETARY REGAN. I thought that was. (Laughter)

Q. No, Delors[17] says that he feels that the United States has adopted a different

16 The reference is to Special Drawing Rights (SDR's) which are artificial international reserve units created by the International Monetary Fund in 1969 to supplement the limited supplies of gold and dollars. SDR is a unit of account whose value is determined by the weighted average of the currencies of the five major industrial countries—United States, Japan, the Federal Republic of Germany, France, and the United Kingdom.

17 Jacques Delors, French Minister of Economy and Finance.

philosophy and you could expect a greater U.S. readiness to intervene in the market. Would you comment on that?

SECRETARY REGAN. The United States has agreed to study intervention to see if it is worthwhile. We have also agreed to abide by something that we've already signed—the International Monetary Fund Agreements. The International Monetary Fund Agreements, Article IV[18] states that a nation should intervene whenever there are disorderly markets. We have agreed to do this and said we are prepared to intervene in disorderly markets.

Q. What is a disorderly market?

SECRETARY REGAN. A disorderly market is not defined under Article IV, it is left up to the nations to decide that.

Q. Will that be defined by that group of five or seven?

SECRETARY REGAN. Will that be defined by the group of five or seven? I am not precluding what will be in the study or won't be. I would think it is something that they would try to make a judgment on.

Q. Mr. Secretary, last night Professor Delors told us that you had agreed to the things that you just mentioned and that you had also agreed to a plan which is called Zones of Likelihood and he said are similar to target zones but less constraining. And he also implied that you had not ruled out intervening against the long-term thrust of the market. Would you comment on that?

SECRETARY REGAN. We have not agreed to any such thing. I don't believe—I am not saying that Minister Delors did or did not say that, but that is not an accurate description of what we have agreed to. I will repeat and go back to exactly what we have agreed to. We have agreed to the study and to participate in the study. We don't know what the study will reveal. We have also agreed that nations of the world should cooperate more in their economies, because if we don't cooperate in our targets in trying to arrive, for example, at low inflation among all our nations, we cannot have stable currencies. You cannot have stable relationships when one country is inflating and the other country is deflating. The currencies have to reflect that.

Now to the extent that we will be cooperating and trying to keep our inflation down, that should not be read to mean that we are ready to intervene in any way that changed the main thrust or main direction that the dollar might be going. If it is a strong dollar we are not going to intervene to weaken it. If it is a weak dollar we are not going to intervene to make it strong. If it is a disorderly market in the dollar we will intervene.

All right, one more right over here.

Q. When President Reagan told the other leaders that a balanced budget was in sight, did he indicate when and would that be under—in a year in which he might perhaps still be President?

SECRETARY REGAN. President Reagan is a man of long vision. (Laughter)

Thank you very much.

Document 91

Transcript of a Press Briefing by the Secretary of the Treasury (Regan), Versailles, France, June 5, 1982 (Extracts)[19]

Issues Raised at the Second Plenary Session: Macroeconomics, Trade, and Investment

MR. SPEAKES. Secretary Regan has been participating in the meetings this afternoon with President Reagan. He is here to brief you and take your questions. It is on the record and, of course, available for radio and television coverage.

SECRETARY REGAN. Thank you, Larry.

This afternoon the session was primarily devoted to the wrap-up of the macroeconomic statements by the heads of state. And then we got into trade, and the subjects lasted most of the day. I told you this morning earlier or early this afternoon what the President had to say about macro.

---

18 Article IV as revised by the Second Amendment of the Articles of Agreement of the International Monetary Fund was approved by the IMF Board of Governors on April 30, 1976, and entered into force on April 1, 1978; for the text of this Agreement and Article IV, see 29 UST 2203.

19 Source: White House Press Release, June 5, 1982, Office of the Press Secretary to the President; printed also in Department of State *Bulletin*, July 1982, p. 3. This briefing took place at L'Orangerie Press Center at 7:41 p.m.

When it came to trade, by that time he had left for his Saturday, live radio show[20] so I did the intervention on trade.

Our points were that we would have to come out strong for free trade and less protectionism during this summit or we might find ourselves going backwards; that the trade among free nations was the hallmark of the post-World War II era and it was up to the summit nations to preserve what had brought prosperity to most nations over the period since that time.

The other points that we made were the need for promoting some type of rules for investment. As you know, there are rules for trade in the GATT. There are rules for money in the IMF, but there are no rules for international investment. And we advocated that the heads of state consider this in their communiqué and give instructions to the finance ministers that they should begin discussions leading eventually toward some such rulemaking.

The other points that came up during the afternoon that might be of interest to you. There was quite an exchange among the Canadian Prime Minister, the British Prime Minister, the German Chancellor and the President of the United States. And the subject was unemployment and inflation, and whether or not there is a tradeoff. If you recall the so-called Phillip's Curve, that is where the more that you have inflation, the more unemployment you'll have; and the less inflation, the less unemployment.

And the President is pretty firm, sticking by his positions as to the fact that while we have high unemployment rate in the United States, we still have at this particular time more employed in the United States. We have gotten our inflation rate down.

The German Chancellor's position was that interest rates and inflation actually started up way back in the time of President Lyndon Johnson and the Vietnam War and the way the United States financed the Vietnam War. And oil prices were not the immediate cause of inflation, but they were just an additive on the road.

The other things that happened during the afternoon; there's another exchange in which the German Chancellor asked the President of the United States at what point he thought that deficits would be coming down in the United States, because he said that psychologically that was, in his judgment, keeping up interest rates. And this was having an adverse effect on the European countries as well as the rest of the world.

And the President replied that the—it's his understanding there'll be a vote in Congress, in the House of Representatives next week—Wednesday probably or sometime around that regarding at least two different budgets. And he was hopeful that with the passage of one of those that a reconciliation between the House and the Senate that the United States would have a budget with deficits trending down.

The British Prime Minister picked up on that and said that in her opinion the trend was the most important thing not the absolute level because we all needed that.

I think those are the highlights of the day. I'll take the questions.

Q. It sounds like they ganged up on the United States.

SECRETARY REGAN. No, no, I said that was just one. The Japanese were referred to many times and they discussed their trade position—

Q. You mean they were victims, too?

SECRETARY REGAN. No, I wouldn't say we're victims. It was just an exchange. This is what President Mitterrand was encouraging—was an exchange rather than formal statements.

Q. Secretary Regan, going to your lunch with the finance ministers,[21] would the United States now accept the OECD formula of May 15th on credit to the Soviet Union?

SECRETARY REGAN. The United States has accepted the Wallen Compromise which is the OECD position of May 15th regarding all credits, not just East-West credits.[22] That's all credits. Let's not confuse the two.

Q. And do you understand that your partners in this conference will also now accept that formula?

[20] For the text of President Reagan's radio address to the nation given from Versailles on June 5 about the purposes of his European trip, June 2–11, see *Weekly Compilation of Presidential Documents,* June 14, 1982, pp. 753–754.

[21] Regan lunched with the other finance ministers on June 5, 1982.

[22] Proposed by Alex Wallen of Sweden, chairman of the Export Credit Group of the OECD, the Wallen Compromise refers to the OECD consensus arrangement on export credits. It is a compromise position between the United States and other countries on one hand and the Export Credit Group (EC) on the other regarding minimum interest rates and other conditions on official export credit. With a few modifications, this compromise was accepted by the OECD on July 1, 1982.

SECRETARY REGAN. I do not understand that. There are still some holdouts on that OECD position. The French have reserved and the English have reserved.

Q. What is their feeling?

SECRETARY REGAN. You'll have to ask them.

Q. Mr. Secretary?

SECRETARY REGAN. Yes.

Q. President Mitterrand gave the impression in his news conference that there has been an acceptance of the view that the United States should intervene—

SECRETARY REGAN. Yes, I heard that question and answer.

Q. It seems to—well, to contradict what you've been saying over the past few weeks—

SECRETARY REGAN. No, he left that—I would amend what the President had to say with a clause, which says, "yes, we will intervene in disorderly markets." But he forgot the "in disorderly markets," which is a part of the text that he referred to. And it is in the text and when you see the final communiqué, you will see that in the text.

That is also the language of Article IV of the International Monetary Fund Agreement to which the United States is a signatory.

Q. It simply boils down then to a disagreement on what constitutes disorderly markets?

SECRETARY REGAN. No, it's that the President overlooked the whole clause. He heard "intervention." He didn't read the fine print.

Q. Your position has not changed?

SECRETARY REGAN. No. Far from it.

. . . .

Q. Given the uncertain state of the American economy, could you believe that the American Congress wholeheartedly supports the position in favor of free trade that you enunciated in the summit?

SECRETARY REGAN. You have an adverb in there, "wholeheartedly." I'm not certain that I could agree with that, no, because I do know that there are at least 100 bills in the Congress advocating some type of protectionism. So I don't think the Congress wholeheartedly agrees with that. A good portion agrees with free trade. Others are a little bit skeptical at this point.

Q. If I may follow up, what ideas do you have to convince your own legislature of the worthiness of your position?

SECRETARY REGAN. We, and in particular Ambassador Brock, are testifying to this and will be testifying before the appropriate committees as these bills come along.

Q. Mr. Secretary, the OECD thing, were you suggesting before that everybody agrees to use the OECD standard for East–West trade, but where the French and the British are withholding their agreement is to apply it to all trade?

SECRETARY REGAN. Well, no; I gave the wrong impression if that is—I would clarify that.

Q. —you made a distinction about all—as opposed to East–West.

SECRETARY REGAN. Well, you have got to remember that OECD is for all trade. It is not just East–West. This is for all trade. It refers to countries other than the Soviet or Eastern bloc countries, because there will be other countries graduating, Israel is one, from Class II to Class I if this new standard is adopted. It goes on a per capita income basis. The graduation of many countries from Class III to Class II is also on a per capita income basis. And there will be countries that will be coming out of the so called LDC area, Class III, into the—a more affluent Class II group. The Soviets will be moving up from II to I. Now, each of those, of course, are going to have a raise in their rates. So what we are talking about as far as the OECD is concerned: two separate subjects; one, how many should graduate, and, two, what the new terms should be for each of the classes: Class I, Class II, and Class III, as far as rates are concerned, as far as maturity of loans is concerned.

Q. What about the East–West trade in that context, doesn't the United States seek even higher rates than the OECD's? The agreement would apply for East–West trade—

SECRETARY REGAN. No; they are not. No; they are going along with the rates that would be suggested for the OECD. This is for governmental rates.

Q. What is the British and French holdup?

Q. Secretary Regan—

Q. Mr. Secretary?

SECRETARY REGAN. I think you should refer to the British and the French for their positions. I think I understand it, but I would not want to give them definitively. Go ahead.

Q. Secretary Regan, how would you characterize on the East–West trade aspect? How would you characterize the position of the U.S. Government and other governments on the export insurance and guarantee question? The OECD comparative study indicates, basically, that the systems are so different that it is very hard to say—there are countries that subsidize it, and others do not. Where are we there on the guarantee and credit insurance question?

SECRETARY REGAN. Well, that is a very technical question. The OECD in the Wallen Agreement are on broader questions than that particular one. I would have to refer back to the text of the OECD, and I am not sure—I do not have it here with me. But we have not been discussing—that subject has not come up.

Q. No; I mean can one infer from that that this is not a sticky political issue between—

SECRETARY REAGAN. I do not think the question of the guarantees in the insurance is a sticky political question; I do not. I think it is rates and graduation.

Q. Sir, the French say your question of East–West trade came up at the luncheon of chiefs of state. It is a little puzzling. They said that Mr. Schmidt and Mrs. Thatcher referred to it and others and President Reagan. It is a little puzzling.

SECRETARY REGAN. I have no knowledge of that. I was not at the luncheon. I did not discuss it with the President as to what was said at his luncheon.

Q. Mr. Secretary, is your study matter still in the intervention thing? Mitterrand made no mention of that study of whether intervention is considered beneficial or not. Is that still part of the agreement that is—

SECRETARY REGAN. Yes; the study has been agreed to by all countries present here, that there should be a study of intervention. The details to be worked out are: who is going to do the study, how quickly, and then how it will be reviewed, and what action, if any, should follow from that study.

Q. Secretary Regan?

SECRETARY REGAN. Go ahead. Right here.

Q. To return to the issue of Western credits to the Soviet Union, it is an important issue to the President. He has stated that. How hard are you going to fight for that here in the time that is left? And what kind of success do you think you will have?

SECRETARY REGAN. I think we are going to fight pretty hard. And think we will have reasonable success.

Q. Reasonable is translated as what?

SECRETARY REGAN. Well, we will have to see just what the wording, and how the wording, will come out. This is a matter of negotiation at this point. There are varying points of view as you can imagine among these nations. To some this has different types of significance, because of their nearness to some of these countries, the amount of trade they do with them vis-à-vis us. It is a question of our own grain trading, where does that fit into the whole picture. So there are many things here, and the best I could characterize it at this moment, and it is an hour before dinner, is reasonable.

Q. Are you going to be horsetrading on this issue?

SECRETARY REGAN. No; we will be trading guips and clauses, not horses. (Laughter)

Go ahead.

Q. If there is no agreement here this weekend on the OECD consensus, are people going to prepare to extend the June 15 deadline?[23]

SECRETARY REGAN. I am not sure that we are. We will have to see what happens. That is a deadline. This was passed by the OECD at our meeting—ministerial meeting on May 5th and 6th. Over a month has passed. We think it time to get on with the decision at this point.

Q. Mr. Secretary, if you get consensus here on the OECD, moving the Russians from category II or Class II to I, how far would that go toward meeting the President's desires?

SECRETARY REGAN. That is part-way. At least they are not being subsidized by official credits to the extent of another full—well, let's see, it would be the difference of a full percentage point—on all the money that they are borrowing. It is the difference 10 and 11 percent.

Q. But that would not go anywhere toward meeting what—the President wants 12.25 percent.

---

[23] June 15, 1982 was one of several deadlines established by OECD for a decision on the Wallen Compromise.

SECRETARY REGAN. Well, if the new rates go into effect, it will. You see the new rates for Class I according to the formula are 12.25, so it would take them up to a Class I at the new rate being 12.25, so that would add about 1.5 percentage points to their current rate.

Q. You would consider that a substantial accomplishment?

SECRETARY REGAN. Certainly.

Q. Mr. Secretary—

MR. SPEAKES. Let's make this the last question, please.

SECRETARY REGAN. I don't know whether you are doing that for their benefit or mine. Thank you. (Laughter)

It is not that I object—it is the heat.

Q. Once you start that trade concern between Europe and the United States, especially in agriculture, what is the nature of that and does that make you more or less optimistic about the trade talks in November?

SECRETARY REGAN. Are you talking there in terms of East–West or are you talking in general West–West trade?

Q. West–West.

SECRETARY REGAN. West–West. Very little came up about the specifics of this. The specifics that most countries referred to, particularly the—Mr. Thorn from the EEC and Count Lambsdorff,[24] in talking to the United States about its trade with specific reference to the challenges that our steel companies have made before the Commerce Department on the dumping of steel by the European Communities. They asked that we reconsider and to be very careful of our decision in this matter because it would so upset them. There are over 200,000 jobs that are at stake in this Community. They have put a lot of money into this. They have done a lot of subsidizing. They feel that they need this for their survival.

Q. What was your response, Mr. Secretary?

SECRETARY REGAN. There was no response to that one. Thank you very much.

---

[24] Otto Graf Lamsdorff, West German Minister for Economics.

Document 92

Statement by the Secretary of State (Haig) at a Press Briefing, Versailles, France, June 5, 1982 (Extract)[25]

The Need for East–West Credit Limits

. . . .

Well, we had a very busy day, and I know Secretary Regan covered in some detail the agenda items that were covered in this morning and this afternoon's sessions which were essentially economic in character involving trade and technology, macroeconomics.[26]

We did have a very lively and very enlightening discussion over lunch with the heads of state in government and the foreign ministers. The discussion ranged essentially from East–West relations in their broadest context to include how best to coordinate political, economic, and security assets of the Western World in an effort to achieve restraint and responsibility in Soviet actions worldwide.

There were discussions on the transition that may take place in the Soviet Union and the implications of that in the period ahead.

President Reagan made a very strong intervention with respect to the subjects I've just touched upon; that is the integration of political, economic, and security assets of the West with the hopes of achieving a moderation in what has been an active period of Soviet interventionism worldwide if you look over the past decade starting with Angola in the mid 70's.

There seemed to be some consensus of view that it was at the same time always necessary that the Soviet leaders know that the West has not been and will not be a threat. And there were then some discussion of arms control, its importance in that context, the initiatives of November 18[27] and the Eureka speech.[28]

---

[25] Source: White House Press Release, June 5, 1982, Office of the Press Secretary to the President; printed also in Department of State *Bulletin*, July 1982, p. 4. This briefing was held at L'Orangerie Press Center at 8:03 p.m.

[26] Regarding Regan's press briefings, June 5, see document 90 and *supra*.

[27] For the text of President Reagan's speech before the National Press Club, November 18, 1981, where he proposed the complete elimination of all longer-range land-based U.S. and Soviet INF missiles, see *American Foreign Policy: Current Documents, 1981*, document 60.

[28] For the text of President Reagan's com-

There was a very keen and lively discussion on East–West trade, technology transfer in which there has been a great deal of progress made following the Ottawa summit and the meetings this past January on COCOM,[29] and the subject which is the focus of some discussion and difference of view here at this summit on the subject of credits and trade in general.

There was an exchange of views on this subject, and there will be a further discussion of that tonight between the foreign ministers and the finance ministers in an effort to resolve differences on a subject which is extremely complex and which is steeped with subjectivity in the sense that anyone involved in dealing with a regime on the credits to the East or the Soviet Union there's always concern that it does not take on discriminatory or punishing overtones for one or the other, because everybody has a different system through which to apply credits. Some don't at all. Some do. It's related to inflation rates, the particular countries and the consensus in the OECD as to what the going rate for inflation is. Some are within that, but some are above it; some are below it. And, of course, these are very complex matters that have to be discussed in great detail, and we'll continue on with those discussions tonight. But I'm optimistic that a consensus will develop from the group to present to the heads of state in government at the table as early as tomorrow.

There were discussions of Poland. Clear recognition that the West is ready and willing and, indeed, anxious to help the Polish economic plight if the conditions established within the Western nations for a resumption to normal relations were to be realized.

There was a brief discussion on the importance of our young people, not as a formal agenda item, but as an exchange of views at the luncheon table, and I am sure that this topic will—which it is scheduled to be on the agenda in the plenary session—will be discussed tomorrow.

. . . .

mencement address at Eureka College, Peoria, Illinois, May 9, 1982, at which he invited Brezhnev to begin START talks, see document 44.

[29] The Coordinating Committee (COCOM) is a committee composed of representatives from all NATO countries (except Iceland) and Japan responsible for compiling lists of strategic goods to be denied to Communist countries. It was created in 1949 with just four members and meets regularly in Paris to review the strategic embargo list. It met in Paris, January 19–20, 1982.

Document 93

Final Communiqué and Statement of International Monetary Undertakings of the Economic Summit, Versailles, France, June 6, 1982[30]

A Pledge to Improve the World Economy

Communique

1. In the course of our meeting at Versailles we have deepened our mutual understanding of the gravity of the world economic situation, and we have agreed on a number of objectives for urgent action with a view to improving it.

2. We affirm that the improvement of the present situation, by a further reduction of inflation and by a return to steady growth and higher levels of employment, will strengthen our joint capacity to safeguard our security, to maintain confidence in the democractic values that we share, and to preserve the cultural heritage of our peoples in all their diversity. Full employment, price stability and sustained and balanced growth are ambitious objectives. They are attainable in the coming years only if we pursue policies which encourage productive investment and technological progress; if, in addition to our own individual efforts, we are willing to join forces, if each country is sensitive to the effects of its policies on others and if we collaborate in promoting world development.

3. In this spirit, we have decided to implement the following lines of action:

—Growth and employment must be increased. This will be attained on a durable basis only if we are successful in our continuing fight against inflation. That will also help to bring down interest rates, which are now unacceptably high, and to bring about more stable exchange rates. In order to achieve this essential reduction of real interest rates, we will as a matter of urgency pursue prudent monetary policies and achieve greater control of budgetary deficits. It is essential to intensify our economic and monetary cooperation. In this regard,

[30] Source: *Weekly Compilation of Presidential Documents*, June 14, 1982, pp. 756–758.

we will work towards a constructive and orderly evolution of the international monetary system by a closer cooperation among the authorities representing the currencies of North America, of Japan and of the European Community in pursuing medium-term economic and monetary objectives. In this respect, we have committed ourselves to the undertakings contained in the attached statement.

—The growth of world trade in all its facets is both a necessary element for the growth of each country and a consequence of that growth. We reaffirm our commitment to strengthening the open multilateral trading system as embodied in the GATT and to maintaining its effective operation. In order to promote stability and employment through trade and growth, we will resist protectionist pressures and trade-distorting practices. We are resolved to complete the work of the Tokyo Round[31] and to improve the capacity of the GATT to solve current and future trade problems. We will also work towards the further opening of our markets. We will cooperate with the developing countries to strengthen and improve the multilateral system, and to expand trading opportunities in particular with the newly industrialized countries. We shall participate fully in the forthcoming GATT Ministerial Conference in order to take concrete steps towards these ends. We shall work for early agreement on the renewal of the OECD export credit consensus.

—We agree to pursue a prudent and diversified economic approach to the U.S.S.R. and Eastern Europe, consistent with our political and security interests. This includes actions in three key areas. First, following international discussions in January, our representatives will work together to improve the international system for controlling exports of strategic goods to these countries and national arrangements for the enforcement of security controls. Second, we will exchange information in the OECD on all aspects of our economic, commercial and financial relations with the Soviet Union and Eastern Europe. Third, taking into account existing economic and financial considerations, we have agreed to handle cautiously financial relations with the U.S.S.R. and other Eastern European countries, in such a way as to ensure that they are conducted on a sound economic basis, including also the need for commercial prudence in limiting export credits. The development of economic and financial relations will be subject to periodic ex-post review.

—The progress we have already made does not diminish the need for continuing efforts to economise on energy, particularly through the price mechanism, and to promote alternative sources, including nuclear energy and coal, in a long-term perspective. These efforts will enable us further to reduce our vulnerability to interruptions in the supply of energy and instability of prices. Cooperation to develop new energy technologies, and to strengthen our capacity to deal with disruptions, can contribute to our common energy security. We shall also work to strengthen our cooperation with both oil-exporting and oil-importing developing countries.

—The growth of the developing countries and the deepening of a constructive relationship with them are vital for the political and economic well-being of the whole world. It is therefore important that a high level of financial flows and official assistance should be maintained and that their amount and their effectiveness should be increased as far as possible, with responsibilities shared broadly among all countries capable of making a contribution. The launching of global negotiations is a major political objective approved by all participants in the summit. The latest draft resolution circulated by the Group of the 77[32] is helpful, and the discussion at Versailles showed general acceptance of the view that it would serve as a basis for consultations with the countries concerned. We believe that there is now a good prospect for the early launching and success of the global negotiations, provided that the independence of the specialised agencies is guaranteed. At the same time, we are prepared to continue and develop practical cooperation with the developing countries through innovations within the World Bank, through our support of the work of the Regional Development Banks, through progress in countering instability of commodity export earnings, through the encouragement of private capital flows, including international arrangements to improve the conditions for private investment, and through a further concentration of official assistance on the poorer countries. This is why we see a need for special temporary arrangements to

---

[31] Regarding the Tokyo Round, see footnote 10 to document 64.

[32] Regarding the March 31, 1982 draft resolution circulated by the Group of 77, see footnote 10 to document 88.

overcome funding problems for IDA VI, and for an early start to consideration of IDA VII.[33] We will give special encouragement to programmes or arrangements designed to increase food and energy production in developing countries which have to import these essentials, and to programmes to address the implications of population growth.

—In the field of balance of payments support, we look forward to progress at the September IMF annual meeting towards settling the increase in the size of the fund appropriate to the coming Eighth Quota Review.

—Revitalization and growth of the world economy will depend not only on our own effort but also to a large extent upon cooperation among our countries and with other countries in the exploitation of scientific and technological development. We have to exploit the immense opportunities presented by the new technologies, particularly for creating new employment. We need to remove barriers to, and to promote, the development of the trade in new technologies both in the public sector and in the private sector. Our countries will need to train men and women in the new technologies and to create the economic, social and cultural conditions which allow these technologies to develop and flourish. We have considered the report presented to us on these issues by the President of the French Republic. In this context we have decided to set up promptly a working group of representatives of our governments and of the European Community to develop, in close consultation with the appropriate international institutions, especially the OECD, proposals to give help to attain these objectives. This group will be asked to submit its report to us by 31 December 1982.[34] The conclusion of the report and the resulting action will be considered at the next economic summit to be held in 1983 in the United States of America.

Statement of International Monetary Undertakings

1. We accept a joint responsibility to work for greater stability of the world monetary system. We recognize that this rests primarily on convergence of policies designed to achieve lower inflation, higher employment and renewed economic growth; and thus to maintain the internal and external values of our currencies. We are determined to discharge this obligation in close collaboration with all interested countries and monetary institutions.

2. We attach major importance to the role of the IMF as a monetary authority and we will give it our full support in its efforts to foster stability.

3. We are ready to strengthen our cooperation with the IMF in its work of surveillance; and to develop this on a multilateral basis taking into account particularly the currencies constituting the SDR.

4. We rule out the use of our exchange rates to gain unfair competitive advantages.

5. We are ready, if necessary, to use intervention in exchange markets to counter disorderly conditions, as provided for under Article IV of the IMF Articles of Agreement.

6. Those of us who are members of the EMS consider that these undertakings are complementary to the obligations of stability which that [*we?*] have already undertaken in that framework.

7. We are all convinced that greater monetary stability will assist freer flows of goods, services and capital. We are determined to see that greater monetary stability and freer flows of trade and capital reinforce one another in the interest of economic growth and employment.

Document 94

Statement by President Reagan, Versailles, France, June 6, 1982[35]

A Commitment to Economic and Political Cooperation

Since World War II our peoples in Europe, Canada, Japan, and the United States

---

[33] Regarding IDA VI, see footnote 24 to document 65. IDA VII negotiations began in November 1982.

[34] The G–77 never submitted a report in 1982 because they could not agree on its contents.

[35] Source: *Weekly Compilation of Presidential Documents*, June 14, 1982, pp. 754–756. This statement was issued at the conclusion of the Versailles Economic Summit Conference. The session took place in the Salle du Congrès at the Palace of Versailles.

have worked together to lay the foundation for global prosperity. Together, we built the international institutions which have seen us through the greatest economic expansion in the history of the world. This weekend at Versailles, that spirit of partnership was very much alive.

In the formal sessions and informal exchanges, the leaders of the major industrial democracies worked on strengthening and solidifying Western cooperation.

We did not ignore the serious difficulties facing our economies. These problems will not go away overnight, but they will be overcome. Beating inflation, convincingly and enduringly, is the key to a strong recovery of growth and employment. This was agreed. And I was pleased to report to my colleagues that in the U.S. we are conquering inflation and are convincing our people that we will not return to the inflationary policies of the past.

In times of economic stress, it is always tempting to seek simple solutions at the expense of others. At Versailles, we resisted this temptation. Instead, we concentrated on ways and means to strengthen our economic performance individually and collectively. We have agreed to reinforce the international institutions which assure cooperation and coordination. In doing so, we are looking to a future with low inflation, greater employment opportunities, rising standards of living through advancing technology, and smoothly functioning international economic relations.

Just to name a few specific areas:

—We will work in association with the IMF to achieve meaningful coordination of medium-term economic policies, aimed at fiscal and monetary discipline and greater reliance on market forces.

—We have dedicated our efforts to a productive ministerial meeting of the GATT, which will address the trade problems of the 1980's.

—We have reaffirmed our commitment, made last year at Ottawa, to ensure that our economic relations with the Soviet Union are fully consistent with our political and security objectives. Specifically, we have agreed to exercise prudence in financial relations with the Soviet Union, including limiting export credits.

—We also agreed to work together to develop the considerable energy potential in the West, as another step in assuring a strong, sustained economic recovery, less vulnerable to energy disruptions.

In our informal political discussions, we addressed the major critical issues before the West. We know that the economic growth we seek would be hollow without the collective capacity to defend our democratic principles and our freedom.

We addressed our shared concerns in East–West relations. The continuing buildup of Soviet military power is a major challenge, heightened by Soviet actions in Poland, Afghanistan, and Southeast Asia—issues I look forward to discussing in greater depth at the Bonn summit.[36] At the same time, we agreed that the serious economic problems and impending succession in the Soviet Union provide us with major opportunities to work out a more constructive East–West dialog.

---

36 For documentation on the NATO summit held in Bonn, June 10, 1982, see documents 180–183.

We must maintain dialog with the Soviet Union, based on reciprocity and restraint. In that spirit, my colleagues have endorsed U.S. initiatives for arms control, particularly the negotiations on reducing strategic arms which will begin on June 29.

The tragedy in the Falkland Islands has been a serious concern to us all. Throughout the crisis, we have all been impressed by the British resolve, and in various ways, we have demonstrated our support for the United Kingdom. The United States continues to believe that we must end the fighting in the South Atlantic and achieve a politial settlement.

On other matters, we urged restraint on all parties in Lebanon. Increasing bloodshed in that region is something we all abhor. We have also called for a political settlement in the Iran–Iraq conflict which would preserve the territorial integrity of both nations. And we agreed to improve our coordinated fight against international terrorism.

Finally, I believe that we should reach out to new generations. The summit nations can invest in the future with expanded exchanges among young people from North America, Japan, and Europe.

A year ago in Ottawa, we ended the first series of economic summits that began in France. With this summit at Versailles, we have begun a new cycle. We thus reaffirm our strong commitment to economic and political cooperation. In the spirit of partnership with our fellow democracies, I want to say that I very much look forward to welcoming these nations to the United States next year.

Chapter 6. United Nations: Developments in International Law

Document 95

Transcript of an Interview With the Representative at the United Nations (Kirkpatrick), April 12, 1982 (Extract)[1]

"There Is a Dynamic in the United Nations Politics Which Tends to Isolate Us"

. . . .

PETER F. KROGH. Well, moving right along to the Middle East, Ambassador Kirkpatrick, we seem to be increasingly isolated alongside Israel at the U.S. [*U.N.*] in the face of various General Assembly resolutions, Security Council resolutions and the rest. How far are we prepared to go in standing almost alone with Israel?

For example, if the General Assembly were to bar Israel from that august body, what would we be likely to do?

JEANE KIRKPATRICK. Well, as you perhaps know, there are resolutions before the Congress just now, both in the House and the Senate, which would in fact require us to withdraw participation and withhold funds from the United Nations if Israel were to be—Israel or any other democracy were to be deprived of their right to participate.

You know, we're not just isolated in the United Nations on questions of Israel. We're isolated in the United Nations on many kinds of questions. Last week, for example, we were isolated, we cast a lone veto against the Nicaraguan complaint. We of course have stood alone on the Law of the Sea Treaty. Not entirely alone but the world thinks we have been standing alone. We cast a lone veto, in a sense we cast the lone "no" vote on the infant formula.[2]

What goes on here? What goes on here is there is a dynamic in the United Nations politics which tends to isolate us. The system I finally figured out works like a legislative body, like a state legislature or Congress, it's got a multiparty system, there are a number of groups that operate like political parties in it and we're a country without a party, and that is basically the reason that we find ourselves, I think, isolated on a good many questions.

PETER F. KROGH. Well, don't we have a party in our alliance system, and particularly in the Atlantic Alliance?

JEANE KIRKPATRICK. That party is not reflected in the votes at the United Nations. Even on issues that concern us as much as, for example, the Salvador elections, we found ourselves there voting alone among NATO powers, that is, without support from any of the other NATO powers, in our support for those Salvador elections.

There was a great deal of support, by the way, there was support from a lot of other sources, including all the Latin American democracies and most of the Latin American nations, and a number of other nations but not our European allies.

PETER F. KROGH. Could we get ourselves a party by being more effective in our diplomacy in the United Nations or do we have to change our policies?

JEANE KIRKPATRICK. I think the only way we're going to get ourselves a party is by linking our bilateral relations much more closely to our multilateral diplomacy in the

---

[1] Source: WETA/26, Washington, D.C., and Jefferson Communications, Inc., Reston, Virginia. The interview was taped on April 12, 1982, as part of the public television series "American Interests." It was broadcast in the Washington, D.C., area on April 13 and nationally on April 14. Kirkpatrick was interviewed by Peter F. Krogh, Dean of the Georgetown University School of Foreign Service and moderator of the series.

[2] Regarding the U.S. veto of the Nicaraguan complaint, which accused the United States of contributing to instability in Central America and asserted that that region was in danger of a U.S. military invasion, see U.N. document S/PV.2347. For documentation on the Reagan administration's policy on the Law of the Sea Treaty, see Chapter 7, Part B, and *American Foreign Policy: Current Documents, 1981*, Chapter 7, Part B. Regarding the U.S. vote in the World Health Organization against an infant formula code, see *ibid.*, document 80.

United Nations and other multilateral bodies. It's not going to be easy, because now there are patterns established.

What happens with our European allies is that they operate as a bloc and the bloc they are part of is the EC 10. They make their decisions in the EC 10, just as the nonaligned make their decisions in the nonaligned, the Africans in the African bloc, et cetera.

PETER F. KROGH. Given the lack of a party and the new majority which can kind of swamp U.S. interests and policies in the United Nations, do you see your job up there as basically just a holding action on American interests?

JEANE KIRKPATRICK. It's a damage limitation, it's a damage limitation operation above all, in fact. That's exactly what the U.S. job at the United Nations is today is a damage limitation operation.

. . . .

Document 96

Statement by the Acting Assistant Secretary of State for International Organization Affairs (Platt) Before Subcommittees of the House Foreign Affairs Committee, April 22, 1982[3]

U.S. Participation in the United Nations

Mr. Chairman, I appreciate the opportunity to appear before you to review U.S. policy toward the United Nations and to address the concerns you have raised about our participation in the organization. I wish to pay special attention in my remarks to the issues that you raised in your letters,[4] that is, to the increasing politicization of U.N. bodies, to the impact of this unfortunate tendency upon the organization's well-being, and to our own countereffort to strengthen the U.N.'s ability to solve the serious problems before it. I will comment as well on House Concurrent Resolution 289.[5]

Let me begin by saying that we in the administration share your disappointment in the performance of the United Nations. We agree with the eloquent sentiments of Congressman Rosenthal in his recent letter to the U.N. Secretary General warning that anti-Israeli vindictiveness in the U.N. is undermining American faith in the institution in a dangerous way.[6] As Ambassador Jeane Kirkpatrick has said, the U.N. is being used to "polarize nations, spread hostility and exacerbate conflict."

I shall not attempt, therefore, to minimize the U.N.'s deficiencies: they are all too glaring. Rather, I hope in what follows both to isolate the U.N.'s defects and to explain how we are trying to deal with them constructively.

It is important at the outset to be clear that much of the U.N. system does what it is supposed to do and often does it very well. Aside from the better published Security Council and General Assembly, the U.N. also comprises the U.N. Secretariat, whose most important function is the implementation of peacekeeping resolutions; the subsidiary U.N. bodies; and the independent specialized agencies. A brief word about each of these U.N. components—and the compatibility of its performance with U.S. interests—is in order.

The Secretariat, first of all, oversees the various U.N. peacekeeping and observer forces, which we consider of great value. In Lebanon, Cyprus, and the Golan Heights, the work of their multinational contingents, albeit imperfect and often restricted, is nonetheless vital. We know of no substitute for the U.N.'s efforts in this sphere. The peacekeeping forces perform professionally and often heroically—the U.N. at its finest.

The subsidiary U.N. bodies and the specialized agencies are another component of the U.N., and their activities in fact consume the major share of U.N. moneys and personnel. The work of these agencies and

---

[3] Source: *U.S. Participation in the United Nations: Hearings and Markup Before the Committee on Foreign Affairs and Its Subcommittees on International Operations in Europe and the Middle East and on Human Rights and International Organizations of the House of Representatives, Ninety-seventh Congress, Second Session* (Washington, 1982), pp. 12–16.

[4] The text of the subcommittees' letters have not been published.

[5] For the text of House Concurrent Resolution 289, which addresses U.S. participation in the United Nations should Israel or any other democratic state be denied its rights in the General Assembly, see *U.S. Participation in the United Nations*, pp. 137–138.

[6] For the text of Rosenthal's letter to Perez de Cuellar, see *ibid.*, pp. 4–7.

conferences is undramatic and gets no headlines. Their debates and reports are often technical and boring. But they provide the world practical benefits in the form of information, technical assistance, uniform rules of operation and conduct, and important coordinating machinery.

Without these institutions our interdependent world would function far less well. Many bear names that are now familiar. UNDP, UNICEF, the World Health Organization, and the U.N. High Commissioner for Refugees, to name but a few. Here, too, the U.N. is working, and often reasonably well.

It is the Security Council and the General Assembly. As Mr. Lantos has said, he will offer an amendment acceptable to the sponsors to broaden the scope of the resolution by extending it to cover specialized agencies as well as the General Assembly. Even here, however, the record is mixed. The Security Council has made crucial contributions to the peace in many cases. U.N. peacekeeping forces, observers, mediators, and special representatives have helped end hostilities and prevent their recurrence in the Congo, Cyprus, Lebanon, and the Golan Heights.

Without these forces in place, the situation in the Middle East and elsewhere would be even more explosive than is now the case. Most members joined the United States in supporting resolutions against the Soviet invasion of Afghanistan and Iran's hostage-taking, although the Soviets vetoed both. Two weeks ago, the Council acted swiftly in calling for withdrawal of forces and an end to hostilities in the Falkland Island crisis, providing a benchmark for negotiations now in progress.[7]

The General Assembly, for its part, has condemned Soviet and Soviet-backed aggression in Afghanistan and Kampuchea and has ordered an investigation of chemical weapons use in these same two countries. It has adopted helpful resolutions on combating international terrorism against diplomats, on the international refugee problem, and on religious intolerance.

Despite these pluses, irresponsible nations have increasingly abused both the Security Council and the General Assembly in ways that do more to inflame grievances than to resolve them. Nowhere is this tendency more pronounced than in the case of the Arab-Israeli dispute. Time and again resolutions on the Middle East, where constructive solutions are so desperately needed, are unbalanced and vindictive; they do not promote peace but hinder it.

Southern Africa is another case in point. Although we no less than others condemn apartheid, we do not believe that sweeping, punitive, unenforceable resolutions contribute to the easing of South Africa's problems; one effect, on the contrary, is to complicate the negotiations now underway for settlement in Namibia. Finally, albeit to a lesser degree, global negotiations and arms control have joined the group of neuralgic issues on which chances for reasoned dialogue seem to grow dimmer.

It is bad enough that the current atmosphere at the U.N. greatly detracts from that forum's efforts to resolve the problems I have mentioned. What is worse, the issues of Israel and South Africa permeate discussion of many other unrelated questions, and not only in the Security Council and General Assembly but in the nonpolitical specialized agencies as well. Organs as disparate and technical as UNESCO, the World Health Organization, and the International Atomic Energy Agency waste time in fruitless, acrimonious debate on Middle East and Southern Africa questions that are irrelevant to their proper function.

As you know, one side effect of the U.N.'s disruptive attachment to a few inflammatory issues is that we ourselves are often under attack. The practice [*price*] we pay for adherence to principle—and to our practice of taking U.N. debate more seriously than do many others—is that we are sometimes isolated within the U.N.'s two major organs on important questions.

It is not an isolation in which we delight, or about which we are smug, and it is harmful to some extent to our bilateral diplomacy on these issues. But the greater detriment is not to the United States but to the U.N. itself, whose capacity to influence events in a constructive way is measurably impaired.

The Reagan administration, like all its postwar predecessors, believes that the U.N. is an important arena in which to pursue and define U.S. interests. We do not believe, therefore, that the answer to the ills I have described is to opt out. The administration has, on the contrary, adopted a forthright, aggressive approach aimed at enhancing our role in the U.N. The policy appears in some degree to be working.

---

[7] For the text of U.N. Security Council Resolution 502, approved April 3, 1982, see document 626.

Our stance is quite simply, to stick to our principles while doing our best to explain our policies to others and to emphasize that we expect a certain measure of support in international organizations from nations that would be our friends. Regarding principle, we have not hesitated to stand alone in the Security Council in recent weeks when our efforts to elicit balanced, constructive resolutions on the Middle East were not successful.

Regarding support from friends, we have made clear to our many friends among the nonalined—most notably following a nonalined movement communiqué last September that was unfairly critical of U.S. policies[8]—that we expect friendly nations who disagree with distorted characterizations of our policies to stand up and be counted.

These efforts are beginning to produce results. Since Cancun, the strident rhetoric which previously surrounded global negotiations has abated. UNESCO has adopted for the time being at least, a moderate and practical approach to communications in the less developed countries instead of accepting radical calls for a "new world information order."[9] Last month the International Labor Organization strongly rebuked Poland and the Soviet Union for their suppression of Solidarity.[10] More recently, the U.N. Commission on Human Rights, for the first time in its history, adopted a resolution condemning human rights violations in an East European country, Poland.[11]

These welcome indications of fresh thinking do not, of course, amount to a sea change at the U.N. But they are nonetheless signs that, in certain important new instances, our viewpoint is being heard. We intend to continue to stand up for our policies, and to expect accountability from our friends in the U.N. The record so far indicates that we will enjoy at least some success.

I wish to turn now to our position on House Concurrent Resolution 289. We welcome the efforts of the Congress on this issue. Your support of Israel's rights within the U.N. system reinforces our own efforts to protect Israel and other democratic states from those who might be tempted illegally to deprive them of their ability to participate in the U.N. General Assembly and in other U.N. bodies.

As you know, we would regard a challenge to Israel's credentials in the General Assembly as a violation of the U.N. Charter, since membership questions must be brought by the Security Council, and would oppose any such challenge in the firmest and most vigorous way. Any action denying Israel's right to participate in the General Assembly would have the gravest consequences for continued U.S. participation including financial support and consequently for the future of the U.N. itself. This position has been an effective deterrent to past threats against Israel.

It should be clear from this that we strongly sympathize with the spirit and intent of House Concurrent Resolution 289, which is designed to deter any challenge to Israel's participation in the U.N. We would have no objection to the measure as a sense of the Congress resolution expressing that sentiment. At the same time, we continue to believe that the administration should not declare specifically in advance what the U.S. reaction would be to a successful challenge to Israel's U.N. membership.

I can assure you that in the frequent private diplomatic consultations which we hold with other U.N. members on this issue, there is no misunderstanding about how strongly we feel on it nor about the impact that expulsion or suspension of Israel would have on our own continued participation. Nor is there any doubt about the

[8] For the text of the communiqué, see U.N. document A/36/566.

[9] The reference is to the International Program for the Development of Communications, a program to bring better technology and training in communications to the lesser developed countries by coordinating international development assistance. The New World Information Order is a concept which had been discussed in UNESCO and other U.N. agencies since the early 1970's. Its goal was to provide the developing countries with the same communications and information capabilities as the developed countries. Proposals ranged from the moderate suggestion to include the improvement of information and communications abilities in overall development efforts to the radical ideas of licensing journalists, developing an international code of journalistic ethics, limiting advertising, and extending individual governments' control over the press. The United States opposed the New World Information Order on the grounds that it would violate First Amendment and free trade principles.

[10] For the text of the 214th Report of the Committee on Freedom of Association of the International Labor Organization, see document GB.219/6/17 of the 219th Governing Body of the International Labor Organization, March 2–5, 1982.

[11] The reference is to U.N. Commission on Human Rights Resolution 1982/26.

President's strong commitment on behalf of Israel.

Mr. Chairman, this concludes my statement. I am ready to answer any questions that you or members of this committee may wish to ask.

Document 97

Prepared Statement by the Representative at the United Nations (Kirkpatrick) Before a Subcommittee of the House Appropriations Committee, May 14, 1982 (Extract)[12]

Achieving Greater U.S. Effectiveness in the United Nations

. . . .

Should we cut our contributions to the UN or renegotiate our annual assessment? These are questions which deserve continuous study. The fiscal discipline in some UN organizations is very lax. Obviously we need to keep a very watchful eye to make sure that our voluntary contributions are used for the purposes we intend. The need to impose more stringent budgetary and fiscal controls is one of the areas on which we and the Soviet Union agree. Similarly, we should press for more effective mechanisms for calculating the annual assessment so that some of the newly wealthy countries pay their fair share and we do not pay more than that. But let me also point out that when contributions to the UN are figured as a percentage of a nation's GNP, some 46 countries paid more to the UN last year than did the United States. At present, we pay four one-hundredths of one percent of our GNP to the UN, and this is a smaller amount than paid by Canada, the UK, Denmark, or Finland, smaller even than some African states such as Burundi, Botswana, or Togo.

In conclusion, let me spell out how I think we should behave in the United Nations. I believe the United States must continue to play a full part in the organization, including the General Assembly, and specialized agencies, and in UN sponsored international conferences. We should try to make that participation more effective. Greater U.S. effectiveness in the United Nations requires, above all, a more systematic integration of our multilateral and bilateral relations. We should be clear and let others be clear that we take the UN seriously, and we take seriously relations between the U.S. and other nations inside the United Nations as well as outside it. We should leave no doubt that attacks on the U.S. inside the UN "count" in U.S. assessment of our bilateral relations. I think we have to go on speaking up for our view of the world, our view of what a just society is, our view of mankind. We should vote our values, listen to other points of view with attention, and not hesitate even when we are a minority of one to remind others that there are alternative analyses of the developmental process, alternative views of freedom, alternative approaches to the Palestinian question, to independence for Namibia without violence, etc. By stating these alternatives clearly and consistently, I think we best do our job which is, as I take it, to represent the legitimate aspirations and goals of the American people.

Regarding the management side of our participation in the United Nations, I know that the Subcommittee's Survey and Investigation Unit has pointed to a number of problems, including the fact that there have been eight Assistant Secretaries of State for International Organizations in the last ten years, along with nine different Deputy Assistant Secretaries. I am told the technical term for this is "personnel turbulence." This same "personnel turbulence" also takes place further down the line, and possibly is even more damaging there. It is something of an anomaly, surely, that the administrative support staff of the U.S. Mission to the United Nations tend to be more or less permanent, but the officers who actually deal with the United Nations and its 157 member nations tend to come and go every two years or so. Exactly the same situation holds true within the Bureau of International Organization Affairs.

In part, our personnel problems at the U.S. Mission stem from the financial unattractiveness of assignment to New York for Foreign Service Officers, or for anyone else whose home is elsewhere. New York is a much more expensive place to live than Washington. Taxes are higher, as are rents,

---

[12] Source: *Foreign Assistance and Related Programs Appropriations for 1983: Hearings Before a Subcommittee of the Committee on Appropriations, House of Representatives, Ninety-seventh Congress, Second Session* (Washington, 1982), Part 5, pp. 95–97. Kirkpatrick spoke before the Subcommittee on Foreign Operations and Related Agencies.

and many officers are unwilling or simply unable to make the financial sacrifice. This is something the Congress can remedy, by the way, by allowing the U.S. Mission to the UN to be treated as we do our embassies overseas as far as allowances are concerned. So far the Congress has declined to do this. As a result, it is often very difficult to find the most qualified officers for vacancies in the Mission.

There are other problems as well, and some even more serious. At the present time, none of the Deputy Assistant Secretaries for International Organizations has ever served at the U.S. Mission to the United Nations, nor has the Acting Director of the Office of United Nations Political Affairs, nor have any of that Office's Deputy Directors. In fact, only two of the twelve officers within the Office of United Nations Political Affairs in State have ever served at USUN, which is what we call our New York Mission. This is exacerbated by the fact that the State Department devotes so little thought and less training to multilateral diplomacy.

The result of all of this is that while we tend to field very large delegations to important international conference[s], and to the General Assembly when it meets each year, a quick look will confirm that only a few people within each of these delegations will be doing the hard work of negotiating positions and lobbying for votes, and even fewer will be doing it effectively.

I want to add a few words on policy coordination. It may come as a surprise to you to learn that I, as the President's appointee to be the U.S. Permanent Representative, in fact play no formal coordinating role with regard to our participation in the work of many of the UN's specialized bodies. It certainly came as a surprise to me. Now I do not wish to intrude on the turf of my colleagues, but it is inescapable that what we do at the UN in New York, and what they do with UN agencies in Paris and Geneva and Vienna, is part of a piece. For example, the strategy we may follow in dealing with an anti-Israel resolution in the General Assembly is linked quite definitely with what we do and say in the case of a similar resolution in the specialized agencies.

In theory, the Bureau of International Organizations is supposed to be the coordinating interface. Often this means simply that, for example, Ambassador Roger Kirk[13] in Vienna and I in New York will receive our instructions from the same relatively junior specialist in the Bureau in Washington. Or sometimes one of us will receive them and the other not. This system, coupled with the lack of true UN specialization, referred to earlier, practically ensures that mistakes in strategy and tactics will occur. There is no person or group which has first-hand experience in UN arenas which routinely plans our overall strategy for managing U.S. participation throughout the UN system. It is badly needed and I think it should be located in the Permanent Mission in New York.

When it comes to cooperation between the U.S. Mission and the State Department other anomalies prevail. There is usually little or no difficulty in the case of a truly important issue. In such a case, there will be frequent discussions with Secretary Haig, or Deputy Secretary Stoessel. National Security Adviser Clark will be involved, and sometimes the President as well. A consensus of views emerges quickly and we all know what we have to do.

But things can go quite differently on what might be called second order issues—matters on which I am reluctant to divert Secretary Haig from all the other important issues with which he must deal. Here there can be quite a lot of bureaucratic foot-shuffling or worse. Dogmatic judgments by those lacking experience in multilateral diplomacy within the special world of the UN point out that they are not equipped to effectively assess what is or is not possible or how to achieve the desired outcome. I recognize that Ambassadors in the field often complain they are overcontrolled from Washington, and that they know best how to deal with the government to which they are accredited. Well, in New York we have to deal with 157 governments, plus the United Nations Secretariat and various other entities. In so complex a situation, group dynamics themselves become as important as anything else. Tactics are important. As in the Congress, it is crucial to know one's colleagues and have a "feel" of the situation. Too often an effort is made to dictate tactics from Washington, by people who have no personal knowledge or "feel" for the politics of the issue.

Years ago, the Murphy Commission which examined the structure and functioning of the State Department concluded that the International Organizations Bureau should be shrunk to a small service office for the US Mission to the UN, with substantive responsibilities being parcelled out among other bureaus on the basis of subject

[13] The reference is to the U.S. Representative to the U.N. Industrial Development Organization.

matter.[14] That recommendation was made at a time when the United Nations was a much smaller constellation of organizations than it is today, and when our problems within it were considerably fewer. I don't know whether that would work today. I know the current system does not work.

I believe the central principle in the Murphy report was correct. The U.S. Mission in New York must have a central role in policy making for the UN system if we are to have coherent policy because New York is the hub of the UN wheel. Policies which are not guided by knowledge and experience can succeed only by luck. And we haven't been all that lucky lately.

Thank you.

Document 98

Statement by the Assistant Secretary of State for International Organization Affairs (Newell), June 4, 1982[15]

U.S. Participation in the United Nations: "A Political, Intellectual, and a Management Challenge"

Chief Justice Burger, Secretary Stoessel, Ambassador Kirkpatrick, friends and colleagues.

A sincere expression of gratitude is in order. To my wife Candilyn, to David and Kendall, to the many of you whose unwavering support has been a constant encouragement, to the President for his confidence and trust, and to the Secretary for his counsel and guidance.

As I approach the task of Assistant Secretary of State, it is with neither pretension nor apprehension but with continuing resolve and commitment to this administration.

Over the course of the past ten years, my professional and political endeavors in close association with those who have borne and now bear responsibilities for world leadership have led me to affirm, in my own mind—without unrealistic expectation—that the future is still ours to fashion.

From an auspicious blend of American realism and idealism, the United Nations was created. We are now no less committed to the principles and ideals of its Charter.

In and through the United Nations we must continue to forge the tools of cooperation among nations while remaining ever alert to any threats to the rights of democratic states to participate in this pursuit of peace.

We will continue to support the United Nations with reason and compassion.

And in and through the United Nations we will continue to uphold American values, express American views and pursue American interests without apology.

This will be a task of extraordinary challenges and disciplined requirements. It is at once a political, intellectual, and a management challenge.

—A management challenge—because the United States is in the forefront urging fiscal responsibility and facing up to economic realities in the UN system. As the largest contributor to the UN budget, we can expect—we must insist—that the same budget restraint that we have applied to our domestic programs in this administration be applied to international activities. This is no more than we have asked of ourselves.

After substantial program growth of recent years, the time has come for sober reflection on the priorities and benefits of the UN system. Of all its agencies and programs we need, therefore, to ask the fundamental questions: How are they serving U.S. policies? How can they become more efficient and accountable? But, above all, how can we in these institutions better promote our values, views and interests?

This challenge reflects the complexities of the system itself and our management task is to find the appropriate combination of ideas, resources, and options to pursue just policies in the United Nations.

—An intellectual challenge—because we must respond to the wide-ranging concerns of the UN system, from peacekeeping to the exchange of scientific knowledge, from the production of food to the protection of children.

Again, an intellectual challenge—because we must also respond to the growing

---

[14] The reference is to *United States Commission on the Organization of the Government for the Conduct of Foreign Policy* (Washington, 1975), a study chaired by Robert D. Murphy.

[15] Source: Department of State files. Newell spoke after being sworn in as Assistant Secretary of State by Chief Justice Warren Burger. Acting Secretary of State Stoessel presided over the ceremony.

anxiety in America about the United Nations itself.

Recent years have seen the steady erosion of American public support for the United Nations. Our initial hopes remain largely unfulfilled, as we have come to acknowledge that while the United Nations has grown, it has not yet matured, and as it has become the sounding board of new and unfamiliar voices, it does not always echo the truth.

—It is, therefore, also a political challenge.

We have been witnessing a trend to politicize the UN system through the insertion of extraneous issues into its agendas, debates, resolutions, and work programs. We see rhetoric replace reason and confrontation win over compromise. Cases in point—ritualistic condemnation of Israel, unhelpful resolutions on Southern Africa, one-sided discussion on disarmament, unrealistic plans for the redistribution of the world's wealth and disguised attempts to muzzle the free flow of information—these are part of our gravest challenge that we must meet—and we are meeting—directly, firmly, and resolutely.

These challenges, among a host of others, cannot be met without the consultation and cooperation and the support of us all: in the bureau, our missions, the respective departments and agencies, and the Congress.

Working in concert, we can give concrete expression to policies that best serve our nation and the peace and security of the world community.

Thank you.

Document 99

Toast by President Reagan at a Luncheon Hosted by the Secretary-General of the United Nations (Perez de Cuellar), New York, June 17, 1982 (Extract)[16]

The United Nations: "American Financial Support Has Not and Will Not Decline"

Well, Mr. Secretary-General, Mr. President, Your Excellencies, honored guests, it is a privilege for me to be with you today because it provides an opportunity to express this country's continued commitment to the principles on which the United Nations was founded some 37 years ago. This body was born out of the brutality and chaos of a terrible war, a war that had engulfed the planet with a ferocity of destruction such as mankind had never known before.

My longevity has given me a perspective on the founding of the United Nations that was useful in the preparation of the remarks that I made today.[17] There has been some attention called to that longevity on occasion, but I do remember the U.N.'s first days and our hopes at that time that this would be a forum for all mankind, replacing armed conflict with debate. We hoped that when necessary, it could do what had to be done to prevent aggression. And yesterday, Mr. Secretary-General, you presided over a convocation honoring the centenary of a great American leader—Franklin Roosevelt. I recall the inspiration of his declaration with Winston Churchill of the Four Freedoms[18] at a time when the freedom-loving people of the world were sorely in need of inspiration. In a very real way, this, an institution dedicated to peace, was his dream. I can assure you today, however imperfect the reality may be, Americans still dream that dream.

Much has happened in these last 37 years. Our countrymen can be proud that from the first day, the United Nations has had from the United States the utmost moral, political and [as] you, yourself, generously remarked, financial support. But I should point out that even in a time of domestic entrenchment, American financial support has not and will not decline.

This institution has not become the panacea for all of mankind's problems as some expected. Nevertheless, it has been and can be a force for great good. While it hasn't

---

[16] Source: White House Press Release, June 17, 1982, Office of the Press Secretary to the President; printed also in *Weekly Compilation of Presidential Documents*, June 21, 1982, pp. 815–816. Reagan was attending the Second U.N. Special Session on Disarmament. His toast concluded at 1:52 p.m.

[17] For the text of Reagan's address before the Special Session, see document 51.

[18] For the text of the Four Freedoms, given in Roosevelt's eighth annual message to Congress on January 6, 1941, see *The Public Papers and Addresses of Franklin D. Roosevelt, 1940 Volume: War—and Aid to Democracies* (New York 1941), pp. 663–672. Roosevelt and Churchill reaffirmed the Four Freedoms in the Atlantic Charter, signed August 14, 1941; for text, see *ibid.*, pp. 314–315.

solved every problem or prevented every conflict, there have been shining accomplishments. More than a few are alive and live decently because of this institution. Perhaps now we have a more mature view of the United Nations. While recognizing its limitations, we don't overlook its real potential and the opportunities—opportunities that for the sake of humanity we cannot afford to waste.

We welcome and support, for example, the sincere and personal efforts made by the Secretary-General to prevent, contain, and resolve the conflicts in the South Atlantic, in Lebanon, and in Iran and Iraq.

You may be new to your job, Mr. Secretary-General, but your vigor and commitment during this trying time have impressed all those who love peace.

As President of the United States, the preservation of peace is a mandate second only to the preservation of my country's freedom and independence. With the destructive power of today's weapons, keeping the peace is not just a goal. It's a sacred obligation. But maintaining peace requires more than sincerity and idealism—more than optimism and goodwill. As you know well, peace is a product of hard strenuous labor by those dedicated to its preservation. It requires realism, not wishful thinking.

For our part, we take the issue of arms control and disarmament—the purpose of this Special Session, very seriously. The tangible proposals we've made and that I spoke of this morning for nuclear and conventional arms reduction should underline our dedication to making this a safer and a more peaceful world. To this end, we seek to reestablish a balance and an actual reduction of strategic weapons. An unpleasant reality, but true nonetheless, is the fact that many words must be spoken before progress between nations can be made. So let us get on with the words. Yet, it has been said that—through their deeds, you shall know men—so let us get on with the deeds of peace as well. So today, I offer you this toast. Mr. Secretary-General, to you, and to this institution and to the need for peace. (Applause)

THE SECRETARY-GENERAL. Peace. (Applause)

(Toasts were exchanged.)

Document 100

Proclamation by President Reagan, September 14, 1982[19]

United Nations Day, 1982

The United Nations was born out of the massive human suffering and destruction caused by the Second World War. From the outset, the United States, one of the principal architects and founders of the United Nations, has worked to make it a forum for debate among all peace-loving nations and to support its purpose of preventing war and conflict through conciliation and cooperation. Because that goal has not been fully achieved and because the U.N. has been misused, today's world is too often fraught with strife, division, and conflict. But, despite the abuse and shortcomings, the United Nations can still be instrumental in facilitating and overseeing agreements to end conflict, in providing a center for reducing tensions through dialogue and debate, and in addressing the problems of underdevelopment which can spur conflict.

Americans can take pride in having provided significant moral, political, and financial support for the United Nations since its inception. That support will be maintained and the United States will continue to play a prominent role in the organization, using it to champion the values and ideals which underlie our own society and which originally helped to inspire the formation of the United Nations.

NOW, THEREFORE, I, RONALD REAGAN, President of the United States of America, do hereby designate Sunday, October 24, 1982, as United Nations Day. On this day I urge all Americans to better acquaint themselves with the activities and accomplishments of the United Nations.

I have appointed Robert Anderson to serve as 1982 United States National Chairman for United Nations Day and welcome the role of the United Nations Association of the United States of America in working with him to celebrate this special day.

IN WITNESS WHEREOF, I have hereunto set my hand this fourteenth day of

[19] Source: White House Press Release, September 15, 1982, Office of the Press Secretary to the President; printed also in *Weekly Compilation of Presidential Documents*, September 20, 1982, pp. 1146–1147. This Proclamation 4970 was filed with the Office of the Federal Register on September 15 at 12:21 p.m.

September, in the year of our Lord nineteen hundred and eighty-two, and of the Independence of the United States of America the two hundred and seventh.

IAEA must cease. The Government of the United States will now reassess its policy regarding participation in the IAEA and its activities.

Document 101

Statement Issued by the Department of State, September 24, 1982[20]

U.S. Withdrawal From the IAEA General Conference

Today in Vienna at the 26th General Conference of the IAEA, the U.S. delegation, led by Deputy Secretary of Energy W. Kenneth Davis, withdrew from the conference following a vote which rejected Israel's credentials. The United States, along with 38 other delegations, voted to accept Israel's credentials.

As our delegate stated on the floor of the conference prior to the U.S. withdrawal,[21] the rejection of the credentials of the Israeli delegation to the General Conference totally ignored that Israel is a member in good standing and that its credentials were properly presented. We consider the action to be illegal and to have resulted from highly irregular voting procedures.

The United States Government believes that great damage has been done to the integrity of the IAEA and the whole U.N. system by the introduction of strictly political issues into a credentials procedure.

The continued politicization of the IAEA, of which this credentials rejection is a symptom, cannot be allowed to go unchecked if the IAEA is to remain a credible tool for the furtherance of our nonproliferation objectives.

It is significant that 15 other delegations also withdrew from the conference.

The pattern of abusing the U.N. system for political purposes is corrosive to the integrity of the system as a whole. The introduction of political issues into specialized international organizations such as the

20 Source: Department of State files.

21 For the text of the U.S. statement, see *U.S. Nuclear Nonproliferation Policy: Hearing Before the Committee on Foreign Relations, United States Senate, Ninety-seventh Congress, Second Session* (Washington, 1983), pp. 4–5.

Document 102

Statement Issued by the Secretary of State (Shultz), October 16, 1982[22]

Israel's Participation in the United Nations

Recently there have been proposals at the United Nations General Assembly in New York and at the Plenipotentiary Conference of the International Telecommunication Union in Nairobi against the continued participation of Israel in those organizations.[23] The United States views these threats with grave concern.

The exclusion of Israel from the General Assembly or the International Telecommunication Union in these circumstances would be contrary to the principles of the United Nations. In the case of the General Assembly, it would be a clear-cut violation of the United Nations Charter. Such action defeats the very purpose of the United Nations—to resolve disputes among nations—by creating further conflict and division. It would do grave damage to the entire United Nations system and it would hurt us all.

The exclusion of Israel from United Nations bodies would also be a serious setback for progress toward peace in the Middle East, to which the United States and virtually all members of the United Nations are committed. It would be a tragic irony, if such moves against Israel in the United Nations system were to succeed just at the

22 Source: Department of State files; printed also in Department of State *Bulletin*, December 1982, p. 63. The statement was made available to news correspondents by Department of State Acting Spokesman Susan Pittman.

23 Documentation from the September 28–November 5, 1982, ITU Plenipotentiary Conference has not yet been published. An amended version of Resolution 120 passed by a vote of 85 to 31 on October 22, 1982. The resolution criticized Israel, but did not eject the Israeli delegation from the conference. Although the United States objected to the resolution, it continued to participate in the conference, since Israel's rights in the ITU had not been breached.

time when there is renewed hope for progress in the Middle East.

The United States has always made clear that any attack on Israel's right to participate in any United Nations organization, if successful, would have grave consequences for our own continued participation and support. As evidence of our determination to oppose such actions we withdrew our delegation from the Conference of the International Atomic Energy Agency following the wrongful rejection of Israel's credentials on September 24, announced that we would reassess our participation in the IAEA, and suspended participation in a broad range of agency activities.[24] Pending the outcome of our reassessment, we are making no further payments to the IAEA.

We will take such action in other United Nations organizations, if there are similar moves.

If Israel were excluded from the General Assembly, the United States would withdraw from participation in the Assembly and would withhold payments to the United Nations, until Israel's right to participate is restored.

We would also withdraw our delegation from the International Telecommunication Plenipotentiary Conference in Nairobi if Israel were excluded and suspend further payments to that organization. The ITU, the IAEA and other technical agencies must not be undermined or destroyed by such political attacks on the rights of member states.

We trust that the majority of nation members of the United Nations and all its agencies recognize the grave dangers of any further attacks on Israel's right to participate in United Nations bodies and will work to turn aside such initiatives.

---

[24] See the statement, *supra*.

Document 103

Prepared Statement by the Alternate Representative at the United Nations (Schwab) Before the Sixth Committee of the U.N. General Assembly, October 27, 1982[25]

The U.N.'s Role in Maintaining International Peace and Security

Mr. Chairman: Our deliberations this year occur at a time of rising doubt over the United Nations' capacity to play a significant role in maintaining international peace and security. Conflict or threat of conflict continues throughout the globe.

Because of this situation, my delegation was heartened by this year's Report by the Secretary General on the Work of the Organization.[26] The report, in our view, is a frank and refreshing appraisal of problems afflicting the United Nations' efforts to settle disputes peacefully, their causes and suggested practical ways of resolving them. We concur with the Secretary General's judgment that the United Nations' peacekeeping role, particularly that assigned to the Security Council, has become paralyzed. Numerous states have chosen to ignore or defy the Organization and the conflict resolution machinery established by the Charter. Some of the causes of this relates to the failure of the Organization or its voting majorities to appreciate the damage which is inflicted on the peace and security potential of the United Nations by partisan posturing on issues; by a condemnatory and divisive rather than constructive approach to problems; by a double standard against disfavored or politically isolated parties; by a growing disrespect for the integrity of language and the truth of the assertions made; and by an all too easy readiness of individual members to cast their vote on an issue in a manner which relates more to the group-dynamics of the

---

[25] Source: U.S. Mission to the United Nations Press Release USUN–102(82), October 29, 1982. Schwab spoke on Peaceful Settlement of Disputes Between States and on the Report of the Special Committee on the Charter of the United Nations and on the Strengthening of the Role of the Organization. For the text of the Report of the Special Committee on the Charter of the United Nations, see U.N. document A/37/33.

[26] For the text of the Report of the Secretary-General on the Work of the Organization, see U.N. document A/37/1.

UN's own political system, but which often does not correspond to the merits of the issue, even as understood by the individual government casting the vote, and does not contribute to the fair and practical resolution of the particular problem at hand. In short, a vital factor in enhancing the UN's effectiveness in dealing with problems of international peace and security is the determination of the majority to make it a forum in which all parties to a dispute can expect a significant degree of objectivity, fairness and evenhandedness.

The report further deserves our serious consideration, because of the Secretary General's emphasis on the desirability for ameliorative measures which could strengthen the United Nations machinery already in existence for promoting peace. His suggestions, in the words of the Permanent Representative of the United States, "demonstrate serious and creative steps that might be taken."[27] Further we concur with the Secretary General's view that "conscious recommitment by Governments to the Charter is needed." That Charter provides a sound and carefully-crafted structure and means for dealing with these world crises. What is needed is the support and determination of all governments to utilize this mechanism effectively. The Special Committee's increasingly important role in this process is obvious, and, in fact, we consider that the Secretary General's report should serve as one of the bases for discussion at the next session of the Special Committee.

Mr. Chairman, before going further into the agenda items on Charter Review and the peaceful settlement of disputes, my delegation would like to thank Ambassador Zachman for his clear and concise introduction of the Report of the Special Committee and for, more importantly, the leadership and impartiality he displayed in chairing the Special Committee at its most recent session.

My delegation believes that the last session of the Special Committee made significant and positive strides toward implementing its mandate. The completion of the draft Manila Declaration on the Peaceful Settlement of Disputes[28] is a noteworthy achievement which, by elaborating this fundamental Charter rule can serve as a useful reminder of the central role of the peaceful settlement of disputes in the Charter context and as a reaffirmation of the allocation among UN organs of authority and responsibility for related functions within that context.

In his recent report, to which we have already referred, the Secretary General also registered his hope that "we can rally once again to the standards of the Charter, beginning with the peaceful settlement of disputes . . . ." It is therefore fitting that the most concrete accomplishment of the Special Committee to date reinforces and undergirds a Charter norm which the Secretary General has so rightly drawn to our attention.

We hasten to note that the Manila Declaration alone is not a panacea; it is a step toward enhancing the principle of the peaceful settlement of international disputes. It can only assist in implementing that principle if member states muster the political will necessary to make use of the Charter based mechanisms dealt with in the Manila Declaration. This determination is absolutely required for the phrases of the Manila Declaration to serve effectively toward improving international relations.

With respect to the question of the maintenance of international peace and security, we remain prepared to discuss any and all proposals aimed at improving the functioning of the United Nations system. The system remains very imperfect and we welcome beneficial change. The most useful suggestions are those which recognize and build on the important strengths of the system and the usefully balanced allocation of authority among the respective organs. We would therefore oppose only those suggestions that would weaken that system, or which would curtail the evolutionary process which is required if the system is to be responsive.

My delegation, does, however wish to register once again its general disappointment at the debate in the Special Committee on the proposals listed under the maintenance of International Peace and Security item.[29] Work on the proposals has proceeded slowly. In part this results from the nature of the issues before the committee. In part, however, it is in the nature of the

[27] Kirkpatrick gave her views on the Secretary-General's report in an interview with Bernard D. Nossiter; see *New York Times*, September 10, 1982, pp. A12–A13.

[28] For the text of the Draft Manila Declaration on the Peaceful Settlement of Disputes, discussed in the Report of the Special Committee on the Charter of the United Nations, see U.N. document A/C.6/37/L.2. The Declaration was adopted as General Assembly Resolution 37/10 on November 15, 1982.

[29] For a record of the debate in the Sixth Committee on these proposals, see U.N. document A/AC.182/SR.59–64.

way the committee has operated. All of the members bear some responsibility for this.

The debate for the most part was a recapitulation of views raised at previous sessions. The exercise again was far removed from what was required of the Special Committee—to prepare a list of proposals enumerating areas of special interest and indicating, in each case, whether general agreement is possible.

What is required to reach this point is an examination of meritorious proposals in a search for common ground. Where suggestions or proposals have awakened particular interest, further and more extensive examination is required in order to distinguish the areas of agreement and of disagreement concerning an item. The rational course remains to focus first on the areas of agreement with a view to implementing immediately that practicable measure of reform and strengthening of the system. We obviously can only maximize the opportunity to achieve meaningful reform by focusing first on these areas and by, thereby, avoiding confrontation; suggestions that stimulate confrontation, in fact, should be quickly identified, in order to devote the time and effort of the Special Committee to areas where real progress is possible.

In this regard, the Special Committee has handled somewhat inexpertly these related, but distinct issues of identifying proposals that "awaken special interest", and of according priority to consideration of those areas on which general agreement is possible. The committee has made certain basic conceptual errors in this regard. Perhaps due to inattentiveness or insufficient concern over the process, members have not honestly appraised the degree of special and meritorious interest spurred by various proposals and have instead succumbed to vigorous lobbying of sponsoring delegations. Similarly, members have failed to assess honestly the possibility of general agreement on proposals with a view to according priority to consideration of such proposals. There has, therefore, been general confusion, first in identifying meritorious "interest" and second, in evaluating the extent to which such interest is sufficiently shared and likely to command a consensus.

These caveats can serve as useful procedures to guide the work of the Special Committee. Bearing them in mind, my delegation remains ready to discuss all proposals, including those submitted at the end of the two most recent sessions of the Special Committee.

With respect to the question of rationalization of existing procedures of the United Nations, my delegation requests that the Special Committee, in due course, consider the proposals made by member states on the question of rationalization of existing procedures of the United Nations and consider also that further work is needed to continue previous efforts to improve the Assembly's functioning. While we fully understand why the Special Committee did not devote any attention to rationalization at its last session, we believe the time is now arriving to review this item.

In conclusion, Mr. Chairman, we wish to reiterate that our own commitment to participate seriously in the Special Committee is based on the Special Committee proceeding in a careful, responsible manner, in accordance with its mandate and in a constructive search for agreement. For this reason, we consider that parallel initiatives duplicative of the Special Committee's work detract from it, since they are undertaken generally in less focused forums that are not carefully structured with a view to achieving the exclusive and unique objectives of the Special Committee. Other bodies, including the main committees of the General Assembly simply cannot consider highly specialized issues of this nature as effectively and efficiently as can the Special Committee. Therefore, in the interest of assuring the continued vitality of the Special Committee, my delegation urges all participants to renew their commitment to the role and mandate of the Special Committee and to work to fulfill its mandate, which, my delegation believes, is eminently sound.

We continue to believe that the Special Committee can achieve much that is useful—the adoption of the Manila Declaration is positive proof of this. However, the committee will continue to serve a useful purpose only if the participants adopt an approach which can contribute toward that end.

Document 104

Remarks by the Secretary of State (Shultz) Before the U.N. Day Concert, October 30, 1982[30]

"We Want the United Nations to Work"

Thank you, distinguished guests.

One of the privileges which comes to a Secretary of State is that of speaking at this annual event, that of the United Nations Association annual concert and dinner. So I do have the privilege of welcoming you here at the 37th anniversary of the UN's founding and I also have the opportunity to congratulate the United Nations Association both for this event and for the contribution it has made over the years to reasoned discussion of foreign policy questions. Also, it is a particular honor to recognize Dr. Halfdan Mahler, Director General of the World Health Organization, to whose agency we are paying special tribute.

This is a commemorative event and on such occasions it is fitting that we recall the origins of the United Nations and the agencies which are a part of the United Nations system.

It is all too easy to forget the circumstances under which the United Nations came into being. The Charter and the structure of the organization were formulated during the dark years of the Second World War. Even as the leaders of the Allied Powers were planning the strategy which led to eventual military victory, they began to plan for the peace that would follow the war. These statesmen considered both the shape of the peace which would follow victory and the institutions required to build and preserve what had been purchased at the cost of millions of lives.

The statesmen of that period succeeded brilliantly. The Charter of the United Nations embodies those principles of state behavior, and those commitments to human rights, peace, and economic progress, which remain the goal of all mankind.

Yet I suspect those same statesmen would look now on the United Nations with some concern and some disappointment. In the wars of this spring, Lebanon and the Falklands, the world could not turn to the United Nations for fear that action there would inevitably end in paralysis. The two peacekeeping efforts of this year, in Beirut and the Sinai, were the work of a collection of individual states working outside the UN framework. And we must all regret the helplessness of the institution as we witness the repression in Poland, invasion in Afghanistan, and occupation in Kampuchea.

Unhappily, in recent weeks we have almost seen the United Nations turn on itself, with efforts in the IAEA, ITU, and the General Assembly to undermine the principle of universality,[31] and of course, in the United States, we couldn't help but notice the attack on the relationship between the United States and Puerto Rico.[32] So, while we marvel at the structure of the United Nations, we must also guard against the erosion of its foundations.

Today, we honor the World Health Organization because it is convincing proof that the ideals of the UN Charter are not hollow. The Director General of that organization, Dr. Mahler, is with us and I want to pay special tribute to him as a physician and humanitarian, a rigorous administrator of complex programs, and, indeed, a visionary who has challenged all countries of the world to achieve a satisfactory standard of health for their people by the year 2000.

It is easy to cite the specific achievements of the World Health Organization—the eradication of smallpox, extensive work on malaria, and important programs applied to a wide range of public health problems worldwide. But to understand what the WHO does, one must get down to the human level of lives lengthened and saved; of children who survive, who grow healthy and strong, and are able to contribute so much more to their societies.

It is to the lives of individuals that so much of the work of the United Nations relates, whether we consider public health, or the right of each individual to expect from his government basic standards of

---

[30] Source: Department of State Press Release 342, November 2, 1982.

[31] Regarding the conflict in the International Atomic Energy Agency, see document 101. Regarding the conflict in the International Telecommunications Agency and in the U.N. General Assembly, see document 102.

[32] The reference is to an attempt by Cuba to include the question of self-determination and independence for Puerto Rico on the agenda of the Thirty-seventh Session of the U.N. General Assembly. The United States opposed this attempt, which eventually failed. Regarding this issue, see U.N. documents A/37/194, A/37/PV.4, and A/37/250.

human decency. A person who has been tortured or committed to internal exile is as much an affront to the human condition and to the principles of the Charter as is a child whose illness could have been prevented by proper medical attention.

Accordingly, tonight it is important that we testify to the continuing validity of the objectives of the United Nations. Whether we speak of its peacekeeping and peacemaking functions, its continuing critical role in achieving Middle East stability, its commitment to health or its assistance to refugees, we must dedicate ourselves to making that organization the constructive global force which its founders envisioned. There is ample room for improvement in the United Nations' performance, and more than adequate grounds for criticism of the behavior of its organizations or its members. But the criticism must be constructive and must be accompanied by commitment. The U.S. commitment is clear. We want the United Nations to work and to live up to the principles upon which it was founded. I pledge to you that we will continue—aggressively and constructively—to insist on those principles and to translate those principles into action.

Document 105

Prepared Statement by the Representative at the United Nations (Gershman) Before the Third Committee of the U.N. General Assembly, November 15, 1982[33]

Restraining the U.N. Budget

Mr. Chairman, the United States has introduced an amendment to Resoultion L.16 on Agenda Item 81 on "policies and programs relating to youth." The amendment to be added as a new operative paragraph 11, reads as follows:

> "Authorizes the Secretary-General to implement the activities approved in this resolution to the extent that they can be financed without exceeding the level of the resources approved in the 1982–83 program budget."

I would like to explain why we have introduced this amendment and why we urge other countries to vote for it.

During the course of the General Assembly, almost every member state has called attention to the dreadful condition of the world economy. Although we believe that recent progress in bringing down inflation and interest rates is preparing the way for economic recovery, this does little to ease the painful situation of the moment.

One of the harshest consequences of the current recession is the budget crisis now afflicting practically every nation in the world. The United States enjoys no immunity from this crisis. We have been compelled to make stringent cuts in our domestic spending programs. So have many of your governments, the governments represented here, done likewise.

United States support for U.N. programs is not at issue. We have succeeded over the past 2 years in maintaining the levels of U.S. voluntary contributions to the leading U.N. development assistance agencies, including UNDP, UNICEF, and UNFPA. We deeply hope to be able to maintain these levels of support for constructive programs.

We are also committed to making the sacrifices necessary to maintain the level of our payments to the assessed budget of the United Nations. But this is as far as we can go. The United States cannot accept continuing increases in the U.N. assessed budget, increases accompanied by no serious efforts at economy. In the last 5 years assessments have risen by 81 percent, well above the rate of inflation. The cost of operating the United Nations today is four times what it was 10 years ago. If this rate of increase continues, expenditures for the program budget of the United Nations will approach $3 billion by 1990. At such a level of expense, member states from every region and every group in the organization would find the cost of their membership unreasonable.

The United Nations will cease to be regarded as a serious institution unless it is able to get its own house in order and face up to the situation in the real world. In the first instance this means that it must get back in touch with economic reality by putting a firm cap on its expenditures. Failure to do so will inevitably lead to growing

---

[33] Source: U.S. Mission to the United Nations Press Release USUN–127(82), November 15, 1982. Gershman spoke in explanation of the U.S. vote on amending Resolution L.16 on Agenda Item 81, on Policies and Programs Relating to Youth. For the text of Resolution L.16, see U.N. document A/C.3/37/L.16. It was adopted as U.N. General Assembly Resolution 37/48 on December 3, 1982, without a vote and without the U.S. amendment.

disillusionment on the part of taxpayers in those countries which are the United Nations' principal donors, and thereby undermine the political support which sustains the life of this organization.

This is not the first time the United States has expressed its deep concern about the need for the United Nations to exercise strict control over its budget. Last year, we took the unprecedented step of voting against the U.N. program budget for the biennium 1982–1983.[34] Our representatives in the Fifth Committee have repeatedly emphasized, in both votes and speeches, our opposition to budgetary increases. And in other committees you all have frequently heard U.S. representatives, after joining in a consensus on a particular resolution, state in explanation the caveat that the resolution must be implemented within existing resources. Yet the budget continues to grow.

By introducing this amendment today—and we are introducing similar amendments in this and other committees where this is necessary—the United States wishes to emphasize that it is very serious about the need to control United Nations' spending.

We can no longer support resolutions which provide for piecemeal extra-budgetary increases. Let me be clear: we do not oppose this program, the program called for in L.16.

We do not oppose new programs in principle.

We do not prefer old programs to new programs.

We do not oppose U.N. spending.

We do believe that a very systematic effort must be made to control budget growth; to phase out old or less efficient programs in favor of new, more timely projects.

We believe that good management practices and the respect for the United Nations in the world, requires that members assist the Secretariat in husbanding our resources for constructive purposes.

Mr. Chairman, my government and the people of the United States fully support the United Nations' decision to declare 1985 International Youth Year, and we acknowledge a debt of gratitude to the Government of Romania for its initiative in this respect. We also approve and support without reservation the IYY themes of *Participation, Development and Peace,* and the content of L.16.

My government has begun to prepare for IYY by encouraging the establishment of a broadly-based organization of nongovernmental youth groups to participate in planning our national activities. Together we hope to develop employment, health, education, juvenile justice, and other programs which will touch the lives of as many Americans as possible. We will follow IYY developments in other nations and regions to make sure that we benefit from the experience of others. We will be informed by the Programme of Measures and Activities adopted by the United Nations General Assembly. We will encourage American youth groups to participate in international and regional meetings. It is our firm intention in this way to make our observance of IYY a tribute to and celebration of the serious purpose, the creative approach and adventuresome spirit of youth, not only in the United States but throughout the world.

It is precisely because my delegation does not want to vote against this resolution that we have formulated an amendment which, if adopted, will permit us to join again in consensus for adoption of the resolution as a whole.

The amendment which the United States proposes to add to the resolution is intended precisely to insure that this organization, that is to say, we ourselves, finally say no to the continuing upward spiral of its expenses.

The paragraph authorizes the Secretary-General to implement the activities approved in the resolution "only to the extent that they can be financed without exceeding" the levels of resources approved in the 1982–1983 program budget. That, let me remind you, provided for expenditures of over one and one-half billion, that is, fifteen hundred million, dollars!

Our amendment is not intended to say no to new or additional activities, but rather to authorize the Secretary-General to make choices on behalf of all of us, to authorize him to manage the resources we have given him in a rational way. In essence, it charges him with the responsibility to establish priorities and to allot the necessary resources to the most important activities first and forego or reduce activities which are superfluous, completed, obsolete, of marginal utility, or ineffective. It charges him to find

---

[34] Regarding the U.S. vote against the 1982–1983 U.N. program budget, see *American Foreign Policy: Current Documents, 1981,* document 105.

and make other economies in the organization, staffing and management of the Secretariat he leads.

If the proposed amendment is not incorporated into the resolution now before us, my delegation will be unable to continue as part of the previous consensus, we must call for a vote on the resolution as a whole and vote against it. We would do so regretfully, solely and strictly to say that we can no longer acquiesce in undisciplined decision-making concerning our resources and programs.

Thank you, Mr. Chairman.

Chapter 7. Oceans and International Environmental and Scientific Affairs

A. General

Document 106

Statement by President Reagan, March 1982[1]

U.S. Support for International Cooperation in the Conservation of Natural Resources

International cooperation in the wise use and conservation of natural resources has become increasingly important as we strive for a better standard of living for all the world. I wish therefore to commend the International Union for Conservation of Nature and Natural Resources for its long, devoted and outstanding efforts in focusing world attention on the vital relationship between conservation and development. Global resources are the ultimate material base for human development as emphasized in IUCN's *World Conservation Strategy.*[2]

The advantages of conservation of rivers and oceans, soils and minerals, forests, grasslands and wildlife, are considerable. The development or improvement of food sources from wild plants and animals, the expanded use of renewable materials for fuel, the discovery of new medicines from wild plants, the preservation of biological diversity, and the protection of the global environment are examples of the human benefits derived from good conservation practices. Approaches developed in one country may have direct application in others, such as the concept of national parks, wildlife refuges and other protected areas, which have been pioneered by the United States and are now used throughout the world by countries with widely different development levels and political systems.

The greatest resource that all nations share is people. The emphasis of our cooperation should focus on developing the knowledge and skills that will help individuals and organizations to formulate sounder policies and programmes. Skilled people are the cornerstone for building institutions that will ensure the long-term success of our development and natural resource conservation efforts. For this reason, training and the continuous voluntary exchange of the newest information and technology must be a central element in our cooperative activities. Training in natural resource management is an important part of our foreign assistance programme. Various United States Government agencies and private organizations are involved in sharing their technical expertise through a variety of multilateral and bilateral programmes.

You can be assured that the United States will continue to lend its experience and energies to the universal quest for a higher standard of living and resolution of global issues of transcending importance to all nations, through the sound stewardship of the earth's resources.

---

[1] Source: International Union for Conservation of Nature and Natural Resources Press Release, March 24, 1982. The Reagan statement, which was prepared in response to an IUCN request, was received on March 17. The IUCN is an independent, international, nongovernmental organization based in Gland, Switzerland.

[2] Reference is to *World Conservation Strategy: Living Resources Conservation for Sustainable Development,* IUCN, Switzerland, 1980.

Document 107

Message to the Congress by President Reagan, March 22, 1982[3]

Annual Report on International Activities in Science and Technology

This report responds to the requirement, embodied in Title V of the Foreign

[3] Source: White House Press Release, March 22, 1982, Office of the Press Secretary to the President; printed also in *Weekly Compilation of Presidential Documents,* March 29, 1982, pp. 352–356. This was the third Presidential report to the Congress as required by Title V of the Foreign Relations Authorization Act, Fiscal Year 1979. (P.L. 95–426; 92 Stat. 982)

Relations Authorization Act, Fiscal Year 1979 (Public Law 95–426), that I report annually on the United States Government's international activities in the field of science and technology. As a supplement to this report, the Department of State, in collaboration with interested departments and agencies, has prepared the attached study which contains a more detailed description and analysis of the Government's international non-military scientific and technological activities.

Since this is my first report under the statute, I would like to discuss the general approach of my administration to our bilateral and multilateral activities in science and technology.

International Cooperation in Science and Technology to Serve National Needs

The United States remains the world's leader in science and technology. We invest more in research and development than any other country. Our total national investment in research and development (R&D) exceeds those of Japan, West Germany, and France combined. We employ more scientists and engineers than any other free world country, and they contribute almost 40% of the world's scientific literature. Over the past decade, American scientists have garnered 57 Nobel prizes compared to 28 from all other countries combined. The magnitude, quality, and diversity of our R&D resources will continue to make cooperation with the United States in science and technology at individual, institutional, and governmental levels highly attractive to other nations.

Yet, we also recognize that, while the United States retains international preeminence in many areas of science and technology, we are no longer in a position to dominate each and every field. Nor do we hold a monopoly on the world's supply of scientific talent. The industrialized democracies of Western Europe, Canada, and Japan have established strong national programs in science and technology. Several other countries, such as Mexico, Brazil, South Korea, the People's Republic of China, and Israel have built their own capabilities for carrying out scientific and technological activities in selected areas of special concern to them. Thus, just as the United States can profit from and be stimulated by vigorous international competition in science and technology, we can also profit through international cooperation, which extends and complements our own efforts and helps us achieve our national objectives.

International cooperation is not simply synonymous with Federally-sponsored cooperation. American scientists and engineers engage in a great many cooperative international ventures. Often, they work through the universities or the industrial firms which employ them, with the Federal Government acting, at most, as a catalyst. An important aspect of this administration's science policy is to encourage such private sector cooperation. American universities have made tremendous contributions to the development of science abroad. International collaboration among industrial firms in areas such as transportation, industrial utilization of space, communications, and energy production can serve important national interests as well as the interests of the firms involved.

Almost every technical agency in the United States Government carries out programs with important international components. Many of the problems with which these agencies deal—such as health, environmental protection, and agricultural production—do not recognize international boundaries. They are worldwide in scope and impact. Governments everywhere invest precious resources in basic and applied research to tackle these problems. Our agencies constantly seek out and are sought out by the best foreign scientists and institutions for collaborative work in areas of common interest. In doing so we build stronger relationships with our partners abroad and help develop common approaches to common problems.

I will illustrate these points by briefly focusing on the National Aeronautics and Space Administration's (NASA) programs. Last year the spectacular voyages of the space shuttle Columbia were among our Nation's proudest achievements. But let us remember that many of our friends abroad made substantial contributions to the shuttle program. Canada provided the remote manipulator system, the "Canadarm," first used on Columbia's second flight, at the cost of $100 million. In December our European Space Agency (ESA) partners presented the first spacelab module to the United States. This billion dollar facility is scheduled to fly aboard the shuttle in 1983. It will enable American and European scientists to carry out astronomical investigations of the Sun and distant parts of the universe, and to perform the most ambitious experiments ever attempted in space's zero-gravity environment.

Thus, the scope and significance of international cooperation in space science are clear and visible. Since NASA's inception, this country's civilian space programs have been open to foreign participation. Almost all of NASA's programs have an international element, and many of them, like shuttle, have a very large foreign component. The Federal Republic of Germany's contribution to the Galileo mission to Jupiter will total approximately $100 million, and ESA's contribution to development of the space telescope will total almost $130 million. Both we and our foreign partners clearly benefit from such collaboration on large-scale, high-cost programs. What each of us may find difficult to do alone, we can accomplish together.

The same is true in many other fields. It is especially true today when fiscal restraint in our agencies' programs is required if we are to restore our Nation's economic health. Since many other nations face similar economic difficulties, it is becoming increasingly important that we all reach beyond our borders to form partnerships in research enterprises. There are areas of science, such as high energy physics and fusion research, where the cost of the next generation of facilities will be so high that international collaboration among the Western industrialized nations may become a necessity. We welcome opportunities to explore with other nations the sharing of the high costs of modern scientific facilities.

We must also work with our partners for less duplication of scientific facilities. Our scientists will travel abroad to make use of unique facilities there just as foreign scientists will come to the United States to work in our laboratories.

I have focused thus far on collaboration with the industrialized democracies of Western Europe, Canada, and Japan. It is to these countries that our government agencies most frequently turn for partners for the simple reason that their capabilities are generally closest to our own. But several other countries, such as Mexico, China, South Korea, Brazil, and Israel, have made impressive strides in developing their own capabilities in science and technology, and they have in selected areas become attractive partners for our government agencies.

In this past year, special emphasis has been placed on the development of our scientific and technological relations with Mexico and the People's Republic of China. Our programs with both of these countries are models of the positive contribution which mutually beneficial scientific cooperation can make to our overall relations with other countries. Both Mexico and China have recognized the importance of building their own scientific institutions. These countries deal with us as equals in areas such as arid lands management and earthquake prediction. I look for cooperation between the United States and these and other rapidly developing countries to expand as their capabilities grow.

The Soviet Union

There is one possible partner for scientific collaboration with whom I have not yet dealt: the Soviet Union. Potentially, American scientific collaboration with the Soviet Union could be highly beneficial to the entire world. It is easy to imagine the problems which might be solved by the cooperative efforts of the two largest scientific establishments in the world, and indeed, it was that vision which prompted President Nixon to launch the cooperative scientific and technological program with the Soviet Union a decade ago.

But that vision never materialized. Unfortunately, both our government agencies and the American scientific community were quickly faced with the stark realities of the Soviet system:

—Many of the best Soviet scientists and institutions are off-limits to foreigners; they work in the vast Soviet military sector, where the Soviet Union has chosen to expand a disproportionate and growing share of its national resources.

—Free exchange of ideas in non-sensitive areas, the norm in the West, is impeded because Soviet scientists face imprisonment for disclosure of unpublished research results.

—Similarly, Soviet scientists are not allowed to travel freely to scientific conferences abroad, and many of the Soviet Union's national scientific conferences are closed to Westerners.

—Jewish scientists, even when they can obtain an education in the Soviet Union, face limited careers.

—The Soviet Government has chosen to imprison, exile, or deny work to some of its most distinguished scientists for the "crimes" of thinking independently or wishing to emigrate. Others are sent to psychiatric hospitals in a flagrant misuse of science in service to the Soviet state.

As a result of all this, many American scientists began independently and personally to boycott the bilateral exchanges with the Soviet Union, and the potential for scientific cooperation with the Soviet Union was diminished even before the Soviet invasion of Afghanistan. That event led to an official curtailment of the level of cooperative activity under the eleven bilateral technical agreements to a small fraction of the pre-invasion level. Following the Soviet involvement in the tragic repression in Poland, I announced on December 29, 1981, that three of our bilateral scientific and technical agreements which come up for renewal in the next 6 months would not be renewed.[4] Furthermore, I requested a complete review of all other exchanges with the Soviet Union. That review is currently underway. Future cooperation with the Soviet Union depends on the steps they take to comply with recognized norms of peaceful intercourse among nations.

Science and Technology for Development

I have dealt so far with those international scientific and technological activities which we undertake as a means of extending our own resources for solving the problems we share with others. We also recognize that science and technology should play a central role in our assistance to developing nations.

Last October I brought to the Cancun summit[5] a program for action inspired by an old proverb: "Give a hungry man a fish and he'll be hungry tomorrow; teach him how to fish, and he'll never be hungry again." I stressed at Cancun the need for the developing countries to strengthen their own productive capacities and the vital role of the private sector—industry, universities and volunteer organizations—in international development.

This administration intends to emphasize the role of science and technology in our bilateral development assistance programs, particularly in the areas of food and energy. Increasing food production in developing countries is critically important. We have always made food and agriculture an important emphasis of our aid programs. In addition to direct food aid we have underwritten successful agricultural research abroad, welcomed thousands of foreign students to our finest institutions, and helped make available throughout the world discoveries of the high-yielding seed varieties of the Green Revolution.

At Cancun I proposed that task forces be sent to developing countries to assist them in finding new agricultural techniques and transmitting to farmers techniques now in existence. It is expected that such task forces, whose expertise has been tailored to address the specific areas identified by the host governments, will visit several countries in 1982. Peru has already been selected as the first country to receive a task force.

The United States will also emphasize energy-related development activities in the years ahead. Our energy bilateral aid program will stress technical assistance rather than resource transfers. We will support intensified energy training programs for technicians from developing countries, and efforts to help developing countries more efficiently utilize their resources.

It is clear that America's greatest resources for assisting developing countries lie in our private sector. Our contributions to development through trade dwarf our direct assistance contributions. The United States absorbs about one-half of all manufactured goods exported by the non-OPEC developing countries to the industrialized world. Our companies have been at the forefront in establishing manufacturing capabilities in the developing countries. Thus, we will work with developing countries to improve the climate for private investment and for the transfer of technology that comes with such investment.

We are also looking to build a stronger, long-term relationship between our universities and the developing countries. The Agency for International Development (AID) is experimenting with several new mechanisms for assuring greater continuity in the involvement of American universities and their scientific talent in development assistance programs. Additionally, more than 150,000 foreign students are enrolled at present in science, mathematics, and engineering programs in American universities. When these foreign students return to their native lands they maintain ties with American institutions, and this becomes a continuing channel for the development of the indigenous scientific and technological capacities of the developing countries.

---

[4] For the text of President Reagan's statement, see *American Foreign Policy: Current Documents, 1981*, document 270.

[5] Reference is to the International Meeting on Cooperation and Development, Cancun, Mexico, October 22–23, 1981. For statements made by Reagan at the conference, see *ibid.*, documents 89 and 90.

FUNDING AND PERSONNEL

My fiscal year 1983 budget has been sent to the Congress. In it I have requested funds adequate to meet our priority research and development and foreign policy needs.

The Department of State plays a central role in ensuring that international scientific activities are consistent with our foreign policy objectives. Over the past year, the Department of State has continued its efforts to upgrade the scientific and technical skills of its officers.

To carry out the commitment to greater emphasis on science and technology in our development assistance program, AID has, over the past year, reorganized and strengthened its science and technology capabilities, and placed a high priority on the effective use of these in planning and implementing its programs. AID established a new Bureau for Science and Technology charged with providing leadership in this area. A new Science Advisor to the Administrator of AID was appointed and a competitive research grants program was started by his office.

THE FUTURE

I believe that the health of the American science and technology enterprise is essential to meeting our principal objectives: sustained economic recovery, enhanced national security, and improved quality of life for our people. The same is true for our friends abroad. International scientific and technical cooperation can help both us and our friends to reach our respective national goals. We intend to continue our participation in international research and development programs on the basis of mutual benefit and mutual interest, and to identify the most fruitful areas for cooperation. And through trade, investment and development assistance we will share the harvest of our scientific enterprise with our friends in need.

Document 108

Statement by the President's Principal Deputy Press Secretary (Speakes), March 29, 1982[6]

U.S. Antarctic Policy

The United States has significant political, security, economic, environmental, and scientific interests in Antarctica. These are reflected in the Antarctic Treaty of 1959.[7] The system established by that treaty has permitted its parties, who maintain different positions concerning claims to territorial sovereignty in Antarctica, to work together to further scientific research and to ensure that Antarctica does not become the scene or object of international discord.

President Reagan has affirmed the United States commitment to a leadership role in Antarctica, both in the conduct of scientific research on and around the continent and in the system of international cooperation established pursuant to the Antarctic Treaty. Following review of a study of U.S. interests in Antarctica prepared by the interagency Antarctic Policy Group, the President has decided that:

—The United States Antarctic Program shall be maintained at a level providing an active and influential presence in Antarctica designed to support the range of U.S. Antarctic interests.

—This presence shall include the conduct of scientific activities in major disciplines; year-round occupation of the South Pole and two coastal stations; and availability of related necessary logistics support.

—Every effort shall be made to manage the program in a manner that maximizes cost effectiveness and return on investment.

The President also decided that the National Science Foundation will continue to budget for and manage the entire U.S. Program in Antarctica, including logistic support activities, so that the program may be managed as a single package. The U.S. Antarctic Program would continue to draw upon logistic support capabilities of other

[6] Source: White House Press Release, March 29, 1982, Office of the Press Secretary to the President; printed also in *Weekly Compilation of Presidential Documents,* April 5, 1982, pp. 404–405.

[7] The United States and 11 other nations signed the treaty on December 1, 1959, and it entered into force on June 23, 1961; for text, see 12 UST 794.

government agencies, including the Departments of Defense and Transportation, on a cost-reimbursable basis.

In another development of direct importance to U.S. Antarctic policy, the United States has ratified the Convention on the Conservation of Antarctic Marine Living Resources.[8] This new agreement will establish international mechanisms and create legal obligations necessary for the protection and conservation of the marine living resources found in the waters surrounding Antarctica. It was adopted at a diplomatic conference in Australia in May 1980. The United States, along with the other Consultative Parties, signed the Convention in September 1980.[9] Last December the Senate gave its advice and consent to ratification and President Reagan signed the instrument of ratification on February 2. That instrument was conveyed to the Government of Australia, the depositary government, on February 18.

The U.S. ratification is the seventh of the eight necessary to bring the Convention into force. The Convention is expected to enter into force within the next few months and the first meetings of the machinery established by the Convention are expected in May and June of this year.

The significance of this Convention lies not only in its environmental and resource management provisions and objectives. It also represents an important example of international cooperation among the Consultative Parties of the Antarctic Treaty.

---

[8] The treaty was ratified February 18, 1982, and entered into force April 7, 1982; for text, see TIAS 10240.

[9] The other 13 Antarctic Treaty Consultative Parties include Argentina, Australia, Belgium, Chile, France, the Federal Republic of Germany, Japan, New Zealand, Norway, Poland, South Africa, the U.S.S.R., and the U.K. The German Democratic Republic also signed the Convention. [Footnote in the source text.]

Document 109

Address by the Under Secretary of State for Security Assistance, Science and Technology (Buckley) Before the International Institute for Environment and Development, May 3, 1982[10]

Ten Years After Stockholm: U.S. International Environmental Perspectives and Interests

In just a few days, we will be celebrating the 10th anniversary of the 1972 Stockholm conference on the human environment.[11] As one who attended that conference, along with Russ Train, Elvis Stahr, and many others of you who are here today, I believe there is genuine cause for celebration. In noting our failure to meet all of the promises of the Stockholm declaration over the intervening years, we all too often forget how ambitious the whole project was and the enormous progress that has, in fact, been made. As I recall, it was widely feared 10 years ago that developing countries would actively resist environmental restraints in the belief that a certain fouling of the nest was the price that had to be paid for economic progress; that to allow themselves to be cajoled into self-imposed environmental disciplines would consign them to perpetual poverty.

But today, in all parts of the globe, there is growing agreement with the basic proposition that sound economic growth is dependent on sound environmental practice; that the proper management of renewable resources and the land and waters on which they depend offers a given society its greatest hope for sustained progress. True, huge areas of the Earth's surface continue to be ravaged today, but thanks to the revolution in world thinking that so many of you here today helped spark, there exists a broad international consensus on environmental priorities that transcends political divisions and ideological cleavages and will support cooperative action in pursuit of common goals.

---

[10] Source: Department of State *Bulletin*, July 1982, pp. 57–59. Buckley delivered his address as part of the Institute's International Environment/Development lecture series in Washington.

[11] Reference is to the U.N. World Conference on the Human Environment, held in Stockholm, Sweden, June 5–16, 1972.

Hence the importance of the commemorative meeting that is about to take place in Nairobi,[12] the "session of special character" that has been convened by the governing council of the U.N. Environmental Program (UNEP). It will be an international event of very great significance and will command broad attention both here and abroad. Not only is its purpose to take stock of how far the international community has come over the decade in response to the spirit and decisions of the Stockholm conference, but it is designed to produce a consensus among the 100 nations expected to participate on the priority problems that need to be met over the balance of this century.

Given the leadership this country has displayed over the last decade in international environmental affairs, our posture and positions in Nairobi will have special importance. I should, therefore, emphasize at the outset that the United States will participate actively and constructively to help insure that the decisions of the conference are responsive to the many future needs and opportunities which lie before the world community in the environmental field. Based on an assessment carried out through our overseas embassies, we know there is considerable interest on the part of other governments in the session of special character. We also find nations appear to share the view that the meeting can be a timely and effective mechanism for both strengthening national commitments to environmental management and promoting improved coordination of international environmental programs.

We anticipate two principal products from the conference: a "declaration" of a general nature along the lines of that developed in Stockholm and a "decision document" setting forth a series of recommendations for future action by governments and international organizations. [13] U.S. interests lie in making certain that these documents present a declaration of purpose and recommendations of a character that will command broad-based international attention and support. It is, therefore, our hope that the assembled delegations will conduct their deliberations in a candid manner but always in a spirit of cooperation and good will. We must avoid both over-simplification and excessiveness in our description of environmental problems and their solutions, avoid setting forth unattainable goals or recommendations, and, above all, avoid irrelevant and extraneous political detours.

We believe that expressions of concern about unfulfilled Stockholm goals, and emerging new problems, should be tempered by recognition of the impressive strides that have been made over the last 10 years. While much remains to be done, we should acknowledge and be encouraged by the rapid expansion of worldwide awareness of the need to manage the global environment, including the natural resource base, on a sound, sustained basis. Not only has this been translated into new policies, laws, programs, and institutions, but we are now witnessing an increasing number of successes in preventing and abating pollution of the air, water, and land, and in maintaining the productive capacity of the resource base.

Our delegation in Nairobi will describe what we have accomplished and learned in working to safeguard the environment here at home because we are proud of what we have managed to do over the past dozen or so years and feel our example and experience can be put to use in the larger international arena.

In discussing our legislative and other initiatives, we will stress the importance of establishing the kind of broad-based commitment to an environmental ethic that has been so critical to our successes here. We could not have made the progress we have without the participation of virtually all sectors of American society—the Federal government; State and local governments; private industry; the scientific community; and, above all, the nongovernmental organizations, the media, and the public. It bodes well for the future that recent polls have indicated that U.S. public interest in solving environmental and resource problems remains at a very high level.

We also intend to call attention to our extensive and productive bilateral environmental relationships with other countries. Among the most important are those with our immediate neighbors, Canada and Mexico. We have also worked closely over the last decade with other developed countries, such as Germany and Japan, to find new solutions to environmental questions. Under our development assistance program, we have been helping a broad array of developing nations to address pollution and resource management problems.

---

[12] Reference is to the Second U.N. World Conference on the Global Environment, held in Nairobi, Kenya, May 10–18, 1982.

[13] The Nairobi conference issued the Nairobi Declaration, UNEP/GC.10/INF.5, May 19, 1982, and the Draft Decision, UNEP/GC(SSC/L.3), May 17, 1982.

But perhaps our most significant efforts to help other nations develop an awareness of environmental purposes and most importantly the knowledge with which to address them has been under the auspices of the U.S. Agency for International Development. It has been a world leader in carrying out environmental reviews of its proposed projects and also in supporting activities specifically designed to address the natural resource management and environmental protection needs of developing countries. In the period between 1978 and 1982, it has increased its environmental budget from $13 million to $130 million with an additional $23 million being requested for fiscal year 1983. I might point out that these expenditures will have been increased by more than $40 million under the Reagan administration. In addition, nearly 5,000 Peace Corps volunteers have devoted attention to a wide range of environmental and natural resource management projects.

Multilaterally, the United States has been present "at the creation" of most of the international environmental organizations in existence today (for example, UNEP, UNESCO's Man and the Biosphere Program, and the environmental bodies of the Organization for Economic Cooperation and Development, NATO, and the U.N. Economic Commission for Europe). In addition to our large financial investments in the programs of these institutions, we have also contributed the time and talents of hundreds of U.S. scientists, technicians, and managers from both the public and private sectors who have provided essential supporting services.

In any assessment of how far the world community of nations has come since Stockholm, recognition must be given to the multitude of important international conventions and treaties negotiated to control pollution and to protect natural resources of common concern. Among these are the London marine dumping convention; the convention on international trade in wild and endangered species; the international whaling convention; the convention for conservation of Antarctic seals; the North Pacific fur seal convention; the agreement on the conservation of polar bears; and the convention on long-range transboundary air pollution.[14] Again, the United States played a prominent role in first developing, and then implementing, these international agreements.

What is more important than establishing how far we have come since Stockholm, however, is the UNEP special session's mandate to set forth "where we need to go from here." Given the fact that identification of future policy direction and program priorities comes at a time of severe resource constraint throughout the world community, all participating nations have a vital interest in seeing that the conference recommendations are sharply focused, realistic, and appropriate.

In this regard, it is important to note one of the major conclusions of a recent U.N. analysis of "changing perceptions" about environmental problems over the last decade: namely, that the interrelationships among individual components of various ecosystems are much more complex than perceived at the time of Stockholm. We will, therefore, press for recognition that there must be a strengthening of our understanding of environmental problems and processes, including improved analysis of environmental trends, as a basis for sound decisionmaking. It is interesting to note that at Stockholm, such important issues of today as PCBs, groundwater contamination from hazardous wastes, the appearance of heavy metals in polar ice cores, stratospheric ozone depletion, and the potential for carbon dioxide-induced climatic change were not recognized.

By the same token, some of the problems that held our attention 10 years ago have either disappeared or moved to the sidelines. For example, high altitude aircraft flights have not emerged as the serious factor in depleting the ozone layer as was then feared. Also, accumulating evidence suggests that many environmental systems, such as coastal areas subjected to major oil spills, are more resilient to stress than had been previously suspected. And, most importantly, we are finding that people's ability to respond and adapt to changing environmental conditions may similarly have been underestimated.

[14] For the text of the London Marine Dumping Convention, entered into force on August 30, 1975, see 26 UST 2403; for the Convention on International Trade in Endangered Species of Wild Fauna and Flora, entered into force on July 1, 1975, see 27 UST 1087; for the International Whaling Convention, entered into force on January 16, 1935, see 3 Bevans 26; for the Convention for Conservation of Antarctic Seals, entered into force on March 11, 1978, see 29 UST 441; for the Agreement on the Conservation of Polar Bears, entered into force on November 1, 1976, see TIAS 8409; and for the Convention on Long-Range Transboundary Air Pollution, entered into force on March 16, 1983, see TIAS 10541.

The U.S. delegation in Nairobi will be addressing a number of other important concerns. These include our continuing desire to see improved coordination and greater efficiency within the U.N. system of organizations. This is especially critical in view of current and projected budget constraints and the ever-present problem of program duplication. Thus, while stressing our continuing support of, and participation in, multilateral programs and institutions, we will, at the same time, note that we will be looking for more in terms of program effectiveness, sound administration, and fiscal responsibility. We will, at the same time, stress the importance of involving private sector institutions in environmental protection programs at both the national and international levels.

The future of UNEP as an institution of course will be considered in Nairobi. A recent U.S. survey suggests that most foreign governments share our view that UNEP should retain and strengthen its catalytic and coordination role but that its program activities should be streamlined and coordinated to a greater degree. Our delegation thus intends to register its continuing support for the original UNEP concept, and call for a narrowing of its program focus, with emphasis on the following:

Environmental monitoring and assessment;

Information dissemination to governments;

Environmental education and training;

The regional seas program;

Management of land and biological resources (forests, arid lands, biological diversity);

Control of potentially toxic substances;

Intra-U.N. program coordination and catalysis, and reduction of country-level operational activities.

As for the conference itself, our great worry is that it may be forced to confront a number of contentious issues of a political nature having little to do with the important business at hand. Certain delegations, for example, may introduce resolutions on such matters as nuclear armaments, the policies of Israel and South Africa, and variations on the new economic order theme. Efforts to inject divisive political issues into world meetings on subjects such as the environment have been all too commonplace of late. We hope, however, that attempts at such diversions will be contained and the deliberations in Nairobi allowed to proceed smoothly and harmoniously to a constructive conclusion.

In our overall approach to the conference, we will be guided by a series of "global environmental principles" developed by an interagency work group chaired by Council on Environmental Quality Chairman Alan Hill.[15] They are grounded in two basic premises: first, that a healthy environment is fundamental to the well-being of mankind and second, that economic growth and social progress are necessary conditions for the effective implementation of environmental policies and programs. Other guiding principles will include the following:

Environmental policy must be based on the needs of both present and future generations;

Careful stewardship of the Earth's natural resource base will contribute significantly to sound economic development;

Biological diversity must be maintained;

Governments should collaborate on addressing problems which extend beyond national boundaries; and

Governments and individuals alike should insure that their activities do not produce environmental degradation.

These "global environmental principles" (which I have presented in abbreviated form) will provide both a philosophical and pragmatic basis for U.S. environmental efforts at home and abroad, efforts which extend well beyond the forthcoming UNEP session of special character.

In conclusion, I would like to highlight the importance of the nonofficial agenda at Nairobi. I speak of the forum for nongovernmental environmental organizations which began there today. As was the case at Stockholm, we anticipate that much of the most important input at the conference will come not from official delegations but from the ideas and concepts that will be generated and discussed by the representatives of the nongovernmental organizations participating in that forum.

Our delegation will be looking forward to reviewing the decisions and conclusions they arrived at and will maintain close contact with the American representatives. The

---

[15] For the full text of the guiding principles, see the statement by Anne Gorsuch, *infra*.

work of these private organizations—of the organizations represented here today—has been of incalculable importance in advancing the environmental cause at both the national and international levels. Given where we were just a dozen or so years ago, we have made extraordinary progress. But we all recognize how very much remains to be done and how late in the day it is.

Therefore, your continuing efforts and support will be more important than ever as we seek to consolidate past gains and to set the agenda for the immediate future. The members of our delegation and I will be looking forward to working with you to achieve these profoundly important goals we share.

Document 110

Statement by the Administrator of the Environmental Protection Agency (Gorsuch), Nairobi, May 11, 1982 (Extract)[16]

U.S. International Environmental Policy

. . . .

We have . . . remained conscious of the international dimension of our environmental concerns. In our bilateral relations with other countries, the United States Agency for International Development (AID) has been the leader in carrying out environmental reviews of its proposed projects. AID has strongly supported activities to address environmental protection concerns of developing countries.

During the past 6 years—from fiscal year 1978 to fiscal year 1983—AID's financial support of environmental programs has increased more than tenfold—from $13 million to $153 million.

This expenditure has been augmented by the people-to-people approach taken by our 5,000 Peace Corps volunteers in approximately 60 developing nations. They have worked among rural residents and small farm producers on programs for human health, environmental protection, and resource management.

These include programs for the protection of surface water systems from contamination, conservation of fuel wood through improved stoves and charcoal production, and many other measures.

Multilaterally, the United States has cooperated wholeheartedly in the establishment of most of the international environmental organizations in existence today, among them:

the United Nations Environment Program;

UNESCO's Man and the Biosphere Program; and

the environmental committees of the OECD, NATO, and the UN Economic Commission for Europe.

The United States has also assisted in framing international conventions and treaties to control pollution and to protect natural resources. Among these agreements are:

The Convention on the Prevention of Marine Pollution by Dumping of Waste and Other Matter (the London Dumping Convention);

The Convention on International Trade in Endangered Species of Wild Fauna and Flora (CITES);[17] and

Other measures to address mutual concerns about the international environment and the life it sustains.

President Reagan has committed his administration to continue an active role in the protection of our domestic environment. The United States shall continue to support sound international environmental practices, building upon the experience that we have acquired and the knowledge that we have accumulated.

Today we have broad international recognition that the global environment, its ecosystems—and their relationships with human factors—are far more complex than we understood a decade ago. In the United States, we have begun to perceive that—at both the national and international levels—there has been inadequate foresight and

---

[16] Source: Environmental Protection Agency files. As head of the U.S. delegation, Gorsuch delivered the major U.S. policy statement to the Plenary of the Session of Special Character, at the United Nations Environment Program, Second U.N. Conference on the Global Environment.

[17] Regarding these conventions, see footnote 14 above.

understanding among policymakers of the long-term costs—as well as benefits—of environmental protection measures.

Many of our actions have failed to take advantage of the natural corrective measures that can work through market forces—if governments allow them to operate. Too frequently, we responded with alarm to pessimistic projections—squandering scarce resources on inappropriate measures—rather than devoting those resources to the careful study of practical and effective ways in which we might improve our world.

Certainly, we are here to commemorate Stockholm and to review the progress of all nations in resolving global environmental concerns, but we would be remiss not to look ahead at what we can add to our accomplishments in the 1980's.

How, then, should the United States and all of us here in Nairobi approach our environmental concerns in the coming years? Let me summarize for you eight principles, discussed at high levels of the United States administration, to provide guidance for our efforts to protect the environment in harmony with an economic prosperity that we can sustain for future generations.

First: A healthy environment is fundamental to the well-being of mankind.

Second: Economic growth and social progress are necessary conditions for effective implementation of policies which will protect the global environment and promote wise use of the Earth's natural resource base.

Third: Environmental policy should be based on the interests of present and future generations. The most successful policies are those which promote liberty and individual rights, as well as protection of the physical environment.

Fourth: Nations should pursue economic development in furtherance of the security and well-being of their citizens in a manner which is sensitive to environmental concerns. Due respect should be given to different approaches which various nations may adopt to integrate environmental considerations into development strategies based on their particular national values and priorities.

Fifth: Careful stewardship of the Earth's natural resources can contribute significantly to sound economic development. Individual ownership of property, free and well-developed markets in products and capital are powerful incentives for resource conservation. These institutions best promote the use of renewable resources and the development of substitutes for nonrenewable resources, ensuring continued resource availability and environmental quality.

Sixth: When environmental problems extend beyond the boundaries of any one nation, all affected nations should participate in investigating the nature of the problem, understanding its implications, and developing cost-effective responses.

Seventh: Governments, like individuals, should act so as to minimize environmental degradation. Decisions on environmental policies and programs should take into account the concerns of those closest to the problems and most directly affected.

Eighth: Increased scientific understanding of environmental problems, and improved methods of forecasting environmental conditions, are needed to address environmental issues in an effective and efficient manner. Ultimately, resolution of environmental problems which are global in nature will be determined by the quality and credibility of our scientific and technical knowledge as well as by the degree of cooperation among nations including the effective involvement of private sector institutions.

These principles will guide the environmental policies of the United States in the coming years. They are a reflection of our deepest beliefs, and derive from the substantial experience that we have accumulated in dealing with environmental matters during this century.

What should be the priorities for the international environmental agenda of the 1980's? In times of budgetary austerity, that agenda must be lean and nonduplicative, concentrating on issues genuinely deserving priority attention. In my government's view, such issues include the following:

(1) Monitoring and assessing of environmental conditions and trends. We must upgrade existing capabilities for anticipating the emergence of new problems, and for monitoring and evaluating changing environmental conditions and interactions as a basis for determining the need for remedial measures.

(2) Natural resources management. Among other priorities, efforts must be intensified to curb excessive deforestation,

to improve the productive capacity of semi-arid and arid lands, and to prevent degradation of prime croplands from erosion, salination and water logging.

(3) Environmental education, training and information dissemination. We must continue to expand popular awareness and knowledge and enlarge the base of trained personnel in the environmental and resource areas.

I wish I could tell you that our experience provides sure cures for everything that might ail our environment. In truth, we have had substantial success in many of our clean-up efforts. On occasion, however, we have rushed to fix things that—as it turned out—we did not adequately understand.

Like good scientists, we must attend to signs that can show us when we might be making mistakes. Nature, after all, has long been managing what we have only recently begun to study.

Once we have acquired improved scientific information, we must devote more of our attention to the dissemination of it through public education, training, and information programs. As President Reagan has observed:

> "The greatest resource that all nations share is people. The emphasis of our cooperation should focus on developing the knowledge and skills that will help individuals and organizations to formulate sounder policies and programs. Skilled people are the cornerstone for building institutions that will ensure the long-term success of our development and natural resource conservation efforts. For this reason, training and the continuous voluntary exchange of the newest information and technology must be a central element in our cooperative activities."[18]

We will proceed in a spirit of confidence that the principles that we have expressed can provide a sound basis to improve the environment and the lives of our peoples. In general, we remain confident that even the most difficult environmental problems will be resolved through the application of human initiative, ingenuity, and the will to address these concerns in an open-minded and technically sound manner.

Above all, we will seek cooperation rather than confrontation between governments, international organizations, private industries, and other concerned groups. Our efforts to promote cleaner air and water, to protect our natural resources, and to provide a healthy and bountiful land for all our peoples deserve and require our most conscientious and cooperative efforts.

We commemorate Stockholm as an important international spark for global environmental concern. Let us work—together—to insure that Nairobi is remembered as the place where we more effectively balanced our concern for the environment with a pursuit of scientific excellence and sustained economic development, an approach that will greatly benefit the future generations who will inherit the world that our decisions shape.

[18] For text, see document 18.

Document 111

Letter From Representative Don Bonker to President Reagan, June 25, 1982[19]

Congressional Support for a Strong U.S. Stand on Whale Conservation

Dear Mr. President: The International Whaling Commission, which will hold its 34th annual meeting from July 19–24, 1982 in Brighton, England, will once again consider the question of adopting an indefinite moratorium on commercial whaling. In view of the mounting scientific evidence against continued commercial whaling, we are hopeful that the IWC will finally act favorably on the U.S.-sponsored moratorium proposal. However, the success of this effort depends upon two critical factors: strong American leadership and U.S. resolve to invoke sanctions against countries which violate IWC agreements.

As you know, the U.S. has been in the forefront of the international movement to bring an end to the commercial exploitation

[19] Source: *Review of the 34th International Whaling Commission Meeting: Hearing Before the Subcommittee on Human Rights and International Organizations of the Committee on Foreign Affairs, House of Representatives, Ninety-seventh Congress, Second Session* (Washington, 1982), p. 82. Bonker was Chairman of the Subcommittee on Human Rights and International Organizations of the House Foreign Affairs Committee. Sixty-four other House members also signed this letter. For the names of additional signatories, see *ibid.*, pp. 82–85.

of whales. Both Democratic and Republican Administrations have supported this policy since 1973, and the Congress has unanimously passed several resolutions endorsing it. Your letter to the 1981 IWC meeting, in which you reaffirmed "the U.S. Government's continuing commitment to whale protection," greatly strengthened the U.S. position.[20] We hope the U.S. Delegation to the 1982 IWC will again work vigorously on behalf of achieving a moratorium on commercial whaling.

Five whaling countries—Japan, Brazil, Iceland, Norway and the U.S.S.R.—have already filed objections to conservation measures adopted at last year's IWC. Their objections represent a blatant challenge to U.S. willingness to invoke the Pelly and Packwood-Magnuson amendments against countries choosing to disregard IWC regulations.[21] These amendments provide that when the Secretary of Commerce, in consultation with the Secretary of State, certifies that a country's activities "diminish the effectiveness" of whale conservation measures, the country automatically loses fifty percent of its fisheries allocation within the U.S. 200-mile zone and may face an embargo on the import of its fisheries products. This year, the whaling nations intend to force the question of whether the U.S. will enforce these laws. Our steadfast resolve to invoke sanctions against any country which violates IWC regulations must be made clear to all IWC member nations.

The success of the decade-long effort to end commercial whaling will be determined by strong U.S. leadership, backed by a firm commitment to enforce the Pelly and Packwood-Magnuson amendments. We encourage you to assure that the U.S. Delegation to the 1982 IWC meeting takes a strong stand in support of whale conservation.

Sincerely yours,

DON BONKER

Document 112

Address by the Representative to the UNISPACE 82 Conference (Beggs), Vienna, August 10, 1982[22]

U.S. Cooperation in the Peaceful Uses of Outer Space

Twenty-five years into the space age, and 14 years after our first U.N. conference on outer space,[23] we again meet in Vienna to consider where we stand and where we are going in the peaceful uses of outer space. The last 25 years have been characterized by extraordinary achievement in space-based activities, not only by the United States but by a growing number of countries throughout the world. Indeed, in a global sense, it is no exaggeration to say that we are on the verge of becoming a space-faring civilization.

The last several decades also have been characterized by U.S. leadership in space science and applications, frequently exercised in broad cooperation with countries throughout the world. To date, the United States has entered into over 1,000 agreements with over 100 countries to share the benefits and adventure of outer space. At the outset of this conference, I want to state categorically that the United States intends to remain the leader in the peaceful uses of outer space and to continue its active and open program of international cooperation.

In this I speak for President Reagan, who is a strong supporter of the U.S. space program and its application to bettering our life here on Earth.

In order to assess where we are and where we should be going in space science and applications, it is constructive to reflect on where we have been. When this conference last met in 1968, there were essentially two significant space powers, with a

[20] For the text, see *Public Papers of the Presidents of the United States: Ronald Reagan,* 1981 (Washington, 1982), p. 634.

[21] References are to an amendment introduced by Congressman Thomas M. Pelly to the Fisherman's Protective Act of 1967, approved on December 23, 1971 (P.L. 29–219; 85 Stat. 786), and to an amendment introduced by Senators Robert Packwood and Warren G. Magnuson to the Fishery Conservation and Management Act of 1976, approved on August 15, 1979 (P.L. 96–61; 93 Stat. 407).

[22] Source: Department of State *Bulletin,* February 1983, pp. 69–72. The Second U.N. Conference on the Exploration and Peaceful Uses of Outer Space (UNISPACE 82) was held in Vienna, Austria, August 9–21, 1982. Beggs was also Administrator, National Aeronautics and Space Administration. Regarding UNISPACE 82, see also U.N. General Assembly Resolution 37/90, adopted without a vote on December 10, 1982.

[23] The First U.N. Conference on the Exploration and Peaceful Uses of Outer Space was held in Vienna, Austria, August 14–27, 1968.

few other countries who aspired to space programs. The United States was in the process of completing its dramatic Apollo project. Twelve Americans walked the surface of the Moon during that program and were brought safely back to Earth. In the course of this program and in the Skylab program that followed, we established the ability of man to function for extended periods in space and vastly increased our scientific knowledge. Since then, there have been additional important achievements by the United States and by a growing number of other countries in the exploration and peaceful uses of outer space.

In the United States, we have completed the testing of the space shuttle and plan to put it into operational service later this year. The shuttle will give us routine, reliable, and cost-effective transportation into space and will continue to open new and broader areas for international cooperation in the future. We have explored many of the planets in our solar system and probably will have visited all except distant Pluto by the end of the decade. We have built and flown communications, weather navigation, and remote sensing satellites that bring untold benefits to all the peoples of the Earth.

Since we last assembled in Vienna, there have been three particular trends which, taken together, are of special relevance to this conference. Because they will continue, they should be kept in mind as we chart our future course.

The advance of technology has been rapid and has shown no signs of slowing. Looking back over the short period we have been in space, the rate of progress in amassing scientific knowledge and in applying space technology has been truly astonishing. Consider, for example, the tiny space capsule in which the first American astronaut, John Glenn, orbited the Earth. Compare it to the space shuttle, launched only two decades later, which is a marvel of sophisticated engineering and promises to be America's primary space transportation system for the balance of this century. The conclusion is inescapable that progress in outer space technology has been dramatic.

There are many more nations with space programs today. Scientific, commercial, and technical incentives have led an increasing number of countries to invest their resources in one aspect or another of space technology and applications. These space programs range from large, very complex enterprises to more modest but nevertheless significant efforts. The United States welcomes this development, the knowledge it generates, and the stimulus it provides to excel in what is still a bright new frontier of human endeavor.

There is a growing emphasis on relating space activity to our needs here on Earth. Innovators in the private sector are incorporating space-related capabilities into countless areas of human activity.

Looking ahead, we can fully expect these trends to continue. It is clear then that among the priority tasks in our agenda of future activities are those which will help us better to understand our own Earth, aid in the development of national economies, and assist in the broader sharing of technological skills. The United States stands ready to do its share to achieve these objectives.

Venturing into outer space provides perspectives not only on other worlds; it helps us better perceive, understand, and deal with conditions affecting life here on Earth. It is clear to the United States, for example, that increased scientific understanding of environmental problems and improved methods in forecasting are needed if we are to enhance our ability to address issues relating to overall global habitability in an effective and efficient manner. We live on a planet characterized by change, and it has been demonstrated that space-based observations are of inestimable value in measuring changes which affect the Earth. The United States today conducts a number of space-based activities directed toward this end, and we note that other governments and international institutions have also undertaken important efforts in this regard.

We believe it is important to begin to think in larger terms with respect to global conditions. Specifically, we envision continued long-term research efforts with international cooperation to expand further the base of data and knowledge from which sound decisions can be made with respect to the environment. By better organized efforts, we can vastly improve the validity and reliability of available information as well as provide more systematic bases for evaluating and responding in long-term global change. Outer space technology will be a more valuable tool in focusing attention on those trends which influence our Earth's habitability.

The United States will be discussing a global habitability concept with other governments and international institutions here at the conference and in the months ahead. We would like to determine whether a more effective, cooperative, long-term effort is feasible on a global basis. My government believes such a cooperative undertaking could benefit all countries of the world, developed and developing.

In addition to gaining better long-term understanding of the Earth's environment, the perspective of outer space can help all countries—and particularly developing countries—to better anticipate and cope with natural disasters. To this end, we propose two projects for consideration.

We suggest that the U.N. Outer Space Division sponsor a working group on disaster assistance communications to examine the possibility of establishing a global emergency space communications system for disaster situations.

To learn how best to bring space technology to bear in coping with natural disasters, the U.S. Agency for International Development (AID) will sponsor a 5-day conference in the spring of 1984 in Washington. The conference would examine current operational systems, regional systems being developed, and future technologies applicable to developing a global disaster monitoring and early warning network.

Finally, in order to encourage a better understanding of the Earth, the United States is also making available to participants in UNISPACE a special LANDSAT index of the best available images collected over the past 10 years by LANDSAT 1, 2, and 3. The indexes are referenced to the new worldwide reference system maps developed by the U.S. Geological Survey.[24] The data available through the LANDSAT program is accessible to every country and is indispensable to understanding and employing earth resources for the benefit of mankind.

There has been a good deal written and spoken about the promise of space technology for national economic development. It is often too easy to give the imagination free play and to ignore the fact that in applying space technology three concepts are fundamental and essential—establishing priorities, allocating scarce resources, and applying the discipline of careful administration. Outer space technology has great promise. And, in its application, much can be done in cooperation with other governments and with the private sector. The process of technology application is not, however, cost-free and should be begun only after deliberate decisions on the part of governments. The United States is prepared to assist in this process through several programs which have proven successful.

The United States, through AID's rural satellite program, has begun work with developing countries to advance the use of satellite communications for development. We are carrying out pilot programs in rural telephone and audio-conferencing, providing training, undertaking research and development, and providing information and advice. To share the results of this effort more widely with others, the United States will hold an international conference on rural satellite communications in 1985.

The United States will shortly begin field testing a combined low-cost satellite ground station and photovoltaic power system, optimized for developing country use. The results and technical data of this test will be widely available through AID's rural satellite program. This effort is a product of cooperation in research and development between the U.S. Government and industry. Its objective is to lower the cost to developing countries of Earth stations and to provide a reliable renewable source for them.

I invite the conference to view the U.S.-sponsored demonstrations of this technology in the Seiten Galerie and the Heldenplatz.

Integral to the success of any of these programs is the spread of the skills necessary to conduct them. The draft report[25] of this conference quite rightly emphasizes the need to expand training programs, particularly for technicians and scientists from developing countries. The United States shares this conviction. Within the context of the work of UNISPACE, and through projects associated with the forthcoming International Telecommunication Union-sponsored World Communications Year,[26] the United States will continue to contribute substantially to training programs and will explore ways of enhancing their quality and availability. My delegation welcomes the views of others on all of the proposals I have made. We will be prepared to elaborate on these and other ideas in committee and in the scheduled poster sessions.

---

[24] Reference is to U.S. Geological Survey, *LANDSAT Worldwide Reference System*, Sioux Falls, S.D., EROS Data Center, 1981.

[25] For the Report of the UNISPACE 82 Conference, see U.N. document A/CONF.101/10, and Corr.1 and 2.

[26] 1983 was the projected year for the World Communications Year.

It is unusual in conferences such as UNISPACE to project dramatic future activities and programs. And, I am confident that future developments in outer space will be every bit as dramatic as those which have occurred since 1968. I say this because I believe we have the human resources, the imagination, the technical capability, and the determination to accelerate the pace of development in the peaceful uses of outer space.

Space has been aptly named the endless frontier, and looking ahead over the next quarter century and beyond, the potential of exploring and exploiting the space environment for the common good is as limitless as the void of space itself.

I am confident the human family will fulfill that potential. New challenges, new adventure, the resources of new worlds are within our reach. It is up to us to grasp them.

The urge to know the unknown is basic to the pioneering spirit that means so much to the world. That urge is alive and well and will continue to thrive so long as man wants to know. And there is much for us to know.

As T.S. Eliot once wrote: "We shall never cease from exploration and the end of all our exploring will be to arrive at where we started and to know the place for the first time."

In that never-ending quest, the United States pledges to work, in cooperation with all nations, to bring peace and prosperity to our generation and to future generations inhabiting this planet.

Document 113

Prepared Statement by the Commissioner of the International Whaling Commission (Byrne) Before a Subcommittee of the House Foreign Affairs Committee, September 16, 1982 (Extract)[27]

Results of Negotiations for the Conservation of Whales

. . . .

Mr. Chairman, 10 years ago, the IWC was a far different organization than it is today. It had 14 members, employed a single staff person year round at half time, and had an annual budget of less than $20,000. It did not regulate whaling in the North Atlantic at all, it had no international observer scheme, it established catch limits in terms of the Blue Whale Unit—a measure of whale oil production rather than a whale conservation concept, and it was responsible for the commercial harvesting of approximately 46,000 whales.

Expressing its grave concern over declining whale stocks and the operation of the IWC, the 1972 United Nations Conference on the Human Environment in Stockholm adopted a resolution calling for a strengthened IWC and a 10-year moratorium on commercial whaling by vote of 53 in favor, none opposed, and three abstentions.[28] At the IWC meeting that was held only 10 days after the conclusion of the Stockholm meeting, the United States proposed the same 10-year moratorium, but the measure was rejected by a vote of only 4 in favor, with 6 opposed, and 4 abstentions.[29] However disappointing this initial result, the United States was not discouraged. We instead initiated a process of reform which continues to this day. The 1972 IWC meeting agreed to abolish the Blue Whale Unit in favor of management by species and, later, by stocks, to implement an international observer scheme, and establish catch limits for the first time for minke and sperm whales in the Southern Hemisphere. In the ensuing decade, catch limits were established for all stocks of large whales worldwide and reduced by some 73 percent, factory ships were prohibited from taking whales other than minkes, a large whale sanctuary was established in the Indian Ocean, and the use of the inhumane cold harpoon was banned. Over the same period, the Commission Secretariat was expanded to include a full time data analysis staff and accommodate the growth of IWC membership to 39 countries. The vast ma-

---

27 Source: *Review of the 34th International Whaling Commission Meeting*, pp. 30–32. Byrne attended the 34th Annual International Whaling Commission Meeting in Brighton, England, July 19–24, 1982. He is also Administrator, National Oceanic and Atmospheric Administration, Department of Commerce.

28 Reference is to Recommendation 33 of the Action Plan for the Human Environment, adopted at the U.N. Conference on the Human Environment, Stockholm, Sweden, June 5–16, 1972, contained in the Report of the Conference; for text, see U.N. document A/CONF.48/14/Rev.1.

29 Regarding the U.S. proposal and the vote, see *Chairman's Report of the 24th International Whaling Commission Meeting, London, England, June 26–30, 1972* (London, 1972).

jority of the current membership, either by change in policy or upon becoming members, has joined the whale conservation cause.

This group of conservation-oriented countries succeeded at the July 1982 meeting in achieving IWC recognition of the need to cease commercial whaling. The poor state of knowledge about whales and the downward trend in IWC catch limits throughout the 1970's clearly supported our view that the available data base and previous IWC Management practices are totally inadequate to manage whales without incurring unacceptable risks.

The moment came on July 23 when the IWC, by a vote of 25 to 7 with 5 countries abstaining, adopted a cessation of commercial whaling to take effect as of the 1985–86 pelagic and 1986 coastal whaling season.[30]

The Commission's decision was taken with the understanding that catch limits will be established during the 3-year transition period in accordance with the recommendations of the Scientific Committee and the provisions of the current management procedures. The postponement of 3 years will provide the industry with the time necessary to cease whaling in an ordinary fashion. The "cessation," as it is called, is to be reviewed by 1990 to determine its effect on whale stocks. I am submitting for the record tables reflecting the newly established catch limits and the trend in catch limits over time.[31]

The goals we are striving for will not be realized until we have successfully implemented the cessation. In the meantime, we will face challenges to maintain the integrity of the IWC while achieving the orderly cessation of all countries from commercial whaling. Affected countries may well file objections to the cessation in the period provided for such action in order to preserve their options while considering measures necessary to comply. None have done so to date. The deferral of the cessation serves to encourage these countries to continue to participate in the IWC as the appropriate forum for whale conservation and makes it possible for us to maintain the dialogues and exert the influence that will be essential to achieve the cessation in practice. We are and should be optimistic. The success achieved in Brighton is the best evidence we could have that whales will receive that protection we have urged for so long.

The July 1982 IWC meeting also devoted substantial effort to the development of guidelines for the establishment of IWC whale sanctuaries. The prime objective set forth in the guidelines is to identify areas in which individual or groups of whale species are protected from whaling for a specified period to provide for long-term conservation. Additional objectives related to research and the collection of information are also articulated. The guidelines will be used to review and assess any proposals for sanctuaries that may be submitted to the IWC in the future and should place the process of establishing IWC whale sanctuaries on a firm basis.

Finally, as a result of determined U.S. efforts since 1979, including intensive work over the past 2 years, the IWC established management principles and procedures to govern aboriginal subsistence whaling. These principles and procedures formally recognize the distinction between commercial and aboriginal subsistence whaling and codify the IWC's practice of attempting, where necessary, to strike a proper balance between the needs of aboriginal people who depend on limited whaling to meet subsistence, cultural, and nutritional needs and the conservation needs of the affected whales. They require the management of such hunting so as to provide for the recovery of depleted whale populations. To assist with the implementation of these procedures at the next meeting of the IWC in July 1983 and thereafter, the Commission agreed to establish a standing subcommittee of the Technical Committee to review aboriginal subsistence whaling needs and provide this information to the Commission in much the same way that the Scientific Committee provides advice. The Alaska Eskimo Whaling Commission contributed substantially to achieving this result and we look forward to its continued contributions in helping to implement the scheme.

Mr. Chairman, our activities since the July 1982 meeting provide an indication of the major issues that can be anticipated for next year's meeting and beyond. As I have indicated, one major challenge for us and our colleagues within the Commission is to facilitate the efforts of the IWC and particu-

---

30 The provision banning commercial whaling, as well as other amendments adopted at the meeting, were incorporated in The Schedule to the International Convention for the Regulation of Whaling as Amended by the Commission, at the 34th Annual International Whaling Commission Meeting, July 19–24, 1982, and entered into force on February 3, 1983.

31 See *Review of the 34th International Whaling Commission Meeting*, pp. 99–100.

larly the whaling countries in implementing the cessation. In this regard, the cooperation of all countries will be required to reflect what we regard as the clear expression of world opinion in favor of a cessation. I have therefore written letters to all Commissioners of countries that joined us on the cessation vote expressing appreciation for their support and urging continued efforts to achieve our common goal. I expressed U.S. commitment to this result and our desire to work intensively with all IWC members to achieve it.

I do not expect any significant changes in the IWC's membership over the next year. We will work with the existing membership to maintain the integrity and viability of the IWC and its decisions. In this regard, my letters to conservation-oriented Commissioners, as well as letters to their counterparts in the whaling countries expressing our desire to facilitate their compliance with the cessation decision, are being reinforced by personal visits by our embassy officials abroad. We have also been in regular contact with the IWC Secretariat to monitor any official reactions to the July 1982 meeting. To date, there has been no such reaction, but we have been able to be of assistance to the Secretary in clarifying the correct text of several decisions reached last July. The 90-day period to object to these decisions expires on November 4.

A second major issue anticipated for the July 1983 IWC meeting is the implementation of the aboriginal whaling management scheme and the establishment of catch limits to govern bowhead whaling in 1984 and beyond. We are working closely with the concerned Federal agencies, particularly the Department of the Interior, and the Alaska Eskimo Whaling Commission (AEWC) to develop information that will be critical to implementing the management scheme. I have been in contact with the chairman of the IWC Technical Committee, whose responsibility it is to establish the standing subcommittee on aboriginal subsistence needs, to express our interest in participating in the planning and conduct of the work of this new body. Within NOAA, we will continue to work with the AEWC to manage the bowhead whale hunt jointly, as provided for under our Cooperative Agreement, with a mind to the need to establish new catch limits for the bowhead whale hunt at the next meeting.

On the matter of sanctuaries, it is too early to predict whether there will be proposals to establish additional IWC whale sanctuaries. I believe, however, that the IWC co-sponsored meeting on the nonconsumptive uses of whales that we proposed should help to develop useful information that complements efforts relating to sanctuaries. This meeting is not yet scheduled but should occur before the July 1983 IWC meeting.

Finally, Mr. Chairman, I would like to make reference to the IWC's ban on the use of cold grenade harpoons to take minke whales. The ban was adopted at the July 1981 IWC meeting and becomes effective beginning with the 1982–83 pelagic and 1983 coastal whaling seasons. The 1982–83 pelagic season starts this November in the Southern Hemisphere. The ban is the subject of objections filed by Brazil, Iceland, Japan, Norway, and the Soviet Union.

The U.S. position on this matter is clear. We supported the ban and continue to do so. We have communicated this position and our concern to each objecting country, urging that every means be explored that would allow the withdrawal of objections. We have also carefully explained the provisions of the Pelly and Packwood–Magnuson amendments[32] which provide for sanctions in the event the Secretary of Commerce determines that a country's nationals are conducting fishing operations, including whaling, in a manner that diminishes the effectiveness of an international fishery conservation program, including that of the IWC.

The achievements at the July 1982 IWC meeting were unmatched in its history. There is a clear and long sought expression of world opinion in the matter of whale conservation. The United States will continue its efforts in the next years to bring the decisions of the IWC into practice and, with the cooperation of all IWC members, enter what I consider to be a bright chapter in the history of conservation.

Mr. Chairman, I want to express to you our appreciation and thanks for your sustained interest and support as we work to achieve the cessation we have sought for so long. We will continue to face challenges to hold the IWC together and to bring into practice the conservation measures already adopted. We will need to rely on the support of the Congress and the American people as we face these challenges.

. . . .

---

[32] Regarding these amendments, see footnote 21 to document 111.

B. Law of the Sea

Document 114

Statement by President Reagan, January 29, 1982[1]

U.S. Announcement to Resume Participation in Law of the Sea Negotiations

The world's oceans are vital to the United States and other nations in diverse ways. They represent waterways and airways essential to preserving the peace and to trade and commerce; are major sources for meeting increasing world food and energy demands and promise further resource potential. They are a frontier for expanding scientific research and knowledge, a fundamental part of the global environmental balance and a great source of beauty, awe and pleasure for mankind.

Developing international agreement for this vast ocean space, covering over half of the earth's surface, has been a major challenge confronting the international community. Since 1973 scores of nations have been actively engaged in the arduous task of developing a comprehensive treaty for the world's oceans at the Third United Nations Conference on Law of the Sea. The United States has been a major participant in this process.

Serious questions had been raised in the United States about parts of the draft convention and, last March, I announced that my administration would undertake a thorough review of the current draft[2] and the degree to which it met United States interests in the navigation, overflight, fisheries, environmental, deep seabed mining and other areas covered by that convention. We recognize that the last two sessions of the Conference have been difficult, pending the completion of our review. At the same time, we consider it important that a Law of the Sea treaty be such that the United States can join in and support it. Our review has concluded that while most provisions of the draft convention are acceptable and consistent with United States interests, some major elements of the deep seabed mining regime are not acceptable.

I am announcing today that the United States will return to those negotiations and work with other countries to achieve an acceptable treaty. In the deep seabed mining area, we will seek changes necessary to correct those unacceptable elements and to achieve the goal of a treaty that:

will not deter development of any deep seabed mineral resources to meet national and world demand;

will assure national access to these resources by current and future qualified entities to enhance U.S. security of supply, to avoid monopolization of the resources by the operating arm of the International Authority,[3] and to promote the economic development of the resources;

will provide a decisionmaking role in the deep seabed regime that fairly reflects and effectively protects the political and economic interests and financial contributions of participating states;

will not allow for amendments to come into force without approval of the participating states, including in our case the advice and consent of the Senate;

will not set other undesirable precedents for international organizations; and

will be likely to receive the advice and consent of the Senate. In this regard, the convention should not contain provisions for the mandatory transfer of private technology and participation by and funding for national liberation movements.

The United States remains committed to the multilateral treaty process for reaching

---

[1] Source: White House Press Release, January 29, 1982, Office of the Press Secretary to the President; also printed in *Weekly Compilation of Presidential Documents,* February 1, 1982, pp. 94–95. For the White House Fact Sheet issued concurrently, see Department of State *Bulletin,* March 1982, pp. 54–55.

[2] Reference presumably is to the statement issued by the Department of State on March 2, 1981. For text, see *American Foreign Policy: Current Documents, 1981,* document 112.

[3] Reference is to the International Seabed Authority, empowered to administer ocean resources under the Law of the Sea Treaty. For draft treaty provisions dealing with the Authority, see the Draft Convention on the Law of the Sea, U.N. document A/CONF.62/L.78, August 28, 1981, Part XI, Section 4, p. 61.

agreement on Law of the Sea. If working together at the Conference we can find ways to fulfill these key objectives, my administration will support ratification.

I have instructed the Secretary of State and my Special Representative for the Law of the Sea Conference, in coordination with other responsible agencies, to embark immediately on the necessary consultations with other countries and to undertake further preparations for our participation in the Conference.

Document 115

Statement by the President's Special Representative for the Law of the Sea Conferences (Malone) Before a Subcommittee of the House Merchant Marine and Fisheries Committee, February 23, 1982 (Extract)[4]

U.S. Negotiating Position in the Law of the Sea Conference

. . . .

In his public statement,[5] the President made clear several points, which I would like to reiterate at this time:

First, it is important that a law of the sea treaty be fashioned so that the United States can join in and support it.

Second, major elements of the deep seabed mining regime as they are now drafted are not acceptable to the United States.

Third, we have six broad objectives with regard to the deep seabed mining regime and we will be seeking changes in the draft treaty in order to achieve them.

Fourth and finally, the United States remains committed to the multilateral treaty process and will support ratification if our six objectives are fulfilled.

Mr. Chairman, we are now consulting with our principal allies, the Soviet Union, the leadership of the Conference, and influential delegates from the Conference, including the leadership of the Group of 77,[6] the Caucus of Developing Nations.

Beginning tomorrow, we will participate in a formal intersessional meeting of the Conference. That will be an important opportunity to explore potential solutions to the problems we have raised with part XI,[7] the deep sea mining portion of the Draft Convention.

During the first week of March, we will assess the results of our consultations and the intersessional meeting, determining whether we believe that it is possible to negotiate satisfactory changes to the Draft Convention which meet the President's objectives. The assessment will describe what the U.S. delegation believes to be an achievable package of improvements in part XI. This assessment will be reviewed carefully before we proceed further.

During the February informal consultations, we have explained our problems with the Draft Convention in a clear and precise and specific way. We have discussed those potential solutions which we believe would meet our national interests and make the treaty acceptable to the United States. I will make available a compendium of the approaches to problems in part XI[8] which we are placing before the Conference leaders in order to evaluate the prospects for successfully negotiating changes that satisfy the President's objectives. Let me, however, now turn to those objectives.

The President stated that we will seek changes necessary to correct unacceptable elements of the draft treaty and to achieve our six objectives:

First, the treaty must not deter development of any deep seabed mineral resources to meet national or world demand.

---

[4] Source: *Law of the Sea: Hearings Before the Subcommittee on Oceanography of the Committee on Merchant Marine and Fisheries, House of Representatives, Ninety-seventh Congress* (Washington, 1982), pp. 130–135. Malone was also Assistant Secretary of State, Bureau of Oceans and International Environmental and Scientific Affairs.

[5] See *supra.*

[6] Reference is to a group of developing nations who first organized in the mid-1960's to set forth a program of action prior to the first meeting of the U.N. Conference on Trade and Development. The group, now expanded to an estimated 121 nations, operates as a developing country caucus on economic matters in the United Nations.

[7] For the text of Part XI, see Draft Convention on the Law of the Sea, U.N. document A/CONF.62/L.78, pp. 49–80.

[8] Reference is to "Approaches to Major Problems in Part XI of the Draft Convention on the Law of the Sea," a paper submitted by the U.S. delegation to the Conference on February 24, 1982.

The United States believes that its interests, those of its allies, and indeed the interests of the vast majority of nations, will be best served by developing the resources of the deep seabed as market conditions warrant. We have a consumer-oriented philosophy. The draft treaty, in our judgment, reflects a protectionist bias which would deter the development of deep seabed mineral resources, including manganese nodules and any other deep seabed minerals such as the polymetallic sulfide deposits which have received considerable publicity recently.

Many different provisions of the draft treaty discourage development of seabed resources. Chief among them are:

The production policies of the International Seabed Authority, which place other priorities ahead of economically efficient resource development.

The production ceiling which limits the availability of minerals for global consumption.

The limit on the number of mining operations which could be conducted by any one country, thus potentially limiting our ability to supply U.S. consumption needs from the seabed.

Broad areas of administrative and regulatory discretion which, if implemented in accordance with the Authority's production policies, would deter seabed mineral development.

To meet the President's first objective, these and other related areas of part XI would require change and improvement.

Second, the treaty must assure national access to those resources by current and future qualified entities to enhance U.S. security of supply, avoid monopolization of the resources by the operating arm of the International Authority, the Enterprise,[9] and promote the economic development of the resources.

The draft treaty provides no assurance that qualified private applicants sponsored by the U.S. Government will be awarded contracts. It is our strong view that all qualified applicants should be granted contracts and the decision whether to grant a contract should be tied exclusively to the question of whether an applicant has satisfied objective qualification standards.

We believe that when a sovereign state sponsors an applicant and certifies that the applicant meets the treaty's qualification standards, the Authority should accept such certification unless a consensus of objective technical experts votes that the applicant's qualifications were falsely or improperly certified.

The Draft Convention also should make specific provision for the rights of private companies that have made pioneer investments in deep seabed mining. We are all aware that a few companies have devoted substantial resources to prospecting for deep seabed minerals and developing new technologies for their extraction. We recognize that there are different views as to the rights which pioneer investors have acquired, but practicality should guide us in this matter. Deep seabed mineral resources will not be made available for the benefit of mankind without the continuing effort of pioneer miners. I am confident, therefore, that the Conference can find ways and means to accommodate their special circumstances.

In addition, the draft treaty creates a system of privileges which discriminates against the private side of the parallel system. Rational private companies would therefore have little option but to enter joint ventures or other similar ventures either with the operating arm of the Authority, the Enterprise, or with developing countries. Not only would this deny the United States access to deep seabed minerals through its private companies because the private access system would be uncompetitive, but under some scenarios the Enterprise could establish a monopoly over deep seabed mineral resources.

To meet the President's second objective, therefore, qualified applicants should be granted contracts, the legal and commercial position of pioneer operators should be accommodated, and the parallel system should be designed to permit private miners to operate independently.

Third, the treaty must provide a decisionmaking role in the deep seabed regime that fairly reflects and effectively protects the political and economic interests and financial contributions of participating states.

The United States has a strong interest in an effective and fair Law of the Sea Treaty which includes a viable seabed min-

---

9 Reference is to the Enterprise, the transporting, processing and marketing organ of the International Seabed Authority. See Draft Convention on the Law of the Sea, Part XI, Section 4, Article 170, p. 74.

ing regime. As the largest potential consumer of seabed minerals, as a country whose private firms could invest substantial amounts in seabed mining, and as potentially the largest contributor to the Seabed Authority and to the financing of the Enterprise, our political and the economic interests in any new international organization are far-reaching and must be clearly protected. The decisionmaking system in the Seabed Authority must reflect these realities.

For example, a treaty which makes American access to natural resources of the seabed dependent upon the voting power either of its competition or of those countries who do not wish to see these resources produced would not meet the President's objectives.

Similarly, the President's objectives would not be satisfied if minerals other than manganese nodules could be developed only after a decision was taken to promulgate rules and regulations to allow the exploitation of such minerals. In our judgment, the development of other seabed minerals should proceed without restraint pending the development of rules and regulations.

We must be candid—many countries do not wish to see new sources of minerals produced from the seabed because they believe that such production will jeopardize their own competitive position in the world markets. We do not criticize them for holding this view, but do expect them to understand that the U.S. national interest is not consistent with impediments to the production of seabed minerals. A seabed mining regime which deters production is antithetical to the interests of all nations in the economically efficient development of resources.

A way must be found to assure that any nation like the United States, having a vital stake in the Authority's decisions, has influence sufficient to protect its interests. The decisionmaking system should provide that, on issues of highest importance to a nation, that nation will have affirmative influence on the outcome. Conversely, nations with major economic interests should be secure in the knowledge that they can prevent decisions adverse to their interests. We will make detailed proposals to the Conference on ways to achieve these objectives.

Fourth, the treaty must not allow for amendments to come into force without approval of the participating states, including in our case the advice and consent of the Senate.

The draft treaty now permits two-thirds of the states parties acting at the Review Conference[10] to adopt amendments to part XI of the treaty which would be binding on all states parties without regard to their concurrence. It has been argued that a state which objects to an amendment has the option to withdraw from the treaty if the amendment is imposed without its consent. This proposal is obviously not acceptable when dealing with major economic interests of countries which have invested significant capital in the development of deep seabed mining in an international treaty regime. We believe there are ways to solve this problem and we will be exploring them during the negotiations.

Fifth, the treaty must not set other undesirable precedents for international organizations.

Most, if not all, of the adverse precedents which would be established by the draft treaty could be avoided by achieving the six objectives set out by the President. Our negotiating efforts, however, should not result in offsetting or replacing one undesirable precedent with another. Our task in returning to the negotiating table is to satisfy all of the President's objectives. The job would not be complete if, for example, adverse precedents related to artificial production limits and protection of land-based minerals are avoided at the price of acquiescence on other issues of principle such as the mandatory transfer of technology.

In solving problems in the draft treaty, we will be alert to the possibility that a particular solution may be viable in the context of a Law of the Sea Treaty but inappropriate as a precedent for some future negotiation. As we proceed to seek solutions to problems in the Law of the Sea negotiations, we will be mindful of the broadest national interests and the relationship of these negotiations to U.S. participation in other global institutions.

Sixth, the treaty must be likely to receive the advice and consent of the U.S. Senate. In this regard, the Convention should not contain provisions for the mandatory transfer of private technology and participation by and funding for national liberation movements.

---

[10] Reference is to a review conference to be convened 15 years after commercial mining of the seabed begins to review the provisions of Part XI and relevant annexes. See Draft Convention on the Law of the Sea, Part XI, Section 3, Article 155, p. 59.

The comprehensive policy review process that has just been completed was initiated because this administration recognized that the Senate could not and would not give its consent to the emerging draft treaty on the Law of the Sea. It is, however, our judgment that, if the President's objectives as outlined are satisfied, the Senate would approve the Law of the Sea Treaty. It would be necessary, of course, to demonstrate very concretely how any renegotiated treaty texts have solved the problems raised by Members of the Congress and the public which led to the review and how they have met the President's objectives.

In this regard, there are certain issues to which special attention must be called. The President highlighted these in his sixth objective. The mandatory transfer of private technology and participation by and funding for national liberation movements create commercial and political difficulty of such consequence that they must be singled out as issues requiring effective solutions. These solutions will have to be clearly defensible as total solutions to the problem.

There is a deeply held view in our Congress that one of America's greatest assets is its capacity for innovation and the invention and its ability to produce advanced technology. It is understandable, therefore, that a treaty would be unacceptable to many Americans if it required the United States, or more particularly private companies, to transfer that asset in a forced sale. That is why the problem must be solved.

I would like to emphasize the President's statement that, if his objectives are successfully met, he will support the ratification of this treaty. We will work with all Members of Congress, particularly those who have shown a special interest in this subject, in order to insure that they will be given the opportunity to give us their advice in advance of any commitments that we make.

We will encourage Members of Congress to participate actively in the work of our delegation and to keep abreast of developments at the Conference. We will continue to work with members of the advisory committee and other interested Americans. We will do everything possible to avoid a situation in which we agree to draft treaty provisions which will later face political opposition.

What we want to do now is return to the bargaining table with a clear and firm position that meets our national interests. We believe that there is a reservoir of good will at the Conference, and we will work cooperatively and diligently at the Conference to seek a result acceptable to all.

. . . .

Document 116

Statement by the President's Special Representative for the Law of the Sea Conferences (Malone) Before the Eleventh Session of the Third U.N. Conference on the Law of the Sea, April 1, 1982 (Extract)[11]

U.S. Reaction to European Negotiating Proposals on Deep Sea Mining

. . . .

The Conference has afforded my delegation an opportunity to raise our concerns with certain aspects of Part XI of the Draft Convention. We have not yet had an opportunity to explore solutions to them which meet the objectives set forth by President Reagan on January 29.[12] I want to express once again our appreciation that other delegations have been both interested and willing to hear us. We are anxious, however, to begin substantive negotiations and await your guidance as to how to proceed.

In your reports to the Plenary on Monday[13] both you[14] and Chairman Engo made reference to a series of proposals put forward by a Group of 11 Heads of Delegation acting in their personal capacities.[15] My

---

[11] Source: Department of State files. Malone addressed the 164th Plenary Meeting. His remarks were summarized in U.N. document A/CONF.62/SR.164.

[12] For text, see document 114.

[13] March 29, 1982.

[14] Tommy T. B. Koh, of Singapore, President of the Conference.

[15] A group of 11 states (Australia, Austria, Canada, Denmark, Finland, Iceland, Ireland, New Zealand, Norway, Sweden, and Switzerland) proposed a set of amendments which they hoped would serve as a basis for negotiations between the United States and the Group of 77 after the latter rejected the U.S. "Proposals for Amend-

delegation joins you and Chairman Engo in welcoming their efforts and we also join them in the hope that the Group of 11 proposals can afford us an opportunity to make progress toward consensus on the difficult issues facing us.

The Group of 11 proposals address many of the issues raised by President Reagan on January 29. They offer suggestions which are related to the following matters of concern to my delegation:

1. The approval of contracts;

2. Production policies including the question of limitations and adjustment assistance;

3. The question of the election to the Council of the seven largest contributors;

4. Decisionmaking;

5. The question of the adoption of amendments to the treaty arising from the Review Conference;

6. The powers of the Assembly and Council—the separation of powers;

7. Transfer of privately-owned technology;

8. The adoption of rules and regulations on minerals other than polymetallic nodules.

On several of these matters the Group of 11 proposals focus on narrower aspects of broader U.S. concerns. With respect to production policies, the Group of 11 proposals may not presently be sufficiently broad to allow negotiations related to the production limitation or adjustment assistance. Similarly, the Group of 11 proposal on decisionmaking addresses only the question of approval of the budget of the Authority without reference to other important problems in the decisionmaking system. The Group of 11 proposals do not seem to contemplate discussion of the relationship of creditors to the Enterprise, an issue on which further consultations would be helpful. We would appreciate some clarification on these points. Finally, the Group of 11 proposals do not address the technical financial terms of contracts or the question of benefits for peoples who have not attained self-governing status.

Mr. President, my delegation greatly appreciates the work of the Group of 11 and hopes, with the clarifications and additions I have suggested, that they can serve as a basis for our continued work. My delegation is eager to pursue these matters and welcomes your efforts to encourage consultations on them. We are prepared to participate in any forum you believe is suitable for further negotiations and we will expend every effort to achieve our common objective of a universally acceptable treaty adopted by consensus at this session. As I mentioned at the outset, Mr. President, if we succeed in this goal the United States will be prepared to expend every effort to fulfill President Reagan's commitment to seek early ratification of a convention on the Law of the Sea.

---

ment to the Draft Convention of the Law of the Sea." After a request by the Group of 77 for specific U.S.-proposed amendments to the treaty, the United States forwarded these proposals on March 11, which were based on the earlier U.S. "Approaches to Major Problems in Part XI" paper. For the amendments proposed by the Group of 11, see U.N. document WG.21/Informal Paper 21 (March 25, 1982).

Document 117

Statement by the President's Special Representative for the Law of the Sea Conferences (Malone) Before the Eleventh Session of the Third U.N. Conference on the Law of the Sea, April 30, 1982 (Extract)[16]

Explanation of U.S. Decision Not To Vote for Adoption of the Law of the Sea Treaty

. . . .

My delegation came to this session willing to work and negotiate with other countries to find mutually acceptable solutions to the problems before us. We proposed a set of amendments[17] that would have satis-

---

[16] Source: Department of State files. Malone addressed the 182d Plenary Meeting. His remarks were summarized in U.N. document A/CONF.62/SR.182. The Law of the Sea Convention was adopted 130 to 4, with 17 abstentions, on April 30. The United States, Israel, Turkey, and Venezuela voted against the treaty. For the text of the United Nations Convention on the Law of the Sea, see U.N. document A/CONF.62/122 (October 7, 1982).

[17] Regarding the U.S.-proposed amendments, see footnote 15 above.

fied our objectives and, in our view, provided a fair and balanced system to promote the development of deep seabed resources. In a spirit of compromise and conciliation, we made a further attempt to find satisfactory solutions by revising our proposed amendments to take into account views expressed by other delegations.[18]

Three misconceptions have arisen about U.S. motivations. I would like to address each of these briefly.

The first misconception has been that the United States was seeking essentially to nullify the basic bargain in the draft treaty. This is not true. Even if all of our proposed changes had been accepted, there would still have been an international regulatory system for the deep seabeds and an international mining entity. We have not tried to destroy the system at all, but rather to structure it in a way that will best serve the interests of all nations by enhancing seabed resource development.

A second misconception has been that the primary interest of the United States in the deep seabed regime related to protecting a few U.S. business interests. That view has drastically misjudged the motivation of the United States and its commitment to certain principles.

Finally, many other countries, and even many people in my own country, have believed that the United States would, in the end, accept an unsatisfactory deep seabed regime because of the navigation provisions that serve other national interests. That view, as well, is false. We have consistently maintained that each part of the treaty must be satisfactory to us.

Mr. President, we came to this session determined to work together to reach improvements that would accord with U.S. objectives and ensure a viable seabed mining regime. I had hoped to be able to say today that we had successfully concluded our task and reached an acceptable outcome. Unfortunately, that is not the case and I cannot make such a report.

Some modest improvements have been made in the draft treaty during this session. However, there has been an unyielding refusal on the part of some to engage in real negotiations on most of the major concerns reflected in the amendments proposed by the United States and cosponsored by Belgium, the Federal Republic of Germany, France, Italy, Japan, and the United Kingdom.[19] We appreciate that others put forward compromise proposals to try to bridge the gap, but these efforts did not succeed.

I do not wish to belabor the problems, but it is important that we understand clearly how far short of our objectives the conference has fallen.

First, we believe the seabed mining provisions would deter the development of deep seabed mineral resources. Economic development of these resources is in the interest of all countries. In a world in which rational economic development is so critical, particularly for developing countries, the treaty would create yet another barrier to such development. It would deny the play of basic economic forces in the market place.

Second, while there have been improvements to assure access to deep seabed minerals for existing miners, we do not believe that the seabed articles would provide the assured access for qualified future miners that is necessary to promote the economic development of these resources. The provisions would also create a system of privileges for the Enterprise that discriminate against private and national miners.

Third, the decisionmaking process in the deep seabed regime does not give a proportionate voice to those countries most affected by the decisions and, thus, would not fairly reflect and effectively protect their interests.

Fourth, the provisions allow for amendments to come into force for a state without its consent. While that may be possible for some political systems, it is clearly incompatible with U.S. processes for incurring treaty obligations. Moreover, after having made substantial investments in deep seabed mining, the choice of either accepting an amendment at some future time or being forced to withdraw from the treaty entirely is not acceptable.

Finally, the deep seabed regime continues to pose serious problems for the United States by creating precedents that are not appropriate. Provisions on mandatory transfer of technology and potential

[18] The U.S. amendments, cosponsored by Belgium, France, the Federal Republic of Germany, Italy, Japan, and the United Kingdom of Great Britain and Northern Ireland, were the result of a compromise between the Group of 11 proposals and the U.S. "Proposals for Amendment"; for the text, see U.N. document A/CONF.62/L.121 (April 13, 1982).

[19] Reference is to *ibid.*

distribution of benefits to national liberation movements, in particular, raise these problems. These and other aspects, like production limitations, are also key problems for the U.S. Congress.

In short, while the other provisions of the treaty are generally acceptable, I can come to no conclusion other than the fact that the treaty before us today does not satisfy any of the U.S. objectives in the deep seabed regime. This is why we were forced to vote against the treaty today, and why I will necessarily report to my government that our efforts to achieve an acceptable deep seabed regime have not been successful. This is not a happy conclusion for the United States.

We recognize that many of us came to these negotiations with different perspectives and diverse interests. Indeed, there are even differences of opinion on the meaning of "the common heritage of mankind"[20] and the consequences that flow from that concept.

Despite our differences, we have held to the conviction that negotiation and compromise could produce a convention serving the interests of all states. Unfortunately, in our view, the treaty before us does not meet those standards. The greatest tragedy of this treaty is that it will not bring more orderly and productive uses of the deep seabeds to reality. It also does not serve the broader goal of bringing the developed and developing countries closer together.

Thus, it is with particular regret that we have had to vote against the adoption of this treaty. We have not done so lightly, but for reasons of deep conviction and principle, which will continue to guide our actions in the future.

Document 118

Letter From the Chairman of the House Foreign Affairs Committee (Zablocki) to President Reagan, June 23, 1982[21]

Congressional Review of the Law of the Sea Treaty

DEAR MR. PRESIDENT: We understand that the Administration is reviewing U.S. policy on the Law of the Sea Convention and the four resolutions[22] adopted on April 30 at the Third U.N. Conference on the Law of the Sea. Because Congress had long recognized the importance of the multilateral treatymaking process and the political, legal, and economic significance of this international negotiation, its Members have attended and closely followed each successive negotiating session and want to participate in the current policy review.

The Committee on Foreign Affairs initiated its recent hearings on U.S. foreign policy to review the results of the most recent session of this Conference.[23] The second hearing in this series, scheduled for June 23, is to be rescheduled for July.

The United States "no" vote on the Treaty package raises critical issues concerning our nation's ability to promote and protect effectively our foreign policy and national security interests in ocean matters. Thus, we strongly believe that a thorough Congressional review of these issues is imperative and that every effort should be made to improve the Treaty prior to its final, official acceptance by the Conference.

Accordingly, we urge you to continue to participate fully in the remaining conference sessions and to initiate and consult with foreign delegations on possible changes in the seabeds text that could serve U.S. interests. Were such changes adopted, they would improve the seabeds text of the Treaty and complement the other sections of the Treaty which the United States, through its long efforts, has been able to fashion into a form acceptable to the Administration.

---

[20] Reference is to Article 136 of the United Nations Convention on the Law of the Sea: "The [Seabed] Area and its resources are the common heritage of mankind." U.N. document A/CONF.62/122, p. 52.

[21] Source: *Law of the Sea Negotiations: Hearing Before the Subcommittee on Arms Control, Oceans, International Operations, and Environment of the Committee on Foreign Relations, United States Senate, Ninety-seventh Congress, Second Session* (Washington, 1983), p. 93. Eighty-four other Representatives also signed this letter. For the additional signatories, see *ibid.*

[22] The four were Resolution I on the establishment of the Preparatory Commission and the International Tribunal; Resolution II governing Preparatory Investment in Pioneer Activities Relating to Polymetallic Nodules; Resolution III regarding Non-self-governing Territories; and Resolution IV regarding National Liberation Movements, adopted together with the Convention on April 30. For the text of these resolutions, see Annex I to the Draft Final Act of the Third United Nations Conference on the Law of the Sea, U.N. document A/CONF.62/121 (October 21, 1982), pp. 23–34.

[23] Reference is to *U.S. Foreign Policy and the Law of the Sea: Hearings Before the Committee on Foreign Affairs, House of Representatives, Ninety-seventh Congress, Second Session* (Washington, 1982). The initial session was held on June 17; subsequent sessions were held on August 12 and September 16, 1982.

At the same time, we also urge you to delay the decision on whether or not to sign the Treaty until Congress has had the opportunity to review fully the 11th session and all of the implications that the United States not signing the Treaty could have on our foreign policy and national security interests in ocean matters.

Sincerely yours,

CLEMENT J. ZABLOCKI

Document 119

Letter From Senator Spark Matsunaga to President Reagan, June 28, 1982[24]

Opposition to the Law of the Sea Treaty Text

DEAR MR. PRESIDENT: The treaty text emerging from the Law of the Sea Conference falls far short of the well considered and highly defensible position you announced on January 29[25] of this year. It also clearly falls short of the Congressional intent expressed in Title II of the Deep Seabed Hard Mineral Resources Act.[26] We feel you correctly instructed the U.S. Delegation to vote against adoption of the treaty text.

We understand that should the treaty nevertheless enter into force, it would establish:

A system of world government in which our political and economic interests and those of our industrial allies were not fairly represented;

A cartel for strategic ocean minerals which would freeze out nearly every American company which decided it wanted to develop the seabed;

A world-wide state owned company which would monopolize ocean mining at the direct expense of American taxpayers who would be called upon to subsidize its operations;

An economic structure built upon production controls, commodity agreements, mandatory transfer of technology and numerous other restrictions which are an anathema to our free enterprise system;

A means by which terrorist groups conceivably could be awarded financial benefits;

Sovereignty threatening precedents applicable to current and future international negotiations;

A de facto system of immediate interim application based upon the mere adoption of resolutions by conference delegates, imposing burdens upon the United States and all other participants, not only prior to the treaty's entry into force, but without the advice and consent of the Senate; and

A means by which amendments to the treaty would become binding on the United States without the advice and consent of the Senate.

You have already clearly identified other features of the treaty as well which would be inimical to U.S. interests and implicitly to those of our industrial allies.

As you know, the United States, the United Kingdom, France and West Germany have already enacted legislation which would establish a legal framework for developing ocean minerals. These nations have already negotiated, pursuant to statutory authority, a Reciprocating States Agreement, which would provide for the harmonization and implementation of their legislation and for the resolution of any conflicts.[27] The agreement has not yet been signed due to a hope that waiting until the conclusion of the Law of the Sea Conference on April 30 would result in an agreement on a Law of the Sea treaty text which all industrialized nations with ocean mining interests could enthusiastically sign and ratify.

Mr. President, the vote on the treaty text at the Law of the Sea Conference confirms that such a prospect has decayed far beyond the point of even the most wishful thinking. We feel that the time has come for a serious rebuilding effort to begin now, based on the model of our domestic legislation and that enacted by the United Kingdom, France and West Germany. Because of the failure

---

24 Source: *Law of the Sea Negotiations*, pp. 92–93. Twenty-nine other Senators also signed this letter; for the additional signatories, see *ibid.*, p. 93.

25 See document 114.

26 Approved on June 28, 1980. (P.L. 96–283; 94 Stat. 553)

27 The reference is to the Agreement Concerning Interim Arrangements Relating to Polymetallic Nodules of the Deep Seabed, which was signed in Washington on September 2, 1982.

of the treaty to meet our national interests, you should withhold signature of the treaty; promptly sign and implement the Reciprocating States Agreement with these nations and then invite any other nation which enacts similar legislation to join with us in such agreement; and commence exploring possibilities for a more acceptable international regime.

We hope that you will see fit to follow such a course.

Respectfully yours,

SPARK MATSUNAGA

Document 120

Statement by President Reagan, Santa Barbara, California, July 9, 1982[28]

"The United States Will Not Sign the Convention"

The United States has long recognized how critical the world's oceans are to mankind and how important international agreements are to the use of those oceans. For over a decade, the United States has been working with more than 150 countries at the Third United Nations Conference on Law of the Sea to develop a comprehensive treaty.

On January 29 of this year, I reaffirmed the United States commitment to the multilateral process for reaching such a treaty[29] and announced that we would return to the negotiations to seek to correct unacceptable elements in the deep seabed mining part of the draft convention. I also announced that my administration would support ratification of a convention meeting six basic objectives.

On April 30 the Conference adopted a convention that does not satisfy the objectives sought by the United States. It was adopted by a vote of 130 in favor, with 4 against (including the United States) and 17 abstentions. Those voting "no" or abstaining appear small in number but represent countries which produce more than 60 percent of the world's gross national product and provide more than 60 percent of the contributions to the United Nations.

We have now completed a review of that convention and recognize that it contains many positive and very significant accomplishments. Those extensive parts dealing with navigation and overflight and most other provisions of the convention are consistent with United States interests and, in our view, serve well the interests of all nations. That is an important achievement and signifies the benefits of working together and effectively balancing numerous interests. The United States also appreciates the efforts of the many countries that have worked with us toward an acceptable agreement, including efforts by friends and allies at the session that concluded on April 30.

Our review recognizes, however, that the deep seabed mining part of the convention does not meet United States objectives. For this reason, I am announcing today that the United States will not sign the convention as adopted by the conference, and our participation in the remaining conference process will be at the technical level and will involve only those provisions that serve United States interests.

These decisions reflect the deep conviction that the United States cannot support a deep seabed mining regime with such major problems. In our view, those problems include:

Provisions that would actually deter future development of deep seabed mineral resources, when such development should serve the interest of all countries.

A decisionmaking process that would not give the United States or others a role that fairly reflects and protects their interests.

Provisions that would allow amendments to enter into force for the United States without its approval. This is clearly incompatible with the United States approach to such treaties.

Stipulations relating to mandatory transfer of private technology and the possibility of national liberation movements sharing in benefits.

The absence of assured access for future qualified deep seabed miners to promote the development of these resources.

We recognize that world demand and markets currently do not justify commercial

---

[28] Source: White House Press Release, July 9, 1982, Office of the Press Secretary to the President; printed also in *Weekly Compilation of Presidential Documents,* July 12, 1982, pp. 887–888. The statement was issued when the President was visiting Rancho del Cielo, his ranch near Santa Barbara.

[29] See document 114.

development of deep seabed mineral resources, and it is not clear when such development will be justified. When such factors become favorable, however, the deep seabed represents a potentially important source of strategic and other minerals. The aim of the United States in this regard has been to establish with other nations an order that would allow exploration and development under reasonable terms and conditions.

Document 121

Address by the President's Special Representative for the Law of the Sea Conferences (Malone) Before the International Law Section of the American Bar Association, San Francisco, August 9, 1982 (Extract)[30]

Prospects for a Future U.S. Oceans Policy

. . . .

In that we are now faced with a treaty that the United States cannot sign, we must focus anew on our national oceans policy. We must examine in particular the actions which the United States should take to protect and enhance its oceans interests outside of the LOS Convention.

It is premature to set forth in detail what our future policies will be, but I believe that we should be prepared not only to meet any challenges to traditional maritime activities, but to take new initiatives to assure the orderly development of ocean resources in response to market forces. It should be understood that the nonseabed provisions of the treaty text reflect compromises which were deemed acceptable in the context of a comprehensive LOS treaty that the United States could sign. We will consult with other countries with common oceans interests, as bilateral and multilateral cooperation will be an essential element of the new policy. Pursuing our policies on a unilateral basis has never been a U.S. goal; that is why we participated to such an extent in the LOS treaty process.

As a leading maritime power with major coastal interests, the United States has played an historic role in the development of international law. As President Reagan stated on July 9,[31] our national policies have defended freedoms of navigation and communication, promoted rights of resource exploration and development, and advanced obligations to protect the marine environment.

It is essential to our national interests to have unimpeded mobility of naval and air forces. Uninhibited mobility of the Nation's commercial and military ships and airplanes furthers the Nation's foreign policy and national security interests and promotes the Nation's economic interests through encouragement of world trade. Under the LOS Treaty and customary international law, the high seas freedoms of navigation and overflight prevail beyond the territorial sea. Innocent passage constitutes the existing passage rights for the territorial sea.

We will continue to emphasize our national interest in ensuring proper management and conservation of the world's fish stocks and in revitalizing our own Nation's coastal and distant water fishing industries.

Freedom of marine scientific research is in our national interest. Unfettered research promotes the well-being of the American people, along with the global community, by producing a better understanding of the effect of the oceans on the world's climate, more effective management programs for the world's living and nonliving resources and more advanced pollution control measures.

Our future oceans policies should emphasize U.S. flag mining of the deep seabed. The United States remains committed to the position that deep seabed mining is a freedom of the high seas, the exercise of which must be respected by all states. I believe that we need to continue to emphasize a deep seabed regime that would encourage investment in deep seabed mining, research and development of the requisite technology, and production and pricing of mineral resources at levels guided by the play of market forces.

At this point, the United States needs to focus on the possibility of establishing a viable alternative regime. The LOS Treaty does not constitute the only means of assured access to seabed minerals. We believe that other means exist. Nations are not bound or ever likely to be, by the LOS Treaty provisions if they do not become

30 Source: Department of State files.

31 See *supra.*

parties to the treaty. In reality, we consider it highly unlikely that there will be investment in seabed mining under the treaty unless governments are willing to heavily subsidize their companies or mining entities.

What rights the United States and others can assert under existing international law are varied. Not only the United States but other potential signatories of the LOS Convention are now evaluating the long-term prospects and costs of participating in the treaty regime, as well as the alternatives to such participation. I cannot speak to their interests, nor do I think it useful to suggest what their future course of action may be. However, I do believe that when their own legislative bodies review the text in detail and weigh the costs against the benefits of participating in the treaty's regime, certain governments might have second thoughts about signing this convention. This would be a great disappointment to those countries, as it was to us, in that we have all worked for years to create conditions which would encourage the development of a new industry that could benefit the nations of the world and sought to establish a mechanism to aid in resolving our conflicts over nonseabed uses of the oceans.

We will continue to consult with our allies. We will continue to ensure that we are aware of each other's concerns and, wherever possible, seek to accommodate them.

Current world demand and markets may not now justify commercial development of deep seabed mineral resources. But when factors become favorable, the deep seabed represents a potentially important source of strategic and other minerals.

For over a decade, we have worked together with the nations of the world to formulate a rule of law that would create a stable, predictable climate for resolving conflicting uses of the oceans. We still believe in this goal; our commitment to world order remains strong. This is precisely why we had to withdraw from the Law of the Sea Conference process, a process that has adopted a treaty based on something considerably less than universally acceptable principles. The Law of the Sea Treaty will only create additional unpredictability and instability and prevent proper development of the oceans resources for the benefit of all. We did not abandon our larger interests of securing a rule of law simply for narrow economic reasons. This treaty is significantly short of the mark and has a good chance of not being ratified by the majority of the participants, thus causing more confusion and uncertainty.

The oceans are still shrouded in mystery. A comprehensive law of the sea program must accommodate the unknown, and must enable us to feel secure in dealing with future uses of the seas and future events, whether they be new mineral finds, food sources, or other discoveries. I feel confident we can meet those challenges, but only if we adhere to our Nation's fundamental principles.

Document 122

Statement by the Deputy Representative at the United Nations (Adelman), Before the U.N. General Assembly, December 3, 1982[32]

Unacceptable Funding Provisions for the Law of the Sea Preparatory Commission

Thank you Mr. President.[33] My delegation has cosponsored an amendment, A/37/L.15/Rev.1, to draft resolution A/37/L.13/Rev.1.[34] It is simple in content and straightforward in concept. It does not address the many serious objections we have to other parts of the resolution. Instead it points to objections we would have regardless of the merits of this resolution. The resolution violates our commitment to fiscal restraint and it does so not only by the extent of the expenditures, but also, and even more seriously, by attempting to convert the expenditures of the Preparatory Commission into expenses of the United Nations Organization itself and assess them against the membership of the United Nations.

As negotiations on the Law of the Sea wound down in April of this year, the issue

---

[32] Source: U.S. Mission to the United Nations Press Release USUN–162(82), December 3, 1982.

[33] Reference is to Tommy T. B. Koh, of Singapore, President of the Conference.

[34] Adelman introduced amendment A/37/L.15/Rev.1 to the draft resolution A/37/L.13/Rev.1 on Preparatory Commission funding; the resolution, with some modification, was adopted 92 to 3 with 19 abstentions the same day. The United States, Israel, and Turkey voted against the resolution.

of funding the Preparatory Commission[35] was dealt with hurriedly and with insufficient reflection. Rather than further protract the process, the Conference passed a resolution which states in part that "the expenses of the Commission shall be met from the regular budget of the United Nations, subject to the approval of the General Assembly of the United Nations." However, we believe that if the members carefully reflect upon the nature of the Preparatory Commission established by the Convention on the Law of the Sea and upon the proper limits of the financial obligations undertaken by states by virtue of adherence to the United Nations Charter, they will agree that the proposal to finance the Preparatory Commission from the regular UN budget is ill advised. Our amendment is designed to correct this potentially serious mistake.

The Preparatory Commission is a temporary commission to formulate the rules and regulations of the two specialized agencies contemplated under the Law of the Sea Convention: the Authority and the International Tribunal. The Authority and Tribunal are entities independent of the United Nations and will be funded outside the United Nations budget. The Preparatory Commission is also an entity distinct from the United Nations Organization. Full participation in the Commission is not a prerogative of members of the United Nations Organization; it is not a right of parties to the United Nations Charter. Instead, to be entitled to participate in the taking of Commission decisions, states must sign an entirely distinct treaty, the Law of the Sea Convention. Since these rights are not rights of states by virtue of membership in the United Nations, the obligations should not be.

This is not merely a question of fairness or reasonableness. The consent of states is fundamental to the international obligations of states pursuant to treaties. It is potentially damaging to the United Nations to attempt to impose upon all its member states responsibility for the expenses of such a separate entity, established under a distinct treaty regime. Consent to such a financial obligation might be presumed if the expenses to be funded through the regular United Nations budget are pursuant to a consensus. However, consent cannot be presumed where, as here, there is and will be no consensus on the activities or funding methods contained in this resolution.

The second serious error is that this draft resolution calls for extravagant and unjustified expenditures. It provides for conferences and secretariat support which for 1983 will cost $4 million. Because these meetings will be held away from United Nations Headquarters, the United Nations can expect to pay a higher amount than if the existing resources in headquarters could be efficiently utilized. To ask the United Nations to pay for a preparatory commission of a separate treaty organization is wrong. To ask it to pay for an expensive conference away from established headquarters is doubly wrong and an additional violation of the principle of fiscal responsibility. The United States, as the largest contributor to the United Nations budget, is deeply concerned that this principle be defended and respected in practice. For the General Assembly to ask states to succumb to such a request is to abandon that principle.

In conclusion, my delegation is convinced that the fiscal approach taken by this draft resolution is a departure from both the spirit of the United Nations Charter and acceptable international practice. Further, it ignores current economic conditions and pays little heed to fiscal restraint. The United States amendment would correct these defects. The United States reserves its legal rights and intends to examine carefully its legal obligations relevant to this draft resolution, within the framework of the Charter, should the resolution be adopted without our amendment.

My delegation urges all member states to support this amendment. We hope each will objectively analyze the grave concerns presented by this draft resolution and give careful and responsible consideration to the vital issues my delegation has identified.

Thank you, Mr. President.

---

[35] For a description of the functions of the Preparatory Commission, see Draft Final Act of the Law of the Sea Conference, Annex I, Resolution I, U.N. document A/CONF.62.121, pp. 23–25.

Document 123

Statement by President Reagan, December 30, 1982[36]

United States To Withhold Funds for U.N. Preparatory Commission

On December 3 the United Nations General Assembly passed a resolution[37] that would, among other things, finance the Preparatory Commission under the Law of the Sea treaty from the regular U.N. budget.

My administration has fought hard to uphold fiscal responsibility in the United Nations system and, in this case, consistently opposed this financing scheme. It is not a proper expense of the United Nations within the meaning of its own Charter, as the Law of the Sea Preparatory Commission is legally independent of and distinct from the U.N. It is not a U.N. subsidiary organ and not answerable to that body. Membership in the U.N. does not obligate a member to finance or otherwise support this Law of the Sea organization.

[36] Source: *Weekly Compilation of Presidential Documents,* January 3, 1983, p. 1674.

[37] Regarding the resolution, see footnote 32 above.

Moreover, these funds are destined to finance the very aspects of the Law of the Sea treaty that are unacceptable to the United States and that have resulted in our decision, as I announced on July 9, 1982,[38] not to sign that treaty. The Preparatory Commission is called upon to develop rules and regulations for the seabed mining regime under the treaty. It has no authority to change the damaging provisions and precedents in that part of the treaty. For that reason, the United States is not participating in the Commission.

My administration has conducted a review of the financing scheme for this Commission. That review has confirmed that it is an improper assessment under the U.N. Charter that is not legally binding upon members. It is also adverse to the interests of the United States. While the United States normally pays 25 percent of the regular U.N. budget, the United States is opposed to improper assessments and is determined to resist such abuses of the U.N. budget.

In this light, I have decided that the United States will withhold its *pro rata* share of the cost to the United Nations budget of funding the Preparatory Commission.

[38] See document 120.

Chapter 8. Refugees, Human Rights, Terrorism

A. Human Rights

Document 124

Statement by the Assistant Secretary of State for Human Rights and Humanitarian Affairs (Abrams) at a Press Briefing, February 9, 1982 (Extract)[1]

Human Rights Progress Report

. . . .

I thought I would begin by discussing the Country Reports Book which we released just recently.[2] We are, of course, very happy with the reaction that, generally speaking, the book has gotten.

Our effort was to do what we had said at the outset we would do which is to tell the truth, and we think we did. We certainly made an effort to be as truthful as we could be and to be balanced in our account of the human rights situation in each of the countries covered.

The introduction to the Country Reports Book is an effort to describe the intellectual underpinnings of our human rights policy. It makes clear that [the] human rights situation around the world is very difficult but on the other hand there is cause for optimism.

The situation was a lot more difficult when the first democratic republic was set up in this country and yet the ideas upon which this republic was based really caught hold around the world so that there are today several dozen fully democratic countries.

There is a problem in talking about human rights around the world because while all of us use the same vocabulary, many people mean different things by it. One can say that the vocabulary of human rights has had a complete victory but the substance of human rights has not. In many countries we hear terms such as peoples democracies used when it is obvious the country in question is not a democracy at all.

What they're doing is in a sense misappropriating the vocabulary of human rights to defend the abuse of human rights. The introduction talks about this now famous question of quiet diplomacy and tries to explain why it is we think it is important in most cases to try diplomatic methods before you turn to other methods.

In the case of friendly countries, as we have said a number of times, where we have substantial diplomatic influence our first recourse would be to use that influence in an attempt to get human rights results through diplomatic methods. In the case of countries where we have very little diplomatic influence, because we have very strained relations, or in some cases none at all, an earlier recourse will be made and in many cases the first recourse will be made to more public means of pressure.

The introduction also makes a point which I think is worth repeating here and that is that prior to the First World War these ideas about human rights, these ideas about liberalization of political regimes, really did have a consensus of all of the major powers of that time. Since then, since the First World War, let's say, the international picture has changed greatly. There are now really only two world powers and they have very different views on human rights. There is certainly no consensus.

In this context, the human rights situation around the world takes on a slightly different character. In our view, the success and the strength of the power that is the leading supporter of human rights around the world becomes very important for the

---

[1] Source: Office of Press Relations, Department of State. The briefing was held at the Department of State.

[2] The reference is to *Country Reports on Human Rights Practices for 1981: Report Submitted to the Committee on Foreign Affairs, U.S. House of Representatives, and the Committee on Foreign Relations, U.S. Senate, by the Department of State,* Ninety-seventh Congress, Second Session (Washington, 1982). For extracts from the introduction, see *American Foreign Policy: Current Documents, 1981,* document 132.

success of the cause of human rights and, similarly, a restriction on the ability of the Soviet Union to export its abuses of human rights around the world is also very important for the success of the cause of human rights throughout the world. This is where we think the East–West questions come into this equation.

We think that the expansion of Soviet power is completely inconsistent with the cause of human rights and its success throughout the world.

Let me stop there and take your questions and see what's on your mind.

. . . .

Document 125

Address by President Reagan Before the Building and Construction Trades National Legislative Conference, April 5, 1982 (Extract)[3]

"We Will Stand Up for Our Ideals and We Will Work for Peace"

. . . .

Your presence at this conference proves that democracy and freedom are alive and well in America. But as you know, America's more the exception than the rule around the globe.

Now, some in this country say, "Freedom is fine for us, but we can't worry about it for everyone else, let's not stick our necks out anywhere."

Have they forgotten that freedom was not won here without the help of others? Have they forgotten that people who turn their backs on friends often lose what they cherish most for themselves? Have they forgotten that freedom is never more than one generation away from extinction?

Your presence at this conference proves that democracy and freedom are alive and well. So we'll just keep it that way. I don't think you've forgotten. You've had to live too often the meaning of struggle, perseverance and unity.

An American, a compatriot of yours once said, "The role of American labor and the struggle for the preservation of human freedom and decency is decisive." No one ever put it better than George Meany did 30 years ago. And he lived up to the responsibility that he gave you.

Today you are needed more than ever to support and sustain the struggle of others whose sacrifices are greater than our own.

In Poland, where citizens must meet in secret to resist military tyranny, courageous workers still struggle underground. Recently, they published a plea for continued resistance. "So that our children do not have to be ashamed of us," they said. So that their children will have a chance to grow up as free and courageous people.

The Polish authorities want the West to close its eyes, accept martial law. The American people will not accept martial law. They demand that Lech Walesa—(applause)—that Lech Walesa and the political—and the prisoners of Solidarity be set free.

Poland's government says it will crush democratic freedoms. Well, let us tell them, "You can imprison your people. You can close their schools. You can take away their books, harass their priests and smash their unions. You can never destroy the love of God and freedom that burns in their hearts. They will triumph over you." (Applause.)

Could I just interject something here that—Our team of representatives from Congress just came back from El Salvador, watching the elections down there led by Senator Nancy Kassebaum.[4] They came in the office to report the other day. And they told me what a thrill it was and how inspiring to see those people stand in line hours for the privilege of voting. And they spoke to a woman. But one woman was wounded by a ricocheting bullet. She refused to leave the line for treatment until she'd voted.

---

[3] Source: White House Press Release, April 5, 1982, Office of the Press Secretary to the President; printed also in *Weekly Compilation of Presidential Documents*, April 12, 1982, pp. 446–447. For the full text, see *ibid.*, pp. 444–450. The President spoke in the International Ballroom at the Washington Hilton Hotel. Omitted portions of his speech dealt with domestic matters and national defense.

[4] For the text of the Statement of the U.S. Official Observer Delegation to the El Salvador Constituent Assembly Elections, March 29, 1982, see document 685.

But another woman said that they had told her personally, the guerrillas, that they would kill her and cut off the finger that had dipped in that visible ink to identify voters, if she voted. And she said she told them just about what I've just said. She said to them, "You can kill me. You can kill my family, but you can't kill us all."

Francis Bacon wrote that "In this theater of man's life, it is reserved only for gods and angels to be lookers on." America will not drift through the 1980's as a spectator. Liberty belongs to the brave. We will stand up for our ideals and we will work for peace.

Never again will we shrink from denouncing the terrible nightmare totalitarianism has wrought: Occupation of an entire section of Europe; genocide in Cambodia; boat people in Vietnam; a bloody invasion of Afghanistan, and everywhere the suppression of human rights and growing want from economic failure.

We will not remain silent when, in Afghanistan, yellow rain is dropped on innocent people, solemn agreements are flagrantly broken, and Soviet helicopters drop thousands of "butterfly" mines which maim and blind Afghan children, who pick them up thinking they are toys. We will condemn these crimes and work for international repudiation.

And we will speak and work for democracy. Winston Churchill said that it was "the worst form of government in the world, except for all the others that have been tried." Yes, we have our warts and our imperfections. But we can be proud that there is so much to love in this land. No nation has worked harder for peace or done more to lift up the downtrodden than the United States of America.

Treasury Secretary, Don Regan, recently told the students at Bucknell University: "We have brought light where before there was darkness, heat where once there was cold, medicines where there was sickness and disease, food where there was scarcity and wealth where humanity was living in squalor."[5] We provide more food assistance each year to developing nations than all the other nations of the world combined.

America has a secret weapon—it's called "trust the people." We're not afraid of free enterprise or free trade unions or freedom of thought. We depend on them. Because only when individuals are free to worship, create and build, only when they are given a personal stake in deciding their destiny and benefiting from their own risks—only then do societies become dynamic, prosperous, progressive and free.

Our democratic dream of human fulfillment through individual equality and opportunity is still the most exciting, successful and revolutionary idea in the world today. But don't take my word for it. Look at Poland where Solidarity captured the hearts and minds of the people. Look at Afghanistan where courageous freedom fighters are battling a 100,000-man army, a Soviet war machine to a standstill. Look at Vietnam where 500,000 boat people have escaped since we left. And look at brave El Salvador, where, in one of the most inspiring demonstrations of personal courage in modern history, one million citizens—a greater percentage of their electorate than turn out for our own elections—risked their lives to go to the ballot box, so they could vote to give freedom a chance.

Let's give El Salvador a chance. Critics question whether we're on the side of right, justice and progress in El Salvador. Well, we found out the answer to that a week ago Sunday.

. . . .

Document 126

Address by the President's Assistant for National Security Affairs (Clark) Before the American Bar Association, San Francisco, August 6, 1982[6]

Personal Liberties and National Security

There was a time, which seems many years ago, when I was a judge in this fair city of San Francisco. During deliberations in that court, I was often aware of an anomaly that you have experienced as lawyers. The fundamental principles of law and justice are simple. All the great codes of justice,

---

[5] The quotation is from Regan's speech, "Morality and Capitalism," at Bucknell University on March 22. (Department of the Treasury News, March 23, 1982)

[6] Source: Department of State *Bulletin*, December 1982, pp. 35–38.

from the Ten Commandments to the U.S. Constitution, are concisely stated. But a sophisticated legal system is required to put the great codes into effect, assuring the faithful transfer of principle into policy. Were that not the case, many of us would be employed in a different profession today.

There is no better illustration of this contrast between the simplicity of basic principles and the complexity of implementation than in dealing with what has been termed "human rights." While that term is of relatively recent derivation, the concept was much earlier recognized by scripture and later in the Magna Carta. Our Founding Fathers called the concept the rights of man and it is, I believe, more aptly described for our purposes as individual and personal liberties.

Like the great codes of justice, the principles of personal liberties are simple and obvious. Murder is wrong. Torture is wrong. Censorship is wrong. In Abraham Lincoln's view, "The leading principle, the sheet-anchor of American republicanism" is that "no man is good enough to govern another man without that other's consent." In other words, totalitarian dictatorships are wrong, and we support democracy and the expansion of democracy as the best vehicle to insure worldwide personal liberty. There can be no real disagreement on these goals here.

But to convert these principles into policy is a complex, difficult task. And it engenders a dispute over method—not the principles themselves. Those who disagree with the administration's current methods of conversion argue that the means they propose are, in fact, as simple and obvious as the principles we all subscribe to. I only wish that it were so.

Today I would like to discuss one vital part of this debate: the complex relationship between promoting the cause of personal liberty and the imperatives of national security. I especially address our government's concerns with personal liberty in those countries where our own national security interests are manifestly at stake.

Notwithstanding assertions by some that conflicting demands of personal liberty and national security are irreconcilable, this is so only in a superficial sense. The administration believes that a strong America—an America whose national security is assured—is good for personal liberties throughout the world. No nation will succeed in pressing for personal liberties if it is seen by the world as weak, retreating, and unsure of itself. In the 19th century, Britain succeeded in eliminating the slave trade because it was at the height of its power and at the peak of its sense of self-assurance. We in the United States achieved one of our greatest victories for freedom—the democratization of Germany and Japan —at a moment of overwhelming strength. Of the two major powers today, only the United States cares about personal liberty in a more than superficial way. The enormous power of the Soviet Union is used to suppress, not encourage, personal freedoms. This fact, it seems to me, is the beginning of geopolitical wisdom in our age. It is verifiable by inquiry—ask the Poles, ask the Afghans, ask the Kampucheans. If the United States were to exercise options that would weaken our national strength, as some would have us do, then the Soviet Union would gain greater worldwide influence and the cause of liberty would suffer all over the world.

A hundred and twenty years ago Abraham Lincoln said: "I hold that while man exists, it is his duty to improve not only his own condition, but to assist in ameliorating mankind's. . . ." We have been fulfilling President Lincoln's commitment. The United States supported positive change toward democracy in Spain and Portugal. The United States strongly supported free elections held in the past year in Honduras, El Salvador, Costa Rica, and the Dominican Republic. The United States strongly supports the Government of Turkey in its plans to reestablish constitutional democracy this coming year.

We have also sought to fulfill our traditional commitment to personal liberties in those areas of the world where our influence is of necessity less readily exercised. Eastern Europe is far removed from us in distance as well as political philosophy. There were those who thought that we would prove indifferent to the struggle for freedom in this area. After four decades of war, occupation, and totalitarianism, Poland was just beginning to emerge into the fresh air of liberty; this movement toward freedom caused the Soviet Union to fear not only the loosening of its grip on Poland but contagion of its whole empire. We responded vigorously to the declaration of war by the Polish Government on its own people. We have put in place sanctions against the Polish Government as well as against the Soviet Government whose bullying was largely responsible for the events of December 13.[7] Our sanctions, however costly they are to the perpetrators of the outrages of Poland, did not come free of charge. The embargoes on critical industrial goods have cost our industries hundreds of millions of dollars, and this at a time of widespread unemployment in this country. Our insistence on strict application of the sanctions has brought us friction with our allies, something we very much wish to avoid at all times. On December 29 we felt we had no choice: At stake are the highest principles. The liberties of the Poles in an indirect but tangible way safeguard our own liberties; their loss is our loss. Sacrificing our commitment to freedom for short-term economic or even political gains would cast us adrift from the very heritage that has made us a strong and admired people.

So that we will understand what is really at stake here, let me read from a Reuters' wire service report with an August 6 dateline:

> "The French Government today instructed its Embassy in Moscow to investigate a report by a Frankfurt-based human rights organization that thousands of Soviet prisoners are working on the new Siberian gas pipeline. The association was quoted as saying about 100,000 prisoners had been put to work in camps set up along the route of the pipeline across Siberia and west beyond the Ural Mountains. Some 10,000 of the prisoners were alleged to be serving sentences for political offenses."

To review my thesis: I hold that the claim of an irreconcilable conflict between personal liberty and national security is misleading, particularly when we examine the ultimate goals of each. American power and strength can achieve as much for humanity and for personal liberties as it does for national security. But these achievements can be realized only if, first, America is strong—militarily, morally, politically, and economically—and, second, other nations perceive our commitment to be firm in the defense of principle, including the defense of personal liberties in the international arena. The record of this administration provides ample evidence of fulfilling that commitment.

I would now like to examine the corollary of the proposition that a strong America is good for personal liberties. That corollary proposition is that our active support for international personal liberties is also good for our national security.

We start with recognition that our most important allies are all democracies, while none of the Soviet Union's allies is. A more democratic world will be a world in which we are likely to find friends and greater assurances for national security.

A word of caution here. We recognize that concepts of freedom are usually deeply rooted in a society's history and politics, and, for that very reason, problems relating to personal liberty cannot be swiftly solved. Attempts at sudden transformation or violent political and social change often lead to even greater violations of personal rights. The Shah, for example, was overthrown quickly, and the Ayatollah immediately set upon a massive suppression of personal liberty. This and other instances, such as Nicaragua, caution us there is no quick fix in building democracy.

To build a democracy for the first time in an emerging country requires comprehensive transformation and political reform. While it is a task requiring patience and dedication, it is also the surest ultimate guarantee of personal liberties. In Spain, for instance, the growth of democracy was gradual, but it was successful—and it was accomplished despite obstacles once regarded as too much for the advocates of democracy to overcome. We need to remember that the most opportune time to work for reform is before a crisis, not in the midst of it. It is unworthy of the United States to discover that personal liberties are being violated only when the alarm bell rings. As in other areas of foreign relations, we must have long-term, consistent policy—one that works quietly to diminish problems before they become acute, and one that will not swerve or reverse in a crisis.

We pause here to note that America's commitment to exercising its power on behalf of personal liberties carries with it special responsibilities, which some smaller countries may well be able to avoid. Frankly, it is easy for countries playing a lesser role in world affairs to urge strident uncompromising perfectionism in situations not directly affecting them. Such countries can—and sometimes do—insist on absolute

[7] The reference is to the imposition of martial law in Poland on December 13, 1981. For documentation on the U.S. reaction to this event, see *American Foreign Policy: Current Documents, 1981*, Chapter 10, Part M. The United States placed sanctions against Poland and the Soviet Union on December 29, 1981; for the text of President Reagan's statement establishing the sanctions, see *ibid.*, document 270.

purity in Turkey or El Salvador or some other country where our security interests are at risk. For these countries the cost of such rhetoric is nil.

Let me relate what I have said to the Reagan administration. When this administration arrived in Washington, extreme views on human rights were prevalent. One extreme said that human rights as practiced in other nations should in no way affect our relations with them. The other extreme said: Disregard our national security concerns in condemning human rights violations within those other nations. The extreme views nevertheless had something in common: They agreed that human liberties and national security impose inconsistent demands and that we were required to choose one to the exclusion of the other.

This administration disagrees. We must seek and do seek to protect our national security even in those areas of the world where there may be regrettable violations of personal liberty. Why? Because our own national security depends on insuring freedom and personal liberties throughout the world.

Let me elaborate on my broad observations about personal liberties and national security by mentioning 7 guidelines this administration looks to in its attempt to encourage individual liberties abroad while adhering to national security needs. They are:

First, a commitment to effectiveness—to accomplish good rather than to look good. Pronouncements and speeches do not alone create an effective policy. I was recently reminded of this by the Vatican Secretary of State who in referring to the Soviet Union said, ". . . human liberty and peace must be more than mere words."

Second, our effectiveness is based on greater use of traditional diplomacy rather than on public condemnation.

Third, commitment that the United States will remain a constant and reliable force in international affairs. Other governments must know we will be a reliable friend and, if need be, a resolute adversary.

Fourth, positive reliance upon human nature to achieve idealistic aims. I stated in an address at West Point last fall:

> "We seek to build on the very features of international life that some seek to abolish—national differences, national interests, and national pride. Properly channeled, these facts of international life can be used to create and support a just and peaceful world order. It is on such constructive use of human nature, rather than repudiation of it, that the major intervals of peace in world history have been based."[8]

We do not wish to remake man or redefine the elements of human intercourse. We seek to appeal to basic human needs and to direct other nations toward peace, democracy, and personal liberty.

Fifth, concern for violations of personal liberties from all sources whether government of otherwise. An opposition group to a government—if it engages in terrorism, murder, torture, suppression of a free press, or interference with the judiciary—is as burdensome to its victims as official suppression. It is a tragic fact that extreme means used by revolutionary movements produce brutality proportional to the means used to attain them. This was understood long ago by Edmund Burke, who said of the textbook revolutionaries of his time, "In the groves of their academy, at the end of every vista, you see nothing but the gallows."

Sixth, commitment to resist the expansion of dictatorship. Direct aggression, guerrilla war, and terrorism are used by the U.S.S.R. and Libya to undermine democracies and to help their brands of dictatorship.

Seventh, commitment to the global campaign for democracy that the President outlined in his recent speech to the British Parliament.[9] We must help strengthen democratic institutions such as the free press, independent judicial systems, democratic political parties, free churches and universities. Democracy is built on free institutions: This is the lesson of our history. Personal liberty policy cannot be just a matter of critiques and sanctions; at its heart must be encouragement and help for those who are actually building democracies throughout the world.

In El Salvador today, people are actually building democracy amid the cruel obstacles of violent insurgency and economic crisis. The long lines of peasants waiting to

---

[8] The quotation is from Clark's speech, "The Human Factor in Shaping Foreign Policy", to the 33d Annual Student Conference on U.S. Affairs at West Point on November 18, 1981. (Department of State files)

[9] For the text of Reagan's June 8, 1982, address before the British Parliament in London, see document 4.

vote in the face of violence and death threats demonstrated that liberties neither should be taken for granted nor seen as a hopeless dream by those who have not heretofore enjoyed them. This administration finds it an honor to assist in the birth of democracy in El Salvador. The right of a people to govern themselves is perhaps the most cherished of personal freedoms. By assisting the people of El Salvador to secure this right, we have a rare opportunity to secure other personal liberties as well. Where democracy prevails there are traditionally fewer violations of other liberties. Again, in the absence of self-government, the fulfillment of personal liberties is never assured.

Let us conclude. American strength and will are essential to the expansion of personal liberty around the globe. These are prerequisites to making the cause of personal liberties a centerpiece of our foreign policy. We adopt a "forward strategy" in this cause. We must be willing to use our influence to promote democratic initiatives in all likely areas of the world. And, in order to maintain our international credibility in all of this, we must avoid idle posturing or fruitless utopianism. We must remember Jefferson's warning: "The ground of liberty is to be gained by inches. We must be contented to secure what we can get from time to time, and eternally press forward for what is yet to get."

In all of this there is one underlying reality: Anyone who wishes to work effectively on behalf of personal liberties must do so with the clear understanding of the greatest threat to those liberties—the growth of totalitarian power and the onrush of an ideology that justifies any violation of personal liberty so long as it is done in the name of the state. It is inconsistent—and this was the great shoal upon which the last administration's well-intentioned human rights policy foundered—to speak of an "inordinate fear of communism" while at the same time promoting the cause of personal liberties. The Marxist-Leninists do not by definition believe in human rights or personal liberties or individual conscience. They believe in the accumulation of state power and the eventual extension of that power to every nation on the face of the Earth. As the President remarked recently in his Captive Nations Proclamation,[10] this attempt at a worldwide repression of freedom is the tragedy of our time and the most important new event of our generation.

This is the central reality that confronts any honest effort to extend personal liberties, the alpha and omega of any intelligent discussion of how best to extend the guarantees of personal liberties to all mankind.

[10] For the text of the proclamation establishing Captive Nations Week, 1982, see *Weekly Compilation of Presidential Documents,* July 26, 1982, pp. 920–921.

Document 127

Prepared Statement by the Representative at the United Nations (Kirkpatrick) Before the Third Committee of the U.N. General Assembly, December 7, 1982[11]

Human Rights in the United Nations

What is the role of the United Nations with regard to human rights? And what should it be? How important is the protection of human rights and human freedom to this institution? These questions were raised in several United Nations arenas last week. They were raised once when the United States noted that the proposed resolution on the Secretary-General's report[12] contained no reference to human rights or freedom, and proposed this addition. The draft resolution had already been expanded beyond the specific subject matter of the Secretary-General's report to embrace broader issues. Our suggestion was not enthusiastically received.

Other nations, we were told, would resist the addition of human rights to the resolution. Its purpose, we were told, was to focus on the Charter and on the purposes stated there.[13] When we pointed out that commitment to human rights and freedom were present in the Charter, it was asserted that the resolution should focus only on the most important purposes of the United Nations—and that protection of human rights did not have the same priority as preserving peace, promoting development, or ending the arms race.

[11] Source: U.S. Mission to the United Nations Press Release USUN–167(82), December 7, 1982.

[12] For the text of the *Report of the Secretary-General on the Work of the Organization,* see U.N. document A/37/1.

[13] For the text of the U.N. Charter, see 3 Bevans 1153.

Furthermore, it was pointed out, human rights involve individuals, whereas the important purposes of the United Nations involve collectivities.

Eventually resisters reconsidered, resistance waned and human rights were included in the resolution.[14] But the initial absence of concern for human rights violations and reticence about their inclusion were significant. They point to an erosion in commitment and clarity concerning human rights and freedom and especially to the existence of ambiguity about their relations to other goals of the Charter and of the United Nations.

The fact is, of course, that the protection of human rights and freedom is identified in the Preamble of the Charter and enumerated among its purposes:

> "We the peoples of the United Nations determined . . .[15] to reaffirm faith in fundamental human rights, in the dignity and worth of the human person, in the equal rights of men and women . . . have resolved to combine our efforts to accomplish these aims. . . ."

"The purposes of the United Nations," says Chapter 1, Article 1, are:

> "to achieve international cooperation . . . in promoting and encouraging respect for human rights and for fundamental freedom for all without distinction as to race, sex, language or religion."

It was entirely natural that persons concerned with the preservation of international peace should have been committed also to the preservation of human rights and freedom because the two are inexorably linked.

In fact, respect for human rights and fundamental freedoms is integrally linked to all major political values, as abuse of human rights and fundamental freedoms is integrally associated with all the most important political crimes.

There are two principal methods of acting politically in both internal and international affairs: these are the method of consent and the method of violence.

In internal affairs the method of consent means governing with permission of the governed. Consent must be given, it cannot be coerced. Consent can be given only when there is freedom to withhold it—to inquire, discuss, disagree. Institutionalized, the method of consent is democracy.

In external affairs, too, the method of consent means respecting the national independence and sovereign equality of all. It means basing relations among nations on persuasion, cooperation, contract, and requires that nations have the right to disagree, to withhold cooperation. Consent is utterly incompatible with conquest.

The method of consent respects human rights. It encourages initiative, innovation, effort. Societies whose governments rely on the method of consent do not produce refugees.

The method of violence stands in sharp contrast to the method of consent. Applied to the internal affairs of a nation, the method of violence bases power on coercion, compels conformity and honors neither law, custom, nor the wishes of the governed. Institutionalized, it is autocracy. In external affairs the method of violence is invasion, occupation, conquest. It respects neither the territorial integrity of nations, nor the right to self-determination nor self-government of peoples. The method of violence produces widespread violation of the human rights of its objects and victims. The clearest expression of the method of violence is war.

"War," wrote its greatest theoretician, Karl von Clausewitz, "is an act of violence intended to compel our opponent to fulfill our will." It occurs in our times when rulers of one nation use physical force to conquer another people. Military force is a means, but as Raymond Aron has noted, "military victory is not the goal." War is not a sport practiced for its own sake. It is a deadly game pursued for political ends.

War, continued von Clausewitz, is "not merely a political act, but also a real political instrument." It is politics conducted by violence—to the end of establishing control over some populace. War is a way of seeking and winning power by conquest, which stands in the sharpest possible contrast to establishing power by consent.

The method of violence seeks to silence, not to persuade. It is more concerned with power than with truth or freedom or law. It values control over consent. It deprives those against whom it is used of basic human rights—of their right to life, liberty, security, due process of law. Today, the

---

[14] Reference is to U.N. General Assembly Resolution 37/67, adopted without a vote on December 3, 1982.

[15] All ellipses appear in the source text.

method of violence deprives the people of Poland of their right to assemble, their right to organize independent trade unions and to bargain collectively, their right to a voice in the basic decisions of the society.

Applied across borders, as in Afghanistan and Cambodia today, the method of violence deprives whole societies of self-determination, security and peace. The method of violence is used against these peoples, their culture, social institutions, religious practices, economies, and governments.

Violence is an assault on the human dignity, human rights, and fundamental freedoms of its objects. It relies on armies, guns, bombs, poison gas, mycotoxins to coerce submission and secure compliance.

The method of violence produces what is here called "mass exoduses," that is, a tragic flow of persons fleeing from their native lands in fear for their lives and freedom. This relationship was recognized in Resolution 309, adopted on March 1, 1980, by the Human Rights Commission, which noted that "large exoduses of persons and groups are frequently the result of violations of human rights," and again, in the recent study of the Special Rapporteur, which asserted:

> "In all the situations taking place during the past decade, violations of this spirit, and frequently of this letter of the Universal Declaration of Human Rights and its Preamble must be recognized. The rule of law, which is the only guarantee of just treatment of the individual, was simply nonexistent in many of the countries from which exodus took place."

Given the incompatibility of violence with human rights and freedom, one might suppose that the U.N.'s concern with human rights would recognize the method of violence in internal and external affairs as incompatible with the Charter and destructive of human rights. With shock, one learns that in many cases the use of force and violation of human rights are not seen as a violation of the Charter relevant to U.N. bodies with responsibility for protection of human rights and fundamental freedoms. Some violations are defined out of existence, some are simply ignored. Only a very limited class of violence and violations are deemed relevant to U.N. purposes today.

Most of the questions of human rights with which United Nations bodies have concerned themselves in recent years are of a single kind. U.N. human rights bodies concern themselves with relatively small, relatively underdeveloped, non-Communist nations, which are not members of any cohesive bloc; which are or have recently been the target of a national liberation movement with important ties to the Soviet bloc; and with countries which have sought to protect themselves by using government violence against guerrilla violence.

Relatively few governments meet all these criteria for attention. There are many small developing countries, but most are protected by their membership in powerful blocs. Furthermore, not all small developing countries are the active objects of revolutionary violence, and not all targeted governments resist violent assaults. Some simply succumb.

Most of the human rights violations singled out for attention in the United Nations are Latin—not, certainly, because the greatest human rights violations of our century have taken place there. The Holocaust, Gulag, Pol Pot's genocidal utopia, Vietnam's labor camps, Idi Amin's slaughterhouse—have won for Europe, Asia, and Africa records of human rights violations unmatched in the Western Hemisphere. Nonetheless, as our Venezuelan colleague noted in this Committee last week, United Nations human rights bodies show a "special taste for those small countries which are apparently lacking in strategic resources of wide political audiences."[16]

An Islamic or African country which becomes the target of violent guerrilla assault would be protected against United Nations human rights action by its involvement in a web of protective alliances—regional organizations, the Non-Aligned Movement, the G–77,[17] or some other bloc.

Even though their records of internal repression and external aggression are

---

[16] Regarding the December 3, 1982, Venezuelan statement in the Third Committee, see U.N. document A/C.3/37/SR.62.

[17] The Non-Aligned Movement refers to a group of countries that since 1955 have chosen not to associate politically or militarily with either the Western or Communist countries. G–77 refers to a group of developing nations which organized to set forth a program of action prior to the first meeting of the U.N. Conference on Trade and Development in 1964. The group, now expanded to an estimated 121 nations, operates as a developing country caucus on economic matters in the United Nations. The Non-Aligned Movement is considered the political voice of the third world, while the G–77 is seen as its economic voice.

clear and well-known, countries linked to the Soviet Union are protected against charges of human rights violations by their membership in the Soviet bloc which, like other blocs, functions as a mutual protection society. The fact that many members of the Soviet bloc are also members of other groups extends their access and influence. Cuba's status as President of the Non-Aligned Movement symbolizes this pattern of overlapping membership and extended influence.

There is another reason that the Soviet Union and its bloc are successful in avoiding the attention of United Nations human rights groups. It is because they have been very successful in selling, here in the United Nations and in influential circles outside this body, a perverse doctrine of violence and human rights which stands traditional conceptions on their heads: where traditionally states have been defined as having a monopoly on the legitimate use of violence, now liberation movements are seen as having a monopoly on the legitimate use of force.

According to this upside-down view of human rights and self-defense, revolutionary violence—that is, violence committed by those linked to the Soviet Union and its clients—is defined as a just protest against an unjust society. Such violence may result in dead civilians, bombed school children, widespread economic destruction, but it will not be considered a violation of human rights if it is committed in the name of revolution against any society whose citizens do not enjoy all the rights listed in the Universal Declaration,[18] that is, most of the societies in the world today. Whole peoples may have their homes and villages burned, their crops destroyed, their cattle killed, may be forcibly "relocated" in camps without provoking any interest or activity in the Third Committee or the Human Rights Commission. People may be invaded, conquered, herded into cities, driven over borders, their fields tainted with toxins, their air poisoned with yellow rain, without them being regarded as victims of human rights violations. They may have their electric plants dynamited, their coffee crops destroyed, their leaders murdered, without being regarded as victims of human rights violations—providing that the perpetrators of this violence, of these gross abuses, are "progressive" national liberation movements, armed, trained, serviced by the professional purveyors of revolutionary violence. Only governments that seek to repress this violence will be cited for human rights violations.

In a recent speech before this Committee, which singled out the governments of Central America for special negative mention, a colleague asserted: "My government opposes violence wherever it occurs, as a method to solve political or social problems. But at the same time we cannot accept the argument that an oppressed people striving for legitimate social and economic reforms of its own society should be automatically classified as terrorists."

Whether a given group is or is not classified as terrorists would, one should think, depend on whether they use terror against civilian populations. During the past year the economy of El Salvador has been devastated, the poor people of that poor nation deprived of the fruits of their labor by repeated, carefully targeted guerrilla attacks—a strange method, indeed, for promoting social and economic reform, but a familiar method of conquest.

Small bands of violent men have discovered in our times that, by the skillful use of violence and propaganda, they can win power against overwhelming numbers. They begin with terror which has been aptly defined as "the deliberate, systematic murder, maiming and menacing of the innocent to inspire fear in order to gain political ends." Such deliberate use of terror to produce a "revolutionary situation" has become the preferred tactic of contemporary revolutionary cadres.

"The process," wrote one student of revolutionary violence, "begins with a small group of individuals working to destabilize a society through assassinations and other violent acts. These are often described as 'pointless,' but in fact they have very astute purposes: intimidation of the general population; destruction of the economy by frightening off capital and skilled workers; and a demonstration to possible political opponents that 'these madmen will stop at nothing'."

Neither the methods nor the goals have changed since they were described in a *Revolutionary Catechism* by nineteenth century nihilists. They are: "to use every means in ((their)) power to foster and spread those wrongs and those evils which will finally break the patience of our people and force them to a general revolt."

In our times, Carlos Marighella's *Minimanual of the Urban Guerrilla* provides a

---

[18] For the text of the Universal Declaration of Human Rights, see Department of State *Bulletin*, December 19, 1948, pp. 752–754.

graphic description of this process of violence, whose aim is to create a situation "where the government has no alternative except to intensify repression. The police roundups, house searches, arrests of innocent people and of suspects, closing off streets, make life in the city unbearable." Marighella continued, in the wake of these repressive measures, "the general sentiment is that the government is unjust, incapable of solving problems, and resorts purely and simply to the physical liquidation of its opponents." Eventually, as repression grows, "the political situation in the country is transformed into a military situation in which the militarists appear more and more to be the ones responsible for errors and violence, while the problems in the lives of the people become truly catastrophic." During this critical period, Marighella counselled, the guerrilla "must become more aggressive and violent, resorting without letup to sabotage, terrorism, expropriations, assaults, kidnappings and executions, heightening the disastrous situation in which the government must act."

This now familiar cycle is accompanied today by a chorus of moral outrage from a self-designated constituency of conscience which deplores all efforts of governments and societies to defend themselves against guerrilla violence.

"Demands for change," said our U.N. colleague, speaking of the beleaguered countries of Central America, "have been met with terror and violence by government forces and groups of the extreme right, supported or condoned by the state power."

One wonders, which demands for change did he mean? Did he mean those communicated by the specialists in violence that destroyed 34 bridges and 145 electrical transmission towers in El Salvador? Or was he thinking of the businesses closed by guerrilla action—putting more than 18,000 Salvadorans out of work—or perhaps the 700 buses destroyed? He could not have been referring to the kidnapping of two soccer teams and 120 spectators from a rural stadium in Salvador, for that was reported in the press only today.

Probably, he was not speaking of El Salvador at all, since that country's democratic elections and broad land reform, carried out under external assault, must inspire admiration.

Furthermore, it is presumably clear to all the world that demands for change can be asserted through Salvador's democratic processes by anyone willing to use the method of consent rather than that of violence.

Perhaps our colleague was talking about Guatemala—Salvador's neighbor, which as recently as 3 years ago had a high growth rate, a growing middle class and good economic prospects—until it, too, became a target of guerrilla violence. This violence was conducted as usual by small guerrilla bands, advised, armed and otherwise assisted by Cuba and bloc countries, infiltrated into that country by well-known routes for the purpose of wreaking violence, sowing destruction, provoking ever-greater repression, fear, alienation, and for the purpose, finally, of coming to power.

The method of violence is applied on a daily basis in Guatemala, where guerrillas make their demands for social justice by bombing bridges, killing provincial police and judges, attacking municipal buildings, burning gas stations, telephone and telegraph installations, mining roads, shooting shop owners, kidnapping businessmen, terrorizing school girls, slaying Indian villagers who resist paying "war taxes" and engaging in an ongoing total war against the Guatemalan people. No reasonable, fair observer could imagine that the method of violence used by Guatemala's guerrillas is merely a reaction to government provocation. It is a brutal, ruthless campaign conducted by specialists in violence determined to seize power and govern by force.

Perhaps in talking of government repression and provocation of a population, my colleague was really thinking of Poland, where the government has used heavy-handed military force against an unarmed population, repressing all moves toward free association, denying all liberties, using the power of the State against the bare hands and simple courage of Solidarity.

He could not really have meant that a society has no right of self-defense against armed bands in its midst: that Uruguay had no right of self-defense against the Tupemaros; that the Federal Republic of Germany had no right to defend itself against the Bader Meinhoff gang; that the Italian Government has no right to defend itself against the Red Brigades; that the Government of Spain has no right to defend itself against Basque terrorists; or Salvador has no right of self-defense against the guerrillas who boycott its elections, that attack its co-ops, murder its peasants; or that the people of Guatemala, who have long suffered under harsh, corrupt governments, must now passively accept new tyrants who, if one can judge by their Nicaraguan comrades-in-arms, will be still more repressive.

The specialists in violence have correctly understood that terrorism and guerrilla war pose extremely difficult problems for organized societies. They do provoke a spiral of repression, chaos, murder. Even strong, sophisticated governments and people, experienced in both the use and restraint of power have difficulty controlling organized political crime.

But a conception of human rights that ignores the guerrilla's war against civilians and focuses exclusively on a government's reprisals is no conception of human rights at all. It is a method of politics which seek victory for a certain kind of Soviet-sponsored "liberation."

Morally serious persons cannot maintain that terror wreaked on a civilian population by revolutionary movements is liberation, while violence committed by a government responding to that guerrilla is repression.

Morally serious persons cannot maintain that national liberation movements have the right to use violence against civilians, economies, societies and governments and that those societies have no right to defend themselves; that violence conducted in the name of revolution is legitimate; that violence used by governments and societies to defend themselves against guerrillas is illegitimate.

It will not wash. The facts are clear—the method of violence is the method of tyranny in internal affairs and aggression in international relations. Modern tyrants use violence against their own people and violence against their neighbors.

In our times, movements which seek total power by terrorist violence, govern by violence.

The continued widespread abuse of human rights in our world constitutes a challenge to all peoples and governments committed to promoting human rights and fundamental freedoms. A serious approach would take account of all deprivations of liberty, law and security committed by organized political groups. A serious approach to human rights would take account of the use of lethal toxins and gases against the H'Mong, of the tens of thousands of Vietnamese imprisoned and held under brutal conditions in labor camps far from home; of the continuing human hemorrhage of refugees from Southeast Asia's Communist nations into the China Sea. A serious approach would take account of the repression and banning of Solidarity, the continuing imprisonment of most of its leaders; of the denial of free association, collective bargaining, free speech, throughout Eastern Europe. It would take account of the Soviet Union's continuing, massive, flagrant violation of the rights and fundamental freedoms of the Afghan people, of the repression of the Helsinki Watch Committee, of the brutal imprisonment of Anatoly Shcharansky, of the abuse of psychiatric treatment, the denial of the right to emigrate, and the repression of Andrei Sakharov.

A serious concern with human rights would also require taking account of the flight of more than 30,000 Ugandans across the border to Rwanda, and of repression in other African states where freedom is denied and due process of law violated. It would take account of apartheid in South Africa.

A serious concern with human rights would take account of the widespread denial of legal and social rights of women and of "untouchables." And, in the context of all those problems, a serious concern for human rights would doubtless also take account of the deprivation of human rights by some groups and governments in some Latin American Republics. It would take account of Chile's exiles, Argentina's desaparecidos, of right as well as left violence in Guatemala and Salvador, and also of the harsh treatment of Nicaragua's Miskito, Suma, and Rama Indians, its repression of press freedom and of the large number of political prisoners in Cuba—some of whom have their sentences arbitrarily resentenced in clear violation of Cuba's own laws and of civilized practice.

The people and government of the United States believe in the method of consent, and we deplore all, I repeat all, recourse to the method of violence in internal and international affairs. We urge, even demand, that societies under attack practice the disciplines of freedom and law even as they defend themselves.

The United States is willing and ready to join with other nations in dealing seriously with these serious problems. Human rights and fundamental freedoms should be our goal and standard, rather than a political weapon used selectively by the strong against the weak, the organized against the unorganized. We will not be a party to the further perversion and selective application of these values. We will not contribute our votes to strengthening those who seek political gain by the method of violence.

We will join our colleagues in any serious, reasonable and fair effort to protect and promote human rights. We are ready when you are.

Document 128

Proclamation by President Reagan, December 10, 1982[19]

Bill of Rights Day, Human Rights Day and Week, 1982

On December 15, 1791, our Founding Fathers celebrated the ratification of the first ten Amendments to the Constitution of the United States—a Bill of Rights which from that moment forward helped shape a nation unique in the annals of history. The Bill of Rights became the formal and legal expression of our liberties and of the principles embodied in the Declaration of Independence.

The Founding Fathers derived their principles of limited government from a belief in natural law, that is, the concept that our Creator had ordained a framework for society giving great importance to individual freedom, expression, and responsibility. They held that each person had certain natural rights bestowed on him by God. As Jefferson put it, "the God who gave us life gave us liberty."

It is with glad hearts and thankful minds that on Bill of Rights Day we recognize and honor this great gift of Liberty bequeathed to posterity by the Founding Fathers.

One hundred and fifty-seven years later, on December 10, 1948, the United Nations adopted the Universal Declaration of Human Rights.[20] By jointly celebrating this anniversary with Bill of Rights Day, we acknowledge the necessary link between human rights and constitutional democracy. As stated in the Universal Declaration, we must staunchly pursue our conviction that freedom is not the sole prerogative of the fortunate few, but the inalienable and universal right of all human beings. Throughout history and from all parts of the globe, man's instinctive desire for freedom and true self-determination have surfaced again and again. Democracy has provided the best and most enduring expression of man's search for individual rights.

We can point to many nations in the world where there is real progress toward the development of democratic institutions. The people of some of those countries have fully demonstrated their commitment to democratic principles by participating in elections under difficult and even life-threatening circumstances. Such displays of courage can only inspire confidence in the future of democracy for all people.

But in December of 1982 our satisfaction in the progress toward human rights is darkened by our realization that one year ago, on December 13, 1981, the Polish military government took steps to extinquish the flames of liberty ignited by Solidarity.[21] As that totalitarian regime moved to crush Solidarity, it laid siege to the dreams and aspirations of a whole people reaching out for freedom, independence, and essential human dignity. The tragedy of the iron suppression of the Polish people transcends the borders of that land and reaches into the hearts of all of us who care for the rights and well-being of people everywhere.

On these important anniversaries let us remember the great and abiding love of freedom that dwells perpetually within the heart of mankind. And let us also hope and pray that the blessings of liberty will one day be shared by all people.

NOW, THEREFORE, I, RONALD REAGAN, President of the United States of America, do hereby proclaim December 10, 1982, as Human Rights Day and December 15, 1982, as Bill of Rights Day, and call on all Americans to observe the week beginning December 10, 1982, as Human Rights Week.

---

[19] Source: White House Press Release, December 10, 1982, Office of the Press Secretary to the President; printed also in *Weekly Compilation of Presidential Documents,* December 13, 1982, pp. 1600–1601. This proclamation, No. 5003, was filed with the Office of the Federal Register at 12:43 p.m. on December 10, 1982.

[20] For the text of the Universal Declaration of Human Rights, see Department of State *Bulletin,* December 19, 1948, pp. 752–754.

[21] The reference is to the imposition of martial law in Poland on December 13, 1981. For documentation on the U.S. reaction to this event, see *American Foreign Policy: Current Documents, 1981,* Chapter 10, Part M.

IN WITNESS WHEREOF, I hereunto set my hand this tenth day of December, in the year of our Lord nineteen hundred and eighty-two, and of the Independence of the United States of America the two hundred and seventh.

B. Campaign for Democracy

Document 129

Address by the Secretary of State (Shultz) Before the Conference on Democratization of Communist Countries, October 18, 1982[1]

"Support for Democracy . . . Is Basic to Our History and Our World View"

I am very pleased to be with you and to have you here considering the questions that you are considering.

Last spring in a speech to the British Parliament,[2] President Reagan announced that our country would redouble efforts to promote the international growth of democracy. That speech, the centerpiece of the President's European trip, provides important clues about the character of the United States.

Support for democracy is not simply a policy of the American Government. It is basic to our history and our world view. The leaders of the American Revolution fought to establish our right to democratic self-determination. The American Civil War reaffirmed that this Nation, conceived in liberty, will forever be dedicated to personal and political freedom. And during the last 40 years, as our nation became more active in international affairs, we made the spread and defense of freedom our central foreign policy goal.

Our efforts, and those of our democratic allies, have borne significant fruit. The cause of political liberty has made great strides since the end of World War II. Scores of colonies won independence and a remarkable number embraced democracy. Elsewhere, vestiges of the authoritarian past disappeared. The U.N. Charter and Universal Declaration of Human Rights[3] established international obligations with respect to personal and political liberties. Today, there is a sense of optimism that democracy can be the wave of the future.

Recent developments in countries under Communist rule also suggest that a new age of democratic reform and revolution lies ahead of us. The weaknesses of Communist societies are becoming increasingly apparent. Popular desires for freedom remain strong. The concessions that Communist regimes make to popular sentiment and to economic necessity may sow the seeds of their transformation. And, of course, that is what worries them.

In Poland, the economic failings of Communism combined with the ever-strong drive for liberty to create the Solidarity movement. Solidarity's meteoric rise and continued impact demonstrate clearly that labor unions and other grassroots organizations can provide an effective vehicle for dispersing power to a broad segment of the population. And I believe they also demonstrate the strong relationship that we can see in our own country and everywhere of free trade unions to a free society.

In East Germany, youths sport an emblem depicting a man beating a sword into a plowshare, showing their opposition to the Communist state's militarism and their continued respect for religious symbols and ideals.

The church survives as an important social institution in several Communist countries. It is a short step from religious commitment to political activism. When churchmen apply the religious principles of individual responsibility and free will to political issues, they demand a more active role in national decisions.

---

[1] Source: Department of State files. The Conference on Democratization of Communist Countries was held on October 18 and 19, 1982, in the Loy Henderson Auditorium of the Department of State. It was organized by the Office of the Under Secretary of State for Political Affairs in response to President Reagan's June 8, 1982, address before the British Parliament in London.

[2] For the text of Reagan's June 8th address, see document 4.

[3] For the text of the U.N. Charter, see 3 Bevans 1153. For the text of the Universal Declaration of Human Rights, see Department of State *Bulletin*, December 19, 1948, pp. 752–754.

In virtually every Communist country a free market thrives, whether with or without official sanction. The system's economic failures drive everyone to the black market—which turns out to be the one efficient market so often. Undoubtedly, official and unofficial market innovations will influence the way Communist countries are governed in the future. Individuals who chart their own economic course will not be satisfied in a society that prohibits the exercise of political rights. So we see economic developments and political developments joined.

In the final analysis, internal forces must be the major factors for democratization of Communist states. Only the people of those countries can muster sufficient pressures for reform. Only they can seize opportunities to determine their own destinies.

We do not seek to foment violent unrest or to undermine Communist regimes. Yet, we will not ignore the individuals and groups in Communist countries who seek peaceful change. It is our responsibility, both moral and strategic, to meet their calls for help. We must aid their struggle for freedom.

The U.S. Government is active on this front.

—Our radio broadcasts serve as the Communist world's surrogate free press. The U.S. Government will spend $44 million this fiscal year as the first installment in a planned billion dollar modernization program to improve the radios' geographic and political impact.[4]

—We are encouraging private sector groups to aid the peaceful struggle for freedom in Communist countries. More organizations must follow the example of the AFL–CIO, which offered strong support for Polish Solidarity.

—American Government leaders will continue to condemn, in words and deeds, Communist human rights violations. We will bring specific cases to public attention and declare our conviction that the people of Communist countries deserve their human rights, and that their drives for freedom will succeed.

—We will continue to press the issue of human rights in public, international forums and will insist that Communist states be held to international standards of behavior. We will hold them to the Helsinki Final Act,[5] as we do in forum after forum and in individual discussion after discussion. We will insist that a single standard be applied to all countries.

These efforts are important, but we must do more to support the emergence of democracy in Communist states. We need new tools, new energies, and new focus to invigorate our efforts.

We called this conference to address a very practical question, "What is to be done?" We look to you for guidance and creative ideas. The President and I are anxious to receive your recommendations.

Some of you here today are political activists from Communist countries; advocates for freedom in your homelands. I believe that history will judge you as the apostles of hope; the forebears of a new age of democracy. We are committed to help you and your countrymen make the dream of freedom a reality.

Document 130

Address by the Secretary of State (Shultz) Before the Conference on Free Elections, November 4, 1982 (Extract)[6]

Conference on Free Elections

I'm very pleased to have this honor of opening the Conference on Free Elections and to welcome you on behalf of President Reagan, the Department of State, and our

---

[4] Regarding the modernization of the international radio system, see document 151.

[5] For the text of the Final Act of the Conference on Security and Cooperation in Europe, signed at Helsinki on August 1, 1975, by the United States, Canada, and 33 European countries, see Department of State *Bulletin*, September 1, 1975, pp. 323–350.

[6] Source: Department of State files; printed also in Department of State *Bulletin*, December 1982, p. 15. Shultz spoke at the opening of the Conference on Free Elections, which was held in Washington, November 4–6, 1982. Sponsored by the Department of State, United States Information Agency, Agency for International Development, and the American Enterprise Institute, the conference was organized in response to President Reagan's June 8, 1982, address before the British Parliament in London. Shultz delivered this speech at the Department of State. Reagan also addressed the participants at a luncheon held later that day at the White House; for text, see *Weekly Compilation of Presidential Documents*, November 8, 1982, pp. 1433–1436.

cosponsors, the American Enterprise Institute.

I'm particularly pleased to greet our honored guests, President Monge of Costa Rica; Prime Minister Spadolini of Italy; and Alhaji Shehu Musa, the personal representative of President Shagari of Nigeria.

President Reagan announced plans for this conference in his speech to the British Parliament last June.[7] In that address, the President held out his hand to join other nations in a global campaign for peaceful democratic change.

Gathered here today are many of the leaders of the "Campaign for Democracy," of which the President spoke, men and women who helped forge institutions in their own countries and who want to help other people lay the foundations for political freedom. This conference will consider what you have accomplished and what we can do together to further the spread of democracy.

We are not here to challenge other countries, but to extend an offer to share our experience and our expertise in making freedom work. Our objective is not to criticize, but to consider what we can do to help other nations realize their democratic aspirations.

In that regard, let me ask you to consider three areas for action: First, we should provide concrete assistance to countries interested in establishing free elections. We can help others learn from our experiences and overcome the initial hurdles of establishing electoral democracy. Some governments and private organizations are already heavily engaged in providing technical assistance to strengthen the electoral process. More are now taking up the challenge.

One month ago in San Jose, eight Central American, Caribbean, and Andean nations resolved to establish a regional elections institute as part of their program for peace and democracy in Central America.[8] Other nations and regions might follow their example. This conference should consider what additional programs might be most effective and how disparate efforts to support the spread of free elections could become more mutually self-supportive.

Second, we need to advocate the right to free elections more actively, and to affirm that political freedom is a human rights issue.

Individuals have a right to participate in their own governance, just as they have the right to be free from state harassment.

The question is not how to create this right, for it already exists. The question is how to put it into practice on the widest possible basis.

We need to expand human rights discussions and activities to include positive steps that foster free institutions. Only free democratic institutions, including elections, the press and labor unions, can break longstanding patterns of human rights violations, assure individual liberty, and satisfy the right to self-government.

Third, we can do more to publicize the success of democracy and draw attention to the comparative performances of democratic and nondemocratic nations.

Democracies have, with few exceptions, enjoyed greater peace, prosperity and stability than their nondemocratic counterparts. Young democratic nations, in particular, can play a key role in making others recognize that democratic government is both desirable and workable. The experiences and success of nascent democracies can be both instructive and encouraging to those who do not yet share political freedom.

Ladies and gentlemen, you have a challenging task before you. You will be considering how the people of this democratic world can help bring liberty to the millions who are not yet permitted to choose their own leaders. We look to you for fresh, creative and concrete ideas that will help translate our beliefs and commitments into action.

. . . .

---

[7] For the text of Reagan's June 8 address, see document 4.

[8] Regarding this agreement, see document 702.

Document 131

Address by the Assistant Secretary of State for Human Rights and Humanitarian Affairs (Abrams) Before the Conference on Free Elections, November 6, 1982[9]

"The Issue of Free Elections Is at the Very Heart of Any Search for Human Rights"

This is the third and final day of our Conference on Free Elections. My purpose this morning is to explain why we believe that the issue of free elections is at the very heart of any search for human rights.

All of us gathered here are struggling in our own countries and throughout the world to advance the cause of human rights. One of these rights is, of course, the right of a people to govern themselves. The very definition of democracy requires that people choose their own rulers and that officials govern with the consent of the governed. We have all put this special emphasis on free elections because they are irreplaceable. A thousand excuses are offered for the failure to hold free elections by rulers who fear that the people in an election would take from them their power. We reject these excuses; they do not represent the views of the citizens of any country, and we must forcefully deny the right of anyone to speak in the name of a people unless he has been freely chosen by that people.

But free elections are not simply a human rights goal. They are also the means which will guarantee that other human rights are also respected. They are, one can say, a catalyst which can transform a political system. Human rights violations are not accidents; they do not come out of nowhere. Many factors can cause the violation of human rights, but the most important is the political system. If you look around the world, you see that democracies tend to have the best human rights practices. Communist regimes and military dictatorships tend to have the worst. This is why free elections should be the very heart of the human rights movement.

Other human rights goals such as an end to physical brutality by the police, or an end to torture, or the right to form free trade unions, can sometimes be gained for a moment without a system of free elections. But without free elections, these gains are ephemeral: they can disappear as quickly as they appeared, for they come only as the gift of the rulers to the ruled. Free elections shift power from the rulers to the citizenry. Thus, respect for human rights becomes not a gift from an enlightened Prince or President or Prime Minister, but a demand which the people enforce through their right to elect those who will govern them.

Too often, in the struggle for human rights, we have reacted rather than acted. That is, we have been concerned only to respond to an abuse of human rights when it occurs, by some form of sanction against the human rights abuser. This is right and we must continue to do it; but we must do more. In our own thinking about human rights, we have come to view as more and more important work which can establish democratic institutions and practices so that human rights abuses can steadily be eliminated. There is an old saying that when you give a man a fish you feed him for a day, but when you teach him to fish you feed him for a lifetime. There is a lesson here for human rights: when we react to an abuse, or pressure a ruler into eliminating a particular abuse, we have helped protect people for a day; but when we help establish a system of free elections, we are helping to protect a people for their lifetime.

This is much more difficult, and all of us, from the experience of our own countries, know it. But we also know that without free elections other human rights can never be guaranteed, for the people lack the ability to replace those who subvert their rights with others who protect them. This emphasis on the spread of democratic systems was inaugurated by President Reagan in his speech to Parliament in June,[10] and his support for this policy remains strong. Free elections are at the core of his human rights policy.

It is this very fundamental significance of free elections for the protection of human rights which teaches us that we must insist on utmost care when we speak about free elections. Every country must have its own forms that meet the requirements of liberty

---

[9] Source: Office of Public Communications, Bureau of Public Affairs, Department of State. Abrams spoke at the Mayflower Hotel in Washington, where the final day of the conference was held.

[10] For the text of Reagan's June 8, 1982, address before the British Parliament, see document 4.

under its own conditions. These fundamental requirements are that the people freely choose the officials who will carry on the tasks of government for them, and, through their representatives, make the laws they will obey. Thus it is sometimes necessary, if the people are to have true participation and to know it, that there be a federal system; in other places it is not necessary. Likewise, liberty may require a system of proportional representation or single-member districts. Special protection for minorities may be necessary. The best forms depend on circumstances; most of you are far better equipped to judge these complex matters than I am. But the varying forms of liberty are all on one side of the great divide separating democracy from despotism. Modern convenience sometimes tries to ignore this divide, maintaining that there can be participation without elections, or that elections in one-party states can be free. These are excuses. We must face the fact that where there are not multiple parties and multiple candidates, there are no free elections. And where there are no free elections, there is no liberty. This is why we are here. We know also how difficult it can be to make the transition to free elections. This can require a variety of practices. But let us never confuse practices aimed at facilitating the transition to free elections, with practices aimed at frustrating that goal. Let us never accept the fraudulent elections which we see in so many countries, as a substitute for letting the people speak. Let us never accept excuses offered in the name of a people when that same people are locked into silence.

There are many abuses of human rights and there are other fundamental rights besides free elections.

But we have chosen in this conference to concentrate on free elections because all of us know that they are fundamental and irreplaceable in the protection of human rights. We look forward to continuing efforts in the international community to allow more and more peoples to taste this fundamental freedom, to choose those who will govern them, and to secure thereby their own liberty.

C. Refugees

Document 132

Statement by the Assistant Secretary of State for Counsular Affairs (Asencio) Before a Subcommittee of the Senate Judiciary Committee, January 25, 1982,[1]

Proposed Change in Immigrant Numbers

Mr. Chairman, if you will also permit me to submit my remarks for the record[2] and give you a very quick summary.

. . . .

As Mr. Nelson indicated, we have proposed a single change in the existing system of numerical limitations, and we do not propose any changes in the preference system. We believe that this proposal, which should be considered in conjunction with the rest of the President's program,[3] will supplement the tools with which this Nation can begin to address the multiple problems posed by illegal immigration.

As Mr. Nelson mentioned, we propose to establish separate limitations of 40,000 each on immigration from our two continental neighbors, Canada and Mexico, and there would be provision for the unused portion of either of the two 40,000 limitations to be used by natives of the other country. The increased limitations for Canada, and particularly for Mexico, would reflect our close relationships with both while providing an additional opportunity to reduce or deter illegal immigration by opening a supplementary channel for legal entry into the United States.

Other than this one change, we are opposed to further changes in the overall

---

[1] Source: *Numerical Limits on Immigration to the United States: Hearing Before the Subcommittee on Immigration and Refugee Policy of the Committee of the Judiciary, United States Senate, Ninety-seventh Congress, Second Session* (Washington, 1982), pp. 8–9.

[2] For the text of Asencio's prepared statement, see *ibid.*, pp. 10–13.

[3] For the text of Alan C. Nelson's statement, see *ibid.* , pp. 2–8. Nelson was Commissioner, Immigration and Naturalization Service, in the Department of Justice. Regarding the Reagan administration's immigration policy, see *American Foreign Policy: Current Documents, 1981*, Chapter 8, Part B.

systems of limitations. Total legal immigration has three components: immediate relatives and special immigrants, preference and nonpreference immigrants, and refugees. Two of these are already subject to numerical limitations. Preference and nonpreference immigrants are subject to a fixed annual limitation, now 270,000. Refugees are subject to the limitation established annually by the President after consultation with the Congress, and the immediate relatives and special immigrants are not subject to a numerical limitation.

With respect to refugees, the Department believes that the existing provisions of law are appropriate and should be retained. The system provides for adequate control over the number of refugees who are actually admitted each year without imposing a rigid ceiling which could inhibit the President's ability to respond to changing foreign and domestic circumstances.

In sum, we believe that the establishment of an absolute ceiling would produce an excessive rigidity in our immigration system. Such a rigidity might be necessary if the figure for the absolute limit were arrived at through scientific analysis. This has not been done, to my knowledge, and I am not certain that it can be done.

Thank you, Mr. Chairman.

Document 133

Statement by the Secretary of State (Haig) Before the National Governors' Association, February 22, 1982 (Extract)[4]

"America Has Not Been Callous"

. . . .

I would like to say a word about immigration. I understand that your task force—and I heard the report here this morning—has recently adopted a policy statement on the matter, and a report of your task force on immigration and refugees was of great interest to me this morning.[5] I know that Senator Simpson, Chairman of the Senate Subcommittee on Immigration and Refugee Policies, discussed this with you yesterday.

These are especially anguishing problems and indicative of the problems we face in today's world. Since 1975, millions of men, women, and children have been forced to leave their homes in Asia, Africa, the Caribbean, and Central Europe. Most of them have fled to avoid Communist repression and aggression.

Our approach is to begin by assuring temporary and secure asylum so that the United States [*Nations*] High Commissioner for Refugees and concerned governments may work an appropriate solution to their particular situation.

With the active support of the United States and other countries, notably Pakistan, most of the African and Afghani refugees have either returned to their homeland or been granted the opportunity to stay where they are. When these solutions are not possible and where we have determined we have a special interest in a particular refugee situation, we have followed our time-honored tradition of granting refuge in this country to the victims of political persecution.

In these instances we have worked closely with like-minded members of the international community—principally the democracies throughout the world—to assure that this burden is shared equitably. For example, in the tragic situation of the Indochinese, this country has resettled 570,000 refugees since 1975, and I would admit to a heavy burden for you, Governor (to Governor Ariyoshi).

Other countries have settled 585,000. So we are not callous, as America has not been callous, and we continue to urge them and remind them of their obligations. I know of your concerns over the financial consequences for the state of refugee resettlement, especially in these times of austerity. Secretary Schweiker understands your problems and is doing what he can to alleviate them.

For our part, I also wish to assure you that in dealing with the refugee crisis over-

[4] Source: Department of State Press Release 75, February 23, 1982. Haig spoke at 11:40 a.m. at a luncheon held in the Hyatt Regency Hotel in Washington.

[5] Reference is to the four-page statement on refugee and immigration policy prepared by the Committee on International Trade and Foreign Relations of the National Governors' Association in February 1982.

seas, the staff of the Department of State is fully cognizant of the economic, financial and social implications of refugee resettlement in this country. Incidentally, Governor (to Governor Clements), we very much welcome the advice and interchange with the State Governors who have been so heavily burdened by this problem. None of us has a monopoly on wisdom, and cross exchange of ideas and solutions is invaluable and indispensable.

As representatives of a large segment of the American people, I urge you to support the President's July initiative[6] which is entirely consonant with the wishes of a large majority of our citizens to regain control of America's borders once again in a manner that is both fair to ourselves and to those whom we would have come to live with us.

We must be careful not to disadvantage people from any area of the world and to avoid damage to our relations abroad as we deal with these difficult and sensitive issues.

. . . .

Document 134

Statement by the Coordinator for Refugee Affairs, Department of State (Douglas), Before the House Foreign Affairs Committee, March 16, 1982[7]

Immigration and Refugee Resettlement Policy

Thank you, Mr. Chairman, members of the committee. I am pleased to appear with my colleagues before the committee this morning.

This is my first appearance before the House Foreign Affairs Committee, and I hope it is the beginning of a long and productive relationship.

As you have noted, Mr. Chairman, accompanying me this morning are Commissioner Alan Nelson, of INS; Ambassador Richard Vine, of the State Department's Bureau for Refugee Programs; on the far left Mr. Joseph Wheeler, the Deputy Administrator of the Agency for International Development; and Dr. Phillip Hawkes, Director of the Office of Refugee Resettlement at the Department of Health and Human Services.[8]

Before providing an overview, I thought that since this is my first appearance, I would say a few words about some of the priorities that my office is looking at at the moment. Our first goal is to preserve America's tradition as a country of opportunity for refugees and immigrants, recognizing there are practical limits to the number of refugees this country can accept at any given time.

My principal objective as the U.S. Coordinator for Refugees will be to address what I consider an urgent need for a new domestic and international balance in our refugee policy. I think we must find this new balance that will continue to be generous in allowing immigrants and refugees into the country, but will more successfully reflect the available domestic resources at the time.

I intend to work very closely with both Houses of the Congress, with the Governors, with the mayors and State and local officials and the private sector to accomplish this goal. I have said consistently since coming into the office that I want to find out firsthand how the resettlement of refugees over the past 5 years or so has affected our local communities, and to that end I intend to travel to those states most heavily affected.

Next week for example, I will be meeting with Governor Graham down in Florida on the Cuban and Haitian problems there.

I would like now to turn briefly to our foreign policy concerns. Our first concern is that forced migration will be with us for a very long time to come. This migration is the product of outside invasion, of civil wars, repressions, and corrupt regimes. Though repression and persecution may surface on the right as well as on the left of the political spectrum, it is an indisputable fact that the major refugee problems in the world today are being caused by Marxist-

---

6 For the text of Reagan's July 30, 1981, announcement of the administration's immigration and refugee policy, see *American Foreign Policy: Current Documents, 1981*, document 134.

7 Source: *Domestic and Foreign Policy Implications of U.S. Immigration and Refugee Resettlement Policy: Hearings and Staff Reports Before the Committee on Foreign Affairs, House of Representatives, Ninety-seventh Congress* (Washington, 1983), pp. 80–82.

8 For the text of Chairman Zablocki's remarks, see *ibid.*, pp. 65–66. For the text of Nelson's remarks, see *ibid.*, pp. 96–98. For the text of Vine's remarks, see *ibid.*, pp. 85–86. For the text of Wheeler's remarks, see *ibid.*, pp. 103–105. For the text of Hawkes' remarks, see *ibid.*, p. 114.

Leninist regimes, and to demonstrate that, let me very quickly call the roll: Afghanistan, with 2½ million refugees; Indochina, 1⅓ million refugees—somewhat less than one-half of them have been or probably will be resettled in the United States—Ethiopia, more than 1 million refugees driven from their homes in that country by a government bent on implementing a Marxist-Leninist style of government; the Soviet Union—the number of Soviet Jews released by the Soviet Union for resettlement has fallen from about 25,000 in 1979 to a projected 6,000 this year; Poland, a story very much in the headlines, a trickle of refugees which could become a flood; Cuba, 1 million refugees, most of them middle class in their country in the 1960's and again in the eighties, the first of the sixties' baby boom; Central America.

Perhaps a few more words on that, for today we are witnessing a turmoil caused by a foreign-induced subversion which could precipitate a whole new tide of refugees into this country. This could be a far more difficult refugee problem for us to manage than those in the past, because of the geographic location of the countries involved and the fact that our southwest border provides easy entry into the United States.

The persistence of these situations carries several important implications for our foreign policy. First, recognizing the refugees are a destabilizing element, particularly for hard-pressed countries of first asylum, it is incumbent upon the United States and other democracies to bear down on countries creating mass exoduses. Still, we have no illusions about the risks and difficulties of persuading other countries to cease the forcible ejection of their citizenry, but we feel very firmly the need to face this is here.

Our second concern is the long-term outlook for the international organization network, chief among them the United Nations High Commissioner for Refugees; the Intergovernmental Committee for Migration; UNRWA, the organization that cares for Palestinian refugees; the World Food Program; and the International Committee of the Red Cross. These organizations have for many years coped with the problems of providing protection and assistance to refugees worldwide. Their business has burgeoned, and we are concerned about their ability to perform the necessary services and to gain the necessary funding in the future.

The third area of our foreign policy concerns, we are convinced—as is the High Commissioner—is the ideal resolution to the refugee problems is voluntary repatriation, but even when this is not possible, it is vital that assistance to countries of first asylum and to third countries be rapid and effective.

Our programs in this area will be explained in Mr. Wheeler's testimony.

Finally, the nurturing of a stable middle class is essential to the ultimate stabilization of the international system. This conviction has already taken concrete form in the President's recent Caribbean Basin Initiative.[9]

Turning to the domestic implications for our refugee policy, we must recognize that, first, by the very act of admitting refugees to this country, we assume a certain level of responsibility for their successful integration into a new culture and our society. At the same time, it is vital that the minorities and the truly needy of this country not perceive refugees as a permanent privileged class of immigrant.

In other words, it is essential in our view to balance the special needs of the refugees with the ongoing needs of our own citizenry. I am convinced that regardless of the progress which we have made in the last several years, our domestic resettlement obligation is deserving of a hard analytical look. We must address some of those major problems, the high dependency rate of certain refugee groups; placement issues; community tensions; and the questions of equity, to mention only a few.

As our other various refugee communities grow in strength and number, I will heed the lessons of the past that immigrants traditionally have helped themselves.

It seems to me well to remember that throughout our history, but particularly in the early decades of this century, when we experienced our largest migrations, national and ethnic associations developed which eased the economic and psychological burdens associated with entry into a new society. New groups now, such as the Indochinese Mutual Assistance Association, are voicing a wish to assume an expanded role for their expatriots. I think we should encourage this and help them do so.

One of my first priorities will be an immediate look at how the Federal Government can help strengthen and to some extent reinvigorate our private resources,

[9] Regarding the Caribbean Basin Initiative, see Chapter 15, Part C.

and how the American welfare system can play the most positive role in giving temporary financial support to refugees seeking that self-reliance.

Mr. Chairman, members of the committee, I have touched several of the major topics presently receiving attention by my office and by the American refugee community within the administration. I will be pleased to answer any questions you may have, and yield now to my colleagues.

Document 135

Prepared Statement by the Director of the Bureau of Refugee Programs, Department of State (Vine), Before a Subcommittee of the Senate Appropriations Committee, May 20, 1982[10]

Fiscal Year 1983 Migration and Refugee Assistance Appropriation Request

It is a pleasure to appear before you today to present the Department of State's request for $419 million for the FY 1983 Migration and Refugee Assistance appropriation. Accompanying me are James N. Purcell, the Senior Deputy Assistant Secretary of the Bureau for Refugee Programs, and Frank Moss, the Director of our Office of Program and Budget Planning.

Before discussing the outline of our budget request, I would like to introduce myself and to bring the members of the committee up to date on the key international refugee relief and resettlement policies being pursued by the Department of State.

I am a career Foreign Service officer. During my career I have had a variety of assignments involving European Affairs, including serving as Deputy Assistant Secretary for the Bureau of European Affairs, and during the previous administration as U.S. Ambassador to Switzerland. I have been with the Refugee Programs for about 6 months.

Concerning the philosophy of our program, a principal State Department policy is to favor solutions to refugee problems that minimize the number of persons resettled in this country. While we cannot deny our special concern and responsibility for refugees from certain areas, we recognize that refugee problems are an international concern and should be resolved where at all possible by voluntary repatriation and resettlement in countries of first asylum. Given this international responsibility, we continue to hold the view that the responsibility for refugee assistance and resettlement is to be shared by the international community as a whole through the services of international organizations, especially the United Nations High Commissioner for Refugees (UNHCR). The UNHCR received the 1981 Nobel Peace Prize in recognition of its efforts to deal with international refugee problems. As a major donor, it is our responsibility to press for continued programmatic and operational improvements in this organization so that it can meet the basic needs of refugees for protection, food, shelter, and medical care while other, more lasting solutions to their plight are being worked out.

The budget request before you is a concrete expression of this philosophy. Whereas, in FY 1980 over 60 percent of our expenditures were for resettlement in the United States, only 38 percent of the FY 1983 budget request is directed towards U.S. resettlement. The number of refugees to be resettled in the United States has fallen from over 210,000 in FY 1980 to an FY 1982 consultations level of 140,000 and to a projected total of only 103,500 in the coming fiscal year. At the same time, we are increasing the proportion of our funding for programs which assist refugees in nations of asylum and for programs of voluntary repatriation and of resettlement in third countries which have not traditionally been engaged in resettlement.

I would like to emphasize, however, that the downward trend in admissions is being managed in a way that is consistent with the humanitarian traditions of the United States and with U.S. responsibilities for refugees of particular concern to the United States. At the same time, we are continuing to provide support for the protection, care and maintenance of refugees abroad, in accordance with the level of need and with U.S. foreign policy interests in the particular program area.

---

[10] Source: *Foreign Assistance and Related Programs Appropriations for Fiscal Year 1983: Hearings Before a Subcommittee of the Committee on Appropriations, United States Senate, Ninety-seventh Congress, Second Session* (Washington, 1983), Part 1, pp. 1024–1031. Vine spoke before the Subcommittee on Foreign Assistance and Related Programs.

Mr. Chairman, the State Department fully understands the significant impacts that refugee resettlement have on some communities in this country. It is our intention to continue to manage refugee resettlement to this country in such a fashion that the concerns of State and local governments are fully considered. We do not accept the faulty premise that the only viable solution to refugee situations is resettlement in a third country, chiefly the United States. We will continue to pursue other alternatives which promise to help resolve refugee situations in a humanitarian manner.

The FY 1983 request for the Migration and Refugee Assistance appropriation totals $419 million, $84 million less than the FY 1982 appropriation. Recently, the President has requested that FY 1982 funding for this program be reduced by $50 million. This proposal was made because of major cost savings in our refugee resettlements program—resettlements to the United States are running lower than the FY 1982 consultations level provides and the enacted appropriation finances. The Department is requesting a supplemental for protective security improvements for American diplomats at selected overseas posts. Because that supplemental and the deferral of refugee appropriation funds coincide, the President proposed to the Congress that transfer authority language be enacted to mitigate the financing of the protective security supplemental. If that language is not enacted, the administration will request a rescission of these funds at a later date.

For U.S. resettlement activities in FY 1983, we are seeking $158,188,000 to finance the resettlement of up to 103,500 refugees, including 72,000 from Southeast Asia. I must stress that this level of refugee admissions is only a projection. The President will determine the admission ceiling after consultations with the Congress prior to the beginning of FY 1983, as required by the Refugee Act.[11] Furthermore, due to such uncertainties as the situation in Eastern Europe, refinements of these admission projections may be required. However, it is my expectation that, unless the refugee situation in the world changes fundamentally between now and when we have our consultations in September, the total admissions ceiling will not exceed this figure, which is 36,500 persons lower than that for the current fiscal year.

Among the 31,500 refugees other than Indochinese, we have projected admissions of 23,000 Soviets and East Europeans, 4,000 from the Near East, 2,000 from the Western Hemisphere and 2,500 from Africa. We are, of course, concerned about the current situation in Poland, and the levels of admissions which we request in September will take into account all factors relevant to this problem.

With respect to funding of relief assistance for refugees, the Department of State is seeking $29,400,000 to support refugee relief operations in Southeast Asia. These funds will support the care and maintenance operations of the UNHCR, as well as the international efforts to care for the 200,000 Khmer who have sought sanctuary along the Thai-Kampuchean border. This finding level is $20,435,000 less than that appropriated for FY 1982, reflecting continued reductions in the number of Indochinese refugees in Southeast Asia, as well as a reduced food program inside Kampuchea. We expect a phase-out of extensive multilateral assistance to the interior of Kampuchea by FY 1983.

The next activity in our budget is resettlement assistance. This program request is a concrete expression of the interest of the Department of State in resolving refugee problems through means other than resettlement in the United States. We are seeking $10 million for this program in FY 1983, an increase of $9 million above the FY 1982 appropriation. The program will finance various voluntary repatriation, local resettlement and third country resettlement projects. It is our expectation that programs funded under this initiative will be organized under the auspices of international organizations or private voluntary agencies. Among the innovative activities funded will be projects involving local permanent settlement in nations of asylum, as well as initiatives to resettle refugees in certain developing nations which are willing to accept refugees for permanent resettlement, but which would be unable to do so without international financial support. These programs are intended to help reduce the number of refugees requiring resettlement in the United States.

The State Department is seeking $12.5 million, the same amount as appropriated in FY 1982, for a contribution to the United Israel Appeal. The contribution will help finance assistance to Soviet and Eastern European refugees who resettle in Israel. Regrettably, the Soviet Union continues to reduce the rate of emigration for its Jewish

---

[11] The reference is to P.L. 96–212, approved on March 17, 1980; for text, see 94 Stat. 102.

citizens, but this program continues at this level in recognition of the long-term costs incurred by Israel in caring for refugees who have arrived in recent years.

For assistance to refugees in Africa, the State Department seeks $76.9 million, which is $30,100,000 below the FY 1982 appropriation. This decrease is accounted for by the one-time appropriation of $30 million to the Migration and Refugee Assistance Appropriation in FY 1982 for longer-term projects to aid refugees and displaced persons in Africa. It was recognized that such longer-term projects are properly the responsibility of the Agency for International Development. In fact, the Congress specified that the FY 1982 appropriation be administered by AID.

Within the $76.9 million that we are requesting for the Africa program, we will continue our current policy of financing one-third of the UNHCR's program in Africa, and will make a $7.9 million contribution to the African programs of the International Committee of the Red Cross. We will also provide up to $8 million for a variety of bilateral and voluntary agency initiatives to address those aspects of refugee problems that are not adequately dealt with by the involved international organizations.

Refugee assistance is provided by this government for both humanitarian and political purposes. These concerns are clearly combined in the Middle East where we are confronted with the human needs of the Palestinians and the Afghans as well as the worldwide political and economic implications of those problems. In order to deal with the needs of the Palestinians, the Department of State is seeking $72 million as a contribution to the United Nations Relief and Works Agency for Palestine Refugees in the Near East (UNRWA). This organization, which provides basic services to the nearly 2 million Palestinian refugees, contributes towards a political atmosphere within the Mideast which is conducive to the long-term peace process. The proposed UNRWA contribution, an increase of $5 million over the FY 1982 appropriation, will help UNRWA deal with the effects of inflation and a constantly increasing population.

The Afghan refugees in Pakistan comprise the largest refugee population in the world. The Government of Pakistan is currently providing asylum to well over 2 million refugees who have fled Afghanistan into Pakistan during the past 3 years. Thousands of refugees continue to flee from Afghanistan because of the ongoing fighting between Soviet forces and the Afghan resistance. Pakistan, I must add, serves as an outstanding example of a nation meeting its international responsibility to provide asylum to refugees. Pakistan has willingly granted asylum with the expectation that the international community will finance the care and maintenance of the refugees, a program expected to require approximately $110 million in FY 1983.

The Department of State requests $38 million to meet our share of this relief effort. Up to $33 million will be provided to the UNHCR to meet 30 percent of the cost of its care and maintenance program. The remaining $5 million will finance a variety of initiatives to meet essential health, relief and transportation needs not addressed through the UNHCR's program. Medical care for persons injured in the fighting in Afghanistan provided by the International Committee of the Red Cross (ICRC) is one example. The $5 million will be used to finance grants to the ICRC, private voluntary agencies and possibly the Government of Pakistan.

Latin America, until recently, was one of the few areas of the world not confronted with a major refugee problem. However, continuing civil disturbances in Central America are forcing increasing numbers of persons to flee across international frontiers to escape fighting and persecution. The Department of State is requesting $5 million to help meet the costs of the international efforts to provide assistance to refugees in Central America. These funds are $1 million less than the amount appropriated in FY 1982 due to nonrecurring costs in the 1982 program. However, given the volatility of the political situation in Central America, these needs are particularly difficult to project. It is clear that we must keep this problem under close review as events unfold.

The State Department requests $9,450,000 in FY 1983 for contributions to various activities of international organizations, an increase of $1 million over FY 1982. We propose to provide a total of $4.7 million to the Intergovernmental Committee for Migration (ICM) in support of that organization's assessed and operational budgets. We will also provide $3.75 million to the ICRC in support of the ordinary budget of the organization and the Political Detainee Protection and Assistance Program. In the case of the ordinary budget we will provide $2 million, an increase of $500,000 above the amount provided in the current year. We are seeking $1,750,000 as a contribution to the Political Detainee Protection and Assistance Program. Previously, U.S. contributions to this activity were obtained through reprograming of other funds in this appropriation. However, because of the importance of this program as an expression of concern by this administration for political prisoners, we are including this item in our FY 1983 appropriation request. We are also seeking $1 million, the same amount appropriated in FY 1982, to support programs of the UNHCR in areas of the world other than those dealt with in the geographic segments of this budget.

The administrative expenses of this program are expected to increase to $7,562,000 in 1983. This is a net increase of only $136,000. This request will finance the salary and operating costs associated with our staff of 98 permanent employees.

This budget request does not include a request for new funding for the United States Emergency Refugee and Migration Assistance Fund. Unobligated carryover balances available in that fund should be sufficient to finance appropriate responses to refugee and migration emergencies during FY 1983.

Mr. Chairman, as you are well aware, refugee situations frequently change between the time that this budget is developed and the new fiscal year. Should any such changes occur affecting our 1983 appropriation, we will attempt to reprogram funds to meet the higher priority needs. I wish to thank this subcommittee for its support during the past two years for our reprograming efforts in order to reallocate our funds to meet new and changing requirements.

This brings me to the end of my prepared remarks. I, and my colleagues, will be pleased to answer any questions you may have.

Document 136

Address by the Assistant Secretary of State for Human Rights and Humanitarian Affairs (Abrams) Before the Tiger Bay Club, Miami, June 2, 1982[12]

Human Rights and the Refugee Crisis

As you know, I am in charge of the Bureau of Human Rights and Humanitarian Affairs. As you may not know, in that capacity I am charged with overseeing for the State Department the granting of asylum to people from all around the world who seek asylum in the United States. Both responsibilities—human rights and the asylum aspect of U.S. immigration policy—obviously give me a great deal to do with Latin America and the Caribbean. What I want to do today is talk about our human rights policy and our foreign policy, and, I hope, help explain our views on a number of problems which face south Florida.

Our human rights policy is, basically, easy to explain: We try to improve the respect for human rights in countries around the world, so that we can improve the lives of the people who live there and so that we continue to make clear America's historic commitment to the cause of liberty. Of course, this is easier said than done, for the problem of human rights violations around the world is profoundly complex. The causes of human rights problems vary from race (as in South Africa) to religion (the Ba'hai in Iran), to factional strife (as between Christians and Muslims in Lebanon), to a wide variety of usually military dictatorships. And the kinds of human rights violations vary from denial of free elections to elimination of the free press or freedom of religion, to arbitrary arrests, to torture and murder.

Needless to say, each situation calls for different tactics for an American effort in the area of human rights. Furthermore, our tactics will vary depending on our relationship with the country in question: whether it is a friend or a foe, whether there exists between us distant relations or a dense network of ties. The tools we use range, of course, from straight diplomatic discussions, to public denunciations, to U.N. votes, to denial of economic or military assistance, and so on.

---

[12] Source: Department of State *Bulletin*, September 1982, pp. 43–45.

Often this administration is accused of doing too little for human rights or of "coddling" friendly regimes while we attack enemies. In fact this accusation is false. We use whatever we think will be the most effective tactic. Where we have good diplomatic ties, common sense tells us to use them. Where we do not have friendly relations, but a regime is very sensitive to its public reputation, we find that public discussions and criticisms are most effective, and we use them—as in the case of the Soviet Union. Our goal, in every case, is to be effective, not to give good speeches but to have a good effect in the real world.

If we are to achieve our human rights goals, it is clear that American power and influence are essential. Few governments around the world are greatly moved by preaching from the United States or anyone else. They change their behavior when American power, American assistance, American commitments, persuade them that it is in their interest to do so. Above all, the intangible force of the American example as a successful example inevitably affects the willingness of other countries to pay attention to our concerns on human rights. The Reagan administration has, it is correctly noted, improved relations between our country and such countries as South Africa and South Korea. It is our view that isolating these countries, driving them away from us, would do nothing but decrease our influence there. Our ability to obtain our goals, including our human rights goals, is sufficient only when America is understood to be an important force.

Thrown into the many complexities I have mentioned is another major one—the role of communism and Soviet power. Why do I single out communism and the Soviet bloc countries, among all the world's dictatorships?

First, because once a Communist government is established, the Soviets make sure that it endures permanently. No efforts by the people of that country will be allowed to win them freedom, as we have just seen in Poland. Unlike Greece or Spain or Portugal, which were dictatorships but are now free, today Communist countries are not permitted to leave the grasp of the Soviet Union and seek freedom.

Second, Communist dictatorships are aggressive. Compare Paraguay and Nicaragua, or Haiti and Cuba, or North Vietnam with the now disappeared South Vietnam. Communist countries not only destroy the human rights of their own population but threaten to export repression to their neighbors and around the world. Most recently we have seen this in Afghanistan, and even now Cuba and Nicaragua are engaged in a massive supply of arms to fuel subversion in Central America.

Third, Communist regimes are incredibly brutal. Let me take but one example. The French group, Doctors Without Frontiers, has sent doctors to Afghanistan to help injured Afghans. They have reported, and these items have been published in several of the leading journals in Paris, that the Soviets drop small mines from planes. They don't explode on landing, but only when picked up by a passerby. They are made to look like matchboxes, and some to look like children's toys. The French doctors report that much of their work in hospitals on the border of Pakistan is surgery performed on children who have lost limbs. And of course, even now the Soviet Union is providing chemical and biological weapons to its proxies and allies in Afghanistan and Southeast Asia—the infamous yellow rain which is outlawed by international treaty and by any sense of human decency.

Obviously, we must take care in our human rights policy to make situations better and not worse. South Vietnam under General Thieu, or South Korea today, present serious human rights problems, but they are as nothing compared to their Communist alternatives. We want to be very sure that in a situation such as that in El Salvador, we do not trade the serious but solvable human rights problems of today for a permanent Communist dictatorship. Resisting the expansion of communism is a key human rights goal.

And here again, American influence in the world is essential to our goals. A strong, confident, vigorous America will be able to help countries resist Soviet subversion. And it will provide a powerful alternative model of a successful, confident people whose freedom leads to prosperity and unity. Needless to say, economic and military strength are essential elements in this picture, which is why President Reagan is determined to restore both.

Now the relevance of all this to the refugee flows you have seen here in south Florida, and to the greater ones you may fear is, I think, clear. People do not flee free, prosperous countries. The largest refugee flows of recent years have come from Indochina and Afghanistan, where, quite simply, people are fleeing communism. The same is true of Cuba. Perhaps the greatest source of refugees throughout history has been, not natural disasters, but misgovernment. When governments have destroyed people's rights and freedoms, and have destroyed the economy, people have voted with their feet.

Our response to the refugee problem of today and the potential problems of tomorrow is necessarily complex. Neither we nor any other wealthy country can accept all of the refugees and immigrants who come to our borders. Neither can we accept immigrants who will constitute a servile class, a class of permanently unequal people such as exists in many countries around the world. Yet our response must have in it a substantial amount of humanitarianism, and we are bound (by international treaty and our own law) to grant asylum to genuine refugees who reach our shores.

But humanitarianism alone will not enable us to deal with a ruler such as Fidel Castro, who with unbelievable cynicism uses his own people as a weapon against foreign countries. He shoots streams of refugees at nearby countries in the way a cannonball is shot out of a cannon. Think of the cynicism, think of the viciousness, of a ruler who would take mentally retarded people and drag them off and shove them into boats to be sent away from their home country. Our foreign policy must make it clear that such behavior is simply unacceptable to us and will not ever again be tolerated.

It is obvious, of course, that this country has many immigration problems that have nothing to do with communism, such as the problem of Haitian migrants you face here in south Florida. But our experience has shown that the most serious refugee problems have political causes and—even more important—that these refugee problems develop much more suddenly than those that have their origin in poverty. Compare the steady flow of migrants from Haiti to the sudden waves from Cuba. Thus they present us with a challenge that the international community has trouble preparing for ahead of time.

In fact, it is Communist rule that has caused the greatest refugee flows of recent years. We can, therefore, have a very firm notion of what the expansion of communism to El Salvador and Guatemala would mean. It has the potential to create a Southeast Asian refugee crisis right here on our doorsteps. Indeed, we have every reason to think that the expansion of communism in Central America would create this kind of incredible problem. I am always amazed when people come to me to voice their concern about refugees from El Salvador, yet who oppose the administration's effort to avoid enlargement of that refugee problem by giving El Salvador the aid it needs to defeat Communist-led guerrillas.

Obviously, the problem of migration and refugee flows is enormously complex, and we must address it in a number of ways. One way is economic assistance. It will help in cases such as Haiti, where poverty leads people to leave home, and it will help in the long run to reduce the opportunities that those seeking political disorder can exploit.

Another way is military assistance. Such aid is essential, for the Soviet Union, through Cuba and now Nicaragua, is deeply engaged in promoting and arming subversion in our hemisphere. If we do not help those who wish to fight and defend themselves, then chances of success are greatly diminished. And if they fail, we can predict that many of their countrymen will flee to our shores.

A third way is our human rights policy, where we seek, by the pressure of America's military and economic power and its reputation in the world, to advance the cause of liberty. We seek to bring about political reforms within many friendly countries, and it is an essential part of this policy to oppose the expansion of communism. In a world of democracies, where human rights were respected, refugee flows would virtually disappear.

A fourth way is our effort to stop the illegal flow of aliens to this country. This involves an improvement in our own enforcement mechanisms, including most recently the interdiction program now in effect with regard to Haiti.

Finally, our laws do not, and none of us would wish them to, exclude all aliens. We have been accepting 800,000 immigrants a year, and we have an active asylum program. When someone who is truly fleeing persecution comes to us, we do not want to send him or her back to the land where the persecution occurred. We cooperate through the U.N. High Commissioner for Refugees, the Red Cross, and other international organizations to help the international community deal with refugee flows. And, of course, we do our share in taking care of the world's refugees. We do so financially, and obviously, as in the case of Indochinese and Cubans, we meet our responsibilities and take a leadership role in the international community.

There is one thing that ties all of these efforts together. There is one thing that will help our human rights policy succeed, help friendly governments resist subversion, help create a safer international climate, and help avoid the creation of new refugee flows. It is, quite simply, American influence. There was a time after the Vietnam war when some Americans came to believe that American power was a force for ill in the world, not for good. I believe most Americans have now come to realize this is a false and dangerous view. Anyone who is seeking to promote and defend freedom, anyone who is wondering whether the future will bring economic and political progress in the Caribbean Basin or will bring more subversion, more violence, more poverty, and more refugee flows, will surely understand that American strength is the essential ingredient. A panacea? No, of course, for the world is not that simple. But let us not be deluded by false complexities. This country remains the greatest friend of freedom in the world, and wherever we go—as with Germany and Japan after the Second World War—we attempt to instill democratic values. An expansion of Communist influence in the Caribbean Basin will inevitably create greater refugee flows. As we know, communism combines political repression with economic failure. It is the perfect recipe for the creation of refugees, and we have only to look at the world around us to see that that recipe has worked only too well.

So for you here in south Florida concerned about the potential refugees of the 1980's and 1990's, for those dealing with human rights issues and concerned about how to promote democratic values and procedures abroad, for those concerned about the fate of liberty in the world at large, let us recall again the common thread that links these issues together: a prosperous and strong America, an America willing to maintain its military strength and willing to make clear to friendly nations and to foes the strength of our values and our commitment to defend them.

Document 137

Prepared Statement by the Attorney General (Smith) Before a Subcommittee of the Senate Judiciary Committee, September 29, 1982[13]

Refugee Consultations

Thank you very much, Mr. Chairman.

As is usual in this area, we subscribe to nearly everything you have just said.[14] As a matter of fact, I should say that we subscribe to everything that you have said, as will be shown, from my remarks here.

I am pleased to appear before the committee today to discuss the administration's proposals for refugee admissions in fiscal year 1983. The discussions today, and over the next weeks, occur in a season of this Nation's life when our country's ability to accept foreigners to our shores, whether as immigrants or refugees, in a rational and humane manner has by some been called into question. This Nation's generous instincts, borne of the immigrant past we are proud to recall, has in some quarters yielded to skepticism and doubt. In large part these concerns arise from the evident fact that we have failed to control illegal immigration to this country. And losing control of our borders to the illegal immigrant has thrown a cloud over legal immigrant and refugee admissions.

This committee has over the past 2 years thoughtfully and comprehensively addressed the questions of illegal migration, asylum, and legal immigrant admissions. The fruit of that effort, the Immigration Reform and Control Act of 1982, passed the Senate on August 17 by the overwhelming bipartisan vote of 80 to 19.[15] Broadly similar to the legislation submitted by the administration 1 year ago, the reform bill will permit this country again to have control of our borders, by deterring illegal migration and regulating legal immigration within fair and realistic limits. This bill, of which the committee and especially Senator

---

[13] Source: *Refugee Consultation: Hearing Before the Subcommittee on Immigration and Refugee Policy of the Committee on the Judiciary, United States Senate, Ninety-seventh Congress, Second Session* (Washington, 1983), pp. 3–6.

[14] For the text of Chairman Simpson's statement, see *ibid.*, pp. 1–2.

[15] For the text of S.2222, which passed the Senate on August 17, 1982, see *Congressional Record*, August 17, 1982, pp. S10619–S10631.

Simpson, whose name has become synonymous with immigration reform, can be justly proud, is in the finest bipartisan tradition of the Congress.

As you know, under the able guiding hand of Chairman Rodino, H.R. 6514,[16] the companion bill in the House, was last week reported favorably by the House Committee on the Judiciary. We must now seize the moment and enact this most important reform legislation before the Congress adjourns. There are few issues of greater importance now facing our people.

We meet today to consult concerning a different, but as I have noted, a closely related subject—refugee admissions to the United States.

When I appeared before the committee last year,[17] I stated the importance that the administration attached to these consultations, carried out under a still new law whose efficacy was yet not fully tested. I want to commend the committee for the thoroughness and understanding with which it has pursued its responsibilities under the Refugee Act.[18] I can say without hesitation that administering the act has depended critically on this committee's discharge of its consultative role.

I would hope also that we in the administration have demonstrated over the course of the year our commitment to true collaboration with the committee, both in setting admissions ceilings and in administering this important program. Others here with me today will report more fully on the past year's progress and challenges that remain, but on behalf of the President, I want to thank you for your most able work.

Regrettably, continued conflict in and among nations has left the world with sustained refugee problems that continue to implicate important humanitarian, foreign policy, and domestic concerns of the United States. The President's proposed refugee admissions reflect our best judgment concerning these sometimes competing considerations. Moreover, as I reported to you last year, in reviewing our program of refugee resettlement, we have thoroughly assessed alternative means of assisting international relief efforts. These include the possibility of voluntary repatriation to the refugee's country of origin, resettlement in a country of first asylum, and resettlement in a third country other than the United States. As a last resort, we admit our fair share of the world's refugees, as part of a genuine international effort.

This is not to understate the important humanitarian and foreign policy interests served by our refugee admissions program. There are certain refugees who are of particular concern to the United States, either by virtue of previous association with this country, of relatives who are already here, or for other reasons. The admission of such persons is the subject of our discussions today.

The U.S. Coordinator for Refugee Affairs and the three agencies charged with administering the refugee program—the State Department, which manages the overseas processing and initial reception and placement of refugees in the United States; the Department of Health and Human Services, which administers the domestic assistance aspects of the program and the INS which interviews and approves each applicant for refugee admission to the United States—have all been working together to insure that the goals of our refugee program be met. These goals are: that the principle of first asylum be preserved; that refugees admitted to this country qualify under the definitions and criteria established in the act; and that those resettled in the United States achieve integration and independence within our society as quickly as possible.

In addition, the administration has been particularly concerned with another aspect of coordinating refugee policy among our various agencies—that equal weight be given the domestic resources available to resettle refugees before deciding upon our admissions recommendations to the Congress. We think our proposals for refugees this year meet these requirements.

This year the President has recommended the admission of up to 98,000 refugees for resettlement in the United States for fiscal year 1983.

Foreign policy and humanitarian considerations have led us to propose that this number be divided among the appropriate geographic regions in the following manner: 3,000 refugees for Africa; 68,000 refu-

---

[16] For a summary of H.R. 6514, see *ibid.*, May 27, 1982, p. H3040. This bill, which was supposed to complement S.2222 above, was not acted on by the House of Representatives in 1982.

[17] For the text of Smith's September 22, 1981, statement, see *Annual Refugee Consultation for 1982: Hearing Before the Committee on the Judiciary, United States Senate, Ninety-seventh Congress, First Session* (Washington, 1982), pp. 8–15.

[18] The reference is to the Refugee Act of 1980, P.L. 96–212, approved March 17, 1980; for text, see 94 Stat. 102.

gees for East Asia; 17,000 refugees for Soviet Union and Eastern Europe; 8,000 refugees for Near East and South Asia; and 2,000 refugees for Latin America and the Caribbean.

In addition to the proposed admissions, the Immigration and Naturalization Service will consider adjusting to permanent resident status up to 5,000 persons who are granted asylum in the United States and have been in the United States for at least 1 year, pursuant to title II, section 209(b) of the Refugee Act of 1980.

I wish to stress that the proposed refugee admissions numbers are ceilings and not a quota. We propose to admit up to that number of refugees, but it is certainly possible that the final number admitted for fiscal year 1983 may be less than 98,000. The underlying principle is that refugee admissions to the United States is an exceptional discretionary act by the United States for those who have no alternatives. It is not the right of a refugee to be admitted to the United States simply because a program has authorized spaces available.

Before turning to my colleagues to make their presentations, I would like to make several points concerning the proposed refugee admissions.

First, as in the past several years, refugees from Southeast Asia will continue to claim the largest share of our potential admissions in 1983. While Ambassador Douglas will elaborate on this point,[19] I would note three conditions justifying this still extraordinary level:

First. The continued repression accompanying the violent reorganization of the Indochinese societies still forces large numbers of person to flee persecution;

Second. Southeast Asian refugees have among the strongest ties to the United States of any refugee population;

Third. Owing to ethnic and cultural animosities in the region, they are among the least accepted in countries of first asylum; and the inability of the first asylum countries to absorb these refugees would result in major foreign policy problems if this situation is not addressed.

In comparison, the proportion of refugee admissions allotted to the countries of Latin America and Africa reflect a positive circumstance—the hospitality and generosity with which these countries accept and care for refugees.

Second, I wish to reiterate that one of the major concerns of this administration is that refugees admitted to this country become independent as soon as possible, and that we do not admit more refugees than our domestic resources permit. With the high levels of refugee admissions in recent years, considerable domestic difficulties have arisen in the resettlement process, accompanied by increasing levels of dependence on cash assistance. Additionally, the refugee admission levels have important budgetary implications both for the Federal Government and for State and local entities as well. This is a matter of concern and careful attention by all concerned agencies and by the President. Proposed admission levels have been set as low as possible in light of urgent foreign and humanitarian policy considerations.

Third, I want to assure the committee that steps have been taken in the course of the last year to insure that the definition of "refugee" contained in the Refugee Act is being administered in a rigorous and evenhanded manner.

As you recall, the question whether certain refugee applicants satisfied the act's definition has been a subject of considerable discussion both within the administration and with the Congress. After reviewing the act and its legislative history, I determined that refugee applications must be reviewed on an individual basis, and determinations made only after such a case-by-case inquiry. Following periodic consultations with this committee and after interagency discussions, guidelines were issued to govern refugee processing and to guarantee their uniformity worldwide.

Fortunately, Mr. Chairman, many refugee problems can be resolved without the resettlement of large numbers of people in third countries like the United States. The development of effective international relief organizations has encouraged countries to continue offering first asylum and to permit humane care for refugees until voluntary repatriation or local settlement is possible.

We expect, however, that the number of refugees in the world will continue to grow in the coming decade of this century.

Resettlement in the United States or other third countries is not the answer to the refugee problem. It is only a partial

---

19 For the text of Douglas' statement, see *Refugee Consultation*, pp. 90–91.

solution of last choice. We must continue to put pressure on those countries who create refugees, and who expel large numbers of their own populations in an effort to forestall change or eliminate political opposition.

This administration is committed to a humane refugee policy, but also recognizes that large-scale migration and resettlement will not solve the injustice and suppression of human rights that is the root cause of massive refugee problems we are seeing in the world today.

In closing, Mr. Chairman, I want again to stress the importance that the President attaches to these recommendations. Certainly, our Nation faces serious problems of both legal and illegal immigration. This administration and this committee take these problems seriously and have acted vigorously concerning them. At the same time, the admission of refugees under the collaborative control of the Refugee Act, though a small part of the overall immigration picture, is a major element in the U.S. leadership of the free world.

The administration is committed to preserving our Nation's traditions of tolerance and freedom, and our willingness to accept to our shores those fleeing oppression. And thus we welcome the opportunity to consult with you under the terms of the act that reflects those enduring principles.

Mr. Chairman, with me today, to join in responding to any questions that you may have, are Kenneth Dam, the Acting Secretary of State; David Swoap, Under Secretary of the Department of Health and Human Services;[20] and Gene Douglas, the U.S. Coordinator for Refugee Affairs.

As you know, our refugee program is thoroughly interdisciplinary, reflecting a host of foreign relations and domestic concerns; and I will, if I may, ask my colleagues to join me at this time.

---

[20] Dam's statement is *infra;* for the text of Swoap's statement, see *Refugee Consultation,* pp. 81–84.

Document 138

Statement by the Acting Secretary of State (Dam) Before the Senate Judiciary Committee, September 29, 1982[21]

Proposed Refugee Admissions

Thank you, Mr. Chairman.

As you know, I was confirmed as Deputy Secretary of State just last week[22] so it is a special pleasure for me to have my first open hearing before this committee, because not only am I a lawyer but it is a committee that in private life I have appeared before on a few occasions; so in a sense I feel right at home here.

I am pleased that this is the first subject I have testified on, because I have had some personal and frankly heartrending experiences in this area, not with the formal program but with individual refugees. To me it is an intensely personal question when one talks about refugees. It is also a foreign policy question, and that is what I would like to talk to you about, the foreign policy aspects of this issue.

I have submitted my statement for the record,[23] and I would like to just talk briefly about a few points.

First of all, I do appreciate the opportunity to consult with this committee on a program of such vital concern to our foreign policy. The program is a measure of our compassion. It is in the nature of our country to be concerned about the refugee problem. It is also very important in the foreign policy arena where the refugee program makes an important contribution to world stability and to our foreign policy objectives.

The suffering—the human suffering—that arises from refugee problems is a serious threat to stability in many parts of the world and frankly a serious threat to peace. We just need to look at the Middle East to see how peace can be threatened by refugee problems.

I think also that the relationship between this country and Southeast Asia has an

---

[21] Source: *Refugee Consultation,* pp. 12–14.

[22] Dam's confirmation hearing before the Senate Foreign Relations Committee will not be published.

[23] For the text of Dam's prepared statement, see *Refugee Consultation,* pp. 16–30.

important dimension, the way in which we have found homes and helped refugees from that area find productive lives in our country.

We are fully aware of the burdens placed by refugee admissions on communities in this country. This is a burden which other countries have shared, where we have, I think, played a particular role of leadership. There are some 7.5 million people in the world that are regarded as refugees. The administration's approach under the Refugee Act,[24] is first of all to seek voluntary repatriation to the country of origin for refugees. Where that is not possible, we seek to find resettlement in the region where the refugees have their own homes. We look to the U.N. High Commissioner for Refugees to take the lead. We help to support the efforts of the United Nations in that respect through voluntary contributions and through our actual physical cooperation with respect to refugees.

The funds that we provide tend to be a way of relieving the burden on our country of the actual admission of refugees, while at the same time relieving the suffering of the individuals involved.

Despite these efforts, it is simply a fact that third country resettlement is the only viable solution in many instances. The neighboring countries where the refugees may first go are not always a place where refugees can escape retaliation of some kind. Often countries are only willing to take refugees for limited periods of time under first asylum principles, and a further third country has to be found for them. It has become a very internationalized activity in the past few years because of these conditions. You mentioned earlier some of the problems that have been faced here in our country by our doing our share in solving this international problem.

Let me talk just a little bit about the numbers, the admission ceilings which we are here to consult with you about. The overall number is 98,000 and, of those, the great bulk come from East Asia. We are recommending the admission of 68,000 Indochinese refugees under these ceilings. The most important country involved is Thailand, a country in which we have a very great foreign policy interest.

The Thais have done a superb job in taking on a very considerable flow of refugees under a first-asylum principle. But it is important for other countries to pitch in and take those people off their hands if they are going to be prepared to continue their practice in this regard. Moreover, Thailand itself has plenty of serious problems, and it is important to keep faith with the Thai people by continuing to ease the burden on them. They are housing a great number of refugees now, and it is essential that we continue to take refugees off their hands to maintain the stability of that country and their willingness to continue to maintain first asylum.

The flow from Thailand has been diminishing and will continue to diminish. It is our judgment that, taking into account other East Asian refugees, 68,000 is the number that we should have for our planning purposes for the coming year.

Another area is the Near East and South Asia. Here the numbers are considerably lower. For the Near East and South Asia, the number is 8,000. The number of refugees there is enormously greater than that, particularly Afghan refugees. At least 2.7 million Afghan refugees are now in Pakistan. We are providing substantial assistance for these refugees, but there are very few Afghan refugees that we anticipate admitting to the United States. We are doing our fair share there of providing aid, but only a tiny percentage of the total number of refugees in that area will be coming to the United States.

I have already referred to the Palestinian refugees and the funding that has been used in that area. In Lebanon, in particular, we have now earmarked $39.5 million for emergency relief and $66 million for long-term reconstruction. The reconstruction of Lebanon is an important issue, and I am now talking about the current situation with regard to funding.

Smaller numbers are proposed for Africa and Latin America; 3,000 for Africa and 2,000 for Latin America. Somewhat larger numbers are recommended for Eastern Europe and the Soviet Union. We contemplate for Eastern Europe, other than the Soviet Union, about 11,000, which would include about 8,000 Poles. About 6,000 are proposed from the Soviet Union, the great bulk of whom would be Jewish.

In connection with these numbers, we plan to try to strengthen our domestic program by attempting to distribute these refugees more evenly throughout the United States, and by trying to promote self-sufficiency through employment and, in gener-

---

[24] The reference is to the Refugee Act of 1980, P.L. 96–212, approved March 17, 1980; for text, see 94 Stat. 102.

al, to do whatever we can to ease the strains that resettlement places on the refugee and on the host communities.

Our refugee programs play a vital role in our foreign policy at the same time that they continue a humane tradition which I believe all Americans have a right to take pride in. We believe that these proposals are, as the Attorney General said,[25] ceilings; they are not quotas. At the same time, they represent our judgment as to the minimums that is [are] needed if we are to encourage continued efforts of other countries. I believe that they are not unduly high and that they take full account as we must of the great burdens that are placed upon our States and communities by the refugee program.

In short, I believe that the proposed levels are prudent and they are balanced. I hope that in this consultation we can discuss these matters, and that in the end, we will have your concurrence.

Thank you.

Document 139

Memorandum From President Reagan to the Coordinator for Refugee Affairs, Department of State (Douglas), October 11, 1982[26]

Presidential Determination No. 83–2

Subject: FY 1983 Refugee Ceilings

Pursuant to Sections 207(a) and 207.1(a)(3) and in accordance with Section 209(b) of the Immigration and Nationality Act (INA),[27] after appropriate consultations with the Congress, I hereby determine that:

—the admission of up to 90,000 refugees to the United States during FY 1983 is justified by humanitarian concerns or is otherwise in the national interest;

—the 90,000 refugee admission ceiling shall be allocated as 64,000 for East Asia; 15,000 for the Soviet Union/Eastern Europe; 6,000 for the Near East/South Asia; 3,000 for Africa; and 2,000 for Latin America/Caribbean; and

—an additional 5,000 refugee admission numbers to be available for the adjustment to permanent residence status of aliens who have been granted asylum in the United States is justified by humanitarian concerns or is otherwise in the national interest.

Pursuant to Section 101(a)(42)(B) of the INA and after appropriate consultations with the Congress, I hereby specify that special circumstances exist such that, for the purposes of admission under the limits established herein, the following persons, if they otherwise qualify for admission, may be considered refugees of special humanitarian concern to the United States even though they are still within their countries of nationality or habitual residence:

—persons in Vietnam with past or present ties to the United States; and

—present and former political prisoners, and persons in imminent danger of loss of life, and their family members, in countries of Latin America and the Caribbean.

You will inform the appropriate committees of the Congress of these determinations.

This memorandum shall be published in the *Federal Register*.

RONALD REAGAN

Document 140

Statement by President Reagan, October 22, 1982[28]

Immigration of Amerasian Children

This is a happy occasion, I think, for all of us here. Today I'm signing into law

---

[25] See Smith's statement, *supra*.

[26] Source: Department of State *Bulletin*, December 1982, p. 61. Copies of this memorandum were also sent to Secretary of State Shultz, Attorney General Smith, and Secretary of Health and Human Services Schweiker.

[27] The reference is to the Immigration and Nationality Act, enacted June 27, 1952 (P.L. 82–474; 66 Stat. 163), as amended on September 21, 1961 (P.L. 87–256; 75 Stat. 535), and on October 7, 1978 (P.L. 95–126; 92 Stat. 992).

[28] Source: White House Press Release, October 22, 1982, Office of the Press Secretary to the President; printed also in *Weekly Compilation of Presidential Documents*, October 25, 1982, pp. 1374–1375. President Reagan spoke at 2:34 p.m. in the Roosevelt Room of the White House.

legislation that comes to grips with a problem that I think should touch every American's heart.

During the last three decades when tens of thousands of our airmen, soldiers and Marines and sailors went to Southeast Asia and Korea to prevent aggression and protect the vital interests of our country, a number of Amerasian children were born.

And when the fathers returned to the United States, far too often innocent children were left without parent or without a country. Through no fault of their own, these children have frequently lived in the most wretched of circumstances and often have been ostracized in the lands of their birth.

Today it gives me great pleasure to sign Senate Bill 1698,[29] a major step toward facing up to the moral responsibility that we can't ignore. This good and humane law—and it is that—recognizes the rightful claim of Amerasian children to American citizenship and permits their entry into our country after arrangements have been made for their care with families or with private organizations.

The sponsors of the legislation, Senator Jeremiah Denton and Congressman Stuart McKinney, deserve a special word of thanks for their efforts to reunite these children with those who will love and care for them. And also my thanks to Father Alfred Kean who worked so hard for this bill. And really he brought it to the government's attention. Now he is not here, but his sister Judy is here, and with her are Julie and Scott Tripp, the adopted children of her sister, and we also have Eddie Chey and Jeannie Choi, who are students at Gonzaga University in Spokane. I'll bet they found out already that that is where Bing Crosby was a student.(Laughter)

Americans have always opened their hearts to those coming from distant lands to make a new life here, to live in freedom and to improve their lot. In this case I think we should go a step further. Instead of saying welcome to these children, we should say welcome home.

And now I am going to sign this bill and make it official.

(The President signs the legislation.)

And I do so with a pen that can only write one word to make sure that it is the only place—And there it is. It is all legal. (Applause)

[29] The reference is to P.L. 97–359, approved October 22, 1982; for text, see 96 Stat. 1716. This legislation amended the Immigration and Nationality Act.

D. Terrorism

Document 141

Remarks by President Reagan, January 18, 1982[1]

"Terrorism is the Hardest Thing to Curtail"

Q. What about the shooting, Mr. President? What about the killing of the American?[2] Is there anything we can do about these outbreaks of terrorism, or are we just helpless?

The President. Well, I think terrorism is the hardest thing to curtail. As a matter of fact, I've said for many years that probably the only defense you have against terrorist attacks is really infiltration to try and find out in advance what their plans are. And in the last few years that's been made more difficult. We're doing our best to try and correct something like that.

Q. Why would anyone want to shoot an obscure lieutenant colonel? What's the advantage?

The President Well, why would anyone want to just park a car with a bomb in a street where they don't even know the people that are going to be killed and blow them up? That's exactly why they have the word "terrorist." Their belief is—there isn't a motive in the individual that they're killing. The great, senseless cruelty and tragedy of it is simply to create terror by making people generally feel unsafe.

Q. Is there enough international cooperation on this issue of terrorism, Mr. President, between countries to try to stop it?

[1] Source: *Weekly Compilation of Presidential Documents,* January 25, 1982, p. 35. President Reagan spoke in the Oval Office at approximately 1:15 p.m. at the beginning of a meeting with Mike Mansfield, U.S. Ambassador to Japan.

[2] The reference is to the assassination of U.S. military attaché Lieutenant Colonel Charles Robert Ray in Paris on January 18, 1982.

THE PRESIDENT. I would say that there is. We've been having the greatest cooperation with Italy so far.

Q. Is General Dozier still alive, in your belief?[3]

DEPUTY PRESS SECRETARY SPEAKES. Thank you.

THE PRESIDENT. What?

Q. General Dozier? Is he still alive?

THE PRESIDENT. We don't know.

Document 142

Statement by the Chairman of the Interdepartmental Group on Terrorism (Sayre) Before a Subcommittee of the House Appropriations Committee, March 18, 1982[4]

Interdepartmental Group on Terrorism

I appreciate this opportunity to testify on behalf of a new program which is the major element of the President's program to combat and deter international terrorism. Specifically, we are requesting authorization, a $5 million appropriation, and five positions for a program of antiterrorism training and assistance for foreign officials.

The objectives of this program are to:

Enhance the law enforcement antiterrorism skills of friendly countries; strengthen our bilateral ties with friendly governments by offering concrete assistance in this area of great mutual concern.

Enhance cooperation in antiterrorism with the developed countries by cultivating ties between their officials involved in combating terrorism and those in the U.S. Government.

Increase respect for human rights by foreign civil authorities by exposing them to modern and humane methods of effective preventive antiterrorism techniques.

Enhance the ability of foreign governments to protect U.S. overseas missions from terrorism attacks.

Contribute to the safety of Americans traveling overseas by lessening the likelihood that they will be caught up in an act of international terrorism such as aircraft hijacking.

The problem is that terrorism has been increasing since 1968. The number has increased from 142 in 1968 to 709 in 1981.

The number of attacks against diplomats have increased from 80 in 1968 to 409 in 1981.

The United States has been the principal target of international terrorist attacks; about one-third have been against American targets. Five American Ambassadors have been murdered in terrorist attacks, more than the number of U.S. Generals killed in action in Vietnam. The murder of Colonel Ray in Paris and the kidnapping of General Dozier are two recent attacks against Americans.[5]

Nor has American business abroad been spared. Between 1968 and 1980 there were 901 attacks against American business executives or facilities.

Some 91 countries have been the target of international terrorist attacks.

MR. LONG. When they get around to Congressmen, I will agree the problem has reached disturbing proportions.

MR. SAYRE. What do we plan to do? Provide training for key civil officials of interested governments. They would include senior police, civil aviation, immigration and other offícals responsible for urban and national civil administration. We plan to concentrate, at least at the beginning of the program, on training of officials who are responsible for crisis management in participating governments.

Based on the participating government's evaluation of its own specific needs, we would provide more specific training for middle manager level officials. For instance, we could offer to train the actual hostage negotiator, the officer directly responsible for airport security, or the official who

---

[3] Regarding the kidnapping and release in Italy of U.S. General James Dozier, see document 230.

[4] Source: *Foreign Assistance and Related Programs Appropriations for 1983: Hearings Before a Subcommittee of the Committee on Appropriations, House of Representatives, Ninety-seventh Congress, Second Session* (Washington, 1982), Part I, pp. 283–285. Sayre spoke before the Subcommittee on Foreign Operations and Related Agencies.

[5] Regarding the assassination of Colonel Ray, see President Reagan's remarks, *supra*. Regarding the kidnapping and release of General Dozier, see document 230.

would be the on-site policy commander for an incident, such as the seizure of an Embassy.

How do we plan to do this?

We intend to provide this training at existing Federal institutions in the United States, using the expertise of several domestic agencies. Primary facilities to be used are the FBI Academy at Quantico, Virginia; the Federal Law Enforcement Training Center at Glynco, Georgia, and the Transportation Safety Institute at Oklahoma City, Oklahoma.

In addition to providing training, we hope to provide some related equipment to complement specific training. For instance, passenger screening equipment for airports might be offered in connection with an airport security course.

With respect to the assistance aspect of the program, training and equipment transfers would be made on a grant or sale basis, depending primarily on the financial situation of each participating country.

The training and advisory services provided by other U.S. Government agencies would be on a reimbursable basis agency-to-agency, with State funding the full additional cost of the services.

On the countries to participate, we do not have a list to suggest today. We consider countries which face a terrorist threat, actual or potential, are committed to participate in combating terrorism; wish to cooperate bilaterally with the U.S. against terrorism; and have a human rights record compatible with U.S. legislative criteria.

We intend to consult with the Congress on the list of countries which we believe meet these criteria, if Congress approves this program. In succeeding years, we would expect to provide Congress with an annual report of participating countries, plus a lot of potential participants for the following year. I would like to emphasize that this program will be completely open and unclassified.

This program will be administered by the Department of State, in a manner similar to training activities conducted in connection with the International Narcotics Control Program.

We intend to provide additional staff to the State Department's Office for Combating Terrorism, which will be the focal point for the Department's management responsibilites.

I would like to submit the whole statement for the record,[6] but those are the high points of what I wanted to say.

Document 143

Address by the Chairman of the Interdepartmental Group on Terrorism (Sayre) Before the Third International Civil Aviation Security Conference, July 21, 1982[7]

U.S. Policy and Organization for Combating Terrorism

Political violence and terrorism are not new. They have been with us since the dawn of recorded history. What is new is the speed with which people and ideas move. You can be in Washington tonight and Paris tomorrow morning. You can sit at your television set and have a front-row seat at the world soccer matches in Madrid. An assassin can attempt to kill the President of the United States on the streets in Washington or the Pope on the streets in Rome, and the television networks will bring the event to you simultaneously and in living color. Political terrorism used to be a national event that seldom had ramifications beyond national borders. Now any attack against any prominent figure or against a commercial aircraft or against an embassy is an international media event. Our ability to travel and communicate rapidly has made it so. Terrorism is international, and, as many say, it is theater.

I would like to be able to tell you that we are doing as well on controlling political violence generally as you are doing in controlling terrorist attacks against commercial aviation. But you are, in a sense, fortunate because you can put people and baggage through a single checkpoint. You can, of course, still be and are the victim of human errors and poor procedures. You have done a remarkable job, at considerable expense, to maintain your safety record.

---

[6] For the text of Sayre's prepared statement, see *Foreign Assistance and Related Programs Appropriations for 1983*, Part I, pp. 285–288.

[7] Source: Department of State *Bulletin*, August 1982, pp. 1–5, 7. The address was given in Washington.

Unfortunately this is not the case for political violence and terrorism generally. We have no way of running all terrorists through a checkpoint or x-raying their baggage. Their methods of attack are myriad, they are clandestine, and they are elusive. They frequently change the names of their organizations and their passports, recruit new faces, send old faces off to different parts of the world, and generally try to confound and confuse the police and security organizations that governments create as defensive mechanisms.

The number of actual terrorist acts increases daily. Every day that passes brings to my desk in the Department of State a new batch of reports about planned terrorist attacks or attacks actually carried out. Diplomats are once again the principal target; and American diplomats are particularly high on the list of victims or intended victims. Some 15 percent of the operating budget of the Department of State goes to pay for protection of our personnel and facilities overseas, and the cost is rising. So while I would like to tell you that the situation is getting better, I must honestly and candidly tell you that it is getting worse. What are we doing about it?

In truth, our problems are not that much different from yours. We have a worldwide operating network and so do the airlines. The difference may be that we are in almost every country, sometimes in several places, whereas your networks are not as extensive. That is a difference in degree and not substance.

We must have an international consensus, and cooperation on security threats to our operation, and so must you.

We must have an understanding with individual governments on how terrorist attacks against us will be handled and so must you. There must be an understanding within our organizations from the President to the security man in the field on how we will react, both in a policy and operational sense, and I am certain that is the case with the airlines.

The first action required of the Reagan administration was a clear and unequivocal statement of policy.

At the very beginning of this administration, President Reagan, in welcoming the Tehran hostages home, articulated U.S. policy on terrorism. He said: "Let terrorists be aware that when the rules of international behavior are violated, our policy will be one of swift and effective retribution."[8]

[8] For the text of the President Reagan's January 27, 1981, statement, see *American Foreign Policy: Current Documents, 1981*, document 139.

We have publicly and repeatedly noted that the United States, when faced with an act of terrorism at home or abroad, will take all possible lawful measures to resolve the incident and to bring to justice the perpetrators of the crime. This policy is based upon the conviction that to allow terrorists to succeed only leads to more terrorism; if they are successful, they will be encouraged to commit more such acts.

We firmly believe that terrorists should be denied benefits from acts such as hostage-holding or kidnapping; thus the U.S. Government does not make concessions to blackmail. We will not pay ransom or release prisoners in response to such demands.

When a terrorist incident occurs outside the United States, we look to the host government to exercise its responsibility to protect persons within its jurisdiction and to enforce the law in its territory. During such incidents, we consult closely with the responsible government, and we offer all practical support to the government concerned.

When a terrorist incident against us is sponsored or directed by a nation, as an instrument of its own policy in an attempt to intimidate or coerce us, we will take all appropriate measures—be they diplomatic, political, economic, or military—to resolve the incident and to resist this form of international blackmail. So the United States has a clearly stated policy.

But a policy is no better than the determination or will to carry it out and the organization established to do so. The problem is international, so the first question is, how effective and determined is the international community?

International organizations, including the United Nations, have sponsored a number of multilateral conventions which deal with particular terrorist crimes to bring them within the criminal law. The United States has strongly supported these efforts over the years.

The most widely accepted conventions are The Hague convention against hijacking and the Montreal convention against aircraft sabotage,[9] which are now

[9] For the text of the Convention on the Suppression of Unlawful Seizure of Aircraft (Hijacking), signed at The Hague on December 16, 1970, and entered into force on October 14, 1971, see 22 UST 1641. For the text of the Convention on the Suppression of Unlawful Acts Against the Safety of Civil Aviation (Sabotage), signed in Montreal on September 23, 1971, and entered into force on January 26, 1973, see 24 UST 565.

adhered to by over 100 states. The international community, through these conventions, has established the principle that aircraft piracy and sabotage, like the maritime piracy they so closely resemble, are universally abhorred international crimes.

Other conventions dealing with additional aspects of the terrorism problem are the New York convention on crimes against internationally protected persons, the Convention Against the Taking of Hostages, and the Convention on the Physical Protection of Nuclear Materials.[10] These agreements establish the obligation among states party to them to submit for prosecution or extradition those alleged to have committed particular crimes.

The United States strongly supports the principle established in these conventions that those who commit terrorist crimes should be brought to justice in accordance with the law, and we continue to urge other nations to become parties to these important agreements.

The United Nations has also considered the effectiveness of the New York convention on attacks against diplomats and other internationally protected persons. The Secretary-General has invited member states to submit reports this year for consideration by the United Nations on actions they have taken to carry out the convention. We welcome this continuing focus on attacks on diplomats which now account for more than half of all terrorist attacks.

In addition to these efforts in the international organizations, the economic summit seven—the United States, Canada, France, the Federal Republic of Germany, Italy, the United Kingdom, and Japan—enunciated a course of action against hijacking. In 1978 the heads of state and government of these seven nations adopted a declaration against hijacking.[11] It was a commitment to take joint action by terminating air service to states which fail to live up to their obligations under The Hague convention on hijackers. Last year the Bonn declaration was implemented against Afghanistan for its conduct during and subsequent to the hijacking of a Pakistani aircraft in March 1981. The United Kingdom, France, and West Germany, the countries of the summit seven with bilateral air service with Afghanistan, gave notice that air links would be terminated this November. We continue to monitor the actions of countries during hijacking incidents and will urge such actions in future cases where it would be appropriate.

At the bilateral level, we have consulted many countries on sharing information on terrorists and their plans. Such exchanges occur systematically, but we need to do more to assure that all members of the world community are aware of specific dangers. I wish to take this opportunity to assure you that when the United States learns that a terrorist act is being planned in any country around the world, we immediately inform the appropriate authorities of the country involved so that innocent lives may be saved. We do not and will not hold back such information. We hope that other countries will adopt a similar policy.

We have also discussed the coordination of policy responses to terrorism. We have urged other countries to adopt a policy similar to ours to deny terrorists the benefits they seek from their crimes and to bring the full force of law enforcement measures to bear on them.

Consultation and coordination of policies are only part of the solution. We have recently submitted legislation to the U.S. Congress which would authorize a program of antiterrorism assistance for foreign government law enforcement personnel. The Congress is now considering this proposal. If authorized, this program would enable us to offer training in antiterrorism security and management skills at our training facilities and to provide equipment, such as security screening devices for airports. Once legislation is passed, we will be contacting selected countries about the possibility of participation in this program. We consider this program as a way to assist countries that may want to learn our techniques of dealing with terrorists. But we also see it as an opportunity to learn by exchanging experiences with all countries that have been victims of terrorist attacks.

As I stated early in my remarks, a principal target of terrorists is the diplomat. Ter-

---

[10] For the text of the Convention on the Protection and Punishment of Crime Against Internationally Protected Persons, Including Diplomatic Agents, signed at New York on December 14, 1973, and entered into force on February 20, 1977, see 28 UST 1975. Neither the International Convention Against the Taking of Hostages, adopted at New York on December 17, 1979, nor the Convention on the Physical Protection of Nuclear Material, with annexes, done at Vienna on October 26, 1979, have been published to date.

[11] For the text of the Joint Statement on International Terrorism issued by the participants in the July 1978 economic summit meeting held in Bonn, see Department of State *Bulletin*, September 1978, p. 5.

rorists have recently turned their attention to foreign diplomats in the United States. We are, therefore, strengthening the protection we provide to foreign diplomats. We have introduced new legislation which will enable the Department of State to carry out its responsibilities more effectively and efficiently in cooperation with State and local authorities. We are hopeful that the Congress will act promptly on this proposal.

Although we have a strong set of policies and laws on terrorism agreed to by the international community, the international community has not been as successful in working out arrangements to give effect to these policies and laws. The countries in Europe have their own working arrangements, and there are occasional conferences such as this one. But multilateral cooperation is extremely limited. If the world community is serious about combating terrorism, then it needs to give more attention to working arrangements that will do that. For its part, the United States stands ready to cooperate to the fullest extent.

Unfortunately there are states which are directly involved in carrying out international terrorist acts. There are also states which find it in their interest to provide arms, training, and logistical support to terrorist organizations. Another problem, then, is that the community of nations needs to face forthrightly the fact that some of its members are promoting terrorism and others have a certain sympathy for terrorist organizations and condone what they do because they are of the same political philosophy and consider terrorism as an effective way to undermine their adversaries.

What is the U.S. Government doing in both its operations and organizations to carry out the strong policy enunciated by President Reagan?

First, I am sure that you would agree that a key to dealing with the terrorist threat is good intelligence. We have recently strengthened significantly our ability to collect, analyze, and use intelligence on terrorism. We have also taken steps to improve the exchange of information with our friends and allies.

It is one thing to have intelligence; it is another to get policy officers to act on it. We have made organizational changes that improve our alert system and response capability. Certainly, on the intelligence side, we are in much better shape today than we were a year or two ago.

Second, soon after the Reagan administration assumed office, it created an Interdepartmental Group on Terrorism—most of you would say interministerial—to serve as the policy formulation and coordination body for the government. It is composed of representatives of Federal agencies with direct responsibilities for combating international terrorism. I am the chairman of that group. Since its inception, it conducted a complete review of U.S. policy and proposed several initiatives. One of the gaps that needed to be filled was a clear operational arrangement to provide support to the President and other key decisionmakers during a major terrorist incident. This has been remedied, and we believe that we are now better organized to get prompt policy guidance so that we can respond swiftly and effectively to a terrorist incident.

The possible use of force to resolve an incident is another important aspect of our response capability. In the United States, most major cities have SWAT teams. Each district of the Federal Bureau of Investigation (FBI) has its own SWAT team. The rescue missions which were conducted at Entebbe, Mogadishu, and the Iranian Embassy in London last year, as well as a number of aircraft incidents, emphasize the need for an effective assault capability. The United States has dedicated military forces for such a purpose. Although we consider the use of force in resolving a terrorist incident a measure of last resort, it is important to have these capabilities should they be needed.

To many of you, terrorism is a domestic problem and you may wonder why the foreign office would head the Federal Government group on terrorism. The answer is quite simple: For the United States, most of the terrorist incidents have been directed against our diplomats or American interests overseas. The Department of State is the "ministry" in the United States most directly affected and best able to respond. We do have terrorist incidents in the United States and when they occur, it is the responsibility of the Department of Justice to take the lead and respond. As all of you attending this conference know, when it is the unique case of an aircraft, it is the responsibility of our Federal Aviation Administration (FAA).

As you might expect, the Department of State has taken many steps over the years to improve our security, especially overseas. We are now engaged in major improvements to many of our embassies which will provide better protection to both personnel and physical facilities. Some 15¢ out of every $1.00 the Department spends on operations is for security. So it is no small matter to us. And other governments which have the responsibility for protecting American Embassies are spending again collectively as much as we do. It is my responsibility to assure that we recommend security policies and programs that provide a prudent level of protection. We are doing that.

We believe we have in place the policies, programs, and organization to deal with terrorism, but we are fully aware that there is much more to be done.

The international community must continue and strengthen its efforts to cooperate more fully on terrorism. The international organizations in particular—the United Nations and the regional organizations—might consider additional conventions to outlaw terrorist tactics, such as assassinations and bombings, and bring these additional tactics under the "prosecute or extradite" obligation. The international community must give special emphasis to working arrangements that will give full effect to these policies and conventions. We are hopeful that we can implement our proposed antiterrorism training program beginning in 1983 and that it will make a significant contribution to more effective working relationships among civil authorities responsible for dealing with terrorism.

Individual countries should redouble their efforts to make clear that terrorism is an unacceptable method for achieving change. No matter what one's ideological preferences, a bomb in a train station or a threat of death against a plane load of civil air passengers is not an acceptable way to bring one's causes to public attention or to overthrow a government. An adequate response requires not only a better intelligence capability so that we are warned of possible terrorist acts, but that the machinery of government is organized from top to bottom so that we act promptly when a terrorist incident occurs. I believe that we in the U.S. Government are now prepared, but it will require constant vigilance, planning, and the exercise of our organizational system to have confidence that we can deal effectively with terrorist incidents.

We must work to establish a world in which peaceful change can occur without violence and terror. We must also be vigilant in our mutual efforts to prevent terrorist attacks. You have a particularly important part to play in prevention. I know that we will continue to work together toward this goal. In that effort, you can be certain that the United States is prepared to be a full and reliable partner.

Document 144

Statement by President Reagan, October 19, 1982[12]

Convention on the Physical Protection of Nuclear Material Implementation Act of 1982

I have signed into law H.R. 5228, the Convention on the Physical Protection of Nuclear Material Implementation Act of 1982.[13]

This step symbolizes our firm commitment both to preventing the spread of nuclear explosives and to fighting the scourge of terrorism. Nuclear proliferation threatens global security, and preventing it is critically important to the United States. Terrorism threatens the fabric of society by indiscriminately aiming violence at the innocent. The commitment of this administration against these global problems has been, and will continue to be, firm and unshakable.

The step I have taken also symbolizes longstanding objectives of the United States people and Congress. The Convention on the Physical Protection of Nuclear Material and the implementing law drew strong, bipartisan support. Such a bipartisan approach is essential for effective action in this area.

The act implements an international convention negotiated at the initiative of the United States and signed in March 1980.[14] This convention calls for adequate physical protection of nuclear material during international transport and for international cooperation in recovering stolen nuclear material and in dealing with serious offenses involving such material. The Senate approved the Convention by 98–0 in July 1981, but deposit of the U.S. instru-

---

[12] Source: *Weekly Compilation of Presidential Documents,* October 25, 1982, p. 1352.

[13] The reference is to P.L. 97–351, approved October 18, 1982; for text, see 96 Stat. 1663.

[14] The reference is to the Convention on the Physical Protection of Nuclear Material, with annexes, signed at Vienna on October 26, 1979. The text has not been published to date.

ment of ratification has awaited enactment of this implementing legislation.

It, too, had overwhelming legislative support. The implementing act amends the Federal Criminal Code to make theft of nuclear material, nuclear extortion, and similar serious offenses involving nuclear material Federal crimes. This fills a gap in U.S. Federal criminal law and establishes jurisdiction over most of these offenses wherever committed, and the offenders are subject to a system of extradition or submission for prosecution. In emergencies, the Attorney General can obtain assistance from the Department of Defense in enforcing the act.

The United States is a leader in the international campaign to prevent nuclear proliferation and terrorism, and the Congress is to be commended for its important contributions in these fields. With respect to the act I have signed, Senators Thurmond, Percy, and Mathias and Congressmen Hughes, Sawyer, Rodino, and McClory, among others, deserve special credit for their efforts. I am pleased that the Congress and the administration are taking this step together.

E. Narcotics

Document 145

Prepared Statement by the Deputy Secretary of State (Stoessel) Before the House Foreign Affairs Committee, April 21, 1982[1]

U.S. Policies on International Narcotics Control

Mr. Chairman: As requested by the committee, I will address policy issues related to international narcotics control. This testimony will complete the review of State Department activities, begun April 21, when Assistant Secretary DiCarlo discussed the programs and strategies conducted by the Bureau of International Narcotics Matters.[2] At that time, Ambassador Boyatt discussed specific policies and programs with respect to Colombia,[3] and, we note that Administrator Mullen discussed the diverse assistance rendered by the Drug Enforcement Administration.[4]

The committee also took testimony from officials of the Justice Department, Treasury, Health and Human Services, the Central Intelligence Agency, and the White House Drug Abuse Policy Office—who provided information on domestic consumption, trafficking, enforcement and prosecution efforts, and other international policy aspects. I will therefore confine my remarks to the responsibilities and policies of the Department of State, although I will note our numerous collaborations with these other U.S. agencies.

Last September, President Reagan said he would establish "a foreign policy that vigorously seeks to interdict and eradicate illicit drugs, wherever cultivated, processed or transported."[5]

The authority for our efforts, which Secretary Haig has affirmed as a high priority for the Department, is Section 481 of the Foreign Assistance Act,[6] which established an international narcotics control function under the direction of the President and the Department of State, on the basis that effective international cooperation is required to eliminate illicit production, trafficking in, and consumption of dangerous drugs.

No nation can cope with drug abuse by relying only on treatment, prevention and domestic enforcement. The supply of heroin, cocaine, marijuana, and other drugs is so great that we simply must reduce production before we can substantially reduce

---

[1] Source: *International Narcotics Control: Hearings Before the Committee on Foreign Affairs, House of Representatives, Ninety-seventh Congress, Second Session* (Washington, 1982), pp. 135–147. Because Stoessel could not attend the hearing, his statement was submitted for the record.

[2] For the text of DiCarlo's oral and prepared statements made the same day, see *ibid.*, pp. 148–186.

[3] For the text of Ambassador Thomas D. Boyatt's testimony, see *ibid.*, pp. 186–191.

[4] For the text of Francis M. Mullen, Jr.'s testimony, see *ibid.*, pp. 191–209.

[5] For the text of President Reagan's address before the International Association of Chiefs of Police in New Orleans, Louisiana, September 28, 1981, see *Public Papers of the Presidents of the United States: Ronald Reagan*, 1981, pp. 839–846.

[6] For the text of section 481 of the Foreign Assistance Act, entitled "International Narcotics Control," which was added to the Foreign Assistance Act of 1971 (P.L. 92–226), see 86 Stat. 21; for the text of section 503 of the Foreign Relations Authorization Act of 1972 (P.L. 92–352), which amended section 481, see 86 Stat. 489.

availability. We must break the grower-to-user chains which stretch across five continents. To do this, we must have a comprehensive program of international control.

The international control function was conferred upon the President, and has been delegated through the Secretary of State to the Assistant Secretary for International Narcotics Matters. I note that the Department of State is the only foreign ministry in which narcotics control has been elevated to the level of a senior policy branch. This function was assigned to the Department of State because the United States believes that other governments should understand that we regard drug abuse as not just a health problem, or an enforcement issue, but as a matter properly integrated into our foreign policy as an issue of government responsibility under international treaties—that should be dealt with as a matter of international obligation and concern.

Accordingly, as the first tenet of its international narcotics control policy, the Department has stressed, through diplomatic and program channels, that each country has the responsibility for demand and supply reduction within its borders.

By virtue of the Single Convention on Narcotic Drugs[7] and the Convention on Psychotropic Substances,[8] signatory nations are required to establish controls limiting the production, manufacture and distribution of scheduled drugs to recognized, legitimate purposes. The Single Convention requires each signatory nation to declare and enforce prohibitions on the cultivation, production and distribution of opium, cocaine, cannabis, and their derivatives. All of the major producer nations are signatories to the Single Convention.

This administration rejects the contention that drug abuse is particularly an American problem, or a problem of Western civilization, and rejects the contention that the United States has the primary responsibility for solving this problem.

We recognize that, because of political and economic considerations, some countries cannot do the job alone, and the second tenet of our narcotics policy is that the international community has an obligation to assist those nations which require help.

As a concerned member of the world community, and as a severely impacted nation, the United States Government supports a program of bilateral and multilateral assistance for crop control, interdiction and demand reduction programs, and we encourage other governments, especially the governments of other industrialized nations, to participate fully in these international control efforts.

As the third tenet of our international control policy, the Bureau is applying more emphasis on crop control at the source in both our bilateral programs and in programs conducted by international organizations which we fund. Current production capability and stockpiles of heroin, cocaine, and marijuana or their base materials, well exceed known consumption. Interdiction through various law enforcement activities is simply not sufficient by itself to reduce availability, given current levels of production.

The fourth tenet of our international policy is that narcotics-related economic assistance, whether rendered by the United States Government or an international organization, should be conditioned on concurrent agreements on control of narcotics production.

There are a number of strategic considerations which link our principal policy positions and our program strategy.

1. While there have been notable achievements in control efforts, success in recent years has been marginal in terms of reducing worldwide availability of heroin, cocaine, and marijuana.

2. Interdiction efforts are not adequate in terms of worldwide effort, given current levels of production and profitability.

3. Comprehensive control programs are not now politically negotiable or operationally feasible in every producer country.

4. Both producer and transit nations are increasingly impacted by domestic drug abuse problems, as are the major industrialized, consumer nations, factors which present improved opportunities for both control agreements and increased international support.

---

[7] For the text of the Single Convention on Narcotic Drugs, signed at New York, March 30, 1961, and entered into force for the United States, June 24, 1967, see 18 UST 1407. For the text of the Protocol amending the Single Convention on Narcotic Drugs, signed at Geneva, March 25, 1972, and entered into force for the United States, August 8, 1975, see 26 UST 1439.

[8] For the text of the Convention on Psychotropic Substances, signed at Vienna, February 21, 1971, and entered into force for the United States, July 15, 1980, see 32 UST 543.

We believe our four fundamental policies—acceptance by governments of producer and transit countries of their national responsibilities under treaties; the need for international assistance from more of the wealthy and industrialized nations; the increased emphasis on crop control; and the insistence on linkage between narcotics-related economic assistance and agreements on reducing production—respond correctly to these strategic considerations.

Let me put these considerations into context.

Our ultimate objective is that production be controlled in all geographic areas, simultaneously.

Our first priority, for both our direct assistance programs and for the projects of international agencies which we fund, is on reducing cultivation and production. Trafficking or interdiction is our second priority, because we are convinced that crop control at the source is the most effective and economical method of reducing supply.

As United States enforcement agencies can confirm, the problems of interdicting drugs in transit are such that only a small fraction is interrupted. Production facilities, financial assets and drug products are highly mobile and cross many national frontiers. Experience has shown that when production declines in one area, drugs from other areas are moved into the market—as has happened with both heroin and marijuana.

However, reductions in cultivation and production through crop control—which can take the form of government bans on cultivation, as in Turkey, or manual destruction as carried out in Peru, or chemical eradication as conducted by the Mexican Government—are very different propositions, country to country, and present different degrees of complexity.

While there have been notable successes in crop control, like Turkey and Mexico, and there are promising control efforts in Peru, Pakistan, and Burma, which we are assisting, the firsthand reality is that worldwide crop control is a long-term objective. The conditions which are considered ideal for mounting and sustaining an effective crop control program include: (1) an awareness of and acceptance by the central government of the national and international impacts of their domestic cultivation and production; (2) a strong central government which has the political will to enforce control and (3) the capability to achieve control of the growing areas; and (4) adequate resources.

With their own material inputs and our resource assistance, Turkey and Mexico met these conditions. But, one or more limitations have to be overcome in other countries. For example, major opium producers like Iran, Afghanistan, and Laos are currently inaccessible politically to the United States. In other instances, like Burma and Pakistan, the central governments do not now have complete control over all the key growing areas. In certain countries, considerations of local economic and political impacts of crop control are such that alternative financial incentives, or control disincentives that create risk for the growers, producers, and traffickers, or both, must be offered before an effective control program can be negotiated or implemented.

Therefore, while the Department believes that crop control should be the end objective sought in all negotiations with producer countries—and we actively seek to assist them in overcoming these limitations, directly or through multilateral assistance, such as United Nations projects—the second reality is that we must have a balanced program of crop control *and* interdiction.

The third reality that must be considered in any assessment of our effort is that the international narcotic control program of the United States—whether the focus be on crop control or interdiction—can only be as effective and comprehensive as are the programs of the governments with whom we negotiate.

The fourth reality is that we face a variety of problems which must be overcome before the problem can be brought under control. I have already mentioned such problems as: the political inaccessibility of certain producer nations; the lack of central government control over growing areas; the political and economic problems encountered by producer and transit nations attempting to exercise control over production and trafficking; and the difficulties inherent in interdiction.

Let me add to our problem list.

First, market profiles change. In just a decade, Turkey, Mexico, and Pakistan have been the major sources, in succession, for heroin entering the United States. While agreements must be negotiated country by country, the control effort must be truly international in scope.

Second, we encounter in dealing with some foreign governments not only a reluctance to accept responsibility for production and trafficking, but we are also challenged by statements that drug abuse is an American problem.

Third, this "American responsibility" syndrome is reflected in international support. It is disturbing to read the list of contributors to the United Nations Fund for Drug Abuse Control and realize that some industrialized and wealthy nations contribute little or nothing to the support of the multilateral international projects sponsored by UNFDAC in critical producer and transit nations.

Fourth, the economics of drug abuse currently favor illicit drug cultivation and production, and present us with some of the most challenging problems. Not only do the profits from the drug trade provide incentives to growers, producers and traffickers, but they impact heavily on local economies in producer and transit nations, as well as the United States, such as in south Florida.

With those realities and problems in mind, I will explain how our principal policies translate into program strategies.

Our diplomatic challenge is to raise international consciousness of the illicit narcotics issue to a level where heightened acceptance of national responsibility becomes an international reality, seen in increased action by affected governments—producer nations, transit nations, and consumer nations.

President Reagan, Vice President Bush, Secretary Haig, the senior officers of the Department, and our Ambassadors are pressing the narcotics issue. They have communicated to the leaders and ministries of key nations the genuine intention of this administration to reduce drug abuse impacts upon the American people. This activity takes many forms—the personal communications by Ambassador Dean to the King and Prime Minister of Thailand; the private talks between Vice President Bush and President Turbay of Colombia; the discussions between Ambassador Corr and Bolivian President Torrelio, the talks Ambassador Boyatt has described with the Colombian Government, and the very recent discussions between the Deputy Secretary and the Jamaican Government. At another level, there are activities such as the recent meetings inaugurated by our Deputy Chief of Mission in Pakistan with key Ambassadors accredited to Pakistan to share information and develop cooperation with the Government of Pakistan on narcotics control.

Assistant Secretary DiCarlo maintains an active continuing dialogue with the leadership of key producer and transit countries. In March, Mr. DiCarlo and Ambassador Corr obtained a commitment from President Torrelio for a coca leaf eradication project in Bolivia which is being developed now. Earlier this year, Mr. DiCarlo met with major donors to UNFDAC to discuss funding priorities and to make explicit the United States position that economic assistance to narcotics producers should be linked to crop reductions. And, the Assistant Secretary and other U.S. officials this year communicated to the members of the United Nations Commission on Narcotic Drugs that we have every intention of urging governments to live up to their commitments—both for their domestic production and trafficking responsibilities and for their support of the international program. There are indications that foreign impacts of drug abuse, human, economic and political, are improving the climate for increased responsiveness by certain governments on both counts.

Because of the diversity of the problems we face, the international effort which State coordinates is a program of many parts. Through our Bureau of International Narcotics Matters, the Department is responsible for coordinating international narcotics activities of the United States Government; for coordinating the Government's international with its domestic activities; for negotiating international agreements; and for ensuring cooperation with the activities of international organizations and foreign governments.

As Dominick DiCarlo and Peter McPherson explained,[9] the Bureau collaborates with the Agency for International Development on economic development projects in such producer nations as Peru, Pakistan, and Thailand. The Bureau works quite closely with the Drug Enforcement Administration on technical assistance and training of foreign professionals—a function in which Customs also participates. The Bureau cooperates with our Bureau of International Organization Affairs in our dealings with United Nations drug control agencies and other international organizations. And, still within the Department, INM's programs are integrated in country policies through close collaboration with our regional bureaus, and with the narcotics coordinators in U.S. Embassies.

---

[9] For the text of the prepared statement by M. Peter McPherson, Administrator, Agency for International Development, submitted for the record in his absence, see *International Narcotics Control*, pp. 209–223.

Secretary Haig is a member of the Cabinet Council on Legal Policy which is addressing the objectives of drug supply reduction. The Secretary is also a member of the South Florida Task Force, chaired by Vice President Bush, which is focused on reducing problems caused by Latin American production and trafficking in cocaine and marijuana.

State and Justice work together on obtaining bilateral agreements on the gathering of information and evidence and rendering it admissible in courts of law in other nations. These two Departments are also negotiating treaties with the Federal Republic of Germany, France, and Italy, similar to the extradition and mutual legal assistance treaties with Colombia[10] and the Netherlands,[11] which the Senate ratified in December. And agreements have been negotiated permitting flag vessels of other nations to be searched if these ships are suspected of transporting drugs to the United States.

Obviously, this diversity of program activity requires close policy coordination. State interacts on narcotics policy development with Justice, Treasury, Commerce, Defense, the Central Intelligence Agency, and other departments through standing and ad hoc committees.

Similarly, State meets regularly with the Oversight Working Group assembled by the White House Drug Abuse Policy Office; these meetings are designed to coordinate the activities of State, Treasury, Commerce, Justice, the National Institute on Drug Abuse, and other agencies involved in both international and domestic drug programs.

In closing, I want to stress certain points.

We have a policy—and we have a strategy, with both short and long-range programs. It is a policy that is designed to ensure that the United States is focusing upon all aspects of the problem internationally—the cultivation, production, and distribution of drugs, the flow of profits, the impacts upon other countries as well as our own, and the development of broad-based, multinationally-supported control programs.

Recent events in several countries, including both new agreements, reductions in crops, and major interdictions, give reason to be optimistic—not that we are solving or eliminating drug abuse—but that we are making significant progress in our more realistic objective of establishing the base for potential control of the production and distribution of major illicit substances. I choose these words carefully; we do not have control, but we have improved the possibility that the world community can gain control.

Document 146

Statement by the Assistant Secretary of State for International Narcotics Matters (DiCarlo) Before a Subcommittee of the Senate Foreign Relations Committee, May 6, 1982[12]

Drug Control Problems in Southeast Asia

The Bureau of International Narcotics Matters has submitted an extensive, formal statement, responding to the detailed requests of the subcommittee. I will therefore, with permission, confine my statement now to a summary of the major issues and our policy and program responses to those issues.

The situation in the Golden Triangle of Southeast Asia is that, after two successive droughts had significantly lowered opium production in the region in the 1979 and 1980 crop years, the area has now produced bumper crops. As a result of the excellent growing conditions for poppies in 1981, the production of opium from the three countries of the Golden Triangle (Thailand, Burma, and Laos) rose from an estimated

---

[10] Reference is to the Extradition Treaty with Annex, signed by the United States and Colombia on September 14, 1979, and entered into force on March 4, 1982. Reference is also to the Mutual Legal Assistance Treaty with exchange of Notes, signed by the United States and Colombia on August 20, 1980. It has been consented to by the United States but not by Colombia. These treaties have not yet been assigned TIAS numbers.

[11] The reference is to the Extradition Treaty with appendix, signed by the United States and the Netherlands on June 20, 1980, and entered into force on September 15, 1983. The reference is also to the Treaty on Mutual Assistance in Criminal Matters, signed by the Netherlands on June 12, 1981, and entered into force on September 15, 1983. These treaties have not yet been assigned TIAS numbers.

[12] Source: Department of State files. This statement was made before the Subcommittee on East Asian and Pacific Affairs. This hearing will not be printed.

200 metric tons in 1980 to an estimated 600–700 tons in 1981—with 1982 production expected to equal or exceed 1981's bumper crop.

The implications of this harvest, while not yet materialized, may well include intensive efforts by traffickers to increase the importation of heroin to the United States. Thanks to the drought-reduced productions in 1979 and 1980, Southeast Asian heroin accounted for an estimated 15 percent of heroin entering the United States in 1980.

The prospect then is for increased competition for the U.S. heroin market between the Golden Triangle heroin and heroin imported from Southeast Asia's Golden Crescent—which has dominated the U.S. market in the 1980's following the reductions in importation of Southeast Asian and Mexican heroin.

The Bureau offers no predictions as to net implications for levels of imports or levels of use. Instead, we recognize that, while much of the opium produced will be consumed in the region and that much of the product could be withheld from the market because prices for raw opium are down, there is the prospect for increased competition and at least the possibility for increased importation.

Whether this increased availability in Southeast Asia directly or proportionately affects the United States is not the sole determinant of our interest and policy. The opium/heroin market is worldwide, and is not compartmentalized by source and market. The lesson to be learned from previous displacements, for example Pakistan heroin for Mexican heroin, is that an increase in Southeast Asian heroin supply could impact indirectly as well as directly on availability of heroin within the United States. For instance, if Southeast Asian heroin displaces southwest Asian heroin in Western Europe, traffickers there could attempt to move additional southwest Asian heroin to our country. Our national interests clearly extend beyond the direct impact of heroin on the United States. The heroin trade threatens the health, economies and, through its corrupting influence, the legal and political fabrics of these friendly countries. Thus, our narcotics control policy reflects these broader foreign policy considerations.

Obviously, much more needs to be done by the governments in Southeast Asia—and by a concerned international community—to ensure that production is stopped at the source. This expansion of opium production in the Golden Triangle confirms the wisdom of the priority the United States assigns to crop control in our negotiations with such governments.

However, the detailed assessment we offer in our formal testimony also confirms that such control will not be quickly or readily achieved.

The opium growing areas of all three countries of the Golden Triangle are remote, trackless and rugged, inhabited by ethnically distinctive tribal people who have grown opium for decades as their major cash crop.

Of our minimum estimate of approximately 600 metric tons of opium, we believe that 500 tons is produced in Burma, 50 tons in Thailand, and 40–60 tons in Laos. At present, while there are reports of heroin refining in Laos, the indication is that Laotian opium products are not entering the international narcotics trade. Our current concern, therefore, is on opium production in Burma and Thailand, opium to heroin refining in Burma and Thailand, and opium and heroin trafficking through Thailand to world markets.

The principal growing areas are not only remote, but in the case of Burma, are beyond the effective control of the central governments. They are, however, controlled by various warlord armies, revolutionary and insurgent groups. These include the Shan United Army, the dominant trafficking group, the Burmese Communist Party, which controls the largest single bloc of opium growing territory in Burma, and, to a lesser extent, Chinese Irregular Forces.

Thailand is a problem in every dimension. Virtually all of the Golden Triangle's heroin passes through Thailand enroute to world markets. Thailand is the major transit country, a producer of opium, a refining base, and a major consumer nation with one of the world's largest heroin addict populations. This substantial domestic consumption provides a significant financial base for the trafficking organizations, independent of profits on the world market.

The Bureau's strategy is (1) to support Thai actions against the refining and trafficking organizations; (2) assist in opium cultivation control; (3) enhance overall Thai narcotics enforcement; and (4) develop a Thai consciousness and response to its own narcotics abuse problem.

Our assessment of the Thai program is mixed. In January, the Royal Thai Government took forceful action against the dominant opium refining and trafficking organization, the Shan United Army led by Chang Chi-Fu. And, as a result of Thai Government efforts, there has been a decline in the availability of precursor chemicals used to refine opium into heroin. Prices have increased, and refineries are reportedly having more difficulty converting their bumper stocks of raw opium into heroin.

On the other hand, the Thai have failed to enforce the opium poppy ban, even in areas which have benefited adequately from the United Nations crop substitution program. While we applauded the government's raid in January, which disrupted production from the 1981–82 harvest, we have advised the Thai Government and it recognizes that additional actions are needed to consolidate and expand this disruption of trafficking.

Burma is slowly emerging from its self-imposed isolation and cooperation on narcotics control issues has been a major aspect of our improved relationship with the Socialist Republic of the Union of Burma. The government places importance on achieving long-term success in reducing the production of opium and heroin, through a combination of rural development and crop substitution with enforcement and eradication. The SRUB reports that sizeable amounts of poppies are manually eradicated each year; however, the government at present is unable to exercise effective control over most of the opium-producing areas—and its efforts are estimated to have destroyed only about 8 percent of the crop.

The Golden Triangle has been the focal point of both bilateral and multilateral programs. In addition to U.S.-funded projects involving our Bureau, the Drug Enforcement Administration, and the Agency for International Development, projects have been supported by the United Nations Fund for Drug Abuse Control, the Colombo Plan organization, the World Bank, and the Governments of Canada, Norway, and the Federal Republic of Germany.

Yet, all too clearly, these efforts by these governments and organizations in support of the Burmese and Thai Governments have not succeeded in containing production in the Golden Triangle.

In the past, the tendency has been to respond to such situations by calling for even greater expenditures of U.S. and international dollars. But, if we have learned anything from our experiences of recent years, it is that successful narcotics control efforts require leadership by strong central governments with both the political will and the capacity to achieve control of the production areas. Both of those essential elements were present in Mexico and Turkey—where narcotics control has had its greatest success to date.

And, that is the critical task in Southeast Asia—to induce Burma and Thailand to intensify their narcotics control efforts. Our policy, with the governments of Southeast Asia, and governments of producing nations around the globe, is that we are willing to entertain requests for additional assistance—conditioned on our obtaining more comprehensive agreements for and host governments commitments to more effective narcotics control programs.

Thanks in part to the adverse impacts being suffered within Burma and Thailand—political, economic, and social impacts, including burgeoning addict populations, the undermining of legitimate economies, and even insurgent threats to the governments themselves—we believe that there is a greater opportunity for increased responsiveness by these governments.

Our government and the governments of other nations that lie on the trafficking routes from Southeast Asia to the United States and Western Europe will intensify their interdiction efforts to meet this latest threat—but the long-term and most effective solution lies in controlling production at the source—and we have made this message unequivocably clear, through President Reagan, through our Ambassadors, through my visits with government leaders in both countries,[13] and through international organizations.

Thank you.[14]

---

[13] On his trip to Asia, January 3–24, 1982, DiCarlo visited Thailand, January 5–6, and Burma, January 6–11.

[14] For DiCarlo's later elaboration of U.S. narcotics policy toward Southeast Asia, see his prepared statement before a subcommittee of the House Judiciary Committee, document 474.

Document 147

Statement Issued by the Secretary of State (Shultz), October 5, 1982[15]

President Reagan and Secretary Shultz Endorse New Federal Drug Abuse Strategy

The Federal Drug Abuse Strategy endorsed today[16] by President Reagan emphasizes foreign policy initiatives and international cooperation as major components of the administration's program to reduce the effects of drug abuse on the American people. I too applaud this emphasis as appropriate and needed; 90 percent of illicit drugs consumed in the United States are of foreign origin.

The Strategy underlines the importance of narcotics control as an international issue. Drug abuse and drug trafficking not only impact negatively on consumer nations like the United States but are undermining the social, political, and economic stability of countries where narcotics are produced or trafficked. The Strategy effectively reviews the administration's efforts to date, the firm resolve with which it has pursued more comprehensive drug control programs, and establishes guidelines for future action. In the international area the concentration is on reducing production and trafficking in heroin, cocaine, and marijuana through a more comprehensive, more cooperative effort involving much wider participation by the international community.

The foundation of our international narcotics policy is that illicit drugs must be controlled at the source. We believe, as explained in the Strategy, that the international community should assist nations in meeting these obligations. Under international convention, each signatory is responsible for controlling production and trafficking in illicit substances within its borders. The United States believes that compliance with these treaty obligations should be a matter of governmental priority for all signatory nations and that other governments should join in integrating narcotics control into foreign policy. We are urging a greater sharing of responsibility and expenditure of both diplomatic efforts and financial resources by other affected nations while continuing to expand our own significant effort.

In sum, the Strategy strikes an essential balance from the foreign policy perspective. As a concerned, responsible member of the international community, the United States is willing to assist producer and transit nations. We recognize and accept the reality of social, political, and economic circumstances which make narcotics control difficult to achieve. But, the United States will increasingly assert that these nations must take greater action to control the harm they export to the world.

---

[15] Source: Department of State files; printed also in Department of State *Bulletin*, November 1982, p. 51. This statement was made available to the press by Department of State Acting Spokesman Alan Romberg.

[16] Reference is to *Federal Strategy For Prevention of Drug Abuse and Drug Trafficking 1982* (Washington, [1982]), which was prepared for the President pursuant to the Drug Abuse Office and Treatment Act of 1972 by the Drug Abuse Policy Office, Office of Policy Development, The White House. This 76-page pamphlet was released by the White House on October 5, 1982.

Chapter 9. International Information, Educational Exchange, and Cultural Affairs Programs

Document 148

Remarks by President Reagan Before the Employees of the Voice of America, February 24, 1982 (Extract)[1]

"Truth . . . a Vital Part of America's Arsenal"

Thank you. Thank you very much. I've just seen a little bit of the workings of your place and read even more of them in the remarkable job that was done on the recent worldwide broadcast.[2] And I stand here filled with mixed emotions. For years now I have been on the Late Late Show and I don't know just what time I am on the air now—(laughter)—and where.

But forty years ago today America opened up a crucial front in its war against the enemies of freedom. It was 79 days after Pearl Harbor and the nation was mobilizing all its resources in the epic struggle that by then had encircled the planet.

In those days, as now, truth was a vital part of America's arsenal. A spirited band of professionals, men and women dedicated to what their country stood for and anxious to do their part, began broadcasting from the fourth floor of a New York City office building. In those early days under the able direction of John Houseman, programs were recorded on acetate disks and then shipped via bomber to England and Latin America for broadcast.

From this humble beginning, the Voice of America has grown into a respected institution of American communication, a global radio network broadcasting 905 hours weekly in 39 different languages.

Though born in war, the Voice of America continued in peace and has made enormous contributions. Today as we witness new forms of inhumanity threatening peace and freedom in the world, the Voice of America can perform an even more vital function.

By giving an objective account of current world events, by communicating a clear picture of America and our policies at home and abroad, the Voice serves the interests not only of the United States but of the world. The Voice of America is for many the only source of reliable information in a world where events move very quickly.

Perhaps today I can outline a news story that you may be hearing about—or as I have already found out, many of you have heard about it already. And that was that a short time ago I announced at a meeting of the Organization of American States a new initiative promoting peaceful economic and political development in Central America and the Caribbean Basin.[3] That area of the world was dramatically affected by the rising price of oil and the subsequent economic uncertainty of the last decade.

There are those who have sought to exploit this instability. We in the United States are concerned not only because of the proximity of those nations but also because we have witnessed on too many occasions the suffering and oppression that invariably follows the establishment of Marxist dictatorships.

In the months and years ahead the United States will work closely with friends in the Western Hemisphere—like Mexico, Canada, Venezuela—to promote economic growth, social stability, and political freedom in the Caribbean Basin and in Central America. On our part, we intend to offer a bold new opportunity for social and economic progress. The centerpiece of the program is a free-trade arrangement for Caribbean Basin products exported to the United States. This will encourage new eco-

---

[1] Source: White House Press Release, February 24, 1982, Office of the Press Secretary to the President; printed also in *Weekly Compilation of Presidential Documents*, March 1, 1982, pp. 223–225. President Reagan made his remarks beginning at 1:31 p.m. in the auditorium of the VOA headquarters following a tour of the VOA newsroom. Following his remarks, James B. Conkling, VOA Director, presented the President with an old microphone as a memento of the occasion.

[2] The reference is presumably to the January 31 worldwide broadcast of "Let Poland Be Poland," sponsored by the U.S. International Communication Agency.

[3] For the text of Reagan's February 24, 1982, address, see document 675.

nomic development and a better life for the people of the area. Also included in the program are incentives for investment and further financial aid; technical assistance also for the area.

We will furthermore seek to encourage the democratic process in the region. All too often extremists from right or left have sought to undermine social and economic progress, hoping to impose their will by brute force. This mentality is unacceptable to the United States and the free people of the Americas. It has no place in this hemisphere.

The United States intends to continue with support to those who are struggling to establish democratic institutions. The Communist-dominated guerrillas of the region offer nothing but the same bankrupt ideas that have imprisoned the populations of Cuba and Vietnam, Afghanistan, and, yes, Poland.

On March 21st free peoples around the world will join in observing Afghanistan Day. In marches, meetings, and rallies, they will express their support for the heroic freedom-fighters of Afghanistan in their brave struggle against Soviet aggression. I am happy to say that the Voice of America will provide thorough international coverage of Afghanistan Day.

Today we celebrate this 40th anniversary of an institution that has given hope to the citizens of those communist regimes and all the victims of tyranny. The challenges we face are no less grave and momentous than those that spawned the Voice 40 years ago. Freedom is no less threatened, and the opposition is no less totalitarian. In this struggle there is no greater weapon than the truth. Free men have nothing to fear from it. It remains the ultimate weapon in the arsenal of democracy.

Now, of course, I know there is a great deal of discussion about the truth as if there are degrees to truth. Well, no, truth can be told, and I remember my first experience because more than 40 years ago, I was a pioneer in radio, a sports announcer, and I found myself broadcasting major league baseball games from telegraphed reports. I was not at the stadium. And a man on the other side of a window with headphones on and a typewriter would hear the dot and dash of the Morse Code and type out and slip under the window, and knowing that there were six or seven other fellows broadcasting the same game—they did it that way in those days; you could take your choice of who you wanted to listen to—you had to keep right up with the play, even though you weren't there. So you'd get a little slip and it would say, "Out. Six to three." Well now, number six on a team is the shortstop—not on his bat; that's the numbered position. Number three is first base, so you knew that had to be a ground-out ground ball to the shortstop.

Now, if the game was rather dull, you could say, "It's a hard-hit ball down toward second base; the shortstop is going over after the ball and makes a wild stab, picks it up, turns, and gets him out just in time." (Laughter) (Applause)

Now, I submit to you, that I told the truth—(laughter)—if he was out from shortstop to first, and I don't know whether he really ran over toward second base and made a one-hand stab, or whether he just squatted down and took the ball when it came to him. But the truth got there, and, in other words, it can be attractively packaged. (Laughter) Also, I should say, in those days of radio—my goodness, they're long-gone—when you had a sound-effects man in the studio and he had a wheel cart, and on it he had every kind of device in the world for your radio dramas, from coconut shells that he beat on his chest to be a galloping horse—(laughter)—to cellophane he could crumple for a fire and everything.

And one day—and I'm only telling this because it shows that there is still room here for initiative—one day we had a play that called for the sound of water falling on a board. Well, this poor fellow during all the rehearsals, he was working—he tried rice on a drum, he tried dried peas on a piece of cardboard, he tried everything, and nothing would give him the sound of water on a board. And finally one day he tried water on a board. (Laughter) And it sounded just like water on a board. (Laughter)

Well, we're justifiably proud that unlike Soviet broadcasts, the Voice of America is not only committed to telling its country's story, but also remains faithful to those standards of journalism that will not compromise the truth.

Recently we celebrated the 250th birthday of George Washington. He understood the power of truth and its relationship to freedom. "The truth will ultimately prevail," he said, "where there are panes to bring it to light." Today we have this responsibility: bringing truth to light in a world groping in the darkness of repression and lies. Let us rededicate ourselves to the task ahead, and like the Founding Father, we can be confident that truth will prevail, and if truth prevails, freedom shall not perish from this earth. Thank you for all that you're doing, and God bless you. (Applause)

Thank you very much.

MR. CONKLING. Mr. President, we'd like to ask you to stay for another moment. It's probably not the appropriate time to discuss our budgets with you—(laughter) but we do have a great deal of antiquated equipment, and we need to do something about it.

This is a microphone. It was invented some time back during one of the wars, perhaps the Civil War. It is something we would like to present to you as a memento to remember us when budget time comes. (Laughter) We had it thoroughly scanned by security for fingerprints and they found yours on there. (Laughter)

THE PRESIDENT. Thank you very much. (Applause)

MR. CONKLING. I do think it is fair to read the inscription. "To President Ronald Reagan on your visit to the Voice of America's celebration of 40 years of international broadcasting on February 24th, 1982." (Applause)

THE PRESIDENT. Thank you. This really dates me, I want you to know. (Laughter) I'm getting vengeance for those budget remarks(laughter). This was the third modernization in my radio days(laughter). We thought it was the newest and most fabulous thing in the world after an old carbon mike where every once in a while you had to turn the game down and then tap it with a pencil to separate the carbon crystals again. (Laughter) We welcome this. And I welcome this and thank you all very much. (Applause)

Document 149

Address by the Under Secretary of State for Security Assistance, Science and Technology (Buckley) Before the Congressional Leadership Group on International Communications of Georgetown University, March 4, 1982[4]

International Communications and Information Objectives

We stand at the dawn of a new era of human history, the full implications of which we cannot yet begin to fathom. Yet under the compelling imperatives of exploding technologies in the communications and computer fields, we will have to work now to develop coherent national policies capable of embracing a growing diversity of increasingly complex enterprises.

In a very real sense, we are embarked upon a uniquely American task, and that is to identify certain fundamental philosophical principles as the underlying and unifying basis for addressing a myriad of yet-to-be-defined practical situations. We have here today representatives of a number of diverse constituencies, loosely gathered under an umbrella labeled "international communications and information." We are legislators, academics, news gatherers, bureaucrats, broadcasters, and transmitters of the electronic impulses by which those incredible machines talk to one another across international borders.

But as Americans, we share a common commitment to the tenets of the first amendment and to the principles of a free and competitive economy. The test that faces us, as we set out to chart policy directives, is how to apply these and other underlying values in addressing the broad objectives that were identified in the summary distributed to you before this meeting;[5] to see how we can best persuade the international community to adopt them; and in doing so, to test our own interpretations of some of our most basic operating principles to determine their real utility in the larger global marketplace. How exportable, for example, is our notion that pornography represents a privileged form of speech?

---

[4] Source: Department of State *Bulletin*, June 1982, pp. 78–79.

[5] For text, see *ibid.*, pp. 79–80.

The objectives described in the summary provide an excellent framework for the work that lies ahead of us in weighing a diversity of views and interests in order to develop sound policy in the variety of areas that fall within the field of international communications and information.

In order to provide some focus for these discussions and to underscore their practical importance, I would like to touch upon just a few of the problems that are currently being addressed in international fora.

In the U.N. Educational, Scientific and Cultural Organization (UNESCO), since the early 1970's, we have been fighting the good fight against the New World Information Order,[6] stoutly defending such fundamental principles of a free press as the media's rights to uncensored news, of access to news sources, and to a work environment free of governmental interference.

Developing countries argue for what they call a better "balance" in internationally distributed news about their countries and their activities. We can and should make an effort to help these nations meet their own legitimate communication needs but never at the expense of free and unfettered reporting by nongovernmental agencies. What we can never concede is that a government—any government—has the right of monopoly on the management and reporting of the news.

In the U.N. Committee on Peaceful Uses of Outer Space, we have been engaged for several years in debating the principles that should govern direct international television broadcasting by satellites. After a great deal of talk, one fundamental issue remains unresolved, and that is whether the government of a receiving country has the right to approve the content of a broadcast before it is transmitted. In this forum, as in UNESCO, our support of the principle of the free flow of information is firmly opposed by the Soviet Union; while more often than not, our Western allies suggest compromise solutions in an effort to bridge contentious issues.

In the Organization for Economic Cooperation and Development (OECD), we began in the early 1970's to consider some of the international implications of advances in computer technology. By 1976, we were reporting to Congress that transborder flows of data[7]—that is to say, the electronic chatter by which computers talk to one another over international telephone lines—that this was an area of growing concern to all the OECD governments. We fought the impulse of our colleagues to impose governmental controls at the outset. We urged the adoption of voluntary guidelines to harmonize national legislation affecting personal privacy and transborder flows of data. At present, we are launching careful studies of the economic and legal problems resulting from the transmission of the nonpersonal data which is rapidly becoming the lifeblood of internationally active companies. The United States has also proposed that the OECD countries adopt a "data declaration" similar to the OECD trade declaration.[8] This would be a commitment to avoid restrictive measures and to maintain an open system of data flows. In these and other ways, we are hoping to head off the premature imposition of controls.

While we undertake these studies in the OECD, we must inevitably come to grips with the few inevitable exceptions that must be made to the rule that we are urging others to adopt. These involve, for example, the special requirements for safeguarding military communications and a showing of a proper respect for the desire of various societies to protect their own distinct cultures and values against a torrent of what they regard as electronic pollution.

But beyond these special exceptions, there lies a cluster of others which, under the banner of "national interest," argue for restrictions on the transborder flows of data that can only be described as classic restraints on trade. In essence, these are efforts to protect developing industries or to shelter government monopolies. One an-

[6] The New World Information Order is a concept which had been discussed in UNESCO and other U.N. agencies since the early 1970's. Its goal was to provide the developing countries with the same communications and information capabilities as the developed countries. Proposals ranged from the moderate suggestion to include the improvement of information and communications abilities in overall development efforts to the radical idea of licensing journalists, developing an international code of journalistic ethics, limiting advertising, and extending individual governments' control over the press. The United States opposed the New World Information Order on the grounds that it would violate first amendment and free trade principles. See also *American Foreign Policy: Current Documents, 1981*, documents 144–146.

[7] Regarding transborder data flows, see *ibid.*, document 144.

[8] The reference is to the OECD Declaration on Trade Policy, adopted on June 4, 1980. (O.E.C.D. Press Release, PRESS/A(80)37, June 4, 1980)

swer to these challenges is to insist on reciprocity. But before we go too far down this road, we should certainly explore other ways of encouraging an unfettered commerce in electronic impluses; such measures, for example, as expanding the scope of General Agreement on Tariffs and Trade[9] to cover trade in services and information as well as in more tangible goods.

Other related concerns, from the American perspective, involve proposals in some countries that telecommunication services be made subject to value-added taxation or burdensome tariffs. These proposals give rise to interesting conceptual problems. As soon all electronically transmitted data will be in the form of bits, how will one distinguish, for tax and other purposes, between bits conveying news, or conveying public information, or proprietary data? Certainly, the attempt to sort them out would create rather significant disruptions. But in any event, as we see in this example, even the most mundane practical considerations would seem to support a presumption in favor of the unrestricted flow of information. Let's let the revenuers look to more readily identifiable areas of economic activity.

To move on to another area, the agenda set for the International Telecommunication Union (ITU) over the next few years will force decisions having a major economic impact on the United States. It is, therefore, of total importance that the ITU remain an effective forum for the international management of the electromagnetic spectrum. All participants must maintain an attitude of full and fair cooperation in determining how best to share this limited resource, as well as that limited ring of space that can be used for fixed-position communication satellites. This means that we cannot allow this forum to degenerate, as have so many other U.N. fora, into an arena for unproductive political brawls.

This is just a sampling of the kinds of issues we need to face and resolve as we move into the new and unprecedented age of instant international communication.

---

[9] For the text of the General Agreement on Tariffs and Trade, signed in Geneva, October 30, 1947, see 61 Stat. Parts 5 and 6.

Document 150

Address by the Secretary of State (Haig) Before Employees of the United States International Communication Agency, March 16, 1982[10]

Communication: "A Crucial Aspect of Living Diplomacy"

You know, I have been looking forward to exchanging views with a group of experts on communication. You know, I consider myself somewhat of an expert on communication. I'm very pleased that your extensive translating facilities will be available to be sure my remarks are understood worldwide, especially in the English-speaking world. (Laughter)

I want you to know also that I've launched a special project here at State, in coordination with ICA. We are going to commence a program to broadcast my morning staff meetings live and in that way, we will save reporters all that time transcribing my senior staff's notes, despite the unfortunate side effect that it might result in greater accuracy. (Laughter)

I do want to express my appreciation that Charlie invited me to say just a very few remarks to the professionals in ICA. You know, it goes without saying that the functions of your Agency are a crucial aspect of living diplomacy, because indeed you present not only America and American policy abroad, but you also elucidate on the underlying reasons which motivate our Nation and other policies.

Beyond that, I think it is important to recognize that ICA also plays an historical role in maintaining the historic memory of America's relationships with the rest of the world, an indispensable role indeed. It is not an unusual fact that in democratic societies, communication with the public and the recognition of the dignity and the great weight that we give to the individual in our society makes this communication essential. You know, at the outset of our republic, our Declaration of Independence was not a confidential code for governmental operations, but a public proclamation of what this Na-

---

[10] Source: Department of State files. Haig spoke at 9 a.m. in the Department of State's Dean Acheson Auditorium following brief introductory remarks by Charles Z. Wick, Director of ICA.

tion stands for, and why it assembled the mechanisms for governing that it did.

I think, day to day, never before has the role of your Agency borne such a tremendous responsibility for the effectiveness of America's worldwide leadership role. In the first instance, of course, you convey the fundamental objectives of American policy, the creation of an international environment that's hospitable to traditional American values, especially the dignity and freedom of the individual.

You find yourselves at a time where the explosion in communications techniques has made this individual-to-individual communication so fundamental, and at a time when totalitarianism has perverted the historic quest for social justice as a vehicle for the imposition of repression and totalitarianism. Especially in the decade ahead, we will have to be more effective in combating, through truth and communication, the growing proclivity for bloodshed, terrorism, and so-called laws of liberation.

It is a unique fact that at this juncture in history, totalitarianism has become the protector of the status quo, and there are new vulnerabilities, if you will, which have yet to be clearly understood in the Eastern world and in Moscow. But it seems to me that an important message, an indirect one, that comes from accurate, precise, truthful and effective communication is that we in the West are no longer vulnerable, and it is indeed the East that is increasingly vulnerable to social change and progress. How important it is that the Soviet leadership begin to grasp this emerging reality, that no longer will it serve their purposes to insist they have the right to intervene in Western spheres of influence in the developing world as the vanguard for social change when the vulnerabilities within their own sphere are becoming increasingly evident day to day—in Poland; the actions which they had to take in Afghanistan to protect the southern, non-Russian loyalties of the Moslem republics of the Soviet Union.

I would like to conclude by stating another word or two, if I may, about the vital role of communication in the exercise of political leadership. You know, even in the military field, the American and democratic style of leadership is very different from that of a totalitarian nation where rigid discipline and mindless adherence to the directive is the style. In democratic societies, precisely the opposite is the approach. What is involved is a very subtle relation of credibility that emerges from truthful dealings, conciseness and accuracy.

When leaders, whether they be nations or individuals, pursue such a style, they develop a sense of confidence and credibility among those over whom they have to exercise influence so that when events occur which make it impossible to explain and to communicate, that fundamental credibility carries you through the crisis. It seems to me, that must be the style of American communication worldwide—honesty, accuracy, objectivity, and the legacy of credibility that that will sustain you, will carry you through the periods of crisis and tension.

I would like to just conclude with another brief comment on the great sense of American accomplishment, I feel, with the cooperation we have had with ICA this past year, whether it was Charlie Wick or Bill [*Gil*] Robinson at our morning staff meetings or the special coordinating groups that we have set up for Poland, for Afghanistan, for Europe, and a host of other functional, critical areas, or whether it has been the day-to-day projection of what we have been attempting to do through your Agency worldwide. I think we can all step back and be both pleased and proud, and this should reinvigorate our approach to the year ahead which is going to be so critically important for our Nation.

Too frequently, Americans in the contemporary analysis of American foreign policy tend to believe that history started this past January. Let me tell you that is not so, because there isn't an issue with which we are dealing today that is not a consequence of the decisions made as much as a decade ago, and which have continued over an extended period of time. It is an unfortunate fact of life that the conduct of foreign policy is an historic process, and so many of our chickens are "coming home to roost." For that reason, this will be a difficult year, as we attempt to reverse the growth of Soviet and Marxist-Leninist interventionism worldwide, which is, of course, the core of our security concerns today—not the exclusive range of our concerns—but the core of our concerns.

I very much look forward, and I welcome that you have taken some time, Charlie, to assess the year's experiences, and to look forward to the months and years ahead. I want you to know that you do it with the respect, the confidence, and the gratitude of the Department of State for all that you have done and will continue to do. Thank you very much.

Document 151

Statement by the Director of the International Communication Agency (Wick) Before the House Foreign Affairs Committee, March 17, 1982[11]

Outline of USIA Programs; Supplemental Budget Request

I am pleased to be here today to present the authorization request for the U.S. Information Agency[12] for fiscal year 1983. President Reagan said during his campaign that he intended to strengthen the U.S. Information Agency, including specifically the Voice of America. When the President appointed me to head the Agency, he asked me to bring together the best minds available both from inside the Government and out, and make the U.S. Information Agency an even more effective and indispensable part of this country's national security structure.

Mr. Chairman[13] and members of the subcommittee, I am pleased with the progress we have made toward fulfillment of the President's mandate. During the past year, we have made many changes and have taken many initiatives which I want to review with you now.

In all that we do to serve the national interests, we in the U.S. Information Agency operate on a principle that the United States must speak the truth clearly, vigorously, and above all, persuasively. We have made important strides over the past year in repositioning the Agency as one of the first line members of the President's foreign policy team. I have been told that never before has this Agency been so closely involved in the formulation and execution of policy as it is today. We are involved in a war of ideas and credibility. Our adversary is the Soviet Union and our weapon is the truth.

I say this not out of any wish to alarm unduly nor to overstate my case, but merely to present a simple fact of international life. In this war of ideas, the U.S. Information Agency is on the front line. Under Project Truth, a U.S. Government-wide effort coordinated by our Agency, we are refuting the massive Soviet campaign of disinformation and misinformation about us and our intentions in the world.

In Western Europe, where I was recently struck by the serious erosion of support for NATO during my visit there, there is a whole new generation, the successor generation which knows nothing of America's role in the Normandy landing, the Berlin airlift, or the need to remain strong in the face of Soviet expansionism. We are trying to reach that generation of people in Europe and elsewhere through Project Truth.

I am pleased to be able to tell you that Project Truth is being administered through existing staff and resources, and does not entail new expenditures of funds.

As the U.S. Government's only means of daily direct communication with peoples of the world, the Voice of America is surely one of the most important activities of the U.S. Information Agency. Despite media stories of the past year suggesting otherwise, we have not waivered in our sworn support for the spirit and the letter of VOA's Charter,[14] nor do we have any plans to do so.

The Voice is and will continue to be an accurate, objective, and comprehensive source of the news. The VOA Charter also requires VOA to present the policies of the United States clearly and effectively, and we have spared no effort to insure that the commentaries do just that. We also seek to reflect the vitality of our Nation in the 1980's, with contemporary relevance to the successor generation of listeners abroad.

As you know, Mr. Chairman and gentlemen, the Soviet Union broadcasts over 2,000 hours a week compared with the 982 weekly planned for the VOA. The need to close this gap and to strengthen already

---

[11] Source: *Fiscal Year 1983 Supplemental Authorization Request for Department of State and United States Information Agency: Hearings and Markup Before the Committee on Foreign Affairs and Its Subcommittee on International Operations, House of Representatives, Ninety-seventh Congress, Second Session* (Washington, 1983), pp. 66–69.

[12] P.L. 97–241, approved August 24, 1982, changed the Agency's name from U.S. International Communication Agency to U.S. Information Agency. For text, see 96 Stat. 273.

[13] Dante B. Fascell, chairman of the Subcommittee on International Operations.

[14] The VOA Charter, first defined on November 1, 1960, was authorized by Congress in P.L. 94–350 and approved July 12, 1976; for text, see 90 Stat. 823.

existing VOA signals is a serious and urgent one. Therefore, a major part of our fiscal year 1983 budget, $115 million, is earmarked for completion of VOA's Botswana shortwave relay station and for the enhancement of the one in Sri Lanka and for improvement of the VOA studios in Washington.

During the past year, we have begun truly effective public communications by satellite transmissions. Our worldwide broadcast, "Let Poland Be Poland,"[15] was a landmark effort. But it was by no means the only use of satellite transmission that we made during the past year. Last November, for example, President Reagan's address on nuclear arms reduction[16] was seen by an estimated 200 million people in 50 countries. We have telecast other statements also by the President and his chief advisers.

We want to continue to make use of the technology of satellite broadcasts, to move America's messages, and are therefore requesting $3 million for additional worldwide television coverage in the coming year.

America's educational and cultural exchange programs are essential to our national interest. They help build bridges of understanding between peoples of the world and the American people, bridges that can withstand the temporary changes of international political winds. Last year, I traveled to China to sign the implementing agreement of the cultural accord between our two countries.[17] I have also traveled to Europe this past year, and have heard world leaders express high praise and support for our exchange program. I am therefore pleased to report that in fiscal 1983 we intend to increase the budget for these programs significantly. We will attain the objective set by the Congress of allocating over $100 million to this program. Let me assure you this marks the beginning of a long overdue upward trend in funding for these valuable programs.

Having discussed some of our program highlights, I would now like to briefly describe the Agency's resource requests.

The continuing appropriations bill, Public Law 97–92,[18] provides $489 million for USIA programs in fiscal 1982. Within that amount, the Agency plans to shift resources in the radio construction and salaries and expenses accounts to cover several new urgent requirements, principally to construct a network of medium wave transmitting facilities in the Caribbean Basin and Central America, to maintain critically needed employment levels, and to transmitting facilities for the Voice of America in Sri Lanka and detailed in two recent reprograming reports submitted to the committee.[19]

The Agency's 1983 request for authorization and appropriations, as reflected in the President's 1983 budget submitted to Congress in February, totals $640 million. This represents an increase of $157.7 million over the amount requested for USICA in March 1981, and approved by the House in H.R. 4814.[20] This increase results from the 1983 budget review concluded in January and the enhanced national security role assigned to the Agency. The major items of change are $113.2 million to complete the construction of high-powered transmittng facilities for the Voice of America in Sri Lanka and Botswana and to meet other technical VOA facility requirements; $44.7 million to cover projected 1983 inflationary increases and other mandatory changes for all Agency programs and activities; and $12 million to restore partially the program cuts implemented in 1982 in exchange programs and overseas missions activities and to enhance other priority programs. These increases are offset, in part, by a reduction of $12.2 million and the salaries and expenses accounts resulting from a decrease of 1982 appropriation as enacted in Public Law 97–92, and partial absorption of the added salary costs related to Federal pay increases in fiscal year 1982.

I realize that the requested budget of $640 million in fiscal year 1983 must be fully justified in the current tight budget situation. We must recognize, however, that

[15] Regarding "Let Poland Be Poland," see footnote 2 to document 148.

[16] For text, see *American Foreign Policy: Current Documents, 1981,* document 60.

[17] The Implementing Accord for Cultural Exchange in 1982 and 1983 Between the United States and the Government of the People's Republic of China will not be published. For the text of the Cultural Agreement Between the Government of the United States of America and the Government of the People's Republic of China, signed at Washington and entered into force, January 31, 1979, see 30 UST 26.

[18] For the text of P.L. 97–92, approved December 15, 1981, see 95 Stat. 1183.

[19] For the text of the report concerning the reprograming of radio construction funds, see *Departments of Commerce, Justice, and State, the Judiciary, and Related Agencies Appropriations for 1984: Hearings Before a Subcommittee on Appropriations, House of Representatives, Ninety-eighth Congress, First Session* (Washington, 1983), pp. 445–456. The report addressing the reprograming of salaries and expenses funds has not been published.

[20] H.R. 4814 became P.L. 97–241, approved August 24, 1982; for text, see 96 Stat. 273.

this Agency is a critical component of our national security apparatus,[21] and that we are waging a war of ideas with our adversaries. Given the state of the world today with all of its attendant dangers to free and open societies, I think we need to ask ourselves what is the most appropriate level of support for our efforts to speak the truth to the world about America in a strong and vigorous voice.

I would suggest that to do less than we are proposing would put at unjustifiable risk not only our ability to deal with the world in turmoil and to explain America to that world, but our capacity to help lead the world and our ability to preserve, to strengthen, and to share the values and the ideals that we hold dearest.

Before closing, I would like to add a word of thanks to the members of this committee for their cooperation in many areas, but especially for the timely passage of the joint resolution which permitted the showing of "Let Poland Be Poland" in the United States, which was shown by 142 PBS stations.

I appreciate the time you have given me today, and I would be pleased to respond to any questions you might have. Thank you.

Document 152

Remarks by President Reagan Before Representatives and Supporters of the Western Youth Exchange Program, May 24, 1982[22]

International Youth Exchange Programs

Well, I am delighted that so many of you were able to be here today. And welcome to the White House.

Behind the headlines of today, steadily chipping away at the obstacles, peace is another, and less sensational, dimension to foreign affairs. It is the network of human relations between our country and other nations around the globe. This network is more than government to government relations, tourism or commerce. It also has been built on the experiences of young people who have lived with families and attended schools or universities in other countries.

I am convinced that one of the best ways to develop more accurate perspectives on other nations and on ourselves is for more Americans to join, for a time, a family and a community in another land. And we cannot hope that other nations will appreciate our country unless more of their future leaders have had the same chance to feel the warmth of the American family, the vitality of an American community, the diversity of our educational system.

Now, sometimes I must admit that last part there has given me some problems. When I was governor, I used to welcome every year those students who were in California from other lands. And I always had one question. I would ask them: "Tell me, now that you have been here and going to our school, is it easier or harder than school in your own country?" And then I would wait two or three minutes for the laughter to stop, which answered the question. (Laughter) They found it somewhat easier. But then, maybe we warmed their hearts a little bit with that too.

But there is a flickering spark in us all which, if struck at just the right age I think, can light the rest of our lives, elevating our ideals, deepening our tolerance, and sharpening our appetite for knowledge about the rest of the world. Education and cultural exchanges, especially among our young, provide a perfect opportunity for this precious spark to grow, making us more sensitive and wiser and international citizens through our careers.

Twenty-two years ago, President Eisenhower, father of the People-to-People Program as you know, said that: "The beginning point of all cooperation between individuals, between groups, within a single society, or between nations is genuine, human understanding." Well, never have we needed this vital ingredient to peace more than in today's world.

Since World War II, the United States has developed many excellent programs for students, scholars, youth, farm, and labor groups. They depend on the cooperation of thousands of American families and hun-

---

[21] Wick commented further on USIA's national security role in response to questions posed by Representative Winn. See *Fiscal Year 1983 Supplemental Authorization Request for Department of State and United States Information Agency*, pp. 78–79.

[22] Source: White House Press Release, May 24, 1982, Office of the Press Secretary to the President; printed also in *Weekly Compilation of Presidential Documents*, May 31, 1982, pp. 692–694. Reagan spoke at 1:45 p.m. in the East Room of the White House.

dreds of schools, universities, and volunteer community organizations. And many of these are represented here today. Still, the total number of young people sponsored by our government is relatively small, especially when compared to sponsored programs of the Soviet Union or even of our allies, West Germany and France.

Early next month I'll go to Versailles to meet with our six major allies.[23] Among both their young people and ours, there's perhaps less appreciation of the values we share than there was 20 or 30 years ago. The successor generations didn't experience our remarkable postwar cooperation and they're less familiar with the ideals which motivated America then and which motivate us now.

I believe that today we have a great opportunity to form new bonds through expanded exchanges among our youth, from all sections of our society. If we're to succeed, if we're to build human bridges across the seas and into the future as an investment for peace, we'll need more private support and cooperation than ever before.

And that, ladies and gentlemen, is why I invited you here today—to forge with me a new kind of cooperation between government and the private sector, between profit and nonprofit organizations, between families across our land and those abroad in an exciting exchange of our young people.

Based on an expanded American program, I plan to discuss with our allies at Versailles greater emphasis on these programs by all our countries. An ancient Chinese proverb says, "If you tell a man, he will forget. If you show a man, he may remember. But if you involve him, he will understand."

I hope we can make a beginning by involving all of you and wonderful families like the Frys and the Gozays here who are with us today in a vast network providing home-stay experience and other support for thousands of young people from abroad over the years to come. To make it work, our corporations, foundations and voluntary organizations across the land will need to take the lead.

I plan to form a presidential committee to advise me and to help Charlie Wick, who is my personal representative for this effort—help them find ways to stimulate greater private involvement across the country.[24] I hope that today's meeting will open a new chapter in our efforts to build the broadest possible base for peace.

I look forward to hearing—or receiving a report from Charlie on the reports of the meeting and the follow-up work. You have my strong support, my sincere best wishes in this new endeavor.

And now at a terrible risk—because I know that I'm getting a reputation for telling anecdotes—(laughter)—I'm going to tell one. I don't know why I just happened to think of this—here today and thinking of the young people in the exchange, and what our young people could do for us. It goes back to just after World War II and I was in England. And you think about these kids of ours being over there and the rest of the world being exposed to them. I was out in the countryside on a weekend, and I wanted to see one of the fabulous—it was my first trip to England, right after the War, and I wanted to see one of the fabulous ancient pubs. The driver that was driving us apologized when he stopped at one that was only 400 years old. (Laughter) He hadn't been able to find a really old one yet.

We went in and it was a mom-and-pop operation. And, you know, the old gentleman there at the bar, and a matronly woman, she came and took our order. And after hearing us for a few seconds, in our talking, she says, "You're Americans, aren't you?" And I allowed as how we were. And she said, "Oh, there were a lot of your chaps staged just down the road during the War." And she said, "They used to come in here, and they'd hold songfests." And she said, "They called me 'Mom' and they called the old man there 'Pop.'" And she said, "It was Christmas Eve"—and by this time she's not looking at us anymore, she's kind of looking off into the distance, and her eyes are beginning to fill up. And she said,"It was Christmas Eve and we were in here all alone." And she said, "The door opened and in they came, and they had presents, Christmas presents for me and Pop." And then she said—by this time the tears were rolling a little bit —she said, "Big strapping lads, they was, from a place called Ioway."

Well, right then I fell in love all over again with "those big strapping lads from Ioway" and from wherever in America. And

[23] For documentation on the Versailles Economic Summit, see Chapter 5, Part F.

[24] Regarding the establishment of the President's Council for International Youth Exchange, see document 155.

you think about them, over there. I think they'd do a lot more than a lot of public relations programs to correct false impressions about the United States.

So, again, thank you all for being here. And Charlie, you tell me all about it. I have to leave. (Applause)

Document 153

Remarks by President Reagan, December 16, 1982 (Extract)[25]

Leading the "Communications Revolution"

Thank you very much. We are delighted to welcome all of you to the White House and it is especially nice to have you with us here at Christmas time. I'm sorry that Nancy isn't here, but as you look around you'll see that she is here with us in spirit. She's been in charge of that department.

You've noticed, I'm sure, that this is the room where we hold the press conferences. I don't mind telling you I'm just as content to be here with your group. (Laughter) At least with you there won't be any failure to communicate.

Many outstanding leaders from different areas of the communications industry are with us here today, and as you know, our administration has asked the private sector to carry the ball for the United States in world communications for the year 1983. We are very grateful for your leadership and initiative.

I know that Bill Ellinghaus[26] has put together a national council with representatives from industry, labor, academia, the media, and professional and trade associations to implement the goals of the United States, and the aim of World Communications Year[27] is to stimulate economic and social progress around the world through accelerated expansion of communications and information services. And I think that this represents a tremendous opportunity for U.S. world leadership. And let's face it, we are the pathbreakers in the most communications-intensive era in history.

The world is in a communications revolution and that revolution is being made right here at home. I think this process grows out of our—or progress, I should say, grows out of our 200-year-old tradition of freedom, freedom like that embodied in our first amendment which gives every citizen the right to express his or her ideas and to act on them politically. We trust the people. Our revolution was born to liberate the individual, and to create economic and social opportunity. It lives in one simple principle, government must rest on the consent of the governed.

This is still the most inspiring and successful and truly progressive political idea in the world today. It always has and always will make tyrants tremble.

Back in the days before we had satellites and electronic hookups, Thomas Jefferson put it this way: "The basis of our Government being the opinion of the people, the very first object should be to keep that right, and were it left to me to decide whether we should have a government without newspapers or newspapers without a government, I should not hesitate a moment to prefer the latter."

Now, I couldn't help noticing something about that kind remark that Jefferson made about the press. (Laughter) He made it before he was President, not during his term. (Laughter) As long as information, though, can flow freely, America can grow and thrive, and democracy itself will be stronger than before. This principle that Jefferson championed is reflected in Article XIX of the 1948 Universal Declaration of Human Rights: "Everyone has the right to freedom of opinion and expression. This right includes freedom to hold opinions without interference and to seek, receive, and impart information and ideas through any media and regardless of frontiers."[28]

---

[25] Source: White House Press Release, December 16, 1982, Office of the Press Secretary to the President; printed also in *Weekly Compilation of Presidential Documents*, December 20, 1982, pp. 1625–1627. Reagan spoke at the signing of Proclamation 5006, which designated 1983 as World Communications Year: Development of Communications Infrastructures. The ceremony began at 11:58 a.m. in the East Room of the White House. For the text of the proclamation, see *infra*.

[26] William Ellinghaus, chairman of the U.S. Council for World Communication in 1983, was also chairman of A.T.&T.

[27] Reference is to U.N. General Assembly Resolution 36/40, adopted on November 19, 1981, which designated 1983 as World Communications Year.

[28] For the text of the Universal Declaration of Human Rights, see Department of State *Bulletin*, December 19, 1948, pp. 752–754.

As we describe the world in which we live today and the world we are building for tomorrow, we see two trends growing side by side, a universal quest for more and better information, and new opportunities and technologies sprouting up to meet this quest almost faster than we can imagine.

We Americans have an unprecedented opportunity. We can embark on a noble journey to reach our dreams and to serve mankind, and we can do it through communications, creating new growth, jobs, and hope for our people and for the rest of the world. This is our challenge for the 1980's.

The development of new technologies such as computers, microchips, satellites, fibre optics has revolutionized our concept of communications over telephone, radio, and television. Each day in the United States our citizens engage in some 400 million telephone calls. That is nearly two for every man, woman and child. And just from being upstairs when Nancy is there, I can tell you, she is ahead of the game. (Laughter)

The world now has over one-half billion telephones and about 140 nations are connected by communications satellites. The majority of these were built and launched in the United States.

Looking ahead to another private sector initiatives effort in 1984, the Olympics in Los Angeles will be carried via satellite transmission to some 2 billion around the globe. There is an international satellite under construction here in the United States that will hopefully be launched by 1986. It will be able to transmit the equivalent of the Encyclopedia Britannica every 3 seconds.

Beyond that we can envision the possibility of building much larger satellites complete with millions of telephone circuits and thousands of television channels. We have opened the door but we have only taken our first small steps into the new age of communications. With faith and confidence in each other, with a commitment to invest more and to invest more wisely in our future, we can create a new era of knowledge and opportunity.

The United States must rededicate itself to development of technology through our private enterprise system. We are one of the few nations of the world in which telecommunications is still controlled by private enterprise. And we shall lead the way. We must continue to share the benefits of this technology with the rest of mankind in keeping with the spirit of Article XIX of the Universal Declaration of Human Rights.

So I thank you very much for your strong personal efforts to help us build our future, a better future of progress, excitement, and hope.

And now, I am pleased to sign this proclamation for World Communications Year 1983. (Applause)

. . . .

Document 154

Proclamation by President Reagan, December 16, 1982[29]

World Communications Year 1983: Development of Communications Infrastructures

The United Nations General Assembly has proclaimed 1983 World Communications Year: Development of Communications Infrastructures.[30] Its purpose is to stimulate accelerated worldwide development of communications infrastructures and to provide an opportunity for all countries to undertake an in-depth review and analysis of their policies on communications development.

Communications systems have taken on an increasingly vital role in every facet of economic, political, and social progress. While there have been remarkable advances in both this technology and its applications—ranging from health care, education, and banking transactions to weather observations and earth resource location—many nations have not been able to benefit appreciably from these capabilities.

Through partnership of United States private businesses, in cooperation with the

---

[29] Source: White House Press Release, December 16, 1982, Office of the Press Secretary to the President; printed also in *Weekly Compilation of Presidential Documents,* December 20, 1982, p. 1627. This Proclamation 5006 was filed with the Office of the Federal Register at 11:43 a.m. on December 17, 1982.

[30] See footnote 27 above.

International Telecommunication Union, we have an opportunity to promote the well-being of people around the globe. I encourage the United States communications industry—with its position of world leadership in this technology—to actively and voluntarily support this effort to stimulate the development of communications infrastructures in all nations.

NOW, THEREFORE, in keeping with the goals of the World Communications Year, I, RONALD REAGAN, President of the United States of America, do hereby proclaim 1983 as World Communications Year: Development of Communications Infrastructures, in the United States.

IN WITNESS WHEREOF, I have hereunto set my hand this sixteenth day of December, in the year of our Lord nineteen hundred and eighty-two, and of the Independence of the United States of America the two hundred and seventh.

RONALD REAGAN

Document 155

Memorandum From President Reagan to the Director of the United States Information Agency (Wick), December 20, 1982[31]

President's Council for International Youth Exchange

On May 24, 1982, I announced the establishment of a program to form new bonds between the United States and other countries through an expansion of youth programs.[32] This program is to involve close cooperation between the Government, nonprofit organizations, and the private sector.

To achieve these goals I request that you form the President's Council for International Youth Exchange and that you serve as my personal representative in this effort. Periodically, I will recommend the names of persons for you to appoint as members of the Council. These members will assist you to stimulate greater private sector involvement in the Youth Exchange Initiative.

The members of the Council will be expected to offer advice to both of us on the various aspects of successfully launching and implementing the program. In addition to this mandate, the members will help you to encourage private participation in the program through the variety of means available to your agency. For example, I expect them to promote the program through personal contacts and by conducting a publicity campaign. Also, their assistance with fund raising for the Initiative is critical.

Because of the importance I place on this program, I request that you exercise your authority to ensure that the members of the Council can adequately assist us in this important endeavor. With USIA providing staff support for the Council, and with the Council members expanding your Agency's capabilities to reach the private sector, I look forward to the beginning of an exciting and successful program.

---

[31] Source: White House Press Release, December 20, 1982, Office of the Press Secretary to the President; printed also in *Weekly Compilation of Presidential Documents*, December 27, 1982, p. 1647.

[32] For text, see document 152.

Chapter 10. Europe and Canada

A. General Policies

Document 156

Prepared Statement by the Deputy Assistant Secretary of State for Economic and Business Affairs (Johnston) Before a Subcommittee of the House Science and Technology Committee, February 9, 1982[1]

Soviet Energy Development and the Western Alliance

I suspect that the drafters of the OTA study on "Technology and Soviet Energy Availability"[2] did not anticipate how timely their work would prove to be. Their report was issued shortly after our discussions last fall with the Europeans on the West Siberian gas pipeline which, of course, is the largest and single most visible example of Western equipment and technology associated with Soviet energy development. Its release also came at a time when the administration was studying a new policy on exports to the Soviet Union of oil and gas equipment and technology.

Since that time, events in Poland took a dramatic turn for the worse and caused us to invoke strong measures against the Soviet Union. One of these actions was to stop oil and gas equipment and technology to the Soviet Union.[3] We have asked our allies to take parallel measures and not to undercut the actions we have taken in response to martial law in Poland.

Energy production is important to the Soviets not only for their domestic use but also for export earnings. I will limit my remarks this morning to the oil and gas sectors of energy because these are the most important sources for Soviet energy consumption and for Soviet exports.

The Soviet Union will seek to import large volumes of Western equipment and technology as it endeavors to develop and exploit its oil and gas reserves in the coming decades.

Even under the most optimistic assumptions about the level of Soviet oil and gas production, it is clear that the days of easy Soviet access to cheap reserves are rapidly drawing to a close.

New reserves, especially in the all-important gas sector, are far from major population and industrial centers. This geographic shift, primarily to the West Siberian region, means that the construction of new gas pipelines will be necessary. The Soviets now depend on Western equipment imports for the key components in pipeline construction—especially large-diameter pipe and compressor stations to drive the gas through the pipes. Which [*Since*?] much of the Soviet equipment imports are not particularly technologically advanced, Soviet indigenous production is currently inadequate to meet Soviet needs, in terms of both quantity and quality.

Perhaps the most notable finding of the OTA study is that the United States alone has little leverage to reduce current and future development of Soviet oil and gas. The study reports that there is no single essential energy equipment or technology area in which the U.S.S.R. must depend on the United States for the long run. In areas where the Soviets now rely on Western imports, there is equipment and technology availability outside this country. The OTA study points out that foreign firms, through research and development, have independently developed their own oil and gas equipment and technology capabilities.

The United States does retain an edge in some oil and gas equipment and technology areas. The OTS study notes that the United States is the sole or preferred supplier in a number of areas, including integrated computer systems and software, submersible

---

[1] Source: *American Technology Transfer and Soviet Energy Planning: Hearings Before the Subcommittee on Investigations and Oversight of the Committee On Science and Technology, U.S. House of Representatives, Ninety-seventh Congress, First and Second Sessions* (Washington, 1982), pp. 207–209.

[2] Office of Technology Assessment, *Technology and Soviet Energy Availability* (Washington, 1981).

[3] For the text of President Reagan's statement of December 29, 1981, where he announced U.S. sanctions against the Soviet Union, see *American Foreign Policy: Current Documents, 1981*, document 270.

pumps, blow-out preventers, and tertiary recovery techniques. But the Soviet Union in recent years has shown a definite reluctance to purchase U.S. energy equipment because of the possibility of export control problems. For instance, the United States has sold no submersible pumps to the Soviet Union since 1978.

Although the United States may have delaying possibilities, we cannot markedly reduce the volume or increase the cost of Soviet energy production through unilateral export controls. However, the West acting in a concerted manner could have a significant effect.

Before discussing possible Western policies towards Soviet oil and gas development, it is important to describe fully the differences of view between the United States and our allies, on the desirability of increased Soviet energy production and expanded East–West energy ties in those areas.

The European perspective is different from ours for a number of reasons. In the first instance, the Europeans are more dependent on imported energy sources than are we. They import approximatley two-thirds of their energy needs, whereas we import only about one-fifth of what we need. Further, given a strong desire to reduce their heavy dependence on Middle Eastern energy imports and to diversify their supplies, and given the Soviet Union's relative proximity to Europe, they view the Soviet Union as an acceptable supplemental supplier. This view is reinforced by the continuing European belief that energy and other trade links with the Soviets serve to moderate Soviet international behavior. It is also reinforced by the perception that European purchases of Soviet oil and gas finance Soviet imports of European technology and manufactured goods.

Another key ingredient in the European and Japanese perspective on Soviet oil and gas development is the opportunity for related energy equipment trade.

These energy, economic, and political factors behind our allies' view of Soviet energy development are, needless to say, not entirely shared by the United States.

These differences in view are not easily bridged. But this administration is committed to working with our allies to ensure that excessive Western dependence on Soviet energy does not develop. In this context, I will briefly discuss the West Siberian pipeline and its implications for Western energy security.

In our discussions with European governments on the pipeline, we have focused on the energy security impact of increased West European reliance on Soviet energy sources. We have stressed the vulnerabilities which could arise from increased imports of Soviet gas, and have emphasized that the volume of energy imports from the Soviet Union is not in itself a sufficient indicator of potential economic and political vulnerability that could arise from expanded energy ties.

Although the six European participants in the pipeline project will be dependent on the U.S.S.R. for only approximately 6 percent of their total energy needs once the pipeline is fully operational, we feel the Europeans must look beyond the aggregate numbers to more fundamental energy security considerations:

First, gas, which is rapidly replacing oil as the chief Soviet hard currency earner, is a difficult fuel to replace in the event of a supply interruption, much more difficult than oil.

Second, certain regions within Europe will be heavily dependent on Soviet gas once the pipeline is completed.

Third, residential and commercial consumers will be particularly dependent on Soviet gas, and a cut-off in these sectors would occasion special and most troublesome domestic political problems and pressures.

We argue that even without a cut-off of Soviet energy flows, the Soviets will possess leverage which could be brought to bear on Western European governments.

In addition to these energy security considerations, we have pointed out that the economics of the pipeline are no longer as attractive as they were when initial negotiations began in 1978. Overall energy growth rates are down, and European gas demands are now being revised downward.

For these reasons, we are continuing to discuss with the Europeans alternatives to the West Siberian project which we believe are more economic and more secure.

In response to our concerns, the Europeans have been firm in characterizing our alternative energy sources as supplementing—but not replacing—increased energy imports from the Soviet Union. But the Europeans have gained through our discussions a better appreciation of the risks inherent in East–West energy trade.

Even before we recently stopped shipments of oil and gas equipment and technology exports to the Soviet Union, we were the only Western country to control the export of such items to the U.S.S.R.

Our unilateral controls can have only a limited effect. In this regard, foreign sources for all equipment and technology required for the West Siberian gas pipeline are either already available or could be developed quickly enough so as not to delay significantly a realistic schedule for putting that project into operation. Therefore, substantial allied cooperation would be needed to deprive the U.S.S.R. of Western equipment and technology.

The OTA study notes that our sanctions program following the Soviet invasion of Afghanistan demonstrated the problems of our allies in imposing trade controls in areas, such as energy, which do not have direct Soviet military applications. Our allies' problems are clearly exacerbated when the incentive of equipment sales to the U.S.S.R. and the goal of energy diversification are added to the equation.

In spite the problems of developing with our allies a multilateral control policy on oil and gas equipment and technology exports to the Soviet Union, our own policy in this area is not and should not be based entirely on our allies' perceptions. We have a leadership as well as a partnership role to play in the alliance. We cannot forge consensus without taking steps ourselves.

Achieving allied cooperation in meeting the problems posed by both Western oil and gas imports from the Soviet Union and oil and gas equipment technology exports to the Soviet Union will not be easy. Our experience with the West Siberian gas pipeline has demonstrated that we have large differences of view with the Europeans. But we shall continue to work cooperatively with our allies to lessen the risks of excessive dependence and potential vulnerability that could stem from Western imports of oil and gas. In the near term, our allies have said they will not undermine our sanctions on exports to the U.S.S.R. Both for now and the more distant future, we must strive to achieve a multilateral approach towards Soviet oil and gas development that will strengthen the alliance.

Document 157

Statement by the Secretary of State (Haig) Before the Conference on Security and Cooperation in Europe, Madrid, February 9, 1982[4]

Soviet Repression in Poland Endangers Security and Cooperation in Europe

Mr. Chairman: We are at a critical crossroads in the postwar history of Europe. Our peoples have invested great hopes in the promise and principles of Helsinki. From Madrid we must send them a clear signal that we are determined to fulfill that promise and to insist upon those principles. Otherwise, the Helsinki Act[5] and the process of reconciliation, which it symbolizes, will be seriously, perhaps irreparably damaged. In 1975, 35 heads of government committed themselves to heal the wounds and divisions of Europe. Respect for the rights of nations and individuals was to form the basis for much greater security and cooperation. A new era of trust, trade, travel, and freedom was to ensue. Europe was to be made whole again.

Now that vision has been fundamentally challenged. As we confront the complexities of the present situation, we might well heed Winston Churchill, who advised that "in critical and baffling situations, it is always best to recur to first principles and

---

[4] Source: Department of State Press Release 52, February 9, 1982; printed also in Department of State *Bulletin*, April 1982, 37–39. The source text is Haig's remarks as prepared for delivery. Haig was in Madrid from February 7 to 10, 1982, to attend the followup meeting of the Conference on Security and Cooperation in Europe, which began on November 11, 1980, and reconvened in Madrid on February 9, 1982. All NATO foreign ministers appeared at this meeting the first week. Their presense reflected the NATO decision of January 11, 1982 to use the Madrid meeting as an effective and unified voice of Western protest against the declaration of martial law in Poland and the threat of Soviet military aggression which preceded it. Haig visited Lisbon from February 10 to 11, Marrakech from February 11 to 12, and Bucharest from February 12 to 13, and returned to the United States on February 13. For the text of the NATO Declaration on Events in Poland, January 11, 1982, see document 171.

[5] For the text of the Helsinki Final Act on Security and Cooperation in Europe, August 1, 1975, see Department of State *Bulletin*, September 1, 1975, pp. 323–350.

simple action." We are indeed in a critical situation. The first principles of the Helsinki Final Act are under attack. My purpose—and indeed the purpose of this conference—must be to defend the Act by speaking clearly about what is happening and why. For more than a year, the American delegation, ably directed by Ambassador Kampelman, has sought with others to build on the promise of the Helsinki Final Act. We have discussed our differences, and we have pursued new initiatives. Throughout, our purpose has been to strengthen security and cooperation in Europe. All of these efforts are now overshadowed by ominous events in the heart of Europe itself. The Polish people, whose destiny has always affected European security, are being denied their right to determine their own affairs. A forcible suppression of the Polish search for dignity in the workplace, for freedom, and for self-determination is underway. The Generals of this war against the Polish people are none other than the Polish regime itself, acting under the instigation and coercion of the Soviet Union. How can these actions be reconciled with Polish and Soviet signatures on the Helsinki Accords?

Nothing endangers security and cooperation in Europe more than the threat and the use of force to deny internationally recognized rights. Nothing endangers the Helsinki Final Act and the Helsinki process more than this willful violation of solemn international obligations. We would be threatening the future peace of Europe if we ignored this dramatic attack on international principles.

Clearly, all countries interested in a more secure, united, and open Europe—the work of this conference—have a responsibility to raise their voices here today. The American people, and other peoples as well, could never countenance a cynical attempt to place the Polish tragedy beyond the reach of the Helsinki Final Act. To the contrary—the Act justifies our concern and demands our protest. Put most simply, the issue is whether we meant what we said in August of 1975.

In Principle I of the Final Act, the signatories said that states had the right to choose and develop their political, social, economic, and cultural systems. Yet through intimidation and interference, the Soviet Union has conspired with the Polish military authorities to deprive Poland of this basic right.

In Principle II, the signatories said that participating states would refrain from the threat or use of force against the territorial integrity or political independence of any state. Yet Soviet and Warsaw Pact military demonstrations and the palpable fear of Soviet military intervention have been used to intimidate the Polish people in their search for reform.

In Principles IV and VI, the signatories said they would refrain from any action against the political independence of any other participating state and from any intervention in their internal or external affairs. Yet the Polish nation has been the victim of a long and vicious campaign. Official statements, some emanating from the highest levels of the Soviet Government, have warned of dire consequences if the Poles persisted in their pursuit of Polish solutions to Polish problems.

In Principle VII, the signatories said they would promote and encourage the effective exercise of civil, political, economic, social, cultural, and other rights and freedoms. But the Polish military authorities, far from promoting and encouraging the exercise of these righs, are suppressing the most fundamental freedoms of the Polish people.

In Principle VIII, the signatories said they would respect the right of peoples freely to determine their political status, without external interference, and to pursue as they wished their political, economic, social, and cultural development. Violation of this principle threatens the entire Final Act. Yet since the beginning of the reform movement in Poland, the Soviet Union has attempted systematically to deny the right of the Polish people to chart their own future.

In Principle X, the signatories said that "in exercising their sovereign rights, including the right to determine their laws and regulations, they will conform with their legal obligations under international law." The suppression of the civil and human rights of the Polish people violates the internationally recognized rights set forth in the U.N. Charter and the Universal Declaration of Human Rights,[6] as well as the specific provisions of the Final Act.

Gentlemen, what I have just described is the Bill of Rights which the Helsinki Act provided Western civilization.

Thus, the Final Act sets forth basic standards by which to judge ourselves and each

[6] For the text of the Universal Delaration of Human Rights, see Department of State *Bulletin*, December 19, 1948, pp. 752–754.

other. These principles were the product of laborious negotiations. They were solemnly undertaken. My own country's attitude was well expressed by President Ford, when he said: "We take this work and these words very seriously. We will spare no effort to ease tensions and solve problems between us. But it is important that you recognize the deep devotion of the American people and their government to human rights and fundamental freedoms and thus to the pledges that this conference has made. . . . "[7] 0

The United States and many other governments represented here today proudly hold ourselves to these standards. The Helsinki Final Act embodies our rejection of the self-serving sovereignty that equates might with right. It reflects the international consensus that all of the principles are equally binding. No state has the right to arbitrary definition. No state has the right to claim selective exemption. Yet, as we meet today, the exercise of arbitrary power and violence has become a pattern.

Together with many others, the American delegation has detailed here since September 1980 the Soviet Union's continuous and utter disregard for the Helsinki Final Act. Afghanistan has been invaded. Soviet citizens trying to monitor the Soviet Union's compliance with Helsinki have been attacked, imprisoned, and placed in mental institutions. Emigration has decreased dramatically. In neighboring Poland, the people now face a ruthless campaign of oppression, instigated and supported by the Soviet Union. These are not random acts but systematic policy. Soviet acts have clearly nullified Soviet commitments.

Such acts of oppression and intervention make it impossible to establish conditions for a more free and secure Europe. To ignore them would condemn this conference as a charade. The Helsinki Final Act would be reduced to a worthless piece of paper.

We cannot accept the fallacious argument that legitimate security interests or alliance systems are threatened by a defense of the Helsinki principles. In fact, peaceful change is essential to any durable framework for security. No legitimate government is threatened by freedom and justice. Solidarity with the Polish people and our support for their rights are essential to the survival of the Helsinki process—and to our own self-respect.

The Polish regime and the Soviet Union know very well that they have violated the Helsinki Final Act. They have taken a path inimical to security and cooperation in Europe. It is up to them to demonstrate that they take seriously the principles to which they are pledged.

—We look for the release from prison of those trade union leaders and others who seek to realize the objectives of the Helsinki Final Act for their people. Promises of good intentions, or the mere movement of prisoners to model camps, are not enough.

—We look for the lifting of martial law. This means the end of repressive conditions.

—We look for reconciliation in Poland. Restoration of internationally recognized rights and a resumption of a process of reform and liberalization provide the only basis for a constructive national dialogue, free from external coercion.

The American people, like those of so many lands, have a special and strong attachment to the people of Poland. No nation has suffered more, nor displayed such enduring courage. Relief from current oppression is not enough—the Polish people want more, need more, deserve more. The United States has decided to join other concerned countries in offering a major program to help Poland overcome its economic problems, including agricultural shortages and massive external debt. This assistance will become available when the basic rights of the Polish people are restored and their quest for a more decent society resumed.

We will not aid tyranny. But if tyranny stands aside, we are ready to help. It is up to the Polish military regime and the Soviet Union to create and to maintain the conditions in which the Polish people can, with Western assistance, rebuild their economy.

As these conditions are restored, we also will be among the first to insist that we return to the job of reaching agreement on moving the Helsinki process forward in both the human rights and security areas. In the meantime, business as usual here at Madrid would simply condone the massive violations of the Final Act now occurring in

---

[7] For the text of President Gerald Ford's address before the Conference on Security and Cooperation in Europe in Helsinki, August 1, 1975, see *Public Papers of the Presidents of the United States: Gerald R. Ford, 1975* (Washington, 1977), vol. II, pp. 1074–1081.

Poland. These violations—part of a broader pattern of Soviet lack of restraint—threaten the very basis of this conference. We cannot pretend to build up the structure of peace and security here in Madrid while the foundation for that structure is being undermined in Poland. How can the United States return to negotiations on new words and new undertakings while existing obligations are being so blatantly ignored?

Today, our deliberations must focus instead on the challenges to the integrity of the Final Act and the CSCE process. To do otherwise would endanger successful negotiations, if and when circumstance permit, on the basis of the constructive proposal table by the neutral and nonaligned states last fall. Even more fundamentally, it would dishonor the Final Act and our commitment to uphold it.

Mr. Chairman, I want to conclude by quoting from the Polish Bishops who wrote recently that "real peace stems from respect for freedom and the correct understanding of everyone's right to freedom." This lies at the heart of the Helsinki process. In the final analysis, peace and security in Europe depend on respect for the freedom of nations and individuals in Europe. Recognition of this fact is the key to the removal of the barriers dividing East from West.

Freedom is the proudest achievement of Western civilization. It was given recent expression in the successful and peaceful transition to democracy in Portugal and here in Spain. The vision of man as a creative and responsible individual has flourished despite the artificial divisions decreed by ideologues and dictators. Western ideals nourish all the nations of Europe, not only those members of the Atlantic world. After a quarter century of Iron Curtain and cold war, the Helsinki Final Act promised a new era because it was based on this unifying vision of man. But the ideals of the West are in danger if their defense is not considered vital by the nations of Europe. The process of reconciliation can be halted if we ignore the acts that betray our faith. The structure of security and cooperation can collapse if we avert our eyes from the undermining of its foundation. Only full observance of the Helsinki Final Act will ensure the solidarity of the nations of Europe. Only respect for freedom will ensure the survival and flourishing of Western civilization.

Document 158

Statement by the Under Secretary of State for Political Affairs (Eagleburger) Before the U.S. Congressional Commission on Security and Cooperation in Europe, March 23, 1982[8]

Current State of the CSCE Process

Mr. Chairman,[9] it is a pleasure for me to appear with Ambassador Kampelman today to give the Commission the Department's views on the recent session at Madrid[10] and, indeed, on the state of the CSCE process as a whole.

As you know, the goal of the United States at Madrid has been to strengthen the process launched at Helsinki nearly 7 years ago. We have sought to do this through a detailed review of implementation of the commitments the signatory states undertook when they signed the CSCE Final Act in 1975.[11] And we have sponsored and supported new proposals that would build on all aspects of the Final Act—in the field of human rights and humanitarian affairs, in economic issues, and in military security. But from the outset, the Madrid conference has been encumbered by actions of the Soviet Union and, in several instances, by other East European governments which are contrary to the spirit and letter of the Final Act.

The Soviet invasion of Afghanistan, repression of human rights activists, jamming of Western radio broadcasts, the decrease in emigration, and the long campaign of Soviet pressure against the reform movement in Poland imposed an oppressive burden upon the Madrid meeting.

In addition, there were difficult negotiating obstacles in the conference itself. The

---

[8] Source: *Implementation of the Helsinki Accords: Hearing Before the Commission on Security and Cooperation in Europe, Ninety-seventh Congress, Second Session* (Washington, 1982), pp. 2–5.

[9] The Chairman of the Commission on Security and Cooperation, Representative Dante B. Fascell.

[10] The Madrid followup meeting of the Conference on Security and Cooperation in Europe which began on November 11, 1980, reconvened in Madrid on February 9 and recessed on March 12, 1982.

[11] For the text of the Helsinki Final Act of the Conference on Security and Cooperation in Europe, August 1, 1975, see Department of State *Bulletin*, September 1, 1975, pp. 323–350.

East has not hesitated to provoke procedural fights intended to quell the dialog CSCE was intended to foster. The East has stubbornly attacked virtually all Western initiatives in the human rights and military security areas.

Nevertheless, by December of last year, the conference had made progress. This was reflected in a draft concluding document developed by the neutral and nonalined states which contained many Western proposals and criteria.[12] This document needed improvements in the human rights and military security areas, but it clearly was a step toward final agreement.

The slow but steady progress was abruptly set back by the Soviet-inspired military crackdown against the democratic reform movement in Poland. Repression in Poland went to the core of the CSCE process. It was obvious that the reconvened Madrid meeting could have only one overriding responsibility—restoring respect for the principles and provisions of the Final Act as the foundation on which greater security and cooperation in Europe could be built.

Thus, with our allies we set the following objectives for the Madrid meeting when it reconvened in February:

First, it was imperative that those who support the Final Act must forcefully condemn those who disdain it. As Secretary Haig told the conference on February 9, and I quote: "The process of reconciliation can be halted if we ignore the acts that betray our faith. The structure of security and cooperation can collapse if we avert our eyes from the undermining of its foundation."[13]

Thus, following up on the January 11 call by the NATO foreign ministers for urgent consideration of the situation in Poland,[14] the Madrid meeting saw the largest gathering of foreign ministers from the participating states since the signing of the Final Act in 1975. Their speeches gave a strong and simple message to the East—stop repression in Poland, start honoring your commitments under the Final Act.

Our second goal was to reaffirm our own commitment to the CSCE process. The Final Act remains, in our view, a valid and important standard for guiding and measuring progress in solving the issues that divide Europe. The CSCE forum is an invaluable opportunity for East–West dialog. The CSCE process must be used to foster a climate of security and cooperation in which movements such as that of the people of Poland can flourish. We went to Madrid in February and will return to Madrid in the fall to further these aims.

Secretary Haig and every other foreign minister who addressed the session stressed the need to make the CSCE process work. In addition, Secretary Haig and other allied ministers declared that we would be ready not only to resume consideration of new commitments in CSCE, but to aid economic recovery in Poland when tyranny is lifted.

Finally, we were resolved not to let the reconvened Madrid meeting resume business as usual; that is, negotiation towards a substantive concluding document, while the Final Act itself was under attack. We did not lightly decide on this course. The initiatives which we and our Allies have worked long and hard to see adopted at Madrid are designed to benefit not only the West, but all the people of Europe. Precisely because we value these proposals, we would not let them be dishonored—and the victims of Soviet repression be ignored—by acting as if nothing had happened. The defense of the Final Act took priority.

The West fulfilled all three of these goals at the reconvened meeting. It did so through an impressive display of unity. Allied delegations—not just the United States, but our Canadian and European colleagues as well—led the way in condemning Eastern offenses against the Final Act; in developing and carrying out tactics for meeting Western objectives, in making sure that the East understood that the West was one in its assessment of the damage wrought by repression in Poland and the long and sorry list of other Eastern violations of the Final Act.

As a result of an initiative by the neutral and nonalined countries, the Madrid meeting recessed on March 12. It is scheduled to reconvene on November 9, and I would like to give you some thoughts on that fall session.

We have not set preconditions for returning in the fall. At the very least, we will want to use the fall session to review the situation in Poland, Eastern compliance generally with the Final Act, and the health of the CSCE process. Whether there can be

---

[12] The reference is (presumably) to the Neutral/Nonaligned (NNA) draft concluding document (RM–39) which was tabled in December 1981.

[13] For the text of Haig's statement to the CSCE meeting in Madrid, Febuary 9, 1982, see *supra*.

[14] For the text of the Declaration issued by the North Atlantic Council, January 11, 1982, see document 171.

progress toward a substantive concluding document depends on the outcome of this review. If there is no improvement in Poland—release of political prisoners, the lifting of martial law, initiation of a process of national reconciliation—then there is no prospect for the comprehensive agreement we long have sought. We do not wish for such a situation. We hope that there will be significant improvement in Poland, principally for its own sake, but also because it would create a climate that would improve chances for agreement on new initiatives under the CSCE process.

Should work resume on the draft concluding document tabled by the neutral nonalined states last December, there would be important East–West differences to overcome regarding human rights and over the mandate for the proposed Conference on Disarmament in Europe. There is no assurance that the East will be any more ready in the fall to accept our proposals than it has been in the past.

As a final note, I would like to pass on Secretary Haig's deep appreciation for the superb performance by Ambassador Kampelman and the members of our delegation in Madrid. For 18 months now—far longer than any of us anticipated—Max's skilled leadership and deep commitment to CSCE have contributed to Western unity and success at Madrid. Throughout the conference, but especially in the recent session, the Commission staff has been a mainstay of our effort in Madrid, both through their participation on the delegation and through their backup work here in Washington.

Let me conclude, Mr. Chairman, by saying a personal word, if I may, which is I think we all recognize the superb performance of Ambassador Kampelman and I think we are all grateful for it, but I would say that it has been an honor to work with a man who has spoken for millions of people who are not themselves able to be heard by the world, and it has been a real pleasure to work with him. Thank you, sir.

Document 159

Statement by the Chairman of the U.S. Delegation to the CSCE Madrid Review Meeting (Kampelman) Before the U.S. Congressional Commission on Security and Cooperation in Europe, March 23, 1982[15]

"The Human Rights Ideal Is a Terribly Powerful Weapon for Our Country . . ."

Thank you very much, Mr. Chairman. I do want to acknowledge with deep appreciation your own comments and those of your colleagues with respect to our performance in Madrid. I am also pleased that Secretary Eagleburger acknowledged the assistance to us from the staff of the Commission, headed by Mr. Oliver, because it was invaluable assistance. It is important that the record reflect that.

As I was listening to Secretary Eagleburger's very fine statement, which encompassed most of the questions that are raised about Madrid, I began to regret the fact that I did not have a prepared statement myself here this morning. Running through my mind was the story of the vicar who appeared before his congregation on a Sunday morning and explained how awfully busy he had been all week. He had simply not had time to prepare his sermon for the morning. He would, therefore, just speak the words that the Good Lord put in his mouth; but that next week he promised to be better prepared.

I cannot claim the lack of time, but mostly I felt if we were going to have a meaningful exchange, it would be important for me simply to give you a quick, broad view and then answer your questions.

Perhaps I should share with you, therefore, some impressions that I had after 18 months in Madrid. During those 18 months, I have probably spent more than 150 hours in private discussions, negotiations with the Soviet delegation. And one draws certain conclusions, as I have, about this kind of experience.

First, let me say that in the broad East–West context, Madrid is a side show, and we

[15] Source: *Implementation of the Helsinki Accords,* pp. 5–7.

all acknowledge that. Any of us who might tend to feel that this is really the main arena has a mistaken notion. On the other hand, even as a side show, one can learn certain lessons from it.

I sense, Mr. Chairman, a kind of arrogance on the other side which I think we must note carefully. I believe it is an arrogance that comes from an acknowledgement of their own power. This is at least my own evaluation of it.

Here we came to Madrid, certainly our delegation and practically every delegation there, in a bona fide search to see what we could do about strengthening the Helsinki Final Act. Prior to Helsinki, the Soviets, at least as a gesture toward the ideals that were implicit in this, the Soviets at least cut back on their radio jamming. Prior to Belgrade, there was an increase in emigration from the Soviet Union. And one would have thought that there would be some kind of a gesture preceding or during Madrid.

What we found was an increase in jamming and a decrease in emigration, and the period of the last 18 months has been a period of continued decrease in emigration, continued violation of human rights, violation of the provisions of the Helsinki Final Act, repression, and a kind of disdain, it seems to me, a kind of "What are you going to do about it?" At least for me, this is the message that I received, whether it was intended to be communicated to me in those terms I do not know. But I think it is important that I share that impression with you.

When we talked about victims of repression, the other side would exclaim, "Why are we so concerned about criminals and scum?" Now, this arrogance cannot be ignored, and I simply note that for what it is and for whatever lessons one wants to draw from it.

Now, I also believe, however, that they thought they might be able to get away with it. I believe they thought that the mood in Europe was such that perhaps the arrogance and their power and their military strength and the fact that they dangled the idea of a conference on disarmament might be enough so that the West would ignore these instances of human rights violations and these other transgressions of the Helsinki Final Act. I think they were surprised to find that this was not the case. Indeed, we have every reason to know from all kinds of conversations in Madrid that they were utterly surprised that Western unity should last for these 18 months.

I think these are lessons also that the United States as a government might learn and has learned. The human rights ideal is a terribly powerful weapon for our country because it is an ideal that is shared by people all over. And if we could identify ourselves and continue to identify ourselves with that ideal, this is all to our benefit.

I also think that standing tough is another indispensable part of our relationship with the Soviet Union because we are not only with the human rights equation highlighting the distinguishing characteristic between a free society and a slave society just by that stand, but if we can remain firm in our views once we establish what our views are on a particular subject, I think that too is very important. This is true for two reasons: the message it gives to the other side, and the feeling of confidence that our friends then begin to develop in the fact that we may have a constant position that they can identify themselves with. I think that is vital to do.

Therefore, I would say that what is necessary is a constancy of message and a consistency of message. I would summarize by saying the message should be: identifying ourselves with the aspirations of the people, which include aspirations for peace, for disarmament, for human rights; identifying ourselves with those aspirations and then challenging the Soviet Union because every single activity of that society runs contrary to those aspirations.

I have very little doubt in my mind that the decisionmakers in Moscow, who are generally slow to react, record that which is done. I also believe, based on previous experience, that they questioned the constancy of our message. They may very well believe that if they wait 6 months, and 8 months, and 10 months, they have now waited 18 months and maybe they have got to wait 24 months, that at some point the West will not be as constant, will not be as consistent, and I think that is something that we must all comprehend.

I didn't mean to go on that long, Mr. Chairman. why don't we throw this open to questions.

Document 160

Statement by President Reagan, June 18, 1982[16]

Extension of Export Sanctions Against the Soviet Union

I have reviewed the sanctions on the export of oil and gas equipment to the Soviet Union imposed on December 30, 1981, and have decided to extend these sanctions through adoption of new regulations to include equipment produced by subsidiaries of U.S. companies abroad as well as equipment produced abroad under licenses issued by U.S. companies.

The objective of the United States in imposing the sanctions has been and continues to be to advance reconciliation in Poland. Since December 30, 1981, little has changed concerning the situation in Poland; there has been no movement that would enable us to undertake positive reciprocal measures.

The decision taken today will, we believe, advance our objective of reconciliation in Poland.

Document 161

Transcript of a White House Press Briefing, June 18, 1982[17]

Expansion of Export Sanctions Against the Soviet Union

Senior Administration Official. As you know from the press statement,[18] the President at the National Security Council meeting this afternoon decided to extend the sanctions on the export of oil and gas equipment to the Soviet Union imposed last December.

Q. Was there a cutoff date? Did it expire?

Senior Administration Official. I'd like to say a few words about that decision and then answer your questions. In the statement, last December 29, President Reagan said that the Soviet Union "bears a heavy and direct responsibility for the repression in Poland."[19]

He noted that for many months the Soviets publicly and privately demanded such a crackdown, that they brought major pressures to bear on the Polish leadership and used other forms of intimidation leading to their open endorsement of the suppression which ensued.

The President said that he had sent a letter to President Brezhnev urging him to permit restoration of basic human rights in Poland as provided for in the Helsinki Final Act. President Brezhnev responded in a manner which made it clear that the Soviet Union does not understand the seriousness of our concern or its obligations under both the Helsinki Final Act and the UN Charter.[20]

The President therefore on December 29 took a series of actions with regard to the Soviet Union, including suspension of the issuance of licenses required for export to the Soviet Union, for an expanded list of oil and gas equipment including pipelayers. He also stated at that time that "if the repression continued, the United States would have no choice but to take further concrete political and economic measures affecting our relationship."

The United States Government was in communication with our friends and allies about measures we were taking then, and has continued to encourage them, as the President did at the Versailles Conference,[21] to support our actions.

Six months have now passed since the President called upon the Soviet Union to recognize the clear desire of the overwhelming majority of the Polish people for national reconciliation, renewal, and re-

---

[16] Source: White House Press Release, June 18, 1982, Office of the Press Secretary to the President; also printed in *Weekly Compilation of Presidential Documents*, June 21, 1982, p. 820.

[17] Source: Office of the Press Secretary to the President. Senior administration officials conducted this background briefing which concluded at 5:12 p.m.

[18] *Supra.*

[19] See footnote 3 to document 156.

[20] The reference is apparently to the correspondence between President Reagan and Soviet President Brezhnev in late December 1981. (*New York Times*, December 28, 1981, p. A1)

[21] For documentation on the Versailles Economic Summit meetings, June 4–6, 1982, see Chapter 5, Part F.

form. Yet, as the President has made clear, little has changed in Poland. Therefore, the President decided this afternoon that the United States should follow the course of action we are announcing today.

Now I'll be happy to answer your questions.

Q. Now will you answer the one I asked you? I didn't realize that when he imposed the sanctions they had a due date, they had a maturity date. What do you mean, "extend" them? Were they to expire?

SENIOR ADMINISTRATION OFFICIAL. No. The President made clear since the inception of the sanctions that we were trying to have movement toward achieving reconciliation in Poland. Six months have passed and there's been no movement of the type that we were trying to advance. Therefore, he felt it indicated to express our deep concern by extending those sanctions.

Q. Are you expanding them?

Q. That's why I asked you again, they weren't going to expire. You want some credit for something which in fact we didn't realize was happening.

Q. Are you expanding those?

Q. You're maintaining the sanctions that were in place and extending those sanctions extraterritorially?

SENIOR ADMINISTRATION OFFICIAL. That's correct.

Q. You're expanding to subsidiaries? It's self-explanatory?

SENIOR ADMINISTRATION OFFICIAL. It's in the statement by the President.

Q. This is specifically aimed at the GE licensing? Is that it?

SENIOR ADMINISTRATION OFFICIAL. This is one of the companies that would be affected. There are others.

Q. Which other companies?

Q. They have been affected, were they not?

SENIOR ADMINISTRATION OFFICIAL. We'll be providing at a later time the list of the companies affected.

Q. But the foreign subsidiaries now come under this. Isn't that what you mean?

Q. What is the practical impact of these?

Q. The foreign subsidiaries did come under this.

Q. No, they didn't.

Q. —Soviet pipeline—

Q. The foreign subsidiaries were exempted. Now, they're included. So, you're expanding it, is that right?

Q. Is that correct?

SENIOR ADMINISTRATION OFFICIAL. Yes.

Q. Can't we get one Q and A going on here?

SENIOR ADMINISTRATION OFFICIAL. Yes.

Q. The foreign subsidiaries had not been under—

SENIOR ADMINISTRATION OFFICIAL.—to answer that question back there. Would you repeat your question?

SENIOR ADMINISTRATION OFFICIAL. Let our colleague respond to the legal point.

SENIOR ADMINISTRATION OFFICIAL. Okay, just one moment. We'll have a legal view of this.

SENIOR ADMINISTRATION OFFICIAL. The sanctions last December applied to U.S. origin goods—the export and the re-export of U.S. origin goods. The extended sanctions now apply to subsidiaries—that is foreign subsidiaries—equipment produced by foreign subsidiaries of U.S. parent corporations as well as to the products of technology that was licensed prior to last December. That is what the extension means.

Q. What does that mean? Products of technology—explain that last—

Q. Explain that—that last part—and the products—

Q. —products of technology.

SENIOR ADMINISTRATION OFFICIAL. It applies to equipment produced under licenses as it says in the statement issued by U.S. companies to foreign companies. There was, in effect, technology that was licensed by a U.S. corporation to a foreign corporation. With those licenses, the foreign corporation produces products. Without the technology license, they would not be able to produce those products.

Q. Can you be specific in the case of the rotors? Tell us the companies involved. Explain to me, if you will and us, how that works now?

SENIOR ADMINISTRATION OFFICIAL. I would not want to comment on that. I was just attempting to give you the legal—

SENIOR ADMINISTRATION OFFICIAL. A couple more legal questions—legal questions?

Q. Let him answer the question. Let this—

Q. But—

Q. —guy answer the specifics.

Q. Yes, how does it work in the case of the rotors?

Q. What's the impact of that? That's what we're after—the impact of this extension. What's it going to do?

SENIOR ADMINISTRATION OFFICIAL. The impact would be to increase the cost, in our view, of the Siberian gas pipeline project which this administration has consistently resisted going forward and would also, according to our reports, further delay construction of this pipeline.

Q. How would it increase the cost?

Q. —how much and delay by how much?

SENIOR ADMINISTRATION OFFICIAL. There are varying reports on what the nature of the delays might be. It's very difficult, for instance, to differentiate between what delays would be caused by the systemic problems of the Soviet Union itself and those caused by the impediments which would presumably result from the—which would result from the extension of extraterritorial controls on this kind of equipment.

Q. Can you give us a range then, both on cost and time? Guesstimates? Best guess?

SENIOR ADMINISTRATION OFFICIAL. The specific costs are very difficult to identify and as far as the delay, it could be from anywhere from say one to three years.

Q. What action is the U.S. Government or is the U.S. Government capable of taking to prevent the subsidiaries or, specifically, the licensees from just going ahead and producing these turbines? What action would you take if that happens?

SENIOR ADMINISTRATION OFFICIAL. The specific measures that the United States has available to it to impede these kinds of issues will be taken up at a later time. But perhaps we can get some insight now.

SENIOR ADMINISTRATION OFFICIAL. The President's action is authorized under the Export Administration Act of 1979.[22] The Commerce Department, in conjunction with the State Department, will be issuing regulations to implement the President's decision.[23]

SENIOR ADMINISTRATION OFFICIAL. Did you have a couple of legal questions for us?

Q. Yes, I did, before you leave. He can't now do this under existing regulations, is that correct? He can't order GE—

SENIOR ADMINISTRATION OFFICIAL. The existing regulations, as I indicated, were directed at the export and re-export of U.S.-origin goods. In other words the lists of items that were subject to specific license issuances by the Commerce Department in December was extended—were expanded to include new sorts of equipment—oil and gas equipment.[24]

Q. But will GE be obliged under law to comply when these new regulations are issued?

SENIOR ADMINISTRATION OFFICIAL. Well, these regulations will have the full force and effect of U.S. law.

Q. Do you expect, however, that they will be challenged in fact in court?

SENIOR ADMINISTRATION OFFICIAL. I would certainly not want to have any speculation on that. I would have no reason to suspect that.

Q. Do you have a precise number of U.S. companies that will be affected?

SENIOR ADMINISTRATION OFFICIAL. Again, I am just attempting to answer your legal questions. I wouldn't know the answer to that.

Q. How can you—legally on—

Q. I have this question here—

Q. —the exact number of U.S. companies that will be affected by this directly?

SENIOR ADMINISTRATION OFFICIAL. Okay, a specific list of those companies will be available at a later time. It is not available—

Q. Do you have a ballpark quess—30, 50, 2,000?

SENIOR ADMINISTRATION OFFICIAL. No, we don't.

Q. Two?

Q. One?

---

[22] For the text of the Export Administration Act of 1979, P.L. 96–72, approved on September 29, 1979, see 93 Stat. 503.

[23] For the text of the Department of Commerce statement on denial orders against two West German firms, October 5, 1982, see document 212.

[24] For the text of the Department of Commerce statement, December 29, 1981, see *American Foreign Policy: Current Documents, 1981*, document 271.

SENIOR ADMINISTRATION OFFICIAL. There are three major—I am not clear whether your questions refer to companies that are not already affected by the existing controls or companies that will be affected by these controls. Is it an add-on that you want?

Q. Ones that have licensing and construction and stuff going on right now.

SENIOR ADMINISTRATION OFFICIAL. Because many of those companies are already affected by our present controls. Once the controls are—expanded is perhaps a better word to use than extended because of this time confusion that existed before—that might at most add two or three companies to the list, so we are now talking about perhaps 15 or 20 in total.

Q. What is the purpose of this?

Q. Are you saying that if something specific happens in Poland that these sanctions will be lifted, and what is it that you want to see happen in Poland? I mean, what is the criteria for lifting them?

SENIOR ADMINISTRATION OFFICIAL. Well, I think the purpose of the decision today was to make clear that no movement to our satisfaction has taken place. We are very anxious to see, naturally, any movement toward reconciliation in Poland. Those moves, when they come—and we are very hopeful that they do come—will be assessed at that time and the President will decide accordingly what commensurate measures, if any, are indicated for our side.

Q. Was the option before the President today to expand the sanctions or did it—did he—was it an act of consideration whether to lift the existing controls?

SENIOR ADMINISTRATION OFFICIAL. Naturally there were a number of options in terms of the December 29th sanctions which were considered. The decision reached today was to extend the sanctions already in place on oil and gas equipment to the U.S.S.R. to encompass, as is stated in the President's statement, to include equipment produced by subsidiaries of U.S. companies abroad as well as equipment produced abroad under licenses issued by U.S. companies.

Q. But was there an option to lift the sanctions altogether that came up?

SENIOR ADMINISTRATION OFFICIAL. There were a number of options that encompassed the full range of possibilities.

Q. Was this the toughest of the options presented to the President?

SENIOR ADMINISTRATION OFFICIAL. Without going into trying to grade the toughness of the options—

Q. No.

Q. Was this the toughest?

SENIOR ADMINISTRATION OFFICIAL. This was an expansion of the action taken on December 29th without—

Q. Excuse me. Were there other options presented to him that would have been even broader? Or was there nothing broader we could have done—let me put it more—

Q. Is this the toughest thing he could have done at this—

Q. Yes, is this the toughest thing possible for him to do?

SENIOR ADMINISTRATION OFFICIAL. The option of lifting the sanctions was one of the options considered and, yes, this was the toughest of the options.

Q. Thank you.

Q. What was the relation between this and the discussions the President had at the summit with the Western allies on further economic steps against the Soviet Union?

SENIOR ADMINISTRATION OFFICIAL. As you know, the administration has pursued a number of policies toward the Soviet Union in all areas, including the economic field. Promoting the advancement of reconciliation in Poland was one of those, and the oil and gas equipment sanctions toward the Soviet Union was designed to address advancing that process.

Another initiative being pursued by the administration has to do with efforts with our allies to restrain officially backed credits to the Soviet Union, which was, as you're aware, one of the items on the agenda at the Versailles summit.

An important first step, in our view, was taken at that time toward that particular objective, but these are being pursued on a parallel basis, if that answers your question.

Q. Reporters were told at the time that this decision would be made partly on the basis of how far the allies were willing to go in what we were asking them to do at Versailles. So what I'm asking is, was this decision made because we didn't get everything we wanted from the allies in terms of credits?

SENIOR ADMINISTRATION OFFICIAL. No, it wasn't. The decision made today was reflecting the President's judgment concerning the lack of movement in Poland.

Q. Al Haig said on-the-record, on *Air Force One* coming back from Europe, that the French agreed to the language in that statement with the—he used the word "linkage"—that there was a link between that and these pipeline parts. So, basically you're saying that you decided to tell the French you're not going to keep that deal. Right?

SENIOR ADMINISTRATION OFFICIAL. There were no deals along these lines. When you're talking about initiatives toward the Soviet Union, they run on a parallel basis, but the decision of the President today was not influenced by the progress on the credit initiative.

We do believe that there has been a very significant first step taken in that area, which is unprecedented. It's the first time that there has been an allied consensus on commercial prudence in financial dealings with the Soviet Union. We think that's very significant and we intend to pursue it. So that we see this as a separate decision.

Q. Can we have a filing break for those who need to file now?

Q. How can we negotiate on a grain deal and then stop this bit of commerce between our allies and the Soviet Union? How do we explain that seeming incongruity?

SENIOR ADMINISTRATION OFFICIAL. The grain policy has had a very—is very different at this time. In the post-Afghanistan, the United States unilaterally self-imposed a grain embargo which was very costly. The grain issue is not connected with this decision today.

Q. Why isn't it? That's the question, why is—

Q. What's the difference?

Q. Why can we sell grain? The question is why we can sell grain and we won't let our allies have this pipeline, delaying it for 3 years?

SENIOR ADMINISTRATION OFFICIAL. Well, in the first place, we are not negotiating a new long-term grain agreement with the Soviet Union at the present time, so that the premise of the question is inaccurate.

Q. What you're telling us about the credits, though, is different from what several administration officials were telling reporters in France at the time of the summit.

SENIOR ADMINISTRATION OFFICIAL. Well, okay, I'm responding now to the question on grain, on the grain agreement, if I may.

Q. Would you address the other question, then? Just—

SENIOR ADMINISTRATION OFFICIAL. As far as our decision with reference to entering into conversation with the Soviet Union with reference to a new long-term grain agreement, that is a decision that has not been made yet. Not doing so is, of course, still our policy because there has been no change on that. That was one of the sanctions that was imposed following the imposition of martial law in Poland.

Q. But you said the premise was inaccurate. But in fact, if we're not negotiating on a new contract, when the current one expires, they are free, then, to come in just as they will in our market.

SENIOR ADMINISTRATION OFFICIAL. That's true.

Q. And there will be an imbalance—that's what the contract was to correct so that we would know how much they were going to buy.

SENIOR ADMINISTRATION OFFICIAL. Yes.

Q. So don't cite that as a strong point.

SENIOR ADMINISTRATION OFFICIAL. I didn't cite it as a strong point.

Q. Yes, but you said the premise was inaccurate. In fact, the premise was accurate.

Q. Did the President not lift the grain embargo—

SENIOR ADMINISTRATION OFFICIAL. The premise was that we are—we are negotiating a new grain agreement, and I'm simply saying we are not at the present time.

Q. But the premise was that we're going to sell them grain—

Q. —not sell them pipeline.

Q. Who's going to bear the cost—this increased cost this gentleman spoke of? Is it going to be the Soviet Union, or is it going to be the four Western countries that are financing the pipeline?

SENIOR ADMINISTRATION OFFICIAL. Well, the increased cost that he was referring to, of course, were the costs of building the pipeline to the Soviet Union.

Q. They will be—they will ultimately bear the increased cost.

SENIOR ADMINISTRATION OFFICIAL. That's correct.

Q. But it will mean higher financing at the moment for the countries that are financing the pipeline, or not?

SENIOR ADMINISTRATION OFFICIAL. There should be no increase in the financing of the—

Q. Do you—

SENIOR ADMINISTRATION OFFICIAL.—the present contracts which exist with reference to the pipeline. Obviously, the longer the pipeline is delayed, as with any project, given inflation and so on and so forth, the eventual cost of the pipeline will be considerably greater than it is now—or than estimates were, initially.

Q. Can we give you another chance to make a better statement, since you haven't really made one, on what appears to be an incongruous policy where you are—where the President has lifted the grain embargo but is imposing one for these companies? And how do you—can you give us a statement on how those fit together into a foreign policy?

SENIOR ADMINISTRATION OFFICIAL. Sure. The President announced a long—a considerable time ago when he lifted the grain embargo that he did not want to impose costs on the agricultural sector of the United States in isolation and that sanctions would be imposed, if they were imposed on agriculture again, with reference to across-the-board embargo on exports to the Soviet Union. There has been no such across-the-board embargo imposed on the Soviet Union. This is strictly oil and gas equipment.

Q. Now you're isolating another sector.

Q. Aren't you penalizing this sector—

Q. Well, wait. I mean, we—(Laughter.)

Q. Let the record show a shrug.

Q. That's a great answer, but it doesn't translate into words.

Q. We can do that. When asked, they went—(Laughter.)

Q. More farmers vote, darling.

SENIOR ADMINISTRATION OFFICIAL. It has to do—it has to do with the fact that we have opposed this pipeline for a very long time in terms of energy security of Western Europe. And as a result, sanctions were applied with reference to this particular sector.

Q. What makes you think this is going to do any good? Politically, what makes you think this is going to do any good—

SENIOR ADMINISTRATION OFFICIAL. Well, I think—

Q. —in even 6 months?

SENIOR ADMINISTRATION OFFICIAL. I think that it demonstrates the will and resolve of the President to insist on movement in Poland or, according to his previous statement when imposing the sanctions, he would take further action that would be detrimental to the Soviet interests, which is obviously in a rather serious economic bind. This has—this move does penalize the Soviet economy.

Q. Does it penalize our West European allies? Might they read it as such? Are you trying to, you know, convince them that it is not meant to penalize them even though they have interests at stake in this?

SENIOR ADMINISTRATION OFFICIAL. No, this isn't meant to convince them of that. There are different, naturally, perceptions between the United States and our West European allies concerning trade with the Eastern bloc. Their trade is considerably more substantial and important to them. Geographic proximity, ethnic ties—there are a whole list of differences that exist. And, therefore, we have made efforts since the Ottawa summit[25] to make progress in closing that perceptual gap concerning our perception of the security dimensions of proceeding with the pipeline project.

THE PRESS. Thank you.

---

[25] For documentation on the Ottawa summit meetings, July 19–21, 1981, see *ibid.*, Chapter 5, Part F.

Document 162

Testimony by the Under Secretary of State for Security Assistance, Science and Technology (Buckley) Before the Senate Foreign Relations Committee, July 30, 1982 (Extract)[26]

Sanctions Signal Soviets That Repression of Poland Must End

MR. BUCKLEY. Mr. Chairman,[27] I want to thank you for the opportunity to join in this discussion of the President's decision to expand sanctions to prevent the export of oil and gas equipment and technology to the Soviet Union.

I intend to address the basis of the President's decision, the effect of the decision, and the reaction of our Western European allies.

On December 29, 1981, the President imposed selected economic sanctions against the Soviet Union because of its role in the imposition of martial law and the suppression of human rights in Poland.[28] Those sanctions included the expansion of export controls on the sale of U.S.-origin oil and gas equipment and technology and the suspension of all licensing of controlled exports to the Soviet Union. At that time, the President made it clear that if the repression in Poland continued, the United States would take further concrete economic and political actions.

Now, some 7 months later, martial law remains in effect, political detainees continue to be held, and the free trade union movement is still suppressed.

As a consequence, the President decided on June 18 to take the further concrete steps he had warned the Soviets about last December.[29] Therefore he expanded the December sanctions covering oil and gas equipment and technology to include the foreign subsidiaries and licensees of American firms. This is an area of critical importance to the economy of the Soviet Union because of its dependence on exports of petroleum and natural gas for hard currency earnings and the significance the Soviets place on the development of a vastly expanded internal gas delivery system.

The June 18 decision was based on the authority granted to the President under the Export Administration Act of 1979[30] to prohibit exports where necessary to further significantly the foreign policy interests of the United States. The act gives the President to [*the*] power to prohibit exports of goods or technology that are subject to U.S. jurisdiction or exported by any person subject to the jurisdiction of the United States.

We have taken note of the subsequent announcement of a slight relaxation of repression in Poland, but as Secretary Olmer has stated,[31] these do not begin to meet our minimum requirements. We are, however, consulting with our allies on the implications of the recent Polish announcement.

The actions taken last December had immediate effect on manufacturers and workers in the United States. U.S. firms have lost a substantial amount of potential business with the U.S.S.R., the impact being spread across a variety of industries supplying parts for the Yamal pipeline, as well as heavy machinery and technology for other construction projects.

However, by only reaching U.S.-manufactured equipment, the December controls left open an important loophole which allowed the Soviet Union to obtain equipment from foreign subsidiaries and licensees of American companies which were subject to the December sanctions. Thus, the recent expansion of those sanctions not only makes them more effective, but more equitable as well.

The obvious focus of the expanded sanctions has been on exports destined for the

---

[26] Source: *Economic Relations With the Soviet Union: Hearings Before the Subcommittee On International Economic Policy of the Committee on Foreign Relations, United States Senate, Ninety-seventh Congress, Second Session* (Washington, 1982), pp. 14–18. Buckley made a similar statement before the International Economic Policy and Trade Subcommittee of the House Foreign Affairs Committee, August 4, 1982. For the text of that statement, see *Export Controls On Oil and Gas Equipment: Hearings and Markup Before the Committee On Foreign Affairs and Its Subcommittees On Europe and the Middle East and On International Economic Policy and Trade, House of Representatives, Ninety-seventh Congress, On H.R. 6838* (Washington, 1983), pp. 96–117.

[27] Senator Charles H. Percy.

[28] See footnote 3 to document 156.

[29] Regarding President Reagan's June 18, 1982, decision to expand the sanctions against the Soviet Union, see document 160.

[30] For the text of 1979, P.L. 96–72, approved September 29, 1979, see 93 Stat. 503.

[31] For the oral and prepared statements of Lionel Olmer, Under Secretary of Commerce, see *Economic Relations With the Soviet Union*, pp. 5–13.

pipeline project. Clearly, the U.S. export control actions of December 29 and June 18 have had a major impact on equipment and the construction timetable for the Siberian gas pipeline to Europe. The U.S. position on the project is well known. We believe European participation in this project to be ill advised and potentially harmful to our joint security interests.

Upon completion, the pipeline will allow the Soviets to earn, through gas sales, some $8 billion to $10 billion per year in hard currency. Such earnings will allow the Soviets to continue purchasing large amounts of critical Western technology for the modernization of the industrial base on which its military power depends, as well as help finance foreign adventurism. It will roughly double European gas dependence on the Soviet Union, and gas is a particularly difficult fuel to replace on short notice.

As you know, the administration over the last year has encouraged the allies to develop alternatives to Soviet gas to avoid any undue dependence which could make them vulnerable to Soviet pressures. The President's decision will clearly impede the construction of the pipeline, which is already behind schedule, and it will increase its cost as well as delay the Soviet Union's plans for a dramatic expansion of its internal gas distribution system.

But, let me emphasize that this impact on the Soviet economy was not in and of itself our primary goal. We are not engaged in economic warfare with the Soviet Union. Above all, we seek an end to the repression of the Polish people. The sanctions imposed against the sale of this equipment increase the internal costs to the Soviet Union of the project and cause an additional strain on already thinly stretched Soviet resources. The President wants to make clear that the Soviets will bear those costs until there is real progress toward a restoration of basic human rights in Poland.

The extension of the sanctions obviously concerns our allies and affects our relationships with them. When the President made his decision to expand the controls, it was clear that it would not be welcomed by key allied governments. Since their expansion, our European allies have voiced their concerns individually and through the Commission of the European Community. Their complaints have centered around their contentions that sanctions will not produce desired results in Poland, that our actions exceed our legal jurisdiction, that they are extraterritorial and retroactive in effect, and that we failed to consult with them before making our decision with respect to the sanctions.

Our allies, of course, attach greater significance to trade with the Soviet Union than we do. In addition, all of Europe has felt the pinch of the current recession. Jobs and investment related to the pipeline project were expected to provide a significant boost for certain hard hit firms in heavy industry.

The President took these considerations into account in coming to his decision. He clearly recognized the effect of the economic sanctions both in Europe and in the United States. Nevertheless, the President decided that in the face of the continuing Soviet support of the repression of the Polish people, the costs of U.S. inaction simply outweighed the sacrifices that would have to be made to bring home to the Soviets our seriousness of purpose. The President had clearly stated that he would be forced to take additional measures if the situation in Poland did not improve. It did not, and he kept his word.

Our allies have questioned the legal basis of our actions. We believe, however, as Secretary Olmer has stated, that our sanctions are proper under international law. We believe that the United States can properly prescribe and enforce controls over exports and re-exports of U.S. goods and technology and over the actions of foreign subsidiaries of U.S. firms.

The provisions in private licensing contracts regarding compliance with U.S. controls demonstrates that the possibility of their being invoked is a familiar and accepted part of international commerce.

With respect to our relations with our allies, many have cited the pipeline decision as the proverbial straw that will break the camel's back and lead to a damaging policy of retaliation through higher tariffs or other measures. We disagree and believe that our differences with our allies can be resolved through continued constructive consultations. We intend to work hard toward that end. And I believe it is clear that our allies wish to work to that end with us.

I would also stress that despite our much-publicized differences, we still share a community of interests far more substantial than the issues which are in dispute at the moment. We certainly share the common goals of helping Poland achieve an end to martial law, the release of all detainees, and the reestablishment of the dialog between the government, Solidarity, and the church.

I hope this overview will provide some useful background regarding the context and effect of the President's decision to expand the sanctions against the Soviet Union for their role in the repression of the Polish people.

I look forward to hearing your views and will do my best to answer such questions as you have.

SENATOR MATHIAS. Thank you very much, Secretary Buckley. Mr. Chairman, do you want to begin?

THE CHAIRMAN. No; go ahead.

SENATOR MATHIAS. Both of you are, I know, familiar with the old legend of the dragon's teeth. Now, when you planted one of the dragon's teeth, a soldier sprang up.

I am wondering if these sanctions might not end up by being a kind of technological version of the myth of the dragon's teeth, that by imposing these sanctions we will be causing new technologies to spring up in other parts of the world where they do not now exist, in order to provide the equipment and the services that we are embargoing, and they will not only ultimately provide what we refuse to sell, but they will remain in existence as permanent competitors to U.S. business, a permanent transfer of jobs that otherwise existed in the United States for years to come.

Is that a possibility?

MR. OLMER. Certainly it is a possibility, Senator, but the question is immensely complicated, and I will try to respond regarding one small part of it, the technology.

There is no question the United States is the world's leader in oil and gas exploration, refinement, production, transmission technology, bar none, and we see no evidence of any competitor on the immediate horizon.

There are a lot of products and technologies of less than great sophistication involved in the building of the 12,000 miles of pipeline in the Soviet Union, no question. Relatively a small proportion, as I think Senator Percy indicated, is what we would call high technology. In the area that we are dealing with presently, the question of rotor sets, the building of turbines with those rotor sets, the building of compressors with those turbines, and the construction of compressor stations from the aggregate, we are talking about some unique American technology which has been licensed abroad.

One of the reasons that competition has not developed is that there just is not a huge market for those kinds of technologies and products. In effect, the world demand has been divided up, the market has been divided up, and some U.S. firms do one thing, and others perform another kind of function in the process of preparing a compressor station.

In my judgment, if others, if foreigners were to develop the competitive ability to beat out the U.S. supplier of these unique parts, it would require several years and a rather major undertaking. In the final analysis, it would be a serious competitive effort between the two to provide the relatively few purchasers of those components with end products.

So I do not think for some time we are going to face that sort of a reality. (a) We are presently the world's leader, and (b) the market for these kinds of goods and services is rather limited. Over time it could happen, but not within the near future.

MR. BUCKLEY. Mr. Chairman, if I might add to those comments, No. 1, technology is not static, and sooner or later people will catch up to our present level of development. But because we are in the lead, we can continue through refinements to stay in the lead. This has been basically true of various oilfield exploration and testing techniques. We simply have been able to stay ahead of the pack and therefore maintain our competitive edge.

I believe this will happen here as well, but in the meantime there is that critical gap spoken of by Secretary Olmer. The period of time in which alternatives would have to be found for these rotors will cause significant delays and disruptions in the process of working to complete the pipeline and meet schedule delivery. The costs of these delays and disruptions to the Soviet economy and to the Soviet earning capacity are very, very significant.

SENATOR MATHIAS. I do not think I have heard anyone deny that this action can cause some delay. But what Mr. Olmer has described is exactly what I think we have to think about. What happens after this period of a couple of years of delay? Suppose our action has driven either the West Europeans or the Soviets themselves to develop some part of this productive capacity in markets which, as Mr. Olmer has described, are very limited markets? Then we have created a situation which will be very difficult, certainly, at the very least, more difficult for us to compete in in the future because the world productive capacity will have been increased, the market presumably will not have been enormously increased, and we will, in fact, have encouraged our own competition.

MR. OLMER. I think that that is a fair statement; yes.

MR. BUCKLEY. But against that, Mr. Chairman, must be balanced what we believe would be the larger costs of remaining passive in the fact of unacceptable Soviet behavior with respect to Poland.

. . . .

Document 163

Transcript of an Interview With the Secretary of State (Shultz), September 23, 1982 (Extract)[32]

"The Sanctions Have Certainly Succeeded in Calling Everybody's Attention to Our View"

. . . .

Q. Again on the pipeline, Mr. Secretary, don't you think that your policy of sanctions has failed to improve the situation in Poland, and failed because it has damaged the relations between the United States and Europe?

SECRETARY SHULTZ. No. I don't. The sanctions have certainly succeeded in calling everybody's attention to our view of the depth and importance of the problem as represented by Soviet behavior in various parts of the world, and most recently Poland.

Poland is not an isolated example. It is a recent example and one that's very close to Europe. The President has felt it important to express himself on the subject in some ways other than with words.

I recognize there's a different opinion in Europe, but it is the view here that the pipeline is not to the advantage of Europe. The sanctions are not an effort to substitute our judgment for yours. We think you're wrong, and that you'll be sorry, and we'll be sorry too; but it is only to say in picking out something on which to register ourselves, we might as well pick out something that we think is wrong.

What the United States has said basically is we don't want to participate in it. Our sanctions tell our U.S. firms that they can't participate, and that their subsidiaries and the flow of patents and licenses and so forth are part of, in a sense, U.S. potential participation.

I think if they didn't mean anything; there wouldn't be so much commotion over them, and at a minimum we have got everybody's attention. People can see, perhaps almost because of the fact that they obviously represent problems—not only in Europe but in the United States—it only underlines the strength of the President's view.

I don't think they have failed at all. What the impacts are in the Soviet Union—there is a certain amount of information about that, but I don't know how precise it can be—but it probably has had some disruptive effect on the pipeline as such, although no one really doubts the capacity of the Soviet Union to deliver gas. They may have to divert it from some place else, but they probably can deliver it.

. . . .

Document 164

Response by a Senior Department of State Official to a Question Asked at an Interview, October 29, 1982 (Extract)[33]

Need to Develop a Strategy in East–West Economic Relations

. . . The pipeline sanctions are a statement on a piece of behavior, directed by the President. That is a kind of statement about

---

[32] Source: Department of State files. Shultz was interviewed by five European journalists from Germany, Great Britain, France, and Italy beginning at 4:32 p.m.

[33] Source: Department of State files. This interview was on background.

a strategy in East–West economic relationships. But of course, it is not a strategy, it is an action. And it is an action that is important in its own right and it is an important statement on the part of the President that in effect, some type of strategy is needed here. And I told the President I am going to do the best I can to express myself about these economic relationships. So what we have been doing, what I have been trying to develop, at the President's directions, the full participation, such that anything that happens will be supported by our allies. But what I have been trying to develop is a more satisfactory and comprehensive and supportive strategy, a (inaudible) economic strategy. And it is, I suppose in some ways surprising that there is not one, after all these years. But at least there is not anything that we can point to and say, here is a thought-through comprehensive way of looking at this that has any kind of a doctrine planted to it. Like we have a military strategy in documents only.

Document 165

Address by President Reagan, November 13, 1982[34]

President Lifts Sanctions Against Soviet Union; Announces Agreement With Allies

My fellow Americans, during the campaign 2 years ago, I spoke of the need for the United States to restore the balance in our relationship with the Soviet Union. For too many years, we had stood still while the Soviets increased their military strength, and expanded their influence from Afghanistan to Ethiopia and beyond.

I expressed a belief, which you seemed to share that it was time for the United States to chart a new course. Since then, we have embarked upon a buildup of our defense forces in order to strengthen our security and, in turn, to strengthen the prospects for peace. We still have a long way to go. But the fact that we have started on a new course has enabled us to propose the most comprehensive set of proposals for arms reduction and control in more than a quarter of a century.

It has always been my belief that, if the Soviets knew we were serious about maintaining our security, they might be more willing to negotiate seriously at the bargaining table. In the near future I will be speaking to you in more detail about this matter of arms control and, more importantly, arms reductions.

But right now, I have something in the nature of news I would like to bring you. The balance between the United States and the Soviet Union cannot be measured in weapons and bombers alone. To a large degree, the strength of each nation is, also, based on economic strength. Unfortunately, the West's economic relations with the U.S.S.R. have not always served the national security goals of the Alliance.

The Soviet Union faces serious economic problems. But we, and I mean all of the nations of the free world, have helped the Soviets avoid some hard economic choices by providing preferential terms of trade, by allowing them to acquire militarily relevant technology, and by providing them a market for their energy resources even though this creates an excessive dependence on them.

By giving such preferential treatment, we have added to our own problems—creating a situation where we have to spend more money on our defense to keep up with Soviet capabilities which we helped create. Since taking office, I have emphasized to our allies the importance of our economic, as well as our political relationship, with the Soviet Union. In July of 1981 at the economic summit meeting in Ottawa, Canada,[35] I expressed to the Heads of State of the other major Western countries and Japan my belief that we could not continue conducting business as we had. I suggested that we forge a new set of rules for economic relations with the Soviet Union which would put our security concerns foremost. I was not successful at that time in getting agreement on a common policy.

Then in December of 1981, the Polish Government at Soviet instigation imposed

---

[34] Source: White House Press Release, November 13, 1982, Office of the Press Secretary to the President; printed also in *Weekly Compilation of Presidential Documents*, November 22, 1982, pp. 1475–1476. This was a radio address given at 12:06 p.m.

[35] Regarding the Ottawa Economic Summit, July 19–21, 1981, see *American Foreign Policy: Current Documents, 1981*, Chapter 5, Part F.

martial law on the Polish people and outlawed the Solidarity Union. This action showed, graphically, that our hopes for moderation in Soviet behavior were not likely to be fulfilled. In response to that action, I imposed an embargo on selected oil and gas equipment to demonstrate our strong opposition to such actions and to penalize this sector of the Soviet economy which relies heavily on high technology, much of it from the United States.[36]

In June of this year, I extended our embargo to include not only U.S. companies and their products but subsidiaries of U.S. companies abroad and on foreign licensees of U.S. companies.[37]

Now, there's no secret that our allies didn't agree with this action. We stepped up our consultations with them in an effort to forge an enduring, realistic and security-minded economic policy toward the Soviet Union. These consultations have gone on over a period of months.

I'm pleased today to announce that the industrialized democracies have this morning reached substantial agreement on a plan of action. The understanding we've reached demonstrates that the Western Alliance is fundamentally united and intends to give consideration to strategic issues when making decisions on trade with the U.S.S.R.

As a result, we have agreed not to engage in trade arrangements which contribute to the military or strategic advantage of the U.S.S.R. or serve to preferentially aid the heavily militarized Soviet economy.

In putting these principles into practice, we will give priority attention to trade in high technology products, including those used in oil and gas production.

We will also undertake an urgent study of Western energy alternatives as well as the question of dependence on energy imports from the Soviet Union.

In addition, we've agreed on the following immediate actions: First, each partner has affirmed that no new contracts for the purchase of Soviet natural gas will be signed or approved during the course of our study of alternative Western sources of energy. Second, we and our partners will strengthen existing controls on the transfer of strategic items to the Soviet Union. Third, we will establish without delay procedures for monitoring financial relations with the Soviet Union and will work to harmonize our export credit policies.

The understanding we and our partners have reached and the actions we are taking reflect our mutual determination to overcome differences and strengthen our cohesion.

I believe this new agreement is a victory for all the allies. It puts in place a much needed policy in the economic area to complement our policies in the security area.

As I mentioned a moment ago, the United States imposed sanctions against the Soviet Union in order to demonstrate that their policies of oppression would entail substantial costs.

Well, now that we've achieved an agreement with our allies which provides for stronger and more effective measures, there is no further need for these sanctions and I am lifting them today.

The process of restoring a proper balance in relations with the Soviet Union is not ended. It will take time to make up for the losses incurred in past years. But, acting together, we and our allies are making major progress. And I'm happy to say the prospects for peace are brighter.

I have just returned to the White House from the Soviet Embassy where I signed the book of condolence for President Brezhnev. New leaders are coming to power in the Soviet Union. If they act in a responsible fashion, they meet a ready and positive response in the West.

'Til next Saturday at this same time, goodbye and God bless you.

---

[36] Regarding President Reagan's statement of December 29, 1981, announcing U.S. sanctions against the Soviet Union, see *ibid.*, document 270.

[37] Regarding President Reagan's June 18, 1982, decision to expand the sanctions against the Soviet Union, see document 160.

Document 166

Statement by the Chairman of the U.S. Delegation to the CSCE Madrid Review Meeting (Kampelman) Before the Conference on Security and Cooperation in Europe, Madrid, November 24, 1982[38]

Condemnation of Soviet Violations of Helsinki Final Act

Mr. Chairman: I believe that the previous interventions this morning have been helpful in serving to clarify some of the issues that we face at our meeting. But, I must emphasize to our Hungarian Colleague that if we are to make progress here, there must be full understanding that the amendments submitted by the Western countries[39] are not a "pretext." It is essential that the seriousness and bona fide nature of the Western proposals be appreciated if we are to find constructive solutions to the serious problems we face here.

In essence, it must be recognized that there are many delegations here, including our own, who believe that there must be an organic connection between words and deeds. Words are suspect if deeds run contrary to them. This is a logical view and if some delegations are skeptical of it, I am at a loss to understand their skepticism. Indeed, we have here the essence of the difficult problem that faces us at this meeting and has been with us for 2 years.

I listened attentively to the statement made by the Soviet delegate yesterday, in response to a statement made by our delegation. I was struck by the fact that he emphasized the compromise nature of the Helsinki Final Act. This is important. We agree. But it must be understood that in our view the essence of the compromise arrived at in 1975 will be destroyed if states here choose only selectively to abide by the commitments made and feel free to disregard other commitments made by them which are of particular importance to that compromise.

When we complain, as we have for 2 years, about Afghanistan, we are told that there was no invasion because Soviet troops were invited by the Afghan authorities. When we talk, as we have since last December, about the Soviet military pressure on Poland, we are told that the Soviets had no role. When we discuss blatant human rights violations, we are told that we are interfering in their internal affairs. In effect, we are told to disregard the very essence of the compromise arrived at in 1975. States must understand that this is not and will not be acceptable to us; and is no basis for reaching an agreement.

The issue of the non-use of force and our Helsinki humanitarian commitments are all issues that are basic to our interests. They are integral parts of the Helsinki compromise of 1975. We insist that these concerns of ours be dealt with around this table. We cannot accept the notion that a pattern of defiant behavior contrary to the provisions of the Accords is consistent with the notion of "détente" or with the letter and spirit of the Helsinki Final Act. It would be a disservice to the objective that we seek if we were to condone or disregard those actions of defiance or in any way make them accepted or acceptable parts of international life.

The amendments introduced by the Western countries to RM–39 are designed to make absolutely certain that we do not in any way unwittingly condone the irresponsibility implicit in these actions. Nor do we want our position to be interpreted as condoning irresponsible behavior that is contrary to the standards of the Helsinki Final Act. It is important that this body understand that we view such behavior as a serious matter. We and many delegations here have been making this statement continually for 2 years or more. It obviously must be repeated. The proposed Western amendments must be viewed in this context.

We opened this meeting on November 9. On that day many people in my country, many in other countries around the world, and many people in the Soviet Union,

---

[38] Source: Commission on Security and Cooperation in Europe Press Release 61, November 24, 1982. Kampelman made this speech before the informal Heads of Delegation Meeting. The Madrid followup meeting reconvened on November 9, 1982, and recessed on December 17, 1982.

[39] The reference is to the amendments to the Neutral/Non-Aligned (NNA) draft concluding document (RM–39) which was tabled in December 1981. The amendments include an affirmation of free trade unionism, a strengthening of the principle that citizens may express themselves freely on Final Act implementation, extending religious freedom, providing for an experts meeting to help solve the humanitarian problems that the Act was intended to meet, providing that there should be public access to missions, a commitment not to jam or otherwise interfere with one another's radio broadcasts, and the assurance of expanded rights of journalists.

marked the sixth anniversary of the founding of the Ukrainian Helsinki Monitoring Group. Out of 30 members of that group, 27 commemorated that occasion behind prison bars. RM–39 was introduced in December of last year. Since then, 3 of these 27 members of that Helsinki monitor group, Yuri Lytvyn and Petro and Vasyl Sychko—a father and son—were sentenced to labor camp and internal exile. This treatment demonstrates vividly the necessity for the language found in Paragraph 2 of RM–39.

In the Final Act, we agreed to deal "in a positive and humanitarian spirit" with the requests of our citizens to be reunited or to visit with relatives in other countries. We all pledged to make extra efforts in cases involving elderly or ill persons. Yet, Francesca Yanson, the 74-year-old cancer-ridden mother of a U.S. citizen, continues to be denied permission by Soviet authorities to join her son.

Seven years ago, the participating states agreed that applicants for family reunification would not be subject to recriminations. Yet, Feliks Kochubievsky, a Jewish refusenik and activist from Novosibirsk, who, together with his wife, has been trying since 1978 to secure emigration approval to join their two sons and his sister in Israel, were arrested on September 10 and charged with defaming the Soviet state.

In Basket III,[40] we agreed to promote tourism and agreed to facilitate freer movement and contacts. Yet, just 4 weeks ago, a train traveling from Kiev to Bucharest was stopped at the Soviet border. There were 11 American tourists on that train. All 11 were hauled off the train, stripped searched, and all their possessions—including bandaids and dental floss—were closely scrutinized. They asked why they were being singled out, out of all the passengers on that train, for such mistreatment. A Soviet border guard answered that it was because tensions between the United States and the USSR were increasing.

It must be understood that such incidents, multiplied by the hundreds and thousands, including one involving the wife of an American Congressman visiting the Soviet Union with her husband, continue to exacerbate relations between our states at this meeting. They lead to our conclusion that the words of the Helsinki Final Act are not consistent with the deeds of the Soviet Union and other delegations here. It is the strong view of many delegations around the table that the words to which we agree must be consonant with our actions. I urge all the delegates around the table to understand that we have serious, bona fide criticisms that will not be swept under the table by more rhetoric and empty words. Where old words are disregarded we question whether we should believe any new promises.

I was pleased to hear Ambassador Van Dongen (Netherlands) on the need to see new positive actions consistent with promises in order to give delegations that confidence. It makes sense to spend time elucidating our position. Otherwise, we have done serious damage to the Act that brings us here.

Thank you, Mr. Chairman.

Document 167

Transcript of a Joint Press Conference by the Secretary of State (Shultz) and the French Foreign Minister (Cheysson), Paris, December 14, 1982 (Extract)[41]

U.S. and European Allies Study Security Dimensions of East–West Matters

. . . .

Q. Could you be more specific in these studies? You refer to OECD and COCOM.[42] Has it been expanded in any

[40] The reference is to the third section or "basket" of the Helsinki Final Act. Basket III is intended to promote the free flow of information, ideas, and people among the participating states. This section contains specific measures which participating states resolve to undertake to foster human contacts, improved access to information, and cultural and educational exchanges. Basket III and Principal Seven of Basket I incorporate the primary human rights provisions of the Final Act.

[41] Source: Department of State Press Release 399, December 21, 1982; printed also in Department of State *Bulletin*, February 1983, pp. 26–30. Shultz was in Europe for meetings with allied and friendly nations. He left Washington on December 6 and visited Bonn, December 7–8; Brussels, December 8–11; The Hague, December 11; Rome, December 11–14; Paris, December 14–15; Madrid, December 15–16; and London, December 16–18. Additional documentation on his trip is in this chapter.

[42] The Coordinating Committee (COCOM) is a committee composed of representatives from all

way? Are you any closer to the umbrella approach you were talking about earlier on this trip?

SECRETARY SHULTZ. Let me say exactly where all these matters stand. There is a series of activities or studies that are underway or about to get underway that are specific to different subjects and I'll identify them.

First, and I think perhaps the most important, is the effort within COCOM to strengthen it in all of its various dimensions. And there is a group that has been working on that with greater intensity now for a few months.

Second, we agreed that there are other types of high technology including possibly in oil and gas technology which may, while not being directly military in their application, nevertheless have a relationship to security issues because of their strategic nature. And we agree that our people engaged in the COCOM exercise should also examine this class of technology and give us their advice and move on and do whatever we think is appropriate in that area.

Third, there was called for at Versailles[43] the establishment of a way of keeping track of the financial and trade flows between the Soviet bloc and the West just as a matter of information so that we had a better information base for any activity and this we hope to get going in the OECD as had been agreed and we should get that off the ground promptly. We will energize the OECD or request the OECD to do that.

Fourth, there is agreement that we should conduct a study about energy alternatives in Europe, but not only in Europe, but for the United States and Japan and we are looking at supply and demand to see just where we stand and where we might go and what would make sense and what would constitute in an East/West sense any potential problem or threat to us and how to deal with it. So that study will be gotten off the ground and our intention (this was agreed to in NATO for example) is to ask the OECD to undertake this effort and they may properly want to use information or resources in the IEA or it's also the case that the governments have all done an extensive amount of work on this subject. The EC Commission has done a lot of work on this so it will be readily possible to put this together.

And finally, we agreed that in view of the fact that we are all spending a lot of money and resources—we can argue enough about whether it is enough or not, but in any case—on our defense effort and that we are doing this principally for the reason that the Soviet Union is putting so much effort into this field and that constitutes a threat to us, that under those circumstances, we shouldn't make, in a sense, gifts of resources to them. Now we will energize the group that studies this general subject in the OECD to tackle it, recognizing that the subject is an exceedingly complicated one. It has lots of angles to it. It is by no means enough to say that we would agree on some rate of interest to charge. That is the tip of the iceberg you might say. So this is a subject that is very complicated and it deserves a lot of attention and study. All those things we have discussed before and we have discussed them today and while no one can be sure where we come out on them, we go into them in good faith and seeing them as related to the basic security concerns that we have.

Now, finally, we have talked before in various fora, including in the NATO meeting and various NATO meetings, about the importance of adequate consultation and coordination among sovereign countries about their overall objectives and strategies in this area of East/West trade insofar as security concerns are related to it. And we agree that it is desirable to make such an effort. It is desirable to have an effective pattern of consultation and that consultation among sovereign countries will work better, if we have some set of objectives against which to hold our discussions and have some understood way or pattern in which the consultations are going to take place. Because we all recognize that there is lots of conversation, but how purposeful—that is the issue. This is designed to make it more purposeful. How in our conversations today we talked about various possible ways to accomplish this objective and places to

---

NATO countries (except Iceland) responsible for compiling lists of strategic goods to be denied to Communist countries. It was created in 1949 with just four members and meets regularly in Paris to review the strategic embargo list. After its meeting in Paris, January 19–20, 1982, the French Ministry of Foreign Affairs issued a press release on January 20, 1982, which stated: "The aim of that meeting was to review together, after more than thirty years of the Committee's existence, the means to ensure the adaptation of its methods to the evolution of the situation, particularly in the technological field of strategic importance. In this respect the Committee reached unanimous agreement. The work was judged successful by all participants."

[43] For documentation on the Versailles Economic Summit, June 4–6, 1982, see Chapter 5, Part F.

put it and I think it is fair to say, Claude, that it was our general view, certainly President Mitterrand seemed to feel that this was the best view, in the light of the fact that what we are talking about here is essentially a security-type issue that the best place to conduct this study is probably in NATO. And we will have to consult with our allies, of course, and develop the more precise contours of what this study would be, but we have agreed that we will raise this together and see if NATO would not be the vehicle for the conduct of this study. And I think we have to recognize as well, and here it is a little difficult to arrange anything these days because you have to describe it constantly before it is all arranged. But in order for this to be effective you have to find a way to associate Japan in the effort. And so we will be in touch with the Japanese and we will be in touch with our allies and we will see if there is some way we can accomplish that and there are various possibilities but at any rate those are the objectives we have in mind. And I think they are good objectives and that the pattern that was identified in our discussions, particularly with President Mitterrand, ought to be quite workable.

Foreign Minister Cheysson. I think I will add something with your permission, George. A number of studies are in course. They will be expedited. Other studies are needed. Instructions will be given by every government to its delegation in the appropriate body in order that it should be started immediately. George Shultz gave the list of such studies. One point which we noted and which we have not recalled now, is that we happen to have a number of political meetings where policy matters could be considered at the end of May and the beginning of June—OECD ministerial meeting, Williamsburg Summit of the industrialized countries, and finally, the Atlantic Council meeting in Paris. So we think that governments should be in possession of the first conclusions of all these studies before that set of meetings, in order that they can then discuss between them. Conclusions of the studies will be sent to each government. Some of them will bear on matters which concern security and this will fall under the constraints of NATO, COCOM, or what. Other conclusions will be sent to governments which will use them within their own policies, but seeing of course that such policies be for each government coherent and compatible with the security concerns that fall under a number of bodies. Where can consultations take place then between the governments on the matters that concern security? NATO, but for one point, which is that Japan is not a member of NATO and cannot be associated with NATO. That is a difficulty. On the matters that fall outside the main security concerns, we shall have to consult when there is an occasion. When there is a political meeting at the very top or at ministerial level. This is not to deny in any manner anything that George has said but to add a few points and particularly the fact that we have noted this convergence of meetings at the end of May and beginning of June.

Q. What will the study in NATO be about? Will it be to pull them all together? Or will it be on military spending?

Secretary Shultz. It is, as I would see it, to set out our objectives as we seem to get some way of collaborating more effectively on East/West trade and financial arrangements. To set out our objectives as they relate to security, our strategy and what that entails is to have some criteria and to examine a variety of fields—some of which are already identified in the ongoing studies but may benefit from looking at them in their relationship to each other so that we have a kind of strategic effort here against which to look at individual events that come along and broad proposals that may come along.

Q. To clarify the point, is this the institutional framework in which the organic or global study of East/West trade will be carried out?

Secretary Shultz. Well, I would prefer not to use words like "organic" or "global." They seem to be words that are difficult, but I would just say that it is an effort to identify by strategic objectives to see what we are trying to accomplish, to separate that from things that we are not trying to accomplish here. After all this has to do with security-related things and most trade with the Soviet bloc does not have directly to do with security things so it's not going to do everything. We are just looking at certain things and we need a strategy to help us coordinate ourselves with respect to that.

Foreign Minister Cheysson. There is one thing which has been forgotten by both of us which is not that important, but still, the economic committee or the economic secretariat of NATO has undertaken a number of studies over the last few years and we have requested them to carry on such studies. They bear on the economic situation in the Eastern bloc. And this would be part of the data and information that would be needed and used by everyone of our governments. On the main point I agree with what George Shultz said. NATO is a proper place to consider, to coordinate action for any matter including economic subjects insofar as they concern security. The only difficulty there is that Japan is not a member of NATO and we will have to find a way to see that the Japanese also take their share of responsibility. After all, they are protected by our security system, although they are not in NATO. They are indirectly protected by the very existence of NATO in its zone of competence so they must be associated some way with the conclusions that will be drawn that concerns security. Because, I repeat, NATO is competent for us only as far as it concerns security.

Q. If it succeeds, won't the result of this study be to slow down East/West exchanges?

FOREIGN MINISTER CHEYSSON. As far as we are concerned we agree with these restrictions in trade with the East if their effect is to reenforce the military potential of trade in the East. Insofar as it concerns security, one more point. But if we consider the evolution of exchanges in the past 2 years, we see that they decreased very rapidly with the exception of trade with the United States and they have decreased with Western Europe for reasons which have nothing to do with security but only due to the lack of monetary credibility of the Eastern bloc.

SECRETARY SHULTZ. I would add one point on this question of: "If you have some procedure doesn't that slow everything down?" Well, it does introduce an element of consultation, however, I think it is likely that the consultation will be fruitful and in the end make the whole process more decisive and with a greater sense of unity behind it. And I would say beyond that, that one of the things that we seek in the COCOM process is to strengthen its administrative capacity a bit so that it is possible for things to be handled more decisively and expeditiously rather than just sort of drag on forever as they had tended to do sometimes as I understand it.

FOREIGN MINISTER CHEYSSON. We agree completely with that.

Q. First, what is your view about the future flow of credits to the Soviet Union? Secondly, what is your view about future purchases of natural gas from the Soviet Union?

FOREIGN MINISTER CHEYSSON. With regard to the flow of credits, there has been no progress in our discussions since Versailles. In other words, we are exactly where we were when we left Versailles. This being said, I'm afraid that since Versailles we noted that the flow of credits was keeping on the decline for the reasons I have already said. Banks are less tempted to open credits to Eastern Europe just now than they were 6 months ago and they were less tempted 6 months ago than they were 12 months ago. When you see the state of the balance of payments of Hungary, of Poland, of Romania and even of the Soviet Union, banks are less inclined to open credits. We should not forget that most of the credits which have been opened to support trade to the Soviet Union and to their partners have been private banking credits. The flow of credits have been on the decline and still are.

With regard to gas, we consider that no one has any right to impose any constraints to any one of our countries with regard to our supplies of energy. We are quite ready to answer questions, to explain why and how we limit the dependence resulting from gas purchases but we feel free to buy gas or to buy any other form of energy from wherever we find it fit. Dependence in the case of France—we consider that our present contracts with the Soviet Union represent a very limited dependence in proportion to our total energy supply—5 percent in toto—this being covered, compensated by the constraints that have been imposed on some of our buyers of gas in France itself, i.e., that they can shift from gas to fuel any time the gas supply will be cut. But this is our problem—our domestic problem—our own policy. What we have said and what we are ready to state again is that it is not our intention to open any new negotiation for gas purchases from the Soviet Union for the time being. But this is our decision, it could be amended if we thought it proper. We don't see why we would enter into such negotiations in the months and even years to come. But, again, this is a decision that we have taken which is our own unilateral decision. It doesn't result from any commitment to anyone.

Q. Is 5 percent a self-imposed ceiling?

FOREIGN MINISTER CHEYSSON. Well, it's a kind of proportion which we found reasonable. It goes a little beyond that. I'm not going to enter into technicalities. But the number of industries that can undertake to shift from gas to fuel overnight, if need be, is limited.

Q. Isn't it the thought, for example, that France will increase its gas imports from the

Soviet Union only to the extent that it reduces other energy imports from the Soviet Union.

FOREIGN MINISTER CHEYSSON. Well, as you know we did import over the last few years, I think, it was 1.5 million tons of crude oil from the Soviet Union and it has always been the intention of the French administration, even before we came to office, that this would progressively be cut. All the more, as it is not sure that the Soviets would be in a position to provide oil in a few years from now. This is half the total of our supplies from hydrocarbons—oil plus gas—coming from the Soviet Union is in fact limited to 5 percent. I told you in addition this 5 percent is quite reasonable due to technical constraints.

Q. You have spoken of 1983 as the most difficult year since the war. Have you discussed this today? Do you feel any better?

FOREIGN MINISTER CHEYSSON. Oh certainly not. Despite my great pleasure to meet my friend, George Shultz, he has not relieved my concerns about 1983. I don't think I put it that way to the Secretary of State in the course of the day so I have to tell him that the two reasons why I consider 1983 will [be] the most difficult year we have known since WW II is: (1) when the December 1979 two-fold decision of NATO will have to be implemented which means either the negotiations in Geneva will succeed or the missiles should be installed. This is the first reason why it will be a very difficult year. There is little doubt that the Soviets will have that very much in mind and will do every effort to try and prevent this installation of Pershings and Cruise missiles. Will you be ready to pay for that noninstallation by a success in the negotiations in Geneva.

This is our hope, but, if not, we repeated it in Brussels in the last few days, then the missiles must be installed as provided for. The second reason is that I consider, and I am not the only one, that the world economic situation has come to its worse possible situation. Purchasing power, facilities for investment, the market is being reduced in all parts of the world, especially in the Third World, which after all was a support for the "relance" (recovery) which took place after the first oil crisis. We do not see where the light can come from. Therefore, we consider 1983 will be extremely difficult in economic terms. Have we reached the threshold beyond which unemployment might become an explosive subject? No one knows. We hope not. But the growth of unemployment is still going. 1983 will be, in the economic field, the most difficult year we have known until then.

Q. How committed is the French Government to President Reagan's zero option? Have you discussed the possibility of a compromise with the Secretary?

FOREIGN MINISTER CHEYSSON. I can answer the first part of the question. The second I leave it to George. The first part of the question—we are not in that negotiation. We rely completely on our American friends to try to achieve success there. We support their position. Their position is option zero. We support option zero. Of course, if we think of possible developments we can't exclude that in the course of the negotiation, there might be slight changes. But a position taken in that negotiation, is option zero—we support that position. Now, was it discussed between the President and Mr. Shultz, I don't know. We did not discuss it together.

Q. Do you believe that the Soviets can or should have the right to negotiate on the basis of the French or British nuclear capability?

FOREIGN MINISTER CHEYSSON. We have never accepted that our own nuclear potential be taken into account. And we haven't changed our mind.

SECRETARY SHULTZ. We didn't discuss any alternatives to the zero option. I think the name Kraft was mentioned once. Our position is that the zero/zero approach is the best approach. It's very desirable to eliminate entirely that class of missiles from the European soil and we think that is a good position. And I don't have any further comments beyond what I made this afternoon on alternative proposals.

Q. Is there any chance the Soviets could accept option zero?

SECRETARY SHULTZ. Well, certainly. It's a good, sensible option. It has many attributes such as, in addition to the obvious merit of eliminating a very threatening form of weaponry, that it is easier than any other option you can think of to verify, keep track of, so it has a lot of attributes and there is a genuine interest in reductions. This is certainly a reduction. So, I think it's worth continuing to advocate it.

Q. Returning to the studies—the decisions based on the studies will be made by the individual governments. Is that correct? Secondly, at Versailles, a pledge was made that no government would undertake commitments that would undercut other governments. Does that pledge still hold?

Foreign Minister Cheysson. On your first question, no, it is not correct to say that decisions will be entirely left to the individual governments when security is concerned. Insofar as it concerns security, we, and I understand every other ally in the Atlantic Alliance, accepts the restraints resulting from the Treaty of Washington and from the COCOM arrangements which are all the time being energized, being put up to date. Yes, your interpretation is correct when the decisions bear on matters which do not concern security. They would consider that every government is free of its choice and decision. Still, even in such cases, we think it's the duty of every government to see that such decisions that they take in their sovereign right be compatible with the undertakings, with the commitments into which they have entered under the security arrangements. We can't have a policy in certain fields which would be completely incompatible with the commitments under NATO.

Q. If differences arise among the Allies over whether a particular action affects security, who will resolve that difference?

Foreign Minister Cheysson. Dialogue is the answer. We are not going to set up a court to decide that George Shultz is right when he says that potatoes are a strategic product because staff soldiers in tanks eat potatoes, and if I say to the contrary, you see. We are not going to set up a court between us.

Q. Suppose the French enter a study group. Is there a commitment at the outset that each government will respect the outcome? Don't you leave plenty of room for escape in the implementation?

Foreign Minister Cheysson. I leave it to George Shultz to answer for the United States. As far as we are concerned, I'd say that when it falls under COCOM, if a conclusion is reached in COCOM unanimously, this is the ruling in COCOM, then it is binding. If a conclusion is reached in a study group in OECD, normally, it is not binding, but the governments can turn it into something binding. That is exactly what happened with the "consensus". At the time when the so-called "consensus" was considered in committees, in meetings in OECD, OECD had no right to decide. The consensus then had to be adopted by all governments, which it was. It was automatically adopted because it had been recommended by a study group. When in COCOM, if the governments sitting in COCOM decide that such a product should be added to the list, then it becomes binding. That's what happened on a number of exports of technologies and what during the last few years.

Q. Do you have a sense of what percentage of decisions fall under COCOM and what under OECD?

Foreign Minister Cheysson. Oh no. No idea.

Secretary Shultz. Relatively speaking, I think it's fair to say that if you take total trade and then you say what proportion of that would be classified as having a security component to it, that the proportion would be probably relatively small. But, of course, to a degree, this is to some extent prejudging what results may emerge from the considerations that will be undertaken here. But I think in answer to your question that a government, certainly the U.S. Government, that started on a study saying whatever the outcome of the majority vote in the study may be, we'll be committed by it, governments don't go about it that way. They undertake, in good faith, to work on a subject together and when a consensus is reached, a general opinion is reached, if a government then undertakes as its policy to do thus and so with respect to that outcome, it will stick by it and be faithful to its commitments.

Q. Mr. Secretary, Mr. Cheysson has made clear where France stands on credits and energy. What is the direction of your thinking on flows of credit and of energy? What would you like to see the studies accomplished?

Secretary Shultz. The object as I see it is to avoid giving them the means to build up their defense capabilities. Because of what the Soviet Union is doing, it makes no sense for us to give them resources. Now, when you say how do you avoid that, what constitutes giving of resources—I'm trying to stay away from the word "subsidize" because I find it is a word that has very special meanings; but in the United States it is the kind of word I would use, but I'm not using it here because it has its own meaning here. But, to express the idea generally, now if that's what you are trying to do to avoid that, then you are undertaking something that is quite complicated and I think there is a tendency and our French friends have brought this out to say all right, we've agreed on an interest rate, that's the policy. Well, if you think about it at all carefully, and if you have been involved in business deals you recognize that that's one part of the price. There are many other dimensions. It's a complicated subject and, so at least as I see it, we will energize this study to confront the true complexity of this issue and try to disentangle it, and I don't know what the answer is at the start of the study. I do know that it is a doggone difficult subject, having struggled with it myself, both as a bidder on major items and as a government person before this in the Treasury, struggling with the credit issue as such. But I think the way in which this is being conceived of, as broader than just an interest rate, is the right way to conceive of it. It's a more accurate way. It makes contact with the subject. So that's about what I can say on it.

On the general subject of energy, I don't have anything to add to what Claude has already said. I think it is generally the case just as he said France does not have an intention of signing new gas contracts right now. That's its own decision made for good and sufficient reasons. My impression is that it is also the case among other countries. In the meantime, however, we will make a comprehensive examination of alternative supplies and what demands may be, and what makes sense and how the kind of hedges that Claude has described, of capacity to switch from one fuel to another, can be built into the system and we will have to see what outcome we get from that. Whether or not Norwegian gas plays a part in this, I don't know the answer to that. If I knew the answer, we wouldn't have to make the study. But, it is certainly a major potential source, so it's one of the things, I presume, will get a lot of attention by the people conducting the study.

FOREIGN MINISTER CHEYSSON. You used a word a little earlier, an expression, which I think is very important in the relations between allies—good faith and I'll take this problem of energy. For the time being, we do not consider that we need more gas than we have contracted for. Maybe, if there were a "relance", new economic growth, that tomorrow we would need more energy imports. Then I think it is most useful that as a result of the study in OECD, as a result of our direct contacts, we should tell our partners: Look [if] we—the Germans, British, Italians, any one of us—need that additional amount of equivalent oil supply, where are we going to find it? And then I suppose that in good faith we can together discuss where that energy can come from. We will see what we can do on the domestic plane and, as you know, the French have been pretty good at that with the development of their nuclear production. What we can't do with our domestic facilities, and what we have to import and we'll see where it has to come from and in what form. It may result by that time that if there is good faith that we find a better solution than importing more gas, than importing more energy from the Soviet Union. This will be seen at the time, and if it is seen in good faith, I'm quite sure that it will result into a contract, into an additional supply that will be considered as reasonable by everyone. But you can't say in advance.

SECRETARY SHULTZ. Recognizing that it is understandable that the questions here tonight would concentrate on East/West economic matters, I'd like to stress again that the relationship between France and the United States covers a wide array of subjects and geographical concerns that we have in common. And that, as we discuss all of these things, our relationship is deepened and strengthened. And this East/West economic matter is an aspect of it. But there are many others and they are very important. We have touched on a few tonight, but not many. I just wanted to make that remark so that the full context of these discussions is seen. And I do think on the East/West economic matters now we have a good understanding, and we will be able to proceed in one way or another, and collaborate in good faith as Claude says.

Q. What is the true value of a study group which reaches conclusions but leaves loopholes to governments to say "it's not for me?"

FOREIGN MINISTER CHEYSSON. This is the rule of the game. We're all allies but none of us can dictate to the others. And we certainly do not accept a machinery that would be in a position to make decisions superseding those of national governments unless it comes under security matters which fall within the purview of NATO or within the contraints accepted under COCOM.

Q. But the Secretary has indicated that security represents a very small percentage of these decisions.

FOREIGN MINISTER CHEYSSON. It isn't a question of percentage. We haven't touched agricultural products. They represent a very large part of the present trade. As a matter of fact it is the United States which now has a very large trade with the Soviet Union to sell agricultural products for something like 90 percent of your total exports. It is a question of dealing with those products, with those technologies which may strengthen the military potential of the Eastern bloc. There we accept the restraints. For the rest we exchange views.

SECRETARY SHULTZ. You wouldn't accept going into a study of something and say, going in before I know anything about what's going to come out of it, bind my sovereign nation. No country would do that. However, when you get to the end of the study, and if it is generally agreed that here is something that is desirable, individual countries may decide in their security interests—yes, we want to make a mutual undertaking to act in such and such a way. And that's what you get out of examining the situation and seeing where you want to go.

Q. Mr. Secretary, it's still not clear to me whether France is ready to participate in this effort to establish an East/West trade strategy.

SECRETARY SHULTZ. If it isn't clear to you by now, it's never going to be clear to you. How many times does he have to say it?

Q. Mr. Cheysson, how are you going to explain these studies to the Soviets? Won't they take offense?

FOREIGN MINISTER CHEYSSON. If they take offense, it's their affair.

SECRETARY SHULTZ. That's a good place to leave it.

Document 168

Statement by the Secretary of State (Shultz) Before the Conference on Security and Cooperation in Europe, Madrid, December 16, 1982[44]

United States Seeks to Strengthen CSCE

Ladies and gentlemen, I am delighted to be here this morning at the site of the CSCE Review Meeting, so ably hosted by the Government and people of Spain.

As you know, I have just met with Ambassador Kampelman and his NATO colleagues. I was greatly impressed by their spirit of cooperation and their dedication to strengthening the CSCE process. Through our mutual efforts to ensure that the promise of Helsinki is fulfilled in practical ways, we are advancing a process that can reduce divisions and improve the human condition in Europe.

Unfortunately, not all of the 35 signatory states have taken the commitments we freely entered into at Helsinki with equal seriousness. In Afghanistan, in Poland and in the Soviet Union, the obligations undertaken in 1975 are being flouted, with grave cost to human life and human dignity.

For the Helsinki Final Act to be a living document, it must be honored by deeds, not just words. This does not mean that we expect the Eastern countries to be like us; but we do expect a sincere effort to abide by commitments freely made: to refrain from the use or threat of force; to honor the right of peoples to self-determination; to respect the dignity and fundamental human rights of individuals at home and abroad.

Events in Poland over the past year strike at the heart of the CSCE process. It was for that reason that Western foreign ministers came to Madrid last February to stand up for the people of Poland and in defense of the Helsinki Final Act. As free nations, we cannot turn our backs on the Polish people's struggle to realize the promise of Helsinki.

We want the Madrid meeting to strengthen CSCE. We seek agreement on a full concluding document which would embody balanced progress on human rights and security issues, including the mandate for a European Security Conference. But failure to honor existing CSCE undertaking is an obstacle to such an outcome. Therefore, we have jointly sponsored new proposals which address these failures. Our proposals—on such issues as labor rights, freedom of religion, and Helsinki monitors—extend the provisions of the Final Act and make the requirement for compliance unmistakably clear.

In making these proposals, we remain mindful that the Helsinki process is more than mere words. The actions of governments are what determine whether that process will flourish or wither away. Here today, I can tell you that the United States pledges to support and promote the standards of Helsinki vigilantly. No state which seeks the goals of peace and stability in Europe can fail to do the same.

[44] Source: Department of State Press Release 392, December 16, 1982; printed also in Department of State *Bulletin*, February 1983, pp. 30–31.

Document 169

Transcript of a Department of State Press Briefing, December 20, 1982 (Extract)[45]

Secretary Shultz's Successful European Trip

SENIOR ADMINISTRATION OFFICIAL. I see there's a great deal of interest in this topic.

In general we were very pleased with the trip. We think it was successful in many respects. It achieved the objectives that we set for it.

I think, as I said before the trip started, that there was clearly a sense of malaise and a sense of crisis within the alliance. We think that the trip itself was the capstone of a process of several months where we have been able to deal effectively with a number of sensitive issues within the alliance.

I think the trip demonstrated the importance of existing transatlantic institutions such as NATO, the EC—the European Community—OECD, and the importance of consultations and what they can accomplish.

More specifically, I think there were four principal tasks that we laid out, and the Secretary accomplished those tasks.

First of all, he advanced the process of implementing the agreement on East-West economic relations, and the work program that was discussed in discussions here and in other areas we think is now going to get underway.

Secondly, we demonstrated allied resolution on the December 1979 INF decision with regard both to deployment in 1983 and continued allied support for the zero-zero negotiating approach that the President unveiled on November 18, 1981. The proposal, as you recall, calls for the elimination of an entire class of weapons.

Thirdly, we think we established on a firmer basis, particularly in the meeting with the five Cabinet Ministers in the EC Commission, a firmer basis for the resolution of transatlantic economic problems, particularly in the area of agriculture—a strong desire on both sides to avoid a disagreement or a trade war concerning agriculture.

And then fourthly, we think we solidified our relationship with a number of new governments in Europe that we held discussions [*with?*] at a high level for the first time: the new Fanfani government in Rome, the Socialist government in Madrid, the new government in The Hague.

I will just stop there and be happy to take any questions you might have.

. . . .

[45] Source: Department of State files. This briefing was conducted on background by a senior administration official beginning at 4:04 p.m.

Document 170

Report by President Reagan Submitted to the Commission on Security and Cooperation in Europe, January 1983 (Extract)[46]

Implementation of the Helsinki Final Act

OVERVIEW

The Final Act of the Conference on Security and Cooperation in Europe (CSCE) represents a framework for the 35 participating states to work to resolve the humanitarian, economic, political, and military issues that divide Europe. The Final Act underscores that each area is of equal importance to genuine security and cooperation in Europe. The Western objective has been to preserve and strengthen this process through a thorough review of implementation of the Final Act and agreement on balanced and constructive steps forward.

The Final Act recognizes that followup conferences are essential for maintaining the Helsinki framework as a vigorous process of addressing problems in Europe. These conferences have two aspects, both of great importance: review of implementation and discussion of new proposals.

The Madrid followup meeting, which began on November 11, 1980, thus far has

[46] Source: *Thirteenth Semiannual Report: Implementation of Helsinki Final Act, June 1, 1982–November 30, 1982*, Department of State Special Report No. 105, January 1983, pp. 2–3.

been unable to reach substantive agreement. Most recently, the gross violations of the Final Act, including the banning of the Solidarity trade union, which have been occurring in Poland since the imposition of martial law on December 13, 1981, have had a serious effect on the negotiations at Madrid. When the meeting resumed on November 9, 1982, the Danish representative, speaking for the West, made clear that the deteriorating record of Eastern compliance with the Final Act continued to be the major obstacle to agreement at Madrid.

Status of the Madrid Meeting

The first phase of the Madrid meeting (to mid-December 1980) was primarily devoted to a review of how well the participating states had fulfilled their obligations under the provisions of the Helsinki Final Act. The focus then shifted to discussion of proposals to further the implementation of the Final Act and to actual drafting of a concluding document. The United States and other Western delegations continued to raise implementation issues as circumstances warranted.

From the outset, two issues have proved particularly contentious: balanced progress on human rights and the mandate for a post-Madrid conference on the military aspects of security. Discussion and progress on these issues was outlined in previous reports. The imposition of martial law on December 13, 1981, and the subsequent suspension of civil rights in Poland brought the negotiations on a draft concluding document to a halt. It became clear that there was no possibility of adopting a concluding agreement in the face of massive violations of existing Final Act commitments in Poland and the Soviet Union. The meeting resumed on February 9[47] with concerted Western attention to repression in Poland and Eastern procedural maneuvers designed to stifle criticism over Eastern violations of the Final Act. It recessed again on March 12 after then Secretary of State Haig and the other Western Foreign Ministers who addressed the Madrid meeting stressed that the meeting could not return to business as usual until there was evidence of Eastern intent to live up to the Final Act, and the Polish people were again free to exercise their rights to self-determination and other fundamental freedoms.

When the meeting resumed on November 9, the United States was prepared to resume the effort to strengthen the Helsinki process if the East made a genuine effort to live up to its existing Final Act commitments, including genuine improvement of the situation in Poland.

Review of Implementation

Review of implementation is necessary both to demonstrate the concerns of the participating states over shortcomings in implementing the Final Act, and to point out areas that require further attention in the discussion of new proposals. The discussion of new proposals provides an opportunity to build on the Final Act.

The United States and other Western countries have used the Madrid meeting for a constructive effort to improve security and cooperation in Europe. The West has raised matters of implementation—particularly the continuing Soviet repression of dissidents and suppression of civil liberties in Poland—as necessary. And there was very tough bargaining on new proposals to insure that agreements reached at Madrid, however modest, involve concrete, balanced, practical, and genuine steps forward.

The Western review of implementation was especially extensive in the field of human rights, with particular attention given to specific issues and cases in the human rights records of a number of countries. Virtually all other Western countries joined the United States in its efforts to examine fully human rights implementation. Many Eastern countries, for their part, addressed human rights questions, thereby strengthening the CSCE mandate of review of implementation.

In the area of implementation, the oppression in Poland constitutes a massive violation of the Final Act for which the Polish authorities and the Soviet Union bear full responsibility. The military regime of General Wojciech Jaruzelski clearly has failed to abide by Principle VII concerning respect for 0 human rights and fundamental freedoms. Soviet complicity in the continuing suppression of the Poles also violates Soviet commitments under the Final Act. Of course, Soviet violations of the Final Act continued in a number of other areas, including the continued military occupation of Afghanistan and repression of the Helsinki "watch groups" that had formed to monitor the Soviet Government's implementation of the Final Act.

When the Madrid session resumed on November 9, there was another forceful demonstration of Western concern over

[47] Regarding the CSCE meeting, February 9–March 12, 1982, see documents 157–159.

Poland. Western delegations, beginning with Denmark representing the EC–10 and the NATO Allies, renewed their criticism of the continuing suppression of Solidarity and the Polish people. The West noted that there had been no significant improvement in Poland nor in Soviet and other East bloc compliance with Final Act obligations in the 8 months since the meeting had recessed in March.

In this situation, the West made clear that the Neutral/Non-Aligned (NNA) draft concluding document (RM–39), tabled in December 1981, needed to be considerably strengthened if the meeting was to result in agreement on a full, substantive, and balanced final document.

To address these concerns, the Western delegations at Madrid proposed significant amendments to the NNA draft calling for, *inter alia,* free and independent trade unions, an end to repression of Helsinki monitoring groups, better treatment of journalists, a ban on jamming of radio broadcasts, and assurances that states would facilitate the exercise of religious freedoms. The West also called for an experts meeting on human contacts, including the important problems of emigration and family reunification. This meeting would be in addition to the experts meeting on human rights sponsored by the NNA countries.

Continuing the practice of the United States delegation, Ambassador Max M. Kampelman gave a series of plenary speeches indicting the East in general and the Soviet Union and Poland in particular for human rights violations, especially continuing repression in Poland, the invasion of Afghanistan, the suppression of Soviet Helsinki monitoring groups, jamming of Western radio broadcasts, continuing decline in Jewish emigration, and the recent cutback in telephone links between the Soviet Union and the West.[48]

Other Western countries also continued to review implementation at the resumed session. The Western Allies unanimously condemned the continuing state of martial law in Poland and made clear to the East that an improvement in compliance with the human rights provisions of the Final Act would improve the chances for a substantive agreement at Madrid, including a mandate for a European Disarmament Conference (CDE).

. . . .

[48] Regarding a speech by Kampelman made on November 24, 1982, to the informal Heads of Delegation Meeting, see document 166.

B. Regional Organizations

Document 171

Declaration Issued by the North Atlantic Council, Brussels, January 11, 1982[1]

NATO Response to the Imposition of Martial Law in Poland

1. The Allied governments condemn the imposition of martial law in Poland and denounce the massive violation of human rights and the suppression of fundamental civil liberties in contravention of the United Nations Charter, the Universal Declaration on Human Rights[2] and the Final Act of Helsinki.[3]

2. The process of renewal and reform which begin in Poland in August 1980 was watched with sympathy and hope by all who believe in freedom and self-determination; it resulted from a genuine effort by the overwhelming majority of the Polish people to achieve a more open society in accordance with the principles of the Final Act of Helsinki.

3. The imposition of martial law, the use of force against Polish workers, with the thousands of internments, the harsh prison sentences and the deaths that followed, have deprived the Polish people of their rights and freedoms, in particular in the field of trade unions. These acts threaten to destroy the basis for reconciliation and

[1] Source: *NATO Communiqués, 1982,* NATO Information Service, Brussels, Belgium, pp. 36–38; printed also in Department of State *Bulletin,* February 1982, pp. 19–20. The United States requested this special ministerial session of the North Atlantic Council held in Brussels, January 11, 1982, to plan an alliance response to the imposition of martial law in Poland. Secretary Haig attended this meeting.

[2] For the text of the Universal Declaration of Human Rights, see Department of State *Bulletin,* December 19, 1948, pp. 752–754.

[3] For the text of the Helsinki Final Act of the Conference on Security and Cooperation in Europe, August 1, 1975, see *ibid.,* September 1, 1975, pp. 323–350.

compromise which are necessary to progress and stability in Poland. They are in clear violation of Polish commitments under the Helsinki Final Act, particularly the principle relating to respect for human rights and fundamental freedoms. Developments in Poland demonstrate once again the rigidity of the Warsaw Pact regimes with respect to those changes necessary to meet the legitimate aspirations of their peoples.[4] This endangers public confidence in co-operation between East and West and seriously affects international relations.

4. The Allies deplore the sustained campaign mounted by the Soviet Union against efforts by the Polish people for national renewal and reform, and its active support for the subsequent systematic suppression of those efforts in Poland. These acts cannot be reconciled with the Soviet Union's international undertakings, and in particular with the principles of the Final Act of Helsinki, especially those dealing with sovereignty, non-intervention, threat of force, and self-determination. The Soviet Union has no right to determine the political and social development of Poland.

5. The Allies call upon the Polish leadership to live up to its declared intention to re-establish civil liberties and the process of reform. They urge the Polish authorities to end the state of martial law, to release those arrested, and to restore immediately a dialogue with the Church and Solidarity. Only with reconciliation and genuine negotiation can the basic rights of the Polish people and workers be protected, and the economic and social progress of the country be secured. Poland could then expect to enjoy fully the benefits of stability in Europe and of constructive political and economic relations with the West.

6. The Allies call upon the Soviet Union to respect Poland's fundamental right to solve its own problems free from foreign interference and to respect the clear desire of the overwhelming majority of the Polish people for national renewal and reform. Soviet pressure, direct or indirect, aimed at frustrating that desire, must cease. The Allies also warn that if an outside armed intervention were to take place it would have the most profound consequences for international relations.

7. In their communiqué of 11th December, 1981,[5] NATO Ministers reaffirmed their commitment to work for a climate of confidence and mutual restraint in East-West relations; what has since happened in Poland has great significance for the development of security and co-operation in Europe. The persistence of repression in Poland is eroding the political foundation for progress on the full agenda of issues which divide East and West.

8. The Allies remain committed to the policies of effective deterrence and the pursuit of arms control and in particular have welcomed the initiatives contained in President Reagan's 18th November speech.[6] The Soviet Union will bear full responsibility if its actions with regard to Poland and its failure to live up to existing international obligations damage the arms control process. A return to the process of real reforms and dialogue in Poland would help create the atmosphere of mutual confidence and restraint required for progress in negotiations in the field of arms control and limitations, including the Geneva talks on Intermediate-Range Nuclear Forces due to resume on 12th January.

9. In view of the grave developments in Poland, which constitute a serious violation of the Helsinki Final Act, the Allies agreed that the Madrid Conference[7] should deal with the situation as soon as possible at the level of Foreign Ministers.

10. The Allies will also intensify their efforts to bring to the attention of world public opinion and international organizations, including the United Nations and its specialized agencies such as the International Labour Organization, the violation of human rights and acts of violence in Poland.

11. Each Ally will, in accordance with its own situation and legislation, identify appropriate national possibilities for action in the following fields:

(a) further restrictions on the movements of Soviet and Polish diplomats, and other restrictions on Soviet and Polish diplomatic missions and organizations;

(b) reduction of scientific and technical activities on non-renewal of exchange agreements.

---

[4] The Greek delegation has reserved its position on this sentence. [Footnote in the source text.]

[5] For the text of the communiqué issued by the North Atlantic Council, December 11, 1981, see *American Foreign Policy: Current Documents, 1981*, document 176.

[6] For the text of President Reagan's speech before the National Press Club, November 18, 1981, see *ibid.*, document 60.

[7] Regarding the meeting of the Conference on Security and Cooperation in Europe in Madrid, February 9–March 12, 1982, see documents 158 and 159.

Meanwhile the Allies emphasise:

—their determination to do what lies in their power to ensure that the truth about events in Poland continues to reach the Polish people despite the obstacles created by the authorities in Warsaw and Moscow in direct contravention of their obligations under the Helsinki Final Act;

—their resolve that the quality of their relations with the military regime in Poland should reflect the abnormal nature of the present situation and their refusal to accept it as permanent;

—their willingness to contribute, with other governments, to the solution of the problem of Polish citizens now abroad and unable or unwilling to return to their own country.[8]

12. The Allies recognize the importance of economic measures to persuade the Polish authorities and the Soviet Union of the seriousness of Western concern over developments in Poland, and stress the significance of the measures already announced by President Reagon.[8]

13. Regarding economic relations with Poland, the Allies:

—noted that future commercial credits for goods other than foods will be placed in abeyance;

—noted that the question of holding negotiations about the payments due in 1982 on Poland's official debts should for the time being, be held in suspense;

—affirmed their willingness to continue and increase humanitarian aid to the Polish people for distribution and monitoring by non-governmental organizations to ensure that it reaches the people for whom it is intended;

—noted that those Allies which sell food to Poland will seek the clearest possible Polish commitments with regard to the use of the food.[8]

14. In the current situation in Poland, economic relations with Poland and the Soviet Union are bound to be affected. Soviet actions towards Poland make it necessary for the Allies to examine the course of future economic and commercial relations with the Soviet Union. Recognising that each of the Allies will act in accordance with its own situation and laws, they will examine measures which could involve arrangements regarding imports from the Soviet Union, maritime agreements, air services agreements, the size of Soviet commercial representation and the conditions surrounding export credits.[8]

15. The Allies will maintain close consultations on the implementation of their resolve not to undermine the effect of each other's measures.

16. In addition to agreeing to consult on steps to be taken in the near future, the Allies will also reflect on longer-term East–West economic relations, particularly energy, agricultural commodities and other goods, and the export of technology, in light of the changed situation and of the need to protect their competitive position in the field of military and technological capabilities.[8]

Document 172

Address by the Director of the Bureau of Politico-Military Affairs, Department of State (Burt), Before the Copenhagen Regional Seminar, Copenhagen, February 5, 1982[9]

In Defense of Western Values

It has become something of a cliche to suggest that NATO is a victim of its own success. Thirty years of peace with freedom have, it is suggested, weakened Western resolve to preserve the former while defending the latter. Western publics have become so accustomed to tranquility that they take it for granted and are unwilling to make sacrifices to insure its continuation.

Following this thesis, the current debate within the alliance is seen as taking place between those who recognize the scope of the external threat and those who do not; between those who appreciate the strategic realities of the Western position and those who remain lulled by illusions of détente.

Yet contrary to this analysis, the major debate within the alliance is not on the

[8] The Greek delegation has reserved its position on these paragraphs. [Footnote in the source text.]

[9] Source: *Current Policy* No. 368, February 5, 1982, Bureau of Public Affairs, Department of State; printed also in Department of State *Bulletin*, April 1982, pp. 65–67.

scope of the Soviet threat but on the form of the Western response. Resistance in Europe to stronger defense measures does not stem, in the main, from complacency. In fact, opinion polls suggest that Europeans as a whole are considerably more worried that a major war may be approaching than are Americans. The strength of the peace movement in Europe demonstrates the level of anxiety. Those who march in opposition to measures designed to strengthen NATO do so, in large measure, not because they think defense no longer necessary, but because they think it no longer possible. Current differences in the alliance thus go well beyond varying perceptions of Soviet capabilities or intentions.

The world has changed significantly in many ways since NATO's inception over 30 years ago. The alliance has changed also but at a slower pace. Consequently, as it now begins its fourth decade, the West faces the need to reinvigorate its security cooperation.

One change of major significance to NATO has been the shift over the last 30 years in the U.S.-Soviet balance of power away from clear American superiority to something closer to parity. Often commented upon, and generally accepted, the consequences of this development for NATO's strategy, doctrine, and force planning are becoming more widely understood. Yet necessary corrective measures have only begun to be undertaken.

More dramatic, less often commented upon, has been the shift in the balance of power between Western Europe and the United States. Thirty-five years ago Europe lay devastated. America produced and consumed half the world's wealth. Today, Western Europe has achieved and in some places surpassed American levels of productivity and consumption. European societies are rich. European economies are dynamic. European systems of governments are solidly based. Europe is more self-reliant and self-assertive than it has been for decades. Europe is more united than it has been for centuries. Yet the patterns of Western defense remain today essentially what they were over 30 years ago.

The single most striking geopolitical change over the past 35 years is not, however, the shift between East and West, or even between the New World and the Old, but rather the shift between North and South, between the First World and the Third. In this brief span of years, the bulk of the world's population, and nearly as much of the world's territory and the world's resources, have moved from Western colonial tutelage to full independence of Western control, and in some cases toward outright hostility to Western interests. Yet the West has fashioned no consensus regarding its response to this revolution; no means for coordinating its relations with the majority of mankind; no concerted policy for defending and promoting its interests in these regions.

The pattern of Western security cooperation was thus set in an era very different from the present. It was set when Europe lay prostrate, when the United States had power to spare, when the only threat to Western interests originated with the Soviet Union, and when the only possible route for aggression was from the East. The security structure established by the West in those early postwar years met the challenges of that era successfully. This structure has continued to evolve and to meet the new challenges of successive decades. But the pace of international change has quickened, the challenges have multiplied, and the structure has begun to develop growing pains.

Throughout the postwar era, deficiencies in European defense efforts have been offset by what amounted to a surplus in American defense capabilities. Today, broadly speaking, American superiority is gone and that surplus is no more. Over the past decade, Europe has taken steps to pick up the slack. The proportional European contribution to NATO's defense has risen significantly. The West is gradually moving toward a new division of labor, one in which Europe assumes greater responsibility. The West is also gradually moving toward a recognition of common security interests extending beyond Europe. But this process still lags behind the real changes in the East–West balance, U.S.–Europe balance, and the North–South balance. Adjustments of the magnitude needed to maintain pace with these changes are bound to be painful. As the process of change within the West accelerates, as the West moves more rapidly toward a new division of labor, occasional signs of discomfort are bound to become evident.

For America, the challenge is to lead a more fractious alliance, in more difficult circumstances, with reduced margins for error, and lessened instruments for persuasion. The United States is and will remain the single most powerful member of the alliance. There is no one else to whom the baton of leadership can be passed. Yet with each passing year the task becomes more difficult; the amount of effort required greater; the end result, in terms of alliance discipline, less. In these circumstances, expressions of impatience and exasperation from Washington are from time to time to be expected.

For Europe, the challenge is to assume responsibilities for Western defense commensurate with the place Europe has attained in the West's economic system and political councils. For 35 years, Europe has gotten more defense than it has paid for. Europeans have become accustomed to relying on the United States for their defense and on the U.S. Government for their defense policies. Assuming greater responsibility for fielding an adequate Western defense will be difficult for Europe. Transferring to Europe greater responsibility for formulating and implementing Western defense policies will be even harder for Europe and for the United States.

For the West, the challenge is to develop a consensus on Western interests in the Third World and to fashion a more effective means to protect and promote them. NATO was established to defend European territory from an attack. It is not designed to deal with threats from other quarters, nor should it be turned to that purpose. Yet these other threats do exist. They endanger us all. They are unlikely to be mastered unless the West responds in a more concerted way than it has done to date.

Agreement on ends should precede discussion of means. The West's withdrawal from colonial responsibilities has left us with a crippling legacy of guilt and despair—guilt over past Western exploitation; despair over future Western ability to influence events in other areas of the world. Western policies toward the Third World thus rest, more often than not, upon little but rhetoric and good intentions and lead to little but hand wringing and inaction. Economic assistance rather than being a primacy for the promotion of Western values and interests is often little more than conscience money, designed to expiate past sins and to excuse a failure to involve ourselves directly in the fate of distant regions and forgotten peoples.

To the extent that the West has had a security policy toward the Third World over the past three decades, it has been one of gradually transferring to the United States the responsibility for protecting residual Western interests. Only 2 years ago, this process culminated in the acceptance by the United States of a unilateral responsibility for preserving Western access to the oil of the Persian Gulf, oil upon which Europe's economy runs.

This process has gone as far as it can. Europe, by reason of its economic power, its historical experience, its cultural links, and its geographic proximity, has a critical role to play in much of the Third World. A new division of labor among Western allies must result in a more equitable sharing of the costs of defending Europe. A new division of labor must also lead to a more equitable sharing of defense commitments in regions of critical importance to the West and a more equitable acceptance of the risks inherent in such commitments.

Another area in which the alliance has failed to keep pace with a changing world is in the relative priorities accorded its conventional and nuclear defense. When NATO was begun in the late 1940s, the memory of World War II was sharp. The fear of a new conventional war was keen. Europeans were willing, indeed eager, to accept a heightened risk of nuclear war to deter the outbreak of any conventional conflict. By threatening the use of nuclear weapons and equipping NATO's forces with them, Soviet conventional superiority was offset and Soviet aggressive designs discouraged.

Gradually, however, the Soviet Union developed a nuclear capability, first against Europe, then against the United States. As a result, the concept that NATO could compensate for conventional weakness with nuclear strength has come under increasing challenge. In the mid-1960's the strategy of flexible response was developed to provide the alliance with alternatives, in responding to aggression, short of nuclear war or surrender. There have since been continuing efforts to strengthen NATO's conventional defenses. But these attempts have not kept pace with European economic potential, with growing Soviet conventional capabilities, or with changes in the strategic balance between the U.S. and the Soviet Union.

Today the Western publics are clearly voicing their desire to raise, not lower, further the nuclear threshold. Certainly there are some who want no defense at all. Yet the vast majority of our peoples recognize the need for defense. They are seeking, however, an approach which reduces the risk of escalation to nuclear weapons while continuing to deter aggression at any level.

Such a defense can be constructed. Nuclear deterrence is not the sole form of dissuasion. In adopting the strategy of flexible response the alliance recognized that a more robust conventional defense, combined with the continued capability for recourse to nuclear weapons, would provide an even more effective deterrent. Faced with a credible conventional and nuclear deterrent, a potential aggressor would need to deal not just with an uncertainty over the exact location of the nuclear tripwire but with the real possibility of initial defeat at the conventional level. Thus in strengthening the alliance's conventional capabilities, we not only make nuclear war less likely, we make any war less likely.

Despite the move to flexible response, however, leaders on both sides of the Atlantic have for too long tended to implicitly accept the common wisdom that Western Europe is indefensible, and that only the threat of nuclear weapons can deter aggression. Certainly nuclear deterrence must remain an essential element of Western defense. But it is time for the problems of conventional defense to be revisited with fresh insights and new approaches. For the past several years the West's military and political leadership, its academic experts, and its journalistic commentators have subjected the nuclear apex of NATO's strategy to the most intense examination. It is time, in my view, we reexamined its conventional base.

If democracy and personal freedom are to thrive, the West requires much more than a military defense. Societies sometimes are conquered from without. Often they first crumble from within. The first bastion in the defense of Western society is that of the intellect. To rejuvenate the structure for Western security, which has kept the peace for over 30 years, the West must first regain that sense of purpose which imbued NATO's creation. The West must once again define its values. It must proclaim them and it must apply them, not just to ourselves but in our dealings with others. What makes Western values unique and worth defending is not their Western origin but their universal application.

Too often we deny the universality of our values. We apply a deadening relativism to our evaluation of other societies and our reaction to events in other regions. In Poland the Soviets are thus said to demonstrate moderation, because they suppress Polish freedom without resort to military invasion. In Afghanistan the Soviet Union is waging a genocidal campaign, employing an arsenal of deadly chemical weapons. In Southeast Asia, the Soviet Union is supplying and controlling the use of toxin weapons against unsophisticated and defenseless people. Have these crimes inspired one march in the West, one demonstration, one dramatic act of protest? I know of none.

Those in our societies who question the necessity for defense need only look East. Those who have difficulty envisaging how the Sovet Union might employ military superiority and geopolitical advantage to dominate a defenseless Europe need only regard the current condition of Poland. Those who doubt the utility of military power in our modern world need only reflect upon the basis for Soviet control of Eastern Europe. those who see little qualitative difference between Eastern and Western forms of government need only note the treatment of Poland's workers.

Yet Western opinion leaders too often regard our democratic forms of government and our free institutions as no more than cultural artifacts, the result of a more or less idiosyncratic historical development particular to Western societies. In consequence we excuse in others what we would never forgive in ourselves. We tend to regard the defense of Western values as a form of parochialism, the spread of those values as a form of aggression. We put ourselves on the psychological defensive from the start. We invite, and half accept, the outrageous arguments of the Soviet Union that the West has intervened in Poland by its expressions of support for Polish independence and liberty.

In fact the West has left the initiative in the ideological field to the Soviet Union for too long. Western values will not survive unless the West propounds them. Ideas, Plato to the contrary, do not exist in some ideal sphere, to be grasped anew by successive generations. Ideas live in the mind of man. If the idea of liberty ceases to light our eyes and to direct our action, then that idea will die. If the spark of liberty is extinguished, it will not soon be rekindled, and in the future all men will live under the varying forms of tyranny which have been the lot of most throughout man's past.

If we harbor any doubts as to whether our values are worth defending, others do not. The world over, men of different cultures, with different histories, fight and die to achieve what we have. Western values represent, as Abraham Lincoln once said of his own country, mankind's last best hope. The worth of what we have to offer is universally recognized. Freedom can remain on offer, however, only so long as we ourselves possess it, are willing to fight to preserve it, and to encourage others who grasp for it.

Document 173

Prepared Statement by the U.S. Trade Representative (Brock) Before a Subcommittee of the Senate Finance Committee, February 11, 1982[10]

European Community Agricultural Policy Harmful to U.S. Farmers

It is a pleasure to be with you this morning to discuss issues that have a significance both in terms of actual trade and in terms of our overall trade policy. The three themes of the subcommittee's hearings today are intertwined because the majority of the Section 301[11] cases that the administration is pursuing today involve the effect on U.S. agricultural interests of agricultural subsidies granted under the European Community's Common Agricultural Policy.

I should say at the outset that we and previous administrations have said that the Common Agricultural Policy, or CAP as it is commonly known, is a domestic agricultural policy and as such is legitimately the domain of the EC. If that policy had no manifestations that affected our trade, we would have no cause to publicly criticize it or to discuss it within the context of the General Agreement on Tariffs and Trade. But, unfortunately, the CAP *does* affect our trade, and we do have just cause for criticism and for bringing certain EC practices before the dispute settlement panels of the GATT.

This subcommittee knows very well the evolution of the European Economic Community from its genesis in the European Coal and Steel Community, so I won't dwell on all of the background. You are also aware that the United States has long favored European integration and as far back as the Eisenhower administration the United States has actively supported the formation of the EC. The original commitment to economic integration in the EC included the gradual establishment of a customs union—the freeing of trade between the members and the establishment of a common customs tariff on imports from third countries. For agriculture, this would mean that it would be necessary to bring some uniformity and centralization to the agricultural programs of the member nations.

Thus, when the Treaty of Rome was signed by the original six member states,[12] the groundwork for the CAP was laid. The original objectives set forth for the CAP are certainly worthy: to increase farm productivity, stabilize markets, ensure a fair standard of living for farmers, guarantee regular supplies, and ensure reasonable prices for consumers. While I find myself in general agreement with these objectives, I am very much in opposition to the ways by which the Community has sought to reach these goals.

We share many of the same goals that the framers of the Common Agricultural Policy had in mind, but we have gone about reaching those goals in a way that we believe is in conformity with our international obligations. The Community, on the other hand, has chosen to undertake a costly series of programs and then shift the burden to other countries. This burden is becoming intolerable.

I don't wish to saddle you with a series of numbers, but it is worthy of note that the cost of the CAP has increased from $7.7 billion in 1976 to $14.4 billion in 1980. These expenditures finance internal programs aimed at improving the structure of agriculture, but they also are designed to act as market supports through intervention purchases, paying for stockpiling, and for

---

[10] Source: *European Communities' Common Agricultural Policy, the Subsidies Code, and Enforcement of U.S. Rights Under Trade Agreements: Hearing Before the Subcommittee on International Trade of the Committee on Finance, United States Senate, Ninety-seventh Congress, Second Session* (Washington, 1982), pp. 22–32.

[11] Section 301 of the Trade Act of 1974 (P.L. 93–618) permits the President to take retaliatory action against a foreign government and allows domestic interests to bring to the Government's attention the fact that foreign practices are adversely affecting U.S. interests; for the text of this section, see 88 Stat. 2041. When the Trade Act of 1974 was amended and it became the Trade Agreements Act of 1979 (P.L. 96–39), Section 301 was augmented to include a list of procedures and actions the President was permitted to take; for the text, see 93 Stat. 295.

[12] The Treaty of Rome established the European Economic Community (EEC or Common Market) which was signed in Rome on March 25, 1957, by Belgium, France, West Germany, Italy, Luxembourg, and the Netherlands; for the text, see 298 UNTS 11.

export subsidies. If the taxpayers and consumers in the Community wish to contribute to the goals set forth in the CAP, they have every right to do so; after all, they elect the officials who provide the EC Commission with its direction. I begin to balk, though, when the U.S. farmer, processor, or exporter is also expected to shoulder that burden.

As an example, in my trip last December to several European capitals,[13] I was told that U.S. exports of nongrain feed ingredients, such as corn gluten, were responsible for many of the woes of the Community. I was told that the United States should voluntarily restrain its exports of such products because they competed unfairly with EC-produced corn and wheat and that the EC had no hope of bringing its expenditures for price supports under control until this "loophole" was closed. The "loophole," as they called it, is the duty-free binding that the United States paid for in earlier rounds of trade negotiations. I pointed this out and mentioned that they actually had the cause and effect reversed. I noted that it was, in fact, the unreasonably high support prices the EC offered that encouraged high priced domestic production. The domestically produced grains are consequently so costly that the feed compounders seek out corn gluten and other lower-cost grain substitutes in order to formulate their feed rations. I suggested that they should be more properly realigning their domestic grain prices than expecting us to cut back our exports.

Since I have mentioned the fact that the Community, through high support prices, induces high price production, I should also mention that this also manifests itself through the need to subsidize exports in order to bring their price down to the world market level. The EC budget is thus hit two ways—the production inducement and the export subsidy, which is euphemistically called a "restitution."

A number of products benefit from this restitution system: wheat, wheat flour, poultry and pasta are only a few examples. As you are aware, we are holding consultations with the EC in an attempt to convince them that the manner in which they are exporting these products is not in conformity with their international obligations. They disagree in several instances, and it appears that we may find it necessary to take several of these disputes to the formal GATT panel process, something we have already done in the case of wheat flour.

Again, I don't wish to burden you with statistics, but I think it worthy of note that in at least one instance we have been able to evaluate the cost to the American farmer of the EC practices. A study undertaken by Michigan State University for wheat showed that in 1981, if the EC had stocked 1 million tons of wheat and exported 7 instead of 14 million tons, the U.S. farmer would have received an additional 50 cents per bushel for his wheat. For 1982 the estimate is that a bushel would bring 35 cents more. The farmers I know would be highly pleased to get 35 to 50 cents more a bushel! *That's* what I mean about bearing the burden of the CAP.

It's not just the export subsidies that bother us, though. The Community has processing subsidies that distort trade; and they also insulate their market from world market price fluctuations through the use of variable levies that come into play when the world market price falls below some calculated minimum import price established by the EC Commission. Further distorting trade is a mechanism that imposes export levies when EC prices fall below the world price. Because the Community is so generous with its support prices, this doesn't happen often; but when it did—in the early 1970's when grain prices around the world were rising at a rapid rate—it contributed to the run up in prices and added to the instability of the world market.

Thus, while the EC has sought to stabilize its internal markets, it appears to be forcing instability on the markets of others. It is for that reason that I think we have an obligation to speak out against the external manifestations of what would otherwise be an internal EC matter.

We're deeply troubled by some of the EC practices that I have mentioned and by the fact that although the fourth CAP reform proposal in the last 6 years is now under review in Brussels, it appears that no meaningful reform is in the cards. There are some who believe that the stronger dollar has removed some of the pressure for CAP reform by making U.S. exports more expensive and consequently reducing

---

[13] Brock left Washington for Europe on December 2, 1981. He attended a conference at Ditchley Park, United Kingdom, December 4–6, and had talks with trade and agricultural officials in London, Paris, Bonn, and Brussels, December 7–12. With Haig and other members of the administration, he met with EC officials in Brussels, December 11–12, and returned to Washington, December 12.

the EC's outlay for export subsidies necessary to match our prices. I'm not certain that this is the case, but it is true that the Community has been able to reduce its payments for restitutions. Whether the freeing up of these funds for other uses has had any effect on the push for CAP reform is not clear. It does appear, though, that this latest attempt at rationalizing the CAP is doomed to failure.

Given the state of affairs described above, we cannot simply stand by while we continue to lose agricultural export markets. And this administration is not standing by—as I noted earlier we are actively investigating a series of complaints brought under Section 301 of the 1974 Trade Act involving EC export and production subsides in such products as wheat flour, pasta, poultry, sugar, and canned fruit and raisins. Most of these cases are in the early consultation stages of the dispute settlement process set forth in the Subsidies Code;[14] the wheat flour case, however, will be heard by a panel during the last week of February.

It is too early to make any definitive judgments about the effectiveness of the Subsidies Code and the dispute settlement process in imposing discipline on the use of subsidies in the agricultural sector. In any international agreement there are ambiguities of language which can only be resolved by testing on a case-by-case basis. This is particularly true of Article 10 of the Subsidies Code relating to export subsidies on primary products where the language is perhaps least precise. As you know the code does not absolutely forbid the use of export subsidies on primary agricultural products. Rather, it forbids their use only when they have certain effects, e.g., where the subsidies result in the exporting country having more than an equitable share of the world export market or in material price undercutting of other suppliers. The cases we are now investigating constitute the first test of the substantive provisions of the Subsidies Code.

However, with regard to procedural aspects of the Code, I can say even at this stage that we have been strongly dissatisfied with EC reaction to our complaints. In every case, the EC has used delaying tactics which interfere with the smooth operation of the dispute settlement process.

Let me give a few examples. In the pasta case, the United States requested consultations on December 1, 1981. The time period for consultations in this case is 30 days. Thus, the consultations should have been completed by January 1, 1982. However, the EC did not even respond to our formal request for consultations until January 25, 1982—almost 8 weeks after our request. Furthermore, they declined to hold consultations. We have replied insisting that they adhere to Code procedures.

Similarly, in the sugar case, the United States requested consultations on October 9, 1981. The EC, claiming that their practice did not constitute a subsidy, refused to consult until the United States supplied further information. We did furnish additional information on December 10, but the EC did not agree to consult until January 25, 1982. Those consultations are now scheduled for next week, more than 2 months after they should have been completed.

It was precisely because of the flagrant use of such delaying tactics in the GATT dispute settlement process that Congress, in the 1974 Trade Act directed U.S. negotiators in the Tokyo Round[15] to seek specific time limits on the dispute settlement process. I have informed EC officials in the high-level consultations held earlier this week that we cannot tolerate the continued flouting of the dispute settlement process of the Code. Furthermore, I made it clear to the EC officials, and wish to assure you, that delays in the international dispute settlement process cannot, and will not, prevent USTR from meeting its deadline to make a recommendation to the President under Section 301.

---

[14] The reference is to the GATT Subsidies Code, one of the agreements signed at the Tokyo Round in 1979 (see footnote 15) which established new rules on subsidies behavior for signatory nations. For the text of the General Agreement on Tariffs and Trade: Interpretation and Application of Articles VI, XVI and XXIII, signed at Geneva April 12, 1979, and entered into force January 1, 1980, see 31 UST 513. Article 10 pertains to export subsidies on certain primary products.

[15] The reference is to the seventh of the major multilateral trade negotiations (MTN) held under the auspices of GATT. The talks which opened in Geneva in October 1973, were called the "Tokyo Round" because they were initiated by a declaration signed in Tokyo in September 1973 at the GATT ministerial level. The agenda for the talks, attended by over 90 countries, placed special emphasis on the export needs of developing countries and also included discussions on nontariff barriers to trade, trade in agricultural goods, and trade protectionism. The talks concluded on April 12, 1979, when 23 countries initialed a comprehensive trade agreement that reduced tariffs an average of 33 percent over the succeeding 8 years and established new codes of conduct regarding nontariff barriers to trade.

This brings me to the question of the effectiveness of Section 301 in responding to policies and practices of foreign governments that are either inconsistent with their obligations under trade agreements or deemed to be unreasonable, unjustifiable or discriminatory and a burden on U.S. commerce. Section 301 is both an authorization to the President to take retaliatory action against a foreign government and a means by which domestic interests can bring to the government's attention the fact that foreign practices are adversely affecting our interests. With respect to the latter I think we must say that 301 is proving effective in light of the number of cases which are now being filed. Since August of 1981, we have received six 301 petitions. Thus, approximately 20 percent of all petitions ever filed under Section 301 since 1975 have been filed in the last 5 months. Of the six recent petitions, five have been accepted for investigation. The sixth, involving production subsidies on specialty steel, is being reviewed and a decision on whether to initiate an investigation will be made by February 26.

With respect to the effectiveness of 301 as a tool of retaliation, let me make several points. First, retaliation is not a preferred result in any 301 case. Rather our goal is to eliminate or modify a foreign practice which is adversely affecting U.S. interests. The authority to retaliate conferred by Section 301 is intended to provide the necessary leverage to obtain this result. In numerous past instances, the knowledge that the United States could retaliate under 301 has led to a settlement of the issue. Where the foreign practice complained of falls into the traditional areas of tariffs and nontariff barriers, we are able to devise an appropriate retaliatory action with relative ease. However, as the scope of the issues raised under 301 broadens beyond the traditional product area, we need to examine the scope of the President's retaliatory authority to determine if it is adequate to meet today's problems.

Specifically, I am referring to foreign practices in the investment and services sectors. Such practices are increasingly viewed as having adverse effects on U.S. economic interests. While Section 301 currently provides the President with specific authority to impose restrictions on services of a foreign country, questions may be raised as to scope of his authority and the methods by which it may be implemented. Furthermore, Section 301 provides no specific authority for the President to retaliate with investment restrictions.

While a product retaliation, for example, a tariff increase, is permissible under domestic law, in an investment or services case, such action might place the United States in violation of its international obligations under the GATT. Therefore, we are currently reviewing the entire scope of retaliatory authority and may come back to Congress to request additional authority. We are examining the legislation introduced recently to expand the President's retaliatory authority to cover investment. This proposed legislation may provide significant new and useful authority, and we will review it carefully.

Our experience with the relationship between the domestic procedures of Section 301 investigations and the Code dispute settlement process is broadening as we proceed with the investigation of the agricultural cases noted earlier. Although these investigations are still in their initial phases, we can already see some areas in which Section 301 needs to be amended.

For example, we have already experienced difficulty with Section 303. That Section requires that we request consultations with a foreign government *on the same day* that we decide to initiate an investigation into the allegations of a 301 petition.[16] The result is that we are required to initiate the dispute settlement process internationally before we've even begun our investigation domestically. In certain Subsidies Code cases, a request for consultations must include evidence of the adverse effect of the subsidy on the complaining U.S. industry. Since evidence is frequently developed in the course of the domestic investigation, we may be in a position where we are *presenting our case* in the international dispute settlement forum *before it has been fully developed.*

In addition, Section 304 differentiates between investigations relating to export and domestic subsidies with regard to the deadline for completion of the investigations. (Section 304 allows 7 months for subsidy cases, and 8 months for domestic subsidy cases.) These time periods were deliberately selected to coincide with the timing of the Code dispute settlement process. However, the Code does not differentiate on the basis of the type of subsidy involved, but rather on the basis of the Code Articles which are alleged to be

[16] When the Trade Act of 1974 (P.L. 93–618, 88 Stat. 1978) was amended and became the Trade Agreements Act of 1979 (P.L. 96–39), new Sections 303–306 were added; for the text, see 93 Stat. 295.

breached. Thus an additional month is provided for consultations where Article 8 is alleged to be violated. Since it is possible that an export subsidy may be in violation of Article 8, the domestic time limits in a 301 investigation do not necessarily match those of the Code dispute settlement process.

While we wish to gain more experience with these cases before recommending any statutory changes, it is likely that we will do so at some future date.

Document 174

Prepared Statement by the Director of the Bureau of Politico-Military Affairs, Department of State (Burt), Before Two Subcommittees of the House Foreign Affairs Committee, February 23, 1982[17]

Alliance Strategy and the Intermediate-Range Nuclear Forces Negotiations

Mr. Chairman, members of the committee: It is a pleasure to appear before you today to discuss this administration's policy on NATO, European security, nuclear deterrence, and arms control. These issues go to the heart of America's relationship with Europe, and to the Atlantic partnership which we have together fashioned. This is a partnership among free nations which share a concept of man's place in society and of the manner in which intercourse between societies should be conducted. By bridging the Atlantic with the pledge that an attack on one is an attack on all, and by giving substance to this pledge through the integration of conventional forces, nuclear forces based in Europe, and strategic nuclear forces into a single continuum of deterrent power, this partnership has allowed its members to live in freedom, peace, and prosperity for over 30 years.

The Soviet Union's ambition—reflected in its force posture, its propaganda efforts to derail NATO modernization and its INF arms control proposal—is to dissolve this partnership, to turn the United States inward, and to turn Western Europe into a nuclear hostage. The United States and its allies will not allow this to happen. By moving ahead with the implementation of both tracks of NATO's 1979 decision, the Alliance is demonstrating its resolve to turn back these Soviet efforts, and to preserve the structure of Alliance security which has maintained the peace for more than three decades.

The December 1979 NATO Decision

The decision of NATO Ministers in December 1979 to deploy new U.S. ground-launched cruise missiles and Pershing II missiles in Europe, and at the same time to engage the Soviets in arms control negotiations involving intermediate-range nuclear forces (INF) provides the framework for any discussion of contemporary NATO nuclear weapons policy.[18] This decision was the culmination of NATO's efforts over several years to come to terms with some fundamental—and troubling—shifts in the strategic environment.

One important aspect of this shift was the gradual erosion of U.S. strategic nuclear superiority over the Soviet Union. Throughout most of its history, NATO has relied for deterrence on a triad of forces—conventional forces, nuclear forces based in Europe, and strategic nuclear forces. The strategy of flexible response defines the relationship between the three legs of this triad. In response to aggression NATO would respond at a level appropriate to the nature of the aggression, and would retain the option of deliberate escalation should the initial response fail to cause the enemy to cease his attack and withdraw. The conventional forces of the Alliance, though inferior to those of the Warsaw Pact, would serve to make a conventional response to nonnuclear aggression credible; nuclear forces based in Europe would make clear the possibility of use of nuclear weapons in response to Warsaw Pact aggression of any kind, and would serve as a visible and credible link to the central strategic forces of the United States, which were, and continue to be, the ultimate deterrent.

---

[17] Source: *Overview of Nuclear Arms Control and Defense Strategy in NATO: Hearings Before the Subcommittees on International Security and Scientific Affairs and on Europe and the Middle East of the Committee on Foreign Affairs, House of Representatives, Ninety-seventh Congress, Second Session* (Washington, 1982), pp. 39–53.

[18] For the texts of the communiqués issued by the special meeting of the NATO Foreign and Defense Ministers on December 12, 1979, and the meeting of the NATO Foreign Ministers on December 14, 1979, see *American Foreign Policy: Basic Documents, 1977–1980*, pp. 494–499.

Up through the early 1970's, NATO had high confidence that this posture would deter Soviet aggression. While the Soviets had conventional superiority on the ground in central Europe, the Alliance had the means to extract a heavy price for any conventional aggression, and held the option of bringing the conflict to the nuclear level, where the West had clear-cut superiority, both in theater nuclear forces, and in strategic nuclear capabilities.

But as we moved into the mid-to-late 1970's the West began to lose this nuclear edge both in theater and in strategic forces. The result of this profound change in the strategic environment was that it was no longer clear that the posture NATO had developed and maintained over the past two decades would suffice indefinitely to deter the Soviet Union. In particular, it was feared that the Soviets could come to believe—however mistakenly—that they could threaten to use nuclear weapons based in the USSR against our European Allies without risking nuclear retaliation against the Soviet homeland.

These fears were substantiated by developments in the Soviet force posture which demonstrated that they were indeed seeking to weaken the link between U.S. strategic forces and European defense. For not only did the Soviets continue their decade-long buildup of conventional and strategic nuclear forces; they introduced in the mid-1970's a new system into their arsenal, the MIRVed SS–20 missile, whose range and mobility was designed to exploit the new strategic relationship between the United States and the USSR, and to expand significantly their capability of launching strikes against our allies from the sanctuary of their own territory. This was only part of an across-the-board nuclear modernization program which included new shorter range missiles and aircraft.

The Alliance recognized that these developments threatened to undermine the central principle upon which the Alliance was formed—that an attack on one member of the Alliance is an attack on all its members—and to decouple the U.S. strategic deterrent from the defense of Europe. The European Allies were the first to express concern about these developments. The United States responded positively. The result was the Alliance decision to deploy in Europe new systems which could reach deep into the Soviet Union, in order to demonstrate that the Soviet Union could not devastate Europe from a Russian sanctuary, and thus to ensure the Soviet recognition that any war in Europe would result in unacceptable damage to the USSR.

When INF modernization is seen in this broader context of Western deterrence strategy, the myths—sometimes expressed here, and frequently expressed across the Atlantic—which have come to surround the Alliance decision of December 1979 melt away.

The deployment of cruise and ballistic missiles to Europe does not move NATO away from its strategy of flexible response. Rather, the deployment decision is essential to sustaining NATO strategy. In particular, it will link more firmly the U.S. strategic deterrent to the defense of Europe.

This deployment was not thrust by the United States upon the Europeans. Rather it represents a considered American response to a widely felt European need for an evolutionary adjustment of NATO's capabilities to take account of the onset of strategic parity and the massive and continuing buildup of Soviet theater forces, such as the SS–20.

The deployment does not give the Alliance a qualitatively new capability. The United States has had systems in Europe capable of striking the Soviet Union since 1952. Rather this deployment will permit NATO to preserve that capability and retain that element of our deterrent strategy despite improvements in Soviet air defense, the aging of our own systems, an increasing need to commit NATO's aircraft resources to conventional roles, and large-scale new deployments of Soviet INF.

This deployment does not increase the Alliance's reliance upon nuclear weapons. Rather, in providing NATO a more balanced nuclear posture, this planned deployment has already permitted a significant net reduction in total nuclear weapons located in Europe.

This deployment does not represent a step toward the development of a NATO nuclear war-fighting capability. It is the Soviet Union which is developing the capability to fight and win a nuclear war in Europe. This deployment will force upon them the realization that NATO will not fight a war on their terms, will not permit them to regionalize a conflict to exclude Soviet territory, and will not permit them to hold Europe a nuclear hostage.

The Role of INF Arms Control

At the same time, NATO recognized that effective arms control could serve the same end—reinforcement of the link between the United States and its allies. When the Reagan administration took office, it recognized that this "track" of NATO's 1979 decision was equally important. In one of the new administration's first foreign policy steps, it announced its intentions to pursue both tracks of NATO's December 1979 decision.

Throughout 1981 the administration conducted an extensive review of U.S. INF arms control policy as part of its overall review of arms control policy. This review, and intense consultations with our NATO allies, culminated in the offer made by President Reagan in his November 18 address, to cancel U.S. plans for deployment of ground-launched cruise missiles and Pershing II missiles in exchange for the elimination of all Soviet SS–20, SS–4, and SS–5 missiles.

The rationale behind this simple and straightforward proposal is simple: If the Soviets are willing to eliminate the systems of most concern to the West, the United States is prepared to forego deployment of those systems the Soviets declare are of most concern to them—the GLCM and Pershing II. This proposal has the full support of the alliance. It provides the basis for the U.S. position in the ongoing INF arms control negotiations between the United States and Soviet Union which began in Geneva on November 30 of last year.[19]

The principles which guided the United States to adopt this position are worth highlighting because they illustrate the place of our INF objectives in our overall national security policy, and underscore our commitment to a militarily meaningful arms control:

—The agreement should focus on the most dynamic and threatening aspect of the threat: longer-range land-based INF missiles. A negotiation which attempted to encompass a wide range of other systems would divert attention away from this threat, and introduce complexities which would impede our effort to achieve agreement.

—Limitations should be global in scope. Because of the range, mobility, and transportability of modern INF missiles, such as the SS–20 missile, limits applied only to those in Europe would not effectively limit the threat to Europe.

—Limits must be equal. Equality between the United States and the Soviet Union is the only acceptable basis for an agreement. The United States cannot permit the Soviet Union to achieve superiority either through negotiation or through military buildup.

—Third-party systems should neither be limited nor compensated for in any agreement. In a bilateral U.S.-Soviet negotiation it would be totally inappropriate to negotiate on systems of countries not present at the negotiating table. The Soviet Union cannot in any case expect to be granted the right to maintain forces as large as all others combined, for the pursuit of total security by any country must result in total insecurity for all the rest.

—Any agreement must be verifiable. Given the smaller size and greater mobility of INF systems, this will be an even greater challenge in INF talks than in those on strategic arms.

The approach chosen by the President, and endorsed by the allies, adheres to these principles.

—The proposal would place limits on those Soviet systems which are of greatest concern to NATO: Longer-range land-based INF missiles such as the SS–20, and on those U.S. systems about which the Soviets have expressed most serious concern, the new ground-launched cruise missiles and Pershing II missiles.

—The proposal calls for limits on a global basis, rather than limits confined to a specific, arbitrary region. In seeking the elimination of ALL SS–20's, SS–4's, and SS–5's, the United States is willing to forego deployment of Pershing II and GLCM in any part of the world.

—The proposal would set equal limits at the zero level. The Soviets claim that they want major reductions and parity; our proposal puts that claim to the test.

—The proposal has been put forth with verification considerations clearly in mind. A total ban on a system, such as the ban we are seeking on longer-range land-based INF missiles, will be easier to verify than any numerical limit above the zero level.

The Soviet Approach

The Soviets have their own two-track approach to INF. On one track they seek to

---

[19] For the text of Secretary Haig's statement announcing the opening of negotiations between the United States and the Soviet Union on intermediate-range nuclear forces, November 30, 1981, see *American Foreign Policy: Current Documents, 1981*, document 62.

decouple the United States from Europe with force deployments. On the other track they seek to do so through arms control and propaganda. Their objective is clearly revealed in the substance of the proposals they have put forward to date.

For years the Soviets refused to place their missiles aimed at Europe on the negotiating table. They argued that since these systems could not strike the United States, but only the European Allies, they should be of no concern to the United States. It was only when faced with the prospect of new INF missile deployments in NATO Europe that they agreed to put their systems on the table at all. They have, for example, proposed a moratorium on the deployment of "medium-range" systems in Europe. This proposal is transparently designed to perpetuate the current Soviet monopoly on longer-range INF missiles, effectively blocking NATO's planned modernization. In addition, it would do nothing to prevent the Soviets from continuing deployments East of the Urals, deployments which would still pose a threat to our allies. First made publicly in October 1979 and repeated in various forms since, this moratorium proposal continues to be put forward by the Soviets, but more recently it has been accompanied by another approach designed to serve the same ends, through somewhat different means.

The Soviets publicly outlined this second proposal in TASS on February 9.[20] It calls for reductions in NATO and Soviet "medium-range systems" down to 600 by 1985, and down to 300 by 1990. Included on the Western side would be U.S. aircraft, including carrier-based and land-based aircraft not in Europe, and French and British systems. On the Soviet side the limits would include SS–20's, SS–4's and SS–5's and Backfire, Badger, and Blinder aircraft in Europe. Excluded would be all Soviet systems outside of Europe, and aircraft in Europe of comparable range and capability to those U.S. aircraft included. This proposal would give the Soviets the right to have, at the end of nearly a decade of supposed reductions, as many as 300 SS–20 launchers with at least 900 warheads in the European USSR alone—a significant increase in Soviet nuclear capabilities, despite their claims of a two-thirds reduction. It would not limit in any way existing Soviet systems outside the European USSR. These would thus be allowed to increase without limit—and could be further augmented under the loophole allowing the withdrawal of allegedly "reduced" systems from the European USSR. An SS–20, it must be noted, is rendered no less threatening if it is moved out of Europe but can still reach alliance territory.

The Soviet proposal, in short, would not require the destruction of a single SS–20 missile. Soviet reductions could be accomplished solely by retirement of older systems such as SS–4's and 5's, which Brezhnev himself has stated have outlived their useful service life. In short, it is anything but a reduction proposal as far as Soviet forces are concerned.

The Soviet proposal rests on the claim that a "balance" in "medium-range" nuclear arms exists in Europe. They cannot support this claim except by manipulation of the facts—for example by including U.S. systems not deployed in Europe, U.S. systems which do not even meet the Soviet criterion for "medium-range systems," as well as U.K. and French independent nuclear forces. The Soviets ignore the fact that if their nuclear-capable aircraft of comparable ranges are also included in the count, the disparity in their favor is made even worse. The Soviet claim that a balance exists is designed to conceal the Soviet monopoly in longer-range land-based INF missiles.

For NATO, on the other hand, the impact of the Soviet so-called reductions proposal would be a severe curtailment of existing capabilities. U.S. longer-range land-based INF missiles would be held to the present level of zero. Other U.S. intermediate-range nuclear forces would be effectively eliminated from Europe.

The proposed outcome is consistent with an apparent Soviet view that the USSR has a right to maintain forces as strong as those of all others combined and therefore must be superior to the United States.

In sum, the Soviet so-called reductions proposal:

—would not result in effective arms control;

—would codify a Soviet nuclear preponderance;

—and would serve longstanding Soviet political ambitions towards Western Europe, with the decoupling of the United States from Europe as an essential first step,

---

[20] Regarding the February 9, 1982, Soviet proposal which called for reductions in NATO and Soviet "medium-range systems" down to 600 by 1985 and to 300 by 1990, see *Current Digest of the Soviet Press*, March 3, 1982, p. 18.

thus turning NATO Europe into a nuclear hostage to the Soviet Union.

Serious negotiations can take place only at the negotiating table. The basic objectives of both sides were made public before the start of talks. The Soviets have since to put details of their negotiating position at Geneva into the public domain, in a transparent attempt to gain public support for their position and to undermine alliance support for the U.S. position. Continued public disclosures must raise doubts as to their true objectives in pursuing these negotiations.

The United States, for its part, remains committed to negotiate seriously and in good faith in Geneva. It remains our conviction that the simple, straightforward U.S. approach, developed in the course of allied consultations, offers the best and most equitable possibility of early agreement leading to real reductions. We have tabled a treaty containing detailed provisions of such an agreement, in an effort to move our discussions in Geneva forward.

Consultations

Mr. Chairman, it is particularly important that the U.S. position in these negotiations enjoy the full support of our NATO Allies. These are unique negotiations. They involve, for the first time in a bilateral negotiation, U.S. systems deployed on the territory of our allies, and Soviet systems designed to strike our allies', not our own, territory. New, truly effective consultative mechanisms have been created within the alliance in response to the unique nature of these issues: the high level group (HLG) and the Special Consultative Group (SCG).

These groups, chaired by the United States and composed of officials from capitals, have ensured a firm Alliance consensus on both tracks of the December 1979 decision. In particular, the position eventually adopted by the United States in Geneva was the result not only of careful work here in Washington, but of extensive discussions within the alliance. Both of these groups continue to meet, in order to sustain allied support for a viable nuclear posture and for a realistic approach to arms control.

It is critical to underscore the importance of maintaining support for both tracks of the December 1979 NATO decision. The modernization program is a response to a challenge to the central basis of the alliance—that an attack on one is an attack on all. Without visible and continuing support for our modernization efforts, the Soviets would have little incentive to negotiate seriously. It was only in the face of continuing alliance unity behind the modernization program that the Soviets agreed to come to the negotiating table in the first place.

Arms control cannot move forward in a political vacuum. The arms control approach chosen by the United States, and supported by the Alliance, offers a serious opportunity for effective arms limitations to eliminate the threat which made this modernization program necessary. But Soviet behavior in Poland cannot but influence the prospects for progress in these negotiations. Events in Poland cast a long shadow over all aspects of East–West relations, and erode the basis for arms control.

The United States remains committed to implementing both tracks of the December 1979 decision and so are our allies. As the depth of this Alliance-wide commitment is made manifest, the Soviets must come to realize that they are to be denied their primary political and military objective: to divide the United States from its allies, and to shatter the unity which has given NATO its strength and resilience for the past three decades. They must be brought to recognize the need to accept substantial limits on their own forces, if they are to achieve comparable limits on U.S. forces of concern to them. It is in the belief that this recognition will come that we must base optimism for the prospects of the negotiations currently underway in Geneva.

Document 175

Statement By the Head of the U.S. Delegation Intermediate-Range Nuclear Forces Negotiations (Nitze), March 31, 1982[21]

U.S. and Soviet Positions on Intermediate-Range Nuclear Forces Negotiations

Well, I have had the opportunity to brief the President in substantial detail about the

[21] Source: White House Press Release, March 31, 1982, Office of the Press Secretary to the President. This statement was made at the opening of a press briefing by Ambassador Paul Nitze and Eugene V. Rostow, Director of the Arms Control and Disarmament Agency, which began at 11:05 a.m. in the White House Briefing Room.

progress of our talks in Geneva. As you know, we began those talks last November.[22] We had a slight interruption during Christmas, and then we agreed to break for a few weeks to return to our capitals to report on the progress of the negotiations thus far.

We lost no time at all in the beginning of the negotiations on the usual questions of agenda, procedures, and so forth. We got through those in a day or two. And we got right to the subject matter, the hard substance of the negotiations.

We have had the opportunity to outline—present to the Soviet side the full basis in fact and in principle and logic of the U.S. position and to outline how we think that the President's proposal of November 18th[23] can best be implemented and carried into practice, and then in February we presented a draft of the text of an agreement—an agreement fully ready for signature.

The Soviets on their side have presented a number of proposals. Basically they are all variations from or implementation of the positions taken by Mr. Brezhnev last fall prior to the beginning of the negotiations, first in his interview in *Der Speigel* magazine[24] and then in his speeches in Bonn when he was meeting with Chancellor Schmidt.[25]

Now the essence of the U.S. position is that the United States is prepared to forego the production and testing and development and deployment of the Pershing II missiles and the ground-launched missiles which are being readied for deployment in Europe pursuant to a NATO decision in 1979, provided that the Soviet Union would forego the deployment of the comparable missiles on its side. In other words, what the U.S. position is, it should be with this range of weapons—should be zero on the U.S. side and zero on the Soviet side.

Now the essence of the Soviet position is that there should be no appreciable restraint upon the 300 SS–20 missiles that they have already deployed on their side, some of them in Europe, some of them in Siberia, and that their deployments in the non-European part of the Soviet Union should be basically without constraints.

Now there are a whole series of secondary issues, and we, I think, have made great—made substantial progress during these negotiations so far in clarifying and dealing with, in a way, these secondary issues. Now there is an awful lot of work which remains to be done and I cannot say that we have made any progress on what I outlined as being the central issue. But nevertheless I am—people generally ask me whether you are optimistic and I consider myself to be a hard-line optimist, so that even though one can realistically see all the differences that remain to be worked out, still I think that we are working at it constructively.

Document 176

Final Communiqué Issued by the North Atlantic Council, Luxembourg, May 18, 1982[26]

NATO Response to Continuing Threats to International Security

The North Atlantic Council met in Ministerial Session in Luxembourg on 17th and 18th May 1982 and agreed as follows:

1. The Allies welcome the impending accession of Spain to the North Atlantic Treaty,[27] which offers fresh evidence of the enduring vitality of the Alliance—a commu-

---

22 The United States began the Intermediate-Range Nuclear Forces Negotiations with the Soviet Union on November 30, 1981. For the text of Secretary Haig's November 30, 1981, statement announcing the opening of these negotiations, see *American Foreign Policy: Current Documents, 1981*, document 62.

23 For the text of President Reagan's speech before the National Press Club, November 18, 1981, see *ibid.*, document 60.

24 For Brezhnev's interview, see *Der Speigel*, November 2, 1981, pp. 34–35, 37, 39, 42, 44, 47, 51, 54–55, 58, 60, 63.

25 Brezhnev visited Bonn for talks with Schmidt, November 22–25, 1981.

26 Source: *NATO Communiqués, 1982*, NATO Information Service, Brussels, Belgium, pp. 17–20; printed also in Department of State *Bulletin*, August 1982, pp. 67–68. The North Atlantic Council Ministerial Meeting was held in Luxembourg, May 17–18, 1982.

27 On December 10, 1981, the Atlantic Council signed a Protocol of Accession inviting Spain to join the Alliance. The Protocol was subsequently ratified by all member countries of the Alliance, a process which was formally completed on May 29, 1982. The Secretary General then invited Spain to adhere to the North Atlantic Treaty. On May 30, 1982, Spain deposited its instrument of accession with the U.S. Government, as called for by Article 10 of the treaty, and it thus became the 16th member of the Alliance.

nity of free countries inspired by the shared values of pluralistic democracy, individual liberty, human dignity, self-determination and the rule of law in conformity with the principles and purposes of the United Nations Charter.

2. The Allies are determined to maintain adequate military strength and political solidarity in order to assure a balance of forces and to deter aggression and other forms of pressure. On this base, in the interest of peace and international stability, the Allies will persevere in their efforts to establish a more constructive East–West relationship aiming at genuine détente through dialogue and negotiation and mutually advantageous exchanges. Arms control and disarmament, together with deterrence and defence, are integral parts of Alliance security policy.

Substantial improvements in East–West relations depend, however, on the readiness of the Soviet Union and the other Warsaw Pact countries to exercise restraint and responsibility in deeds as well as in words. The continued build-up of Soviet forces across the full spectrum of military capability, the Soviet Union's aggression against the people of Afghanistan, its encouragement and support for martial law in Poland and its destabilizing activities elsewhere in the world contradict Soviet claims to peaceful intentions and weigh heavily on East–West relations.

3. The continued oppression of the Polish people violates the United Nations Charter and the Helsinki Final Act. The Allies recall their Declaration of 11th January 1982[28] and again urge the Polish authorities to end the state of martial law, release all those detained and restore genuine dialogue with the Church and Solidarity. Hopes of progress in this direction were disappointed when recent limited relaxation of certain measures taken under martial law was followed so quickly by new repressive measures. The Polish authorities should refrain from forcing Polish citizens into exile.

4. The increasing Soviet aggression against Afghanistan is meeting growing resistance by the Afghan people. The toll of death and destruction is mounting, more than three million Afghans are refugees and the stability of the region is endangered. This Soviet behaviour is unacceptable. The Allies again emphasize their support for the proposals, put forward by the United Nations and other international bodies and repeatedly ignored by the Soviet Union, for a political solution based on the total withdrawal of Soviet troops and respect for the independence, sovereignty and non-alignment of Afghanistan. They express the hope that the mission of the United Nations Secretary General's Personal Representative for Afghanistan will help to find a solution in accordance with these principles.

5. Soviet policies confirm the need for the Allies to make all necessary efforts to maintain a strong and credible defence. The Allies can preserve peace only if they have the capability and the will to defend themselves at any level in any region of the North Atlantic Treaty area. This requires a wide range of conventional and nuclear forces designed to persuade any potential aggressor that an attack would be repulsed and would expose him to risks out of all proportion to any advantages he might hope to gain. Deterrence has kept the peace in Europe for over thirty years, and this policy is still valid today. Moreover this policy is essential to bring the Soviet Union to negotiate seriously on the reduction and control of armaments.

6. Members of the Alliance have put forward a broad series of proposals aimed at achieved concrete and far-reaching progress in a number of arms control and disarmament negotiations:

—in the context of CSCE, to seek confidence and security building measures covering the whole of Europe from the Atlantic to the Urals;

—in the framework of MBFR, to establish equal collective ceilings to be achieved by manpower reductions on the basis of agreed data;

—as regards negotiations on nuclear arms, to eliminate totally United States and Soviet intermediate-range land-based missiles and to make substantial reductions in their inter-continental strategic nuclear systems.

The Allies urge the Soviet Union to respond, without further delay, in a positive way to these proposals which are designed to improve security and achieve a military balance at the lowest possible level of forces.

7. The Allies welcome President Reagan's proposal to President Brezhnev to begin the Strategic Arms Reductions Talks

[28] See document 171.

(START) by the end of June[29] and urge the Soviet Union to respond positively. The United States intention to seek significant reductions in the strategic armaments of the two countries, particularly in the most destabilizing systems, is a far-reaching but realistic offer that would lead to a significant increase in strategic stability and thereby strengthen peace and international security. Within the START framework, and pursuant to the December 1979 decision on intermediate-range nuclear forces modernization and arms control,[30] the United States is continuing to negotiate with the Soviet Union in Geneva on the basis of an imaginative proposal for the limitation of their respective intermediate-range systems.

The United States negotiating approach offers the chance for fair and effective agreements. The Allies, who remain in close consultation with the United States, support its efforts to reach such agreements.

8. The Allies participating in the Vienna talks on Mutual and Balanced Force Reductions reaffirm their determination to work for an agreement that strengthens security and peace in Europe through force reductions to equal collective manpower levels in the area of reductions. For negotiations to succeed, it will be necessary for the East to co-operate in reaching agreement on existing force levels, and on adequate associated measures to enhance stability and to verify compliance.

9. The Allies remain committed to developing and strengthening the CSCE process but recognize the severe obstacles posed by persistent Eastern violations of the principles and provisions of the Helsinki Final Act, most recently and flagrantly in Poland.

They hope that by the time the Madrid CSCE Follow-up meeting reconvenes in November, faith will have been restored in the implementation of the Final Act and that it will be possible to adopt a substantive and balanced concluding document covering all areas of the Final Act, including human rights, human contacts and information. They reaffirm their support for a Conference on Security and Disarmament in Europe and for adoption at the Madrid meeting of a precise mandate for negotiations in an initial phase of confidence and security building measures that are militarily significant, binding, verifiable and applicable throughout the whole of Europe from the Atlantic to the Urals.

10. The Allies intend to play a constructive part at the forthcoming Second United Nations Special Session on Disarmament.[31] They hope that discussion there will take full account of the need for openness and adequate verification provisions in all areas of arms control and disarmament. In the Committee on Disarmament in Geneva, the Allies will continue to work for concrete and verifiable agreements, including a total ban on all chemical weapons.

11. The maintenance of the stable situation in and around Berlin remains for the Allies an essential factor in East–West relations.

The Allies recall their statement in the Rome Communiqué of 5th May 1981[32] and express the hope that the continuation of the dialogue between the Federal Republic of Germany and the German Democratic Republic will lead to increased direct benefits for Berlin and for the people in the two German states.

12. Economic exchanges have an important role in the development of a stable East–West relationship. The Allies reaffirm their intention which they expressed in their Declaration of 11th January 1982[33] to review East–West economic relations, bearing in mind the need for such relations to be mutually advantageous and to take full account of security considerations, particularly in the technological, economic and financial areas, including export credits. In particular, they acknowledged the dangers involved in transfers of militarily relevant technology to the Warsaw Pact countries.

13. The recovery of the economic health of Allied countries is essential and integral to their defence effort. Allied governments

---

29 For the text of President Reagan's commencement address at Eureka College, Peoria, Illinois, May 9, 1982, when he invited Chairman Brezhnev to begin START talks, see document 44.

30 In this connection, Greece reserved its position and expressed its views which were recorded in the Minutes. [Footnote in the source text.]

31 The Second Special Session of the U.N. General Assembly on Disarmament was held from June 7 to July 9, 1982. For the text of President Reagan's address before this Assembly, June 17, 1982, see document 51.

32 For the text of the communiqué issued by the North Atlantic Council, May 5, 1981, see *American Foreign Policy: Current Documents, 1981*, document 157.

33 The Greek Delegation recalled its positions on various aspects of this Declaration. [Footnote in the source text.]

will work together both bilaterally and through competent organizations to further the prosperity of their peoples and the world economy. The Allies recognize the need for continued support for programmes intended to benefit the economies of the less favoured Allied partners in keeping with Article 2 of the North Atlantic Treaty.[34]

14. In view of the fundamental importance which they attach to the principle that the use of force to resolve international disputes should be resolutely opposed by the international community, the Allies condemn Argentina for its aggression against the Falkland Islands and Dependencies and deplore the fact that after more than six weeks she has still not withdrawn her forces in compliance with Mandatory Resolution 502 of the Security Council.[35] They call for a continuation of the efforts to achieve a satisfactory negotiated settlement in accordance with this Resolution in its entirety.

15. The Allies are profoundly concerned over the acts of terrorism which recur in several of their countries. They strongly condemn all such acts and solemnly appeal to all governments to wage an effective struggle against this scourge and to intensify their efforts to this end.

16. The Allies recognize that certain developments outside the Treaty area can have consequences for their common interests. They will consult together as appropriate, taking into account their commonly identified objectives. Member countries of the Alliance, in a position to do so, are ready to help other sovereign nations to resist threats to their security and independence.

17. The Allies will work together with others to strengthen and maintain the sovereignty and independence of countries in the Third World. They respect genuine non-alignment and support economic and social development in the Third World which contributes to world stability and can help to provide protection against outside interference. The Allied countries will continue the struggle against hunger, poverty and under-development.

18. Ministers agreed to intensify their consultations. They will hold an informal meeting in Autumn 1982, taking advantage of their presence in North America on the occasion of the next regular Session of the United Nations General Assembly. In this connection, they noted with pleasure the invitation of the Canadian Government to hold that meeting in Canada.

19. The next regular meeting of the North Atlantic Council in Ministerial Session will be held in Brussels in December 1982. Ministers accepted with pleasure the invitation of the Government of France for the Spring 1983 Ministerial Council meeting to take place in Paris.

Document 177

Transcript of an Interview With President Reagan, May 21, 1982 (Extract)[36]

President Praises European Willingness to Base Intermediate Missiles

. . . .

Q. Mr. President, in a few days you will be visiting the four major European partners of the United States in the Atlantic Alliance.[37] Three of these, West Germany, Britain, and Italy pledged to go ahead and modernize the nuclear weapons of NATO,

---

[34] For the text of the North Atlantic Treaty, signed at Washington, April 4, 1949, see 4 Bevans 828. Article 2 states that the Parties "will contribute toward the further development of peaceful and friendly international relations by strengthening their free institutions" and "will seek to eliminate conflict in their international economic policies and will encourage economic collaboration between any or all of them."

[35] For the text of U.N. Security Council Resolution 502, April 3, 1982, see document 623.

[36] Source: Office of the Press Secretary to the President; printed also in *Weekly Compilation of Presidential Documents*, May 31, 1982, p. 715. For the full text of the interview, see *ibid.*, pp. 710–717. President Reagan was interviewed by four representatives of West European publications: Marc Ullman of *Paris Match*, Nicholas Ashford of *The Times of London*, Thomas Kielinger of *Die Welt*, and Marino De Medici of *Il Tempo*.

[37] Reference is to President Reagan's forthcoming trip to European capitals, June 2–11. He visited Paris and Versailles to attend the eighth economic summit, June 4–6; Rome and Vatican City, June 7; London and Windsor, June 7–9; and Bonn and Berlin, June 9–11, to attend the North Atlantic Council summit in Bonn, June 10. Documentation on these visits is in this Chapter. Documentation on the Versailles Economic Summit is in Chapter 5, Part F.

a decision that was taken in December 1979. In fact, my country has already started work on our cruise missile bases. How do you assess the contribution of Italy and generally what's the prospect for productive negotiations in the area of intermediate nuclear forces?

THE PRESIDENT. I must tell you we're very grateful to Italy for its forthrightness with which it stepped forward with regard to preparations for basing of those intermediate missiles.

We know why the missiles have been requested of us by NATO. There are 900 warheads on 300 SS–20 missiles the Soviets have targeted on all of Europe and nothing comparable to counter them. The NATO decision came for Pershing missiles and cruise missiles as a deterrent to prevent the Soviets continuing that monopoly. I know that politically in Europe this was a great problem in a number of countries because of the peace movement. Some people can't quite see that unilateral disarmament is not the road to peace. But Italy was very forthright in coming forth on the preparations. We appreciate it very much. I must also salute the West German, the British, and the Belgian Governments for their leadership on this critical issue. President Mitterrand also shares our deep concern over the Soviet buildup.

The very fact that countries of Western Europe have said they were willing to base these missiles and we were willing to provide them is why the Soviets agreed to go to Geneva to meet when I proposed—why don't we negotiate a total elimination of such weapons in Europe? We won't put in the Pershings and cruise missiles if they'll do away with the SS–20's. I don't think they would have ever come to negotiate had it not been for the imminence of that proposal—the fact that we are all going forward.

I would hope that before all those missiles are in place on our side, we would have negotiated an agreement in which they'll be unnecessary and the Soviets will remove theirs.

. . . .

Document 178

Transcript of a White House Press Briefing, May 27, 1982 (Extract)[38]

The Versailles and Bonn Summits to Build a Foundation for Alliance Policies

SENIOR ADMINISTRATION OFFICIAL. My purpose as it's been explained to me is to thoroughly confuse you for 5 minutes so that these gentlemen can straighten me out afterward.

I think in trying to understand the purposes and the emphasis of the two summits, it's important to understand that from our point of view this administration came into office seeing in the past decade an alliance that had gone through a series of ups and downs, which included, obviously, Vietnam, Watergate, the agonies of that period; and some confusion in the previous 4 years with regard to the U.S. position with regard to Europe.

It was also a decade in which Henry Kissinger's Year of Europe had been misunderstood in Europe, and some of the aftermath of that still pertains. It was a period in which the blossoming of the U.S.-Soviet relationship in the early 1970's evoked European concerns over condominium, even at the same time that it was paralleled by a European rush to develop their own economic and political ties with Moscow.

It was a decade in which the 1973 war and the ensuing oil crisis brought serious differences to the surface, and worsened economic strains resulting from endemic worldwide inflation.

Despite this very bumpy decade, Europe wasn't quite prepared for this administration. In particular, whereas President Reagan was elected at least in part because of the bitter disappointment in this country with the process of détente, most Europeans continued to view détente as a success, according to their narrow view and their low expectations.

---

[38] Source: Office of the Press Secretary to the President. This briefing, which was conducted on background by senior administration officials, took place at 1:05 p.m. at the Old Executive Office Building. It was transmitted to the press in Santa Barbara where President Reagan was preparing for his forthcoming trip to Europe, June 2–11.

I say narrow view in the sense that what they saw as détente was a process which was attempting in the heart of Europe to reduce tensions. We saw détente as a worldwide process, and this led to a great deal of misunderstanding between the Europeans and ourselves.

The first year of this administration was, then, admittedly, a rocky year. It was a rocky year, but it was a year that we expected to be rocky. We believed that a major transition was needed in the way the West dealt with the East. In contrast, the Europeans, notwithstanding their dissatisfaction with our earlier leadership, clung to the process of continuity. This, itself, contributed to the first year of rocky relationships between us.

I believe very strongly, however, that the transition period, that first year of this administration, has been completed and that we are on a new course. We have major and sustained increases in [the] U.S. defense effort well underway and there is no question now, I think, either in Europe or in Moscow, where the United States stands with regard to the Soviet Union, Soviet proxies, and their activities around the world.

Having established our resolve and having begun to recover our strength, it's been possible for the United States, then, to reengage the Soviets in arms control negotiations. A watershed was the November 18th speech of the President which established a framework and launched an initiative in the area of military competition of most concern to the Europeans, that's the intermediate-range nuclear forces.

That, now, has been followed by the President's Eureka speech[39] which filled out more of the program by proposing to begin the START talks.

Thus, by now, the Europeans should be adapted to our new, firm approach toward the Soviets, while also relieved to see that the aim of this approach is not open-ended confrontation and military competition. They should now see that we are in a stronger position because of the President's policies to achieve significant arms control, to restrain the Soviets, and to protect our interests and theirs if the Soviets are not constrained.

Thus, these summits, this trip in general, should be seen, I think, as a watershed. We are emerging from a transition period and, we hope, building a foundation for alliance policies, especially toward the East, that will get us through this decade in better shape and with greater steadiness than we were when the President took office.

Obviously, a major fly in the ointment is the economic situation of the West in general. All of the major Western powers are in to one degree or another, economic difficulties. As a result, there is a real blame-thy-neighbor trend which could easily become a beggar-thy-neighbor approach.

The Europeans blame our high interest rates for their economic malaise. They blame Japanese trade practices for industrial problems. And there's a real danger of rampant protectionism which will, of course, not help us collectively climb out of the slump that we are all in.

The economic problems also affect allied willingness to accept our prescriptions for dealing with the East. First of all, of course, they will be reluctant to increase defense spending to correct conventional force deficiencies so long as their own economies are in difficulty. They will, as well, be reluctant to constrict credits to the Soviet Union when they need the profits and the jobs from the exports that those credits will make possible.

Thus, in a way, Versailles is the more critical of the two summits. We need to emerge with all the partners more confident that we can pull out of the slump. We need to arrest the protectionist trends that we all see. If there is more confidence about Western economic management and growth, we should be able to get what we need on credits and greater support for sustained, conventional defense efforts.

In sum, our basic themes for the trip and for the summits will be that we want to set the stage for a decade of peace and prosperity with growth, with a strong dose of common values, reminding the Western Allies that we do, after all, stand for some things that no one else in this world stands for and that we will symbolize the strength of the NATO Alliance by the entry of Spain into that alliance which we hope will demonstrate to all that this still is a growing alliance and one which can accept new members into its ranks. . . .

With that, I think I will pass to my colleague who will talk about the summit itself, the Bonn summit.

Senior Administration Official. Thank you.

---

[39] For the text of President Reagan's commencement address at Eureka College, Peoria, Illinois, May 9, 1982, see document 44.

I will be brief so that you can also listen to my colleague talk a little bit about the summit, and then we can take some questions.

I think that the previous speaker has presented a good overview, or provided us a good overview for thinking about the Bonn summit, because I think that the Bonn summit is a bit different than Versailles. . . .

But a NATO summit is really more of a culmination of a day-to-day process that is, of course, underway all the time. NATO is a going entity. It is an alliance, and all the NATO Allies are represented in Brussels of course. And a great deal of work that will be represented in the summit itself will really reflect the day-to-day work that has been underway for months beforehand, and the discussions and problems that the Alliance normally has to deal with.

So, while I think that my colleague is correct in calling this a watershed, it is also, I think, the capstone, so to speak, of what this administration has been doing and the other allies have been doing over the last year or so. And I think, probably, the best way to talk specifically about the NATO summit is to give you some themes, I think, of what we have emphasized in our policy in NATO over the last year or so, and then tell you how I think these are going to be reflected in the summit.

I think the first theme I would stress is consultation. That is a buzz word in NATO jargon. It has been a word that has been used for years. Sometimes it is never well discussed, and frequently, never been too frequently honored. I want to emphasize this morning that I think that this administration, because of necessity and I think because of belief, has carried out and has been committed to closer consultations with the allies than any previous administration since the formation of the Alliance itself.

I think one good example of that is in the area of INF, intermediate-range nuclear forces, where we have not only created new formal mechanisms to discuss these issues that take a really multilateral approach to negotiating with the Soviets on intermediate-range forces and discussing the deployment of those systems if negotiations fail, but where there has been a great deal of informal consultation on a regular basis. And not simply informal consultation on lower levels of the government, but at the very highest levels. And I think the INF area, the degree of consensus behind the December 1979 decision to seek negotiations and to move forward with the deployment of systems in the face of continuing Soviet SS–20 deployments, is simply a reflection of a more general process of consultation which has emerged in this administration, which involves, as I said, [not simply] lower-level officials, but the Secretaries of State and Defense and the President in terms of the degree to which they now get on the phone, write letters, and discuss issues informally before they stake out positions formally, and we find ourselves at loggerheads frequently on questions.

I think the emphasis on consultations is simply going to be reflected in the NATO communiqué,[40] where we think we will see a greater degree of consensus and unity on the issues directly before the Alliance and a broader array of global issues than has been the case in many, many years.

The second theme I would stress would be the question of U.S. sensitivity to the concerns of the allies. My colleague pointed out that we now feel that we are ready to begin negotiations on the reductions of strategic arms with the Soviets. We have begun negotiations on intermediate-range nuclear forces. In fact, the President very early on, recognizing the political concerns generated by nuclear weapons in Europe, committed himself to seeking negotiations by the end of the year, last year on intermediate-range nuclear forces. And I think we are going to see an agenda of arms control initiatives on START, support for the ongoing INF negotiations, discussions on a fresh approach to the long-stagnating mutual balance force reduction talks in Vienna, and other arms control initiatives that recognize our sensitivity to the real concerns of the Europeans over both limiting the risks of war in Europe and having a constructive dialogue with the Soviets.

If sensitivity is a theme, I think a third theme, though, will be American leadership. Because, while I think we have been sensitive to the Europeans, particularly in the arms control area and to their concerns about limiting war, I think we have achieved much in recent months with the Europeans in recognizing the essential role of adequate defenses, in both the success of our arms control negotiations as well as working out a constructive dialogue with the Soviets.

---

[40] For the text of the North Atlantic Council Summit Declaration, June 10, 1982, see document 180.

We feel very strongly that the maintenance of the military balance, the regeneration and restoration of the military balance, and a special emphasis in the Alliance on improved conventional defenses, is a precondition, a prerequisite to success in arms control, as well as a precondition to achieving reciprocity and restraint in our relations with the Soviet Union.

I think in demonstrating sensitivity to the allied concerns on arms control, we think we have been able to exercise leadership on getting the allies to recognize the crucial role that enhanced defenses play in bringing about progress in arms control and constructive dialogue with the Soviets.

But arms control is only one area, defense is only one area, where the United States, I think, has succeeded in exercising leadership, and we hope will succeed at the NATO summit.

We will want to reaffirm our existing position on Poland and the three conditions that we have laid out as a united alliance on the restoration of stability and reconciliation in Poland. We will not ignore the continuing Soviet presence in Afghanistan, and there we will make it very clear to the Soviets that we are unprepared to accept the status quo.

Technology transfer to the East, the fact that the transfer of high technology to the Soviet Union does provide the Soviet Union with the military means to enhance their capabilities, and we will want that reflected in our discussions with the allies.

Finally, the last theme, and my colleague mentioned this briefly, the theme of values.

We will want strong recognition of the fact that NATO is not simply an alliance or a marriage of strategic convenience, but that it does reflect shared values: a consensus on the role of the individual within society, a strong reaffirmation that this is an alliance of democratic countries.

And I think this will be reflected in two ways: in the discussions on the ongoing developments in Poland, and our concerns in Poland and Eastern Europe more broadly; and equally, in Spanish accession to NATO.

I want to stress Spanish accession to NATO because I think it's been taken for granted, to some extent, seen as really a ceremonial event. But we need to emphasize the fact that Spain as a democratic country, a country that has chosen the democratic path, has asked for membership in a democratic alliance and has been accepted for that membership. I think it reflects the fact that this is an alliance, again, that is robust; it's vital; and it's an alliance based on shared values.

. . . .

Document 179

Address by President Reagan Before the Bundestag, Bonn, June 9, 1982[41]

"The Soil of Germany, and Every Other Ally, Is of Vital Concern to Each Member of the Alliance"

Thank you very much. (Applause) Thank you. Mr. President, Chancellor Schmidt, members of the Bundestag, distinguished guests, perhaps because I've just come from London, I have this urge to quote the great Dr. Johnson who said, "The feeling of friendship is like that of being comfortably filled with roast beef." (Laughter) Well, I feel very much filled with friendship this afternoon and I bring you the warmest regards and good will of the American people. (Applause)

I'm very honored to speak to you today and thus to all the people of Germany. Next year, we will jointly celebrate the 300th anniversary of the first German settlement in the American colonies. The 13 families who came to our new land were the forerunners of more than 7 million German immigrants to the United States. Today more Americans claim German ancestry than any other.

These Germans cleared and cultivated our land, built our industries, and advanced our arts and sciences. In honor of 300 years of German contributions in America, President Carstens and I have agreed today that

---

[41] Source: White House Press Release, June 9, 1982, Office of the Press Secretary to the President; printed also in *Weekly Compilation of Presidential Documents*, June 14, 1982, pp. 775–780. The President spoke at 4:22 p.m. He was in Bonn from June 9 to 10 for meetings with German and NATO leaders, and visited Berlin on June 11, 1982.

he will pay an official visit to the United States in October of 1983 to celebrate the occasion. (Applause)

The German people have given us so much, we like to think that we've repaid some of that debt. Our American Revolution was the first revolution in modern history to be fought for the right of self-government and the guarantee of civil liberties. That spirit was contagious. In 1849 the Frankfurt Parliament's statement of basic human rights guaranteed freedom of expression, freedom of religion, and equality before the law. And these principles live today in the basic law of the Federal Republic. Many peoples to the east still wait for such rights. (Applause)

The United States is proud of your democracy, but we cannot take credit for it. Heinrich Heine, in speaking of those who built the awe-inspiring cathedrals of medieval times, said that, "In those days people had convictions. We moderns have only opinions, and it requires something more than opinions," he said, "to build a Gothic cathedral." Well, over the past 30 years the convictions of the German people have built a cathedral of democracy—a great and glorious testament to your ideals. We in America genuinely admire the free society that you have built in only a few decades, and we understand all the better what you have accomplished because of our own history.

Americans speak with the deepest reverence of those Founding Fathers and first citizens who gave us the freedom that we enjoy today. And even though they lived over 200 years ago, we carry them in our hearts as well as in our history books.

I believe future generations of Germans will look to you here today and to your fellow Germans with the same profound respect and appreciation. You have built a free society with an abiding faith in human dignity—the crowning ideal of Western civilization. This will not be forgotten. You will be saluted and honored by this Repuplic's descendants over the centuries to come.

Yesterday, before the British Parliament,[42] I spoke of the values of Western civilization and the necessity to help all peoples gain the institutions of freedom. In many ways, in many places, our ideas are being tested today. We are meeting this afternoon between two important summits, the gathering of leading industrial democracies at Versailles[43] and the assembly of the Atlantic Alliance here in Bonn tomorrow.[44] Critical and complex problems face us, but our dilemmas will be made easier if we remember our partnership is based on common Western heritage and a faith in democracy. (Applause)

I believe this partnership of the Atlantic Alliance nations is motivated primarily by the search for peace, inner peace for our citizens and peace among nations. Why inner peace? Because demoracy allows for self-expression. It respects man's dignity and creativity. It operates by a rule of law, not by terror or coercion. It is government with the consent of the governed. As a result, citizens of the Atlantic Alliance enjoy an unprecedented level of material and spiritual well-being, and they are free to find their own personal peace.

We also seek peace among nations. The Psalmist said, "Seek peace and pursue it." Well, our foreign policies are based on this principle and directed toward this end. The noblest objective of our diplomacy is the patient and difficult task of reconciling our adversaries to peace. And I know we all look forward to the day when the only industry of man [*war*] will[45] be the research of historians.

But the simple—the simple hope for peace is not enough. We must remember something that Friedrich Schiller said, "The most pious man can't stay in peace if it doesn't please his evil neighbor." (Applause) So there must be a method to our search, a method that recognizes the dangers and realities of the world. During Chancellor Schmidt's State visit to Washington last year,[46] I said that your Republic was "perched on a cliff of freedom." I wasn't saying anything the German people do not already know living as you do in the heart of a divided Europe, you can see more clearly than others that there are governments at peace neither with their own peoples nor the world.

---

[42] For the text of President Reagan's address before the British Parliament, June 8, 1982, see document 4.

[43] For documentation on the Versailles Economic Summit, June 4–6, 1982, see Chapter 5, Part F.

[44] For information on the NATO Heads of Government meeting in Bonn, June 10, see documents *infra* and 181–183.

[45] White House correction.

[46] For information on the official visit of Chancellor Helmut Schmidt to the United States, May 20–23, 1981, see *American Foreign Policy: Current Documents,* 1981, documents 183 and 184.

I don't believe any reasonable observer can deny that there is a threat to both peace and freedom today. It is as stark as that gash of a border that separates the German people. We're menaced by a power that openly condemns our values and answers our restraint with a relentless military buildup.[47]

We cannot simply assume every nation wants the peace that we so earnestly desire. The Polish people would tell us there are those who would use military force to repress others who want only basic human rights. The Freedom Fighters of Afghanistan would tell us as well that the threat of aggression has not receded from the world.

Without a strengthened Atlantic security, the possibility of military coercion will be very great. We must continue to improve our defenses if we're to preserve peace and freedom. (Applause) This is—Is there an echo in here? (Laughter) (Applause)

But this preserving peace and freedom is not an impossible task; for almost 40 years we have succeeded in deterring war. Our method has been to organize our defensive capabilities, both nuclear and conventional, so that an aggressor could have no hope of military victory. The alliance has carried its strength not as a battle flag, but as a banner of peace. (Applause) Deterrence has kept that peace and we must continue to take the steps necessary to make deterrence credible. This depends in part on a strong America. A national effort, entailing sacrifices by the American people, is now underway to make long-overdue improvements in our military posture. The American people support this effort because they understand how fundamental it is to keeping the peace they so fervently desire.

We also are resolved to maintain the presence of well-equipped and trained forces in Europe, and our strategic forces will be modernized and remain committed to the alliance. By these actions, the people of the United States are saying, "We are with you Germany. You are not alone." (Applause) Our adversaries would be foolishly mistaken should they gamble that Americans would abandon their alliance responsibilites, no matter how severe the test.

Alliance security depends on a fully credible conventional defense to which all allies contribute. There is a danger that any conflict could escalate to a nuclear war. Strong conventional forces can make the danger of conventional or nuclear conflict more remote. Reasonable strength in and of itself is not bad; it is honorable when used to maintain peace or defend deeply held beliefs.

One of the first chores is to fulfill our commitments to each other by continuing to strengthen our conventional defenses. This must include improving the readiness of our standing forces and the ability of those forces to operate as one. We must also apply the West's technological genius to improving our conventional deterrence.

There can be no doubt that we as an alliance have the means to improve our conventional defenses. Our peoples hold values of individual liberty and dignity that time and again they've proven willing to defend. Our economic energy vastly exceeds that of our adversaries. Our free system has produced technological advances that other systems, with their stifling ideologies, cannot hope to equal. All of these resources are available to our defense.

Yet, many of our nations currently are experiencing economic difficulties. Yet, we must nevertheless guarantee that our security does not suffer as a result. We've made strides in conventional defense over the last few years despite our economic problems, and we've disproved the pessimists who contend that our efforts are futile. The more we close the conventional gap, the less the risks of aggression or nuclear conflict. The soil of Germany and of every other ally is of vital concern to each member of the alliance. And this fundamental commitment is embodied in the North Atlantic Treaty. But it may well be an empty pledge unless we ensure that American forces are ready to reinforce Europe, and Europe is ready to receive them. (Applause)

I am encouraged by the recent agreement on wartime host-nation support. This pact strenthens our ability to deter aggression in Europe and demonstrates our common determination to respond to attack. Just as each ally shares fully in the security of the alliance, each is responsible for shouldering a fair share of the burden. Now, that, of course, often leads to a difference of opinion, and criticism of our alliance is as old as the partnership itself. But voices have now been raised on both sides of the Atlantic that mistake the inevitable process of adjustment within the alliance for a dramatic divergence of in-

[47] "At this point, two members of the audience began heckling the President. The heckling continued intermittently during this part of the President's address." (Explanatory note in *Weekly Compilation of Presidential Documents*, June 14, 1982, p. 776)

terests. Some Americans think that Europeans are too little concerned for their own security. Some would unilaterally reduce the number of American troops deployed in Europe. And in Europe itself we hear the idea that the American presence rather than contributing to peace, either has no deterrent value or actually increases the risk that our allies may be attacked. These arguments ignore both the history and the reality of the transatlantic coalition. Let me assure you that the American commitment to Europe remains steady and strong. Europe's shores are our shores. (Applause) Europe's borders are our borders, and we will stand with you in defense of our heritage of liberty and dignity. (Applause)

The American people recognize Europe's substantial contributions to our joint security. Nowhere is that contribution more evident than here in the Federal Republic. German citizens host the forces of six nations. German soldiers and reservists provide the backbone of NATO's conventional deterrent in the heartland of Europe. Your Bundeswehr is a model for the integration of defense needs with a democratic way of life, and you have not shrunk from the heavy responsibility of accepting the nuclear forces necessary for deterrence.

I ask your help in fulfilling another responsibility. Many American citizens don't believe that their counterparts in Europe, especially younger citizens, really understand the United States presence there. Now, if you'll work toward explaining the U.S. role to people on this side of the Atlantic, I'll explain it to those on the other side. (Applause)

In recent months, both in your country and mine, there's been renewed public concern about the threat of nuclear war and the arms buildup. I know it's not easy, especially for the German people to live in the gale of intimidation that blows from the East.

If I might quote Heine again, he almost foretold the fears of nuclear war when he wrote, "wild, dark times are rumbling toward us, and the prophet who wishes to write a new apocalypse will have to invent entirely new beasts, and beasts so terrible that the ancient animal symbols will seem like cooing doves and Cupid in comparison." The nuclear threat is a terrible beast. Perhaps the banner carried in one of the nuclear demonstrations here in Germany said it best. The sign read, "I am afraid." Well, I know of no Western leader who doesn't sympathize with that earnest plea. To those who march for peace, my heart is with you. I would be at the head of your parade if I believe marching alone could bring about a more secure world. And to the 2,800 women in Filderstadt who sent a petition for peace to President Brezhnev and me, let me say I, myself, would sign your petition if I thought it could bring about harmony. I understand your genuine concerns.

The women of Filderstadt and I share the same goal. (Applause) The question is how to proceed. We must think through the consequences of how we reduce the dangers to peace.

Those who advocate that we unilaterally forego the modernization of our forces must prove that this will enhance our security and lead to moderation by the other side—in short, that it will advance, rather than undermine, the preservation of the peace. The weight of recent history does not support this notion.

Those who demand that we renounce the use of a crucial element of our deterrent strategy must show how this would decrease the likelihood of war. It is only by comparison with a nuclear war that the suffering caused by conventional war seems a lesser evil. Our goal must be to deter war of any kind. (Applause) And those who decry the failure of arms to control efforts to achieve substantial results must consider where the fault lies. I will remind them that it is the United States that has proposed to ban land-based intermediate-range nuclear missiles—the missiles most threatening to Europe. It is the United States that has proposed and will pursue deep cuts in strategic systems. It is the West that has long sought the detailed exchanges of information on forces and effective verification procedures. And it is dictatorships, not democracies, that need militarism to control their own people and impose their system on others. (Applause) To those who've taken a different viewpoint and who can't see this danger, I don't suggest that they're ignorant, it's just that they know so many things that aren't true.

We in the West—Germans, Americans, our other allies, are deeply committed to continuing efforts to restrict the arms competition. Common sense demands that we persevere. I invite those who genuinely seek effective and lasting arms control to stand behind the far-reaching proposals that we've put forward. In return, I pledge that we will sustain the closest of consultations with our allies.

On November 18th, I outlined a broad and ambitious arms control program. One element calls for reducing land-based, intermediate-range nuclear missiles to zero on each side. If carried out, it would eliminate the growing threat to Western Europe posed by the U.S.S.R.'s modern SS–20 rockets, and it would make unnecessary the NATO decision to deploy American intermediate-range systems. And, by the way, I cannot understand why among some, there is a greater fear of weapons NATO is to deploy than of weapons the Soviet Union already has deployed. (Applause)

Our proposal is fair because it imposes equal limits and obligations on both sides and it calls for significant reductions, not merely a capping of an existing high level of destructive power. As you know, we've made this proposal in Geneva, where negotiations have been underway since the end of November last year. We intend to pursue those negotiations intensively. I regard them as a significant test of the Soviets' willingness to enter into meaningful arms control agreements.

On May 9th we proposed to the Soviet Union that Strategic Arms Reductions Talks begin this month in Geneva. The U.S.S.R. has agreed and talks will begin on June 29th. (Applause) We in the United States want to focus on the most destabilizing systems, and thus reduce the risk of war. And that is why in the first phase we propose to reduce substantially the number of ballistic missile warheads and the missiles themselves. In the second phase we will seek an equal ceiling on other elements of our strategic forces, including ballistic missile throw weight, at less than current American levels. We will handle cruise missiles and bombers in an equitable fashion. We will negotiate in good faith and undertake these talks with the same seriousness of purpose that has marked our preparations over the last several months.

Another element of the program that I outlined was a call for reductions in conventional forces in Europe. From the earliest post-war years the Western democracies have faced the ominous reality that massive Soviet conventional forces would remain stationed where they do not belong. The muscle of Soviet forces in Central Europe far exceeds legitimate defense needs. Their presence is made more threatening still—(applause)—more threatening still by a military doctrine that emphasizes mobility and surprise attack. And as history shows, these troops have built a legacy of intimidation and repression. In response, the NATO allies must show they have the will and capacity to deter any conventional attack or any attempt to intimidate us. Yet we also will continue to search for responsible ways to reduce NATO and Warsaw Pact military personnel to equal levels.

In recent weeks we in the alliance have consulted on how best to invigorate the Vienna negotiations on mutual and balanced force reductions. Based on these consultations, Western representatives in the Vienna talks soon will make a proposal by which the two alliances would reduce their respective ground force personnel in verifiable stages to a total of 700,000 men and their combined ground and air force personnel to a level of 900,000 men.[48]

While the agreement would not eliminate the threat nor spare our citizens the task of maintaining a substantial defense force, it could constitute a major step toward a safer Europe for both East and West. It could lead to military stability at lower levels and lessen the dangers of miscalculation and a surprise attack, and it also would demonstrate the political will of the two alliances to enhance stability by limiting their forces in the central area of their military competition.

The West has established a clear set of goals. We as an alliance will press forward with plans to improve our own conventional forces in Europe. At the same time, we propose an arms control agreement to equalize conventional forces at a significantly lower level.

We will move ahead with our preparations to modernize our nuclear forces in Europe. But, again, we also will work unceasingly to gain acceptance in Geneva of our proposal to ban land-based intermediate-range nuclear missiles.

In the United States, we will move forward with the plans I announced last year to modernize our strategic nuclear forces,[49] which play so vital a role in maintaining peace by deterring war. Yet, we also have proposed that Strategic Arms Reductions Talks begin. We will pursue them determinedly.

In each of these areas, our policies are based on the conviction that a stable military balance at the lowest possible level will

---

[48] Regarding the draft MBFR treaty tabled by the NATO Allies in Vienna on July 8, 1982, see document 185.

[49] For the announcement of the program to modernize U.S. strategic nuclear forces made by President Reagan and Secretary Weinberger, October 2, 1981, see *American Foreign Policy: Current Documents, 1981*, documents 45 and 46.

help further the cause of peace. The other side will respond in good faith to these initiatives only if it believes we are resolved to provide for our own defense. (Applause) Unless convinced that we will unite and stay united behind these arms control initiatives and modernization programs, our adversaries will seek to divide us from one another and our people from their leaders.

I'm optimistic about our relationship with the Soviet Union if the Western nations remain true to their values and true to each other. (Applause) I believe in Western civilization and its moral power. I believe deeply in the principles the West esteems. And guided by these ideals, I believe we can find a no-nonsense, workable, and lasting policy that will keep the peace.

Earlier, I said the German people had built a remarkable cathedral of democracy. But we still have other work ahead. We must build a cathedral of peace, where nations are safe from war and where people need not fear for their liberties. I've heard the history of the famous cathedral of Cologne—how those beautiful soaring spires miraculously survived the destruction all around them, including part of the church itself.

Let us build a cathedral as the people of Cologne built theirs—with the deepest commitment and determination. Let us build as they did—not just for ourselves but for the generations beyond. For if we construct our peace properly, it will endure as long as the spires of Cologne.

Thank you very much. (Applause)

Document 180

Declaration Issued by the North Atlantic Council, Bonn, June 10, 1982[50]

"We . . . Set Forth Our Program for Peace in Freedom"

We, the representatives of the 16 members of the North Atlantic Alliance, reaffirm our dedication to the shared values and ideals on which our transatlantic partnership is based.

2. The accession of Spain to the North Atlantic Treaty,[51] after its peaceful change to parliamentary democracy, bears witness to the vitality of the Alliance as a force for peace and freedom.

3. Our Alliance has preserved peace for a third of a century. It is an association of free nations joined together to preserve their security through mutual guarantees and collective self-defence as recognised by the United Nations Charter. It remains the essential instrument for deterring aggression by means of a strong defence and strengthening peace by means of constructive dialogue. Our solidarity in no way conflicts with the right of each of our countries to choose its own policies and internal development, and allows for a high degree of diversity. Therein lies our strength. In a spirit of mutual respect, we are prepared to adjust our aims and interests at all times through free and close consultations; these are the core of everyday Allied co-operation and will be intensified appropriately. We are a partnership of equals, none dominant and none dominated.

4. The Soviet Union, for its part, requires the countries associated with it to act as a bloc, in order to preserve a rigid and imposed system. Moreover, experience shows that the Soviet Union is ultimately willing to threaten or use force beyond its own frontiers. Afghanistan and the Soviet attitude with regard to the Polish crisis show this clearly. The Soviet Union has devoted over the past decade a large part of its resources to a massive military build-up, far exceeding its defence needs and supporting the projection of military power on a global scale. While creating a threat of these dimensions, Warsaw Pact governments condemn Western defence efforts as aggressive. While they ban unilateral disarmament movements in their own countries they support demands for unilateral disarmament in the West.

5. International stability and world peace require greater restraint and responsibility on the part of the Soviet Union. We for our part, reaffirming the principles and purposes of the Alliance, set forth our Programme for Peace in Freedom:

(a) Our purpose is to prevent war and, while safeguarding democracy, to build the

---

[50] Source: *NATO Communiqués, 1982*, NATO Information Service, Brussels, Belgium, pp. 39–41; printed also in Department of State *Bulletin*, July 1982, pp. 9–10. President Reagan attended the North Atlantic Council meeting, June 10, 1982. He participated in the morning and afternoon plenary sessions held at the Schaumberg Palace.

[51] See footnote 27 to document 176.

foundations of lasting peace. None of our weapons will ever be used except in response to attack. We respect the sovereignty, equality, independence and territorial integrity of all states. In fulfilment of our purpose, we shall maintain adequate military strength and political solidarity. On that basis, we will persevere in efforts to establish, whenever Soviet behaviour makes this possible, a more constructive East–West relationship through dialogue, negotiation and mutually advantageous co-operation.

(b) Our purpose is to preserve the security of the North Atlantic area by means of conventional and nuclear forces adequate to deter aggression and intimidation. This requires a sustained effort on the part of all the Allies to improve their defence readiness and military capabilities, without seeking military superiority. Our countries have the necessary resources to undertake this effort. The presence of North American armed forces in Europe and the United States strategic nuclear commitment to Europe remain integral to Allied security. Of equal importance are the maintenance and continued improvement of the defence capabilities of the European members of the Alliance. We will seek to achieve greater effectiveness in the application of national resources to defence, giving due attention to possibilities for developing areas of practical co-operation. In this respect the Allies concerned will urgently explore ways to take full advantage both technically and economically of emerging technologies. At the same time steps will be taken in the appropriate fora to restrict Warsaw Pact access to Western militarily relevant technology.

(c) Our purpose is to have a stable balance of forces at the lowest possible level, thereby strengthening peace and international security. We have initiated a comprehensive series of proposals for militarily significant, equitable and verifiable agreements on the control and reduction of armaments. We fully support the efforts of the United States to negotiate with the Soviet Union for substantial reductions in the strategic nuclear weapons of the two countries, and for the establishment of strict and effective limitations on their intermediate-range nuclear weapons, starting with the total elimination of their land-based intermediate-range missiles, which are of most concern to each side. We will continue to seek substantial reductions of conventional forces on both sides in Europe, and to reach agreement on measures which will serve to build confidence and enhance security in the whole of Europe. To this end, those of us whose countries participate in the negotiations on Mutual and Balanced Force Reductions in Vienna have agreed on a new initiative to give fresh impetus to these negotiations.[52] We will also play an active part in wider international talks on arms control and disarmament; at the Second United Nations Special Session on Disarmament which has just opened in New York, we will work to give new momentum to these talks.

(d) Our purpose is to develop substantial and balanced East–West relations aimed at genuine détente. For this to be achieved, the sovereignty of all states, wherever situated, must be respected, human rights must not be sacrificed to state interests, the free movement of ideas must take the place of one-sided propaganda, the free movement of persons must be made possible, efforts must be made to achieve a military relationship characterised by stability and openness, and in general all principles and provisions of the Helsinki Final Act in their entirety must be applied. We, for our part, will always be ready to negotiate in this spirit and we look for tangible evidence that this attitude is reciprocated.

(e) Our purpose is to contribute to peaceful progress world-wide; we will work to remove the causes of instability such as under-development or tensions which encourage outside interference. We will continue to play our part in the struggle against hunger and poverty. Respect for genuine non-alignment is important for international stability. All of us have an interest in peace and security in other regions of the world. We will consult together as appropriate on events in these regions which may have implications for our security, taking into account our commonly identified objectives. Those of us who are in a position to do so will endeavour to respond to requests for assistance from sovereign states whose security and independence is threatened.

(f) Our purpose is to ensure economic and social stability for our countries, which will strengthen our joint capacity to safeguard our security. Sensitive to the effects of each country's policies on others, we attach the greatest importance to the curbing of inflation and a return to sustained growth and to high levels of employment.

While noting the important part which our economic relations with the Warsaw

---

[52] See document 185.

Pact countries can play in the development of a stable East–West relationship, we will approach those relations in a prudent and diversified manner consistent with our political and security interests. Economic relations should be conducted on the basis of a balanced advantage for both sides. We undertake to manage financial relations with the Warsaw Pact countries on a sound economic basis, including commercial prudence also in the granting of export credits. We agree to exchange information in the appropriate fora on all aspects of our economic, commercial and financial relations with Warsaw Pact countries.

6. Nowhere has our commitment to common basic values been demonstrated more clearly than with regard to the situation in Germany and Berlin. We remain committed to the security and freedom of Berlin and continue to support efforts to maintain the calm situation in and around the city. The continued success of efforts by the Federal Republic of Germany to improve the relationship between the two German states is important to the safeguarding of peace in Europe. We recall that the rights and responsibilities of the Four Powers relating to Berlin and Germany as a whole remain unaffected and confirm our support for the political objective of the Federal Republic of Germany to work towards a state of peace in Europe in which the German people regains its unity through free self-determination.

7. We condemn all acts of international terrorism. They constitute flagrant violations of human dignity and rights and are a threat to the conduct of normal international relations. In accordance with our national legislation, we stress the need for the most effective co-operation possible to prevent and suppress this scourge.

8. We call upon the Soviet Union to abide by internationally accepted standards of behaviour without which there can be no prospect of stable international relations, and to join now with us in the search for constructive relations, arms reductions and world peace.

Document 181

Statement Issued by the North Atlantic Council, Bonn, June 10, 1982[53]

Agreement on Integrated NATO Defense

As indicated in the Declaration of today,[54] we, the representatives of those members of the North Atlantic Alliance taking part in its integrated defence structure hereby set out our detailed positions on defence. We welcome the intention of Spain to participate in the integrated defence structure, and the readiness of the President of the Spanish Government to associate himself with this document, while noting that the modalities of Spanish participation have still to be worked out.

Pursuant to the principles set out in the Programme for Peace and Freedom, we agree that, in accordance with current NATO defence plans, and within the context of NATO strategy and its triad of forces, we will continue to strengthen NATO's defence posture, with special regard to conventional forces. Efforts of our nations in support of the decisions reached at Washington in 1978[55] have led to improved defensive capabilities. Notwithstanding this progress, it is clear, as documented in the recently published comparison of NATO and Warsaw Pact forces, that continuing efforts are essential to Alliance security. Against this background, we will:

—Fulfill to the greatest extent possible the NATO Force Goals for the next six years, including measures to improve the readiness of the standing forces and the readiness and mobilization capability of reserve forces. Note was taken of the recently concluded agreement between the United States and the Federal Republic of Germany for wartime host nation support.[56]

---

[53] Source: *NATO Comminqués, 1982*, NATO Information Service, Brussels, Belgium, p. 44; printed also in Department of State *Bulletin*, July 1982, p. 11.

[54] *Supra.*

[55] For the text of the Final Communiqué of the NATO Ministerial Meeting, Washington, May 31, 1978, where the allied leaders agreed to strengthen and modernize the alliance, see *American Foreign Policy: Basic Documents, 1977–1980*, pp. 479–483.

[56] Regarding this agreement for wartime host nation support concluded between the United States and the Federal Republic of Germany, April 15, 1982, see document 211.

—Continue to implement measures identified in the Long-Term Defence Programme designed to enhance our overall defence capabilities.

—Continue to improve NATO planning procedures and explore other ways of achieving greater effectiveness in the application of national resources to defence, especially in the conventional field. In that regard, we will continue to give due attention to fair burden-sharing and to possibilities for developing areas of practical co-operation from which we can all benefit.

—Explore ways to take full advantage both technically and economically of emerging technologies, especially to improve conventional defence, and take steps necessary to restrict the transfer of militarily relevant technology to the Warsaw Pact.

Noting that developments beyond the NATO area may threaten our vital interests, we reaffirm the need to consult with a view to sharing assessments and identifying common objectives, taking full account of the effect on NATO security and defence capability, as well as of the national interests of member countries. Recognising that the policies which nations adopt in this field are a matter for national decision, we agree to examine collectively in the appropriate NATO bodies the requirements which may arise for the defence of the NATO area as a result of deployments by individual member states outside that area. Steps which may be taken by individual Allies in the light of such consultations to facilitate possible military deployments beyond the NATO area can represent an important contribution to Western security.

Document 182

Statement Issued by the North Atlantic Council, Bonn, June 10, 1982[57]

NATO Endorsement of U.S. Arms Control Initiatives and Objectives

As indicated in our Declaration of today,[58] we, the representatives of the 16 members of the North Atlantic Alliance, hereby set out our detailed positions on Arms Control and Disarmament.

Militarily significant, equitable and verifiable agreements on arms control and disarmament contribute to the strengthening of peace and are an integral part of our security policies. Western proposals offer the possibility of substantial reductions in United States and Soviet strategic arms and intermediate-range weapons and in conventional forces in Europe, as well as of confidence-building measures covering the whole of Europe:

—In the forthcoming Strategic Arms Reductions Talks (START), we call on the Soviet Union to agree on significant reductions in United States and Soviet strategic nuclear forces, focussed on the most destabilizing inter-continental systems.

—In the negotiations on Intermediate-range Nuclear Forces (INF) which are conducted within the START framework and are based on the December 1979 decision on INF modernization and arms control[59], the United States proposal for the complete elimination of all longer-range land-based INF missiles of the United States and the Soviet Union holds promise for an equitable outcome and enhanced security for all.[60]

—Those of us participating in the Vienna negotiations on Mutual and Balanced Force Reductions (MBFR) will soon present a draft treaty embodying a new, comprehensive proposal designed to give renewed momentum to these negotiations and achieve the long-standing objective of enhancing stability and security in Europe.[61] They stress that the Western treaty proposal, if accepted, will commit all participants whose forces are involved—European and North American—to participate in accordance with the principle of collectivity in substantial manpower reductions leading to equal collective ceilings for the forces of Eastern and Western participants in Central Europe, based on agreed data, with associated measures designed to strengthen confidence and enhance verification.

—In CSCE, the proposal for a Conference on Confidence-and Security-building Measures and Disarmament in Europe

---

[57] Source: *NATO Communiqués, 1982*, NATO Information Service, Brussels, Belgium, pp. 42–43; printed also in Department of State *Bulletin*, July 1982, pp. 10–11.

[58] See document 180.

[59] In this connection Greece reserves its position. [Footnote in the source text.]

[60] The reference is to President Reagan's speech before the National Press Club, November 18, 1981; for text, see *American Foreign Policy: Current Documents, 1981*, document 60.

[61] See document 185.

as part of a balanced outcome of the Madrid CSCE Follow-up Meeting would open the way to increased transparency and enhanced stability in the whole of Europe from the Atlantic to the Urals.

At the same time, we are continuing our efforts to promote stable peace on a global scale:

—In the Committee on Disarmament in Geneva, the Allies will actively pursue efforts to obtain equitable and verifiable agreements including a total ban on chemical weapons.

—In the Second Special Session on Disarmament of the United Nations General Assembly now in progress, we trust that new impetus will be given to negotiations current and in prospect, especially by promoting military openness and verification, that the need for strict observance of the principle of renunciation of force enshrined in the United Nations Charter will be reaffirmed, and that compliance with existing agreements will be strengthened.

We appeal to all states to co-operate with us in these efforts to strengthen peace and security. In particular we call on the Soviet Union to translate its professed commitment to disarmament into active steps aimed at achieving concrete, balanced and verifiable results at the negotiating table.

Document 183

Transcript of a Press Briefing by the Secretary of State (Haig), Bonn, June 10, 1982 (Extract)[62]

NATO Heads of Government Meeting Reflects "A Solid Consensus"

Secretary Haig. Good afternoon, ladies and gentlemen. I would describe this as a historic day for the NATO Alliance due primarily but not exclusively to Spain's formal entry into NATO. It is a step of vital importance to both the alliance and to Spain. The entry of Spain is a clear demonstration of the continuing appeal and vitality of the alliance of some 33 years' life span.

This summit meeting and the documents that were adopted by the meeting today[63] also demonstrate that NATO represents Western values at their very best. I'm particularly pleased with the communiqué and the associated documents that were released on arms control and the strengthening of our conventional defenses. They reflect a year of very solid work within the framework of the alliance on a number of key areas and I think it was appropriate that they should be. All of the considerations contained in those documents—and I would urge you to study them carefully—are a keen reflection of the views of the U.S. Government as well as a manifestation of a solid consensus within the framework of the alliance itself.

I think we have here a framework for the decade of the 1980's which has been established, which is both contemporary in its recognition of needs in the area of balanced defenses for the alliance; the need for arms control and integration of the political, economic, and security assets of the Western world to elicit what we hope will be an era of restraint and responsibility on the part of the Soviet Union under a framework which is coordinated, integrated, and fully accepted by all member states. And I think that's extremely important.

Now, I want to say a word about the summit declaration itself which sends the strongest message in memory to the Soviet Union—in recent memory. It clearly contrasts how NATO is fundamentally different from the Warsaw Pact. Our alliance is an open partnership based on consensus and democracy. Its diversity is also its strength. The Warsaw Pact is a strained association—a forced marriage dominated by a single government. It is unresponsive in many ways to the needs of the peoples that it is designed to protect. It is afraid of freedom, chary of diversity. The West has again called on the U.S.S.R. to show restraint and responsibility in its behavior and that's a clear message and signal throughout the communiqué.

The statement on defense, which we consider to be especially significant and important, reaffirms NATO's strategy at a

---

[62] Source: White House Press Release, June 10, 1982, Office of the Press Secretary to the President; printed also in Department of State *Bulletin*, July 1982, pp. 11–13. Haig was in Bonn to attend the North Atlantic Council meeting with President Reagan, June 10. This briefing took place at 7 p.m.

[63] See documents 180, 181, and *supra*.

time when it has become fashionable to question something that has kept and preserved the peace in Western Europe and indeed in an East-West sense for the 33-year life span of the alliance itself.

It reflects top level agreement on the need to improve NATO's conventional defense posture, including the rapid deployment and reserve forces. It emphasizes full employment of emerging technologies; a need to protect our Western technological advantage. You'll recall that that surfaced earlier in both Ottawa[64] and subsequent NATO ministerial meetings.

It emphasized the importance of growing cooperation by the Allies to ensure security and stability in critical regions elsewhere in the world. And, here again, it was an anathema some years ago to speak an alliance parlance of anything. Outside this strict geographic confines of the alliance itself, we have now developed a consensus of agreement that, like it or not, the alliance is increasingly influenced by events outside of the geographic confines of the alliance and therefore those nations with essential interests must coordinate and consult together in dealing with them, not within the alliance framework but as a framework for watching briefs and continuous exchange of information.

There's also a very important statement on arms control. It makes absolutely clear that it is the Western Alliance which has the ideas and the initiatives in seeking a dialogue with the East in this very important area.

The document itself strongly endorses the major aspects of President Reagan's own peace program. It supports U.S. objectives in START and the U.S. approach to the Geneva negotiations on intermediate-range nuclear forces based on the December 1979 decision.

It announces Western readiness to invigorate the Vienna negotiations on mutual [and] balanced force reductions now in their ninth year.

Through a new approach aimed at lower and more equal force levels in Central Europe: 700,000 for ground; 900,000 for the aggregate ground, sea and air. And it signals a strong Western interest in the possibilities for a constructive dialogue offered by the United Nations Special Session on Disarmament and other arms control fora.

As important as these Western initiatives—as important as they are—the appeal that NATO has made today once again to the Soviet Union to match its professions of peaceful intentions with actions leading to results I think is a very important theme in the overall deliberations. As the Danish Prime Minister said today, "The searchlight is now on Moscow."

I think for many of us the highlight of the summit—which was a very well-prepared summit, and therefore permitted the heads of state in government to make their own separate interventions without a great deal of what I call "heated dispute" about remaining controversies, and that says something for the quality of the preparations that were made—was President Reagan's intervention at the conclusion this afternoon. It was an ad-libbed, if you will, or unstructured, personal intervention. It ran about 10 minutes I'd say, I think, give or take. And it clearly summarized the President's own view on East-West relations. It was both powerful, as it was extemporaneous. (Laughter) It was—it reiterated in clear terms the President's willingness to have a genuine dialogue with the Soviets but one based on Soviet restraint.

Q. Give us a quote.

SECRETARY HAIG. It talked about the experiences we'd had in the decade of the 1970's with the 1970 interpretation of détente, a formula through which we witnessed increasing Soviet interventionisms worldwide: in Africa, the Middle East, the Yemens, Afghanistan, Southeast Asia, and, once again, in this Western Hemisphere.

And you will note that the language in the communiqué refers to something different than the classic 1970 version. It refers to genuine détente. In other words, there's no abandonment of the principle of dialogue and the desire to reach agreements and the meeting of the mind with the Soviet Union, but to do so, not with words, but by a continuous assessment of actions. The heavy emphasis on reciprocity.

I think the President's intervention—he referred to the situation in Hungary and Czechoslovakia and Poland. He painted clearly a picture of hope for the future by emphasizing the demographic assets available to the Western World if properly integrated and orchestrated. He referred to those in political terms, our essential democratic values, in economic terms, the vast superiority of Western industrialized societies, and, of course, the security assets of the collection of alliance members all in-

---

[64] Regarding the Ottawa Economic Summit Conference, July 19–21, 1981, see *American Foreign Policy: Current Documents, 1981*, Chapter 5, Part F.

tegrated. I think the President drew the conclusion, as many of us have, that, if we abandon the self-consciousness of the recent decade, the sense of inadequacy or perhaps even inevitability, and apprise with full frankness and openness what we have going for us, and apply those assets intelligently, moderately, but with vision and steadiness of purpose, that there is indeed hope. The President referred to his communication with Mr. Brezhnev at the time that he was convalescing from his wound,[65] how he suggested to Mr. Brezhnev that if the governments themselves could step aside and that the peoples could communicate each other's wishes, aspirations, and desires that clearly a new world structure for peace and stability would be an inevitable outcome. And he decried the continual manipulation of the wishes and desires of the people by insensitive government.

Now, all in all, as I would like to emphasize that I personally feel extremely pleased with the outcome of this summit meeting. I suppose it is because of my own NATO background; understandable. As I say, it reflects a year of solid, positive work and progress in consensus building. It confirms that the alliance is itself not only alive and healthy, but that it has never been better.

Now, there were other meetings today on the margin. There were discussions about the Middle East. There was a registration of support for Great Britain's actions in the Falklands. The President had bilaterals with the Prime Minister of Spain, with the Prime Minister of Greece, and he met after the conclusion of the summit with Foreign Minister Saud of Saudi Arabia.

. . . .

[65] Reference is to President Reagan's letter to Soviet Chairman Brezhnev, April 24, 1981. This letter has not been released, but President Reagan quoted several paragraphs from it in his speech on arms control to the National Press Club on November 18, 1981. For the text, see *ibid.*, document 60.

Document 184

Address by President Reagan to the People of Berlin, West Berlin, June 11, 1982[66]

President Reagan's Berlin Initiative to Reduce Danger of Nuclear Accidents

Thank you. Mr. Governing Mayor,[67] Mr. Chancellor,[68] Excellencies, you ladies and gentlemen, it was one of Germany's greatest sons, Goethe, who said that "there is strong shadow where there is much light." In our times, Berlin, more than any other place in the world, is such a meeting place of light and shadow, tyranny and freedom. To be here is truly to stand on freedom's edge and in the shadow of a wall that has come to symbolize all that is darkest in the world today, to sense how shining and priceless—and how much in need of constant vigilance and protection our legacy of liberty is.

This day marks a happy return for us. We paid our first visit to this great city more than 3 years ago, as private citizens. As with every other citizen to Berlin or visitor to Berlin, I came away with a vivid impression of a city that is more than a place on the map—a city that is a testament to what is both most inspiring and most troubling about the time we live in.

Thomas Mann once wrote that "A man lives not only his personal life as an individual, but also consciously or unconsciously the life of his epoch." Nowhere is this more true than in Berlin where each moment of everyday life is spent against the backdrop of contending global systems and ideas. To be a Berliner is to live the great historic struggle of this age, the latest chapter in man's timeless quest for freedom. (Applause)

As Americans, we understand this. Our commitment to Berlin is a lasting one. (Applause) Thousands of our citizens have

[66] Source: White House Press Release, June 11, 1982, Office of the Press Secretary to the President; printed also in *Weekly Compilation of Presidential Documents*, June 14, 1982, pp. 786–789. The President spoke at 11:35 a.m. in front of the Charlottenburg Palace. The source text is the text as delivered.

[67] Berlin Mayor Richard von Weizsacker.

[68] Helmut Schmidt.

served here since the first small contingent of American troops arrived on July 4, 1945, the anniversary of our independence as a nation. Americans have served here ever since—not as conquerors but as guardians of the freedom of West Berlin and its brave, proud, people. (Applause)

Today I want to pay tribute to my fellow countrymen, military and civilian, who serve their country and the people of Berlin and, in so doing, stand as sentinals of freedom everywhere. I also wish to pay my personal respects to the people of this great city. My visit here today is proof that this American commitment has been worthwhile. Our freedom is indivisible. (Applause)

The American commitment to Berlin is much deeper than our military presence here. In the 37 years since World War II, a succession of American Presidents has made it clear that our role in Berlin is emblematic of our larger search for peace throughout Europe and the world. Ten years ago this month, that search brought into force the Quadripartite Agreement on Berlin.[69] A decade later, West Berliners live more securely, can travel more freely and, most significantly, have more contact with friends and relatives in East Berlin and East Germany than was possible 10 years ago. These achievements reflect the realistic approach of Allied negotiators who recognized that practical progress can be made even while basic differences remain between East and West.

As a result—as a result, both sides have managed to handle their differences in Berlin without the clash of arms, to the benefit of all mankind. The United States remains committed to the Berlin Agreement. We will continue to expect strict observance and full implementation in all aspects of this accord, including those which apply to the Eastern Sector of Berlin. But if we are heartened by the partial progress achieved in Berlin, other developments made us aware of the growing military power and expansionism of the Soviet Union.

Instead of working with the West to reduce tensions and erase the danger of war, the Soviet Union is engaged in the greatest military buildup in the history of the world. It has used its new-found might to ruthlessly pursue its goals around the world. As the sad case of Afghanistan proves the Soviet Union has not always respected the precious right of national sovereignty it is committed to uphold as a signatory of the United Nations Charter. And only one day's auto ride from here, in the great city of Warsaw, a courageous people suffer because they dare to strive for the very fundamental human rights which the Helsinki Final Act[70] proclaimed. (Applause)

The citizens of free Berlin appreciate better than anyone the importance of allied unity in the face of such challenges. Ten years after the Berlin Agreement, the hope it engendered for lasting peace remains a hope rather than a certainty. But the hopes of free people—be they German or American—are stubborn things. (Applause) We will not be lulled or bullied into fatalism, into resignation. We believe that progress for just and lasting peace can be made—that substantial areas of agreement can be reached with potential adversaries—when the forces of freedom act with firmness, unity and a sincere willingness to negotiate.

To succeed at the negotiating table, we allies have learned that a healthy military balance is a necessity. Yesterday, the other NATO heads of government and I agreed that it is essential to preserve and strengthen such a military balance.[71] And let there be no doubt: the United States will continue to honor its commitment to Berlin. (Applause)

Our forces will remain here as long as necessary to preserve the peace and protect the freedom of the people of Berlin. For us the American presence in Berlin, as long as it is needed, is not a burden. It is a sacred trust.

Ours is a defensive mission. We pose no threat to those who live on the other side of the Wall. But we do extend a challenge—a new Berlin initiative to the leaders of the Soviet bloc. It is a challenge for peace. We challenge the men in the Kremlin to join with us in the quest for peace, security, and a lowering of the tensions and weaponry that could lead to future conflict.

We challenge the Soviet Union, as we proposed last year, to eliminate their SS–

---

69 For the text of the Quadripartite Agreement on Berlin, signed on September 3, 1971, and entered into force on June 3, 1972, see 24 UST 283.

70 For the text of the Helsinki Final Act of the Conference on Security and Cooperation in Europe, August 1, 1975, see Department of State *Bulletin*, September 1, 1975, pp. 323–350.

71 For the text of the Declaration issued by the NATO Heads of Government, June 10, 1982, see document 180.

20, SS–4, and SS–5 missiles. If Chairman Brezhnev agrees to this, we stand ready to forego all of our ground-launched cruise missiles and Pershing II missiles. (Applause)

We challenge the Soviet Union, as NATO proposed yesterday, to slash the conventional ground forces of the Warsaw Pact and NATO in Central Europe to 700,000 men each and the total ground and air forces of the two alliances to 900,000 men each. And we challenge the Soviet Union to live up to its signature its leader placed on the Helsinki Treaty so that the basic human rights of Soviet and Eastern Europe[an] people will be respected.

A positive response to these sincere and reasonable points from the Soviets, these calls for conciliation instead of confrontation, could open the door for a conference on disarmament in Europe. (Applause)

We Americans—we Americans are optimists, but we are also realists. We're a peaceful people, but we're not a weak or gullible people. So we look with hope to the Soviet Union's response. But we expect positive actions rather than rhetoric as the first proof of Soviet good intentions. We expect that the response to my Berlin initiative for peace will demonstrate finally that the Soviet Union is serious about working to reduce tensions in other parts of the world as they have been able to do here in Berlin.

Peace, it has been said, is more than the absence of armed conflict. Reducing military forces alone will not automatically guarantee the long-term prospects for peace.

Several times in the 1950's and 1960's the world went to the brink of war over Berlin. Those confrontations did not come because of military forces or operations alone. They arose because the Soviet Union refused to allow the free flow of peoples and ideas between East and West. And they came because the Soviet authorities and their minions repressed millions of citizens in Eastern Germany who did not wish to live under a Communist dictatorship.

So I want to concentrate the second part of America's new Berlin initiative on ways to reduce the human barriers—barriers as bleak and brutal as the Berlin Wall itself—which divide Europe today. (Applause)

If I had only one message to urge on the leaders of the Soviet bloc, it would be this: Think of your own coming generations. Look with me 10 years into the future when we will celebrate the 20th anniversary of the Berlin Agreement. What then will be the fruits of our efforts? Do the Soviet leaders want to be remembered for a prison wall, ringed with barbed wire and armed guards whose weapons are aimed at innocent civilians—their own civilians? Do they want to conduct themselves in a way that will earn only the contempt of free peoples and the distrust of their own citizens?

Or do they want to be remembered for having taken up our offer to use Berlin as a starting point for true efforts to reduce the human and political divisions which are the ultimate cause of every war. (Applause)

We in the West have made our choice. America and our allies welcome peaceful competition in ideas, in economics and in all facets of human activity. We seek no advantage. We covet no territory. And we wish to force no ideology or way of life on others.

The time has come, 10 years after the Berlin agreement, to fulfill the promise it seemed to offer at its dawn. I call on President Brezhnev to join me in a sincere effort to translate the dashed hopes of the 1970's into the reality of a safer and freer Europe in the 1980's.

I am determined to assure that our civilization averts the catastrophe of a nuclear war. (Applause) Stability depends primarily on the maintenance of a military balance which offers to [*no*?] temptation to an aggressor. And the arms control proposals which I have made are designed to enhance deterrence and achieve stability at substantially lower and equal force levels. At the same time, other measures might be negotiated between the United States and the Soviet Union to reinforce the peace and help reduce the possibility of a nuclear conflict. These include measures to enhance mutual confidence and to improve communication both in time of peace and in a crisis.

Past agreements have created a hot line between Moscow and Washington, established measures to reduce the danger of nuclear accidents,[72] and provided for notification of some missile launches.[73] We are

[72] For the text of the "hot line" agreement, June 20, 1963, see 14 UST 825; for the text of the agreement to reduce the risk of outbreak of nuclear war, September 30, 1971, see 23 UST 1590.

[73] Article 16 of the SALT II Treaty, signed on June 18, 1979, but not ratified, provided for advance notification to the other party of all planned ICBM launches except for those not planned to extend beyond its national territory.

now studying other concrete and practical steps to help further reduce the risk of a nuclear conflict which I intend to explore with the Soviet Union.

It is time we went further to avert the risk of war through accidents or misunderstanding. (Applause)

We shortly will approach the Soviet Union with proposals in such areas as notification of strategic exercises, of missile launches and expanded exchange of strategic forces data. Taken together, these steps would represent a qualitative improvement in the nuclear environment. They would help reduce the chances of misinterpretation in the case of exercises and test launches. And they would reduce the secrecy and ambiguity which surround military activity. We are considering additional measures as well.

We will be making these proposals in good faith to the Soviet Union. We hope that their response to this Berlin initiative, so appropriate to a city that is acutely conscious of the costs and risks of war, will be positive.

A united, resolute Western Alliance stands ready to defend itself if necessary. But we are also ready to work with the Soviet bloc in peaceful cooperation if the leaders of the East are willing to respond in kind. (Applause)

Let them remember the message of Schiller that only "He who has done his best for his own time has lived for all times." Let them join with us in our time to achieve a lasting peace and a better life for tomorrow's generations on both sides of that blighted wall. And let the Brandenburg Gate become a symbol not of two separate and hostile worlds, but an open door through which ideas, free ideas and peaceful competition flourish.

My final message is for the people of Berlin. Even before my first visit to your city, I felt a part of you, as all free men and women around the world do. We lived through the blockade and airlift with you. We witnessed the heroic reconstruction of a devastated city and we watched the creation of your strong democratic institutions. (Applause)

When I came here in 1978, I was deeply moved and proud of your success. What finer proof of what freedom can accomplish than the vibrant, prosperous island you've created in the midst of a hostile sea? Today, my reverence for your courage and accomplishment has grown even deeper.

You are a constant inspiration for us all—for our hopes and ideals, and for the human qualities of courage, endurance and faith that are the one secret weapon of the West no totalitarian regime can ever match. As long as Berlin exists, there can be no doubt about the hope for democracy.

Yes, the hated Wall still stands. But taller and stronger than that bleak barrier dividing East from West, free from oppressed, stands the character of the Berliners themselves.

You have endured in your splendid city on the Spree, and my return visit has convinced me, in the words of the beloved old song that "Berlin bleibt doch Berlin"—Berlin is still Berlin. (Applause)

We all remember John Kennedy's stirring words when he visited Berlin. I can only add that we in America and in the West are still Berliners, too, and always will be. And I am proud to say today that it is good to be home again. (Applause)

God bless you. Dankeschoen.

Document 185

Transcript of a Press Conference by the Director of the Arms Control and Disarmament Agency (Rostow), July 8, 1982 (Extract)[74]

NATO Allies Table Draft MBFR Treaty

MR. ROSTOW. Good morning, ladies and gentlemen. We have some news from Vienna.

In his speech at the Bundestag in Bonn on June 9th,[75] President Reagan said that the alliance had agreed on a new proposal designed to give new life to the Vienna negotiations on mutual and balanced force reductions in Central Europe.

At their recent summit meeting, the NATO leaders announced that the Western participants in the MBFR would soon present a draft treaty embodying a new, comprehensive proposal designed to give re-

---

[74] Source: Department of State files; printed also in Department of State *Bulletin*, August 1982, p. 53. The press conference was held at 11:30 a.m.

[75] See document 179.

newed momentum to those negotiations and to achieve the longstanding objective of enhancing stability and security in Europe.[76]

This morning in Vienna's Hofburg Palace, where the MBFR plenary sessions take place, the West formally tabled its draft treaty. This new initiative is the result of an effort by this administration to develop an arms control approach on the question of conventional forces in Central Europe, an approach which calls for substantial reductions—reductions, which if implemented, could reduce the risk of war in Central Europe. The U.S. delegation in Vienna is headed by Ambassador Richard Staar.

As the President stressed in his speech to the Bundestag, this new Western approach on conventional force reductions is an important complement to previous American initiatives taken in the talks on intermediate-range nuclear forces and in the strategic arms reduction talks, both of which are now in session in Geneva. Thus, the comprehensive arms control program launched by President Reagan in his November 18th speech of last year has now culminated in these three specific proposals in the categories he listed. These proposals all meet the criteria set forth in that speech of last November, namely, that there must be substantial militarily significant reductions in forces, equal ceilings for similar types of forces, and adequate provisions for verification.

The primary Western objective in MBFR continues to be the establishment of parity at significantly lower levels of force in Central Europe.

Currently, the Warsaw Pact has some 170,000 more ground forces in Central Europe than the West. This disparity is one of the most destabilizing factors in the military situation in Europe. Its elimination, through the establishment of parity, could reduce the capability for sudden aggression and thereby lessen the risk of war, including nuclear war, in Europe.

The new initiative differs from previous Western proposals in that it provides for one comprehensive agreement in which all direct participants would undertake, from the outset, a legally binding commitment to take the reductions required for each side to decrease to the common collective ceiling of 700,000 ground force personnel for each side. This reduction would take place in stages, and would be completed within 7 years. Each stage of reductions would have to be fully verified. Under this new approach, the West will be making stronger reduction commitments than we have ever proposed before.

There is no change in the Western position that the sides must agree on the number of troops present in the area and subject to reduction before signature of any treaty. Without agreement on the size of the forces to be reduced and limited, an MBFR treaty would be neither verifiable nor enforceable. In the draft treaty, starting force levels for each side would be identified at the time of signature.

The Western draft incorporates the package of confidence-building and verification measures proposed by the West in 1979.[77] These measures are designed to help verify reductions and limitations and to enhance security and stability by reducing the risks of miscalculation and misperception.

In sum, the draft treaty tabled by the West in Vienna takes into account Eastern arguments and interests while making this administration's requirement that arms control agreements result in real reductions to equal levels. It offers the opportunity for achieving concrete results in the negotiations in furtherance of the agreed objectives of enhancing stability and security in Europe, and it complements our efforts in other arms reduction negotiations.

This is the first time that a Western proposal in the MBFR negotiations has been tabled in the form of a draft treaty. Doing so underscores Western seriousness in the negotiations and readiness to bring about substantial reductions.

I'll be glad to have your questions.

Q. I have a question. On the numbers in your statement you say currently the Warsaw Pact has some 170,000 more ground forces in Central Europe and in the release we just got you say there are 160,000 more. The question is, how many are really more and how do you identify them and how come in the last 7 years you haven't been able to find a more common ground? Could you identify a little more explicitly what you think those 160,000 or 170,000 increased

---

[76] For the text of the NATO statement on arms control and disarmament, June 10, 1982, see document 181.

[77] Regarding the Western initiatives on MBFR in 1979, see *American Foreign Policy: Basic Documents, 1977–1980*, pp. 462–464.

forces of the Warsaw Pact, what this is; what you have in mind on that?

A. Well, I'll take your last question first. The reason we have been unable to reach agreement on these force statements over the last 7 or 8 years is simply that the Soviet Union has refused persistent Western efforts to reach agreed data figures.

We hope we've made some progress in the direction of resolving that problem but [it] is not yet resolved.

The essence of this treaty approach is to combine the Western concern with verification and the responsibility for data. That is, the Soviet assumption of responsibility for data with the concept of a common collective ceiling, and the problems are not resolved.

What we are saying here with regard to these figures is that we are presenting only our own Western estimate and not agreed figures. That is, we have not achieved agreed figures with the Soviet Union as yet on what their force levels are.

So the figures I've presented and the figures on the basis of which this press release and press guidance are constructed is that we are talking now about our own figures, not about agreed figures.

. . . .

Document 186

Transcript of a Department of State Press Briefing, New York, October 3, 1982 (Extracts)[78]

NATO Foreign Ministers Confirm Need for a Comprehensive and Global Policy To Manage East–West Relations

SENIOR DEPARTMENT OFFICIAL. Just a few brief points to make about La Sapiniere: The meeting was very successful.[79] The Secretary of State was particularly pleased with the outcome and felt that the informal setting of the meeting itself was a key to the beneficial results. We believe that the discussions did result in an important meeting of the minds on several fundamentals about the alliance.

There was a strong consensus at La Sapiniere on the essential importance of maintaining the East–West military balance. The ministers there recognized the need for continuing military modernization of the alliance's defense posture, both for its own sake and in creating an environment that will maximize prospects for progress in arms control in the INF negotiations, START negotiations and others. As part of this consensus, the ministers stressed the importance of arms control generally and the CSCE process, in particular—this is the European Conference on Security and Cooperation.

The ministers also agreed on the need for a comprehensive and global policy to manage East–West relations, including its economic dimensions. Reflecting that fact, they agreed on basic considerations for East–West economic policy.

In addition, on other subjects they discussed the problem of international terrorism and resolved to increase cooperation on that problem. They also discussed the GATT ministerial session which is scheduled for next November,[80] and emphasized their determination for that meeting to succeed with ministers understanding the need to come to grips with forces of protectionism within the Western economic system.

I'll be happy to answer any of your questions.

Q. Can you explain what was meant by an "East–West economic policy"—a basic global policy to deal with East–West economics?

A. There I just think that they all recognize that a basic consensus on East–West economic relations is necessary to enhance the overall security of the alliance, and that kind of consensus needs to flow from a comprehensive and global approach.

---

[78] Source: Department of State files. This briefing, which was conducted on background by a senior Department of State official, took place at the United Nations Plaza Hotel at 8 p.m.

[79] An informal meeting of NATO Foreign Ministers and NATO Secretary General Joseph Luns took place at La Sapiniere, Quebec, October 2–3, 1982.

[80] For information on the GATT Ministerial Meeting in Geneva, November 24–29, 1982, see document 76.

I don't necessarily want to get into semantics here because I obviously wasn't there, and I'm not sure exactly what "global" means here. I tend to think . . . it means more of a broad approach to East–West economic relations.

Q. Would COCOM be the instrument or would there be a new instrument?

A. COCOM would certainly be part of a comprehensive East–West economic policy. COCOM focuses on trade with the Soviet Union that could directly enhance Soviet military potential. That certainly is one of the areas that was discussed this weekend.

Q. By dealing with the future and dealing with the needs of the future, did they, in effect, simply put the pipeline behind them?

A. As I understand it, the pipeline was not a major issue addressed by the participants this weekend. There was a desire, I think, to move ahead and discuss broad issues of East–West economic relations.

Q. In that connection, MacGuigan of Canada told people up in Quebec that members had agreed to make studies of credits and technology to the Soviet Union and their effect on security. They indicated that individual nations would make these studies.

Q. Are we making a study? Is there a particular portion of this that has been assigned to members? How will these studies be done?

A. Every nation will participate in the studies. Some of these studies are already underway. For instance, there is a meeting that begins tomorrow in Paris of the COCOM countries, and we and other members of COCOM have been preparing for that meeting.[81] We have looked at existing lists of technology that are administered by COCOM and examining whether that list needs to be modified.

In the area of credits, there has already been a substantial amount of work done, and we have had discussions with the Allies on the subject. These are two areas—militarily-relevant technology as well as credit flows to the East—that we are very interested in; and we hope to achieve a consensus within the alliance on how to manage it.

. . . .

[81] The meeting of the COCOM countries took place in Paris, October 4–5, 1982.

Document 187

Statement by the Secretary of Commerce (Baldrige) at a White House Press Briefing, October 21, 1982[82]

Steel Trade Arrangement Concluded With the Commission of European Community

As the President announced this morning,[83] we have successfully negotiated a withdrawal of the American Steel Industry's countervailing duty and dumping suits against some 40 European companies. The withdrawal comes after complex months-long negotiations that have resulted in agreements under our trading laws on steel and that both parties find preferable to continuation of the suits. The arrangements cover over 90 percent of steel exports to the United States from Europe.

This settlement has many advantages. First, it will be a shot in the arm to employment in the U.S. steel industry, which has been severely damaged. Second, it will stop the subsidized export of European steel unemployment to this country.

Finally, it removes one of the most severe trade frictions between the United States and the European Community and demonstrates that we can work together for an amicable settlement of difficult disputes in an atmosphere of cooperation, understanding and friendship. European unity was strengthened by the participation in the agreement by Germany, Luxembourg, and the Netherlands, who had small or no subsidies.

All of the major producers in the U.S. industry have informed us that this settlement will permit them to withdraw their lawsuits.

Specialty steel, about 5 percent of the total, was not included in the agreements since those companies have filed most of

[82] Source: Department of Commerce files. This statement was made at 11:45 a.m.

[83] For the text of the President's announcement of these successful negotiations, see *Weekly Compilation of Presidential Documents*, October 25, 1982, pp. 1366–1367.

their suits under Section 301 of the Trade Act of 1974,[84] which means separate dispostions must be made. The administration is deeply concerned about the distressed state of the U.S. specialty steel industry. The antidumping and countervailing duty cases filed by that industry, and any cases that may be filed, will be pursued just as vigorously as we pursued these cases that are being withdrawn. And I know that Ambassador Brock is doing the same with the specialty steel industry's petitions filed under Section 301.

The settlements announced today will help the steel industry, but they are by no means the answer to all of the industry's problems. Productivity increases have not kept up with wage increases and plant modernization programs must be continued.

This was a long, tough road. All parties worked very hard to reach this arrangement. More than 70 people in this Department alone have worked on nothing but these cases for 10 months and I want to take a moment to thank them for their dedication.

I'll be glad to take any questions.

Document 188

Transcript of a Department of State Press Conference, November 9, 1982 (Extract)[85]

U.S.–E.C. High-Level Consultations

. . . .

UNDER SECRETARY WALLIS. Thank you. I've had the pleasure during the last day and a half of participating with Vice President Haferkamp and his delegation in these consultations which occur twice a year.

We have during this time reviewed the entire range of economic issues that concern us both. These meetings . . . [go] back to 1970, and they provide a valuable opportunity for the United States and the Commission of the European Communities to exchange views and to take stock of those problems which require further attention.

Let me make clear that we have not engaged in negotiation on any issue. That's not the purpose of these regular consultations.

It's well known that in the past year, since the last session of the high-level consultation in November of'81, that the last year has been a difficult one for the global economy and also for U.S.-European economic relations.

High unemployment here and in Europe tempts us all to look for remedies which may ease the political pressures to do something, but inevitably will weaken our economies and hurt our standards of living over the long haul. Many of these so-called "remedies" seek to help one country's situation at the expense of others. All of them basically seek to help one group in a country at the expense of the rest of the people in that country.

Managing this pressure hasn't been easy, but so far it has been successful. The recent steel agreement[86] is a concrete example of our ability to crack even a pretty tough nut.

These consultations took place with the GATT ministerial—the General Agreement on Tariffs and Trade meeting of ministers—scheduled only 2 weeks from now.[87] That meeting presents an exceptionally important opportunity to renew and strengthen our mutual resolve against protectionism.

We talked about our views of how this can best be done. For the United States I indicated that there are several essential ingredients that we will be seeking at the GATT ministerial meeting.

---

[84] Section 301 of the Trade Act of 1974 (P.L. 93–618) permits the President to take retaliatory action against a foreign government and allows domestic interests to bring to the government's attention the fact that foreign practices are adversely affecting U.S. interests; for the text of this section, see 88 Stat. 2041.

[85] Source: Department of State files. The press conference, which was conducted by W. Allen Wallis, Under Secretary of State for Economic Affairs, and Wilhelm Haferkamp, Vice President of the Commission of the European Communities, took place at 11:30 a.m. after the U.S.–E.C. High-Level Consultations on November 9 and 10 at the Department of State were completed.

[86] Regarding the October 21, 1982, arrangement between the United States and the European Economic Community on a 3-year plan establishing a voluntary quota on EEC steel exports to the United States beginning November 1, 1982, see *supra*.

[87] Regarding the GATT Ministerial Meeting in Geneva, November 24–29, 1982, see Chapter 5, Part B.

First, a strong political commitment to a healthy international trading system founded on free-market principles.

Second, understandings on safeguards and dispute settlement.

Third, a framework for serious discussions on agricultural trade.

Fourth, work programs on new issues such as services which will achieve an increasing prominence in the coming decade.

We agreed that we can't afford failure at Geneva. We all have in front of us the specter of the 1930's to reflect upon if our governments can't make the often difficult and unpopular political choices needed to strengthen the trade system.

We recalled the devastating consequences of a vicious cycle of protection and retaliation on the economic well-being of our countries and on the health of the relationships that bind the industrial democracies together.

In addition to the GATT issues, the agenda for our consultations covered questions of East–West economic relations: energy and bilateral trade issues, and a review of the economic outlook in the United States and Europe.

Contacts between the United States administration and members of the Commission have never been as frequent and intense as in recent months. These include the discussions President Thorn had with our four U.S. Cabinet officers last December in Brussels, and I'm pleased to announce here that Secretary Shultz will be joined in Brussels this December by Secretaries Regan, Block, and Baldrige, as well as by Ambassador Brock, for another session of consultations at the ministerial level.[88]

These ministerial meetings are clear evidence of the will on both sides to work together not only to solve problems, but especially to prevent them.

I would like now to ask Vice President Haferkamp, who has been the cochairman of these meetings with me, for his comments.

MR. HAFERKAMP. Ladies and gentlemen, since our last high-level U.S.–E.C., relations have gone through a difficult year. There have been and there are a number of serious problems, but in a major relationship like ours and in difficult times like these, problems are only natural and can be expected to continue to arise in one form or another.

What matters is our handling of these problems and whether we can fix [them] one by one as we go along.

I believe that we are just doing this, which is why in bad times the transatlantic relationship is in such basic good shape. So the steel issue has now been resolved, and I hope that the pipeline problem, which is still under careful consideration between the principal—by some parties concerned, will also soon be satisfactorily resolved.

We have carefully gone over the ground for the GATT ministerial meeting. Here, too, there has been something of a meeting of minds. We both share the same objective: The successful GATT meeting to uphold the free world open trading system.

Looking further ahead, there will be the followup to the Geneva ministerial, including the delicate issue of agricultural trade.

Europe and America will have to hang together in all this if they are not to hang separately. We in the European Community look to our opposite numbers in Washington to resist growing protectionist pressures inside the United States in such areas as specialty steel, footwear, domestic content legislation, and the rest.

Back in Brussels we shall be holding the line with our own protectionist special groups. We have also had a comprehensive technical exchange of views on energy matters, including the oil market outlook, gas security, and the development of indigenous energy supplies.

The point here lies not too much in details. The essential thing is that we are sharing information and endeavoring to concert our politics, whatever the occasion offers.

All in all, as I said just now, I think the U.S.–E.C. dialogue is in good shape. Sometimes we have spectacular public results, but more frequently we are working away behind the scenes on a host of detailed issues in difficult international economic circumstances. This is exactly as it should be.

At the general political level, we need to keep in frequent contact. This week's high-level consultations have permitted me, as Commission Vice President for External

[88] This meeting took place on December 10, 1982.

Relations, to take the political pulse here in Washington.

In 4 weeks' time, as Secretary Wallis has just announced, it will be the E.C.'s turn to welcome in Brussels Secretary Shultz and other senior representatives of the executive to carry the political dialogue forward into 1983. Thank you.

. . . .

Document 189

Testimony by the Under Secretary of State for Political Affairs (Eagleburger) Before the Senate Foreign Relations Committee, November 30, 1982 (Extract)[89]

Withdrawal of U.S. Troops From Europe Detrimental to NATO and Arms Control Negotiations

. . . .

I welcome the opportunity to testify today on the American role in NATO. Too often in foreign policy, as elsewhere, we take the most important things for granted. Too rarely do we examine the foundations of our security and our role in the world.

This is an important time for the United States to examine and state clearly our policies toward European security. We are now almost 2 years into the Reagan administration.

In the Soviet Union, a new leadership has just taken up the reins of power. While it is unlikely that Mr. Andropov and his associates will veer far from existing Soviet policies, they are undoubtedly now studying the opportunities and constraints they face. They are sizing up our resolve and our steadiness, and, in particular, our ability to maintain a unified Western Alliance.

In Europe, we and our allies are succeeding in putting behind us contentious questions regarding the Siberian gas pipeline and are about to start an effort to shape a coordinated Western approach to East-West economic relations for the rest of this decade and perhaps beyond.

Against this backdrop we are now hearing voices in this country calling for a scaling down of the American role in NATO. Most disturbingly, we are facing specific proposals in the Senate and the House which would, among other things, reduce the level of U.S. forces in Europe and interfere with our ability to meet our commitment to modernize NATO's nuclear forces.

When such views surfaced in the past, the national commitment to a strong Atlantic Alliance prevailed. Having fought two wars to defeat aggression in Europe, the American people know that our interests cannot be insulated from events across the Atlantic. We decided after the second of those wars—as we should decide again now—that alliance with the other Western democracies is vital to our national security and prosperity. If we have learned anything from the history of this century, it is that we cannot retreat to a fortress America, nor safely disengage from European affairs.

Europe has become more, not less, important for us over the three decades since the Alliance was formed. The European and North American economies are now so tightly knit together that neither can grow without the other. The allied countries are our main export market. American direct investment in Europe is an important positive factor in our balance of payments and contributes heavily to the profitability of American business.

The United States and Western Europe are more than simply trading and political partners, however. Our security is unalterably linked with theirs. Western Europe is quite literally our first line of defense. It is the center of our global competition with the Soviet Union and by far the most alluring object of Soviet ambitions.

NATO's strength and cohesion have protected Western freedom and democracy and kept Europe peaceful for over three decades, despite a menacing Soviet military presence. If we sometimes forget that our European allies stand face to face with Soviet tanks and with Eastern totalitarianism, if the Soviet challenge sometimes seems distant to us, it is because NATO has been effective.

---

[89] Source: *NATO Troop Withdrawals: Hearing Before the Committee on Foreign Relations, United States Senate, Ninety-seventh Congress, Second Session* (Washington, 1982), pp. 9–15.

In recent years, Soviet military might has grown more rapidly than ever. Soviet foreign policy has become more assertive and aggressive. The invasion and occupation of Afghanistan is Moscow's first attempt since the end of the second world war to expand by force the area under its direct control. The assault on the people of Poland shows that the Soviet leaders will not permit free institutions in countries where it has military dominion.

The new leadership in Moscow faces basic choices about the Soviet role in the world. If they see an America drawing inward, a demoralized Western Alliance, and our European partners in doubt about the U.S. commitment, their incentive to act with greater restraint will be diminished.

The need for a strong Atlantic Alliance based on unity of purpose and steady American leadership has never been more critical.

The Reagan administration is particularly concerned, therefore, by the prospect of legislation that would cast doubt on the steadiness of the U.S. commitment to NATO. The current Senate defense appropriations bill, which contains provisions to cut back American participation in NATO defense programs, would, if passed, signal a broad U.S. retreat from its responsibilities and its leadership.

Passage of this legislation would be a fundamental departure from the historical bipartisan post-war U.S. approach to national security. Never has the American role in the defense of Western Europe been reduced through legislation. Never has the United States backed away from its NATO commitments. And never have the elected representatives of the American people voted not to stand by our allies and back up our defense commitments.

Are we really ready now to take such a fateful step? Do we really want to greet the new Soviet leadership with a sharp deviation from the policies that have so successfully preserved Western security and American leadership in Europe?

The provisions that have been inserted in the Senate version of the proposed appropriations act that would be most damaging are: first, the reduction by 18,900 troops of the American force planned for the end of fiscal year 1983; second, the elimination of funds to procure heavy equipment for prestocking at two sites provided by Belgium and the Netherlands; third, the elimination of the American portion of the funding for 93,000 German reservists who will support our units in wartime under the Host Nation Support program; fourth, cuts in funding for the ground-launched cruise missile, which would force us to stretch our deployment schedules; and fifth, restrictions on transatlantic defense cooperation and trade.

Let me emphasize one point right away. This administration, like the Congress, is seriously concerned about the budget. We recognize that a sound economy is the necessary foundation for a successful foreign policy. But the provisions I have just outlined have almost nothing to do with budgetary austerity. The total saving contemplated by these anti-NATO proposals before the Senate is about $150 million, which is less than one-tenth of 1 percent of the total defense budget.

If the political consequences of these measures were as insignificant as the budgetary savings, I would not be here today. But the impact of these measures on our security would be out of all proportion to their budgetary significance.

I am aware that this legislation reflects a concern about the fairness of the distribution of defense burdens within the Alliance. Like you, we want the allies to do more for the common defense. And it is true that U.S. defense spending is now growing faster than that of the allies. But let me remind you that we in the United States neglected military programs for nearly a generation and that only today are we repairing the resulting gaps in our forces. We must sprint now because we went so slowly for so many years.

In contrast, the allies have kept up a strikingly steady performance. During the 1970's, their defense spending rose at a rate of 2 percent per year in real terms. Our defense spending declined in real terms by 1 percent per year during the same period. If we had matched the allied growth rate during the 1970's, we would not need to accelerate now. Conversely, had the allies failed to maintain their steady effort in those years—had their defense spending decisions been dominated by considerations of what some here in the United States now call "equity" rather than need—the alliance would not be as secure as it is today.

In any case, it would be a tragic mistake to allow concerns about burden-sharing to prevent us from doing what is necessary for our own security. Following that policy would allow those whose defense performance is weakest to set the standard. We are fortunate that the allies did not adopt such an attitude during a time of less-than-adequate U.S. performance.

After all the arguments and counterarguments about burden-sharing have been heard, we must, at the end of the day, ask ourselves one basic question. Will the United States be more or less secure if these provisions are enacted? I believe the answer is clearly "less secure." Let me outline the effects I foresee.

First, the American commitment to NATO would be placed in doubt. I do not see how the advocates of this legislation could dispute this or argue that causing doubts about our commitment would advance our interests. Nothing could weaken the alliance more than the perception in Europe that the United States is not determined to preserve European security.

Our allies would take little comfort in the fact that the amount of money involved is small. They would see passage of these cuts as a statement of U.S. intentions; they would interpret it as the beginning of a more general American retreat from Europe.

The Soviets would undoubtedly try to exploit the inevitable doubts and fears of the Europeans. Dividing us from our allies and pushing us out of Europe are, of course, central goals of Soviet foreign policy. The administration has, as you know, recently made progress in healing divisions and rebuilding consensus and confidence in the alliance. This legislation could undo what has been achieved.

Second, reductions, especially reductions in the number of American troops in Europe, would send the worst possible signal to European publics about the importance of a strong defense. NATO and U.S. leaders have been warning Europeans that the Soviet threat is growing. Reducing American forces or abandoning planned improvements would make these warnings sound hollow and undermine European public and Parliamentary support for defense expenditures.

Proponents of this legislation may claim that our doing less would jolt our Allies into doing more. I see no basis for such wishful thinking. U.S. cuts would have the opposite effect. If we do less, the Europeans will do less, and we will all be less secure.

Third, these cuts, while small in dollar amounts, would hit priority, cost-effective programs especially hard. The proposed troop cuts could leave our combat forces undermanned, or force the withdrawal of other essential units. Reductions in funding for prepositioning combat equipment and our share of the host nation support agreement would compound the difficulties and costs of wartime deployment.

We are constantly striving to make our dollars buy more fighting strength. These programs enhance our combat capacity by improving what is sometimes called our "teeth-to-tail" ratio. The proposed cuts would therefore reverse a major effort to improve our forces' effectiveness, while saving very little money. Moreover, they would not simply penalize our allies but our own forces as well, by denying them the means to carry out their rapid reinforcement mission.

Fourth, these cuts would damage the very programs in which allied performance has been especially good. The Europeans have joined the host nation support and prepositioning programs with the clear and correct understanding that we would match or supplement them. If we now back down on our side of the bargain, we will not only lose the benefits of these programs but will undermine our credibility for the development of any future cooperative efforts.

In 1978, at a summit meeting in Washington, alliance leaders agreed to a long-term program providing, among other things, for rapid U.S. wartime reinforcement of Europe.[90] Since then, our allies have fulfilled their commitment. For example, Belgium and the Netherlands, both small and densely populated countries, have gone to considerable effort and expense to obtain the land required to store prepositioned U.S. equipment.

The Federal Republic of Germany has allocated half the funds for 93,000 additional German reservists to support U.S. deployments. The proposed appropriations bill would threaten both of these programs. Is this a sensible way to respond when the allies have done just what we proposed that they do?

If restrictions on our contributions to the long-term defense program stand, the entire program will atrophy. We will turn a notable success into failure. We will cancel

---

[90] Regarding the North Atlantic Council Meeting in Washington, May 30–31, 1978, and the Final Communiqué, May 31, 1978, see *American Foreign Policy: Basic Documents, 1977–1980*, pp. 193–194.

out much of what we and the allies have already achieved and paid for.

Last June in Bonn, President Reagan and his allied counterparts committed themselves in a special summit charter to specific plans for improving NATO's conventional capabilities.[91] This charter called for the achievement of demanding force goals, and identified priority programs. I cannot now guarantee that this charter will be implemented in every detail, though we will work very hard to that end. But I can say with absolute confidence that if these cuts are legislated, that charter will not be translated into concrete improvements.

Let me restate unequivocally our agreement that the allies need to do more. This administration has made that clear at every opportunity, here and abroad, and is working to produce a greater allied contribution to our common defense effort.

Our attempts to foster better cooperation, better coordination of United States and European defense spending, and to have our allies take greater responsibility for our common defense are bearing fruit, but only if we ourselves keep the commitments that we have made can we count on the allies to improve their performance.

Finally, a legislated, unilateral U.S. pullback from our military commitments to NATO would damage prospects for arms control. Unilateral U.S. troop withdrawals would remove any incentive for the Soviets to agree to mutual reductions that would lower the threat and ease the military confrontation in the heart of Europe.

At the MBFR talks in Vienna we are seeking to negotiate the new Western draft treaty[92] put forward by the President last spring. That treaty would correct the present imbalance between Soviet and Western forces in Central Europe through significant verifiable reductions to equal levels.

A cut in funding for the ground-launched cruise missile and the deletion of funds for the deployment of the Pershing II missile, which has been voted in the House, would dash our hopes for a negotiated solution to the problem posed by the Soviet SS–20 intermediate range nuclear missiles. In the INF talks in Geneva, we have proposed a treaty that would ban this whole class of Soviet and U.S. intermediate range nuclear missiles, but only if we and our allies show that we are resolved to deploy U.S. missiles in Europe can we get to the Soviets to negotiate seriously.

The advocates of this legislation owe it to us all to explain how it would help arms control and thus contribute to reduction of the threat. Is there any evidence that unilateral limits and cuts can have anything other than a destructive effect on negotiated arms control? Should we not be more concerned about reducing the threat than about reducing our ability to counter it?

Let me conclude with a few basic points. The Atlantic Alliance has provided well for Western security for 30 years. That alliance is built upon the forces that we and our allies have deployed in Europe and the conviction that the United States is fully committed to the defense of Europe. When those forces and that conviction are strong, deterrence in Europe is sturdy and we are secure. We weaken them at our peril.

The world will be dangerous enough in this decade. It is not in our interest to tamper with North Atlantic security.

Thank you, Mr. Chairman.[93]

THE CHAIRMAN. Thank you very much, indeed, Mr. Secretary. We will go on a 10-minute rule this morning.

Just to be sure we know exactly what the Appropriations Committee proposal would do, we had actually in Europe in troop strength on September 30th, 1982, 355,600 troops. To bring down the level to 331,700, as they propose, the level of September 30th, 1980, would mean a reduction of 24,000 troops.

We have certainly both agreed that there would be a disastrous reaction in Europe. I have seen that in the talks that I have had with members of 16 countries now. Is there anything that has happened in Europe that would justify a 24,000-man reduction? Is there any lessening of the military threat that we have from the Soviet Union to Western Europe?

You mentioned the recent change of command. Is there any reason we have to believe that the threat is any less than would justify any withdrawal?

SECRETARY EAGLEBURGER. Mr. Chairman, I don't myself see any reason to believe that the threat has lessened. And indeed, I would argue that in the political area, there

91 Regarding the statement on Integrated NATO Defense, June 10, 1982, see document 181.

92 Regarding this Western draft treaty tabled at the MBFR plenary session in Vienna, July 8, 1982, see document 185.

93 Senator Charles H. Percy.

are factors which argue that we need now to be particularly careful. One is that there has been a change in the leadership in the Soviet Union, and I think we have to be very careful about the sorts of signals we send at this time of transition.

Second, as I indicated, we are in the midst of negotiations on intermediate range nuclear forces in Geneva, and it seems to me that we need to be terribly cautious about the signals we send now to the Soviets in terms of how they may act or react in those negotiations. We should not be reducing our ability to negotiate in Geneva, and I think all of these steps would in fact do that.

. . . .

Document 190

Final Communiqué Issued by the Nuclear Planning Group of the North Atlantic Treaty Organization, Brussels, November 30, 1982[94]

Nuclear Forces Remain Essential Part of NATO's Deterrent

The NATO Nuclear Planning Group (NPG) held its thirty-second Ministerial meeting at NATO Headquarters, Brussels, on 30th November, 1982. Ministers addressed a wide range of security matters including the trends in the balance of nuclear forces of NATO and the Warsaw Pact, the preparations for NATO's Intermediate-range Nuclear Forces (INF) missile deployments and the status of negotiations between the United States and the Soviet Union on strategic nuclear forces and on intermediate-range nuclear forces.

Ministers reaffirmed that the purpose of deterrence is to preserve security, peace and freedom by conveying to a potential adversary that the cost of any aggression against NATO would far exceed any conceivable gains. To do this successfully, NATO must possess a spectrum of forces to demonstrate that it has both the will and the ability to defend itself. For its strategy to be credible, the Alliance must maintain an interlocking triad of forces: strategic nuclear forces, intermediate-and short-range nuclear forces and conventional forces. No one part of the NATO triad can be a substitute for another. In this context, Ministers reiterated the importance of maintaining adequate nuclear forces as an essential part of NATO's deterrent.

The United States Secretary of Defense led a discussion on the status of strategic nuclear forces. Ministers noted the consistency and continuity of the United States nuclear policy designed to enable the Alliance to carry out its deterrence strategy more effectively. In the face of a significantly increased Soviet threat, Ministers stressed the importance of maintaining the effectiveness of NATO's strategic nuclear forces from the standpoint of deterrence and stability. From this standpoint the significance of the recent decision on MX basing which was designed to enhance the survivability of NATO's strategic nuclear forces was emphasized. Ministers recognized that stability would be further enhanced and that the security of all countries concerned would be greatly improved by an equitable and verifiable agreement which would substantially reduce strategic nuclear systems and ballistic missile warheads, as the United States had proposed at the Strategic Arms Reduction Talks (START) in Geneva. They welcomed the recent United States proposals to negotiate with the Soviet Union expanded nuclear confidence-building measures aimed at further enhancing international safeguards in this area.

Ministers noted with concern that the Soviet Union continues to improve the entire spectrum of its nuclear forces from strategic to short-range. These overall improvements to the Soviet nuclear arsenal, particularly in the field of longer-range INF, have taken place in spite of the decade of restraint shown by the Alliance. Since the publication by NATO of "NATO and the Warsaw Pact—Force Comparisons" in May 1982, more SS–20 missiles have become operational. The Soviet Union now has 324 SS–20 launchers deployed and operational world-wide, comprising 972 warheads; when these are combined with the SS–4 and SS–5 missiles still operational, the Soviets have more than 1,200 longer-range land-based INF missile warheads compared with none deployed by NATO.

Against this background, NATO's INF modernization programme is moving ahead

---

[94] Source: *NATO Communiqués, 1982,* NATO Information Service, Brussels, Belgium, pp. 23–24; printed also in *NATO Review,* vol. 30, No. 6, 1983, pp. 27–28.

with development and flight testing of Ground-Launched Cruise Missiles (GLCMs) and Pershing II missiles in the United States and preparation for deployment in the European basing countries. Ministers reiterated that, in the absence of a concrete arms control agreement, these deployments would begin according to schedule at the end of 1983.

Ministers discussed the negotiations between the United States and the Soviet Union on intermediate-range nuclear forces and welcomed the continuous and close consultation on the progress of the negotiations, particularly in the Special Consultative Group (SCG). They reiterated their strong support for the United States negotiating position, developed in close consultation with the allies, which calls for the elimination of all existing and planned Soviet and United States longer-range land-based INF missiles, thus resulting in the elimination of an entire category of nuclear weapons. Ministers stressed the importance of a successful outcome to the negotiations; they noted, however, that while there had been some progress in them, the Soviets have not yet made any move on the central issue and are maintaining their position which would permit them to retain their SS–20s while precluding NATO from deploying any longer-range INF missiles. In addition, the Soviets' position calls for the withdrawal of almost all United States dual-capable aircraft from NATO Europe, which are an important element in NATO's conventional defence. The result of this position would be to erode seriously the linkage between the United States strategic nuclear deterrent and the defence of NATO Europe and lessen NATO's conventional and nuclear defence capabilities. Ministers again welcomed the fact that the United States remains prepared to give full consideration to any serious Soviet proposals which would enhance chances for effective and verifiable arms control agreements and would take into account legitimate Western security concerns.

Ministers also discussed the progress in the important ongoing work of the High Level Group, which, as a matter of priority and against the background of INF arms control negotiations, is examining the precise nature, scope and basis of the adjustments which would be required by longer-range INF deployments as well as the possible implications of these deployments for the balance of roles and systems in NATO's nuclear armoury as a whole.

Ministers reaffirmed that NATO's nuclear posture in no way represented a policy of seeking to fight and win a nuclear war, and underlined their firm commitment to the existing policy of collective deterrence including a nuclear component, designed to prevent war and to protect the territorial integrity and independence of Alliance member countries. Ministers restated that NATO's strategy of deterrence remained unchanged; the Alliance does not threaten anyone and none of its weapons will ever be used except in response to attack.

Greece has expressed its views on the issues discussed in a statement included in the minutes.

Document 191

Final Communiqué Issued by the Defence Planning Committee of the North Atlantic Treaty Organization, Brussels, December 2, 1982[95]

NATO's Strategy of Flexible Response Essential to the Maintenance of Peace

The Defence Planning Committee of the North Atlantic Treaty Organization met in Ministerial Session in Brussels on 1st and 2nd December, 1982. Ministers recalled the Programme for Peace in Freedom declared by their Heads of State and Government in Bonn in June of this year.[96] This programme rests equally on the imperatives of maintaining strong deterrence through defence modernization and the need to achieve, through constructive negotiation, agreements on militarily significant, equitable and verifiable arms reductions. The Bonn Summit emphasized the Allied commitment to the prevention of war, to the preservation of democracy and to building the foundations for peace. The Allies expressed their collective determination both to maintain adequate military strength and political solidarity and to seek more constructive East–West relations whenever Soviet behaviour makes this possible.

---

[95] Source: *NATO Communiqués, 1982,* NATO Information Service, Brussels, Belgium, pp. 25–28; printed also in *NATO Review,* vol. 30, Nov. 6, 1983, pp. 26–27.

[96] For the text of the Declaration issued by the North Atlantic Council, June 10, 1982, see document 180.

2. On the previous day Ministers participating in the Nuclear Planning Group reviewed a wide range of nuclear and arms control issues, and noted with concern that the Soviet Union continues to improve the entire spectrum of its nuclear forces from strategic to short-range. Ministers turned their attention in the Defence Planning Committee meeting to a review of NATO's defence programme as a whole against the background of the continuing numerical superiority of Soviet conventional forces and the growing application of advanced technologies.

3. Modernization and expansion of Warsaw Pact conventional forces continue to accelerate and include the addition of advanced aircraft, surface ships, submarines, a full range of armoured vehicles and artillery and other systems. In this context, and recognizing particularly the need for strong conventional forces, Ministers discussed the results of the 1982 Annual Defence Review, adopted the NATO Force Plan for 1983–1987, and agreed to provide resources to implement the necessary force improvements. Ministers noted the considerable progress achieved by nations in 1982, but acknowledged that there is still much to be done, including the pursuit of measures originally identified by the Long-Term Defence Programme.

4. As a further important contribution to the credibility of NATO deterrence, Ministers approved a plan for the rapid reinforcement of Europe as necessary in a crisis. The improved capability to reinforce and augment Allied forces in the forward areas, implicit in this plan, extends the range of options open to the Alliance.

5. In reviewing the status of the collective security efforts of the Alliance in the 1980s, Ministers reaffirmed their strong conviction that, over and above the importance of reinforcements, the continuing and undiminished presence of United States and Canadian forces in Europe is essential to NATO's defence and deterrence strategy and serves the interests of all the members of the Alliance. These forces play a unique and essential rôle in the integrated defence posture and as a concrete demonstration of the cohesion and will of the Alliance. In like fashion, the efforts by European members of the Alliance to maintain and improve their defence capabilities are essential elements in this common demonstration of cohesion and will. In this context, Ministers reaffirmed the intent expressed at the Bonn Summit to continue to give due attention to fair burden-sharing and developing areas of practical co-operation.

6. It is clear that all countries are making sacrifices to meet their defence commitments. However, Ministers noted the extent to which Greece, Portugal and Turkey rely on Allied assistance to carry out their missions more effectively to the advantage of all. Ministers agreed to continue to explore the possibilities for further support and assistance.

7. Recalling the important declaration on arms control and disarmament issued at the Bonn Summit.[97] Ministers expressed strong support for the position taken by the United States in the Strategic Arms Reduction Talks (START) to seek substantial reductions in the strategic arsenals of both the United States and the Soviet Union through an equitable and verifiable agreement. Ministers also reiterated their strong support of the position taken in the negotiations on Intermediate-Range Nuclear forces by the United States, which was developed in close consultation with its Allies, and which calls for the elimination of all existing and planned Soviet and United States long-range land-based intermediate-range nuclear missiles, thus resulting in the elimination of an entire category of nuclear weapons. They also reiterated their adherence to both tracks of their December 1979 decision as the firm foundation of these negotiations.[98] Recalling the Bonn Summit initiatives on Mutual and Balanced Force Reductions (MBFR) and the tabling of a draft Western Treaty in Vienna, Ministers expressed the hope that the East would respond in an equally serious and constructive manner.

8. Ministers stressed their common interest in the security, stability and sovereign independence of countries outside the NATO area: respect for genuine non-alignment is important for international stability. While recognizing that the purpose of NATO is to preserve the security of the North Atlantic Area, Ministers acknowledged that developments beyond the NATO area might threaten the vital interests of members of the Alliance. They agreed to take full account of the effect of such developments on NATO security, defence capabilities, and the national interests of member countries, and recalled the Bonn Summit at which the need to consult and to share assessments on the basis of commonly identified objectives was reaffirmed. Recognizing that the policies which

[97] See document 182.

[98] Greece reserves her position. [Footnote in the source text.]

nations adopt outside the NATO area are a matter for national decision, Ministers stated that those countries such as the United States, which have the means to take action outside the treaty area to deter threats to the vital interests of the West, should do so in timely consultation with their allies, as defined in the Bonn Summit documents. Ministers acknowledged that other individual allied nations, on the basis of national decision, would make an important contribution to the security of the Alliance by making available facilities to assist such deployments needed to strengthen deterrence in such areas. Ministers acknowledged the need for increased co-operative planning, noting that the Alliance authorities are studying a report on the implications for NATO of United States plans for the Rapid Deployment Joint Task Force.

9. Ministers endorsed the need to seek ways to redress escalating defence costs by more effective application of national resources to defence, particularly in the conventional field. Some improvements can be achieved through the rationalization and better co-ordination of NATO defence planning aimed at a greater harmonization of such planning activities as those involving infrastructure, armaments and logistics. In this context Ministers emphasized the special importance which they attach to armaments co-operation within the scope of the transatlantic dialogue and especially with regard to the concept of families of weapons.

10. Consistent with the Bonn Summit mandate, Ministers received a United States paper on taking advantage of emerging technologies to improve conventional capabilities and thereby enhance deterrence and defence.[99] They agreed that NATO should actively seek ways to exploit these technologies within the co-operative defence planning process and endorsed the pursuit of NATO efforts to look for the economical and efficient application of emerging technologies.

11. Similarly, effective steps to restrict the transfer of militarily relevant technology to the Warsaw Pact will serve to preserve the West's technological advantage, particularly in the development of conventional armaments. In this regard, Ministers noted the recent progress made in this area and urged continued strong support of common efforts to stem the leakage of Western technology to the East.

12. Ministers welcomed the growing public debate in the West about how best to preserve peace with freedom over the coming years. They acknowledged the responsibility of democratic governments to ensure that these debates were carried forward in full recognition of all the facts. Fundamental to any such discussion must be a recognition of the defensive nature of the Alliance. Equally, in the face of the continuing build-up of armaments by the Warsaw Pact, there must be a recognition of the need, if peace is to be preserved, for NATO to maintain a strong, modern and flexible triad of forces. NATO must maintain conventional forces at a level sufficient to ensure that a potential aggressor could not count on any quick or easy gain. In view, however, of the capabilities of both the nuclear and conventional forces of the Warsaw Pact, conventional defences alone cannot deter aggression.[1] It is therefore essential to have available intermediate-and short-range nuclear forces and the strategic nuclear forces of the United States and the United Kingdom as indispensible parts of the interlocking triad of forces.[1] A potential 0 aggressor would have to take into account that an attack on any member of the Alliance would run the risk of escalation making the price of aggression higher than any conceivable gain. This is the essence of NATO's strategy of flexible response that has been—and remains—essential to the maintenance of peace.

13. Ministers reaffirmed that continued adherence to this strategy backed up by strong defence efforts, including nuclear and conventional force modernization, holds the greatest promise of creating a climate conducive to substantial, equitable and verifiable reductions in the level of nuclear and conventional arms and to the achievement of genuine détente.

---

[99] For the text of the Programme for Peace in Freedom, outlined in the June 10, 1982 Declaration of the NATO Heads of Government which states that they should explore ways to take advantage of emerging technologies to improve defense, see section 5 b of document 180.

[1] Greece reserves her position. [Footnote in the source text.]

Document 192

Address by the Ambassador to the Federal Republic of Germany (Burns) Before the Deutsche Atlantische Gesellschaft, Bonn, December 9, 1982[2]

The Economic Health of the Western Alliance

I wish to thank the Deutsche Atlantische Gesellschaft for the opportunity to address your members and friends this evening. Since its establishment a quarter of a century ago, your society has faithfully supported the fundamental objectives of the North Atlantic Alliance. You have never wavered in your devotion to peace or in your efforts to espouse the principles of individual freedom and democracy that constitute the moral foundation of NATO. In so doing, you have earned the gratitude of enlightened citizens of both your country and mine.

My purpose this evening, beyond expressing appreciation of your contribution to preserving international peace and freedom, is to discuss some of the economic issues that have recently been troubling the Western alliance.

Economic factors inevitably have a significant impact on political attitudes that prevail in our respective countries, and they in turn can be decisive for the military effectiveness of the alliance. In view of the immense role of the United States in world affairs, I shall concentrate on the economic relations between the United States and its European Allies. That these relations have been rather strained of late is a matter of common knowledge. That is reason enough for trying to see the American-European relationship in a sound perspective. Beyond that, it is vital to our alliance to consider how well its economic underpinnings are being maintained and protected.

Since the end of 1979, both the United States and Western Europe have been experiencing considerable economic sluggishness or actual recession. That Western economies are vastly stronger than the economies of the Soviet bloc is a matter of considerable importance, but this can hardly justify complacency on our part. What needs to concern us is the state of our own economic health—how best to preserve and improve it. My first task this evening, therefore, is to examine briefly the sources of recent difficulties in the West.

The oil price shocks of 1973 and 1978 have certainly contributed to our economic problems. So too have other developments in the international marketplace, particularly the increasing challenge of Japan to some of our key industries as well as the new competition for a variety of Western manufacturers from the more advanced of the developing nations. These external influences, however, have been less important for Western economies than difficulties of our own making.

During the early decades of the post-war period, the fiscal and monetary policies of Western democracies were highly successful in maintaining reasonably full employment and in improving social conditions. These very successes tempted governments during the 1970's to respond to the never-ending public pressures for governmental benefits by risking large budget deficits and easy money in the hope of expanding social welfare programs still further as well as attending to new environmental concerns. But by attempting to extract more and more goods and services from our economies without adding correspondingly to our willingness to work and save, we in the West inevitably released the destructive forces of inflation.

Under these conditions, it should not be surprising that tensions over economic issues have at times seriously tested the harmony that has generally characterized the political relations between the United States and its European Allies. When our individual economies are booming, there is little pressure on governments from their business or agricultural communities to protest or counteract activities being pursued in other countries. Such pressures tend to mount, however, in times of economic adversity. Difficulties that would be passed over under prosperous conditions then take on some importance—occasionally even a large importance. Gentle voices of spokesmen of economic interests are then apt to become loud and strident, and even the customary composure of academicians and high government officials tends to suffer. Human nature being what it is, that has been the usual experience of mankind and we have not escaped it this time.

There is, first of all, the issue of American interest rates. There can be no dispute

---

[2] Source: Department of State files; printed also in Department of State *Bulletin*, February 1983, pp. 35–40.

over the fact that these rates have been extraordinarily high in recent years. Nor can it be denied that they served to attract funds to the United States from other parts of the world, that this movement of funds tended to raise interest rates in some European countries, and that business investment suffered to some degree as consequence. If European complaints had stopped at this point, no one could reasonably quarrel; but many Europeans, including prominent government officials, at times went further and either stated or implied that American interest rates were responsible for the economic troubles in their countries. That line of thinking overlooked the fact that high American interest rates could not be responsible simultaneously for the still higher interest rates in France and the drastically lower interest rates in Japan. Needless to say, factors indigenous to individual countries—among them, the propensity of the public to save and the state of governmental budgets—always exercise some influence on interest rates.

Much of European criticism of American interest rates also stemmed from a misunderstanding of American policy objectives. Seeking to end the havoc wrought by inflation, our authorities proceeded on a principle that has been tested across the centuries—namely, that stoppage of inflation requires curbing the growth of money supplies. It is, of course, true that the high interest rates were in large part a result of our restrictive monetary policy. That does not mean, however, that we sought high interest rates.

On the contrary, the immediate effects of the restrictive monetary policy on interest rates and economic activity were by no means welcome, but this policy did achieve its fundamental purpose of curbing inflation in the United States. Since 1979, when the consumer price level rose more than 13 percent, the rate of inflation has moved steadily lower. By coming down to less than 5 percent this year, the inflation rate in the United States is now one of the lowest in the world.

The success of monetary policy in subduing inflation eventually made it possible for American interest rates to move to lower levels—partly through the inner workings of the marketplace and partly through adjustments of policy. The slowing of inflation encouraged the authorities to reduce monetary restraints, and the deepening of recession impelled them to do so. Economic conditions in the United States were, of course, primarily responsible for the subsequent decline of interest rates, but our monetary authorities were also mindful of the benefits that the lower rates could bring to Europe. Since last year, when the rate that commercial banks charge their prime borrowers reached 21½ percent, the prime rate has fallen to 11½ percent. Open-market short-term rates have been cut in half. Long-term rates on corporate bonds and home mortgages declined less, but they too have fallen materially. The greater part of these interest rate adjustments has occurred since June, and European rates followed American rates downward—although not to the same degree. As these financial developments unfolded. Europeans joined Americans in wishing that interest rates would move even lower, but what had previously been a significant source of friction within the alliance virtually ceased being troublesome.

Another recent irritant to some members of the alliance was the stand taken by the American Government on intervention in foreign exchange markets. The effectiveness of such maneuvers in stabilizing foreign currencies had long been a subject of serious debate among financial experts, including central bankers. Nevertheless, governments of leading countries kept intervening with some frequency during the 1970's, in the hope of smoothing out some of the short-run fluctuations in the exchange market. Being critical of these policies, the Reagan administration announced soon after it came into power that, in its judgment, foreign currencies are best left to the free market and that it would therefore refrain from intervening except under highly exceptional circumstances. Not a few financiers and government officials welcomed this decision, and even some who questioned it were more concerned with the political consequences of nonintervention than with its intrinsic economic merits. There were, nevertheless, some determined European critics of the new American policy, and they made their influence felt—most notably at the summit meeting held this June at Versailles.[3]

While Americans held to their basic position at that meeting, they did propose that a committee of international experts study the results of past experience with intervention. By agreeing to such a study, all participants tacitly admitted the possiblity that some of their views on intervention might need to be revised. Since then, the United

---

[3] Regarding the Versailles Economic Summit, June 4–6, 1982, see Chapter 5, Part F.

States has gone further in the direction favored by its critics by actually intervening several times—albeit on a modest scale—in the market. There is reason for hoping that the foreign exchange study now under way may further contribute to narrowing the differences between the United States and some of its allies. And if good will should be aided by good fortune, so that both interest rates and inflation kept coming down in our respective countries, the fluctuations of exchange rates would of themselves narrow and thus reduce both the impluse to intervene and the inclination to fret over the issue.

A far more serious conflict between the United States and its allies was stirred by the decision of several European countries to support the construction of a Siberian natural gas pipeline. This conflict reached a climax when the American Government, feeling morally outraged over the Soviet Union's role in suppressing the newly won freedoms of the Polish people, proceeded to forbid shipments by American firms of materials and equipment needed to build the pipeline. This prohibition was later extended to European subsidiaries and licensees of American firms.[4] These actions led to acrimonious charges and debates, and some political observers on both sides of the Atlantic felt that American reaction to the crisis in Poland may have given rise to a crisis of the alliance.

That danger, fortunately, was surmounted. Not only was damage to the alliance kept down, but the pipeline controversy actually helped to steer Western thinking about foreign policy onto a sounder track.

In the course of pondering the sanctions imposed against the Soviet Union, the American Government undertook a review of Western economic relations with the Soviet Union in the hope of developing a policy that, unlike the pipeline sanctions, could prove of lasting benefit to the alliance. It soon became clear that this would require more resolute dealing with elements of incoherence in Western foreign policy. The reasoning that led to this conclusion was straightforward. On the one hand, NATO countries were devoting, year after year, vast resources to our common defense against the Soviet threat. Simultaneously, however, partly through private banks and partly through government agencies, we in the West kept lending during the past decade vast sums of money to the Soviet Union and its satellites. At times, this was even being done at subsidized interest rates. In view of the high priority that the Soviet Union assigns to its military establishment, the financial resources that the West so liberally put at the disposal of the Soviets thus indirectly helped to strengthen their already formidable military establishment. To make matters worse, the Soviet Union continued to take advantage of the weaknesses in our controls on the export of militarily related products and technology.

These considerations were persistently pressed by the American Government on its allies during the past year. For a time, they were resisted by European governments, partly because of displeasure over the pipeline sanctions, partly also because of concern that the American initiative could lead to an East–West trade war. But as the American Government made clear that its basic aim was simply to steer Western policy onto a path that was more consistent with allied security interests, controversy and recrimination gradually yielded to quiet voices of reason.

On November 13, President Reagan was able to announce that agreement had been reached on the need to consider allied security issues when making trade arrangements with the Soviet Union.[5] More specifically, the United States and its partners agreed, first, that new contracts for Soviet natural gas would not be undertaken during the course of an urgent study of alternative sources of energy; second, that existing controls on the transfer of strategic items to the Soviets will be strengthened; third, that procedures for monitoring financial relations with the Soviets will be promptly established; and fourth, that the allies will work to harmonize their export credit policies. In the eyes of the American Government, these measures will promote allied interests more effectively than the pipeline sanctions. The President therefore concluded his statement by announcing their removal. Long and difficult negotiations on ways of carrying out the agreed measures are undoubtedly still ahead of us, but the pipeline crisis as such has fortunately come to an end.

In other areas of economic policy—particularly defense burden-sharing and trade

---

[4] For the text of President Reagan's statement extending export sanctions, June 18, 1982, see document 160.

[5] For the text of President Reagan's speech where this agreement was announced, November 13, 1982, see document 165.

issues—the United States continues to have major differences with its European partners. Difficulties of this type have troubled the alliance almost from its beginning, and in one form or another they are likely to remain troublesome in the years ahead. Even here, however, we have generally managed to work out our problems, and we have had some limited successes during the past year that are noteworthy.

The distribution of defense burdens among allies inevitably raises difficult questions of equity. Many Americans, especially members of Congress, have long felt that the United States is bearing an excessive part of the heavy costs of the alliance. In view of the financial stringency that has developed in my country, such criticisms of Europe have recently intensified. Our NATO partners usually respond by reminding us that their spending on defense rose steadily during the 1970's while real American spending kept falling off. That is entirely true, but it does not tell the whole story. Official statistics indicate that defense spending reached 7.9 percent of the gross domestic product in the United States during 1970. The highest corresponding figure for each of our major allies fell short of 5 percent in that year. While the defense outlays of the United States decreased during the 1970's, this gap has never been closed. Confronted with these facts, European governments are inclined to observe that monetary figures fail to capture all costs involved in the defense area, particularly the conscription of soldiers that exists in most of their countries. Such remonstrances, however, are not always accepted by Americans, as the lively discussions that have been resounding in our congressional halls indicate.

Whatever the merits of ongoing debates among members of the alliance, the Reagan administration recognizes that some of the military proposals now before Congress would seriously weaken the alliance. Not only that, they would also encourage the Russians to remain unyielding in the vital arms control negotiations now underway in Geneva. Those dangers have not escaped the attention of European leaders. In fact, many Europeans have long shared the widespread American belief that Europe is not doing enough for its own or for the common defense. Financial stringency is nowadays no less a problem in Europe than in the United States. In spite of that, the German Government has recently taken steps that should help Americans to see the problem of defense burden-sharing in a better perspective. Several months ago the Federal Republic signed a treaty with the United States under which it agreed to commit 90,000 reservists in support of American combat forces in the event of war.[6] More recently, Minister Manfred Woerner announced that the new German budget provides a significant additional contribution for constructing vital NATO military facilities in Europe. These measures had long been urged by Americans on the German Government. The fact that they have been adopted at a difficult time should certainly help to quiet American concerns.

Differences between the United States and its allies over international trade issues also have a long and checkered history. From the end of World War II through the 1970's the broad trend of Western policy has been towards increasing liberalization of international trade and investment, and there can be little doubt that this trend contributed enormously to the prosperity of the West and other parts of the world. While the United States led the world toward an open trading system and unrestricted foreign investment, this policy—except for agriculture—was generally supported in Europe, particularly in the Federal Republic of Germany. Unfortunately, but not surprisingly, the deep recession of recent times has by now stirred up strong protectionist sentiment in many European countries and also in the United States.

The Reagan administration has stoutly resisted congressional moves toward protectionism—thus far with considerable although incomplete success. During the recent ministerial meeting of the parties to the General Agreement on Tariffs and Trade,[7] the United States fought especially hard for an unequivocal commitment by the world's trade ministers to phase out existing measures restricting international trade and to refrain from taking new restrictive measures. The debates over this principle and on specific trade issues were protracted and at times bitter, but at the end American initiatives brought only modest results. Assuming professorial garb, Mr. Brock, the American trade representative, judged the result as deserving hardly more than a grade of "C"—an assessment that few informed observers have questioned.

---

[6] Regarding the agreement between the United States and the Federal Republic of Germany for host nation support, concluded on April 15, 1982, see document 211.

[7] Regarding the GATT Ministerial Meeting in Geneva, November 24–29, 1982, see Chapter 5, Part B.

From an American viewpoint, the most disappointing aspect of this meeting was the failure to convince the European Community to modify some aspects of its agricultural policy. For many years the Community has maintained farm prices above the world level. Surpluses therefore developed, and in order to move them into world markets the Community subsidized their export. As long as this policy was confined to protecting farm sales within the Community, the United States accepted it—although not without protest. But once the subsidization led to large exports to third-country markets, a more serious problem arose for American farmers and agricultural exporters of other countries. With farm incomes in the United States currently at their lowest level since the 1930's, American protests against the Community's agricultural policy have become increasingly insistent. The Community, however, has refused to budge, maintaining among other things that the issue of its subsidies had already been settled in earlier negotiations. This and other arguments of the Community have not softened American attitudes; and unless this agricultural controversy is soon settled, there is a serious possibility that the Congress will pass retaliatory legislation next year. This would be so damaging for both the United States and Europe that I continue to believe that some mutual accommodation will be worked out.

Such a result, indeed, was achieved in connection with another trade dispute that for a time resisted every attempt at resolution. For many years the world steel industry has suffered from excess capacity and, as so often happens under such conditions, various countries—including some in Europe—made export subsidies available to their steel producers. As a consequence, large quantities of steel produced with the benefit of government subsidies have penetrated the American market in recent years. American steel manufacturers, who do not receive subsidies, sought to limit this vexing competition. They took advantage of a law that enables an industry to veto certain governmental efforts to work out trade arrangements with other countries. Despite this formidable obstacle, the American Government finally reached an agreement with the European Commission that imposes moderate quotas on exports of various steel products to the United States.[8]

To me, as to other confirmed free traders, this agreement has brought little joy. However, the practical choice that both Americans and Europeans faced in this instance was not between protectionism and free trade, but rather between degrees and kinds of protectionism. If the negotiations on steel quotas had failed, existing American law would have required prompt imposition of punitive duties on steel imports. Worse still, it seemed likely that in that event the Congress would legislate still more drastic protectionist measures. The negotiated settlement clearly violated the salutary principle of free trade, but it also forestalled more serious consequences. To this extent, it is not only a tolerable arrangement, but one that has served to reduce political tensions between the United States and its allies.

The conclusion that I feel can justly be drawn from my review of the recent steel and other economic disputes within the alliance is reassuring. To be sure, there have been excesses of political rhetoric on both sides of the Atlantic and, occasionally, misguided actions as well. Nevertheless, the United States and its European Allies have succeeded in working out—or at least in muting—most of their troublesome differences over economic issues. Our ability to accomplish this mutual accommodation under difficult conditions demonstrates that the moral, political, and security interests that unite us are strong enough to overcome even divisive economic issues. That at any rate has proved to be the case thus far, and from that we can surely draw encouragement for the future.

We must temper, however, any feeling of optimism that international economic conditions will improve so much in the near future that they will be unlikely to cause or intensify political strains within the alliance. It is by now widely recognized that the weakness of the international economy during the past 3 years is the aftermath of the inflationary pressures released during the 1970's. It is not so clearly understood, however, that our recent econômic difficulties reflect more than the normal vicissitudes of the business cycle. They reflect also a certain loss of business dynamism—that is, a gradual weakening of the underlying forces of economic growth in the Western World.

Liberal fiscal and monetary policies had served us well over a long generation in fostering full employment and improving the social environment. They might have continued to work beneficially if they had

---

[8] Regarding the October 21, 1982, arrangement between the United States and the 0 European Economic Community on a 3-year plan establishing a voluntary quota on EEC steel exports to the United States beginning on November 1, 1982, see document 187.

not been carried to excess. But, unfortunately, traditional rules of financial prudence were thrown to the winds. As a result, our Western economies have become so highly sensitive to the dangers of inflation that liberal financial policies can no longer be counted on to perform their earlier constructive function.

Of late, government and business thinking in the Western World has focused on creating an environment that is more conducive to business innovation and private capital investment than it has been in recent years. Responsible leaders in our respective countries frequently emphasize not only the need to practice moderation in the monetary area, but also the need to bring about some reduction from the high levels that both government spending and taxes have reached relative to the size of our respective national incomes. Even France, which moved for a while in another direction, has recently adopted a rather restrictive monetary policy, besides announcing the intention to restrain further expansion of budgetary deficits. With earlier economic policies now in general disrepute in the West, and the newer policies not yet fully tested, deep concern about the economic outlook has spread during the past year or two in the United States as well as throughout Western Europe.

Such pessimism can be overdone. In the United States at least, the aggregate output of the economy has remained virtually unchanged during the past 6 months or so, and there are now numerous indications that the groundwork for recovery has been laid. As noted earlier, both inflation and interest rates have come down sharply. Stock and bond prices have risen dramatically, thereby adding hundreds of billions of dollars to the net worth of individuals and business entities. Of late, consumer spending for goods and services has increased modestly. Residential construction has been moving upward again this year; home sales have recently revived; and the financial condition of mortgage-lending institutions has improved. The upward climb of wages has slowed materially; industrial productivity has recently perked up; and corporate profits have begun to increase. These improvements have been offset thus far by sharp deterioration of merchandise exports and business investment in new plants and equipment. Nevertheless, it seems likely that a gradual recovery of aggregate production and employment will get under way in the United States within the next few months.

With the possible exception of Great Britain, the immediate outlook for Europe is less favorable, in large part because of the greater rigidity of its labor markets. But it is reasonable to expect that any improvement in the American economy also will be felt before too many months pass in Western Europe.

Unemployment, nevertheless, will remain high in the West for an uncomfortable period, since the pace of recovery is likely to be slow in the present instance. There are compelling reasons for this gradualness.

First, there are as yet hardly any signs that contracts for business contruction or orders for business equipment have begun to increase either in the United States or in Western Europe.

Second, most of the larger banks throughout the West must now realize that their lending policies, both at home and abroad, were excessively liberal during the 1970's. They will consequently be more cautious lenders—perhaps excessively cautious lenders—in the years immediately ahead. Third, many of the less developed countries—not only Mexico, Brazil, and Argentina, which lately have figured so heavily in the press—are at present unable to make timely payments of the interest or principal that is due on their overextended indebtedness. These financial difficulties constitute a grave, but I believe still manageable, danger to the international banking system. Under the best of circumstances, however, great austerity will need to be practiced in many of the less developed countries, and their reduced imports will inevitably restrict the pace of Western economic recovery over the next 2 or 3 years, if not longer.

If my assessment of the economic outlook is anywhere near the mark, political tensions on account of economic difficulties may well continue to trouble the alliance. To make progress on economic issues in the years immediately ahead, it is particularly important that every country avoid "beggar-thy-neighbor" policies. We cannot afford to think in terms of winners and losers when it comes to solving our common problems. It is essential, therefore, that member countries of the alliance mobilize the vast economic and political statesmanship that is at their disposal. Cooperation among economic ministries, finance ministries, central banks, private commercial banks, and international financial agencies, which has not always been close, must become very much closer. The heads of Western governments, who thus far have been reasonably successful in controlling the disease of protectionism, must work still more earnestly towards this vital objective. Meetings among members of the foreign policy and defense establishments of the alliance must occur still more frequently, and become more thorough as well as more timely, so that misunderstandings among their governments are kept to a minimum.

These, ladies and gentlemen, are the paths to confidence in the security and prosperity of the industrial democracies that are joined in the brotherhood of the Atlantic Alliance.

Document 193

Final Communiqué Issued by the North Atlantic Council, Brussels, December 10, 1982[9]

NATO Reaffirms Its Strength and Determination To Preserve North Atlantic Security

The North Atlantic Council met in Ministerial Session in Brussels on 9th and 10th December 1982 and agreed as follows:

1. The Atlantic Alliance, based on the ideals and values of democracy, has through its strength and cohesion succeeded in preserving peace and independence for the free and equal members of this partnership. On this solid foundation, the Heads of State and Government reaffirmed at their meeting in Bonn on 10th June 1982 the Alliance's policy of a strong defence and of East–West dialogue. Moreover, they set forth their Programme for Peace in Freedom, emphasising their resolve to develop substantial and balanced East–West relations aimed at genuine détente based on the effective application of the principles and provisions of the United Nations Charter and the Helsinki Final Act.

2. The Allies will maintain a firm, realistic and constructive attitude towards the Soviet Union on the basis of mutual acceptance of the principles of restraint and responsibility in the conduct of international affairs. They desire to improve relations with the member states of the Warsaw Pact and to extend areas of co-operation to their mutual benefit.

The Allies look to the Soviet leadership for tangible evidence that it shares their readiness to act in this spirit. They expect the Soviet Union to honour its obligations and to show respect for the sovereignty and independence of other states. In face of the continuing and massive Soviet arms build-up, the legitimate security concerns of the Allies remain and must be recognized. But the Allies are open to all opportunities for dialogue, will welcome any positive move to reduce tension, and desire, if Soviet attitudes allow, to co-operate in re-building international trust.

3. The violations in Poland of the Helsinki Final Act and of the Conventions of the International Labour Organization, in particular by the banning and dissolution of trade unions including Solidarity, continue to cause the gravest concern.

The Allies call upon the Polish authorities to abide by their commitment to work for national reconciliation. Recalling their declaration of 11th January 1982,[10] the criteria of which are far from being fulfilled, the Allies have noted the recent release of a number of detainees and continue to follow closely developments in Poland, including possible relaxation of military rule. They emphasize that in this regard the actions of the Polish authorities will be judged by their practical effects. The Allies consider that the improvement of relations with Poland depends on the extent to which the Polish Government gives effect to its declared intention to establish civil rights and to continue the process of reform. Freedom of association and the rights of workers to have trade unions of their own choice should not be denied to the Polish people. The dialogue with all sections of Polish society must be resumed. The Allies call on all countries to respect Poland's fundamental right to choose its own social and political structures.

4. In violation of the United Nations Charter and despite repeated calls from the General Assembly, the Islamic Conference and other international bodies, the Soviet

[9] Source: *NATO Communiqués, 1982*, NATO Information Service, Brussels, Belgium, pp. 29–33; printed also in Department of State *Bulletin*, February 1983, pp. 15–17.

[10] The Greek Delegation recalled its position on various aspects of this declaration. [Footnote in the source text.]

Union continues its military occupation of Afghanistan in the face of determined resistance by the Afghan people. The Allies call upon the Soviet Union to accept a political solution which would bring an end to the sufferings of the Afghan people and allow the return to their homeland of over 3 million refugees who have been forced into exile. This solution must be based on the withdrawal of Soviet forces and respect for the independence and sovereignty of Afghanistan which would thereby be enabled to exercise its right of self-determination and to return to a position of genuine nonalignment.

5. In unremitting pursuit of its military build-up, which has long passed the level required for defence, the Soviet Union is increasing its superiority in conventional arms and expanding its naval power. It is simultaneously strengthening its nuclear capability, particularly through the deployment of intermediate-range missiles. As stated in their Bonn Declaration, the Allies are left no choice but to maintain an effective military deterrent adequate to meet their legitimate security concerns in a changing situation. It therefore remains essential for the Allies to preserve the security of the North Atlantic area by means of conventional and nuclear forces adequate to deter aggression and intimidation. To that end they agree to continue their efforts towards greater co-operation in armaments and, in particular, to take full advantage of emerging technologies and to continue action in the appropriate fora restricting Warsaw Pact access to Western militarily-relevant technologies.

The presence of North American forces on the European continent and the United States strategic nuclear commitment to Europe are essential to Allied security. Equally important are the maintenance and continued improvement of the defence capabilities of the European members of the Alliance.

6. Arms control and disarmament together with deterrence and defence are integral parts of Alliance security policy and important means of promoting international stability and peace.

Firmly committed to progress over arms control and disarmament, the Allies have initiated a comprehensive series of proposals for militarily significant, equitable and verifiable agreements, which are designed to lead to a balance of forces at lowest possible levels. They seek from the Soviet Union a constructive and serious approach in current negotiations.

7. In the Strategic Arms Reductions Talks (START), the Allies fully support the efforts of the United States to negotiate with the Soviet Union significant reductions in United States and Soviet strategic forces emphasising the most destabilizing systems in the first phase of the negotiations. The Allies urge the Soviet Union to contribute in a concrete way to speedy progress in these important negotiations.

8. The Allies underline the importance of both parts of the decision of 12th December 1979 which provided for a limited modernization of United States Intermediate-range Nuclear Forces (INF) combined with a parallel offer of negotiations on United States and Soviet weapons of this kind. This decision, which was prompted, in particular, by the deployment of SS–20 missiles, led to the current INF talks in Geneva within the framework of negotiations on strategic arms reductions.[11]

The Allies fully support the United States efforts to enhance security through the total elimination of all existing and planned Soviet and United States longer-range land-based INF missiles. The United States proposal was developed in close consultation within the Alliance among the member countries concerned. The Ministers of these countries welcomed the continuing United States commitment to serious negotiations, and to consider carefully with these Allies any serious Soviet proposal.

Ministers reiterated that, in the absence of concrete results, INF deployments would begin according to schedule at the end of 1983.[11] 0

9. The Allies welcomed the recent proposals by President Reagan for new confidence-building measures in the nuclear field between the United States and the Soviet Union intended to enhance stability.

10. The Allies participating in the Mutual and Balanced Force Reduction (MBFR) talks in Vienna are confident that the comprehensive approach embodied in the draft Treaty text presented by Western negotiators has given new momentum to the negotiations. This Western initiative is aimed at achieving real progress towards substantial reductions of ground forces, leading to parity in combined ground and air force manpower at equal collective levels in Central Europe. Western participants

---

[11] Greece reserves its position on these two paragraphs. [Footnote in the source text.]

in the negotiations call upon the East to respond adequately to the need for prior agreement on data for current Warsaw Pact force levels and to agree to effective associated measures for verification and confidence-building.

11. The Allies also attach great importance to efforts in the United Nations to secure improved verification procedures, wider availability of information on defence spending and other measures likely to enhance transparency and thus build confidence.

12. The Allies are gravely concerned about strong evidence of continued use of chemical weapons in South-East Asia and Afghanistan in violation of international law, including Soviet involvement in the use of such weapons.[12]

They stress the need for progress in the Committee on Disarmament towards a convention on the prohibition of development, production and stockpiling of chemical weapons and on their destruction, with appropriate provisions for verification including on-site inspection.

13. At the Madrid CSCE follow-up meeting the Allies have deplored infringements of the principles and provisions of the Final Act.[13] They noted in this respect that the situation in Poland remained a source of concern. The Allies are continuing their efforts to arrive at a substantial and balanced concluding document and they regard the draft submitted by the Neutral and Non-Aligned States in December 1981 as a good basis for negotiations. They have introduced a number of amendments to bring it up-to-date with realities in Europe and to call for progress on human rights, free trade unions and the freer movement of people, ideas and information. To facilitate a positive outcome in Madrid, the Allies urge the Soviet Union and other Warsaw Pact states to abide by the principles and provisions of the Final Act.

As part of a substantial and balanced concluding document, the Allies reaffirm their support for a conference on confidence and security building measures and disarmament in Europe on the basis of a precise mandate to negotiate in a first phase militarily significant, politically binding and verifiable confidence and security building measures applicable to the whole of Europe, from the Atlantic to the Urals. They will also strive to achieve significant progress in the important humanitarian aspects of East–West relations.

14. Economic recovery in the West is essential both for Allied defence efforts and for social stability and progress. The Allies reaffirmed the need for effective cooperation bilaterally and in the appropriate fora towards this end, including programmes in keeping with Article 2 of the North Atlantic Treaty which are intended to benefit the economies of the less favoured partners.

15. The Allies recognize that mutually advantageous trade with the East on commercially sound terms contributes to constructive East–West relations. At the same time they agree that bilateral economic and trade relations with the Soviet Union and Eastern Europe must also be consistent with their broad security concerns which include the avoidance of contributing to Soviet military strength. Studies are underway or will soon be undertaken on several aspects of East–West economic relations and Ministers will consider these issues again, on the basis of these studies, at their next meeting.[14]

16. The strict observance and full implementation of the Quadripartite Agreement of 3rd September 1971[15] and the maintenance of an undisturbed situation in and around Berlin remain essential elements in East–West relations. The Allies welcome the efforts of the Federal Republic of Germany to strengthen the economy of the city in particular by ensuring long-term employment prospects.

Recalling their Rome statement of 5th May 1981,[16] the Allies express the hope that the continuation of the dialogue between the Federal Republic of Germany and the German Democratic Republic will contribute to the strengthening of peace in Europe and will bring direct benefits for Berlin and the German people in both states.

17. Peaceful progress world-wide is a goal to which the Allies remain committed.

---

[12] Greece has expressed its views on this sentence, which were recorded in the record of the meeting. [Footnote in the source text.]

[13] Regarding the Madrid CSCE follow-up meeting which began November 11, 1980, see document 170.

[14] Greece recalled its position on various aspects of this paragraph. [Footnote in the source text.]

[15] Regarding the Quadripartite Agreement, see footnote 69 to document 184.

[16] For the text of the communiqúe issued by the North Atlantic Council, Rome, May 5, 1981, see *American Foreign Policy: Current Documents, 1981*, document 157.

They consider that genuine non-alignment—an important element of international peace and stability—contributes to this goal, as does the aid which the Allies give bilaterally and multilaterally to the development of Third World countries. They reaffirm their readiness to co-operate with Third World countries on a basis of equal partnership. The Allies call upon all states to make an effective contribution to the struggle against under-development and to refrain from exploiting those nations' economic and social problems for political gain.

The Allies recognize that certain events outside the Treaty area may affect their common interests as members of the Alliance. Allied consultation on such events will be based on the recognition of those common interests. Those Allies in a position to do so may respond to requests by sovereign nations whose security and independence are threatened. It is in the interest of the Alliance as a whole to ensure that sufficient capability remains in the Treaty area to maintain deterrence and defence.

18. The Allies again strongly condemn the crime of terrorism, which is a menace to democratic institutions and the conduct of normal international relations. They appeal to all governments to examine the possibilities of increased co-operative efforts to stamp out this scourge.

19. The Alliance's efficiency in pursuing its policies depends upon continued cohesion and solidarity taking into account the natural diversity of its sovereign member states. Recognizing in this connection the value of their informal meeting in Canada, Ministers agreed that similar meetings could usefully be held in future.

20. The Spring 1983 meeting of the North Atlantic Council in Ministerial Session will be held in Paris on 9th-10th June.

Note: The Minister for Foreign Affairs of Spain has informed the Council of the Spanish Government's purpose regarding the Alliance and reserved his Government's position on the present communique.

Document 194

Transcript of a Press Conference by the Secretary of State (Shultz) and the President, Commission of the European Communities (Thorn), Brussels, December 10, 1982[17]

United States and European Communities Define Common Strategies and Goals

EC PRESIDENT GASTON THORN. Ladies and gentlemen. Let me first tell you that we had the pleasure, my colleagues from the Commission and myself, to welcome this afternoon Secretary of State Shultz, his colleagues from the American administration, Mr. Donald Regan, Mr. John Block, Mr. Malcolm Baldrige and Mr. Bill Brock. We had a real exchange of views covering, I believe, all topical issues. We thought that the timing of this meeting and discussion of these problems was particularly appropriate. First, because we find ourselves in a very delicate political and economic situation—the most difficult economic situation we've known since the end of the war—and particularly because, in this context, the United States and the Community, which account for approximately one-third of world trade, have specific responsibilities and particular interests in coordinating their goals. I will tell you that the exchanges were frank and straightforward, but they were so mainly because we did not talk about the past and difficulties that we may have encountered. But right away we turned to the problems at hand and we tried to define some strategies and to seek a few points where it is in our interest to cooperate together in the future, and even in the

[17] Source: Department of State Press Release 376, December 14, 1982; printed also in Department of State *Bulletin*, February 1983, pp. 19–22. Shultz was in Europe for meetings with allies and friends of the United States. He left Washington on December 6 and visited Bonn, December 7–8; Brussels, December 8–11; The Hague, December 11; Rome, December 11–14; Paris, December 14–15; Madrid, December 15–16; and London, December 16–18. Additional documentation on this trip is in this chapter.

While in Brussels, Shultz attended the Commission of the European Communities Meeting on December 10 along with his Cabinet colleagues Donald Regan, John Block, and Malcolm Baldrige, and William Brock, all of whom were present at this press conference.

very near future. It is of no interest to anyone, nor does it benefit anyone, to talk about the past; but it is absolutely imperative that we take action and that action replace words; that we emphasize our common interests and that we try to face them. It is in this spirit that we have tackled the following topics which I will only mention, allowing Mr. Shultz to add the introductory remarks that he wishes.

We have discussed trade matters, i.e., essentially the GATT and what is known as its follow-up. Then, of course, we discussed agricultural problems; we discussed East–West relations and then talked about the economic and financial situation such as we assess it on both sides of the Atlantic. These are the four main topics that have been brought up until now, excluding what might be discussed tonight during dinner. So much for my introduction.

SECRETARY SHULTZ. I think that is a good statement of the general scope of our discussion. Maybe the thing to do is just to respond to questions.

Q. I address my question to the Agriculture Secretary, Mr. Block. I'll skip the diplomatic niceties and ask roughly, if I may, whether the two sides were able to work out a compromise on the agriculture issues or will there be an agricultural trade war?

MR. BLOCK. First of all, there will not be an agricultural trade war. I don't think we should talk about trade wars. We need to solve problems. My appraisal of the outcome is that there have been some concrete actions agreed to; there is a joint appreciation that the internal farm program policies can have an impact on international trade and they can have, occasionally, a destructive impact on international trade. The European Community appreciates the need to harmonize internal prices and the world price. It was agreed, and this is most important, that we sit down and, in specific terms, review what can be done to solve our trade frictions—what can be done within the maneuvering room that the Community has. And we're going to do that within a time frame; with the first meetings early in January, continuing if necessary with a report back and review sometime in March. And I think I said that correctly.

Q. Can Mr. Regan illustrate his views on the reform of the international monetary system?

SECRETARY REGAN. I discussed just briefly at the meeting some of the thoughts that I have that there is a need for a better structure in the international monetary system to handle many of these problems that crop up very quickly that are very serious and need many different organizations for their solution. I offered no specific antidotes for these problems. I would say that what I am trying to do more than anything else is to encourage discussion of these items because I don't think there is anyone that has the best solution or the only solution. I think there can be many solutions, but the more we discuss them within various types of organizations, I think the quicker the chance will be that we can solve some of these problems rather than going in for ad hoc solutions.

Q. Question to President Thorn, I suppose. Mr. Block has referred to the Europeans accepting at least in part that their internal farm policies can have a disruptive effect on world trade. In which areas of internal EEC farm policy is the disruptive effect on world trade evident in your view? What are the concrete actions agreed to and referred to by Minister Block? And if I could ask a brief question to Secretary Regan, are you more worried now than you were 6 months ago about the danger of a world banking crisis?

SECRETARY REGAN. I'm less worried at this moment than I was 6 months ago. You will recall that in this period of time we have successfully handled several countries that are large debtors by renegotiating their loans, by temporary bridging loans, government-to-government or through the BIS, and as a result these nations are now on IMF programs. The more that happens and the more successful we are, the less dangers there are and the less threats there are to the international banking system.

MR. THORN. As for the question John Palmer addressed to me, and for which I am thankful to him in as much as it will perhaps give me the chance to detail our views on that matter. What I think John said and what I would like to confirm as far as I am concerned, is that we thought we should definitely avoid upheavals in the world market in regard to agriculture and that we both said that we definitely wanted to take steps to avoid that, each of us in the context of his own policy. To that purpose we said that we should keep in mind, as much on the American side as on the European side, that when faced with decisions in agricultural matters, we must prevent decisions from having these negative effects which we would like to avoid—also and notably as regards certain subsidies which could be granted and how far one could go, all the while respecting the policies of both partners. We therefore said that we would have the most extensive exchanges of views possible with our collaborators as of January, on actions that we might be led to take when making the inventory of specific issues. This is not a reevaluation of our policy, but rather a matter of seeing what concrete examples of problems there are in Europe and the United States, and then let us attack them immediately as of January. We will see in March, as my American colleague said, how advanced these studies will be; to what level, or if we have achieved some results. We also have examined some examples from the American side; our interlocutors have explained, for example, the measures that the President of the United States proposed last night—on the American side—to deal with that problem.

On our side, we have brought up, for instance, the measures that we have taken regarding products such as sugar, as well as those to reduce surpluses; and it is this analysis that we intend to pursue as soon as possible, which is to say after the holiday season.

Q. This is a follow-up to this question. Mr. Block, you just talked about respecting the space of maneuver of the European Community. Does it mean that the United States has now (garbled) the common agricultural policy as it is, meaning for instance subsidies for exports, and secondly, when you say there will not be a trade war on agriculture, means that you are not going to dump any food in a short time on the world market?

SECRETARY BLOCK. In response to the first question, we do not and have not quarreled with the common agricultural policy. Our quarrel has been with the spillover of that policy into the international markets, and it is our contention that it has created problems for us and other trading countries. The effort that the European Community intends to make and we intend to review with them how they can accomplish it, is to bring their internal prices, or see internal prices, and world prices more in harmony, or when they come close together or together, once this happens, it is a fact that export subsidies, but this would cause it to happen, and I think it is an appropriate approach. And the question of my statement that there would be no trade war—and I don't expect a trade war—trade wars would be bad for everyone concerned—that is a fact. It is also a fact that we did not give up. We did not agree that we would necessarily withhold any actions to compete on a favorable basis with the European Community in the export market.

Q. I would like to ask a question to the Commission, to the representative of the Commission, again on agriculture. I would like to know if you have any commitments regarding agriculture and an eventual modification of the policy followed until now. Can we speak of a commitment, and, if so which one?

And then a question to Mr. Block. It seems totally illusory to imagine that European prices could match world prices. In which case, what conclusion do you draw?

MR. THORN. Regarding the first part, I thought I had answered it by saying, twice, that naturally the cap was not negotiable. I believe you all heard that against and over the cap, but that we were both anxious to respect each other's policy—but that it's time to establish a list of concrete problems, as quickly as possible and then to discuss them together at the beginning of next year. No negotiation commitment, and no commitment to a result, has been taken at this stage and cannot be taken since we are only now initiating discussions.

SECRETARY BLOCK. In answer to your question you suggest that, in view of the circumstances, it's illusory to expect the common agricultural prices to harmonize with the world prices. I don't accept that necessarily. I don't think that the European Community accepts that and that is what we are going to sit down and look to when we have our meetings in January to see how that can come about.

Q. This is to both Mr. Block and Mr. Dalsager.[18] Was there any discussion here or has there been any discussion about cooperation in world agricultural marketing of major commodities to help you get over short term surpluses?

SECRETARY BLOCK. I guess I'll go first. We didn't talk in specific terms about cooperation. I guess I don't know what you mean specifically by cooperation in marketing these commodities. Yet we did talk about looking at the impact of the markets, of the exports, of the problems we both face. So certainly in that respect we're looking at cooperation. I'm a little concerned when you say cooperation. If you're talking about market sharing, and we really are not going to go out and divide up the markets if that's what you're suggesting, but we are going to

[18] Paul Dalsager, EC Commissioner for Agriculture, Denmark.

cooperate together to find solutions to some of the problems that we have the best we can anyway.

Mr. Dalsager. Yes, but the answer has already been given in detail on what we do with different products in detail and it has been overall discussion where we have decided to go into a further discussion after the new year to start to take up all the problems.

Q. I would like to address my question to Mr. Shultz and Mr. Regan. Mr. Shultz, you were Treasury Secretary when the Bretton Woods system finally was pulled apart. Now it sounds to me as though the new administration is—I don't say looking for a new Bretton Woods—but at any rate, changing very dramatically its view about the need for international cooperation and linkage of monetary, trade and financial banking measures. The question for you is whether your experience in those 10 years has affected your view on how to go about these things and whether you support this approach now? And the question for Mr. Regan is what has led to this change in the administration's approach?

Secretary Shultz. As for me, I try to learn as I go along, but yet I don't abandon my old ideas; but I'll let Secretary Regan handle where the outlook is.

Secretary Regan. The opinions that I expressed earlier this week are my own. This is not necessarily an administration position. I have not changed my opinion that there is a need for handling problems in the international community. What I am suggesting is that our experience of the last few months certainly has led us to a realization—by those of us who have had to deal with these on a daily and sometimes hourly basis—has led us to the conclusion that there might be a better way to handle this. Each case as it has come up now has been handled in a different fashion. I am suggesting that not only those of us who have been engaged in this type of endeavor but also those who have been observing us do it might have suggestions as to a better way to handle this. Now I am not suggesting that we should have some type of international rescue agency, because I think that banks have a right to be the victims of their own folly if indeed they have been foolish. And on the other hand, I think that every nation that has been profligate should not be rescued by the international community. But I think that when there are emergencies that there should be some type of apparatus to deal with that emergency in a better fashion than we're currently doing it.

Q. I'd just like to follow up on that. You did mention in your briefing or your informal meeting earlier this week the possibility of some kind of international federal reserve system. How do you see that possibility and how does this fit into the picture of your plans?

Secretary Regan. I would like to correct an impression you have. I did not call for an international federal reserve; I asked a rhetorical question: What is the bank of last resort behind the Eurodollar mechanism? Here is a market with many hundreds of billions of dollars in it if not a trillion dollars, yet as far as I know there is no bank of last resort. I asked that as a rhetorical question without any answer, nor did I suggest that there be a Federal Reserve for that at the same time, what I was suggesting was that in the international markets change is coming about and coming about very quickly. Domestically in the United States we're finding new fashions in finance almost every day. This is coming into the international markets also, and as things change in the financial markets and in the monetary system, I'm suggesting there is also a need for institutions to modernize and to stay up with these changes.

Q. This is for Secretary Block. Mr. Secretary, I understood you to say that you do not want to have a trade war, but I don't understand what you said about dumping butter. Is that something you are still considering or have you decided not to do that now?

Secretary Block. We did not agree at this meeting today to withhold actions on the part of the United States or to take actions. We didn't specify what we would do. We leave that open. There's no decision on that at this time.

Q. I would like to follow up with a question which has just been raised. President Thorn has brought up the reciprocal efforts to try to dissipate the agricultural difficulties between the United States and the Community. But I have only heard Mr. Block speak of the efforts that were contemplated on the European side to bring domestic prices closer in line with world prices. I would like to know what efforts the Americans themselves are contemplating to reduce these differences. Would there be an end to blank credits, the lifting of sugar import quotas, a self-limitation on corn gluten feed, etc? Can this question be answered?

Secretary Block. I think it's important that countries around the world be responsible at a time when we have large volumes of crops. The United States today has one half of the world's supply of grains. And the efforts we are making—the major effort was just announced yesterday by the President—and what he announced was that we will be going forward with a payment-in-kind program where we will make grain available to farmers if they will cut their production. We will take grain out of government stocks, give it to farmers if they will cut their production of that grain. This will reduce the stocks in the United States and yet keep plenty available for export to countries that are needing the grain. Furthermore, we are taking the steps to work with Congress to freeze our target prices later on, because high supports encourage excessive production. They distort the demand of the country. Secondly, in the area of dairy, in two years we have frozen prices, and, indeed, this year we have cut the price of dairy—to the dairymen—by $1 per hundredweight, which is about an 8 percent cut. That's a cut, an absolute cut in money to the farmer. Furthermore, we have instituted policies this year to expand our storage. Of course, I have explained all the storage of grain we have. We have enormous stocks of grain and we have lots of storage, and the government has helped to store it. We have tremendous stocks of dairy products. These are the efforts we are making to try and cope with the situation that we all face in agriculture. These are large stocks overhanging the markets. And in the United States certainly anyway, where the price fluctuates with the world market, it's a serious problem for us because prices are very low.

Q. I would like to know from Mr. Thorn or Mr. Shultz or maybe Mr. Haferkamp or Mr. Baldrige what the talks about East–West trade were about, what agreements or at least consensus has been reached here. Was it only about procedural questions or was it also about details for the forthcoming negotiations in international bodies?

SECRETARY BALDRIGE. We discussed the initiatives that have already been started, and some of the cases on the agreements reached in November on East–West trade, credit and financial arrangements, some of that work has already been done in the OECD, alternate energy sources. There'll be studies on that. How we integrate overall economic policy between the West and the East. The EC has participated where it has been appropriate in the past. They have told us they will participate where it's appropriate in the future. For example, in COCOM, that's not an EC kind of initiative. We're doing that through other sources: the tightening of COCOM at the top, the more technical and sophisticated potential exports, and the loosening at the bottom of the kind of exports that aren't really that strategically important.

Q. I have a second question for Secretary Shultz. Regarding the alliance, I gather this afternoon you mentioned that one of your hopes was that the dispute in agriculture would not spill over and undermine the alliance. I wonder if you could expand a bit on the dimension and the importance of this agreement that we seem to be moving toward in agriculture as it affects the alliance on one hand and how it relates to the East–West issue, or issues? Are they likely to emerge as contentious an issue and, if so, how do you plan to deal with that in the coming weeks in the transatlantic relationship?

SECRETARY SHULTZ. I don't see that these issues affect the alliance. The alliance is strong and it has its own bases. The discussions we've had here and elsewhere on East–West trade seem to be moving in a positive direction. And you've heard the report of the discussions we had this afternoon in the field of agriculture, which have not solved the problems, but they've set us in the road to trying to do so. So I think the thing adds up to a great big plus.

Q. For Mr. Regan, a lot of the issues you've been discussing here today relate in some way or other to the problems of monetary instability and high interest rates. The view on this side of the Atlantic is that you and the President have been very slow to wake up to your international responsibilities through tolerating an excessive budget deficit and perhaps a rather dubious monetary and fiscal mix. Have you any reassuring words to offer today about your efforts to reduce the budget deficit, and, in particular, have you anything reassuring to say about the future of American interest rates?

SECRETARY REGAN. I deny that either one of us has been asleep. As far as the international situation is concerned, you will recall at the time of Ottawa, at Versailles and again at Cancun, we were asked by the summit participants to do various things. I think we carried that out pretty well. We were asked to get inflation down in the United States. That was the number one problem that we had to address as an administration. Inflation was causing all kinds of international problems for our trading partners, for our allies and the like. I submit that we have done rather well with inflation. It was 12½ percent when we came in. This year it looks like it's going to run somewhere in the neighborhood of just below 5 percent. We were asked later to get our interest rates down, that high interest rates were the cause of the problem worldwide. When we took over, interest rates—prime rate at least—in the United States were running somewhere in the neighborhood of 21½ percent. Currently, it's at 11½ and hopefully on its way down further. So I think that we've done rather well there. The next complaint was that we had too strong a dollar. First of all it was a weak dollar in 1980. That was causing problems. We strengthened the dollar. And now the complaint is that the dollar is too strong, and would we mind weakening the dollar. I submit that over the past couple of months the dollar has been weaker, and perhaps will get even weaker as time goes on. I think that we have been living up to our international responsibilities rather well when you look at the record. As far as whether or not we—I don't like to use the word "locomotive"—but at least can we be the leader in getting the nations of the world back on the recovery path from the current recession that all of us are wallowing in, I would say that we should have—and this I told to the participants this afternoon—that we should have a good year next year with real growth in the United States of somewhere from 3 to 4 percent, and that we were hopeful that 1984 would be an even better year.

If that proves to be the correct scenario, then we think that our trading partners will benefit from the recovery in the United States.

Document 195

Statement Read by the President's Principal Deputy Press Secretary (Speakes), December 16, 1982[19]

United States Rejects Soviet INF Proposal

As you know the U.S. Government has proposed total elimination of U.S. and Soviet land-based, longer-range INF missiles, the zero-zero solution. As you know from the Soviet public statements the Soviets have proposed that after 5 years the USSR and NATO reduce to a ceiling of 300 medium-range nuclear missiles and aircraft located in or intended for use in Europe, to include British and French forces.[20]

This longstanding position, which is basically unchanged, would allow them to maintain their monopoly over the United States in longer-range INF missiles, especially their mobile triple-warheaded SS–20 missile in Europe and the Asian part of the Soviet Union.

The number of deployed SS–20's currently stands at 333 Launchers. A missile subceiling, mentioned in the recent press accounts, would at most require the reduction of some of those highly mobile systems in or intended for use in Europe while requiring the United States to cancel entirely our deployment of Pershing II and ground-launch cruise missiles, planned to begin in December 1983.

This would leave the Soviets with a substantial monopoly over the West in long-range land-based INF systems and would not constrain overall levels of the Soviet system and would draw into bilateral negotiations the nuclear forces of other countries and is patently inadequate as the solution to the INF issue since it would not eliminate the political and military threat to the alliance posed by the Soviet longer-range INF missiles.

We will continue the negotiations on a serious basis. During these negotiations we and the Soviets have elaborated our positions in both formal and informal contexts. We will continue to study the Soviet position and it will be among the things we will be discussing when the next round begins January 27th.

We have kept our allies fully informed about negotiations as they have occurred. We and our allies have reaffirmed in recent NATO meetings at the foreign minister or defense minister level that the zero-zero solution remains the best arms control result since it would eliminate the systems of greatest concern to both sides.

The President and his administration are fully convinced of the reasonableness of this carefully-developed proposal. Nothing could be fairer to all concerned.

---

[19] Source: Office of the Press Secretary to the President; printed also in *Weekly Compilation of Presidential Documents,* December 20, 1982, p. 1628. Speakes read this statement at a White House press briefing beginning at 12:55 p.m.

[20] On December 11, 1982, the United States revealed a Soviet offer to reduce to intermediate-range missile force by more than half if the United States agreed to forego planned missile deployments in Europe.

Document 196

Transcript of a Department of State Press Briefing, December 21, 1982 (Extract)[21]

Andropov's INF Proposal Unacceptable to the United States

. . . .

MR. HUGHES. And we'll have copies of this. The *on-the-record* statement is this:

The President has proposed to eliminate all land-based INF missiles at the Geneva talks. This proposal has been reaffirmed in recent days by the defense and foreign ministers of the NATO Alliance.[22]

The Soviet proposal contained in Mr. Andropov's speech today[23] is unacceptable because it would leave the Soviets with several hundred warheads on SS–20's, while denying us the means to deter that threat.

We cannot accept that the United States should agree to allow the Soviets superiority over us because the British and French maintain their own national deterrent forces.

Nor can we agree that INF limits should apply only in Europe. This would leave the Soviets free to threaten our Asian friends as well as to maintain a highly mobile missile force that can be moved at any time into position to threaten NATO.

In sum, we hope the Soviets will now come to realize that we cannot give up the means to counter the nuclear threat they pose to NATO unless the threat is eliminated all together.

That's the end of the *on-the-record* statement.

. . . .

Q. What are the key elements of this latest proposal, and is there anything in the newest proposal about dismantling missiles as opposed to simply removing them from the range of Western Europe?

FIRST OFFICIAL. Let me clarify one thing. First of all, the negotiations in Geneva are confidential, and we have tried to keep to the rule of confidentiality.

Mr. Andropov, in his speech, has talked about aspects of what is the Soviet proposal. I don't think it's appropriate for us to go beyond what Mr. Andropov has said.

I can say that so far in the negotiations we have not received a concrete Soviet proposal. So when we use the word "proposal," we're talking about an idea or an approach, elements of which were discussed in the last round of the negotiations, both in the negotiations and on the margins. So we were generally familiar with the ideas that were contained in Mr. Andropov's speech today. There were also newspaper articles talking about an approach like this, as you know.

We have discussed this approach within the government so we were not in any way surprised by the ideas contained in the speech today. We were able to discuss these ideas with the allies, as our statement noted.

My colleague may want to say a little bit about the discussions in Brussels with the defense ministers. We held a meeting of the NATO special consultative group during the foreign ministers meeting in Brussels recently, so we have fully discussed these concepts with the allies. And as the communiqués produced by the defense ministers' and foreign ministers' meetings have shown, there is total support for the President's position in the negotiations.

I don't want to characterize the other governments' attitudes toward proposals. They speak for themselves, but you've seen now a statement by the French. We've seen, I think, a statement by the British. I haven't seen it myself. I think, generally speaking,

---

21 Source: Department of State files. The first part of this briefing, by John Hughes, Department of State Spokesman, begun at 2:45 p.m., was on-the-record. The second part, by senior Department of State officals, was on background.

22 For the text of the communiqué issued by the NATO Defense Planning Committee in Brussels, December 2, 1982, see document 191. For the text of the communiqué issued by the North Atlantic Council in Brussels, December 10, 1982, see document 193.

23 For excerpts from Andropov's speech given on December 21, 1982, in which he proposed that the Soviet Union would reduce its medium-range missiles in Europe from over 600 to 162, the number of missiles maintained by Britain and France, if the United States and its allies abandoned plans to deploy 572 medium-range missiles in Europe, see *New York Times*, December 22, 1982, p. A14.

the alliance recognizes that this is a one-sided proposal.

What the Russians are proposing here is that they will be able to maintain a massive force of SS–20's targeted against our European Allies and the United States would get zero. If you want to see it as a variant, it's a Soviet-zero option. That is, we get nothing and they get to maintain a complete monopoly in this class of weapons.

Q. How many missiles?

A. I can just simply quote what Mr. Andropov has said is that—I think he said they would be prepared to size their force on the size of the British and French forces.

Q. Would they dismantle the remaining missiles or simply remove them from the western part of the U.S.S.R.?

A. It's not completely clear, but if they were only going to remove them and not dismantle and destroy them, then they would be in the position of being able at any time, not only to reach parts of the alliance from the Far East—and I want to remind you that you can reach places like Norway and Turkey from very far into Soviet Asia—but they could also, because these are highly mobile and transportable systems, at any time they can move these forces back into the western portions of the Soviet Union and could threaten the alliance.

Let me ask my colleague to comment.

Q. Let me just nail this down. Are you saying that we don't know if they're referring to dismantling or simply removing?

A. I think our assumption is that they are probably only referring to removing, but that's why I made my original point. Mr. Andropov has made some statements in a speech; elements of that speech were discussed in the last round. We expect that we will see some kind of formal proposal in the next round, but we have not been given a formal, detailed proposal.

Second Official. If I might add one point. Even if the Soviet proposal were in fact to entail the destruction of those SS–20's West of 80 degrees East, in excess of the 162 systems that they attribute to the British and French, even [if] they were to dismantle all of the remaining ones and if they were to keep only those that are presently deployed in the Far East and in Central Asia, they would still have under this proposal more SS–20's than they had when the talks began.

So what has been characterized as a proposal to cut Soviet forces in half has conveyed a very misleading impression that this would substantially alter the Soviet deployment.

We didn't like the situation we faced when the talks began, and hence the decision to carry forward on the deployment on the NATO side.

Q. Why does the United States need its own missiles there if the British and French maintain their own deterrent force?

First Official. Because the purpose of NATO strategy and the purpose of American strategy is to defend the entire alliance. The purpose of those missiles is to make it very clear to the Soviet Union that any major aggression against the alliance entails risk of escalation. That has been NATO's strategy for 30 years, and these missiles play an important role in that strategy as long as this massive SS–20 force exists.

Here, I think it's a very important conceptual point. The role of these missiles is different than the independent nuclear deterrence of Britain and France.

Britian maintains an independent deterrent; France maintains an independent deterrent. Those are independent, sovereign forces. They are not part of the so-called NATO triad of forces that have been the bedrock of NATO strategy for many years.

Q. If I may, don't you run the risk of utterly making arms control impossible if the Soviets can sit there and say their forces are their own independent—

A. I can only tell you that throughout the period of the 1970's when we negotiated on strategic forces, with the United States and the Soviet Union, the Soviet Union in several junctures said that the British and French forces had to be limited or taken into account. We never accepted that; we argued that these were bilateral negotiations, that we had no right nor ability to negotiate for someone else who is not at the table, and we were able to achieve agreements without limiting British and French forces.

I just don't understand why at this juncture we have to accept the concept that we're going to limit British and French forces when the experience of arms control has demonstrated very clearly that we can negotiate equal agreements with the Soviet Union bilaterally.

I'll make just one other point along these lines. I think that if you accept the Soviet position, that we have to limit British and

French forces, you're really saying, and as well, that you leave Asian forces—Soviet Asian forces out of the equation, you're saying that the Soviet Union has the right to be equal to the entire combination of its potential adversaries. Putting it differently, you're saying that the Soviet Union has the right to be superior over any one of those adversaries.

In other words, the Soviet Union has the right to have more forces than the United States, and we simply don't accept that concept.

The President of the United States has said many times that we have to negotiate on the basis of equality. There are all kinds of variables that can be brought into the negotiations if you're not interested in a serious negotiating outcome.

I'll give you an example: The Soviet Union is adjacent to Western Europe. Being adjacent to Western Europe, it enjoys several important geographical and strategic advantages in terms of being able to bring its power to bear on Western Europe. We're 4,000 miles away from Western Europe though we haven't asked in negotiations to be compensated for the fact by the existence of geography. And that's essentially what the Soviet Union is asking here.

We think that experience has demonstrated that when the two—United States and the Soviet Union—are willing to negotiate seriously and get down to business, that you can negotiate on the basis of equality.

Q. The proposal is not acceptable, but is it considered a serious effort to get negotiations going? Is this a serious move that's been made by the Soviet Union or is it just totally unacceptable?

SECOND OFFICIAL. It's a repackaging of the proposal that they have made from the very beginning with one minor change, which is not a significant one, and that is they are now talking about a subceiling on missiles. Whereas, previously they talked about limitations on missiles and aircraft together.

Q. Didn't that also include a subceiling in there by 1990?

SECOND OFFICIAL. Initially, they were talking about 300 systems on both sides, missiles and aircraft. Now they're talking about 300 on both sides, missiles and aircraft, of which no more than 162 could be missiles. So it is essentially a repackaging, a variant, if you will, of their original position.

But, to repeat, if we were to accept the most optimistic interpretation of what the Soviets have proposed, which is that they would dismantle everything above the 162 and the number now in the Far East, they would be left with more SS–20's than they had on the day these negotiations began.

FIRST OFFICIAL. Which was already much too high.

. . . .

Let me just make one other point, going back to the balance in Europe, because sometimes I think that arms control and the negotiations tend to create an artificial idea of the reality of the balance in Europe. I think it's worth making two points: when one thinks about military stability in Europe, you're not talking only about nuclear weapons; you're talking about the conventional forces. We've got to remind ourselves constantly of the tremendous imbalance in conventional capabilities that exists in the alliance.

We also have to remind ourselves about the other nuclear weapons in Europe or that could be used against Europe. This goes back to the British and French forces. The NATO Alliance undertook a study last year of that overall nuclear balance and found that the Soviet Union could have as many as 8,000 aircraft that could be used to deliver nuclear weapons against targets in Europe;[24] and that right now, 2,500 aircraft, operationally, could be used by the Soviet Union and its Warsaw Pact allies. I think this compares to, I'd say, 400 similar aircraft on the NATO side, so it's impossible to argue that if you include British and French forces in an overall assessment of the nuclear balance in Europe, that somehow there is a balance. There just isn't. Depending on exactly how you count it, NATO is at a disadvantage of 3 to 6 to 1 in overall nuclear systems in Europe.

Q. Does this speech leave you more pessimistic about prospects in the next round of the INF talks?

FIRST OFFICIAL: No, we're not pessimistic, and we are going to continue to negotiate seriously. But we believe what is vital to the success of the negotiations is for the European Allies and the United States to-

---

24 The reference is to the NATO publication *NATO and the Warsaw Pact: Force Comparisons*, issued in 1982 and subsequently reprinted by the Government Printing Office in 1983.

gether to demonstrate that in the absence of an acceptable agreement, that we will go ahead and deploy on schedule beginning at the end of 1983. We believe that once the Soviet Union believes that and recognizes that fact, that we will have a better chance of obtaining an agreement.

. . . .

C. United Kingdom

Document 197

Statement by the President's Principal Deputy Press Secretary (Speakes), March 11, 1982[1]

Sale of Trident II Missiles to the United Kingdom

Today in London the British Government is informing the House of Commons of its decision to purchase from the United States the Trident II (D–5) missile system, rather than the Trident I (C–4) system. When the President decided in October 1981, that the U.S. Navy would develop the Trident II missile, he informed the British Government that it would be available for purchase by the United Kingdom. In an exchange of letters today,[2] Prime Minister Thatcher formally requested that the United States sell the Trident II missile, and the President agreed.

Beginning during the Second World War, the United States has cooperated intimately with the United Kingdom on nuclear matters. In President Roosevelt's administration, American and British scientists began working together on the development of nuclear weapons. In 1962 at Nassau, President Kennedy agreed to assist the British in the development of their strategic nuclear forces by selling Polaris missiles to the United Kingdom.[3] Today's announcement signals a continuation of this longstanding cooperation, which is a central element in the close cooperation between the United States and the United Kingdom.

The primary reason for the British choice of the Trident II missile over the Trident I is to maintain commonality with the United States Navy. Although the performance of the Trident I was adequate for British purposes, there would be a long term logistic and cost penalty associated with the uniqueness of the system once the United States Navy made the transition to the Trident II missile.

The administration believes the independent British strategic nuclear force which is assigned to NATO makes an important contribution to the ability of the North Atlantic Alliance to deter Soviet aggression. For this reason, the President has decided to continue to assist the United Kingdom in the maintenance of a modernized independent British deterrent force into the twenty-first century. In addition, the President's letter welcomes the Prime Minister's commitment to use savings from cooperation in the strategic nuclear field to strengthen British conventional forces, which are also vital to the NATO deterrent.

Document 198

Letter From British Prime Minister Thatcher to President Reagan, March 11, 1982[4]

Purchase of Trident II Missiles by the United Kingdom

DEAR MR. PRESIDENT: I wrote to your predecessor on 10 July 1980[5] to ask whether the United States Government would be ready to supply Trident I missiles, equipment and supporting services to the United Kingdom on a similar basis to that on which the Polaris missiles were supplied under the Polaris Sales Agreement of 6 April 1963.[6]

---

[1] Source: White House Press Release, March 11, 1982, Office of the Press Secretary to the President; also printed in *Weekly Compilation of Presidential Documents,* March 15, 1982, p. 287.

[2] See documents *infra* and 199.

[3] Regarding the Nassau agreement of 1962, see *American Foreign Policy: Current Documents, 1962,* p. 635.

[4] Source: Office of the Press Secretary to the President; also printed in *Weekly Compilation of Presidential Documents,* March 15, 1982, pp. 287–288.

[5] See *American Foreign Policy: Basic Documents, 1977–1980,* p. 522.

[6] 14 UST 321.

President Carter replied on 14 July[7] confirming that the United States Government were prepared to do so, subject to and in accordance with applicable United States law and procedures.

In the light of decisions taken by the United States Government in 1981 to accelerate their own programme to procure Trident II missiles, and to phase out the Trident I programme earlier than had hitherto been intended, the United Kingdom Government have carried out a review on their nuclear deterrent programme. In the light of this review, I am now writing to ask whether in place of Trident I missiles the United States Government would be ready to supply Trident II missiles, equipment and supporting services on a continuing basis and in a manner generally similar to that in which Polaris was supplied. The United Kingdom Government would wish to purchase these missiles complete with multiple, independently targettable reentry vehicles but without the warheads themselves. I propose that, as in the past, close co-ordination should be maintained between the executive agencies of the two governments in order to assure compatibility of equipment.

Like the Polaris force, and consistent with the agreement reached in 1980 on the supply of Trident I missiles, the United Kingdom Trident II force will be assigned to the North Atlantic Treaty Organization and except where the United Kingdom Government may decide that supreme national interests are at stake, this successor force will be used for the purposes of international defence of the Western Alliance in all circumstances. It is my understanding that co-operation in the modernisation of the United Kingdom nuclear deterrent in the manner proposed would be consistent with the present and prospective international obligations of both parties.

I would like to assure you that the United Kingdom Government remain wholly committed to the strengthening of the Alliance's conventional forces. The United Kingdom Government have in recent years substantially increased their defence spending and further increases are planned for the future in order to sustain the United Kingdom's all-round contribution to allied deterrence and defence. The economies made possible by the United States Government's co-operation with respect to the supply of the Trident I missile system will be used in order to reinforce the United Kingdom Government's continuing efforts to upgrade their conventional forces.

If the United States Government are prepared to meet this request, I hope that as the next step you will be prepared to receive technical and financial missions to pursue these matters using the framework of the Polaris Sales Agreement where appropriate.

Yours Sincerely,

MARGARET THATCHER

Document 199

Letter From President Reagan to British Prime Minister Thatcher, March 11, 1982[8]

Sale of Trident II Missiles to the United Kingdom

DEAR MADAME PRIME MINISTER:[9] Thank you for your letter of March 11.[10]

I am pleased to confirm that the United States Government is prepared to supply to the United Kingdom Trident II missiles, equipment and supporting services as proposed in your letter, subject to and in accordance with applicable United States law and procedures.

The United States' readiness to provide these systems is a demonstration of the great importance which the United States Government attaches to the maintenance by the United Kingdom of an independent nuclear deterrent capability. I can assure you of the United States' willingness to cooperate closely with the United Kingdom Government in maintaining and modernizing that capability.

I attach great importance to your assurance that the United Kingdom Trident II force will be assigned to NATO and that the economies realized through cooperation

---

[7] See *American Foreign Policy: Basic Documents, 1977–1980*, pp. 522–523.

[8] Source: Office of the Press Secretary to the President; printed also in *Weekly Compilation of Presidential Documents*, March 15, 1982, p. 288.

[9] In *Weekly Compilation of Presidential Documents*, the salutation reads, "Dear Margaret."

[10] *Supra.*

between our two governments will be used to reinforce the United Kingdom's efforts to upgrade its conventional forces. Such nuclear and conventional force improvements are of the highest priority for NATO's security.

I agree that, as the next step, our two governments should initiate the technical and financial negotiations which you propose.

Sincerely,

RON

Document 200

Letter From the Secretary of Defense (Weinberger) to the British Secretary of State for Defence (Nott), March 11, 1982[11]

Sale of Trident II Missiles to the United Kingdom

DEAR JOHN: In the exchange of letters between the President and the Prime Minister of today's date,[12] it was agreed that the United States Government would supply Trident II missiles to the United Kingdom. I am writing now to record our joint understanding on specific aspects of the agreed arrangements for the sale of the Trident II (D–5) missile system and associated equipment.

It is understood that the Polaris sales agreement of 1963 and its implementing agreements will be the general pattern for the sale of the Trident II (D–5) missile system.

It is agreed that the United Kingdom will pay a total contribution to research and development for the Trident II (D–5) system equivalent to $116 million in Fiscal Year 1982 dollars, subject to actual payments being adjusted to reflect an agreed inflation index.

It is understood that the United Kingdom acknowledges that waiver by the United States of all charges (other than the administrative charge) in excess of $116 million will fully satisfy the requirement that the United States Government give defense assistance to the United Kingdom defense budget in return for manning by the United Kingdom of Rapier air defense of United States Air Force bases in the United Kingdom, and support and servicing for these Rapier systems. In addition it is understood that the United Kingdom will employ additional savings represented by the remainder of the United States waiver to reinforce its efforts to upgrade its conventional forces.

With respect to procurement of the Trident II (D–5) weapon system, the Department of Defense is prepared to undertake, subject to compliance with United States law and national policy:

—to permit United Kingdom manufacturers to compete on the same terms as United States firms for subcontracts for Trident II (D–5) weapon system components for the program as a whole;

—to ensure that Department of Defense procedures bearing on such competition for such Trident II (D–5) weapon system components are consistent with this general principle; and

—to designate appropriate United States staff in both countries to provide a point of contact for United Kingdom manufacturers, and to offer advice and briefing.

The United States attaches great importance to the maintenance by the United Kingdom Government of an independent nuclear deterrent. I am, therefore, pleased that it has been possible to reach this agreement between our two countries. I regard this arrangement as a significant contribution to the maintenance of stability and peace.[13]

With warm regards,

CAP WEINBERGER

---

[11] Source: Office of the Press Secretary to the President; printed also in *Weekly Compilation of Presidential Documents,* March 15, 1982, p. 289.

[12] See documents 198 and *supra.*

[13] In a letter of March 11 to Secretary Weinberger, Secretary Nott confirmed his agreement with the understandings enumerated in this letter. (*Weekly Compilation of Presidental Documents,* March 15, 1982, p. 289)

Document 201

Transcript of an Interview With the British Ambassador (Henderson), April 25, 1982[14]

U.S.–U.K. Relations and the Falklands Crisis

MR. BRINKLEY. Coming next, our interview with Sir Nicholas Henderson, British Ambassador to the United States, in a moment.

(Announcements)

MR. BRINKLEY. Mr. Ambassador, we are glad to have you with us today. Thank you for coming in. Here with me with questions at the ready are George Will, ABC Analyst, and Sam Donaldson, ABC News White House Correspondent.

Mr. Ambassador, there are some in this country, including some in Congress, who would like to see the U.S. Navy join with the British Navy in the South Atlantic. Would you welcome that?

AMBASSADOR HENDERSON. It's for the United States to say what they want to do and what they think they should do. We haven't asked or sought or needed any military support from the United States in carrying out this obligation we have under the Security Council resolution.[15]

MR. BRINKLEY. But you wouldn't reject it if offered?

AMBASSADOR HENDERSON. No, we would not.

MR. WILL. Do you have sufficient military capability in the area, and are you going to have it in the next few weeks, to make, for example, an amphibious landing and reconquer the Islands?

AMBASSADOR HENDERSON. We are, as you know, determined that the Argentine forces should withdraw from the Islands, in keeping with the Security Council demand, international opinion.

We want to do it by peaceful means, by negotiation, and I hope that that is still possible. But we are confident that we can bring it about by other means if necessary.

MR. DONALDSON. Many people are saying, on both sides of the Atlantic this weekend, that your strategy is to first take that little island of South Georgia, the island off which apparently this naval action with the Argentine submarine occurred. Is that correct?

AMBASSADOR HENDERSON. Yes, but incidentally I would like to say, I heard twice earlier, just now and on the television, that hostilities have started or action has broken out. This isn't true. Of course, it started 3 weeks ago with the Argentinian attack on the Falkland Islands. What we are doing is an act of self-defense, under Article 51 of the Charter, to restore the situation where it was. And incidentally we gave them warning, not simply the setting out of the maritime inclusion zone but we gave the Argentinians warning on the 23d of April, 2 days ago, that any vessel, including submarines, specified, that came—that looked like being able to threaten any of our forces or naval vessels would be dealt with appropriately.

MR. DONALDSON. But my question was, is your strategy to take this little island of South Georgia as a show of force? Apparently you can do this.

AMBASSADOR HENDERSON. Our intention, which has been stated, is to ensure the withdrawal of the Argentine forces from the territories they have occupied, and if they aren't—they have been told to do so now for 3 weeks—and we have the methods of ensuring that if they don't do so peacefully.

MR. DONALDSON. The answer is yes, to my question?

AMBASSADOR HENDERSON. Well, the obvious answer is that this is our intention.

MR. BRINKLEY. Mr. Ambassador, the negotiations, including Mr. Haig's transatlantic shuttle, have been going on for some time. Now that there has been some shooting, what hope do you have for further negotiations?

AMBASSADOR HENDERSON. Well, as I say, there has been some shooting. There was a much more military action 3 weeks ago by the Argentinians. They will, they will negotiate when they realize that they cannot leave their forces with impunity on those islands. That is the time they will be prepared to negotiate.

MR. WILL. Might they not be also more inclined to negotiate if you had a blockade

---

[14] Source: ABC News. The interview with Sir Nicholas Henderson was conducted in Washington by David Brinkley, George F. Will, and Sam Donaldson on the ABC program, "This Week With David Brinkley."

[15] The U.N. Security Council passed resolution 502, calling for Argentine withdrawal from the Falklands, on April 3. For the text of the resolution, see document 623. Documentation on the Falkland crisis is in Chapter 15, Part B.

which shut off commercial maritime traffic, including the export of Soviet grain from Argentina, and is that among your plans?

AMBASSADOR HENDERSON. I wouldn't—I am afraid I couldn't—I don't think it would be responsible to give you the steps by which we will carry out what we believe to be our obligations in support of the self-determination of the Islands and in support of the U.N. Charter. But the methods by which we do it, the timing, and the various stages, I don't think you could expect me to give in detail now.

MR. DONALDSON. Mr. Ambassador, you have just apparently laid down a very hard line in suggesting that there are no negotiations still in progress—

AMBASSADOR HENDERSON. No, I haven't said that. No, I didn't say that.

MR. DONALDSON. All right, let me ask you, then, we understand that Secretary Haig now has some proposals from your government and that Argentina's Foreign Minister, Costa Mendez, is going to see him this afternoon, isn't there still a chance that you might come to some resolution of the sticky problem of how this interim period should occur?

AMBASSADOR HENDERSON. I think there is. Our Foreign Secretary was here for 2 days, had long talks, and following those now Secretary Haig will be talking to the Argentine Foreign Secretary and I think that we are by no means at the end of the road in negotiation. It certainly is the road we want to take and I don't think you can use words "optimistic" and "pessimistic" but the negotiations are still going on and could resolve this thing—

MR. DONALDSON. What happens tomorrow if somehow the OAS invokes the Treaty of Rio?[16] That may not be likely, but Argentina may ask for it. What happens then? That's the treaty that, for listeners—

AMBASSADOR HENDERSON. Well, two things on that. First of all, the Rio Treaty's first article says no members of the Treaty shall resort to force in settlement of disputes and shall resort to peaceful means. Secondly, another article of the Rio Treaty says that nothing that is done under the Rio Treaty can take the place of the overriding authority of the United Nations, and the United Nations has taken, excuse me, the Security Council, to call upon the Argentinians to withdraw. That is what holds the field.

MR. DONALDSON. I suppose, for viewers who don't know, the vital section that Argentina will claim under the Treaty of Rio is one that suggests that all the signatories, including the United States, must come to the aid of anyone else who is attacked within or without the hemisphere.

AMBASSADOR HENDERSON. Yes, but it also says, the Rio Treaty says, two or three times, that nobody shall resort to aggression for settlement of disputes.

MR. BRINKLEY. Mr. Ambassador, if I may go back a week, 2 or 3 weeks, to the beginning of this and the first reaction from the United States when President Reagan said he was neutral and was friends of both sides. How did you react to that?

AMBASSADOR HENDERSON. I think people in U.K. and in Europe generally were a bit worried and, as you know, the European opinion has been very stalwart and come out categorically in support of us in calling upon the Argentinians to withdraw. But we, the government, understand perfectly well that you are involved in a go-between exercise of a negotiation or possibly an arbitration at some stage, and we understand that if that breaks down through Argentine intransigence and they continue to occupy the Islands against the authority of the world community we have no doubt which side you will be on.

MR. WILL. Is it the case, however, that your fleet actually took its sweet time in getting there in order to give Secretary Haig more time in which to operate? In other words, has not the Secretary been acting really in congruence with British policy?

AMBASSADOR HENDERSON. Well, all one can say is that the Argentinians had 3 weeks, 3 weeks, of negotiation and have remained intransigent, and you know, that has been perfectly clear, that what they were meant to do in that time.

MR. BRINKLEY. We will have more questions for the Ambassador of Great Britain, in a moment.

(Announcements)

MR. BRINKLEY. Mr. Ambassador, obviously you would not wish to discuss whatever military strategy the British have worked out in the South Atlantic, but let me ask you this about the negotiating. There's been a great deal of it, many messages back and

[16] For the text of the Rio Treaty, signed September 2, 1947, see 4 Bevans 559.

forth by way of Secretary Haig, your own diplomatic service, and other means. What is the best offer the Argentines have made to Britain?

AMBASSADOR HENDERSON. They haven't made any offer direct to us because it has been Haig, Secretary Haig—

MR. BRINKLEY. Well, through Haig or otherwise, what's the best they have offered?

AMBASSADOR HENDERSON. That is—I don't think they have completed. As you know, they have been extremely slow in sticking to any particular idea, and I think we still don't know what they are prepared to accept. They know, I think, very clearly what we are prepared to go along with, what we can wear, and obviously what we can't wear is the tolerance of condoning of smash and grab on the Falkland Islands.

MR. DONALDSON. But can you wear eventual sovereignty guaranteed to Argentina?

AMBASSADOR HENDERSON. What we can wear, very clearly, is a complete, the free discussions on what the ultimate relationship between the Islands and Argentina is. But it cannot simply cast aside the wishes of the inhabitants, any more than—we have given independence, as you know, to a fourth of the whole world's population since the end of the War. In no case did we say that you have got to be incorporated in a third state, and we couldn't suddenly do that just because they are a small people miles away.

MR. BRINKLEY. Well, let me be clear on the previous question. Do I understand you to say that the Argentines have made no clear, specific offer of any kind?

AMBASSADOR HENDERSON. Well, I don't know—if you ask me what the Argentine bottom line is, at the moment I do not know.

MR. WILL. Mr. Ambassador, British opinion has been remarkably unanimous behind your government—

AMBASSADOR HENDERSON. Yes.

MR. WILL.—both in Parliament and out. However, it has become neither bloody nor boring yet, this crisis. Is it possible that the United States, if it weighed in on Mrs. Thatcher's side, could wind up being more British than the British? That is, is your public prepared to stay the course?

AMBASSADOR HENDERSON. Oh, yes. I think—I mean, I haven't—I am not there so I can only go on what I hear second-hand, but everybody tells me that there is a firmer, more united spirit on this than anything since 1940.

MR. WILL. Why?

AMBASSADOR HENDERSON. I think that it's—you have all sorts of psychosis in your history, Pearl Harbor, getting involved in another Vietnam—and we have one which I call the Munich trauma. There we let down a small country in 1938, Hitler, and we condoned aggression or a threat of aggression, and that is a governing factor in our lives ever since, my generation, the people who run my country.

MR. WILL. You had another trauma, some people think, in 1956, over Suez, when the United States did not back your joint Israeli-French-Anglo invasion of Egypt. Is this part of what—the backdrop against which the United States operates? Is there a lingering suspicion that we have, as the economists put it, alliance a la carte on the part of the United States?

AMBASSADOR HENDERSON. Well, that was a bitterly controversial action in the United Kingdom and the country wasn't united on it in 1956—

MR. WILL. Suez, you mean.

AMBASSADOR HENDERSON.—not at all united as it is now. And the United States, I think they could have, they had every right to question the way we did it, without consulting them. But nevertheless, it did produce great bitterness in the United Kingdom because it's when you make a mistake or when you are in trouble that you need an ally. So that did leave residues of bitterness.

MR. WILL. But given that backdrop, if the United States should not be with you in some sense, about which you have not chosen to be specific, would this not undermine the British and hence the European attachment to the alliance itself?

AMBASSADOR HENDERSON. If the negotiations broke down because the Argentinians were intransigent and refused to withdraw, in the face of world opinion, I think—and then the United States remained completely on the sidelines—there would be this bitterness. But I don't think they will. It is not for me to tell you what your government is going to do, but I have no doubt about where their solidarity lies.

MR. DONALDSON. Mr. Ambassador, what would a war, a real war, with a lot of casualties on both sides—as we have heard someone already say on this broadcast, a lot of young men die—what would it accomplish if in the end, if in the end, Argentina gets sovereignty, somewhere down the line, of the Falklands?

AMBASSADOR HENDERSON. We don't want it to be a fullscale, wide-ranging war. Our aim is limited to getting the Argentinians off these islands, which they have occupied. That is what we are confined to doing.

MR. DONALDSON. Can wars always be limited?

AMBASSADOR HENDERSON. It is a difficult thing to do. Once you start a war, it is a very, very dangerous thing, and you never know where it is going to go. That's why no aggression should be taken and no aggression should be condoned.

MR. DONALDSON. Is there any possibility that the Soviets might come into this more than they have? And to what extent do you think they have?

AMBASSADOR HENDERSON. I think the Soviet role is important. They are a key trading partner with the Argentines, now since the Afghan crisis. They have taken over a big role in providing grain and foodstuffs. They concluded four agreements only 10 days ago, including nuclear enrichment and nonfishing rights. And they are, as you know, your State Department, your Defense Department announced that they are providing them with important surveillance information on our fleet.

So the danger is that if by chance the military dictatorship, the Argentines got away with it, Russia would complain that was thanks to them and they would demand some quid pro quo and that is a dangerous thing.

MR. DONALDSON. But if shooting starts, would the Soviets dare enter it?

AMBASSADOR HENDERSON. I should be extraordinarily surprised if they would, but you are now getting into the realms of strategy, and what you might call—I'm not going to be a Sunday morning quarterback or armchair scientist.

MR. DONALDSON. Oh, yes, that's why you are here today. You must indeed.

AMBASSADOR HENDERSON. I wouldn't think so.

MR. BRINKLEY. Mr. Ambassador, we've all heard 9,000 opinions about this and I am sure you have heard even more. One is that it has reached something of an impasse. Galtieri cannot back down and survive. Prime Minister Thatcher cannot back down and survive. So, where do we go from here?

AMBASSADOR HENDERSON. It isn't, incidentally, only Mrs. Thatcher who couldn't back down. No British Government could take office or stay in office if it didn't try to defend, and feel it had an obligation to defend the people who have been simply occupied and overthrown by a military dictatorship.

What Galtieri is going to do—he started the thing. It isn't our business to save his face.

MR. WILL. Mr. Ambassador, the Island of Gibraltar is a lot closer to Spain than the Falklands are to Argentina, and the Spanish military is every bit as restive over the last century or so. Are you afraid that unless you get your Union Jack back on those islands that Gibraltar will be in increased danger?

AMBASSADOR HENDERSON. The Spaniards, since the beginning of the 18th century, have realized that we are there in the military possession and capable of defending it. And we moved on to—I lived in Spain for 4 years and I know the bitterness of this dispute and don't deny that the Spaniards feel very strongly about it. I am quite sure we can get a negotiated settlement on that and that is what we are trying to do. So I don't think, really see the military threat hanging over there.

MR. DONALDSON. Mr. Ambassador, speaking of government survival, why isn't it fair to ask why your government hasn't fallen because of not paying attention to the intelligence data which you had which might have enabled you to forestall an Argentine invasion of the Falklands?

AMBASSADOR HENDERSON. Well, Carrington, as you know, did resign because, he said, I made a mistake in not drawing deductions from such information as perhaps we had, but I don't think—

MR. DONALDSON. But where does the buck stop in—

AMBASSADOR HENDERSON.—I think there is a great misunderstanding about this. I was involved in this, very much in this town. I don't think that until that Wednesday night, which was the 30th of April, the 30th of March, the 30th of March,[17] I don't think any of us, certainly your government, until

[17] March 30, 1982, was a Tuesday.

then had no reason to believe that they were going to invade. Certainly your government was behind ours in that conviction.

MR. BRINKLEY. Mr. Ambassador, thank you very much for being with us today. We have enjoyed having you.

Document 202

Remarks by President Reagan and British Prime Minister Thatcher, June 23, 1982[18]

Visit by Prime Minister Thatcher to the United Nations

THE PRESIDENT. It's been good to welcome the Prime Minister to Washington even if for only an afternoon's visit. I was delighted that we could continue our conversations from Paris, London, and Bonn,[19] on a whole host of issues where our cooperation is so close. In that connection, incidentally, I note that we have now met four times in this month in as many cities. It's customary when two political figures get together to describe their talks as far-ranging. But in our case, that statement is both figuratively and literally true. I'm going to have to check the history books, but four separate meetings in four different places in less than 4 weeks may well be unprecedented in our bilateral relations.

Seriously, I did have, as I always do, an exceptionally useful discussion with the Prime Minister which covered a number of critical issues. The fighting in the South Atlantic has stopped since we last met. We believe that a fundamental principle of international society—that force not be used to settle disputes was at stake in that conflict. We also discussed other issues including a number of economic questions, the future of East–West relations and the crucial role played by—the events in Poland. We share the commitment to arms control negotiations with the Soviet Union. We also agreed that the work accomplished at the two summit meetings in which we participated earlier this month, Versailles and Bonn, demonstrated anew the vitality and cohesion of the Western democracies.

Clearly, there's much more in our free and pluralistic societies that unites us than divides us and that's our major strength when we face a determined and totalitarian adversary.

With respect to the tragic situation in the Middle East, we consulted about what we could do to promote a lasting and just peace in that region that's so important to us—especially in Lebanon and to bring an end to the human suffering there.

The Prime Minister has come to us at a particularly auspicious moment—the birth of an heir to the throne of the United Kingdom. And we have every hope that she will carry back to London our fondest good wishes, those of the American people, Nancy and myself, to their Royal Highnesses, the Prince and Princess of Wales, and to their little son. And so, we're most grateful to you for making the extra effort to come down here and see us.

PRIME MINISTER THATCHER. Thank you very much. Mr. President—can I just add a few words to what the President has already said—I was very anxious to come and talk to the President so that we could get up to date with a number of things that have happened since we last met on his very highly successful visit to Europe and his particularly successful visit to Britain.

As he pointed out, since then, the fighting in the Falkland Islands has been concluded which was a tremendous relief to us all. And we hope that things will steadily continue to improve there. We also discussed matters as—such as Lebanon where there is a great tragedy taking place which is of concern to us all. And naturally, of course, we discussed East–West matters and a number of economic things.

I've just noticed today that in some of the questions I have been asked by some of you

---

[18] Source: White House Press Release, June 23, 1982, Office of the Press Secretary to the President; printed also in *Weekly Compilation of Presidential Documents,* June 28, 1982, pp. 833–834. Prime Minister Thatcher was in the United States to address the Special Committee on Disarmament at the United Nations. She met with President Reagan in the Oval Office. These departure remarks on the South grounds of the White House began at 6 p.m.

[19] The references here are to conversations President Reagan held with Prime Minister Thatcher during the President's trip to Europe. In Paris, President Reagan met with Mrs. Thatcher prior to the Versailles Economic Summit, June 5–6. The two met in London, June 7–9, and again in Bonn at the NATO summit, June 9–11. For documentation on the Versailles Economic Summit, see Chapter 5, Part F. For the text of President Reagan's speech to the British Parliament on June 8, see document 4. Documentation on the NATO summit is in Chapter 10, Part B.

ladies and gentlemen and some others there's often been a little bit of an attempt to try to indicate some differences either between the United—between the United States and Britain or some sort of attempt to divide us on some things. I can only report to you that those attempts will never succeed because we can't be divided. Our relationship and the Alliance is far too staunch and far too deep for that.

I'm just very grateful, too, for what the President said about the new Royal birth. It does indicate the great continuity that there is in Britain, the tremendous patriotism which one gets in almost all countries, but it's a patriotism in a way of the kind we have here in the States as well; not only love of your country because you belong to it but because it stands for certain things and it's those that make you patriotic.

I will, of course, take back your very warm message to our people, and I'm certain they will be delighted with your good wishes.

Now, I think, ladies and gentlemen, that I'm due to be cross-examined by a number of you elsewhere. I look forward to that, and I hope you do, too.

And thank you, Mr. President, for your warm hospitality and for the opportunity of talking to you.

Q. Mr. President, sir, do we still support negotiations in the South Atlantic dispute as provided for in U.N. resolution 502?

THE PRESIDENT. This is a photo opportunity, Sam. Fall back on that. I think that we have—we've made our position plain and clear on what we've tried to do there.

PRIME MINISTER THATCHER. We're very grateful to the President for everything they've done to help.

Thank you very much. Thank you.

THE PRESIDENT. Thank you.

Document 203

Transcript of a Press Briefing by the Secretary of State (Haig), June 23, 1982[20]

Meeting With Prime Minister Thatcher

SECRETARY HAIG. It's a very newsy day, the clean-up hitter.

Now, I'll just say a few remarks about the meetings this afternoon with Prime Minister Thatcher. As you know, this is her second visit to Washington.[21] But as the President noted in the Garden,[22] it's the fourth meeting he's had with her in as many weeks. And I would suppose that that plus the commonality of problems that we've been engaged with have created a very unusual relationship, one of great informality, a great directness in communication, and one that permits because of its informality an intimacy. It enables both leaders to do a great deal of work very, very quickly, unlike some.

Now, as you know, the Prime Minister was here for the special conference—second Special Conference on Disarmament where she delivered a speech today. And as the President noted out in the Garden, as the Prime Minister stated in her press conference a few moments ago, there was focus on the Falklands question. The Prime Minister updated the President on the current state of affairs in the Falklands; the exchange of prisoners, some 10,000 of which have been returned to Argentine control; the situation on the island itself—islands themselves, which will require a great deal of rehabilitation and some demilitarization in the case of mines.

Anticipating some of your questions on the future of the situation there, of 502[23] and other related questions, I think the Prime Minister has stated that very clearly, both on national television this morning on two occasions and again this evening.

The situation in Lebanon was discussed, and the President brought the Prime Minister abreast of the diplomatic activity now under way, which is at a very critical stage, through Ambassador Habib in Beirut where he's been in contact with the Committee of National Salvation in an effort to put in place a clear set of arrangements which will meet United States and, above all, Lebanese Government aspirations for the future of their country.

That involves, as you know, the cessation of all hostility. There has been yet another

---

[20] Source: White House Press Release, June 23, 1982, Office of the Press Secretary to the President. The press briefing, which recounted the meeting between President Reagan and Prime Minister Thatcher earlier in the afternoon, began at 7:10 p.m.

[21] For President Reagan's meeting with Mrs. Thatcher in Washington on February 26, 1981, see *American Foreign Policy: Current Documents, 1981*, documents 178 and 179.

[22] See the departure remarks, *supra*.

[23] For the text of U.N. Security Council Resolution 502, see document 623.

cease-fire put in place today, and as I understand, it's still holding at the moment.

It also involves the withdrawal of foreign forces, and it involves the necessary assurances to Israel that there will not be a repetition of the attacks against Northern Galilee from Lebanon, which had brought the crisis to its current state.

There was an exchange of views between the two leaders on the peace process and the urgency of moving in the wake of the Lebanon crisis into a comprehensive settlement which gives clear recognition to the aspirations of the Palestinian people.

The East–West relations were discussed in some detail. The situation in Poland, Afghanistan. The Prime Minister raised the question of the recent broadening of U.S. sanctions against Poland. And, in one instance, that has a severe impact on one British industrial firm.

The President pointed out that he recognizes clearly and did before the decision that this would place a burden not only on our allies but it is already, and will continue, to place a serious burden on American industrial interests both based here at home and subsidiaries abroad.

At the same time, the President reiterated to the Prime Minister that, in announcing his decision on 29th December,[24] he made it clear that were there not an improvement in the human rights situation in Poland that there would be a continuation of U.S. sanctions and a strengthening and an expansion of them. And that the clear solution to this problem is progress towards the three conditions established, not only by the United States, but by the ten, the NATO Alliance and the Western industrialized states, including Japan, for a release of prisoners, a termination of martial law and the, above all, institution of a dialogue between the church, state and the labor movement.

There was a discussion of the recent decisions by U.S. courts on steel which, of course, poses a very serious threat to transatlantic trade relationships. And while the President—while we ran out of time on that particular subject, I know the President would have reassured Mrs. Thatcher that it is this government's policy to attempt to negotiate a satisfactory resolution of this problem between ourselves and the economic community in Europe because it is recognized to be a threat to escalating protectionist measures on both sides. And, therefore, there's a certain degree of urgency and a great deal of importance on this subject.

And, finally, the President, as he did outside, congratulated the Prime Minister on the birth of the heir and first son of the Prince and Princess of Wales, to get back where we started from. (Laughter).

Now, I welcome your questions.

Q. Mr. Secretary, on the Falklands, Prime Minister Thatcher mentioned practical help that she was seeking from the United States, the rehabilitation and the mine fields. One, will that involve any American personnel on the Falklands or in the area?

SECRETARY HAIG. No.

Q. And two, what kind of material help are you talking about?

SECRETARY HAIG. What kind of —

Q. What kind of practical help, material help, are you talking about in this case?

SECRETARY HAIG. Well, clearly there is technology available that can assist in mine clearance operations, and we look very promptly and urgently into our inventory of potentially useful devices for that. And you know the kind I am talking about that had their genesis in the Second War where you have a roller or a detonator precede a vehicle to attempt to clear mine fields.

Q. But no people.

SECRETARY HAIG. No, no, no.

Q. Mr. Secretary, did the President ask the Prime Minister to do anything at all on the Falklands situation that she is not presently doing or intends to do?

SECRETARY HAIG. No; I think both leaders know very well the state of play of the situation at this time, and there are still a number of uncertainties that must be resolved before other matters are considered. Among those uncertainties are the cessation of the state of conflict which is still unresolved, and the emergence of a constitutional authority which is in a state of transition in Buenos Aires to give you confidence that whatever assurances that have been provided if any are viable and one can have confidence in them, a return of the prisoners, the rehabilitation and clean-up of the island itself. And I think the Prime Minister has discussed this question at length here in the United States today.

---

24 See *American Foreign Policy: Current Documents, 1981,* document 270.

Q. Mr. Secretary, did we ultimately favor negotiations to settle the long-running dispute between Britain and Argentina over the Falklands?

SECRETARY HAIG. Well, I think it is a premature question because there are a number of uncertainties yet to be resolved before I think we feel it would be appropriate to make such a statement or make such a judgment.

Q. Does that U.N. resolution, in our view, call for that, ultimately—that we voted for—

SECRETARY HAIG. Yes; but I think the Prime Minister said something about a—

Q. Well, she takes the position that, because they did not withdraw, it is null I suppose.

SECRETARY HAIG. No; I think she took the position that the resolution itself was not accepted by the Argentine side and, therefore, that the provisions of that resolution—in other words, that all of the sacrifices had to [be] made and a determination of a military outcome was what resolved the problem.

Q. Do we agree with her?

SECRETARY HAIG. I would defer any comment on it at this juncture because what our interest is is to be whatever help we can to bring this whole situation in the South Atlantic to a satisfactory conclusion.

Q. What is that? What is our ultimate goal?

SECRETARY HAIG. I think the Prime Minister discussed the British point of view and we are going to withhold on ours.

Q. So, we're not discussing our point of view at the time? Is this what you are saying?

SECRETARY HAIG. No, our point of view at this time is, above all, to get a state of peace and stability and have a direction. Now, I think the Prime Minister is very clear that we wouldn't expect anyone to tell us how to deal with our property and we're not going to presume to tell her how to deal with hers.

We do feel, along with the British, a sense of responsibility for the damage that the events which have occurred have caused in the hemisphere and our relationship with various nations. But I also share the Prime Minister's view that when we put a template over Latin America and describe it as some kind of a homogenous mass, why, we are making a serious geopolitical misjudgment. Each nation has their own aspirations, their own national interest, and their own attitudes on this situation. Yes?

Q. Mr. Secretary, are the sanctions against—the military sanctions against Argentina by the United States still in force and how long will that remain?

SECRETARY HAIG. They are still in force and—

Q. How long will that remain?

SECRETARY HAIG.—we are reviewing those sanctions now. The decision on them will depend on a number of the factors that I raised earlier about the Falkland situation—the ultimate solution, the cessation of hostilities, the evolution and emergence of a viable government in Buenos Aires.

Q. Mr. Secretary, when Mrs. Thatcher said that the Falklands are British, that sovereignty is not an issue, that 502 is no longer operative, did President Reagan say to her what you just said now—

SECRETARY HAIG. No.

Q. —that, well, we reserve judgment on that or did he—

SECRETARY HAIG. No, the subject of sovereignty did not come up in the discussion this afternoon.

Q. Mr. Secretary, when the subject—

SECRETARY HAIG. Did not come up. Yes?

Q. On the subject of the pipeline, did Mrs. Thatcher in any way suggest that this government had misled her and the other allies at the summit talks—

SECRETARY HAIG. No.

Q. —on what the President was abut to do regarding the pipeline—

SECRETARY HAIG. No, no.

Q. Can I follow—

Q. Well, what was the tone of the—

SECRETARY HAIG. She expressed concern about the interest of one of her corporations and I think she referred to it very lightly in her press conference and there is a heavy contract impact on one of the Scottish-based British industries.

Q. And the President's only response was that domestic American companies are hurting also and that he felt that—

SECRETARY HAIG. No, no. His response was that—he took a position on sanctions as a matter of principle, that—when human rights were trampled in Poland, aided and abetted by the Soviet Union, he announced certain actions. He made it clear at the time of that announcement that were those conditions to not improve, then he would consider additional steps. And he took those steps. This is a matter of principle with the President. And I think just as Mrs. Thatcher has her principles, our President has his.

Q. Mr. Secretary—

Q. Can I follow that?

SECRETARY HAIG. Yes.

Q. Is it—where was the situation left? I mean, she and her companies are going to abide by his decision or—

SECRETARY HAIG. Well, there remains to be—

Q. —she expects an exemption? She implied—

SECRETARY HAIG. That did not come up, but clearly there will be some legal consequences to the decisions that were announced on Friday last week.[25] And that will involve a number of litigations potentially.

Q. Mr. Secretary, does your question about reviewing sanctions apply to economic as well as military sanctions, all sanctions that we now have, apparently, against Argentina?

SECRETARY HAIG. Against Argentina?

Q. Yes.

SECRETARY HAIG. Oh, yes, but they are, of course, of very different character.

Q. But you said we're reviewing—we're reviewing the sanctions. Were you—does that apply to—does that apply to all sanctions?

SECRETARY HAIG. To military assistance?

Q. Yes.

SECRETARY HAIG. Well, it does, but it's in a separate category. And I don't mean to suggest by my answer that we're contemplating some very early change in our current situation there.

Q. Earlier on—

SECRETARY HAIG. I think that's what you were asking, isn't it?

Q. I was trying to understand your answer. I mean, is there—are there any sanctions that we have against Argentina that are being reviewed with the view to whether or not they should be continued at this time or lifting sanctions? There have been reports—there have been published reports that sanctions would be lifted in the near future. I was trying to understand what your answer—what you were trying to tell us by your answer.

SECRETARY HAIG. Yes. What I'm saying is: The whole subject is under review, but there are certain aspects of the situation that will need to be clarified before a decision is made. And I think I outlined what those aspects were. I hope I've answered your question.

Q. May I follow up on that? Mrs. Thatcher referred to sanctions that have been in place on military sanctions all the way back to 1978. Is President Reagan reviewing those sanctions, or just the sanctions that he imposed after the beginning of the outbreak of conflict in—

SECRETARY HAIG. Let me say that we are constantly reviewing our relationships in those areas where there are prohibitions. But they are in an entirely different category, I am sure that you understand what I am saying. And the sanctions that were applied in the wake of the Falkland invasion are very different from those which relate to the 1978 human rights violation sanctions.

Q. Are you and Judge Clark now at odds?

SECRETARY HAIG. Not at all.

Q. No, I mean seriously—

SECRETARY HAIG. Not at all. That is nonsense.

Q. Was any of this meeting one-on-one between the two leaders?

SECRETARY HAIG. No.

Q. Mr. Secretary, do you feel that Judge Clark is undermining somehow your approach to foreign policy?

SECRETARY HAIG. Not at all. Why do you ask this question?

Q. I refer to the printed columns that you have read in—

SECRETARY HAIG. You know, it is the greatest fun in this town. (Laughter.) One more question now that we are getting to the nerve. (Laughter.)

---

25 On Friday, June 18, President Reagan announced the extension of sanctions on the export of oil and gas equipment to the Soviet Union to include equipment produced by subsidiaries of U.S. companies abroad, as well as equipment produced abroad under licenses issued by U.S. companies. (*Weekly Compilation of Presidential Documents*, June 21, 1982, p. 820)

Q. Mrs. Thatcher was very confident that this had not had quite as adverse an impact—the whole Falklands thing—on relations with Latin America, and she cited Brazil. Are you concerned about that and are you—

SECRETARY HAIG. Of course we are concerned, and there is no question that this has damaged relationships between the United States and Latin America, and between Great Britain and to some degree Europe and Latin America. But there is a great spectrum of difference from nation to nation, as you would expect. And some are very slightly disturbed. Others are very seriously disturbed.

Q. Is the United States going to undertake any new effort to try to repair that?

SECRETARY HAIG. Already started.

Q. With Argentina as well?

SECRETARY HAIG. Well, now there is more to be clarified in the Argentine case, and it is still—it is our ultimate objective, of course, to have good, strong, cordial and cooperative relationships with Argentina, but there are a number of uncertainties that make the exploration and development of that still premature.

Q. Did the President say what you just said just now, that American relations with some Latin American countries had been damaged? Did he say that to Mrs. Thatcher?

SECRETARY HAIG. Well, both leaders understand that thoroughly and the general inference of the discussion was an update for the President on the current situation.

Q. Mrs. Thatcher would appear to disagree is why I ask.

SECRETARY HAIG. How do you mean?

Q. Well, in her news conference she seemed to—

SECRETARY HAIG. Are you one of those guys she talked about out there that is spending myopic preoccupation with creating differences between two friendly nations? (Laughter.) I really don't know where the difference was. If there was, it was probably my answer.

Q. I am asking about her press conference—after her meeting.

SECRETARY HAIG. Yes, what did she say?

Q. That there were some nations in Latin America where it was a vast overstatement to say that relations with other countries were damaged—

SECRETARY HAIG. I hope I said the same thing in different words. There is a great spectrum of difference. Some countries are very, very concerned about first use of force.

Q. She didn't say the first thing, that relations with Latin America were hurt either for the United States or Britain.

SECRETARY HAIG. Oh, she knows that, and the President knows that.

God bless you. You are a loveable gang. (Laughter.)

THE PRESS. Thank you.

Document 204

Remarks by the British Foreign Secretary (Pym), July 29, 1982[26]

Meeting With Secretary of State Shultz

FOREIGN SECRETARY FRANCIS PYM. I want to say that I have had an extremely useful two hours of talks with Secretary of State Shultz. I wanted to come over and share views with him and discuss problems at the earliest moment and he suggested this afternoon and these talks have now taken place. I think we covered the main problem areas of the world, including particularly the Middle East, but we also discussed the problems that have arisen in Europe and I think we have a much greater understanding of each other's point of view. And I want to say that we are resolved to settle those differences one way or another and make sure that the Alliance continues in the future as it has for the past 33 years in a state of great coordination and cohesion. And I think, as I have said, this has been a very useful visit. I also had the chance of seeing Vice President Bush at lunch time where we also discussed other problems. So, although this is a short visit to the United States where I am very glad to be again, I think it has been immensely valuable from my point of view and I think, and I hope, from the American point of view as well.

---

[26] Source: Department of State files. Foreign Secretary Pym made his remarks in the lobby of the Department of State after meeting with Secretary Shultz. Secretary Pym was in Washington to meet with Secretary Shultz.

Q. What are the prospects for resolving the dispute over the Soviet pipeline?[27]

PYM. We didn't set about trying actually to solve that problem, but we went round the course. We discussed the issues and how it looks to the United States. And I was able to explain how it looks to Britain and how it looks to Europe. And I hope by exchanging views on a very frank basis that will provide a way in which progress can be made to all to resolve the differences.

Q. Just how serious is the disagreement?

PYM. I wouldn't want to underestimate it but I want to say very emphatically it's very limited. It's limited to this one issue of the pipeline; on quite a different issue there are problems over steel where negotiations have begun already today in Brussels between the European community and the United States and it's really limited to this one thing and therefore don't get it out of proportion. But equally let us realize that it is quite serious and I hope that between us we will be able to solve it quite soon.

Q. Has there been an improvement in this relationship as a result of this visit?

PYM. The relationship between the United States and the United Kingdom is very deep—we have a very great friendship—and I don't believe that recent events have in any way disturbed that friendship. It is if you like more of a family difference between the United States and Europe. Our relationship is excellent. This is the first meeting of any length I've had with the new Secretary of State and I think it's been a very, very valuable one and I look forward to all dealings with him in the future. So our partnership, ancient friendship, is in exactly as good a state as it was before and I'm very glad about that.

Q. Did the issue of the Falklands come up?

PYM. Yes, indeed we discussed the Falklands and Latin America. I think we touched every continent in the course of the afternoon. So I think it was very valuable.

Q. Any reason for optimism as far as the Middle East is concerned?

PYM. Well, there is room certainly for some optimism. We hope that the negotiations now going on in Beirut will bear fruit. I think it would be a terrible thing if the war were to continue. We want a withdrawal of all forces, but the United States and Mr. Habib are doing the best they can to achieve it and we are giving every support we can to him.

Thank you very much.

[27] For documentation on the trans-Siberian natural gas pipeline, see Chapter 10, Part A.

Document 205

Transcript of a Joint Press Conference by the Secretary of State (Shultz) and the British Foreign Secretary (Pym), London, December 17, 1982[28]

Relations Between the United States and the United Kingdom

SECRETARY PYM. I've had the pleasure of welcoming Secretary Shultz in London. Any visit by a United States Secretary of State is important and always welcome to Britain. It is particularly so in this case because in 6 months Mr. Shultz has made a major mark upon the world, and I have met him many times and he's certainly put his stamp on United States foreign policy. We have had a very useful and interesting talk. I am very glad that he arranged his European visit in such a way that he concluded it here in London. We have discussed this morning East–West relations, including the change of leadership in the Soviet Union, including the arms control talks and the CSCE talks in Madrid, and also the economic aspect.[29] We have also talked about the NATO alliance and defense issues and particularly the issues that face the alliance in 1983. We also had a discussion on the world economy. This is, of course, primarily a matter for Western leaders and finance ministers, but as foreign ministers we are inevitably involved in many discussions on the world economy which bears on how we do our business; and we exchanged our views

[28] Source: Department of State Press Release 398, December 22, 1982; also printed in Department of State *Bulletin*, February 1983, pp. 32–35. Secretary Shultz was in London at the end of a trip that took him to Bonn, December 7–8; Brussels, December 8–11; The Hague, December 11; Rome, December 11–14; Paris, December 14–15; Madrid, December 15–16; and finally London, December 16–18.

[29] Documentation on the Soviet Union is in Chapter 10, Part M; on arms control talks in Chapter 4; and on the CSCE in Chapter 10, Part A.

about that and looked forward to the next economic summit in May. We also exchanged views on the situation in the Middle East where, of course, the United States is playing a leading role and we are giving every support to the beginning of the peacemaking process based on the Reagan plan which we regard as an opportunity that is absolutely vital and must not be missed. We had a brief discussion about Namibia and also about Central America. They were certainly, for me, and for us, extremely useful talks and I feel that we have advanced our understanding on many matters. We are always in very close touch, I think the United States and Britain have always been like that, and Mr. Shultz and I have certainly always kept in very close touch and we are certainly going to do that in the future. So thank you for coming and thank you for taking part in these discussions.

SECRETARY SHULTZ. Well, thank you. As always when you have made a statement describing something you leave little else for me. I think your description is accurate and comprehensive. I don't have anything to add to it except to say that I am very pleased to have a chance to be here and talk with you, and this evening with Mrs. Thatcher and your colleagues. It is a little bit like coming home to me because London is where I started out as Secretary of State-designate. This is where President Reagan gave me the news that my life was going to change, so it is kind of fun to come back here and see London again in this perspective.

Q. You said that you had discussed defense issues and NATO issues. Could I ask you about the issue of the Cruise and Pershing missiles which may be deployed in this country later on next year? Is your government prepared to allow an element of joint control over the operation of those missiles, and if not, why not?

SECRETARY SHULTZ. Well, of course, Mr. Pym briefed me on the discussions that you have had here in this country on that issue and we agreed that the arrangements for a joint decisionmaking that have been going on here for some 20 years and have covered U.S. nuclear systems in the United Kingdom work well. The December 1979 decision[30] was taken by the alliance as a whole and so all INF issues continue to be discussed in the alliance, and we had discussed in the NATO ministerial meeting and in bilateral discussions, but nevertheless within the context of the alliance, all manner of issues. Now, of course, Mr. Pym and I will be in touch on this issue and a full range of issues and there are very many, particularly in the year 1983, and talk about them continuously. But as I said, from all that I can hear and sense the way in which this has been handled has worked well but I'll leave it up to Mr. Pym.

SECRETARY PYM. No, I agree with that. It certainly has worked well for over 20 years now.

Q. But could I just follow that through. I think the demand being made in some quarters here, and I think the Foreign Secretary himself has said it would be highly desirable to have some kind of joint key arrangement or dual key arrangement as it's called. Some actual decision that has to be taken by both governments before those missiles could be fired.

SECRETARY SHULTZ. Well, dual key is a kind of a phrase that casts up an image. I don't think that image accurately describes any arrangements that have literally existed in the past, but there have been a wide variety of arrangements and they vary by countries and I think that we have to look upon this as an alliance matter and discuss it on that basis and not get into further detail about it right at this point.

Q. Mr. Secretary Shultz, the President has given an interview that has just been published that is being portrayed as bringing new pressure, heavy pressure, on Israel in connection with withdrawal from Lebanon.[31] Mr. Secretary, can you amplify on that aspect of the reported interview and can you tell us after your talks with Mr. Pym whether the United States can do anything beyond what it is already doing to bring about the withdrawal of all foreign forces from Lebanon?

SECRETARY SHULTZ. Well, that is our objective—one of our objectives—to help bring about the withdrawal of all foreign forces from Lebanon. That is not the only objective. It is also our objective to help the Lebanese, the Government of Lebanon, develop itself and take control of its country and develop its own armed forces so that they can be effective throughout the rela-

---

[30] December 12, 1979; see *American Foreign Policy: Basic Documents, 1977–1980*, pp. 494–496.

[31] Reference is to an interview with President Reagan, on December 16, summarized in the *Washington Post*, December 17, 1982, pp. A1, A27. The edited text of the interview is *ibid.*, December 19, 1982, p. A8. For an extract of the interview, see document 421.

tionships among the confessional groups and in the physical arrangements of Lebanon into the vibrant and thriving country that it once was. Now as far as the steps that we are taking in Lebanon are concerned, as you know, Phil Habib and Maury Draper are back in the Middle East. They met with Prime Minister Begin yesterday, they are in Beirut today and I think that they are in the process of conducting this renewed effort on our part and I would leave any commentary or coloration of that to them.

Q. What about the President's interview and the way that it's being portrayed as new and heavy pressure on Israel. Could you amplify on that, sir?

SECRETARY SHULTZ. Well, I think there is clearly pressure being felt by everybody to bring this result about. I had the privilege of talking again with the Foreign Minister of Lebanon and he certainly feels—as do others in Lebanon—that not only do we want to have this result but it is a matter of urgency to bring it about speedily so that on the one hand the foreign forces don't get unduly dug in, and on the other that the emerging capacity of the Government of Lebanon to exert its authority can continue to be realized.

Q. Mr. Secretary, to what extent do you recognize that in these talks about Lebanon the Israelis want them to be much more than talks about just withdrawal but the real direct political negotiations leading to a new relationship between Lebanon and Israel?

SECRETARY SHULTZ. Well, we read and we listen so we realize that there are broad objectives involved and there are also definite realities involved about the importance of an atmosphere that allows these confessional groups to come together and for Lebanon to construct itself as a country. And, of course, beyond that you have to say what does it mean to have a new kind of relationship with a country until that country has been able to form itself and get some coherence and have a capacity for deciding what it wants to do. But I would say more generally that the objective of a peaceful situation between Israel and her neighbors is one that we, of course, are doing everything we can to help bring about, not only with respect to Lebanon but with respect to all of her neighbors in the Middle East. Having peace with justice and reasonable conditions is the objective, just as it is in the efforts that the United States and our allies are making in other parts of the world, that's what we are standing for, peace and justice.

Q. Secretary Shultz, obviously in the weeks leading up to your coming here the peace movements have played an important part in your own country and in this country and in Western Europe. How important a part did that kind of public disquiet about nuclear questions—how important was that at your talks today?

SECRETARY SHULTZ. Well, everyone, I think, shares the hope that we can somehow construct a world that is at peace, that has an increasing element of justice in it, and which allows people to live without an overhang of fear that's generated by awesome weapons. There is no difference of opinion about that. We all share that view. The question is what do you do about it? Because, unfortunately, we are not the only people around the world who have awesome weapons. We are seeking to reduce the level of these weapons. We are seeking to restrict the matter of their use. We are seeking to solve problems regionally around the world. Arms control is not the only thing that you have to do, you have to remove the reasons why people would want armaments. And everywhere you turn, I think I'm fairly stating it, the United States is on the side of the solution not on the side of the problem, and so that is our objective. We listen to people in our own country. And elsewhere and it's been very useful for me in coming here and elsewhere in Europe and talking with not only with my counterparts but many other people, and I have gone out of my way to try to see people not in the government as well as people in the government to get a feeling for how people view things. And we are, we understand the fears that people have, but we also understand that when you are confronted with a strong aggressor the worst thing that you can do is let your own defenses decline and let fear lead you into appeasement. That is a key and I feel on this trip in discussions certainly here, and elsewhere—everywhere, without any exception, a great sense of reassurance in the depth of understanding, the subtleties of understanding and the sense of determination, unity and cohesion that I felt in our alliance.

Q. Do you feel that the peace movements constitute a threat to the United States policy or NATO?

SECRETARY SHULTZ. Well, they ought to present a reminder of the strength of conviction behind what we all presumably want, namely the kind of peace that has justice right in it.

Q. According to reports coming from Jerusalem, the Israeli Defense Minister claimed yesterday to have achieved a major breakthrough in the talks with Lebanon. You met yesterday with the Lebanese Foreign Minister; do you share this view?

SECRETARY SHULTZ. Well, we did not have any information about that statement that Mr. Sharon made, and I don't have any comment about it except to say that any genuine breakthrough, however derived that will bring about a withdrawal of all foreign forces from Lebanon and contribute to the reconstruction of Lebanon is something that we will welcome.

Q. Secretary, you said that the arrangements for the last 20 years had worked well over control of nuclear weapons which has been the single American control here. But surely in the 1980's there was the joint U.S./British control over Thor missiles in this country. Why are you not prepared to allow a return to that system?

SECRETARY SHULTZ. Well, as I understand it, there have been a variety of arrangements and what has happened is, bilaterally and now, of course, we have to consider this as an alliance matter as well as a bilateral matter. We keep confronting new situations and I think the answer that I have given may be interpreted as meaning that somehow we have been able to work these problems out and the result has worked well in everybody's eyes and we feel that the arrangements that were made in 1979, those were mutually agreed and we are proceeding on that basis, but we are constantly talking not only about this, but a wide variety of other issues as we move along in this process.

Q. Can I ask Mr. Pym under what conditions he would ask the United States for joint control over the firing of these weapons?

SECRETARY PYM. Well, the arrangements which Mr. Shultz has referred to are in fact joint decisionmaking. That has been the basis of our arrangement for the last 20 years and those are the arrangements to which Mr. Shultz has referred. I have talked to him about the views that were expressed in the House of Commons and elsewhere and he is quite right that these are matters that have been decided by the alliance and are considered in that context as well as bilaterally.

Q. Mr. Secretary Shultz, I am a Yugoslav journalist. When you have been nominated you have been explained as highly educated Soviet expert. I am interested, are you going to change a policy toward the Soviet Union because they are expecting so and a lot written about that probably the relations between Soviet Union and the United States are going to be better than during Nixon?

SECRETARY SHULTZ. The policy of the United States toward the Soviet Union, and I believe that broadly speaking it is the same policy that the North Atlantic alliance has toward the Soviet Union as I see it, consists of four parts. First, that we must be realistic in our appraisal of what is taking place. The worst thing in the world you can do is allow wishful thinking to lead you into failure to realistically appraise what is taking place, so realism is the first point. The second point is that in the face of the buildup and the level of Soviet strength and the demonstrated willingness to use it, as for example in the invasion of Afghanistan, just an example, tell you that to be successful you must be strong. To defend your own values and to defend peace and to defend liberty and freedom you must be strong. Third, in the kind of world we live in, with the awesomeness of the threats particularly that have been mentioned here earlier, we are all aware of, we must also be willing to be ready to solve problems and to work constructively for better relationships and for solutions to problems, and we are, and we have negotiations taking place now as is well-known in Geneva and Vienna and elsewhere. So we are ready to solve problems and fourth, that we do so in the belief that if these problems can get on their way to solution and a more constructive relationship emerges, we can all have a better world with less fear and many other better attributes. Now with new leadership of the Soviet Union we, and I think our allies, have all sought to underline the third point so that they wouldn't miss that it's there. But we should not allow ourselves because of our interest and desire for peace and for freedom and for constructive dialogue to lose sight of the importance of being realistic and being strong. Those are the keys to peace and freedom.

Q. Secretary of State Shultz, at the end of your tour of Europe do you now reckon that you have a clear policy umbrella governing relations with the Soviet Union and its allies, particularly on the economic front?

SECRETARY SHULTZ. Well, I think we have long had, and continue to have, a very good strategy umbrella if you want to call it that, in the form of the NATO alliance and it is strong, it is unified it has cohesion and I think at least as I felt, as I said before, a lot of reassurance on that point. We have been struggling together to find a better sense of strategy—set of objectives—on the security aspects of East–West trade and financial flows. And I do think now we have going, or propose to go, forward with a pretty unified view, a general unified view, the studies and the activities that we feel are the necessary ones to construct that strategy, and we think that one of the great benefits of getting an overall strategy identified is that we will minimize the problems that may be caused by misunderstandings which often go under the label of you did not consult enough or we did not consult with each other. We all know that there is an immense amount of conversation, there is no lack of that and at least I feel what we need is some sort of overall set of objectives and strategy then when we consult with each other we have some standards against which to talk, and our consultation can be more purposeful and therefore more fruitful and I think we have got that identified now and will start in on constructing that study.

Q. Sir, if you have one overriding objective for 1983 what would that be?

SECRETARY SHULTZ. If you want to speak about it in broad terms I think we are looking for peace with justice and prosperity. We have not had any commentary here about the economic situation but I think we want to see the world economy expand and see progress in that sense. Those are our main objectives.

Q. Mr. Secretary Shultz, could you possibly be trying to help Prime Minister Begin with your recent attacks on Israel. If not, what is the public pressure in aim of?

SECRETARY SHULTZ. I have made no attacks on Israel and I have made no comments designed to help or hinder or in any way be a part of the internal political flow of events and opinion in Israel. That is strictly for Israel to determine. I have not hesitated to say when I think that something is wrong or that something is right. Now when it appeared to me that the requiring of university professors to sign special oaths otherwise dismissed came to my attention I said I thought that was wrong and I do think it is wrong. I've also commented on the dismissal of mayors from the West Bank. It also was the case when moves were made to deny Israel credentials to the United Nations that in the United States, and I was pleased to speak for the President on this, that we said that if the United Nations votes to do that we will withdraw. We support Israel. So I think that we, I certainly and the President certainly, support Israel, the security of Israel, the purposefulness, the idea and the ideal of Israel. I've been there, I know many people there, but that doesn't mean that no matter what Israel does or says we are going to applaud it. I think we have to say if they do something we think isn't right. Maybe we are good enough friends to be able to say so.

Q. This is to Foreign Secretary Pym. As a result of these talks this morning, has the situation in regard to control of the Cruise missiles changed from what it was two nights ago when you were questioned about it in Parliament, and if not, is it likely to change in the future as a result of these conversations?

SECRETARY PYM. No, it has not changed. As Secretary Shultz said, we discussed this point and I told him the views that were expressed in our debate the day before yesterday. And the fact of the matter is that the decision we took in 1979 was taken by the alliance and included these joint decision arrangements with the United States that had existed before. But anyway we discussed that aspect but we discussed many other aspects of INF and so there is no change in the situation. Is it likely to change, well there is no particular likelihood of any change, as I say, we exchanged views about it but the position remains as it was.

Q. Mr. Secretary Shultz, if I understood correctly the readout of the meeting yesterday with the Lebanese Foreign Minister, he expressed concern that continued Israeli presence in Lebanon in effect was leading to annexation of part of Lebanon. Do you share that concern, is that a real possibility?

SECRETARY SHULTZ. I didn't make that comment, so I don't know where your readout comes from. I only made the comment about the sense of urgency but I do think that it must be a matter of concern, and I am not referring to the meeting I had with the foreign minister, that you have foreign troops in your country and they stay there and they stay there longer, and they stay there longer, and when they stay they get embedded and they have developed an infrastructure and so on, so this is one of the reasons why I think there is an urgency to getting the foreign forces out. Not just the Israeli forces. The Israeli forces are the most recent entrants, the PLO has been there for quite a long time, established a state within a state and was very disruptive of the ability of Lebanon to operate as a country, and the Syrians have been there for a long time. So it is all foreign forces that we are seeking to get out of the country.

Ladies and gentlemen, thank you very much.

D. West Germany

Document 206

Transcript of a Department of State Press Briefing, January 4, 1982[1]

Visit of Chancellor Helmut Schmidt of the Federal Republic of Germany

Mr. Fischer. Okay, I think we are ready to go. The speaker will be on background unless he indicates otherwise.

Senior Department Official. Let me first give you a little bit on the schedule. I know you've got most of it, but one thing is new. Mr. Genscher will be arriving tonight. He will fly directly from Brussels where there is a meeting of the EC Ten Foreign Ministers and will join Mr. Schmidt in the meeting. We can't tell you exactly what time he'll get in yet because we're not sure exactly what time he's going to be leaving Brussels, but he will be getting in some time this evening.

Depending on what time he gets in, he will probably have a meeting with Secretary Haig tonight and certainly another one tomorrow morning before the rest of the schedule moves on.

The Secretary will meet Mr. Schmidt at the airport tonight and will have a meeting with Mr. Schmidt in Blair House this evening after the Chancellor's arrival.

Tomorrow the Chancellor will have a breakfast with Congressional leaders on the Hill; a meeting with the Vice President; followed by a meeting and a lunch with the President. In the afternoon he will meet with the Secretary of Defense. He, the Chancellor, will have a breakfast with Secretary Haig on Wednesday morning[2] and depart shortly thereafter for Dulles Airport.

I think those are the highlights of the schedule. Now let me talk a little bit about the visit. I know this will come as a tremendous shock to you all but obviously the major, but I think not the only, subject of the meetings between Mr. Schmidt and the President and Secretary are [*is*] going to be Poland. I would suspect that there will be some conversation on other subjects as well. Probably the international economic situation. I would assume there would be some discussion of NATO military strength and defense budgets and things of that sort. And we'll give you a read-out on what is in fact discussed after the meetings, but clearly the focus is going to be on Poland.

And I think on the Polish question we have to see the Schmidt visit fortuitously because you all know, I'm sure, that the visit was set up long before the Polish situation captured all of our attention. But I think we now have to see the Schmidt visit as it relates to Poland as part of the whole consultative process on how to handle that subject. It's part of a process which has included long and detailed discussions in NATO for over a year of a number of economic and political steps that might be taken in the event of a Soviet invasion of Poland. It's in the context of my own trip to Europe several weeks ago where I covered Rome, Bonn, Brussels, Paris, and London, followed some days thereafter by the President's announcement on steps that will be taken against the Soviet Union[3]; messages between Foreign Ministers that have followed that Presidential announcement; now the Schmidt visit, which is accompanied as well by the meeting of EC Ten Foreign Ministers on the subject of Poland, and we'll all have a better read-out on what went on at that meeting after Mr. Genscher gets here to brief us on it; and there will be a ministerial meeting in Brussels of the NATO Alliance on the 11th of January.[4]

So this visit is part of that process. It is not our purpose during this visit to arrive at

---

[1] Source: Department of State files. The briefing was on background and took place in the Department of State beginning at 10:05 a.m. Chancellor Schmidt visited Washington, January 4–6, after vacationing in Florida.

[2] No records of any of the meetings mentioned here, except that with the President, have been found. The statement issued after the meeting with the President is *infra*.

[3] President Reagan made the statement on December 29, 1981; for text, see *American Foreign Policy: Current Documents, 1981*, document 270.

[4] For documentation on this meeting, see Chapter 10, Part B.

a series of agreements with the Chancellor on how to handle the Polish situation. Our purpose is to discuss with him how we see the situation, how he sees it, to exchange views on what is going on in Poland, and indeed to discuss what steps might be taken by the West with regard to the Polish situation.

We will want very much, I think, to look for examples during the visit of the Chancellor at [*of*] how the Soviets have been dealing with the United States on this subject and what they have been saying to the Federal Republic on the same subject of Poland because it is very much our view and our impression that the Soviets have been taking one line with us, which is quite hard, and a much less hard line in their discussions with officials of the Federal Republic of Germany, and that's one of the things we're going to want to talk about with the Chancellor and sort of exchange information on what has been said to us and to them by the Soviet Union.

As you all know, our general position with regard to our sanctions against the Soviet Union is that we hope for parallel action from our allies where possible, recognizing that in all cases the situations are not the same, and we would hope in those cases for at least complementary steps, but under any circumstances we believe that our allies should not undercut the steps we have taken against the Soviet Union, and I'm sure that that will be part of the discussions that will take place over the course of the next several days.

Now, since I know you will all ask me, because I read the newspapers too, "What about the difference between the Federal Republic of Germany and the United States on what's going on in Poland and on the question of Soviet involvement in what is going on in Poland?" Let me start by highlighting for you, please, Foreign Minister Genscher's December 31 press conference,[5] which I would suggest is worth taking a look at again. It is, in our view, the definitive statement at the present moment of the Federal Republic's attitude on the Polish circumstances and on Soviet involvement in those circumstances, and I must say from our view it's a fairly precise statement.

I do not deny, and I do not intend to deny at this point that there may well be differences of perspective on what's going on in Poland, or some elements of it, but I think there has been a tendency to overdraw those, and it's why I highlight for you Mr. Genscher's interview.

I would point out that with regard to how we handle Poland there seems, in my view, to be closer identity of views than has often been noted. For example, the United States Government has said that we will not provide further government-to-government assistance to Poland so long as circumstances in that country remain as they are. It's my clear understanding that, in effect, that is what the Government of the Federal Republic has also done with the statement that no further aid would be forthcoming without the approval of the Bundestag. I think there's a fairly general community view that with regard to humanitarian assistance to Poland it should continue but it should continue with guarantees that the aid will in fact go to the people for whom it is intended. I might also add that the U.S. Government is at this moment looking at ways in which we might provide further humanitarian assistance to Poland, consistent with the guarantees we insist on, however, from the Polish Government.

I think as well there's a fair degree of similarity of view between the Federal Republic and ourselves on what ought to happen in Poland; namely, three things: martial law ought to be ended; the detainees ought to be released; and the three parties in Poland; that is, the Church, the Government authorities, and Solidarity ought to return to the negotiating table.

I think, finally, there is strong understanding both on the part of our German friends and certainly here in Washington as well that the last thing we need to do is turn this crisis in Poland caused by the Soviet Union's involvement with the Polish authorities in repressing the workers' movement into a crisis within the Western community, and I think that is neither our intention, nor is it the intention of the Federal Republic of Germany, and it is with this critical point as background that I think both sides will be going into these discussions over the next several days.

I'll be glad to answer questions as long as you understand I don't want to try to get into a prediction as to what specifically is going to come out of these meetings, but I'll be glad to try to answer your questions.

Q. Could you expand a bit . . . on the difference in which the Soviets have been talking to the Germans and the way they've been talking to us?

A. Well, essentially no. Let me just say that it is clearly our impression that the

[5] For a summary of this press conference, see *Washington Post*, January 1, 1982, p. A12.

Soviet Union—well, the President, for example, described in essence Mr. Brezhnev's reply to him as negative.[6] Our general impression, and you've seen, I think—I think the Soviets have released the text of Mr. Gromyko's letter to Mr. Haig[7]—the Soviet communications with us have been extremely negative, extremely harsh. It is our impression that the Soviets have talked a somewhat different language to the Federal Republic and been a good bit softer in their style at least. I don't say in substance. I'm not sure there's much difference on the substance. But at least in terms of the style. And it's one of the things we're going to want to discuss with Mr. Schmidt to try to get some analysis of whether our impression is in fact correct and, if so, why they've dealt with the two of us somewhat differently.

Q. In the last 18 months have there been no consultations on what in fact happened; that is, internal repression rather than external, within the Western Alliance?

A. No. Look, again, the greatest amount of concentration within the alliance has clearly been in terms of what might the allies do in the event of a direct Soviet intervention? There's no question about that. And the long list of items that we came up with, not as a contract but as items that would be looked at in the event of a Soviet intervention, were debated and discussed and arrived at in NATO, but against the focus of a Soviet intervention. Within NATO there has been a good bit of discussion over a fairly long period of time about this gray area—what we call the gray area—with a fairly substantial agreement that in fact it would be the most difficult case to deal with, and a lot of discussion about what might be done with regard to it. But there's no sense hiding from the fact that after the consultations and discussions on that subject were completed the general view within the NATO Council was that the gray area scenarios were so imprecise and might run such a tremendous gamut that there simply was no way that the 15 nations were going to be able to come to agreement on steps that might be taken in that gray area situation. So I'm not hiding from the fact that there was never agreement on what might be done under those circumstances, but I strongly dispute anybody who argues that it wasn't discussed in Brussels because it was in some great detail.[8] Nor should we, I think, assume that discussions that took place with regard to what might be done in the event of a Soviet intervention were all a waste of time, because in fact some of those steps we in fact used several of them last week. There is at least a fairly common view within the alliance of what some of those steps might mean. The issue is one of when we plan to use them and now when in fact we are using them.

Q. Can you talk some about what your latest reading of the situation in Poland is as you go into the conversations with Schmidt?

A. Yes. And I must say I haven't read anything this morning, so I'm dealing with what I saw on Saturday. I don't think it has changed much. I think there's no doubt that General Jaruzelski and his coup on December 13 have, for now, succeeded in establishing his definition of law and order. But I think it's much too early to assume that that is going to be any sort of a long-term situation or condition. And I'm now speaking personally, but I think it's a view shared by a number of people in this building that we should not forget, first of all, that the economic situation before the December 13 coup was not good. What has happened since then has certainly made it worse. On the basis of past history, we all know that economic conditions have had a great deal to do with political instability—if you want to call it that—within Poland. I personally do not think that the General has succeeded in establishing a situation in which you can count for any long period of time on tranquility and peace in Poland. I think it's almost inevitable that there will be passive resistance. I think you will probably see that factories that used to produce X number of tractors per week are now producing X minus whatever. I think production is going to be reduced simply as a process of passive resistance.

Whether it gets any worse than that in the short run I don't know. I think it is important though, particularly in terms of discussions with the Chancellor. It's important that we all in the West recognize that if we're going to reestablish any sort of a situation in Poland where stability over a longer period is possible that can only be done, in our view, by eliminating martial

---

[6] See *New York Times*, December 28, 1981, p. A1.

[7] The letter from Foreign Minister Gromyko to Secretary Haig has not been further identified.

[8] The reference here is to the NATO Foreign Ministers meeting in Brussels, December 10–11, 1981; for text of the communiqué issued at its conclusion, see *American Foreign Policy: Current Documents, 1981*, document 176.

law, letting the detainees go, and getting back to the negotiating table. And we don't see how it is possible to negotiate with the leaders of Solidarity when they are in jail or detained. That's not normally considered a way in which you're dealing with a free agent. And I think we will make the point very clearly in our conversations with the Chancellor. But as I indicated earlier, and certainly in Mr. Genscher's statement on the 31st, they support those same three conditions with regard to Poland.

Q. I get the impression from reading German statements that their feeling is the quickest way to bring those things about is to stop the punishment scenario and to try to discourage the passive resistance and encourage people to get back to work so that we can get on about reviving the economy, and that our view is it's nice to see this passive resistance.

A. Well, I don't know that I would say it's nice. I think what we're saying is it's almost inevitable. But I think certainly if you read the statements of some German officials there is no question that that's a view that some take. I would have to say other statements—and again I refer you to the Genscher statement—don't make that distinction quite so clearly. I think there may well be a good bit of discussion in the next several days over how we both see the situation in Poland, how we see General Jaruzelski. Do we see him as his own agent, or is he an agent of the Soviet Union? And I frankly at this point can't predict to you what the German view on this is going to be. I can only say that on the basis of what I've read out of Bonn over the course of the last several weeks you can get a different view depending on who you read.

Q. . . . (inaudible) . . . General Jaruzelski met with the ECK people today. Has he requested, or has the U.S. Ambassador requested, a similar meeting in Warsaw?

A. Not to my knowledge, . . . Ambassador Meehan met with the Deputy Foreign Minister last week, but I don't know of any since then. I'm told he's seeing Czyrek this afternoon, the Foreign Minister.

Q. How much value do you attach to the analysis the Catholic Church, the Vatican, has of the situation in Poland? How close are you in touch, and what is your assessment of their analysis? Because the Germans attached their story on that very strongly.

A. We've been in quite close contact with the Vatican. As you know, the President has been in communication with the Pope on the subject. There is no question that we value very much the Church's view on what's going on in Poland and the view of what the approach in Poland ought to be from the point of view of the Church.

I must say in my own trip there a couple of weeks ago—and I think this situation has changed a bit now—but it was clear to me at that point that communications between the Polish Church and the Vatican were not terribly good. Since then we've had our Bishop Dabrovski and Archbishop Poggi back and forth, so they have a better understanding, I think, now of what the Primate and the Polish Church think. But to a degree the Vatican is going to have to depend on what it gets out of the Polish Church, and that depends to a great degree on the ability to communicate, and I gather that's not terribly good.

Q. Mr. Secretary, will the United States continue to support Poland's application for membership in the International Monetary Fund?

A. The question is now under review. I can't give you a definitive answer at this point, but I should point out to you that under any circumstances that application does not really become a major issue for about 6 months. It's not something that's likely to be moved on by the IMF within the next week or two. There's a good bit of time before the IMF will move on the application anyway, but it's a question that's now under review.

Q. To come back to the German-American aspects of this story, how helpful do you think German attempts at bridge-building are? We have noticed from Bonn a great sense of relief when Secretary Haig says several times that in times of crisis you have to have particularly good contacts and community dialogue. The Germans are using that line, have been using it for some time to continue talking at high level with Brezhnev, they had Rakowski in Bonn. Do you think this is helpful or do you think it allows the East to separate Germany into departing more from a concerted Western policy?

A. The proof of that pudding will be in the eating. There is no question that lines of communication need to be kept open, and there is no question, for example, that the Rakowski meeting in Bonn gave us a point of view, as briefed to us by the German officials, that is worth having. Bridge-building is not, I think, the term I would use so much as the Federal Republic's role in keeping the lines of communication open and finding out what they're thinking in Poland, and so forth, is obviously worth while.

Should the Soviet Union or the Poles succeed—and I do not think they will—in convincing any one, two, or three members of NATO that the situation is different than other members of NATO believe it to be, then we obviously would have a problem, but communications between the parties involved is, I think, by and large, a good thing, so we don't have any problem with it.

Q. I believe you said at one point that at a minimum we should expect that our allies would not take action to undercut that that [*sic*] we have decided to do. What is your latest reading on the extent of cooperation you are getting from them? I'm thinking of what happens, for example, if the Germans or some other countries sell pipeline equipment which we have decided not to sell.

A. . . . in general—and again you all must keep in mind this NATO meeting on the 11th because an awful lot is going to be a lot clearer after that meeting. The whole question of the attitude of the allies and how close we are with the allies is something of a moving target, so you have to start with that. I have seen—and I don't want to detail the countries, largely because I can't remember how much of it was confidential and how much of it is open—but I have seen at least three countries that I can recall from within NATO who have already made it clear that they will not take actions to undercut our sanctions. In all three cases they were major members of the alliance. It is clearly a subject that will be a part of our discussions with the Chancellor over the next 2 days, and we'll have a better fix on German attitudes with regard to that subject then. The definitive answer to that, I think, will come after the meeting on the 11th.

Q. In the interview with Reston in the *Times* over the weekend,[9] the Chancellor had an interesting line in which he complained about the rhetoric coming from Washington which gave the impression of a prewar situation rather than a postwar situation. Would the United States be willing to tone down its rhetoric toward Moscow as a price for greater German or allied cooperation?

A. As I remember that particular quote, it was in the context of IMF, wasn't it? I don't think it was in the context of the Polish situation. Not that that's necessarily relevant.

How do I answer your question? As long as we're not talking about the Polish situation, we, I think, feel very strongly that the world needs to know our view of Soviet and Polish repression of the workers' movement of some 10 million people and our view of what's going on in Poland with regard to detaining people, continuation of martial law, and so forth.

Now, that is not to say that I'm arguing for heightened rhetoric. What I am saying is I think we are going to continue to talk about the Polish situation as we see it and continue to make it clear our abhorrence of what is going on there, and continue to make it clear it is our firm belief that the Soviets must permit the Polish people to get back to the negotiating table and that the Polish authorities need to move quickly to do the same thing.

Q. Can you assume that there wouldn't be any further American unilateral action until after the January 11 meeting, or may we do some more things before that on our own?

A. The answer to that is there is no way I can give you a definitive answer. Again speaking totally personally, I would be very surprised if the situation in Poland doesn't change. I mean if things don't change between now and the 11th. I would personally be surprised if we would be taking any further steps until we have completed our conversations with the allies.

Q. Did I understand you to say that General Jaruzelski for now has succeeded in establishing his definition of law and order, and it's a long-term problem however it is going to be resolved? You seem to be taking a position which sounds as if you think he has got the immediate problem there in better shape than most of the noises that have been coming out of this building in the past week or so. Is this based on some new sense of what they are able to do in Poland? Is it based on just the fact that time has run [out] now and nothing more has happened or the country is getting back to work? How do you reach that judgment?

A. . . . I should start by saying I did not, in fact, intend it to sound like something different than we've been saying over the last couple of weeks. My own view is that in fact things are not—if I were General Jaruzelski I wouldn't be happy at all. I do have to make the point, however, that the number of strikes has been reduced. You

[9] See *New York Times*, January 3, 1982, p. I14.

know, if you decapitate the Solidarity leadership, close off all lines of communication so the people can't converse back and forth, you can accomplish a fair amount in terms of bringing things to a dead halt, and that's, I think, what he has succeeded in doing, and I guess in that sense, to answer your question, the course of the last 3 or 4 days has made it clear that there aren't going to be, at least immediately, any massive strikes, there isn't going to be any countrywide uprising or anything of that sort. But I would make the point . . . that one of the things that closing down the lines of communications has also done is made it far more difficult to manage the economy. And once you begin to let up so that the economy can begin to move again you also are permitting people to start communicating with each other, and I therefore think what we may see is in fact a more difficult situation in Poland in the future. I don't know when, but, as I say, if I were Jaruzelski I would not feel at all confident that I had really solved my problem.

Q. There have been repeated reports that Soviet troops are actually in Poland wearing Polish uniforms. Has the State Department here been able to verify any of those reports?

A. As far as I know, no.

Q. Do you want to persuade the Chancellor to terminate the gas pipeline deal or postpone it, or would that not be a subject at all any more?[10] I mean it has been discussed in the past many times.

A. You people had almost disappointed me. It has gone 35 minutes before the pipeline really came up. Let me answer that question by saying that the view of the U.S. Government with regard to the pipeline is clear. It hasn't changed. Obviously it is in the last analysis a decision to be made by sovereign governments, but everybody, I think, knows what our view is, and I would expect that should the opportunity arise we will express during this visit our view of the pipeline.

Q. May I follow that question up? I'm not sure I understand our view. As I understand our view, it was that we can't stop the pipeline but let's at least urge the Europeans not to get too heavily involved in Soviet sources of energy. I just want to make sure that's the position, or is it the position they shouldn't go ahead with the pipeline?

A. . . . our view has always been we don't think they should go ahead with the pipeline. Then you go from that to say, "However, we also recognize that it is not a decision we can make," and you proceed with the description as you stated it. But our view is that the pipeline is a mistake, and it has always been that.

Q. I want to make sure I understand when you said earlier that you don't want the Europeans to undercut our sanctions, one of the sanctions was that you would not allow licenses for any equipment in helping build the pipeline. Could that be enlarged upon to say that if the Germans go ahead with the pipeline that's cutting into the American sanctions?

A. I want to be careful how I answer that, . . . but I will say that you're right we have taken steps to suspend any U.S. sales to the Soviet Union some of which would affect the pipeline, and our position is with regard to our allies that they should not undercut the sanctions we have taken, and I don't want to go beyond that.

Q. You said that the Soviets have now a much harsher language to the United States than to Germany. I suppose it is not very surprising for you. So I would like to know what do you expect to hear from Chancellor Schmidt about that? Apparently you are concerned that it would be working.

A. As I say, we want to talk about that subject because I think it would be interesting for both sides to exchange views. First of all, I should say we want to find out whether our impression is in fact correct that the line they have taken with us and the line they have taken with Bonn are different at least in tone. If that proves to be the case—and in the conversations we should be able to establish that—it would be interesting for us together to try to analyze why there have been those differences in tone and to think a little bit about the implications of why the Soviets would be talking to us one way and to Bonn somewhat differently.

Q. Do you expect anything in the way of a communiqué or some kind of a statement of facts[11] that are agreed by both parties after that meeting, or are you waiting until after January 11?

A. January 11th is not really relevant to this. The practice has varied a bit from visit

[10] For documentation on the Trans-Siberian natural gas pipeline, see Chapter 10, Part A.

[11] For text of the statement issued after Chancellor Schmidt's meeting with President Reagan on January 5, see *infra*.

to visit, so at this point I can't predict to you whether we'll have a communiqué or sort of a noncommuniqué like we did, I think it was in March, or whether anything at all will be released. I just don't know that, and I won't know until we've had a chance to talk to the Germans.

Q. One other question on the pipeline, you said the U.S. position hasn't changed, but in fact the circumstances have changed in that the Germans went ahead and signed this contract. Now it is the U.S. position that they should get out of the contract, cancel it, abrogate it in some way?

A. There are some other circumstances which have changed, one of which is that Poland has happened. Again, I don't want to get terribly specific because this is something that is going to have to be discussed. I would like to stand on my statement that we've always had a view of the pipeline. It is, obviously, in the last analysis, not a decision for us to take, but as you say, some circumstances have changed with regard to signing contracts, but also some circumstances have changed in Europe itself—particularly in Poland. Our view of the pipeline has not changed.

Q. Can I follow that up again, because the political dimension of the pipeline has been referred to by columnists and others—and I think it's accurate—as tantamount to the farmers' lobby in this country against the grain embargo.

The United States in its sanctions obviously did not take the really tough political issue dealing with the farmers, and yet you're asking the Germans to take the really tough one dealing with a contract already signed. How do you respond to something like that?

A. . . . at this point, I'm not saying we're asking anybody to do anything other than to recognize that this is a subject worth thinking about in the context of what has happened in Poland and against the background of our desire that nothing be done to undercut the sanctions we've taken. I don't want to go any further than that right now.

Q. Can I ask you, you said that one of the preoccupations on both sides, you believe, is to make sure that the crisis in Poland doesn't become a crisis in the alliance, whether this administration wishes to scream at the Europeans as the last one did or not. If the facts don't change, are you concerned that there will be, on the Hill for one place, and others, basically what turns into a crisis in the alliance?

A. Instead of answering the question, the point is, if the facts don't change, and again, . . . as I said, it's a moving target. We are already closer together than we were 2 weeks ago. I don't know where we will be on the 11th and so forth, but I think, to answer the question in a different way, if we were not to receive support from our allies for the steps we've taken, obviously, this would be a serious matter insofar as this alliance of ours is concerned. There is no question about that. I don't think that that is what is going to happen.

Q. I wonder whether you can tell us what you make of the apparent disagreement between your own position and that of the Chancellor as regards Yalta[12] and its implication for the current situation. Obviously, in the interview the Chancellor gave you Sunday, he made a great deal out of the fact that Yalta is still there, that it is insurmountable, and we cannot sweep it under the carpet, whereas out of here, we hear more about Helsinki.[13]

Is that likely to come up in the debates? Are we going to have a philosophical agreement [*argument?*] as to what extent Yalta is still relevant or not relevant, and whether it can be used as a means to not do as much as you might hope to?

A. Whether it will come up or not, I cannot be certain. I think it is clear that in our view the Helsinki Final Act is an important, but not the only important, element in the whole question of looking at the legal situation, if you will, as it regards Poland. Obviously, the U.N. Charter is also involved. There is a whole series of international agreements that are important. I think it would tend to be very quickly a sterile debate if we are arguing over whether Yalta still applies or whether Yalta has been amended by the Helsinki Final Act and all of this. I wouldn't expect it would take a great deal of our time.

What is important, when everything else is said and done, is that Poland is in the heart of Europe. In terms of the long-term stability of Europe, it is our very strong view that Poland will be, in the long run, a more stable country if the forces in Poland can

---

[12] The reference here is to the accords worked out at Yalta in February 1945 by President Roosevelt, Marshall Stalin, and Prime Minister Churchill concerning the post-war shape of Europe.

[13] The reference here is to the Final Act of the Conference on Security and Cooperation in Europe, signed at Helsinki on August 1, 1975; for text, see Department of State *Bulletin*, September 1, 1975, p. 323–350.

get back to the negotiating table and can establish some community of view, and return to the reform process that was going on up until the 13th of December.

I find it difficult, on the basis of 35 years of looking at Polish history, to believe that a repressed Poland is a Poland that contributes to stability in the heart of Europe, and that is, when we are all through with it, what we are all talking about.

Q. . . . does the United States plan to go back to the Madrid conference[14] when it resumes with full participation without any sort of protest or anything like that?

A. I have to give you the same answer to this one that I gave you to the last one. It's a question that's under review and I can't give you any firm answer on that now. It will obviously depend to some degree at least on the events between now and the scheduled resumption of the Madrid meetings.

Q. Is that the same with the Haig meeting with Gromyko? Is that also under review?

A. Yes.

Q. Getting back to what . . . asked earlier, there is a column in one of the newspapers this morning saying that while the President plans to talk softly and reasonably he is going to lay great stress on the fact that if there's a wide gap that continues between us and Bonn it's likely to have a very, very adverse effect within Congress. Can you elaborate a little bit on that?

A. Again, I don't want to predict what the President is going to say or how he is going to say it. And I'm not sure I know how some articles have arrived at that. But as I said in answer to . . . question, if you take the worst possible outcome, which is no agreement, obviously it is going to have an impact on attitudes in the United States, public opinion in the United States, I would assume on public opinion in Europe. I don't think that's what's going to happen, but, at the same time, as I indicated in my opening remarks, I think both we and the Germans are going to come into this meeting fully conscious of the fact that we have got to be careful not to let what has been an issue created in Poland by Poles and Soviets become an issue of major debate within the West, and I think we both approach it with that point in mind.

[14] For documentation on the Madrid review conference on implementation of the Helsinki Final Act, see Chapter 10, Part A.

Q. Have you heard from Congressmen and Senators? Is the administration getting any kind of feedback from these people even though they are not here now?

A. I haven't. That doesn't mean that others haven't. But with the Congress in recess I have not heard. I've had a couple of conversations with Congressmen, and I have seen a statement I think by Senator Moynihan, but that's all I've seen.

Q. You said that a repressed Poland doesn't contribute to the stability in Europe. But do you think that a more democratic Poland, a less Communist Poland, could contribute to stability in Europe?

A. I believe very strongly that a more democratic Poland can contribute to the stability in Europe, yes.

Q. Okay, thank you.

A. Thank you.

Document 207

Joint Statement Issued by President Reagan and West German Chancellor Schmidt, January 5, 1982[15]

Visit by Chancellor Schmidt of the Federal Republic of Germany

The President and the Chancellor on January 5, 1982 held extensive talks in which Secretary of State Haig and Foreign Minister Genscher participated. The Chancellor also met with Vice President Bush, Secretary Weinberger, and senior administration officials and with leaders of Congress.

The President and the Chancellor had a thorough exchange of views on the situation in Poland. They expressed grave concern about the imposition of martial law, which has resulted in the suppression of the fundamental rights of Polish citizens in violation of international agreements, including the Final Act of Helsinki, the United Nations Charter and the Universal Declaration on Human Rights.[16]

[15] Source: Office of the Press Secretary to the President; printed also in *Weekly Compilation of Presidential Documents*, January 11, 1982, pp. 6–7.

[16] For the text of the Helsinki Final Act, see Department of State *Bulletin*, September 1, 1975, pp. 323–350; for the text of the Universal Declaration on Human Rights, see *ibid.*, December 19, 1948, pp. 752–754.

The Chancellor informed the President about the final communiqué issued by the Foreign Ministers of the member countries of the European Communities on January 4.[17] The President welcomed this statement.

The President and the Chancellor agreed on their analysis of the Polish situation. They noted that contrary to the undertaking of the Polish leadership to reestablish liberty and the process of reform, repression and violation of basic human rights in Poland continues.

The President and the Chancellor call again on the Polish authorities to end the state of martial law, to release those arrested and to restore the dialogue with the Church and Solidarity.

The President and the Chancellor agreed that developments in Poland demonstrate once again the obvious inability of the Communist system to accept those changes necessary to meet the legitimate aspirations of their peoples. This endangers public confidence in cooperation between East and West and seriously affects international relations and stability.

They both noted the responsibility of the Soviet Union for developments in Poland and expressed concern about the serious pressure it is bringing to bear against Polish efforts for renewal. They insist Poland be allowed to resolve its problems without external interference.

The President and the Chancellor reiterated their position that any military intervention in Poland would have the gravest consequences for international relations and would fundamentally change the entire international situation.

The President explained the economic measures taken by the United States with regard to the Soviet Union. The Chancellor informed the President that the Federal Republic, together with its partners in the European Community, will undertake close and positive consultations in this regard with the United States and with other Western states in order to define what decisions will best serve their common objectives and avoid any step which could undermine their respective actions. They welcomed the agreement of the NATO Allies to hold a special Foreign Ministers' meeting in Brussels next week[18] for further discussion of these matters.

The Chancellor drew the President's attention to the resolution passed on December 18, 1981,[19] in which the Bundestag, in agreement with the Federal Government, decided to hold in abeyance official economic aid to Poland as long as the present regime continues its oppression of the Polish people. The President reiterated his previous statement that further assistance by the United States to the Government of Poland is not possible under present circumstances. The President and the Chancellor expressed their hope that the course of developments in Poland would permit their countries to review these decisions.

The President and the Chancellor expressed their solidarity with the Polish people and their readiness to continue humanitarian aid provided that it directly benefits the people. In this context, the President informed the Chancellor that American labor and other private groups are working together to organize a day of solidarity with the Polish people on January 30.

In view of the grave developments in Poland, which constitute a serious violation of the Helsinki Final Act, the President and the Chancellor agreed that the Madrid Conference on the implementation of the Helsinki Final Act should deal with the situation as soon as possible at the level of Foreign Ministers. They will take action as appropriate within the framework of the United Nations with a view to denouncing the violation of human rights as well as acts of violence. Other measures will be considered as the situation in Poland develops.

They welcomed the initiatives by the European Parliament and the U.S. Congress to establish March 21 as "Afghanistan Day" to express common hope and support for the people of Afghanistan, agreed that the Soviet occupation of Afghanistan must end, and demanded the withdrawal of Soviet troops from Afghanistan and respect for the right of the Afghan people to choose an independent and nonaligned government.

The President and the Chancellor underlined the significance of arms control as an indispensable element of their common security policy. They reaffirm their determination to continue their efforts for effective arms control. In this context the Chancellor expressed his deep appreciation of the President's speech of November 18, 1981,[20]

---

[17] For the text of this communiqué, see *New York Times*, January 5, 1982, p. A7.

[18] For documentation concerning this meeting, see Chapter 10, Part A.

[19] Regarding this resolution, see *New York Times*, December 19, 1981, p. 7.

[20] For the text of this speech, see *American Foreign Policy: Current Documents, 1981*, document 60.

and welcomed the initiatives for a comprehensive arms control policy it contains.

The President and the Chancellor also stressed the great importance of current economic issues. In this context, the Chancellor referred to the danger of a worldwide depression and ensuing far-reaching political hazards that may arise if the industrial countries fail to agree on a common strategy to combat unemployment. The Chancellor emphasized in particular the strategic significance of social and economic stability in the industrial countries of the West as an important element in the maintenance of a stable East–West balance.

The President and the Chancellor agreed that protectionism is to be rejected and stated their resolve to work for a maximum degree of freedom in international trade.

They also noted that their governments were following policies aimed at reducing significantly the level of interest rates through control of budget deficits, combatting inflation and overcoming the recession.

The two leaders emphasized the importance of close bilateral and multilateral consultations at all levels between the members of the Western Alliance.

The President and the Chancellor underlined the close and trusting relationship between the United States and the Federal Republic of Germany. They agreed on the need to maintain and deepen U.S.-German friendship by furthering and broadening mutual contacts and, in particular, a better understanding among the members of the younger generation.

To this effect, they noted with satisfaction that Secretary of State Haig and Foreign Minister Genscher have named coordinators in their respective departments for American-German relations. In the State Department the duties have been assigned to Lawrence S. Eagleburger, Assistant Secretary of State for European Affairs. In the Foreign Office the duties will be assumed by Minister of State, Dr. Hildegard Hamm-Bruecher.

Document 208

Transcript of an Interview With the Secretary of State (Haig) and the West German Foreign Minister (Genscher), March 8, 1982[21]

Visit by Foreign Minister Genscher to the United States

Q. (Interpretation) Mr. Secretary Haig, Republican Senator Stevens, of Alaska, has threatened to introduce a resolution in the Senate with the goal of effecting the withdrawal of American troops from Germany.[22] What measures are available to you in the Executive to prevent this resolution?

SECRETARY HAIG. I do not anticipate that this viewpoint represents a very strong attitude in the American Congress today. After all, the presence of American forces in Europe has served two fundamental purposes: first, the vital interests of the United States in the protection of its national security; and it is also, of course, the bedrock of the unity of the Western community of nations which has been the shield that has preserved it since the inception of NATO. And I do not contemplate any such proposals getting prominence in our policy.

Q. Mr. Genscher, in Washington there is more and more dissatisfaction because of the pipeline dealings with the Soviet Union because of German restraint on economic sanctions.[23] Some say East–West trade is more important to the Germans than the principle of unity in NATO. How can you deal with this dissatisfaction here in the United States?

MR. GENSCHER. I believe we must concentrate more on the public opinion of the

---

[21] Source: Department of State files. The interview by correspondents of German television took place beginning at 1:55 p.m. at the Department of State. Foreign Minister Genscher was in Washington, March 7–9, primarily to discuss preparations for the NATO summit in Bonn in June. A note on the source text indicates that Genscher's responses were in German and were interpreted into English for transcription.

[22] The proposal under reference was in fact introduced as an amendment to the Defense Appropriations Bill for 1983. For a discussion of the proposal, see *NATO Troop Withdrawals: Hearing Before the Senate Foreign Relations Committee, United States Senate, Ninety-seventh Congress, Second Session* (Washington, 1982).

[23] Regarding the Trans-Siberian natural gas pipeline, see Chapter 10, Part A.

United States, and that the government and the opposition know our positions well. I think this visit makes a further contribution to explain the objectives of German policy. Also, we have the common goal that the Versailles and Bonn summits[24] will be an expression of Western unity and solidarity.

Q. Mr. Haig, isn't it true that both of you two Ministers demonstrate the traditional unity, but that in reality you are deeply worried about certain neutralist and pacifistic tendencies of the Federal Republic of Germany? And don't you ask yourselves whether the Germans are still reliable partners?

SECRETARY HAIG. Well, I have seen some of these suggestions in the media and speculation among journalists, but I remain profoundly confident that the imperatives that underline the good relationships enjoyed today between Bonn and Washington, and those between the Atlantic community of nations at large, remain the overriding imperative for policies on both sides of the Atlantic, and I am very confident.

One could really draw some lessons from the recent Polish experience, where Western unity and consistency of policy has been remarkable for the very character of that unity.

Q. (Translation) If I may ask you again, Mr. Haig, of course, the official picture of the relations looks very positive, but when you read the American newspapers and you hear American Congressmen and Senators too, then you see that there is spreading a growing skepticism and distrust vis-à-vis the Germans.

SECRETARY HAIG. Again, I don't want to overemphasize it, but I think it does suggest that perhaps the time has come for a strengthening of the coordinating mechanisms between the United States and our partners in Europe, through improved consultation—perhaps even by a broadening of the political dimension of the alliance itself to be sure that these questions that have been raised are dealt with through effective two-way communication.

Q. (Interpretation) Mr. Genscher, would the image of America of many Germans be more positive if the Reagan administration would show greater willingness for a dialogue with the Russians?

MR. GENSCHER. (Interpretation) I think the speech in November by President Reagan[25] on the question of arms control has given some clear signals, and we also have acted in the common conviction that we do not wish to break off the CSCE process, but rather continue it; and this shows that Europeans and Americans know very well how valuable this process is for East–West relations. What is involved here, and both of us have stated this here, conscious of the great responsibility that Germany and the United States have for Western unity, that we must come to an even closer concertation [*sic*] of American and German policy, and in this context must pay even closer attention to the political dimensions of the alliance and to enlarge them. I think this would greatly help to present a clearer picture of our common objective. I would hope that the most recent opinion polls in the United States on the attitude of Europeans towards the alliance, towards the United States, towards our common security policy will show when they are published that the picture which has been painted by the Government of the Federal Republic of Germany on the attitude of the majority of the German population was absolutely correct.

Q. (Interpretation) Mr. Secretary, when will the American-Soviet negotiations on the limitation, on the reduction of strategic nuclear weapons start? And why does Washington hesitate to schedule for this year a summit meeting between Chairman Brezhnev and President Reagan?

SECRETARY HAIG. First, with respect to arms control negotiations, as you know, we have (inaudible) those negotiations in Geneva on the regional systems. We are now completing a year of very intense efforts of preparing our position on strategic talks, the so-called START talks. And I would feel that in a matter of weeks, not months, those positions will be completed. Then it merely remains to insure that the conditions are right for the launching of such talks.

It is important that your viewers recognize that we have not delayed on this, but have taken great care to be sure that we do not have a repetition of the SALT II experience, where an agreement was arrived at, but where that agreement was not supported by the American Congress; and that is even more disastrous to East–West relations and arms control progress than to

---

[24] For documentation regarding the Versailles Economic Summit, see Chapter 5, Part F; concerning the Bonn NATO summit, see Chapter 10, Part A.

[25] For the text of President Reagan's speech, November 18, 1981, see *American Foreign Policy: Current Documents, 1981*, document 60.

hastily rush into talks that are not well prepared.

With respect to the summit question, the President has made it very clear that he feels summitry must be well prepared, there must be an outcome visualized and achievable or it merely raises euphoric expectations which are dashed on the rocks of disappointment and the worsening of East–West relations when a summit is not well prepared.

At this time, the situation in Poland certainly does not lend itself to a successful summit outcome. It does not mean that we do not continue our communications with the Soviet leadership. I've met once this fall and in January with Gromyko,[26] and I have had continuing discussions with the Soviet Ambassador here in Washington, and they will continue in the days ahead.

Q. (Interpretation) Mr. Genscher, how do you feel about President Reagan's receiving the opposition leaders, Mr. Kohl and Mr. Strauss, but not former Chancellor Willy Brandt, Chairman of the Social Democratic Party, who holds a Nobel Prize, when he was in Washington recently?

Mr. Genscher. (Interpretation) I do not know why this meeting did not take place, but we welcome all contacts between people from all sectors who hold political responsibility. Incidentally, we handle it in Bonn the same time [*way*?], when opposition leaders come from the United States. I think it is important that one gets to know the full spectrum of the political opinions of another country.

Q. (Interpretation) Mr. Haig, President Reagan will travel to Europe in June.[27] My question to you is, why is he not going to visit a location which is of such great point to Americans and Germans alike? I'm referring to West Berlin.

Secretary Haig. I think it is too early to judge whether he will or will not go. I know Foreign Minister Genscher will raise this with President Reagan tomorrow. It's too early to say. If a decision was made not to go, it would be strictly in the context of available time, and should not be misread as to some lack of enthusiasm for the importance of such a visit. As you know, I was there recently myself.

Q. (Interpretation) So you would say there is still a good opportunity the President might come to Berlin?

Secretary Haig. I think it is still under consideration, and it will be viewed with increased intensity in the days ahead.

Q. (Interpretation) Herr Genscher, don't you have the impression that especially with American Congressmen and Senators, there is a certain lack of information on our foreign policy and its principles? And how do you think this information deficit can be removed in a convincing fashion?

Mr. Genscher. (Interpretation) Well, I am using this visit for meetings with a number of Americans outside the administration proper and also with representatives of the mass media, and I agree that more information must be offered; but all in all, I would say that during the meetings which I have had so far I have gained the conviction that during our forthcoming meetings in Bonn, we shall come to common positions, not only on alliance policies, but that, beyond that, it will become very clear that it is the consensus of all the countries of the alliance that we shall offer to the Soviet Union our willingness for cooperation, and that the Soviet Union must realize that it would be very much in its own interest to cooperate with us, and that for that reason the Soviet Union should refrain from everything which constitutes a burden to (inaudible).

Q. (Interpretation) Mr. Haig, the gas pipeline deal with Moscow is a most sensitive point in German-American relations. When do you believe the American Government, everybody in the American Government, will give up their resistance to this gas pipeline deal?

Secretary Haig. I doubt that they will give up their concerns about the deal. Our position on that question has been longstanding, and has not changed in a number of months. That notwithstanding, I think Americans understand that certain commitments have been made and contracts signed, and that today we are engaged in a very important question with respect to Poland.

I would hope—and I do not anticipate—that the pipeline will get engaged in those important discussions, which after all involve vital matters of future East–West relations.

Q. (Interpretation) Mr. Genscher, do you believe that the Federal Government

---

26 For the text of Secretary Haig's press conference following his January 26 meeting with Foreign Minister Gromyko, see document 252.

27 President Reagan visited Paris, London, Bonn, Berlin, and Rome, June 2–11, 1982.

will be able to sustain the pipeline deal if the Soviet Union should send its own troops into Poland?

MR. GENSCHER. (Interpretation) Our policy is trying to prevent such an outcome, and I think the Soviet Union will understand that such a step would change the world situation fundamentally. I would like to continue a policy which tries to stimulate interest and cooperation with the West, and not take such steps. We understand that the Federal Republic keeps its contracts, and is going to have to keep this one, too.

INTERVIEWER. Thank you, gentlemen.

Document 209

Remarks by the Secretary of State (Haig) and the West German Foreign Minister (Genscher), March 9, 1982[28]

Foreign Minister Genscher's Meeting With the President

SECRETARY HAIG. Good afternoon, ladies and gentlemen. I just want to take a few moments and emphasize that we've just completed a very successful and encouraging visit by our distinguished Foreign Minister of West Germany, Hans Dietrich Genscher, an old friend.

Our discussions here, starting Sunday evening carried through yesterday, and have just concluded with a detailed discussion with President Reagan. They included topics of East–West relations, the Polish situation, the measures preparatory to the upcoming summits, the economic summit in France and the NATO summit in Bonn this coming spring. They involve a number of bilateral issues—to include the details of the President's visit to Bonn in conjunction with the NATO summit which now will probably be expanded to include a visit to West Berlin. Details of this visit are to be worked out in the period ahead.

And in summary, I just want to say again before introducing our distinguished guest, that as always the discussions with our German colleagues confirm the convergence of views on the major issues of the day between Bonn and Washington. And now I'll turn it over to Minister Genscher.

FOREIGN MINISTER GENSCHER. During these 2 days, we had extensive talks with the President, with the Secretary of State, with the Secretary of Defense, and with a number of Senators. And all these talks have reaffirmed my view that the United States of America like the Federal Republic of Germany are aware of the vital importance this relationship has for the efficiency of the Western Alliance. And we are acting accordingly and correspondingly. When we discussed international issues, such a great measure of agreement was reflected that the question may be permitted, why occasionally people were trying to use a microscope to find questions in areas where we haven't reached yet a common position.

We are determined—firmly determined on the basis of our membership—common membership in this alliance, on the basis of our relations, to continue to work in friendship to continue to work with a common will to defend and uphold self determination and freedom.

Q. Does that mean you're both in agreement on everything?

SECRETARY HAIG. Almost anything you want to mention, Helen. (Laughter.)

Q. What about the pipeline? Mr. Secretary, what about the pipeline?

SECRETARY HAIG. I would say including the pipeline from the standpoint of our current policies. The American position on that pipeline is well-known and longstanding.

Q. You oppose the pipeline.

SECRETARY HAIG. We have always been in opposition to that pipeline starting with the discussions we had in Ottawa this past summer.[29] Our concerns continue with respect to that pipeline anyway.

SECRETARY HAIG. The Germans have been committed to that pipeline for a number of years. I think the original discussion started in the mid-70's.

Q. Well, then why do you say you have a convergence of views?

FOREIGN MINISTER GENSCHER. I think you should also be aware of the fact that it's

---

[28] Source: White House Press Release, March 9, 1982, Office of the Press Secretary to the President. The session began at the White House at 3:35 p.m.

[29] For documentation on the Ottawa Economic Summit, June 1981, see *American Foreign Policy: Current Documents, 1981*, Chapter 5, Part F.

in line with the common convictions and common views of all Western partners that contracts that have been concluded should also be honored.

SECRETARY HAIG. Thank you very much. I'll take one more question, that's all.

Q. Mr. Secretary, does that mean although you agree, you said, on current policy regarding the pipeline, what about any further sanctions that this country is contemplating? What is the German position on that?

SECRETARY HAIG. We've had a number of discussions over the last two days and they've been going on, incidentally, since the Polish crisis. As you know, we have moved very, very closely with our European partners on the subject of sanctions. We have a visit to Western Europe coming the end of this week from Under Secretary of State Buckley in which we will be looking at the subject of future credits to the East and, as has been the case in the past, I think our policies will tend to converge in this area as well. Thank you.

Q. Why is the President going to West Berlin? Why?

SECRETARY HAIG. This has to be the last question because it's the kind I think I can wrestle with, Helen. (Laughter.)

Q. Especially with Helen. (Laughter.)

SECRETARY HAIG. Now, there's a line, Helen. (Laughter.) Every American President, of course, makes every effort to visit West Berlin which constitutes a very special city in the context of free world determination to preserve our freedoms and this would be the first visit of President Reagan to West Germany. And I think it would be appropriate if at all possible and the schedule permits, and it looks like it will, that he visit West Berlin. Thank you and good bye to you as well, my friend. (Laughter.)

Document 210

Prepared Statement by the Ambassador to the Federal Republic of Germany (Burns) Before a Subcommittee of the House Foreign Affairs Committee, April 5, 1982[30]

U.S. Relations With West Germany

My message today is simple: While there are problems in our relations with the Federal Republic of Germany, the majority of Germans remains supportive of the United States and cognizant of the broad range of values and objectives we have in common.

Let me turn to some of our problems. Complaints on both sides of the Atlantic attest to an accumulation of tensions. Americans were disappointed in the Federal Republic's delay in deciding to boycott the Moscow Olympics after the Soviet invasion of Afghanistan. They frequently ask why Bonn seems reluctant to pay more to improve billets of American troops in Germany. They were disturbed by the initial reluctance of the Federal Republic's leaders to recognize publicly the Soviet role in the military takeover in Poland. They are puzzled by German criticisms of American policy with regard to El Salvador and Nicaragua. On their side, again to give some examples, Germans have complained in recent years about "zigzags" in American foreign policy and indicated that they wanted stronger U.S. leadership. Now many Germans worry about what they regard as bellicosity in Washington and overemphasis on military solutions.

Although economic problems have played a part in the friction between our two countries, it is largely the result of political and psychological forces. There is increasing anxiety among the German public, particularly among young people, about the world in which they live. The sources of this anxiety are legion. Many Germans feel that their country has become a pawn in the struggle for supremacy between two superpowers—the Soviet Union and the United States. Fears of a nuclear war fought on German soil are widespread. Environmental concerns, especially with regard to reliance on nuclear fuel, are pronounced.

---

[30] Source: *Current Policy*, No. 385, April 5, 1982, Bureau of Public Affairs, Department of State. Burns' statement was made at a briefing and was not printed by the subcommittee.

There is now some fear of a harsher economic environment and a sagging social safety net. There is also a feeling of alienation among young people, as well as among intellectuals at all ages, stemming from concerns about the role of technology and large impersonal organizations in their society. Many young people, furthermore, have come to believe that it is morally wrong to live in affluence when millions in the Third World are starving. Speaking more generally, many Germans nowadays feel that a coherent purpose in life has been eluding them.

Since the United States is frequently identified with things that trouble many Germans—notably superpower rivalry, rampant technology, and militarism—concern has arisen in the Federal Republic about America's international role, more particularly about our ability to manage East-West relations wisely. The Soviet Union has found it useful to exploit European fears of armaments. It has done this with skill and energy, especially in West Germany. Soviet propaganda pictures the United States as a restless, bellicose power lacking a true desire for peace and willing to risk the nuclear destruction of Europe. At the same time the Soviet Union presents itself as working tirelessly in behalf of international peace and order. The massive peace offensive mounted by the Soviets seeks to drive a wedge between us and our European allies—an exercise in which they have been to some degree successful.

I must say, however, that media concentration on "anti-Americanism" in West Germany strikes me as overdrawn and wide of the mark. The basic national interests of the United States and the Federal Republic have for many years been very similar and they are so recognized by a majority of the German people. In Germany we have a staunch ally. Nevertheless, German anxieties and the differences in perceptions that exist between us and the Federal Republic require careful attention on both sides of the Atlantic if we are to promote successfully our common interests.

Before addressing these issues, I wish to emphasize the need to get our economic houses in order. The element of friction between the United States and the Federal Republic is being worsened by economic difficulties in our two countries. Financial stringency largely accounts for Germany's disinclination to increase defense outlays at this time. Nevertheless, it even now appears that there will be some progress in German willingness to provide additional finance for NATO infrastructure.

Partly because of our own economic problems, we want Germany to bear a larger burden in supporting American forces in the Federal Republic and in providing aid to common allies like Turkey. But Germany right now is preoccupied with difficulties of its own—high interest rates, rising unemployment, and budget constraints—which, though less intense than our economic troubles, are quite disturbing to German people. The Bonn government believes with some justification that Germany has made a steady, substantial contribution to NATO defenses during the past decade when the United States was downgrading its defense priorities. Bonn feels it must now tighten its belt. We should encourage that effort and try to understand that a healthier German economy will enable the Federal Republic to bear in the future the larger defense burden which we regard as its rightful share.

Politically, we must try harder to understand the interests that motivate the Federal Republic. In our admiration for Germany's postwar recovery, its economic strength, and its increasing role in Europe, we sometimes fail to perceive the limitations that the Germans feel keenly—their status as a divided nation with millions of families having relatives or close friends in East Germany; their role as a European country with limited world responsibilities; their dependence on the good sense of the United States as a nuclear-protecting power but one whose dependability has been called into question by Vietnam, Watergate, and occasional contradictory statements of policy emanating from Washington. Moreover, the Germans are troubled by their geographic proximity to the Soviet Union and the hazards attaching to the lonely outpost of Berlin.

Because of factors such as these, the Federal Republic takes a different view toward détente than we do. To us detente was another approach to the old question of dealing with the Soviets—an approach that in the end has benefited us little. The Germans, on the other hand, feel that détente has resulted in reduced tensions in Europe and in a stabilized political situation in and around Berlin. In addition, the Germans have gained through détente closer contacts with their compatriots in the East, also improved trade relations and a better lot for the 17 million Germans who reside in the German Democratic Republic.

To be sure, as we all know, detente did not lead the Soviets to abandon their foreign adventurism or their military buildup.

Soviet aggression in Afghanistan and the military takeover in Poland have inevitably called into question the basis of détente and the future of *Ostpolitik*. Fortunately, the Reagan administration has taken major steps to correct our response to Soviet actions. In general, the Government of the Federal Republic approves our decision in this respect. It believes in firmness toward the Soviets. But it also believes that firmness must be coupled with continued dialogue to reduce tensions and to prevent jeopardizing the gains of *Ostpolitik*. It further believes, perhaps naively, that through a process of friendly communication we in the West can over time encourage respect by the Soviets for human rights as well as some restraint in their international behavior.

There are important differences in the geopolitical roles of the United States and the Federal Republic that influence the world outlook of each. Germany is essentially a regional power. The United States, on the other hand, has global interests and responsibilities. We need to make hard decisions on numerous questions in which the direct interests of the Federal Republic are quite limited. Many Germans and Americans seem not to appreciate that difference. At times this failure leads to German resentment of our attitude toward their country and to a feeling that we ignore German interests. On the other hand, not a few Americans expect generous economic contributions for our sponsored projects in Asia, the Middle East, Latin America, and other places from a country that is not yet pursuaded that it has a global responsibility.

It would be wise for the Germans to consider more carefully the complexities that the United States often faces in providing leadership for the alliance and in taking actions in other areas of the world. From an American viewpoint, the German Government has not been helpful on some issues where American interests are directly and heavily involved, as in the case of El Salvador. The American Government feels that Germany needs to do more, together with other allies, to show displeasure over the repression engineered by the Soviets in Poland. We have also been troubled about the Federal Republic's caution in involving itself in some problems outside NATO's boundaries, particularly in the Persian Gulf area. We feel that the Federal Republic, being heavily dependent on imports of Middle Eastern crude oil, should play a larger role in support of American policies in that area. Our government is also inclined to believe that the German leadership should assume a larger burden of political responsibility in explaining agreed alliance policies to its own public.

The United States and the Federal Republic can only achieve a better mutual understanding at the policy level through extensive and effective consultations. The approach to the arms control negotiations at Geneva exemplifies the value of good consultations with our NATO allies. From our frequent conversations with the Germans during the preparatory period we gained important insights that helped us plan for our discussions with the Soviets. I think it is important for the German public, and not only those involved in the peace movement, to recognize that their government has had and is having a real voice in the formulation of alliance policy on armaments control. Just as we have been doing in the armaments negotiations, so our two governments must strive for improved dialogue on other policy issues. To be a shade more specific, we should alert each other to emerging problems at an early stage and thus reduce the kind of misunderstanding that develops when one side thinks it is consulting and the other feels it is only being informed after the decisions have been taken. We certainly need to avoid situations where our efforts at genuine consultation are mistaken by the Germans as still another test of their loyalty.

Obviously, the administration must take a leading role in shaping our relations with the Federal Republic, but there is also much that the Congress could do. This is especially true in the area of improving understanding of basic policy perceptions and interests of our two countries. One way to do this is in the context of the newly created German-American group in the *Bundestag*. I urge your support of their effort. Get to know your German counterparts. Telephone them if necessary to get their views on issues under consideration here and convey to them your views about subjects of interest to the United States that are being discussed in Germany. I am assured by German parliamentarians that they are most eager to work closely with Members of our Congress.

One issue currently under discussion with the German Government is the administration's effort to restrain the flow of public credit to the Soviet Union. We are concerned that by extending credits on a liberal scale, European and some other governments have been strengthening the economic potential of the Soviet Union, and that they have thereby been helping indirectly to build up in some degree its military machine. The private market now recognizes the financial difficulties faced by the Soviet bloc and is, as a result, sharply curtailing its lending. The present American initiative is designed to parallel this reduction in private credits by seeking restraints on officially subsidized credits and export credit guarantees. The reduction of credits and credit guarantees will either cause a contraction in Soviet imports from the West or will require payment in hard currency for what the Soviets choose to purchase.

Our effort to restrict credit to the Soviet Union is perceived by some in Germany and elsewhere as "waging economic warfare." That is by no means the administration's intention. We merely seek, as far as the Soviets are concerned, to have international financial markets work without undue interference by governmental financial agencies. Of course, our objective is to reduce the provision of advantageous financing to the Soviets so as not to undermine our efforts to strengthen the common defense. I urge you to understand this administration effort and to help explain it to your German colleagues.

We must also try to stem the growing deficiency in understanding between our two countries that is reflected in a drifting away of young people from what had previously been a shared belief in our common moral and cultural heritage. Parents, teachers, journalists, and parliamentarians on both sides of the Atlantic have neglected their responsibilities in preparing the new generation of Americans and Europeans to take over the reins of power. The leaders in this rising "successor" generation in our two countries are often uninformed or, worse still, ill-informed about their respective peers. I sense, for example, in young Germans a lack of interest in the study of history—hence their lack of understanding of how the world got where it is. And I find in young Americans a lack of interest in the study of foreign languages and cultures. One of the more important objectives of the public policies of our two countries must, therefore, be an extension and deepening of the intellectual contact between the young people of our respective societies, so as to rekindle appreciation of each other's values and historic experiences and thus achieve a better understanding of our spiritual, economic, and political interdependence.

We already have a substantial and successful academic exchange program—the Fulbright program—which brings German teachers and university students to the United States and sends American counterparts to the Federal Republic. I am convinced that this program is a vital element in our long-term bilateral relationship. I suggest that we now devote additional attention to an exchange program involving young people at a formative age—that is, well before their prejudices have become ingrained.

I am always loath to suggest additions to the Federal budget and am again reluctant to do so here. But I am certain that a show of congressional intent and support—perhaps a redirection of some of the funds already available for our overseas information and cultural programs and a concerted appeal to the private sector for support of this program—will be a worthwhile investment for our country. Experience has shown that long-term exchanges of young people, such as those conducted by the American Field Service and Youth for Understanding, pay lifetime dividends in understanding and appreciation of the culture and moral values of the country and the people visited. I, therefore, urge you to give suitable support to German-American youth exchanges.

I am convinced this will prove to be a good investment, not only because the Federal Republic is a key country in Europe but also because it is a loyal, dependable ally whose basic interests and values are essentially supportive of our own. This fact was borne home once again in a poll released recently in which West Germans expressed high confidence in and appreciation for the United States. I believe that with greater sensitivity on our part and better understanding in Germany, our two countries can continue to work effectively together in furtherance of the moral, economic, and cultural values that constitute the essence of Western civilization.

Document 211

Joint Statement Issued by the Governments of the United States and the Federal Republic of Germany, April 15, 1982[31]

U.S.-West German Wartime Host Support Agreement

The Governments of the United States of America and the Federal Republic of Germany today concluded a bilateral agreement under which the German Government intends to make available certain personnel and assets in support of U.S. forces which would deploy to the Federal Republic of Germany in crisis or war.[32] The agreement was signed at the German Foreign office in Bonn by Hans-Dietrich Genscher, Foreign Minister of the Federal Republic of Germany, and by Dr. Arthur F. Burns, American Ambassador to the Federal Republic of Germany.

This Wartime Host Nation Support Agreement represents a visible demonstration of the agreed principle of division of labor within the alliance. The agreement is also a strong reaffirmation of the U.S. commitment to the defense of the Federal Republic of Germany and NATO Europe. Under the terms of the agreement, the United States intends to carry out the rapid reinforcement in crisis or war of its ground and air forces in the Federal Republic of Germany to more than twice their present strength. The agreement will result in an enhanced early deterrent force in Europe and thus strengthen effective forward defense of the alliance area.

For its part, the Federal Republic of Germany intends to train and equip some 93,000 Bundeswehr reservists who will provide support to U.S. forces in the areas of transportation, supply, airfield repair, logistics, and security of U.S. Army facilities. The German military reserve manpower required will be made available from the general reserve manpower pool, and will not detract from the current or proposed German reserve military structure, nor will it in any way diminish the combat effectiveness of the Bundeswehr.

Under the agreement, the Federal Republic of Germany also undertakes to make available additional civilian support in the form of transportation, material handling, facilities and other services.

The agreement is a significant step towards the implementation of the long-term defense program of the alliance. It will have the important benefit of reducing strategic airlift requirements on the United States for support forces, thereby making it possible for the United States to provide a higher percentage of combat troops in an emergency. For this reason, and because of the intensified use of in-country assets, the agreement will result in increased cost-effectiveness within the alliance context.

A U.S.-German joint committee has been established to implement the agreement, and detailed plans are being made to begin activating the necessary German reserve units in 1983 and to have the necessary German military and civilian support activities organized and the required training well underway by 1987.

The investment costs of the wartime host nation support program will be approximately 570 million U.S. dollars. These costs, and all operating expenses, will be shared equitably by the United States and the Federal Republic of Germany.

Document 212

Statement Issued by the Department of Commerce, October 5, 1982[33]

U.S. Denial Orders Against West German Firms

The Commerce Department today issued temporary denial orders prohibiting export of all U.S. oil and gas equipment, services and related technology to the West German firms AEG-Kanis Turbinenfabrik GmbH, of Essen and Nuremberg, and Mannesmann Anlagenbau AG, of Dusseldorf.

The Mannesmann Anlagenbau order also applies to two subsidiaries of that com-

[31] Source: Department of State files; also printed in Department of State *Bulletin*, June 1982, p. 61. The statement was made available to news correspondents by Department of State Acting Spokesman Alan Romberg.

[32] The text of the agreement has not yet been published. It has been designated TIAS 10376.

[33] Source: Department of Commerce files.

pany which are engaged in oil and gas exploration, production, transmission, or refinement: Essener Hochdruck-Rohrleitungabau GmbH, of Essen, and Kocks Pipeline Planning GmbH, of Dusseldorf. Essener manufactures high pressure pipeline commodities and Kocks provides pipeline architectural services.

AEG-Kanis is under contract to produce gas turbines containing U.S. parts and technology for the Trans-Siberian pipeline. Mannesmann Anlagenbau is one of the prime contractors for the northern segment of the pipeline and a party to the three-party gas turbine supply contract that includes AEG-Kanis and the Soviet foreign trade organization, Machinoimport.

AEG-Kanis and Mannesmann Anlagenbau are under investigation by the Commerce Department because of the export of two gas turbines manufactured by AEG-Kanis to the Soviet Union contrary to the Export Administration Act of 1979.[34] Investigation of Mannesmann Anlagenbau's contractual relationship with AEG-Kanis and Machinoimport has led to its inclusion under the temporary denial order. Investigation of these shipments continues.

The terms of today's temporary denial orders are identical in scope to the denial orders in effect against John Brown Engineering Ltd., Nuovo Pignone S.P.A., Dresser (France), and Creusot-Loire S.A., which are also under investigation for shipping pipeline turbines contrary to the Act.

The temporary denial orders issued against AEG-Kanis and Mannesmann Anlagenbau and the other denial orders prohibit the export to them and the two named subsidiaries of Mannesmann Anlagenbau of U.S. origin equipment and technology and services for, or relating to, oil and gas exploration, production, transmission or refinement. Mannesmann Anlagenbau, Creusot-Loire and Nuovo Pignone are prime contractors for the Trans-Siberian natural gas pipeline. AEG-Kanis, John Brown Engineering and Dresser (France) are subcontractors.

In announcing the latest Commerce Department action to enforce the President's policy on oil and gas controls, Secretary Malcolm Baldrige emphasized that the temporary denial orders issued today against these German firms, like the earlier actions, were taken to enforce the department's export regulations. He stressed that "this action is not punitive, but was taken with the purpose of facilitating investigations into suspected violations."

On June 22, President Reagan, under authority granted by the Export Administration Act of 1979, extended the export controls on oil and gas equipment to the Soviet Union[35] imposed the previous December. Through adoption of new regulations, the government prohibited all oil and gas equipment (including turbines and compressors), services and technology from being exported or reexported to the Soviet Union by U.S. companies, their subsidiaries or foreign licensees. The President said on that date: "The objective of the United States in imposing the sanctions has been and continues to be to advance reconciliation in Poland." Baldrige noted that, "There has been little movement in the Polish situation since last winter. The Polish Government and the Soviet Union are still far from meeting the three conditions set forth by NATO last January."

Document 213

Joint Statement Issued by President Reagan and West German Chancellor Kohl, November 15, 1982[36]

Visit of Chancellor Kohl to the United States

During the visit of the Chancellor of the Federal Republic of Germany, Helmut Kohl, he and President Reagan held detailed talks in Washington on current political and economic issues on November 15, 1982. The Chancellor is also meeting with Secretary of State Shultz, Secretary of Defense Weinberger, Secretary of the Treasury Regan, high-ranking administration officials, and leading members of the Senate.[37]

---

[34] P.L. 96–72, September 29, 1979; 93 UST 503.

[35] For the extension of sanctions on June 18 (not June 22), see document 160. June 22 was the date of National Security Decision Directive Number 41 announcing the decision.

[36] Source: White House Press Release, November 15, 1982, Office of the Press Secretary to the President; printed also in *Weekly Compilation of Presidential Documents*, November 22, 1982, pp. 1480–1485. Chancellor Kohl visited the United States from November 14 to 16, 1982.

[37] No records of Chancellor Kohl's discussions with any other U.S. officials have been found.

The discussions attested to the depth and the breadth of German-American friendship. The United States and the Federal Republic of Germany are partners as well as friends, sharing common ideals, human and democratic values. In today's uncertain world, this commitment has become more important than ever. Our shared values form the unshakeable foundation for our joint efforts to maintain the freedom and prosperity of the Western world.

The discussions were based on a determination to work together as closely as possible to meet the challenges of the closing decades of the twentieth century.

These challenges are as critical as those which faced the great statesmen who founded our partnership more than 3 decades ago. During the past 30 years the Atlantic partnership has been successful in guaranteeing to our peoples more freedom, security, and prosperity than at any time in history. The President and the Chancellor reaffirmed during their discussions their common view on the central role played by the Atlantic Alliance in the foreign policies of their respective governments.

A major reason for success of the Atlantic Alliance has been the close relationship which has developed between the United States and the Federal Republic of Germany. German-American ties are deeper than simple calculations of national interest.

After World War II and after the destruction caused by it in Germany, these ties originated from the generous humanitarian aid and the political support which the United States granted to the German people and their young democracy. German-American relations are based on a close affection among our two peoples and are supported by intimate personal and familial ties between Americans and Germans. Ours is a relationship based on mutual support and open discussion between equal partners.

During the discussions it was agreed that high level consultations between the United States and the Federal Republic of Germany will be continued during a visit to Bonn by Secretary of State Shultz in early December.[38]

An example of the close ties between our two nations are the more than 50 million Americans of German descent. German Americans have provided major contributions to every aspect of American life and form one of the foundations of American society. The President and the Chancellor anticipated with pleasure the joint celebration in 1983 of the Tricentennial of German immigration to the United States. President Reagan announced today the formation of a Presidential commission to help prepare American commemoration of this important event. Chancellor Kohl described plans for celebrations in the Federal Republic of Germany. They stressed that the Tricentennial should be a joint celebration among the peoples of their two nations and reaffirmed the intention of President Reagan and President Carstens to meet in the United States in October, 1983, to highlight the American celebration.

The wider the understanding of the commonality of the issues facing the United States and the Federal Republic of Germany, the stronger our partnership will become. For this reason President Reagan and Chancellor Kohl were pleased to reaffirm their support for the initiatives to broaden U.S.-German contacts and to set up a multilateral youth exchange among Western industrialized democracies. The purpose is to pass on to the younger generations in our nations the sense of partnership which the older generation feels so deeply.

The President and the Chancellor reaffirmed the Alliance's overall concept for successfully safeguarding peace in Europe as embodied in the declaration made by the heads of state and government of the Atlantic Alliance in Bonn on June 10, 1982.[39] As stressed in that declaration, they agreed that in accordance with current NATO defense plans, and within the context of NATO strategy and its triad of forces, they will continue to strengthen NATO's defense posture, with special regard to conventional forces.

The Alliance has demonstrated that it serves the cause of peace and freedom. Even in difficult situations, it has been able to do so because its members have acted in a spirit of solidarity. The Alliance does not threaten anyone. Nor does it aspire to superiority, but in the interests of peace it cannot accept inferiority either. Its aim is, as before, to prevent any war and safeguard peace and freedom. None of the weapons of the Alliance will ever be used except in response to attack.

---

[38] Concerning this visit, see document 215.

[39] For the text of this declaration, see document 180.

The Chancellor paid tribute to the crucial contribution that the United States renders to the joint security of the Alliance through the indispensable presence of American troops in Europe. The President and the Chancellor agreed that a unilateral reduction of American troops would have a destabilizing effect and, at the same time, would undermine efforts for negotiated force reductions.

The President expressed his great appreciation for the significant and uninterrupted German contribution to the common defense. In particular, he paid tribute to the German-American agreement of April 15, 1982 on Wartime Host Nation Support,[40] which entails considerable additional expenditure by the Federal Republic of Germany and the United States of America for common defense.

The President and the Chancellor stressed the need for close, comprehensive, and timely consultations to strengthen the Alliance's cohesion and its capacity to act. They attached particular importance to German-American cooperation. They hoped that informal meetings of the foreign ministers of the Alliance would be continued.

The President welcomed the resolve of the Government of the Federal Republic of Germany to strengthen European unification. The President and the Chancellor paid tribute to the important role of the European Community and all its member states for economic and political stability in Europe and the world. The development of a united Europe will strengthen cooperation between Europe and the United States and, hence, also reinforce the Alliance.

The President and the Chancellor paid tribute to the close agreement and cooperation between the Federal Republic of Germany and the Three Powers in all matters relating to Berlin and Germany as a whole. They concurred in the view that the preservation of trouble-free conditions in and around Berlin was an essential element of East–West relations and of the international situation as a whole.

The President reaffirmed American support for the political aim of the Federal Republic of Germany to work for a state of peace in Europe in which the German nation will regain its unity through free self-determination.

A major subject discussed during the meetings was relations with the Soviet Union. The values and goals of the Soviet Union do not correspond to our own. The USSR restricts freedom on its own territory and in countries under its influence, and has shown that it is ready to use force or the threat of force to achieve its foreign policy aims. Security of Western societies requires constant attention to the military threat posed by the USSR. The Federal Republic of Germany and the United States of America gear their policies in East–West relations to the concept of renunciation of force, human rights, and the right of nations to self-determination.

The President and the Chancellor called upon the Soviet Union to comply with internationally recognized rules of conduct. This required respect for the principles enshrined in the Charter of the United Nations and in the Helsinki Final Act[41] as well as a worldwide policy of moderation and restraint.

In this spirit, the President and the Chancellor underlined their desire to improve relations with the Soviet Union. They are ready to conduct relations with the new leadership in Moscow with the aim of extending areas of cooperation to their mutual benefit if Soviet conduct makes that possible. It is especially important at present for the West to approach the Soviet Union with a clear, steadfast and coherent attitude which combines the defense of its own interests with the readiness to pursue constructive relations, dialogue, and cooperation with the leadership of the Soviet Union.

In this regard, the President and the Chancellor greeted with satisfaction the recent agreement on measures leading to a broader consensus on East–West economic relations.[42] They attached the greatest importance to a common approach to this issue. Close consultation and cooperation on East–West economic issues is as vital to Western interests as is the traditional cooperation on political and security questions.

It is the purpose of our common efforts that trade with the Soviet Union and Eastern Europe should be conducted on the

[40] See Document 211.

[41] For the text of the Helsinki Final Act on Security and Cooperation in Europe, see Department of State *Bulletin*, September 1, 1975, pp. 323–350.

[42] The allied agreement on economic strategy toward the Eastern bloc was part of an accord that called for loosening the pipeline sanctions against the Soviet Union. President Reagan announced the agreement in a radio address on November 13. For text, see document 165.

basis of a balance of mutual advantages. While noting the important part which our economic relations with the Warsaw Pact countries can play in the development of a stable East–West relationship, the President and the Chancellor agreed that those relations should be approached in a prudent and diversified manner, consistent with our political and security interests.

The Chancellor expressed his appreciation for the lifting of the embargo on oil and gas technology and equipment, which he considered as evidence of successful efforts on the part of all concerned for improved coordination of Western policy in the economic field.

The President and the Chancellor agreed that developments in Poland, which continued to cause great concern, had an adverse effect on efforts to promote security and cooperation in Europe. They drew attention once more to the Soviet Union's responsibility for the events in Poland. They called upon the Polish leadership to lift martial law in Poland, to release all detainees, to reverse the ban on the trade union Solidarity and, through serious dialogue with the Church and appointed workers' representatives, to seek national consensus which is the only way to lead Poland out of its present crisis, free from any external interference. They hoped that the release of Lech Walesa will promote these objectives. The President and the Chancellor welcomed the numerous initiatives for humanitarian aid for the Polish people. They agreed that this aid should be stepped up wherever possible.

The President and the Chancellor agreed on the importance of the CSCE process initiated by the Helsinki Final Act and advocated that it be continued. It is a long-term process which has been gravely affected by events in Poland. It can prove successful only if the participating countries observe the principles and provisions of the Final Act in their entirety. They expressed support for the new proposals, responsive to events in Poland and the USSR, put forward by the West in the resumed Madrid session, as reasonable and essential elements of a balanced outcome.

The President and the Chancellor agreed that the CSCE review conference, which was resumed in Madrid on November 9, 1982,[43] should agree on a substantive and balanced final document which leads to progress in the important humanitarian field of East–West relations and contains a precise mandate for a Conference on Disarmament in Europe (CDE), envisaging militarily significant confidence and security building measures covering the whole of Europe, from the Atlantic to the Urals.

The President and the Chancellor noted that arms control and disarmament as well as defense and deterrence were integral parts of NATO'S security policy. They agreed that significant progress towards reduction of the levels of nuclear and conventional forces through balanced and verifiable agreements would be an important contribution to the reduction of international tensions. The incessant unilateral increase in Soviet armaments in recent years has threatened the security of the Alliance and international stability and made even more urgent the need to establish a balance of forces between East and West. The goal of the United States and the Federal Republic of Germany remains to achieve a stable balance of both nuclear and conventional forces at the lowest possible level.

The President and the Chancellor recalled the comprehensive program of arms control proposals put forward by the United States on the basis of close consultation and adopted by the entire Alliance at the Bonn summit on June 10, 1982.[44] They stressed their common belief that this program provides the best hope for true reductions in arsenals of both intermediate and intercontinental strategic weapons. They rejected the proposals to freeze existing levels of nuclear weapons, or for one-sided reductions by the West, as inadequate for substantive arms control and as harmful to the security of the Atlantic Alliance. They noted also that the Soviet Union had in recent years refused to reciprocate the unilateral restraint in this field by the United States. They expressed the strong judgment that true reductions in nuclear armaments would be possible only when the Soviet Union is convinced of the determination of the West to maintain its defenses at the level necessary to meet the threat posed by massive increases in Soviet nuclear forces.

In this connection they attached particular importance to negotiations on reductions of strategic arms and of intermediate range nuclear forces now underway be-

[43] For documentation on the Review Conference, see Chapter 10, Part A.

[44] For the text of the arms control statement issued on June 10 at the NATO summit, see document 181.

tween the United States and the Soviet Union in Geneva. President Reagan reaffirmed his determination to do his utmost to achieve true reductions in nuclear armaments through balanced and verifiable agreements. The President and the Chancellor pointed out that negotiations in Geneva are serious and substantial. At the same time they expressed concern at the refusal of the Soviet Union to take into account legitimate Western security concerns.

In conformity with their policy for actively safeguarding peace through firmness and negotiation, the President and the Chancellor reaffirmed their commitment to both parts of the NATO dual-track decision of December 12, 1979,[45] consisting of a program of INF modernization and an offer to the Soviet Union of arms control negotiations on INF. An important aspect of Western security policy remains the common determination to deploy modernized longer-range INF missiles in Europe beginning at the end of 1983 if negotiations on this subject now underway in Geneva do not result in a concrete agreement making deployment unnecessary. The President and the Chancellor noted that the decision to deploy the systems in Europe was based on a unanimous finding by members of the Atlantic Alliance that increases in Soviet weapons, in particular introduction of SS–20 missiles, had endangered the security of Western Europe and thus of the entire Alliance. They stressed that the complete elimination of Soviet and United States land-based, longer-range INF missiles, as proposed by the United States, would be an equitable and fair result and would be a substantial contribution to serious arms control. They called upon the Soviet Union to negotiate seriously toward this end. The Chancellor restated his full confidence in the American negotiating effort in Geneva and welcomed the close and continuous process of consultations within the Alliance.

President Reagan described the ideas behind his Berlin initiative of June 10, 1982, for an agreement between the United States and the Soviet Union on measures to help avoid the danger that accident or miscalculation could lead to a nuclear exchange between East and West.[46] He stated that the United States was preparing proposals for nuclear confidence building measures which would be presented by American representatives at the Geneva negotiations. The Chancellor and the President expressed their hope that the Soviet Union would join with the United States in progressing rapidly to an agreement on such measures. They also remain committed to halting the spread of nuclear weapons through the pursuit of vigorous nonproliferation policies.

The President and the Chancellor underscored their undiminished interest in substantial reduction in conventional forces in central Europe. They recalled the new draft treaty which the Western participants had presented at the Vienna negotiations on mutual and balanced force reductions.[47] This proposal provides an excellent foundation for a balanced agreement on reduction of conventional forces in Europe. The President and the Chancellor called upon Warsaw Pact participants to react positively.

They stated that agreement on a comprehensive and fully verifiable ban on chemical weapons in the Geneva committee on Disarmament remained a prime objective of their policies.

They also attached great importance to efforts in the United Nations to secure transparency by promoting military openness, verification, and wider availability of information on defense spending.

The President and the Chancellor were in complete agreement on the requirement for special attention to Alliance needs on the Southern Flank. They emphasized in this connection their resolve to support the Turkish Government in its efforts to lead Turkey back to democracy.

The President and the Chancellor expressed confidence that our free societies would overcome the current difficult economic situation. They attached paramount importance to restoring the conditions for sustained growth through higher investments, in order to reduce unemployment and to maintain price stability.

The economic policies of industrial nations must be closely coordinated. Each country must bear in mind the effects that its political and economic measures will have on other countries. These factors will also have an important effect on the eco-

---

[45] Concerning this decision, see *American Foreign Policy: Basic Documents, 1977–1980*, pp. 494–496.

[46] Reference is to President Reagan's initiative in his Berlin speech on June 11, not June 10. For text, see document 184.

[47] Concerning the draft treaty proposal presented at the MBFR talks on July 8, see Chapter 10, Part B.

nomic summit to be held in Williamsburg at the invitation of the United States. Both sides reaffirmed the importance of conducting the discussions at this summit on the basis of openness, trust, and informality.

The President and the Chancellor discussed the dangers posed by rising protectionism to world trade and the economic well being of nations. They reaffirmed their commitment to the multilateral trading system, looking forward to a successful GATT Ministerial meeting in Geneva this month.

The President and the Chancellor agreed that it is imperative to respect and promote the independence of the countries of the Third World and that genuine nonalignment is an important element of stability and world peace. The President and the Chancellor reaffirmed their readiness to continue to cooperate with Third World countries on the basis of equal partnership.

The continuing Soviet occupation of Afghanistan is a strain on international relations. The President and the Chancellor deplored the fact that the Soviet Union continued to defy international opinion and ignored United Nations resolutions calling for the withdrawal of foreign troops from Afghanistan, as well as the right to self determination for Afghanistan and restoration of its nonaligned status. Afghanistan remains an acid test of Soviet readiness to respect the independence, autonomy, and genuine nonalignment of Third World countries and to exercise restraint in its international behavior.

The Chancellor welcomed President Reagan's proposal of September 1, 1982,[48] as a realistic attempt to promote the peace process in the Middle East. They agreed that negotiations between Israel and its neighbors in the framework of U.N. Resolutions 242 and 338 offer the best opportunity for peaceful resolution of disputes in that area. The United States and the Federal Republic of Germany, together with its partners in European Political Cooperation, will, as before, seek to ensure that the American and European efforts for a comprehensive, just, and lasting peace in the Middle East, on the basis of existing achievements, are complementary to each other. They called for early withdrawal of all foreign forces from Lebanon. They continued to urge that the sovereignty and unity of Lebanon be restored and expressed their support for the reconstruction of Lebanon.

[48] Concerning President Reagan's September 1 proposal, see document 318.

Document 214

Transcript of a White House Press Briefing, November 15, 1982[49]

Meeting Between Chancellor Kohl and President Reagan

MR. ALLIN. If we could get started. I think most of you have a copy of the joint statement.[50] Is that right? Well, there are some, I think, in the bins for those of you that don't.

The briefing on the visit between the President and the Chancellor will be conducted on a background basis, attributable to senior administration officials. For your information, but not for mention in your stories, the briefers are . . . .

SENIOR ADMINISTRATION OFFICIAL. Thank you, Mort. What I thought I'd do, especially since, I guess, either you don't yet have the joint statement of you've just gotten it, I'd walk you through it quickly—I promise quickly—and then take questions.

But let me begin by saying that the President and the Chancellor met together for a little over two hours, that the discussions were quite informal. Indeed, having myself been an observer of a lot of such discussions, there was an informality and intimacy which I think—Sorry. Can you hear?

Q. Yes.

SENIOR ADMINISTRATION OFFICIAL. All right. An informality and intimacy which was quite unusual. One of the reasons for that, incidentally, was the superb translation that was going on simultaneously so there wasn't the usual gap in such circumstances.

What I'd like to do now is just go quickly through the joint statement and I won't go through it all or we'll be here all afternoon.

Q. Hear, hear.

SENIOR ADMINISTRATION OFFICIAL. Hear, hear, yes. The second paragraph picks up

[49] Source: Office of the Press Secretary to the President. The briefing was on background and was conducted by senior administration officials. It began in the Briefing Room at 2 p.m.

[50] *Supra.*

themes that both the President and the Chancellor have made for years in their political pronouncements, that is to say, the importance of the common ideals, human and democratic values that the two societies share.

Then, skipping on down a couple of paragraphs, one of the common themes of the discussion which they returned to in several different ways was the view that the central role of the Atlantic Alliance is crucial to the foreign policies of two governments.

The last paragraph is a description of two different interventions by the Chancellor describing his own boyhood experiences with the Americans in Germany which I found, in fact, quite moving and which you've heard him say on other occasions.

Turning the page, the second paragraph is a description of the Tricentennial Commission which the President announced a few minutes ago.

And the next paragraph indicates the initiative to broaden U.S.-German contacts and set up a multilateral youth exchange program.

The next paragraph is a description of the conviction in the Bonn summit communiqué, repeated here, of the importance of strengthening NATO conventional forces.

Moving right along, I would call your particular attention to the last sentence of the first paragraph on page 3, which, in some sense, symbolizes the policies of both the Federal Republic, the United States and the alliance. None of the weapons of the alliance will ever be used except in response to attack.

The next paragraph is a plea against unilateral American troop withdrawal, as you can see, to which both the Chancellor and the President attached themselves.

Near the end of the page is a paragraph on Berlin, carrying the idea that stability in Berlin was an essential element of East–West relations.

Page 4, you'll notice several paragraphs here on relations between the West and the Soviet Union. In fact, almost all of the lunch, which went on for nearly an hour and a half, was taken up with a discussion of East–West relations and the essence of it here, I think, is in the sentence in the paragraph that begins, "In this spirit", the second sentence, "They are ready to conduct relations with the new leadership in Moscow, with the aim of extending areas of cooperation to their mutual benefit if Soviet conduct makes that possible."

The next three paragraphs have to do with the recently announced consensus on East–West economic relations. You can follow those on through.

The next paragraph is a paragraph on [page] five on Poland. I don't think you'll find anything surprising there. There's no disagreement whatever. In fact, I can't think of an issue on which the two gentlemen disagreed.

The next two paragraphs are on the CSCE meeting in Madrid.

Then—I'm now on [page] 6—I suggest you read carefully the second paragraph which describes our arms control objectives and the President's arms control proposals as endorsed by the Bonn summit of last summer.

And then beginning at the last of that page, there's a paragraph on INF, the two-track decision, indicating that the decision in the first instance was based on a finding by all the members of the alliance, that such a decision was necessary in view of the increases in Soviet weapons, in particular the introduction of the SS–20, and calling for the complete elimination of these weapons systems in Europe, the zero option and the Chancellor stating his confidence in the American negotiating effort in Geneva and welcoming the consultations.

The next paragraph indicates that we are preparing proposals flowing from the President's Berlin speech[51] on nuclear confidence building measures which we will be presenting in Geneva to the Soviets.

The next paragraph is an MBFR paragraph.

Page 8. There are two paragraphs on the international economic situation and its implications for national economies, indicating the confidence of the two gentlemen that our free societies would overcome the current economic difficulties, a reference to the importance of the GATT ministerial meeting, a paragraph beginning at the end on Afghanistan and saying that this is an acid test of—how the Soviets conduct themselves there is an acid test of Soviet readiness to respect Third World genuine nonalignment and a test of whether they're

[51] For the text of the President's Berlin speech, June 11, 1982, see document 184.

willing to exercise restraint in international behavior.

And finally, a paragraph on the Middle East, in which the Chancellor welcomes the President's September 1 proposal.

I'll take questions.

Q. Any discussion of the Chancellor's joy with lifting of the pipeline sanctions? Was that discussed at all?

Senior Administration Official. Well, I wouldn't—the Chancellor said to the President he thought this was a—as the language in the communiqué indicates, thought that this was appropriate, given the agreement which had been reached on East–West economic issues. That's described in the communiqué. There wasn't an extended discussion on this, though.

Q. Any discussion of the French reaction to it?

Senior Administration Official. They—Let me confine myself to saying that the essence of the discussion was an agreement that the West would profit from much greater coordination on economic relations with the East, that the announcement that the President made last Saturday was an important contribution to this, which the Chancellor fully supported, and that we would go on to implement that agreement.

Q. Was there any discussion of West Germany's trade relationship with the Soviet Union?

Senior Administration Official. No, not that I recall.

Q. Any concern expressed by the President about opening up too much for the Soviet Union?

Senior Administration Official. Well, they discussed at lunch the economic prospects of the Soviet Union, but not really in that context. I guess I could inferentially say that both of them behind what they were saying were expressing the now familiar idea that East–West economic relations should fit into an overall political strategy with respect to the Soviet Union.

Q. Was this joint statement prepared before the Chancellor's visit?

Senior Administration Official. No.

Q. Well, why doesn't it mention seeing Secretary Shultz and others?

Q. Right. I mean, obviously—

Senior Administration Official. Because—Well, if you'll look at the tense, which is drafted carefully, he will be—he is also meeting with, in English, means tomorrow morning. But, no, it wasn't prepared before they came.

Q. —the Soviet Union paragraph, sir, did the gentlemen discuss the likelihood or otherwise of a summit meeting between the American and Soviet—

Senior Administration Official. Didn't come up.

Q. Did not come up?

Senior Administration Official. Did not come up.

Q. Not advanced by Mr. Kohl as a—

Senior Administration Official. Did not come up.

Q. In your previous answer, you implied some linkage in what Kohl said between the lifting of the pipeline sanctions[52] and the accord on East–West agreement. Is it your understanding that there is a connection?

Senior Administration Official. Well, I just refer you to the President's radio broadcast.[53]

Q. Well, that's why I'm asking because—

Senior Administration Official. Let me just say that the purpose of this briefing is not that subject. The purpose of this briefing is to discuss the meeting that just took place. And that particular issue is being addressed other places. And I would prefer not to address it here.

I would be delighted to discuss with you what just occurred in the Oval Office. But I really do not want to go beyond that.

Q. But just to clarify, to clarify what you just answered.

Senior Administration Official. As I say, I just ask that you look at what the communiqué says and what the President said on Saturday, which is our definitive position.

Sir?

Q. Was there any area of less than total agreement?

Senior Administration Official. I do not know. They did not look at one another

[52] Concerning the Trans-Siberian natural gas pipeline sanctions, see Chapter 10, Part A.

[53] The reference here is to President Reagan's radio broadcast on Saturday, November 13, in which he announced the lifting of sanctions on oil and gas equipment to the Soviet Union. For text, see document 165.

every 10 seconds and say—Did you agree? Did you agree? But what was striking to me was the shared assumptions with respect to the Soviets, the need for a strong defense, but, also, the requirement that we do everything possible to reach arms control agreements with them, the hope for a better relationship with the Soviet Union if their conduct globally makes that possible.

All I am saying is that I was not struck by—as one sometimes is in meetings—any particular issues of dispute.

Yes?

Q. Did they mention any of the concerns of possible renewed or intensified Soviet appeal to the peace movement in Germany, and what effects that might have?

SENIOR ADMINISTRATION OFFICIAL. The Chancellor described the activities of Soviet propaganda in the Federal Republic at some length. In fact, in terms which are quite familiar to you all, because he has, also, described them publicly.

Yes?

Q. In this page 4—the paragraph about relations with Moscow, which, presumably, means the new leadership, are you talking about—assuming there are areas of cooperation, that has been a theme for several days—what areas of cooperation do you want to extend? What areas did they talk about in terms of improved relations with the Soviets?

SENIOR ADMINISTRATION OFFICIAL. One does not have to be, particularly, a genius to go down—there are really two categories. You can think of the arms control negotiations where the President has a set of proposals, which, obviously, we would think it was a step forward if the Soviets were more responsive in the future than they have been in the past. There are a number of regional issues where the same thing is true—Afghanistan, Southeast Asia, and what have you.

But I do not want to mislead you. That particular issue was not discussed at any length. They did agree that we should be alert for opportunities to improve relations if Soviet behavior allows.

Q. What did the Chancellor commit himself to, or comment upon, regarding his defense spending? Did he tell the President that he was going to have to cut his defense spending because of economic situations?

SENIOR ADMINISTRATION OFFICIAL. No; he did not. The discussion of defense spending was quite general, and really referred not so much to their budget or our budget, but the necessity, over the long-term, to address the adverse trends in the balance.

Q. Did they compare notes on Andropov—what they knew about him?

SENIOR ADMINISTRATION OFFICIAL. A bit. Not a great deal. It was not so personalized. They were talking about—it was more of a philosophical discussion about various past trends in Soviet succession—what happened in the past, what we could expect in the future in a, kind of, structural sense rather than a personal sense.

Yes?

Q. Page 8, paragraph 3—about the special attention to the southern flank of NATO and supporting the new Turkish Government?

SENIOR ADMINISTRATION OFFICIAL. Yes.

Q. Could you tell me whether they discussed the new bases in Turkey?

SENIOR ADMINISTRATION OFFICIAL. They did not.

Q. Did the President express his hope that the German aid to Turkey, which at the moment seems to be put in abeyance by the Parliament, would go forward in the foreseeable future?

SENIOR ADMINISTRATION OFFICIAL. It really was not put like that. The idea was a more general idea that both sides would do everything they could to assist the Turkish Government to return Turkey to democracy.

Yes?

Q. When you said that there was a general discussion about defense spending, was there any specific discussion about Germany's commitment to NATO?

SENIOR ADMINISTRATION OFFICIAL. The Chancellor began like that. When you say—"Germany's commitment to NATO"—and this, in fact, is described in the paper; the Chancellor was very concerned to assure the President that Germany was not drifting away, that Germany was solidly within the NATO framework, that it had been so in the past, that it would remain so in the future, only in that sense.

But, again, it is a theme that the Chancellor has mentioned since he has come to Washington on several occasions.

Yes?

Q. With respect to the Soviet trade situation—was there any specific mention made of credit, and of the technology problem?

SENIOR ADMINISTRATION OFFICIAL. No; they did not get into that detail.

Q. How about Poland?

SENIOR ADMINISTRATION OFFICIAL. About Poland, there was a—

Q. Question?

SENIOR ADMINISTRATION OFFICIAL. I am sorry. The question was about Poland.

I think it is basically described in the communiqué—that both of them hope that the release of Lech Walesa is going to prove to be a step toward national reconciliation. And you will notice that the three conditions which the alliance adopted nearly a year ago, now are, also, mentioned and continue to be a benchmark for our joint approach and that of NATO to the evolution of events in Poland.

THE PRESS. Thank you.

Document 215

Toast by the Secretary of State (Shultz), Bonn, December 7, 1982[54]

Visit by Secretary Shultz to Bonn

Mr. Minister, my friend, my host, my colleague in the world of foreign affairs.

I might say that I am senior to you in that you have just been reappointed Foreign Minister, but I am very junior to you in so many respects that the opportunity to be here at the start of my visit to Europe and talk with you and the Chancellor and President Carstens, not only about our relationships together as two countries, but also about our alliance, is of great importance to me. But I would like to first say how grateful I am to you and Mrs. Genscher and distinguished quests here for joining us and in extending this wonderful warmth and hospitality that is so clear here this evening and has been clear to me throughout the day as I have had the privilege of talks with members of your government. That warmth and hospitality is very important to us.

I might say also that the discussions that we have had have been very productive, full of content, as your very gracious toast suggests. We have covered an awful lot of ground in a comprehensive way and in a probing way. I suppose that is just what is appropriate for two countries that have as many things that pull us together as our countries do. There are a million or perhaps a little more—Americans on your soil. For the most part they are military people and their families. We think they are here on a mission of peace. We think they are here in the interests of the United States and in your interests, our shared interests. And that is the way we look at it and that is the faith that we will keep.

I have heard that on the order of 25 percent of the residents of the United States, the citizens of the United States, in one way or another can trace their roots to Germany. Now I don't know about a figure like that and I hesitate to use a number of that kind in the presence of my teacher and the great Arthur Burns, because Arthur is a stickler for numbers and whenever you use a number in Arthur's presence he will come around later and say to me, "George, where did you get that number?" But I have the perfect answer on this occasion. I'll say: "Arthur, you gave it to me."

But I might say it is a measure of the respect and friendship that we have, and that President Reagan has, that we are able to persuade and able to send you such a distinguished person as Arthur Burns and Helen Burns. I feel very strongly about this personally because I have had the privilege of working with and for Arthur for a great many years. And I know there is no person in the United States who stands taller and is more respected, he is more than an ambassador here. He is a very distinguished American and a very distinguished citizen of the world. So when I have a number from Arthur I know that I am in very safe hands.

I said that our discussions have been comprehensive and productive, as is suggested by the wide range of topics that were brought up in your own remarks here this evening, Mr. Minister. And I don't want to try to review them here in any detail, but it is quite clear that they have to do with our

---

[54] Source: Department of State Press Release 372, December 9, 1982; also printed in Department of State *Bulletin*, February 1983, p. 14. Secretary Shultz was in Bonn, December 7–8, on the first leg of a trip that took him to Brussels, December 8–11; The Hague, December 11; Rome, December 11–14; Paris, December 14–15; Madrid, December 15–16; and London, December 16–18.

alliance, where you and I are going as Ministers to the NATO Ministerial meeting. I think it is very well for us all to keep in our minds that this alliance has been and remains today one of the greatest alliances in history. It is an alliance for peace. There has been no war in Europe while this alliance has been in being although there have been tensions. There have been incidents or whatever you may want to call them all over the world, much bloodshed all over the world; but I think, in very considerable part due to the alliance, that has not been true here. So it is something that we prize and we work on and we develop together. We have, as we all recognize, the dual track decision[55] which you and the Chancellor affirmed very positively to me today as the most recent expression of the things that we share together and recognize as important.

Outside this sphere of the alliance and the concerns that go with it, of course, we have our economic relationships to think about. And it was, I think, significant to notice in your remarks that you brought forward both the importance of an economic strategy in our East–West relationships which we are together determined to work out to our mutual benefit, but also what we share in the importance of the trading community around the world.

We had a meeting in the GATT here recently,[56] and how it should be evaluated I suppoose depends on your point of view. There is [a] gap on rating things going around these days. I was asked by a reporter as we were winding up our South American trip with the President recently, on a scale of one to ten, how would you rate the trip? Of course, I immediately said "eleven." But nevertheless it is important to recognize that with all of the difficulties we face in our economies and in the world economy, there were positive assertions of the importance of open trade, and at least the beginning of a sensitivity to the emergence of that great miscellany now called "services," but which I predict will sooner or later be called such words as "banking" and "insurance" and "engineering," and so on, the real parts of this word. There is a recognition of this new and emerging and very important aspect of trade and the necessity for dealing with it. So that is a positive element.

At any rate, the point is that as we worked on this matter of the greatest difficulty I know that we found that the representatives of your country and mine found much in common, perhaps most of all found a philosophic base in common which made it possible for us to work fruitfully together.

Finally, I might say and I could practically pick up and read and welcome your own comments about the truly significant base of our relationship and that has to do with the values that we share. The human values, the democratic values, that sustain us and sustain our alliance and make us, as we look perhaps at other parts of the world, recognize what a good deal we really have in having a situation of freedom and a sort of progress and a sense of humanity that characterizes your world here and mine in the United States.

So, again I am most grateful to you for this warm and hospitable greeting and even more for what it stands for—the strength of our relationship, the content of it, the ability to talk and discuss, share views on important issues. So these matters are of tremendous significance to me and benefit to me and my job, even more of great significance to my countrymen and to President Reagan, who has asked me to express to this gathering, as I did to Chancellor Kohl, his very best wishes.

So in that spirit I would like to ask you all to join me in a toast to my host and hostess, Minister and Mrs. Genscher, and to the continued friendship and well-being of our countries and their relationship to each other.

E. France

Document 216

Joint Communiqué Issued by the Secretary of Defense (Weinberger) and the French Minister of Defense (Hernu), January 7, 1982[1]

Franco-American Defense Cooperation

Minister of Defense Charles Hernu of France and Secretary of Defense Caspar

---

55 Concerning the dual-track decision of December 1979, see *American Foreign Policy: Basic Documents, 1977–1980*, pp. 494–496.

56 Concerning the GATT meeting, November 24–29, see Chapter 5, Part B.

1 Source: *Public Statements of Secretary of Defense*

Weinberger of the United States met on 7 January in the Pentagon, Washington, D.C. The Ministers discussed security issues of mutual concern with particular attention to the grave situation in Poland.[2] The Ministers affirmed both governments' strong stand in condemning the imposition of martial law in Poland and reviewed the concrete actions both have taken to demonstrate the seriousness of their concerns. Both noted the responsibility of the Soviet Union for developments in Poland and expressed concern about the serious pressure the Soviets are continuing to apply against Polish efforts for reform. They agreed that Poland must be allowed to resolve its problems without such external interference, and without the use of force and intimidation. In light of the Soviet role in the suppression of human rights in Poland contrary to the provisions of the Final Act of the Helsinki Conference,[3] Secretary Weinberger noted the direct actions the United States has taken against the Soviets in an effort to bring home to them the costs of continuing repression in Poland and Minister Hernu recalled the French Government's total disapproval of the events in Poland and its intention to study appropriate measures supporting the European Community's decision to assure that U.S. actions not be undermined. Minister Hernu added that the French Government shall continue its humanitarian aid to the Polish people.

The transfer to the Soviet Union of advanced technology with eventual military application was also discussed. Both France and the United States believe that an unchecked flow of such technology would afford the Soviets a windfall advantage in their programs for expanding their military forces and would be a major contributing factor in the rapid improvement in the sophistication and capability of Soviet forces relative to those of the West. To this end issues such as improving controls over computers and microelectronics, key elements in Soviet military improvements, were discussed. The Ministers agreed on the need for both France and the United States to remain in close communication with regard to this important problem.

The Ministers also discussed a number of armaments cooperation measures. Symbolic of this cooperation both Ministers noted that re-engining of U.S. Air Force KC–135 aircraft with a jointly-developed engine is fully funded for 1982. Note was taken of United States plans to field a jointly developed French/German surface-to-air missile system designated ROLAND with the Rapid Deployment Force. Other areas of existing and potential cooperative ventures were also discussed. For his part, Secretary Weinberger expressed willingness to work for removal of the restriction on specialty metals voted by the Congress.

The Ministers agreed that the protection of the freedom and independence of both the United States and France require the maintanance of strong deterrent forces, both nuclear and conventional, and solidárity among the democracies of the West.

Weinberger, 1982. Hernu visited Washington on January 7 for talks with Secretary of Defense Weinberger and senior officials of the Department of State. Omitted portions deal with the gas pipeline from the Soviet Union to Western Europe, Poland, U.S. grain sales to the Soviet Union, and European steel and agricultural exports to the United States.

[2] For documentation on the U.S. response to the repression of civil liberties in Poland, see *American Foreign Policy: Current Documents, 1981*, Chapter 10, Part M.

[3] For the text of the Helsinki Final Act, signed August 1, 1975, see Department of State *Bulletin*, September 1, 1975, pp. 323–350.

Document 217

Transcript of the Department of State Daily Press Briefing January 25, 1982 (Extract)[4]

Soviet-French Gas Supply Agreement

. . . .

Q. Have you said anything about this French-Soviet Union deal on gas?[5]

A. I don't have any report other than that which has come from the press as yet. Assuming that the report is true, as an administration official accompanying the

[4] Source: Office of Press Relations, Department of State. Alan Romberg, Department of State Acting Spokesman, conducted the briefing which began at 12:37 p.m.

[5] On January 23 France and the Soviet Union signed a 25-year agreement under which the Soviet Union would supply France with 8 billion cubic meters of natural gas annually. In return the Soviet Union received French loans to cover 85 percent of the cost of French-made components for the pipeline which would carry the gas to Western Europe.

Secretary or on the Secretary's plane said, "We were disappointed by this development." But, beyond that, I don't have any comment.

Q. The French didn't tell the United States they were going to do this?

A. I have nothing to indicate other than what I've just given you.

Q. Alan, what were you saying a moment ago on possible new U.S. sanctions? Is the United States considering additional sanctions of its own or we're not, we're just waiting to see what our allies do?

A. I think it's been made clear in the past that we have left open the door to taking further sanctions as we deem appropriate. I don't want to go beyond that at this point.

. . . .

Document 218

Statements by President Reagan and French President Mitterrand. March 12, 1982[6]

"Our Exchange . . . Was . . . Frank and Productive"

THE PRESIDENT. This has been a very unusual friend-to-friend meeting and one for which I'm very grateful. President Mitterrand and I have had a very productive day. In the Oval Office and during our working lunch, we covered a very broad range of subjects which naturally included our preparations for two major summit meetings in June.

President Mitterrand will host this year's economic summit in Versailles,[7] and we are, along with the other participants, committed to a conference which will help the industrial democracies deal more effectively with today's economic challenges. With that in mind, I look forward with special pleasure to my visit to France, America's oldest ally.

We also touched on the Atlantic Alliance summit and the need to demonstrate allied unity and resolve in response to Soviet expansionist pressures. I will attend that summit in Bonn[8] with the greatest of interest and commitment.

As I indicated a moment ago, our talks were comprehensive. Since President Mitterrand has just returned from Israel,[9] I was particularly interested in his assessment of the peace process in the Middle East.

Regarding Central America, I believe that President Mitterrand now has a better understanding of United States policy objectives in that troubled region. Our discussion on this subject was particularly candid and thorough. President Mitterrand shares my concern that the failure to promote the evolution of democratic government in this region would have the most serious consequences. The principles and goals that we share suggest that we will be able to work together on this problem in the months ahead.

Our exchange of views on the economic concerns of our two countries was equally frank and productive. President Mitterrand made a forceful and thorough presentation of his government's views on outstanding trade and financial issues. While it would be impossible to resolve our economic differences in one day, I think we've made tangible progress toward better communications on these important issues.

And now let me just repeat my personal thanks to President Mitterrand for coming to Washington. *Merci beaucoup.*

PRESIDENT MITTERRAND. Ladies and gentlemen, the first thing that I would like to say is to thank President Reagan for the welcome extended here in Washington to the President of the French Republic. The welcome extended to us was as is in the very nature of things, of course, both friendly, open, and frank. We were able to talk about a number of problems. Some of them had been prepared, of course, by the continuous exchanges which exist among our min-

[6] Source: White House Press Release, March 12, 1982, Office of the Press Secretary to the President; also printed in *Weekly Compilation of Presidential Documents,* March 15, 1982, pp. 293–295. The two Presidents spoke at the South Portico of the White House beginning at 1:43 p.m., immediately before President Mitterrand's departure for France.

[7] For documentation on the June 4–7 Versailles Economic Summit, see Chapter 5, Part F.

[8] For documentation on the June 9–11 NATO summit, see Chapter 10, Part B.

[9] Mitterrand visited Israel, March 3–4.

isters, our embassies, and representatives of all kinds.

But direct talks such as these, after I had recently had opportunities of meeting a number of European political leaders and following my recent visit to Israel and in the light of the events that take place each day in Europe, in Africa, in Latin America—because of all these reasons, it was natural that our talks today were brought to bear on a number of very topical problems, and indeed such talks are in themselves very fruitful.

And indeed this certainly fully justified making this trip. Now, the prime reason for my visit to the United States was to prepare, in more specific terms, the so-called "summit" of the industrialized nations which will be meeting in Versailles, in France at the beginning of June. And the conference will be an opportunity of considering the economic, monetary, and financial problems that our countries have to face. And that the purpose [of] the exercise being that we should harmonize our goals so as to be able to lend each other mutual assistance and not hindrance. And it is clear that in that we see very much eye to eye.

Then we talked of the other summit meeting that will take place a few days afterwards in Bonn which will be the summit meeting of the Atlantic Alliance. And so, naturally, that led us to discuss East-West problems and in particular relationship with the Soviet Union; and the need to demonstrate our force so as to be able to further the possibility of negotiations; and so as to be able to work towards peace while asserting our rights and the rights of the peoples of the world and in particular of Europe.

And as President Reagan has just said, we also talked about Central America. And I repeated what I have often stated in France and in Europe that our first duty is to fight against poverty and the exploitation of human beings and the domination on the part of bloody dictatorships. And as it just has been said, the search for the—we must work in order to find the way of furthering, and this is not always an easy path to discover, but the way of furthering the cause of democratic government. And there, there is something that we have in common and that leads to a meeting of the minds between us.

And I feel that we should do everything that can enable the democratic powers of the West to achieve a better understanding and to be able to give more assistance to the peoples that are rebelling against their fate and that can lead to peace, civilian peace, and more freedom, is a good thing. And, as I said when I was receiving Chancellor Schmidt,[10] that I appreciated the economic proposals made in the context of the Caribbean plan[11] which would also apply to Central America. It is clear that what is needed is more aid and consistent aid. And I think that what is being suggested is a step in the right direction. The path to be followed will clearly be a long one, but everything that is done that can show us where that path lies and can enlighten us in that respect can but be a good thing.

And as far as the Middle East is concerned, I was in the area recently. And only last week, I indicated what my feelings were on the subject.[12] And it was, therefore, only natural that, in talking with the President of the United States, that we should, in fact, also discuss those very serious questions. And we found that the assertion of the rights of Israel and the rights of all peoples of the region should make it possible to define, with patience and tenacity, the policies that will lead to peace. Now, our two countries are not the ones to pass judgment on such policies, but they are policies which should be of interest and concern to the countries directly involved in the area.

Now, lastly, on bilateral matters, well there, we were talking among friends. And there, of course, that is a long story that goes back many years. But we were able to discuss these matters frankly as friends and allies whose calling it should be, in the world, to express their views clearly, so as to be able to bring them closer together when they are not the same. And in order to be able to assert them with greater force when ones positions do converge, so as to be able to give the right kind of orientation to the peoples of the world who are waiting with anxiety for the outcome. Now, as to the hospitality that has been extended to me, I would like to say that it is [*has*] given me, again, the opportunity of feeling the real depth of the ties between our two countries. And I certainly intend, on the next occasion, which will be in my own country, to continue along the very same lines. In such talks, we have been able to discuss matters.

---

[10] Mitterrand met with Schmidt during the latter's visit to France on February 25.

[11] For documentation relating to the Caribbean Basin Initiative, see Chapter 15, Part C.

[12] Apparent reference to Mitterrand's March 4 speech to the Israeli Knesset in which he called for recognition of the right of both Israelis and Palestinians to a national homeland.

And we must continue to do so, to talk about these issues with method. In order to be able to indicate, clearly, the areas on which we can move forward together. And in order to be able to serve, to the best of our ability, the cause of world peace. So my last words will be to say thank you. And I turn, particularly, to the President of the United States in order to extend to him, directly, my heartfelt thanks.

Document 219

Remarks by the Secretary of State (Haig) and the French Foreign Minister (Cheysson), March 12, 1982[13]

The State of U.S.-French Relations

SECRETARY HAIG. Good afternoon, ladies and gentlemen. I just want to say a few brief remarks following the very unusual and unprecedented visit of President Mitterrand and his discussions this morning with President Reagan.[14] This wasn't an unusual visit—it was one we had talked about and was in preparation for some weeks now. I want to emphasize that it was a very personal kind of a meeting to permit a broad exchange of views among friends and Western leaders. It provided an invaluable opportunity for us to prepare for the upcoming summit in Europe this spring—the economic summit in Versailles[15]—and the Atlantic Alliance summit in Bonn.[16] And it also provided us an invaluable opportunity for the two leaders to discuss a full array of bilateral, global and regional issues of mutual concern for both of our governments and both of our nations. I was very, very pleased with the outcome of these discussions and I hope my French colleague was equally pleased. We were especially grateful for the kind of exchange the two leaders had on the situation in this hemisphere. They were able, I think, to clearly approach a convergence of views on the significance and the best ways of dealing with this situation and especially in its socio-economic aspects. Now, we also had an opportunity to hear firsthand about the very successful visit of President Mitterrand to Israel[17] and to exchange views on the peace process which was very helpful. Now both Presidents spoke at length this morning at the White House but I suspected that if we had walked out of here without saying a word to you [you] would have read something into that but I think the two Presidents spoke for the full scope and character and progress achieved today. I would like to invite my counterpart and my colleague and friend, Claude Cheysson, to say a word or two so again you don't misread the character of our departure.

FOREIGN MINISTER CHEYSSON. I shouldn't think I have forgotten my English completely. Well, after the Secretary of State, I would like to say that this is the tone of the relations as should be between France and the United States. It's been the tone of our relations and Al can confirm it since I came to office, we have seen one another very often—no protocol—when there is a problem I call him on the phone or he calls me. We exchange letters. But this should not be limited to the foreign secretaries. France and the United States are friends; everyone says so and has said so for a very long time; therefore, they should be able to meet like this—at very short notice or as this time after a careful preparation but forgetting about protocol. Yes, it is unusual that the French President should cross the Atlantic to have lunch with his American counterpart and why not? Why shouldn't we do so? We have things to say to one another. The best way is to exchange views directly. I'm not going to tell Americans that they can decide on relations between friends and I'm very pleased as it's concerned today.

SECRETARY HAIG. We have time for just a couple of questions.

Q. Mr. Cheysson, could you explain where the two countries have had a convergence of views on the situation in Central America?

FOREIGN MINISTER CHEYSSON. There is remarkably a convergence of views between France and the United States on the most fundamental issues. I remember the first time I came here that was 3 weeks, I think,

[13] Source: Department of State files. Haig and Cheysson spoke in the C Street Lobby of the Department of State. Cheysson accompanied President Mitterrand on his March 12 visit to the United States.

[14] See the March 12 statements of Presidents Reagan and Mitterrand, *supra*.

[15] For documentation on the June 4–7 Versailles Economic Summit, see Chapter 5, Part F.

[16] For documentation on the June 9–11 NATO summit, see Chapter 10, Part B.

[17] Mitterrand visited Israel, March 3–4.

after we had come into the government; it was June 1981.[18] And already then I stressed our agreement on the most fundamental issues—defense. Defense because we defend the same values and we have the same ideals about the organization of defense. Market economy because this is the only type of economy that can work in the free world—in a world where the human being has his rights—approach of some of the most difficult problems in the world. In the Middle East, we believe that every people, every state has a right to exist, to live in peace, and we may have different tactical approaches but we have the same fundamental reactions. Since then when on December 13, General Jaruzelski imposed the constraints which hinder on the Polish people, we had, I think I can say, the exact same reaction. We denounced what was happening out there in the same terms. So on all fundamental issues there is agreement. There may be, in some parts of the world, a different assessment because geographically we are not placed at the same place, because we haven't got the same power, in many cases we don't have exactly the same interest and it's all the more important that we should compare our assessment of the situation.

Q. Mr. Secretary, what sort of convergence or disagreement of views is there with France regarding arms sales to Nicaragua?[19]

SECRETARY HAIG. Well, I think we discussed this at some length. We make no secret of the fact that it concerns us. We had a good exchange of views on that today and I think both sides left reassured with respect to the nature of it and the future situation as well.

Q. Are you any less concerned about it as a result of conversations with the Minister?

SECRETARY HAIG. Well, if you mean by that: Do we welcome it? We didn't at the time; we don't today but we had an exchange of views that was very positive and constructive with respect to that and the future situation. Thank you very much.

Q. —where this convergence of views were on the subject—

SECRETARY HAIG. Well, no, he didn't but I think if you listened to President Mitterrand today, he talked with great support for the socio-economic approach and we're pulling together. But there was real progress.

Q. How about the López Portillo thing?[20] Did you get into that?

SECRETARY HAIG. It was discussed.

Q. Are you any closer to a decision on what to do about it?

SECRETARY HAIG. Well, as I told you we're exploring it in depth but we're exploring a number of other alternatives as well and I'll continue this discussion in New York this weekend with Castenada[21]—carry them forward and we'll have something to say after that.

Q. Mr. Secretary, did you discuss Lebanon with the French Foreign Minister?

SECRETARY HAIG. Yes.

Document 220

Statements by President Reagan and French President Mitterrand, Paris, June 3, 1982[22]

"Our Common Goals"

THE PRESIDENT. Mr. President, Madame Mitterrand, Prime Minister and Madame Mauroy, Ministers and honored guests and dear friends, Nancy and I are very pleased to be with you tonight in this lovely home of Ambassador and Mrs. Galbraith, our gracious hosts.

I hope you all realize that we know, of course, France has great appreciation for fine wines and that's why we decided to treat you to some California wine tonight. (Laughter.)

---

[18] Regarding Cheysson's visit to the United States, June 4–7, 1981, see *American Foreign Policy: Current Documents, 1981*, document 188.

[19] Reference is to the French announcement in January that it would sell "nonoffensive weapons" to Nicaragua.

[20] Apparent reference to the proposal of Mexican President Jóse López Portillo that his nation mediate between the United States and Mexico. For documentation, see Chapter 15, Part C.

[21] Jorge Castenada, Foreign Minister of Mexico.

[22] Source: White House Press Release, June 3, 1982, Office of the Press Secretary to the President; also printed in *Weekly Compilation of Presidential Documents*, June 7, 1982, pp. 744–747. President Reagan visited France, June 2–7, during a four-nation European tour which included the economic summit at Versailles, June 4–7, and the NATO heads of government meeting at Bonn, June 9–11. The Presidents began speaking at 10:22 p.m. Paris time.

I speak not just for Nancy and myself but for so many of our countrymen when I express the joy that we Americans feel in returning to France and seeing again her special jewel—"Paree". Mr. President, I am grateful to have the opportunity to continue our dialogue and to meet with Madame Mitterrand, members of your government, and so many of your fine citizens.

I've enjoyed getting to know you this past year and have benefited from your wise counsel during our several discussions. This will be our second economic summit together. You may be sure I'll work with you to help make it a success. I come to Europe and to this summit with a spirit of confidence.

Our administration has embarked upon a program to bring inflationary government spending under control, restore personal incentives to revive economic growth and to rebuild our defenses to ensure peace through strength. This has meant a fundamental change in policies and understandably the transition has not been without difficulties.

However, I'm pleased to report that these policies are beginning to bear fruit. Inflation is down, interest rates, I'm very happy to say here, are falling and both personal savings and spending are improving and we believe that economic recovery is imminent.

We also are moving forward to restore America's defensive strength after a decade of neglect. Our reason for both actions are simple: a strong America and a vital unified alliance are indispensable to keeping the peace now and in the future just as they have been in the past.

At the same time, we've invited the Soviet Union to meet with us to negotiate for the first time in history substantial, verifiable reductions in the weapons of mass destruction, and this we are committed to do.

You and your country have also been working to set a new course. While the policies you've chosen to deal with economic problems are not the same as ours, we recognize they're directed at a common goal: a peaceful and a more prosperous world.

We understand that other nations may pursue different roads toward our common goals, but we can still come together and work together for a greater good. A challenge of our democracies is to forge a unity of purpose and mission without sacrificing the basic right of self-determination. At Versailles, I believe we can do this. I believe we will.

Yes, we in the West have big problems and we must not pretend we can solve them overnight. But we can solve them. It is we, not the foes of freedom, who enjoy the blessings of constitutional government, rule of law, political and economic liberties, and the right to worship God. It is we who trust our own people rather than fear them.

These values lie at the heart of human freedom and social progress. We need only the spirit, wisdom and will to make them work. Mr. President, just as our countries have preserved our democratic institution, so have we maintained the worlds oldest alliance.

My true friends, who may disagree from time to time, we know that we can count on each other when it really matters. I think there's no more fitting way to underscore this relationship than to recall that there are more than 60,000 young Americans, soldiers, sailors, and Marines who rest beneath the soil of France.

As the anniversary of D-Day[23] approaches, let us pay homage to all the brave men and women, French and American, who gave their lives so that we and future generations could live in freedom. In their memory let us remain vigilant to the challenges we face standing tall and firm together.

If you would allow me, there was a young American. His name was Martin Treptow who left his job in a small town barbershop in 1917 to come to France with the same "Rainbow Division" of World War I. Here on the Western front he was killed trying to carry a message between battalions under heavy artillery fire.

We're told that on his body was found a diary. And on the flyleaf under the heading, "My Pledge," he had written that we must win this war. And he wrote, "Therefore I will work. I will save. I will sacrifice. I will endure. I will fight cheerfully and do my utmost as if the issue of the whole struggle depended upon me alone."

The challenges we face today do not require the same sacrifices that Martin Treptow and so many thousands of others were called upon to make. But they do require our best effort, our willingness to believe in each other and to believe that

[23] The June 6, 1944, invasion of Nazi-occupied France by British, U.S., Canadian, and Free French armies.

together, with God's help, we can and will resolve the problems confronting us.

I pledge to you my best effort. Let us continue working together for the values and principles that permit little people to dream great dreams, to grow tall, to live in peace, and one day to leave behind a better life for their children.

St. Exupéry wrote that a rock pile ceases to be a rock pile the moment a single man contemplates it bearing within him the image of the cathedral. Mr. President, let us raise our glasses to all the cathedrals yet to be built. With our friendship, courage, and determination, they will be built.

Vive la France et vive l'Amérique, des amis ce soir, demain et toujours. Would you like to translate that for the Americans. (Laughter). (Applause). All right. Thank you.

(Toasts are exchanged).

President Mitterrand.[24] Mr. President, Madame, I would like to say welcome, welcome to our country. And our country is a country which enjoys receiving a visit from friends. And we're also proud that you should be here and that you should be here on the occasion of your first trip to France and, indeed, your first trip to Europe.

So during this visit we will keep you here with us for three days and the Prime Minister and myself, we will then have the privilege of seeing you again in Bonn.

Now, the French who are here with me, here today, during those days when you will be here in France, we will try to insure that this visit, which I know is a visit which is dedicated to work and activity but also be a visit for—of pleasure, a pleasure that one finds among friends.

We have had several occasions already to meet and to talk together and we will move forward towards—(inaudible)—each other. And we have been able to talk of the matters which are important for our countries and, indeed, for the whole world. And I have always appreciated, Mr. President, your wise counsel, the very marked attention that you have devoted to what has been said around you and your open mindedness. And it is clear that when the fate of mankind is at stake and also, well, mankind to some extent for which we are responsible, you and I, it is on those occasions that your attention is particularly dedicated.

It is not a matter of chance that we should in fact be the members of the oldest alliance in the world. Think of the time that has elapsed. Generations have gone by—the events that have taken place—the contradictions, perhaps, in our approaches to the things of the world, and yet despite all of these differences, when the time and need came we were there, both of us, in order to defend the cause of liberty, the liberty for the individual citizen within each country and the liberty for all the citizens in the whole world, and the liberty, in fact, of friends.

It is not a matter of pure chance nor a matter of simply a combination of various interests which led to the presence of French soldiers by the side of American soldiers when it was a question of fighting for the independence and liberty of your country. Nor was it a matter of chance out of interest merely when many years later American soldiers fought side by side with French soldiers for the independence and the liberty of France.

It is because perhaps tonight really realizing it during those two centuries many people reacted and reflected in the same way as the almost synonymous hairdresser that you were mentioning earlier who later became a soldier in fact felt that on their shoulders rested the weight of the whole world.

It was simply because they felt that they were responsible and this man alone realized in his innermost conscience and awareness that in fact what he decided in his intimate knowledge of himself and his—and what was right in his eyes, that in fact that that would govern the way the rest of the world would think likewise.

And where else really does one learn responsibility? Surely it is only in the political democracies where in fact one entrusts to no one else the decisions that have to be taken by each and every individual. And who can really be fully responsible more than the person who realizes and fully appreciates that it is the force of the mind that is decisive and that it can always win the day over the forces—over the mechanical forces, however powerful they may be—even the forces of economics.

One can say that the world can be built if the world thinks right and if one wants it. And we have an excellent opportunity of proving this in the next three days—without too much ambition—but all the same we need a lot of ambition in the positions that arise.

Now the least we can do, of course, is to discuss economics. And if the seven coun-

[24] As interpreted. [Footnote in the source text.]

tries which will be meeting with the European Economic Community are to attain the strength that they need in order to defend the ideas which they consider to be right, then it is important not to divorce the economic powers from the other resources that there are. It is important that we should be able to guarantee peace which, after all is based on agreement among ourselves, but in order to be able to do that, it is essential that we should not be, in fact, fighting among ourselves.

I, as you are yourself, I am confident that we can, in fact, control and dominate the crisis that we are living. The methods that we may employ within our countries may indeed be somewhat different. But the aims are the same, and our methods can and must in fact converge in the form of common actions that we can engage in together.

Yes; I am confident that we will win the battle of peace, although, sometimes the methods that we would employ within our countries may be different. But we will always agree on the essential goals. And so it is that, for over a year now, we have indeed moved forward together, hand in hand, in full agreement about the goals that we were striving to achieve. Now, by the presence of force and power, we should be able to view with equanimity and indeed serenity the threats that may be before us. But at the same time, we would only use force in order to ensure the protection and the appeasement of the peace which is so necessary.

So it is that force must be there in order to first, start the necessary negotiations, and that indeed is what you have just done, saying what you have said just before the opening of the very important talks concerning disarmament, talks that are to be held with the very great power that—with you and with others, such as ourselves—is responsible for the state of the world.

And I hope that we will be able to extend our efforts too, further, in order to help those millions of human beings who are no longer really the Third World, but a sort of world which is in the process of moving towards development, a world which needs us just as we need them in order that our century should have a future.

Well, my dear Ron, perhaps the remarks that you were making yourself earlier have taken me somewhat far afield from the tone that should be the tone of this evening that is continuing, because it has not yet reached its end. And it is a tone, of course, of happiness, the happiness of being together, the joy of being together. And so in a moment, I will be raising my glass to your health, to the health of Mrs. Reagan. And I have had the very great pleasure of having long talks with Mrs. Reagan. We started our talks in London,[25] as you will recall, and indeed we also talked about you—(laughter)—and also raise my glass to the people of the United States, friends, our faithful friends, just as we are their loyal allies. And it is our function to say on all occasions what we think, just as it is our duty to at all times show our wholehearted solidarity.

And also I raise my glass to the health of the Ambassador and Mrs. Galbraith, representing the United States here in France. And it is to you, Madame, that we owe these very pleasant moments.

And I am honored to speak on behalf of the French guests present here tonight who represent what you might call in American terms, as far as the political scene is concerned, we call them proxies. (Laughter.)

But vis-à-vis the President of the United States and indeed the world, they are representatives of the whole nation of France and it is on their behalf, on behalf of everyone present, I would like again to raise my glass to your health and I would say, good luck to your action and also good luck to the work that we are going to undertake in the next 2 days—the conquest of liberty and peace. (Applause)

Document 221

Transcript of a Press Briefing by the Secretary of State (Haig), Paris, June 3, 1982[26]

"The First Series of Working Meetings . . . in Europe"

Secretary Haig. Good evening, ladies and gentlemen. I'm going to make a very

[25] During the ceremonies surrounding the July 29, 1981, wedding of Prince Charles and Lady Diana.

[26] Source: Department of State Press Release 189, June 11, 1982; Secretary Haig's opening remarks were also printed in Department of State *Bulletin*, July 1982, p. 15. The briefing took place in the Meridian Hotel Press Center in Paris. Haig accompanied President Reagan on his four-nation European tour, June 2–11.

few remarks about the first series of working meetings today on the—our first day in Europe.

They took place at a working luncheon with President Mitterrand, President Reagan that lasted about an hour and a half and which covered a broad range of regional, security-related issues and bilateral issues between the two governments and peoples.

Now, as you know, the summit[27] officially begins tomorrow so both leaders were reluctant to deal in any depth with the subjects which should be included on the agenda when all seven of the leaders of the Western industrialized nations, including Japan, convene at Versailles tomorrow evening.

Instead, they used this opportunity to extend the very warm personal relationship and rapport that has developed between the two leaders—this being the fourth meeting between the two men since they both assumed their responsibilities, the last being a personal visit by President Mitterrand to Washington this past March. They used it as an opportunity and, of course, because of the extensive rapport already established and the warmth of friendship, to move to issues of mutual concern in the domestic scene in both countries and to exchange insights on several important global situations of a regional character.

That included the Falkland question[28]—its near-term consequences and its long-term consequences. It involved an exchange of views on the Middle East with a very special focus on the conflict between Iran and Iraq[29] and the concern of both leaders that this conflict not expand, that the territorial integrity of the countries involved be preserved and that international attention be focused on international efforts to bring this conflict to a peaceful conclusion.

With respect to the Falklands, of course, both leaders are concerned that the bloodshed terminate at the earliest possible date and that that conflict be resolved within the framework of U.N. Resolution 502,[30] which from the outset, has enjoyed the support of both governments and which has been the fundamental premise upon which the United States has conducted its policies towards this very difficult situation in the South Atlantic.

Now, in the exchange of domestic issues, it is clear that both leaders approach economic issues from a different philosophic base. Nevertheless, they are seeking common objectives—the reduction of inflation, the reduction of excess levels of federal central government spending and high levels of employment in the return to a cycle of prosperity.

Now, the President, President Reagan, noted the success that his administration had achieved in bringing down the very high levels of inflation that he found upon assuming office. He also expressed some disappointment that he was unable to arrive in Europe with a budget compromise in hand[31]—one that would have brought the projected American deficits in the period ahead down substantially and, thereby, influence more substantially the interest rates which are of such concern on both sides of the Atlantic today.

I think in sum, and it's important, to characterize these first of two series of meetings. There'll be further meetings this evening with President Mitterrand at a dinner as an extension of an unusual relationship that has developed between the two leaders, one of intimacy and mutual confidence, and one of frankness in their exchange of viewpoints.

All in all, I think it was a very successful first day of what is going to be an increasingly busy schedule of activity in Versailles and, subsequently, in Rome, in Bonn, and Berlin.[32]

Now, I welcome your questions.

Q. We're getting the impression that there is a difference, at least of degree, between the United States and France in their support for the present course that Great Britain has taken in the Falkland crisis. Is that impression correct?

SECRETARY HAIG. No, I would not characterize—

---

[27] For documentation on the June 4–7 Versailles Economic Summit, see Chapter 5, Part F.

[28] For documentation on the Falklands crisis, see Chapter 15, Part B.

[29] For documentation on the Iran–Iraq War, see Chapter 11.

[30] For the text of this resolution, approved April 3, which called for the end of fighting in the Falklands and a diplomatic resolution of the crisis, see document 623.

[31] The reference is to efforts to effect a compromise between budget resolutions offered by the Democratic and Republican leaderships of the House of Representatives. On June 10, the House approved the Republican version, 220 to 207.

[32] President Reagan visited Rome on June 7, Bonn from June 9 to 11, and Berlin on June 11.

Q. The question?

SECRETARY HAIG. The question was, are there differences developing or in some degree, between France, on the one hand, United States on the other with respect to their support for Britain in the Falkland crisis?

I think it's important to emphasize that—and I can't and won't presume to speak for the French Government, other than the exchanges I overheard today and the exchanges I've had with Foreign Minister Cheysson. But I think both governments have been strong advocates of U.N. Resolution 502. They have been strong advocates of the principle which guides that resolution—that resort to force to solve political differences is not acceptable, and that aggression must not be rewarded. I think that is a very common framework. Beyond that, of course, both governments are sensitive to their historic and longstanding relationships and their alliance relationship with Great Britain. But I want to emphasize, above all, the principle which is the underlying, common thread in a number of converging threads.

Now, I'm not aware of any differences. None appeared today either in my discussions with the Foreign Minister or in the discussion, more importantly, between the two leaders.

Q. A followup on that question. When the Presidents, Reagan and Mitterrand, expressed their concern about the earliest possible cessation of hostilities, can that be taken to mean that it would be desirable if the hostilities ended before the final assault on Port Stanley[33] and is that likely to be discussed with Prime Minister Thatcher tomorrow?

SECRETARY HAIG. Well, I think it's difficult to say. I think both leaders, and the United States, certainly, have always advocated a negotiated solution in the framework of U.N. Resolution 502 which calls for a cease-fire, the withdrawal of Argentine forces from the island, and a political solution to the differences.

Now, the question that you've posed involves decisions to be made by the Argentine Government in coordination with the British Government. We would all hope—and I think Mrs. Thatcher made some comments yesterday in that regard, that she would hope there would be a withdrawal of Argentine forces.

Q. But don't—we're not asking for any cease-fire without a withdrawal, no standstill cease-fire—

SECRETARY HAIG. We continue to be advocates of U.N. Resolution 502. There's been no deviation from that, recognizing that the situation has changed somewhat. We would hope that there would be a manifestation of withdrawal on the part of the Argentine Government. Then the consequences your question suggested would not come about. But this is something that we have no judgment on in the context of the question that was asked.

Q. If I may continue the followup on that. When Mrs. Thatcher talked about a 10–14-day period in which Argentina might withdraw,[34] do you take that to mean that she will wait that period of time to see whether Argentina will withdraw?

SECRETARY HAIG. I wouldn't presume to put words in Prime Minister Thatcher's mouth. She's very capable and has been very clear. I think she said that if they were to withdraw in that time frame, that would be adequate for British purposes.

And, incidentally, that's a time frame that from the very outset experts have concluded on both sides—probably would be adequate to provide for complete evacuation.

Q. Sir, you know there are stories that President Reagan, in his phone-call tour,[35] suggested that he might like to see a wait that length of time so that he might not be embarrassed while he was in Europe.

SECRETARY HAIG. It is not right, but I am not going to indulge in public expositions on discussions between two leaders. It is inappropriate and wrong and it just ain't good style. (Laughter.)

Q. Mr. Secretary, if there is some kind of a multination force set up for the future administration of the Falklands, would the United States be willing to take part in such a force?

---

[33] At the beginning of June, British forces surrounded the Argentine garrison in the Falkland's capital, Port Stanley.

[34] In a May 20 statement to Parliament, Prime Minister Thatcher revealed that on May 17 the British Government proposed allowing Argentina 10 to 14 days to withdraw from the Falkland Islands as part of a peaceful settlement under U.N. auspices.

[35] An apparent reference to telephone calls which the President made to President Gualtieri of Argentina and Mrs. Thatcher at the outbreak of the crisis on April 1.

SECRETARY HAIG. Well, I think it is too early to say. I think the United States is anxious to do anything it can to make any contribution it can to bring about a peaceful, long-term solution to the situation. But the answer to your question is hypothetical and I would far prefer to wait and see what conditions might develop to enable me to refine an answer for that, and, certainly for the President.

Q. Do you personally believe it will take more than one nation to defend the Falklands in the future?

SECRETARY HAIG. Well, now that is a question that I hope will not be an appropriate question if a long-term solution is found.

Q. You said the two leaders discussed the long-term consequences of what is happening in the Falklands. Can you shed any light for us on that?

SECRETARY HAIG. No, I think we are dealing with two aspects. The question is, what are the long-term aspects of the Falklands Islands question that were discussed between the two leaders today, and the answer to that is, you know as well as I that there are near-term problems and there are long-term problems. The long-term problems involve a return to stability in the South Atlantic and hopefully a long-term settlement of what has been a historic dispute.

Q. Mr. Secretary of State, do you think it is possible or desirable to try to persuade Mrs. Thatcher to delay the final assault on Port Stanley in order to give time for diplomatic maneuvers to get withdrawal of the Argentines?

SECRETARY HAIG. I think that would be a presumptuous observation for me to make, for third parties to make, other than as we have from the outset expressed our concern that the fighting be terminated at the first practical date, that a peaceful solution be found. But as you know, once force has been employed it becomes a very different set of parameters that guide the situation, and certainly those involved on the ground are best able to answer that kind of question.

Q. Have there been any discussions between the two Presidents yet on President Reagan's disarmament proposals, and has there been any discussion of the American defense budget with all the political and economic implications?

SECRETARY HAIG. The question was, was there any discussion today on the disarmament proposal made recently by President Reagan at Eureka College,[36] and I assume also November 18th,[37] and was there any question about the record level of American defense spending projected in the American budget. And the answer to both questions is "no" except in general terms. I have had discussions with the Foreign Minister on the subject of the arms control initiatives. I think we have had all kinds of diplomatic traffic on this subject ever since the President's speech with all of the governments. All the governments of Western Europe have expressed strong support and affirmation for the President's initiatives, and they are in agreement with those initiatives.

Q. Towards the defense budget?

SECRETARY HAIG. The defense budget, no, other than—again you will recall we are fresh from the meeting at Luxembourg in the NATO family where of course defense improvements were discussed in detail and are reflected—and I would refer you to the communiqué that came out of the North Atlantic Council Foreign Minister's meeting[38] where it is very explicit in that area and we are all very pleased with its degree of detail and its thrust.

Q. Sir, did they discuss the credit question on East–West trade?

SECRETARY HAIG. No, this was not discussed today by the two leaders. There have been discussions for an extended period between the two governments.

I had some discussions with Foreign Minister Cheysson on that topic today, and there are others being conducted within the economic family.

Q. Did they discuss turn-key intervention, Mr. Secretary?

SECRETARY HAIG. Not yet, no. These are subjects, incidentally, that will clearly be on the agenda for Versailles. And I think both leaders are extremely sensitive not to look like we are developing a condominium between Paris and Washington with which to face our other partners. So they're sensitive, and for that reason they are avoiding subjects which will be on the Versailles agenda.

---

[36] For the text of President Reagan's May 9 speech, see document 44.

[37] For the text of this speech, see *American Foreign Policy: Current Documents, 1981*, document 60.

[38] For the text of the NATO foreign ministers' final communiqué, May 18, see document 176.

Q. You said, Mr. Secretary, that they approach economic issues from a very different base—economic base. On what did you base that—

SECRETARY HAIG. Well, I think the philosophic bases we are talking about is an approach to government at large. And I don't have to tell you that President Reagan comes from one philosophic set of roots, and the Socialist Government of President Mitterrand comes from another. Now, this is the fact of our alliance, that kind of a potpourri, if you will, of philosophic roots.

But the great strength of that alliance is the shared values and the overall objectives that all of our governments—despite their philosophic form of government. And that's the very strength of the alliance. We like it.

Q. With respect to the Middle East, Mr. Secretary, were your viewpoints identical with those of the French or were there differences concerning the Middle East?

SECRETARY HAIG. I would say that the general level of exchange on that subject—there was a great deal of convergence. I think historically that has not been the case between the United States and France, as you know. But we find that it is in greater balance today than it has been historically.

Q. Mr. Secretary, is the President proposing to Mitterrand any kind of a joint action to carry out what you mentioned here with regard to avoiding the spread of the Iran–Iraq war? You seem to be concerned that this might also lead to—

Q. Question.

SECRETARY HAIG. The question: Was there any specific set of proposals for dealing with the Iran–Iraq conflict? And the answer to that question is no. There was an extensive exchange of views on the character of the conflict, the number of seeming contradictions, and above all, the grave consequences of the outcome of the spread of this conflict.

Q. Do you think there is a danger of that spread? How do you—

SECRETARY HAIG. Well, I think everyone is very sensitive and concerned about that. I addressed it recently in a speech in Chicago.[39] We've been in close touch with our moderate Arab friends; our friends from the Islamic world, and as well as our Western European partners.

Q. Mr. Secretary, while you were in Ankara,[40] did you ask the Turkish Government to mediate between Iran and Iraq? This week there is going to be an Islamic summit meeting that they are going to participate in.

SECRETARY HAIG. No, we have not made such a request. While I was in Ankara recently, I had a very good exchange of views with both the Foreign Minister and with President Evren—or General Evren on this subject. As you know, Turkey enjoys a rather unique posture on this question in that it maintains good relationships with both governments.

Q. Mr. Secretary, back to the Falklands for just a moment. Could you give us some indication as to the thrust of the American approach when Mr. Reagan meets with Mrs. Thatcher tomorrow? What is it we really want to see happen?

Q. Question.

SECRETARY HAIG. The question is: What will occur at the meeting between President Reagan and Mrs. Thatcher tomorrow, as it involves the Falkland question? I'm confident there will be more to discuss than simply the Falkland question, but I think this is a good opportunity for a more detailed exchange of views. Bringing one another abreast of each other's thinking on this subject is very difficult in either transatlantic telephone conversations or the exchange of diplomatic messages, to really get to the heart of complex questions and therefore, this is going to be a very beneficial meeting. But I do not want to characterize it as a meeting in which two sides have lined up opposing views or necessarily even converging views, but rather an opportunity for both leaders to plumb in depth the attitudes of each other on this subject.

Q. Mr. Secretary, can you clear up the credit issue? A senior French official today said that it is not on the agenda, the issue of Western credits to the Soviet bloc, and that he hoped very much that the issue would not in any way be a spoiler or be a divisive issue at the economic summit.

SECRETARY HAIG. Well, I think we all hope that the issue will not be a spoiler or a divisive issue here at Versailles. I'm rather confident that it will not be.

Now, I'm not making a comment on an unnamed official. You know, there's noth-

[39] For the text of Haig's May 26 speech, see document 303.

[40] For documentation on Haig's May 13 to 15 visit to Ankara, see Chapter 10, Part L.

ing more dangerous because you don't know who they are sometimes. It's even dangerous when you do. (Laughter.)

Thank you very much.

Document 222

Transcript of an Interview With President Reagan, St. Louis, July 22, 1982 (Extract)[41]

French Sale of Technology to the Soviet Union

. . . .

MR. HUNTER On the international scene, were you surprised this morning when France announced that it was going to go ahead and give U.S.-developed technology to the Russians for the development of that Russian pipeline,[42] and have you and your foreign policy advisors determined some sort of way to dissuade France from taking that action?

THE PRESIDENT What really they are doing is going forward with contracts that were already signed. I have talked with President Mitterrand about his situation. He said when he came there he found the contracts already agreed to and signed by the previous administration, and they feel legally bound by those.

What I have asked our Commerce Department to do is a study, and come back to me with a report on what our situation is; because where it involves us—with our sanctions that we have imposed against the Soviet Union—where it involves us is what is our legal position with regard to subsidiary companies in France and in the other European countries owned by American firms, and whether they are legally bound, possibly, by contracts that were made before.

MR. HUNTER. What are your options that are available to dissuade France?

The President. We tried our best in the meetings over there.[43] I think they know what we were going to do because we had announced what we were going to do way last December. They, as I say, had gone forward with the contracts. We have been investigating, with some of the European countries, the possibilities of energy sources closer, and that would not have the two problems which we are very concerned about with our European allies. Number one, making themselves dependent on the Soviet Union, and putting themselves in a position to be blackmailed by the Soviet Union if they decide to shut off the gas.

There are sources in the North Sea, in Norway, in the Netherlands. We would be happy to help them with the development of those. The other one is, they would be cash customers. The Soviet Union has poured so much money into its great military might that we are now trying to get reduced that they are up against the wall. They do not have cash for those purposes the way they did. This would give them $10 or $12 billion a year in cold, hard cash for doing this. And these are the things that we tried to point out.

Our allies, on the other hand, pointed out to us that they had already gone forward to the point that they did not feel they could retreat from that. Although, they did join us in shutting off, or reducing credit. So that we, at least, are not helping finance a potential adversary.

. . . .

---

[41] Source: White House Press Release, July 22, 1982, Office of the Press Secretary to the President; also printed in *Weekly Compilation of Presidential Documents,* July 26, 1982, pp. 946–947. The President was interviewed by Julius Hunter of KMOX-TV in his hotel suite at the Marriot Pavillion. The interview began at 5:32 p.m.

[42] The pipeline equipment was produced by Dresser Industries, a French subsidiary of a U.S. corporation.

[43] During the President's visit to France, June 2–7.

Document 223

Transcript of an Interview With President Reagan, August 6, 1982 (Extract)[44]

The State of U.S.-French Relations

. . . .

Q. All along your European tour last June[45] you insisted that, contrary to the disarray in the Atlantic Alliance at the time of the Carter administration, the relationship between Europe and the United States had never been better. Then came the dispute over the gas deal. What is now your judgment on the state of the alliance?

THE PRESIDENT. I believe the alliance is strong. The fundamental values and shared interests which have always united us are, and will remain, much more important and enduring than the issues over which we differ from time to time. Differences of view are not new within the alliance; they are the hallmark of consultations among free and sovereign states.

The issues which have bothered Europe recently are primarily economic; they do not affect directly the fundamental interests—in security and related issues—on which NATO is based. I don't want to underestimate the seriousness of these economic issues; but I do think we will successfully resolve them.

Let's not forget that we made real progress at Versailles and subsequently in a number of important economic areas. We initiated a new process of economic policy coordination, undertook a joint study of the effectiveness of exchange market intervention, agreed to a new OECD export credit arrangement which reduces export credit subsidies—including those to the Soviet Union—and narrowed our differences on important North-South issues. Meantime, the allied consensus on security, arms control, and defense is intact; in fact, that consensus was strengthened at the Bonn summit and has been reaffirmed in our discussions since then.

Q. In this same context how do you assess the relationship between your country and France? Originally it seemed America had no partner more faithful than Socialist France. Because of the gas issue the French Government has returned to its familiar dissenting role in the alliance. Cheysson is much blunter than his European colleagues when he warns of a looming "divorce"[46] between Washington and Europe. What is your answer to such pessimism?

THE PRESIDENT. I don't even think we face a trial separation. To be serious, I remain optimistic, and I believe there are sound historic reasons for my optimism. France and America have close bilateral ties that go back to the times of our respective revolutions and we have always been the strongest of allies. Of course, our relations have had their ups and downs. But the United States highly values its alliance with France as I value my excellent relationship with President Mitterrand. We've had a number of very useful and productive meetings and just recently I received an exceptionally warm and personal message from him in response to my congratulatory note on the occasion of Bastille Day. With respect to the gas pipeline issue, I agree with Chancellor Schmidt's characterization of this as a "family quarrel".[47] Like family issues, this one can and will be resolved. It is not "grounds for divorce". Close, constructive and private consultations are in order, but we start with the advantage that discussions of our differences build on deep bonds of common interest and values that far transcend isolated problems.

. . . .

---

[44] Source: Office of the Press Secretary to the President. The interview was conducted by Charles Lambroschini of *Le Figaro* in the White House.

[45] Reference is to the President's four-nation European tour, June 2–11.

[46] In a July 21 interview with French radio, Cheysson spoke of a "gradual divorce" between the United States and its European allies as a result of U.S. indifference to European interests.

[47] An apparent reference to comments made by Schmidt during a July 23 radio interview.

Document 224

Transcript of a Press Conference by the Secretary of State (Shultz), Paris, December 14, 1982 (Extracts)[48]

Discussions With President Mitterrand

SECRETARY SHULTZ. My colleague Foreign Minister Cheysson gave me the courtesy of meeting me at the airport and driving in with me. Then I had an opportunity for a lengthy meeting with President Mitterrand, the two of us, for an hour or so and then we had a luncheon joined by the French Ambassador to the United States[49] and the Foreign Minister and our own Ambassador[50] and Assistant Secretary Burt. I have been delayed in my schedule ever since.

But I would say in terms of topics and approach that, as you might expect knowing the very large array of places and subjects in which the interests of France and the United States intersect, that we went across the board through military issues, regional issues and economic issues of various dimensions so that our discussions truly were comprehensive. I believe that in that process we deepened and strengthened and broadened the relationship that we have and, of course, which has been in existence for so many years.

I imagine that everybody somehow puts the subject of East–West economic matters at the top of your list, although I do think that somehow it has to be seen in the full perspective of this panoply of relationships we have with our friends in France. I would only say on that, that we discussed, both in my private meeting with President Mitterrand, and in the larger meeting, the full array of the activities and studies that have been referred to in our discussions earlier and I think in the process explored some of the points that have to be developed if those efforts are going to be truly fruitful. Some have more ambiguity than others, particularly the subject of credits. But in any case both with respect to those studies and the importance from all of our standpoints of in some manner finding a way to develop our overall objectives, what we are trying to accomplish, what we are not trying to accomplish and in finding a manner of consulting properly about activities that any nation might plan to undertake in the general East–West trade area, narrowed, of course, to the aspects of what we are talking about here, we will find a way to do that. Obviously anything that we discuss here in France that might go forward is something that we need to consult with among all of our allies. But of course anything that we are able to agree to here, I'm sure everyone will be interested in, so we'll be engaging in that process. I consider in general that the discussion was a very fruitful and worthwhile one. No questions?

Q. What is the French position on the issue of deployment of missiles—the freeze versus the zero option.

SECRETARY SHULTZ. Well, one of the few things that I really learned is that when it comes time for somebody to express the French position on something, particularly when I'm in Paris, I should leave it to the French to do that—

Q. Reports from Washington indicate the United States is planning to reject the Soviet suggestion for reduction of missiles. Is this the final decision and what would you recommend?

SECRETARY SHULTZ. I believe all that has been said is that the idea of a reduction in a number of missiles in this immediate theatre, leaving the United States with none but the Soviets with some large number—enough to hit all the targets that they are looking at while what missiles they remove are not destroyed but simply taken out of the theater, remembering that these are very readily moved—is not a very interesting proposition.

Q. What about a middle position—a counter proposal?

SECRETARY SHULTZ. I don't have any comment on that.

Q. Mr. Secretary are you happy with the French position?

SECRETARY SHULTZ. We have worked very closely and effectively with the French on this whole range of military matters and their attitude toward the IMF [*INF*] deployment, the conduct of negotiations and so on. We haven't had any differences of view and in fact I think we have been mutually supportive.

Q. What is the field in which there is a serious lack of understanding between the United States and France?

---

[48] Source: Department of State Press Release 384, December 15, 1982. Shultz visited Paris at the conclusion of the NATO Foreign Ministers meeting in Brussels, December 8–11, and a trip to Rome, December 11–14. The omitted portion is an exchange on Namibia.

[49] Bernard Vernier-Palliez.

[50] Evan Galbraith.

SECRETARY SHULTZ. Well I don't know that there is any deep, serious lack of understanding. There are a number of really complicated issues. The position of France and the United States is not identical with respect to them and so in any effort to coordinate on an aspect of them, like those parts of trade and financial flows, East–West, that have a security orientation to them, any effort to coordinate is going to pose some difficulties. But that doesn't mean they can't be overcome. What we have been struggling for is the right framework and manner for developing that cooperation. I think that we'll be able to find it all right. I think it is perhaps reassuring to find that there are a number of existing institutions and somewhere within the framework of these institutions we should be able to get done what we need to get done, remembering that this is all not simply a question of what France and the United States want to do, but we have many other countries that are of great importance to us both with whom we need to coordinate our actions.

Q. President Mitterrand recently suggested the United States was in some way assisting the franc. Are we doing so?

SECRETARY SHULTZ. The question of actions of government in exchange markets is a question that is best left to those conducting it and to the markets. I know when I was Secretary of the Treasury I would never comment and if somebody else did I didn't appreciate it. I remember once when one of my colleagues had some comments to make when I was in Tokyo; I said, "Tell Mel Laird to keep his cotton-picking hands out of economic policy." So I'll forego any comment.

Q. Based on your discussions here today, would you say that the French are going to do studies on East–West trade,[51] studies that you would like to see?

SECRETARY SHULTZ. Well, of course, there are quite a few things going on right now and I think as these evolve and develop and the whole process emerges we should be able to find a satisfactory way of conducting the studies and the activities. Now, when you say you are going to study something that doesn't mean that you know what you are going to come out with in the end. We have some ideas, they have some ideas and others do too. So people of honesty and imagination undertake a study in good faith and we'll see where we come out. But I think the idea of making these efforts is one that is generally accepted and certainly that seems to be the case here today. Under those circumstances I think we'll be able to see some good work coming out.

Q. President Mitterrand has indicated that on military policy, France and the United States are very close, but on economic, fiscal, trade, commercial policy there has not been enough consultation. Is this your position?

SECRETARY SHULTZ. Well I certainly wouldn't make a comment on anything that President Mitterrand has said but I would say that it is important for us as two close friends and allies, not only for the United States and France but all our other friends, to be in close contact with each other about what is going on in fields of our own interests, such as the one we are talking about. I also think that the way you make such consultation effective is not just by talking to each other. Because obviously we do that a tremendous amount. I think the various governments involved probably support the international airlines for the number of people transported back and forth all the time—I think the consultation is more effective if you have a process that sets out and develops what it is that we are trying to achieve. So it sets out a little more clearly than we have been able to so far in this area what the object of consultation is. If we can accompany that with a somewhat better system of consultation then it will all be more effective and I think we all desire that.

Q. Are you discussing ways of doing this?

SECRETARY SHULTZ. Yes, oh yes, that's what we—talked about that.

Q. Did you speak to President Mitterrand about the Middle East and Lebanon? Was there agreement on forces in Lebanon?[52]

SECRETARY SHULTZ. Well I'm sort of immersed in my discussions I guess, between those that I have had with the Foreign Minister, the Defense Minister as well as with President Mitterrand. Obviously the subjects of Lebanon and many other areas of the world came up. We are both in Lebanon together in the multinational

---

[51] For further discussion by Secretary Shultz of these studies, see document 167.

[52] For documentation on the three-nation peacekeeping force in Lebanon, to which the United States and France supplied contingents, see Chapter 11, Part C.

force. I might say that as an example of outstanding cooperation and collaboration, it is working very well; we are tightly coordinated and I think have been effective together there. We agree that as developments take place in Lebanon and as it may emerge that new and additional missions for the multinational force might be put on the table we both said we are quite ready to look at these. We'll look at them in a consultative fashion and, of course, each nation, as sovereign nations, will make its own decision but will do it through a process of consultation, in the United States of course, also in consultation with the Congress. But it is a good example of just what I was talking about earlier. In Lebanon we have defined our objectives reasonably carefully; we have set up a way of consulting about them and everybody has done so—the French, the Italians and the United States. That operation has worked very well indeed.

Q. Recently President Reagan announced an allied agreement on the framework for East-West trade.[53] But there was confusion on whether France is a participant. Can you clarify?

SECRETARY SHULTZ. Well, I don't want to go back over all of that material. I think the point is that the various things that we want to talk about—we and our allies, all of us—are now going on in various places in OECD and COCOM principally or getting started there. We will be going forward with additional efforts to assess overall objectives and we'll find the right framework for that. So as far as the substance of what we have been talking about together is concerned I think we are seeing that gradually emerge. The question of whether who agreed to what and so forth I think is becoming—I was going to say—academic, but being an old academic I don't like to think that is irrelevant.

. . . .

Q. To what do you attribute the recent trouble in Franco-American relations?

SECRETARY SHULTZ. Oh, I don't know. I think there are probably some differences in perception, in fact, and so these can easily lead to misunderstandings. That suggests the importance of trying to talk them out. I think it is also fair to say that the United States is a proud and sovereign country. So is France, so is every other country as far as I can see. There are no exceptions to that rule, but it is possible occasionally to have some public misunderstanding and I hope that perhaps we can put those behind us but at any rate we'll be trying.

Thank you.

[53] For the text of President Reagan's November 13 radio address on East-West trade, see document 165.

F. Portugal

Document 225

Transcript of a Press Conference by the Secretary of State (Haig), Lisbon, February 11, 1982 (Extracts)[1]

U.S.-Portuguese Relations

SECRETARY HAIG. Thank you. Good morning ladies and gentlemen. I just want to say a brief, few remarks about this very, very compressed and much too brief visit to your country, Portugal. This visit was, as you know, at the invitation of my colleague and the Foreign Minister of the Government of Portugal, Goncalves Pereira, with whom I have had very close associations since assuming my position as Secretary of State. The visit itself I found to be extremely fruitful. It was a continuation of long-going and close consultations between our two governments. Its focus involved regional and alliance affairs, the coordination that has become so essential at a time of the suppression of freedoms and liberties in Poland.[2] It involved a host of discussions related with the CSCE Conference in Madrid,[3] on-going Western actions related to

[1] Source: Department of State Press Release 62, February 19, 1982; printed also in Department of State *Bulletin*, April 1982, pp. 43–45. Haig held this press conference at the Lisbon Airport upon his departure from Portugal. He had visited Portugal after addressing the CSCE conference in Madrid, February 9. For the text of this address, see document 157. The omitted portion deals with violence in northern Syria and arms sales to Jordan.

[2] For documentation on the U.S. response to the Polish crisis, see Chapter 10, Part M.

[3] For documentation on the CSCE conference, see Chapter 10, Part A.

the crisis in Poland. It involved also other regional discussions in areas of common interest between the Government of Portugal and the Government of the United States and it included extensive discussions on the situation in southern Africa[4] where Portuguese experience and influence has historically played a very important role and whose advice and counsel with respect to the provisions of UN Resolution 435[5] and the sought-after independence of Namibia is invaluable to me. And thirdly, it focused on bilateral relationships. As you know, we have had historic and extensive bilateral relationships between the people of Portugal and the people of the United States, between our two governments. This involves cooperation in a host of political, economic, and security-related matters in this regard. Of course, the United States has been keenly interested in the progress of the Portuguese Government since the turbulent days of 1974[6] and the creation of a democratic institution and a democratic process which remains the bedrock of our relationship. During this visit I had an opportunity to extend, on behalf of President Reagan, an invitation for your Head of State to visit the United States in the latter half of this coming year and we would also, of course, welcome a similar visit from your Prime Minister, dates to be worked out in the not too distant future.[7] Now, in sum, I want to emphasize once again the highly constructive and fruitful character of our very, very brief visit and they've underlined once again the friendship, the cooperation and mutuality of interests that have been demonstrated by the Government of Portugal in a host of recent strategic situations—the Afghanistan crisis, the American hostage crisis in Iran, and the most recent situation where freedom is in jeopardy in Poland. And in that context, I leave here greatly encouraged and enthusiastic about the days ahead. Now I welcome your questions.

Q. Mr. Haig, I'm working for Radio France. Do you believe that Portugal must be associated to the solution of the Namibian question and if yes, how?

SECRETARY HAIG. The Namibian question?

Q. Yes.

SECRETARY HAIG. Well, I think all member governments of the United Nations have a very keen interest in accordance with the Resolution 435 involving the desirability and the necessity for the independence of Namibia. As you know, the U.S. Government working with the contact group, (inaudible) does not include Portugal, have very special responsibilities, and, as you know, the United States has been leading an effort within the contact group to establish an early progress, hopefully in the coming year, in 1982, to establish a schedule and a firm realization of the objectives of the UN Resolution 435. In that regard we have repeatedly pointed out that there is an empirical relationship between the situation in Namibia and the continuing Cuban and Soviet presence in Angola. We continue to work on this problem and we have made substantial progress in the last month. We are now dealing with a set of constitutional principles which we have run through the interested parties, the front line states, the internal parties in Namibia, the South African Government and the contact group and I hope to have in the near future a finalization of that first effort. We will then turn to the other two aspects of the problem which involve the UN presence in Namibia and the final schedule for South African withdrawal.

Q. Mr. Secretary, considering that Spain is coming into NATO,[8] how do you see as a major NATO partner the new strategic role of the Iberia bloc, especially on the position of Portugal in the Atlantic Islands?

SECRETARY HAIG. Well, as you know, I have been a great advocate myself in my past role as supreme allied commander to be very active in the integration of the Portuguese forces, the Portuguese Brigade, for example. Now, the command relationships are, of course, a matter for NATO authorities and sometimes, to my regret, I am no longer a NATO authority. But as you know also, the alliance works on a consensus and in that context consensus is equivalent to unanimity. So that whatever arrangements are ultimately worked out for the Iberian command structure, it would be with the complete approval and acceptance of the Government of Portugal.

---

[4] For documentation on the Namibia issue, see Chapter 14, Part B.

[5] For the text of U.N. Security Council Resolution 435 (1978) on Namibia, see *American Foreign Policy: Basic Documents, 1977–1980*, p. 1205.

[6] Reference is to the April 25, 1974 revolution which established a democratic regime in Portugal.

[7] President Eanes did not visit the United States in 1982. However, Prime Minister Pinto Balsemão visited Washington, December 14–15, for meetings with President Reagan. For information on that visit, see documents *infra* and 227.

[8] Spain formally joined NATO on May 30, 1982.

Q. Mr. Secretary, can Portugal be a link between Washington and Luanda?[9]

SECRETARY HAIG. Can it be a link? Well, we have been in direct contact with Luanda. However, we very highly value the advice we receive from the Government of Portugal on the situation in all of southern Africa, including Angola.

Q. Are you going to meet Mr. Savimbi[10] in Morocco?

SECRETARY HAIG. No, I'm not.

Q. Another question. Can your visit here be seen as a support for Portuguese Government as it is facing a popular discontent?

SECRETARY HAIG. I specifically and very vigorously avoid any involvement in the internal affairs of the sovereign government of Portugal. And anyone who would interpret my visit here as contributing in any way to the internal situation from one point of view or another, would be guilty of, not only misjudgment but probably mischievous misjudgment.

Q. Mr. Secretary, what kind of new military facilities do the United States intend to get here in Portugal or in Portuguese territory do you intend to assure that the rapid deployment force would probably scale the Azores Airbase without consulting previously with the Portuguese Government?

SECRETARY HAIG. Well, it would be inconceivable to me and I'll answer your question, that any utilization of sovereign Portuguese territory could or would occur without the complete cooperation and coordination with the Portuguese Government. That would be inconceivable. It has not been done in the past and it would not be done in the future. Now with respect to the rapid deployment force, there are no definitive plans at this time, but I think you know that the employment of the rapid deployment force would be, as always, in the basic interests of fundamental western concern, whether they be energy related or in more (inaudible) strategic concerns. And again, no utilization of sovereign territory of Portugal could nor would occur without the full agreement and support of the Portuguese Government.

. . . .

[9] Reference is to the capital of Angola.

[10] Jonas Savimbi, leader of the National Union for the Total Independence of Angola (UNITA), which was waging a war against the Government of Angola.

Q. Mr. Secretary, do you foresee further steps of the Portuguese Government in supporting the American position against the Soviet Union in Poland? Did the Portuguese Government tell you they will take new measures in this important problem?

SECRETARY HAIG. Well, I would rather than talk about new measures, suggest that convergence of views between the Government of Portugal and the Government of the United States on the Polish question is rather complete and thorough and identical, and in the period ahead we will be considering whatever steps are necessary in the light of whatever changes may or may not occur in the unsatisfactory situation in Poland.

Q. Mr. Secretary, could the relationships between Portugal and its ancient colonies have a great importance for the United States? What's the importance of the good relationships between Portugal and its ex-African colonies for the United States?

SECRETARY HAIG. Well, I wouldn't want to answer that question with specificity because it would suggest a point of view that I don't think we have explored in the depth that it requires and that you might have as a journalist. In general, it has always been the United States view that Portugal has had a great deal of historic experience in Africa and that that experience can make a major contribution to the democratic development of the nonaligned and new governments of Africa and I think that is a matter, of course, for the sovereign decision of the Government of Portugal and its relationships with the various governments of southern Africa. But in general, we are not only comfortable with increasing relationships, we see advantages to both developing states themselves and to the Portuguese people as well.

Q. Did you discuss the use of the Porto Santo Island to store nuclear arms? The United States possible wish to store nuclear arms on the Porto Santo Island?

SECRETARY HAIG. On where?

Q. Near Madeira Island?

SECRETARY HAIG. Well, first let me say as a matter of policy, and longstanding policy, American officials never discuss such sensitive issues involving nuclear weapons, but in order to set your mind at rest, let me assure you there were no discussions of any kind during my visit here in Lisbon that had to do with deployment, stationing or positioning of nuclear weapons.

Q. Mr. Secretary, yesterday night in your speech at the official dinner[11] you said that totalitarian pressure continues now in Portugal. What were you referring to?

SECRETARY HAIG. I said what?

Q. You said that totalitarian pressures are remaining in Portugal.

SECRETARY HAIG. Well, I think again without casting any particular label there are certain worldwide movements that are influenced and controlled extensively from Moscow. You have such a movement here in Portugal and therefore any party that takes instructions from outside the borders of the sovereign nation in which it's playing its role would be a matter of concern in that regard.

Q. Is that an internal question, sir?

SECRETARY HAIG. Well it's an internal question for Portugal, but it's an external question as far as East–West relations are concerned and the activities of the Soviet Union and its extension through Marxist/Leninist parties to the degree that those parties are subservient under whatever concept you care to refer to, democratic centralism, Stalinist loyalty, or whatever.

Q. Mr. Haig: Are you any nearer U.S. recognition of Angola and has the importance your administration attaches to UNITA been criticized by Portuguese leaders? Has the importance that the Reagan administration attaches to UNITA been criticized by the present Portuguese administration?

SECRETARY HAIG. Well, I don't know what importance you're referring to. We receive many, many visitors from many, many countries and that does not suggest any particular value judgment one way or the other. I met recently with Felipe Gonzalez from Spain, a Socialist leader. I have met leaders from African splinter groups and African opposition groups, I have done that with Western European groups. We think it's a value to keep an open mind, to listen to all points of view and I think that's part of the democratic process. It should not be interpreted as a subjective value judgment one way or the other, but hopefully an educational experience which will refine the important judgments that governments must make. Now with respect to any concerns here, no because they would not be justified. The United States does not have a relationship with UNITA or Mr. Savimbi. As a matter of fact, in terms of support, we are specifically prohibited from such activity under the provisions of the so-called Clark amendment.[12]

Q. Are you any nearer U.S. recognition of the Angolan Government?

SECRETARY HAIG. Well, we are talking and dependent on their future actions, orientations and independence of policy, we of course would welcome continuing improvement in our relationships. Thank you very much.

Document 226

Statements by President Reagan and Portuguese Prime Minister Balsemão, December 15, 1982[13]

"The Relationship . . . Is One of Common Values, Mutual Respect and Broad Cooperation"

THE PRESIDENT. Prime Minister Balsemao and I first met last June at the NATO Summit in Bonn.[14] This, however, has been our first opportunity to talk at length and we've had a lot to discuss. Our exchange

---

[11] In a toast at a dinner hosted by Prime Minister Pinto Balsemão on February 10, Haig said: "Having thrown off authoritarian rule, you have also resisted successfully thrusts from the extreme left and totalitarianism and even as I arrived here in your capital today, those pressures continue . . . ." He was referring to reports that Portuguese police had foiled a plot to overthrow the government in connection with demonstrations called by the Portuguese Communist Party.

[12] For the text of the Clark amendment, Section 404 of the International Security Assistance and Arms Export Control Act of 1976 (P.L. 94–329), enacted June 30, 1976, see 90 Stat. 757. Changes in the Clark amendment were made in Section 118 of the International Security and Development Cooperation Act of 1980 (P.L. 96–533), enacted December 16, 1980. For the text of the revisions, see 94 Stat. 3141. The Clark amendment prohibited security assistance to Angola without specific congressional authorization.

[13] Source: White House Press Release, December 15, 1982, Office of the Press Secretary to the President; also printed in *Weekly Compilation of Presidential Documents*, December 20, 1982, pp. 1623–1624. The two leaders spoke at the Diplomatic Entrance to the White House beginning at 12:27 p.m.

[14] For documentation on the NATO summit, June 9–11, see Chapter 10, Part B.

was exceptionally useful and harmonious. After these discussions it is now even more clear why our two countries have been such hard and fast allies for so many years.

The relationship between Portugal and the United States is one of common values, mutual respect and broad cooperation. In our meeting and the working lunch which followed, we covered a broad range of international topics and found substantial agreement.

Among other subjects, we discussed our defense cooperation which goes back many years. We're now in the process of negotiating a new security cooperation agreement to broaden and strengthen our collaboration on our common defense objectives.

Portugal and the United States share a common responsibility for the defense of the West. And our security relationship is important to both countries, as well as to the NATO alliance.

The Prime Minister has explained to me the various military modernization needs of his country and I have reaffirmed the U.S. commitment to help Portugal to meet these goals.

We also discussed the economic assistance which the United States has provided to Portugal over the years. This continuing assistance is an important expression of our desire to befriend and help the Portuguese people. We agreed that the current negotiations on the security cooperation agreement should lead to an early and mutually satisfactory conclusion.

We also discussed each country's initiatives in southern Africa and the unique perspective that Portugal brings to these issues, especially in view of its historic ties with Angola and Mozambique.

The Prime Minister and his government have been most generous in sharing with us some valuable insights drawn from their extensive experience in the area.

We shall continue to consult our Portuguese friends in the future.

Finally, and perhaps above all, as one democratic leader to another, I've expressed to the Prime Minister my personal admiration and that of all Americans for the continued progress of democracy in Portugal.

The Portuguese experience has shown how, given a chance, people will choose freedom. That the progress [*process*?] worked so well in Portugal is a tribute to the Portuguese people with their love of freedom, their high ideals and high civic and political responsibility.

We're delighted with their success and we certainly are proud to continue calling them friends and very happy to welcome the Prime Minister here today.

PRIME MINISTER BALSEMAO. Thank you very much, Mr. President.

I'm thankful to President Reagan for the invitation he addressed to me to come to Washington, providing a timely opportunity to discuss bilateral relations between Portugal and the United States and to exchange views on international items and matters of mutual interest.

The summary of our talks was brilliantly given by the President and so this allows me to concentrate only on some of the points which were raised.

First, I would like to fully endorse the President's assessment of our relationship and of the principles on which it is based.

It is not by sheer coincidence that a sound friendship between Portugal and the United States has existed for 200 years. And it is still showing a dynamic vitality, as we all know and as this visit demonstrates.

We in Portugal look forward to working in close cooperation with the United States and for that effort we count very much on the strong Portuguese-American community living and working here in the United States.

Our interests and concern about the evolution of the situation in southern Africa has led us to express our viewpoint that peace and stability in that area can be achieved only through balanced economic development and respect for the security of all countries concerned.

I was also very interested in hearing the President's assessment of his recent trip to South America[15] and in exchanging views on this region, which is also of particular interest for Portugal.

I had the opportunity to fully brief the President on the recent political evolution of the situation in Portugal, on our economic situation, also, and on the development of our negotiations to join the European Economic Community.

In the present political stability of my country, opens new perspectives for more

[15] For documentation on President Reagan's visit to Latin America, November 30–December 4, see Chapter 15.

cooperation and more constructive cooperation with the United States and with the free world.

We also discussed in detail our security cooperation regarding which we have been engaged in extensive negotiations. These talks have now reached an important stage as we have just begun to renegotiate the Azores agreement. Portugal is a reliable partner which wants to fully assume its responsibilities in secure terms, [and] expects within this context a clear understanding from its American alliance. Thank you.

Document 227

Transcript of a White House Press Briefing, December 15, 1982[16]

The Visit of Prime Minister Balsemão

Senior Administration Official. Thank you. I think, as you know, the Prime Minister met first this morning with the Acting Secretary of State, Kenneth Dam. And then he came for a meeting with the President in the Oval Office. There was a working lunch in the Oval Office—or in the White House—and then there was a separate meeting after that with the Vice President.

And the Prime Minister's just left to go up to the Hill. He will be seeing separately Secretary Weinberger and Secretary Regan, both of whom were at the lunch as well.

I don't know how many of you have had a chance to look at the statements that were released at the end of the conversation between the President and the Prime Minister.[17] But I might just very quickly emphasize and read a few parts of them which sums up, I think, the essence of the substantive nature of the discussions.

The President said that after the talks today it was even more clear to him why our two countries have been such hard and fast allies for so many years, the relationship between Portugal and the United States being "one of common values, mutual respect and broad cooperation."

There was a considerable discussion, both in the meeting with the President in the Oval Office at the lunch and then again in the meeting with the Vice President, of our security cooperation, which is, I think you know, is a cooperation that goes back very many years and is quite intimate and intense and cooperative.

And there was an agreement on the part of both gentlemen to broaden and strengthen our cooperation on these common defense objectives.

The Prime Minister discussed at length in several of these sessions the military modernization needs of Portugal, and the President reaffirmed our commitment to help Portugal meet those goals.

Perhaps an important operational sentence in the statement the President read after his meeting was the one that states, "We agreed that the current negotiations on the security cooperation agreement should lead to an early and mutually satisfactory conclusion."

Finally, the President closed his statement with a reaffirmation of our—of our admiration for the development of Portuguese democracy. Perhaps I'll be courageous enough to say that in a conversation the Prime Minister in describing what has happened in Portugal in the last 6 or 7 years, which has been an extraordinary success story, I think, as you know of the triumph of a people's desire for freedom and liberty—the Prime Minister wryly noted that often good news is no news, so that this wasn't a particularly popular theme in the press, but it was well understood by the President and our side how important a development this was and how we should all be delighted by it.

In addition, in the lunch there was a rather extended discussion between the two sides of the current global economic situation. And the President expressed his confidence in the underlying strength of the American economy.

Both at the lunch and then subsequently with the Vice President—there was an extended discussion both of the Middle East, where both sides agreed that it was time for action with respect to the withdrawal of all foreign military forces from Lebanon and concerning Africa and especially southern Africa, where, as you know, Portugal has a

---

[16] Source: White House Press Release, December 15, 1982, Office of the Press Secretary to the President. This background briefing was conducted by a senior administration official and began at 2:32 p.m.

[17] *Supra.*

special interest because of its relationship with its former colonies there. I think I'll end with that and take your questions.

Q. What is the status of the Azores treaty—base treaty?[18]

SENIOR ADMINISTRATION OFFICIAL. There—it expires in February. And negotiations concerning a renewal of the agreement are taking—have begun in Lisbon with our Ambassador there, Ambassador Alan Holmes, leading the U.S. side and discussions with Portuguese authorities. Those discussions will continue, in fact, next week, I believe. And it's the desire of both sides to have them concluded before the present agreement runs out in early February.

Q. For how many years is it being negotiated?

SENIOR ADMINISTRATION OFFICIAL. That's under discussion. That's one of the issues which is being discussed.

Q. And the current treaty is 5 years?

SENIOR ADMINISTRATION OFFICIAL. That's right and it expires on, I believe, it's the fourth of February.

Q. What are some of the issues in that agreement that are being discussed?

SENIOR ADMINISTRATION OFFICIAL. Well, you'll excuse me if I don't go through the issues. These are confidential discussions. I characterize the political will on both sides to reach an early agreement and I think I'll leave it at that.

Q. The Prime Minister said he'd briefed the President fully on political developments in Portugal meaning, I suppose, the political crisis he's left behind.[19] Can you give us something—

SENIOR ADMINISTRATION OFFICIAL. No, that, really—I understand that that's how you can interpret that but that isn't what, in fact—when he said "political developments" he was really describing the developments since'74 which he went into in considerable length—and the evolution of Portuguese democracy. There was not a discussion of the current political situation in Portugal. I could see how you could misinterpret that but what he meant was that he discussed with the President what's happened in these years since the Portuguese revolution.

Q. Can you talk about the President—was the military relationship discussed? I didn't quite understand it when you—

SENIOR ADMINISTRATION OFFICIAL. Yes, it was.

Q. Can you be specific on the details of that?

SENIOR ADMINISTRATION OFFICIAL. I've said as much, I think, as I want to say about it. They agreed that this was a relationship which was mutually beneficial to the two sides, which was very longstanding and which both sides very much want to be continued.

Q. Do they want anything? Did they ask for anything in terms of weapons?

SENIOR ADMINISTRATION OFFICIAL. They're in the process of modernizing their armed forces and there are continuous discussions between their Ministry of Defense and ours but if you're asking did specific weapon systems come up, no, they didn't.

Q. The President reaffirmed the U.S. commitment to help Portugal with its modernization program. What is the United States really willing to do? What in terms of money, equipment, sophisticated systems?

SENIOR ADMINISTRATION OFFICIAL. As I said, my purpose here is to brief on what the discussions this morning entailed. But what we're willing to do is do everything we can, as the President said when he made his statement a few minutes ago, to assist Portugal as others are doing in the modernization of its military force. And we are going to do everything we can to ensure that that occurs in an expeditious fashion.

Yes?

Q. Has the United States provided military and economic aid to Portugal over the past few years and can you give us an idea of the ballpark figure?

SENIOR ADMINISTRATION OFFICIAL. Yes, it has—for 4 years. I can tell you that in'82, the figure which emerged from the Congress was $10 million in grants, $45 million in guaranteed credits, and $20 million in economic assistance and then another $10 million was added in a supplemental—are—the current figures up on the Hill for the'83

---

[18] For the text of the agreement regarding U.S. use of Azores base facilities, signed in Lisbon, September 6, 1951, and entered into force that day, see 5 UST 7236. For the text of the June 18, 1979, amendment to this treaty, see TIAS 10050.

[19] Apparent reference to divisions within the Social Democratic Party and within the Balsemão coalition government which led to the Prime Minister's resignation on December 19.

budget are $37.5 in grants, $52.5 in guaranteed credits and $20 million in economic assistance.

Q. Is that likely to continue to go up at a substantial rate?

SENIOR ADMINISTRATION OFFICIAL. I think I'll just confine myself to repeating that we are going to do everything we can to assist the Portuguese in modernizing their armed forces and it's a goal which we believe is important both with respect to their NATO obligations and with respect to the important role that Portugal and its facilities play in the defense of the West.

Thank you very much.

THE PRESS. Thank you.

G. Spain

Document 228

Transcript of a Press Conference by the Secretary of State (Haig), Madrid, February 10, 1982 (Extract)[1]

Spanish-American Relations

SECRETARY HAIG. Good morning ladies and gentlemen. I want to state at the outset that the purpose of this press conference is to focus on Spanish-American bilateral relationships having conducted a press conference yesterday on the Madrid CSCE conference[2]—a conference which is proceeding as expected with very clear and full Western unity, with the focus on the situation in Poland and the impact that that has on the entire CSCE process, and I anticipate that that focus will continue in the days ahead.

So turning now to Spanish-American bilateral relationships, I want to emphasize that I've had extremely productive discussions here in Madrid. First with His Majesty King Juan Carlos; with Prime Minister Calvo-Sotelo; and with my counterpart, Foreign Minister Perez Llorca.

In these discussions I emphasized that the United States is committed to the democratic process in Spain, admires immensely the strength and vigor of the democratic institutions that have been established and which are now thriving in Spain and views democracy in Spain as the guiding principle of Spanish-American relationships.

We welcome Spain's movement toward full membership in Western institutions. We consider Spain a valuable international partner and welcome and fully support Spain's decision to enter NATO. With respect to NATO, we see the alliance moving rapidly to ratify Spanish entry. Canada and Norway have already done so. The United States and two or three others will do so in the immediate future and we look forward to full ratification sometime this spring by all member governments. The United States also seeks to build in the period ahead stronger and more intimate bilateral relationships with Spain, and in this regard the on-going base negotiations and the United States security assistance program with Spain will reflect this American objective. In conclusion, I consider this visit to have been highly beneficial in the context of the Spanish-American relationships. I welcome your questions.

Q. The question is, Mr. Secretary, you have referred to Spanish-American relations in a very vague way. I wonder if we could ask you to be a bit more specific as to the negotiations. Do you believe that they will be ended, that they will conclude at the same time as the conclusion of the ratification process for the entry of Spain into NATO and if that is the case do you believe that this entire process will climax with the visit of President Reagan to this country in July?

A. Well, first let me emphasize that we are very, very pleased with the current conduct of the base negotiations. We do see somewhat interrelationship between the completion of the ratification process, the program for American security assistance that will be submitted to the Congress for fiscal year '83 and the timely conclusion of the base negotiations by May of this year. I remain very optimistic that all of those events will happily in an interrelated way coincide. The question of a future visit from President Reagan is one that only he can

---

[1] Source: Department of State Press Release 59, February 16, 1982; also printed in Department of State *Bulletin*, April 1982, pp. 42–43. Haig was in Madrid to address the opening session of the CSCE. The omitted portion relates to the U.S. and other Western nations' positions on Poland and the Soviet-Western Europe gas pipeline.

[2] For a transcript of Haig's statement at this press conference, see document 157. The entire transcript is printed in Department of State *Bulletin*, April 1982, pp. 39–42.

answer. There is no current plan for such a visit. I don't have to tell you however, and I could not overemphasize the great regard that the President has for American-Spanish relationships and for his relationships with the officials here in Madrid. We've had a very successful visit from His Majesty recently in Washington[3] which the President has described as one of the highlights of his first year in office, and it was indeed that for all of us.

Q. The question, Mr. Secretary, is that in your conversations with Spanish authorities have you considered the possibility of a government of Spain headed by Socialists, and I say in a medium term span, and if that were the case what variations would that represent for the four year relationships with this country, and what new situations would you envision under those circumstances?

A. Well I think it would be highly inappropriate for a visiting official from the United States to comment in any way on the sovereign internal affairs of the Spanish people and I don't intend to do so. It would be wrong, self-defeating and counterproductive.

Q. Mr. Bernard Kalb, NBC. Mr. Secretary since Spain and the United States were on the same side in the debate yesterday at the conference, I hope you will allow me to ask a question that reflects on the conference. Why do you think the morning after, the Soviets and Poland were so determined to cut off Western denunciations of the crackdown in Poland?

A. Well, Mr. Kalb, I suppose that many of us have spent a good part of our lives trying to fathom Soviet and Eastern motivation. One could look very intensely at the Soviet media this morning, *Izvestia* in particular, which suggests that there was an orchestrated unanimity in the Western interventions yesterday on the topic of Poland. One could also question the tactic of accepting interventions by a number of Western spokesmen and then rather belatedly snuffing off, through a trumped-up parliamentary procedure, the intervention of other ministers who had traveled so far. It clearly underlines in my view the weakness and the incompatibility of the current policies of Moscow and Poland in Afghanistan and in the broader areas of implementation of human rights obligations and I consider it to have been a rather unfortunate misjudgment of neutral, nonaligned and Western attitudes with respect to these violations. And as I said yesterday there is no question in my mind that the truth will out, that Western spokesmen and nonaligned and neutral spokesmen as well will indeed have their opportunity to speak in the days ahead and have every right to insist on this opportunity.

Q. The question is, Mr. Secretary, everybody knows the great admiration and friendship felt by the President of the Socialist Party of Spain for Fidel Castro. And my question is did the United States Government, in receiving Felipe Gonzalez recently,[4] receive him as a representative of these guerrillas, as a President of the Socialist Party, or as a member of the Socialist International?

A. Well, (laughter) without accepting any of the premises of your question necessarily (laughter), the visit, the recent visit of Felipe Gonzalez to Washington was predicated on his recent visit to Central America as the Vice-President of the Socialist International[5] and our desire to discuss with him his own observations during that visit and the report that hopefully he would make to the upcoming meeting of the Socialist International. I would describe that discussion, which was essentially of the character I just said, as one that reflected Mr. Gonzalez's concern, which parallels my own, about the internal developments in Nicaragua which clearly manifest a trending toward a militaristic, totalitarian Marxist/Leninist model, which we consider to be unacceptable and a serious threat to peace and stability in the Western Hemisphere.

. . . .

---

[3] For documentation on King Juan Carlos' visit to the United States, October 12–16, 1981, see *American Foreign Policy: Current Documents, 1981*, Chapter 10, Part G.

[4] Secretary Haig met with Socialist Party Secretary General Felipe Gonzalez on January 8 at the Department of State.

[5] Gonzalez visited Nicaragua, Panama, and Cuba during a December 1981 Latin American trip.

Document 229

Statements by the Secretary of State (Haig) and the Spanish Foreign Minister (Perez Llorca), May 5, 1982 (Extract)[6]

Progress in U.S.-Spanish Negotiations

SECRETARY HAIG. Good afternoon, ladies and gentlemen. I want to use this opportunity to welcome my distinguished colleague, the Foreign Minister of Spain Perez Llorca who [is] with me here this morning on a long-scheduled visit to discuss the soon-to-expire, after having been extended, American and Spanish agreements,[7] and we've had very productive discussions on that subject. But I think also this visit has provided the very timely opportunity for us also to discuss the crisis in the South Atlantic.[8] As you know, Spain has a very special interest in this crisis, and our discussions today brought forth some very helpful and important ideas from my colleague which I hope will serve and assist in the political resolution of the crisis. Now, I'd like to introduce my colleague.

FOREIGN MINISTER PEREZ LLORCA. Good afternoon. As the Secretary of State has said, we have had [a] long time of friendly discussion and the main question has been discussed, have been (inaudible) we are [making] every effort to be accumulated to make it possible to find a political solution to the crisis and a peaceful one. We have had an important exchange of impressions and that of information and we have also discussed about bilateral relations—the future of our relations, and the new agreement which is to be signed covering the relations of the two countries within the Atlantic context—the context of the Atlantic Alliance. The progress in these talks has been very positive, too, and I think we have made it possible for the two delegations to work in the very early future—the very near future in a very productive way.

. . . .

[6] Source: Department of State files. The statements were made at the outset of a brief press conference following their meeting.

[7] For the text of the mutual defense agreement signed at Madrid on September 26, 1953, see 4 UST 1876. For the text of the agreement regarding the grant of defense articles and services under the Military Assistance Program, enacted by an exchange of notes of August 30, 1979, see 30 UST 7238.

[8] Reference is to the Falklands/Malvinas crisis. For documentation, see Chapter 15, Part B.

H. Italy

Document 230

Statement by the President's Assistant for National Security Affairs (Clark), January 28, 1982[1]

Release of General Dozier

It is a pleasure to report that General Dozier has been rescued, after 42 days captivity, by Italian police in the city of Padua, and is in top condition after his ordeal. President Reagan was notified of the rescue by me at 10 minutes of 7 this morning. We had early reports that the rescue had been carried out, but it was necessary to confirm that the General was safe.

The President said to me that a lot of peoples' prayers have been answered and that he finds it difficult to express his joy at this turn of events.

The President talked with Italy's President Pertini later this morning. He expressed our admiration for the efficiency of the Italian police who made the rescue.

When he was freed, General Dozier was barefoot and was still bearded, as some of the photos distributed by the Red Brigade indicate.

It is my understanding that he spoke to his wife by telephone from the police station in Padua after the rescue.

The rescue was carried out, according to reports we are receiving, by a special paramilitary group of the regular Italian police force. When they broke into the hideaway in Padua, firing one shot in the process, they seized five members of the Red Brigade.

The Italian police report that they had to overpower one guard who was holding a gun at General Dozier's head when the rescue took place.

The first unconfirmed report was received in Washington at 5:50 a.m., and at

[1] Source: White House Press Release, January 28, 1982, Office of the Press Secretary to the President.

6:07 a.m. Mr. Peter Bridges, our Deputy Chief of Mission in Italy, talked with Dozier. At that point I notified the President.

Document 231

Statements by President Reagan and Italian President Pertini, March 25, 1982[2]

"The Close Ties Which Bind Our Two Peoples and Countries"

THE PRESIDENT. Ladies and gentlemen, I've just completed extremely useful talks with a man who embodies the essential qualities we have in mind when we mention such terms as principle, staunchness, courage, and most important, friend.

I refer to the distinguished President of the Italian Republic, Sandro Pertini. President Pertini in a very real sense not only symbolizes but indeed helps forge the close ties which bind our two peoples and countries.

In our talks this morning, I made a point of reiterating to President Pertini the deep admiration which Americans feel for the constructive and courageous role Italy is increasingly playing on the world stage.

Our country, of course, has special reasons for appreciating that role. We applaud Italy's consistently strong support for the Atlantic Alliance. We applaud her decision to participate actively in the search for a Middle East peace. We are deeply moved by the tireless battle she is waging against the scourge of international terrorism—a battle so recently dramatized for us with the heartlifting liberation of General Dozier by Italian security forces.[3]

President Pertini's long and sometimes lonely fight against the evils of totalitarian oppression give him exceptional credentials as a man of integrity and resolution. He was among the first to speak out publicly against Soviet actions in Poland.[4] For this reason, I welcome the chance to share his insights on a number of critical international issues including the Polish crisis—the continuing Soviet occupation of Afghanistan and our joint determination to defeat international terrorism; the situation in Central America and the status of the peace process in the Middle East.

It's a great honor to have President Pertini with us and I look forward to seeing him again when I visit his country in June.[5]

PRESIDENT PERTINI. I am very pleased with my meeting with President Reagan, which I have looked forward to for a long time and which has fully met with my expectations. I was certain that we would immediately understand one another. Our talk was characterized by that cordiality and frankness which marks the relationship between our two countries.

Even before leaving on this trip I had had the opportunity to emphasize to you, members of the press, how sincerely we Italians share with the other Europeans, possibly to an even greater degree, the deep appreciation for the decisive help given us by the Americans during the last two world conflicts, to defend the independence and liberty of our continent. How deeply we feel the need to keep alive the common ideals of our Western civilization, a love of freedom, of social justice, of peace, of human rights, and therefore the reciprocal understanding between these two shores of the Atlantic.

I have also recalled how there exists between Italy and the United States still another deep bond, as sentimental as it is real, that of the presence in America of so many citizens of Italian origin. All these reasons for a strong and lasting understanding, based on common ideals, have been recalled by President Reagan and me in our meeting today, a meeting which, from the very beginning has engendered between us a spontaneous flow of friendship.

We have also reviewed those political and economic issues most relevant to the current international climate, which will be discussed in depth by Secretary of State

---

[2] Source: White House Press Release, March 25, 1982, Office of the Press Secretary to the President; also printed in *Weekly Compilation of Presidential Documents*, March 29, 1982, pp. 388–389. President Pertini visited the United States, March 24–April 1. These statements were made beginning at 11:47 a.m. on the South Grounds of the White House following their meeting.

[3] For the text of a statement on Dozier's release, see *supra*.

[4] Apparently a reference to Pertini's condemnation of the repression of the Polish people in his December 31, 1981, New Year's message to the Italian people.

[5] For the statement issued on President Reagan's June 7 visit to Italy, see document 233.

Haig and Foreign Minister Colombo. We will be able to continue our warm and fruitful exchange of ideas when President Reagan returns my visit in Rome next June. I am looking forward to furthering my direct contact with the dynamic American way of life, here in Washington and in my successive visits to other great cities in the United States.

I will be happy to meet first-hand the generous American people, for whom I have deep admiration, and who have moved me with the warmth of their welcome.

(In English) Thank you very much.

Document 232

Transcript of a White House Press Briefing, March 25, 1982[6]

President Reagan's Discussions With Italian President Pertini

SENIOR ADMINISTRATION OFFICIAL. Good morning or afternoon, as the case may be.

Q. It's afternoon.

SENIOR ADMINISTRATION OFFICIAL. Thank you, sir. We're very happy to [be] back with you again. We're getting to be sort of a—. . . two-step routine here. The—the meeting between the two Presidents, President Pertini of Italy and—and President Reagan of the United States, went extremely well. This was one of those occasions which some people think are—are rather rare when the—the public statements that the two leaders[7] give—their very, very close relationship to what was actually said and—and discussed during the meetings.

I think—I think it's fair to say the general theme of the strength of the U.S.-Italian bilateral relationship and the mutual expression of admiration and gratitude for what these two countries are doing for each other was—was the highlight in these talks.

On our side, President Reagan reiterated the very strong feelings of American respect—respect and gratitude for the very key contributions Italy has made in a number of areas of great—of great concern and interest to us.

The NATO Alliance was talked about. The efforts that Italy is making to help pursue a settlement in the Middle East peace process was also touched upon. We see eye-to-eye on Poland and Afghanistan. And that was a cause for particular appreciation on our side. And, of course, the fight that Italy is waging against terrorism, and, as the President mentioned out on the South Lawn, a fight that was dramatized for us by the release of General Dozier[8] in which President Pertini takes very justifiable—takes justifiable pride.

They—on President Pertini's side, he reiterated some of the remarks that he had made during the arrival ceremonies. He reminisced a bit about his own long career and association with Americans beginning in World War I when he was just a young—young officer, 18 years old and had—had worked with Americans of all kinds and had, at that period in his time, already become very impressed by what he called, "The American spirit of generosity, of selfless devotion to peace."

He made the point that Americans had come to the aid of European peoples in two major conflicts and they came to Europe, not for purposes of conquest but out of impulses that had to do with preservation of liberty and justice.

And as I say that took—that really—taking time for translations which were necessary, that consumed a good bit of the meeting.

There was one rather significant, substantive point that came up apart from the general theme. I think I'll let . . . address that. It—it had to do with the issue of Central America.

Q. Well, President Reagan said they talked about the Mideast, if I'm not mistaken.

SENIOR ADMINISTRATION OFFICIAL. They did. They talked about the Mideast. They talked about Afghanistan. They talked about Poland—talked about mutual contributions to the Atlantic Alliance—but not at any extended length. These are—these are two fellas who really see eye-to-eye on these things and there was no—

---

[6] Source: Office of the Press Secretary to the President. Senior administration officials conducted the briefing, which began at 12:06 p.m. in the White House Briefing Room.

[7] *Supra.*

[8] See the January 28 statement of the Assistant to the President for National Security Affairs, document 230.

Q. —speculate as to whether Israel will actually give back the Sinai?

SENIOR ADMINISTRATION OFFICIAL. No.

Q. How long was the meeting altogether?

SENIOR ADMINISTRATION OFFICIAL. Let's have the senior administration official address the—

Q. —move on.

Q. Tell us what the substance is.

Q. Tell the substance.

SENIOR ADMINISTRATION OFFICIAL. All-right. On—on Central America, the President described the background, historical background, to our involvement there. He described the purposes of our policies with particular emphasis on Salvador. And in reply, and here I should note that—that Foreign Minister Colombo replied because of the separation of powers between the Presidency and the Governor—he replied—gave a substantive reply in which he—he explained that there was a lot of concern in Italy about the situation in Central America with particular reference to Salvador. There was division of opinion with respect to—with—

Q. What?

Q. —division.

SENIOR ADMINISTRATION OFFICIAL.—division of opinion in Italy with respect to the revolution in Salvador and with respect to the elections. But he gave particularly strong emphasis—Foreign Minister Colombo gave particularly strong emphasis to the Caribbean Basin Initiative,[9] which he applauded, which he says is strongly supported by the Italian Government. He believes that this is an important effort to get at the social and economic problems which are at the root of political disaffection in Central America and he suggested even that European countries should support the Caribbean Basin Initiative and get involved in its implementation.

Q. Did he express the Italian Government's view on—the Government's view on the situation in El Salvador or you said he expressed a difference of opinion in Italy but, I mean, what is the government's view?

SENIOR ADMINISTRATION OFFICIAL. The government—he expressed the point of view that the government understands the United States goals in El Salvador and is strongly supportive of the Caribbean Basin Initiative.

Q. Were there any comments by President Pertini, himself, on the Central American situation?

SENIOR ADMINISTRATION OFFICIAL. No, there were not.

Q. Are you suggesting that he softened his criticism—

SENIOR ADMINISTRATION OFFICIAL. I beg your pardon?

Q. Are you suggesting that he had softened his previous criticism of Central America?

SENIOR ADMINISTRATION OFFICIAL. Who?

Q. President Pertini.

SENIOR ADMINISTRATION OFFICIAL. President Pertini did not—during the meeting that I was in. I was not in the first part of the meeting in the Oval Office where a senior administration official was present. But in the Cabinet Room, the part that I was in, he did not express himself on Central America.

Q. You're leaving us with the impression that the Government of Italy simply understands American goals in El Salvador. They didn't express any reservations as foreign minister speaking for the government?

SENIOR ADMINISTRATION OFFICIAL. The foreign minister says that the Italian Government understands American policy and goals in El Salvador and strongly supports the Caribbean Basin Initiative.

Q. The Government of Italy has already gone on record, has it not, in opposing some of the things we're doing in Central America?

SENIOR ADMINISTRATION OFFICIAL. What are you referring to? Would you cite them for me?

Q. No, I can't cite them chapter and verse but I believe Colombo, himself, in a speech, what, a month ago,[10] complained that the United States might be intervening in Central America in a way that would be destructive to a peaceful process.

SENIOR ADMINISTRATION OFFICIAL. I'm not aware of that speech.

---

9 For documentation on the Caribbean Basin Initiative, see Chapter 15.

10 Apparently a reference to a February 10 statement by Colombo during a debate on foreign policy in the Italian Chamber of Deputies.

Q. I'll see if I can find it but—

SENIOR ADMINISTRATION OFFICIAL. I'd be interested if you can find it to send it to me.

Q. I'll look for it.

SENIOR ADMINISTRATION OFFICIAL. Okay.

Q. Does he mean by the initiative the United States initiative to be specific?

SENIOR ADMINISTRATION OFFICIAL. Yes—

SENIOR ADMINISTRATION OFFICIAL. Yes, in the Caribbean Basin.

SENIOR ADMINISTRATION OFFICIAL. Yes, the Caribbean Basin Initiative, yes.

SENIOR ADMINISTRATION OFFICIAL. Unequivocally.

Q. Would you characterize how the, in fact—the meeting go? They were alone together at the beginning and then people—

SENIOR ADMINISTRATION OFFICIAL.—how long—

Q. —talked. How long was it too?

SENIOR ADMINISTRATION OFFICIAL. Do you want to take that?

SENIOR ADMINISTRATION OFFICIAL. Yes, sure. Essentially, back-to-back, I think the meeting ran about an hour and a half and in three stages, although there was a certain fluidity between these stages—the first stage the two Presidents were alone. They were in the Oval Office and this was during the time when the photo opportunities were taking place. So, they had, I would reckon, about 10, 15 minutes of discussion side-by-side by the fireplace.

After the photographers had all left, there was then a period when they were joined by the Vice President and the foreign ministers and Judge Clark.[11] And there was additional conversation and this was—at least this was—that's the only part I heard. . . .

And then this went on for about probably a good half hour perhaps a little bit longer. And then . . . into the Cabinet Room for the larger group with about—I'd say, nine on either side.

Q. Did they discuss the President's forthcoming visit in June?

SENIOR ADMINISTRATION OFFICIAL. No, only—no, they did not discuss it in any detail—only that the President said he was very much looking forward to coming to Rome[12] and President Pertini said we're really happy to have you coming and looking forward to it.

Q. Did they discuss Japan and Asia in any way?

SENIOR ADMINISTRATION OFFICIAL. No.

Q. Because he had just been there.

SENIOR ADMINISTRATION OFFICIAL. No, did not come up.

Q. Did they discuss the pipeline deal?

SENIOR ADMINISTRATION OFFICIAL. No.

Q. Did they discuss Western credits to the Soviet Union?

SENIOR ADMINISTRATION OFFICIAL. No. Understand in this sense, President Pertini would not really have been empowered to deal with that subject. They could have discussed it, obviously, if they had wanted to, but it didn't come up.

Q. Did President Reagan reminisce at all as President Pertini reminisced about his career or—

SENIOR ADMINISTRATION OFFICIAL. To a certain extent, yes. In the Oval Office, he, as I mentioned, talked about how as a young officer in the Italian Army he had first met Americans—this was World War I and then when he fought with the partisans in World War II and in the battle for the liberation of Florence he was involved in that and he came back to this point. He emphatically stated on at least three—

Q. No, I meant did President Reagan reminisce and in a similar vein?

SENIOR ADMINISTRATION OFFICIAL. I don't know. He may have in their private—when they were sitting in the two chairs together in the Oval Office. But I didn't hear that.

Q. You were saying—

SENIOR ADMINISTRATION OFFICIAL. Excuse me.

Q. —that he kept going back to one point—Pertini?

SENIOR ADMINISTRATION OFFICIAL. Yes, saying that the Italian people will never forget the sacrifices that America had made for Italy in—and the cause of freedom in Europe.

---

[11] William Clark, the Assistant to the President for National Security Affairs.

[12] President Reagan visited Rome on June 7.

This was a leitmotif that permeated their exchange.

Q. I'd like to raise a question that I base on your background briefing a couple of days ago on Sicily,[13] where I was never [?] granted a cavalier response, actually.

The response that you made was that you don't think that there's any threat from the Sicilian separatist movements and that you don't think that there's any particular danger from the massive demonstration planned against the NATO base on April 4th.[14]

The reason I want to raise this now is there was a parliamentary inquiry raised in the Italian Parliament yesterday on this situation and they do seem to consider it somewhat serious. The separatists, of course, are completely funded by Qaddafi and have been a problem for quite some time. And the European Peace Movement leaders recently met with Qaddafi and discussed plans for the actions in Sicily on April 4th.

I'm wondering if I can't get just some response of any sense of seriousness of the situation or are you monitoring it closely? Just something beyond what you said the other day, which just dismissed—

SENIOR ADMINISTRATION OFFICIAL. Well, first of all, I think I will turn that over to my colleague who really addressed the question in the last briefing, as I recall. And—

SENIOR ADMINISTRATION OFFICIAL. I'm the one that dismissed it. (Laughter)

SENIOR ADMINISTRATION OFFICIAL. He's the one who dismissed it and I dismiss it with him.

But, no, anything more you want to elaborate—

SENIOR ADMINISTRATION OFFICIAL. I really don't have anything to add to what I responded the other day. According to the information we have, the separatist movement, if you could even call it that, is not regarded in Italy as a serious threat to the solidarity of the country.

SENIOR ADMINISTRATION OFFICIAL. Yes, I would add, I think we have about as much concern in the context of the President's visit about dangers from a separatist movement in Sicily that we do from, say, a—you know—the Breton separatist movement in France. I mean, I—we don't—well, we don't—

Q. Do you know that the projections now by the Peace Movement are that they will have 50,000 people from throughout Europe converging on that NATO base? And that's not any—

SENIOR ADMINISTRATION OFFICIAL. I'd have no idea what numbers, but I'm sure we would be foolish to think that people are not going to try to mobilize as many peace demonstrators as they can.

THE PRESS. Thank you.

Document 233

Joint Statement Issued by the Governments of the United States and Italy, Rome, June 7, 1982[15]

"A Productive Exchange of Views"

At the invitation of the President of the Italian Republic, Sandro Pertini, the President of the United States of America, Ronald Reagan, paid a visit to Rome on June 7th, 1982. The visit provided an opportunity for the two Presidents to have a productive exchange of views. Two useful meetings were held between President Reagan and the President of the Council of Ministers, Giovanni Spadolini. President Reagan took the opportunity to thank President Pertini for his recent state visit to the United States and conveyed to him the warm good wishes of the American Government and the American people. President Pertini expressed to President Reagan his appreciation for the warm reception he enjoyed in the United States.

Presidents Reagan and Pertini reviewed the threat which international terrorism presents to the free world and noted with satisfaction the successes of the Italian and other Western governments in combatting this menace. The two Presidents also reviewed international trouble spots includ-

---

[13] March 23. At this briefing, reporters were given biographical information about President Pertini.

[14] Major demonstrations in the area of Comiso, Sicily, were planned and held on April 4.

[15] Source: White House Press Release, June 7, 1982, Office of the Press Secretary to the President; printed also in *Weekly Compilation of Presidential Documents*, June 14, 1982, pp. 763–764. The text of the statement was released in London.

ing Afghanistan, Poland, and Central and South America; the two reaffirmed their strongest commitment to the preservation and restoration of freedom and justice for all men. They noted their shared hope for a cessation of hostilities in the South Atlantic. The two Heads of State concluded their meeting with an affirmation of the strength of U.S.-Italian bonds and a review of those common values on which the two societies have been built.

Prime Minister Spadolini and President Reagan, first between themselves and then along with Minister of Foreign Affairs Emilio Colombo and Secretary of State Alexander Haig, reviewed a number of questions facing the two countries, including the 1979 decision by NATO to place intermediate-range nuclear forces in Europe,[16] together with the offer to the Soviet Union for simultaneous negotiations on control and limitation of such weapons, and the overall Middle East situation, with special attention to the two most urgent questions in that area at the moment; the Lebanese situation where it is of the utmost urgency to bring a cessation of the fighting. On the Iran–Iraq conflict—the two sides agreed on the need for a political settlement respecting the territorial integrity of both nations.

In addition they reviewed the validity of both countries' participation in the Sinai multinational force and the prospects for the dialogue on Palestinian autonomy. They also examined East-West relations, including questions of trade and credit and issues related to economic and monetary cooperation between the two countries. The two Heads of Government reaffirmed their commitment to a policy aiming at a growing level of economic and commercial relations between the two countries in order to fight against inflation, promote growth and thereby employment.

President Reagan reviewed his proposals for the worldwide reduction of strategic nuclear weapons and for the reduction of intermediate-range nuclear forces in Europe. Prime Minister Spadolini noted with approval the recent announcement that the START talks will begin in Geneva on June 29.[17] The two said they shared the aspirations of many of the young people who were marching for peace, took note of the institutions and policies which have kept the peace in Europe for almost forty years, and urged the Soviet Union to respond positively to proposals which have been made by the United States.

The Prime Minister and the President viewed with pleasure the new initiative for the exchange of young students between their countries which will begin in 1982.

The two governments agreed to begin regular meetings to discuss cultural and information matters with the desire to improve cultural programs and in order to examine means of strengthening relations in these fields. The first cultural and information talks will be held in Washington in October.

The two sides concluded their talks by welcoming recent decisions to strengthen mutual consultations as an expression of the special and close relationship which Italy and the United States enjoy.

Document 234

Statements by President Reagan and Italian Prime Minister Spadolini, November 3, 1982[18]

"The United States Has No Better Friend . . . Than Italy"

THE PRESIDENT. Ladies and gentlemen, Prime Minister Spadolini and I have had productive and harmonious discussions today covering a wide range of important issues. Our discussions confirmed the wide ranging accord that exists between our two countries on matters affecting world peace, Western solidarity and international economic cooperation. And this is only fitting, as between allies as close as the United States and Italy. On the key issues of East-West trade, Prime Minister Spadolini and I

---

[16] For the text of this statement, see *American Foreign Policy: Basic Documents, 1977–1980*, pp. 494–496.

[17] For the text of the May 31 speech in which President Reagan announced the beginning of START talks, see *Weekly Compilation of Presidential Documents*, June 7, 1982, pp. 730–731. For the text of the brief joint announcements by the U.S. and Soviet Governments, May 31, on the beginning of formal START negotiations, see *ibid.*, p. 731.

[18] Source: White House Press Release, November 3, 1982, Office of the Press Secretary to the President; also printed in *Weekly Compilation of Presidential Documents*, November 8, 1982, pp. 1430–1432. Prime Minister Spadolini visited Washington, November 2–4. The President spoke in the Rose Garden beginning at 1:23 p.m., following their meeting.

agree that the United States, Italy and the other allies must pursue discussions aimed at establishing a broad transatlantic consensus. Our trade and financial relations with the Soviet Union must take into account the nature of the Soviet conduct toward its neighbors. The Prime Minister shared with me Italy's special perspective in this regard.

We discussed the current situation in the Middle East where our two countries are working closely both to guarantee the peace which prevails in the Sinai and to assist the Government of Lebanon in securing withdrawal of all foreign forces and restoring its full authority throughout the territory. The Prime Minister stated a readiness in principle to support the expansion of Italy's contribution to the multinational force in the context of broadening the force's mandate and its composition.

And I want to take this occasion to extend my personal appreciation to the Prime Minister for his vigorous and constructive contributions that Italy is making for the promotion of peace and stability in that critical region.

We also discussed the importance of the aerospace industry in strengthening the technological capability of the West, and we've agreed to instruct the appropriate authorities in our respective governments to facilitate cooperation in this sector. In this connection the Prime Minister and I agree that our governments would establish working groups to explore the means of future cooperation between our two nations. During our discussion of Western security issues, I expressed appreciation to the Prime Minister for Italy's indispensable contribution to the December 1979 NATO decision on the intermediate-range nuclear forces.[19] I reaffirm to him my commitment to pursue vigorously negotiations leading to the elimination of such forces by both sides and to the deep reduction in strategic nuclear forces as well.

I'd like to close on a personal note. This was my fourth meeting with the Prime Minister[20] and my admiration and respect for him has grown with each encounter. The United States has no better friend in the world than Italy, and the West has no more erudite and distinguished a leader than my friend, Giovanni Spadolini. After our meetings in Europe, it was a great pleasure for me to receive him here at home, and I look forward to seeing him once again when he returns to the United States for the economic summit that will be held in Williamsburg next spring. Welcome.

PRIME MINISTER SPADOLINI. I have come today to see President Reagan together with Foreign Minister Colombo not only in behalf of Italy, but, also, as the interpreter of the concerns and common feelings of Western Europe—that Europe that finds itself in the values of freedom and tolerance and of respect of man for man, which are part and parcel of the Atlantic community.

I have told President Reagan about the absolute need to find a global strategy in the economic and trade relations with the Eastern countries. The misunderstandings of the last months must be replaced by a new relation of partnership on a basis of equal dignity and a mutual understanding based on the agreements of Versailles and on which the Italian contribution was determined.

As Italians, we feel that in consistency with the approach adopted at Versailles, the Western world must find and define a common approach based on a greater strictness of an economic nature in its relations with the Eastern world, and based on and inspired by the following four points.

First, no undue gift to the Soviet Union as far as credits are concerned. Second, greater strictness in the transfer of technologies to the Soviet Union. Third, implementation of a security net within the Western system so as to reduce the dependence on the Soviet Union concerning raw materials and energy products. Fourth, the contracts that have already been signed by European countries concerning the pipeline must be honored so as not to prejudge the credibility as far as the trade of the Western world is concerned.

But I think that, amongst these four points, we also feel that it is indispensable to have a prejudicial position that would effect in a legitimate manner the past, or that would create obstacles for the future.

Following the first meetings that I have had here in Washington, the United States has made a further step forward toward the solution of this problem through a formula which will be presented this evening to the ambassadors of the countries concerned. And within this perspective, an awareness of the need of the lifting of sanctions as a

---

[19] For the text of the NATO statement, December 12, 1979, see *American Foreign Policy: Basic Documents, 1977–1980*, pp. 494–496.

[20] President Reagan met with Spadolini in Versailles, June 4–7; in Rome, June 7; and in Bonn, June 9–11.

consequence of the new agreement, Italy will continue to commit itself to find a conclusion and a solution so as to have a global agreement—a solution which I think is very near.

I will, also, present this same position in Paris in the very close meeting that I will have with President Mitterrand.[21] The political solidarity between Europe and the United States that we want to defend at all costs, also, implies the overcoming of these conflicts which are not necessary, and that we are having because of the Soviet Union.

Italy is and will always be coherent to the principles that have been inspiring for more than 30 years its foreign policy and which are based on the strengthening of the bonds with its partners of the Western world and first and foremost with the United States, which is the essential premise to start, once again, and on the basis of a guaranteed security, the East–West dialogue which is undergoing new tensions today which torment us and concern us very much. I am thinking in particular of the situation in Poland and in Afghanistan. This is why, in spite of the international difficulties—and I think that because of these difficulties we are convinced more than ever about the fact that we should pursue in the negotiations undergoing in Geneva for the control—for a balanced control and reduction of armaments.

I have reaffirmed to President Reagan the conviction that Italy has, that to find peace in the world it is necessary to also act for the development of a policy which would favor the dialogue between the North and the South in our planet. And I am referring in particular to the difficult areas of the Mediterranean. And it is in this framework that I am thinking of satisfaction of the joint action of our two countries, first in the Sinai and today in Beirut, an action that we want to strengthen, in agreements between our two governments, and that in the next days will find a further development with the parallel decisions which will increase our presence in Lebanon, always with the aim of giving to that torn country a condition of true independence and stability.

Within the framework of bilateral collaboration, which is developing in all fields from the economic to the cultural, and within the framework of our collaboration, also, in the fight against terrorism and against narcotics, I have told President Reagan about the Italian decision which will have to be now defined in the competent fora, to buy from the American industry three[22] McDonald–Douglas DC–980 aircraft.

I have also conveyed to President Reagan the warm greetings of the President of the Italian Republic, Mr. Sandro Pertini, seeing with satisfaction that in the last 2 years Italy has confirmed its role amongst the most industrialized countries of the Western world. And this is why I've been able to come here expressing the voice of an Italy which is determined to respect its international commitments and to, therefore, begin working from the strengthening of defense in the Atlantic Alliance; to struggle, therefore, against economic difficulties which are common to the whole Western industrialized world. And we are doing this in a very strict and steadfast manner.

All Europeans know how much they owe to the United States that twice has given back freedom to our continent. And I, therefore, have been interpreter of these feelings to my friend, President Ronald Reagan, a man that I admire very much for his loyalty, dedication, to individual freedoms of the whole world.

Thirty—I'm sorry. It was 30 and not 3 aircraft.

Document 235

Transcript of a Joint Press Conference by the Secretary of State (Shultz) and the Italian Foreign Minister (Colombo), Rome, December 13, 1982 (Extract)[23]

Talks With Italian Leaders

SECRETARY SHULTZ. In keeping with the courtesy extended to me and my party throughout this visit, the Foreign Minister has invited me to make the first statement,

---

[21] Spadolini's scheduled meeting with Mitterrand was canceled after a domestic political crisis led to the fall of the Italian Government.

[22] Thirty. [Footnote in the source text.]

[23] Source: Department of State Press Release 383, December 14, 1982; printed also in Department of State *Bulletin*, February 1983, pp. 24–25. Shultz visited Rome on December 12 and 13 for talks with Italian leaders, Pope John Paul II, and Egyptian President Hosni Mubarak. The omitted portion was a question and answer on Secretary Shultz's meeting with President Mubarek.

and I think what I might say is simply that in the series of meetings I have had here with Prime Minister Fanfani,[24] with President Pertini and with my friend Foreign Minister Colombo, it has been a very worthwhile and enlightening day for me. I know that you would prefer to ask questions than have me give lectures so I will simply let it go at that except for one incident in the discussion with Prime Minister Fanfani. I told him that Mr. Colombo was the first Foreign Minister to call on me and that he had taken me under his wing and given me some instructions. I said that he had also told me the tricks of the trade, and Mr. Fanfani thought about that for a minute and said, "I hope he didn't tell you all of them."

FOREIGN MINISTER COLOMBO. First of all, I would like to take this opportunity to once again convey words of welcome and greeting on my own behalf and on behalf of the Italian Government to Secretary of State Shultz. I would also like to say that this day of talks has been a very intense and a very fruitful one. I could add at this point fruitful as always in all the talks that I have had the pleasure of having with Secretary of State Shultz since he came into office. Our talks have covered a wide range of problems starting with East–West relations, especially in view of the recent evolution of our policy vis-à-vis the Eastern countries. We have exchanged our views on the Polish situation; we have discussed the INF and the START negotiations; we have discussed the Middle East, both Lebanon and the general negotiations as a whole; we have had discussions on international terrorism and also a discussion on bilateral problems, a discussion which we will be able to continue this evening.

Q. My question is directed to Mr. Shultz. Mr. Secretary, my question is in regard to Poland; the announcement by General Jaruzelski.[25] Does the United States at this point regard those announcements as cosmetic?

SECRETARY SHULTZ. I think the general answer is that we are looking closely at what has been said, that we are consulting with our allies, but in a preliminary way. What we have seen so far are some words, but nothing of substance has actually been done. But we will continue to observe the situation and consult—it is hard to say at this point. We do not see that there is anything that substantial as to cause us to think a major change has taken place. There may have been some development during the day of which I am not aware because I have been in one meeting after another, but I think that the Minister and I discussed this and we basically see this the same way.

Q. With respect to your conversations on the antiterrorism problems, could you tell us how much concern there is in your country with respect to the investigation of the assassination attempt on the Pope and links or attempts to link it to Bulgarians?[26]

FOREIGN MINISTER COLOMBO. We are following with great concern the evolution of this situation. The data that we do have at the moment is not complete, and not everything has been confirmed. We will give a political assessment when all the necessary data has been collected and, most of all, confirmed. Of course, we consider the situation to be a very serious one, and if the data that will be collected will correspond to what is assumed at the moment, Italy will reflect very seriously on the conclusions to be drawn. And just as today we have discussed this problem with Secretary of State Shultz, so in the same manner, if this data is confirmed and also if this data is on a broader basis than what it is at the moment, we will also inform and speak about this to our NATO allies.

Q. Secretary Shultz, what can you tell us from your visit with the Pope;[27] what his feeling is about what's happening in Poland; how does he feel about events there now?

SECRETARY SHULTZ. I don't think it is appropriate for me to comment on things that the Pope may have told me about Poland beyond saying that he is obviously following the matter very closely and we did talk about it. I did raise with Cardinal Casaroli[28]—I asked him what he thought about it and he said, "Well, you must talk with our resident expert." So certainly His Holiness' views are ones we all are very interested in, but I don't think it is appropriate for me to quote him.

Q. You mentioned that, on the subject of the Bulgarian investigation, you were

---

[24] Amintore Fanfani became Prime Minister on November 30, following the resignation of Giovanni Spadolini.

[25] Reference is to the announcement that martial law would be lifted in Poland.

[26] Reference is to the arrest by Italian security forces of Antonov, an employee of the Bulgarian State Airlines. Antonov has been charged with directing convicted terrorist M. Ali Agca in his May 1981 assassination attempt on Pope John Paul II.

[27] Shultz met with Pope John Paul II on December 12. No public statement regarding their meeting was released.

[28] Vatican Secretary of State.

going to consult with your NATO allies. Does that suggest that you think there might be a link with the Soviet Union?

FOREIGN MINISTER COLOMBO. First of all, this information would only take place if the data collected would prove this information to be necessary, and second, what you say is not necessarily so because if there is one problem that concerns one of the countries of the Warsaw Pact, therefore, we would discuss this at NATO as we have always discussed this type of thing: that is, a collaboration within NATO to fight against terrorism. Well, if I may express myself freely, I don't feel that you can draw the conclusions in the direction you seem to be going.

Q. Mr. Secretary, today in your talks with various representatives of the Italian Government, have you also discussed the problem of an eventual crisis in the Persian Gulf and what the Italian contribution could be to such a crisis, bearing in mind that this crisis in the Persian Gulf would be a threat for the security of NATO?

SECRETARY SHULTZ. We discussed Middle East developments, Lebanon, West Bank/Gaza issues, and matters of that kind. We did not discuss the Gulf area as such, so I can't say that we had any discussions on that point.

I would add more generally, however, that I did say to each of the Italian Government officials I talked to that the contributions of Italy to peace in the world, to constructive behavior, for example in the Sinai, for example in the multinational force in Lebanon, in its determination to deploy the INF weapons, to support the negotiations in Geneva, and in many, many respects all the way through, Italy has been a great friend and ally and we welcome this behavior on the part of Italy very warmly and applaud it.

Q. If evidence were to bear out some of the speculation concerning the Bulgarian connection, what implications would you derive from this with regard to the future of the East–West dialogue?

SECRETARY SHULTZ. I don't think it is well to speculate excessively on this and I would only echo what Foreign Minister Colombo has just said, that it is a serious investigation with important implications and we'll await the developments of the investigation. The Government of Italy has said that it will keep us informed. We'll rest at that.

Q. Was the question of the Siberian gas pipeline addressed in the course of the discussions? Could you give us an indication as to whether, in the event that evidence were to throw further conclusive light on the Bulgarian connection, would this tend to slow matters down also with regard to the issue of the Siberian pipeline?

SECRETARY SHULTZ. We didn't discuss that subject. We did, however, discuss the subject of East–West economic relationships and the desirability of finding together a firm strategy for conducting those relationships and a method of consulting about that strategy. Those of you who were at the NATO Ministerial meeting remember that we did agree there to energize the OECD and COCOM and in various respects stimulate a variety of studies and activities. Minister Colombo and I, in our discussion, agreed that it would be desirable to have some overall strategic umbrella, you might say, over these individual activities. And, in one way or another, we are both determined to find our way to the answer of how to construct that—we haven't got the answer yet.

FOREIGN MINISTER COLOMBO. I confirm that we have not discussed the problem of the Siberian pipeline, and I confirm that we have discussed an East–West strategy, especially the problem of security for the Western World which includes also economic behavior and conduct vis-à-vis Eastern countries. This coordination will take place in studies that are going to be carried out in the appropriate fora such as OECD and COCOM. Then, once these studies are made, there will be coordination which will bring about a coordinated policy.

. . . .

I. Vatican

Document 236

Statements by President Reagan and Pope John Paul II, Vatican City, June 7, 1982[1]

"I Leave This Audience With a Renewed Sense of Hope and Dedication"

The President. Your Holiness, Your Eminences, Your Excellencies, members of the clergy, and ladies and gentlemen, on behalf of myself and for all Americans, I want to express profound appreciation to you Your Holiness and to all of those from the Holy City who made it possible for us to meet in Vatican City.

This is truly a city of peace, love, and charity where the highest to the humblest among us seek to follow in the footsteps of the fishermen. As you know Your Holiness, this is my first visit to Europe as President, and I would like to think of it as a pilgrimage for peace, a journey aimed at strengthening the forces for peace in the free West by offering new opportunities for realistic negotiations with those who may not share the values and the spirit we cherish.

This is no easy task, but I leave this audience with a renewed sense of hope and dedication. Hope, because one cannot meet a man like Your Holiness without feeling that a world that can produce such courage and vision out of adversity and oppression is capable, with God's help, of building a better future. Dedication, because one cannot enter this citadel of faith, the fountainhead of so many of the values we face in the—or that we in the free West hold dear without coming away resolved to do all in one's power to live up to them.

Certain common experiences we have shared in our different walks of life, Your Holiness. And the warm correspondence we have carried on also gave our meeting a special meaning for me. I hope that others will follow. Let me add that all Americans remember with great warmth your historic visit to our shores in 1979.[2] We all hope that you will be back again with your timeless message: "Ours is a nation grounded on faith, faith in man's ability through God given freedom to live in tolerance and peace as faith in a Supreme Being guides our daily striving in this world." Our national motto, In God We Trust, reflects that faith.

Many of our earlier settlers came to America seeking a refuge where they could worship God unhindered. So our dedication to individual freedoms is wedded to religious freedom as well. Liberty has never meant license to Americans. We treasure it precisely because it protects the human and spiritual values that we hold most dear: the right to worship as we choose, the right to elect democratic leaders, the right to choose the type of education we want for our children, and freedom from fear, want and oppression. These are God-given freedoms not the contrivances of man.

We also believe in helping one another through our churches and charitable institutions or simply as one friend, one good Samaritan to another. The Ten Commandments and the Golden Rule are as much a part of our living heritage as the Constitution we take such pride in. And we have tried, not always successfully, but always in good conscience to extend those same principles to our role in the world.

We know that God has blessed America with the freedom and abundance many of our less fortunate brothers and sisters around the world have been denied. Since the end of World War II, we have done our best to provide assistance to them; assistance amounting to billions of dollars worth of food, medicine and materials. And we'll continue to do so in the years ahead.

Americans have always believed that in the words of the Scripture, "Unto whomsoever much is given, of him shall be much required." To us in a troubled world, the Holy See and your pastorate represent one of the world's greatest moral and spiritual forces.

We admire your active efforts to foster peace and promote justice, freedom and compassion in a world that is still stalked by the forces of evil. As a people and as a

[1] Source: White House Press Release, June 7, 1982, Office of the Press Secretary to the President; also printed in *Weekly Compilation of Presidential Documents,* June 14, 1982, pp. 758–761. The President visited the Vatican during his four-nation European tour, June 2–11. The President and Pope spoke in the Papal Library, beginning at 12:41 p.m.

[2] Pope John Paul II visited the United States, October 1–7, 1979.

government, we seek to pursue the same goals of peace, freedom and humanity along political and economic lines that the Church pursues in its spiritual role. So we deeply value your counsel and support and express our solidarity with you.

Your Holiness, one of the areas of our mutual concern is Latin America. We want to work closely with the Church in that area to help promote peace, social justice and reform, and to prevent the spread of repression and godless tyranny.

We also share your concern in seeking peace and justice in troubled areas of the Middle East such as Lebanon. Another special area of mutual concern is the martyred nation of Poland—your own homeland. Through centuries of adversity, Poland has been a brave bastion of faith and freedom in the hearts of her courageous people, yet not in those who rule her.

We seek a process of reconciliation and reform that will lead to a new dawn of hope for the people of Poland, and we'll continue to call for an end to martial law, for the freeing of all political prisoners, and to resume dialogue among the Polish government, the Church and the Solidarity movement which speaks for the vast majority of Poles.

Denying financial assistance to the oppressive Polish regime, America will continue to provide the Polish people with as much food and commodity support as possible through church and private organizations.

Today, Your Holiness, marks the beginning of the United Nations special session on disarmament. We pledge to do everything possible in these discussions, as in our individual initiatives for peace and arms reduction, to help bring a real, lasting peace throughout the world. To us, this is nothing less than a sacred trust.

Dante has written that, "The infinite goodness has such wide arms that it takes whatever turns to it." We ask your prayers, Holy Father, that God will guide us in our efforts for peace on this journey and in the years ahead and that the wide arms of faith and forgiveness can some day embrace a world at peace with justice and compassion for all mankind.

THE POPE. Mr. President, I am particularly pleased to welcome you today to the Vatican. Although we have already had many contacts, it is the first time that we have met personally.

In you, the President of the United States of America, I greet all the people of your great land. I still remember privately the warm welcome that I was given by millions of your fellow citizens less than 3 years ago. On that occasion, I was once more able to witness first-hand the vitality of your nation. I was able to see again how the moral and spiritual values transmitted by your Founding Fathers find their dynamic expression in the life of modern America.

The American people are indeed proud of their right to life, liberty, and the pursuit of happiness. They are proud of civil and social progress in American society as well as their extraordinary advances in science and technology.

As I speak to you today, it is my hope that the entire structure of American life will rest evermore securely on the strong foundation of moral and spiritual values. Without the fostering and defense of these values, all human advancement is stunted and the dignity of the human person is endangered.

Throughout the course of their history, and especially in difficult times, the American people have repeatedly risen to challenges presented to them. They have given many proofs of unselfishness, generosity, concern for others, concern for the poor, the needy, the oppressed.

They have shown confidence in that great ideal of being a united people with a mission of service to perform.

At this present moment in the history of the world, the United States is called above all to fulfill its mission in the service of world peace.

The very condition of the world today calls for a farsighted policy that will further those indispensable conditions of justice and freedom, of truth and love that are the foundations of lasting peace.

Mr. President, my own greatest preoccupation is for the peace of the world, peace in our day.

In many parts of the world, there are centers of acute tension. This acute tension is manifested above all in the crisis of the South Atlantic,[3] in the war between Iran and Iraq and now in the grave crisis provoked by the new events in Lebanon.[4]

This grave crisis in Lebanon likewise merits the attention of the world because of

---

[3] For documentation, see Chapter 15, Part B.

[4] For documentation on the crisis in Lebanon, see Chapter 11, Part C.

the danger it contains of farther provocation in the Middle East with immense consequences for world peace.

There are, fortunately, many factors in society that today positively contribute to peace. This positive factor includes an increasing realization of the interdependence of all peoples, the growing solidarity with those in need, and a growth of conviction of the absurdity of war as a means of resolving controversies between nations.

During my recent visit to Britain[5] I stated in particular that the scale and the horror from all the warfare, whether nuclear or not, makes it totally unacceptable as a means of settling differences between nations.

And for those who profess the Christian faith, I offer up as motivation the fact that when you are in contact with the Prince of Peace, you understand how totally opposed to His message are hatred and war.

The duty of peace calls especially upon the leaders of the world. It is up to the representatives of governments and peoples to work to free humanity not only from wars and conflicts, but from the fear that is generated by evermore sophisticated and deadly weapons.

Peace is not only the absence of war; it also involves reciprocal trust between nations, a trust that is manifested and proved through constructive negotiations that aim at ending the arms race and at liberating immense resources that can be used to alleviate misery and feed millions of hungry human beings.

All effective peacemaking requires foresightedness, for foresightedness is a quality needed in all peacemakers. You—your own great nation is called to exercise this foresightedness as far—all the nations of the world. This quality enables leaders to commit themselves to those concrete programs, which are essential to world peace—programs of justice and development, efforts to defend and protect human life, as well as initiatives that favor human rights.

On the contrary, anything that wounds, weakens, or dishonors human dignity in any aspect imperils the cause of the human person and at the same time the peace of the world.

The relations between nations are greatly affected by the development issue—issue, which reserves its full relevance in this day of ours. Success in resolving questions in the North-South dialogue will continue to be the gates of peaceful relations between values, political communities, and continue to influence the peace of the world in the years ahead.

Economic and social advancement linked to financial collaboration between peoples remains an apt goal for renewed efforts of the statesmen of this world.

A truly universal concept of the common good for the human family is an incomparable instrument in building the edifice of the world today. It is my own conviction that a united and concerned America can contribute immensely to the cause of world peace through the efforts of our leaders and the commitment of all her citizens. Dedicated to the high ideals of her traditions, America is in a splendid position to help all humanity enjoy what she herself is intent upon possessing.

With faith in God and belief in universal human solidarity may America step forward in this crucial moment in history to consolidate her rightful place at the service of world peace. In this sense, Mr. President, I repeat today those words that I spoke when I left the United States in 1977. My final prayer is this; that God will bless America so that she may increasingly become and truly be and long remain one nation under God, indivisible, with liberty and justice for all.

Thank you.

Document 237

Statement Issued by the Department of State, December 22, 1982[6]

U.S. Involvement in the Investigation of the Papal Assassination Attempt

Q. Has the United States received any requests from Italy for assistance in the investigation into the attempted assassination of Pope John Paul II? If so, what assistance have we rendered?

A. In October 1982, the Italian magistrate investigating the assassination attempt

[5] May 28–June 2, 1982.

[6] Source: Office of Press Relations, Department of State; posted statement. The statement was posted in response to a question taken at 12:20 p.m. at the December 20 Department of State Daily Press Briefing.

requested U.S. assistance in facilitating interviews with several American citizens who were eyewitnesses to the crime. In response to this request the Department of Justice assisted Judge Martella in arranging interviews with and taking depositions from a number of people in the Washington area and around the United States. We are not aware of any other specific request from the Italian authorities for assistance in this investigation. We continue to follow the investigation with great concern and, of course, stand ready to offer whatever assistance we might appropriately provide.

J. Greece

Document 238

Transcript of a Press Conference by the Secretary of State (Haig), Athens, May 16, 1982[1]

"These Relationships . . . Involve Deep Mutual Respect and . . . Shared Values"

SECRETARY HAIG. Good morning, ladies and gentlemen. I apologize for getting you out early on a Sunday morning.

I think at the outset I want to express a "sas efharisto"[2] to President Karamanlis, Prime Minister Papandreou, and to my counterpart, the distinguished Foreign Minister of Greece.[3]

I think in reflecting back on what has been a very busy although a very compressed schedule that I would describe our visit here in Greece as being a very good one marked by cordiality, constructive and far ranging discussions, all of which set a very positive tone and framework for which to deal with a number of longstanding and difficult questions.

Yesterday was a very busy one. We started out with 3½ hours of discussion in the first hour with the Prime Minister alone followed by 2½ hours with our respective teams, concluded by a 3-hour dinner last night in which substantive discussions continued and, of course, a very special privilege for me, a 1-hour meeting with President Karamanlis, an individual I have known over many years and who is rapidly becoming the elder statesman of Europe, based both on his vast experience, his adherence to the democratic values of the Western World, and his unusual contributions over many, many years. I think the trip itself underscores President Reagan's and his administration's attachment to the importance of our relationships with the Government and the people of Greece. These relationships of over a century standing involve a deep mutual respect and are built on the shared values, the historic Greek perception of the role of the individual, his dignity, his creativity, and the need to preserve the freedom of the citizens within the state. These shared perceptions and values have always generated mutual benefits for the American and Greek peoples as manifested by a continuing alliance in two conflicts in this century and understanding relationships in peace as well.

I think in summary the visit itself, while not focused on making specific decisions on particular questions, did establish a very positive framework for the improvement of our bilateral relationships, including the defense sector. They underlie Greece's vital role in assuring peace and stability in the southern region of the Atlantic Alliance. Specific topics included a number of global issues, East–West issues, the topic of arms control, and the recent initiative taken by President Reagan to achieve for the first time substantial reductions in nuclear armament.

We had an opportunity to discuss the ongoing and continuing crisis in Poland,[4] the Falkland crisis,[5] and, of course, the question of Cyprus.[6] I emphasized the support for the continuation of the intercommunal talks under the auspices of the Unit-

---

[1] Source: Department of State Press Release 172, May 19, 1982; printed also in Department of State *Bulletin*, August 1982, pp. 62–64. Secretary Haig visited Ankara, May 13–15, and Athens, May 15–16, prior to attending a NATO Foreign Ministers meeting in Luxembourg, May 16–18.

[2] Thank you.

[3] Ioannis Haralambopoulos.

[4] For documentation on the Polish crisis, see Chapter 10, Part M.

[5] For documentation on the crisis in the South Atlantic, see Chapter 15, Part B. 0

[6] For information on the situation in Cyprus, see documents 240–242.

ed Nations Secretary-General. We discussed the Greek-Turkish question, and this was particularly valuable because I have, as you know, just proceeded from Ankara where similar discussions were held and, as always, I encouraged a resolution of these questions on a bilateral basis.

We also discussed what the Prime Minister referred to as the triangular question—Greece, Turkey, and NATO related issues. Here, of course, these are appropriately dealt with in NATO itself but, as a member of the alliance and as a good friend to both Greece and Turkey, we have always some constructive contributions to make.

We, of course, focused on Greek-American bilateral relationships to include our defense relationships and the issue of U.S. facilities in Greece. Again, not to seek to make decision but I think we arrived at a consensus of view on how to deal with this issue in the period ahead. So all in all the visit was very positive and I think its results justify optimism. There will be progress in the days ahead on a number of longstanding and difficult questions in the areas that I touched upon. Now I welcome your questions.

Q. Mr. Secretary, what is your line on Mr. Papandreou's request for a guarantee for the eastern frontier of Greece?

SECRETARY HAIG. The question was how was the topic of a guarantee to Greece, a longstanding question, dealt with in our discussions, and I think it suffices to say that this question arose in both capitals. We are sensitive to the issue. We believe, regardless of the future treatment of this question, that its fundamental character is best assured by a full participation of the member states in the alliance, of a resolution of longstanding questions among member states on a bilateral basis.

I know yesterday the question came up on certain letters that have been exchanged in the past between both President Carter and the Government of Greece, and the Foreign Ministers of the United States and Greece in an earlier period.[7] We recognize those letters are in the file and the task ahead now is to get on to resolve the issues which create understandable concerns, and we intend to work as actively as we can to be a catalyst in that effort.

Q. Mr. Secretary, let me try a different way on this question of the security guarantee. You have stressed the need for peaceful resolutions between the two parties, between Greece and Turkey, on the Aegean question. Would the United States actively and unequivocably oppose military action by either side in resolving that dispute?

SECRETARY HAIG. Well, I think it goes without saying that the United States view is no different than it is in the Falkland question. We reject and oppose first use of force to resolve disputes no matter what their nature, except the reaffirmation of U.N. Security Council Resolution 51[8] which provides for the right of self-defense. This is a matter of principle, and just as the United States has subscribed to that principle in the Falkland crisis—although, we have and seek to maintain good relationships with, of course, Great Britain and Argentina—we cannot recoil from stating unequivocably our adherence to rule of law and peaceful change in the resolution of political disputes.

Q. Your excellency, since the United States requested departure from the Falkland Islands of the Argentine troops, why do they not ask the departure of the Turkish troops from the island of Cyprus where they are for 8 years?[9]

SECRETARY HAIG. Well, it has been the United States position, continues to be the United States position, that the best way to deal with the non-Cypriot forces on the island of Cyprus is through the prompt continuation—with active movement on the side of the two communities—to arrive at a settlement through the intercommunal talks. We believe that progress in that area will necessarily include progress in dealing with the subject of non-Cypriot forces. I am very pleased that the discussions I had in both Ankara and Athens suggest that both parties are willing to subscribe to progress under the auspices of the U.N. Secretary-General shortly after my return to Washington this week.

Q. In your discussion here you said you have arrived at a consensus of view dealing

---

[7] A reference to an April 10, 1976 letter from Secretary of State Henry Kissinger to Greek Foreign Minister Demetrios Bitsios (in response to a letter from the latter of April 7), which stated that the United States opposed the use of force in settling disputes in the Mediterranean and would work for a just settlement of the Cyprus dispute.

[8] Reference apparently is to Article 51 of the U.N. Charter which provides for the right of self-defense; for text, see 3 Bevans 1165.

[9] Turkish troops landed in Cyprus in July 1974 after a coup which overthrew the government of President Makarios and eventually occupied approximately 37 percent of the island.

with the question of U.S. facilities and bases in Greece. What do you mean by that?

SECRETARY HAIG. Well, I think the consensus was on how to deal with this subject in the period ahead, primarily with respect to timing and initial discussions. I don't want to go beyond that because it would suggest that we actually got into the substance of these discussions. We did not. We merely discussed how to treat them in the period ahead.

Q. Mr. Haig, I would like, concerning Greece's participation in the military wing of NATO, Mr. Papandreou said recently "for the time being we are neither in nor out."[10] I would like to know your opinion today after the talks with Papandreou.

SECRETARY HAIG. The question was the topic of Greece's role in the integrated military structure of the alliance.

I am not a novice on this subject. But there is a danger, because I am not a novice, of portraying myself as an active official in the resolution of the remaining questions on the command structure here in the Aegean. I am not. This is a NATO question. It should be dealt with within the NATO framework. We did, however, have a very good exchange of views on the subject and, as the Prime Minister pointed out yesterday, this is not an area in which I have a lack of background. I know specifically what the remaining questions are. I believe they are resolvable within the NATO framework and am optimistic they will be resolved in the period ahead. This is going to take some careful work as in the past it has as well, but I think enough said.

Q. Mr. Secretary, can you say after your visit to Ankara and Athens now whether or not as a result of your visit the tensions between Greece and Turkey have somewhat been ameliorated?

SECRETARY HAIG. I think it would be wrong to make such a suggestion as a result of a brief visit of the kind we have just had, and I wouldn't even presume to draw such a conclusion. However, I think I leave the visits in both capitals with an enhanced sense of optimism. In the period ahead these questions can be positively resolved.

Q. Mr. Secretary, you have stated that the United States believes that the only solution for the Cyprus issue is the dialogue that will take in the withdrawal of the Turkish military forces. But at present time it has been accepted that the dialogue is between Nicosia and Ankara. In case that the dialogue between the two is not successful, what do you see as being the alternative to this?

SECRETARY HAIG. Well, I think it serves no useful purpose to indulge in speculations about failure on a political effort that should be undertaken with increased vigor. It is still underway, as you know. There has been the U.N. assessment of the situation. There was some movement some months ago. I think it is very important that we do not indulge in speculation which visualizes failure because sometimes it contributes to failure. What we are after is a successful outcome that will meet the interest of the communities not only in a contemporary sense but in the future as well. And this is an important and delicate issue as it has been for a number of years. What is important is to establish a broad political framework and to get progress within that framework. When one becomes too preoccupied with contemporary aspect—and incidentially the Falkland question is much the same, and it isn't quite as simple as the question that was posed to me earlier. We are not just talking about the withdrawal forces from the Falkland Islands. We are not just talking about the withdrawal of non-Cypriot forces from the Islands, as desirable as that is. We are talking about a broad framework which will meet the fundamental interests of the peoples on Cyprus and their children and this is going to take, as it always does in such difficult questions, patience and care.

Q. Mr. Secretary, I wonder if you could make some general observations about the kind of welcome the Greek Communist Party had prepared for you, particularly at a time when the President has called for an initiative on nuclear affairs and you are about to proceed into discussions with your NATO colleagues.

SECRETARY HAIG. Well, I think that since I had not been exposed to the demonstration and only had access to the Greek press on that, I prefer to take my lead from them and I think their descriptions of the situation covering a broad spectrum of political views give a very adequate reply to you and I would not presume to.

Q. Sir, could you tell us what dates the talks about the bases will start and whether there will be a special meeting between Papandreou and President Reagan in Bonn?[11]

---

[10] Reference is to a December 10, 1981, press conference statement by Papandreou following his return from a meeting of NATO Defense Ministers. Papandreou also holds the defense portfolio in his government.

[11] For documentation on the June 9 to 11

SECRETARY HAIG. With respect to the first question, I would prefer to let events unfold on that. I think we have a general commonality of view on how to approach these questions on timing and venue. But I think it is preferable to let that unfold. With respect to the upcoming summit in Bonn, of course, I think there are only one set of bilaterals discussed that are now scheduled between President Reagan and the Chancellor of West Germany as the host government for the summit. This does not preclude whatever discussions will occur on the margins and during the frequent opportunities that occur during breaks and social events which I am quite confident will afford an opportunity for discussion.

Thank you very much.

Document 239

Remarks by the Prime Minister of Greece (Papandreou), October 18, 1982 (Extract)[12]

"We Are Not Looking for a Confrontation But for a Solution"

Q. You caused a stir over the weekend by saying that an agreement on U.S. bases there would have to be reached in a certain time limit.[13]

A. The time limit will be arranged by the two parties. The present state of affairs, established in 1953, is not acceptable, so we must ask for an early termination of the talks—perhaps 6 months. We will have a chance to arrive jointly at a common date.

Q. Is this an ultimatum?

A. No. This is exactly what we don't do. I have made it clear we will not take singlehanded action. We are sure the United States will deal with us in a fair way. We are not looking for a confrontation but for a solution. From all evidence from the administration, the climate is very positive. Our position is that the bases should not endanger our relations with other countries with which we have good relations. A second point, we are very concerned about our national security—a threat from Turkey.

Q. Do you think a hard line by Greece will push the United States and NATO into the arms of Turkey?

A. It is something one must take into account. We don't deal under pressure. We deal as equals—moral equals.

. . . .

K. Cyprus

Document 240

Letter From President Reagan to the Speaker of the House of Representatives (O'Neill), May 25, 1982[1]

Status of Intercommunal Negotiations

DEAR MR. SPEAKER: In accordance with the provisions of Public Law 95–384,[2] I am submitting the following report on progress made during the past 60 days toward reaching a negotiated settlement of the Cyprus problem.

In the course of continuing discussion of the United Nations "evaluation"[3] of the

---

NATO Heads of Government meeting in Bonn, see Chapter 10, Part B. President Reagan and Papandreou did have a brief bilateral meeting at that time.

[12] Source: NBC News. The interview with Prime Minister Papandreou was conducted by Bryant Gumble on the NBC "Today" show.

[13] In an interview with *New York Times* correspondent Marvin Howe, Papandreou stated:

"Either there will be an agreement, or else we have finished with the status of the bases. In other words, supposing that we do not reach an agreement within a period of 6 or 9 months, no matter what it may be, if we fail to agree on this, it does not mean that the bases will remain as they are. It means that they must go."

The Papandreou interview is in *New York Times*, October 17, 1982, p. I21.

[1] Source: White House Press Release, May 25, 1982, Office of the Press Secretary to the President; also printed in *Weekly Compilation of Presidential Documents*, May 31, 1982, pp. 702–703. An identical letter, with the salutation "Dear Mr. Chairman," was addressed to Senator Charles Percy, Chairman of the Senate Foreign Relations Committee.

[2] For the text of P.L. 95–384, the International Security Assistance Act of 1978, approved September 22, 1978, see 92 Stat. 729.

[3] Reference is to a U.N. document dated November 18, 1981, enumerating points of agreement and disagreement between the parties to the Cyprus dispute.

intercommunal negotiations, the Greek Cypriot and Turkish Cypriot negotiators met on April 14, 21, and 30 and May 4, 6, 11, 13 and 18. The negotiators have continued to focus their discussion on elements of the United Nations "evaluation" of the intercommunal negotiations. Having completed their initial review of many of the "points of coincidence," the communities are now beginning examination of "points of equidistance" including such issues as the freedoms of movement, settlement and property ownership in any future agreement. The negotiating sessions continue to be useful and constructive discussions with good relations between the participants.

United Nations Secretary General Perez de Cuellar met in Rome on April 4 with Cypriot President Kyprianou and in Geneva on April 9 with Turkish Cypriot leader Denktash. These meetings provided a thorough review of the status of the negotiations and both sides agreed to accelerate the pace of the talks and hold two meetings per week. The negotiating parties also agreed to meet again with the Secretary General in New York in June for a further review of the negotiating process.

We believe that the intercommunal negotiations are firmly established as a strong and effective tool to promote progress toward resolving the Cyprus problem. I wish to congratulate both the United Nations Secretary General and his Special Representative on Cyprus, Ambassador Hugo Gobbi, for their commitment to bringing the Cyprus problem to a just and lasting settlement. They have my full support for their efforts. We hope that the negotiators will seize the opportunities offered by the United Nations "evaluation" to make progress toward resolving outstanding differences between the communities.

Sincerely,

RONALD REAGAN

Document 241

Letter From President Reagan to the Speaker of the House of Representatives (O'Neill), July 21, 1982[4]

Recent Discussions Regarding the Cyprus Dispute

DEAR MR. SPEAKER: In accordance with the provisions of Public Law 95–384,[5] I am submitting the following report on progress made during the past 60 days toward reaching a negotiated settlement of the Cyprus problem.

In the course of continuing discussion of the United Nations "evaluation"[6] of the intercommunal negotiations, the Greek Cypriot and Turkish Cypriot negotiators met on May 18, 25 and 27, June 1, 3, 24 and 29 and July 1, 6 and 8. The negotiations are now in recess with the next session scheduled for early August. Throughout recent discussions, the negotiators have carefully reviewed elements of the United Nations "evaluation" dealing with *inter alia* the possible organization of the executive structure of a federal system and the organs and powers of a federal government. The intercommunal negotiations are continuing in a serious and constructive manner.

United Nations Secretary General Perez de Cuellar met in New York on June 8 and 10 with Cypriot President Kyprianou and on June 9 with Turkish Cypriot leader Denktash. These meetings provided a further opportunity for useful discussion of the status of and developments in the intercommunal talks.

The United Nations continues to pay close attention to the Cyprus problem. In his June 1, 1982 report to the Security Council on Cyprus,[7] a copy of which is attached,[8] the Secretary General reviewed recent developments and emphasized that

---

[4] Source: White House Press Release, July 21, 1982, Office of the Press Secretary to the President; also printed in *Weekly Compilation of Presidential Documents,* August 2, 1982, p. 937. An identical letter, with the salutation "Dear Mr. Chairman," was addressed to Charles Percy, Chairman of the Senate Foreign Relations Committee.

[5] See footnote 2 above.

[6] See footnote 3 above.

[7] For the text of this report, see U.N. document S/15149.

[8] Not printed.

"the intercommunal talks continue to represent the best available method for pursuing a concrete and effective negotiating process." He noted that negotiations are proceeding at "a deliberate but reasonable pace" and while major substantial problems are still to be resolved, "they are being systematically reconsidered, reformulated and reduced." The Secretary General also noted the prospective need for devising solutions to unresolved constitutional and territorial issues and urged the communities to give "earnest thought" to the requirements for an agreement. We fully endorse the efforts and observations of the Secretary General and his special Representative on Cyprus, Ambassador Hugo Gobbi.

I also note with pleasure that on June 15, 1982, the Security Council unanimously passed a resolution extending the mandate of the UN Peacekeeping Force on Cyprus (UNFICYP) to December 15, 1982.[9] We share with other Security Council members the judgment that the continued presence of UNFICYP adds a valuable dimension of security and stability conducive to productive intercommunal negotiations.

Sincerely,

RONALD REAGAN

Document 242

Letter From President Reagan to the Speaker of the House of Representatives (O'Neill), November 30, 1982[10]

"The Parties Are Engaged in a Genuine Dialogue"

DEAR MR. SPEAKER: In accordance with the provisions of Public Law 95–384,[11] I am submitting the following report on progress made during the past 60 days toward reaching a negotiated settlement of the Cyprus problem.

Intercommunal negotiations resumed on November 9 following a one and one-half month recess and continue to focus on various elements of the U.N. Secretary General's evaluation document.[12] The two parties remain committed to these U.N.-sponsored talks and to working for progress in this forum. We continue to believe that it represents the most fruitful course for negotiating progress. The parties are engaged in a genuine dialogue which has made it possible for each side to define its positions.

On October 6, Secretary Shultz and Cypriot President Kyprianou met in New York during the United Nations General Assembly and exchanged views on efforts to reach a settlement to the Cyprus problem.[13] In addition, Mr. Christian A. Chapman, a senior Foreign Service Officer newly appointed by the Secretary of State as U.S. Special Cyprus Coordinator,[14] traveled in early November to Cyprus[15] where he met with President Kyprianou, Turkish Cypriot leader Denktash, the intercommunal negotiators, and U.N. Special Representative Gobbi. Mr. Chapman will coordinate our support for the efforts of the Secretary General and Ambassador Gobbi.

I wish once again to affirm my commitment, and that of this Administration, to the search for a just and lasting solution to the problems of the people of Cyprus.

Sincerely,

RONALD REAGAN

---

[9] For text, see U.N. Security Council Resolution 510.

[10] Source: White House Press Release, November 30, 1982, Office of the Press Secretary to the President; also printed in *Weekly Compilation of Presidential Documents,* December 6, 1982, pp. 1553–1554. An identical letter, with the salutation "Dear Mr. Chairman," was addressed to Charles Percy, Chairman of the Senate Foreign Relations Committee.

[11] See footnote 2 above.

[12] See footnote 3 above.

[13] Kyprianou met with Shultz on October 6 to discuss the status of the U.N.-sponsored intercommunal talks and bilateral issues. The Cypriot President was in New York to deliver an address to the U.N. General Assembly, October 7.

[14] Chapman's appointment was announced on October 26.

[15] Chapman visited Cyprus from November 7 to 11.

L. Turkey

Document 243

Statement Read by the Department of State Acting Spokesman (Romberg), January 29, 1982[1]

Terrorist Assassination of Turkish Official

Yesterday morning in Los Angeles the Consul General of Turkey, Kemal Arikan, was brutally murdered by gunmen. An anonymous caller has claimed that the Justice Commandos of the Armenian Genocide carried out this assassination. The Justice Commandos are a well-known terrorist organization which has been killing Turkish diplomats and their families around the world for the past few years. Kemal Arikan is the 21st victim of this savage campaign. The Justice Commandos also claimed responsibility for the Columbus Day 1980 bombing in New York, which severely damaged the Turkish U.N. Mission and adjacent buildings and injured a number of innocent pedestrians.

President Reagan, Secretary Haig, and Acting Secretary Stoessel have extended their condolences to the Government of Turkey and the family of Mr. Arikan. They have also expressed shock and outrage at this vicious and cowardly act. We are deeply gratified to learn that authorities in California were able promptly to take several suspects into custody.

Terrorism is a hideous crime which violates the norms of decent human behavior. It cannot be tolerated by the civilized community of nations. Those who practice it must find no excuse and no haven. The murder of Kemal Arikan is a sharp reminder to all nations of the need to redouble their efforts to stamp out the worldwide menace of terrorism.

---

[1] Source: Office of Press Relations, Department of State. The statement was read at the Department of State Daily Press Briefing beginning at 12:31 p.m.

Document 244

Transcript of an Interview With the Deputy Secretary of State (Stoessel), April 5, 1982[2]

U.S.-Turkish Relations

MS. TUNA. Today I am going to talk to you about the Reagan administration at the present time.

My first question is, since the Reagan administration took office, various Turkish officials have visited Washington, the last one being Defense Minister Bayulken,[3] and they all said that the present aid level is insufficient to modernize the Turkish Armed Forces.

Will the United States administration fund modernization of the Turkish Air Force which is, I think, the most vital at this point?

SECRETARY STOESSEL. I would say certainly we're aware of the Turkish needs and their interests. We will be giving more assistance in'83 than in'82, and this is in general for maintenance of present equipment, acquisition of new equipment, and also economic assistance.

The Air Force question is a very special one.[4] We've had a special expression of interest on that, and I would say we're considering that. It does get into a lot of money. It's a big program. There is the question of coproduction, coassembly. That has to be looked at too. So I can't give a definite answer, but we're aware of the interest, and we want to be as helpful as we can.

MS. TUNA. Do you think the administration would take a step and have an additional aid which would come from the White House for Turkey in the near future? Because the last time such an act has happened was after the Guadaloupe summit meeting of then President Carter with the European leaders, and he had returned and asked additional aid from the Congress on and above what was already in the aid package.[5]

---

[2] Source: Department of State files. The interview, which began at 3:40 p.m., was conducted by Koprulu Tuna of Turkish radio.

[3] Bayulken last visited the United States in July 1981.

[4] In January the Government of Turkey requested permission to purchase nearly 300 military aircraft from the United States.

[5] Reference is to the support provided by the United States and other OECD donors, the IMF, and the World Bank to Turkey's economic stabilization program which was begun in 1980 at a period of severe economic crisis.

SECRETARY STOESSEL. As I say, we've got a big aid package now, and we will be increasing it at our request in'83, and this is against the background of very severe economic stringency in this country. So I think what we're doing now is already quite a bit.

Turkey, I guess, is the third largest recipient of aid for the United States, so I doubt really that an additional, special program would be feasible. But we are doing a lot, and we want to continue that.

Of course, we want to encourage other countries also to be of assistance.

MS. TUNA. The other two are saying we're the third largest recipient, and the other two—mainly Israel and Egypt—they too receive aid levels of more than $5 billion, so the third one is $815 [million]. Doesn't that have a big gap in between, saying the largest third?

SECRETARY STOESSEL. It's still pretty big.

MS. TUNA. I would like to follow up the Greek-Turkish relations with you. America has been following a wait-and-see policy toward Greece since the election time.[6]

This situation makes the Greek Government more aggressive toward Turkey, as you are well aware of, I think. And the Greek Government perceives the United States as supporting that performance at this time.

What would you do to prevent any inconvenience between the two parties?

SECRETARY STOESSEL. We have said that we want as good a relation as possible with the Greek Government. We hope to work with them. We certainly hope that that does not increase any tendencies on their part to be aggressive.

We have urged restraint on all parties in the eastern Mediterranean, and we feel that it's very important that both Greece and Turkey try and work out their problems as members of the alliance. That membership in the alliance itself is the best guarantee of security, and that's what we would stress.

As I say, we hope that between the two, they can work out their problems.

MS. TUNA. Do you think the agreement of Bern in 1976[7] is obeyed by both parties at the present time? Because they have come to an agreement in Bern that several items which are to be followed have now been violated by the Greek side.

As I remember the other day, Mr. Dillery was, of course, witnessing at the subcommittee hearing at the House Foreign Relations,[8] and the American Congressmen are asking questions and they're asking about certain declarations of the Greek Foreign Minister which comes one day and then the next day is rejected type of thing. It even happened in the last NATO meeting. As you recall, they had signed a communiqué, and the next day the communiqué signature changed and their minister, I believe, was recalled back to Greece.[9]

I mean, there is kind of a—how should I say it—like Secretary Eagleburger said the other day, "hanky-panky going on in Congress."[10]

Don't you think there is some kind of evidence already in sight which maybe people are not aware of?

SECRETARY STOESSEL. I don't know. I know there have been some problems of this kind, and there have been charges and countercharges. I wouldn't want to get into the specifics about it. As I say, we hope that these can be overcome, and that there can be a dialogue between Turkey and Greece. We've been encouraged by the contacts which have taken place, and we hope this process can continue.

MS. TUNA. Do you think this attitude of the United States, as a little bit supportive toward Greece, is understood as supportive by Greeks?

SECRETARY STOESSEL. As I say, we want to be positive in our attitude toward Greece as toward all members of the alliance, and we hope for as good a relationship as possible. We certainly hope that that will not have any adverse effect on the neighbors.

MS. TUNA. My last question is about Cyprus. What is the U.S. position on Cy-

---

6 A reference to the October 1981 Greek elections won by the PASOK party of Prime Minister Andreas Papandreou.

7 Reference is to 1976 discussions between Turkey and Greece over control of Aegean flight space and the continental shelf. In the November 1976 Bern Agreement both sides agreed to continue negotiations and exercise restraint on these issues.

8 For the text of the April 1 testimony of Edward Dillery, Director of the Office of Greek, Turkish, and Cypriot Affairs, Department of State, see *Foreign Assistance Legislation for Fiscal Year 1983, Hearings and Markup Before the Committee on Foreign Affairs, House of Representatives, Ninety-seventh Congress, Second Session* (Washington, 1982), pp. 135–142.

9 Reference is to the January 5 dismissal of the Greek Deputy Foreign Minister, Asimakis Fotilas, after he signed an EEC communiqué on Poland without consultations with his government.

10 Not further identified.

prus, and are you against the so-called internationalization of the issue?[11]

Secretary Stoessel. I would say here that we support the intercommunal talks under the auspices of the United Nations and feel that that is where the attention of the parties should be directed, and we do not see at this time that internationalization would be advisable.

Ms. Tuna. You think that the evaluation of the United Nations—last November 1981[12]—the U.N. evaluation was a positive step to go forward with the intercommunal talks?

Secretary Stoessel. We thought it was, and since then, we saw some progress. We hope it can continue in that direction.

Ms. Tuna. That's about all I can ask. I think I probably did finish in 15 minutes—rather, 13 minutes.

Document 245

Transcript of a Joint Press Conference by the Secretary of State (Haig) and the Turkish Foreign Minister (Turkmen), Ankara, May 15, 1982 (Extracts)[13]

The State of U.S.-Turkish Relations

Foreign Minister Ilter Turkmen. I wish to speak very briefly and leave the floor as soon as possible to the Secretary of State. May I say, first of all, that we are extremely pleased with the visit of Mr. Haig to our country. I think that the talks we have had here have shown that there is a complete mutual understanding and mutual trust between Turkey and the United States. Secretary Haig also visited our Prime Minister,[14] an old friend, again. He visited the President of the Consultative Assembly, Mr. Irmak, and we had extensive talks on many subjects with the Secretary. The Secretary of State had the opportunity to meet and to talk with the members of the National Security Council; he had a chance to talk to Deputy Prime Minister Ozal, Minister of State Aztrak, and Defense Minister Bayulken. We have, of course, taken up with priority the bilateral relations between Turkey and the United States. We have dealt extensively with the defense and economic cooperation between the two countries. I think we agree that the high-level committee on defense and cooperation is a very useful and effective instrument for promoting our defense cooperation.

We have explored the possibilities of furthering our economic, commercial, technological and scientific cooperation. We have had a large exchange of views on international problems, particularly on the sources of tension today. I think that we are in full agreement on the broad principles and the main approaches towards these problems.

We have reiterated together our strong support for NATO solidarity. We discussed the problem of international terrorism and there is an agreement between us that there should be an effective fight against this evil. We reviewed the situation in the Middle East with particular emphasis on the Arab-Israeli conflict and the war between Iraq and Iran. We have naturally discussed the relations between Turkey and Greece, and the Cyprus problem. On Turkish-Greek relations we have explained our point of view to the Secretary. We have emphasized that we are always ready to negotiate our differences with Greece but that, of course, we are equally opposed to any faits accomplis or unilateral acts. On the Cyprus problem we have reiterated our strong support for the inter-communal talks and we have underlined to the Secretary that we were ready to deploy all efforts in order to facilitate and promote these talks.

I think on the whole we can say, as the Secretary pointed out yesterday, that the relations between Turkey and the United States are excellent, that we have reached in our relationship the age of maturity and that we are looking forward to increased cooperation and partnership between Turkey and the United States. Thank you.

---

[11] Reference is to Papandreou's suggestion that the Cyprus issue be debated in the United Nations and other international forums. Since 1980 the forum of discussion has been intercommunal talks between representatives of the Greek and Turkish Cypriots.

[12] A reference to proposals presented by the U.N. Secretary-General's representative at the intercommunal talks held on November 18, 1981.

[13] Source: Department of State Press Release 170, May 18, 1982; printed also in Department of State *Bulletin*, August 1982, pp. 60–62. Haig visited Turkey, May 13–15, and Greece, May 15–16, before attending the NATO Foreign Ministers meeting in Luxembourg, May 16–18. The omitted portion is a question and answer on the Falkland Islands controversy.

[14] Bulend Ulusu.

SECRETARY HAIG. Thank you very much, Minister Turkmen. I want to reiterate and underline the great sense of enthusiasm and satisfaction that I feel as a result of this all-too-brief visit here in Turkey. This is the first time I've had an opportunity to return to Turkey since my days as Supreme Commander in the spring of 1979[15] and I was especially gratified that it could be in the year of the centennial of the great Ataturk who is the founder of modern Turkey and whose influence is so pervasive today in all that is Turkish.

I think I was able to use the opportunity of this visit to underline once again the great sense of dedication that the United States feels to its relationship with Turkey, and its recognition that Turkey is the vital anchor of the southeastern flank of the alliance. Turkey also plays an indispensable role in the stability of the eastern Mediterranean region and indeed southwest Asia as well. This visit afforded me an opportunity to convey to General Evren,[16] an old friend, President Reagan's determination to continue the level of economic and military assistance to Turkey and to build and strengthen our ties in the months and years ahead.

As Foreign Minister Turkmen mentioned, during the visit we had an opportunity to exchange views on the blight of international terrorism and I, of course, used the opportunity to convey the deep sense of regret and sorrow that every American feels for the recent tragedies in our own country as a result of terrorist, vile terrorist acts against Turkish officials.[17] In this sense we are working now at the Federal, State and local levels to deal with this situation, to bring prompt and firm justice to perpetrators of these acts. One of the most encouraging aspects of the visit for me was to see the changes that have occurred here in Turkey since my last visit. I speak of the return to law and order, the suppression of terrorist activity that Turkey was plagued by in the late 1970's, early 1980's, which I had an opportunity to witness firsthand as the Supreme Allied Commander. To see the elimination of that kind of activity is very encouraging to me.

And it goes without saying I was also able to witness firsthand, through the briefings and information that were provided to me and my party, the high level of improvement that has occurred as a result of Turkey's economic reform program, both in the area of internal economic inflation, where the reductions have been very encouraging and in the increase in exports that Turkey is realizing as a result of the disciplined and effective and visionary planning of the Evren regime. We, of course, had an opportunity to discuss the timetable for the return to representative democracy here in Turkey[18] and I was able to reassure General Evren that the United States has full, total and unquestioning confidence in the adherence to the schedule which we support and believe is wholly reasonable and practical.

We did have an opportunity also to discuss Greek-Turkish relationships, the Cyprus question and problems in the Aegean. As you know, it is United States policy to favor a peaceful solution of whatever disputes occur, by the parties. And I will go on to Athens where I am sure there will be further discussions about these subjects.

All in all, I want to emphasize and reiterate the deep sense of satisfaction I had with this visit. It is especially so because I have known and respected Turkey so well over the years. To see the kind of progress that is so evident today, and to a visitor who has been away for some time, I think this progress is even more sharply evident. Again, I want to thank you, Mr. Minister, General Evren, Prime Minister Ulusu, and the general staff, with whom I've worked in the past, as well as the other officials of the government, for the hospitality and great benefit that this visit afforded me and my colleagues. Thank you. I will take your questions.

Q. It is reported that you advised the Turkish Government to improve its somewhat strained ties with the European countries. In your opinion, what could and should Turkey do to improve them?

A. Well, as a matter of fact, I did not advise my Turkish hosts to improve their ties. I have encouraged our European friends to continue their high level of support and cooperation with Turkey. I don't think it is the role of a friend and ally to be pedantic in the context of your question. I

---

15 Haig visited Ankara on April 3, 1979, in connection with negotiations for the reintegration of Greece into the NATO military command structure.

16 Kenan Evren, Turkish Head of State.

17 A reference to the murder of Kemal Arikan on January 28, 1982 (see document 243), and Orhan Gundaz on May 4, 1982, by terrorists.

18 A reference to a December 30, 1981, statement by the Turkish Government which promised a referendum on a new constitution by the end of 1982 and parliamentary elections in late 1983 or early 1984. For the Department of State's initial reaction to that statement, see *American Foreign Policy: Current Documents, 1981*, document 213.

have no question that the overwhelming membership of the alliance is fully cognizant of the vital role and indispensable role that Turkey plays today, and they will continue their high level of cooperation with Turkey.

Q. Mr. Secretary. In 1976 the Greek Government's demand for a guarantee against Turkey was answered by a letter signed by Mr. Kissinger.[19] Today the present Greek Government seems to be asking for the same type of a letter from the American side. I wonder whether you consider this Kissinger letter still valid and whether you will make a reference to it when asked.

A. Well, I think that United States policy on this subject is well-known and longstanding. It involves our interest in seeing disputes in the Aegean between Greece and Turkey solved through peaceful means through communication among the parties. That has been and remains American policy and I am confident that these two valuable members of the NATO alliance, who have willingly joined the alliance to meet their own securities through that partnership and that participation in the alliance. And I think enough said on that subject.

Q. Mr. Secretary, are you still committed to the Rogers Plan for the allocation of defense responsibilities in the Aegean?[20]

A. As you know, I have a certain degree of my own energies and activities involved in the Rogers Plan, if that's what the proper term is these days. We, of course, feel that it is vitally important to be full, total participants in the alliance, full members. Whatever the vehicle that's employed to achieve that in the light of recent history is something that would have our support.

Q. Mr. Secretary, how does your administration interpret these European misconceptions about Turkey and how valid are these perceptions in Europe and the United States toward Turkey?

A. Well, I think that it's not for me to be the official observer of these things. I can speak for my own government and reemphasize again our full confidence in the leadership here in Turkey and the great admiration we have for what this leadership has accomplished. I sometimes regret that memories are too short. All of which has happened is a source of satisfaction to me and I am fully confident and I have no reservation about the return of Turkey to representative democracy under the time schedule announced by the Evren government last year. I would hope that our European partners would share that sense of confidence.

. . . .

Q. Mr. Secretary, it seems like the Greek Government's policies are against NATO principles—asking for guarantees against another NATO ally, and putting reservations in the joint declarations. Do you think that Greece is causing a crack in NATO right now?

A. Well, I would not. I don't think it's appropriate for me to make any observations along these lines. As you know, I will be moving from here this morning to Athens and I'm sure there will be further discussions there. I have outlined for you the general policy of the United States on this subject. I am aware that there is a letter of the kind referred to in the files, and that's where it is.

Q. Mr. Secretary, Turkey is ready to start negotiations again. Do you believe that you will be able to convince the Greek Prime Minister to start the negotiations?

A. On Cyprus?

Q. Not on Cyprus. Between Turkey and Greece.

A. Well, I understand there is some discussion already underway in a sporadic sense on some of the narrower issues. There is some underway on the question of territorial waters. We, of course, think these are matters to be discussed and resolved either bilaterally or under international agreement.

Q. Mr. Secretary, in light of Deputy Prime Minister Mr. Turgut Ozal's statement on Thursday[21] that political parties in Turkey will be allowed to start functioning as from the middle or end of 1983, are you still confident that the regime can stick to its timetable of holding elections in late 1983 or early 1984?

---

[19] Regarding this letter, see footnote 7 to document 238.

[20] In 1980 General Bernard Rogers, SACEUR, negotiated an agreement which permitted the return of Greece to NATO's military structure under conditions acceptable to both Turkey and Greece.

[21] A reference to a May 13 statement by State Minister and Deputy Prime Minister Turgut Ozal to the Consultative Assembly in which he outlined plans for reform of local government structures.

A. My discussions here convinced me that the timetable established by the government is satisfactory, is on schedule and is proceeding as anticipated. I have no basis for questioning that. I have no doubt that it will be pursued as outlined.

Q. Mr. Secretary, did you discuss specifically the case of Mr. Ecevit?[22] There is a lot of opinion in Europe that he should be released from prison.

A. It's not my role nor would it be appropriate for me to make any public comment on an internal matter which is being pursued in accordance with existing Turkish law, and I'm not going to do that this morning.

Q. Mr. Secretary, did you discuss the question of Mr. Ecevit with the Turkish authorities?

SECRETARY HAIG. I didn't discuss it but it was discussed with me by Turkish officials.

Q. Mr. Secretary, is the Kissinger–Bitsios letter valid or not?

SECRETARY HAIG. Almost in dental fashion, you have tried to extract everything you can on that subject. I said it's a letter that's in the files. I told you what our policy is in the administration today. That is, that these are matters to be worked out peacefully by the governments concerned and I'm talking about tensions in the Aegean. Only last week somebody said I feel like a lemon in service to 20 martinis.

Q. Are you satisfied with the explanation you received concerning Turkey's close ties with Libya?

SECRETARY HAIG. Well, I certainly understand clearly the Turkish-Libyan relationship. It is somewhat different than that between the United States and Libya. The great strength of this alliance is that we are all different and we pursue sovereign policies of the member states and that's as it should be. We are not a Warsaw Pact where all march in tandem—most of the time.

---

[22] Former Prime Minister Bulent Ecevit was arrested on April 11 for violations of Turkish martial law.

Document 246

Statement Issued by the Department of State, July 9, 1982[23]

Council of Europe Application Against Turkey

Q. Please comment on the human rights application filed against Turkey by five members of the Council of Europe.

A. On July 1, five European governments—Sweden, Denmark, France, The Netherlands, and Norway—filed with the European Commission of Human Rights in Strasbourg, a body of the Council of Europe (COE), an application concerning the human rights situation in Turkey.

—Reportedly, that application expresses concern that the basic principles of the European Convention on Human Rights are not being satisfactorily implemented by Turkey.

—According to the Turkish press, the GOT has withheld comment on this application, pending study of the official documents.

—The European Human Rights Convention spells out a detailed procedure for reviewing applications of this kind. That procedure gives all concerned governments the chance to state their views.

—The United States is not a party to the European Convention on Human Rights or the application filed on July 1.

—While there are human rights problems in Turkey, it would be shortsighted to forget that the current government has nearly eliminated the human rights violations due to terrorism that were rapidly eroding the viability of democracy in Turkey.

—Reports of torture continue, but the government has punished many offenders; it is the first Turkish Government to move vigorously against this problem. Restrictions on political and press freedom exist, but the U.S. Government is confident that the Turkish Government is moving in good faith to implement its schedule for a return

---

[23] Source: Department of State files. The statement was made available to news correspondents following the Department of State Daily Press Briefing beginning at 12:33 p.m.

to stable parliamentary democracy and full constitutional freedoms.

—We question whether filing applications of this kind is the best way to promote human rights in Turkey.

Document 247

Transcript of the Department of State Daily Press Briefing, November 8, 1982 (Extract)[24]

The Progress of Democracy in Turkey

. . . .

Q. Do you have anything on Turkey, either the referendum or the story about new bases?[25]

A. I have something on the referendum for you. The United States has welcomed the effort of the military government in Turkey to return peace and stability to an important ally, as well as that government's decision to return Turkey to democratic, constitutional government in accordance with its established timetable.

We believe the constitution provides the basis for a democratic system of government and are confident that as the process of reestablishment of democracy proceeds, strong, viable, civilian political institutions will emerge.

. . . .

---

[24] Office of Press Relations, Department of State. John Hughes, Department of State Spokesman, conducted the briefing which began at 12:16 p.m.

[25] In a November referendum on a proposed new constitution, 92 percent of the Turkish people voted in favor of the document. The "story about the new bases" has not been further identified, and Hughes subsequently in the briefing said he had "[n]othing on the bases."

M. Soviet Union and Eastern Europe

Document 248

Statement Read by the Department of State Spokesman (Fischer) January 7, 1982 (Extract)[1]

U.S.-European Consensus on the Polish Question

. . . .

The United States has not softened its stance on the need for a Western response to the Polish situation. In fact, the United States is exercising its leadership through the example of its own actions and in consultations with the allies.

Progress is being made. The EC Foreign Ministers' communiqué[2] was the strongest statement yet out of Europe. There was further convergence of views as a result of the visit of Chancellor Schmidt to Washington.[3]

Our aim now in the NATO ministerial meeting on Monday in Brussels[4] is to create a U.S.-European consensus as well as a common strategy. This will provide a basis for coordinated action.

We have never expected the allies to take the same steps as we at precisely the same time. We are moving in the same direction together with our allies. The United States will continue its leadership effort as long as the situation in Poland requires it.

. . . .

[1] Source: Office of Press Relations, Department of State. The statement was read at the Department of State Daily Press Briefing, which began at 12:38 p.m.

[2] For the text of the communiqué issued by the European Community Foreign Ministers meeting in Brussels on January 4, see *Keesings*, April 30, 1982, pp. 31457–31458.

[3] For the text of the joint statement, much of which dealt with the Polish situation, issued by President Reagan and West German Chancellor Helmut Schmidt on January 5 at the conclusion of the latter's visit to Washington, see document 207.

[4] Documentation on the special session of the NATO Foreign Ministers in Brussels, January 10–11, is in Chapter 10, Part B.

Document 249

Address by the Secretary of State (Haig), Brussels, January 12, 1982[5]

Poland and the Future of Europe

The beginning of a new year is always a moment for reflection and resolve. As we in the West reflect upon our societies and resolve to improve them, we should recall the principles that sustain our governments, our law and our behavior toward each other. Our idea of a just community is founded upon respect for the rights of the individual, including freedom of expression, freedom of choice and freedom of association.

We believe that the rights of free men sustain the creativity of civilization. The arts, science and technology of the West flourish because creative talents can develop undisturbed. And our enormous material abundance comes from the cooperative efforts of free men and women working together.

An ancient scholar once wrote that "history is philosophy drawn from examples." The philosophy of freedom that unites the Western community of nations is an enduring theme of European history. Already in this decade, Poland, a nation steeped in a thousand years of European culture, has given us an example of the link between liberty and creativity. The Polish people sought the dignity of the workplace through free association in their union Solidarity in order to resolve their mounting economic problems. Such dignity meant above all respect for the individual, his talents and his right to a just reward for his work.

The Polish search for reform was a peaceful movement. Solidarity respected both Poland's geographic situation and the imperatives for social progress. This example of peaceful change in the world's most heavily armed continent would surely have contributed to a more legitimate and secure international order.

After 18 months of achievement, Solidarity is now being violently suppressed. In a grotesque parody of their own propaganda, the Communist authorities are employing the police power of the state to oppress the very workers they are pledged to protect. Fear is widespread. Thousands remain in jail. Tens of thousands are being forced to violate their consciences, a practice described by His Holiness the Pope as "the most painful blow inflicted on human dignity." Once again, a knock at the door heralds the arrival of the secret police. Poland today exemplifies the historic failure of Soviet-style communism to produce either bread or freedom.

Poland's future now hangs in the balance. Will there be reform or reaction, a renewal of hope or a deepening of despair? This is not a question for Poland alone. The poet Schiller wrote that "world history is the world's court of judgment." The historic events in Poland with their far-reaching implications demand a judgment by the West.

We must not let our judgment be confused by four myths about Poland: first, that Solidarity brought about its own suppression through excessive ambition; second, that the Soviet Union did not intervene in Poland and is therefore not accountable; third, that Poland's rulers are acting out of laudable national considerations; and fourth, that the West can and should do nothing because what happened in Poland is strictly an internal affair. Each of these myths is belied by reality.

The first myth is that the brutality which began on December 13 was provoked by the excesses of Solidarity itself. The reality was different. For months prior to the sudden imposition of martial law, Solidarity worked strenuously to halt strikes and prevent chaos. Lech Walesa traveled from city to city, from factory to factory, calling for people to return to work. His call was heard. After March 1981, strikes in Poland never exceeded a small fraction of the work force. After August 1981, the Polish Government's own statistics recorded increasing production.

Solidarity's search for stability was not reciprocated. The Jaruzelski government had planned a different course. Its only contribution to the call for national dialogue was the introduction of a law to forbid strikes, making confrontation inevitable.

---

[5] Source: Department of State Press Release 15, January 12, 1982; printed also in Department of State *Bulletin*, February 1982, pp. 20–23. The address was made at the International Press Center. Haig was in Brussels to attend the special session of the NATO Foreign Ministers, January 10–11.

The contrast could not be greater between the victims and the conspirators. On the one side, the Solidarity leaders, representing a free association of workers, were caught virtually intact in a single building. On the other side, a government claiming to protect the workers prepared so well to impose martial law that its plans have been accurately described in the Soviet Union as "brilliantly conspired."

The second myth is that the Soviet Union did not intervene in Poland and therefore should not be held accountable. The reality was different. After August 1980, Poland was subjected to a continuous campaign of Moscow's pressures, threats and intimidation—including military maneuvers. All of these actions were intended explicitly to halt the process of reform.

The secret preparations were even more ominous. It is known that as early as last March the Soviets were arguing for the imposition of martial law. In September, the martial law decree itself was printed in the Soviet Union. And the Commander of the Warsaw Pact forces, a Soviet marshal, was positioned in Poland both prior to martial law and during its execution.

Can anyone seriously be surprised by the Soviet role? Have we forgotten earlier episodes in Poland, East Germany, Hungary, and Czechoslovakia? The use of force on a nationwide scale against the Polish people today takes place only because the Soviet Union instigated it, supports it and encourages it.

The third myth is that we are witnessing a Polish attempt to establish law and order in the hope of forestalling an otherwise inevitable Soviet military intervention. In a cruel paradox, we are asked to believe that martial law, like Solidarity itself, is a purely national phenomenon, inspired by a high national purpose. It follows therefore that we must somehow be prepared to accept what is happening in Poland today because it is a lesser evil.

The reality is different. Regardless of motivation, a Soviet-trained military man is suppressing his own people under the pressure of the Soviet Union. As the Polish bishops put it: "Our suffering is that of the entire nation, terrorized by military force." The loss of liberty in Poland is no less keenly felt because a Polish general, rather than a Soviet general, is in charge.

The fourth myth is that Poland's misfortunes are strictly an internal affair, that the West has no right to judge the situation nor to take any action that might affect it. The reality is different. The Soviet Union and Poland both signed the Helsinki Final Act of 1975.[6] All the signatories were obligated to nurture conditions of freedom and diversity, thereby encouraging our peoples to resolve the problems dividing Europe. The standards of freedom and diversity established at Helsinki have been violated. The process begun at Helsinki has been put in jeopardy. We have both a right and an obligation to point out this danger.

For centuries the Poles have known the bitterness of aggression. Instigated, aided and abetted by the Soviet Union, the suppression of Poland's search for social justice is taking place today. Once again the dictates of a foreign power are determining the shape of Polish society.

The people of Poland are now looking to the West. We must give them clear and unequivocal evidence of our support. But our policies must be practical as well, taking into account Polish and Soviet realities. We want real progress, not just empty posturing.

My President and other Western leaders have therefore stated that we seek an end to martial law and repression, release of political prisoners, and the restoration of those rights, as promised in the Helsinki Final Act, that protect the independence of a trade union movement and the church. Only in this way can the basis be established for reconciliation through negotiation within Polish society.

The outcome of such a negotiation is entirely a matter for the Polish people. Nonetheless, under the Helsinki accord, we must counter the external and internal pressures which impede the reconciliation and reform so clearly desired by the citizens of Poland.

These are realistic objectives based on both the situation in Poland and East–West relationships. The desire for dignity in the workplace, embodied by Solidarity, cannot be eradicated. The brutal suppression of Poland's first free union has provoked profound outrage throughout Polish society. Resistance exists.

The Polish economy will not revive without the cooperation of the Polish worker,

---

[6] For the text of the Final Act of the Conference on Security and Cooperation in Europe signed at Helsinki, August 1, 1975, see Department of State *Bulletin*, September 1, 1975, pp. 323–350.

upon whom the brunt of the repression has fallen. And the growing problems of Poland cannot be resolved alone. The Polish Government should not expect our assistance while repression continues. Moscow can also be made aware of the benefits of restraint. Neither assumption of Poland's economic burdens nor military intervention are easy decisions for a Soviet Union with such problems as a weakening economy, and war in Afghanistan. Clearly, Moscow wants to sustain economic and other elements of cooperation with the West.

Prudent Western leadership can help to achieve a greater degree of moderation in Poland so that the necessary process of reform may continue. With this in mind, President Reagan has taken serious steps to signal both the Polish and Soviet Governments of our concern. He has also reserved additional action in the hope of deterring both further repression and Soviet intervention.

—All future credits and government-to-government assistance will be denied the Polish regime until progress resumes. At the same time the United States will continue to provide food, medicine, and other humanitarian assistance through private institutions or other arrangements that guarantee delivery to the Polish people and not the regime. The President has also stated that we are prepared to offer significant help if the path of reconciliation and reform is chosen and pursued—of course with meaningful acts and not just gestures to delude the West.

—President Reagan brought to President Brezhnev's attention our fundamental concerns; the response was negative. The United States has therefore initiated a number of actions, primarily in the economic field, which will penalize the Soviet Union. The President is prepared to go further, if necessary. At the same time, Moscow has been informed of our desire to pursue a more constructive path, if the Soviet Union will reciprocate.

The United States is not alone. Yesterday, the North Atlantic Council condemned developments in Poland. In a special Ministerial declaration,[7] they made clear that both the Soviet Union and the Polish Government have violated the Final Act of Helsinki and other international standards. The Allies left no doubt that repression in Poland is eroding the foundation for East–West progress.

The United States and its partners stated that the current situation in Poland is bound to affect their economic relations with both Poland and the Soviet Union. They stressed the significance of the measures already announced by President Reagan. In this spirit, the members of the Council resolved not to undermine the effect of each other's measures. And they agreed to identify appropriate national possibilities for action across a broad front, including an examination of the course of future economic and commercial relations with the Soviet Union.

Thus it is clear that events in Poland have a significance beyond the tragic fate of that country. A repressed Poland is not a factor for stability in Europe. Only respect for internationally recognized rights can form the basis for national reconciliation and reform to rescue Poland from the abyss of despair.

Once again, the Polish events have revealed a faultline in the political geography of the East. Once again, an ideology has been discredited. Fundamental disregard for individual rights has brought about a basic failure in social creativity. The attempt to ignore this prevailing weakness in Soviet-style communism by resort to force is a source of great danger in the nuclear era.

Far from being inconsistent with constructive East–West relations, reform in the East is the basis for greater legitimacy, stability and security throughout Europe.

The Polish situation also challenges the credibility of the West. We also stand at a crossroads. Do we want a world characterized by growing freedom, cooperation and security, or increasing repression, confrontation and fear? Are we going to see free nations acting to help expand liberty and peace, or will international change be dominated by totalitarian forces?

For well over a year, the alliance has stated that there would be serious consequences if the Soviet Union intervened to reverse an entirely peaceful dialogue in Poland. Soviet responsibility for present events is clear. A Western failure to act would not only assist the repression of the Polish people but also diminish confidence about our reactions to future events in Poland and elsewhere. Stable relations between East and West depend upon what Chancellor Schmidt has called "calculability." The Soviets must know that there can be negative or positive consequences, depending on their conduct. Poland is a test case, and European history teaches that the

---

[7] For the text of the special NATO declaration, see document 171.

greatest mistake in dealing with heavily armed aggressors is to ignore their violations of international agreements and to act as though nothing had happened.

Beyond the fate of Poland, beyond East–West relations, we must ultimately ask ourselves what these developments mean for our self-respect if we do not respond together. The West is often accused of being merely a collection of consumer societies. Are we so sated or intimidated that we fear to defend the values that make life worth living?

The Soviet Union has proclaimed for many years that there is no contradiction between the pursuit of détente and ideological competition. And Moscow has always supported the spread of Marxism-Leninism.

Are freedom and democracy less a part of our policy? Do we imagine that we can purchase peace by silence and inaction? Poland should remind us that in the battle for the minds of men, the best arguments are to be found on our side. The existence of successful industrial democracies in the West is a striking rebuke to Soviet style communism. Our persistent progress, even with all of our faults, means that the Soviet system is neither necessary nor inevitable. After all, the Polish people sought nothing more than free association, the dignity of labor and respect for the individual, rights that we in the West sometimes take for granted.

Poland should also change our thinking about world affairs. For over 60 years, each new Marxist-Leninist regime has been greeted by some in the West with fresh hopes and expectations. Then, as the urge for social justice and freedom which helped bring them to power in the first place was suppressed, disillusionment set in. It took 20 years or more of Stalinism before many Western observers saw the reality of the Soviet Union. It took just a year after the North Vietnamese takeover of South Vietnam and Kampuchea for understanding of that supposedly progressive regime. We are still learning about this brand of totalitarianism as the evidence mounts of the yellow rain of terror in Southeast Asia and Soviet complicity. Some still do not understand what is happening in Nicaragua or what is at stake in El Salvador.

The greatest danger to the West today may be the tendency to apply different standards to the behavior of the East and the West. No matter how much Communist repression, no matter how many Soviet nuclear missiles, no matter how many Afghanistans and Polands, some would still put pressure on the West to improve relations with the Soviet Union—rather than to demand from Moscow the moderation of its behavior.

The common sense of our citizens rejects this double standard.

Above all, the crime against the Polish people has outraged the workers of the world. A state supposedly founded on the workers movement is actively suppressing a worker's movement 10 million strong. The Polish workingman is the target—and the victim. His voice has been silenced. His productive energies have been sapped. His labor is being forced. His chosen leaders have been imprisoned. His hopes are being sacrificed because they do not fit with Soviet plans for maintaining absolute control over the countries of Eastern Europe.

It is therefore appropriate that our unions are taking the lead—with churches and other private groups—to honor the Polish people on January 30. This gesture of mass solidarity will represent a major expression of moral support. It will also demonstrate to the Soviets and their friends that the crushing of human rights will not be ignored. Such an expression of moral support will be equally important as a celebration of freedom.

My country is a child of European civilization. The American people share your outrage about the trampling of a nation in the center of Europe, because it has dared to assert its Europeanness. We can disagree about which events in the world are central to the security of the alliance and which are peripheral to its purposes; but surely there can be no disagreement that events in Poland touch the core of the conscience of the alliance.

We have spoken with one voice about these events. Yesterday, we created a clear and united framework for action. Now we must act.

Winston Churchill once observed that "the world is divided into peoples that own the governments and governments that own the peoples." Poland challenges us to remember our values and to advocate them. In the final analysis, only we, the people of the world that own the governments, are the guarantors of both peace and freedom.

Document 250

Remarks by President Reagan, January 19, 1982 (Extract)[8]

Effect of U.S. Sanctions Against the Soviet Union

. . . .

Q. Mr. President, it's been 3 weeks now since you announced the sanctions against the Soviet Union in connection with Poland.[9] What effect, if any, have they had? If they haven't had any effect, what next and when?

THE PRESIDENT. Well, I think they have had an effect, although there's no question that the situation in Poland is deteriorating. They have tried to present it as moderating. It isn't. The people are still imprisoned. There is no communication with Solidarity or between the military government and the people and the military law is still in effect.

We think, however, that there has been an impression made and we have held back on some things additionally that we can do, things that we will consider that can add to the steps that we've already taken.

I've had a lengthy communication from the Pope.[10] He approves what we've done so far. He believes that it has been beneficial and, yet, we're not going to wait forever for improvement in the situation there. We have other steps that we can take. . . .

. . . .

[8] Source: White House Press Release, January 19, 1981, Office of the Press Secretary to the President; also printed in *Weekly Compilation of Presidential Documents*, January 25, 1982, p. 40. For the full text of this press conference in the East Room of the White House beginning at 2 p.m., see *ibid.*, pp. 39–46.

[9] For the text of President Reagan's announcement of sanctions against the Soviet Union, December 29, 1981, see *American Foreign Policy: Current Documents, 1981*, document 270.

[10] This communication has not been further identified.

Document 251

Proclamation by President Reagan, January 20, 1982[11]

Designation of January 30 as Solidarity Day

Solidarnosc, the Polish free trade union Solidarity Movement, was born not only of the failure of the Polish Government to meet the needs of its people but also from a tradition of freedom preserved and nourished by the proud Polish people through two centuries of foreign and domestic tyranny.

Solidarity symbolizes the battle of real workers in a so-called workers' state to sustain the fundamental human and economic rights they began to win in Gdansk in 1980—the right to work and reap the fruits of one's labor, the right to assemble, the right to strike, and the right to freedom of expression. Solidarity sought to address and to resolve Poland's deep-rooted economic ills; it acted in good faith and pursued a path of constructive dialogue with the Polish Government.

Despite these peaceful efforts on the part of Solidarity, a brutal wave of repression has descended on Poland. The imposition of martial law has stripped away all vestiges of newborn freedom. Authorities have resorted to arbitrary detentions, and the use of force, resulting in violence and loss of life; the free flow of people, ideas and information has been suppressed; the human rights clock in Poland has been turned back more than 30 years. The target of this repression is the Solidarity Movement but in attacking Solidarity its enemies attack an entire people. Ten million of Poland's thirty-six million citizens are members of Solidarity. Taken together with their families, they account for the overwhelming majority of the Polish nation. By persecuting Solidarity, the Polish military government wages war against its own people.

History shows us that stability in Europe is threatened when Poland is suppressed. The hearts and minds of free people every-

[11] Source: White House Press Release, January 20, 1982; office of the Press Secretary to the President; printed also in *Weekly Compilation of Presidential Documents*, January 25, 1982, pp. 46–47. This proclamation, No. 4891, was filed with the Office of the Federal Register at 11:42 a.m. on January 20, 1982.

where stand in Solidarity with the people of Poland in the hour of their suffering.

We hold in high esteem the leadership and objectives of Lech Walesa, the head of Solidarity, and we express our grave concern for his present well-being. As Americans we feel a special affinity with Solidarity and the basic human values it seeks to uphold, in keeping with the long tradition of Polish-American friendship and freedom. President Wilson's advocacy of self-determination for the Polish people helped to bring about a rebirth of the Polish nation earlier in this century. America stands ready today to provide generous support and assistance to a Poland which has returned to a path of genuine internal reconciliation.

There is a spirit of Solidarity abroad in the world today that no physical force can crush. It crosses national boundaries and enters into the hearts of men and women everywhere. In factories, farms and schools, in cities and towns around the globe, we the people of the Free World stand as one with our Polish brothers and sisters. Their cause is ours.

NOW, THEREFORE, I, RONALD REAGAN, President of the United States of America, do hereby designate January 30, 1982, as Solidarity Day. I urge the people of the United States, and free peoples everywhere, to observe this day in meetings, demonstrations, rallies, worship services and all other appropriate expressions of support. We will show our Solidarity with the courageous people of Poland and call for an end to their repression, the release of all those arbitrarily detained, the restoration of the internationally recognized rights of the Polish people, and the resumption of internal dialogue and reconciliation in keeping with fundamental human rights.

IN WITNESS WHEREOF, I have hereunto set my hand this twentieth day of January, in the year of our Lord nineteen hundred and eighty-two, and of the Independence of the United States of America the two hundred and sixth.

RONALD REAGAN

Document 252

Transcript of a Press Conference by the Secretary of State (Haig), Geneva, January 26, 1982[12]

Haig–Gromyko Meeting

SECRETARY HAIG. Good evening, ladies and gentlemen. It's quite late, so I hope we can keep this thing very brief and crisp—in my usual fashion. We have just completed a 7¾ hour, one-on-one discussion with Foreign Minister Gromyko. The discussions were divided into a morning and an afternoon session. They were far-ranging, in-depth discussions on all of the areas of concern to the Western governments, and they included, of course, areas of concern to the Soviet Union, as well. It was clear that the situation in Poland cast a long and dark shadow over all of the discussions involving East–West relations. There was discussion of that subject, in both the morning and the afternoon session. We also discussed the topic of arms control, the ongoing negotiations on INF being conducted here in Geneva, under the American representative, Ambassador Paul Nitze, on the American side. I explained in some detail the logic and rationale underlying President Reagan's initiative for zero levels of medium-range missilery, a proposal designed to achieve the elimination of the major source of nuclear tension here in Europe.

We also discussed the subject of START—the former strategic arms control talks. I emphasized that the U.S. side is actively engaged in preparations which would lead to the initiation of talks in this area, which we will be prepared to initiate when conditions permit.

The other areas of discussion included, *inter alia*, Central America, and Cuba; the continuing situation in Afghanistan; southern Africa; and a host of bilateral issues, with focus on humanitarian problems, of citizens in the Soviet Union, and their relationship with human rights.

All in all, the discussions were very sober; as I said at the outset, extremely detailed and I believe, beneficial from the standpoint of necessary communication at

---

[12] Source: Department of State Press Release 34, January 27, 1982. Secretary Haig departed Washington on January 24 for a visit to the Middle East, stopping in Geneva en route from January 25 to 27.

the ministerial level between the Soviet Union and the United States, a necessity that does not decline in times of tension and stress.

I welcome your questions.

Q. Mr. Secretary, you said you were prepared to start talks under certain conditions?

SECRETARY HAIG. Well, I think it's clear, as I said at the outset, that the current situation in Poland casts a long and dark shadow over the full range of East–West relations, including the subject of strategic arms talks or START talks.

Q. In other words, martial law would have to end?

SECRETARY HAIG. I am not giving you a litmus test of conditions, but merely a broad statement of the influence of the Polish situation on the current environment.

Q. Mr. Secretary, you did not mention summitry; did that come up at all?

SECRETARY HAIG. No.

Q. You said there was discussion on Poland. You emphasized your standpoints, but did you actually have a discussion on Poland?

SECRETARY HAIG. Well, he emphasized that again in the sessions, but within the context of the clear attitude of the Soviet Union that this is an internal affair. Yes, we had a two-sided discussion.

Q. Did you detect an improvement in Soviet-American relations as a result of the meeting or are they the same as they were before?

SECRETARY HAIG. I do not think the purpose of these talks was to improve U.S.-Soviet or East–West relationships in general. Quite the contrary. They were designed to provide the American side with an opportunity to express clearly a number of areas of concern, primarily our concern with respect to the situation in Poland. I think in that sense the discussions were more than justified, and I left them with a feeling of satisfaction that it was indeed the right time to hold such discussions. But I would describe our relationships as affected essentially, as I mentioned, by the long, dark shadow cast by the situation in Poland.

Q. Did the Soviets, represented by Mr. Gromyko, say anything on other issues—on Afghanistan, Central America, or anything in which you saw some new flexibility on their—

SECRETARY HAIG. Well, I don't like to go into value judgments of particular areas of discussion. In some areas, our differences remain wide, and in others there are obvious prospects for solutions.

Q. You said the discussions were valuable and necessary. Did you agree to meet again?

SECRETARY HAIG. No, we did not.

Q. Why not?

SECRETARY HAIG. Well, I don't think the opportunity presented itself, and it does not represent a judgment one way or the other; it is a very easy thing to arrange at the appropriate time.

Q. Mr. Secretary, is arms control one of the areas in which there are prospects for solutions with the Soviet Union?

SECRETARY HAIG. Well, I like [to] think that there are prospects for solutions in the INF discussions. We are very confident that our proposals, which are put forth with the greatest sincerity, provide an opportunity to relieve East and West of the kind of level of tensions associated with nuclear missilery here in Europe. But I would be somewhat disingenuous were I to suggest that there are not many differences that remain and many obstacles to overcome.

Q. Do you think the zero levels proposal is realistic now?

SECRETARY HAIG. Well, we think it's very realistic, and we also think it's the proper solution for a problem which was brought about by the deployment of SS–20 missiles by the Soviet Union.

Q. Could you go into any more detail on what it is you asked Mr. Gromyko to do about Cuba because there is a lot of speculation about the sale of MIG–23's?

SECRETARY HAIG. We had extensive and detailed discussions on the Cuban situation—not just the level of Soviet armaments, including the question you've touched upon; but perhaps even more important, the character of Soviet activity worldwide, in Africa and in the Central American region especially. And, as I say, this occupied a very extensive portion of our exchanges today, and it was very detailed.

Q. When you said Soviet, did you mean Cuban?

SECRETARY HAIG. Cuban—don't interpret that as pure Freud. (Laughter)

Q. Mr. Secretary, did you mention human rights and the question of Jewish emigration, specifically the case of Mr. Shcharansky?

SECRETARY HAIG. We had discussions in the bilateral area of all of the human rights and humanitarian issues—that particular case—the emigration of Soviet Jewry—the Pentecostalists currently in the American Embassy, a number of other cases, but family cases.

Q. Did you get the impression that there is any specific field where the Soviets will give anything away?

SECRETARY HAIG. I don't like to walk away from meetings of this significance and give value judgments of that sensitivity. I would emphasize again that the main focus of my concern and President Reagan's concern, is the situation in Poland, which influences across the entire spectrum of our relationships with the Soviet Union.

Q. Mr. Secretary, would you say that this was a meeting almost totally of confrontation—of you giving your views and Mr. Gromyko putting his—or was there any area where you can indicate any agreement at all?

SECRETARY HAIG. Well, again I don't want to describe it as an area that was seeking agreement, but I think there were important exchanges of views that contributed to the ability of both sides to understand the concerns of the other. And on that basis alone, especially in view of the Polish situation, I think the meeting was both timely and important and valuable.

Q. You met last September in New York.[13] Did you cover any of the same topics with Foreign Minister Gromyko? In the light of your statement that the shadow of the Polish situation is falling on American-Soviet relations. Could you give us some indication of how the character of these discussions that you had today differed now, after Poland, from what you had in September?

SECRETARY HAIG. I would say it varied. Some of the discussions were carried forward in a constructive way and some found themselves on the rocks of disagreement.

Q. Was there any question of a summit meeting between Mr. Brezhnev and Mr. Reagan?

SECRETARY HAIG. No, there was no discussion of such a meeting.

Q. You said there will be no START talks under [*until*?] conditions permit, and that things would have to change in Poland. Did you give Mr. Gromyko any specific set of criteria of what would have to happen in Poland?

SECRETARY HAIG. No, I think it's sometimes laborious to state the obvious to get too detailed. I think these are issues of broad substantive character, and I also want to make it very clear that it is the position of President Reagan that he is very anxious to get on with START talks, and to achieve substantial reductions or meaningful reductions in the levels of nuclear armaments. But the political backdrop under which these talks are to be conducted has an important impact on any hopes for progress and success. And I'll have one more question.

Q. Did you have any discussion on trade relations and embargoes which might affect them?

SECRETARY HAIG. There was some discussion on the subject of sanctions. But I'll leave that for the private minutes.

Q. Thank you.

Document 253

Statement Issued by the Department of State, January 28, 1982[14]

Polish Defectors to the United States

Q. Has the United States experienced masses of Poles defecting?

A. To speak of masses of Polish defectors and refugees seeking asylum in the United States following recent events in Poland overstates the case considerably. There has been a small number of Polish officials, such as the Polish Ambassador here and in Japan[15] who have sought politi-

[13] Regarding Haig's meetings with Foreign Minister Gromyko in New York on September 23 and 28, 1981, see the extract from the interview with Haig on October 29, 1981, *American Foreign Policy: Current Documents, 1981*, document 254.

[14] Office of Press Relations, Department of State; posted statement. The statement was posted in response to a question asked at the Department of State Daily Press Briefing of January 25, 1982.

[15] On December 20, 1981, the Polish Ambassador to the United States, Romuald Spasowski, requested asylum in the United States. A similar request was made by the Polish Ambassador to Japan, Zdzislaw Rurarz, on December 23, 1981.

cal asylum in the United States. It is difficult to provide a precise figure as to the number of Poles who have requested asylum or refugee status around the world since the imposition of martial law, but our estimate would be in excess of 2,000. This figure includes a considerable number of seamen.

We will have no comment on press reports that a Polish General has defected to the United States and has provided sensitive information on recent events in Poland.

Document 254

Address by the Secretary of State (Haig) Before a Solidarity Day Rally, Chicago, January 30, 1982[16]

Solidarity Day

Thank you very much.

Distinguished officials, guests on the dais, my fellow Americans, friends of Poland, and lovers of freedom: (Applause) Just under 2 hours ago I left President Reagan in our Nation's capitol. How I wish he could have been here personally to feel, as I have, the support of the great citizens of the City of Chicago for the dreadful crisis we are witnessing today in Poland!

The President has asked me, in his behalf, to read to you his own personal message dictated for this occasion, and I will do so now. (Applause)

I quote:

"I am very proud to join with all the freedom-and peace-loving people in this celebration of Solidarity Day. There is a spirit of Solidarity abroad in the world today that no physical force can crush. It crosses national boundaries, and enters into the hearts of men and women everywhere. In factories, farms, and schools, in cities and towns around the globe, we the people of the free world stand as one with our Polish brothers and sisters. (Applause) Their cause is ours. (Applause)

"I have urged my fellow Americans and other free nations to observe this day in meetings, demonstrations, rallies, prayer services, and all other appropriate expressions of support, just as they are doing. By our actions, we demonstrate our solidarity with the courageous people of Poland, and call for an end to their repression, for the release of all those arbitrarily detained, for the restoration of the rights of the Polish people, and for the resumption of an internal dialogue.

"Nancy and I add our hopes and prayers to yours in the great cause of freedom. Thank you." (Applause)

It is with a deep sense of pride and humility that I address this gathering. Throughout the United States, Americans are showing that Poland matters to them. Not only Americans of Polish descent, but their neighbors and friends care about events in a far-off country. Not only Americans but peoples in many states around the world are marking this moment in behalf of Poland.

We know that Poland is a nation steeped in a thousand years of European culture. It has nourished the civilization from which we draw our own roots as Americans. And our youth stand guard in Europe today, defending our freedom and the freedom of our allies for posterity.

What happens in Poland is therefore not the affairs of a distant country of which we know nothing and care less. In an age of materialism, when statistics and machines seem to matter most, the people of Poland remind us of the simple dignity of the workplace that is the birthright of every worker. In a time when philosophers debate the best social system for mankind, the people of Poland remind us that man requires freedom if he is to be truly creative. In a world thirsting for change, the people of Poland have shown that change can be most promising when it is peaceful.

What was the achievement of Poland known as Solidarity? It embodied an entire nation's search for dignity in the workplace, for freedom, for self-determination. It offered hope that the release of creative talents long suppressed could rescue Poland from its mounting economic problems. It seemed possible at last that in the midst of the world's most heavily armed continent, Poland would emerge as a symbol of hope instead of tragedy.

After 18 months, Solidarity has been violently suppressed. December 13, 1981,

---

[16] Source: Department of State Press Release 39, February 2, 1982; printed also without Secretary Haig's introductory remarks and the President's personal message in Department of State *Bulletin*, March 1982, pp. 32–33. The Secretary was in Chicago to participate in a Solidarity Day rally. Similar rallies were held in many other U.S. cities.

began the descent for Poland and for the world. The Communist authorities, mocking their own propaganda, threw the armed machinery of the state against the worker. The results are clear for all to see. Instead of dignity, there is degradation. Instead of truth, there is violation of conscience. Instead of freedom, there is fear.

The Polish Government and its ally, the Soviet Union, have been unable to produce either bread or freedom. They have been more adept at producing falsehoods. First, we are told that Solidarity itself brought about its own suppression through excesses that endangered Poland's entire economy. Has the Polish Government forgotten its own statistics, which recorded increasing production after August of 1981? Does it expect the world to forget the heroic figure of Lech Walesa, who declines to cooperate in the soiling of Solidarity's record?

Second, we are told that the Soviet Union did not intervene in Poland and had nothing to do with the suppression of Solidarity. But does Moscow expect the world to forget its pressures, threats and intimidation—including its military maneuvers? Can we forget that these actions were intended explicity to halt the progress of reform? Can we ignore the evidence of secret preparations for martial law, including the printing of the decree itself in the Soviet Union? The use of force against the Polish people today takes place because Moscow wanted it, because Moscow supports it, and because Moscow encourages it.

Third, we are told that General Jaruzelski's regime deserves support because the "state of war" in Poland is the act of Polish nationalists, concerned that something worse will happen unless Communist-style law and order are established. Let us listen instead to the Polish Bishops who described the entire nation as terrorized by military force. Is this terror more justifiable because a Polish General, rather than a Soviet General, signs the decrees?

Fourth, we are told that Poland's misfortunes are none of our business, that we have no right to judge the situation nor to influence it. Let us listen instead to the voice of reason, the voices of Polish intellectuals and artists who wrote "we declare that the decision to introduce the state of war in Poland on December 13, 1981, has broken the basic principle of international law for self-determination." This judgment of the Polish intellectuals is well-founded. The Helsinki Final Act of 1975,[17] signed by both Poland and the Soviet Union, is based on this principle. It sets standards of freedom and diversity. Can we afford to forget that the violation of this act affects the very basis of East–West relations? Can we afford to ignore the pattern of intervention and violence that marks Soviet policy not only in Eastern Europe but in Afghanistan and elsewhere?

As we stand here today, the people of Poland look to us for support in their hour of need. We must give our support not only because it matters to them but also because it matters to us. We must set practical policies with realistic objectives.

President Reagan and other Western leaders have declared that we seek a restoration of those rights, as promised in the Helsinki Final Act, that protect the independence of the union movement and the church. Only in this way can the basis be established for reconciliation through negotiation within Polish society.

These are not foreign demands made in America or elsewhere to be imposed on Poland. Since the imposition of the state of war, the men of reason in Poland have demanded an end to confrontation with the nation. The men of faith have demanded to know the truth behind the suppression of liberty. The men of solidarity have demanded that General Jaruzelski fulfill his statement before the National Assembly that "trade unions in Poland will be as the working people wish them to be."

We must face the fact that today both the Polish and the Soviet Governments are ignoring these just demands of the Polish people. They seem determined to plunge further into the abyss. But their course is not without cost. And when they reckon the cost, a degree of moderation may be possible.

The United States has made clear that we will not do business as usual with either Poland or the Soviet Union while repression in Poland continues. We have also made evident that Poland is not merely an incident to put behind us. It has cast a long and dark shadow over East–West relations.

The United States is not alone. Our allies in the North Atlantic Council have already

---

[17] For the text of the Final Act of the Conference on Security and Cooperation in Europe signed at Helsinki, August 1, 1975, see Department of State *Bulletin*, September 1, 1975, pp. 323–350.

taken some steps. They have begun the task of identifying possibilities for action across a broad front, including an examination of the course of future economic and commercial relations with the Soviet Union. At the same time, the West has indicated its readiness to help revive Poland's shattered economy when the Polish people regain their rights.

Make no mistake. These tragic events in the East have a profound meaning for us in the West. Our progresses, despite all of our faults, is a striking rebuke to the Soviet system. After all, what the Polish people sought was no more than we take for granted, as natural to us as the air we breathe.

This cruel suppression of freedom reminds us, as the Polish Bishops wrote, that "real peace stems from respect for freedom and the correct understanding of everyone's right to freedom." As the trustees of peace and freedom, it is only through our strength and resolve, our passion for the defense of our liberties, that we earn the right to say to the Polish people—the day will dawn after the terror of the night.

Ladies and gentlemen, Poland has not perished. Poland cannot perish. The exponents of Marxist-Leninism in Warsaw or Moscow, who pride themselves on knowledge of the laws of history, have ignored this basic truth. The sight of a peaceful people seeking peaceful change has terrified them. But the actions of these fearful men will not deprive the Poles of their faith, their courage, or their secret dreams. Change will come. Hope will be reborn. And Poland will truly be Poland again.

Jeszcze Polska nie zgnieya. (Poland has still not perished.)

Document 255

Transcript of a Department of State Press Briefing, February 5, 1982[18]

Poland's Indebtedness to the West

MR. ROMBERG. The briefing will be on the record in terms of the statement to be made. Q's and A's following will be on background, attributable to a senior administration official.

The statement will be made by Marc Leland, Assistant Secretary of the Treasury for International Affairs, and for your guidance, he will also be taking your questions on background.

Copies of his statement will be available before we leave.

MR. LELAND. The subject of this briefing is the two issues of the Polish debt and the recent subject of the CCC credits, for those of you following it.

Basically, the President has decided that maximum pressure can be put on Poland by insisting on repayment rather than declaring a default now. A declaration of default might be used by the Polish Government as an excuse to relieve itself of its obligations to make repayments.

The U.S. Government has fulfilled its legal obligations to U.S. banks. The U.S. Government, through the Commodity Credit Corporation, guaranteed loans made by U.S. banks for the sale of agricultural commodities to Poland.

In 1981, when the Poles did not pay the banks the amount due on these loans, the U.S. Government fulfilled its obligation by making payments to the banks. We are, of course, doing the same in 1982. These payments in no way relieve Poland of any of its obligations. The only difference now is that Poland owes the money to the U.S. Government instead of U.S. banks.

A lot of questions have been raised which we will try to deal with, and maybe I will just kind of go through them to give general answers, and you can ask more things about them if you want.

1. Are payments to the banks on the Commodity Credit Corporation loans a bail out of the banks?

No. The U.S. Government guaranteed these loans and it is obligated to honor the obligations.

2. Is this payment to the banks letting the Poles off the hook?

No. The obligation is now owed to the U.S. Government instead of to the banks, and we will do everything possible to collect it.

3. Did the payment to the banks prevent them from declaring Poland in default?

No. The banks are owed amounts on nonguaranteed loans for which they have

---

[18] Source: Office of Press Relations, Department of State. The briefing, much of which was conducted on background by the Assistant Secretary of the Treasury for International Affairs, Marc E. Leland, concluded at 5:10 p.m. Leland was introduced by Department of State Acting Spokesman Alan Romberg.

not declared default but can declare default any time they wish.

4. Would a formal declaration of default force the Soviets to pay the amount due by the Poles?

No. It is an obligation incurred by Poland and not guaranteed by the Soviet Union.

5. Wouldn't a declaration of default keep further credits from going to Poland?

No. Private banks are not lending to Poland. The Polish debt situation prevents further credits from going to Poland. Some funds are coming from Poland to the West toward satisfying previous Polish obligations while no new credits are going to Poland.

6. Would a declaration of default stop credit from going to the Soviet Union?

No. Unguaranteed private bank credit unrelated to short-term trade transactions has not been going to the Soviet Union. This is because of the debt situation of Poland and other countries in Eastern Europe, as well as other economic and financial difficulties faced by the Soviet Union itself.

7. Can we declare a default on the Soviet Union?

No. They are current on all of their obligations to the United States.

8. Finally, the basic question, will the U.S. Government ever declare Poland in default?

Default always remains an option, to be used any time we see fit.

Does that answer all your questions? Are there any left? Have I thought of every possible question?

On Background

Q. What would the consequences of default be, for both the Western financial community and in its foreign policy implications?

A. Basically, Poland is in arrears. I mean, the fact that Poland is not paying its debt is a fact. Whether or not you go up and announce you are in default or whether you don't announce you are in default, they have not been paying their debts.

Therefore, as far as the Western banking community, at such time as it is determined by banking examiners, and so forth, that there is no chance of Poland paying back its debt, we will have to set aside reserves for that debt. To some degree, we will have to write them off.

Our understanding is that no U.S. banks will be faced with any grave problems about it. A few European banks which have other troubles may find it more troubling, because they will have these debts, but the amounts there are probably something that they can handle themselves, as well. And this is something that may happen by the banking examiners, whether or not a formal default ever is declared, if they see that the debt is not going to be repaid.

Q. Can you go through the numbers with us? What is the total debt owed to the United States? How much to the government and how much to the banks?

A. Well, let's see, the banks—I think the total amount to the United States is about $3.2 billion, of which about $1.3 billion is owed to the banks.

Q. The rest to the government?

A. The rest to the government. To make that clear, I should explain, the loans that we make, that went to Poland, were made often in the form of bank loans guaranteed by the U.S. Government. That is with these CCC credits. So when I give you that division, I count the CCC credit loans as U.S. Government loans, because we guarantee them, and I count the others as unguaranteed loans.

Q. The $1.3 is unguaranteed?

A. Unguaranteed loans, yes.

Q. Are these loans going to be coming due monthly? In other words, will this be a decision to be faced monthly, or quarterly, or exactly how?

A. Yes. I mean, basically, these are loans that we are talking about there that were made 3 years ago in most cases. Now they are coming due, and they come due quarterly, usually, and some of them monthly, but basically they will be coming due over the next years, over the period of time that we made the loans.

Q. While we are at this thing, how often does this decision have to be faced? How frequently?

A. The point is, it isn't really a decision to be faced. I mean, the point is, we have a lot of government-guaranteed programs. I mean, Exim Bank has had all kinds of guarantees, and when the bank comes in and says, "The debtor didn't pay, you pay," it is not particularly a decision that you have got to take. They submit it to you. You are the guarantor, you pay it. So, as it comes due, if the Poles aren't paying it, we pay it.

Q. When is the next one due?

A. I think there will be some next month again. Basically, I think it is more quarterly. But you will have amounts coming [that] the banks will submit to us under their guaranteed debt, and say, "Please pay this."

Q. How many banks are involved in both the guaranteed and the nonguaranteed portion?

A. The total number of banks involved in the Polish debt is all of 90. There are really 60 that have any amount that you could call sizable, and then there are those—there are really only about 20—that have any really sizable amount.

Q. How many U.S. banks?

A. I am talking about U.S. banks. There are 450 worldwide banks.

Q. Is that list available anywhere?

A. I am not sure. I don't think it is. I don't think it is a public document now.

Q. Have you ascertained that the banks have done all in their power to collect this money, and how have you done that?

A. We are in constant contact with the banks, and they are doing everything they think they can possibly do to collect the debt. They want to be paid. They have put all the pressure that they know how to put on the Poles to get them to pay.

They have refused to reschedule the 1981 debt until they get the full interest payment on the 1981 debt, and the amount that you read about that they have been receiving is the amount on the 1981 debt.

Q. But there are assets in this country and in other parts of the world that they could apply against this debt rather than have U.S. funds applied against it.

A. As I understand it, minimal. If there were, there would be no question that that is what you should go after. We are owed money, the U.S. Government is owed money on the 1981 rescheduling, so they owe the U.S. Government money, Poland, so if there were assets around, you would go attach them. Banks would, too, if there were something that they could grab onto. There aren't any.

Q. Is there a possibility that a Chrysler-like situation could develop here, where the banks may be requested to make certain concessions in the national interest, which they normally might not make using the normal business standards?

A. No. I don't see any possibility of that happening, particularly under these circumstances. . . .

Q. Have you got a system in which the private debts of the Polish Government are being transferred to the U.S. Government rather than the private banks with which they are contracted? Does that not decrease the heat on the Poles to repay their debts? Wouldn't they rather have it in the hands of the U.S. Government than in the hands of private creditors?

A. No. What I was trying to explain is, when the banks made these loans, they primarily looked to the debtor, the U.S. Government, not to Poland. If Poland was looked upon as the debtor—and that is the way they were received, with the U.S. Government guarantee.

It is not as if the government—you are a guarantor of a loan, you don't have any choice as to whether you want to pay it or you don't want to pay it. It is your obligation. It is the U.S. Government's obligation to pay the bank every bit as much as it is Poland's.

Now, with us holding the debt, the leverage on them—or if you want to put it—the pressure is just as great if not greater with the government pressing together as it would be from the banks.

The banks are owed other unguaranteed amounts on which they are putting tremendous pressure to get payments, and if the banks determined—as I say here, if they wanted to declare a default, that they thought was a better way of getting paid here, if they thought there was some asset that they could attach, and that was a better way, they would do so, because no pressure is or isn't envisioned to be put on them by the government.

Q. The fourth question that you have concerning formal declaration of default force the Soviets to pay. It seems to me that the answer is rather legalistic. In a formal sense, a legal sense, the Soviets wouldn't be forced to pay. But what is the determination of the political cost of the Soviets not extending that so-called umbrella to take care of Poland? I mean, look at it in the political sense as opposed to the formal sense.

A. I agree that the answer reads in that form, but I think it's meant in both senses.

Poland's debt to the West is $26 billion. In 1982 10-some billion dollars are going to be owed, interest and principal. Now, the Soviet Union is not that size amount with the default[?] The Soviet Union doesn't have or going to come with to pay it[?] Their answer is simply going to be, "You made the loan to them. You didn't get our guarantee. We are not paying it."

I think you are correct that the umbrella theory, because of the fact that the Soviets have not—I mean if the Soviets were planning to do that they would continue making much more substantial payments for Poland now in order to forestall any possibility that they would have to come up with the whole amount. I think the fact is that in the troubles that other parts of Eastern Europe are having come from the fact that some people are realizing that the umbrella theory is just a theory and that in practice the concept that they can just turn and give the debt to the Soviet Union won't happen.

Q. In your statement you say that, "In 1981, when the Poles did not pay the banks the amount due on these loans, the U.S. Government fulfilled its obligation by making payments to the banks." In other words, the $71 million is not the first time?

A. No. We did the same thing in 1981.

Q. Could you give us the amount involved in 1981?

A. I think in the neighborhood of $380 million.

Q. That was through the refinancing, wasn't it?

A. No, the private banks have not rescheduled their debt at all for 1981. But they weren't being paid, and they came, and we paid them.

VOICE. Make that $340 million.

A. Well, on the 1981 debt of CCC-guaranteed loans—now those would have been loans made 3 years prior to that date—there is about $340 million paid by the U.S. Government prior to martial law, of course.

Q. Last week you and Mr. Hormats testified for a couple of hours before the European Subcommittee of the Senate Foreign Relations Committee[19] on the Polish debt, and the question of the guaranteed loans never came up directly. Then there was no discussion of the fact that the U.S. Government was about to have to make good the guarantees of $71 million. Then in Monday's paper, following that hearing, we read about it. It was in Mr. Safire's column in his story in the *Times*.[20] Why didn't you bring it up during those hearings?

A. To be quite candid, because I never saw the thing as being a major issue. When you read it looking in hindsight, maybe I should have. The papers had come through before. It wasn't, I wasn't even absolutely certain. It had to go through the whole line of chain of people, and I wasn't sure at what date exactly how the thing was going to finally be done. It certainly wasn't a secret. Anything you notify 90 banks of there is no secret, and you're not even trying to keep it a secret. There wasn't any concept of doing it. We had done it in'81 and we were doing it again in'82. We owed it to the banks, and nobody kind of thought that there was any major thing to mention. If somebody had asked about it we would have answered that that was what we were planning to do. I mean the exact date of when it was going to be done was really only in the knowledge of the Agricultural Department. Had they been there I suppose that would have been more on people's mind. In Bob's and my mind I don't think either of us was aware at that moment exactly at what time that was going to happen. It was a very normal procedure.

Q. Was there not an interagency consultation going on that week?

A. There were interagency discussions of how to handle it for the next year. That's it.

Q. The truth of the matter is that now the United States is involved here in something not very short of half a billion dollars in bad debt which it guaranteed and which it has paid.

A. Already, and a lot more that's owed to it to come.

Q. What do you see as the ultimate realistic figure?

A. As I said, there is $3.2 billion owed to the U.S. private and public sector, $1.3 to the private banks and $1.9. It all depends—

Q. Does the $1.3 include that which you have already guaranteed and paid off?

A. No, no. That's what I say. The $1.9 is a figure that is due to the government, and

[19] For this testimony on January 27, see *The Polish Economy: Hearing Before the Subcommittee on European Affairs of the Committee on Foreign Relations, United States Senate, Ninety-seventh Congress, Second Session* (Washington, 1982), pp. 4–31.

[20] *New York Times*, February 1, 1982, p. A15.

$1.3 to the private banks. That is the U.S. exposure so to speak.

Q. Of your exposure of $1.9 do you foresee virtually all of it being paid to the banks?

A. It's over a 3 year period. To predict what's going to happen over a 3-year period in making those payments, it would be overly speculative. Given the Polish financial situation, our hope and expectation is that they are going to have to make some payments. They are going to have to keep up the interest and try to get them to pay some money on principal. But it's impossible to know when that will happen or whether or not we'll have to pay the banks and then go after the Poles later on.

Q. What kind of exchange have you been having with the Polish Government concerning this question? What kind of assurances, if any, have they been giving to you regarding their best efforts to pay? Have there been discussions about the political situation in connection with the debt? Could you fill us in a little bit on this?

A. We had extensive discussions with the Poles on this matter prior to December 16. There were constant meetings. There were debt reschedulings and debt rescheduling meetings on how are we going to pay this. As I said, in August we rescheduled the'81 debts. The private banks—we have said that we are not going to reschedule any debt or consider it is going to be repaid until the banks do their 1981 rescheduling whatever that is, and they are under the most extreme pressure to come up with that couple of hundred million dollars. So the most contact with them on that basis has been with the private banks to fulfill that previous debt because no one will consider anything until that date, but you've got ourselves and the Europeans pressuring them with the idea that they owe us this money and that they've got to find a way to come up with it. Their answer is always, of course, to say that they are going to make their best efforts, and what you have is every week or so some money dribbling into the banks to pay off part of the debt, and they say, "That's the best we can do," and one keeps pressuring them, as you do any debtor.

Q. What about the other West European governments which are owed money? Has what you're doing today been coordinated with the other West European governments?

A. Definitely. In January, prior to martial law, there had been a meeting scheduled in January by ourselves, by the 16 basic creditor nations and the Poles. Because of martial law the determination was to have that meeting with all the creditors and not with the Poles. We didn't want to meet with them when there was no purpose. And everybody is taking the same policy, which is the $250 million I'm talking about isn't just due to our banks, it's due to banks all over, and all the governments are trying to use whatever pressure they can to say, "Come up and pay the debts." And in addition, one should add not giving them any new credit.

Q. If the Polish Government does not make any payment this year what will be the total U.S. Government obligation?

A. What do you mean?

Q. In terms of what additional funds you have to come up with under the guaranteed loan program.

A. Well, I think for this year under the guarantee program it's more in the $500 to $700 million of those that were made, again, 3 years ago that are coming due.

Q. Five to seven hundred million dollars this year?

A. Yes, this year.

Q. You said that, in effect, by paying the $71 million and I guess $340 million before that you were transferring Poland's indebtedness from the private banks to the government. Since this situation is ultimately a political situation, why not transfer it—I guess. . . [21] suggested—the entire indebtedness and take over the private indebtedness and use that as a political lever in dealing with the Poles.

A. That would be a bail-out of the banks. They made loans that were unguaranteed. Let them try to collect those debts and wait and let them do it. Why would the U.S. Government go and buy their debts. Poland owes $26 billion, about half, or a little over half, to the government and a little over half privately.

Q. That's sufficient leverage one has to give up anyway isn't that?

A. That isn't true. There's $1.3 billion that the taxpayer is not going to pick up.

Q. Well, if they write it down it comes off their profits.

A. You can say that with any business; why don't you just take over any obligation

[21] Ellipsis appears in the source text.

that any business has to anybody that they aren't going to get paid?

Q. You don't have to pick it up at the full dollar on a dollar, but you can pick it up at something less than that.

A. I don't see how by doing that you would increase your leverage. What you are doing is you are putting your leverage on from two places. The fact that they owe the Western governments over $14 billion, given the Polish economy where it is, seems to be pretty sufficient leverage. If you add to that another $10 billion I don't see that that is going to add much to it.

Q. Will the United States support the Polish application for membership in the IMF as long as they owe the government money?

A. That is one of the (inaudible) even from dealing with the Polish. No determination has been made on Polish membership or what eligibility, whether they will meet the requirements of the IMF. What will happen to that is quite some time off.

Q. If I could back up a minute. Of that $1.9 billion owed to the government, is that all bank-guaranteed debt?

A. Mostly. It is done by banks making loans under CCC credit program and our guaranteeing it.

Q. And the provisions for a government guarantee was authorized by Congress as part of the CCC program?

A. Yes.

Q. Was it authorized specifically for the case of the Polish loans, or is it part of the general?

A. No, it's part of the general. They authorized the CCC program, and then the decision is made, the loans are made separately.

Q. You said the $500 to $700 million due this year is under the CCC credit?

A. Basically, most of that, that's what most of their obligation is.

Any other questions?

Q. Thank you.

Document 256

Statement Issued by the Department of State, February 10, 1982[22]

Visit to Washington of Yugoslav Vice President Dragan

At the invitation of Secretary of Commerce Malcolm Baldrige, Zvone Dragan, Vice President of the Federal Executive Council of the Socialist Federal Republic of Yugoslavia, paid an official visit to Washington from February 7 to 10, 1982.

Vice President Dragan was received by Vice President George Bush for an exchange of views on the further promotion of bilateral relations between the two countries, and on current international issues. Satisfaction was expressed at the development of relations and cooperation between the two countries. Vice President Dragan conveyed through Vice President Bush President Kraigher's greetings to President Reagan.

Vice President Dragan also held discussions with Donald T. Regan, Secretary of the Treasury; Malcolm Baldrige, Secretary of Commerce; William E. Brock, U.S. Trade Representative; Paul A. Volcker, Chairman, Board of Governors of the Federal Reserve system; Walter J. Stoessel, Jr., Acting Secretary of State; Guy Fiske, Acting Secretary, Department of Energy; William H. Draper III, President, EXIM Bank; Murray L. Weidenbaum, Chairman, Council of Economic Advisers; and Craig Nalen, President, Overseas Private Investment Corporation.

During the talks, note was taken of the strong efforts to overcome present economic difficulties in Yugoslavia, with a view in particular to stemming the high inflation rate and dealing with balance of payments problems. Some obstacles to better functioning of the economy remain, but an overall improvement of economic performance is evident, including reduction of the balance of payments deficit. The Yugoslav interest in expansion of economic relations with the United States and in the import of U.S. equipment and technology was also noted. Both sides expressed an interest in finding means to further cooperation in economic and other areas.

---

[22] Source: Office of Press Relations, Department of State; posted statement.

Document 257

Transcript of a Press Conference by the Secretary of State (Haig), Bucharest, February 13, 1982[23]

Haig's Visit to Romania

SECRETARY HAIG. Ladies and gentlemen, we have just concluded some 4¼ hours of discussion with President Ceausescu and his Foreign Minister Andrei, to include a working lunch during which I held this morning with the Foreign Minister and his colleagues from the Foreign Office, from the Ministry. I would describe these discussions as cordial, and with the same degree of frankness that has characterized discussions between our two governments for over a decade. I did have an opportunity to deliver a letter from President Reagan to President Ceausescu which was a response from the President to an earlier piece of correspondence from the Romanian President,[24] and which dealt with the current situation in Poland.

During our discussions this morning and this afternoon we focused on inter-European questions, including the Polish question, broader East–West matters with a very clear focus on disarmament, both the discussions underway on the IMF in Geneva, and the strategic arms discussions as well. We discussed the current conference in Madrid, the CSCE conference, Latin America, the Middle East, southern Africa and a broad range of mutual bilateral questions involving political, economic, cultural, scientific, [and] technological exchanges between our two countries. There were some differences on the Polish question as they pertained to sanctions against the Polish Government, but a general convergence of view on the need for normalization, immediate normalization, of the situation in Poland to include lifting of international law and the elimination of the state of siege.

Now this visit to Romania, as you know, has been a response to a longstanding invitation to visit Bucharest first extended to me by Foreign Minister Andrei on behalf of President Ceausescu when the Foreign Minister visited Washington in May of last year.[25] President Ceausescu's invitation had been reiterated several times since then, and most recently about 3 weeks ago. It is the President's view, President Reagan's view, that at a time of increased East–West tension, it is particularly important to talk with those Eastern European countries which are open to such talks, and Romania certainly must be included among those nations to seek ways together to reduce tension and to continue to seek constructive relationships on the basis of respect and mutual benefit.

Romania has for years pursued a relatively independent foreign policy. On many issues, in fact, our foreign policy objectives are quite similar. On the commercial level we have had increased two-way trade from barely 300 million in 1973 to over 1 billion annually in just the short period of over 7 years. Within the context of generally good relations, that I have just described, we have been able to discuss with Romania human rights, emigration, and family reunion cases. There has been progress in some individual cases; nonetheless, some problems continue. But I believe that our visit here will help to alleviate those remaining problems. I think the hallmark of mature relations between countries is not the absence of problems which do exist. That has been and will continue to be the nature of our relationship with Romania. We demonstrated by this visit that we are prepared to continue our constructive relationship with the Government and the people of Romania. Romania's policy on issues ranging from arms control to the Middle East, the foreign economic policies and attitudes toward national independence are both longstanding and well known, and were discussed in detail with President Ceausescu today.

In sum, Romania is a nation which, ever mindful of its geography, has courageously sought to assert its independence and full sovereignty. We welcome that, we have constructed with the Romanians a network of political, commercial, cultural and scientific ties which have operated to our mutual benefit. And this is a relationship which should continue to broaden and deepen in the days and months ahead.

Thank you for your attention. I welcome your questions. Somebody reminds me that

---

[23] Source: Department of State Press Release 69, February 17, 1982; printed also in Department of State *Bulletin*, April 1982, pp. 47–50. The Secretary visited Romania, February 12–13, as the last stop of a four-nation trip to Europe and North Africa.

[24] These letters have not been further identified.

[25] Foreign Minister Andrei visited Washington, May 14–16, 1981.

I might have said "international" law, but lifting of "international" law, I meant to say the lifting of "martial" law. I don't know what I'd do without my press secretary.

Q. From my notes you said that there were some differences on the Polish question as to sanctions. But you didn't say anything about the sanctions that the United States has imposed on the Soviet Union. Did that matter come up for discussion today, and what was the attitude of the Romanian Government on that?

A. I think President Ceausescu made it very clear that he felt sanctions against the Polish Government might be counterproductive in this environment. He raised no concerns about sanctions with respect to the Soviet Union, and it was not discussed in the very terms that the Polish question was.

Q. Did the Romanians ask for any help, economic help, to cover their short-term situation?

A. As you know, like so many of our industrialized nations, and even more importantly our developing nations in the Third World, the current economic climate worldwide has had a severe impact. There are a number of contributors to that: High energy costs, the impact of high American interest rates with the dollar such a heavily-employed currency, declining productivity, increasing levels of unemployment, and they're high here in Romania today as they are in our own country and throughout Western Europe. This all has caused a problem here in Romania in terms of their fluidity and the need for cash assets to keep economic growth moving in a positive direction. There are longstanding requests in that regard to the IMF and World Bank, and these questions were discussed at great length and great detail, with a view towards finding near-term solutions.

Q. Mr. Secretary, if you could give us some feeling—did the Romanian President raise concerns about the status of East–West relations; in other words, did he feel that the sanctions and the refusal to start the strategic arms talks were hurting the atmosphere and urge you to drop the sanctions and begin the talks and if so, what was your response on what we were doing?

A. I don't like to go into too much detail on discussions that were held in a mutually, confidential atmosphere. I think President Ceausescu has been a longstanding advocate of progress in arms control, as has President Reagan. I would not suggest that our discussions this morning focused on the contradiction imposed by the Polish question and our longstanding tensions in the arms control area. I would say that the concerns here involve the impact that sanctions against the Polish Government can have toward the rapid normalization of the situation in Poland. And that was the focus of the concerns that were expressed. On the other hand, we had rather far-ranging discussions on the question of the maintenance of normal relations among those states in the East and worldwide, indeed, that may belong to the Socialist system, who conduct independent and sovereign policy, and I think we had a meeting of the minds on that subject.

Q. Let me rephrase Bernie's question just now and ask you whether or not, given the fact that he feels, the Romanian President, sanctions are counterproductive, and we know the U.S. decision on that, does that amount to a stalemate, insofar as the U.S.-Romanian positions vis-à-vis Poland?

A. No not at all. As I've pointed out, I think that both President Reagan, as I know his position to be, and President Ceausescu, believe that it is vitally important that a normal condition be established in Poland, that martial law be lifted, that is whether or not economic or matériel sanctions against Poland, as distinct from the longstanding American and Western policy to continue humanitarian assistance to the Polish people, where we are assured that that assistance gets to the people, and is not utilized by repressive government action or to reinforce further repression. So there is just a minor difference here and I would describe it in terms of this tactical question, with the Polish side believing that it would be useful to help Poland in this crisis.

Q. Mr. Secretary, did President Ceausescu hear of the American view that ultimately it was the Soviets who were responsible for the imposition of martial law?

A. I must say that we did not discuss that question in the context in which it was asked.

Q. Can anybody else know the contents of that letter from President Reagan to President Ceausescu?

A. Well, the nature, and there again I don't think that it's appropriate for me to publicly air communications between two Heads of State, but clearly I've talked about where our differences are on the sanction question.

Q. Mr. Secretary, did President Ceausescu express any concern about a disruption or possible discontinuation of the CSCE process?

A. Yes, we had a very good exchange on that subject. I think we have a convergence in our broad objectives there, and that is the desirability of maintaining confidence in and continued progress on the implementation of the final act. As you know, it is our view that that continuation will require very clear clarifications on the human rights violations that are occurring in Poland today, and that have thus far remained unanswered by the Soviet Union and the Polish participants in the conference. I would think I would interpret President Ceausescu's view as one that we should nevertheless persevere and seek a meaningful outcome of those current talks. And these again are tactical differences which underline the concerns of both the Romanian and the U.S. Government that the Helsinki process should be preserved and protected. It is the American view that it's in jeopardy in this current climate while these fundamental violations of the obligations of the final act of Helsinki are underway in Poland today, and that there has to be some reckoning on these questions.

Q. Sir, was the question of Soviet involvement in the situation in Poland brought up at all in these discussions?

A. It was a one-sided discussion in which I laid out very clearly the facts that the United States holds on Soviet involvement.

Q. Mr. Secretary, for the Romanian televiewers, how would you appreciate the role that the United Nations can have and must have in primarily the matter of disarmament, the reduction of tensions, the solving of differences among states, and obviously, for the promotion of free economic cooperation?

A. I suppose the past record of the United Nations in that regard is a mixed bag, replete with limited successes and many failures. That is not to suggest that the U.N.'s role has not been of incalculable value in a host of other areas of international cooperation not the least of which is the convening of the representatives of the member governments each year repeatedly to discuss and address and to exchange views on such questions. I would hope as an individual to see past inadequacies and the failures to be able to deal with the more profound questions you asked somehow strengthened the resolve within the United Nations. Thus far, they haven't done too well, as you know, but that is not to be taken as necessarily a criticism, but a revelation of fact.

Q. Mr. Secretary, does President Ceausescu also condemn the martial law imposition in Poland in the first instance like the United States does?

A. I can't speak for him on that, and I prefer to let him speak for himself on that. That's a rather finely honed question. I think he would see greater justification than perhaps he would see from the U.S. point of view.

Q. Mr. Secretary, please, did you discuss the possibility of a direct or indirect participation of the European countries to the negotiations in Geneva?

A. No, we did not.

Q. Mr. Secretary, from your discussions with President Ceausescu, how far did he go in agreeing with you that there should be a return to dialogue on Poland among church, Solidarity, and government?

A. Well, I think there are different views on how one would describe, would outline the best ways to return to normalcy, and what we call a reconstruction in the Polish scene. I think basically all recognize that there are elements in Poland that have to have a voice within their proper sphere of responsibility. And I'd say in general there was a convergence there. Conditionality in specific terms would probably not be enthusiastically supported here in Romania.

Q. Did President Ceausescu raise the question of a European disarmament conference, and if so, what is the American reaction to such a proposal?

A. Yes, we discussed that, as of course the current focus of attention before the Polish situation, there was the Madrid Conference itself, and I think both governments recognize that a great deal of progress has been made in Madrid on the area of confidence-building measures under the original French proposal of a zone extended from the Atlantic to the Urals, and the need to develop mutual confidence-building arrangements for that zone. But from our point, and from my point of view, I emphasize that business as usual, a continuation of business as usual, on these talks, would make a mockery of the fundamental obligations of the Helsinki Accords themselves, through which all signatory governments committed themselves in the basic principles of the final act to a host of obligations which are clearly being violated today by both the Polish Government and the Soviet Union in Poland.

Q. Mr. Secretary, does the President feel that the sanctions by the United States against Poland and not the Soviet Union would harm the dialogue that Washington wants with this government?

A. No, I don't think so. I think that there was no inference of that kind in discussions that were held today which, on the bilateral side of course focused on the continuing need for cooperation and the question of credits and trade and the cultural/scientific exchanges and the like.

Q. Mr. Secretary, did you by any chance suggest that the U.S. administration would like to see the most-favored-nation clause extended over a period of—into a multi-year—

A. This did not come up in the discussions. I was prepared to discuss them, and as you know, we have certain legislative requirements in the United States, which means that we do have to annually review these questions. As a matter of principle, we would not have any concern about such a multi-year approach, but we do have our internal regulations.

Q. Mr. Secretary, in 1968, after the Soviet invasion of Czechoslovakia, there was a great deal of apprehension and fear about the possibility of the Russians coming here. Did you sense any continuing apprehension that that sort of thing might happen?

A. No.

Q. Mr. Secretary, did you get any impressions from President Ceausescu that any worsening of tensions between East and West might cause a general Soviet clampdown and try to assert its authority throughout the Warsaw Pact nations?

A. I think any responsible leader near the East or West today is concerned about a host of repercussions from continuing repression in Poland. And I would suggest that they include a whole range of possible consequences which would further add to international tensions, and I wouldn't discount the one you raised, but I do not want to suggest that it was raised specifically by our Romanian hosts while we're here.

Q. Thank you, Mr. Secretary.

Q. Mr. Secretary, I would like to return to the Romanian economic problem. Was there any specific agreement reached on any way in which the United States could help Romania regain full capacity, do you think?

A. We've had an on-going dialogue on this question, and I think our visit today helped to clarify a number of issues related to it, IMF, the area of CCC credits, and a host of related trade issues. I wouldn't say that any magic light was turned on that is going to suggest that all of these difficult problems will be instantaneously solved, but I do think we have improved the climate for finding solutions to these problems, especially the most urgent and immediate ones of them.

Q. Thank you very much.

Document 258

Transcript of an Interview With the Secretary of State (Haig), February 14, 1982 (Extract)[26]

Linkage in U.S.-Soviet Relations

. . . .

MR. GEORGE WILL. Secretary Haig, someone said earlier on the show that U.S.-Soviet relations were bad.[27] Some people complain that they're too good. That is, that we're now entering the third—

SECRETARY HAIG. I know there's some here.

MR. WILL.—the third month of the so-called Polish crisis, they're getting our grain, the American taxpayers are subsidizing their empire's loans, they're getting the International Harvester sale, negotiations are proceeding in Geneva as though no one believes in linkage any more.

What has changed in U.S.-Soviet relations?

SECRETARY HAIG. George, I understand the concern of serious people in the light of the crackdown in Poland, but I think memories are rather short. I recall the reaction in the West at the time of Hungary, Czechoslovakia, East Germany.

---

[26] Source: Department of State Press Release 67, February 16, 1982. The Secretary was interviewed on the ABC television program, "This Week With David Brinkley," by David Brinkley, Sander Vanocur, and George Will, all of ABC News. The interview began at 11:05 a.m.

[27] Apparently a reference to comments made earlier in the program by Stanislav Menshikov, Soviet Central Committee Spokesman in Moscow, who was interviewed via satellite.

On this occasion we've had a rather remarkable unanimity of condemnation on the part of all Western nations, a willingness to support one another in sanction actions that are underway, some of which have already been announced and others which will be announced.

I just came back from Madrid,[28] and I thought the Soviet-Polish actions on the first day of the resumption of that conference were appalling. It not only confirmed the unity of the Western world in condemning what is going on in Poland and refusing to conduct business as usual, but it brought a very strong decibel of sympathy from the nonaligned and neutral nations participating in this conference.

I think the Soviet Union and Poland are isolated internationally today on this Polish question, and I think the impact of Western and perhaps even nonaligned and neutral opposition to what is going on far exceeds what might be otherwise desirable unilateral American sanctions which could, if improperly handled, have the practical consequence of turning an Eastern failure into a Western failure.

MR. WILL. The President has said that there are other sanctions that may be triggered, but he has been unclear about the trigger. He's said, on the one hand, if things don't get better, they will be triggered; and, on the other hand, if things get worse. There's a difference there.

What are the criteria by which we will decide whether or not to proceed with other sanctions and those involving the Soviet Union?

SECRETARY HAIG. In the first place, George, it makes no sense to lay out a scenario of actions that are currently being contemplated. I do believe that you're as familiar as I with the range of economic and trade sanctions available to the United States. They involve grain and future credits; they involve the question of default which has been getting such attention in our press.

But, again, I emphasize to you that our analysis confirmed beyond a shadow of a doubt that unless there is a unified, uniform approach to this problem, unilateral U.S. steps could be less than significant, even in the category of grain where we have had an experience that confirmed that it was a self-defeating imposition of unilateral U.S. sanctions.

So we're trying to avoid that, and we're trying to keep the Western world together. I know of no situation that has changed the strategic environment in such a way that we Americans in the period ahead can afford unilateralism.

If that's the alternative to working systematically with our allies as we have been doing—and with considerable success, especially when compared with past experiences—then I think a degree of prudence and careful handling is in order.

MR. WILL. Very quickly, isn't it unilateralism for the French to go ahead with the huge gas deal?

SECRETARY HAIG. Absolutely. And it is not a step which we favor or condone, and which we are quite appalled by. This, however, is conducted in the channel that it should be conducted and not in the front pages of our press.

MR. BRINKLEY. You don't want to try in any way to stop it, as I understand it. Is that right? The pipeline deal.

SECRETARY HAIG. I think that's an absolute specious interpretation of my position. I have been a longstanding force for opposition to the gas pipeline.

MR. BRINKLEY. But do you want the U.S. Government actively to try to stop it?

SECRETARY HAIG. Of course, and we have been doing so. But what I do not want done, David, is to suddenly seize the anguish of the Polish situation to attempt to accomplish what has been a longstanding U.S. policy, and that is to convince our allies that there are other alternatives and above all to avoid blackmailing those allies on this very sensitive issue.

There's no question about America's condoning the pipeline. There may be some differences in and out of the government as to how best to achieve that.

. . . .

---

[28] Secretary Haig attended the Conference on Security and Cooperation in Europe, which resumed in Madrid on February 9 after being adjourned on December 18, 1981, in the wake of the imposition of martial law in Poland. Documentation on the Madrid conference is in Chapter 10, Part A.

Document 259

Remarks by President Reagan, Feburary 18, 1982 (Extract)[29]

Leverage on the Polish Government

. . . .

Q. Sir, there's another due date coming for the interest payments on Poland's loans to the West. Last month, your government bailed Poland out by paying interest payments to Western banks. Are you going to do it again?

THE PRESIDENT. I don't know what the situation will be or what our move will be, but we didn't bail Poland out in doing that, we retained our leverage because default would mean great financial hardship for a great many people and a great many institutions here in the West. Default literally is like bankruptcy and they're absolved of their debts. And we felt that in this way, we could hold that back to where if that becomes a useful alternative, we can make use of it. But the default as it stands right now, we believe, would simply throw Poland more dependent on the Soviet Union and we would rather not have that happen.

Q. You'd probably pay it again, sir?

THE PRESIDENT. What?

Q. You will probably pay it again?

THE PRESIDENT. I said we haven't made a decision on that. . . .

. . . .

[29] Source: White House Press Release, February 18, 1982, Office of the Press Secretary to the President; printed also in *Weekly Compilation of Presidential Documents*, February 22, 1982, pp. 194–195. For the full text of this press conference, which began at 2:02 p.m. in the East Room of the White House, see *ibid.*, pp. 187–196. The press conference was broadcast live over nationwide radio and television.

Document 260

Transcript of the Department of State Daily Press Briefing, February 25, 1982 (Extract)[30]

Repayment by Romania of Commodity Credit Corporation Credits

. . . .

Q. Do you have anything on Romania, particularly regarding the *Post* story[31] today?

A. Yes. The question I assume you have in mind is any information we can provide about the $5.8 million that it owes the United States.

Q. Yes.

A. For the specific details on the procedure for repayment of the CCC credits through private U.S. banks acting as agents, I have to refer you to the Department of Agriculture.

The State Department first learned of this report late yesterday. We've instructed our Embassy in Bucharest to seek a full explanation from the Romanians on why they are late with these payments, and we will be asking the same question of the Romanian representatives here in Washington today.

We will be asking that they bring their payments up to date immediately.

Q. Are you confirming that that $5.8 million figure is correct and that the U.S. Government has indeed paid banks that amount?

A. As I say, we learned of the report late yesterday. We will be discussing that issue with the Romanians both in Bucharest and here today.

Q. Do you mean this possibility never came up in the talks that Secretary of State Haig held in Bucharest?

A. The possibility specifically I can't speak to, but I did mention on Monday[32]

[30] Source: Office of Press Relations, Department of State. The briefing, which began at 12:28 p.m., was conducted by Department of State Spokesman Dean Fischer.

[31] *Washington Post*, February 25, 1982, p. A1.

[32] February 22.

that the Secretary informed the Romanians in Bucharest that any further consideration of their longstanding request of CCC guarantees would have to await the outcome of their discussions with private banks as well as the IMF, plus the resolution of their current financial difficulties.

Q. Let me make sure I have this straight. What you're saying is that you are going to ask them to immediately make their accounts good? In other words, you're going to seek that $5.8 million from the Romanian Government?

A. Yes, indeed. We're asking them to bring their payments up to date immediately.

Q. And what if they don't? Are they then automatically in default, or is there some other process where they have to be declared?

A. At this point neither the United States nor the private banks have declared Romania in default. The situation simply is that Romania is in arrears in payment to both the government and to the banks.

Q. Did the CCC actually repay the banks what was due them?

A. For this I have to refer you to the Department of Agriculture.

Q. I'm still not quite clear about your previous answer. Did not the Secretary and President Ceausescu discuss this whole problem while the Secretary was there?

A. I acknowledged that. But in specific response to a question, did this particular payment arise in the discussions, I don't have any information for you.

Q. Yes. But the specific figures and the specific payment aside, did not Ceausescu warn the Secretary that they might have to default on some of their payments or get an extension?

A. I don't have any information on any warning given the Secretary by Ceausescu. The information I have on the meeting is what I gave you.

Q. What about the meeting with the Foreign Minister? Did he not point out that they might have to do this?

A. I just can't confirm that, Bob.

Q. Are you likely to have something on this after you complete your discussions this afternoon?

A. Later today?

Q. Yes.

A. I don't know. I don't know precisely what time these meetings are planned to be held.

Q. Can you tell us who's doing the meeting?

A. I can find out, yes.

Q. Just a point about this Romania issue again. Why is it that the administration is taking this line on Romania and taking a different one on Poland when Romania has not experienced the upheavals that Poland has in the last 3 months.

A. A different line?

Q. Yes.

A. We haven't declared Poland in default.

Q. No. I understand that. Is that what you're doing now in Romaina?

A. No. I'm not saying that we are—

You're asking that the Romanians—

Q. What I am asking you is, what is the difference in the line?

As I understand what you're saying, the Romanians are being asked to pay up now and you're going to talk to them here and in Bucharest.

A. Yes.

Q. The Poles are in debt to the United States for a lot more than $5.8 million. Have you made a similar request to the Polish Government to pay up today? Are you alerting them that they have to pay today as well?

A. No.

Q. Why the difference?

A. The answer to that question is that we are not asking Poland to pay up today, but I don't see what the basic difference is here in our approach to the two countries.

Q. The U.S. Government was paying the interest payments on the Polish debt, but it is not prepared to do so with the Romanian debt.

A. The point is that we first learned about this late yesterday, and we are having meetings today. Until those meetings are held, I can't give you any indication as to what will be the decision in the future based on those meetings.

Q. But you said that you are going to tell the Romanians that they have to pay up to date.

A. We will be asking that they bring their payments up to date.

Q. Have you ever said that to Poland?

A. I will have to take that question.[33] I don't know the answer to that.

Q. Isn't it clear that there are two different approaches here?

A. The problem I have with this is that we haven't yet had the meetings with them, and so I'm not sure that I can accept the premise that somehow there is a difference of approach until we've had communication with them directly.

Q. I don't want to belabor it, but obviously you have not asked the Poles and you are asking the Romanians, and it appears just on the face of it to be two different approaches, and I was asking you what—

A. I can't confirm, without checking, that we haven't asked the Poles to do this.

Q. You didn't the last time it came up. The U.S. Government paid the money.

A. I understand that.

Q. Are you saying that the Secretary, when he came back from Bucharest, had no inkling that Romania would default on its next payment?

A. No. I am not saying that at all. I can only repeat what I did say which was that the Secretary informed the Romanins that any further consideration of their requests for guarantees would have to await the outcome of discussions with banks as well as the IMF.

Q. I know, but we're talking about a payment coming due. Did he know that was not going to be paid?

A. This I cannot confirm.

Q. Dean, does their inability to make this payment in any way jeopardize any future consideration for CCC credits?

A. Again, I think we have to await the outcome of the meetings today before we can prejudge what might be the situation as a consequence of those meetings.

Q. Can you at least say whether they are State Department meetings, or are Agriculture Department officials meeting with Romanian officials?

A. No. I will have to look into who is meeting on our behalf.

Q. Did you already say or were you asked when these meetings are? What time?

A. No. I don't know the precise times.[34]

. . . .

Document 261

Remarks by the Deputy Secretary of State (Stoessel), March 3, 1982 (Extract)[5]

Poland in the Context of East–West Relations

. . . .

First, on the Soviet Union, clearly the relationship is a very important one for the United States. The Soviet Union is the other superpower and the only other power in the world capable of directly threatening our own security. We have to take the relationship very seriously. We are sometimes accused in this administration of being obsessed by the Soviet Union and

---

[33] On February 26 the Department of State issued the following statement in response to this question:

"On March 26, 1981, the then Polish authorities notified their creditors that they would no longer be able to guarantee payment of their external debt. Subsequently, creditor governments and private banks responded to the Polish notification by agreeing to enter into debt rescheduling negotiations. Separate debt rescheduling exercises were organized by the official and private creditors. Fifteen official creditor nations (later increased to sixteen with the addition of Spain) concluded negotiations with the Government of Poland and a multilateral debt rescheduling agreement was signed in Paris on April 27, 1981. Throughout these discussions and subsequently, we made it clear to the Polish authorities that we expect them to repay their obligations in full." (Office of Press Relations, Department of State; posted statement)

[34] During the Daily Press Briefing on February 26, Fischer said that the Romanian Government had not yet responded to U.S. inquiries about the payments owed on the CCC loan. Deputy Assistant Secretary of State Thomas Niles had met on February 25 with Romanian Ambassador Nicolae Ionescu to discuss the matter and the U.S. Chargé in Bucharest had been instructed to make a parallel approach on February 26. (Office of Press Relations, Department of State)

[35] Source: Department of State files. Stoessel spoke at a foreign policy briefing for the United Jewish Appeal in the Old Executive Office Building. The briefing began at 3 p.m.

believing that all of the problems of the world are traceable to the Soviets. Clearly, that is a gross exaggeration. The problems of the world are infinitely complex. We do know that the Soviets profit by instability, and that we must take very seriously their pattern of military buildup and increasing activism around the world.

I believe Mr. McFarlane[36] talked about the military buildup, and this is something which is of grave concern. We are trying to do something about it, to reverse the trends, which have been very dangerous, and to create a better balance to serve as the deterrent.

We have also been very concerned about a pattern of Soviet activism, going back at least to 1975 with the introduction of Cuban troops with Soviet help into Angola, then Cubans in Ethiopia; the takeover in South Yemen; the use of Libya as a surrogate; the activities of the Soviet Union in supporting Vietnam in the invasion of Kampuchea; the use of Soviet forces directly in Afghanistan—the first time since the war that Soviet forces have been used outside the Warsaw Pact; the activities in Central America of Cuba, supported by the Soviet Union; and the long period of pressures, military and otherwise, on Poland leading up to the December 13th takeover. So this is a record of activism of a dangerous kind, which is of great concern to us.

We do seek a moderation in this behavior—greater restraint on the part of the Soviet Union. We are communicating with the Soviets on many levels—through our Embassy in Moscow and through Ambassador Dobrynin here in Washington, who has now been here, I guess, almost 20 years and is a very well-known figure in this town. Secretary Haig has had two conversations with Gromyko, one last fall at the United Nations and one just in January in Geneva,[37] where we had the opportunity to present in detail the whole catalog of problems, as we see them, with the Soviet Union.

I can't say that we have been encouraged to believe there will be immediate changes in Soviet behavior, but we have been encouraged that the dialogue is a useful one. There was an absence of polemic on the part of Gromyko, a willingness to consider our views. We think that the exchanges have been useful and constructive in the sense of exposing very frankly and very directly our concerns.

I might mention that, as you would expect, the Secretary, in talking with Gromyko raised the general question of emigration from the Soviet Union and mentioned Jewish emigration, in particular, which has been, this past year, at the lowest level it has been for over a decade. He also took up a number of special cases, and made very clear the depth of our concern and the President's concern about these cases.

We are communicating also with the Soviets in other fields. The talks about intermediate-range nuclear weapons are continuing in Geneva. We are preparing for the strategic arms talks on an interagency basis, and will be ready within a few weeks with our position on the strategic arms talks. We have not felt it appropriate, given the situation in Poland, to name a date for beginning those talks; but with some improvement in the Polish situation, we would hope that that could be within the fairly near future.

The Soviet Union itself, of course, is a vast country and a very powerful country. It has many, many problems internally and with all the problems we have in this country, I'm always grateful that we don't have the Soviet problems. We know that their economy is in bad shape; their agriculture is not productive; and they are clearly having great difficulty within their Eastern European empire.

At the same time, they are having all these problems, one has the impression that they are already in a succession period, that Brezhnev himself is failing and the intimations of mortality must be quite acute, with a number of the older members of the leadership dying in recent months, so this also adds to the complex of problems affecting the Soviet Union. While we can observe these, I don't think we should take undue satisfaction from them. In a way, we could be in a more dangerous period than we ever have been, with the tremendous military strength of the Soviet Union combined with these weaknesses within the Soviet Union and the Soviet empire. That is a dangerous mix, and we have to be on our guard about it.

I have mentioned the problems within Eastern Europe. Poland is the most obvious example of that, and all of us have been

---

[36] Robert C. McFarlane, Deputy Assistant to the President for National Security Affairs.

[37] Regarding Secretary Haig's conversations with Gromyko in New York on September 23 and 28, 1981, see *American Foreign Policy: Current Documents, 1981*, document 254. For a transcript of a press conference by Haig in Geneva on January 26, 1982, regarding his discussions that day with Gromyko, see document 252.

deeply concerned by what occurred December 13, with the imposition of martial law, the repression of the Solidarity Free Trade Union organization, the arrest of many Solidarity leaders and independent thinkers, and the repression and chaos which has occurred in the economic organization in Poland.

We have made this concern very clear in a number of ways. The President has taken steps: He will impose sanctions on the military regime in Poland while continuing to improve humanitarian—the shipment of food aid. We have also imposed sanctions with regard to the Soviet Union. We have encouraged our allies to do the same thing, all with the idea of imposing pressures on the Soviet leadership and on the Polish regime to move back—probably it is unrealistic to think you could get back in Poland to the situation which existed before December 13—but at least to a lifting of the martial law, a release of the prisoners, and a renewed dialogue with the church and the Solidarity trade union.

Within the alliance, the response on sanctions in some respects has not been satisfactory. There has been reluctance on the part of some of the countries in Europe to impose stringent economic sanctions against the Soviet Union. However, there has been unity within the alliance with regard to an assessment of the situation in Poland and the Soviet responsibility for it. We have felt—and I think the Secretary felt when he saw Gromyko in Geneva—that the Soviets themselves have been very surprised by the degree of unity which has existed within the alliance. A number of countries have taken steps on sanctions, which were not exactly parallel to our own, but steps which give some bite to their concern. And I would expect that we will see more of this in the future.

As we look at this whole problem, we are concerned to preserve the alliance. We do not want to make out of an Eastern problem a Western crisis, and thereby serve the Soviet aim of splitting off Europe from the United States. So it is a rather fine line we have to draw.

We will be sending a mission to Europe next week led by Jim Buckley,[38] the former Senator, for further discussions and consultations with Europe concerning sanctions, the question of the pipeline, the question of future credits and subsidized interest rates as we deal in trade with the Soviet Union. We have long felt that there should be a better organization of the West looking to trade with the Soviets, that there should be a tool which we could employ for our own policy purposes in the West, and with the effect that we do not subsidize the Soviet economy to our own detriment and to the benefit of the Soviet military machine. We will be pursuing those aims through Under Secretary Buckley's mission.

. . . .

Document 262

Statement Read by the Department of State Spokesman (Fischer), March 11, 1982 (Extract)[39]

U.N. Human Rights Commission Resolution on Poland

. . . .

. . . [O]n the 10th of March the U.N. Commission on Human Rights, meeting in Geneva, adopted a resolution which expressed its deep concern over the widespread violations of human rights and fundamental freedoms in Poland.[40] The 43-member Commission adopted the resolution by a vote of 19 in favor, 13 opposed, with 10 abstentions and one nonparticipation.

The resolution affirms the rights of the Polish people to pursue their political and economic development, free from outside interference.

It calls for the end of measures restricting human rights and fundamental freedoms, release of prisoners detained without

---

[38] Under Secretary of State Buckley's mission, consisting of senior officials from the Departments of Defense, Commerce, the Treasury, and the National Security Council, visited Bonn, Paris, London, and Rome from March 13 to 20, 1982.

[39] Source: Office of Press Relations, Department of State. The statement was read at the Department of State Daily Press Briefing which began at 12:35 p.m.

[40] U.N. Commission on Human Rights Resolution 1982/26.

charge, and a review of sentences proposed under martial law.

It also requests the Secretary-General to undertake a thorough study of the human rights situation in Poland and present a comprehensive report to the next annual session of the commission.

This action by the U.N. Human Rights Commission was an important event. It was the first time in 38 years that the Human Rights Commission has spoken out on human rights violations in an Eastern European country. It demonstrates that Poland is not an East/West issue, but a matter of worldwide concern. The resolution received support from all regions. The sponsors of the resolution were all European nations. And many small countries courageously resisted Soviet pressure to vote against the resolution.

This action by the Human Rights Commission is a victory for human rights and for the Polish people. It represents an important expression of deep international concern through a United Nations body, for the plight of the Polish people who are struggling against the deprivation of their human rights and fundamental freedoms.

. . . .

Document 263

Transcript of the Department of State Daily Press Briefing, May 3, 1982 (Extracts)[41]

Brezhnev's Suggestion of an October Summit Meeting

. . . .

Q. Can you clarify whether, in fact, the United States has told the Soviet Union that it will take part in this summit meeting in October?

A. I saw some reports to that effect. First, I would note that President Reagan's offer to meet with President Brezhnev in New York this June[42] remains on the table. This is a serious offer to expand U.S.-Soviet high-level dialogue, and we regret that the initial Soviet response was not positive. We hope the Soviet side will reconsider, and that Presidents Brezhnev and Reagan will be able to meet in June in New York.

With regard to a full-fledged summit in October, we will carefully consider this possibility in the light of events and the substance of our bilateral dialogue with the Soviet Union over the coming months. President Reagan has made it clear that our longstanding criteria for a formal summit meeting remain in place. That is, it would have to be carefully prepared, it would have to be justified by the overall state of our relations at the time, and hold reasonable prospects for positive results. There are currently no specific preparations for such a meeting.

Q. Dean, what are you responding to there? Is that still the *Pravda* interview that Brezhnev gave where he suggested this thing,[43] or have the Russians followed it up with a formal invitation?

A. No. There has been other press speculation in the American press to the effect that President Reagan had agreed to a summit with President Brezhnev.

Q. That's not my question. My question is, when you respond about your interest in an October summit, had the Russians proposed to you formally that there be a summit in October or are you still responding to the way that that was originally floated, which was a Brezhnev—

A. Yes, of course. That's the original source for the report.

Q. You have not gotten any formal invitation from the Russians to a summit in October?

A. Not to my knowledge.

Q. Have you said to the Russians more or less what you're telling us today, that we will carefully consider the possibility of such

---

41 Source: Office of Press Relations, Department of State. The briefing, which began at 12:26 p.m., was conducted by Department of State Spokesman Dean Fischer.

42 The President's offer was made during a question-and-answer session with reporters on April 5; for the text, see *Weekly Compilation of Presidential Documents*, April 12, 1982, pp. 440–444.

43 Brezhnev made the proposal for an October summit meeting in an interview published in *Pravda* on April 18, an English translation of which is printed in *Current Digest of the Soviet Press*, May 19, 1982, p. 6.

a summit, or has the United States or the President put it more affirmatively that we will go to such a summit—that we are willing to go to such a summit?

In other words, is your language here, "We will carefully consider the possibility of such a summit" what has been communicated to the Soviets?

A. Well, we've been continuing to discuss all aspects of our relations with the Soviets, through our respective embassies here and in Moscow.

Q. You're saying there is no agreement to hold a summit in October?

A. That is correct.

Q. There is no agreement to hold a summit in October?

A. That is correct.

Q. Can I just clear up something? Maybe it's a tonal thing that is not possible at a briefing to clear up. But our colleagues at the White House, by talking to Mr. Speakes this morning, have certainly written stories suggesting the White House has confirmed the report that there is an agreement.[44]

A. But I don't believe that was based on anything Mr. Speakes said.

Q. I'm not breaking any confidence because as one wire report said, "Mr. Speakes was asked if he was knocking down the *Post* story?" and he shook his head negatively, that he was not.

A. I've given you what I have to say on the subject.

. . . .

Q. Dean, could you be a little bit more helpful on the summit thing, as we've got two somewhat contradictory stories? The White House stories, as reported by the wires, are that the United States and the Soviet Union have agreed that there will be a summit in October. You seem to be saying that there has been no Soviet invitation, there has been no agreement, although we will consider that.

A. That's right.

Q. Has there been an informal agreement with the Russians that we would both aim for a summit by October?

A. I would repeat that there are apparently no specific preparations for a summit meeting in October.

Q. Preparations. But actually has there been an agreement that we would both aim—to prepare for a summit is one thing. To agree that there will be a summit is another thing. Have we agreed with the Soviets that there should be a summit in the fall sometime, in October, in September?

I'm trying to understand why there is evident contradiction between what you're saying and what the White House seems to be saying.

A. It seems to me that when I say we will carefully consider this possibility, and that at present there are no preparations underway for such a meeting, that it obviously precludes agreement on such a meeting.

Q. It precludes agreement?

A. Yes.

Q. At this point?

A. Yes.

Q. That there has been no agreement?

A. That's right.

Q. Can you define for me what the distinction is between the meeting proposed in June and the summit proposed in October?

A. Make the distinction in what terms?

What sort of scale meeting do you have in mind for June as opposed to October?

A. I think the President addressed this the other day.[45] He said he would not describe it in terms of a full-fledged summit meeting, but an opportunity to get together with President Brezhnev.

. . . .

---

[44] During the extensive discussion of the possibility of an October summit meeting at the White House press briefing that morning, Deputy Press Secretary Larry Speakes said, "There are currently no specific plans or preparations for such a meeting." (White House Press Release, May 3, 1982, Office of the Press Secretary to the President)

[45] Apparently a reference to the President's comment at his press conference of April 20 that he did not intend the proposed June meeting to replace a "full summit meeting" later. (*Weekly Compilation of Presidential Documents,* April 26, 1982, p. 515)

Document 264

Transcript of the Department of State Daily Press Briefing, May 13, 1982 (Extract)[46]

Retaliation for Poland's Expulsion of Two U.S. Officials; Suspension of Joint Scientific Research Programs in Poland

. . . .

MR. ROMBERG. A statement finally on Poland: On May 10 the Polish Government demanded that two American diplomats, John Zerolis, Scientific Attaché, and J. Daniel Howard, Cultural Affairs Officer, leave Poland by May 14 for allegedly "promoting destabilizing activity" by visiting a Polish scientist who had recently been released from detention.

The actions of the Polish authorities in illegally detaining diplomats, who had identified themselves, and manhandling and searching them were a clear violation of diplomatic practice.

We have therefore told the Polish Embassy that before midnight, May 17, Mr. Andrzej Koroscik, Attaché for Science and Technology, and Mr. Mariusz Wozniak, Political Officer of the Polish Embassy in Washington, should leave the United States. This action is being taken in retaliation for the Polish Government's expulsion of our diplomats.

In addition, officials of the Polish Government have been alleging in the Polish press that visiting American scientists are engaged in espionage activities. These untrue accusations threaten the continuation of the jointly financed program of scientific research in Poland.

This program over many years has built up close and valuable contacts between the scientific communities of the two countries. It has provided useful research conducted in Poland in such important fields as agriculture, public health and energy. both countries have benefited.

In light of the attitude adopted by the Polish martial law regime toward these American visitors, we have found it necessary to suspend travel by participants in ongoing, jointly financed research projects between our two countries until the matter can be carefully reviewed and the Polish Government's attitude clarified.

Q. Can we get copies of that?

A. You can get copies.

Q. Which way is that travel? Is that from them to us, or—

A. No. These are, as I said, research programs conducted in Poland.

Q. How many people are involved in it?

A. The personnel exchanges involved about 100 people per year per side.

Q. Are there any Poles here at the moment in this program?

A. I do not know whether there are any Poles who are here or not.

Q. Does this mean that the people who are there now should leave or just people who are planning to go there will not be able to go?

A. The latter. Let me just take a look here in terms of people here. If anybody who's listening in can provide information while we're doing the briefing, it would be helpful. But it looks to me like it's entirely in Poland because the entire fund under the programs that have been carried have been in Polish currency.

Q. You're suspending travel and reviewing the program, or suspending the program?

A. Travel under this program or with regard to the projects is being suspended. There is an agreement. Let me go into this a little bit just to help, if I may. I hope I'm not going to confuse you.

In 1974 the two countries signed an agreement which provided they would conduct cooperative scientific research in areas of mutual interest and benefit.[47] They set up a joint fund for this and a joint board to manage the fund and to determine the areas of research which would be undertaken.

That agreement expired on December 31, 1981. Prior to its expiration both sides

---

[46] Source: Office of Press Relations, Department of State. The briefing, which began at 12:28 p.m., was conducted by Department of State Acting Spokesman Alan Romberg.

[47] An agreement of funding of cooperation in science and technology, with related letters, was signed at Washington, October 8, 1974. For the text of the agreement, see 25 UST 2572.

decided the program was mutually beneficial and they desired to continue it beyond 1981, and accordingly they met in Warsaw in order to negotiate a new agreement to accomplish this.

Both sides had intended to sign the new agreement prior to January 1, 1982, but since the imposition of martial law in Poland, we have suspended discussion with the Polish authorities on this matter.

Nonetheless, the 1974 agreement contains a clause which permits projects agreed upon under it to continue to completion even though the agreement itself may expire, so that work on uncompleted projects has continued since January 1, although travel has been minimal in fact because of the conditions in Poland.

Q. Are you suggesting that Marius Wozniak and Andrzej—I'm sorry, I didn't get his second name—did anything improper, or is this strictly retaliatory?

A. This action is in retaliation.

Q. Would you spell those names for us?

A. Sure. Although you're going to get the statement, I think, and we'll make it available.

Q. Is it in there?

A. We'll make it available. It is spelled out.

Q. Was this fund a soft currency fund from some sort of concessional agricultural sales, or was it a hard currency fund that paid for this?

A. The entire fund is in Polish currency. In the 1950's and 1960's, the United States sold Poland large amounts of surplus U.S. agricultural products for which we accepted Polish money which is not usable outside Poland, as you know,—these are known as P.L.-480 funds—and by the early 1970's the United States owned large amounts of Polish currency which were not spendable outside of Poland. In 1972 we agreed with the Polish authorities that one useful purpose could be to finance such scientific programs of mutual benefit; and further agreed the Polish side would match all U.S. contributions.

Q. Is there any special theme to the research? That is to say, is it medical in nature or is it over the wide spectrum of science and technology?

A. I think I said that it has included such important fields as agriculture, public health and energy.

Q. When was the Polish Embassy, and in what manner, informed that their two people have to leave?

A. I don't know the answer to that.

Q. Can you find out?

A. Yes. I'll find out.

Q. Have there been other incidents other than the Howard and Zerolis fracas?

A. Other incidents?

Q. In Poland, involving American diplomats?

A. I'm not aware of any of this particular sort. Obviously, in terms of martial law there have been problems with moving around and occasionally there have been other problems, but not of this—

Q. Have any of the American scientists visiting Poland been harassed or accused of improper activities?

A. Specifically, I don't know. Again, as the statement says, officials of the Polish Government have been alleging in the Polish press that visiting American scientists are engaged in espionage activities. So in the general sense, yes. I do not know whether any specific instances have been cited.

Let me just say: Three categories, I am told, are suspended: U.S. travel to Poland, Polish travel here, and scientific projects there—that is, in Poland—which are pending review. I'm not sure I quite understand the last category, but anyway—

Q. Is there any parallel toughening in the economic area in U.S. relations with Poland?

A. There is nothing new I have to announce on this at this point. These actions are being taken specifically for the reasons stated.

. . . .

Document 265

Remarks by President Reagan, May 21, 1982 (Extract)[48]

Timeliness of U.S.-Soviet Summit Meeting

. . . .

Q. Part of the question of how well NATO is doing seems to be tied into the question of East-West relations in general. And we have heard that you now favor a summit with your Soviet counterpart. You used to tie this to the condition that some summit meetings should have a tangible outcome or result.

Do you feel the time has come where such a meeting could accomplish something concrete?

THE PRESIDENT. I would hope so because I think that the Soviet Union also has some very real problems. Maybe it's time for someone to point out to them that their attitude of hostility, their worldwide aggression, their denial of human rights, whatever it's based on—whether it is a concern that they are threatened by the Western world or whether it is just determination to pursue the Marxist-Leninist theory of world domination—point out to them that the road to peace and giving up that aggressive attempt might be helpful to them with their own economic problems.

If there is any truth to the belief of some that the Soviet Union is motivated by fear of the West, that they think the West is going to threaten them—I don't think there's anyone in the West who believes that for one minute. They could have a guarantee of peace tomorrow if they themselves would follow the words of Demosthenes 2,000 years ago in the Athenian marketplace when he said, "What sane man would let another man's words rather than his deeds tell him who is at peace and who is at war with him." So far, it is the West that has to feel that the Soviet Union is at war with us on the basis of their great military buildup. I don't think they can point to anything from our side that indicates that.

What if back some years ago after World War II when our country was the only one with the nuclear weapon and really the only one left undamaged by war, in a position to do as we did, to go to the aid of our allies and even our former enemies; what if the situation had been reversed and the Soviet Union had had that bomb and not anyone in the West? If we had an aggressive intent wouldn't we have acted then when we could have done so easily? I think that's the greatest guarantee that it isn't the West that threatens the world with war.

. . . .

[48] Office of the Press Secretary to the President; also printed in *Weekly Compilation of Presidential Documents*, May 31, 1982, p. 714. For the full text, see *ibid.*, pp. 710–717. These remarks were made during an interview by Marc Ullman, *Paris Match;* Nicholas Ashford, *The Times of London;* Thomas Kielinger, *Die Welt;* and Marino De Medici, *Il Tempo.*

Document 266

Statement by the Under Secretary of Agriculture for International Affairs and Commodity Programs (Lodwick), Paris, May 22, 1982[49]

U.S.-Soviet Grain Consultations

We have just concluded the second semiannual session of regular grain consultations for the sixth year of the U.S.-USSR Grain Agreement,[50] which extends through September 30, 1982. During the two-day meeting, we discussed in detail the world grain supply-demand situation, U.S. supplies and possible Soviet import needs. We reviewed the substantial progress in the rebuilding of grain trade which has occurred, partly through our working closely together in these meetings which resumed in June 1981.[51]

During the talks, the Soviets confirmed that thus far they have purchased 6.14 million metric tons of U.S. wheat and 7.6

[49] Department of Agriculture, *Major News Releases and Speeches*, May 21–28, 1982, pp. 36–38.

[50] Reference is to the U.S.-Soviet grain agreement signed on October 20, 1975, which provided for the purchase by the Soviet Union of 6 to 8 million tons of U.S. grain yearly. For the text of the agreement, see 26 UST 2971.

[51] Regarding the June 1981 grain consultations, see *American Foreign Policy: Current Documents, 1981*, document 237.

million tons of U.S. corn for shipment in the sixth year of the agreement. They also confirmed that shipments of these purchases are now scheduled for completion by the end of this month. When we met last fall,[52] the Soviets informed us that their total grain import program, from all origins, amounted to about 20 million tons during January–June of 1981 and would likely be somewhat larger in July–December of 1981. At this meeting, it was indicated that last fall's prediction for the July–December 1981 period was correct and that the total import volume reached about 21 million tons.

For the current January–June period, the total Soviet grain import program now is likely to exceed 24 million tons, not including any processed products, soybeans or grains for re-export. The Soviets indicated they are taking continued measures to facilitate prompt unloading and inward transport of grain. In the past three months, they achieved a rate of 190 thousand tons per day. With the steps being taken, they also expect to be able to take more during the winter months than they previously achieved. As for the July–September 1982 quarter, the Soviets indicated the flow of imports is likely to decline but that would depend on prospects for the current Soviet crop, credit and the overall availability of funds.

As for the year ahead, the Soviets indicated that, with a reasonably good harvest such as 200 to 210 million tons, wheat and wheat flour imports would not likely remain at the 1981–82 level. Import of feedgrains, however, could be as large or possibly even larger because of the continued emphasis being placed on maintaining herd numbers and feeding programs and also because of likely reduced dependence on imported meat.

During the meeting, I emphasized the abundant exportable stocks of wheat, corn and other commodities now available from the U.S. and that our prices are unusually competitive with those from other origins. I also reviewed the further advantages of dependability of U.S. grain in light of our farmer reserve policy and the unmatched ability of our marketing system to respond with prompt shipment, handling of large vessels and other services to serve the Soviet market most efficiently. I pointed out that the size of Soviet purchases, especially in the next few weeks, could be an important signal for U.S. farmers as to the size of crops they should produce in both 1982 and 1983.

After reviewing the Soviet import situation and Soviet purchases to date of U.S. grain, it was concluded that the 23 million tons of U.S. wheat and corn which have been available to the USSR since the consultation last October remained adequate at this time for likely Soviet needs. It was agreed, however, that the two sides will remain in close contact and the U.S. indicated that, should Soviet purchases for the sixth year begin to increase sharply over the next few weeks, the U.S. would promptly propose further consultations, as provided for in the agreement, to review supply availabilities again so the agreement could avoid any possibility of serving as a limitation on trade. We also indicated we would welcome purchases of U.S. grain for delivery after October 1, which could begin at any time.

The U.S. side also noted that some recent Soviet purchases have been accompanied by private credit arrangements. We indicated that we have no problem with these arrangements, as such matters are entirely up to the purchasers and private sellers.

The Soviets cited a number of continuing concerns about the quality of U.S. grain. We agreed to continue our work with the Soviets and grain companies in an effort to improve the arrival quality of U.S. grain.

Under the terms of the five year U.S.–USSR Grain Supply Agreement, which began in October 1976 and was extended for a sixth year, the Soviet Union buys at least 6 million tons of U.S. grain—3 of wheat and 3 of corn—annually and, without prior consultations, may buy up to 8 million tons.

This was the eleventh regular session of consultation under the agreement.

The Soviet delegation was headed by Deputy Minister of Foreign Trade Boris Gordeev. We followed the same agenda covered in past consultations under the agreement.

---

[52] These meetings were held in Moscow, September 30–October 1, 1981.

Document 267

Transcript of an Interview With the Secretary of State (Haig), May 23, 1982 (Extract)[53]

Soviet Agricultural Problems; Linkage in U.S.-Soviet Relations

. . . .

MR. PIERPOINT. Mr. Secretary, to go back to the discussion of our relations with the Soviet Union, you obviously have to take into account domestic problems within the Soviet Union when you are evaluating how much they are willing to give in certain areas. Today the *Washington Post* has a very interesting report, which I'm sure you've seen, saying that Soviet agriculture is once again, still, and yet in deep trouble, and that as a result of this, they expect some changes at the higher levels of the Kremlin during Politburo meetings that start tomorrow.[54]

What is your evaluation of this report and of the possible changes in the Soviet hierarchy?

SECRETARY HAIG. Mr. Pierpoint, this is an historic, almost organic, failure of the Marxist-Leninist system and the Soviet model. From the outset, the Soviet Union has been unable to meet the food requirements of its people—this despite the fact that they have placed greater and greater concentration on that sector of their society. They have applied more human effort and more technology, but they still, through systematic failure, have failed to "turn the corner," so to speak.

I think that it is perfectly natural that there are always scapegoats in such failures, and periodic meetings provide an opportunity to make some changes. It's just that simple.

MR. HERMAN. Speaking of the hierarchy, what do you see about the impact on the Soviet Union's relations with the West if it's going to be so dependent for food on the outside world?

SECRETARY HAIG. I've always made the point that the United States and the West at large, if they maintain especially their unity in their dealings with the Soviet Union, have a great deal of political and economic leverage with which and through which to insist on greater restraint and responsibility on the part of Soviet leaders.

MR. GWERTZMAN. Do you think we're sending the wrong signal by agreeing or even urging the start of the strategic arms talks without any conditions attached to it—in other words, without any direct linkage?

SECRETARY HAIG. No. I think we've made it very clear that linkage continues to be an active aspect of American foreign policy—indeed it does. But the President has also made it clear that arms control is a very special area of East-West relations, and one in which we seek our own vital interests to be realized.

MR. PIERPOINT. You're really saying that linkage is dead.

SECRETARY HAIG. Not at all. I said just the opposite. I said it is not dead; it remains a very active part and will remain an active part. It's a fact of life. It's not a question of an option of policy. It is a fact of life that international behavior of nations that have relationships with one another effect the full range of their relationships in all—

. . . .

---

[53] Source: Department of State Press Release 176, May 24, 1982; printed also in Department of State *Bulletin*, July 1982, pp. 54–55. For the full text, see *ibid.*, pp. 52–55. Secretary Haig was interviewed on the CBS television program, "Face the Nation," by George Herman, CBS News; Bernard Gwertzman, *New York Times*; and Robert Pierpoint, CBS News.

[54] *Washington Post*, May 23, 1982, p. A1. The article was based on a Soviet Government report made public in Moscow describing the decline in the Soviet Union's ability to feed itself and calling for extensive Agricultural reforms.

Document 268

Transcript of an Interview With the Secretary of State (Haig), June 13, 1982 (Extract)[55]

Economic Sanctions Against Poland and the Soviet Union

. . . .

MR. WILL. Mr. Secretary, last week on this program, Secretary Regan, the Treas-

---

[55] Department of State Press Release 198, June

ury Secretary, was a very good soldier. He came on and said that the agreement at Versailles to limit credits to the East bloc really implied that credits would be cut.

Is it your understanding that the Versailles communiqué[56] will be violated unless credits will be cut to the East bloc by our allies?

SECRETARY HAIG. Not necessarily. I don't think the seven at Versailles control the full mechanism of credit management with the East, let alone the Soviet Union. As you know, the OECD put forward some proposals recently which involve an increase in the interest rates and, in effect, on the time for repayment.

They visualize that by moving the Soviet Union into a Category I recipient. That will have the effect of raising the price of credits to the Soviet Union, and we hope that by the 15th—the time the mandate would run out for the implementation of that by the OECD—it will be implemented.

What was done at Versailles was to put together for the first time a comprehensive mechanism to begin to assess the whole range of East–West trade, credit transfer, and to do so with assessments on 6-month intervals so that we can be sure that we are not overexposed.

MR. WILL. But 2 days after the Versailles meeting ended, the *New York Times* carried a headline reporting that the Poles are now threatening us with default, that they will go into default unless they get more loans to pay the interest on their old loans.[57]

When you were on the show, Mr. Secretary, about 6 months ago,[58] the question was asked, "What in the world could be done by the Poles to provoke the United States into calling their default, default.?"

Your answer was that, "Unless things get better, we will get tougher." Things have not gotten better, and we have not gotten tougher.

Is there any likelihood that we'll call them into default?

SECRETARY HAIG. It's still too early to say. I wouldn't suggest we haven't gotten tougher because the pervasive impact of the cutoff of credits to Poland has been substantial and has had a grievous effect on the economic development of Poland today, and we hear it every day.

MR. WILL. One other short question. One other bit of lobbying that was done at Versailles and has gone all over this town is that the Japanese are lobbying for a waiver from the sanctions against the Soviet Union imposed after Poland so that they can sell energy technology for yet another Soviet energy project.

Is the Reagan administration going to grant this waiver?

SECRETARY HAIG. We're talking about some $2 million of energy related equipment to this Sakhalin pipeline?

MR. WILL. Yes.

SECRETARY HAIG. The President has not made a decision on this question, just as he has not made a decision on the spare parts associated with the East–West pipeline and the extraterritoriality question on existing contracts.

I would anticipate he will make this in the very near future in the wake of his assessment of—

MR. WILL. Is it a hard call? I mean, this is punching holes in sanctions that are fairly porous to begin with.

SECRETARY HAIG. It is a hard call. It's a hard call because I think the President's been very, very strong in attempting to exercise leadership in Western Europe and in Japan. And, incidentally, we've had very good cooperation on the whole from Japan on this question, and the question of whether or not the results of the decision really have a meaningful impact as a sanction against the Soviet Union to influence their behavior at the price of considerable sacrifice to American industry, jobs, and future markets.

So it's not an easy problem, and of course that's why it's been prolonged for so long. Easy ones are settled very easily, George.

. . . .

16, 1982; printed also in Department of State *Bulletin*, July 1982, pp. 56–57. For the full text of this interview, see *ibid.*, pp. 55–58. Secretary Haig was interviewed on the ABC television program, "This Week With David Brinkley," by Sam Donaldson, ABC News; Sander Vanocur, ABC's Chief Diplomatic Correspondent; and George Will, ABC news analyst.

[56] For the text of the final communiqué issued on June 6 at the conclusion of the eighth economic summit of the industrialized nations at Versailles, see document 93.

[57] Apparently a reference to the headlines in the *New York Times*, June 8, 1982, p. D1.

[58] The Secretary had appeared on the program on November 22, 1981.

Document 269

Transcript of a Press Conference by the Secretary of State (Haig), New York, June 19, 1982[59]

Haig–Gromyko Meeting

SECRETARY HAIG. Good afternoon, ladies and gentlemen. Sorry to dig into your weekend so deeply.

We have just completed 9¼ hours of discussions with Foreign Minister Gromyko; 5 yesterday and 4¼ this morning and early this afternoon.

I'll just say a few words about those discussions and then touch upon some issues related both to the discussions and the activities of this past week here in New York.

I would describe the meeting itself as full, frank and useful. The topics ranged from the broad principles that should seek to underline East–West relations in general and U.S.-Soviet relations, in particular. We went through the full range of global and regional issues of mutual importance and interest to both governments. And we also conducted discussions on a number of bilateral issues between the United States and the Soviet Union. One of the major areas of the discussions of yesterday was on the broad subject of arms control.

In that regard I would like to make some broad observations about the activities of the past week here at the Disarmament Conference: the position of President Reagan on this vitally important subject.

The President's policies, as you know, are based firmly on deeply rooted principles, and I'm talking now in the broad sense of East–West relationships and then arms control—deeply rooted principles of international conduct in order. As a people, we Americans have always believed in rule of law, the settlement of disputes by peaceful means and nonuse of force except for self-defense. These are the principles that guide our approach to the various regional conflicts that confront us as a nation today.

It is the President's sincere desire to put the U.S.-Soviet relationship on a stable, constructive, long-term basis. We see important potential advantages for both countries in every area of our relationship but this cannot be achieved without Soviet willingness to conduct its international affairs with responsibility and restraint.

It is clearly, squarely up to the Soviets to determine what sort of relationship they want to have with the United States in the months and years ahead. The United States, for its part, is prepared for constructive and mutually beneficial relations if the Soviet Union is prepared to join us in acting with the rsponsibility necessary in the nuclear age.

We have made serious and realistic proposals to achieve this end. The objective of the United States remains an overriding interest in the maintenance of peace and stability.

I would like to say a word about arms control, in particular. With the negotiations on strategic arms reduction beginning later this month, the topic of arms control is clearly very high on the agenda of U.S.-Soviet relations. The full range of President Reagan's arms control initiatives are now well known. They're all on the table.

They are proposals which mark the way to the first significant reductions in the arsenals of the two major superpowers.

With respect to START first. The President's proposals provide an equitable basis for real and significant reductions of strategic nuclear weapons, beginning with the most destabilizing systems.

East and West—especially the United States and the Soviet Union—have important reasons to curb weapons that threaten their retaliatory capabilities. We will consider most seriously the Soviet proposals, and the President has stated that nothing—and I repeat, nothing—is excluded from the upcoming START negotiations.

In short, our approach to START is not one-sided but it is designed with mutual benefit and mutual stability in mind. Now is the time to get on with serious negotiations devoid of public posturing. Similarly, on the intermediate range missile question, the INF talks, the seriousness of the President's proposals for total elimination of landbased intermediate ranged missiles is very clear. It

---

[59] Department of State Press Release 203, June 21, 1982; printed also in Department of State *Bulletin*, July 1982, pp. 58–60. The press conference, which concluded at 3:30 p.m., took place at the U.S. Mission to the United Nations. Secretary Haig and Gromyko were in New York to attend the U.N. General Assembly's Second Special Session on Disarmament.

is our conviction that this proposal is an equitable and realistic approach to the threat to peace created by the imbalance in such systems which now favors the Soviet Union.

Last week's discussions, and the week before in Europe,[60] underlied the fact and confirmed that the entire NATO Alliance stands four square behind the proposals put forth and underscores the alliance's commitment to proceed with the deployment of the 1979 decision—that's for the II's Pershing and the GLCM's—in the absence of an arms control solution.

Finally, President Reagan's initiative to reinvigorate the long-stalled negotiations on reducing conventional forces in Europe, his proposals to reduce the risk of accidental nuclear war and to convene an international conference on arms expenditures, are now on the table for prompt responsive action by the Soviet Union.[61]

Together, all of these proposals represent a carefully thought through, integrated approach to arms control, and its is fitting that it has come together at a time of the United Nations Special Session on Disarmament.

It certainly stands in sharp contrast to the various cosmetic arms control proposals such as that as the non first-use proposal made this week. Our position on this proposal remains clear: The United States stands for the non use of force of any form except in legitimate self-defense.

The United States, together with its Allies, intends to deter all war, conventional or nuclear. As the President said in his November speech of November 18th, "No NATO weapons, conventional or nuclear, will ever be used in Europe except in defense against attack."[62]

So, in sum, the President has now put forward a comprehensive agenda for arms control which is balanced and equitable and which, for the first time, offers a way to reducing the burden of armaments at every level. We hope that the Soviet Union will negotiate seriously with us on the agenda now before us. We will do our part and we look to the Soviet Union to turn from posturing to serious talks in the interest of peace. We also call upon the Soviet Union to match its words about arms control with concrete actions demonstrating its seriousness.

I would note, for example, that only a few days after the speech here at the United Nations given by Mr. Gromyko,[63] with emphasis on arms control in outer space, the Soviet Union has undertaken an unusually high-level of strategic activity, including an anti-satellite test, two ICBM launches, an SS–20 launch, an SLBM launch, and two ABM intercepts. Such activity belies by specific action the words put forth to the world audience here in New York this week.

I welcome your questions.

Q. Mr. Secretary, two questions: One, do you have any apparent explanation for this increased strategic activity you just talked about and, two, did you discuss with the Foreign Minister the possibility of a summit meeting between Presidents Brezhnev and Reagan?

SECRETARY HAIG. I have no explanation with respect to the first part of your question other than to suggest that the best measure of the real state of relationships between East and West and the Soviet Union and the United States is the criteria of action and not words, as the President has repeated in the recent past, especially in his recent trip to NATO, Europe.

The question of summitry was discussed in the meetings with Foreign Minister Gromyko but I have nothing to put forward on that subject today.

Q. Can I pick up on that Mr. Secretary?

SECRETARY HAIG. Yes.

Q. You addressed arms control which presumably occupied you yesterday. Could you take us through today in any greater detail?

SECRETARY HAIG. There was some discussion today on that topic but the bulk of today's discussions dealt with a range of

---

60 Apparently a reference to the discussions which took place at the U.N. General Assembly's Second Special Session on Disarmament which opened in New York on June 7 and which was addressed by several world leaders, including President Reagan on June 17, and to the meeting of the North Atlantic council in Bonn, June 10. Documentation on the latter is in Chapter 10, Part B.

61 Regarding the initiatives on conventional forces and accidental war in President Reagan's speech in Bonn, June 9, see document 179. For his proposal on arms expenditures in his address to the United Nations, June 17, see document 51.

62 For the text of this address, see *Amerian Foreign Policy: Current Documents, 1981*, document 60.

63 For a translation of the text of Gromyko's speech on June 16, see U.N. document A/S–12/PV.12.

regional problems and a very extensive range.

Q. Mr. Secretary, the strategic activity you referred to, I understand these are in the area of tests. Are any of them prohibited by treaties or other agreements?

SECRETARY HAIG. I would leave that observation until later. It's clear that they are not consistent with the words that are being used.

Q. Mr. Secretary, in these strategic tests, what kind of activity does this compare to in the past? We have no basis for which to say this is heavier or lighter than usual?

SECRETARY HAIG. Unprecedented.

Q. Mr. Secretary you said that you discussed regional issues. Was anything said about what is going on in Lebanon? Also, in the last talks there was said to be some stress because of the Soviets' imposing martial law in Poland. Was there any—

SECRETARY HAIG. Yes. Well, I'm very happy to tell you the topics that were touched upon. By mutual agreement with my counterpart, I will not go into the character of the substance. That is the position we have followed—this is the third of the series of the discussions we've had.

Of course, the Middle East was discussed, as was the other topic you mentioned.

Q. Mr. Secretary, do you think that this strategic activity relates to any particular situation in the world, in Lebanon, for example?

SECRETARY HAIG. No.

Q. Did you discuss this strategic activity with Mr. Gromyko?

SECRETARY HAIG. No.

Q. Why not?

SECRETARY HAIG. I think there are several reasons for it. We have had very extensive discussions on the topic of arms control. Some of the details of the activity I've described were not clear at the time I went into the discussions—they have become clear since. I believe they do underline the character of the difference sometimes between words and actions.

Q. Your discussions began with him, as you know, yesterday. Do you mean that the evidence of this strategic activity was just within the last 24 hours?

SECRETARY HAIG. I mean it is very recent activity, and the integration of the various components of it have just been pulled together this morning—overnight.

Q. Mr. Secretary, to clarify an earlier response, did you mean to give the impression that there is some possibility that some of these tests may have been in violation of either of—

SECRETARY HAIG. No. I meant to give an indication that they run rather counter to the speech given here this week—

Q. And nothing else?

SECRETARY HAIG. And repeated calls for restraint in outer space.

Q. Just to back up, when you say, "It runs counter to what was said," what was said at the speech was that the Soviet Union would like arms control agreements, and they made a pledge not to be the first to use nuclear weapons.

Could you just embroider what you mean—why it runs counter to Gromyko's speech?

SECRETARY HAIG. I prefer not to go into an extensive "Who shot John?" on this. I put this information forward because it does represent a significant first in both the scope and integration of activity and capability.

Q. Mr. Secretary, has there ever been any period of American testing that compares to this? To put this thing in further perspective, is there a way to put it in percentages?

SECRETARY HAIG. No, I prefer not to do that other than to suggest that this is a first in the context of the activities by either the East or the West.

Q. Mr. Secretary, could you help us understand the way these meetings go? If you are clearly troubled by the evidence that you are presenting to us here—you tell us it came together in the middle of the night; you've been talking to them for 4¼ hours this morning. Why didn't you raise it with them?

SECRETARY HAIG. I think the point I just made was that it was not available to me in its entirety before I started these meetings, but rather subsequent thereto. That is not to suggest I would have raised it in the meeting, in any event.

Q. Is this the kind of thing that does get raised?

SECRETARY HAIG. Probably, but not necessarily.

Q. I get the feeling that your having come out of this meeting, and made this rather discouraging—from your standpoint—announcement, that the meeting itself didn't accomplish much? Is that right?

SECRETARY HAIG. No. I described the meeting as useful, and I think it is always useful—

Q. Why?

SECRETARY HAIG.—to conduct far-ranging discussions with my counterpart in the Soviet Union. They inevitably bring about consequences which are favorable, and I don't view this meeting as any exception.

Q. Mr. Secretary, just prior to the meeting you had described the Soviet's approach to the Middle East in the communications you have had, as cautious. On the basis of the last 2 days, would you still say that that is their general approach to the situation?

SECRETARY HAIG. Concerned and cautious, yes.

Q. Mr. Secretary, I'm still not quite clear on what you mean by the integration of these various strategic tests. What—

SECRETARY HAIG. I think I called them "strategic activity."

Q. What relationship is there between these? For example, are the two ABM intercepts related to the two ICBM launches?

SECRETARY HAIG. Integrated.

Q. Did they involve (inaudible) or explosions?

SECRETARY HAIG. I didn't hear—

Q. Can you tell us which test ranges?

SECRETARY HAIG. No. No, no, I can't do that.

Q. Mr. Secretary, how do you interpret this? What does it mean, this activity?

SECRETARY HAIG. It shows the level of interest, skill, and technological advancement that should be of concern.

Q. Is a summit meeting between the two leaders likely by the end of the year, would you say?

SECRETARY HAIG. I don't want to comment on that. I'm sure the President will comment on the subject in the months ahead. I think both sides clearly have made their position clear on summitry, and they are surprisingly convergent, and that is that summitry for summitry's sake is to be avoided; but rather summitry that has been well prepared, that will result in a positive movement forward is far preferable to an ad hoc kind of summitry in which expectations rise before—sometimes in the past, we have seen even euphoric expectations that were only dashed following such ill-prepared summits. I don't think either side wants to go into such (inaudible).

Q. Mr. Secretary, you said that the United States favors the rule of law in the settlement of disputes except in legitimate self-defense. Would you include the Israeli actions in Lebanon this past week to be covered by that rubric?

SECRETARY HAIG. Clearly, there is a great deal in support of that. A number of objective observers might question the scope of the counteraction and the character of it. We have, as a government, not made a ruling on that as yet.

Q. Mr. Secretary, would you expect to either protest or to inquire about these strategic activities once you are—

SECRETARY HAIG. I would like to wait until we have had an opportunity to consider what we will do with respect to it. It might be a decision to do nothing.

Q. There is a possible further response to it?

SECRETARY HAIG. Possibly.

Q. Mr. Secretary, can you run through with us what progress, if any, has been made in your effort to strengthen the cease-fire in Lebanon?

SECRETARY HAIG. Well, Phil Habib has been intensely engaged in the whole framework of the crisis in Lebanon, both in search of a permanent and lasting cease-fire and in creating the conditions by which the sovereignty of the Central Government of Lebanon will be enhanced and strengthened as a consequence of this tragedy. I think while this activity is underway, it sometimes is counterproductive to become too specific on how; but he has been in touch with all the internal parties and with the external parties involved as well. And we have been backstopping here in Washington on an hourly basis and throughout the night.

That situation has not changed from the beginning of this crisis; especially the President has personally followed it moment by moment. I just spoke to him at Camp David, and it is clear that the United States is doing all within its power to have a situation in which the bloodshed terminates, and the conditions for a long-term settlement are enhanced.

Q. Do you find that the Soviet policy, as best you understand it now, works in the same direction as America's?

SECRETARY HAIG. I would not describe it that way. On the other hand, I would not indict recent Soviet activity as particularly troublesome or counterproductive.

Q. Mr. Secretary, on that strategic activity, do you regard that as an acceleration of some of the past activities that they've had, or is this, given the integrated nature as you characterized it, is this something that involved an entirely new effort by the Soviets?

SECRETARY HAIG. I think there has been enough said on this subject. Clearly, I wanted you to have the information as quickly as it was available and releasable. We've done that, and I think I'd just like to let it drop there.

Q. Sir, would you be kind enough, so we don't botch this up, could you run through exactly what you said about this strategic activity?

SECRETARY HAIG. All right—and I do refer to it as "activity."

Q. Mr. Secretary, you didn't answer the question about the nuclear explosions?

SECRETARY HAIG. I'm about to. Oh, no; no nuclear, no.

I will repeat what I said on this subject. I would note, for example, that only a few days after the speech at the United Nations which touched upon outerspace arms control, the Soviet Union has undertaken an unusually high level of strategic activity, including an anti-satellite test, two ICBM launches, an SS–20 launch, an SLBM launch, and two ABM intercepts.

Q. Thank you, sir.

Q. Mr. Secretary, you mentioned earlier that you had not taken a position on whether this Israeli activity in Lebanon is in self-defense or not. Can you say, first of all, why you have not taken a position on that? And secondly, the United States had maintained that it wants all the foreign troops out of Lebanon. Was that a similar Soviet point of view? And is the U.S. thinking of a particular time-frame on the withdrawal of such troops from Lebanon?

SECRETARY HAIG. I don't know what the Soviet view is on the subject of foreign forces in Lebanon. The U.S. view is, of course, that we would like to see ultimately all foreign forces out of Lebanon so that the Central Government can conduct the sovereign affairs of a sovereign government within internationally-recognized borders.

With respect to the other question, it is clear that there was a sequence of events that has been going on for an extended period involving actions and counteractions, terrorist activity, across-the-border shelling, and rocket attacks, and a series of air and counteractions. Clearly, this recent crisis is the culmination of a long period of unacceptable instability in southern Lebanon and perhaps throughout Lebanon. I think there will have to be a very careful analysis of events associated with this recent crisis before the kind of valued judgment you've asked for would be appropriate.

Q. Thank you, Mr. Secretary.

Document 270

Transcript of an Interview With the Secretary of Defense (Weinberger), July 11, 1982 (Extract)[64]

Rationale for U.S. Sanctions Against the Soviet Union

. . . .

MR. NELAN. Mr. Secretary, I'd like to ask you about the pipeline that's supposed to be built to bring Siberian gas to Western Europe. There was a report a couple of days ago that the administration is considering withdrawing its sanctions on the export of technology and is looking for some sort of gesture from the East. Is this correct?

A. No, sir, that is certainly not correct. It is like too many reports that keep floating around from time to time. The President's decision was not lightly taken.[65] It was made

---

[64] Source: *Public Statements of Secretary of Defense Weinberger*, 1982. Secretary Weinberger was interviewed on the NBC television program, "Meet the Press," by Bill Monroe, NBC News; Richard Valeriani, NBC News; Bruce W. Nelan, *Time;* William Beecher, *Boston Globe;* and Rowland Evans, *Chicago Sun-Times.*

[65] Reference is to the extension of export sanctions against the Soviet Union on June 18 to include equipment produced by subsidiaries of U.S. companies abroad as well as equipment produced abroad under licenses issued by U.S. companies. For the text of President Reagan's statement announcing this extension, see document 160.

with a great deal of care and deliberation on his part, and it did not differ in any way from the decision that he had made last December, and that was based upon the fact that there was repression in Poland, intimidation of Poland, and that it was vital to have some improvement in that situation. And that's essentially—the situation has not been changed.

There has not been any improvement in the situation in Poland at all, and the President's statements and feelings still stand. So, stories that he's about to change on the basis of some gesture that hasn't even been defined, a decision which he made very carefully, with full awareness of the fact that it was a critically important decision, those stories just aren't right.

Mr. Nelan. Now, your own opposition was not, as I understand it, primarily based on Poland. It was a question of the possibility of the Soviet Union earning about $10 billion a year in hard currency by selling that gas.

A. Well, that was part of it, and the other part was the fact that it put a rather dangerous and unwise reliance in Europe on the Soviet Union for some additional portions of their energy requirement, and that we would be doing all this at a time when the Soviets were taking action in and around Poland which the world, as a whole, strongly disapproves.

Mr. Nelan. Are you in favor of economic warfare against the Soviet Union? Are you trying to hurt their economy?

A. Well, that's such a broad term that I think we would have to define it and go into it much more on a specific, case-by-case basis. Certainly, I do not favor the assistance to the Soviet Union in acquiring $10 billion a year in hard currency. They're very short of hard currency. They use almost all of their resources that they get of any kind—with a high first priority on military strength. One of the reasons our defense budget has to be as high as it is is because of the threat they pose and because of the way they have used so much of their resources, including technologies that they've taken from us, or that we have given them, for military purposes. So, that has to be a factor.

And when you say economic warfare, why, that could mean anything from stopping all trade which I don't think is necessary. What I do think is necessary is not economic warfare, it's a realistic appraisal of how much benefit we can give the Soviet military machine unless we're very careful of what we transfer.

. . . .

Document 271

Remarks by President Reagan, July 19, 1982[66]

Proclamation of Captive Nations Week

The President. Thank you very much. Thank you. I heard all that applause that you were getting. I almost didn't come out. (Laughter)

Six weeks ago when I visited our friends and allies in Europe,[67] I found a warm response to this nation's call for a global campaign for freedom. Our straightforward criticism of totalitarianism regimes and our willingness to promote the ideals of individual liberty and representative government struck a responsive chord among Europeans and I believe many other millions of people around the globe.

Yet, even as I expressed our confidence that the ideals of freedom and the aspiration of self-government would ultimately triumph over those who wished to subordinate the individual to the state, I was confronted with the hard evidence of just how difficult this struggle will be.

In Berlin, a grey, grim monument of steel and stone stands as a reminder of

---

[66] Source: White House Press Release, July 19, 1982, Office of the Press Secretary to the President; printed also in *Weekly Compilation of Presidential Documents*, July 26, 1982, pp. 918–920. The President spoke at 11:45 a.m. at the signing ceremony in the Rose Garden of the White House. For the text of the Captive Nations Week 1982 Proclamation, dated July 19, 1982, see *ibid.*, pp. 920–921.

[67] President Reagan visited several European capitals, June 2–11. Documentation on his visit to Paris and Versailles to attend the eighth economic summit of industrialized nations is in Chapter 5, Part F. Documentation on the President's visit to Rome and Vatican City on June 7 is in Chapter 10, Part H. Documentation on his visit to London and Windsor, June 7–9, is *ibid.*, Part C. Documentation on his visit to Bonn (to attend the North Atlantic Council summit) and to Berlin, June 9–11, is *ibid.*, Parts B and D.

those whose self-proclaimed goal is the domination of every nation on Earth.

The tragedy of our time is that this goal has been so widely achieved. Throughout the Baltic States, Eastern Europe and Asia, now in Africa and Latin America, nation after nation has fallen prey to an ideology that seeks to stifle all that's good about the human spirit, even as it attempts to justify Communist rule.

This extension of totalitarianism has not come about through popular movement or free elections. It's been accomplished instead by military force or by subversion practiced by a tiny revolutionary cadre whose only real ideal is the will to power.

It hasn't meant, as promised, a new classless society or the dictatorship of the proletariat. It has, instead, meant forced labor and mass imprisonment, famine and massacre, the police state and the knock on the door in the night.

And it's also meant the growth of the largest military empire in the history of the world. An empire whose territorial ambition has sparked a wasteful arms race and whose ideological obsession remains the single greatest peril to peace among the nations.

The ominous growth of this danger, the human suffering that it's caused, is clearly the most important news event of our generation. And it is, as I've said, the tragedy of our time.

In 1959, the Congress of the United States, spurred on by the ruthless and bloody attack in 1956 on the free Hungarian Government first decided to commemorate the heroism and fortitude of those living in nations in which the right of self-determination has been denied.[68]

Today, in this Captive Nations Proclamation, and at this first public signing of this proclamation, we keep faith with this tradition and with those to whom it is intended to give hope and moral substance.

Today, we as a nation, also remind ourselves of the preciousness of our own freedom, renew our sacred resolve that someday all the people of the Earth will enjoy the God-given rights of free men and women. (Applause)

We renew especially our hope that those countries of Eastern Europe, Asia, Africa, and Latin America now under Communist domination will someday regain their national sovereignty and, again, enjoy the dignity of their own national traditions. (Applause)

Since that—since that first Captive Nations Resolution passed by the Congress, we've seen equally distressing examples of the assault on the human spirit. The independent people of Afghanistan are giving their lives resisting aggression of the bloodiest kind. And, again, in Poland, the suppression of the rights of Polish workers, the imprisonment of the leaders of Solidarity. All of this, sustained and directed by Soviet military might, is another tragic chapter in the quest of the Polish people for freedom and national sovereignty.

We in the West must do more than merely decry attacks on human freedom. The nature of this struggle is ultimately one that will be decided, not by military might, but by spiritual resolve and confidence in the future of freedom especially in the face of the decaying and crumbling dreams of Marxism/Leninism. (Applause)

Lenin advocated resorting to all sorts of strategems, artifices, maneuvers, illegal methods, evasions, and subterfuges. We in the West have at our command weapons far more potent than defeat, deceit, and subterfuge. We have the power of truth. Truth that can reach past the stone and steel walls of the police state and create campaigns for freedom and coalitions for peace in Communist countries.

How long can one simple fact be ignored or overlooked: that only the totalitarian states mark their borders with walls and barbed wire to keep their people from fleeing the "worker's paradise."

Some months ago I received a letter from Solidarity leaders who were in the free world during the crackdown by the ruling military junta.[69] These leaders pointed out that totalitarian regimes can be "eroded only from within by nonviolent, popular pressure. Our Polish experience shows how efficient such a drive for change can be. Our adversary is fully aware that our resistance cannot be sustained without a free flow of information and ideas."

These leaders went on to say, "We appeal to you for the same appreciation of the power of ideas and the effectiveness of broadcasting as their carrier. In the long

---

68 S.J. Res. 111, July 17, 1959. For text, see 73 Stat. 212.

69 This letter has not been further identified.

run it may prove to be the least expensive and the most effective option at your disposal."

Today let met make it clear that we intend to move forward consistent with budgetary requirements with a program to modernize our primary means of international communication, our international radio system. (Applause) In carrying out this vital element in our forward strategy for freedom we will be redeeming the pledge I made to the American people during the campaign, a pledge deeply felt at the time and deeply felt today. This plan of modernization for a relatively modest expenditure over a number of years will make it easier for millions of people living under Communist rule to hear the truth about the struggle for the world going on today between the forces of totalitarianism and freedom.

The sad fact is that the Voice of America, Radio Free Europe, and Radio Liberty have been neglected for many years. Their equipment is old and deteriorating, their programing resources strained. Little has been done to counter the jamming that has intensified in recent years.

The Soviets, I think you should know, spend three to four times more to jam foreign broadcasts than we spend to transmit them. And somebody—we can only speculate as to their identity—perpetrated a devastating bombing of Radio Free Europe and Radio Liberty's headquarters last year.

I want to extend my appreciation to the Congress for agreeing recently to reorganize the management of these international broadcasting channels, and I especially want to urge them today to approve the funds so desperately needed to bring to the people of Cuba through Radio Marti the truth about the struggle between freedom and totalitarianism. (Applause)

We can fully appreciate the fear of those who do not want the truth to reach the people of the Communist world, those who are willing to violate flagrantly the Helsinki Agreements or even to engage in terrorist violence to stifle the truth. For the events in Poland during the last two years show that when given air time and a little breathing space the truth becomes a powerful weapon, one which even the most repressive police states must fear.

We are confident that in Poland, Afghanistan, and in all the Captive Nations the forces of totalitarianism have won only a temporary fleeting victory. Against the appeal of democratic ideas, against the hunger and thirst of men and women who would be free, the threat of martial law, imprisonment, or any of the other artful forms of repression can never win lasting triumph.

In an interview that was published here before his imprisonment[70] Lech Walesa spoke of "the wheat that can grow on the stones," of how brutal repression only seems to strengthen the hope and hunger of those who long for freedom. And he said, "Our souls contain exactly the contrary of what they wanted. They want us, the Communist rulers, not to believe in God, and our churches are full. They wanted us to be materialistic and incapable of sacrifices. We are anti-materialistic and capable of sacrifice. They wanted us to be afraid of tanks and of the guns. And instead, we do not fear them at all." (Applause) The love of liberty, the fire of freedom burns on in Poland just as it burns on among all the peoples of the Captive Nations.

To the leaders of Solidarity, to the people of Poland, to all those who are denied freedom, we send a message today. Your cause is not lost. You are not forgotten. Your quest for freedom lives on in your hearts and in our hearts. (Applause) God willing, we will see a day when we shall speak together of the joys of freedom and of the wheat that grows on stones. (Applause)

Now, I better—

Q. Mr. President?

THE PRESIDENT. What?

Q. "God Bless America," would you sing it with us?

THE PRESIDENT. You will have to start.

(The President joins the assembled in singing "God Bless America.")

THE PRESIDENT. Thank you. (Applause) Thank you very much.

Now, I am going to sign this before you all catch cold. (Laughter)

(The President signs proclamation. Applause)

Thank you all. Thank you very much. Now get in the shade.

---

[70] This interview has not been further identified.

Document 272

Transcript of the Department of State Daily Press Briefing, July 28, 1982 (Extracts)[71]

60th Anniversary of U.S. Recognition of the Baltic States; Use by Soviet Diplomats of Recreational Facilities in Glen Cove, New York

MR. FISCHER. I have a couple of statements.

Today is the 60th anniversary of the U.S. recognition of the independent States of Estonia, Latvia, and Lithuania.

The three republics were invaded and illegally annexed by the Soviet Union in 1940. The United States has never recognized the forcible and unlawful incorporation of the Baltic States into the Soviet Union.

To mark this anniversary of 60 years of continuous recognition, Deputy Secretary of State Walter J. Stoessel, Jr., and Deputy Assistant Secretary of State for Human Rights and Humanitarian Affairs Melvin Levitsky met this morning with the Chargé d'Affaires of Estonia, Latvia, and Lithuania.

The U.S. Government wishes to draw attention to the continuing Soviet violation of the human rights of the citizens of the Baltic republics. The Soviet policies of control of their politics, religion, and culture maintain an atmosphere of harsh repression in the three countries of Latvia, Lithuania, and Estonia.

Q. Can we have a copy of that?

A. Yes.

Secondly, I have an announcement on the—

Q. Before you go on, I can't recall your ever marking, for example, the 50th anniversary of these diplomatic relations.

A. I know I didn't. (Laughter) Q. So I'm curious as to why the administration chooses to mark this event.

A. Let me say that we believe the circumstances of the Baltic States merits today's statement. Latvia, Lithuania, and Estonia were independent sovereign nations from 1918 to 1940. The United States recognized them dejure on July 28, 1922.

Their incorporation into the Soviet Union was a unique and tragic event in modern history. The Soviet policies of political, religious and cultural domination in the three countries are striking and should serve as a reminder to the free world of the actual nature of the Soviet treatment of non-Russian peoples.

Q. Does the United States regard this as a colonial issue worthy of the attention of the decolonization committees of the United Nations?

A. I don't know that we're necessarily pursuing it in that particular forum.

Q. The logical extension of what you're saying is that you would like the annexation to be reversed—the annexation that took place in 1942?

Q. 1940.

A. I think it's fair enough to conclude that, yes, of course. But I think the statement speaks for itself.

. . . .

Q. Do you have anything on the action taken at Glen Cove where there was a vote to ignore the State Department's request to lift the ban on allowing Soviet diplomats to use local recreational facilities in the area?[72]

A. We're obviously disappointed that the city of Glen Cove is continuing to discriminate against resident representatives to the United Nations, since this impinges on the conduct of foreign relations.

Q. Do you have any reaction to the Glen Cove assessment that the Russians are, in fact, using their mission there for spying?

A. I have no specific reaction to give you on that question, but I just indicated our disappointment.

---

[71] Source: Office of Press Relations, Department of State. Dean Fischer, Department of State Spokesman, conducted the briefing which began at 12:29 p.m.

[72] In May 1982 the town of Glen Cove, New York, banned Soviet diplomats from public beaches, tennis courts, a golf course, and other parks. The action was taken following reports that Soviet diplomats were using their summer retreat in Glen Cove for espionage. The city government said it would lift the ban if the Soviet Government would pay local taxes, despite Federal laws exempting from taxation property owned by foreign representatives accredited to the U.S. Government or the United Nations.

Q. On the face of it, it would seem that the city council's position would be consistent with that of the Reagan administration of getting tough with the Soviet Union. (Laughter)

Do you have any reaction to that?

A. Not all parallels are precise.

Q. Where does it go from here?

A. As far as we're concerned, we intend to consult with the Department of Justice.

Q. Has this situation resulted in any retaliation of our people in the Soviet Union?

A. No, not to my knowledge. I'm not aware of any such reports.

Q. What would be the purpose of talking to the Justice Department?

A. We think that's the appropriate agency to address the situation as it now stands.

Q. Do they have the authority to change that city's actions?

A. I'm not going to get into the question of what steps the Department of Justice might choose to take, but that's the appropriate Department.

. . . .

Document 273

Transcript of the Department of State Daily Press Briefing, August 6, 1982 (Extracts)[73]

Status of Pentecostalists Residing in the U.S. Embassy in Moscow; Soviet Retaliation for the Glen Cove Incident

. . . .

Q. You suggested a couple days ago that you would have some comment on the Davies' article on Poland.[74] Is that available yet?

Do you know what I am referring to? Excuse me, I am way off. I mean the Pentecostalists. Sorry about that.

A. There is rather extensive guidance. What is your specific question, though?

Q. Davies in his article quotes the Department of State as having certain attitudes. What I really want to know is, is he quoting you correctly?

A. I don't have the article. Let me just address it in these terms, since he did, I believe, talk about H.R. 2873[75] as the vehicle for providing permanent resident alien status.

We have not been requested, first of all, to provide our views on H.R. 2873. However, we understand that it is identical to Senate Bill 312 which recently passed the Senate and we did provide our views on that bill.

While we are in complete agreement with the sponsors of the legislation in their efforts to help the Vashchenko and Chmykhalov families who have been living in our Embassy in Moscow for over 4 years, we do not believe that granting the families permanent resident alien status will further their goal of emigrating from the Soviet Union.

We believe that the legislation, which will not affect their status in Soviet eyes, will only harden the Soviet position which presently is that the families must return to their hometown in Siberia before their applications to emigrate will be considered.

Q. But this doesn't address the Department's basic problem which I would have thought was the acute embarrassment of a great nation not being able to do anything about nearly a dozen—seven or eight—Pentecostalists cluttering up the Embassy.

A. I wouldn't put it in those terms. Ever since June 1978, we have been making repeated approaches to the Soviet Govern-

---

[73] Source: Office of Press Relations, Department of State, Dean Fischer, Department of State Spokesman, conducted the briefing, which began at 12:39 p.m.

[74] A column by R. T. Davies, a retired Foreign Service officer and the Director of the Research Center for Religion and Human Rights in Closed Societies, in the *Washington Post*, August 5, 1982, p. A19.

[75] H.R. 2873, which is identical to S.312, was legislation to provide private relief for the Vaschenko and Chmykhalov families who have been living in The American Embassy in Moscow for four years. S.312 passed the Senate on July 13, 1982, but neither bill became law in the 97th Congress.

ment regarding these families. We continue to urge—

Q. And they haven't moved.

A. We continue to urge the Soviet Government to resolve the case, and we reject emphatically Ambassador Davies' contention that we disclaim any responsibility beyond giving them refuge in the Embassy.

It should be clear to anybody who is familiar with the record or reviews the record that the U.S. Government has long since recognized its moral responsibility to the Pentecostalists, contrary to the allegations Ambassador Davies makes in another portion of the article.

We have spent thousands of man hours working on this case and have addressed it at virtually every foreign policy level of the government. We have supported the families with food, clothing, medical care, and housing for over 4 years—

Q. Can you give me that in a written form?

A. —and we will continue to do so until such time as they voluntarily depart the Embassy. Our efforts to support them will indeed continue until the Soviet authorities can be convinced to allow them to emigrate.

I will be happy to give that to you, not precisely in those words, but close to it.

. . . .

Q. Do you have anything on the latest escalation of the battle of Glen Cove?

A. The battle of Glen Cove.

I think it has been noted that the Soviets have now reacted by banning American diplomats from the so-called "diplomat beach" near Moscow.

Let me say, we reject any linkage for reciprocity purposes between the Soviet Missions to the United Nations and the U.S. Embassy in Moscow. We regret the Soviet decision to take actions against U.S. diplomats in Moscow in retaliation for the actions of the City of Glen Cove, especially when the U.S. Government is making every effort to have the prohibition by Glen Cove authorities lifted.

Q. If they don't, will we retaliate at, say, Jones Beach and other places in Long Island?

We hope that the situation in Glen Cove will be worked out.

. . . .

Document 274

Statement Issued by the Department of Agriculture, Des Moines, August 20, 1982[76]

Extension of U.S.-Soviet Grain Agreement

Secretary of Agriculture John R. Block said today the Soviet Union has agreed to President Reagan's offer to extend the Long-Term Grains Sales Agreement[77] for 1 year.

"This extension will allow American farmers to continue rebuilding this important market which was thrown away to our competitors during the partial embargo imposed on U.S. agricultural sales to the Soviet Union in January, 1980," Block said. "The willingness of the Soviet Union to accept this extension is proof that they believe the President's pledge that the United States will again be a reliable supplier."

Block said the acceptance was delivered in writing to the American Embassy in Moscow today. It is the second extension[78] to the original 5-year agreement negotiated in 1975. It provides that the Soviet Union must purchase 6 million metric tons of grain, plus they can purchase up to 8 million metric tons without consultations with the U.S. During the current year, United States has offered an additional 15 million metric tons to the Soviet Union.

"In keeping with the President's wishes, I will be contacting the Soviet Union immediately to determine a date for discussing additional grain sales during this second extension," Block said.

---

[76] Source: Department of Agriculture, *Major News Releases and Speeches*, August 20–August 27, 1982, p. 2.

[77] For the text of the October 20, 1975 agreement, see 26 UST 2971.

[78] The first extension was agreed to on August 5, 1981.

Document 275

Transcript of an Interview With the Secretary of State (Shultz), August 22, 1982 (Extract)[79]

Possible Reagan–Brezhnev Summit Meeting; Effectiveness of U.S. Sanctions Against the Soviet Union and Poland

MR. GWERTZMAN. Mr. Secretary, yesterday you had a meeting with a number of experts on the Soviet Union. I'd like to ask you about some aspects of policy toward the Soviet Union. There has been talk before of a possible summit, perhaps by the end of this year, between President Reagan and President Brezhnev. Do you think this is at all likely or should be sought?

SECRETARY SHULTZ. Well, it depends upon whether or not there are some identifiable constructive results to be obtained from the summit, and if there are, then probably it would be constructive. If not, I don't really see that there is that much point in it.

MR. GWERTZMAN. Do you plan to meet with Mr.—

SECRETARY SHULTZ. And I believe that's been the President's position all along.

MR. GWERTZMAN. Well, do you plan to discuss this possibility with Mr. Gromyko at the United Nations this fall?

SECRETARY SHULTZ. I hope to meet Mr. Gromyko in the United Nations, expect to, although there hasn't been any time worked out, and quite possibly the subject might come up.

MR. GWERTZMAN. On another area of Soviet-American difficulties which involved the allies, it's the question of American sanctions against the Soviet Union over Poland. You yourself have written, before you took office, of course, that such sanctions are hardly likely to be successfully used as a lever against the Soviet Union. Have you changed your position any, or are you trying to educate the administration along your position?

SECRETARY SHULTZ. Well, when you read that, it sounded like the word such was describing or referring to the sanctions that President Reagan has imposed. That wasn't the case. That article was written several years ago, and was referring to some other sanctions that were put on, taken off, put on, taken off, back and forth in a matter of a few months, and that I labeled light-switch diplomacy and said it wouldn't work.

In the case of the sanctions imposed by President Reagan, they have had a very broad purpose, particularly focusing on Poland, but other similar things that the Soviet Union—Soviet Union behavior, and I fully support the idea of expressing ourselves in this manner.

MR. GWERTZMAN. But do you see any way of resolving this growing dispute with the allies over this question, barring a relaxation of tensions in Poland?

SECRETARY SHULTZ. Well, that is the way that we would hope it would occur.

. . . .

Document 276

Transcript of an Interview With the Secretary of State (Shultz), September 5, 1982 (Extracts)[80]

Effectiveness of U.S. Sanctions Against the Soviet Union

. . . .

MR. PIERPOINT. But, Mr. Secretary, the United States sits down and talks with the

[79] Source: Department of State Press Release 260, August 24, 1982; printed also in Department of State *Bulletin*, October 1982, pp. 8–9. For the full text of the interview, see *ibid.*, pp. 7–10. The Secretary was interviewed on the NBC television program, "Meet the Press," by Bill Monroe and Marvin Kalb, NBC News; Rowland Evans, *Chicago Sun-Times;* Karen Elliott House, *Wall Street Journal;* and Bernard Gwertzman, *New York Times.*

[80] Source: Department of State Press Release 270, September 7, 1982; printed also in Department of State *Bulletin*, October 1982, p. 13. For the full text of this interview, see *ibid.*, pp. 10–13. The Secretary was interviewed on the CBS television program, "Face the Nation," by George Herman, Leslie Stahl, and Robert Pierpoint, all of CBS News.

Soviet Union across the board, and yet the Soviet Union exports revolution all over the world wherever it can. In fact it does more than that, it carries out military conquest in places like Afghanistan and Poland, and we still have closer relations with the Soviet Union than we do with Cuba.

What is the reason for this?

SECRETARY SHULTZ. The reason is that Cuba has violated all sorts of conditions that we would attach to tolerable behavior in the international arena, in Central America, in the Caribbean, in its efforts throughout South America, in the presence of Cuban troops in Africa. There are many examples of behavior.

I'm not talking about what somebody says. I'm talking about what they do—behavior that is disruptive—and we register our views about that, and I think we're on the right track.

As far as the Soviet Union is concerned, I think the President has made it very clear what his views are there. The behavior in Afghanistan and the events that we see in Poland very recently stand behind the President's very firm intention to register a view about the reprehensible manner of that behavior, and he's done so.

MR. HERMAN. There's been talk that you're looking forward to a meeting with Mr. Gromyko at the United Nations.

SECRETARY SHULTZ. I am planning to have a meeting with Mr. Gromyko in the United Nations, and there are many important things that we need to talk about, I'm sure.

. . . .

MR. HERMAN. Secretary Shultz, I'm a little confused about the Cubans have [*having*?] to change their ways before we'll talk to them; the Russians apparently don't. There's no sign, I gather, that the sanctions that we have placed on the companies of our allies has changed Soviet behavior in Poland. In fact, if anything, their behavior—the Polish military government under Soviet stimulus—has been even more rigorously repressive.

How can you call this a success? How can you say that they're modifying their behavior?

SECRETARY SHULTZ. What is happening in Poland is a very discouraging, but at the same time a dramatic, illustration of the bankruptcy of the Soviet system.

The Polish people are wonderful people, productive people. There are great resources in that country, and the placement on it of the Soviet system has brought it to its knees. It's a terrible indictment of their system.

MR. HERMAN. But this happened after we began our sanctions.

SECRETARY SHULTZ. No. This has been happening for many, many years—

MR. HERMAN. But it continues to happen after our sanctions.

SECRETARY SHULTZ.—and it has continued. It's very discouraging that it continues, but the Polish people have not given up, and we certainly should stand—

MR. PIERPOINT. Let's talk about the sanctions themselves. What good have they really done except to benefit the Soviet Union, because it's split us from our allies?

SECRETARY SHULTZ. I'm sure that they have imposed a cost on the construction of that pipeline. They have dramatized our strong feelings about the subject, and, to a degree one can say that because they have had costs in the United States and costs to our allies, they only dramatize how important the President feels this is and how strongly he feels about it.

MR. HERMAN. Let me just take that a step further. The allies are so disturbed they've been holding a meeting on it. Do you plan to send some senior State Department official—yourself or anybody else—to talk to our allies about reducing these sanctions?

SECRETARY SHULTZ. I'm sure the President will hold firmly to the strategy implied by the sanctions. To the extent that you can view the sanctions as an important tactic, if we can work out things that are more effective and have all of our allies with us, we're certainly willing to look at them.

MR. HERMAN. Thank you very much, Mr. Secretary. Sorry to interrupt. Thank you for being with us on "Face the Nation."

Document 277

Transcript of an Interview With the U.S. Trade Representative (Brock), September 12, 1982 (Extracts)[81]

Rationale for U.S. Sanctions Against the Soviet Union

. . . .

MR. ROWEN. Well, Mr. Ambassador, one of the elements of growing tension is the situation that exists between the United States on one side and our European allies on the other in a number of trade matters. And most specifically and recently, that relating to the Russian natural gas pipeline to Europe. Our country has put into effect sanctions against European companies and subsidiaries of American companies that are delivering equipment for that pipeline. Mrs. Thatcher, one of our strong allies, has said that this is unacceptable. So have other countries.

Do you see any possibility that the administration might ease its stance and allow some of those contracts to be fulfilled without penalties?

AMBASSADOR BROCK. I guess people too often miss the basic reason that we are doing what we are doing. Back when the imposition of martial law was placed on Poland, the President said that we were going to use sanctions to raise the penalty on the Soviet Union for the actions they had undertaken, and we're not going to change those sanctions until martial law is lifted, until there is a greater discourse between Solidarity, the church, and until those people are freed that are political prisoners. We care a lot about it. The President feels very strongly about it. And we—When we tried to reach a common approach to deal with that problem and were not quite successful, then we had to act on our own initiative, as we have done.

I think ultimately this will be a good example of the need for common action and I think that's what's going to happen. We will have a more effective program when we are joined by our European allies. I hope that will happen.

MR. ROWEN. But our European allies and some critics of policy in this country say that what is really happening, Mr. Brock, is that the pipeline is going to go forward. The only danger, the only damage that is being done is to our relationship with Europe. It comes at a time when Europe is in a deep recession. And it's also hurting American companies because in the future, others are likely to say how can you rely on American commitments because they can be changed at a political stroke. Isn't this a great danger?

AMBASSADOR BROCK. Sometimes I wonder if this country can ever do anything right. When our interest rates are too high, we were criticized. When interest rates are too low, we are criticized. When the dollar is too weak, we're criticized. When it's too strong, we're criticized. We're mostly criticized for not being effective leaders.

Well, the President has demonstrated leadership, and it's a very strong and effective leadership. I think that the bottom line is that while we do have some temporary agony at the moment, the important thing is the achievement of a unified approach. I believe that's what's going to occur, and if it does we will all be better off.

. . . .

MR. ELLIS. Mr. Ambassador, when President Reagan recently extended the grain sale agreement with the Soviets for 1 year, Secretary of Agriculture Block said that this was proof of the President's pledge that the United States once again would become a reliable supplier.[82]

Now under President Reagan's sanctions on the pipeline, the Caterpillar Tractor Company lost a $90 million firm contract for 200 pipelaying machines which the Japanese rapidly snapped up. And one of the complaints, as I talked with Caterpillar officials was that no longer would foreigners think of Caterpillar as a reliable supplier.

How do you find logic in all of this?

AMBASSADOR BROCK. We have under the six Presidents that I have known in the time that I have been in this business of politics,

[81] Source: NBC News. Brock was interviewed on the NBC television program, "Meet the Press," by Bill Monroe, NBC News; Hobart Rowen, *Washington Post;* Boyd France, *Business Week;* and Albert Hunt, *Wall Street Journal.*

[82] See the announcement by the Department of Agriculture, August 20, 1982, document 274.

we have always made a distinction between national security and strategic or critical materials of that sort and the kind of materials that would generally be classified as agricultural goods, consumer goods. The fact is that we have maintained that policy under this administration, which is—you know, granted it is changed from the former administration, because they did put an embargo on grains. But this President has committed not to do that and I think as long as we keep our focus on the very narrow description of the kinds of goods that we do restrain in the sale to the Soviets, we will over a period of time by staying with that policy, establish the credibility of that policy. It's going to take some time, but it can be done.

You know, the bottom line is that we just have to do certain things in this country to demonstrate our conviction that people have a right to join a church or a labor union, or whatever else, whether it's in Poland or around the world. And if we don't stand up for some basic principles, we have no leadership role at all.

MR. ELLIS. You spoke earlier in response to a question from Mr. Rowen about this was a time for common action by the United States and the European allies, are we in a sense being diverted by the pipeline issue which causes great pain to a number of firms in Europe and to a number of governments, including our own? Are we being diverted that what we really are trying to find is a common Western approach to trade and credits to the Soviet Union? And might I ask further, is the search for such a common purpose and policy now centering on trade and credit policies, because the Europeans consistently subsidize the exports of their goods to the Soviet Union; we do not?

AMBASSADOR BROCK. They do and that's one of the real concerns, because when you subsidize a country like the Soviet Union you're not subsidizing their consumers, the people that eat the food; you're subsidizing the military and they've had the biggest military buildup in the history of the world. And that does threaten us and causes us to—to have to respond to it to maintain our own security. But I think the—the obvious gist of this problem came about because maybe for too long now we've just been moving apart by inches, but there has been a difference in perception between Europe and the United States as to how to respond to this sort of event, to the constant abuse of other countries by the Soviet Union. And perhaps one of the most important things that must come out of this and will is a greater sense of how valuable we are to each other, how important we are to each other, and the need to work in common purpose.

MR. MONROE. Mr. France?

MR. FRANCE. Mr. Ambassador, as you say, the President's policy on sanctions was adopted in a hope of persuading the Soviet Union to permit more freedom in Poland. Have you any indication at all that that policy is working, that that result may be achieved? As you know, critics say that all the sanctions have done is to ignite a flaming crisis in—within the NATO Alliance, which provides a further strong incentive to Moscow to hang tough in Poland.

AMBASSADOR BROCK. Well, I guess one of the things I did in the last four years in a different occupation was spend a lot of time criticizing the previous administration for constantly shifting ground. I don't think the Russians or even our friends really were very secure in knowing what we were going to do next. There is a difference with President Reagan. They do know what he is going to do. He is very open and aboveboard. And I think the consistency of that policy is awfully important. We will achieve some results if we stay with it. But the worst thing you could do is to have a policy and then pull off because there's some criticism, and then try something else and then pull off, that—that will not work. We have to have a general, solid, straightforward, continuous approach.

MR. FRANCE. On that very point, European officials often have complained that the administration speaks with different voices on this—this sanctions issue. In fact, specifically there were complaints last week that U.S. Secretary of Defense Weinberger, when you were in London discussing this, gave different perceptions to the Europeans as to what our policy is.

Is—Does this reflect a continuing conflict within the administration on the issue of sanctions and where to go from here?

AMBASSADOR BROCK. No. The President has made a decision. Every member of this administration is going to make that decision stick. We're going to make it work. We are going to speak with one voice, act with one voice, and it's going to be effective.

MR. FRANCE. In answer to one of Mr. Rowen's questions you seemed to suggest that there is no basis for a compromise with the Europeans on the sanctions issue short of a—an ending or great softening of martial law in Poland. Is that what you're saying? That there are no grounds—There is nothing they could do to penalize the Soviet Union economically in some other way which would persuade us to lift or modify the sanctions?

AMBASSADOR BROCK. I think we've said throughout that we would not only be willing, but we would be delighted to listen to—to any suggestion they might have as to what approach they might take with us that would be more effective than that which we have had to do by ourselves for the moment.

MR. FRANCE. And were they to tighten credit terms to the Soviet Union significantly, would that meet that criterion?

AMBASSADOR BROCK. I don't know that I would want to try to describe any one thing, because I'm not sure it would be. But I do think the need to work together is obvious and the—the effectiveness of working together is obvious.

MR. MONROE. Mr. Ambassador, part of Mr. France's first question had to do with whether you see any signs that the sanctions are having any effect on the Polish situation. I take it the fact that you didn't address yourself directly to that represents a concession that you don't see any signs that it is having any effect on the Polish situation.

AMBASSADOR BROCK. No, I can't say that there's been any change. As a matter of fact, there may be signs that there's even more repression in the last few weeks. But if you did your policy on the basis of signs week-to-week, you'd never have a policy, you'd just be all over the lot, and that's the one thing you must not do.

MR. MONROE. Well, are you advocating sticking with a policy whether it works or not?

AMBASSADOR BROCK. (Laughter) No. I'm saying for gosh sakes, give it time to work.

. . . .

Document 278

Testimony by Central Intelligence Agency Officials Before the Senate Select Intelligence Committee, September 28, 1982 (Extract)[83]

Soviet Leadership Succession

MR. DIAMOND. Thank you, Senator.

It is a pleasure to appear before this committee on the subject of Soviet succession. I am Douglas Diamond, the Office of Soviet Analysis, and I have with me several colleagues who are expert on various related topics to the succession issues.

Mr. Barry Stevenson will lead off with a presentation that will run close to probably a half hour. Of course, he and others stand ready to respond to questions at any time.

MR. STEVENSON. Before I begin, I will just drop a copy of the Politburo apparatus in front of people since at times it is hard to tell the players without a program.

A quick glance at the top of the list will give you the rundown of the current Politburo, although I think it still has Suslov on it. He died recently, so it hasn't been changed since.

We understand that there is some interest in how a succession actually takes place in the Soviet Union and who plays the major role. I will therefore begin with an assessment of Mr. Brezhnev's political fortunes as we see them at the moment, and the informal rules that govern the succession process. From there, I will touch on the role of the various institutions in a succession environment, the attitudes of a couple of men who we see as the likely successors to Brezhnev, and conclude with a few comments on what we see as the major policy issues confronting the new Soviet leaders and what we know about their attitudes.

---

[83] Source: *Soviet Succession: Hearing Before the Select Committee on Intelligence of the United States Senate, Ninety-seventh Congress, Second Session* (Washington, 1982), pp. 28–43. The text is a declassified version of a closed committee hearing. Testifying for the Central Intelligence Agency were Douglas B. Diamond, Deputy Director, Office of Soviet Analysis; Barry Stevenson, Chief, Current Support Division, Office of Soviet Analysis; Kay Oliver, Office of Soviet Analysis; and James Barry, Chief, Policy Analysis Division, Office of Soviet Analysis. They were accompanied by Mary Brown, Legislative Liaison.

On the surface, Brezhnev is still the preeminent party and state leader, and it would probably still be very risky for anyone to mount an open challenge against him. But for the first time since he consolidated his power, well over a decade ago, we believe there are indications of a substantial disparity between his formal authority and power and the amount of power he really wields behind the scenes. We believe his health is deteriorating over time, that he is more vulnerable politically than ever before, and that his Politburo colleagues have begun individually and probably even collectively to prepare for a future without him.

We believe, in short, that the political succession is underway in the Soviet Union, even if Brezhnev is still in power, and we would not have said that 1 year ago.

We believe there are several reasons for this. The first is the state of his health. When he was alert and active, his consensual style of leadership provided a piece of the political action and job security for the colleagues he came into power with. With his stamina failing and his mortality increasingly evident, it becomes prudent for these same colleagues to begin to make preparations for their futures without him. Available evidence indicates that this is exactly what they are doing.

Second, the passing of the old guard has begun to crack the facade of leadership unity that we have seen for a long time. If you think back to the past decade of the senior Soviet leaders, you tend to think of Brezhnev, Kosygin, Podgornly, Suslov. The only one of these that is left is Brezhnev.

The most important recent event was the passing of the senior party ideologist—in some senses the conscience of the Soviet party—Mikhail Suslov, last January. His removal took a pivotal figure out of the core of the Soviet leadership and it necessitated personnel moves to take over his duties that opened up political maneuvering that we see continuing today.

Brezhnev's role in decisionmaking has apparently lessened to some extent recently. The roles of several others of his Politburo colleagues have expanded. We now have derogatory rumors floating around the Soviet Union and getting to foreigners about Brezhnev's children, about corruption in Brezhnev's family. There is indirect public criticism of Brezhnev himself. And all of these things suggest some breakdown in party discipline, and particularly, an erosion of Brezhnev's image within the country.

More importantly—and this is where this sort of thing translates into action—we believe that Brezhnev has been unable to dictate some very key personnel decisions lately. Some examples: Yuriy Andropov, the former head of the KGB, has moved out of the KGB into the powerful Party Secretariat where he is able to challenge Brezhnev's very close ally and protege, Konstantin Chernenko. His replacement as head of the KGB could easily have been the First Deputy Chairman of the KGB, whom we know to have been a longtime Brezhnev ally, but it wasn't. They pulled a regional official out of the Ukraine who, we are getting increasing reporting, has career ties to Andropov, and made him the KGB chief. His name is Fedorchuk.

As a consequence of these and other personnel changes, we believe that Brezhnev's control of the KGB, which is essential to any Soviet leader's security, no longer seems to be assured. There have been indications, as well, of opposition to some of Brezhnev's domestic policies recently, and perhaps of leadership conflict or indecision on several areas of foreign policy as well.

Now, in recounting this, I don't mean to imply that Brezhnev is now only a figurehead or even that he is a negligible factor in Soviet policy. This is clearly not so.

What we are seeing is that, for the first time, Brezhnev's political vulnerability is on the increase, and his influence is waning, and we do not expect either of these trends to change.

Now, regarding the succession itself, as you are undoubtedly aware, when the time comes for a change at the top in the Soviet Union, one of the basic flaws and weaknesses of their system is a lack of any constitutional procedure for the transfer of power. In effect, once you get power in the Soviet Union, you hold onto it until you can't anymore and someone takes it away from you. That can create a lot of problems at the time that taking away occurs.

It doesn't mean, however, that anything can happen. There are limits to what can happen. There are a number of collectively shared understandings that govern the behavior of Soviet leaders in a succession environment and define the limits of politically possible succession outcomes.

In the first place, the Politburo will choose the new leader from among its own. No member can seize power and make himself the leader as such although, of course, by adroit political maneuvering, he can help shape the outcome. In their selection of a successor, the top leadership is influenced by various organizations and institutional groups, including their own party and government constituencies and the military hierarchy.

The potential consequences of backing a loser are no longer what they once were in the Soviet environment. If you back a loser, you can lose your perquisites of office, but you are not going to lose your life in the current environment, which does create a bit more order to the process.

Competition among contenders, therefore, takes place among a certain amount of self-imposed constraints. The leaders have a collective interest in seeing that the arena for debate is confined to the Politburo, I mean, just for sheer self-interest and for increasing their own political advantage and in keeping the process from seeping out into the public or among other elite groups.

So while there are no constitutional procedures for changing, there still are informal agreements that will be in effect and will influence what happens.

Now, if Brezhnev should die in office, an inner core of leaders on the Politburo will meet immediately and it will be shortly followed by a meeting of the whole 13-member Politburo. The chart you have has 14 members because we haven't put a new chart out since Suslov died.

Brezhnev's death, arrangements for his funeral would be publicly announced, probably by the Central Committee, which would meet a few days to ratify the Politburo's choice of a successor.

The Stalin precedent, which was near-panic among the remaining leaders, is simply not relevant today. The suddenness of Stalin's death, his dictatorial style, made the event much more traumatic than it will be today. Brezhnev's consensual approach to decisionmaking and his long-deteriorating health have given his colleagues plenty of time to prepare.

If Brezhnev were to be—yes, sir.

SENATOR MOYNIHAN. Mr. Stevenson, the Politburo doesn't have a Chairman as such, but it does have a General Secretary.

MR. STEVENSON. That's correct. He acts as Chairman.

SENATOR MOYNIHAN. So the real choice is for General Secretary.

MR. STEVENSON. That's right. That's what they are choosing.

SENATOR MOYNIHAN. But in effect, the Politburo will make that choice as the Secretariat is subsidiary to it.

MR. STEVENSON. As the Secretariat is the administrative arm, so the Politburo indeed will make that choice.

SENATOR MOYNIHAN. And the General Secretary presides at the Politburo.

MR. STEVENSON. That's correct, that's correct. And as in any organization, if you can chair it, you can certainly go a long way in affecting what it does, as witness—if his colleagues decided to remove Brezhnev, if he did not die in office, any maneuvering to build support for this action would have to be done covertly. The party rules prohibit factionalism, which gives the leader the advantage of moving against anyone who tries to put a cabal together against him. Premature exposure of any such maneuvering would enable Brezhnev, using his powers as Chairman, in all likelihood to defeat it.

But once the Politburo reached a decision as a whole, covertly, to remove Brezhnev, it would be too late for him to reverse the verdict, providing his opponents had made some arrangement to control his ability or his ability to communicate with others.

They failed to do that in 1957 when they tried to remove Khrushchev. Even though there was a majority on the Politburo to remove him, he was able to appeal to the Central Committee as a whole where he had greater support, where he had majority support, and he succeeded and saved himself. That's the only time that has ever occurred, and I am sure the lesson was well learned by any who are on the Politburo today and would want to remove Brezhnev.

But it is just such a situation that makes firm control of the KGB and its warning apparatus essential. And as I noted a couple minutes ago, we have reason to believe that Brezhnev's control of this organization is not as tight as it once was. And that is one of the reasons why we feel he is more politically vulnerable today than previously.

Now, it is unlikely that Brezhnev would step down of his own volition. In over 20 successions in the Communist regime since 1917, there has not been a single one that was—a single case in which a party head had relinquished power on his own, and we are quite doubtful that they would begin with Brezhnev.

It is possible, though, that his colleagues, if he became so infirm that he couldn't carry on, would choose to remove him, and would give him the option of stepping down with honors and making it look like it was his own retirement. There is a chance he would acquiesce in this. He is a very vain and proud man and very conscious of his place in history. So we could have a situation that looked as though he retired voluntarily. We doubt that he would do so.

As far as the institutions that have an influence in the succession period, the Secretariat, which you have just made reference to, Mr. Senator, does not play a direct role in the process, as you had suggested, but the succession contenders on the Politburo who are secretaries have a significant advantage, and that is that the Secretariat is responsible for the appointment and removal of party regional and central officials, and therefore, the members who are on the Secretariat have a strong power base and a lot of patronage, and it is for this reason that we think that the secretaries on the Politburo have the signal advantage over the others, and this has proven to be the case in past Soviet successions.

SENATOR MOYNIHAN. And yet when Andropov moved up, he dropped out.

MR. STEVENSON. No; he dropped his chairmanship of the KGB, which is a state organization, and became a secretary.

SENATOR MOYNIHAN. Became a secretary. I see. We don't have this.

MR. STEVENSON. I'm sorry. This is a chart that has not been brought up to date.

MS. OLIVER. Senators, the way it usually works—not to get too much into detail—is that there are three, four, or five senior secretaries who hold membership on the Politburo as well. They supervise the work of a group of junior secretaries who have more specific responsibilities, so that Suslov, for example, supervised several junior secretaries, one of whom dealt with domestic ideology and propaganda. Another dealt with relations with foreign Communist parties in countries outside of Eastern Europe. non-ruling Communist parties. in other words, That is Ponomarev. Another who dealt with relations with Communist parties in Eastern Europe.

MR. STEVENSON. As for nonparty institutions in the succession, in differing ways, the government, the KGB, and the military all have influence in the succession outcome. But none of these three groups pose any credible alternative to party rule at this time.

There are strong limitations on the KGB's influence, for instance.

THE CHAIRMAN.[84] You mentioned military and KGB. May I ask you, is there any indication which of those two groups have the most power?

MR. STEVENSON. I guess, without putting too fine an edge on it, one would almost have to say how you would define power. The military certainly has—well, to give a simple answer, my answer would be the military, and I could go into a number of different reasons for giving that answer, and one or another of my colleagues might even disagree with me, but I would say the military, for a lot of different reasons.

THE CHAIRMAN. Does the fact that their old military leaders have been dying off, and they haven't been engaged in military actions enough to develop new ones, had any effect on this?

MR. STEVENSON. I will pass that question to my colleague here who can speak very well to that.

MR. BARRY. Thank you.

Senator, the military has done a somewhat better job than the party hierarchy of rejuvenating its own ranks. There are a number of younger and very vigorous military officers who seem to have gotten themselves into good positions, not only in terms of upholding their own professional interests, but in terms of good relations with the Politburo and party rulers.

The Minister of Defense, Dmitriy Ustinov, who is about a year younger than Brezhnev, is not a professional military man. He is a former party secretary, and he came up through the supervision of defense industries. Below Ustinov, there are a number of senior officials in the Ministry of Defense itself that have moved into their positions relatively recently. There are a number of hangers-on, people who have hung on for some time, but there are a few more recent entrants.

I suppose that the most prominent of these has been Ogarkov, the Chief of the General Staff, who has been a rather vocal proponent of Soviet military power, rather prolific writer, and we think continues to enjoy high level political support as well as staunch support from the military establishment.

MR. STEVENSON. And was a member of the first Soviet SALT delegation, too, I might add.

---

[84] Senator Barry Goldwater.

Excuse me.

SENATOR MOYNIHAN. Just a question. Does the military command in the Soviet Union begin with the Minister of Defense?

MR. BARRY. We usually define the military high command to begin with the Minister of Defense. Unlike the organization for military operations in this country, I believe the Minister of Defense generally is considered to be an integral part of the high command.

I think basically in response to your earlier question, the Soviet military does indeed face a challenge of rejuvenating its leadership. There is a prospect of impending generational change, but the military establishment itself seems to have been somewhat better rejuvenated in recent years than the political establishment.

THE CHAIRMAN. Let me inject a thought here. It has been my feeling for some time that the younger element in the Soviet Union are beginning to move up, and to me that is encouraging. Are you encouraged in any way to think that a new leader, whoever that might be, would be a younger man? I am speaking of someone below 70, someone in his 50's, possibly.

MR. STEVENSON. We do not see a new leader right now in his 50's. Almost certainly, the new leader to replace Brezhnev is going to come out of the inner core of older men now in the Politburo.

Now, it is conceivable you could get into a real deadlock in the fighting for the job and there could be a younger, compromise candidate somewhere. But we would feel that at this point, that is a long shot, a very long shot. Brezhnev was very cautious in his personnel policies. He regulated Soviet cadre policy very carefully, in reaction, in part, to the wild swings in policy under Khrushchev, which made an awful lot of party officials very nervous about their security, and for the most part you could say that in the hard-core cadre, Soviet party jobs, right down through the party, for the last 15 years or so, no one has been leapfrogging anyone else. Someone who is a party secretary, when he dies, his first subordinate moves up one notch, and his subordinate moves up one notch. The result is that the age of the Soviet elite organs—the Central Committee, the Central Auditing Commission, and so on—are far the highest they have ever been.

SENATOR MOYNIHAN. The only member of the Politburo under 60 is Romanov.

MR. STEVENSON. Gorbachev now, since Gorbachev has moved up. Gorbachev is in his 50's.

SENATOR MOYNIHAN. I want to claim right now my candidate for General Secretary is Romanov. The fact that his first name happens to be Aleksandr is—

MR. STEVENSON. Well, people have opined that having a Romanov back in charge of the Soviet Union would be a refreshing thing, but he has got some powerful hurdles in front of him.

In a couple of minutes, we pretty much have believed that at the moment there are two clear front runners, and these two are Andropov and Chernenko. For the last decade, Andre Kirilenko, who, you will note on your chart, is the secretary in charge of heavy industry, has acted as Brezhnev's deputy in effect.

For the last year or so, we have seen a lot of indications, in fact, over a year, that Kirilenko's political stature has been slipping. He has had severe health problems for the first time. Politically, it has become pretty apparent that Brezhnev has been moving Chernenko, who has been close to him for a long, long time, into the fore, and Kirilenko has been slipping out of sight.

At the time that Suslov died, there was a lot of evidence that Brezhnev attempted to move Chernenko forward very quickly. We feel that it was in part reaction to that, that we have seen Andropov moving ahead.

We believe that Andropov and Chernenko are the two prime contenders right now. They are both secretaries, central secretaries. They are both on the Politburo. Romanov suffers from the problem that he is still out of town. He is still over in Leningrad. He is not at the center where he can elbow and jockey and gouge and fight his own interests better.

I will finish up with a few comments on that, just as far as the roles of the organizations in the succession. I think Kay put her finger on the KGB's primary role. Its influence expands at the time of a succession because of what it does control. That doesn't necessarily hold. Soviet leaders learned their lesson from Beria's use of the KGB in 1953, and after they executed him, they moved an awful lot of Komsomal and party officials into the KGB and put them in positions of power and not just KGB official career operatives, and they have been very careful to maintain that situation since.

The new head of the KGB is out of the Ukraine. He is not a Politburo member. He is not even a member of the Central Committee.

SENATOR MOYNIHAN. What is his name.

MR. STEVENSON. His name is Fedorchuk. It is F-e-d-o-r-c-h-u-k.

We cannot see him playing an independent role in the succession.

As for the military, it is not likely to act unilaterally in a succession environment. It has no tradition of Bonapartism in the Soviet Union. Marshall Zhukov's flirtation with power in 1957 was an exception, not at all the rule, but it can play an important facilitating role in a transition period, either if Brezhnev is ousted or if he dies. In 1957, when the cabal against Khrushchev almost succeeded, Khrushchev was able to get Zhukov to have the military to fly Central Committee members in from all over the Soviet Union and assemble them for the vote which saved him.

Now, certainly everyone remembers that precedent, and that would be guarded against in any attempt to remove Brezhnev now.

But the military's influence is largely due, I would say, to the substantial congruence of outlooks and objectives between it and the top political leaders in the Soviet Union. Ustinov is held in very high regard by his Politburo peers, and he is also, of course, the Minister of Defense.

As Kay mentioned, by defining national security interests—with access to information that allows him to do that—the military, it is not hard to imagine at all putting up an objection to one of the contenders' platforms.

So it has grown in prestige under Brezhnev. I mean, it has grown in funding under Brezhnev. The heightened Soviet international role and so on, we would expect, would give the military considerable influence in a succession environment, but not control and not as a challenger to the party for power.

Now, regarding the players which I just mentioned a little earlier on, there are a couple of interesting things about the current cast of characters. For one thing, there is no one to play the role of senior executive and statesman that Suslov apparently played in 1964. That removes a bit of a moderating influence on the struggle for succession. There is also no really well qualified candidate to replace Brezhnev.

If we look at previous Soviet leaders, they have been rich in party organizational experience. They have run—they have had line party duties. They have run significant party organizations. They have had experience in the economic area as well. Nobody on the scene now in the Politburo has the breadth of experience that Khruschchev had in 1953 or that Brezhnev had in 1964, not the kind of experience that traditionally we feel makes for a Soviet leader.

Precedent nevertheless suggests that the successor will be one of the senior secretaries in the center, and at this particular time, that is Andropov, Chernenko, Kirilenko, Gorbachev, and each of these men has significant liabilities.

As I mentioned earlier, evidence indicates that at the moment, only Andropov and Chernenko are the really serious contenders, so I will just discuss the two of them specifically at the moment. If you have any questions about any of the others, we will be happy to try to answer them.

Andropov's KGB background could work either for or against him. Nothing is ever neat and clean in politics, as we all know. It depends on how he is able to play it.

In past years, we said that Andropov could not be a serious contender for power until he left the KGB role, in effect, until he had been laundered out of his KGB role. Well, that of course has now happened. He has left it; he is on the Secretariat. But memories of the purge years still run strong in the Soviet Union. You know the age of the senior people. We all know about the violence of the purge eras, and there is no question that they remember this. Some might remember it enough to make Andropov's ascendancy distasteful.

On the other hand, right now we have a situation in the Soviet Union when there is a heightened concern over popular discontent, over lack of ideological preparation. You hear a lot of Soviets saying, "what this country needs is another good boss, you know, good old Joe Stalin. By God, when we had him, we had someone in charge."

Well, Andropov's KGB background could benefit him in that kind of an environment. So on balance, I think we come down believing that his KGB background probably won't really hurt him, and it could help him.

Chernenko originally was seen by a lot of people, and apparently is still seen by a lot of Soviets as just Brezhnev's creature. He has provided him his staff support throughtout his chairmanship, but he has also been involved in a pretty wide range of party activities in recent years which have necessitated a good deal of responsibility. All the other contenders, we think, have more serious handicaps.

Now, whoever does take over after Brezhnev, and at some future time, if Brezhnev lives longer, some other contender might move further forward than he is now, we doubt that—he won't come in with all the power that Brezhnev has acquired himself over a period of time.

SENATOR MOYNIHAN. None does.

MR. STEVENSON. That's right, that's right. It just isn't going to be that way. The fact that none of them has a really strong, clear claim to succeed him probably also is going to work against him. They might have to strike a lot of compromises.

SENATOR MOYNIHAN. None of them does. It is a characteristic of the system.

MS. OLIVER. But we think this successor will have less power than any previous successor at the time he succeeded.

MR. STEVENSON. Both Brezhnev and Khrushchev had a lot more experience and a lot more patronage and people accountable to them out there on which they could build support than we see any of the people right now who are positioned to replace Brezhnev having.

We figure it takes at least 5 years, and it has been in every case for any leader to really pull it all together. But in addition, it might be tougher for any leader to freewheel than previously. Brezhnev, as I indicated earlier, institutionalized an awful lot of cadre policies. Debate and handling of issues was much more formalized under Brezhnev than under any other leader. By putting restraints on the most blatant kinds of patronage, he probably made it more difficult for a new leader quickly to hand out a lot of plums and build support.

So we think that the contender probably has a tougher row for this variety of reasons to build his support fast and take charge quickly than either Brezhnev or Khrushchev did.

Now, there's a number of problems that Brezhnev is leaving behind that are probably going to make it pretty tough for him to handle without being able to accrue a lot of power pretty quickly. Brezhnev's chief legacy, I would say, certainly as we see it from the West, and I think probably as they see it from the Soviet Union, is an ambitious policy of military spending that made the Soviet Union a genuine world power and world factor but which is increasingly difficult for the Soviet Union to support economically.

With the removal of the terror and the waning of the influence of ideology domestically, he also tried to buy popular quiescence and support through incremental improvements in the populations's well-being, and when we look at the Soviet Union's economic problems today, we have got to remember that for most of his period in power—and this goes back to 1964—Brezhnev succeeded in providing a Soviet version of guns for the state and butter for the populace. The standard of living in the Soviet Union increased significantly in Brezhnev's era, along with that significant buildup that we are all so well aware of.

The problem is that with the slowing in economic growth over the last several years and the consequent near stagnation of per capita income and consumption has translated into what we see as a general malaise in Soviet society, and one that shows.

It is mainfest in a lot of ways, the growing consumption of alcohol, the severe alcohol problem in the country, increasing labor turnover. We are getting reports of sporadic strike activity, I mean, nothing like Poland. We can't jump to that, but nevertheless, in flourishing black-market corruption and cynicism. You talk to Soviets, and it is amazing how consistent the reports are that, well, things were getting better for a long time, but they sure don't seem to have gotten better recently. And many, in fact, think that they have slipped.

. . . .

Document 279

Address by President Reagan, Santa Barbara, California, October 9, 1982[85]

U.S. Intention to Suspend Most-Favored-Nation Status for Poland in Response to the Polish Government's Outlawing of Solidarity

My fellow Americans, yesterday the Polish Government, a military dictatorship, took another far-reaching step in their persecution of their own people. They declared Solidarity, the organization of the working men and women of Poland, their free union, illegal.

Yes, I know Poland is a far away country in Eastern Europe. Still, this action is a matter of profound concern to all the American people and to the free world.

Ever since martial law was brutally imposed last December, Polish authorities have been assuring the world that they're interested in a genuine reconciliation with the Polish people. But the Polish regime's action yesterday reveals the hollowness of its promises. By outlawing Solidarity, a free trade organization to which an overwhelming majority of Polish workers and farmers belong, they have made it clear that they never had any intention of restoring one of the most elemental human rights—the right to belong to a free trade union.

The so-called "new trade union legislation" under which this contrary and backward step has been taken claims to substitute a structure and framework for the establishment of free trade unions in Poland. But the free world can see this is only a sham. It is clear that such unions, if formed, will be mere extensions of the Polish Communist Party.

The Polish military leaders and their Soviet backers have shown that they will continue to trample upon the hopes and aspirations of the majority of the Polish people. America cannot stand idly by in the face of these latest threats of repression and acts of repression by the Polish Government.

I am, therefore, today directing steps to bring about the suspension of Poland's most-favored-nation tariff status as quickly as possible. This will increase the tariffs on Polish manufactured goods exported to the United States and thus reduce the quantities of these goods which have been imported in the past.

The Polish regime should understand that we're prepared to take further steps as a result of this further repression in Poland. We are also consulting urgently with our allies on steps we might take jointly in response to this latest outrage. While taking these steps, I want to make clear as I have in the past that they are not directed against the Polish people. We will continue to provide humanitarian assistance to the people of Poland through organizations such as Catholic Relief Service and Care as we have since the beginning of martial law.

At the same time, I stand by my earlier offer to provide recovery assistance to help the Polish economy back on its feet once Warsaw restores to the Polish people their human rights.

There are those who will argue that the Polish Government's action marks the death of Solidarity. I don't believe this for a moment. Those who know Poland well understand that as long as the flame of freedom burns as brightly and intensely in the hearts of Polish men and women as it does today, the spirit of Solidarity will remain a vital force in Poland.

Surely, it must be clear to all that until Warsaw's military authorities move to restore Solidarity to its rightful and hard-won place in Polish society, Poland will continue to be plagued by bitterness, alienation, instability, and stagnation.

Someone has said that when anyone is denied freedom, then freedom for everyone is threatened. The struggle in the world today for the hearts and minds of mankind is based on one simple question: Is man born to be free, or slave? In country after country, people have long known the answer to that question. We are free by divine right. We are the masters of our fate, and we create governments for our convenience. Those who would have it otherwise commit a crime and a sin against God and man.

There can only be one path out of the current morass in Poland, and that is for the

[85] Source: White House Press Release, October 9, 1982, Office of the Press Secretary to the President; printed also in *Weekly Compilation of Presidential Documents*, October 18, 1982, pp. 1289–1290. The President spoke at 9:06 a.m. on nationwide radio from his residence at Rancho del Cielo.

military regime to stand up to its own statements of principle, even in the face of severe outside pressure from the Soviet Union, to lift martial law, release Lech Walesa and his colleagues now languishing in prison, and begin again the search for social peace through the arduous but real process of dialogue and reconciliation with the church and Solidarity.

I join with my countrymen, including millions of Americans whose roots are in Poland, in praying for an early return to a path of moderation and personal freedom in Poland.

Thanks for listening. I'll be back next week. Let Poland be Poland. God bless you.

Document 280

Transcript of the Department of State Daily Press Briefing, October 15, 1982 (Extract)[86]

Consideration of Most-Favored-Nation Status for Romania

. . . .

Q. Can you comment on the *New York Times* article 0 today that said Romania was able to insure continued MFN?

A. I have something on that for you.

The story said that Romania was able to insure continued most-favored-nation status.

Assistant Secretary Abrams was in Bucharest October 6 and 7 for discussions of Romanian emigration procedures. During last summer's congressional consideration of MFN for Romania, the Government of Romania stated that it would engage in such discussions and would improve its emigration procedures.

The talks last week made real progress but reached no final accords and most-favored-nation status for Romania for next year is not assured. The President will not decide on whether to recommend MFN for Romania until next spring, and his recommendation will depend not on Romania's pledges but Romanian performance on human rights issues.

The U.S.–Romania Governments will continue discussions on Romanian emigration procedures in the coming months, and we will watch carefully to see if the delays and harassment which applicants for migration have faced are now being eliminated.

. . . .

Document 281

Transcript of a White House Press Briefing, October 25, 1982 (Extract)[88]

President's Intention to Suspend Poland's Most-Favored-Nation Status

. . . .

MR. SPEAKES. . . . Okay. Now, Flo has in hand here the Executive order designating the Secretary of State to report to the Congress on the payment of the Polish debt.[89] This is a routine thing that has been done quarterly under the law. Here's—P.L. 97–257, which is the FY'82 Supplemental Appropriations Act.[90] In order for the United States to make any payment on credits extended to Poland, the President must either declare Poland in default or say why such payments would be a national interest.

By this piece of paper, the President is delegating the authority on this to Secretary Shultz who will act, following discussions between the White House, State Department, USDA, and the Treasury Department.

---

[86] Source: Office of Press Relations, Department of State. John Hughes, Department of State Spokesman, conducted the briefing which began at 12:22 p.m.

[87] See *New York Times*, October 15, 1982, p. A8.

[88] Source: Office of the Press Secretary to the President. Deputy Press Secretary Larry Speakes conducted the briefing which began at 6:03 p.m.

[89] For the text of Executive Order 12390, dated October 25, see *Weekly Compilation of Presidential Documents*, November 1, 1982, p. 1389.

[90] For text, see 96 Stat. 818.

This action is similar to the previous actions taken. And he will make the designation from the State Department.

The payments are made by the U.S. Government without any specific action by the President required. The CCC takes a step on its own. So this is routine.

Now, the question of MFN, that is a proclamation and that will be—the President has made up his mind to move forward. The President has decided to move forward on that. The language of the proclamation has been reviewed by the Special Trade Representative and is being reviewed by the Justice Department, has not been signed, but possibly will be done as early as tomorrow.[91]

Now, the question came up this morning about the number of countries that had CCC loan guarantees.[92] There are 20 other countries.

MR. ALLIN. Approximately.

MR. SPEAKES. Approximately. Okay. Now, the Eastern European countries, who have MFN status are Hungary and Romania in addition to Poland. Also, you will recall that the People's Republic of China in 1974 was granted the most-favored-nation status.

Now, the figure in the *Times, Washington Times,* this morning of $346 million, that is the total amount of contingent liabilities for all of FY'83. These debts come due at various times throughout the fiscal year.

Now, if Poland were not to resume paying its debts, the U.S. Government is obligated to make good on these guaranteed loans to banks and exporters.

Poland has an outstanding debt of approximately $900 million in direct U.S. Government credits; $244 million of that, Export-Import Bank and $656 million CCC.

There is an additional $800 million in U.S. Government guaranteed CCC credits through private banks and exporters. An additional $1.3 billion owed to private U.S. banks.

And that's the extent of my knowledge, such as it is.

Q. Do you know what the figure is on the amount that's been paid out so far to date on the Polish debt? On the CCC credits?

MR. SPEAKES. By the U.S. Government in guarantees, no, I don't.

MR. ALLIN. I think it is about $450 million.

Q. And how much more have they—

MR. ALLIN. And we paid the last 2 years.

Q. How much have we gotten from the Polish Government? Have they paid us anything back?

MR. ALLIN. There may have been some payments last year. I don't think there have been any this year. There have not been payments on the direct—which Larry mentioned there in the $900 million that is outstanding.

Q. So $450 million has gone out of the U.S. Treasury?

MR. ALLIN. Well, they are still obligated to pay that to us. They now owe that money to us whereas in the question of direct credits, that is—excuse me, in the question of liabilities that have not come due, they owe that money to banks and exporters.

Q. Yes, but the U.S. Government has paid that much out and has not—I mean again for Poland? Correct?

MR. ALLIN. We paid it out because under the obligations of the guaranteed loan to the bankers and exporters we have that requirement.

Q. But you are saying we haven't gotten anything back this year and maybe a little bit last year?

MR. ALLIN. Yes, not to my knowledge.

Q. Out of the $346 million for FY'83, has the United States paid any of that back to the banks and exporters yet?

MR. ALLIN. No, no. That is FY'83. To my knowledge I don't know if any of it has come due. It comes due at different times through the year.

Q. But that is money that has not yet gone from the U.S. Treasury?

MR. ALLIN. Right.

Q. Do they pay them interest, and how much is the interest?

MR. ALLIN. That is principle and interest.

Q. Principle plus interest.

. . . .

---

[91] For the text of the proclamation issued on October 27 terminating Poland's most-favored-nation status, see *Weekly Compilation of Presidential Documents,* November 1, 1982, p. 1397.

[92] The question was raised at the White House Press briefing that had begun at 12:37 p.m.

Document 282

Statement by the Under Secretary of Agriculture for International Affairs and Commodity Programs (Lodwick), Vienna, October 29, 1982[93]

U.S.-Soviet Grain Consultations

We have just concluded the first session of regular, semi-annual grain consultations for the 7th year of the U.S.–USSR grain agreement,[94] which extends through September 30, 1983. During these talks, we followed the same basic agenda covered in past consultations, including a thorough review of the world supply/demand situation, U.S. supplies, possible Soviet import needs, and the record of purchases and shipments thus far for this year.

The Soviets confirmed that they purchased and shipped about 6.1 million metric tons of wheat and about 7.6 million metric tons of corn from the United States during the 6th year and that thus far, purchases for the 7th year delivery total about 1.6 million metric tons of corn. It was reported that purchases of grain from all origins for shipment in the July–December 1982 period total around 12 to 13 million metric tons, but that there could yet be some further purchasing for that shipment period. This slow-down had been projected by the Soviets during the previous consultations. No specific indication of the 1982 crop size was given but it was noted that this was the fourth consecutive year of disappointing outturn.

A key point is that during these talks we officially advised the Soviet Union that, in addition to the 8 million metric tons provided for in the agreement, the United States would make available an additional 15 million metric tons for Soviet purchase during the 7th agreement year (October 1, 1982–September 30, 1983), without the necessity of further consultations. (No proportion of wheat and corn was specified.)

We also stated that for any Soviet purchases made against the 15 million metric tons during November and shipped within 180 days, the United States is extending the same assurances that are now given under Article 2 to the basic 8 million metric tons of trade. It was explained that the Soviets do not need to complete purchases of the basic 8 million metric tons before they buy against the 15 million metric tons and take advantage of these additional supply assurances. At this time, the Soviets have contracted for 1.6 million metric tons of the basic 8 million metric tons. The remaining 6.4 million metric tons may be purchased at any time during the year and will be covered by Article 2 assurances throughout the year.

At this stage, and particularly this year, it is simply too early to judge what total Soviet grain import requirements for the current October–September year will be or what amount may come from the United States Based on our talks, however, I do believe that, in view of both the steps being taken to resume expansion of livestock feeding and the continued improvement of handling capacity for importing grains, large imports will continue. The Soviets indicated that their imports in the coming year are very unlikely to exceed the past year's level and perhaps might be noticeably less, depending upon their crop and the availability of funds. They said that any decline might be larger for feedgrains than for wheat, depending on the final outcome of their corn crop. It was indicated that their 1982 wheat crop was larger but poorer in quality than last year. They added, however, that their long-term plan is to become gradually self-sufficient in wheat but would require continued substantial imports of feedstuffs.

Prospects for our own trade, I believe, are very good. With regard to trade above 8 million metric tons, the Soviet side indicated that the United States had moved in the right direction but they asked a number of clarifying questions and showed particular concern about the limited duration of the offer of extra supply assurances. My impression is that these steps will enable the Soviets to take a larger portion of their grain imports from us this year than would otherwise have been the case. Moreover, supplies from certain other origins are limited this season and the Soviets are well-aware that with our marketing system they can be certain of getting competitive prices, the types of grain they want, unmatched flexibility in loading, delivery and vessel size, as well as other services to accommodate the Soviet market most efficiently. I think there is a good chance that the volume

[93] Source: Department of Agriculture, *Major News Releases and Speeches*, October 29–November 12, 1982, pp. 19–22.

[94] For the text of the agreement signed on October 20, 1975, see 26 UST 2971.

of our trade could exceed any previous October–September level, especially if Soviet needs should hold at the 40 million metric ton level or if the Southern Hemisphere corn corp is disappointing next March–April.

During the meeting, I indicated that the additional supply assurances available on grain purchases above the basic 8 million metric ton level would also apply to any other U.S. agricultural products purchased by the Soviet Union during November and shipped within 180 days. At the same time, I emphasized that there are abundant exportable crops, not only of wheat and corn but of rice, soybeans and other commodities as well, which are now available from the United States. We also pointed out the size of the Soviet purchases could be important not only as a signal for U.S. farmers as to the size of crops they should produce in both 1983 and 1984 but also as a key longer-run factor in the evolution of U.S. farm programs and in the general availability of grain on the world market at prices reflecting most efficient production.

It was agreed that the two sides will remain in close contact over the coming months. The United States indicated that, should Soviet purchases for the 7th year begin to approach the 23 million metric ton level now available, the United States would promptly propose further consultations, as provided for in the agreement, to review supply availabilities and Soviet needs again.

This would be done to assure that the agreement, at all times, serves the purpose of facilitating trade. In addition, it was tentatively agreed that the next regular session of consultations will be held during the last week of March 1983.

The Soviets cited a number of continuing concersn about the quality of U.S. grain. We agreed to continue our work with the Soviets and grain companies in an effort to improve the arrival quality of the U.S. grain. Specifically, plans were confirmed for a team of Soviet specialists to visit the United States for about 10 days beginning November 16 to study the wheat scab situation.

Under the terms of the 5-year U.S.–USSR grain supply agreement, which began in October 1976 and was recently extended for a 7th year, the Soviet Union buys at least 6 million metric tons of U.S. grain (3 of wheat and 3 of corn) annually.

This was the twelfth regular session of consultations under the agreement. The Soviet delegation was headed by Deputy Minister of Foreign Affairs Boris Gordeev.

Document 283

Letter From the Assistant Secretary of State for Congressional Relations (Moore) to Senator William Armstrong, November 4, 1982[95]

Soviet Use of Forced Labor in the Construction of the Trans-Siberian Pipeline

DEAR SENATOR ARMSTRONG: Conference Report No. 97–891 dated September 29[96] accompanying H.R. 6956[97] directed the Secretary to undertake an investigation into allegations that forced labor is being employed, and human rights violated, by the Soviet authorities in the construction of the Trans-Siberian gas pipeline.

There is clear evidence that the Soviet Union is using forced labor on a massive scale. This includes the use of political prisoners. We have information from a variety of sources which confirms that the Soviets routinely employ a portion of their 4 million forced laborers, the world's largest forced labor population, as unskilled workers on domestic pipeline construction. It cannot yet be conclusively established whether such labor is being used specifically on the export pipeline project, but a number of reports suggest that forced labor has been used in some of the site preparation and other preliminary work on the export pipeline including clearing the forests, leveling the right-of-way, building roads, and constructing living quarters.

There is, in fact, a long history to the use of forced labor in the Soviet Union. This has included the use of forced labor—including thousands of political prisoners—on numerous large-scale development pro-

[95] Source: Department of State files.

[96] *Making Appropriations for the Department of Housing and Urban Development and for Sundry Independent Agencies, Boards, Commissions, and Corporations and Offices*, Conference Report on H.R. 6956, Ninety-seventh Congress, Second Session, House of Representatives Report No. 97–871 (Washington, D.C., 1982).

[97] For text of H.R. 6956 (P.L. 97–272), Department of Housing and Urban Development Independent Agencies Appropriations Act, 1983, enacted September 30, 1982, see 96 Stat. 1162.

jects. The Baikal-Amur rail line, the Bielomorsk and Volga-Don canals, the Moscow subway, and the Kama River truck plant are a few of the better known Soviet projects built with forced labor. Among the groups that Soviet authorities traditionally press into forced labor are political prisoners and prisoners of conscience convicted for "anti-Soviet agitation" or under broadly-worded "hooliganism" and "parasitism" laws. For nearly thirty years, complaints have been registered in the International Labor Organization, and in other international bodies, against the use of such laws to punish and exploit political and religious dissidents in the Soviet Union.

The Soviet authorities not only have failed to provide responses satisfactory to the ILO on any of these complaints, but also have attacked the ILO supervisory machinery itself. Their continuing refusal to cooperate with the ILO authorities puts the burden of proof on the Soviet Union with regard to the numerous and grave charges of forced labor lodged against them. We strongly believe that the Soviet authorities should open all of their labor camps and large-scale labor brigades to independent international investigation.

We welcome Congressional interest in this question. Forced labor in the USSR is a human rights issue of deep concern to the administration, as expressed most recently in our official statement of September 22.[98] Decency compels us to express our distress at the Soviet Union's exploitation of forced labor. For those who believe in the promotion of world peace through law, it is crucial that the international community investigate and demand remedial action when confronted with serious charges of violations of international agreements. Obviously, the closed nature of Soviet society renders difficult the discovery of facts on this issue, as well as the production of convincing evidence. But be assured that we will continue diligently to conduct this investigation. We also are pursuing this issue vigorously through the ILO.

As our preliminary report, I am transmitting under this cover a copy of the administration's statement of September 22 and a packet of reports and documents which will provide for you the status of our efforts up to now. This packet includes a historical summary of Soviet forced labor questions before the ILO; a study entitled "The Soviet Forced Labor System," which includes maps and graphics of the pipeline network and forced labor camps; documentation and testimony from hearings sponsored by the Frankfurt-based International Society for Human Rights; and a summary of actions by other governments and international labor bodies.[99] Intelligence information pertinent to the issue will be made available through the House and Senate Intelligence Committees.

Sincerely,

Powell A. Moore

Document 284

Transcript of a Press Conference by President Reagan, November 11, 1982 (Extracts)[1]

Brezhnev's Death; Comparison of U.S. and Soviet Ways of Life

The President. Before taking your questions, I want to share with you just briefly my reflections on the important events that we've witnessed today. From Moscow, we've learned of the death of President Brezhnev—a man who played a major role in world affairs for more than 2 decades. Here in the White House, I met with Phil Habib about our plans to help bring peace to the Middle East where the opportunity for progress has been fundamentally improved by recent developments in that region. And also today, the space shuttle was successfully launched.

Once again, we will expand mankind's opportunities for enriching the human experience through peaceful exploration of the universe. Those events could have a critical impact on our future—a future we face with confidence and resolve. If there is

[98] For text of this statement, see Department of State *Bulletin*, November 1982, p. 41.

[99] None of these reports or documents is printed.

[1] Source: White House Press Release, November 11, 1982, Office of the Press Secretary to the President; printed also in *Weekly Compilation of Presidential Documents*, November 15, 1982, pp. 1457, 1459–1460, 1462, 1464. For the full text, see *ibid.*, pp. 1457–1465. The press conference, which began at 8 p.m., took place in the East Room of the White House.

a lesson for us, it is that we, as a free people, must always be prepared for change so that when it comes we're ready to meet new challenges and opportunities. Our system of government is unique and best able to adapt to change and move forward without disruption or break in continuity of purpose.

I want to underscore my intention to continue working to improve our relationship with the Soviet Union. Our two nations bear a tremendous responsibility for peace in a dangerous time—a responsibility that we don't take lightly. Earlier this year, we put forth serious and far-reaching proposals to reduce the levels of nuclear and conventional forces. I want to reconfirm that we will continue to pursue every avenue for progress in this effort. But we shouldn't delude ourselves. Peace is a product of strength, not of weakness—of facing reality and not believing in false hopes.

Today we honor American veterans—men and women who, by their courage and dedication, protected our freedom and independence. In the wake of events in the Soviet Union, we remain hopeful for a better relation. Conscious of our national interest and determined to remain a free people, I can think of no better day than Veterans Day to rededicate ourselves to peace and to do those things necessary to maintain the peace and to preserve our freedom.

Now, Jim, I believe you—

Q. Mr. President, who will be leading the U.S. delegation to Leonid Brezhnev's funeral? If you won't be going, how come? And also, aside from your personal hopes for peace, do you have reason to believe that the next coming months might see the new Soviet leadership flexing its muscle a bit and a period of increased tension coming about?

THE PRESIDENT. Well, answering the last part first. No, I don't anticipate that as they make this transition. And we certainly can hope that there won't be anything of the kind. But with regard to the service, we've had no direct official word yet on anything about the service, although we are in communication directly with them. And it was just a plain case of looking at schedules and my own scheduling calling for visits here by a head of state next week and it was felt that it would be better for George[2] to head that delegation. But it will be an appropriate and a very distinguished delegation.

Q. So it will be—

THE PRESIDENT. That what?

Q. It will be the Vice President then who will be heading the delegation?

THE PRESIDENT. This is what we're considering now. No final decisions have been made because, as I say, we're waiting to hear some word about the services.

Q. If there is a period of tension, how would you respond?

THE PRESIDENT. Well, we've had periods of tension before and I—I can just—you can't guess that in advance or what the answer would be, except that I think we'd—We must remember that our goal is and will remain a search for peace and we would try to find the best way to achieve that. And, incidentally, I believe that we can continue that search without my attendance at the services.

. . . .

Q. Mr. President, the Polish Government announced that they are about to free Lech Walesa. And as you've mentioned, Mr. Brezhnev is dead and a new Soviet leadership is coming into power. Is there any thought in your mind that this would be a good time for you to take some big step—even a symbolic step—to—that would lead to the lessening of tensions between East and West? And are you thinking of taking any initiatives that would give the world a signal that you would like that to come about?

THE PRESIDENT. We have been trying to do that in the area of quiet diplomacy, tried in the summit conference, tried in the NATO conference, of various things. We are prepared and ready—and they know that—about trying to have a better relation. But it's going to require some action, not just words. For 10 years détente was based on words from them and not any deeds to back those words up. And we need some action that they—it takes two to tango—that they want to tango also.

Q. But are you willing to take the first step at this stage, at this juncture?

THE PRESIDENT. Well, there are some people that have said I took the first step with lifting the grain embargo. Have we gotten anything for it?

. . . .

[2] Vice President George Bush.

Q. Sir, you like to describe yourself as an optimist—a man who sees opportunities instead of problems. And in that light, I would like to hear what you think are the opportunities that the United States now has with the death of President Brezhnev?

THE PRESIDENT. I don't think that the death of President Brezhnev is a factor in this—of what opportunities we might have. I have felt for a long time that we have an opportunity because while the entire world, including the Soviet Union and ourselves, is involved in a deep recession and deep economic problems—all of us—it would seem to me that out of those troubles, that might be a time where, in a cooperative sense, we could find out that we'll all be far better off if we decide to get along with each other instead of one pursuing an aggressive policy and the other one resisting that and so forth.

So, I am optimistic that—and would have been without his death today—continue to be optimistic that we can get together.

. . . .

Q. Mr. President, in 2 weeks the United States will celebrate Thanksgiving. Given the passing of Brezhnev, inevitably there are comparisons between the two systems. Could you take just a minute to tell Americans why at this time they especially should be thankful for their blessings and give a comparison of the two systems?

THE PRESIDENT. Yes, because I think the comparison is so obvious and you don't even have to use our own country. Turn to some of the newer and the developing countries, and those that have chosen our way, the free way, free trade, democracy, are so far ahead in standard of living and the happiness of their people than the others that have chosen the other, the controlled, the authoritarian way, and I think here is —Lincoln said it then and it is truer even today, this is the last best hope of men on Earth. We are freer than any other people, we have achieved more than any other people, and if you looked around this room—I thought the other day, when we had all those representatives from all over the world, all of those representatives in this room, who were here to look at our election, to learn how they could spread the word about that kind of freedom in their own countries and in other countries on the other continents, I thought that we could have a meeting of Americans in this room, and the ethnic heritage of the Americans in this room would be as diverse and there would be as many represented as there were in those hundreds of people who have come from foreign lands here today, and here we all live together proudly as Americans, in spite of that difference in birth. There just isn't any comparison with what we have and what we have to be thankful for . . .

. . . .

Document 285

Statement by the Vice President (Bush), Moscow, November 14, 1982[3]

Condolences on Brezhnev's Death

On behalf of the President of the United States, I wish to express the condolences of the American people to the Soviet people on the death of President Leonid Il'ich Brezhnev. We wish to convey our deep sympathies to the late President's family.

Leonid Brezhnev was the leader of the Soviet Union for nearly two decades. He was a strong man, a fierce fighter for his deeply held convictions. Now, the enormous burdens and responsibilities of leadership will be passed on to others who will navigate the Soviet Union's ship of state in the years to come.

I have led this American delegation to Moscow on this solemn occasion to symbolize my nation's regard for the Soviet people at this moment of loss and to signify the desire of the United States to continue to work for positive relations between our two countries.

It is in this spirit of seriousness and hope that we have come to Moscow. We have come to declare to the Soviet leaders, to the Soviet people and to the world, that the

---

[3] Source: Press Release, November 14, 1982, Office of the Press Secretary to the Vice President. Bush's statement was made upon his arrival in Moscow where he was to head the U.S. delegation attending the funeral of President Brezhnev on November 15. The Vice President came to Moscow from Nigeria, the third stop in his projected seven-nation African tour that had begun on November 10.

United States is devoted to the pursuit of peace and a reduction of global tensions. We seek a world of greater harmony, not only between the two great super powers, but for all nations. It is our fervent hope that today's massive expenditures for arms can be reduced and that the world's standard of living, especially for the impoverished, can be greatly improved.

In all of this, we are realistic. Fears, suspicions, and distrust must be replaced by hope, by trust, by mutual cooperation. The barriers that now divide nations and regions can be dismantled and discarded. To accomplish these lofty goals we must look to strong men and women, men and women of courage, patience, and perseverance. Fortunately, they are human characteristics that can and must be brought to the fore.

This spirit of hope, which I mentioned before, is with us all. As we pay our respects to a renowned leader, let us also take this occasion to give serious thought to the great and positive opportunities that are before us all.

Document 286

Transcript of a Press Conference by the Secretary of State (Shultz), Moscow, November 15, 1982[4]

U.S. Policy Toward the Soviet Union

Q. Mr. Secretary, I wonder if you would address yourself to the question of what should be understood by the high level of American representation at Mr. Brezhnev's funeral. And should it be taken in context with other events such as the end of the pipeline sanctions[5] and Mr. Reagan's message to the effect that he would like to see an improvement in relations after the transition period in the Soviet Union.[6] What does your visit and Mr. Bush's visit here signify? Is it a signal?

SECRETARY SHULTZ. Exactly what the President said. It is an expression on the one hand of our respect for a human being and condolences being expressed to President Brezhnev and the peoples of the Soviet Union. It is also an expression (also like the President said) that if constructive behavior emerges on the part of the Soviet Union, the United States is prepared to respond and is prepared for a more constructive relationship than we've had in past years.

Q. Mr. Secretary, the Soviets have in one form or another been publicizing a rather long list of grievances as regards U.S. foreign policy even before October 27 but certainly since President Brezhnev's October 27 speech.[7] Are you bringing any sort of message from the Government of the United States, the President of the United States, that there is room for conciliation, negotiation, change on both sides?

SECRETARY SHULTZ. Well, I can't really imagine why anyone would have grievances against our policies and our foreign policies. They are constructive. Our efforts are for problem-solving all around the world. We must of course maintain our strength, our strength in our defense capabilities, the strength of our economy, our will power. These are things which are present and at the same time, as we have demonstrated, all over the world, we have a constructive point of view—we are part of the solution, not part of the problem and our message here is the same.

Q. Mr. Shultz, how would you characterize Yuri Andropov? I am wondering what this administration thinks about him—personally, as a man.

SECRETARY SHULTZ. I don't think it's useful for me to speculate about the nature of various Soviet personalities, including Mr. Andropov. I've never met him so I think it's better to let that emerge.

Q. Mr. Secretary, what do you feel are the possibilities for an improvement in U.S.-Soviet relations now that there is a change of leadership?

SECRETARY SHULTZ. There is the same possibility that there has been. United States policy has been clear, it has not changed. It is a policy of realism, of strength, of willingness to work on prob-

---

[4] Source: Department of State Press Release 349, November 15, 1982; printed also in Department of State *Bulletin*, January 1983, pp. 59–62. The press conference took place at Spaso House.

[5] For the text of President Reagan's address, November 13, lifting the sanctions, see document 165.

[6] The President's remarks were made at his press conference on November 11; for extracts, see document 284.

[7] For the text in English translation of Brezhnev's speech on October 27 to Soviet military officials in the Kremlin, see *Current Digest of the Soviet Press*, November 24, 1982, pp. 1–3.

lems together and the expectation if that can be done successfully, everyone will be better off as a result. That's been our policy. That is our policy, and we want to make it clear to the new Soviet leadership that that remains in place.

Q. Mr. Secretary, have you been offered any high-ranking meetings while you are here?

SECRETARY SHULTZ. We have just arrived and in my brief meeting with Ambassador Dobrynin in Washington when I went to the Soviet Embassy to sign the book of condolences we talked briefly about it and I simply said I would be here, the Vice President would, I wasn't sure of his precise schedule at the time, and that if it were possible to see people in the Soviet leadership we would like to do that. But we can also understand that it is a busy time and it might not be possible, so as of right now I know of no appointments.

Q. I believe your predecessor, General Haig, referred to the Carter grain embargo as a blunder and some people now refer to the pipeline sanctions as blunder. Will you please comment on that?

SECRETARY SHULTZ. I would only comment without connecting the two that we now have the basis for a broader strategic approach to our economic relationships with the Soviet Union, and the emergence of a substantial agreement with our allies, one that has provided the occasion for the lifting of those sanctions. The sanctions, I think certainly did call attention to the problem, have registered the President's very strong feeling that the events in Poland in particular are events that we must register ourselves on beyond just talking about them, and at this point we are very pleased. Our allies have joined us, we have joined with them, it is a mutual thing to develop a broad economic strategy here.

Q. Mr. Secretary, I wonder if I could ask you a question here which goes, it seems to me, to the heart of the relationship with this country. For about 21 months the Reagan administration has done a variety of things specifically in the field of security—increasing the budget and so forth—to what the Soviets regard as tremendous proportions. They have been waiting for some time and now they have cranked themselves up just before Mr. Brezhnev died to start to reciprocate.

Do you think that you and Mr. Bush by coming here have something concrete to tell these people? That something can be done to stop this vicious circle, or is there anything else you can say on this particular matter?

SECRETARY SHULTZ. Obviously, something can be done to moderate behavior all around. I would say first of all I think your account of the sequence of things is not the way I see it—quite the reverse. The steady, relentless buildup of Soviet military capacity has in effect forced the United States after quite a period of not pushing its defense establishment forward powerfully, has in effect forced us to look to our defenses and our strength and I might say that I believe everybody knows that we have it. We have a tremendous economy, a very productive economy, so we are able to do that and sustain that. It is not a question of us suddenly increasing our efforts in this regard and the Soviets deciding that they better do so also. It is quite the reverse. Their efforts have been very strong and sustained. And we have had to raise our sights and we will continue to do so and we will maintain the strength of our defenses. Now, I presume that everyone, not only ourselves, but our allies would prefer a world in which we do not have to spend so much of our efforts on purely military means. And if so, we are ready to work at that, as is evidenced by the President's arms reduction proposal, as an example.

Q. Mr. Secretary, a top American diplomatic source said that we must try to be as forthcoming as possible with the Soviets now. Could you elaborate on that, other than what that means?

SECRETARY SHULTZ. The Ambassador is here and we will let him elaborate.

AMBASSADOR. This is a collaborative operation here. We are talking to a new leadership here and we are reiterating our position. It is very clear to the new leadership.

SECRETARY SHULTZ. I don't think the message is complicated. That is what makes it a good message. It is a simple message. And it is that we are realists. We will stay that way, we are strong, we will stay that way, we are constructive and we are ready to solve problems and we will continue ready to do so, ready to respond, and if that takes place then the world can be better for everyone.

Q. Mr. Secretary, that means your happening to be here is not necessarily to carry a new message but to restate a standing message from the United States. You are not bringing anything new in the way of proposals from the administration for easing the situation between us.

SECRETARY SHULTZ. I think our basic policy is clear. We have sought to make it clear. The President has and we have emphasized, particularly right now, our readiness to work for a more constructive relationship than the one we have had in the recent past. You might say that is point three in the four-point list that I gave. All four points are there, I only sought to put a little emphasis on number 3.

Q. Mr. Secretary, could you bring us up to date on the status of the two negotiations going on in Geneva on arms limitations issues.

SECRETARY SHULTZ. I don't know that there is too much to be said there. They are going on. They are going on in a businesslike manner. The people who are conducting the negotiations are professionals—skillful people. We know that our negotiators are such and they tell me that their estimate of the Soviet negotiators is that they are professional, competent people who are businesslike in their approach so the negotiations are going on and I don't think that I want to characterize them further.

Q. If I may follow up for just a moment and make my question more precise, I think the real question is do you see any progress in these talks or are they just at a stage where both sides are just exchanging positions without any give occurring on either side?

SECRETARY SHULTZ. Well, I think there is an intensive exchange of positions which I suppose in the process of explaining tends to develop them in more richness and detail, so that's where I will leave that.

Q. Mr. Secretary, can you explain the *quid pro quo* from the lifting of the pipeline sanctions? Apart from promising to make studies on East-West trade, it's not exactly clear what concrete commitments the Western Europeans have taken in response to our lifting the sanctions.

SECRETARY SHULTZ. Well, we haven't conducted our discussions with the Europeans along that line at all. We haven't discussed the sanctions as I have discussed these matters with the Foreign Ministers going back to the New York U.N. Session when I started with them. And while they were talking with me about it, and at the La Sapiniere meeting of the NATO Foreign Ministers—our efforts were to find the basis for a common strategic understanding of how we would conduct our economic relationships with the Soviet Union. The general idea is that we're not looking for a trade war, however, we are looking to focus on certain aspects of trade and finance—aspects of trade that are related to the military capability of the Soviet Union, to the strategic posture of the Soviet Union, and in view of the huge expenditures that we and our Allies are undertaking for our defense. The only reason we're undertaking them is that the level of defense effort in the Soviet Union is so great. In view of that it makes no sense to subsidize the Soviet economy. So, based on those principles, we will work together to develop a strategy in the meantime. The COCOM list is being examined and strengthened and a stronger administrative capacity is being connected to it. An intensive study of energy alternatives will be undertaken. In the meantime, the governments involved have undertaken not to have any additional purchases of Soviet gas while people look around and reflect and see what the alternatives are. The agreement at Versailles[8] to examine the flows of trade and finance will be implemented in an administrative capacity. There is renewed emphasis on working out export credit arrangements. So, there are a whole series of things that are involved. Some are in the nature of immediate action, some are in the nature of a work program. I think in the long long run, well, of course, you can not say what a work program will produce. It is always possible that it won't produce anything, except my own estimate is that the effort to find a better strategic posture is likely to be a very productive and worthwhile effort in the long run.

Q. Excuse me, Mr. Secretary, for interrupting you. Does the change in leadership in the Soviet Union increase in any way your view of the possibility of a summit meeting?

SECRETARY SHULTZ. Our attitude toward a summit meeting remains as being in favor of one if it is well prepared so that it is possible to imagine that something constructive might come out of it. And I think the same would hold now with a new Soviet leadership. We will just have to see, but in principle the President is willing to have such a meeting but only if it can be a constructive one and have a constructive outcome.

---

[8] For the text of the final communiqué issued on June 6 at the conclusion of the eighth economic summit of the industrialized nations at Versailles, see document 93.

Q. Mr. Secretary, a recent Soviet speech seems to say that the way to peace is through military might.

SECRETARY SHULTZ. Soviet military might has been increasing. That is a description of their policy. We can speak about our own policy which is to be strong, to develop our strength, to see that it is based solidly on a very strong and productive economy and at the same time to say beyond that, if you want to try to work toward a world that is less tense, that has more constructive possibilities in it, that includes the possibilities of reductions in armaments, we are prepared to do so.

Q. Mr. Secretary, is it present U.S. policy to encourage American trade with the Soviets and will you please comment on the visit this week of hundreds of American businessmen to Moscow?

SECRETARY SHULTZ. I think the fact that the U.S. delegation [is] coming to Moscow, as large as it is and I might say as distinguished as it is (there are some very important and strong business leaders included in that delegation), is an indication of the fundamental interest and goodwill of the American people. And in a sense that complements the message that President Reagan enunciated in his various statements which have been quoted here—that we are ready to work with the Soviet Union if the circumstances are right. I think the fact of the matter is that the circumstances have not been right, they have not been conducive to the expansion of trade particularly but along the lines of the answers to various questions here, if the circumstances change, the fact that so many high level businessmen are coming suggests the interest and the potential for a response. When people come here, that is not trade, that is an exhibition of a willingness to trade. For an actual trade to take place, it requires a lot more. I might say that there is an interesting closing of the circle here. I believe that the last time I was in Moscow in 1973—almost 10 years ago—that was the meeting at which the first American business group met with the governmental counterparts to start this process. That is still in existence although it has been on a very slow track in recent years.

Q. Mr. Secretary, when you speak of these circumstances, what exactly do you have in mind. Can you just speculate?

SECRETARY SHULTZ. We have expressed our concerns in various ways. There are a variety of human rights concerns that the President and the American people generally feel very strong about. We really do care a lot about human beings in the United States. There are regional issues of various dimensions, there is arms control, there is a variety of things through which progress conceivably could be made, and progress has to change the atmosphere.

Q. Mr. Secretary, I was wondering if in the last 2 or 3 days if the Soviet leadership has done or said anything that will make you hope for an improvement in relations between the two countries. Is there any sign at all?

SECRETARY SHULTZ. I think it is really too early in the emergence of a new leadership to be trying to read the tea leaves that way. They are in the process of getting organized. We will see what comes forward. In the meantime, we will try to express our own viewpoint. The President has, and supplementing and complementing his view, there is the fact that the Vice President has broken off from a very important trip to Africa, to which he will return, and he will complete all of the visits. But nevertheless, he broke off from that visit to come here—all as an expression of the importance that the United States attaches to the Soviet Union and to our relationship with the Soviet Union.

Q. Can we perhaps meet with you again before you leave Moscow?

SECRETARY SHULTZ. It depends upon the schedule. Everything hangs on the schedule. We have some meetings tomorrow morning. I do not know, I cannot speak for the Vice President's schedule. I do not know, precisely, when he will return. So there is a lot of uncertainty there but if there is anything to say as a result of whatever happens here, we will certainly want to get you together and tell you what it is. I have always been taught by John Hughes, "If you have any news, do not sit on it." Chances are it is very unlikely that we will have any news. But if we do we will see that you get it.

Q. Did you say who these meetings are with tomorrow morning?

SECRETARY SHULTZ. They are not with Soviet officials. Mr. Pym has gotten in touch with me and I hope I can get together with him. He has made the request and Mr. Genscher of the Federal Republic of Germany has also requested that I talk with him. As you know, Mr. Kohl is in Washington so I suppose since we are not in Washington we had better have our own meeting to see what we think, and there may be some others.

Q. Will you be trying to meet with the Chinese before you leave sir?

SECRETARY SHULTZ. I do not have any scheduled meetings and I doubt that it is possible. We checked schedules.

Document 287

Transcript of a Press Conference by the Secretary of State (Shultz), November 18, 1982 (Extacts)[9]

U.S.-Soviet Relations

SECRETARY SHULTZ. Good afternoon. Anyone have a question? (Laughter)

GREG NOKES, AP. Mr. Secretary, now that there is a new leadership in the Soviet Union, and you have met with the new leader, Yuri Andropov, can you tell us what opportunities exist for improved U.S.-Soviet relations and discuss our strategy for dealing with Moscow in the post-Brezhnev era?

SECRETARY SHULTZ. First, I think, it's important to emphasize that we have had a policy with respect to the Soviet Union. That policy is in place and will continue in place.

The policy is, first, to be realistic about what is going on both in terms of military capacity, its use, the human rights aspects of the situation and other things.

Second, to be fully alert to the importance of our own strength and the strength of our alliance in the face of Soviet behavior.

Third, to be willing, always, to work on problems and to try to work them out and to solve problems. The United States has always been in the forefront as part of the solution in the many problems that we have around the world. And we know, finally, that if problems can be solved, there are opportunities for a better world.

The President, with the emergence of new leadership in the Soviet Union, has made a number of statements emphasizing, let's say, the third point in that set of points. But I think we have to remember that the whole set of points are there. We stand ready to solve problems, work on them, but we also continue to be realistic, to regard the things that represent solutions of problems, not to be simply rhetoric, but to be deeds, and that will be our posture.

Q. Mr. Secretary, what would you regard as a meaningful signal from the new leadership in the Kremlin; a meaningful signal in the direction of easing relations?

SECRETARY SHULTZ. I hear this word "signal" all the time. It goes from little things that affect the way you're treated, and I might say that the Vice President and I and Ambassador Hartman were treated with great courtesy throughout our visit to the Soviet Union. People say that's a signal, and perhaps it is. But I think the things that we are really looking for, after all the signaling has taken place, is the substance of change in behavior on important matters.

Now, we are engaged in an active negotiation for arms reduction in Geneva and in Vienna. We are engaged, with our European allies, with the Soviet Union, and others, in active discussions in Madrid. So those are two settings, or three settings where discussions are going on right now and where we would welcome movement.

So those are in a sense the things that we want to see happen, and signals are fine, and indications that people are ready to sit down and talk seriously are fine, and we have given those signals ourselves. I think, as we move ahead, we will look for substantive responses.

Q. Could you please be specific about what—

SECRETARY SHULTZ. Let him follow, and then I'll come back to you.

Q. Would you expect to see within the foreseeable future another—are you talking about meetings and sitting down, would you expect to see any kind of summit meeting?

SECRETARY SHULTZ. The President has always been ready for a summit meeting if there is something worthwhile to be accomplished by the meeting. A meeting for the sake of a meeting doesn't really get you a lot. I think there does have to be a prospect of some genuine, positive result, and that has been the President's position and it remains so now.

Q. Could you specifically outline what steps the United States expects the Soviet

---

[9] Source: Department of State Press Release 351, November 18, 1982; printed also in Department of State *Bulletin*, January 1983, pp. 54–57. The press conference began at 4 p.m. and concluded at 4:31 p.m.

Union to take in the forums you just mentioned or elsewhere before improved relations can occur and what specific steps the United States is prepared to take to improve relations?

SECRETARY SHULTZ. As far as the details of steps are concerned, of course, we'll conduct our negotiations in those fora rather than this way. But, obviously, if you are engaged in a negotiation, the process of give-and-take is something that you look for and sense. We would be looking for those signs and that kind of movement, but I don't want to try to specify any explicit point.

Q. Mr. Secretary, a number of Soviet spokesmen this past week have argued that the United States is using trade as a political weapon. Do you believe that the United States has been doing this; do you believe that the United States sees trade as part of a larger political picture, and can you see trade possibly being divorced from politics?

SECRETARY SHULTZ. We must think of our relationships with the Soviet Union—you know, all of their dimensions, and while they aren't linked in any kind of tight way, certainly, they are related to each other. We have made that point; the pipeline sanctions, in a way, made that point, the political dimension of an economic relationship. And in our discussions with our friends in Europe and Japan, we have also been working with them on that very point to see if we can develop—and I believe we can and we are well on our way to doing so—a better sense of strategy for our economic relationships with the Soviet Union and her satellites.

That doesn't mean that all trade is subject to this kind of examination, but in certain critical categories and aspects we believe that it must be.

. . . .

Q. Mr. Secretary, very few American officials have had a chance to meet the new Soviet leader, Mr. Andropov, as you have. There are stories that he likes American food, American music, Chubby Checker records, that he speaks English; can you give us a little bit of your reaction to the man? (Laughter)

SECRETARY SHULTZ. There were Soviet soft drinks and Soviet food on the table where we sat. If he likes another kind of food, I can't say anything about that. There was no evidence of the things that you mentioned in the course of the meeting that we had.

What impact he will have as a leader of the Soviet peoples is something that, of course, we are very interested in and watching, and that remains to be seen.

Q. How did he strike you? Did he strike you as a man who had taken charge?

SECRETARY SHULTZ. Yes.

. . . .

Q. Mr. Secretary, could you give us some assessment of the recent diplomatic contacts between the Soviet Union and China?

SECRETARY SHULTZ. Well, of course, these developments have been taking place. We've been watching them and reading about them. I'm not privy to them, of course—don't know just what is taking place.

I do know some of the concerns the Chinese have. They are concerned about the Soviet presence in Afghanistan, and have said so; they are concerned about the behavior of the Soviet proxy state Vietnam and Kampuchea. So if through their discussions, they can persuade the Soviet Union to get out of Afghanistan and in effect get out of Kampuchea, so much the better.

Q. Mr. Secretary, in an earlier question, you seemed to hold out some hope that at some point a summit might be arrangeable. Were you suggesting that now—just to tie it down—it is premature?

SECRETARY SHULTZ. The discussion of a summit has kind of emerged out of thin air, as far as I can see. There has been no direct discussion with the Soviet Union representatives that I know of. It didn't come up in my discussion with Mr. Gromyko in New York, whenever that was, a couple of months or so ago;[10] and it didn't come up in the meeting the Vice President had with Mr. Andropov.[11]

That doesn't rule it out; it doesn't rule it in. It is exactly where I said it was. If there is

[10] Shultz met with Gromyko in New York on September 28 during the 37th session of the U.N. General Assembly.

[11] Vice President Bush met with Andropov in Moscow on November 15. For Bush's impressions of the meeting, see his remarks before the American Enterprise Institute, December 6, document 289.

something constructive and positive to be accomplished, the President is always willing, but he is not looking for a trip or a meeting for the sake of a trip or a meeting.

Q. Does that same criterion apply to your own meetings with Mr. Gromyko, and do you have any such meetings planned in the near future?

SECRETARY SHULTZ. We don't have a meeting planned in the near future, but it is always conceivable that one might take place.

Q. Mr. Secretary, going back to the question of trade with the Soviet Union, do you see the possibility that freer trade with the United States might be an inducement to the Soviet Union to behave in a way that you would like them to, as previous administrations have offered?

SECRETARY SHULTZ. I don't think it is worthwhile to think of things on a kind of a one-for-one basis like that. You have to think of the whole relationship, which is complicated and interrelated, and there are many important dimensions to it. We can all spell out what those are, and the potential of trade is one of them, but only one.

Q. Mr. Secretary, both the United States and the Soviet Union seem to be exchanging what you might describe as conciliatory "mood music," each side waiting for the other to take specific steps.

How long can just the mood music last?

SECRETARY SHULTZ. We'll have to see what takes place. I was, of course, at the funeral, standing on Red Square for 2½ hours, watching what was taking place. Of course, there is the "mood music" that everybody seems to have focused on, namely the statements that the President has made and like statements made on the other side.

There was other "mood music." It was quite startling. I don't know how many of you watched the funeral on television, but after the body of Mr. Brezhnev was put in the ground, and the members of the Politburo came up on top of that structure where they stand, it was as though somebody threw a switch, and suddenly martial music and a long march-by of troops. That was "mood music," too, I thought.

I think there are all of these dimensions, and we must remember the military strength that they have, and remember not to, in any way, allow what I think you perhaps properly call "mood music" to delude us or take us away from our own convictions that we must do what is necessary for our own defense.

Q. In your discussions, what discussion was there of the Reagan proposals for Middle East peace? Was there any discussion at all of Soviet Jewish emigration?

SECRETARY SHULTZ. I don't want to discuss the internal content of the discussion the Vice President and the Secretary General of the Soviet Union had.

Q. Was the topic raised at all?

SECRETARY SHULTZ. I said I don't want to discuss the content of the discussion. Those topics have been discussed a lot in other fora, and generally speaking, we always raise, particularly, the human rights concerns in any discussion that we have with a Soviet official; but I don't want to say more than that.

. . . .

Q. Mr. Secretary, in your discussion earlier of what specific steps the Soviets could take, you discussed the two arms control negotiations in Geneva, the MBFR talks in Vienna, and the CSCE conference in Madrid.

You didn't mention the regional issues which in the past you've put on your kind of hope list.

SECRETARY SHULTZ. They're on my list of things that we're concerned about. It's my concern list. But we don't have any talks going on with them about Afghanistan, for example.

We don't have any direct talks going on other than the conversations that we have had with their leadership, but there's no sort of negotiation as in the case of Geneva. That's why I didn't mention that.

Q. But would a Soviet withdrawal of some consequence from Afghanistan be a—I hate to use the word "signal"—but at least a sign that they're interested in a better relationship?

SECRETARY SHULTZ. It would be a fact, and a fact that would be a piece of constructive behavior. If things like that occur, if you add them up, they would add up to opportunities for much improved relationships.

Q. Is it positive, Mr. Secretary, if the Soviets were to reduce their troops along the Chinese frontier, would you regard that as a negative or a positive step?

SECRETARY SHULTZ. That's a matter for the Chinese and the Russians to discuss, and I don't have any comment on that.

. . . .

Q. Mr. Secretary, as a word of clarification, please, is it your intention for this news conference to end, leaving us with the impression that the U.S. position is that the Soviets will have to make the first substantive move before there can be a real change in U.S.-Soviet relations?

SECRETARY SHULTZ. We look for changes in behavior or indications of a willingness to discuss them. We have said we're willing to do so. I think if you look at the problems that are before us, on the whole they're problems that they have created, and so a willingness to be less creative is what is called for here.

But we're ready to get in and discuss and try to work things out in a careful, thoughtful way. You've been wanting to get a question in, so go ahead.

. . . .

Document 288

Remarks by the Secretary of Defense (Weinberger), Dubrovnik, Yugoslavia, December 3, 1982[12]

Weinberger's Visit to Yugoslavia

I really prefer the title Admiral, but they tell me that the correct address is Mr. Secretary, so I will use that, as I see it, somewhat lesser title.

We enormously appreciated and enjoyed the opportunity that we had to visit Yugoslavia, and for me it is the first time and an occasion that I've looked forward to for many, many years. I always worry when I come to a country that I know has made very nice preparations for our visit. Today I worried even more because I knew how rapidly and how skillfully you had to change the arrangements that had previously been made and I think it's a very convincing, and a very effective, demonstration of your skills in contingency planning. Whatever it was, it came out to be an extremely happy and a very fruitful visit and we have enjoyed ourselves thoroughly and are delighted that we came.

Our President asked me to convey, particularly, not only his greetings to the Presidency, but to the people of Yugoslavia. He carries on a tradition of all of his predecessors because every American President since the end of World War II has felt and expressed the very warm and deep admiration and appreciation of the qualities that have made Yugoslavia great; a fierce independence, an enormously effective and firm determination to preserve your independence, and your territorial integrity, and a willingness to make enormous sacrifices to achieve the goals of peace and freedom.

We all watched with enormous admiration the heroism that was exhibited from the very beginning of World War II, when you, almost alone of the subjugated nations, regained your independence and freedom against enormous odds. You spoke very eloquently and very correctly of the fine and warm relationships that have existed, and continue to exist, between our two countries, particularly between the military of the two countries.

It is our hope and belief, particularly on the basis of today's very helpful discussions, that perhaps our visit will have the effect of not only continuing but of strengthening and deepening the warmth of that relationship, not only between military and military, but now between personal friends. Among the other things about your great country that we have long admired was the magnificent leadership of your world statesman, Marshal Tito. When our plane was circling Belgrade this morning I was thinking about some of the events that were planned and I wrote out a little statement that I was going to put in the memorial book at Marshal Tito's memorial tomb. I hope I'll have an opportunity to do that tomorrow. But in the event that I don't, I have it with me here, and I would like permission to read it.

"In memory of Joseph Broz Tito, A world statesman who led his people in

---

[12] Source: *Public Statements of Secretary of Defense Weinberger*, 1982. Weinberger's remarks were made at a dinner given by the Yugoslav Federal Secretary for National Defense, Admiral Branko Mamula. Following his attendance at the meetings of the NATO Nuclear Planning group and NATO Defense Planning Committee in Brussels, November 30–December 2, Secretary Weinberger was making a one-day official visit to Yugoslavia, during which time he met with Defense Minister Mamula and President Petar Stambulic.

war and peace, and who, with far-sighted wisdom, successfully preserved an independent path for his country, and whose achievements and accomplishments will live long after him."

Now I would like all of you to rise and join with me in a toast to the President of Socialist Federal Republic of Yugoslavia, to long lasting friendship between our two countries.

Document 289

Address by Vice President Bush Before the American Enterprise Institute, December 6, 1982 (Extracts)[13]

Bush's Attendance at Brezhnev's Funeral; Impressions of Andropov

. . . .

My trip took me to seven African countries. About halfway through, I was diverted north, to attend a funeral service in Moscow.[14] Life often lays unexpected detours and juxtapositions in front of us. This time the juxtapositions were as striking as they were consciousness-raising. In a 48-hour period, we went from Nigeria to Moscow to Zimbabwe.

A few days ago on a morning television show I was asked what "struck" me about the funeral. Well, everything struck me; it was sheer sensory overload; the austere pageantry of the Kremlin, the goose-stepping soldiers, the immense beauty of the music; the body being drawn through Red Square—not, incidentally, by horses, but behind an armored personnel carrier. But what struck me most, after the images had subsided into memory was the fact that from start to finish there was not one mention of—God.

As you know, we Vice Presidents attend a lot of funerals. So as professional mourners, we tend to notice these things. Well—should it surprise, this lack of spiritual dimension? No; and yet, it did. It made a tremendous impact on me.

Shortly after returning to Africa from Moscow, I attended a dinner where I sat spellbound listening to an African Chief of State deliver one of the most spirited renditions of grace I have ever heard. He gave it first in Swahili; and then in English. The English was a courtesy to us, he explained, since God probably does not listen to prayers said in English.

This moving rendition of grace, I must say, was a kind of objective correlative. It drove home the remarkable change of atmosphere, scene, sentiment and spirit from Red Square.

. . . .

I know you want to hear a little about Mr. Andropov. Well, following the funeral, I spent about 40 minutes with him. Everyone's curious about Mr. Andropov, as well they should be. There's already been a spate of journalistic psychoanalyzing of the man, speculation about his alleged predilection for Chubby Checker, tennis, and Harold Robbins. As we all know, in the end, such speculation will not get us very far. This is uncertain stuff, too flimsy to allow us to extrapolate very much from so little. There's an excellent essay on the subject, incidentally, in last week's *Time* magazine, by Roger Rosenblatt. It's called "Looking For Mr. Goodpov."[15]

My impressions of him are naturally sketchy, inasmuch as we had less than an hour in which to size each other up. Since I was once Director of Central Intelligence and he was for 15 years head of the KBG, we were at least able to speak as spook to spook.

It's said that Soviet leaders fall into two categories: peasant and grandfather, Khrushchev and Brezhnev being, respectively, representatives of the genres. Mr. Andropov and I spoke through an interpreter, so there were no telling nuances of language that often give us a more revealing glimpse of a man than the words themselves.

But this much was clear: he is neither peasant nor grandfather. As head of an intelligence and secret police service for 15

---

[13] Source: Press Release, December 6, 1982, Office of the Press Secretary to the Vice President. The address was made at a luncheon at the Mayflower Hotel in Washington.

[14] Bush interrupted his African trip, November 10–24, to attend the funeral of Chairman Leonid I. Brezhnev in Moscow on November 15.

[15] *Time*, December 6, 1982, p. 100.

years, he had access to all foreign Soviet Reporting. He is well versed in Western methods and minds. In this sense he is a highly sophisticated man. Whether or not this will prove to be to our advantage, or cause for even deeper concern, remains to be seen.

Many have written of the KGB connection as totally negative. Without sounding defensive, let me suggest that anyone who had access to all the intelligence, all the reporting, might be well equipped to comprehend the true intentions of a foreign power than one who had had no experience in foreign affairs.

You and I know that we do not intend war—and yet we are often told: the Soviets, dealing from insecurity seasoned by vivid memories of wars fought on their home soil with enormous loss of blood, simply feel they can't trust our intentions.

I am convinced that anyone who has had access to all the data must objectively know that if a country goes in peace, it has absolutely nothing whatsoever to fear from the United States of America.

George Shultz and the President have ably and clearly stated what the tenor of our policy toward the Soviet Union will be: we will take them more at their actions than at their words. The President has said, "We are ready for a better relationship anytime they are." And so we are.

At the same time, the Secretary of State announced several days ago that the United States now holds conclusive proof that the Soviets have been waging chemical warfare in Afghanistan,[16] in direct violation of the 1925 Geneva Protocol on chemical warfare and the 1972 Biological and Toxin Weapons Convention. He called on other nations to deplore this. An editorial in the *Washington Post* noted, "An international public that could weep for Lebanon surely can mourn the evident thousands of victims of Soviet chemicals in Afghanistan, Laos and Cambodia . . . the cause needs help."[17]

Yet there is Georgi Korniyenko, First Deputy Foreign Minister, writing in *Newsweek*, ". . . we are for peaceful coexistence and the right of nations to choose independently what social systems they prefer."[18]Such, such are the antipodes.

Where Soviet chemical warfare in Afghanistan is concerned, I have this to say: the use of these toxins severely undermines our ability to deal confidently with the Soviet leadership in other areas. It is extremely difficult to negotiate in an atmosphere of trust and confidence with a nation that flaunts world opinion through the use of such egregiously inhumane weapons. If, on the other hand, the Soviets were to cease using them, this would be a signal which we would note and to which we could respond.

To call attention to Soviet chemical warfare, to Soviet expenditures on nuclear weapons, to Afghanistan, to Vietnam, to Angola, to Ethiopia, to South Yemen, to Libya, to the spread of terrorism throughout the world—does it all just amount to rhetoric?

We have been charged by some with having spoken too loudly while carrying not a big stick, but a twig. It would, I think, be an interesting research project for the AEI to undertake a comparison of actual U.S. and Soviet official language. My guess is that the researchers would discover no shortage of exuberant Soviet rhetoric. I remember the day President Reagan decided, in the face of abundant Soviet conventional force facing Western Europe, to proceed with the production—not, repeat, not deployment—of the neutron bomb. He was called "barbaric," "criminal," "inhuman," and "cannibalistic." But of course that was merely the Soviet press speaking, not the government.

A quasi-related aside. When I was sent to live in China, it took me weeks to get used to the heated anti-American rhetoric carried almost daily in the so-called "Red News," an English language summary of propagandistic outbursts often leveled at the United States of America. I got used to it, but I never liked it.

Rhetoric has its uses and abuses. Our purpose, in speaking frankly about the Soviets, has never been to humiliate them, but instead to use our ultimate weapon, a weapon more fearsome than the MX, than B–52's or Trident submarines; truth. It's considerably cheaper than missiles or sub-

---

[16] Shultz transmitted a report entitled "Chemical Warfare in Southeast Asia and Afghanistan: an update" by letter to Congress on November 29, 1982. The letter and The report dated November 1982 are printed, in full in Department of State *Bulletin*, December 1982, pp. 44–53. For the text of the section of the report on Afghanistan, see document 443.

[17] For the editorial entitled "Soviet Chemical War Goes On," see *Washington Post*, December 1, 1982, p. A26. This and following ellipsis of three periods appear in the source text.

[18] For the text of Korniyenko's article "A Plea for Good Relations," see *Newsweek*, November 29, 1982, p. 41.

marines, and needs no spare parts. On the walls of a building I once used to work in, there were these words inscribed: "You shall know the truth, and the truth shall set you free." Words men and women can at least try to live by; words that nations, too, can be guided by.

We will not refrain from speaking the truth; just as we will not refrain from responding to positive signals from the Soviet Union. That's a point we've made time and time and time again; but a point I find prudent to reiterate every chance I get.

At the same time, I do agree with a certain former Secretary of State that we need a kind of armistice—dare I call it détente? At least I'm among friends—here at home, between those who reject all negotiations as a trap and every agreement as a surrender and those who insist that most of our dangers are self-induced, to be remedied by unremitting pressure on our own government, and also those who want unilateral disarmament, what I call "preemptive surrender."

In the days ahead, as we, all of us, turn to Kremlinology, as we watch and wait and hope for encouraging signs, such an armistice here at home would accomplish much. There will be tremendous public pressure to seize on every puff of smoke, to read great significance into tea leaves and vodka splotches. There will be public pressure for fast and frequent administration comment on each of these portentous or unportentous developments. But too much talk might work against such an armistice: might create illusory expectations, high and low. This is a good time to be taciturn. Conservatives, meanwhile, need not fear: a softer voice doesn't presage a lighter stick, doesn't mean we're entertaining illusions about either the Soviet Union or Mr. Andropov. It might just mean that instead of giving speeches, we're quietly building bridges to Africa and other parts of the world that are turning to us, not only for what we have to offer them, but because of things we already have—like spiritual values, and a belief in God. As I think back to that cold November day in Moscow, it occurs to me that those are weapons that we just possibly might have more of here than they do at the Kremlin.

Thank you very much.

Document 290

Transcript of a Press Conference by the Secretary of State (Shultz), December 6, 1982 (Extract)[19]

Western European Views on U.S.-Soviet Relations

. . . .

Q. Mr. Secretary, in attempting to put together a strategy for dealing with the new Soviet leadership, do you bring with you any new approach, fresh ideas, or new initiatives that you expect to present as the American view as to how precisely this ought to move ahead?

SECRETARY SHULTZ. We continue to have the view that allied strength is the key to strengthened unity in all of its various dimensions, and so that's an important part of the objective of my trip, and it was of Cap Weinberger's trip.[20] And I don't see any reason to alter our thinking about that being a fundamental. We do have to keep in mind realistically the various things about East-West relationships and they consist in part of the military dimension and that highlights the importance of arms control negotiations. But they also include so-called regional issues and—I don't know how to describe the Madrid issues or human rights issues. So these are things that are in the picture. And we'll be comparing notes and seeing the extent to which there is a prospect for progress on these issues.

Q. It was on this trip a year ago when martial law was declared in Poland.[21] I wonder if you think, there have been reports now out of Warsaw for a couple of weeks, that the Polish Government may be about to propagate some kind of liberalization, real or otherwise. First of all, are you expecting something like that? Second of

---

[19] Source: Department of State Press Release 403, December 28, 1982. The press conference took place on board the Secretary's plane en route Andrews Air Force Base, Maryland, to Bonn, Germany. The Secretary was embarking on a seven-nation European trip, December 7–19, including attendance at the NATO ministerial meeting in Brussels, December 8–11.

[20] Regarding Weinberger's trip to Europe, see footnote 12 to document 288.

[21] Martial law was declared in Poland on December 13, 1981, while Secretary of State Haig was in Brussels for the North Atlantic Council ministerial meeting.

all, is the alliance in a position to deal with that, without it becoming as divisive an issue as martial law was in the first place?

SECRETARY SHULTZ. No, I don't think martial law was divisive. I think there was a united reaction from the alliance on those moves in Poland. Whatever is done by the Polish Government or announced by the Polish Government, is a better way to put it, will bear some analysis because you have a need to look beyond any announcement and see what reality has transpired. And you can lift martial law and then do other things and take away the effect of that or maybe not. So, I don't think that the moment somebody makes an announcement you try to react but you try to look into what it truly means and construct a thoughtful response and that's what was done in the first place. That's been done in various points in time between last year about this time and now. And no doubt that's what will be done again.

Q. Will you be talking about this with the allies?

SECRETARY SHULTZ. Oh, yes. We'll share perceptions and be ready to analyze and see about reactions we should take. But I think we all recognize that it is desirable to the extent we possibly can, to have a generally unified response.

Q. What would you regard as a mark of true liberalization, of true change in Poland?

SECRETARY SHULTZ. Well, there have been three main things that I think summarize pretty well the sorts of actions that we all would like to see. We would like to see people released from jail. We would like to see a legitimate dialogue taking place between the church and Solidarity and the government, and we would like to see martial law lifted, which means that people have a much greater measure of freedom and there is more openness in the society than is allowed by martial law. So what I am saying on that last part is that there are the words stand for,[?] and if you remove the words you have left the reality of what they stand for and that needs to be examined.

Q. Mr. Secretary, in point two, you are talking about dialogue between church (inaudible).

SECRETARY SHULTZ. Solidarity is an organization as such and it is also an idea that people have work, have rights to express themselves about the conditions of work, and have an impact on them as well as other aspects of their society. So I think that's the sense in which I mean that Solidarity still exists as an organization.

Q. Sir, a question on relations with the Soviet Union. You have said that before relations could be significantly improved there needs to be substantive actions by the Soviet Union, such as on arms control, Afghanistan, etc. Are the allies in agreement that we need to see substantive actions before relations can improve?

SECRETARY SHULTZ. Let me try to put it in a little different way, because there seems to be in people's minds an idea that our thought is that we just sort of sit there and the Soviet Union should do acts (inaudible) and at some point will decide yes there's been enough substance so that relationships can improve. That's not the way relationships improve. If there is an improvement it will take place as a result of a process. The process will be one, if it takes place through which discussions going on about important issues start resulting in outcomes that we agree on. If such a process takes place, that is in a sense that definition of an improved relationship (inaudible). So, we do have areas where we are negotiating, two in Geneva, one in Vienna, in Madrid. We have contacts, some of which we're not directly involved in, on other regional issues. It is said that the Chinese are concerned about Afghanistan, for instance, so they are talking to the Russians about it. I read that in your columns all the time. Well, if they succeed, that's a plus. So I think there has emerged this idea that we're just sitting there and we're looking for all sorts of actions and at some point we would say relationships have improved. But, as I say, I don't think that's the way that things happen, either happen in a plus direction or a negative direction. They happen as a result of a process and you get a gradual shift.

Q. Under that heading (inaudible) are you detecting any such shifts on the part of the Soviets in Vienna, Madrid, Geneva? And are we for our part indicating any shifts to the Soviets since it's always a two-way operation?

SECRETARY SHULTZ. I would only say this. People are saying the same things that they have said before but in the part before where we have said and they have said we would like to see negotiations be successful—there's been a tendency to underline that desire. But nobody's substantive decisions have shifted.

Q. It's been a tendency to underline?

SECRETARY SHULTZ. To say in the messages that we have sent, and that they have sent, there is perhaps a little bit more emphasis put on it that we would like to see these negotiations succeed. But in answering your question—

Q. (Inaudible)

SECRETARY SHULTZ. No, there isn't anything. On the other hand say we say we want to have these negotiations succeed. We like to see a zero-zero (inaudible). We would like to see major arms reductions, we really would. We are ready to negotiate.

Q. (Inaudible)

SECRETARY SHULTZ. I think it (this emphasis on willingness to negotiate) is basically most noticeable in recent weeks; and one can't help but believe that the last days of Mr. Brezhnev's life were preoccupied with other things. For example, in the meeting that I had with Mr. Gromyko in New York,[22] he didn't raise the question of a summit and neither did I because it is obviously not something in the cards and when I talked with leaders of other countries who visited Moscow recently and asked them about the situation they reported there was an air of succession in Moscow—

. . . .

Document 291

Remarks by President Reagan, December 10, 1982[23]

Anniversary of the Imposition of Martial Law in Poland

I have before me, as I'm sure you know, two documents that speak to freedom and especially to Polish freedom.[24] And their contents, particularly at this time—because Monday marks the first anniversary of the repression of Polish freedom by the military government there. And this repression, carried out under the intense Soviet pressure and using tactics of brute force and intimidation, has sparked anger and sadness throughout the world.

No people were more saddened and more angered than those who share with the Polish people close and enduring ties of blood, tradition and affection—the people of the United States of America.

Before the tragic crackdown by the military authorities the American people watched with approval and growing excitement the democratic gains that were won by Solidarity. We observed with awe and admiration the courage of political [Polish] workers as they sought to reclaim the right to self-government and their nation's ancient heritage of liberty. All this they did peacefully, without shedding one drop of blood.

These days of light and hope are over and the cold night of repression has descended on Poland. But, despite the threats, the provocations and the imprisonments, the spirit of independence and resistance to tyranny, a spirit that has characterized the Polish people for more than a thousand years, still burns brightly in Poland today. It is the fervent hope of the American people that that spirit will again, someday soon enjoy full expression. It is the fervent hope of the American people that the Warsaw authorities will realize, and sooner rather than later, that continued repression can only prolong the political alienation and economic stagnation that characterizes Poland today.

In recent months we've seen partial steps taken toward this recognition by the Warsaw authorities—Lech Walesa and a number of other internees released. We welcomed the release of these people and, of course, we hope that the Polish Government will take other actions necessary to genuinely transform the existing climate of repression in their country.

In introducing sanctions against Poland last December I noted that those sanctions

---

[22] Shultz met with Gromyko in New York on September 28 during the 37th Session of the U.N. General Assembly.

[23] Source: Office of the Press Secretary to the President; printed also in *Weekly Compilation of Presidential Documents*, December 13, 1982, pp. 1599–1600. The President spoke at the ceremony of his signing of the Human Rights Day Proclamation which took place in the East Room of the White House beginning at 9:40 a.m.

[24] One of the documents was a proclamation of December 10 as Human Rights Day and December 15 as Bill of Rights Day. The other was a proclamation of Sunday, December 12, as a Day of Prayer for Poland and Solidarity With the Polish People. For the text of the Former, see document 128. For the text of the latter, see *Weekly Compilation of Presidential Documents*, December 13, 1982, pp. 1601–1602.

[25] Correction in the text printed *ibid.*, p. 1599.

were reversible and this remains the case. But I cannot and will not remove the sanctions until the Polish Government shows with its actions that it intends to live up to the obligations it assumed when it signed the U.N. Universal Declaration of Human Rights and the Helsinki Final Act.[26] (Applause) Reports reach us that further steps in this direction may be taken by the Polish Government in the coming weeks and months. I will stress today the United States is prepared to respond to genuine liberalizing actions by the Polish Government. Any such actions will be the subject of careful discussions with our allies. I repeat, if the Polish Government introduces meaningful liberalizing measures, we will take equally significant and concrete actions of our own. However, it will require the end of martial law, the release of political prisoners and the beginning of dialogue with truly representative forces of the Polish nation such as the church—(applause)—and the freely formed trade unions to make it possible for us to lift all the sanctions.

The United States can only respond to deeds, however, and not to words. We're not interested in token or meaningless acts that do nothing to fundamentally change the situation in Poland today—or to replace one form of repression with another.

As I've often said, the United States Government and its people are deeply concerned about the plight of the Polish people. We will continue to supply humanitarian aid to them through such voluntary and private relief agencies as the Catholic Relief Services and CARE.

Furthermore, as I stated last December 23d,[27] if the Polish Government will honor the commitments it has made to human rights, we in America will gladly do our share to help the shattered Polish economy just as we helped the countries of Europe after both world wars.

As a further sign of affection and solidarity felt by the American people toward the Polish people, I am signing today these two proclamations. The first is a bill of rights—Human Rights Day Proclamation—that takes particular note of the current tragedy of Polish freedom and reminds Americans and millions of people all over the world the fate of freedom in Poland affects the fate of freedom everywhere.

Through the proclamation, we remember today the Polish people—the millions of others who struggle against the brute force of despotism and all those who seek freedom and self-rule. Our nation was conceived in liberty and we have always understood that the fate of our own freedom is tied to the fate of freedom in the world.

The flourishing of liberty, democracy, and constitutional government is the goal of this administration as it is the greatest wish of Americans and that Americans have for all peoples of the world. We pray that we'll all come to enjoy what we consider our greatest treasure—freedom.

Second, I am signing a proclamation asking Americans to join together Sunday in solidarity with the Polish people and to pray for ultimate success in their quest for freedom. Lech Walesa long ago spoke of the wheat that grows on the stones, of how freedom sometimes grows from repression, how repression only serves to strengthen the determination of those who live in the darkness of tyranny to someday be free and the ideals and heroism exemplified by the Polish people and the members of Solidarity. The world has seen splendid affirmation of the desire for human freedom that springs from deep religious faith.

On Sunday, let us pray with confidence—confidence that wheat will someday grow on the stones in Poland and the other suffering lands under the brutal repression of today will be remembered only as a prelude to times of freedom and peace and independence. This Sunday let us remember the cause of freedom and let us, with the Polish people and all oppressed peoples everywhere, remind ourselves of the words of *Isaiah*, "They that wait upon the Lord shall renew their strength. They shall mount up with wings as eagles. They shall run and not be weary." I shall now sign these proclamations. (Applause) (The President signs the proclamations.) (Applause)

And I understand that someone is placing a cross of flowers on Kosciuszko's monument in commemoration of the first anniversary of martial law. And—(Applause)

("Sto Lat" [May You Live 100 Years][28] is sung.) (Applause)

---

[26] For the text of the U.N. Universal Declaration of Human Rights, signed December 10, 1948, see Department of State *Bulletin*, December 19, 1948, pp. 752–754. For the text of the final act of the Conference on Security and Cooperation in Europe signed at Helsinki on August 1, 1975, see *ibid.*, September 1, 1975, pp. 323–350.

[27] For the text of the President's address of December 23, 1981, see *American Foreign Policy: Current Documents, 1981*, document 265.

[28] Bracketed note appears in the source text.

I've said this before—you know, I didn't realize until just a few years ago, but when I did realize it, I was filled with mixed emotions and a feeling of challenge that we have to meet—that our own national anthem is only one I know that ends with a question, "Does that banner still wave o'er the land of the free and the home of the brave?" We must always be able to answer that question affirmatively.

N. Canada

Document 292

Statement by the Deputy Assistant Secretary of State for European Affairs (Niles) Before a Subcommittee of the Senate Foreign Relations Committee, February 10, 1982[1]

Acid Rain

Thank you very much, Mr. Chairman.

I am Thomas Niles, Deputy Assistant Secretary of State for European Affairs. In that capacity I am the U.S. Chairman of the United States-Canadian Coordinating Committee on Transboundary Air Pollution.

I thought I would use this occasion to report briefly to you on our negotiations to date with the Canadians on the subject of transboundary air pollution, a highly sensitive and important issue in our relations with our close friend and ally to the north.

As you know, the ties between the United States and Canada cover a broad range of cooperative activities, political, economic, cultural, commercial, and defense.

Our relationship with Canada is broader than with any other foreign country. The two governments work closely together, consult regularly on bilateral and international issues. As long-time friends and allies we share the same basic goals.

During his first year in office, President Reagan met five times with Canadian Prime Minister Trudeau, which certainly confirms the important place which Canada occupies in U.S. foreign policy, and the President's personal commitment to and interest in the United States-Canadian relationship.

In the defense sphere we and Canada are close allies in NATO and partners in the defense of North America. The North American Aerospace Defense Command [NORAD][2] the joint command with a U.S. Commander and a Canadian Deputy Commander, provides for aerospace surveillance, warning of possible attack by bombers or missiles, and air defense. The two Governments are assisted in managing the broad range of defense relations by the Permanent Joint Board on Defense, established in 1940.

United States-Canadian bilateral trade and investment is far and away the largest we have with any foreign country. Two-way trade in 1981 was in the range of $83 billion, and at the end of 1980, U.S. investment in Canada and Canada's investment in the United States totaled $54 billion.

We cooperate very closely with the Canadians in energy. An important step ahead in the energy area was the congressional action last fall of approving the President's proposal to remove roadblocks to private financing of the Alaska natural gas pipeline, a project which we hope will now be possible under private financing.

We also have very close and intensive relations with the Canadians in the fisheries area. Here the dispute arising from our overlapping boundary claims off the east coast has been submitted to the International Court of Justice in The Hague for binding adjudication.[3]

Finally, turning to the specific subject we are considering today, environmental issues are of great importance in the United States-Canadian relationship.

The United States–Canada International Joint Commission has worked since 1909 on transboundary problems and it continues to monitor and assist in the solution of bilateral pollution issues. The United States and Canada have accomplished a great deal in cleaning up water pollution under the Great Lakes Water Quality Agreement of 1972 and subsequent agreements.[4]

---

[1] Source: *Acid Rain: Hearing Before the Subcommittee on Arms Control, Oceans, International Operations and Environment of the Committee on Foreign Relations, U.S. Senate, Ninety-seventh Congress, Second Session* (Washington, 1982), pp. 98–101.

[2] Bracketed note appears in the source text.

[3] Regarding this referral, see document 298.

[4] For the 1972 agreement, signed April 15, 1972, see 23 UST 301; this agreement was superseded by the Great Lakes Water Quality Agreement, November 22, 1978, 30 UST 1383.

Today, the question of transboundary air pollution is of particular importance to both countries. We approach this problem with an acute awareness of the high level of concern in Canada about acid rain and acidification of lakes, rivers, and streams. We know that many areas in the United States have similar concerns and problems, and indeed we should remember that the original impetus for a bilateral approach on this issue came from the U.S. Congress.

In the fall of 1978, the Congress adopted a resolution calling upon the President, "To make every effort to negotiate a cooperative agreement with the Government of Canada aimed at preserving our mutual airshed so as to protect and enhance air resources and insure the attainment and maintenance of air quality protective of public health and welfare."

As a result of that resolution, informal bilateral discussions with Canada were begun in 1978. We also organized in that same year the bilateral research consultative group.

Discussions with Canada continued in 1979. In July of that year, the United States and Canada issued a joint statement on transboundary air quality, recognizing that both countries contribute to transboundary air pollution and announcing the intention to develop a cooperative agreement on air quality.[5]

As a result of further discussions, the United States and Canada signed a memorandum of intent in August 1980,[6] agreeing on procedures to be followed in preparing for and negotiating an agreement on transboundary air pollution.

The memorandum provided for the creation of a United States–Canada Coordinating Committee and under it five joint work groups composed of United States and Canadian Government representatives from scientific, technical, and legal areas.

The U.S. membership of about 50 is drawn from 8 different Federal agencies. The Canadian membership is comparable. The objective of the United States–Canada work groups has been to develop as much mutual understanding of the causes and effects of transboundary air pollution as possible. The work groups have been hard at work for more than a year now. Their reports are to be ready at the end of March, at which time they will be subjected to peer review and will serve as a technical basis for use in the negotiations.

During his first visit to Canada in March of last year,[7] the President confirmed our commitment to open negotiations on transboundary air pollution, as called for in the memorandum of intent. The President noted U.S. support for the ongoing cooperative scientific work to better understand the problem. He also indicated his expectation that the negotiations would prove lengthy.

Our interest in an agreement with Canada stems from the fact that the only sensible approach to the problem is a cooperative one with our northern neighbor, as the Congress has recognized.

In addition, we want Canada to adopt stricter air pollution control regulation now in effect in the United States. At present, the Canadian Federal Government is generally able only to recommend pollution regulation to the Provinces, which have final authority to implement environmental programs.

We would like to see improved emissions control technology applied to Canadian smelters and major powerplants. For instance, there are more than 100 sulfur dioxide scrubbers now in operation or in final stages of construction at powerplants in the United States, while there are no such scrubbers on powerplants in Canada.

Further, U.S. standards for control of automobile emissions are three times stricter than those in Canada. We believe that achieving an equivalent level of pollution control in the two countries should be our mutual objective.

Because of the importance of the issue with Canada, and its complexity, we believe transboundary air pollution can best be addressed in bilateral negotiations, whether we work toward a treaty or an executive agreement. This is a common problem and we believe it requires a joint solution. We would foresee difficulties in concluding an agreement with Canada if either country, or both, were inclined to act unilaterally now.

We held our first two formal negotiating sessions with Canada last year in June and

---

[5] For the text of the joint statement, July 26, 1979, see Department of State *Bulletin*, November 1979, pp. 26–27.

[6] August 5, 1980; TIAS 9856.

[7] For documentation concerning President Reagan's March 1981 visit to Ottawa, see *American Foreign Policy: Current Documents, 1981*, Chapter 10, Part N.

November. These meetings were devoted in part to review the progress of the work groups and to developing further guidance for their work.

We have also exchanged a series of technical papers and have begun discussions on the nature of an eventual agreement. At our next session, planned for February 24 here in Washington, we expect to begin discussion of the agreement text. I personally believe as the head of the U.S. delegation that the negotiations are going well, and we intend to push ahead as fast as the degree of our scientific understanding of the issue will allow.

I can assure you that we do care about and are concerned about Canadian concerns on air pollution, and that we are indeed committed to working out an agreement mutually acceptable and balanced in its provisions to deal with this problem.

The Canadians have made clear that they believe the two countries should enter into an interim program to control transboundary air pollution.

Sorry, my time is up. Let me just say that this is an area where we should continue the negotiations, continue the scientific work, and hope that as the scientific work is concluded this will give us a good basis on which to conclude an agreement.

Thank you, sir.

Document 293

Prepared Statement by the Assistant Secretary of State for Economic and Business Affairs (Hormats) Before a Subcommittee of the Senate Foreign Relations Committee, March 10, 1982[8]

U.S. Economic Relations With Canada

It is my pleasure to be here today to discuss the current state of United States-Canadian economic relations. This comprises a broad group of issues to which we give regular and high-level attention.

The United States-Canadian Interparliamentary Group, involving many of your colleagues, convened last week in Florida[9] and addressed most, if not all, the issues I plan to raise here.

There are few countries so interdependent economically as the United States and Canada. Let me start, therefore, by putting issues between us in a broad perspective which reflects the depth, and the mutual benefit, of our relationship. With this as background, I will then discuss the economic differences between our two nations which have increased in the last year or so.

TRADE

In 1981, two-way trade exceeded US$83 billion, accounting for over 17 percent of U.S. total foreign trade and more than 60 percent of Canada's total international trade. More than one-sixth of U.S. exports go to Canada, nearly twice that which go to Japan, our next largest customer. Canada sends us a number of important products—including not only raw materials such as minerals and wood products, but also an increasingly wide range of manufactured goods. The U.S./Canadian auto pact,[10] which was the framework for a total exchange of automotive products in 1980 or $19 billion, has produced significant benefits for the United States and Canadian auto industry.

While United States-Canadian trade remains vitally important and beneficial to both sides, we have problems in specific fields. For example, Maine's problems with Canadian potatoes from the eastern provinces. These problems arise and can disturb our trade relations; but for the most part, they do not become major issues and are resolved in ways satisfactory to parties on both sides of the border.

ENVIRONMENTAL ISSUES

Canada and the United States share concerns about the preservation of our environment; both countries recognize that we must work together to achieve this goal.

The massive program to clean up the Great Lakes, begun a decade ago, con-

---

[8] Source: *U.S. Economic Relations with Canada: Hearing Before the Subcommittee on International Economic Policy of the Committee on Foreign Relations, U.S. Senate, Ninety-seventh Congress, Second Session* (Washington, 1982), pp. 6–13.

[9] For a report on the meeting of this group, see *Twenty-third Meeting of the Canada–U.S. Interparliamentary Group, March 4–8, 1982*, Print of the Committee on Foreign Affairs, House of Representatives, Ninety-seventh Congress, Second Session (Washington, 1982).

[10] April 16, 1965; 17 UST 1372.

tinues. With the assistance of the International Joint Commission, the United States and Canada have succeeded in reversing a pattern of deterioration in the lakes which could have led to their biological death. The results of this massive effort are already evident.

Similarly, we recognize that we can deal with transboundary air pollution, our principal environmental concern, only by working together. Five United States–Canada work groups were established over a year ago to define the dimensions of this problem and to assemble scientific data. Negotiations on a United States–Canada agreement on transboundary air pollution were opened last year. Canadian concerns will be very much in the minds of American policymakers during the renewal of the Clean Air Act.[11] When we consider the work that lies ahead on air pollution, we must remember that the road to improved water quality in the Great Lakes was long.

DEFENSE

In defense, we are the closest of allies. The defense of this continent must be shared if it is to be effective, and it is being shared. The principal bilateral defense tie, the North American Aerospace Defense Agreement,[12] goes beyond our joint undertakings within NATO. Policies are coordinated regularly in the Permanent Joint Board on Defense. Canadian and American forces as well as civilian personnel work and train together at bases in both countries. Cooperation in defense procurement benefits both economies.

FISHERIES

Fisheries issues have been particularly important in recent years. In 1979, the United States and Canada signed fisheries and boundary agreements concerning the Gulf of Maine. Convinced that the fisheries agreement could not receive the approval of the Senate, the President withdrew it, just prior to his trip to Ottawa last March. Canada and the United States have now ratified the boundary treaty, and it is in effect. As provided for in that treaty, the World Court has established an Ad Hoc Chamber to determine the boundary. The Court's findings will be binding on both parties.[13]

In the west coast fishery, careful negotiation and a cooperative approach by both sides permitted the resolution—in 1981—of significant differences. In 1979, Canada had seized U.S. albacore tuna boats, and the United States had embargoed tuna imports from Canada. In a treaty which both countries ratified last July, Canadian and U.S. vessels are permitted to fish for albacore tuna along each other's coasts and to land their catches at designated ports in the other country.[14]

ALASKAN GAS PIPELINE

A joint project of the greatest importance to both our countries passed an important stage late last year when, on December 10, the Congress passed legislation submitted by the President to facilitate the private financing of the Alaska Gas Pipeline.[15] This prodigious undertaking would afford the lower 48 States access to 12 percent of America's natural gas reserves and provide the equivalent of 400,000 barrels of oil per day, for at least 20 years. It will stimulate exploration which could lead to major new finds. Canada and the United States already have moved ahead on the construction of the southern portions of the pipeline—linking Alberta to the U.S. West and Midwest markets.

Cooperation such as this has been customary in United-States-Canadian economic relations. Canada has benefited greatly from the openness of the U.S. economy, and from major resources provided by U.S. investors. U.S. exporters and investors have benefited from the Canadian market. The prosperity of both countries has been enhanced by extensive trade, flows of energy resources, and flows of capital. Canadian economic policy has undergone some important changes, however, and these are a source of much of the current friction. Before I describe those changes, I would like to clearly state our policy in one key area.

U.S. INVESTMENT POLICY

United States investment policy has, for many years, been based on the fundamental

---

[11] P.L. 91–604, December 31, 1970; 84 Stat. 1676.

[12] The most recent agreement on this topic was signed on March 11, 1981; TIAS 10111.

[13] Regarding the boundaries and fisheries agreements, see *American Foreign Policy: Current Documents, 1981*, Chapter 10, Part N. Regarding referral of the boundary question to the World Court, see document 298.

[14] Signed May 26, 1981, ratified July 29, 1981; TIAS 10057.

[15] P.L. 97–93, December 15, 1981; 95 Stat. 1204.

premise that an open international investment system provides the most efficient allocation of global resources. When capital is free to move without hindrance, many nations can benefit through expanding world output. As a corollary, U.S. Government policy is to minimize intervention in the private sector decisionmaking process.

Two basic tenets, which we have strongly supported, are the national treatment and most-favored-nation principles. And we insist, of course, that investment be treated in a fashion consistent with international law. The national treatment principle holds that foreign investors should be treated no less favorably than domestic investors in like situations. The most-favored-nation principle holds that the investors of one foreign country should be treated no less favorably than the investors of any other foreign country. The two principles have the common characteristics of reducing instances of discrimination directed at foreign investment. We have worked bilaterally and multilaterally to gain wide acceptance of these principles and to extend the application of such treatment to a wider range of enterprises.

A particularly important step in this process took place in 1976 when the United States joined other OECD member governments in participating in the consensus adopting a Declaration on International Investment and Related Decision on national treatment. The Declaration and Decision were reviewed and reaffirmed in 1979 by a consensus of OECD countries in which the United States also participated.

The adoption of restrictive investment and trade policies by our neighbor and largest trading partner is a matter of particular concern which poses fundamental issues for the members of the OECD, particularly the United States.

Our concerns center on two areas, the restrictive and discriminatory policies in the National Energy Program (NEP), now being established and the activities of the existing Foreign Investment Review Agency (FIRA). In addition, Canada just announced a new set of mineral policy proposals which I will mention briefly.

NATIONAL ENERGY PROGRAM (NEP)

Canada proposed its National Energy Program, or NEP, in October 1980. The basic policy is to be implemented by two major pieces of legislation, the Canada Oil and Gas Act, ("Bill C–48") and the Energy Security Act, or ESA. The Canada Oil and Gas Act passed the Parliament in December. The ESA has just been introduced in the Parliament.

Our key concern about the NEP is not its objective—the well publicized "Canadianization"—but the means used to achieve the objective, especially what we believe to be discriminatory and unfair treatment of foreign investors. The elements of the program which are of most concern are:

The 25 percent crown share, or "back-in," in existing oil and gas discoveries in Federal, or "Canada," lands. This changes the rules of the game for foreign firms which have already invested in exploration and development of Canadian energy resources. The Canadian Government now plans to pay a portion of the exploration costs incurred by the companies in Canada lands (which include the Northern Territories and offshore areas), calling these "ex gratia" payments. We believe the decision to make these payments was a positive step. But it is only a very small step; and it is not adequate to compensate for the value of what was taken.

The old system of depletion allowances available to all producing firms has been replaced by the Petroleum Incentives Program (PIP). Under the PIP, the level of Canadian ownership determines the amount of exploration grants awarded to a company—with the maximum grants awarded to companies with Canadian ownership of 65 percent or higher. Moreover, qualifying firms must meet strict control tests which verify that the enterprise is controlled and directed by Canadians. The Canadian ownership rate rules concern us because they embody an overtly discriminatory regime based on nationality to award financial grants to explore in Canada. The control status test troubles us because of the large degree of subjective discretion—rather than objective criteria—that confronts firms. The plans for the Petroleum Incentives Program have been modified twice since their intital appearance, most recently on February 9. These changes were intended to clarify the calculation of the ownership rate and to lessen the record-keeping burden on smaller companies. However, the firms are still uncertain as to where they stand because the depletion allowance system has been cancelled but companies still are awaiting final regulations governing the PIP.

We are also concerned by the constrained shares provision of the ESA, which gives Canadian corporations the means to achieve and maintain a certain level of Canadian ownership in order to qualify for the petroleum incentives grants. We have had initial discussions with the Canadians on this issue, and voiced certain concerns. For instance, a two-thirds vote of holders of a class of shares can restrict eligibility for ownership of that class of shares. This provision is potentially discriminatory; it could depress prices of stock in foreign hands since non-Canadians could be excluded as potential shareholders. We intend to make our concerns clear to the Canadians.

The Committee on Megaprojects Industrial and Regional Benefits, or CMIRB, has as its objective to increase the participation of Canadian firms in major projects and to increase procurement of Canadian goods and services in the energy sector. Depending on how the program is administered, its operations may be in conflict with the provisions of the General Agreement on Tariffs and Trade (GATT), particularly Article III, regarding national treatment for imported products.

Production licenses for oil and gas on Canada lands will only be available to companies with 50 percent or greater Canadian ownership. Thus, U.S. companies which have explored on Canada lands, and made an exploitable discovery, would be forced to join with a Canadian partner holding at least 50 percent interest, before receiving a license to produce.

The Canada Oil and Gas Lands Administration (COGLA) has just been established by the Canada Oil and Gas Act to redistribute exploration rights already held by private companies. We are seeking more information on this. On the basis of what we know, we have a number of initial concerns. By requiring the owners of existing exploration interests to negotiate new exploration agreements with the Government of Canada or to apply for provisional leases, the COGLA will have significant discretion in controlling ongoing exploration operations. The actual guidelines for the organization are still being drawn up. We have learned that firms may be asked to relinquish a large share of their exploration acreage as a condition for receiving a new exploration agreement (although in cases where leases had already expired, new conditions may have been anticipated). The stated purpose is "to meet an objective of substantially increasing crown reserves (and) to provide for new entry into the frontier areas." We will make it clear that this should not become another retroactive measure. COGLA is also supposed to increase Canadian industrial, employment, and social benefits from oil and gas activities on Canada lands. (It is not clear how this agency will combine with the CMIRB to enforce "Buy Canadian" policies on energy enterprises.) The COGLA also seeks to help meet "Canadian government objectives of increasing equity participation by Canadians and Canadian companies" and to achieve "the objective of increased government participation." Depending on how it is administered, COGLA raises many potential concerns.

FOREIGN INVESTMENT REVIEW AGENCY (FIRA)

I would now like to turn to the Foreign Investment Review Agency, or FIRA, and describe those elements which concern us most.

The FIRA is a legislatively-mandated screening agency which must approve incoming investments. We have not challenged FIRA's existence or its basic promise—to review inward investment—although we have stressed, and Canada itself has acknowledged, that it is an exception to the national treatment principle (Canada has notified this to the OECD). Our problems center on FIRA's operations.

First, in judging an application by a foreign investor, FIRA applies a vague and highly subjective standard: whether there is significant benefit to Canada. Second, FIRA in many cases extracts undertakings from prospective investors before approving an investment proposal. These are legally enforceable agreements, or performance requirements, such as undertakings requiring purchase in Canada, export commitments, import restrictions, requirements to hire specified levels of Canadian management and labor, obligations to move productive facilities from the United States to Canada, obligations to transfer patents and know-how to Canada without charge, and other commitments which run counter to generally accepted international practices. These measures can seriously distort investment and trade flows between the United States and Canada. Moreover, because of the way FIRA now operates, its very existence undoubtedly discourages many would-be investors.

The FIRA is essentially aimed at new investment. But it also reviews changes in ownership of Canadian subsidiaries of foreign firms. This might occur when two American firms merge or when an American firm wishes to sell its Canadian subsidiary to another non-Canadian firm. These transfers are frequently disapproved by FIRA, even in situations where there is no change in the level of Canadian ownership. This FIRA policy can have the effect of depressing the value of U.S. firms' assets in Canada.

Despite Canadian Government claims of a high rate of approval by the FIRA, its statistics present an incomplete picture. Many foreign investment applications are either never presented, withdrawn before disapproval, or are greatly modified to accommodate FIRA-mandated performance requirements.

NATIONAL MINERALS POLICY

Canada announced on March 8 a set of new minerals policy proposals. These were the subject of a joint Federal-Provincial Ministers meeting in mid-January. Though we have made only a very preliminary review of the proposals, I should note that the level of foreign ownership in the Canadian minerals sector is about 36 percent, considerably lower than in the energy sector. The new proposals refer to maintenance of "stability" in taxation and the investment climate and do not appear to contain specific reference to a Canadianization goal like that in the NEP. We have also noted that there is a reference to increasing procurement of mining machinery from Canadian sources. It is not clear precisely how this would be implemented; we will need to monitor this aspect.

U.S. RESPONSE TO THE CANADIAN INVESTMENT POLICIES

The rising concern in the United States regarding discriminatory Canadian investment and energy policies has engendered wide ranging and vigorous discussion on how we should respond. The concerns over Canadian investment policies expressed here in Congress, and by U.S. business and labor groups, are valid and we share them.

NEP—BILATERAL

We have met with Canadian officials on a bilateral basis on numerous occasions to enumerate—with the frankness characteristic of our countries' relationship—our concerns on the NEP. The President, Secretary Haig, Secretary Regan, Ambassador Brock, and other Cabinet officers, and other senior officials have been actively involved in this dialogue. Secretary Haig has had several meetings and conversations with External Affairs Secretary MacGuigan. Secretary Regan headed a small delegation to Ottawa last October to discuss investment and energy policies. More recently, on December 16. I led an interagency delegation to Ottawa and we presented our case against the "back-in" provision. Ambassador Brock visited Canada in late January for further discussion, including a meeting with Prime Minister Trudeau.

We concentrated our talks initially on the NEP provisions, such as the back-in, contained in the Canada Oil and Gas Act. The Canadian Parliament passed this legislation on December 18. During the course of our discussions, lasting more than 1 year, the Canadians decided to make "ex gratia" payments for the crown share. But these payments cannot be regarded as adequate, and there have not been any significant modifications in other elements of the legislation of concern for foreign investors.

The Energy Security Act (ESA) contains other objectionable provisions, such as the Petroleum Incentives Program (PIP), which I mentioned earlier. That legislation was formally introduced in Parliament about 2 weeks ago. A Canadian team visited Washington on March 1 to brief U.S. officials on this legislation. The ESA introduces a number of complex changes to Canadian energy policy, and we have raised a number of important concerns about it. We are studying the effects of the ESA on U.S. interests and will have further discussions with the Canadian Government on the issues raised by ESA.

NEP—MULTILATERAL DISCUSSIONS AND CONCERNS

In addition to bilateral contacts, we have had numerous consultations on the NEP in multilateral fora, in the OECD Committee on International Investment and Multinational Enterprises (CIME) and the International Energy Agency.

In the CIME, several other member countries have joined us in criticizing the discriminatory aspects of the NEP which depart from national treatment. We first presented our concerns in the March 1981 meeting of the CIME under the consultations provisions of the 1976 investment instruments. (This was the first formal use of these provisions.) The discussions continued in subsequent meetings of the Committee and its Working Group on International Investment Policies. The United States and the other countries not only raised the specific, substantive aspects of the NEP which depart from the national treatment principle, but also noted that Canada's discriminatory policies could disrupt efforts within the OECD aimed at expanding and strengthening the national treatment principle and could undermine acceptance of the principle by the developing countries.

In response, the Canadian Government described the NEP to the CIME members and reaffirmed its commitment to the national treatment principle. The Canadian Government promised to notify to the OECD the elements of the NEP which are national treatment exceptions. On the other hand, Ottawa has not, in our view, adequately reconciled its current energy policies with its OECD commitments. Also, the Canadian Government has not, to date, fully responded to the various specific concerns raised by the other OECD countries during the consultative process. Thus, the results of these consultations have not been fully satisfactory. However, they have been a useful indication to Canada that the NEP is not solely a U.S. concern, but one which is widely shared among OECD member countries.

In the IEA, the effects of the NEP pricing, taxation, and production policies on Canadian energy supplies have been the subject of multilateral discussions. We have raised questions about the potential negative supply consequences of the NEP on Canada's ability to meet its IEA undertakings. These include placing maximum reliance, as practicable, on market forces to promote production and conservation.

A positive development was the statement in the Canadian budget message of November 12 that "the special measures being employed to achieve more Canadian ownership and control of the oil and gas industry are not, in the Government of Canada's view, appropriate for other sectors." On the basis of this assurance, we expect that the Canadian Government will not extend NEP-type discriminatory measures. Such measures would introduce disturbing new shocks in our bilateral economic relations.

FIRA

As with the NEP, we have had extensive consultations with the Canadian Government on FIRA's practices and its impact on U.S. investors. The Canadian Government is keenly aware of our views, but to date has shown little willingness to make any significant modifications to meet our specific concerns. Therefore, we reluctantly concluded that we must take our case to the GATT for those elements of FIRA's policies which we consider to be GATT violations.

GATT Article XXII provides for consultation between Contracting Parties on any matter covered by the GATT. At our initiative, consultations under this Article took place in Geneva on February 17. Observers from the European Community delegation were also in attendance. At this meeting, we argued that the export and local contents requirements imposed by FIRA in the investment approval process are contrary to GATT articles regarding (1) quantitative or other restrictions on imports, (2) national treatment and (3) import substitution. The Canadian side heard our case but asked for an adjournment so they could seek instructions from Ottawa on their response.

If the results of these consultations are not satisfactory, we would likely seek a GATT Article XXIII proceeding. This is a more formal process, consisting of an international panel. The decision is binding. In that proceeding, we would base our case on the points described above, but would also argue that FIRA's practices nullify the benefits of earlier trade agreements and concessions.

The November Canadian budget message promised a review of FIRA's administration and deferred, at least for the present, an earlier proposal to expand FIRA's mandate to review and monitor already-established foreign investments in Canada. This is certainly a positive development. An expansion of FIRA's mandate would have been a serious new derogation from international norms. We were told in the fall that the FIRA was considering adopting a policy of more explicitness and openness in its decisionmaking process—in particular, publicly explaining the reasons for disapprovals. There were also indications that size criteria would be applied, granting small businesses special treatment. While certain of our important concerns would remain, these would be positive steps. We have not, however, seen actual signs of such new policies. Foreign investors continue to face complex and difficult FIRA performance requirements.

We have an ongoing effort to obtain information on individual companies' experiences with FIRA. This is needed as a basis for presenting our views on FIRA's effects to Ottawa and to international organizations which oversee investment matters. We, of course, avoid jeopardizing individual companies' relations with the Canadian Government. Thus it is sometimes difficult to obtain a complete picture through the fact-finding process.

OTHER ISSUES

In a related area, one of my deputies, Matt Scocozza, visited Ottawa last week to hear Canadian views on the access of U.S. trucking companies to the Canadian market. We are seeking to determine the effect of Canadian Provincial regulations and the FIRA on U.S. trucking firms. In the United States, Canadian firms have benefited equally with U.S. firms from the recent liberalization of U.S. laws. The ICC has halted action on applications by Canadian trucking firms to operate in the United States, at least until it can investigate the issues.

At the discussions last week, involving several U.S. agencies and Canadian Provincial and Federal officials, we gathered information regarding the relationship of the Provincial and Federal authorities about U.S. truckers' access to the Canadian market. This information indicated that provincial regulation did not appear to be unfair to American trucking. The ICC will consider this information in their investigation, and we will maintain our active involvement in the issues.

Finally, because the National Minerals Policy proposals have just been announced, we have not had an opportunity to assess their implications for U.S. interests, but they appear to raise a number of new issues. We will probably need to seek consultations with the Canadian Government. If these proposals are adopted in ways which are detrimental to U.S. interests, we will take whatever steps are appropriate.

MINERAL LANDS LEASING ACT

The NEP and FIRA raised questions about whether Canada should still be considered a "reciprocal country" under the terms of the Mineral Lands Leasing Act of 1920,[16] thus permitting continued access to U.S. Federal mineral lands to companies owned wholly or in part by Canadians. In February, after a public comment period and after soliciting the views of other interested agencies, Interior Secretary Watt ruled that Canada's status as a "reciprocal" country under the terms of the Mineral Lands Leasing Act should not be changed. Interior took into account public comments on factual questions to aid in interpreting whether the MLLA's provisions were met. Interior based its decision on a two-part test: (1) whether U.S. citizens are precluded by Canada from investing in Canadian corporations and (2) whether U.S. investors are discriminated against by exclusion from access to Canadian mineral resources. The Interior Department determined that U.S. citizens may make such investments and that they have access to Canadian mineral resources. It is worth emphasizing that this determination was made in the narrow context of complying with a specific U.S. law, and does not address, or prejudice, our position on broader Canadian investment and energy policies.

FUTURE U.S. RESPONSES

As a result of the extensive discussions we have had with Ottawa, I think that it is fair to say that the Canadian Government has a heightened awareness of U.S. congressional, executive branch, and public concerns about the discriminatory and unfair elements of the NEP and FIRA. For our part, we understand somewhat better—although we continue to have major problems with—the Canadian rationale for these programs. And we have a much better knowledge of the administrative details of these policies and how they may affect U.S. investors in Canada.

At the same time, substantial differences remain between the United States and Canada over the efficacy and fairness of these Canadian investment and energy policies and their potential impact on the international norms to which most developed nations adhere, as well as the impact on our bilateral economic relationship. Because the NEP is still evolving, and because the laws and regulations regarding both NEP and FIRA allow for a large measure of administrative discretion in implementation, we cannot accurately forecast the full impact yet. I would now like to describe some of the potential future actions which are available to us on these issues.

First, I think it is essential that we continue and intensify bilateral pressure. The implementing regulations and administrative procedures for the NEP are not all in

---

[16] P.L. 66–85, February 25, 1920; 41 Stat. 437.

place. Some new governmental agencies with potentially wide-ranging mandates have been created in the Canadian energy area, and the scope of operations of these agencies is just being developed. By staying in close touch with Ottawa, we will be better able to gauge the impact of the NEP on U.S. investors as it evolves and to press for changes in those aspects which have an unfair or harmful impact.

Second, we should vigorously pursue our GATT case on FIRA and initiate a case against the NEP if it is implemented in ways which are contrary to Canada's GATT obligations. This is important, not only to seek redress for our specific problems with FIRA and the NEP, but also to enlist the support of others and test the ability of the current GATT framework to deal with trade-related investment issues.

Third, we need to continue to encourage Canada to live up to its OECD commitments on national treatment. The OECD investment instruments are not binding in the sense that they contain enforcement procedures or sanctions. But Canada as much as the other OECD countries has benefited from the kind of open international investment regime that the OECD is seeking to foster. The Canadians need to recognize the potentially harmful effects of their policies both within and outside the OECD. In this regard, we expect the Canadians to notify to the OECD all NEP-related national treatment exceptions, as they have agreed to do, and to move to conform to a greater degree with OECD standards.

Fourth, we will continue to stay in close touch with U.S. investors in Canada in order to obtain their views of Canadian actions and legislation, to monitor the impact of the NEP as it develops, and to be aware of changes in the operations of FIRA. This is particularly important in view of the administrative discretion for Canadian officials provided for under both NEP and FIRA regulations.

Fifth, we are prepared to intercede with the Canadian authorities when we believe it necessary or when requested to do so by U.S. firms on specific problems which arise under either the NEP or FIRA. When there are instances of harmful or discriminatory treatment based on nationality of an enterprise, we will respond promptly and strongly.

CONCLUSION

In dealing with these investment, energy, and minerals concerns, both Canada and the United States need to keep in mind the importance of resolving our problems in ways consistent with our broader relationship. And we also need to recognize these problems as part of a troubling international progression of investment restrictions. To counter this trend, the United States has sought international discussion of a number of investments issues—notably national treatment and the imposition of performance requirements similar to those mandated by FIRA—in a number of organizations, including the World Bank, the GATT, and the OECD. In the Executive Committee of the OECD in January, for example, we gained the agreement of other members to reinvigorate the OECD's work on investment. In our preparations thus far for the Versailles Summit and the fall GATT Ministerial meeting, we are encouraging other governments to consider a more rigorous international approach to investment problems.

Just as we expect that, over time, the deleterious effects of the NEP and FIRA will become clear to Canada, so do we hope that the positive value of international understandings to reduce or eliminate unfair or harmful investment policies will also become clear. In a period of rapid change and uncertainty, our mutual interests are best served by national policies which attempt to remove distortions to trade and investment flows and which have the effect of strengthening global allocation of resources according to economic criteria.

Document 294

Statement by the Assistant U.S. Trade Representative for Investment Policy, U.S. Trade Representative Office (Bale), Before a Subcommittee of the Senate Foreign Relations Committee, March 10, 1982[17]

U.S. Economic Relations With Canada

Thank you, Mr. Chairman.

I welcome the opportunity to come before you and your subcommittee to address the subject today.

---

[17] Source: *U.S. Economic Relations with Canada*, pp. 26–28.

My prepared testimony[18] and that of my colleagues deal rather thoroughly with energy investment related issues, which today are the major contentious problems in United States-Canadian economic trade relations.

In regard to these relations on the positive side, the United States–Canada trading and investing relationship is the largest and most extensive of any two countries in the world. In 1981, two-way trade approached $87 billion, accounting for almost 20 percent of United States world trade and more than 70 percent of Canada's total trade.

There is a high degree of economic integration between our two countries, and this is exemplified by the large volume of duty-free trade. In 1979 more than three-quarters of United States imports from Canada entered the United States duty free, while 70 percent of United States exports to Canada were accorded duty-free treatment.

The average United States tariff applied to Canadian imports has been 1.3 percent, compared to an average Canadian tariff rate of 4.3 percent applicable to United States exports. As a result of the concessions agreed to in the Tokyo round,[19] duty-free trade between our two countries should approach 80 to 90 percent by 1987.

I think what this represents, Mr. Chairman, is an extensive volume of duty-free trade without a formal free trade agreement between our two countries but the effects of an evolution between our two countries.

On the negative side, major problems have been created for the United States by FIRA and its practices of engaging in legally enforceable performance standards that distort trading investment, FIRA's screening of inward investment and its interference with the transfer of foreign-held Canadian assets.

We are also very much concerned about the national energy program with its discriminatory, retroactive, and inadequate compensation features.

Now, on the Canadian side there is great political sensitivity about foreign ownership of Canadian assets, which in the manufacturing sector approaches 50 percent and in the energy sector exceeds 60 percent. In addition, the current Canadian Government appears bent on increasing the Canadian Government's role in the Canadian economy.

The real issue before the United States is how can we, how should we, and how do we intend to best deal with these problems. We must deal with them not only because of the particular problems that Canada's policies present to our interest but also because of the example Canada is setting in not living up to its international obligations that we would rather not have other countries follow.

In terms of the methods of approach to this problem, we do have a bilateral problem. We are utilizing bilateral techniques. We have had, as other speakers have mentioned, frequent bilateral discussions and communications for more than 1 year with some, albeit quite limited, success. We should, however, continue such an approach.

Second, in a bilateral context we have taken some of Canada's practices to the GATT. We are utilizing GATT procedures to bring the attention of the GATT to what we think are clear violations of several articles of the GATT and the practices of the Foreign Investment Review Agency.

Under these procedures we are probably headed toward an arbitration panel, although at any point along the road a settlement could be reached if Canada meets our concerns. The Canadians themselves appreciate the use of the GATT. They have in the past and now are in the process of bringing GATT cases against the United States, and on this issue Canadians at the highest level of their Government have told Ambassador Brock and others that they will abide by the GATT decision process.

We must recognize that the GATT will not deal with all or perhaps not even most of our problems, but for the first time, we have taken a trade-related investment issue to the GATT, and this is an important precedent. The problem we are having with Canada is illustrious of a broader multilateral weakness in the international economy.

The problem is that Canada is under no international sanctions according to any existing and binding rules in the investment field regarding its policies that are cleary in

---

[18] For Bale's prepared statement, see *ibid.*, pp. 28–33.

[19] The Tokyo Round, which was the seventh set of multilateral trade negotiations since the Second World War, concluded at Geneva on April 12, 1979. Among the many agreements concluded were two with Canada, the first a Memorandum of Understanding, TIAS 9978, the second an agreement on cheese, TIAS 9980. For further documentation on the Tokyo Round, see *American Foreign Policy: Basic Documents, 1977–1980*, Part V, section B.

violation of certain agreed principles of treatment of international investment. Canada has multilateral obligations under the OECD, and the United States as well as other countries have raised the problem of the massive derogation that Canada's national energy program represents from the 1976 Declaration on National Treatment[20] to which Canada is a party.

However, there are no sanctions under the OECD other than under international pressure, and while international pressure may be effective in certain circumstances, in many other cases it may not be. We need to explore in the 1980's new forms of international rules for investment. A start can be made in the GATT Ministerial in the fall in addressing the trade-related investment practices.

Canadian problems are not unique to Canada. National treatment, barriers to investment, and trade-distorting performance requirements are widespread among both developed and developing countries. While working both bilaterally and multilaterally to arrive at solutions to our problems, we will have to continue to evaluate the impact of Canada's investment and energy policies and United States economic and commercial interests and assess what we can do under United States law to address our concerns.

In the administration we are continuing to explore possible further approaches to the investment and energy problems that we have with Canada. Certainly one thing we should take into account, however, is that Canadian policy will clearly be affected by the Canadian Government's evaluation of the internal cost of its current and prospective policies.

There appears to be mounting internal concern in Canada about these policies. For example, the president of a major Canadian company recently said,

> "Because of the NEP, the Canadian energy industry is smaller and weaker and less capable of finding the new energy sources that Canada will need to achieve to arrive at self-sufficiency."

In addition, some of the Canadian press have stated that—

> "Ottawa's pursuit of the Canadianization objective has had a devastating impact on the Canadian dollar, and the National Energy Program and the attitude of the Canadian Government towards investment, both domestic and foreign, have resulted in a huge outflow of capital from Canada."

I should note in passing that despite Canada's internal need for investment capital, according to OECD and U.N. sources, since 1973 Canada has had a net outflow of direct investment. Canada will have to choose between its current political and long-term economic needs.

Various members of the administration believe that positive solutions are possible. We need to work hard to find them and we should do this in order to preserve the extensive and generally good economic and trade relations that Canada and the United States have for so long enjoyed.

Thank you, Mr. Chairman.

Document 295

Letter From the Canadian Secretary of State for External Affairs (MacGuigan) to the Secretary of State (Haig), April 23, 1982[21]

Financing for the Alaska Natural Gas Pipeline

Dear Al: I have been alerted to what could become a critical impasse in the discussions on financing of the Alaskan segment of the Alaska Natural Gas Transportation System.

As you well know, in addition to the bilateral agreement of 1977,[22] our two Governments have jointly invested substantial efforts in support of this pipeline, which we have agreed is in the long-term security and energy interests of both our countries. The Canadian Government remains committed to the early completion of the project, based on private financing, but I am concerned that the various parties involved in the financing negotiations may fail to appreciate fully the implications of any sig-

[20] The "Declaration on National Treatment" is Section II of the OECD "Declaration on International Investment and Multilateral Enterprises," June 21, 1976. For text, see Department of State *Bulletin*, July 19, 1976, p. 83.

[21] Source: Department of State *Bulletin*, July 1982, p. 54. This letter and the one following were released jointly by the U.S. and Canadian Governments.

[22] September 20, 1977; 29 UST 3581.

nificant delay on the willingness or ability of the Canadian Government and the Canadian companies involved to proceed with it at some later date.

The Canadian Northern Pipeline Commissioner, the Honourable Mitchell Sharp, is planning to convene a meeting of the producers and the sponsors of the Alaska portion next week in order to apprise them of the views and concerns of the Canadian Government. I am sure that a reiteration by you of the USA Government's support of the project, preferably in a public statement, would have a positive influence.

I am prepared to release this letter as a clear statement for the public record of our Government's position.

Yours sincerely,

MARK MACGUIGAN

Document 296

Letter From the Secretary of State (Haig) to the Canadian Secretary of State for External Affairs (MacGuigan), April 27, 1982[23]

Financing for the Alaska Natural Gas Pipeline

DEAR MARK: Thank you for your letter of April 23 regarding the financing of the Alaska Natural Gas Transportation System (ANGTS).

We shared the Government of Canada's concerns about recent developments which could delay significantly completion of the pipeline. The United States Government remains fully committed to the Alaska Natural Gas Transportation System based upon private financing, and believes it would be unfortunate if its construction were subject to another, perhaps indefinite postponement.

As you know, this Administration has taken an active role in reducing legal and regulatory impediments that have complicated efforts in the private sector to arrange the necessary financing. Upon submission of the waiver of law to Congress October 15, 1981,[24] President Reagan reaffirmed this Government's basic commitment to ANGTS when he stated,

> "My Administration supports the completion of this project through private financing, and it is our hope that this action will clear the way to moving ahead with it. I believe that this project is important not only in terms of its contribution to the energy security of North America. It is also a symbol of U.S.-Canadian ability to work together cooperatively in the energy area for the benefit of both countries and peoples."

Through the cooperative efforts of the Administration and Congress, the waiver was approved December 15, 1981.[25]

We continue to believe ANGTS offers Americans the most realistic option to obtain secure and reliable access to some 13 percent of America's natural gas reserves which is currently inaccessible. Once in operation, the project promises to provide the energy equivalent of some 400,000 barrels of oil a day which will help Americans lessen their energy dependence on uncertain foreign sources. Moreover, the pipeline's early completion would be an important step toward further reduction of our energy vulnerability.

Sincerely,

ALEXANDER M. HAIG, JR.

Document 297

Statement Issued by the Department of Commerce, July 15, 1982[26]

New York MTA Purchase of Canadian Subway Cars

The Commerce Department today started an investigation to determine whether

[23] Source: Department of State *Bulletin*, July 1982, p. 54.

[24] For the complete statement by President Reagan, October 15, 1981, see *Public Papers of the Presidents of the United States: Ronald Reagan, 1981*, pp. 934–935.

[25] P.L. 95–93, December 15, 1981; 95 Stat. 1204.

[26] Source: Department of Commerce files. For exhaustive hearings on this subject, May 28, 1982,

the Canadian Government is subsidizing exports of subway cars to the United States.

The investigation follows a petition by Budd Company of Troy, Michigan which charges that the Canadian Government has offered preferential financing to the New York City Metropolitan Transit Authority in order to help Bombardier Company Quebec compete unfairly in the U.S. market.

"The Tariff Act of 1930[27] requires the Commerce Department to investigate charges of government subsidization of exports if a petition submitted by a domestic manufacturer is accompanied by sufficient information. This investigation is being undertaken as a result of such a petition," Lawrence J. Brady, Assistant Secretary for Trade Administration, said.

The contract awarded to Bombardier Company calls for delivery of 825 subway cars valued at $659 million. Budd charges that the Export Development Corporation of Canada, a government agency, is providing financing for 85 percent of the contract at 9.7 percent.

The case has been referred to the U.S. International Trade Commission which must make a preliminary determination by August 9 whether the imports threaten injury to the domestic industry. If injury is found, Commerce must make its preliminary determination by September 17.[28]

---

see *New York MTA Purchase of Canadian Subway Cars: Hearing Before the Committee on Finance, U.S. Senate, Ninety-seventh Congress, Second Session* (Washington, 1982). This hearing includes statements by Deputy Secretary of the Treasury R.T. McNamar, Deputy Assistant Secretary of Commerce for Import Administration Gary N. Horlick, and General Counsel of the U.S. Trade Representative Donald E. DeKieffer.

[27] P.L. 71–497, June 17, 1930; 46 Stat. 590.

[28] The International Trade Commission ruled on August 3 that the Canadian export financing subsidy was causing injury to U.S. industry. On November 22, the Department of Commerce announced in a preliminary finding that Canada was unfairly subsidizing the sale of subway cars, a finding which, if made final, would require MTA to pay penalty duties on the cars.

Document 298

Statement Issued by the Department of State, September 27, 1982[29]

Maritime Boundary With Canada

On September 27, 1982, the United States filed its first written pleading (Memorial) with the International Court of Justice, in the The Hague, in the "Case Concerning the Delimitation of the Maritime Boundary in the Gulf of Maine Area" between Canada and the United States. Canada also filed its first pleading on the same date.

The case is before the Court as the result of a boundary settlement treaty between the United States and Canada which entered into force on November 20, 1981.[30] The Court has already established a Chamber of five judges to hear the case. The Members of the Chamber are Judge Roberto Ago of Italy, as President, Judge Andre Gros of France, Judge Hermann Mosler of the Federal Republic of Germany, Judge Stephen Schwebel of the United States, and Judge *ad hoc* Maxwell Cohen of Canada.

The Court will establish the single maritime boundary between the two countries that will divide their continental shelf jurisdictions and 200-nautical-mile fishery zones in the Gulf of Maine area. At stake is approximately 15,000 square nautical miles of resource-rich ocean off the New England coast. This Atlantic area includes a rich fishery developed by the United States on Georges Bank, a site of significant cod, haddock, scallop, and other catches. The Bank may also contain valuable oil and gas resources.

The boundary proposed by the United States claims U.S. jurisdiction over all of Georges Bank. New England fishermen developed the fisheries of Georges Bank during the 19th century and fished the area exclusively until the late 1950's when an influx of foreign fishermen began. Over the last 200 years, the United States has undertaken the primary responsibility for surveying and charting the area, the maintenance of other navigational aids, the provision of search and rescue services, the conduct of

---

[29] Source: Department of State Press Release 300, September 27, 1982.

[30] Regarding this treaty, see *American Foreign Policy: Current Documents, 1981*, Chapter 10, Part N. It was designated TIAS 10204.

scientific research, and defense. The boundary proposed by the United States respects the natural divisions in the marine environment of the area by taking into account the Northeast Channel, which separates the Georges Bank ecological regime from the separate ecological regime of the Scotian Shelf.

The next round of written pleadings is expected to be filed in the spring of 1983. Oral argument is currently contemplated to begin in the fall of 1983.

The Agent of the United States directing the case is Davis R. Robinson, the Legal Adviser of the Department of State. A chart depicting the boundary claimed by the United States is attached.[31]

Document 299

Transcript of a Press Conference by the Secretary of State (Shultz), Ottawa, October 17, 1982 (Extracts)[32]

U.S.-Canadian Relations

MR. ROBINSON. Good morning gentlemen. It's a pleasure to welcome you to our press meeting today, and to start it off I would like to introduce John Hughes, Assistant Secretary of State for Public Affairs, who will lay out the ground rules.

MR. HUGHES. Well, thank you, Mr. Ambassador. The ground rules are very simple. We just thought it would be a useful idea to have a little breakfast session with a number of leading Canadian journalists.

The rules are very simple, we thought we might as well make it on the record and the other rule is we will have to leave before 9 o'clock.

MR. ROBINSON. Thank you very much, John. Gentlemen, it is a pleasure to introduce the Secretary of State. As you may know, this is his first official visit as Secretary of State outside of the United States. As you may also know, this is his fourth Cabinet position, having previously been the Secretary of Labor, and then Director of the Office of Management and Budget, and then Secretary of the Treasury and now Secretary of State. In addition to his knowledge of Canada, it goes a long way back to his academic days as well as his business days. So, it's a pleasure to introduce my boss, George P. Shultz.

MR. SHULTZ. Thank you, Mr. Ambassador. I believe there are questions, so why don't you proceed.

Q. Can you start, Mr. Secretary, by telling us whether you actually did teach Allan MacEachen economics at university?

A. I think we taught each other—it was usually sitting around in the evening puzzling over something or other. I think we were both interested in industrial relations as much as economics—that aspect of economics, and the Department of Economics at M.I.T. in those days had an industrial relations group that was a very interesting one and a very good one, and they still do. So, it was a combination of those things and it has struck me, in looking back at it, that the combination of economics as a formal discipline that has a kind of relentless logic to it, on the one hand, and the study and work on industrial relations problems which get you into reality immediately, is a pretty good combination; and both Allan and I had that combination tossed at us at M.I.T. after World War II.

Q. How do you feel about the Canadian attitude on foreign investment now? Do you sense a softening? Do you sense that your visit here and other things that are going on represent a change in the attitude of the Canadian Government?

A. I don't think my visit represents any change on the part of the Canadian Government at all.

Q. . . . on the part of your government?

A. There has been, well on the part of my government, I'm merely following the President's lead. He's met with the Prime Minister seven times since he's been in office—that's a little less than 2 years' time—and has considered that the United States has a tremendous stake in its neighborhood where we live, just as you do, and that we should be paying attention to our neighborhood. It seems to me the President is absolutely right about that and I've just been following his lead in coming here

---

[31] Not printed. A similar map showing the identical boundary proposed by the United States is printed in Department of State *Bulletin*, August 1983, p. 58.

[32] Source: Department of State Press Release 336, October 27, 1982. Secretary Shultz visited Canada, October 24–27, to discuss a wide variety of issues of mutual interest. All ellipses of three periods are in the source text.

and it's my own natural instinct anyway. I've been here many times and know lots of people here. So the visit is really in keeping with that idea.

As far as the economic relationships between the two countries are concerned, there are certain areas of strain. If you put the whole thing in context, I think we have to keep reminding ourselves there's a huge amount of trade between the two countries. Canada is, by far, the biggest trading partner of the United States and the same is true in the other direction. There is very large foreign investment in Canada and I don't have the figures on this but I'd be surprised if it weren't true, that Canadian foreign investment is overwhelmingly oriented to the United States, and there's a lot in the United States . . . lots of Canadian investment in the United States. So there are many strong relationships there.

As far as the Foreign Investment Review Act[33] is concerned, that's a question I'll undoubtedly be talking with Mr. MacEachen about. But there are some problems in it for the United States. But it seems to me that we all have to recognize that every country has certainly a complete sovereign right to decide on the rules for investment and what foreigners, I think, properly can ask is that the rules be applied fairly, be applied expeditiously and be applied, let's say prospectively, rather than retroactively. So that you don't get the rules changed on you after you have made an investment. Then, once an investment is made according to the rules, that that Canadian dollar of investment, whether it comes from inside or outside, be treated the same way—nondiscriminatory treatment. Those are, I think, fairly standard items and those are the things that we would tend to look for.

Q. Mr. Secretary, you were referring to the retroactive features that the United States might object to. For a country like Canada, with a huge disproportionate amount of foreign investment, are you suggesting that we remain locked into that framework?

A. Well, the future is a long time. So, if you change things prospectively, over a period of time that can make a change. Let me make a pitch in the other direction. We'll take all of the Canadian investment we can get. The United States, under President Reagan, is doing everything it can to make itself attractive to investment—whether it's from inside or outside. We've been trying to stimulate the pool of savings in the United States. Our savings rate is lower than we think is desirable. We've been trying to enlarge that and we all know that in the end you can't save what you—you can't invest what you haven't saved. So one way of dealing with that problem is to attract, in effect, the savings from outside your country to come in. And so we have been doing everything we can to make ourselves as attractive as possible to the flow in of investment from other countries. So let me plug the United States as a place for you Canadian investors to take a look around and consider if you don't get a good rate of return and find it attractive.

Q. That doesn't seem to have been the attitude of the U.S. Congress last year.

A. In general, I think the United States is very receptive to foreign investment.

Q. I suggest a view in Canada, which is very common, several takeovers, takeover attempts in the American economy by Canadian interests that set off a wave of reaction in Congress that has led to almost record numbers of what we might view here as anti-Canadian bills.

A. I don't think that takeovers, as such, are the . . . are a problem. We've become accustomed to a lot of that kind of activity in our economy. It's a question of whether or not takeovers take place on a special basis. If a takeover is sponsored by government, that's a problem. As a matter of fact, I believe myself, and I'm getting out of my jurisdiction, if I were Secretary of the Treasury again I might talk more about this. But I think the takeover of a private company by a government from another country, that you have to scratch your head about. We had the Kuwait Government take over one of our companies, Santa Fe International, and I think the Canadians and the French played chess with some of our companies, and its gone ahead. But it's not thrilling to have that happen. But that's different from private investment entirely.

Q. Mr. Secretary, earlier this year there were harsh words said by officials on both sides of the border. Have you and Mr. MacEachen considered any—I guess I would use the word institutional arrangements—to anticipate, iron-out, whatever, these kinds of problems?

A. Well, we've had three moments of conversation so far, in New York, La

[33] The Canadian Parliament passed the Foreign Investment Review Act, which established the Foreign Investment Review Agency, in 1974.

Sapiniere,[34] and here. In the first two settings we were part of the groups and we didn't really have a chance to talk intensively with each other, and in our schedule of talks here we sort of divided the times into different subject matter areas.

The one yesterday was concentrated on common international and diplomatic matters, you might say. So we didn't get into that, but I think it's a good subject and I know that when I was in the government before, I worked quite hard with my Canadian counterpart, who was at the time, John Turner, Minister of Finance. We tried, not through some formal mechanism, but through informal means, to develop an atmosphere where we could . . . that did not eliminate problems but it made it possible for us to discuss them immediately, quickly, candidly and decide how we were going to deal with them together.

On the whole, I think that the record would show that after we got going on that the financial area between the United States and Canada went along quite smoothly in spite of the fact that we had some very tough problems to contend with. So, maybe there is some formal thing, we'll probably talk about it. But I think, surely, we have already said to each other that we want to pay attention to each other, we want to stay in touch, we want to create an atmosphere of easy discussion and consultation. I am certain that we can do that—there's no problem at all, and we will.

Q. Mr. Secretary, a great deal has been written lately, at least in this country, about the low ebb of U.S./Canadian relations, but I was in Washington 20 years ago—I guess this weekend—when the Cuban missile crisis began. I wonder if you could try to put in some kind of historical perspective the relationships, at that time, compared with now. Specifically, how the Reagan administration would be likely to respond to that kind of situation and whether it would—what sort of response you would expect from Canada, diplomatically? Militarily?

A. You're positing some problem with the Soviet Union and then how would the United States and Canada relate to it. Is that what your question is?

Q. Yes, or something more specifically, like the Cuban missile crisis, a threat to this hemisphere.

A. Oh, I don't want to speculate about possible threats to the hemisphere. I would say that, as a general proposition, the defense arrangements between the United States and Canada are outstanding. Strong, collaborative, and I think if there were some major problem that constituted a threat to this hemisphere we would, undoubtedly, work on it together.

Q. Would you be satisfied today with the kind of response that the Diefenbaker government gave the Kennedy administration?

A. You're too good an historian for me. I don't want to . . . I know there's been a lot of TV things on the missile crisis lately, but one of the problems of this job is that I don't have much chance to look at things like that, I'm so busy reading memos, and things. So I do not want to make comparisons with that time. I'm just not up on it enough.

Q. You mentioned, sir, the defense arrangements between the two countries being strong and I know there's quite a lot of concern in the United States that Canada isn't doing as much as it should be to maintain its NATO and defense commitment. Could you . . . ?

A. I think, in general, we believe in the United States that the Alliance should be doing more to build and maintain its strength. We are critical of ourselves and critical of the whole thing. Somehow we have had a period of a decade or so, in which we did not adequately pay attention to the importance of our military capabilities. There has been a tremendous effort in the Reagan administration to look to the amount and the quality of our defense capability. We have made a lot of noise about that all over the world. We have talked in Europe about the importance of it, here, Japan, and elsewhere. So I think that it is true, that we wish that Canada would do more and we think that Canada should do more. We believe the United States should do more. We think the European countries should do more. We believe that all of us have confronting us a very threatening situation that comes out of the huge buildup of the Soviet Union, and the demonstrated willingness of the Soviet Union to use that strength, ruthlessly and without compunction. And so we have in front of us Afghanistan and Poland. I read the paper this morning about Lech Walesa and how he is being treated. Imagine in Canada treating a trade union leader like that? You cannot even imagine it. It is so completely outside the realm of possibility. But all of this is

[34] The reference to conversations in New York has not been further indentified. La Sapiniere is a lodge at Val David, Canada, where the NATO Foreign Ministers met on October 2 and 3, 1982, to discuss various alliance issues.

backed by the formidable military capability and we have to look to our own capability if we are going to adequately defend and look after our interests. So that is the point of the whole thing.

. . . .

Q. (Inaudible)

A. Canada has been very supportive in a general way, and that's been quite helpful. Of course, working on something like this has many dimensions to it. We've got, for example, the Arab onslaught to get Israel removed from the United Nations has not been particularly helpful. And, as you know, we have fought very hard about that. Canada has been right there. So, we have worked in tandem on that subject.

Q. Canada has been supporting—

A. I'm sorry, I couldn't understand.

Q. Canada has been supportive of the peace plan—

A. Yes.

Q. —in very general terms, it is agreed to be specifically supportive of the peace plan.

A. Well, I have the feeling from the talks I've had with Mr. MacEachen so far that if there's something specific that needs to be done, it's possible to consider it. But, I don't know what you have in mind, if there is some particular thing that you are asking about.

Q. Did you take that to mean that Canada would be willing to provide troops for the multinational force, or—

A. That subject didn't come up. What the mission for the multinational force will be as this process unfolds is still being talked about. We have had discussions with the French and the Italians with whom we are partners there in that multinational force. Each country has not committed itself to do anything different than it is now doing, but each has said that it's willing to consider having its forces used if there is some definable, constructive mission—and everyone will take a look at that. Amin Gemayel has asked that the numbers in the multinational force be increased very substantially, by as much as ten times the current amount. That's quite a lot and I think it's a question of whether that's really necessary. But there are some additional things that need to be done and probably a role for somewhat expanded forces and there's also a question of what the UNIFIL force will do. All those things would be looked at.

There have been several countries that have indicated to us that they would be willing to consider contributing to that force.

. . . .

Q. Are you going to be talking about the Middle East with Mr. MacEachen or are you going to be talking about bilateral issues?

A. We talked some in our first session about the Middle East and I'd doubt that we'd spend much more time on that—it may be—I understand that the Prime Minister may well be at lunch—he may want to discuss it some—in which case we would.

Q. In your discussion of bilateral issues, going back to where we started—could you describe how intense you regard the problems you describe with FIRA—

A. There are a great variety of problems. It seems to me any two major countries that are as large as our two countries and with as much interaction between them and interdependence between them as ours—there's going to be a continuing flow of problems through time. It seems to me there are two aspects in working on those problems.

First is to address yourself to the general atmosphere within which an individual problem is worked out. And, then second, to work on that individual problem separate from all the other problems. So, on the one hand, I'm sure Mr. MacEachen and I will look at these various issues and talk about them some, although, we don't have the time to sort of go into each one in a lot of detail, but we are also trying to construct a general umbrella—you might say—of constructive spirit and outlook that has historically been the case between the United States and Canada and is today and we can improve on it so that we create an atmosphere within which those who are going to take up these individual issues can do so in a constructive spirit.

Q. It is my understanding that that constructive spirit does not now exist—problems are rather more intense than—

A. No, I don't think that's a fair statement. It is, the amount of aggravation and tension over things varies as time goes along. Perhaps it's a little higher than it has been—than usual, but when you compare the relationship between the United States and Canada with the relationship of most neighboring countries that have a lot of interdependence with each other around the world, our relationship, relatively speaking, looks terrific. So, it can go up and down somewhat, but basically it's a good, strong relationship and sometimes in our preoccupation with individual issues—not that those aren't important and not that they shouldn't fight about them—but it can cause us to lose the perspective of the overall picture. And we need to keep that in front of us once in a while. I'm a great believer, incidentally, that you don't improve a relationship by failing to represent yourself strongly in the discussion of particular issues. The worst thing in the world that I could do is to say, "Well, in the interests of better S.-C=C=U.S.-=S.-C=Canadian relationships, I'll forget about some issue that is of great importance to the United States and U.S. interests." That's the way in the end to undermine a relationship. I'm sure the Canadians would feel the same way. We have to put these issues up on the table and confront them and work at them and argue about them and eventually resolve them. That's the way to build a strong relationship, in fact, it's the measure of a strong relationship that you can surface problems and argue about them—and the relationship remains strong.

This goes back to the subject that Allan MacEachen and I studied together years and years and years ago—labor relations problems—the same thing between labor and management and the woods are full of relationships between a union and the management that were superb and people became so enamoured with what a good relationship it was that they wouldn't discuss any issue—even though it was an important issue—because they didn't want to spoil the relationship. And in the end that's what brings a relationship down. So, I think the way to have a good and strong relationship is that you do discuss the problems—but you discuss them within the framework of the expectation that our ties and our involvement with each other are so strong and enduring that in the end we'll find answers to these things.

Q. You and MacEachen have a totally different philosophy, I submit you may have gone to the same school. You're much more a private enterpriser than he is. Reagan is much more a private enterpriser than Trudeau is. So, you start talking—now, how do you agree to disagree on the mixed sort of economy we have and your dedication to private enterprise?

A. We're not trying to tell you how to run your country—and don't you try to tell us how to run ours. But, each running our countries the way we want—we nevertheless have successfully worked at the issues that come up between us. The fact of the matter is that with whatever differences there have been—there has been a very worthwhile and constructive—for everybody—relationship between these two countries. Lest we overemphasize whatever philosophic differences there may be—and I don't expect that they're that great—let's not forget the tremendous commonality of basic values; of democratic values; of concern for the individual human being; of religious freedom—shall we note the right of people to form unions, just to contrast with it some other countries, and to assemble and to express themselves and all of these things that we have in common. And, when you look around the world today and ask yourself how many major countries are there that share these values, I wish the number were higher. So we have tremendous, deep values in common that we both cherish and that we want to see flourish.

Thank you very much.

Chapter 11. The Middle East

A. Regional Developments and General Policies

Document 300

Responses by the Department of Defense to Supplemental Questions Submitted by the House Foreign Affairs Committee (Extract)[1]

Foreign Military Sales Programs in the Middle East

Q. The administration has requested $1,739 billion in concessional direct credits for fiscal year 1983 ($900 million in forgiveness for Egypt and Israel, and $839 million in direct credits for a number of other countries). With respect to this $839 million, couldn't the same degree of concessionality be achieved at much lower budgetary cost, by providing that a mix of 50 percent grants and 50 percent off-budget concessional credits be given instead of the direct credits? My understanding, based on the administration's testimony last year, is that this 50/50 mix would have the same concessionality as direct credits, but would require only half the outlays ($420 million instead of $839 million). Is this so, and, to the extent it is, is there any reason why the committee shouldn't use this approach, given the budgetary savings?

A. FMS credit budgetary outlays in a given year depend upon a number of variables including: timing of disbursements, the borrowers' requirements, and prior year sales commitments. Therefore, it cannot be assumed that outlays will be cut in half by adopting the 50/50 formula adopted in fiscal year 1982. The budget authority (BA) requirements, e.g., new appropriations required, provide a more useful benchmark for responding to your question.

The administration's proposed FMS credit program includes $950 million in forgiven loans (for Israel, Egypt, and Sudan) and $789 million in concessional loans. Conversion to a 50/50 mix would result in a forgiven loan program of $1345 million (950+395) and a shift of an additional $394 million to the off-budget guaranteed loan program. Fiscal year 1983 budget authority for the FMS credit program, therefore, would drop from $1739 million to $1345 million. It should be pointed out that while the guaranteed loan program is off-budget, the impact on the U.S. economy is identical to that of the on-budget direct loans.

A comparison of the "degree of concessionality" to the recipient associated with these two approaches depends upon the assumptions one makes with respect to length of repayment period, interest rate, and grace periods associated with direct and guaranteed loans.

The possible combinations of these factors are infinite. This said, our calculations indicate that under the most commonly offered terms, the 50/50 formula approximates the concessionality in the administration's proposal for direct credits, over the life of the loan. We would note, however, that where the borrower receives a grace period on the repayment of principal (and virtually all proposed credit recipients require grace periods) the repayment in the early years is significantly less than the administration's proposal—$24 million (3 percent of $789 million) vs. $55 million (14 percent of $394 million). This is an important consideration for countries with hard-pressed economies which may improve in future years.

Q. You have stated several times that no request for improved HAWK missiles has yet been received from Jordan. To the extent that such a sale is even being contemplated, however, what arguments can be advanced in support of it? In particular,

---

[1] Source: *The Role of International Security Assistance in U.S. Defense Policy, Hearing Before the Committee on Foreign Affairs, House of Representatives, Ninety-seventh Congress, Second Session* (Washington, 1982), pp. 65–66. Representative Stephen J. Solarz submitted the supplemental questions following testimony by Secretary of Defense Weinberger on March 10. For Weinberger's testimony on arms transfers, see *ibid.*, pp. 39–41, 58–61.

whereas an argument could conceivably be made that the sale of I–HAWKS would be justified if the Jordanians, as a quid pro quo, cancelled the purchase of SAM 8's from the Soviet Union, in view of the fact that the Jordanians have announced that the Soviet arms deal will not be cancelled, this argument is simply inapplicable. Is there any other rationale for the sale?

A. We have received no request for this kind of equipment from Jordan. If Jordan formally submits a request for additional air defense systems, such a request will be examined by the administration in the light of Jordan's legitimate defense requirements, the impact on Israeli security concerns, our own interest in assuring that our friends in the area have the capability to defend themselves, and the need to bring peace to the region. You may be assured that any decisions on future arms sales to Jordan would be made only in the context of full consultation and supporting rationale with the Congress. We have a long-standing military supply relationship with Jordan which serves U.S. interests in the region, and we want it to continue. It is in our interest to treat Jordanian concerns for legitimate self-defense seriously. With respect to the King's decision to go ahead with the Soviet weapons purchase, it is hardly in our interest to have other nations, less interested in Israeli concerns for peace and security, supply weapons to Jordan.

Q. Why was the amount of grant assistance for Israel reduced from $550 million to $500 million, at the same time that grant assistance to Egypt was increased by $200 million? Isn't it true that Israel's already staggering debt burden increased during the past year, and that Israel's debt per capita is the highest in the world?

A. The recent AID paper, Report on the Israeli Economy and Debt Repayment Prospects, transmitted to Congress on March 9, concludes that current and proposed aid levels and terms are adequate to meet Israel's needs and avert a serious debt problem. We concur with that paper. Our proposed grant level of $500 million is consistent with that judgment.

Q. Why has the administration requested a tripling of military assistance to Morocco?

A. The proposed higher level of FMS credit more realistically aligns our tangible support of Morocco with our security objectives for the country and region. Morocco occupies a strategic location on the Straits of Gibraltar and has demonstrated over many years a loyal and active friendship for us. During Secretary Haig's recent visit to Morocco,[2] a dialogue was begun on en route access for the RDJTF. We have agreed to establish a Joint Military Commission (JMC). Morocco is in a vastly inferior military position relative to neighboring Algeria, which is Soviet-supplied, and to Libya, whose support of terrorism and adventurism we all know only too well. Our increased FMS program derives from these factors, and will also serve as a signal that we intend to stand behind our loyal and trusted friends, particularly in time of need.

Q. What specific military equipment will be financed by this assistance?

A. We have not as yet elaborated a final program. Further planning will be done during the inaugural session of the JMC, which we expect will meet this spring. However, in general, we expect a major portion of the FMS credits will be used to finance supply support arrangements for previously acquired U.S. systems, such as F–5 and OV–10 aircraft, Chapparal missiles and Vulcan AA guns. Also, Morocco may decide to purchase other major systems such as the M–60 tank and the Maverick antitank weapon, or to further enhance its Westinghouse radar aerial defense system.

Q. Is this equipment suitable for use in the conflict in the Western Sahara, or will it be used only for the defense of Morocco itself?

A. Our security assistance program for Morocco is designed to assist Morocco defend itself from external threats. The answer to your question will, of course, depend principally on the precise items finally purchased. We would assume that most of the equipment to be purchased would be suitable for use by Moroccan forces in various battle situations. To a large extent, what equipment ultimately is used in the Western Sahara will depend on what the Polisario do there. Since they have elected to escalate this conflict in its technological dimension by introducing armor and sophisticated surface-to-air missiles, we think we must assume that the Moroccans will continue to respond with whatever weapons they have which will best deal with such threats.

. . . .

---

[2] Haig visited Morocco on February 11 and 12, 1982; see documents 425–427.

Document 301

Statement by the Assistant Secretary of Defense for International Security Affairs (West) Before the Senate Armed Services Committee, March 12, 1982 (Extract)[3]

U.S. Defense Policies in Southwest Asia and the Persian Gulf

. . . .

Basically, the mission of the RDJTF is to conduct the planning, joint training and exercises and to be prepared to deploy designated forces to the Southwest Asian region. The RDJTF is programed to counter the most serious threat to the area, that of a Soviet invasion. But the Department is not unmindful that other threats require other security-related instruments of policy.

Our basic goals for the region are, first, to insure the security of Israel while promoting the continuation of the peace process; second, to support moderate states against overt attack by radical states; third, to support moderate states against the spillover of regional conflicts and subversion aided or directed by outside powers; and fourth, to limit the Soviet military influence and leverage in the region and to deter a Soviet mission.

The primary mission of the RDJTF relates to this fourth goal.

The first goal is insuring the security of Israel. President Reagan has reaffirmed the U.S. policy that Israel's qualitative technological advantage will be maintained and that we will be mindful as well about Israeli concerns with respect to quantitative factors and their impact upon Israel's security. Our military assistance to Israel exceeds that of any other nation and continues to rise. At $1.7 billion, the fiscal year 1983 request is 21 percent above fiscal year 1982 and accounts for 44 percent of U.S. military grants worldwide and 25 percent of the U.S. military credit worldwide.

Our second goal, that of supporting moderate states against overt attack by radical states, relates to the fact that interstate rivalries and conflicts independent of the Arab-Israeli dispute are a major threat which the Soviets can exploit. In some cases—Libya and Tunisia, Ethiopia and Somalia, People's Democratic Republic of Yemen, and Oman—the moderate state with whom the United States has good relations is deficient in military equipment compared to its adversary.

That brings us to the issue of security assistance. The leadership and the policy guidance in security assistance matters rests with the Secretary of State. The Department of Defense fully and very enthusiastically supports the State Department's fiscal year 1983 Security Assistance budgetary request; that is, a request for $5.6 billion of foreign military sales of which $950 million is grant, or forgiven loans; another $800 million are loans at concessional terms; and $3.9 billion are loans at prevailing interest rates, approximately 14.5 percent today.

Egypt, Turkey, Israel, and Spain comprise about 70 percent of the FMS request; 40 other countries share the other 30 percent. In constant dollars we are allocating less in military grant assistance today than at practically any time since the end of World War II; yet as a nation we have grown richer while our friends in many lesser developed countries are growing poorer, and the Soviet Union is providing to their allies and the LDC's at least twice our level of military grant assistance.

Overall, we simply are not devoting too much to military assistance, nor are we overemphasizing military assistance at the expense of economic assistance. I have another chart in my testimony that illustrates that while 30 percent of our own Federal budget goes to defense, only 20 percent of our grants overseas are for military assistance, while the other 80 percent are for economic assistance.

The Department of Defense plays an active role in security assistance through three means. First, the Secretary of Defense, under the direction of the President, has primary responsibility for the determination of military end-item requirements. Second, to meet any urgent requests the services must take from their own stocks the time for security assistance. Otherwise, a hard-pressed nation must queue up for as much as 2 to 4 years.

This is so because for several years Congress forbade procurement in anticipation of foreign military sales. Hence, there were no items on the shelf. In 1981 the service in

---

[3] Source: *Department of Defense Authorization for Appropriations for Fiscal Year 1983, Hearings Before the Committee on Armed Services, United States Senate, Ninety-seventh Congress, Second Session* (Washington, 1982), Part 6, pp. 3714–3719.

general, and especially the Army, were remarkably forthcoming in responding to Secretary Haig's initiatives in the Middle East and southwest Asia following the assassination of President Sadat.

Third, Congress in fiscal year 1982 authorized a Special Defense Acquisition Fund to permit anticipatory procurement. Funding, at $300 million per year, is to come from recoupments from prior year sales. It will be a revolving fund to be replenished from its own sales. Oversight and authorization of the fund will be the joint responsibility of the Senate Foreign Relations Committee and, through referral, the Senate Armed Services Committee and the respective committee in the House. The Department is looking forward to consultations with these committees.

The fund is a major step forward because security assistance is complementary to the RDJTF. One is not a substitute for the other. Each faces a different task and confronts a different aspect of the Soviet threat.

Our third primary goal is to support moderate states against the spillover of regional conflicts and subversion which may be aided or directed by outside powers. Radical fundamentalist movements backed by foreign military aid and aggression are a genuine threat to the integrity of the region. Examples include the Libyan attempts at subversion in Egypt, Sudan, and Somalia, and the Iranian-backed effort at a coup in Bahrain. Many regional states are militarily weak and all depend on external support to equip and supply their armed forces.

These sorts of threats argue for greater diplomatic and economic measures in conjunction with support for security assistance and discussions through joint military commissions. Through such discussions the United States gains a better appreciation of the threats while the regional states better understand ways in which we can assist them.

It is when we come to the fourth goal, Senator, that of limiting Soviet influence and deterring a Soviet invasion, that we speak primarily about the missions of the RDJTF. The interrelated economies of the United States, Europe, and Japan, of course, cannot do without Persian Gulf oil. Soviet control of the gulf oil would totally change the political and economic shape of the world. The prime U.S. defense objective in southwest Asia, therefore, is to prevent Soviet military hegemony. Nations in the region will shape their policies at least partly in accord with their perceptions of the prevailing military balance between the superpowers. The United States must not be perceived as wanting in either the will or the capability to defend Western interests, interests we share with the regional states.

To deter a Soviet invasion in southwest Asia, the capability of and funding for the Rapid Deployment Joint Task Force have been increased. Employment of the RDJTF in furtherance of U.S. strategy has three time dimensions. First, given warning and timely political decisions, we would move forces as close as possible to the area of potential conflict. This would signal to the Soviets that we consider vital Western interests at stake and that further movement on their part would risk a war between the two superpowers. Should deterrence fail, the second dimension involves our ability to fight in the region. We must deploy forces rapidly to interdict and blunt a Soviet attack, although we would not be compelled to respond only at the Soviet point of attack. Third, this strategy must take into account how we would cope with the potential of a wider war. Conflict with the Soviets may not be contained to the region, and the United States would have to be prepared for a global confrontation.

A principal objective is to deny the Soviet Union the notion that it can necessarily confine a conflict to a region or fight in a manner of its own choosing. The Soviets would have to take into account the possibility of a long, widespread, costly, and ultimately unwinnable war. This would affect Soviet calculations of potential gains and risks involved with persevering with their invasion. The Soviet decisionmakers must calculate how to terminate a war, not just how to begin it.

A limited clash with the Soviet Union, followed quickly by a cease-fire, is a possibility. But equally possible is a global war if the United States enters the combat to protect its vital interests. Academic restraints on assumptions about combat cannot repeal the facts of geography. Soviet combat aircraft fly regular sorties from Cuba, Angola, Ethiopia, South Yemen, Vietnam, and other places and are thus astride our lines of communications to southwest Asia. Soviet submarines, aircraft, and surface combatants routinely intermingle with our carrier battle groups. The Soviet Union today is a global superpower. In times of crisis, we have not seen the Soviets withdraw their worldwide forces to their homeland; instead we have seen them, as careful military planners, posture to strike effectively in many theaters if war came. In World Wars I and II, the battle could not be confined to one theater. It would be imprudent to assume that in the 1980's war against the other global superpower to protect a vital interest of the West could be confined to one battlefield of our choosing.

Senator, as you said to the committee last year:

> "It is difficult to envision any major shooting war between the United States and the Soviet Union confined or confinable to the gulf alone. In all probability such a conflict would spill over into at least the European theater."[4]

Now, perhaps the Soviets would stand down all their forces worldwide with the exception of one place and allow us to move 10,000 miles unimpeded. Perhaps they would withdraw their fleets from the oceans of the world. But such assumptions have not in the past been the basis of U.S. defense planning.

Let there be no confusion. Discussions in prior years about a "1 and ½ wars" strategy or a "NATO war" were discussions about a global war. While verbal and resource emphasis was given to one theater, military planners were still taking into account combat at varying levels of intensity in the Pacific, in Korea, in the Indian Ocean, in southwest Asia, in Africa, in the Atlantic, in the Caribbean, in the Mediterranean, on NATO's southern and central fronts, in the Norwegian Sea, and on NATO's northern flank.

In recent years we have come to recognize the genuine peril of Soviet aggression, outside NATO boundaries, against Western access to oil. One can assume and plan for a limited, direct defense in southwest Asia, with U.S. lines of communication unchallenged, with no simultaneous buildup in NATO, with no dedication of forces to cope with Soviet overseas bases. Prudently, however, one should also plan for a wider war, because the choice of war may not be ours.

Service representatives testified to an Armed Services Subcommittee last week[5] that even the very substantial fiscal year 1983 to 1988 Defense budget plan may not in all cases result in the forces required to obtain all national security objectives. The reason is not diffuse global commitments. The Reagan administration expects priorities among theaters to be set. As Senator Nunn has said, there is always a gap between strategy and resources. Recent defense funding efforts, in the assessment of General Jones, Chairman of the Joint Chiefs of Staff, "have begun to arrest and, in some cases, reverse the unfavorable trends, but much more must be done if the United States and its allies are to reduce the risks to an acceptable level." What we are talking about are sustained increases for the long haul. Our 5-year budget plan is intended to restore a tolerable balance of military power.

Assessments of capabilities, of course, are a different matter than assessment of defense policy and strategy. A strategy of global flexibility does not necessarily mean simultaneous, intense conflict worldwide. Quite the opposite. It means assessing the opponent's strength on the entire global chessboard, assessing the capabilities of allies and of theater criticalities, and assigning priorities and moves and countermoves designed to terminate the conflict speedily and with minimum escalation, while protecting the vital interests of the United States and its allies. If we say the Soviet Union is a mature global superpower in the 1980's then we must think globally.

The RDJTF has developed excellent logistics plans for quick movement to the southwest Asia theater. In terms of developing flexible means of responding quickly, we are moving on several fronts, although these assets are not exclusive for the RDJTF. In my statement I have a chart which shows that in fiscal year 1982 Congress has allocated and in fiscal year 1983 we have requested substantial funds for military construction in southwest Asia, a variety of sealift and airlift assets, and tactical and strategic airlift.

The purpose of such speed is to make it crystal clear to the Soviets that no cheap blitzkrieg—presenting the West with a fait accompli in terms of control of the oil—is possible. Instead, such an invasion would be a land war fought laboriously through narrow defiles, mountain pass after mountain pass. The Soviets, hence, must calculate the unpredictable course, scope, and consequences of a long war. The Soviets would also have to weigh the possibility of United States moves where we held a domi-

---

[4] Senator William S. Cohen made this statement on March 9, 1981. See *Department of Defense Authorization for Appropriations for Fiscal Year 1982, Sea Power and Force Projection: Hearings Before the Committee on Armed Services, United States Senate, Ninety-seventh Congress, Second Session* (Washington, 1981), Part 4, p. 1700.

[5] See *Department of Defense Authorization for Appropriations for Fiscal Year 1983, Preparedness: Hearings Before the Committee on Armed Services, United States Senate, Ninety-seventh Congress, Second Session* (Washington, 1982), Part 5.

nant advantage or where we could prepare well for later combat. Those moves would be intended to change the political calculus of the Soviet decision-makers. In our planning and programming, therefore, we do not look at southwest Asia in isolation.

In conclusion, Senators, the mission of the RDJTF is to deter Soviet aggression in southwest Asia, particularly as it threatens access to oil, and to prevent the threat of Soviet military power being used as a tool of political coercion. This requires the ability for rapid movement of substantial American forces. It requires planning for direct defense in the theater, and it requires planning on a global basis.

The capabilities of the RDJTF are increasing substantially, but this should not divert efforts to cope with the more likely threats in the region. So the Department strongly supports the President's request for security assistance and other means of assisting moderate, friendly states.

Hence, our policy is to: Strengthen the RDJTF; maintain a military presence in the area; expand access to facilities both in the region and en route; integrate the RDJTF into broader military options; and support security assistance and other measures aimed at more likely but less militarily demanding threats.

. . . .

Document 302

Prepared Statement by the Assistant Secretary of State for Near Eastern and South Asian Affairs (Veliotes) Before a Subcommittee of the House Appropriations Committee, March 31, 1982[6]

Foreign Assistance Requests for Fiscal Year 1983

I welcome this opportunity to discuss with you our policy toward the Near East/South Asian region in the context of the administration's FY'83 budget requests. Since I will be followed by AID Assistant Administrator Antoinette Ford,[7] I shall concentrate my brief opening remarks on a political overview into which our requests fit. This can serve as a framework for our subsequent discussion.

Under Secretary Buckley in his appearance before you March 11[8] has sketched the overall foreign policy framework into which our Near East/South Asian policy fits. He has spoken of the need for a safer future in which all nations can live in peace free from pressures such as that exerted by Soviet presence in Afghanistan. He has also spoken of our desire to promote peaceful solutions to regional rivalries and hostilities. There is no question that persistent pursuit of a comprehensive and balanced U.S. policy in the Near East/South Asian region is critical to these goals. It is critical:

—to preserving a global strategic balance which will permit free and independent societies to pursue their aspirations;

—to checking the spread of Soviet influence in this strategic region;

—to fulfilling our responsibility to assist in the resolution of conflicts which threaten international security and the well-being of the nations and peoples in the region;

—to assuring the security and welfare of Israel and other friendly nations in the region;

—to preserving free world access to the region's oil;

—to supporting other major economic interests such as assisting the orderly economic development of some of the needy countries in the region, cooperating with wealthier states to maintain a sound international financial order, and generally maintaining access to markets for American goods and services.

There are two central themes to our approach which can be summarized in the words "peace" and "security" for the region. Both promote our own policy and the welfare of the region's people. In this context:

—We are continuing to pursue vigorously a just and comprehensive Middle East peace within the framework of the Camp

---

[6] Source: *Foreign Assistance and Related Programs, Appropriations for 1983: Hearings Before the Subcommittee on Foreign Operations and Related Agencies, Committee on Appropriations, House of Representatives, Ninety-seventh Congress, Second Session* (Washington, 1982), Part 4, pp. 335–344.

[7] *Ibid.*, pp. 346–364.

[8] For Buckley's statement, see *ibid.*, Part 1, pp. 134–149.

David Agreements, which in turn derive from UN Security Council Resolution 242.[9] Arrangements are nearly complete for emplacement of the Multinational Force and Observers and its assumption of responsibility to monitor the security provisions of the peace treaty between Egypt and Israel. We are confident that both Egypt and Israel are committed to the continued strengthening of their relationship.

—We are also continuing with negotiations on the establishment of an autonomy regime for the West Bank and Gaza. These negotiations look to achievement of an agreement which will serve as the basis for the Palestinian participation necessary for successful conclusion of arrangements to permit establishment of a transitional regime in the West Bank and Gaza.

—We are continuing our support for the Government and people of Lebanon in working their way—with help from other Arab States—toward national reconciliation and greater security. We are committed to the independence, sovereignty, and territorial integrity of Lebanon and strongly support the constitutional process which calls for the election of a new President later this year. As you know, Ambassador Habib has just returned from another trip to the region, and his discussions encourage us to believe that the cease-fire agreement he worked out last July can and will continue to hold, thus winning time for the internal conciliation process in Lebanon, which offers the best prospect for a phased, orderly withdrawal of Syrian forces.

—Moving to another serious conflict in the area, we support the resolution of the war between Iraq and Iran—which has already caused so many human casualties and extensive physical destruction. The continuation of this war, we believe, serves the interests of neither Iraq nor Iran. It endangers the peace and security of all nations in the gulf region. Consistent with our policy of neutrality toward this conflict, we have refused to sell or authorize the transfer of U.S.-controlled defense articles and services to either Iran or Iraq. And we have urged that others avoid actions which will have the effect of prolonging or expanding the conflict. We have welcomed responsible international efforts to bring the fighting to an end and the parties to negotiations. We consider a peaceful settlement, reaffirming the independence and territorial integrity of both Iran and Iraq, to be essential to the security and well-being of the region.

—We also support the return of peace to the suffering peoples of Afghanistan. But this must be peace in the context of the withdrawal of Soviet military forces, the restoration of Afghanistan's independence and nonaligned status, the right of the Afghan people to form a government of their own choosing, and creation of conditions which will permit the 3 million Afghan refugees to return to their homes.

This brings me to my second theme of security. Under Secretary Buckley in his own presentation spoke of the importance of southwest Asian security and the relationship of this concern to Middle East peace. We share with friendly states their concern about threats to security throughout this region posed by factors such as the Soviet invasion of Afghanistan, the uncertainty surrounding Iran, the Soviet position in the Horn of Africa and in South Yemen, Libyan support for terrorism and pressures against neighboring states, and efforts to magnify such threats through the Libyan alliance with Ethiopia and South Yemen.

Indeed, both in our efforts to move further with the Middle East peace process and in our efforts to encourage the return of peace with security and national sovereignty elsewhere in the region, we recognize that the necessary spirit of accommodation can grow more easily if the states concerned feel secure and confident of U.S. support.

We have taken important steps to build the confidence of key states in our commitment to their security. At a time of budgetary stringencies, we have, with considerable sacrifice, increased the national resources for our own military, to develop their capability to deter threats to the region.

We have at the same time significantly increased our security and economic assistance to friendly and strategically located states in the region so that they can better provide for their own defense, resist external pressures, improve their own economies, and thus enhance the prospects for orderly progress. I shall briefly list for you the highlights of our assistance programs for the countries in the Near East/South Asian region (NEA).

The NEA FY'83 foreign assistance request will fund six major programs. These include:

—development assistance totaling $287.243 million for the region to seven

---

[9] For the text of U.N. Security Council Resolution 242 (1967), see *American Foreign Policy: Current Documents, 1967*, pp. 616–617.

countries, of which over $200 million goes to the three poorer countries of South Asia (India, Bangladesh, Sri Lanka);

—P.L. 480[10] totaling $619.513 million ($420 million Title I, $99.513 million Title II), provided to 13 of the 15 NEA foreign assistance recipient countries;

—Economic Support Fund (ESF) of $1768 million, of which a substantial proportion goes to Israel and Egypt, our partners in peace;

—Foreign Military Sales (FMS) financing totaling $3660 million, $1030 million of it in direct concessional loans, $500 million and $400 million as forgiven loans for Israel and Egypt respectively;

—International Military Education and Training (IMET) totaling $11.1 million;

—and peacekeeping operations (PKO) totaling $34.474 million, in support of the Middle East peace process.

These programs total $6380.33 million for FY'83, which the administration believes is the minimal required to the United States to protect its interests and achieve its policy goals in this vital region.

I would now like to offer a few comments on each of our FY 83 proposals.

Israel: We are committed to Israel's security and well-being. Security support for Israel is central to our Middle Eastern policy. The $1.7 billion in FMS that we are proposing will help Israel maintain its technological edge in overall military capability in the region. We are also requesting $785 million in ESF to reflect U.S. support tangibly and facilitate a modest rate of economic growth.

Egypt: Egypt is key to much of what we hope to accomplish in the Middle East, in terms of both regional peace and regional security. The $1.4 billion FMS program contributes to Egypt's ability to defend itself and help its neighbors, in the face of the various threats I have mentioned. It replaces a small portion of Egypt's aging, deteriorating military matériel. The Economic Support Fund request for Egypt totals $785 million, which is designed to provide direct support for economic stability in the near-term while building the base for improved economic productivity and equity upon which long-term stability must depend. The requested P.L. 480 program consists of $250 million in P.L. 480 Title I and $9.9 million Title II in support of private voluntary agencies.

Pakistan: Pakistan is a key frontline state which remains steadfast in resisting great pressures from the Soviets in Afghanistan. Our FY'83 proposal of $275 million in FMS loans is the first FMS increment of the $3.2 billion 5-year assistance package. This will help fund F-16 aircraft, armored vehicles, artillery and associated equipment ordered in FY'82 as well as follow-on orders for additional quantities of similar equipment later. Our assistance to Pakistan is in no way intended against India, good and mutually beneficial relations with whom remain our high priority goal. A total of $200 million in development assistance and ESF will be concentrated in the agricultural sector with activities also in the fields of population, health, energy, and private sector development. We are requesting $50 million for P.L. 480 Title I.

Morocco: The proposal of $100 million in FMS credit to Morocco would permit support of major U.S. combat systems which Morocco has already acquired, together with an ongoing modernization program. Concessional terms for 50 percent of this FMS are recommended to alleviate a heavy debt burden related to economic difficulties largely beyond Morocco's ability to control (e.g., drought and world inflation). Development assistance of $13.5 million will fund programs in agriculture, family planning, renewable energy resource development, and low cost housing. The requested level of P.L. 480 is $25 million for Title I and $10.5 million for Title II.

Tunisia: Tunisia, under direct threat from Libya, requires a military modernization program with heavy initial costs. Our FMS credits of $140 million, half of which we are requesting in concessional terms, are intended to cushion the shock of such large expenditures. The FY'83 levels would help fund the acquisition of F–5 aircraft, M60 tanks, and Chaparral missiles, which the Tunisians intend to order in FY'82. We are requesting $10 million for P.L. 480 Title I and $1.8 million for Title II.

Jordan: We propose an increase in FMS for Jordan by $25 million to a total of $75 million. We seek, through our continued support, to enhance Jordan's security and ability to remain a viable, independent, and constructive actor in the region. A stable Jordan supports our objective of building

---

[10] Formerly entitled the Agricultural Trade Development and Assistance Act, enacted July 10, 1954, P.L. 480 provided for the donation of U.S. agricultural surpluses to friendly governments; for text, see 68 Stat. 454, and subsequent amendments.

peace in the region and assisting countries in acquiring the capability of resisting outside aggression and regional subversion. We are also preparing $20 million in ESF to assist the development of critical water and waste water programs, health programs, and agricultural and irrigation projects. There is also a $256,000 P.L. 480 Title II program.

Yemen: North Yemen is presently being challenged militarily by an armed, Marxist-led insurgent group backed by Soviet-sponsored South Yemen. The North Yemeni military requires essential additional training and operational assistance effectively to utilize U.S. equipment funded by Saudi Arabia. Further, it requires increased and sustained economic and military assistance if we are going to provide credible support to the central government in the face of this persistent outside threat. We are asking for an additional $5 million in FMS to a total of $15 million and a modest increase in IMET over FY'82. Development assistance of $27.5 million is requested to meet basic human needs in one of the poorest nations of the region.

Oman: The $40 million in FMS will in part be applied against continuing payment for U.S. equipment acquired over the past 2 years. In light of a tightening internal budget, the remaining amount will be used to offset the cost of the continuing and essential Omani force modernization effort. Oman continues to play an important role in regional security and in the defense of the southern gulf Indian Ocean region. And we are requesting $15 million in ESF which will support dam construction, fisheries, and other projects identified by the U.S.–Oman Joint Commission.

Lebanon: Small increases in our proposed FMS loan program for Lebanon of $15 million, up $5 million from the FY'82 level, reflect our continued desire to see the Lebanese Government develop the capability to reduce and eventually eliminate civil conflict, and work for restoration of essential public services and a return to normalcy of life in that very troubled country. An ESF program of $8 million will include support for humanitarian purposes and will assist the programs of the Council of Redevelopment and Construction.

For the poorer countries of south Asia, we are proposing development assistance of $87 million for India, $76 million for Bangladesh, $40.3 million for Sri Lanka, and $13.5 million for Nepal. In general their programs seek to increase food production and rural employment as well as health and family planning programs. As for P.L. 480, we are requesting $111 million in Title II for India; $60 million in Title I and $20.5 million in Title II for Bangladesh; and $2.5 million Title I and $5.8 million Title II for Sri Lanka.

In short, Mr. Chairman and members of the subcommittee, both through our foreign military sales credits and through our economic assistance to the countries of this region, we seek to strengthen security and stability, promote the peaceful solution of old or new conflicts, and assist those countries to provide a better life for their peoples. To these goals we remain committed.

Document 303

Address by the Secretary of State (Haig) Before the Chicago Council on Foreign Relations, Chicago, May 26, 1982[11]

Peace and Security in the Middle East

The Middle East today is a severe testing ground for constructive diplomacy. Deeply rooted rivalries and historic animosities mark its politics. The region's strategic value as a bridge linking three continents is amplified by its vast natural wealth. And in the nuclear age, the interplay of local and superpower competition takes on a special edge of danger.

As a consequence, no other region is less forgiving of political passivity than the Middle East. So many interests are at stake and so many factors are at work that the alternative to shaping events is to suffer through them. We are at such a juncture today. We must shape events in the Middle East if we are to continue to hope for a more peaceful international order, one characterized by peoples living in peace and the resolution of conflicts without resort to force.

Ever since the 1973 war, the daunting task of achieving peace between the Arabs and Israel has been among America's highest priorities. Despite the reluctance of the American people to expand their interna-

[11] Source: Department of State Press Release 177, May 26, 1982; printed also in Department of State *Bulletin*, July 1982, pp. 44–47.

tional commitments during the decade of the seventies, the efforts of our diplomats were supported by an increasing volume of economic and military assistance. Clearly, the safeguarding of our interests in the Middle East through the peace process has merited and enjoyed both bipartisan support and popular consensus.

The efforts launched by the United States in those years have borne substantial fruit. Two American Presidents and Secretary of State Kissinger laid the groundwork for progress through the disengagement agreements. The Camp David Accords became the living testimony to the vision of the late President Sadat, Prime Minister Begin, and President Carter that the cycle of war and hatred could be broken. The United States will always be proud of its crucial role in this process. By 1981, however, the challenges to American policy had multiplied far beyond the self-evident necessity to prevent another Arab-Israeli war:

—The Soviet Union and its allies increased their influence, particularly along the sea lanes and vital approaches to the region. Local conflicts and ambitions ranging from North Africa to the Horn of Africa, the Yemens to Afghanistan, offered the context. Arms, Cuban mercenaries, and Soviet soldiers themselves in Afghanistan were the instruments. The United States seemed slow to recognize that this pattern of events was undermining the regional security of our friends, prospects for peace, and vital Western interests.

—Iran, a close American ally and a force for stability in the Persian Gulf, was convulsed by revolution as the Islamic Republic rejected the diplomacy and modernizing program of the Shah. In the face of this upheaval, the United States found it difficult to pursue its interests or to achieve a constructive relationship with the new government. Meanwhile, Iraq invaded Iran. Fueled by Soviet arms to both countries, this conflict threatened ominous consequences for the future security of the area and Western interests in the flow of oil.

—The once prosperous and peaceful state of Lebanon was shattered by civil conflict and the intervention of outside forces. Continuous tension sapped the authority of the Lebanese Government, aggravated inter-Arab relations and threatened to involve Israel and Syria in war.

—Meanwhile, the peace process itself had reached a dangerous impasse. Egypt and Israel were divided over the role and composition of the Multinational Force and Observers, crucial to the Israeli withdrawal from Sinai and the peace treaty itself. The negotiations for Palestinian autonomy were in recess. The other Arab States, American friends in Saudi Arabia and Jordan among them, were opposed to the Camp David Accords and Egypt's peace with Israel. The Palestinian Arabs themselves were still adamantly against either joining the peace process or recognizing explicitly Israel's right to live in peace.

These developments required an American approach to the problems of the Middle East that not only pressed the peace process forward, but also enlarged the security dimension of our relations with the states of the area. Peace and security had to move in parallel. Local leaders understood that the inevitable risk-taking for peace would be vitally affected by the strategic context of the region. Lack of confidence in the United States and fear of the Soviet Union or radical forces would paralyze the prospects for progress, not only in the Arab-Israeli conflict but other regional problems as well.

Our previous policies had to be strengthened by building on a consensus of strategic concern over Soviet and radical activities that already existed among our friends in the Middle East. It was not enough to say that we opposed Soviet intervention and Soviet proxies. We had to demonstrate our ability to protect our friends and to help them to defend themselves. We had to take initiatives on the peace process and other regional conflicts that would prevent the Soviet Union from exploiting local turmoil and troublemakers for its own strategic purposes. In short, the United States had to be receptive, useful, and reliable in helping our friends to counter threats to their security.

The President, therefore, set in motion a broad-ranging attempt to create more effective security cooperation in the Middle East.

—We established a fresh basis for cooperation with Pakistan, a traditional American friend, a key state on the northern tier of the Middle East and, with the Soviet occupation of Afghanistan, at the front line of danger;

—We have improved relations with Turkey, a staunch member of NATO, and long a barrier to Soviet expansion;

—We have worked together with our friends to counter the activities of Libya in Africa and the Middle East.

In addition, the United States has sought and will continue to seek practical arrangements with such countries as Morocco, Egypt, Sudan, Somalia, Jordan, Oman, and Saudi Arabia that enhance security. We are also working with Israel, a strategic ally, to whose security and qualitative military superiority we have long been committed.

In undertaking these efforts, we recognize that for many countries formal and elaborate security structures are no longer appropriate. We have not tried to create interests where none exist. Though we shall take full account of local sensitivities, no country can be given a veto over the pursuit of our best interests or necessary cooperation with others.

The United States, working with its local friends despite their sometimes conflicting concerns, can be a responsive partner in the achievement of greater security for all. Our strong naval forces and the determination of the President and the American people to improve our defense posture despite economic austerity, are also essential to our credibility in the Middle East.

Greater cooperation in the field of security will increase measurably the confidence that our local friends repose in the United States. If properly managed, such cooperation reinforces American diplomacy. And today the United States must address three issues: First, the Iraq–Iran war; second, the autonomy negotiations, and third, the crisis in Lebanon.

Each of these issues is characterized by a mixture of danger and opportunity. Moreover, they have begun already to affect each other. If we are to succeed in advancing our goals throughout the region, then we must coordinate our approaches to all of them.

First the Iran–Iraq war. Iraq has justified its invasion and seizure of Iranian territory by referring to longstanding border claims and Iranian calls for the overthrow of its government. Iran has responded that the 1975 Algiers agreement[12] settled such claims and accuses Iraq of deliberate aggression intended to bring down the Islamic Republic. It is clear that disregard for the principle that international disputes should be settled peacefully has brought the region into great danger, with ominous implications for Western interests.

Both Iran and Iraq, though wealthy in oil, have been badly drained of vital resources. There is great risk that the conflict may spill over into neighboring states and it has already aggravated inter-Arab relations. It may lead to unforeseen and far-reaching changes in the regional balance of power, offering the Soviet Union an opportunity to enlarge its influence in the process.

The United States does not have diplomatic relations with either Iraq or Iran. From the beginning of the war we have stressed our neutrality. We have refused and we shall continue to refuse to allow military equipment under U.S. controls to be provided to either party.

Neutrality, however, does not mean that we are indifferent to the outcome. We have friends and interests that are endangered by the continuation of hostilities. We are committed to defending our vital interests in the area. These interests—and the interests of the world—are served by the territorial integrity and political independence of all countries in the Persian Gulf. The United States, therefore, supports constructive efforts to bring about an end to the fighting and the withdrawal of forces behind international borders under conditions that will preserve the sovereignty and territorial integrity of both Iran and Iraq. In the weeks ahead, we shall take a more active role with other concerned members of the international community as efforts are intensified to end this tragic war.

Second the autonomy negotiations. President Sadat of Egypt, who gave his life for peace, once described the barriers to Arab-Israeli peace as primarily psychological. He recognized that the profound antagonisms dividing Arab and Israeli were deeply reinforced by lasting suspicion. Politics—the art of the possible—could succeed only after psychology—the science of perceptions—had done its work.

Our initial task was to make sure that both the psychology and the politics of the peace process continued. While we were prepared to take the initiative on the autonomy negotiations, it soon became evident as the Sinai withdrawal date approached that the best way to sustain confidence in the peace process was to help both Egypt and Israel fulfill the terms of their peace treaty. After prolonged American diplomatic effort, the Multinational Force and Observers (MFO) was established. It is safeguarding the peace in Sinai today. The President's decison to offer U.S. troops for the force was a tangible recognition of the

---

[12] On March 26, 1975, Iran and Iraq reached an agreement under which Iraq abandoned its claims to the Shatt al-Arab waterway and accepted land frontiers that predated the British presence. Iran in return abandoned its support for a rebellion in Kurdistan.

interrelationship between peace and security. Such a demonstration of our commitment to the treaty helped to secure broader participation, including units from some of our European allies. This truly multinational peacekeeping force testifies to international support for peace.

Only 1 month ago, the final arrangements were put into place. On that occasion, President Reagan spoke for all Americans when he praised the courage of both Egypt and Israel.[13] Sinai, so often the corridor for armies on the way to war, was at last a zone of peace. But we cannot allow the peace process to end in the desert.

The signatories of the Camp David Accords, of which we are the witness and full partners, wisely entitled their work, "A Framework for Peace in the Middle East." Basing their diplomacy on United Nations Security Council Resolutions 242 and 338,[14] which provide for peace between Israel and all of its neighbors, including Jordan and Syria, both Egypt and Israel were not content to establish peace only with each other. They recognized the necessity to go beyond their bilateral achievement in the search for a just, comprehensive, and durable settlement of the Arab-Israeli conflict. They have, therefore, been engaged for over 3 years, not only in the execution of the treaty of peace but also in negotiations aimed eventually at the resolution of the Palestinian problem in all its aspects.

These negotiations, known as the autonomy talks, have been the subject of much misunderstanding and criticism. For many Israelis the process threatens to go too far, leading toward a Palestinian state which they fear would deny Jews access to the historic areas of ancient Israel, threaten Israeli security, and offer the Soviet Union a fresh opportunity for influence. For many Arabs, including until now the Palestinians themselves, autonomy does not seem to go far enough. In their view, it is only a formula for an Israeli domination they resist and that they fear will lead to further radicalization of the entire region. Israeli settlement activities in the occupied territories have exacerbated these fears.

We must all face the reality that autonomy in and of itself cannot entirely alleviate the fears on either side. But we should also realize that autonomy is only one stage of a process. It is an opportunity, not a conclusion. The beginning of autonomy actually initiates a transitional period to last no longer than 5 years, in which a freely elected self-governing authority would replace the Israeli military government and civilian administration. Furthermore, negotiations are to commence not later than the third year of the transitional period, on the final status of the West Bank and Gaza and its relationship with its neighbors. A peace treaty between Israel and Jordan is also an objective of this negotiation.

Ample opportunity is provided in every phase for the participation, in addition to the present partners in the peace process, of Jordan and the Palestinian Arabs. These arrangements are to reflect both the principle of self-government by the inhabitants and the legitimate security concerns of all the parties involved.

The Camp David process, which is based firmly on United Nations Resolutions 242 and 338, remains the only practical route toward a more comprehensive Middle East peace between Israel and all of its neighbors, including Jordan and Syria. No other plan provides for movement despite the conflicting interests and fears of the parties. No other plan embodies so well the necessity for progress despite the inherent imperfections of a transitional arrangement. As Churchill put it, "The maxim—nothing avails but perfection—spells paralysis."

The United States has been heartened by the public and private declarations of both President Mubarak of Egypt and Prime Minister Begin of Israel to press forward toward the early and successful conclusion of an autonomy agreement. As we proceed, it is important that we conduct ourselves with several considerations in mind:

—Autonomy is transitional, not the final word. The genius of Camp David was to provide for the possibility of progress, despite crucial, unresolved issues such as the ultimate status of Jerusalem. These, too, must be negotiated but first we must establish a self-governing authority that will enable Israelis and Palestinians to work together. Public statements that fail to recognize the temporary nature of autonomy and negotiating positions that mistake autonomy for final status do nothing but hinder forward movement.

—Unilateral actions by any party that attempt to prejudge or bias the final out-

---

[13] For the White House statement on the Israeli withdrawal from the Sinai Peninsula, see document 312.

[14] For the text of U.N. Security Council Resolution 338(1973), see Department of State *Bulletin*, November 12, 1973, pp. 598–604.

come of the process serve only to raise suspicions and aggravate relationships. Truly all of our ultimate hopes for peace depend in the end upon the achievement of mutual respect and friendly relations between Arab and Israeli. A heavy responsibility will be borne by those who darken these hopes without regard for either Israel's long-term interests or legitimate Palestinian aspirations.

—Refusal to participate in the talks by those most affected by the conflict risks the loss of the best chance for the achievement of a lasting peace. Fifteen years have passed since the 1967 war and the initiation of Israeli's military government over the West Bank and Gaza. Autonomy is the vital first step in the historic opportunity to change this situation and to begin the painful but necessary process of resolving the Palestinian problem. A settlement cannot be imposed but peace can be negotiated. History will judge harshly those who miss this opportunity.

Despite all of the obstacles confronting a broader Middle East peace, there has been a change in the polemic over the Arab-Israeli conflict in recent months. Many are recognizing at last that "No war, no peace" is not good enough. Increasingly, disagreement concerns the terms of peace, not the fact that peace itself must come.

The United States long has believed that the risks and sacrifices required for settlement of the Arab-Israeli conflict do not admit of any ambiguity on the basic issue that genuine peace is the objective. That is why, for example, we shall neither recognize nor negotiate with the Palestine Liberation Organization until it accepts United Nations Resolutions 242 and 338, and recognizes Israel's right to live in peace.

Now is the time to redouble our efforts to make the peace process under the Camp David framework continue to work. I have said that great intellectual ingenuity and political courage will be required by all parties if an autonomy agreement is to be reached. Our delegation, led by Ambassador Fairbanks, will continue to work closely with Egypt and Israel as we intensify our effort to achieve success.

The peace process has already accomplished what would have been considered a utopian fantasy only a few short years ago. But none of us should be under any illusions. The failure to negotiate an autonomy agreement, and to negotiate one soon, will squander the best chance to act in the best interests of all parties. Inevitably, such a failure will invite more dangerous alternatives.

Third, and finally, the crisis in Lebanon. Lebanon today is a focal point of danger. All of those conditions are present in abundance that might be ignited into a war with far-reaching consequences. The lives of the people of Lebanon are at stake. The life of the state itself is at stake. And the stability of the region hangs in the balance.

The recent history of Lebanon is a grim tale. Over the last 6 years, many of the country's most striking achievements have been lost. Once stable enough to be the center of Middle Eastern finance, its economy has been wracked by internecine warfare and foreign intervention. Tragically, Lebanon, once extolled as a model in a region of suffering minorities, is now a byword for violence.

Lebanon's unique position as a marketplace for the ideas of the Arab world has given way instead to a marketplace for the violent conflicts of inter-Arab and regional rivalries. Its representative government has been endangered. The Arab deterrent force, now consisting entirely of Syrian troops, with its mission to protect the integrity of Lebanon, has not stabilized the situation.

The story on the Lebanese-Israeli border is no different. Once the most peaceful point of Arab-Israeli contact, southern Lebanon turned into a battleground between Israel and the PLO even as the peace process proceeded. In this part of the country as well, intercommunal relations have suffered badly. The central government's authority has been challenged by the variety and military strength of contesting groups. The brave units of the U.N. force, faced with an enormously difficult and dangerous task, have saved many lives, but have not succeeded entirely in establishing the security of daily life.

Over the past year, deteriorating conditions in Lebanon have required extraordinary efforts to avoid war. In April of 1981, Ambassador Habib, at the President's direction, worked successfully, to avoid military confrontation in Lebanon. His efforts culminated in the cessation of hostilities in the Lebanese-Israeli area.[15] A fragile cease-

---

[15] For the announcement of a cease-fire in Lebanon on July 24, 1981, see *American Foreign Policy: Current Documents, 1981*, documents 374 and 375.

fire has survived for more than 10 months. While all parties remain fundamentally interested in maintaining it, the danger is ever present that violations could escalate into major hostilities.

These measures have deterred war. But conflict cannot be managed perpetually while the problems at the root of the conflict continue to fester. The world cannot stand aside, watching in morbid fascination, as this small nation with its creative and cultured people slides further into the abyss of violence and chaos. The time has come to take concerted action in support of both Lebanon's territorial integrity within its internationally recognized borders and a strong central government capable of promoting a free, open, democratic, and traditionally pluralistic society. The President has, therefore, directed Ambassador Habib to return to the Middle East soon to discuss our ideas for such action, with the cooperation of concerned states.

The Middle East today is a living laboratory for the political experiments of the twentieth century. A multitude of nations have emerged from the disintegration of empires, their dreams of a better future sustained by memories of a glorious past. The modern nation-state has been imposed upon traditions that transcend both secular loyalties and well-defined borders. The quest for modernization competes uneasily with religious and ethnic identities that long predate the industrial revolution of the West.

Clearly, the peoples of the Middle East are embarked upon the most rapid social transformations in their history. Nonetheless, the past strongly permeates both their attitudes toward the future and the texture of their daily life. The ruins of ancient times remind them and us that the region has always played a vital part in the advance of civilization.

There are other ruins, too, that remind us of another aspect of the Middle East. Philosophers and artists, merchants and travelers, statesmen, and scholars have made their impact throughout the ages. But the soldier, with his vast monuments to destruction, is perhaps overly represented in the archaeology of this region. The violence of war is all too often the point of contact between the history of the Middle East and its contemporary struggles.

By the standards of this ancient region, the United States is a country still in its infancy. But by virtue of our power and our interests, our relationships, and our objectives, we are uniquely placed to play a constructive role in helping the nations of the area in their quest for peace and security. Now is America's moment in the Middle East. As Americans, let us hope to be remembered by the peoples of the Middle East not for the monuments of war but for the works of peace.

B. The Arab-Israeli Dispute

Document 304

Statement Read by the Department of State Spokesman (Fischer), February 1, 1982[1]

United States Welcomes European Participation in the Multinational Force and Observers

We are very pleased that the Israeli Government yesterday formally accepted the participation of Italy, the United Kingdom, the Netherlands, and France in the Multinational Force and Observers in the Sinai. The Israeli acceptance of European participation sets the stage for contingents from Australia and New Zealand to join this Force. We warmly welcome the participation of all these states in this vital peacekeeping force, and we believe that their presence enhances its overall credibility and its effectiveness.

We wish to express our thanks to the governments of these states as well as to the Governments of Fiji, Colombia, and Uruguay, which previously agreed to participate. We look forward to the deployment of this peacekeeping Force on March 20, this year, as called for in the Egypt–Israel Protocol establishing the Multinational Force and Observers.[2]

---

[1] Source: Office of Press Relations, Department of State. The statement was read at the Department of State Daily Press Briefing held at 12:35 p.m.

[2] For the text of the Egyptian-Israeli Protocol of August 3, 1981, establishing the Multinational Force and Observers, see *American Foreign Policy: Current Documents, 1981,* document 311.

Document 305

Testimony by the Secretary of State (Haig) Before the Senate Foreign Relations Committee, February 2, 1982 (Extract)[3]

Status of the Camp David Peace Process

. . . .

Since assuming office, we have worked to support the Egyptian-Israeli Peace Treaty[4] and to facilitate the talks on Palestinian autonomy. We have at long last resolved the remaining issues concerning the deployment and composition of the multinational force and observers in the Sinai.

We were also able to ease Israeli concerns over freedom of navigation in the Straits of Tiran by confirming the role of the MFO in that area—with Egyptian agreement. The force itself should be deployed by March 20, resulting in final Israeli withdrawal on April 25.

Another purpose of both visits[5] was to urge both Egypt and Israel to intensify their efforts to reach agreement on autonomy. In 30 hours of intense discussion, I worked with the leaders of Egypt and Israel to make progress on a declaration of principles. This declaration would establish a framework for inviting the Palestinian Arabs to join with us in negotiating the detailed agreement to a self-governing authority—as specified in the Camp David accords.[6]

After analyzing the issues and differences, my trip last week gave me the opportunity to suggest certain ideas on how gaps between Egypt and Israel might be bridged. These ideas now are being considered by the parties. Hard work and intellectual ingenuity will be required by both sides to bridge the great differences that now divide them. We have agreed together to strive for a declaration of principles as soon as possible, but without artificial deadlines.

Both President Mubarak and Prime Minister Begin have pledged to join with us in good faith to achieve success. To encourage momentum the President has approved my proposal to ask former Assistant Secretary for Congressional Relations Richard Fairbanks to work full time on this effort. His experiences on my second visit have already introduced him to the complexities of this vital negotiation.

These visits have also been useful in easing friction between Egypt and Israel. As the Sinai withdrawal date approached, both sides began to doubt each other's intentions. Israel has been reassured that both the United States and Egypt are firmly committed to Camp David beyond April and the withdrawal date. Egypt has been reassured that Israel will withdraw on schedule and that the United States will be a full partner in the autonomy negotiations.

My trips to Cairo also provided the opportunity for intensive and wideranging discussions with President Mubarak on matters of mutual concern. The President's dedication to the welfare of his people is matched by his dedication to peace. His meeting with President Reagan this week, starting today,[7] will mark another significant step in the development of a close partnership between our countries.

. . . .

SENATOR BOSCHWITZ. . . . I also noted that the Israelis seem to have announced through the press some of their efforts, some of their plans with respect to the negotiations now occurring on autonomy.[8] I would presume that announcing these in a public way is going to constrict the ability to move forward on that. Would you agree

[3] Source: *East–West Relations: Hearing Before the Committee on Foreign Relations, United States Senate, Ninety-seventh Congress, Second Session* (Washington, 1982), pp. 5, 6, and 34.

[4] For the text of the Treaty of Peace between Egypt and Israel, signed at Washington, March 26, 1979, see *American Foreign Policy: Basic Documents, 1977–1980*, pp. 669–683.

[5] Reference is to Secretary Haig's visits to Egypt and Israel, January 12–15, 1982, and to Israel and Egypt, January 27–29, 1982.

[6] For the texts of the two Camp David Accords, "Framework for Peace in the Middle East," and "Framework for the Conclusion of a Peace Treaty between Egypt and Israel," both dated September 17, 1978, see *American Foreign Policy: Basic Documents, 1977–1980*, pp. 653–657.

[7] Regarding the state visit of Egyptian President Mubarak, February 2–5, see Chapter 11, Part C.

[8] Israeli proposals for autonomy for the West Bank and the Gaza Strip were published in the *Jerusalem Post* on February 1, 1982. See Foreign Broadcast Information Service, *Daily Report: Middle East and Africa*, February 1, 1982, pp. 13–16.

with that? Would you wish to comment on that?

SECRETARY HAIG. Well, first, Senator, you always have to sort out what is an official Israeli Government position and what you read in the Israeli press. The Israelis enjoy the same very open approach to that as we do, and I wouldn't have it otherwise. But I think you are talking specifically about the document that was released, I think this morning or yesterday evening, which laid out their concept of autonomy and the authorities that they are prepared to turn over to the populations of the West Bank and Gaza, some 13 of them.

Now, I was aware of this document and asked them to hold up on releasing it publicly initially. That was during my first trip 3 weeks ago. I urged them to be sure that they didn't just drop it under the public perception without having provided the Egyptian Government a copy of that paper. I think they have done all that.

Therefore, I don't think it is a counterproductive step, but rather a step that I would support, because it does show for the first time a degree of real flexibility has been brought to bear on the question of autonomy. It doesn't answer all the questions, and I told that, frankly, to the Israeli Government. There are a lot of unstated aspects of the autonomy question that will continue to be a source of paranoia, but on balance I would say it is a constructive step, although your observations are not without value.

SENATOR BOSCHWITZ. I also noted that it did show some flexibility, but it wasn't clear to me whether or not showing that flexibility in the press would hinder or allow the negotiations to proceed more swiftly.

SECRETARY HAIG. In a coalition and in an open society like that there are no secrets, even when you don't put it in the press.

SENATOR BOSCHWITZ. Oh, yes, perhaps even less so than here.

. . . .

Document 306

Statement by the Representative at the United Nations (Kirkpatrick) Before the U.N. General Assembly, February 5, 1982[9]

U.S. Opposition to U.N. General Assembly Resolution on the Golan Heights Situation

Mr. President, the resolution before this emergency special session of the General Assembly is profoundly objectionable to the United States.[10] We oppose it because it does not contribute to peace in the Middle East: It will make peace harder to achieve.

We oppose the end it seeks—which is revenge and retribution, not conciliation and compromise.

We oppose the means it recommends: which are unreasonably punitive and ill-suited to accomplishing any constructive purpose.

We oppose the use of the United Nations involved here because this body was and is meant to be devoted to building peace and security, and this resolution seeks neither. Instead, it uses this body as an instrument to deepen divisions and exacerbate conflicts.

We oppose this resolution because, like any other cynical use of power, it will leave this body weaker than it already is, less fit to achieve its noble purposes.

By damaging the prospects for peace, this resolution undermines the integrity—indeed, the very raison détre—of the United Nations.

Last month in the Security Council the United States voted against a resolution on Israel's Golan Heights legislation[11] because

---

[9] Source: U.S. Mission to the United Nations Press Release USUN 03(82), February 5, 1982.

[10] U.N. General Assembly Resolution ES-9/1(1982) condemned Israel's annexation of the Golan Heights as an illegal and invalid act of aggression. It stated that Israel's activities showed that it was not a peace-loving state and called on all states to suspend military assistance to Israel and to sever diplomatic, economic, and cultural relations with it. The resolution was approved on February 5, 1982, by a vote of 86 to 21 (including the United States), with 34 abstentions. For text, see *UN Chronicle*, April 1982, pp. 11–12.

[11] In the U.N. Security Council on January 20,

as we stated at the time, the resolution constituted "a perversion of the very purpose which the Security Council is called upon by Chapter VII of the United Nations Charter to perform." That purpose is to prevent "an aggravation of the situation." The resolution before us today, like the previous resolution, does not prevent an aggravation of the situation: it is itself a source of aggravation. It is also procedurally flawed in that it seeks to assign to the General Assembly responsibilities that Chapter VII of the Charter properly and solely invests in the Security Council.

The United Nations has discussed the Golan Heights legislation now for nearly 2 months. As my delegation made clear at the outset, we opposed this legislation because it purported or appeared to alter unilaterally the international status of the Golan Heights. Therefore, on December 17th the United States joined other members of the Security Council in passing Resolution 497,[12] thereby making clear our disapproval of the Israeli Government's action in extending its civil law over the Golan Heights. We communicated the same message in our bilateral relations.

As we have stated often, the future of the Golan Heights, like that of all the occupied territories, can be resolved only through negotiations pursuant to Security Council Resolutions 242 and 338. Accordingly, we have called upon Israel to rescind its legislation and—most importantly—to reaffirm its commitment to a negotiated solution. In its letter of December 29th to the Secretary-General, Israel did, in fact, reaffirm its readiness to enter into unconditional negotiations with the Syrians over the international legal status of the Golan.

At that point, the only constructive role for the United Nations was to facilitate such negotiations, in accordance with Resolutions 242 and 338.[13] But the resolution before the Security Council did not even mention these resolutions and, needless to say, the current draft resolution doesn't either.

Mr. President, we must go back to basics. Israel is accused of threatening peace. Yet peace is not the situation that prevailed between Israel and Syria before Israel's Golan Heights legislation was adopted. Security Council Resolution 338, which was the basis for the 1973 cease-fire, called upon the parties to "start immediately" to negotiate the implementation of Resolution 242 so that Israeli withdrawal could be effected in exchange for recognition of Israel's existence within "secure and recognized" borders. But no such negotiations took place.

There is no one in this chamber who does not know which party has refused to negotiate peace or even to accept Resolution 242. Yet the resolution before us today and the speeches we have heard take no account of this reality.

Mr. President, the United States greatly desires to have cordial, cooperative, good relations with all the states in the region. My country has devoted enormous effort, in this administration and under previous administrations, to finding a basis for peace and reconciliation. We also want very much a strong United Nations acting in fidelity to the principles of its Charter. For these very reasons we are appalled by this resolution which distorts reality, denies history and inflames passions.

The draft resolution before us calls the Israeli legislation an act of aggression. But no shots were fired, no soldiers were brought into place. And the future of the Golan Heights is no less negotiable than before.

It describes the Israeli legislation as an annexation. It is not. The United States has not recognized it as such. The Security Council in Resolution 497 did not recognize it as such. To now call it annexation only creates an artificial obstacle to negotiations.

This resolution calls for comprehensive sanctions against Israel and for Israel's total isolation from the rest of the world. But can anyone truly believe that such proposals, advanced in a spirit of vindictiveness, will make a constructive contribution to peace?

Mr. President, the United States objects to this resolution because it makes the search for peace more difficult, and because it weakens this body. We also object to it for less disinterested reasons—we object to the

---

1982, the United States vetoed a Jordanian draft resolution that called the Israeli action "an act of aggression" and urged member states to consider effective measures and refrain from aid to Israel. On January 28, the Security Council voted 13–0 (with the United States and the United Kingdom abstaining) to convene a special session of the U.N. General Assembly, which began the next day.

[12] For the text of U.N. Security Council Resolution 497 (1981), see *American Foreign Policy: Current Documents, 1981*, document 329.

[13] Regarding U.N. Security Council Resolutions 242 and 338, see this Chapter, Part A, footnotes 9 and 14.

barely veiled attack on the United States present here in the paragraph that "strongly deplores the negative vote by a permanent member. . . ."[14]

The right to cast a veto is vested by the Charter in the five permanent members of the Security Council. The sole purpose of this provision is to permit one of the permanent members to block a proposed action of the Council if for any reason this action is deemed seriously flawed. The United States used the veto for the purpose for which it was intended—to block action which we deemed ill-conceived and imprudent and, moreover, one incompatible with the pursuit of international peace and security to which this body is dedicated. It is not at all appropriate that an action taken in conformity with the spirit and the letter of the Charter should be deplored.

Furthermore, as everyone present understands, this resolution raises basic questions which go to the heart of the relationship of a member state to the United Nations. This is a profoundly serious matter, filled with ominous portent. Questions of membership in this body and its associated agencies should not, indeed cannot be settled by majority passions. The United Nations or any similar organization can only exist if the principle of majority rule is balanced by respect for minority rights. This resolution strikes twice at the principle that minorities also have rights: first when it deplores our use of the veto, and second when it attempts to submit questions of membership to the General Assembly. Respect for the United Nations means respect for its Charter.

We hope that the authors and supporters of the resolution will think deeply about this aspect of their approach, for the health, even the survival of the United Nations depends on respect for both majority rule and minority rights. Nothing is more clear than this.

Mr. President, suppose this resolution passes, as regrettably I suppose it will, what will this exercise have achieved?

—An Israeli withdrawal from the Golan? Of course not.

—An embargo of economic, technological, military goods destined for Israel? Of course not.

—A restoration of the occupied territories? Of course not.

—A resolution of the problems of Palestinians? Of course not.

—Peace in the Middle East? Of course not.

—Will it intimidate the United States, causing it to abandon its Middle East policy, its friendship with Israel, its search for peace in the region? Of course not.

What then, will this resolution accomplish?

What has already been achieved by these weeks of harsh, seemingly endless attacks on Israel, on the United States, on the spirit of reason, moderation, on peace itself? To raise the question is to answer it.

There is, in my country, a child's rhyme, sticks and stones may break our bones but words will never hurt us. The rhyme is profoundly mistaken. Words have consequences.

Words express the ideas, the values and the truths we live by. They are the principal means available for reason to explain purposes and dispel misunderstandings. The United Nations was conceived as a place of reason, a place where reason would replace violence as the tool for settling disputes.

This miserable resolution before us today demonstrates the sad truth that any instrument can be made to serve purposes remote from its raison détre: words can be used as weapons; ploughshares can be turned into swords, and the United Nations itself can be used to polarize nations, spread hostility, and exacerbate conflict.

The use made of the United Nations in this resolution and in the weeks preceding it is indeed worth "strongly deploring" and my government strongly deplores it.

Naturally we shall vote no.

---

[14] Ellipsis appears in the source text.

Document 307

Letter From President Reagan to the Speaker of the House of Representatives (O'Neill), March 19, 1982[15]

Mission and Deployment of U.S. Forces in the Multinational Force and Observers

DEAR MR. SPEAKER: On December 29, 1981 I signed into law Public Law 97–132,[16] a Joint Resolution authorizing the participation of the United States in the Multinational Force and Observers (MFO) which will assist in the implementation of the 1979 Treaty of Peace between Egypt and Israel. The U.S. military personnel and equipment which the United States will contribute to the MFO are now in the process of deployment to the Sinai. In accordance with my desire that the Congress be fully informed on this matter, and consistent with Section 4(a)(2) of the War Powers Resolution,[17] I am hereby providing a report on the deployment and mission of these members of the U.S. Armed Forces.

As you know, the 1979 Treaty of Peace between Egypt and Israel terminated the existing state of war between those countries, provided for the complete withdrawal from the Sinai of Israeli armed forces and civilians within three years after the date of the Treaty's entry into force (that is, by April 25, 1982), and provided for the establishment of normal friendly relations. To assist in assuring compliance with the terms of Annex I to the Treaty, so as to enhance the mutual confidence of the parties in the security of the Sinai border area, the Treaty calls for the establishment of a peacekeeping force and observers to be deployed prior to the final Israeli withdrawal. Although the Treaty called on the parties to request the United Nations to provide the peacekeeping force and observers, it was also recognized during the negotiations that it might not be possible to reach agreement in the United Nations for this purpose. For this reason, President Carter assured Israel and Egypt in separate letters that "if the Security Council fails to establish and maintain the arrangements called for in the Treaty, the President will be prepared to take those steps necessary to ensure the establishment and maintenance of an acceptable alternative multinational force."[18]

In fact, it proved impossible to secure U.N. action. As a result, Egypt and Israel, with the participation of the United States, entered into negotiations for the creation of an alternative multinational force and observers. These negotiations resulted in the signing on August 3, 1981 by Egypt and Israel of a Protocol for that purpose. The Protocol established the MFO and provided in effect that the MFO would have the same functions and responsibilities as those provided in the 1979 Treaty for the planned U.N. force. Included are: the operation of checkpoints, reconnaissance patrols, and observation posts; verification of the implementation of Annex I of the Peace Treaty; and ensuring freedom of navigation through the Strait of Tiran in accordance with Article V of the Peace Treaty. By means of an exchange of letters with Egypt and Israel dated August 3, 1981, the United States agreed, subject to Congressional authorization and appropriations, to contribute an infantry battalion, a logistics support unit and civilian observers to the MFO, as well as a specified portion of the annual costs of the MFO. The U.S. military personnel to be contributed comprise less than half of the anticipated total MFO military complement of approximately 2,500 personnel.

In Public Law 97–132, the Multinational Force and Observers Participation Resolution, Congress affirmed that it considered the establishment of the MFO to be an essential stage in the development of a comprehensive settlement in the Middle

---

[15] Source: White House Press Release, March 20, 1982, Office of the Press Secretary to the President; also printed in *Weekly Compilation of Presidential Documents*, March 29, 1982, pp. 349–350. An identical letter was sent to George Bush, President of the Senate.

[16] For the text of P.L. 97–132, see *American Foreign Policy: Current Documents, 1981*, document 332.

[17] Section 4(a)(2) of the War Powers Resolution requires the President, in the absence of a declaration of war, to report to Congress within 48 hours of the introduction of U.S. Armed Forces equipped for combat into the territory, airspace, or waters of a foreign country except for deployments which relate solely to supply, replacement, repair, or training of such forces. For the text of the War Powers Resolution, P.L. 93–148, passed over President's veto on November 7, 1973, see 87 Stat. 55.

[18] For the texts of President Carter's letters of March 26, 1979, to President Sadat of Egypt and Prime Minister Begin of Israel, see *American Foreign Policy: Basic Documents, 1977–1980*, p. 683.

East. The President was authorized to assign, under such terms and conditions as he might determine, members of the United States Armed Forces to participate in the MFO, provided that these personnel perform only the functions and responsibilities specified in the 1979 Treaty and the 1981 Protocol, and that their number not exceed 1,200 at any one time.

In accordance with the 1981 Egypt–Israel Protocol, the MFO must be in place by 1300 hours on March 20, 1982, and will assume its functions at 1300 hours on April 25, 1982. Accordingly, the movement of U.S. personnel and equipment for deployment to the Sinai is currently under way. On February 26 five unarmed UH–1H helicopters (which will provide air transportation in the Sinai for MFO personnel), together with their crews and support personnel, arrived at Tel Aviv; on March 2 approximately 88 logistics personnel arrived at Tel Aviv; on March 17, the first infantry troops of the First Battalion, 505th Infantry, 82nd Airborne Division arrived in the Southern Sinai; and by March 18 a total of 808 infantry troops, together with their equipment, will have arrived. These troops will be equipped with standard light infantry weapons, including M–16 automatic rifles, M–60 machine guns, M203 grenade launchers and Dragon anti-tank missiles.

The duration of this involvement of U.S. forces in the Sinai will depend, of course, on the strengthening of mutual confidence between Egypt and Israel. The U.S. contribution to the MFO is not limited to any specific period; however, each country which contributes military forces to the MFO retains a right of withdrawal upon adequate prior notification to the MFO Director-General. U.S. participation in future years will, of course, be subject to the Congressional authorization and appropriations process.

I want to emphasize that there is no intention or expectation that these members of the U.S. Armed Forces will become involved in hostilities. Egypt and Israel are at peace, and we expect them to remain at peace. No hostilities are occurring in the area and we have no expectation of hostilities. MFO forces will carry combat equipment appropriate for their peacekeeping missions, to meet the expectations of the parties as reflected in the 1981 Protocol and related documents, and as a prudent precaution for the safety of MFO personnel.

The deployment of U.S. forces to the Sinai for this purpose is being undertaken pursuant to Public Law 97–132 of December 29, 1981, and pursuant to the President's constitutional authority with respect to the conduct of foreign relations and as Commander-in-Chief of U.S. Armed Forces.

Sincerely,

RONALD REAGAN

Document 308

Transcript of an Interview With President Reagan, New York, March 23, 1982 (Extract)[19]

"The Answer to Israel's Security is Long-Term Peace"

. . . .

Q. Could we turn to international—this is an international question, also, as you recognize a New York question.

How could you assure the Jews of the city, this city, who came out very strongly for you in the election, how could you assure the—that you haven't abandoned them and Israel? You know, many of the Jews in this city feel very hurt. And now maybe the lines are crossed, but that's the way we hear it.

THE PRESIDENT. I think they are and we've tried to meet with leaders of various groups and organizations in the Jewish community to explain, particularly last year over the AWACS, what it was that we were trying to do. And I can assure you, in fact it will be in my remarks tonight, that we remain without qualification pledged to the security and the support of Israel.

---

[19] Source: White House Press Release, March 24, 1982, Office of the Press Secretary to the President; also printed in *Weekly Compilation of Presidential Documents*, March 29, 1982, pp. 376–377. The President was interviewed at the New York Hilton Hotel by members of the *New York Post* Editorial Board. Present were: executive editor Roger Wood, editorial page editor Bruce Rothwell, metropolitan editor Steve Dunlavy, Washington bureau chief Niles Lathem, City Hall bureau chief George Arzt, and columnist Joey Adams.

Q. Then you do feel the lines have been somewhere crossed?

THE PRESIDENT. Yes. Let me take the AWACS issue to begin with. Here is Israel, virtually one of the smallest of the nations, outnumbered a 100 to 1; basically by countries that—other than Egypt—have still, until Saudi Arabia softened its position, declaring that Israel does not have a right to exist as a nation. So Israel retains a military capacity that is backbreaking for them.

The answer to Israel's security is longtime peace. The United States is dedicated—and was before I ever got here, as witnessed at Camp David—to helping in this process. I think that one of the only ways we can bring this about is if we can persuade, particularly the more moderate Arab nations, to see this situation as Egypt did—and Egypt was the one that was at war. And to bring them into where we sit down and they can recognize that we intend to be fair as an outsider in here trying to help.

So what we have been—this is one of the reasons we have been trying to develop this relationship and let them know that we want peace for everybody there.

Q. If we could, Mr. President—previous to that, that the American Government was so—to coin a phrase—pathologically tied into Israel, that the—even the moderate Arab countries felt they were so threatened, not so much by Israel but by the so-called almighty American arm and got scared into something and doing something that they would not have normally done. And then by—what you're saying is by balancing it, we both have a right hand and a left—

THE PRESIDENT. No, I don't think that—I think that you'll find among those same moderate nations that they have much more of a concern of a threat of the Soviet Union in the Middle East. And Egypt certainly did not. Sadat did not change because of any pressure from us. He—you know, he had inherited the alliance with the Soviet Union. Then he finally had it out to here with them, and he kicked them out. And then made that great overture that led to where we are today.

But, no, I believe it is a case of—and Prime Minister Begin, when he visited Washington, I told him this and what we were going to do and I told him that we were allies and that in my view it was a two-way street, that we derived benefit as well as they did from the relationship, and that we were completely dedicated to the preservation of the State of Israel. And the—this was the only supposed arm-twisting and everything that took place and the AWACS thing. This was all that I said—

Q. —arm-twisting. (Laughter)

THE PRESIDENT.—this was all that I said with the Senators. I told them that I believed that this was the most useful step in a pursuit of peace. And many of them—they were—and I must say, the Senators that I talked to are most sincere in this, even the ones that—their concern with the security of Israel. And I got their votes when I was able to persuade them that it was equally my concern. I remember one day one of them, he stood up after we talked and he said well, he said I'm going out of here and do some praying. And I said well if you get a busy signal, it's me in there ahead of you. (Laughter)

Q. Mr. President, you also sent those Senators, I think I recall correctly, into the Congress, a letter in which you pledged that the planes would not be—the deal wouldn't go through unless certain conditions were fulfilled. One of which was that the United States would share in the intelligence gathered and have a say in the supply of that to any third party.

THE PRESIDENT. You mean of the information from the Saudis, the AWACS.

Q. Right.

THE PRESIDENT. Yes, yes.

Q. And I presume, of course, that that is still the case and that, either it's been achieved or is in the process of being achieved.

THE PRESIDENT. That is being worked out, yes.

Q. And positively? That is you'll be able to fulfill it.

. . . .

Document 309

Statements by the Secretary of State (Haig) and the Director-General of the Multinational Force and Observers (Hunt), March 26, 1982[20]

The United States Signs the MFO Agreement

SECRETARY HAIG. We are present here this morning to both celebrate peace and to carry peace forward with this signing. Some three years have passed since the momentous Egyptian-Israeli peace treaty agreement of March 26, 1979. In the intervening period, the roots of peace and normalization have begun to take hold and over three decades of tension and animosity between two great nations have steadily declined, and normalization has begun. Today's event carries forward that momentum and that deepening of the peace process and the breadth of participation of the nations involved in the Multinational Force and Observers is testimony first to the vision and the wisdom of the leaders and the people of both Egypt and Israel. But it is also testimony to the continuing American support not just for the peace treaty between Egypt and Israel itself but for the peace process. I think Americans can today take just pride in the fact that they have been full partners in this momentous and historic process. Today's events are also testimony to the splendid work of Director-General Hunt and his staff who in a relatively brief period have brought an ephemeral concept into a practical reality, and I want to congratulate you, Mr. Director-General, and all those who have worked with you so successfully and have put together this MFO which is being formalized today. Thank you, Mr. Director-General.

DIRECTOR-GENERAL HUNT. Mr. Secretary, Your Excellencies, ladies and gentlemen, it's a real pleasure to sign this treaty with the United States for the U.S. participation in the Multinational Force and Observers. This is the last agreement we have signed. It completes our efforts to bring 11 nations into the force. It has been a long 6 months; it seems more like 6 years. We have finally accomplished a great deal. As of the moment we have some 2,400 soldiers in the Sinai. Eleven units are on the way, and we expect by the early part of next week to have the full force there. The troops have started their training orientation. They will on April 25 take up their peacekeeping duties and get accompanying responsibilities under the Protocol. We are confident that we can do the job that Egypt and Israel has asked us to do, confident with this kind of international effort that we will be able to stay in the Sinai to continue to help these two important countries phrase [*phase in*?] the confidence-building process to continue the normalization toward full peace that they seek. Mr. Secretary, and the people in this room who have assisted the MFO a great deal, during the last 6 months we have continued support (inaudible) so many places that it would be difficult to really comment on the things that have been done for us, but I would like to thank you personally for it—your continued support and efforts that you have made to bring together the 11 nations that now make up the MFO. We look forward to our responsibilities and let me assure you that we will carry them out. Thank you very much.

[20] Source: Department of State Press Release 155, May 3, 1982. The statements were made at the ceremony of the signing of the Agreement Relating to Participation of U.S. Military and Civilian Personnel in the Multinational Force and Observers of March 26, 1982 (TIAS 10557). The date of March 25, 1982 for these statements is erroneously given on the source text.

Document 310

Statement by the Alternate Representative at the United Nations for Special Political Affairs (Lichenstein) Before the U.N. Security Council, April 2, 1982[21]

Explanation of the U.S. Vote on Security Council Draft Resolution on the Situation on the West Bank

Mr. President, the recent events on the West Bank have been a source of deep

[21] Source: U.S. Mission to the United Nations Press Release USUN 16(82), April 2, 1982. Draft U.N. Resolution S/14943, introduced by Jordan, denounced Israeli measures imposed on the population of the West Bank, especially the disbanding of the elected municipal council of El Bireh and the removal from office of the mayors of Nablus and Ramallah. The vote on the draft resolution was 13 to 1 (United States, a veto), with one abstention.

concern to the government and people of the United States. In the last few days the level of tension and violence has somewhat subsided, but, of course, we are aware of the danger of a resurgence and of a renewed crisis in this complex and emotional situation. For this reason, we believe that the Security Council's primary role in the present context should have been to urge restraint on the parties to avoid any new outbreak of violence which could endanger international peace and that its other equally essential role should have been to take a step, at least, on the road to a secure and lasting peace.

We do not believe that the Jordanian resolution achieved either objective.

I wish to address the dismissal of the three elected West Bank mayors referred to in the resolution. My country was founded on, and is proud of its support for, the concept of government by freely elected officials. We are always concerned when elected officials are no longer able to serve their constituents. At the same time, it is useful to recall that the present situation on the West Bank is that of belligerent occupation, subject to the rules laid down for such regimes in the Fourth Geneva Convention.[22] It is a carefully drawn and balanced set of rules seeking to serve the interests of the occupier and the occupied alike.

There is no provision in the Geneva Convention for the election of public officials, which Israel nonetheless permitted in 1972 and 1976, thereby going beyond the requirements of the Convention. In any event, Article 54 of the Geneva Convention gives the occupying power the unrestricted right to dismiss public officials, whether they may be appointed or elected. As we would not wish Israel to be selective in its own application of the Convention to the occupied territories, so we should not be selective in our criticism—denouncing Israel for violations where, in fact, no violations of the Convention have taken place.

But the goal, of course, is to move beyond belligerency to a state of peace. This is the higher duty, indeed, the highest duty of the Security Council.

Fortunately, in this respect Council Resolutions 242 and 338, forged by this body in past years after full debate and consultation, provide an available, a ready-made internationally approved basis for a just and lasting settlement of the outstanding issues. These resolutions are the foundation of the Camp David framework, and they remain the only existing basis for a negotiated solution leading to a resolution of the conflict. We deeply regret that this resolution makes no reference to 242 or 338.

We would have preferred, Mr. President, to have had before us a resolution that we could have supported, one that expressed in a non-condemnatory way the Council's great concern about the recent tragic events which have resulted in injury and loss of life on both sides. Instead, the resolution we were called on to vote on this evening uses strongly denunciatory language and does not take into account the complexity of the problem. Nor would it lead us closer to a solution. On the contrary, it would lead us away from an ultimate solution. Since this resolution, in our judgment, did not promote, will not promote, the cause of peace which should always be the paramount concern of this Council, the United States was compelled to vote no.

Thank you, Mr. President.

[22] Reference is to the Geneva Convention Relative to the Protection of Civilian Persons in Time of War of August 12, 1949; for text, see 6 UST 3516.

Document 311

Statement Issued by the White House, April 16, 1982[23]

Incident at the Dome of the Rock Mosque

The President today met with six Ambassadors delegated by the Islamic countries represented in Washington. On this occasion, he expressed his deep personal sorrow and that of all Americans over last Sunday's violence at the hands of a deranged individual in an area sacred to three of the world's great religions.

[23] Source: White House Press Release, April 16, 1982, Office of the Press Secretary to the President; also printed in *Weekly Compilation of Presidential Documents*, April 19, 1982, pp. 490–491. On Sunday, April 11, Alan H. Goodman, an American-born immigrant to Israel, shot and killed two Arabs and wounded nine others at the Dome of the Rock Mosque in Jerusalem. The incident led to rioting among Arabs in East Jerusalem and the occupied territories.

The President expressed his sympathy with the concern of the Islamic world over the disruption of the tranquility of one of its most holy shrines. This concern is shared by the members of all faiths. He reiterated his conviction that the peace of the holy places of Jerusalem must be maintained and confirmed the dedication of the United States to encouraging the conditions necessary for the well-being of all those who draw their spiritual inspiration from that city.

The President called upon all the governments and peoples of the Middle East to work to decrease tensions in the area and prevent further acts of violence and loss of life.

The six Ambassadors were:

Ambassador Omer Salih Eissa, Sudanese Ambassador to the United States

Ambassador Ali Bengelloun, Moroccan Ambassador to the United States

Ambassador Faisal Alhegelan, Saudi Arabian Ambassador to the United States

Ambassador Ejaz Azim, Pakistani Ambassador to the United States

Ambassador Azraai Zain, Malaysian Ambassador to the United States

Ambassador Andre Wright, Niger Ambassador to the United States

---

Document 312

Statement Issued by the White House, April 25, 1982[24]

Israeli Withdrawal From the Sinai Peninsula

We note today the successful completion by Israel of the withdrawal of its forces from the Sinai Peninsula and the reestablishment there of full Egyptian sovereignty. The President believes that withdrawal represents a truly major sacrifice by Israel, and he admires its courage in taking the great risks which true peace requires. He admires as well the courageous Egyptian initiative without which peace with Israel would not have been achieved.

Israeli withdrawal from Sinai marks the beginning of a new era in the peaceful relations between Israel and Egypt, peaceful relations which should be taken by us all as the model for the future in that troubled region. The President is determined that the United States, together with Egypt and Israel, will continue to pursue the course of peace, under Camp David, with renewed vigor and dedication. It will not be an easy task but, with the example of Egypt and Israel before us, it can be achieved.

Document 313

Executive Order 12361, Issued by President Reagan, April 27, 1982[25]

Reporting Functions of the Multinational Force and Observers

By the authority vested in me as President of the United States of America by the Multinational Force and Observers Participation Resolution (Public Law 97–132, 95 Stat. 1693)[26] and Section 301 of Title 3 of the United States Code, it is hereby ordered as follows:

Section 1. *Delegation of Functions.* The reporting function conferred upon the President by Section 6 of the Multinational Force and Observers Participation Resolution (22 U.S.C. 3425) is delegated to the Secretary of State.

Sec. 2. *Interagency Coordination.* In the exercise of the function conferred on the Secretary of State by Section 1 of this Order, the Secretary of State shall consult with the Director of the Office of Management and Budget, the Secretary of Defense, the Director of the United States Arms Control and Disarmament Agency, the Assistant to the President for National Security Affairs, and the heads of other Executive agencies as appropriate.

RONALD REAGAN

---

24 Source: *Weekly Compilation of Presidential Documents,* May 3, 1982, p. 528.

25 Source: White House Press Release, April 27, 1982, Office of the Press Secretary to the President; also printed in *Weekly Compilation of Presidential Documents,* May 3, 1982, p. 540.

26 For the text of the Multinational Force and Observers Participation Resolution, approved on December 29, 1981, see *American Foreign Policy: Current Documents, 1981,* document 332.

Document 314

Message to the Congress by President Reagan, May 26, 1982[27]

Final Report of the U.S. Sinai Support Mission

I am pleased to transmit herewith the Thirteenth Report of the United States Sinai Support Mission.[28] It covers the Mission's activities during the 6-month period ending April 26, 1982. This report is provided in accordance with Section 4 of Public Law 94–110 of October 13, 1975.[29]

This is the final report on the Mission's peacekeeping operations, which ended on April 25, 1982, when Israel completed its withdrawal from the Sinai and Egyptian sovereignty was reestablished in accordance with the 1979 Peace Treaty. At that time the Sinai Field Mission, the Support Mission's overseas arm, relinquished its treaty verification responsibilities to the new Multinational Force and Observers. Established by the August 3, 1981, Protocol to the Peace Treaty, the Multinational Force is now supervising implementation of the Treaty security arrangements.

The Congress appropriated $5 million for the conclusion of the Sinai Support Mission's activities in Fiscal Year 1982. By careful financial and technical planning to minimize its phase-out costs, the Mission expects to complete its activities at this minimal funding level. No funds are being requested for Fiscal Year 1983.

The Field Mission's base camp in the Sinai is expected to be closed by June 1982 and the fixed assets turned over to the Government of Egypt at that time as authorized in Section 6 of the Special International Security Assistance Act of 1979 (P.L. 96–35). The movable assets are being made available to the United States Embassies in Egypt and Israel and to the Multinational Force and Observers on a nonreimbursable basis under authorities contained in the Federal Property and Administrative Services Act of 1949, as amended (40 USC 511 et seq). In accordance with Executive Order 12357 of April 6, 1982,[30] the Sinai Support Mission will conclude its activities no later than September 30, 1982, at which time the Department of State will assume responsibility for any residual actions necessary to complete activities initiated by the Mission.

The Congress and the American people can take pride in the successful completion of this unique peacekeeping initiative that combined Government and private sector talents to carry out on very short notice a sensitive and complex series of missions in an isolated and distant environment. In meeting these challenges, the men and women of the Sinai Support and Field Missions have made a major contribution to our continuing efforts to bring a just and lasting peace to the troubled Middle East.

[27] Source: White House Press Release, May 26, 1982, Office of the Press Secretary to the President; also printed in *Weekly Compilation of Presidential Documents,* May 31, 1982, p. 708.

[28] For text, see *United States Sinai Support Mission, Message From the President of the United States Transmitting the Thirteenth Report of the United States Sinai Support Mission, Pursuant to Section 4 of Public Law 94–110,* House Document No. 97–188, Ninety-seventh Congress, Second Session (Washington, 1982), pp. 15–29.

[29] For text, see 89 Stat. 572.

Document 315

Statement by the Secretary of State-Designate (Shultz) Before the Senate Foreign Relations Committee, July 13, 1982 (Extract)[31]

Position Concerning the Lebanese and Palestinian Questions

. . . .

Mr. Chairman,[32] during my individual visits with members of this committee, many expressed a strong interest in my views on problems and opportunities in the Middle East, particularly as related to the conflict between Israel and the Arabs. Responsive to this interest but even more to the importance of developments in this

[30] For text, see *Weekly Compilation of Presidential Documents,* April 12, 1982, p. 452.

[31] Source: *Nomination of George P. Shultz: Hearings Before the Committee on Foreign Relations, United States Senate, Ninety-seventh Congress, Second Session* (Washington, 1982), pp. 10–12. For the full text, see *ibid.,* pp. 6–12.

[32] Senator Charles H. Percy.

area, I will conclude my statement today by a brief discussion of my views.

I start with the terrible human tragedy now taking place in Lebanon. Violence on a large scale has come once again to a region whose strategic importance inevitably guarantees that any local conflict will receive global attention, with all the dangers for world peace that implies.

In late 1974 I visited Beirut, at the time a beautiful and thriving city, even then marked, however, by the presence of Palestinian refugees. But since then, Lebanon has been wracked by destruction, enduring the presence of armed and assertive PLO and other forces. Coherent life and government are impossible under these conditions, and inevitably Lebanon became a state in disrepair. The Lebanese deserve a chance to govern themselves, free from the presence of the armed forces of any other country or group. The authority of the Government of Lebanon must extend to all its territory.

The agony of Lebanon is on the minds and in the hearts of us all, but in a larger sense, Lebanon is but the latest chapter in a history of accumulated grief stretching back through decades of conflict. We are talking here about a part of the globe that has had little genuine peace for generations, a region with thousands of victims, Arab, Israeli and other families torn apart as a consequence of war and terror.

What is going on now in Lebanon must mark the end of this cycle of terror rather than simply the latest in a continuing series of senseless and violent acts. We cannot accept the loss of life brought home to us every day, even at this great distance, on our television screens; but at the same time, we can as Americans be proud that once again it is the United States, working most prominently through President Reagan's emissary, Ambassador Philip Habib, in my judgment a genuine hero, that is attempting to still the guns, achieve an equitable outcome and alleviate the suffering.

Mr. Chairman, the crisis in Lebanon makes painfully and totally clear a central reality of the Middle East: the legitimate needs and problems of the Palestinian people must be addressed and resolved, urgently and in all their dimensions. Beyond the suffering of the Palestinian people lies a complex of political problems which must be addressed if the Middle East is to know peace.

The Camp David framework calls, as a first step, for temporary arrangements which will provide full autonomy for the Palestinians of the West Bank and Gaza. That same framework then speaks eloquently and significantly of a solution that must also recognize the legitimate rights of the Palestinian people.

The challenge of the negotiations in which the United States is, and during my tenure will remain, a full partner is to transform that hope into reality. For these talks to succeed, representatives of the Palestinians themselves must participate in the negotiating process. The basis must also be found for other countries in the region in addition to Israel and Egypt to join in the peace process.

Our determined effort to stop the killing in Lebanon, resolve the conflict and make the Government of Lebanon once again sovereign throughout its territory underscores the degree to which our Nation has vital interests throughout the Arab world. Our friendly relations with the great majority of Arab States have served those interests and, I believe, assisted our efforts to deal with the current Lebanon crisis.

But beyond the issues of the moment, the importance to our own security of wide and diverse strengthening ties with the Arabs is manifest. It is from them that the West gets much of its oil. It is with them that we share an interest and must cooperate in resisting Soviet imperialism. It is with them as well as Israel that we will be able to bring peace to the Middle East.

The brilliant Arab heritage of science, culture, and thought has a fresh dynamism. Working together with us, our Arab friends can contribute much, not only to our bilateral interests and those of the region but to the global future and the world economy as well. I will do all in my power to sustain these relationships and to further them.

Finally and most important, Mr. Chairman, the Lebanese situation is intimately linked to the vital question of Israel's security. Israel, our closest friend in the Middle East, still harbors a deep feeling of insecurity. In a region where hostility is endemic and where so much of it is directed against Israel, the rightness of her preoccupation with matters of security cannot be disputed, nor should anyone dispute the depth and durability of America's commitment to the security of Israel or our readiness to assure that Israel has the necessary means to defend herself.

I share in this deep and enduring commitment, and more. I recognize that democratic Israel shares with us a deep commitment to the security of the West. Beyond that, however, we owe it to Israel in the context of our special relationship to work with her to bring about a comprehensive peace acceptable to all the parties involved, which is the only sure guarantee of true and durable security.

America has many often competing concerns and interests in the Middle East. It is no secret that they present us with dilemmas and difficult decisions. Yet we must, using all the wit and compassion we possess, reconcile those interests and erase those contradictions, for it is in the last analysis peace we are seeking to create and nurture.

Today's violence should not cause us to forget that the Middle East is a land of deep spirituality where three great religions of our time were born and come together even today. Some have suggested that it was only natural in a land of such vast, harsh and open space that men should be drawn toward the heavens and toward the larger sense of life's meaning. Whatever the reasons, the force of religion in this region is as powerful today as ever, and our plans for peace will be profoundly incomplete if they ignore this reality.

Let me close by recalling to you President Reagan's definition of America's duty in this region. "Our diplomacy," he said, "must be sensitive to the legitimate concerns of all in the area. Before a negotiated peace can ever hope to command the loyalty of the whole region, it must be acceptable to Israelis and Arabs alike."

Mr. Chairman, I pledge to you and this committee that if I am confirmed as Secretary of State, I will do my best to help the President carry out the task so clearly defined in his statement. We must dare to hope that with effort and imagination, we can arrive at an agreement that will satisfy the vital security interests of Israel and the political aspirations of the Palestinians, meet the concerns of other parties directly involved, and win the endorsement of the international community.

Document 316

Responses by the Secretary of State-Designate (Shultz) to Additional Questions Submitted by the Senate Foreign Relations Committee, July 1982 (Extracts)[33]

Questions on U.S.-Arab Relations

. . . .

Question 7. Do you believe that Saudi Arabia has directly or indirectly supported or funded terrorist acts against Israel?

A. Saudi Arabia, in common with all of the Arab States, recognizes the Palestinian Liberation Organization as the "sole representative of the Palestinian people." At the Rabat Arab summit in 1974, the Saudis committed themselves to an annual contribution to the PLO, making it a substantial financial supporter.

At the same time, however, Saudi Arabia has publicly condemned "terrorism in all its forms," and has persistently argued that the Palestinians should reject the use of international terrorism as a policy instrument and should, instead, seek their objectives through political means including negotiations. In this context, the Saudis have, through the years, used their influence with the Palestinians to strengthen the hand of the more moderate elements within the PLO.

Question 8. Do you believe Camp David accords were a positive step toward peace in the Middle East?

A. Yes. Camp David led directly to the first peace treaty between Israel and an Arab State, Egypt. This in itself was a major achievement. Camp David also provides a vehicle for resolving the Palestinian problem and establishing peace between Israel and the Palestinians, Jordan, and Syria.

Question 9. How can we help get Israel's neighbors, who are still at war with her, to negotiate peace with her?

A. The Palestinians, Jordan, and Syria ought to join in the peace process on the

[33] Source: *Nomination of George P. Shultz*, pp. 118–119. For the full text, see *ibid.*, pp. 117–120. No date for these questions and answers is given on the source text, but Senator Carl Levin submitted the questions and inserted the answers of Secretary-designate Shultz in the *Congressional Record*, July 15, 1982, p. S8370.

basis that Camp David is founded on UNSC Resolutions 242 and 338, which all but the Palestinians have accepted. We understand their doubts about Camp David and their concerns that Israel is not prepared to be flexible enough to meet any of the Palestinians' aspirations. We would hope that the arrangements we will be seeking for the traditional period, a truly full autonomy, will change their perceptions and encourage them to join us.

Question 10. Describe the specific portions, if any, of the President's speech of [*before*] the B'nai B'rith in 1980[34] in which you did not occur [*concur*].

A. As I said in my July 13 testimony before the SFRC, "My job is to help the President formulate and execute his policies."[35] The President and I have discussed his Mideast policy in general terms and I can assure you that I will have no difficulty in supporting his policies in this as in other areas.

. . . .

Question 17. Do you support the anti-boycott legislation aimed at reducing the impact of the blacklisting by certain Arab countries against firms doing business with Israel?

A. Yes. I participated in a business roundtable group led by Irving Shapiro[36] which developed ideas on the Export Administration Act Amendments adopted in 1977,[37] and I think it is a reasonable law.

. . . .

---

[34] On September 3, 1980, Republican Presidential nominee Reagan addressed the B'nai B'rith in Washington. He called Israel "a major strategic asset" and criticized the Carter administration for neglecting Israel's security, selling arms to Arab countries, and refusing to call the PLO a "terrorist organization."

[35] *Nomination of George P. Shultz*, p. 7.

[36] Chairman and chief executive officer of E. I. Dupont de Nemours and Company since 1974. See *Arab Boycott: Hearings Before the Subcommittee on International Finance of the Committee on Banking, Housing and Urban Affairs, United States Senate, Ninety-fifth Congress, First Session* (Washington, 1977), pp. 465–489.

[37] P.L. 95–52; 91 Stat. 235.

Document 317

Transcript of an Interview With the Secretary of State (Shultz), August 22, 1982 (Extracts)[38]

The Middle East After Lebanon

. . . .

MR. EVANS. Let me ask you, sir, a different question, and that is a very long statement by the President of Egypt today published in the *Washington Post*. Mubarak said, "The right of the Israeli people to live in their country does not contradict the right of the Palestinian people to live in their country."[39] Do you agree with that as a general starting point for trying to get Camp David back on the track?

SECRETARY SHULTZ. Well, I read President Mubarak's article, and I thought it was a very constructive contribution to discussion on this issue, and I think gave a good indication of his own attitude toward moving these discussions along, and precisely what position various people will take on that question, among others, remains to be seen. But I do think that the establishment of a situation where the Palestinian people can have some sense of dignity and control over their lives is very important and an essential part of any agreement.

MR. EVANS. Well, you're not going to tell us whether you agree with that statement by Mr. Mubarak?

SECRETARY SHULTZ. Not categorically yes or no to—

MR. EVANS. Let me then try it this way, sir.

SECRETARY SHULTZ.—the various questions you might ask me.

MR. EVANS. Let me try it this way. You said yourself, sir, in your testimony before

---

[38] Source: Department of State Press Release 260, August 24, 1982; printed also in Department of State *Bulletin*, October 1982, pp. 8–10. For the full text, see *ibid.*, pp. 7–10. Secretary Shultz was interviewed on the NBC television program, "Meet the Press," by Bill Monroe and Marvin Kalb of NBC News, Rowland Evans of the Chicago *Sun-Times*, Karen Elliott House of the *Wall Street Journal*, and Bernard Gwertzman of the *New York Times*.

[39] Reference is to Mubarak's article, "Can the Camp David Peace Process Be Restored?", *Washington Post*, August 22, 1982, p. C7.

the Senate Foreign Relations Committee several weeks ago, "The legitimate needs of the Palestinian people must be addressed in all their dimensions."[40] Is self-determination one of those dimensions, and, if it is, do they have the same right as the Jewish people had to set up the State of Israel?

SECRETARY SHULTZ. Well, certainly they should have a part in determining the conditions under which they're governed. The word self-determination somehow in this word game in the Middle East, I've discovered, has come to be the equivalent of a Palestinian state, which has a lot of implications about military forces and many other things, so I'm not going to bite on that one, but rather say that the main point is that the Palestinian people have a voice in determining the conditions under which they're governed.

MR. MONROE. Mrs. House?

MRS. HOUSE. You said in your press conference[41] that there is a lot of room for flexibility in the language of Camp David. Are there points of dispute between Egypt and Israel in the autonomy talks where you think an addition of American views would be helpful and, if so, what are they?

SECRETARY SHULTZ. Well, I think that as this process resumes—and I think we have to bear in mind it's been pretty much stopped for some period of time now—we will be putting forward views, others will be, and as I see it there is a delicate interplay between, you might say, substance and process here. So we'll want to be trying as best we can to manage that from our standpoint in a way designed to give a constructive result.

MRS. HOUSE. One of the areas of dispute has been what would be the potential for a final solution on the West Bank.

SECRETARY SHULTZ. Yes.

MRS. HOUSE. And Israel has made it very clear that while Camp David says that the process is based on U.N. Resolution 242 that they do not interpret that resolution to mean that Israel must withdraw from that territory. Do we interpret 242 to mean that Israel must withdraw from some of the West Bank and Gaza or all?

SECRETARY SHULTZ. I should think—I should think so, yes.

MRS. HOUSE. Why hasn't anyone in this administration said that?

SECRETARY SHULTZ. Oh, I think that's been said.

MRS. HOUSE. Can you say it today?

SECRETARY SHULTZ. I've said it just now.

MRS. HOUSE. That we do—we do believe it means withdrawal?

SECRETARY SHULTZ. Well, I think 242 has that implication in it, myself. That's a matter of interpretation, no doubt, and various points of view have been taken. Having said that leaves still lots of room for negotiation. The language of the Camp David itself, I think, when you read it obviously can be interpreted many ways, but certainly one of those ways is that some shift in what are the practical borders now will take place.

MRS. HOUSE. Do you believe that you can get those talks going again between Egypt and Israel, or do you have to get some broader Arab participation before the Egyptians are willing to return?

SECRETARY SHULTZ. Well, we'll have to see what we can bring about in this process, and I don't want to make a forecast, but obviously—I would say obviously—for there to be a genuine peaceful outcome that is widely accepted in the region, there have to be more countries involved than Egypt, Israel, and the United States.

. . . .

MR. KALB. Mr. Secretary, do you regard—back on the Middle East again—do you regard Israel, in light of what has happened in Beirut, as a true and trusted friend and ally of the United States?

SECRETARY SHULTZ. Oh, yes, and I believe that we must in all of the things that we do be always cognizant and careful about the security of Israel.

. . . .

MR. KALB. On the Mubarak statement, again, in the *Washington Post* today, you've called it very constructive and yet the Egyptian President said that it would be, quote, most difficult for Egypt to resume the autonomy talks or revive the peace process [unquote], and then he cited three preconditions: "Unless first the United States recognizes the right of the Palestinians to self-determination"—and he's quite specific that it must take place in the West Bank and the Gaza Strip. Are you going to be able to move it on that one point?

[40] See document 315.
[41] For the text of Secretary Shultz's press conference, August 20, see document 393.

SECRETARY SHULTZ. Well, I'm sure we'll want to talk with President Mubarak directly and others about their views and what it takes to get this process moving, and I think that we'll be able to do it.

MR. KALB. Well, you seemed to make an assumption in answer to another question that you already have Egypt and Israel and you're seeking others for the autonomy talks. This—

SECRETARY SHULTZ. No, I said—

MR. KALB. No?

SECRETARY SHULTZ.—that for the kind of result that we would all like to see out there take place, you have to have more parties to it than the three countries.

MR. KALB. Do you—do you right now have in your mind even a general plan on how you're going to proceed on the autonomy talks?

SECRETARY SHULTZ. Well, we've thought about it a lot and we've heard a lot of advice from people, so I suppose it's fair enough to say that there is a—there are general ideas that we have in our minds, but we're not freezing onto anything, because, as I said in response to an earlier question, I think success here involves a sort of delicate interplay between the processes that are involved and the substance that your're trying to achieve.

MR. KALB. Well, at the end of the framework, the general idea that you have in mind, is there a homeland for the Palestinian people on the West Bank and the Gaza Strip?

SECRETARY SHULTZ. Well, certainly that is a place that many of them call home, and a place that they'll live and they should have a participation in determining the conditions under which they live.

MR. KALB. Can I assume that the answer is yes to that question, then, sir?

SECRETARY SHULTZ. Well, I tried to give an answer in my own words.

MR. MONROE. Mr. Evans?

MR. EVANS. Mr. Secretary, following up Marvin Kalb, you said recently—I don't know where it was, but I have the quote—you said that the Israeli settlements in the West Bank, quote, have not reached a conclusion, unquote, but, you said, they are not constructive. Have you told Mr. Begin that you want the Israelis to stop creating new settlements, Jewish settlements, on the West Bank?

SECRETARY SHULTZ. I'm the new man on the block here—

MR. EVANS. Well, you've been here for 6 weeks, sir.

SECRETARY SHULTZ.—and I've been struggling with the Beirut problem and I did respond to that question yesterday at the press conference or day before yesterday, having thought about it quite a bit, and having listened to the President talk about it, and I believe my response was that I'd heard the President say that whether the settlements were legal or illegal, they were not constructive.

MR. EVANS. Well, you said—you've also said, sir, "I am a quiet person, but I do believe in saying what I think." Could you tell us what you think about Israeli settlements on the West Bank?

SECRETARY SHULTZ. I agree with the President.

MR. EVANS. Let me ask you about another question that involves this whole West Bank-Palestinian problem. You have said you hate to see—you used the word hate—Israel—the Israeli Government fire all those mayors of Palestinian cities and towns on the West Bank. Have you expressed that sentiment to the Israeli Government?

SECRETARY SHULTZ. I have expressed myself publicly several times, I think, in my confirmation hearings, and I have expressed myself privately. Whether—I'm just trying to recall literally whether I said that in so many words to an official of the Israeli Government, and I can't recall precisely whether I have, but I certainly do feel that way, that these are people who achieved a certain legitimacy as representatives of Palestinians living on the West Bank, and one of the things that we're looking for, we must be looking for if this negotiation is to succeed, are Palestinians who are legitimate to represent them.

MR. EVANS. Do you think, sir, that the Israeli Government has any right under—as an occupying power to prevent the Mayor of Bethlehem, who is not a member of the PLO, is not even very enthusiastic about the PLO, from appearing on this program that you're on today, "Meet the Press"?

SECRETARY SHULTZ. Well, I think it's unfortunate that that took place.

MR. EVANS. Why is it unfortunate?

SECRETARY SHULTZ. Because he should be allowed to come and express his views. I think we all gain from an open expression of views, and that's a person who has some.

MR. EVANS. Is that worth following up?

SECRETARY SHULTZ. There's no reason to shut that out.

MR. EVANS. Is that worth following up as Secretary of State?

SECRETARY SHULTZ. Well, there are many things worth following up. I don't want to have a tone left in the interchange between you and I that all of the problems here represent problems created by Israel. There are many problems in the area, and you've identified some of them. There are many others. There are a lot of violations of the cease-fire taking place by the Palestinians in Lebanon right now that I don't consider to be very constructive under the circumstances. So we can go and list a lot of things that we would rather see not happen.

. . . .

MR. GWERTZMAN. I have some more questions on the Middle East, Mr. Secretary. You said earlier that you interpreted 242 as meaning Israel had to make some withdrawals, but, of course, the Camp David Agreement tries to, I think, finesse this question by setting up an interim Palestinian autonomy for 5 years and then a negotiation on the ultimate outcome of the whole area. I just wanted to make sure that you weren't trying to indicate a desire to revise that basic principle of the Camp David framework agreement?

SECRETARY SHULTZ. Not a bit. I think the Camp David framework, as I read it and have heard about the background of it, Resolutions 242 and 338 are ample bases and good bases for any ongoing negotiation, and what they do, I think, is make these questions that you've raised open questions and open for negotiation.

MR. GWERTZMAN. On the question of PLO recognition, which has been a sore point, Dr. Kissinger in'75 said the United States would not recognize or negotiate with the PLO until it met certain conditions, such as the right of Israel to exist.[42] Now, certainly the United States has been negotiating with the PLO, albeit indirectly, over the last 2 months. The Kissinger statement did not seem to make a distinction between indirect or direct. I just wondered if you think it's worth maintaining that agreement, which, of course, arouses emotions in Israel and elsewhere, when in fact it's really been breached in the literal sense of negotiation?

SECRETARY SHULTZ. Oh, I think that the President's position on this has been well stated, and we'll maintain it and I think it's important to maintain it. It isn't vitiated in any way by the practical fact that if you are, for example, going to be successful in having the PLO depart from West Beirut under these circumstances, you have to have some method of being in touch with them, and the way that it has been done is Phil[43] has talked to various representatives of the Government of Lebanon, and they've talked to the PLO leaders and so forth, as you know.

MR. GWERTZMAN. Can we expect you to name a chief negotiator on these broad questions of Palestinian autonomy or other things in the near future, someone of the stature of Dr. Kissinger or something like that?

SECRETARY SHULTZ. It remains to be seen just how we think the best way will be to conduct the U.S. aspect of these negotiations. We do have Ambassador Fairbanks[44] who's helping me on this and who's very knowledgeable.

. . . .

Document 318

Address by President Reagan, Burbank, California, September 1, 1982[45]

Middle East Peace Initiative

My fellow Americans, today has been a day that can make us proud. It marks the

---

[42] Reference is to the Memorandum of Agreement between Israel and the United States on the Geneva Peace Conference, September 1, 1975. (TIAS 9829)

[43] Ambassador Philip C. Habib, the President's Special Emissary to the Middle East.

[44] Richard M. Fairbanks III, Special Middle East Peace Negotiator.

[45] Source: White House Press Release, September 1, 1982, Office of the Press Secretary to the President; also printed in *Weekly Compilation of Presidential Documents*, September 6, 1982, pp. 1081–1085. President Reagan spoke from KNBC-TV Studios at 6 p.m. His address was broadcast live over nationwide radio and television.

end of the successful evacuation of the PLO from Beirut, Lebanon. This peaceful step could never have been taken without the good offices of the United States and especially the truly heroic work of a great American diplomat, Ambassador Philip Habib.

Thanks to his efforts I am happy to announce that the U.S. Marine contingent helping supervise the evacuation has accomplished its mission. Our young men should be out of Lebanon within 2 weeks. They, too, have served the cause of peace with distinction and we can all be very proud of them.

But the situation in Lebanon is only part of the overall problem of conflict in the Middle East. So over the past 2 weeks while events in Beirut dominated the front page America was engaged in a quiet, behind-the-scenes effort to lay the groundwork for a broader peace in the region. For once there were no premature leaks as U.S. diplomatic missions traveled to Mideast capitals and I met here at home with a wide range of experts to map out an American peace initiative for the long-suffering peoples of the Middle East—Arab and Israeli alike.

It seemed to me that with the agreement in Lebanon we had an opportunity for a more far-reaching peace effort in the region and I was determined to seize that moment.

In the words of the scriptures, the time had come to follow after the things which make for peace. Tonight I want to report to you the steps we have taken and the prospects they can open up for a just and lasting peace in the Middle East.

America has long been committed to bringing peace to this troubled region. For more than a generation successive United States administrations have endeavored to develop a fair and workable process that could lead to a true and lasting Arab-Israeli peace.

Our involvement in the search for Mideast peace is not a matter of preference, it is a moral imperative. The strategic importance of the region to the United States is well known, but our policy is motivated by more than strategic interests. We also have an irreversible commitment to the survival and territorial integrity of friendly states. Nor can we ignore the fact that the well-being of much of the world's economy is tied to stability in the strife-torn Middle East. Finally, our traditional humanitarian concerns dictated a continuing effort to peacefully resolve the conflict.

When our administration assumed office in January of 1981 I decided that the general framework for our Middle East policy should follow the broad guidelines laid down by my predecessors. There were two basic issues we had to address. First, there was a strategic threat to the region posed by the Soviet Union and its surrogates, best demonstrated by the brutal war in Afghanistan, and, second, the peace process between Israel and its Arab neighbors.

With regard to the Soviet threat, we have strengthened our efforts to develop with our friends and allies a joint policy to deter the Soviets and their surrogates from further expansion in the region, and, if necessary, to defend against it.

With respect to the Arab-Israeli conflict, we have embraced the Camp David framework as the only way to proceed. We have also recognized, however, solving the Arab-Israeli conflict in and of itself cannot assure peace throughout a region as vast and troubled as the Middle East.

Our first objective under the Camp David process was to ensure the successful fulfillment of the Egyptian-Israeli Peace Treaty. This was achieved with the peaceful return of the Sinai to Egypt in April 1982. To accomplish this, we worked hard with our Egyptian and Israeli friends, and, eventually, with other friendly countries to create the multinational force which now operates in the Sinai.

Throughout this period of difficult and time consuming negotiations we never lost sight of the next step of Camp David—autonomy talks to pave the way for permitting the Palestinian people to exercise their legitimate rights. However, owing to the tragic assassination of President Sadat and other crises in the area, it was not until January 1982 that we were able to make a major effort to renew these talks.

Secretary of State Haig and Ambassador Fairbanks made three visits to Israel and Egypt early this year to pursue the autonomy talks. Considerable progress was made in developing the basic outline of an American approach which was to be presented to Egypt and Israel after April.

The successful completion of Israel's withdrawal from Sinai and the courage shown on this occasion by Prime Minister Begin and President Mubarak in living up to their agreements convinced me the time had come for a new American policy to try to bridge the remaining differences between Egypt and Israel on the autonomy process.

So, in May, I called for specific measures and a timetable for consultations with the Governments of Egypt and Israel on the next step in the peace process. However, before this effort could be launched, the conflict in Lebanon preempted our effort.

The autonomy talks were, basically, put on hold while we sought to untangle the parties in Lebanon and still the guns of war. The Lebanon war, tragic as it was, has left us with a new opportunity for Middle East peace. We must seize it now, and bring peace to this troubled area so vital to world stability while there is still time. It was with this strong conviction that over a month ago, before the present negotiations in Beirut had been completed, I directed Secretary of State Shultz to again review our policy, and to consult a wide range of outstanding Americans on the best ways to strengthen chances for peace in the Middle East.

We have consulted with many of the officials who were historically involved in the process, with members of the Congress, and with individuals from the private sector. And I have held extensive consultations with my own advisors on the principles that I will outline to you tonight.

The evacuation of the PLO from Beirut is now complete. And we can now help the Lebanese to rebuild their war-torn country. We owe it to ourselves, and to posterity, to move quickly to build upon this achievement. A stable and revived Lebanon is essential to all our hopes for peace in the region. The people of Lebanon deserve the best efforts of the international community to turn the nightmares of the past several years into a new dawn of hope.

But the opportunities for peace in the Middle East do not begin and end in Lebanon. As we help Lebanon rebuild, we must also move to resolve the root causes of conflict between Arabs and Israelis. The war in Lebanon has demonstrated many things, but two consequences are key to the peace process.

First, the military losses of the PLO have not diminished the yearning of the Palestinian people for a just solution of their claims; and, second, while Israel's military successes in Lebanon have demonstrated that its armed forces are second to none in the region, they alone cannot bring just and lasting peace to Israel and her neighbors.

The question now is how to reconcile Israel's legitimate security concerns with the legitimate rights of the Palestinians. And that answer can only come at the negotiating table. Each party must recognize that the outcome must be acceptable to all and that true peace will require compromises by all.

So, tonight I'm calling for a fresh start. This is the moment for all those directly concerned to get involved—or lend their support—to a workable basis for peace. The Camp David agreement remains the foundation of our policy. Its language provides all parties with the leeway they need for successful negotiations.

I call on Israel to make clear that the security for which she yearns can only be achieved through genuine peace, a peace requiring magnanimity, vision and courage.

I call on the Palestinian people to recognize that their own political aspirations are inextricably bound to recognition of Israel's right to a secure future.

And I call on the Arab States to accept the reality of Israel—and the reality that peace and justice are to be gained only through hard, fair, direct negotiation.

In making these calls upon others, I recognize that the United States has a special responsibility. No other nation is in the position to deal with the key parties to the conflict on the basis of trust and reliability.

The time has come for a new realism on the part of all the peoples of the Middle East. The State of Israel is an accomplished fact; it deserves unchallenged legitimacy within the community of nations. But Israel's legitimacy has thus far been recognized by too few countries and has been denied by every Arab State except Egypt. Israel exists; it has a right to exist in peace behind secure and defensible borders; and it has a right to demand of its neighbors that they recognize those facts.

I have personally followed and supported Israel's heroic struggle for survival, ever since the founding of the State of Israel 34 years ago. In the pre-1967 borders Israel was barely ten miles wide at its narrowest point. The bulk of Israel's population lived within artillery range of hostile Arab armies. I am not about to ask Israel to live that way again.

The war in Lebanon has demonstrated another reality in the region. The departure of the Palestinians from Beirut dramatizes more than ever the homelessness of the Palestinian people. Palestinians feel strongly that their cause is more than a question of refugees. I agree. The Camp David agreements recognized that fact when it spoke of the legitimate rights of the Palestinian people and their just requirements. For peace to endure it must involve all those who have been most deeply affected by the conflict. Only through broader participation in the peace process, most immediately by Jordan and by the Palestinians, will Israel be able to rest confident in the knowledge that its security and integrity will be respected by its neighbors. Only through the process of negotiation can all the nations of the Middle East achieve a secure peace.

These, then, are our general goals. What are the specific new American positions and why are we taking them? In the Camp David talks thus far both Israel and Egypt have felt free to express openly their views as to what the outcome should be. Understandably their views have differed on many points. The United States has thus far sought to play the role of mediator. We have avoided public comment on the key issues. We have always recognized and continue to recognize that only the voluntary agreement of those parties most directly involved in the conflict can provide an enduring solution.

But it has become evident to me that some clearer sense of America's position on the key issues is necessary to encourage wider support for the peace process. First, as outlined in the Camp David Accords, there must be a period of time during which the Palestinian inhabitants of the West Bank and Gaza will have full autonomy over their own affairs. Due consideration must be given to the principle of self-government by the inhabitants of the territory and the legitimate security concerns of the parties involved.

The proof is in the 5-year period of transition which would begin after free elections for a self-governing Palestinian authority to prove to the Palestinians that they could run their own affairs, and that such Palestinian autonomy poses no threat to Israel's security. The United States will not support the use of any additional land for the purpose of settlement during the transitional period. Indeed, the immediate adoption of a settlement freeze by Israel, more than any other action, could create the confidence needed for wider participation in these talks.

Further settlement activity is in no way necessary for the security of Israel and only diminishes the confidence of the Arabs that a final outcome can be freely and fairly negotiated.

I want to make the American position well understood. The purpose of this transitional period is the peaceful and orderly transfer of authority from Israel to the Palestinian inhabitants of the West Bank and Gaza. At the same time, such a transfer must not interfere with Israel's security requirements.

Beyond the transition period, as we look to the future of the West Bank and Gaza, it is clear to me that peace cannot be achieved by the formation of an independent Palestinian state in those territories, nor is it achievable on the basis of Israeli sovereignty or permanent control over the West Bank and Gaza. So the United States will not support the establishment of an independent Palestinian state in the West Bank and Gaza. And we will not support annexation or permanent control by Israel.

There is, however, another way to peace. The final status of these lands must, of course, be reached through the give and take of negotiations. But it is the firm view of the United States that self-government by the Palestinians of the West Bank and Gaza in association with Jordan offers the best chance for a durable, just, and lasting peace. We base our approach squarely on the principle that the Arab-Israeli conflict should be resolved through negotiations involving an exchange of territory for peace.

This exchange is enshrined in United Nations Security Council Resolution 242, which is, in turn, incorporated in all its parts in the Camp David Agreement. U.N. Resolution 242 remains wholely valid as the foundation stone of America's Middle East peace effort. It is the U.S. position that, in return for peace, the withdrawal provision of Resolution 242 applies to all fronts, including the West Bank and Gaza.

When the border is negotiated between Jordan and Israel, our view on the extent to which Israel should be asked to give up territory will be heavily affected by the extent of true peace and normalization, and the security arrangement offered in return.

Finally, we remain convinced that Jerusalem must remain undivided. But its final status should be decided through negotiation. In the course of the negotiations to come, the United States will support positions that seem to us fair and reasonable compromises and likely to promote a sound agreement. We will also put forward our own detailed proposals when we believe that they can be helpful. And, make no mistake, the United States will oppose any proposal from any party and at any point in the negotiating process that threatens the security of Israel. America's commitment to the security of Israel is ironclad. And I might add, so is mine.

During the past few days, our Ambassadors in Israel, Egypt, Jordan, and Saudi Arabia have presented to their host governments the proposals, in full detail, that I have outlined here today. Now, I am convinced that these proposals can bring justice, bring security, and bring durability to an Arab-Israeli peace. The United States will stand by these principles with total dedication. They are fully consistent with Israel's security requirements and the aspirations of the Palestinians. We will work hard to broaden participation at the peace table as envisaged by the Camp David Accords. And I fervently hope that the Palestinians and Jordan, with the support of their Arab colleagues, will accept this opportunity.

Tragic turmoil in the Middle East runs back to the dawn of history. In our modern day, conflict after conflict has taken its brutal toll there. In an age of nuclear challenge and economic interdependence, such conflicts are a threat to all the people of the world, not just the Middle East itself. It's time for us all—in the Middle East and around the world—to call a halt to conflict, hatred, and prejudice. It's time for us all to launch a common effort for reconstruction, peace, and progress.

It has often been said—and regrettably too often been true—that the story of the search for peace and justice in the Middle East is a tragedy of opportunities missed.

In the aftermath of the settlement in Lebanon, we now face an opportunity for a broader peace. This time we must not let it slip from our grasp. We must look beyond the difficulties and obstacles of the present and move with a fairness and resolve toward a brighter future. We owe it to ourselves—and to posterity—to do no less. For if we miss this chance to make a fresh start, we may look back on this moment from some later vantage point and realize how much that failure cost us all.

These, then, are the principles upon which American policy toward the Arab-Israeli conflict will be based. I have made a personal commitment to see that they endure and, God willing, that they will come to be seen by all reasonable, compassionate people as fair, achievable, and in the interests of all who wish to see peace in the Middle East.

Tonight, on the eve of what can be a dawning of new hope for the people of the troubled Middle East—and for all the world's people who dream of a just and peaceful future—I ask you, my fellow Americans, for your support and your prayers in this great undertaking. Thank you and God bless you.

Document 319

Letter From President Reagan to the Mayor of Bethlehem (Freij), September 5, 1982[46]

Response to the President's Peace Plan

Mr. Mayor: I wish to express to you my deepest gratitude for your message[47] of support for the proposals which I outlined in my address on September 1.[48] It is particularly important to have your endorsement of my approach to peace. You are not only a recognized and respected Palestinian leader, but you represent Bethlehem which has been a glowing symbol of peace and brotherhood throughout the world for the past two thousand years. May God bless you and your efforts on behalf of your people and peace and security for all in the region.

Ronald Reagan

---

[46] Source: *Weekly Compilation of Presidential Documents*, September 13, 1982, p. 1092.

[47] Mayor Freij had written to President Reagan:

"I wish to convey to you, Mr. President, from the little town of Bethlehem, our support for your plan to find a comprehensive solution to end the sufferings of the Palestinian people and to bring peace and security for all nations in the Middle East. Please be assured of our sincere desire for peace with freedom and for peace with a homeland. May God give you strength and wisdom to fulfill our expectations." *Ibid.*

[48] *Supra.*

Document 320

Final Declaration of the 12th Summit Conference of Arab Heads of State, Fez, Morocco, September 9, 1982 (Extract)[49]

The Arab League Peace Plan

. . . .

I. *The Arab-Israeli Conflict*

The Summit paid homage to the resistance of the forces of the Palestinian revolution, of the Lebanese and Palestinian peoples, of the Arab Syrian Armed Forces and reaffirms its support to the Palestinian people in its struggle for the recovering of its inalienable national rights.

The Summit, convinced of the strength of the Arab nation for the achievement of its legitimate objectives and for putting an end to the aggression, on the basis of fundamental principles laid down by Arab Summits and out of Arab countries' concern to carry on the action by all means for the achievement of a just peace in the Middle East, taking into account the plan of His Excellency President Habib Bourguiba who considers the international legality as a basis for settling the Palestinian issue and the plan of His Majesty King Fahd Ibn Abdelaziz,[50] related to peace in the Middle East, and in the light of discussions and remarks made by their Majesties, their Excellencies, and their Highnesses, the Kings, Presidents and Emirs, the Summit has agreed upon the following principles:

1) The withdrawal of Israel from all Arab territories occupied in 1967, including the Arab Al Qods (Jerusalem).

2) The dismantling of settlements established by Israel on the Arab territories after 1967.

3) The guarantee of freedom of worship and practice of religious rites for all religious in the holy shrines.

4) The reaffirmation of the Palestinian people's right to self-determination and the exercise of its imprescriptible and inalienable national rights under the leadership of the Palestine Liberation Organization (PLO), its sole and legitimate representative and the indemnification of all those who do not desire to return.

5) Placing the West Bank and Gaza Strip under the control of the United Nations for a transitory period not exceeding a few months.

6) The establishment of an independent Palestinian state with Al Qods as its capital.

7) The Security Council guarantees peace among all states of the region including the independent Palestinian state.

8) The Security Council guarantees the respect of these principles.

. . . .

Document 321

Statement by the Secretary of State (Shultz) Before the House Foreign Affairs Committee, September 9, 1982[51]

Prospects for Peace in the Middle East

I appreciate this opportunity to discuss with you recent developments in the Middle East. These developments are of immense importance. The positive, bipartisan support for President Reagan's peace initiative has been evident to us and is deeply appreciated. That support is essential to the conduct of a vigorous and creative foreign policy and, accordingly, your willingness to meet with me on short notice is especially significant.

In recent weeks the world's attention has focused on the Middle East, and particularly on our diplomatic efforts there to end the bloodshed and to bring a deeper and lasting peace to the area.

With the successful evacuation of the PLO from Beirut, we have turned our atten-

---

[49] Source: Embassy of the Kingdom of Morocco Press Release, September 9, 1982. The 12th Arab summit met at Fez, Morocco, November 25, 1981, and September 6–9, 1982.

[50] For the text of the Saudi Arabian peace proposal of August 8, 1981, see *American Foreign Policy: Current Documents, 1981,* document 312.

[51] Source: *The Situation in Lebanon: U.S. Role in the Middle East: Hearing Before the Committee on Foreign Affairs, House of Representatives, Ninety-seventh Congress, Second Session* (Washington, 1982), pp. 3–8. For the full statement, see *ibid.*

tion to the next steps necessary for peace: The withdrawal of all foreign forces from Lebanon and the restoration of central authority in that country and, of prime importance, the reinvigoration of the Camp David peace process, designed to fairly resolve the underlying Arab-Israeli dispute.

Lebanon, of course, has suffered grievously over the last several months, let alone the last several years. Phil Habib's and Morris Draper's[52] successful negotiation of the withdrawal of the PLO from Beirut can only be regarded as the first phase of our approach to the problem in Lebanon.

As the President announced, the U.S. Marine contingent of the multinational force will begin withdrawing from Beirut tomorrow.[53] The Government of Lebanon, meanwhile, is working carefully but surely to reestablish authority over all parts of Beirut, with the Lebanese army and police increasingly assuming security responsibilities in the city.

A second phase in our Lebanon diplomacy is now before us. As all of you know, the President is sending Ambassador Draper to Lebanon to begin the next phase of negotiations on withdrawal of foreign forces from that country.

The President has made it clear that he personally intends to stay fully engaged in efforts to bring about a strong, free, united and healthy Lebanon, sovereign throughout all its territories within internationally recognized borders.

The withdrawal of all foreign military forces from Lebanon must be accompanied by the creation of conditions in southern Lebanon to preserve Israeli security. In the immediate future, we will seek a further stabilization in the situation in Beirut.

We must create an environment in Lebanon that will allow the newly elected Lebanese Government, free of outside pressure or imposed solutions, to carry on with its task of national reconciliation. The desperate need for economic reconstruction can be well served through such reconciliation and the withdrawal of foreign forces.

The United States is a staunch friend of the Lebanese people and will be a good partner in Lebanon's courageous effort to rebuild its economy and to strengthen its national institutions.

[52] Special Negotiator for Lebanon.

[53] See document 397.

We will exercise our responsibility and duty to give every opportunity to the Lebanese themselves to recreate a united but pluralistic society behind strong leadership from their newly elected president.

We also look forward to cooperating with appropriate international institutions in the effort to ameliorate the destruction caused by the long and most unfortunate fighting.

These efforts to rebuild Lebanon and strengthen its institutions can only be helped by progress in the overall search for a Middle East peace. The problems of Lebanon are distinct and must be addressed whenever possible separately from our Middle East peace initiative, but both tasks must be carried on without delay.

The President will therefore dispatch Ambassador Draper to Lebanon this weekend, while we also continue to work on the overall peace initiative.

The President's statement last week began a fresh start on the Arab-Israeli dispute.[54] The fundamental problems involved are of universal concern not just to the people of the region, but to the United States and other countries as well.

The events of the last month have demonstrated once again that we Americans have a special responsibility in the efforts to bring peace to the area. No one else has the credibility—and therefore the ability—to provide the crucial link to all sides.

The President's Middle East peace initiative is based on an intensive and detailed review of the problem by the President and his advisers. We have discussed the issues in detail with members of this committee and others in the Congress, with former Government officials and many other knowledgeable people.

The paramount conclusions of that review are that first, it is time to address, forcefully and directly, the underlying Palestinian issues, and second, genuine success depends upon broadening participation in the negotiations to include, as envisaged in the Camp David Accords, Egypt, Israel, Jordan, and representatives of the Palestinian people.

In taking this initiative the President established two conditions: We will remain firmly committed both to the principles of the Camp David Accords and to the security of Israel.

[54] See document 318.

The Camp David framework has one key element that all other peace plans lack: It has been successful. It produced the only treaty of peace between Israel and an Arab country and the completion of the disengagement and return of the Sinai.

Moreover, the Camp David framework has the necessary room for negotiations to fulfill the legitimate rights of the Palestinian people and to reach peace treaties between Israel and her neighbors.

As President Carter said a week ago, the day after the President's speech:

> "There is absolutely nothing in the President's speech . . . [55] nor in the information he sent to the Israelis which is contrary to either the letter or the spirit of Camp David. It is absolutely compatible with the Camp David agreement."[56]

Our initiative will give the provisions of Camp David their full meaning and a new dynamism.

This renewed dynamism for the Camp David negotiations will insure Israeli security, and we emphatically will require the product of the negotiations to do so. As the President's speech noted, this country, this administration, and the President personally are committed to Israel's security.

This same renewed dynamism also will provide appropriate regard to the "legitimate rights of the Palestinian people and their just requirements." That is in quotation marks here. Those words are lifted literally from the Camp David Accords.

Camp David itself calls for the residents of the West Bank and Gaza and other Palestinians, as agreed, to participate in negotiating the two primary means of achieving those rights: A 5-year transitional period of autonomous self-government and final status after the 5-year transitional period.

By renewing the process, we seek to fulfill the hope of Camp David: Israel and her neighbors, Jordan, Egypt and the Palestinians, engaged in fair, direct and successful negotiations on how they will all live together.

The Camp David Accords provide that these negotiated arrangements on final status must be "just, comprehensive . . . durable" and "based on Security Council Resolutions 242 and 338 in all their parts."

Security Council Resolution 242 sets forth the two key principles:

> "(i) Withdrawal of Israeli armed forces from territories occupied. . . .
>
> "(ii) Termination of all claims or states of belligerency and respect for and acknowledgment of the sovereignty, territorial integrity and political independence of every state in the area and their right to live in peace within secure and recognized boundaries free from threats or acts of force."

As it has often been summarized, peace for territory.

I think it is worthwhile, Mr. Chairman,[57] to go back and reread and refresh our memories on some of these things that have been agreed to, both in Resolutions 242 and 338 and in the Camp David Accords because the language, when you read it, is very revealing.

We believe these principles apply on all fronts, but our position on the extent of withdrawal will be significantly influenced by the extent and nature of the peace and security arrangements being offered in return.

Israel, Jordan, Egypt, and the elected representatives of the inhabitants of the West Bank and Gaza will negotiate the final boundaries, recognizing Palestinian legitimate rights and securing what Resolution 338 calls a "just and durable peace." We will support positions in these negotiations which we believe are fair. Those positions include:

First, Israeli sovereignty/Palestinian state: It is the President's belief that the Palestinian problem cannot be resolved through Israeli sovereignty or control over the West Bank and Gaza. Accordingly, we will not support such a solution.

We will also not support the formation of a Palestinian state in those negotiations. There is no foundation of political support in Israel or in the United States for such a solution and peace cannot be achieved by that route. The preference we will pursue in the final status negotiations is some form of association of the West Bank and Gaza with Jordan.

Second, self-determination: In the Middle East context, the term "self-determination" has been identified exclusively with the formation of a Palestinian state. We will not support this definition of self-determination.

---

[55] All ellipses appear in the source text.

[56] See *Washington Post* September 2, 1982, p. A23.

[57] Representative Clement J. Zablocki.

We do believe that the Palestinians must take a leading role in determining their own future and fully support the provision in the Camp David agreement providing for the elected representatives of the inhabitants of the West Bank and Gaza to decide how they shall govern themselves consistent with the provisions of their agreement in the final status negotiations.

Third, Jerusalem: We will fully support the position that Jerusalem must be undivided and that its status must be determined through negotiations. We do not recognize unilateral acts with respect to final status issues.

Fourth, settlements: The status of Israeli settlements must be determined in the course of the final status negotiations. We will not support their continuation as extraterritorial outposts, but neither will we support efforts to deny Jews the opportunity to live in the West Bank and Gaza under the duly constituted governmental authority there, as Arabs live in Israel.

Negotiations on the final status of the area will not start until a self-governing authority for the territories is firmly in place. This is just out of Camp David.

Negotiations about the transitional phase have been in progress for the last 3 years. In those negotiations we have consistently expressed our views to our negotiating partners, Israel and Egypt, as issues arose.

Most recently, we informed our partners of how these separate expressions fit into the overall view of Palestinian self-government during a transitional period.

In our view, the objective of the transitional period is the peaceful and orderly transfer of authority from Israel to the Palestinian inhabitants, while insuring that all necessary measures are taken to assure Israeli security.

We have emphasized that this period is a transitional status, not final, and that, therefore, the provisions relating to it should not prejudice the final status. In light of those views, we have told our partners that we have supported and will continue to support:

The definition of full autonomy giving the Palestinian inhabitants real authority over themselves, the land, and its resources subject to fair safeguards on water;

The inclusion of economic, commercial, social and cultural ties between the West Bank, Gaza, and Jordan;

Participation by the Palestinian inhabitants of east Jerusalem in the election for the West Bank/Gaza authority;

Progressive Palestinian responsibility for internal security maintaining internal law and order based on capability and performance.

Using those same standards, we have opposed and will continue to oppose dismantlement of existing settlements, provisions which represent a threat to Israel's security.

As the President noted in his speech, we are attempting to reinvigorate the autonomy negotiations. That effort would be assisted to a great extent by a freeze of the Israeli settlements in the occupied territories, which was requested during the Camp David negotiations. Our concern is not with their legality or illegality, but with their effect on the peace process.

The President's initiative follows over 3 years of active negotiations, continuous discussions of the issues involved over the same period and, most recently, two trips to the Middle East by the Secretary of State this year and additional trips by Ambassador Fairbanks and by others working on the negotiations.

We have put these ideas in some detail to the Israelis and the key Arab States, including Jordan and Egypt. They are now examining the proposals. It would be surprising if they liked or disliked all of them.

We have received reactions from some of our interlocutors. We are studying those reactions. We confidently expect to continue our discussions.

Mr. Chairman, after the President's speech Chairman Zablocki was quoted as commending the President for having said "what must be said." Those words are most apt, for we are articulating a reasonable basis for a negotiated compromise among the parties.

We emphasize that any agreement must be based on the free give-and-take of the negotiating process. We do not guarantee to any party the outcome of the negotiations on any issue.

The President has now stated publicly some U.S. positions on key issues. We now call for the parties contemplated by the Camp David agreement to join us in seeking peace.

In launching this initiative, the President determined that he would stay fully involved and fully committed to the principles he enunciated. We will be working hard over the next weeks in light of the new dynamic the initiative introduces to bring the peace process forward.

I pledge to you that we will be exercising the creativity, the persistence, and the dogged determination to succeed which marked the successful effort in Beirut. I also emphasize to you that we recognize that our effort is to bring a lasting, effective and just peace to this area.

That goal can hardly be accomplished in a few short weeks. We ask you to stay with the President in his determination to sustain this effort and to look for the long-term, just solution.

We believe, deeply and purposefully, that peace can come between Arabs and Jews. No greater purpose can be placed before us all than a just and lasting peace.

Document 322

Address by the Secretary of State (Shultz) Before the United Jewish Appeal, New York, September 12, 1982[58]

The Quest for Peace

My friends and fellow Americans: No theme is more appropriate for my first speech as Secretary of State than the theme of peace. No objective we share is more worthy or more elusive: to attain it requires realism, strength, the capacity to run risks, and the ability to gather trust. It takes sustained good will to build up that trust. And it takes serious, fair, and direct bargaining at the negotiating table to hammer out workable and durable agreements.

If we needed any reminder, events of this year make it clear that we do not live in a world of peace. Scarcely a region of the developing world—where peace is crucial for social and economic growth—has been spared. From Indochina to the Horn of Africa, from the Persian Gulf and Afghanistan to the tip of South America, wars raged with frightening intensity and tragic results. Some cases, such as the Soviets' imperialistic war in Afghanistan, are new conflicts where one nation is seeking to extend its power and control. But much of the violence we witnessed this year, including the war over the Falklands,[59] represented only the latest outbreak of long-smouldering disputes. Mankind has advanced his capacity to wage war. But his ability to settle disputes peacefully and to prevent violence remains primitive.

We have clear codes of international morality and law. From the words of the prophets to the rhetoric of 20th century statesmen, mankind has set out standards for individual and international behavior. Over the last two centuries, nations have formed international bodies to adjudicate disputes, resolve conflicts, and promote peace. But the ideal of a world at peace has remained, and will remain, a mirage until nations pursue, as a matter of course, policies rooted in mutual respect and aimed at forging and fostering a just international order.

The formula for peace often requires that we convince our adversaries of the strength of our forces and of our will to defend liberty and security. That same formula demands that we stand prepared to meet with our adversaries and work with them to bridge differences. Despite the catalogue of troubles around the world, there are great opportunities and practical possibilities before us today.

The pursuit of peace with freedom, security, and justice is the essence of America's foreign policy. Our country's commitment to peace is beyond doubt, based on our creative, unrelenting efforts in that cause.

The past year has been a year rich in American efforts for peace. At the President's direction, and with the commitment of American peacekeeping forces, Secretary Haig took the lead in creating the multinational force that helped make good on the historic Israeli move for peace: withdrawal from the Sinai. Deputy Secretary of State Walter Stoessel worked intensively in the crucial final weeks to assure that achievement. Ours was the nation that made a major effort to head off the tragic war in the South Atlantic. We have continued the effort to find peaceful and just settlements to the fighting in Indochina and Afghanistan. With all America behind him—including, once again our dedicated men in uniform—Phil Habib used every ounce of his legend-

[58] Source: Department of State Press Release 278, September 13, 1982; also printed in Department of State *Bulletin*, October 1982, pp. 1–4.

[59] Documentation on the War in the South Atlantic is in Chapter 15, Part B.

ary skill and stamina to prevent a tragic denouement of the war in Lebanon. We are currently engaged in a major diplomatic effort to achieve Namibian independence and lasting security in southern Africa. We have provided vigorous backing for the international efforts that secured Libya's withdrawal from Chad. And to ease the dangers of nuclear war, the President has proposed major reductions of U.S. and Soviet nuclear weapons, and has offered new proposals to advance the talks on the reduction of conventional forces.

International institutions and resolutions for peace need practical efforts to give them life. Mankind has made astonishing technological and material leaps in the last 40 years. But we must make equally dramatic gains in the political realm if we are to bequeath a safe and secure world of peace to our children.

I believe we can make those gains. Strength of arms and of will are essential, but no more so than the ability to find that winning mixture of courage and realism. No matter what the obstacles, we must persevere—for there are no more noble nor important goals than peace, freedom, and security.

These principles apply fully to that set of goals foremost in our thoughts today—peace in the Middle East, and security and success for Israel and her Arab neighbors. No one who has walked the streets of Jerusalem and Tel Aviv and who has talked at length with as many Israeli people as I have can doubt that they want peace and security, and I am dedicated to helping them achieve both.

Against the backdrop of confrontation, despair, and fear that have characterized the search for peace in the Middle East, three key documents spell out how peace might be made a reality:

The first is U.N. Security Council Resolution 242, which established the basis for a negotiating process founded on the idea of an exchange of territory for real peace.

The second is the Camp David Accords, which—in the Egypt–Israel Peace Treaty—led directly to the realization of such an exchange of territory for peace. Camp David calls for a "just, comprehensive, and durable" Middle East peace based on Resolution 242, but builds on it as well by calling for a solution that recognizes "the legitimate rights of the Palestinian people and their just requirements" and a "resolution of the Palestinian problem in all its aspects."

And third, there is the President's speech of September 1. This historic address builds on the earlier documents by stating categorically that our approach to peace will continue to be based on Resolution 242, with its concept of an exchange of territory for peace, and the Camp David Accords, which provide for Palestinian self-government with full guarantees for Israel's security.

While I cannot summarize for you the totality of a rich and complex speech, I would like to review four important points made by the President.

—First, there should be full safeguards for Israeli security, both internal and external, throughout the transitional period and beyond. The President has made this forcefully clear.

—Second, as stated in Camp David, there should be a transitional period of 5 years during which the Palestinians of the West Bank and Gaza should be permitted to exercise full autonomy.

—Third, the United States believes that peace cannot be achieved on the basis of Israeli sovereignty over the West Bank and Gaza, but must be based on Resolution 242's formula of an exchange of territory for peace. Our preference is for self-government by the Palestinians in association with Jordan, with the extent of withdrawal determined by the quality of peace offered in return.

—Fourth, the United States also believes that peace cannot be achieved by the creation of an independent Palestinian state on the West Bank and Gaza. The President has stated clearly and unequivocally that we will not support an independent Palestinian state in the territories.

One section of the President's speech especially deserves reading tonight word for word, because it did not appear in the text printed in the *New York Times.* But don't blame the *Times.* The passage was inserted by the President at the very last minute—after the press had received their copies. It was put in because the President wanted to speak from his heart to the people of Israel.

The President said this:

"I have personally followed and supported Israel's heroic struggle for survival ever since the founding of the State of Israel 34 years ago. In the pre-1967 borders, Israel was barely 10 miles wide at its narrowest point. The bulk of Israel's population lived within artillery range of hostile Arab armies. I am not about to ask Israel to live that way again."

Those words represent the President's, and America's, fundamental commitment to Israeli security and to genuine peace. Our commitment grows out of a sense of moral obligation but also out of strategic interest. A strong, secure Israel is in our interests and the interests of peace. There will be no peace without Israeli security, but Israel will never be secure without peace. Our vision of the future on the West Bank is one guided by a vision of a secure Israel living with defensible borders and by our abiding belief that it is not in Israel's long-term interests to try to rule over the more than one million Palestinians living in the West Bank and Gaza.

Approval for the President's initiative is gathering force and momentum, both here at home and abroad. I believe it will gather more and more support as people read and study that speech carefully. The same is true of the Camp David Accords on which the President's speech is based. Those who do take the time to read those historic documents soon recognize the genius of Camp David. It is an accomplishment that is a tribute to the statesmanship of the leaders of three great nations—Prime Minister Begin, the late President Sadat, and our own President Carter.

Despite the many dark periods of stagnation, setback, and delay since 1967, a look at the long-term trend in the Middle East is encouraging. After a quarter-century of sterile conflict and confrontation, the past decade has seen a building momentum toward peace. Three negotiated disengagement agreements have been signed. President Sadat paid his historic and stirring visit to Jerusalem. There was the great achievement of the Camp David framework; and the signing in 1979 and fulfillment this past April, of the first treaty of peace between Israel and an Arab neighbor—a treaty that is a tribute to the willingness of the people of Israel and of Prime Minister Begin to take risks for peace. I say the first treaty because there must be—and there will be—more to come. For only in the context of true peace, freely negotiated, can there be true security for Israel and her neighbors.

Nothing is more crucial than building on this momentum. But, as has been obvious to all, the stalemate in the autonomy talks over the past 2 or more years, and the outbreak of major military conflict this past summer, pose a grave threat to further progress.

In these circumstances, President Reagan decided that the time had come for renewed American leadership. He acted, as well, because the Middle East today is at a moment of unprecedented opportunity: Israel, the moderate Arab States, the Palestinians, and the United States are all affected, and all now face the choice between hope and frustration, between peace and conflict.

—Israel has demonstrated once again, at tragic cost, that it will not be defeated militarily. If Israel's adversaries want peace and justice they must recognize, clearly and explicitly, the right of the State of Israel to exist, and they must enter, as President Reagan said, "direct, hard, and fair" negotiations with Israel. When they do, Israel then has the chance to translate military strength into peace, the only long-term security.

—For the moderate Arabs, there is the opportunity to demonstrate that the course of negotiations can produce results and serve their vital interests. For Lebanon, there is now a second chance; the chance once again to be free, prosperous, and democratic, posing no threat to its neighbors and serving as a stable bridge between the West and the Arab world.

—The Palestinians now confront a great decision: whether to continue down the self-destructive road of armed struggle, which has only produced tragedy for the Palestinian people, or to seize the opportunity to affect their destiny by way of the peace process. The Camp David framework upholds the importance of self-government for the Palestinians of the West Bank and Gaza. And it provides Palestinian representatives the right to participate in the determination of their future at every step in that process.

—For the United States, the brilliant, dogged diplomatic achievement of Presidential emissary Phil Habib has shown America's determination and ability to promote just and peaceful solutions to the problems of the area. His work is but the latest evidence of how crucial is the help of the United States if the peoples and nations of the region are to stop the fighting, construct solid agreements, and prevent wars between Arabs and Israelis from again threatening to become the focal point of global conflict.

In his historic address to the Israeli Knesset,[60] Anwar Sadat spoke of "moments

[60] President Sadat addressed the Knesset on November 20, 1977; for text, see *American Foreign Policy: Basic Documents, 1977–1980*, pp. 625–632.

in the lives of nations and peoples when it is incumbent upon those known for their wisdom and clarity of vision, to penetrate beyond the past, with all its complexities and vain memories, in a bold drive toward new horizons." The present is such a moment for us all.

The President has offered a challenge—the challenge of peace—to Israelis and Arabs alike. Everyone talks so much about peace that it requires some effort to stop and comprehend what it really can mean. Relief from the horrible burden of war can unleash the full development of human potential, promising even greater creativity in the arts and sciences. Peace offers new economic possibilities—when the defense burden is lightened—to build a better life at home and contribute to the prosperity of the region and the world. Peace can mean fruitful economic cooperation between Israel and her neighbors. Imagine how the genius of the Israeli nation could flourish if it were freed from the physical and psychological burdens imposed by the continuing state of conflict. Imagine the enormous contribution that the peoples of this region—so rich in spiritual strength—could make to all mankind.

The challenge that the President has offered to Israel is to extend its hand to welcome wider participation in the peace process. Israel has demonstrated once more its military strength and bravery. But we all recognize that while true peace requires military strength, strength alone is not enough; true peace can only be achieved through lasting negotiated agreements leading ultimately to friendly cooperation between Israel and her neighbors.

In the 1948 War of Independence Israel lost 6,000 dead, out of a population that was much smaller than it is today; it lost nearly 200 dead in 1956; nearly 700 in 1967, and hundreds more in the War of Attrition that lasted until 1970; 2,800 young Israelis were killed in the 1973 war; and more than 300 in 1982.

That terrible cycle of death and suffering must end. The evacuation of the PLO from Beirut and the forceful demonstration of Israeli capability make this an altogether unique moment, a moment of opportunity to end this cycle. Triumphs of statecraft are decisions which join opportunity with action. If this opportunity is allowed to pass it may never come again.

The challenge Israel faces now is to combine diplomacy with power to build an enduring political settlement. There is nothing that says that Palestinian self-government in association with Jordan must lead inevitably to a Palestinian state. The President has said that we will not support such an outcome. It is not beyond the reach of diplomacy to create, nor Israeli military power to ensure, that agreed arrangements for the West Bank will not erode over time. U.S. determination that concrete, iron-clad arrangements for the security of Israel accompany the ultimate resolution of the Palestinian question is heightened, not diminished, by the fact that we have views on a desirable direction for the negotiations.

The crucial point is that when it comes to safeguarding the long-term security of Israel, the friendship and resolve of the United States are second in importance only to Israel's own resolution and strength. And, in the final analysis, that friendship and resolve deserve, in return, to be reciprocated by a willingness to listen with an open mind to the views of others. But let me be clear: we have a right to be heard but we have no intention of using our support for Israel's security as a way of imposing our views.

We must not underestimate the dilemmas and risks that Israel faces in opting for negotiations, but they are dwarfed by those created by a continuation of the status quo. The United States recognizes its obligations, as the principal supporter of Israel's security, to be understanding of Israel's specific circumstances in the negotiating process. The President has urged consideration of his proposals in the context of negotiations, to be undertaken without preconditions and with no thought of imposed solutions.

That is why the United States particularly asked that the parties themselves not preclude possible outcomes by concrete and perhaps irreversible actions undertaken before the process of negotiation is completed. While we support the right of Jews to live in peace on the West Bank and Gaza under the duly constituted governmental authority there—just as Arabs live in Israel—we regard the continuation of settlement activity prior to the conclusion of negotiations as detrimental to the peace process.

The President has offered a fundamental challenge to the Arabs as well. It is time for the Arab world to recognize the opportunity provided by Camp David. The path of rejection has achieved nothing but tragedy, particularly for the Palestinians. Surely, the pattern of agonies of this capable and courageous people must not be repeated. Alternatively, the Camp David process and the President's fresh start offers a promise of resolution with honor and justice to those with the wisdom to join the peace process. But it also implies a corollary: those who fail to join will miss a precious opportunity—an opportunity for peace that may not come again soon.

The absence of Jordan and representatives of the Palestinian inhabitants of the occupied territories from the negotiations has been the crucial missing link in the Camp David process. Success in the peace process depends on Arab support for these vital missing partners to join the negotiations and become partners for peace. We trust that support will be forthcoming soon. Our consultations with the Arab world will be designed to encourage such support. We recognize the risks to all parties, but the risks of failure are even greater. The Arab nations missed one chance for peace when they rejected the 1947 U.N. partition plan. Then, for nearly two decades, they rejected the legitimacy of the boundaries within which Israelis lived so insecurely prior to 1967. In 1978 they refused to support Egypt when the Camp David Accords were signed. Today, the Arabs again have great opportunities: to move from belligerency to negotiation to peace and to work realistically and practically for the rights of the Palestinians. But these opportunities, like the previous ones, will not last forever.

Thus for the Palestinians and other Arabs, and for Israel, this is indeed the moment, as the President said, for a "new realism." An element in that realism is that the United States has decided to state publicly where it stands on critical questions. There will be, as I have said, no imposed solutions: any point agreed by Israel and its Arab neighbors will not be opposed by us. But at the same time, the United States is now obligated, by reality and morality alike, to make known its views on what we believe is needed to reach a fair, workable, and lasting solution. This the President did on the first of September. The President's initiative contains firm American principles; we will not depart from them. As we move ahead the United States, as a full partner, will reserve the right to support positions on either side when we feel this is likely to promote fair agreement. And we will put forward our own proposals when appropriate, to the same end. I reiterate, however, that no specific negotiated result is ruled out: that is the essence of the process.

We must also recognize another reality: the positions now held by the potential partners in negotiations are widely at variance. The point however is this: any participant in this process—including the United States, as a full partner—is free to have and to enunciate its positions. Once views are expressed, the place, indeed the only place, to thrash out differences is at the bargaining table. If there were no differences of opinion, there would be no need for negotiations.

The issues are complex, the emotions deep, the forces in the Middle East contentious, and the stakes so great. The wisdom of the peace process must spring from recognition of these facts. Bitterness dies hard, while trust grows slowly. President Reagan has now set out the lines of a fair and realistic solution; together with the other parties we should all come together to discuss and negotiate these matters.

There is no need now to agree on any principle but one—that is the need to come together at the bargaining table. To talk. To talk about differences; to talk about aspirations; to talk about peace. But in all events to talk. We ask for nothing more of any of the participants at the beginning of the process. And we have the deepest duty and obligation to ask for no less.

If it takes more time, we are prepared for that. But there are limits—this opportunity must not be lost. One hundred and twenty years ago, Abraham Lincoln, speaking to the Congress of the United States, said that "the dogmas of the past are inadequate to the present. The occasion is piled high with difficulty, and we must rise with the occasion. As the case is new, so we must think anew and act anew . . . ."[61]

In this spirit, and with the vision, self-confidence, and mutual trust that has marked our relationship at its best moments, Israel and America—and our Arab friends, now and in the future—can shape a life of dignity, justice, and true peace.

---

[61] Ellipsis appears in the source text.

Document 323

Address by Vice President Bush Before the Washington Press Club, September 23, 1982 (Extract)[62]

"All Arab Nations Must State With Clarity . . . That Israel Has a Right to Exist"

. . . .

The subject is the Middle East. And the events in Lebanon culminating in the horrifying massacre over the past weekend,[63] graphically demonstrates the incendiary nature of the Middle East in crisis, a crisis that has continued for far too long.

Almost 40 years ago, the United States applauded as Israel was founded in a hopeful attempt to build on the ashes of the Holocaust a new state in the at once new and ancient homeland of the Jewish people. Israel's legitimacy was proclaimed by its people's history, by the world community and by the blood that Israel expended to defend that new independence.

But that legitimacy was not recognized by Israel's Arab neighbors. Tragically, memories of the past 40 years are punctuated by five successive wars.

This ever-escalating violence in the Middle East must end.

And we shall be true to our enduring commitment to the security of Israel. We're bound to Israel by moral as well as strategic interests. Just as important, Israel is the single democracy in the Middle East that subscribes in its everyday life to the democratic process and to these principles on which the American Republic is based.

And yet these same values that form the basis of our alliance with Israel force us to express sorrow and regret at the continued Syrian and Israeli occupation of a weak and divided Lebanon. We must express our honest dismay and our opposition when the capital of Lebanon itself is seized. We must express profound horror and outrage when helpless women, children and men are massacred in the capital city of Beirut.

We believe the people of Lebanon have an opportunity now to reestablish their freedom and identity. But first the bloodshed and the occupations must end. And we must, with all the power we can muster, attempt to bring peace to this troubled land.

Israel's borders must be protected. Lebanon's borders must be protected. Innocent Israelis must be protected from the bombs and the rockets and the terror which have been inflicted upon them since the State of Israel was created. Not one bit less protection is deserved by a Lebanese mother or a Palestinian child. And the steps toward peace that President Reagan has proposed are significant,[64] significant guideposts along the road to a point where such protection will be not only assured but taken for granted by all of the people who live in the Middle East.

We must not permit ancient passions that afflicted the Holy Land of three great religions to further endanger human survival. America's friendship for the peoples of the Middle East is permanent and it is substantial. And our relationship with the people in Israel, in particular, is deeply entwined in the precepts that have shaped each of our peoples through the course of history. We share a bond rooted in the passion for democracy and justice.

Today, Palestinians are scattered throughout the whole region. The Lebanese people remain uprooted by war. The people of Israel are still threatened by military aggression and they live in fear of terrorism. And it is against this backdrop of reality in the region that the few with the boldness and courage to wage peace too often meet the same fate as those who live by the sword. Despite this threat, the Middle East needs more courageous statesmen who will take the great risks to bring peace and dignity to millions. Terrorists may have murdered President Sadat but the olive branch that he brought home from Jerusalem is now firmly rooted along the Nile River.

And today in an attempt to cool passions and tensions, and hopefully give democracy

---

[62] Source: White House Press Release, September 23, 1982, Office of the Press Secretary to the President. Vice President Bush gave the address at the Watergate Hotel. Omitted portions are Bush's brief introductory remarks and the question-and-answer session following his address.

[63] On September 16–18, 1982, Lebanese Phalangist militia massacred approximately 700–800 Palestinian civilians in the Sabra and Shatila refugee camps south of Beirut. See documents 401 and 402.

[64] See document 318.

an opportunity to work, American ships are again steaming to Lebanon carrying American Marines. These young men are returning to a land they left just three weeks ago. And they're coming to Beirut not as policemen, but rather to provide a presence which will help the Lebanese Government restore its sovereign authority over the Beirut area. In this way, our Marines along with their counterparts from France and Italy will further the efforts of the Lebanese themselves to ensure the safety of the people of Beirut and bring an end to the violence. Their stay in Beirut is going to be limited. But I'm persuaded that it will make an indispensable contribution to the process of achieving a free, united, secure Lebanon at peace with all of its neighbors.

Today Lebanon inaugurated a new President, Amin Gemayel. The American people extend to him our congratulations—our full support. We are hopeful that the new leaders will be given the time and the support by all factions to begin the reconstruction of Beirut and of Lebanon, itself, as well as the opportunity to form a government representative of all of the Lebanese people.

Peace and security simply cannot be gained by military force alone. The cowardly work of the assassin and the terrorist breed more violence and build upon already existing hatreds. Peace and security can only be realized by negotiation, through discussion, through arduous days and weeks and months of face to face talk.

In the aftermath of Beirut, some see tensions that lead to war. In this regard, we believe now is the time to actively pursue peace. All parties must agree to certain basic objectives if we are going to be helpful in bringing stability to Lebanon. First, a permanent cessation of hostilities. Secondly, establishment of a strong and representative government. Thirdly, a withdrawal of all foreign forces: PLO—now mainly Syrian and Israeli. Fourth, a restoration of control of the Lebanese Government—throughout the entire country. And, fifth, the establishment of conditions under which Lebanon no longer can be used as a launching pad for attacks against Israel in the Northern Galilee or anywhere else.

Lebanon must be free from the pressures and violence of outside forces if it is to have any chance of restoring the democratic form of government that it knew in the not so distant past.

In the larger context of bringing permanent peace and stability to the region, all nations and parties must fully understand that Israel is there to stay. The United States is committed to the security of Israel and its need for peace. And the Palestinians and Arab nations must accept the reality of this situation.

In return, Israel and the Arab States must recognize that the Palestinian people have legitimate rights that have not been satisfied and are not today satisfied. Palestinians can no longer be left in squalid camps, scattered throughout the region which only foster conditions that build deeper hatreds and nurture frustrations that turn young men into absolute, total fanatics.

Ironically, perhaps, it is Israel, more than any nation today that recognizes the history of injustices perpetuated in a wandering and homeless people. And in this respect, we must encourage Israel as well to help solve the Palestinian tragedy. But this cannot be a one-way street. Palestinians must accept the reality and the legitimacy of Israel. Palestinians must understand that the satisfaction of their legitimate rights is directly tied to their recognition of Israel's right to exist.

The recent Fez proposal of the Arab states[65] provides an implicit recognition of Israel by calling for the United Nations Security Council to guarantee peace among all states of the region. But it isn't enough. Guarded references or allusions, and code words are not going to suffice while the conflict festers. All Arab nations must state with clarity, as Egypt has done, that Israel has a right to exist. Peace cannot be achieved by parties who, like the ostrich, refuse to face reality.

And President Reagan's proposal is really a catalyst. It's intended to catalyze action. We certainly aren't forcing it on anybody. We couldn't if we wanted to. Our hope is to spur broader participation and progress toward peace within the Camp David framework—that's been forged by Prime Minister Begin, President Sadat, and President Carter. We strongly believe that ours is a bold proposal—one that can be used both as a point of departure for reducing immediate tensions and as a negotiating proposal that's going to bring stability and peaceful opportunities for millions of people that have too long been victimized by war. More than anything else, it represents our vision of a future settlement—one that recognizes and responds to Israel's legitimate needs

---

[65] For the Arab League peace plan, see document 320.

for secure and defensible borders and the legitimate rights of the Palestinian Arabs. It is not in Israel's interest to rule over 1.3 million West Bank and Gazan Arabs. It is long past time for Israeli and Arab to sit together, face to face, as they did at Camp David.

We've learned painfully and too often from modern history that the ultimate result of Israelis and Arabs refusing to sit together, face to face, is the resumption of war. After each of the past five wars, world leaders have called for the parties to prepare for peace. Instead, too much blood has been shed and too many lives have been lost. But here we are again, faced with the same ugly situation that we've looked at too often in the past. Israelis, Palestinians, Syrians, Lebanese, Jordanians—all must recognize that the continuation of hatreds, jealousies and bigotries will lead more men, women, and children to death's door. And it's only face to face negotiations that can uproot those deadly forces.

Since last weekend, we've had the opportunity to work closely with the President and Secretary of State and others in reviewing the massacre—the situation in Lebanon and the entire region. I can report on several major concerns that the President expressed during these meetings.

The President is more determined than ever to bring peace or to be a catalyst for peace to the entire region. He believes that stability in Beirut is an essential first step. But he also believes now is the time to push forward to have all foreign troops peacefully withdraw from Lebanon. In addition, the President is concerned about anonymous stories that he or anyone in this administration, particularly in the top of the administration, would want to interfere in internal Israeli politics. I can't emphasize strongly enough that that is not true. The President strongly respects Israel—respects its democratic processes. And for our part, we will work even harder for peace that will protect the borders of Israel. But now is the time for Israel to signal that it too intends to accelerate the drive for peace.

The President's proposal, at the very least, has given new hope to many in the region. The opening bids from both Israel and from the Arabs have been tough. But peace and reason can prevail. The leaders of the region must exhibit the bravery and vision that characterized President Sadat's trip to Jerusalem and Prime Minister Begin's return of the Sinai. If they do not, I fear that once again, we will all relive the terror of Sabra and Shatila, of Ma alot, of Munich, of indiscriminate shelling of innocent people in the Northern Galilee. And these sad memories have got to be seared in the consciousness of the Mideast's leaders as they contemplate their future and President Reagan's call for peace.

. . . .

Document 324

Transcript of a Press Conference by President Reagan, September 28, 1982 (Extracts)[66]

Israel and the Reagan Peace Plan

. . . .

Q. Mr. President, it has been reported that you believe that Israel is sabotaging your peace initiative, and also that you now believe that Israel has become the Goliath in the Middle East, and that the other countries, the Arab countries, are the David. Did you say that? Do you believe that?

The President. I didn't say it exactly that way. In fact, I didn't say that I thought they were the Goliath. I said that one of the things, as the negotiations approach and we proceed with this peacemaking business, that Israel should understand, as we have come to understand from talking to other Arab States, that where from the very beginning all of us including Israel, have thought of it as a tiny country fighting for its life surrounded by larger states and hostile states that want to see it destroyed, that their military power has become such that there are Arab States that now voice a fear that they are expansionist, that they may be expansionist, and they have the military power. So all I was referring to was that.

The first part of your statement there, though, about Israel and trying to un-

---

[66] Source: White House Press Release, September 28, 1982, Office of the Press Secretary to the President; printed also in *Weekly Compilation of Presidential Documents*, October 4, 1982, pp. 1223–1224. For the full text, see *ibid.*, pp. 1219–1227. The press conference was held in the East Room of the White House beginning at 7:30 p.m.

dermine—no, I don't believe that. I think that both sides have voiced things that they feel very strongly about, and contrary to what I have suggested in my proposal, and having been a long-time union negotiator, I happen to think that some of that might be each side staking out its position so as to be in a better position when it comes time to negotiate.

. . . .

The President. . . . you said you had a follow-up and I cut you off. Did you?

Q. That's very kind of you. I just wanted to ask you since you said you didn't think that Israel was trying to undermine your peace initiative whether you are less optimistic about its chances since the massacre and the tragedy in Beirut?

The President. No, I'm not less optimistic. I'm also not deluding myself that it's going to be easy. Basically what we have, I think, in this peace proposal is a situation where on one side territory is the goal and on the other side security. And what has to be negotiated out is a kind of exchange of territory for security and I meant what I said when I proposed this plan and that is this country will never stand by and see any settlement that does not guarantee the security of Israel.

. . . .

Document 325

Statement by the Department of State Spokesman (Hughes), October 18, 1982[67]

U.S. Position on the PLO

We are aware of press reports to the effect that a PLO official will accompany the Fez summit follow-up committee to the United States; but as we have already said, we have made it clear we will not receive a PLO official, and we have no reason to expect that the Fez Committee would disregard our wishes on this matter.

Beyond this, we can only repeat for you that our position on talks with the PLO has not changed. We will not recognize or negotiate with that organization until it has accepted U.N. Security Council Resolutions 242 and 338, and recognized Israel's right to exist.

[67] Source: Office of Press Relations, Department of State. Hughes made the statement at the Department of State Daily Press Briefing, which began at 12:17 p.m.

Document 326

Remarks by President Reagan and King Hassan II of Morocco, October 22, 1982[68]

Visit of the Arab League Delegation

The President. Our meeting today with King Hassan and the Delegation is an important milestone along the road toward a common objective, a just and lasting peace in the Middle East. His Majesty King Hassan and his colleagues were forthright and helpful to us in clarifying the positions of the Arab League adopted last month in Fez, Morocco. I've clarified for His Majesty and the Delegation a number of points concerning the peace initiative that I announced September 1st.

We listened to one another's views in the spirit of good will, understanding, and mutual respect. Peace in the Middle East means achieving security for all the states in that troubled region—security for the Arab States and security for Israel and a sense of identity for the Palestinian people. We must pursue these goals rigorously, thoughtfully, and in close consultation with all here.

[68] Source: White House Press Release, October 22, 1982, Office of the Press Secretary to the President; also printed in *Weekly Compilation of Presidential Documents*, October 25, 1982, pp. 1373–1374. King Hassan II headed the delegation from the Arab League which met with President Reagan on October 22. The other members of the delegation were: Arab League Secretary General Chedli Klibi of Tunisia, Moroccan Foreign Minister Mohammed Boucetta, Algerian Foreign Minister Ahmed Taleb Ibrahimi, Jordanian Foreign Minister Marwan al-Kasem, Saudi Arabian Foreign Minister Prince Saud al-Faisal, Syrian Deputy Prime Minister and Foreign Minister Abdel Halim Khaddam, and Tunisian Foreign Minister Beji Caid Essebsi. The President spoke at 1:45 p.m. at the Diplomatic Entrance on the South Grounds of the White House.

And like our guests today, we all share the hope of peace. Our mutual goal of peace and the road to it lies through a negotiating process which I hope can be resumed in the very near future. I hope they realize—all the Delegation and His Majesty—how welcome they are here in the United States and how much we appreciate their coming here.

KING HASSAN.[69] Mr. President, I and my colleagues, I would like to assure you, we express our gratitude for this wonderful reception we received today and the hospitality which we have received here today.

We also would like to thank you for the depth and the good will which we have witnessed here today as we reviewed with you the hopes of the Arabs and their objectives, which is peace with justice and dignity. I personally believe that we will find in the framework of Security Council Resolution 242 and in 338 and your program—your plan for peace—and the decisions of the Fez conference, we will find in all these, which will save us a lot of time in order to achieve our noble aim and objective which is peace and coexistence and construction for the welfare of the region and all mankind.

Thank you very much again, Mr. President.

Document 327

Statement by the Department of State Acting Spokesman (Romberg), November 4, 1982[70]

Additional Israeli Settlements on the West Bank

The United States regards this latest announcement of Israel's intention to begin work on additional settlements[71] as most unwelcome. As we have previously stated, we cannot understand why, at a time when we are actively seeking broader participation in the peace process, Israel persists in a pattern of activity which erodes the confidence of all, and most particularly the Palestinians of the West Bank and Gaza, in the possibilities for a just and fairly negotiated outcome to the peace process.

Settlements activity raises questions about Israel's willingness to abide by the promise of Resolution 242 that territory will be exchanged for true peace.

Document 328

Interview With the Assistant Secretary of State for Near Eastern and South Asian Affairs (Veliotes), November 9, 1982 (Extracts)[72]

Jordan and the Middle East Peace Process

. . . .

[ANDERSON.] I understand that the United States is very eager to have Jordan enter the negotiations, but the question I kept being asked in the Middle East was, "what is the United States prepared to do to make it easier or possible for King Hussein to join the negotiations." In other words, what pressure is the United States willing to put on Israel for example to stop the settlements?

VELIOTES. Obviously, in order to have a successful negotiation, you have to have the relevant parties to the negotiation. In the Middle East peace context, this means Jordan and the Palestinians. Given the various facts of life in the Middle East, King Hussein therefore becomes the key element with respect to broadening these peace negotiations. We believe that the President's September 1 proposals are in themselves sufficient encouragement for the Jordanians and the Palestinians to agree to join

---

[69] King Hassan II spoke in French, and an interpreter translated his remarks.

[70] Source: Office of Press Relations, Department of State. Romberg made the statement at the Department of State Daily Press Briefing, which began at 12:14 p.m.

[71] On November 3, 1982, Israeli Housing Minister David Levi announced plans to establish five new settlements on the West Bank. See Foreign Broadcast Information Service, *Daily Report: Middle East and Africa*, November 4, 1982, pp. I7 and I8.

[72] Source: Department of State files. Veliotes was interviewed on "Voice of America" by Jim Anderson of United Press International, Jon Wrightenburg of *Frankfurter Allgemeine*, and Dan Sutherland of *Christian Science Monitor*. William McCrory was the moderator.

the negotiations. These proposals have been discussed at great length. The recent exchanges between the Fez Delegation, the Arab League, led by King Hassan and President Reagan went into them in great detail. They are on the table. They are fair, and they seem to us to be a basis for a just and stable peace which would not only achieve the rights of the Palestinians but also achieve security for everyone in the area.

ANDERSON. Well, the Jordanians, the ones I've talked to at least, would not agree with you that the proposals of September 1 are in themselves sufficient. They think that what has to be done first is that the United States has to reestablish its credibility to maintain its commitments to the Arab world. Specifically, the Arab world is looking for some sign from this administration that it is prepared to return to a more even-handed approach. In that context, what is the United States prepared to do to make it easier for King Hussein to join?

VELIOTES. The problem with the position that you are outlining is that it smacks of additional preconditions before coming to the table. Now you mentioned settlements. Obviously, settlements are a very important issue. The settlements are, as we have made clear and the President has made clear, a major obstacle to the peace process,[73] it's psychological conditioning as well as facts on the ground. Our position on this is very well known. We believe that the most effective way in the near term, to significantly affect the Israeli practices on the West Bank including settlements to which the Arabs object and to which we object, is to get the negotiations started. Right now, we are dealing—continuing to deal—in, if you will, a theoretical vacuum. We do not have the additional Arab parties who have said clearly that they are prepared to come to the table to negotiate peace. And although not—I don't want to argue that the United States has no responsibilities beyond the President's plan and that one wasn't my point—I am concerned lest a growing set of preconditions from either side push us back further from the prospect of early negotiations. And as we keep reminding people, and I'm a little surprised that it's always the United States that has to keep reminding people, that there are 1⅛ million Palestinians who would like us all to be more effective in a more urgent manner to help them solve their problems, which is, of course, the military occupation.

WRIGHTENBURG. Mr. Secretary, the problem involved in this is also, is it not, which Palestinians are going to be participants at the future negotiating table. I wonder what you think about King Hussein's own problem vis-à-vis the PLO in that context? Do you think the King is more or less forced to represent the position which he did before that the PLO has to be part of this or have things somewhat changed since the Lebanese war?

VELIOTES. We have always understood King Hussein's position that before he could join the negotiations, he would have to have broader Arab support. That's well understood and during the Fez discussions here, King Hassan made clear that for the Arabs a Palestinian, a PLO, concurrence for Jordanian participation was a prerequisite. The President's response to that was "O.K. we understand that. Let's make this happen fast." The facts of life are that if the PLO comes to a negotiating table, the Israelis won't be there. Now, that obstacle, if you will, has to be overcome. We believe that the way to overcome it, is for agreement with Jordan so that Jordan can come with appropriate Palestinians who are readily acceptable under the Camp David agreements, those inhabitants of the territories, and get the process started. We don't see why it should take so long to just move through these preliminary procedures, while understanding fully the position of the Arabs and King Hussein's requirements.

WRIGHTENBURG. An additional question, sir. Would that then mean that you would hope that King Hussein would be able to bring some of those Palestinians along to the negotiating table about whom one talked already to you on the Camp David process. That is to say the mayors, some mayors of the West Bank, who might also be acceptable to the Israelis, for instance?

VELIOTES. Well, according to the Camp David Accords, inhabitants of the territory, obviously non-PLO, could join either the Jordanian or the Egyptian delegations. That's the fastest way to get things started. Presumably, the mayors would be widely accepted as legitimate representatives of Palestinian nationalism. And that should solve the issue.

. . . .

WRIGHTENBURG. Mr. Secretary, former President Nixon has very recently made some remarks to this whole Middle Eastern situation and in his usual blunt way he said

---

[73] See documents 318 and *supra*.

that obviously the other key person in this whole process would be Prime Minister Begin. I think if I quote Mr. Nixon correctly, he said at one point, in his view, Mr. Begin would finally come around to go to such a negotiating process as was done in Camp David in respect to the peace between Israel and Egypt. He would do that too finally in the Palestinian question because it was in Begin's own interest. Or else Mr. Nixon said, Begin would only be remembered as the man of the Beirut massacre.

Mr. Begin is coming back to this country pretty soon. Could one expect, reasonably expect that the President will be, President Reagan that is, blunt with Mr. Begin in the amount that this is now required in order to get this process moving?

VELIOTES. Well, I think the President will, as usual, speak clearly with respect to American policy and American interests. With respect to your first comments, I don't think the issue is would an Israeli Prime Minister agree to negotiate peace if we could find those other parties that we have been looking for so avidly, to announce their willingness to come to the table. I have no doubt that there will be Israelis at the table as well. That is not the same as saying that the various parties would agree with each other with respect to their coming to the table. But I think if you take a look at what the elements are at issue, you find that there are two major points with respect to the Palestinian issue. And they are both covered very well under Camp David. Unfortunately too many people talk about the Camp David Accords and they don't read them.

The first element which is of vital importance to a million and a half people, is the circumstances whereby the Israeli military occupation will get off their backs. Now, that is called the interim period, the transitional period, the autonomy period. There is general agreement. There should be a transition period. There is general agreement that that should be a time of confidence building. We would ask all of the parties to resolve to come to the table to work out those arrangements and hold off injecting into these negotiations the so-called final status issues where the differences are vast. And until or unless you have a confidence-building period I don't think that you are going to find an ability to make the necessary compromises on those issues. So all of the differences being expressed really are over final status issues and we would like to get the focus back to the first step, which [is] of such importance to the people actually living under the military occupation.

Q. There again you would come back to what you said earlier in this program, Mr. Secretary, that it would be good if there were no preconditions. And that goes for both sides, doesn't it?

VELIOTES. Yes. No preconditions other than acceptance of the basic rules of the peace process which is the basis for Camp David.

MODERATOR. Mr. Sutherland.

SUTHERLAND. I wonder if you find any encouragement or whether you have any interest in a statement which the PLO has made a number of times recently to the effect that there ought to be a mutual and simultaneous recognition between the Israelis and the PLO. I don't know whether this comes under your category of a final status-type issue or not. When they first started making that kind of statement last summer people said it was a trial balloon and didn't carry much authority. But most recently I heard it from Kalid Hassan, the PLO man who was standing by here when the Fez group went in to see the President recently.

Does that offer any encouragement that they are moving in the direction we like. Is it something new or is it simply an old statement full of loaded conditions?

VELIOTES. Well, we hear about this in two respects. The first is in the context of the PLO meeting the American conditions, which we believe should be viewed as a standing offer on the table for a direct dialogue. And incidently that was reconfirmed to King Hassan by President Reagan here during their talks. And the answer we get consistently on that, unfortunately in my view, is well we can't do that. That's the last card to be played. And we can only do that if Israel recognizes us. Well, since Israel is not going to recognize the PLO in any time frame that I can see, that means that the PLO will not do what is required, if this thesis holds forth, to open up a great dialogue with the United States and obviously that is their choice. The other aspect—and they are related—is the question of negotiations. Under what circumstances would the PLO get a seat at the table. And we say to them, we can't guarantee a seat at the table for you. You are unacceptable to Israel. We've got to move on with this process in the interests of the Palestinians, and everyone else out there. So, you get this formula which as far as I'm concerned and since I've heard it for so long, is a formula for no progress in any direction. And I'm very sorry about that.

Q. So, you don't see anything particularly new, you don't see any movement in that kind of statement.

VELIOTES. No, that is a move backwards.

MODERATOR. Mr. Anderson.

ANDERSON. Do you believe that the Israeli government, the present Israeli government, still accepts U.N. Security Council Resolution 242 as applying to the West Bank and Gaza?

VELIOTES. Well, that is an issue, a question that I think ought to be put to the Israelis themselves. As you know, there has been some question raised in this respect. And it is a very troublesome subject.

ANDERSON. Well, are you operating on the understanding under the belief that the Israelis do or don't accept it.

VELIOTES. Well, until or unless proven to the contrary, we operate on the belief that they do accept 242 as applying on all fronts and that includes the Golan.

ANDERSON. And Jerusalem?

VELIOTES. And Jerusalem. This is an integral part of Camp David. I keep coming back to Camp David because so few people seem to take the time to see what is there. There is a very interesting exchange of letters on Jerusalem which expresses American policy.

ANDERSON. I did take your advice and I went to the Israelis. The answer they come back with is yes we accept 242 as modified by Camp David in effect saying that Camp David has changed the basic formula of 242.

VELIOTES. We don't accept that at all. And the President has made that clear in his September 1 peace proposals.

. . . .

Document 329

Transcript of a Press Conference by the Secretary of State (Shultz), November 18, 1982 (Extracts)[74]

Israeli Policies on the West Bank

. . . .

Q. Mr. Secretary, to what degree is economic aid to Israel linked to the settlements policy of the Government of Israel?

SECRETARY SHULTZ. There hasn't been any link made. We have been very clear, I think, from the beginning that we think the settlements and the expansion of them are not constructive at all, not a contribution to the peace process. So the President has been very clear in opposing them, just as I think some of the conditions on the West Bank are certainly not a constructive contribution to the peace process.

I suppose I speak about it, in part, because I am fundamentally a university man, and the idea of asking people who come to teach and work in a university setting, which is, after all, a setting where we expect to have freedom of thought and to encourage freedom of thought, signing oaths is just not the way to go about it. So those are some things that are going on that we think are just not constructive at all.

. . . .

Q. Mr. Secretary, a moment ago, you expressed special concern about the professors on the West Bank who have been asked to sign a pledge against the PLO or leave. Do you have any realistic expectation that the United States, in consultation with Israel, can bring about a reversal of that action?

SECRETARY SHULTZ. I think we should speak unequivocally about it, and people in the intellectual community particularly who have been through this. You remember, we had the episode of the loyalty oath—maybe

---

[74] Source: Department of State Press Release 351, November 18, 1982; also printed in Department of State *Bulletin*, January 1983, pp. 55–56. For the full text, see *ibid.*, pp. 54–62. Shultz held this press conference in the Department of State beginning at 4 p.m.

some of you are too young to remember those days, but I remember them—ought to speak up, including people in universities in Israel. It's the same problem. It's a problem of freedom—freedom of thought.

. . . .

C. Egypt

Document 330

Statements by President Reagan and Egyptian President Mubarak, February 4, 1982[1]

Pursuit of a Comprehensive Peace in the Middle East

THE PRESIDENT. Ladies and gentlemen, President Mubarak and I have just completed a most fruitful and wide-ranging set of meetings. Our discussions were frank and cordial and covering a number of matters of mutual concern.

President Mubarak's visit demonstrates more clearly than any words the continuity of American-Egyptian relations and reflects the strong ties that bind us together.

Foremost among these ties is our belief in and commitment to a peaceful solution to the Arab-Israeli dispute. President Mubarak has assured us that Egypt remains committed to a peaceful solution of this conflict. And to that end, we'll spare no effort to achieve a comprehensive peace as set forth in the Camp David agreement.

During our talks, we reaffirmed our commitment to press ahead with the autonomy talks in order to reach agreement on a declaration of principles which is the best means of making tangible progress toward a solution of the Palestinian problem in all its aspects as envisaged by Camp David.

We reviewed our mutual concerns about the strategic threats to the region and reconfirmed our identification of views on the need to work closely together. We discussed in some detail our economic and military assistance programs. We agreed to consult regularly on methods of implementing and improving them. These consultations have, in fact, already been or begun, I should say, among our principal advisers.

And, finally, let me just say that it has been a pleasure having this opportunity to further my personal relationship with President Mubarak. I'm confident that we will be working closely together to achieve those many goals that are in the mutual interest of our two countries.

Thank you very much and, President Mubarak, we've been delighted to have you here.

PRESIDENT MUBARAK. Thank you. Ladies and gentlemen, I'm very pleased with the outcome of my talks with President Reagan. As he just stated, the discussions we held were frank and cordial. They were very fruitful as well.

I welcome the reaffirmation, the continuation of the U.S. role as a full partner in the peace process. We are determined to pursue our peace efforts until a comprehensive settlement is reached according to the Camp David Accords.

I intend to maintain close cooperation and consultation with President Reagan and his administration. And we are looking forward to seeing him in Cairo.

Thank you very much.

Document 331

Statement of Principle by the Governments of Egypt and the United States, February 4, 1982[2]

U.S.-Egyptian Economic Cooperation

WHEREAS:

—Egypt and the United States have been full partners in the pursuit of peace in the Middle East;

[1] Source: White House Press Release, February 4, 1982, Office of the Press Secretary to the President; printed also in *Weekly Compilation of Presidential Documents*, February 8, 1982, pp. 115–116. Presidents Reagan and Mubarak spoke to reporters at the South Portico of the White House beginning at 11:05 a.m.

[2] Source: White House Press Release, Febru-

—Egypt and the United States are full partners in the pursuit of regional stability and in the continuation of peace in the Middle East;

—The United States has cooperated in the economic development of Egypt through a program of assistance to the Egyptian Government in recognition of the sacrifices made by the Egyptian people;

—The Government of Egypt has announced its intentions to undertake its own program of economic reform that utilizes the initiative and capabilities of the Egyptian people;

—Egypt has, with substantial U.S. assistance and the infusion of other external resources, strengthened its economy and rebuilt much of the capital and social infrastructure base;

—Egypt has entered a period of economic progress that will require its own management of substantial external resources, including continued U.S. assistance;

—It is in the interest of both Nations to assure the success of the economic reform program in Egypt in a manner that recognizes the substantial capabilities of the Government of Egypt to accomplish its intentions and the continuing commitment of the United States to provide resources that may be utilized to this end.

Now, therefore:

—The United States endorses the intentions expressed by the Government of Egypt to acknowledge the continued need for economic reform and progress and to undertake necessary measures towards that end;

—The Government of Egypt expresses appreciation for U.S. assistance and the significant contribution it is making to Egypt's present stage of development and to the enhancement of living conditions in Egypt;

—Both Nations recognize Egypt's commitment to improving the efficiency with which it uses its human and financial resources;

—Both Nations are now embarking on a new phase of greater interest in economic progress in Egypt with a view toward making U.S. assistance, as permitted by U.S. law, be of an optimum impact and to assure Egypt a more active role in the allocation and disbursement of the U.S. assistance.

Accordingly:

1. The two parties agree that directing U.S. economic resources into program assistance in support of Egypt's sectoral strategies can significantly improve overall sectoral efficiency and therefore they shall seek means for increasingly programming resources in this manner. Under sectoral funding Egypt shall be responsible for the design, implementation and evaluation of specific activities, the allocation of resources to those activities, and related policy objectives within each sector.

2. The use of incremental budgeting *can* increase the flow of assistance and expand its effectiveness. The current program and planned new activities will be reviewed to apply this budgeting principle. To the maximum extent consistent with Egypt's sectoral strategy and specific nature of the financing of capital projects, U.S. assistance will be provided on an incremental basis, thus assuring maximum current distribution of the resources transferred.

3. The two parties agreed that the Commodity Import Program can play an important role not only for financing imports of consumption and intermediate commodities but also for investment in productive enterprises and to support structural program adjustment. Both parties agreed to consider additional means for using the CIP in support of development objectives. Specifically, the parties agree to consider programming $350 million for CIP in FY 1982, of which $300 million will be obligated immediately, and to consider an increasing level of CIP financing in future fiscal years.[3]

4. Egyptian professional and technical experts shall have wider opportunity to participate in the design and implementation of all projects and programs funded through U.S. assistance programs.

5. In recognition that the assistance pipeline of obligated but undisbursed funds represents a substantial resource available for economic progress in Egypt, both parties agree to develop effective ways to accelerate the utilization of these funds.

---

ary 4, 1982, Office of the Press Secretary to the President; also printed in Department of State *Bulletin*, April 1982, p. 79. The statement of principle was signed by Fouad Iskaudar, Egypt's Under Secretary of the Ministry of the Economy, and Bradshaw Langmaid, Jr., Acting Assistant Administration for the Near East, AID.

[3] The Commodity Import Program agreement was signed on February 5 (TIAS 10347), together with an agreement authorizing $75 million in additional financing of U.S. agricultural exports to Egypt under the P.L.–480 program (TIAS 10328).

Document 332

Transcript of a Press Conference by the Secretary of State (Haig), February 5, 1982[4]

Assessment of U.S.-Egyptian Relations Following President Mubarak's Visit

SECRETARY HAIG. First, let me welcome some of our Egyptian colleagues we're delighted to have with us here today. I do want to say a few words on the record, summarizing our assessment of the about-to-be-completed visit of President Mubarak and his colleagues here to the United States. This, as you know, is the first visit of President Mubarak, as President. He was here, I think about 4 months ago, in behalf of President Sadat.

I think in summary we can say that the visit has deepened and broadened the relationship between the United States and Egypt begun under President Sadat. It confirmed the continuing conformity of views on peace, justice, and security and strengthened that convergence of views.

We in the United States, of course, have great admiration for the Egyptian people, for the strength of their institutions, and for the leadership of President Mubarak which have been so clearly confirmed by the successful transition in Egypt following the recent national tragedy.[5]

All in all, I think the visit can be described as a highly successful one at all levels from personal to strategic. It is clear that the visit reinforced the U.S. conviction that it will remain a full partner in the peace process begun at Camp David.

In that regard the Egyptian Government and the U.S. Government at the Presidential level have renewed their mutual commitment to the Camp David peace process and to work with Israel to bring full autonomy for the Palestinians on the West Bank and Gaza as the first stage described in the Camp David accords itself with the following language: "The resolution of the Palestinian problem in all its aspects."

The United States reaffirmed the value of its relationship with Egypt and will work closely with Egypt and President Mubarak to bring a better life to the people of Egypt through cooperative economic efforts.

The United States fully understands Egypt's desires for flexibility in economic assistance programs, and in that regard yesterday afternoon an agreement between the representatives of the two governments was arrived at which will establish a framework to provide greater flexibility in the administration and conduct of American economic aid programs for Egypt.[6]

The United States believes that a strong Egypt is essential to the peace and security in the Middle East. In that regard we consider and continue to support programs designed to modernize Egyptian Armed Forces. This is part of a broad regional effort which will be conducted in FY '83 and reflected in our program for FY '83 in the region.

This issue was, of course, discussed in detail not only between the President and President Reagan, but between President Mubarak and myself, and between President Mubarak and Defense Secretary Weinberger in separate meetings.

I think it's important to say that President Reagan especially appreciated the opportunity afforded by this visit to discuss the full range of regional bilateral issues and issues related to the peace process in the Middle East personally with President Mubarak. There is no question but that the conclusion of this important visit leaves President Reagan with a deep sense of confidence and optimism that the period ahead of Egyptian-U.S. relationships will progress on a sound and solid basis to the mutual benefits of the American and Egyptian people.

I welcome your questions.

Q. Mr. Secretary, do you now have a clearer idea of what President Mubarak meant by a national Palestinian entity? For example, does it mean Palestinian authority over the land as well as the people—population?

---

[4] Source: Department of State Press Release 51, February 5, 1982; also printed in Department of State *Bulletin*, April 1982, pp. 80–83. The press conference took place after the State visit of Egyptian President Mubarak.

[5] Reference is to the assassination of Egyptian President Anwar Sadat on October 6, 1981.

[6] Reference is to the U.S.-Egyptian Statement of Principle of February 4, 1982, *supra*.

SECRETARY HAIG. I think you're referring to the language of the Camp David agreements.

Q. I'm referring to a phrase he used in his arrival statement on Wednesday at the White House where he talked of the creation of a Palestinian national entity.[7]

SECRETARY HAIG. That is the focal point of the discussions on full autonomy with respect to the West Bank and to Gaza. It is, of course, the focal point of the autonomy talks themselves, the power and authorities, and the multitude of arrangements which provide first for a transition arrangement in this regard which would ultimately lead to a final settlement of these problems and the character of the entity to which you refer.

I think it's premature to go beyond the point of the language of Camp David itself and the ongoing discussions which I do not think it's helpful to engage in here on the topic of autonomy. But I do want to emphasize that what we are talking about is a transition period where confidence can be structured on both sides and where the ultimate outcome will reach, in the words of Camp David itself, the resolution of the Palestinian problem in all of its aspects.

Q. Mr. Secretary, may I follow that up, please? I just want to follow up Jim's question. Could that, in the U.S. view, encompass the possibility of a national entity of some kind emerging from this process?

SECRETARY HAIG. I think it's important that those of you who have questions on that subject—and it's a sensitive area—go back to the language of Camp David. That provides, if you will, an overall framework to which the participants have committed themselves.

There are other aspects of this question which are to be determined in the context, first, of an agreement in principle for the transitional period, then a detailed autonomy agreement, and then an ultimate solution. And some of these nettling questions have been deferred until the final stages, so I think you're asking a question for which there is no timely or contemporary answer.

Now let me turn to our guests.

Q. Mr. Secretary, I understand clearly your statement concerning the right of the Palestinians and the full solution of the problem of Palestine. But let me put this question:

President Mubarak repeated several times his appeal for a dialogue between the American Government and the Palestinians.

How do you figure this can be implemented? What kind of Palestinians? How can you do it? Are you going to do it or not, sir?

SECRETARY HAIG. The question was, President Mubarak had referred repeatedly to the desirability of a dialogue between the Palestinian people and the Americans as a partner in the peace process.

I think President Mubarak was equally careful in not putting out any road maps, any specific formula for this. We know we have the question of the PLO, and the U.S. position on that question is clear and has not changed.

With respect to discussions with the Palestinian inhabitants of the West Bank and Gaza, these lines of communication have been exercised, not in a formal sense because the structure for that does not exist, but in the recent trips that I made. In the first trip I had a discussion with the Mayor of Bethlehem. Assistant Secretary Veliotes had additional discussions, not only with the Palestinian inhabitants of the territories but also with other friendly Arab States in the region.

So I think that's the answer to your question with an underlying emphasis on the conditions which have been stated previously with respect to the PLO.

Q. Mr. Secretary, do you think it's realistic to continue this policy of refusing to entertain the possibility of conversations with PLO representatives?

SECRETARY HAIG. I don't think it's a question of realistic. I think there's nothing that suggests we're not prepared to do that when the PLO is prepared to meet its obligations as a participant in such discussions, and we've made those positions very clear.

Q. You're talking about changing their covenant? Is this specifically what you refer to?

SECRETARY HAIG. I wouldn't refer to it as changing a covenant. I would call it certain obligations or certain commitments with respect to Israel's right to exist.

Q. Mr. Secretary, the President offers the PLO as an entity, to which you an-

---

[7] For President Mubarak's arrival statement, Wednesday, February 3, see *Weekly Compilation of Presidential Documents*, February 8, 1982, pp. 109–110.

swered—you also made very clear that the Palestinian peoples have the right for self-determination.

Could you interpret your understanding of self-determination within the context of the Camp David that you are saying.

SECRETARY HAIG. As I say, you sharpies that deal with this subject every day know even better than I the risks of greater specificity in that area. After all, we are talking about the establishment of full autonomy for the populations on the West Bank and Gaza.

This is going to be the product, hopefully, of an agreement in principles which will spell out those details with the mutual agreement of the participants in the peace process, and I'm not going to unilaterally get out with interpretative statements on a subject that is so sensitive and controversial.

Q. Sir, how close are we to a declaration of principles now?

SECRETARY HAIG. I said in my recent trip my own assessment was that we had a further distance to go than we had already traveled. I want to point out, however, that that shouldn't sound quite as grim as it might be interpreted.

One must remember that we in January entered into a situation in which the whole process was stalled, not only autonomy but the framework for return of the Sinai this coming April was stalled, and there were a number of profound disagreements.

Some of them have been bridged. For example, I don't know of any issues on the return of the Sinai as part of the Camp David process which now will pose an obstacle. I think all those things have been solved, and I must say they were not easy to solve, but they have been done.

With respect to autonomy, as a result of the two trips we've taken, the work of the specialists established by the two governments with our full participation which we're going to upgrade somewhat as you know, we've now gotten to the point where we are not discussing differences on many key issues but rather are discussing solutions to differences.

We've said that we'd do this without establishing deadlines, and we have none, and we are going to continue to work. It's, I think, encouraging that the leaders of both Israel and Egypt and specifically during this visit at the Presidential level, President Mubarak committed himself to the full engagement of the resources of Egypt. We've had that commitment from Israel, and we've made it ourselves to continue to work the problem.

Q. Mr. Secretary, you spoke earlier about a program of modernization of armed forces for not only Egypt but the region in fiscal year 1983.

Could you tell us some of the details of what you envision?

SECRETARY HAIG. I've seen a lot of press speculation on it, and it won't be very long before it's all in the public venue, but it's not appropriate for me to get out ahead of it.

Let me just say that the ongoing discussions—and they've gone on for many months and many venues—Defense to Defense, State to Foreign Office, and President to President—leave me with a great deal of confidence that the framework we have put together for 1983 is responsive to Egypt's needs and will further enhance regional security and stability.

You know as well as I do that some figures have been bandied around, and there have been some improvements in those figures. I think we have to wait until we formally submit them.

Q. Mr. Secretary, do you intend to intensify your contacts with the Palestinians? With whom, when and how, and do you consider, as President Mubarak said, the (inaudible) organization as a moderate Palestinian?

SECRETARY HAIG. Oh, my golly. (Laughter) I just love to have our visiting Egyptian press corps here.

Q. It just means one man, sir, on the West Bank.

SECRETARY HAIG. I think what you say is that however you answer it, somebody will be mad. That's what you mean, because that's the truth of it, and I'm going to skip the answer, skirt it.

Q. But in the West Bank are you planning to intensify your contacts with the Palestinians?

SECRETARY HAIG. It's always been our policy, for example, in Jerusalem, to have our Interests Section be in close contact with the inhabitants of the city, and we have maintained contact with the inhabitants.

Q. How can we get them to agree to a principle or to the autonomy or anything like that without contact?

SECRETARY HAIG. I think I said we are maintaining that contact, but I think you will recall that at the time of Camp David, those agreements were arrived at based on the conscience of the participants. We will carry that process forward with great sensitivity, with the objective of a reasonable autonomy agreement.

Q. Mr. Secretary, in light of these visits and your travel out there, can you talk about what you see now as the biggest threat in the, I guess, southwest Asia/Middle East region? I mean what concerns you now?

SECRETARY HAIG. The greatest threat?

Q. The biggest problem or whatever.

SECRETARY HAIG. Well, I said threats, like beauty, are in the eye of the beholder; and I think that varies. Clearly, there is an interrelationship between external threats and threats to internal stability supported and abetted by external threats; and I'm talking of the Soviet Union and their adherents. There are threats associated with radicalism. That has a distinctly threatening character in its own right to incumbent regimes. There is the continuing instability associated with the Palestinian question and the Arab/Israeli peace process.

Now, all three of these threats, if you will, are independently serious and are, at the same time, interrelated in that one draws sustenance from the other, and perhaps direction and aggravation. And, again, as we go back to the so-called "strategic consensus" that we talked about last spring, clearly this issue is not a substitute for our concern about the peace process and achieving progress in the peace process; and I said that at the time and repeated it at the time. I find a preoccupation in some of the writings that have occured that these are alternative problems. They are not alternative problems. They are intimately interrelated in that progress with one, as I have said, contributes to progress in the other, and a deterioration of one aggravates the possibility of progress in the other.

And I hope I've answered your question.

Q. Can I ask you to be specific then by asking: One of our Arab friends in the area, King Hussein, has just, you know, asked for volunteers to go to Iraq. Are you concerned in any new level with the Iraq–Iran war, what the Soviets are doing in Iran?

SECRETARY HAIG. Well, let me reiterate again American policy with respect to that conflict. We are concerned by any policy which would drag that conflict on.

Q. Do you think the Soviets are pursuing a policy that drags that conflict on?

SECRETARY HAIG. Well, I think we all know that both of the combatants-are the recipients of military equipment and assistance from the Soviet Union and that the provision of such armaments can only contribute to a continuation of the conflict.

We would hope to see an early negotiated termination of that conflict. Its continuation serves no one's interest. And we would hope that success would soon be arrived there, although I must say I have no basis for expressing optimism in that regard.

Q. Mr. Secretary, just to follow that up a little bit, there are reports that the Soviets have recently provided Palestinian units with fairly sizable amounts of military hardware, including some ground-to-ground missiles.

First of all, is that correct? And, secondly, what do you make of it; what impact is it likely to have?

SECRETARY HAIG. Well, this is a very key aspect of the cessation of hostilities in Lebanon, southern Lebanon. We view the provision of such armaments to Palestinian elements in southern Lebanon as an aggravation to the efforts we have been engaged in to prevent the outbreak of conflict. It is true that there are reports of levels of both tubed artillery, and rocketry, moving through Lebanon to the Palestinian forces in southern Lebanon.

This is one of the areas that is a focus of Ambassador Habib to achieve a termination of these destabilizing actions and in the period ahead we clearly have additional work to do in that area.

Q. Does it seem to remain a problem for new fighting in southern Lebanon?

SECRETARY HAIG. It has that potential, of course.

Q. Mr. Secretary, there were reports before President Mubarak came that the President said that President Carter had made a sacred promise in 1978 to have Israel and Egypt make their military aid compare. Would this new FY '83 plan that you were not going to tell about—will it bring them closer together or would they now be comparable in the military aid that they will get from the United States?

SECRETARY HAIG. Well, you know, there are a number of evaluations that go into that kind of comparability commitment: absorption, capacity, needs, current equipment levels—a host of contributory factors that have to go into such an assessment—but to answer your question in an uncharacteristically blunt way, I would say that comparability has been increasingly the direction in which our assistance levels to Egypt have been moving, and this next year's program will be a further continuation of that.

Q. Will it satisfy President Mubarak?

SECRETARY HAIG. Well, I can't speak, and I would not presume to speak, for President Mubarak. All I can say is that I think our discussions were both fruitful and successful this past week here in Washington.

Q. Mr. Secretary, after meeting with President Mubarak, do you have any thought that President Mubarak is much more independent of the United States than President Sadat?

SECRETARY HAIG. Well, I wouldn't presume to make a value judgment of that kind either other than to—you know, I've know President Mubarak, I suppose, since the mid-seventies, and I think he's pledged himself, with respect to the peace process and mutual assessment of the dangers to the region, the cooperation in the security and economic areas, to pursue the policies that his predecessor committed Egypt to. I have seen nothing, and I've discovered nothing, in our many hours of discussion that would change that assessment on my part.

Now, there are a number of related questions associated with the costs of Camp David to Egypt in the Arab world which are not necessarily in conflict with the basic character of the relationship between the United States and Egypt; and I would expect that in affairs among nations and regions that they will always be dynamic.

Q. Mr. Secretary, specifically with regard to the Palestinians, it does look as though—or manages to look as though—these talks, this particular series of talks, did not really work. Is that a fair assessment?

SECRETARY HAIG. I'm really not sure I understand it.

Q. With regard to the Palestinian issue and all its ramifications, these talks got you nowhere. Is that a fair assessment?

SECRETARY HAIG. Not at all. Precisely the opposite.

Q. Where is the progress?

SECRETARY HAIG. I think I described the progress. In some areas we have come very close, I think, to a consensus of view. In other areas we have narrowed the differences.

In other areas we have at least launched a process of ingenuitive and creative thinking for solutions, and the months ahead and weeks ahead will demonstrate whether or not we succeed.

Again, I don't want to characterize my attitude on the situation as one of excessive optimism. There are many problems. But I am confident that I can state without exaggeration that we have made progress, and I anticipate that we will continue to in the period ahead.

Q. Mr. Secretary, can you tell us what you expect to achieve through the declaration of principles that you are working on? Do you think it will be a kind of Camp David II?

SECRETARY HAIG. Do I think it will be a kind of what?

Q. Camp David number II?

SECRETARY HAIG. No, no. I don't anticipate a Camp David II.

Q. What do you hope to achieve through this declaration of principles in specific terms?

SECRETARY HAIG. Well, what we hope to achieve is the establishment of a transition process which will ultimately lead to a resolution of the Palestinian problem in all of its aspects, and that's the objective of Camp David.

With respect to the issue and the process itself, Camp David was agreed to 3½ years ago. Certain very difficult questions were deferred in those agreements, such as the ultimate status of Jerusalem. That deferral was a conscious deferral. And the differences that existed then and continue to exist today then are approached in an autonomy agreement in principle.

Now, we can either choose in our efforts to achieve an autonomy agreement to solve those problems that could not be solved at Camp David or to continue on with a conceptual approach that visualizes an evolutionary solution through mutual confidence-building and the establishment of a framework which will get that process started; and I have said that if the participants in this peace process seek to make the principles that we are seeking to achieve agreement on to be a leg up on the final outcome rather than a solution, to providing a framework that will permit that confidence-building, that experience and that evolution, then it makes the problem all the more tractable, and I think you gather what I'm saying.

Q. Mr. Secretary, in Italy recently, one of the investigators who has been looking into the sources of Italian terrorism—Judge Imposinato—has declared that the Red Brigades were being controlled by factions within the PLO within the Israeli side and, within Egypt, Egyptians who had assassinated President Sadat.

Now, also in Italy, the head of military intelligence has charged recently that these same sources, the controllers of the Red Brigades, had been depositing into numbered Swiss bank accounts money which was then used for the payoff of certain U.S. officials.

What he was talking about particularly was his predecessor in military intelligence who was a member of Italy's propaganda to the Masonic Lodge which was linked to terrorism and, according to *La Republica*, the Italian newspaper, the American official who was paid off with this news was Michael Ledeen. And I wonder if you can tell me what the purpose of this was or whether you can confirm it.

SECRETARY HAIG. I'm so confused, I'm not sure I know where to start. (Laughter)

If you mean by that am I appalled by international terrorism, the answer is "yes;" and is it the policy of President Reagan's administration to work actively to stamp out this international plague, the answer is "yes" again.

Q. But the specific charge that was made—

SECRETARY HAIG. I never got it amongst the other charges. (Laughter)

Q. Specifically, that the head of Italian military intelligence, according to the newspaper *La Republica* says that Michael Ledeen was paid off by propaganda too.

SECRETARY HAIG. Well, I would reject that without knowing anything about it as inconceivable to me, and I've never heard of such a thing, and it's probably because I don't read the same Italian papers that you may read.

I leave it to you to ask it where the answer may be more forthcoming.

Q. Mr. Secretary, does Mr. Fairbanks have any new proposals to accelerate the momentum of the autonomy talks with regard to the meetings?

SECRETARY HAIG. Is Mr. Fairbanks going to carry any new proposals?

Q. Yes.

SECRETARY HAIG. He's going to put forth, as a full partner in this process, ideas and suggestions that we have that might provide solutions to existing differences. As I said, at the end of my first trip 3 weeks ago—it's almost 4 now—we were going to gather facts. We would come home and assess those facts. We would come back and, on a bilateral basis, suggest to both governments certain ideas or approaches—no formula and no blueprint, no "Made in America" solution but, what I would term, catalyzing suggestions.

We've done that, and that process is going to continue in the weeks ahead, and Mr. Fairbanks will engage in it very actively.

Q. Mr. Secretary, how significant is the current resolution under consideration in the General Assembly regarding Israel's Golan Heights legislation; and what happens after it's approved, in the U.S. view?

SECRETARY HAIG. I looked very carefully yesterday at the current draft, and we consider it basically unacceptable not only [in] its own right but in the context of the direction to which it might lead.

MR. ROMBERG. Thank you very much, Mr. Secretary.

SECRETARY HAIG. Fine. They tell me I've run out of time, and it's my disappointment and your pleasure.

Thank you.

D. Iran and Iraq

Document 333

Transcript of the Department of State Daily Press Briefing, January 20, 1982 (Extract)[1]

Implementation of the Algiers Accords

. . . .

Q. Do you have any response to a charge by an Iranian official that the United States

---

[1] Source: Office of Press Relations, Depart-

is reneging on the agreement which was signed a year ago?

A. The short answer to your question is no, we are not. I will give you a longer answer, if you would like.

Some $8 billion in Iranian assets were transferred to an escrow account with the Bank of England last January. $2.8 billion went to Iran and the rest has been paid to U.S. bank claimants, or will be as settlements are concluded.

A further $2 billion was transferred to the Central Bank of the Netherlands in August, from which $1 billion was placed in a security account for payment of awards made by the U.S.–Iran Claims Tribunal in The Hague, and $1 billion was returned to Iran.

While there are relatively minor issues to be resolved through negotiation or arbitration, the record is clear that the United States is living up to its obligations under the Algiers Accords.[2]

Q. You say an additional $2 billion. That is $2 billion in addition to the $8 billion, or in addition to the $2.8 [billion]?

A. The $8 billion was transferred to an escrow account with the Bank of England in January. That's right. I would say it has to be other—I will go back and double-check this, but the guidance says $2.8 billion went to Iran, and the rest has been paid to U.S. bank claimants, or will be as settlements are concluded.

Then we go on to talking about a further $2 billion. I have to conclude that logically that is an additional $2 billion, beyond the $8 [billion].

Q. On top of the $8 [billion]?

A. On top of the $8 [billion]. Let me ask you to double-check with us later, and I will double-check with the appropriate people.

Q. As I understand it, the burden of the Iranian complaint is that the United States is not being diligent enough in researching the family assets of the Pahlavi family. Do you have anything to add to what was said a year ago?

A. No, I have nothing on that.

Q. Do you have anything in a general way, given that this is the anniversary of the release, as to how U.S.-Iranian relations are, where they stand at this point? Can you characterize them?

A. We continue to support the independence and territorial integrity of Iran. While the U.S. Government recognizes the Iranian revolution, this does not mean that we approve of all that is taking place in Iran at present. Obviously we deplore the summary executions and continuing bloodshed stemming from the revolutionary turmoil in that country.

However, U.S. policy must rest primarily on a careful calculation of how Iran might affect vital U.S. interests in the region, and it must be clear to all that we cannot remain indifferent to the fate of Iran.

Q. What do you mean by indifferent?

Q. Are you worried about the Russians moving in?

A. Obviously instability in Iran and efforts to export revolution are potential threats to U.S. interests, and any change in Iran would make it less of a buffer between the Soviet Union and the Gulf, and that would clearly heighten the direct and indirect threats that we confront in the area.

. . . .

---

ment of State. Alan Romberg, Department of State Acting Spokesman, conducted the briefing, which began at 12:42 p.m.

[2] For texts of the Algiers Accords, also known as the Hostage Release Agreements, see *American Foreign Policy: Current Documents, 1981*, documents 341–344.

Document 334

Transcript of the Department of State Daily Press Briefing, May 14, 1982 (Extract)[3]

U.S. Policy Toward the Iran–Iraq War, and Toward Exports to Iraq

. . . .

Q. . . . do you have any position on the new developments in the Iran–Iraq war?

[3] Source: Office of Press Relations, Department of State. Alan Romberg, Department of State Acting Spokesman, conducted the briefing, which began at 12:30 p.m.

A. I don't really have anything on any new developments. I could reiterate for you, though, our attitude towards it which I think might be appropriate as this all progresses.

U.S. policy with regard to the Iran–Iraq war has been clear and consistent since the outbreak of the hostilities 20 months ago. The policy enunciated when Iraqi forces entered Iran remains our policy today. The United States supports the independence and territorial integrity of both Iran and Iraq as well as the other states in the region. In keeping with our policy worldwide, we oppose the seizure of territory by force. We see the continuation of the war, as we have repeatedly said, as a danger to the peace and security of all nations in the Gulf region and we have therefore consistently supported an immediate cease-fire and a negotiated settlement. We have maintained a firm policy of not approving the sale or transfer of American military equipment and supplies to either belligerent, and we have welcomed constructive international efforts to bring an end to the war on the basis of each state's respect for the territorial integrity of its neighbors and each state's freedom from external coercion.

Q. Is there a new turn in the war now that has changed your attitude?

A. No. Our policy remains consistent on this.

Q. Do you have any comment on the action by the House Foreign Affairs Committee refusing to take Iraq off this list of terrorism-banned countries?[4]

A. Yes, I do have something on that. Let me address the amendment as a whole as it was adopted yesterday.

The amendment would impose the controls that were removed by the administration in February.[5] The decisions to remove Iraq from the terrorism list to accept civil aircraft for civil airlines from controls for antiterrorism purposes and to adjust the controls for South Africa were made after a lengthy review which is required annually. The review took into account the compatibility of the controls with U.S. foreign policy objectives, the reaction of other countries to the controls, and the likely effect of continuing controls on U.S. export performance. All is required by the Export Administration Act.

We oppose the restrictions the amendment would impose. Fixing controls by legislation reduces our flexibility to respond to changes in the international arena and to insure that export controls further our foreign policy objectives as is required by the Export Administration Act itself. Changing course at this time will also confuse foreign governments and call into question the credibility of the United States as a reliable supplier.

. . . .

Document 335

Statement Issued by the White House, July 14, 1982[6]

The Iran–Iraq War

The United States Government has remained from the beginning, and will remain, neutral in the war between Iran and Iraq. We remain deeply concerned, however, about the continuation of this conflict and the attendant loss of life and destruction. The United States supports the independence and territorial integrity of both Iran and Iraq, as well as that of other states in the region. In keeping with our policy worldwide, we oppose the seizure of territory by force. We urge an immediate end to hostilities and a negotiated settlement. We support constructive international efforts for a peaceful solution to the conflict on the

---

[4] On May 13, the House Foreign Affairs Committee passed an amendment to the foreign aid authorization bill that would have restored Iraq to the list of countries described as supporting international terrorism. The amendment was not enacted.

[5] On February 26, the Department of Commerce formally announced the extension, with some modification, of the foreign policy export controls required by section 6 of the Export Administration Act of 1979 (P.L. 96–72; 93 Stat. 515). The announcement stated, among other things: "The Secretary of State has determined that Iraq's improved record warrants removal from the list of countries covered by anti-terrorism controls." For text of the formal announcement, see *Federal Register*, Vol. 47, March 4, 1982, p. 9201.

[6] Source: White House Press Release, July 14, 1982, Office of the Press Secretary to the President; also printed in *Weekly Compilation of Presidential Documents*, July 19, 1982, p. 903. The statement was handed out at the press briefing conducted by Larry M. Speakes, Deputy Press Secretary to the President, beginning at 10:46 a.m.

basis of each state's respect for the territorial integrity of its neighbors and each state's freedom from external coercion. In keeping with this policy we have joined with other members of the United Nations Security Council in 1980 and on July 12 of this year[7] in resolutions calling for an end to the conflict.

Our support for the security of friendly states in the region which might feel threatened by the conflict is well known and the United States is prepared to consult with these states on appropriate steps to support their security.

Document 336

Message to the Congress by President Reagan, November 1, 1982[8]

Financial Aspects of the Crisis With Iran

Pursuant to Section 204(c) of the International Emergency Economic Powers Act (IEEPA), 50 U.S.C. Section 1703(c),[9] I hereby report to the Congress with respect to developments between my last report of May 6[10] and mid-October 1982, concerning the national emergency with respect to Iran that was declared in Executive Order No. 12170 of November 14, 1979.[11]

1. The Iran–United States Claims Tribunal established at The Hague pursuant to the Claims Settlement Agreement of January 19, 1981,[12] is now actively engaged in the process of arbitrating the several thousand claims filed before it by the January 19, 1982 deadline. Although it has only recently begun to schedule significant numbers of prehearing conferences and hearings on the merits, the Tribunal has rendered decisions on twelve claims of U.S. nationals against Iran. Eight of those decisions approved settlements reached by the parties directly concerned; two more represented adjudications in favor of the U.S. claimants. The remaining two resulted in the dismissal of claims for lack of jurisdiction. In total, the Tribunal has made awards of more than $7.6 million in favor of U.S. claimants. The Department of State, with the assistance of the Departments of the Treasury and Justice and other concerned government agencies, continues to coordinate the presentation of U.S. claims against Iran as well as the U.S. response to claims brought by Iran, and also assists U.S. nationals in the presentation of their claims against Iran.

2. The Tribunal rendered its decision on the four issues concerning the $1 billion security account held by the N.V. Settlement Bank of the Netherlands to pay Tribunal awards against Iran. As indicated in the last report, those issues, which had not been resolved in the negotiations leading to the establishment of the security account in August 1981, involved (1) the disposition of the interest accruing on the funds in the account; (2) indemnification of the Settlement Bank and its parent, the Netherlands Central Bank, against any claims relating to the management of the security account; (3) payment of the administrative fees of the Settlement Bank; and (4) payment of settlements reached directly between U.S. claimants and Iran.

The Tribunal decided the last question first, ruling on May 14 that such settlements may be paid from the security account if the Tribunal determines that it has jurisdiction over the underlying claims and accepts the terms of the settlement agreements as the basis for rendering an award on agreed terms.

The decision on the other three issues was rendered August 3, 1982. The Tribunal decided that interest earned on the security account should continue to be credited to a separate suspense account established pursuant to the interim arrangements under which the security account had been managed since it was established. The Tribunal further decided that any such interest may be used by Iran to fulfill its obligation to replenish the security account whenever the payment of awards causes the balance to fall

---

[7] For the text of U.N. Security Council Resolution 479 (1980), unanimously adopted on September 28, 1980, calling for an end to the Iran–Iraq War, see *American Foreign Policy: Basic Documents, 1977–1980,* p. 606. On July 12, 1982, the U.N. Security Council unanimously adopted Resolution 514 (1982), calling for a cease-fire between Iran and Iraq, and a mutual withdrawal of forces to internationally recognized boundaries.

[8] Source: White House Press Release, November 1, 1982, Office of the Press Secretary to the President; printed also in *Weekly Compilation of Presidential Documents,* November 8, 1982, pp. 1423–1425.

[9] P.L. 95–223, approved December 28, 1977; for text, see 91 Stat. 1627.

[10] For text, see *Weekly Compilation of Presidential Documents,* May 10, 1982, pp. 590–591.

[11] For text, see *American Foreign Policy: Basic Documents, 1977–1980,* pp. 739–740.

[12] For text, see *American Foreign Policy: Current Documents, 1981,* document 342.

below $500 million. The decision thus prevents the diversion of the interest to any purpose other than payment of awards in favor of U.S. claimants, without the agreement of both the United States and Iran, until all claims are decided and all awards paid.

On the questions of management fees and indemnification, the Tribunal decided that fee payments should be shared equally by the two Governments and that indemnification should be joint and several, leaving open until an actual case arises the question of how ultimate responsibility for indemnification should be allocated between the United States and Iran.

3. The January 19, 1981 agreements with Iran[13] also provided for direct negotiations between U.S. banks and Bank Markazi Iran concerning the repayment of nonsyndicated loans and disputed interest from the $1.418 billion escrow account presently held by the Bank of England. The U.S. banks and Bank Markazi Iran continue to negotiate concerning payments out of this account.

4. Since my last semiannual report submitted to the Congress in May, there have been no transfers of assets to Iran by or through the U.S. Government under the January 19, 1981 agreements with Iran. However, I attach herewith five excerpts from the *Federal Register* that deal with the Iranian Assets Control Regulations.[14] The first, published on May 24, 1982, is a requirement that holders of tangible property in which Iran had or asserted any interest report on such property to the Office of Foreign Assets Control. The purpose was to obtain information for use in promoting the resolution of disputes with Iran, preparing submissions for the Iran–United States Claims Tribunal, and formulating policies to deal with the tangible properties. The second, published on June 8, 1982, contains additional information with respect to the tangible property reports. The third was published on June 10, 1982. It is a directive license to the New York Federal Reserve Bank to deduct 2 percent of award amounts it receives from the security account for payment to U.S. claimants who have received awards from the Iran–United States Claims Tribunal. That 2 percent is for deposit in the U.S. Treasury to reimburse the U.S. Government for costs incurred for the benefit of U.S. nationals with claims against Iran. On September 14, 1982, the administration submitted to the Congress a bill[15] that deals with this deduction and also gives authority to the Foreign Claims Settlement Commission of the United States to receive and determine the validity and amounts of certain claims of U.S. nationals against Iran. Also, the bill authorizes the Secretary of the Treasury to reimburse the Federal Reserve Bank of New York for expenses incurred by the Bank in the performance of fiscal agency agreements relating to the settlement or arbitration of claims pursuant to the January 1981 agreements with Iran. The fourth *Federal Register* item revoked any authorizations for the permanent disposition, by means of a final judicial judgment or order, of interests of Iran in any standby letter of credit or similar instrument. The purpose was to preserve the status quo to permit resolution of claims involving those interests through either the Claims Tribunal or negotiations with Iran. Iran has filed more than 200 such claims with the Tribunal, and U.S. nationals also have filed a large number of claims concerning the same issues or related undertakings. U.S. account parties are still able to prevent payments to Iran by obtaining preliminary injunctions or other temporary relief, short of final dispositions, or by using procedures set forth in the Iranian Assets Control Regulations. Finally, on July 22, 1982, the Office of Foreign Assets Control published a new provision of the Iranian Assets Control Regulations that sets forth a licensing procedure for the sale and disposition of tangible property that is currently blocked because of an interest of Iran in the property. The purpose is to conserve the value of the assets and to permit the satisfaction of certain claims against the property. Licenses for such sales may be issued after a case-by-case review of license applications.

5. Several financial and diplomatic aspects of the crisis with Iran have not yet been resolved and continue to present an unusual challenge to the national security and foreign policy of the United States. By separate action, I am extending the emergency with respect to Iran beyond the November 14, 1982 anniversary. I shall continue to exercise the powers at my disposal to deal with these problems and will continue to report periodically to the Congress on significant developments.

---

[13] See *ibid.*, documents 341–344.

[14] Not printed here; for texts, see *Federal Register*, Vol. 47, May 24, 1982, p. 22361; June 9, 1982, p. 25003; June 10, 1982, p. 25243; July 7, 1982, p. 29528; July 22, 1982, p. 31682.

[15] S. 2967, introduced by Senator Percy on September 29, 1982, was referred to the Senate Foreign Relations Committee without further action. For a later statement on the claims question, see document 338.

Document 337

Message to the Congress by President Reagan, November 8, 1982[16]

Continuation of the National Emergency With Respect to Iran

Section 202(d) of the National Emergencies Act (50 U.S.C. 1622(d) provides for the automatic termination on the anniversary date of a declaration of emergency, unless prior to the anniversary date the President publishes in the *Federal Register* and transmits to Congress a notice stating that the emergency is to continue in effect beyond the anniversary date. I have sent to the *Federal Register* for publication the enclosed notice stating that the Iran emergency is to continue in effect beyond the November 14, 1982 anniversary date.[17] Similar notices were sent to the Congress and the *Federal Register* on November 12, 1980 and November 12, 1981.

The crisis between the United States and Iran, which began in 1979, has eased, but it has not been fully resolved. The internal situation in Iran remains uncertain. The war between Iran and Iraq continues, and the Soviet Union still occupies Afghanistan. The international arbitral tribunal established for the adjudication of claims of United States nationals against Iran and by Iranian nationals against the United States continues to function. Full normalization of commercial and diplomatic relations between the United States and Iran will require more time. In these circumstances, I have determined that it is necessary to maintain in force the broad authorities that may be needed to respond to the process of implementation of the January 1981 agreements with Iran and the eventual normalization of relations.

[16] Source: White House Press Release, November 8, 1982, Office of the Press Secretary to the President; printed also in *Weekly Compilation of Presidential Documents*, November 15, 1982, p. 1447.

[17] For text of the notice sent by President Reagan on November 8, 1982, see *ibid.*, p. 1448.

Document 338

Statement by the Deputy Legal Adviser of the Department of State (Michel) Before a Subcommittee of the House Foreign Affairs Committee, December 7, 1982[18]

Operations of the Iran–United States Claims Tribunal

MR. MICHEL. Thank you. Mr. Chairman, members of the subcommittee, it is a privilege to appear before you today to testify in support of the proposed legislation relating to the settlement of claims against Iran.

I have a prepared statement, which has been submitted to the subcommittee. I believe that this contains some useful background information, but it is a bit lengthy and with your permission—

MR. BINGHAM. Without objection, your full statement will appear in the record, and you may summarize it or give us highlights as you see fit.

MR. MICHEL. Thank you, Mr. Chairman.

The statement covers four areas. It provides some background on the Algiers Accords which created the present claims settlement process; it describes the operations of the Iran/United States Claims Tribunal at The Hague, which is empowered by the accords to adjudicate these claims; it describes costs incurred by the U.S. Government in performing claims-related functions; and it discusses the proposed legislation which provides standby authority for the Foreign Claims Settlement Commission and authorizes a fee to recover some of the Government's costs.

Beginning with the basis for this claims arbitration, the Algiers Accords of January 1981, among other things, established the Iran–United States Claims Tribunal as an international arbitration forum to decide claims of U.S. nationals against Iran.

[18] Source: *Claims Against Iran: Hearing Before the Subcommittee on International Economic Policy and Trade of the Committee on Foreign Affairs, House of Representatives, Ninety-seventh Congress, Second Session* (Washington, 1983), pp. 1–7. Michel was testifying on behalf of H.R. 7473, a bill to facilitate the adjudication of certain claims by American citizens against Iran. A brief interruption of Michel's statement by subcommittee members on an unrelated procedural matter is not printed. For Michel's prepared statement, see *ibid.*, pp. 7–19.

The tribunal also has jurisdiction over claims of Iranian nationals against the United States and certain claims by the two Governments against each other.

The tribunal consists of nine members: three appointed by the United States, three appointed by Iran, and three selected by the six party appointed arbitrators. It has divided itself into three chambers with that tripartite makeup in order to handle better the caseload that it has before it.

The accords provide for a security account established at an initial level of $1 billion from Iranian assets that had been frozen in the United States, and imposes a duty on Iran to replenish that account whenever it falls below $500 million.

The accords also establish a basic framework requiring claims to be filed, in effect, by January 19, 1982. It provided that the tribunal would follow the rules of the U.N. Commission on International Trade Law, UNCITRAL, except as modifications might be necessary.

It established The Hague as the seat of the tribunal, and provided that expenses of the operation would be borne equally by the two Governments.

It also provided a distinction between large claims of $250,000 or more, which are to be presented directly by the claimants to the tribunal, and the small claims of under $250,000 which are to be presented to the tribunal by the claimant's government.

The tribunal first met in May 1981. Nine people, sitting in a room that was borrowed from the Permanent Court of Arbitration in the Peace Palace at The Hague, had to create a new international institution. They had to establish a registry, a court clerk system in effect; they had to hire staff, including interpreters and translators because there were two official languages involved; they had to review the UNCITRAL rules of procedures and decide how modifications might be needed to facilitate their work; and they were presented very soon after the tribunal was established with a number of threshold issues of jurisdiction and interpretation on which the two Governments had been unable to agree.

Since the deadline for filing claims passed on January 19, 1982, we have been able to get some idea of the tribunal's workload. Over 4,000 claims have been filed. That includes almost 2,800 small claims, about 650 large claims of U.S. nationals against Iran; about 100 contract disputes between the two Governments; a number of other claims, including Iranian bank claims based on letters of credit and other bank disputes, and several hundred claims of various kinds raised by Iran or by Iranian nationals.

The individual claimants will be heard by the three chambers of the Tribunal and a decision by a chamber will be the decision of the Tribunal. The full Tribunal will meet and sit en banc to consider interpretation disputes, implementation disputes between the two Governments, and major legal issues common to a number of claims.

The Tribunal is laboring under difficult circumstances in the absence of diplomatic relations between the United States and Iran, and with an ongoing revolution and external war in Iran. However, the arbitrators have made considerable progress during the past year and a half. They have ruled on several major issues which set a framework for the future.

The Tribunal has decided, among other things, that the Tribunal did not have jurisdiction over claims by a government against a national, except in the context of a counterclaim. This resulted in a large number of Iranian claims being withdrawn by the Government of Iran.

The Tribunal also made decisions on settlements, on how interest earned on the security account should be disposed of, and decided how to deal with jurisdiction over contracts providing that only Iranian courts could hear disputes arising from those contracts.

With a number of these interpretive issues resolved, the Tribunal has now turned its attention primarily to the individual claims and seems to be focusing on the large claims.

The pace has been slow in this regard. The Tribunal has been presented with repeated Iranian requests for extensions of time, a number of procedural and jurisdictional disputes and questions and generally, I think it is fair to say, delaying tactics by Iran which probably reflect both the real burden that country faces with so many claims to respond to, and also a desire not to have the Tribunal reach the merits of the claims that Iran contests.

There has been some progress in recent months, and in particular, we see a less automatic willingness on the part of the Tribunal to approve requests for time extensions.

The Tribunal has assigned all 650 of the large claims to the chambers. It has set dates for Iranian responses to those claims in almost all of the cases. About 250 statements of defense have been filed. By the end of this year, we expect that the chambers will have conducted about 75 prehearing conferences, and more than 20 hearings on the merits.

The Tribunal has issued awards in individual claims in 13 cases, 11 awards in favor of American claimants, 9 of which have approved settlements, and has dismissed two claims brought by U.S. nationals for lack of jurisdiction.

The Tribunal is also beginning to deal with the small claims and has now served all of those statements of claims on Iran. The Tribunal is considering how best to proceed with the small claims in a manner that will be expeditious and at the same time will not create unreasonable interference with the other business of the Tribunal.

The U.S. Government in all of this has incurred substantial costs. The total of these costs will depend on the lifespan of the Tribunal and the extent to which claims can be settled by negotiation.

These costs fall into five basic categories. First of all, contributions to pay the expenses of the Tribunal, are made by both Governments on an equal basis. These are presently running a little over $2 million a year for the United States, and we expect that there will be some form of expansion of the Tribunal in the next year or two and that this will require some corresponding increase in the contributions of the two Governments.

There are, second, management fees by the subsidiary of the Dutch Central Bank that manages the security account. These fees are $1.8 million a year to manage the billion-dollar account and our share is one-half, or about $75,000 a month.

Third, the Federal Reserve Bank of New York, acting as fiscal agent for the United States, has incurred substantial costs in marshalling Iranian assets and has a role in the payment of awards. If the Tribunal decides in favor of a U.S. claimant and issues an award, that award is communicated to the Central Bank of Algeria, the escrow agent, which then notifies the Dutch bank holding the money, and that bank pays the New York Federal Reserve Bank, which then in turn distributes the payment to the U.S. claimant. We expect the New York Fed to incur $20,000 to $40,000 a year in the processing of these awards.

The Department of State has incurred significant costs. This arbitration is one of the top priorities of the Office of the Legal Adviser. There are billions of dollars in dispute. There are significant questions of international commercial law and public international law at stake in this arbitration.

In addition to dealing with the official and government-to-government claims and disputes, the Department of State has devoted substantial resources to the presentation of U.S. positions to the Tribunal on matters that are of concern to the U.S. claimants.

I have brought with me, as examples, a few of the memorials we have filed on such questions as Tribunal jurisdiction over claims of dual nationals and claims by Iran to entitlement to the interest on the security account. We can make these materials available to the subcommittee staff for perusal. We are engaged in quite an arduous task of legal research and writing on very complex issues with substantial consequences.

. . . .

The Office of [the] Legal Adviser and Office of Iranian Claims within that office monitors Tribunal activity, analyzes Iran's arguments before the Tribunal, acts as a coordination point for American claimants, and analyzes and distributes Tribunal decisions and information about the Tribunal.

We also maintain an agent in The Hague, as provided for in the Algiers Accords, who receives and serves Tribunal documents. Service is made through the agent and not directly from the Tribunal to the claimant.

The agent is our on-the-scene representative to the Tribunal and is there every day, and so is in a position to familiarize claimants and their representatives with procedural issues and attend the proceedings of the Tribunal, so that he is in a position to address issues of a general nature that inevitably arise, and that may be something totally new and mysterious to the individual claimant who is appearing there 1 day only.

The office is also, of course, preparing for the presentation of the 2,795 small claims to the Tribunal. Our costs are running over $1 million annually.

Last, other U.S. Government agencies, and in particular the Treasury and Justice Departments, have responsibility for assuring U.S. compliance with the Algiers Accords. There is the Treasury foreign assets control program and the Justice Department has responsibility for litigation that arises in the United States arising out of Iranian claims matters.

We rely heavily on the expertise of those agencies in formulating positions for use in the Tribunal, and the Treasury Department also plays a major coordinating role in dealing with the U.S. banks and their customers.

With this background, I would then like to turn to the legislative proposal before the subcommittee.

This bill[19] would authorize the Foreign Claims Settlement Commission to adjudicate categories of claims by U.S. nationals against Iran which might be settled by lump-sum agreement and would authorize the Secretary of the Treasury to make the payments to individual claimants in accordance with the adjudications by the Commission. The exercise of those authorities will depend on the ability of the two Governments to come into agreement on some settlement.

We expect claimants with large claims to negotiate directly with Iran on an individual case-by-case basis. Those kinds of settlements would not be affected by this legislation. We do hope, however, to avoid for all concerned the time, effort, and expense of arbitrating individually more than 2,700 small claims. While we are prepared to go forward with such an arbitration and to represent the claimants vigorously, there are obvious advantages to a settlement. If such a settlement can be achieved, then we believe the fastest, most economical, and fairest way to divide the amount received would be through adjudication of the individual small claims by the Foreign Claims Settlement Commission, which has unique capability to carry out that function, and it is an existing agency.

The proposed legislation also provides authority and procedures for reimbursement to the U.S. Government of expenses, such as those I have described, incurred by the Departments of State and Treasury, Federal Reserve Bank and other Government agencies, for the benefit of U.S. nationals who have claims before the Tribunal.

This cost recovery would be achieved by deducting 2 percent from each arbitrable award against Iran paid from the security account to a successful claimant. Those who would contribute this cost recovery would be those who used the Tribunal and benefited from that use of the Tribunal by winning an award.

We have transmitted with the administration's draft bill a detailed section-by-section analysis. Chairman Bell, who is here today, is prepared to address the issue of granting standby authority to the Foreign Claims Settlement Commission.

With respect to the cost recovery, let me just say that the legislation is intended to help finance an effort we have undertaken to provide American claimants with an appropriate and effective forum for the resolution of their disputes, and that the amount the bill seeks to recover is expected to approximate the costs the Government will have incurred.

In sum, we think that the Tribunal can provide American claimants with an effective forum for the resolution of their financial disputes with Iran. The Department of State and other agencies are providing substantial services to the claimant and are incurring significant costs. We believe that the proposed legislation will facilitate the arbitrable process and will fairly allocate among the claimants the costs of providing this forum.

That ends my submission, Mr. Chairman.

---

[19] H.R. 7473 was introduced on December 6 by Representatives Zablocki, Bingham, Broomfield, and Lagomarsino. No action was taken on the bill before the end of the Second Session of the 97th Congress.

E. Israel

Document 339

Letter From President Reagan to Israeli Prime Minister Begin, February 16, 1982[1]

"America's Policy Toward Israel Has Not Changed"

DEAR MENACHEM: Recent press reports have presented incorrect and exaggerated

[1] Source: White House Press Release, February 16, 1982, Office of the Press Secretary to the President; printed also in *Weekly Compilation of Presidential Documents*, February 22, 1982, pp. 184–185.

commentary regarding U.S. military assistance policies for the Middle East.

I want you to know that America's policy toward Israel has not changed. Our commitments will be kept. I am determined to see that Israel's qualitative technological edge is maintained and am mindful as well of your concerns with respect to quantitative factors and their impact upon Israel's security.

The policy of this government remains as stated publicly by me. Secretary Haig's and Secretary Weinberger's statements on the public record are also clear. There has been no change regarding our military supply relationship with Jordan, and Secretary Weinberger brought me no new request. Any decision on future sales to Jordan or any other country in the region will be made in the context of my Administration's firm commitment to Israel's security and the need to bring peace to the region.

Israel remains America's friend and ally. However, I believe it is in the interest of both our countries for the United States to enhance its influence with other states in the region. I recognize the unique bond between the United States and Israel and the serious responsibilities which this bond imposes on us both.

Sincerely,

RON

Document 340

Prepared Statement by the Deputy Assistant Secretary for Near Eastern and South Asian Affairs (Draper) Before a Subcommittee of the House Foreign Affairs Committee, March 23, 1982[2]

Fiscal Year 1983 Assistance Requests for Israel

Mr. Chairman, I am here today to testify in support of our military and economic assistance programs in Israel for fiscal year (FY) 1983. The administration is proposing a funding level of $1.7 billion—up $300 million from last year—in foreign military sales (FMS) financing and $785 million in Economic Support Funding (ESF). If approved by the Congress, the overall level of $2.485 billion in combined military and economic assistance for Israel would be the largest U.S. bilateral assistance program.

Military Assistance

In a fundamental sense, our proposal for $1.7 billion in military assistance reflects our intention that Israel be assisted so as to maintain its technological edge and its qualitative military advantage in the region. We expect that Israel would use some of the $300 million in added funds primarily to purchase U.S.-produced aircraft, although in the end Israel may make other choices. The bulk of the military assistance funding would be used to purchase artillery, missiles, tanks, APC's, and aircraft engines from the United States. We are proposing that $500 million of this total financing be in the form of forgiven credits and that the remainder—$1.2 billion—be in the form of a 30-year loan.

Economic Assistance

We are proposing for 1983 FY a level of $785 million in ESF, which is identical to the pattern of the past few years (actual amounts programed in the past 2 years have fluctuated, owing to "borrowings" by the United States and "pay backs"). The program is essentially a cash transfer program, although we are proposing a return to the traditional mix of two-thirds grants and one-third concessional loans, rather than the full grant programs of the last 2 fiscal years.

Israel's political and economic stability is important to U.S. policy. Our economic assistance program in effect provides balance-of-payments support in order to meet short-term balance-of-payments requirements and to import certain civilian goods and services without undue reliance on high cost commercial borrowing and drawdowns of essential foreign exchange reserves.

Israel's Debt Burden

---

[2] Source: Department of State files; also printed in Department of State *Bulletin*, July 1982, pp. 74–75. This statement was submitted to the Subcommittee on Europe and the Middle East of the House Foreign Affairs Committee but was not printed. For Draper's testimony that day before the subcommittee, see *Foreign Assistance Legislation for Fiscal Year 1983: Hearings and Markup Before the Subcommittee on Europe and the Middle East of the Committee on Foreign Affairs, House of Representatives, Ninety-seventh Congress, Second Session* (Washington, 1983), Part 3, pp. 32–68.

Israel's growing debt repayments to the United States have been a source of concern to many Israeli officials, who naturally would prefer that the grant component of our assistance program be much larger. We carefully reviewed the debt burden before submitting the security assistance proposals to Congress. Our review also had to take into account our own budget stringencies. In reaching our conclusions we attempted to put all factors—including needs, priorities, and resources—into sensible balance. As our separate report to the Congress should make clear, we believe Israel will be able to handle the additional debt burdens implicit in the FY 1983 funding levels.[3]

Conceptual Approach

Let me outline briefly some of the major elements of the conceptual framework within which our assistance proposals for Israel have been formulated:

—First of all, our support for Israel's security and economic well-being is a basic and unshakable tenet of American foreign policy in the Middle East. It is also a critical element in our strategy toward the region as a whole. While Israel cannot hope to keep up with its potential adversaries in quantitative military terms, with U.S. assistance at our proposed levels it can continue to maintain its qualitative and technological superiority over any potential combination of regional forces.

—Our support for Israel grows out of a longstanding moral commitment to a free and democratic nation which has been a haven and which shares many of our own social and democratic traditions. Israel has been a steady friend of the United States.

—The perennial Arab-Israeli conflict and the need to achieve a broad, just, and lasting peace in the region have been at the forefront of U.S. foreign policy concerns for many years. Israel has sought peace and in the process has agreed to the Camp David understandings and signed the historic treaty of peace with Egypt.

—Our large military and economic assistance programs for Israel tangibly support the unfinished business of the peace process and give Israel the confidence to continue. Israel is making important sacrifices for peace—including the forthcoming full withdrawal from the Sinai Peninsula in the last week of April—and our matériel as well as moral and political support over the years have provided some compensation.

—Our assistance programs for Israel complement the two mutually reinforcing goals of American policy in the region: first, the search for a just and lasting peace; and, second, the assurance that our friends in the region will be able to maintain their security against threats from the outside and from radical forces within the region. These programs are also consistent with the premise that economic progress and advancement of the welfare of the peoples of the region will help promote stability.

—In addition, a strong Israel has been a good investment as we look to the strategic picture and to potential Soviet and Soviet-supported challenges to our interests in the region. We know that we can count on Israel for cooperation and understanding.

—We are, however, in the midst of an extremely tense period, affecting not only Israel but the entire region. The political and security environment in the region has changed, and mostly for the worse. The Iran–Iraq war, the Soviet occupation of Afghanistan, the tripartite pact between Libya, South Yemen, and Ethiopia,[4] and continued Russian mischief-making—directly and through proxies—present threats and challenges. Lebanon remains a powder-keg. Israel's full cooperation has been indispensable in preserving and strengthening the cease-fire in the Israeli-Lebanese arena, which has held since last July and which has seen no loss of life yet through cease-fire violations.

—The presentation and examination of our foreign assistance proposals are taking place at a particularly sensitive juncture in Israel itself. Israel is experiencing a genuine domestic crisis in the process of completing preparations for its final withdrawal from the Sinai next month. The Israeli Government has been facing tremendous pressure from many of its own citizens, yet is faithfully carrying out its commitment to bring back into Israel the settlers and squatters from the settlements in the Sinai before Israel's final withdrawal.

---

[3] For the "Report on the Israeli Economy and Debt Repayment Prospects," see *ibid.*, Part 3, pp. 196–207. The continuing appropriations for fiscal year 1983 (P.L. 97–377, approved December 21, 1982) provided $785 million in economic aid, $750 million in military grants, and $950 million in military credits for Israel. For text of this law, see 96 Stat. 1830.

[4] The treaty between Libya, Ethiopia, and the People's Democratic Republic of Yemen (PDRY), signed in Aden on August 25, 1981, provided for the deployment of the armed forces of the signatories in each other's territory under certain circumstances.

These tensions show why it is so important that Israel continue to have confidence in our determination, in our policies, and in the quality and credibility of our friendship.

Document 341

Transcript of a Press Conference by President Reagan, September 28, 1982 (Extracts)[5]

U.S. Relations With Israel

. . . .

Q. Mr. President, shortly before the Israeli invasion of Lebanon, the administration informally notified Congress that it was planning to send more F–16's to Israel.[6] There's been no formal notification since then. Is the delay linked to difficulties in relations with Israel? When do you think formal notification will go up and under what conditions?

THE PRESIDENT. They're still on tap and we haven't sent the formal notification up. And, very frankly, it was simply because in the climate of things that were going on, we didn't think it was the time to do it. However, there has been no interruption of those things that are in the pipeline, the spare parts, ammunition, things of that kind. The only thing that we have actually withheld after the controversy that came on in Lebanon was the artillery shell, the so-called cluster shell.

. . . .

Q. Mr. President, I seem to get the impression from what you are saying about our relationship with Israel that nothing has really changed in the wake of the massacre in Beirut or the temporary rejection, anyway, of your peace plan. Is that correct? Is there no change at all?

THE PRESIDENT. There's no change in the sense that we are still going with everything we can, we're going to try and persuade the Arab neighbors of Israel to do as Egypt once did, and Israel, to negotiate out a permanent peace solution, in which Israel will no longer have to remain an armed camp, which is making their life economically unbearable, and at the same time, an answer must be found that is just and fair for the Palestinians. And I don't think anything has happened to change that, if I understood your question correctly. Nothing has changed in our feeling of obligation to bring about, if we can, such a result.

Q. Sir, I really meant our relationship with the Begin government. Is it as cordial and friendly? Is it now tense? Is it—what is the situation?

THE PRESIDENT. I can tell you one thing it isn't. It isn't what some of you have said or written, that we are deliberately trying to undermine or overthrow the Begin government. We have never interfered in the internal government of a country and have no intention of doing so, never have had any thought of that kind, and we expect to be doing business with the Government of Israel and with Prime Minister Begin, if that's the decision of the Israeli people. I think that Frank Reynolds last night voiced something that we believe, and that is that the Israeli people are proving with their reaction to the massacre that there is no change in the spirit of Israel. They are our ally, we feel morally obligated to the preservation of Israel, and we're going to continue to be that way.

. . . .

---

[5] Source: White House Press Release, September 28, 1982, Office of the Press Secretary to the President; also printed in *Weekly Compilation of Presidential Documents*, October 4, 1982, pp. 1225–1226. The press conference took place in the East Room of the White House, beginning at 7:30 p.m.

[6] On May 24, the Reagan administration notified the Congress of its intention to sell 75 advanced F–16 aircraft to Israel with associated support, test, and repair equipment valued at $2.7 billion. First delivery of the aircraft was scheduled to begin in late 1985.

F. Jordan

Document 342

Remarks by the Secretary of Defense (Weinberger), Amman, February 13, 1982 (Extract)[1]

Additional Arms Sales to Jordan

Good morning. We had a very fine visit here in Jordan. We have been very warmly received by His Majesty, who is certainly one of the oldest friends the United States has in the region. He has been extraordinarily cordial and warm in his reception of us as indeed have all the members of his government, and General Bin Shaker particularly, who has been very hospitable, very warm and a very good friend.

We've been delighted to have the opportunity to have these discussions. We discussed a number of areas of common interest and discussed some of the needs of Jordan and some of the ways in which we believe that the United States may be able to be of assistance. These matters I will convey to the Government at home and to the President. There will be unquestionably, discussions at high levels back home about these matters and we believe and hope that we will be able to be helpful in the maintaining and sustaining and, in fact, deepening the warm and friendly relations that have always existed between our countries. I will take back very happy memories of a very fine visit that has been marked by the warmth and hospitality and the cordiality of the discussions which we've had. Thank you.

Q. Do you regard the sale of weapons to Jordan, say a mobile missile or maybe another fighter as a threat to Israel, Mr. Secretary? They are saying they will fight it tooth and nail.

A. No. I have no feeling that matters of that kind would do anything more than strengthen a good friend in this area. But these are values that would be [considered?] in Washington when requests are received. No requests are pending and so any discussion of them now would be just hypothetical.

Q. Mr. Weinberger, do you think any Israeli objections to a U.S.–Jordan arms deal will make it more difficult to get the U.S. congressional approval to proceed?

A. Oh, I wouldn't want to estimate any eventualities from the United States. We, in our Department, would discuss the military needs and necessity and present these to the proper people in Washington and discussions with them would take place.

Q. What is the status of the F–16 request, or is there a request? Are you taking back any formal request?

A. No, as I said, there are no formal requests of any kind pending. We've had preliminary discussions and the joint military commission here will have further discussions. If recommendations come out of that, why then we would consider them. My talks were of a more general nature and I had an opportunity to see and discuss the Jordanian military forces which I find to be very, very strong and very effective.

Q. You have indicated you will very definitely go back to Washington with a favorable impression from Jordan and try to argue Jordan's case. Is that not true?

A. Well, I wouldn't put it quite that way. I will simply go back to Washington with a very favorable impression of the strength of Jordan, the effectiveness of His Majesty and the warmth of the relationships that exist between our countries. I will certainly report that, yes.

Q. Do you have any indication that there will be any roll-back or change in Jordan's order of Soviet anti-aircraft missiles?

A. No, I don't have any indications of that matter at all.

Q. What do you think you have achieved in this trip to the Middle East which you are just concluding now?

A. Well, I think one thing has been a greater understanding of the problems of the region and certainly greater personal friendships which are extremely important in these matters when you are dealing with the problems of a country. I think it is very important to have a personal knowledge of the people involved, and that has been enhanced, and I've been delighted to do that. I've also encountered very warm feelings for the United States and of the impor-

---

[1] Source: *Public Statements of Secretary of Defense Weinberger*, 1982. Weinberger made the remarks just prior to his departure. He had arrived in Jordan on February 10, after visiting Saudi Arabia and Oman. See document 430. Omitted are Weinberger's responses to questions on the Iran–Iraq War and El Salvador.

tance of maintaining peace in this whole region. I've acquired a very, as I say, substantial education in the strength of the countries that I've had an opportunity to visit and the importance of maintaining warm and strong and continuing good relations between these countries and the United States.

. . . .

Document 343

Transcript of an Interview With the Secretary of Defense (Weinberger), February 16, 1982 (Extract)[2]

Proposed U.S. Arms Sales to Jordan

MR. CHRIS WALLACE. As we reported earlier, the Israeli Parliament yesterday voted to oppose a U.S. arms sale to Jordan and Prime Minister Begin said it would violate President Reagan's pledge to maintain Israel's military superiority in the region. What's your reaction?

A. Well, I think that that's a little preemptive action perhaps because there is no pending sale to Jordan. There have been discussions of things that I had with them[3] as to what their military needs were, which of course is one of the statutory responsibilities of the post I have now. In the course of these discussions they mentioned the fact that to be effective anti-aircraft defense, such as the Hawk missile, needs to be mobile which is of course accepted and standard fact. It is also by definition, by nature, by name, a defensive weapon. We had discussions of that. They have no request pending. If a request comes in, it would be considered by the President and the National Security Council. It would then, if favorably approved, would have to go to the Congress. So talk of an arms sale to Jordan, because we had discussions in Jordan about it, is, I think, really quite premature.

Q. Do you believe though that the sale of anti-aircraft missiles and of F–16 fighters would in some sense jeopardize Israel's military superiority in the region?

A. No, I think Israel's margin of superiority is very great and the President, the administration, are pledged to maintain a margin of superiority. I do think that there is quite a difference between an anti-aircraft missile and an advanced fighter plane. But I don't think there's any suggestion that there would be anything other than careful consideration given, including consideration of Israel's interest and of the pledge of that—the administration has always had to maintain that strategic superiority, strategic edge that they have. What is important, however, is that the United States have more than one friend in the Mideast. And adding strength to other countries in the Mideast can really only serve the best interests of all of the countries in the Mideast, specifically including Jordan, and certainly including ourselves, by the means of protecting the Mideast against incursions by the Soviets or other threats.

Q. Let me ask one more question about the Jordanian possible arms sales. Mr. Begin talks of your "strange and astonishing statements" but says, well, perhaps you're not speaking for the President. Does Mr. Reagan share your view about the need to beef up Jordan's air defense?

A. I think President Reagan is going to have to, and certainly is fully capable of, speaking for himself on all of these issues. I have not expressed any administration opinion or anything of the kind. All I've done is, in discussions with the Jordanians, learn that they feel they need additional anti-aircraft defensive strength. If they should make a request for that, that is making the Hawk that we sold them earlier more mobile and more useful and thus preclude the necessity of their getting Soviet equipment, then we would certainly want to discuss that. And if we agree that that should be done, make the request to Congress. That's a long way down the road.

Q. You talk about the Israeli reaction as if its an over reaction. But let me ask you about a number of statements that came out of your trip to the Middle East, most of them attributed to a senior official, who most people at least in this town think it was you.

A. And many of them very inaccurate I have to say.

---

[2] Source: *Public Statements of Secretary of Defense Weinberger*, 1982. Chris Wallace interviewed Secretary Weinberger at the Pentagon on the NBC "Today" television program. The source text is incorrectly dated February 15, 1982.

[3] Between February 4 and 13, Weinberger visited the United Kingdom, Saudi Arabia, Oman, Jordan, and the Federal Republic of Germany. He was in Jordan from February 10 to 13.

Q. Let me ask you about some of them and I'll read you some of the quotes. "The administration has given up trying to deal with Begin and is getting tough with Israel."

A. Absolutely wrong. All that was ever said on the trip was that it was important that the United States have many friends in the Mideast, more than one friend, that we not be perceived as having a willingness to have only one friend and that it was important to us, it was important to the Mideast and to Israel, for us to add to the strength of a number of countries in that region so that they would be able to resist incursions by the Soviets. I sometimes get the feeling that the desire is to have sensational story rather than to say what was actually said. But in any event, I hope I've set that to rest.

. . . .

Document 344

Letter From the Secretary of State (Shultz) to King Hussein, August 11, 1982[4]

The Thirtieth Anniversary of King Hussein's Accession to the Throne

YOUR MAJESTY, It is my pleasure to extend best wishes to you and to the people of Jordan on the thirtieth anniversary of your accession to the Throne. The length and success of your reign ranks as one of the great achievements of modern statesmanship. Seven Presidents and ten Secretaries of State have benefitted from the wisdom of your counsel and from the strength of your support for our shared objectives.

You became King at a most difficult period for your country and for your region. Jordan has since made long strides on the road to economic and social development and is today one of the examples of success held out to those just setting out toward creating prosperity for their people. You have done this with strength, great economic freedom and willpower, characteristics Americans greatly admire.

Despite all of our best efforts, however, these are still very difficult times for the cause of peace. We will not rest until we have achieved a just and comprehensive peace in your troubled area. As we have so often in the past, we will look to you for advice and support as we pursue our goal.

On this auspicious occasion it is also appropriate to note again that the Government and people of the United States support the territorial integrity, soveriegnty and independence of Jordan, as well as Jordan's unique and enduring character. These principles have formed the basis of our mutually beneficial relationship for 30 years. You may rest assured that they are the rock upon which our future relations will be built as well.

I trust that in the years ahead the dreams we hold in common come to life for our two peoples and for all of those whose lives are touched by our deeds.

Sincerely,

GEORGE P. SHULTZ

[4] Source: Department of State *Bulletin*, October 1982, p. 45. The letter was released to the press by Department of State Acting Spokesman Alan Romberg after the August 11 Daily Press Briefing.

Document 345

Statements by President Reagan and King Hussein, December 21, 1982[5]

Commitment for Peace in the Middle East

THE PRESIDENT. One of the nicest customs in the Middle East is the traditional greeting, "Peace be upon you." King Hussein's visit with us comes at a time of the year when thoughts of peace are very much in our minds. And in our meeting today, His Majesty and I have had a chance to reaffirm personally the continuing friend-

[5] Source: White House Press Release, December 21, 1982, Office of the Press Secretary to the President; also printed in *Weekly Compilation of Presidential Documents*, December 27, 1982, pp. 1647–1648. The remarks were made on the South Lawn of the White House at 1:32 p.m., following the first meeting between President Reagan and King Hussein. King Hussein visited Washington, December 18–23, to meet with President Reagan and other U.S. Government officials.

ship between our two countries and to share with each other our hopes and dreams about our common goal of a just and lasting peace in the Middle East.

As trusting friends, we've spoken to one another as we always do—with candor and good will. And I told the King of my personal commitment to see peace in the Middle East become a true and lasting reality and of my equally deep commitment to the proposals that we made September 1st to Israel, to the Palestinians, and to the Arab States.

I also expressed America's gratitude to the King for his own important actions in support of our initiative over these past few months. His Majesty eloquently described his vision of peace and reviewed for us what he's been doing to help give peace a chance to take root—particularly his efforts to encourage the Palestinians to join him in efforts to take bold steps toward peace.

Together, we've also shared our thoughts on what remains and must be done by each and all of us to give life to this common goal. We share a sense of urgency to succeed at this commitment. Our discussion today has led to further meetings between our staffs over the next 2 days and I look forward to meeting with the King again before he leaves Washington.

Your Majesty, welcome.

KING HUSSEIN. I thank you, sir, for the warmth of your welcome, for the privilege and pleasure I and my colleagues have had of meeting with you, sir, and with our friends and for the opportunity to discuss many problems of mutual concern and interest and many challenges that lie before us.

We look forward, sir, to continuing our discussions in the coming days and this is an opportunity for me to reaffirm a long-life commitment for the establishment of a just and durable peace in the Middle East. May we hope and pray that we will succeed in making a contribution for a better future for generations to come in our part of the world and for the cause of world peace.

We'll continue to do our utmost and we value very much, indeed, the atmosphere of friendship, honesty, and candor that has characterized our relations and particularly, sir, the friendship that exists between us. I thank you very, very much indeed, sir, for your many kindnesses and for the privilege and pleasure of being with you and with our friends. Thank you, sir.

Document 346

Statements by President Reagan and King Hussein I, December 23, 1982[6]

Dialogue for Peace in the Middle East

THE PRESIDENT. Your Majesty, we've had extremely—and productive talks and I think we've made significant progress toward peace. We have initiated a dialogue from which we should not consider turning back.

Much work remains to be done and the road ahead is tough. But it's the right road and I remain optimistic that direct negotiations for a just resolution of the Palestinian problem in the context of a real and enduring peace is within our reach.

Your visit has served as a reminder that the bonds of friendship that link Jordan and the United States are as strong as ever. And I am gratified as well by the warmth and good will which characterizes our personal relationship.

I hope we can build on these bases in the weeks and months ahead to achieve the objective, enduring peace, which we and our people so fully share.

Your Majesty, I wish you a safe trip and look forward to our next meeting.

KING HUSSEIN. Mr. President, I thank you once again, sir, for the privilege and pleasure I've had, together with my party from Jordan, of meeting you, sir, and being with our friends at this very important, historical point in time in terms of our common hopes, in terms of the future of the area I come from and the future of generations to come.

To the skeptics, I would like to say that it has been, in my view, a very successful visit. I believe, sir, that we have an understanding

---

[6] Source: White House Press Release, December 23, 1982, Office of the Press Secretary to the President; also printed in *Weekly Compilation of Presidential Documents*, December 27, 1982, pp. 1661–1662. The remarks were made on the South Grounds of the White House at 2:46 p.m., following a meeting between the President and the King in the Oval Office with a group of U.S. officials and then in the Cabinet Room with members of the Jordanian delegation, prior to the King's departure.

of each other's views better than at any time in the past.

I can also seek to advise our friends that Jordan has been committed for the cause of establishing a just and durable peace. It has been our record since'67. This was reemphasized by the first [*Fez*] summit,[7] representing the view and the consensus of the entire Arab world. And I hope that I've been able on this visit to assure you, sir, and our friends of our determination to do all in our power for the establishment of a just and durable peace in the Middle East.

We will go back to our area. We will be in close contact and—over the coming period with our brethren there. There is much that we will take back with us. And we hope to be in touch again—I hope to have the privilege and pleasure of being with you, sir, before too long.

Rest assured of our commitment to the cause of future generations, their rights to live in peace and security in our entire area. I hope that we can contribute our share for a better, safer, more stable life for generations to come in the Middle East.

Thank you so much, sir, for your many kindnesses and your warm welcome. And may I also wish you a very Merry Christmas and a very Happy New Year, sir.

G. Lebanon

Document 347

Statement by the Representative at the United Nations (Kirkpatrick) Before the U.N. Security Council, February 25, 1982[1]

Enlarging the U.N. Interim Force in Lebanon

Mr. President,[2] for the past week the Government of the United States has worked alongside other governments in this body and alongside you to negotiate a text that would have the support of the Government of Lebanon, the troop contributors and others who support this important peacekeeping operation. We have also sought a text that would be acceptable to Lebanon's neighbors and respect the vital national interests of all concerned. We believe that the Council has succeeded in negotiating such a resolution. An observer of the Council's activities might wonder why, in fact, it has been so difficult to find consensus on a question about which there was so little disagreement, the question of whether the Council should or should not support General Callaghan's[3] request that 1000 troops be added to the UNIFIL contingent. And we do regret that the Council could not take the simple, straightforward step of enlarging the UNIFIL forces without adding to the resolution some elements that seemed to us extraneous to the basic purpose of the resolution. We regret that it is so difficult here to take constructive action without obstructive, ad hominem attacks on one another.

Mr. President, the Government of the United States is nonetheless pleased to support this resolution which provides General Callaghan the additional 1,000 troops for the UNIFIL forces which he has said he needed to accomplish his task, to provide the soldiers under his command with the reinforcement and the leisure that they require. My government is committed to the task of extending and reinforcing peace in this deeply troubled area. We are committed also to restoring the sovereignty and the territorial integrity of the Government of Lebanon. We believe that the cycle of violence that afflicts the area is profoundly dangerous to the security, peace, and well-being of the region and should be addressed in all its aspects and complexities. We expect that the reinforced troops of UNIFIL will be able more effectively to deal with the incursions and violations of all kinds and from all sources. To help achieve these goals, the Government of the United States offers its moral, political, financial, diplomatic support. We also work through our bilateral and regional diplomacy to achieve these goals. We desire to express our gratitude and admiration of the efforts of the distinguished representative of the

---

[7] See footnote 49 to document 320.

[1] Source: U.S. Mission to the United Nations Press Release 05(82), February 25, 1982. This statement was made after adoption of U.N. Security Council Resolution 501 (1982) by a vote of 13 (including the United States) to 0, with 2 abstentions on February 25, 1982. The resolution authorized an increase in UNIFIL's troop strength from 6,000 to 7,000. For text, see *U.N. Chronicle*, April 1982, pp. 18–19.

[2] Sir Anthony Parsons, Permanent Representative of the United Kingdom to the United Nations, served as President of the U.N. Security Council during February 1982.

[3] Major General William Callaghan, Commander, U.N. Interim Force in Lebanon.

United Nations Secretariat for his hard work on behalf of peace in this troubled region. Finally, we offer our best, warm wishes to General Callaghan and the UNIFIL troops as they continue their terribly important task.

Thank you, Mr. President.

Document 348

Testimony by the Deputy Assistant Secretary of State for Near Eastern and South Asian Affairs (Constable) and the Director of the Office of Lebanon, Jordan, Syria, and Iraq Affairs, Bureau of Near Eastern and South Asian Affairs (Howell), Before a Subcommittee of the House Foreign Affairs Committee, March 3, 1982 (Extract)[4]

Efforts to Maintain the Cease-Fire in Lebanon

. . . .

MR. HAMILTON. All right, sir. Let us begin with Lebanon and the Habib mission.[5]

What is the objective for Mr. Habib this time around with regard to Lebanon?

MR. CONSTABLE. Well, the principal objective of Ambassador Habib's mission on this occasion is to try to strengthen the cessation of hostilities which has been in place since last July.

That cessation of hostilities had been under a certain amount of pressure. There have been discussions and rhetoric about a possible breakdown. We think it has been a major achievement of our policies in the area that the cessation of hostilities has endured since last July. Countless lives have been saved through this process and we hope that Ambassador Habib's current trip will result in its strengthening and consolidation.

MR. HAMILTON. Do we think there is a real danger of a collapse of that cease-fire?

MR. CONSTABLE. I think in that part of the world, which is rather volatile, the danger always exists.

MR. HAMILTON. Is it greater now than it has been?

MR. CONSTABLE. It has been our impression that in recent weeks there has been perhaps a greater danger than previously.

MR. HAMILTON. Do we see chances of an Israeli attack on Lebanon soon?

MR. CONSTABLE. I think the Israelis have made it pretty clear that in the event of some sort of provocation they would respond to that. So that there is a danger in the first instance of a breakdown across the border toward Israel and, in that event, of an Israeli response.

So, there is a certain fragility in it and Ambassador Habib is there to try to see if he can make it stronger and persuade all of the parties concerned that the cessation of hostilities is worth preserving and that the costs of a breakdown would be great and in no one's interest.

MR. HAMILTON. Is it our impression that the Palestinians are building up their weapons in South Lebanon at the present time?

MR. CONSTABLE. We believe there has been some increase in armaments since the cease-fire came into place. We understand Israeli concerns over this and we share them. But our principal interest is that there be a strengthening of the cease-fire. This is valuable in itself, it saves lives and we hope that neither side will take steps that would affect and undermine or break that cessation of hostilities.

MR. HAMILTON. When you say there has been some buildup, could you be more specific than that?

MR. CONSTABLE. We are aware of the introduction of some additional artillery. The problem of counting is a very difficult one for us and I would not try to be very precise about numbers because I do not think we can be in a way that is really sound.

MR. HAMILTON. Where does it come from?

MR. CONSTABLE. It comes from different directions. The PLO gets its weapons sometimes from Syria, sometimes from outside. The Libyans have occasionally supplied weaponry to parts of the PLO, to some of the splinter groups.

MR. HAMILTON. Do we consider that buildup a violation of the cease-fire or the spirit of the cease-fire?

---

[4] Source: *Developments in the Middle East, March 1982: Hearings Before the Subcommittee on Europe and the Middle East of the Committee on Foreign Affairs, House of Representatives, Ninety-seventh Congress, Second Session* (Washington, 1982), pp. 2–5.

[5] Ambassador Habib visited Lebanon, Israel, Syria, and Jordan, February 26–March 10, 1982.

MR. CONSTABLE. Well, the cease-fire itself, of course, speaks of movement across the border in either direction, from Lebanon into Israel, from Israel into Lebanon.

The cessation of hostilities language and agreement does not address the question of buildup of weapons. Obviously, anything that raises tensions in the area can undermine the spirit of the cease-fire, can undermine the commitment to the cessation of hostilities and so, that in itself would be dangerous.

MR. HAMILTON. Now, the Syrian missiles are still there, are they not, and that was one of the triggering factors?

MR. CONSTABLE. Yes.

MR. HAMILTON. Why have not the Syrians taken those out?

MR. CONSTABLE. Well, I would rather not get right into that at this point. Some of these issues are very much what Phil Habib will be talking about in his discussions at various stops along the way, and I would not want to say anything here in open session that might prejudice his efforts to work on these problems.

MR. HAMILTON. Will Ambassador Habib be seeing Mr. Assad?

MR. CONSTABLE. He has seen him, yes.

MR. HAMILTON. He has already seen him?

MR. CONSTABLE. He has seen him today.

MR. HAMILTON. Are we getting cooperation from the Saudis in defusing the situation there?

MR. CONSTABLE. Well, the Saudis have been very interested in the Lebanon problem and were very cooperative in the process of bringing about the cessation of hostilities last July. They have been cooperative in the Arab followup committee's efforts to bring about some reconciliation among the Lebanese factions.

One of the stops that Ambassador Habib will be making is in Saudi Arabia and he will be discussing with the Saudis our mutual interest in trying to improve the Lebanon situation.

MR. HAMILTON. So, they are still actively interested and involved.

MR. CONSTABLE. They continue to be interested and they find some aspects of it as frustrating as we do.

MR. HAMILTON. What about the role of the Lebanese Army here? Have they extended their writ to any noticeable extent?

MR. CONSTABLE. That remains an objective of the central government. I think that that has not happened in recent months in the particular expansions.

MR. HAMILTON. Not in southern Lebanon.

MR. CONSTABLE. Not at this point. That is one of the things they would like to do.

MR. HAMILTON. Now, we recently turned down a request from the Lebanese Government for some tanks. What was the reason for that decision?

MR. CONSTABLE. If I may ask Mr. Howell to address that.

MR. HAMILTON. Yes.

MR. HOWELL. The request actually was for the transfer of some tanks from a third country. It is not a question of us turning them down, but it is a question of the Lebanese Government making arrangements with the other country and then getting our approval for the transfer.

MR. HAMILTON. They were not American tanks?

MR. HOWELL. They are originally American tanks. Of course, the Lebanese Government would be a government to which we would have no problem in principle with the transfer. But it is not a question of the U.S. Government having turned down the request.

MR. HAMILTON. Would they have gotten the tanks had we not intervened?

MR. HOWELL. I am not sure I understand the question.

MR. HAMILTON. I am not sure I understand the situation. [Laughter]

Where are the tanks coming from?

MR. HOWELL. Sir, I am not sure that I am prepared to say at the present stage in this forum.

MR. HAMILTON. In open session?

MR. HOWELL. Yes, sir.

MR. HAMILTON. All right.

Mr. Findley.

MR. FINDLEY. Mr. Constable, last Friday, I believe, the State Department said it was not aware of any major infusion of arms into southern Lebanon.[6] Is that still the position of the Department?

---

[6] Reference is to a statement by Department of State Spokesman Dean Fischer at the Department of State Daily Press Briefing on Friday, February 26, 1982.

MR. CONSTABLE. Our position is that there have been additional arms brought into Lebanon. I do not think it is very useful to try to get into discussions about major and minor and so on, but the central point is that anything that threatens the stability of the cessation of hostilities is something that has to concern us. It concerns the Israelis, too, and we share that concern.

MR. FINDLEY. Am I incorrect in my statement that the State Department said that it was unaware of any major infusion?

MR. CONSTABLE. I believe that was said by the spokesman.

MR. FINDLEY. Do you have reason to modify that?

MR. CONSTABLE. I am not trying to modify it, I am trying to shift the emphasis to the central issue as we see it, which is the cessation of hostilities rather than the debate about how many weapons have come in.

MR. FINDLEY. It is a very important item because you are aware, I am sure, of what Mr. Arens has said about the likelihood of the Israeli movement there, the need to preempt or to prevent attack.[7]

If our Government sees a major infusion of arms, that would certainly give the Israelis a basis for a decision to attack. So, it is timely and it is of great importance to this committee.

MR. CONSTABLE. What my major point is, and what we are saying to the Israelis and all parties involved in this is that we do not see any developments that would justify breaking the cessation of hostilities, and letting that very important achievement which has saved so many lives over these past months and brought at least a fragile kind of tranquility to the area—

MR. FINDLEY. Is it our opinion that the PLO has not broken the cease-fire?

MR. CONSTABLE. We believe that there was at least a technical violation of the cease-fire in the penetration involved with members of Fatah moving from Lebanon through Syria, through Jordan in an attempt to target Israeli facilities or personnel—we are not quite sure what the target was. But we believe that was indeed a violation.

MR. FINDLEY. What were they targeting?

MR. CONSTABLE. We do not know what their final objective was, they were intercepted.

MR. FINDLEY. Did they move into Israeli territory at any point?

MR. CONSTABLE. They were on the West Bank when they were apprehended.

MR. FINDLEY. They were on the West Bank?

MR. CONSTABLE. But they were not there with an innocent purpose.

MR. FINDLEY. They were not within pre-67 Israel.

MR. CONSTABLE. No; but it was pretty clear that they were moving towards Israeli targets. They came out from Lebanon.

MR. FINDLEY. Does our Government view with concern statements such as that made by Mr. Arens, indicating that it is only a matter of time before Israel moves into Lebanon?

MR. CONSTABLE. In all our discussions with all of the parties we encourage that that cessation of hostilities be maintained.

. . . .

Document 349

Statement and Remarks by the President's Special Emissary to the Middle East (Habib), March 18, 1982 (Extract)[8]

U.S. Support for "An Independent, United, Integral Lebanon"

. . . .

[AMBASSADOR HABIB.] During my recent trip to the Middle East,[9] I was concerned

[7] Moshe Arens, the Israeli Ambassador to the United States, told reporters on February 25, 1982, that an Israeli invasion of Lebanon was "a matter of time." (*Facts on File, 1982*, Vol. 42, p. 121F2)

[8] Source: White House Press Release, March 18, 1982, Office of the Press Secretary to the President. Habib made his statement and remarks on the South Lawn of the White House at 2:31 p.m. after reporting to President Reagan.

[9] Regarding Habib's trip, see footnote 5 above.

principally with two tasks assigned to me by President Reagan: First, to do what I could to strengthen and reinforce the cessation of hostile military action which we helped to bring into existence last July; second, to see what the United States could do with regard to the Lebanese situation itself.

I reported to the President that all parties realize more than ever the grave implications of a major breakdown of the cease-fire. However, the situation should still be described as fragile, despite the fact that cease-fire violations have been of minor significance compared with the situation that existed last spring. We believe that any move which could lead to a breakdown of the cease-fire must be avoided. Military actions would serve no useful purpose and would be extremely damaging to the peace process in the Middle East.

As for the internal Lebanese situation, it is a matter of deep interest to the United States. I made it clear during my trip that the United States strongly supports an independent, united, integral Lebanon, sovereign within its internationally recognized borders. We have welcomed the expansion of the UNIFIL forces—the U.N. forces—by 1,000 men, which will help stabilize the situation in the southern part of the country. We continue to support efforts to order political consensus and national reconciliation within Lebanon and seek to enlist the support of Arab States for this process.

We strongly support the constitutional process which calls for the free election of the next president of Lebanon, which will take place later this year. We believe the Lebanese themselves, if they are not subjected to undue pressures and influence, will be able to get together in a way that will strengthen their national sovereignty.

To sum up, I informed the President that pursuant to his instructions, we have been able to underline the strong and abiding American interest and concern with the future of Lebanon and the need to maintain the cease-fire, which has unquestionably saved many lives. Thank you.

Q. Did you get a promise from Israel that they would not invade southern Lebanon?

AMBASSADOR HABIB. What I received was a clear indication that they wish to abide by the cease-fire.

Q. Ambassador Habib, Dean Fischer made a point today[10] of saying that the cease-fire extends the action that might originate in Lebanon and go through Syria and Jordan. Why was that specific point made?

AMBASSADOR HABIB. That's always been the case. There's nothing new about that. The cease-fire terms, which were always—as you know, were never written—there was never a signed agreement—cease-fire terms are—always involved action from Lebanon into Israel or from Israel into Lebanon and it also included the enclave in the south to and from. So there's nothing—there's nothing extraordinary about that. It's just that the question was raised and defined in those terms. That's always been the clear understanding on my part.

Q. Are the Syrian missiles in Lebanon, which at one time Prime Minister Begin was threatening to take out, a problem any longer?

AMBASSADOR HABIB. They're still a problem. The Israelis still consider that they should leave. And we took up that problem on both sides. I would say at the moment that the cease-fire was of more immediate interest and its affirmation—the affirmation of the cease-fire in light of recent events was—sort of overtook that one a little bit.

Q. You say Israel gave you the clear understanding that they wish to abide by the cease-fire.

AMBASSADOR HABIB. That is correct.

Q. Do you take that to mean that they will unless there is some provocation? And can you—

AMBASSADOR HABIB. They will not attack.

Q. They will not attack?

AMBASSADOR HABIB. That is correct. That's my understanding. Not be the first to attack, anyway.

Q. Ambassador Habib, is there some reason to believe—some assurances or evidence that the Palestinians would slow a buildup in southern Lebanon that the Israelis say they are concerned about?

AMBASSADOR HABIB. Those are questions that we discussed in various places. I don't think it would be—I don't think I'm in a position to say anything very positive about something like that, other than to say that I would hope that nothing occurs which creates any provocative appearance and nothing occurs which would produce any provocative actions.

. . . .

10 Department of State Spokesman Dean Fischer made this observation during the Department of State Daily Press Briefing on March 18, 1982.

Document 350

Statement Read by the Department of State Acting Spokesman (Romberg), June 4, 1982[11]

U.S. Reaction to the Attempted Assassination of Israel's Ambassador to the United Kingdom

The despicable assassination attempt on the Israeli Ambassador in London[12] has once again set off a new spiral of violence in the Middle East. We have been receiving reports of Israeli air strikes in and around Beirut today. These air strikes have now ceased, according to our latest information.

We also have press and other reports that just a little while ago rockets launched from southern Lebanon began hitting northern Israel.

The United States would be deeply and profoundly concerned over any loss of innocent lives caused by this threatening spiral of violence.

We call on all parties in the strongest terms to refrain immediately from any further acts of violence. This would only bring the loss of innocent lives. We call on all with influence on the parties to use their best efforts to bring this violence to an end immediately.

---

[11] Source: Office of Press Relations, Department of State. The statement was read at the Department of State Daily Press Briefing held at 12:48 p.m.

[12] On the evening of June 3, Shlomo Argov, Israel's Ambassador to the United Kingdom, was shot and seriously wounded outside the Dorchester Hotel in London. Israel attributed the attack to the PLO, although a Palestinian faction associated with Abu Nidal (code name for Sabri Khalil al-Banna) later claimed responsibility.

Document 351

Resolution 508 (1982), Adopted by the U.N. Security Council, June 5, 1982[13]

Appeal for a Cease-Fire in Lebanon

The Security Council,

Recalling Security Council resolutions 425 (1978),[14] 426 (1978)[15] and the ensuing resolutions, and more particularly, Security Council resolution 501 (1982),[16]

Taking note of the letters of the Permanent Representative of Lebanon[17] dated 4 June 1982 (S/15161 and S/15162),

Deeply concerned at the deterioration of the present situation in Lebanon and in the Lebanese-Israeli border area, and its consequences for peace and security in the region,

Gravely concerned at the violation of the territorial integrity, independence, and sovereignty of Lebanon,

Reaffirming and supporting the statement made by the President and the members of the Security Council on 4 June 1982 (S/15163), as well as the urgent appeal issued by the Secretary-General on 4 June 1982,[18]

Taking note of the report of the Secretary-General,[19]

1. *Calls upon* all the parties to the conflict to cease immediately and simultaneously all military activities within Lebanon and across the Lebanese-Israeli border and no later than 0600 hours local time on Sunday, 6 June 1982;

2. *Requests* all Member States which are in a position to do so to bring their influence to bear upon those concerned so that

---

[13] Source: U.N. Security Council Resolution 508 (1982); also printed in Department of State *Bulletin*, September 1982, p. 14. The resolution was adopted unanimously.

[14] For text, see *American Foreign Policy: Basic Documents, 1977–1980*, p. 789.

[15] For text, see Department of State *Bulletin*, May 1978, p. 51.

[16] See footnote 1 to document 347.

[17] Ghassan at-Tueni.

[18] For text, see U.N. document SG/SM/3292, June 4, 1982.

[19] For the text of the U.N. Secretary-General's report to the Security Council on hostilities in Lebanon, see U.N. document S/PV.2374, June 5, 1982.

the cessation of hostilities declared by Security Council resolution 490 (1981)[20] can be respected;

3. *Requests* the Secretary-General to undertake all possible efforts to ensure the implementation of and compliance with this resolution and to report to the Security Council as early as possible and not later than forty-eight hours after the adoption of this resolution.

Document 352

Statement Read by the President's Deputy Press Secretary (Speakes), Versailles, France, June 6, 1982[21]

Ambassador Habib's Mission to Lebanon

The President has summoned Ambassador Philip Habib to Versailles to discuss the Middle East situation. At the President's direction, Ambassador Habib will come at 3:30 this afternoon, where he will meet in the President's suite with the President and Secretary Haig.

Ambassador Habib's mission, as outlined by the President, will be to offer the assistance of the United States Government in the cause of peace in the Middle East.

During this meeting, the President will discuss the current escalation of violence in the Middle East and will determine Ambassador Habib's role in the coming days at the conclusion of the meeting.

In connection with the escalation of violence, the United States Government has ordered a reduction in force of U.S. Embassy personnel in Beirut. In the next 72 hours, all dependents will leave, and an Embassy staff of approximately 50 will be reduced by one-half.

The President last night sent a personal letter to Prime Minister Menahem Begin of Israel expressing the President's hopes that the Government of Israel would seriously consider that no further action be taken that could widen the conflict.

We have made similar appeals to every government in the area with some influence over the situation or the parties which have been engaged in the fighting. I would characterize it as we have pulled out all stops to bring about an end to the fighting and a restoration of the cessation of hostilities which was arranged by Ambassador Habib in July of 1981.

We have strongly supported the call by the United Nations Security Council and the Secretary-General for a cessation of the hostilities at dawn this morning. We continue to be deeply and profoundly concerned by the mounting loss of lives caused by this ongoing spiral of violence and counterviolence.

We renew our call on all parties to refrain at once from further violence. We continue to call on all with influence on the parties to exert all their efforts to effecting a speedy end to this tragic violence. We will continue to confer closely with all parties to bring an end to the fighting. I can assure you we're exerting ourselves to the utmost to restore peace to the region.

Document 353

Statement by the Secretary of State (Haig) at a Press Briefing, Versailles, France, June 6, 1982 (Extract)[22]

Efforts to Limit the War in Lebanon

. . . .

We have been watching this situation moment by moment as it unfolds. The

---

[20] This resolution, calling for an end to armed attacks and reaffirming the U.N. Security Council's commitment to the sovereignty, integrity, and independence of Lebanon, was unanimously approved by the Security Council on July 21, 1981.

[21] Source: *Weekly Compilation of Presidential Documents,* June 14, 1982, p. 754. Speakes read this statement at a White House press briefing held in the L'Orangerie Press Center beginning at 12:34 p.m. President Reagan was attending the eighth economic summit conference at Versailles, June 4–6. For documentation, see Chapter 5, Part F.

[22] Source: Department of State Press Release 192, June 16, 1982; also printed in Department of State *Bulletin,* July 1982, p. 7. For the full text of the statement, see *ibid.,* pp. 7–9. Secretary Haig accompanied President Reagan to Versailles for the eighth economic summit conference, June 4–6. The omitted portion relates to developments on economic questions at the Conference and a subsequent question-and-answer session.

President has followed it throughout the day, and has shared with his colleagues during the plenary session the updates that we had as they developed to include the fact of his communication very early this morning with Prime Minister Begin and the response received later this afternoon from Mr. Begin.

Now, that response was consistent with the decision made by the Israeli Cabinet and announced in Jerusalem which reads as follows:

> "The Cabinet took the following decision, first, to instruct the Israeli defense forces to place all civilian population of the Galilee beyond the range of the terrorist fire from Lebanon where they, their bases, and their headquarters are concentrated. The name of the operation is Peace for Galilee. During the operation, the Syrian army will not be attacked unless it attacks the Israeli forces. Israel continues to aspire to the signing of the peace treaty with an independent Lebanon, its territorial integrity preserved."

That is the brief text, which you may or may not have seen from Israel.

Now, we are, of course, extremely concerned about the escalating cycle of violence. The President, yesterday afternoon, asked Ambassador Habib to proceed here posthaste.[23] He met with Ambassador Habib this afternoon, and decided to send him directly to Israel as his personal representative to conduct discussions on an urgent basis with Prime Minister Begin. The President also dispatched an urgent message to Prime Minister Begin telling him of his decision to do so.

I anticipate that Phil will proceed on to Rome this evening, and, hopefully, will arrive in Israel early tomorrow morning.

In the last 48 hours at the President's direction, we have been engaged in an intense degree of diplomatic activity in the United Nations in New York, where we firmly supported the resolution urging an immediate cease-fire.[24] And as you know, President Reagan joined this morning with the other members of the summit in issuing a statement urging a responsive reaction to the U.N. resolution.[25]

We have been in touch with the Government of Israel for a prolonged period on the situation in Lebanon, always urging restraint. And always hoping, as we continue to hope, that the cease-fire can, even at this late date, be reinstituted. As of now, we are informed that there are two Israeli military columns that crossed into Lebanon from Israel, one proceeding along the coast road in the direction of Tyre, and the other through the Upper Galilee Panhandle. The penetration in the later case has been approximatley 10 kilometers, in the former case perhaps three or four.

We are extremely disturbed by the loss of innocent lives in this fighting on the Israeli-Lebanese border. It has involved, as you know, the exchange of artillery and rockets for a prolonged period preceding the Israeli ground penetration.

We are concerned also that the fighting not be expanded into a broader conflict and are acutely conscious of the presence of Syrian forces in fairly close proximity to the eastern penetration.

We will do our best to convey to the Government of Syria the stated intentions of the Government of Israel not to engage unless engaged by Syrian forces.

. . . .

Document 354

Resolution 509 (1982), Adopted by the U.N. Security Council, June 6, 1982[26]

Demand for an Israeli Withdrawal From Lebanon

The Security Council,

Recalling its resolutions 425 (1978) of 19 March 1978 and 508 (1982) of 5 June 1982,

Gravely concerned at the situation as described by the Secretary-General in his report to the Council,

Reaffirming the need for strict respect for the territorial integrity, sovereignty and po-

---

[23] See *supra*.

[24] See document 351.

[25] For the text of the statement on the Middle East fighting issued by the leaders of the United States, France, United Kingdom, Italy, Canada, West Germany, and Japan on June 6, see *New York Times*, June 7, 1982, p. A14.

[26] Source: U.N. Security Council Resolution 509 (1982), also printed in Department of State *Bulletin*, September 1982, p. 14. The resolution was adopted unanimously.

litical independence of Lebanon within its internationally recognized boundaries,

1. *Demands* that Israel withdraw all its military forces forthwith and unconditionally to the internationally recognized boundaries of Lebanon;

2. *Demands* that all parties observe strictly the terms of paragraph 1 of resolution 508 (1982) which called on them to cease immediately and simultaneously all military activities within Lebanon and across the Lebanese-Israeli border;

3. *Calls* on all parties to communicate to the Secretary-General their acceptance of the present resolution within 24 hours;

4. *Decides* to remain seized of the question.

Document 355

Statement by the Alternate Representative at the United Nations (Lichenstein) Before the U.N. Security Council, June 6, 1982[27]

Link Between Israeli Withdrawal and Cessation of All Hostilities

Thank you, Mr. President. This resolution[28] focuses on two elements as a means of ending the present military confrontation in Lebanon: A cessation of hostilities by all of the parties and the withdrawal of Israeli forces from Lebanon. Operative paragraphs one and two of this resolution seek to accomplish these two interrelated objectives. We wish to emphasize, Mr. President, that these two objectives are in fact inextricably linked and that their implementation must be simultaneous. This, in our view, is the clear, logical, and necessary meaning of the resolution.

I need only add, Mr. President, that it is the fervent hope of my government—which has devoted so much effort to the resolution of this conflict, which even at this very moment is carrying forward its commitment to this task—it is the fervent hope of my government that the bloodshed be ended immediately and that the conditions be established for a just and enduring peace in the region. Thank you.

---

[27] Source: U.S. Mission to the United Nations Press Release USUN 42(82), June 6, 1982.

[28] *Supra.*

Document 356

U.N. Security Council Draft Resolution, Vetoed by the United States, June 8, 1982[29]

Demand for a Cease-Fire and an Israeli Withdrawal From Lebanon

The Security Council,

Recalling its resolutions 508 (1982) and 509 (1982),[30]

Taking note of the report of the Secretary-General (S/15178) of 7 June 1982,

Also taking note of the two positive replies to the Secretary-General of the Government of Lebanon and the Palestine Liberation Organization contained in document S/15178,

1. *Condemns* the non-compliance with resolutions 508 (1982) and 509 (1982) by Israel;

2. *Urges* the parties to comply strictly with the regulations attached to the Hague Convention of 1907;[31]

3. *Reiterates its demand* that Israel withdraw all its military forces forthwith and unconditionally to the internationally recognized boundaries of Lebanon;

4. *Reiterates also its demand* that all parties observe strictly the terms of paragraph 1 of resolution 508 (1982) which called on them to cease immediately and simultaneously all military activities within Lebanon and across the Lebanese-Israeli border;

---

[29] Source: U.N. document S/1585; also printed in Department of State *Bulletin*, September 1982, p. 14. This draft resolution failed of adoption by a vote of 14 in favor to 1 (United States) against, a veto. In explanation of the U.S. vote, Ambassador Jeane J. Kirkpatrick stated before the U.N. Security Council on June 8, 1982, that the resolution was "not sufficiently balanced to accomplish the objectives of ending the cycle of violence and establish the conditions for a just and lasting peace in Lebanon." For text of her statement, see Department of State *Bulletin*, September 1982, p. 15.

[30] For text, see document 354.

[31] Reference is to the Convention Respecting Laws and Customs of War on Land, With Annex of Regulations, signed at The Hague, October 18, 1907, and entered into force for the United States, January 26, 1910. For text, see 1 Bevans 631.

5. *Demands* that within six hours all hostilities must be stopped in compliance with Security Council resolutions 508 (1982) and 509 (1982) and decides, in the event of non-compliance, to meet again to consider practical ways and means in accordance with the Charter of the United Nations.

Document 357

Transcript of a Press Conference by the Secretary of State (Haig), Bonn, June 9, 1982 (Extracts)[32]

Hostilities in Lebanon

. . . .

I'll say a brief word about Lebanon. It's clear that over the last 24 hours, the intensity of fighting has continued at a heavy pace. One might say the situation has worsened. Last night the United States vetoed a U.N. resolution,[33] feeling that it lacked the necessary balance that the preceding resolutions that we had supported—508 and 509—offered.

We believe, and continue to believe, the major emphasis must be on the achievement of the termination of bloodshed, the [end] of violence, and to restore full international respect for the sovereignty and territorial integrity of Lebanon at its recognized international borders.

The military action today was heavy in the Bekaa Valley where there was apparently a substantial air engagement. There may have been missile activity as well associated with the air engagement. There coutinue to be reports of the westward movement of Syrian Armed Forces.

Ambassador Habib, at the direction of the President, following his extensive discussions with Prime Minister Begin, proceeded this morning to Damascus in the further effort to halt the cycle of violence.

I think that's the essence of today's—

Q. Has Habib seen President Assad yet?

SECRETARY HAIG. He has been in touch, I believe, with the Prime Minister,[34] and I don't know that he's seen Assad yet.

Q. By missile activity, do you mean missiles fired at aircraft, or do you mean also an aircraft destroying missiles on the ground?

SECRETARY HAIG. I would say ground to air.

Q. The reported clashes between the Israelis and the Syrians reached the point where you are concerned about the involvement—

SECRETARY HAIG. We've been very concerned about this from the outset and I think you know that I have reiterated that here. I would say it looks somewhat more ominous in that regard after the last 24 hours than it did at the time of yesterday evening's report. But it still does not contain evidence of a clear intent on either side to engage one another in a substantial way.

Q. What is our understanding of the Israeli intention, how long do they plan to stay in Lebanon; what is their objective; and when are they going to withdraw, if they are going to withdraw?

SECRETARY HAIG. We feel that Israel has largely achieved the objectives that it has set for itself, at least in the initial exposition of those objectives in terms of geographic penetration and it has, in fact, substantially exceeded them.

The question of duration, of course, is directly related to the other objective—that Israel put forth at the time of its decision. And I would recall for you, that decision was justified by the Israeli Government in the wake of heavy artillery and rocket firing into the Galilee area. And that objective, so stated by the Government of Israel, is to eliminate that threat.

I think it would be hard to say at this juncture, despite the speed and apparently devastating character of the Israeli penetration that that objective is yet achieved.

Q. Do you see the kind of protracted negotiations ahead in obtaining Israel's withdraw[al] from this territory that has characterized other negotiations?

SECRETARY HAIG. You mean the'78 incursion? That was not too protracted, you'll recall. It moved rather rapidly. We would hope that this would move very speedily

---

[32] Source: Department of State Press Release 196, June 16, 1982. Secretary Haig accompanied President Reagan on a state visit to Bonn, June 9–11, 1982.

[33] For text, see *supra.*

[34] Reference is to Prime Minister Abd al Ra'uf al-Kassem of Syria.

and result in the withdrawal of Israeli forces and a reestablishment of the ceasefire and that's what we're working to do.

Q. How can it move speedily, Mr. Secretary, unless the United Nations or the United States or somebody is beefing up the peacekeeping force there so that the Israeli security concerns will be met? Is anything going on in that area?

SECRETARY HAIG. Yes, of course. There is all kinds of diplomatic activity associated with potential solutions to this problem, but it serves no useful purpose to air them publicly. In fact, it may put progress in jeopardy so I—

Q. Mr. Secretary, can you explain why the 7,000 UNIFIL troops were not an important military factor in this situation?

SECRETARY HAIG. I don't think I can do anymore than cite for you previous history in that area. Clearly, their own political instructions at the time they were put in place could be questioned.

Q. In other words, were they instructed to avoid contact with the Israelis?

SECRETARY HAIG. No, but I think if you go back and look at the mandate of the UNIFIL force in southern Lebanon, you'll see that it left a great deal to be desired and that is, unfortunately, the part of developing an international consensus. I hope we've all learned from it.

Q. Mr. Secretary, without spelling out how much a force could be changed in the future, what other ideas do you have in general that could be put in place that could stop this kind of thing of coming back on it year after year?

SECRETARY HAIG. Again, I would refer you to the speech I gave in Chicago when I highlighted the fact that this is one of three critical areas of tension and perhaps the most immediate—as a threat to peace.[35] And I talked about the overall need to strengthen the central government of Lebanon—to enhance its capability to provide security for its own territories; to reduce the level of foreign involvement in Lebanon and to provide an interim assured security force through both geographic buffer and physical presence. In that context, one might conceive of a number of possibilities—the EMFO [MFO] approach, a U.N. approach, a combination of both, perhaps, with a strengthened central government military capability.

As you know, the Christian elements in the south under Major Haddad[36] are not an inconsequential force. They might in some way be included.

All of these things are under intense review through diplomatic channels, and, as I say, I prefer to avoid laying out any format other than to assure you that intense activity is underway with respect to all.

Q. Mr. Secretary, in terms of foreign forces, would it be helpful if the Syrian troops were out of Lebanon as well?

SECRETARY HAIG. I think it would be helpful if they substantially modified their current disposition.

. . . .

Q. Mr. Secretary, why is it if the Israelis are—have these limited objectives that they stated, and if the Syrian armies and the Israeli forces were avoiding each other which they seemed to be earlier in the week, why is it that the Israelis in your view attacked the missile sites today? Could you give us some readout on that? Are they trying to engage the Syrian Army—

SECRETARY HAIG. No, I think there was an infusion of additional Syrian missiles into the Bekaa Valley, a rather substantial number in the last 48 hours.

Q. Did the Israelis attack the missile sites?

SECRETARY HAIG. We have some evidence of that, but I cannot confirm it. And I assume that you have something harder—

Q. Mr. Secretary, the United States has contributed to the peacekeeping force in the Sinai, can you imagine circumstances under which it would contribute troops to UNIFIL?

SECRETARY HAIG. I think it's too early to say. I think it's not too different than the response I would give to the Falkland peacekeeping role. It would depend fundamentally upon the mission, the composition of the force, the political mandate under

[35] On May 26, 1982, Haig addressed the Chicago Council on Foreign Relations on the theme of peace and security in the Middle East. See document 303.

[36] Reference is to Major Saad Haddad, commander of the "Free Lebanon Army." This Lebanese Christian force had, with Israeli support, controlled an enclave immediately north of Israel's border since April 1979.

which such an American contribution might evolve. It isn't something that I think we're leaning heavily in the direction of at all. But we are gravely concerned about a return to stability in Lebanon. And that is going to require more than just a return to status quo ante. After all, we've been living for a number of years with a fragile arrangement which clearly over time was going to break down. It's unfortunate that it did before we were able to deal with more profound, long-term elements of instability.

Q. Does the United States support Israel's objective?

SECRETARY HAIG. The United States voted in favor of U.N. Resolution 508 which called for the cessation of hostilities and the withdrawal of Israeli forces from Lebanon. Now, I think that would suggest in no way was there either collusion or a foreknowledge or support.

Q. Well, then is it fair to say we disagree with what they are doing?

SECRETARY HAIG. I think it's fair to say that we have supported a U.N. resolution which asks for their early withdrawal from southern Lebanon.

Q. Mr. Secretary, related to that, are you beginning to have any doubts about the Israeli objective as stated by Israel? That in light of the military activities, they may have another objective in mind.

SECRETARY HAIG. We would look at that in two ways. The first is that they have moved very rapidly and one could consider very clearly tactical expansions on original objectives for tactical purposes. The other way you would look at it is the possibility of Syrian engagement in which clearly there would be a change.

Q. What do you mean?

Q. Could you be a little more precise about—

Q. What do you mean by that—there could be a change in what?

SECRETARY HAIG. The question was do we see a change in the originally stated objectives of the Government of Israel? You remember the 40 kilometers, the assurance of no vulnerability from PLO attack within that zone. They have gone beyond that zone. And the question was, "Under what circumstance—or would you foresee a change in their basic objectives?" My answer to that is we could look at it from two points of view. Perhaps these are tactical extensions of the basic objectives which have not modified and which will be adhered to. We could look at it from the other point of view and that is that Syrian forces become engaged. If Syrian forces become engaged, then clearly there's a whole new character to the nature of this conflict.

Q. Mr. Secretary, does the Israeli advance beyond its stated objective make it more likely that the Syrian forces will become engaged? And does it make Mr. Habib's mission any more difficult or—

SECRETARY HAIG. I think in both cases the answer is clearly yes.

Q. Does it make it necessary at this point that they have gone beyond their original objectives for the United States to begin making that value judgment about their role and their use of these—

SECRETARY HAIG. That is a process that has been underway from the outset of our assessments and our diplomatic activity.

Q. Well, what is your current assessment?

SECRETARY HAIG. Not to be divulged.

Q. What was your answer to that?

SECRETARY HAIG. I am not going to add any more to what I said earlier.

Q. Yesterday you said the Habib talks with Begin were initially profitable.[37] Do you still feel that way?

SECRETARY HAIG. Yes.

Q. And in what manner would it be profitable?

SECRETARY HAIG. We have a much better grasp of the thinking of the Israeli Government, its purposes and its objectives and its own motivations and requirements that have to be met as we looked—

. . . .

---

[37] Reference is to Haig's press conference held in London on June 8. (Department of State Press Release 194, June 16, 1982)

Document 358

Transcript of an Interview With the Secretary of State (Haig), June 13, 1982 (Extract)[38]

U.S. Policy and Lebanon

. . . .

[MR. DONALDSON.] Secretary Haig, Israel says it will not withdraw immediately from Lebanon, as demanded by U.N. Resolution 508 that we voted for. So let's just say it out loud, if we mean it: Is that all right with us, or do we want an immediate withdrawal?

SECRETARY HAIG. It's too early to say, Mr. Donaldson. I think the key aspects of the resolution you refer to are, for the moment, to get a cessation of the hostilities and the bloodshed, and the President's focus thus far has been on that.

Clearly, no one would welcome a return to status quo ante in Lebanon with all of the instabilities that we've experienced since 1976.

MR. DONALDSON. It's too early to say, as you put it, because you don't believe the cease-fire has been tested long enough. But let me ask the question: After a cease-fire clearly is in place, do we want an immediate Israeli withdrawal?

SECRETARY HAIG. I think we are going to want and to work to achieve adjustments in the withdrawal of all foreign elements from Lebanon. After all, this has been a country that's been wracked by internal elements not under the authority and control of the Lebanese Government, as well as a nation that's been occupied by Syrian forces for too long.

MR. DONALDSON. You ducked the question, Mr. Secretary.

SECRETARY HAIG. I'm sometimes very good at that, Sam, but why don't you ask it again?

MR. DONALDSON. I'm really trying to find out if we want to back up our vote in the U.N. Security Council?

SECRETARY HAIG. Of course.

MR. DONALDSON. Do we want an immediate Israeli withdrawal?

SECRETARY HAIG. Of course. The vote that the United States stood behind and joined the other nations in putting forward was a very clear picture that ultimately there must be a withdrawal of all foreign forces from Lebanon.

MR. WILL. Two short questions: To facilitate an Israeli withdrawal, to fill the vacuum that has been their objective to create in that part of Lebanon, would you be willing to see American troops put into a peacekeeping force?

SECRETARY HAIG. I think, Mr. Will, it's still a hypothetical question.

MR. WILL. But you're not really—

SECRETARY HAIG. We have not given serious thought to U.S. participation in the peacekeeping in Lebanon. However, I think in the hours and days ahead we're going to have to look very, very carefully at what will be necessary to provide a stable situation in southern Lebanon to relieve the tensions which have brought about this disaster in the first place.

MR. WILL. Might it be useful, as a precondition to having whatever settlement we come to in that area, to have a referendum in which the people of that part of Lebanon are asked if they want the PLO and the Syrians back?

SECRETARY HAIG. I wouldn't discount a referendum. I wouldn't discount any step that would strengthen the authority of the central government and bring about a rapprochement, if you will, of the various factions in Lebanon, that is, the Lebanese factions, toward a strengthened central government.

MR. VANOCUR. Mr. Secretary, I take it from the tenor of your remarks today and in the past week that the U.S. Government and, indeed, most of the countries involved, are not too unhappy about the developments.

In other words, the dirty little secret which has existed for some time is that nobody really wants the PLO in Lebanon.

SECRETARY HAIG. I wouldn't suggest there's a dirty little secret because the next question that would be asked is, "Did the United States collude, were we acquiescing in the actions?"

Nothing could be farther from the truth. We regret very much that the situation has

---

[38] Source: Department of State Press Release 198, June 16, 1982; also printed in Department of State *Bulletin*, July 1982, pp. 55–56. For the full text, see *ibid.*, pp. 55–58. Secretary Haig was interviewed on the ABC television program, "This Week With David Brinkley," by Sam Donaldson, Sander Vanocur, and George Will.

resulted in the violence that we've witnessed. On the other hand, I think it's very clear that you must not and cannot have enclaves of separate authority in a sovereign nation and expect the seeds for stability to grow. They will not.

MR. VANOCUR. No. I wasn't suggesting collusion, Mr. Secretary, but I'm suggesting now a question that goes to the heart of what happens next. Is the United States willing to see whatever Israel is trying to do, whether it's playing the Jordanian option or a homeland for the Palestinians?

How far is the United States going to go in symmetry, [with] what seems to be Israeli objectives in the Middle East?

SECRETARY HAIG. It's too early to say. I think our first priority must and must continue to be a cessation of the hostilities and the humanitarian aspects of this problem have got to be dealt with on a most urgent basis.

We've got to work with all of the nations in the region. There are some of those in Western Europe who are concerned to seek to provide a long-term solution in which the sovereignty of Lebanon will again be established.

MR. VANOCUR. Can I just follow up? Work with other European nations. Does that mean Camp David is dead and you're back to the Geneva Conference which would include the Russians?

SECRETARY HAIG. No. Not at all. Camp David is not dead. As a matter of fact, I would hope that these tragic circumstances in Lebanon today would offer new opportunities for a reinvigorating of the Camp David process and to moving forward as we intend to do.

MR. DONALDSON. When the fighting first broke out, you and other American officials were worried that somehow the Soviets might come in, that the whole thing could escalate into that kind of a very dangerous confrontation.

This morning can you say that that now has receded—that danger—that it looks like we'll have a situation where the Soviets will not in any way intervene?

SECRETARY HAIG. Of course, we've been concerned about that from the outset. There have been exchanges between the President and Mr. Brezhnev—exactly two sets of exchanges during the period. I would describe the Soviet attitude thus far as being encouragingly cautious.

The holding of the cease-fire which started 2 days ago—it broke down yesterday with respect to the PLO, which we worked on all night, and again this morning—it appears that the local collapse of the cease-fire in the Beirut area has again been reestablished—the cease-fire has.

So I would hope that all of these circumstances would make it clear to the Soviet leadership that they have no business in intervening or becoming involved in this situation other than to urge those with whom they exercise influence to exercise restraint.

MR. DONALDSON. I didn't realize there were two sets of exchanges. Can you describe them? When did they come? I thought Mr. Brezhnev sent a letter to President Reagan and he replied. When was the second exchange?

SECRETARY HAIG. There was a subsequent communication and reply. A reply went out last night.

MR. DONALDSON. What kind? Can you characterize it?

SECRETARY HAIG. I would characterize it as essentially concerned, but cautiously concerned.

MR. DONALDSON. Concerned but cautiously in what sense? In other words, does this second exchange mean that the Russians were telling us, and we were telling the Russians, "Okay, we've cooled it, it looks like the heat's off?"

SECRETARY HAIG. No. Not in the context of that question. I think it was a continuing expression of concern on the part of the Soviet leadership about the potential dangers of a spreading of the violence, and we share that concern ourselves. It doesn't mean that we accept the Soviet view as to why these conditions occurred, but thus far I would say that the situation is cautious on both sides.

MR. WILL. I'm struck by the fact that you said earlier that no one really wants the status quo ante. When you add to this the fact that two Soviet clients, armed by the Soviet Union and trained by the Soviet Union have been decisively bested in battle by an American ally with American training and American arms, isn't this a tremendous thing? I mean, aren't you really pleased? How can we possibly be displeased about that?

SECRETARY HAIG. Mr. Will, no one is pleased when circumstances involve the loss of innocent lives, and there's been too much of that in Lebanon today. The longer term strategic aspects of this question remain to be seen.

. . . .

Document 359

Statements by the Egyptian Deputy Prime Minister and Foreign Minister (Ali), June 16, 1982 (Extract)[39]

Egypt's Views on the Conflict in Lebanon

. . . .

DEPUTY PRIME MINISTER ALI. Thank you. I've just met with President Reagan and delivered to him a message from President Mubarak. My visit to Washington had been planned for some time, to come and assess the situation in the area in the light of the developments in the Iran–Iraq war as well as on how to enhance the peace efforts following the completion of the Israeli withdrawal from Sinai.

Egypt felt we were on the threshold of achieving progress to bring about peace between Israel and all our Arab brothers, a just and lasting peace based on the fulfillment on the national aspirations of the Palestinians and the achievement of security for everyone in the region, including Israel.

We were all shocked by the second turn of events when the Israeli—when the Israelis decided to invade Lebanon. Since the fifth of June we have seen tragedies taking place there with the loss of life of thousands and the situation of tens of thousands. What we have, a refugee problem to settle from'48 onward, has now been compounded with Palestinians as well as Lebanese becoming new refugees in a destructed land.

Higher risks of larger conflict loom over the horizon. The situation in Lebanon and especially around Beirut is unacceptable. Israeli forces must withdraw from its vicinity. This besieged Arab capital and its government must become free to handle its own destiny.

Today, I have impressed on the President the feeling in our country and in the area for the needs of a determined U.S. leadership and efforts to bring bloodshed to an end, for sanity to prevail, for combatants to treat their prisoners of this tragic war with humanity and according to international law and convention. That now, above all, is the time for the United States to do everything possible so that war comes to an end and peace could prevail.

I found the President deeply concerned. He assured me that the United States will deploy every effort to bring about a ceasefire respected and enduring, that the United States [will] stand by its vote on Resolutions 508 and 509 of the Security Council calling on Israel to withdraw its forces from Lebanon.

I found him convinced that the Lebanese people must be left to themselves to form a strong central government that can assure the safety, stability, and territorial integrity of Lebanon that must be respected by everyone in the area and beyond.

He assured me, as well, that the United States will continue to play the full partner role in their efforts to bring about a comprehensive peace in the Middle East, that more than ever before he was convinced that the Palestinians must have hope about their future. We count on that active leadership role in the days and weeks ahead.

Peace, stability, prosperity—the Middle East needs it. Interests of the United States call for it.

Thank you.

. . . .

---

[39] Source: White House Press Release, June 16, 1982, Office of the Press Secretary to the President. The remarks were made in the West Wing Driveway of the White House at 3:10 p.m., following a meeting with President Reagan. Omitted are Secretary Haig's introduction of Ali and responses to questions by Haig and Ali following Ali's statement.

Document 360

Resolution 511 (1982), Adopted by the U.N. Security Council, June 18, 1982[40]

Extension of the UNIFIL Mandate for Two Months

The Security Council,

Recalling its resolutions 425 (1978), 426 (1978), 427 (1978), 434 (1978), 444 (1979), 450 (1979), 459 (1979), 467 (1980), 483 (1980), 488 (1981), 490 (1981), 498 (1981), and 501 (1982),

Reaffirming its resolutions 508 (1982) and 509 (1982),

Having studied the report of the Secretary-General on the United Nations Interim Force in Lebanon (S/15194 and Add.1 and 2) and taking note of the conclusions and recommendations expressed therein,

Bearing in mind the need to avoid any developments which could further aggravate the situation and the need, pending an examination of the situation by the Council in all its aspects, to preserve in place the capacity of the United Nations to assist in the restoration of the peace,

1. *Decides* as an interim measure, to extend the present mandate of the Force for a period of two months, that is, until 19 August 1982;

2. *Authorizes* the Force during that period, to carry out, in addition, the interim tasks referred to in paragraph 17 of the Secretary-General's report (S/15194/Add.2);[41]

3. *Calls on* all concerned to extend full co-operation to the Force in the discharge of its tasks;

4. *Requests* the Secretary-General to keep the Security Council regularly informed of the implementation of resolutions 508 (1982) and 509 (1982) and the present resolution.

Document 361

Resolution 512 (1982), Adopted by the U.N. Security Council, June 19, 1982[42]

Appeal for Humanitarian Assistance to Lebanon

The Security Council,

Deeply concerned at the sufferings of the Lebanese and Palestinian civilian populations,

Referring to the humanitarian principles of the Geneva Conventions of 1949[43] and to the obligations arising from the regulations annexed to the Hague Convention of 1907,

Reaffirming its resolutions 508 (1982) and 509 (1982),

1. *Calls upon* all the parties to the conflict to respect the rights of the civilian populations, to refrain from all acts of violence against those populations and to take all appropriate measures to alleviate the suffering caused by the conflict, in particular, by facilitating the dispatch and distribution of aid provided by United Nations agencies and by non-governmental organizations, in particular, the International Committee of the Red Cross (ICRC);

2. *Appeals* to Member States to continue to provide the most extensive humanitarian aid possible;

3. *Stresses* the particular humanitarian responsibilities of the United Nations and its agencies, including the United Nations Relief and Works Agency for Palestine Refugees in the Near East (UNRWA), towards civilian populations and calls upon all the parties to the conflict not to hamper the exercise of those responsibilities and to assist in humanitarian efforts;

---

[40] Source: U.N. Security Council Resolution 511 (1982); also printed in Department of State *Bulletin*, September 1982, p. 15. The resolution was adopted by a vote of 13 (including the United States) to 0, with 2 abstentions. For Ambassador Kirkpatrick's statement supporting Resolution 511, see *ibid.*, p. 16. Further extensions were made for 2 months by U.N. Security Council Resolution 519 (1982) of August 17 and for 3 months by U.N. Security Council Resolution 523 (1982) of October 18, 1982. The United States voted for these resolutions also.

[41] UNIFIL's interim tasks involved attempting to provide protection and humanitarian assistance to the Lebanese population.

[42] Source: U.N. Security Council Resolution 512 (1982); also printed in Department of State *Bulletin*, September 1982, p. 16. The resolution was adopted unanimously.

[43] For the texts of the four Red Cross conventions, dated at Geneva, August 12, 1949, entered into force for the United States, February 2, 1956, see 6 UST 3114, 3217, 3316, and 3516.

4. *Takes note* of the measures taken by the Secretary-General to co-ordinate the activities of the international agencies in this field and requests him to make every effort to ensure the implementation of and compliance with this resolution and to report on these efforts to the Council as soon as possible.

Document 362

Statements by President Reagan and Israeli Prime Minister Begin, June 21, 1982[44]

Israel's Need for Security Before Withdrawal From Lebanon

The President. It has been worthwhile to have Prime Minister Begin at the White House again. All of us share a common understanding of the need to bring peace and security to the Middle East.

Today, we've had an opportunity to exchange views on how this cause can be advanced. On Lebanon, it's clear that we and Israel, both, seek an end to the violence there and a sovereign, independent Lebanon under the authority of a strong, central government.

We agree that Israel must not be subjected to violence from the North, and the United States will continue to work to achieve these goals and to secure withdrawal of all foreign forces from Lebanon.

And, now, our guest, Prime Minister Begin.

Prime Minister Begin. Thank you, Mr. President.

Mr. President, ladies and gentlemen. Good afternoon.

I'm deeply grateful to my friend, the President of the United States, for his invitation to come to visit with him again after my first visit in September 1981[45] in the White House, and all the discussion—a very fruitful discussion with the President and his advisors.

Everybody knows that we face now a situation in the Middle East which calls for activity, great attention and understanding. I have read in some newspapers in this great country that Israel invaded Lebanon. This is a misnomer. Israel did not invade any country. You do invade a land when you want to conquer it, or to an exist [annex it?], or, at least, to conquer part of it. We don't covet even one inch of Lebanese territory. And, vehemently, we will withdraw our troops—all of our troops and bring them back home as soon as possible. As soon as possible means as soon as arrangements are made that never again will our citizens—men, women and children be attacked, maimed and killed by armed bands operating from Lebanon, and armed and supported by the Soviet Union and its satellites.

There is hope to believe that such arrangements will be made, and that all foreign forces without exception will be withdrawn from Lebanon. And there will be an independent, free Lebanon based on its territorial integrity. And the day's near that such a Lebanon and Israel will sign a peace treaty and live in peace forever.

Thank you.

Document 363

Statement by the Alternate Representative at the United Nations (Lichenstein) Before the U.N. Security Council, June 26, 1982[46]

Call for Elimination of Armed Palestinians From Lebanon

Mr. President, the fundamental basis of the policy of the United States is now and

---

[44] Source: White House Press Release, June 21, 1982, Office of the Press Secretary to the President; printed also in *Weekly Compilation of Presidential Documents*, June 28, 1982, pp. 823–824. President Reagan spoke to reporters on the South Grounds of the White House at 1:56 p.m., after a private meeting with Prime Minister Begin in the Oval Office and lunch in the Residence. The Prime Minister visited Washington, June 20–22, 1982.

[45] Regarding this visit, see Secretary Haig's statement, September 10, 1981, in *American Foreign Policy: Current Documents, 1981*, document 357.

[46] Source: U.S. Mission to the United Nations Press Release USUN 48(82), June 26, 1982; also printed in Department of State *Bulletin*, September 1982, p. 17.

has consistently been to contribute to the restoration of the Government of Lebanon's full authority throughout its land and its sovereignty and territorial integrity.

My government is deeply moved by the suffering of the Lebanese people in the present crisis.

We had hoped that the draft resolution before the Security Council tonight would have reflected this basic concern.[47] Unfortunately, the draft resolution, while containing many elements we support, fails to call for the essential requisite for the restoration of the authority of the Government of Lebanon—that is, the elimination from Beirut and elsewhere of the presence of armed Palestinian elements who neither submit to nor respect the sovereign authority of the Lebanese Government. The omission of this requisite, in our view, thus, is inconsistent with the essential goal of restoration of Lebanese sovereignty. This, we believe, is a fatal flaw.

The resolution does contain many elements that we support—namely, 1) a call for an immediate cease-fire, 2) a call for simultaneous withdrawal of Israeli and Palestinian forces from the area of Beirut, and 3) the proposal that U.N. observers, upon the request of the Government of Lebanon, monitor the cease-fire.

The members of this Council are well aware of the threat which armed foreign elements pose to the authority of the Government of Lebanon and to stability throughout the region. We deeply regret that this essential factor was not accorded the weight we believed it must have in the draft resolution before us.

Thank you, sir.

---

[47] The U.N. Security Council draft resolution, introduced by France, called for a cease-fire by all parties, withdrawal of Israeli forces to 10 kilometers from Beirut as a first step to complete Israeli withdrawal from Lebanon, and withdrawal of armed Palestinian forces from Beirut to existing camps. (U.N. document S/15255/Rev. 2) The draft resolution failed of adoption by a vote of 14 in favor to 1 (United States) against, a veto, on June 26.

Document 364

Resolution ES–7/5, Adopted by the U.N. General Assembly, June 26, 1982[48]

Demand for Israeli Withdrawal From Lebanon

The General Assembly,

Having considered the question of Palestine at its resumed seventh emergency special session,

Having heard the statement of the Palestine Liberation Organization, the representative of the Palestinian people,[49]

Alarmed by the worsening situation in the Middle East resulting from Israel's acts of aggression against the sovereignty of Lebanon and the Palestinian people in Lebanon,

Recalling Security Council resolutions 508 (1982) of 5 June 1982, 509 (1982) of 6 June 1982 and 512 (1982) of 19 June 1982,[50]

Taking note of the reports of the Secretary-General relevant to this situation, particularly his report of 7 June 1982,[51]

Taking note of the two positive replies to the Secretary-General by the Government of Lebanon[52] and the Palestine Liberation Organization,[53]

Noting with regret that the Security Council has, so far, failed to take effective and practical measures, in accordance with the Charter of the United Nations, to ensure implementation of its resolutions 508 (1982) and 509 (1982),

Referring to the humanitarian principles of the Geneva Convention relative to the

---

[48] Source: U.N. General Assembly Resolution ES–7/5, June 26, 1982; also printed in Department of State *Bulletin*, September 1982, pp. 18–20. This resolution was adopted by a vote of 127 to 2 (including the United States). In explaining the U.S. vote against the resolution, Charles M. Lichenstein, Alternate Representative at the United Nations, characterized it as "an unbalanced statement which may well have the effect of heightening the underlying animosities in Lebanon and actually increasing the danger of a wider conflict." For the text of this statement before the U.N. General Assembly, June 26, see *ibid.*, pp. 17–18.

[49] See A/ES–7/PV.22. [Footnote in the source text.]

[50] See document 360.

[51] S/15178. [Footnote in the source text.]

[52] *Ibid.*, para. 3]Footnote in the source text.]

[53] *Ibid.*, para. 4. [Footnote in the source text.]

Protection of Civilian Persons in Time of War, of 12 August 1949,[54] and to the obligations arising from the regulations annexed to the Hague Conventions of 1907,[55]

Deeply concerned at the sufferings of the Palestinian and Lebanese civilian populations,

Reaffirming once again its conviction that the question of Palestine is the core of the Arab-Israeli conflict and that no comprehensive, just and lasting peace in the region will be achieved without the full exercise by the Palestinian people of its inalienable national rights,

Reaffirming further that a just and comprehensive settlement of the situation in the Middle East cannot be achieved without the participation on an equal footing of all the parties to the conflict, including the Palestine Liberation Organization as the representative of the Palestinian people,

1. *Reaffirms* the fundamental principle of the inadmissibility of the acquisition of territory by force;

2. *Demands* that all Member States and other parties observe strict respect for Lebanon's sovereignty, territorial integrity, unity and political independence within its internationally recognized boundaries;

3. *Decides* to support fully the provisions of Security Council resolutions 508 (1982) and 509 (1982) in which the Council, *inter alia,* demanded that:

(*a*) Israel withdraw all its military forces forthwith and unconditionally to the internationally recognized boundaries of Lebanon;

(*b*) All parties to the conflict cease immediately and simultaneously all military activities within Lebanon and across the Lebanese-Israeli border;

4. *Condemns* Israel for its non-compliance with resolutions 508 (1982) and 509 (1982);

5. *Demands* that Israel comply with all the above provisions no later than 0600 hours, (Beirut time) on Sunday, 27 June 1982;

6. *Calls upon* the Security Council to authorize the Secretary-General to undertake necessary endeavours and practical steps to implement the provisions of resolutions 508 (1982), 509 (1982) and 512 (1982);

7. *Urges* the Security Council, in the event of continued failure by Israel to comply with the demands contained in resolutions 508 (1982) and 509 (1982), to meet in order to consider practical ways and means in accordance with the Charter of the United Nations;

8. *Calls upon* all States and international agencies and organizations to continue to provide the most extensive humanitarian aid possible to the victims of the Israeli invasion of Lebanon;

9. *Requests* the Secretary-General to delegate a high-level commission to investigate and assess the extent of loss of human life and material damage and to report, as soon as possible, on the result of this investigation to the General Assembly and the Security Council;

10. *Decides* to adjourn the seventh emergency special session temporarily and to authorize the President of the latest regular session of the General Assembly to resume its meetings upon request from Member States.

Document 365

Statement by President Reagan, June 30, 1982[56]

Authorization of Humanitarian Assistance to Lebanon

I am signing into law today H.R. 6631,[57] a bill which authorizes emergency humanitarian assistance to the unfortunate victims of the hostilities in Lebanon. Providing help to people in need is a tradition in which the American people should take great pride. The suffering in Lebanon continues to mount even as an international humanitarian effort, of which the United States is a part, attempts to aid the hurt, hungry and homeless people in Lebanon.

[54] United Nations, *Treaty Series,* Vol. 75, No. 973, p. 287. [Footnote in the source text.]

[55] Carnegie Endowment for International Peace, *The Hague Conventions and Declarations of 1899 and 1907* (New York, Oxford University Press, 1915). [Footnote in the source text.]

[56] Source: White House Press Release, June 30, 1982, Office of the Press Secretary to the President; printed also in *Weekly Compilation of Presidential Documents,* July 5, 1982, p. 847.

[57] As enacted, H.R. 6631 is P.L. 97–208, approved June 30, 1982; for text see 96 Stat. 138.

I am grateful to the Congress for acting so quickly to authorize assistance for Lebanon, and hope that it will soon make available the $20 million I requested on June 16 [9?] for the relief effort.[58] In the meantime, I have authorized the use of $2 million from the Refugee Emergency Fund and the State Department is reprogramming another $10 million of appropriated funds to meet the most urgent relief needs. As the full impact of this tragedy becomes known, the United States will continue to do its share in the international effort to relieve the suffering of the people in Lebanon.

Document 366

Transcript of a Press Conference by President Reagan, June 30, 1982 (Extracts)[59]

Policy Goals in Lebanon

. . . .

Q. Mr. President, there are some who say that by failing to condemn the Israeli invasion of Lebanon and refusing to cut off arms to the invading armies, the U.S. and Israeli policies have become—and goals—have become identical. Is there a difference, what is it?

Also, is there a difference between the Soviet slaughter of Afghans, which the United States has condemned so often, and the killing of Lebanese and the displaced people of Palestine? If so, what's the difference?

THE PRESIDENT. Helen, you've asked a question that—or several questions that I have to walk a very narrow line in answering.

There's no question but that we had hoped for a diplomatic settlement and believed there could have been a diplomatic settlement in the Middle East, in that situation.

We were not warned or notified of the invasion that was going to take place.

On the other hand, there had been a breaking of the cease-fire, which had held for about 11 months in that area.

I think there are differences between some of these things that are going on and things like just the outright invasion of Afghanistan by a foreign power determined to impose its will on another country. We have a situation in Lebanon in which there was a force, the PLO, literally a government within a government and with its own army. And they had pursued aggression themselves across a border by way of rocket firing and artillery barrages.

But the situation is so complicated and the goals that we would like to pursue are what are dictating our conduct right now. We want the bloodshed to end, there's no question about that. We didn't want it to start. But we've seen Lebanon for 7 years now divided into several factions, each faction with its own militia, not a government in control. We have seen, as I've said, this PLO and we've seen the invasion of other forces, the presence of the Syrians as well in Lebanon.

Right now, our goals are, as for the first time in 7 years the Lebanese seem to be trying to get together and their factions have come together seeking a way to have a central government and have control of their own country and to have a single Lebanese army. That is one of the goals we would like to see.

The other goal would be the guaranteeing of the southern border with Israel, that there would be no longer a force in Lebanon that could, when it chose, create acts of terror across that border.

And the third goal is to get all the foreign forces, Syrians, Israelis, and the armed PLO, out of Lebanon. And we're—

Q. People have been displaced in Palestine.

THE PRESIDENT. Yes, and I signed a bill this morning for $50 million in aid for Lebanon there,[60] where several hundred thousand of those Palestinians are. I don't think they were all displaced from one area and they have been refugees now into ongoing generations.

---

[58] On June 9, President Reagan made available $5 million in emergency relief assistance to Lebanon, and asked Congress to provide an additional $20 million for relief and rehabilitation. (*Weekly Compilation of Presidential Documents,* June 14, 1982, p. 780) On June 18, he authorized an additional $10 million, to be drawn from existing appropriations. (*Ibid.,* June 21, 1982, pp. 819–820)

[59] Source: White House Press Release, June 30, 1982, Office of the Press Secretary to the President; also printed in *Weekly Compilation of Presidential Documents,* July 5, 1982, pp. 850–857. The press conference was held in the East Room of the White House, beginning at 8 p.m.

[60] See *supra.*

I think, when I say PLO one has to differentiate between the PLO and the Palestinians. And out of this, also, we have another goal, and it's been our goal for quite some time. And that is to, once and for all—when these other things are accomplished, once and for all, to deal with the problem of the Palestinians and settle that problem within the proposals and the suggestions that were made in the Camp David Accords.

. . . .

Q. Mr. President, many Arab States are saying that if Israel invades Beirut—West Beirut, it can only be because you have given Israel a green light to do so. Have you done so? Will you? And what will be your attitude if Israel goes into West Beirut?

THE PRESIDENT. Sam, again this is the type of question in which, with the negotiations at the point they are, that I can't answer. I would like to say this: No, I've given no green light whatsoever. And an impression that I know some of the neighboring states there have had from the beginning is that somehow we were aware of this and we gave permission or something. No, we were caught as much by surprise as anyone, and we wanted a diplomatic solution and believe there could have been one.

Q. But, sir, if I may, last week your Deputy Press Secretary said that when Prime Minister Begin was here, he promised you that Israel would go no further into Beirut.[61]

THE PRESIDENT. I think also—his not having heard the conversation between Prime Minister Begin and myself, that what he called a promise actually was in a discussion in which, to be more accurate, the Prime Minister had said to me that they didn't want to and that they had not wanted to from the beginning.

Q. So it was not a promise not to do it.

THE PRESIDENT. No.

. . . .

Q. Mr. President, some Israeli officials have acknowledged in recent days the use of cluster bombs in the war in Lebanon.[62] How much does this concern you?

THE PRESIDENT. It concerns me very much, as the whole thing does. And, Judy, we have a review going now, as we must by law, of the use of weapons and whether American weapons sold there were used offensively and not defensively, and that situation is very ambiguous. The only statement that we have heard so far with regard to the cluster bomb was one military official—Israeli official—has apparently made that statement publicly and we know no more about it than what we ourselves have read in the press. But the review is going forward and the review that would lead to what the law requires, that we must inform the Congress as to whether we believe there was a question of this being an offensive attack or whether it was in self defense.

When I said ambiguous you must recall that prior to this attack Soviet-built rockets and 180 millimeter cannons were shelling villages across the border in Israel and causing civilian casualties.

. . . .

Document 367

Remarks by President Reagan, Los Angeles, July 1, 1982 (Extracts)[63]

The Israeli Invasion of Lebanon

. . . .

Q. Mr. President, you said yesterday that Mr. Begin's pledge to you that came during

[61] Reference is to a statement by Larry M. Speakes, Deputy Press Secretary to the President, at the 12:20 p.m. White House Press Briefing on June 24, 1982.

[62] In a statement broadcast on the Jerusalem Domestic Service on June 28, 1982, Major General Aharon Yariv, serving with the Northern Command, Israeli Defense Forces, acknowledged that Israeli forces had used cluster bombs and shells against Syrian troops in Lebanon. (Foreign Broadcast Information Service, *Daily Report: Middle East and Africa,* July 1, 1982, p. I10)

[63] Source: White House Press Release, July 1, 1982, Office of the Press Secretary to the President; also printed in *Weekly Compilation of Presidential Documents,* July 5, 1982, pp. 860–863. President Reagan spoke during a meeting with editors and broadcasters of the western region in the Beverly Hills Room of the Century Plaza Hotel, beginning at 1:22 p.m.

the meeting last week had been mistakenly reported as a promise that Israel would not invade further into Lebanon, that in fact he had said only that he hoped that Israel would not have to invade further into Lebanon.[64] If that is true, number one, how could that have happened? And number two, why was the erroneous report allowed to go uncorrected for so long?

THE PRESIDENT. On the pledge idea, I did not know—he had several conversations with other people. And when I first heard that he had made this promise, I was going to check with the State Department to see had he said it there. It turned out that it—and how it could happen was, I think, explainable. It was a case of the second-hand repeating—maybe even third-hand—within the shop of the conversation that I had had with him, which was a conversation just between the two of us and at which he had expressed the fact that he did not want to invade Lebanon. This had never been his intention. And how the cease-fires kept being broken and so forth and it arrived to that threatening place. And so, as soon as I realized that it was based on my conversation with him, I corrected the fact that, no, he had not promised. He had said that that had not been his intention, and he did not want to if he could avoid it.

. . . .

Q. Thank you, Mr. President. Jeanne Innerson from King Television in Seattle. It was reported today the Egyptian Foreign Minister said that your administration knew about Israel's pending invasion of Lebanon and didn't do anything about it in return for Israeli promise of support for Mr. Haig's presidency in 1984.[65] Could you comment on both parts of that question? (Laughter)

THE PRESIDENT. You say the Egyptian Ambassador said that?

Q. No, it was said by the Egyptian Minister of State for Foreign Affairs today. He also said that it is the widespread perception among Arab countries.

THE PRESIDENT. Oh, he needs to be talked to. (Laughter) No, and we do know—and this is very troublesome—it is very difficult for me to comment—and I have been grateful that there haven't been more Lebanon questions because the negotiations are so delicate right now that, as I said last night in the press conference, that there is very little that I can answer. But this I can answer. We know that the Arab States—and many of which we've been trying to establish a bond with them so that we can bring them into the peacemaking process with Israel. And we've called it "create more Egypts." This is the only way we're going to settle that particular problem in the Middle East, is if we can get more Arab nations that are willing to come forward as Egypt did and establish a peace treaty, recognize the right of Israel to exist. And we've been doing this.

We're terribly disturbed, because it has come to our attention that for some reason they are convinced that we—if we did not actually connive and give our consent, that we were aware of it and did nothing about it. We were caught as much by surprise as anyone.

We've had Phil Habib there who, as you know—and God bless him, if there's ever a hero—Phil Habib, as you know, created, when we first sent him there, and has kept alive for 11 months until this latest tragedy the cease-fire in the Middle East. He's done a superhuman job. And he's still there and negotiating. And that's why I don't want to do anything to louse up his act.

But we knew that they had gone up to the border as a threat. We knew they'd mobilized; the whole world knew that and were all writing and talking about it. And it is true that the PLO from across the border had shelled and rocket-attacked some of the villages in Israel. And—but when they crossed the border—and presumably to go only 40 kilometers and then form a line to protect their border against these artillery attacks, that was a surprise. Then when they did not stop—and they justified that on the basis that once they tried to stop, they were under attack, and they had to keep pursuing the enemy—no, this is—was not done with our approval or our consent.

And I will have to say on behalf of Al Haig—number one, I don't believe he has such ambitions, and, number two, believe me, he's served his country too long to have done anything of that kind. He never would have. And we're—we're continuing with everything we can do now—we've been 5 days in the present cease-fire, and we're just hanging on that—that we can maintain and that the negotiations will be successful. And

---

[64] See *supra*.

[65] Reference is to a July 1, 1982 report of a statement by Butrus Ghali, Egyptian Minister of State for Foreign Affairs; see Foreign Broadcast Information Service, *Daily Report: Middle East and Africa*, July 2, 1982, p. D1.

as I said last night—I'll repeat them—the three goals are: For Lebanon to create a stable government which they haven't had for 7 years. They've had several factions, each with its own militia—but a single united Lebanese army and Government controlling its own territory, guaranteeing the border between Israel—because so far they've had another government and army living within their midst, the PLO—changing that; and then all the other countries getting out of Lebanon. And we're working as hard as we can to that end.

But anything you can all do to convince the Arab States—we're trying our best. But, no, we were not a party to that.

. . . .

Document 368

Resolution 513 (1982), Adopted by the U.N. Security Council, July 4, 1982[66]

The Alarming Violence Against Civilians in Lebanon

The Security Council,

Alarmed by the continued sufferings of the Lebanese and Palestinian civilian populations in South Lebanon and in West Beirut,

Referring to the humanitarian principles of the Geneva Conventions of 1949 and to the obligations arising from the Regulations annexed to the Hague Convention of 1907,

Reaffirming its resolutions 508 (1982), 509 (1982) and 512 (1982),

1. *Calls* for respect for the rights of the civilian populations without any discrimination and repudiates all acts of violence against those populations;

2. *Calls further* for the restoration of the normal supply of vital facilities such as water, electricity, food and medical provisions, particularly in Beirut;

3. *Commends* the efforts of the Secretary-General and the action of international agencies to alleviate the sufferings of the civilian population and requests them to continue their efforts to ensure their success.

Document 369

Statement by President Reagan, Los Angeles, July 6, 1982 (Extract)[67]

Agreement in Principle to Contribute U.S. Personnel for Peacekeeping in Beirut

Thank you all very much. And before turning to the question of Federalism, I know that many of you here today share our great concern about the tragedy that's been occurring in Lebanon. And I thought I might give you just a brief update.

In recent days Ambassador Habib and others have been working tirelessly to bring peace to that troubled region. We're dealing with extremely delicate and fast-moving negotiations to save West Beirut and to bring the withdrawal of all forces from Lebanon. The situation is too sensitive for detailed discussion, but I can report to you that this weekend in discussions with Mr. Habib the Government of Lebanon told us that a multinational force might be essential for a temporary peacekeeping in Beirut and informally proposed that the United States consider making a contribution to that force.

The Lebanese Government has not made a formal proposal, but I have agreed in principle to contribute a small contingent of U.S. personnel subject to certain conditions. The United States has pledged to do all that it can do to bring peace and stability to the Middle East and we must keep that pledge.

Obviously, there's much work still to be done. I can't overemphasize the delicacy of

---

[66] Source: U.N. Security Council Resolution 513 (1982); also printed in Department of State *Bulletin,* September 1982, p. 20. The resolution was adopted unanimously.

[67] Source: White House Press Release, July 6, 1982, Office of the Press Secretary to the President; also printed in *Weekly Compilation of Presidential Documents,* July 12, 1982, p. 876. President Reagan spoke during a meeting with State and local Government officials in the Beverly Hills Room at the Century Plaza Hotel, beginning at 11:04 a.m. The omitted portion is the President's remarks on federalism.

these negotiations. I can only say that in coming days we'll press forward. And I can, once again, praise the work of Ambassador Habib who has labored heroically in recent days.

. . . .

Document 370

Transcript of the Department of State Daily Press Briefing, July 6, 1982 (Extract)[68]

The Israeli Blockade of West Beirut

. . . .

Q. Dean, what is the administration's position on the total blockade being imposed against West Beirut by the Israelis? I understand today that the blockade continues, and all the crossing points, all services have been stopped—water, electricity, food, medication, and all the others.

A. We have the deepest concern about the human dimension of this conflict. We urge, as we have urged, that power and water service be restored to West Beirut as soon as possible. I am informed that water service has been restored, and electricity has not yet been restored.

More than that, through seeking to maintain the cease-fire and to bring about a peaceful solution, we are trying to prevent actions that endanger the lives and welfare of innocent civilians. We are engaged, in cooperation with international relief agencies, in a significant effort under the President's Lebanon relief coordinator, Mr. Peter McPherson, to relieve the suffering of affected civilian populations in Lebanon.

As you know, last weekend we joined other members of the Security Council in adopting Resolution 513 calling for protection of civilian populations in Lebanon without discrimination, and the restoration of the normal supply of vital services.[69] We urge all parties to the conflict to respect the rights of all civilians affected by the situation in Lebanon, and further to cooperate with relief efforts.

. . . .

[68] Source: Office of Press Relations, Department of State. Dean Fischer, Department of State Spokesman, conducted the briefing, which began at 12:39 p.m.

Document 371

Transcript of a White House Press Briefing, July 16, 1982 (Extracts)[70]

Israeli Use of U.S.-Supplied Arms in Lebanon

. . . .

Q. What about the letter that was sent to Congress on Israel?

MR. SPEAKES. We can confirm there was a letter sent to Congress regarding that situation but its contents are classified so we do not have any further comment.

Q. What is the situation—

MR. SPEAKES. The situation in Israel and Lebanon and the Middle East. Signed by the Acting Secretary of State Stoessel.[71]

Q. The letter says there may have been substantial violations of U.S. arms sales agreements in the use of American-made arms for purposes other than those provided for in the agreements.[72] Can you confirm that?

MR. SPEAKES. Cannot confirm that. Classified.

Q. Do you deny that?

[69] See document 368.

[70] Source: Office of the Press Secretary to the President. Larry Speakes, Deputy Press Secretary to the President, conducted the briefing, which began at 12:33 p.m.

[71] Walter J. Stoessel, Jr., Deputy Secretary of State, served as Acting Secretary of State from July 5 to 16, 1982.

[72] The Mutual Defense Assistance Agreement of July 23, 1952, between Israel and the United States sets forth the purposes for which Israel may use U.S.-supplied defense articles. For text, see 3 UST 4985.

MR. SPEAKES. Don't deny it; don't confirm it. Don't do anything on it.

Q. Does the President feel he's fulfilled his obligations now under the law to make a determination?[73]

MR. SPEAKES. Determinations are required by the law. That does then mean that Congress has the opportunity to either make a finding or that the President can make a finding. Neither of those have been done at this time.

. . . .

Q. Have we heard from Israel on the cluster bomb issue?

MR. SPEAKES. We have not. We've made repeated inquiries and have not.

Q. Are we still seeking more information from Israel or does this sending of the letter close it as far as you're concerned?

MR. SPEAKES. I just wouldn't want to get into that. We are seeking more information from Israel on the cluster bomb—alleged use of cluster bombs.

Q. Let me ask you something—just to follow up on that. Am I correct that there is a separate 1978 agreement that effects—that pertains to cluster bombs being used?

MR. SPEAKES. That's true.

Q. Which has a higher standard—a different standard than the—

MR. SPEAKES. Yes, I couldn't—that agreement is also classified but there are different restrictions on the use of cluster bombs and other weapons.

Q. Does that require another letter—a separate letter—

MR. SPEAKES. No, not necessarily, no.

Q. Why is the United States having such difficulty nailing down this cluster bomb question?

MR. SPEAKES. We have not had a response from the Israelis.

Q. —an Israeli military official who publicly acknowledged that they had used them, General Yariv.

MR. SPEAKES. That's true, Curtis, but that was not in any capacity as an official. That, in fact, is the only acknowledgement from the Israelis of this matter. And that was not—

Q. He announced it publicly in a press briefing at the Defense Ministry in Tel Aviv.

MR. SPEAKES. That's true. But that did not constitute any official reply to our official request.

Q. You haven't gotten anything official from them?

MR. SPEAKES. No.

Q. Are we notifying them that our patience is running short—our time is running out and we want an answer?

MR. SPEAKES. I wouldn't characterize it in that fashion but we have made repeated requests to the Israelis.

. . . .

Document 372

Transcript of a White House Press Briefing, July 19, 1982 (Extracts)[74]

The Lebanon Conflict and U.S. Arms Deliveries to Israel

MR. SPEAKES. . . . The President is reviewing the reply from Israel received here on Friday and associated factors. The review is taking place by an interagency group. They will make recommendations to the President.

---

[73] Section 304 (B)(1) of the Arms Export Control Act (P.L. 94–329, approved June 30, 1976) directs the President to report to Congress promptly upon receipt of information on violation of any agreement on the use of U.S.-supplied defense articles. It also provides that a country may be deemed ineligible for credit or cash sales of defense articles in case of a violation, if the President so determines and so reports to Congress, or if Congress so determines by joint resolution. Notwithstanding a Presidential determination of ineligibility, cash sales and deliveries pursuant to previous sales may be made if the President certifies in writing to the Congress that a termination would have significant adverse impact on U.S. security, unless Congress adopts or has adopted a joint resolution with respect to such ineligibility. For text, see 90 Stat. 754.

[74] Source: Office of the Press Secretary to the President. Larry Speakes, Deputy Press Secretary to the President, conducted the briefing, which began at 2:13 p.m.

In making his decision, he will, of course, consider the recommendations of his advisors.

Until that review is completed, there will be no shipments of artillery projectiles or other CBU-related materials—cluster bomb unit-related materials.

Q. That includes the air-dropped units as well as the artillery units? Is that right?

MR. SPEAKES. Any cluster bomb unit-related materials, which would include that.

Now the major item here that you see is artillery projectiles. Now while we are continuing our overall review of the entire question of the use of U.S.-supplied arms—

Q. Entire question of—

MR. SPEAKES.—other materials will continue to be shipped.

Q. Why make the difference?

MR. SPEAKES. That was the President's judgment on that one item.

Q. What are the other—

Q. Does this reflect the belief up front that there may be more evidence of a misuse of the cluster bombs than of the other matériel?

MR. SPEAKES. No, I wouldn't indicate that, Sam. I indicated that there were certain items that were currently—or near the point of being shipped and these were those.

. . . .

MR. SPEAKES. We are getting into an area, Curtis, I guess where we are skirting on what we have got classified and what we have not. We acknowledged on Friday[75] that there was a letter that went up to the Hill. We did not reveal its contents due to the sensitive nature of the negotiations.

Q. What about F–16's that have been used in bombing Beirut? Is that a claim? Has anybody raised that, officially, as a misuse of U.S.-made weapons?

MR. SPEAKES. Whenever there is activity of the type that has taken place since June 6th in Lebanon, we do look at all aspects of the matter. And we said that beginning in Paris when the outbreak of fighting occurred. But we now have acknowledged that a letter went forward to the Hill. But we did not reveal its contents.

Q. Let me follow this up on the F–16's. What is the status of the next shipment of F–16's? Is that under review?

MR. ALLIN.[76] I do not know when there are anymore F–16's to go, if there are indeed any in the current shipment.

Q. They are sending 75 more.

MR. ALLIN. That is not a shipment. That is a notification to Congress which deals with planes that were scheduled to go in 1985.

Q. You informally notified Congress that you were going to do this?

MR. SPEAKES. That is right, and we did not send the formal notification pending the President's decision. And he has not made a decision.

Q. What is the status of it? Is it under review?

MR. SPEAKES. No; the President has not made a decision as to when this notification goes forward, the timing of the notification. And, when he makes a decision, he will.

Q. What is the delay?

MR. SPEAKES. We are waiting on the President to make his mind up.

Q. I understand that there are 11 F–15's still due Israel under existing agreements.

MR. SPEAKES. John, I do not have those kinds of details.

Q. Larry, would you say that the only thing that differentiates the CBU from all of the other matters under review is the fact that the CBU's were about to be shipped?

MR. SPEAKES. I would characterize that as an error.

MR. ALLIN. The fact of the CBU's is that they are sold to Israel under restrictions that vary somewhat from other equipment. Unfortunately for both us and for you, those restrictions are classified. We cannot go into them. But they are separate from other U.S.-supplied equipment. And for that reason, this review is being conducted separately.

Q. Larry, if this weapon is apparently so repulsive in its use, why is the United States making such a weapon?

MR. SPEAKES. I do not really know how to answer that.

. . . .

[75] See the White House Press Briefing, *supra*.

[76] Lyndon K. (Mort) Allin, Deputy Press Secretary to the President.

Document 373

Transcript of a White House Press Briefing, July 20, 1982 (Extracts)[77]

Visit of the Saudi Arabian and Syrian Foreign Ministers

. . . .

[SENIOR ADMINISTRATION OFFICIAL.] The meeting began at 11:15 a.m. and present on the U.S. side were the President, the Vice President, Secretary Shultz, Judge Clark, and Ambassador Veliotes and members of the NSC staff.

And from the Saudi side, there were Prince Saud, Ambassador Alhegalan, and Dr. Shawaf from Saudi Arabia.

And from the Syrian side, the Minister of Foreign Affairs; the Syrian Ambassador, Mr. Jouejati; and Dr. Sabah Qabammi.

The meeting, as you know, was scheduled to go from 11:15 a.m. to 12 p.m., in fact, ran over 20–25 minutes and I think indicative of the seriousness of the discussions we had.

. . . .

[SENIOR ADMINISTRATION OFFICIAL.] The meetings were primarily dedicated to the situation in Lebanon. There was a good exchange of views. A follow-on to the—oh, almost 3 hours of discussions that Secretary Shultz had had yesterday in the State Department and the fact that the President personally has spent so much time today on this issue is another indication of his personal commitment in this matter and his support of Ambassador Habib and his mission.

We did exchange views, some new ideas, which are going to form the basis of further discussions. In addition to discussing Lebanon both in the White House and in the State Department yesterday, of course, we discussed the overall Palestinian issue. This was touched on in the White House because you can't discuss the current problem in Lebanon without quickly getting to the core issue which is the Palestinian problem itself.

In that respect, to the extent these discussions touched on that issue, the President reiterated our commitment to making progress, a renewed commitment, if you will, in light of the situation in Lebanon within the framework of the Camp David Accords.

The other side reiterated their own well-known concerns for the Palestinian—on the Palestinian issue in the context of Lebanon and beyond.

. . . .

Document 374

Transcript of the Department of State Daily Press Briefing, July 26, 1982 (Extract)[78]

U.S. Congressional Delegation Meets With Yasir Arafat

. . . .

Q. Is there anything in our agreement with Israel which would preclude us from encouraging the PLO to take the steps that we have outlined?

A. Anything in our position which you say would—

[77] Source: Office of the Press Secretary to the President. The briefing was conducted on background in the Briefing Room of the White House by senior administration officials, beginning at 1:05 p.m. The Saudi and Syrian Foreign Ministers comprised one of five different teams that met with different permanent members of the U.N. Security Council following an Arab League meeting. Saudi Arabian Foreign Minister Prince Saud al-Faisal was accompanied by Ambassador Sheikh Faisal Alhegalan and by Sheikh Hassan Shawaf, Director of the Office of the Foreign Minister. Syrian Foreign Minister Abd al-Halim Khaddam was accompanied by Ambassador Rafic Jouejati and by Sabah Qabammi, Director of American Affairs and Ambassador to the United States from 1974 to 1980.

[78] Source: Office of Press Relations, Department of State. Dean Fischer, Department of State Spokesman, conducted the briefing, which began at 1:02 p.m.

Q. Would preclude us from encouraging the PLO to take the sort of steps which you have outlined?

A. I think it's up to the PLO to decide when or if they are going to meet our conditions in order for us to open up a dialogue with them.

Q. At a breakfast this morning with reporters, Ashraf Ghorbal, the Egyptian Ambassador, said that to minimize what Arafat has done now is to lose opportunities. He would have liked to have seen the United States encourage Arafat rather than, in his words, "to treat with more of a welcome what Arafat has done." Do you have any reaction to that?

A. No specific reaction to that. It seems to me that there should be no doubt in Mr. Arafat's mind about what it is that we expect of them if we are to have any dialogue with them.

Q. Do you view the phenomenon of an American Congressman getting involved in Mideast diplomacy as a positive development?

A. Let me say that the State Department does not comment on the activities of individual Congressmen during the course of their meetings with foreign officials and persons.

I would simply have to refer you to Congressman McCloskey for elaboration on his recent remarks.[79] As I understand it, our Embassy in Beirut played no role whatsoever in arranging the meeting between the congressional delegation and Mr. Arafat. The meeting was arranged privately by the congressional delegation.

Ambassador Dillon briefed the delegation fully on U.S. policy toward the PLO, and further advised them of the security risks involved in traveling to West Beirut. As you know, members of Congress are free to meet with whomever they please.

. . . .

Document 375

Transcript of the Department of State Daily Press Briefing, July 27, 1982 (Extract)[80]

Suspension of Cluster Munitions Deliveries to Israel

. . . .

Q. Dean, do you consider the matter of Israeli use of cluster bombs on civilians in Lebanon as a closed case, or is it still under review by the U.S. Government?

A. No, it is not a closed case. We may have something on that subject for you later in the day.

As if on cue, I can tell you on the subject of cluster bombs, or rather CBU's, the Department yesterday sent to Congress a letter with information specifically on the use of CBU's supplementing its earlier letter on Israeli use of American weapons. Since it is a classified communication, I cannot get into its contents. However, without getting into the contents, I can confirm that the President has suspended the delivery to Israel of 155 mm artillery ammunition which employs a cluster munition concept similar to air-delivered CBU's.

. . . .

Document 376

Transcript of a Press Conference by President Reagan, July 28, 1982 (Extracts)[81]

Progress of the Habib Mission

. . . .

Q. Mr. President, I would like to stay with foreign policy, but turn to the Middle

[79] On July 25, Representative Paul N. McCloskey announced on CBS News that he and four other members of a U.S. congressional delegation had met with PLO leader Yasir Arafat in Beirut. He claimed that Arafat signed a document accepting various U.N. resolutions that included Israel's right to exist. Arafat later qualified this statement, saying that he accepted U.N. resolutions "dealing with the Palestinian question." (Foreign Broadcast Information Service, *Daily Report: Middle East and Africa*, July 26, 1982, pp. A1–A4)

[80] Source: Office of Press Relations, Department of State. Dean Fischer, Department of State Spokesman, conducted the briefing, which began at 12:41 p.m.

[81] Source: White House Press Release, July 28,

East. And I wondered what effect you believe the constant, day-after-day bombing by the Israelis and shelling by the Israelis in Beirut is having on your efforts and your special envoy Mr. Habib's efforts to try to bring some kind of a settlement?

And, secondly, Mr. Habib has been there nearly 7 weeks.[82] And can you give us some idea what progress, if any, he is making?

THE PRESIDENT. John, there's nothing we would like more than to see an end to the bloodshed and the shelling. But I must remind you it's also been two-way. The PLO has been, and in some instances has been the first to break the cease-fire. That we would like to see ended, of course. And we still stay with our original purpose, that we want the exodus of the armed PLO out of Beirut and out of Lebanon. Mr. Habib has been making a tour of countries to see if we can get some help in temporary staging areas for those people. We want the central government of Lebanon to once again, after several years of almost dissolution—to once again be the authority with a military force, not several militias belonging to various factions in Lebanon. And then we want the foreign forces, Israeli and Syrian both, out of Lebanon.

Ambassador Habib has been doing a magnificent job. I don't comment on specifics because I know how sensitive these negotiations are and sometimes you lose some ground that you think you gained, and sometimes you gain again. I still remain optimistic that the solution is going to be found.

As I say, he has returned from that trip to other countries, some of the other Arab States and to Tel Aviv. Contrary to some reports or rumors today, there are no deadlines that have been set of any kind. There is an unsubstantiated report now that another cease-fire has gone into effect. Let's hope it will hold.

But he continues to believe it is worthwhile to continue the negotiations and I think he's entitled to our support.

Q. Sir, you said that you wanted the bombing stopped, if I understood you correctly. Have you conveyed your feelings to Prime Minister Begin?

THE PRESIDENT. When I say that, what I should say is, we want the bloodshed and the conflict to stop. And I am hesitant to say anything further about where we are in those on who might be providing the stumbling block, now, to the steps that I just outlined that are necessary to bring peace there. So I can't go beyond that except to say that unless and until Ambassador Habib would tell me that there's nothing more to be negotiated and he can't solve it, I'm going to continue to be optimistic.

. . . .

Q. As you've said before and as your spokesmen have been saying, the PLO Chief Arafat has not yet met the conditions that the U.S. Government has set for direct talks with you. However, do you think that Mr. Arafat is moving in that direction? And would you welcome such a development?

THE PRESIDENT. Well, I think it would be a step forward in progress if the PLO would change the position it has had—and that is that Israel must be destroyed or that it has no right to exist as a nation. And what that would require is agreeing to abide by the U.N. Resolutions 242 and 338, agreeing that Israel is a nation and does have a right to exist. Then I would feel that the United States could enter into discussions with the PLO. I'm not speaking for Israel. That's up to them, and we could not speak for them. But we're there as an intermediary offering our services to try and help bring about peace in the Middle East.

Q. Would you also, then, support an independent Palestinian state, which is what the PLO wants?

THE PRESIDENT. That, again, I think is up to the negotiators. We wouldn't impose anything on them, but Egypt and Israel—under the Camp David agreement, they are supposed to enter into now an area of talking of autonomy for the Palestinians. And that, again, is something that has been delayed because of this tragedy in Lebanon. But I think that is up to them as to how that autonomy develops and what they see as a proper solution to the Palestinian problem.

. . . .

1982, Office of the Press Secretary to the President; also printed in *Weekly Compilation of Presidential Documents,* August 2, 1982, pp. 965–969. The press conference was held in the East Room of the White House, beginning at 8:01 p.m.

[82] Ambassador Habib had begun his mission to the Middle East on June 6, 1982. On July 28, he was conferring with Israeli officials in Jerusalem.

Document 377

Statement by the Representative at the United Nations (Kirkpatrick) Before the U.N. Security Council, July 29, 1982[83]

"A One-Sided Appeal in a Two-Sided Conflict"

Mr. President, the United States is never indifferent to the sufferings, insecurity or deprivations of human beings caught in war, occupation or natural disasters. Certainly, we have been deeply concerned with the hardships visited on the people of Lebanon during the current conflict. The Lebanese people, we know, have too long suffered violence at the hands of unwanted intruders, unwelcome invaders and occupiers. The concern of my government for the people of Lebanon has been and is being actively expressed in the large contributions for emergency humanitarian aid made by my government, by the appointment of a special administrator for aid and by implementation of extensive, humanitarian aid programs in the region. President Reagan has asked the Congress to provide a total of some $65 million in humanitarian emergency aid for the people of Lebanon. The President's special envoy, Ambassador Phillip Habib, has worked indefatigably in his efforts to restore peace to Lebanon and a degree of territorial integrity and sovereignty that the government has not enjoyed for too many years.

Mr. President, there is no room for doubt among reasonable men and women, I believe, about the commitment of the United States Government to the peace, independence, and sovereignty of Lebanon; indeed, for our commitment to peace, national independence, and sovereignty of all nations. Yet, we see serious problems with the resolution proposed by my friend and distinguished colleague, the representative of the Government of Spain,[84] for the following reasons: First, because of inadequate time either to gather or confirm the facts about the situation in Beirut and the problems of access; second, because of an inadequate opportunity to consult with our government; and third, because this resolution, we believe, is lacking in a certain, serious balance which would give it greater weight. It is, surely, in the first instance, the Palestine Liberation Organization that imposes itself on the civilian population of Beirut. But, the resolution proposed by my distinguished colleague from Spain does not ask that that armed force abandon its occupation of Beirut or desist in its military activities. It calls only on Israel. Yet everyone understands that Israel seeks to affect supplies to the PLO forces, not to the civilian population of Beirut.

Mr. President, the United States welcomes the concern of the Security Council and of the humanitarian agencies of the United Nations for the suffering in Lebanon, as we welcome the concern of this body for an end to human suffering everywhere. But, Mr. President, we feel that a one-sided appeal in a two-sided conflict suggests purposes that are political as well as humanitarian, and we cannot support these. Certainly, we cannot support them on the basis of inadequate notice and inadequate information. We call, therefore, upon the Council to take the time necessary for more careful, balanced consideration of this most serious, wrenching problem. I ask the suspension of this session to permit consideration and consultation with our governments.[85]

Thank you Mr. President.

---

[83] Source: U.S. Mission to the United Nations Press Release USUN 59(82), July 29, 1982; also printed in Department of State *Bulletin*, September 1982, pp. 20–21.

[84] Jaime de Piniés, Permanent Representative of Spain to the United Nations.

[85] Ambassador Kirkpatrick's proposal to suspend the meeting for 2 hours to allow delegates to consult with their governments did not obtain a majority; there were 6 votes for, 6 against, and 3 abstentions. The Security Council then approved Resolution 515 by a vote of 14 to 0, with the United States not participating. For text of U.N. Security Council Resolution 515 (1982), see *infra*.

Document 378

Resolution 515 (1982), Adopted by the U.N. Security Council, July 29, 1982[86]

Demand That Israel Lift the Blockade of West Beirut

The Security Council,

Deeply concerned at the situation of the civilian population of Beirut,

[86] Source: U.N. Security Council Resolution

Referring to the humanitarian principles of the Geneva Conventions of 1949 and to the obligations arising from the regulations annexed to the Hague Convention of 1907,

Recalling its resolutions 512 (1982) and 513 (1982),

1. *Demands* that the Government of Israel lift immediately the blockade of the city of Beirut[87] in order to permit the dispatch of supplies to meet the urgent needs of the civilian population and allow the distribution of aid provided by United Nations agencies and by non-governmental organizations, particularly the International Committee of the Red Cross (ICRC);

2. *Requests* the Secretary-General to transmit the text of this resolution to the Government of Israel and keep the Security Council informed of its implementation.

Document 379

Transcript of a White House Press Briefing, July 30, 1982[88]

The Visit of Egyptian Foreign Minister Ali

Senior Administration Official. The meeting today between the President and the Deputy Prime Minister and Foreign Minister of Egypt lasted approximately 45 minutes. I am sure that the White House will make available to you all of the participants.

There were two basic issues discussed: the current situation in West Beirut and the future of the peace process.

With respect to the current situation in West Beirut, both sides obviously welcomed the published six-point declaration of the Arab follow-up committee[89]—saw it as a positive step. We also discussed ways in which Egypt could be helpful in resolving the immediate crisis in West Beirut. And naturally we briefed on the current status of the Habib mission.

With respect to the broader subject of the future of the peace process, both sides agreed on the need to redouble efforts in the near future to move the peace process forward, to work for a comprehensive peace, with the priority on an early solution of the Palestinian problem in all of its aspects.

Okay, I will take some questions and then I will have to—

Q. Did Egypt agree to—at least in principle—to accept a large number of the Palestinians now in Beirut?

Senior Administration Official. I don't want to get into who has agreed to what. We have been in discussions with the Egyptians and they have always indicated a willingness to help. The exact terms under which this could be worked out are still under discussion.

Q. There was a report a couple of days ago—I am not asking you to confirm the numbers—but the report said that they would take 3,000 if the United States committed itself to pursuing a homeland for the Palestinians. Does this meeting—was this a meeting to state that commitment and did the President fulfill the requirements that the Egyptians were seeking?

Senior Administration Official. To the extent that we have differences with the Egyptians, I would describe them as differences in tactics, not overall goals, and in this context we have to remember that Egypt is really our foremost friend in the Middle East working not only as a partner for peace but with respect to the mutual contributions that can be made for the stability and security of that broader area. And that is the general atmosphere in which these discussions were held. There is not a complete identity of views on all aspects of how best to resolve the West Beirut problem and we will be continuing these discus-

---

515 (1982); also printed in Department of State *Bulletin*, September 1982, p. 20. The resolution was approved by a vote of 14 to 0, with the United States not participating. See footnote 85 above.

[87] Reference is to the most recent Israeli blockade that began on July 22, 1982.

[88] Source: Office of the Press Secretary to the President. The briefing, conducted on background in the Briefing Room of the White House by a senior administration official, began at 11:08 a.m.

[89] On July 28 and 29, the Foreign Ministers of Saudi Arabia, Lebanon, Syria, Kuwait, and Algeria, plus a representative of the PLO, met in Jiddah, Saudi Arabia. They signed a six-point plan calling for the evacuation of the PLO from Beirut in return for an end to the Israeli siege, safe passage from Beirut, and guarantees for the security of Palestinian civilians in Lebanon. For text, see Foreign Broadcast Information Service, *Daily Report: Middle East and Africa*, July 30, 1982, pp. C2–C3.

sions in depth in the meeting this afternoon in the State Department with Secretary Shultz.

Q. It sounds to me as though you are saying that whatever happened does not satisfy what they said was their requirement for taking in the PLO. Is that a fair—

SENIOR ADMINISTRATION OFFICIAL. I wouldn't establish—let me caution you, not an established and such an exact linkage. They definitely believe, as they, I believe, have stated publicly, that there should be a form of linkage, the more explicit the better, between the solution of this current crisis in West Beirut and the future of the peace process. Now just how that impacts—

Q. We don't believe that?

SENIOR ADMINISTRATION OFFICIAL. Well, I think that we share the belief that the lesson of Lebanon—really the essential lesson is the need to move ahead quickly on the Palestinian issue. The goals are not a problem with us.

Q. Well, what's the problem?

SENIOR ADMINISTRATION OFFICIAL. I guess we have to continue to discuss the tactics of achieving what we both believe is necessary. That's the solution to West Beirut, as well as how best to move ahead on the Palestinian problem.

Q. In line with the tactics, did Minister Ali ask for U.S. support for the French-Egyptian resolution and the Security Council, or did he seek ways in which this could be made more agreeable to the United States?[90]

SENIOR ADMINISTRATION OFFICIAL. He discussed it, but not in the terms, John, that you've suggested—not seeking American support to vote for this Security Council. Discussing it, explaining it from Egypt's point of view and it was helpful.

I really have to run. Let me take one from the Israeli press.

Q. Yes. The Egyptian Foreign Minister just said outside that there was again a reaffirmation of the PLO, so he said in the United Nations yesterday, of acceptance of all the U.N. resolutions. Is there any development?

SENIOR ADMINISTRATION OFFICIAL. I'm really not up to speed on that. I don't know what happened yesterday in the United Nations. Just—I haven't had time to find out; that's all.

Q. Will the United States—

SENIOR ADMINISTRATION OFFICIAL. And I don't know. I mean—

Q. Just to follow up—what you said—

SENIOR ADMINISTRATION OFFICIAL. Yes.

Q. Can you tell us anything about the memo that Habib allegedly received from—was transmitted by Arafat to Habib?

SENIOR ADMINISTRATION OFFICIAL. No.

Q. As you read the six-point plan, does it require the Israelis to pull back before the plan is implemented?

SENIOR ADMINISTRATION OFFICIAL. Those are the things that are going to be worked on. I can't—

Q. Has Israel accepted 242 and 338?

SENIOR ADMINISTRATION OFFICIAL. A long time ago. It was somewhat—

Q. Are they still accepting them?

SENIOR ADMINISTRATION OFFICIAL. Yes.

Q. Good.

Q. What was that, . . . ?

Q. He said yes—yes.

THE PRESS. Thank you.

Document 380

Resolution 516 (1982), Adopted by the U.N. Security Council, August 1, 1982[91]

Demand for a Cease-Fire in Beirut

The Security Council,

Reaffirming its resolutions 508 (1982), 509 (1982), 511 (1982), 512 (1982) and 513 (1982),

---

[90] On July 28, the French and Egyptian representatives to the United Nations introduced a draft resolution calling for a withdrawal of Israeli forces around Beirut and a simultaneous withdrawal of Palestinian forces within the city as a first step toward the removal of all foreign armed forces from Lebanon. The Security Council did not vote on this proposal, but adopted instead Resolution 515 (1982). See documents 377 and *supra.*

[91] Source: U.N. Security Council Resolution 516 (1982); also printed in Department of State *Bulletin*, September 1982, p. 21. The resolution was adopted unanimously.

Recalling its resolution 515 (1982) of 29 July 1982,

Alarmed by the continuation and intensification of military activities in and around Beirut,

Taking note of the latest massive violations of the cease-fire in and around Beirut,

1. *Confirms* its previous resolutions and demands an immediate cease-fire, and a cessation of all military activities within Lebanon and across the Lebanese-Israeli border;

2. *Authorizes* the Secretary-General to deploy immediately on the request of the Government of Lebanon, United Nations observers to monitor the situation in and around Beirut;

3. *Requests* the Secretary-General to report back to the Council on compliance with this resolution as soon as possible and not later than four hours from now.[92]

Document 381

Remarks by President Reagan, August 1, 1982[93]

"The Bloodshed Must Stop"

Q. Mr. President, what about the fighting in Israel [sic]? We've heard so much about the fighting in Israel [sic]. They have a cease-fire now,[94] but there was terrible fighting over the weekend.

THE PRESIDENT. Yes, and I've been in touch with our ambassador all the time that I've been gone. And a resolution, as you know, has been adopted in the United Nations,[95] which we supported, calling for a cease-fire that will stay. And I think it is absolutely imperative that this cease-fire, at this stage of the negotiations, must not be violated by anyone.

Q. Foreign Minister Shamir said that there was something happening in the negotiations, that we were close to a breakthrough. Are we?

THE PRESIDENT. Well as I say, you know I don't comment on those things, only to say I think it's imperative that this cease-fire not be violated.

Q. Tomorrow, when you see Foreign Minister Shamir, is it time to get tough with Israel on breaking cease-fires?

THE PRESIDENT. Let me say I'll be firm as I've just been here. Yes, this must be resolved, and the bloodshed must stop.

Q. Are you going to be tough with Shamir tomorrow? Is it time to get tough with Israel?

THE PRESIDENT. If I answered it that way you'd say, "The President says he's going to get tough."

Q. I can say that?

THE PRESIDENT. No. You can just say that we're going to have a very serious discussion, and I think they will understand exactly how we feel about this.

Q. Are you losing patience? Are you frustrated?

THE PRESIDENT. I lost patience a long time ago.

Q. Must the PLO leave Lebanon, or just Beirut?

THE PRESIDENT. I don't think there will really be a solution or the other forces leave Lebanon until the PLO does.

Q. They must leave Lebanon?

THE PRESIDENT. Leave Lebanon, yes.

Q. [Inaudible][96]—think you're close to it?

THE PRESIDENT. I said before that there have been times when there has been reason for optimism, and I almost feel as if I might jinx things if I gave any expression of that. But there has been progress made.

REPORTERS. Thank you.

---

[92] For the text of the U.N. Secretary-General's reports on compliance with U.N. Security Council Resolution 516 (1982), see U.N. documents S/15334, August 1, 1982; and S/15334/Add. 1, August 3, 1982.

[93] Source: *Weekly Compilation of Presidential Documents*, August 9, 1982, p. 981. This exchange with reporters took place at 4 p.m. at the South Portico of the White House after President Reagan returned from Camp David, Maryland.

[94] Reference is to a cease-fire arranged by Ambassador Habib that went into effect in Beirut at 5 p.m. local time, ending a weekend of fighting.

[95] See *supra*.

[96] Bracketed note appears in the source text.

Document 382

Statement Issued by the White House, August 2, 1982[97]

President Reagan's Meeting With Israeli Foreign Minister Shamir

The President met with Israeli Foreign Minister Shamir this morning. The focus of the discussion was Lebanon. The President reaffirmed his support for Ambassador Habib and his mission, which is based on the policies, expectations, and hopes of the Government of Lebanon. The President emphasized that an early diplomatic settlement of the current problem of west Beirut is the essential first step in ending the trauma of Lebanon, beginning the process for a better future for this ravaged country, and moving on to the broader peace process. The President stressed the need for a complete end by all parties to the hostilities in and around Beirut as a prerequisite to allow Ambassador Habib to pursue his urgent work. The world can no longer accept a situation of constantly escalating violence. The President highlighted the humanitarian needs of the large civilian population of west Beirut, with emphasis on the need to maintain essential services and to assure adequate supplies of food and medicines.

Document 383

Statement by President Reagan, August 4, 1982[98]

Call for an Israeli Cease-Fire and PLO Withdrawal From Lebanon

Last night, Israeli forces moved forward on several fronts from their cease-fire lines around Beirut. These movements were accompanied by heavy Israeli shelling and came only a day after I had made clear to the Israeli Government, in my meeting with Foreign Minister Shamir,[99] that the United States placed great importance on the sustained maintenance of a cease-fire in place—to avoid further civilian casualties and to secure the prompt withdrawal of the PLO forces in Beirut.

This is a necessary first step toward our goal of restoring the authority of the Government of Lebanon, a goal Ambassador Habib is earnestly working toward with the full cooperation of the Government of Lebanon.

Through governments which have direct contact with the PLO, I have expressed my strong conviction that the PLO must not delay further its withdrawal from Lebanon. At the same time I have expressed to the Government of Israel the absolute necessity of reestablishing and maintaining a strict cease-fire in place so that this matter can be promptly resolved.

Document 384

Resolution 517 (1982), Adopted by the U.N. Security Council, August 4, 1982[1]

Censure of Israel for Noncompliance With U.N. Resolutions on Lebanon

The Security Council,

Deeply shocked and alarmed by the deplorable consequences of the Israeli invasion of Beirut on 3 August 1982,

---

[97] Source: *Weekly Compilation of Presidential Documents,* August 9, 1982, pp. 981–982; also printed in Department of State *Bulletin,* September 1982, p. 22. Israeli Foreign Minister Yitzhak Shamir visited Washington, August 2–4, 1982. A note to the source text indicates that Vice President George Bush, Secretary of State George P. Shultz, National Security Adviser William P. Clark, U.S. Ambassador to Israel Samuel Lewis, and Israeli Ambassador Moshe Arens were present at the meeting in the Cabinet Room at the White House.

[98] Source: White House Press Release, August 4, 1982, Office of the Press Secretary to the President; also printed in *Weekly Compilation of Presidential Documents,* August 9, 1982, p. 1000.

[99] See *supra.*

[1] Source: U.N. Security Council Resolution 517 (1982); also printed in Department of State *Bulletin,* September 1982, p. 21. The resolution was approved by a vote of 14 to 0, with the United States abstaining. In a statement before the U.N. Security Council on August 4, 1982, Carl Gershman, the U.S. Alternate Representative, said that the resolution "has one fatal flaw. It does not explicitly and unequivocally call for the withdrawal of the PLO from Lebanon," and was therefore "inconsistent with the balanced policy set forth in President Reagan's statement" of August 4. (U.S. Mission to the United Nations Press Release USUN 60(82), August 4, 1982)

1. *Reconfirms* its resolutions 508 (1982), 509 (1982), 512 (1982), 513 (1982), 515 (1982) and 516 (1982);

2. *Confirms once again* its demand for an immediate cease-fire and withdrawal of Israeli forces from Lebanon;

3. *Censures* Israel for its failure to comply with the above resolutions;

4. *Calls* for the prompt return of Israeli troops which have moved forward subsequent to 1325 hours EDT on 1 August 1982;

5. *Takes note* of the decision of the Palestine Liberation Organization to move the Palestinian armed forces from Beirut;

6. *Expresses* its appreciation for the efforts and steps taken by the Secretary-General to implement the provisions of Security Council resolution 516 (1982), and authorizes him, as an immediate step, to increase the number of United Nations observers in and around Beirut;

7. *Requests* the Secretary-General to report to the Security Council on the implementation of the present resolution as soon as possible and not later than 1000 hours EDT on 5 August 1982;[2]

8. *Decides* to meet at that time if necessary in order to consider the report of the Secretary-General and, in case of failure to comply by any of the parties to the conflict, to consider adopting effective ways and means in accordance with the provisions of the Charter of the United Nations.

Document 385

U.N. Security Council Draft Resolution, Vetoed by the United States, August 6, 1982[3]

Demand for Cessation of Military Aid to Israel

The Security Council,

Deeply indignant at the refusal of Israel to comply with the decisions of the Security Council aimed at terminating the bloodshed in Beirut,

1. *Strongly condemns* Israel for not implementing resolutions 516 (1982) and 517 (1982);[4]

2. *Demands* that Israel immediately implement these resolutions fully;

3. *Decides* that, in order to carry out the above-mentioned decisions of the Security Council, all the States Members of the United Nations should refrain from supplying Israel with any weapons and from providing it with any military aid until the full withdrawal of Israeli forces from all Lebanese territory.

Document 386

Transcript of a White House Press Briefing, August 12, 1982 (Extract)[5]

President Reagan Appeals to Prime Minister Begin for a Cease-Fire

[MR. SPEAKES.] The President was shocked this morning when he learned of the new heavy Israeli bombardment of West Beirut.

As a result, the President telephoned Prime Minister Begin concerning the most recent bombing and shelling in Beirut.

The President expressed his outrage over this latest round of massive military action. He emphasized that Israel's action halted Ambassador Habib's negotiations for the peaceful resolution of the Beirut crisis when they were at the point of success.

---

[2] For the Reports of the U.N. Secretary-General in Pursuance of Security Council Resolution 517 (1982), see U.N. documents S/15345 and S/15345/Add. 1, August 5, 1982, and S/15345/Add. 2, August 6, 1982.

[3] Source: U.N. document S/15347/Rev. 1. The draft resolution, sponsored by the Soviet Union, failed of adoption by a vote of 11 in favor to 1 (United States) against, a veto, with 3 abstentions. Charles M. Lichenstein, U.S. Alternate Representative, characterized the draft resolution as "unbalanced" and unlikely to promote a peaceful settlement. (U.S. Mission to the United States Press Release USUN 61(82), August 6, 1982)

[4] *Supra.*

[5] Source: Office of the Press Secretary to the President. Larry Speakes, Deputy Press Secretary to the President, conducted the briefing, which began at 1:01 p.m. in the Briefing Room of the White House. His statement was also printed in *Weekly Compilation of Presidential Documents,* August 16, 1982, p. 22.

Q. That was the point.

MR. SPEAKES. The result has been more needless destruction and bloodshed.

The President made it clear that it is imperative that the cease-fire in place be observed absolutely in order for negotiations to proceed.

We understand the Israeli Cabinet has approved a new cease-fire which is in effect. It must hold. That's—hold on a second—that's the end of the statement. Now, did you need more—is anybody not clear on—

Q. What time was this phone call?

MR. SPEAKES. Let me give you the whole sequence now if you will listen very carefully.

The first action taken on behalf of the U.S. Government this morning was Ambassador Lewis, on instructions from Washington, had delivered to Prime Minister Begin a message indicating the President's attitude on this matter, which has been reflected in the statement. At the time the Prime Minister was in the Knesset. The message was not delivered personally in the Knesset. He caused it to be delivered.

Between 10 a.m. and 11 a.m. this morning—

Q. Washington time?

MR. SPEAKES. Washington time—the President placed a telephone call to the Prime Minister—instructed that the telephone call go forward. It was not completed at that time. I will come to that in a second. Meanwhile the President received a telephone call at 10:50 a.m. from King Fahd of Saudi Arabia expressing his concern over the situation in West Beirut.

Q. What time was this, Larry?

MR. SPEAKES. At 10:50 a.m. Now at 11:10 a.m. the President's phone call—

Q. Did he talk to Fahd?

MR. SPEAKES. Yes. At 11:10 a.m. the President's phone call to Begin was begun and lasted for 10 minutes, until 11:20 a.m. And shortly before this phone call we had learned that an order had gone out to cease the bombing in West Beirut. Now at 11:40 a.m. Prime Minister Begin called back to the President and the information contained in this phone call was that a cease-fire—a complete cease-fire had been ordered. Now it is our—as far as we know at this moment, the negotiations between Ambassador Habib and the Lebanese officials have not begun again, but it is our hope and our belief that if the cease-fire holds then they will be able to resume—

Q. Well, when Mr. Begin told the President that he had ordered a complete cease-fire, did he say or give any indication that he intended to maintain the cease-fire?

MR. SPEAKES. Yes.

. . . .

Document 387

Resolution 518 (1982), Adopted by the U.N. Security Council, August 12, 1982[6]

Demand for Israeli Observance of Earlier Security Council Resolutions

The Security Council,

Recalling its resolutions 508 (1982), 509 (1982), 511 (1982), 512 (1982), 513 (1982), 515 (1982), 516 (1982), and 517 (1982),

Expressing its most serious concern about continued military activities in Lebanon and, particularly, in and around Beirut,

1. *Demands* that Israel and all parties to the conflict observe strictly the aterms of Security Council resolutions relevant to the immediate cessation of all military activities within Lebanon and, particularly, in and around Beirut;

2. *Demands* the immediate lifting of all restrictions on the city of Beirut in order to permit the free entry of supplies to meet the urgent needs of the civilian population in Beirut;

3. *Requests* the United Nations observers in and in the vicinity of Beirut to report on the situation;

---

[6] Source: U.N. Security Council Resolution 518 (1982); also printed in Department of State *Bulletin*, September 1982, p. 21. The resolution was adopted unanimously. In a statement to the Security Council, Ambassador Lichenstein called the resolution "constructive" and urged the Council to avoid any initiatives that might imperil negotiations in progress in Lebanon. (U.S. Mission to the United Nations Press Release USUN 62(82), August 12, 1982)

4. *Demands* that Israel co-operate fully in the effort to secure the effective deployment of the United Nations observers, as requested by the Government of Lebanon, and in such a manner as to ensure their safety;

5. *Requests* the Secretary-General to report soonest to the Security Council on the implementation of the present resolution;[7]

6. *Decides* to meet if necessary in order to consider the situation upon receipt of the report of the Secretary-General.

Document 388

Transcript of a Press Briefing by President Reagan, August 13, 1982 (Extracts)[8]

The President's Efforts To Obtain A Cease-Fire in Beirut

. . . .

Q. Mr. President, why didn't you take the kind of highly-publicized public action to stop the bombing in Beirut before you did yesterday?[9] Perhaps hundreds of thousands could—or thousands anyway—could have been saved. Why not be—why not go public, no matter what you may have said in private, sir?

THE PRESIDENT. Well, much of what we said—and we weren't silent or idle in all this time that Habib has been working—but the sensitivity of the negotiations were such that I avoided, as you know, anything that might interfere with those negotiations or in some way injure what Ambassador Habib was trying to accomplish. However, yesterday the situation was that the negotiations were down. We had general agreement by all parties finally to the arrangement, and the negotiations were down to the logistics, the technicalities of getting the people—getting the PLO moving and so forth and those negotiations, literally, were broken off by the extent of that bombing and shelling. The delegates couldn't even get to the negotiation meetings and I have to be fair and say that, in my first call, I was informed then by Prime Minister Begin that he had ordered a cessation of the aerial bombing and so, we discussed the artillery shelling from then on.

Q. Mr. President, why don't you tell us a little bit of how you felt in these 9 weeks with people being bombarded and your continuing to send weapons to inflict this horror on them? I mean, what has been your personal feeling?

THE PRESIDENT. As I say, this was a matter of great concern and we were trying to get an end to it. On the other hand, I think that perhaps the image has been rather one-sided because of the Israeli capability at replying, but in many instances—in fact, most of them—the cease-fire was broken by PLO attacking those Israeli forces.

Q. Well, they were the invaders, were they not?

THE PRESDIENT. Are they the invaders or are the PLO the invaders? Lebanon is the country,—

Q. As of June 6th.

THE PRESIDENT.—but, on the other hand, if we look now at the stories that are beginning to come out and that some have been public, the PLO was literally a government and an armed force in another nation and beholden in no way to that other nation which was one of the reasons why you didn't hear more protest from the Lebanese government about the Israeli presence.

Q. Mr. President, you said that yesterday you did have a general agreement and then, there was this firing. Where—are we back on track today? Do we still have a general agreement? And would you go along with some forecasts that say the PLO evacuation will begin sometime next week?

THE PRESIDENT. I'm reasonably optimistic. Now, see, I didn't say "cautiously". I'm reasonably optimistic about this because I believe that this time the cease-fire is going to hold and, as I say, the negotiations now are not the case of trying to persuade agreement on the part of the various parties. The negotiations are on the technicalities, the logistical move that must be made in get-

---

[7] For the text of the Secretary-General's Report in Pursuance of Security Council Resolution 518 (1982), see U.N. document S/15362, August 13, 1982.

[8] Source: Office of the Press Secretary to the President; also printed in *Weekly Compilation of Presidential Documents*, August 16, 1982, pp. 1023–1026. For the full text, see *ibid.*, pp. 1024–1027. The President spoke at 2 p.m. in the White House Briefing Room.

[9] See the White House Press Briefing, August 12, 1982, document 386.

ting them out. And so, I think there's reason for, great reason for hope.

Q. The PLO—would the evacuation start next week? As early as that?

THE PRESIDENT. I can't—again, I don't want to speculate on that because I'm not there at the negotiating table.

Here, and then, I've got to get back there into those back lines there.

Q. Mr. President, yesterday your spokesman said you were outraged by what had happened. Can you tell us a little bit about what happened in your phone call with the Prime Minister, specifically, did you raise your voice and what was the tenor of the conversation?

THE PRESIDENT. This is something that I don't do. I won't comment on my communications, whether written or spoken, with other heads of state. I don't think that's proper, so I won't do that.

. . . .

Q. Mr. President, has the Israeli action in Lebanon, often against U.S. wishes—the massive retaliation for violations of the cease-fire by the PLO, has that changed in any way the special relationship between Israel and the United States? And has it changed your own personal views toward Israel?

THE PRESIDENT. No, I think and I was concerned also that—the reason for the call, that it could endanger that—the manner in which it's being portrayed, there's been less emphasis on the provocation and more emphasis on the response. And, yes, I did and have voiced the opinion that the response many times was out of proportion to the provocation that—but we can't deny that the Israelis have been taking casualties from those cease-fire violations themselves. I think the figure now is 326 dead of their own military from being attacked in the breaking of the cease-fire.

Q. Has it changed your own attitude?

THE PRESIDENT. What?

Q. Has it changed your own attitude toward Israel?

THE PRESIDENT. I still believe that this country has an obligation to pursue the peace process that was started in Camp David and that this country has an obligation to ensure Israel's survival as a nation.

. . . .

Document 389

Note From the Lebanese Deputy Prime Minister/Foreign Minister (Boutros) to the Ambassador in Lebanon (Dillon), Beirut, August 18, 1982[10]

Lebanese Proposal for a U.S. Contribution to a Temporary Multinational Force in Beirut

YOUR EXCELLENCY: I have the honor to refer to the many conversations between their Excellencies the President of the Republic of Lebanon, the Prime Minister and myself on the one hand, and with Ambassador Philip C. Habib, Special Emissary to the President of the United States of America, on the other hand, as well as to the resolution of the Council of Ministers passed today.[11] I have the honor to refer to the schedule set up by the Government of Lebanon, after consultations with interested parties, in order to assure the withdrawal from Lebanese territory of the Palestinian leaders, offices and combatants related to any organization now in the Beirut area, in a manner which will:

(1) assure the safety of such departing persons;

(2) assure the safety of the persons in the area; and

(3) further the restoration of the sovereignty and authority of the Government of Lebanon over the Beirut area.

In this context, the Government of Lebanon is proposing to several nations that they contribute forces to serve as a temporary Multinational Force (MNF) in Beirut. The mandate of the MNF will be to provide appropriate assistance to the Lebanese Armed Forces (LAF) as they carry out the foregoing responsibilities, in accordance with the annexed schedule. The MNF may undertake other functions only by mutual agreement. It is understood that, in the event that the withdrawal of the Palestinian

---

[10] Source: Department of State *Bulletin*, September 1982, p. 4.

[11] This resolution is summarized in Foreign Broadcast Information Service, *Daily Report: Middle East and Africa*, August 19, 1982, pp. G1–G2.

personnel referred to above does not take place in accord with the predetermined schedule, the mandate of the MNF will terminate immediately and all MNF personnel will leave Lebanon forthwith.

In the foregoing context, I have the honor to propose that the United States of America deploy a force of approximately 800 personnel to Beirut, subject to the following terms and conditions:

The American military force shall carry out appropriate activities consistent with the mandate of the MNF.

Command authority over the American force will be exercised exclusively by the United States Government through existing American military channels.

The American force will operate in close coordination with the LAF. To assure effective coordination with the LAF, the American force will assign liaison officers to the LAF and the Government of Lebanon will assign liaison officers to the American force. The LAF liaison officers to the American force will, inter alia, perform liaison with the civilian population and manifest the authority of the Lebanese Government in all appropriate situations.

In carrying out its mission, the American force will not engage in combat. It may, however, exercise the right of self-defense.

The American force will depart Lebanon not later than thirty days after its arrival, or sooner at the request of the President of Lebanon or at the direction of the U.S. Government, or according to the termination of the mandate provided for above.

The Government of Lebanon and the LAF will take all measures necessary to ensure the protection of the American force's personnel, to include securing the assurances from all armed elements not now under the authority of the Lebanese Government that they will comply with the cease-fire and cessation of hostilities.

The American force will enjoy both the degree of freedom of movement and the right to undertake those activities deemed necessary for the performance of its mission or for the support of its personnel. Accordingly, it shall enjoy all facilities necessary for the accomplishment of these purposes. Personnel in the American force shall enjoy the privileges and immunities accorded the administrative and technical staff of the American Embassy in Beirut, and shall be exempt from immigration and customs requirements, and restrictions on entering or departing Lebanon. Personnel, property and equipment of the American force introduced into Lebanon shall be exempt from any form of tax, duty, charge or levy.

I have the further honor to propose, if the foregoing is acceptable to your Excellency's government, that your Excellency's reply to that effect, together with this note, shall constitute an agreement between our two governments, to enter into force on the date of your Excellency's reply.

Please accept, your Excellency, the assurances of my highest consideration.

FUAD BOUTROS

Document 390

Note From the Ambassador in Lebanon (Dillon) to the Lebanese Deputy Prime Minister/Foreign Minister (Boutros), Beirut, August 20, 1982[12]

The U.S. Acceptance of Lebanon's Proposal for a Temporary Multinational Force

EXCELLENCY: I have the honor to refer to Your Excellency's note of August 18, 1982 requesting the deployment of an American force to Beirut.[13] I am pleased to inform you on behalf of my Government that the United States is prepared to deploy temporarily a force of approximately 800 personnel as part of a Multinational Force (MNF) to provide appropriate assistance to the Lebanese Armed Forces (LAF) as they carry out their responsibilities concerning the withdrawal of Palestinian personnel in Beirut from Lebanese territory under safe and orderly conditions, in accordance with the schedule annexed to Your Excellency's note. It is understood that the presence of such an American force will in this way facilitate the restoration of Lebanese Government sovereignty and authority over the Beirut area, an objective which is fully shared by my Government.

---

[12] Source: Department of State files; also printed in Department of State *Bulletin*, September 1982, p. 4.

[13] *Supra.*

I have the further honor to inform Your Excellency that my Government accepts the terms and conditions concerning the presence of the American force in the Beirut area as set forth in your note, and that your note and this reply accordingly constitute an agreement between our two governments.

Accept, Excellency, the renewed assurance of my highest consideration.

ROBERT S. DILLON

Document 391

Agreement by the Governments of Lebanon, the United States, France, Italy, and Israel, and by the Palestine Liberation Organization, August 20, 1982[14]

Plan for the Departure of the PLO From Beirut

1. Basic Concept. All the PLO leadership, offices, and combatants in Beirut will leave Lebanon peacefully for prearranged destinations in other countries, in accord with the departure schedules and arrangements set out in this plan. The basic concept in this plan is consistent with the objective of the Government of Lebanon that all foreign military forces withdraw from Lebanon.

2. Cease-fire. A cease-fire in place will be scrupulously observed by all in Lebanon.

3. U.N. Observers. The U.N. Observer Group stationed in the Beirut area will continue its functioning in that area.

4. Safeguards. Military forces present in Lebanon—whether Lebanese, Israeli, Syrian, Palestinian, or any other—will in no way interfere with the safe, secure, and timely departure of the PLO leadership, offices, and combatants. Law-abiding Palestinian noncombatants left behind in Beirut, including the families of those who have departed, will be subject to Lebanese laws and regulations. The Governments of Lebanon and the United States will provide appropriate guarantees of safety in the following ways.

The Lebanese Government will provide its guarantees on the basis of having secured assurances from armed groups with which it has been in touch.

The United States will provide its guarantees on the basis of assurances received from the Government of Israel and from the leadership of certain Lebanese groups with which it has been in touch.

5. "Departure Day" is defined as the day on which advance elements of the multinational force (MNF) deploy in the Beirut area, in accordance with arrangements worked out in advance among all concerned, and on which the initial group or groups of PLO personnel commence departure from Beirut in accord with the planned schedule (see page 9).[15]

6. The Multinational Force. A temporary multinational force, composed of units from France, Italy, and the United States, will have been formed—at the request of the Lebanese Government—to assist the Lebanese Armed Forces in carrying out their responsibilities in this operation. The Lebanese Armed Forces will assure the departure from Lebanon of the PLO leadership, offices, and combatants, from whatever organization in Beirut, in a manner which will:

(A) Assure the safety of such departing PLO personnel;

(B) Assure the safety of other persons in the Beirut area; and

(C) Further the restoration of the sovereignty and authority of the Government of Lebanon over the Beirut area.

7. Schedule of Departures and Other Arrangements. The attached schedule of departures is subject to revision as may be necessary because of logistical requirements and because of any necessary shift in the setting of Departure Day. Details concerning the schedule will be forwarded to the Israeli Defense Forces through the Liaison and Coordination Committee. Places of assembly for the departing personnel will be identified by agreement between the Government of Lebanon and the PLO. The PLO will be in touch with governments receiving personnel to coordinate arrival and other arrangements there. If assistance

---

[14] Source: Department of State *Bulletin*, September 1982, pp. 2, 3, and 5. The text of this departure plan was made public by Department of State Acting Spokesman Alan Romberg.

[15] Reference is to the schedule of departures attached to the plan but not printed here. For text of the schedule, see *ibid.*, p. 3.

is required the PLO should notify the Government of Lebanon.

8. MNF Mandate. In the event that the departure from Lebanon of the PLO personnel referred to above does not take place in accord with the agreed and predetermined schedule, the mandate of the MNF will terminate immediately and all MNF personnel will leave Lebanon forthwith.

9. Duration of MNF. It will be mutually agreed between the Lebanese Government and the governments contributing forces to the MNF that the forces of the MNF will depart Lebanon not later than 30 days after arrival, or sooner at the request of the Government of Lebanon or at the direction of the individual government concerned, or in accord with the termination of the mandate of the MNF provided for above.

10. The PLO leadership will be responsible for the organization and management of the assembly and the final departure of PLO personnel, from beginning to end, at which time the leaders also will all be gone. Departure arrangements will be coordinated so that departures from Beirut take place at a steady pace, day by day.

11. Lebanese Armed Forces Contribution. The Lebanese Army will contribute between seven and eight army battalions to the operation, consisting of between 2,500–3,500 men. In addition, the internal security force will contribute men and assistance as needed.

12. ICRC. The International Committee of the Red Cross (ICRC) will be able to assist the Government of Lebanon and Lebanese Armed Forces in various ways, including in the organization and management of the evacuation of wounded and ill Palestinian and Syrian personnel to appropriate destinations, and in assisting in the chartering and movement of commercial vessels for use in departure by sea to other countries. The Liaison and Coordination Committee will insure that there will be proper coordination with any ICRC activities in this respect.

13. Departure by Air. While present plans call for departure by sea and land, departures by air are not foreclosed.

14. Liaison and Coordination:

The Lebanese Armed Forces will be the primary point of contact for liaison with the PLO as well as with other armed groups and will provide necessary information.

The Lebanese Armed Forces and MNF will have formed prior to Departure Day a Liaison and Coordination Committee, composed of representatives of the MNF participating governments and the Lebanese Armed Forces. The committee will carry out close and effective liaison with, and provide continuous and detailed information to, the Israeli Defense Forces (IDF). On behalf of the committee, the Lebanese Armed Forces will continue to carry out close and effective liaison with the PLO and other armed groups in the Beirut area. For convenience, the Liaison and Coordination Committee will have two essential components:

(A) Supervisory liaison; and

(B) Military and technical liaison and coordination.

The Liaison and Coordination Committee will act collectively; however, it may designate one or more of its members for primary liaison contact who would of course act on behalf of all.

Liaison arrangements and consultations will be conducted in such a way as to minimize misunderstandings and to forestall difficulties. Appropriate means of communications between the committee and other groups will be developed for this purpose.

The Liaison and Coordination Committee will continually monitor and keep all concerned currently informed regarding the implementation of the plan, including any revisions to the departure schedule as may be necessary because of logistical requirements.

15. Duration of Departure. The departure period shall be as short as possible and, in any event, no longer than 2 weeks.

16. Transit Through Lebanon. As part of any departure arrangement, all movements of convoys carrying PLO personnel must be conducted in daylight hours. When moving overland from Beirut to Syria, the convoys should cross the border into Syria with no stops en route. In those instances when convoys of departing PLO personnel pass through positions of the Israeli Defense Forces, whether in the Beirut area or elsewhere in Lebanon, the Israeli Defense Forces will clear the route for the temporary period in which the convoy is running. Similar steps will be taken by other armed groups located in the area of the route the convoy will take.

17. Arms Carried by PLO Personnel. On their departure, PLO personnel will be allowed to carry with them one individual

side weapon (pistol, rifle, or submachine gun) and ammunition.

18. Heavy and Spare Weaponry and Munitions. The PLO will turn over to the Lebanese Armed Forces as gifts all remaining weaponry in their possession, including heavy, crew-served, and spare weaponry and equipment, along with all munitions left behind in the Beirut area. The Lebanese Armed Forces may seek the assistance of elements of the MNF in securing and disposing of the military equipment. The PLO will assist the Lebanese Armed Forces by providing, prior to their departure, full and detailed information as to the location of this military equipment.

19. Mines and Booby Traps. The PLO and the Arab Deterrent Force (ADF) will provide to the Lebanese Armed Forces and the MNF (through the Lebanese Armed Forces) full and detailed information on the location of mines and booby traps.

20. Movement of PLO Leadership. Arrangements will be made so that departing PLO personnel will be accompanied by a proportionate share of the military and political leadership throughout all stages of the departure operation.

21. Turnover of Prisoners and Remains. The PLO will, through the ICRC, turn over to the Israeli Defense Forces, all Israeli nationals whom they have taken in custody, and the remains, or full and detailed information about the location of the remains, of all Israeli soldiers who have fallen. The PLO will also turn over to the Lebanese Armed Forces all other prisoners whom they have taken in custody and the remains, or full and detailed information about the location of the remains, of all other soldiers who have fallen. All arrangements for such turnovers shall be worked out with the ICRC as required prior to Departure Day.

22. Syrian Military Forces. It is noted that arrangements have been made between the Governments of Lebanon and Syria for the deployment of all military personnel of the Arab Deterrent Force from Beirut during the departure period. These forces will be allowed to take their equipment with them, except for that—under mutual agreement between the two governments—which is turned over to the Lebanese Armed Forces. All elements of the Palestinian Liberation Army, whether or not they now or in the past have been attached to the Arab Deterrent Force, will withdraw from Lebanon.

Document 392

Statement by President Reagan, August 20, 1982[16]

Announcement of an Agreement for the Withdrawal of the PLO From Beirut

Thank you all, and let me just say in advance, I will be taking no questions, because Secretary Shultz, a little later today, will be having a full press conference.[17] So you can take everything up there with him.

Ambassador Habib has informed me that a plan to resolve the West Beirut crisis has been agreed upon by all the parties involved.[18] As part of this plan the Government of Lebanon has requested and I have approved the deployment of U.S. forces to Beirut as part of a multinational force.

The negotiations to develop this plan have been extremely complex and have been conducted in the most arduous circumstances. At times it was difficult to imagine how agreement could be reached, and yet it has been reached. The statesmanship and the courage of President Sarkis[19] and his colleagues in the Lebanese Government deserve special recognition, as does the magnificent work of Ambassador Habib. Phil never lost hope, and in the end his spirit and determination carried the day and we all owe him a debt of gratitude.

The parties who made this plan possible have a special responsibility for insuring its successful completion, or implementation. I expect its terms to be carried out in good faith and in accordance with the agreed time table. This will require meticulous adherence to the cease-fire. Violations by any party would imperil the plan and bring renewed bloodshed and tragedy to the peo-

---

[16] Source: White House Press Release, August 20, 1982, Office of the Press Secretary to the President; also printed in *Weekly Compilation of Presidential Documents,* August 23, 1982, pp. 1048–1049. President Reagan made his statement in the Rose Garden at the White House, beginning at 9:50 a.m.

[17] For the transcript, see *infra.*

[18] See the departure plan, *supra.*

[19] Elias Sarkis, President of Lebanon until September 23, 1982.

ple of Beirut, and under no circumstances must that be allowed to happen.

As you know, my agreement to include U.S. forces in a multinational force was essential for our success. In the days ahead, they and forces from France and Italy will be playing an important but carefully limited noncombatant role. The parties to the plan have agreed to this role, and they have provided assurances on the safety of our forces.

Our purpose will be to assist the Lebanese Armed Forces in carrying out their responsibility for insuring the departure of PLO leaders, officers, and combatants in Beirut, from Lebanese territory under safe and orderly conditions. The presence of U.S. forces also will facilitate the restoration of the sovereignty and authority of the Lebanese Government over the Beirut area. In no case will our troops stay longer than 30 days.

The participation of France and Italy in this effort is further evidence of the sense of responsibility of these good friends of the United States. Successful resolution of the West Beirut crisis by responsible implementation of the plan now agreed, will set the stage for the urgent international action required to restore Lebanon's full sovereignty, unity, and territorial integrity; obtain the rapid withdrawal of all foreign forces from that country; and help insure the security of northern Israel.

We must also move quickly in the context of Camp David to resolve the Palestinian issue in all its aspects, as well as the other unresolved problems in the Arab-Israeli conflict.

Only when all these steps are accomplished can true and lasting peace and security be achieved in the Middle East.

Document 393

Transcript of a Press Conference by the Secretary of State (Shultz), August 20, 1982 (Extracts)[20]

Prospects for Peace in Lebanon After the Departure of the PLO

SECRETARY SHULTZ. Good morning. The President today announced[21] that a plan to resolve the crisis in West Beirut has been agreed upon by all the parties, and that in connection with that plan the Government of Lebanon has asked the United States, and the President has agreed, to the deployment of U.S. forces as part of a multinational force to help the Government of Lebanon to implement the plan.

He also expressed his admiration and his thanks to Phil Habib, and I would like to take this occasion to add my thanks to Phil, a truly great American.

The President also said that I would answer the questions, so here I am.

MR. MYERS, UPI. Mr. Secretary, have American-Israeli relations suffered because of the Israeli invasion of Lebanon; and on a broader scale, how do you judge the impact of the fighting on American-Arab relations?

SECRETARY SHULTZ. The Israeli-U.S. relationship remains a strong one. We are completely committed to the support of the security of Israel. Certainly there have been some strains during this period. The United States opposed the entry of Israeli troops into Lebanon. There were some occasions when it seemed to us that the Israeli military actions were excessive, and we said so. So those times presented great strains. But underneath it all the relationship between the United States and Israel remains a strong one.

There's no question about the fact—turning to the second part of your question—that our relationships with our friends in the Arab world have been strained, and understandably so, as they have seen the suffering in Lebanon and the

---

[20] Source: Department of State Press Release 257, August 20, 1982; also printed in Department of State *Bulletin*, September 1982, pp. 8–13. The press conference began at 1 p.m. Omitted here are the portions of the press conference covering other Middle East as well as European issues.

[21] See the President's statement, *supra*.

great destruction in Beirut. We seek to resolve those issues. I think the constructive role that the United States has played in the development of this plan, and Phil Habib's actions, show the fundamental commitment of the United States to peaceful solutions and the ability of the United States to be a constructive force in the region.

Q. Mr. Secretary, following withdrawal of Palestinian forces from West Beirut, do we expect the Israelis to attack other Palestinian and Syrian forces in the country, and what, if anything, are we trying to do to prevent that from happening?

SECRETARY SHULTZ. What we expect and what we hope for is that as this process unfolds the Government of Lebanon will be able to take control, first in Beirut, then increasingly throughout the country and that the forces of Israel, the forces of Syria, the forces of other armed groups in the country will withdraw or lay down their arms and Lebanon will become a country free of foreign forces.

I might note that in the plan, if you look at the first section, which is labeled "Basic Concepts," you'll see that this notion is explicitly stated as being consistent with the objectives of the plan.

Q. I wonder if you could amplify what the President said. He said that if American forces were shot at, there would be a recall of U.S. forces. In that sort of violent environment, it is possible for stray bullets to be flying. Would a single shot result in an American call-back?

SECRETARY SHULTZ. The President was not referring to some stray shot by some kook that might be fired. We're talking about a situation in which all the parties have agreed to a cease-fire and have agreed to establish the conditions under which the departure of the PLO can take place with safety. We are there to help in that process, help the Government of Lebanon in that process.

We will stay there as long as that process is going forward and as long as the basic conditions envisaged for our forces remain in effect.

Q. Mr. Secretary, we've heard a lot about Ambassador Habib's role in all of this. What do you envision as his role in the next phase which is the evacuation of all foreign troops from Lebanon?

SECRETARY SHULTZ. He's a very skillful man. He's been over there since early June, and I think he deserves a good night's sleep. But he's very skillful and very capable, and he told me on one occasion that he never says no to a President. So I imagine his talents will be called upon from time to time in the future.

Q. Has the Government of Israel given you any assurances that they intend to withdraw from Lebanon in the near future?

SECRETARY SHULTZ. When Foreign Minister Shamir was here, I asked him that question directly. He told me that Israel does not covet one inch of Lebanese territory and plans to withdraw from Lebanese territory. I looked at him and I said, "We will take you at your word."

Q. On the previous question on Mr. Habib. Is it contemplated that Mr. Habib will conduct the next round of negotiations on the withdrawal of all foreign forces from Lebanon, and do you have any timeframe in mind, and the venue, on how and when these talks should begin?

SECRETARY SHULTZ. I think that it is important to be working strongly not only for the withdrawal of foreign forces from Lebanon, but for that to happen in such a manner that the Government of Lebanon has strength and the security concerns of Israel and its northern border are adequately safeguarded.

Beyond that, I think, we must recognize that there has been a tremendous amount of destruction and displacement in Lebanon. The extent of it varies widely in peoples' estimates but even the most modest estimates show that it's considerable. We and others around the world need to address ourselves to those problems and start thinking in constructive terms about what needs to be done to help the people of Lebanon reconstruct their land and bring it back to the conditions that it once enjoyed.

Q. Will Mr. Habib actually do the negotiating for the United States?

SECRETARY SHULTZ. Phil's precise role has not been determined. As I said, he has been at it for a couple of months of very tiring work, and it's time for him to get a good night's sleep. We do plan to have a Lebanon Task Force in the government and Morris Draper, who has been Phil's assistant, will head that up; Peter McPherson, the head of AID, is going to take on the special concern of the reconstruction and development aspects of this plan. Some other people are being put in place to work on this. I don't say that Phil will have no role in it. He's a very constructive and able person, but I do think at this point that he'll obviously want to see the departure go on in a good way. But at some stage of the game, as I say, we have to give him a good night's sleep.

Q. Mr. Secretary, it's not clear to me, in the way you answered some of the earlier questions, whether you expect further negotiations to take place to obtain the withdrawal of the Syrians and the Israelis or whether you expect them to do that voluntarily, without any further diplomatic activity. Could you clarify that a little bit?

SECRETARY SHULTZ. I'm sure that the Syrians must feel that they, having been invited in by the Government of Lebanon, would expect to hear from the Government of Lebanon about its wishes. Again, I was told by the Syrian Foreign Minister that they were there at the request of the Government of Lebanon and when the Government of Lebanon requested them to leave, they would do so.

So I think what we are looking at here is a process in which the Government of Lebanon increasingly takes control; and as that happens and as security arrangements on Israel's northern border can be adequately developed, we should expect to see these forces withdraw. I can't tell you that all that can take place in an easy, uncomplicated way. There's no doubt about the fact that it will be complicated and difficult.

Q. How long do you think it will take?

SECRETARY SHULTZ. I can't tell you.

Q. Mr. Secretary, there is talk of an Israeli-Lebanese peace treaty as the next step after withdrawal. Will the United States actively support such a peace treaty?

SECRETARY SHULTZ. I think it is constructive to have peace in that part of the world. With the emergence of a strong and legitimate Government of Lebanon, that is certainly something we would hope they would consider very strongly.

Q. But will we actively support it?

SECRETARY SHULTZ. Sure.

Q. Mr. Secretary, what is the possibility of the use of American troops in some type of multinational force such as is going into Beirut now to facilitate the withdrawal of Israeli and Syrian troops from Lebanon itself?

SECRETARY SHULTZ. We don't have any plan for that at all.

Q. Will this be used as a precedent, do you think?

SECRATARY SHULTZ. No, I don't think so.

Q. Do you foresee the formation of a Palestinian state at some point? If so, when, and what are you going to do with all these Palestinians that you are splitting up and sending to all these various countries, just leave them there?

SECRETARY SHULTZ. The Palestinians that are departing from West Beirut probably number in the range of 6,000 to 7,000, and that is a number that can be assimilated. Where they go eventually, of course, remains to be seen. I do think, and have emphasized before—and practically everybody who talks about the subject emphasizes—the importance of turning to the problems of the legitimate rights of the Palestinian people, working at that, and negotiating about that.

My own observation is that the language of Camp David is quite worth reading in that regard. So we would expect to be moving on that front, as I'm sure others will too, because it represents an underlying issue of great importance and is one that is at the center of all this.

Q. Mr. Secretary, since you brought up Camp David, sir, could you give us, as best you can foresee it now, the start-up again of the autonomy talks, the timetable, including whether or not you are going to appoint a new special negotiator at any time in the near future?

SECRETARY SHULTZ. I can't really comment with any clarity on those questions. Obviously, the parties to those talks are heavily engaged in their thinking in the West Beirut problem. It will take some time and a lot of effort to construct a suitable negotiating situation, and I don't want to put down some sort of marker on it.

Q. Ambassador Habib is quoted as telling Prime Minister Begin that he thought it was Israel's military pressure which brought the PLO to agree finally to leave Beirut. Do you agree with that assessment?

SECRETARY SHULTZ. I'm not going to try to analyze what may or may not have brought the PLO to agree to leave West Beirut. Fairly early on they had made a statement in principle that they would withdraw. We went through a long period of trying to identify where they would go, and during that period there were many doubts expressed about whether in the end they would go. We felt that they had said they would, and we would take them at their word and expect that they would.

Q. But the greatest progress was made in the negotiations, wasn't it, after August 1 when the heaviest Israeli bombings took place?

SECRETARY SHULTZ. The discussions that gave more and more assurance as to where they would go materialized obviously as these negotiations went on. It was quite a struggle at first, and became more definite.

Q. Mr. Secretary, how do you intend to try to blend, or what is your own sense of priorities about resolving the rest of the issues in Lebanon, getting the foreign forces out, etc., and dealing with the Palestinian problem on the West Bank and Gaza?

SECRETARY SHULTZ. Both issues are important. There is, obviously, some connection between them, but they are also separate issues. I think we, obviously, have to work—it's my opinion obviously, any way—on both. It is difficult to lay down a timetable, but both are matters of urgency. I think that this moment in time, with the bloodshed and the damage done in Lebanon freshly in peoples' minds, is a time to work hard on this, because people must be able to see that the alternative to a reasonably peaceful situation in the Middle East is not a pleasant thing to contemplate at all. So perhaps it is a moment when people can turn their eyes from the problems of war to the problems of peace—at least I hope so—and that is going to be our effort.

. . . .

Q. Mr. Secretary, next month is the deadline within the Lebanese constitutional framework for a Presidential election. Security is one of the reasons cited why the election was put off until next week and might be put off again.

Obviously, in general, the United States has a lot of influence in a situation like this right now. It has gained more influence; it's having forces coming in there which will help provide security.

What are your views on the holding of the Lebanese Presidential election? Should it be in the next month, as originally planned?

SECRETARY SHULTZ. I think, basically, the conduct of an election in a country, the development of its own governmental processes, and the identification of the President and other officials of the country are matters for that country. The role of the United States is, as we are, to be helpful to the Government of Lebanon, at their request, as they seek to take control of Beirut and the country generally. Beyond that, I think the issue of the election of a new President and other related matters are essentially a matter for the Government of Lebanon, not for us.

Q. Mr. Secretary, in the wake of what Menachem Begin calls a great victory, what would make you believe that Israel would become more flexible in terms of dealing with the Palestinian problem? And has the Government of Israel given us any assurances that they would be willing to discuss this more amenably?

SECRETARY SHULTZ. What the outcome of discussions will be and how much flexibility will be shown by various parties to it remains to be seen. I think that the prospect of peace, particularly in the light of the conflict in Lebanon that we've seen recently—and for that matter, the conflict in Lebanon that has been going on since 1975—should convince people that if there is any genuine prospect of peace, it should be seized. Perhaps that will be an incentive for everyone to give and take, and try to construct something that might work.

Q. Mr. Secretary, do you believe that the PLO has any role to play in the negotiation process, or do you think that it does not represent the Palestinian people and is better not involved?

SECRETARY SHULTZ. As far as the United States is concerned, the President has set out well-known conditions for any contacts between the United States and the PLO directly, and we stand by those conditions. If the PLO meets those conditions, obviously the United States would be willing to talk with them. Whether others would be willing to talk with them, those others will have to say for themselves.

I think it is quite clear that if there is to be a negotiation that has as one of its center objectives meeting the legitimate concerns of the Palestinian people, there have to be representatives of the Palestinian people involved in those negotiations. No one accepts a result that they didn't have any part in. Who that should be remains to be seen. I don't know the answer to that question, but I know that an answer to it needs to be found.

Q. Mr. Secretary, could you give us an idea of how much U.S. funding is going to be involved in the evacuation and whether or not we will be reimbursed?

SECRETARY SHULTZ. I don't think that what funding we supply we will be reimbursed for. We have, I think, committed around $2 million by now for the chartering of ships and things of that kind, and perhaps we will spend a little bit more money on that sort of thing. Others will also bear some expense as they receive the PLO contingents that come to their countries, so it will be a shared expense. That is the order of magnitude, and I don't see where any reimbursement would come from.

Q. Your fact sheet[22] states United States troops will go in probably 5 or 6 days after the evacuation begins.

SECRETARY SHULTZ. That's right.

Q. Is there a trigger mechanism for that to happen? Is there some condition to be met before those U.S. troops go in?

SECRETARY SHULTZ. Just that we observe that the conditions precedent to the whole operation are in force and the departures are taking place as scheduled and there is a basically non-hostile environment.

. . . .

Q. Mr. Secretary, during this news conference I've been informed that President Carter has charged that—

SECRETARY SHULTZ. I think it's a little tough on me—

Q. I know.

SECRETARY SHULTZ.—that you get some information—

Q. I apologize that it's only happened—

SECRETARY SHULTZ.—that comes in while I'm here that I don't have access to it. It's like sitting in front of the Senate for confirmation. All those fellows are going in and out—and ladies—all the time, and I'm just sitting there. I don't know what has happened.

Q. I will explain to you what has happened, as far as I know—

SECRETARY SHULTZ. You're blind-siding me.

Q. —and I don't think you'll be totally blind-sided because it's not the first time we've heard this charge, but I've been told that President Carter—and I cannot vouch for the truth of whether he actually said it or not—has charged that Washington gave the go-ahead to Israel for the invasion of Lebanon.

I'm sure that I'm not blind-siding you because that you've heard from other sources before.

Can you answer that charge?

SECRETARY SHULTZ. It is not correct.

Q. Did not Secretary of State Haig, your predecessor, know in advance that Israel was going to strike into Lebanon?

SECRETARY SHULTZ. My understanding is that the U.S. Government was not informed, and the U.S. Government was and is on the record as having opposed that invasion. Whether somebody came through here and talked about it as a possibility, I don't know. People talk about all kinds of possibilities.

Q. Mr. Secretary, who goes in first? Who's the advance element that's spoken of, if it's not American forces?

SECRETARY SHULTZ. You mean in the Beirut situation?

Q. In Beirut, right.

SECRETARY SHULTZ. I think that's in all the fact material. The first element of the multinational force is the French with about 350. Let me correct that. It basically is the responsibility of the Government of Lebanon and their armed forces to provide for the safety of these departures, and of course to take control of the city and their country. The multinational force is there to assist the Government of Lebanon.

The first contingent is the French contingent of about 350 who will be stationed, I think, in the immediate port area in the beginning. The U.S. troops, the balance of the French and the Italian will enter about 5 days after the departures start.

Q. Mr. Secretary, you just talked about the necessity of addressing the legitimate rights of the Palestinian people in the next phase after Beirut.

Are you willing to tell us whether those legitimate rights include the rights for self-determination and independence? In other words, what's your definition of these legitimate rights for the Palestinians?

SECRETARY SHULTZ. Precisely what that will wind up meaning will have to emerge from a negotiation, I'm sure. The words "self-determination" seem to have taken on terms of art. But I would say, as I've indicated earlier, if people are going to accept some solution, they have to have a part in forming it. Certainly one would expect, as the language of Camp David makes clear,

———

[22] For text, see Department of State *Bulletin*, September 1982, pp. 5–6.

that the Palestinians should have a role in determining the conditions under which they will be governed.

Q. Mr. Secretary, in going through the agreement, I don't see anything mentioned about verifying that the PLO has in fact left Beirut. Maybe I just passed over it, but I wondered if you could address that problem?

SECRETARY SHULTZ. Arrangements have been made to, in effect, check off people as they leave so that there is a verification of how many people have left and so on, and where they have gone. That process will be undertaken, and I believe that is basically a responsibility of the Government of Lebanon to do.

Q. You just mentioned in one of your answers that Arab-American relations are now strained. It doesn't seem to have passed on to some of those Arab governments that when the United States made clear to Israel what the United States wanted, Israel did stop the bombing.

Looking to the future, do you intend again to make clear to Israel to really pursue a negotiated solution which will be acceptable to all parties in the Middle East?

SECRETARY SHULTZ. My hope is that everyone will look at what has happened in the last few weeks and feel that it means that we must all concentrate on creating a just peace.

This shining objective will be the principal motivating force for everyone.

Q. Mr. Secretary, can I just come back to Camp David? You've talked a lot about peace and rights of Palestinians, and you also talked about Camp David.

Before the Lebanon crisis erupted, Secretary Haig was about to launch into an intensified effort to revive the talks between Egypt and Israel on the ground rules for the self-governing authority, as it's called, As well as other leftover points that hadn't been negotiated.

Are you looking for ways beyond this, or are you willing to continue that negotiating track which has been on and off for the last several years as a first step toward this interim solution which is called for in Camp David?

I'm not sure whether you want to stay with Camp David or not.

SECRETARY SHULTZ. The language of Camp David, as I read it, has lots of room for ideas as to how the situation might be arranged. I have been listening to many people. You mentioned Dr. Kissinger and others—Sol Linowitz, Irving Shapiro, Larry Silberman, members of Congress—talking with the President. We're trying to form our ideas about what we think in a general way should be a reasonable outcome and what kind of process will get us there.

As I said at the beginning of this statement, there is a lot of room within the Camp David language, and I think when you see a situation like that it's worthwhile to preserve that.

Q. A lot of room for what, sir?

SECRETARY SHULTZ. A lot of room for many different interpretations as to what that language means, but it's just the kind of language that is generally used, and I recognize that different people put different meanings on it.

Q. Mr. Secretary, your fact sheet that your Department handed out about the sending of these forces suggests strongly that you plan to report to Congress under the War Powers Act under a provision which is not binding in the sense that the troops are not required to be out after 60 days.

As you know, the Chairman of the House Foreign Affairs Committee, Mr. Zablocki, and of the Senate Foreign Relations Committee, Mr. Percy, argue that it should be under the more binding provision because of both the situation and the precedent involved.

In that view is it correct that you're planning, as this suggests, but doesn't exactly say, to go under the nonbinding provision and, if so, why?

SECRETARY SHULTZ. The President will make a decision about what section of the War Powers Act to use at the time of the introduction of American forces. I believe under the law he's required to make that statement within 48 hours of their deployment, and I'm sure that he will do so. He'll have to decide at the time what is the right section.

I would say this: That, first of all, the President has stated explicitly that we have a 30-day time limit here, and that is right in the plan, rather than 60 days as your question suggested.

Second, if we have a basically peaceful departure situation in West Beirut and this government announces that its forces are going in under what it considers conditions of imminent hostility, I wonder what the message is?

I think we have to be cognizant of what the real facts are on the ground and suit our determination to that. I believe the President will certainly be doing that, and I don't want to prejudge what decision he will make..

But I think the basis for the decision should be the conditions on the ground rather than some notion about the number of days or something of that kind.

The President has already specified the limit on the number of days.

MR. JOHN HUGHES. This is the last question.

SECRETARY SHULTZ. If nobody else will end this press conference, Mr. Hughes, who works for me, will. (Laughter)

Q. Mr. Secretary, would you just finish up the Camp David questions that have been brought up?

What evidence is there today that President Mubarak is as anxious to proceed along the framework of Camp David, no matter how you work within this large framework, as was his predecessor?

There's some evidence he is not that keen, is there not?

SECRETARY SHULTZ. I think that, as we noted earlier, people throughout the Arab world are very upset about the events in Lebanon, and it has had a profound effect on their attitudes. I know that. That will represent a problem that we'll have to contend with.

As we go along here we certainly expect to work with President Mubarak and the Egyptians. They have been an essential part of this whole peace process, and I would have every expectation that in the end they will still want to be a part of the peace process.

Q. Thank you very much, Mr. Secretary.

Document 394 0

Transcript of a Department of Defense Press Briefing, August 20, 1982[23]

Deployment of U.S. Marines in Beirut

This morning, following a briefing of congressional leaders, the President announced his decision to send U.S. Marines to Lebanon as part of a multinational force. Earlier this afternoon, Secretary of State Shultz gave further details of the Habib peace agreement. We're now going to give you as many details as we can of the actual military mission. If you'll permit me, I'll give you a narrative summary before we open to the floor for questions.

As most of you already know, the multinational force committed to the Habib plan and requested by the Government of Lebanon will consist of approximately 400 Italian, 800 French and 800 U.S. military.

The U.S. contribution to the Multinational Force will be comprised of Marines of the 32nd Marine Amphibious Unit, or MAU, presently serving with elements of the Sixth Fleet on duty in the Eastern Mediterranean.

Command of the U.S. force ashore in Lebanon will be through normal military command channels starting with the National Command Authority here in Washington, going through the U.S. European Command, to the Commander of the Amphibious Task Group.

There will be no overall Multinational Force Commander; however, the U.S. Marines will coordinate their activities through the U.S. Ambassador in Lebanon and through the Lebanese Armed Forces. Coordination with the other multinational forces and the Lebanese Forces will be achieved through a liaison and coordinating committee and by an exchange of liaison officers between the U.S. contingent and the Lebanese Armed Forces.

Their mission will be to assist the Lebanese Armed Forces in carrying out their responsibilities for the safe and orderly departure from Lebanon of the PLO in a manner which will ensure the safety of other persons in the area.

---

[23] Source: Department of Defense files. Henry E. Catto, Jr., Assistant Secretary of Defense for Public Affairs, conducted the briefing, which began at 3 p.m.

The exact date that U.S. Marines will go ashore is not precisely known but it will be a few days after the PLO withdrawal begins. The U.S. Marines, the Italian forces and the balance of the French will enter Lebanon at the same time. The Marines will take up positions in the vicinity of the Port of Beirut. The exact definition of that area of responsibility will be known later.

They will go ashore from 6th Fleet ships by way of landing craft and helicopters. The exact location of their landing is yet to be determined. They will take ashore field equipment, such as tents, in which to live.

The U.S. Marines will wear their standard camouflage utility uniforms plus have available flak jacket, helmet, canteen, cartridge belt and first aid kit. The normal weapon for the enlisted man will be the M–16 rifle; officers will carry 45 caliber pistols, and pilots will carry 38 caliber pistols. They will not take ashore heavy weapons such as artillery and tanks, but they will have weapons such as machine guns, mortars, and such antitank weapons as Dragons.

While the plan includes provisions for scrupulous observance of the cease-fire, and we consider that provisions are adequate for the safety of our men, our troops ashore will have the assurance that they are backed by elements of the Sixth Fleet including the Carrier *Independence* and its Battle Group stationed just off shore. Individual marines may use their weapons, if necessary, in self-defense.

Let me say here that we will not be discussing the specific rules of engagement. To do so could jeopardize the safety of our men if an adversary sought to take advantage of these rules. Suffice it to say that the rules of engagement are adequate to protect our forces if they are fired upon.

At the end of 30 days or less, the Marines will resume their duties with the Sixth Fleet.

I will be pleased to try to take questions.

Q. The President said that if the Marines are shot at they'll withdraw, is that the case?

A. Certainly a shot by a single deranged person or something like that is not going to terminate the mission. What might terminate it, what will terminate it, is the violation of the agreements that Habib has negotiated.

Q. You mean if they came under sustained fire, they would pull out?

A. I'm not going to go into speculative answers, but any basic violation of the agreement as negotiated by Ambassador Habib will cause the multinational force to withdraw.

Q. Do you expect any casualties in this operation and do you have provisions for medical treatment with the group in Beirut?

A. We certainly do not expect any casualties, but prudent arrangements have been made in case there should be.

Q. Are you deploying tanks and artillery on shore to be held in a holding area, or are those being held on the ships?

A. No, there are no tanks and artillery being deployed on shore.

Q. You said that a Marine could shoot back in self-defense if necessary. Does he have to ask the Secretary of Defense through the European Command whether he can or not? It's a serious question.

A. I understand that, and the answer is no.

Q. Who can authorize them to return fire?

A. Fire can be returned, if a person is fired upon he can return the fire.

Q. He himself can make that judgment?

A. He has the right to self-defense.

Q. Henry, you said that the Marines would be deployed around the Port of Beirut, is that correct?

A. Yes.

Q. Who will go into the central city of Beirut?

A. Well, it depends on what you mean by the central city. The port area more or less encompasses that general area where the piers and docks and so forth are. First of all, the French will go into the port area and then, as the second phase of the operation begins and the Italians and the Americans and the rest of the French come in, then the French will move down toward the central part of the city, toward the museum area which is a major crossing point and toward a gallery that is also a major crossing point. The Italians will be down in the area of the airport which is also an area of major traffic crossing. Let me hasten to say that most of the deployments of all of the forces will be in the eastern sector of Beirut.

Q. Say that again, please.

A. Most of the deployment, 95 percent, for example, of the American position will be in eastern Beirut. This is a rough figure, but the vast majority will be in eastern Beirut.

Q. What physically will the marines do?

A. The marines will be available to assist the Lebanese Armed Forces should they be called upon.

Q. Physically to do what?

A. We simply don't know yet. We don't know under what circumstances the Lebanese might call on us for help, so there's no way of telling in advance what circumstances will arise.

Q. There have been reports that the marines will be asked to disarm the Palestinians boarding boats.

A. Not correct.

Q. Will they have any interaction with the Palestinians at all or are they there just as a presence?

A. They are there as a presence. I foresee no interaction with the Palestinians. The Lebanese basically are the key factor in bringing this about.

Q. —establishing checkpoints of any kind through which Palestinians need to pass?

A. I can't answer that. That is something that will have to be determined.

Q. I just want to be sure we all understand that correctly. You say there will be no contact between American forces and the Palestinians?

A. Not that I am able to foresee. That is subject to change. We all have to keep in mind that this is not the kind of thing that can be rehearsed in advance, and the key word has to be flexibility, based upon what the Lebanese need and upon what the Ambassador and the Embassy staff feels is prudent and necessary and what the Commander feels is within the—

Q. It seems to me your flexibility is quite limited by the intent to keep our people out of any shooting situation. I'm just interested in what form of assistance, appropriate assistance as the term is used here, we can provide and under what circumstances. What's left after you bar a fire-fight possibility?

A. Somebody down here a minute ago said, and I think that pretty well sums it up, the presence of observers from Italy, France, the United States, of troops from Italy, France, and United States, I mean, lends a sense of security and stability. As to specific activities during the course of the day, as I said, I'm not in any position to say how that is going to develop.

Q. Is it envisioned then that the Lebanese will be handling all the logistical aspects of moving the PLO, getting them to the port, making the lists, and checking them twice?

A. That is correct.

Q. And no one else? Not the French or the Italians or the Americans?

A. It is anticipated that the Lebanese will be the ones that are in charge of moving of the PLO, of the supervision of their evacuation.

Q. Could we get into, and you might want to refer to somebody here who specializes, into the tactics of the marines once they land? Are they going to set up a perimeter defense? Are they going to dig up any mines that may be in the area of operations? Are they going to sleep in totality out in the open in their tents? I mean, how are they going to operate on the ground once they get there?

A. That is going to be hard to do in advance. You ought to keep in mind that the French will have been in this area before the Americans get there. I do not believe that it is anticipated that there will be any kind of search for mines or anything like that at all. The French undoubtedly will have taken care of that in advance. And the Lebanese Army will have the basic responsibility for it.

Q. How about the bivouac? Are they going to all sleep in tents or take over buildings?

A. I suspect that will be, here again, a matter to be determined once they get on the ground and see. The anticipation is that they will sleep in tents. I have no idea as to whether or not that will change.

Q. Just one last thing, are we going to deploy in regular infantry company formations, or how are we going to go in?

A. I have no detailed information on that for you.

Q. Haven't many of these details been worked out by the advance party that's been there for a couple of weeks now? I mean, the site of the tent encampment, the logistical arrangements, some of the tactical movements George mentioned?

A. I think it's safe to assume that most of the possibilities have been considered and decisions undoubtedly have been made subject to what the situation on the ground is as it develops.

Q. Henry, if an American soldier finds himself at gunpoint and believed to be at risk, what is his response to be?

A. Well, as I say, he has the right to defend himself if that becomes necessary.

Q. If they shoot him, now if suppose he cannot initiate firing, is that it? In other words, he has to be fired at?

A. He has the right for self-defense.

Q. But that doesn't necessarily mean somebody shot at him. If he thinks he's in danger—

A. I'm not going to get into the hypothetical question area. I just don't think there's anything to be gained by that. The thing to keep in mind is that our guys will have the right of self-defense.

Q. Certainly the soldier will have this clarified for him, won't he? I mean, my Lord, you're not going to send him into Beirut and tell him that if somebody points a gun at him you can or cannot fire?

A. By all means, they will be fully apprised of what their rules of engagement are.

Q. Are they going to wear flak jackets?

A. I can't answer that. I don't know.

Q. If the decision is made to withdraw the marines from Beirut, how long would that take to get them all off the Lebanese coast?

A. You mean at the successful completion of the mission?

Q. I'm talking about if the decision is made because an incident occurs which requires the withdrawal of the multinational force, how quickly could the marines be out of Lebanon?

A. That, there again, is the kind of speculative question that it's impossible to answer. It would certainly depend upon the circumstances under which the decision was taken for the mission to terminate, who's standing between them and a withdrawal. It's just—

Q. Do we have enough helicopters to pull them all out at once?

A. There again, I'm sure, sufficient equipment of all kinds to handle any contingencies that may arise.

Q. Can you say how far off shore the five amphibious ships of this group will be during this operation? One mile, two miles, five miles?

A. No, I'm not going to be able to precisely go into that kind of detail.

Q. Even the backup force, the carrier group, how far will they be off shore?

A. Close enough to do the job.

Q. Henry, are you trying to paint this force as really just a group of reserves that are just being thrown in there rather than front line—

A. I wouldn't dare call active marines just reserves.

Q. That's the mission that you seem to be laying out for them—not an active mission at all.

A. Well, there certainly is no thought that this will be anything but a totally pacific mission—a mission of peace and assistance in the evacuation of the PLO from Beirut.

Q. You cannot tell us at this point, even that they're going to do anything at all? You're just sending them there and if something comes up, they'll do it?

A. They are a presence to be there and to assist as appropriate in the completion of this mission.

Q. Who would be in charge of departure of the agreed number of the PLO from Beirut?

A. That is the kind of detail that has to be answered at the State Department. We just don't have that kind of information.

Q. Henry, did you say when and how the PLO will start withdrawing?

A. When and how?

Q. When they will start and how they will leave, yes.

A. As I understand it, the withdrawal will begin immediately, as soon as the French are there and on shore and able to lend their presence.

Q. You said that 95 percent will be deployed in East Beirut, but in fact your arch extends well into West Beirut.

A. My artistic ability is sharply limited as is my cartographic ability and the idea that I drew here was just to show you where the port area is.

Q. My question is, the port area itself is somewhat of a no-man's land, or it's been a contested territory. Do the Americans go in as far as the area of eastern control is assured, or will they go into some of the no-man's land?

A. The area that the Americans will be in will be in the general area of the port. I'm not prepared to say it will go down to First Street and Roosevelt Avenue, because we have no knowledge of that yet.

Q. Henry, you don't know how the PLO [will leave], that was the other part of my question.

A. The PLO will leave for the most part on board ships. Some will perhaps go overland, and there remains, of course, the possibility of aerial departure as well, or a combination thereof.

Q. Will there be any U.S. Navy escorts for these chartered Red Cross evacuation ships?

A. Should that be requested, that would be available.

Q. What sources are available in that area?

A. The 6th Fleet.

Q. Requested by whom?

A. Well, that's not entirely clear in my mind, whether it would come through the International Red Cross or through the Lebanese Government. Perhaps through both.

Q. Why is there no *overall* commander?

A. That I can't tell you. I have no background on why the decision was made to leave each of the three national forces autonomous.

Q. Was the decision made to delay the entry of the marines into the area because of the opposition expressed to their being there at all in this country?

A. No.

Q. If they're going to provide a presence, why don't they go in the beginning instead of 5 or 6 days later then?

A. The decision to stage it the way they have was made by Ambassador Habib and the people involved and I have no details for you on the problems that were faced in making that decision.

Q. Is this a decision that was supported enthusiastically by the Joint Chiefs of Staff?

A. I wouldn't want to characterize the emotional state of the Joint Chiefs.

Q. What exactly will cause the United States to go in, you say 5 or 6 days, a few days, and what are you looking for that's going to—

A. The trigger in other words.

Q. I don't like to use that word, yes.

A. Fair enough. The thing that will cause the balance of the force to move in [is] when the authorities involved on the scene decide that the time is right. When Ambassador Habib and Ambassador Dillon and the military commanders and the Lebanese think that it is appropriate to move into this second phase, it will begin. In other words, there is no specific action that will bring it about.

Q. And what limits are being placed upon the type of assistance that we can give the Lebanese forces? If they ask for assistance we're giving it to them. Is that a blank check?

A. No, certainly not. It will depend upon whether it is appropriate within the parameters of the agreement.

Q. So you do know at this point if they'll be landing at port facilities or what the arrangements are?

A. Yes, I think it is anticipated that they will sail into a dock, not hit the shore or anything like that.

Q. If asked by the Lebanese Government, would the marines have the authorization to have some kind of direct contact with the PLO?

A. I don't think that that kind of political question is going to arise. And if it does, it's the kind of thing that will have to be decided on the spot.

Q. What can you tell us, a little more specifically, about the PLO withdrawal, and do you have a, let me start with the second question first. Do you have an estimate of how many PLO, you call them combatants, there are here?

A. The general guess is 6,000 to 7,000.

Q. Are they going to march out? Are they going to ride out in jeeps? How are they going to arrive at the port?

A. I have no information on precisely what the mode of transportation to the port area is going to be. I'm sure it will depend on how far away they are.

Q. And lastly, if you're a marine and you're fired upon by an Israeli, I suspect you can fire back?

A. The right of self-defense is not limited by nationality.

Q. Henry, you say, again I'm trying to get a better idea of when this withdrawal will start. You say immediately, as soon as the French are there. Is this tomorrow we're talking about?

A. That's hard to say, Fred, in advance, because we're not positive as of this hour precisely when things are going to get underway.

Q. How many in the French advance party?

A. Oh, 350, maybe.

Q. Several weeks ago the Soviets warned against sending any American troops into Lebanon. Anything that you can say about that now?

A. Yes, the Soviets have been apprised of precisely what is going on and of the very limited nature of what is going on.

Q. Have they responded to that information?

A. For a specific answer to that, you'd have to talk to the State Department, but I'm unaware of any objections on their part. But there again, that's a State Department question.

Q. Does the State Department expect any problems with the Soviets in this operation?

A. No.

Q. Henry, there have been some questions on the arms situation. Now as the PLO board the ships in port, are they going to have any arms at all on board ship?

A. My understanding is that as they get on board ship they will check their arms for the duration of the voyage.

Q. That is with the crew of the ship?

A. Whether it be left with the crew or with Lebanese escorts, I just don't know.

Q. Marines are not going to be involved?

A. No sir.

Q. Can you give us at least the name of the commander who will be in charge of the land force of the Marine Group, the 800 Group or the Aviation Group?

A. The Commander of the 32d MAU is Colonel James Mead, U.S. Marine Corps, of Boston.

Q. Can you spell Mead?

A. M–E–A–D.

Q. Does this group have any special name or [are] they just known as the Marine—

A. It's the 32d MAU.

Q. That's all?

A. Yes.

Q. Is Colonel Mead therefore the local commander for the United States?

A. No, we will have for you names of who the commanders who go ashore will be when they go ashore.

Q. How about a military officer here in the building who will be responsible from this end?

A. Searching for sources, Walter?

Q. No, I'm just searching for information.

A. No, I do not know.

Q. Could you go back over the change of command as you rattled through it at the very beginning?

A. Command of the United States force ashore in Lebanon will be through normal military command channels starting with the National Command Authority here in Washington, going through the United States European Command to the commander of the Amphibious Task Force.

Q. The 6,000 or 7,000 people you're talking about are PLO not including the Syrian Army that's in there, or does that include the Syrians?

A. I do not believe that includes the Syrian Army but I would have to check that.

Q. How many Syrians do you believe—

A. I don't know.

Q. What will the remaining 1,200 amphibious unit marines be doing off shore?

A. Their customary duties that they do when they are at sea.

Q. You have a statement here on financing—the United States is going to underwrite the entire initial cost?

A. No, that's not my understanding.

Q. The United States is prepared to provide initial funding from State Department funds, and estimates regarding the cost of $2 to $4 million.

A. Yes.

Q. Who else is going to share in those costs?

A. I really don't have that information yet.

Q. The United States is not going to underwrite the entire cost?

A. That's my understanding, that we're not going to underwrite the entire cost. The Red Cross is going to pick up a big chunk of the bill and I'm sure that there will be contributions by French and Italian sources as well.

Q. Will there be any forces on board these evacuation ships and would any American forces be allowed on board?

A. No, my understanding is that that is not to happen.

Q. Could you tell us what sort of aid is envisioned that the Lebanese might ask for that we would be willing to give them? You say that we're—

A. No, it's just impossible to tell what is going to happen on the ground in a situation like this.

Q. Well, you're authorized to give them some kind of assistance. I'm just curious as to what they may be asking for.

A. I just have nothing for you at all on precisely what form it might take.

Q. Do you know if there are going to be any Arabic speakers in the U.S. military contingent?

A. I do not know for a fact, but it would seem very likely.

Q. Do you know whether they will be identified in any particular way, with a special arm band or any other sort of—

A. The Arab speakers?

Q. The marines.

A. Well, the marines will certainly be identified by their uniforms.

Q. But there is no multinational force—

A. Not to the best of my knowledge.

Q. Have I got this right? Eight hundred marines wearing camouflage field uniforms and carrying M–16's are going to get on boats and helicopters and go into the port area of Beirut and set up tents. That is all you've told us they are going to do in the course of this 30 days, isn't it? Have you told us a single thing that they are going to do while they're there?

A. You are quite correct. I have not told you a single thing that they are going to do while they are there because it is, at this stage of the game, quite simply impossible to know in advance precisely what is going to be—I've told you some things they're not going to be doing. They're not going to [be] looking for mines and they're not going to be disarming PLO and that kind of thing.

Q. Does it follow from that that nobody knows of anything that they're going to do?

A. The full range of possibilities has undoubtedly been discussed but I have nothing for you—no decisions have been made until they get on the ground and see what the situation is.

Q. This has been going on for 11 weeks or something of this sort. In July, Mr. Habib requested from the President the possible commitment of troops. There must be a purpose in it. There must be a list of things known to someone. Can you reassure us that, while you can't tell us, somebody does know what they are going to do?

A. Sure, Charlie. The main thing is that the presence of the Americans, the Italians, and the French will be seen as a guarantor and as a safety mechanism that will make the Palestinians feel comfortable in a withdrawal situation. A situation that is inherently militarily dangerous and which obviously gives the Palestinian Commanders pause at the thought. They have felt apparently, and Ambassador Habib has felt that there is justification in the way they felt, that there was a need for an outside presence to stabilize the situation and to provide the comfortable knowledge of the existence of outsiders there to see to it that nothing was likely to go wrong.

Q. One more question, forgive me. Is what you have just said then, that the purpose of the American and other forces is to see that Israeli troops do not bother the Palestinians when they are leaving?

A. What I'm saying is that in a situation like this, the withdrawing forces realizing that their rear is vulnerable, feel the need of assurance.

Q. How are you going to secure their safety when most militias in Lebanon have the same camouflage uniforms like your marines that are going to be landing there?

A. I dare say there are going to be some differences in the uniforms.

Q. There is another aspect though to this whole operation and that is the stated purpose of assisting the Lebanese Government in restoring its sovereignty and authority in its own capital city. That would seem to indicate to the casual reader that there is some more active role that the Marine Corps would play in assisting the Lebanese Armed Forces than standing around looking imposing. What kinds of things might be done to help restore Lebanese authority in Beirut?

A. Well, there won't be anything, as far as I understand it, specific done to help restore Lebanese authority except the very key first step, which is to remove the PLO fighters from the Lebanese capital. That in itself will contribute to the restoration of the authority of the Lebanese Government.

Q. That begs the question that if not all of them choose to go there might be some problem in restoring that—

A. Well, here again, you have moved into the speculative realm and there's just no way for us to know and no reason to assume that the negotiations worked out by Ambassador Habib are not going to work.

Q. Henry, you've touched on some of this before, but please go over it once more. Under what conditions would the United States Marine Corps contingent we're discussing here terminate their mission before its natural end and leave?

A. All of the multinational force have made it very clear that they would terminate their mission before its natural end and leave if there were a violation of the agreements which Ambassador Habib has negotiated.

Q. That is, such things as the PLO declines to leave on schedule?

A. Who knows what form the violations might take. But a violation would result in termination.

Q. Do you understand that to include the cease-fire itself?

A. Oh yes. If the cease-fire were to collapse I think that would certainly be—

Q. The President said this morning that the troops would withdraw if they were shot at. Secretary Shultz tried to clarify that by saying he did not, the President did not mean a stray shot, something similar to what you said earlier, but it still leaves the impression that if the Marine Corps contingent comes under fire from anything greater than a stray shot from a roof or whatever, Secretary Shultz said, they would pick up and leave.

A. No, a determination that the terms of the Habib agreement had been violated would result in the departure of the multinational force.

Q. It's very germane. You keep saying that the troops provide a sense of stability and a sense of security yet if we don't [*sic*]; I mean one gets the impression that all you have to do is set off some fire crackers and the 800 marines run back to the ships.

A. No, my best understanding of the Habib agreement does not cover the explosion of fire crackers.

Q. Let's say you get five or six guys to start a small fire fight, and there you have something that could be interpreted by—

A. Here again, Jack, you're going to have to see what the situation is on the ground, and decisions will have to be made when this hypothetical situation takes place. There is no way in advance to know.

Q. You've got to lay down the rules, so you're saying that it could be more than a kook and they still won't necessarily leave. But something less than that might not—

A. I'm just not willing to go any further into the realm of the speculative to say what, how many millions of ways can things fall apart. There are lots.

George, your turn.

Q. I'd like to get this straight. Let's say that the PLO troopers or whatever are on an American ship on the way to somewhere.

A. That is not going to happen.

Q. Will they ever be in our custody?

A. No.

Q. We will never do anything but be a screen force, right?

A. I wouldn't want to call it a screening force, but we will not have in our custody PLO fighters.

Q. Will the marines have any authority for any kind of interface with the PLO offensive, defensive?

A. I'm sure they will have authority to respond to "Say, buddy, will you give me a light?" or something like that, but there is no contemplation that we will deal directly with them.

Q. In a legal sense, are these PLO troops, what are they considered? Are they considered citizens of Lebanon, prisoners of war, detainees?

A. As I understand it, they carry a number of different national passports, many of them, from Arab countries.

Q. For our purposes, if I were a U.S. Marine, and I'm told you have to consider these people prisoners of war, detainees or foreign troops or—

A. They won't be in the hands of the U.S. Marines.

Q. I was just wondering what their legal status is in our eyes?

A. Do you have anything to add to what I said?

VOICE. State Department.

MR. CATTO. That's the kind of thing that State Department can much better address. (Laughter)

Q. Will the multinational force be providing any special protection or special accommodations for the PLO leadership?

A. No, not to the best of my knowledge.

Q. Can you tell us anything about coordination with Israeli forces? Will there be any?

A. Undoubtedly there will be full cooperation and coordination with the Israelis under the agreement.

Q. Is it a formalized liaison, et cetera?

A. I do not know the precise methods of communication that will be set up, but of course there will be.

Q. Will we have the authority to decide whether there was a violation—Habib or, who makes the—

A. Undoubtedly, the people on the scene including Ambassador Habib, Ambassador Dillon, the military authorities, the coordinating committee among the countries and the Lebanese, the key people, the Lebanese.

Q. Do you expect while this is going on next week to see Mr. Sharon here in Washington? He has a scheduled visit here this week.

A. I've seen nothing about that. Can anybody throw any light on that?

VOICE. No.

MR. CATTO. I've seen nothing about it.

Q. It sounds to me like most of your dependence is on the Lebanese Armed Forces and they are only armed with M–16's and rifles and machine guns. How do you expect them to do the job with that kind of weaponry?

A. I listened to Secretary Shultz for a clue to the answer to that and didn't get anything definitive. He made the very germane point that Habib is undoubtedly very weary of the whole thing, having worked around the clock as long as he has, but my guess would be, and it would be strictly a guess, that he will continue to be available to the President should he be needed.

Q. Yassir Arafat, when will he be evacuated, where will he go, and under whose auspices?

A. I have absolutely no information on where the PLO will be going.

Q. I'm not talking about the PLO, I'm talking about him, Arafat—

A. Where the leadership will go, to which countries or anything, I just don't know. I don't know if that has been finalized.

Q. Can we assume that there will be some special measure to expedite his departure from Beirut or will he just walk out with all his—

A. It's outside my area of knowledge, Rick, I just don't know. There again, that's the kind of question the State Department will have to get into.

Q. How many PLO will be left when the marines finally come in? What is the criteria for these first waves that are going out and what ships are going to be actually used to transport them?

A. There will be Red Cross chartered ships to transport them away from Lebanon; many to Cyprus and then on to their final destination, either by ship or by air.

Q. How many will be physically gone?

A. I do not know offhand what the schedule is going to be of numbers per day or where they'll be going or that sort of thing. I don't have anything for you on that.

Q. Henry, there's a period in the first days when the Syrians are moving out of Beirut and it would appear that they must leave Beirut before the Americans and the Italians come in, is that correct?

A. I cannot answer that. That again deals with the details of the agreement and will have to be answered by the State Department.

Q. Is there a certain amount of movement that has to take place before the

French move on to their second area and then the Americans come in?

A. I am unaware of any specific numerical point at which A will cease to happen and B will begin to happen.

Q. One other thing, do the Israelis have any right, opportunity, provisions to oversee the departure? Will any Israelis be in the port area during their departure?

A. Not to the best of my knowledge, no. They will stay at the line of furthest advance to which they had originally arrived.

Q. Since the marines will be in the port area nowhere near West Beirut where all the PLO is, and since they're there to assist the Lebanese, if the Lebanese get shot at and ask for assistance, is it part of the mission that the Americans or the Italians or the French would go to their aid?

A. There again you have a speculative situation which I can't address, but I do want to make one thing clear because you said "because they are not going to be in West Beirut where the PLO is." Part of the generally demarcated port area is going to lap over into West Beirut. Exactly where it is going to be, I don't know. The port area that the French first and later the Americans will occupy, is not entirely in East Beirut. Part of it is in West Beirut.

Q. If the Lebanese get into trouble, can they call on the French and the Americans and the Italians to help them?

A. Here again, that is the kind of speculative "what if" question that I'm just not going to be able to address.

Q. Can I ask a political question?

A. From me?

Q. The President himself made the announcement that American troops were going in and Secretary Shultz held his first press conference. I was just wondering why the Secretary himself didn't hold this briefing?

A. Well, this is the kind of nuts and bolts thing that I don't think is appropriate for him to have to worry about. That's what I get paid for.

Q. Will the U.S. Marines ever move out of the port area as such? Will they be deployed along the green line or at any of the check points or along the Beirut–Damascus highway or is that—

A. No, no. The Americans will stay in the port area.

PRESS. Thank you.

MR. CATTO. Thank you all.

Document 395

Letter From President Reagan to the Speaker of the House of Representatives (O'Neill), Santa Barbara, August 24, 1982[24]

Notification to Congress Regarding the U.S. Role in the Multinational Force

DEAR MR. SPEAKER: On August 18, 1982, the Government of Lebanon established a plan for the departure from Lebanon of the Palestine Liberation Organization leadership, offices, and combatants in Beirut. This plan has been accepted by the Government of Israel. The Palestine Liberation Organization has informed the Government of Lebanon that it also has accepted the plan. A key element of this plan is the need for a multinational force, including a United States component, to assist the Government of Lebanon in carrying out its responsibilities concerning the withdrawal of these personnel under safe and orderly conditions. This will facilitate the restoration of Lebanese Government sovereignty and authority over the Beirut area.

In response to the formal request of the Government of Lebanon, and in view of the requirement for such a force in order to secure the acceptance by concerned parties of the departure plan, I have authorized the Armed Forces of the United States to participate on a limited and temporary basis. In accordance with my desire that the Congress be fully informed on this matter, and consistent with the War Powers Resolution, I am hereby providing a report on the deployment and mission of these members of the United States Armed Forces.

On August 21, in accordance with the departure plan, approximately 350 French military personnel—the advance elements of the multinational force—were deployed in Beirut together with elements of the Lebanese Armed Forces, and the departure of Palestinian personnel began. To date,

[24] Source: White House Press Release, August 25, 1982, Office of the Press Secretary to the President; also printed in *Weekly Compilation of Presidential Documents*, August 30, 1982, pp. 1065–1066. An identical letter was also addressed to Strom Thurmond, President pro tempore of the Senate.

Palestinian personnel have departed Lebanon in accordance with the terms of the plan.

On August 25, approximately 800 U.S. Marines began to arrive in Beirut. These troops are equipped with weapons consistent with their non-combat mission, including usual infantry weapons.

Under our agreement with the Government of Lebanon, these U.S. military personnel will assist the Government of Lebanon in carrying out its responsibilities concerning the withdrawal of Palestinian personnel under safe and orderly conditions. The presence of our forces will in this way facilitate the restoration of Lebanese Government sovereignty and authority in the Beirut area. Our forces will operate in close coordination with the Lebanese Armed Forces, which will have 2,500–3,500 personnel assigned to this operation, as well as with a total of approximately 800 French and 400 Italian military personnel in the multinational force. Transportation of the personnel departing is being carried out by commercial air and sea transport, and by land. According to our agreement with the Government of Lebanon,[25] the United States military personnel will be withdrawn from Lebanon within thirty days.

I want to emphasize that there is no intention or expectation that U.S. Armed Forces will become involved in hostilities. They are in Lebanon at the formal request of the Government of Lebanon. Our agreement with the Government of Lebanon expressly rules out any combat responsibilities for the U.S. forces. All armed elements in the area have given assurances that they will take no action to interfere with the implementation of the departure plan or the activities of the multinational force. (The departure has been underway for some days now, and thus far these assurances have been fulfilled.) Finally, the departure plan makes it clear that in the event of a breakdown in its implementation, the multinational force will be withdrawn. Although we cannot rule out isolated acts of violence, all appropriate precautions have thus been taken to assure the safety of U.S. military personnel during their brief assignment to Lebanon.

This deployment of the United States Armed Forces to Lebanon is being undertaken pursuant to the President's constitutional authority with respect to the conduct of foreign relations and as Commander-in-Chief of the United States Armed Forces.

[25] See documents 389 and 390.

This step will not, by itself, resolve the situation in Lebanon, let alone the problems which have plagued the region for more than thirty years. But I believe that it will improve the prospects for realizing our objectives in Lebanon:

—a permanent cessation of hostilities;

—establishment of a strong, representative central government;

—withdrawal of all foreign forces;

—restoration of control by the Lebanese Government throughout the country; and

—establishment of conditions under which Lebanon no longer can be used as a launching point for attacks against Israel.

I also believe that progress on the Lebanon problem will contribute to an atmosphere in the region necessary for progress towards the establishment of a comprehensive peace in the region under Camp David, based firmly on U.N. Security Council Resolutions 242 and 338.

Sincerely,

RONALD REAGAN

Document 396

Statement by the Administrator, Agency for International Development (McPherson), Beirut, August 31, 1982[26]

Relief and Rehabilitation Assistance to Lebanon

This is my second visit to Lebanon in the past 2 months. During my current visit, I met senior officials of the Lebanese Government, including the President and the President-elect, representatives of the voluntary relief agencies and international organizations, and officers of the U.S. Embassy. These discussions indicate that the immediate needs for disaster relief in Lebanon are largely being met, although continuous monitoring is required, and shelter will need to be provided for about 60,000 people before the fall rains. The question of rehabilitation, however, is another matter,

[26] Source: AID Press Release, September 2, 1982. McPherson made this statement upon the conclusion of a 2-day visit to Beirut.

both in West Beirut and in the south. The extent of devastation in West Beirut is clearly very great. However, an on-the-ground assessment is required before we can determine the damage and the necessary response.

The Lebanese Government will provide the leadership in the rehabilitation. We also expect Lebanon's other friends to give support. This is going to be an international effort.

As for our own role, the President has requested $65 million for relief and rehabilitation in Lebanon. Fifty million of this money must be voted by Congress. The first priority of this money is for relief, and about $13.5 million has been spent, largely for relief.

I discussed the further needs with Secretary Shultz and the White House before I left Washington and have had several discussions here. Pursuant to these discussions, we are now announcing 30 million additional dollars of U.S. Government guarantees for repair or reconstruction of power, sewer, and water facilities damaged by the recent hostilities. These guarantees are from authority already voted by Congress. Details are to be worked out.

I will report to the President and the Secretary of State upon my return on my findings here.

Document 397

Remarks by President Reagan and the President's Special Emissary to the Middle East (Habib), September 8, 1982 (Extract)[27]

"The Next Phase of U.S. Diplomacy in Lebanon"

THE PRESIDENT. Good afternoon, ladies and gentlemen. I asked Phil Habib to come by today in order to discuss the next phase of the U.S. diplomacy in Lebanon and the prospects for our Middle East initiative. I want to begin by reaffirming our principal objectives in Lebanon—first, the removal of all foreign, military forces from Lebanon; second, the strengthening of the central government and the establishment of its authority throughout the country; third, Lebanon must not again become a launching pad for attacks into Israel. Indeed, the security of all the states in the area can only be guaranteed through freely negotiated peace treaties between Israel and its neighbors. And, finally, I call on all the parties in Lebanon to maintain the cease-fire so that diplomacy can succeed.

In the course of his briefing, Phil told me that a peaceful resolution of the Beirut crisis would not have been possible without a multinational force that included the U.S. forces. With the evacuation complete and the authorities asserting their control throughout Beirut, I am pleased to announce that the multinational force will commence its withdrawal from Beirut, Friday, September 10th, day after tomorrow. And the U.S. marine contingent should be among the first to leave. We are, therefore, keeping our commitment to have them out within 30 days.

I'll remain fully and personally engaged in support of the next phase of our diplomacy in Lebanon. I also am announcing the formation of an interagency steering group on Lebanon. This group, under the chairmanship of the Deputy Secretary of State, will coordinate the political, economic, and security assistance dimensions of our policy. Peter McPherson, Director of AID, will assume responsibility for reconstruction efforts in addition to his role as my personal representative for relief in Lebanon. And Morris Draper, Phil's right hand in Lebanon, has been accorded the personal rank of Ambassador and he will manage the political working group and shortly return to Lebanon to continue his work. And I want to express my appreciation to him for what he has done and what he is going to continue doing.

And once again, I want to extend my heartfelt congratulations to Phil Habib for his superhuman efforts throughout the past year and a half. Phil's successful diplomacy is one reason why we are now able to inject a fresh start into the peace process.

Phil would like to make some remarks, I know, and I know many of you would like to ask him questions. So, I'm going to leave

---

27 Source: White House Press Release, September 8, 1982, Office of the Press Secretary to the President; also printed in *Weekly Compilation of Presidential Documents,* September 13, 1982, pp. 1104–1105. For the full text, see *ibid.* President Reagan spoke to reporters on the South Grounds of the White House at 3:28 p.m. after meeting in the Oval Office with Secretary Shultz and Ambassadors Philip C. Habib and Morris Draper. On September 7, President Reagan awarded Habib the Presidential Medal of Freedom in a ceremony in the East Room of the White House. (See *Weekly Compilation of Presidential Documents,* September 13, 1982, pp. 1094–1095)

Phil and Morris to you and I have a date back in the office that I must now keep and return to work. So, thank you for being here. And, Phil, again, thank you. God bless you.

AMBASSADOR HABIB. Thank you for everything, Mr. President.

AMBASSADOR DRAPER. Thank you very much, Mr. President.

THE PRESIDENT. Morris, thank you.

Q. Mr. President, before you go, can you just tell us what you think about Prime Minister Begin saying to the Knesset today that the West Bank would be a Jewish homeland forever?

THE PRESIDENT. I think that I—I think that I'll let these gentlemen handle the questions—and take a question from that, my own personal reaction is that, because I stressed negotiations as the settlement to many of these troublesome issues there, I think that we have to understand sometimes that maybe positions are being staked out with those negotiations in mind.

Q. But do you think Israel will change, sir? Do you think this initial reaction can be modified in the future?

THE PRESIDENT. That's up to the negotiators.

Q. He's gone now. Tell us everything. (Laughter)

AMBASSADOR HABIB. No. It's—first of all, it's kind of nice to be able to talk to you fellows without having to just wave as I go by.

But I'm particularly gratified that the President is continuing his personal interest in the Lebanese situation. It's going to require continued high-level attention in our government as we pursue the objectives that the President has laid down for us. And in that regard he and Secretary Shultz have given Morris and myself our instructions. Morris has his marching orders. He'll be taking off very shortly. And then later in the month I'll go out for the inauguration of the new President[28] and spend a few days with him.

But, basically, we're going to be trying to build upon the initial—I wouldn't call them successes as much as I would call them the initial progress that's been made in the Lebanese situation. There is a fair, good chance that we can see a sovereign, integral, free, pluralistic Lebanon, once again sovereign within its own territories. And that's what we're basically going to be working for.[29]

. . . .

Document 398

Statement and Remarks by the Department of State Spokesman (Hughes), September 15, 1982 (Extract)[30]

Efforts To Restore the Authority of the Lebanese Government

[MR. HUGHES.] We deplore the shocking assassination of President-elect Gemayel.[31] This latest violent tragedy only reemphasizes the need for urgency in the search for peace in the Middle East. The central government of Lebanon remains in place. We will be consulting with President Sarkis, Prime Minister Wazzan, and other Lebanese Government officials to explore ways we can support their efforts to maintain stability.

We have been in frequent touch with senior officials of the Government of Lebanon and with other prominent Lebanese personalities. Ambassador Draper is in Lebanon today for meetings with Lebanese officials. Our support for their efforts to maintain order is clear. We have also contacted Israeli officials in Beirut, Washington, and in Israel. We have urged they do nothing to increase tensions, and we again call on all parties to exercise restraint.

President-elect Gemayel's death underscores the need that we not lose sight of the

---

[28] On August 23, 1982, the Lebanese Chamber of Deputies elected Bashir Gemayel, a Maronite Christian, to a 6-year term as President of Lebanon, beginning September 23. Gemayel received 57 votes on the second ballot, with 5 blank ballots being cast.

[29] Here follow questions and answers reproduced only in the press release.

[30] Source: Office of Press Relations, Department of State; also printed in Department of State *Bulletin*, November 1982, p. 48. The statement and remarks were made at the Department of State Daily Press Briefing held at 12:15 p.m.

[31] President-elect Bashir Gemayel was assassinated by a bomb explosion in East Beirut on September 14, 1982. He had been scheduled to take office on September 23.

important objectives which Lebanon has set for itself. The restoration of central government authority remains the key to Lebanon's future. We will do everything we can to assist this process through this difficult period in the country's history.

Ambassador Draper has the full support of the President, and will continue to work closely with the Government of Lebanon in pursuit of its objectives. Those objectives parallel our own support for the withdrawal of all foreign military forces from Lebanon, the strengthening of the central government and the reestablishment of its authority throughout Lebanon, the creation of conditions which ensure that Lebanon will never again be a launching pad for attacks against Israel, and the promotion of national unity and reconciliation along with strengthening of all national institutions, including the army. We will continue to pursue the goals we share with the Government of Lebanon of internal unity and withdrawal of all foreign forces. The United States intends, as well, to press ahead vigorously with the President's initiative to broaden the participation at the Middle East peace talks.

Q. What that doesn't say is what impact do you think the death of Gemayel is going to have on the situation.

A. As the President said in his statement,[32] this was a shocking development, a cowardly assassination, but I think the President also indicated that we have to continue to move forward vigorously with both the objectives in Lebanon and on this overall question of a Middle East peace settlement, and that despite the human tragedy which, obviously, has deeply moved him, this should not be allowed to deter us from these goals.

. . . .

---

[32] In a statement issued on September 14, President Reagan said, "The United States Government stands by Lebanon with its full support in this hour of need." (*Weekly Compilation of Presidential Documents,* September 20, 1983, p. 1145)

Document 399

Statement Read by the President's Deputy Press Secretary (Speakes), September 16, 1982[33]

Call for Israeli Withdrawal From West Beirut

It appears from press reports and eyewitness accounts that the Israelis have now moved into strategic positions throughout West Beirut and control much of that sector of the city. This is contrary to the assurances given to us by the Israelis both in Washington and in Israel.

We fully support the Lebanese Government's call for the withdrawal of Israeli forces, which are in clear violation of the cease-fire understanding to which Israel is a party. There is no justification in our view for Israel's continued military presence in West Beirut, and we call for an immediate pull-back.

Document 400

Resolution 520 (1982), Adopted by the U.N. Security Council, September 17, 1982[34]

Demand for Israeli Withdrawal From West Beirut

The Security Council,

Having considered the report of the Secretary-General of 15 September 1982 (S/15382/Add. 1),

Condemning the murder of Bashir Gemayel, Lebanon's constitutionally selected President-elect, and every effort to disrupt by violence the restoration of a strong, stable government in Lebanon,

Having listened to the statement by the Permanent Representative of Lebanon,[35]

---

[33] Source: *Weekly Compilation of Presidential Documents,* September 20, 1982, p. 1160. The statement was read at a White House press briefing held at 12:20 p.m.

[34] Source: U.N. Security Council Resolution 520 (1982); also printed in Department of State *Bulletin,* November 1982, p. 55. The resolution, sponsored by Jordan, was adopted unanimously.

[35] For the text of the statement by Ghassan at-

Taking note of Lebanon's determination to ensure the withdrawal of all non-Lebanese forces from Lebanon,

1. *Reaffirms* its resolutions 508 (1982), 509 (1982) and 516 (1982) in all their components;

2. *Condemns* the recent Israeli incursions into Beirut in violation of the cease-fire agreements and of Security Council resolutions;

3. *Demands* an immediate return to the positions occupied by Israel before 15 September 1982, as a first step towards the full implementation of Security Council resolutions;

4. *Calls again* for the strict respect for Lebanon's sovereignty, territorial integrity, unity and political independence under the sole and exclusive authority of the Lebanese Government through the Lebanese Army throughout Lebanon;

5. *Reaffirms* its resolutions 512 (1982) and 513 (1982) which call for respect for the rights of the civilian populations without any discrimination and repudiates all acts of violence against those populations;

6. *Supports* the efforts of the Secretary-General to implement Security Council resolution 516 (1982) concerning the deployment of United Nations observers to monitor the situation in and around Beirut and requests all the parties concerned to cooperate fully in the application of that resolution;

7. *Decides* to remain seized of the question and asks the Secretary-General to keep the Council informed on developments as soon as possible and not later than twenty-four hours.[36]

Tueni, Lebanese Permanent Representative to the United Nations, before the U.N. Security Council on September 16, 1982, see U.N. document S/PV.2394.

[36] For the Report of the U.N. Secretary-General in Pursuance of Security Council Resolution 520 (1982), see U.N. document S/15400, September 18, 1982.

Document 401

Statement by President Reagan, September 18, 1982[37]

Massacre at the Sabra and Shatila Palestinian Refugee Camps in West Beirut

I was horrified to learn this morning of the killing of Palestinians which has taken place in Beirut.[38] All people of decency must share our outrage and revulsion over the murders, which included women and children. I express my deepest regrets and condolences to the families of the victims and the broader Palestinian community.

During the negotiations leading to the PLO withdrawal from Beirut, we were assured that Israeli forces would not enter West Beirut. We also understood that following withdrawal, Lebanese Army units would establish control over the city. They were thwarted in this effort by the Israeli occupation that took place beginning on Wednesday.[39] We strongly opposed Israel's move into West Beirut following the assassination of President-elect Gemayel both because we believed it wrong in principle and for fear that it would provoke further fighting.[40] Israel, by yesterday in military control of Beirut, claimed that its moves would prevent the kind of tragedy which has now occurred.

We have today summoned the Israeli Ambassador[41] to demand that the Israeli Government immediately withdraw its forces from West Beirut to the positions occupied on September 14. We also expect Israel thereafter to commence serious negotiations which will first lead to the earliest possible disengagement of Israeli forces from Beirut and second, to an agreed framework for the early withdrawal of all foreign forces from Lebanon.

---

[37] Source: White House Press Release, September 18, 1982, Office of the Press Secretary to the President; also printed in *Weekly Compilation of Presidential Documents,* September 27, 1982, p. 1177.

[38] During September 16–18, 1982, an estimated 700 to 800 Palestinian civilians were massacred in the Sabra and Shatila refugee camps at the southern edge of West Beirut.

[39] September 15, 1982.

[40] See document 399.

[41] Moshe Arens.

Despite and because of the additional bloody trauma which adds to Lebanon's agonies, we urge the Lebanese to unite quickly in support of their government and their constitutional processes and to work for the future they so richly deserve. We will be with them.

This terrible tragedy underscores the desperate need for a true peace in the Middle East, one which takes full account of the needs of the Palestinian people. The initiative I announced on September 1[42] will be pursued vigorously in order to achieve that goal.

Document 402

Resolution 521 (1982), Adopted by the U.N. Security Council, September 19, 1982[43]

Condemnation of the Massacre in Beirut

The Security Council,

Appalled at the massacre of Palestinian civilians in Beirut,

Having heard the report of the Secretary-General (S/15400),

Noting that the Government of Lebanon has agreed to the dispatch of United Nations observers to the sites of greatest human suffering and losses in and around that city,

1. *Condemns* the criminal massacre of Palestinian civilians in Beirut;

2. *Reaffirms* once again its resolutions 512 (1982) and 513 (1982) which call for respect for the rights of the civilian population without any discrimination and repudiates all acts of violence against that population;

3. *Authorizes* the Secretary-General as an immediate step to increase the number of United Nations observers in and around Beirut from 10 to 50 and insists that there shall be no interference with the deployment of the observers and that they shall have full freedom of movement;

4. *Requests* The Secretary-General, in consultation with the Government of Lebanon, to ensure the rapid deployment of those observers in order that they may contribute in every way possible within their mandate, to the effort to ensure full protection for the civilian population;

5. *Requests* the Secretary-General as a matter of urgency to initiate appropriate consultations and in particular consultations with the Government of Lebanon on additional steps which the Council might take, including the possible deployment of United Nations forces, to assist that Government in ensuring full protection for the civilian population in and around Beirut and requests him to report to the Council within forty-eight hours;[44]

6. *Insists* that all concerned must permit United Nations observers and forces established by the Security Council in Lebanon to be deployed and to discharge their mandates and in this connexion solemnly calls attention to the obligation on all Member States under Article 25 of the Charter to accept and carry out the decisions of the Council in accordance with the Charter;

7. *Requests* the Secretary-General to keep the Council informed on an urgent and continuing basis.

Document 403

Statement by President Reagan, September 20, 1982[45]

Announcement of a New Multinational Force Deployment in Beirut

The scenes that the whole world witnessed this past weekend were among the

---

[42] For President Reagan's Middle East peace initiative, see document 318.

[43] Source: U.N. Security Council Resolution 521 (1982); also printed in Department of State *Bulletin,* November 1982, pp. 55–56. The resolution was adopted unanimously.

[44] For the Report of the U.N. Secretary-General in Pursuance of Security Council Resolution 521 (1982), see U.N. documents S/15408, September 20, 1982; S/15408/Add. 1, September 27, 1982; and S/15408/Add. 2, September 30, 1982.

[45] Source: White House Press Release, September 20, 1982, Office of the Press Secretary to the President; also printed in *Weekly Compilation of Presidential Documents,* September 27, 1982, pp. 1182–1184. The President delivered this statement from the Oval Office at the White House on nationwide radio and television at 5 p.m.

most heartrending in the long nightmare of Lebanon's agony. Millions of us have seen pictures of the Palestinian victims of this tragedy. There is little that words can add. But there are actions we can and must take to bring that nightmare to an end.

It is not enough for us to view this as some remote event in which we ourselves are not involved. For our friends in Lebanon and Israel; for our friends in Europe and elsewhere in the Middle East; and for us as Americans—this tragedy, horrible as it is, reminds us of the absolute imperative of bringing peace to that troubled country and region. By working for peace in the Middle East, we serve the cause of world peace, and the future of mankind.

For the criminals who did this deed no punishment is enough to remove the blot of their crime. But for the rest of us there are things that we can learn and things that we must do:

—The people of Lebanon must have learned that the cycle of massacre upon massacre must end. Children are not avenged by the murder of other children.

—Israel must have learned that there is no way it can impose its own solutions on hatreds as deep and bitter as those that produced this tragedy. If it seeks to do so, it will only sink more deeply into the quagmire that looms before it.

—Those outsiders who have fed the flames of civil war in Lebanon for so many years need to learn that the fire will consume them too if it is not put out.

—And we must all rededicate ourselves to the cause of peace. I reemphasize my call for early progress to solve the Palestinian issue and repeat the U.S. proposals which are now even more urgent.

For now is not the time for talk alone. Now is a time for action. To act together to restore peace to Beirut; to help a stable government emerge that can restore peace and independence to all of Lebanon; and to bring a just and lasting resolution to the conflict between Israel and its Arab neighbors, one that satisfies the legitimate rights of the Palestinians who are all too often its victims.

Our basic objectives in Lebanon have not changed, for they are the objectives of the Government and people of Lebanon themselves. First and foremost, we seek the restoration of a strong and stable central government in that country, brought into being by orderly constitutional processes. Lebanon elected a new President two short weeks ago only to see him murdered even before he could assume his office. This week a distressed Lebanon will again be electing a new President. May God grant him safety as well as the wisdom and courage to lead his country into a new and happier era.

The international community has an obligation to assist the Government of Lebanon in reasserting authority over all of its territory. Foreign forces and armed factions have too long obstructed the legitimate role of the Government of Lebanon's security forces. We must pave the way for withdrawal of foreign forces.

The place to begin this task is in Beirut. The Lebanese Government must be permitted to restore internal security in its capital. It cannot do this if foreign forces remain in or near Beirut. I have consulted with our French and Italian allies. We have agreed to form a new multinational force similar to the one which served so well last month, with the mission of enabling the Lebanese Government to resume full sovereignty over its capital and the essential precondition for extending its control over the entire country.

The Lebanese Government, with the support of its people, requested this help. For this multinational force to succeed it is essential that Israel withdraw from Beirut. With the expected cooperation of all parties, the multinational force will return to Beirut for a limited period of time. Its purpose is not to act as a police force, but to make it possible for the lawful authorities of Lebanon to do so for themselves.

Secretary Shultz, on my behalf, has also reiterated our views to the Government of Israel through its Ambassador in Washington. Unless Israel moves quickly and courageously to withdraw, it will find itself ever more deeply involved in problems that are not its own and which it cannot solve.

The participation of American forces in Beirut will again be for a limited period. But I have concluded that there is no alternative to their returning to Lebanon if that country is to have a chance to stand on its own feet.

Peace in Beirut is only a first step. Together with the people of Lebanon, we seek the removal of all foreign military forces from that country. The departure of all foreign forces at the request of the Lebanese authorities has been widely endorsed by Arab as well as other states. Israel and Syria have both indicated that they have no territorial ambitions in Lebanon and are prepared to withdraw. It is now urgent that specific arrangements for withdrawal of all foreign forces be agreed upon. This must happen very soon. The legitimate security concerns of neighboring states, including particularly the safety of Israel's northern population, must be provided for, but this is not a difficult task if the political will is there. The Lebanese people must be allowed to chart their own future; they must rely solely on Lebanese armed forces, who are willing and able to bring security to their country. They must be allowed to do so—and the sooner the better.

Ambassador Draper, who has been in close consultation with the parties concerned in Lebanon, will remain in the area to work for the full implementation of our proposal. Ambassador Habib will join him, will represent me at the inauguration of the new President of Lebanon and will consult with the leaders in the area. He will return promptly to Washington to report to me.

Early in the summer our government met its responsibility to help resolve a severe crisis and to relieve the Lebanese people of a crushing burden. We succeeded. Recent events have produced new problems and we must again assume our responsibility.

I am especially anxious to end the agony of Lebanon because it is both right and in our national interest. But I am also determined to press ahead on the broader effort to achieve peace between Israel and its Arab neighbors. The events in Beirut of last week have served only to reinforce my conviction that such a peace is desperately needed and that the initiative we undertook on September first is the right way to proceed. We will not be discouraged or deterred in our efforts to seek peace in Lebanon and a just and lasting peace throughout the Middle East.

All of us must learn the appropriate lessons from this tragedy and assume the responsibilities that it imposes upon us. We owe it to ourselves and to our children. The whole world will be a safer place when this region which has known so much trouble can begin to know peace instead.

Both our purpose and our actions are peaceful and we are taking them in a spirit of international cooperation. So, tonight, I ask for your prayers and your support as our country continues its vital role as a leader for world peace—a role that all of us, as Americans, can be proud of.

Document 404

Transcript of an Interview With the Secretary of State (Shultz), September 21, 1982 (Extract)[46]

Mission of the Second Multinational Force

. . . .

[MR. GUMBEL.]. . . Mr. Secretary, I'd like to start this off by alluding to something we heard earlier today, earlier on this program. King Hussein suggested that further moves in addition to the sending in of marines into Lebanon by the United States, such as sanctions, would be needed to keep U.S. credibility among Arabs in the area.

My question to you is, are such sanctions under consideration, or will the marines be the extent of the administration's reaction, for the time being?

SECRETARY SHULTZ. The point in the Middle East is first to stop the bloodshed in Lebanon. That seems to be coming to an end. The marines and the multinational force are designed to help in that regard. Second, to get a stable central government of Lebanon, first, taking control of its own capital in Beirut, and then, and promptly, strongly, and urgently to clear Lebanon of foreign forces so that the country can be governed by its own government, and to set to work on the basic peace process which must address the basic needs, problems, and aspirations of the Palestinian people. That's what our priorities must be on.

MR. KALB. Mr. Secretary, let me ask you in that connection, since we just heard from King Hussein, he is a key player in trying to get the peace process going.

SECRETARY SHULTZ. Yes.

MR. KALB. You've tried to involve him. What success have you had so far?

SECRETARY SHULTZ. King Hussein has made a number of comments about the

---

[46] Source: Department of State Press Release 291, September 21, 1982; also printed in Department of State *Bulletin*, November 1982, pp. 42–43. For full text, see *ibid.* Secretary Shultz was interviewed by Bryant Gumbel and Marvin Kalb, both of NBC News, on the "Today" television program.

President's fresh-start proposals. They have been basically favorable and positive. He has been trying to get himself into a position where he has some support in the Arab community for coming to discussions, and so I think, basically, there has been a lot of progress there.

MR. KALB. Do you feel that he is able to break loose of the commitment of 1974 of Rabat, and be able to negotiate on behalf of the Palestinians?

SECRETARY SHULTZ. That, of course, is what we would like to see happen. I think it certainly is possible. It depends upon his generating support among Palestinians and other Arabs.

MR. KALB. The Israeli Cabinet is meeting, I think, as we're speaking right now. Have you had any word at all on whether they will agree formally to the introduction of the multinational force once again into Beirut?

SECRETARY SHULTZ. We have had a number of indirect suggestions about what might happen, but since the Cabinet is meeting and is going to make a decision on this, I think it is best to await their decision.

MR. KALB. You do expect a positive response? We are going to proceed with this plan, are we not?

SECRETARY SHULTZ. We are planning to proceed with it, and I think that we can have some reason for hoping that the response will be a positive one from Israel.

MR. KALB. Because our NBC sources in Jerusalem say that they have agreed, that the Cabinet has indeed agreed.

SECRETARY SHULTZ. We'll wait and hear what the government has to say, much as I respect NBC sources. You're probably right. I hope you are.

MR. KALB. Mr. Secretary, let me ask you this: The President is described today as believing that Israel cannot be trusted in the search for peace right now in the Middle East. I wonder if you would comment on that?

SECRETARY SHULTZ. Israel is clearly a very important part of the peace process—right in the center of it—and we will work with the Government of Israel, and that's the President's intent. So we certainly intend to work with the Government of Israel on the peace process.

MR. KALB. But is there any underlying effort on the part of the administration now, based upon the stories that have been appearing in the last 48 hours, that indeed you would like to see a change of government in Israel, a somewhat more moderate regime?

SECRETARY SHULTZ. The decisions about what the Government of Israel should be are up to the citizens of Israel. It's a democracy; they have their processes for choosing their government. That is up to them. As far as the United States is concerned, when we deal with Israel, we deal with the Government of Israel, just as when we deal with any other country, we deal with the duly-constituted government of that country.

MR. KALB. Mr. Secretary, how long will the marines stay in Beirut? You really are not clear about that as yet.

SECRETARY SHULTZ. It isn't that we're trying to dodge the question or anything like that; it's just that when you sit here right now, and you say that they should be there to help the Government of Lebanon create stability and govern in the city of Beirut, you don't know how long that is going to take. It could come about very quickly—it could take a matter of more days. So I can't tell you here today what the situation is going to be like 10 days from now, 20 days from now, 30 days from now, 40 days from now—I just don't know. So I think it is a mistake to set yourself up right now and say as of some date, we're going to leave because the situation may not be propitious at that moment.

MR. KALB. But just to be clear, it's not open-ended, or is it?

SECRETARY SHULTZ. No. It is intended to be, and will be I'm sure, of limited duration; but we don't want to get in the position of putting some number on it.

MR. KALB. Let me ask you this, sir. During the deliberations on sending marines back, did any of you—you yourself, perhaps—have the feeling that you were getting on a slippery slope? Did any memories of Vietnam come to mind?

SECRETARY SHULTZ. No, I don't think this has any analagous aspect of Vietnam at all.

MR. KALB. None? Because so many people up on the Hill wonder about whether you are in for 10 days, 40 days, 40 months. What is your sense of that?

SECRETARY SHULTZ. I don't want to put down some number of days because then we might somehow be in the position of doing something that wasn't appropriate at the end of that number of days, or we might feel that it is propitious to leave well before that, and people would then say, "Why don't you stay longer?" So it is a mistake to put yourself into that trap.

MR. GUMBEL. Mr. Secretary, I might, since we're winding down on time, one final note: A lot of people with perfect hindsight are now suggesting that the troops, in departing on the 10th, left too early. Do you agree?

SECRETARY SHULTZ. No, I don't agree. The situation was stable, and the new Government of Lebanon was in the process of taking over. The President, Bashir, was in the process of bringing about a reconciliation. So the conditions that were presumed at the time we came in had been met, and so we left, and I think properly so.

MR. GUMBEL. Secretary Shultz, Marvin Kalb, gentlemen, thank you very much for joining us.

Document 405

Letter From President Reagan to Lebanese President-elect Gemayel, September 22, 1982[47]

Election of Amin Gemayel as President of Lebanon

DEAR MR. PRESIDENT-ELECT: The American people join me in congratulating you upon your election as President of Lebanon.[48] We are proud to stand beside your courageous nation as our friends in Lebanon again overcome adversity in exercising the democratic and constitutional tradition that our nations share.

In my September 20 address to the American people,[49] I restated the basic objectives of the U.S. relationship with Lebanon. "First and foremost," I said, "we seek the restoration of a strong and stable central government" in Lebanon, "brought into being by orderly constitutional processes." Your election as President sets Lebanon firmly on the path to national reconciliation behind a strong government with a broad mandate from the people of Lebanon.

You have our pledge that the United States will remain a staunch partner and friend to Lebanon as you set out upon the difficult and challenging tasks ahead. The American nation and I extend to you and all Lebanese our very best wishes for the future.

Sincerely,

RONALD REAGAN

Document 406

Statement by the Deputy Representative at the United Nations (Lichenstein) Before the U.N. General Assembly, September 24, 1982[50]

"The Resolution Now Before Us . . . Will Prolong and Embitter Conflict Rather Than Assist in Its Resolution"

President Ronald Reagan spoke for all Americans last Monday night[51] when he expressed his horror and revulsion over the killing of Palestinian civilians in West Beirut. Regarding the heart-rending scenes of the slaughter which were witnessed by the whole world, he said: "There is little that words can add, but there are actions we can and must take to bring that nightmare to an end."

The Government of the United States has demonstrated by word and deed its total commitment to the goals enunciated by the President: to restore peace to Beirut;

---

47 Source: White House Press Release, September 23, 1982, Office of the Press Secretary to the President; also printed in *Weekly Compilation of Presidential Documents*, September 27, 1982, p. 1194.

48 Amin Gemayel, older brother of the late President-elect Bashir Gemayel, was elected President of Lebanon by a special session of the Lebanese Chamber of Deputies on September 21, 1982. There were 77 votes for Gemayel and 3 abstentions. Gemayel was inaugurated on September 23.

49 For text, see document 403.

50 Source: U.S. Mission to the United Nations Press Release 70(82), September 24, 1982. The resolution was adopted by a vote of 147 to 2 (United States and Israel). For text, see *infra*.

51 For text, see document 403.

to help a stable government emerge in Lebanon that can secure the withdrawal of all foreign forces from Lebanon and restore peace and independence to that long-suffering country; and to bring a just and lasting resolution to the conflict between Israel and its Arab neighbors—one that satisfies the legitimate rights of the Palestinians, who are all too often the victims of this conflict.

Taken as a whole, we do not regard the resolution now before us as a means to these ends. It will prolong and embitter conflict rather than assist in its resolution.

However, the United States is ready to join with other members of the Security Council in support of any inquiry into these tragic events which the Government of Lebanon and the members of the Council find constructive. For this reason, we have requested a separate vote on operative paragraph 2 and will vote in favor of that paragraph.

Because of unacceptable language in several other paragraphs, we will vote against the resolution itself. In so doing, we would like to emphasize our firm intention to work with others, in other contexts, toward the positive ends stated by President Reagan and in a manner that will serve the ultimate goal of peace.

Document 407

Resolution ES–7/9, Adopted by the U.N. General Assembly, September 24, 1982[52]

The U.N. General Assembly Condemns the Beirut Massacre

The General Assembly,

Having considered the question of Palestine at its resumed seventh emergency special session,

Having heard the statement of the Palestine Liberation Organization, the representative of the Palestinian people,[53]

Recalling and reaffirming, in particular, its resolution 194 (III) of 11 December 1948,

Appalled at the massacre of Palestinian civilians in Beirut,

Recalling Security Council resolutions 508 (1982) of 5 June 1982, 509 (1982) of 6 June 1982, 513 (1982) of 4 July 1982, 520 (1982) of 17 September 1982 and 521 (1982) of 19 September 1982,

Taking note of the reports of the Secretary-General relevant to the situation, particularly his report of 18 September 1982,[54]

Noting with regret that the Security Council has so far not taken effective and practical measures, in accordance with the Charter of the United Nations, to ensure implementation of its resolutions 508 (1982) and 509 (1982),

Referring to the humanitarian principles of the Geneva Convention relative to the Protection of Civilian Persons in Time of War, of 12 August 1949,[55] and to the obligations arising from the regulations annexed to the Hague Conventions of 1907,[56]

Deeply concerned at the sufferings of the Palestinian and Lebanese civilian populations,

Noting the homelessness of the Palestinian people,

Reaffirming the imperative need to permit the Palestinian people to exercise their legitimate rights,

1. *Condemns* the criminal massacre of Palestinian and other civilians in Beirut on 17 September 1982;

2. *Urges* the Security Council to investigate, through the means available to it, the circumstances and extent of the massacre of Palestinian and other civilians in Beirut on 17 September 1982, and to make public the report on its findings as soon as possible;[57]

3. *Decides* to support fully the provisions of Security Council resolutions 508 (1982) and 509 (1982), in which the Council, *inter alia*, demanded that:

---

[52] Source: U.N. General Assembly Resolution ES–7/9. For the U.S. position on this resolution, see Lichenstein's statement, *supra*.

[53] See A/ES–7/PV.32. [Footnote in the source text.]

[54] S/15400. [Footnote in the source text.]

[55] United Nations, *Treaty Series*, vol. 75, No. 973, p. 287. [Footnote in the source text.]

[56] Carnegie Endowment for International Peace, *The Hague Conventions and Declarations of 1899 and 1907* (New York, Oxford University Press, 1915). [Footnote in the source text.]

[57] This paragraph was adopted by a vote of 146 (including the United States) to 0, with no abstentions and 9 absent (including Israel).

(a) Israel withdraw all its military forces forthwith and unconditionally to the internationally recognized boundaries of Lebanon;

(b) All parties to the conflict cease immediately and simultaneously all military activities within Lebanon and across the Lebanese-Israeli border;

4. *Demands* that all Member States and other parties observe strict respect for the sovereignty, territorial integrity, unity and political independence of Lebanon within its internationally recognized boundaries;[58]

5. *Reaffirms* the fundamental principle of the inadmissibility of the acquisition of territory by force;

6. *Resolves* that, in conformity with its resolution 194 (III) and subsequent relevant resolutions, the Palestinian refugees should be enabled to return to their homes and property from which they have been uprooted and displaced, and demands that Israel comply unconditionally and immediately with the present resolution;

7. *Urges* the Security Council, in the event of continued failure by Israel to comply with the demands contained in resolutions 508 (1982) and 509 (1982) and the present resolution, to meet in order to consider practical ways and means in accordance with the Charter of the United Nations;

8. *Calls upon* all States and international agencies and organizations to continue to provide the most extensive humanitarian aid possible to the victims of the Israeli invasion of Lebanon;

9. *Requests* the Secretary-General to prepare a photographic exhibit of the massacre of 17 September 1982 and to display it in the United Nations visitors' hall,

10. *Decides* to adjourn the seventh emergency special session temporarily and to authorize the President of the latest regular session of the General Assembly to resume its meetings upon request from Member States.

---

[58] This paragraph was adopted by a separate vote of 149 (including the United States and Israel) in favor to 0 against, with no abstentions and 5 absent.

Document 408

Note From the Lebanese Deputy Prime Minister/Foreign Minister (Boutros) to the Ambassador in Lebanon (Dillon), Beirut, September 25, 1982[59]

Lebanese Request for a U.S. Contingent in the Second Multinational Force

YOUR EXCELLENCY: I have the honor to refer to the urgent discussions between representatives of our two governments concerning the recent tragic events which have occurred in the Beirut area, and to consultations between my government and the Secretary General of the United Nations pursuant to United Nations Security Council Resolution 521.[60] On behalf of the Republic of Lebanon, I wish to inform Your Excellency's Government of the determination of the Government of Lebanon to restore its sovereignty and authority over the Beirut area and thereby to assure the safety of persons in the area and bring an end to violence that has recurred. To this end, Israeli forces will withdraw from the Beirut area.

In its consultations with the Secretary General, the Government of Lebanon has noted that the urgency of the situation requires immediate action, and the Government of Lebanon, therefore, is, in conformity with the objectives in U.N. Security Council Resolution 521, proposing to several nations that they contribute forces to serve as a temporary Multinational Force (MNF) in the Beirut area. The mandate of the MNF will be to provide an interposition force at agreed locations and thereby provide the Multinational presence requested by the Lebanese Government to assist it and the Lebanese Armed Forces (LAF) in the Beirut area. This presence will facilitate the restoration of Lebanese Government sovereignty and authority over the Beirut area, and thereby further efforts of my government to assure the safety of persons in the area and bring to an end the violence which has tragically recurred. The MNF may undertake other functions only by mutual agreement.

---

[59] Source: Department of State files; also printed in Department of State *Bulletin*, November 1982, pp. 50–51.

[60] See document 402.

In the foregoing context, I have the honor to propose that the United States of America deploy a force of approximately 1200 personnel to Beirut, subject to the following terms and conditions:

—The American military force shall carry out appropriate activities consistent with the mandate of the MNF.

—Command authority over the American Force will be exercised exclusively by the United States Government through existing American military channels.

—The LAF and MNF will form a Liaison and Coordination Committee, composed of representatives of the MNF participating governments and chaired by the representatives of my government. The Liaison and Coordination Committee will have two essential components: (A) Supervisory liaison; and (B) Military and technical liaison and coordination.

—The American Force will operate in close coordination with the LAF. To assure effective coordination with the LAF, the American Force will assign liaison officers to the LAF and the Government of Lebanon will assign liaison officers to the American Force. The LAF liaison officers to the American Force will, inter alia, perform liaison with the civilian population and with the U.N. observers and manifest the authority of the Lebanese Government in all appropriate situations. The American Force will provide security for LAF personnel operating with the U.S. contingent.

—In carrying out its mission, the American Force will not engage in combat. It may, however, exercise the right of self-defense.

—It is understood that the presence of the American Force will be needed only for a limited period to meet the urgent requirements posed by the current situation. The MNF contributors and the Government of Lebanon will consult fully concerning the duration of the MNF presence. Arrangements for the departure of the MNF will be the subject of special consultations between the Government of Lebanon and the MNF participating governments. The American Force will depart Lebanon upon any request of the President of Lebanon or upon the decision of the President of the United States.

—The Government of Lebanon and the LAF will take all measures necessary to ensure the protection of the American Force's personnel, to include securing assurances from all armed elements not now under the authority of the Lebanese Government that they will refrain from hostilities and not interfere with any activities of the MNF.

—The American Force will enjoy both the degree of freedom and movement and the right to undertake those activities deemed necessary for the performance of its mission for the support of its personnel. Accordingly, it shall enjoy the privileges and immunities accorded the administrative and technical staff of the American Embassy in Beirut, and shall be exempt from immigration and customs requirements, and restrictions on entering or departing Lebanon. Personnel, property and equipment of the American Force introduced into Lebanon shall be exempt from any form of tax, duty, charge or levy.

I have the further honor to propose, if the foregoing is acceptable to Your Excellency's Government, that Your Excellency's reply to that effect,[61] together with this Note, shall constitute an agreement between our two governments.

Please accept, Your Excellency, the assurances of my highest consideration.

FOUAD BOUTROS

Document 409

Note From the Ambassador in Lebanon (Dillon) to the Lebanese Deputy Prime Minister/Foreign Minister (Boutros), Beirut, September 25, 1982[62]

U.S. Agreement to Participation in the Second Multinational Force

YOUR EXCELLENCY: I have the honor to refer to Your Excellency's note of 25 September 1982 requesting the deployment of an American Force to the Beirut area.[63] I am pleased to inform you on behalf of my Government that the United States is pre-

[61] *Infra.*

[62] Source: Department of State files; also printed in Department of State *Bulletin*, November 1982, p. 51.

[63] *Supra.*

pared to deploy temporarily a force of approximately 1200 personnel as part of a Multinational Force (MNF) to establish an environment which will permit the Lebanese Armed Forces (LAF) to carry out their responsibilities in the Beirut area. It is understood that the presence of such an American Force will facilitate the restoration of Lebanese Government sovereignty and authority over the Beirut area, an objective which is fully shared by my Government, and thereby further efforts of the Government of Lebanon to assure the safety of persons in the area and bring to an end the violence which has tragically recurred.

I have the further honor to inform Your Excellency that my Government accepts the terms and conditions concerning the presence of the American Force in the Beirut area as set forth in your note, and that Your Excellency's note and this reply accordingly constitute an agreement between our two Governments.

R[OBERT] D[ILLION]

Document 410

Transcript of a Press Conference by President Reagan, September 28, 1982 (Extracts)[64]

The U.S. Effort to Establish Security for Lebanon and Israel

. . . .

Q. Mr. President, when the Palestinian fighters were forced to leave Beirut, they said that they had America's word of honor that those they left behind would not be harmed.

Now comes U.N. Ambassador Jeane Kirkpatrick who says that America must share in the blame for these massacres.[65]

My question to you is do you agree with that judgment? And I'd like to follow up.

THE PRESIDENT. Helen, I think the manner in which Jeane said that, and she's talked to me about it, was one about the responsibility of all of us back over a period of time with regard to the separation and divisions in Lebanon, the whole matter of the Middle East, and not doing more to bring about the peace that we're trying so hard now to get.

I don't think that specifically there could [be] assigned a responsibility on our part for withdrawing our troops. They were sent in there with one understanding. They were there to oversee and make sure that the PLO left Lebanon. And that mission was completed, virtually without incident, and they left.

Then, who could have foreseen the assassination of the President-elect that led to the other violence and so forth.

Q. Well, why did you give orders to our Representative at the United Nations to vote against an inquiry to find out how it happened and why?[66]

THE PRESIDENT. As I understand it, there were things additional in that inquiry, things that we have never voted for and will not hold still for, such things as sanctions and such things as voting Israel out of the United Nations.

Now, I can't recall exactly now what it was that caused our vote to be negative on that. But the Lebanese and the Israelis are apparently going forward with such an inquiry.

. . . .

Q. Mr. President, do you have a plan for getting the United States out of Lebanon if fighting should break out there, or could the marine presence there lead to another long entanglement such as Vietnam?

THE PRESIDENT. No, I don't see anything of that kind taking place there at all. And the marines are going in there into a situation with a definite understanding as to what we're supposed to do. I believe that we are going to be successful in seeing the other foreign forces leave Lebanon. And then at such time as Lebanon says that they

---

[64] Source: White House Press Release, September 28, 1982, Office of the Press Secretary to the President; also printed in *Weekly Compilation of Presidential Documents*, October 4, 1982, pp. 1221–1224. For the full text, see *ibid.*, pp. 1219–1227. The press conference was held in the East Room of the White House beginning at 7:30 p.m.

[65] Reference is to a speech made by Ambassador Kirkpatrick to the Public Policy Forum in Washington, on September 24, 1982.

[66] Reference presumably is to U.N. General Assembly Resolution ES–7/9, September 24, 1982. For text, see document 407.

have the situation well in hand, why, we'll depart.

Q. Sir, if fighting should break out again, would you pull the marines out?

The President. You're asking a hypothetical question, and I've found out that I never get in trouble if I don't answer one of those. (Laughter)

. . . .

Q. Mr. President, it has been reported that you believe that Israel is sabotaging your peace initiative, and also that you now believe that Israel has become the Goliath in the Middle East, and that the other countries, the Arab countries, are the David.[67] Did you say that? Do you believe that?

The President. I didn't say it exactly that way. In fact, I didn't say that I thought they were the Goliath. I said that one of the things, as the negotiations approach and we proceed with this peacemaking business, that Israel should understand, as we have come to understand from talking to other Arab States, that where from the very beginning all of us including Israel, have thought of it as a tiny country fighting for its life surrounded by larger states and hostile states that want to see it destroyed, that their military power has become such that there are Arab States that now voice a fear that they are expansionist, that they may be expansionist, and they have the military power. So all I was referring to was that.

The first part of your statement there, though, about Israel and trying to undermine—no, I don't believe that. I think that both sides have voiced things that they feel very strongly about, and contrary to what I have suggested in my proposal, and having been a long-time union negotiator, I happen to think that some of that might be each side staking out its position so as to be in a better position when it comes time to negotiate. . . .

. . . .

Q. . . . I just wanted to ask you since you said you didn't think that Israel was trying to undermine your peace initiative whether you are less optimistic about its chances since the massacre and the tragedy in Beirut?

The President. No, I'm not less optimistic. I'm also not deluding myself that it's going to be easy. Basically what we have, I think, in this peace proposal is a situation where on one side territory is the goal and on the other side security. And what has to be negotiated out is a kind of exchange of territory for security and I meant what I said when I proposed this plan and that is this country will never stand by and see any settlement that does not guarantee the security of Israel.

. . . .

Q. Mr. President, you've told us that you're sending marines to Lebanon for a limited amount of time and yet you haven't told us what the limit is. Can you give us a general idea of how long you expect them to stay there and tell us precisely what you would like to see them accomplish before they withdraw.

The President. I can't tell you what the time element would be. I can tell you what it is that they should accomplish and I hope sooner rather than later.

One, they're there along with our allies, the French and the Italians, to give a kind of support and stability while the Lebanese Government seeks to reunite its people, which have been divided for several years now into several factions, each one of them with its own army, and bring about a unified Lebanon with a Lebanese Army that will then be able to preserve order in its own country. And during this time, while that's taking place, the withdrawal, as quickly as possible, to their own borders of the Israelis and the Syrians.

Now there, we've had declarations from both countries that they want to do that. So I am reasonably optimistic about that. I have no way to judge about when the Lebanese Government—the Lebanese Government will be the ones that tell us when they feel that they're in charge and they can go home.

Q. Are you then saying that they will remain there until all foreign forces are withdrawn?

The President. Yes, because I think that's going to come rapidly. I think we're going to see the withdrawal—our marines

---

[67] Unidentified White House officials told reporters on September 22, 1982, that President Reagan "had come to regard Israel as the 'Goliath' rather than the 'David' of the Middle East." (*Facts on File, 1982,* Vol. 42, p. 715 C2)

will go in tomorrow morning, as I've said, because the Israelis have agreed to withdraw to that line south of the airport. . . .

. . . .

Document 411

Letter From President Reagan to the Speaker of the House of Representatives (O'Neill), September 29, 1982[68]

Use of U.S. Armed Forces in Lebanon

Dear Mr. Speaker: On September 20, 1982, the Government of Lebanon requested the Governments of France, Italy, and the United States to contribute forces to serve as a temporary Multinational Force, the presence of which will facilitate the restoration of Lebanese Government sovereignty and authority, and thereby further the efforts of the Government of Lebanon to assure the safety of persons in the area and bring to an end the violence which has tragically recurred.

In response to this request of the Government of Lebanon, I have authorized the Armed Forces of the United States to participate in this Multinational Force. In accordance with my desire that the Congress be fully informed on this matter, and consistent with the War Powers Resolution,[69] I am hereby providing a report on the deployment and mission of these members of the United States Armed Forces.

On September 29, approximately 1200 Marines of a Marine Amphibious Unit began to arrive in Beirut. Their mission is to provide an interposition force at agreed locations and thereby provide the multinational presence requested by the Lebanese Government to assist it and the Lebanese Armed Forces. In carrying out this mission, the American force will not engage in combat. It may, however, exercise the right of self-defense and will be equipped accordingly. These forces will operate in close coordination with the Lebanese Armed Forces, as well as with comparably sized French and Italian military contingents in the Multinational Force. Although it is not possible at this time to predict the precise duration of the presence of U.S. forces in Beirut, our agreement with the Government of Lebanon makes clear that they will be needed only for a limited period to meet the urgent requirements posed by the current situation.

I want to emphasize that, as was the case of the deployment of U.S. forces to Lebanon in August as part of the earlier multinational force, there is no intention or expectation that U.S. Armed Forces will become involved in hostilities. They are in Lebanon at the formal request of the Government of Lebanon, and our agreement with the Government of Lebanon expressly rules out any combat responsibilities for the U.S. forces. All armed elements in the area have given assurances that they will refrain from hostilities and will not interfere with the activities of the Multinational Force. Although isolated acts of violence can never be ruled out, all appropriate precautions have been taken to ensure the safety of U.S. military personnel during their temporary deployment in Lebanon.

This deployment of the United States Armed Forces is being undertaken pursuant to the President's constitutional authority with respect to the conduct of foreign relations and as Commander-in-Chief of the United States Armed Forces.

I believe that this step will support the objective of helping to restore the territorial integrity, sovereignty, and political independence of Lebanon. It is part of the continuing efforts of the United States Government to bring lasting peace to that troubled country, which has too long endured the trials of civil strife and armed conflict.

Sincerely,

Ronald Reagan

---

[68] Source: White House Press Release, September 29, 1982, Office of the Press Secretary to the President; also printed in *Weekly Compilation of Presidential Documents*, October 4, 1982, p. 1232. An identical letter was addressed to Senator Strom Thurmond, President pro tempore of the Senate.

[69] Reference is to the Joint Resolution Concerning the War Powers of Congress and the President (P.L. 93–148), passed over President Richard M. Nixon's veto, November 7, 1973. For text, see 87 Stat. 555.

Document 412

Transcript of the Department of State Daily Press Briefing, September 30, 1982 (Extract)[70]

When Did U.S. Officials Learn of the Sabra and Shatila Massacre?

. . . .

Q. Alan, reports in the *New York Times* and *Washington Post* today detail the purported involvement of high Phalange force officers in the massacre in West Beirut. Another report from Israel states that U.S. officials were aware of the slaughter on Friday, September 17, and asked for the Phalange forces to withdraw.

Are you aware of those reports? Do you have a comment on them?

A. I don't have any comment on the reporting in the papers this morning about who might have been involved specifically.

As far as the charge that the United States knew that a massacre was going on and so on, that simply is just utterly false. What we knew, when we knew it, how and when we acted on the information are as we have provided, I think, to you in earlier guidance, which I can read to you if you want. I see a nod in the back.

On Friday afternoon, September 17, we started to receive fragmentary information that something was amiss in the Shatila and Sabra refugee camp areas of Beirut. We did our best to find out what was happening. It was not until Saturday morning, September 18, that an Embassy officer was able to enter the Shatila camp and observe directly the evidence of a massacre. A report of this eyewitness account was sent to the State Department and received here at about 5 a.m. EDT the same day. In short, we had no advance word. When we heard that something might be happening, we acted upon it immediately.

. . . .

[70] Source: Office of Press Relations, Department of State. Alan Romberg, Department of State Acting Spokesman, conducted the briefing, which began at 12:27 p.m.

Document 413

Remarks by President Reagan and Lebanese President Amin Gemayel of Lebanon, October 19, 1982[71]

Visit of President Amin Gemayel of Lebanon

THE PRESIDENT. Our talks have covered a full range of issues with particular focus on our shared objective of prompt withdrawal of all foreign forces from Lebanon.

We also discussed Lebanon's goals in restoring authority and control of [the] central government in all parts of the country. In this regard I reaffirmed the U.S. support for the sovereignty, unity, territorial integrity, and freedom of Lebanon. And I am pleased to have had the opportunity to establish a close working dialogue with President Gemayel who deserves all of our support as he and the people of Lebanon work to rebuild their nation.

President Gemayel can rely upon the help of the United States. It is my hope that our mutual efforts will lead to restored peace and prosperity for all the people of Lebanon and indeed all the Middle East.

He has been most welcome here and we are pleased to have had him with us.

Mr. President.

PRESIDENT GEMAYEL. I am honored to be the first President of Lebanon to make an official visit to the United States. The Lebanese people deeply appreciate and will never forget your gracious and decisive efforts to help bring an end to the suffering of my country. American commitment to the sovereignty and territorial integrity of a free democracy in Lebanon has been fundamental to our survival. We see the U.S. role as the indispensable ingredient to bring peace not only to Lebanon but also to the whole region as well. We firmly believe that President Reagan's initiative has created unprecedented opportunities for peace.

[71] Source: White House Press Release, October 19, 1982, Office of the Press Secretary to the President; also printed in *Weekly Compilation of Presidential Documents*, October 25, 1982, pp. 1352–1353. The two Presidents spoke on the South Grounds of the White House, beginning at 10:18 a.m., following their meeting. President Gemayel visited New York, October 17–18, to address the United Nations on October 18. He visited Washington, October 18–19, where he met with President Reagan and other officials.

We in Lebanon intend to be active in the search for peace with all nations of the region. The relation between the United States and Lebanon is not only between our two governments; it is between our two peoples who share the same heritage and adhere to the same values and principles of democracy and liberty.

The 2½ million Lebanese have[an] almost equal number of close relatives in the United States. We value enormously the unique tie provided by these American Lebanese, among the most loyal of all Americans, and we believe they have a leading role in keeping our two countries together. Lebanon has been the most recent, and for us, the most painful example of the assault upon free men by the forces of darkness and occupation. We have fought to retain our freedom and the strength of our resistance has earned for us not only a restated pride in ourselves but also a re-entry into the ranks of the free world.

With equal resolve, I together with my people am committed to the immediate removal of all foreign forces from our soil and to work hand in hand with all sectors of Lebanese society to build a nation in which all citizens have equal privileges, rights, and responsibilities.

The historic U.S.–Lebanon relationship is the cornerstone of building this new Lebanon. America's friendship and assistance not only in peacekeeping and peacemaking but also in reconstruction and rebuilding our armed forces are vital.

We, on our part, intend to carry our share of the responsibility of this partnership by a full and reciprocal contribution to all U.S. goals in its many noble endeavors as the leader of the free world.

Thank you.

Document 414

Transcript of a Press Conference by the Secretary of State (Shultz), Ottawa, October 25, 1982 (Extract)[72]

"We Had a Very Good Visit With Amin Gemayel"

. . . .

Q. The Middle East has been desperately volatile all spring and summer and is likely to continue that way. You may not be able to comment too much, but, can you tell us—give us some insight as to how you think—how you hope things are going to develop in resolving the serious problems that exist there?

A. There are plenty of problems in the Middle East, and we shouldn't forget that there is a war on between Iraq and Iran. When you say Middle East, you are probably thinking about the Arab/Israeli conflict in Lebanon and so on; but I remind you that there is that problem, and it has a lot of repercussions to it. But, swinging over from that and in the Middle East—I don't know whether you include Afghanistan and that set of problems and the implications for what surrounds the Gulf, but I just put those markers out there in case you think I've forgotten about them. But, as far as Lebanon is concerned—I will comment on that first.

We had a very good visit with Amin Gemayel last week. And, of course, we have been working with the Lebanese and others to help get the foreign forces out of Lebanon and help the government take control—put together a reconciliation of the various confessional groups in Lebanon and start the process of rebuilding and reconstructing their culture and economy and life. You couldn't help but feel good about your exposure to Amin Gemayel. He has a tremendous amount of faith in his people and told the President and told others that you just give Lebanon half a chance and you'll be amazed at what the people of Lebanon can do and how they will

---

[72] Source: Department of State Press Release 336, October 27, 1982, pp. 15–18; also printed in Department of State *Bulletin*, December 1982, p. 16. For the full text, see *ibid.*, pp. 13–18. Secretary Shultz visited Ottawa, October 24–25, 1982.

rebuild and become again a crossroad to commercial and transportation and cultural centers in the Middle East. And I believe they will, but they need a chance. So we have set in our minds an objective of trying to get the foreign forces out of Lebanon by the end of this year. And that's a do-able proposition—I don't mean by that to say it's easy, or that it's probable, but it's do-able. And it's a good objective and we are going to try hard to help in every way we can to bring that off. There are many angles to that and I don't know—I'd be glad to talk about them if you like. I don't know how much you want to do that.

Among the things that Gemayel is very conscious of and talked about a lot, was the importance of the basic peace process. And if you think about it for a second, it's easy to see why—because of all the countries in the Middle East that have been hit hard by the lack of a solution to the Palestinian problem and the conflict resulting from it, Lebanon has been the one that's been hurt the most—almost an innocent bystander. But they have been clobbered by all of that. Going way back for almost 10 years now. So, he has and feels a great stake in the peace process and was quite forthcoming in the strength of his support for President Reagan's initiatives. Now, the interest in the peace process is very much alive. The visit that we had in Washington on Friday from King Hassan[73] as a leader of an Arab League delegation that included a complete spectrum of views in the Arab world was evidence of that and I would say the over-all result of that meeting was a constructive one, and it was evidence that on the Arab side they are very much interested in trying to work out a peace. I'm sure the Israelis are interested in peace.

We're always being asked about our strategy and what sort of leverages are we going to be using as whatever help we can give in bringing about a peaceful situation. The President, though, puts up front in that the big lever is peace. If you've lived in an area that has been—seen lots of war, seen lots of bloodshed and the ravishing of the countryside, and you live in that atmosphere all the time, the possibility of peace is a big thing. We're so accustomed to it here in Canada and the United States that we take it for granted like air. But, if you live out there you don't take it for granted and you think that, if there's a possibility of that, it's just terrific. So, that we count on as the big objective and the more we can get that possibility up into people's minds and consciousness, the better chance, I think, we'll have of people being willing to make the compromises and take the chances and risks that they have to take if a peaceful resolution is to emerge.

Q. You found Gemayel impressed?

A. Yes, sir.

Q. More so than you would have found his brother—

A. Well, I never met his brother. His brother is said to be—was a very impressive and strong person. So, it's a tragedy that he was killed. Anyway, Amin Gemayel is the President of Lebanon. He's a good person and a person with a great amount of strength and understanding. He has a very positive outlook on the prospects for his country. So, we're working with him.

. . . .

[73] King Hassan II of Morocco led an Arab League delegation that visited Washington on October 22 and 23 and met with President Reagan and Secretary Shultz on Friday, October 22. See document 326.

Document 415

Transcript of a Press Conference by the Secretary of Defense (Weinberger), October 28, 1982 (Extracts)[74]

The Extent and Duration of U.S. Military Assistance to Lebanon

. . . .

Q. . . . What's your view on expanding the U.S. presence in Lebanon or expanding the size of the multinational force?

A. My views are that it is very necessary for us to do everything we can to strengthen the Lebanese Government and help them strengthen the Lebanese Armed Forces so that they can maintain security and the sovereignty and the sanctity of their bor-

[74] Source: *Public Statements of Secretary of Defense Weinberger*, 1982. This press conference was held at the Pentagon.

ders and not allow their country to be used as a platform for any shelling or bombing of any other country or to be used as a maneuver ground for foreign forces. To do that, their armed forces are going to need some assistance and the country's going to need some assistance, economically and militarily and every other way.

The multinational force is designed to try to ensure that during the withdrawal of all foreign forces, which is an absolutely essential first part of the whole process, that that withdrawal can take place without the various parties concerned feeling that one or the other may take advantage of them. The desire is to do that in as quick a time as possible and with a minimum number of forces. We will certainly contribute and have taken a strong lead in the whole attempt to bring peace to the Mideast; not just to Lebanon and Beirut but to the whole Mideast. That's what the President's peace initiative is all about. We would want to carry our share of the burden that is necessary to try to accomplish that.

Q. Mr. Secretary, do you see Lebanon, and particularly the Bekaa Valley as a flashpoint for a new war there and therefore may there be a need for the United States to station its own forces in that area beyond the withdrawal of other foreign forces?

A. There are two questions and I don't really think they're related if you'll permit me to say so. The Mideast and the whole area has for many many years, centuries, been an area of substantial tensions and wherever those tensions build up, there is more likelihood of armed conflict breaking out as indeed has taken place there, so often in the past few years, particularly.

I don't think that it is because of that it is essential to try to remove the causes of that and the causes of it are the things that are addressed in the President's initiative. The thing that's going to bring peace to the Mideast is not stationing U.S. Forces in the Mideast or anything of that kind. The thing that ultimately will bring peace is the thing the President is trying to accomplish and that is to remove the tensions and have the ability to maintain peace be based on good and growing and improving relationships between all those countries by removing as many of the points of differences as you possibly can.

So you're not going to maintain peace by manning the borders with ever larger forces. So I would think that the principal effort that we want to make is to bring peace to that area and to bring it by strengthening the Lebanese Government so that it can prevent its territory from being used in any way that would foster war and then at the same time through the President's peace initiative, with the relationships in the West Bank and Jordan and the Palestinian people and all the other elements to it, trying to remove the forces that have driven all those countries apart for so long.

. . . .

Q. Mr. Secretary, do you still doubt that we will increase the size and mission of our marine force, or of our military peacekeeping force in Lebanon?

A. It isn't a question of doubting or supporting or opposing or anything of the kind at the moment. We're trying to do three things at once. We're trying to get as much as we can over to strengthen the Lebanese Armed Forces and the Lebanese Government, and the country—militarily and economically—and we've already started some of that. Some howitzers going over and some armored personnel carriers and things of that kind and we'll continue that flow, to the extent that Congress will permit us to do so, and I hope they will. It's a very important priority.

We're also trying to get all the foreign forces out of Lebanon as quickly as possible in conjunction with the Lebanese Government's stated desire to do this.

And finally, we're trying to get the President's peace proposal, the longer-range proposal, adopted and in force.

At the moment, we've made a significant contribution to the multinational force. We have a marine amphibious group reinforced battalion, but we've also contributed a carrier battle group, and that's a fair sized contribution. We are going to, as the situation changes, as the foreign forces begin to leave Lebanon as they've all said they want to do, there may be additional tasks and missions for a multinational force. That can be handled in two ways.

It can be handled by increasing the number of nations that contribute to that force; it can be handled by temporary expansions of that force by the nations that are now contributing to it. As the foreign forces withdraw, the size and mission of the multinational force can become smaller and more limited. So I can't really say today what we'll be doing 3 or 4 weeks from now. It depends on the progress of the negotiations in which we're engaged at the moment.

Q. Mr. Secretary, the actual number of U.S. troops in Lebanon then is open-ended, is that right?

A. No, it isn't open-ended at all. We have not open-ended resources in this country, sadly. All of these things will have to be measured by a combination of judgments with respect to our own requirements and our own resources, our own abilities to help. We have made major, substantial contributions already. It is an enormously important cause, and we will continue to support it. The precise details of how we'll support it will remain to be worked out when we know the way in which the foreign forces will withdraw, when they'll withdraw, how quickly the Lebanese Armed Forces can be strengthened.

They've got four brigades now, but they're somewhat under strength. They need additional brigades; they need additional equipment and training, and we certainly expect to continue helping to supply both equipment and training. But it isn't an open-ended commitment, and it isn't anything that is going to be done to any greater extent than is absolutely necessary. By the same token, we've made significant progress toward achieving peace in the Mideast by the President's actions, and we don't want to lose the momentum of that.

Q. I want to ask you a follow-up on that. If it's not open-ended, is there some limit that our resources can handle, in other words, can we say today that under no circumstances would there be more than 20,000 or 50,000 or—

A. Well, we aren't anywhere near that point because we just don't know the requirements; we don't know how many other nations will want to join in this effort. As I've said before, there are a great many other nations that have the same interest we do in having a strong and stable and sovereign Lebanon. There's just no way of trying to predict what we may do on any given day. But it's always going to be a fluctuating thing. If we got up to 1201 one day, why we might be down to 900 the following week, depending on how fast the forces move out and so forth, and so on. So, it wouldn't be fair to you for me to give you any kind of specific number.

. . . .

Q. Back to Lebanon. With what other countries are you discussing contributions to the MNF, and the other part of that, are you also considering a buildup in numbers and mandate of the U.N. forces?

A. With respect to the first part, we are not conducting any negotiations and should not with other countries with respect to whether or not they will or will not contribute. We respond to questions; we furnish information and we work with the State Department in any negotiations they might have.

With respect to the U.N. force, I'm not aware of any pending activity to build up UNIFIL or to change it. It's mandate was recently extended and I'm not aware of any other plans in connection with it.

. . . .

Q. . . . You don't want to talk about troop numbers, perhaps you'll talk about the length of stay of the troops.

A. Well, again it's the same problem. What we need is a multinational force until certain conditions have been achieved. Nobody knows when those conditions can be achieved. It is not an open-ended commitment for any one unit. We're rotating the marine forces today because they've been over there a long time. We don't know how long a multinational force will be needed. Everybody agrees that the less time that is needed the better.

Q. There were reports that they might be needed as much as 2 years.

A. No, I think that what—I don't know what reports, I don't see all the reports, but basically the idea is that the training, the full training for the full expansion necessary of the Lebanese Armed Forces will take quite a while, but this isn't to say that there has to be a multinational force there all that time. The Lebanese Armed Forces can perform significant duties while they're being trained and while they're being expanded and while they're being equipped. So that there isn't any date or deadline that anybody has in mind and it's also impossible to say how long the troops of any one country will have to be there because you don't know how many other countries will come in and how much rotation will be possible.

Q. Are we talking weeks, months or years?

A. I'm talking as soon as possible.

. . . .

Document 416

Remarks by President Reagan, Brasilia, December 1, 1982 (Extract)[75]

Consideration of Lebanon's Request for an Increased Multinational Force

. . . .

Q. Sir, what about the Lebanon situation?

THE PRESIDENT. Lebanon has made a request. They believe that a bigger multinational force would speed up and help them in removing the other foreign forces that are in Lebanon. This has been talked about for some time. It's not a new idea presented to us. And we will be talking to friends and allies about that and taking it up with them, because we want to do whatever we can to help get the foreign forces out of Lebanon. That's the first important step for beginning—

Q. When do you think you can get the foreign forces out?

Q. When can you get them out now, and how soon could you bring them home?

THE PRESIDENT. We're not discussing that now. We're discussing how the multinational force can aid the Lebanese Government in getting control of its own country and getting the Syrians, the PLO, and the Israelis out of Lebanon.[76]

Q. A few more troops, would that help? If we offered a few more troops, would that help?

THE PRESIDENT. Well—[inaudible][77]—not only for ourselves. The request has simply been made for the multinational force—but to see if there are other nations that would like to join in that force.

. . . .

[75] Source: *Weekly Compilation of Presidential Documents,* December 13, 1982, p. 1555. For the full text; see *ibid.*, pp. 1555–1556. These remarks were made to reporters at the Palacio do Planalto, beginning at 11:32 a.m., following meetings with President Joao Baptista de Oliveira Figueiredo of Brazil. President Reagan visited Brazil, November 30–December 3, 1982.

[76] President Reagan had declined to place a time limit on the MNF deployment during his press conference on November 11, 1982. See *ibid.*, November 15, 1982, pp. 1463–1464.

[77] Bracketed note appears in the source text.

Document 417

Transcript of a Press Conference by the Secretary of State (Shultz), Brasilia, December 1, 1982 (Extracts)[78]

Possible Expansion of the Size and Scope of the Multinational Force

. . . .

Q. Are we willing to send more troops to Lebanon?

SECRETARY SHULTZ. The question was are we willing to see more troops in Lebanon or U.S. forces, I assume you are saying, in Lebanon.

The answer is this: The President has said that he wants to see Lebanon emerge as a country that can take care of itself and rule itself. He wants to see the foreign forces, all the foreign forces removed from Lebanon. And we are part of the multinational force there now and we are willing to consider proposals that may come along as part of a plan for bringing those things about. The Government of Lebanon has stated its belief that additions to the multinational force are desirable. And so I am sure that the President will consider that.

But, of course, we will want to consider it in its relationship to a plan for accomplishing all of the things that are wanted to be accomplished there. At this point, nothing explicit of that kind has come to the President. And I would say beyond that, that there would not be any commitment before consultations with the Congress had taken place.

[78] Source: Department of State Press Release 361, December 3, 1982; also printed in Department of State *Bulletin,* January 1983, pp. 8–9. For the full text, see *ibid.*, pp. 7–9. Secretary Shultz accompanied President Reagan on his official working visit to Brazil, November 30–December 3, 1982.

So the brief answer is, certainly, the President is willing to consider additions if that will be helpful in this process. And in terms of when would a U.S. commitment be made and all of that—well, we have to see a specific proposition. We have to consult with the Congress and so on.

Q. What sort of conditions would we want to see agreed to before we would make a commitment?

. . . .

SECRETARY SHULTZ. We would want to see, no doubt, the structure of some sort of program that is going to achieve the goals that we and others seek. And then see how the multinational and the U.S. part in it fits into that program. That is the object—not just to have a lot of people there. And you can see, in a general way, the sorts of things that might be done. And there have already been some potential missions identified. But there is not yet an overall plan to fit into. So this is something that will be emerging.

Q. Mr. Secretary, what about consultations with other governments like France and Italy? Are they going on?

SECRETARY SHULTZ. Oh, yes. We are constantly in consultation with the Governments of France and Italy who are partners with us in the multinational force. Part of the agreement in going in is an agreement for close consultation as we consider it is, also, possible that other countries may wish to contribute to the forces there. But at the same time, I think it all is contingent on developing some sort of a program, because people do not want to send forces in without knowing what for.

. . . .

Document 418

Address by the Deputy Secretary of State (Dam) Before the Chicago Law Club, Chicago, December 2, 1982 (Extract)[79]

Securing a Peaceful Future for Lebanon

. . . .

A short time ago, the President charged me with responsibility for coordinating our work in Washington on one such issue, the future of Lebanon. What I'd like to do this evening is talk about that one issue, because it represents in a microcosm many of the things we're trying to accomplish in the world in general.

With regard to Lebanon, some Americans may wonder why we are concerned about such a small country so far away. Others may ask why U.S. troops are in Lebanon and how long they must stay. Americans are right to ask these questions; so tonight let me address them in turn: Why is America in Lebanon? What are our goals? And, what must we do to secure a peaceful future for Lebanon?

The desolation in Beirut today belies its past role as the Paris of the Arab world. The occupation of Lebanon by foreign forces contradicts its deep tradition of democracy and sovereignty. Our dismay at the resulting division of the country is deepened by the promise of what might have been, and by the knowledge that Lebanon's future was engulfed by its neighbors' disputes.

The Arab-Israeli wars of 1948 and 1967 brought thousands of embittered Palestinian refugees into Lebanon, straining the social fabric of that country. In 1970, these Palestinians were joined by large numbers of PLO fighters that had been expelled from Jordan. Lebanon became an armed camp. Civil war broke out in 1975 among PLO, Christian, and Muslim forces. Syrian troops entered and remained under an Arab League mandate to maintain order. But order was not restored. PLO fighters harassed northern Israel; Israeli defense forces retaliated; Syrian and Christian

---

[79] Source: Department of State Press Release 362, December 6, 1982; also printed in Department of State *Bulletin*, January 1983, pp. 73–75. Dam's introductory remarks are omitted.

forces clashed. Lebanese civilians—and Lebanese sovereignty—were caught in the crossfire. And a nation's agony became an international crisis.

This was the situation the Reagan administration faced in the spring of 1981, when Ambassador Philip Habib, at the President's direction, negotiated a cease-fire in southern Lebanon. Last spring, however, destabilizing forces prevailed and the cease-fire disintegrated. Israel then sent its forces into Lebanon in order, in the words of the Israeli Cabinet, "to place all the civilian population of the Galilee beyond the range of the terrorist fire from Lebanon."[80] The fighting advanced to the threshold of Beirut, and Ambassador Habib was called on again. The peaceful departure of PLO forces from Beirut last August was a tribute to his efforts and to the Multinational Force that stood guard over the evacuation. Indeed, those who complain about a lack of cooperation among the Western democracies should note how American, French, and Italian troops stood together to assist the Lebanese. Those soldiers were truly soldiers of peace.

But triumph was followed by tragedy. In quick succession, Lebanon's newly-elected President, Bashir Gemayel, was assassinated, and Palestinians were slaughtered in their camps.

Why are we involved? This is a sad history. The Lebanese sought peace, and found destruction; they sought freedom, and found occupation. This led Lebanon's new President, Amin Gemayel, to plead before the United Nations, "We have had enough, enough of bloodshed, enough of destruction, enough of dislocation and despair."[81]

In October our nation once again sent marines to Lebanon in response to Gemayel's request and the plight of his people. Together with French and Italian forces those marines are there to assist the Lebanese Government in restoring peace. In meeting this moral obligation, they reaffirm what President Reagan has termed our "irreversible commitment to the territorial integrity of friendly states" and our "traditional humanitarian concerns" for those who suffer injustice.[82]

---

[80] For the text of the Israeli Cabinet's communiqué of June 6, 1982, see Foreign Broadcast Information Service, *Daily Report: Middle East and Africa,* June 7, 1982, p. I4.

[81] For the text of President Gemayel's address to the U.N. General Assembly on October 18, 1982, see U.N. document A/37/PV.35.

[82] The quotations under reference are from President Reagan's address of September 1, 1982, on U.S. policy for peace in the Middle East. For text, see document 318.

Our commitment to Lebanon, however, is consistent not only with our sense of morality, but also with our national interest. Peace—the solution to Lebanon's suffering—is also the solution to our strategic and diplomatic concerns in the Middle East.

The future of Lebanon is linked strategically to the entire Middle East region. Located at the vital eastern end of the Mediterranean, bounded by the oil-rich nations of Africa and Asia, that region lies in the shadow of vast Soviet military power. To the extent that Lebanon is a flashpoint for regional conflict, it is also a potential source of international conflict. Promoting stability in Lebanon and the Middle East is thus vital to our security and that of other industrial democracies.

Diplomatically, the United States plays a central role in the Middle East because Israel and the Arab states recognize that America is the only credible catalyst for a wider peace. We must, however, demonstrate our ability to sustain this role by resolving the Lebanese crisis. Such a resolution would contribute to the long-term security of Israel, and to the momentum for a comprehensive peace created by the President's historic initiative of September 1. There should be no mistaking the fact that there are others, whose interests are inimical to ours, who are prepared to exploit our failure to resolve these issues.

These are the concerns—moral, strategic, and diplomatic—that underlie our policy in Lebanon, and that led to the presence of U.S. Marines in Beirut. What, then, is the objective of that policy, and the mission of those troops?

Objective. Our objective is straightforward. We seek to restore Lebanese sovereignty and ensure Israeli security. These are not separate objectives. A stable, sovereign Lebanon and a secure Israel are two sides of the same coin. The threat to Israel does not come from the Lebanese people, but from foreign forces that have usurped Lebanese sovereignty and are still camped on Lebanese soil. It follows that a peaceful Lebanon, free of all foreign forces and sovereign over all its territory, will make a major contribution to Israeli security. To achieve this objective, we and the responsible international community support a three-part strategy in Lebanon:

First: withdrawal forthwith of all foreign forces from Lebanon.

Second: restoration of Lebanese Government sovereignty and strengthening of the Lebanese Armed Forces.

And, third: reestablishment of a Lebanese national consensus and reconstruction of the Lebanese economy.

This strategy in support of the Lebanese Government is designed to achieve peace and security for both Lebanon and Israel. The withdrawal of all foreign forces will remove a threat to Israel's border. Restoring Lebanon's sovereignty and strength, and rebuilding its economy, will prevent that threat from returning. The United States is moving now to implement all three parts of this strategy. Let me address each of those efforts in detail.

What are we doing to implement our strategy?

First, the withdrawal of foreign forces.

America's diplomatic energy is focused now on bringing about the immediate withdrawal from Lebanon of all foreign forces—Israeli, Syrian, and PLO. To succeed, we must meet the legitimate interests of each of the parties through practical security arrangements. Three sets of negotiations will be involved: negotiations between Lebanon and Israel, between Lebanon and Syria, and between Lebanon and the PLO.

The United States will participate directly at the table in the first set of negotiations—between Lebanon and Israel. In these talks we will seek security arrangements that will permit Israel to withdraw its forces with the knowledge that southern Lebanon will never again be used to launch assaults on Israeli citizens.

Israel also desires establishment of normal relations with Lebanon as a way of safeguarding the peace. This is an important goal. But progress toward more normal relations must be approached carefully lest it undermine Lebanon's credentials in the Arab world. Moreover, ill-timed or forced normalization may actually threaten Israel's security if it should lead to the breakdown of the Lebanese national consensus, thereby inviting the return of hostile forces.

The second set of negotiations—between Lebanon and Syria—is designed to achieve Syrian troop withdrawal. The Syrians, citing their 1975, [*1976*] Arab League mandate[83] to maintain order in Lebanon, have said they will not withdraw unless Israeli forces are also withdrawn. Although we will not be directly involved in these talks, Ambassador Habib will play a role with interested parties. We expect that agreement for withdrawal of Israeli forces will also lead to Syrian agreement to withdraw.

We will not be involved in the third set of negotiations—between Lebanon and the PLO—because it is U.S. policy not to "recognize or negotiate with the PLO so long as the PLO does not recognize Israel's right to exist and does not accept U.N. Security Council Resolutions 242 and 238." We will, however, make our views known through friendly governments. As in the case of the withdrawal of PLO fighters from Beirut, the United States is prepared to provide its good offices in bringing about the withdrawal and resettlement of the PLO forces still in Lebanon. Such withdrawal will be facilitated if Palestinian civilians in Lebanon feel secure. The Lebanese Government must provide such security. To this end, we will help strengthen Lebanese Government authority and the Lebanese Armed Forces.

It is a fact that none of these talks has begun. The Israeli-Lebanese negotiations could provide a stimulus for the others, but they have been stalled by debate over the level and location of the talks. Last week President Gemayel proposed a compromise solution on the diplomatic level of these negotiations. The Israeli Cabinet recently adopted that solution, but the Cabinet remained firm in its insistence that talks take place in Beirut and Jerusalem.

The current Israeli position is unacceptable to the Lebanese Government. The success and stability of that new government depends on the support of those within Lebanon and throughout the Arab world for whom the status of Jerusalem remains a crucial issue. The United States acknowledges the importance of Jerusalem to Israel and to all Arab States. But insistence on a Jerusalem venue should not be made an obstacle to negotiations on the withdrawal of external forces from Lebanon.

The present situation is clearly intolerable. Syrian, PLO, and Israeli forces remain poised in the field. The continued occupation of Lebanon by foreign forces—forces that imperil Lebanese sovereignty and threaten Israeli security—is dangerous and should be unacceptable to the parties. The task is to get the dispute out of the trenches and onto the table. Wrangling over procedures must end, and substantive negotiations must begin.

---

[83] The Arab League Council agreed to authorize a symbolic peacekeeping force in Lebanon on June 10, 1976. At a summit meeting in Riyadh, October 17–18, 1976, five Arab States and the Palestine Liberation Organization resolved that the symbolic security forces (2,500 men) be strengthened into a deterrent force of 30,000 men. An Arab League summit meeting in Cairo, October 25–26, 1976, endorsed the decision and established a special fund by Arab League members to finance the Arab Deterrent Force.

Second, restoring Lebanese sovereignty and strengthening their armed forces.

The withdrawal of foreign forces from Lebanon could leave an internal vacuum. To prevent the reinfiltration of those who would threaten Lebanon or Israel or both, withdrawals must be accompanied by steps to restore Lebanese Government sovereignty and strengthen the Lebanese Armed Forces.

The United States will join the international community in this effort. We have offered to help provide equipment and training to the Lebanese Armed Forces for four brigades by February, and seven brigades thereafter. It is our judgment that this force structure will be sufficient to maintain internal security and protect Lebanese sovereignty.

While the Lebanese Armed Forces are being strengthened, the international community will have to help maintain stability. An expanded Multinational Force, including U.S. participation and additional national contingents, may well be necessary. Indeed, we have already received such a request from the Lebanese Government.

As in the case of the present U.S., French, and Italian troops, any expanded multinational force would bolster the parties' confidence in security arrangements to facilitate the withdrawal of foreign forces. The Lebanese Armed Forces will continue to provide internal security, and the United Nations International Force in Lebanon (UNIFIL) should retain its crucial peacekeeping role. As the effectiveness of the Lebanese Armed Forces increases, the tasks of the MNF will decrease, permitting a phased withdrawal.

Third, economic reconstruction and national reconciliation.

Lebanese sovereignty and Israeli security, however, cannot be achieved by military measures alone. The economy of Lebanon has been shattered. To bring about a peace that is not merely the absence of fighting, but the well-being of the people, withdrawal of foreign forces must be coupled with an effort to reconstruct the Lebanese economy. The challenge seems staggering. But all that is needed is a period of political tranquility and some help in rebuilding Lebanon's roads, its water system and its schools. The Lebanese people—with their entrepreneurial skill, spirit and resilience—can take care of the rest themselves.

It is impossible to cite an exact figure for total reconstruction costs. The U.S. Government, however, stands ready to cooperate with the efforts of the Lebanese and of the international community. Since June we have made available $82 million in emergency relief and rehabilitation funds. We are planning to authorize another $30 million to guarantee housing and services for the poorest communities. This money is an investment in stability. It indicates American support for Lebanese national reconciliation and strengthens Lebanon's central government.

Further aid should come from Arab and Western donors, including the World Bank. Indeed, the World Bank is already taking an active role in assessing priorities for all potential donors and is willing to coordinate the matching of donor resources and Lebanese needs. It sent a reconnaissance team to Lebanon, and its report should be available by January 1983.

Now for my conclusion: The challenge of rebuilding a peaceful Lebanon, free of all foreign forces and sovereign over all its territory, is a daunting one. But the President is determined not to allow the opportunity for peace to slip away and the spark of war to be ignited again.

The objective of our Lebanon policy is, and I repeat, a fully sovereign Lebanon and a secure Israel. We pursue this objective because it is both right and in our national interests. We have seen that our responsibilities did not end with the mere cessation of hostilities. America alone has the power and credibility, and hence the duty, to help bring to Lebanon a stable and lasting peace that answers the basic security needs of Lebanon's neighbors. After all, Lebanon seeks and deserves what America already has, even though we may not always appreciate our blessings.

The sovereignty of the Lebanese Government must extend to the borders of the state. We have a name for that: We call it freedom. The opportunities of the Lebanese people must be made commensurate with their aspirations, and we have a name for that: We call it democracy. And the lives of their children must be made secure and full of hope. We have a name for that: We call it peace. (Sustained applause)

Document 419

Transcript of a White House Press Briefing, December 9, 1982 (Extracts)[84]

Ambassador Habib Reports on Progress Toward the Withdrawal of Foreign Forces From Lebanon

. . . .

[AMBASSADOR HABIB.] Ambassador Draper and I had the opportunity to review the situation in the Middle East, and particularly the situation in Lebanon with the President. We have, as is normal in these matters, taken this occasion to take a look at where we have been and where we are going, have a chance to have our instructions refreshed.

Obviously, we are working within the President's policies with respect to the situation in Lebanon regarding the earliest possible withdrawal of all external forces from that country so that our policy of general support for the sovereignty and integrity of Lebanon can be sustained.

Secondly, of course, we discussed and received anew the President's views with respect to the initiative, which he set forth in his speech on September 1st, and which is ongoing in accordance with its purposes. We are, both of us, returning to the Middle East in just a few days. We will be there next week to continue the discussions that we have been having with the relevant parties on those issues. And in particular, in this case, we will start with trying to accelerate the process on the Lebanese situation.

Q. Mr. Ambassador, viewed from this perspective, it sure looks like both the President's peace initiative and the withdrawal of foreign forces from Lebanon are really stalled.

AMBASSADOR HABIB. No. I just could not agree with you less. I think that you are presuming more than you should. In the first place, when this thing started out, nobody expected this to be an exercise of a couple of weeks. All of you who are familiar with the problems of that part of the world know that you have got a great deal of talking to do. You are dealing with a complex situation. You are dealing with a lot of parties. And call it ambitions we may have, you always find yourself having to go through a process of thorough discussion. The United States just does not have the authority to just decide within deadlines. You have to convince people. And that is what we are in the process of doing.

I think that there has been considerable success in narrowing the issues. And I suspect that we will have to go a little further along that road.

Q. Do you agree with President Gemayel that the withdrawal will not work unless you increase the number of troops—double the number of American forces?

AMBASSADOR HABIB. I think that the question of whether or not there will be a necessary increase in the multinational force, not just in American forces, is a question that we should address at the time when and if—when and if such a need is evident. Now, such a need is not evident at this moment, because you have not yet gotten to the position of full agreement on the withdrawal. I would say, when you get that, then you have to take that into account. And at such time, of course, the matter will be discussed in the normal ways.

Q. Then you disagree that it is needed now. He is asking for now, is that right?

AMBASSADOR HABIB. I would say that he is asking in anticipation of certain things. I think, at the moment—I would argue at this moment that we should maintain that anticipation. But we do not have to give a response immediately. And I think that he understands that. This is not, basically, a difference of opinion between us.

Q. What sort of an arrangement would be necessary and agreeable to give Israel a buffer zone, if any, in southern Lebanon?

AMBASSADOR HABIB. That is part of the negotiations, Sam. It is quite clear that the United States has been, and will be, and is committed to the security of Israel. And

---

[84] Source: White House Press Release, December 9, 1982, Office of the Press Secretary to the President. Philip C. Habib, the President's Special Representative for the Middle East, conducted the briefing. Morris Draper, Deputy Assistant Secretary of State for Near Eastern and South Asian Affairs, also took part in the briefing, which began at 1:09 p.m. in the White House Briefing Room after a luncheon with President Reagan. Omitted portions deal with Habib's and Draper's informal banter with the press and their refusal to answer questions on the September 18 Beirut massacre and on Israeli Prime Minister Begin.

there is no question about that. The arrangements that are going to have to be made—and I use the arrangements with respect to southern Lebanon—are a matter that are going to have [to] be resolved between Israel and Lebanon. And we, of course, will be of assistance in the resolution of that problem. I do not think that that is a major hurdle that cannot be resolved. On the basis of the work that Morris has been doing and my own conversations, I would say that I can see our way clear to resolving those kinds of issues. I'll take one or two more.

Q. We've been reading about a north bank. You know, they're calling southern Lebanon Israel's north bank.

AMBASSADOR HABIB. I would—I wouldn't accept that characterization.

Q. Mr. Ambassador, does the President feel that Israel has been forthcoming in this process?

AMBASSADOR HABIB. Well, I think the President, like ourselves, is—understands that this is a process of negotiation. And I don't think that—I haven't gotten any sense of characterization at this point. . . .

. . . .

Q. My question is on the external forces. In negotiating to get Israelis out, either you or Ambassador Draper will go to Jerusalem. In negotiating to get the Syrians out, you go to Damascus. With whom do you negotiate to get the PLO out?

AMBASSADOR HABIB. The process of negotiation is a question of getting the word from the right person to the right person. There are different ways it can be done. For example, when we arranged the evacuation of the PLO from west Beirut, which you'll recall was done through an American participation in the negotiating process, we managed without too much difficulty to find someone who could play that role of intermediary in the negotiations in such a manner that there was [*were*] very clear channels and clear understandings of what would happen. I can assure you we have the same capacity and the Lebanese have the same capacity today as we had then. So, I don't anticipate any problem in communication.

. . . .

Q. There has been a lot of talk earlier about getting all of the marines out by the end of the year. Is that now by the boards?

AMBASSADOR HABIB. I don't think anybody's setting that kind of deadline at this point. I think that it's fairly well recognized that it's purpose, function, and utility that count and you don't need to set that kind of deadline.

. . . .

Document 420

Letter From Fourteen Members of the Senate Foreign Relations Committee to President Reagan, December 15, 1982[85]

Congressional Responsibility Under the War Powers Resolution With Respect to U.S. Troops in Lebanon

DEAR MR. PRESIDENT. As Members of the Senate Foreign Relations Committee, we have a particular concern for the situation in Lebanon and a particular responsibility under the War Powers Resolution[86] with respect to the commitment of U.S. Armed Forces abroad. We are convinced that it is in the national interest of the United States to work toward a stable and independent Lebanon as part of a broader peace settlement in the Middle East. We also recognize that the current Multinational Force in Lebanon has played a constructive role in preventing further violence in and around Beirut and that the U.S. Marine component of that force has performed admirably under difficult circumstances.

In reintroducing U.S. Armed Forces into Lebanon on September 29, you reported under the War Powers Resolution that there was "no intention or expectation that

---

[85] Source: *Congressional Record,* December 18, 1982, p. S15482. Charles H. Percy, Chairman of the Senate Foreign Relations Committee, inserted the letter into the *Congressional Record.* Three members of the committee did not sign the letter: Senators Howard H. Baker, Jr., Alan Cranston, and Jesse Helms.

[86] Reference is to the Joint Resolution concerning the war powers of Congress and the President, passed over President Richard M. Nixon's veto (P.L. 93–148), November 7, 1973; for text, see 87 Stat. 555.

U.S. Armed Forces will become involved in hostilities".[87] Individual members of Congress, including members of our Committee, have disagreed with your assessment of the risks inherent in the Beirut operation and, therefore, with your interpretation of the War Powers Resolution in this case. No member has chosen to contest the issue through Congressional action at this time. Under the procedures set out in the War Powers Resolution, Congress reserves the ability to direct the removal of such forces at any time they are engaged in hostilities if it should determine that the circumstances no longer justify a U.S. military presence.

As the Beirut operation continues, and as discussions proceed regarding its possible extension or expansion, we want to ensure that the Congress has an adequate opportunity to consider the full implications of any extended commitment of U.S. forces and to fulfill its responsibilities in this area. We recognize the difficulties in developing longer-term proposals for such a multinational force until the negotiations for the departure of all foreign forces have progressed. However, we would expect Congress to be involved at the earliest possible stage in the development of such proposals and that formal Congressional authorization would be sought before undertaking long-term or expanded commitments or extending indefinitely the present level of operations.

In the longer term, it may be appropriate to consider more general legislation to clarify the respective roles of the President and the Congress in undertaking the commitment of U.S. Armed Forces to such operations. We look forward to further discussions with you and the members of your Administration in the exercise of our joint responsibilities in this area.

Sincerely, Charles H. Percy, Richard G. Lugar, Nancy Landon Kassebaum, Paul E. Tsongas, S. I. Hayakawa, John Glenn, Charles McC. Mathias, Jr., Claiborne Pell, J. R. Biden, Jr., Larry Pressler, Edward Zorinsky, Christopher J. Dodd, Paul Sarbanes, and Rudy Boschwitz

[87] See document 411.

Document 421

Transcript of an Interview With President Reagan, December 16, 1982 (Extract)[88]

Call for Withdrawal of Foreign Forces From Lebanon

. . . .

Q. On Sept. 1, you called for withdrawal of all foreign forces from Lebanon. What are you prepared to do to bring this about?

A. Well, we have Ambassador [Philip] Habib and Ambassador [Morris] Draper over there right now. . . .[89] They're meeting with them. We think the time is now for action. We made the proposal in September, a complete proposal leading toward a peaceful settlement for all the problems in the Middle East. But it begins with recognizing the sovereignty of Lebanon after all these several years of division and, I say, warlords with their own militias at odds with each other in Lebanon. The Government of Lebanon should be sovereign over its own territory.

We think the time has come now for the foreign forces that are in there—Syria, Israel and the remnant of the PLO that is in there—to get out. And that's why the multinational force was sent—to, in a sense, help give some stability while the new Lebanese Government established itself. For those countries to delay in getting out now places them in the position of being occupying armies. Because it was one thing to be in by invitation of Lebanon. It's another thing to cross a border because that border has been violated and other forces were attacking Israeli targets. But now that the Lebanese Government has enough confidence in itself that it has asked them to leave, then to not leave is, as I say, they make themselves occupying forces.

. . . .

[88] Source: *Washington Post*, December 19, 1982, p. A8. President Reagan was interviewed by Lou Cannon and David Hoffman, both of the *Washington Post.*

[89] Brackets and ellipsis of three points appear in the source text.

Document 422

Transcript of an Interview With President Reagan, December 18, 1982 (Extract)[90]

Planning the Removal of "Armies of Occupation" From Lebanon

. . . .

Q. Mr. President, you have King Hussein of Jordan coming in here next week.[91] He has been described as the linchpin in your Middle East peace initiative, because of your proposal for the Palestinian entity. What do you think are the prospects of bringing him on board the Camp David process at this point?

THE PRESIDENT. King Hussein is not only a very intelligent and responsible leader, but I think that he is very sensitive to all of the problems that are involved, and very sincerely desirous of peace in the Middle East and a resolution of this problem. And I think that he will be cooperative. And I think we can count on him for that. But the main thing right now that we have Ambassadors Habib and Draper working on in the Middle East is to get what now constitute armies of occupation—the PLO, the Syrians, and the Israelis—out of Lebanon, and let the Gemayel government have the sovereignty of their own country.

I call them armies of occupation, because there was a time in which Lebanon, with all of its troubles and its divisions, did have to welcome them in, in an effort to create order. But now, that government has had enough confidence to ask them to leave. For them to continue to stay against the will of Lebanon makes them, technically, armies of occupation. And we are working on that. That is the first step.

And then we move to the peace process, involving the Palestinian problem, Israel, and guaranteeing the security of Israel's borders.

Q. There is a report today, sir, that you have told President Gemayel of Lebanon that the United States will guarantee the withdrawal of all foreign forces by the end of February. Is there any truth to that?

THE PRESIDENT. No. There is none. We have set no date, no timetable. But I will say this—Ambassador Habib will be reporting to me Monday.[92] But, when I sent him on this most recent trip over there, I told him that no longer are we talking about a peace plan. We are now talking about action—a plan for action. Let's get it done and let's get the forces withdrawn so that we can proceed with the other steps.

. . . .

[90] Source: White House Press Release, December 18, 1982, Office of the Press Secretary to the President; also printed in *Weekly Compilation of Presidential Documents,* December 27, 1982, pp. 1646–1647. For the full text, see *ibid.*, pp. 1640–1647. The interview, which was held at 12:15 p.m. in the Roosevelt Room of the White House, with Frank Sesno of Associated Press, Bill Groody of Mutual News, Ted Clark of National Public Radio, Joe Ewalt of RKO Radio Network, Bob Ellison of Sheridan Broadcasting Network, and Gene Gibbons of United Press International, was broadcast live on the participating radio networks.

[91] For information regarding the U.S. visit of King Hussein I of Jordan, see documents 345 and 346.

Document 423

Statement by the President's Special Negotiator for Lebanon (Draper), Khalde, Lebanon, December 28, 1982[93]

The Opening Session of Negotiations Between Israel and Lebanon

This is indeed a moving occasion. I am pleased to be here today to represent the United States at the opening of these important negotiations. As a close friend of both Israel and Lebanon, the United States will do all it can to assist efforts to achieve agreement.

[92] The President met with Ambassador Habib on Tuesday, December 21.

[93] Source: Department of State files. Draper made the statement at the Lebanon Beach Hotel in Khalde, Lebanon, at the first session of negotiations between Israel and Lebanon that were intended to bring about the withdrawal of foreign forces from Lebanon and to determine future relations between the two countries. The second session was held in Qiryat Shemona, Israel, on December 30. Future sessions were to be held alternately in Lebanon and Israel.

The United States has made clear on frequent occasions its sympathy and support for many of the key objectives of the parties at this table. The United States believes strongly that the legitimate security interests of Israel should be addressed and satisfied to the maximum extent possible. At the same time, the United States supports Lebanon's independence, national unity, and integrity, and the restoration of full sovereignty throughout its territories.

There is a good basis for confidence that the negotiations will be productive. For its part, Israel has affirmed that it does not covet a single inch of Lebanese territory and that it wants to withdraw its military forces. For its part, Lebanon has affirmed that it does not intend to allow its territory to become again a base for hostile actions directed against Israel.

Israel, Lebanon, and the United States also all agree on the need for the quickest possible withdrawal of all external military forces from Lebanon. The initiation of these negotiations is a major and indispensable step towards the achievement of this goal held in common.

Peace and security, however, are as always basic issues with two nations which are destined by history and geography to live together. Will we be destined to see a repetition of the violence, the instability, and the suffering of the past? Or, will we see imagination and vision on the part of the representatives at this table? We have an historic opportunity to set the stage for a future filled with hope.

I am sure that all of us would agree that we must proceed rapidly and cooperatively—and with a sense of the good will which I know is present—to bring about an early and successful conclusion to the negotiations. With that outcome—in combination with arrangements for the withdrawal of external military forces from Lebanon—Israel will be assured that its fundamental security interests will have been met and Lebanon will be able to embark confidently on a long overdue course of national recovery.

I pray that God blesses our efforts.

H. Libya

Document 424

Statement Read by the Department of State Spokesman (Fischer), March 10, 1982[1]

U.S. Economic Measures Against Libya

President Reagan, after consultations with Congress and discussions with appropriate foreign governments, has decided to prohibit imports of Libyan oil into the United States and to ban selected exports of U.S.-origin items to Libya.[2]

We are taking these measures in response to a continuing pattern of Libyan activity which violates accepted international norms of behavior. Libya's large financial resources, vast supplies of Soviet weapons, and active efforts to promote instability and terrorism make it a serious threat to a large number of nations and individuals, particularly in the Middle East and Africa.

Our policy towards Libya has been under careful review for over a year. We have moved in a measured way to address the Libyan challenge by strengthening states in the region threatened by the Libyan Government and supporting peacekeeping initiatives such as the OAU force in Chad.[3] We have previously taken steps to demonstrate that we are no longer prepared to tolerate Libyan misbehavior, such as closing the Libyan People's Bureau in the United States last May.[4]

We have seen no evidence of a significant, lasting change in Libyan behavior; Libyan efforts to destabilize U.S. regional friends has continued. Accordingly, the administration has decided that further measures are appropriate at this time to underline our seriousness of purpose, and reas-

---

[1] Source: Office of Press Relations, Department of State; also printed in Department of State *Bulletin*, June 1982, pp. 68–69. The statement was read at a Department of State Special Briefing on Libya which began at 1 p.m.

[2] For the text of Presidential Proclamation 4907, see *Weekly Compilation of Presidential Documents*, March 15, 1982, p. 280.

[3] For U.S. logistical support for the OAU peacekeeping force in Chad, see *American Foreign Policy: Current Documents, 1981*, document 646.

[4] See *ibid.*, document 378.

sure those threatened by Libya. The specific measures we will take are as follows:

Prohibiting imports of Libyan crude oil, thus ending U.S. reliance on Libya to meet a part of our crude oil needs and cutting off our flow of dollars to Libya. This step would be taken under Section 232 of the Trade Expansion Act of 1962.[5]

Requiring validated licenses for all U.S. exports to Libya, except for food and other agricultural products, medicine, and medical supplies. This step would be taken for foreign policy reasons under Section 6 of the Export Administration Act.[6]

A general policy of denying licenses for the export to Libya of items now on the Commodity Control List for national security purposes. Under this policy, we would be prohibiting the sale to Libya of dual-use, high technology items.

A general policy of denying licenses for the export to Libya of U.S.-origin oil and gas technology and equipment that is not readily available from sources outside the United States.

In implementing these new export controls, we will seek to minimize to the extent feasible their extraterritorial impact on third countries and their effect on preexisting contracts.

We believe that these measures will focus attention on the fact that Libya is able to threaten its neighbors and international order because of the revenues it derives from its oil trade. We will no longer be providing the dollars or the technology to Libya which can be used for activities that threaten international stability. We recognize that these measures may have only limited economic impact on Libya, but feel that they are necessary to complement other measures for dealing with this problem, such as support to regional states and efforts to reduce the underlying instability which Libya exploits.

---

[5] P.L. 87–794, approved October 11, 1962; 76 Stat. 877.

[6] Reference is to Section 6 of the Export Administration Act of 1979, P.L. 96–72, approved September 29, 1979; for text, see 93 Stat. 513.

I. Morocco

Document 425

Statement by the Secretary of State (Haig), Marrakech, February 12, 1982[1]

Establishment of a U.S.-Moroccan Joint Military Commission

We have agreed that it would serve our mutual interests to establish a joint military commission which will meet periodically for consultations. The agreement to establish this commission stems from the growth in the U.S.-Moroccan military relationship to the point where a more formal structure is required to address security matters of mutual interest.

The establishment of this joint military commission is symbolic of the traditional and longstanding close friendship between Morocco and the United States. The first meeting is planned in the spring in Rabat.

Document 426

Transcript of a Press Conference by the Secretary of State (Haig), Marrakech, February 12, 1982 (Extract)[2]

"Fruitful and Far-Ranging Discussions" in Morocco

SECRETARY HAIG. Good Morning, ladies and gentlemen. I just have a few brief remarks to make to cover the essence of our visit here—all too brief visit—in Morocco.

This is my first visit to the Kingdom of Morocco, having had to cancel an earlier planned visit at the time of the Polish suppression in December. And as brief as this

---

[1] Source: Department of State *Bulletin*, April 1982, p. 46. Secretary Haig visited Marrakech, February 11–12, 1982, during a trip to Europe and North Africa.

[2] Source: Department of State Press Release 66, February 19, 1982; also printed in Department of State *Bulletin*, April 1982, pp. 45–47. The omitted portion is a question and answer on the Polish crisis.

visit has been, it has given me the opportunity to meet at length with His Majesty, King Hassan, with the Prime Minister[3] and the Foreign Minister[4] and their colleagues, and to conduct very fruitful and far-ranging discussions.

The main focus of the extensive discussions with His Majesty were, of course, strategic in character and were a reflection of the great experience and leadership that His Majesty has demonstrated over the years. He has been both a witness and a participant in global affairs and has been a very knowledgeable counselor to American leaders over many decades.

Of course, the primary focus of these discussions were the restoration of global and regional peace and stability. In this regard, His Majesty has a unique perspective and offered sage advice. He has been, as you know, an advocate of the achievement of a comprehensive and just peace in the Middle East, at the earliest possible date, and he has also been an advocate for a peaceful solution to the war in the Western Sahara through a peaceful process proposed by His Majesty and facilitated recently at the OAU Meeting.[5]

An additional purpose of mine, of course, was to underline and reiterate President Reagan's support and friendship for His Majesty and the Government and people of Morocco.

U.S.–Morocco cooperation in the political, military, economic, educational and cultural areas was discussed, and we signed, just a few moments ago, an agreement establishing a permanent binational commission for educational and cultural exchange.[6] Of course, a very specific focus was on the security threats to this region which are evident, only too evident, in the Northern African region. In this regard, we agreed it would serve our mutual interests at this time to establish a joint military commission periodically to review our security cooperation. And I think our statement with respect to that is available to the press here this morning.[7] We also discussed the potential availability of transit facilities for U.S. forces on sovereign Moroccan soil and early discussions will commence with the possible realization of such objectives.

I want to emphasize that no decisions were made with respect to this question, but that positive and affirmative communication was established with the objective of leading to the availability of such facilities.

We also reviewed His Majesty's plan to visit Washington the first half of this year before this coming summer. This visit is one which President Reagan very much looks forward to as an opportunity for a working, sleeves-up discussion of the strategic situation, globally and regionally. Finally, before turning it over to your questions, I want to express the appreciation of Mrs. Haig and myself and our party for the hospitality and warmth of our reception here, and nothing could contribute more to that than the beautiful setting in which this visit occurred here at Marrakech.

Now, I welcome your questions.

Q. Mr. Secretary, will your talks on the transit facilities perhaps involve the reactivation of some U.S. military bases which were closed over the years?

SECRETARY HAIG. I think, as you know, there has been discussion on two specific possible facilities for American transit use. Nothing has been discounted; nothing has been specifically approved, but I think in the very near future detailed discussions will focus on these facilities.

Q. Mr. Secretary, did you discuss with the King the projected American military credits that would be available to his government in the next fiscal year, and could you give us some idea of what that might be?

SECRETARY HAIG. There were, of course, broad discussions on future American plans in the security assistance area. I think it's too soon for me to pinpoint a specific level that is contemplated for FY–83. I think the experience of FY–82 was, from my point of view, somewhat disappointing. I wish we had been able to do better, and I hope we will be able to do better in FY–83, and I would anticipate that will be the case.[8] Be-

---

[3] Maati Bouabid, Prime Minister of Morocco.

[4] Mohamed Boucetta, Moroccan Minister of State in Charge of Foreign Affairs.

[5] On June 27, 1981, the Organization of African Unity (OAU) adopted a resolution calling for a cease-fire, to be followed by a referendum to determine the future status of the Western Sahara. For the text of the resolution, see *American Foreign Policy: Current Documents, 1981*, document 393.

[6] Reference is to the Agreement Establishing a Binational and Cultural Exchange, signed at Marrakech, February 12, 1982, entered into force May 20, 1982. (TIAS 10407)

[7] *Supra.*

[8] The military aid program for Morocco in fiscal year 1983 consisted of a grant of $25 million and guaranteed loans of $75 million; see P.L. 97–377, approved December 21, 1982; for text, see 96 Stat. 1830. Morocco had received a total of $30 million in military assistance during fiscal year 1982.

cause, as we look today at the African Continent, as we witness the activity of Libya, the high level of armaments that have been provided to the Government by the Soviet Union, the appearance of these armaments in various destabilizing actions, together with funds and resources from the Libyan Government, it's been clearly a destabilizing offensive underway. And I think it's extremely important that the advocates of international peace and stability cooperate together more closely in the period ahead to deal with this destabilization.

Q. Sir, can you tell us what you learned about the prospect for a settlement in the Western Sahara, and would those prospects be greatly complicated with Qaddafi expected to take over as head of the OAU?

SECRETARY HAIG. I think the distinguished Foreign Minister of Morocco had a brief press conference this morning in which he discussed the recently concluded OAU-sponsored conference.[9] I think we are all encouraged by the fact that a framework was put together which broadens responsibility in the region specifically to include Mauritania, Algeria, as well as Morocco, in the direction of a cease-fire and time certainly will be established to continue with this process and that in the interim all responsible participants will refrain from undertaking actions which would put the realization of the referendum and the maintenance of a cease-fire in jeopardy. In that regard, one cannot draw any encouragement whatsoever from the rejection by the Polisario elements of the OAU proposals.

Q. How about the second part of the question, sir, on the role that Mr. Qaddafi might play in the settlement after he becomes head of the OUA? Will that complicate the situation or does there need to be a settlement before that time?

SECRETARY HAIG. I wouldn't want to speculate about that. Clearly, the U.S. concerns about Mr. Qaddafi's activity for an extended period—his support of international terrorism, the level of armaments that have been introduced into Libya, the appearance of those armaments elsewhere in the region—are all matters of concern. There has been no indication in the recent past of any moderation in Mr. Qaddafi's activity. I would hope that his responsibilities within the OAU would offer a refreshing departure from his past activity.

Q. Could I just go back to the discussion on the transit rights for American forces and the press release that is coming out on this joint commision? Now, Mr. Weinberger recently, I think, reached agreement on a joint commission with the Saudi Arabians on a similar trip. Can you discuss—is there a broad administration effort to get this kind of joint commission or closer ties with friendly countries in the region now going on? Is this part of a larger effort?

SECRETARY HAIG. I think you will recall my first trip to the region last spring[10] when we talked about the desirability of greater cooperation, and the development of a commonality of view to the dangers from external sources to stability of the region, and externally directed internal threats to the security of the region. I think I recall at the time and in the period since, a great deal of skepticism about this from some of your colleagues in the press. That does not make it any less desirable, and what you are witnessing is further steps in that direction. I would emphasize again as I did at the outset of our discussion about this objective, that this in no way runs counter to our continuing efforts in the direction of achieving a comprehensive settlement of longstanding Arab-Israeli disputes. As a matter of fact, I have always described these as mutually reinforcing objectives. And when progress is achieved in one area, it contributes to progress in the other. Just as when a setback occurs in one area, it makes the achievement of progress in the other more difficult.

. . . .

Document 427

Statements by President Reagan and Moroccan King Hassan II, May 19, 1982[11]

U.S.-Moroccan Discussion of Bilateral Relations

THE PRESIDENT. His Majesty, King Hassan II of Morocco, and I met this morning,

---

9 On February 8–9, 1982, an OAU-sponsored committee met in Nairobi and proposed that a mixed UN/OAU commission should be sent to the Western Sahara at least a month before a cease-fire to organize the referendum to determine the territory's future status. (*Keesing's Contemporary Archives,* May 14, 1982, p. 31489)

10 Haig visited Egypt, Israel, Jordan, Saudi Arabia, Italy, Spain, the United Kingdom, France, and West Germany, April 4–11, 1981.

11 Source: White House Press Release, May 19,

and he was my guest lunching. He's a firm friend of the United States and his working visit to Washington gives us an opportunity to build on two centuries of cordial diplomatic relations between our two countries.

It is a real personal privilege and pleasure to have His Majesty as our guest.

King Hassan is the leader of a great nation at the crossroads of two continents lying on NATO's southern flank at the entrance to the Mediterranean. It has deep ties to Africa, Europe, the Middle East and the whole Islamic world. We, therefore, discussed not only bilateral relations but a wide range of regional and global issues.

I deeply value the depth of experience and breadth of vision that His Majesty brings to the issues of profound mutual concern.

His Majesty briefed me on the latest developments in his efforts to reach a peaceful settlement of the conflict in the Western Sahara. And I expressed my admiration for his support of the OAU, Organization of African Unity, referendum.

We discussed opportunities for continued progress in the Middle East and agreed to continue a strategic dialogue on security issues.

We reviewed the progress that we've achieved in augmenting our bilateral relations, the Binational Committee for Economic Relations that Secretary Baldrige chaired last January,[12] the Joint Military Commission that held its first meeting last month and the agreement establishing a binational commission for cultural and educational exchange that Secretary Haig signed in Morocco in February.

We considered other opportunities for closer cooperation between our two countries in private investment, trade, and other areas.

And I expressed to His Majesty the great value the United States places on cooperation with him and on friendship with Morocco, a country that stood with us at our independence, fought at our side during the Second World War and joins with us today in a quest for world peace and security.

Your Majesty, we're honored to have you here and we bid you welcome.

King Hassan. Mr. President, I shall try to be understood against—and even my very bad English. But I shall try to speak the language of the heart to thank you very deeply, you and your government and your people, for your hospitality.

And I can assure you that from yesterday in the afternoon until now I really felt that I was between very strong and loyal friends.

Naturally, the nature of the problems of the United States and the nature of our problems in Morocco, they have not the same volume and they are not at the same level. But the nature is the same. Our problems, like your problems, are to live in the dignity, in the freedom and in the way of life which our people choose for themselves and for the future.

A big ocean is between the United States and Morocco. But we must each day after each day, we must try to build a bridge of solidarity and understanding. We can—or you could sometime, you and I, have not the same analysis or the same position for one functioning situation in the world. That is the sign of your independence and our independence and the sign of our free exercise of our sovereignty as you are free to exercise your sovereignty.

But the importance is to see and to know that always, as before, Moroccan people and American people are ready and will be ready always to fight for the same ideal and to mix their blood for the dignity of man and the freedom of the countries.

Again, Mr. President, I thank you very warmly for your hospitality and I wish for your country prosperity and glory and for yourself, health and success. Thank you. (Applause)

1982, Office of the Press Secretary to the President; printed also in *Weekly Compilation of Presidential Documents*, May 24, 1982, pp. 672–673. The remarks were made on the South Lawn of the White House at 1:48 p.m. King Hassan visited Washington, May 18–21, 1982.

[12] A U.S. trade and investment mission led by Secretary of Commerce Malcolm Baldrige visited Morocco, January 19–20, 1982, during a 12-day tour of four African countries (Ivory Coast, Nigeria, Cameroon, and Morocco), January 9–20, 1982. On January 19, 1982, Baldrige chaired the first formal meeting of the U.S.-Moroccan Joint Committee for Economic Relations, established by an agreement signed at Washington, September 25, 1980.

Document 428

Statement Read by the Department of State Spokesman (Fischer), May 21, 1982[13]

Visit of King Hassan II of Morocco

The discussions with His Majesty King Hassan II have been most satisfying and thorough, covering a broad range of subjects. Perhaps the most important outcome of the visit was the opportunity for the President and King Hassan to have face-to-face discussions on the major issues of common concern and our respective positions on them.

Secretary Haig and Foreign Minister Boucetta, in the presence of the King, exchanged the instruments of the ratification of the agreement establishing a binational cultural and educational commission on the 20th of May. Secretary Haig signed the agreement in Marakech in February and the rapidity with which the whole process was completed, testifies to its importance to both countries.

We also had a chance to review economic issues of common interest. In order to promote U.S. investment in Morocco, an investment working group in the U.S.-Moroccan Economic Commission will be established to begin operations soon, and we've held discussions on the possibility of negotiating on a bilateral investment treaty. We also discussed a cooperative venture in dryland agricultural development. It is our hope to be able to provide around $200 million in assistance over the next 5 years for this effort which could cushion Morocco against the effects of another devastating drought.

We reviewed the important security aspects of our relationship. Morocco and the United States have had a long tradition of close cooperation on security issues which has been strengthened recently with an expanded strategic dialogue. The joint military commission is an important vehicle for continuing discussions between our respective military establishments.

Both sides also stressed the importance of our security assistance relationship. We are proceeding with negotiations in which Morocco will grant U.S. Forces access to Moroccan transit facilities in special contingencies of concern to both countries. A detailed agreement will now be worked out, and we expect agreement on a text before His Majesty departs the United States.

We discussed the implications of the OAU actions taken toward the Western Sahara. The King's initiative taken at Nairobi last year calling for a cease-fire and referendum continues to be the basis of our policy. After the excellent beginnings of the implementation committee of this year, we hope that the OAU will persist in its activities.

Finally, we had a productive exchange on the Middle East situation. We very much value the views of King Hassan and the constructive approach that he has traditionally taken toward that issue. We reiterated U.S. determination to press forward with the autonomy talks. We look forward to a continuing dialogue with Morocco on this vital matter.

Document 429

Statement Read by the Department of State Spokesman (Fischer), May 27, 1982[14]

Agreement on U.S. Use of Moroccan Airfields

I have a statement regarding the Facilities Agreement signed by the United States and Morocco. The United States and Morocco have reached agreement on the use and transit by the U.S. Forces of agreed airfields in emergencies and for periodic training.[15] The United States will not permanently station armed forces or establish U.S. military bases in Morocco in connection with carrying out this agreement. It will have an initial term of 6 years and will continue thereafter unless terminated on 2-years' notice by either party.

---

[13] Source: Office of Press Relations, Department of State; printed also in Department of State *Bulletin*, August 1982, p. 70. The statement was read at the Department of State Daily Press Briefing held at 12:40 p.m.

[14] Source: Office of Press Relations, Department of State. This statement was read at the Department of State Daily Press Briefing held at 12:20 p.m.

[15] Reference is to the Agreement Concerning the Use of Certain Facilities in Morocco by the United States, effected by notes exchanged at Washington, May 27, 1982. (TIAS 10399)

J. Saudi Arabia

Document 430

Statement and Remarks by the Secretary of Defense (Weinberger), Dhahran, Saudi Arabia, February 9, 1982 (Extracts)[1]

Establishment of a Saudi-U.S. Joint Committee for Military Projects

. . . .

SECRETARY WEINBERGER. . . . I would like to express the great appreciation that we all feel, my party and I, for the warmth and hospitality that has been extended to us and the warmth of the greetings and importance of the statements made to us by His Majesty, the King, the Crown Prince, His Highness Prince Sultan, and His Highness Prince Saud, Foreign Minister.

During the course of these meetings we have been impressed repeatedly with the great desire on both sides for a warm and continued friendly relation between our two great countries. I would particularly like to thank the Saudi people for the way in which they manifested their great friendship for the United States for so many years.

During the course of these meetings we agreed to establish and oversee a Saudi-U.S. Joint Committee for Military Projects, which will deal with military matters of mutual interest to our two countries. And, of course, His Highness is correct that it is not the only area in which we would want to have cooperation. We are also very interested in doing things to help other nations. We have both been very generous in our aid and assistance to other countries and we want to work to continue that in a mutually beneficial way.

We also have had a most helpful exchange of views on the immediate problems that are facing both of our countries in this area and we have discussed the arrangements for completing the sale of the AWACS to Saudi Arabia and for the continued presence of the AWACS in the Kingdom until the Saudi AWACS arrive.[2] And as a result of these discussions, I am happy to say we have agreed on all the measures that are necessary for the sale of the AWACS to Saudi Arabia.

I would like to express my great appreciation in that [*what*] I feel that I know all the members of my party feel for the warmth of our welcome, for the friendship of the Saudi people and for His Majesty's Government and for all the people who have been so cordial and helpful to us, and certainly Prince Sultan has been foremost in the hospitality and the cordiality that he has extended to us.

. . . .

Q. Mr. Secretary, can you give us some detail—first of all the joint committee that was set up with the Saudis, and number two, was the Gulf Cooperative Council[3] brought up and does the United States have any intention to specifically help countries as a result of your talks here today, specifically help those countries with military aspects of their—

SECRETARY WEINBERGER. The Joint Commission will essentially be designed to follow up and follow on with work that has been already underway. We will obviously take up anything the Joint Committee for Military Projects wants to take up. His Highness and I will be cochairmen and we will meet annually, once in one country and again in the other country and experts on our staff will be meeting more often than that. We would be primarily concerned with

---

1 Source: *Public Statements of Secretary of Defense Weinberger*, 1982. Between February 4 and 13, Weinberger visited the United Kingdom, Saudi Arabia, Oman, Jordan, and West Germany. He arrived in Saudi Arabia on February 7, and made these remarks prior to his departure. The omitted portions are the introductory remarks by Prince Sultan Ibn Abdul Aziz, Saudi Arabian Minister of Defense and Aviation, and his and Weinberger's responses to questions on the U.S. position toward Israel in the Middle East peace process, U.S. and Saudi Arabian cooperation in the fields of technology and industrial development, and Afghanistan.

2 That is, the U.S. Air Force AWACS aircraft deployed to Saudi Arabia in 1980 would remain there until 1985. For documentation concerning the proposed sale of AWACS to Saudi Arabia, see *American Foreign Policy: Current Documents, 1981*, Chapter 11, Part J.

3 On February 4 and 5, 1981, the Foreign Ministers of Bahrain, Kuwait, Oman, Qatar, Saudi Arabia, and the United Arab Emirates met in Riyadh to establish a Cooperation Council of the Arab Gulf States. The heads of state of the member countries held their first meeting in Abu Dhabi, May 25–26, 1981.

following up on the necessary actions on various military projects. With respect to the second part of your question, the Gulf Cooperation League was mentioned from time to time, not in any special connection. We are helping with other Arab countries in military assistance and economic assistance and we certainly plan to continue that as long as it is desired and it is desired so far as we know.

. . . .

Document 431

Testimony by the Deputy Assistant Secretary of State for Near Eastern and South Asian Affairs (Constable) Before a Subcommittee of the House Foreign Affairs Committee, March 3, 1982 (Extract)[4]

Saudi Arabia and the Middle East Peace Process

. . . .

MR. SHAMANSKY. How about the Saudis?

MR. CONSTABLE. The Saudis take the posture that they are prepared to go along with what the Palestinians want on the issue of the West Bank.

MR. SHAMANSKY. Unrelated to their supplying them with money?

MR. CONSTABLE. They supply their money because they are sympathetic to the Palestinian cause. They are not prepared to try to dictate or to attempt to dictate to the Palestinians how they define their own tactical position. If the Palestinians, the PLO would say, "Yes, we will recognize Israel," the Saudis would be very happy with that outcome.

MR. SHAMANSKY. But we do not do anything to suggest that the Saudis should suggest it to the PLO.

MR. CONSTABLE. We have a lot of discussions with the Saudis about all of these issues. Now, the point at which we make suggestions to them or the line between suggestions and telling them what our position is and what we think would be helpful to the process, is a fine one.

MR. SHAMANSKY. But there are no untoward consequences for the Saudis not to do that, as far as our policy is concerned.

MR. CONSTABLE. We have a variety of relationships with the Saudis and a variety of interests which we seek to advance.

MR. SHAMANSKY. Can you tell us what the Saudis are doing to try to defuse the situation in Lebanon, and to what extent they can pressure or they have pressured the Syrians to withdraw those missiles?

MR. CONSTABLE. They were very, very helpful in producing the cessation of hostilities last July when Ambassador Habib undertook on behalf of the President to organize that. The Saudis engaged in that effort and were very helpful in it and very constructive.

They have also participated in the so-called Bayt ad-Din process to try to bring together, reconcile, the factions in Lebanon that would strengthen the central government in a way that would enable the whole Lebanese crisis to be defused.

That process had, I think, constructive Saudi support and interest. It has not gone ahead as well as any of us had hoped that it would. Ambassador Habib will be in Saudi Arabia in the next few days talking again with the Saudis about the Lebanon question and ways in which some of these efforts might progress further.

MR. SHAMANSKY. Why have the Saudis reestablished relations with Libya?

MR. CONSTABLE. They did it at a time after the annexation of the Golan when there was a kind of a drawing together in the Arab world.

Now, I can only speculate on what all of their motives were. But they were undoubtedly urged to do this by other Arab nations who wanted to see a solid front develop in reaction to Israeli annexations.

I do not think the re-establishment of relations has led to very much. The Libyan Embassy has not been reopened in Saudi Arabia. Just before coming over here I saw a ticker today that Qadhafi is blaming all of the gulf leaders for supporting high production of oil and low prices, and they are causing other Arabs such as themselves great difficulties. According to the ticker

---

[4] Source: *Developments in the Middle East, March 1982: Hearings Before the Subcommittee on Europe and the Middle East of the Committee on Foreign Affairs, House of Representatives, Ninety-seventh Congress, Second Session* (Washington, 1982), pp. 21–23.

the Saudi response to this was, "Qadhafi is a nitwit."

So, it does not suggest that the relationship is going very far.

MR. SHAMANSKY. Do you see the Saudis working with other Arab States to make the Fahd plan[5] an alternative to—I do not want to say an alternative to the Camp David, but at least getting some movement?

MR. CONSTABLE. Let me make it clear, certainly we do not see it as an alternative. Since the Fez summit failure[6] the Saudis have been, I think, considerably less active on the Fahd plan. Whether they intend to pursue it further in the future I do not know. Some Arab leaders continue to talk about its importance and believe that it should be pursued. But I think it remains to be seen.

MR. SHAMANSKY. What was the motivation for proposing it in the first place because it was an aberration in their previously rather low profile.

MR. CONSTABLE. It was part of the pattern of, perhaps, greater Saudi assertiveness, greater involvement in the Lebanon crisis. Perhaps a feeling that it was time to develop a new Arab position on the issues of an Arab-Israeli settlement, that the Arab positions had been rather stagnant and unproductive.

Now, whether they saw it genuinely in terms of an alternative or a process of defining Arab positions in a more constructive way is not entirely clear to me.

MR. SHAMANSKY. What have you concluded as to Saudi Arabia's acceptance of the continued existance of Israel and an acceptance in the area as a state?

MR. CONSTABLE. Yes, we think that that was what they were saying. There had been contradictory statements off and on since that, but the latest thing that I am aware of would lead me to believe that that was their intent.

MR. SHAMANSKY. In other words, that they have accepted it. I mean, in terms of de jure, not just de facto.

MR. CONSTABLE. That they are prepared to accept it.

MR. SHAMANSKY. Yes, that should be the collective Arab position.

MR. CONSTABLE. Yes, with definition of borders still to be decided.

MR. SHAMANSKY. Yes, yes because frankly, we have heard them say with respect to one of the eight points that if the Israelis were concerned about changing the border, say, from 10 km to 20 km, they could understand that because of the narrowness of the country.

At least it is my conclusion that is a rather key element if not the basic one in the whole area. Are they doing anything to lobby their fellow Arab States?

MR. CONSTABLE. Well, they worked pretty hard on it before the Fez summit. The effort was unsuccessful. My sense is that they are still interested in this effort. There is no date for a new summit yet, but I would expect when that issue is resolved when a new summit will be held, that one will see some resumption of this activity in some form.

. . . .

Document 432

Statement by Vice President Bush, Riyadh, Saudi Arabia, June 16, 1982[7]

Death of King Khalid of Saudi Arabia

We have mourned with the people of Saudi Arabia the death of a wise King and

---

[5] On August 8, 1981, Crown Prince Fahd of Saudi Arabia proposed an eight-point plan for peace in the Middle East. For the text of the plan, see *American Foreign Policy: Current Documents, 1981*, document 312.

[6] The Arab League scheduled a summit conference in Fez, Morocco, for November 25 to 28, 1981. Only 8 out of 21 heads of state attended the conference, which adjourned on November 25 without adopting a common diplomatic strategy toward Israel.

[7] Source: Press Release, June 16, 1982, Office of the Press Secretary to the Vice President. Vice President Bush made the statement before returning to the United States after attending the funeral of King Khalid of Saudi Arabia, who died on June 13, 1982. Other members of the U.S. delegation included: Secretary of Defense Caspar W. Weinberger; Senator Charles H. Percy; Senator J. Bennett Johnston; Representative William S. Broomfield; Representative Clement J. Zablocki; General Lew Allen, Jr., Air Force Chief of Staff; Robert C. McFarlane, Deputy Assistant to the President for National Security Affairs; and Joseph Twinam, Deputy Assistant Secretary of State for Near Eastern and South Asian Affairs. For President Reagan's statement on the death of King Khalid, see *Weekly Compilation of Presidential Documents*, June 21, 1982, p. 795.

noble man. He will be greatly missed. We have been honored with the opportunity to pay our respects to His Majesty King Fahd, His Royal Highness Crown Prince Abdullah, His Highness Prince Sultan and their distinguished colleagues and counselors in this hour of grief. We have affirmed the deep friendship and esteem of the people of the United States, and indicated our government's desire to have the benefit in the days ahead of their counsel. The friendship between our two nations is old and strong. It is built on mutual respect and shared interests, a friendship we value, and one that will grow and endure in the years ahead.

In our meeting, His Majesty King Fahd impressed upon me the depth of feeling that he and the Saudi people feel about the situation in Lebanon. As a man of peace representing stability in the region, he shares with the United States the dual objectives of cease-fire and withdrawal responsive to the will of the Lebanese people. I emphasized to him the commitment of President Reagan to U.N. Resolutions 508 and 509. The reestablishment of peace in the area is a goal that we both seek and pursue.

On my return to the United States, I will convey the commitment to peace of the leaders of Saudi Arabia to President Reagan.

The President and our hosts here in Saudi Arabia share the same objectives—that the time has long passed for differences to be settled by the guns of war and that the peace process and stability in the region must be advanced by diplomatic discussions, not by continued death and destruction.

Despite the crisis which now involves us all, we have not lost hope that this area of the world can indeed be one of peace and one of prosperity for the millions of people who are suffering and those who have suffered so much.

K. Tunisia

Document 433

Remarks by President Reagan and Tunisian Prime Minister Mzali, April 29, 1982[1]

Visit of Prime Minister Mohamed Mzali

THE PRESIDENT. Prime Minister Mzali and I met at 11:30 today and we have just lunched together. And I welcome this opportunity to meet the Prime Minister. His visit to Washington has initiated a personal exchange of views that I look forward to continuing.

I was particularly gratified by his visit because I didn't have the opportunity to meet with Tunisian President Habib Bourguiba when he visited the United States privately earlier this year.[2] It's a special pleasure to meet with the leader of a country with which our relations have been and are characterized by continuing trust and friendship.

I'm proud that the United States has been able to play a role in the outstanding economic growth and development of Tunisia. And I have told the Prime Minister that he can count on us as Tunisia faces the external threats that have emerged in the past few years. He and I renewed our hope for an increased level of trade and commerce between our nations as a means of benefiting our peoples and sealing our friendship.

We exchanged views on the Middle East, and I reassured the Prime Minister of our determination to spare no exertion in seeking to bring a just and lasting peace to the Middle East.

I regret only the shortness of his visit. Mr. Prime Minister, you certainly are most welcome here in the United States.

THE PRIME MINISTER. I had the honor to be received this morning by President Rea-

---

[1] Source: *Weekly Compilation of Presidential Documents,* May 3, 1982, p. 545. The remarks were made on the South Portico of the White House at 1:17 p.m., following a meeting in the Oval Office and a luncheon in the State Dining Room of the White House. Prime Minister Mzali made an official working visit to Washington, April 26–30, 1982.

[2] President Bourguiba made a private visit to the United States, January 17–30, 1982.

gan, to whom I brought the very friendly greetings of President Bourguiba and to whom I expressed our thanks for the efforts that the United States has made to contribute to the social and economic development of Tunisia.

The contribution of the United States began right at independence and has assumed different forms and has been carried out at different levels. I'm very happy and very satisfied to note that as a contribution to the success of our Sixth Plan, Tunisia can continue to count on the assistance of the United States.

I was happy to listen to the views of President Reagan on a number of issues effecting world peace and the situation in different regions of the world, especially the Middle East—the situation on the Iraqi-Iranian border and the situation in the Mediterranean. We exchanged information. We exchanged viewpoints. It was a very interesting meeting.

In conclusion, I should like to express my full gratification at the very warm and friendly welcome which was extended to myself and to my colleagues who traveled with me. We received a very warm welcome not only from President Reagan and members of his Cabinet and the senior officials of his government but also from Members of the Senate and the House of Representatives.

I hope very much that my visit will have strengthened the traditional bonds of friendship between our two countries and that it will be further strengthened by future contacts at all levels.

Thank you very much.

Chapter 12. South Asia

A. Regional Policies and Developments

Document 434

Statements by the Deputy Assistant Secretary of State for Near Eastern and South Asian Affairs (Schneider) Before Subcommittees of the House Foreign Affairs Committee, December 9, 1982[1]

Balancing Strategic Interests and Human Rights in South Asia

Thank you, Mr. Chairman. I also wish to express my thanks for the opportunity of appearing before these subcommittees to discuss a crucially important subject. I commend the committees for setting forth the issue in this manner of balancing strategic interests and human rights. In my case, I will comment on this issue in regard to the countries of South Asia.

Our objective in South Asia is to promote human rights in conjunction with strategic interests. We also do not see these as mutually exclusive; rather, we see them as complementary parallel objectives.

Speaking in general terms, we see that the strength of the United States, the strength of U.S. security in the world, is an important requirement for creating the kind of world in which human rights can prosper. Therefore, our strategic interests are related in that way to human rights.

Similarly, we see in our experience that countries which have a developed system of political communication, representative institutions and which observe human rights, are more stable and therefore are better able to cooperate with us in pursuit of our security interests.

We see no single model for representative government or for observation of human rights which we would prescribe for our friends. But we do consider that there are certain general values, overall principles, which are generally applicable.

With regard to our strategic interests in South Asia, there too, but in very specific form, our major strategic interest is to deter Soviet expansion, to deter Soviet aggression. We have been made quite aware of the crucial nature of this objective by Soviet aggression in Afghanistan almost 3 years ago.

Closely associated with this objective is our purpose of promoting political and economic development, and through promoting this development, to promote the stability of the countries in the region. And I should explain I do not like that term "stability" very much because it suggests we want to keep things the same as they are. By stability I mean orderly change, because change, of course, is necessary. Indeed it is a requirement for the very stability of which we speak.

These efforts on our part, both to deter Soviet expansion and also to promote political and economic development are aimed at creating conditions under which human rights can be better observed. Therefore, we have complementary, reinforcing objectives.

I might very briefly mention something of our positions on countries in South Asia. India, for example, has a remarkable record of participatory democracy: Seven general elections, five peaceful changes of national government within three decades. In fact, it is the peaceful change, the peaceful transition from one government to another which is the ultimate test of representative institutions.

---

[1] Source: *Reconciling Human Rights and U.S. Security Interests in Asia: Hearings Before the Subcommittees on Asian and Pacific Affairs and on Human Rights and International Organizations of the Committee on Foreign Affairs, House of Representatives, Ninety-seventh Congress, Second Session* (Washington, 1983), pp. 440–452. Schneider testified before a joint session of the two subcommittees. Representative Sam Gejdenson, a member of the Subcommittee on Human Rights and International Organizations, presided during Schneider's presentation. Stephen J. Solarz, Chairman of the Subcommittee on Asian and Pacific Affairs, joined the discussion which followed the presentation. The exchange between Schneider and the members of the subcommittees which grew out of the presentation is *ibid.*, pp. 453–476. For an extract, see document 447.

The United States can be proud of the role which it has played over the years, not in rewarding India for achievement—I think it is demeaning to suggest that we would in some way pay off a country for forms of government it has developed itself—but the United States can be proud of the contributions it has made in India which have helped India proceed along the lines which it has determined on its own.

We have been the largest aid donor. The achievements of Indian agriculture, in particular, have been crucial for the success of Indian development. And we have played a major role in that. We have thousands of Indian students in the United States every year who have returned to India with a clear knowledge of how American democracy functions and put that knowledge into practice at home.

We have small, but what we think are terribly important military training programs in which Indian military personnel who are familiar with their version of the control of the civil over the military, learn how we do it here. We have had any number of additional contacts, business and cultural, which reinforce both democracies.

The administration has responded to Indian success in a number of ways, by recognizing the importance of India: Mrs. Gandhi's visit, the initiatives that took place then, the revitalization of our joint commission,[2] the political dialog that our Under Secretary recently took up in Delhi.[3] In a number of ways we have shown our appreciation of Indian achievement.

Let me speak also briefly of Pakistan. As we know, from the President of Pakistan, who is now a guest of the United States in this country[4]—he has left Washington only this morning—Pakistan faces a severe threat from the Soviet Union, a threat from the Soviet Union through Afghanistan. This is a real threat, and it is in the United States strategic interest that Pakistan be enabled to meet this threat with confidence. It is in our interest, first, because of events in Afghanistan and the manner in which Pakistan in various fora around the world has supported the principle of a free Afghanistan and has argued strongly for the withdrawal of Soviet troops. It is important because of the security of Pakistan itself, which is of great importance to us. It is important because of the Soviet threat which reaches beyond Pakistan to the Gulf, to the Arabian Sea, to areas of vital importance to the United States.

And it has been for this reason that the United States has agreed with Pakistan on a 6-year program of assistance,[5] subject to annual congressional appropriation, designed to assist Pakistan to meet that threat, but also to develop the Pakistani economy, because we recognize both of these are important for the stability and confidence which Pakistan must have in order to evolve some sort of representative institutions.

In regard to these human rights interests of the United States, we think it is important to examine Pakistan in terms of the difficulties it has had over the years of its independence in evolving parliamentary constitutional institutions, problems of national identity, the relationship between religion and government, social, political, economic, regional, and ethnic differences within the country. Pakistan has indeed had difficulty in evolving governmental forms, of which it has tried a number.

Our human rights policies should take into account both this history and our security interests. And it is within this context that the U.S. Government has sought to encourage representative government within Pakistan with a view that such government would help Pakistan deal with some of these pressures.

Mr. Chairman, I have tried briefly to summarize my remarks. I would be delighted to answer questions and go into any of these subjects in greater detail. Again, let me express appreciation for the opportunity to appear here.

[Mr. Schneider's prepared statement follows:][6]

Chairmen and members of the committees: I am pleased to have this opportunity

---

[2] Prime Minister Indira Gandhi visited the United States from July 28 to August 4, 1982. For documentation relating to the visit, and the consequent reestablishment of a joint Indo-U.S. commission dealing with science, economics, and culture, see Chapter 12, Part D.

[3] Under Secretary of State Lawrence S. Eagleburger visited India in November 1982 during a trip which also took him to Korea, Japan, Pakistan, and the Sudan.

[4] President Zia ul-Haq visited the United States from December 6 to December 14, 1982. He was entertained by President Reagan in Washington, December 6–9. For documentation on the Zia visit to Washington, see Chapter 12, Part E.

[5] For documentation relating to the development of this long-term program of assistance, see *American Foreign Policy: Current Documents, 1981*, Chapter 12, Part E.

[6] Bracketed note appears in the source text.

to testify on the problem we face in balancing our strategic interests and human rights concerns in the countries of South Asia: Afghanistan, Bangladesh, India, Nepal, Pakistan, and Sri Lanka.

As Mr. Shoesmith[7] has said, our objective is to promote and protect human rights—not against our strategic interests, but in conjunction with them. This administration believes that in the long run American Human Rights concerns and strategic interests point generally in the same direction. The development of stable democratic institutions, greater tolerance for free speech, popular participation in government, and respect for fundamental human rights will lead to enhanced stability and prospects for peace.

In South Asia our strategic interests focus on deterring Soviet expansionism in a region whose geographic proximity to the Persian Gulf and the sea lanes leading to it have highlighted its importance to us. To this end we cooperate in various ways—whether through diplomatic dialogue or security assistance—to promote the security of the region. Concurrently, we support economic growth and political stability aimed at fostering strong and independent South Asian nations which can accord basic human rights to their citizens. South Asian countries are among the very poorest in the world, making all the more critical the interrelationship of our security, developmental, and human rights goals.

President Reagan has committed the United States to make a greater effort internationally to assist the development of democracy. The President believes that support for the growth of democracy should be an important dimension of the foreign relations of the United States and other democratic nations. There is no single model that is applicable to all countries. However, democracies no matter what shape are built upon a set of basic principles which we believe are valid in most societies—and, where followed, have resulted in nations with relatively stable political and economic systems flexible enough to meet a complex, changing international environment, and respect for human rights.

While each country must find its own way toward representative institutions, we have fostered an understanding of democratic values and processes in South Asia in a variety of ways, including our development programs and information and visitor exchange. We have quietly used our diplomacy to encourage broader participation in government. We are now exploring the possibilities for specific activities to help enhance representative systems in India, Sri Lanka, and Nepal and to promote such systems in the other nations of South Asia.

A discussion of specific countries in South Asia will serve to highlight our approach to promoting both U.S. strategic interests and human rights.

India is a key nation in a region of the world important to U.S. strategic interests. It is the largest nation in South Asia in terms of its population, economy, and military strength. India has a remarkable record of over three decades of democratic rule—seven general elections; five peaceful changes of national government. Indian democracy has endured almost to the point at which the world takes it for granted. In fact, the administration attaches great importance to maintaining constructive relations with India and has sought ways to expand its dialogue with India and to work together more closely. The visit of Prime Minister Gandhi here this summer and the solid progress made on the initiatives announced at that time demonstrate the interest on both sides in seeking a better understanding and finding ways to strengthen the already extensive ongoing ties. As a part of this process the Indo-U.S. Joint Commission, with its subcommissions on science and technology, economics and commerce, agriculture, and education and culture have been revitalized. As a result of a decision at the time of Mrs. Gandhi's visit, our political dialogue has been intensified by the recent visit to India for bilateral talks of Under Secretary Eagleburger. The Government of India has issued a special invitation to Secretary Shultz to visit New Delhi.

In particular, we see good scope for enhanced cooperation in the economic, commercial, and scientific areas. We are encouraging U.S. firms to take advantage of new opportunities in India which are the result of the improved business climate there. American companies can thereby contribute their unique talents and technology to assisting India's development efforts through private sector to private sector collaboration. The President's Science Advisor led a senior group to India last month to lay the groundwork for enhanced joint cooperation in certain specialized fields of science. We recently invited a group of Indian Parliamentarians, including the Speaker, to observe the congressional elections.

---

[7] Thomas P. Shoesmith, Deputy Assistant Secretary of State for East Asian and Pacific Affairs. For the text of the statement made by Shoesmith earlier in the hearing, see document 463.

Since India won independence in 1947, the United States has admired its vigorous democratic process and has been the major foreign contributor to Indian economic development. Our two countries have worked closely in bringing about remarkable success in Indian agriculture. Over the years there has been extensive interaction between our nations including the education of tens of thousands of Indians in American universities. We also have a modest military cooperation program with India (some cash sales of equipment and training of a few military officers), which supports our security and democracy objectives. The issue of civilian supremacy over the military does not arise in India, which stands as a model throughout the world for its scrupulous adherence to the principle of civilian control.

Sri Lanka is strategically located astride the major ocean trade routes of the Indian Ocean and offers access for U.S. Navy vessels. Our substantial economic development program, training for military students, and active political dialogue serve to demonstrate strong U.S. support for this strategic and democratic country. Since independence Sri Lanka has a history of free elections and active popular participation. Sri Lanka's current government also favors a market-oriented, free enterprise economic approach. In addition to helping fund two of the three lead projects in Sri Lanka's development strategy, we are encouraging U.S. firms to consider investing in the country's free trade zone.

Nepal forms an important buffer between India and China. U.S. interests center on its strategic location and on our consequent interest in orderly economic development and the evolution of stable political institutions which provide for public participation in government. While Nepal's constitution specifies that the king is the sole source of authority for all government institutions, the country has recently made dramatic progress toward its own sort of representative institutions. By referendum Nepal chose the partyless panchayat form of representation and the country has now launched its own experiment in participatory government. Accompanying this has been a trend toward broader enjoyment of a wide range of human rights.

Our commitment to assist Nepal's economic development goes back to 1951 when the country ended its self-imposed isolation. We also provide training in the United States for two Nepali military officers, exposing them to American attitudes toward the role of the military in society.

Bangladesh was born in conflict in 1971, a time when political turmoil threatened the security and stability of the entire subcontinent. In the decade since independence, the country has suffered from severe political and economic difficulties. Events during the past year have returned this struggling country to military rule. We have welcomed and encouraged the stated intention of the present government to return the country to civilian rule. Economic development and political stability are inextricably linked in Bangladesh, and we view a return to representative government as a key element of political stability. Our assistance program has evolved from emergency relief to long-term development, which we hope can foster stability and encourage civilian representative rule. Our military training program (IMET—$225,000) exposes Bangladeshi officers to American democratic values and is important to our policies in that country because of the influential role the military plays in government.

I would now like to turn to Pakistan, the country most directly threatened by recent aggressive Soviet moves in the region and of critical importance in regard to U.S. strategic interests in the Persian Gulf–Indian Ocean area and to our goal of stability in South and Southwest Asia. In 1981, the United States reached agreement with Pakistan, subject to annual appropriation by the Congress, to provide $3.2 billion in foreign military sales credits and economic assistance over a period of 6 years. We take this action in support of Pakistan's strong, principled stand against the Soviet invasion of Afghanistan and its leading role in international efforts to induce withdrawal of Soviet forces from Afghanistan. Our assistance programs are intended both to help Pakistan modernize its military forces and to promote internal stability through economic development. Our security commitment is a major element in assuring that Pakistan will be able to sustain its stand against Soviet aggression and thereby protect vital U.S. strategic interests in this crucial region.

During its 35 years of independence, Pakistan has sought effecitve government through a variety of regimes. This history has been influenced by a number of factors. Throughout its history, Pakistan has been preoccupied with a search for its national identity and, in particular, a definition of the position of Islam in its national character. In addition, the social, political, economic, regional, and ethnic differences which characterize Pakistan's diverse society have frequently led to political turmoil. Pakistan's human rights problem derives from this difficult experience.

We believe it important that our policies toward Pakistan take into account these causes of instability as well as our national security interests in the area. Within this context we have sought to encourage the evolution of representative government in accordance with the view that such institutions would help Pakistan to deal with the conflicting pressures it faces. Nevertheless, we recognize Pakistan's right to try to evolve its own forms which take into account its traditions and problems. We also recognize that, while there are undeniably human rights problems, in many ways this regime is moderate in comparison to some of the previous ones.

We have, of course, discussed these human rights issues with the Pakistani leadership and will continue to do so. While our dialogue on human rights has for the most part been a private one, our Ambassador in Pakistan has also sought to gain public understanding of our support for more representative forms of government.

Another factor which we believe our policies must take into consideration is our interest in the human rights situation in the region as a whole. Here, of course, I refer to Afghanistan. It has been with great economic and political sacrifice and no little strain that Pakistan has welcomed into its territory almost 3 million Afghan refugees who have been forced to seek temporary asylum from the Soviet assault on their freedom and independence. The phenomenon of masses of refugees fleeing from political oppression is a common one in the contemporary world. No nation, however, has shown greater hospitality and tolerance to such a flow than Pakistan. Further, despite the threat to Pakistan itself, the Pakistanis have bravely offered their support in international fora around the world to the Afghan freedom fighters and the concept of a free and independent Afghanistan. Pakistani support is important to the reestablishment of human rights in Afghanistan, a major U.S. cause.

Our security assistance to Pakistan is not extended in support of any particular government in power. It is aid to Pakistan as a nation. We believe the Pakistani people understand it in this light and support our policies.

Mr. Chairman, I have sought to review briefly how we seek to take into account both our strategic interests and our human rights concerns in the South Asian region. I believe we can take pride in the achievements of the countries located there. Their record, whether in the development of democratic government or in the support to an oppressed neighboring people is deserving of our support—and it has our support.

B. Afghanistan

Document 435

Statement by the Deputy Secretary of State (Stoessel) Before the Senate Foreign Relations Committee, March 8, 1982[1]

March 21: Afghanistan Day

Thank you very much, Mr. Chairman.

It is a great pleasure for me to appear before your committee today on the joint congressional resolution adopted unanimously by the Senate and by the House of Representatives designating March 21 as Afghanistan Day.[2] I wish to congratulate you for the action you have taken to pay tribute to a valiant people struggling for their freedom against foreign aggressors. Our European allies who conceived of this initiative and other countries around the world will also be observing Afghanistan Day.

The President will sign the proclamation of Afghanistan Day this Wednesday at a White House ceremony.[3] The same day the State Department will brief and host a reception for representatives of ethnic groups in the United States from Eastern Europe, South and Southeast Asia, and the Caribbean on the commemoration. The President fully supports and endorses the purpose of Afghanistan Day, as do former

---

[1] Source: *Situation in Afghanistan, Hearing Before the U.S. Senate Committee on Foreign Relations, Ninety-seventh Congress, Second Session* (Washington, 1982), pp. 2–6. Charles H. Percy was the chairman of the committee.

[2] Senate Joint Resolution 142, enacted on March 4, 1982. For text, see *Congressional Record,* 97th Congress, Second Session (March 4, 1982), pp. H688–H689.

[3] See document 437.

Presidents Carter, Ford, and Nixon and former Secretaries of State Muskie, Vance, Kissinger, and Rusk.

The President has requested former Secretary of State William Rogers to coordinate private American observance of this date. Over the next several days Secretary Rogers will be outlining various nongovernmental activities which will be undertaken in our observances here. We hope that these activities by concerned private groups will help focus American public attention on what is happening in Afghanistan today.

The vernal equinox, March 21, has traditionally been celebrated as the beginning of the Afghan New Year. The worldwide observance of Afghanistan Day will signal to the Afghan people that they enjoy the solidarity of the free world. We believe that it is of the utmost importance that the international community also signal to the Soviet Union that the passage of time has not dimmed the concern of free men everywhere over Soviet aggression, nor diminished demands that the Soviet Union withdraw its troops from that country. We must not forget the Afghan people's struggle. We must not allow the Soviets to believe that their aggression is accepted as a fait accompli.

December 27, 1979, was a watershed in post-World War II history. On that date, for the first time Soviet forces invaded an independent country which was not a member of the Warsaw Pact. This act was one of outright aggression, even more pronounced than recent Soviet actions in Poland. Today we estimate that as a result of Moscow's augmentation of its forces in Afghanistan since November, the Soviets may have as many as 100,000 troops in Afghanistan.

The saga of Afghan resistance to Soviet occupation is one of personal courage and heroism against great odds. The hardships and losses which the Afghan people have suffered in this unequal battle have been high. Thousands of innocent civilians have been killed or maimed as the Soviets and the puppet Afghan army have destroyed villages and crops, strewn antipersonnel mines over trails and inhabited areas, employed lethal chemical weapons and forcibly impressed young Afghans in the armed forces.

Just recently Soviet troops surrounded Afghanistan's second largest city, Kandahar, and subjected it to a savage artillery and air bombardment in which hundreds of innocent civilians lost their lives. After the bombardment, Soviet forces entered the city and engaged in wanton looting and killing among the civilian population.

Many of the city's buildings were seriously damaged. Two-thirds of its population fled. Soviet forces also moved against Afghanistan's fourth largest city, Herat, with similar ruthlessness, causing great suffering among its population.

I would like to refer to a particularly heinous aspect of Soviet military actions in Afghanistan. The use of chemical weapons in war is a violation of the 1925 Geneva Protocol[4] to which the U.S.S.R. is a party and the rules of customary law which apply to all nations. Analysis of all the information available leads us to conclude that attacks have been conducted with irritants, incapacitants, nerve agents, phosgene oxime, and perhaps micotoxins, mustard, lewisite, and toxic smoke.

Afghan military defectors have provided information on chemical weapons containing lethal nerve agents, where they were stockpiled, and where and when they have been used. This information generally corresponds with refugee reports and recorded military operations. As a result of chemical attacks, over 3,000 deaths attributed to 47 separate incidents between the summer of 1979 and the summer of 1981 have been reported.

Today, the Soviet Union maintains the fiction that the regime of Babrak Karmal is a legitimate government. However, it is the Soviets who not only make policy in Kabul, but who also make the day-to-day political, administrative, and military decisions of government. Moreover, it is commonly accepted that the Karmal regime would not last until nightfall without the presence of Soviet troops.

The Soviet suppression of Afghan political freedom is paralleled in all other aspects of life. For example, the Soviets are currently imposing their brand of judicial system and the Soviet model of education in Afghanistan. At Kabul University, medical school degrees are no longer granted and medical students are required to obtain their degrees in the Soviet Union.

Despite regime efforts to cloak itself in religious piety, concern for the preservation

[4] For the text of the 1925 Protocol for the Prohibition of the Use in War of Asphyxiating, Poisonous or Other Gases, and of Bacteriological Methods of Warfare, ratified by the United States in 1975, see 26 UST 571.

of Islamic values remains at the heart of the anti-Communist resistance.

The most basic human right, to life itself, is being violated daily by the Soviets and their puppets in Afghanistan. There are thousands of political prisoners. We have frequent reports of torture, of summary executions, and a long list of other violations which testify to the brutality of the Afghan regime and its Soviet masters.

About 3 million Afghan refugees have fled their homeland seeking freedom, principally in neighboring Pakistan. Almost one-fifth of the preinvasion population of Afghanistan, the largest group of refugees in the world, has so voted with its feet.

Although conditions in refugee camps are hard, the United Nations High Commissioner for Refugees, aided by resources from many countries, including our own, has done a commendable job of assisting these innocent victims of Soviet aggression. The Government and people of Pakistan have also displayed a generosity and hospitality of the highest order in welcoming these refugees to their country.

The plight of the Afghan refugees is one which deserves our help. We will continue to support the U.N. High Commissioner for Refugees with funds and with food assistance.

Mr. Chairman, it is the very concept of freedom which is on the line today in Afghanistan—the freedom of a people to determine its own destiny, to form a government of its own choosing, to practice freely its religion and to enjoy full sovereignty and independence. Historically, Afghanistan existed, sometimes uneasily, between the expanding Czarist Empire and British India. On three occasions when external powers sought to expand their influence in Kabul through military action, they were rebuffed as Afghans united to repel the foreign invader.

I recall this history to highlight a major characteristic of the Afghan people—their fierce determination to retain their freedom despite the misfortune of a geography which places them on the border of a powerful, expansive neighbor. To achieve this, various Afghan Governments adopted a policy of nonalignment. We accepted this policy, which also seemed to serve the interests of the Soviet Union, until it was destroyed overnight by a decision made in Moscow.

Soviet aggression in Afghanistan has been viewed with particular concern by other nonaligned nations, who rightly see it as an example of superpower imperialism. This has been reflected in overwhelming votes in the U.N. General Assembly and other U.N. bodies and a wide variety of international organizations.

The Islamic countries have felt a special empathy for the fate of their Muslim brothers. On four separate occasions, the 43-member Islamic Conference has passed resolutions calling on the Soviets to withdraw their forces, for restoration of Afghanistan's neutrality and nonalignment, for the right of the Afghan people to form a government of their own choosing, and for conditions which will permit the Afghan refugees to return to their homes.

In South Asia, the Government of India and other regional states have called on Moscow to withdraw its forces, whose presence in Afghanistan has changed the regional strategic equation.

The 99 members of the nonaligned movement, meeting in plenary session in New Delhi 1 year ago, made a similar plea. Last fall, 116 countries, 54 more than the previous year, endorsed a U.N. General Assembly resolution along similar lines.[5] This was the third such resolution overwhelmingly adopted by the U.N. General Assembly since the invasion.

Mr. Chairman, our Government earnestly wants to see a political solution to the Afghanistan conflict which brings the violations of human rights and the sufferings of the Afghan people to an end. We have consistently made it clear to the Soviets that we are ready for serious discussion on Afghanistan which might promote a Soviet withdrawal and a political settlement on terms acceptable to the Afghan people.

Let me outline some of the actions which we and others have taken in a search for a political solution. Secretary Haig made clear to Soviet Foreign Minister Gromyko during their recent meeting in Geneva[6] that the Soviet occupation remains a major impediment to prospects for improvement of United States-Soviet relations. Unfortunately, the Soviet side has not demonstrated a willingness to seriously discuss a peaceful settlement of the Afghan conflict.

We will continue to raise this matter in our high-level contacts and in our normal

---

[5] Resolution 36/34, adopted by the U.N. General Assembly, November 18, 1981; for text, see *American Foreign Policy: Current Documents, 1981*, document 431.

[6] Held on January 26.

diplomatic dialog with Moscow. Our hope is that eventually the Soviet Union will remove its forces from Afghanistan, thereby reducing a major barrier to better East–West relations.

International efforts to achieve a Soviet withdrawal are also in progress. The U.N. Secretary-General Perez de Cuellar has appointed a personal representative to continue discussions with the concerned regional nations about a political solution. We support this effort by the Secretary-General, though we must point out that the source of the problem is not in Islamabad, Tehran, or Kabul, but in Moscow. It is there that a solution ultimately must be sought.

The European community last June proposed a two-stage international conference on the Afghan conflict.[7] Regrettably, the Soviet Union has chosen to reject this important initiative. We note that it remains on the table, a serious proposal which we will continue to urge the Soviets to pick up.

Mr. Chairman, in closing let me praise the courage and heroism of those Afghan freedom fighters who refuse to accept foreign domination of their homeland. Their courage, steadfastness of purpose and determination have earned the admiration of all who cherish freedom. Let us also remember the Afghan refugees in Pakistan who have been forced to flee Soviet oppression.

The joint resolution is a fitting tribute to these Afghan patriots from a people who also guard their freedom zealously. It forcefully reminds the Soviet Union that the Afghan conflict is at the very heart of the increase of international tension and that a negotiated settlement will serve the genuine security interests of all parties, including the Soviet Union.

Thank you, Mr. Chairman. This concludes my remarks. I will be very pleased to answer any questions that you may have.

---

[7] Statement issued by the Council of the European Economic Community, June 30, 1981; for text, see *American Foreign Policy: Current Documents, 1981*, document 427.

Document 436

Remarks by President Reagan on Signing Proclamation No. 4908, March 10, 1982[8]

"Nowhere Are Basic Human Rights More Brutally Violated Than in Afghanistan Today"

I can't help but—say thank you all very much—but I can't help but recall that I was in Iran on the day that the first coup took place by the Soviet Union and their overthrow there of the government.

I take particular satisfaction in signing today, a Proclamation[9] authorized by Joint Resolution No. 142, which calls for the commemoration of March 21st as Afghanistan Day throughout the United States.

This resolution testifies to America's deep and continuing admiration for the Afghan people in the face of brutal and unprovoked aggression by the Soviet Union.

A distinguished former Secretary of State, William P. Rogers, is coordinating the observance of Afghan Day in the United States. He not only has my strong support but that of former Presidents Carter, Ford, and Nixon and former Secretaries of State Muskie, Vance, Kissinger, and Rusk.

The Afghans, like the Poles, wish nothing more, as you've just been so eloquently told, than to live their lives in peace, to practice their religion in freedom and to exercise their right to self-determination.

As a consequence, they now find themselves struggling for their very survival as a nation. Nowhere are basic human rights more brutally violated than in Afghanistan today.

I have spoken on occasion of the presence of unsung heroes in American life. Today, we recognize a nation of unsung heroes whose courageous struggle is one of the epics of our time. The Afghan people

[8] Source: White House Press Release, March 10, 1982, Office of the Press Secretary to the President; also printed in *Weekly Compilation of Presidential Documents*, March 15, 1982, pp. 280–282. The President began speaking at 12:01 p.m. in the East Room of the White House.

[9] *Infra.*

have matched their heroism against the most terrifying weapons of modern warfare in the Soviet arsenal.

Despite blanket bombing and chemical and biological weapons, the brave Afghan freedom fighters have prevented the nearly 100,000-strong Soviet occupation force from extending its control over a large portion of the countryside.

Their heroic struggle has carried a terrible cost. Many thousands of Afghans, often innocent civilians, women and children, have been killed and maimed. Entire villages and regions have been destroyed and depopulated. Some 3 million people have been driven into exile. That's one out of every five Afghans. The same proportion of Americans would produce a staggering 50 million refugees.

We cannot and will not turn our backs on this struggle. Few acts of international aggression have been so universally condemned. The United Nations has repeatedly called for the withdrawal of Soviet forces. The Islamic Conference, deeply troubled over this assault in Moslem religion, has four times condemned the Soviet occupation. The nonaligned movement has added its voice to the demands for withdrawal of foreign troops. Most recently, as you've been told, the European Parliament took the leadership in advancing the idea of a worldwide commemoration of Afghanistan Day.

On behalf of all Americans, I want to thank the members of the European Parliament for this action and welcome today the participation of Egon Klepsch, Vice President of the European Parliament and his distinguished colleagues.

I also want to express the hope that people the world over will respond with eagerness and determination. And in that connection, I want to express my particular appreciation that we're joined here today by members of the Parliaments of Japan, Kenya, Panama, Thailand, and Austria.

We must go beyond public condemnation of the Soviet puppet regime in Kabul to bring relief and an early end to the Afghan tragedy.

We have a human responsibility to the Afghan refugees. The United States has given generous support to the U.N.'s refugee effort. And I'm pleased to announce today an additional commitment of $21.3 million-worth of food. This contribution will bring the total U.S. support for the refugees to over $200 million in the past 2 years. But I ask that all Americans supplement these funds with personal donations to organizations which work with Afghan refugees and the cause of a free Afghanistan. (Applause)

Beyond this, the United States is determined to do everything politically possible to bring the Soviet Union to the negotiating table. We and our allies have made clear that Afghanistan will remain a central issue in U.S.[-Soviet][10] Government and East–West relations as long as Soviet forces continue to occupy that nation.

We have used, and will continue to use, every available opportunity, including the last meeting between Secretary Haig and Soviet Foreign Minister Gromyko, to urge the Soviets to enter into genuine negotiations for a peaceful settlement of the Afghan crisis.

In that spirit I want to address the claim made by the Soviet Union—that its troops entered Afghanistan and must remain there as a result of foreign intervention against the Kabul government. The world is well aware that this is nothing more than propaganda designed to divert international attention from the sordid reality. The foreign interference in Afghanistan comes from the nearly 100,000 Soviet armed invaders. (Applause)

The United States has consistently followed a policy of noninterference in Afghanistan's internal affairs. We similarly supported the nonalliance character of the previous Afghanistan Government.

The fire of resistance in Afghanistan is being kindled and sustained not by outside forces but by the determination of the Afghan people to defend their national independence.

We and most other members of the international community have repeatedly stressed to the Soviets both publicly and privately that we have no objectives in Afghanistan beyond those set forth in the U.N. General Assembly resolutions. These are the withdrawal of the Soviet forces, the free exercise of self-determination for the Afghan people, the restoration of Afghanistan's nonalliance status, and the safe and honorable return of Afghan refugees to their homes.

Unfortunately, the Soviet Union has to date rejected all attempts to move toward

---

10 White House correction. [Footnote in the text of *Weekly Compilation of Presidental Documents.*]

an internationally acceptable solution. In 1980 it refused to receive emissaries of the Islamic Conference, who were to travel to Moscow to discuss a political solution. In 1981 it was the British Foreign Minister who was rudely rebuffed when he presented a very sensible proposal of the European Community for a two-tiered international conference which is still on the table.

Finally, the Soviets have evaded the issue, insisting that the U.N. Secretary General seek a solution in Kabul, Islamabad, and Tehran rather than at the source of the aggression in Moscow.

The Soviet Union bears a grave responsibility for the continuing suffering of the Afghan people, the massive violations of human rights and the international tension which have resulted from its unprovoked attack. The Soviet Union must understand that the world will not forget—as it has not forgotten the peoples of the other captive nations from Eastern Europe to southwest Asia—(applause)—who have suffered from Soviet aggression. (Applause)

This is the meaning of Afghanistan Day, that the Afghan people will ultimately prevail.

Coincidentally, the day after Afghanistan Day, this country plans to launch the third Columbia space shuttle. Just as the Columbia, we think, represents man's finest aspirations in the field of science and technology, so too does the struggle of the Afghan people represent man's highest aspirations for freedom. The fact that freedom is the strongest force in the world is daily demonstrated by the people of Afghanistan.

Accordingly, I am dedicating on behalf of the American people the March 22 launch of the Columbia to the people of Afghanistan. (Applause)

And in that same spirit I call on all Americans to observe Afghanistan Day in their thoughts, their prayers, their activities, and in their own renewed dedication to freedom. With the help of those assembled here today, the unanimous backing of the Congress and the support of the American people, I'm confident that this day will mark a true celebration and not just for freedom in Afghanistan but for freedom wherever it is threatened or suppressed the world over. (Applause) Now, I shall sign the proclamation. (Applause)

Document 437

Proclamation by President Reagan, March 10, 1982[11]

Designation of March 21, 1982 as Afghanistan Day

In December 1979, the Soviet Union invaded Afghanistan without provocation and with overwhelming force. Since that time, the Soviet Union has sought through every available means, to assert its control over Afghanistan.

The Afghan people have defied the Soviet Union and have resisted with a vigor that has few parallels in modern history. The Afghan people have paid a terrible price in their fight for freedom. Their villages and homes have been destroyed; they have been murdered by bullets, bombs and chemical weapons. One-fifth of the Afghan people have been driven into exile. Yet their fight goes on. The international community, with the United States joining governments around the world, has condemned the invasion of Afghanistan as a violation of every standard of decency and international law and has called for a withdrawal of the Soviet troops from Afghanistan. Every country and every people has a stake in the Afghan resistance, for the freedom fighters of Afghanistan are defending principles of independence and freedom that form the basis of global security and stability.

It is therefore altogether fitting that the European Parliament, the Congress of the United States and parliaments elsewhere in the world have designated March 21, 1982, as Afghanistan Day, to commemorate the valor of the Afghan people and to condemn the continuing Soviet invasion of their country. Afghanistan Day will serve to recall not only these events, but also the principles involved when a people struggles for the freedom to determine its own future, the right to be free of foreign interference and the right to practice religion according to the dictates of conscience.

NOW, THEREFORE, I, RONALD REAGAN, President of the United States of America, do hereby designate March 21, 1982, as Afghanistan Day.

---

[11] Source: White House Press Release, Office of the Press Secretary to the President; also printed in *Weekly Compilation of Presidential Documents*, March 15, 1982, pp. 282–283. This proclamation, No. 4908, was filed with the Office of the Federal Register at 3:54 p.m., March 10, 1982.

IN WITNESS WHEREOF, I have hereunto set my hand this tenth day of March, in the year of our Lord nineteen hundred and eighty-two, and of the Independence of the United States of American the two hundred and sixth.

RONALD REAGAN

Document 438

Statement by President Reagan, March 20, 1982[12]

Appeal to Soviet President Brezhnev for Peace in Afghanistan

The Afghan New Year which begins today dawns on a nation in turmoil. The traditional celebration on March 21, 1982 will be stifled by the stark reality of the suffering of a people under occupation or in exile from the intolerable conditions in their homeland. The year ahead appears to offer the prospect of a continuing bitter struggle and even wider devastation, rather than the blessings of peace and prosperity which are the natural right of the Afghan people. Our heart goes out to the Afghan people in these terrible times.

We cannot accept the transparent Soviet rationale for their invasion of Afghanistan, namely, that they were invited in by the Afghan Government. How can the Soviets explain the mysterious death of the President who supposedly invited them in and his replacement by a Soviet nominee who had conveniently been living in Eastern Europe? Nor can we accept the Soviet claim that the cause of the conflict in Afghanistan is external interference on the part of powers other than the Soviet Union itself. There has, indeed, been external interference in Afghanistan. But that interference has been committed by the Soviet Union itself, which, utterly without provocation, invaded that free and nonaligned nation and imposed its will on an independent people.

Nevertheless, let me make clear that, to the extent that legitimate Soviet security interests may be engaged along the Soviet border with Afghanistan, we are confident that these interests can be adequately protected through negotiated understandings. Virtually the entire community of nations is already on record as supporting the concept of a return to the previous status quo in which Afghanistan was a nonaligned nation threatening no one.

The war against Soviet aggression is a hard and lonely struggle. It is waged in remote mountain valleys far from the reach of international media. We want to penetrate that wall of silence with the powerful Voice of America. Therefore I have decided the Voice will begin broadcasting as soon as possible in Pushtu, complementing the broadcasting we are already doing in Dari. The brave men and women most directly involved in the fighting need to know we are with them. We will now be communicating with them in the two major languages of Afghanistan.

On this solemn occasion I would like to appeal directly to President Brezhnev to join with us and other like-minded nations in a genuine and intensive search for a peaceful resolution of the tragic conflict in Afghanistan. A sensible and creative proposal was put forward last year by the European Community for a two-stage international conference on Afghanistan. Obviously the principal purpose of such a conference—or of any realistic negotiations—would be to engage the Soviet Union in a serious discussion of a settlement involving the prompt withdrawal of their occupation force from Afghanistan. For this reason, we and others were particularly disappointed that the Soviet Union rejected this proposal. Today I call on Mr. Brezhnev to reconsider that rejection.

The tragedy of Afghanistan must not be allowed to drag on endlessly. This conflict imperils the stability of the region. It has seriously poisoned the international environment. Afghanistan itself is being brutalized. The suffering of the Afghan people is immense. I earnestly hope that the Soviet Union will join with us in an urgent effort to bring a swift withdrawal of its forces to end this needless conflict.

---

[12] Source: White House Press Release, March 20, 1982, Office of the Press Secretary to the President; printed also in *Weekly Compilation of Presidential Documents*, March 29, 1982, pp. 351–352.

Document 439

Statement by Vice President Bush at Afghanistan Day Commemoration, March 21, 1982[13]

"The Soviet Union Has Shown Only Contempt for the Universal Condemnation of its Invasion of Afghanistan"

What I have in my hand is a Soviet mine. It's called a "butterfly" mine, because when it's dropped from Soviet helicopters, it flutters softly to the ground. At that point any resemblance to one of nature's most gentle creatures ends. This device isn't meant to kill—at least immediately. It's meant to maim—to blow off feet, a hand, the flesh from someone's face, the eyes. To someone injured by one of these, death from infection can be a slow agony, far from medical care.

The Soviets dropped thousands of these devices on Afghanistan. The freedom fighters and most of the adult population know what they are, and avoid them. But children, not knowing better, do not, and so most of the victims of the butterfly mines are children—children who, if they survive, will live their entire lives blind, disfigured, or lame.

Tens of thousands of people have died since the Soviets invaded Afghanistan 2 days after Christmas, 1979. Butterfly mines are by no means the cruelest way they have devised of killing. All evidence indicates that the Soviets have opened Pandora's box of modern warfare. They've used chemicals—nerve agents, phosgene oxime, perhaps mycotoxins, and others. Over 3,000 deaths alone have been attributed to these.

The United Nations General Assembly has twice called for the withdrawal of Soviet troops,[14] the first time by a vote of 104 to 18, the second by a vote of 111 to 22. Similar resolutions have been passed by the U.N. Human Rights Commission, the Foreign Ministers of the Association of Southeast Asian Nations, the European Economic Community, and the Islamic Conference.

All of this has had no effect on the Soviet Union, which has twice vetoed resolutions in the U.N. Security Council deploring its armed intervention.

The Soviet Union has shown only contempt for the universal condemnation of its invasion of Afghanistan. In the face of this, how can the world be asked to take seriously their talk of peace?

The occasion we're observing here today was conceived of by our European allies as a way of demonstrating our continued support for the Afghan people.

Not much news has been coming out of Afghanistan, for the simple reason that Western journalists are finding it virtually impossible to get permission to enter the country, thereby making it impossible to cover the atrocities. Tyranny fears a free press, because tyranny fears the truth.

Instead, news of the continuing struggle trickles out. Freedom House, the New York organization that has brought many of the developments there to light, published in 1980 in a letter from Afghanistan. I want to read you a few lines from it:

> "Since about a week ago, all the streets and corners of Kabul have been swarming with young men armed with Russian rifles . . . [15] they seize boys and young men between the ages of 15 and 26, and assemble them at various Army posts. From these posts, the young men are sent in trucks to the airport, from where they are dispatched to places nobody knows.
>
> "During these dreadful nights and days of cold winter, many parents are living in a state of agony and mourning. They can do nothing but pray to God."

The Soviets can really no more allow a free press in Afghanistan than they can in their own country. If they did, the horrors of the war would play across our newspapers and television screens every day and every night.

Almost more distressing is the refusal to allow representatives of the International Red Cross into Afghanistan. Adolf Hitler

---

[13] Source: Press Release, Office of the Press Secretary to the Vice President, March 21, 1982. The Vice President made these remarks at 4:30 p.m. at the Kennedy Center.

[14] As of the Vice President's statement, the U.N. General Assembly had passed three resolutions calling for the withdrawal of foreign or Soviet troops from Afghanistan. See the texts of U.N. General Assembly Resolutions ES-6/2, January 14, 1980, and 35/37, November 20, 1980, in *American Foreign Policy: Basic Documents, 1977–1980,* pp. 831–832, 884–885, and U.N. General Assembly Resolution 36/34, November 18, 1981, in *American Foreign Policy: Current Documents, 1981,* document 431.

[15] Ellipsis appears in the source text.

allowed the Red Cross—albeit selectively—into Germany during the Second World War.

The Soviets justified their invasion from the beginning with a farcical explanation, saying they were invited. This is nonsense, and everyone knows it. They told their own troops that they would be fighting against Chinese and American troops, but in fact they are fighting only one enemy: the natives of the country they invaded. The Kremlin has not even been telling the whole truth to Soviet mothers, whose sons have been dying by the thousands in a war they can never hope to win.

The charades persist. Babrak Karmal, whose regime would not last until nightfall without Soviet troops, recently awarded President Brezhnev Afghanistan's highest order—The Sun of Freedom. This is a remarkable honor indeed to bestow on one whose troops have forced 3 million Afghan refugees to flee their country. That medal now hangs from President Brezhnev's chest, even as he makes speeches about his country's desire for a lessening of world tension, for arms limitation, for peace among men.

It was a Frenchman, the Marquis De Custine, a counterpart to De Tocqueville, who observed that we must not blame the Russians for being what they are, only for pretending to be what we are.

The Afghans are a brave people, and a determined people. The Soviets are not losing their war, in the sense that they are killing a great number of Afghans. But neither are they winning their war. The freedom fighters, 2¼ years later, still control most of the country. Considering the almost overwhelming technological odds against them, their bravery and endurance are extraordinary.

What can we do? What is said here today matters little. But the very worst that could happen would be that we forget the Afghan freedom fighters. Their struggle is not on the front pages every day. In the midst of our own liberty, we should not forget their lack of it. The Soviet Union should be made to answer for their crimes every day before the Councils of the world. Every day, someone, somewhere, should ask, when are you getting out of Afghanistan? In that spirit, let me say to the Soviet leaders: end the suffering. Take your troops out of Afghanistan.

The Vernal Equinox traditionally marks the start of the new year in Afghanistan. This year will bring more killings, more brutality, more butterflies—more suffering children.

It's my hope, and the hope of all of us here, the hope of all those across this country and across the world who today are demonstrating their solidarity with the Afghan people, that this year will bring something else.

Today, President Reagan made a direct appeal to President Brezhnev.[16] He said that this conflict has "seriously poisoned the international environment." He noted that the European Community put forward last year a sensible and creative proposal for an internaional conference on Afghanistan; and he said that we and others were particularly disappointed that the Soviet Union rejected the European proposal.

Finally, he asked President Brezhnev to join with the United States and many other nations in a "genuine and intensive search for a peaceful resolution" of the tragedy that has come to Afghanistan.

There is a saying: Afghanistan Ahzod. It means, "Free Afghanistan."

Perhaps on this day, a year from now, we will be celebrating a free Afghanistan, instead of commemorating the struggle of a people to survive.

Thank you.

Document 440

Report by the Department of State Submitted to the Congress, March 22, 1982 (Extracts)[17]

Chemical Warfare in Afghanistan

. . . .

Afghanistan. Soviet forces in Afghanistan have used a variety of lethal and nonlethal

---

16 See *supra.*

17 Source: *Chemical Warfare in Southeast Asia and Afghanistan,* Department of State Special Report No. 98, March 22, 1982, pp. 6, 15–17. The report was transmitted to the Congress by an undated letter from Secretary Haig, which is printed *ibid.*, p. 2. For extracts from the report on Southeast Asia as well as details on the methodology of the study, discussion of the findings, and analysis of the motivations for the use of chemical weapons in these areas, see document 477.

chemical agents on *mujahidin* resistance forces and Afghan villages since the Soviet invasion in December 1979. In addition, there is some evidence that Afghan Government forces may have used Soviet-supplied chemical weapons against the *mujahidin* even before the Soviet invasion. Although it has not been possible to verify through sample analysis the specific agents used by the Soviets, a number of Afghan military defectors have named the agents brought into the country by the Soviets and have described where and when they were employed. This information has been correlated with other evidence, including the reported symptoms, leading to the conclusion that nerve agents, phosgene oxime, and various incapacitants and irritants have been used. Other agents and toxic smokes also are in the country. Some reported symptoms are consistent with those produced by lethal or sublethal doses of trichothecene toxins, but this evidence is not conclusive.

. . . .

Afghanistan

Attacks with chemical weapons against the *mujahidin* guerrillas in Afghanistan were reported as early as 6 months before the Soviet invasion on December 27, 1979. The information specifies that Soviet-made aircraft were used to drop chemical bombs, with no clear identification of Soviet or Afghan pilots or of the specific agents used. On November 16, 1979, chemical bombs reportedly were dropped along with conventional air munitions on targets in Farah, Herat, and Badghisat Provinces by Soviet-supplied Afghan IL–28 bombers based at Shindand. A number of Afghan military defectors have stated that the Soviets provided the Afghan military with chemical warfare training as well as supplies of lethal and incapacitating agents.

For the period from the summer of 1979 to the summer of 1981, the U.S. Government received reports of 47 separate chemical attacks with a claimed death toll of more than 3,000 (see Table 3).[18] Of the 47 reports, 36 came from Afghan Army deserters, *mujahidin* resistance fighters, journalists, U.S. physicians, and others. For 24 of the reported attacks, there is additional independent evidence supporting allegations of chemical attacks. In seven instances, further individual reporting exists. Evidence for 20 of the reported incidents comes from information on Soviet or Afghan Army combat operations in progress in areas and at times approximating those of a reported chemical attack (see map[19]).

The reports indicated that fixed-wing aircraft and helicopters usually were employed to disseminate chemical warfare agents by rockets, bombs, and sprays. Chemical-filled landmines were also reportedly used by the Soviets. The chemical clouds were usually gray or blue-black, yellow, or a combination of the colors.

Symptoms reported by victims and witnesses of attacks indicate that nonlethal incapacitating chemicals and lethal chemicals—including nerve agents, phosgene or phosgene oxime, possibly trichothecene toxins, and mustard—were used. Medical examinations of some of the victims include reports of paralysis, other neurological effects, blisters, bleeding, and sometimes death. While none of the agents being used in Afghanistan has been positively identified through sample analysis, there is no doubt that the agents being used are far more toxic than riot-control agents such as CN and CS or even adamsite.

Several descriptions of the physiological action of a chemical agent or of the condition of the corpses of victims were particularly unusual. In one, victims were rapidly rendered unconscious for 2–6 hours and had few aftereffects. In another, the bodies were characterized by abnormal bloating and blackened skin with a dark-reddish tinge, and the flesh appeared decayed very soon after death. In a third incident, three dead *mujahidin* guerrillas were found with hands on rifles and lying in a firing position, indicating that the attacker had used an extremely rapid-acting lethal chemical that is not detectable by normal senses and that causes no outward physiological responses before death.

Shortly after the Soviet invasion, many reports were received that both Soviet and Afghan forces were using various types of chemical agents. Ten separate chemical attacks, resulting in many deaths, were reported in the first 3 months of 1980. These reports came from northeastern Afghanistan and provide the highest percentage of reported deaths. During the mid-January to February 1980 period, helicopter attacks were reported in northeastern Afghanistan

[18] Not printed.

[19] Not printed.

in which a grayish-blue smoke resulted in symptoms similar to those described by the H'Mong refugees from Laos (e.g., heavy tearing or watering of eyes; extensive blistering and discoloration of the skin, later resulting in large sheetlike peeling; swelling in the areas affected by the blister; and finally numbness, paralysis, and death). Medical reports from examinations in Pakistan of refugees from a large attack in the upper Konar Valley in February 1980 described red skin and blisters containing fluid described as "dirty water." Refugees estimated that about 2,000 people were affected after contact with a dirty yellow cloud.

By spring and summer of 1980, chemical attacks were reported in all areas of concentrated resistance activity. Many reports from different sources strongly support the case that irritants were used to drive the insurgents into the open to expose them to attack with conventional weapons and incapacitants to render them tractable for disarming and capture. On several occasions in April 1980, for example, Soviet helicopter pilots dropped "gas bombs" on insurgents, evidently to drive them from caves.

A Dutch journalist, Bernd de Bruin, published an eyewitness account of two chemical attacks occurring in the Jalalabad area on June 15 and June 21, 1980 (*Niewsnet*, August 2, 1980). He filmed an MI–24 helicopter dropping canisters that produced a dirty yellow cloud. A victim with blackened skin, discolored by extensive subcutaneous hemorrhaging, was photographed in the village 5 hours after the attack. The journalist evidently was exposed because he developed blisters on his hands and a swollen and itchy face. He also was exposed in the second attack, and it took about 10 days for him to recover from skin lesions, nausea, diarrhea, and stomach cramps.

An Afghan insurgent provided an eyewitness account of a July 6, 1980 attack on a village 10 kilometers east of Darae Jelga in Vardak Province. He reported that a Soviet MI–24 helicopter gunship dropped a bomb that, upon explosion, released a lethal chemical. A separate report confirmed that Soviet bombing attacks on villages in Vardak as well as Lowgar and Parvan Provinces were taking place during this period. In August 1980, information surfaced on a Soviet attack with chemical bombs on the village of Sya Wusan, 30 kilometers southeast of Herat, leaving 300 dead. It was during this time that the Soviet chemical battalion at Shindand set up an operational decontamination station.

Reports of chemical weapons use in 1981 essentially parallel 1980 reporting with respect to frequency and location of attack. Soviet helicopter units participated in chemical attacks from April 20 to April 29, 1981, in areas east and west of Kabul and in the Konar Valley, according to eyewitness accounts. These attacks were intended to drive personnel from sanctuaries, such as caves, in order to engage them with conventional fire. The munitions were described as Soviet 250-kilogram RBK cluster bombs. The Soviets have such a munition, which can be filled with chemical agents. Other reports described similar operations by helicopters north of Qandahar on April 24 and April 26, 1981.

A former Afghan MI–8 helicopter pilot said Soviet forces had used chemical weapons in Badakhshan, Qonduz, and Konarha. Chemicals in canisters that contained toxic gas, tear gas, and antirespiratory gas, which has an incapacitating effect by causing choking and difficulty in breathing, were manually pushed from the cargo compartment of helicopters. The pilot said that there also was a specific gas that is absorbed by the body and leaves the skin so soft that a finger can be punched through it. In one case, there was a wind shift, and Soviet and Afghan forces were seriously affected. Other sources also have described an incident where Soviet and Afghan forces were victims of their own gas attack.

The following sequence occured in a small valley in Qandahar Province in early June 1981. According to an Afghan exile, Soviet combat groups engaged rebel forces in that valley during a 2-week period. The situation worsened for the Soviets, and an air-strike was conducted. The exile stated that a Soviet helicopter delivered a single rocket, releasing a chemical that killed 16 insurgents. Nearly all reports state that chemicals were delivered by aircraft or helicopters; a few reports describe chemical artillery rounds.

Before a sweep operation in the Konar Valley in September 1981, resistance leaders were told by an Afghan officer that the Soviets had four agents available but would use only the incapacitant which they could defend against with wet rags over the face. During the operation, Soviet helicopters conducted gas attacks in 25 different areas, using cylinders about 1.5 meters long and 60 centimeters in diameter that exploded 4–5 meters above the ground, releasing the incapacitating gas. Some victims lost consciousness, were paralyzed, and recovered, but others died, and unprotected areas of their skin turned dark green to blue-green.

An Afghan tribal leader recently described a Soviet chemical attack against a large resistance force in October 1981 near Maruf, about 100 kilometers east of Qandahar. Soviet helicopters dropped green cylindrical canisters (18 inches long, 3–4 inches in diameter) which, upon hitting the ground, emitted a greenish-yellow gas. According to the report, victims felt faint and dizzy; later their skin began to itch, and many lost consciousness. About 300 persons were affected by the gas and many died. Soviet ground forces captured many of the survivors. Other information on Soviet and *mujahidin* activities in the Qandahar area during this period confirms that this incident did in fact take place.

In February 1982, a member of the resistance, with considerable knowledge of Soviet weapons, told a U.S. official that the Soviets were using irritants, a hallucinogenic gas, and what he said was an apparent nerve gas. He described the "nerve agent" as an off-white powdery substance dispersed from helicopters generally during artillery or bombing attacks. Victims realize they have been exposed to chemical attack only when they become faint and dizzy. Subsequently, they begin to vomit and bleed from the eyes, nose, and mouth. Death occurs within a short time. The corpses are extremely relaxed, with no evidence of rigor mortis. Flesh and skin frequently peel off if an effort is made to move the bodies.

According to this account, survivors suffer aftereffects for about 6 months, including chest congestion and pain, dizziness, and mental agitation. The powder-like substance is more effective at lower altitudes where there is less wind to dilute the poison, and *mujahidin* groups have experienced fatality rates as high as 70%. Many survivors of chemical attacks in Laos and Afghanistan have exhibited the same long-term health problems described in this account.

Chemical defense battalions—standard in all Soviet divisions—are deployed with the three Soviet motorized rifle divisions operating in Afghanistan at Qonduz, Shindand, and Kabul. Soviet operational personnel decontamination stations were observed at several locations, and chemical decontamination field units were deployed during a sweep operation of the Konar Valley in eastern Afghanistan and near Shindand in the west in 1980. The operational deployment of decontamination units for personnel and equipment suggests that chemical battalions have supported offensive chemical use. In addition, Soviet personnel have been observed wearing chemical protective equipment. The Soviets have specifically tailored their forces in Afghanistan, in part because of logistical constraints; 5,000 troops and "nonessential" combat equipment were withdrawn, but the chemical battalions remain.

A Soviet military chemical specialist, captured by the *mujahidin*, gave his name as Yuriy Povarnitsyn from Sverdlovsk. During an interview, he said that his mission was to examine villages after a chemical attack to determine whether they were safe to enter or required decontamination. An Afghan pathologist who later defected described accompanying Soviet chemical warfare personnel into contaminated areas to collect soil, vegetation, and water samples after Soviet chemical attacks. According to first-hand experience of former Soviet chemical personnel, the Soviets do not require decontamination equipment in an area where chemical bombs are stored or loaded onto aircraft. Thus, deployment of this equipment in Afghanistan must be assumed to be associated with the active employment of casualty-producing chemical agents.

Afghan military defectors have provided information on ammunition and grenades containing phosgene, diphosgene, sarin, and soman and have described where and when some of them have been used. They also have revealed locations where these agents were stockpiled. The agents used, plus the time and location of the attacks, correspond with the refugee reports and recorded military operations.

The Soviet Union has stocked a variety of toxic chemical agents and munitions to meet wartime contingencies. Weapons systems capable of delivering chemical munitions available to Soviet forces in Afghanistan include artillery, multiple rocket launchers, and tactical aircraft.

. . . .

Document 441

Statement by the Representative at the United Nations (Kirkpatrick) Before the U.N. General Assembly, November 24, 1982[20]

"The Afghan People Are Fighting for Their Own Survival, But Their Struggle Has a Much Broader Meaning"

Once again the issue of Afghanistan is before the General Assembly. Once again, in what is by now a familiar exercise, one representative after another will come before this body to decry the Soviet invasion of Afghanistan and the continuing and increasingly brutal attempt to subjugate the Afghan people. And once again we will consider, and hopefully adopt by another overwhelming majority, a resolution calling for the withdrawal of the Soviet occupation force, respect for Afghanistan's right of self-determination, restoration of Afghan independence and nonalignment, and the return of the Afghan refugees to their homes in safety and honor.

The familiarity of this exercise must not be allowed to detract in any way from its extraordinary significance. Of all the issues before this Assembly, none has more far-reaching implications than the issue of Afghanistan. The aggression committed by the Soviet Union in Afghanistan and its proxies elsewhere has had and continues to have a great impact upon the climate and course of East–West relations. Such aggression ominously affects the entire fabric of international relations and the future of the state system based upon respect for the principles of territorial integrity, national independence, and political sovereignty. These actions bear directly upon the capacity of states, especially those most vulnerable, to retain their unique identities and to fulfill their aspirations in peace and security.

The Afghan people are fighting for their own survival, but their struggle has a much broader meaning. If a small, relatively defenseless, nonaligned country like Afghanistan is allowed to be invaded, brutalized, and subjugated, what other similarly vulnerable country can feel secure? If the fiercely independent and incredibly courageous people of Afghanistan are uprooted, economically ravaged, culturally annihilated, and eventually subdued, the survival of other peoples—even those equally resilient—will be endangered.

The effort to subjugate the Afghan people and to impose upon them a form of alien and totalitarian rule has been marked by a degree of violence against the population that is exceeded in the recent past only by the terrible tragedy in Cambodia. The crimes against the Afghan people have taken place far from the eye of world publicity, behind a tight curtain of totalitarian disinformation and thought control. Still, the story of the brutality has come out—as it often does in such situations—from refugee accounts and from reports of journalists and doctors who have ventured into the country.

One measure of the extent of the violence inflicted upon the Afghan people is the number of refugees uprooted from their homes and forced to flee to neighboring countries. When the illegitimate regime of Babrak Karmal was installed as a result of the Soviet invasion, the number of refugees in Pakistan had already reached 400,000. These refugees had fled the reign of terror unleashed against Afghanistan by the earlier Communist regimes of Taraki and Amin. Babrak promised an end to the methods of terror used by his predecessors. But in the less than 3 years of his rule, the number of Afghan refugees in Pakistan and Iran has increased nearly tenfold to over 3 million, almost one-quarter of the estimated 1978 population of Afghanistan. This is the largest single refugee mass in the world for any one national group.

Even these figures fail to convey the full extent of the dislocation and suffering of Afghanistan, since there have been many hundreds of thousands of internal refugees who have fled from the rural areas where the fighting has been most intense. The depopulation of the countryside, it appears, has been the deliberate goal of Soviet scorched earth policies in rural areas controlled by the resistance. As a result of the fighting in these provinces, many farmers have been unable to gather their crops and there is a danger this winter of famine.

The last General Assembly called upon the Soviet Union to withdraw its forces

---

[20] Source: U.S. Mission to the United Nations Press Release USUN 146–(82); also printed in Department of State *Bulletin*, January 1983, pp. 78–83. Ambassador Kirkpatrick made this statement before the plenary of the Assembly on Item 25, the Situation in Afghanistan.

from Afghanistan. Far from respecting the decision of the Assembly, the Soviets over the past year have augmented their forces in Afghanistan to approximately 105,000, and they have conducted their most ruthless, wide-ranging, and systematic offensive of the entire war. The heightened aggressiveness of the Soviet forces became evident in January when the Soviets bombarded, shelled and occupied the resistance stronghold of Qandahar, Afghanistan's second largest city located some 250 miles southeast of Kabul. The brutal action in Qandahar, which resulted in high civilian casualties, was repeated 2 months later in Herat and Mazar-E-Sharif, and later in the spring against the northeastern town of Tashkurghan. In the early summer the town of Aq Gozar in the far northwest was rendered unfit for human habitation by systematic air and tank strikes.

As brutal as these attacks have been, the main thrust of the Soviet offensive took place closer to Kabul in the spring and summer of this year. The principal targets were villages in the Panjsher and Logar Valleys and the Shomali region, and districts near Kabul, particularly the mountain town of Paghman located only 12 miles northwest of the capital. These attacks have been marked by indiscriminate bombardments of villages resulting in thousands of civilian casualties, many of them women and children. Survivors also relate that Soviet troops, frustrated in their search for resistance fighters, have committed numerous acts of terrorism against civilians.

In Qandahar, for example, accounts of rape and plunder by Soviet troops following last January's bombing shocked and alienated even the most enthusiastic apologists of the Babrak regime. According to eyewitness reports from the Shomali region, in one village all males over the age of 10 were shot in the presence of their female relatives. The Swedish journalist Borje Almquist, who visited the Logar Province in July and August, has described similar incidents in that area, as indeed such incidents have been reported from all over Afghanistan. According to Almquist, women, children, and old men were dragged into the street and executed, while civilians with their hands tied behind their backs were used instead of sand sacks for protection in street fighting. He also reported the burning of harvests, the poisoning of food and drinking water, and the plundering of homes and shops.

The Soviets also continue to use antipersonnel "butterfly bombs" and boobytrapped objects such as toys, cigarette packs, and pens, in gross violation of an international convention outlawing such weapons which they themselves signed in 1981. Earlier this year a team of French doctors which had returned from as far inland as the central highlands of Hazarajat charged that the Soviets scatter such mines over fields, villages, and mountain paths, causing heavy casualties among inhabitants, especially among children who are the least wary. "We have treated many children whose hands and feet are blown up by such mines," said Dr. Claude Malhuret, a member of the French medical team. He also revealed that the Soviets, fearing that the French doctors might speak about what they had seen, destroyed their hospitals in an attempt to drive them out of the country.

Boobytrap mines are not the only outlawed weapons used by the Soviets against the people of Afghanistan. They continue to use chemical weapons in violation of both the Geneva Protocal of 1925 and the 1972 Biological Weapons Convention which they, along with 110 other countries, have ratified.[21] Earlier this year the United States listed 47 known chemical attacks in Afghanistan.[22] They began as early as 6 months before the invasion and have resulted in over 3,000 deaths. These attacks have continued. Just last September a Soviet soldier captured by the resistance, Anatoly Sakharov, said that he knew of three types of chemical agents used by the Soviets in Afghanistan. His testimony about the effects of one of them, a particularly deadly agent which he called "smirch," corresponds closely to reports given to the U.N. experts team by doctors working with refugees in Pakistan. The doctors noted that on several occasions after attacks on villages, "bodies had quickly decomposed, and limbs had separated from each other when touched." Sakharov also described a chemical attack on resistance fighters in which the Soviet soldiers had been ordered to use gasmasks.

Next week the United States will make public an updated report on chemical and biological weapons which will contain new information regarding the Soviet Union's continued use of these illegal weapons in Afghanistan as well as in Laos and Kampuchea.[23]

---

[21] The Biological Weapons Convention was signed in London, Washington, and Moscow on April 10, 1972, and entered into force on March 26, 1975; for text, see 26 UST 583.

[22] For a brief summary of these attacks, see *supra*.

[23] Apparent reference to the updated report; see document 443.

Nothing more clearly demonstrates the courage and resilience of the Afghan freedom fighters, or the Afghan people's universal hatred of the Soviet occupation, than the fact that the resistance forces remain intact and active throughout the country despite the massive violence that the Soviets have used against them. In the Panjsher and in Paghman, for example, the Soviets were able to establish footholds as the Mujahidin melted into the hills. But as soon as the main invading force withdrew, the resistance overran the newly established government outposts and regained control of these positions. Similarly, savage bombardments in the Shomali temporarily drove the Mujahidin back from the main roads but in no way broke their organization. Even in the devastated city of Qandahar the freedom fighters have been able to mount operations against the occupying forces, the most notable being a spectacular jailbreak and freeing of prisoners last August. Destroyed Soviet tanks and transport vehicles litter the roadsides throughout Afghanistan, testimony to the Soviets' continuing inability to establish security in the countryside or control over the population.

The most glaring and revealing failure of the Soviets has been their inability to build the various branches of their puppet regime's armed forces into effective units that could take over the brunt of the fighting. To date it appears that no progress has been made in this key area. Recent measures to overcome the critical manpower shortage in the Afghan Army—including the toughest draft decree yet issued, indiscriminate arrests and beatings of those resisting conscription, and incentive payscales for recruits almost equal to sub-cabinet salaries—have been fruitless. As a consequence, press gangs have returned to the streets of Kabul and provincial cities, and young men have been forcibly conscripted in house-to-house searches. The futility of these various measures was demonstrated during the summer fighting when large-scale defections, surrenders, and desertions by Afghan soldiers led to a net loss of military personnel.

The failure of the Soviets to break the resistance by military means, and the self-evident fact that the Soviet aggressors and their Afghan proxies are rejected by the Afghan people, have not caused the Soviets to relent in their desire ultimately to subjugate the country. Instead, they show every sign of pursuing a long term strategy, looking on the one hand to the gradual wearing down of the resistance through attrition, and on the other hand to the military, economic, and social integration of Afghanistan into the Soviet sphere.

The Soviets have already taken significant steps in this direction. They have consolidated their military, transport, and communications infrastructure, including the expansion of existing air fields and the completion of the bridge across the Amu Darya River. They have tightened their grip on the strategic Wakhan corridor which rests on Pakistan's northernmost border and links Afghanistan with China, and they have tied Afghanistan's economy tightly to those of the Soviet bloc through a proliferation of economic and trade agreements.

Perhaps most significant is the Soviet effort to reshape Afghan culture and to replace the decimated intellectual and middle classes with a new elite trained in the Soviet mold. Thousands of Afghans, including even children between the ages of 6 and 9, are being trained in the Soviet Union and other bloc countries, while the Afghan educational system itself is being restructured along Soviet lines. The Sovietization of Kabul University is made evident by the presence of Soviet advisers at all levels of administration and instruction and in the preference given to party activists in admissions. The curriculum of Afghanistan's primary education system has been redrawn to promote indoctrination in Marxist-Leninist ideology and to prepare young Afghans for further study in the Soviet Union.

It is in light of these policies—and the continuing, escalating, savage Soviet military involvement—that we must view Moscow's repeated claim that the Great Saur Revolution of April 1978 is "irreversible." But what, one may legitimately ask, gives the Soviet Union the right to insist that the violent overthrow of a nonaligned government constitutes an "irreversible" revolution? According to what tenet of international law, on the basis of which article of the United Nations Charter, do they base their position? One would think that it is the Afghan people, and only the Afghan people, who have the right to determine whether the events of 1978 are or are not "irreversible."

In fact, the Afghan people made their decision—long ago. They rejected a revolution whose chief accomplishment before the Soviet invasion was the arrest, torture, and execution of tens of thousands of Moslem clerics, teachers, civil servants, doctors, and engineers. They rejected a revolution whose cruelty and sadistic violence is best symbolized by the mass burial pits outside Pol-e Charkhi prison and the massacre at Kerala. They rejected a revolution which systematically assaulted Islam and Afghan nationhood and turned their proud country over to its predatory northern neighbor.

They expressed this rejection in the form of a spontaneous, countrywide resistance movement. By invading Afghanistan in order to crush this resistance and maintain in power a hated, Marxist regime, Moscow took a momentous step which signaled the expanding scope of its political and territorial ambitions. In effect, for the first time it was claiming the right to apply the Brezhnev Doctrine[24] to a previously nonaligned, Third World country.

The world has not permitted this act of expansion and aggression to go unchallenged. It has rejected the claim advanced by Soviet propaganda that it is providing "fraternal assistance" to Afghanistan with its "limited military contingent." These words ominously echo assurances which were given to Afghanistan itself 60 years ago when it protested the entry of Soviet troops into two of its neighbors, the independent Moslem states of Khiva and Bokhara. Let me quote from a letter which the Soviet Ambassador in Kabul sent to the Afghan Ministry of Foreign Affairs on February 20, 1922:

> "Concerning the question of the independent status of Khiva and Bokhara, this has been provided for in the treaty agreed to and signed by the two Governments of Russia and Afghanistan. The Government which I represent has always recognized and respected the independence of the two Governments of Khiva and Bokhara. The presence of a limited contingent of troops belonging to my Government is due to temporary requirements expressed and made known to us by the Bokharan Government. This arrangement has been agreed to with the provision that whenever the Bokharan Government so requests, not a single Russian soldier will remain on Bokharan soil. The extension of our friendly assistance in no way constitutes an interference against the independence of the sovereign State of Bokhara."

Today, 60 years later, the Soviet Union provides the same justification and the same assurances with respect to its invasion of Afghanistan. It is useful, therefore, to reflect upon the ultimate fate of Khiva and Bokhara. Two years after the Soviet Ambassador gave his assurances to the Government of Afghanistan, the Soviet Union annexed Khiva and Bokhara. Their languages, Turkish and Persian, were abolished and replaced by pseudo-languages fabricated by Soviet linguists. These languages, Uzbek and Tadzhik, were mere dialects of Turkish and Persian, but were transcribed into Latin and later Cyrillic script. Mosques were closed or changed into museums and Koranic education was abolished. The surviving members of the local factions the Soviets had supported with their invasion were executed on charges of "bourgeois nationalist deviationism" and replaced by young bureaucrats trained in new Soviet schools.

Is history repeating itself today in the case of Afghanistan? If we are to judge from Soviet actions to date, it is hard not to conclude that they intend that history shall repeat itself, if not through the formal annexation of Afghanistan, then through its de facto absorption into the Soviet empire. And if this is allowed to happen, can anyone be reasonably assured that this will be the end of the process, that there are not future Khivas and Bokharas and Afghanistans that await a similar fate?

It is not, therefore, simply moral considerations and human solidarity that link us to the fate of the Afghan people. At stake in their struggle is respect for the principles of the United Nations Charter, the principles of the nonuse of force, respect for the territorial integrity, national independence, and political sovereignty of states. Without this respect, world politics would succumb to anarchy and domination by the most ruthless, expansionist predator.

We cannot—we must not—permit this to happen.

The Soviet leaders undoubtedly believed when they launched their invasion of Afghanistan that they could deal with the international reaction by waiting patiently for the world's outrage to subside. the General Assembly can take great credit for frustrating this strategy. Passage of time has not served the aggressor. Indeed, the adoption of resolutions on Afghanistan by in-

---

[24] The Brezhnev Doctrine derives from a speech Leonard Brezhnev gave to the Polisle United Workers Party in Warsaw on November 12, 1968, just a few months after the Soviet Union's invasion of Czechoslovakia. In this speech he asserted that the Soviet Union had the right to protect Communist regimes from internal and external threats.

creasingly large majorities over the last 3 years shows that the world's outrage is growing.

We now have an opportunity to reaffirm once again our commitment to the liberation of Afghanistan. In so doing, we can help remind those in the Kremlin who ordered the Soviet invasion that their strategy has failed. We cannot afford, either as individual states with our own security concerns, or as a world organization dedicated to maintaining world peace, for the Soviet leaders to have any doubts on this score.

The resolution before us today offers an honorable course for ending the Afghanistan crisis. Its objective is a peaceful, negotiated settlement leading to the withdrawal of Soviet forces, the restoration of Afghan self-determination, independence, and nonalignment, and the return of the refugees to their homeland. By adopting this resolution, the United Nations General Assembly will be impressing on the Soviets the necessity to negotiate an end to their misadventure. Hopefully, this will speed the day when real negotiations on a settlement can begin.

In this context, the United States wishes to express its appreciation to Secretary-General Perez de Cuellar for his effort to probe the opportunities for a settlement which would implement the General Assembly resolutions. We support these efforts and urge the Soviets to cooperate with them. We also recognize, as the Secretary-General said in his report to the General Assembly this year, that "time is of the essence." If the Soviets truly desire to negotiate, they must come forward quickly or the rest of the world will be forced to conclude that they have no serious interest in reaching a settlement.

The alternative to a negotiated settlement is a continuation of the conflict, with far-reaching and long-lasting consequences for world peace. The Afghan people, unbowed and unbroken despite repeated and relentless hammer blows, have shown that they will not submit to aggression—not now and not ever. They have proved themselves to be a strong, proud, heroic people. With our support and solidarity, they shall also once again become a sovereign and independent people, permitted, as President Harry Truman once said, to work out their own destiny in their own way. This is all that they seek. It is all that we, the member States of the United Nations, seek for them.

Document 442

Resolution 37/37, Adopted by the U.N. General Assembly, November 29, 1982[25]

The Situation in Afghanistan and its Implications for International Peace and Security

The General Assembly,

Having considered the item entitled "The situation in Afghanistan and its implications for international peace and security",

Recalling its resolutions ES–6/2 of 14 January 1980,[26] 35/37 of 20 November 1980[27] and 36/34 of 18 November 1981,[28] adopted at the sixth emergency special session, the thirty-fifth session and the thirty-sixth session, respectively,

Reaffirming the purposes and principles of the Charter of the United Nations and the obligation of all States to refrain in their international relations from the threat or use of force against the sovereignty, territorial integrity and political independence of any State,

Reaffirming further the inalienable right of all peoples to determine their own form of government and to choose their own economic, political and social system free from outside intervention, subversion, coercion or constraint of any kind whatsover,

Gravely concerned at the continuing foreign armed intervention in Afghanistan, in contravention of the above principles, and its serious implications for international peace and security,

Noting the increasing concern of the international community over the continued

---

[25] Source: U.N. General Assembly Resolution 37/37; also printed in Department of State *Bulletin,* January 1983, p. 80. The resolution was adopted by a vote of 114 (United States) to 21, with 9 absences or abstentions.

[26] For text, see *American Foreign Policy: Basic Documents, 1977–1980,* pp. 831–832.

[27] For text, see *ibid.,* pp. 884–885.

[28] For text, see *American Foreign Policy: Current Documents, 1981,* document 431.

and serious sufferings of the Afghan people and over the magnitude of social and economic problems posed to Pakistan and Iran by the presence on their soil of millions of Afghan refugees, and the continuing increase in their numbers,

Deeply conscious of the urgent need for a political solution of the grave situation in respect of Afghanistan,

Taking note of the report of the Secretary-General,[29]

Recognizing the importance of the initiatives of the Organization of the Islamic Conference and the efforts of the Movement of Non-Aligned Countries for a political solution of the situation in respect of Afghanistan,

1. *Reiterates* that the preservation of the sovereignty, territorial integrity, political independence and non-aligned character of Afghanistan is essential for a peaceful solution of the problem;

2. *Reaffirms* the right of the Afghan people to determine their own form of government and to choose their economic, political and social system free from outside intervention, subversion, coercion or constraint of any kind whatsoever;

3. *Calls* for the immediate withdrawal of the foreign troops from Afghanistan;

4. *Calls upon* all parties concerned to work for the urgent achievement of a political solution, in accordance with the provisions of the present resolution, and the creation of the necessary conditions which would enable the Afghan refugees to return voluntarily to their homes in safety and honour;

5. *Renews its appeal* to all States and national and international organizations to continue to extend humanitarian relief assistance, with a view to alleviating the hardship of the Afghan refugees, in coordination with the United Nations High Commissioner for Refugees;

6. *Expresses its appreciation and support* for the efforts and constructive steps taken by the Secretary-General in the search for a solution to the problem;

7. *Requests* the Secretary-General to continue these efforts with a view to promoting a political solution, in accordance with the provisions of the present resolution, and the exploration of securing appropriate guarantees for non-use of force, or threat of use of force, against the political independence, sovereignty, territorial integrity and security of all neighbouring States, on the basis of mutual guarantees and strict non-interference in each other's internal affairs and with full regard for the principles of the Charter of the United Nations;

8. *Requests* the Secretary-General to keep Member States and the Security Council concurrently informed of the progress towards the implementation of the present resolution and to submit to Member States a report on the situation at the earliest appropriate opportunity;

9. *Decides* to include in the provisional agenda of its thirty-eighth session the item entitled "The situation in Afghanistan and its implications for international peace and security".

[29] U.N. document A/37/482-S/15429.

Document 443

Report by the Department of State to the Congress and Member States of the United Nations, November 1982 (Extract)[30]

An Update on Chemical Warfare in Afghanistan

. . . .

Afghanistan

Evidence indicates that the Soviets have continued the selective use of toxic agents in Afghanistan as late as October 1982.[31] For the first time we have obtained convincing evidence of the use of mycotoxins by Soviet forces through analyses of two contaminated Soviet gas masks acquired from Afghanistan. Analysis and quantification of material taken from the outside surface of

[30] Source: *Chemical Warfare in Southeast Asia and Afghanistan: An Update*, Department of State Special Report No. 104, November 1982, pp. 4–5. The report was transmitted by a letter from Secretary Shultz to the Congress and the member states of the United Nations, which is *ibid.*, p. 2. The report is printed in full in Department of State *Bulletin*, December 1982, pp. 44–53. For portions of the report primarily on chemical warfare in Southeast Asia, see document 477.

[31] See document 439. For an earlier Department of State report presenting evidence of chemical warfare in Afghanistan, see document 440.

one mask have shown the presence of trichothecene mycotoxin. Analysis of a hose from a second Soviet mask showed the presence of several mycotoxins. In addition, a vegetation sample from Afghanistan shows preliminary evidence of the presence of mycotoxins. (See Annex A.[32])

Our suspicions that mycotoxins have been used in Afghanistan have now been confirmed. Reports during 1980 and 1981 described a yellow-brown mist being delivered in attacks which caused blistering, nausea, vomiting, and other symptoms similar to those described by "yellow rain" victims in Southeast Asia. Because of limited access to survivors who still exhibited symptoms, as well as great difficulties in collecting environmental and other physical samples from attack sites, we were unable to conclude with certainty in the March 22 report that mycotoxins were being used in Afghanistan. We have now concluded that trichothecene mycotoxins have been used by Soviet forces in Afghanistan since at least 1980.

A number of reports indicate that chemical attacks are continuing in 1982. While we cannot substantiate every detail, the pieces of evidence in these reports add up to a consistent picture. For example, a physician in a facility treating casualties among the *mujahidin* (resistance fighters) has reported that he treated 15 *mujahidin* for red skin lesions that he said were caused by Soviet chemical attacks in Qandahar Province in May–June 1982. Three *mujahidin* within 12 hours of one attack in the general area of Maharijat south of Qandahar. The *mujahidin* claimed that Soviet helicopters fired rockets that emitted black, yellow, and white gases on impact. The physician said that the surviving victims failed to respond to conventional medical treatment.

We have received reports that on September 20, 1982, Soviet soldiers poisoned underground waterways in Lowgar Province south of Kabul where the *mujahidin* were hiding. According to a *mujahidin* commander in Pakistan, a similar event occurred in the same province on September 13, 1982, resulting in the deaths of 60 adults and 13 children. These two independent accounts described a Soviet armored vehicle pumping a yellow gas through a hose into the waterways.[33]

According to the accounts of the September 1982 attacks, the victims' bodies decomposed rapidly, and the flesh peeled away when attempts were made to move the bodies. Since 1979, *mujahidin* resistance leaders, refugees, journalists, and Afghan defectors have described chemical attacks causing almost identical symptons. Most reports have described the skin as being blue-black after death. Although such symptoms seem bizarre, the large number of reports from a variety of sources since 1979 suggests that they cannot be dismissed (see our March 22 report, p. 16).[34]

In 1982, a Soviet soldier who defected to the *mujahidin* said in an interview with a British journalist that a Soviet toxic agent, termed "100 percent lethal," causes the flesh to become very soft. The Soviet defector stated that the Soviets maintained stores of "picric acid" (probably chloropicrin, a potentially lethal tear gas), the "100 percent lethal" agent, and an incapacitating agent near the cities of Qonduz and Kabul. The defector also reported that:

Unidentified toxic agents had been used in June 1982 on the highway between Termez and the Salang Pass north of Kabul;

The "100 percent lethal" agent was delivered by rockets; and

"Picric acid" and an incapacitating agent were delivered by air-dropped canisters.

The defector stated that the Soviets have been preoccupied with protecting the roads and that chemicals were sprayed by planes along the areas adjacent to highways. Chemical grenades reportedly have been used, but the data are inadequate to allow us to hypothesize about the contents, although some symptoms are indicative of mycotoxins.

The reports of rapid skin decomposition as quickly as 1–3 hours after death continue to concern us. There is no recognized class of chemical or biological toxin agents we know of that could affect bodies in such a way. If we assume occasional inaccuracies in reporting by journalists and survivors of attacks, it is possible that phosgene or phosgene oxime could cause such effects after 3–6 hours but with much less softening of tissues than is consistent with stories of "fingers being punched through the skin and limbs falling off." The reported medical effects of other toxic agent attacks are consistent with use of the nerve agent

---

[32] The tables and annexes are not printed.

[33] We know from other sources that Soviet chemical agent delivery methods include this technique, as reported, for example, by a Cuban emigré trained by the Soviets in the use of chemical weapons. [Footnote in the source text.]

[34] See document 440.

tabun. We have information that both phosgene oxime and tabun are stored by the Soviets in Afghanistan.

The British journalist, who interviewed the Soviet defector, also reported on two attacks described to him by the *mujahidin*, which have not yet been confirmed. One was an attack in the spring of 1982 on Kaiba, where Soviet soldiers reportedly shot victims already rendered unconscious by a gas; the other was in the summer of 1982 near Herat where Soviet troops reportedly loaded the bodies from a gas attack onto a truck and removed them. Reliable information indicates that the Soviets used chemical bombs against *mujahidin* forces in late September 1982 and in early October 1982 in Baghlan Province.

Our earlier findings are reinforced by several reports received this year about earlier attacks not covered in our March report:

According to a former Afghan Army officer, in September 1981 a Soviet helicopter sprayed a yellow mist in Paktia Province (Sheikn Amir) causing 16 deaths. The survivors had bloody noses and tears; extensive bleeding was reported in those who died. The Afghan officer described a similar attack in Nangarhar Province during the same month in which four persons were killed.

In early December 1981, according to interviews with survivors, 15 refugees attempting to escape to Pakistan were attacked by a helicopter using gas; four or five people were killed (the youngest and the eldest), while the rest became unconscious for 5–6 hours. The attack occurred about 60 kilometers northwest of Jalalabad.

According to a Soviet soldier who served in Afghanistan in 1980 and personally observed the use of chemical weapons, the Soviets dispersed chemicals from fighter-bombers and assault helicopters. He said that an aircraft or helicopter first would drop a container and then, on a second run, drop a bomb, resulting in a mixture of two different chemicals that killed everything within the contaminated area. We believe that the soldier may have been describing the delivery of two separate chemical agents, an occurrence described by other eyewitnesses.

An Afghan veterinarian recently has described an incident in May 1979 in which 20 people and a number of sheep were killed near Qandahar. Soviet lab technicians explained that the incident resulted from anthrax, but the doctor knew that the explanation did not fit the effects observed. Local Afghans told the veterinarian that Soviet vehicles had been in the area spraying a yellow/white powder before the incident.

In June 1980, an airport official described seeing 200–300 gas containers painted in greens and browns at Qandahar Airport. The containers averaged 35–40 inches high and 26–30 inches in diameter. A subordinate reported three types of gases in the containers: one causing burning in the throat as well as suffocation; one causing what looked like smallpox and blistering; and one making victims tired and sleepy and unable to run or fight. Further, the subordinate stated that the containers were placed in special casings that were dropped from aircraft and exploded on impact, emitting a large cloud of smoke, usually yellow but sometimes other colors. He said he had heard *mujahidin* describe these gas attacks and had himself seen animals that had been killed by the gases. We lend credence to this report because we know from other evidence that chemicals are stored at Qandahar Airport, which is an important staging area for Soviet military operations.

Finally, information received this year revealed that a Soviet adviser inspecting sites for housing Soviet troops before the Afghan invasion indicated that Soviet chemical defense forces entering Afghanistan would bring in extensive stores of toxic materials. The adviser indicated that a proposed garrison in Kabul would be inappropriate for the Soviet chemical defense unit because the materials it transported could devastate the city if an accident occurred.

. . . .

Document 444

Transcript of the Department of State Daily Press Briefing, December 17, 1982 (Extract)[35]

"We Are Always Alert for Evidence of a Soviet Willingess to Negotiate a Settlement in Afghanistan"

. . . .

Q. Alan, does the Department or the government have any reason to believe that the Soviet Union is looking for a way out of Afghanistan?

A. That's a rather sweeping question. Let me address the *Pravda* editorial[36] which, I think, probably gives rise to that question.

We are always alert for evidence of a Soviet willingness to negotiate a settlement in Afghanistan which will lead to the withdrawal of their troops, a political settlement allowing for the establishment of an independent and nonaligned Afghan Government chosen by the Afghan people themselves, and an honorable return of the refugees.

We would welcome concrete Soviet moves in this direction. We do not, however, see evidence of concrete change in the Soviet position as expressed in yesterday's *Pravda* editorial. Moreover, I would note we are hesitant in any case to try to divine Soviet policies from this type of article which has clearly generated conflicting interpretations, if nowhere else, in the press.

Q. Have there been any signs—leaving *Pravda* out of it, for the moment—any signs of flexibility, direct or indirect, by the Soviet Union, even through the United Nations?

A. I think I would leave it where I just have. We haven't seen evidence in the position as expressed yesterday in the *Pravda* editorial. I don't think I want to go beyond that.

One other thing I think is worth noting in that editorial: On the question of hot pursuit, or pursuing Mujaheddin across the border into Pakistan, we would view with grave concern anything that threatens Pakistan or risks enlarging the war.

Q. Do you have anything to suggest whether Soviet military activity in Afghanistan in recent weeks and months has increased or decreased, whether they are bringing in more matériel and troops?

A. I don't have anything that would change qualitatively what we last said about that. I think we've indicated the troop levels in a range—I would refer you back to what we've said about it—but I don't think there has been a qualitative change in that.

Q. Are you implying by that that there has been some quantitative shift?

A. No. What I'm saying is, whatever small shifts that might have taken place one way or another—and I'm not suggesting there necessarily have been—but obviously, there would be movement back and forth of replacements and so on. But there is nothing basic.

. . . .

Document 445

Transcript of the Department of State Press Briefing, December 22, 1982[37]

Afghanistan: Three Years After the Soviet Invasion

MR. HUGHES. Good afternoon. This is an *on-the-record* session on Afghanistan by Under Secretary Eagleburger. Mr. Eagleburger.

UNDER SECRETARY EAGLEBURGER. Since December 27 marks the third anniversary of the Soviet invasion of Afghanistan and since we have just completed a visit by the President of Pakistan here[38] in which the Afghan

---

[35] Source: Office of Press Relations, Department of State. Alan Romberg, Department of State Acting Spokesman, conducted the briefing which began at 12:25 p.m.

[36] Editorial in *Pravda*, December 16, 1982, a condensed text of which is in *Current Digest of the Soviet Press*, January 12, 1983, pp. 1–4.

[37] Source: Department of State files. Paragraphs 3 through 10 of this briefing are also printed as a statement in the Department of State *Bulletin*, February 1983, p. 62. The briefing, which was conducted by under Secretary of State for Political Affairs Eagleburger, began at 2:30 p.m.

[38] For documentation on President Zia Ul-Haq's state visit to the United States, December 6–14, 1982, see Chapter 12, Part E.

subject was discussed at some length with the President, and lastly because I just took a visit there, we thought it might be useful if we reviewed with you briefly where we see the situation in Afghanistan at the moment, the U.S. views thereon, and then try to answer any of your questions.

I would like to begin with just a brief resumé of the situation as we see it. Three years after the Soviet invasion, the struggle for freedom in Afghanistan still continues. The military situation can best be described as a stalemate. The augmentation of Soviet forces to 105,000 and a greatly intensified Soviet offensive during the past spring and summer have produced only very limited gains, if any.

After 3 years of increasingly harsh and destructive occupation, and even with the use of chemical warfare, the Soviet Union has not been able to accomplish what it set out to do—namely, to strengthen the Marxist-Communist government in Kabul and eliminate the resistance.

This is due to the incredible spirit, courage, and tenacity of the Afghan people. They deserve the admiration and support of free people everywhere. I don't know of any other example in the world today where a small and ill-equipped people has stood up to the might of a tremendous military power with such effectiveness.

As you know, this administration views the Soviet invasion and continuing occupation of Afghanistan in a broad strategic context. It is an example of Soviet willingness to use its growing military might beyond its borders and in ways that threaten American interests, the interests of the West in general in an area of great strategic importance to us, the interests of the Islamic world, and the interests of the subcontinent.

For these reasons, we believe it is absolutely essential that Soviet aggression in Afghanistan be checked. The world must not forget Afghanistan. In the United Nations General Assembly, under Pakistan's leadership, another resolution on the Afghanistan situation was passed by an overwhelming majority at the end of November. In other meetings such as the Islamic Conference, resolutions calling for Soviet withdrawal remain agenda items of the greatest importance. In Moscow, Afghanistan was a major item of discussion with the new Soviet leadership following President Brezhnev's funeral. In Washington, a few days ago, President Reagan and President Zia of Pakistan had a searching discussion of Afghanistan. I might add that the United States and Pakistan policies remain close and compatible. In brief, the Soviet invasion of Afghanistan remains an issue of primary world importance, as it should be.

The position of the United States Government in regard to Afghanistan is clear. We seek the total withdrawal of Soviet troops from Afghanistan in the context of a negotiated settlement, which will also provide for the self-determination of the Afghan people, the independent and nonaligned status of Afghanistan, and the return of the refugees with safety and honor. These elements of a settlement have been spelled out in four United Nations General Assembly resolutions.

In order to achieve a negotiated settlement we, like Pakistan, feel that every reasonable avenue must be explored. Thus, we support the efforts of the U.N. Secretary-General's personal representative, Diego Cordovez, as he prepares to continue his indirect talks in the region in January. We understand that Mr. Cordovez will carry with him a draft or outline of a possible framework for a settlement. We have not seen it and therefore I cannot comment on what he will be suggesting as the basis for discussion. We have said we will support the U.N. process as long as it is consistent with the UNGA resolutions on Afghanistan and does not tend to legitimize the Babrak regime.

Since the leadership change in Moscow, there has been a great deal of press speculation and comment on the possibility of Soviet flexibility toward a negotiated solution in Afghanistan. Thus far, we have had no meaningful indications of Soviet intentions. We would welcome signs of Soviet willingness to work seriously for a negotiated settlement that will return Afghanistan to the Afghan people.

I will be glad to answer any questions, if I can. If I can't, we have several people here who I'm sure can.

Q. You say you've seen no meaningful indications, but there have been signs, public signs from Moscow that they are willing, at least, to discuss the U.N. framework. Isn't that meaningful or in some way hopeful?

A. Whether it's meaningful remains to be seen. I doubt yet that it's hopeful. The Soviets, as I think we indicated at the time that the Secretary saw Mr. Gromyko in New

York,[39] indicated that they were prepared to continue with the U.N. discussions. But they have also indicated on any number of occasions that there can be a settlement in Afghanistan only after all outside interference, as they describe it, has ended and that the withdrawal of Soviet troops is an issue between Afghanistan and the Soviet Union.

I will admit that there were some blips on the radar screen, if you will, in the period immediately after the death of President Brezhnev that looked like they might indicate some change of view, but I think we have to put alongside those the recent *Pravda* article which, at least in my reading, indicates no change whatsoever in the Soviet view and, indeed, in a way tended to go further in the other direction by at least hinting at the danger of hot pursuit into Pakistan, and therefore I thought was at least as negative a signal as anything positive that might have occurred in the previous several weeks.

So by and large, again, I think our judgment is that at this point we haven't seen any meaningful signs of a desire for a Soviet progress on Afghanistan but we remain hopeful that we will find something in the cards soon.

Q. Mr. Secretary, during President Zia's visit, was there any discussion at all, in terms of coordinating what the U.S. side and the Pakistani side would find as an acceptable solution in terms of a regime in Kabul, a successor regime? There have been reports that there's some divergence; the Pakistanis are softening. They would accept something less than a popularly elected government.

A. There was a lot of discussion between the two Presidents, and during President Zia's visit. Coordination of positions would be going too far. But I can say that there was no indication—these reports of a divergence between Pakistan and the United States on a settlement are not true. I indicated in my statement what our objectives are with regard to a settlement. Those remain, as far as we know, the objectives as well of the Pakistan Government, so I don't think there's any disagreement there at all.

We did make it clear to the Pakistanis that we do support the U.N. effort, and we'll do what we can to further it but, again, with the understanding that we have certain specific objectives we think that U.N. effort ought to seek as well.

Q. By self-determination, do you mean a plebiscite or some sort of a referendum or actual election in Afghanistan in order to come up with a legitimate successor regime?

A. I wouldn't want at this point to try to go further than a general statement. I tried to describe how we would see that issue determined or settled, I think, remains for the negotiations, and there are any number of ways in which it could be solved. I wouldn't want to try at this point to come down in favor of any specific one.

Q. Is that general statement available?

A. It will be as soon as he gets it typed up.

Q. In addition to the Soviet troops, there have been reports that there are troops from the East European bloc. Could you confirm this or discuss this?

A. I've seen the reports. I have not seen anything that would confirm it, but let me check.

Do we have any confirmation? I've seen the reports but no confirmation of it.

Q. In the report it talks about heavy Soviet casualties. Do you have any numbers, estimates?

A. Bernie, we can give you an estimate which is, since the fighting began, somewhere between 10 and 15 thousand casualties. I should emphasize this is, from everything we've been able to pick up, this would be on the very conservative side of the estimate. But between 10 and 15 thousand casualties.

I heard when I was on my visit in Pakistan[40] that the estimates there were that it was about 5,000 killed, 10,000 injured or ill, particularly from hepatitis. But those are estimates. I don't think anybody can be absolutely sure.

Q. Following that for just a minute, there have also been—Defense Secretary Weinberger has been quoted with some higher figures than the ones you used on the number of troops. Perhaps as high as 120,000 Soviet troops in Afghanistan.[41]

A. The way that works out, and I think in a sense we're both right, is that our judg-

[39] Apparent reference to the Shultz–Gromyko meeting of September 29, 1982.

[40] Eagleburger visited Pakistan in November 1982 during a trip which also took him to Korea, Japan, India, and the Sudan.

[41] See Secretary Weinberger's interview in the *Washington Times*, December 28, 1982, p. 2.

ment is that there are about 105,000 Soviet troops in Afghanistan and there are approximately another 30,000 in the Soviet Union right along the border with Afghanistan that on occasion have crossed the border and have been used in operations in northern Afghanistan.

But permanently assigned in Afghanistan, our figure is about 105,000. Let me just check again.

Q. On the matter of casualties, do you now have a firmer fix on that tunnel episode?

A. Not that I know of.

Come up here if anybody has an answer to that. Is there anything more on that?

STAFF. I think the final estimates have been between, say, 700 and a 1,000. The figures came down in the beginning. They were terribly exaggerated, and as more facts came out they have been scaled down.

Q. That's total Afghans and Soviets?

STAFF. Yes.

STAFF. And furthermore there may not have been any reports about closing the ends of the tunnel, and the resistance activities that might have led to the incident may not have been correct.

Q. If the Afghan operation threatens U.S. interests, as you said, why hasn't the United States provided aid to the resistance?

A. The United States has spent a great deal of money in trying to support the Afghan refugees. The United States has done a great deal in public fora in the United Nations and so forth to try to keep the issue before public opinion and before world opinion.

With regard to the question of support for the Afghan freedom fighters beyond that, they seem to be doing quite well with the arms they pick up in Afghanistan from the Soviets and from the Afghan army defectors.

Q. The figure of a 105,000 is 25,000 more than the figure we had the first year, which seemed to be [a] stable number. In other words, there has been some creep or there has been a revision of figures.

Has there been an incremental addition?

A. Yes.

Q. Does it continue?

A. Our estimate was that at the beginning of this year there were approximately 85,000 Soviet forces in Afghanistan. That has increased over the course of the year to 105,000 by our estimate.

You have to assume, at least, that this is an indication that the Soviets have not been satisfied with their ability to act militarily within Afghanistan; that they felt they had to increase their forces. Nevertheless, even with that increase in force, it's our judgment that by and large while the Soviets can hold the cities and the main highways, they do not control the countryside and in order to be able to do so would require a major reenforcement of of great magnitude.

Q. Does this add-in to forces continue to this day? Do you expect it to continue?

A. I think it got to 105,000 earlier this year, and I haven't seen any increase since. I don't think it's gone up recently.

Q. Can you be more precise than earlier this year?

STAFF. By the time of the spring and summer offensive, by the summer it was at about 105,000—(inaudible).

STAFF. By the end of January. Actually, it went up from 85 to 90 a year ago December. We announced a year ago in December it was 90.[42]

A. Early this year, apparently, was the major jump.

Q. When this invasion first occurred, it was the assessment of the administration that was then in power here in Washington that this was some sort of an effort to get to the Persian Gulf, to menace the Persian Gulf, and this caused a lot of evaluations of U.S. strategic policy in the area.

You stated that the Soviet army seems to be bogged down in a statemate. Do you still think that this Soviet action in Afghanistan presents a threat to the Persian Gulf?

A. Absolutely. What I tried to indicate in my opening statement was that the Afghan invasion, Soviet invasion of Afghanistan, is from our point of view a strategic question of major importance; that Soviet entry into Afghanistan, much less Soviet conquest of Afghanistan, would present a serious threat to the Gulf. All you have to do is look at the map. It would put them some 300 miles from the entrance to the Persian Gulf. It would create tremendous pressures on Pakistan. It would create even further pressures on Iran.

---

[42] See the statement by President Reagan, December 27, 1981, *American Foreign Policy: Current Documents, 1981*, document 432.

It is an extremely important area, and the Soviet success in that area would be a real blow strategically to us.

Q. Have they continued with any sort of effort to destabilize Pakistan? What evidence is there that they've tried to do anything to Pakistan since they've been in Afghanistan?

A. It depends on what you mean by "destabilize." There have been a number of incidents—as I mentioned before—the question of hot pursuit, where they have crossed the Pakistani border in attacks on what they claim to be Afghan rebels, freedom fighters who were crossing into Pakistan from Afghanistan.

I don't know that there is any evidence that the Soviets have been trying to do anything internally within Pakistan to overthrow the Zia regime.

Q. Are you prepared at this time to share some information about U.S. military support to the freedom fighters?

A. The question of support to the freedom [fighters?] is an issue that I think, as I indicated earlier, our evidence is that the Afghan freedom fighters obtain most of their weapons from captured Soviet equipment or from defecting regular Afghan soldiers; and with regard to the supply to Afghanistan freedom fighters of weapons from anywhere else, I wouldn't want to make any comment.

Q. I wondered if you could discuss the sort of complexion of the troops in Afghanistan to some extent? How long the Soviet troops stay there at any given time, the morale of the troops? Do you have any evidence that the Soviets are having some trouble with their own troops there?

I mean, it is the invisible war everywhere, including in the Soviet Union. Do you have any reason to comment why?

A. I think there are several points to be made, the first of which is we have some, but I think not very many, indications of some Soviet defections. They are probably Soviet Moslems. There have been some few defections. I wouldn't want to exaggerate that.

Certainly, when I was in Pakistan a month or so ago, the reports I got from a great many people were that the Soviets really were extremely wary of getting off the main highways out into the countryside, that they tended to stand back in the fire fights. Whether that is true or not, I can't obviously say from my own knowledge, but that was common talk in Pakistan at the time.

I think the other self-evidence fact is that the Soviet people themselves know virtually nothing about this war, and so in terms of an impact within the Soviet Union, I would guess I would have to say there apparently hasn't been a great deal.

Q. Do you know, are the troops being brought from completely different areas in the Soviet Union? Have they stopped sending Soviet Moslems in now? Do you have any information on that?

A. I'll double check this with the experts over here, but my understanding is that there has been a shift; that while they began with troops from the area near Afghanistan, there have been substantial shifts in the units. Is that correct?

STAFF. Yes.

A. Yes. I'm told that's true. Yes, sir. I missed you.

Q. Larry, are there any U.S. personnel assisting in the training of any Mujahedin?

A. Not to my knowledge, no, and I think the answer to that is clearly no.

Q. What is your assessment of the diplomatic costs to the Soviet Union of this campaign in Afghanistan, their costs in the Third World, the United Nations?

A. I think the costs originally were very great on a worldwide basis. I think there has been a tendency in the West, here in the United States and in Western Europe, for Afghanistan to sink a bit from sight, partly because of Polish events; and I think it is now not quite the issue in Western public opinion that it used to be, but I think it has continued to be a major element in Third World opinion, and particularly within the Islamic world.

It's constantly discussed, it's constantly referred to, and if you look at the vote in the UNGA this last month, I think you get an indication of the degree to which it is still a major issue with a lot of countries; and I think it has continued to hurt the Soviets, particularly in the Third World and Moslem context.

Q. What is your estimate as to the capacity of either side to continue the stalemate, and are there any signs that the Mujahedin are weakening or that the Soviets may decide at a certain point to end it?

A. I think, Barrie—and again I partly put this on the basis of my own visit—but the feeling in the area, and I think the judgment of most of our people, is that, (1) it is a stalemate, and (2) it is likely to continue for a long time, barring a major Soviet investment of resources and forces; and no evidence whatsoever that the Mujahedin are in any way weakening in their resolve or in any way prepared to contemplate giving up the struggle.

In fact, again, not to get too personal about it, but when I went to the refugee camps, I came away a very impressed fellow, because the one thing that came through out of that—I had a meeting with some of the Afghan refugee leaders—and I have seldom seen as dedicated people. You felt it. You didn't have to understand them. You could just feel it. I don't think that's changed at all, and therefore I think our estimate would be that under current conditions that war is going to go on for a long time.

Q. Did these leaders ask anything of the United States?

A. Yes. They asked for support, understanding and support, in the way of arms and aid to the refugees.

Q. How did you respond?

A. I responded that the United States was actively engaged in doing what we could to help with regard to supporting the refugees, and that we were actively engaged in searching for a peaceful, diplomatic solution to the conflict.

I didn't make any promises, if that's what you're asking.

Q. Not even on background?

A. Not even on background. Not even off the record. (Laughter)

Q. What about the sanctions that were initially leveled with regard to Afghanistan? We had the Olympics, we had a grain embargo, we had other sanctions imposed.

Those seem to have dropped away as time has gone on. Are there any thoughts being given to reimposing any sanctions to give the Soviets more of a strong feeling that the United States wants them out of Afghanistan?

A. No. No thought that I am aware of to any new sanctions at all.

Q. Are we going to boycott the Olympics?

A. We're not going to boycott the Olympics. No. (Laughter)

Q. Mr. Secretary, there was some thought when Yuri Andropov became General Secretary, that because he had been in the KGB and supposedly he had opposed the Afghan action, that this might cause some change in Soviet policy.

First of all, is that true, as far as you know? And, number two, do you think it might have a bearing on Soviet actions in Afghanistan?

A. Any answer I give to that question has to be pure speculation, but I'm more than prepared to speculate a little with you.

I will tell you that, you know, the first leaks don't come out of the Kremlin the way they come out of Washington; and, therefore, when we got the report that the KGB had in fact been opposed to the Afghan adventure, there were at least some of us who thought, ah ha, maybe this indicates something. What is yet to be seen, but we ought to watch it. And I would be prepared to concede to you, I was one of those, and I suppose it is still something we have to watch.

But I would have to say that the evidence since then—let's not talk about Mr. Andropov for the moment and what his personal views on the question may be, because that would be total speculation—but the evidence since then and most particularly that *Pravda* editorial of I think a week or so ago tells me that if there was some thinking in the Kremlin about a change of approach on the subject, that the debate that has taken place since then has led to a reevaluation of the Soviet attitude on any compromise.

This is all speculation. I don't say that any of this even took place, and we may have read much too much into that first leak. I think what is important is to look at that *Pravda* piece which came out after the reports of President Zia's discussions here and his talk in New York about his view of the question.[43] And I have to read that at least as a fairly clear signal from Moscow at this point that they want the world to know that their view has not changed with regard to Afghanistan.

I have to hope that that is not something that will continue, but that's certainly my own judgment on the basis of where we stand now.

Q. On the basis of—just by way of kind of a simple explanation to me and to any-

---

[43] See document 439.

body else who might read or listen to your comments, could you explain what the difference is between the U.S. approach to Poland and the U.S. approach to Afghanistan?

Why is it that the United States is conducting a PR campaign and a refugee aid campaign in Afghanistan, but has taken a whole series of economic steps with regard to Poland?

A. I suppose that, one, there were a series of economic steps taken after the Afghan invasion, but I guess the basic answer to your question is that they are different situations. You have approximately 3 million Afghan refugees to deal with. You don't have 3 million Polish refugees. So you've got that element of a difference.

Soviet forces are in and fighting in Afghanistan against indigenous forces within the country. There is an active warfare going on in Afghanistan.

In the Polish case, while there is no question that the Polish regime took its decisions on the basis of advice and counsel with Moscow, it is the Polish regime doing this to the Poles, and again without any direct military confrontation going on in Poland, so you have to deal with the situation in a totally different circumstance.

What we have tried to do in the Polish case is make it clear both to General Jaruzelski and his regime and to the Soviet Union that their conduct in Poland is not something that we will accept without some counter steps, as indeed we took counter steps in Afghanistan. But the situations really are quite different I think.

Q. Thank you, Larry.

Document 446

Statement by President Reagan, December 26, 1982[44]

Third Anniversary of the Soviet Invasion of Afghanistan

At this holiday season when most Americans are warmed and comforted by their family relationships and the blessings of this country, it is hard for us to realize that far away in a remote and mountainous land a valiant people is putting up a fight for freedom that affects us all. No matter how far removed from our daily lives, Afghanistan is a struggle we must not forget.

Afghanistan is important to the world, because the Afghan people are resisting Soviet imperialism. Three years ago on December 27, 1979, the Soviet Union invaded Afghanistan and installed a new Communist leader to head the Marxist regime that had taken power in 1978. For the first time since the immediate aftermath of World War II, the Soviets used a large-scale military force outside their borders and Eastern Europe to try to impose their will. If this aggression should succeed, it will have dangerous impact on the safety of free men everywhere.

Three years after the invasion, the Soviet occupation of Afghanistan is not a success. Even with the augmentation of their forces to close to 105,000 men this year, the Soviets, with the puppet Karmal regime, have not been able to control the countryside or secure many cities. They have failed to rebuild the Communist-controlled Afghan Army and to create an effective government.

This is due to the spirit and will of the majority of the Afghan people, and to the *mujahidin,* the freedom-fighters, who continue to resist the Soviet invaders. In the face of repeated offensive campaigns during the spring and summer of 1982, the *mujahidin* were able to drop back and then regain their positions once the Soviet forces had withdrawn. Their forces and their will remain intact.

We must recognize that the human costs of this struggle are immense. With the more intense fighting in 1982, casualties on both sides rose, and the civilian population suffered more than ever before. Crops and fields were destroyed by the Soviets, trying to deny to the *mujahidin* the support of the local population. Homes, and even entire villages, were leveled. We have convincing proof chemical weapons have been used by the Soviets against the afghans. The refugee population has continued to grow, both in Pakistan and in Afghanistan, as peasants flee the destruction of war. It is a sad but inspiring story.

The United States does not intend to forget these brave people and their struggle. We have said repeatedly that we support a negotiated settlement for Afghani-

---

[44] Source: *Weekly Compilation of Presidential Documents,* January 3, 1983, pp. 1666–1667.

stan predicated on the complete withdrawal of Soviet troops. We joined the vast majority of the world community at the United Nations again in November in support of a resolution calling for a settlement along these lines. Just a few weeks ago, during his visit to the United States, I discussed with President Zia of Pakistan the need for a solution to the Afghanistan problem. We are both committed to a negotiated settlement that will return Afghanistan to the ranks of independent, nonaligned nations.

We in the United States sincerely hope that the new leadership of the Soviet Union will take advantage of the opportunities the new year will no doubt offer to achieve a solution for Afghanistan. The American people do not want to see the suffering and deprivation of the Afghan people continue, but we will not grow weary or abandon them and their cause of freedom.

It is our hope for 1983 that a free, independent Afghan nation will again find its place in the world community. We will not cease to support Afghan efforts to that end.

C. Bangladesh

Document 447

Transcript of the Department of State Daily Press Briefing, March 24, 1982 (Extracts)[1]

Reaction to the Coup in Bangladesh

. . . .

Q. On Bangladesh—

. . . .

A. Again, we're keeping this situation under review. As you know from reports, martial law was imposed early in the morning on the 24th of March.[2] We understand the military takeover was peaceful. No violence has been reported. All Americans are safe.

I would further add to that that ever since the establishment of Bangladesh a decade ago, we have had the deepest humanitarian concern for the welfare of its people.

Q. How many people were arrested under martial law?

A. I don't have any figures on that.

Q. You don't?

A. No.

Q. You don't know about the President, the former regime—President Sattar?

A. There is no information to suggest he is anywhere other than in Bangladesh.

Q. Dean, they just had an election there. What's our attitude toward a coup with respect to elections?

A. I think I've addressed that question.

Q. In yesterday's? But, no, seriously, I saw a State Department statement[3] that reflects some disapproval with respect to this specific coup in Bangladesh.

A. We did address that. I have nothing to add to it.

. . . .

---

[1] Source: Office of Press Relations, Department of State. Dean Fischer, Department of State Spokesman, conducted the briefing which began at 12:35 p.m.

[2] On the morning of March 24, the Bangladesh military overthrew the government of President Abdus Sattar, seized control of the country, and established martial law. Sattar was placed under house arrest. Army Chief of Staff Lt. Gen. H. M. Ershad was proclaimed Chief Martial-Law Administrator, chief executive, and head of the new government.

[3] There was no reference to Bangladesh in the daily press briefing on March 23, but a statement issued by the Department of State in response to the coup stated: "We regret that constitutional processes in Bangladesh, which the late President Zia reintroduced so carefully, have been overturned . . . . We hope that there can be a return to constitutional government at the earliest opportunity." (*Washington Post,* March 24, 1982, p. A14)

Document 448

Testimony by the Deputy Assistant Secretary of State for Near Eastern and South Asian Affairs (Schneider) Before Two Subcommittees of the House Foreign Affairs Committee, December 9, 1982 (Extract)[4]

"At the Time That the Coup Took Place, We Were Encouraging the Continuation of Constitutional Government"

. . . .

MR. SOLARZ.[5] I know you have to go in just a few minutes. Let me ask briefly just one or two other questions.

Mr. Schneider, when the coup took place in Bangladesh sometime ago in which the elected government was overthrown and replaced by a military government, was anyone in our Embassy, or was any American official consulted in advance by the military officers responsible for the coup as to whether or not we would approve such an undertaking?

MR. SCHNEIDER. The best of my recollection is that there was no such consultation.

MR. SOLARZ. And what was our policy with respect to the coup?

MR. SCHNEIDER. Our policy was and is one at the present time of encouraging a return to representative institutions, and we favored the continuation of the peaceful transition which was then taking place.

MR. SOLARZ. Were we opposed to the coup at the time that it took place?

MR. SCHNEIDER. At the time that the coup took place, we were encouraging the continuation of constitutional government.

MR. SOLARZ. So we were presumably opposed to the coup at the time it took place?

MR. SCHNEIDER. It depends on how you put it, yes.

MR. SOLARZ. Well, the way I put it?

MR. SCHNEIDER. Yes.

MR. SOLARZ. The answer is: Yes.

Now, in other words, if any American diplomat encouraged the plotters or indicated to them that we would not be opposed to the coup, they were acting outside the framework of American policy?

MR. SCHNEIDER. There was no such encouragement, to my knowledge.

MR. SOLARZ. Yes. And have you ever heard any allegations to that effect?

MR. SCHNEIDER. No.

MR. SOLARZ. Do you have any reason to believe that that might have happened?

MR. SCHNEIDER. No.

. . . .

[4] Source: *Reconciling Human Rights and U.S. Security Interests in Asia: Hearings Before the Subcommittees on Asian and Pacific Affairs and on Human Rights and International Organizations of the Committee on Foreign Affairs, House of Representatives, Ninety-seventh Congress, Second Session* (Washington, 1983), pp. 471–472. For Schneider's initial testimony and prepared statement, see document 433.

[5] Stephen J. Solarz was chairman of the Subcommittee on Asian and Pacific Affairs.

D. India

Document 449

Transcript of the Department of State Daily Press Briefing, March 25, 1982 (Extract)[1]

Attack on the U.S. Consulate General in Bombay

. . . .

I have a statement on an attack that took place against our consulate in Bombay, India. At approximately 4:45 p.m., March

[1] Source: Office of Press Relations, Department of State. Dean Fischer, Department of State Spokesman, conducted the briefing which began at 12:37 p.m.

25, which is 6:15 a.m. today, Washington time, the American consulate general in Bombay, India, was attacked and damaged by about 50 Indian demonstrators.

There were no injuries to either American or Indian employees of the consulate. One demonstrator was killed by Bombay police and 29 others arrested. The demonstrators threw fire bombs, burned 10 vehicles, and caused considerable damage to the front exterior of the main consulate building. They did not gain access to the interior of the building. Local police brought the situation quickly under control.

The demonstrators carried pamphlets addressed to President Reagan. Printed in Hindi, the pamphlets identified the group as the "Azad Hind Sena," which translates into Free India Army, a group about which little is known. The pamphlet contained anti-American rhetoric but it gave no specific reason for the attack.

. . . .

Document 450

Remarks by President Reagan and Indian Prime Minister Gandhi, July 29, 1982[2]

Visit of Indian Prime Minister Gandhi

THE PRESIDENT. Prime Minister Gandhi, Nancy and I are delighted to welcome you to the White House. And let me add a personal note. It is good to see you here again as leader of the great Indian democracy which provides a unique opportunity for us to broaden and deepen the dialogue we began last autumn in Mexico.[3]

Through our talks, we can help to reach a renewed recognition of the mutual importance of strong, constructive ties between India and the United States. In searching for words to describe the focus of your visit to Washington this week, I came upon a statement that you had made in Delhi when Roy Jenkins visited in 1980. And at that time, you said, "The great need in the world today is to so define national interest that it makes for greater harmony, greater equality and justice, and greater stability in the world." That is more than an eloquent description of enlightened national interest. It can also serve to describe the foundation of the relationship between the United States and India—a relationship we seek to reaffirm this week. A strengthening of that relationship based on better understanding is particularly important at this time.

Your father once said that the basic fact of today is the tremendous pace of change in human life. The conflicts and the tensions of the 1980's pose new challenges to our countries and to all nations which seek, as India and the United States do, freedom in a more stable, secure, and prosperous world. As leaders of the world's two largest democracies, sharing common ideals and values, we can learn much from one another in discussing concerns and exploring national purposes. From this understanding can come greater confidence in one another's roles on the world's stage and a rediscovery of how important we are to one another.

Prime Minister Gandhi, we recognize that there have been differences between our two countries but these should not obscure all that we have in common for we are both strong, proud, and independent nations guided by our own perceptions of our national interests. We both desire the peace and stability of the Indian Ocean area and the early end of the occupation of Afghanistan. We both seek an equitable peace in the Middle East and an honorable settlement of the Iran–Iraq conflict. We both seek a constructive approach to international economic cooperation, building on the strong links even today being forged between the economies of the United States and India. Beyond that, India and the United States are bound together by the strongest, most sacred tie of all, the practice of democratic freedoms denied to many peoples by their governments.

My devout hope is that, during this visit, we can weave together all these threads of common interest into a new and better understanding between our two countries.

---

[2] Source: White House Press Release, July 29, 1982, Office of the Press Secretary to the President; also printed in *Weekly Compilation of Presidential Documents*, August 2, 1982, pp. 971–972. Prime Minister Indira Gandhi made an official visit to the United States, July 28–August 4, 1982. It was Prime Minister Gandhi's first visit to the United States in 11 years. She was in Washington, July 28–31, where she met with President Reagan and other U.S. Government officials. The remarks printed here were made during a welcoming ceremony on the South Lawn of the White House which began at 10:10 a.m.

[3] For information on President Reagan's meeting with Prime Minister Gandhi at Cancun, Mexico, in October 1981, see *American Foreign Policy: Current Documents, 1981*, document 438.

Welcome to the United States. (Applause)

PRIME MINISTER GANDHI. Mr. President and Mrs. Reagan, to me every journey is an adventure. And I can say that this one is an adventure in search of understanding and friendship.

It is difficult to imagine two nations more different than ours. As history goes, your country is a young one. Over the years, it has held unparalleled attraction for the adventurous and daring, for the talented as well as for the persecuted. It has stood for opportunity and freedom. The endeavors of the early pioneers, the struggle for human values, the coming together of different races have enabled it to retain its elan and dynamism of youth. With leadership and high ideals, it has grown into a great power. Today, its role in world affairs is unmatched. Every word and action of the President is watched and weighed and has global repercussions.

India is an ancient country. And history weighs heavily on us. The character of its people is formed by the palimpsest of its varied experiences. The circumstances of its present development are shadowed by its years of colonialism and exploitation. Yet, our ancient philosophy has withstood all onslaughts, absorbing newcomers, adapting ideas and cultures. We have developed endurance and resilience.

In India, our preoccupation is with building and development. Our problem is not to influence others, but to consolidate our political and economic independence. We believe in freedom with a passion that only those who have been denied it can understand. We believe in equality, because many in our country were so long deprived of it. We believe in the worth of the human being, for that is the foundation of our democracy and work for development. That is the framework of our national programs.

We have no global interests. But we are deeply interested in the world and its affairs. Yet, we cannot get involved in power grouping. That would be neither to our advantage, nor would it foster world peace.

Our hand of friendship is stretched out to all. One friendship does not come in the way of another. This is not a new stance; that has been my policy since I became Prime Minister in 1966.

No two countries can have the same angle of vision, but each can try to appreciate the points of view of the other. Our effort should be to find a common area howsoever small on which to build and to enhance cooperation. I take this opportunity to say how much we in India value the help we have received from the United States in our stupendous tasks.

I look forward to my talks with you, Mr. President, and getting to know the charming Mrs. Reagan. I thank you, Mr. President, for your kind invitation, for your welcome, and your gracious words. I bring to you, to the First Lady, and to the great American people the sincere greetings and good wishes of the Government and people of India. (Applause)

Document 451

Transcript of a White House Press Briefing, July 29, 1982[4]

Meeting Between President Reagan and Prime Minister Gandhi

SENIOR ADMINISTRATION OFFICIAL. I'll make a very few remarks about the setting of the meeting and then my colleague will go into deeper background on the substance.

The President and Mrs. Gandhi met alone from 10:30 a.m. to 10:55 p.m. in the Oval Office. During these talks, they set the stage for the more detailed discussions that followed. The plenary session in the Cabinet Room lasted from 10:55 a.m. to 11:55 a.m. The President was joined by the Vice President, Secretary Shultz, Secretary Regan, Judge Clark, Ambassador Barnes, and State and NSC officials.

The Prime Minister was joined by Mr. Parthasarathi, who is advisor to the Prime Minister, P.C. Alexander, the Principal Secretary to the Prime Minister, Ambassador Narayanan, and other Indian officials.

The talks were friendly, relaxed, informative and constructive and Mrs. Gandhi extended an invitation to the President to visit India. Both delegations expressed their

[4] Source: Office of the Press Secretary to the President. The briefing began at 2:43 p.m. and was conducted on background by senior administration officials.

desire to further improve U.S.-Indian relations.

The major subjects discussed included U.S.-Indian economic relations, the U.S.-Soviet relationship in the context of Afghanistan and U.S. relations with both India and Pakistan.

And now, my colleague will go into more detail on these subjects for you.

SENIOR ADMINISTRATION OFFICIAL. All right, I'll give you a rundown of the talks today between Prime Minister Gandhi and senior Indian officials on the one hand and President Reagan and senior U.S. officials on the other.

As I told many of you on Monday,[5] we have viewed this visit as an opportunity for India and the United States to better understand just how important we are to one another and in that context to give Mrs. Gandhi and the President and opportunity to develop the personal relationship that they began in Cancun.

In the discussions today which involved an exchange of views on a broad range of global, regional and bilateral issues, there is no question but that the two leaders gained a greater appreciation than they previously had of each other's viewpoints. They discussed topics such as the U.S. security relationship with Pakistan, its relevance to the Soviet occupation of Afghanistan, India's own bilateral relations with Pakistan and China as well as efforts, which we support, which India has been making to improve those relations, the Iran–Iraq War and what might be done to bring about a peaceful resolution of that conflict, the Middle East and the U.S. role in resolving the current situation in Lebanon, and a general review of East–West relations from our perspective including our views on the need to have meaningful negotiations on arms control with the Soviets, based on a position of strength.

There were also exchanges on a number of economic issues. Mrs. Gandhi and her colleagues briefed the President and his senior colleagues on efforts India has been making to strengthen its national economy. Mrs. Gandhi was assured of our commitment to continue to assist India's economic development. And, in this regard, we said we would work—we would continue our support of the Multilateral Development Bank lending to India, which we recognize is of vital importance to Indian development needs.

They also discussed ways to strengthen international economic cooperation and international development efforts through the global economic problems which beset developed and developing countries alike. And they particularly noted the importance of liberalizing the international trading system at the upcoming GATT ministerial.

Now, clearly, we did not, necessarily, agree on everything. Although, the discussions were extremely cordial. There were differing points of view without any sharp disagreements. I suppose that is the best way to put it.

With regard to our security assistance to Pakistan, for example, Mrs. Gandhi expressed her concern about the possibility of the weapons that we are supplying to Pakistan being used against India. She was assured that our assistance is being provided for defensive purposes only, to meet the threat to Pakistan posed by the 100,000 Soviet troops in Afghanistan.

Mrs. Gandhi made very clear that India's traditional policy was friendly [*firmly*?] opposed to any foreign troops in occupation of any country, and that certainly included Afghanistan.

The President and the Prime Minister also considered ways in which India and the United States might cooperate in further strengthening our already extensive collaboration in fields as varied as science technological transfer, agriculture, trade, and educational exchange. They agreed on a number of activities where both countries can focus their attention in the months ahead to bring about a strengthening of our bilateral relationship. The State Department Spokesman will have more to say on this tomorrow.[6] But I will mention now that among these activities is the establishment of a blue ribbon panel of eminent scientists from both countries to determine priority areas for collaboration.

I will take your questions.

Q. Are you saying that the United States justified its arms relationship with Pakistan on the Soviet troop presence in Afghanistan? And, if that is true, if there is a solution in Afghanistan and the Soviet troops come out, does that mean that the United States will scale down its military relationship with Pakistan?

SENIOR ADMINISTRATION OFFICIAL. We were discussing this matter with Mrs. Gan-

---

[5] On Monday, July 26, senior administration officials conducted a preliminary background briefing in conjunction with the Gandhi visit.

[6] See document 453.

dhi and her colleagues in the context of well-known Indian concerns that the arms provided to Pakistan under this renewed security relationship with the United States might be used against India. Now, that was the context, and that was the context of our reply. We have a multiyear program—economic and security assistance to Pakistan which I would expect would be fulfilled and which we hope would add to, not detract from. The purpose is to add to the stability of the subcontinent in the context of Afghanistan.

Q. I'm also trying to drive at the exclusivity of the Afghanistan situations being the reason. In other words, was it explained to her that there were other reasons for arming Pakistan?

SENIOR ADMINISTRATION OFFICIAL. This was the context of the discussion, . . . and in that context we have discussed with the Indians another fora, broader policy considerations involving the Gulf, but we didn't go into this at this time. Yes.

Q. And from what you say—

SENIOR ADMINISTRATION OFFICIAL. Yes.

Q. —it appears that both India and the United States—there's no disagreement between the two countries that the solution should be drawn from Afghanistan. Now, where is the difference between the two countries—where is the difference in their position of fighters which are to attack us before a political solution is devised?

SENIOR ADMINISTRATION OFFICIAL. We really didn't go into any detail today in discussing the differences. Mrs. Gandhi explained her perception from her own discussions with the parties involved with the Soviets in particular as to what their concerns were, not in the context of justifying the Soviet troop presence.

We explained that we had continuing contacts with the Soviets on this issue, and we would imagine that we would continue to probe where appropriate and possible to see if there was a chance for a peaceful resolution. We frankly noted that as of now we were not encouraged that the Soviets were seeking any solution which could be stable there and which was other than a Soviet-imposed puppet regime, which is what you have now.

Q. On the Tarapur thing,[7] with the French supplying the fuel, will the safeguards be exactly the same as if the United States were to supply the fuel?

[7] See Veliotes' statements, *infra*.

SENIOR ADMINISTRATION OFFICIAL. It's my understanding, and unless I'm corrected by some of my colleagues here who know more about this than I do in details, that all aspects of the 1963 agreement[8] will stay in effect in all other respects, including the provision for the IAEA safeguards.

Q. So then why is it necessary to go through the devise of having a third country supply it?

SENIOR ADMINISTRATION OFFICIAL. If I can very briefly remind you of what we talked about on Monday, the issue in the American-Indian nuclear relationship has never been the safeguards on the Tarapur reactor. According to our nonproliferation legislation of 1978,[9] we can't continue to provide fuel or have any nuclear relations with a country that does not have all of its nuclear facilities under full-scope safeguards. That's correct, isn't it?

And therefore—there is a waiver procedure[10]—I don't want to go into this in too much detail, but in late 1980 we won by two votes in the Senate and it was clear we would never get through again on this issue. So, at that point, we and the Government of India tried to find another way that would solve India's legitimate requirement for fuel; to fuel this nuclear generator of electricity for western India. And our requirements, the requirements of our Act plus the provisions for safeguards of this agreement. So, it's—we believe it's a very happy resolution—a potentially very thorny problem.

Q. What does the settlement say about the reprocessing of spent fuel?

SENIOR ADMINISTRATION OFFICIAL. I believe that issue was raised with the Indian briefer today and I won't go beyond what he said on that.

[8] For the text of this agreement between the United States and India regarding nuclear fuel, see 14 UST 1484.

[9] For the text of the Nuclear Non-Proliferation Act of 1978, P.L. 95–242, adopted on March 10, 1978, see 92 Stat. 120.

[10] Section 126 b (2) of the Atomic Energy Act of 1954, as amended (42 USC 2155 (b) (2)), provides that the President may waive a finding by the Nuclear Regulatory Commission that an export license for nuclear material cannot be granted. The waiver procedure is based upon a certification by the President that denial of the license would be seriously prejudicial to the achievement of U.S. nonproliferation objectives and would jeopardize the common defense and security. As established by Section 130 g of the Atomic Energy Act of 1954, as amended (42 USC 2159 (g)), Congress has 60 days in which to respond to the waiver.

Q. But they say they haven't agreed to it. You say they have. There's a tremendous contradiction here.

SENIOR ADMINISTRATION OFFICIAL. No, there's no tremendous contradiction. The terms of this—

Q. Can it be done by India—or a joint determination to a study?

SENIOR ADMINISTRATION OFFICIAL. This is an issue that will be the subject of continuing discussions between us but it does not affect this agreement that I have described.

Q. Where does it stand now?

SENIOR ADMINISTRATION OFFICIAL. I am going to read you a statement in answer to your question.

With regard to reprocessing, the agreement provides that any special nuclear material produced at the Tarapur Atomic Power Station may only be reprocessed in Indian facilities—

Q. Can you repeat—

SENIOR ADMINISTRATION OFFICIAL.—may only be reprocessed in Indian facilities upon a joint determination by the parties—both India and the United States that the article of the agreement that includes safeguards provisions may be effectively applied.

It is clear that there must be a joint determination and the United States has not agreed to such a determination or delegated the authority to agree to such a determination.

No reprocessing of Tarapur spent fuel in India may thus occur without United States agreement which has not been given. We look forward to a continuing discussion between the United States and India on any differences in interpretation with a view to assuring that implementation of the 1963 [Agreement] for Cooperation proceeds in a mutually satisfactory manner.

Q. Would you read that sentence again, please?

SENIOR ADMINISTRATION OFFICIAL. Now, this—I'll even hand it out for you. Now, this satisfies us. It satisfies the Indians and it does not detract in any way in our perspective from the success—

Q. There is a question—

SENIOR ADMINISTRATION OFFICIAL. Would you let me finish, please?

Q. Yes.

SENIOR ADMINISTRATION OFFICIAL. Thank you—the successful resolution of the Tarapur issue.

Now, let me—one more question and then I'll ask someone else.

Q. One more question.

SENIOR ADMINISTRATION OFFICIAL. Fine.

Q. If this discord continues—from lack of—is this supply from the French subject to an agreement or independent of—

SENIOR ADMINISTRATION OFFICIAL. These are issues, I'm sure that you should be pursuing down the road through the years and I suggest you start with your government.

Q. Mrs. Gandhi in her statement this morning[11] on the lawn back here spoke of her country—

SENIOR ADMINISTRATION OFFICIAL. Wait a minute, did you want to add anything to any of—

Q. —spoke of her country's position of having more than one friend. In the talks today, either here or at the State Department, did she go into a further explanation of India's relationship to the Soviet Union? Did the United States have any comments to make about India's relationship to the Soviet Union?

SENIOR ADMINISTRATION OFFICIAL. The fact that India has more than one friend is well known. And I should note that it's not only India that has more than one friend in this world.

There was—I think that's taken as a given if what you're referring to is—Indian relationship with the Soviets. To the extent it was mentioned, it was mentioned in the context of a given situation.

Q. United States has nothing to say about it?

SENIOR ADMINISTRATION OFFICIAL. I'm not sure what we could say, honestly.

Q. Just a question of fact as to whether he did or not.

SENIOR ADMINISTRATION OFFICIAL. No, I mean not—no, not in a critical sense or anything.

Q. Was the idea that they have a friendship with the Soviet Union and we have one with Pakistan related to each other—as hav-

[11] *Supra.*

ing more than one friend? Is that what you're trying—

SENIOR ADMINISTRATION OFFICIAL. But that's a good analogy.

Q. I thought you were trying to say that.

SENIOR ADMINISTRATION OFFICIAL. I wish I had thought of that.

Q. I thought you just said it.

SENIOR ADMINISTRATION OFFICIAL. No, I was thinking of other situations but, of course, this is relevant.

Q. This didn't come up in—

SENIOR ADMINISTRATION OFFICIAL. No, not in that sense, although we made clear that in the context of our renewed security relationship with the Pakistanis, we were urging that both sides improve their relations. In that sense, what you've described did come up. I'm sorry.

Q. A clarification—there is actually not only a request for fuel but also for spare parts. Will the spare parts also go through? This will go from the United States?

SENIOR ADMINISTRATION OFFICIAL. We have received from the Government of India their list of requirements on spare parts and we're now considering that list.

Q. This is no problem, I think. I mean, there's no problem because of the U.S. law?

Q. A legal problem.

SENIOR ADMINISTRATION OFFICIAL. That's all we can say at this point.

Q. Can I just make sure I understand. The French are supplying the fuel but we are saying that it cannot be reprocessed until we agree to it and we haven't agreed to it and so we and the Indians are going to continue talking about who can reprocess the fuel, whether it's French supplied or—

SENIOR ADMINISTRATION OFFICIAL. Yes. That's—

Q. You mention support for the Multilateral Development Bank lending to Indians. Does that include any commitment to increase the U.S. contribution? Because, as I understand it, the Indian concern is over reduction.

SENIOR ADMINISTRATION OFFICIAL. Well, the Indian concern is a concern which I think is shared throughout the developing world and the contributor world, if you will. That is, every one dollar reduction in U.S. contribution to these institutions sets a model for other donors—it doesn't have to, but the facts are, practical matter it does. So each one dollar reduction results in a total of four dollars reduction. And in that sense, our Indian friends urged us to do our best to keep our contributions up. And—

Q. The contribution comes down dramatically next year, as I understand it.

SENIOR ADMINISTRATION OFFICIAL. I think one thing—given the fact that we're both rather active democracies, I believe Mrs. Gandhi and her colleagues understand the role of the Congress in this country and that they will understand that the President, through his personal intervention, was able to get IDA 6[12] through. There are those who argue it's not enough. Without agreeing or disagreeing, if the President had not taken the strong action he did, it wouldn't have been at that level.

And that's understood. That is the context in which the Indians made their presentation on the subject.

Q. But he didn't make any commitment to go back and ask for more next—

SENIOR ADMINISTRATION OFFICIAL. Well, these are things that are going to be handled within the context of our own internal processes.

Q. Did Mrs. Gandhi come up with any new ideas for solving Afghanistan? Any proposals?

SENIOR ADMINISTRATION OFFICIAL. No, I don't think that you could say that she did. We weren't expecting that anyone would come up with any magic new solutions. We just discussed the issues and the problems primarily.

Q. What's the Indian concern about the Iraq–Iran War and what does she suggest doing about it?

SENIOR ADMINISTRATION OFFICIAL. Well, the Indians, Mrs. Gandhi expressed, you know, shared our interest. First, our concerns and our general objective that the war end as soon as possible, hopefully through mediation. Serious concern about the spil-

---

12 Established in 1960 as an affiliate of the World Bank, the International Development Association (IDA) provides low interest loan assistance to low income developing countries. In order to replenish its capital base, the IDA has met regularly with its membership to secure donations, mainly from the developed nations. IDA VI marked the sixth round of such replenishment negotiations, during which $12 billion was added to the institution's lendable funds.

lover impact of the continuation of a war. India is dependent on those gulf sources of supply. Any significant new tightening in the market in which the prices shoot up have a direct and major negative impact on India's development which is India's top priority, as it should be.

It was in this context that we had a discussion on the issue.

Q. The poor performance of Soviet weaponry and our own interest may be in some American weaponry as a result?

SENIOR ADMINISTRATION OFFICIAL. No.

Q. As far as Soviet weaponry—

Q. Didn't it come up?

Q. As far as Soviet weaponry is concerned, is India buying an aircraft carrier from the Soviet Union? Is that correct?

SENIOR ADMINISTRATION OFFICIAL. I don't know. I'm told no. I never heard of it.

Q. Just MIG's. Right? That's what it would predominantly be?

SENIOR ADMINISTRATION OFFICIAL. Well, I think they buy a variety of end items from the Soviets, including MIG's. But I don't have before me the—

Q. —ask the question of are there arm[ed] intervention in Afghanistan—discussed—Mrs. Gandhi discussed?

SENIOR ADMINISTRATION OFFICIAL. There was a general discussion on this.

Q. Sorry.

SENIOR ADMINISTRATION OFFICIAL. I know what you're asking, but I'm not going to talk about details of the discussion.

Q. I'm asking, was the situation of Afghanistan seen only as a Soviet occupation problem or was there any other external interference problem also?

SENIOR ADMINISTRATION OFFICIAL. Not in the sense that you are asking, no.

Q. Did Mrs. Gandhi or any member of her party request and/or receive reassurances on Pakistani use of U.S.-supplied weapons?

SENIOR ADMINISTRATION OFFICIAL. Yes, we said we understood the concerns that she had stated. We do. They are longstanding Indian concerns. And we assured her that these arms are provided to Pakistan for defensive purposes and, as I mentioned earlier in the context we were talking about, we noted this was the Soviet occupation of Afghanistan and the pressures that this put the Paks under.

Q. Better relations between India and Pakistan—was there any discussion on what the United States might do to influence Pakistan to promote more harmony on the subcontinent?

SENIOR ADMINISTRATION OFFICIAL. Not in any specific in the sense that Mrs. Gandhi told us, you have to do one, two, three, four. I don't think that there is any question of doubting our motives in this relationship. There is a question in expressing concern as to the results.

Q. Was there any discussion on reaching General Zia and trying to negotiate some sort of political settlement with the existing regime in the country?

SENIOR ADMINISTRATION OFFICIAL. This kind of detail we did not get into.

Q. On the Pakistani arms thing, you say Mrs. Gandhi was assured the defensive nature of the arms that the United States has given?

SENIOR ADMINISTRATION OFFICIAL. Yes.

Q. In light of the Lebanese experience and the U.S. inability or unwillingness to enforce the defensive provisions there, why should she take that seriously?

SENIOR ADMINISTRATION OFFICIAL. Well, in the first instance I don't think there is any parallel between the two situations. When you take a look at the Israeli military operation in Lebanon, it is an overwhelmingly superior Israeli military force marching on Lebanon. I don't see where you see—I don't see that parallel in the Pakistani-Indian equation. I don't want to suggest that our response was—reassured our Indian friends. I think that—at least I hope that they understand that this is our policy and this is what we intend and we will exert all of our efforts to insure that this is indeed what happens.

Q. In an administration that is dedicated to curb the flow of high technology, how does the technological arrangement with India that is proposed going to be—

SENIOR ADMINISTRATION OFFICIAL. This is—I don't think that is correct—what you have just stated. The administration is concerned seriously about the proliferation of nuclear weapons and nuclear-weapons-producing capability. We are in the forefront of trying to encourage practical technological transfer amongst the countries from the developed to the developing world, which is a whole theology of its own that I hope we don't get into. And the proposals that I noted about a committee of scientists is thoroughly consistent with this as is [*are*] such things as our Joint Commission on Economic and Business Affairs, and certainly the Indo-American Business Council, which in many respects is in the technological transfer field. And the Indians would welcome a transfer of technology in the economic area.

Q. Could I follow that? You said something about some spare parts—that they have given a list of spare parts and things to us for the reactors and so forth. What other items do they want from us and what else do they seek from us in the way of assistance?

SENIOR ADMINISTRATION OFFICIAL. Well, we have already covered—one of your colleagues asked about the multilateral banks.

They would, of course, like to see us increase our own contributions, because it works with the multiplier of three. And the Indians are in a highly successful economic development program. Everyone recognizes this. They are in a critical period now for the next decade. And they are very concerned about the availabilities of concessional lending being cut down.

Q. So was that the main thing; nothing else?

SENIOR ADMINISTRATION OFFICIAL. Basically, this was the kind of discussion. But, also, not that they were asking for anything, they were explaining their position, which represented the position of, basically, the developing world, and noting that this kind [of] assistance is in the interest of the United States and the other developed countries who are interested in creating stability.

Q. Was there any discussion of what—resumption? Was there any reference—the United Nations General Assembly—

SENIOR ADMINISTRATION OFFICIAL. May I add one point to that last question?

The Prime Minister did say, toward the end of our discussions this morning, that she hoped very much a group of American business representatives would come to India to see what the opportunities now are for increased collaboration with—

Q. A little louder, please?

SENIOR ADMINISTRATION OFFICIAL. She hoped she could have a group of American business representatives come to India to see what the prospects are for increased collaboration between American firms and Indian firms. It would involve some transfer of technology among other things.

Q. On this assistance and support for multilateral aid, will that extend to support for the next vote on the IMF funds needed?

SENIOR ADMINISTRATION OFFICIAL. We had a discussion of that. And I think we made clear our satisfaction and, I would say pleasure, with the documentation that the Indians have given to the IMF in support of the subsequent tranches.

Q. Has India showed any interest in American arms—acquiring American arms?

SENIOR ADMINISTRATION OFFICIAL. This was not a subject of these meetings. We addressed this earlier in this forum and, I believe, elsewhere. Mr. Stoessel was asked this question a week ago on the record. And we said we are prepared to consider any interest expressed by India on a case-by-case basis.[13]

Q. Has there been any interest?

SENIOR ADMINISTRATION OFFICIAL. None was expressed here at this time.

Q. You seem to be—

SENIOR ADMINISTRATION OFFICIAL. None was expressed during the meeting.

Q. But on the trip.

SENIOR ADMINISTRATION OFFICIAL. Oh, on the trip. I am sorry. I do not mean to play games.

Q. You seem to be leaving it open.

SENIOR ADMINISTRATION OFFICIAL. I do not mean to.

Q. Okay.

SENIOR ADMINISTRATION OFFICIAL. There was none expressed during the meetings held today, either the meeting with the President alone, or the larger one with us,

---

[13] Acting Secretary of State Walter Stoessel briefed Indian correspondents in Washington on July 22 in regard to the forthcoming visit of Prime Minister Gandhi. On July 27, Department of State Spokesman Dean Fischer commented, at the daily press briefing, on news reports growing out of what he said was a misinterpretation of Stoessel's remarks on July 22. Stoessel had indicated, in response to a question, that the United States "would be prepared to consider" any Indian requests for the purchase of U.S. arms, but that did not mean, Fischer noted, that the United States had expressed a willingness to sell F–16 fighter planes to India. (Transcript of the Department of State Daily Press Briefing, July 27, 1982, Office of Press Relations, Department of State)

or the Secretary's subsequent working lunch. You know, wrap it all up. I am not hiding anything.

Q. Pardon me. On the loans, was there a figure expressed?

SENIOR ADMINISTRATION OFFICIAL. No; they know what we have put into the IDA. And they would like more.

Q. Just more.

SENIOR ADMINISTRATION OFFICIAL. And hell, we tried to get more, too.

Document 452

Statement Read by Assistant Secretary of State for Near Eastern and South Asian Affairs (Veliotes), July 29, 1982[14]

Agreement on the Supply of Uranium to the Tarapur Power Station

In the context of Prime Minister Gandhi's visit this week the Governments of India and the United States have significantly enhanced the friendly relations between the two countries by agreeing to resolve the matter of supply of low enriched uranium to India's Tarapur atomic power station.

The two governments, after consulting with the Government of France, have reached a solution which envisages the use of French-supplied low enriched uranium at Tarapur while keeping the 1963 agreement for peaceful nuclear cooperation in effect in all other respects, including provision for IAEA safeguards. This solution will serve nonproliferation interests and meet India's need for nuclear fuel for the Tarapur station.

An exchange of notes formalizing this solution will take place during the forthcoming visit to the United States of Dr. H. N. Sethna, Chairman of the Atomic Energy Commission of India.

---

[14] Source: Department of State *Bulletin*, September 1982, p. 58. The statement was read to reporters at the Department of State.

Document 453

Transcript of the Department of State Daily Press Briefing, July 30, 1982 (Extract)[15]

"Additional Initiatives That Will Supplement the . . . Activities Linking Our Two Nations"

. . . .

One other statement: As a result of Indian Prime Minister Indira Gandhi's meetings with President Reagan and other administration officials, the Indian and American sides have agreed upon additional initiatives that will supplement the extensive ongoing activities linking our two nations.

Among these is the establishment of a blue-ribbon panel of eminent scientists from both countries to determine priorities for expanded collaboration in agricultural research, biomass energy and health. They also agreed that 1984 and 1985 would be designated a period of special focus to intensify and highlight cultural and educational exchange.

In addition, they have decided to reinstitute annual official-level talks between the Department of State and the Ministry of External Affairs, promote commercial relations through trade missions, and an OPIC mission in early 1983 to study opportunities for joint business ventures and consult closely to insure the success of the GATT ministerial to be held in November 1982.

. . . .

---

[15] Source: Office of Press Relations, Department of State. Alan Romberg, Department of State Acting Spokesman, conducted the briefing which began at 12:43 p.m.

E. Pakistan

Document 454

Statements by the Acting Deputy Assistant Secretary of State for Near Eastern and South Asian Affairs (Schneider) Before a Subcommittee of the House Foreign Affairs Committee, March 25, 1982[1]

Pakistan: A Frontline State

I would welcome also dispensing with the reading of my statement.

If I could have a few minutes for an oral summary, what I would like to do is to say something of the impressions which I brought back from a trip to South Asia, from which I returned just 1 week ago Sunday.[2] So this is a timely occasion for me, and in the context of some of the things mentioned in my statement.

The continent, as seen from Islamabad, brings home very clearly to one that Pakistan is, indeed, a frontline state. The Soviet threat is close by, with the Afghan border not far from Islamabad. One becomes quite aware of the strategic location occupied by Pakistan, not simply along the Afghan border but also along the border of Iran to the south and also commanding access to the Persian Gulf along critically important areas of the Arabian Sea. Therefore, from that vantage point, it was particularly apparent to me that the United States has major interests in a strong and stable Pakistan occupying this strategic location.

I also viewed the United States relationship with Pakistan from this perspective, and from the perspective of my discussions within the Embassy and discussions with Pakistani officials. This relationship has now been established by the administration and with, I want to emphasize, the responsible support of this committee and the Congress, because this has been a cooperative endeavor.

I found that we have made a good beginning in establishing a relationship with confidence. As you recall, agreement was reached with the Government of Pakistan on the components of the relationship when Under Secretary Buckley visited South Asia in September.[3] Since then there have been letters of offer and agreements signed with regard to the F–16 aircraft, in regard to certain ground forces equipment, and there has been an appropriation of $100 million ESF.

I found that confidence had been established. There was a good basis for the achievement of our objectives, and those objectives are important. First let me mention a few.

First, of course, is Pakistani security against the Soviet threat. Second, and an important objective of this committee, is to give the United States influence over Pakistani nuclear policy. I might mention a third objective—and there are many that could be mentioned—the objective of cooperation in regard to both the eradication and enforcement concerning narcotics.

However, I want to emphasize one thing, and that is that this relationship has just begun. The moneys of the $100 million ESF were just made available by OMB and, in fact, the waiting period before the Congress was finished on March 15. This is, in fact, the first full year of the relationship. I think we have made a beginning in establishing the confidence which is necessary, confidence which had been eroded, rightly or wrongly, because of questions about our reliability in the past. This confidence is essential if Pakistan is to be able to stand up to the Soviet threat and is to be able to withstand the diplomatic intimidation and military intimidation which it is subjected to every month.

Therefore, I do want to emphasize that it is essential that we continue to approve the full program of assistance which the administration is asking for—for two reasons. First, because each element of that program fulfills a specific purpose, whether it is in economic assistance to support the economy of Pakistan, or in military assistance to

---

[1] Source: *Foreign Assistance Legislation for Fiscal Year 1983: Hearings and Markup Before the Subcommittee on Asian and Pacific Affairs, Committee on Foreign Affairs, House of Representatives, Ninety-seventh Congress, Second Session* (Washington, 1982), Part 4, pp. 32–47. Schneider was testifying in support of the administration's foreign assistance proposals for Pakistan. For the text of the question-and-answer session with the subcommittee which grew out of Schneider's testimony, see *ibid*, pp. 49 and 52–61.

[2] March 14.

[3] Under Secretary of State Buckley outlined the new security relationship established with Pakistan in the autumn of 1981, and the administration's proposed 5-year program of economic and military assistance for Pakistan, totaling some $3 billion, in testimony before the Senate Foreign Relations Committee on November 12, 1981. For the text of this testimony, see *American Foreign Policy: Current Documents, 1981*, document 460.

bolster the Pakistani Army. But second, because there is a high symbolism to this entire package. The President made a commitment to seek from the Congress every year the full program of assistance for a 5-year program. We will be judged on that performance. If we fail to meet the President's commitment, although it is understood by the Pakistanis that we must seek annual appropriation, we will be judged accordingly, and not only by the Pakistanis but by their neighbors as well.

Well, there were certain other things which I observed and which I can comment on during questions, if you will, but I will not take your time. They include United States–India relationships, which we also consider of great consequence; certain specific issues about Pakistan: Internal developments, economic developments, the narcotics situation, the nuclear situation. But I want to conclude once again by indicating the importance, both because of the use of the components of the program, but also because of the high symbolism of the program, of each element of this first year of our 5-year program.

Thank you.

[Mr. Schneider's prepared statement follows:][4]

Mr. Chairman and members of the committee: It is a pleasure and a privilege for me to be invited to speak before the subcommittee today concerning our assistance proposals for Pakistan in FY 1983. This hearing is particularly timely for me personally since I have recently visited Pakistan and other countries in South Asia in connection with a conference in New Delhi of our ambassadors to South Asian countries. To my satisfaction I found that we have already gone a considerable distance toward establishing a relationship of confidence and trust with Pakistan, one which can support that country against the severe threat it faces from the Soviet Union in Afghanistan. I found Pakistan firm in its condemnation of Soviet aggression in Afghanistan and determined to seek a peaceful settlement of that conflict, when such a settlement is feasible, under which Soviet troops would be withdrawn, an independent and nonaligned Afghanistan would be reestablished with a government responsive to the desires of the people, and the 3 million Afghan refugees could return to their homes.

In India there was continued disagreement regarding our relationship with Pakistan but I found, nonetheless, a desire for better communications and friendly cooperative relations. I found that the smaller countries of South Asia were reassured by the firm position we had taken regarding Afghanistan and the strength of our relationship with Pakistan. I will summarize my personal findings in greater detail in my opening oral presentation.

U.S. Policy Toward Pakistan and the Region

In the hearings held concerning Pakistan last year, under Secretary Buckley spelled out in detail our policy objectives. I believe that it would be useful to recapitulate this policy.

With the Soviet invasion of Afghanistan, Pakistan found itself thrust into the unwelcome status of a frontline state subject to all the hazards that have been the common experience of other countries which find themselves in the same neighborhood with the Soviet Union or its proxies. Pakistan had the option of succumbing to pressures to accept the status quo or resisting them. Pakistan elected to condemn the occupation of Afghanistan, and has accepted our help in bolstering its defenses even though this has already resulted in both Soviet military and diplomatic pressures and has created a near-term threat of retaliation.

The administration attaches the greatest importance to the new relationship which we developed with Pakistan during the course of 1981. Pakistan's strategic location athwart the sea lanes to the Persian Gulf and along the Iranian border has gained added importance with the advance of Soviet forces through Afghanistan. A strong, stable and independent Pakistan is an essential anchor of the entire southwest Asian region. The 430,000-man Pakistan Army is a highly professional force. It has the discipline and the will to protect Pakistan's independence and territorial integrity. Currently, however, Pakistan's military forces are not adequately equipped to defend this independence and the critical portion of the approaches of the Persian Gulf which Pakistan commands.

Our proposed military assistance has two objectives: to give Pakistan the ability to handle, with its own resources, incursions and limited cross-border threats from Soviet-backed Afghan forces and to keep the Soviets from thinking they can coerce or subvert Pakistan with impunity. We fully recognize that, even with our proposed assistance, Pakistan cannot acquire an independent capability to confront the full wave of a direct and massive Soviet attack. Our

[4] Bracketed note appears in the source text.

intention is to raise the cost of potential aggression and to demonstrate that a strong security relationship exists between the United States and Pakistan which the Soviet Union must take into account in its calculations.

Soviet Threat

Mr. Chairman, the threat to Pakistan remains very real. Soviet troop strength in Afghanistan is now as many as 100,000 men as contrasted with the 85,000 which were present when under Secretary Buckley last testified before this committee. While the Pakistan border region with Afghanistan has been relatively free in recent winter months from armed ground and air incursions from the other side, with the coming of warmer weather renewed incursions are a distinct possibility. During 1981 alone, there were over 300 aerial penetrations of Pakistan air space, including 12 with firing. Additionally, there were at least two ground incursions.

Aside from these direct attempts at intimidation of Pakistan, the Soviet Union has also continued its not always subtle diplomatic effort to induce Pakistan to acquiesce in its invasion of Afghanistan. In neighboring Iran, the Soviets are using propaganda and other measures to fan the Khomeini regime's hostility toward the United States while at the same time increasing Soviet and bloc country presence. Moscow recently signed an agreement strengthening its economic and commercial ties with Iran and Eastern European countries are following suit.

At this point, when the Soviets are stalemated in their military takeover of Afghanistan, it is more important than ever that the United States demonstrate its support for Pakistan tangibly so that the Soviet Union understands clearly that we will not permit further Soviet adventurism and encroachments in this vital region.

Proposed Assistance

In assessing Pakistan's needs we have given equal weight to economic as well as military considerations. We propose, with the cooperation of the Congress, to address both the economic sources of national strength and Pakistan's direct requirements for a credible military deterrent.

For FY 1983, we are requesting of the Congress the following assistance for Pakistan: $175 million in Economic Support Funds; $25 million in Development Assistance; $50 million in P.L.–480 Title I Loans; $275 million in Foreign Military Sales financing; and $800 thousand for IMET. Our proposed $3.2 billion assistance program for FYs 1982–1987 is described in considerable detail in a document which has been distributed to the committee.

With regard to economic assistance, you will recall that in the authorization bill adopted last year the Congress earmarked $200 million in ESF for Pakistan for FY 1983. With the concurrence of the Congress and the Office of Management and Budget we propose that $25 million of this amount be provided as Development Assistance. We had originally proposed $75 million in DA. However, this would have threatened distortions in AID's Asian Bureau programs and a $25 million figure is now recommended. We wish to point out that both the ESF and Development Assistance Funds will be carefully devoted to helping sound development programs in accordance with strict AID criteria. Our determination to program substantial amounts of economic assistance funds is an important confirmation that we are resuming our longstanding support for economic development and that we view Pakistan's needs as much in an economic as a security/political context.

Our proposed economic assistance would be used in the following activities: financing agricultural inputs; agricultural production, distribution and storage; farm-to-market roads; energy development; water management; agriculture education, research and extension; population and health; private sector mobilization; small-scale public works in the sensitive tribal areas of the Northwest Frontier Province and Baluchistan with a focus on efforts to reduce opium poppy production in the former. We anticipate that the P.L.–480 would be used to import vegetable oil. Title III may be utilized if appropriate policy reforms can be negotiated.

The proposed $275 million in FMS would be in the form of guaranteed loans. As you know, the interest on guaranteed loans is that charged by the Federal Financing Bank which is based on the cost of money to the bank plus a small administrative charge. There is, therefore, no budget authority required and there will be no cost to the U.S. taxpayer. We believe that this is an important consideration at this difficult economic and budgetary juncture.

These FMS funds would be used to continue payments in FY 1983 for items already ordered by Pakistan in FY 1982. Major items include: additional payments on the F–16 program, M–110A2 and 155mm howitzers, AH–IS helicopters and M88A1 recovery vehicles. The proposed assistance would provide approximately one-half of the payments in FY 1983. The balance is being financed directly by Pakistan from its own sources of funds. Items for which LOA's have been signed are included later in this statement. The proposed IMET funds would be used to provide training for 54 Pakistani military personnel in the United States, primarily on those new systems and equipment which Pakistan has purchased. As in the case of other countries, IMET is an important means of strengthening service-to-service contacts between our own services and those of the recipient country.

Mr. Chairman, as I indicated earlier, it is of vital importance to U.S. national interests that the Congress approve the assistance which we have requested. The funds we have requested for FY 1983 will be the first year of our proposed 5-year assistance program which we negotiated and which was agreed to by both our governments. It is clearly understood that funds for each year's assistance will have to be approved by the Congress. We negotiated a *package* of assistance over this entire period under which the President undertook to seek those levels from the Congress in each future year. Failure to provide the initial funds would result in a severe setback to the U.S.-Pakistani bilateral relationship and would be taken by Pakistan as proof of the unreliability of the United States—a sentiment which has, rightly or wrongly, marred our relations in the past. Equally important, our credibility would be undermined in the southwest Asia region—in Saudi Arabia, and in other friendly countries in that region.

There is no way that reallocations within FMS levels could be achieved without doing irreparable damage to some vital country programs. The total FMS program authorized for FY 1983 is inadequate for meeting minimum requirements.

Now, let me turn to some of the specific questions which you have posed.

Arms Sales

To date in FY 1982, Paskistan has signed Letters of Offer and Acceptance for $1.6 billion in military equipment. Major equipment purchases are: F–16 aircraft, M–48A5 tanks, M109A–2, M–110A2 and 155mm howitzers, APC's, AH–IS helicopters, trucks and ammunition. In FY 1983, payments will continue on most of these items and, depending on Pakistan's cash position, it is possible that Pakistan might procure additional tanks, howitzers and helicopters as well as other systems which have been the subject of discussions between our two governments.

Indo-Pakistan Relations and U.S-Indian Relations

India strongly objected to our arms sales—particularly sale of the F–16 fighter—and our security relationship with Pakistan on grounds that these would inject great power rivalry into the South Asian subcontinent and, moreover, would upset the power balance in the region. Under Secretary Buckley and others have spoken before you at some length about why we believe our policies are correct and are not a threat to India.

As you will recall, the Government of Pakistan proposed to the Indian Government discussions looking towards a "no-war" pact between the two countries. The Indian Government accepted this proposal and discussions were held in New Delhi in late January and early February. Further discussions were to be held in March but, regrettably, they have been postponed. We are hopeful that the promising dialogue which began earlier will be resumed. We strongly believe that better understanding and improved relations between India and Pakistan are not only in the interests of both countries, but in the interest of the region and the United States.

Despite India's criticism of our relationship with Pakistan, we have consistently indicated to India that our aid to Pakistan is directed entirely against the Soviet threat from Afghanistan and that we wish to maintain a constructive and friendly relationship with that country, the world's largest democracy. While not changing their position on our relationship, Indian officials have indicated that India too is desirous of maintaining friendly relations. There is particular interest on both sides in developing areas of mutual interest such as the interrelationship between our two economies. It was therefore significant that, for example, there was very good rapport during Assistant Secretary Hormats' visit to New Delhi earlier this month in connection with the sixth session of the Indo-U.S. Subcommission for Economic and Commercial Affairs. Both sides sought to strengthen and expand the significant commercial ties between our two countries and are already undertaking followup actions. We consider that India has an important role to play in both regional and global affairs. Consequently we attach importance to our relationship with India and we intend to seek improvement in both communications and cooperation with India.

Internal Developments

I would now like to review briefly developments in Pakistan since Under Secretary Buckley met with you last November. At the end of 1981, Pakistan removed prior censorship of newspapers and other publications. President Zia also announced the formation of a Federal Advisory Council with appointed councilors representing Pakistan's four provinces and a cross-section of Pakistani society, including minorities. The Federal Advisory Council was to act as an interim body pending national elections which as you recall were postponed indefinitely in 1979. Several of you will have had an opportunity to meet with some of the members of the Council who were in the United States on a study visit earlier this month. The Council has met several times and has been the scene of active discussion of domestic as well as foreign policy issues. It is too early to tell what role the Council may play in Pakistan's political future. The Government of Pakistan has made clear its intention ultimately to return the country to constitutional government. We agree that such a government with broad participation is important to long-term stability in Pakistan.

More recently, there have been a series of apparently disconnected developments in Pakistan. In mid-February, the government arrested possibly as many as several thousand persons in a crackdown on what it termed criminal elements in the country. More recently there have been protests in Peshawar in the wake of the assassination of a local political leader and there have also been disturbances in several of Pakistan's universities, most of which have been closed. The disturbances in the schools appear to derive not from national political issues but largely from internal student factional disputes or disputes between students and administrative authorities and have not to date had an antigovernment focus. Finally, this past week about 20,000 Pakistani teachers struck for higher salaries. These developments have led Pakistani authorities to reaffirm existing restrictions on the right of assembly and to issue warnings to several prominent opposition politicians. We are, of course, following these developments closely. There are no indications that they represent more than expressions of social and economic conditions in Pakistan.

We continue to monitor human rights developments in Pakistan closely as indicated by our 1981 human rights report to the Congress.[5] We have discussed our human rights policies and human rights conditions with Pakistani officials and will continue to do so—on the basis of private diplomacy—as we do with other countries.

Mr. Chairman, you have asked whether our proposed assistance has generated an anti-American backlash in Pakistan. The answer is an unequivocal no. While our proposed assistance has been criticized by a few as support for the government in power, most Pakistanis, including many in the political opposition, have welcomed U.S. efforts to bolster Pakistan's independence and its capabilities to defend itself.

Economic Developments

Despite some recent short-term problems which have cropped up, the outlook for Pakistan's economy remains essentially favorable, assuming that projected foreign assistance levels materialize. Delayed winter rains have upset prospects for another record wheat crop. Severely depressed international markets in Pakistan's two key exports—rice and cotton—have resulted in an abrupt leveling off in export performance after dramatic growth over the last several years. Fortunately, import growth is easing at the same time, so the country's overall balance of payments, while continuing to experience considerable pressure, should remain within the order of magnitude originally envisaged in the strategy for international support from the IMF, World Bank and bilateral donors.

Pakistan continues to exercise fiscal and monetary discipline in accordance with its IMF-prescribed structural adjustment program, and to pursue other economic reforms. Recent notable events include a delinking of the rupee from the dollar, resulting so far in a de facto devaluation of roughly 10 percent, which should help export performance; and some increases in producer prices for petroleum and natural gas. A recently discovered new oil field has gone into commercial production, increas-

[5] *Country Reports on Human Rights Practices for 1981, Report Submitted to the Committee on Foreign Affairs, U.S. House of Representatives, and the Committee on Foreign Relations, U.S. Senate, by the Department of State,* Ninety-seventh Congress, Second Session, Joint Committee Print (Washington, 1982), pp. 1072–1082.

ing domestic oil supply by around 10 to 15 percent.

Narcotics Program

The Government of Pakistan instituted a complete ban on the growing of opium poppies in 1979, after a combination of very high prices and ideal weather pushed opium production to an estimated 600 to 800 tons. Since that time, the ban has been completely successful in those areas of the country over which the government has full administrative control. However, a significant production—in the range of 100 to 120 tons—continued in the less settled areas of the Northwest Frontier Province where Government authority is weak.

With training, advisory, and financial support from DEA, the Customs Service and the State Department's Bureau for International Narcotics Matters, the Government of Pakistan has begun to increase the effectiveness of its enforcement efforts in both the growing and trafficking aspects of the problem. The number of narcotics seizures has increased notably in the past year. The GOP late last year successfully enforced the cultivation ban for the first time in a limited region of the less controlled areas of the NWFP (Buneer).

However, this progress is only a beginning. Estimates for the current opium crop are for only 50 to 80 tons. This favorable result is due both to depressed prices and poor weather and the growing ban. Enforcement will become more difficult when higher prices increase the incentives to grow poppies. A particularly disturbing development during the past year was the discovery of clandestine heroin factories in tribal areas. Senior GOP officials have assured us that a long-awaited comprhensive narcotics law, which will greatly strengthen the government's ability to control narcotics, will be promulgated in the near future. We have been assured at the highest levels of the full commitment of the Government of Pakistan to vigorous enforcement. This is obviously crucial to a successful control program, and we are engaged in ongoing consultations with the GOP at the highest levels to ensure effective implementation of that commitment.

A successful program also requires the provision of economic alternatives and benefits in the traditional growing areas. In this regard, the State Department is financing a prototype development program package for the Malakand Agency, on which a professional design team is currently at work in Pakistan. USAID is actively planning development project activities in the tribal areas of the NWFP with close attention to their impact on reducing poppy cultivation.

Nuclear Program

Mr. Chairman, before closing I would like to touch briefly on one aspect of Pakistan's nuclear program. As you know, the Pakistan Government and the International Atomic Energy Agency have held confidential discussions since last summer concerning enhancing safeguards at the Karachi Kanupp nuclear reactor. We understand that progress has been made in these confidential negotiations. We have and will continue to urge Pakistan to cooperate fully with the Agency in this matter.

In sum, we have made a good beginning in establishing a relationship of trust and confidence with Pakistan which will bolster that country against the Soviet threat from Afghanistan. We have made efforts and intend to continue those efforts to improve our relations with India, despite that country's differences with us. The smaller countries of the region have gained reassurance from our strong position on Afghanistan. Our programs for Pakistan have, however, just begun after a period of interruption. We believe it essential that funding for those programs be approved in full, any other course would place at risk our entire relationship with Pakistan and the very important strategy which it is intended to support.

I will now try to answer any questions which you may have.

Document 455

Transcript of a White House Press Briefing, December 6, 1982[6]

State Visit of President Zia ul-Haq of Pakistan

Senior Administration Official. I'm just going to make a few remarks about the schedule and then my colleague will go into the background of the visit, the objectives and what we hope to accomplish.

---

[6] Source: Office of the Press Secretary to the President. The briefing began at 10:04 a.m. and was conducted on background by senior administration officials.

As you know, President Zia will be making his first state visit to the United States beginning today. He arrives this morning and will meet with the Secretary of State this morning and have a luncheon with him. He will then have further meetings this afternoon, including Mr. Clausen at the World Bank.

The official visit begins tomorrow with the arrival ceremony at the White House at 10 a.m., followed by a meeting in the Oval Office with the President at 10:30 a.m., to be followed by a plenary session.

There will then be a meeting in the Pentagon with Mr. Weinberger followed by a luncheon at the Pentagon.

In the afternoon tomorrow, the President will meet with representatives of the Senate Foreign Relations Committee, the House Foreign Affairs Committee and with the Attorney General. This will be followed by the State Dinner here at the White House.

On Wednesday, he will be meeting with, among other people, the Secretary of the Treasury. He will address the National Press Club, on Wednesday, that is. He will then meet with Peter McPherson of AID and with John Block, Secretary of Agriculture.

There will be a return dinner on Wednesday evening hosted by President Zia in honor of the Vice President at the Madison Hotel. He will also meet on Wednesday with the Vice President and John Tower.

He then departs from Washington on Thursday for New York and will have meetings, among others, with the Secretary-General of the United States [*Nations*] and will stay in New York until Saturday when he leaves for Houston and after a couple of days in Houston, departs for San Francisco and will leave the United States for Pakistan on Tuesday, December the 14th.

That, in essence, is the schedule, a fairly routine one.

Q. Why is he seeing the Attorney General?

SENIOR ADMINISTRATION OFFICIAL. Why is he seeing the Attorney General? Well, among other things, and my colleague can go into more detail here, as you know, we are cooperating with Pakistan to try to curb the opium traffic and this will clearly be a subject of conversation.

SENIOR ADMINISTRATION OFFICIAL. Right. And the Attorney General himself visited Pakistan last month to discuss refugees and to discuss, even more importantly, as my colleague has said, the narcotics issue. And we anticipate that would be the focus of their talk.

SENIOR ADMINISTRATION OFFICIAL. This is the first meeting that the President will have had with President Zia, although he did come to Washington, as you know, on a working visit in the last year of the Carter administration, but that was not a state visit.

Q. Is he going on to Canada after the United States?

SENIOR ADMINISTRATION OFFICIAL. Yes, he is.

SENIOR ADMINISTRATION OFFICIAL. He is?

SENIOR ADMINISTRATION OFFICIAL. Yes.

SENIOR ADMINISTRATION OFFICIAL. Oh, okay.

SENIOR ADMINISTRATION OFFICIAL. Yes, he flies from San Francisco up to Ottawa on the 14th.

SENIOR ADMINISTRATION OFFICIAL. I'm sorry about that. Yes, that's true. Why don't you take over.

SENIOR ADMINISTRATION OFFICIAL. Sure. Yes, my colleague apologizes for not being here. Your favorite Assistant Secretary is getting ready—is even now meeting Zia out at the airport. And—

Q. Tell him we'll forgive him.

SENIOR ADMINISTRATION OFFICIAL. You will, huh? I will.

Q. Hope you'll be more informative. (Laughter)

SENIOR ADMINISTRATION OFFICIAL. No comment on that.

Let me say a few things about the visit. As my colleague has said, this is his first state visit to the United States. It's also the first high level discussion that we've had with the Pakistanis since we revived the security relationship last September.

We feel this meeting is important as a further effort to consolidate the relationship and to build what we hope will be a more confident—more confident and reliable ties between the two countries, whose relations, let's face it, have had their ups and downs over the last 20 years.

We also see this as an opportunity to discuss with Zia a number of key issues. We will be particularly focusing on Afghanistan, where the Pakistan Government plays a really crucial role in the effort to counter Soviet—the Soviet invasion. We will be talking about other regional issues such as India–Pakistan relations, about the Iran–Iraq war in which the Pakistanis have sought—so far unsuccessfully—to play a useful role. The Pakistanis also will be interested in hearing what we have to say about the Middle East, where they have been particularly concerned about U.S. policy in light of their own Muslim character.

Then there will be other issues—you might call them somewhat controversial—nonproliferation; narcotics, already alluded to. We will also want to hear what the President of Pakistan has to say about his plans, which he has discussed publicly from time to time, to bring a restoration of democratic and civilian rule in Pakistan.

But we look forward to this very much as do the Pakistanis. He has got a tremendously busy schedule. I think the protocol people have told me that the 119-page book which has now been issued is about the heaviest they have published in the last few years. And what I am impressed by is the President of Pakistan's great interest in getting Pakistan's position across to the administration, to Congress, and to the American people.

So with that as an opening note, I will take your questions.

Q. How do you feel about all the stories that have been written sort of as a prelude to his visit which are so devastating in terms of torture, human rights abuses—feeling that there is a real lack of sincerity in his promise to hold elections and so forth? I mean, does this bode well for his visit?

Senior Administration Official. I think that he is in no doubt about how we feel about the importance of restoring democratic institutions in Pakistan and about this administration's clear-cut concern on human rights issues. We have talked to the Pakistanis quietly, which is the style and policy of this administration, on human rights issues and will continue to do so.

Q. Could I just follow that up? I realize that because of the importance that the administration puts on the strategic relationship of Pakistan that you are not going to raise what we might consider to be some extremely crucial issues, but I am wondering if I should at least isolate one and find out if you are planning to put pressure on him, and that is the situation involved in the daughter of the person—the last democratically elected leader of the country, Mr. Bhutto, who was killed by Zia, who is now in prison within Pakistan—is recognized as the leader of the Pakistan People's Party which was of course the last democratic party in that country. She is imprisoned—there is an international effort for her release. I noticed on the wires that her party is going to be holding a press conference with the Secretary-General in protest of these abuses and so forth. And here these are not rebels. This was the democratically elected party that was governing the country when Zia overthrew it.

Senior Administration Official. Could you ask the question?

Q. My question, since you didn't bring up these facts—I thought I had better—

Senior Administration Official. Yes, I am familiar with that. You don't quite know the facts. She is not in prison, she is under house arrest.

Q. She is under house arrest—fine. She would like to leave the country and I am wondering since—

Senior Administration Official. I did not hear that she wanted to leave the country. But in any event, I was not aware that she wanted to leave the country. But again I would have to fall back on the administration policy. We discuss human rights issues privately, but it would certainly be a contravention of the policy for me to say now whether we will or will not be discussing Benadir Bhutto's case with President Zia when he gets here.

Q. Well, could I just ask if the administration would think of it as a positive step if she were released—if you were to understand that she wanted to leave the country?

Senior Administration Official. I cannot respond to that.

Q. Have there been any positive steps in the prelude to this visit on his part? I mean, has your quiet diplomacy come to any fruition at all in terms of saving lives?

Senior Administration Official. I would mention one recent case. I think we did speak quietly. I keep stressing that word to the Pakistan Government regarding the interest of the young lady's mother, Mrs. Bhutto, in leaving Pakistan to receive medical care overseas. The government had set up a medical board to consider whether such care outside Pakistan was required.

Two of its members were her own nominees, her own doctors.

And they did decide to let her go, whether our discussions with them and that of others had any influence, of course, I'm not in a position to say.

Q. What is Pakistan doing about the Afghanistan invasion and what more would you like?

SENIOR ADMINISTRATION OFFICIAL. They are doing a great deal. For one thing, they are taking the diplomatic lead, if you consider that there are various elements in the policy which we and Pakistan basically share. One of them is—and they're all designed to continue to put pressure on the Soviet Union with a view towards persuading the Soviets to agree to a peaceful settlement which will involve their withdrawal, the reestablishment of an independent and nonaligned Afghanistan, self-determination for the Afghan people, and a return to Afghanistan of the 3 million plus refugees in safety and honor.

Pakistanis have spearheaded the diplomatic effort here. They were the principal sponsor of the resolution, which once again passed by an overwhelming vote at the U.N.G.A. the week before last, a vote of 114 to 21.[7] They have provided hospitality to something on the order of 2.7 to 2.8 million Afghan refugees, an important measure at Pakistan's own expense. They have allowed the various elements of the Afghan resistance to headquarter in the border city of Peshawar. They have generally been supportive of the efforts of the resistance inside Afghanistan.

They have also been very helpful in working with us and others in trying to keep the Afghan issue before the international public. Obviously what the Soviets would like would be for the world to forget about Afghanistan. But the Pakistanis and others, especially including us, are resisting that. We want to keep that a fresh idea.

Q. In what ways have they supported the resistance within Afghanistan? And if you'd answer the second part of my question, is there anything else we'd like them to be doing?

SENIOR ADMINISTRATION OFFICIAL. There isn't—let me answer the second part of your question first. There is nothing specific beyond what they are now doing that we would like them to do and I do not anticipate, for that reason, that this is going to be a point which will be raised.

I think we're, as I've suggested, very satisfied with what they're doing. We think it's courageous in light of frequent Soviet bullying. We think that the security relationship that we have worked out with Pakistan encourages Pakistan to continue to stand up to Soviet bullying or—and this is the alternative to Soviet blandishments.

Q. What do you—

SENIOR ADMINISTRATION OFFICIAL. Now, wait a minute. I've got to answer the other part of his question.

As far as what Pakistan specifically is doing, I've mentioned a number of things, but I think that question had best be put to the Pakistanis, who, as I've told you will be very anxious to—will be anxious to talk about everything. They'll be particularly keen, I think, to talk about Afghanistan.

Q. What do you think of the report in the *New York Times*[8] which says that there's split, between Pakistan and the United States in the approach to Soviet—negotiating the Soviets out of Afghanistan, that we are too hardline, that we want the Soviets out, and that the Pakistanis are willing to be a little more compromising to leave the present government in and so forth if they'll agree to pull out and let the refugees go back.

SENIOR ADMINISTRATION OFFICIAL. I do not see any significant difference between the Pakistan and the U.S. positions on this. We are fully supportive of the effort at indirect talks between the Babrak Kamal regime in Kabul and the Pakistan Government with the Iranians being kept informed which have been mounted by the United Nations, a senior officer there, Diego Cordovas. He will be visting the area—Kabul, Teheran, and Islamabad—once again early in the new year. We will be supportive at that time. So I would just discount reports that there are any significant differences as to either how to proceed or what we want at the end of the line.

Q. How much would Pakistan's nuclear program weigh in, specifically in today's talks with the Secretary and tomorrow will

---

[7] For the text of U.N. General Assembly Resolution 37/37, adopted on November 29, 1982, which renewed the call for the Soviet Union to withdraw from Afghanistan, see document 442.

[8] The reference is to an article by Selig G. Harrison entitled "Pakistan's Role on Kabul." (*New York Times*, December 6, 1982, p. A23)

the President bring it up and raise it in a significant way?

SENIOR ADMINISTRATION OFFICIAL. I would expect that the proliferation and nonproliferation issue will come up. The administration, as you know, considers preventing the spread of nuclear weapons to be a major foreign policy objective. Pakistan is well aware of our concerns about certain of their nuclear activities and about the importance we attach to nonproliferation.

To repeat a position which we have frequently taken, we believe that our program of military and economic assistance will help Pakistan meet some of its genuine security needs and, thus, reduce the incentive to explore a nuclear weapons option in the future.

Q. Well, this is a follow-up to that. I mean, will we actually say to them, "If you detonate a nuclear device, we will cut off this $3 billion program", or whatever it is?

SENIOR ADMINISTRATION OFFICIAL. I am not going to get into that, but I think you will find, if you look at the legislation, that were Pakistan to detonate a nuclear device we would be obliged to cut off assistance.

Q. There have been reports that Pakistan is looking for help in Western Europe for a nuclear, another nuclear power reactor. Have you any reason to think he's going to, President Zia's going to make that request here among either the government or private industry?

SENIOR ADMINISTRATION OFFICIAL. We are not permitted under U.S. law to assist the Pakistan civilian nuclear program because Pakistan is not a signatory to the Non-Proliferation Treaty, nor has Pakistan accepted full-scope safeguards. I think that the issue may come up in the sense that Pakistan may be interested in what our position is, but there is nothing under the law now that we can do.

Q. Would you review the actual numbers for FY 1983 in terms of aid and what they want?

SENIOR ADMINISTRATION OFFICIAL. Sure. Now, we have to look at this as part of a 5-to 6-year program involving a total of $3.2 billion, roughly divided between military and economic assistance. The figures that we want to provide them in FY 1983 are for, on the security side, FMS guaranteed credits to the tune of $275 million. On the economic side, economic assistance of $200 million and P.L. 480 assistance amounting to $50 million. That totals $525 million.

Now, we recognize and have discussed this with the Pakistanis that it will be difficult, given the budgetary constraints that the administration faces for us to come up with those figures.

This could be a particular problem on the FMS side because we did not have any foreign military sales to Pakistan last year. Under the terms of the continuing resolution we have to get, we have to notify appropriate congressional committees that we intend to reprogram funds for Pakistan. We have so notified Senate and House committees that we wish to reprogram $150 million in FMS during the present period covered by the continuing resolution.

I understand that Congressman Long has asked that—has put a hold on this as he's able to do within the 15 days following the notification. The notification was made on December 1st and we will be prepared, if necessary, of course, to go up and testify. We actually would welcome the opportunity to testify and to explain to him why we think it's important to proceed.

Q. Where do they want to use the $275 million for—

SENIOR ADMINISTRATION OFFICIAL. This will be used for various purchases including the F–16's. There is a particular need for them to get the $150 million early on because they do have some payments coming due this month on the F–16's.

Q. How many—

SENIOR ADMINISTRATION OFFICIAL. The total number of F–16's, as you know, is 40 and we will—

Q. Forty?

SENIOR ADMINISTRATION OFFICIAL. Forty—4-0.

Q. What? That we have committed to or they want or what?

SENIOR ADMINISTRATION OFFICIAL. We are committed to the sale of 40 F–16's.

Q. Is there any new military equipment beyond what we know or new aid that they are requesting that you expect to be discussed or settled on this trip?

SENIOR ADMINISTRATION OFFICIAL. No, I don't. The thorny issue of the timing of the delivery of the first six F–16's has now been resolved and so it will not come up as an issue between the two Presidents.

Q. When will they be delivered?

SENIOR ADMINISTRATION OFFICIAL. Let me read the press guidance.

Discussions have been held over the last few days between the U.S. authorities and the representatives of the Government of Pakistan regarding the avionics configuration of the first six F–16's to be delivered to Pakistan. Agreement has been reached on this subject and the first six F–16's will leave for Pakistan shortly.

Q. Was that a revision of their original order of the upgrading of the avionics?

SENIOR ADMINISTRATION OFFICIAL. No, let me put it this way. There was a misunderstanding between ourselves and the Pakistanis as to what the nature of the U.S. commitment was. This has now been worked out. They will be getting the F–16's.

Q. Which ones? I mean, will they have the advanced equipment or not? Wasn't that the dispute?

SENIOR ADMINISTRATION OFFICIAL. That was the dispute and I can't go beyond what I have said. But I can say that the Pakistan Government is pleased with the result of the discussions.

Q. Just to elaborate on that. The dispute—to simplify it greatly—the dispute was between the more advanced technology and the less advanced technology, was it not?

SENIOR ADMINISTRATION OFFICIAL. Yes.

Q. And the dispute has been resolved in their favor?

SENIOR ADMINISTRATION OFFICIAL. Let me say it's been resolved to their satisfaction.

Q. What is the amount of their payment?

SENIOR ADMINISTRATION OFFICIAL. What?

Q. What is the amount of their payment? You said their payment was coming up.

SENIOR ADMINISTRATION OFFICIAL. I don't know that. It's around $150 million. That's why they need the $150 million now.

Q. Payable to whom?

SENIOR ADMINISTRATION OFFICIAL. Payable to the contractor.

Q. Payable to whom? The contractor—you say the contractor?

Q. It's General Dynamics.

SENIOR ADMINISTRATION OFFICIAL. Yes, General Dynamics down in Fort Worth.

Q. When was the original order—this apprehension for—

SENIOR ADMINISTRATION OFFICIAL. I don't quite understand that.

Q. When was the original order for the F–16's? What time did that take place?

SENIOR ADMINISTRATION OFFICIAL. I'm not precisely sure but it would have followed the decision of September 1981 to go ahead with the security program.

Q. Can you just tell us a little bit about where they stand on the narcotics issue, what they're doing, what we want them to do?

SENIOR ADMINISTRATION OFFICIAL. Yes, the narcotics issue is an important one between us because something like 55 percent of the heroin reaching this country comes from opium in the southwest Asian countries. That would include Iran, Afghanistan, and Pakistan.

Pakistan has become increasingly a source of heroin as heroin labs have been opened there. What we would like them to do basically are two things. One is to further implement the ban on poppy growing which they promulgated in 1979. It's been difficult for them to do so. And one can easily understand why because some of the poppy growing takes place in tribal areas where the writ of the Government of Pakistan either does not run or does not run very solidly.

The second thing which we think it's important for them to do is to bust up the heroin labs. We're satisfied that progress on both scores has taken place. Part of this may reflect our efforts, spearheaded in November by Attorney General Smith, but, also, I think the Pakistanis themselves are recognizing that addiction is becoming an increasing problem in their own country. So it is for their own benefit to try to control the problem.

Q. Say "heroin lab"—

SENIOR ADMINISTRATION OFFICIAL. I've got to go—I'm sorry. I've got to go over now—

MR. ALLIN. Want to take one more?

SENIOR ADMINISTRATION OFFICIAL. It's a lab where heroin is manufactured from opium.

Q. One question on Afghanistan. When President Zia came away from his talks with Yuri Andropov, he characterized those talks as disclosing a new freshness of the Soviet position. And he went in an interview with the FT to admit that, indeed, now he was prepared to take the Soviets at his word, whereas in the past he wasn't.

I'd like to ask whether anything has come to your attention, either through the talk that was held with Andropov and Bush or through any other channels that would incline you to think there is a new freshness in the Soviet position over Afghanistan or new flexibility?

Senior Administration Official. Well, of course, we'll be talking—the President, specifically, will be talking to President Zia about his impressions from the Andropov visit.

The Pakistanis, leaving aside from what was said or what the atmosphere of the 40–45 minute discussion was, were very pleased that General Zia was among the few singled out. I am rather skeptical that there has been any—any evidence of a significant change in what until now has been a hard-line, inflexible Soviet position.

I would like to hope that this will change. But as far as the Soviets moving toward a position which we will find acceptable, the Pakistanis would find acceptable or the people, 114 countries which voted for the resolution the other day, will find acceptable, I just don't see yet.

Q. Can I follow that up?

Senior Administration Official. No, you can't. I've got to go over to the Shultz talks now.

Document 456

Statement Issued by the Department of State, December 7, 1982[9]

Democracy in Pakistan

Q. Can you comment on the remarks which were reportedly made by Ambassador Spiers that the United States is not interested in the elections in Pakistan, but in the integrity of Pakistan?

A. We believe that the record of the U.S. Government and Ambassador Spiers in support of democratic institutions, in Pakistan as elsewhere, is clear and requires no amplification. In a widely publicized speech in Karachi, for example, Ambassador Spiers observed that the United States "has the greatest political affinity with other democracies" and that Pakistan's continued martial law "has been a source of continuing reservation" about Pakistan in the United States. The comment referred to in this question appears to be one which was published in Pakistan earlier this year and which was the subject of a clarification issued by the U.S. Embassy in Islamabad at that time. Ambassador Spiers did not say that the United States is not interested in elections in Pakistan. He said that, despite the lack of elections, the threat to Pakistan's security and stability posed by the Soviet invasion of Afghanistan necessitates and justifies the renewed U.S. security relationship.

Document 457

Remarks by President Reagan and Pakistani President Zia, December 7, 1982[10]

A Visit Which "Symbolizes and Strengthens the Close Ties Which Exist Between Our Two Countries"

The President. Mr. President, Begum Zia, it is a great pleasure for Nancy and me to welcome you to Washington today. Your visit to the United States this week both symbolizes and strengthens the close ties which exist between our two countries. As you arrive here the world, and your region in particular, are passing through a critical phase. We confront serious challenges that by choice and necessity will draw our peoples ever closer. It is vital that those nations committed to peace and progress work diligently together to achieve those goals.

One of Pakistan's founding fathers, Prime Minister Liaquat Ali Khan, visited

---

[9] Source: Office of Press Relations, Department of State; posted statement. The statement was posted in response to a question taken on December 6 at the Department of State Daily Press Briefing.

[10] Source: White House Press Release, December 7, 1982, Office of the Press Secretary to the President; also printed in *Weekly Compilation of Presidential Documents*, December 13, 1982, pp. 1581–1583. The remarks were made during a welcoming ceremony on the South Lawn of the White House which began at 10:15 a.m.

Washington in 1950. And speaking before the United States Senate, he described our continuing challenge. He said, "This is the century of great awakenings in all parts of the globe. And it depends entirely on the leaders of the world whether mankind will awaken to the horrors of darkness or to a glorious dawn." Well, his words ring true even now.

Pakistan today stands in the front rank of the nations shouldering a great responsibility for mankind. Your courageous and compassionate role in giving shelter to millions of Afghan refugees is well known to the American people and will long be remembered. We're proud to stand with you, Mr. President, helping to provide for these tragic victims of aggression, while, at the same time, seeking a peaceful resolution of the circumstances which brought them to your country.

We also applaud your efforts and those of the Indian Government to reconcile your differences. The steps you take today to deter these relations will bring incalculable benefit to all the people of the subcontinent and will be memorialized in improvement of their lives.

Similarly, Pakistan's positive response to peace efforts in the Middle East have contributed to our confidence that our two countries can work together for peace and stability. After many years of disappointment, there is growing recognition in the Middle East that a continuation of violence can only breed a worsening conflict. This cycle must be broken. We're gratified to know that we can count on Pakistan's cooperation in confronting these perplexing problems.

We believe that the program of economic and security assistance on which we embarked last year will contribute to the tranquillity and progress of the entire region and it's our hope that reinvigoration of the relationship between our two countries will enable Pakistan to maintain its courageous stand on behalf of peace and amity of nations.

The United States-Pakistani friendship which stretches back over 30 years has been tested by time and change. It has endured and, because of the substantial agreement between us on the great issues of peace, development and security, it grows stronger daily.

Underlying our ties, however, is something which is even more critical in an enduring relationship and that is the warmth and understanding that exist between the people of our countries. This friendship is based on the mutual warmth and affection which have developed between our people, something which no government can mandate and which is indeed a cherished possession.

When you leave us and leave the United States next week, Mr. President, we want you to return home secure in the knowledge that the American people support close ties with Pakistan and look forward to expanding them in the coming years. We hope the friendship and hospitality that you receive during your stay will underline our good will and the permanence of our bond.

Mr. Prsident, Begum Zia, welcome to the United States. (Applause)

PRESIDENT ZIA. Mr. President, Mrs. Reagan, distinguished guests, ladies and gentlemen. Sir, may I thank you most sincerely for your very kind words of welcome, for the warmth with which we have been received and the generous hospitality that has already been extended to me, my wife and the members of my delegation since we arrived in your great country.

Mr. President, I am no stranger to the United States. I've had the honor of coming here a few times before. But each time I have felt that it was a new experience for me. Perhaps this is because of the perpetual freshness, the vibrant dynamism and the ceaseless forward movement which characterizes this great nation of yours.

My visit this time, Mr. President, is not just one of discovery or rediscovery. I take it as one of my—as a visit of great importance for renewal and reaffirmation, renewal of a friendship that has to us many ups and downs and reaffirmation of those shared values and perceptions on which our relationship is based. I, therefore, look forward to the strengthening of our ties as the years go by.

Mr. President, west and southwest Asia from the eastern Mediterranean to Afghanistan is today in ferment. Armed aggression, military intervention, conflicts, disregards for universally accepted principles of international conduct, have all combined to present a serious challenge to the security of the countries of this region.

This in turn threatens to undermine the whole structure of international relations upon which the peace of the world ultimately rests.

Mr. President, sir, Pakistan's continued commitment to the principle of nonalignment and to the objectives of the Islamic Conference are the fundamental postulates of its foreign policy. Pakistan is endeavoring to contribute effectively to the peace and stability of a troubled and turbulent region. But we cannot ourselves long remain immune from the dangers around us, Mr. President, nor have we in fact escaped their consequences.

The responsibility for providing refuge and a safe haven for nearly 3 million fleeing the repression in Afghanistan has been shouldered by our people as a humanitarian duty in the spirit of Islamic brotherhood. Nevertheless, the burdens are there, especially for a developing country like Pakistan.

But at the same time I must emphasize that we have borne these burdens ungrudgingly and we will continue to do so enshallah. We are conscious of the security implications of the great developments across our border. The qualitative change brought about by these developments and their impact on the entire region have evoked a response from the United States which, Mr. President, we appreciate.

It was as a result of our common concern that there were two governments decided on a program to enhance Pakistan's potential to withstand external forces of disruption and continue to play a stabilizing role in the region.

Mr. President, sir, it's our consistent endeavor to find equitable and humane solutions to the conflicts in our region.

This task can only be accomplished through negotiation and mutal accommodation within the framework of the principles and resolutions of the United Nations.

It must also inevitably entail the proper regard for the individual and collective dignity of the peoples involved.

In this endeavor, we have been fortunate, Mr. President, to have your understanding. What is more, sir, I claim that we have your friendship as well. A friendship mature enough to withstand differences of opinion and mirrored by the very candor and sincerity of our mutual exchanges. For all this, we are indeed very grateful to you.

Mr. President, I have come here to deepen and strengthen this friendship. I'm looking forward to our talks later this morning. And I have no doubt that they will lead us to this goal and that our respective efforts on behalf of peace and stability in our region and in the world in general, enshallah, shall bear fruit.

Indeed, Mr. President, borrowing your own words, it will be in the fitness of the things for me to conclude by saying, sir, that you and I have a rendezvous with destiny. I thank you. (Applause)

Document 458

Transcript of an Interview With Pakistani President Zia, New York, December 12, 1982 (Extract)[11]

Relationship Between the United States and Pakistan

. . . .

Mr. Smith. Mr. President, in seeking support for its $3.2 billion air program the Reagan administration has stressed the strategic relationship with your country. I'd like to ask specifically, would you be willing to commit Pakistani forces in the event of hostilities in the Persian Gulf?

President Zia. We have always maintained that the security of the Gulf is the responsibility of the Gulf States. Pakistan is the backyard of the Gulf; that's what we claim. And if we protect the backyard, you can rest assured that the Gulf will be as secure by themselves as they can.

Mr. Smith. Are you prepared to allow units of the U.S. Rapid Deployment Force to use Pakistani bases or ports?

President Zia. We say that we are 84 million people, not a small nation. If there is anything we could do to maintain peace in the world, Pakistan will be too glad to offer its services with their own men and weapons.

Mr. Smith. That is to say you do not accept the idea that the Rapid Deployment Force could use Pakistani bases and ports?

President Zia. For the time being, sir, this is not our policy.

---

[11] Source: National Broadcasting Company. The text is from a transcript of the NBC radio and television program "Meet the Press", which was taped in New York on December 12. Bill Monroe of NBC News was the moderator of the program. The reporters involved were Marvin Kalb of NBC News, Milt Frudenheim of the *New York Times*, Marcia Gauger of *Time* magazine, and Richard Smith of *Newsweek*.

MR. SMITH. What about electronic surveillance stations? As you know, the United States lost some of these units in Iran. Would you be prepared to let the United States establish similar stations in Pakistan?

PRESIDENT ZIA. We have enough resources ourselves. If we can share some information, we'll be too pleased to do so.

MR. SMITH. From—From your perspective then, in strategic terms, if these three points we've talked about are not acceptable, what is the nature of the strategic relationship with the United States?

PRESIDENT ZIA. If I were you, sir, I'll ask a very frank question. What is the quid pro quo? There is no quid pro quo. And only quid pro quo which the American administration has very kindly accepted is the strength and importance that Pakistan has. And if it fulfills the security requirements of the region, I think it indirectly and directly assists the United States administration in achieving their strategical objectives.

MR. SMITH. What did President Reagan and other members of the administration stress when they spoke to you about the strategic relationship?

PRESIDENT ZIA. They agreed with me totally that the relationship must be credible and durable, and that's what our efforts are.

MR. MONROE. Mr. President, billions of dollars in U.S. aid to the Shah of Iran eventually backfired because he became a dictator and the target of popular illwill. Yet you ruled by martial law for 5 years, no elections; you have the power in your own right to alter the Constitution. Your critics, opponents get thrown in jail and according to Amnesty International, frequently get tortured and ill-treated. Why should the United States bet billions of dollars more on a country right next to Iran that apparently is an undemocratic, one-man regime?

PRESIDENT ZIA. Mr. Monroe, if all of what you said was true, I wouldn't have been here today. If I can say, these are exaggerated reports. It is a military regime. We have no inhibitions about this. I am not elected representative of the people. But I think I can very proudly say that we command the confidence of 84 million today and that's why we are here. Otherwise, by now this government would have been thrown out. And I think we have our objectives; we have our aims; we have our policies. And one of the main basic aims is to have a peaceful transfer of power from the military to the civil regime, and also to increase Islamic democracy, which incidentally is not something which can come out from the air. All the basic principles are well-known to you and it is my effort to do what I can, and thereby pass the baton to the next runner for the lap.

. . . .

Chapter 13. East Asia

A. Regional Policies and Developments

1. General Statements of U.S. Policy in Asia

Document 459

Address by the Secretary of Defense (Weinberger) Before the Japan National Press Club, Tokyo, March 26, 1982[1]

Pillars of U.S. Asian Policy

It is most appropriate here in Japan to talk about Asia because Asia is such a dynamic and hopeful continent, and Japan is one of the most impressive features of Asia. I don't want to talk about the Soviet threat to Asia, not because it isn't important—it is, unfortunately, an extremely serious threat—but because I think this challenge is becoming more clearly recognized. I want to talk instead about Asia outside of the Soviet empire, the vibrant and forward looking part of Asia in which the United States has a very positive interest.

Ambassador Mansfield has said that the 21st century will be the Asian Century, and his rationale is not difficult to understand. Except for the politically and economically tragic situations in Soviet Asia, North Korea, Vietnam, Laos and Kampuchea, one sees spectacular modernization. The United States, as a Pacific power, has a natural, important connection with this exciting part of the world. A peaceful Pacific Ocean is the great highway whose sea-lanes presently travel over $100 billion of commerce each year. Interruption of those sea-lanes has brought major war in the past. And yet the importance of the Pacific today is greater than ever. As the Pacific links the United States and Asia, we are intensely interested in our relationships with that continent.

There are six pillars of America's Asian policy, pillars supporting a bridge across the Pacific if you will, which is serving and, we hope, will continue to strengthen Asia-American relations well into the 21st century.

First, the United States will remain a Pacific power, our dependence on overseas resources dictates our involvement which is, therefore, not totally unselfish. The American commitment, however, is larger than we would like because of the magnitude of the area to be covered and the aggressive growth of the Soviet challenge. Our Pacific Command includes the Indian Ocean, where access to oil is as important to Japan and Western Europe as it is to us. The United States has no imperialistic ambitions, and we are not committed to one world under our economic system. I pledge to our Asian friends and allies that, as they have all requested, the United States will, within its means, do as much as is necessary to ensure that the Pacific–Indian Ocean sea-lanes remain open for the free passage of trade of all seagoing nations.

Japan has become one of our most important allies. Japan's economy has virtually equalled that of the Soviet Union. And there is no question as to which will grow faster in the future. Although Japan and the United States are competing seriously in the economic sphere today, our culturally different nations are the two most politically and economically vibrant democracies in the world.

The treaty of mutual cooperation and security,[2] which is the linchpin of our relationship, is an arrangement which should remain. While the treaty obviously helps Japan, it also provides the United States with bases without which our ability to meet our Pacific security concerns becomes more costly and difficult. Some Americans, as well as some Japanese, have tried to link Japan's defense efforts to trade issues. While such linkage has obvious emotional appeal, we do not believe that action on

---

[1] Source: *Public Statements of Secretary of Defense Weinberger,* 1982. Secretary Weinberger visited Japan, Korea, and the Philippines between March 25 and April 2.

[2] Signed at Washington on January 19, 1960; for text, see 11 UST 1632.

trade problems resolves our concerns with defense—or vice-versa. Clearly, we hope that Japan will continue to widen access to its market by removing barriers which still make meaningful outside participation in the Japanese miracle difficult. Equal access, rather than an absolutely equal balance as [of] trade, will allow Japan and the United States to coexist as friendly economic competitors.

The defense relationship between Japan and America is already very close. I am here as the guest of Minister Ito, continuing a series of meetings conducted annually since 1977. Since 1978, the "Guidelines for Defense Cooperation" have linked Japan Self-Defense Forces with U.S. Forces in Japan in planning studies for the defense of Japan, in more and better bilateral military exercises, and most recently in studies of cooperation on Far Eastern contingencies outside of Japan impacting on Japanese security.

Japan's self-defense efforts are in my estimation frequently misunderstood and sometimes underestimated. We cannot ignore the substantial efforts Japan is already making to improve its defense capabilities. Our concern lies with the pace of these efforts.

We understand why Japan, recognizing its increasing vulnerability, has increased its strength to the present level. In May 1981, Prime Minister Suzuki and President Reagan acknowledged the appropriateness of a rational division of labor between Japan and the United States.[3] The Prime Minister stated that Japan could, within the limits of its constitution, defend its own territory, the seas and skies around Japan, and its sealanes to a distance of 1,000 miles.[4]

Yet, the Japanese forces today have not yet reached the point of being able to carry out their constitutional missions fully. Thus, they would have difficulty defending Japan. The defense of Japanese air space and sealanes out to 1,000 miles will require substantial improvements in military capabilities. To satisfy those critical defense missions will require increases in defense spending substantially greater than the current annual growth rate.

Although Japan cannot carry out its defense role fully today, if it's in its interest, it could with its economic vitality improve and increase within this decade its armed forces to the levels necessary to provide self-defense to the levels mentioned by the Prime Minister. Such actions by Japan would complement the buildup being undertaken by the United States and would contribute to Japan's own security and the stability of the entire free world.

Of course, no one in the United States wants to see Japan become a military superpower. But Japanese forces capable of providing sea and air defense in the Northwest Pacific could complement U.S. strategic and conventional forces in the area. If these Japanese and American elements are supplemented by U.S. sea control and projection forces in the Southwest Pacific and Indian Oceans, the vital arteries of free commerce in the Pacific would be strongly defended. Thus, Japan can, within the constraints of self-defense, contribute to her own and indeed to global security. This Japanese-American defense partnership on which free trade in the Pacific may increasingly depend, constitutes the second pillar of our Asian policy.

The third is our dedication to the principle of freedom and independence for the Korean Peninsula. The economic growth of the Republic of Korea from ashes in the mid-1950's is postwar Asia's second major success story. While the United States and Japan gave economic assistance to the Seoul Government, the United States shed its own blood to ensure that Korea remained free following independence. The Korean people themselves have shown the largest measure of willingness to sacrifice on behalf of their freedom from totalitarianism.

The suffering of the Republic of Korea did not end in 1945 or in 1954. Following occupation and attack from the North, it bravely fought back and built an impressive, industrialized country despite the fact that most industry was originally located in Northern Korea. The Republic of Korea provided forces to fight for freedom in Vietnam. It suffered economic stress resulting from skyrocketing energy costs in the 1970's and an expected shock when the United States announced an intention to withdraw its troops. President Reagan has put an end to Korean anxiety that it might have to stand alone against the North Korean threat.

President Reagan welcomed President Chun as our first head of state visitor in the new Administration. I will be in Seoul next

---

[3] For text of the joint communiqué issued by President Reagan and Prime Minister Suzuki on May 8, 1981, see *American Foreign Policy: Current Documents, 1981*, document 514.

[4] For a statement to this effect made by Prime Minister Suzuki at a news conference at the National Press Club on May 8, 1981, see *ibid.*, document 515.

week to participate in our annual security consultative meeting, witness our armed forces training together, and observe the 100th anniversary of Korean-American relations. The United States will continue to support the independence of the Republic of Korea. We are confident that the government is pursuing a course which will promote stability and economic growth, maintain a strong deterrent against aggression from the North and at the same time hold open the door to talks with Pyongyang should the North Koreans eventually see the logic of negotiations.

No development in recent years has so profoundly altered the strategic picture as our fourth pillar—the increasing rapprochement of the People's Republic of China with the United States and our allies in support of global peace and regional stability. In recent years, and especially since normalization of Sino-Japanese and Sino-American relations, China has moderated its foreign policies and evidences a real desire to improve state-to-state relations with its Asian neighbors.

Our policies toward China are predicated on the belief that a strong, secure and progressing China is in our national interest and that of our allies. We are prepared to contribute in a responsible way to China's modernization, both for the benefit of China and of the United States, and we want to do so in ways which enhance our own security and that of our allies and friends.

China and the United States share a common concern about the Soviet threat to stability. And we recognize that our individual efforts can be mutually reinforcing. China's leaders have welcomed our efforts to improve U.S. military capabilities in the Pacific as evidence of our intent to stand firm against Soviet expansionism.

Although there are issues on which we differ, there is a growing range of interests which we share. We seek to build an enduring relationship with China that recognizes our common interests and our differences and which permits us to take complementary actions when our common interests are challenged.

The fifth pillar of our Asian policy is our support for the Association of South-East Asian Nations (ASEAN). The viability and maturation of this vital political and economic group of nations located between East and West Asia can, if sustained, greatly aid regional stability.

We are linked by a Mutual Security Treaty[5] and by the Manila Pact[6] to the Philippines. Our access to Philippine bases is essential for maintaining the military balance in Southeast Asia. The bases provide key transshipment points for U.S. logistic resupply efforts to the Western Pacific and Indian Oceans and are important to the maintenance of military access to the region. Implementation of the 1979 Amendment to the Military Bases Agreement[7] has gone smoothly and the United States continues to enjoy unhampered use of the facilities. I look forward to visiting the Republic of the Philippines next week and meeting with my Philippine colleague, Minister Enrile.

In addition to continuing its longstanding defense ties with the Philippines, the United States cooperates on a bilateral basis to strengthen the self-defense capabilities of Indonesia, Malaysia, and Singapore. We welcome their contributions to regional stability.

Our other Southeast Asian ally, Thailand, faces hostile forces across its border. We will continue to provide the Thai with assistance to bolster self-defense improvements.

The sixth and newest pillar of United States Asian policy is our relationship with Southwest Asia. We are determined to preclude disruption or hostile control of Middle East oil reserves which are even more critical to East Asia and Western Europe than to ourselves. Indeed, if the Soviets did succeed in denying access to the oil fields, it could be disastrous to Japan. Since the invasion of Afghanistan we have maintained a strong naval presence in the Indian Ocean to maintain the sealanes of communication and to assure access to the Persian Gulf. We have arranged for increased funding for facilities in Southwest Asia because of our concern for regional stability. We will be improving our long-range airlift capabilities in order to lessen our disadvantage in projecting power in the vital Middle East and Persian Gulf region.

Progress in the development of our capabilities for operations in Southwest Asia is reflected in the continuing evolution of the

---

[5] The U.S.–Philippine Mutual Defense Treaty, signed at Washington on August 30, 1951; for text, see 3 UST 3947.

[6] The Southeast Asia Collective Defense Treaty, signed at Manila on September 8, 1954; for text, see 6 UST 81.

[7] Signed at Manila on January 7, 1979; for text, see 30 UST 863.

Rapid Deployment Joint Task Force (RDJTF). Because of the great range of possible threats in the region, prudent military planning requires the capability to deploy and employ a balanced and flexible U.S. projection force that combines the unique capabilities of each of our military services. A number of exercises have been conducted to evaluate progress. Operation Bright Star 82, conducted in October–November 1981, was the largest U.S. exercise ever conducted in the Southwest Asia region. Segments of the exercise involved forces deployed in the countries of the region. The continuing development of the RDJTF signifies the depth of the U.S. commitment to the defense of its interests in Southwest Asia.

In sum, I have tried to describe the importance the United States attaches to Asia, an importance that grows every day. Much of Asia is modernizing at an impressive rate, and not coincidentally, I am proud enough to say, those parts of Asia which have close ties with the United States are doing the best while those who are aligned with our adversary are suffering as a result. The United States seeks no domination and will continue to support Asia's dynamic growth and vitality. We will do our best to continue to strengthen our bridge across the Pacific and to keep the seas beneath that bridge open for use by all. I am pleased to make these remarks here in Tokyo, the capital of this impressive Asian democracy. Working together with our Asian allies and friends we hope to insure that the 21st century is bright for both Asians and Americans alike.

Document 460

Statement by the Assistant Secretary of State for East Asian and Pacific Affairs (Holdridge) Before a Subcommittee of the House Appropriations Committee, March 30, 1982[8]

U.S. Assistance Programs in East Asia

As always, I am very pleased to be here and present to you our budget estimates for fiscal year 1983. The area for which I am responsible, I believe, is one of the more crucial ones in the world today. It contains some very important elements of U.S. foreign policy. Japan, in the economic sense, is a very vital area of concern to us. We are very much concerned about the stability of the Korean Peninsula. There is the China situation which is one of my principal concerns as well.

And, finally, we are concerned about stability in Southeast Asia. Let me say Japan, of course, is our number two customer in the world. That is extremely important for the United States economy, and I think you are aware of some of the situations that we are following now in the defense area, and trade with Japan.

China has become our sixteenth largest customer, fifth in East Asia. The fact that it has been a friendly country over these last 10 years has been of enormous strategic value to us.

ASEAN has become our fifth largest customer. Last year the trade was 22.5 million. American investment is at least five billion. I think it is probably increasing.

Now it is a relatively stable area, all things considered. This is in the face of what one might call a remarkable buildup of Soviet military power in Northeast Asia; the extension of the military force along its southeast border, air power in the projection of the northeast region, which extends all the way down to Vietnam. It supports Vietnam in its invasion of Kampuchea, and projects its force through the Malacca straits, all the way into the Indian Ocean.

There is, of course, a continuing North Korean military threat, very significant, and very serious, that we have to take into account.

As I mentioned, in Southeast Asia there is this continual Vietnamese presence in Kampuchea, efforts to stifle the resisting forces and establish a puppet government in Phnom Penh and which at this very moment is threatening Thailand. The threat exists of a spillover of war into Thai-

---

[8] Source: *Foreign Assistance and Related Programs Appropriations for 1983: Hearings Before a Subcommittee of the Committee on Appropriations, House of Representatives, Ninety-seventh Congress, Second Session* (Washington, 1982), Part 4, pp. 269–272. Holdridge testified before the Subcommittee on Foreign Operations and Related Agencies. For the full text of his testimony, see *ibid.*, pp. 269–332. Holdridge's prepared statement, which he summarized before the committee, is *ibid.*, pp. 273–299.

land. Nevertheless, this has remained a remarkably stable area and I would like to credit our own presence there militarily as one of the factors for the stability. Another factor which has contributed to the stability is our security assistance and our development assistance programs throughout East Asia. These have helped, I think, markedly in furthering the United States national interest.

Now, what are we trying to accomplish in that part of the world? We are intent on strengthening our ties with our friends and our allies. This has been something which has been going on steadily. I think it is very productive in terms of having other countries see eye to eye with us in terms of national interest and following complementary courses in the international arena.

We are helping these countries maintain their independence and their territorial integrity against threats which in the case of Thailand, as I mentioned, are very active. This is also true in the case of Korea. We are able to maintain access to vital raw materials for which the region is a significant source; tin and rubber and petroleum products, just to name a few.

We are able to help protect key sea lanes in the region, especially those that link East Asia to the Indian Ocean and the Middle East. I mentioned the Soviet extension of power. It is critical to Japan, which gets 70 percent of its energy from the Middle East, that these sea lanes remain open.

We are able to enhance the stability of friendly governments. This has a number of ancillary purposes. These countries can serve as forces for peace and development. They can act in ways, with a friendly relationship with us, which furthers our own interests. Stability enables them to address human rights and to improve their own handling of this important problem, and to make progress in this particular field.

Our assistance programs enhance stability by mitigating poverty, addressing inequality, securing the forces against threats, and serving as a political symbol of the United States commitment. They help us to maintain our strong military presence, and I refer most specifically to the U.S. military bases in the Philippines which are at this point indispensable in terms of maintaining the balance of power in the Indian Ocean, and into the Middle East.

Let me deal with the three areas of concern in more specific terms. In Northeast Asia we are out to strengthen the Korean armed forces. I mentioned the threat from the North Koreans. They enjoy a strong military advantage which North Korea has now and which they probably will maintain for years to come.

Our programs in Korea are intended to address this disparity.

Now, let me mention China. In our requested fiscal year 1983 foreign aid and security assistance authorizing legislation there are proposed amendments which call for removing some existing wording which cuts China in the category of the Soviet Union as a Communist bloc country, which is antithetical to the interests of the United States.

What we are trying to do, and the President decided last year we would do, is to amend anachronistic laws that group China with the Soviet Bloc. The President, last year, decided that we should amend those laws which are arbitrary and anachronistic.

The foreign aid bill contains two proposals to end such discriminatory treatment. One, elimination of the prohibition on foreign assistance for China, and two, clarification that China is not ineligible for Public Law 480 programs. These are important proposals, designed to bring our laws into line with our critically important relationship with China, and start treating China just as we do any other friendly country.

Let me explain, Mr. Chairman, we have no intention of instituting a Public Law 480 program with China, nor an AID program with China. These changes are to remove China from the categories of countries along with the Soviet Union which we have regarded as hostile to our interests. It is not intended to open up a wide and major assistance program for the People's Republic.

Now, in Southeast Asia, one of our purposes is to maintain unity and confidence in the United States commitment, and this, given the threat Thailand faces, assumes a position of major importance. Thailand is a frontline state in our judgment. It does have a military threat to confront from Vietnam, across the Thai-Kampuchea border, and our failure to assist Thailand would cast doubt on our commitment.

We have a military security relationship with Thailand under the Manila Pact, and for us not to act to strengthen Thailand under such circumstances would certainly be regarded by other countries in ASEAN and elsewhere in Asia as the United States retreating from a commitment. And just at this moment, the Vietnamese military activity on the Thai border has reached a level which is the highest for several years, and there have been a number of instances in which Vietnamese troops have actually crossed the Thai border in minor incursions.

It is not beyond the realm of the possible that the Vietnamese could cross in force. One must take into account the threat against Thailand.

In our programs, in general, we have tried to address the areas of greatest concern, Korea is one where we have a force improvement program. Thailand is another. The third largest area of increase in our security assistance is Indonesia, which while not facing a direct threat, faces a typical threat from the Soviet Union as it moves down into those waters, and from Vietnam and its Asian capability.

The Indonesians are going through a process of trying to upgrade 100 battalions. Their military has lagged far behind. The income that the Indonesians have had from oil has gone essentially into economic development. The military has lagged behind, and we believe it is important to assist the Indonesians.

Let me say, in conclusion, we have tried to balance the need for budgetary constraint with the realities of Soviet pressure against our increasingly resource constrained East Asian friends and allies. Again, let me say, that we believe that our programs have been instrumental in helping to maintain security and economic progress, and that we hope that you will support us in these programs this year, and in the years to come.

Document 461

Statement by the Acting Secretary of State (Stoessel) Before the Senate Foreign Relations Committee, June 10, 1982[9]

Allied Responses to the Soviet Challenge in East Asia and the Pacific

Thank you very much, Mr. Chairman.[10] I appreciate this opportunity to discuss the allied response to the Soviet challenge in East Asia and the Pacific. I have a formal statement which I will submit for the record and I would now like to highlight some of the principal points in that statement.

Assistant Secretary Holdridge discussed the Southeast Asia situation before Senator Hayakawa's subcommittee last Tuesday.[11] Today, I will limit my remarks to northeast Asia and the South Pacific countries.

The contributions of East Asian and Pacific nations to the vitality and strength of the free world have grown enormously over the last 10 years. All evidence indicates that they will continue to do so over the next decade.

The largest and longest sustained economic growth rates for advanced, middle-income, and less developed countries are now found in Asia. Japan, Australia, New Zealand, and Korea have not only achieved outstanding success but have stimulated growth throughout the region by transferring resources and technology through assistance programs, investment, and trade. They also have made important contributions to economic growth in the Middle East and in African nations where the United States has vital interests.

This economic vitality is, of course, an intrinsic defense strength. Many East Asian and Pacific countries have embarked on military modernization programs while continuing to improve living standards. More important, perhaps, is the marked contrast between these societies and those

---

[9] Source: *East–West Relations; Focus on the Pacific: Hearings Before the Committee on Foreign Relations, United States Senate, Ninety-seventh Congress, Second Session* (Washington, 1982), pp. 3–5. For the full text of Acting Secretary Stoessel's testimony, see *ibid.*, pp. 1–16. His prepared statement is *ibid.*, pp. 5–10.

[10] Senator Charles H. Percy.

[11] See document 470.

of North Korea and Vietnam, whose immense armed forces are a great strain on mismanaged, stagnant economies. This contrast has been noted by the people in the area. It has helped bring about a near collapse of the export market for revolution in East Asia.

The Soviet objective in East Asia is to seek positions of maximum geopolitical strength from which to project power and influence. As in other areas, Moscow has used military force as its chief instrument, perhaps because of its inability to compete in the economic, political, and cultural areans. Specific Soviet objectives in the region include neutralizing Japan in any future conflict by intimidation and by undermining the United States–Japan alliance, diminishing the security of the sea lanes by positioning forces to interdict the shipment of petroleum and other key commodities, increasing access to Vietnamese air and naval facilities as a means of projecting Soviet military power, and limiting external assistance to China's modernization.

The aggressive use of power by the U.S.S.R. has increased the awareness among Asian nations of the danger posed by the buildup of Soviet forces. Each of our friends has reacted in its own way to the problem. The Japanese have taken what they called a comprehensive security approach to the threat. They believe they can best contribute to regional security through a combination of political, economic, and defense measures. These actions strengthen Japan's security at home and improve its cooperation with industrial democracies in the Third World.

Our security dialog with Japan focuses on a rational division of labor to meet our common strategic concerns. This concept of burdensharing covers several fields and envisages strengthened self-defense forces that enable Japan to assume primary responsibility for its own defense as well as for the protection of neighboring sealanes—more effective cooperation between American and Japanese forces under the Mutual Security Treaty.

Japan provides us bases that are indispensable to our strategy of forward deployment in the Asia–Pacific region. Cooperation includes joint planning for the defense of Japan and for Japanese facilitative assistance to our forces in meeting emergencies elsewhere in the Far East; joint exercises which have grown in frequency and in scope; technological cooperation in weapons development; and international cooperation on such issues as Afghanistan, Poland, refugees, and arms control, where Japan's position has been very close to our own.

Turning now to our ANZUS allies, Australia and New Zealand stand guard over a lengthy, secure line of communication between the Pacific and Indian Oceans. Australia, which is in the midst of a 5-year defense modernization program, will soon have a potent naval force backed by modern aircraft and a small but well-equipped and well-trained army. Its contribution to the alliance is an important one, both in terms of defending its island continent and maintaining peace in the region.

New Zealand and Australia have taken active roles in promoting security in the neighboring Southeast Asian and Pacific island nations. Both participate in the five-power defense arrangement and furnish development as well as military assistance to a number of regional states. Their contributions in this respect are very generous in relation to their resource base.

At the annual ANZUS ministerial meeting—which I will attend next week in Canberra—we plan to impress upon Australia and New Zealand our continued commitment to the alliance and to the maintenance of security in the Pacific and Indian Ocean area.

The maintenance of a credible deterrent to North Korean aggression is a key element in preserving peace and security in northeast Asia. In view of the significant advantages North Korea possesses in manpower and equipment, the Republic of Korea's unremitting commitment to force modernization is an indispensable component of this stability. The maintenance of a U.S. military presence in South Korea and the provision of adequate foreign military sales credit are necessary to the Republic of Korea's own defense efforts.

The Republic of Korea maintains an armed force of more than 600,000, backed by a large, ready reserve. To support this level of preparedness, it spends some 6 percent of its gross national product on defense.

Finally, continued good relations with China greatly enhance security and stability in East Asia. We share important strategic interests with the People's Republic of China as well as a common perception of Soviet ambitions worldwide. Our relations are currently at a sensitive juncture due to the Taiwan arms sales issue. We are attempting to resolve this problem through a continuing dialog with Beijing.

The recent visit of Vice President Bush to China[12] demonstrated this administration's desire to bridge differences and to strengthen cooperation. The Chinese welcomed Vice President Bush and showed a spirit of willingness to work toward resolution of our differences. I understand the Vice President himself has just briefed members of the committee on his visit.

The visit to China last week by Senate Majority Leader Baker further contributed to this spirit and certainly enhanced Chinese understanding of congressional views on the sensitive issues before us.

Let me conclude by noting that our allies and friends in East Asia and the Pacific are assuming an ever-increasing share of the defense burden of the area. It is essential that together we transmit a strong and unremitting signal of our resolve to protect our immense interests there.

Thank you, Mr. Chairman.

Document 462

Statement by the Under Secretary of Defense for Policy (Iklé) Before the Senate Foreign Relations Committee, June 10, 1982[13]

The Soviet Challenge in the Pacific and the U.S. and Allied Response

I am indeed happy to have this opportunity to discuss the Soviet challenge in the Pacific and the response of the United States and its allies. We believe there is good reason to expect that United States interests in Asia and the Pacific, already of vast importance, will become more important as the region's economic activity and potential continues to grow.

During the past decade and a half, the Soviets have taken disturbing steps to enlarge their military capabilities and expand their influence throughout the region. These efforts continue unabated. Soviet ground forces east of the Urals, including those on the sino-Soviet border, have increased since 1965 from 150,000 to almost half a million today. Recently issued modern equipment provides these forces increased mobility and fire power and improves their command and communications systems.

Soviet air forces in the four easternmost military districts are equipped with more than 3,000 combat aircraft, and the Soviets have approximately 100 SS-20 missiles, one-third of their SS-20 missile force deployed in Asia where they can strike United States and allied installations throughout the region.

The significant growth of modernization of the Soviet Pacific fleet has been of special concern to us. It is the Soviet Union's largest fleet, and contains roughly—Good morning, Mr. Chairman.[14] I am just summarizing the statement which I will submit in full.

THE CHAIRMAN [presiding].[15] Thank you.

DR. IKLÉ. The Soviet Union's Pacific fleet is the Soviet Union's largest fleet, and contains roughly one-third of all Soviet submarines, one-fourth of its principal surface combatants, one-third of all naval aircraft. Let me give you a feel for the size of the Soviet Pacific fleet. There are more than 80 principal service combatants, about 120 submarines of all types, dedicated land-based aviation, including—let's not forget—the nuclear capable backfire bomber. All this gives the Soviet Union a significant naval capability. Soviet use of ports and airfields in Vietnam aids their Indian Ocean deployments and improves, of course, their surveillance capabilities in the Pacific.

Mr. Chairman, we must also not forget the Vietnamese, with the largest, strongest, and most battle-tested military force in Southeast Asia. They are a significant threat, independent of the Soviets. Then there is North Korea, which maintains a large, formidable, highly trained military establishment supported by continuing defense expenditures which we estimate total at least 20 percent of their gross national product.

---

[12] For documentation concerning Vice President Bush's trip to China, May 5–9, see Chapter 13, Part D.

[13] Source: *East–West Relations: Focus on the Pacific*, pp. 17–20. For the full text of Under Secretary Iklé's testimony, see *ibid.*, pp. 16–30; for the text of his prepared statement, which he summarized before the committee, see *ibid.*, pp. 20–24.

[14] Senator Percy, who had left the hearing during Acting Secretary Stoessel's testimony, returned at this point.

[15] Bracketed note appears in the source text.

It is our policy to help maintain peace in the region and to encourage and support the stability and independence of friendly nations. We have now stopped the trend of the 1970's which saw our Pacific force structure reduced to well below the pre-Vietnam, that is to say, the 1960 levels. The force structure of the Pacific Command has remained relatively constant over the past year, and has benefited from the recent improvements in readiness, sustainability, and modernization of equipment.

In particular, the Naval force improvements include the introduction of the *Perry*-class guided missile frigates, continued addition to the fleet of *Los Angeles*-class attack submarines and *Spruance*-class destroyers, and introduction to the Pacific this fall of the first Trident fleet ballistic missile submarine.

In Korea, we are replacing older F–4D fighter bombers with newer F–16's, and have introduced a squadron of A–10 close air support aircraft. Our Army division in Korea has been provided new antitank helicopters and long-range artillery.

The 1982 budget and the proposed 1983 budget provide for increases in war reserves, fuel, ammunition, supplies, and other readiness enhancing improvements. However, they do not provide for the type of force structure increases which would enable the Pacific Command to meet its responsibilities simultaneously and adequately without reinforcement. Priority requirements in Europe and Southwest Asia are likely to perpetuate shortfalls in resources available to the Pacific.

We have requested funds to lease land in the Northern Marianas which, with our facilities in Guam and land in Palau now provides us critically needed training areas, and will insure that we retain a major alternative basing option should a change in our Pacific strategy or in our access to other facilities require it. Congress needs to act quickly, because the land-lease option expires on January 9, 1983, just 100 days into the new fiscal year. A failure to fund this 50-year lease, which would be renewable for another 50 years, would throw away an option that might be of tremendous value in the future. Funding the lease option would signal that the United States intends to remain a Pacific power.

Mr. Chairman, I realize this is a very small item in the budget, but I think it is of long-term strategic importance and value.

The cornerstone of our Asian security policy is our defense policy with Japan, based on the Treaty of Mutual Cooperation and Security. Recent years have seen a stronger recognition in Japan of the need for a stronger defense. Prime Minister Suzuki enunciated the role for Japanese forces when he stated in May 1981 that defense of Japan's territory, its surrounding seas and skies, and its sealanes out to 1,000 miles are legal under Japan's constitution and are, in fact, national policy.

However, we are concerned that in the Japanese defense program for 1983–87, which is now in its final stages of preparation, the Japanese Government might set only modest force levels as its 1987 goal. United States and Japanese defense officials agree that while achievement of these levels would substantially increase Japanese capabilities, it would not provide air and naval forces adequate to defend Japan's sealanes against the threats of 1990. Thus, we believe the less ambitious levels should be achieved as quickly as possible in the 1983–87 defense plan, so that Japan can move beyond them to acquire the forces needed to carry out the mission stated by the Prime Minister.

Japan's record is better on host nation support. Without our bases in Japan, our presence in the western Pacific would become far more costly and exceedingly difficult, if not impossible. Japan contributes annually about $1 billion to the costs of U.S. forces in Japan. This averages over $21,000 for each of the approximately 46,000 U.S. military personnel in the country, a contribution higher than that from any other U.S. ally.

The trends and magnitude of the military threat to Japan do not permit further procrastination. Mr. Chairman, Japan should assume the full responsibilities of national sovereignty. The time has come for that great nation to move toward a defense effort commensurate with its economic capability and responsive to the threat to its integrity.

Let me briefly touch on the Republic of Korea. That nation spends about 6 percent of its GNP on defense and, of course, provides substantial support for U.S. forces that are stationed there. The potential ramifications of another Korean conflict on the relationship of the great powers and the threat it would pose to the security of Japan make Korea's self-defense improvements a substantial and important contribution to peace in the region. We should therefore help the Koreans to increase their capabilities more rapidly by providing more FMS credits and at better terms.

Secretary Weinberger's April visit[16] underscored the importance we place on our security relationship with Korea, Japan, and a third staunch Pacific ally, the Philippines. Our unhampered use of facilities at Clark Air Base and Subic Naval Base is very important for the security of the Pacific. The Secretary's discussions helped set the stage for the late 1983 review of the Philippine basing agreement.

The People's Republic of China, although, of course, not an ally, seems to share our view of the danger from Moscow's expansionist drive into Asia. Indeed, the growing convergence of Chinese and American strategic interests has been the primary reason for the steady improvement of our bilateral relations over the past decade. Increasingly, we have found that where our common interests are threatened, it is useful to take parallel actions.

The People's Republic of China appears to have decided that containment of Soviet expansionism and the maintenance of a global balance of power depends for the the foreseeable future on the viability of U.S. military power and America's alliances throughout the world. As a result, as you know, Mr. Chairman, the Chinese actively support our security partnership with Japan. They are enthusiastic supporters of NATO, and they support a continued U.S. military presence in the Philippines and the western Pacific.

To wrap up this overview, in the South Pacific, the efforts of our ANZUS allies with the island nations and Southeast Asian nations are important contributions to the common defense. Australian forces cooperate with ours to maintain a strong Western presence in the Indian Ocean. Joint United States-Australian facilities enhance U.S. global command and control systems, and U.S. B–52's are permitted to transmit through Darwin on Indian Ocean reconnaissance missions. New Zealand and Australia enhance Western presence in Southeast Asia by conducting combined training with other members of the five-power defense arrangement.

Both Australia and New Zealand are valued by the South Pacific island nations as friends, sources of aid, and guarantors of security. They therefore help in denying the Soviets access to facilities in the South Pacific.

Mr. Chairman, our Asian allies have been generally supportive of our Indian Ocean deployments, even though these deployments take resources previously committed to the western Pacific. Our allies have been responsive to our arguments that we need a more rational division of labor, but this could change if they were to suspect that we are not arguing for burden sharing, but are actually seeking to reduce our commitments.

In the Pacific, our commitment as a minimum, is to maintain our forward deployed forces. At the same time, we must update the plans and procedures for allied cooperation in wartime. Through our security assistance programs, we must help our less developed friends and allies to improve their own capabilities for self-defense. We can show by our actions that our allies with us can and must do more so that our combined capabilities for the common defense will safely preserve the peace.

Thank you, Mr. Chairman.

[16] See footnote 1 to document 459.

Document 463

Statement by the Deputy Assistant Secretary of State for East Asian and Pacific Affairs (Shoesmith) Before Two Subcommittees of the House Foreign Affairs Committee, December 9, 1982[17]

Balancing Strategic Interests and Human Rights in Asia

Thank you very much, Mr. Chairman.[18]

I am, of course, pleased to be here today to testify at the conclusion of the series of hearings on balancing U.S. strategic interests and human rights in Asia which these two subcommittees have been conducting over these past few months. I, of course, will be speaking only from the perspective of East Asia, and my colleague

[17] Source: *Reconciling Human Rights and U.S. Security Interests in Asia: Hearings Before the Subcommittees on Asian and Pacific Affairs and on Human Rights and International Organizations of the Committee on Foreign Affairs, House of Representatives, Ninety-seventh Congress, Second Session* (Washington, 1983), pp. 432–435. For the complete text of Shoesmith's testimony, see *ibid.*, pp. 431–474. His prepared statement, which he summarized before the committee, is *ibid.*, pp. 435–440.

[18] Representative Sam Gejdensen, a member of the Subcommittee on Human Rights and International Organizations, was presiding.

Ambassador Schneider will cover South Asia.[19]

Let me begin, Mr. Chairman, by reemphasizing what Assistant Secretary Holdridge said in his testimony before these two subcommittees just 1 year ago.[20] On that occasion he pointed out that human rights is an integral part of this administration's foreign policy to be considered along with, and not against, other factors.

In following this policy direction, we in the East Asia and Pacific Bureau and in our embassies abroad view human rights improvement as a goal to be pursued in tandem with our security, political, and economic commercial interests.

A strong human rights policy strengthens our overall foreign policy by distinguishing us from our adversaries and by making it clear that American interests are based on American values and beliefs. One cannot define U.S. strategic interests without touching on all these elements of policy.

In its broadest terms, our principal strategic interest is, of course, in deterring the increasingly assertive Soviet presence in East Asia and the Indian Ocean. This can best be achieved by supporting the growth and stability of the region through a variety of security, political, economic, and commercial programs.

The contrast between the dynamic free market economies of East Asia and the seriously flagging Communist economies has been among our greatest strengths in the area. The success of free market economies has been, and should continue to be, a bulwark against Communist penetration in the area.

We have additional strategic objectives: Those of maintaining access to vital raw materials, for which the region is a significant source; protecting key sealanes of communication in the region and those that link East Asia to the Indian Ocean and the Middle East; and enhancing the stability of friendly governments of the area so that they may act in ways that further our mutual global security and other interests.

In this latter context, we believe that stable, self-confident governments based on popular consent and support will be more inclined to undertake actions which will improve the human rights situations and the humanitarian services in their countries.

We likewise believe that human rights abuses undermine governmental legitimacy and may thereby become a destabilizing factor tending to vitiate other components of our strategy to foster peace, stability, and prosperity in the region.

As I believe I have indicated in these few remarks, we do not believe that a line can be drawn or should be drawn between human rights interests and strategic interests. On the one hand, we cannot be indifferent to the adverse effects on our strategic interests of a pattern of persistent and gross violations of human rights within a country with which we are allied or whose cooperation we seek in the pursuit of such interests.

On the other hand, we must be concerned to exercise such influence as we can bring to bear in redressing human rights abuses in such a way as to maintain an effective working relationship with the government concerned. Without such a relationship, we will be unable to pursue either our strategic interests or our human rights concerns.

Perhaps the manner in which we have attempted to follow this balanced approach will be clear in discussing some of the specific questions which have been raised in the letter from Chairman Solarz and Chairman Bonker to the Under Secretary of State. I do not believe, Mr. Chairman, that quiet diplomacy can fairly be described as silent diplomacy. While we prefer to rely on diplomatic channels where relations with the government permits serious discussions of human rights problems, we do not shy away from speaking out when this approach can be most effective.

Our human rights reports, which are widely read, attempt to describe the human rights situation in the various countries of Asia in an accurate and objective manner. These reports I believe constitute the administration's assessment of the human rights record of nearly every government in

---

[19] David T. Schneider, Deputy Assistant Secretary of State for Near Eastern and South Asian Affairs, also testified at the hearing; see document 434.

[20] Holdridge testified before the two subcommittees on November 17, 1981, on the subject of U.S. human rights policy in East Asia and the Pacific. For the text of his testimony, see *Implementation of Congressionally Mandated Human Rights Provisions: Hearings Before the Subcommittees on Europe and the Middle East, on Asian and Pacific Affairs, on Human Rights and International Organizations, and on Africa of the Committee on Foreign Affairs, House of Representatives, Ninety-seventh Congress* (Washington, 1982), pp. 98–136.

the world and, I believe, have their effect in support of our human rights concerns.

Regardless of whether a government is popular or unpopular, it is often the case that our efforts to work together with a particular government in other areas can give rise to resentment by opposition groups against the United States. The fact, however, that our bilateral relations are necessarily conducted with a government concern is not indicative of our support for all of the domestic or foreign policies of that government.

Further, we also have contacts and discussions with groups or individuals in a country who do not agree with every aspect of that country's government's policy. And we try to make it a point to keep in touch with responsible opposition leaders and groups in order to listen to their points of view, to explain our policies, and to indicate where we can give them support. Our ambassadors and their staffs engage in this kind of activity on a regular basis.

On another point raised in the letter, I would like to comment that we do not feel it is useful to list successes and disappointments of any administration in the human rights field, since this contradicts the purpose of quiet diplomacy. A major drawback, of course, is that relying on traditional diplomacy or quiet diplomacy to advance our human rights interests is not as visible as public diplomacy.

But we believe the former is generally more effective, particularly when we have good relations with a particular government. Either to condemn or to take credit publicly would in our view undermine our ability to use our influence to promote general progress on human rights and to deal with specific cases.

In addition to the human rights reports, we do, however, make public statements during the year designed to complement our diplomatic channel.

In short, a careful mix of the two approaches, quiet diplomacy and public diplomacy, seems to us to be necessary.

Mr. Chairman, in my prepared statement, I have commented on the strategic interests and on the human rights situation in several of the countries—Korea, the People's Republic of China, Taiwan, and the Philippines—that were of particular interest to these subcommittees in my area. I will in the interest of time not at this point read these concerns in my prepared statement, but will be prepared, of course, to answer any questions which you or other members of the committee may have on those particular countries or particular problems in those countries.

Let me close then, Mr. Chairman, by saying that we welcome the support of you and these subcommittees, the support that has been given to our efforts to improve human rights conditions in East Asia and the Pacific. Your interest has helped stimulate, I believe, many governments in this region toward practices which promote both personal liberty and security for their societies as a whole.

I welcome the opportunity to be here today, and would be pleased to respond to any questions which you may have. Thank you very much, Mr. Chairman.

---

2. The ANZUS Pact

Document 464

Communiqué Issued Following a Meeting of the ANZUS Council, Canberra, June 22, 1982[1]

Thirty-first Meeting of the ANZUS Council

The 31st meeting of the ANZUS Council was held in Canberra on 21 and 22 June 1982.[2] The Hon. Warren Cooper, Minister of Foreign Affairs, New Zealand; Ambassador Walter J. Stoessel, Deputy Secretary of State, United States; The Hon. Tony Street, Minister for Foreign Affairs and the Rt. Hon. Ian Sinclair, Minister for Defence, Australia, represented their respective governments. Also participating were senior foreign affairs and defence officials of the three governments.

The Australian Minister for Foreign Affairs welcomed the other Council members

---

[1] Source: Department of State files.

[2] For a report on the ANZUS Council meeting by Assistant Secretary of State for East Asian and Pacific Affairs John Holdridge, see *U.S. Policies and Programs in Southeast Asia: Hearings Before the Subcommittee on East Asian and Pacific Affairs of the Committee on Foreign Relations, United States Senate, Ninety-seventh Congress, Second Session* (Washington, 1982), pp. 151–152.

and noted that 1982 marked the thirtieth anniversary of the entry into force of the ANZUS Treaty.[3] In the course of those three decades many challenges had confronted the treaty partners and a wide variety of issues had been taken up at the annual Council meetings. Throughout the period, there had been a preoccupation with threats to international peace and stability, both globally and in the region covered by the treaty. It was a disturbing reflection that the basis for this concern was as strong now as at any time in the recent past. The Soviet invasion and continuing occupation of Afghanistan, its increased military presence in Indochina and assistance to Vietnamese occupying forces in Cambodia, and the imposition of martial law in Poland demonstrated that the Soviet Union retained ambitions outside its own borders which could not fail to lead to a deterioration in the climate of international security. He added that the annual meetings of the Council formed a most significant part of continuing discussion at all levels between the three partners on the central issue of international security and other matters of mutual concern. The other Council members agreed with this assessment.

The Council members reaffirmed their strong commitment to the ANZUS Treaty and expressed satisfaction with the level of military co-operation established among the partners. They observed that, in addition to the continuing free flow of technical information and strategic intelligence among the partners, there was an active programme of exercises, exchanges and visits involving the partners' armed services. In particular they confirmed the high priority each partner placed upon a regular and comprehensive programme of naval visits to each other's ports, as well as to friendly ports in the Asia/Pacific region generally. They recognized the importance of access by United States naval ships to the ports of its Treaty partners as a critical factor in its efforts to maintain strategic deterrence and in order to carry out its responsibilities under the terms of the Treaty. In this regard the Australian and New Zealand members declared their continued willingness to accept visits to their ports by United States naval vessels whether conventional or nuclear-powered. They noted and accepted that it is not the policy of the United States Navy to reveal whether or not its vessels are armed with nuclear weapons.

The Council members noted the participation by the forces of each partner in exercise Kangaroo 81 and at the recent highly successful RIMPAC'82. The Council members reiterated the importance they attached to defence co-operation programmes arranged on a bilateral basis with countries of the region. While regretting that circumstances continued to require a military presence at the current high level in the Indian Ocean area, they noted measures taken there by the United States and Australia on an independent national basis, commensurate with the threats to security in the area, in particular from Soviet naval and land-based forces.

Noting that the Second Special Session of the General Assembly devoted to disarmament was currently proceeding in New York, the Council members reaffirmed their commitment to the negotiation of effective, balanced and verifiable measures of arms control, including reductions of nuclear armaments. They reaffirmed that the maintenance of national security continued to be the basis upon which all disarmament and arms control proposals needed to be evaluated.

The Council members welcomed, in particular, the agreement between the United States and the USSR for the opening of negotiations on strategic arms reductions, which they saw as constituting a positive approach towards the achievement of a stable strategic nuclear balance. They commented that President Reagan's proposals offered a practical and realistic basis for negotiations and expressed the hope that the Soviet Union would approach the START negotiations in the same spirit.

The Council members also stressed the need for continuing international efforts to inhibit the spread of nuclear weapons. They noted with concern the apparent trend of developments in several regions and reaffirmed their commitment to the Treaty on the Non-Proliferation of Nuclear Weapons. They reaffirmed that they would continue to consult among themselves and with other like-minded countries about ways in which the international non-proliferation regime could be strengthened. They welcomed the fact that agreement had been reached on the establishment of a working group within the Committee on Disarmament to examine verification and com-

[3] Signed at San Francisco on September 1, 1951, and entered into force on April 29, 1952; for text, see 3 UST 3420. For an account of the origins of the treaty, see Edward C. Keefer, "The Origins of the ANZUS Treaty and Council," Department of State *Bulletin*, August 1982, pp. 46–49.

pliance aspects of a Comprehensive Test Ban Treaty.

The Council members expressed their concern at persistent reports of the use of chemical weapons against civilian populations in South East Asia and Afghanistan.[4] They underline the need for a continuing international effort to investigate these reports and reaffirmed the need for continuing action by the international community towards the conclusion of a verifiable and effective ban on chemical weapons.

The Australian and New Zealand members were briefed by the United States members on the recent North Atlantic Treaty Organization summit meeting in Bonn. The Council members welcomed the NATO decision to engage in co-operative efforts to promote peace, progress and stability in regions outside the North Atlantic Treaty area.

The Council members emphasised their support for the Association of South East Asian Nations (ASEAN)[5] and noted with satisfaction the continued impressive development of co-operation between ASEAN member countries. They noted the importance of sustained economic progress for the security of the region and agreed to continue to provide economic and technical assistance to ASEAN countries. They also reaffirmed their support for ASEAN member countries' efforts to strengthen peace and security in the region and agreed to maintain close consultation with them.

The Council members reiterated their support for United Nations General Assembly Resolution 36/5[6] which calls particularly for the withdrawal of all foreign forces from Cambodia, and for ASEAN members' continuing efforts to implement it. They noted the positive contribution towards the resolution of the Cambodian problem made by the International Conference on Kampuchea in July 1981 and the *Ad Hoc* Committee of that conference.[7] They reaffirmed their conviction that the conflict in Cambodia should be settled by peaceful rather than military means, and that any such settlement should reflect the wishes of the Cambodian people themselves. A neutral, non-aligned Cambodia would pose no threat to its neighbors. The Council members noted the negotiations taking place to form a coalition of Khmer nationalist factions, and expressed the hope that the formation of a coalition would contribute to a political solution.

The Council members expressed once again their concern that any settlement should provide adequate guarantees of the security and territorial integrity of Thailand. They noted that the Soviet Union was stepping up its activity in the Asia/Pacific region; this was another factor tending to destabilize peaceful relations among regional states.

The Council members further agreed to continue essential humanitarian assistance to the Khmer people. The Council once again acknowledged the contribution made by ASEAN members in providing refuge and processing facilities for refugees fleeing from Indo-China.

The Council members expressed satisfaction with the continuing stability of the South Pacific region. They recognised the difficulties faced by many island states in the light of adverse external economic conditions and the paucity of their own resources. The Council members further recognized the need, in the light of continuing global security uncertainties, to encourage the maintenance of a stable security environment in the South Pacific as a necessary pre-condition for regional development. They pledged their commitment to continue and to expand practical co-operation with countries of the region in support of the maintenance of regional security and development.

The Council members emphasised the importance of the ANZUS partners' programmes of continuing development assistance, and they noted the complementary Australian and New Zealand Cooperative Defence Assistance Programs. The tripartite arrangements made by the United States, Australia and New Zealand for geoscientific research in the South Pacific under the Consultative Committee for Offshore Prospecting in the South Pacific represented a tangible demonstration of their co-operation in the development of the region.

The Council members agreed that effective regional co-operation was fundamental to the continuing development of the South Pacific region. They reaffirmed the impor-

---

[4] For documentation concerning this subject, see Chapter 13, Part A–5.

[5] For documentation relating to the Association of Southeast Asian Nations, see Chapter 13, Part A–4.

[6] Adopted by the U.N. General Assembly on October 21, 1981; for text, see *American Foreign Policy: Current Documents, 1981*, document 552.

[7] For information concerning the International Conference on Kampuchea held in New York, July 13–17, 1981, see *ibid.*, documents 547 and 548.

tance of the South Pacific Forum as a focus for discussion amongst heads of government of major issues affecting the area, of the South Pacific Bureau for Economic Cooperation in fostering common approaches to economic issues and of the South Pacific Commission in helping promote social and economic development in the island countries. They also welcomed the continued development of more specific, functional regional cooperation. In this regard the Australian and New Zealand members expressed continuing support for the development of the Pacific Forum Line on a sound economic basis, and for the work of the Forum Fisheries Agency and welcomed the various measures being undertaken under the auspices of the Commonwealth Secretariat in areas of high priority to developing island economies.

Council members welcomed the increased participation in South Pacific regional activities of the Micronesian entities and the progress being made in the status of negotiations between the entities and the United States leading towards the termination of the trusteeship.[8]

The Council discussed the Law of the Sea Convention, adopted in New York on 30 April 1982.[9] The Australian and New Zealand members noted with particular satisfaction that the draft convention would consolidate and reinforce traditional high seas freedoms and the right of innocent passage through the territorial sea and establish rules for passage through straits, archipelagoes and exclusive economic zones. They emphasised the importance for Western security interests of free movement of naval vessels in accordance with international law. They outlined the importance of the convention as a peaceful and orderly regime for the world's seas and their resources, and emphasised its significance for the straits and archipelagic states to their north and for the island countries of the Pacific region. They urged that the United States should most carefully consider these aspects before deciding its attitude towards signature of the convention. The United States member noted these views, and undertook that his government would consult closely with its friends and allies on the matter.

The Council welcomed China's continued commitment to economic modernisation and to a peaceful environment. The Council noted the important contribution of China to the political stability and strategic outlook of the Asia/Pacific region. The Council members emphasised the value of close relations between the United States and China. They expressed the hope that as a result of the discussions currently being held between the two countries, they would be able to resolve their differences.[10]

The Council noted with regret that, in North Asia, the Korean Peninsula remained an area of tension and armed confrontation. In the face of the threat from the North, the Council reaffirmed its support for the political integrity of the Republic of Korea. The Council called upon the DPRK to renounce hostile intentions towards the ROK and to enter into real and direct negotiations with it as essential prerequisites to the reduction of tension in the region.

The Council welcomed the Government of Japan's willingness to play an active and constructive role in the political and economic affairs of the Pacific region. The Council reaffirmed its support for the Japanese Government's commitment to upgrade its self-defence capability, as reflected in the priority given to defence expenditure in the 1979–84 budgets, and welcomed efforts by Japan towards assuming greater responsibility for its own defence and that of its maritime surroundings. Council members valued highly the fact that Japan was implementing its pledge to double development assistance in the period 1981–85, and that increased aid was being made available.

The Council members welcomed the cease-fire in the Falkland Islands and expressed the hope that it would lead to an early end to all hostilities in the South Atlantic. Members noted that the British Government, in making its decision to use force to recapture the Falkland Islands, was exercising its inherent right of self-defence under Article 51 of the United Nations Charter and upholding the principle that the unprovoked use of force should not be allowed to go unchecked.

The Council members reaffirmed their concern over the continuing Soviet occupation of Afghanistan and its destabilizing international effects, particularly in the

[8] For documentation relating to these negotiations, see Chapter 13, Part A–3.

[9] The U.N. Convention on the Law of the Sea; for text, see U.N. document A/CONF.62/122 (October 7, 1982). The United States did not sign the convention.

[10] For the U.S.–China Joint Communiqué of August 17, 1982, and related documentation, see Chapter 13, Part D.

South Asian region. They stressed that the Soviet invasion of Afghanistan was a flagrant violation of the fundamental principles governing international relations and, as had been demonstrated in many forums, was totally unacceptable to the international community. They noted in particular that the Soviet Union continued to carry out harsh, repressive action against the people of Afghanistan, including bombing of cities and villages, destruction of crops and livestock and the detention of thousands of citizens. This had led to the creation of the largest single refugee problem in the world, with over 3 million refugees in Pakistan and Iran. Treaty partners believed that there could be no lasting peaceful settlement and political solution to the situation in Afghanistan without the Soviet Union withdrawing all its forces, so that Afghanistan could regain its sovereign, independent and nonaligned status. The Council members noted the continuing efforts of the United Nations Secretary-General in seeking to bring about a negotiated and peaceful settlement.

The Council members discussed recent developments in the Middle East. They expressed their support for Security Council Resolutions 508 and 509[11] calling for an immediate cessation of military activities and demanding that "Israel withdraw all its military forces forthwith and unconditionally". The Council members also expressed their full support for the Lebanese Government, for the sovereignty and territorial integrity of Lebanon, and for early steps which would enable the withdrawal of all foreign military forces from Lebanese territory. The Council members also emphasized the importance to the world's economy, and its security, of stability in the Gulf region. They hoped that the Iran–Iraq conflict would rapidly be resolved.

The Council members welcomed the completion of Israel's withdrawal from the Sinai and noted that the Sinai Multinational Force and Observers (MFO) represented a significant contribution to the development of a sense of mutual security between nations in the Middle East. Council members underlined the importance of finding a way to satisfy Palestinian political aspirations while ensuring the security of all states in the region as called for in Security Council Resolution 242.[12] They called for a determined effort by all to move forward in a constructive search for a just and lasting peace.

The Council members discussed global economic prospects, the outcome of the recent Versailles Economic Summit and a range of current international development issues. They noted that the world economic situation remained seriously depressed with continuing high levels of inflation and high real interest rates in most countries, sluggish growth and high unemployment, stagnation in world trade and large external current account imbalances. On the positive side, it was noted that inflationary pressures in a number of developed countries had eased and they agreed that a continued decline in inflation and inflationary expectations was essential for renewed and sustainable economic growth and a fall in real interest rates. They agreed on the need to strengthen their efforts to stop the slide towards protectionism, including agricultural protectionism, to support measures to dismantle protectionist barriers and to strengthen and improve the multilateral trading system. In this regard, they supported strongly the Summit participants' resolve to address these and other major international trade issues at the forthcoming GATT ministerial meeting, and commended to that meeting the Australian Prime Minister's recent proposals to halt the trend to protectionism, to reduce levels of protection and to eliminate export incentives and subsidies over a period of 5 years.

The Council members welcomed the resolve of the major industrial countries at the Versailles summit to pursue fiscal and monetary policies aimed at reducing inflation, promoting economic growth and more stable exchange rates and to intensify their economic and monetary cooperation. They welcomed the commitment shown by the major Western Alliance governments to pursue economic relations with the USSR and Eastern Europe consistent with political and security interests and on the basis of financial caution and commercial prudence. They endorsed and welcomed the decision to exchange information in the OECD and other appropriate forums on all aspects of economic, commercial and financial relations with these countries. They also welcomed the summit participants agreement to the launching of global negotiations as a major political objective.

The Council members noted that the present easing of the oil market and the temporary halt in oil price increases would assist global economic recovery. They

[11] Adopted June 5 and 6, 1982; for texts, see documents 351 and 354.

[12] Adopted November 22, 1967; for text, see *American Foreign Policy: Current Documents, 1967*, pp. 616–617.

agreed nonetheless that the treaty partners should not be deflected from their longer-term policies of energy conservation and development of alternative energy sources.

Following their discussion of the problems confronting the developing countries, the Council members noted that developed countries have a very real interest [in] assisting the developing countries to overcome their development problems and to participate for mutual benefit in the Western economic system. An important element in this process would continue to be the provision of adequate official development assistance, but it was also vital for the economic development process that trade relations between developed and developing countries expand rapidly in a liberal international trading environment. Council members also recognised the need for continuing grant or other aid to smaller developing countries particularly in the South Pacific. Continuing efforts were also required to assist developing countries and to improve the international economic system.

The Council members agreed to meet again in Washington in 1983 at a date to be decided.

---

3. The Southwest Pacific

Document 465

Letter From the Representative at the United Nations (Kirkpatrick) to the U.N. Secretary-General (Perez de Cuellar), November 18, 1982[1]

Request for U.N. Observation of Micronesian Plebiscites

In accordance with rule 3 of the rules of procedure of the Trusteeship Council, my Government hereby requests the convening of a special session of the Trusteeship Council at which my Government will request the Council to organize and dispatch a mission or series of missions to observe plebiscites in Palau, the Marshall Islands and the Federated States of Micronesia.

It is my pleasure to inform you that my Government has recently completed negotiations with three duly elected constitutional Governments of the Trust Territory of the Pacific Islands—the Governments of Palau, the Marshall Islands and the Federated States of Micronesia—on their future political status.

The agreed arrangements are incorporated in a document known as the Compact of Free Association and a series of subsidiary and related agreements, copies of which this Mission has recently furnished to the President and the Secretary of the Trusteeship Council.

These documents are now being committed to a process of consideration and approval by each of the four signatory Governments in accordance with their constitutional processes and by the voters of Palau, the Marshall Islands and the Federated States of Micronesia by plebiscites in which the voters will be invited either to approve the Compact of Free Association or to ask their Government to negotiate independence or a closer relationship with the United States.

The Administering Authority and the Micronesian Governments envisage that this process will lead to the termination of the trusteeship. It has long been their wish that this important act of self-determination should be conducted under the observation of the United Nations, and they so agreed in 1978. The Trusteeship Council followed such a procedure in sending a mission to observe the act of self-determination carried out in the Northern Mariana Islands in June 1975.

In carrying forward the process of self-determination, the United States as Administering Authority is continuing to observe and implement Article 76 *b* of the Charter of the United Nations which provides that the basic objectives of the trusteeship system are "to promote the political, economic, social, and educational advancement of the inhabitants of the Trust Territories, and their progressive development towards self-government or independence as may be appropriate to the particular circumstances of each territory and its peoples and the freely expressed wishes of the peoples concerned, and as may be provided by the terms of each trusteeship agreement" and Article 6 of the Trusteeship Agreement for the Trust Territory of the Pacific Islands.

Given the limited character of the special session, my Government believes that the

---

[1] Source: U.N. document T/1844.

30-day period of notification referred to in rule 4 of the Council rules which, "as a rule", is to precede the date of a session of the Council might, in this instance, be abridged. Should that prove impossible, my Government requests that, in any event, and for reasons of convenience and economy, the special session of the Trusteeship Council be held before the conclusion of the current session of the General Assembly.

I should like to request that this letter be circulated as an official document of the Trusteeship Council.[2]

Document 466

Prepared Statement by the President's Personal Representative for Micronesian Status Negotiations (Zeder) Before a Subcommittee of the Senate Foreign Relations Committee, December 10, 1982[3]

Micronesian Political Status Negotiations

1. HISTORY

Negotiations began in 1969. The United States offered territorial status to the people of the Trust Territory of the Pacific Islands, which their elected representatives generally rejected in favor of a looser, but still close, relationship known as free association. (The United States has administered the islands since World War II and, since 1947, under a Trusteeship Agreement with the United Nations.)[4]

The exception was the people of the Northern Mariana Islands, who in 1972 began separate negotiations with the United States for territorial status, completed in 1975 in the "Covenant to Establish a Commonwealth . . . in Political Union with the United States" (Public Law 94–241 of March 24, 1976).[5]

Negotiations for this status of free association, which the Micronesians themselves had proposed, continued throughout the 1970's under three administrations. By 1978, as the result of action by the remaining districts of the Trust Territory on a draft constitution for a unified Micronesia, three separate entities had emerged—Palau, the Marshall Islands, and the Federated States of Micronesia (FSM)—and the United States had agreed to negotiate with each of them for a common relationship[6]

---

[2] Regarding these negotiations and the resulting agreements, see *infra*.

[3] Source: *Micronesian Status Negotiations: Hearing Before the Subcommittee on East Asian and Pacific Affairs of the Committee on Foreign Relations, United States Senate, Ninety-seventh Congress, Second Session* (Washington, 1983), pp. 7–10. For the complete text of Ambassador Zeder's testimony, see *ibid.*, pp. 2–22.

[4] For text, see 12 Bevans 951.

[5] For text, see 90 Stat. 263. Ellipsis appears in the source text.

[6] The Statement of Principles signed by representatives of the United States and the three Micronesian Political Status Commissions in Hilo, Hawaii, April 9, 1978, reads as follows:

"1. An agreement of free association will be concluded on a government-to-government basis and executed prior to termination of the United Nations trusteeship. During the life of the agreement the political status of the peoples of Micronesia shall remain that of free association as distinguished from independence. The agreement will be subject to the implementing authority of the United States Congress.

"2. The agreement of free association will be put to a United Nations observed plebiscite.

"3. Constitutional arrangements for the governance of Micronesia shall be in accord with the political status of free association as set forth in these principles.

"4. The peoples of Micronesia will enjoy full internal self-government.

"5. The United States will have full authority and responsibility for security and defense matters in or relating to Micronesia, including the establishment of necessary military facilities and the exercise of appropriate operating rights. The peoples of Micronesia will refrain from actions which the United States determines after appropriate consultations to be incompatible with its authority and responsibility for security and defense matters in or relating to Micronesia. This authority and responsibility will be assured for 15 years, and thereafter as mutually agreed. Specific land arrangements will remain in effect according to their terms which shall be negotiated prior to the end of the trusteeship agreement.

"6. The peoples of Micronesia will have authority and responsibility for their foreign affairs including marine resources. They will consult with the United States in the exercise of this authority and will refrain from actions which the United States determines to be incompatible with its authority and responsibility for security and defense matters in or relating to Micronesia. The United States may act on behalf of the peoples of Micronesia in the area of foreign affairs as mutually agreed from time to time.

"7. The agreement will permit unilateral termination of the free association political status by the processes through which it was entered and set forth in the agreement and subject to the continuation of the United States defense authority and responsibility as set forth in Principle 5, but any plebiscite terminating the free association political status will not require United Nations observation.

"8. Should the free association political status

whose provisions would be set forth in a document known as the Compact of Free Association.

The Compact and its first several related agreements were initialed, but not signed, in October and November 1980.[7]

This administration, upon assuming office, conducted a comprehensive review of policy toward the Trust Territory and in September 1981 determined that the Trusteeship should indeed be terminated and that the political status negotiations should be concluded on the basis of the initialed Compact.

Negotiations resumed in October 1981 on some revisions to the initialed Compact and on the remaining agreements related to it. The negotiations were essentially concluded when I signed the Compact and its related documents with the President of the Marshall Islands on May 30, 1982, and with the chief negotiators for Palau and the Federated States of Micronesia on August 26 and October 1, 1982, respectively.[8]

2. WHAT THE COMPACT PROVIDES

The relationship of free association has no precedent in U.S. constitutional practice and few precedents in international law. Essentially, it would create three sovereign states in the western Pacific which would enjoy full internal self-government and very substantial authority in foreign affairs but would have vested in the United States full responsibility and authority for their defense for minimum periods of 15 years (in the cases of the Marshall Islands and the FSM) or 50 years (in the case of Palau).

The United States would provide agreed amounts of grant financial assistance and certain Federal programs and services, for the same minimum periods. Forty percent of the grant funding (which in turn is the major part of the Compact funding) would be earmarked for economic development, a provision which the administration believes would give each of the three states a reasonable chance of achieving economic self-sufficiency.

The basic relationship of free association would be indefinite in duration, subject to termination by mutual agreement or by the unilateral action of any of the governments. The economic and defense provisions described above would be subject to renegotiation and renewal at the end of their specified minimum periods.

The Compact's funding scheme provides for the diminution of U.S. grant assistance after the 5th and 10th years, but on the other hand a system of partial adjustment for inflation tied to the performance of the U.S. domestic economy would help to maintain the value of the funding over the years.

The estimated cost of the United States over the initial 15-year period would be approximately $2.2 billion before adjustment for inflation. Funding for Palau during the 16th through 50th years would be provided entirely out of an initial investment of $60 million made during the first year.

This figure of $2.2 billion over 15 years compares with a projected cost of $3.1 billion for continuing the Trusteeship over the same period, assuming that the same kinds of programs now in operation in the Trust Territory were to continue. Because a number of specific Compact grants would be funded in the first 2 or 3 years of free association, there would be no saving in those years. From the 4th year onward, however, the annual savings would begin to accrue.

The Compact and its subsidiary agreements provide that the United States will continue to provide the services of the Federal Aviation Administration, the Civil Aeronautics Board, the National Weather Service, and, in the event of natural disasters, of the Federal Emergency Management Agency. In addition, the United States Postal Service would continue to provide international postal service, although as the result of a modification negotiated just this year each of the three governments would assume responsibility for its domestic postal operations. The costs of these services are included in the figures mentioned above.

---

be mutually terminated the United States' economic assistance shall continue as mutually agreed. Should the United States terminate the free association relationship, its economic assistance to Micronesia shall continue at the levels and for the term initially agreed. If the agreement is otherwise terminated the United States shall no longer be obligated to provide the same amounts of economic assistance for the remainder of the term initially agreed. An early free association agreement based on the foregoing eight principles shall be pursued by the parties." (Department of State *Bulletin*, June 1978, p. 49)

[7] For an announcement of the initialing of the Compact, see *American Foreign Policy: Basic Documents, 1977–1980,* pp. 962–964.

[8] For a summary of the Compact and its related agreements, see U.N. document T/1851: *Report of the United Nations Visiting Mission to Observe the Plebiscite in Palau, Trust Territory of the Pacific Islands, February 1983,* pp. 3–10.

Returning for a moment to defense matters in more detail, the Compact and its subsidiary agreements would permit the United States to continue to operate the Kwajalein Missile Range for a period of up to 30 years and would provide us contingency use-rights in Palau for military purposes: specifically, a small exclusive-use area and a larger, adjacent nonexclusive-use area for military training; joint use of two existing airfields; and use of a portion of the harbor. It should be stressed that these are contingency rights and that the United States has no present intention to establish military facilities in Palau. There is no comparable reservation of use rights in the FSM.

In addition, the United States undertakes in the Compact to defend the Freely Associated States as the United States and its citizens are defended for the minimum period mentioned earlier: 15 years in the cases of the Marshall Islands and the FSM, and 50 years in the case of Palau. For the same minimum periods the United States would have the right, after consultation, to disapprove action by any of the governments which in our view compromised our ability to provide such defense.

Further, the United States under the Compact has the right to foreclose use of the territory of the Freely Associated States by the military forces, or for the military purposes of, any third nation. That right would extend in each jurisdiction until otherwise mutually agreed, and in return the United States would for the same period guarantee the defense of each of the states on basis comparable to that which underlies our mutual security agreements with our closest allies. The intent of this provision is to ensure that the territory of Micronesia may never again be used for purposes of aggression against the United States, or against the Micronesians themselves, as it was in World War II.

Other agreements subsidiary to the Compact of Free Association deal with such matters as telecommunications, extradition, the turnover of Federal property to the Micronesian governments, the status of U.S. forces who may be stationed in Micronesia (including personnel at Kwajalein and the Military Civic Action Teams which now operate in Palau and three of the four states of the FSM), and other technical matters.

[3.] SPECIAL NEGOTIATING ISSUES

The constitution adopted by the electorate of Palau in July 1980 contained three provisions which, if literally applied, would have made it impossible for the United States to enter into free association with Palau. They concerned the banning of nuclear, chemical, biological and other substances; a very extensive claim of maritime sovereignty which would have brought Palau into conflict with neighboring states; and the use of the right of eminent domain by the Government of Palau. The Palauan Constitution itself provides remedies for the first two of those issues, which have been resolved through signed agreements related to the Compact. The third issue is resolved in the agreement on Military Use and Operating Rights, whose contingency use provisions are summarized above. (An administration position paper attached to this outline treats these issues in greater detail.)[9]

In the case of the Marshall Islands, the Compact undertakes to make a comprehensive settlement of all claims arising out of the nuclear testing program which the United States conducted at Bikini and Enewetak Atolls in the northern Marshalls from 1946 to 1958, as well as to meet the intent of existing U.S. legislation on medical treatment of the persons affected by the program and to continue to provide supplemental food to them for a number of years. The subsidiary agreement to this effect provides about $150 million in payments and programs and, if approved in the Marshalls and funded by the Congress, would also have the effect of mooting about $7 billion in claims against the United States and its contractors now pending in the Federal courts. The administration regards the signed agreement as entirely satisfactory, but President Kabua of the Marshalls has proposed revisions to it. I am leaving Washington tommorrow to meet with him, members of his staff, and some of the affected people and their legal representatives to try to reach agreement on a revision of this agreement. It is the only major piece of unfinished business in the negotiations.

[4.] THE APPROVAL PROCESS

The Compact provides that it must be approved by the three Micronesian governments in accordance with their constitutional processes (which includes action by their legislatures) and by their voters in a plebiscite.

The original intention was to hold the plebiscite simultaneously in all three ju-

[9] For text, see *Micronesian Status Negotiations*, pp. 10–13.

risdictions, but this eventually proved impossible because of the differing pace of their respective negotiations with us. We have therefore acceded to the idea of different dates. The first plebiscite will take place in Palau on Tuesday, January 11. We hope that plebiscites can follow soon after in both the Marshall Islands and the FSM—certainly within the first few months of 1983.

In each jurisdiction there will be a voter information program leading up to the plebiscite. The program in Palau began in early September and is going full tilt. I saw it in operation when I was there a few weeks ago. The organizers of the program are using public meetings, published materials including translations of the Compact into Palauan and two other local languages, and daily radio and television broadcasts to inform the voters of the issues before them.

The plebiscite in Palau, and those to follow in the other two jurisdictions, will be acts of self-determination to which we will want to point with pride when we approach the United Nations about terminating the Trusteeship. We and the Micronesian negotiators agreed long ago that the United Nations should be invited to observe the plebiscites (as it did the plebiscite on the Northern Marianas Covenant in 1975). Accordingly, we have asked for a brief special session of the U.N. Trusteeship Council at which we can present our formal request for the dispatch of all three plebiscite observer missions. That session will begin in New York next Thursday, December 16.[10]

The other portion of the approval process will take place here in Washington, when the administration presents the Compact to the Congress for consideration. We intend to present it as a Joint Resolution for enactment as a Public Law of the United States, which is the same way the Northern Marianas Covenant was presented and approved. Majority approval of both Houses would be required, for the Compact will constitute a multi-year authorization and will amend numerous domestic laws. The Compact would thus be an Executive-Congressional Agreement and contain international obligations.

We expect to submit the Compact early in the life of the 98th Congress, although we realize that the relevant Committees may choose to give it no more than preliminary consideration until the voters of Micronesia have spoken in the plebiscites. We consider the Compact's path through the Congress to be a matter entirely within the purview of the Senate and the House of Representatives, respectively.

5. Terminating the Trusteeship

The 1947 Trusteeship Agreement prescribes no procedures for its own termination, and there is no real precedent in U.N. practice because this one is the only strategic trusteeship ever established. Ultimate responsiblity for it therefore rests with the Security Council, whereas in the cases of the other ten trusteeships—all now terminated—the body with ultimate responsibility was the General Assembly. Like the General Assembly, the Security Council has (under Article 83(3) of the U.N. Charter)[11] availed itself for the assistance of the Trusteeship Council in overseeing our administration of the Trusteeship.

To date we have said only that we will take up the matter of termination with the appropriate United Nations bodies—the Trusteeship and Security Councils—at the appropriate time. We will decide our precise course of action closer to the event.

There has been much speculation over the years that our attempt to terminate the Trusteeship might be frustrated by a veto in the Security Council. We believe that no nation or group of nations could in good conscience object to, or attempt to obstruct, the free exercise of the right of self-determination by the peoples of the Trust Territory. In the exercise of our responsibility as Administering Authority under the Trusteeship Agreement, we will seek to prevent procedural maneuvers aimed at obstructing the realization of that right.

---

[10] The Trusteeship Council met in special session, December 16–20, 1982. At its 1543d meeting, on December 20, the Council adopted Resolution 2174 (S–XV), by which it decided to send visiting missions to Palau, the Marshall Islands, and the Federated States of Micronesia to observe the plebiscites. The resolution was adopted by a vote of 3 (United States, United Kingdom, and France) to 1 (Soviet Union); for text, see U.N. document T/L.1233.

[11] For text, see 3 Bevans 1153.

4. Developments Affecting Southeast Asia

Document 467

Statement by the Deputy Secretary of State (Stoessel) Before the Fourth Ministerial Meeting of the United States and the Association of Southeast Asian Nations, March 9, 1982.[1]

ASEAN–U.S. Dialogue

I am delighted to welcome you to the fourth ASEAN–U.S. dialogue. It is especially gratifying for me to meet with representatives of a regional group which has achieved an unqualified success in bringing progress, stability, and international prestige to its member countries. The cooperation which your nations have attained in the economic and political fields, both among yourselves as well as with the rest of the world, is a glistening example for the rest of us.

I am particularly proud of the close partnership which my country has established with ASEAN. It is a model for the way in which nations can work together on common problems for the common benefit. I can assure you that this administration is determined to continue the high level of cooperation, friendship, and openness which has been established with the ASEAN states; to listen carefully to your concerns; and to respond positively to the very best of our ability.

The meeting which begins today is part of a diverse and constructive U.S.–ASEAN interaction which has been crucial to our mutual efforts to deal with many difficult issues. The process has taken place through the formal dialogue meetings, through participation by Secretaries of State in post-ASEAN ministerial consultations with dialogue partners, through the ASEAN Washington committee, and through frequent get togethers on many subjects. This fruitful day-by-day exchange truly demonstrates, as Philippine Foreign Minister Romulo stated at the last dialogue meeting that ASEAN and the United States share long-range concerns for the continued stability and sustained growth of the ASEAN region.

The dialogue process has helped ASEAN achieve some very impressive accomplishments.

First, and particularly impressive, is ASEAN's resolute effort to achieve a peaceful solution to the tragic situation in Vietnam-occupied Kampuchea, which the United States has strongly supported and will continue to support. ASEAN's effectiveness in marshalling international support for its position, and in keeping the pressure on Vietnam to agree to a negotiated settlement which allows the Cambodian people self-determination under U.N.-supervised elections, has provided conclusive evidence of the strength, diplomatic skill, and maturity of the ASEAN nations.

Another impressive accomplishment facilitated by the dialogue process has been the successful effort to deal, in humanitarian fashion, with the inundation of Indochina refugees, which only 3 years ago posed a severe crisis for ASEAN. ASEAN efforts, including establishment of regional processing centers and cooperation with the international community on refugee relief and resettlement, have converted this into a manageable, though still difficult, problem. It is doubtful that this could have been accomplished without the existence of ASEAN and the dialogue process. The United States is continuing to support ASEAN and to live up to its humanitarian obligations by accepting large numbers of Southeast Asian refugees for resettlement.

The dialogue process has brought about concrete and practical improvements in economic and commercial relations between ASEAN and the United States. The second dialogue meeting in 1978 contributed to the U.S. decision to support negotiation of the common fund. The United States signed the resulting agreement and is prepared to take further steps toward ratification provided that commodity agreements decide to associate with the fund. The United States also signed the International Rubber Agreement and played a central role in the establishment of its headquarters in Malaysia, an important ASEAN goal. We have cooperated in an ASEAN development program, which addresses crucial regional problems by sharing our technology and experience. These programs are moving forward at a good pace. We intend to build on these programs to further advance ASEAN regional development.

In the trade field, ASEAN has been given status as a regional association eligible for

---

[1] Source: Department of State *Bulletin*, May 1982, pp. 45–46. The meeting was held in Washington at the Department of State from March 9 to 11, 1982.

cumulative treatment under GSP rules of origin, and Indonesia has become eligible for GSP. ASEAN is a major beneficiary of this program and is showing an expanding ability to make use of GSP concessions. We have been able to discuss GATT and other trade issues with creativity and candor because of the relationship built up through the dialogue.

This administration is particularly conscious of the importance of the private business sector to development and mutually beneficial commerce. The ASEAN–U.S. Business Council, which has arisen out of the dialogue process, is proving to be one of its most important accomplishments in terms of long-run economic progress and increased trade and investment. President Reagan strongly believes in the effectiveness of the private enterprise contribution to economic development, and the Business Council is a concept we wholeheartedly support. The impressive success of market-oriented ASEAN economies is eloquent testimony to the progress which private enterprises can achieve. We are exploring ways in which the U.S. Government can further strengthen the U.S. private sector contribution to ASEAN's development.

I would like to say a few words about the broader global aspects of U.S. foreign policy, particularly in the East Asian region. All of you in this room today will understand how the U.S. global responsibilities influence our regional activities and capabilities. We can deal harmoniously and productively with economic issues only in a climate of security and freedom from external threats. Indeed, the world trading system is predicated on the absence of hostilities and aggression. It is precisely to preserve a peaceful world system in which all can prosper that the United States has to focus on threats to that system. In this regard, we are determined to continue to play a major role in assuring peace and security in East Asia.

To help ASEAN withstand the threat created by Vietnam's invasion of Kampuchea and an expanding Soviet naval presence, the United States is increasing its military assistance to individual ASEAN countries, especially Thailand, the frontline state. We recognize and accept the independent status of ASEAN, however, and we will continue to provide our support in ways fully acceptable to your governments.

It is in this broader context that the United States places such high value on its relationship with ASEAN. You are independent, self-reliant, and economically dynamic. We will continue to support this favorable situation with trade, investment, development cooperation, and military assistance.

This administration also is engaged in a major effort to revitalize the U.S. economy. As we proceed, we may not always be able to respond immediately to your desires for increased access to the U.S. market or for increased U.S. financial support. But we are committed to an open global trading system and will strongly resist the winds of protectionism. Most importantly, the renewed health of the U.S. economy will have major benefits for international trade, including improved markets for the commodity exports of the developing world.

The Agenda for the fourth dialogue is well thought out and unusually appropriate in view of the upcoming GATT Ministerial. The discussions will influence how both sides proceed in the global context. We are especially aware of your concerns about the outlook for your commodity exports, as well as your interest in increasing the benefits from GSP. We will give careful consideration to your views on these subjects during the course of the dialogue.

We are also extremely interested in thoroughly exploring with you ways in which we can increase our investment and financial cooperation, including transfer of technology and increased access to U.S. capital markets. The dynamism of ASEAN economies has led OPIC, the Eximbank, and the trade and development program to count ASEAN as one of their prime customers, and we are prepared to consider what further participation these U.S. agencies can make.

The meeting you are about to begin will play an important role in achieving mutual understanding of economic problems and concerns on both sides. We have assembled our leading experts on trade, finance, and development as well as leaders from our private business sector, to discuss your concerns and aspirations thoroughly. I am convinced that the results will lead to a further strengthening of the dynamic and fruitful relationship between our countries, leading to greater prosperity for all.

Document 468

Joint Press Statement Issued by the Fourth Ministerial Meeting of the United States and the Association of Southeast Asian Nations, March 11, 1982[2]

Accomplishments of the Dialogue

The fourth meeting of the ASEAN–U.S. dialogue took place in Washington, D.C., March 9–11 in the Department of State.

The ASEAN delegations were led by H.E. Atmono Suryo, Director-General, ASEAN-Indonesia; H.E. Mohd. Yusof bin Hitam, Director-General, ASEAN-Malaysia; H.E. Vicente B. Valdepenas, Jr., Deputy Minister of Trade and Industry, Philippines; H.E. Sime D. Hidalgo, Director-General, ASEAN-Philippines; H.E. Punch Coomarasawamy, Ambassador of Singapore to the United States; and H.E. Vudhi Chuchom, Director-General, ASEAN-Thailand. H.E. Vicente B. Valdepenas, Jr., leader of the Philippine delegation, was the ASEAN spokesman. H.E. Narciso G. Reyes, ASEAN Secretary General, and members of his staff were also present.

The U.S. delegation was led by Anthony C. Albrecht, Deputy Assistant Secretary of State for East Asian and Pacific Affairs. The U.S. delegation was made up of representatives of the Departments of State, Commerce, the Treasury, Agriculture, the U.S. Trade Representative, AID, Council of Economic Advisors, OPIC, and the Eximbank.

The meeting opened with a welcoming statement by Walter J. Stoessel, Deputy Secretary of State. The Deputy Secretary reaffirmed the close and friendly ties between the United States and ASEAN, the increasingly prosperous effective grouping of five nations in Southeast Asia. Secretary Stoessel went on to state that this Administration is determined to continue the high level of cooperation, friendship, and openness which has been established with the ASEAN states. The dialogue process has helped ASEAN achieve some very impressive accomplishments, including concrete and practical improvements in the economic and commercial relations between ASEAN and the United States. Regarding the role of the private sector, the ASEAN–U.S. Business Council is proving to be most important in promoting long-run economic progress and increased trade and investment.

Anthony C. Albrecht, Deputy Assistant Secretary of State for East Asian and Pacific Affairs and head of the U.S. delegation, in introductory remarks, noted the importance of ASEAN as the fifth largest trading partner with the United States, the total trade having reached $22 billion in 1981 and that U.S. investment in the region was now over $5 billion with more to come. He referred to $2.2 billion in Exim loans and guarantees over the past 5 years. OPIC has provided $314 million of insurance on 16 projects in ASEAN.

Dr. Vicente B. Valdepenas, Jr., as the ASEAN spokesman, welcomed the fourth dialogue as an opportunity for both the United States and ASEAN to resolve their common concern and hoped that the dialogue would further strengthen the partnership between ASEAN and the United States.

Both sides noted with satisfaction the progress of the ASEAN–U.S. dialogue as evidenced by the expanding development cooperation program, cultural, educational, joint narcotics control activities, and the increasing flow of technicians and officials between the two sides.

International Economy

There was a wide-ranging discussion of the issues facing the world economy. Particular reference was made to the importance of revitalizing the U.S. economy in order to restore the prosperity and the growth of the world trading system, including the ASEAN area. The United States welcomed the continuing vigorous growth exhibited by the ASEAN economies, expressing the view that the role of the private sector was one of the major elements in their prosperity.

The ASEAN side reassured the U.S. side that ASEAN states have always taken a positive attitude in searching for a healthy international political and economic environment. However, the ASEAN delegations expressed concern over certain recent developments such as the U.S. policy on commodities of interest to ASEAN particularly tin and sugar; on the integrated program for commodities; U.S. policy on multilateral development banks; economic cooperation in developing countries activities; and the U.S. position on global negotiations. Nonetheless, ASEAN is hopeful that

[2] Source: Department of State *Bulletin*, May 1982, pp. 47–48.

the spirit of genuine cooperation and meaningful consultations fostered at the Cancun summit, which has characterized the ASEAN–U.S. dialogue and its activities, would result in mutually beneficial and cooperative endeavors.

Trade and Commodities

Both sides discussed the results of the MTN including the reduction of tariffs and the agreements on nontariff measures. Both sides noted that slow economic growth and unemployment led to rising protectionist sentiment in many countries and pointed to the advantages of maintaining an open international trading system and the need to resist protectionist trends.

Both sides referred to the importance of the upcoming GATT ministerial meeting and view it as a forum to improve the multilateral trading system.

The ASEAN side expressed appreciation for the U.S. GSP scheme which has benefitted ASEAN exports, particularly of manufacturers, and welcomed the U.S. efforts to further improve the scheme as well as assist ASEAN countries in better utilizing the scheme. The ASEAN side further stressed the importance of making the GSP scheme a permanent feature of the U.S. trade policy.

The ASEAN side emphasized the importance of basic commodity exports in their respective economies. They expressed their concern at the slow progress of the integrated program for commodities in the establishment and operation of effective international commodity agreements which will contribute to the stabilization of prices. The ASEAN side reiterated their strong concern with regard to GSA release of tin onto the world market.

The U.S. side recognized the views of ASEAN on commodities and reiterated its policy of support for a case-by-case approach toward commodity matters. The United States cited its active participation in the International Natural Rubber, Sugar, and Coffee Agreements. The U.S. side felt that GSA sales had not disrupted the tin market but expressed its understanding of the ASEAN concern with regard to GSA sales of tin and in this context offered to hold special consultations with ASEAN countries. At the same time the U.S. Government wished to assure tin producers that it would cooperate with the sixth ITA and expects that consumers and producers would join even though for well-known reasons the United States would be unable to participate in the agreement.

The ASEAN side expressed serious concern on the possible adverse effects of the Caribbean Basin initiative on ASEAN exports to the United States, in particular sugar, a substantial portion of which have been subject to full tariff duties and fees not only on account of their being ineligible under the U.S. GSP but also due to the U.S. sugar price support program. The ASEAN side believed that the tariff benefits that would be accorded beneficiary sugar exporting countries under the Caribbean Basin initiative would result in a competitive disadvantage for ASEAN sugar exports. The U.S. side indicated that an objective of the overall Caribbean Basin initiative is to encourage diversification away from sugar and that the U.S. does not expect that Caribbean sugar exports to the United States will rise significantly above historical levels.

Investment and Finance

Both sides recognized the vital role of private capital in economic development and stressed the importance of maintaining a favorable investment climate.

The ASEAN side requested the United States to facilitate ASEAN's efforts to raise financing for their development projects, to organize investment seminars, and to undertake other measures to promote U.S. investment in the ASEAN countries. On financial cooperation, ASEAN requested the United States first, to encourage U.S. financial institutions to work on ASEAN industrial project financing; second, to make available technical expertise of financial issues; third, to organize programs such as seminars, study tours, and on-the-job training to assist ASEAN access to the U.S. capital market; fourth, to organize study tours or training programs on insurance; and finally, to encourage the U.S. Eximbank to continue its effort to promote ASEAN development.

The U.S. side indicated that they understood and supported the economic development objectives which underlay these proposals, and they would give serious consideration to them. In particular, regarding seminars, investment missions, and feasibility studies, the United States agreed to make further proposals. The U.S. representatives pointed to the programs of several U.S. Government agencies—including the U.S. Eximbank, OPIC, the Department of Commerce, Agency for International Development, and the trade and development program—which are active in the ASEAN region in support of U.S. investment. The

Eximbank has sizable commitments in the ASEAN region and is prepared to increase these commitments. Similarly, the United States noted that OPIC had been active in providing insurance, loan guarantees, and feasibility studies grants in the ASEAN area; still there is considerable scope for expansion of OPIC activities in the region.

ASEAN–U.S. Business Council

Both sides welcomed the special presentation closely related to trade and investment issues made by Mr. William E. Tucker, chairman of the U.S. section of the ASEAN–U.S. Business Council. His reference to the training and technology transfer opportunities offered by U.S. firms for the ASEAN area was welcome. Both sides considered that the possibility of future participation by private sector representatives in appropriate dialogue sessions, by invitation, would be desirable.

Development Cooperation

Both sides expressed satisfaction with the progress made in six ongoing ASEAN–U.S. development projects in the fields of agriculture, energy, public health, and academic training and research. ASEAN–U.S. projects are now underway or planned in all five member countries.

The growing success of the cooperation between ASEAN and the United States with AID funding was underlined by the signing of the seventh project agreement between the U.S. Government and ASEAN during the dialogue by AID Administrator M. Peter McPherson on behalf of the United States, and Ambassador of the Republic of Indonesia to the United States, D. Ashari, on behalf of ASEAN. The agreement provides $1 million of AID assistance over 3 years. This is the second energy project between ASEAN and the United States in the very important area of energy planning and development.

The first ASEAN–U.S. development cooperation agreement was signed in 1979 and since then AID has committed $16.5 million in economic assistance to ASEAN regional projects.

Other topics discussed during the meeting included narcotics control, cooperation in science and technology, agriculture, education, cultural affairs, and shipping. On ocean shipping policy ASEAN requested the U.S. Government to approve as soon as possible its proposed legislation to exempt the shipping lines of developing countries from being classified as controlled carriers. Both sides agreed to study carefully the proposals and suggestions exchanged in the various fields during these discussions with the aim of strengthening ASEAN–U.S. cooperation.

Document 469

Statement Issued by the Department of State, March 15, 1982[3]

Clarification on Increased U.S. Military Aid to Southeast Asia

Q. This morning Deputy Secretary Stoessel spoke about stepped-up military aid to countries in Southeast Asia.[4] Do you have any specifics on that—whether or not it is something new above and beyond programs that have already been announced?

A. No. I have nothing to add to what the Deputy Secretary said.

Clarification.

Deputy Secretary Stoessel was referring to administration decisions to increase the levels of military assistance in the FY 1982 programs in certain key countries in Southeast Asia. For instance, Thailand, the frontline ASEAN state, faces Vietnamese forces across its border in Kampuchea. Thailand is modernizing its armed forces to meet this threat, while at the same time maintaining its commitment to continued economic growth. In support of this effort the United States increased its overall security and development assistance to Thailand from approximately $47 million in 1979 to $101 million in 1982. Security assistance alone for FY 1982 included $62.5 million in military sales credits, $4.5 million grant military aid, $5 million in grant economic support funds, and $1.45 million in grant assistance for military education. Assistance provided in FY 1981 and 1982 to the members of the Association of Southeast Asian Nations is shown on the attached table.

---

[3] Source: Office of Press Relations, Department of State; posted statement. This statement was posted in response to a question asked at the March 9 Daily Press Briefing.

[4] The reference is to his remarks to the Fourth U.S.–ASEAN ministerial meeting; see document 475.

ASEAN ASSISTANCE LEVELS (dollars in thousands)

Country	FMS Financing		Economic Support Fund		International Military Education & Training		Development Assistance	
	FY81	FY82	FY81	FY82	FY81	FY82	FY81	FY82
Indonesia	30,000	40,000	—	—	1,823	2,200	68,800	67,300
Malaysia	10,000	10,000	—	—	300	500	—	—
Philippines	50,000	50,000	30,000	50,000	591	1,000	39,700	38,858
Singapore	—	—	—	—	7	50	—	—
Thailand	53,400	67,000*	2,000	5,000	795	1,450	24,180	27,600

*Included $4.5 million in MAP

Document 470

Prepared Statement by the Assistant Secretary of State for East Asian and Pacific Affairs (Holdridge) Before a Subcommittee of the Senate Foreign Relations Committee, June 8, 1982[5]

Favorable Trends and Current Challenges in Southeast Asia

Mr. Chairman, I greatly welcome your invitation to speak on U.S. policy toward Southeast Asia. This hearing is timely as Deputy Secretary Stoessel and I will next week be meeting with the ASEAN Foreign Ministers in Singapore,[6] where many of the issues I will mention today will undoubtedly be addressed.

FAVORABLE TRENDS

Few would have thought 20 years or even 10 years ago that Southeast Asia would be described this year in the financial section of the *New York Times* as "the most upbeat area of the world." Although I have not measured Southeast Asia's claims to this distinction against those of other parts of the globe, several important developments, in my view, justify an overall positive assessment both of developments in the region and of our relationships there.

Particularly encouraging is the successful manner in which many Southeast Asian nations have carved out for themselves increasingly important roles in the world's free market. The economic growth of most of our Southeast Asian friends to which I drew attention in my appearance before this Subcommittee last summer, has continued despite a less than favorable international environment, particularly as regards demand for their principal export commodities. The ASEAN states in particular have both drawn strength from—and lent strength to—the world market economy.

Another positive feature is the effectiveness with which ASEAN countries continue to rally international support for resolution of the Kampuchean problem. They have met continued Vietnamese intransigence with resolution and resourcefulness. ASEAN's success has been reflected in another decisive vote on Kampuchea in the U.N. General Assembly last fall,[7] equally broad support for its approach to a political solution to the Kampuçhea problem spelled out in the Declaration of last July's International Conference on Kampuchea,[8] and

[5] Source: *U.S. Policies and Programs in Southeast Asia: Hearings Before the Subcommittee on Asian and Pacific Affairs of the Committee on Foreign Relations, U.S. Senate, Ninety-seventh Congress, Second Session* (Washington, 1982), pp. 5–7.

[6] For Deputy Secretary Stoessel's speech to the ASEAN Foreign Ministers' Meeting in Singapore, June 18, 1982, see document 473.

[7] The reference is to U.N. General Assembly Resolution 36/5, adopted on October 21, 1981; for text, see *American Foreign Policy: Current Documents, 1981*, document 552.

[8] Adopted on July 17, 1981, at the Conference on Kampuchea held in New York. For text, see *ibid.*, document 547.

broad cooperation in applying strong economic pressure on Vietnam to help persuade it to negotiate a comprehensive political solution in Kampuchea as outlined by ASEAN in the International Conference.

We can also point to favorable trends in popular political participation paralleling the emphasis that a market economy approach places on freeing individual initiative. Three of the five ASEAN states held national elections this year and the other two held important bi-elections, adding to the foundation of democratic development. While progress in this area may be regarded by some as uneven, the trend is encouraging when viewed over the long term. Certainly prospects are bright when contrasted with conditions in Indochina, which possesses the region's principal alternative governing system.

CURRENT CHALLENGES

When we meet with ASEAN Foreign Ministers in Singapore later this month, the focus will be less on past accomplishments, of course, than on challenges that lie before us—and there are many.

The ASEAN governments are particularly concerned about the current state of the world economy, which has placed strains on them and on their relationship with us. As we are all aware, economic growth such as many ASEAN countries have experienced often increases popular expectations faster than actual incomes, and the depressed market for certain export commodities has had a widespread effect within their domestic economies. Some governments are under pressure to withdraw from competition through restrictive and thus ultimately self-defeating trade arrangements. There is a widespread fear that the United States itself might turn to protectionism. We will stress our commitment to get our own economy into order, to resolve trade and investment problems in a manner which will deepen attachments to the market economy, and to contribute to balanced growth through investment, trade and development assistance programs. Improving the global economic climate will also be important in this respect and I think that we will soon be able to point to some positive movement arising from the Versailles Summit. We will ask in return for ASEAN's continued cooperation in assuring that the world market from which we all have drawn our strength remains competitive and thus efficient.

Continued Vietnamese intransigence on Kampuchea and the threat Vietnamese forces pose to our good friend, Thailand, are also matters of immediate and great concern to ASEAN and the U.S. alike. The repressive measures used by the Indochinese regimes to control their own people including the use of lethal chemical agents against civilian populations is an additional disturbing element. Pressing for a political solution to the Kampuchea problem while strengthening the military forces of Thailand and its friends in the area are parallel, complementary measures to meet this challenge. We will reassure the ASEAN states that they can rely on our firm support for their efforts to promote a Kampuchean settlement based on the declaration of the International Conference on Kampuchea. We believe ASEAN governments should continue to take the lead on this issue because of their demonstrated success in marshalling international support and because of their sound approach to the problems involved. At the same time, we will stress the reliability of the United States as a treaty ally to Thailand, as a counterweight to the growing Soviet military presence in Indochina, and as a reliable supplier of credit, equipment and training for the modest military modernization programs of friendly Southeast Asian countries.

While Indochinese refugee flows have fortunately diminished markedly in past months, they remain a problem for the first asylum countries. It is important that the residual refugee population in Thailand, Malaysia and Indonesia continue to decrease, and we will work with other resettlement countries toward this end.

The lack of a complete accounting for U.S. servicemen missing in action in Vietnam and Laos is a bilateral problem to which we assign highest priority. We will continue strenuous efforts to obtain the cooperation of the governments of Vietnam and Laos on this matter, as a humanitarian issue to be handled expeditiously and separately from other concerns.

CONCLUSIONS

Mr. Chairman, Southeast Asia has for many years been known as the home of some of the world's most intractable and dangerous problems. Many of them are still with us. Today, however, Southeast Asia is also the home of some of the world's more effective problem-solving governments—and this has made a difference.

I think we might sum up the sources of favorable developments in Southeast Asia by singling out three characteristics of our friends there. First, they have strived hard to compete in the world market economy. Their overall growth rates, which are far above the world average, testify to the efficiency and strength they have gained from such competition. Second, they have sought to cooperate in preserving the economic system which gives them this growth. ASEAN, which found common economic goals for countries whose economies are not complementary and which has now become a potent constructive force in world political councils, is proof of their success in this field. Finally, they have recognized and demonstrated that local initiative is the basic building block for economic development, social progress and security.

The United States has great interest in assuring that this competitive spirit, cooperative attitude and local initiative continue to thrive. Our objectives, therefore, remain much as I described them to you in last year's hearing.[9] In cooperation with our ASEAN friends we will seek to curb the security threat posed by Vietnamese aggression and the Soviet military presence, and to alleviate the economic pressures caused by the current world slump and imbalances within our system. The progress and stability of our friends and allies in ASEAN are the heart of our policy since they form the foundation for the favorable trends we have thus far witnessed in Southeast Asia.

In pursuing these goals, Mr. Chairman, I feel certain that we will have the continued cooperation of your subcommittee and other Members of Congress.

Document 471

Prepared Statement by the Deputy Assistant Secretary of Defense for East Asian and Pacific Affairs (Armitage) Before a Subcommittee of the Senate Foreign Relations Committee, June 8, 1982[10]

The Security Threat to Southeast Asia

Mr. Chairman, I, like Ambassador Holdridge, have been pleased at the many positive trends we see in Southeast Asia and at the growing strength of the friendly governments in the region. They stand in dramatic contrast to the economic and social tragedies spawned by the Communist regimes of Indochina.

Unfortunately, when we turn to consideration of the security threat, I cannot say that the picture has been much relieved from when I was privileged to come before this distinguished committee last year at this time. I pointed out then that after the events of 1975, events which went very much against our interests, the unfraternal Communists of Vietnam and Kampuchea fell into a bloody and, thus far, unrelenting struggle—a struggle, which like an open fire, threatens still the peace and security of the region. I also reported that these events had once again opened the region to the rivalries of the great powers, rivalries which the countries of the region strongly wish to avoid.

Today, the Vietnamese divisions remain at their work attempting to "pacify" Kampuchea. The fighting between the Vietnamese and the Khmer resistance groups along the Thai/Kampuchean border, if anything, has been more intense than in past years. The tragic byproduct of this upheaval, the flow of refugees out of Indochina, continues. Above all, the fighting puts at risk the stability of this region, which has seen far more than its share of trouble, and which is of abiding importance to our own national interests.

If I may, I would like to call your particular attention to two countries, the Philippines and Thailand, which stand as our principal security partners in upholding the interests of the free world in Southeast Asia.

Thailand continues a gradual military modernization given day-to-day impetus by the events along her eastern border. When Thailand's Prime Minister, Prem Tinsulanon, came to Washington last October in a very successful visit. President Reagan, noting Thailand's status on the front lines, reassured him of this country's firm adherence to the security guarantees we gave Thailand in the 1954 Manila Pact.[11] We have backed these assurances with foreign military sales and the provision of military training (IMET), both at expanded levels. By this assistance, we play a major role in upgrading Thai forces.

---

9 The reference is to statements by Holdridge before the Senate Subcommittee on East Asian and Pacific Affairs, July 15, 1981. See *ibid.*, document 472.

10 Source: *U.S. Policies and Programs in Southeast Asia*, pp. 10–13.

11 Also known as the Southeast Asia Collective Defense Treaty, signed September 8, 1954; for text, see 6 UST 81.

We do not expect that Thailand can become a military match for the Vietnamese, who, after all, have the fifth largest military force in the world. But we are certain that, if pressed, the Thai Armed Forces would give a good account of themselves in the event of invasion of their homeland. In slowing down a Vietnamese assault, they would buy the time for Thailand's friends to come to her assistance.

We conduct periodic training exercises with the Thai and with other friends in the region. Just two weeks ago, U.S. Navy and Marine units together with corresponding units in the Thai Armed Forces took part in a large combined military training exercise, Operation "Cobra Gold." Out in the Gulf of Siam and along the beaches of the southern Thai peninsula, this exercise combined what had previously been a number of individual exercises into a comprehensive array of naval and marine maneuvers. Also, over the last several months, we have worked to increase the Thai Armed Forces' inventory of especially needed military equipment. In January, we provided air defense weapons long requested by the Thai Government. In the last several weeks, we airlifted 155mm howitzers and expedited the shipment of M48 tanks. These items had been the subject of urgent Thai Government requests for speeded up delivery.

In our presentations to the Congress earlier this year for security assistance to Thailand in fiscal year 1983, we asked for foreign military sales allocations of $50 million in direct credit and $41 million in guaranteed loans. We have asked for another $25 million in fiscal year 1982 supplemental funds. These are, at least in the East Asia region, large amounts. It is our intention to do all that we can to meet the needs of this ally in acquiring the means of self-defense.

The military situation on the border, particularly in the dry season months just past (the late winter and early spring of this year) has brought about an acceleration of Vietnamese attacks on the several Kampuchean resistance groups standing between Vietnamese forces and the Thai border. These attacks have been pressed more stringently than in past years. The nature of the fighting in western Kampuchea, however, is such that fast moving, lightly equipped guerrilla groups have, in fact, many advantages over the more conventionally operating and numerically superior Vietnamese. The military situation shows every sign of continuing as it is; essentially a cyclical pattern of fighting adding up to a stalemate for some time to come. The Vietnamese have by no means wiped out the resistance; these groups seem as determined as ever not to acquiesce in the Vietnamese dominance of Kampuchea. Indeed, the seeds of Khmer nationalism have proved very resistant to eradication.

I cannot leave a discussion of Indochina without mentioning another important and continuing U.S. interest in that area. That is our concern for nearly 2,500 Americans missing as a result of the Vietnam war. In the nearly 9½ years since the Paris agreement was signed,[12] we have seen little improvement in the cooperation of the Communist governments of Indochina. We know they can be more forthcoming on the PW/MIA issue and we are committed to seeking every possible assistance from them to obtain the fullest possible accounting for those who remain missing. Because it is a humanitarian matter, resolution of the accounting issue is not linked to progress or lack of progress on other contentious issues between the United States and the Indochina governments. The United States Defense Department looks forward to national PW/MIA recognition day on July 9 as an opportunity [to] show again that we have not forgotten.

In my statements last year I referred to the Republic of the Philippines as a vital irreplaceable ally. I am more than ever convinced that the Philippines is the keystone in our structure of defense arrangements in Southeast Asia. The Philippines provides the platform on which our forces would stand and from which they would operate in the event of emergencies in East Asia, the Indian Ocean area or southwest Asia. Without this platform our ability to back up our interests would be much lessened.

I'm happy to say that over the last year our relations in the political/military field with the Philippines have advanced markedly. We have had a series of high level visits, capped, if you will, by that of Secretary Weinberger to Manila in late March.[13] With all our Defense Department visitors has gone the message that Philippine cooperation in our concert of defense arrangements is respected and appreciated.

Over the years, our relationship with the Philippines has come to be known as a "special relationship". This signifies that

---

[12] Signed at Paris on January 27, 1973; for text, see 24 UST 1.

[13] See document 526.

the United States does more than count the Philippines among its friends in the region. The Republic of the Philippines was our first ally in Asia. The U.S.–Philippines Mutual Defense Treaty, signed in 1951,[14] predates our bilateral defense pacts with Korea and Japan, as well as our multilateral pact with Australia and New Zealand and the Manila Pact which includes Thailand.

General Ramas, commanding general of the Philippine Army, pointed out to me during a recent visit that the terrible suffering endured by the Philippine people during the Second World War was totally unlike the experiences of other colonial peoples of Southeast Asia. The Filipinos fought against the Japanese invaders, while their country was still a dependency of the United States. Unlike the history of neighboring Indochina, Malaysia and Indonesia, there was no anticolonial movement to throw the Americans out at the end of the war. The Filipinos had been promised their independence and they got it, on time, in 1946. General Ramas made the point that both our countries shared many of the same values and had roughly the same ideas about free societies. Therefore, we fought together under the same flag as brothers—indeed, a special relationship.

Situated at the geographic hinge between our Pacific area military resources and the petroleum-rich areas of southwest Asia, the Philippines are strategically vital in any event. We recognized early that the Philippines was key to an American military presence in the western Pacific. Together with our military facilities in northeast Asia, Subic Bay Naval Base and Clark Air Base provide the forward positions from which we can respond as required to threats throughout this large region.

I do not mean to say that our facilities in the Philippine bases are irreplaceable. Facilities which could provide much of what is already at Subic and Clark could, indeed, be constructed in Guam and other locations in the islands under our jurisdiction in the western Pacific. These facilities, however, would be farther from the hinge and would, in most cases, have to be built up from present rudimentary facilities or built up from scratch.

Particularly as the Soviet use of bases in Vietnam becomes more apparent and, unfortunately, more regular we believe the Philippine Government sees our use of facilities in the bases as contributing directly to the defense of their homeland. Similarly, we have heard expressions of other friends in the Southeast Asia region that our use of facilities in the Philippine bases makes a contribution to the stability of the whole region.

We do not wish to see renewed and increased military rivalries in Southeast Asia. While American economic interests have proceeded to grow steadily in the region and our political relationships have continued strong, we have not sought to build up a military presence beyond what we felt necessary for the protection of our standing interests, including the defense of our two treaty allies in the region.

Since 1978, however, the Soviets have introduced their ships and planes to bases along the coast of Vietnam, concommitant with major growth in Soviet naval and naval air strength in the whole Pacific region. They have deployed SS–20 missiles to areas of the Soviet Far East. The region has come under an increasing potential threat which shows no signs of abating.

Moreover, as I pointed out in my testimony this time last year, the Soviet Union appears in many respects to have its own agenda in the Indochina countries. It is not just backing up the enterprises of its surrogate. Soviet aid, approximately two-thirds in basic food stuffs and one-third in military equipment, continues to flow to the Hanoi government—aid which translates directly into Hanoi's ability to continue the fighting in Kampuchea. But of perhaps greater importance, Soviet long range reconnaissance aircraft are permitted in return to operate out of Vietnam to carry out surveillance missions over the South China Sea.

The sea lanes from the Indian Ocean through the Strait of Malacca, around Singapore and up through the South China Sea are the petroleum lifeline of our friends in East Asia. Any potential adversary's ability to choke off these narrow seas must be, inevitably, of abiding concern to our friends in that part of the world. We have seen, since 1978, the product of what must be a determined Soviet intent to establish this kind of potential choking grip.

As we seek to protect our interests in the region and those of our friends and allies against the growing potential threat, we believe that our policies and approach enjoy inherent advantages over those of the Soviet Union and its surrogates. The Soviets appear to believe that a country must be remolded in the Soviet image if it is to be a reliable friend. Others must be intimidated

[14] 3 UST (part 3) 3847.

by military power. Our interests, however, are not threatened by true independence and diversity. Our policies support independence, strengthen the capabilities and confidence of our allies and friends to resist intimidation, and do so without demanding conformity. Our force presence in the western Pacific offers reassurance that we can come to the aid of our friends against external threats which are too big for them to handle alone. Our security assistance helps each country strengthen its own self-defense capabilities, reducing the probability that it would need to ask for help from outside military forces. At the same time, security assistance, combined exercises, and military-to-military contacts make the military forces of our friends in the region more able to operate with our own and thereby more capable of effective combined operations were they ever required.

We have healthy bilateral defense relations with Indonesia, Malaysia, and Singapore as well as with our treaty allies, Thailand and the Philippines. We also encourage and support—without seeking to dominate or, unless asked, even participate in—the various arrangements for mutual cooperation established by the nations of the region. We see as in our interest, as well as theirs, the evolution of ASEAN from purely economic cooperation toward political cooperation, most notably in their concerted policies toward Vietnamese occupation of Kampuchea.

We are also pleased to see the continuation of the five-power defense arrangement, a defense agreement which includes the commonwealth partners—Malaysia, Singapore, Australia, New Zealand, and Britain. They hold a series of military exercises involving the small but important Australian and New Zealand air and ground units which are maintained in Malaysia and Singapore and the increasingly competent forces of those two countries. Because it strengthens the ability of its members to resist Soviet and Vietnamese intimidation, the five-power defense arrangement is an excellent example of regional cooperation in which our interests, as well as those of its members, are served without our participation.

The pattern of defense cooperation in the region is that of multiple bilateral U.S. relationships and regional arrangements in which our efforts play a supporting role. Within this loose framework of defense relationships among the countries of Southeast Asia there is a recognition of the need for the United States to play a responsible and sustainable role in upholding the stability of the region. Our ability to play a sustainable role depends, in the main, on the support the American people and the Congress give to this effort. The continuation of an American commitment to this region, to our two treaty allies especially, cannot stand without firm roots here at home. We have, since the Second World War, spent immeasurable amounts of blood and treasure in this part of the world. We have seen, particularly over the last decade, American economic interests in these resource-rich, fast-developing countries grow steadily. We know that particularly in the ASEAN group there are some of the most vibrant economies in the world today. This region is not one we can walk away from. We are tied by treaties, by friendly relations, and by our self-interest to the success of our friends there.

Document 472

Prepared Statement by the Deputy Assistant Secretary of State for East Asian and Pacific Affairs (Albrecht) Before a Subcommittee of the Senate Foreign Relations Committee, June 10, 1982[15]

U.S. Economic Relations With Southeast Asia

Mr. Chairman, I am pleased to be with you today to discuss our economic relations with Southeast Asia. Our ties with ASEAN are increasing in importance as our economic interdependence with this dynamic region expands and demands priority attention.

Our contacts with the Burmese Government have expanded significantly since our cooperative narcotics program began in 1974. AID programs, beginning in 1980, have further expanded these contacts at the same time that Burma has been refusing lucrative approaches by the Soviet Union. Although we do not expect a change in Burma's basic commitment to neutrality, it is in our interest to encourage a continued, quiet Burmese opening toward the United States and the West. Brunei, a small, oil rich country on the north coast of Kalimantan

[15] Source: *U.S. Policies and Programs in Southeast Asia,* pp. 72–75.

(Borneo) will become fully independent next year, and will probably be invited to join ASEAN at that time. With respect to Vietnam, the United States has actively cooperated with the ASEAN efforts to restrict multilateral development aid so long as Vietnamese forces continue their occupation of Cambodia.

U.S. ECONOMIC RELATIONS WITH ASEAN

Since its establishment in August 1967, the Association of Southeast Asian Nations (ASEAN), comprising Indonesia, Malaysia, Singapore, the Philippines and Thailand, has emerged as a growing economic and political force in Southeast Asia and on the world scene. ASEAN's announced goals are to strengthen regional cohesion and self-reliance while promoting economic development. The organization developed slowly during the first decade of its existence due to the diverse background of its member states and the competitive nature of their economies. But it gained rapid momentum following the first Summit Conference of ASEAN leaders in Bali in 1976. Since that time its political cohesiveness has strengthened and regional cooperation activity [has?] greatly expanded. Our cooperation with ASEAN on Kampuchea has become especially important.

Agriculture and the production of basic commodities remain the principal economic activities in ASEAN, with the notable exception of the highly industrialized city state of Singapore. As a result, commodity market issues such as price stabilization and market growth are of vital importance. Tin, natural rubber, vegetable oils, tropical timber and sugar are especially important. Our decision not to join the Sixth International Tin Agreement and GSA sales of excess tin stocks have become especially contentious issues over the past year.

The real annual GNP growth of over 7 percent over the past decade has earned ASEAN a well deserved reputation as one of the most promising growth areas in the developing world. The private sector has played a key role in this economic dynamism. The ASEAN countries recognize that private enterprise must be involved in the development process and that foreign investment should play an important role. ASEAN looks to the United States, as well as to other developed nations, for support and cooperation in providing market access, investment capital and economic assistance to help promote its economic development goals.

The ASEAN nations now must cope with lagging sales of export commodities, increasing costs in financing investment and slower growth in the OECD countries. ASEAN needs a prosperous and open U.S. market if it is to continue to grow—but we also need ASEAN for vital raw materials, as a growing market for U.S. exports, and as an attractive home for U.S. private investment.

IMPORTANCE OF ASEAN

The population of ASEAN is about 256 million people, comparable to that of the United States and Canada combined. Estimated per capita GNP's range from $420 in Indonesia to $4,480 in Singapore. ASEAN's total GNP is nearly $200 billion. It is rich in natural and human resources and occupies a key strategic position astride vital sea lanes.

ASEAN countries are important suppliers of essential U.S. imports. For example, in 1980, 89 percent of our natural rubber, 65 percent of our tin, 6 percent of crude petroleum, 28 percent of our hardwood lumber, as well as 99 percent of our palm oil and 95 percent of our coconut imports came from ASEAN. Most of our tantalum/niobium and much of our tungsten is imported and the region is a vital supplier of these minerals. But ASEAN is not only a source of key resources needed by the United States to assure our security and prosperity, ASEAN is likewise an important and rapidly growing market for a wide range of U.S. machinery, chemicals and foodstuffs. Thus, in 1981 our exports reached nearly $9 billion, an increase of 30 percent since 1979. Total two-way U.S. trade with the ASEAN countries was about $22 billion last year, making ASEAN our 5th most important trade partner. Total trade has more than doubled since 1977. The U.S. Export-Import Bank, with an exposure of over $2 billion, has fostered increased exports to ASEAN.

The ASEAN countries appreciate that their economic advance requires close cooperation with and financial support from foreign investors. We estimate that total U.S. investment in ASEAN, including the expenditures of U.S. oil companies in exploration and development in oil and gas production-sharing arrangements with Indonesia and Malaysia, now amounts to about $10 billion.

ASEAN–UNITED STATES BUSINESS COUNCIL

Because all of the ASEAN governments perceive a major role for business and strive to foster it, cooperation within ASEAN and with the international business community has grown rapidly. The ASEAN Chambers of Commerce and Industry are playing an increasingly important role in ASEAN. The ASEAN–U.S. Business Council, which joins the business communities of the United States and ASEAN in the fostering of trade, investment and cooperative projects, has given a new and important dimension to our relationship with Southeast Asia. We look increasingly to the Council to help promote closer ties with ASEAN and consider its activities to be an important complement to the official dialogue. Recognition of this role was emphasized by Secretary Haig in his address before the UN General Assembly last September when he pointed out that the "ASEAN–U.S. Business Council is a model of how our private sectors can work together for mutual benefit."[16]

We will continue to support and encourage the Business Council. It carries out activities and programs which governments cannot do, especially in the fields of training and technological transfer. It also fosters direct contacts and cooperation between business people which results in increased trade and investment and greater understanding.

Since its establishment in July 1979 the Council has undertaken various programs which have increased the flow of information, people and ideas between the United States and ASEAN. Among the more notable accomplishments were an ASEAN–U.S. Seminar on Science and Technology for Development held in Singapore in October 1980; and a seminar on ASEAN–U.S. automotive developments held in Detroit in June 1981. Working groups on technology, education and training to facilitate technology transfer between the United States and ASEAN have been formed, and a financial conference was held in Kuala Lumpur in November 1981. We look forward to the fall meeting of the ASEAN–U.S. Business Council which will bring about 100 of ASEAN's leading business figures to Washington. A brief description of the Business Council is attached as Annex I.[17]

CONSULTATIONS WITH ASEAN

The United States has found that it works well with ASEAN and that we are able to cooperate to promote economic growth and to solve mutual problems because our approach to most basic economic issues is similar. At the June 1981 meeting of ASEAN Foreign Ministers, Secretary Haig stressed that U.S. policy toward ASEAN rests on three important commitments: To economic development and commerce for mutual benefit, to fruitful bilateral relations, and to a genuine dialogue between equals on matters of common concern.[18] Indeed the term "dialogue" has been the name given to the special kind of relationship ASEAN carries on with its major world partners. Our economic dialogue with ASEAN is a continuous operation at all levels. Since 1977 the United States and representatives of the ASEAN nations have had four formal meetings at Ministerial or sub-Ministerial level to discuss common concerns and to seek solutions to problems in the economic, social and cultural spheres. Unlike many international conferences, our ASEAN dialogues have been characterized by straight talk and an honest attempt to deal with issues that trouble both sides. For example, at the recent March 1982 dialogue in Washington,[19] ASEAN representatives clearly and frankly told us of their serious concern over our GSA tin disposal policy and the new Caribbean Basin Initiative (CBI). On tin, we were able to offer further consultations, and we are willing to discuss modification in GSA sales practices that may go some way to meet their concerns. On the CBI, we explained U.S. goals carefully and tried to reassure them that their interests would not be neglected in the pursuit of our Caribbean efforts.

That meeting also reviewed our cooperative regional development assistance program with ASEAN, as well as special educational/cultural exchanges. We now cooperate to enhance regional institutions in areas of nonconventional energy, tropical medicine, plant quarantine, and agricultural development planning. We are looking at the possibility for new ways to cooperate such as in marine science and to promote small- and medium-scale industry. A copy of the Joint Press Statement of the March 1982 ASEAN–U.S. dialogue is attached at Annex II.

Because the nature of ASEAN as an organization may not be fully understood, I

---

[16] As quoted in Secretary Haig's speech to the U.N. General Assembly, September 19, 1981; for text, see *American Foreign Policy: Current Documents, 1981*, document 82.

[17] None of the annexes are printed.

[18] See Haig's statement to the ASEAN Foreign Ministers, June 20, 1981, *American Foreign Policy: Current Documents, 1981*, document 474.

[19] See document 467.

want to conclude with a brief view of how it operates and where we perceive ASEAN to be going. Most importantly ASEAN should be seen as a pragmatic, cooperative organization that is sui generis. It is not like the European Community, and its success should not be judged by criteria applied to the EC. It has a wide variety of cooperative economic and technical activities and joint industrial projects and there are increasing efforts to lower trade barriers within ASEAN. ASEAN functions mainly through regular meetings of its Foreign Ministers and Economic and other Ministers, through national secretariats in each of the Foreign Ministries, and through a series of technical intergovernmental committees in areas such as food and agriculture, finance and banking, and industry, minerals and energy. There is a small ASEAN Secretariat in Jakarta, but the governments have until now strictly limited its size and role.

The ASEAN Secretariat and most of the committee structure is focused on the original nonpolitical goals of the organization as outlined in the ASEAN Declaration of 1967: Fostering of collaboration in "economic, social, cultural, technical, scientific and administrative fields." In addition, ASEAN government representatives have tended to work together as a group to formulate common positions in UN and other international fora on issues such as commodity policy, global negotiations, refugees and Kampuchea. Their ability to take common positions has been a source of enhanced strength and influence for the ASEAN nations. Though clearly associated with the so-called "Third World" group, the ASEAN countries have tended toward a moderate role on most North/South issues, a factor of great interest to us as we strive for their resolution. ASEAN has also operated as an effective unit and enhanced its bargaining power by establishing bilateral economic dialogues with third countries such as the United States, Japan, Australia, New Zealand, Canada and with the EC.

ASEAN's future seems bright. ASEAN's rich resource base and its proven economic vitality and success make it a leading candidate for strong economic growth in the next decade. While there are no major proposals for an economic union of the five, ASEAN Economic Ministers have agreed recently to study establishment of an ASEAN-wide free trade area.

But regardless of what organizational forms it takes and how cooperative efforts evolve in ASEAN, we feel confident that the ASEAN–U.S. economic relationship will continue to be one of increasing interdependence. There will be problems typical of any close relationship. In a period of slower world growth, there will be protectionist pressures on both sides, which must be resisted. However, in the light of our shared goals and our common interest in an open world economic system and our common approach toward peace and stability in Southeast Asia, it is in the U.S. interest to continue to support the demonstrated independence, self-reliance and economic dynamism of ASEAN.

Document 473

Address by the Deputy Secretary of State (Stoessel) Before the Foreign Ministers of the Association of Southeast Asian Nations, Singapore, June 18, 1982[20]

Consultations With ASEAN

I most appreciate this opportunity to meet with the Foreign Ministers of the Association of South East Asian Nations (ASEAN). My government places great importance on your organization and on our relations with each of its individual members.

The front pages of newspapers these days may lead some to believe that the United States is so busy fighting brush fires and larger conflagrations around the world that it does not place value on its longstanding relations in noncrisis areas. As a brush fire fighter for the Reagan administration, I wish to disagree. Not far from us here today are areas with dangerously low flashpoints. These concern us all very deeply, and I will say more about them later. But I want first to pay tribute to the dynamic, well-tended societies of ASEAN.

While we must deal with crises and threats to protect our common interests and preserve peace in the world, we must also sustain and strengthen these relationships which are not necessarily tried by daily crisis. As Prime Minister Lee Kuan

---

[20] Source: Department of State *Bulletin*, October 1982, pp. 27–29. Stoessel met with ASEAN Foreign Ministers from June 17 to 18, 1982, in consultations following an ASEAN ministerial meeting.

Yew so eloquently pointed out, ASEAN is an exception in the Third World by reason of its success and its stability.

The emphasis that ASEAN has placed since its inception on cooperation for economic and social development has improved not only your peoples' standards of living but also their security. Today we find ASEAN growth rates to be among the highest and longest sustained in the world. Clearly you have a great deal to be proud of—and to protect.

We place value not just on economic growth rates themselves, of course, but also on the system from which they spring. Foreign Minister Ghazali has well-focused our thoughts on the central importance of the private enterprise system characteristic of your societies and mine. Indeed, there is one remarkable factor about the phenomenal economic growth we witnessed earlier in Northeast Asia and are seeing today in Southeast Asia. Each successful country has competed within the world market in its own way without sacrificing the key values that comprise national identity. Competition has been within the context of cooperation between like-minded states. The system which provides these mutual benefits has thus been maintained.

My words describing your accomplishments reflect some of the basic values which underlie all Americans' thinking and which have been given particular emphasis by the Reagan administration. Primary among these is the belief that both social and economic progress depends in great part on giving free rein to local initiative. We believe this is a system which is on the one hand competitive, and thus efficient, and on the other cooperative, and thus constructive.

The success of our Asian—and particularly ASEAN—friends reinforces this belief. Nowhere has the effectiveness of local initiative been more salient than in the ASEAN countries' individual records of raising their populations' standard of living and, more recently, in their cooperative endeavor to focus the world's attention on a peaceful solution for Kampuchea.

My government recognizes that threats to which I have labeled our cooperative, competitive system can come from within, that imbalances can lead nations to withdraw from both competition and cooperation.

The current world slump highlights the exposed situation of those lesser developed countries overly dependent on the export of commodities with volatile prices. It increases the temptation to enter into cartels in situations where such measures are certain to be self-defeating. It dramatizes the need to make room for the exports of those countries newly moving into industrial production. It accentuates the harmful aspect of long-term trade imbalances between developed countries. In particular, I would note that we, too, are very concerned by the growing tendency toward protectionism.

We fully realize the degree to which the massive U.S. economy affects the world environment. In good part for this reason, the Reagan administration has placed top priority on getting its domestic economy into order. In so doing, we have eschewed controls in favor of incentives for local initiative and competition. At a time when pressures for increased protectionism have escalated in most countries, leaders of the world's major economic powers in their just concluded Versailles summit firmly committed their nations to keep the system open. We look forward to the GATT ministerial in the fall, where our goal is to extend the multilateral system for a still freer flow of trade, services, investment, and technology—all matters of importance to your countries as well as ours. We look to these and other actions in the coming months to bring a turn-around in world economic prospects.

My government is seeking means of strengthening our trade relationship with ASEAN, which, as a group, is already our fifth largest partner. This was, of course, a focus of our dialogue with ASEAN in Washington last March when I was pleased to be able to meet and talk with your delegations. We wish to work out the differences which naturally arise from our role as a major consumer of commodities, of which some of the ASEAN countries are principal producers.

Although free market economies may now be going through one of the most difficult periods of the postwar era, the lead they have long held over Communist economies is growing even greater. Nowhere is this more evident than in Asia, where Vietnam's and North Korea's misdirected and mismanaged economies contrast starkly with the prosperity of their neighbors. The extraordinary difficulty of presenting these systems as a model for economic and social development in Asia has brought the export market for revolution near to collapse.

There is, nevertheless, more reason for concern than complacency. Totalitarian regimes have established a clear historical pattern of compensating for economic failure with military adventurism. And the poor market for revolution can well lead certain states to take more direct routes to their goals.

The Soviet Union, in many respects, has deepened its confrontational cast. Military arms constitute its leading foreign exchange earner as well as, overwhelmingly, the largest component of its foreign assistance. Domestic growth of the Soviet military sectors has kept pace with arms exports.

This has been particularly evident in Asia, where the Soviet Pacific fleet is characterized by greatly improved capabilities. Formidable Soviet land forces are backed up by over 3,000 aircraft. Access to bases in Vietnam has extended the Soviet military reach, which could now challenge sea passage between the Pacific and Indian Oceans. We are also deeply concerned by the export of Soviet chemical warfare technology to Laos and Vietnam and the use of lethal chemical agents by those regimes against civilian populations.

The United States remains dedicated to meeting the Soviet challenge. We will address our difficult problems of economic recovery—yet we will continue to accord our defenses high priority. Our policy, however, is not one of confrontation in purely military terms but of demonstrating to the Soviet Union the need for moderation and restraint in the international arena.

Mutual reduction of nuclear armaments is one important route toward reduction of tensions. President Reagan and Secretary Haig are this week in New York at the U.N. Special Session on Disarmament to pursue this goal which, we are convinced, is far preferable to unrestrained nuclear competition. We shall continue this endeavor while remaining militarily strong.

Vietnam's intransigence and aggressiveness remain one of our principal concerns and the major destabilizing element in the region. The aging Vietnamese leadership has shattered its own promises and its talented peoples' dreams of peaceful reconstruction. Their misallocation of resources for militaristic foreign adventures has badly hurt the Vietnamese economy. Persecution, corruption, and despair still drive thousands of Vietnamese to seek refuge outside their homeland. Vietnamese policies and military forces deny the other peoples of Indochina the same independence and freedom which, according to Ho Chi Minh, the Vietnamese cherish for themselves. Their ambitions have aligned them with external powers, not their natural neighbors in ASEAN, and introduced Sino-Soviet rivalry to Southeast Asia.

The United States has followed ASEAN's lead in seeking a comprehensive political solution to the Kampuchean problem which would result in a withdrawal of Vietnamese forces from Kampuchea and Khmer self-determination. We will continue to support you strongly because we believe your approach is correct and, over time, effective. We share your view that continued international pressure is required to induce Vietnam to negotiate a settlement based on the declaration of the international conference and repeated U.N. General Assembly resolutions. We share your support for efforts to the Khmer to form a coalition to facilitate realization of the conference's declaration.

ASEAN has had many successes in carrying out its strategy on Kampuchea. The U.N. General Assembly resolution on Kampuchea last fall, the well-attended international conference on Kampuchea in New York, and the postponement of OPEC and other multilateral assistance to Vietnam are excellent examples. You have been very effective in assembling international support for your position, particularly from the nonaligned states.

Neither you nor we wish to bleed or punish Vietnam. They have brought their suffering on themselves through their actions. Last year, Secretary of State Haig stated that Vietnam has a choice. We believe that choice remains available to that country. It can agree to consider the rights of the Khmer people to live free from foreign domination and to determine their own future. It can consider the just concerns of ASEAN and its other neighbors in the region. Or it can continue to bear the severe consequences of its self-imposed diplomatic and economic isolation. We hope that Hanoi will eventually realize that its own national interests would be served best by seeking a solution to the Kampuchea problem which meets the legitimate interests of all concerned countries.

In any event, ASEAN can continue to count on full American support for ASEAN's strategy for dealing with the Kampuchea problem. As Foreign Minister Dhanabalan pointed out, patience and perseverance in this effort are essential.

Bilaterally with Vietnam, we will continue to seek a complete accounting for the U.S. servicemen missing-in-action in Laos and Vietnam. President Reagan has a personal abiding interest in resolution on this issue.

The Vietnamese Government has said it accepts our position that this is a humanitarian issue which is not linked to political and economic matters. We can only hope that the Vietnamese will take actions in accordance with this principle. We would welcome assistance of the ASEAN nations by whatever means.

The continued granting of first asylum to Indochinese refugees by neighboring countries is a humanitarian response to tragedy which earns worldwide respect. The United States will share this heavy burden by continuing its resettlement programs and, with the U.N. High Commissioner for Refugees (UNHCR), by urging other resettlement countries to do their fair share.

The United States, as well as some other principal resettlement countries, seeks an enlargement of the orderly departure program so that potential refugees will not have to resort to dangerous clandestine flight. Some progress has been made in this direction, and we want more. We also strongly support the UNHCR's efforts to establish agreements leading to voluntary repatriation of refugees. But until orderly departure is a realistic option for potential refugees, and voluntary repatriation is a reasonable choice for actual refugees, first asylum clearly is needed.

In the same way, the United States will continue to support humanitarian relief to the Khmer people. We are convinced that current emergency needs in the interior of Kampuchea are being met. Requirements for those people in the border areas persist, however. We urge other donors to contribute on a timely basis to meet this need.

The emergence of common purpose from common geography is not, as we are all aware, a common occurrence. The unity ASEAN has achieved is all the more impressive when one considers your very different histories and the legacy of misunderstanding and quarrels left from earlier eras.

You have demonstrated the power of constructive local initiative, which we believe to be the key to peace as well as economic and social development. For this reason, we do not push forward our own solutions to the regional issues we face together. This is not, I would emphasize, a sign of indifference or neglect. It is a testimony of our trust and respect as well as our recognition that ASEAN, with its unique consensus approach, has forged a leadership role in the region. Through meetings such as these and other increased contact, we will be following closely your plans and sharing our own with you. We will strive to insure that the efforts of the United States and of ASEAN are mutually reinforcing. It is our hope that in difficult times as in good, you will have no cause to doubt our support.

Document 474

Prepared Statement by the Assistant Secretary of State for International Narcotics Matters (DiCarlo) Before a Subcommittee of the House Judiciary Committee, December 14, 1982[21]

U.S. International Narcotics Control Policy in Southeast Asia

Mr. Chairman,[22] the international narcotics control policy of the United States Government, endorsed by the President and the Secretary of State, is expressed in the recently released Federal Strategy. This policy contains four basic elements:

1. The major narcotics producer nations are all signatories to the Single Convention on Narcotic Drugs,[23] under which each country has responsibility for controlling the cultivation, production, and trafficking in narcotics.

2. The international community should assist those nations which need help in controlling production and distribution of illicit substances.

3. Crop control, which can be achieved through government bans, chemical or manual eradication at the source, or controlled reductions to legitimate quotas, is the most effective, efficient, and economical means of reducing the availability of opium, cocaine, cannabis, and their derivatives. Our corollary policy for the psychotropic

---

[21] Source: *Drug Enforcement Activities in Southeast Asia: Hearing Before the Subcommittee on Crime of the Committee on the Judiciary: House of Representatives, Ninety-seventh Congress, Second Session* (Washington, 1983), pp. 6–17.

[22] Representative William J. Hughes.

[23] Signed in 1961 and entered into force in 1967; for text, see 18 UST 1407.

drugs, which are controlled by a separate international convention, is to seek limits on imports and exports, and to curtail illicit diversion.

4. Narcotics-related economic assistance, by the United States Government or international organizations, should be conditioned on concurrent agreements on the control of narcotics production.

When implementing these policies, there are a number of considerations which affect and influence our program strategy for each country and worldwide. The principal considerations, all of which are relevant to our strategy for Southeast Asia, are:

1. While there have been notable achievements in crop control and interdiction efforts, these successes in recent years have been marginal in terms of reducing worldwide availability of heroin, cocaine, and marijuana.

2. Interdiction efforts, which include arrests, seizures of drugs in transit, and capturing of financial assets, are not adequate in terms of worldwide impact, given current levels of production and profitability.

3. Comprehensive crop control programs are not now politically negotiable or operationally feasible in every producer country.

4. Both producer and transit nations are increasingly impacted by domestic drug abuse problems—as are the major industrialized, consumer nations—factors which present improved opportunities for both control agreements and increased international support.

SOUTHEAST ASIA

Production

Opium and heroin are the target drugs for both United States and foreign government control activities in Southeast Asia. Two successive droughts significantly lowered Southeast Asian production from its estimated levels of 550 to 660 metric tons per year to an estimated 180 metric tons in 1979 and 210 metric tons in 1980, resulting in steep price increases for opium at the farm gate and the displacement of Southeast Asian heroin in both European and American markets.

However, we estimate that, with excellent growing conditions in the 1980–81 and 1981–82 crop years, Golden Triangle production may have reached record harvests of 600 to 700 tons.

The changing market profile for Southeast Asian heroin is shown in the following chart:

These data, when fitted with reports from other growing sectors, especially Mexico and Southwest Asia, underscore critical points about the U.S. heroin market.

In the years following the peak importation of 7.5 tons of heroin in 1975, the United States experienced a decline in heroin imports, due in part to declining demand and concurrent with the successful Mexican opium eradication program and to the drought in Southeast Asia. These latter supply factors altered the profile of U.S. imports. In 1979, Southwest Asia passed Southeast Asia as the prime source of U.S. heroin, and subsequently has dominated the U.S. market. Total imports of heroin from all sources have stabilized at approximately 4.5 tons of heroin per year. While drought, low prices and a government ban on cultivation sharply reduced Pakistani production in 1980, 1981, and 1982, there is still a considerable stockpile from a 1979 Pakistani harvest of 700–800 tons and a continuing flow of opium from Afghanistan.

Thus, with this current increased Southeast Asian availability, there is at least the possibility of increased importation from all three sectors—including Mexico, where cultivation has reportedly expanded. There are indications that traffickers connected with Southeast Asian producers are attempting to recapture markets in the United States and Europe, while expanding markets in Southeast Asia, and seeking new markets in Australia and New Zealand. At present, an estimated 10 percent of heroin imported into the United States originates in the Golden Triangle; the prediction is that this figure will increase to 15 percent in 1983. Southeast Asian heroin dominates the Canadian market and its availability there is increasing.

Lessons can be inferred from these data. First, despite some expansion in crop control and increased interdiction efforts, the U.S. heroin market remains vulnerable to changes in production levels and distribution patterns—which, like the droughts in

---

[24] Year-to-year comparisons of estimates may be useful in identifying trends, but these data reflect ongoing refinements of estimating methodologies. [Footnote in the source text.]

[25] The Thai production estimates for 1979–82 were based on a comprehensive aerial survey, rather than on an estimative methodology. [Footnote in the source text.]

PRODUCTION OF 1976–82 METRIC TONS OF OPIUM[24]

	1976	1977	1978	1979	1980	1981	1982
Burma	400	300	325	125	160	500–600	500–600
Thailand	50	45	70	17	12	50	[25]60–70
Laos	60	50	50	40	40	40–60	50
Total	510	395	445	182	212	590–710	610–720

the two Asian areas, are more influential at present on that market than our enforcement efforts. Second, to achieve our ultimate objective of reducing heroin imports into the United States, international narcotic control activities must be directed comprehensively and simultaneously at all three of the major opium producing areas. Third, greater emphasis must be placed on crop control, given the limitations on interdiction and other enforcement efforts to cope with production at these levels. And fourth, given political and economic realities, we must recognize that control of production in Southeast Asia will not be easily or quickly achieved.

Growing areas

Opium is grown in northern Thailand, the Shan State of Eastern Burma and the Kachin State of Northeastern Burma, and Western Laos—the area known as the Golden Triangle. The United States has had limited information about Laotian narcotics activity since the formation of the Socialist Government, and except as specifically noted, the references to the Golden Triangle in the ensuing discussions pertain to Burma and Thailand.

The opium growing areas of all three countries of the Golden Triangle are largely remote, trackless, and rugged, inhabited by ethnically distinctive tribal people—hill tribes which have grown opium for decades as their major cash crop. These hill tribes people (Shan, Kachin, Karen, Lisu, and Lahu, among others) have historically practiced a "slash and burn" method of agriculture which exhausts the soil and destroys the natural erosion control of trees and plants so that much of the area is no longer arable. In addition to providing a guaranteed, although labor intensive, cash crop, opium has historically satisfied their medicinal requirements.

In Thailand the principal opium growing areas are in Chiang Mai, Chiang Rai, Mae Hong Son, and Nan Provinces, with lesser amounts grown in adjacent northern provinces. The Burmese area of intensive cultivation spans a region of mountains and jungle encompassing most of the Shan Plateau running from the Eastern Kachin State along the China border down nearly 600 miles into the Kayah State, with the most intensive area of cultivation east of the Salween River and north of Kengtung. This area has traditionally provided a stable, cheap, and plentiful supply of opium for the international market.

Trafficking organizations

Trafficking in opium in the Golden Triangle is controlled by various ethnically based insurgent, revolutionary and warlord groups. The Burmese Communist Party, the Shan United Army, the Lahu National Liberation Army, and others have turned increasingly to narcotics production and trafficking to finance their activities. Several of these groups control the refining of opium into heroin.

Warlord armies control the majority of the narcotics trafficking in the Golden Triangle and the refining in the Thai-Burma border area. Most of these groups masquerade as ethnic insurgents, are well armed, and are organized along military lines. The soldiers may be Shan, Aka, Lahu, or Lisu; most of the leaders are Chinese, Sino-Thai, or Sino-Burmese. Many have a history of involvement with the Kuomintang military units, some with ties reaching back to World War II. In Burma, several of these units were Kha Kwe Yei, the so-called Burmese militia units deputized by Rangoon in 1967 to fight the Burmese Communist Party. All of these groups were officially outlawed by 1973. Today, their activities cover a broad range of illegal enterprises ranging from narcotics trafficking and refining to smuggling consumer goods into Burma. Over the past decade, the most significant trafficking groups have been the

Chinese Irregular Forces (CIF) and the Shan United Army (SUA).

From the early 1950's to about 1975, most of the Golden Triangle narcotics trafficking was controlled by the Third and Fifth Chinese Irregular Forces (CIF), which were headquartered in Thailand at Tam Ngop and Mae Salong, after their bases were forced out of Burma in 1961. These groups, which are currently estimated to have 2,500–3,000 men in arms are the remnants and descendants of Nationalist Chinese groups which retreated into Burma and Thailand from 1948 to 1952. In 1972, the United States supported a Thai Government effort to remove the CIF from the narcotics trade. In exchange for the CIF's promise in 1972 to refrain from further involvement in narcotics, the Thai Government provided financial assistance and permission for legal residence in Thailand. Subsequently, it has become clear that, while some CIF narcotics activity may have been reduced, the CIF has not ended its involvement as promised.

In 1972–73, warlord leader Lo Hsing Han made a major attempt to supplant the CIF, in alliance with other insurgent and warlord groups, including the Shan State Army. Lo's effort to control the narcotics trade was aborted with his arrest in 1973 by the Thai Government and extradition to Burma for trial and imprisonment. In 1975, the first of the Burmese Government's "Mohein" military operations seized the most important of the CIF's narcotics refineries and stockpiles, dealing a serious blow to CIF domination of the narcotics trade.

Burmese Government military operations during the 1973–1977 period also brought an end to the immense mule caravans that formerly transported opium south out of Burma and across mountainous ridges into Thailand. To avoid increasingly vigorous Burmese attacks and to reduce the chance of detection, traffickers began using smaller caravans, and resorting to human carriers.

Warlord Chang Chi-Fu (or, Khun Sa) took advantage of the disruptions caused by these Burmese anti-narcotics measures against other larger and established trafficking groups, and after 1975 expanded his narcotics operations. Described as a rebellious former Burmese militia commander, Chang Chi-Fu was under Burmese confinement from 1969 to 1975, when he escaped. By 1978–79, Chang Chi-Fu and the SUA had secured control of about two-thirds of Golden Triangle heroin production. Headquartered in the Thai border town of Ban Hin Taek, Chang built up an extensive network of contacts in Thailand as security against attacks by the Thai Government. He also attempted to develop a propaganda image as a popular Burmese ethnic insurgent leader, and an image as a security bulwark for Thailand against advances by the Burmese Communist Party. (These efforts were far more successful in the West than in Burma.) Chang occasionally provided soldiers to the Thai military for counter-insurgency operations. Chang, who has periodically entered into extensive business arrangements with the Burmese Communist Party, is now a prime target for the anti-narcotics actions of the governments in Rangoon and Bangkok.

In February 1980, the Burmese Government, which outlawed the 3,500-man SUA army in 1971, attacked SUA narcotics refineries in the Lao Lo Chai area. Over the border, the Royal Thai Government, after several less effective measures against Chang, offered the equivalent of a $25,000 reward for his arrest, and then increased efforts to ensure Thai control over the area around Ban Hin Taek. These efforts culminated in the January 21, 1982 assault by Thai Border Patrol Police and the Thai Air Force on Ban Hin Taek. This military operation resulted in the destruction of SUA barracks and Chang's home, and in the capture of significant amounts of military and communications equipment, arms, and munitions. While large quantities of opium or heroin were not seized, there was some disruption of the last stages of the opium harvest in the Chang Rai area and some interruption of refinery operations. While the raid succeeded in driving most of the SUA out of Thailand, Chang Chi-Fu was not captured.

However, the raid, the loss of life (16–17 Thai police and a greater number of the SUA), and the resultant publicity have apparently raised the consciousness of the Thai Government and public to the dangers of allowing narcotics traffickers to control significant portions of Thai territory. When the SUA attempted to reestablish itself in Thailand, the Thai responded with a second military action in May, which again sent Chang Chi-Fu's forces across the border into Burma. A third, extensive assault involving Tahan Prahan Irregulars, the BPP, and the Air Force occurred in October/November. It resulted in destruction of the SUA's third headquarters in less than a year, destruction of a refinery, and seizure of some opiates as well as lab equipment.

We expect continued pressure by both the Thai and the Burmese against the SUA. The Thai Government has assured the United States that it will continue to pursue Chang and prevent his establishing an army again in another area of Thailand.

At the same time, the Thai have targetted other warlord groups/heroin traffickers, such as the Shan United Revolutionary Army and the 3rd and 5th CIFs, and we expect the Thai and Burmese Governments to continue their pressure, particularly against other trafficking groups which may attempt to replace the SUA. The Burmese Government is keeping a close watch on Lo Hsing Han, freed in a 1980 amnesty, to prevent his reinvolvement with narcotics.

An important factor in the current assessment is the full-scale move by the Burmese Communist Party into narcotics after 1978–79. Narcotics trafficking by BCP elements prior to 1978 appears to have been the work of individuals without explicit approval by the party leadership. However, in 1978–79, the BCP appears to have begun compensating for a sharp reduction, if not elimination, of Chinese assistance by resorting to party-sponsored and centrally-directed cultivation of and trading in opium—including association with the SUA. Today, the BCP has an estimated armed strength of 10,000 to 12,000 men (with a 30,000-man militia as well), and controls large areas of Burma, particularly in the Shan Plateau, which are centers of opium poppy cultivation. The BCP has moved closer to the Thai/Burmese border recently, and has involved itself more directly in the refining and trafficking of opium and heroin, as well as cultivation.

The anticipation is that the BCP will attempt to expand its narcotics operations and profits at the expense of other groups. This has brought it into direct conflict with the SUA, in what has historically been a constantly shifting pattern of alliances, betrayals, and realignments among trafficking groups.

In addition to the narcotics trafficking by warlord, revolutionary, and insurgent groups, there are a number of smaller syndicates, and independents, who from time to time are involved in trafficking or refining or both. Often they pay a percentage fee to one of the major trafficking groups for refining facilities or protection.

Refining

Narcotics refining in the Golden Triangle occurs primarily in Burma. Many of the refineries are located a few kilometers of the Thai border, allowing ready movement of the facilities and their products into Thailand as the need arises.

An understanding of the nature and character of this refining process is as important to assessing the difficulties of controlling Southeast Asian production as is the understanding of the trafficking system and the principal traffickers. The typical refinery is located in rough terrain dominated by jungle-covered ridges, near small streams. The equipment is easily dismantled, and fairly primitive: enameled pots or copper vats, strainers and filters, pans, trays, and a simple heating source, usually a charcoal-fueled stove. The chemicals, particularly acetic anhydride, are primarily supplied illegally through Thailand or Malaysia. The heroin chemists are generally ethnic Chinese who reside at the refineries.

The laboratories refine the morphine base (pit'zu) into either heroin number 3 (smoking variety) or heroin number 4 (which is 95 percent pure and suitable for intravenous injections). The raw opium, particularly from Burma, is reduced to morphine base very close to the poppy fields for convenience of travel, since the process reduces the opium by a factor of 10 to 1.

Recently, a refined form of heroin base—a step between pit'zu and heroin 3 or 4—has been discovered by narcotics agents, especially in Hong Kong. This heroin base is particularly prized by the professional narcotics trafficker because it can be refined by a relatively simple process into heroin 3 or 4.

Distribution

The vast majority of the narcotics moving out of the Golden Triangle continues to cross the Thai/Burma frontier, which remains the primary site of the region's heroin refineries—but, today, trafficking is often accomplished by truck or river boat. While most Golden Triangle narcotics are transported out of Burma's Shan State and across Thailand to reach the outside world, new routes have also been developed along the Burmese Tenassirim coast to Malaysia, or south through central Burma to the Andaman Sea, and then to Malaysia and Singapore. Because of its long seacoast, extensive river system, and large numbers of fishing boats, it is quite difficult to control narcotics traffic in, around, and through Thailand.

Many syndicates or combinations of syndicates and individuals control the international trafficking. Big-time traffickers usually are well-connected and successful in avoiding arrest. Hong Kong, Penang, Kuala Lumpur, and Singapore, as well as Bangkok, provide way stations for international narcotics traffic and banking facilities for "laundering" the enormous amounts of money generated by the narcotics trade. Procedurally, established trafficking groups control the refining operations, while groups of financiers pool their resources to purchase a quantity of heroin from a refinery. They then locate a courier to carry the narcotics to a point of debarkation and additional couriers are found to smuggle the shipment to the country of destination. In addition to these organizations there are casual overseas purchasers, frequently addicts, who come to Thailand to make a purchase and attempt to smuggle it out of Thailand.

Major international airports remain the preferred departure areas for traffickers, although Customs seizures significantly increase the risks. In an effort to deceive Customs officials, couriers are taking circuitous routes, which include the People's Republic of China.

SOCIAL, POLITICAL, AND ECONOMIC FACTORS

While the patterns of narcotics production and trafficking have modernized since the mid-1970's, when opium caravans transversed Burma and Thailand almost without interruption, there have also been important changes in the impact this production and trafficking have had on governments, economies, and indigenous populations—social, political, and economic impacts that, to some still undetermined degree, represent new motivations for increased narcotics control activities.

One of the most significant factors affecting the attitudes of some Thai and Burmese leaders toward narcotics is the recognition that their own people have developed serious addiction problems. While opium consumption and addiction have been traditional and generally tolerated, addicts are no longer relegated to opium dens in "China Town" or in the hill tribes—and there are now large heroin-using populations, including young, primarily urban, addicts.

The Thai Government estimates its heroin addict population at 300,000 to 500,000 people, out of a population of 48 million. In addition, marijuana is readily available throughout the country, and there are increasing reports of misuse of tranquilizers, barbiturates, amphetamines, and morphine. It is estimated there are over 100,000 opiate addicts in Burma which reports 32,000 registered opiate addicts. Malaysia, a major consumer of Golden Triangle narcotics, has from 100,000 to 300,000 heroin addicts out of a population of 14 million; 69,000 of these addicts are registered. These heroin addict populations are proportionately higher than that of the United States, which has an estimated 450,000 addicts out of a population of 230 million people.

The fact that much of the Golden Triangle's narcotics production is consumed within the region has important implications for the Burmese and Thai Governments as well as our own. It creates a significant hidden economy which evades taxation, frustrates economic policies, and distorts economic activities. The funds derived from this local consumption provide a resource and financial base independent of the large profits from the overseas trade, and finances insurgencies and terrorism.

The growing domestic addict populations add immeasurably to internal social and health care problems, and debilitates users, many of whom are youths. The welfare costs are also significant.

Narcotics refining and trafficking feed on corruption and encourage it. The corruption of public officials provides disincentives for a stable national policy and economy and discourages positive action against other criminal activities often linked to narcotics.

Cities in Asia, like Bangkok, Kuala Lumpur, and some areas of Hong Kong, have serious crime problems, and, while a direct connection between addiction and street crime is not always easy to substantiate, narcotics activities are often interconnected with other criminal activities such as prostitution and gambling.

REGIONAL STRATEGY

The Department believes that a multifaceted approach is essential to achieving our narcotics reduction objectives in Southeast Asia.

Our narcotics control strategy for the Southeast Asian region is to stimulate governments to take effective action against illicit drug production and major trafficking that will achieve the objective of reducing the availability of Southeast Asian narcotics in the United States.

Diplomatically, we impress upon governments in this region (and all other regions) their national responsibilities under treaties to control illicit narcotic cultivation, production, and trafficking. We recognize that some governments need assistance in fulfilling these obligations, and we provide bilateral assistance for crop control and interdiction programs on a country-specific and regional basis—as well as support through multilateral United Nations programs. This assistance not only encourages governments in the region to undertake programs but is critically important to the success of those initiatives.

The United States recognizes that crop control can impact on local economies in producing countries—which are generally under-developed and resource-poor—and we therefore provide or stimulate income replacement projects where appropriate.

The United States also provides technical assistance for demand reduction programs, and, through funding for training by the Drug Enforcement Administration and U.S. Customs, we provide training to foreign law enforcement personnel.

While our regional strategy is heavily focused on Thailand and Burma, the Bureau also supports program initiatives to other countries through our East Asian regional project.

Our Bureau of International Narcotics Matters (INM) has budgeted $7,700,000 for programs in East Asia in fiscal year 1983. Expenditures totaled $9,257,000 in fiscal year 1982. The higher fiscal year 1982 figure chiefly represents a one-time replacement of aircraft for the Burmese program.

In the balance of our testimony, we provide details—on a country by country basis—on host country programs in crop control, interdiction and demand reduction, as well as data on the assistance provided by United States agencies, international organizations, and other foreign governments. These country reports include our assessments of the effectiveness of these efforts, the problems encountered, and prospects for future effectiveness.

THAILAND

Overview

Thailand is a grower of opium, a producer of refined opiates, and the major country of transshipment for Southeast Asian heroin. It also has a large addict population.

The U.S. Government's drug effort in Thailand focuses on opiates (opium, morphine base, and heroin), although cannabis is also grown in Thailand. There is no licit production of opium, coca, methaqualone, cannabis, amphetamines, or chemicals for conversion or refining of opium. There is some licit production of barbiturate pills or capsules from imported powder.

The primary goal of the United States is to assist the Royal Thai Government [RTG][26] in reducing as rapidly as possible the amount of opiates produced in and transmitted through Thailand.

Social, economic, and political environment

Although opium has historically been an economic and sociological fact of life in Thailand, international trafficking of finished narcotics from Thailand (and other countries in Southeast Asia) began in the 1960's in large part as a result of the buildup of U.S. military forces in Indochina. U.S. military personnel in Thailand and Vietnam provided a ready market for No. 4 injectable heroin, while No. 3 smoking heroin was being produced for local consumption and for shipment to newly expanded markets in Europe. Although the withdrawal of U.S. forces from Southeast Asia from 1973 through 1975 caused a temporary curtailment of the No. 4 heroin market, a replacement market made up of the indigenous populations in Thailand, Burma, and Malaysia developed rapidly, as did new markets in Europe and the United States.

Thai officials historically were relaxed about narcotics grown, refined, transported through, or shipped from their country since there was little perceived narcotics problem among ethnic Thai. Opium smoking (primarily limited to the Chinese in the cities and hill tribes in the countryside) was banned by the King in the early 1960's but the extensive sales of 90 percent pure heroin to American military in Thailand did not arouse major official Thai concern. However, in the ten years since the withdrawal of U.S. forces, a serious local drug abuse problem has developed and concern has increased.

The narcotics problem in Thailand has not been given the highest priority by the RTG. Problems of internal security, refugees, relations with Cambodia, Laos, and Vietnam, and the economy are of more immediate concern to both the Thai Government and the public. On the other hand,

[26] Bracketed note appears in the source text.

the RTG does devote considerable amounts of funding and manpower to anti-narcotics efforts. Unfortunately, the results have not always been consistent with the amounts of time, money, and manpower expended.

Efforts at drug control to date

The United States objective of reducing the production in and transshipment through Thailand of opium and heroin can be achieved by thorough, efficient and effective Thai enforcement of the ban on opium growing, supported by interdiction and other law enforcement programs, alternative crop substitution, treatment rehabilitation, and prevention education. An immediate goal of the United States is to assist in the development of Thai institutional capabilities to deal with the narcotics problem. Narcotics control assistance since fiscal year 1972 has amounted to some $23 million; INM has budgeted $2,475,000 for Thailand in fiscal year 1983.

Law enforcement

The Thai National Police has been the primary narcotics suppression body in Thailand. Police General Pow Sarasin, Secretary General of the Office of Narcotics Control Board (ONCB), and his deputy, General Chavalit Yodmani, are the key officials coordinating narcotics control policy and programs. Since 1973 Special Police Narcotics Suppression Centers have had units in Chiang Mai, Bangkok, and Haad Yai. In addition, the Bangkok Metropolitan Narcotics Unit is a specialized unit in the capital. The Thai Border Patrol Police have traditionally conducted narcotics operations, primarily in the North along the Thai-Burma and Thai-Lao borders. Royal Thai Customs has special units at international embarkation/debarkation points.

The United States has provided both equipment and training to Thai law enforcement entities. Thai Customs narcotics units increased from 7 to 84 members in the last few years. Customs and DEA training in methods of narcotics interdiction, investigation techniques and teaching methodology is geared toward assisting the Thai enforcement agencies to become self-sufficient in narcotic law enforcement.

The Thai Government realized in early 1982 that its ad hoc efforts to suppress the heroin trafficking groups based in Thailand and operating along the Thai/Burma border needed to be placed on a continuous basis. The Department, by reprograming funds available almost entirely within the Thai program budget, was able to respond to a Royal Thai Army request for material and operational support of five to six companies, which would provide sustained suppression of these trafficking groups. Begun last June, this force has now been trained and is deployed in the most contested area of the Thai/Burma border. The results of these activities and expectations of ongoing action were detailed earlier. Reprogramed fiscal year 1983 funds bring the total budget for this project to $2.1 million for the 12 months ending May 1983.

There has been a recent decline in the availability of precursor chemicals such as acetic anhydride used to refine opium into heroin, as a result of Thai enforcement of a "chemical free zone" in Northern Thailand. The amount of acetic anhydride reaching the northwest border refineries by traditional routes has dropped significantly, while prices have increased, and some refining activities have apparently moved to both sides of the Thai/Malaysia border.

U.S. collaborative programs in narcotics production control, demand reduction and enforcement are largely programmed with the ONCB which is the coordinating agency on narcotics matters, working through the Department of Technical and Economic Cooperation (DTEC), the agency designed to represent the RTG in matters relating to grant assistance programs with donor countries.

Crop substitution eradication

Thai Government crop substitution efforts have been carried out for over 15 years, originating with the "King's Project," in Chiang Mai Province. Eight years ago, the United Nations Fund for Drug Abuse Control (UNFDAC) became involved in the programs. Our objective is to support the UNFDAC efforts and a U.S. Agency for International Development (USAID) rural development project in the Mae Chaem watershed area.

For many opium farmers in the hill tribes of northern Thailand, opium has been the principal and sometimes only cash crop. Rice production in many areas is insufficient to meet subsistence requirements. While there has been some limited success with such new crops as potatoes, beans, and coffee, new crops have not "caught on" sufficiently either in interest or market value to be a disincentive to poppy cultivation. Although the programs have been successful in introducing new crops to limited numbers of farmers, they have, thus far, had very limited success in reducing the numbers of acres planted with opium poppies, since the Thai Government has yet to take effective action in enforcement of its opium growing ban. We now have a commitment from the Thai to develop, by early 1983, a comprehensive opium eradication strategy. Without adequate enforcement of the ban—including destruction of opium fields—opium will continue to be grown by the hill tribes because it is a guaranteed, remunerative cash crop with returns that have increased significantly over the years.

A promising recent development has been the voluntary surrender of opium stockpiles and a pledge by a few hill tribe villages to abandon cultivation in return for specific transitional assistance. We have undertaken to support Thai civil-military authorities in two such cases, and are seeking a firm commitment on a third case.

Demand reduction

Demand reduction programs in Thailand include prevention, treatment, and rehabilitation. The Thai Government actively supports demand reduction, as demonstrated by a relatively high level of cooperation and coordination between the Bangkok Metropolitan Health Department, the ONCB and the Ministry of Health. The overall project goal is to reduce the demand for narcotics in Thailand, prevent further spread of drug abuse to rural areas, and stimulate increased cooperation with law enforcement agencies through increased public and official awareness of the social impact of addiction.

The U.S. program provides training, technical assistance, and a modest amount of equipment for treatment and prevention. This project agreement on prevention, which emphasizes increasing Thai awareness of its drug abuse problems and preventive education by the schools and media, is to continue the program through fiscal year 1984.

Other government agencies

The U.S. Department of Agriculture has been funding crop substitution, research and extension activities in Thailand since 1973; this program is funded at $500,000 in 1981 and 1982. The program objective is to identify viable alternative agricultural cropping systems to replace income from opium poppy production. The USAID Mae Chaem project of rural development in an opium growing watershed was signed in August 1980 to raise the standard of living of the hill tribe people in the area. The initial U.S. contribution was $4.2 million, but a total U.S. contribution of $10 million is anticipated over a 7-year period. The Thai Government has agreed to provide $11 million as its contribution to the agreement to control opium poppy cultivation in the project area. The U.S. Information Agency supports U.S. narcotics control objectives through a modest information program on prevention, and by dissemination of policy and program information.

International organizations and other countries

As noted, the United Nations Fund For Drug Abuse Control (UNFDAC) has an active pilot crop substitution program which has received logistical and agricultural resource support from the USDA and State Department narcotics program in Thailand. The UN contribution is $2.4 million for 5 years matched by $1,235,800 in Thai funds. UNFDAC recently evaluated this project and extended it for two years, with greater Thai involvement. UNFDAC is implementing several programs for treatment, rehabilitation, prevention and research, projected at almost $2 million with $9 million matching Thai funding over a 4-year period. This program would build upon U.S. programs in demand reduction.

The Colombo Plan spends $10,000 annually, primarily in training and conferences. The Thai contribute $5,000 per year to the Plan.

The Federal Republic of Germany has initiated a crop substitution project in Northern Thailand with the orientation phase cost of almost $90,000 to be matched by an RTG contribution of almost $73,000.

An $80 million World Bank rural development project in Northern Thailand will include several opium growing areas, but has not yet been implemented.

Canada has provided $200,000 for narcotic related projects in health and crop substitution and training. The United Kingdom has provided some commodities, a coffee expert, and $50,000 each year to Thai law enforcement. New Zealand, France, and Japan provide funds for educational grants and other crop substitution programs. In recent discussions, we have encouraged the Japanese to provide assistance to advance narcotics control.

Other U.S. assistance

In Fiscal year 1982, the United States contributed $79 million to Thailand for military assistance programs, $27 million for development assistance, $5 million in economic support funds (ESF), and $2 million for U.S. Peace Corps activities.

Prospects for the future

Although the U.S. narcotics assistance program has been active in Thailand for some time, success, particularly in terms of controlling the "choke points" of entry of refined heroin from Burma, has not been in keeping with the amount of funds expended. Recent military/police actions against the SUA represent a major breakthrough, demonstrating a determined Thai commitment to suppress the heroin trafficking organizations on the Thai/Burma border. We are assured of continued, expanded suppression efforts. However, there has been limited success in interdiction. The United States is hopeful that many Thai will increasingly understand the importance of controlling opium production, refining, and heroin trafficking—for their own social and economic well-being, and to overcome the international notoriety of being the primary conduit for illicit drugs in East Asia.

Thus, while we applaud the Government's military actions against the SUA, and look forward to the opium control strategy promised for early 1983, we are disappointed that the Thai have thus far failed to enforce the opium poppy ban effectively, even in areas which have benefitted from the United Nations crop substitution program.

BURMA

Overview

Burma is the primary opium growing area in Southeast Asia. The United States objective is to reduce the flow of Burmese opium and heroin into the international and U.S. markets. Our bilateral program of assistance is very important to the Burmese; the dangers both of domestic narcotics abuse and international narcotics traffic are well understood by the highest officials of the Socialist Republic of the Union of Burma and throughout most elements of Burmese society.

Burma is committed to eliminating domestic drug abuse, reducing opium production, and destroying organizations which grow and traffic in narcotics. The Burmese have developed programs involving military and paramilitary operations in narcotics source areas against narcotics caravans and refugees, as well as route interdiction, law enforcement, treatment, rehabilitation, crop substitution and destruction, education, and propaganda programs.

Social, economic, and political environment

For the Burmese Government, illicit narcotics pose a combination of social, political and security problems—all interrelated.

The social problem of narcotics in Burma is both historical and modern. Opium usage and addiction in Burma are not a recent phenomena. The hill tribe growers of the area historically have consumed the opium for medicinal purposes as well as for general addiction. In 1942, when the British evacuated Burma in the face of the advancing Japanese Army, there were 50,000 registered opium addicts.

The increasing world focus on the role played by Burma's opium crop in international trafficking has led to concern by the government over its international image. In 1974 Burma passed a strict Narcotics and Dangerous Drug Law. Since then, anti-drug efforts have been given a high priority by the government and the general population. The Burmese enforcement agencies and courts enforce narcotics laws vigorously and generally impose severe sentences on convicted offenders. Sentences of 5 years' imprisonment for illegal narcotics usage are not uncommon. Convicted peddlers and traffickers inevitably receive long prison sentences, with 10 years generally the minimum. On December 15, 1980, the Burmese Government issued an order establishing rewards for seizures of narcotics and other contraband. This reward system may increase the amount of narcotics seized in Burma.

Burma's narcotics problem is intertwined with the insurgency problem. Since independence in 1948, the Rangoon government has been plagued by rebellious groups seeking national power (BCP) and by ethnic minorities seeking autonomy for their regions (the Shan, Kachin, and Lahu insurgency groups, to name a few). To these groups have been added several powerful armed bands of narcotics traffickers, usually ethnic Chinese, at least in leadership. As previously noted, these groups are heavily dependent upon the opium trade for their income, arms purchases, and other activities.

A significant reduction in opium production and trading would affect some areas of Burma more than others. The economy in the Eastern Shan State appears to be heavily dependent upon opium revenues. For some hill tribes, opium in the past has been an acceptable and valued cash crop. The recent prohibition against opium growing and the subsequent Burmese eradication programs have taken away some disposable income from growers, but the majority of growers were rarely dependent upon opium for their total livelihood.

Efforts at drug control to date

United States assistance has been significant in supporting Burmese anti-narcotics efforts—some $47 million over the last 10 years. INM has budgeted $5 million for Burma in fiscal year 1983.

American-Burmese cooperation against illicit narcotics began with a June 1974 bilateral agreement, effected by an exchange of notes between the American Ambassador and the head of the Burmese People's Police. Under the terms of this agreement, and subsequent amendments, and the current project agreement, the United States provides Burma with helicopters, fixed-wing aircraft, communications equipment and associated training and equipment-maintenance support. The bulk of our current budget is dedicated to aircraft maintenance contracts for previously supplied equipment. Additionally, to assist the Burmese Government in developing replacement means of income for former opium growers, the United States has provided limited assistance in development of alternative agriculture and livestock projects. Our crop substitution program has included special beekeeping and swine/poultry training at Ohio State University for 20 Burmese students.

Burmese programs

Narcotics in Burma is a multifaceted problem and the country has developed an integrated strategy for dealing with it. The Burmese Central Committee for Drug Abuse Control (CCDAC), chaired by the Minister of Home and Religious Affairs, consists of eight deputy ministers from other concerned government ministries. Responsibilities of the CCDAC are nationwide and include all aspects of the government effort, including enforcement, crop/income substitution, and treatment/rehabilitation:

(1) Enforcement—A basic part of the Burmese enforcement strategy focuses upon interdicting narcotics caravans and destroying refineries and base camps operated by trafficking groups. Burmese police and military personnel have been active both in major operations against the BCP narcotics activities and the poppy eradication programs.

(2) Crop Substitution/Eradication—The Burmese Government estimates that it eradicated more than 10,000 acres of opium poppy in the 1981–82 season that could have produced as much as 40,000 to 45,000 kilograms of opium. While this represents about 8 percent of the total acreage under poppy cultivation in Burma, it almost doubled the previous year's destruction.

A Burmese crop substitution program supported by UNFDAC is making progress in distributing coffee and tea plants, seeds for spices, and medicinal herbs, and improved livestock to farmers in areas in which opium was formerly grown. The (CCDAC) is establishing a multisectoral livestock, horticultural, and demonstration center at Pekhon in the southern Shan State. The purpose of this center will be to provide training and to demonstrate viable crop substitution and livestock production. The INM program has provided bees, quail, and related equipment and training to support pilot programs for crop substitution. However, the full impact of these programs on opium production must await more hospitable conditions in poppy producing areas.

(3) Treatment, Rehabilitation, Training, and Information—The Burmese Ministeries of Health and Social Welfare have responsibility for addict treatment and rehabilitation programs, respectively. Treatment centers have been established in each of the major urban centers with addict population problems. Larger hospitals have treatment wards; district and township hospitals have a basic capability for treating addiction. Rehabilitation centers have been established in Kengtung, Namla, Rangoon, Mandalay, and Lashio. Both treatment and rehabilitation centers have been improved and expanded by UNFDAC.

The Burmese Government conducts a continuous program of narcotics information through the government-controlled news media, in schools, posters, and public and party indoctrination sessions.

Other programs

As indicated, UNFDAC has several programs in Burma. Between 1976 and early 1981, UNFDAC assisted Burma through financing a large multisectional drug abuse control program involving activities in law enforcement, crop and income substitution, education, health, and vocational rehabilitation at a total cost of $5,571,000 over the 5-year period. Phase II of this program was agreed upon in June 1981 for 5 years at a cost of $5,042,000. Development aid funds for this program have been provided by the Government of Norway.

Other U.S. assistance

The United States resumed economic assistance to Burma in 1980 after an absence of 15 years. The AID/Burma funding level has increased from initial amounts of $2 million in fiscal year 1980 and $3 million in fiscal year 1981 to $7.5 million in fiscal year 1982, assistance concentrated in agricultural and public health projects. Additionally, the United States provided $150,000 in fiscal year 1982 for military training under our security assistance program.

Prospects for the future

When considering the future of narcotics suppression in Burma, one must remember that it is essentially a Burmese program, not an American one. The ultimate success or failure of the program (used in the broadest sense of the term) will depend upon Burmese efforts prompted by Burmese perceptions of national priorities.

The United States has assisted and cooperated with the Burmese by providing some needed enforcement equipment (i.e., the purchase of, and maintenance funding for, telecommunications equipment, a small fleet of helicopters and fixed-wing aircraft) and modest support for Burmese pilot programs for crop substitution in opium growing areas. In addition, the United States has provided training for Burmese officials with responsibilities for customs and narcotics enforcement.

Our programs have helped sharpen the Burmese focus on their narcotics problems and our material assistance and training have given them the tools for the job at hand. Politically, our narcotics cooperation has fostered a unique (for neutralist/isolationist Burma) bilateral relationship in which our assistance relates to a sensitive Burmese domestic issue. U.S. assistance supports the narcotics control objective which is consistent with Burma's objective of securing its territory. By any measure, the number of acres of opium crop destroyed and amount of opiates seized is significant. In addition, the continuing Burmese efforts in fields not directly supported by U.S. assistance are a measure of their commitment to the overall goals of narcotics control.

Nevertheless, the narcotics program in Burma must be viewed as an integral part of the Golden Triangle narcotics phenomena. As long as Burmese warlords/insurgents/bandits know that they can enjoy even temporary safe haven in Thailand and Burma, the Thai and Burmese police/military actions and threats will be limited in their effectiveness. Greater Burmese/Thai cooperation and coordination is an essential long-term goal. In the last analysis, however, real progress in Burma will depend on greater Burmese authority in the poppy growing areas.

OTHER EAST ASIAN PROGRAMS

INM supports other program activity in East Asia through its East Asian regional budget and through funding and other support for the Colombo Plan project.

A specific goal of the Bureau's East Asian regional activity is to support programs among Association of Southeast Asian Nations (ASEAN) members which are designed to impede illicit narcotics production, processing, trafficking, and consumption. The INM regional program includes law enforcement, prevention, education, and technical assistance in treatment and rehabilitation. The Bureau has budgeted $225,000 for its regional projects in fiscal year 1983.

For example, in Malaysia, which is both a major narcotics consumer as well as an important transshipment center, the Bureau has just concluded a technical assistance program which developed a drug counseling and rehabilitation program within the Malaysian prison system, and assisted in the development of a national strategy on drug control and an after-care program.

Similarly, in Indonesia, where our objective is to assist that government in preventing the country from becoming either an alternative opium growing area or a major transshipment point, the Bureau's agreement is to provide commodities, training and personnel exchange—at an estimated cost of $50,000 through 1984—to stimulate the Indonesian Government to take more comprehensive actions on its own initiative, in both supply reduction as well as demand reduction.

CONCLUSION

The specific commitments and actions which we seek on a country-by-country basis are integral to the success of our Southeast Asian strategy. However, the United States is also seeking greater cooperation within the region, and believes that such internal cooperation is also essential to achieving narcotics control objectives in Southeast Asia.

In this regard, we are supporting ASEAN, and we are encouraging regional and bilateral contacts, which we believe should include Burma and Hong Kong.

Throughout the region, we are seeking wider adoption of precursor chemical controls, as well as agreements on seizures of financial assets, and on legal cooperation.

The United States cannot, in the final analysis, control opium production in Southeast Asia. We can only facilitate the achievement of control by the producing and transit nations. We are employing, therefore, a strategy that not only provides these governments with the capacity to act, but encourages and sustains them in the will to act.

Nor can we succeed with just a bilateral effort. As cultivation and refining sites multiply, and the number of trafficking organizations and routes expand, in keeping with worldwide demand, the conclusion is inescapable that, more than ever, ultimate success depends on achieving comprehensive, simultaneous control in the many key growing areas. The United States is actively enlisting the participation of other victim and donor nations. We are encouraging greater contributions to bilateral and multilateral control projects. We are attempting to internationalize the response to a global problem.

---

5. The Question of Chemical Warfare

Document 475

Transcript of an Interview With the Secretary of State (Haig), February 14, 1982 (Extract)[1]

"There's No Question in Our Minds That Such [Chemical] Weapons Have Been Used and Are Continuing to be Used"

. . . .

MR. WILL. You heard Mr. Menshikov[2] say a moment ago that there's no evidence whatever that he knows that they're using "yellow rain," so-called chemical weapons.

You've been beaten up roundly by the *Wall Street Journal* and others for not making enough of an issue of this. Do you agree with them?

SECRETARY HAIG. I raised this issue in Geneva.[3] With every passing day, Mr. Will, we get more incontrovertible evidence of the use of mycotoxins in Afghanistan, Laos, and Kampuchea.

We now even have specific estimates of casualties of noncombatants which are in the range of scores of thousands in all three target areas.

---

[1] Source: Department of State Press Release 67, February 16, 1982. This interview was broadcast on the ABC News television program "This Week With David Brinkley," beginning at 11:05 a.m.

[2] Stanislav Menshikov, the Spokesman on Arms Control and Disarmanent of the Soviet Union's Central Committee, was interviewed on the same program just prior to Secretary Haig. Menshikov denied that his government had used chemical weapons and he stated that the United States "has made a decision to resume or expand the production of chemical weapons. . . ." He also stated that the Soviet Union and the United States "should get together and settle the question of chemical weapons." The complete text of Menshikov's remarks is in the ABC News transcript of the February 14 program, "This Week With David Brinkley."

[3] At a January 26 meeting between Secretary Haig and Soviet Foreign Minister Andrei Gromyko.

There's no question in our minds that such weapons have been and are continuing to be used.

MR. WILL. Mr. Secretary, if there were the slightest hint that the United States ever did a thing like that, you can imagine the uproar in the world. There was an uproar because there were five rifles on television in El Salvador now.

SECRETARY HAIG. I agree with you.

MR. WILL. Why is this country incapable of making more of a ruckus over poison gas?

SECRETARY HAIG. We are doing this with a great deal of a ruckus, so to speak. We have brought all of the information to the United Nations committee which is investigating it. We have been somewhat disappointed by their initial reaction, but we've given them far more extensive evidence in recent weeks.

I have raised it in the most unequivocal way with Mr. Gromyko, and we have briefed the press repeatedly. It just is a question that I would share your frustration about. I sometimes wonder why we focus more on the pecadillos of the Western World than the tragic policies being pursued in the East.

MR. WILL. Is the Soviet Union in violation of the treaty regarding chemical and biological weapons? And, if so, why don't we renounce the treaty?

SECRETARY HAIG. There are two aspects to this question, and they have difficult, technical roots. One is that mycotoxins themselves are controversial as to whether they are chemical or biological.

We have a firm agreement on biological. We do not have as firm an agreement on chemical as Mr. Menshikov expressed. There have been ongoing discussions for a number of years that have led nowhere because of Soviet unwillingness to accept verification that we feel is essential.

MR. BRINKLEY. I agree with George—I'm sure you do—that if the United States were accused of this, there would be crowds in the streets in Europe carrying signs. There aren't any there about it now.

Thank you, Mr. Haig, for being with us today. I hope you come again.

Document 476

Statement by the Deputy Secretary of State (Stoessel), March 22, 1982 (Extract)[4]

"The Chemical and Toxin Weapons Which the Soviet Union Has Developed, Used and Supplied to its Clients Are a Cheap and Effective Way to Terrorize and Exterminate Defenseless Peoples"

Thank you, Dean. Good morning, ladies and gentlemen.

This morning Secretary Haig transmitted to the Congress a report on chemical warfare in Southeast Asia and Afghanistan.[5]

The report is also being provided to the Secretary-General of the United Nations and to each member government of that world organization.

This report contains the most comprehensive compilation of material on this subject available and presents conclusions which are fully shared by all relevant agencies of the U.S. Government. The judgments contained in this study were arrived at through a rigorous, analytical process. Every relevant piece of information available to the U.S. Government was reviewed.

All the test data on physical evidence, including environment samples and background controls were gone over again. A scientific report on toxins was prepared. The medical evidence was analyzed. Extensive consultations were held with government and nongovernmental scientists and medical authorities, many of whom were asked to review the evidence. This information was then correlated.

The testimony of eyewitnesses, date, place, and type of attack was matched

---

[4] Source: Department of State files. Stoessel made the statement at the opening of a Department of State briefing which began at 11 a.m. Omitted is Stoessel's introduction of Richard Burt, Director of the Bureau of Politico-Military Affairs, who conducted the subsequent question-and-answer session.

[5] For an extract, on chemical warfare in Southeast Asia, see *infra*.

against information from defectors, journalists, international organizations, and sensitive sources and methods. Information dating back to 1975, reviewed, analyzed, and correlated in this manner has led the U.S. Government to conclude that in Laos selected Lao and Vietnamese forces under direct Soviet supervision have employed lethal trichothecene toxins and other combinations of chemical agents against Hmong resisting government control and their villages since at least 1976.

Trichothecene toxins have been positively identified but medical symptoms indicate that irritants, incapacitants, and nerve agents also have been employed. Thousands have been killed or severely injured. Thousands also have been driven from their homeland by the use of these agents.

In Kampuchea, Vietnamese forces have used lethal trichothecene toxins on democratic Kampuchean troops and Khmer villages since at least 1978.

Medical evidence indicates that irritants, incapacitants, and nerve agents also have been used. Toxins and other chemical warfare agents have been developed in the Soviet Union provided to the Lao and Vietnamese, either directly or through the transfer of know-how and fabricated into weapons with Soviet assistance in Laos, Vietnam, and Kampuchea.

In Afghanistan, Soviet forces have used a variety of lethal and nonlethal chemical agents on resistance forces and Afghan villages since the Soviet invasion in December 1979. In addition, there is some evidence that Afghan Government forces may have used Soviet-supplied chemical weapons against the freedom fighters even before the Soviet invasion.

The implications of these findings are far-reaching. The use in war of lethal chemical or toxin weapons is forbidden by one of the oldest arms control agreements still in force, the Geneva Protocol of 1925,[6] and by the customary international law which has grown out of that agreement.

The possession, manufacture, storage, and transfer of toxin weapons is forbidden by one of the most recent arms control treaties now in force, the Biological and Toxin Weapons Convention of 1972.[7]

As this report documents, the Soviet Union and its allies are flagrantly and repeatedly violating international law and international agreement.

Chemical warfare thus poses a threat not only to its immediate victims but to the entire international community and particularly to those nations least able to defend themselves against such weapons. For the chemical and toxin weapons which the Soviet Union has developed, used, and supplied to its clients are a cheap, convenient, and effective way to subdue, terrorize, and exterminate defenseless peoples.

If the world community fails to halt this activity in Laos, Kampuchea, and Afghanistan, it will have little chance to prevent its repetition in other lands against other peoples.

As the report states, only an alert and outspoken world community, intent to maintain those standards of international behavior it has so painfully achieved and so tenuously established, can bring sufficient pressure to bear to halt these violations of law and treaty.

With the publication of this report, the world community has been alerted. The United States will continue to be outspoken. We are confident other nations, as they recognize the danger, will do likewise.

. . . .

Document 477

Report by the Department of State Submitted to the Congress, March 22, 1982 (Extracts)[8]

Chemical Warfare in Southeast Asia

. . . .

This study presents the evidence available to the U.S. Government on chemical warfare activities in

[6] For the text of the 1925 Protocol for the Prohibition of the Use in War of Asphyxiating, Poisonous or Other Gases, and of Bacteriological Methods of Warfare, ratified by the United States in 1975, see 26 UST 571.

[7] The Biological Weapons Convention was signed in London, Washington, and Moscow on April 10, 1972, and entered into force on March 26, 1975; for text, see 26 UST 583.

[8] Source: *Chemical Warfare in Southeast Asia and Afghanistan*, Department of State Special Report No. 98, March 22, 1982, pp. 4, 6–8, 10–11, 13–14, 17–18. For the portions of the report primarily on chemical warfare in Afghanistan, see document 440. Omitted from the report printed here are Secretary Haig's undated transmittal letter to the Congress, a chronology, several maps, tables, and figures, the sections on Afghanistan, and five annexes.

Laos, Kampuchea, and Afghanistan through January 1982 and examines the Soviet involvement in those activities. It is based on a massive amount of information, from a variety of sources, which has been carefully compiled and analyzed over the years. The paper is accompanied by annexes and tables that provide details of the medical evidence and sample analyses, a technical description of trichothecene toxins, and other supporting data.

INTRODUCTION

Nearly 7 years ago, reports of the use of lethal chemical weapons began to emerge from Laos. In 1978, similar reports started to come from Kampuchea, and in 1979 from Afghanistan. Early reports were infrequent and fragmentary, reflecting the remoteness of the scene of conflict and the isolation of those subjected to such attacks. In the summer of 1979, however, the State Department prepared a detailed compilation of interviews with refugees from Laos on this subject. That fall, a U.S. Army medical team visited Thailand to conduct further interviews. By the winter of 1979, the United States felt that it had sufficiently firm evidence of chemical warfare to raise the matter with the governments of Laos, Vietnam, and the Soviet Union. All three governments denied that a basis for concern over the use of chemical warfare agents existed.

Dissatisfied with these responses, and possessing further reports that lethal chemical agents were in use in Southeast Asia and Afghanistan, the U.S. Government in 1980 began to raise the issue publicly in the United Nations, with the Congress, and in other forums. In August of that year, the State Department provided extensive documentation containing evidence of chemical weapons attacks to the United Nations and also made this material publicly available. In December, as a result of efforts by the United States and other concerned nations, the U.N. General Assembly voted to initiate an international investigation into the use of chemical weapons.[9] This investigation is still underway. To date, the U.N. investigating team has been denied admission to any of the three countries where these weapons are in use.

Despite the volume of information on chemical warfare in Southeast Asia which had become available by 1980, there remained one major unresolved issue—the exact nature of the chemical agents in use. Collection of physical samples was hindered by the remoteness of the then principal areas of conflict—as many as 6 weeks by foot to the nearest international border. Tests for known chemical warfare agents on those samples that were obtained proved consistently negative.

In order to identify the chemical agents in use, U.S. experts in late 1980 began to go back over all the reporting—as far back as 1975—looking for new clues. In particular, they sought to match the reported symptomatology of victims—which commonly included skin irritation, dizziness, nausea, bloody vomiting and diarrhea, and internal hemorrhaging—with possible causes. As a result of this review, the U.S. Government in mid-1981 began to test physical samples from Southeast Asia for the presence of toxins. These substances are essentially biologically produced chemical posions. Although they have never before been used in war, this was a technical possibility, and it was noted that certain toxins could produce the sorts of symptoms observed in Southeast Asian victims of chemical warfare.

In August 1981, unnatural levels and combinations of lethal trichothecene toxins were detected in the first sample to be tested by the United States for such agents. This consisted of vegetation taken from a village in Kampuchea where an attack occurred in which people had died after exhibiting the symptoms described above. In succeeding months, further samples, taken from the sites of attacks in both Kampuchea and Laos, yielded similar results. So did samples of blood taken from victims of a chemical attack in Kampuchea.

Despite a continued flow of reports, dating back over 7 years, of chemical warfare in Southeast Asia and more recently Afghanistan, and despite the still mounting physical evidence of the use of trichothecene toxins as warfare agents, doubts as to the conclusive nature of the available evidence have persisted. These doubts have arisen for several reasons. For one, the evidence of the use of lethal chemical weapons has become available over a period of several years and from a variety of sources. Few governments, journalists, or interested members of the public have been exposed to all of this evidence, nor has it been available in any one place. A second difficulty has been the inevitable need for the U.S. Government to protect some of the relevant information, often gathered at personal risk to individuals who secured it, or obtained through the use of highly sensitive methods.

---

9 U.N. General Assembly Resolution 35/144C, adopted December 12, 1980.

This report represents an effort of the U.S. Government to correct the first deficiency and to ameliorate the second to the extent possible. In preparation of this report, all of the information available to the U.S. Government on chemical weapons use in Laos, Kampuchea, and Afghanistan was assembled in one place. This information was again reviewed, analyzed, cross-indexed, and organized in a coherent fashion. Based upon this comprehensive analysis, a set of conclusions were drawn, conclusions which have since been reviewed and agreed on without qualification by every relevant agency of the U.S. Government.

The evidence upon which this report is based is of several kinds, including:

Testimony of those who saw, experienced, and suffered from chemical weapons attacks;

Testimony of doctors, refugee workers, journalists, and others who had the opportunity to question large numbers of those with firsthand experience of chemical warfare;

Testimony of those who engaged in chemical warfare or were in a position to observe those who did;

Scientific evidence, based upon the analysis of physical samples taken from sites where attacks had been conducted;

Documentary evidence from open sources; and

Intelligence derived from "national technical means."

These sources provide compelling evidence that tens of thousands of unsophisticated and defenseless peoples have for a period of years been subjected to a campaign of chemical attacks. *Taken together, this evidence has led the U.S. Government to conclude that Lao and Vietnamese forces, operating under Soviet supervision, have, since 1975, employed lethal chemical and toxin weapons in Laos; that Vietnamese forces have, since 1978, used lethal chemical and toxin agents in Kampuchea; and that Soviet forces have used a variety of lethal chemical warfare agents, including nerve gases, in Afghanistan since the Soviet invasion of that country in 1979.*

The implications of chemical warfare in Afghanistan and Southeast Asia are painful to contemplate but dangerous to ignore. This activity threatens not only the peoples of those isolated regions but the international order upon which the security of all depends. Those who today suffer chemical warfare against their homelands are powerless to stop it. The prohibitions of international law and solemn agreement are not self-enforcing. Only an alert and outspoken world community, intent to maintain those standards of international behavior it has so painfully achieved and so tenuously established, can bring sufficient pressure to bear to halt these violations of law and treaty. It is hoped that publication of this report will be one step in this process, the end result of which will be the cessation of chemical warfare and the strengthening of the rule of law in the affairs of nations.

KEY JUDGMENTS

Laos. The U.S. Government has concluded from all the evidence that selected Lao and Vietnamese forces, under direct Soviet supervision, have employed lethal trichothecene toxins and other combinations of chemical agents against H'Mong resisting government control and their villages since at least 1976. Trichothecene toxins have been positively identified, but medical symptoms indicate that irritants, incapacitants, and nerve agents also have been employed. Thousands have been killed or severely injured. Thousands also have been driven from their homeland by the use of these agents.

Kampuchea. Vietnamese forces have used lethal trichothecene toxins on Democratic Kampuchean (DK) troops and Khmer villages since at least 1978. Medical evidence indicates that irritants, incapacitants, and nerve agents also have been used.

. . . .

The Soviet Connection. The conclusion is inescapable that the toxins and other chemical warfare agents were developed in the Soviet Union, provided to the Lao and Vietnamese either directly or through the transfer of know-how, and weaponized with Soviet assistance in Laos, Vietnam, and Kampuchea. Soviet military forces are known to store agents in bulk and move them to the field for munitions fill as needed. This practice also is followed in Southeast Asia and Afghanistan, as evidenced by many reports which specify that Soviet technicians supervise the shipment, storage, filling, and loading onto aircraft of the chemical munitions. The dissemination techniques reported and observed evidently have been drawn from years of Soviet chemical warfare testing and experimentation. *There is no evidence to support any alternative explanation, such as the hypothesis that the Vietnamese produce and employ toxin weapons completely on their own.*

METHODOLOGY

The judgments of this study were arrived at through a rigorous analytical process.

Every relevant piece of information on reported chemical warfare incidents was reviewed, recorded, and tabulated. Numbers of attacks and deaths were screened for possible duplication. Extensive data on the Soviet chemical and biological warfare program also were reviewed.

All the test data on physical evidence available to the U.S. Government—including environmental samples and background controls—were reviewed.

A scientific report on toxins, which concluded that trichothecenes probably were among the agents used in Southeast Asia, was prepared.

The medical evidence was analyzed, drawing on all available information from Southeast Asia and Afghanistan and incorporating the findings of a Department of Defense medical team, which concluded that at least three types of agents were used in Laos.

Extensive consultations were held with government and nongovernment scientists and medical authorities, many of whom were asked to review the evidence. Experts from other countries also were consulted.

After the data were organized to permit comparative analysis, the study focused on three separate questions.

Have lethal and other casualty-producing agents been used in Southeast Asia and Afghanistan?

What are these agents, and how and by whom are they employed?

Where do these agents originate, and how do they find their way to the field?

Although the evidence differs for each country, the analytical approach was the same. Testimony of eyewitnesses—date, place, and type of attack—was matched against information from defectors, journalists, international organizations, and sensitive information that often pinpointed the time and place of chemical attacks. In addition, information on military operations in the areas where chemical attacks had been reported was examined to establish whether air or artillery strikes took place or whether there was fighting in the areas where chemical agents reportedly were used. *In all three countries, instances were identified in which eyewitness accounts could be correlated directly with information from other sources on military operations in progress.*

There is no evidence of any systematic propaganda campaign by either the H'Mong in Laos or the Afghan resistance forces to promote the allegation that chemical agents have been used on their people. On the other hand, there were early indications that Pol Pot's Democratic Kampuchean resistance did engage in an organized propaganda campaign on chemical agent use. These indications made U.S. Government analysts cautious about accepting DK allegations, which increased markedly after the chemical attacks in Laos were publicized. For Kampuchea, therefore, special efforts were taken to confirm such allegations by analyzing sources of information that in no way could be considered part of a propaganda or deception campaign.

DISCUSSION OF FINDINGS

In September 1981, the U.S. Government declared publicly that toxins—poisonous chemical substances extracted from biological material—probably were the mysterious lethal agents used for many years in Laos and Kampuchea.[10] The statement was prompted by the discovery of high levels of trichothecene toxins in a vegetation sample collected shortly after a March 1981 Vietnamese chemical attack in Kampuchea. This conclusion, however, rested on a much broader base of evidence than analysis of one sample.

By April 1980, the U.S. Government had already concluded that lethal agents almost certainly had been used against H'Mong tribespeople in Laos. There was less certainty then about the use of lethal agents in Kampuchea, mainly because of the already mentioned suspicions about the propaganda campaign of Pol Pot's Democratic Kampuchean forces, although their claims subsequently were shown to be valid. It was also concluded that chances were about even that lethal agents had been used in Afghanistan. There was little doubt by April 1980 that riot-control agents and some

---

10 See the statement by Under Secretary for Political Affairs Stoessel, September 14, 1981, *American Foreign Policy: Current Documents, 1981*, document 476.

form of incapacitants had been used in all three countries. Since that April 1980 assessment, additional evidence has allowed a much firmer conclusion. There is now no doubt that casualties and deaths have resulted from chemical attacks in all three countries.

What Chemical Agents Are Being Used?

As soon as it was determined that chemical agents had been used, an effort was made to identify the specific agents. To do this it was necessary to collect and analyze at least one of the following: environmental samples contaminated with agents, the munitions used to deliver agents, or biological specimens from victims of an attack. A study by medical-toxicological experts of symptoms exhibited by individuals exposed to toxic agents provides a good indication of the general class of chemical agent used. Thus, the range of clinical manifestations from chemical agents, as reported by a U.S. Army investigative team in Thailand, resulted in the determination that nerve agents, irritants such as CS, and highly toxic hemorrhagic chemicals or mixture of chemicals were used in Laos.

Other medical-toxicological personnel who reviewed the evidence and conducted their own investigation reached the same conclusion. They further indicated that toxins such as the trichothecenes were a probable cause of the lethal hemorrhaging effect seen in Kampuchea and Laos. In many cases, symptoms reported by the Democratic Kampuchean forces in Kampuchea and the *mujahidin* in Afghanistan were similar to those reported by the H'Mong in Laos. Moreover, symptoms reported from Afghanistan and Kampuchea indicated that a highly potent, rapid-acting, incapacitant "knockout" chemical also was being used. *Mujahidin* victims and witnesses to chemical attacks reported other unusual symptoms, including a blackening of the skin, severe skin irritation along with multiple small blisters and severe itching, severe eye irritation, and difficulty in breathing—all of which suggests that phosgene oxime or a similar substance was used.

Collecting samples possibly contaminated with a toxic agent during or after a chemical assault is difficult under any circumstances but particularly when the assault is against ill-prepared people without masks or other protective equipment. Obtaining contaminated samples that will yield positive traces of specific chemical agents depends on many factors. These include the persistency of the chemical, the ambient temperature, rainfall, wind conditions, the medium on which the chemical was deposited, and the time, care, and packaging of the sample from collection to laboratory analysis.

Many traditional or known chemical warfare agents are nonpersistent and disappear from the environment within a few minutes to several hours after being dispersed. Such agents include the nerve agents sarin and tabun; the blood agents hydrogen cyanide and cyanogen chloride; the choking agents phosgene and diphosgene; and the irritant phosgene oxime. Other standard chemical warfare agents—such as the nerve agents VX and thickened soman and the blistering agents sulfur mustard, nitrogen mustard, and lewisite—may persist for several days to weeks depending on weather conditions.

The trichothecene toxins have good persistency but may be diluted by adverse weather conditions to below detectable concentrations. To maximize the chances of detection, sample collections need to be made as rapidly as possible after a chemical assault; as with many agents, this means minutes to hours. Under the circumstances of Southeast Asia and Afghanistan, such rapid collection has simply not been possible. Although many samples were collected, few held any realistic prospect of yielding positive results. It is fortunate that trichothecenes are sufficiently persistent and in some cases were not diluted by adverse weather conditions. Thus we were able to detect them several months after the attack.

Samples have been collected from Southeast Asia since mid-1979 and from Afghanistan since May 1980. To date, about 50 individual samples—of greatly varying types and usefulness for analytical purposes—have been collected and analyzed for the presence of known chemical warfare agents, none of which has been detected. Based on recommendations by medical and toxicological experts and findings of investigators from the U.S. Army's Chemical Systems Laboratory, several of the samples have been analyzed for the trichothecene group of mycotoxins. Four samples, two from Kampuchea and two from Laos, were found to contain high levels of trichothecene toxins. In addition, preliminary results of the analysis of blood samples drawn from victims of an attack indicate the presence of a trichothecene metabolite of T–2, namely HT–2.

A review of all reports indicates the use of many different chemical agents, means of delivery, and types of chemical attacks. The use of trichothecene toxins has been identified through symptoms and sample analysis. In some cases, however, the symptoms suggest other agents, such as nerve gas, which have not been identified through sample analysis. Significant differences as well as similarities have surfaced in the reports from the three countries. The evidence from each country, therefore, is described separately, with attention drawn to similarities where appropriate.

Laos

Reports of chemical attacks against H'Mong villages and guerrilla strongholds in Laos date from the summer of 1975 to the present (see Table 1[11]). Most of the reports were provided by H'Mong refugees who were interviewed in Thailand and the United States. More than 200 interviews were carried out variously by U.S. Embassy officials in Thailand, a Department of Defense team of medical-toxicological experts (see Annex B[11]), U.S. physicians, Thai officials, journalists, and representatives of international aid and relief organizations. According to the interviews, Soviet AN–2 and captured U.S. L–19 and T–28/41 aircraft usually were employed to disseminate toxic chemical agents by sprays, rockets, and bombs. In some cases, Soviet helicopters and jet aircraft were said to have been used.

The reports describe 261 separate attacks in which at least 6,504 deaths were cited as having resulted directly from exposure to chemical agents. The actual number of deaths is almost certainly much higher, since the above figure does not take account of deaths in attacks for which no specific casualty figures were reported. The greatest concentration of reported chemical agent use occurred in the area where the three provinces of Vientiane, Xiangkhoang, and Louangphrabang adjoin (see map[12]). This triborder region accounted for 77% of the reported attacks and 83% of the chemical-associated deaths. Most of the reported attacks took place in 1978 and 1979. Since 1979, the incidence of chemical attacks appears to have been lower, but reported death rates among unprotected and untreated victims were higher. Only seven chemical attacks were reported in the fall of 1981, for example, yet 1,034 deaths were associated with those incidents.

The medical symptoms reportedly produced by the chemical agents are varied. According to knowledgeable physicians, the symptoms clearly point to at least three types of chemical agents—incapacitant/riot-control agents, a nerve agent, and an agent causing massive hemorrhaging. The last-named was positively identified as trichothecene toxins. This was announced publicly by Secretary Haig in September 1981.[13]

In a number of the refugee reports, eyewitnesses described attacks as consisting of "red gas" or a "yellow cloud." Red gas was considered the more lethal. A former Lao Army captain stated that the "red gas" caused the H'Mong to die within 12 hours. An employee of an international organization interviewed victims of a September 15, 1979 attack in which nonlethal rounds preceded an attack by five or six "red gas" bombs that covered a 500-meter area. Persons within 30–100 meters of the circle died in 10 minutes after severe convulsions. Others had headaches, chest pains, and vomiting but did not die.

Every qualified interrogator who systematically interviewed the H'Mong refugees concluded that they had been subjected to chemical attacks. A U.S. Government medical team returned from Thailand in 1979 convinced that several unidentified chemical warfare agents had produced the symptoms described by the refugees. This evidence was expanded by testimony from a variety of sources, including that of a Lao pilot who flew chemical warfare missions before defecting in 1979. His detailed description of the Lao, Vietnamese, and Soviet program to use chemical agents to defeat the H'Mong resistance helped dispel any lingering suspicions that the refugees had fabricated or embellished the stories. The Lao pilot described the chemical rocket he had fired as having a more loosely fitting warhead than a conventional rocket. (His account appears in Annex A.)[14]

In 1977, a H'Mong resistance leader found a U.S. 2.75-inch rocket[15] with a modified Soviet warhead that fits the Lao pilot's description. Other sources reported that U.S. 2.75-inch rockets were fitted with Soviet-supplied lethal chemical warheads by Soviet and Vietnamese technicians at facilities

[11] Not printed.

[12] Not printed.

[13] Reference is to Secretary Haig's address before the Berlin Press Association, September 13, 1981; for text, see *American Foreign Policy: Current Documents, 1981,* document 15.

[14] Not printed.

[15] During withdrawal of U.S. forces from Vietnam, thousands of these fell into Vietnamese hands. [Footnote in the source text.]

in Vientiane as well as in Xiangkhoang and Savannakhet Provinces. Munitions storage facilities suitable for storing chemical agents and weapons have been identified in each of these provinces. The aircraft types—AN–2s, L–19s, and T–28/41s—most often reported by the H'Mong refugees as being used to deliver chemical agents have been identified as based on airfields in northern Laos throughout this period. A special Lao Air Force unit is responsible for chemical rockets. The unit is commanded by a Soviet-trained Lao and has a Soviet rocket expert attached as an adviser.

Obtaining additional data for Laos has been difficult because of the nature of the fighting there. There have been few major operations. The reports reflect numerous minor engagements between the opposing forces. In nearly all cases, the chemical use reported has been directed against villages, in the absence of obvious combat operations. This lends support to the Lao pilot's claim that the Vietnamese and Lao military commands were engaged in a "H'Mong extermination" campaign.

Of particular interest are the circumstances surrounding the collection of two physical samples found to contain lethal toxins. The first was collected after a March 13, 1981 attack on a village between the villages of Muong Chai and Phakhao in the Phou Bia region. In this case, a large two-engine plane reportedly sprayed a mist of a moist, yellow, sticky substance; two villagers and all village animals died. The second sample is from Ban Thonghak, another village in the Phou Bia region, collected following an April 2, 1981 attack in which a jet aircraft reportedly sprayed a yellow substance; 24 of the 450 villagers died. In the spring of 1981, seven separate chemical attacks, resulting in 218 deaths, were reported to have occurred in this region.

It is significant that these attacks took place following a period of escalation in overall resistance activities in the Phou Bia area in the winter of 1980–81. During that period, joint suppression operations by Lao People's Liberation Army and Vietnamese Army forces had achieved only limited success, perhaps spurring both forces on to greater effort. The more intense use of chemical weapons may have been part of this effort.

Evidently the fact that chemical agents were being used in Laos was not widely known among units of the Lao Army. In June 1981, a group of refugees from a village in Vientiane Province reached Thailand and described attacks against them carried out a month earlier by helicopters "dropping poison" into their water supply. Lao feld units subsequently entered the village and were surprised at the sight of many villagers still suffering from symptoms of acute poisoning. According to a villager, when the Lao military personnel saw the "small yellow grains" spread around the village, they were convinced that toxic chemicals had been used on the village and requested medical assistance for those villagers still suffering from nausea and bloody diarrhea.

In a December 15, 1981 press conference in Beijing, former Lao Health Ministry Bureau Director Khamsengkeo Sengsathit—who had defected to China—confirmed that chemical weapons were being used "in the air and on the ground" in Laos, killing "thousands." He asserted that the Vietnamese alone were using such weapons, keeping the matter secret from the Lao. He also stated that 3,000 Soviet advisers were in Laos and "have taken control" of the Lao Air Force, while 40,000–50,000 Vietnamese troops had "reduced Laos to the status of a colony."

Kampuchea

Since October 1978, radio broadcasts, press releases, and official protests to the United Nations by the Democratic Kampuchea leadership have accused the Vietnamese and the Hanoi-backed People's Republic of Kampuchea regime of using Soviet-made lethal chemical agents and weapons against DK guerrilla forces and civilians. DK allegations for a time were the only source of information concerning chemical warfare attacks in Kampuchea. In November 1979, however, the guerrilla forces of the Khmer People's National Liberation Front reported that the Vietnamese had attacked them with a tear gas which, from their description, resembled the riot-control agent CS. Subsequently, Thai officials, Democratic Kampuchea informants and refugees, Vietnamese Army defectors, U.S. and Thai medical personnel, officials of international aid and relief organizations, and Canadian and West European officials also have implicated the Vietnamese in the offensive use of lethal and incapacitating chemical agents in Kampuchea.

There are reports of 124 separate attacks in Kampuchea from 1978 to the fall of 1981 in which lethal chemicals caused the deaths of 981 persons (see Table 2[16]). The mortality figure represents a minimum because some reports state only that there were deaths and do not provide a number. The earliest reports cite attacks in Ratanakiri Province, in the northeastern corner of the country (see map). Reports from 1979 to the present show the use of lethal chemicals primarily in the provinces bordering Thailand. The greatest use of chemical agents apparently has been in Battambang Province, with 51 reported incidents; Pursat Province has experienced the next highest frequency, with 25 reported incidents. These numbers are consistent with the overall high level of military activity reported in the border provinces.

A review of information from all sources provides direct and specific support for 28 of 124 reported attacks. There is, in addition, some evidence that in all reported instances some form of attack took place. This evidence includes reports of troop movements, supply transfers, operational plans, postoperation reporting, and air activity. It indicates that military activity took place at the time and place of every incident reported to involve lethal chemical agents. In some cases, it provides strong circumstantial evidence that the action involved chemical substances—for example, the movement of chemicals and personal protection equipment into the area.

There is no doubt that in late 1978 and 1979 the Vietnamese, and what later became the People's Republic of Kampuchea forces, made at least limited use of riot-control chemicals and possible incapacitating agents against both Communist and non-Communist guerrilla forces in Kampuchea. The chemicals used probably included toxic smokes, riot-control agents such as CS, and an unidentified incapacitating agent that caused vertigo and nausea and ultimately rendered victims unconscious with no other signs or symptoms.

In March 1979, during Vietnamese operations against Khmer Rouge forces in the Phnom Melai area, a Vietnamese Army private, who later defected, observed the following activities related to chemical warfare. During the fighting, all regiment (740th) troops were issued gas masks. However, the 2nd Battalion, a "border defense unit," was not issued masks. This unit was in the Phnom Melai area and was virtually surrounded by Khmer Rouge forces. At another point in the battle, the regiment's troops were ordered to don masks. The Vietnamese Army private reported that he saw two Soviets (Caucasians) fire a DH–10 (a hand-held weapon identified by the private's comrades). He was about 50 meters from the firing point. The weapon at impact, which he was able to observe from his position, gave off clouds of white, gray, and green gas/smoke. His signal unit subsequently passed a message reporting that there were 300 dead, including the unprotected Khmer Rouge and Vietnamese of the border defense forces' 2nd Battalion. The corpses reportedly had traces of white and green powder on their faces and clothes. Their faces were contorted, with eyes wide open. No blood was seen. (A H'Mong resistance leader described an incident in 1981 in which two Soviet soldiers fired a hand-held weapon that dispersed a similar lethal agent.)

Starting in February 1980, reports revealed that the Vietnamese were using 60 mm mortars, 120 mm shells, 107 mm rockets, M–79 grenade launchers filled with chemical agents, as well as munitions delivered by T–28 aircraft. According to the DK, the chemicals used were green and yellow and powderlike in appearance. In some instances the gas was described as yellow or white. The symptoms described were tightening of the chest, disorientation, vomiting, bleeding from the nose and gums, discoloration of the body, and "stiffening" of the teeth. In July 1980, the DK described artillery attacks that produced a black smoke causing itchy skin, weakness, skin lesions, and in some cases decaying skin and blisters. In December 1980, the Vietnamese were once again firing chemical artillery shells, and it was believed that poison chemicals were being brought into Thailand's border region. By March 1981, the Democratic Kampuchea forces had reported numerous attacks directed against them with lethal chemical agents and the poisoning of food and water.

U.S. analysis of contaminated vegetation samples collected within hours of a March 1981 attack showed high levels of three trichothecene toxins in a combination that would not be expected to be found in a natural outbreak in this environment. At the levels found on the vegetation, the three trichothecenes would produce vomiting, skin irritations and itching, and bleeding symptons. Water samples taken from the area of the same attack also contained trichothecene toxins. Control samples from nearby areas confirmed that these toxins were not indigenous to the locale. (Details

[16] Not printed.

on the sample analysis appear in Annex D.)[17]

There also is ample evidence of military activity at the place and time of the acquisition of the samples. Vietnamese Army defectors described plans for multiregimental sweep operations to be conducted along the border in northwestern Battambang Province before the end of the dry season in May. Actual fighting, however, continued to be characterized by guerrilla tactics on both sides, including, according to a Vietnamese Army defector, "staging ambushes, laying minefields, and use of deception." Indeed, Democratic Kampuchean resistance forces were ordered to avoid large-scale operations and to limit combat operations to scattered sapper attacks. Such information is consistent with other reports of Vietnamese Army forces spreading toxic chemicals in streams, along roadsides, and around villages and firing toxic gas shells against enemy positions. The Phnom Melai sector, where Phnom Mak Hoeun is located, was described as an "anthill of DK activity," and actions reported during March were "sporadic firefights" around Phnom Mak Hoeun involving the Vietnamese Army's 2nd Battalion, 2nd Border Security Regiment.

In Kampuchea, as in Laos, the period of late 1980 through spring 1981 was one of intensified Vietnamese operations to suppress the resistance and break the will of the opposing forces. In July 1981, trucks loaded with blue sacks filled with white powder were being moved by the Vietnamese into the Pailin, Battambang, and Siem Reap areas. Vietnamese soldiers told villagers that the chemicals caused blindness, hemorrhaging, and vomiting.

Additional evidence was derived from blood samples drawn from victims of Vietnamese chemical use that occurred on September 19, 1981 in the Takong area. Takong is in the same general area as Phnom Mak Hoeun—that is, the central region of Battambang Province near the Thai border. Although there is no independent confirmation of the accounts of the attack, American medical personnel visiting a DK field hospital examined the victims and obtained the blood samples. Analyses of these samples suggested the use of trichothecenes. (Blood analysis results also appear in Annex D.)

According to the DK soldiers affected, the chemicals used in the September 19 Takong attack were dispersed as a gas or powder and as a poison to water. The gas or powder was released from containers by tripwires in the area of the rear forces. This description is consistent with the other reporting for this area and time.

Thailand also has been concerned about chemical attacks against its own forces and civilian population. In March 1981, one Thai died from poisons placed by Vietnamese troops, and others became ill after suffering bleeding from the nose and mouth. In May 1981, Thai forces captured two Vietnamese as they were attempting to poison the water supply in a Kampuchean relocation camp in Thailand. The poison was analyzed by the Thai and found to contain lethal quantities of cyanide. Many reports indicate that it is common practice for Vietnamese units to poison water and food used by the DK forces.

The Soviet Connection in Southeast Asia

Much of the Soviet interest in Southeast Asia is dictated by their rivalry with China and their close alliance with the Vietnamese. Regional Communist forces have been strengthened to contain Chinese influence and deter military incursions. The area of northern Laos between Vientiane and the Chinese border—where the H'Mong hill tribes have stubbornly resisted and harassed Vietnamese forces—is strategically significant to the Vietnamese because it adjoins a hostile China. In the last few years the Vietnamese have expanded their military construction and strengthened their forces in Laos which now number 50,000.

Initially there was a tendency to interpret the Soviet role as strictly advisory. Now, however, there is considerable evidence to suggest that the Soviets are far more involved in the Lao and Vietnamese chemical warfare program than was assumed earlier. An estimated 500 Soviet military advisers provide maintenance assistance and technical support, actually running the Lao Air Force, and give advanced training to Lao personnel in conventional as well as chemical warfare.

The Soviets have had advisers and technicians working in Vietnam and Laos for many years and in Kampuchea since 1979. However, it was not until early 1979 that evidence surfaced on the Soviets' direct involvement in chemical warfare activities. For example, the Lao Army chemical section in Xiangkhoang prepared Soviet-manufactured chemical items for inspection by a Soviet military team on February 7, 1979. A seven-man team of Soviet chemical artillery experts, accompanied by Lao

[17] Not printed.

chemical officers, inspected chemical supplies and artillery rounds at the Xeno storage facility in Savannakhet on June 1, 1979. One report stated that the Soviets would be inspecting the same chemical explosives used to suppress the H'Mong in the Phou Bia area.

In addition to this information, H'Mong accounts have described Soviet advisers and technicians participating in the preparation of the chemical weapons for the attacks on the H'Mong villages. H'Mong eyewitnesses claim to have seen "Caucasian pilots" in aircraft, and one H'Mong report states that a downed Soviet aircraft was discovered in the jungle along with a dead Soviet pilot. In November 1981, a H'Mong resistance leader described how Soviet soldiers fighting with the Lao Army fired handheld weapons that dispersed a lethal agent over a 300-meter area. Several Lao defectors have reported seeing Soviet advisers present when aircraft were loaded with chemical-agent rockets.

In July 1981, a Soviet shipment of wooden crates filled with canisters described by the Vietnamese as "deadly toxic chemicals" was unloaded at the port of Ho Chi Minh City. This incident further corroborates the judgment that the Soviets have been shipping chemical warfare matériel to Vietnam for some time. During the unloading, Vietnamese soldiers were caught pilfering the wooden crates containing the canisters. The soldiers dropped one of the wooden cases and intentionally broke it open; they wanted to determine if its contents were edible or valuable for pilferage. When a soldier broke the nylon seal and attempted to pry open a canister, special security personnel isolated the area and told the soldiers that the canisters contained deadly toxic substances from the U.S.S.R. The wooden crates, each weighing 100 kilograms, were loaded on military trucks and taken under special guard to the Long Binh storage depot.

This incident is only one in a series involving Soviet chemical warfare matériel dating back several years. In 1975, for example, a Soviet captain of a diving support craft engaged in salvaging a sunken ship in the Black Sea, which had been transporting Soviet military supplies to Vietnam, said that his divers came in contact with toxic chemicals, and a special Soviet salvage unit took over the operation after the divers became very ill. The salvage operations, conducted by the ASPTR–12 Salvage, Rescue, and Underwater Technical Services Group based in Odessa, were monitored by high-ranking Soviet naval officers.

The operation began with the removal of tractors and helicopters which cluttered the deck of the ship and prevented access to hold hatches. Once the surface clutter was removed, the divers attempted to enter the holds. At this point, however, operations had to be suspended temporarily because of a violent outbreak of chemical poisoning among the divers. Contact with the unidentified chemicals resulted in reddish welts 1–3 centimeters in diameter on exposed skin and was accompanied by severe headaches, nausea, and a general feeling of fatigue. The symptoms disappeared on their own after 3–5 days of rest. At this point, military authorities took over from the ASPTR–12 divers, who were temporarily withdrawn from the project. Soviet naval divers were sent down and determined that the source of poisoning was chemical seepage from an open hatch of one of the holds. The hatch was promptly sealed, and the salvage operation was once more assigned to ASPTR–12 divers who resumed work and retrieved ammunition and an assortment of other equipment. Once this was done, the military took over permanently. The ship was raised without removing the poisonous chemicals and towed to an Odessa shipyard where the chemicals were unloaded by military personnel. The ship was then broken up and scrapped. The entire operation took about 3 years to complete.

As another example of Soviet involvement, two Vietnamese corporals, from the 337th and 347th Vietnamese Army divisions, have stated that Soviet-supplied chemical weapons were stored in caves near Lang Son in February 1979. Although their Vietnamese units were issued gas masks, they were told that Soviet-supplied chemical weapons would not be used unless the Chinese initiated chemical warfare. As late as February 1981, a team of uniformed Soviet military advisers was attached to the corps headquarters. The team leader was a senior Soviet colonel. The Soviets were involved in training corps personnel in the use of Soviet-supplied weapons and equipment, including chemical artillery shells and gas masks. The Soviet team often inspected defensive positions and observed training maneuvers.

. . . .

Motivation for Using Chemical Weapons

In the course of this analysis, the question has been posed: Is there a military-strategic or tactical rationale for the systematic use of chemical weapons by conventional forces in Laos, Kampuchea, and Afghanistan? The military problems faced in these countries—viewed from the perspective of the Soviets and their allies—make the use of chemical weapons a militarily effective way of breaking the will and resistance of stubborn anti-government forces operating from relatively inaccessible, protected sanctuaries.

The Soviets have made a large investment in insuring that Vietnam and its clients succeed in extending their control over Indochina. For Vietnam, the H'Mong resistance in Laos is a major irritant to be removed as quickly and cheaply as possible. The use of chemical agents has played a major role in driving the H'Mong from their mountain strongholds, relieving Vietnamese and Lao ground forces of the need for costly combat in difficult terrain. Much of the H'Mong population that lived in the Phou Bia mountain region has been driven into Thailand, killed, or resettled.

In the mountainous areas of Afghanistan, where rebels are holed up in caves or other inaccessible areas, conventional artillery, high-explosive bombs, and napalm are not particularly effective. Many reports indicate that unidentified chemical agents have been used on such targets. Caves and rugged terrain in Laos and thick jungles in Kampuchea also have frustrated attempts to locate and destroy the resistance forces. Chemical clouds can penetrate the heavy forests and jungle canopy and seep into the mountain caves. Persistent agents linger in the area and cause casualties days and sometimes weeks after the attack. Unprotected forces and civilians have little or no defense against lethal agents like toxins, nerve gas, or blister agents.

Trichothecene toxins, which are known to have been used in Southeast Asia, have the added advantage of being an effective terror weapon that causes bizarre and horrifying symptoms. Severe bleeding, in addition to blisters and vomiting, has instilled fear in the resistance villages. Not only have the villagers and their animals been killed in a gruesome manner, but the vegetation and water also have been contaminated. Survivors are reluctant to return to their inhospitable homes and instead make the long and dangerous trek to camps in Thailand.

There is no clearcut explanation of why trichothecene toxins have been used in addition to irritants, incapacitants, and other traditional chemical warfare agents. Speculation suggests that they are probably cheaper to make and are readily available from Soviet stocks; they are probably safer and more stable to store, transport, and handle in a Southeast Asian environment, and they may require less protective equipment when being prepared for munitions. They are difficult to trace as the causative agent after an attack—as demonstrated by the length of time it took for the United States to detect them. Few laboratories in the world have the analytical capability to identify precisely the type and amount of trichothecene toxin in a sample of vegetation, soil, or water.

The Soviets may well have calculated that they and their allies could successfully deny or counter charges that chemical weapons had been used, recognizing that it would be especially difficult to compile incontrovertible evidence from inaccessible areas of Southeast Asia and Afghanistan. With respect to Kampuchea, they may also have calculated that, in view of the lack of international support for Pol Pot's resistance, chemical weapons could be used on his troops without significant international outcry.

In addition, the Soviet military very likely considers these remote areas as providing unique opportunities for the operational testing and evaluation of chemical weapons under various tactical conditions. Years of aerial and artillery chemical dispersion have undoubtedly provided the Soviets with valuable testing data. Southeast Asia has offered the Soviets an opportunity to test old agents that had been stockpiled for many years as well as more recently developed agents or combinations of agents. This conclusion is supported by information from foreign military officers who have attended the Soviet Military Academy of Chemical Defense in Moscow. According to their Soviet instructor, three types of chemical agents may be used during the "initial stages" of local wars: "harassing agents (CS, CN, DM), incapacitants such as psychochemicals (BZ) or intertoxins [*sic*—possibly enterotoxins],[18] and herbicides." During the "decisive phase, lethal agents can be employed under certain circumstances." In a local war, "chemical weapons can be used to spoil enemy efforts to initiate operations, even if the enemy has not used them first." The foreign officers' accounts, including detailed descriptions of the Soviet chemical warfare program, support the conclusion that the Soviets consider chemical weapons an effective and acceptable means of warfare in local conflicts.

---

[18] Bracketed note appears in the source text.

Insight into the Soviet bloc military perspective on the use of toxins is provided in the following passage from a 1977 East German military manual entitled *Textbook of Military Chemistry.*

> "Toxins are designated as toxic agents which are produced by biological organisms such as micro-organisms, plants, and animals, and cannot themselves reproduce.
>
> "By the middle of 1960 the toxins selected for military purposes were included among the biologic warfare agents. In principle, this was understood to mean only the bacterial toxins. Today it is possible to produce various toxins synthetically. Toxins with 10–12 amino acids can currently be synthesized in the laboratory. Toxins are not living substances and in this sense are chemicals. They thus differ fundamentally from the biological organisms so that they can be included among chemical warfare agents. As a result of their peculiarities they are designated simply as "toxin warfare agents." They would be used in combat according to the same principles and with the same methods used for chemical warfare agents. When they are used in combat the atmosphere can be contaminated over relatively large areas—we can expect expansion depths of up to 6 kilometers before the toxin concentration drops below lethal concentration 50 . . . the toxin warfare agents can be aerosolized. They can be used primarily in micro-bombs which are launched from the air or in warheads of tactical rockets. Toxin warfare agents concentrates can be applied with aircraft spray equipment and similar dispersion systems."

The Soviet designation for several pathogenic *Fusarium* products is "IIF (*iskusstvennyy infektsionny fon*), which stands for "artificial infection background." IIF devices are used in the Soviet Union deliberately to contaminate soil in experimental agricultural test areas with spores of disease-producing fungi. We are not certain if the IIF compounds include trichothecenes. Nor are we certain as to the intent of this agricultural research program. It is possible that these programs are designed to colonize soil with pathogenic organisms either to determine which crop varieties are most resistant to disease or, alternatively, to test eradication and control methods in infected soils. Elsewhere in the Soviet agricultural research program, however, it is known that there is widespread use of certain trichothecenes, including sprays from light aircraft. A capability exists within the Soviet Union for multi-ton production of light aircraft spray-delivered microbial products such as those described above.

Evidence accumulated since World War II clearly shows that the Soviets have been extensively involved in preparations for large-scale offensive and defensive chemical warfare. Chemical warfare agents and delivery systems developed by the Soviets have been identified, along with production and storage areas within the U.S.S.R. and continuing research, development, and testing activities at the major Soviet chemical proving grounds. Soviet military forces are extensively equipped and trained for operations in a chemically contaminated environment. None of the evidence indicates any abatement in this program. The Soviets have shown a strong interest in improving or enhancing their standard agents for greater reliability and effect. Their large chemical and biological research and development effort has led them to investigate other kinds of chemical warfare agents, particularly the toxins.

None of the four countries considered in this report—Vietnam, Laos, Kampuchea, and Afghanistan—has any known large-scale facility or organization for the manufacture of chemical and biological materials. Nor are they known to have produced even small quantities of chemical warfare agents or munitions. The technical problems of producing large quantities of weapons-grade toxins, however, are not so great as to preclude any of the four countries from learning to manufacture, purify, and weaponize these materials. It is highly unlikely, however, that they could master these functions without acquiring outside technical know-how.

. . . .

Document 478

Statement by the Deputy Director of the Bureau of Politico-Military Affairs (Dean), November 29, 1982 (Extract)[19]

New Evidence on the Use of Chemical Warfare

Good afternoon, ladies and gentlemen. This morning Secretary Shultz transmitted to the Congress and the United Nations an updated report on Chemical Warfare in Southeast Asia and Afghanistan.[20] The report presents new evidence on chemical and toxin warfare in Laos, Kampuchea, and Afghanistan that has become available to us and to the United States Government since publication of the special report on the same subject on March 22 of last year.[21] The new evidence includes both information on events occurring since the first of this year and additional information from a variety of sources on activities described in the earlier report.

We have compiled this report as carefully and as conscientiously as we know how. The same rigorous, analytical process employed in our earlier report and outlined in detail there has been followed to arrive at our current judgments. Every report of chemical and toxin weapons use has been carefully checked. Sample collection procedures, physical examinations, and documentation have been improved. The conclusions are fully shared by all relevant agencies of the United States Government. The most important conclusion to be drawn from the new evidence is that chemical and toxin warfare is continuing in Afghanistan and Southeast Asia.

Despite the worldwide attention that has been given to this issue, the evidence available to us shows that Soviet forces in Afghanistan, Vietnamese and Lao forces in Laos, and Vietnamese forces in Kampuchea have continued, during 1982, to use chemical and toxin weapons against the people of those countries. Our latest evidence indicates that attacks with chemical or toxin weapons were continuing in all three countries as recently as last month.

Our analysis has also led to one significant new discovery. Our earlier report showed that mycotoxins were being used in Laos and Kampuchea by Vietnamese and Lao forces acting under direct Soviet supervision. The evidence available to us at that time, however, did not permit us to show conclusively that mycotoxins were also being used by Soviet forces in Afghanistan.

We now have such evidence. We have received two gas masks used by Soviet forces in Afghanistan. Analysis of the surface of one of these gas masks has revealed the presence of T–2 mycotoxin. These results have been confirmed by two other laboratories. Similar analysis of material from the other Soviet gas mask which was removed from the head of a dead Soviet soldier in Afghanistan revealed the presence of mycotoxins, as well. We believe, accordingly, that these masks were worn by Soviet soldiers during operations in Afghanistan in which a toxin agent was used.

Other judgments we have reached on the basis of the new information include the following: First, reports of chemical attacks from February through October 1982 indicate that Soviet forces continue their selective use of chemicals and toxins in Afghanistan. Moreover, new evidence collected in 1982 on Soviet and Afghan Government forces' use of chemical weapons from 1979 through 1981 reinforced the previous judgment that lethal chemical agents were used on the Afghan resistance during those years.

Second, Vietnamese and Lao troops, under direct Soviet supervision have continued to use lethal and incapacitating chemical agents and toxins against the H'Mong in Laos through at least June of 1982. We have incomplete reports on further attacks as recent as October 17, 1982, in Laos.

Third, Vietnamese forces have continued to use lethal and incapacitating chemical agents and toxins against Kampucheans through at least June 1982. As in Laos, we are also examining more recent reports, as yet incomplete, of further attacks as recent as the last week of October in Kampuchea.

Fourth, trichothecene toxins were found in the urine, blood, and tissues of victims of yellow rain attacks in Laos and Kampuchea

---

[19] Source: Department of State files. Robert Dean made this statement at the beginning of a Department of State briefing which began at 2:30 p.m. Omitted are Dean's mentioning of the names of the "group of experts", who helped put together the updated report referred to in his statement and who were at the briefing, and the subsequent question-and-answer session.

[20] For an extract, see *infra.*

[21] Reference is to the report, dated March 22, 1982. For extracts, see *supra.*

and in samples of residue collected after attacks in both countries.

Fifth, we continue to find that a common factor in the evidence is Soviet involvement in the use of these weapons in all three countries. Our judgment is based both on our newly acquired information and on continued analyses of prior data about Soviet mycotoxin research and development, chemical warfare training in Vietnam, the presence of Soviet Chemical Warfare advisers in Laos and Vietnam and the presence of the same unusual trichothecene toxin in samples collected from all three countries.

The implications of these findings are far-reaching. The use of chemical and biological weapons in war is prohibited by the 1925 Geneva Protocol. The 1972 Biological and Toxin Weapons Convention prohibits the possession of toxin weapons. Therefore, the fact that such weapons are, nevertheless, being used in Afghanistan and in Southeast Asia raises the most serious questions. Our purpose in calling attention to these issues is not to engage in polemics, but to obtain a halt in the use of chemical and toxin weapons.

This is now a second report on chemical warfare in Southeast Asia and Afghanistan. We hope that it can be our last and that we will be able to report a few months hence that the use of these weapons has ceased. Until that happens, however, we will continue to present evidence and to take steps to insure that the world does not ignore the continuing plight of today's victims of chemical and toxin weapons. We believe that all who are concerned about respect for human rights and upholding the integrity of international agreements should join in seeking a halt to the use of such weapons. In particular, we invite those who may have evidence of their own to come forward with their evidence and their conclusions.

. . . .

Document 479

Report From the Secretary of State (Shultz) to the Congress and Member States of the United Nations, November 1982 (Extracts)[22]

An Update on Chemical Warfare in Southeast Asia

This report presents conclusions based on further evidence about chemical and toxin warfare activities in Laos, Kampuchea, and Afghanistan that has become available to the U.S. Government since publication of the special report on this subject on March 22, 1982.[23] *The evidence includes new information on events occurring since the first of this year as well as additional information from a variety of sources on activities described in that report. The current report is accompanied by tables listing recent and newly reported attacks and annexes providing additional sample analysis results, medical evidence, and other supporting data.*

UPDATED FINDINGS

Based on a thorough analysis of this new information, we are able to conclude the following:

Reports of chemical attacks from February through October 1982 indicate that Soviet forces continue their selective use of chemicals and toxins against the resistance in Afghanistan. Moreover, new evidence collected in 1982 on Soviet and Afghan Government forces' use of chemical weapons from 1979 through 1981 reinforces the previous judgment that lethal chemical agents were used on the Afghan resistance. Physical samples from Afghanistan also provide new evidence of mycotoxin use.

Vietnamese and Lao troops, under direct Soviet supervision, have continued to use lethal and incapacitating chemical agents and toxins against the H'Mong resistance in Laos through at least June 1982.

Vietnamese forces have continued to use lethal and incapacitating chemical agents

---

[22] Source: *Chemical Warfare in Southeast Asia and Afghanistan: An update,* Department of State Special Report No. 104, November 1982, pp. 3–4, 5–8; also printed in full in Department of State *Bulletin,* December 1982, pp. 44–53. For portions of the report primarily on chemical warfare in Afghanistan, see document 443. Omitted from the report printed here are Secretary Schultz's transmittal letter to the Congress, table of contents, and all tables and annexes.

[23] See document 477.

and toxins against resistance forces in Kampuchea through at least June 1982.

Trichothecene toxins were found in the urine, blood, and tissue of victims of "yellow rain" attacks in Laos and Kampuchea and in samples of residue collected after attacks.

We continue to find that a common factor in the evidence is Soviet involvement in the use of these weapons in all three countries. Continued analysis of prior data and newly acquired information about Soviet mycotoxin research and development, chemical warfare training in Vietnam, the presence of Soviet chemical warfare advisers in Laos and Vietnam, and the presence of the same unusual trichothecene toxins in samples collected from all three countries reinforce our earlier conclusion about the complicity of the Soviet Union and about its extent.

INTRODUCTION

Our March study showed that casualties and deaths resulted from chemical attacks in Southeast Asia and Afghanistan and that trichothecene toxins were used in both Laos and Kampuchea. The new evidence shows that these attacks are continuing in all three countries and that trichothecene toxins have been used in Afghanistan as well.

The same rigorous analytical processes employed in our March study, and outlined in detail there, were followed to arrive at the judgments contained in this update. In light of the widespread publicity given the March report, special efforts were made by U.S. Government analysts to preclude being led astray by any possible false reports that might be generated for propaganda or other purposes and to eliminate the possibility of making erroneous judgments about the chemical or toxin agents involved because of tampering or improper handling. Every report has been carefully checked.

The evidence in the March study was based on a broad range of data, including testimony by physicians, refugee workers, journalists, and others. Although some of the new reports are anecdotal, we have been able to corroborate most of them by other sources and sample analysis. Moreover, personal testimony tends to add credence to other accounts which, taken together, form a coherent picture. The material presented in this report represents only a relatively small amount of the total accumulated evidence. This additional information is examined in greater detail in the annexes. Improved sample collection procedures, a better quality of medical histories and physical examinations, documentation including photographs of lesions and hospital charts from Southeast Asia, and interviews by trained personnel have reinforced our earlier conclusions and led to new discoveries.

As international concern about this subject has increased, based on the development of evidence from many countries, independent analyses have been initiated by foreign chemical warfare experts, physicians, journalists, and independent nongovernmental scientists and laboratories. Analysts in the United States have found this research very helpful both in supporting their own conclusions and, more importantly, in expanding on them.

. . . .

Laos

H'Mong refugees, recounting details of toxic agent attacks and exhibiting severe medical symptoms from exposure to the agents, fled to Thailand every month from January through June 1982. They brought out more samples contaminated by a yellow, sticky substance described as a "yellow rain" dropped by aircraft and helicopters on their villages and crops. We have preliminary reports on attacks as recent as October 1982. We now know that the yellow rain contains trichothecene toxins and other substances that cause victims to experience vomiting, bleeding, blistering, severe skin lesions, and other lingering signs and symptoms observed by qualified physicians. Experts agree that these people were exposed to a toxic agent and that no indigenous natural disease, plant, or chemical caused these unique physical effects.[24]

Laboratory analyses of blood samples from these victims and studies on experimental animals have shown that trichothecene toxins are retained in the body for much longer periods of time than previously thought. Scientific research has shown that the multiple-phase distribution pattern in animals includes a secondary half-life of up to 30 days. We believe that

[24] See Canadian report to the United Nations: "Study of the Possible Use of Chemical Agents in Southeast Asia," Dr. H. B. Shiefer, University of Saskatchewan. [Footnote in the source text.]

the severe skin lesions observed on victims by doctors are also relevant. Victims whose blood proved on analysis to have high levels of trichothecene mycotoxins exhibit such skin lesions.

Descriptions of the 1982 attacks have not changed significantly from descriptions of earlier attacks. Usually the H'Mong state that aircraft or helicopters spray a yellow rain-like material on their villages and crops. In some reports the symptoms are similar to those described in our March 22 study, and we attribute them to the use of trichothecene toxins. However, in many cases there was no bleeding, only abdominal pains and prolonged illness. These symptoms, described in previous years, suggest that another agent or combination of agents is still being used. The explanation is complicated because different symptoms are ascribed to men, women, children, and animals. It is possible that different agents, lower concentrations of the same agents, or climatic conditions have affected the efficacy of the agents.

Medical personnel in Lao refugee camps in Thailand were much better organized in 1982 to screen victims than in past years. Doctors now routinely use extensive questionnaires and conduct comprehensive medical examinations, including some on-site, preliminary blood analysis. Skilled paramedical personnel oversee preparation of blood and serum samples for proper transport and shipment to the United States or other countries for chemical analysis. Some patients with active symptoms are now being monitored extensively over time.

A number of blood samples have been collected from Laos for analysis in the United States. All biological specimens were drawn by qualified medical personnel, and samples were refrigerated until analyzed in the United States. Analysis of these samples shows that trichothecene mycotoxins continue to be used against H'Mong villages. In addition to blood and urine specimens from victims exposed to chemical warfare, we have collected additional physical samples this year. These physical samples consist of more residue of yellow rain containing mycotoxins from the same attacks that yielded human biological specimens positive for these same toxins. (See Annex A).

The number of reported attacks in Laos in 1982 did not differ significantly from the frequencies reported for comparable periods in the years 1977 through 1981. Reported fatalities per attack during 1981 and 1982 showed an apparent decrease, suggesting the possibility that less lethal toxic agents, or lower concentrations of the same agents, are now being used. This apparent decrease, however, was not statistically significant and could have been caused by a number of other factors, including the following:

Due to emigration and the high number of fatalities since at least 1976, the H'Mong were living in smaller, more scattered communities.

H'Mong survivors still in Laos were warier and quicker to take cover and to use rudimentary protective measures at the first sign of attack.

The H'Mong were not taking time to count victims—this is supported by the existence of very few reports that indicate the precise number of people affected by a toxic agent attack.

As stated in the March report, the Soviet Union maintains in Laos significant numbers of advisers who provide maintenance assistance, technical support, and training in both conventional and chemical warfare. A former Lao transport pilot who defected early this summer has described the aerial movement, under Soviet supervision, of toxic agents within Laos.

Kampuchea

Most reports of toxic attacks in Kampuchea for the period 1978–June 1982 come from Democratic Kampuchean (DK) sources, including interviews with DK military personnel. Evidence from other sources confirmed most of these reports. In 1982, most reported attacks occurred near the Thai border, making it easier to obtain samples and other direct evidence of toxic agent use.

In the first 6 months of 1982, the number of reported toxic agent attacks in Kampuchea was about half the number reported during the same periods in 1980 and 1981. The number of reported deaths per attack also decreased, but data were insufficient to determine if this decrease was statistically significant. We also have preliminary reports on attacks through early November 1982.

In February and March 1982, several attacks occurred just across the Kampuchean border in Thailand. Analysis of samples collected from the attacks was performed in Canada, Thailand, and the United States. Although differing sampling techniques give rise to significant sampling error and lead to slightly different analytical results, both the U.S. and Thai analysts, using different analytical techniques, found trichothecene mycotoxins in their samples.[25] The Canadian team investigating these attacks has published a detailed medical assessment of the victims' symptoms; it concluded that illness had in fact occurred and was caused by a toxic agent, although preliminary tests for trichothecenes proved inconclusive in the Canadian sample.

Blood and urine samples from Kampuchean victims of a toxic agent artillery attack on February 13, 1982, contained trichothecene toxins (Annex A). In addition, post-mortem tissue from a victim of this same attack confirmed the presence of trichothecene toxins (Annex B). Analysis of additional samples showing the presence of trichothecenes taken from other attacks is also found in Annex A.

The Vietnamese conducted toxic agent attacks this year against another resistance group, the Kampuchean People's National Liberation Forces. On several occasions in March–May 1982, the resistance camp at Sokh Sann was hit with toxic artillery shells and bombs. Samples of contaminated vegetation and yellow residue from these attacks are now being analyzed. Attacks occurred in Kampuchea through June 1982, providing new samples; qualitative tests indicate that the presence of trichothecenes is probable. The results of confirmatory analyses are pending.

Several Vietnamese military defectors from Kampuchea have provided valuable information in 1981 and 1982 on chemical weapons use and on the Vietnamese chemical warfare program and have reported that some types of agents are supplied by the Soviet Union. Information from other sources also confirms our earlier view that the Vietnamese possess toxic agent munitions and are equipping their own troops with additional protective equipment.

. . . .

[25] It was thought initially that a harmless yellow powder had been dropped on Thai villages as part of a disinformation campaign attempting to discredit U.S. sample analysis results. Within days of such an attack, the Thai Ministry of Health announced that only ground-up flowers had been found. However, Thai officials later stated that further analysis showed traces of toxin and that the earlier Health Ministry announcement was based on incomplete investigation. [Footnote in the source text.]

B. Australia

Document 480

Remarks by Vice President Bush, Melbourne, May 1, 1982[1]

Vice President Bush's Visit to Australia

Barbara and I have been the recipients of so many kindnesses since we arrived here 2 days ago. The hospitality seems to go on and on, seems to be as endless as the great stretches of territory we flew over since our first stop in Darwin and here. Once again, so many thanks.

I want to tell you how pleased Barbara and I are to have had the chance to visit Melbourne, your city, Mr. Prime Minister. I see why it is called Australia's "Garden City." On our visit here we've seen one beautiful city after another. I must say, I think John Batman knew a bargain when he saw one—if he bought all this for 200 pounds of trinkets. When your great past Prime Minister and fellow Victorian Robert Menzies visited us in the United States back in 1950, he said that except in the jaundiced eye of the law, Americans are not regarded as foreigners in Australia. I have managed on my visit to keep out of the way of your law. You've made us feel wonderfully at home.

Our two countries have passed so many tests in this century. We fought together in four wars—World Wars One and Two, Korea, and Vietnam. If, as Hazlitt said, prosperity is a great teacher, but adversity is a greater one—then we've learned much, both from our hardships, and from the way we shared them.

For the past 30 years, our ANZUS Mutual Defense Treaty[2] has helped to keep the peace. That treaty is the cornerstone of our security in the southwest Pacific, and the foundation for our search for peaceful resolutions to heated conflict worldwide.

[1] Source: Press Release, May 1, 1982, Office of the Press Secretary to the Vice President; also printed in Department of State *Bulletin*, August 1982, pp. 43–44. Vice President Bush's remarks were made at a dinner hosted by Australian Prime Minister Malcolm Fraser. The Vice President visited Australia from April 29 to May 3.

[2] Signed at San Francisco, September 1, 1951; for text, see 3 UST 3420.

Thirty years later, it has endured in a way far beyond the vision of those who put their signatures to that document. The cooperation of Australian and U.S. forces in contributing to the Sinai peace force shows how far our collaboration has taken us. In a world in which there are too few peace processes, our standing together in that part of the world, far from our own shores, should give us great satisfaction. In these perilous times, President Reagan is determined to do all he can to maintain the intimacy between our countries on which ANZUS thrives.

It was Sir Percy Spender, the Australian statesman, who once told our House of Representatives that "So far as it is possible, it is our objective to build up with the United States somewhat the same relationship that exists within the British Commonwealth. That is to say, we desire a full exchange of information and experience on all matters of mutual interest."

Well, our discussions of the past 2 days can only be described as very friendly and productive. Yesterday in Canberra, we had a long and straightforward session around the Cabinet table with the Prime Minister and members of his Cabinet. Many subjects were raised with so few disagreements. It's not the stuff that banner headlines are made of, but that's the way it is with friends. That's the way it must be in this dangerous world. And for the free nations of the world, that's big news.

Our talks ranged around the entire world—Japan, China, the Falklands, the Soviet Union, the ASEAN nations, the nations that comprise the Caribbean. We discussed President Reagan's deep and abiding desire to reduce nuclear weapons throughout the world. And as the Prime Minister said in the meeting, we saved to the last the sweetest subject of all—sugar.

There is very little going on in our world today that is not of mutual interest to both our countries. As partners in the free world, we have done, and will continue to do our all, to ensure that those who have given everything they had in the defense of freedom, shall not have done so in vain; and that those who come after us will be able to say that we worked for peace on their behalf.

Document 481

Remarks by President Reagan and Australian Prime Minister Fraser, May 17, 1982[3]

Visit of Australian Prime Minister Fraser

The President. It's been a great pleasure to welcome the distinguished Prime Minister of Australia, Malcolm Fraser, on his latest visit to Washington. As you know, he was here last June[4] and this meeting, like that one, has been most valuable.

Prime Minister Fraser graciously hosted the very successful visit of Vice President Bush to Australia a few weeks ago. Australia and the United States have been partners, friends, and allies for more than 40 years. I've had the benefit today of the Prime Minister's views on matters that may arise at the Versailles and Bonn summit meetings and we've discussed other matters of concern such as the Falkland Island crisis and the East–West issues. Through consultations such as these, our individual efforts are made mutually supportive.

The Prime Minister will be in New York tomorrow before leaving for Seoul and Tokyo. We wish him a good trip. I've asked him to carry my greetings and those of the American people back home with him to the Australian people.

Welcome, we're delighted to have you here even for the brief visit.

Prime Minister Fraser. Mr. President, I'd like to say how much I appreciate the opportunity for the kind of discussions and consultations that have been made possible through the period of your administration—the discussions that we had only a short while ago with Vice President Bush were very useful and we were delighted, indeed, to have the Vice President in Australia, especially for the time that he was there during Australia-American Week

---

[3] Source: White House Press Release, May 17, 1982, Office of the Press Secretary to the President; also printed in *Weekly Compilation of Presidential Documents*, May 24, 1982, pp. 666–667. The President and Prime Minister spoke at 4 p.m. to reporters assembled on the South Grounds of the White House.

[4] For the text of statements made by President Reagan and Prime Minister Fraser after their meeting on June 30, 1981, see *American Foreign Policy: Current Documents, 1981*, document 486.

which each year commemorates the Battle of the Coral Sea which was the occasion which secured and made Australians understand that they would be free from the threat and fear of invasion. And ever since then, that particular week has been celebrated in Australia and to have Vice President Bush with us through those celebrations on this occasion was particularly appreciated. And the discussions that I and my colleagues had with the Vice President were obviously useful. But those discussions set our minds at work and we know, Mr. President, the importance of the meetings that you will be participating in next month in Versailles and at Bonn—the economic meetings and the meetings of the heads of government of the NATO powers. And while we're not a party principal to these discussions, as with other free societies, we're obviously affected by the outcomes of those discussions.

And we know that the role that you'll be playing at both meetings is going to be critical to their success. And for that reason in particular, Mr. President, I value the opportunity for an exchange of views with you today which, I believe, have been very constructive and useful and I'd like to thank you for the opportunity at relatively short notice when I know you must be preparing for those meetings in Europe.

I'd like to wish you good fortune in your visit to Europe because much will be depending upon it. Much will be depending upon the outcomes, not only for the principal participants, but for free peoples wherever they are.

So, thank you very much, indeed, Mr. President.

C. Burma

Document 482

Testimony by the Assistant Secretary of State for East Asian and Pacific Affairs (Holdridge) Before a Subcommittee of the House Foreign Affairs Committee, March 25, 1982 (Extract)[1]

"We don't Want Burma to Come Out of Its Shell in Another Direction"

. . . .

MR. SOLARZ . . . . But in the case of Thailand and Burma, please persuade me, so that I can see if there is any possibility of persuading others, why, at a time when the administration is asking for cutbacks in a whole range of domestic programs, many of which really are quite important, we should increase the level of military assistance in Thailand by $50 million and development assistance to Burma by $5 million? I understand that's desirable and all that, but if we didn't approve of this particular increase, would this constitute a severe blow to American interests in Asia?

MR. HOLDRIDGE. I would say yes, Mr. Chairman. Burma is a relatively modest sum, an increase of $5 million over fiscal year 1982. But this $5 million does shown real interest on the part of the United States for Burma's economic development, at a time when Burma, after years of traveling the Burmese road to socialism, is now beginning to cast around for some outside inputs to help it out, no longer trying to do everything on its own. We would like to see the Burmese go in directions, as I said, which are consonant with U.S. interests, and this, in a relatively modest way, will show that the United States is concerned over how Burma approaches its economic problems.

It is a matter which is of considerable interest to Burma. The $5 million will go for food. It's an oil seeds program.

---

[1] Source: *Foreign Assistance Legislation for Fiscal Year 1983: Hearings and Markup Before the Subcommittee on Asian and Pacific Affairs of the Committee on Foreign Affairs, House of Representatives, Ninety-seventh Congress, Second Session* (Washington, 1982), Part 4, pp. 50–51.

MR. SOLARZ. Let me be blunt. Why is it in our interest for Burma to come out of its shell?

MR. HOLDRIDGE. Certainly we don't want Burma to come out of its shell in another direction, which is a possiblity. It is right there at the meeting point of several different political persuasions. The Soviet Union is interested in Burma. There is an active insurgency in the north. We have our narcotics interest in Burma, trying to grapple with that problem, with narcotics flowing out into Thailand and other parts of Asia and to the United States from the Golden Triangle. I think now that the Burmese have shown a disposition to look for outside help, I would rather have them turn to the United States than have them turn to other interests which are now particularly—

MR. SOLARZ. Well, have they turned to the Soviet Union?

MR. HOLDRIDGE. They have not so far. The Soviets have been kept out of it, and I would just as soon see the Soviets kept out.

MR. SOLARZ. Why haven't they turned to the Soviets?

MR. HOLDRIDGE. I think they are very suspicious of the Soviet Union, but if they consider themselves as extremists, if they're not getting the results that they need from us, they may.

MR. SOLARZ. And is there any relationship between this aid program in Burma and the narcotics efforts there?

MR. HOLDRIDGE. Certainly, if we want the Burmese to continue cooperating with us on areas of great concern, of which narcotics has got to be one, it makes much sense to be responsive to Burmese concerns.

MR. SOLARZ. Are they cooperating with us?

MR. HOLDRIDGE. They are cooperating, yes. In fact, we have another program for narcotics cooperation. You will probably be hearing from others about our whole narcotics program in which we are being helpful to them as well. But still, it is a mindset, an attitude toward the United States as a friendly rather than not neutral or unfriendly power. If the Burmese are friendly toward us, I think we can get more from them in the areas that we want.

MR. SOLARZ. Is their cooperation with us on the narcotics program producing any results?

MR. HOLDRIDGE. Some. I think we can do more. I think, again, the attitude of the Burmese toward the United States will be helpful in getting the Burmese to do more.

MR. SOLARZ. What is this $5 million for?

MR. HOLDRIDGE. It's for an oil seeds project over a period of some years.

MR. SOLARZ. Oil seeds?

MR. HOLDRIDGE. Oil seeds.

MR. SOLARZ. What are oil seeds?

MR. HOLDRIDGE. Oil seeds are used for cooking oil, Mr. Chairman. This is of extreme importance in an Asian society, seasame oil, I believe, and it is the basis for much of the cooking in that part of the world.

. . . .

D. China

Document 483

Statement Read by the Department of State Acting Spokesman (Romberg), January 11, 1982[1]

No Sale of Advanced Fighter Aircraft to Taiwan

Since the beginning of this administration, the President has been conscious of the need to carry forward the unofficial people-to-people relationship between the United States and Taiwan, and he has expressed on many occasions his personal concern for the continued well-being of the people of Taiwan.

This administration has attached a high value to fulfilling the longstanding policy of the U.S. Government with respect to providing such defense articles as may be necessary to enable Taiwan to maintain a sufficient self-defense capability.

Concerned agencies of the U.S. Government, including the Departments of State

---

[1] Source: Office of Press Relations, Department of State; also printed in Department of State *Bulletin*, February 1982, p. 39. The statement was read at the Department of State Daily Press Briefing held at 12:29 p.m.

and Defense and other national security elements, have been addressing the question of Taiwan's defense needs over a period of many months, and have taken into careful consideration the many factors which bear on the judgments which must be made in implementing this policy.

On the basis of this study, the administration has already taken steps to sell Taiwan items necessary for self-defense. We anticipate further steps of this sort.

A judgment has also been reached by the concerned agencies on the question of replacement aircraft for Taiwan. Their conclusion is that no sale of advanced fighter aircraft to Taiwan is required because no military need for such aircraft exists.

Taiwan's defense needs can be met as they arise and for the foreseeable future by replacing aging aircraft now in the Taiwan inventory with comparable aircraft, and by an extention of the F-5E coproduction line in Taiwan. The details have not yet been worked out. The President has approved these recommendations.

Document 484

Transcript of an Interview With the Secretary of State (Haig), February 5, 1982 (Extract)[2]

"Extremely Sensitive Discussions"

Q. Despite the decisions on not selling advanced jets to Taiwan, the Chinese still seem to be hammering away on the question of Taiwan and infringements on their sovereignty. How do you see Chinese-American relations developing? Are they deteriorating as the Chinese press seems to make out?

A. I think our first principle is to recognize we highly value good relations with China. That is our policy, and I think also you have to make the point that a great deal has been achieved over the decades since the Shanghai communiqué,[3] in which I myself was intimately involved, and that we are determined to do all we can to preserve these achievements.

We have taken a number of important initiatives to advance the relationship with the People's Republic of China. It goes without saying that since the beginning of this administration, we have also had to face continuing disagreement with Peking over our arms sales to Taiwan. We made clear in a bipartisan spirit the United States position at the time of normalization, and the Chinese Government went ahead, knowing our intentions. Still the United States recognizes this is an area to be approached with prudence and discretion.

We carried forward the policy enunciated at the time of normalization, but any examination of our actions will show that we have taken a very careful account of Chinese concerns.

We have also undertaken extremely sensitive discussions with Peking since Foreign Minister Huang Hua visited Washington last October,[4] including Assistant Secretary Holdridge's visit to China last month.[5]

It would be counterproductive to go into details because things are at a delicate stage; but speaking candidly, some difficult issues are involved. We are now making a major effort to bridge these differences. I will be just as frank when I tell you I am not in a position to predict the outcome.

Q. Are there still plans to have talks with the Chinese on arms sales to them? Are they in abeyance?

A. It is clear that that subject is hostage, in effect, to a resolution of these differences I have talked about.

---

[2] Source: *New York Times*, February 7, 1982, p. I12.

[3] For the text of the joint United States–People's Republic of China statement issued at Shanghai, February 27, 1972, see *Public Papers of the Presidents of the United States: Richard Nixon, 1972* (Washington, 1974), pp. 376–379.

[4] Chinese Vice Premier and Foreign Minister Huang Hua visited Washington, October 29–31, 1981. For a partial text of the transcript of a press briefing by Secretary Haig and Huang, see *American Foreign Policy: Current Documents, 1981*, document 500.

[5] Assistant Secretary of State for East Asian and Pacific Affairs John H. Holdridge visited China from January 10 to 14.

Document 485

Exchange of Letters Between President Reagan and Chinese Premier Zhao, February 28, 1982[6]

Tenth Anniversary of the Shanghai Communiqué

ESTEEMED MR. PRESIDENT: On the occasion of the tenth anniversary of the issuance of the Joint Communiqué in Shanghai by the People's Republic of China and the United States of America, I wish to extend, on behalf of the Chinese Government and people and in my own name, our cordial regards and good wishes to Your Excellency and the Government and people of the United States.

The Joint Communiqué issued by China and the United States a decade ago was a historic document, which started the process of normalization of relations between China and the United States and subsequently led to the establishment of diplomatic relations between them. During this period, our two sides have had extensive contacts and exchanges in many fields, thus enhancing the understanding between the governments and deepening the friendship between the peoples. The development of Sino-U.S. relations is not only in the fundamental interests of our two peoples, but also conducive to the maintenance of peace and stability in Asia and the world as a whole.

Both the Chinese and American peoples hope that Sino-U.S. relations will continue to move ahead in the years to come. I believe that these relations will continue to develop so long as both governments adhere to the principles jointly established in the Shanghai Communiqué and the Communiqué on the Establishment of Sino-U.S. Diplomatic Relations[7] and overcome the obstacles currently existing in the relations between the two countries. The Chinese Government is willing to make efforts together with the U.S. Government towards this end.

Sincerely,

ZHAO ZIYANG

DEAR MR. PREMIER: Ten years ago today the United States of America and the People's Republic of China issued the Shanghai Communiqué. In the ensuing decade, and particularly since the establishment of full diplomatic relations between the two countries on January 1, 1979, our relations with your government and people have greatly expanded, and our contacts have embraced almost all areas of human endeavor.

Our bilateral ties now encompass trade, banking, maritime affairs, civil aviation, agriculture, educational and scientific exchange, technology transfer and many other fields. Well over one hundred thousand Americans and Chinese now flow back and forth between the two countries each year, and our relations continue to develop through both people-to-people and diplomatic channels.

These concrete manifestations of good relations between the people of the United States and China are not only in the interests of the two countries. They enhance the prospects for peace and stability throughout the Asia-Pacific region, and beyond.

As we enter the second decade since the issuance of the Shanghai Communiqué, our desire is to build an even stronger bilateral and strategic framework for long term friendship between our two nations. It is appropriate for me, at this time, to reaffirm the positions agreed to by both sides in the Shanghai Communiqué and the Joint Communiqué on the Establishment of Diplomatic Relations between the United States of America and the People's Republic of China and to declare my government's willingess to work with our counterparts in Beijing to overcome differences and deepen U.S.-China ties.

On behalf of the American people, I extend the hand of friendhsip and warmest wishes to the Government and people of China on this historic anniversary.

Sincerely,

RONALD REAGAN

---

[6] Source: White House Press Release, March 1, 1982, Office of the Press Secretary to the President; also printed in *Weekly Compilation of Presidential Documents,* March 8, 1982, pp. 242–243. Department of State Spokesman Dean Fischer stated at the Department's Daily Press Briefing on March 1 that the President's letter had been sent on February 26 and that the Premier's reply had been received on February 28.

[7] For the text of the Joint Communiqué issued on December 15, 1978, which established diplomatic relations between the United States and the People's Republic of China as of January 1, 1979, see *American Foreign Policy: Basic Documents, 1977–1980,* pp. 967–968.

Document 486

Letter From President Reagan to the Vice Chairman of the Chinese Communist Party (Deng), April 5, 1982[8]

U.S. Interest in Resolving U.S.-Chinese Differences

DEAR MR. VICE CHAIRMAN: The establishment of diplomatic relations between the United States and China was an historic event which improved the prospects for peace and served the interests of both our peoples. Yet we now find ourselves at a difficult juncture in those relations.

I am writing to you because it is important for the leadership of both our countries to resume the broad advance to which you have contributed so much. This is particulary important today, as we face a growing threat from the Soviet Union and its satellite nations throughout the world. Though our interests and thus our policies are not identical, in Afghanistan and Iran, in Southeast Asia, in my own hemisphere, and in the field of nuclear weaponry, your nation and mine face clear and present dangers, and these should impel us toward finding a firm basis for cooperation.

We have come far together in a very short time. I strongly support the continuation of this progress. We must work together to expand the benefits to both our countries. My administration has taken a number of initiatives to further this process, and we intend to do more.

Clearly, the Taiwan issue has been a most difficult problem between our governments. Nonetheless, vision and statesmanship have enabled us in the past to reduce our differences over this issue while we have built a framework of long-term friendship and cooperation.

The United States firmly adheres to the positions agreed upon in the Joint Communiqué on the Establishment of Diplomatic Relations between the United States and China. There is only one China. We will not permit the unofficial relations between the American people and the people of Taiwan to weaken our commitment to this principle.

I fully understand and respect the position of your government with regard to the question of arms sales to Taiwan. As you know, our position on this matter was stated in the process of normalization: the United States has an abiding interest in the peaceful resolution of the Taiwan question.

We fully recognize the significance of the nine-point proposal of September 30, 1979.[9] The decisions and the principles conveyed on my instructions to your government on January 11, 1982[10] reflect our appreciation of the new situation created by these developments.

In this spirit, we wish to continue our efforts to resolve our differences and to create a cooperative and enduring bilateral and strategic relationship. China and America are two great nations destined to grow stronger through cooperation, not weaker through division.

In the spirit of deepending the understanding between our two countries, I would like to call your attention to the fact that Vice President Bush will be traveling to East Asia toward the end of April. The Vice President knows and admires you. He is also fully aware of my thinking about the importance of developing stronger relations between our two countries. If it would be helpful, I would be delighted to have the Vice President pay a visit to Beijing, as part of his Asian trip, so that these matters can be discussed directly and personally with you and other key leaders of the People's Republic of China.

Sincerely,

RONALD REAGAN

---

[8] Source: Press Release, May 10, 1982, Office of the Press Secretary to the Vice President; also printed in Department of State *Bulletin*, August 1982, p. 45. The text of the letter was released following Vice President Bush's visit to China, May 5–9.

[9] The reference is to the nine-point proposal set forth on September 30, 1981, by Ye Jianying, Chairman of the Standing Committee of the National People's Congress. For the text of the nine points, see *American Foreign Policy: Current Documents, 1981*, footnote 25 to document 499.

[10] The reference is apparently to the statement of January 11; see document 483.

Document 487

Letter From President Reagan to Chinese Premier Zhao, April 5, 1982[11]

"In the Context of Progress Toward a Peaceful Solution, There Would Naturally Be a Decrease in the Need for Arms by Taiwan"

DEAR MR. PREMIER: The present state of relations between our two countries deeply concerns me. We believe significant deterioration in those relations would serve the interests of neither the United States of America nor the People's Republic of China.

As the late Premier Zhou Enlai said in welcoming President Nixon to China in 1972, "The Chinese people are a great people, and the American people are a great people."[12] We are strong, sovereign nations sharing many common interests. We both face a common threat of expanding Soviet power and hegemonism. History has placed upon us a joint responsibility to deal with this danger.

The differences between us are rooted in the longstanding friendship between the American people and the Chinese people who live on Taiwan. We will welcome and support peaceful resolution of the Taiwan question. In this connection, we appreciate the policies which your government has followed to provide a peaceful settlement.

As I told Vice Premier Huang in Washington,[13] we welcome your nine-point initiative.

As I also told the Vice Premier, we expect that in the context of progress toward a peaceful solution, there would naturally be a decrease in the need for arms by Taiwan. Our positions over the past 2 months have reflected this view. We are prepared, indeed welcome, further exchanges of view in the months to come. I hope you share my conviction that the United States and China should work together to stengthen the prospects for a peaceful international order. While our interests, and thus our policies, will not always be identical, they are complementary and thus should form a firm basis for cooperation.

In my letter to Vice Chairman Deng,[14] I have suggested that a visit to Beijing by Vice President Bush at the end of April could be a useful step in deepening the understanding between our two countries. The Vice President will be traveling in Asia at the time, and could visit Beijing if you feel it would be useful.

Sincerely,

RONALD REAGAN

Document 488

Transcript of the Department of State Daily Press Briefing, April 7, 1982 (Extract)[15]

Sale of Spare Parts to Taiwan

. . . .

Q. Also on China, do we have any report to confirm something in the *Wall Street Journal* today which was that the Chinese have told us that they will not downgrade the Embassy if the parts sale goes through.[16]

---

[11] Source: Press Release, May 10, 1982, Office of the Press Secretary to the Vice President; also printed in Department of State *Bulletin,* August 1982, p. 45. The text of the letter was released following Vice President Bush's visit to China, May 5–9.

[12] The reference is to a toast made by Premier Zhou at a dinner on February 21, 1972; for text, see *Public Papers of the Presidents of the United States: Richard Nixon, 1972,* pp. 369–370.

[13] The reference is to Vice Premier Huang's visit to Washington in October 1981; see footnote 4 to document 484.

[14] *Supra.*

[15] Source: Office of Press Relations, Department of State. Alan Romberg, Department of State Acting Spokesman, conducted the briefing, which began at 1 p.m.

[16] *Wall Street Journal,* April 7, 1982, p.3. The reference is to an anticipated sale of spare parts to Taiwan, of which the administration had informally notified Congress on December 11, 1981; see *American Foreign Policy: Current Documents, 1981,* document 503. On April 13, the Department of Defense announced that the administration had formally notified Congress of its approval of a $60 million transaction for the sale of spare parts to Taiwan. The announcement stated that the sale would provide the spare parts necessary for Taiwan to maintain its U.S. origin aircraft, that it represented the estimated annual logistical support requirements, and that it would not affect the basic military balance in the region.

A. I don't have anything specific to offer on that particular point.

I might note, prehaps in that regard, that back in December, to set the record straight with regard to that issue, shortly after our informal notification to Congress, we told the Chinese essentially three things:

One was that the transfer involved no weapons whatsoever;

Secondly, that the transfer was part of a longstanding arrangement concluded many months before, and before the President met with Premier Zhao at the Cancun summit;[17] and

Third, that we contemplated no new decisions on arms sales during the next few months when our talks were underway.

Q. In the same report, you say that the United States has agreed to stop new military transfers to Taiwan after the spare parts deal goes through.

Could you also confirm this?

A. I would refer you to what I have just said.

. . . .

Document 489

Letter From President Reagan to the Chairman of the Chinese Communist Party (Hu), May 3, 1982[18]

Vice President Bush to Discuss Issue of U.S. Arms Sales to Taiwan

DEAR MR. CHAIRMAN: The visit of Vice President Bush to China affords a welcome opportunity to convey my regards to you.

As sovereign nations, our two countries share a common responsibility to promote world peace. We face a grave challenge from the Soviet Union which directly threatens our peoples and complicates the resolution of problems throughout the globe. It is vital that our relations advance and our cooperation be strengthened.

Vice President Bush is visiting China as my personal emissary. He is prepared to discuss a wide range of issues of mutual concern. My sincere hope is that we can achieve, through discussions, enhanced mutual understanding, at the highest levels of our governments.

Among the issues the Vice President will address is the question of United States arms sales to Taiwan. This remains an area of residual disagreement, as our governments acknowledged at the time of U.S.–China normalization. I believe, so long as we exercise the statesmanship and vision which have characterized our approach to differences over the past decade, we will be able to make progress toward the removal of this issue as a point of bilateral contention.

In the meantime, as stated in my recent letters to Vice Chairman Deng and Premier Zhao, the United States will continue to adhere firmly to the positions agreed upon in the joint communiqué on the establishment of diplomatic relations between the United States and the People's Republic of China. Our policy will continue to be based on the principle that there is but one China. We will not permit the unofficial relations between the American people and the Chinese people on Taiwan to weaken our commitment to this principle.

On this basis, and with good faith on both sides, we are confident that a means can be found to resolve current differences and deepen our bilateral and strategic cooperation. It is my hope that you and I will have an opportunity to meet soon. Please accept my best wishes in your efforts to build a secure and modernizing China.

Sincerely,

RONALD REAGAN

---

[17] President Reagan met with Premier Zhao in Cancun, Mexico, on October 21, 1981; see *ibid.*, document 498.

[18] Source: Press Release, May 10, 1982, Office of the Press Secretary to the Vice President; also printed in Department of State *Bulletin*, August 1982, p. 45. The text of the letter was released following Vice President Bush's visit to China, May 5–9.

Document 490

Toast by Vice President Bush, Beijing, May 7, 1982[19]

Visit Symbolizes U.S. Efforts to Bridge Differences

Premier Zhao Ziyang, I want to first thank you for a superlative dinner and magnificent hospitality. These are among the hallmarks of China.

Barbara and I have a special regard and personal friendship for the people of China. We feel at home in Beijing. During our stay here[20] we spent a great deal of time on our bicycles touring the city. We also never experienced anything other than the utmost courtesy and genuine friendship of the people.

Those were happy days. They were good days. Important days. We were part of the dramatic process which brought our two countries back together and set us on the road to full normalization of relations between the United States and China. President Reagan, in his letter to Premier Zhao at the close of the first decade following the Shanghai Communiqué, rightly observed that our relationship now extends into almost every field of human endeavor.

Your late Premier and esteemed statesman, Zhou Enlai, in welcoming President Nixon to China more than 10 years ago commented that, "The Chinese people are a great people and the American people are a great people." Premier Zhou's words are as correct today as they were then.

As representatives of two great peoples we not only have the opportunity but the obligation to make major contributions to the cause of global peace. It must be remembered that we share not only a common interest in the face of hegemonist expansionism, but we share a common responsibility.

We live in a time when the Soviet Union continues its brutal occupation of Afghanistan. It exerts unconscionable pressures on the people of Poland, suppressing their will to be free. It continues to sponsor aggression, subversion and violence in Kampuchea and other places throughout the globe.

In the face of such blatant expansionism, the United States and China have vital roles and responsibilities in doing all that we must to bring about and maintain global peace.

We in the United States believe that our real strength as a nation lies not so much in military forces or the size of our national economy. It rests in the decency and compassion of our people. It also rests in the value of our word.

The President asked me to come to China because of the vital importance he places on United States/China relations and because of his strong personal commitment to building an enduring relationship—one based on equality and mutual trust and understanding.

We recognize that there are issues of difference to be discussed and important ideas to be exchanged. My visit is a symbol of the good faith with which we seek to bridge differences and preserve and strengthen our important strategic relationship.

My discussions here will be conducted with one important principle in mind. The United States acknowledges the Chinese position that there is but one China and that Taiwan is part of China. We stand by the principles agreed upon by our governments in the joint communiqué on the establishment of diplomatic relations.

We respect China's sovereignty and territorial integrity. My visit is not intended to resolve all areas of disagreement between us, but all discussions will be based on these unalterable premises.

This afternoon I met for 2 hours with Huang Hua. While the discussions were frank and candid, they were conducted in an atmosphere befitting old friends. I stressed that we believe the relationship between our two countries is of fundamental importance in strategic, cultural and economic terms.

I believe that events of the past decade have confirmed time and time again that American and Chinese friendship and cooperation will flourish through the rest of this century and beyond.

Now I wish to express my great appreciation to Premier Zhao Ziyang and to propose

---

[19] Source: Press Release, May 7, 1982, Office of the Press Secretary to the Vice President. The toast was made at a banquet at the Great Hall of People.

[20] Vice President Bush was Chief of the U.S. Liaison Office in the People's Republic of China, 1974–1975.

a toast to his good health. Also join me now as I propose a toast to the health of all of China's leaders, to friendly relations between our two peoples, and to good, productive relations between our two countries.

Document 491

Statement by Vice President Bush, Beijing, May 9, 1982[21]

"A Clarification of Thinking on Both Sides"

During the past 3 days, in private discussions and public statements, I have stated again and again that my visit to China is a symbol of the Reagan administration's good faith in seeking to build upon the strength of our friendship and the strength of our important strategic relationship.

I have attempted to impress upon the leaders of China the depth of President Reagan's commitment to building an enduring relationship—a relationship based on mutual trust and understanding.

Frankly, I feel good about the discussions I have had during the past days. I feel that some progress has been made, and I believe that recent personal correspondence by the President to the Chinese leaders has done much to help advance the process.

Differences between us remain, to be sure. But as we seek to resolve them we must be certain that the positive elements in our relationship are reinforced and that the problems do not determine the course of our relationship.

We have a clarification of thinking on both sides on the Taiwan issue and other bilateral and global concerns. And we have agreed that United States and China representatives will continue to hold talks on the main question before us. I am also pleased by the positive way in which the Chinese leaders have presented my visit and the talks to the Chinese people. These are good signs.

When I came to China, I came with the purpose of conveying and explaining in detail the President's position on bilateral, regional and global issues. I believe that has been accomplished. I am confident that in the weeks and months ahead, the friendship and relations between our governments will grow. I know that the President, and those officials of the United States who work constantly to enhance our relationship, will do everything to ensure that.

[21] Source: Press Release, May 9, 1982, Office of the Press Secretary to the Vice President. The Vice President made the statement at Beijing Airport at the time of his departure from China.

Document 492

Report Issued by the Senate Foreign Relations Committee, May 28, 1982 (Extract)[22]

Chinese Eligibility for U.S. Assistance Programs

. . . .

Sec. 110—Eligibility of the People's Republic of China for Assistance

Section 110 adds a new Section 620(y) to the Foreign Assistance Act.[23] It is an amendment proposed by Senators Hayakawa and Glenn which would allow the President to authorize foreign assistance to the People's Republic of China provided the President certifies to the Congress that such assistance is important to the security of the United States. The provision overrides the prohibition against foreign assistance to China contained in Section 620(f). The Hayakawa/Glenn amendment substituted for an administration proposal which would have struck the People's Re-

[22] Source: *International Security Enhancement Act of 1982,* Report of the Committee on Foreign Relations on S. 2608, Ninety-seventh Congress, Second Session, Report No. 97–464 (Washington, 1982), pp. 17–20.

[23] The Foreign Assistance Act of 1961, or P.L. 87–195 (approved 0 September 4, 1961; 75 Stat. 424). For the text of the proposed Section 620(y), see International Security Enhancement Act of 1982, p. 53. Section 602 of H.R. 6370, reported out of the House Foreign Affairs Committee on May 13, was similar to Section 110 of S. 2608; for text, see *Foreign Assistance Legislation for Fiscal Year 1983: Markup Before the Committee on Foreign Affairs, House of Representatives, Ninety-seventh Congress, Second Session* (Washington, 1982), Part 8, pp. 349–350. Neither S. 2608 nor H.R. 6370 was adopted.

public of China and Tibet from the list of prohibited nations.[24] The Committee, in making this change, recognizes that the People's Republic of China, although it has a communist form of government, is a non-allied nation which plays a helpful strategic role.

The Committee received assurances in a letter, dated May 13, 1982, signed by Assistant Secretary of State Powell A. Moore that no military assistance program is being contemplated for China. The letter further states that if, in the future, the initiation of military assistance is contemplated, the Senate Foreign Relations Committee will be consulted and the administration will proceed through the normal statutory process before funds can be expended. The Committee has been further assured that the administration does not contemplate using reprogramming authority to provide military aid to China. It is the Committee's understanding, based on these assurances, that further congressional action is required beyond that taken in this legislation for China to become a recipient of U.S. military aid. The text of the Committee letter requesting assurances on military aid and the administration's response are as follows:

U.S. SENATE,
COMMITTEE ON FOREIGN RELATIONS,
Washington, D.C., May 3, 1982.

Hon. Alexander Haig, Jr.,
Secretary of State,
Washington, D.C.

DEAR MR. SECRETARY: We are writing in regard to the administration's request that China be made eligible for foreign assistance. As you know, the administration has proposed changes in the foreign assistance legislation to achieve this purpose.

Our understanding is that the administration plans no bilateral assistance programs, Public Law 480 programs, or military assistance programs to China at this time, although the administration would like to invite China to participate in several exchange and multilateral technical assistance programs proscribed by current law.

In principle, we do not object to the administration's plans. But there are some concerns about the extensiveness of future programs to China and their effect on other ongoing assistance programs in an increasingly austere aid budget. We also have reservations about extending military assistance to China.

Bilateral assistance programs, as well as military assistance, for China would have to be considered by Congress through the normal authorization and appropriations processes. On the issue of military assistance, we would like assurance that the administration will not use reprogramming authority to provide military assistance to China without first going through the normal authorization and appropriations processes, thus requiring further Congressional action beyond that taken this year.

Sincerely,

CHARLES H. PERCY,
Chairman.
S.I. HAYAKAWA,
Chairman, Subcommittee on East Asian and Pacific Affairs.
CLAIBORNE PELL,
Ranking Minority Member.
JOHN GLENN,
Ranking Minority Member, Subcommittee on East Asian and Pacific Affairs.

DEPARTMENT OF STATE,
Washington, D.C., May 13, 1982.

Hon. Charles H. Percy,
Chairman, Senate Foreign Relations Committee.

DEAR MR. CHAIRMAN. I have been asked to respond to the letter which you and Senators Hayakawa, Pell, and Glenn sent to Secretary Haig on May 3 concerning China and amendments to the existing legislation on foreign assistance. I wish to reaffirm the assurances given your Committee on April 26 in testimony by Acting Assistant Secretary for East Asian and Pacific Affairs Thomas P. Shoesmith[25] and to assure mem-

[24] The administration's proposal, incorporated in proposed foreign assistance legislation for fiscal year 1983, included provisions which would have amended the Foreign Assistance Act of 1961 and the Agricultural Trade Development and Assistance Act of 1954, or P.L. 480 (approved July 10, 1954; 68 Stat. 454), in order to remove prohibitions against assistance to the People's Republic of China. For the text of a statement concerning the proposed legislation which Assistant Secretary Holdridge made on March 30 before a subcommittee of the House Appropriations Committee, see document 460.

[25] For the text of Shoesmith's testimony, see *Fiscal Year 1983 Security Assistance: Hearings Before the Committee on Foreign Relations, United States Senate, Ninety-seventh Congress, Second Session, on S. 2227, A Bill to Amend the Foreign Assistance Act of 1961 and the Arms Export Control Act to Authorize Additional Security and Development Assistance Programs for Fiscal Years 1983 and 1984, and for Other Purposes* (Washington, 1982), pp. 315–352.

bers of your Committee that no military assistance program is being contemplated for China.

Let me emphasize that the administration's proposal to make China eligible for foreign assistance and Public Law 480 should in no way be construed as a request for the authorization or appropriation of funds. The request has no budgetary impact and is not designed to provide military assistance to China.

Rather, our intent was to remove outdated prohibitions which are inconsistent with our foreign policy and with our treatment of China as a friendly, non-allied country with which we share important strategic interests. The administration has no present intention of proposing a Public Law 480 program, or an economic or military assistance program for China. If the prohibition on assistance is eliminated, however, we do intend to consider Chinese participation in certain on-going technical assistance programs for which funding is already available. We have already provided your Committee a paper describing the types of programs in which China might participate.

If, in the future, we should contemplate initiating assistance programs for China, we would at that time consult with the appropriate Committees of the Congress. Following such consultations, it would of course be necessary to proceed through the normal statutory process before funds could be expended.

With respect to your question on reprogramming, you can be assured that the administration does not contemplate using the reprogramming authority to provide military assistance to China. If, at a future date, we propose to initiate military assistance to China, we would provide the details of such assistance in connection with our request for the authorization of foreign assistance funds for that year. The Congressional action we are requesting at this time is designed only to establish treatment for China consistent with our treatment of other friendly, non-allied nations.

I trust this letter responds to the concerns raised by you and your colleagues.

With cordial regards,

Sincerely,

POWELL A. MOORE,
Assistant Secretary for Congressional Relations.

The Committee commends the Agriculture Committee for its timely consideration of the administration's proposal regarding Public Law 480 Food for Peace and supports the Agriculture Committee's decision to write report language which would state that the administration's proposed amendment making China eligible for Public Law 480 is unnecessary.[26] It is the Agriculture Committee's judgment that if the President believes that China neither dominates nor is dominated by a world Communist movement, he is free to designate China as a "friendly country" and, therefore, eligible for Public Law 480 under existing law.

The Committee found that, from a foreign policy point of view, the Agriculture Committee's views noted above are consistent with the Foreign Relations Committee's views. Because initiation of a Public Law 480 program would have important foreign policy implications, not only in regard to U.S.–PRC relations, but also in regard to its potential effects on other foreign nations, the President should also notify the Committee on Foreign Relations at least 90 days in advance of implementation of any Public Law 480 program with China. In a situation where Public Law 480 title II might be used to respond to a specific emergency, the Committee recognizes that it might be impossible to provide notification the full 90 days in advance and would accept the administration's best efforts to provide prior notification.

. . . .

Document 493

Address by the Deputy Secretary of State (Stoessel) Before the National Council on U.S.–China Trade, June 1, 1982[27]

Developing Lasting U.S.–China Relations

It is a great pleasure to be here today. I know that you and the other members of

[26] For comments on Section 108(b) of S. 2227 by the Senate Committee on Agriculture, Nutrition, and Forestry, together with a letter of May 13 from Senator Jesse Helms, chairman of the committee, to Senator Percy, see *International Security Enhancement Act of 1982*, pp. 34–39.

[27] Source: Department of State *Bulletin*, July 1982, pp. 50–52. The address was given in Washington.

the National Council on U.S.–China Trade have been deeply involved in developing a strong, mutually beneficial relationship between the United States and China. I can honestly say that without your constructive approach and persistent efforts, we would not have come as far as we have in our bilateral relations.

Fostering a lasting relationship between the United States and China has been a vitally important bipartisan objective for the last four administrations. A strong U.S.–China relationship is one of the highest goals of President Reagan's foreign policy.

Strong U.S.–China relations are not only critical for our long-term security but also contribute to Asian stability and global harmony. The United States and China are both great countries, strong and vigorous, with tremendous potential for promoting world peace and prosperity. As President Reagan noted in his letter to Premier Zhao commemorating the 10th anniversary of the Shanghai communiqué, "our contacts have embraced almost all areas of human endeavor."

We view China as a friendly country with which we are not allied but with which we share many common interests. Strategically, we have no fundamental conflicts of interests, and we face a common challenge from the Soviet Union. In areas such as trade, tourism, banking, and agriculture and in scientific, technological, and educational exchanges, a close, cooperative relationship has resulted in a productive flow of people and ideas between our two societies. It is for these reasons that the Reagan administration believes it essential that we develop a strong and lasting relationship.

During the decade-long process of normalizing our relations, a number of principles upon which we base our China policy have emerged. These principles, which President Reagan has strongly endorsed, include our recognition that the Government of the People's Republic of China is the sole legal government of China and our acknowledgment of the Chinese position that there is but one China and that Taiwan is a part of China.

They also include a firm acceptance that the U.S.–China relationship, like all relationships between equal, sovereign nations, should be guided by the fundamental principles of respect for each other's sovereignty and territorial integrity and noninterference in each other's internal affairs. The relationship should be based on a spirit of consultation, cooperation, and strong efforts to achieve mutual understanding on the wide range of issues of interest to both of our countries.

The Reagan administration is committed to pursuing a durable relationship with China based on these principles. President Reagan values the relationship highly and believes it is important to work together to expand the benefits to both countries. As he said in a recent letter to Vice Chairman Deng Xiaoping, "China and America are two great nations destined to grow stronger through cooperation, not weaker through division."

It is because of the importance that President Reagan places on the U.S.–China relationship that Vice President Bush recently visited Beijing as the President's personal emissary. We were highly pleased with the outcome of the Vice President's trip, both in terms of the reception he received and in terms of the clarity and quality of the high-level communication which it produced. We believe that both the United States and China saw in this visit the opportunity to demonstrate the high value each places on the relationship. We also believe that good progress was made in addressing the one serious issue that threatened good relations—Taiwan arms sales.

We are continuing our discussions with the Chinese on this complex, historical issue. We believe that so long as both sides demonstrate the statesmanship, vision, and good will that have characterized our relationship, we will be able to overcome our difficulties. Indeed, anything other than a successful outcome would be a great misfortune for both sides. The only beneficiary would be our common adversaries.

It is not my purpose to address the Taiwan arms sale issue today. Indeed, public attention on this issue has tended to obscure the continuing progress which this administration has made in carrying out important China policy initiatives. These steps play an important role in removing residual impediments to a relationship based on mutual trust. They will further strengthen the foundation for a durable long-term partnership between the United States and China.

These initiatives grew out of a thorough review of all aspects of U.S.–China relations conducted during the first 5 months of the Reagan administration. They were launched just 1 year ago, when Secretary Haig visited Beijing. During his meetings, the Secretary reaffirmed our common strategic perceptions and announced new steps aimed at deepening our bilateral relationship.[28] The subsequent implementation of this policy focused on four main areas—technology transfer, arms transfers, legislative restrictions, and consular relations. In the 11 months since the Secretary's visit, important progress has been made on all fronts.

We have substantially liberalized our export control policy toward China.[29] This initiative has reflected not only a desire to expand business opportunities but also our strong national interest in contributing to China's modernization. We recognize that a secure, modernizing China is important to the United States from a global and strategic perspective. We strongly believe in supporting Beijing's ambitious efforts to improve the quality of life of more than one-quarter of the world's population.

Over the past year, there has been a dramatic rise in approvals of export licenses for China. Since July of 1981 through March of this year, 1,203 license applications were approved. This represented an increase of nearly 40% over the prior 9-month period.

A recent White House directive reaffirmed this policy of substantial liberalization, emphasizing that U.S. export policy "should support a secure, friendly, and modernizing China" and underscoring the importance of "prompt and full implementation" of the President's June 4, 1981 decision. This new directive should give additional impetus to our efforts to expand trade relations. I fully expect that as U.S.–China relations continue to advance, there will be important further progress.

Another area in which we have opened the way to future cooperation is in arms transfer policy. During his June 1981 visit to Beijing, Secretary Haig announced that we were prepared to cooperate with China in this area on the same case-by-case basis governing U.S. arms transfers to all other nations. In December 1981, we lifted the historical bars on munitions sales to China.[30]

The administration also recognized that the increasing flow of businessmen, tourists, and students between the United States and China made it imperative that we establish regular consular relations. Accordingly, Secretary Haig rapidly concluded negotiations on a consular convention which was ratified last fall and came into force this year.[31] Since the differing social systems of the two countries at times lead us to take differing views on some issues involving our citizens, the convention provides important protections for Americans in China. We intend vigorously to uphold its provisions, not only in letter but in spirit.

The administration conducted a thorough review of legislation affecting our relationship with China. The review identified three areas in which outdated laws discriminated against China in ways inconsistent with our current strategic relationship. These were: eligibility for foreign assistance, P.L. 480,[32] and the importation of seven previously banned furskins.[33]

Congressional reaction to these proposals has been positive. We have no plans to extend P.L. 480 and are only contemplating limited technical assistance through Chi-

[28] For information concerning Secretary Haig's visit to Beijing, June 14–17, 1981, see *American Foreign Policy: Current Documents, 1981*, documents 491–493.

[29] On July 8, 1981, Deputy Assistant Secretary of Commerce for Export Administration Bo Denysyk announced changes in the administration's policy on the export of dual-use, high-technology products to China. He stated that all validated licenses not requiring review by the Coordinating Committee for Multilateral Export Control (COCOM) would be processed by the Department of Commerce without interagency review, that there would be a presumption of approval for most products with technical levels twice those previously approved, and that cases above the double threshold would be considered on a case-by-case basis. (Department of Commerce, International Trade Administration, Press Release, July 8, 1981)

[30] An amendment to the International Traffic in Arms Regulations, December 14, 1981, deleted the People's Republic of China from the list of countries denied licenses and other approvals for U.S. Munitions List exports; for text, see *Federal Register*, December 14, 1981, p. 60820.

[31] The reference is to the U.S.–China consular convention signed at Washington on September 17, 1980; for text, see *Public Papers of the Presidents of the United States: Jimmy Carter, 1980–81* (Washington, 1982), II, pp. 1807–1822. Notes exchanged at Beijing on June 16, 1981, provided for the establishment of additional U.S. and Chinese consulates general; see *American Foreign Policy: Current Documents, 1981*, footnote 15 to document 493.

[32] See the Senate Foreign Relations Committee report, *supra*.

[33] Section 11 of the Trade Agreements Extension Act of 1951 (P.L. 50, approved June 16, 1951; 65 Stat. 72) prohibited the importation of seven types of furskins from the People's Republic of China and the Soviet Union. Section 101 of H.R. 6867, originally introduced as H.R. 5707, would have repealed this prohibition with respect to China. H.R. 6867 was passed by the House of Representatives on September 22, 1982, but was not adopted by the Senate.

nese involvement in established programs. However, these are important symbolic gestures, which we hope will contribute to a relationship based on equality, mutual benefit, and mutual respect.

I would now like to share with you some of my thoughts about the value of the U.S.–China relationship, both past and future. We have made tremendous strides and will seek continued progress in the years ahead.

To start with, the strategic benefits that we see now—some 10 years after the beginning of rapprochement—have been substantial. It is an obvious but often overlooked and vitally important fact that the United States and China no longer face each other as hostile adversaries and no longer need to deploy forces against one another. This has made a tremendous difference to both nations and will continue to be of critical importance to planners on both sides.

The relationship has been important to our entire global strategy. U.S. and Chinese security policies are basically compatible. The relationship has supported our alliance structure and enhanced China's ability to deal with challenges to its security. In many areas of the world our economic assistance and political relationships have been mutually reinforcing.

To turn to specific areas, our consultations with the Chinese on Kampuchea have been an important complement to our cooperation with the ASEAN nations in attempting to turn back Vietnamese aggression. In Afghanistan and Southwest Asia, the United States and China have maintained closely parallel policies, recognizing that the entire region is threatened by a southern thrust from the Soviet Union.

Indeed, even where we disagree, the very fact that we can maintain a high-quality dialogue on international issues is an important byproduct of the relationship. In one area which we approach in different ways—the Korean Peninsula—our good relations have been an important factor fostering regional stability.

Bilaterally, of course, there have been major benefits. U.S.–China trade is of tremendous importance to our nation. Its volume has increased dramatically, and its potential for further expansion remains great. We were pleased, for example, to see Premier Zhao Ziyang receiving important American businessmen recently even at a time of difficulty elsewhere in U.S.–China relations. The Premier's reception of Mr. Phillips[34] and Mr. Tappan[35] are strong indicators that the importance we continue to attach to building a long-term commercial relationship is reciprocated at the highest levels in China.

It is impressive to note the levels of cooperation that already exist between our two countries.

The volume and value of bilateral trade have been increasing dramatically. China is now our 14th largest trading partner.

U.S. agricultural sales to China were around $2 billion in 1981. China has thus become our fifth largest market for agricultural products.

There are currently over 8,000 Chinese students in the United States. They are now the largest group of students from another country to be studying here. Hundreds of Americans have also studied or done research in China.

Tourism and other travels between the two countries have grown to massive dimensions. Tens of thousands of Americans visit China annually. Official delegations are already numerous and are increasing.

At last count some 80 American companies have established permanent offices in Beijing. Many companies with representatives in Hong Kong or Tokyo are also involved in frequent business discussions with the Chinese.

Opportunities for joint ventures are growing. The Chinese recently adopted a joint venture law that establishes a legal framework for such undertakings. Under the auspices of the U.N. Industrial Development Organization, the Chinese have announced 130 joint ventures open to foreign participation.

Our two governments have begun to explore the possiblity of a bilateral investment treaty which would further facilitate U.S. investment in China.

We have also been conducting discussions with the Chinese on the possibility of an agreement for peaceful nuclear cooperation, which would enable us to compete commercially in the development of China's nuclear power program.

Exchanges have increased substantially in the science and technology area. During

[34] Christopher H. Phillips, President, National Council of U.S.–China Trade.

[35] David S. Tappan, Jr., President and Chief Operating Officer, Fluor Corporation.

1981 dozens of delegations were exchanged, and three new protocols were signed—bringing the total number of protocols under our bilateral science and technology agreement to 17. The benefits to both sides in this area, which span a wide variety of fields ranging from health to earthquake studies, have proven to be even more impressive than we had foreseen.

In conclusion, I would like to emphasize again that the Reagan administration values the U.S.-China relationship very highly. That relationship must be based on the principles of equality and mutual respect. We will continue to work closely with the Chinese leadership with the objective of resolving the Taiwan arms sales issue. We will seek to expand cooperation with China in areas where our interests are parallel or complementary.

American foreign policy is sometimes accused of being shortsighted and of operating in a 4-year context. It is clear from the record of four administrations that this is not the case with China. U.S. foreign policymakers clearly recognize that it is not in our interest to perpetuate the hostility that existed between the United States and China but to look ahead to decades of close Sino-American cooperation.

I believe that the coming years will see the development of an even deeper and more extensive relationship between our two great countries. We at the State Department would welcome your thoughts on areas that remain to be explored and initiatives for the future. With your help we can forge a lasting relationship of mutual benefit to both the United States and China that will take us well into the 21st century.

Document 494

Transcript of a Press Conference by President Reagan, July 28, 1982 (Extract)[36]

"We Are Not Going to Abandon Our Longtime Friends and Allies on Taiwan"

. . . .

Q. Mr. President, what role do you envision for Mainland China in American strategic planning in East Asia and along the Soviet border and what are your plans for arms sales to Taiwan?

THE PRESIDENT. We want to continue developing the relationship that was started some years ago by President Nixon with the People's Republic of China. But at the same time, they know very well our position and it has not changed. We are not going to abandon our longtime friends and allies on Taiwan. And I'm going to carry out the terms of the Taiwan Relations Act.[37] And this has been made clear. And we have no secret agreements of any other kind or anything that should cause the Government or the people of Taiwan to have any concern about that. It is a moral obligation that we'll keep.

. . . .

Document 495

Joint Communiqué Issued by the Governments of the United States and the People's Republic of China, Washington and Beijing, August 17, 1982[38]

U.S. Arms Sales to Taiwan

1. In the Joint Communiqué on the Establishment of Diplomatic Relations on January 1, 1979, issued by the Government of the United States of America and the Government of the People's Republic of China, the United States of America recognized the Government of the People's Republic of China as the sole legal government of China, and it acknowledged the Chinese position that there is but one China and Taiwan is part of China. Within that

---

[36] Source: White House Press Release, July 28, 1982, Office of the Press Secretary to the President; also printed in *Weekly Compilation of Presidential Documents*, August 2, 1982, p. 966. For the full text, see *ibid.*, pp. 963–971. The press conference, held at the White House and broadcast live on nationwide radio and television, began at 8:01 p.m.

[37] P.L. 96–8, approved April 10, 1979; for text, see *American Foreign Policy: Basic Documents, 1977–1980*, pp. 989–994.

[38] Source: White House Press Release, August 17, 1982, Office of the Press Secretary to the President; also printed in *Weekly Compilation of Presidential Documents*, August 23, 1982, pp. 1039–1040. The text of the joint communiqué was released at 7 a.m., eastern daylight time.

context, the two sides agreed that the people of the United States would continue to maintain cultural, commercial, and other unofficial relations with the people of Taiwan. On this basis, relations between the United States and China were normalized.

2. The question of United States arms sales to Taiwan was not settled in the course of negotiations between the two countries on establishing diplomatic relations. The two sides held differing positions, and the Chinese side stated that it would raise the issue again following normalization. Recognizing that this issue would seriously hamper the development of United States–China relations, they have held further discussions on it, during and since the meetings between President Ronald Reagan and Premier Zhao Ziyang and between Secretary of State Alexander M. Haig, Jr., and Vice Premier and Foreign Minister Huang Hua in October 1981.

3. Respect for each other's sovereignty and territorial integrity and noninterference in each other's internal affairs constitute the fundamental principles guiding United States–China relations. These principles were confirmed in the Shanghai Communiqué of February 28, 1972, and reaffirmed in the Joint Communiqué on the Establishment of Diplomatic Relations which came into effect on January 1, 1979. Both sides emphatically state that these principles continue to govern all aspects of their relations.

4. The Chinese Government reiterates that the question of Taiwan is China's internal affair. The Message to Compatriots in Taiwan issued by China on January 1, 1979,[39] promulgated a fundamental policy of striving for peaceful reunification of the Motherland. The Nine-Point Proposal put forward by China on September 30, 1981, represented a further major effort under this fundamental policy to strive for a peaceful solution to the Taiwan question.

5. The United States Government attaches great importance to its relations with China, and reiterates that it has no intention of infringing on Chinese sovereignty and territorial integrity, or interfering in China's internal affairs, or pursuing a policy of "Two Chinas" or "one China, one Taiwan." The United States Government understands and appreciates the Chinese policy of striving for a peaceful resolution of the Taiwan question as indicated in China's Message to Compatriots in Taiwan issued on January 1, 1979, and the Nine-Point Proposal put forward by China on September 30, 1981. The new situation which has emerged with regard to the Taiwan question also provides favorable conditions for the settlement of United States–China differences over the question of United States arms sales to Taiwan.

6. Having in mind the foregoing statements of both sides, the United States Government states that it does not seek to carry out a long-term policy of arms sales to Taiwan, that its arms sales to Taiwan will not exceed, either in qualitative or in quantitative terms, the level of those supplied in recent years since the establishment of diplomatic relations between the United States and China, and that it intends to reduce gradually its sales of arms to Taiwan, leading over a period of time to a final resolution. In so stating, the United States acknowledges China's consistent position regarding the thorough settlement of this issue.

7. In order to bring about, over a period of time, a final settlement of the question of United States arms sales to Taiwan, which is an issue rooted in history, the two governments will make every effort to adopt measures and create conditions conducive to the thorough settlement of this issue.

8. The development of United States–China relations is not only in the interests of the two peoples but also conducive to peace and stability in the world. The two sides are determined, on the principle of equality and mutual benefit, to strengthen their ties in the economic, cultural, educational, scientific, technological and other fields and make strong, joint efforts for the continued development of relations between the governments and peoples of the United States and China.

9. In order to bring about the healthy development of United States–China relations, maintain world peace and oppose aggression and expansion, the two governments reaffirm the principles agreed on by the two sides in the Shanghai Communiqué and the Joint Communiqué on the Establishment of Diplomatic Relations. The two sides will maintain contact and hold appropriate consultations on bilateral and international issues of common interest.

[39] For the text of the message of the Standing Committee of the National People's Congress to compatriots in Taiwan, see Foreign Broadcast Information Service, *Daily Report: China,* January 2, 1979, pp. E1–E3.

Document 496

Statement by President Reagan, August 17, 1982[40]

Administration Position on the Joint Communiqué

The U.S.–China Joint Communiqué issued today embodies a mutually satisfactory means of dealing with the historical question of US arms sales to Taiwan. This document preserves principles on both sides, and will promote the further development of friendly relations between the governments and peoples of the United States and China. It will also contribute to the further reduction of tensions and to lasting peace in the Asia/Pacific region.

Building a strong and lasting relationship with China has been an important foreign policy goal of four consecutive American administrations. Such a relationship is vital to our long-term national security interests and contributes to stability in East Asia. It is in the national interest of the United States that this important strategic relationship be advanced. This communiqué will make that possible consistent with our obligations to the people of Taiwan.

In working toward this successful outcome we have paid particular attention to the needs and interests of the people of Taiwan. My longstanding personal friendship and deep concern for their well-being is steadfast and unchanged. I am committed to maintaining the full range of contacts between the people of the United States and the people of Taiwan—cultural, commercial, and people-to-people contacts—which are compatible with our unofficial relationship. Such contacts will continue to grow and prosper, and will be conducted with the dignity and honor befitting old friends.

Regarding future U.S. arms sales to Taiwan, our policy, set forth clearly in the communiqué, is fully consistent with the Taiwan Relations Act. Arms sales will continue in accordance with the Act and with the full expectation that the approach of the Chinese Government to the resolution of the Taiwan issue will continue to be peaceful. We attach great significance to the Chinese statement in the communiqué regarding China's "fundamental" policy; and it is clear from our statements that our future actions will be conducted with this peaceful policy fully in mind. The position of the United States Government has always been clear and consistent in this regard. The Taiwan question is a matter for the Chinese people, on both sides of the Taiwan Strait, to resolve. We will not interfere in this matter or prejudice the free choice of, or put pressure on, the people of Taiwan in this matter. At the same time, we have an abiding interest and concern that any resolution be peaceful. I shall never waver from this fundamental position.

I am proud, as an American, at the great progress that has been made by the people on Taiwan, over the past three decades, and of the American contribution to that process. I have full faith in the continuation of that process. My administration, acting through appropriate channels, will continue strongly to foster that development and to contribute to a strong and healthy investment climate, thereby enhancing the well-being of the people of Taiwan.

[40] Source: White House Press Release, August 17, 1982, Office of the Press Secretary to the President; also printed in *Weekly Compilation of Presidential Documents,* August 23, 1982, pp. 1040–1041. The statement was released at 7 a.m., eastern daylight time.

Document 497

Statement by the Spokesman of the Chinese Ministry of Foreign Affairs, Beijing, August 17, 1982[41]

Chinese Statement on the Joint Communiqué

1. Following discussions, the Government of the People's Republic of China and the Government of the United States of America have reached agreement on the question of United States sale of arms to Taiwan. The two sides have released the joint communiqué simultaneously today.

The United States sale of arms to Taiwan is an issue which affects China's sovereign-

[41] Source: Foreign Broadcast Information Service, *Daily Report: China,* August 17, 1982, p. V1. The source text is an August 17 report in English by Xinhua (New China News Agency). The spokesman is not further identified.

ty. Back in 1978, when the two countries held negotiations on the establishment of diplomatic relations, the Chinese Government stated in explicit terms its opposition to the U.S. arms sales to Taiwan. As this issue could not be settled at that time, the Chinese side suggested that the two sides continue discussions on the issue following the establishment of diplomatic relations. It is evident that failure to settle this issue is bound to impair seriously the relations between the two countries.

With a view to safeguarding China's sovereignty and removing the obstacle to the development of relations between the two countries, Premier Zhao Ziyang held discussions with President Ronald Reagan on this issue during the Cancun meeting in Mexico in October 1981. Subsequently, Vice Premier and Foreign Minister Huang Hua continued the discussions with Secretary of State Alexander M. Haig, Jr., in Washington. As from [*of*?] December 1981, the two sides started concrete discussions through diplomatic channels in Beijing. During this period, U.S. Vice President George Bush, entrusted by President Reagan, paid a visit to China in May 1982, when he held discussions with the Chinese leaders on the same subject. The joint communiqué released by the two sides today is the outcome of repeated negotiations between China and the United States over the past 10 months. It has laid down the principles and steps by which the question of U.S. arms sales to Taiwan should be settled.

2. The joint communiqué reaffirms the principles of respect for each other's sovereignty and territorial integrity and noninterference in each other's internal affairs as embodied in the Shanghai Communiqué and the joint communiqué on the establishment of diplomatic relations between China and the United States. Both sides also emphatically state that these principles continue to govern all aspects of their relations. That is to say, the question of U.S. arms sales to Taiwan must be settled on these principles. Needless to say, only by strictly observing these principles in dealing with the existing or new issues between the two countries will it be possible for their relations to develop healthily.

3. In compliance with the above principles governing the relations between the two countries, the U.S. arms sales to Taiwan should have been terminated altogether long ago. But considering that this is an issue left over by history, the Chinese Government, while upholding the principles, has agreed to settle it step by step. The U.S. side has committed that, as the first step, its arms sales to Taiwan will not exceed, either in qualitative or in quantitative terms, the level of those supplied in recent years since the establishment of diplomatic relations between the two countries, and that they will be gradually reduced, leading to a final resolution of this issue over a period of time. The final resolution referred to here certainly implies that the U.S. arms sales to Taiwan must be completely terminated over a period of time. And only a thorough settlement of this issue can remove the obstacles in the way of developing relations between the two countries.

4. In the joint communiqué, the Chinese Government reiterates in clear-cut terms its position that "the question of Taiwan is China's internal affair." The U.S. side also indicates that it has no intention of infringing on Chinese sovereignty and territorial integrity, or interfering in China's internal affairs, or pursuing a policy of "two Chinas" or "one China, one Taiwan." The Chinese side refers in the joint communiqué to its fundamental policy of striving for peaceful reunification of the motherland for the purpose of further demonstrating the sincere desire of the Chinese Government and people to strive for a peaceful solution to the Taiwan question. On this issue, which is purely China's internal affair, no misinterpretation or foreign interference is permissible.

5. It must be pointed out that the present joint communiqué is based on the principle embodied in the joint communiqué on the establishment of diplomatic relations between China and the United States and the basic norms guiding international relations and has nothing to do with the "Taiwan Relations Act" formulated unilaterally by the United States.

The "Taiwan Relations Act" seriously contravenes the principles embodied in the joint communiqué on the establishment of diplomatic relations between the two countries, and the Chinese Government has consistently been opposed to it. All interpretations designed to link the present joint communiqué to the "Taiwan Relations Act" are in violation of the spirit and substance of this communiqué and are thus unacceptable.

6. The agreement reached between the Governments of China and the United States on the question of U.S. arms sales to Taiwan only marks a beginning of the settlement of this issue. What is important is that the relevant provisions of the joint

communiqué are implemented in earnest, so that the question of U.S. arms sales to Taiwan can be resolved thoroughly at an early date. This is indispensable to the maintenance and development of Sino-U.S. relations.

Document 498

Statements by Members of the Senate Foreign Relations Committee and by the Assistant Secretary of State for East Asian and Pacific Affairs (Holdridge), August 17, 1982[42]

"Our Policy Is Predicated on China's Commitment . . . to a Peaceful Approach"

The committee met, pursuant to notice, at 2:20 p.m., in room 4221, Dirksen Senate Office Building, Hon. Charles H. Percy (chairman of the committee) presiding.

Present: Senators Percy, Helms, Hayakawa, Mathias, Pressler, Pell, Glenn, Tsongas, and Dodd.

THE CHAIRMAN. It is a pleasure to welcome back once again Ambassador Holdridge to the committee.

It is my understanding, Ambassador Holdridge, that you have come to explain to us and elaborate on the President's announcement this morning concerning our relations with China and Taiwan.[43] We particularly welcome your appearance this afternoon on this subject.

As you know, over the period of almost a year the committee has been in contact with you and other officers of the Department on the administration's policy toward China and Taiwan. These sessions have been most helpful to the members of the committee in understanding the problems you confront in pursuing U.S. interests in our dealings with China and Taiwan.

I commend you, former Secretary Haig, Secretary Shultz, and the President on your forthright and candid approach toward the committee. The approach has greatly assisted the committee in fulfilling its constitutional role in the field of foreign affairs.

Our discussions on U.S. policy toward China and Taiwan over the past year have been a model of the consultative process of which both branches of our Government can be justifiably proud. I thank you for your role in that process.

Our sessions during this process, however, in deference to the administration's wishes, have been in executive session and classified to protect the confidentiality of your discussions with the Chinese. While we understand the need for confidentiality in diplomatic discussions, I believe we have made clear that many of us have had reservations about the administration's reluctance to expose its China–Taiwan policy to public discussion and debate.

As I said to you during our meeting in June, it is only as a result of public discussion that general bipartisan support of our policy emerges. Only through public debate can you be assured the administration has defined a national interest which must underlie any enduring policy in a way that is satisfactory to the country as a whole.

Today we begin this practice, and the policies you have devised must stand the test of that debate and time. The committee intends to hold hearings subsequent to this one on our relations with China and Taiwan in an effort to encourage the development of a consensus, and we seek your assistance in doing so. We anticipate further hearings in the near future.

In considering the President's announcement this afternoon we want to give particular attention to two areas. First, we have undertaken certain solemn obligations to the people on Taiwan as embodied in the Taiwan Relations Act overwhelmingly passed by the Congress in 1979. These obligations must be upheld. A policy statement cannot change a public law.

Second, we as a Nation value our relationship with the People's Republic of China. We have a number of strategic interests in common. Our relationship has expanded over the last decade. Although our trade with Taiwan is double that with the PRC, trade with the PRC has increased many times over, and this growth promises to continue.

In my view, our relationship with China is to our benefit and should continue to

---

[42] Source: *U.S. Policy Toward China and Taiwan: Hearing Before the Committee on Foreign Relations, United States Senate, Ninety-seventh Congress, Second Session* (Washington, 1982), pp. 1–15.

[43] See documents 495 and 496.

expand and improve. I realize that this is a difficult problem. These two objectives can sometimes be in conflict. Under these circumstances a certain amount of ambiguity may be helpful as long as it does not undermine our basic, fundamental objectives or prejudice what we might want to do in the future. There may be ambiguity in the communiqué, but there can be no ambiguity in implementing the Taiwan Relations Act. We must assure that Taiwan's legitimate defense needs are met as the Taiwan Relations Act requires of us.

We look forward, Ambassador Holdridge, to your views on how we can achieve these ends and to your explanation of some of the wording in the communiqué, which on the face of it appears troublesome.

Senator Pell.

Senator Pell. Mr. Chairman, I want to second your excellent opening statement. The points you raise are important. I would add that at first blush the joint China–United States communiqué seems fair. However, on further examination I find myself very concerned with the interests of the native Taiwanese, some 16 million people out of a total Taiwan population of 18 million, or pretty close to 90 percent of the people. Too often our discussions of China–Taiwan policy assume that the hopes, dreams, and aspirations of the native Taiwanese are shared by the mainland Chinese authorities in power on both sides of the Taiwan strait. In fact, nothing could be further from the truth.

The evidence of this is the martial law that has remained, in effect, in Taiwan for over 30 years. The results of this are apparent when you talk to native Taiwanese without any chaperones or advisers around. And I think we should bear in mind the old idea of self-determination. We fought World War I with that as one of our goals. We have forgotten it in many places since.

I believe that given a free choice, the Taiwanese would opt for a separate identity—a free and independent Taiwan. Unfortunately, I conclude after having read the communiqué and examining it more carefully and noting the inherent contradiction between "peaceful reunification," mainland China's position, and "peaceful resolution," our hope, that it could make it more difficult, if not eliminate the possibility altogether, for the people on Taiwan to choose a free, independent democratic government. And when I say independent I mean independent of mainland China.

I hope I am wrong but if not, I believe we cannot stand by and condone PRC pressures on Taiwan to bend to its desires. This must be a choice freely made not by the Government on Taiwan governing by martial law, but by the people of Taiwan.

Thank you.

The Chairman. Senator Glenn.

Senator Glenn. I would like to make a short opening statement.

Along with the chairman and other members of the committee I helped draft the legislation which became known as the TRA;[44] so we, better than most perhaps, know what we intended to accomplish in that act. And I can tell you that in my considered judgment the communiqué announced today does undermine the spirit and intent of the TRA.

Three years ago the executive branch appeared before this committee arguing that the United States intended to sell arms to Taiwan indefinitely, but that this need not be mentioned in the legislation we were considering at that time, the Taiwan Relations Act. Administration spokesmen went further and indicated that the President might, in fact, veto a bill that contained specific arms sales assurances for Taiwan. I am glad to say that Congress failed to blink in that confrontation.

In President Reagan's words 2 years ago, the Congress was clearly unwilling to buy the Carter plan which it believed would have jeopardized Taiwan's security. The TRA that passed the Congress with almost unanimous support contained our pledge that:

> "The United States will make available to Taiwan such defense articles and defense services in such quantity as may be necessary to enable Taiwan to maintain a sufficient self-defense capability, and the President and Congress shall determine the nature and quantity of such defense articles and services based solely upon their judgment of the needs of Taiwan."

The legislative history demonstrates beyond a doubt that the intent of this passage was to insure that arms sales decisions, albeit prudent and cautious, would be made in Washington, not in Peking or Taipei.

Now, because we anticipated the PRC would pressure us to end or limit Taiwan arms sales, we provided in the act a framework for the executive branch to resist such

[44] The Taiwan Relations Act.

pressures. Without these written assurances and confidence that the President would faithfully carry out the TRA, I seriously doubt that the Congress would have been prepared to go along with normalization and the PRC demand that we terminate the Mutual Defense Treaty with Taiwan.[45]

The communiqué announced today discards that very carefully crafted framework, the heart of the TRA, in favor of an arms sales formulation negotiated under Chinese threats of a retrogression of United States–PRC relations.

As you might expect, under such circumstances the new restrictions on arms sales leave much to be desired. President Reagan indicates that based upon the Chinese statements, particularly the statement that, "Peaceful reunification" is a "fundamental policy of the PRC," he was able to impose further restrictions on arms sales to Taiwan.

These new restrictions include: No. 1, agreeing that the United States "does not seek to carry out a long-term policy of arms sales to Taiwan." No. 2, "Arms sales to Taiwan will not exceed, either in qualitative or quantitative terms, the level of those supplied in recent years." No. 3, that the United States "intends to reduce gradually its sales of arms to Taiwan." And No. 4, this will lead "over a period of time to a final resolution."

I should also note in passing that President Reagan's concessions came just 2 years after candidate Reagan pledged that he"would not impose restrictions which are not required by the Taiwan Relations Act and which contravene its spirit and purpose."

Not only do these restrictions contravene the spirit and purpose of the TRA, they are exactly the sort of PRC-imposed conditions we sought to avoid when we drafted the act. Moreover, the restrictions set forth in the communiqué unfortunately do not resolve the fundamental differences between the United States and the PRC on Taiwan arms sales questions. They merely postpone the day of reckoning. I think that is a very important point. The Chinese continue to oppose arms sales, asserting it infringes on their sovereignty and is an interference in their internal affairs.

Under these conditions, agreeing on limits to gradually reduce and ultimately end arms sales puts us in an impossible position. Soon the Chinese will return with more demands and insist we finally resolve the issue, and we can expect that. We will be in the unfortunate position of having limited our argument to when, not if, a cutoff should occur. Based upon past precedent, I anticipate we will not have to wait long before the PRC makes these new demands known.

Let me close by issuing a communiqué of my own. I can assure you there will be a retrogression in this committee's relations with the Bureau if the action the executive branch has taken results in any major or significant change in the relative military balance that exists today between Taiwan and the PRC.

We want that balance to be maintained, and if implementation of the communiqué causes a deterioration in Taiwan's capability and an improvement in the PRC's relative military advantage, as a starter I would like your commitment you will not orchestrate a reduction of Taiwan's military capabilities and will notify us on each occasion you are required to disapprove U.S. industry contacts with Taiwan or deny an arms sales request made by the authorities on Taiwan.

As I indicated a few weeks ago, obviously we must be prudent and cautious in our arms transfer decisions. Gratuitous sales protect no one. But when we appear to bend to Chinese pressures on each and every sale we make to Taiwan, it is inevitable that Taipei begins seriously to doubt whether we will live up to our solemn responsibilities.

A State Department spokesman has urged me not to worry and indicated that "our relations with China are predicated on our expectation that the Taiwan issue will be resolved peacefully by the Chinese people themselves." In fact, they are so confident the issue can be resolved peacefully, they state that it is in this context that we have been and will continue to judge Taiwan's defense needs.

Unfortunately, I am not quite so sanguine. If Taiwan decides it wants to reunify with the mainland, everything will work out fine. But what if the present or future leaderships decide reunification is not in the island's interest? What then?

Warren Christopher told the Foreign Relations Committee during the TRA debate that:

---

[45] The Mutual Defense Treaty between the United States and the Republic of China, signed at Washington, December 2, 1954; for text, see 6 UST 433. On December 15, 1978, the United States announced its intention to terminate the treaty; for text of the U.S. statement, see *American Foreign Policy: Basic Documents, 1977–1980*, p. 968.

"It is our position that if there is to be a reunification, it is of great importance that it be peaceful and not be destabilizing in the area. But we do not have a position of encouraging the people on Taiwan to do something against their will."[46]

That was an excellent policy then; it is one I fully endorse today. However, if maintaining Taiwan's free choice means supplying needed and selected defensive arms to the island to maintain the balance we have tried to maintain, even over Peking's objections and in the face of threats to downgrade United States–PRC relations, then so be it.

Mr. Chairman, I would harken back to President Reagan's statements when he was a candidate. On August 25, 1980, he stated: "We should not impose restrictions which are not required by the Taiwan Relations Act and which contravene its spirit and purpose." He went on to comment by a use of examples of the Carter administration where they refused to open consulates on behalf of Taiwan; yet just last month we postponed a Boston consulate opening. He said the Carter administration had a 1-year moratorium on arms sales. Yet, we have not sold arms in this administration either.

He talked about the difficulty the Carter administration had caused by refusing to train Taiwan military officers here. We are not now doing that. He went on to state:

"I recognize the PRC is not pleased with the Taiwan Relations Act which the U.S. Congress insisted on as the official basis for our relationship with Taiwan. This was made abundantly clear to Mr. Bush and I am told clear to the Carter administration. But it is the law of our land."

Then at a later point he said:

"As President, I will not accept the interference of any foreign power in the process of protecting American interests and carrying out the laws of our land. To do otherwise would be a dereliction of my duty as President."[47]

---

[46] Then-Deputy Secretary of State Christopher made this statement in testimony before the committee on February 5, 1979; *Taiwan: Hearings Before the Committee on Foreign Relations, United States Senate, Ninety-sixth Congress, First Session, on S. 245, A Bill to Promote the Foreign Policy of the United States Through the Maintenance of Commercial, Cultural, and Other Relations with the People on Taiwan on an Unofficial Basis, and for Other Purposes* (Washington, 1979), p. 64.

[47] For extracts from the statement, which then-candidate Reagan issued at a press conference on August 25, 1980, see *New York Times*, August 26, 1980, p. B7.

Thank you.

THE CHAIRMAN. Thank you very much.

Secretary Holdridge, the Chair will break the precedent of having opening statements by just the Chair and ranking minority member in this case.

We have met with you for over a year. Members have observed silence as a result of coming out of those meetings. And I think in the exchange that we have had, and the confidential nature of that exchange, it is well now to permit all members who want to make statements to make their views known publicly on this important issue.

Senator Pressler, I will call on you next to rotate sides.

SENATOR PRESSLER. Mr. Chairman, I will be brief.

Let me say that this announcement by the administration at this time is very ill conceived, because it does not achieve any foreign policy objectives. The point is that we have had trade with both Chinas. We have had relations with both.

I recently visited both. We were going along quite well. If a change of this magnitude occurs, which as my colleague has pointed out violates our law, it should be for some clear foreign policy objectives. And I would like to hear in public what the immediacy of this was, what caused us to do this now, what foreign policy objectives are we achieving.

Let me also say that I have felt for some time that we did not have a need for change, that things were going well; and granted the People's Republic of China was making some alleged threats, but China needs the trade, and China wants the relationship with us. Both countries do. I do not think we should have yielded to those threats, if we did so at this time. I fear that down the road there are those in the State Department who would like to see us engage in the sale of arms to the PRC or be involved in an aid program there or some sort of relationship such as that. I am opposed to that. I am for trade and a two Chinas policy, but we already have that.

Let me also say that although I respect our chairman's analysis that this was a model of consultation, I would have to politely disagree. Most of the consultations we have had have been under the ground rules that they were confidential, and the options presented to us in the timing of this decision were very ambiguous. I would not agree that this is a model for consultation with Congress in advance of a decision, because we were under very great restrictions not to repeat or analyze in public some of the things said.

Also, it came as a complete surprise to me that this was going to occur at dawn today. In fact, I found out about it from a phone call at 6:30 this morning; but that is, I guess, the way it was done. The point is, if I saw a clear foreign policy objective that we were achieving with this decision, I would probably go along with it because I believe in real politics. I have served in the Army in that area of the world. I think that we are abandoning one of our best friends, in essence, in terms of the way this will be perceived.

If the decision helped to achieve something in trade or achieve something in terms of our national interest objectives, I would probably be for it, but I cannot see why it is being done at this time and in this fashion.

Mr. Chairman, I yield back the balance of my time.

The Chairman. Thank you very much.

Senator Hayakawa.

Senator Hayakawa. Thank you, Mr. Chairman.

The unveiling of the latest joint communiqué between the United States and the PRC leaves much to be desired. As a semantic purist I am somewhat disturbed by the lack of clarity in the language. I am afraid unless one looks very closely at the whole document and what is said and what is not said, it appears as though the United States is turning its back on the people of Taiwan. However, I believe there is enough ambiguity so that no one need take any offense.

The wonderful thing about language is its ability to mean whatever we may want it to mean. As a psychologist I recognize that what we have here is a situation not uncommon in human affairs: a totally ambiguous situation. In one sense Taiwan and China are one country because they both say so. Taiwan says China is one country, and the PRC says China is one country. But in another sense they are not one country.

There are many ambiguities in everyday life with which one lives. Often we condemn them as hypocrisies, but life always puts us into situations in which we have to live with these hypocrisies and endure them, hoping that some day a consistent or rational point of view can prevail, perhaps even with a solution which is not yet thought of.

If you look at the present situation between Taiwan and China where they are making totally inconsistent and incompatible assertions about each other, the PRC is saying that Taiwan is really one of our provinces, and we have complete authority over Taiwan, so that if you, the United States, sell them arms, you interfere in our internal affairs. But we go ahead and sell Taiwan arms, and the PRC does not start a war over it. They do nothing more than make a big squawk and accept what is essentially an illogical situation.

I think that we will have to live with this ambiguity for some time to come. Insofar as any of us on any side of this problem insist we be perfectly logical about it, we will perpetrate some awful injustice on somebody. The only way to guarantee a minimum of justice for perhaps a few decades to come is to accept this ambiguity, to accept this, shall we say, hypocrisy on all sides.

It seems to me that this joint communiqué is just another one of the necessary ways of enduring this illogic, and even though it has been called another temporary palliative, it may have positive, permanent consequences insofar as it places the burden on the PRC to resolve their differences with Taiwan only through peaceful means; and that we have asked them to underline, and they have. Nonetheless, the United States must still be diligent about assessing the intent of the PRC. We must look to what they do and not just what they say. And we, too, must live by this same standard and watch what we do and what we say.

The American people through President Reagan have given assurances to the people of Taiwan that we will not abandon them, and we must make sure that we keep our word and continue to abide by these assurances.

Thank you, Mr. Chairman.

The Chairman. Thank you, Senator Hayakawa.

Senator Tsongas.

Senator Tsongas. Mr. Chairman, I am curious about the Secretary's position. I have just an observation.

Last night before the Red Sox game there was a fellow on television who bore an uncanny physical resemblance to President Reagan, and he called for tax increases that outrages supply side economists and have been enthusiastically endorsed by the ADA. And today we consider a communiqué involving Taiwan and the PRC and the United States, which, if promulgated by a liberal Democrat, would have had this place surrounded by hostile elements all day long.

I guess you have to conclude in Washington if you wait long enough, anything is possible. And I would be curious as to the Secretary's position.

I would also like to read the analysis of the statement by those who were here today, because I do not understand them either; and I would be curious as to how those in our midst who are not from the United States interpret what has been said today to their own people. I would be rather curious.

Thank you.

THE CHAIRMAN. Thank you, Senator Tsongas.

Senator Mathias.

SENATOR MATHIAS. Mr. Chairman, I wait with breathless anticipation for the testimony of the witnesses today. I will just say that I think Senator Hayakawa has given us an interesting historical perspective on this problem and has, I think, said it in the kind of context in which we must view it.

A two-China policy was, I suppose, a comforting concept to some Americans, but it aroused only contempt in both the People's Republic of China and in Taiwan. And if a two-China policy is not a reality in China, then it is only an illusion, and the sooner we clear our vision of it, the better off we will be.

Thank you, Mr. Chairman.

THE CHAIRMAN. Thank you, Senator Mathias.

That is as good a buildup as any witness has ever had. It is a challenge to you, I am sure. We will be anxious to hear from you.

STATEMENT OF HON. JOHN H. HOLDRIDGE, ASSISTANT SECRETARY, BUREAU OF EAST ASIAN AND PACIFIC AFFAIRS, DEPARTMENT OF STATE, ACCOMPANIED BY WILLIAM F. ROPE, DIRECTOR OF THE OFFICE OF CHINESE AFFAIRS; AND DONALD C. FERGUSON, TAIWAN COORDINATION ADVISER, BUREAU OF EAST ASIAN AND PACIFIC AFFAIRS

Thank you very much, Mr. Chairman. I appreciate the chance to meet the challenge.

I would like to introduce, on my right, Mr. William Rope, the Office Director for China, and on my left, Mr. Don Ferguson, the Office Director for Taiwan. I am straddling in the middle. I guess I am in the middle of the Taiwan Strait here. [Laughter]

Let me say, Mr. Chairman, I much appreciated your words yesterday about consultations and again today, and I want you to know that we will do everything in our power to meet the continued obligation to consult with you on matters such as this which we regard as being of transcendental importance, and we will try to keep the standard up as high as you said it was. Let me continue.

Mr. Chairman, this morning the United States and the People's Republic of China simultaneously issued a joint communiqué. Now, during yesterday's hearing and on prior occasions, members of the committee have expressed the view that public hearings on the course of our policies toward China should be held at the earliest possible date. I agreed with that view and I am glad to be able to continue our discussion of these issues in a public forum.

I would also like to express our appreciation for the way the committee has cooperated with us in maintaining the confidentiality of our discussions with the Chinese. This has been vital, and without this confidentiality, I don't know whether we would have reached the state we reached today in terms of issuing a joint communiqué. We are very appreciative of the confidentiality which was maintained.

Mr. Chairman, I think you have stated the problem we face very accurately. As we went into these negotiations, we had two things in mind, our historic obligations to the people of Taiwan and our important and growing relations with the People's Republic of China. Throughout the entire period of our discussions with Beijing, we were guided by these dual considerations. It is a fundamental national interest of the United States to preserve and advance its strategic relations with China. At the same time we have, as you said, obligations to old friends and we will not turn our backs on them.

I am glad we have been able to arrive at a communiqué with the Chinese that demonstrated their recognition of our determination on this score despite the difficulties it obviously causes them and that they, too, because of the important interests involved for them, were willing to join with us in a modus vivendi which will enable us to continue our relationship.

Again, as you and I have pointed out, such an outcome is of vital importance to our national interest. Three administrations before us have worked very hard to establish and expand this relationship, and we would have been derelict if we had not made every effort to find a way around the problem threatening it.

Mr. Chairman, I think it would be useful to take a few minutes to examine the reasons we valued this relationship so highly. One of the major reasons is strategic. Prior to 1971, we had a hostile relationship with China. It was costly. We fought the Chinese in Korea. We almost came to a major war over Quemoy and Ma-tsu. The Chinese worked hand-in-hand with the Soviets against us in Vietnam. We had to maintain a naval presence between Taiwan and the mainland.

China identified itself with support for guerrilla movements on the soil of many of our allies and friends. Furthermore, a large part of our defense resources were allocated on the premise of a hostile China. Lastly and perhaps most importantly, these 1 billion people were not identified with our interests as we faced the Soviet Union.

Starting in 1971, we changed the situation. Thanks to a productive relationship between the United States and China, Taiwan has never been more secure and prosperous. We no longer have to plan for China as an enemy. We can now think of China as a country with which we might cooperate in certain significant areas. China's relations with our allies in Asia have improved.

These 1 billion people are cautiously moving into the mainstream of the world's cultural and economic life. Their isolation is dissolving. Trade has increased. Eight thousand Chinese students are now studying in the United States. Investment opportunities are opening and our parallel interests in containing the Soviet Union have been repeatedly reaffirmed.

As an illustration of one of the benefits to both parties of this relationship, I want to introduce into the record as a part of my statement an article by Christopher Wren in this morning's *New York Times.* It describes the contributions to mutual understandings of United States-Chinese cooperation in the field of management training in Dalian, China.[48]

[48] *New York Times,* August 17, 1982, p. A6. The text of the article which follows in the source text is here omitted.

All of these things represent solid benefits to our security and well-being, Mr. Chairman. We were not going to let these achievements disappear into rancor and hostility if we could avoid it. We went after both of the objectives you have outlined, and I believe we have succeeded.

Let me turn to this morning's communiqué It reaffirms the fundamental principles which have guided United States-Chinese relations since the inception of the normalization process over 10 years ago. This reaffirmation is significant. It illustrates the strength and durability of these principles. On this foundation the United States established relations with China which have been economically beneficial to us and which have greatly enhanced our vital strategic interests.

At the same time, we have maintained and strengthened our commercial and cultural relations with the people of Taiwan. We have achieved these important goals without impairing the security of the people of Taiwan, and indeed, because of these improved relations between China and the United States, Taiwan has never been more secure.

The communiqué also addresses an issue which was not resolved at the time of normalization of relations, the question of U.S. arms sales to Taiwan. During discussions leading to normalization, China demanded that arms sales be terminated. We refused. China agreed to proceed with normalization despite this disagreement but reserved the right to raise this issue again.

I can say here, Mr. Chairman and members of the committee, I believe it is well known that the normalization negotiations almost foundered on this whole question of continued U.S. arms sales to Taiwan, and it was only at the last minute by, I would say, a very statesmanlike decision on the part of the leadership of the People's Republic of China that the decision was made to go ahead, but it really was touch and go.

When China agreed to proceed with normalization despite disagreement on arms sales to Taiwan, it reserved the right to raise the issue again. When it did so last year, we agreed to engage in discussions to determine whether an understanding could be reached. The alternative to our agreeing to hold such discussions would clearly have been the beginning of a process of deterioration in our relations, deterioration that could have led us back toward hostility. Since the issue itself was volatile and basic, we would have been irresponsible had we allowed such a process to start.

To address Senator Pressler's question, our foreign policy objective was to preserve a valuable relationship which otherwise might well have and probably would have undergone a serious and possibly fatal deterioration. We undertook these discussions, therefore, with the hope that a formula could be found which would permit the continued growth of our relations with China, but also with the firm resolve that there were principles regarding the security of Taiwan which could not be compromised.

Those principles embodied in the Taiwan Relations Act commit the United States to sell to Taiwan arms necessary to maintain a sufficient self-defense capability. Aware of our consistent and firm opposition to the use of force against Taiwan, the Chinese during these discussions, and I mean the most recent ones, agreed to state in very strong terms their policy of pursuing a peaceful resolution of the Taiwan issue, and eventually came to describe this policy as "fundamental."

The Chinese insisted, however, that we agree to the ultimate termination of arms sales. We refused because the level of our arms sales must be determined by the needs of Taiwan, and we could not agree to a termination date as the Chinese demanded which might impair our ability to meet those needs. At the same time, we recognized that China's peaceful policy bore directly on the defense needs of Taiwan. So long as the policy continued, the threat to Taiwan would be diminished.

As I have noted, assurances of such continuity were provided when the Chinese began to describe their peaceful policy on the resolution of the Taiwan question as, as I have said, "fundamental," which contains the connotation of unchanging and long term. Let me say this again: which contains the connotation of unchanging and long term. We were thus able to consider a policy under which we would limit our arms sales to the levels reached in recent years and would anticipate a gradual reduction of the level of arms sales.

We were not willing, however, to adopt such a course unconditionally. While the Chinese were willing to state their peaceful policy in strong terms, they at first resisted any relationship between that policy and our arms sales to Taiwan. The Chinese resisted this relationship because of their view that the sale of arms to Taiwan constitutes an interference in China's internal affairs. We rejected any language to this effect in the communiqué.

We also stressed that as a matter of fact and law, any adjustments in our arms sales to Taiwan had to be premised on a continuation of China's peaceful policy. We therefore maintained, and the Chinese ultimately agreed, that the statement of our policy in paragraph 6 of the joint communiqué be prefaced by a phrase that related it to the continuation of China's peaceful approach.

This is the genesis and purpose of the phrase "having in mind the foregoing statements of both sides" which precedes our statements in that paragraph. Thus, our policy is predicated on China's commitment in paragraph 4 to a peaceful approach and our acknowledgment of that approach in paragraph 5.

Let me say this again. Our policy is predicated on China's commitment in paragraph 4 to a peaceful approach and our acknowledgment of that approach in paragraph 5. Let me summarize the essence of our understanding on this point. China has announced a fundamental policy of pursuing peaceful means to resolve the longstanding dispute between Taiwan and the mainland.

Having in mind this policy and the consequent reduction in the military threat to Taiwan, we have stated our intention to reduce arms sales to Taiwan gradually and said that in quantity and quality we would not go beyond levels established since normalization. This follows from a literal reading of the communiqué.

While we have no reason to believe that China's policy will change, an inescapable corollary to these mutually interdependent policies is that should that happen, we will reassess ours. Our guiding principle is now and will continue to be that embodied in the Taiwan Relations Act, the maintenance of a self-defense capability sufficient to meet the military needs of Taiwan, but with the understanding that China's maintenance of a peaceful approach to the Taiwan question will permit gradual reductions in arms sales.

During our meeting yesterday, questions were raised concerning whether the wording of the communiqué adequately conveys the meaning which we ascribe to it. I believe it does or I would not have recommended its approval. The present wording evolved from 10 months of intense negotiation in which fundamental principles were at stake on both sides. The language necessarily reflects the difficult compromises which were reached.

We should keep in mind that what we have here is not a treaty or an agreement but a statement of future U.S. policy. We fully intend to implement this policy in accordance with our understanding of it. I hope I have made that point abundantly clear in my remarks today. I can further assure you that, having participated closely in the negotiations, I am confident the Chinese are fully cognizant of that understanding.

Turning to the document itself in more detail, let me recapitulate and emphasize a few key features, and then I will be happy to take your questions. First, the document must be read as a whole since the policies it sets forth are interrelated. Second, as I previously noted, the communiqué contains a strong Chinese statement that its fundamental policy is to seek to resolve the Taiwan question by peaceful means, paragraph 4. In this context, I would point out again that the reference to their "fundamental" policy carries the connotation in Chinese of unchanging and long term.

Third, the U.S. statements concerning future arms sales to Taiwan, paragraph 6, are based upon China's statements as to its fundamental peaceful policy for seeking a resolution to the Taiwan question, and on the "new situation" created by those statements, paragraph 5. This situation is new because for the first time, China has described its peaceful policy toward Taiwan in the terms I have outlined. Thus, our future actions concerning arms sales to Taiwan are premised on the continuation of China's peaceful policy toward a resolution of its differences with Taiwan.

This is indicated by the words at the beginning of paragraph 5 that "having in mind the foregoing statements by both sides, the U.S. Government states." We have no reason to think the Chinese will change this fundamental policy, but if they should, we would, of course, reexamine our position.

Fourth, we did not agree to set a date certain for ending arms sales to Taiwan, and the statements of future U.S. arms sales policy embodied in the communiqué do not provide either a timeframe for the reduction of U.S. arms sales or for their termination. The U.S. statements are fully consistent with the Taiwan Relations Act and we will continue to make appropriate arms sales to Taiwan based upon our assessments of their defense needs. So much for what is in the actual communiqué.

Over the past several months there has been considerable speculation about the substance of our discussions with the Chinese. As you know, we have not felt free to comment on such speculation while our talks were underway. Therefore, it might be useful at this point to clarify our stand on a number of issues which have surfaced in such speculations.

As to our position on the resolution of the Taiwan problem, we have consistently held that it is a matter to be worked out by the Chinese themselves. Our sole and abiding concern is that any resolution be peaceful. It follows that we see no mediation role for the United States nor will we attempt to exert pressure on Taiwan to enter into negotiations with the PRC.

I would also like to call your attention to the fact that there has been no change in our longstanding position on the issue of sovereignty over Taiwan. The communiqué, paragraph 1, in its opening paragraph simply cites that portion of the joint communiqué on the establishment of diplomatic relations between the United States and the PRC in which the United States acknowledged the Chinese position on this issue; that is, that there is but one China, and Taiwan is a part of China.

It has been reported in the press that the Chinese at one point suggested that the Taiwan Relations Act be revised. We have no plans to seek any such revisions.

Finally, in paragraph 9 the two sides agree to maintain contact and hold appropriate consultations on bilateral and international issues of common interest. This should be read within the context of paragraphs 8 and 9, which deal with the two sides' desire to advance their bilateral and strategic relations. It should not be read to imply that we have agreed to engage in prior consultations with Beijing on arms sales to Taiwan.

We hope and expect that this communiqué and the step forward it represents in the resolution of United States-Chinese differences on this issue will enhance the confidence of the people of Taiwan, whose well-being and prosperity continue to be of the utmost importance to us.

From the President down, we have acted in a way which seeks to enhance the future security and prosperity of the people of Taiwan, and I call your attention to the emphasis on this matter in the President's statement which was released simultaneous with the release of the joint communiqué this morning.

Removal of the arms question as a serious issue in United States–China relations will help assure both countries can continue to cooperate on mutually shared international objectives: For example, deterring Soviet aggression in East Asia and the removal of Vietnamese troops from Kampuchea. It will ease fears by American friends and allies that the general peace and stability in the Asia Pacific region could be undermined. By defusing the difficult issue of arms sales, we will open the way for an expansion of United States-Chinese relations on a broad range of economic, cultural, scientific, and technological areas as well as in people-to-people contacts.

In conclusion, I would like to quote a paragraph from a statement issued by the President this morning:

> "Building a strong, lasting relationship with China has been an important foreign policy goal of four consecutive American administrations. Such a relationship is vital to our long-term national security interests and contributes to stability in East Asia. It is in the national interest of the United States that this important strategic relationship be advanced. This communiqué will make that possible consistent with our obligations to the people of Taiwan."

Thank you very much, Mr. Chairman.

Document 499

Statement by the Chairman of the House Foreign Affairs Committee (Zablocki) and Testimony by the Assistant Secretary of State for East Asian and Pacific Affairs (Holdridge) Before the House Foreign Affairs Committee, August 18, 1982 (Extracts)[49]

Questions Raised by the Joint Communiqué

The committee met at 11:20 a.m. in room 2172, Rayburn House Office Building, Hon. Clement J. Zablocki (chairman) presiding.

CHAIRMAN ZABLOCKI. The committee will please come to order.

We meet today to hear from the administration justification of the policy decision, announced yesterday by the President, affecting United States relations with the People's Republic of China and Taiwan.

That policy decision, made public in the form of a communiqué issued jointly by the authorities in the People's Republic of China and in the United States, essentially pertains to the question of Taiwan. It sets out policies of both countries toward Taiwan.

In light of the obligations under the Taiwan Relations Act, this joint communiqué is understandably causing controversy. Therefore, we have invited an administration spokesman, the Honorable John H. Holdridge, Assistant Secretary of State for East Asian and Pacific Affairs, to appear today to explain the circumstances that surround this important foreign policy action and to answer questions that the committee members may have.

Frankly, in my opinion the joint communiqué raises serious questions and concerns.

First, procedurally, the way the communiqué was negotiated and drafted seems to have violated the spirit if not the letter of the Taiwan Relations Act. That act makes clear United States policy statements on how United States policies would be formulated. It clearly states that the nature and the quantity of the defense materials sold to Taiwan would be determined soley—and I emphasize solely—by the judgment of the U.S. President and the U.S. Congress.

Indeed, many Members of Congress agreed to adopt the provisions of the Taiwan Relations Act in the spring of 1979 only with the clear understanding that the People's Republic of China would in no way have veto power over United States decisions affecting Taiwan's security needs and defense equipment requirements.

Yet, the joint communiqué issued yesterday—almost entirely devoted to matters of great security important to Taiwan—was apparently the product of secret negotiations between the United States and the People's Republic.

Second, the joint communiqué in substance makes several U.S. policy commitments—for example, to deny a long-term policy of arms sales to Taiwan, to set qualitative and quantitative ceilings on arms sales to Taiwan and, ultimately, to reduce arms sales to Taiwan entirely.

---

[49] Source: *China–Taiwan: United States Policy: Hearing Before the Committee on Foreign Affairs, House of Representatives, Ninety-seventh Congress, Second Session* (Washington, 1982), pp. 1–19.

In this regard, the Taiwan Relations Act makes it U.S. policy to accomplish the very opposite, to assure that Taiwan remains eligible to receive U.S. arms of a defensive character and in such quantity so as to enable Taiwan to maintain sufficient self-defense capability.

The joint communiqué seems to prejudge future security needs of Taiwan, to rule out enhancement if needed for its defensive capability. It seems to leave Taiwan with no better prospect than obtaining obsolete equipment from the United States in progressively smaller amounts.

It was always my impression that the Carter administration, which negotiated the joint communiqué of January 1, 1979, also envisioned that arms sales would continue with no discriminatory restraint applied to Taiwan, except for the calendar year 1979 during which the security treaty was being terminated and no new arms sales commitments would occur.

This being the case, the decision made public yesterday in Washington and Peking seems to represent a new foreign policy departure. As reported in the press, the People's Republic of China believes, they have really dictated to us and have won their case.

Secretary Holdridge, we look forward to your testimony regarding these concerns. There remains great anxiety about U.S. policy toward Taiwan that this decision only further excites.

We welcome you today and expect your help in explaining the reasoning behind this policy decision and how you expect U.S. policy will be followed in the future. If you will proceed, Mr. Secretary.[50]

. . . .

CHAIRMAN ZABLOCKI. Thank you, Mr. Secretary.

Apparently the very basis of this communiqué is what you described as China's "fundamental" policy. It is your understanding, and hopefully, it will be the case, that they will resolve their differences with Taiwan in a peaceful manner.

You do say repeatedly that "should" there be reason to believe that China's policy will change from what is now the understanding in the communiqué, we will reassess our policy. How long will it take to reassess and make a determination?

MR. HOLDRIDGE. I would imagine, Mr. Chairman, that such a reassessment could occur quite rapidly.

CHAIRMAN ZABLOCKI. On the basis of the track record in the executive branch, in other areas, we wait 6 weeks sometimes.

MR. HOLDRIDGE. Well, again, Mr. Chairman, I am quite sure that we would respond in a timely manner to any shift in China's policy.

Let me say again here that we have no reason to believe that China's fundamental policy of peaceful resolution of the Taiwan question would in fact change.

CHAIRMAN ZABLOCKI. On the basis of this communiqué, what is the status of the prospective aircraft sales to Taiwan which were under consideration for several months?

MR. HOLDRIDGE. That notification will go to the Congress before the Congress goes into recess. The paperwork is now underway and I would anticipate that the notification could go forward as early as tommorrow.[51]

CHAIRMAN ZABLOCKI. Now, on the basis of the communiqué, if it is determined that Taiwan indeed does need certain upgrading of, for example, their communications,

---

[50] Holdridge's statement, here omitted, was almost identical with his statement before the Senate Foreign Relations Committee the day before (see *supra*). For the text of his prepared statement, see *ibid.*, pp. 8–17.

[51] On August 19, the Department of Defense announced that the administration had formally notified Congress of its approval of the sale of 60 F–5E and F–5F aircraft to be coproduced in Taiwan, at an estimated cost of $240 million. The announcement read in part as follows:

"The Taiwan Relations Act states that the United States will make available to Taiwan defense articles and services in such quantity as may be necessary to enable Taiwan to maintain a sufficient self-defense capability. The proposed sale of 60 additional F–5E/F is consistent with U.S. law and policy.

"Improvement of its air defense is one of Taiwan's highest military priorities. The proposed sale would sustain Taiwan's air defense capability and thus contribute to both Taiwan's security and the maintenance of regional stability. The relative power balance in the Taiwan Strait area has not changed appreciably since normalization of relations between the United States and China. However, attrition of aging F–100, F–104, and F–5A/B aircraft between now and 1986 could degrade Taiwan's air defense capability. Accordingly, Taiwan relies increasingly on the F–5E/F and needs to procure additional aircraft to compensate for these projected losses.

"The sale of this equipment and support will not affect the basic military balance in the region." (Department of Defense files)

or transportation, or indeed some military equipment, would upgrading be possible?

MR. HOLDRIDGE. Well, let me say that we are fully confident, Mr. Chairman, that within the provisions of the joint communiqué and in accordance with the Taiwan Relations Act, we will be capable of meeting Taiwan's needs.

CHAIRMAN ZABLOCKI. In paragraph 7 of the joint communiqué, there is the statement that "the two governments"—meaning the United States and China, the People's Republic of China—"will make every effort to adopt measures and create conditions conducive to the thorough settlement of this issue"; that is, the arms sales issue concerning Taiwan.

What would "conducive conditions" be?

Mr. Holdridge. I would put it in simple terms, Mr. Chairman. We can say that each side will continue to do what it says it is going to do. That is, the Chinese would continue to maintain and pursue their fundamental policy of peaceful resolution of the Taiwan question, and we would carry out the policies that we have outlined in paragraph 6.

CHAIRMAN ZABLOCKI. And how would you, Mr. Secretary, answer concerns expressed on Taiwan? I am sure there was some reaction. For example, how would you respond to the concerns expressed by Premier Sun that peace proposals from Peking, particularly the nine point proposal, are just other forms of Communist struggle and that they presume that Taiwan is a subordinate provincial government, not an equal negotiating partner?

MR. HOLDRIDGE. I would like to draw your attention, Mr. Chairman, to the fact that we have a distinction between what the Chinese state in paragraph 4, and what we state in paragraph 5. They talk about a policy, a fundamental policy of peaceful reunification of Taiwan with the motherland. We talk about the peaceful resolution of the Taiwan question.

Our wording was accepted in the joint communiqué by the Chinese side, so that in effect we are not committed to supporting any particular content of what the People's Republic of China should propose. We look at this, their two statements about their fundamental policy of peaceful resolution of the Taiwan question, as we put it, in just those terms. We do not take any position on how the resolution of this dispute should be accomplished.

As I mentioned, we are not trying to put any pressure on Taiwan to do anything or to take any particular position. Our only role in this matter is to maintain that the resolution of the differences should be by peaceful means.

CHAIRMAN ZABLOCKI. On page 10 of your statement you say:

> "By defusing the difficult issue of arms sales, we will open the way for an expansion of United States–China relations in a broad range of economic, cultural, scientific, and technological areas as well as in people-to-people contact."

Is there any security cooperation implication in the communiqué?

MR. HOLDRIDGE. Well, we did not address the question of security, Mr. Chairman, in the course of our discussions.

You may recall that as of last year we announced a revision in the policy which would permit the Chinese to come to us if they wanted to purchase weaponry. We said that we would consider any such request on a case-by-case basis, and this would be done in conjunction with consultations with the Congress and also taking into account the views expressed by friends and allies.

The ball is still in the Chinese court, they have not responded to this proposal and the matter still rests in limbo. And, as I said, we did not address the question of a security relationship in our discussions leading to the joint communiqué.

CHAIRMAN ZABLOCKI. Thank you, Mr. Secretary.

. . . .

Document 500

Transcript of an Interview With the Secretary of State (Shultz), October? 1982 (Extract)[52]

"Our Decision to Have a Strong Relationship With the Chinese Stands on Its Own Feet"

. . . .

Q. Mr. Secretary, are you concerned about recent meetings between the Soviets and Chinese[53] and the possibility of rapprochement between their countries?

A. Our decision to have a strong relationship with the Chinese stands on its own feet as something desirable to do. It is desirable regardless of their relationship with the Russians, whatever that might be. Of course, we're interested in Sino–Soviet relations. If, for example, as a result of those negotiations there is an improvement in the situation in Cambodia or Afghanistan, we're for that. China and Russia have been at odds in those two places for some time.

Q. But do you see danger that Russia and China could draw so closely together again that it would jeopardize our interests?

A. We could sit here and play "20 Questions" and conjure up all sorts of things. I won't play that game.

The question is: What is going on now? They are having discussions about many things. For example, we know that the Chinese are very concerned, as we are, about Russian activities, directly and indirectly, in Cambodia and Afghanistan. If, through their discussions, Vietnamese and Russian influence is removed from Cambodia, we're for that. If the Russians leave Afghanistan, we're for that.

Q. How far, in your view, should we go to strengthen ties with China? Should we go to the extent of seeking some form of strategic cooperation or wider economic cooperation?

A. We want to build up a strong relationship with China. And if you take the perspective of the last 10 years, we are gradually doing that. It's an important country, and the Chinese people are a marvelous people. So we want to have our relationship with them develop on economic fronts and strategic fronts.

. . . .

[52] Source: *U.S. News and World Report,* November 8, 1982, p. 30. For full text, see *ibid.*, pp. 28–30. Also printed in Department of State *Bulletin,* December 1982, pp. 19–21. The interview took place well before November 8, but the exact date has not been identified.

[53] Hu Yaobang had announced on October 17 that Chinese and Soviet Vice-Foreign Ministers Qian Qichen and L.F. Ilichev had been holding discussions in Beijing and that ongoing Sino-Soviet talks would be held in alternating capitals. (Foreign Broadcast Information Service, *Daily Report: China,* October 18, 1982, pp. C1–C2)

Document 501

Address by the Assistant Secretary of State for East Asian and Pacific Affairs (Holdridge) Before the National Council on U.S.–China Relations, New York, December 13, 1982[54]

Assessment of U.S. Relations With China

I have been one of those fortunate enough during much of my professional career to be able to share in the high points and cope with the low points as the course of our relations with China dramatically shifted course. And during the past 2 years with the State Department's Bureau of East Asian and Pacific Affairs, which maintains operational responsibility for our China policy, I have been intimately involved with the continued evolution of this policy.

At this juncture—and we are at a juncture, in terms of U.S.–China relations—it is gratifying to have this occasion to look back and take stock: to see what hurdles we've already surmounted, to assess whether we are on the course, and to plot the direction and challenges that still line the track ahead.

In the early days of this administration, then-Secretary Haig sketched the broad

[54] Source: Department of State *Bulletin,* February 1983, pp. 7–9.

outlines of the China policy-to-be in an interview published in *Time* magazine.[55] Following the direction set by President Reagan, Haig stated that we would continue efforts to expand our relations with the People's Republic of China. The Secretary characterized this relationship and its development as "a fundamental strategic reality and a strategic imperative . . . of overriding importance to international stability and world peace." We would adhere to the communiqués associated with U.S.–China normalization, he said, and we would maintain unofficial relations with the people of Taiwan. He made clear then—as did I and others in the administration from the President on down—that we would seek to restore dignity to the conduct of these people-to-people relations with Taiwan, but that we would observe the agreements regarding the nature of these relations contained in the U.S.–China Joint Communiqué on normalization and embodied in our domestic law.

In June 1981, Secretary Haig visited China, the first such visit by a Secretary of State since 1977. Haig used the occasion to inform the Chinese of President Reagan's conviction that U.S. policy toward China should reflect the friendly and cooperative nature of our relationship and of the administration's plans to translate that into practical and meaningful terms in the form of a three-pronged initiative designed to give teeth to the relationship.

First, the President would issue a directive substantially increasing the level of technology to be routinely approved for sale to China, reflecting our intent to treat China as a friendly, non-allied state.

Second, the President would suspend the prohibition on arms sales to China embodied in our arms control legislation, permitting the consideration on a case-by-case basis of requests to export munitions list articles to China, a procedure we follow with all friendly countries.

Third, the President would propose to Congress that it amend those laws that treated China in the same manner as the Soviet Union and its satellites, to make clear that we do not consider China a potential adversary and to remove legal impediments to our further cooperation.

---

[55] The interview was published in *Time* magazine, March 16, 1981, pp. 24–25. For an extract, including the statement here quoted, see *American Foreign Policy: Current Documents, 1981,* document 489.

The administration has registered significant progress in implementing this policy on all three counts.

This is the framework from which we began nearly 2 years ago to manage and direct the course of the immensely important U.S.–China relationship. It was gradually discovered, however, that a keystone in the foundation had never been set in place. We faced, we learned, the threat of collapse of the entire structure unless we could devise a way of inserting and devising a proper fit for that keystone. I am referring, of course, to the issue of arms sales to Taiwan and the continuing U.S.–China discussions on this issue which culminated in the August 17 joint communiqué.

The arms sales issue was one deeply rooted in history, touching on the most basic principles and the deepest sensitivities of both the Chinese and ourselves. For that reason, previous U.S. administrations and the Chinese had largely skirted the issue as we worked our way respectively toward normalization. The Chinese, however, had always reserved the right to raise the issue, and in the fall of 1981, we found we could sidestep it no longer.

I need not review in detail the 10-month-long negotiating process or period leading up to the issuance of our August 17 joint communiqué. It was an especially difficult and sensitive time for both sides. The sentiment in this country on not "abandoning" Taiwan is well known, and the Chinese, for their part, have repeatedly made reference to the feelings of China's "1 billion people." The utility of the communiqué is that it has provided both the Chinese and ourselves with a means of handling the problem in a way that allows us to continue, and hopefully advance, our bilateral relations without compromising important principles on either side. On the basis of policy statements enunciated by both governments in the communiqué, I believe that we have found that good fit that will firm up the foundation and allow for the development of a sound and solid relationship in the period ahead. In essence, the communiqué establishes a formula whereby the Chinese state that they will strive for a peaceful solution to the Taiwan question, and we accordingly state that under those circumstances we will gradually reduce the level of our arms sales to Taiwan. This position of ours is entirely consistent with the Taiwan Relations Act, which predicates U.S. arms sales to Taiwan on our judgment of Taiwan's military needs.

Since the communiqué, both of us have been taking a brief respite these past few months, turning our attention to pressing domestic concerns. We have had an election campaign; the Chinese have had their 12th Party Congress in September and a National People's Congress in December; and other international trouble spots and relations have demanded concern. During this period, however, there has been an unfortunate tendency for rhetoric to dominate the headlines, perhaps with domestic constituencies in mind. Moreover, reflecting the fact that the communiqué process was painful and difficult, a certain uncomfortable aftertaste was left behind. In this same period, the Chinese have been widening their options somewhat, developing an independent foreign policy line which stresses identification with the Third World and even resuming a dialogue with Moscow. This alignment with the Third World is not a new policy—we have watched it evolve for at least 2 years, as witness the speeches by China's representatives in the U.N. General Assembly—but it has received even greater emphasis lately. The Sino–Soviet dialogue is a more recent development.

The period of respite is ending. Secretary Shultz will be visiting Beijing in the not-too-distant future for what we hope will be serious, constructive, and wide-ranging talks with the Chinese leadership. It is time now to drop the rhetoric. We must get on with the practical action and statesmanship necessary to advance the relationship for the benefit of both our peoples.

Good relations with China have served our interests well over the past decade. I need not attempt to convince this audience of the benefits which have accrued, both strategic and otherwise. China's 1 billion people are entering the mainstream of the international economic system. The volume and value of bilateral trade between our two countries has grown tremendously in the past few years. China is now our 14th largest trading partner and 5th largest market for agricultural products. And China, with its extraordinarily rich cultural tradition and so much to contribute, has moved out of its former isolation, much to our and the world's benefit. More than 9,000 Chinese students are now enrolled at U.S. educational institutions. More than 500 Americans study in China each year, and tens of thousands more are availing themselves of the opportunity for an incomparable travel experience. The reciprocal benefits to China as it embarks on its ambitious program of modernization are incalculable.

The strategic element has always been fundamental to the development of our relations as well. President Reagan, as recently as August, has said that:

> "Building a strong and lasting relationship with China has been an important foreign policy goal of four consecutive administrations. Such a relationship is vital to our long-term national security interests and contributes to stability in East Asia. It is in the national interest of the United States that this important strategic relationship be advanced."

In addition, however, we have since normalization maintained that China's concentration on economic normalization is beneficial to world peace, and we wish to assist in this modernization process.

Our perceptions of many of the world's more troublesome problems are in close tandem. We endorse the Chinese view that the Soviets need to prove with deeds, not words, their desire to make progress toward a peaceful solution of the problems they have done so much to create and aggravate. The Chinese have undertaken a series of negotiations with the Soviets and have specifically aimed at progress on the issues of Soviet troop reductions on the Sino-Soviet and Sino-Mongolian borders, Soviet withdrawal from Afghanistan, and a halt to Soviet support for the Vietnamese occupation of Kampuchea. Both sides must overcome a bitter legacy of military confrontation if they are to reduce tensions. It is too early to speculate on prospects. In general, we would welcome developments that would reduce regional and global tensions. We would also welcome genuine—not simply cosmetic—reductions in Soviet armed forces that threaten neighboring states. The Chinese, however, should be under no illusions as they proceed with these talks, and they must be well aware of the continuing Soviet deployment of advanced weaponry, including SS–20's and Backfire bombers, east of the Urals.

Besides shared views on Afghanistan and Kampuchea, our views remain close in international issues ranging from U.S.–Japan defense arrangements to U.S. deployments in the Indian Ocean, U.S. missile deployments in Europe, and the need for a strong NATO.

In areas where we have at times differed—the Middle East, southern Africa, and Third World issues—we have in the past been able to conduct a constructive dialogue, and my hope is that we will be able to continue so in the future. We will, in addition, work to live up to our part of the understandings expressed in the August 17 communiqué, as we will expect the same of the Chinese.

We have not—indeed, we could not—ignore some of the more simplistic rhetoric that has been emanating from Beijing of late. To put it bluntly, we take exception to Chinese references to us as "hegemonists" and expect better from the Chinese than being lumped together with the Soviets as the cause of all the world's ills. Given the complexity of international issues which confront us today, a "Xiu Shou Panguan" [to stand off to the side—literally, with arms folded and hands in the sleeves][56] approach will no longer do. We know, on the basis of our past dialogue with Chinese leaders, that they are fully at home with more sophisticated and constructive analyses. As Secretary Shultz prepares for his visit to China, I am confident that we can realize a successful return to the kind of active, serious, constructive, statesmanlike dialogue that is necessary for our two important nations to conduct in the interest of regional and global peace.

At the same time, we cannot afford to overlook the differences between us. Each side will be closely watching the other's performance under the August 17 communiqué, which we on our side, of course, intend to honor fully. China, for its part, will be looking for us to provide more in the way of technology transfer and support of its economic modernization. There has been some disappointment on this score, perhaps generated by unrealistic expectations.

I am upbeat on the future of U.S.–China relations. The very fact that we were able to overcome the obstacles on the path to the communiqué is an excellent indication of how highly each side values the relationship. The momentum is now building for renewed progress. Secretary Shultz's visit will provide a needed shot of adrenalin. It will be preceded by an important session of the U.S.–China Joint Economic Commission opening today in Washington under the chairmanship of Treasury Secretary Regan and attended on China's part by Finance Minister Wang Bingqian. We are looking forward to other exchanges of high-level visits. In short, the wheels have already begun to turn and we're heading out of the station moving off in the right direction again.

With the foundation now hopefully well repaired and proceeding on the basis of equality, mutual benefit, and mutual trust, our two nations which have so much to learn from and so much to offer each other are ready to rechart the course of their relations. I believe we are on our way to making 1983 a good year for U.S.–China relations.

In closing, if I may, I would like to look at one brief moment in the past and then ahead to the coming decades. Just over a decade ago in the Great Hall of the People, welcoming President Nixon to China, the late Premier Zhou Enlai stated to the world that "the Chinese people are a great people, and the American people are a great people." These were simple words, but they had a great impact on me as he called upon the two nations to bring to an end a long and bitter period of estrangement.

As we look to the future, we must recognize that the world has grown even smaller in the 10 years since, and the challenges facing both nations, in terms of meeting our peoples' needs and safeguarding the security of our planet, are greater than ever. With cooperation, hard work, and a sense of vision, the United States and the People's Republic of China can accomplish much as they face these challenges. Together we can make a profound contribution to the region and the world as we pursue the overall goal of world peace.

[56] Bracketed note appears in the source text.

E. Indonesia

Document 502

Statement by the Assistant Secretary of State for East Asian and Pacific Affairs (Holdridge) Before a Subcommittee of the House Foreign Affairs Committee, September 14, 1982[1]

Recent Developments in East Timor

Thank you very much, Mr. Chairman.

It is a pleasure to be before you and the other members of the committee. I am

[1] Source: *Recent Developments in East Timor: Hearing Before the Subcommittee on Asian and Pacific Affairs of the Committee on Foreign Affairs, House of Representatives, Ninety-seventh Congress, Second Session* (Washington, 1982), pp. 48–52.

pleased to have this opportunity to discuss with you the situation in East Timor. This is the fifth time the State Department has testified before the House of Representatives on this specific subject since March 1977.

The most recent such occasion was in June 1980, before the Subcommittee on International Operations.

In addition, I commented on the situation in East Timor as part of a joint hearing on human rights in East Asia, held in November 1981 by your subcommittee and the Human Rights and International Organizations Subcommittee.

It is important as we examine this complex situation in East Timor that we give due note both to the progress that has been achieved in meeting the humanitarian needs of the Timorese people as well as to the problems that remain.

We don't want to disguise the fact there are problems and that these need to be addressed on a continuing basis. U.S. policy with regard to East Timor has been consistent through three administrations. We accept the incorporation of East Timor into Indonesia, without recognizing that a valid act of self-determination has taken place there.

We simply say it is impossible and impractical to turn back the clock. Our efforts now are concentrated on doing what we can to improve the welfare of the Timorese people. Particularly, we have found that progress can be achieved only by working closely with the Indonesian Government and with the international organizations active in East Timor.

In addition to our concern regarding East Timor, there are a number of other important elements in our relationship with Indonesia.

I wouldn't want to submerge these in our concerns about the situation in East Timor. We value highly our cooperative relationship with Indonesia and expect it to continue.

In fact, we are looking forward to the visit of President Suharto of Indonesia next month.

Let me proceed by outlining our view of current conditions in East Timor.

Any consideration of the current food and health situation in East Timor must begin by acknowledging the major relief effort undertaken jointly by the Indonesian Government, international agencies and the United States and other donors from mid-1979 to early 1981.

By April 1981, the involved international agencies concluded that the emergency situation had been overcome and that the long-term needs of the Timorese people could best be met by shifting emphasis from relief to development.

In the last year, there have been reports that the food situation was again deteriorating and East Timor was facing the threat of famine.

Since the economy and agricultural base of East Timor are extremely fragile, the United States has been quick to look into any reports of food shortages.

Based on our monitoring, it is our view that East Timor is not now facing a famine situation, nor the threat of famine in the near future.

However, in some isolated areas, particularly in the southeast portion of the island, there are food shortages. These areas demand and are apparently receiving immediate attention.

Serious health problems remain in East Timor. Malaria is a particularly acute problem, affecting large numbers of the population.

The Indonesian Government and the international agencies have ongoing programs to address both food and health problems, and we are supportive of those.

With regard to the military situation, Fretilin, the Timorese guerrilla group does not seriously threaten overall Indonesian authority.

Fretilin does, however, retain the capability to conduct occasional, limited operations. Its operations continue to result in some Indonesian and Fretilin casualties.

There are unconfirmed reports of a recent upsurge in Fretilin activity, perhaps designed for propaganda impact in advance of the upcoming UNGA session. This is a characteristic we have noted in past years.

It is noteworthy that the people of East Timor turned out in large numbers in May of this year to participate for the first time in Indonesian national elections.

The elections in the province were carried out without disruption, in a completely peaceful atmosphere.

We remain concerned about reports of abuses in connection with military operations. One of the more extreme charges made is that Indonesian forces have engaged in a systematic effort to kill innocent Timorese. We have found no evidence to support such a charge.

There are also recurring charges of disappearances and mistreatment of Timorese. While any abuse of human rights is deplorable, the number of allegations of physical mistreatment and disappearance has declined since the period of fiercest fighting between Indonesia and Fretilin forces in 1976–78.

Nevertheless, we are continuing to follow allegations of military abuses of this sort.

Detainees

Another positive development is that there is more information available to the international community on the numbers and conditions of detainees in East Timor as a result of the increased international access permitted by the Government of Indonesia to the principal places of detention: Comarca Prison in Dili and Atauro Island off the coast of East Timor.

An ICRC team visited East Timor in February to begin a program of prison visitation and visited both sites.

Most persons suspected by the Indonesian Government of supporting, or sympathizing with Fretilin are detained on Atauro Island.

The ICRC team, on its February trip, spent 4 days on Atauro and reported 3,737 persons had been temporarily relocated to the island. Most of these people had been sent to Atauro during military sweep operations in 1981.

We have no reliable information on the precise, current population on Atauro, but have no reason to believe it has dramatically changed in recent months.

A recent Embassy visitor indicated conditions on Atauro have improved considerably since the ICRC began its prison visitation program in February.

Let me now report on what is being done to address the humanitarian and economic development problems that remain in East Timor.

By far the most active and important role is being undertaken by the Government of Indonesia itself, which has significantly expanded its development activities in East Timor each year since 1976.

This Indonesian effort is even more striking when viewed in the context of that country's overall development needs. Although faced in each of its 26 far-flung Provinces with enormous socioeconomic problems, the GOI has given top development priority to East Timor. This year it will spend more per capita on development in East Timor than in any other Province.

It also must be noted that the Government's development effort must, by necessity, be concentrated at this stage on fundamental infrastructure projects, since there were almost no basic facilities at the time of the Portuguese withdrawal.

I might add I have gone into this question of what the Indonesian Government is doing in greater detail in my prepared statement.

Supplementing the Indonesian Government efforts, the international organizations have made a major contribution to improving the welfare of the Timorese people. Going about their tasks in a nonpolitical, nonpolemical way, they have succeeded where a confrontational approach would surely have failed.

The International Committee of the Red Cross [ICRC][2] has five ongoing activities in East Timor. First, it is continuing to provide technical assistance to the Indonesian Red Cross in support of food and health programs in East Timor.

Second, ICRC is serving as the intermediary for family reunification of persons with immediate relatives in Portugal and elsewhere.

Third, it has administered a tracing program to assist Timorese, both in Timor and abroad, to locate missing or displaced relatives.

Fourth, as already noted, in February 1982, the ICRC began a program of prison visitations.

Finally, food and medical supplies provided through ICRC since March to detainees on Atauro have had a significant positive effect on the conditions of detention. This program is continuing.

Catholic Relief Services [CRS], which had the largest program in East Timor during the international relief effort, has turned its attention to agricultural development.

---

2 This and following bracketed notes appear in the source text.

It is administering a 5-year, $5-million river basin development plan.

A third international agency, the United Nations International Children's Emergency Fund [UNICEF], has recently begun work in East Timor.

UNICEF will work with the Indonesian Red Cross in providing primary health care services to the women and children in seven villages where health conditions are poorest.

All three of the agencies listed above have expatriate staff in Djakarta who travel frequently to East Timor and enjoy good access throughout the province.

In addition to the international agency programs, the U.S. Agency for International Development [USAID] is working directly with the Indonesian Government in implementing a malaria control program under a $3.6 million agreement signed in mid-1980 to cover the entire island of Timor, both East and West.

When the project is complete, an estimated 45 percent of the population of East Timor will be protected against malaria.

Another area of U.S. concern is access to East Timor. While international access to East Timor remains limited, there has been major improvement in recent months.

In addition to a continuation of the improved access to East Timor enjoyed by U.S. mission and international agency personnel, there has been an increase in the number of journalists and diplomatic personnel allowed to visit the island. Among these have been a U.S. academic group, including Stanley Roth of Chairman Solarz' staff in November 1981; former Australian Prime Minister Gough Whitlam in February of this year, journalists from the *Philadelphia Inquirer;* Asian *Wall Street Journal;* and Reuters News Agency in May/June; members of the Djakarta diplomatic community in early August; and an American Jesuit official in late August 1982.

Indeed, one of the reasons for the recent flurry of press articles on East Timor is precisely because the Indonesian Government has been increasingly willing to let outsiders into the Province to take a look at the situation firsthand.

Increased access to East Timor is one of the best examples of how quiet efforts are most effective in addressing Indonesian human rights concerns.

Our Embassy in Jakarta also has followed closely the matter of family reunions and repatriation of Portuguese citizens from East Timor, the majority of whom have been proceeding for residence either in Portugal or Australia.

Progress is being made, but details have not generally been made public.

In conclusion, the record shows progress in many areas.

The Indonesian Government has demonstrated a willingness to come to grips with some of the most disturbing problems, as evidenced by increased international access, the beginning of the prison visitation program, and the entry of UNICEF into the province.

We will continue to follow events in East Timor closely, taking every appropriate opportunity to continue our quiet dialog with Indonesians who are capable of influencing developments in the province and fostering the kind of humanitarian progress which is our common goal.

I want to say, Mr. Chairman, in conclusion, that we are not going to minimize the fact that problems continue to exist in East Timor, I am simply saying that we are doing our best through our own efforts, to see what we can do to improve this situation.

Thank you very much.

Document 503

Transcript of a Department of State Press Briefing, October 8, 1982 (Extracts)[3]

Upcoming State Visit of President Soeharto

Senior Department Official. Let me fill you in, if I may, on the background of the Soeharto visit to the United States, the reasons why we have indeed invited President Soeharto to pay an official visit to the United States.[4]

First, Indonesia is a very interesting developing country. It is beginning to real-

---

[3] Source: Department of State files. This background briefing, which began at 4:30 p.m., was conducted by a senior Department of State official.

[4] President Soeharto visited the United States from October 12 to 15, 1982; see documents *infra* and 505.

ize its potential now after a period of some 12 or so years of concentrating on capital investment; this capital investment is beginning to pay off. Those of you who have visited Indonesia over the years as I have, I think will begin to see some rather startling changes in the whole way of life, certainly in the areas where the development has been most concentrated, the areas around Java, Sumatra, and Kalimantan (or Borneo) where again, you're beginning to see the payoff of long years of investment and very large big-ticket capital projects.

Indonesia is going to be a very important country by the end of this century. Already of course, by virtue of its population—150 million people—it is, incidentally, the largest Islamic country in the world. It's strategic location, the Malacca Straits, Sunda Straits, and Lombok, put it right astride the very strategic oil lines, the lines of communication especially for oil between the Middle East and Japan.

It is also a very integral part of ASEAN. The ASEAN countries today are totalling a population of some 250 million. Indonesia is a very important trading partner of the United States. We have very large investments there. Economically, politically, and in the security sense, we regard our relationship with Indonesia as being extremely important.

Let me talk a little bit about the ASEAN aspect, that Indonesia is indeed a very key member of ASEAN. The Indonesians like to harken back to 1975 or 1976, when after a period of some years of languishing, it began to move ahead very vigorously, and its movement ahead was in part stimulated by President Soeharto, who had convened a summit meeting of all the ASEAN Heads of State at Bali, in January 1976. I think you can legitimately [say?] it was that Bali meeting that started the momentum again for ASEAN and turned it into the kind of an organization which exists today.

The Indonesians take great pride in the fact that they were instrumental in getting ASEAN going again, and President Soeharto, I know, regards his relationship with the ASEAN countries [as?] very important; and ASEAN is, in fact, a very key element in Indonesian foreign policy. Of course, in that regard, we, the Indonesians and the rest of ASEAN all see eye-to-eye. Our policy in Southeast Asia takes ASEAN as its keystone, and we want to be very supportive of what ASEAN is trying to do.

I might mention that ASEAN has, of course, in the last several years played a very key role in the whole question of Kampuchea and the Vietnamese occupation of that country. The events of this year at the United Nations General Assembly bear out the fact that ASEAN continues to play a very, very important part in the whole process of trying to get the Vietnamese out of Kampuchea. As I said, we're very supportive of what ASEAN is trying to do in this regard as well as in other matters.

Apropos of ASEAN in general, the 250 million people in ASEAN together represent the United States fifth largest trading partner. Last year, our total volume of trade both ways was over $21 billion. Together with Indonesia, the other countries of ASEAN also occupy a very strategic position as well as an economic position in our scale of things.

Finally, let me talk about one other aspect. President Soeharto has now been President of Indonesia for 16 years. He is acknowledged as a very major figure on the world scene, something of a world statesman. It is President Soeharto, really, who has led Indonesia away from the chaos that characterized the Sukarno era, and got Indonesia away from the very disasterous economic policies of that time onto the development track which I mentioned to you earlier, where Indonesia is really making very striking progress.

President Soeharto is a friend of the United States—we regard him as such—and we want to reinforce that friendship. His last official visit to the United States was in 1970—that's 12 years ago; his most recent trip was a very informal, very quick one to Camp David in 1975. But it is, in our view, the best way to show how high we value the relationship with the country and the people, is through an official visit by a Chief of State as indeed we're anticipating beginning next week.

Now I'd be very happy to answer any questions that you would like to throw my way.

Q. You used the phrase "strengthening the relationship." What do you all mean by "strengthening the relationship?" Is it a vague term or is it a specific one—you want to strengthen specific military relations?

A. I'm not talking about this in, shall I say, military terms. On the contrary, we're not regarding our relationship with Indonesia as having any kind of specific military application. What I am talking about is just a degree of understanding—you might say rapport—which exists between the two countries, that if there are some differences in our approach to international issues, one way to address these differences is through person-to-person contact at the highest level. Understanding is then increased thereby. This is the kind of concept that we have in mind.

Although there will be other things that will be addressed as well, I think the basic point to get across here. . . is the kind of the understanding, the strengthening of the understanding, the rapport, which exists between the two countries.

Q. What are some of the things on which the two countries disagree?

A. I would say that being an Islamic country, we would find some differences of approach in Indonesian policy with respect to the Middle East situation, but obviously, not of a magnitude to interfere with the other factors that I've talked about. And we are looking to a very successful visit of President Soeharto to the United States.

Q. What is the U.S. assessment of oil production coming from Indonesia in the long term?

A. That is a debatable point. At the moment, Indonesia is producing about 1.3 million barrels per day. That's the figure assigned to it by OPEC. They could do more. I think they could probably go up to 1.6 or 1.7 without any strain.

It's anybody's guess how long they could maintain, say, total production up around the 1.7 million barrels-per-day level. I recall when I was in Singapore a few years ago, there were some projections which suggested that Indonesian production might start to taper off later on in the 80's. However, there has been a sufficient amount of exploration and development on the part of the oil companies—and there are a number of finds which have been located which haven't even begun exploitation yet.

I think at this point we would be very reluctant to predict when there might be a sloughing off of Indonesian oil production. It looks like it will go at present levels, capable of going well into certainly the next decade, at the production level that it is occupying right now.

Q. There has been some dissent in Indonesia about the OPEC policies. Do you see any splits there whatsoever, political splits with other oil-producing nations?

A. I would judge that Indonesia is probably beset by the same differences or differences of interpretation that affect OPEC as a whole, that we have a situation worldwide where the consumption has not been up to what OPEC had predicted in areas of oil glut.

I might add that Indonesia, knowing that there are problems in this regard, that is as far as oil production, is looking around for other sources of energy. One of the areas where they are beginning to develop rather markedly is in coal, both in Sumatra and in Borneo—Kalimantan.

Q. Let me just follow that up? I realize that they have the same problems as the other oil-producing countries. But what I'm asking about specifically is, do you see them staying within the guidelines set down by OPEC as far as low production, or do you think they want to go their own way? Do you see any signs of that?

A. I haven't seen any sign that Indonesia is prepared to go off in [*on*] a course independent from the rest of OPEC.

Q. Indonesia's Ambassador yesterday was asked whether or not his country saw American foreign policy toward Asia as being coherent and unified. His reply, as I recall, was generally along the lines that his country seeks clarification from the United States on some key points, including the U.S. backing for an expanded Japanese defense force and the concept that that defense would extend 1,000 nautical miles to sea, and also the American encouragement of an expanded Chinese or perhaps U.S. sales to China.

Do you expect this to come up? And what would be the U.S. attitude toward these questions?

A. If the Ambassador said that those are questions likely to be raised, I would accept that, and we are prepared to address both those questions. Let me talk about Japan first: I, personally, have had some contacts with senior Indonesian officials over the last several weeks, most recently in New York, and previous to that time also since the ASEAN post-ministerial meeting in Singapore last June, so we are aware of the concerns that the ASEAN's as a group have about the possibility of, say, Japan's being used by the United States as a surrogate, and our turning over the security of East Asia to the Japanese.

Well, (a) we have no intention of doing that. When we are talking about an expansion in the Japanese military role, what we are hoping for is nothing more than Japan's living up to the objective which Japan has set for itself, that is defense of the air and sea approaches of Japan out to a distance of 1,000 nautical miles. The line would fall between Taiwan and the northern Philippines, the Bashi Channel.

Q. Excuse me. Where do you measure the 1,000 nautical miles from?

A. Well, the Japanese have done this. I suppose you'd draw it out from Tokyo Bay. But at least I can tell you this, it does not extend any farther south than the Bashi Channel, and that it is all defensive. The accent is on *defense* of the sea and air approaches to the home islands out to this distance.

We are not interested in turning Japan into a new military power in East Asia. What we're hoping for is Japan's picking up some of the slack in the defensive situation in East Asia caused by the added roles and missions which our Seventh Fleet has had to assume into the Indian Ocean as a consequence of the developments in the Middle East, especially since the Iran–Iraq and Afghan situations developed.

The Japanese military posture, from all accounts, is to be defensive. All we're asking is that they fill out the blanks, so to speak, in the requirement of 1,000 nautical miles.

Q. Did I understand you correctly to say "pick up some of the slack in Southeast Asia caused by the new roles of the Seventh Fleet"?

A. In East Asia. You know, the Seventh Fleet was originally designed to maintain a power balance in East Asia, but now some of its ships and aircraft are spending a good part of their time in the Indian Ocean, which does leave the rest of the area somewhat more vulnerable. In that, we would like to have the Japanese help out, do more, in defense of the home islands, as a consequence.

Q. The reason I asked where you measured, the Ambassador expressed some concern that if you measured from Okinawa, then it would fall into Indonesian waters.

A. As far as I know, there is no intention of going beyond the Bashi Channel. It is not our intention to rearm Japan, to give Japan a security responsibility beyond the mission which the Japanese have set for themselves.

Q. What kind of trade or economic issues do you expect will come up next Tuesday?

A. I suppose, just in general terms, the economic issues would probably concern more than the North South type. The Indonesians, being a developing country, are much interested in the whole North–South concept and the developed countries providing the kind of assistance to the developing countries which will meet their needs. I think that the Presidents will probably talk in broad and general terms against issues such as that.

There are other lesser issues which might come up about, say, levels of American assistance, or other matters such as investment, or what-have-you. But I would expect those would be taken up outside the Presidential level. With President Soeharto is coming Minister Widjojo and others who are amply qualified to talk about these other issues, and they will be doing so, in my judgment.

Q. Will he speak with Baldrige or Regan?

A. Yes, yes.

Q. At what forum, at the Shultz luncheon, perhaps?

A. Yes, at the Shultz luncheon for some and special calls for others.

Q. Is the United States at this point ready to consider increased levels of American assistance?

A. What we're considering is some increase, Congress being willing, in our foreign military sales program to Indonesia, but our economic levels are remaining roughly the same. As I said, we just pledged somewhere around—what was it?

OFFICIAL. Almost $100 million.

SENIOR ADMINISTRATION OFFICIAL. Almost $100 million at the IGGI meeting in Amsterdam, and our aid levels will fall roughly in at a sort of a mixture of development assistance and P.L.–480; and they will stay at about the same level.

They have been at that same level for several years, and I don't anticipate any major shift.

Q. What magnitude do you expect to be considered in the FMS?

A. The FMS is in the neighborhood of $40 million.

Q. Now. And what will it be?

A. We hope to get it up above that, but again that depends on a whole lot of factors, not the least of which is Congress.

Q. Is that fiscal '83, this number?

A. Yes. That will be for FY '83.

. . . .

Q. Is there any weakening of ASEAN on the question of Kampuchea and how does Indonesia—

A. On the contrary. I think that ASEAN has stayed remarkably firm. . . .

Q. So that's not likely to be a major—

A. I don't think so, although I suspect that we will indeed congratulate the Indonesians for the role which they've played in ASEAN and in turn the role which ASEAN is playing with respect to the Vietnamese occupation of Kampuchea.

Q. Are they asking us to do more in terms of military support or other kinds of support for them?

A. I think they understand our position: That we've made it very plain that we're not going to provide military assistance, and that while we are prepared to consider in concert with ASEAN—keeping in touch with them, how we might be helpful in other ways—our assistance will not go to anyone except the non-Communist elements in the coalition. That would be to Prince Sihanouk and to Son Sann.

. . . .

Q. Does the administration on that point have any response to, I believe it's Senator Tsongas' group in Congress that has written the President, asking for a consideration of aid?

A. The response would be the one that I gave to Congressman Solarz in his East Asia subcommittee of the House Foreign Affairs Committee very recently.[5]

I just happen to have the texts here, and if any of you are interested, you can pick them up on the way out. But that—

Q. The policy hasn't changed?

A. The policy hasn't changed since I testified before the Solarz subcommittee.

Q. Getting back to something . . . asked earlier that was the second half of the question about Japan, it would be—

A. I forgot to mention China, didn't I? Let me talk about China, too.

I'll refer you to what Deputy Secretary Stoessel said in Singapore at the post-ministerial ASEAN meeting—that was last June—that we regard ASEAN as the keystone of our policy toward Southeast Asia, and we would not let the relations with any other country, such as China and including China, get in the way of our relationship with the ASEAN countries.[6]

We will carry out our relationship with China in such a way that it will not be detrimental to the interests of the ASEAN countries.

Q. Nonetheless, did you encounter some wondering concern on those grounds?

A. Less now rather than earlier, I think. We've been talking this matter over for quite some time, and I've noticed that without mentioning what particular representative of what particular country, they said that knowing the difficulties that we had since last October and the question of reaching agreement on a joint communiqué,[7] they understand full well the nature of our relationship with China and they're not as concerned about it surely now as they were then, having seen the difficulties that we had.

Q. Although a formal security arrangement with Indonesia is nowhere in sight, is it fair to assume that over the years the two countries will be drawn closer in unofficial situations?

A. Do you mean the United States and Indonesia?

Q. The United States and Indonesia.

A. Certainly, we're not going to seek a formal relationship, but we do—certainly we respond to their security concerns by providing FMS, and we hope that we can provide more, and we're also providing something called IMET. I think you're probably familiar with it—International Military Educational Training.

I think Indonesia is now one of the largest recipients—second.

. . . .

[5] See *supra.*

[6] See Stoessel's address, June 18, document 473.

[7] Regarding the U.S.–China communiqué, August 17, see document 495.

Q. But do they have specific weaponry in mind?

A. They're thinking of air patrol aerial surveillance and naval vessels capable of keeping an eye on all the many islands which they have in the Indonesian territory.

Q. The Indonesians have expressed some interest in providing for the security of their own sea lanes toward the mid-1990's based on a system of land-based missiles.

I wonder if that has come to your attention whether the United States would encourage them in that direction?

A. We wouldn't want to tell them what they should do in their own defense. That's a judgment that they, themselves, are going to make, and we will be supportive where we can. That's point number one.

Point number two: That's an element which we have not discussed.

Q. What kind of planes would they use for aerial patrol?

A. I have an understanding that they're interested in a variant of some commercial aircraft which could be used both for transports and also for aerial surveillance.

Q. This IMET increase doesn't envision American trainers and what-not on the ground there, does it?

A. No. It means Indonesians coming to the United States and going to American service schools and American technical training schools.

Q. Is there any concern in this administration about the fact that there is no present U.S. Ambassador?

A. We're working [on] the problem.

Q. Can you give us a status report on that?

A. I can't give you a status report. All I can say is the problem is being addressed.

Q. Isn't Mr. Kane's [*Crane's*] nomination about to be announced?

A. I can't comment on that.

Q. Do you expect any kind of announcement during this visit?

A. I wouldn't want to predict. It's all something that is being handled at the White House level, and from where I sit I wouldn't be able to add anything to it.

Q. You know Indonesia's in a bit of an economic bind right now—

A. Yes. I do know that.

Q. —and I was wondering whether, although a State visit is not necessarily a time for gift-giving, would there be some kind of a—you know, some balm that will come out of this?

A. I wouldn't want to think that every time a State visit occurs that there's some kind of a quid pro quo or they could expect some kind of a gratuity from us. No.

Again, let me go back to what I said at the beginning. We want to reinforce the degree of understanding and rapport between the two countries and the two leaders, and I would not wish to encourage you in thinking that there's any kind of a largesse involved.

Q. The Ambassador said that Indonesia is interested in selling more of its nontraditional exports, and I think there are two things on the table—there's the textiles and there's the GSP.

A. All right. We're willing to take a look at that. GSI [*GSP*] is especially designed for developing countries, and those that have reaching [*reached*] graduation, while this might be something of a problem, in our judgment Indonesia, which now has a per capita income of something around $550 per annum, is hardly reaching that level. So Indonesia does qualify for GSP, and we would support Indonesia in its interest in developing a further range of goods for export and developing markets for them.

Q. You know, Indonesia will be the first Third World country to go into this syndication market since the Mexican financial crisis. They're in for $250 million.

Although this issue will probably pertain to Japan because the Japanese Minister of Finance really sits in the bank and tells him what to do, do you think that there could be some arguments made for—with the Treasury to, you know, be nice to Indonesia this particular time?

A. I really haven't heard that matter discussed. Frankly, it's the first I've heard of it.

Q. Could I ask you more broadly—[what?] not just Indonesia but the other ASEAN countries—seem to think about these recent overtures between the Soviet Union and China?

Do they take them very seriously, or are they concerned about what the implications are, or do they think it's just atmospherics?

A. I would say they're watching with considerable interest. Some of the ASEAN's do have diplomatic relations with China, and I would presume that they probably asked the Chinese if anything can be expected.

The line which is going around—and the Chinese expect deeds, not words, and when you ask about deeds, I think the four points that have been well known and understood for quite some time are still there. That is a reduction of Soviet troops along China's borders to the pre-1964 levels; withdrawal of Soviet forces from Mongolia; cessation of Soviet support for Vietnam, especially with reference to Kampuchea; and, finally, withdrawal of Soviet forces from Afghanistan. That's for openers. (Laughter)

Q. What do you expect to come out of these talks?

A. Again, I just refer you to those four points, and all I would say is that based on my personal knowledge of Soviet past interests in performances and policies, I would find the Soviets might find any or all of those four points a little hard to accommodate.

Q. Would you amplify on your remarks earlier about the U.S. willingness to do whatever possible to enlarge Indonesia's access to markets for their non-oil products?

A. Let me say this: That we have a program now in our AID and supported by other government agencies, including the State Department, and that is to try to see if we can't develop additional markets. That is, areas where American investment might take place overseas.

Of course, if American investment does take place, there would be products coming out of this, and there would be need for our consideration of what markets there might be.

Let me say here that we're very interested in the role of the private sector in economic development of other countries, and this particular office in AID is specifically designed to encourage the private sector participation in economic development.

Q. Does the United States take the view on Indonesia's policy of counterpurchases?

A. We don't like it.

Q. And are you likely to bring it up?

A. If it comes up, we're prepared to discuss it.

Q. And what would you say?

A. . . . I think we would make plain at other levels our views on this as being in effect perhaps would get in the way of the kind of investment that I've just been talking about.

Q. What about a bilateral investment treaty?

A. That's something which we would be willing to discuss with them.

Q. And Indonesian participation in a North–South round in Geneva in November?

A. We're all looking forward to GATT. We want to make sure that GATT isn't just a kind of a talk session but there is really something of a concrete nature coming out of it.

We have been discussing with a number of countries how we might make the GATT ministerial in November a very useful function.

Q. Did I understand you to say that there is an investment treaty on the table now?

A. No. I said we would be prepared to consider one if the Indonesians are so interested.

Q. Okay. Thank you.

A. You're very welcome. Again, if anybody has any questions about our policy in East Timor, there it is.

Document 504

Remarks by President Reagan at the Arrival Ceremony for Indonesian President Soeharto, October 12, 1982[8]

"As a Senior Statesman of Asia, Your Views on World Affairs Carry Special Authority"

THE PRESIDENT. Mr. President, I take particular pleasure in welcoming you and

---

[8] Source: White House Press Release, October 12, 1982, Office of the Press Secretary to the President, October 12, 1982; printed also in *Weekly Compilation of Presidential Documents*, October 18, 1982, pp. 1295–1296. The ceremony began at 10:10 a.m. on the South Lawn of the White House.

Madam Soeharto to the United States and to the White House. And Mrs. Reagan joins me in extending personal hospitality on this important occasion.

You are no stranger to these shores, Mr. President, having visited the United States twice before as leader of your great nation. As one of the world's longest serving Chief Executives, indeed, as a senior statesman of Asia, your views on world affairs carry special authority and add special meaning to our discussions today. Your viewpoints and wise council will be greatly appreciated.

I warmly recall my last meeting with you, Mr. President. My visit to Jakarta and private talks with you in 1973 were among the highlights of my international experience as Governor of California. And, although I have not had the opportunity to visit your country since then, I know of the great strides made by Indonesia in national building under your leadership.

I am sure that our talks during your State Visit will further strengthen the bonds of friendship and mutual respect between our two countries. The United States applauds Indonesia's quest for what you call "national resilience." No nation in our era has shown itself more firmly committed to preserving its own independence than Indonesia. And yet, no nation has pursued that goal in a more responsible manner.

Indonesia has lived by and brought credit to the concept of genuine, constructive nonalignment. The United States, too, fought for its independence and over the years has jealously guarded certain, fundamental principles. We, consequently, understand the striving of Indonesia for national resilience. We wholeheartedly respect it. It is this respect which lies at the heart of our excellent bilateral relationship.

President Soeharto, the challenges confronting our nations are great indeed. Both strive for world peace whether in important areas of Asia such as Kampuchea, or in the Middle East where particularly vexing problems await lasting solutions. The United States regards Indonesia as an important force for peace, stability, and progress. We value our bilateral relationship with your country most highly, and we hope to broaden and deepen that relationship.

On the economic front, I believe it is in the clear interest of both our countries to maintain and improve our economic and trade relations. Mutually beneficial economic cooperation, equitable two-way trade, and investment in enterprises which involve the transfer of technology to meet your country's pressing development needs are part of the fabric of healthy U.S.-Indonesian economic relations.

The United States will, also, continue to provide appropriate development and food assistance in the framework of the Intergovernmental Group of Indonesia. I am proud to say this consortium has had wholehearted American backing since its founding. Let me, also, assure you that the United States wishes to pursue actively joint collaboration in science and technology for the economic development of your country.

It is particularly fitting today to make special mention of the Association of Southeast Asian Nations, ASEAN, and of Indonesia's important role in it. The success which ASEAN has enjoyed during the 15 years—or 16 years—of its existence would have been impossible without Indonesia's farsighted and enthusiastic participation. As one of ASEAN's founding fathers, Mr. President, you deserve a great measure of credit for the accomplishments of that organization in the economic and social areas. These accomplishments have far surpassed the expectations of most observers a decade and a half ago when ASEAN was established.

Since that time, the most important milestone for ASEAN has been the 1976 summit meeting in Bali which demonstrated your personal commitment. Indeed, ASEAN now stands as a model for regional cooperation and, if I may use your term, Mr. President, of regional resilience. Let me assure you that support for ASEAN has been and will continue to be the keystone of American policy in Southeast Asia.

As we pursue our overall policy in Asia and the Pacific, we will never lose sight of ASEAN's concerns, or neglect our commitments to the ASEAN countries. Let me, also, stress our full support for the important initiatives which ASEAN has undertaken to resolve the tragic situation in Kampuchea.

I also extend a special warm welcome to Madam Soeharto. Her good works on behalf of charitable organizations, for handicapped, needy, and disadvantaged people are recognized at home and abroad. These activities are in line with the spirit of volunteerism which Mrs. Reagan and I have encouraged in our own country.

And, once again, I welcome you, President Soeharto, and you, Madam Soeharto, in a spirit of friendship and respect. Mrs.

Reagan and I are personally delighted with your visit. Welcome to Washington; and again, welcome to the White House. (Applause)

Document 505

Transcript of a Press Conference by the Secretary of Defense (Weinberger), Jakarta, Indonesia, November 3, 1982[9]

Secretary Weinberger's Meetings With President Soeharto and Defense Minister General Mohammed Jusuf

SECRETARY WEINBERGER. Good afternoon ladies and gentlemen. We've had a successful visit, a series of meetings with the President and with the Defense Minister and we've had an opportunity to discuss matters of mutual interest, matters that affect the security of both our countries. I found them [an] extremely interesting and very valuable continuation of the meetings and discussions that we had in Washington somewhat earlier with Minister Yusuf,[10] and just a short time ago with President Suharto.[11] We are very glad indeed that we came. We think they are very useful and we want to continue these discussions. I will be glad to take your questions now.

Q. Mr. Secretary, in the Pentagon's threat perception, how serious is the presence of the Soviet Union in East Asia?

A. I think the Soviet Union's presence has been increasing both in strength and in numbers. They are positioning more naval units here. They are positioning greater air strength up in the regions near Japan and overflying a lot of these regions. They also have increased their attempts at gathering intelligence. As you know, several countries here have expelled Soviet espionage people. I think there is every evidence that they are attempting to increase their strength and certainly they have increased their presence in Vietnam. I think Vietnam's whole ability to survive now is based upon or bolstered by very large continued Soviet contributions and that, I think, contributes to some of the things that Vietnam is undertaking now in Cambodia.

Q. Sir, could you please quantify the increase in the Soviet naval buildup in East Asia and would you say also please how many Soviet naval ships are using Cam Ranh Bay?

A. Well, a great many ships are using Cam Ranh Bay. I don't have an ability to share with you precise numbers. Of course, they shift from day to day. But they are using Cam Ranh Bay on a very large scale as well as other bases in Vietnam and they have added a number of ships to their presence in the Pacific, particularly in the North Pacific. I am not able to quantify it. All the information is not fully available and much of it is classified, but on a steady basis they are clearly increasing their naval and their air presence in the area and are attempting to make increasing use of permanent bases such as Cam Ranh Bay.

Q. Mr. Secretary, have you been able to successfully placate fears in the Asia region, and Indonesia particularly, about possibly involving Japan in regional security?

A. I would hope so. We feel that Japan has identified for itself a suitable and entirely self-defensive role, protecting their homelands and the air and sea space around them and the sea lanes out to a thousand miles are [*as*?] measured from the home island. Our concern primarily is that Japan will have to do a very great deal more than they are now doing to fulfill this entirely self-defensive role. I don't think there is any indication whatever that they have any militaristic or offensive desires and certainly no capabilities at this time. Our reason for urging them to do more in their own self-defense is very simple. It would free some of our units—some of the fleet and air units—to do more in other parts of the Pacific and the Indian Ocean and the China Sea and elsewhere.

But we don't see anything that resembles any kind of major Japanese military offensive strength at all or any desire to do that. We see quite the contrary—that thus far there hasn't been enough effort made to carry out the full self-defensive role which we think is entirely appropriate. There are a number of reasons for that. They have some economic problems. They have con-

---

[9] Source: *Public Statements of Secretary of Defense Weinberger,* 1982. Weinberger was on a tour of five East Asian nations, Australia, New Zealand, Thailand, Singapore, and Indonesia, from October 29 to November 9, 1982.

[10] Yusuf is a varient transliteration of Jusuf.

[11] Suharto is a varient transliteration of Soeharto.

stitutional provisions, none of which would be violated by the role that they are to play. But a self-defensive role is an appropriate one, I think. They are going to have to do a lot more to reach that. Meanwhile, we don't see any basis for any fears or anything else. We understand perfectly the reason for the fears. Anyone who participated in any way in World War II or has any familiarity with it is bound to understand completely the concern that would be felt in Indonesia, or in Thailand or in the Philippines in that connection. So we don't discount the depth of the feeling. We understand it completely and the reasons for it. We think at the moment that Japan's not in any way taking steps that would indicate they have any offensive designs in mind.

Q. Sir, you have been urging Japan to increase its defense capabilities in the region. Have you been urging ASEAN countries to do likewise?

A. No, it hasn't been in any way necessary. We think the ASEAN countries are devoting a very large percentage of their gross national product (to defense) and have a full awareness of the importance of doing that for their own defense and or the defense of the region. This trip of mine has primarily been for the purpose of demonstrating the great importance that we attach to this part of the world and to discuss matters of mutual security interest and areas where the countries involved—Indonesia, Singapore, Thailand—feel that we can be most helpful. But we haven't found it necessary to urge any greater attention to security matters.

Q. In view of the increased Soviet threat to the Asia/Pacific region, will the United States make a radical change in defense policy toward this region and at the same time will the United States increase its logistical support to some of the Asia/Pacific countries?

A. The basic policy of the United States is to, first of all, recognize the nature of the threat and the source of the threat and try to do the best we can to acquire enough strength to deter any attack from any quarter. That requires a substantial addition to our military strength and it requires substantial willingness to give assistance to countries in ways which they feel will be most helpful—logistical and additional arms supplies, discussions of ways in which we might work out any sort of joint activities that would be considered useful. All of those things. So that is a policy of the United States Government. It is a policy which the President is very firmly attached to and one that we will continue to follow.

Q. Could you give us your comments on the Sino-Soviet talks that began recently?

A. I don't have any information about those that we can share. Those talks in one way or another are nothing really new. They've been going on for quite a long time. Different participants at different levels participate from time to time, but I don't have any results of those talks. It is important to note that they have been going on for a long time and, obviously, it's an important subject for us all to follow very closely.

Q. There are some people who feel that the presence of the enemy's troops in Cambodia should be viewed in larger context—that of a proxy war between the Soviet Union and China. What is your view of this? That's my first question. Second, proxy war or not—as one gentlemen has already pointed out—the Chinese and Soviets are engaging in talks. Some people feel that because Cambodia is of far greater strategic importance to China than say Afghanistan, the Chinese might be willing to tone down or even cease its condemnation of the Soviet presence in Afghanistan if the Soviets are willing to tone down and cease support of Vietnam. Is there a possibility of such a private deal between the Chinese and the Soviets?

A. Well that's a very speculative, long-range type of question, and I'm not at all sure that I'm qualified to guess about it. I think you've guessed pretty well and maybe that's a pretty good guess. I don't really know. I do think that the activities in Cambodia present a threat; I think that the ASEAN nations in the resolution that was adopted by the United Nations and incidentally, very skillfully managed in the United Nations by the ASEAN nations, represents our policy. And it is very important that the aggressive activities of Vietnam in Cambodia be brought to a halt, and we would very much hope that the United Nations action and the policies would have that result. I couldn't really go on and try to anticipate what might happen—but it's an interesting thesis.

Q. Sir, what do you expect from Indonesia and what can Indonesia expect from your side? And what do you think about the possibility of Red China's infiltration and subversion to Indonesia?

A. Well, take the first part. We don't, as you put it, expect anything of anybody. We believe that there is a very great mutual advantage to the United States and Indonesia continuing to maintain and strengthen the friendship that we feel we have. President Reagan was extremely good foundation on which to build [*sic*]. We are not, as I say, expecting anything of any country; we are very anxious to be as helpful as possible and we have in mind through these talks ways of finding our different actions that we can take that would be found to be useful and in our mutual interest. And it is very much to the interest of both countries to continue to work closely together. We will certainly consider that any kind of infiltration of or attack on the sovereignty of Indonesia would be something that we would regard very seriously and something that we would feel—that we would want to assist the Indonesian nation in any way they felt we might should it ever take place.

Q. In your talks here did the Indonesians ask for military aid? Do they plan to buy more armament from the United States?

A. No, we didn't talk in any kind of specifics of that sort at all. We just talked in terms of the kinds of things that might be done that would be of assistance. We were pleased that we have been able to increase the military programs for Indonesia in our own budget, and we hope that Congress continues [to] do that. But we did not go into specific weapons systems or anything of that kind. We discussed in general terms the mutual advantage there is to both countries for us to maintain the kind of working relationship, that can discuss such matters as weapons systems that are found to be important, any kind of opportunities that we would have to work together to get a better understanding of the procedures and the techniques of the various weapons systems, things of that kind, and also set the foundation for continuing these talks. Defense Minister Jusuf and I met in Washington; we've met again here today; we hope to meet again in Washington soon—so that we'll have a continuing on-going dialogue about these matters.

Q. Thank you, Mr. Secretary.

F. Japan

Document 506

Statement by the Assistant Secretary of State for East Asian and Pacific Affairs (Holdridge) Before a Subcommittee of the House Foreign Affairs Committee, March 1, 1982[1]

U.S. Relations With Japan

Thank you very much, Mr. Chairman. I will indeed take the opportunity to run down the high spots of my prepared text. Let me say it is always a pleasure to be before this subcommittee. I think that the hearings that you have had with respect to China, for example, have been very useful, and I certainly welcome the opportunity to be here with you to discuss the issues that exist in our relationship with Japan.

Speaking from my position as Assistant Secretary for East Asian and Pacific Affairs, I certainly can't take exception to the point that you make that the Japanese-American relationship is our most important bilateral relationship in the world, although I think some of my colleagues in the Department of State with their own perspectives might have a somewhat different view. But certainly I don't think there is anything that occupies our attention more continually than the question of United States-Japanese relations. And of course from the standpoint of trade and defense we are to a perceptible extent interrelated in our conceptions. This does have a bearing on the relationships that we have with the rest of the world. So therefore, as I said, I welcome this opportunity to come and testify before the subcommittee.

With respect to the question of defense let me say that we were very impressed by

[1] Source: *United States–Japan Relations: Hearings Before the Committee on Foreign Affairs, House of Representatives, and its Subcommittees on International Economic Policy and Trade and on Asian and Pacific Affairs, Ninety-seventh Congress, Second Session* (Washington, 1982), pp. 4–9. The hearing was held by the Subcommittee on Asian and Pacific Affairs, the chairman of which was Representative Stephen J. Solarz. Holdridge testified along with the Assistant Secretary of Defense for International Security Affairs, Francis J. West, Jr. (see his statement, *infra*), and the Deputy U.S. Trade Representative, David R. Macdonald. For the complete transcript of their testimony, see *ibid.*, pp. 1–87. The text of Holdridge's prepared statement is *ibid.*, pp. 9–16.

the staff study prepared by William Barnds and Vance Hyndman,[2] and we think this is precisely the kind of additional input which is going to be very useful in the situation.

Now I will start off with the evolution of United States-Japanese relations. Certainly we can say since World War II there has been a remarkable metamorphosis in the relationship which now exists between Japan and the United States, and indeed Japan's relationship with the world as a whole. Starting in 1945 a country devastated by war with an economy frankly nonexistent at that time and very much dependent on the relationship with the United States, Japan has progressed to being at least a regional power. And now I guess we can say quite fully that Japan is, as I just mentioned, a real world power.

What it does in an economic way has an effect on countries worldwide and, therefore, Japan has to be considered a world power. And in our own relationship with Japan we have moved from a position where Japan had a relationship of dependency to one in which we have, I would say, an equal partnership; that we and Japan treat each other as equals. We address our problems as equals and, of course, we have to admit in this equal partnership there cannot but be certain elements of competition.

There are a lot of good reasons why we and Japan have to stay on the same cooperative track. First of all, there is the strategic situation in East Asia. We and Japan want very much to see the military status quo, the balance of power being maintained; and, consequently, we are working together toward this end. Northeast Asia is a place where Japan, the United States, the Soviet Union, and China all have security interests which overlap, and it is very important for us to work very closely with the Japanese in regard to maintaining, as I said, the military balance of power.

In addition, we have a lot of economic interests together. There is no one that denies that in this room. Our trade with Japan is two way. In 1981, it was $60 billion; that is about 35 or 40 percent of our total trade with East Asia. This trading relationship, of course, is of enormous value to us both.

In addition to the trading or economic relationship, however, we have—let me go back to the joint communiqué issued when Prime Minister Suzuki was here last May.[3] It cited shared values of a democratic way of life, and rules of law. Our values are very similar in this regard. In addition, we understand each other. There are benefits of scientific and technological and cultural exchange which we have to maintain.

So despite the current and serious problems which exist between us, we do obviously perceive the overriding advantage of maintaining this degree of close cooperation.

Now let me talk a little bit about the security relationship. The U.S. ability to maintain forces and bases in Japan permits power projection elsewhere in Asia if needed. We are not thinking simply now in the current situation in terms only of the balance of power, and the maintenance of that balance in East Asia, but regrettably, because of the world scene we have had to move a considerable part of our 7th Fleet from time to time out of the region of the Western Pacific all the way into the Indian Ocean. And I have to say that were it not for our bases in Japan and the support which we enjoy from the Japanese Government in the military security sense, we would be unable to maintain this burden.

Japan, in addition, has helped us considerably in the stability of the region, maintaining economic stability by helping out in the economic development of Korea, and also all of the countries of Southeast Asia. Wherever one goes one can see that the Japanese presence is very marked, and yet this presence is not necessarily antithetical to our interests but in fact is very supportive in helping to build economic stability and providing security.

In short, our relationship with Japan, symbolized by the mutual security treaty[4] which we have, is supportive of our policy throughout East Asia and helps give the region a sense of confidence.

Let me turn to some of the problem areas which exist between us. It is extraordinary, as you mentioned, Mr. Chairman, that despite our great differences in culture and tradition and language, nevertheless, we

[2] The reference is apparently to a draft of a report published in May 1982: *United States Relations with Japan and Korea: Security Issues*, Report of a Staff Study Mission to Japan and Korea, July 23–August 15, 1981, to the Committee on Foreign Affairs, U.S. House of Representatives (Washington, 1982).

[3] For the text of the joint communiqué of May 8, 1981, see *American Foreign Policy: Current Documents, 1981*, document 514.

[4] The Treaty of Mutual Cooperation and Security, signed at Washington, January 19, 1960; for text, see 11 UST 1632.

have managed to maintain over the years a remarkable degree of similarity in policy. And we have maintained, as I said, a partnership in our relationship, but there are the strains which you have mentioned.

Earlier on we were subjected to a considerable amount of criticism in Japan over the mutual security treaty. A lot of Japanese feel that the security treaty involved Japan perhaps more so than it wanted to be in the world scene, military tensions and rivalries, and served U.S. interests more than it served Japanese interests.

I should say that since the reversion of Okinawa, the ending of the Vietnam war, the U.S. rapprochement with China, and the consolidation of our military presence in Japan to a relatively few number of bases has eased a lot of the tensions. The criticisms over the mutual security treaty have diminished considerably. This situation has changed indeed over to a positive support for the mutual security treaty and, in more recent years, with the buildup of Soviet military power, and in particular, the Soviet invasion of Afghanistan and I should add also the presence of Soviet military forces in the northern territories of Japan.

However, there still are these problems which you have outlined. There are questions in the minds of many people in the United States; the feeling in the United States that Japan has failed to assume an equitable share of the defense burden over the years, that we ourselves seem to be doing the major part of the military outlay and Japan has been providing only a fragmented part, a fractional part of this total expenditure.

The other major source of friction, of course, lies in the region of trade. In the past our trade problems seem to focus essentially on certain items such as color TV sets, automobiles, or steel. But now we are getting into something which in our judgment involves the very basic nature of the Japanese economic system; that is, the Japanese attitude toward exports and imports and whether or not Japan will in fact, as we see it, participate in the worldwide international free trade system.

The perception is prevalent that Japan, the second largest economic power in the free world, is unwilling to do its share in carrying the burden of the free trade system. And we are particularly concerned at this time, moving away from the single item problems that existed in the past to continuing regulations and practices in Japan which limit American access to the Japanese market.

Nontariff barriers and tariff barriers, both these are still in existence, and we believe that they are inequitable in terms of giving Americans access to Japan equivalent to the access which Japan enjoys in the American market.

The situation regarding trade could be one of the most serious challenges to United States-Japanese relations in the postwar period.

Now against this background what are our policy objectives? In trade, first we want to expand our two-way trade and investment while correcting the inequities in the relationship as we perceive them. Let me say we do not foresee a precise balance in our bilateral trade. In fact, I should say here if the Japanese indeed do make some of the adjustments which we have called on them to make, we would not be able to see an $18 billion trade deficit disappear overnight. What we are looking to see is progress in the direction of reducing these obstacles to free trade so that we will get equal access to the Japanese markets commensurate to the degree of access to the American market enjoyed by Japan. And in a related matter we hope Japan will accept a greater responsibility worldwide for helping to maintain the free trade system.

Now on defense, our objective is an equitable sharing of roles and missions. That is our focus rather than defense expenditures, per se. We don't wish to become bogged down in discussion of percentage points of the defense budget in Japan or percentage of GNP. What we would like to see is the Japanese filling out their part of a relationship, assuming certain roles and certain responsibilities for the defense of Japan and the Japanese home islands. And within this framework, we agree with the position espoused by Prime Minister Suzuki when he was here last May, that Japan should assume responsibility for the defense of the home islands out to a distance of about 1,000 nautical miles.[5] This would mean air defense and protection of sealanes, in particular,. although I wouldn't want to neglect the ground force role in this situation.

Now there has been, in our judgment, rather notable progress. Joint military planning is proceeding smoothly, and cost sharing support for our Forces is increasing

[5] Prime Minister Suzuki made a statement to this effect at a news conference in Washington on May 8, 1981; for text, see *American Foreign Policy: Current Documents, 1981*, document 515.

rather significantly, we believe, over the last several years, and joint exercises are being expanded. I will let my colleague, Assistant Secretary West, deal with this subject.

Nevertheless, despite the progress we remain concerned about the pace of the Japanese buildup in response to the growing Soviet threat. In our judgment there is an urgency now, and I think that some of you have heard me give a rundown on the growth of Soviet military power in East Asia. We feel, therefore, that we have to respond more urgently. And we would feel it incumbent upon our friends in the East Asian area to respond in the same light.

Let me turn now to foreign aid. We do not regard foreign aid as a substitute for defense, but it is certainly complementary. When the Japanese Government, Prime Minister Suzuki, speaks about comprehensive security, we do not challenge this concept. That is, increased economic assistance overseas, increased political and diplomatic activity, and increased defense expenditures at home. But again let me say that we do not regard overseas development assistance as a substitute for defense. We fully support and encourage Japan's expansion of foreign aid, which is fourth in the world in absolute terms, as contributing to peace and stability in Asia and elsewhere.

Let me just remark here that in fiscal year 1982 Japan is projecting a $4.3 billion foreign aid expenditure. In fiscal year 1981 Japan already has spent $4 billion in overseas development assistance, and we support Japan's decision to broaden the range of its support to countries in politically sensitive areas such as Egypt, Turkey, and Pakistan.

Very early in this administration Japan donated $10 million to Jamaica, and we would like to see further Japanese expenditures in the Caribbean area.

Let me turn to United States–Japan international cooperation. As I have indicated, across the broad range of international relations, while hardly identical, Japanese policies generally support or are consummate with our own. We maintain frequent consultations with Japan both in Japan and in the United States. I think personally I must have seen over 150 Diet Members this last year, and we are constantly meeting our counterparts at all levels of the U.S. Government.

We share interests and values, and Japan closely identifies with the Western industrial democracies in shaping its policies.

Mr. Solarz. Mr. Secretary, how many House Members have you seen in the last year?

Mr. Holdridge. I have seen quite a few who are interested in East Asian affairs, Mr. Chairman. I usually see Japanese in larger groups, maybe 20 or 25 at a time.

We are especially grateful for Japanese supports and consultations with regard to crisis areas, such as Iran, Afghanistan, and Poland, where Japanese support has equaled or surpassed that of some of our other allies.

Looking ahead, the U.S. bilateral relationship with Japan is one of our most important in the world—and it is of advantage to both of us—and we understand that on both sides. But it would be a mistake to take for granted a projection of our close cooperation into the indefinite future. Our relationship requires careful and constant attention on both sides of the Pacific. The fundamental danger facing us during the next few years is the likelihood of growing disparity between United States expectations of Japan in the economic and defense areas and Japan's ability or willingness to meet these expectations.

Additionally, as Japan assumes greater international responsibilities, we will no doubt benefit from continued cooperation. But here, too, there is a potential for friction in response to adjustments in relative power and influence. Should Japan lose confidence in the credibility of the United States security guarantee or should the United States lose patience with what we perceive to be Japan's failure to take more responsibility for its own defense, basic changes in the relationship could occur.

Similarly, should we on our side change our position with respect to maintaining and expanding a liberal international trading system, our relationship also could be radically altered.

None of this seems likely at this point. Security, economic, and political ties are strong, but clearly careful handling is necessary on both sides of the Pacific.

A high degree of emotionalism envelops the discussion of trade, and to a lesser extent, defense issues. Therefore, to assure future relations and preserve these relations will require the exercise of considerable initiative and understanding on our parts, on both our parts.

Thank you very much, Mr. Chairman.

Document 507

Statement by the Assistant Secretary of Defense for International Security Affairs (West) Before a Subcommittee of the House Foreign Affairs Committee, March 1, 1982[6]

U.S.-Japanese Defense Cooperation

Thank you, Mr. Chairman. I have been frantically trying to cut out things from it, and I will try to summarize it as briefly as possible.

I am pleased to be here this afternoon to discuss the evolution of the U.S.-[Japanese] defense cooperation and the U.S. policy on this issue. I have prepared answers to your specific questions, and I would just like to make a brief summary at this time.

U.S. security interests and strategic objectives in the East Asian-Western Pacific area are to maintain regional stability on our western security perimeter and to prevent increasing Soviet forces in the area from taking advantage of internal theater conflicts.

Japan is the cornerstone of the U.S. forward defense strategy in the Asian-Pacific region. Although the United States and Japan fought fiercely in World War II and are competing seriously in the economic sphere today, our culturally different nations are the two most politically and economically vibrant democracies in the world. Our bilateral trade amounts to over $50 billion annually; Japan is the United States second largest customer, and the United States is by far Japan's largest trade partner.

After the United States, Japan is the strongest non-Communist country militarily in all the Asian-Pacific area. Although attention frequently focuses only on Japan's so-called "free ride" or "cheap ride" because it spends less than 1 percent of its GNP on defense, it is instructive to note that its budget is third largest in the world among nonnuclear armed nations.

Japan's self-defense forces today include: 13 army divisions, even though the direct threat of invasion is fairly minimal; 50 destroyer-type vessels, over twice as many as our 7th Fleet, which has responsibilities for the Western Pacific and Indian Oceans; almost as many antisubmarine warfare aircraft as we have in the Eastern and Western Pacific Command, which also includes the Indian Ocean; and approximately 400 tactical fighter aircraft, more than the Republic of Korea's Air Force or the U.S. Air Force has in Japan, in the ROK, and in the Philippines combined.

If Japan should decide it is in its interest, it could with its economic vitality do significantly more for its own self-defense than any other U.S. ally in the world. Such actions would have meaningful results for Japan's own security and for the stability of the entire free world.

The United States and Japan share many common interests and goals which tend to overshadow differences in language and customs. The most fundamentally similar characteristic is our island status, resulting in a common need to maintain free access to the broad Pacific Ocean which lies between us. Also, because of resource dependencies and thriving economies, both countries need to use other oceans of the world as well.

As Thomas Jefferson so accurately foresaw in 1785, those nations which frequent the sea will "be principally exposed to jostle with other nations"; but, because of their free people's desire, their governments must preserve the right to employ the oceans for transportation, fishing, and other uses. Mr. Jefferson continued by saying that the result of the exercise of that freedom would be "the necessity of some naval force."

Although the Imperial Japanese Navy was a major combat force which briefly ruled the Pacific, it and all other Japanese military forces were disbanded by fiat of the Allied Occupation; and Japan's present Constitution, written with considerable American influence, banned all armed force with the exception of that absolutely necessary, exclusively for self-defense.

Almost immediately, however, the desire of the occupiers and the occupied for the Japanese to continue to use the seas for transportation, coastal commerce, and fishing required the reinstitution of, at first, paramilitary naval forces for minesweeping and, finally, self-defense forces to play a limited role for legitimate defense needs.

At the time of the discussion of a peace treaty in 1951, the United States expressed

[6] Source: *United States–Japan Relations*, pp. 17–21. For the text of West's prepared statement, see *ibid.*, pp. 22–46.

a desire for a significant military buildup by Japan, which was unable to do so for both financial and psychological reasons. The Japanese Constitution, written in 1947, became a symbol of sometimes bitter political determination not even to consider military options. Japan's history documented tensions which had continued with the Soviet Union; but post-1952 Japanese governments preferred to rely on the military power of the United States and to permit rent-free U.S. miliary bases on Japanese soil, sometimes used in ways the Japanese people did not support, rather than act themselves to insure free use of the seas which Japan needed in order to prosper.

At the urging of the United States, Japan created the Self-Defense Forces in 1954; wrote a defense policy in 1957 to rely on the United Nations, the United States, and only marginally on its own defense forces for its well-being; and went through the motions of four defense buildup programs which gradually developed the force levels I have described earlier. Despite the numbers of these forces, they are still fundamentally unable to provide effective, meaningful self-defense against the threat facing Japan in the 1980's.

Following the initial, unsuccessful efforts in the 1950's of John Foster Dulles, who negotiated the peace treaty, to get Japan to build defense forces of meaningful size, U.S. efforts vis-à-vis Japan became less direct. Successive attempts were made to convince Japan to do more in terms of defense forces. But defense was a sensitive political issue in Japan, and there were occasional references to the possible danger of resurgent Japanese militarism.

American and Japanese friends and allies in Southeast Asia have still not completely abandoned such fears. Because Japan's defense base was so small, and because the early 1970's were colored by hopes of détente, U.S. policy largely left Japan to decide for itself what it wanted to do in the defense area. That being the case, the Japanese Government chose an understandable course—reliance on the United States to carry the majority of the expensive and politically sensitive military load.

The rapid relative change in status between the United States and the U.S.S.R. in the 1970's, however, at least slightly concerned the Japanese public, which had gained a large measure of self-confidence with the advent of unprecedented economic prosperity. In 1976, Japan set forth force level goals to provide for sufficient military capability to prevent limited aggression; but the threat against which these forces were to defend was not specified; and the goals have not yet been achieved in 1982.

The United States still did little more than vaguely urge Japan, largely through Defense Department channels, to do more in air defense and antisubmarine warfare, while we decreased our presence in the Western Pacific.

In 1978, the United States and Japanese defense establishments concluded the guidelines for defense cooperation, which authorized bilateral military planning studies; but it was the Soviet invasion of Afghanistan which gave actual impetus to renewed high level U.S. interest in meaningful Japanese self-defense efforts. In fact, in 1980 Japan was publicly and strongly criticized by the Secretary of State and again by the Secretary of Defense for not raising its defense budget sufficiently in percentage terms.[7] Still unclear, however, was the meaning of "steady and significant increases" urged by the U.S. Government.

The Japanese could say honestly that they were already making these efforts in the 1970's from a statistical point of view, because Japan's defense budget had grown in the decade by about 8 percent annually in real terms.

The Reagan administration adopted a policy of not criticizing its allies in public and of discussing defense cooperation on the basis of roles and missions rather than on arbitrary statistical indices such as percentages of GNP, which by themselves are not necessarily meaningful.

On March 4, 1981, Secretary Weinberger told the Senate Armed Services Committee that a rational division of labor between Japan, the United States, and our NATO allies would be a central thrust of the administration's defense policy.[8]

The United States–Japan defense dialog began in earnest the same month when the Secretary met Japan's Foreign Minister.[9]

---

[7] See the statement of December 30, 1980, by Secretary of Defense Harold Brown, *American Foreign Policy: Basic Documents, 1977–1980*, p. 1043.

[8] For the text of Secretary of Defense Weinberger's testimony, see *Department of Defense Authorization for Appropriations for Fiscal Year 1982: Hearings Before the Committee on Armed Services, United States Senate, Ninety-seventh Congress, First Session, on S. 815* (Washington, 1981), Part 1, pp. 544–610.

[9] Foreign Minister Ito visited Washington from March 22 to 24, 1981; for the text of a press conference held jointly by Ito and Secretary of State Haig on March 24, see *American Foreign Policy: Current Documents, 1981*, document 506.

Mr. Weinberger stated that in the Northwest Pacific the United States would provide the nuclear umbrella, offensive projection forces as necessary, and assist the Republic of Korea in the defense of its territory. In the Southwest Pacific and Indian Oceans the United States would provide the nuclear umbrella, projection forces as necessary, and sealane protection forces.

President Reagan and Prime Minister Suzuki met in May, and defense was a major issue at the head-of-state level. The two leaders acknowledged the appropriateness of a rational division of labor; and the Prime Minister stated that Japan could, within the limits of its Constitution, defend its own territory, the seas and skies around Japan, and its sealanes to a distance of 1,000 miles.

He also stated that Japan would take additional measures to alleviate the financial burden of U.S. Forces in Japan. In 1982 the GOJ support figure is over $1 billion.

The United States supported these roles, which would enhance Japanese self-defense as well as contribute meaningfully to peace and stability in the Northwest Pacific.

Today, unfortunately, Japan cannot carry out these roles. By its own public analyses, its self-defense forces cannot sustain its army divisions, destroyers, and tactical aircraft in combat due to very limited supplies of ammunition, torpedoes, and missiles. The size and modernization of Japan's air and naval forces are not adequate to defend its airspace and sealanes to 1,000 miles against the Soviet force levels of the 1980's, which even the Japanese Government now identifies as potentially threatening.

Thus our defense dialog is continuing. For now the burden of the meaningful defense of Japan still rests largely with the United States, owing to the deficiencies which the Japanese publicly acknowledge. Owing to these shortcomings the self-defense forces do not constitute effective deterrence. But meaningful United States-Japanese defense burden-sharing goals have been set and publicly acknowledged at the highest levels for the first time in the post-1945 era.

In its 1982 budget which is presently under deliberation and expected to take effect in April, the Japanese Government took a meaningful first step by giving defense a significantly higher priority than all other ministries and agencies including social welfare, another postwar first.

If Japan is to be able to carry out the meaningful roles which its Government has said are legitimate, substantially more significant efforts will be required in each of the next 5 years of the defense planning period. The content of the 5-year plan is expected to be announced later this year.

The decision on the future course rests with the Japanese Government. Several U.S. congressional resolutions of last year proposed measures such as Japanese patrols to the Indian Ocean, revision of the Treaty of Mutual Cooperation and Security, Japanese payment of a $20 billion security tax to the United States, and a minimal expenditure of Japanese GNP. The Reagan administration feels that the dialog on roles and missions has made considerable progress in barely a year's time and should be continued.

Patrols to the Indian Ocean, other than at token levels, are not possible for the foreseeable future, even with significant Japanese defense increases, and could be unwelcome by United States and Japanese friends in South Asia. The United States–Japan treaty has been revitalized by the Reagan–Suzuki communiqué and need not be revised to allow for meaningful self-defense missions in the Northwest Pacific by Japanese forces.

Spending of 1 percent or more of GNP is only significant if such expenditures are properly programed for effective defense capabilities. The administration hopes Japan will spend what is necessary to provide forces adequate to carry out its legitimate defense roles within this decade.

We are optimistic that our defense dialog will continue to prosper, and we hope the Congress and this committee will participate and play a significant role in convincing Japanese leaders of the wisdom of substantive United States–Japan defense cooperation under a roles-and-missions approach.

Thank you, Mr. Chairman.

Document 508

Transcript of a Department of State Press Briefing, March 23, 1982 (Extract)[10]

Visit of Japanese Foreign Minister Sakurauchi

SENIOR STATE DEPARTMENT OFFICIAL. I'm happy to be here to discuss what I

[10] Source: Department of State files. The brief-

thought was an extremely useful and very fruitful visit. You've heard the word fruitful before, and I don't want to belabor you with a cliché, but when the Secretary of State said in the lobby out there that they were far-ranging, that was absolutely the case.

You will notice that the meeting was originally scheduled to begin at 11. It did not start promptly at 11, but it was scheduled to end at 1:15, so by the time the Foreign Minister actually got out the door we were over an hour later. That does illustrate the depth to which the various questions were addressed—global matters, regional matters, bilateral issues—and among the various elements that were touched upon: The situation in East Asia, Poland, arms control—which I should say was a very important matter for the Japanese—Afghanistan, the Middle East, and a number of other elements all attached thereunto. When you talk about the Middle East, one has to discuss also Lebanon and the situation in the Persian Gulf and so on. So there were indeed global, regional, and far-ranging [questions].

Let me say something about the atmospherics. That we had, I thought, one of the more friendly and really productive sessions that I've seen for a long time. We've been working with the Japanese in a very close relationship for a long period of time now, and we would certainly have to say that the Japanese are among our closest friends. I think that that closeness of attitude was reflected in the way the discussions went this morning.

There were a number of bilateral issues that were discussed, of course. Both today and yesterday we touched a bit upon such things as trade in the bilateral sense. There was also the question of defense which was addressed, and some bilateral issues particularly of importance to Japan: Whales, whaling, fisheries, and we also touched upon the civil air talks.

With that, I think I'll stop, and I'll let you ask questions.

Q. You talked about more productive [sessions?] than you've seen in a long time. Can you go beyond the generalities and provide us some specifics?

A. No. I can't get into the substance, naturally, but I would say this: That the depth of the discussions, the extent that we went into various matters—let me say, for example, when talking about Poland or Afghanistan, the question of sanctions came up. In this case we talked about how important it was for all the countries of the West, and it was very implicit in talking about the West that Japan was considering itself a part of this relationship, the importance of maintaining a unified position.

Q. But is there anything you can give us in the way of specifics, particularly, for example, on trade?

A. All right. On trade—

Q. Sometimes we have a feeling of a cosmetic visit.

A. It was not cosmetic, but it was not one of these things in which you might say there are recriminations. There were not. On the question of trade, the point was expressed yesterday by the President,[11] for example, how important it would be for Japan to open up its market further—not just from the standpoint of American businessmen, but also from the standpoint of the Europeans who are also having their economic troubles—and that Japan, by opening up its markets further to imports from outside Japan, would in fact be contributing very markedly to the preservation of the world free trade system.

Q. Did you get any assurances that made you happier about tariff barriers or nontariff barriers?

A. Certainly, the Japanese—the Foreign Minister said that Japan was aware of the problem, had already been working hard, and in this case some of these steps Japan has already taken—were cited—such as the 67 items, nontariff barriers, which have already been addressed, and the creation of the ombudsman. Then Mr. Sakurauchi went on to say, yes, Japan would look to see what it could be doing more in that regard, bearing in mind that the Versailles summit will be coming up and that, again, there will be high-level discussion of all of these problems involving not just the bilaterals with the United States but the European heads of state or government too. So, in effect, what I thought was a very positive response from the Japanese was signified.

Q. Did he warn against reciprocity?

A. When you say "he," who?

---

ing, conducted on a background basis by a senior Department of State official, began about 2:15 p.m. Foreign Minister Sakurauchi visited Washington from March 20 to 24. The briefing was held after a meeting between the Foreign Minister and Secretary of State Haig.

[11] President Reagan met with Foreign Minister Sakurauchi on March 22.

Q. The Japanese Foreign Minister.

A. That did not come up in the context of the conversations, no.

Q. Did the Minister indicate whether or not Japan was planning to take any further major steps before the Versailles summit as has sometimes been suggested?

A. The Japanese made it very plain that they would do as much as they thought they could, that they would approach this in a very positive spirit; and while no ironclad guarantees were given in this regard, I would say that the attitude was very responsive to the position that was expressed, and that I'm sure, and in fact the Secretary of State expressed confidence, that the Japanese would do everything that they could.

Q. Given what he did say, would this lead you to believe that they will take some further step between now and the Versailles summit or—

A. Let me be a little bit cautious here. I don't want to be pinned to the mat on whether they will or will not. All I can say—and I think this was the impression that the Foreign Minister intended to convey—that Japan would approach this problem in a very positive and constructive manner and look into ways and means to indeed show that it would be doing more to demonstrate that it would be doing more, bearing in mind that there is this point in time coming up when the question will be addressed again at high levels.

Q. Did the Japanese express to you any of the frustration that they have expressed elsewhere that their efforts in this direction so far haven't been acknowledged or given enough—

A. I did not detect any sense of frustration coming through in the conversations today. Again, let me stress that they were extremely positive.

Q. Did they ask the United States to make their case for them a little better with the American public?

A. This is not something that I heard in the discussions that I participated in yesterday and today. I can't tell you what may transpire in the remaining talks that the Foreign Minister is going to have while in Washington, but yesterday with the President and today with the Secretary of State, that did not come up.

Q. He didn't mention reciprocity at all? Here he put out a 10-page argument against it.

A. I think at this particular point you're dealing with people who know the issues well on both sides, and that it doesn't help in a situation such as that to go over the ground which people know very well indeed. Again, it's my impression that the Japanese, as represented by the Foreign Minister, intend to approach this matter in a very positive way.

Q. You say that arms control was mentioned and that it's a very important matter to the Japanese, but obviously the area of their defense spending has been a difficult area between us. How much was that discussed?

A. These two are sort of mixing apples and oranges. When you talk about Japanese defense spending, that does not enter into the realm of arms control and the area that we're concerned with, which gets into—let me check my notes here for you—arms control in this context means the intermediate nuclear forces, the START talks, and the Japanese also expressed considerable interest in the U.N. Special Session on Disarmament coming up.

Q. Did they speak about the pressure that the United States is putting on—

A. There was no word about pressure. In fact, yesterday the President made a point of expressing appreciation to the Japanese for what they have done already and increasing their attention to defense—the effort that they're making in that field. That was also, as I understand, second hand, the gist of what Deputy Secretary of Defense Carlucci had to say yesterday, although the point was made by the President, and certainly by the others, that Japan certainly can do more, and that's it.

. . . .

Document 509

Address by Vice President Bush Before the Foreign Correspondents' Club of Japan, Tokyo, April 24, 1982[12]

Vice President Bush's Visit to Japan

I've come to Japan in the interests of harmony, friendship, and peace. I've come

---

[12] Source: Press Release, April 24, 1982, Office

to learn, and I've come to listen. The day is past when America seeks to dominate the agenda of the countries of the free world.

The free world will survive, as a concept and reality, only if the partnerships that make it up remain intact and vibrant. As we enter the eighties and approach the millennium, America will guard its old friendships carefully, even as it seeks new partners in the free world.

If I come in the interests of harmony, it is at a time when the affairs of the world are increasingly disharmonious. The Soviet Union's appetite for the freedom of other peoples is as rapacious as ever. Lech Welesa languishes in confinement as his countrymen contend with martial law, having only the fleeting encouragement of the broadcast of Radio Solidarity.

An army of occupation continues its ruthless campaign against the Afghan people; continues to kill innocent men, women, and children with chemicals outlawed by all decent societies. Soviet leaders have given homilies on their desire for nuclear disarmament as SS–20 missiles sprouted overnight like fields of asparagus. Old wounds persist in the Middle East, though tomorrow will witness a decisive, historic, and courageous step for peace when Israel completes its withdrawal from the Sinai.

We are reminded every day that liberty is on trial, and that darkness has descended over many parts of the world. In Eastern Asia, it has descended on North Korea, Vietnam, Laos, Soviet Asia, Kampuchea. One of the most enduring symbols of the injustices of the 20th century may be those people who have braved the dangers of the sea in open boats.

There is much to mourn. But there is also much to celebrate. Which brings me to my visit. In the next three weeks, Japan and the United States will observe two important anniversaries. April 28th, just a few days from now, will mark the 30th anniversary of the San Francisco Peace Treaty[13] and the end of postwar occupation.

The last 30 years have seen the historically unprecedented boom of postwar Japan. Not surprisingly is this known as "the miracle of Japan."

No Eastern bloc countries will be celebrating such anniversaries this year—or next year, or the year after. That is a sad fact; and the heart of the West goes out to those millions of people who will continue to live under the threat of Soviet armies, and under the blight of Marxist mismanagement.

On May 15th, Japan and the United States will observe the tenth anniversary of the reversion of the Island of Okinawa. Many brave men fought and died there. The soil that absorbed their blood is now a shrine to their memory. I hope Okinawa will now be remembered not so much as a battleground, but as a symbol of how our two nations worked together to heal the wounds of war.

It's true that these two anniversaries come at a time of some bilateral problems between our two countries. But I haven't come here to emphasize them, or to dramatize them. If my presence here today dramatizes anything, it's what joins us, not what separates us.

Obviously problems exist. They're no secret and they are important problems for us both but just as obviously we're all anxious to work out solutions. Together. Partners consult; they don't dictate to each other. We've got a vigorous dialogue going, and there's no need to suspect it will grow any less vigorous over the years.

Our Japanese friends can expect from us what all our friends can expect from us: open lines of communication. A determination to overcome obstacles, and consistency. To them I would say: There will be no unpleasant surprises in your relations with us.

Japan now enjoys an unquestioned prominence among the nations of the world. She has a global role to play in the affairs of the 20th century, a role that will expand in the 21st. As she assumes a greater role, her responsibilities will grow in proportion. There are clear indications the Japanese people have a growing awareness of their country's new global role, and of the obligation and responsibilities that accompany great economic strength.

To paraphrase penetrating analysis by the present Chief Cabinet Secretary, Kiichi Miyazawa, the Japanese were not ready, in the 1970's, to assume their full share of global responsibility; even though Japan, as Mr. Miyazawa pointed out, "became increasingly conscious of the need to play a large role in the international economy, and

---

of the Press Secretary to the Vice President; also printed in Department of State *Bulletin*, August 1982, pp. 39–41. Vice President Bush visited Japan from April 23 to 25.

[13] The Peace Treaty with Japan, signed at San Francisco, September 8, 1951, entered into force for the United States on April 28, 1952; for text, see 3 UST 3329.

made considerable efforts to do so." Japan's performance should be measured in her context as the second largest economic power among the industrialized democracies. Today, her political role is growing—as it should. As a pillar of the industrialized democracies, Japan cannot avoid that role; and I for one can think of no nation more qualified to assume it.

Japan, meanwhile, has been demonstrating that she is willing to cooperate with her Western friends in all areas, including matters of defense and trade. Prime Minister Suzuki's statements on behalf of increased defense goals, along with recent increases in Japan's defense budget attest to Japan's good faith.

We are conscious, too, that the question of Japan's defense spending is much more complex than the black-and-white terms in which it is too often discussed. Let me say that the United States is grateful for the progress so far on the defense issue.

We would, of course, be grateful for continued progress, knowing as we do that Japan will make her own decisions. We have confidence in the wisdom and global perspective of Japan's leaders and her people, just as we have confidence that we will continue to cooperate in this crucial area. At the same time, we recognize the contributions of Japan's foreign aid program, much of which goes to critical parts of the world, where both our countries are working toward the same goals.

There is no question that some friction exists between the United States and Japan in the matter of trade. Many visitors from Japan, as well as my and Japan's great friend, former Ambassador Robert Ingersoll, have recently remarked on the danger of protectionism, and the extent to which sentiment has been aroused in all quarters on trade issues. My own sense is that we both want to achieve the same goals: free trade, and fair trade. But here I want to make a point that I cannot emphasize enough, namely that we cannot allow trade disagreements to dominate our dialogue. Some newspapers have drawn the conclusion that our two countries are moving toward a "head-on collision" on trade. I disagree. I think, happily, that we're moving toward some head-on decisions on trade.

Long before the dilemmas of the post-modern age, Simón Bolívar said that ". . . the majority of men hold as a truth the humiliating principle that it is harder to maintain the balance of liberty than to endure the weight of tyranny."[14] However vexatious our disagreements may be, we live at a time when we ought never to take for granted the special comfort of our friendship.

The difficulties abound, but we have the will and the wherewithal to overcome them. The historical imperative demands that we do. It is, for instance, no secret that the United States has had difficulties pursuing our relations with the People's Republic of China. But we are absolutely resolved to strengthen our relationship with the People's Republic, and in cooperating in her development. We thoroughly appreciate the importance of that relationship to all Asia. Strengthening it will of course require the efforts on both sides. But I am greatly confident of a successful outcome.

There are many other challenges facing the United States. President Reagan is deeply committed to arms reduction. He is willing to explore all reasonable—and verifiable—approaches to the question of how to reduce the world's arsenal of nuclear weapons. His zero-option proposal of last November[15] was the single most sincere and dramatic overture to the Soviet Union in a long, long while. He's been earnest and aggressive in pursuing talks with the Soviets. But there has been a great deal of confusion and misunderstanding on the matter.

No one is more interested in maintaining peace between the Soviet Union and the United States than Ronald Reagan. He seeks no confrontation there. He seeks to reduce tensions—tensions caused in no small part, by the Soviet Union's international behavior.

President Reagan will do everything he can to convince the Soviet Union to cooperate with the United States in agreeing to arms reduction. And he will keep America strong. To pursue new policies does not mean old ones will be abandoned. Make no mistake: he will maintain our deterrence.

Our secret weapon in the protracted conflict against totalitarianism lies not in underground silos, but in our free marketplaces. I say secret because the leaders of the totalitarian regimes cannot afford to impart the knowledge of the triumph of capitalism to their people. What Russian

---

[14] Ellipsis appears in the source text.

[15] For the text of the President's address of November 18, 1981, see *American Foreign Policy: Current Documents, 1981,* document 60.

worker, fully informed of the status, condition and rights of his counterpart in the United States, or Japan, or in any of the other industrialized democracies, would not run to the nearest Aeroflot office and get himself and his family on the next flight out. But alas: *Pravda* does not print the whole story, Aeroflot does not accept reservations from just anyone.

Irving Kristol once addressed the question of why democracies live and die. For over 2,000 years, he said, political philosophers rejected democracy because they believed that it inevitably degenerated into chaos and dicatatorship. But:

"What changed the attitude of political philosophers," wrote Kristol, "was the emergence of modern capitalism, with its promise of economic growth—of an economic system in which everyone could improve his condition without having to do so at someone else's expense. It is the expectation of tomorrow's bigger pie, from which everyone will receive a larger slice, that prevents people from fighting to the bitter end over the division of today's pie."

Japan and the United States need each other to grow. We depend on each other to grow. Our combined national products account for one-third of the world's output. That is a formidable weapon against the adversaries of freedom. We owe it to ourselves, to our friends in the free world, and moreover to those who may someday be free, to resolve our differences, so that, together, we can build on a past that promises great things to come.

Thank you.

Document 510

Transcript of a Press Briefing by the Secretary of State (Haig), Paris, June 4, 1982 (Extract)[16]

Meeting Between President Reagan and Japanese Prime Minister Suzuki

. . . .

Now, we also had a very busy day with several bilaterals—the first with Prime Minister Suzuki of Japan and the second with Prime Minister Thatcher of Great Britain.[17] With respect to the Suzuki bilateral, it was a very detailed and subjective and tightly programmed one hour of discussion between the two leaders and their representatives. The focus was on trade. In these discussions, President Reagan very much welcomed the recent announcement of the Government of Japan on the further liberalization of Japanese trade practices.[18] The President described it as a positive step in the direction of greater liberalization.

This involved the recent decisions by the Japanese Government to liberalize tariff and nontariff restrictions and an improvement in Japanese import regulations. During these discussions, Prime Minister Suzuki pledged to support the further enhancement of free trade at the upcoming GATT Conference next fall—a pledge which, of course, was welcomed by the United States as it is parallel to and consistent with U.S. objectives and intention at that upcoming meeting.

The President also welcomed the announcement made earlier this afternoon by the Japanese Government of the completion of an interim agreement on civil aviation between the United States and Japan. As you know, this has been under discussion for an extended period and a breakthrough was achieved largely as a result of the initiative of Prime Minister Suzuki himself.

The President in those discussions this afternoon warmly endorsed the recent decision of the Suzuki government to increase its level of defense spending to almost 8 percent—increase real term spending for the coming year, the only sector, incidentally, of the current Japanese budget to receive such an enhanced allocation of resources.

During the discussions, Prime Minister Suzuki warmly endorsed and welcomed President Reagan's recent initiatives in arms control ranging from the November 18 speech on INF and the talks at Geneva and the more recently announced decision

---

[16] Source: Department of State Press Release 191, June 16, 1982; printed also in Department of State *Bulletin*, July 1982, pp. 18–19. President Reagan and Secretary Haig were in Paris for the Versailles Economic Summit meeting.

[17] For Haig's statement on the meeting with Prime Minister Thatcher, see *ibid.*, p. 19.

[18] The eight-point package of measures to reduce import restrictions which the Japanese Government had announced on May 27 is summarized in *New York Times*, May 28, 1982, p. A1.

on START talks which will resume on the 29th—negotiations themselves which will resume on the 29th of this month in Geneva.[19]

Prime Minister Suzuki welcomed the position of the United States with respect to mobile, intermediate-range missiles in our Geneva discussions, in which they were dealt with in global terms. Of course, there would be great concern in the Far East that missiles now directed at Western Europe might be shifted to the Far East.

In conclusion, there were some detailed discussions as they wound up their meeting of the recent visit of the Premier of the People's Republic of China to Tokyo and Prime Minister Suzuki's impressions, important impressions with respect to this visit. As the meeting broke up, the Prime Minister described the current state of U.S.-Japanese relations as never better and on the highest plain in his memory, particularly singling out the leadership of President Reagan in this difficult time of international crisis and confusion.

. . . .

Document 511

Statements by the Chairman of the Senate Foreign Relations Committee (Percy), the Deputy U.S. Trade Representative (Macdonald), and the Under Secretary of Agriculture for International Affairs and Commodity Programs (Lodwick) Before the Senate Foreign Relations Committee, September 14, 1982[20]

U.S. Trade Relations With Japan

THE CHAIRMAN. [presiding].[21] I want to welcome this afternoon our distinguished guests. This afternoon we will be continuing a hearing begun this morning on United States–Japan trade relations. We heard from private industry witnesses this morning and will hear from Government witnesses this afternoon. We have heard a large number of examples of areas where Japan is successful in erecting barriers to American goods, both manufactured and agricultural. This afternoon we will explore U.S. Government efforts to reduce and eventually eliminate those barriers.

We look forward to hearing first from Mr. David Macdonald, U.S. deputy trade representative, who will give us an overview of the situation and discuss ongoing negotiations with the Japanese on trade issues. Mr. Seeley Lodwick, Under Secretary of Agriculture for international affairs and commodity programs, will then discuss U.S. efforts to expand American sales of farm goods.

I would like to announce that I will have to leave at 3 o'clock. If we have not finished the hearing by then, Senator Hayakawa has thoughtfully agreed to join us at that time and take up the chair. We will try to move right along. Thank you very much.

Let us start with you, Ambassador Macdonald.

AMBASSADOR MACDONALD. Thank you very much, Mr. Chairman. As you requested, I have a complete statement, which I will file with the committee as part of these hearings.

THE CHAIRMAN. Your complete statement will be incorporated in the record.

AMBASSADOR MACDONALD. I have about a 10-page double-spaced summary, if you can put up with that.

The economic relationship between the United States and Japan is one of the major underpinnings of the world trading system today. After Canada, Japan is our single most important trading partner. But while our trade has brought us many benefits, both as producers and consumers, it has also become a source of friction between us. That friction has arisen, in part, because of the frustration that many Americans, especially American business leaders, have felt at the impediments that have kept the Japanese marketplace relatively closed by comparison to our economy to foreign goods, services, and investment.

This frustration has created a race against time for Japan, although the Japanese may not be totally aware of it. While

---

[19] For President Reagan's announcement on May 31 of the beginning of START talks, see *Weekly Compilation of Presidential Documents*, June 7, 1982, pp. 730–731.

[20] Source: *U.S. Trade Relations with Japan: Hearing Before the Committee on Foreign Relations, United States Senate, Ninety-seventh Congress, Second Session* (Washington, 1982), pp. 77–81, 88–93. For the complete text of Macdonald's and Lodwick's testimony, see *ibid.*, pp. 77–111; for the texts of their prepared statements, here omitted, see *ibid.*, pp. 81–88 and 93–96.

[21] Senator Charles H. Percy. Bracketed note appears in the source text.

Japan has undertaken numerous trade liberalizing reforms and has, in fact, completed several, the pace of Japan's progress appears to lag behind the advance of anti-import legislation in this country and the anti-import actions of Japan's other trading partners.

Nevertheless, we have made some progress with Japan, albeit slow in pace. And I would like to take the opportunity to review this progress with you today.

The concerted efforts of the administration and its predecessors over the past decade and more to induce Japan to dismantle its network of obstacles to foreign products, services, and investment have brought about slow but steady results.

The Japanese economy is now more open than it ever has been. Much of the progress that has occurred has taken place during the past year, which it is our sincere hope will prove to have been a watershed year in terms of finally putting Japan firmly and fully on the path of real liberalization of her markets.

But if that is to be the case, the momentum for open markets that has begun in Japan must be continued and increased. It must reach down from the verbal commitments of top political leaders into the practical actions of the bureaucracy, customs officials, standards inspectors, and others in the Japanese Government, whose acts can impede or facilitate the flow of imported goods.

What is most hopeful in our recent trade discussions with the Japanese is the realization among Japan's top leadership that changes are necessary. The realization indeed was given utterance in the important statement issued by Prime Minister Suzuki on the occasion of Japan's announcement of its latest package of trade initiatives last May 28.[22]

The Prime Minister made a direct appeal to his people and, particularly, to the government officials and corporate decision-makers whose attitudes and actions will be all important in this respect, to extend a welcoming hand to foreign goods and investment. Such a statement is an unusual step for a nation's leader to take. What remains to be seen is whether the Prime Minister's appeal translates into change in the attitudes and actions of his countrymen.

Mr. Chairman, if I may, let me review for the committee what our objectives in trade policy toward Japan have been, what progress we have made in achieving them, and what remains on our agenda.

The United States has four principal objectives in its trade policy with Japan: first, equivalently free access to the Japanese economy in goods, services, and investment; second, a balanced trade composition between manufactured goods and raw materials; third, the avoidance of protectionist measures by both countries; and fourth, inducing the Japanese to exercise leadership in free trade commensurate with the Japanese economic strength.

As I suggested in my introductory remarks, securing access to the Japanese economy for American goods, services, and investment on an equivalent basis to that which the Japanese enjoy in the U.S. economy has been the keystone of our trade policy. Over the past year, we have pursued our trade policy objectives with Japan through a dialog in which we have sought removal of many Japanese impediments to our exports. In response to these efforts, the Government of Japan has undertaken a series of trade liberalizing measures in November 1981 and January and May 1982.

After the publication of the May package, Ambassador Brock announced publicly that we were requesting the Japanese Government to work with the U.S. Government for the purpose of initiating a continuing program designed to resolve difficulties that may arise in implementing the package. In the first week of August, a subgroup of United States–Japan Trade Subcommittee inaugurated a series of visits to Tokyo. Those visits will probably be carried out monthly.

The August visit revealed substantial progress in some areas, such as customs procedures, and the easing of access to the insurance market. A number of standard issues appear to be on the track for early resolution. The promised system of business consultants has indeed been set up and is in operation. And the Japanese Fair Trade Commission—that is their antitrust

---

[22] The reference is to a statement issued by Prime Minister Suzuki on May 28, following the Japanese Government's May 27 announcement of a package of measures to reduce import restrictions. Suzuki's statement declared that the Japanese Government had taken various steps to open the Japanese market to foreign trade but that for these steps to bring about concrete results, an attitude welcoming foreign products and foreign investment was necessary; he asked the Japanese "to be even more clear and forthcoming in taking the attitude of extending a welcoming hand to foreign products and investments and not discriminating against them." (U.S. Trade Representative files)

enforcement body—has begun to take a more assertive role both in beginning its promised monitoring of the distribution of foreign goods and in proclaiming its opposition to legislation expanding exemptions to Japan's antimonopoly laws, specifically regarding cartels.

These are positive steps representing tangible improvements. However, the May package has produced no major new opening of the Japanese market, nor has completely resolved any major problem. While the Japanese are moving in the right direction, I am afraid they are not moving far enough fast enough.

From our perspective, at least four major issues are still outstanding involving impediments to U.S. access in areas where there is very significant trade potential and where our firms are highly competitive.

The first issue is that of the remaining onerous tariffs. I should hasten to add that these tariffs are entirely legal. Nevertheless, emphasis will continue to be placed by us on securing reductions in Japan's tariffs, as this is an area in which the Japanese Government has strong and direct control. In our monthly visits to Japan, we will continue to press for significant tariff reductions on a wide range of products not addressed in the May 28 package.

The second issue that was barely addressed in the May package is that of agricultural import barriers. While we recognize that Japan is our largest single country market for agricultural exports, it is our belief that Japan would purchase even more of our competitive agricultural products if it eliminated its quotas, tariff quotas, high duty levels, and other nontariff barriers to agricultural trade. Bilateral agricultural consultations with the Japanese are now scheduled. We intend at that time to ask the Japanese what action they plan to take on the remaining quota items as well as to discuss general agricultural trade estimates.

As you know, the three quota items that are of the most concern to us are those on beef, oranges, and citrus juices. Import levels on these products were negotiated during the Tokyo round of Multilateral Trade Negotiations, and those agreements last until March 31, 1984.

As part of the agreement, it was decided that negotiations on future levels of imports would not begin until the second half of the Japanese fiscal year 1982. So therefore, we have the first session of those negotiations scheduled for October 20. The United States will press for the phased elimination of trade barriers on these products during that meeting.

The third major impediment to U.S. firms is that of a state monopoly, the Japan Tobacco and Salt Monopoly. Manufactured tobacco products are an industry sector in which the United States is extremely competitive. U.S. industry estimates of our potential share of the Japanese market in the absence of any barriers range upward from 25 to 50 percent. Since each percent of market share is roughly equal to $50 million in sales, the potential value of increased U.S. exports in this sector is significant.

The combination of significant U.S. trade potential being frustrated by barriers that are, in essence, directly controlled by the Government of Japan justifies this issue as a significant place on our list of priorities. We have also been conducting intense bilateral negotiations on tobacco and have another such set of negotiations scheduled in the near future.

A final major issue not adequately addressed in the May package is that of Japanese business practices that make it difficult for U.S. exporters to penetrate the Japanese market. These are particularly crippling in the area of high-technology products. American high-technology companies have long protected [*protested*] that a pattern exists to limit or deny access to Japanese markets to foreign firms at the leading edge of the technology until Japanese firms have become firmly established in the technology and possessed a world-scale production capacity.

Foreign firms with a significant lead in product or process technology have, in many instances, either been denied permission to manufacture in Japan or required to transfer their technology or to accept Japanese joint venture partners. The effect in each case has been to ensure that the foreign firms are unable to achieve a significant share of the Japanese market at its inception and, hence, are denied the competitive advantage that accrues to the early market leader.

In response to these problems, and in view of the vital importance of high-technology industries to both the United States and Japan, it was decided in April to form the United States–Japan High-Technology Work Group. The group met in July and August and has addressed issues such as transfer of technology, market access, trade distortions in high-technology goods and services, and joint research and development. It will develop a series of recommendations to be made to each government in October 1982 and a work program will also be developed.

When the best efforts of our bilateral discussions fail to overcome the differences between our two positions, this administration is determined that the United States should avail itself of GATT remedies. We have recently taken such action in one area and informed the Japanese of our decision to take it in another; and we are making the preparations necessary to do so in a number of other areas of unresolved difficulties.

The first case, where we have already commenced our complaint under the Standards Code in the GATT, is on the issue of Japanese certification of manufacturing plants located outside of Japan. The case we have picked to exemplify this issue is softball bats. Since this was first raised in July 1981, little progress has been made. The refusal by Japanese officials to permit U.S. suppliers direct access to the required safety mark in violation, in our view, of the Standards Code [*sic*].

Another area where we have informed Japan of our intention to move into formal dispute settlement is that of leather. This case involves a quota system on leather and also the means of allocating licenses to license holders in Japan. As of this date, the United States has informed Japan of its intention to reopen its complaint under article XXIII of the GATT in the absence of an acceptable agreement.

Mr. Chairman, in your invitation to me to testify before this committee, you also requested that I address the issue of the dollar-yen relationship. Criticisms have been raised that Japan maintains an undervalued yen. The yen has depreciated against the dollar—in fact, by quite a bit, 30 to 40 percent—as have all major currencies. And certainly, this depreciation has enhanced the price competitiveness of Japanese exports.

There are a number of practical restraints that the Japanese impose on capital flows, both by their own citizens and by foreigners. This fact seriously weakens the argument that the value of the yen is not being maintained at an artificial level. Nevertheless, recent Japanese exchange market intervention operations and interest rate increases have been designed to strengthen, not weaken, the yen.

Recent U.S. trade frictions with Japan have been caused by Japanese barriers to foreign access to the Japanese economy, not by exchange rate fluctuations. Nevertheless, as long as the Japanese capital and goods markets are perceived to be relatively restricted, the perception will also remain that the value of the yen is an artificially manipulated currency. It will continue to be a prime U.S. policy objective, therefore, to bring about liberalization of Japan's capital markets, with the idea that the yen then would seek its own level against other currencies.

In my testimony, I have described for the committee the administration's position with respect to various pieces of legislation currently pending before Congress. In conclusion, Mr. Chairman, if we are to maintain a new partnership with Japan, the dynamic of that partnership must be one of a common consideration of our mutual interests in preserving and expanding free access to each other's markets.

The chronic pattern of our past relationship, with the United States in the unwanted aggressive role of having to demand time and again Japanese market openings and the Japanese responding with reluctant and partial openings, seen as concessions, has caused irritation and an erosion of goodwill on both sides.

The time is ripe for a new beginning, for the emergence of an era in which Japan joins with the United States in taking a new international trading system. But like any opportunity that is ripe, it must be grasped quickly before it deteriorates in a mass of recrimination, if not retaliation. We are not yet sure that the Japanese are prepared to move with the necessary speed. Thank you, Mr. Chairman.

. . . .

The Chairman. I want to thank you very much. I would like to comment on two aspects of your testimony, Ambassador Macdonald. I thought it was important that you did quote the Japanese Prime Minister, Mr. Suzuki, when he did, after his most recent effort to remove trade restrictions, appeal to his own people. I hope they were listening to him.

He was wise when he said that the Japanese should extend a welcoming hand to foreign goods and investment. I also appreciated your own reiteration and statement to Japan that Japan must be persuaded to act to head off this threat to the free trading system, to act in a positive and constructive manner to remedy its own protectionism and exclusivity, not simply to protest American protectionist responses.

I would like to talk directly to my friends in Japan, and I do consider myself a friend of Japan. We have the Japanese media here, and I will take the opportunity to talk through them directly to our friends in Japan. I haveconsidered myself a supporter of free flowing international trade since the midfifties, when Dwight Eisenhower asked if I would help found the Committee for National Trade Policy. I was head of the legislative committee for the committee.

I was the head of a highly protected company and industry. The tariffs in the photographic industry were 40 percent. And every time I would come before the Finance Committee in the Senate and the Ways and Means Committee in the House to argue and debate against our trade associations that were building the stability of our industry on protectionism, I would say that those tariffs ought to come down. We ought to be competing in the free market.

I did not feel comfortable selling so much in Hong Kong, where it is a free market, with the domestic industry hiding behind a wall of protectionism. And the industry survived as the tariffs came down and down and down. I do not know what they are now, 5 percent or something like that. And the Japanese photographic industry has become quite prominent.

But we were fair. And we gave them a chance, and we gave them access to our markets. So I can talk with a clear conscience when I say that I have been a freer trader all of my industrial life and all of my public life.

But I find myself changing inside. And I want my Japanese friends to know it. I think it would be a catastrophe for us to go protectionist. But I think it would be an even worse catastrophe for us to stand still and do nothing about the gross unfairness of what is being done to the American worker.

I just returned last night, having spent several days home in Illinois, where we have the second highest unemployment in the country. We had manufacturers from Illinois testifying this morning about the gross unfairness and the lack of access that they have for their products in Japan. We need jobs for Americans. We open our markets to create jobs for Japanese, yet their market is closed as far as some of our products are concerned.

If there is no other way to get the point across, if we cannot do it through persuasion and reason, then we will have to go the route that many of my colleagues are advocating and just put the lid down. We will have to shut the door. We take one-quarter of Japanese exports, as you have said. What would happen if Japanese firms had to start laying people off?

I know. I operated a factory and built one in Japan. It is pretty hard to lay people off over there. You do not lay them off, but you are going to have to do something with those goods, like we are doing something with our goods. We are "eating" them. If you cannot sell them, you have to do something or you just stop producing and lay people off.

The Japanese have less flexibility than we have. We may have to turn the tables. I hope, therefore, that the reasoning which you have described, which is a sound, rational argument that this administration is putting forward, will be listened to. I hope they recognize what is behind the alternative if those efforts are not successful.

I applaud what they have done to date. Japan has made progress, but not fast enough. Not fast enough at all. The momentum of resentment is building up across the board at the grass-roots level and at the very top echelons of corporate America today as well as in the leadership of the House and the Senate.

So I think what you have said is good, sound advice. They are words of wisdom, and I hope they will be listened to by our friends in Japan.

AMBASSADOR MACDONALD. As you know, Mr. Chairman, that is the message that we have carried over on your behalf to officials of Japan in the past. It has been most effective.

THE CHAIRMAN. I thank you very much. We want to work closely with them. We have been friends with the Japanese for decades. We have so many friends there. But I think it is because of friendship that we can talk frankly to them. They cannot underestimate the feelings as exemplified by the *Los Angeles Times* survey of the American attitude toward Japan's trade policy now.

Mr. Secretary, we warmly welcome you. You were lauded this morning by the President of the American Farm Bureau Association. So we are happy to have you here today.

MR. LODWICK. Thank you, Mr. Chairman. I appreciate very much the opportunity to discuss with you today U.S. agricultural trade relations.

THE CHAIRMAN. Excuse me. I wonder if you would mind assuming the chair for just a second, Senator Dodd? Secretary Shultz and I have been going back and forth, and we are finally together on the phone now. Thank you.

SENATOR DODD. Certainly, Mr. Chairman.

Please proceed, Mr. Secretary.

MR. LODWICK. Thank you, Mr. Chairman, let me say it is a privilege to be here this afternoon with Ambassador Macdonald. We together have worked closely trying to work with these problems, and we see some daylight.

I would also commend you and your associates for the timing of this hearing, because it is the last of this month and the 20th and 22d of this next month that we will be visiting one-on-one across the table, if you will, with the Japanese, attempting to work out a solution to these problems.

If it would be satisfactory, we would certainly carry your message to them as to the feeling that you and the committee have on these matters.

My purpose today is briefly to review the status of our agricultural trade relations with Japan and to discuss the issues that confront us and what we hope to gain in the negotiations that are scheduled next month.

There is no question that agricultural trade between the United States and Japan is mutually beneficial. Japan has imported more U.S. agricultural products than any other country in the world every year since 1964. Last year we shipped a record of $6.7 billion worth of products to Japan. This was 15 percent of our total farm exports and represents the production for more than 14 million acres of cropland; incidentally, an area larger than the total cropland available in Japan itself.

Japan, in turn, relies on imports to meet an estimated 50 percent of its caloric needs. The United States has been its most dependable, largest supplier, providing more than 90 percent of its soybeans, 55 percent of its wheat, 65 percent of its feedgrain requirements in the past decade.

In all, Japan has looked to the United States for more than a third of its food and fiber requirements. So there are benefits for both countries in a stable and expanding trade.

Our principal trade concerns with Japan at this point is one of access for high-value U.S. products: beef, citrus, nuts, canned and frozen foods, and other processed and consumer-ready products.

The problem is rooted in Japan's domestic agricultural policy. Japan protects its agriculture because of its small size and inefficiency. The average farm size is only about 2½ acres. And while yields are quite high, agricultural labor productivity is among the lowest of the developed countries. Agricultural production is maintained and stimulated by high domestic support prices which are protected by erecting import barriers to insulate Japan's domestic agriculture from international competition.

Over the years, with abundant supplies of imported grains and soybeans and limited arable land, Japan has moved toward the production of high-value specialty crops such as livestock and fruits. Therefore, Japan applies its import protection selectively, with an eye to insuring foreign supplies of the commodities it needs to supplement its own agriculture, such as feed grains for its livestock industry, while restricting entry of competing products.

This is done in a variety of ways, including the use of import quotas, tariff quotas, high tariffs, state trading, administrative guidance, and restrictive product standards. As a result, about 85 percent of the value of U.S. agricultural exports to Japan consist of raw materials, such as feed grains, wheat, soybeans, cottons, hides. The rest is in high-value products, and they are far short of their market potential.

While we have been concerned with the trade restrictive effects of all of Japan's barriers, we are particularly interested in eliminating its import quotas, which we firmly believe are in violation of the General Agreement on Tariffs and Trade. There are now 22 such quotas affecting agricultural and marine products, some of which are of significant trade interest, most notably beef, oranges, citrus fruits. And despite some Japanese steps to reduce tariffs and expand quotas, we continue to face quantitative restrictions on the same 22 items that we did 10 years ago.

Well, as the chairman knows, we have for over the past year intensified our efforts to improve access to the Japanese market. But to date, the Japanese have announced only limited measures to reduce restrictions on agricultural imports.

The first of these positive, if limited, responses occurred last December, when Japan announced its intention to advance by 2 years tariff reductions negotiated in the Multilateral Trade Negotiations on 1,653 items, both agricultural and industrial. This was followed in January by disclosure of 67 actions Japan said it would take to facilitate trade by removing or reducing the effects of various nontariff trade barriers.

Now, some of these measures, such as the intention to improve grading practices for imported sake, to increase the number of inspectors for U.S. cherry and papaya shipments, and to revise plywood standards could favorably affect U.S. agricultural trade. However, no quota items were addressed in either package, and although the announcements represented a step in the right direction, they represented very small steps.

We continue to apply pressure at the March, United States–Japan Trade Subcommittee meetings in Tokyo. This was the third meeting of the subcommittee since September 1981. At this meeting the Japanese agreed to begin negotiations on beef and citrus quotas in October 1982, the earliest possible date under the MTN agreement, and to discuss in April their GATT justification for the 22 import quotas affecting agricultural and marine products.

At the April meeting, held here in Washington, the Japanese made what we thought was a weak defense of the import quota system. We indicated it might be necessary to exercise our rights under GATT in response to their continued reluctance to eliminate trade restrictive policies.

On May 28 Japan announced a "second" trade liberalization package in anticipation of the Versailles Economic Summit. Measures affecting agricultural products included expansion of import quotas on prepared and preserved pork, hi-test molasses, canned pineapple, tariff reductions on 15 agricultural items, amendment of tariff classifications to allow the importation of wild rice and improvement in certain import procedures.

Well, after seeking clarification on these measures, we found out that our gains again were minimal. Japan had chosen to act only on those quota items of least significance to us. Since May we have undertaken further steps towards the elimination of Japan's quotas and other trade barriers. In late July the administration decided to pursue an Article 23 GATT action against Japan's restrictive import practices on leather. We informed the Japanese of this decision in our bilateral talks of August 2–7, and are currently considering their response before seeking recourse under the GATT.

Well, in addition, we are setting up a tobacco study group to discuss reduction of high Japanese tariffs and other restrictive marketing policies on imported cigarettes, cigars, and pipe tobacco. We have also voiced our concern and are paying careful attention to discussions by Japan's lumber industry regarding the formation of an importer's cartel that could curtail imports of U.S. lumber.

At every other opportunity, including my recent visit to Japan last month, we have been emphatic that Japan must quit temporizing and move boldly toward liberalization in agricultural products.

One thing we try to make clear is that agricultural trade liberalization will not destroy Japan's agriculture. Instead, it will make it more efficient and viable in the long run. We believe to allay the fears in the Japanese agricultural community, we must as soon as possible increase the dialogue with them on possible adjustment alternatives in their foreign sector.

We are now developing our strategy for the beef and citrus talks next month. Without question, these will be the most important bilateral discussions of agriculture with the Japanese since the conclusion of the MTN in 1978. We are hopeful that the October meetings will lead to full liberalization by Japan of its beef, orange, and citrus juice markets by 1984. These markets are important to us. Since the partial liberalization achieved in the MTN, the value of exports of these three commodities together has increased by a factor of 3. U.S. beef exports, mostly high-quality beef, increased from 7,000 tons in 1977 to 26,000 tons last year. And there is the potential for further expansion.

The great discrepancy between the Japanese wholesale and import prices is indicative of that potential. Last year Japanese wholesale prices were more than four times the average price of imported beef. Under a liberalized situation, consumption and imports would increase, probably quite substantially. And U.S. high-quality beef would do very well. As internal prices fell, Japanese consumers would likely substitute higher quality cuts for those of lower quality.

In the case of fresh oranges, import prices in wholesale Japanese citrus prices are fairly close, indicating that the Japanese citrus industry is competitive and does not need the protective shield of high tariffs and import quotas.

Imports of processed food items like juices are often restricted because the raw materials with which they are made are protected. If oranges were liberalized, then orange juice should also be liberalized. Grapefruit juice should have been liberalized long ago, when the fresh grapefruit imports were opened up in 1972.

We expect success in the beef and citrus negotiations, but the challenge is formidable, and there is strong opposition in Japan. Considering the size of Japan's beef and citrus industries in relation to the whole economy, the producers of these commodities would not seem likely to be a significant political force. Most beef producers have very small herds and derive much of their income from other farm or nonfarm activities. Beef is not a staple in the Japanese diet, and neither beef nor citrus can be linked to food security interests.

Nevertheless, beef producers, representing 460,000 households, and that is out of a total of about 4,700,000 households, and citrus growers, with 300,000 households, have substantial political clout. Furthermore, a powerful cooperative organization, Zennoh, has large sums invested in slaughter, packaging, storage, and marketing facilities that depend on local beef production. And the Government of Japan itself has invested much political capital in persuading farmers to shift resources out of rice and into other crops, including citrus.

Thus, although we are optimistic, we have no illusions about the difficulties we face in the negotiations next month. And we are prepared to meet them. We recognize that Japan is our largest agricultural customer. But at the same time, with a population of well over 100 million and per capita income approaching $10,000, the Japanese market offers significant export growth potential if the barriers to agricultural trade are removed. With the continued support of the Congress and the agricultural community, we are confident that they will be removed.

That concludes my statement, Mr. Chairman. I will be glad to answer questions. And again I thank you very much for this opportunity.

Document 512

Transcript of the Department of State Daily Press Briefing, December 30, 1982 (Extract)[23]

U.S. Interest in Increased Japanese Defense Spending

. . . .

Q. Any comment about Japanese defense budget?[24]

A. Yes. Last year we applauded the Japanese defense increase as demonstrating a commendable awareness of the need for Japan to play a greater role in its own self-defense.[25]

The United States hoped that the 1982 effort represented an important step in the direction of meaningful Japanese self-defense capability, and toward an effective and significant Japanese-American division of labor dedicated to preserving peace and security.

Due to domestic financial difficulties, which faced the new Japanese Cabinet upon taking office in late November, this year's defense increase falls short of the meaningful further step which seems necessary if Japan were to achieve, within a reasonable

---

[23] Source: Office of Press Relations, Department of State. Department of State Acting Spokesman Alan Romberg conducted the briefing, which began at 12:10 p.m.

[24] Tokyo news agency Kyodo reported on December 30 that the Japanese budget for fiscal year 1983 provided for a 6.5 percent increase in defense spending.

[25] At the Daily Press Briefing on December 30, 1981, Romberg made the following statement:

"Let me say that with regard to the decision taken on the Japanese defense budget, we welcome the result which was an increase of 7.754 percent over last year.

"We welcome that as an indication of shared responsibility in the security area, in keeping with the joint communiqué between the President and Prime Minister Suzuki last May.

"We realize that in a period of budget austerity, it required strong political leadership to achieve such an outcome at a time when increases in domestic programs were being held down, just as in this country." (Office of Press Relations, Department of State)

period of time, the defense goals it has set for itself.

The United States agrees with Prime Minister Nakasone's positive statements on the need for increased Japanese defense capabilities, and we welcome the personal efforts of the Prime Minister in achieving a real increase of over 4 percent and putting emphasis on defense capability despite reductions in other government ministries. Nonetheless, we believe that more significant progress toward achieving the self-defense capabilities proposed by the Japanese Government needs to be made. The United States will, of course, continue its defense dialogue with its Japanese ally in earnest. Japan is our most important ally in the Pacific, and we look forward to working with the Japanese Government in building a more effective and equitable defense partnership.

. . . .

G. Kampuchea

Document 513

Transcript of the Department of State Daily Press Briefing, June 22, 1982 (Extract)[1]

The U.S. Position on Military Assistance to the Coalition of Khmer Groups Resisting Vietnamese Occupation

. . . .

Q. Dean, do you have any comment on the agreement reached by the three anti-Vietnamese resistance groups in Cambodia?[2]

A. Yes, I think there is something here.

We are very pleased to learn of the formation of a coalition of Khmer groups resisting the Vietnamese occupation of Kampuchea.

It is a positive step forward in providing the framework for leadership against the Vietnamese occupation, and for the ultimate self-determination for the Khmer.

This is a very important development which we welcome.

Q. Dean, will the United States offer any assistance to this coalition?

A. As you know, our position on assistance is well-known. We have given political and moral support to the non-Communists. We have also contributed heavily to international programs of emergency humanitarian relief for the Khmer people no matter where they are located.

What we do beyond that will depend on further developments and our own assessment.

I want to reiterate that we do not plan to offer military assistance, nor will we provide support of any kind to the Khmer Rouge.

Q. Can you say why? I mean, if we welcome this move, and the problem in Cambodia is the Vietnamese military occupation, why will the United States not offer military assistance?

A. Because we do not feel that conditions are appropriate at this time to justify a change in our longstanding policy.

. . . .

---

[1] Source: Office of Press Relations, Department of State. Dean Fischer, Department of State Spokesman, conducted the briefing which began at 12:42 p.m.

[2] In Kuala Lumpur on June 22, 1982, the three principal Khmer resistance leaders, Prince Norodom Sihanouk, Khieu Kamphan, and Son Sann, signed a joint declaration creating the Coalition Government of Democratic Kampuchea. Sihanouk was named president of the coalition; Son Sann became prime minister; and Khmer Rouge leader Khieu Kamphan became vice-president with responsibility for foreign affairs. The coalition government issued a declaration calling for a common struggle against Vietnamese occupation, restoration of Khmer sovereignty, and implementation of relevant U.N. General Assembly resolutions on Kampuchea. The new government pledged to operate under "principles of tripartism, equality, and nonpreponderance." The text of the coalition agreement is in Foreign Broadcast Information Service, *Daily Report: East Asia*, June 28, 1982, pp. H1–H2.

Document 514

Statement by the Assistant Secretary of State for East Asian and Pacific Affairs (Holdridge) Before Two Subcommittees of the House Foreign Affairs Committee, September 15, 1982[3]

Review of U.S. Policy Toward Kampuchea

Thank you very much, Mr. Chairman.[4] I am very pleased to appear before both subcommittees to review the administration's policy toward Kampuchea, including the Kampuchean seat in the United Nations.

Since 1970, the Khmer people have suffered immeasurably through the consequences of a destructive war, a complete restructuring of society, and now the invasion and occupation of their country by the forces of a stronger, neighboring country. I welcome the opportunity to review U.S. policy toward Kampuchea before you today.

At each U.N. General Assembly since the Vietnamese invasion and occupation of Kampuchea in 1978, Vietnam and its allies have challenged the credentials of the representative of Democratic Kampuchea. The ultimate goal of Vietnam and its friends is to seat the Heng Samrin regime, which Vietnam installed and controls. In every case, the challenge has been defeated easily through the efforts of the ASEAN governments, supported by much of Western Europe and the nonalined world, Japan, and the United States.

After careful consultation with our friends and allies, particularly the Southeast Asian countries whose interests are most threatened by the Vietnamese invasion of Kampuchea, the United States has again decided to support the position of ASEAN to continue accrediting the Democratic Kampuchea representatives. Our stand remains as in the past based on the technical ground that, having granted credentials to a representative, the U.N. can withdraw them only if there is a superior claimant to the seat.

The DK credentials have been accepted since its assumption to power in 1975, and there still is no superior claimant. The Heng Samrin regime is not a superior claimant because it was created by Vietnam, is controlled by Vietnamese officials, and is maintained in Phnom Penh only by the Vietnamese armed forces that continue to occupy Kampuchea in violation of the U.N. Charter and in defiance of General Assembly resolutions. Three in a row, Mr. Chairman.

Support for seating the Heng Samrin regime would indicate international acceptance of a government imposed by foreign aggression in violation of the U.N. Charter, Further, if Vietnam's invasion of Kampuchea were sanctioned by seating the Heng Samrin representatives in the U.N., the incentive would be reduced for a negotiated settlement, as called for by successive U.N. General Assembly Resolutions on Kampuchea since 1979 as I stated, and by the Declaration of the U.N.-sponsored International Conference on Kampuchea in July 1981.

It is important to note that those U.N. resolutions, which call for the withdrawal of Vietnamese troops and self-determination for the Khmer people, were proposed by the Third World countries of ASEAN and supported by the majority of the Third World and nonalined nations. The small and weak nations of the world clearly share ASEAN's determination to defend the principles of national integrity and noninterference, which continue to be so blatantly violated by Vietnam.

The broadening of the Democratic Kampuchea regime into a coalition of leading indigenous and independent Kampuchean political elements opposed to the Vietnamese occupation and domination of Kampuchea and broadly representative of the Khmer people should increase support for the DK claim to the U.N. seat and ASEAN's approach within and outside the U.N. this year. The coalition was achieved with significant encouragement by ASEAN.

Although the United States has not been directly involved, we welcome and endorse the coalition's formation. The coalition obviously strengthens ASEAN's strategy of gaining acceptance for the credentials of Democratic Kampuchea in the U.N., while denying the seat to the Vietnamese-controlled regime in Phnom Penh, but this is by

---

[3] Source: *The Democratic Kampuchea Seat at the United Nations and American Interests: Hearing Before the Subcommittees on Asian and Pacific Affairs and on Human Rights and International Organizations of the Committee on Foreign Affairs, House of Representatives, Ninety-seventh Congress* (Washington, 1983), pp. 15–21.

[4] Representative Stephen J. Solarz, Chairman of the Subcommittee on Asian and Pacific Affairs, presided at this hearing.

no means the only reason that the coalition is important for Kampuchea.

The coalition provides a domestic and international platform for the non-Khmer Rouge nationalist Kampucheans like Prince Sihanouk and Prime Minister Son Sann and could allow them to expand significantly their domestic and international status and support as true representatives of the Khmer people. The fact that Prince Sihanouk and His Excellency Son Sann will address the U.N. General Assembly and lead the Kampuchean delegation is an important step forward.

We believe it of major significance that the coalition gives the non-Communist Khmer the platform to play a leading role in any political settlement of Kampuchea. The Khmer people now have the hope of an eventual choice other than the Vietnamese-controlled Heng Samrin regime or the return to power of the Khmer Rouge.

Let me add here, Mr. Chairman, the allegation has been made that the coalition simply gives the Khmer Rouge a certain amount of additional status, a figleaf of respectability. We would put it the other way around, that this gives an additional democratic component to the DK, puts a democratic component into the anti-Vietnamese resistance, and therefore is capable of mobilizing a much greater degree of popular support throughout Kampuchea.

The most recent reporting from State Department officials who have interviewed Khmer who have just arrived at the Thai border reinforces this view and indicates that many Khmer are aware of the coalition, pleased with the reemergence of Prince Sihanouk and Prime Minister Son Sann, and hopeful that they will lead the country again.

I might say that I was personally in Thailand in the camps along the Cambodian border last June, and the coalition was just at that time coming into being. And I found among the people in those camps a great deal of interest and potential support for the coalition.

The formation of the coalition is another significant development in the overall ASEAN strategy of applying political, diplomatic, and economic pressure on Vietnam to negotiate a comprehensive solution to the Kampuchea problem. It is an arrangement which has as its stated purpose implementation of the Declaration of the International Conference on Kampuchea (ICK) which outlines a formula for Vietnamese military withdrawal and restoration of Khmer self-determination through full U.N. supervised elections. It is not a permanent government. Therefore, for the United States the question of recognizing the coalition does not arise. Nonetheless, I would reiterate that we welcome the formation of the coalition.

The United States has given moral and political support to the non-Communist Khmer, and will continue to do so. We have had and will continue to have regular contact with the non-Communists. We look forward to welcoming Prince Sihanouk and His Excellency Son Sann during their upcoming visits to this country. We are carefully watching developments in Kampuchea, and in close consultation with ASEAN and others are considering how we can be of further help. We do not plan to offer military aid to the coalition or any of its members. Under no circumstances would we provide any support to the Khmer Rouge, and we do not intend to deal directly with them.

Our support for the non-Communist Khmer notwithstanding, I would like to stress that our decision on the Kampuchean U.N. credentials in no way implies any support for or recognintion whatsoever of the Khmer Rouge. Our opposition to the Khmer Rouge has been open and strong. The U.S. Government has frequently and emphatically condemned the Khmer Rouge's heinous record of oppression and misrule. There should be no doubt in anybody's mind about U.S. policy toward the Khmer Rouge regime. The administration opposes the return to power of the Khmer Rouge.

In a communiqué issued July 7, Vietnam announced that as an "act of good will" it would withdraw an unspecified number of its occupying forces in Kampuchea during July, and that further partial withdrawals would depend on steps by Thailand to "reestablish peace and stability" on the Thai-Kampuchean border.

While tactically somewhat different and procedurally somewhat more flexible in tone and style, Vietnam's offer unfortunately represents no change in its essential position. It does not address the central problem in Kampuchea—Vietnamese forces occupy the entire country and Vietnamese control of the Phnom Penh authorities prevents the Khmer from exercising their basic right to independence and self-government. Total withdrawal is still tied to "ending the China threat" as Hanoi alleges, and the key issue of Kampuchea, according to Heng Samrin officials, would not be discussed under Vietnam's proposal. The proposal would permit the Heng Samrin regime to participate in the conference as if its legitimacy were a fait accompli. Accepting a partial Vietnamese withdrawal as a step toward a solution could appear to legitimize the continued presence of the remaining Vietnamese troops. In addition, Hanoi's sincerity on its intentions about withdrawal of troops from Kampuchea is highly questionable to put it mildly, Mr. Chairman. Vietnam has offered no proof of its initial "unilateral" troop withdrawal or a net reduction in Vietnamese troops in Kampuchea. We and others have concluded that the alleged withdrawal was designed only to take advantage of a planned, seasonal rotation of troops.

We still have no sign that Hanoi has abandoned its pursuit of an outdated colonialist ambition to dominate its near neighbors and inherit the mantle of hegemony of France in Indochina. While Hanoi obviously wishes to reduce the costs of its ambitions in Indochina—and their recent diplomatic offensive shows that Hanoi wishes to escape its isolation—there is no sign that the Vietnamese are prepared to abandon their goal of political and economic domination of Kampuchea and Laos, and to integrate as closely as feasible those economies into that of Vietnam. Hanoi does not appear to have realized that its colonialist ambitions undermine rather than bolster its national security.

ASEAN and most of the international community including the United States believe that the International Conference on Kampuchea [ICK][5] provides the framework for negotiation of a comprehensive political settlement in Kampuchea which could be acceptable to all concerned governments and groups and beneficial to the Khmer people. China also accepts the ICK Declaration. A just settlement on that basis would address the security concerns of all states in the region, including the ASEAN countries and Vietnam. Through the ICK Declaration ASEAN and the international community have offered Vietnam an honorable way out of its self-created dilemma and a framework to protect its own national security—in short, a way out of Kampuchea, and we support that.

With a few exceptions, the situation inside Kampuchea remains as it has been since the Vietnamese invasion in 1978. Backed by a Vietnamese occupation force, the Heng Samrin regime continues its attempts to establish legitimacy through the establishment and expansion of its administrative structure and a variety of state institutions. With implementation of a compulsory military service, it is also attempting to build an indigenous army, but with only limited success. Desertions and draft evasion, poor performance and training, as well as local accommodation with resistance units hinder these efforts. The emergency economic and agricultural conditions appear to be over largely through the efforts of the international community and the Khmer people themselves, and the regime is seeking the means to move from relief and rehabilitation to reconstruction and development in the economic sphere. International relief experts are cautiously optimistic on the current food situation, but note the probability of pockets of food shortages. Food production has been hampered by increasing efforts to collectivize production.

Until now the Phnom Penh regime has gained, at best, only the tacit acquiescence of its subjects, who generally are politically apathetic but fear a return of Khmer Rouge rule. The Heng Samrin regime skillfully exploits that fear, claiming that it and a close association with Vietnam represent the only alternative to the re-emergence of the Khmer Rouge, but there are signs that this tactic may be losing its effectiveness. The Heng Samrin regime is seen as a Vietnamese creation, and the public believes that the Vietnamese are increasing their influence and control. Fear of undisciplined Vietnamese troops, increasing suspicions of Vietnamese motives in Kampuchea, and a resurgence in Khmer nationalism are causing resentment toward the Vietnamese presence to rise. Forced labor and conscription have heightened popular disaffection toward the regime and the Vietnamese. It will be difficult for the Phnom Penh regime to generate popular enthusiasm or attract dedicated administrators to solve the staggering economic, social, and political problems still facing the country. The participation of Prince Sihanouk and Son Sann in the coalition further makes it difficult for the Heng Samrin regime to consolidate its control and to establish a claim to legitimacy.

The Vietnamese manage their occupation of Kampuchea heavily supported by Soviet supplies and are engaged in military operations throughout the country. We believe that Hanoi recently has increased its

[5] All bracketed notes appear in the source text.

military strength by upgrading its equipment and improving its logistics, particularly in the Thai border area. Vietnamese military and political objectives are to eliminate or neutralize the Khmer resistance and consolidate the position of the Heng Samrin regime, including its domestic and international acceptance.

Khmer Rouge forces were unable to recover all of the territory in western Kampuchea taken by the Vietnamese during the previous dry season. Popular support for the Khmer Rouge has not increased, and is unlikely to do so. The Khmer Rouge, however, remain the principal military resistance to the Vietnamese occupation, and while pressed hard during the dry season earlier this year, their units remain intact, strong, and a problem for the Vietnamese.

The Khmer People's National Liberation Front [KPNLF] remains the largest and most active noncommunist resistance group operating in Kampuchea. The number and efficiency of Prince Sihanouk's military forces have increased in recent months. Both non-Communist groups have numerous sympathizers. Both groups say material shortages have inhibited efforts to increase their military and popular support and their activities. Although they have attempted to increase their military activities to a limited degree, they are aware of their current limitations and have not sought a major combat role.

It is still too early to assess fully the impact of the coalition on popular support for the resistance or the Heng Samrin regime. Initial reports from inside Kampuchea suggest that many Khmer are taking a wait-and-see attitude, but that they are aware of the coalition's formation, pleased with the more active role being taken by Prince Sihanouk, and hopeful that the coalition may offer them an alternative to a Kampuchea under a Vietnamese-controlled or Khmer Rouge regime. There is a tremendous reservoir of popular support for Prince Sihanouk among rural Khmer, which has improved Khmer perceptions of the coalition. There is also strong sympathy for Son Sann among those urban, educated, and civil servant groups that survived the Khmer Rouge purges. The potential support for these two Khmer nationalists and for the coalition is strong, but it remains to be fully mobilized. The coalition is not likely to affect popular distrust for the Khmer Rouge, which remains an anathema to most Khmer.

The Heng Samrin regime has reacted vehemently and defensively to the formation of the coalition. It is going to great lengths to discredit the coalition and its members. Its criticism of Prince Sihanouk has been especially harsh. Khmer suspected of association with any of the resistance groups in some cases appear to be imprisoned summarily without trial or recourse.

As I mentioned in my statement before this committee last July 15,[6] the ASEAN states are in firm agreement that their goals regarding Kampuchea are total withdrawal of Vietnamese troops and a neutral, independent Kampuchea. Their goal is a political, rather than military, settlement of the problem.

ASEAN is the keystone of U.S. policy toward Kampuchea and Indochina. We fully support ASEAN's strategy and respect ASEAN's leadership role in the region. We share ASEAN's goals as elaborated in the ICK Declaration and work with ASEAN to realize its objectives. We, too, strongly favor a comprehensive political settlement.

Like ASEAN, we remain convinced that Hanoi itself must realize the disastrous results its policies have produced and that those policies must be changed to reconcile Vietnam's ambitions with its interests. We cannot predict when such a change of mind might occur in Hanoi. The choice for Hanoi does exist, nonetheless. In the meantime, the international community must continue to stress the unacceptability of Hanoi's behavior and the durability of our opposition to its occupation of Kampuchea.

Thank you very much, Mr. Chairman.

---

[6] Holdridge made this statement in a hearing on July 15, 1982. See *U.S. Policies and Programs in Southeast Asia: Hearings Before the Sub-Committee on East Asian and Pacific Affairs of the Committee on Foreign Relations, U.S. Senate, Ninety-seventh Congress, Second Session* (Washington, 1982), pp. 147–152.

Document 515

Transcript of the Department of State Daily Press Briefing, October 8, 1982 (Extracts)[7]

Prince Sihanouk and Son Sann Meet With Vice President Bush and Secretary of State Shultz

. . . .

Finally, a statement regarding the visit of Prince Sihanouk and Prime Minister Son Sann.

The Secretary met with Khmer non-Communist resistance leaders Prince Sihanouk and Prime Minister Son Sann in New York on October 6. This morning they were the guests of the Vice President at breakfast. Both the Secretary and the Vice President emphasized our support for ASEAN's strategy on Kampuchea, including the implementation of the Declaration of the International Conference on Kampuchea, which calls for the total withdrawal of foreign forces from Kampuchea and the restoration of Kampuchean independence.

The Vice President and the Secretary also indicated our moral and political support for the non-Communist Kampucheans and expressed appreciation for Prince Sihanouk's and Prime Minister Son Sann's leadership. Prince Sihanouk and Prime Minister Son Sann expressed the appreciation of the Khmer people to the United States for its humanitarian support for the Kampuchean refugees.

I'll be happy to take your questions.

Q. Was there any discussion of assistance to the non-Communist Kampucheans?

A. They did not ask for assistance.

. . . .

Q. On the meetings with Prince Sihanouk, since he and Son Sann have both previously asked for aid from outside parties, can you at least give us an explanation why the United States only gives moral and political support?

A. We have also contributed to international programs of emergency humanitarian relief for the Khmer people. I don't have a specific response to you beyond that except to emphasize that in any event we don't plan to provide military assistance, and, of course, we will provide no assistance to the Khmer Rouge.

. . . .

[7] Source: Office of Press Relations, Department of State. Alan Romberg, Department of State Acting Spokesman, conducted the briefing which began at 12:33 p.m.

Document 516

Statement by the Representative at the United Nations (Kirkpatrick) Before the U.N. General Assembly, October 25, 1982[8]

Explanation of the U.S. Vote on the Credentials of Democratic Kampuchea

The United States continues to support the credentials of Democratic Kampuchea on technical grounds. Democratic Kampuchea's credentials are clearly in compliance with the General Assembly's rules of procedure. This fact has been recognized by the Secretary General in his report to the Credentials Committee,[9] which has accepted the Khmer credentials. The past three General Assemblies also have affirmed this.

The United States support for Democratic Kampuchea's credentials is based on

[8] Source: U.S. Mission to the United Nations Press Release USUN 92 (82), October 25, 1982. The U.N. General Assembly voted (90 (United States) to 29 with 26 abstentions) on October 25, 1982, to seat the representatives of Democratic Kampuchea by rejecting an amendment by Laos in U.N. document A/37/L.8 to approve the report "except with regard to the credentials of Democratic Kampuchea."

[9] According to the First Report of the Credentials Committee, October 14, 1982, the Secretary-General reported to the committee on October 5 that as of that date Democratic Kampuchea was one of 90 Member States to have submitted its credentials in accordance with the General Assembly's rules of procedure. (U.N. document A/37/543)

the ground that, in the absence of a superior claimant, there is no basis for rejection of Democratic Kampuchea's credentials, which have been accepted since 1975. There is no superior claimant. Certainly the Heng Samrin regime is not a superior claimant. It was created by Vietnam's invasion of Kampuchea 4 years ago, and is sustained by Vietnam's occupation force. It is controlled by Vietnamese officials both in Phnom Penh and in Hanoi. The Vietnam which would have us reject Democratic Kampuchea's credentials is also, we would underscore, the Vietnam which continues to defy three successive General Assembly resolutions on Kampuchea as well as the Declaration of the International Conference on Kampuchea, all of which call for the withdrawal of her troops and the end of her occupation of Kampuchea.

Support by the United States for the credentials of Democratic Kampuchea does not diminish our concern for human rights violations in Kampuchea, particularly from 1975 to 1978 during Khmer Rouge rule. The United States has repeatedly spoken against these heinous abuses and gross misrule of the Khmer Rouge and will continue to disassociate itself from those responsible for them.

However, this year the United States welcomes the broadened base on which Democratic Kampuchea rests as a result of the formation last June of the Coalition of Democratic Kampuchea. Now, with the inclusion of Prince Sihanouk as President and Mr. Son Sann as Prime Minister, the Coalition of Democratic Kampuchea is clearly more representative of the Kampuchean nation.

We welcome the participation of Prince Sihanouk and Prime Minister Son Sann in the deliberations of the General Assembly. We have been impressed with the response given to this new leadership by the Khmer people who have an alternative to the grim choice between the Khmer Rouge and a regime imposed by Vietnam. The inauguration of the Coalition also constitues a major step in implementing the General Assembly's basic policy for a resolution of the Kampuchean crisis—that embodied in the Declaration of the International Conference on Kampuchea held in July, 1981 and in GA Resolutions 34/22, 35/6 and 36/5.[10]

Prince Sihanouk, in addressing this assembly 3 weeks ago,[11] put succinctly Kampuchea's plea to the United Nations:

> "We ask but restoration of our national sovereignty, our territorial integrity, and once that is achieved, we solemnly commit ourselves to live in perfect, peaceful coexistence with all our neighbors, and amongst the first with Vietnam, as will all other countries who respect us, no matter what their political and social systems may be. Is this an unreasonable demand, an impossible pretension?"

My government believes it is neither unreasonable nor impossible. It is rather the minimum that this body must support in line with its own past commitments, with the principles of the United Nations Charter, and with the peace and stability of Southeast Asia.

Thank you, Mr. President.

Document 517

Statement by the Alternate Representative to the Thirty-seventh U.N. General Assembly (Sherman) Before the U.N. General Assembly, October 27, 1982[12]

"Vietnam's Action Against Kampuchea Gravely Violates the Charter of the United Nations"

Mr. President, for the fourth consecutive year the General Assembly is considering the matter of Kampuchea's military occupation by neighboring Vietnam, a situation denying the Kampuchean people their right to self-determination. Vietnam's action against Kampuchea gravely violates the Charter of the United Nations. Its aggression in Kampuchea also poses a threat to its other neighbors in Southeast Asia. Vietnam persists in defiance of resolutions of the last three sessions of the General Assembly and of the Declaration of the International Conference on Kampuchea, brought together

[10] For U.N. General Assembly Resolution 34/22, adopted on November 14, 1979, see *American Foreign Policy: Basic Documents, 1977–1980*, pp. 1052–1053; for Resolution 35/6, adopted October 22, 1980, see footnote 7, *ibid.*, p. 1052; for Resolution 36/5, adopted October 21, 1981, see *American Foreign Policy: Current Documents, 1981*, document 552.

[11] For the full text of Prince Sihanouk's address before the Assembly, September 30, 1982, see U.N. document A/37/PV.11.

[12] Source: U.S. Mission to the United Nations Press Release USUN 96 (82), October 27, 1982.

under the leadership of the Association of Southeast Asian Nations and sponsored by the United Nations. Indeed, it is no overstatement to say that Vietnam's aggression against a smaller, weaker neighbor—if it continues unchecked in this time of threatening international anarchy—undermines the security of weaker states everywhere.

In Phnom Penh there is a Kampuchean dictator installed and maintained in office only by the presence throughout the country of some 180,000 soldiers of the Socialist Republic of Vietnam. Vietnam in turn is heavily dependent upon supplies from the Soviet Union, and the services of some 10,000 Soviet military advisers in Vietnam, in order to maintain its military occupation of Kampuchea.

The regime installed by the Vietnamese Army in Phnom Penh denies its subjects fundamental freedoms of speech, press and association. Free elections are unknown under the rule of the figurehead leader, Heng Samrin. Outspoken opponents and others merely suspected of dissent have been imprisoned or have disappeared. This regime strictly curtails the freedom of the Kampuchean people to pursue the economic, social, and cultural development of their families, of their towns and villages, and of their nation.

As a regime of foreign occupation, the so-called "People's Republic of Kampuchea" is breaking apart Kampuchean cultural and national integrity in favor of an elaborate system of Vietnamese colonial domination. A number of former high-ranking functionaries of the Heng Samrin regime have cast aside their privileges and risked their very lives to become refugees at the Thai border. From Hanoi one hears that occupied Kampuchea actually is "liberated" Kampuchea, and it is true that Hanoi's armies drove the Khmer Rouge from Phnom Penh. But let us not forget that Hanoi, together with its allies in Moscow and elsewhere, materially and enthusiastically supported the coming to power of the Khmer Rouge. Hanoi provided training to Khmer Rouge cadre before the Khmer Rouge capture of Phnom Penh in 1975, and Hanoi supported the Khmer Rouge regime's program of mass murder and ideological nihilism until the Khmer Rouge became, from Hanoi's hegemonistic perspective, too independent.

If the Vietnamese in Kampuchea are truly liberators, then we must ask why nearly 180,000 Vietnamese troops are required to keep the Kampuchean people from overthrowing it. We must ask why the Vietnamese occupation authorities will not allow the safe, legal, and orderly repatriation of those Kampuchean peasants now displaced in Thailand, who are willing to risk returning to their farms. We must ask as well why the Vietnamese occupation forces continue to shell heavily civilian concentrations of nationalist Khmer near the Thai border. We must ask why the Vietnamese, following the example given in Afghanistan by their Soviet patrons, are employing chemical weapons against Khmer freedom fighters.

Mr. President, we have stressed the hardship and injustice imposed on the Kampuchean people by the Vietnamese invasion, and we have underlined also the threat this aggressive behavior poses to the other states of the region. In fairness we should also take note of the hardship Vietnam's occupation of Kampuchea is causing the Vietnamese people themselves. Already one of the 20 poorest nations in the world, Vietnam has amassed the world's third largest standing army. The heavy price for this policy of military aggression is being paid for not only by the beleaguered draftees of the Vietnamese Army, but also by the heavily taxed farmers and laborers of Vietnam, and the dependent mothers and children of that unhappy and unfree country.

Mr. President, while the Kampuchean people now living under the Vietnamese-imposed dictatorship suffer a lack of freedom to pursue personal, social and economic fulfillment according to their abilities, some Kampucheans have fled and remain outside the control of Heng Samrin and the Vietnamese simply in order to enjoy some greater degree of freedom to pursue their aspirations. The people and Government of the Kingdom of Thailand, at no small sacrifice to their own economic and social needs, temporarily have given harbor to hundreds of thousands of Kampuchean refugees fleeing oppression and famine induced by totalitarian policies. Thailand deserves our profound thanks. Moreover, the United Nations system, supported by free, generous, and civilized people and their governments, deserves great credit. It has provided generous and ready assistance to Kampucheans who fled their homes in order to find their way back to the ground of freedom and dignity.

Special recognition should be accorded to His Excellency, Mr. Poul Hartling, the United Nations High Commissioner for Refugees, for the outstanding and indispensable work he and his office have performed in protecting and sustaining the refugees in Thailand and in assisting in the resettlement of many of the Kampucheans to third countries. The Secretary General and his special representative for humanitarian assistance to the Kampuchean people, Sir Robert Jackson, deserve our praise for mounting a complex joint mission in international aid for desperately hungry and needy Kampucheans in Thailand, in the border area, and in the interior of Kampuchea itself.

Generous assistance from free world governments and voluntary agencies has helped to banish famine from Kampuchea. The Kampucheans seeking haven in Thailand and at the border, however, clearly will require international assistance for some time, and it remains imperative for the well-being of these refugees and displaced persons that the Secretary General continue to lead the coordination of this assistance, and that governments continue to contribute to the effort.

Mr. President, we have before us a resolution offering the framework for a comprehensive settlement of the political situation that has imposed such great suffering upon the Kampuchean people.[13] The resolution, offered by members of the Association of Southeast Asian Nations and more than 40 other United Nations members, reaffirms declarations by the past three sessions of this Assembly. The essential elements of the ASEAN nations' proposal for a settlement in Kampuchea are simple: first, the withdrawal of all foreign forces; and, second, the enabling of the Kampuchean people freely to choose their government. We have in the past indicated our strong support for the course which ASEAN members have proposed; we are pleased to do so again today.

The pending resolution reaffirms not only these principles, which are essential for peace anywhere, but also the framework for a just Kampuchean settlement established last year in New York at the International Conference on Kampuchea. If followed in good faith by the responsible parties, the prescriptions of the International Conference would bring about the supervised withdrawal of all foreign forces, guarantees of public authorities' respect for the fundamental human rights of the Kampuchean people; a process of free elections to let the Kampuchean people choose a truly Kampuchean Government; and safeguards to respect the sovereignty, independence, and neutrality of the Kampuchean nation. The United Nations would be given the solemn responsibility of guaranteeing the fairness, openness, and honesty of each of these processes.

The International Conference on Kampuchea provides a fair and honorable mechanism for the Vietnamese to withdraw from Kampuchea. In contrast, Vietnam has put forward a counterproposal calling for a regional peace conference that blandly ignores the greatest violation of peace in the region, Vietnam's occupation of Kampuchea. Vietnam makes claims that it has withdrawn some of its troops, but all information is to the contrary. Vietnam has made no reduction of its forces in Kampuchea, but simply has traded units and in the end has reinforced its army of occupation. With the other participants in the International Conference we reiterate our call for Vietnam to move away from this sterile and uncooperative posture and to join in good faith a resumed International Conference on Kampuchea.

Mr. President, my delegation regards with appreciation the appearance in this Assembly of His Royal Highness Prince Norodom Sihanouk and of His Excellency, Mr. Son Sann, representatives of Kampuchean people struggling for the restoration in their country of national independence, personal freedom, the democratic process and the rule of reason and law. Their participation in the coalition of democratic Kampuchea gives substance to hopes that popular, democratic, nationalist Kampuchean movements will provide the Khmer with an alternative to the grim choice between the Khmer Rouge and a Vietnamese-dominated Kampuchea.

Prince Sihanouk expressed a love of peace and a will toward understanding shared by civilized people everywhere when he told this Assembly:

> "I feel no hate towards Vietnam. I have never ceased to recognize that the geographical position of our two countries make them neighbors to the end of time and that they are, because of this, compelled to understand each other and to listen to each other. This understanding, however, can only be established between equals and not between servant and master."

As Prince Sihanouk has made clear, and as the leaders of ASEAN have affirmed, the resolution before us today in no way threat-

[13] For text as adopted, see *infra*.

ens the independence and security of Vietnam, Laos, the Soviet Union, or any other nations globally or regionally concerned with the situation in Cambodia. On the contrary, restoring respect for the sanctity of international borders in Southeast Asia and for the fundamental human rights of the people of Kampuchea, will enhance the peace, stability, and well-being of that vital and tormented region, and beyond it, of all regions torn by armed conflict between states.

Mr. President, at this General Assembly, many of us have called attention to the United Nations' failure to deal resolutely and effectively with international aggression. The pattern of aggression is sadly familiar to us all: The aggressor acts swiftly; he overwhelms his weaker adversary; and then he defies the international community to act. The aggressor's hope is to present us with a fait accompli. Over time, he expects that our concern with the fate of his victims will diminish, that our opposition to his "irreversible situation" will ebb. Eventually, the aggressor expects that we will all return to "business as usual."

If we in the General Assembly truly wish to strengthen peacekeeping efforts of the United Nations, I can think of no better place to begin than in Kampuchea. Over the past 3 years, the General Assembly has stood firm against Vietnam's aggression, has supported the constructive efforts of ASEAN, and has insisted that Vietnam totally withdraw from occupied Kampuchea. This year, we have an opportunity, in the form of this resolution on the situation in Kampuchea, to renew our commitment to the goal of an independent and free Kampuchea as well as to the principles of the United Nations Charter which defend all U.N. members against aggression and the world against anarchy. My government asks all United Nations members truly desirous of strengthening our institution to join us in support of the resolution.

Document 518

Resolution 37/6 (1982), Adopted by the U.N. General Assembly, October 28, 1982[14]

The Situation in Kampuchea

The General Assembly,

Recalling its resolutions 34/22 of 14 November 1979, 35/6 of 22 October 1980 and 36/5 of 21 October 1981,

Further recalling the Declaration on Kampuchea and resolution 1 (I) adopted by the International Conference on Kampuchea, held at United Nations Headquarters from 13 to 17 July 1981, which offer the negotiating framework for a comprehensive political settlement of the Kampuchean problem,

Taking note of the report of the Secretary-General on the implementation of General Assembly resolution 36/5,[15]

Noting the recent developments resulting in the coalition with Samdech Norodom Sihanouk as President of Democratic Kampuchea,

Deploring that foreign armed intervention and occupation continue and that foreign forces have not been withdrawn from Kampuchea, thus causing continuing hostilities in that country and seriously threatening international peace and security,

Greatly concerned that the continuing deployment of foreign forces in Kampuchea near the Thai-Kampuchean border has maintained tension in the region,

Gravely disturbed that the continued fighting and instability in Kampuchea have forced Kampucheans to flee to the Thai-Kampuchean border in search of food and safety,

Recognizing that the assistance extended by the international community has continued to reduce the food shortages and health problems of the Kampuchean people,

Emphasizing that it is the inalienable right of the Kampuchean people who have sought refuge in neighbouring countries to return safely to their homeland,

---

[14] Source: U.N. General Assembly Resolution 37/6. This resolution was introduced by 49 nations and was adopted by a vote of 105 (United States) to 23 with 20 abstentions.

[15] U.N. document A/37/496.

Emphasizing further that no effective solution to the humanitarian problems can be achieved without a comprehensive political settlement of the Kampuchean conflict,

Convinced that, to bring about durable peace in South-East Asia, there is an urgent need for a comprehensive political solution to the Kampuchean problem which will provide for the withdrawal of all foreign forces and ensure respect for the sovereignty, independence, territorial integrity and neutral and non-aligned status of Kampuchea, as well as the right of the Kampuchean people to self-determination free from outside interference,

Convinced further that, after the comprehensive political settlement of the Kampuchean question through peaceful means, the countries of the South-East Asian region can pursue efforts to establish a zone of peace, freedom and neutrality in South-East Asia so as to lessen international tensions and to achieve lasting peace in the region,

Reaffirming the need for all States to adhere strictly to the principles of the Charter of the United Nations, which call for respect for the national independence, sovereignty and territorial integrity of all States, non-intervention and non-interference in the internal affairs of States, non-recourse to the threat or use of force, and peaceful settlement of disputes,

1. *Reaffirms* its resolutions 34/22, 35/6 and 36/5 and calls for their full implementation;

2. *Reiterates its conviction* that the withdrawal of all foreign forces from Kampuchea, the restoration and preservation of its independence, sovereignty and territorial integrity, the right of the Kampuchean people to determine their own destiny and the commitment by all States to non-interference and non-intervention in the internal affairs of Kampuchea are the principal components of any just and lasting resolution to the Kampuchean problem;

3. *Takes note with appreciation* of the report of the *Ad Hoc* Committee of the International Conference on Kampuchea[16] and requests that the Committee continue its work, pending the reconvening of the Conference;

4. *Authorizes* the *Ad Hoc* Committee to convene when necessary and to carry out the tasks entrusted to it in its mandate;

5. *Reaffirms* its decision to reconvene the Conference at an appropriate time in accordance with Conference resolution 1 (I);

6. *Renews its appeal* to all States of South-East Asia and others concerned to attend future sessions of the Conference;

7. *Requests* the Conference to report to the General Assembly on its future sessions;

8. *Requests* the Secretary-General to continue to consult with and assist the Conference and the *Ad Hoc* Committee and to provide them on a regular basis with the necessary facilities to carry out their functions;

9. *Expresses its appreciation once again* to the Secretary-General for taking appropriate steps in following the situation closely and requests him to continue to do so and to exercise his good offices in order to contribute to a comprehensive political settlement;

10. *Expresses its deep appreciation once again* to donor countries, the United Nations and its agencies and other national and international humanitarian organizations which have rendered relief assistance to the Kampuchean people, and appeals to them to continue existing arrangements to assist those Kampucheans who are still in need, especially along the Thai-Kampuchean border and in the holding centres in Thailand;

11. *Reiterates its deep appreciation* to the Secretary-General for his efforts in co-ordinating humanitarian relief assistance and in monitoring its distribution, and requests him to continue such efforts as are necessary;

12. *Urges* the countries of South-East Asia, once a comprehensive political solution to the Kampuchean conflict is achieved, to exert renewed efforts to establish a zone of peace, freedom and neutrality in South-East Asia;

13. *Reiterates the hope* that, following a comprehensive political solution, an intergovernmental committee will be established to consider a programme of assistance to Kampuchea for the reconstruction of its economy and for the economic and social development of all States in the region;

14. *Requests* the Secretary-General to submit to the General Assembly at its thirty-eighth session a report on the implementation of the present resolution;

15. *Decides* to include in the provisional agenda of its thirty-eighth session the item entitled "The situation in Kampuchea".

---

[16] U.N. document A/CONF.109/6.

H. Korea

Document 519

Joint Communiqué of the Fourteenth Annual Republic of Korea–United States Security Consultative Meeting, Seoul, March 31, 1982[1]

U.S.–Republic of Korea Security Consultations

The Fourteenth Annual Security Consultative Meeting between the Republic of Korea and the United States of America was held in Seoul on March 30 and 31, 1982.

Minister of National Defense Choo Young Bock and Secretary of Defense Caspar W. Weinberger led their respective delegations, which included senior foreign affairs and defense officials of both countries. Prior to the meeting, the chairman of the Joint Chiefs of Staff of the two countries presided over the ROK–U.S. Military Committee meeting on March 29, 1982.

Secretary Weinberger, during his stay in Korea, paid a courtesy call on President Chun Doo Hwan. The Secretary visited major military bases and observed the ROK–U.S. joint military exercise, "Team Spirit'82."

On the centennial of Korean-United States relations, the two delegations, noting with satisfaction that the traditional ties of security cooperation have been steadily promoted between the two countries, pledged to develop further such cooperative relations in the interests of the peace and stability of Northeast Asia and the Pacific region.

Reviewing the security situation in Asia and the Pacific area with special reference to Korean Peninsula, the two delegations agreed in their appraisal of the threat to security in the region. The discussion included the possible impact of the regional situation on the security interests of both the Republic of Korea and the United States.

In particular, Minister Choo and Secretary Weinberger shared the view that the continuing military buildup of North Korea and its aggressive posture posed a major threat to the security of the Republic of Korea as well as to peace and stability in the region. In this connection, they had full deliberations on combined ROK–U.S. measures to deal effectively with the North Korean threat.

The two sides reaffirmed that the security of the Republic of Korea is pivotal to the peace and stability of Northeast Asia and, in turn, vital to the security of the United States.

Secretary Weinberger, reaffirming that the United States will remain a Pacific power, reiterated the firm commitment of the United States to render prompt and effective assistance to repel armed invasion against the Republic of Korea—which constitutes a common danger—in accordance with the Korean-United States Mutual Defense Treaty of 1954.[2] He also confirmed that the United States nuclear umbrella will continue to provide additional security to the Republic of Korea.

Minister Choo and Secretary Weinberger agreed that the reinforced U.S. forces in Korea not only attest to the United States firm resolve to help defend Korea, but render a significant contribution to the peace and stability of Northeast Asia.

Minister Choo and Secretary Weinberger, expressing satisfaction with the effective functioning of the ROK–U.S. combined force command, agreed to continue common efforts to enhance further the ROK–U.S. combined defense capabilities.

Secretary Weinberger outlined the ongoing efforts to upgrade U.S. ground combat forces and deploy A–10's and F–16's in Korea and pledged to carry on the modernization of U.S. forces in Korea.

The two sides agreed to continue to improve their early warning capabilities, to broaden the exchange of strategic information and to further develop ROK–U.S. joint military exercises.

Minister Choo and Secretary Weinberger reviewed the progress of the Republic of Korea's force improvement plan and the development of the Korean defense industry. Minister Choo and Secretary

[1] Source: *Public Statements of Secretary of Defense Weinberger,* 1982.

[2] Signed at Washington, October 1, 1953; entered into force, November 17, 1954; for text, see 5 UST 2368.

Weinberger, noting with satisfaction the ROK–U.S. cooperation to date in this area, had close consultations on concrete steps to widen the scope of such cooperation.

Secretary Weinberger assured Minister Choo that, subject to consultations with and the approval of the Congress and other appropriate agencies, the United States would continue to seek to improve the terms for the provision of FMS credits to the Republic of Korea.

Minister Choo and Secretary Weinberger agreed to further step up mutual cooperation for the development of Korean defense industry including the use of Korean facilities for the maintenance of United States defense equipment.

Minister Choo and Secretary Weinberger agreed to update and continue to develop the current wartime resupply requirements study and jointly to augment stockpiles of war reserve material with a view to enhancing combat readiness in the event of a contingency on the Korean Peninsula. To this end, they signed an agreement covering the expeditious transfer of war material to the Korean Government in the event of emergency.

Minister Choo and Secretary Weinberger shared the view that it is essential for the establishment of lasting peace of the Korean Peninsula to ease tensions and create an atmosphere for national reconciliation through dialogue between the South and the North of Korea.

Particularly, Secretary Weinberger expressed his full support for the far-reaching "proposal for democratic reunification through national reconciliation" put forward by President Chun Doo Hwan on January 22, 1982.[3]

Both sides reconfirmed that the effective functioning of the United Nations Command as a peace keeping mechanism holds continuing importance until alternative arrangements can be agreed upon to ensure lasting peace on the Korean Peninsula.

Minister Choo and Secretary Weinberger supported the United Nations Command's proposal that each side of the military armistice commission invite the other to observe major military exercises on the Korean Peninsula.

[3] President Chun's proposal was made in an address to the National Assembly in Seoul; for text, see Foreign Broadcast Information Service, *Daily Report: Asia & Pacific,* January 26, 1982, pp. E1–E11.

The two delegations agreed to continue close consultations through the year on security matters of mutual concern.

Both sides reconfirmed the importance of the Annual Security Consultative Meeting and agreed to hold the next meeting in the United States of America in 1983.

Secretary Weinberger expressed the sincere appreciation of the U.S. delegation for the courtesy and hospitality of the Government of the Republic of Korea and for the excellent arrangements which led to a productive and successful meeting.

Document 520

Address by Vice President Bush Before the Republic of Korea National Assembly, Seoul, April 26, 1982[4]

"We Will Remain a Faithful Ally"

Speaker Chung, Vice Speakers Choe and Kim, distinguished members of the National Assembly. This is my first visit to Korea. I hope it will not be my last. On arriving I was struck by two things. The first was how close we are here to the DMZ; and the realization of how much a part of everyday life in Seoul that proximity is. The second was how amazed and touched I was by the warmth of the public reception. I have always heard about Korean hospitality and graciousness. Yesterday, what had only been general knowledge became a firsthand experience. Please thank the people you represent. They made me feel very welcome, just as you have by inviting me to speak to you today.

We celebrate this year a century of friendship between the Government and peoples of the United States and Korea—100 years. That is not such a long time, perhaps, in the march of human history; but 100 years is one-half of the United States life as a nation. That we have been friends so long, in a world that, in those 100 years has seen enough conflict and hatred to last a millenium, is cause for great joy.

I carry with me the greetings and the friendship of the people of the United

[4] Source: Press Release, April 26, 1982, Office of the Press Secretary to the Vice President; also printed in Department of State *Bulletin,* August 1982, pp. 41–43.

States and of President Reagan. What I have to say here today I say on their behalf. I am glad to be able to give my message to you, representing as you do the Korean people. I am honored that you called this body into special session in order to hear it.

Legislative bodies such as this National Assembly are where the people's business should be conducted. I myself am well enough acquainted with legislative branches to know that they are not always tranquil. Indeed, sometimes they are rather noisy.

Long ago, Simon Bolivar, one of the great liberators of the Western Hemisphere, said that " . . . the majority of men hold as a truth the humiliating principle that it is harder to maintain the balance of liberty than to endure the weight of tyranny."[5] This is even true of our own times. Our own Congress is sometimes full of noise. But we would have it no other way.

In the North, there is no truly representative Congress. Instead only a great silence: the silence of despotism and one-man rule. This silence is broken by the occasional sounds of violence, as it was last week when four who sought freedom were killed by their own countrymen as they made their way to freer soil.

The occasion of 100 years of relations is a fitting time to emphasize the continuity of our friendship. We will remain a faithful ally. We will remain a reliable ally. We are partners in the non-Communist world. That especially makes our bond a sacred one. If America once lectured her friends and apologized to her adversaries, that day is over.

During the height of the Vietnam war, a message was passed to President Nixon. It was from Henry Kissinger, then a professor at Harvard. The message said, "The word is going out that it may be dangerous to be America's enemy, but it is fatal to be her friend." As long as Ronald Reagan sits in the Oval Office of the White House, no one will be able to say this about the United States.

We live in a world full of tensions, tensions which complicate our search for a lasting peace. The United States is a Pacific power, and Korea is one of our most vital allies. The purpose of America's presence in Korea is to protect and preserve the peace which both our countries fought so hard to bring about. The United States will remain a power in Korea only as long as we are welcome. It is not our desire to dominate the non-Communist world; only to be a vital partner in it, and to be a friend upon whom our friends can rely.

The United States is proud to have as its friend and ally a country such as Korea, where economic miracles occur. Twenty years ago, this was a poor country.

Political scientists study South Korea as a model for economic development. Kim Kyung Won has explained part of the Korean success this way: "It is," he said, "the culture of discipline and postponing immediate satisfaction for the future—even for posterity."

According to an international labor organization study, South Koreans work longer hours than any other people on earth. This industriousness has given you one of the most dynamic economies of the 20th century. Between 1970 and 1980, the volume of trade between our two countries has increased hugely: from $531 million to $10 billion.

The United States is, of course, a vital market for Korean goods; and vice versa. President Reagan has made it clear that he will do all he can to keep the U.S. market open. There are few other advocates of free trade as ardent as he. And naturally his job in persuading those who regulate the market to keep it open will be made easier if our trading partners are prepared to make the same pledge. Korea is our ninth largest trading partner, and we expect it will become even more important in the years ahead. Because, among other things, your economy is expanding so rapidly. Your growth rate last year was 14 percent. By sharp contrast, the North has one-fourth the output of the South. One-half of the North's work force is required to feed its people; in the South, little more than one-third is needed to fulfill that task. Your hard work and determination to bring about these economic successes have validated, in the eyes of the world community, the United States decision to help you sustain your freedom.

Against this background of extraordinary economic achievement, the opportunities for pluralism are strong. President Chun, the first Head of State President Reagan received at the White House, spoke of a new era in the Republic of Korea, an era of "renewal of the spirit of national harmony, replacing the old chronic and internecine battles between those who take rigid and extreme positions." He spoke of

[5] All ellipses appear in the source text.

an era of "dialogue" and "consensus-building." He spoke of a "freer, more abundant, and Democratic society in our midst."[6]

We support this philosophy with all our heart. And we look to President Chun and to this Assembly to build on such a commitment, the foundation stones of which have already been laid.

In a Democracy, legislatures are the only true means of determining the will of the people. Democracy, as President Abraham Lincoln defined it for us long ago, consists of " . . . government of the people, by the people, for the people." To be sure, the people speak with many voices; but in free countries, as someone once observed, every man is entitled to express his opinions, and every man is entitled not to listen.

Some countries have a fear of pluralism, and only the preordained few control the destinies of the many. One country in our own hemisphere, Nicaragua, overthrew an autocratic, repressive regime, promising that the new order would be pluralistic and Democratic, promising that all Nicaraguans would have a voice in their new government. Unfortunately, the rulers of that new Nicaragua subsequently found one excuse after another for postponing elections, closing down the newspapers, and jailing the opposition. The United States regrets this, just as it regrets the suppression of Democratic practices in all countries, friend or foe. We see political diversity as a source of strength, not weakness.

There is an ancient Chinese curse that says, "May you live in interesting times." We live today in interesting times—though I think that is more a challenge than a curse. The most important task facing us as partners is preserving peace.

The very close cooperation between the United States and Korea is a matter of record. The United States will try to build on new relations, such as the one we have with the People's Republic of China, but not at the expense of our longstanding friendships.

A great American poet once wrote that, "Most of the change we think we see in life is due to truths being in and out of favor." The policy of deterrence has served us well in the past; why should it not continue to serve us well in the future? I sympathize with those intellectual quarters who devote themselves to the search for new solutions.

But that does not mean the old solutions are no longer valuable. The essence of deterrence is that where there is balance, there is safety. This policy has kept the peace in Korea since 1954. The world has seen a great many wars in our time. Since NATO was founded in 1948, for instance, about 150 wars have broken out. In this troubled century, 28 years of peace on this peninsula amounts to a proud legacy.

The quest for lasting peace involves more than merely maintaining the status quo. This is why President Reagan has been trying hard to encourage the Soviet Union to work with the United States in finding a way to bring about real and verifiable nuclear arms reduction. And that is also why the United States so strongly supports the bold and imaginative initiative of President Chun toward a reunification of the two Koreas.

I would take this opportunity to urge Kim Il-song to respond to President Chun in the same spirit. The United States will be glad to discuss new ideas with the North, in conjunction with the South. We have no intention of talking to the North alone.

Here let me make an important point about the foreign policy of Ronald Reagan: he is anxious to pursue all avenues toward dialogue, believing as he does that the best way to bring about dialogue is to seek it from a position of strength. It is a truism of foreign policy that an adversary is more likely to negotiate if it is to his advantage to negotiate. If, for instance, the United States were to remove its military force from all over the world, what incentive for restraint in international behavior would remain for the Soviets? Thus, until the day comes when the Soviet Union, and other Communist nations such as Vietnam, decide to respect international law and to reduce international tension, the United States has little choice but to remain strong. And so we shall.

Kim Il-song, to judge from his rather lengthy speeches—lengthier, even, than my own—is adamant on the subject of withdrawal of the United States peacekeeping forces from Korea. I should like to take this opportunity to admonish him to redirect his rhetorical energies elsewhere.

Too many men and women, Korean and American, have already given their lives protecting this land from his troops. He desires reunification, but as we saw all too recently in Vietnam, reunification, in Com-

[6] The reference is to a toast made by President Chun at a luncheon given by President Reagan on February 2, 1981; see *American Foreign Policy: Current Documents, 1981,* document 557.

munist terms, means the horrors of new wars, "re-education," camps, and hundreds of thousands of people driven to the sea in open boats.

The United States has no intention of stepping aside in Korea so Kim Il-song can launch another invasion and set the clock back 32 years.

It is our earnest hope that he eventually will see the logic of negotiations. But we in the United States as you in the Republic of Korea, are prepared to wait for that day patiently, and to prosper in the meantime as we begin our second hundred years of friendship.

Thank you very much.

Document 521

Proclamation by President Reagan, May 10, 1982[7]

United States–Korea Centennial

On May 22, 1982, representatives of the United States of America and the Kingdom of Korea concluded a Treaty of Peace, Amity, Commerce, and Navigation providing for the opening of diplomatic relations and the establishment of permanent resident missions in each capital.[8] This treaty marked a new chapter in the history of northeast Asia and was the auspicious beginning of an enduring partnership between the United States and Korea.

The intervening century has witnessed enormous change and progress in our two nations. Our relationship began when both of our nations were largely isolated from the main currents of world life. A century later, Korea and the United States are heavily engaged in all aspects of international endeavor. We have undergone remarkable social and economic transformations as well—from largely rural agricultural societies 100 years ago to the urban industrial economies of today. And, in the process, we have come to enjoy unprecedented levels of prosperity.

Americans are proud of the role they have played in Korean history, especially during these last 100 years. In 1945, American soldiers were crucial to the restoration of this ancient land's independence. Just 5 years later, Americans fought side-by-side with Korean soldiers in the struggle against the Communist invasion of 1950. Korea, in turn, made a major contribution to the United States efforts to defeat Communist aggression in Vietnam.

Throughout this period, Americans and Koreans have enriched each other's cultures through the exchange of teachers, scholars, and missionaries, and each other's economies through trade and scientific and technological cooperation. The United States applauds and welcomes the valuable contributions that citizens and residents of Korean ancestry have made and continue to make to our society.

Today Americans share many common values with the people of Korea. We believe that only in an atmosphere of freedom can full human potential be realized. We both have set high standards for education and achievement. We believe that an environment of free enterprise encourages initiative and innovation. And we both believe that hard work and diligence will lead to a better life and a better world for our children.

As we enter this second century of our relationship, we can look with satisfaction on our past accomplishments and with anticipation to the future. We will stand by our friends in Korea. In so doing we reaffirm our dedication to the principles of freedom and democracy as the basis of our continued strength and friendship. It is fitting then, that we now reflect upon our relations with this great nation and its people.

NOW, THEREFORE, I, RONALD REAGAN, President of the United States of America, do hereby proclaim the week of May 16 through May 22 as a week of national observance of the centennial of the establishment of diplomatic relations between the United States and Korea and of the ties of friendship that bind our two peoples.

IN WITNESS WHEREOF, I have hereunto set my hand this tenth day of May, in the year of our Lord nineteen hundred

---

[7] Source: White House Press Release, May 11, 1982, Office of the Press Secretary to the President; also printed in *Weekly Compilation of Presidential Documents*, May 17, 1982, pp. 626–627.

[8] For text, see 9 Bevans 470. Regarding its negotiation and signing, see Harriet D. Schwar, "The Establishment of Korean-American Relations: A Centennial," Department of State *Bulletin*, June 1982, pp. 1–15.

and eighty-two, and of the Independence of the United States of America the two hundred and sixth.

RONALD REAGAN

Document 522

Transcript of the Department of State Daily Press Briefing, July 1, 1982 (Extract)[9]

Visit of Republic of Korea Foreign Minister Lee

. . . .

Q. The South Korean Foreign Minister is now visiting Washington, and he had meetings with Mr. Haig and Mr. Stoessel.

Could you tell us what they discussed and what they agreed upon?

A. As you know, this is the Foreign Minister's first visit to Washington since his appointment earlier this month and was at the invitation of Secretary Haig.

In his meeting with the Foreign Minister on Tuesday, the Secretary assured Minister Lee that there would be no change in our policy toward Korea and that our commitment to the security of the Republic of Korea and maintenance of peace and stability on the peninsula would endure.

The Secretary and Foreign Minister Lee exchanged views on the situation in East Asia and the Pacific in which both our countries are vitally interested, and where the ROK is playing an increasingly prominent role as well as on other international issues.

The Secretary also pledged continued U.S. support for ROK efforts to open a dialogue with North Korea, notably President Chun's proposals of January 22.

Many of these same subjects were reviewed by the Foreign Minister and Deputy Secretary Stoessel during the luncheon hosted by the Deputy Secretary on Wednesday.

Minister Lee's visit confirmed a high degree of understanding between our two governments toward important international issues.

His meetings with the Secretary and Deputy Secretary took place in an atmosphere of warmth and friendship, reflecting the excellent state of our bilateral relations.

We were particularly pleased that the Foreign Minister could come to Washington during the Centennial Year of U.S.-Korean Relations.

. . . .

Document 523

Transcript of the Department of State Daily Press Briefing, December 16, 1982 (Extract)[10]

U.S. Reaction to the Release of Kim Dae Jung[11]

. . . .

Q. Regarding the report that the Korean Government might allow Mr. Kim Dae Jung to visit the United States for treatment, has the Government of the United States given this permit of residence to Mr. Kim and his family; and, if so, are there any conditions

---

[9] Source: Office of Press Relations, Department of State. Department of State Acting Spokesman Alan Romberg conducted the briefing, which began at 12:45 p.m.

[10] Source: Office of Press Relations, Department of State. Department of State Acting Spokesman Alan Romberg conducted the briefing, which began at 12:30 p.m.

[11] Korean dissident leader Kim Dae Jung had been sentenced to death on September 17, 1980, upon his conviction by a military tribunal on charges of sedition; his sentence had been commuted to life imprisonment by President Chun on January 23, 1981. The Korean Government announced on December 16 that he had been released from prison so that he could obtain medical treatment; for the text of the announcement, see Foreign Broadcast Information Service, *Daily Report: Asia & Pacific*, December 16, 1982, p. E1. For previous statements relating to Kim's case, see *American Foreign Policy: Basic Documents, 1977–1980*, p. 1082, and *American Foreign Policy: Current Documents, 1981*, documents 555 and 556.

attached to this permit? For instance, would he be allowed to engage in political activities while in residence here?

A. Let me first give you a reaction to the release of Mr. Kim, and then try to respond as much as I can to your question.

We very much welcome the release of Mr. Kim Dae Jung from prison on December 16 and take particular note of the government's statement that possible further steps include allowing Mr. Kim to come to the United States for continuing medical treatment.

We also welcome the government's statement that it is reviewing the cases of others connected with Mr. Kim and the Kwangju incident of 1980.[12] We note the Korean Government's statement that the measures it has taken were based both on President Chun's humanitarian concerns and on a desire to promote a sense of national unity. We believe these measures will make an important contribution to political harmony in Korea.

As far as any application to come here is concerned, I can only say that we will review the case promptly, but I don't have any further specifics about the timing of that other than "promptly," and I don't have any kind of conditions that might be attached to that.

. . . .

Document 524

Transcript of the Department of State Daily Press Briefing, December 27, 1982 (Extract)[13]

U.S. View of Korean Political Process

. . . .

Q. Do you have anything on the comments of Mr. Kim,[14] whose release was secured by the United States, but who nonetheless says the United States hasn't done enough for human rights and democracy in Korea?

A. I believe the U.S. relationship with the Republic of Korea has benefited both countries. The United States and the Republic of Korea fought together to help preserve the independence of Korea and to lay the foundation for the development of democracy there. That has remained our goal ever since.

The United States has made known publicly and privately its hope that there would be continued progress toward a more open political system and greater respect for human rights in Korea as in other countries around the world.

We believe President Chun's decision to release Mr. Kim contributes to that end, and have welcomed it.

For the record, I would note that simultaneously with Mr. Kim's release the Government of the Republic of Korea announced the release of 47 other prisoners held in politically-related cases.[15] We welcome those releases as well which reflected a spirit of reconciliation and will, we hope, contribute to political harmony in Korea.

Q. Can we get a copy?

A. Yes.

Q. I don't understand. You say that the United States hopes that the political process will become more open and you think that Kim's release contributes to that? Wouldn't it be logical that if he were allowed to stay and participate in the political process there, that would be a step in that direction?

A. I have no particular comment or knowledge, in fact, of Mr. Kim's future objectives or plans or what the Korean Government might permit, so I don't have a comment on that.

Q. Do you have any understanding with respect to the conditions under which he was freed? His wife was complaining last week that he would not be freed unless he agreed to come to this country.

A. I don't know what discussions took place between the Government of Korea and Mr. Kim. As far as we're concerned, he applied for a visa and was granted one. We

---

[12] For a statement of May 22, 1980, of U.S. concern at the civil strife in Kwangju, Korea, see *American Foreign Policy: Basic Documents, 1977–1980*, pp. 1081–1082.

[13] Source: Office of Press Relations, Department of State. Department of State Acting Spokesman Alan Romberg conducted the briefing, which began at 12:07 p.m.

[14] Kim Dae Jung had come to the United States on December 23; his comments were reported in the *New York Times*, December 27, 1982, p. A1.

[15] For text of the announcement, see Foreign Broadcast Information Service, *Daily Report: Asia & Pacific*, December 27, 1982, p. E1.

discussed that last week, and also indicated that there were no particular restrictions which applied to his visa here.

Q. Would the U.S. Government welcome his eventual return to Korea?

A. I don't think that's a matter for us to comment on in specific terms. It gets us into the internal affairs more specifically than I think would be appropriate.

. . . .

I. New Zealand

Document 525

Remarks by Vice President Bush, Wellington, May 3, 1982[1]

Vice President Bush's Visit to New Zealand

It's very good, finally, to be in New Zealand, Mr. Prime Minister,[2] and I want to thank you sir for your kind invitation. Barbara and I have been looking forward very much to this part of our journey for a long, long time. I've never been here before, but back home the beauty of New Zealand is well known, as is the innate and legendary graciousness of New Zealanders.

I'm looking forward enormously to our talks, and to those with other members of your government.

I've come to New Zealand to reaffirm the friendship between our two countries. Just a few days ago we marked the thirtieth anniversary of the entry into force of the Anzus Treaty,[3] which marked the beginning of our formal, postwar alliance. The spirit of Anzus is strong, stronger even than the vision of those who put their signatures to the document in 1951. As the world has evolved, so has our friendship. The United States has learned that, as Emerson put it long ago, "The best way to have a friend is to be one."

Ours is much more than a security alliance. Our ties are cultural and economic, and grounded in the conviction that Democracy has given us the means and the power to attain our prosperity—and our peace.

Our friendship goes back long before Anzus. I've come not only to celebrate our past, but, I hope, to inaugurate our future. In America we place great value on the comradeship and the self-sacrifice that characterized the origins of our partnership. And we place equally great value on a friend who continues to stand for those values that sustain and nourish the free world.

Lest I overstay my welcome within only minutes of my landing here in Wellington, let me conclude by simply saying, thank you for this warm welcome. Thank you for having us here, Mr. Prime Minister.

[1] Source: Press Release, May 3, 1982, Office of the Press Secretary to the Vice President; also printed in Department of State *Bulletin*, August 1982, p. 44. Vice President Bush, who visited New Zealand, May 3–5, made these remarks on his arrival.

[2] Robert Muldoon.

[3] Signed at San Francisco, September 1, 1951; for text, see 3 UST 3420.

J. Philippines

Document 526

Statement by the Secretary of Defense (Weinberger), Clark Air Force Base, the Philippines, April 2, 1982[1]

"The Defense of the Philippines . . . Is a Very Big Job"

Good afternoon, ladies and gentlemen.

I have a few remarks I want to make about the trip, particularly the part in the Philippines. I won't be able to take any questions except highly technical questions related to the F–4, F–5, and the C–5, because I have been a bit out of touch with

[1] Source: *Public Statements of Secretary of Defense Weinberger*, 1982. Secretary Weinberger, who visited Japan, South Korea, and the Philippines from March 25 to April 2, 1982, made his remarks upon his departure from Clark Air Force Base.

day-to-day events. But I did want to say before leaving the Philippines what a very fine trip I think we have had, and what very warm hospitality the President, Minister Enrile and all of the Philippine officers and the Philippine military have extended to us and to our party.

I think it was particularly useful because it enabled me to convey from President Reagan the message of full support for the defense of the Philippines that the President was anxious to have conveyed to President Marcos.

President Marcos will be calling on the President and visiting Washington in the fall. And I have invited Minister Enrile to come to Washington so that we can have an opportunity to continue the discussions that we have begun here. I think it's very important to continue those discussions particularly on the basis of the personal friendship of the kind that we have had an opportunity to establish here.

I find the morale of both the Philippine and American forces extremely high, and I found the spirit in which we are all working together particularly good and encouraging.

The defense of the Philippines, the defense of the free world, is a very big job. It will require a great deal of effort by every one concerned with preserving freedom. The threat that we face is very real and very near, as we found in Korea, and I find here the full recognition of that and the willingness to make the sacrifices necessary to meet that kind of threat. This willingness is particularly evident among the troops involved, whose morale I found to be excellent and whose proficiency I found to be very high. I am always delighted to have a chance to talk with men and women in uniform and to find the great enthusiasm in all the countries that they have for their equipment and for the task that is assigned.

Lastly, I would just like to say to Minister Enrile how much we have appreciated and enjoyed the hospitality and the friendship and this opportunity to renew the deep ties which have bound together the Philippines and the Americans for many, many years. And, of course, on a personal note it was a very happy return for me and I have enjoyed every minute of it.

Document 527

Remarks by President Reagan, September 16, 1982[2]

"Our Two Peoples Enjoy a Close Friendship—One Forged in Shared History and Common Ideals"

THE PRESIDENT. Mr. President, Mrs. Marcos, it gives me special pleasure to welcome you to the United States. Mrs. Reagan and I have been long looking forward to returning the hospitality you showed us on our 1969 visit to your country.

Our two peoples enjoy a close friendship—one forged in shared history and common ideals. In World War II, Americans and Filipinos fought side by side in the defense of freedom—a struggle in which you, Mr. President, personally fought so valiantly.

The values for which we struggled—independence, liberty, democracy, justice, equality are engraved in our constitutions and embodied in our peoples' aspirations. Today our ties remain strong, benefiting each of us over the full range of our relations. Politically we tend to view many world issues the same general way. Yours, Mr. President, is a respected voice for reason and moderation in international forums.

The Philippines with its ASEAN partners has taken the lead in search for self-determination for the people of Kampuchea. In that vein, let me also pay tribute to you and Mrs. Marcos' personal leadership and commitment to the care of refugees in Southeast Asia. Under your direct sponsorship, the Philippines' refugee processing center has become a model of its kind in encouraging the development of self-sufficiency and the restoration of human dignity.

The Philippines and you, Mr. President, play an important role in addressing the problems of economic development in the

[2] Source: White House Press Release, September 16, 1982, Office of the Press Secretary to the President; also printed in *Weekly Compilation of Presidential Documents*, September 20, 1982, pp. 1162–1163. President Reagan made these remarks on the South Lawn of the White House at the arrival ceremony beginning at 10:15 a.m. for President and Mrs. Marcos who made a state visit to the United States, September 15–21, 1982.

world. At Cancun, we made a new start toward a more effective and practical dialogue and improved cooperation among industrial and developing countries.[3] Your leadership in that area, Mr. President, is vital and widely respected. Under your leadership at home, the Philippines can boast a record of solid economic growth over the past decade attributable in significant part to its hospitable attitude toward free enterprise and private initiative.

Your country's dedication to improving the standard of living of your people is an effort in which we've been delighted to participate through bilateral and multilateral economic assistance. Your continuing interest in better nutrition has led the Philippines to achieve self-sufficiency in food grain production.

You can also point with pride to the success of your rural electrification program now bringing benefits to an increasing number of remote regions. And I find it a matter of personal satisfaction that your country and my home state of California are both pioneers in developing geothermal power to replace expensive energy imports.

The United States remains the Philippines' leading trading partner and American firms are the largest foreign investors in your country, reflecting their confidence in your progress and prospects for economic growth.

We have welcomed the growing two-way trade between our nations and have been pleased that we've been able to keep our markets for the products of your growing manufacturing and industrial sector the most open of any country in the industrialized world.

America considers itself especially fortunate to have nearly one million persons of Filipino heritage now residing in our country. They bring with them their energy and their talents and they contribute enormously to the rich diversity of American society.

Similarly, thousands of Americans, enchanted with the beauty of your nation and by its people have chosen to live in the Philippines.

Our security relationship is an essential element in maintaining peace in the region and is so recognized. This relationship, one of several we have in the Western Pacific, threatens no one but contributes to the shield behind which the whole region can develop socially and economically.

Mr. President, under your leadership the Philippines stands as a recognized force for peace and security in Southeast Asia through its bilateral efforts and through its role in ASEAN which is the focus of our regional policies in Southeast Asia.

Mr. President and Mrs. Marcos, the United States deeply values its close friendship and alliance with the Philippines. We seek to use this visit to further strengthen our ties with your country.

Nancy and I are personally delighted that you are here. And we say, "Welcome to the United States. Welcome to our national home." (Applause).

Document 528

Transcript of a White House Press Briefing, September 16, 1982[4]

President Marcos' Discussions With President Reagan

Senior Administration Official. I'll be fairly brief because there are other meetings that are currently taking place [at] which I'm expected to be present.

I would characterize the meeting as one that was extremely amiable, as you would expect between friends and allies. This was not a meeting to negotiate major problems. It was a meeting between the leaders of countries that have a good deal of common business and whose policies have been quite complementary.

It was a meeting focused on ways of consolidating an already strong relationship. The President—President Reagan and President Marcos both affirmed the value of our security relationship. It was agreed that the review of our military base arrangements which, under the 1979 amendment[5]

[3] For documentation on the economic conference held at Cancun, Mexico, October 22–23, 1981, see *American Foreign Policy: Current Documents, 1981*, Chapter 5, Part F.

[4] Source: Office of the Press Secretary to the President. This background briefing, which began at 12 noon and ended at 12:14 p.m., was conducted by senior administration officials.

[5] For the text of the January 7, 1979, amendment to U.S.–Philippines Bases Agreement, see *American Foreign Policy: Basic Documents, 1977–1980*, pp. 1087–1088. For the text with its four annexes, see 30 UST 863.

is to take place within 5 years, will commence next April—that is, April 1983.

It was also agreed that we will regularize our consultations between the Defense Ministers. You'll remember that Defense Minister—Defense Secretary Weinberger visited Manila last April.[6] Minister Enrile, his counterpart, will come to Washington later in the year, I believe in December, to continue discussions between our highest defense official. At that time, I'm sure one subject that will be taken up will be ways in which the United States can continue to be helpful in modernizing the armed forces of the Philippines.

There were a number of political issues that were discussed. The focus was, principally, upon Asian questions. President Reagan, of course, emphasized our strong support for ASEAN. There was discussion of the Kampuchean question in which both acknowledged an important matter of principle at stake in the continued occupation by the Vietnamese of a neighboring country and our resolve to bring that occupation to an end, if possible. There was discussion of our respective policies toward China and Japan. The Middle East was discussed. The Philippine Government welcomed President Reagan's recent initiatives on the Middle East and there was some discussion of recent developments in Lebanon.

With respect to economic questions, the United States affirmed its continued interest in providing what support we can to the development of the Philippines. The Philippine economy, as you know, has experienced difficulties as have we in recent years and their difficulties have been a function, in part, of commodity prices, slack commodity prices, the high cost of money and so forth.

We did indicate that we could be helpful on one issue—namely the financing of the Bataan Nuclear Power Plant where the President of Ex-Im Bank recommended to the board and found board approval for the provision of an additional $204.5 million financial guarantees for that power reactor. That is, of course, subject to congressional concurrence, but it was a favorable recommendation made by the executive branch and a favorable action by the board.

Q. How much—

Senior Administration Official. $204.5 million financial guarantees.

Q. From what bank?

Senior Administration Official. From the Export-Import Bank.

It was also agreed that we would develop a more regularized forum for treating bilateral economic issues that come up. I expect the Treasury Department will take the lead on this. The Deputy Secretary of [the] Treasury regularly visits the Philippines in connection with the Asian Development Bank meetings in the spring. But it was agreed that we would discuss ways in which his presence in the Philippines could be supplemented by other experts from our government and their government to provide an early warning network for problems and to provide a forum for discussing issues that have been festering and require a solution.

Those, I think, were the principal points covered. And I can take a few questions.

Q. On this Ex-Im Bank loan, was this—is this the first President Marcos had heard of the approval? Surely not.

Senior Administration Official. No, but I think the dimension—the decision was reached at the board, I believe, on September 14th, so it's a fairly recent decision.

Q. Is this regarded as festering right now?

Senior Administration Official. Well, I wouldn't say festering, but there have been questions related to textile—expansion of textile exports, Philippine desires to get additional exports into the United States under the generalized system of preferences.

Q. Was there any discussion of human rights?

Senior Administration Official. Human rights was not discussed in any kind of detail. You should not assume, incidentally, that any discussion of human rights is a critical discussion. You will recall—

Q. It's got to be—

Senior Administration Official. You will recall that the President's remarks on the South Lawn made appropriate reference to a very important contribution which the Philippine Government has made for several years to the handling of refugees from Indochina.[7] That's an appropriate—

Q. —the internal human rights in the Philippines.

---

[6] See document 526.

[7] See *supra*.

Senior Administration Official. There was no extensive discussion of that. I think the President commented in a brief exchange on the ramp out here.

Q. Did he discuss it with the President of the Philippines, sir?

Q. With him? Did he discuss it at all with him?

Senior Administration Official. This issue, as I say, was not discussed in any detail.

Q. Was it discussed at all?

Q. Was there any talk—

Q. Was it discussed at all?

Q. Excuse me. We've got a question up here on the—

Q. We've got a question—

Q. Question. Wait a minute.

Q. Did they talk about it at all?

Q. Did they discuss it at all? You keep saying it wasn't discussed in detail. Was it brought up at all?

Senior Administration Official. This question was not discussed this morning.

Q. Thank you.

Q. Was there any talk of increasing the Philippine—the American contribution for the use of the bases in the Philippines?

Senior Administration Official. No, we didn't get into that kind of discussion. As I say, the focus of the base question was when the review will start. The agreement in 1979 was that—within 5 years we would review the base agreement to be sure that it continues to serve the mutual interests of both governments. The 5 years is up essentially in January—early January 1984. And the question was when we'll begin to review the base agreement. We agreed we'll commence in April.

Q. Do they need—

Q. Would you expect a question of increased compensation to come up at all during this visit?

Senior Administration Official. Would I expect it to? I would expect that would be a question to be taken up in the review itself.

Q. What's the problem with the extradition treaty? The signs out on the sidewalk seem to be against an extradition treaty for the Philippines. What is the difficulty there?

Senior Administration Official. I'm not sure precisely what the question is. The—

Q. Is there a problem right now—we don't have an extradition treaty or they want to make a stronger one or—

Senior Administration Official. No. In conjunction with an effort to modernize extradition arrangements with many countries, a treaty was negotiated with the Philippines. There are comparable treaties with virtually identical language on key provisions with Colombia, Mexico, the Netherlands, and a number of others I've forgotten at the moment. But this is within that framework.

The problem—it's not a problem. The reason why it hasn't moved forward is that there is domestic legislation before the Congress concerning extradition. And as between the House and Senate bills, there have been some differences on key provisions. It seemed sensible to work out our own domestic law before moving forward on the treaty, because the domestic law will have some bearing on the terms of our international agreements.

Q. Did they meet alone at all?

Senior Administration Official. Just very briefly before they went into the group meeting.

Q. And who conducted the main conversation on this, dialogue on this—on everything?

Senior Adminstration Official. The two Presidents with a good deal of participation by the Cabinet members on both sides.

Q. Was Mrs. Marcos present?

Senior Administration Official. Yes. I think you can—

Q. During the whole meeting?

Senior Administration Official. Yes.

Senior Administration Official.—probably—you can probably provide the members who were present.

Senior Administration Official. Yes, we'll get you a list—

Q. Did she add anything to the conversation?

Q. Was there any—excuse me. Was there any discussion of credit to the Philippines on commodities or other imports from the United States, credits on prices or credits on interest?

SENIOR ADMINISTRATION OFFICIAL. No. The only question that came up along this line was the Ex-Im—this is financial guarantees, by the way. It's not credits.

Q. Did Mrs. Marcos—

SENIOR ADMINISTRATION OFFICIAL. That involves guarantees against default and it facilitates borrowing in the market.

Q. In that the State Department's human rights report[8] did find some difficulties with the Philippines situation, why was it decided not to bring it up at all? These things usually are brought up in these kinds of meetings.

SENIOR ADMINISTRATION OFFICIAL. Well, this is not the only contact—I mean, President Marcos is here for several days. He will be seeing the President. He will be having other meetings around town, so—

Q. Will it be brought up?

SENIOR ADMINISTRATION OFFICIAL. I don't have a comment.

Q. Well, can you tell us why it wasn't brought up here today?

SENIOR ADMINISTRATION OFFICIAL. I don't have a comment.

I think the President—what I would say is the President conveyed his own view that there has been progress since the dismantling of martial law, relaxation of press constraints, the reintroduction of greater freedom for assembly, the reintroduction of habeas corpus—restoration of habeas corpus, restoration of the right to strike, a variety of developments of a positive character.

Q. But President and Mrs. Marcos still continue to fly in separate airplanes, drive in separate automobiles? Why is that?

SENIOR ADMINISTRATION OFFICIAL. I don't—it's probably for security reasons.

SENIOR ADMINISTRATION OFFICIAL. I think you should address that to the Philippine spokesman, . . .

SENIOR ADMINISTRATION OFFICIAL. Thank you.

THE PRESS. Thank you.

---

[8] Apparent reference to *Country Reports on Human Rights Practices for 1981*, Report Submitted to the Committee on Foreign Affairs, House of Representatives, and the Committee on Foreign Relations, U.S. Senate, by the Department of State, Ninety-seventh Congress, Second Session (Washington, 1982), pp. 661–674.

Document 529

Statement Issued by the Department of State, September 20, 1982[9]

Results of President Marcos' State Visit to Washington, D.C.

The President of the Philippines, His Excellency Ferdinand E. Marcos, met with President Reagan at the White House on September 16. In addition, during the course of his state visit to Washington, President Marcos met with the Vice President, Secretary Shultz, Secretary Weinberger, congressional leaders, and other prominent U.S. Government officials. Other members of his party, including Mrs. Marcos, Prime Minister Virata, and Foreign Minister Romulo, also met with Secretary Regan, Secretary Baldrige, U.S. Trade Representative Brock, and other administration leaders.

The two Presidents reaffirmed the strong traditional ties between the United States and the Philippines, as well as their commitments under the Mutual Defense Treaty. They reviewed the international situation, with special attention to the Pacific and Southeast Asia. They also reviewed the full range of bilateral, political, economic, and security issues. President and Mrs. Marcos are proceeding today to New York and other stops in the United States.

The Government of the United States and the Republic of the Philippines have agreed to begin the scheduled 5-year review of the military bases agreement in April 1983 in Manila. The review will entail an examination of the provisions of the military bases agreement to insure that they continue to meet both countries' current needs and interests. Agreement was also reached on conducting periodic strategic consultations at the ministerial level, beginning with a visit to the United States by Philippine Minister of Defense Juan Ponce Enrile in February 1983.

The two countries took action on several specific economic matters during the visit,

---

[9] Source: Department of State *Bulletin*, November 1982, p. 25. John Hughes, Department of State Spokesman, made this statement available to news correspondents at the September 20, 1982, Department of State Daily Press Briefing.

including exchanging instruments of ratification of a tax treaty, completing a civil aviation agreement,[10] concluding an agreement for the promotion of tourism, and signing an agricultural cooperation agreement. The Export-Import Bank of the United States agreed, subject to final congressional concurrence, to provide additional financial guarantees in the amount of $204.5 million for the U.S.-designed Philippine nuclear power plant at Bataan, a project intended to move the Philippines closer to energy self-reliance.

As a further cooperative action, the U.S. Department of the Treasury has agreed to continue the wider dialogue begun during this visit through annual consultations with the Philippine Ministry of Finance on financial and related issues of mutual concern. An agreement recently signed providing $50 million in economic supporting fund assistance to improve economic conditions for the people living near the U.S. military bases was also noted. The U.S. Agency for International Development and the Philippine Government agreed to explore new cooperative measures to reduce loss of life and property due to typhoons by using the most advanced tracking and warning technologies. The U.S. Government also agreed to organize an investment mission of U.S. businessmen to the Philippines and other ASEAN countries in 1983.

The state visit by President Marcos was a significant milestone in the relations between the two countries symbolizing the close and constructive relationship which has long existed between the United States of America and the Philippines.

K. Singapore

Document 530

Remarks by Vice President Bush, Singapore, April 27, 1982[1]

Meeting With Prime Minister Lee Kuan Yew

I'm pleased to be in Singapore, an important friend of the United States.

I've come to discuss a full range of matters of international importance. While I'm here I also hope to learn about and profit from the extraordinary economic policies that have made this Republic such a landmark in prosperity.

I began my trip through East Asia and the Pacific in Japan and Korea where I had excellent discussions with those countries' leaders. I'm looking forward enormously to meeting again with Prime Minister Lee Kuan Yew. I speak for President Reagan when I say that the United States attaches great importance to his views. I expect we'll have a frank and open exchange with him and with other members of Singapore's leadership.

We value highly our close and cooperative relationship with Singapore, just as we value our ties to all of the ASEAN countries. Their close and cooperative spirit has made possible progress toward resolution of a number of regional problems. This spirit, in a world that lives with the everyday specter of Communist aggression, cannot be taken for granted, or overemphasized.

Document 531

Transcript of a Press Conference by the Secretary of Defense (Weinberger), Singapore, November 2, 1982[2]

Discussions With Prime Minister Lee Kuan Yew and U.S. Interest in Singapore

I will make a short opening statement. I'd just like to say we had a very fine trip and

---

[10] Regarding these two agreements, see *ibid.*, p. 28.

[1] Source: Press Release, Office of the Press Secretary to the Vice President. The Vice President spoke at 2:10 p.m. local time upon his arrival in Singapore. Vice President Bush was in East Asia from April 22 to May 9, 1982. He visited Japan, Korea, Australia, New Zealand, China, and Singapore (April 27–29). For text of his dinner toast in Singapore, April 27, 1982, see Department of State *Bulletin*, August 1982, p. 43.

[2] Source: *Public Statements of Secretary of Defense Weinberger*, 1982. Secretary Weinberger was on a tour of five East Asian nations, Australia, New Zealand, Thailand, Singapore, and Indonesia, from October 29 to November 9, 1982. This press conference took place at the VIP Complex, Changi Airport, prior to the Secretary's 9 a.m. departure from Singapore.

visit in Singapore. I have been greatly impressed with the economy, the prosperity, the strength of the country and the developments that have been made under the Prime Minister's direction. I came with the intention of showing the importance that the United States attaches to this part of the world. There have been very few visits by Secretaries of Defense to these countries for many years, in some cases not at all, and we wanted to correct that as quickly as we could. I also had a message from the President of the United States for the Prime Minister. The President has the greatest admiration for Prime Minister Lee. We had a great visit with him earlier in the year[3] and the President wanted to express that personally, as well as other messages that were conveyed. We also had the opportunity to reaffirm our support of all of our commitments under the Manila Pact. I'd be delighted to take your questions.

Q. What was the message?

A. Well, if anybody is going to discuss the message with you, it should be Prime Minister Lee.

Q. Secretary, can you tell us about what your commitments under the Manila Pact would be?[4] If there's an attack, for example, by Vietnam on Thailand.

A. Well, the particular response would be whatever would be appropriate to the purpose, whatever was desired by the nations involved, and whatever was specifically authorized by our political processes. The general intention and purpose of the Pact is to demonstrate, that is to state, that the signatories to that pact are committed to support one another; and that is what would be done, that commitment would clearly be kept. However, the actual nature of the response would depend on particular circumstances at that time, whatever seemed to be appropriate, and whatever was desired by the countries involved.

Q. If Vietnam forces came across the border, would you commit ground forces to—

A. Oh, that's a very hypothetical question and involves a great many other considerations under the United States constitutional processes.

Q. Secretary, you were quoted as saying to Singapore Government leaders yesterday that "the more we can cooperate the stronger our deterrent ability will be."

A. I think that's right, yes. It's one of those few quotations that's absolutely correct.

Q. Do you have any proposals for strengthening defense cooperation between the United States, ASEAN countries, Australia and New Zealand? Or did Mr. Lee in his discussions with you yesterday make any such proposals?

A. Well, again, the discussions I had with the Prime Minister, I would always consider confidential and it would be entirely up to him to discuss what took place specifically there. But in response to the other part of your question, we have considered and discussed with representatives of many of the countries the ways in which we could be helpful to each other and that includes joint exercises and furnishing equipment, arms, and weapon systems that seem to be desired for specific assignments. Those are always matters of consideration. We have always felt in the United States that we can best serve our own defense interests and those of our friends and allies if we work closely together in connection with the development and use of arms that can be used interchangeably and that are appropriate for particular purposes at given times. So, those are always part of the discussions and they will indeed be part of the discussions I will be having in the other countries—Thailand, Indonesia, Australia, and New Zealand.

Q. When you say joint exercises, do you mean bilateral or wider?

A. Either way. Again, it depends on the wishes of the countries involved, and with the ASEAN nations, our exercises have been entirely bilateral—by wish of the nations involved. It just depends on what the wishes are. Our feeling is that the joint exercises are very helpful and so far, they have worked out well from a technical, professional point of view and we hope to continue them.

Q. Mr. Secretary, what if anything was said with regard to the defense guidance paper made public last June[5] and if anything was discussed on that?

A. Well, the defense guidance paper from our Department of Defense is a con-

[3] Apparent reference to Vice President Bush's visit; see *supra*.

[4] Also known as the Southeast Asia Collective Defense Treaty, signed September 8, 1954. For text, see 6 UST 81.

[5] Reference presumably is to the 125-page, DOD study, "Fiscal Year 1984–1988 Defense Guidance," which was summarized extensively in the *New York Times*, May 30, 1982, pp. I1, I12.

fidential document. It was not made public. Various bits and pieces of it were printed in unauthorized fashion because the whole document is of course classified. And because of its classified nature, it's a little hard to discuss the whole thing without breaking the basic rules. They have been partially broken by the publication already and I don't want to add to that. If you are referring to the thing most frequently quoted, about a protracted nuclear war, that is the whole problem with partial disclosures. What was actually said in the guidance on that point was that the Soviets have developed a very clear capacity for extended protracted nuclear war and in order for our deterrent to remain effective, we have to develop a flexibility of response that will enable us to respond to this new capability and to respond to this apparently continuing, as we think, very erroneous belief by the Soviets that a nuclear war is winnable. All of that discussion, because it proceeded from sort of half truths and half inaccurate unauthorized statements in the defense guidance, caused a great deal of misunderstanding.

Q. Mr. Secretary, are you asking the Government of Singapore to increase defense spending?

A. Well, in Singapore's case, we have nothing but admiration for the willingness of the country to commit the necessary amount of its resources to building a very strong defense. We point out in some other areas, not necessarily on this trip at all, but in some other areas that it is very much to a country's advantage to increase the contributions that it makes to its own defense. Because we frankly can't think of a higher priority particularly in view of the increasing nature of the Soviet threat. We get additional evidence of that everyday from the additions they have made to their armed forces and the fact that those additions are almost always offensive in character, for offensive warfare. And that threat is clearly increasing in the Pacific and it's obviously one of the things we discuss with each of the countries. But, of course, each country must decide the contributions that it can make. Singapore is a very fine example of a very strong contribution to national defense because of the realistic and accurate views of the Prime Minister as to the nature of the threat.

Q. Earlier this year, Prime Minister Lee suggested that because of this increased threat from the Soviet Union, and increased responsibilities of the Seventh Fleet, that perhaps an additional fleet should be organized and supplied from the United States. Was this discussed? Is it possible, is it desirable?

A. Well, again, on whether or not it was discussed I will have to defer to the Prime Minister. And he can tell you whatever he wishes to about the discussions. The American fleet strength is growing. We will have a 600-ship fleet by 1990. We have asked the Congress specifically to authorize two carriers this year and we have great flexibility in the disposition of the fleet now. We don't feel it is necessary to have particular portions of the fleet permanently based in any one area. It is a very rapidly changing world. And we have now a fleet disposition plan under which we have great flexibility—the ability to cover portions of the Indian Ocean, the ability to cover the Mediterranean as needed and the western and southern Pacific. We will continue to position our forces so that we can try to deal with whatever appears to be the greatest need at the greatest time. In order to do that, we obviously need additional naval strength and that we are gaining, and have gained in the last 2 years. The use of that naval strength is one of the things that we've talked about with our friends in Japan—about how important it is for the defense of the Japanese home islands and for areas a thousand miles out from the home island to be covered by Japanese efforts. When this is done, then this can free parts of the U.S. Fleet for assistance in other parts of the world, particularly the sealanes in the southern Pacific regions.

Q. Taking you up on a point about the expanding role by Japanese maritime forces. There has been concern in some ASEAN countries that this might take place. How do you intend to meet that concern, Mr. Secretary?

A. Well, the concern I understand perfectly. And I think anyone who participated in World War II understands that completely in this part of the world. The concern, I think, is not well founded because I see no disposition whatever on the part of the Japanese, and we talk to them frequently, and I was there earlier this year, to regain any kind offensive, military strength nor anything remotely resembling a militaristic spirit. It is clear that they can very well serve the cause for which we all work by increasing their ability to defend their own home islands and the air and sealanes. And that's a role that they have concluded is entirely appropriate for themselves and we fully share that feeling. We understand the worries of other countries, but we try to make very clear that we don't have any—we have not picked up the slightest indication of any kind of feeling on the part of the Japanese Government or people that they want any such militaristic role again, ever again.

Q. Sir, considering your flexibility, is it not feasible for anyone to expect another carrier force in this particular region?

A. Well, it is feasible for people to expect another carrier force in this region from time to time. Because conditions keep shifting very rapidly and the carrier forces are very mobile, very flexible, very powerful and that is indeed why we feel it is important to have them. But at any given moment, there might be needs in various other parts of the globe or needs here. And what our flexible position and flexible disposition of the fleet is designed to do is to enable us to be in the areas where its strength can serve as a deterrent to attack on ourselves or on our friends. That is the whole purpose of everything we do. If we are completely successful in everything we do, we will never have to use any of the strength that we feel it is necessary to acquire because it will have a successful deterrent capability.

You have had one (question), maybe if I can see if someone else has one and then we'll come back to you.

Q. There is a feeling in the Southeast Asian countries that there is a congruence of interests between the Soviet, I'm sorry, China and the United States because of their anti-Soviet approach. Do you think that there has been any change in this perception, as a result of the recent talks in Peking between the Soviet Union and China attempting to reach some normalization?

A. No, I don't really think so. Those talks have been going on in a rather desultory fashion, off and on, for a number of years. We don't have anything definitive on it, but it wouldn't appear that there has been any major change in the basic Chinese policy with respect to the Soviet Union.

Q. Sir, we hear a lot in this region about Soviet use of the base at Cam Ranh Bay in Vietnam but these reports are usually very short on details as to exactly what happens in Vietnam. Can you tell us if you think it is a permanent base of the Soviet Naval/Air Forces or is it merely a refueling stop?

A. Well, I think it is as permanent as the Vietnamese will allow it to be, and so far they have shown no disposition to do anything other than allow full and complete Soviet use of it. The Soviets are making very substantial use of it. It's a very important and very well developed base. They are there and we don't have any idea how permanent the relationship between Vietnam and the Soviet Union is, but it does seem rather permanent so far.

Q. I'll just follow up on that. In what ways does the use of this base complicate the mission of the Seventh Fleet and American allies in the region?

A. Well, it just makes it all the more apparent and necessary for the U.S. Fleet to have places where it can operate and can have the necessary facilities for its operation if it is to perform its mission of deterring attack and safeguarding the sealanes of communications that are so vital to all of the countries in this region.

Q. Mr. Secretary, do you see a kind of interlocking relationship between the Manila Pact, the ANZUS alliance and the Five-Power Defense arrangement?[6]

A. Well, I think they all are expressive of the common interests that the United States and the countries involved in those pacts and agreements that you mentioned have. We do have a common interest. It is entirely to the benefit of the United States as well as all of the other countries involved in those pacts, we think, to stay together, to keep close and warm relationships, and to discuss military matters of mutual interests so as to enable us to be as effective as possible. The more that is done, the more a deterrent to attack is built and the more it is perceived that there is sufficient strength to deter an attack. That is the way in which we believe the peace is kept all over the world, from the point of view of strategic intercontinental range weapons, conventional weapons and everything else. The alliances are a critically important part of the defense of freedom in the world because they pool mutual strength. It is very essential not to use those strengths, but to have them available to deter attack.

LTC Burch, closes conference: No more, then thank you, Mr. Secretary.

Secretary Weinberger. Thank you very much indeed.

---

6 The Five-Power Defense arrangement was an agreement signed in 1971 by Singapore, the United Kingdom, Australia, Malaysia, and New Zealand for consultation to decide what matters should be taken jointly or separately in the event of an attack or threat of an attack on one or more signatories.

L. Thailand

Document 532

Statement Read by the Department of State Acting Spokesman (Romberg), January 27, 1982[1]

U.S. Appreciation of Thailand's Campaign Against the Narcotics Trade

Thailand: I would like to note a major step taken by the Royal Thai Government against the narcotics trade. On January 21, Thai forces began operations against the base areas of the chief heroin trafficking group in the Golden Triangle, the so-called Shan United Army led by warlord Chang Chi-fu. We view this as a courageous, forceful action on the part of the Thai Government and greatly appreciate this important blow against heroin production and trafficking.

We want to express our thanks to the Royal Thai Government for this action, and our regret at the casualties which were suffered by the Thai forces in this operation.

[1] Source: Office of Press Relations, Department of State. This statement was read at the Department of State Daily Press Briefing, which began at 12:40 p.m.

Document 533

Prepared Statement by the Director of the Bureau of Refugee Programs, Department of State (Vine), Before a Subcommittee of the House Foreign Affairs Committee, April 29, 1982[2]

The United States, Thailand, and Piracy in the Gulf of Thailand: A New International Approach

Thank you for inviting me to appear today before this subcommittee to discuss pirate attacks against Vietnamese boat refugees in the Gulf of Thailand, and actions to combat them.

The refugee victims of piracy have aroused the concern and compassion of people throughout the world. But bare statistics on piracy hardly reflect the degree of human suffering they undergo. They are first robbed of their meager material possessions, then, of their human dignity, and sometimes, of their lives. We may never know of those who suffered and died in incidents in which the attackers senselessly or by design made certain there were no survivors. What we do know from surviving victims is an appalling account, abhorrent to all civilized people.

But condemning piracy and sympathizing with its victims is not the same as combatting it. The international community, the United States included, has found it difficult to translate its humanitarian concern into effective action. The reasons for this are many and complex.

Piracy has been endemic in these waters for hundreds of years; while refugees are a recent human phenomenon in this region, pirates are not. But refugees are an especially vulnerable target; as they flee they bring some money or other possessions with them, but because they flee, they have no protection from their homelands. They cannot arm themselves for self-protection. Thus the pirates become bolder and more

[2] Source: *Piracy in the Gulf of Thailand: A Crisis for the International Community: Hearing Before the Subcommittee on Asian and Pacific Affairs of the Committee on Foreign Affairs, House of Representatives, Ninety-seventh Congress, Second Session* (Washington, 1982), pp. 6–13.

numerous. Acts of piracy against refugees have been reported both within and outside territorial waters and on either side of an international water boundary. Who bears responsibility for the maintenance of safe passage when the adjacent maritime states are admittedly unable to do so?

Moreover, there are operational problems in mounting efforts to combat piracy, most notably the difficulty in distinguishing pirate craft from the thousands of other small boats similar in appearance but engaged in harmless, legitimate activities. Simply stated, some pirates may be sometime fishermen, but not all fishermen are sometime pirates; indeed, fishermen in the area have in many instances assisted refugees by providing them fuel, food, water, and sailing directions.

Notwithstanding these difficulties, the Department has since early 1980 sought to focus international attention on pirate depredations against refugees and to promote action to counter them. An early attempt in that year by UNHCR to develop a regional approach to the problem was unsuccessful, so the United States sought to develop with the Royal Thai Government a bilateral effort. Following agreement in September 1980 on a $2 million bilateral antipiracy arrangement,[3] the Royal Thai Navy formally inaugurated its program on February 6, 1981, having provided a P–3 surveillance aircraft until the arrival of two O–2 spotter aircraft under the U.S. program on that date. Communications equipment and spare parts, and the refurbishment of an aging Coast Guard cutter which already belonged to the Thai Navy were also covered by the agreement. In addition, the United States reimbursed the Royal Thai Government for the per diem costs of Thai Navy personnel involved in the program. The Department has already furnished to the subcommittee a written report summarizing the operational plan and evaluating the results of the bilateral arrangement.[4] Here I only wish to repeat the Department's judgment that the program had beneficial effects, not so much in terms of the numbers of pirates apprehended *in flagrante* or frightened away from their intended victims but more importantly, though in unidentifiable ways, by deterring would-be pirates and by increasing the receptivity of the RTG and the Thai public to antipiracy activities.

I should note at this point that the United States Navy also provided relief to the boat refugees transiting this area through the P–3 overflight program. In July 1979, the President authorized the dedication of P–3 aircraft specifically to survey the South China Sea for refugees in distress on the high seas, including refugees under attack by pirates. These aircraft were able to communicate via radio with passing merchant ships about refugee boats and thereby assisted in the rescue of hundreds of refugees. And in at least two instances, P–3 aircraft were able to scare off pirate attackers. This special program was terminated in September 1980 as the bilateral program came to function. Additionally, Navy ships and aircraft continue to be under specific instruction to rescue refugees at sea. Last week, for example, the USS *Indianapolis* picked up 30 refugees at sea.

As the 6-month U.S.-Thai program approached its termination date of September 30, 1981, the United States offered another $600,000 to sustain operations for an additional 6 months. The RTG believed, however, that its Navy could not perform the antipiracy task credibly and creditably without substantially increasing its scope and intensity, with more equipment and operational funds. And during this period the International Committee of the Red Cross (ICRC) had called for effective *international* action to combat this menace. Spurred by that call, last September the UNHCR convened the first of a number of meetings of countries believed interested in the piracy problem, including all of the countries which eventually became donors to the program which emerged. UNHCR initiated preliminary contacts with the Thai Government and, by late fall, reached agreement with the RTG on the broad outlines of a $3.67 million, 1-year antipiracy program. Twelve developed nations have pledged to finance the effort, with the United States contributing $1.04 million, or roughly 30 percent of the total.

The operational details of the UNHCR-Thai arrangement are still under active negotiation and, while full agreement should be achieved shortly, it is not appropriate for me in this forum to discuss the

---

[3] For text of the exchange of notes at Bangkok, September 30, 1980, see TIAS 9886. For the Department of State announcement of the agreement, January 2, 1981, see *American Foreign Policy: Current Documents, 1981*, document 574.

[4] "Thai-United States Antipiracy Program," printed in *Foreign Assistance Legislation for Fiscal Year 1983: Hearings and Markup Before the Subcommittee on Asian and Pacific Affairs of the Committee on Foreign Affairs, House of Representatives, Ninety-seventh Congress, Second Session* (Washington, 1982), Part 4, pp.67–68.

program except in general terms. Under the new agreement, the Thai Navy is to patrol the same area of the Gulf of Thailand as under the former bilateral program, that area being most infested with pirates. Importantly, however, surface patrols will double in intensity with the addition of two fast patrol boats and two decoy vessels ("Q–Boats") to the antipiracy flotilla. The O–2 aircraft will also be employed as they were during the U.S.-Thai bilateral program. Also under the UNHCR plan, Thai boat owners will be required to register their vessels with the RTG. Registration data will be computerized and used in identifying suspects in piracy incidents and other illicit activities. The United States and other donor countries look to the UNHCR to perform day-to-day monitoring functions for the program. The donor countries, meeting regularly as the Joint Consultative Committee, will advise and, as necessary, assist the UNHCR in the overall program management and evaluation tasks.

For the present, the Department believes that the most important item on the antipiracy agenda is to put the UNHCR program into operation as soon as possible: the lives of helpless refugees may be at stake. We are under no illusion that the program, even if implemented to perfection, can "solve" the piracy problem. We are also aware that the UNHCR plan has been criticized as "too little, too late," and that other, more elaborate and expensive proposals have been advanced. Whatever the merit of such assertions, however, the fact is that the UNHCR program presently under negotiation with the RTG is the only mechanism for fighting piracy that can be put into action in the near future, in time to save lives and prevent suffering now and in the several months ahead. Should it be necessary to extend the program beyond its originally anticipated 1-year life span, improvements can and will be made in design and implementation based on the experience gained during the initial 12 months.

But as I have indicated, it is the refugees, not the pirates, who are the new phenomenon in the area. The Department of State has worked very closely with the UNHCR to establish an Orderly Departure Program from Vietnam. This program was resumed last fall for departures for the United States and our expectation is that with the active cooperation of the Vietnamese authorities, it can provide a safe, legal means by which substantial numbers of Vietnamese may leave their country. With this avenue available, it does not in my view make sense for persons to place their lives in jeopardy not only to the normal hazards of the sea but, for those who cross the Gulf of Thailand toward southern Thailand and northern Malaysia, also to the virtual certainty of attack by pirates.

It is difficult to say if the existence of the ODP by itself will lead to a decrease in clandestine boat departures. I should point out however, that a comparison of boat refugee arrivals between August 1981 through March 1982 to the same period of time in 1980–81 shows a 27 percent decrease in refugee arrivals and this is the period of time in which the ODP resumed. An additional factor may have been, however, the increased severity of punishment for those refugees who were caught trying to escape. Whatever the reason, it is our view that the ODP is a going and viable means for Vietnamese to depart safely and legally; this is preferable to the clandestine departures; and if these people do so choose the ODP route, there should be a continuing decrease in the boat refugee flow.

I am prepared to receive any questions you have at this time.

Document 534

Statement Issued by the Department of State, September 25, 1982[5]

The Visit of the Thai Foreign Minister to Washington

Thai Foreign Minister Air Chief Marshal Siddhi Savetsila has completed 3 days of discussions with high-level officials here on a broad range of issues. The Foreign Minister met with the Vice President, the Secretary and Deputy Secretary of State, and the Deputy Secretary of Defense. He also met with congressional leaders.

During the discussions with Foreign Minister Siddhi, both sides reviewed the situation with regard to ASEAN, Kampuchea, the U.S.-Thai security relationship,

[5] Source: Department of State *Bulletin*, November 1982, p. 33. This statement was made available initially to news correspondents by John Hughes, Department of State Spokesman.

and other political and economic matters including the refugee issue. As ASEAN standing committee chairman, Foreign Minister Siddhi requested U.S. Government support on the Kampuchea issue at the United Nations. He also expressed the continuing concern of the ASEAN governments over the threat to peace and stability in the region caused by the continued presence of Vietnamese forces in Kampuchea.

Secretary Shultz reiterated the full support of the United States for the ASEAN approach on the Kampuchea issue, including full withdrawal of Vietnamese forces from Kampuchea and establishment of an independent and neutral government. Secretary Shultz also reaffirmed to Foreign Minister Siddhi the clear U.S. Government commitment to the security of Thailand embodied in the Southeast Asia Collective Defense Treaty and U.S. support for Thailand as the ASEAN frontline state.

During the visit, arrangements were concluded for an additional $9.9 million in foreign military sales (FMS) guarantees, increasing the level for 1982 to more than $75 million in FMS guaranteed credits and grants. These funds will promote further modernization of Thai forces and are another demonstration of the strong security relationship between Thailand and the United States.

The Secretary particularly welcomed this opportunity for a first meeting with Foreign Minister Siddhi, one of Asia's leading statesmen.

Document 535

Transcript of a Press Conference by the Secretary of Defense (Weinberger), Bangkok, November 3, 1982 (Extracts)[6]

Discussions With Thai Officials

. . . .

Q. Can you tell us the main topic of conversations between you and the Thai authorities and General Prem?

A. I think generally they wanted to have our views on the nature, extent and size of the Soviet threat and the firmness of the United States commitment, and also with respect to the threat that might arise should the Vietnamese utilize the dry season to move into Cambodia and perhaps continue on across the border here. We did reassure him that we regarded the Manila Pact[7] and the additional communiqué issued by Secretary of State Rusk and Thanat many years ago[8] to be completely valid and binding on the United States. We also discussed the possibilities of additional arms systems that the government felt might be welcome. The details of the talk, of course, should come from the Prime Minister himself. These were matters that we generally considered.

. . . .

Q. Mr. Secretary, there is no question that the countries of Southeast Asia have both the material and the moral support of the United States, but for the past 5 or 6 years there has been some question about how far the American people, more particularly the U.S. Congress, were willing to go with the manpower support in this area. Do you think that the Congress and the country as a whole have sufficiently recovered from what was termed "post-Vietnam syndrome" that Southeast Asia can again be considered a part of the world where the U.S. military and U.S. Government can again take action if need be?

A. I think this part of the world is clearly one of the most important parts of the globe as far as the United States and the interests of our friends is [*sic*] concerned. We certainly are fully prepared to do everything that we can that seems to be required to maintain the interests of our friends, allies, and ourselves in these areas. They have not thus far indicated any kind of requirement for commitment of military manpower. They have indicated a requirement which we are carrying out now for increased naval activity, increased aerial activity, and those things we are doing.

My own feeling is that given sufficient awareness of the nature of any particular

---

6 Source: *Public Statements of Secretary of Defense Weinberger*, 1982. Secretary Weinberger was on a tour of five East Asian nations, Australia, New Zealand, Thailand, Singapore, and Indonesia, from October 29 to November 9, 1982.

7 Also known as the Southeast Asia Collective Defense Treaty, signed September 8, 1954; for text, see 6 UST 81.

8 Reference is to the Joint Statement issued by Secretary of State Dean Rusk and Thai Foreign Minister Thanat Khoman on March 6, 1962. For text, see *American Foreign Policy: Current Documents, 1962*, pp. 1091–1093.

threat at a given time, the Congress and American people will respond and will respond very quickly to anything that should actually be required. By the same token, I think we would certainly want to make sure that whatever was called for was indeed required for our own interests.

I would hope that we would never again move into any kind of military situation where it was not so vitally necessary for us to do so. That was the great crime, I think, of Vietnam. We entered a war we did not intend to win and that was, I think, a very grave mistake, certainly a terrible thing to ask Americans who participated so very valiantly.

But I think that the votes in the Congress in the last 2 years have demonstrated that they are perfectly willing to add very substantially to American military strength because they are convinced that we required that. I hope that will be the same feeling over the course of the next 2 years because the only way in which a nation can regain the strength that it needs to deter war, is to stay on this kind of very difficult and expensive and basically unpopular sort of path for a number of years. It is unpopular because people in democracies would much rather talk about and think about things other than regaining necessary military strength. We believe, however, in the basic message that it is necessary to do so, and that it is the very best way to maintain the peace. If you do have a situation in which, in concert with your allies and nations of similar interests, you can deter any kind of attack and that is essentially what we are trying to do [*sic*]. So far we believe the recovery is going very well.

. . . .

M. Vietnam

Document 536

Questions Submitted by a Subcommittee of the House Foreign Affairs Committee and Answers by the Department of State, Undated[1]

The Vietnamese Threat to Southeast Asia and the U.S. Response

Q. Review the threat to the United States and ASEAN interests posed by the increased Soviet presence in Southeast Asia and by their Vietnamese clients.

A. From Indochina Moscow can influence regional developments and advance their claim to be an important Asian power. Specifically:

The Soviet military presence in Vietnam underlines Moscow's commitment to back Vietnam's confrontation with China, thus raising the specter of a Sino-Soviet conflict on two fronts.

From Indochina the USSR can project its power more directly in Southeast Asia, to counter U.S. commitments in the region, and to offset Japanese and Western political and economic links with the members of the Association of Southeast Asian Nations.

The increased Soviet military presence near the main sea route between the Pacific and Indian Oceans puts Japan and other Asian states, which depend heavily on seaborne commerce, on notice that the USSR intends to play a major role in Asia, and enables the Soviets to threaten their sea lanes.

Vietnamese facilities afford stops for crew rest, resupply, and minor repairs, thus avoiding costly and time-consuming returns to home ports in the USSR. Moscow can also deploy specialized support ships to

---

[1] Source: *Foreign Assistance Legislation for Fiscal Year 1983: Hearings and Markup Before the Subcommittee on Asian and Pacific Affairs of the Committee on Foreign Affairs, House of Representatives, Ninety-seventh Congress, Second Session* (Washington, 1982), Part 4, pp. 97–98. The questions were submitted by the Subcommittee on Asian and Pacific Affairs. Though the questions and answers were undated, the hearings took place on March 25 and April 21, 1982.

Cam Ranh, making them available for quick reaction support for naval units in potential combat zones.

The Soviets have increased the range, duration and responsiveness of their maritime patrols and now conduct long-range air reconnaissance of U.S., Chinese, Australian, and New Zealand forces in the region.

Soviet forces are now better positioned to threaten the Philippine air and naval bases.

The Soviets have provided their Vietnamese ally with late-model MIG–21 interceptors plus ground attack fighters. The Vietnamese Navy has gained over a dozen patrol boats (some of them missile armed), antisubmarine warfare helicopters and a number of smaller minesweepers.

Moreover, on the ground in Kampuchea the Vietnamese military forces have stepped up their activities against the Kampuchean resistance forces and have been making force improvements in their combat capabilities, e.g., command and control, and target acquisition.

Q. What are the implications of an increased Soviet air and naval presence in Vietnam at Cam Ranh Bay and Da Nang, in the South China Sea and recently even in the Gulf of Thailand? What is the U.S. strategy to counter this heightened Soviet effort?

A. From Vietnam, the Soviets could threaten both our Pacific and Indian Ocean sea lines of communication, and for the first time threaten the Philippines. The Philippines have the only U.S. bases near mainland Asia which are not vulnerable to combined Soviet air and naval attack from existing bases in the Soviet Far East.

In addition to an increased sea lane threat by Soviet forces per se, the USSR has provided its Vietnamese ally with greater air and naval capabilities. The Vietnamese air forces have received late-model MIG–21 interceptors, plus ground-attack fighters. The Vietnamese Navy has gained over a dozen patrol boats (some of them missile armed), anti-submarine warfare helicopters and a number of smaller minesweepers.

A long-term U.S. measure to counter the increased Soviet threat to our global and sea lines of communcations is the administration's well known effort to build up the U.S. Naval Fleet to some 600 ships. The sea lanes in East Asia should benefit from this increased U.S. capability, both in the obvious military sense and politically as our East Asian friends perceive the U.S. buildup as an indication of U.S. resolve to counter the increasing Soviet threat.

Beyond increasing the American military capability, the United States has been helping its East Asian friends and allies to increase their own military capabilities through its security assistance programs. Militarily, the sale of certain naval and air weapons systems has directly increased the capabilities of our friends to provide sea lane security. Training provided at U.S. military schools, either through cash purchase or under the International Military Education and Training (IMET) program further enhances the military capabilities of friendly countries. Politically, U.S. security assistance programs serve as a symbol of the U.S. resolve to remain a Pacific power, and thereby, stiffen the resolve of East Asian countries to resist Soviet encroachments into the region. The demonstrated U.S. commitment provides a milieu which enhances the unity among East Asian countries to meet a common threat, e.g., ASEAN political unity on the Kampuchean question.

Moreover, the United States has been encouraging the Japanese to gradually assume a more active role in their own defense generally, and specifically for the security of their own sea lanes out to approximately 1,000 nautical miles.

Document 537

Transcript of the Department of State Daily Press Briefing, June 14, 1982 (Extract)[2]

Willingness of the United States to Accept Vietnamese Political Detainees

. . . .

Q. Do you have any comment on the Vietnamese offer on television here to send all its political detainees here?

[2] Source: Office of Press Relations, Department of State. Dean Fischer, Department of State Spokesman, conducted the briefing which began at 12:40 p.m.

A. This was the CBS "Sixty Minutes" program?[3]

Yes. As Minister Thach certainly knows, Vietnamese may leave their country for resettlement in the United States in a legal manner through the Orderly Departure Program negotiated with the SRV by the United Nations HCR.

Many Vietnamese now held in re-education camps probably would be eligible for consideration and many have been accepted for this program because of their special ties to the United States, but Hanoi has not issued them exit permits.

The State Department added that it had signified to the Vietnamese that the United States is willing to receive up to 1,000 eligible refugees a month under the Orderly Departure Program.

. . . .

Document 538

Transcript of the Department of State Daily Press Briefing, September 24, 1982 (Extract)[4]

The United States Welcomes Vietnam's Offer to Cooperate on Resolving the Missing-in-Action Issue

. . . .

Q. John, do you have any comment on the reported comments by Vietnamese officials to the effect that they would be willing to cooperate on the missing-in-action issue if the United States were prepared to improve relations with Hanoi?

A. Yes, we do have something on that. We have read the report of Vietnamese Foreign Minister Thach's statement suggesting that four official U.S. teams a year would be allowed to go to Vietnam to discuss the POW/MIA issue.

The United States Government has a longstanding proposal to the Vietnamese that Joint Casualty Resolution Center personnel and representatives of the Vietnamese Office for Seeking Missing Persons meet regularly, preferably in Hanoi, to discuss resolution of the POW/MIA issue. We welcome Mr. Thach's statement and are awaiting official confirmation from the Government of Vietnam.[5]

. . . .

Document 539

Transcript of the Department of State Daily Press Briefing, October 14, 1982 (Extract)[6]

Return of Remains and Documents of Americans Missing-in-Action by the Socialist Republic of Vietnam

. . . .

Q. The MIA transfers in Vietnam, do you have anything to offer us on that, for

---

[3] An interview given Mike Wallace of CBS by Nguyen Co Thach, Foreign Minister of the Socialist Republic of Vietnam, had been broadcast on "Sixty Minutes" the previous day. When Wallace asked Thach about political prisoners, the Vietnamese Foreign Minister offered to send all political detainees to the United States if the U.S. Government would take them.

In a subsequent interview, Thach confirmed that the offer still stood, but that the United States must take all prisoners without exception. (*Indochina Chronology*, Vol. I, No. 2, April–June 1982, p. 8)

[4] Source: Office of Press Relations, Department of State. John Hughes, Department of State Spokesman, conducted the briefing which began at 12:16 p.m.

[5] At the Department of State Daily Press Briefing on October 1, Department of State Acting Spokesman Alan Romberg read the following statement:

"The Government of the Socialist Republic of Vietnam, on September 30, confirmed its acceptance of U.S. technical visits to discuss in Hanoi matters concerning Americans unaccounted for in Vietnam. We appreciate this response to our longstanding proposal for such visits. Vietnamese have agreed to four visits annually, the first [of?] which could take place before the end of this year." (Office of Press Relations, Department of State)

[6] Source: Office of Press Relations, Department of State. Alan Romberg, Department of State Acting Spokesman, conducted the briefing which began at 12:05 p.m.

instance, the specifics of what was transferred, to whom it was transferred, and is this the first fruit of a recent agreement to deal with searches?

A. First of all, the remains of five U.S. servicemen and identity documents on three U.S. servicemen were turned over to a Department of Defense recovery team which flew to Hanoi, October 14, today.

I might note that we understand from the Vietnamese that they are the remains which were mentioned previously to the Vietnam Veterans Association.

Obviously, we welcome the return of the remains and are prepared to receive them from any source. We regard government-to-government channels as the most effective and appropriate manner for the return of remains.

In terms of first fruit of discussions and so on, I don't know how to address that except to say that we have been dealing with the Vietnamese on this issue for many years. We welcome this development. Continued progress will depend on the cooperation of the Government of Vietnam, but I would have to refer further questions on it to DOD. I just don't have any more details on this.

Q. I guess I was just getting at the apparent breakthrough that occurred last month when the North Vietnamese said they would welcome a team, a regularly-spaced team,[7] and I wondered if this was part of that; or is this outside of that, and those arrangements have not yet been completed or not yet progressed beyond where they were.

A. I have given you everything I've got on it.

. . . .

---

[7] See *supra.*

Chapter 14. Africa

A. General Policy

Document 540

Testimony by the Assistant Secretary of State for African Affairs (Crocker) Before a Subcommittee of the House Foreign Affairs Committee, March 9, 1982 (Extract)[1]

U.S. Human Rights Policy Toward Africa

. . . Do we really have a human rights policy in Africa?

A. Yes, we do. Human rights is an integral part of our overall foreign policy, the goal of which is the defense and promotion of liberty in the world. A human rights policy, like all policies, is ultimately judged on its effectiveness. This administration decided that traditional diplomacy would be the most effective means to pursue our human rights concerns with countries with which we have friendly relations. As previously noted, we have raised our concerns about human rights problems with the countries mentioned and with other countries in Africa. We believe traditional diplomacy allows for full and frank expression of our concerns, and allows other governments to take remedial actions without fear of seeming to bow to U.S. pressure. We have expressed our opposition to apartheid and encouraged South Africa along the road of peaceful evolution away from apartheid. We have and will continue to make our human rights concerns known to the governments of African countries.

. . . .

[1] Source: *Implementation of Congressionally Mandated Human Rights Provisions (Volume II): Hearings Before the Subcommittees on Europe and the Middle East, on Asian and Pacific Affairs, on Human Rights and International Organizations, and on Africa of the Committee on Foreign Affairs, House of Representatives, Ninety-seventh Congress* (Washington, 1982), p. 325. Crocker's answer was sent under cover of a letter dated August 12 from Assistant Secretary of State for Congressional Affairs Powell A. Moore to Representative Howard Wolpe, Chairman of the House Subcommittee on African Affairs, in response to written questions submitted by Wolpe during the March 9 hearings on human rights in Africa. For the text of Crocker's testimony of March 9, see *ibid.*, pp. 225–253.

Document 541

Prepared Statement by the Deputy Assistant Secretary of State for African Affairs (Bishop) Before a Subcommittee of the House Appropriations Committee, March 17, 1982 (Extract)[2]

U.S. Goals in Africa

I appreciate the opportunity to appear before this Committee to present the Bureau of African Affairs' FY'83 budget request.

We are seeking to achieve the following goals, which reflect our major concerns on the African Continent. In east Africa and the Horn, we seek to protect our strategic interests in maintaining access both to the Indian Ocean and the Persian Gulf. We, therefore, view the establishment of economic stability in such countries as Sudan, Kenya, and Somalia as vital to the development of their ability to resist increasing threats from countries such as Ethiopia and Libya. In west Africa, we have strategic interests to protect which involve access to key military and communications facilities, as well as access to the region's mineral resources. Nigeria, for example, is one of our largest suppliers of oil. In southern Africa we seek to achieve objectives corresponding to a wide range of U.S. interests, including ensuring continued Western access to key strategic minerals and reducing opportunities for Soviet and Cuban adventurism.

[2] Source: *Departments of Commerce, Justice, and State, the Judiciary, and Related Agencies Appropriations for 1983: Hearings Before a Subcommittee of the Committee on Appropriations, House of Representatives, Ninety-seventh Congress, Second Session* (Washington, 1982), pp. 683–687.

In seeking to achieve these basic foreign policy objectives in Africa, the Bureau of African Affairs recognizes the enhancement of political and economic stability and development to be of great concern to the United States. Regional stability in Africa obviously affects our security interests in terms of continued access to essential facilities, fuel, and strategic minerals. It is a necessary environment for the effective promotion and development of American trade and commercial interests in Africa, and it directly impinges on our ability to initiate appropriate dialogues on such issues as human rights and proper consideration of the concerns of American citizens in Africa, be they businessmen or tourists, students or scholars.

Our determination to achieve the goal of regional stability has had several positive results over the past year. We and our Western Contact Group allies are in the midst of promising negotiations with the frontline states, South Africa, SWAPO, and the internal political parties of Namibia which could lead to independence for that state and withdrawal of Cuban combat forces from Angola in the foreseeable future. Thanks, in large measure, to the initiatives of the Africans themselves, the Libyan military presence in Chad has ended, and we are assisting the OAU peacekeeping force presently in that country with logistic support. Continuing consultations and cooperation with Liberia's postrevolutionary government have maintained our cooperative relationship with that nation. Similarly, we have moved to strengthen our political and military ties with other key west African states. We have further expanded our warm political and security relationship with the strategically vital nations of eastern Africa and the Horn. We have also continued to encourage a steady peaceful evolution toward social, political, and economic justice in South Africa.

Many problems remain unresolved on the continent. The Soviets, their surrogates and the Libyans continue to pose a threat to the stability of many countries. Conflicts still exist in Eritrea, Angola, and Mozambique. The solutions to the political problems of Chad have not yet been found. And a democratically elected government in Ghana has been replaced by a revolutionary regime.[3] Nonetheless, the Africans themselves have successfully met and overcome many other problems: a radical coup in the Gambia was suppressed with Senegalese assistance;[4] as noted above, African pressures led to the Libyan pullback from Chad; Uganda's economy is reviving, and its political stability, although fragile, has improved; and many nations are trying to face up to the monetary dislocation caused by external and internal events during the past decade and to put their economies back on safer tracks.

All of our efforts look toward the long term, as well as the short term, interests of the United States and our ability to represent best those interests in Africa. Our ability to respond to the needs of an American tourist or businessman who is confused, or perhaps even distraught, by his first contact with an unfamiliar culture very much depends on effective American representation. Our ability to lend support to meeting those strategic requirements that are inseparable from our national security interests, and our ability to assess and deal with future political, economic, social, and military problems in strategically important countries such as Sudan and Liberia, all depend on effective American representation. That effectiveness, in turn, is dependent on our willingness to make what we believe to be a well-reasoned commitment of personnel and of resources to a continent which brings us face to face with great complexities and difficulties on one hand and with great possibilities on the other.

We in the Africa Bureau believe that the growing awareness on the part of the American public has been amply demonstrated for many members of Congress by the numerous inquiries they have begun to receive from all quarters—and often have passed on to us—regarding developments in Africa. The future holds more American business interests in Africa, more American visitors to Africa, more American students and scholars in Africa. It also brings with it questions of how we may best safeguard our access to facilities and resources crucial to our national strategic and security interests. What reception American concerns in these matters will encounter is really at the heart of the question of that relationship with Africa which we seek to develop and encourage.

. . . .

[3] On December 31, 1981, former Ghana Air Force Lieutenant Jerry Rawlings overthrew the government of Hilla Limann. For further information, see *Washington Post*, January 1, 1982, p. A15, and *New York Times*, January 1, 1982, p. 1.

[4] See document 596.

Document 542

Address by the Assistant Secretary of State for African Affairs (Crocker) Before the Conference on Trade and Investment in Africa, Boston, April 14, 1982[5]

Enterprise in Africa

The purpose of this conference is to discuss opportunities for U.S. business in Africa. The motive of the government cosponsors—the Departments of State and Commerce—can be stated simply. First, we believe the future peace and stability of Africa depends in substantial measure on economic growth, and that this can be achieved only by an increase in mutually advantageous trade and investment.

We are of course aware that stability does not always flow automatically from economic development. Growth creates new realities and, at times, new challenges to political leadership. But this is not the problem we face in most of contemporary Africa. Although some countries are making solid progress, more are close to economic crisis, beset by problems both of their own making and beyond their control. African states need greater U.S. trade and investment to help reverse no-growth trends, to broaden their chances for self-reliance, and to strengthen the prospects for genuine economic security. If present trends continue, the risk of spiraling instability can only grow.

Second, we in government are convinced—as I am certain you are—that the United States requires in its own self-interest a more activist commercial diplomacy in Africa. In the past this has been less urgent. But we have learned much in the first two-plus decades of African independence. Contracts do not necessarily go to the lowest bidder, or to the premier technology. Foreign trade and foreign policy cannot be effectively sanitized from each other. Despite obvious comparative advantages favoring many U.S. products and technologies, our trade imbalance with African nations has mushroomed. Opportunities remain little more than that unless talented and dedicated managers and salesmen know how to translate them into reality. We in government are determined to do our share.

Until today my remarks at gatherings such as this one have usually emphasized the economic policy initiatives undertaken by this administration to stimulate U.S. trade and investment in Africa and elsewhere. As most of you are aware, these initiatives have covered a spectrum of activities. We have reduced or eliminated some needless disincentives to business, such as the excessive income tax previously paid by Americans abroad. In the same vein, we are working to legalize export trading companies, and to rationalize the Foreign Corrupt Practices Act.[6]

New aid initiatives are underway which will facilitate increased investment (both foreign and local) and help develop indigenous entrepreneurs. Our aid programs have been reshaped to help wherever possible those governments which are willing to take the often difficult steps necessary to create incentives for private trade and investment.

American Ambassadors have been instructed to place highest priority on helping U.S. businessmen, only one symptom of a more general determination to eliminate the traditional mind set which assumes an adversary relationship between American Government and American business. Abroad, we have initiated a candid dialogue with governments on how they can create or improve conditions that will attract investment. In Africa our new approach was both symbolized and reinforced by an unprecedented Cabinet-level trade and investment mission in January led by Secretaries Baldrige and Block.

In short, the administration's new private-sector strategy is now clearly discernible and beginning to yield results. Among other things, we in government have engaged as never before in a dialogue with business, both in the United States and at our Embassies abroad. We are beginning to learn something about the ingredients of success in the African environment.

Based on that experience, and at the risk of presumption, I would like to shift ground slightly. With your permission, I would like to venture a few thoughts not about what government hopes to do for you, but about what you, as businessmen, might do for yourselves in order to help achieve our

[5] Source: Department of State files.

[6] For text, see P.L. 95–213, approved December 19, 1977; 91 Stat. 1503–1508.

shared goal of a stronger U.S. economic presence in Africa. (I would note at the outset that you are of course welcome to reciprocate by sharing with me and my colleagues your views on U.S. foreign policy—indeed it is my hope that we can keep the dialogue going on both levels.)

I would like to organize my remarks under four general headings: first, the importance of American business presence; second, concern for African development aspirations; third, getting more mileage from the government-business relationship; and fourth, taking full advantage of the great diversity—in products, personnel, and organizations—that characterizes American capitalism.

Presence comes first because it is probably most important. At every stop on the recent high-level trade mission, Africans asked, "Where are the American businessmen? We want to see more of them." In Africa as elsewhere, business success begins with awareness and ends with acceptance. But in most societies, and particularly in Africa, this process involves personal contact. Businessmen who succeed in Africa repeatedly tell us that personal contact, both with local businessmen and with responsible local officials, is in most cases far more effective than that much over-discussed subject, bribery.

Presence takes time, and you will rightly observe that time is money. We are very much aware of the expense factor, estimating as we do that the start-up cost of placing one official American in an African capital runs into six figures. Effective presence involves cultural sensitivity (and, in the francophone areas, ability to speak French). It means recruiting managers who enjoy the special challenge of doing business in a developing country.

In short, persistence and specialized skills are necessary corollaries of presence. The necessary effort makes little sense unless it is regarded as a long-term investment in a continent with great potential for further growth. We believe that Africa's great resource potential—in oil, minerals, timber, and agriculture—does justify such a long-term approach, notwithstanding such here-and-now problems as a shortage of skilled labor, shortage of physical and management infrastructure, and (in some cases) investment policies which deter all but the most adventurous of entrepreneurs.

My second theme is concern for development aspirations. This is partly but not entirely a matter of tone. Increasingly, even Socialist African governments are anxious for more U.S. trade and investment. They know full well it won't happen unless the foreign businessman makes a fair profit. But they also want the kind of business activities which will most obviously and immediately contribute to their own development goals. To the extent that businesses generate employment and/or foreign exchange they contribute to development. Because food production is the number one economic problem of the continent, there is a particularly keen and widespread interest in agribusiness, a field where, as I need not tell you, the United States remains without peer.

One of the most successful participants in the recent high-level trade mission was an American agribusinessman proffering two kinds of projects—integrated poultry production and mechanized mass production of cassava, a starchy African staple which has up to now been largely untouched by modern technology. To the Africans this man could say, "I am relevant to your problems. I can help you to produce better food at a fraction of what it costs you at present. In the process I will make a profit and you will learn a new technology, reduce food imports, and improve the quality of life of your population." To virtually any African leader such a message is well nigh irresistible, and the businessman in question was almost mobbed by would-be joint venturers at every stop on the trip.

There are many ways in which business can appeal to Africa's development aspirations. Investment proposals which emphasize the role for a joint venture partner are sometimes necessary and always more saleable. Training is another relevant area—and it can take many forms. The manager of a profitable joint venture tire factory in a very underdeveloped central African country tells us that his happiest and most successful expatriate managers are people who naturally enjoy teaching on the job. Of course, multinational companies can achieve tremendous developmental impact through more formal technical educational initiatives in the United States or in Africa. In several developing countries, U.S. firms have assisted or even created institutions of learning. For example, Union Carbide built and equipped a technical college in Queque, Zimbabwe, to help offset loss of technical skills through emigration. In Latin America, U.S. firms contribute equipment to a regional food processing and packaging training institution in Mexico City, an idea with obvious potential for application to Africa.

Many recent development studies, including the World Bank's report entitled "Accelerated Development in Sub-Saharan Africa," have called for more training of Africans, especially in management, as interns or research assistants with banks and multinational corporations. There is no reason why the costs of such training cannot be shared between private and public sector entities; it is another concept ripe for further development.

My third theme, the government-business relationship, could be boiled down to two words: "exploit us," and by "us" I mean Congress as well as the executive branch. As I mentioned earlier we feel we've made a fair beginning in developing a new economic policy framework. We need to know from you whether we're on or off target. We would like to hear from specific sectors of the business community—the bankers, for example—as well as from those who are concerned with particular regions or countries. We want to know how you feel about government programs and institutions and in what ways they could be doing more to encourage greater U.S. competitiveness abroad. If you want maximum effectiveness you should convey your views on specific topics to the Congress as well as the executive branch. I would note that one of the best ways to make your views known is through business organizations, including both bilateral business councils abroad and such groups as the American Chamber of Commerce in the United States. In other parts of the world—the ASEAN region of Southeast Asia[7] is a good example—such organizations have become a highly effective vehicle for government–business dialogue and cooperation. In Africa the recent formation of a U.S.–Nigeria bilateral business council is a solid achievement in this important area.

Speaking as a representative of the State Department, I would also remind you that our Embassies are a rich source of information on doing business in African countries, particularly for a first-time visitor. They can provide free risk assessment as well as economic data. They are familiar not only with U.S. aid programs, and how these may be relevant to your concerns, but also with the usually larger programs of the World Bank and other multilateral institutions. If they don't know the answers to your questions they can generally put you in touch with someone who does.

We have been gratified by recent reports that businessmen working in Africa have noticed a positive change in the attitude of U.S. Embassies toward advising and assisting them. We appreciate that feedback, and are confident that the warming trend will continue. In Washington, we in the Africa Bureau at the Department of State have instituted an "open door" policy toward U.S. businessmen and their concerns. Whether at home or abroad, this administration is willing to get involved on your behalf, subject only to the constraints imposed by law.

My fourth theme is the diversity of American society—our private sector writ large—and the almost limitless ways in which this diversity can help stimulate business activity. Two general aspects of American diversity are especially relevant in this connection. The first is the sheer size of the U.S. market, which has stimulated an enormous range of goods and services with unexploited potential for export to, or replication in, developing countries. The second aspect is the wealth of private voluntary and trade-related activity which gives American capitalism a unique developmental dimension.

Let me mention three subtopics and some specifics which will barely scratch the surface of this vast area.

First: industrial conventions, professional symposia and trade fairs. All these activities can provide Africans and others with high-level exposure to U.S. products and the latest developments in particular fields. A typical opportunity would be for American pharmaceutical firms active in west Africa to jointly select, invite, and pay the expenses of key west Africans to attend an Atlanta conference on drug treatment for tropical dermatological disorders.

More developing country attendance at U.S. trade fairs is another example. For example, our largest agricultural trade fair, held annually at Moultrie, Georgia, shows products in action in a way that forcefully impresses developing country viewers. Business sponsorship of more African attendance at such events would be worthwhile. Developing country representation at industrial conventions of such obviously relevant organizations as the Irrigation Association, the Solar Energy Association, or the National Water Well Association, is another activity with great potential. The Department of Commerce foreign buyers program is actively promoting LDC attendance at such conventions.

---

[7] The Association of South East Asian Nations (ASEAN) is comprised of Thailand, the Philippines, Indonesia, Malaysia, and Singapore.

Second: "relevant technology." U.S. firms can publicize equipment which has special application in developing countries. For example, John Deere has helped the Iowa-based Self-help Foundation to display its small tractor—"The next step up from oxen"—at a fair in Mexico City. The fair itself was organized by Appropriate Technology International, a Washington private voluntary organization which operates with AID support.

R&D divisions of U.S. corporations occasionally turn out goods or processes that are not applicable to the U.S. market but have real potential for developing countries. A large Missouri chemicals manufacturer, for example, developed a laundry detergent process that was too small for North America but exactly what was needed in a small west African country. Another Missouri company points to advances in metallurgy which would be "marvelous for blacksmiths—if we had any blacksmiths." Africa has thousands.

Because of the obvious need for better information about such opportunities, the National Technical Information Service, in cooperation with Control Data Corporation of Minneapolis, is organizing a data base which, drawing on both U.S. Government and private sector information, will be available to service developing country requests, channelled through U.S. Embassies, for advice on appropriate technology.

Third: volunteer advisers. The United States has a unique wealth of individuals and organizations who provide voluntary services to assist with business education and management advice. An outstanding example, one which has produced success stories from all corners of the globe, is the International Executive Service Corps (IESC), through which retired business executives, free from the demands and schedules of former jobs, devote 1 to 3 months abroad advising on projects which demand precise kinds of expertise. The Peace Corps is also devoting new and increased attention to programs which will stimulate the development of local entrepreneurship, concentrating on activities which have maximum impact on small businesses and rural areas.

I could go on citing the almost endless variety of U.S. organizations, institutions, and industrial processes which are relevant both to Africa's development and to the further development of U.S. trade and investment; the main point is that if we are serious about competing abroad, U.S. awareness and support for the private voluntary—educational—technology transfer dimension of our presence is neither marginal nor a form of charity.

I would end by emphasizing that we in government are not urging American business to replace government aid programs. We are fully aware that for the private sector, a reasonable assurance of profit must remain the essential prerequisite for further involvement, in Africa as anywhere else. It is for that reason that through our aid programs, and in every other way possible, we are encouraging and supporting efforts on the part of the Africans themselves to improve the investment climate and reduce growth-inhibiting overregulation of trade.

Yet it is also a fact that private resource flows are already by far the most important dimension of our economic involvement in Africa. Since there is no realistic prospect for dramatic increases in official aid flows, the relative importance of our private sector to our official economic policy objectives will increase in the years ahead. As a result, there is no more room to question that the interests of government and business are linked.

Your efforts in Africa can provide the margin between success or failure in two interrelated areas. These are, first, competing in a difficult but expanding market with the other industrialized democracies; and second, helping Africa achieve the increased level of prosperity necessary to political health and stability. It is my hope that we can keep working together with increased effectiveness to achieve these goals.

Document 543

Prepared Statement by the Assistant Secretary of State for African Affairs (Crocker) Before a Subcommittee of the House Foreign Affairs Committee, April 20, 1982[8]

Proposed Foreign Assistance Budget for Africa

Mr. Chairman, members of the committee, I appreciate this opportunity to discuss

---

[8] Source: *Foreign Assistance Legislation for Fiscal*

with you the integrated foreign assistance budget for Africa which the President has proposed for Fiscal Year 1983. We view our foreign assistance as vitally important since it represents the principal tool the U.S. Government has at its disposal for effecting its goals in the foreign policy area in African countries.

Under Secretary Buckley has already discussed with the House the worldwide increases the administration is requesting above those levels already authorized by Congress for FY 1983.[9] That authorization was made without the benefit of the administration's views, and it is to present those views as they pertain to Africa that my colleagues and I are here today.

The administration has made major strides to improve and intensify the American dialogue and partnership with key African states. While we respond in part to humanitarian motives, these programs cannot be conceived of as charity. They are in the American national interest and they buttress American policies and goals: enhancing regional security in the face of destabilizing adventures; strengthening threatened economies that could slide into heightened political instability; expanding growth possibilities in which U.S. exporters, workers, and investors will be direct beneficiaries; and enhancing the prospects for negotiated solutions to the dangerous conflicts of southern Africa. We believe our credibility as a regional partner and world leader is dependent on the strength of our bilateral assistance efforts. The assistance programs which we are carrying out are designed to address both economic and security goals, for we recognize that sooner or later political security and economic security are interdependent sides of the same coin.

We expect that our efforts, combined with those of other Western and multilateral donors, will achieve further progress. Clearly the process will not be quick or easy, for reasons that are well known. Africa has the worst economic growth rate of any continent. It contains two-thirds of those countries certified by the United Nations as being the very poorest. It is also the only continent with declining per capita food production. Last year Africa's food import bill alone rose by 7% or $1 billion, an amount roughly equivalent to our total bilateral aid program. Many African nations are caught in the merciless squeeze of high oil prices, stagnating export production, and ever mounting debt.

All too often governments have opted for economic policies which work against sustained, real economic growth. We are encouraged, however, by a growing awareness among Africans themselves that an improved economic policy climate, combined with increased trade and investment, is the real key to economic growth, and that without growth equity will remain elusive. It is our judgment that economic policymaking in a number of African nations is at a watershed, and in the balance rest our shared hopes for a brighter economic future and our interest in growing participation in African development.

I said that our African programs are not charity programs. In every case, the development and security measures which we support with our aid require resource commitments and often tough decisions by the Africans themselves. Our economic programs, funded by DA, ESF and P.L. 480,[10] encourage and support the self-help efforts of the Africans and are designed to complement the much larger resource flows provided by multilateral institutions (chiefly the World Bank) as well as the economic stabilization programs of the IMF. Our military assistance programs, constituting less than one-quarter of our total 1983 budget, provide a credible level of response to our friends who face external threats. We recognize that security programs cost money which in a perfect world could be devoted to economic programs. Our FY 1983 FMS credit request seeks to restore direct credits so that we can ease the repayment burden by offering concessional terms. We are proposing that $210 million of our total FMS program of $234 million be in direct credit. In Africa, as in the United States, where security needs exist they must be addressed.

Our total proposed FY 1983 Africa assistance program is divided as follows:

Year 1983: Hearings and Markup Before the Subcommittee on Africa of the Committee on Foreign Affairs, House of Representatives, Ninety-seventh Congress, Second Session (Washington, 1982), Part 7, pp. 6–16.

[9] Reference is to Buckley's testimony of April 1, 1982. For the text of this testimony, see *Foreign Assistance Legislation for Fiscal Year 1983: Hearings Before the Subcommittee on International Security and Scientific Affairs of the Committee on Foreign Affairs, House of Representatives, Ninety-seventh Congress, Second Session* (Washington, 1982), Part 2, pp. 2–28.

[10] Title I of P.L. 480 authorizes the sale of agricultural commodities to foreign countries on credit terms. For the basic legislation, see 68 Stat. 454 and subsequent amendments.

1. DA	$324 million
2. ESF	$325 million
3. P.L. 480–I	$117 million
4. P.L. 480–II	$75 million
5. FMS	$234 million
6. IMET	$9 million
TOTAL:	$1.083 billion

In the following remarks, I will address our programs under the ESF, FMS, and IMET titles. Mr. Ruddy will concentrate primarily on our DA and P.L. 480 programs.[11]

ESF

The largest component of our African assistance budget is the $325 million in ESF. The quick disbursement and flexibility of ESF is particularly important to promote economic and political stability in key countries where the United States has security interests. In several of these countries we also have DA programs to promote basic, long-term economic growth. Present world economic conditions and the fragile infrastructure of many African countries, however, result in situations like the one in Sudan which urgently requires short-term, balance-of-payments assistance if economic development and political stability are to be achieved. Liberia, Somalia, and to a lesser degree Kenya all face similar problems. Our ongoing ESF programs are designed to bridge the gap between their short-term needs and long-term development goals.

In southern Africa we are again proposing ESF to fulfill our commitment to assist Zimbabwe as it seeks in the early independence years to meet popular aspirations while also encouraging a healthy mixed economy, the retention of skills and an open political system. Our assistance to Zambia, Botswana, and in the regional program demonstrate interest in promoting the political and economic stability of the mineral rich but volatile southern Africa region. Moreover if we are to continue to make progress in negotiating the interrelated issues and conflicts in Namibia and Angola we need to demonstrate consistently and concretely our support for the area.

This year we are proposing three new ESF programs: Senegal, Niger, and Zaire. The two west Africa countries are strategically located, friendly to the United States, and threatened by economic instability and Libyan adventurism. The small ESF commodity import programs coupled with our other assistance are designed to assist these two nations to meet these threats. Both countries have excellent records in use of economic development resources. Senegal is currently tackling some difficult but basic economic reforms to reduce subsidies, improve prices to farmers, and eliminate inefficient operations. It also plays an important regional security role through participation in peacekeeping efforts. Providing these resources will show our support of good economic management and our recognition of the special security threat posed in this region.

Our proposed $15 million ESF program is small against the magnitude of the problems facing Zaire; nevertheless, we feel that financing essential imports for the private sector is a key factor in both assisting the economy and encouraging needed structural reform. We are working closely with the IMF and other donor countries to impress on the Zairian Government the need to restructure its economic policy. Direct help to the private sector reinforces that message and stimulates economic activity in depressed areas of Zaire's economy.

Security Assistance

The military assistance component of our assistance program, which accounts for roughly one-quarter of the total, is founded on both the security needs of the countries concerned and our own regional security concerns. The bulk of this assistance, with the obvious exception of the new programs, is to fund efforts already begun which were the product of careful consultations and planning both with our African interlocutors and among the executive agencies concerned. I have provided charts along with this statement which detail our FY 1983 budget proposal and review the FY's 1981 and 1982 actual program allocations.

FMS represents our principal tool for responding to the very real defense needs of a number of African countries. You will also note as we discuss the details of these programs that they are essentially defensive in nature, and provide basic military equipment and training and some support items such as housing and communications equipment. In Africa as elsewhere the United States simply cannot be a credible partner or reliable friend if we turn a deaf ear to those who turn to us with legitimate military requirements; we cannot ignore the presence and activity in Africa of forces hostile to both our friends and to us. We are also sensitive to the severe economic bind in which many of our African friends and potential friends find themselves, and thus we are seeking to the greatest degree possi-

---

[11] See the prepared statement, *infra.*

ble concessional terms for the FMS funds we are requesting. We appreciate the efforts of the Congress in passing legislation in FY 1982 which authorized concessional credit. I strongly urge the Congress to authorize additional concessional terms for 1983 in order to bring consistency to our development and security assistance efforts.

Our major FMS programs continue to be Kenya, Liberia, Somalia, Sudan, and Zaire. The only new program for FY 1983 is in Zimbabwe.

For Kenya we are requesting $28m in ESF, $35m in FMS direct credits, and $1.5m in IMET. These levels are programmatic and if approved will allow Kenya to continue programs already begun and perhaps begin needed logistic and communications programs. Kenya continues to be among our strongest friends in sub-Saharan Africa and one of our most consistent political allies. With the exception of ESF there are no significant changes here from our FY 1982 allocations.

For Liberia we are requesting $32m in ESF, $15m in FMS direct credits, and $800,000 in IMET. These levels reflect continuations of programs already begun. The FMS program consists primarily of the military housing project, which addresses the kind of problems which helped spark the military takeover in 1980. The remainder of FMS and IMET provides basic equipment and training for the Liberian armed forces. We need to continue our assistance levels in order to help promote stability and encourage continued progress and reform.

We have come a long way in our relationship with Somalia and we are now seeing some positive results of the patience shown on both sides and of our willingness to provide assistance. Our request for FY 1983 is much the same as our FY 1982 allocation. We are requesting $25m in ESF, $30m in FMS direct credits, and $550,000 in IMET. The FMS credits will be used to complete programs already begun, primarily early warning radar, ground transportation, and communications.

Sudan continues to be our largest program. Strategically located as a bridge between the Middle East and Africa, and between the Horn of Africa and Libya, Sudan is experiencing extremely severe economic problems. These problems will continue, but we hope they will be less severe than they are at this moment. We are requesting $100m in FMS direct credits and $1.5m in IMET. Although these are, objectively speaking, large numbers, they nevertheless will only allow the Sudanese to continue the programs begun in 1982. These programs will include rounding out the tank battalion, adding to the F–5 program, completing the early warning radar program and adding equipment to the combat engineer, communications, and transportation programs. The Sudanese also hope to begin a modest naval modernization program in 1983.

In Zaire, as in other countries, we have based our military assistance levels on continuation of ongoing programs. The FMS credits will go toward supporting the C–130 and ground vehicle programs, and toward modernization of some of the ground force units. We are also working on logistics and communication improvements. We will continue to use both technical assistance and mobile training teams to the fullest. Our efforts in Zaire are aimed at preventing disorganization of the armed forces and destabilization in the Shaba region. Our efforts parallel those of the French and Belgians in the military assistance field. Without the modest increase proposed we cannot expect to be successful in our effort to strengthen the capacity for self-defense of this critically located and vast African nation.

Our only new FMS program is for Zimbabwe where we are proposing a modest program of $3m in FMS credit. Our overall commitment to Zimbabwe's total development, which I cited earlier, compels us to look favorably on appropriate requests for nonlethal military assistance. We anticipate that Zimbabwe will wish to use those credits for ground transportation, uniforms, boots, and some communications equipment. We are continuing our IMET program and are proposing $150,000 for Zimbabwe in 1983.

IMET is a program which produces invaluable results for an extremely modest outlay of funds. We are requesting just under $9m for a program which not only keeps us in close touch with the military establishments of the countries concerned, but also gives us a unique opportunity to expose the future leaders of those establishments to American methods, values, equipment, and society, and thus gain from the beneficial aspects inherent in any cross-cultural exchange. Our proposed new programs for the IMET budget are Zambia, Guinea, and Madagascar. The largest programs are proposed for Kenya, Liberia, Sudan, and Zaire.

We are not requesting any funds in this budget for the peacekeeping force in Chad.

As you may know, a recent OAU special meeting on Chad held in Nairobi[12] resulted in a decision to withdraw the PKF at the end of June. Nevertheless, it is possible that the PKF could be needed beyond June to help protect a political reconciliation process. The OAU is planning a request to the United Nations for voluntary contributions to the PKF. Should further U.S. help be needed, we will have to examine with the Congress how such requirements can be met.

Mr. Chairman, I know that many critics of the administration have the perception that the U.S. Government is somehow shifting its foreign assistance emphasis from the developmental field to the military field, that we are actively seeking to become the major arms supplier in Africa. That is very far from the truth. The United States has no such ambition. We account for no more than about 4% of African arms imports, while the USSR accounts for approximately 60%. Although Mr. Ruddy will discuss developmental assistance with the committee, the figures I mentioned at the beginning of this statement should give you a very clear idea of the relationship within the Africa budget of economic assistance to military assistance: the ratio is about three to one. It is true that the strictly "military" portion of this year's budget is a larger percentage of the total than last year, but I believe the bulk of that increase can be accounted for by programmatic increases, the expensive nature of some types of equipment and the request for conditionality I mentioned previously. I believe a better characterization of what distinguishes our 1983 program from some of its recent predecessors and what differentiates this administration's approach to the broader foreign assistance policy we must take is that the U.S. Government is now actively seeking to be a reliable partner, a sympathetic and helpful friend who no longer looks askance at the very real security requirements of friends in need, and a realistic world power capable of evaluating threats to its friends and to itself. We are also, I believe, readier to be responsive to foreign policy opportunities, and to do so with all the instruments at our disposal, including security assistance which in the recent past was seen to be "off limits" for reasons founded more in a misreading of history than in a realistic appraisal of U.S. interests. This administration has launched important initiatives and sought to strengthen key partnerships in Africa—a region of growing importance in global politics. We are conducting an active African policy that takes into account the full range of regional and global factors that impinge upon Africa and our interests there. To do less would be to discourage our friends or to force them to turn to sources of help that would be destabilizing and against our interests in a peaceful continent. To do less would be a signal that this country has not yet grasped the extent of its interests in this region and is prepared to ignore its challenges and opportunities, its needs and potential.

Mr. Chairman, I would be happy at this time to discuss these programs in more detail.

Document 544

Prepared Statement by the Assistant Administrator for Africa, Agency for International Development (Ruddy), Before a Subcommittee of the House Foreign Affairs Committee, April 20, 1982[13]

AID's Proposed Economic Assistance Request for Africa

FY 1983 Request

Thank you for the opportunity to discuss AID's FY 1983 economic assistance request for Africa.

For FY 1983 the Africa Bureau is requesting a total of $648.4 million, a 7 percent increase over the FY 1982 level of $606.1 million. The Development Assistance request of $323.4 million is virtually unchanged from the FY 1982 level of $327.5 million. The FY 1983 request of $325 million for ESF is 17.3 percent higher than the $276.7 million in FY 1982.

The $323.4 million in Development Assistance for FY 1983 will concentrate on the following areas: $142 million for agriculture and rural development activities; $32.4 million for health activities; $30 million for education and human resources development programs; $20 million to address se-

[12] The OAU ad hoc committee on Chad met in Nairobi on February 10–11, 1982.

[13] Source: *Foreign Assistance Legislation for Fiscal Year 1983,* Part 7, pp. 19–33.

lected development problems; and $7 million for population planning (including $2 million in population activities in the Sahel Development Program). The Sahel Development Program, which is a separate functional account, for which $93.8 million is requested, focuses on food production, environmental reclamation, health, population and related training. In addition to Development Assistance, $325 million in Economic Support Funds is requested primarily for programs in Southern Africa and the Horn. $191.7 million in P.L. 480 assistance is requested, including $43 million in Title III. The FY 1983 request, if appropriated, will be used to address a series of economic and social problems throughout Africa.

Overview of Trends in Africa

From what we can observe over the last decade, economic development in sub-Saharan Africa is becoming more difficult and urgent. After moderate but steady growth and development in the 1960's and early 1970's, the economic performance of Africa has declined, and projections for the 1980's are not bright. At present, average annual growth in per capita GNP is projected between 1 percent and negative 1 percent between 1980 and 1990.

The downturn in African economic performance is taking place against a background of population growth, relatively slow rates of technological change, and the fact that in many areas the limit of cultivation has been reached.

While Africa's population is estimated to be growing at an average annual rate of about 2.8 percent, food production has not kept pace. Throughout the seventies, the average annual per capita growth rate in agriculture, Africa's most important economic activity, was minus 1.4 percent for all crops. Per capita food production was minus 1.2 percent. Overall production increases, such as they have been, were attained almost exclusively by expanding the areas under cultivation. Food yields per hectare in Africa have been at a lower level than in other regions.

Potential and Progress in Africa

Notwithstanding what we are witnessing in sub-Saharan Africa, the region has substantial long-term economic promise. Africa has the potential for increasing annual production of cereals by 16 million metric tons from rainfed land and by 9 million metric tons from irrigated land, for an annual production increase of 25 million metric tons. This compares to a total production of 42 million metric tons in the period 1977–79. The potential average annual increase in livestock products is estimated at 1.04 million metric tons.

Sub-Saharan Africa has nine major river basins running through several countries in the Sahel, central and southern Africa. Irrigation potential can be compared to the American West. The basins offer the possibility of putting some 14 million hectares under irrigation. Africa is estimated to have over one-third of the world's potential hydropower resources. Energy from hydropower is one of Africa's greatest underutilized resources. The natural highways which are formed by the rivers can serve as low-energy alternatives for moving agricultural products to markets and supplies to producers.

The Sahel region alone could put 2 to 6 million hectares under irrigation, and about 1.8 million of that could be under irrigation by the year 2000. This alone would mean a 50 percent increase in food produced. Significant production increases could be achieved through intensification of dry land production, application of different farm technologies and opening of new lands through onchocerciasis and other disease control programs.

While distribution among countries is very uneven, Africa is a major producer of minerals such as copper, cobalt, chrome, and uranium. There has also been a steady increase in the number of oil deposits located, particularly in coastal waters. Only a small portion of the land has been surveyed in detail and the potential is believed far greater than current production levels would suggest.

With respect to progress, Africa's absorptive capacity has been rapidly enlarging. Today, an estimated 60 percent of all school age children are in primary schools. Since mid-1960 annual secondary and higher education enrollment have increased by 9.8 percent, and 11.1 percent, respectively. Conditions are being created which will increase Africa's ability to use its greatest resource, its population.

In the area of food production, new hybrid cereal varieties have been developed, seed multiplication activities replicated and agriculture research activities initiated. A number of African countries are beginning to reexamine food pricing, parastatal and other policies affecting food and agriculture production. As a result of a joint assessment in Senegal, a declaration was issued calling for the abolishment of two major parastatals, reorganizing rural development agencies and promoting private cooperatives. The government also plans to undertake new pricing policies and revamp the farm credit system. In Somalia parastatals are being disbanded. Private voluntary organizations are continuing to play a significant role, especially at the grass roots level, in the implementation of AID-funded activities. Under a rural enterprise development project in Upper Volta, business practices of 80 entrepreneurs have been upgraded, loans granted to 120 entrepreneurs, and a demonstration farm established, introducing new technology such as hand mills, peanut presses and other implements.

Description of the FY 1983 Program

The FY 1983 request concentrates the Agency's efforts on a small number of key interrelated problems facing the African continent. AID assistance will continue to stress the production aspects of agriculture with particular emphasis on small holders. In that context, special emphasis will be placed on institutional development, policy reform, and building and supporting the private sector wherever appropriate.

Private Sector Activity

AID is placing special emphasis on support of the private sector of African economies, particularly for indigenous small-and medium-size enterprises. We are now reviewing projects to assure that wherever appropriate the private sector is used and supported. For example, in Sudan approximately two-thirds of the foreign exchange associated with our CIP program will be reserved for imports for the private sector to assure that it will be able to update its plant and equipment and operate efficiently. We are also actively developing projects to be funded out of the counterpart funds which will be designed to promote and assist small-and medium-size entrepreneurs. Wherever possible we will, in association with AID's Private Enterprise Bureau, be alert to opportunities for the U.S. private sector to participate in African development activities.

We believe that support of the private sector is an efficient way to expand employment and productivity. Moreover, maximizing use of the private sector will lessen the burden of already overextended governments.

We expect PVO grants of approximately $31 million in Africa in FY 1983. This includes $25 million from DA and $6 million from ESF funds. We believe that AID/PVO cooperation is an effective means for enhancing the impact and effectiveness of our efforts.

Agriculture

Helping African nations increase their food and agricultural production and improve food distribution is the major emphasis of AID's development assistance program in Africa.

In response to the food deficit problem, AID has implemented a food/agricultural sector assistance strategy. Its three major components are:

1. Assist in creating national policies and programs that give farmers adequate incentives to expand agricultural output, especially of food.

2. Assist in building self-sustaining institutions that provide appropriate technology, inputs, and services at the time and in the quantity necessary for effective production and distribution of food products.

3. Support institutional and human resource development programs that provide the means for greater participation by farmers in the development process, including policy planning, to build popular support and acceptance of programs necessary for self-sustaining growth.

To improve efficiency in the employment of both AID and host country resources, AID has placed an increased emphasis on host country economic policies. This effort is being implemented at two levels. At the macroeconomic level AID seeks to insure that its country programs are consistent with the intent of International Monetary Fund and/or World Bank reform agreements with host countries. Where possible AID measures will actively reinforce host countries' efforts to comply with these agreements. At the sector level AID will seek to collaborate with host countries on devising ways to improve specific policies. AID is especially interested in obtaining adjustments in host countries which will increase the influence of market forces in the determination of agriculture prices, liberalize marketing arrangements and expand the role of the African private sector in agriculture-related activities. Private enterprise activities such as a new agribusiness development project in Kenya, along with ongoing activities on the manufacture of farm implements in Uganda and Niger, as well as training, are proposed for funding in FY 1983.

Health

The goal of the Africa Bureau health sector development program is to assist the countries of the region to address their health problems on a national and regional basis. Health programs are supported for the most part in four general categories:

Primary Health Care—These multidisciplinary projects provide support for systems of health services for rural communities. Projects usually consist of training village health workers and their supervisors and providing logistic support. Seven basic services are recommended for primary health care systems. $13.9 million is proposed.

Health Planning, Management and Manpower Development—Training and technical assistance are provided to countries and regional organizations to develop national capabilities to manage national primary health care programs. Bilateral, regional, and multilateral projects address Africa's main constraint to health development—lack of health manpower. $2.3 million is proposed in the category.

Water and Sanitation—Support is provided for developing safe water sources in rural communities, and maintaining environmental safeguards. Education of communities is an important aspect of these projects. $4.7 million is proposed.

Endemic Disease Control—Bilateral, regional, and multilateral projects address the tropical disease problems of vast geographic areas. Diseases such as malaria, schistosomiasis, onchocerciasis, and trypanosomiasis are endemic in most of Africa. Programs include surveillance, sector control, treatment, chemoprophylaxis, and immunizations. A budget of $10 million is proposed.

Population Program

In Africa, progress in the population sector has been slow. As Haven North and others of my predecessors have noted before me, the population issue in Africa has to be approached with great care and sensitivity. It must be carefully integrated with the provision of health services, with the opportunities for improvement in income and in general economic growth and employment opportunities. Otherwise it will be distorted and backfire on efforts to establish programs.

The implementation of a family planning program is a slow and difficult process: In part it is a matter of establishing the systems for delivery of health services in conjunction with family planning; in part, it is institutional and a lot is attitudinal. It is a matter of what people want, because AID cannot force countries to accept population programs.

Seven sub-Saharan African nations (Botswana, Ghana, Kenya, Mauritius, Rwanda, Senegal, Uganda) have declared national population policies. Several others, including Nigeria and Sudan, have recently established national population councils. Twenty-three countries in the region now provide family planning services in government clinics.

Energy and the Environment

AID must continue to address the high cost and increasing scarcity of energy resources, deforestation and ecologically unsound agriculture and livestock practices if Africa's productive capability is to be preserved and expanded. AID will support afforestation, range and soil conservation efforts. These activities will be designed as integrated components of agriculture production systems. In Mali, Senegal, and Burundi projects will focus on fuelwood renewable energy technology.

Education and Human Resource Development

In FY 1983, AID will help expand Africa's human resources capacity. Attention will be devoted to: (1) development administration and technical skills training, as preconditions to institutional development and the transfer of technology; (2) strengthening indigenous private voluntary organizations (PVO's) and the commercial private sector by helping them develop management and entrepreneurial skills, and (3) expanding training opportunities in the United States through the Africa Manpower Development Project.

An example of technical skills training and development administration is the Agricultural Education Project in the Cameroon, which will create an agricultural university capable of training managers, researchers, planners, and teachers who can effectively staff the agricultural support institutions of Cameroon.

Sahel Development Program

The Sahel Development Program was initiated in FY 1978 as a regional effort through which eight African countries cooperate with Western donors and oil producing countries of the Middle East (OPEC). Led by the United States and France under the Club du Sahel, 20 bilateral donors are now active contributors to a range of programs and projects to help the Sahel countries become self-sufficient in food and to construct economic infrastructures which will assure sustained economic growth and a better and more secure life for their people. Donor assistance has increased from $1.1 billion in 1976 to $1.5 billion in 1980.

Twenty years from now, the Sahel can be feeding itself. Our long-term economic objective is to assist the countries in the Sahel region to increase agricultural production to levels where basic food imports will not be necessary. Sound economies in the region will contribute to the stability of the countries and provide opportunities for U.S. investments as well as access to mineral resources such as uranium (Niger), phosphates (Upper Volta), iron (Mauritania), bauxite (Mali).

As a result of a development strategy agreed to by the donors and recipient countries, progress is being made. Agricultural research programs have been expanded and strengthened; extension services are reaching the farmer; new agricultural technologies are being introduced; range management and animal health improvements are being applied. The agriculture policy picture is starting to improve. In Senegal and Mali, cereal marketing through the private sector is now being encouraged. The Governments of Senegal, Niger, Mali, and Upper Volta are adjusting cereal pricing policies to provide more incentive to the farmer for both production and marketing.

In the FY 1983 program, AID will continue to support the Sahel development strategy and direct resources to the agricultural sector, and particularly toward rainfed agriculture which constitutes the mainstay of Sahelian agriculture. AID is providing technical assistance and key inputs to assist in developing Sahelian agriculture capacity.

AID is also supporting long-range strategies to develop water resources in the Senegal and Gambia river basins. AID is supporting other donor efforts through its regional program which concentrates on institutional development and basins planning, and through the development of small scale irrigated perimeters which have an impact in the individual countries. Of the $93.8 million request in FY 1983, $27.6 million will be allotted to regional programs directly benefiting the individual countries in the basin area. The balance will be allotted to seven countries in the region under bilateral programs.

Our assistance to Chad has been limited to relief and rehabilitation together with other donors. The civil war has brought extensive damage to Chad's economy. Nevertheless, we propose to continue monitoring the situation, looking for improvements before undertaking any extensive or long-term development projects.

Sahelian problems with financial management of AID funds continue to be a matter of serious concern. Steps have been taken to correct serious deficiencies in the accounting and management systems. Host country documents are being verified and accounting systems have been examined to determine their adequacy for certification by AID officials as a precondition to disbursement of funds. To correct the deficiencies, training programs, workshops, and teams have been developed to improve the financial management of the local institutions concerned with the Sahel programs and projects. Donor and recipient countries have acknowledged the seriousness of the problem and collaborative efforts are underway to assure efficient use of funds and accurate accountability.

The Economic Support Fund Program (ESF)

The FY 1983 request for $325 million is intended to provide the United States with the resources necessary to stem the spread of further economic and political disruption and to support the efforts of friends and allies to deal with threats to security and independence. Economic Support Funds totaling $325 million are requested for Sudan, Somalia, Kenya, Mauritius, Seychelles, Djibouti, Zimbabwe, Zambia, Botswana, the Southern Africa Regional Program, Liberia, Niger, Senegal, and Zaire.

These countries are currently experiencing a broad range of economic and political problems, such as balance-of-payments and budgetary deficits, external debt burdens, deteriorating terms of trade and declining output, and the threat of political instability.

In addition to the political and security objectives of these funds, AID makes every effort to assure that they have developmental effect as well. For instance, in Zambia and Kenya our Commodities Import Program is targeted on agricultural inputs; in Zimbabwe 80 percent of the CIP is reserved for the private sector, with local currencies supporting development in traditional areas. ESF funds are a particularly versatile development instrument when used as program assistance in support of policy reform.

P.L. 480

The FY 1983 program request for P.L. 480 is $191.7 million of which $117 million will be allocated to the Title I category. Within Title I, $43 million will be directed to Title III. The $74.7 million balance of the request will be devoted to Title II.

By legislation, P.L. 480 embodies several objectives, among them the economic and social development of P.L. 480 recipient countries. The Africa Bureau is committed to fostering sustained development as the objective of its assistance through P.L. 480 food resources. Specifically, the Africa Bureau seeks to utilize P.L. 480 resources (sales revenues and/or commodities) to address and alleviate the underlying causes of the need for food assistance, particularly in the agricultural and rural sectors. The Administrator has instructed our field missions to enhance the effectiveness of P.L. 480 food aid by: a) seeking policy dialogue with host governments on ways to alleviate the constraints to improved food security; and b) increasing the degree of integration of P.L. 480 programs within the total AID development assistance program.

Self-help measures, under Title I use of local currency sales revenues, and policy dialogue, or integration with other forms of nonfood assistance are intended to enhance the development impact of Title I. The Title III program will be continued in Sudan and Senegal and a new program may be initiated in Somalia.

Title II grant commodities have been traditionally channeled into direct food distribution programs through maternal-child health centers, school feeding programs and food for work projects, all of which are administered by U.S. registered private voluntary organizations or by the World Food Program. similarly under Title II, Section 206, we are undertaking programs for food for development in Cape Verde, Mauritania, and Upper Volta.

Other Donor Coordination

As the Berg report[14]noted, donor coordination deserves special emphasis at this time. The serious problems faced by many African countries can only be met by integrated projects and programs. Moreover, as certain governments find themselves less and less capable of meeting the recurrent costs associated with various projects, project and program planning requires an assessment of total donor activities as well as those of individual donors.

[14] Reference is to *Accelerated Development in Sub-Saharan Africa: An Agenda for Action,* prepared by Elliot J. Berg for the World Bank in 1981.

The extent of the problem is illustrated by the fact that although the United States is a major aid contributor in Africa, our assistance accounts for only 7 percent of total official development assistance. There are no less than 52 bilateral donors in sub-Saharan Africa; the 17-member Development Advisory Council (DAC) of the OECD, 7 Arab/OPEC, 9 Arab multilateral, 12 other multilateral, and 7 East bloc. In addition, there were 34 American PVO's associated with AID alone in FY 1981. Each of these donors has its own policies, procedures, and programs.

AID is promoting greater cooperation among donors in several ways by encouraging ongoing cooperative efforts in such donor groups as CDA (Cooperation for Development in Africa, formerly CADA) and the Sahel program, and through cooperative efforts with African groups such as ECOWAS and SADCC. We are also seeking opportunities for cofinancing with other donors, both bilateral and multilateral. Thank You.

Document 545

Prepared Statement by the Assistant Secretary of the Treasury for International Affairs (Leland) Before a Subcommittee of the House Banking, Finance and Urban Affairs Committee, April 27, 1982[15]

The Case for U.S. Participation in the Replenishment of the African Development Fund

Mr. Chairman. I am pleased to testify today in support of authorization legislation for U.S. participation in the third replenishment of the African Development Fund (AFDF). As you know, final negotiations for the replenishment agreement were com-

[15] Source: *The African Development Fund: Hearing Before the Subcommittee on International Development Institutions and Finance of the Committee on Banking, Finance and Urban Affairs, House of Representatives, Ninety-seventh Congress, Second Session* (Washington, 1982), pp. 6–17. On December 21, 1982, Congress approved $50 million for the African Development Fund; see P.L. 97-377, Continuing Appropriations for Fiscal Year 1983 (96 Stat. 1831).

pleted in February this year. This is the first multilateral development bank replenishment to be negotiated by this administration.

The provisions of the agreement fit within the budgetary planning parameters established for the multilateral development banks. The agreement also fits within the framework of the assessment on U.S. participation in the banks which we have recently completed. One of the cardinal principles of the assessment is that concessional assistance should be targeted toward the poorest and least developed countries. That is certainly the case with regard to Africa, which contains two-thirds of the countries currently classified as "low income." The administration has consulted with Congress during the course of negotiations for this particular replenishment over the past year.

We are requesting authorization for $150 million. This is a relatively modest sum in terms of U.S. subscriptions and contributions which have been made to other multilateral development banks. It represents a small increase in nominal terms over the $125 million which was authorized by Congress in June 1980 for our contribution to the second replenishment of the AFDF, but constitutes little if any increase in real terms when considering the rate of inflation in the years between the last replenishment and this one.

The funds to be authorized under this legislation would be appropriated in three equal annual installments of $50 million each in FY 1983–85. Actual expenditures of funds would lag that schedule by several years because drawdowns are tied to disbursements required for implementation of specific projects. Prior experience with African Development Fund drawdowns suggests that budgetary outlays arising from this request will be minimal over the next several years. Our current estimate is that only about $40 million of the $150 million total will have been expended through the end of FY 1987.

This request would provide funds for the U.S. share of a replenishment totaling about $1060 million. The U.S. share of the replenishment would be 14.2 percent. This is a decrease from our 16.5 percent share of the current replenishment. The United States would be the largest single contributor of new resources, closely followed by Japan which is contributing $140 million, or 13.3 percent of the total. On a cumulative basis, however, Japan would remain the largest single contributor of Fund resources, taking account of contributions made under the initial mobilization and the first two replenishments. Other significant contributors to the replenishment include the members of the European Economic Community, who are together providing 34.5 percent of the total, and Canada, which is providing nearly 8 percent of the total. In addition, a number of OPEC countries and some developing countries from outside the region, including Argentina, Brazil, Korea, and India are making contributions to the replenishment. Altogether there are 24 donor countries in addition to the African Development Bank, itself, which will be contributing $26.3 million to the replenishment.

The resources to be provided under the replenishment will be used to finance African Development Fund projects over the period 1982–84. Lending by the Fund during the period will continue to emphasize projects designed to increase food production for domestic consumption and the production of agricultural commodities for export. Other sectors which will receive emphasis are transportation (primarily the upgrading of rural roads and tracks); public utilities (primarily potable water supplies and sewage); and health and education.

African countries confront some of the most basic developmental problems and the lending program of the Fund is oriented toward making a significant contribution in such areas. For example, in some parts of the Sahel, financial help is needed to build deeper wells with concrete liners and covers in rural villages so that a supply of water will be available on a reliable basis through the dry season and be kept reasonably clean from infestation by rodents and contamination by trash.

Education and vocational training programs are badly needed to relieve shortages of personnel who are qualified to implement development programs. This shortage of trained individuals has been a very serious bottleneck to further economic progress in that area. In addition, more programs are needed to reduce endemic diseases and to raise the level of health care in both urban and rural areas.

U.S. support for the African Development Fund is based on a wide and rapidly expanding spectrum of interests which this country has on that continent.

U.S. economic interests in Africa have increased at a rapid rate in recent years. Private investment by U.S. firms and individuals in sub-Saharan Africa is now approaching the $6 billion level. Our exports to all of Africa in 1981 totaled $11 billion and our imports were $27 billion. Although the majority of this trade has been with South Africa and Nigeria, there is a large potential for further growth in trade with a number of other African countries.

I should also point out, on the supply side, that sub-Saharan African countries are a source of minerals considered essential for our own national development and defense. These minerals include critical quantities of chrome for our automobile and defense industries, manganese for steel, cobalt for jet engines and mining equipment, as well as copper, industrial diamonds, and mica. I believe it is also important to remember that Nigeria, which became our principal supplier of foreign oil during the 1973 oil embargo, remains the second largest foreign source for us today, and that Angola and Gabon have also begun to export oil in greater quantities.

The U.S. interest in Africa is very much a humanitarian one. Most of the countries in sub-Saharan Africa have extremely low per capita incomes and very limited ability to provide even the most basic services for their people. Progress has been made in all economic sectors over the past two decades throughout the continent. However, that progress has been painfully slow and most countries in the region have been extremely hard hit by economic reversals in recent years as a result of international economic developments. These include slower growth in developed countries, higher energy prices, the relatively small increase in trade in primary products, and adverse terms of trade for copper and iron ore exporters. In 1979, per capita income in the region was $411 ($329 if Nigeria is excluded). Death rates in Africa are the highest in the world and the life expectancy of 47 years is the lowest. Fifteen to twenty percent of all children die by their first birthday and only 25 percent of the people are able to have clean water.

There is a longstanding and widely accepted tradition in our country of providing assistance to those most in need and our participation in the African Development Fund is an important means of helping to alleviate the destitution which prevails in most of Africa.

U.S. participation in the African Development Fund is not the only way for us to advance U.S. interests in Africa. Our participation is, however, a highly visible way for us to demonstrate our willingness to work cooperatively with other donor countries and with African countries toward the solution of their economic problems. The African Development Bank group, of which the Fund is part, is the largest of the regional economic institutions on the continent and it has active lending programs in more than 40 of its member countries.

From an administrative and operational viewpoint, the African Development Bank group is less effective and efficient than the other multilateral development banks. However, its management has recognized the problems it has in these two areas and is taking a number of steps to improve the situation. They have, for example, made a concerted effort to recruit more highly qualified staff and to increase training opportunities for staff members who are already on board. Upgrading of staff has been carried out through overseas training assignments with the World Bank and the Asian Development Bank as well as through on-the-job training which is supervised by technical experts from developed countries. We will continue to monitor the progress made by the Bank group in this area as well as in the area of operations and encourage them to make further improvements.

I should also emphasize our belief that government economic policies in some African countries have had the effect of impeding economic growth. The World Bank's *Accelerated Development in Sub-Saharan Africa: Agenda for Action* makes this point abundantly clear. It indicates that inappropriate trade and exchange rate policies have overprotected industries, held back agriculture, and absorbed too much of the limited administrative capacity. The report points out that too little attention has been paid to administrative constraints in mobilizing and managing resources for development programs and that there has been a consistent bias against agriculture in terms of price, tax, and exchange rate policies. We agree with this assessment and we also believe that greater emphasis should be placed on the role of the private sector in the development process in Africa.

Clearly, the African Development Bank group cannot play the primary role in encouraging the African countries to move away from inappropriate economic policies which they are now following. That role belongs to the World Bank and the International Monetary Fund. However, we believe the African Development Bank group can be an important actor in this process and we will be encouraging them to take a larger role.

To sum up, the economic conditions which exist in most African countries are a compelling argument for U.S. participation in this replenishment of the African Development Fund. We believe that we can make a useful contribution, not only in financial terms but also in terms of improving the administration and operation of the Fund and in making it a more viable force for development. We are also confident that we can work within the African Development Fund to encourage African countries in the direction of sound, market-based strategies for development. We hope that congressional approval of this replenishment request will be forthcoming in order to assure the continued work of the African Development Fund to improve the conditions of life in Africa.

Document 546

Address by the Deputy Assistant Secretary of State for African Affairs (Lyman) Before the Conference on Continuity and Change in Africa, Monterey, California, May 1, 1982[16]

Changes in Africa and Challenges for U.S. Policy in Africa

In my address tonight, I want to speak of some underlying changes taking place in Africa and the challenges they present to American foreign policy.

I am aware that trying to capture a sense of significant trends, to extricate oneself enough from the problems that are at the front of our attention at the moment, in order to gain a larger historical perspective, is risky. What seems to be an emerging trend today may prove to have been but a flash-in-the-pan a few years from now, yet I believe we can identify very significant changes taking place in Africa and at least speculate on their implications.

There are six areas of change that I would emphasize:

The first is the passing of the first independence generation. This is an incomplete process, one going on before our eyes, and for that reason all the more fascinating; Senghor, Nkrumah, Kenyatta, are gone. And those other major figures of that same era, Haile Selassie and Tubman, are also gone. A small band of elder statesmen—Houphouet, Nyerere, Kaunda, Banda, Ahidjo, Sekou Toure—are still on the scene and playing significant roles. But their significance arises in part because their own role has evolved and is changing before our eyes.

For example, the older Marxists—those who seemed so formidable in their Marxist commitment in the past—have "mellowed" (if I can use that phrase—the Soviets would have another). Several such leaders are no longer enamored of the brotherhood of the Socialist bloc, have long since ended their enmity toward conservative neighbors, warn in fact against radicalism in the OAU, and actively seek Western private investment. Guinea is one such state, and in its wake, other long-time Marxist states—Congo, Equatorial Guinea—have begun to move in the same direction. A subtle process is evident in these outward manifestations of change: The dream of African socialism which several prominent early independence leaders articulated, has become tarnished by the grim reality, after two decades, of terribly limited progress.

While the leadership and some of the early themes of African independence are changing, however, the new generation has not revealed a clear and distinct pattern. There are in fact contrasting tendencies. We would be wise to avoid generalizations. Nevertheless, I think it is prudent to expect that this new generation as a whole has a world view much at variance with that of their predecessors in the sixties and seventies. They have no direct experience with the colonial period. Yet many have even stronger views on neocolonial, black/white, social, and economic issues than many of their predecessors. The role of this new generation will be especially marked in the military, where young officers and noncommissioned officers are anxious to have greater—if not total—influence over the course of national life. Perhaps more important in terms of the new leadership's dealings with the rest of the world, is the fact that it is a generation which is somewhat disdainful of the postindependence generation, and finds the latter's policies toward and relationships with other countries as well as toward economic development, either irrevelant or at least open to serious question. This will cut both ways, toward associations with the West and models of development fashioned by that as-

---

16 Source: Department of State files.

sociation, and—as already noted—toward associations with the Soviet bloc.

The second significant change in Africa is that the newer independent states, those which gained independence in the 1970's, are more radical than almost any of their predecessors. There is an irony here that radicalism should burst forth in these states as its ardor fades in earlier radical states. In the first flush of this phenomenon—the coming to power of Frelimo in Mozambique, the MPLA in Angola, and equally significant as part of this same period, the revolution in Ethiopia—the new radical states appeared as possibly the "model" for the new generation, replacing the romantic image of Nyerere or the quasi-charismatic appeal of Nkrumah. Today one can question that, as these states exhibit continued civil war, failures in development, and heavy dependence on the Soviets.

Yet their radical philosophy stands as an alternative for some of today's new generation, especially those disillusioned with a generation of more conservative policies that produced their own failures. As such, it is a vital part of the dynamic of today's Africa. In Ghana, one can literally feel the tension from this dynamic: Intense young reformers—radicals for sure—convinced that it is possible, indeed, imperative, to make a "new Ghanaian", and seeking to utilize those tactics of mass mobilization—people's defense committees, kebeles, what have you—to obtain direct participation of the masses, and to "educate" them for this purpose. Against these tendencies stand others, also reformers, but clinging to a more pragmatic, Western-oriented model of development, hoping that there is redemption still in that process, and justifiably fearful of the authoritarian imperatives that hover behind the propositions of their radical rivals. How much more experimentation, how much more suffering, is necessary before these tensions are resolved is not certain, but Ghana suggests not a little.

Third is the economic crisis that now is spreading across Africa—gripping, like a vice, the economies of Zambia, Sudan, Liberia, Zaire, Tanzania, and Ghana, which lurch now from crisis to crisis, but spreading too to Senegal, Kenya, and indeed Ivory Coast. As commodity markets continue weak, debt burdens are reaching impossible levels, production as well as prices continue to fall, and the terms default and bankruptcy are heard with ominous frequency. It has become fashionable in some quarters to speak of the predictability of this crisis; that it comes almost as divine retribution for 20 years of misguided African policies, narrow urban-based political favoritism, and reckless acquisition of debt. All these factors are indeed very relevant to today's crisis. But outsiders played their role too, sometimes contributing to these very tendencies, at best only mildly critical of them. The fact is that, aside from a few Cassandras, who always will predict disaster, few if any of us involved in African development over the last decade or two anticipated the extent of the economic crisis now facing Africa.

And perhaps most unsettling for those of us who participated in development programs and projects over the last two decades, we see what progress we thought was being made disintegrating before our eyes; roads falling apart, clinics and hospitals growing filthy and lacking in even a semblance of drugs, buildings in every capital growing shabbier and peeling apart every day. And this is not a thing of recent origin. I recall studying a rural roads proposal in Ethiopia in 1977, a project to construct ten roads, and was crestfallen to find that seven of the ten were not new roads at all, but roads built by the Italians 30 years before that had virtually disappeared from lack of care. We were not building anew, but simply tapping out an old pattern on the surface of a problem we did not yet understand.

In summary, the crisis in Africa is one whose origins go deeper than today's world recession. As such it is of a different character than that which grips much of the rest of the Third World. Africa enters this recession, after two decades of independence, without one country—with the possible exception of the Ivory Coast—having reached the point of industrialized take-off of a Taiwan, South Korea, or Singapore, let alone having achieved the social infrastructure of a Sri Lanka.

Africans and donors alike must now recognize that there were fundamental flaws in the policies, theories, emphases, and experiments which we pursued over the past 20 years. Perhaps, as Uma Lele suggested in a recent article,[17] we all grossly underestimated the importance of human resource development—including and especially at the policy level. Perhaps, as the World Bank has recently argued, the fault is in policies and programs which subsidized inefficient industries at the expense of agriculture,

[17] See "Rural Africa: Modernization, Equity, and Long-term Development," *Science* magazine, February 6, 1981, pp. 547–553.

high exchange rates at the expense of exports, urban consumption over rural production, and state bureaucracies at the expense of the private sector. Perhaps, as one observer has remarked, the political kingdom—of ideologies, urban-based politics, fragile political systems—destroyed the framework of economic rationality.

If so, this crisis, which now rocks nearly every country in Africa, and which is cutting back the budget of nearly every development activity started in the last 20 years, is having enormous political consequences in turn. One is that countries are experiencing, with galling bitterness, a new dependence—this time on the institutional mechanism of the IMF—a dependence not only on its funds, but on its blessing of its policies. Elements of policy—right or wrong—which were considered privileges of sovereignty: credit, budgets, exchange rates—but even more, choice of political-economic philosophy—are now the province of international technocrats. Twenty-two African countries have approached the IMF—triple the number 2 years ago. It is the savior, and it has become, alas, the new symbol of neocolonialism.

Second, the economic structural changes that are demanded in this crisis are tearing up the economic support of African political systems as we have known them, forcing an end to cheap urban food, protected industry, cheap credit. The political framework of these societies is threatened, as the riots in Sudan,[18] the coup in Ghana, the threat of left-wing authoritarianism in other countries all attest, as does the increasingly heard cry in Africa that it is better to return to the bush than submit to the regimen being demanded. For the United States, unwilling anymore to subsidize uneconomic policies, unable to finance a painless transition to new economic structures, yet reluctant to see its friends threatened by unrest and instability, the crisis is also of great consequence.

The fourth underlying change is the growth of defense as a major factor in African national priorities. Africanists and idealists alike hoped to shelter Africa from that element of modern nationhood. But defense concerns have grown—Tanzania, Ethiopia, Nigeria, Angola, Mozambique, Sudan, Zambia, and now increasingly Kenya, Botswana, Senegal, and others are accepting large defense expenditures as an unavoidable part of national independence. The threats vary, as do the degree of outside influence, but the pattern is clear. With growing defense concerns, old barriers on weapons systems are broken. Armaments, once prohibitively expensive for any African country, are steadily becoming part of the common arsenal. Ground-to-air missiles, sophisticated radar, tanks, air transport, modern forms of night weaponry, jet fighters—all are finding their way into African military establishments. There is no overall mechanism to control it, no structure to limit it. The Soviets supply 60 percent of the arms to Africa, but once they are there, there is a secondary market in Soviet parts and replacements in which Egypt, Sudan, and Somalia—to say nothing of Libya, China, North Korea, and North Vietnam—can actively participate. With the growth of defense comes also an even greater role of the African military.

Fifth, events since 1974 have changed dramatically the dynamics of southern Africa, that area that contains two-thirds of Africa's GNP and the most controversial and far-reaching elements of African politics. In 1974, the Portuguese colonial empire collapsed suddenly and dramatically. In the wake of that collapse, the relationship between South Africa and the region around it changed. Militantly Marxist regimes came to power where there had been a colonial buffer, the liberation movement assumed power in the once companion state of Rhodesia. Into this cauldron of changing forces and new conflicts, the USSR and Cuba inserted themselves, with greater degree, and risks, of direct involvement than ever before in sub-Saharan Africa, competing in effect with South Africa to control the future of the region.

The result is that while three colonial territories have gained independence, removing one great source of instability, the region is now more fraught with the danger of major violence—and perhaps large-scale military activity—than ever before. Tensions are high, and the dangers are enormous, not only for African states of the region but for the long-term political and economic interests of the West.

This situation lends a whole new urgency to Western engagements in the region. Only the Western powers can broker a

[18] On January 3, 1983, students in Khartoum rioted to protest the increase in sugar prices. On January 4, Sudanese police arrested 21 leading southern Sudanese politicians charging them with forming an illegal party, the Council for the Unity of South Sudan. For further information, see *Keesing's Contemporary Archives*, April 16, 1982, p. 31444; *New York Times*, January 9, 1982, p. 2; and *Washington Post*, January 13, 1982, p. A18.

situation of peaceful and constructive relationships between black African states and South Africa while supportive of changes within South Africa—and only the West can counter Soviet and Cuban influence, if the counterweight is not to be the growing use of South African military power with all the implications that would have for the independent states on its borders. Thus there has been a new and far more intensive involvement of the United States in this region since 1975. And while focused today on Namibia and the search for an internationally accepted solution to that problem, this engagement cannot stop once that issue is resolved. Nowhere else in Africa are we likely to be, and required to be, so intensively involved diplomatically and economically over the next decade, drawing on as wide an array of foreign policy instruments as we can to address the complex of political, military, economic, and social issues there; all of which impinge upon our interests and our objectives.

Sixth and finally, Africa has become, beyond just southern Africa, increasingly enmeshed in global politics including superpower rivalry. That has always been a two-edged sword for those who liked to argue for Africa's importance in terms of its minerals and strategic location, but tried at the same time to deny that superpower competition should have a role. However, the geopolitical realities in Africa cannot be denied—or ignored. Africa's East Coast is part of the strategic struggle for control of the Indian Ocean and the oil transport lanes of southwest Asia. Soviet arms in Zambia and Botswana, and with SWAPO and the Katangan rebels, Cuban troops in Angola and Ethiopia, Russian reconnaissance planes covering the South Atlantic from bases in Africa—these are realities that neither Africa nor the West can ignore. In turn, American access agreements in Somalia and Kenya,[19] Western allied cooperation in the defense of Zaire, French and American support of OAU peacekeeping forces in Chad, American military exercises in Liberia and Sudan all have a basis in both Western and African security. No longer can anyone say Africa is not part of the total crosscurrent of major international rivalries.

And Africans, if bemoaning the fact on the one hand, seek it on the other. Partly out of perceived needs of their own, but partly too because African nations do indeed see themselves as part of global politics, they have sought out superpower involvement, asked for superpower protection, and not infrequently sided in superpower conflicts out of their own convictions.

Given these important changes taking place in Africa, what are the changing responses demanded of U.S. policy? I will only sketch them.

1. First, U.S. policy in Africa has to reflect both the realities of Africa and the realities of our global interests. No U.S. policy in Africa is sustainable without both elements.

I would submit, in this context, that the present administration's policy in southern Africa is especially realistic in this regard. I will not describe that policy here in detail. But I submit that the basic premise, which sees a de facto and necessary policy relationship between the issues of Namibia, the Cuban presence in Angola, the mode of our relationships with the South African Government, and our support for Zimbabwe and other majority-ruled states in that region—all bearing on an underlying threat of major, long-term violence in the region and growing Soviet influence—I submit that this framework is the only realistic one and the only one with a chance to succeed. By success, I mean a policy to which the United States will remain committed and to which it will lend its full weight and one which will achieve the Africans' objectives of an independent Namibia, a peaceful and prosperous region, and progress toward equality within South Africa.

2. Second, we need to create a far more effective management for our international economic policy. It is ironic that as we argue with Africa that its real future lies with the trade, aid, and investment of the West, we are so poorly equipped to mobilize and deploy those very strengths of ours. The need is all the more urgent as Africa enters this era of economic crisis. Today, we are bound by legislation and by bureaucratic structure from considering questions of debt and investment in a single framework. More broadly, we have not faced up fully to the economic and political dilemmas inherent in the IMF "recipes" for economic health. We have been ineffective in linking formulas for stabilization with programs for growth and development, instead separating out institutionally and even more in resource deployment, our efforts in these

---

19 Regarding the U.S. and Somalia Access Agreement, signed on August 22, 1980, see *American Foreign Policy: Basic Documents, 1977–1980*, pp. 1237–1238. Regarding the U.S. and Kenya Access Agreement, signed on June 26, 1980, see Department of State *Bulletin*, September 1980, p. 80.

regards. We talk of private investment but we have a limited range of tools to promote actively such investment in the economically troubled countries of Africa. Clearly for some countries there will be unavoidable pain and instability. And no country will attract investment where there are no prospects for profit. But our own political interests demand that we try to help our friends manage this transition better. And that requires us to improve our own instruments of economic and commercial diplomacy.

Further, we will need, once again, to reexamine our aid and development assumptions in terms of how these problems can be addressed more effectively. There will have to be a reexamination of "basic human needs" and of other approaches that guided us in the past. This must not mean a lurching to sudden new panaceas, but a willingness on the part of all concerned to critique old assumptions.

3. Third, and quite appropriately on the heels of my comments on economic policy, we also have to be prepared to participate in the defense side of the African equation. This administration has taken what I believe is a realistic attitude toward requests for military assistance. We have no intention of becoming the arms warehouse for the continent, but we are no longer unwilling to consider requests for such assistance from African countries, as we were just a short while ago. Obviously, once one enters this arena, careful management of the process and our resources becomes paramount—avoiding overemphasis on military might as a solution to African problems or the waste of inappropriate and unsupportable equipment.

But here again, the United States is ill-equipped to play this role well. In an effort to control the use of military assistance, and today to control the level of budgetary outlays, Congress has refused to authorize very much military assistance on concessional terms. We are therefore in the anomalous position of offering Africa military assistance, at market rates of interest, in the midst of the greatest economic crisis Africa has experienced in 20 years.

4. Fourth, we will need to bring to our African policy a great deal more sophistication and coherent management than in the past.

As Africa is becoming an increasingly important part of the global system, it also becomes apparent that Africa is a matter for high-level policy concern, one deserving of a significant portion of total foreign policy resources.

As we work our way through this coming decade of economic travail, political upheaval, and changing generations, we will need to avoid simple stereotypes or hopes for quick-fix solutions to Africa's problems. We will be working with one major advantage. The new generation of leaders—whatever rhetoric they choose—will be struggling with problems that in large part only the West can help them solve.

But we have to be on guard against making promises we cannot keep. Our resources will be limited as far ahead as one can see. The private sector will not go to African countries—short of scarce mineral resources—which are unstable, insolvent, and unfriendly to foreign investment. Nor can we sustain cooperative relationships with countries that participate in the subversion of other states important to us. In summary we will have to be realistic and candid in our dialogue with Africa on our prospective role, even if it means postponing in some cases the kind of relationships and cooperation that seem a desirable outcome.

Above all, we need more sophisticated management of policy. In southern Africa today we have come closer to doing that than perhaps ever before in Africa. We are following a comprehensive and integrated deployment of all our assets (political, military, economic, commercial). Many do not understand it, shooting at one or another piece of it, sometimes threatening the integrity of the policy itself. I do not deny for a moment the very high risks involved and the difficulties ahead in achieving our several objectives there. Nevertheless, in the best sense, it is a very serious effort.

It is not necessary to mobilize the same intensity of U.S. influence or level of resources in all other regions of Africa, but it will be necessary to approach this degree of comprehension and coherence in our policy throughout the continent if we are to meet fully the challenges and changes of the next decade.

5. Finally, as we work and share experiences with the new generation of Africans, we should be wary of jumping too quickly between extremes and of missing what is perhaps one of the most important lessons of the past 20 years.

It would be a mistake in calling attention to the new wave of radicalism, and the criticisms of the past, to think that the only "models" open to the next generation in Africa are left-wing authoritarianism, or inefficient legacies of the past. Indeed, out of the tension and competition of the kind one sees in Ghana today, and in the witnessing of the terrible human price being paid in the name of revolution in countries like Ethiopia, there may be growing appreciation among the new generation of the path of not a few states in Africa which have maintained a tradition of openness, tolerance, overall respect for human rights, and quite respectable economic progress. Senegal, Cameroon, Ivory Coast, Kenya, Botswana, and others present this third alternative. Perhaps the lesson that is emerging is that we must protect these values, and these models, if the alternatives of barbarous authoritarianism or political decay are not to predominate in the next decade.

Document 547

Address by the Assistant Secretary of State for African Affairs (Crocker) Before the National Business League, Dallas, September 17, 1982[20]

Development in Africa

It is an honor to have this opportunity to discuss the administration's view of the economic prospects and problems of Africa before the National Business League—the oldest national business organization and the largest association of minority business people in America. It is a pleasure to be here in Texas speaking on the subject of Africa. At first glance the two have a good deal in common. Both are vast in area. Both are frontiers. Both are endowed with great mineral and agricultural resources. Both are marked by human diversity. There are many differences as well, but one stands out. Texas, by any standard, is very, very rich. Africa, by comparison with other continents, is distressingly poor.

Today I would like to discuss with you Africa's economic plight, its implications for U.S. foreign policy, what we in government are attempting to do about it, and how this effort can involve you, as representatives of the private sector.

Africa, more than any other region, is gravely threatened by economic crisis. It is the only area of the world where national growth rates are often negative, with more of the same predicted for the rest of the eighties unless there is rapid improvement. It is the only continent characterized by declining per capita food production, the consequence of the highest population growth rates in the world combined with stagnating agricultural production. Increased requirements for food imports, combined with the soaring cost of imported oil, have pushed several important countries close to bankruptcy. Normally a situation where a nation's debt payments amount to more than one-quarter of export earnings is considered dangerous. But in two major African countries, Sudan and Zaire, debt payments due in 1983 will exceed available export earnings, leaving nothing for essential imports. Either the countries will default, which is unlikely, or their debt will be "rolled over," or rescheduled. Neither alternative is satisfactory. Even Africa's more successful economies are, in general, faced with unhealthy debt burdens and insufficient rates of growth.

I could spend the next hour explaining the causes of the African economic crisis. They include a difficult, disaster-prone environment, the afterglow of political instability in many countries, and a varying mixture of counterproductive policies and institutional weaknesses. During the sixties, Africa was shielded from the effect of structural economic weaknesses by relatively high commodity prices combined with relatively generous flows of foreign aid. These conditions also encouraged some African countries to borrow heavily from private commercial banks.

With the onset of world recession, however, the prices of African commodities plummeted, while the cost of most imports remained relatively high. Aid flows leveled off as the industrialized countries, including the United States, tightened budgetary belts. But the debts still had to be paid—indeed new borrowing was often imperative.

It is now generally recognized, by Africans as well as by foreign observers, that Africa's special vulnerability to world recession was usually exacerbated by misguided economic policies. For example, pricing systems have typically been geared to keep food prices low, penalizing farmer-producers in order to benefit urban consumers whose political support is usually critical for regime survival. Overvalued cur-

---

[20] Source: Department of State files; printed also in Department of State *Bulletin*, November 1982, pp. 12–15.

rencies have, in effect, taxed (and discouraged) exports of all kinds, resulting in chronic balance-of-payments crises.

From colonial predecessors, new African governments often inherited networks of state-owned businesses and marketing boards. Originally designed to channel colonial products to the mother country, these so-called "parastatals" have all too often assumed a new primary function of providing employment, leaving productivity a secondary consideration. The classic example is the crop marketing board in an east African country which now pays its employees more than it budgets to purchase crops!

Foreign aid programs have accomplished much of positive and enduring value in Africa, including the elimination of several major diseases, the provision of roads and railroads to market crops and minerals, and the creation of much invaluable educational infrastructure in a continent which at the time of independence was almost totally lacking in universities and technical training facilities of all kinds. At the same time, however, aid donors, ourselves included, sometimes contributed unwittingly to the growing economic problem by subsidizing inefficient state corporations and underwriting elaborate government programs and "pilot projects" which (when the aid flows stopped) governments often could not afford to operate or maintain.

Africa's economic crisis has a multiple impact on U.S. interests which are increasingly related to our most vital concerns. For example, I am now heavily engaged in negotiations which will, if successful, achieve a peaceful settlement in Namibia and Angola and pave the way toward reduced conflict and expanded economic growth in southern Africa. If we fail, we may witness a spiral of turmoil that could destroy a number of southern African countries and would directly benefit our Cuban and Soviet adversaries. Either way, the repercussions will be global. Africa is no longer on the policy sidelines.

By threatening the stability of some of our oldest friends and partners on the continent, the African economic crisis threatens virtually all of our broader goals, including the search for peace in southern Africa. It endangers U.S. and allied access to valuable resources, including the oil fields of west Africa and the vital strategic minerals of southern Africa. All too often, economic distress generates starvation and refugees, problems which can only be addressed through expensive emergency relief programs. While our government will respond generously to humanitarian imperatives of this kind, we certainly prefer to spend money in a manner more conducive to long term development. The economic collapse or default of a major African country would pose an additional threat to the integrity of the international financial system, already under worrisome pressure elsewhere.

Our African economic policy is influenced by three fundamental facts:

—First, U.S. aid to Africa, although substantial and increasing, is unlikely (given budgetary pressures) to experience dramatic growth. The same goes for other aid donors.

—Second, as mentioned earlier, inadequate economic policies are one critical impediment to development in many African countries.

—Third, the present and potential contributions of the private sector (both foreign and indigenous) to African economic growth vastly outweigh anything that foreign aid can contribute.

The various elements of our policy flow naturally from consideration of these basic facts. Let me elaborate briefly:

As a matter of highest priority, the United States continues to take the lead in helping—and mobilizing others to help—human beings imperilled by strife and starvation in Africa. The United States has been foremost in assistance to international refugee programs and in providing opportunities for third-country settlement. (Several thousand African refugees will come to the United States this year.) The Congress has recently approved $30 million for new activities designed to provide refugee-related development opportunities, so that long-term refugees will not be forced to live perpetually on the dole. Our refugee aid to Africa totaled about $110 million in FY 1982, a quadrupling of the amount expended in 1978, mainly for programs in Somalia, Sudan, and Zaire, and for persons displaced by conflict in Chad.

Second, under more normal conditions we are using our aid to encourage the process of policy reform, which is another way of saying that we intend wherever possible to help those who have demonstrated a willingness to help themselves.

I might note that despite budgetary constraints, U.S. economic aid to Africa requested for fiscal 1983 is $840 million, compared to the $737.6 million requested in 1981 (not including the refugee assistance and emergency food aid which I mentioned earlier). In addition to our bilateral programs, we are maintaining a vigorous commitment to the World Bank and the African Development Bank and Fund. We are encouraging the World Bank to devote an increasing share of its "soft loan" IDA funds to Africa, and are now completing arrangements to join the African Development Bank, recently opened to non-African membership. Including our share of aid disbursed through these multilateral institutions, total U.S. economic assistance to Africa is well in excess of $1 billion annually. (By contrast, total military aid requested for fiscal 1983 is only one-fifth of this amount.)

Exactly how can we best deploy our aid to encourage better economic policies in Africa? This question taxes our diplomatic skills, and those of our colleagues in AID, on a daily basis. I can assure you it is not a matter of bribing foreign governments to go against their own inclinations. Reforms must come from each governments' own political will. Even in the poorest countries we have neither the vast sums of money required, nor the inclination, to "buy" changes of policy.

Our approach involves working with Africans to identify potentially successful programs and policies and then using our resources to support them. Often, as we well know from our own domestic experience, the initial phases of an economic reform measure involve expense and dislocation. Properly deployed, our aid can ease such burdens for those governments courageous and enlightened enough to assume them.

Encouraging policy reform also means working closely both with other donors and with the World Bank and International Monetary Fund. Because of their great resources, expertise, and impartiality as international institutions, these multilateral organizations often take the lead in proposing and supporting economic reforms. That is why their continued health is vital to our own efforts.

Having told you that the private sector figures heavily in our policy, it is important that you understand what we mean by that term in the African context. Our definition is broad; it includes everything that is not government-owned, and it most emphatically covers African as well as foreign enterprise.

Africa's private sector is overwhelmingly a realm of small operators—farmers, fishermen, artisans, cooperatives. The archetype is that dynamo of small-scale capitalism, the woman market entrepreneur who dominates much indigenous retailing, the so called "informal sector", in west Africa. All too often such small producers and merchants have been ignored or discouraged by proliferating and sometimes predatory bureaucracies—and there is little doubt that, on a per capita basis, Africa has more bureaucracy than any other continent. More than any other factor, government-run marketing schemes combined with government-set prices have denied the farmer a fair return for his produce, and that in a nutshell is why Africa today spends even more on imported food than on imported oil.

For many reasons foreign or multinational enterprise is a less significant element in Africa than such small-scale local capitalism. In many countries markets are too small, skills and infrastructure too scarce, to attract and sustain big business. Nevertheless, American trade and investment is already by far the most significant element in our economic presence in Africa, and it has great potential for further growth.

I should dwell on that word *growth* for a moment. It is in large part because we recognize the overwhelming importance of helping Africa achieve higher economic growth rates that we want to encourage the private sector. For it is only through the private sector, whether large or small, indigenous or foreign, that significant growth will occur. If African experience over the last decade proves anything, it is the folly of assuming that one can achieve popular welfare goals via purely government actions, while neglecting growth. Redistributing poverty is a dead end.

Let me now describe an imaginary African case and illustrate for you a few of the ways in which our policy can respond, partly by engaging and supporting the private sector. Our hypothetical country has just agreed to embark on a tough economic stabilization program. Debts have been rescheduled and currency devalued in order to restore balance-of-payments equilibrium. While temporarily free from the threat of default, capital resources are perilously scarce. The government has imposed tough limits on domestic spending to keep down inflation. Although these austerity measures are essential to restore and maintain stability they involve great hardship, limiting investment both in development projects and in private enterprise. At least for the moment, business firms are starved for foreign exchange.

In this kind of situation there are a number of ways that aid donors can help. They can provide some of the capital needed for development projects. Through commodity import programs, they can ease the damaging impact of foreign exchange constraints on private firms by channeling assistance directly to the most growth-oriented sectors of the economy. In short, external assistance can help both to alleviate and to achieve the transition from austerity to growth. It can thereby demonstrate our awareness of the effort and sacrifice being made by a friendly government and our willingness to help.

Once economic stability is achieved and growth resumes, additional measures become relevant. We can provide a range of more traditional aid, including technical assistance and institution building measures which will help small-scale African farmers and entrepreneurs. As opportunities for larger-scale investments develop, there will be an expanding role for U.S. firms and for the various programs—including the Overseas Private Investment Corporation and the Export-Import Bank—which are available to encourage U.S. trade and investment. As they interact with their African partners, U.S. firms can provide much additional technical and managerial expertise, all of it relevant to the achievement of economic growth and welfare. It is for this reason that African leaders across the political spectrum, from market-oriented moderates to old line Marxists, are today increasingly eager, both in public and private, for additional U.S. trade and investment.

That, painted in very broad strokes, is the new dimension of our strategy. Now I would like to turn briefly to the implications for you, as black Americans and businessmen. I don't want to gloss over the difficulties imposed by world recession and Africa's economic crisis. Although there are some very significant exceptions and bright spots, Africa is not in general an easy place to do business, even for the largest of multinational firms. It takes perseverance, a great deal of careful preparation and dialogue with African decisionmakers, and an underlying faith in Africa's long-term growth potential. But you do have a role to play and one which may increase sharply in the future.

To begin with, I would note that the sympathetic interest of black Americans in Africa is extremely important as a sustaining factor in our policy. It encourages Congress to provide the aid resources we need and it sharpens awareness of Africa in the minds of senior policymakers. So even when black Americans outside government disagree with the executive branch on specific issues, as is sometimes the case, we can only welcome and encourage their interest.

And despite the present difficulties which I have described, Africa should engage your interest as businessmen. Black American firms such as Johnson Products of Chicago are already involved in Africa. President Hagans of the National Business League was among those who participated in the first Cabinet-level trade mission to Africa last January. Mayor Ferre of Miami is involved in organizing a trade fair which will introduce African entrepreneurs to minority businessmen in Florida, with the aim of encouraging trade between the United States and Africa, and joint venture partnerships between Africans and Americans. Both the Commerce Department and AID maintain offices which are charged with encouraging the increased participation of minority firms in our export and foreign assistance programs. Congressional approval of the administration-supported bill legalizing export trading companies[21] would make it much easier for small and medium businesses of all kinds to operate in Africa, by enabling smaller operators to share the often great overhead costs involved in African operations.

Among the innovations launched by this administration is AID's new Bureau of Private Enterprise, established specifically to help increase development-oriented private sector resources in the LDC's. The Bureau's program includes new methods of financing private enterprise projects, a wide range of advisory services, and funding of feasibility studies through the closely associated Trade and Development Program, which may be of particular interest to small and medium U.S. businesses.

Finally, I would underline that the impediments imposed by world recession will be lessened as our own domestic economy recovers, increasing the range of business opportunities for all Americans in Africa. U.S. recovery will help to benefit all developing countries by expanding markets for African as well as other Third World

[21] Reference is to P.L. 97-290, the Export Trading Company Act of 1982, approved on October 8, 1982; for text, see 96 Stat. 1233.

exporters. The United States currently takes about half of all the manufactured goods exported by the non-OPEC developing countries to the industrialized world. As President Reagan stated before the Cancun conference, every 1 percent reduction in U.S. interest rates due to lower inflation improves the balance-of-payments of the LDC's by $1 billion.

In concluding, I would like to reemphasize the extent to which both Americans and Africans will gain from accelerating African economic growth. It has become a truism that more than ever before, U.S. prosperity depends on trade with developing countries. Today we export more to them than to Europe and Japan combined. However, the developing nations in question are largely the middle income, high growth countries—the Brazils, Mexicos, Singapores, and Taiwans. Our total exports to sub-Saharan Africa, including South Africa, still amounts to less than 3 percent of our global total and less than one-tenth of our total exports to the LDC's.

Nevertheless, for a number of reasons we can be optimistic about the future. Although still relatively small, our trade with Africa has been growing at a high rate compared to other areas. Africa's future potential is undeniable given its enormous resources of minerals, energy, and unexploited, arable land.

It is important to remember that several of today's more dramatic LDC success stories faced apparently insoluble economic problems only a few years ago. In 1960, to cite two examples, many American observers regarded South Korea as a hopeless case, deprived both of natural resources and necessary entrepreneurial skills by the ugly fact of partition. In India it appeared that we were pouring our aid dollars into an economic quagmire, destined for perpetual dependency on others. Only a few years ago, speeches written in my own Bureau of African Affairs habitually illustrated Africa's food problems by drawing gloomy parallels with India.

Today it seems that things have changed. The Indians have virtually achieved food grain self-sufficiency and are increasingly capable of financing development needs by borrowing from private capital markets. The Koreans have achieved one of the economic miracles which inflates LDC trade statistics. Their rapid expansion into new industrial export sectors is a challenge to even the most sophisticated market economies. These cases are not unique; a number of other former recipients of massive U.S. aid have achieved or are approaching self-sustaining growth, providing in the process a better standard of living for their citizens and a healthy stimulus to world trade.

The African states are at an earlier stage of the same process, often still in the most profoundly difficult stage of post independence and far less well equipped by their colonial experience to make a smooth transition to prosperity. Yet there can be no doubt that the transition is already underway. Our challenge is to speed up the process, for to the extent that we do so, we will be among the beneficiaries.

Document 548

Address by Vice President Bush Before the Plenary Session of Cooperation for Development in Africa, October 26, 1982[22]

U.S. Support for Africa's Economic Growth and Prosperity

I am honored to open the fourth policy-level meeting of the Cooperation for Development in Africa.

The opportunity to address this distinguished audience is particularly timely, as I am looking forward to going back to Africa to visit seven countries next month.[23] In 1972, when I was United States Ambassador to the United Nations, I visited ten countries in Africa. I am anxious to go back to see firsthand the changes and to learn what key African leaders are thinking and to make clear that the United States knows what its interests are and who our friends are. I am also anxious to see the economic and social development opportunities which are the subject of recent studies, discussions, and concerns in our councils of government, and which are in part the concern of this conference.

---

[22] Source: Press Release, October 26, 1982, Office of the Press Secretary to the Vice President. Bush spoke in the Loy Henderson Conference Room of the Department of State.

[23] Regarding Vice President Bush's visit to Africa, November 10–14 and 16–22, 1982, see documents 550–552, 571, 574, 589–590, 594, 601, 602, 612, 613.

The worldwide transition of peoples from colonies to free and independent states, which began decades ago, has been referred to as "the revolution of rising expectations." The aspirations of this "revolution" unfortunately remain unfilled in many of the sub-Sahara African countries. Africans are concerned that, while the "winds of change" still prevail, the rate of change in the social and economic order has not been satisfactory.

In Africa the rate of economic growth, particularly in the agricultural and industrial sectors over the last two decades, has been disappointing. With the help of newfound wealth, some African countries have made great progress in building their national economies, and in sustaining their varied and valuable cultures. Others—not so fortunate—still depend upon substantial external assistance to help them meet the needs of their people.

The aspirations and goals of the African countries have been elaborated in the Lagos Plan of Action, which was adopted by the heads of African states in April 1980.[24] One of the purposes of this conference is to explore additional ways of attaining those goals through coordinated actions among the African and CDA member countries. In doing so, we will also strive to harmonize our development efforts with those of the World Bank and the other multinational banks and donors.

The task to be accomplished is formidable. It will require the most determined efforts of all of us. The scope and structure of our challenge is outlined in the recent World Bank Report of 1981 entitled "Accelerated Development in Sub-Saharan Africa". Appropriately, it reminds us of Africa's great promise, as well as of the magnitude of the task before us.

Africans are proud and practical people; proud of their independence; proud of their self-reliance. We Americans have applauded and encouraged the growth of political and economic freedom in Africa. That is our heritage, too.

As practical people, we understand that we all live in an interdependent world. Nations are linked by history, trade, personal experiences, and by common necessity—each to the other.

We all recognize the value of developing and adapting technologies in agriculture, education, industry, and in the administration of government.

As representatives of the principal donors to Africa, gathered here under the auspices of the CDA in Africa—you conference delegates have a key role to play. This collaboration should seek to make the most efficient use of the technical and financial resources provided under our respective bilateral programs. This can best be achieved through well-planned and timely coordination by the donors, among themselves, with the African governments and with regional institutions. I see this effort as an important partnership—a partnership which the United States takes most seriously and which it will continue to support.

The United States, therefore, reaffirms—for the decade of the 1980's—its continued concern and support of Africa's economic growth and prosperity.

Our economic development efforts are not based solely on pious hopes, but on fundamental principles which we believe are practical guides. These are:

—to help African nations attain self-sustaining economic growth;

—to support the development of productive human capacities and institutions;

—to stimulate trade by facilitating access to markets;

—to develop strategies and policies tailored to the specific needs and potentials of individual countries, thus recognizing that each nation's approach to development will reflect its own cultural, political, and economic heritage;

—to direct assistance toward the most productive activities—especially in the crucial areas of food production and energy;

—to help improve the climate for private investment, and to help develop the indigenous private sector in an environment of free and fair markets;

—and finally, to support a democratic political atmosphere in which practical economic solutions can flourish.

One year ago, on October 22, 1981, President Reagan reaffirmed the American commitment to the global needs for development at the International Meeting on Cooperation and Development held in Can-

---

[24] The Lagos Plan of Action was adopted by a special economic summit conference of OAU heads of state and government at Lagos on April 29, 1980.

cun, Mexico. This conference brought together government leaders representing 22 nations from both the industrial and the developing countries, to discuss global development issues. In his speech the President made several important observations which are noteworthy for those who are dealing with matters of public policy and economic development issues. The President observed:

—first, that history demonstrates that economic growth and human progress make their greatest strides in countries that encourage economic freedom;

—second, that responsible government has an important role to play in building the economic foundations for society. The critical test is whether the governments are genuinely working to liberate individuals by creating incentives to work, to save and to succeed;

—finally, President Reagan observed that individual farmers, laborers, traders, and managers are the heart and soul of development. Trust them. When they have a personal interest in deciding the conditions of life for themselves and their children, they will create and they will build. It is only then that societies become dynamic, prosperous, and achieve progress.

The United States under President Reagan recognizes Africa's needs and has responded by increasing the resources devoted to sub-Saharan Africa from 1981 to 1983 from $463.3 million to $638 million—a full 40 percent. In addition, the administration is requesting $220 million in food assistance in 1983. We intend to increase our commitment again for fiscal year 1984.

Some of the CDA member countries represented at this conference have had a long relationship with the people in Africa. With the end of the colonial period, the United States has quickly established diplomatic relations and initiated economic development programs to help in meeting the social and economic needs of the newly independent countries.

But the task is not completed. In historical terms, it has just begun. Strategies, policies, and programs must focus on productivity and self-sustained growth. They must be realistic. They must be designed for the long haul, if they are to succeed and stand the test of time.

The deliberations of the CDA delegates during this 3-day meeting are of particular importance to the Africa of today and of the future:

—The present international economic situation has created some extremely difficult problems for the developing countries in sub-Saharan Africa.

—The donor countries represented here, and the development institutions they are affiliated with, have at their disposal many of the key instruments which are so important to the development process.

I am proud to have this opportunity to meet with you. I welcome you to Washington, and I assure you of my respect for the great work we are undertaking here together.

Thank you.

Document 549

Address by the Assistant Secretary of State for African Affairs (Crocker) Before the Baltimore Council on Foreign Relations, Baltimore, October 28, 1982[25]

The Challenge to Regional Security in Africa: The U.S. Response

Dr. Burd, ladies and gentlemen, thank you for your generous welcome. I commend you for the formation and success of the Baltimore Council on Foreign Relations, which is a singularly appropriate organization for our Nation's third largest port city. Baltimore is an international commercial hub that is symbolized in such a practical fashion by this impressive World Trade Center in which we have the pleasure of meeting. I must add that I am honored to have been invited by the Council to participate in a speakers program that in only 2 years has attracted so many distinguished leaders.

You in Baltimore do not have to be told about the economic interdependence of nations or about our need to expand trade links in the Third World, which has been the main area of expansion for American exports in recent years. Yet in considering today the security problems facing Africa, we are also discussing the interaction of

[25] Source: Department of State files; printed also in Department of State *Bulletin*, December 1982, pp. 22–25.

political, economic, and security factors that comprise American interests in Africa. Security is one component of an equation.

We too often consider our relations with the 50 nations of Africa in one of two highly simplistic ways. The globalists would have us believe that events in Africa are explainable as reactions to initiatives and manipulations from the key centers of world power. African goals, motives, and dynamics are, in this view, of only minor importance. Conversely, the regionalists stress the complex array of strictly African factors to explain events in the region. They suggest that the role of external motivations and power relationships is superficial and ephemeral. Both views are seriously flawed and—when pressed to extremes—potentially dangerous. Most African events are obviously explainable in local terms, and to ignore or be insensitive to these factors is folly. Yet it is equally true that Africa is a full participant in the global economic and political system. Africa is directly influenced by—just as it also helps shape—the competitive arena of world politics.

Just to state that we have security interests in Africa is not to say that we seek to promote East–West confrontation there, which we do not. We have no mandate to be the gendarme of Africa nor do we seek that role. Certainly we have no economic or political interests in Africa that are served by local arms races or by instability itself. On the contrary, our interests are best served by political and economic stability, which foster the peaceful development of modern African economic and political institutions that can interact with our own to mutual advantage. Our overarching strategic goal in Africa is to help establish the rules of the game that will limit and discourage the application of outside force in African conflicts.

There is a security challenge in Africa because there are real security threats to individual African nations and regions. Internal instability, often in tandem with external adventurism, plagues many African countries. Border struggles, which have often evolved from uncertain colonial arrangements, create serious regional problems. Ethnic rivalries have precipitated civil wars, sometimes leading to cross-border violence. The mere management of modest security forces overtaxes the meager resources of many states. These circumstances are often exploited by outside powers unfriendly to us, and in this manner a problem having clearly African roots can acquire broader global implications.

When this occurs, we face a new factor in the global balance we cannot ignore. Neither we in the West nor African states can gain when one outside power seeks unilateral advantage through the projection or application of military force in Africa. Africa, like the West, is the loser when regional actors are encouraged to pursue violent rather than negotiated solutions. In such circumstances, we believe that unilateral self-denial by Western countries cannot strengthen African security or nonalignment; instead it erodes the climate of confidence necessary to achieve them. The United States cannot be a credible partner if it ignores friendly African states who turn to us in real defensive need. The solution to conflicts in Africa does not rest with U.S. abstinence, while others rush in to exploit regional strife. This administration stands ready to help bolster the security of countries so affected.

The sobering fact is that it is not the West but the Soviet bloc that has supplied Africa with 60–70 percent of its arms. In 1981, the United States was only in fifth place as a source of arms for Africa. Instead we continue to emphasize economic over military assistance at a ratio of 3 to 1. Next fiscal year we have planned roughly $1 billion assistance for sub-Saharan Africa. Of this, only $243 million is for military sales and training. This contrasts sharply with the Soviet bloc's overwhelming preponderance of military over economic assistance.

Peaceful development is the only way Africa will find solutions to the critical social and economic challenges it faces. Africa is struggling to survive its worst economic crisis since World War II. This explains our emphasis on economic assistance. We clearly recognize that even minimal conditions of security in Africa will be elusive unless African states can stabilize their economies and regain the path of development. But instability and insecurity frustrate this effort. When insecurity is fueled by external forces, we promote African, as well as our own, interests in helping African friends to resist and overcome it.

This is the key to an effective policy, the fact that Africans and we both seek peaceful change and the security conditions needed for development and nation-building. This is an essential element in our support for the Organization of African Unity (OAU), whose charter and foreign policy principles we endorse. The OAU is dedicated to protecting Africa's territorial integrity and defending the continent from external aggression and subversion. We give strong support to its mediation and peacekeeping activities within Africa, as do our allies.

Our cooperative efforts with the OAU have paid off. For example, U.S. policy toward Chad, aimed at countering Libyan military adventurism, has yielded important dividends over the past 12 months. In 1980, 7,000 Libyan troops intervened in the Chadian civil war, and quickly became a major source of regional instability, posing a direct threat along Sudan's border and creating great worry among the other states bordering Chad. Seriously concerned by the Libyan presence, we and others encouraged the Chadians to ask for Libya's withdrawal and to seek OAU help in solving internal problems. In late 1981, the then provisional Chadian Government, headed by former President Goukouni, called upon Libya to remove its military force. We then worked closely with the OAU to prepare the way for an African peacekeeping force to maintain order in Chad once the Libyans left. An African peacekeeping force, organized by OAU Chairman, Kenya's President Daniel arap Moi, was subsequently deployed into Chad in record time, before serious factional violence could break out in the void left behind by the Libyans. This remarkable achievement reflects favorably on Chairman Moi and the troop donor countries, Nigeria, Zaire, and Senegal.

For our part, the United States moved directly to facilitate and support this peacekeeping effort. We allocated $12 million to support the Nigerian and Zairian contingents with nonlethal equipment and aid transport of supplies to Chad. We also supported OAU efforts to promote reconciliation among various Chadian factions. By June 1982, Goukouni, who refused reconciliation efforts proposed by the OAU, had been forced out of Chad and replaced by his principal rival, Hissene Habre. The OAU concluded that its troops could be withdrawn. For the past 4 months Habre has consolidated his control over the entire country and actively pursued the goal of internal political reconciliation. The United States has been responding to the urgent humanitarian needs in Chad with emergency food shipments, air transport of food to hard-hit areas in rural Chad and provision of emergency assistance.

Chad's problems are far from over. Libya still occupies a band of territory which it claims across the north of the country[26] and seems prepared to support insurrection again. The country's economy and infrastructure are shattered and the political fissures from many years of civil war will not be breached overnight.

Chad's reconstruction and reconciliation must proceed apace if Libya is to be denied another opportunity for foreign meddling in a sensitive area. Recognizing this, the United States has just signed an agreement to provide $2.8 million in rehabilitation assistance over the coming year.[27] We will also be supporting an international donors' conference which the U.N. and OAU are organizing to get urgently needed economic assistance flowing. The initial international response to Chad's plight has been heartening, particularly the massive international food airlift which took place in September, and certainly was responsible for saving many hundreds, if not thousands, of lives.

Perhaps nowhere in Africa have our security concerns, and our security policies, been more intensely engaged than in southern Africa. This region, from Zaire to the Cape of Good Hope, contains the bulk of Africa's mineral wealth, its most developed industrial structure, and almost two-thirds of the continent's GNP. It is also a region threatened with the prospect of heightened violence and polarization that could lead to great-power confrontation. It is precisely to avoid that possibility of violence and confrontation that we have fashioned a major effort to bring about regional peace and security.

Southern Africa is a complex region and its many characteristics and conflicts cannot be easily summarized. But two major sources of tension dominate the scene. One is that South Africa, the richest and most powerful state in the region, governed by a white minority that has erected a structure of legally entrenched racial separation to protect itself, feels surrounded and threatened by its black-ruled neighbors. South Africa believes that it must preempt any armed threat—guerrilla or conventional—from its neighbors, and is prepared to use its military superiority to that end. Until there develops a structure of understanding—some reciprocally understood basis for coexistence—between South Africa and its neighbors, this situation will remain a major source of instability and could result in growing violence across borders. To say

[26] The Aozou Strip.

[27] The agreement to provide $2.8 million in reprogrammed economic support funds was signed on September 30, 1982.

this is not to downplay the urgency or the gravity of South Africa's own domestic agenda. Movement toward a system based on consent, shaped by South Africans of all races, is essential for that country's stability and survival. But that process is unlikely to occur peacefully in conditions of heightened international violence across South African borders.

The second great source of tension came with the collapse of the Portuguese empire in southern Africa in 1974–75 and the decision of the USSR to inject its power into the vacuum that resulted. Soviet arms had been fed to insurgent movements in this part of Africa for many years, but in 1975 the USSR supported the deployment of 25,000 Cuban troops to Angola. This direct injection of Soviet and proxy military force in southern Africa posed a challenge to the future of the region. It exacerbated South Africa's feelings of threat from its neighbors, and it threatened long-term Western access to the region's mineral and economic resources. Without question, it raised to a new threshold the tension between South Africa and its neighbors, and affected the calculations of all who live in this region.

It is not overstatement to note that the political future of Africa will be shaped by the ways in which the deep tensions and problems of southern Africa are eventually resolved. It is for these reasons that this administration has adopted a policy of constructive engagement in southern Africa. The search for a more stable, secure, and prosperous southern Africa will be a long and arduous process, but there is no other responsible course for American policy. There are many aspects to this effort, but we judged that the place to start was with the interrelated conflicts in Namibia and Angola.

A year ago, we were in the initial stages of the revived negotiations on Namibian independence on the basis of U.N. Security Council Resolution 435.[28] Working closely with our Western Five Contact Group partners and the other parties to the negotiations, we have come a long way since then. On July 12, we were able to conclude Phase I of the negotiations—agreement on a set of principles concerning the Constituent Assembly and the constitution for an independent Namibia. Since then, we have also made considerable progress on remaining questions, including the impartiality of all parties in U.N.-supervised elections and the size, deployment, and composition of UNTAG—the United Nations Transition Assistance Group, which would be responsible for monitoring implementation of the U.N. plan for Namibian independence embodied in Security Council Resolution 435. With the exception of the electoral system for the Constituent Assembly and final agreement on the battalions for UNTAG, we are close to implementation of the U.N. plan.

At the same time, we have always made clear that there is also a vitally important Angolan agenda which must be addressed. Seven years after Angola's independence from Portugal, thousands of Cuban combat forces and a substantial number of Soviet advisors remain in that country, as participants in a tragic and prolonged civil war. The presence of these forces has—since their introduction in 1975—profoundly affected the balance of security in the region and has inevitably shaped the security calculations of other countries in southern Africa.

From the outset, we have recognized that Namibia does not exist in a vacuum, and that in practice the chances for a negotiated settlement of the Namibian question would be decisively influenced by parallel progress toward withdrawal of the Cuban troops from Angola. This is not an issue which we contrived on our own. The South African Government which, all parties agree, holds the key to a settlement, has long made clear its deep concern over the presence of these forces.

It would be idle to argue that the United States has no interest in ending the presence of Cuban troops in southern Africa. The introduction of Cuban combat forces into Angola changed strategic reality and upset the delicate fabric of reciprocal restraint maintained since World War II in the developing world. It was one of a series of events—all of us know too well—that led us to the period of aggravated tension we face with the Soviet Union today. Regaining that balance is in Africa's interest, our interest, and in the interest of a more stable and positive U.S.-Soviet relationship as well.

We have, for nearly a year now, been engaged in an intensive, high-level dialogue with the Angolan Government in an effort to reach a broadly acceptable formula for Cuban withdrawal. These bilateral discussions have been held outside the framework of Security Council Resolution 435 and are

---

[28] For the text of U.N. Security Council Resolution 435 (1978), see *American Foreign Policy: Basic Documents, 1977–1980,* p. 1205.

not part of the Contact Group's mandate. Our efforts have attempted to respond to Angola's security concerns while dealing squarely with the reality of South African concerns as well. We believe that this is a viable means of achieving the goal to which we are profoundly committed: a stable and peaceful regional context in which Namibia can achieve its independence under the free and fair process envisaged in the U.N. plan.

We have achieved real progress in our talks with the Angolans, and we will spare no effort in continuing our quest for a comprehensive, peaceful settlement. However, this complicated and difficult effort involves fundamental issues and choices for both sides, and it will take time. In the final analysis, there will be no agreement unless the key security concerns of the principal parties are dealt with. We have sought and will continue to seek an understanding that meets the basic concerns of all parties and opens a new and brighter chapter in southern Africa's troubled history.

East Africa and the adjacent Indian Ocean area represent another region which is of major concern to the United States in global security terms. The states in this region realize that their first priority is to overcome serious economic problems that hobble development and interfere with productive political relations. The United States and other Western countries, together with the World Bank, the International Monetary Fund, and other international financial institutions are currently working with countries in east Africa to overcome their severe economic difficulties. We consider this effort, which will require painful reform by the countries themselves and extraordinary steps by their creditors as well as the donor community, to be our most important long-term "security" program. It is to this effort that the overwhelming part of our assistance goes.

We are working closely with our allies on these problems. France, Great Britain, and Italy also have important interests in the region. Moreover, these countries have considerable experience in east Africa and are prepared to devote substantial resources to assist the development of the region. Several friendly Middle Eastern countries are also prepared to assist. European and Arab economic assistance to east Africa is significant, and is often larger than that provided by the United States.

Serious political problems exist in the region, however, which cause instability and unrest. Last summer we witnessed attempted coups in Kenya[29] and the Seychelles,[30] and major clashes between Ethiopia and Somalia. In Uganda, years will be needed to overcome the debilitating consequences of former President Idi Amin's tyranny. Ethiopia, second only in Africa to Nigeria in population, is still in the throes of insurgency and civil war in parts of its territory. These local problems are especially troublesome because of this region's considerable strategic significance to the West. East Africa and the Arabian Peninsula lie astride the Red Sea and the major oil tanker lanes leading to Europe.

An important example of regional security concern is the Horn. Tensions within this strategically important part of Africa, an area astride key transport routes through the Red Sea, go back at least to the 19th century. They are sustained by foreign intervention, domestic civil strife, and ethnic irredentism that pose a grave challenge to the African structure of order enshrined in the Charter of the OAU. In recent years, this source of tension has sparked major outside involvement. Somalia, in 1977, attacked Ethiopia in an effort to take over the Ogaden region and Ethiopia called upon Moscow and Cuba for assistance. Today, 11,000 Cuban troops remain in Ethiopia, and the USSR has established a position of influence in Ethiopia through massive arms shipments totaling around $4 billion in 5 years. In return, the USSR has acquired naval and air facilities in Ethiopia.

The United States has an important interest in this region. Following upon the revolution in Iran[31] and the threat to oil supplies in the Middle East, the United States entered into a series of agreements with countries in Africa and the Middle East for use of facilities to support our rapid deployment force. Somalia is one of those countries. At the same time, the United States has consistently supported the OAU position of the sanctity of colonial borders and has limited our military assistance to Somalia to quite modest levels geared to the defense of internationally recognized Somali territory.

But security in the region is now threatened from the Ethiopian side. With the

---

[29] Regarding this coup, see footnote 4 to document 613.

[30] See *American Foreign Policy: Current Documents, 1981,* document 622.

[31] During September to December 1978, internal opposition and unrest against the Shah intensified. The Shah departed Iran on January 16, 1979, for Egypt on what was officially described as a vacation, but was actually exile.

massive shipments of Soviet arms, and a major expansion of its military forces, Ethiopia now has the largest standing army in sub-Saharan Africa, and is far superior to Somalia in numbers and weapons. In 1981, Ethiopia signed a treaty with Libya and South Yemen[32] which has led to Libyan-Ethiopian cooperation in subversion and armed attack against both Sudan and Somalia. This past summer, Ethiopian regular troops, supporting a smaller number of Somalia dissidents trained and armed in Ethiopia, occupied two Somali towns. Evidence indicates that Ethiopian actions are intended to foster instability and insurrection in Somalia and the overthrow of the Somali Government.

African security is not served if Soviet arms, Cuban reserve forces, and Libyan money and arms are combined to overthrow legitimate governments in the Horn. The United States has acted quickly in this situation. We have airlifted several shipments of arms to Somalia and indicated that we are not prepared to countenance subversive action and armed aggression against our friends in the region. Our actions, together with Somali nationalist sentiment against the Ethiopian attacks, has served to strengthen Somalia in this crisis, though several areas remain occupied by Ethiopian forces. We are at the same time looking at a wider basis for resolution of the tensions in this region. We have no intention or desire to refuel Somali ambitions against Ethiopia, nor do we wish to see Somalia and Sudan have to allocate greater resources to defense when their economic needs are so great. We are making clear to all the parties in the region that we are interested in promoting a modus vivendi among the countries in the area, and are doing everything within our power to encourage better relations among those countries with which we have close ties, e.g., Somalia and Kenya. We would welcome signs from Ethiopia that it too seeks a better structure for relationships in the region, and an end to policies of confrontation. As a clear indication of where we think priorities should be placed, during this same period, we have been actively engaged with our allies in Europe and with the international financial institutions such as the IMF and the IBRD to promote more comprehensive economic programs for Sudan, Kenya, and Somalia.

In summary, we have provided a limited but important and timely military assistance response to a serious security threat in the region. We will not shrink from helping our friends, nor from defending our own strategic assets in the region. But our policy objectives are broader. We are not building up threatening forces. We are giving our full weight to the accepted African position on borders, and are making ourselves available for diplomatic efforts that can reduce the security threats in the area.

In west Africa as well, the United States has important political and security interests to protect. Most countries in this region are moderate in outlook and Western oriented. They comprise a large block of votes in the U.N. and other international bodies. Their views are important factors in reaching an African—or OAU—consensus on issues of great importance to the United States and the West. Additionally, our strategic interests include access to petroleum. Nigeria is our second largest foreign supplier of oil—only Saudi Arabia provides us more.

But these countries are facing severe economic problems, which can result in political instability, outside adventurism, and the loss to the West of some supportive and moderate friends. In Ghana, for example, a deteriorating economic situation eroded support for a weak but pro-Western democratic government and led directly to its downfall.

In Liberia, rampant corruption and an economic crisis led to a military coup in 1980.[33] As one of its earliest acts, the Reagan administration developed a program of sustained support for the new government to resist the blandishments of the Soviets and their surrogates designed to destroy the special relationship which has existed between Liberia and the United States for almost 150 years. Our assistance, primarily economic but including military loan credits, has increased tenfold during the last 4 years.

Other west African nations confront real and serious external security threats, notably those emanating from Libya. As neighbors of Colonel Qadhafi, several west African countries have suffered his adventurism and destabilizing efforts. For example, Qadhafi has publicly threatened the moderate Government of Niger as his next target for subversion. Similarly, his government is engaged in the training of dissidents who are helped to return to their home countries to work against established governments.

[32] See footnote 8 to document 604.

[33] President William R. Tolbert was overthrown on April 16, 1980.

The United States has been responsive to requests for help against such threats. In Niger, we have established a modest foreign military sales loan program and a military training program. We have also asked the Congress to approve a small balance-of-payments grant to help Niger meet its budget shortfall stemming from the collapse of the uranium market, the country's leading foreign exchange earner.

All these U.S. security programs in sub-Saharan Africa are in support of our strategic goal of helping to establish and maintain the limits of outside force that is applied in Africa. We are not Africa's self-appointed policeman but we are its partner in economic growth and nation-building. As such we cannot ignore the real security threats facing our African partners, especially when these are prompted or fueled by our global adversaries. Moreover, the presence of Soviet bloc forces and bases in parts of Africa that would threaten our communications with the Middle East and the gulf are a serious challenge to vital U.S. security interests. The answer is neither to ignore the problem nor to overreact and provoke an essentially East–West arms race in Africa. The proper answer is for the United States and our allies, in close consultation with our African friends, to provide just the amount of security assistance to afflicted African nations for them and us to achieve our mutual strategic goals.

We Americans—especially in leading commercial centers—have become increasingly sophisticated in our appreciation of our major stake in the economic success of Africa and the rest of the Third World. We know that we cannot afford unlimited amounts of economic assistance to countries unable to support themselves, that we need a number of commodities only they can provide in abundance, and that our future prosperity depends in large part on the growth of their economies. This is why the Reagan administration believes it is equally important for all of us to understand the critical role that security considerations play in the economic development equation. It is a challenge that we and our African friends must meet and overcome. Thank you.

Document 550

Remarks by Vice President Bush, Lagos, November 13, 1982 (Extract)[34]

"We Affirm Our Support . . . for the Objective of the Organization of African Unity"

. . . .

Q. (AP)—In 10 days time, the OAU will be meeting. There have been other scheduled meetings that did not hold. What will be your comments on the venue of the upcoming meeting?

VICE PRESIDENT. Our comments about the venue of the meeting is that the members of the Organization of African Unity should determine that, and they don't need any help from us. (Laughter) Or any advice. And I don't believe that that would be appropriate for the United States to interject ourselves into their workings. We affirm our support, our broad support, for the objective of the Organization of African Unity, but we cannot and, I'll be honest, we have expressed our own reservation as a sovereign nation about when we have differed with some conclusions stated by individual members of OAU. But we don't think that we should prejudge a meeting that looks like it will now go forward with a relative degree of unity.[35] And so I just can't help you in terms of the venue. I really think that it would be inappropriate for me to come to Africa, sit amongst friends and try and indicate what we feel the Organization of African Unity should address itself to. We have stated and, again, you're at disad-

---

[34] Source: Press Release, November 13, 1982, Office of the Press Secretary to the Vice President. Bush's remarks were made at a press conference prior to his departure from Nigeria.

[35] In August 1982, the OAU Ministerial meeting collapsed for lack of a quorum as a consequence of a dispute over the seating of a delegation representing the Saharawi Arab Democratic Republic (the Polisario Front). The second attempt to convene the annual OAU summit—following the voluntary withdrawal of the Western Sahara delegation—also failed for lack of a quorum on November 25, because of the conflict over which of two delegations from Chad to seat. This effectively forestalled Qaddafi's succession to the chairmanship of the OAU.

vantage without the text, but we have reaffirmed our general support for its deliberations, sir.

. . . .

Document 551

Address by Vice President Bush Before the Kenya Chamber of Commerce, Nairobi, November 19, 1982[36]

A New Partnership With Africa

Mr. President, members of the Kenya Chamber of Commerce, ladies and gentlemen: You do the United States a great honor in receiving me this evening. I bring you the greetings of the President of the United States and of millions of my fellow citizens who are sincerely interested in America's longstanding friendship with the continent and people of Africa. I bring also special greetings to President Danial arap Moi, and to all Kenyans. Your country is an old friend of the United States and is dear to us all.

The past 10 days have been important to me. President Reagan asked me to carry our message of friendship of and deep commitment to a true partnership with the nations of Africa. We are determined to work with the leaders of this continent in the quest for peace and progress. My visit has been particularly satisfying. It has permitted us to see old friends and make new ones.

I have exchanged views with some of Africa's most impressive leaders. I have had an opportunity to see and feel at firsthand the diversity of this beautiful continent and to sense its great promise. In several days, I will be able to share with President Reagan and my fellow Americans the thinking of Africa's leaders on the major issues important to us.

It should come as no surprise to you that President Reagan thought it especially important for me to visit Kenya. Since Kenya's independence, close ties have bound our two countries and peoples. Your nation has been admired in the United States for its political and economic record.

We share important values—democratically elected governments, civilian rule, freedom of press and religion, a multiracial society, and an economy guided by the principles of free enterprise. Kenya has been a strong advocate for peace in the world. Your country and its distinguished President have led the Organization of African Unity during a year in which Africa faced many problems. Because Kenya has served this year as spokesman for Africa's aspirations, I am especially pleased to speak from the city of Nairobi to all the people of Africa. I particularly wish to speak about the hopes and values which grew up during Africa's struggle for independence, and which will guide Africa as she faces the future. Chief among these values is the desire for freedom—freedom of nations from outside pressures and freedom of people within nations. That desire gave birth to the OAU, thanks to the recognition that—without regional cooperation—the peace, progress, and independence of Africa would not be maintained. Such cooperation is not an easy goal given the great variety of peoples, circumstances, and cultures in Africa. This tremendous diversity, coupled with the harsh impact of today's global economic recession, underscores more than ever the importance of African regional cooperation for common purposes.

There is no justification for despair about Africa's future. Despite trials and setbacks, the history of Africa since the independence era has included significant progress, especially in the development of human resources. Education, talent, and energy, such as that represented by this very audience, prove that Africa has the capacity to make good the promise of its enormous potential in spite of the many problems it faces. Thanks to the abilities and values which men and women, like ourselves, bring to the everyday task of national development, Africa can enter its third decade of independence with confidence in the future.

Because we believe that Africa has the capacity and will to be master of her destiny, President Reagan has over the past 20 months, worked to forge a new and mature partnership with the nations and people of Africa. We speak of a partnership that begins with mutual respect. We speak of a partnership that includes honest discus-

---

[36] Source: Press Release, November 19, 1982, Office of the Press Secretary to the Vice President; printed also in Department of State *Bulletin*, January 1983, pp. 45–49. Bush spoke at the Hilton Hotel.

sions. We speak of a partnership which recognizes that each nation must do its part if the goals we share are to be achieved. Partnership is a two-way street based on shared goals, common principles, and mutual interests.

These principles have guided our administration's policies toward Africa. The time is ripe for the sort of candid dialogue I have been privileged to experience on this trip. And I have learned a lot. A top priority in our diplomacy is southern Africa, where the choices between regional strife and regional cooperation are stark. The inescapable need for peaceful change is challenged by a climate of fear, distrust, foreign intervention and cross-border violence.

The United States is committed to the search for constructive change in southern Africa. In cooperation with our allies and in direct response to the will of Africa's leaders, the United States has engaged its influence and resources in the effort to bring Namibia to independence. We are determined to help turn the sad tide of growing conflict and tension in southern Africa. We are fully committed to work for a settlement that will enhance regional security and assure Namibia's early independence on terms acceptable to its people, Africa and the world at large.

Let me state again, we are fully committed to an independent Namibia.

I can assure you that significant progress has been made. A year ago the settlement effort was relaunched with vigor. Since then the United States and its Western Contact Group partners have worked closely and intensively with all parties. This past July, agreement was reached on the principles which will guide Namibia's Constituent Assembly. Since then substantial progress has been made on remaining issues concerning the implementation of Security Council Resolution 435.[37] We are close to agreement on implementation of the U.N. plan. Remaining issues can be resolved.

From the outset of this administration's engagement in the peace process, we have emphasized that there are vitally important issues arising from the situation in Angola which must be resolved if Namibia's independence is to be achieved. For 7 years Angola has been engulfed in war, its territory invaded, its progress toward a better economic future stalled. Thousands of Cuban troops remain in Angola. Wouldn't Angola and the region itself be better off with all foreign forces out of that country, South African forces and Cuban forces?

The history of foreign conquest in Africa is replete with examples of armed foreigners who came with the professed purpose of helping others but who stayed in order to help themselves. The withdrawal of Cuban forces from Angola in a parallel framework with South Africa's departure from Namibia is the key to the settlement we all desire. In the final analysis, it is also the surest way to guarantee Angola's long-term security and independence. The United States wants the earliest possible independence for Namibia. At the same time the United States wants an end to Angola's suffering and to the dangerous cycle of violence in the region. My government is not ashamed to state the U.S. interest in seeing an end to the presence of Cuban forces in Angola. Their introduction 7 years ago tore the fabric of reciprocal restraint between the United States and the Soviet Union in the developing world. Such restraint is vital if African regional security and the global balance are to be maintained.

We recognize there will be no agreement unless all the parties know that their security is protected. We also recognize there will be no settlement unless each party is prepared to make the concessions necessary. If the challenge is accepted we believe peace can be achieved and a brighter future for southern Africa can begin. The substantial progress already made is based on a diplomatic partnership of equals in which all parties share burdens. That partnership remains vital in our continuing efforts for peace. In the search for that peace, the United States seeks constructive relations with all the states of southern Africa. We are building bridges of communication to each nation in the region, including South Africa. However, we will not ignore or disguise our strong belief in the importance of justice and equality before the law. Apartheid is wrong. It is legally entrenched racism—inimical to the fundamental ideals of the United States. America's history and America's future can only be understood in terms of our commitment to a multiracial democracy in which all citizens participate and from which all benefit. The rule of law, the principles of consent and participation in the political process, and the right of every human being to citizenship which reflects these principles are to Americans a sacred trust. We will not betray this trust.

---

[37] For text of U.N. Security Council Resolution 435 (1978), see *American Foreign Policy: Basic Documents, 1977–1980,* p. 1205.

Nor can we escape reality; if there is to be security in southern Africa, South Africa must be involved in shaping it: If there is to be constructive change in South Africa, South Africans of all races—not foreigners—must be the ones who shape the pattern of that change. The United States is working for constructive change in ways that benefit all South Africans. Our actions match our words as our deepening involvement in expanding educational, social, and economic opportunities for black South Africans demonstrates. We also believe there is a relationship between the security of southern Africa and the pace of peaceful change within South Africa. We do not believe that armed conflict must be the road to justice, and we doubt that it can be the road to lasting freedom and well-being.

The United States believes that it can be helpful in advancing the frontier of freedom and observance of human rights, not only in southern Africa but in Africa as a whole. Without respect for human rights, there is a great risk that Africa's enormous human potential will be wasted. Fear and intimidation keep people from working to achieve their aspirations, from contributing to the common good and from pursuing the democratic principles and ideals that are denied for too many in the world today. Narrowing political participation by their citizens can be highly counterproductive. African nations that have devised their own national democratic institutions broaden public participation in government, protect the integrity of the individual, and expand the frontier of economic freedom for the ultimate good of all.

In Kenya, respect for individual rights is written in your constitution. Democratic institutions that embody the democratic process have been established. They are an essential framework for lasting stability. Experience in Africa and elsewhere clearly demonstrates that the abuse of power, the suppression of diversity, and the denial of individual rights only leads to instability and a loss of confidence at home and abroad. My visit to Africa has shown me encouraging examples of African nations that are building their own institutions to broaden political participation and advance the frontier of freedom. We realize, however, that nations cannot reap the benefits of individual freedom in an environment of insecurity. We attach high importance to strengthening Africa's security and are prepared to be Africa's partner in building the necessary conditions for security.

We have no interest in an East–West confrontation in Africa; such a confrontation increases the threat to world peace. The goal of the United States in Africa is to help establish a framework for restraint and broad rules of conduct which discourage the use of outside force in African conflicts and encourage peaceful settlement of conflicts in the region. In this area our goal is consistent with the goals enshrined in the charter of the Organization of African Unity.

At the same time the United States is deeply sensitive to the threats which individual nations and the regions of this continent face and probably will continue to face. Internal stability, often fueled by outside interference, and longstanding border and ethnic disputes tax heavily the resources of African governments. The United States has no mandate to act as a policeman in Africa and it seeks no such role. But neither do we believe that the sovereignty of African nations will be preserved if the West is unable or unwilling to respond to the legitimate defense needs of its friends in Africa. The United States intends to be a reliable partner both in working with our friends on a long-term basis to meet these needs, and in responding to their urgent requirements in emergency situations. We have done so in the past; we are doing so today; let there be no doubt about our determination and capability to do so in the future. At the same time, our overall concern including the concern that guides our military assistance is to dissuade countries from undertaking military solutions and to encourage negotiated settlements of differences between them. We believe negotiated solutions are possible for even the most difficult and longstanding disputes on the continent. We are ready to lend whatever support we can to those efforts in Africa and to give them the highest priority. In this view, we believe that Africa's capacity for collective security deserves our help. We will, when asked, support multinational peacekeeping forces that Africa creates in its own defense. The record of the United States in support of the OAU peacekeeping role in Chad is the most recent illustration of the importance we attach to regional security. We want African nations to be able to defend their interests and resolve their problems without foreign intervention.

Real security, and with it the confidence that can enhance prospects for peace, cannot be achieved without sustained economic growth. During my travels, I have seen Africa's most serious economic crisis in more than 40 years. Because African countries are often dependent on one or two export commodities, and because they have borrowed heavily to spur growth and meet the costs of higher oil prices, they have been vulnerable to commodity fluctuations, high interest rates, and to the impact of world recession. There has been a long, slow decline in per capita food production; population has increased rapidly and balanced growth has not occurred. Many nations have experimented with subsidies, centralized economic direction, and extensive public ownership of industry and commerce. Those strategies have proved costly.

The present state of the global economy is not of Africa's making. In the world economic system, the United States has a special responsibility not only to put its own house in order but to help rekindle growth in other lands. We are deeply committed to that task and, to achieve it, the American people are making real sacrifices. We are confident that when we are successful Africa will benefit quickly and significantly.

At the most fundamental level, we will remain concerned about those imperiled by strife and starvation. We have taken the lead both in mobilizing international relief efforts to help African refugees, and in providing emergency assistance. In the past 2 years the United States has provided Africa $187 million for such programs. But we are equally concerned about the underlying problems which produce refugees and other forms of human misery. As we all look at these problems, we can see that the next few years in Africa will be critical. The current economic situation is forcing austerity on all African nations. It points to the need for a reexamination of economic strategies and national economic policies. It would be a mistake to view this period as only a temporary phenomenon, and to believe that as the world recession begins to ease, Africa will be able to resume an easy path of growth and diversity. On the contrary, in the current situation, many fundamental decisions must be made about the future of African development, about the priorities of agriculture and other sectors and about the degree of sacrifice that should be demanded of the various elements of the population. How these decisions are made will affect the future of African development for decades to come.

We in the United States admit that there are serious differences among experts over the best path to development. We believe that there should be a full exchange among all those involved in African development. We must reach a common agreement regarding the kinds of programs which must be developed, financed, and mobilized. Discipline and self-reliance are necessary. Courageous leadership is necessary. Now is the time for fresh thinking, an eschewing of old ideologies that have not passed the test of experience.

We are prepared to help give African governments the wherewithal, and the international political and financial backing, to take the steps where necessary to restructure their economies.

During the past 2 years, a growing number of African countries have applied to the IMF for assistance in meeting immediate balance-of-payments crises. This has led to difficult adjustments in exchange rates, budgets, and other aspects of economic policy.

Recognizing the fundamental nature of the development crisis, we have encouraged a more comprehensive approach by both donors and multilateral agencies in Africa. We have urged that reform be supported with short-term foreign exchange and development assistance adequate to fuel the recovery process. We are fully aware of the importance of debt in this equation, where countries are making serious efforts to restructure their economies. Relief from heavy debt must be part of the exchange program. For our part, we are committed to participating in the difficult process of recovery.

The United States, despite the fact that its resources are under special strain in this time of economic adversity, still remains committed to Africa's stabilization and growth. Our bilateral economic aid for all of Africa now totals approximately $800 million a year, and extends to 46 countries throughout Africa. It encompasses a variety of programs, including fast-disbursing balance-of-payments support, food aid, and development assistance. Including the U.S. contribution to multilateral programs, our total economic aid to sub-Saharan Africa is in excess of $1.4 billion annually. Of the multilateral portion, the largest share by far—almost $300 million per year—goes to the soft-loan programs of the World Bank's International Development Association (IDA).

The Reagan administration has placed a new emphasis on the role of private enterprise in development. In Africa, as elsewhere, we define "private sector" broadly to include small businesses and farmers, as well as large corporations. Our aid planners are seeking new ways to help develop market institutions and more effective incentives for farmers. Wherever possible, we are encouraging mutually beneficial partnerships between large and small American companies and their African counterparts. The recent enactment of export trading legislation supported by President Reagan will make it possible for small and medium U.S. firms to pool expenses, and thereby play a more active economic role in Africa.

The economic task that you and we face is enormous. But it is far from impossible if we all work together in a wise and understanding partnership. The exact nature of that cooperation will be as varied as the countries of Africa, but it will have some common elements. We, the industrialized countries, must help Africans manage their debt burden so that private credit, which is so essential to growth, can resume and increase. We must support successful economic policies at both the national and regional levels. We must seek greater coordination among Africa's friends who wish to finance development. The importance of Africa's economic future demands that we do no less.

As we all look to the future and decide how Africa and the United States can work together, the agenda of issues we face is long. It includes essential issues of security, peacemaking, human rights, and economic progress. It calls for advancing the frontiers of freedom.

The United States is a friend who respects your potential and shares your commitment to maintaining the hard-won prize of freedom. With respect to that freedom our nations are equals who must be prepared to work together, making sacrifices and making tough decisions at the same time. Each of us has a share of the burden to carry; each has a contribution to make. All have a better future to gain. This is the meaning of a true partnership.

Thank you for your kind hospitality.

Document 552

Address by Vice President Bush Before the American Enterprise Institute, December 6, 1982 (Extract)[38]

Results of African Visit

. . . .

Shortly after returning to Africa from Moscow,[39] I attended a dinner where I sat spellbound listening to an African Chief of State deliver one of the most spirited renditions of grace I have ever heard. He gave it first in Swahili; and then in English. The English was a courtesy to us, he explained, since God probably does not listen to prayers said in English.

This moving rendition of grace, I must say, was a kind of objective correlative. It drove home the remarkable change of atmosphere, scene, sentiment, and spirit from Red Square.

The experience stayed with me for the rest of the African trip, reinforced by more prayers at more luncheons and dinners in other countries. Along the way my thoughts were constantly triangulating between three points: the Soviet Union, Africa, and the United States. Please note that I avoided using the word trilateral.

Let me briefly sketch for you what I found in Africa. Great economic hardship, requests for more economic aid—of course. I found a lot of differences on how to gain independence for Namibia—but no difference at the bottom line: we all want to see that independence soon. I found a lot of young countries looking for advice, for an example to follow, and for respect as sovereign nations. And they are learning to look more to the West—and less to the East—for respect, for economic assistance, for trade, investment, and technology; and for friendship.

Africa is not a big chessboard on which we and the Soviets move pieces. Africa means something important, vibrant, culturally relevant to us. All the Soviets have to

[38] Source: Press Release, December 6, 1982, Office of the Press Secretary to the Vice President. Bush spoke at the Mayflower Hotel.

[39] Bush was in Moscow, November 14–15, 1982, as head of the delegation attending the funeral of Leonid Brezhnev. Regarding his impressions of his Moscow visit, see document 285.

offer are cheap, used weapons, tractors that don't work, Cuban mercenaries, and an opportunity to have your government infiltrated with people who want to take over and then order you around like servants.

It wasn't Americans who pushed the Russians out of Egypt, the Sudan, Somalia, or Guinea. It was the people who live in those countries.

And that's all we ask of any country in Africa; protect your independence, and give your people the basic human rights that will encourage them to work hard and build prosperity. We do not ask other nations to copy us or to agree with us on everything. Genuine nonalignment is just fine. African nationalism is our greatest ally against Soviet and Cuban interference in Africa's internal affairs. Most Africans are proud of their independence and not about to sell their souls to communism, to the God that failed.

So my conclusion is that Africa is a continent of opportunity, but no longer for the Soviet Union. They've had their chance. And the signs now point toward increasing irrelevance where Soviet influence in Africa is concerned.

True, this may not be the general impression the American public gathers from some of the rhetoric at the United Nations, as in Africa itself.

The United States comes in for a lot of fire over there. In some countries there they've got a press corps that makes Mary McGrory sound like John Lofton. But beneath these layers of public disregard is a desire for partnership with the United States; I'd go so far as to say verges on the fervent. They view us an essential partner for development.

I'm talking here obviously of personal impressions; but unless I was badly deceived, they want our friendship. They'd much rather deal with us than the Soviets. This is motivated in part by a kind of cultural kinship; in part by vicissitude. They view us as the catalyst for peace, not the Soviet Union. But don't take my word for it. Next time you're in Harare, ask Mr. Mugabe.

While in Africa, I uttered thousands of words dealing specifically with our constructive efforts in Namibia and Angola, and they were constructive. We are on the right track—indeed, at this juncture, we are on the only meaningful track.

. . . .

B. Southern Africa

Document 553

Testimony by the Secretary of State (Haig) Before the House Foreign Affairs Committee, March 2, 1982 (Extract)[1]

Prospects for a Namibian Settlement

. . . .

MR. GOODLING. . . . The first question I have is you mentioned in your statement, in passing, Namibia,[2] because you had so much to cover, and of course I have a real concern that with all of the other problems we are facing all over the country, that this might be put on the back burner. You say in your statement that we could have a breakthrough in 1982.

How strongly do you feel about that? Is there anything that you can tell us publicly that will give us encouragement along those lines?

SECRETARY HAIG. I think we have approached the Namibian independence under U.N. Resolution 435 in three phases. We are largely through the first phase, which involves the acceptance of arrangements for constituent assembly and bullion arrangements and parliamentary procedure. We are now working with the frontline states to try to deal with some concerns they have expressed on the voting framework, which is in their view somewhat complex in that it takes the German model rather than the simple one-man, one-vote, one-time approach.

---

[1] Source: *East–West Relations—U.S. Security Assistance: Hearing Before the Committee on Foreign Affairs, House of Representatives, Ninety-seventh Congress, Second Session* (Washington, 1982), p. 26.

[2] Reference is to Haig's statement, which reads as follows: "We have helped to revive the negotiations on Namibia that had effectively collapsed before this administration took office, and we are actively engaged with our allies, the frontline states, and South Africa in a realistic effort to obtain a settlement that could lead to independence for Namibia in 1982." *Ibid.*, p. 5.

The contact group, the European nations worked with us in preparing the set of principles for the constituent assembly and parliament, and I am hoping we are going to get those resolved within a matter of weeks, and then we will go into another very quick second phase, which would be to determine the U.N. presence and the introduction of the U.N. forces for peacekeeping forces. Then the third phase would be a decision on a date certain for withdrawal of South African forces.

Now, from the beginning we, Mr. Goodling, have emphasized the de facto empirical interrelationship between the withdrawal of South African forces and the full independence of Namibia and the continuing and threatening presence of Cuban forces in Angola, and we are beginning to develop an international consensus in a very broad way, and that there is indeed an empirical interrelationship and that simultaneity in phased withdrawals is both doable and perhaps desirable.

We are continuing to build on that consensus and I hope that we will have a successful outcome very shortly.

Document 554

Remarks by the Deputy Secretary of State (Stoessel), February 24, 1982 (Extract)[3]

Why the United States Does Not Recognize Angola

. . . .

SECRETARY STOESSEL. I'm not sure I got the whole question. Why we do not recognize Angola?

Q. That's right. You are the only country in the Western alliance that doesn't recognize Angola. All your allies recognize Angola. In spite of the fact that there are enormous business interests by members of the U.S. Chamber of Commerce and business community, your government has (inaudible) mutually agreed documents recognizing (inaudible).

SECRETARY STOESSEL. I think that one clear reason is that Cuban troops are present in Angola. The Government of Angola has been, at least in the past and up to the present, dependent on those troops for its existence, and under these circumstances we have not felt it desirable or appropriate for us to recognize Angola in a formal sense.

As you mention, we have large business interests there, and in recent months we have had a number of official contacts with Angola, particularly in connection with this Namibia problem which I mentioned in my remarks.[4]

On the Assistant Secretary level, we have had a number of discussions, and Secretary Haig has met with the Foreign Minister of Angola. We have found these talks to be constructive and quite promising for the future. So I think that's all I can say at the moment on this. I would emphasize that we are in contact and we are discussing problems of mutual concern.

. . . .

Document 555

Testimony by the Secretary of State (Haig) Before a Subcommittee of the House Appropriations Committee, March 4, 1982 (Extracts)[5]

Trade With South Africa

. . . .

MR. GRAY.. . . I wonder if you could perhaps comment on what events in South

---

[3] Source: Department of State files. Stoessel addressed the U.S. Chamber of Commerce International Forum.

[4] Reference is to Stoessel's address preceding his remarks, wherein he stated:

"The situation, of course, is complicated by the presence of Cuban troops in neighboring Angola. Any lasting solution to the Namibian problem must include the withdrawal of those troops, and this is also part of our consideration."

[5] Source: *Foreign Assistance and Related Programs Appropriations for 1983: Hearings Before a Subcommittee of the Committee on Appropriations, House of Representatives, Ninety-seventh Congress, Second Session* (Washington, 1982), pp. 115–117. The hearing was before the Subcommittee on Foreign Operations and Related Agencies.

Africa led the administration to believe that a change in this restrictive policy was warranted.[6]

And, secondly, one of the officials of the State Department who was unnamed said that the sales would not be used to enforce apartheid and I am wondering how you are going to monitor that.

SECRETARY HAIG. Well, first, Mr. Gray, I do not think it takes any undue decibel on my part today in reiterating the clear policies of President Reagan with respect to apartheid.

We are opposed to it. We are appalled by it. Let there be no question about that.

And, secondly, with respect to the recent decision on the conduct of trade in non-security related trade, I think you know, Mr. Gray, we have attempted to work somewhat differently with the government of South Africa than the preceding administration.

There are a host of reasons for that. But one of the more consequential is, of course, our efforts to engender cooperation from that government in the promise of seeking progress in Namibia under United Nations Resolution 435. I think in hindsight over this past year, when one considers that no progress was made in the preceding 2 years on that subject, none, despite our high level of rhetoric and condemnation against the issues you have asked about and as a result we have made great progress, substantial progress, and with a great deal of cooperation from the Government of South Africa, which is itself presiding over a tightly balanced constituency which contained those who are concerned about the things you and I are concerned about and those that are opposed, and I think in recent weeks you have seen some manifestations of that controversy.

I want to answer your question simply by saying, of course, foreign policy abides by contradictions. It is inherent in the process. It has always been. It does not necessarily constitute a value judgment if the greater good tolerates in some instances still onerous evil. We live that way in the very complex world. I am sorry it is so, but it has been necessary for generations.

. . . .

[6] Reference is to the February 26, 1982, announcement (effective March 1) of a relaxation in the export controls that the Carter administration had imposed on trade with South Africa.

MR. GRAY. . . . Of course, I am well aware, that there are contradictions in foreign 0 policy. But, at the same time, I find it tremendously disturbing that this administration can light candles for those suffering under oppression in Poland rightfully so, by the way, and yet seem to not be able to strike a match for those suffering from repression and apartheid fascism in South Africa. To be told that we are bringing them along carefully and slowly, when all of the evidence that has come to my attention shows that there is not that reform in South Africa.

. . . .

SECRETARY HAIG. Mr. Chairman, I think it is important that Mr. Gray's—the premises of his question which I reject out of hand, are not left in the record unchallenged.

It is not the policy of this administration to condone, support, sweep under the rug or accept with equanimity any violations of human rights to which we subscribe wholeheartedly, and I have made my statements about apartheid.

You are posturing.

MR. GRAY. Computer sales to South Africa will enforce apartheid, and yet you say you are opposed to apartheid.

SECRETARY HAIG. Why will that enforce apartheid?

MR. GRAY. Because we will be selling computers to the Department of Manpower Utilization which operates for black labor, for bureaus recruiting blacks, for white hiring under the 11-month rule, and more relaxations of those restrictions. Yet you told me—

SECRETARY HAIG. There has been a movement in the direction of improvement in the area which both you and I are appalled by, and it is always important that we deal with these questions in an enlightened way, with a view towards the outcome we seek, and not to just posture for positions that perhaps make us feel good, but just do not accomplish the objectives.

. . . .

Document 556

Testimony by the Assistant Secretary of State for Human Rights and Humanitarian Affairs (Abrams) and the Assistant Secretary of State for African Affairs (Crocker) Before Two Subcommittees of the House Foreign Affairs Committee, March 9, 1982 (Extracts)[7]

Export Controls and Apartheid in South Africa

. . . .

MR. CROCKETT. . . . My question to each of you gentlemen is: What is the State Department 0 doing to oppose apartheid in South Africa and, hopefully, to bring that Government around to recognizing basic human rights for the 20 million blacks and the 2 million coloreds who live within the geographic limits of South Africa?

MR. ABRAMS. Perhaps I will begin. I think the first thing you said, Congressman, was that, except for an offhanded remark, we did not have much to say about apartheid. I would like, for the sake of the record, to point out the remarks that were made at the U.N. Human Rights Commission by Warren Hewitt in a formal speech addressed to that question,[8] and by Ambassador Edelson [*Adelman*] at the U.N. in New York also discussing apartheid.[9] I do not think it is the case that the Government has had nothing more than a line or two to say about the subject.

The key question, it seems to me, is the one that you raised; that is, what do we do about it? That is, what is and what should be U.S. Government policy? To us, that question as it regards South Africa is similar to the question we ask about any other country in which there are human rights abuses.

We do not believe that a policy of constant public attack upon what we consider to be a friendly government is an effective way of influencing its internal policies. I do not believe that the policy that was followed by the Carter administration, which I think was a lot closer to that model than we would like to be, was effective, in fact, in achieving the kind of progress of which you speak in South Africa.

It is our view that in the case of South Africa and a number of other friendly governments, we are going to have a lot more influence through private discussions, through diplomatic channels, than we are through repeated public criticism. And I think myself that the record will bear that out.

I did not see 4 years of steady progress during the Carter administration either in South Africa or in a number of other countries which were subjected to that kind of policy. It is our hope and our belief that the policy we are following is going to prove to be more effective in maximizing American influence.

MR. CROCKER. Congressman, could I add just a note about the effort of this administration to get the facts as we see them on the record?

We are not seeking opportunities for what I would term gratuitous comment on each incident that takes place or each event or each development that may occur. But we have, for example, in the human rights report[10] that you recently received, provided, I think, what can only be described as a full, extensive, and objective treatment of the situation in that country as we see it from all the sources available to us.

I think, in a nutshell, and I am certain there are followup questions you will want to pursue, but we assess South Africa as being a country which is undergoing change. We think that there is no possibility of debate about the fact that South Africa is in the midst of change. If one wanted the most recent tangible example of that, one

---

[7] Source: *Implementation of Congressionally Mandated Human Rights Provisions: Hearings Before the Subcommittees on Europe and the Middle East, on Asian and Pacific Affairs, on Human Rights and International Organizations, and on Africa of the Committee on Foreign Affairs, House of Representatives, Ninety-seventh Congress,* (Washington, 1982), Volume II, pp. 238–241. Abrams and Crocker testified before the Subcommittees on Human Rights and International Organizations and on Africa.

[8] Reference is to Hewitt's address before the U.N. Commission on Human Rights in Geneva on February 16, 1982. For text, see U.N. document E/CN.4/1982/SR.23, February 18, 1982.

[9] Reference is to Ambassador Adelman's address before the General Assembly on December 17, 1981. For text, see *American Foreign Policy: Current Documents, 1981,* document 623.

[10] Reference is to *Country Reports on Human Rights Practices for 1981: Report Submitted to the Committee on Foreign Affairs, U.S. House of Representatives, and the Committee on Foreign Relations, U.S. Senate, by the Department of State* (Washington, February 1982), pp. 232–258.

would simply have to point to the ferment within the governing party of South Africa, which is a direct result of commitments made by its senior leadership to a process of reform and change.

Now, there can be and there should be, debate about how extensive is the change, how serious, how soon, and all the rest, and who is participating in it. But the fact that there is a degree of change underway and that it is important, I think most observers would agree on.

. . . .

MR. CROCKETT. I take it the State Department does support the approach of the United Nations with respect to apartheid in South Africa, and that it was because of that that you joined them in the embargo that they called for.

I note, however, that as of March 1 you are retreating from that embargo. You have taken off the list of embargoed products manufactured items that now can be used by the military and the police forces in South Africa. Is that right?

MR. ABRAMS. That is untrue, Congressman. The United States is not retreating one step from the United Nations embargo,[11] with which we have always been completely in compliance and with which we will continue to be in complete compliance.

MR. CROCKETT. Why was it necessary to in effect soften the terms of the embargo?

MR. ABRAMS. I think we should distinguish first of all between the United Nations embargo and additional controls on exports which the United States—

MR. CROCKETT. I am talking about our embargo, not the United Nations. You cannot possibly change the United Nations embargo.

MR. ABRAMS. No. And I want to make it clear that we will continue to comply fully with the United Nations embargo. Dr. Crocker can comment on this in more detail. I think the question to ask about export controls with respect to any country is: Are those kinds of controls of commerce going to have a beneficial impact upon the domestic policies which we seek to influence?

Now the controls which were put on by the Carter administration to which you refer made it impossible, for example, to sell carpeting, tomato juice, or paper cups to the South African defense forces. It is hard for me to see how that kind of extensive control has any impact upon the enforcement of apartheid.

MR. CROCKETT. Is that why we changed the terms of the embargo, so we could sell carpet and tomato juice to South Africa? [Laughter.]

MR. ABRAMS. We changed the terms of the embargo so that these goods, which have absolutely nothing to do with the enforcement of apartheid, with policing in South Africa, for example, were not excluded from sale.

Now, I would point out that not only are we in compliance with the United Nations embargo, we continue to embargo other goods. We have a stronger export control with respect to South Africa (a) than the U.N. insists on, and (b) than our allies in Europe have. I believe, in fact, we have more controls with respect to exports to South Africa than any other country, any other major Western country.

MR. WOLPE. Will the gentleman yield?

MR. CROCKETT. Yes.

MR. WOLPE. What is really frightening, Mr. Abrams, is that you really believe what you just said—that there is no relationship between the changes that were made in our export controls and the extent to which this country will be perceived as essentially sanctioning or encouraging the acceleration of repression in South Africa.

I do not doubt your sincerity for a moment. I mean, I think you really thought that what we were doing in the export controls was totally independent of the human rights situation in South Africa. I think the ultimate tragedy of this administration, which by its actions, sometimes well-intentioned, ends up reinforcing the most intransigent elements, and the most repressive elements in the societies with which we deal.

. . . .

MR. ABRAMS. Congressman, no one can doubt that there will be people—and you are clearly one of them—who perceive that change in export controls as having an extraordinarily large symbolic point to make.

[11] Reference is to U.N. Security Council Resolution 418 (1977), adopted on November 4, 1977. For text, see *American Foreign Policy: Basic Documents, 1977–1980*, pp. 1185–1186.

MR. WOLPE. You do not?

MR. ABRAMS. Oh, I think it is symbolic, but it is not symbolic of American approval of apartheid. I think the question to ask about those controls is: Is American policy which is aimed at, in part, maximizing American influence in South Africa, going to be effective or is it going to be ineffective? I think that is the question that should be asked about the export controls. I do not see how the continuation of those export controls helps or hurts the enforcement of apartheid in South Africa.

. . . .

Document 557

Testimony by the Assistant Secretary of State for African Affairs (Crocker) Before a Subcommittee of the Senate Judiciary Committee, March 22, 1982 (Extracts)[12]

Communist Influence in Southern Africa

DR. CROCKER. Mr. Chairman, I want to thank you first for the opportunity to be the leadoff witness in hearings which I understand will extend over 5 days.

As I understand it, the topic that will be the principal focus of the hearings will be the role of Communist influence in southern Africa. The scope will include not only external Communist influence in the area—the role of the Soviet Union, its Warsaw Pact associates, and Cuba—but also Communist influence in political movements indigenous to the area, including the South West Africa People's Organization and the African National Congress. Consideration of Communist influence in southern Africa would also include the question of relations of various Communist countries with the independent states of the area, all of which consider themselves to be nonalined nations.

It is an indisputable fact, faced squarely in policy terms by President Reagan's administration beginning in January 1981, in consultation with our Western allies, that a wide range of vital Western interests and U.S. interests in particular are engaged in the southern African region. The 10 nations of southern Africa comprise an area of great mineral wealth, including resources critical to Western strategic interests. Angola, South Africa, Mozambique, and the territory of Namibia are all littoral states on the strategic Cape sea route, a lifeline of Western commerce. U.S. two-way trade with the countries of southern Africa amounted in 1980 to some $7.2 billion and U.S. direct investment in the region is estimated at $2.3 billion.

All of these factors obviously make southern Africa an area of great interest also to the Soviet Union and to its surrogates. In recent years, we have detected a substantial increase in Soviet interest and involvement in the area. In Angola and Mozambique the number and range of activities of Soviet, Cuban, and other foreign Communist advisers and technicians, in the civilian and military domains, has increased, implying concomitant political and economic influence. The Soviet Union has concluded arms agreements with Zambia and Botswana, complementing those countries' previous arms supply relationships with Western nations. Zimbabwe recently requested North Korea to train and equip a brigade, although that country continues to work closely with Great Britain as its primary foreign source of military equipment and training. Other countries of the region and of Africa, in general, have remarked with concern the increase in Soviet activity in the region, noting particularly that the Soviet Union has concentrated its efforts there on military assistance, showing little interest at all in contributing to the economic development of the region.

It is also clear that the Soviet Union has continued to play a very active role in southern African political and military organizations such as SWAPO and the ANC, on whose activities the hearings will focus. SWAPO is the primary external Namibian organization seeking power in Namibia. Its military elements are based primarily in Angola and other neighboring countries and carry out some actions within Namibia itself. It exists also as a political structure, inside and outside Namibia, and is one of the parties—with the Western Contact Group, the African frontline states, South Africa, the United Nations, and other

---

[12] Source: *The Role of the Soviet Union, Cuba, and East Germany in Fomenting Terrorism in Southern Africa: Hearings Before the Subcommittee on Security and Terrorism of the Committee on the Judiciary, United States Senate, Ninety-seventh Congress, Second Session* (Washington, 1982), pp. 6–9, 12–13, 15.

Namibian political organizations—to the present negotiations underway to reach a settlement of the Namibia issue. We estimate that SWAPO receives some 90 percent of its military support and some 60 percent of its overall support from Communist sources. It also receives direct assistance from African states, Western states other than the United States and from some U.N. bodies.

The ANC, which seeks to replace the present government in power in South Africa by violent as well as other means, receives comparable percentages of its military and other support from Communist and other sources. It is basically an African nationalist organization with a long history, founded in 1912, 5 years before the 1917 revolution in Russia. A main thread in the history of the ANC over the years is the varying degrees of internal and external Communist influence that have characterized what is basically an African organization. These conflicts within the organization have often been very bitter and have resulted in various segments and individuals breaking with the ANC at different points in time.

We categorically condemn all terrorist and other violent acts that either of these organizations take to try to bring about change in Namibia and South Africa. Our policy in relationship to both seeks to channel the impetus toward change into peaceful channels. We seek in general in pursuing our objectives in southern Africa to strengthen and make more viable the possibilities of peaceful change. As we have repeatedly stated in the Namibia–Angola context, we believe the spiral of violence is a two-way street, and we deplore it. In doing so, we seek to obviate the necessity for terrorism that some parties involved in developments in the region choose to perceive.

In Namibia, we have been working very actively since last April to arrive at a negotiated settlement of the Namibia issue that would bring that territory to an internationally recognized independence based on U.N. Security Council Resolution 435. We are pursuing a carefully crafted, three-phase negotiating process, with coordination at all stages with all of the interested parties, including South Africa, SWAPO, and other Namibian political elements.

In South Africa, we are pursuing a policy of constructive engagement, encouraging the government of Prime Minister P.W. Botha and other elements in South African society to move away from apartheid toward a South Africa changed, modern, and strong, with bright prospects for stability and development rooted in justice, free of the problems that now stand in the way of closer United States-South African relations. We believe that a process of peaceful, evolutionary change promises a much better immediate and long-term future for all South Africans than the protracted, bloody terror and violence that is the alternative for that nation.

Speaking directly to the purpose of these hearings, I believe that the policy that the administration is pursuing under President Reagan's leadership is one calculated to meet head-on the intentions that the Soviet Union may have in southern Africa. These objectives would represent not only a serious threat to our own interests there but are objectives which would also push the people of that area deeper into an environment of chaos, violence, and disorder, the antithesis of the peaceful economic development that I believe the leaders of the countries of southern Africa seek for their people. We proceed on the basis that the Soviet Union does not have a grand design for southern Africa, but that it is, in fact, taking advantage of targets of opportunity that present themselves to act counter to Western interests. The Soviet Union alone has a vested interest in keeping the region in turmoil. It is to no one else's advantage, neither to that of the South Africans, the other southern Africans, nor certainly to the United States and the West.

We seek a settlement in Namibia that will permit a fair and democratic expression of the will of the Namibian people and will bring to power a constitutional government not only with the support of the Namibian people but also with solid long-term prospects for stability.

We seek an end to the guerrilla warfare that has continued in northern Namibia and southern Angola for 15 years now and which has cost the lives of many people in the area, most recently in the South African attack on SWAPO in southern Angola this month.[13]

In seeking to resolve the Namibian problem through negotiations, we strip the Sovi-

---

[13] Reference is to the South African raid into Angola of March 13, 1982, in which some 201 guerrillas were killed. South Africa claimed that the Cambeno Valley area, where the raid took place, was a SWAPO base for guerrilla operations into Namibia. See *Washington Post*, March 17, 1982, p. A10, and *New York Times*, March 17, 1982, p. A3.

et Union and its surrogates of any excuse they have to continue to fuel violence in southern Africa through military aid to SWAPO and through the Cuban forces in Angola.

We seek an end to the conflict between political elements in Angola which has preoccupied that country since 1974.

We seek the withdrawal of all Cuban combat forces from Angola. Their continued presence in Angola represents a threat to regional security that is an obstacle to resolution of the Namibian issue. Their removal can also be part of a process of national reconciliation among Angolans that can result in time in a unified, peaceful Angola whose leaders can concentrate the country's efforts on national economic and social objectives.

We seek, through our own programs of assistance and cooperation, alternatives to Soviet involvement in and attempts to dominate the national security structures of independent southern African nations.

Finally, in seeking to encourage South Africans to resolve their problems through peaceful, evolutionary change, we strip the Soviet Union not only of any justification that it may put forth to justify its efforts to fan tensions within South Africa itself into racial war, but we also make it clear to the people of other African nations and to the world the gravity with which we view developments in southern Africa and the strength of our own policy.

I think it is important that we all understand that in southern Africa the world faces a dangerous conjunction of factors. Vital Western interests are involved, vital American interests are involved. The Soviet Union is involved. The region itself is severely troubled by problems that inevitably carry with them general instability. South Africa is strong, economically and militarily. But the momentum of events in the area, whether it be toward independence for Namibia, national unity and peace in Angola, or toward change within South Africa itself, is also strong and vital. We believe that the diplomacy that the United States is pursuing in southern Africa can be a key factor in the outcome of these developments and that our diplomacy is, in fact, essential if hope for a peaceful solution of southern Africa's problems is to remain alive.

Mr. Chairman, the Department of State will pay the closest attention to the information that will be brought to light by these hearings. I appreciate your giving me the opportunity to present to you at the beginning of the hearings the policy context within which the administration conducts our diplomacy toward southern Africa.

. . . .

Senator Denton. . . . In your view, why are the Soviets and other Communist states providing this assistance, and what quid pro quo will they exact if SWAPO comes to power in Namibia?

Dr. Crocker. Mr. Chairman, these are difficult judgmental questions. The first part of the question, why are they doing it, I think I would suggest that the reason basically has to do with a desire for influence in several different spheres: influence, in the first place, over the military aspects of the conflicts that they get themselves involved with, over doctrine, over training, over arms, where they do have, as I have indicated before, a kind of comparative advantage because they tend to specialize in the instruments of coercion. They do it, second, because they hope thereby to get statements of strong support for Soviet foreign policy from the movements themselves, as you have indicated in your opening comments,[14] and from other states in the region who generally support the concept of freedom in Namibia or greater equality in South Africa.

And by putting themselves in this position, they are able thereby to seek to get greater support from many Third World nations and other nations for what they are doing; even if it's only rhetoric, they get that at least—they get U.N. speeches, they get public declarations, they get rhetorical support from the nonalined movement, that kind of thing.

I suppose also they are hoping that this support will lead to future influence or affinity with an independent government, if that government should be heavily influenced by or controlled by the movements they support.

The second part of your question, Mr. Chairman: what quid pro quo would they exact—is a trickier one. It is easy for them to get a quid pro quo today in terms of public statements of support. It is less obvi-

---

[14] For Senator Denton's opening comments, see *The Role of the Soviet Union, Cuba, and East Germany in Fomenting Terrorism in Southern Africa*, pp. 2–6.

ous what the quid pro quo will be when and if, let us say, SWAPO were to gain a measure of power in Namibia. This depends on the choices available to SWAPO, and many other factors.

. . . .

SENATOR DENTON. Considering the situation as it now exists, and the forces and trends within SWAPO, what is your assessment? Are you considerably concerned that there will be more development of Communist influence or that it has already reached an alarming degree and must be a matter of our hope and aim that it be decreased? How would you discuss that?

DR. CROCKER. Mr. Chairman, I think the influence that we are referring to is quite substantial at the present time. SWAPO is, for the most part, at least as a military organization, in exile in neighboring countries; it is dependent in terms of hardware, advice, and training, as I have indicated, very substantially on the Soviets and their surrogates. Although that influence is not 100 percent, it is fairly significant.

As one looks toward the future, and just as a matter of hypothesis or speculation at this point, much would depend on the nature of the transition process that led to the independence of Namibia. It is for this reason that we have sought through our diplomacy to provide certain general guidelines, if you will, or constraints, concerning the future constitutional development of Namibia, for example.

We are convinced that the nature of that transition to independence will have an effect on the degree to which those committed to minority domination—if you want to call them the Communist minority—would be limited, would be hampered in seeking to control that process and dominate the government that came out of it.

A second factor that will influence the extent of Communist influence, were SWAPO to come to power, is the nature of the problems a new Namibian Government would face. And in that connection, sir, I would emphasize that much will depend in turn on the options available to that Government, and to different elements within that Government. As we have said, SWAPO consists of a coalition, if you will, or alliance of some kind, and once we see what an independent government would like, if indeed SWAPO gets to power, I think a lot would depend on the kind of options that it would face, the choices it has, and who is prepared to have a role vis-à-vis the new Namibia. If South Africa, for example, remains part of the picture, if we offer support in various ways, this would have some effect.

. . . .

Document 558

Statement by the British Representative at the United Nations (Parsons) Before the U.N. General Assembly, March 29, 1982[15]

Contact Group Objects to Appointment of Commissioner for Namibia

I have the honour to speak on behalf of the delegations of Canada, France, the Federal Republic of Germany, the United Kingdom and the United States. We are speaking now because of our long involvement in the negotiations that we hope will lead this year to the implementation of Security Council Resolution 435 (1978).

Our Governments are engaged in intensive consultations with all the parties concerned. Later this week high-level delegations from the Five will be visiting Luanda and Cape Town in an effort to complete the present phase and to move the negotiations forward.

The consultations leading to the nomination of the Commissioner for Namibia have been hasty and inadequate.[16] Neither the Council for Namibia nor the Commissioner has a part in the negotiations to implement Security Council Resolution 435 (1978). Our responsibility in these negotiations, as authors of the settlement proposal, has led us to warn that the appointment of a

---

[15] Source: U.N. document A/36/PV.109, p. 4.

[16] On March 29, 1982, the U.N. General Assembly appointed Brajesh C. Mishra United Nations Commissioner for Namibia. On April 13, Prime Minister Botha informed the Secretary-General that South Africa did not recognize the "provocative" appointment. See U.N. document A/37/176 (S/14977), April 14, 1982.

Commissioner at this time is potentially damaging. The course we have set for ourselves, and in which we hope that the Africa countries most closely concerned also continue to believe, is the peaceful negotiated settlement of the Namibia question.

Document 559

Address by the Deputy Assistant Secretary of State for African Affairs (Wisner) Before the Conference on Ethics, May 14, 1982[17]

Southern Africa: The Responsible Use of American Power

I welcome the opportunity to stand in for Assistant Secretary Crocker. I will deliver the remarks he would have made and discuss with you our policy toward southern Africa. It is fitting that he is absent from us today for meetings with the South Africans in Geneva and with the Western Contact Group in Paris on Namibia. The negotiating effort he is engaged in is one of the centerpieces of President Reagan's southern African policy. In another sense, however, despite the focus of attention that has been on the Namibia negotiations, they are only part of a broader southern African policy. That policy is, equally, a part of our overall foreign policy. What we are doing in southern Africa can be examined with reference to the general theme of this second annual Conference on Religion and Politics. In view of what is at stake in southern Africa this conference and its theme, "The Responsible Use of American Power", is an excellent setting in which to examine the issues.

What we are out to achieve in southern Africa represents a very responsible effort on the part of the United States to perform a task for which this administration is uniquely prepared, which responds to the needs and interests of the people of the region and Africa as a whole, and the fulfillment of which is fully consistent with the interests of this nation. In that sense the activism of the effort is responsible and, above all, moral.

By the time of the 1980 American Presidential elections, U.S./South African relations had reached a level of mistrust where very little practical could be accomplished between the two governments. A similar level of mistrust prevailed between the Western Contact Group and South Africa in the Namibia negotiations which did, in fact, grind to a halt in the inconclusive Geneva conference of January 1981. A spirit of collaboration existed between the African frontline states and the Western Contact Group which was enhanced by the achievement of independence for Zimbabwe in 1980 through negotiations. The African states clearly consider the independence of Namibia to be their highest international political priority. Thus, the Western Allies and the African states were very eager to pursue the negotiation process, seeking to find a way past the impasse that the failure of the Geneva conference had produced. Given our broad interests in a strong and positive relationship with Africa—a continent with which we are bound by history, deep friendship, and current economic and political realities—and given the importance we attach to the views and interests of our allies, we had to consider these wishes very seriously.

President Reagan was inaugurated in January; in April, South African Prime Minister P.W. Botha's party was returned to office with a fresh mandate.[18] The door was open to creative diplomacy and the stage was set for potentially very fruitful developments in our southern African relationships with broad regional and perhaps global consequences.

The new administration engaged in a sharp and searching review of America's overall southern African policy that lasted for almost 4 months. As part of that review, Assistant Secretary Crocker met with many of the leaders of southern Africa in their own capitals. The French, German, Canadian, and British Governments told us of the urgency they attached to rapid progress in southern Africa and their intention of working with us. That period also included a visit by South African Foreign Minister Botha to the United States, during which he met with the President and with Secretary Haig. The review also included careful reflection on the African policies of previous administrations since continuity in our policies is necessary. It provides our Western Allies as well as the nations of the region themselves confidence that an unchanging desire for good relations with them remains the bed-

[17] Source: Department of State files.

[18] The South African National Party won the April 29, 1981 elections.

rock upon which new strategies in our African policy are constructed.

This review produced a new southern African policy, appropriate to our fundamental stake in seeing long-term peace and stability in the region, given our strategic and economic interests there. The spread of violence in southern Africa does not serve our interests as it would deeply complicate our relations in the area and open it to an expansion of Soviet influence. A lessening of tensions and the eventual emergence of a broad modus vivendi in the region accords with our interests.

In pursuit of these basic objectives the United States would:

(1) build upon the constructive relations existing between the United States and its allies and the frontline states of the region;

(2) add the balance that would permit us to play the role of mediator by seeking to improve relations with South Africa, consistent with the long-term best interests of both countries;

(3) in tandem with (1) and (2) seek to work with the South African Government and other parties to the negotiations to achieve the independence of Namibia as soon as possible, perhaps even in 1982;

(4) seek means of bringing about the end of the conflict in Angola which has preoccupied that nation for 7 years by devising an agenda to deal with the problems of Cuban troop presence, national reconciliation, and long-term development needs;

(5) seek to work with elements within South Africa, including the newly elected government of Prime Minister Botha, to bring about the peaceful change in conditions in that country which constrain our relations with South Africa; and

(6) to pursue a policy of strong economic cooperation with the nations of southern Africa, doing what we can to strengthen the economies of the region, through aid and through the investment and trade activities of the U.S. private sector. We were, in short, ready to undertake a broad and constructive policy of engagement and collaboration with the region and all its member states.

Let me note that in some ways the elements in the southern African policy that resulted from review represented a departure from the policy of the previous administration, especially our decision to improve relations with South Africa. At the same time, it is our judgment that there was no realistic hope of achieving the third and fifth objectives—independence for Namibia and the effective encouragement of peaceful change in South Africa itself—unless South Africa was prepared to accept the United States as an honest and concerned broker.

The policy furthermore differs from that of the previous administration in the emphasis which we gave to Angola and the issues of Cuban troop withdrawal and national reconciliation. Namibia will not be settled, the security of southern Africa will not be assured, and dangers of confrontation with our global adversary will continue if a way is not found to resolve the Angola problem. The sixth element—economic cooperation—represents a departure from previous policy only in its emphasis on the constructive role that the U.S. private sector is capable of playing in the region. We recognize that official aid flows cannot by themselves meet the needs of the region; private capital and technology are required if southern Africa is to develop to its potential.

One year later, what has been achieved? We have engaged ourselves fully with the states of the region. With Zimbabwe, Zambia, Botswana, and Tanzania we have an active diplomatic dialogue and extensive bonds of bilateral and regional cooperation. With Zimbabwe we have met our post-Lancaster House pledge[19] and have committed $225 million in bilateral assistance in addition to an important effort to stimulate private sector activity.

Relations with South Africa are better. There are still rough spots—for the most part due to a fundamental difference of views between our two countries on the subject of apartheid. At the same time, there has been a very substantial improvement in our ability to communicate with the South African Government on all issues, including those which are most sensitive.

In the field of education, cooperation has increased. Scholarship aid which we pro-

---

[19] Reference is to the pledge made by President Carter on November 14, 1979, that sanctions against Zimbabwe–Rhodesia would be lifted when a British Governor assumed authority in Salisbury and a process toward impartial elections began. Following the December 12, 1979 arrival of a British Governor and the fulfillment of the conditions stipulated, Carter ordered sanctions lifted as of December 16, 1979. See *American Foreign Policy: Basic Documents, 1977–1980*, pp. 1230–1231.

vide to disadvantaged, black South Africans has been augmented substantially. In the nuclear field, we are seeking South African acceptance of full-scope safeguards and signature of the Nuclear Non-Proliferation Treaty.[20] In this regard we have worked more closely with South African nuclear bodies to seek to persuade South Africa that it can develop the peaceful uses of its nuclear capacity acting entirely within the safeguarded international nuclear community. We have sought to rationalize regulations relating to trade with South Africa, preserving full observation of the arms embargo and our distance from South African institutions that administer apartheid, while removing impractical constraints on American exporters and South African buyers of American products.

Most importantly, we have also instituted a frank, direct, diplomatic dialogue with South Africa on matters of political interest to our two governments. Communication has improved greatly and [*now*?] that we are paying much closer attention to each other's views. The progress we have made thus far in advancing the Namibian process is a clear example of the positive results of quiet diplomacy.

On the Namibia negotiations, developments are breaking very fast. Assistant Secretary Crocker met with the South Africans in Geneva, May 10–11, and completed yesterday 2 days of discussions in Paris with his counterparts from the other members of the Western Contact Group—Canada, France, the Federal Republic of Germany, and the United Kingdom. These talks took place against a background of South Africa having agreed to the constitutional principles that constituted Phase One of the three-phase negotiations. In contrast the African frontline states have not yet agreed to move from Phase One to Phase Two. They have supported the objections of SWAPO which has so far refused to accept the electoral formula proposed in the principles. SWAPO and the frontline have said they want a settlement and rapid progress. A delay in the process that would bring peace and independence to Namibia benefits no one. If the negotiating process moves forward, implementation of U.N. Security Council Resolution 435—the final countdown to independence—can begin this year. That is what we seek and I am hopeful that the Geneva and Paris deliberations will lead to new momentum. Such momentum is sorely needed if the diplomatic opportunity which we have developed is to remain open and if Namibia's independence is to be secured. An historic responsibility now lies with the parties directly involved in the dispute.

As regards Angola, we have opened a dialogue. The Secretary met the Angolan Foreign Minister last fall and Assistant Secretary Crocker has met with senior Angolan officials on three occasions.[21] We have spelled out a range of ideas which cover regional security, peace in Angola itself, and the Namibian settlement. Questions of bilateral interest have also been addressed. We have been clear in expressing our belief that a simultaneous withdrawal of Cuban and South African forces is necessary if there is to be an overall settlement. We also believe that national reconciliation in Angola is essential to long-term stability in Angola and peace in the region at large. We await the response of the Angolan representatives. At the same time we have opened communications with UNITA. Its President, Jonas Savimbi, visited the United States in December[22] to discuss his views and made it clear to us that he supports fully the settlement effort. He too has a part to play in the overall process. He has influence in the war-torn southern area of Angola and a vital stake in national reconciliation.

One criticism of our overall southern African policy has been that we have concentrated all of our energy on the Namibian and Angolan issues and have simply lost interest or decided to pay little attention to internal developments within South Africa. I would like to speak to that point directly. Another line of argument, sometimes from within South Africa itself, is that the United States is seeking improved relations with South Africa only to bring about Namibian independence, with the corollary that, as soon as that is achieved, we will then begin pounding on South Africa itself.

I find these two arguments equally flawed in their only partial comprehension of our overall policy. We see constructive engagement with South Africa—like we seek constructive engagement with all

---

[20] For the text of the Treaty on the Non-Proliferation of Nuclear Weapons, see 21 UST 483.

[21] The reference is to Crocker's meetings with Angolan Foreign Minister Paulo Jorge in Paris on January 15 and 16, and March 4 and 5, 1982, and in Luanda on April 1, 1982, where he also met with SWAPO leader Sam Nujoma.

[22] See *American Foreign Policy: Current Documents, 1981*, document 633.

states in the region—as a wide-ranging approach to U.S. relations with that country. The Namibia negotiations provide both countries with an opportunity to work closely together to resolve a serious international problem which is in both nations' interests to solve. The opportunity exists because it is in both countries' interests to resolve the problem. If we do so together successfully, we may then conclude together that the experience of resolving problems by peaceful means gained in those negotiations might be relevant to a common approach to other problems. I would underline that the United States has a long-term interest in peace, security, and the general economic and political health of southern Africa. That interest will not flag.

Finally, to address squarely the theme of this conference, the question of the responsibility of the use of American power that pursuit of our southern African policy represents, I repeat that what we are doing in southern Africa is right and it is in the national interest. It is right because we are seeking peace in the broadest sense—in Namibia, in Angola, in southern Africa, and, in the sense of defusing an issue of potential East/West tension, in the world. It is right in that success in our effort will create conditions in the region which will permit a concentration of national and international resources on economic development—meeting the economic needs of the people of the region. It is right because we seek a resolution of the problems of the region that would remove foreign troops from national soil—the South Africans out of Namibia and the Cubans out of Angola. It is right because we have not compromised our beliefs or principles. Finally, it is right from our point of view since the achievement of these goals—peace in the region, economic development, removal of constraints on national sovereignty—is fully consistent with our principles as well as with our national interests. Policy in consonance with American principles and American interests is good policy.

Document 560

Communiqué Issued by the Contact Group on Namibia, Luxembourg, May 17, 1982[23]

Continuing Efforts in Pursuit of a Settlement in Namibia

The Foreign Ministers of Canada, France, the Federal Republic of Germany, the United Kingdom and the United States of America met in Luxembourg on May 17, 1982, to pursue their efforts to achieve an early settlement of the problem of Namibia in accordance with Security Council Resolution 435.

The Ministers noted the replies received from the parties concerned to the Five's proposal for constitutional principles for the Namibian constituent assembly. In the light of these replies, Ministers instructed their officials to accelerate the resolution of outstanding issues with a view to maintaining their target of beginning implementation of UNSCR 435 during 1982. They expect soon to present proposals to the parties concerned notably on impartiality and UNTAG.

They stressed the need for positive and flexible responses to these proposals when they are presented, in order to achieve early implementation of UNSCR 435. The Ministers agreed to keep under review additional negotiating mechanisms which might prove useful as matters develop.

Document 561

Transcript of a Department of State Press Briefing, Luxembourg, May 17, 1982[24]

Update on Namibian Independence Negotiations

SENIOR DEPARTMENT OF STATE OFFICIAL. I think the main points are pretty well stated

[23] Source: Department of State files.

[24] Source: Department of State files. The briefing was conducted on background by a senior Department of State official following the Luxembourg meeting of the Ministers of the Western Five Contact Group on Namibia.

in the communiqué.[25] All five Ministers were there.[26] We had a very good meeting. There was unanimity on all the key points in terms of where we are in this initiative. I think there is a strong feeling that we are anxious to continue to stick to our timetable which we have laid out from the beginning as leading to the beginning of implementation in 1982. That's a form of art, those words, and I want to make sure people are clear on it.

When we say that we want to get a beginning of implementation, we are talking about implementation of U.N. Security Council Resolution 435 which itself, takes many months to run. We are trying to get that process started in 1982. And we have said that from the beginning; we have said it since our Contact Group mission first tabled these proposals last September and October. We continue to believe, despite the delay that there has been on Phase I, that that is achievable, and we want to make certain that we achieve it. So that's what the words mean—that middle paragraph there.

I guess you could say that we have been delayed for several months on Phase I. Basically, the constitutional principles are agreed by everybody with the exception of the electoral law for the elections for the constitutent assembly, and that's the one issue we've been sticking on.

As you know there were meetings this past 10 days or so. U.S. meetings with the senior South African delegation in Geneva followed immediately by a Contact Group meeting at my level in Paris. If you want dates on that, the South African meetings were 10th and 11th of May and Contact Group, 12th and 13th of May at the Africa directors level and then leading right into the ministerial here.

So we have, as I said, a wide agreement, a unanimous agreement I would say, on where we are and what to do next to keep the process moving ahead. I think I'll stop there and take any questions you have.

Q. Does SWAPO have objections to this electoral process? Will you get into that?

A. Yes. The frontline states and SWAPO met together in Dar Es Salaam on the 4th of May, having been presented with ideas, approximately a month earlier, that were designed to meet their concerns about the electoral system. As a result of that meeting on the 4th of May, we were informed by SWAPO and the frontline jointly, that they continue to reject the dual electoral system—combined system that we have proposed which as been accepted by South Africa.

Q. Is there an alternative electoral formula? Or did they just reject the one you proposed?

A. No. They have said that they would be prepared to accept either proportional representation outright, that is 100 percent proportional representation, or single member districts which is the other possibility—100 percent single member districts.

Q. What do the South Africans have to say about that?

A. We never presented those two alternatives to the South Africans. We have presented them the combined system.

Q. (inaudible)—were you better off?

A. This is an interesting phase because we are very—we feel it's kind of a puzzling situation that so much emphasis will be placed on this one issue, and that it will be characterized as something that was unfair to SWAPO. That is certainly not its intention, and any analysis of the electoral possibilities in Namibia could demonstrate that it would not have that result. So our proposal remains on the table and we are exploring, obviously, the possibilities for moving this issue to a successful conclusion as rapidly as possible. We are determined to do so, and we expect to get into Phase II this month. So we believe that there are grounds to think that we can move ahead rapidly.

Q. When you speak of unanimity on what to do next—?

A. Yes. Within the Five.

Q. (inaudible) push ahead with this particular proposal?

A. To push ahead with our effort. Yes. SWAPO has dug in on this particular proposal.

Q. Do you think you can (inaudible) SWAPO to a minimum persuasion?

A. We think that there are ways to deal with the problem, put it that way. That's as far as I can go. We think there are ways to deal with the problem. I'm not saying that we are asking SWAPO to reconsider yet again, this proposal has been on the table

---

25 *Supra.*

26 The Foreign Ministers were as follows: Alexander Haig, the United States; Francis Pym, the United Kingdom; Claude Cheysson, France; Mark MacGuigan, Canada; and Hans-Dietrich Genscher, the Federal Republic of Germany.

since January, and they have continued to reject it.

Q. Is there any objection within the Contact Group to doing either all proportional representation or either all (inaudible) member of (inaudible)?

A. Within the Contact Group?

Q. Yes.

A. Well it isn't us. We don't have any hangups about any particular system.

Q. You said you haven't tried it?

A. We did not present it to the South Africans, our proposal originally was the combined system.

Q. Supposing you were to present it to the South Africans (inaudible) okay with us? Is that just what you will do?

A. But that isn't the point. The point is that we have a negotiation—a very complex one—with South Africans dealing with the internal parties on behalf of them, and in effect, frontline states and SWAPO, we've got many different parties here. We put an idea forward. One side accepted it. So we are not, obviously, anxious to be in a position where we are going back to the one party that has accepted something and saying, "Okay, unaccept it and consider something else." So we are not eager to do that.

Q. Well, you discussed this surely with the South Africans in your meeting a week ago today, would you say perhaps on *deep background* whether the South Africans are interested in one or the other alternatives that you mentioned which have not been rejected by SWAPO?

A. The South Africans have not shown any interest in either one of the other two alternatives. We haven't, as I say, gone beyond our previous discussions.

Q. Are you trying to say that they are hostile toward the other types of proposals?

A. They feel that they have said "yes" to what we put forward.

Q. Are they amenable to other ideas?

A. That's not for me to say.

Q. It's not clear to me how you expect to move rapidly forward if the objective appears to be to try to change SWAPO's mind on this.

A. Our objective is to simply make clear to everybody, despite the apparent logjam, that we believe that there are strong grounds for optimism that this thing can be brought to a conclusion in 1982, that we can get an implementation underway in 1982, that we hear from all the parties that they are sick of delay. We get accused here and there of seeking to encourage delay; that is not our objective. So we sense that the African side of the equation, the frontline and SWAPO, want rapid movement. We also believe, on the South African side, that there is a desire for rapid movement. So if that's the case, if that's where people are coming from, there's got to be a way to get beyond this and very soon to the issues of Phase II which involves the question of impartiality on the one hand and the military component of UNTAG on the other hand. These in practice are more complicated issues than Phase I issues. So we need to get cracking on them right away.

Q. We've been hearing for several months now that there was this hangup over the electoral system, right?

A. Right.

Q. It didn't seem to be insoluble and does not (inaudible) explanation or elaboration and persuasion, but SWAPO and the frontline states could come around and accept it. Now they, in effect, disavow pretty much catagorically your proposal more strongly than ever before (inaudible). Don't you reach a point where somebody could say, "Well, they are not going to buy this," and we'll have to get a new plan and go back in?

A. When we reach that point we will announce it.

Q. In other words, you don't feel that despite what they did in Dar es Salaam (inaudible)?

A. We think it's got to be kept on the table for the time being, yes.

Q. It's got to be kept on the table; you don't have to persuade them. SWAPO doesn't have to be swung around. It sounds like there is a tight manuever here which the purpose escapes me.

A. The only manuever involved is that we are seeking independence for Namibia as rapidly as we can. I'm not here with any miracle that I pulled out of a hat. But we do believe, as I indicated, that parties have boxed themselves in to some extent and that we have to find a way to unbox them because they all say they want to move rapidly. We are going to do precisely that, find a way to unbox them.

Q. Well, is the strategy to beat this on the table and say, "Well, if you really want to move quickly, you better accept it," or, "You would be wise to accept it?"

A. I'm not going to indicate *on background* or anything else what it is we are saying to SWAPO and the frontline; what it is we are saying to South Africa in our next cables. I mean, that's—because these parties all have their domestic constituents, and it would be most unhelpful for me to do that. All I'm saying is that I think we can break the logjam and soon.

Q. As you understand it, what were the motivations for this SWAPO–frontline rejection of your proposals?

A. Well, there are many possible explanations. The first, the charge that we faced was that this proposal was overly complicated for the people of Namibia who were simple people—these were not my words, their words—largely unschooled people—and a proposal that had in effect two votes for each citizen, each voter, would complicate people's minds. Specifically, in response to that we simplified the procedure by making it instead of being one man two votes, making it one vote counted twice. So you have a single ballot paper and you would mark your X in a single spot and it would count locally for the candidate and nationally for the party.

So we thought we had addressed that issue of complexity. There were other kinds of complaints or charges that were made. That it might lead to the over representation of minorities and that it was cooked up for that specific purpose. But in practice, if you know anything about election systems, you know that it would have the precise opposite effect. If you wanted to maximize representation of minorities, you would have all PR. Portional representation is the system that best maximizes minorities. If you wanted to maximize the interest of regional or local sentiment, you would have all single member districts and as many of them as possible. So we have sought to compromise that and make it the mixed system.

Q. Based on that rationale, one would think that South Africa would be willing to embrace the other alternatives, and this would enhance minority group representation.

A. Well, their interests are also somewhat complicated because they have a number of different constituents to listen to. They are not speaking for any one element in Namibia. The South African Government has to listen to a number of different parties which may have different interests.

Q. Was that the reason given by the Africans on May 4?

A. Pretty much. In addition, there were arguments that this phase-by-phase approach was designed to delay things, as though there was some speedy way to cut through in one bold stroke. That it was a device with which the Contact Group was protecting South Africa from taking tough decisions. That was in their reply. Not a whole lot of substantive discussion frankly of the merit of the system itself.

Q. But on the face of all this, you still think that this problem can be resolved?

A. I think we can solve the problem one way or the other, yes.

Q. Thank you.

Document 562

Transcript of a Department of State Press Briefing, June 10, 1982 (Extracts)[27]

The Status of the Namibia Negotiations

SENIOR DEPARTMENT OFFICAL. . . . We have been for the past month or more in a period of great diplomatic activity. I'll just touch on some of those different diplomatic contacts so that you have a bit of a framework.

There is currently in Zambia, Angola, and Tanzania a mission of the Contact Group at the Africa Director level. General Walters has just completed his trip, which was the United States working alone, where he also met with Heads of State of Tanzania, Zambia, and Angola.

Assistant Secretary Chester Crocker returned recently from a meeting in Bonn with President Sam Nujoma of SWAPO—that was just about 10 days ago—whose results, I think, are pretty well known. There were public statements given here as well as the press conference given by President Nujoma in Bonn at that time.[28] A little

---

27 Source: Department of State files. The briefing was conducted on background by a senior Department of State official.

28 Reference is to the June 2, 1982 statement by Nujoma in Bonn, in which he rejected Western proposals for a one-man, two-vote election system put forth during the Contact Group meetings in Bonn. (*New York Times*, June 3, 1982, p. A3)

earlier, there was an extensive set of discussions between an American delegation and the South African delegation in Geneva. That was May 10th and 11th, followed immediately by the Contact Group meeting in Paris that I made reference to earlier.

The new South African Ambassador to Washington, Bran Fourie, who has been the leader of just about all South African discussions with us over the past year and a half and who has been involved in the Namibian negotiations for many years, has now arrived in Washington, which further facilitates expediting this negotiation—the fact that he is physically here in Washington.

Assistant Secretary Crocker and his counterparts from other countries in the Contact Group will also be active up in New York tomorrow (June 11), over the weekend and next week with frontline states Foreign Ministers and others involved in an effort to move the negotiations forward as rapidly as we can.

I might say a word about what leads us to think that things are in an active phase. I think all parties agree that nothing much is to be gained by continuing a sterile stalemate, an argument over one issue which has been the source of our delay for the past 4 months on the Namibia negotiations, and that is the electoral system for the first election, that is, the election to the Constituent Assembly for Namibia.

I think there is consensus on all sides that too much time has been taken with this problem, that it puts at risk too much and that the time is ripe, in fact, to find a way to move forward.

There's a broader feeling, I think, as well, that the time may be ripe, in general, for a settlement. The South African Government has made it clear that it wishes to go ahead as rapidly as possible. We are persuaded that South Africa does not want the Namibia question to be an element that lingers for the indefinite future in the evolving political calculus within South Africa. By the same token, we are very much of the view that the frontline state leaders and SWAPO want a settlement sooner rather than later.

The regional climate in southern Africa is today, as it has been for some time, dangerous. The way to get that danger under control is to get a handle on this particular question.

I think the recent meeting of Prime Minister Botha and President Kaunda of Zambia[29] was more than anything else a clear indication, despite the differences that do exist, of the consensus on the need to get the problems of regional security in southern Africa under better control.

There are, of course, differences, but we believe these differences have narrowed and that there is interest in trying to find a solution.

How are we going to do this? Let me indicate where we are on the substantive issues in the negotiations. As I've indicated, on the Phase I questions, which concern a set of constitutional principles which we first tabled with the parties last fall, there is consensus that the negotiations should not fail or become indefinitely bogged down over the question of an electoral system.

So what we are going to do is to put the electoral issue aside for resolution later, in accordance with the procedures originally spelled out in U.N. Resolution 435. We do not intend to push, therefore, at this moment, for agreement on an electoral system, and we have so told the parties. We believe the issue can be resolved to everyone's satisfaction in a more positive context at a later time.

So we are not asking any of the parties to abandon their stated positions. We are simply asking for agreement from all sides to finesse this one question for now.

On the Phase II questions, which revolve around the role of the United Nations in the transition period, specifically the question of impartiality toward all the political parties in Namibia, on the one hand, and the U.N. Transitional Assistance Group, UNTAG, on the other hand, we believe also the differences are narrowing.

There is a recognition on all sides that the United Nations has a job to do and it must have the resources to do that job effectively. There is also recognition that sensible and appropriate steps will be re-

[29] Reference is to the meeting held on April 30 between South African Prime Minister Botha and Zambian President Kaunda at Kopfontein Gate, on the border between South Africa and Botswana, to discuss independence for Namibia and other issues. For further information, see *New York Times*, May 1, 1982, p. 2, and May 21, 1982, p. A2; *Washington Post*, May 1, 1982, p. A14; and Foreign Broadcast Information Service, *Daily Report: Middle East and Africa*, April 29, 1982, pp. U1–U4; April 30, 1982, pp. U1, U4–U5; and May 3, 1982, pp. U1 and U3.

quired on the issue of impartiality to assure a workable degree of confidence in the United Nations on all sides.

As I mentioned a moment ago, there is a Contact Group team presently in Africa talking to some of the key parties about our preliminary ideas on Phase II as we sit here today.

Looking to the future in the very near term, we expect to conclude Phase I, recognizing that all of the constitutional principles have been accepted by the parties except for the electoral system. That is a clear position on the part of all as was reaffirmed in Bonn by President Nujoma of SWAPO and all the other parties.

We expect in the near future to be coming up with Contact Group proposals on Phase II issues which, we hope, will be able to narrow differences and lead to agreement on those as well, with appropriate involvement of the U.N. Secretariat, which, of course, is involved in implementing such proposals and, therefore, has a role to play as well.

We think it is not an insignificant accomplishment that the constitutional principles, which are some three plus pages of specifics about the way a constitution would be drawn up, have been agreed upon and that the one unresolved issue is this electoral system. But all attention having been focused on the electoral system, we think there's been perhaps a lack of recognition as to what has been agreed to.

If things move according to the kind of timetable that we have in mind, it is foreseeable that we could, within the next several months, be in a position where the parties can agree on a date for implementation, and that that date could be in the next few months as well. That would enable us to make up for the lost time that has been spent on the electoral question, the question of the electoral law, so that we could, as we have said from the outset of these negotiations, be able to see the beginning of implementation of U.N. Resolution 435 in 1982.

And as I have just indicated, implementation, in our view, could, if things go well, and the differences are narrowing, begin as early as in the next few months.

We have also, from the beginning of these negotiations, made clear that we believe there is a close interrelationship between the questions of Namibia and Angola and that the two questions, if there is to be success, must be addressed and resolved in tandem.

As those of you who followed these discussions before are aware, we have said from the beginning this is not an American precondition. This is a fact of life. It reflects the reality on the ground. It reflects the close geographic relationship of the Angola conflict and the Namibia conflict and the close political interrelationship as well.

To assure success on Namibia, we need a commitment from the Angolan Government that Cuban combat forces will depart from Angola in a way coordinated with the departure of South African forces from Namibia as foreseen in U.N. Resolution 435. Without that, I cannot say that this negotiation will succeed.

Our views on Angola and on the Angolan issues have been conveyed up to now in the diplomatic channel, where they will remain. So I'm not going to go into any further detail on background or any other basis. We have had extensive discussions with the Angolan Government as we have, indeed, with President Savimbi of UNITA.

General Walters met recently with President Dos Santos of Angola in Luanda to discuss the full range of issues that I am describing here as well as bilateral questions.

It would suffice for me to say that we are seeking to play the role of catalyst in a very complex negotiation; for that to succeed, it must have something in it for everybody and that is the basis on which we are proceeding.

We are not asking any party to commit suicide and we seek constructive relations with all the parties involved.

I think I'll stop there.

. . . .

Q. When you talk about the notion that you can't ask any party to commit suicide and also the relationship between Namibia and Angola, what now do you see is the role of UNITA and whether that is part and parcel of a Cuban withdrawal?

A. We have made clear, and it continues to be our view, that it's difficult to envisage an overall regional solution that does not take into account the interests of the major parties. Clearly, UNITA and the people it represents are major parties. Having said that, we have no blueprint or any model for national reconciliation in Angola. We do not believe it is for us to mediate or to negotiate, and we have made that clear as well to all the parties. But we find it difficult to envisage the possibility of a regional solution that did not include some discussion leading eventually to some understanding between the key parties in Angola.

Q. Can I follow up on that? When you use the word "we" now are you speaking of the U.S. Government or as the Contact Group; is that a consensus?

A. I'm speaking as the U.S. Government.

. . . .

Q. I get the impression here that the attitude here is that some is better than none. What about the completion of Phase I? I don't understand what the stumbling block seems to be in getting Phase I completed and finished.

A. Phase I consisted of a complete set of constitutional proposals, including an electoral law for the first election, that is, the election of the Constituent Assembly. We have agreement on everything but that electoral law and so what we are seeking to do and are going to do is to complete Phase I without agreement on the electoral law, and move ahead to Phase II.

Q. I understand, but what are you looking for to complete Phase I? What are you looking for to tie up that electoral—

A. I see your question. We are simply consulting at this stage, doing a final round of consultations with all the parties as to the procedural means by which we terminate Phase I, which will involve communication between the Five and the U.N. Secretary-General.

. . . .

Q. Is it your hope, then, that there will be enough give in the positions, especially of the South Africans, in Phase II that would allow SWAPO to accept the Phase I electoral proposals as they are now, or do you envisage a situation where the electoral proposals will be changed at a later date?

A. It's too early to predict that. But we are not asking anyone to change their position, and, as you know, the frontline states and SWAPO have met—they met on May 4th in Dar es Salaam—and announced at that time that the mixed electoral system which we had put forward was unacceptable to SWAPO.

We are not asking at this stage—we are not asking SWAPO to go back again and look at it again, that is, the position on the electoral issue.

Q. But you might be, after the conclusion of Phase II?

A. We are not asking anyone to reconsider. We are deferring this issue, and the U.N. Security Council Resolution 435 spells out a procedure for deciding that issue at the appropriate time.

. . . .

Q. Is it a fair inference that you—now speaking of "you" as the U.S. Government you—have a fair degree of confidence—maybe that's not the word, but I'll say confidence—that Angola can be brought to agree to a withdrawal of the Cubans? And if not, why go through this whole exercise only to be foiled in the end?

A. I don't think it's particularly helpful at this stage for us to indicate our view of the likelihood of decisions that may be forthcoming in a matter of weeks or months on the part of other parties. But I would say this: that we believe that what we have put forward is in the spirit of our playing a role of good faith catalyst, broker, if you will, in the middle of a great number of parties in a highly complex negotiation.

We wouldn't be doing it if we thought it was a fatuous exercise. We also wouldn't be doing it if we didn't think it was in the interest of all the parties who live in southern Africa, and that that may be increasingly recognized.

Q. Is there any indication of what the Soviet attitude is toward this?

A. It has been our view from the beginning that we are both superpowers; we are both great powers. We have, perhaps, responsibilities that are rather special for peace and security in the world. It's also been our view that we would not win popularity contests by seeking to negotiate the future of southern Africa bilaterally between the United States and the Soviet Union, and that the parties in the region were not encouraging us to do that. So we have been talking directly with the parties concerned, but from time to time these regional questions, like others, are discussed between our two governments to keep each other informed in general.

. . . .

Q. This is a kind of a procedural question. You expressed that, without agreement by the Angolans for a phased withdrawal on some basis, the process may come to naught. My question is, is the question of Angola and the withdrawal of Cubans specifically on the agenda that the Contact Group brings up with the frontline states and with South Africa?

Does it come under Phase I, Phase II, or is it simply a kind of understood notion that everybody agrees it has to be determined while Phase I and Phase II are being negotiated?

A. No. I think that's an important point to clarify. The Contact Group exists in order to negotiate the independence of Namibia. It is the Contact Group which all along for the past 4 plus years has developed the proposals that led to the Western plan, or the U.N. plan, Resolution 435, and everything that has followed since, and the Contact Group negotiates on that issue.

For a statement of the position of other members of the Western Five on the Angola question, I think it's probably most appropriate to address that question to them directly. It is our understanding that all of us are fully aware of the importance of the Angolan agenda and that, as a matter of our objective assessment of the situation, there is a high degree of consensus that this is, indeed, going to be an important aspect of the overall solution. But the Contact Group is not putting forward proposals on Angola. That is not its role, and the U.N. plan does not involve Angola in any way.

. . . .

Q. Would you talk some on this electoral procedure which seems to be a sticking point of Phase I? Would you give us your assessment of where Nujoma is? Presumably, if you conclude Phase I and Phase II goes smoothly, is it your sense that Nujoma then will feel more comfortable about this two-tier or this double vote that's involved in Phase I? Is it really an issue of substance or an issue of attitudes, because suspicions run deeply on this issue? And how much room did Nujoma, in terms of Crocker's talks with him, give him, if everything else goes well, in terms of resolving this problem?

A. When Assistant Secretary Crocker met with President Nujoma in Bonn, I think both agreed that it was the path of wisdom not to debate the past and to find ways, as best they could, to improve communication both between us and the Contact Group and SWAPO in general which we are quite confident can be done.

Secretary Crocker did not, in Bonn, ask him yet again to reconsider—make a proposal which his organization has on several occasions rejected. Secretary Crocker did not leave him the impression that he would be coming back to him later and asking him to reconsider the mixed electoral system.

But in the spirit of not debating the past, I'm not sure what purpose would be served by my going into detail about the past, except to say that we don't believe there was anything unfair or undemocratic about our proposal. But SWAPO had a number of objections to it—objections of principle. We are not arguing the point, and that's where it stands for now.

. . . .

Q. I'm talking about Phase II. Could you give us some sense of where the differences are? Is it on the composition of the UNTAG force, the role of it, or the size of it?

A. There has been for some time a considerable concern in the minds of both people who live in Namibia and the South African Government that [*of*] the ability of the United Nations to play a proper, impartial role in that transition, given the long-standing practice in various U.N. organs of taking a position that SWAPO is the sole legitimate representative of the Namibian people.

At the same time, there is a recognition that the United Nations has a responsibility for Namibia and must play a role in that transition. So what we're seeking to do is to narrow differences on that point to find ways in which it can be clearly demonstrated that the United Nations is impartial, that there is impartiality in general during the transition—it's not strictly and solely a U.N. issue—so that all parties do have equal treatment in terms of public relations and access to media and so forth.

On the issue of the U.N. force for Namibia, there were many issues from the past that were never fully resolved. There is a misperception, I believe, that UNTAG was all signed, sealed, and delivered in 1978–1979. It was never the case. There were outstanding issues never resolved then concerning the role and deployment and composition of the U.N. force. So some of these are legacies from the past.

In addition, I think it is well known in the public record after the failed Geneva meeting of January 1981. There had been public announcements from the South African side that U.N. troops were unacceptable. And, as I've indicated, differences on that issue have, of course, narrowed substantially, and we believe there is a possibility now to put forth proposals which will be in the ballpark from the standpoint of all parties.

. . . .

Q. Why, after all these years, what do you think is the key that's made South Africa willing to loosen its grip on Namibia?

A. I don't believe it is the South African position that it wants a settlement at any price. This is a very tough decision. As we have said many times before, people talk about concessions and who's making concessions. The big concession in this exercise, if you look at it and take the long view, is the decision to withdraw, to decolonize.

So I'm not saying that it is our assessment for a minute that the South African Government is eager for a settlement in the abstract; a settlement on terms it can live with, yes. But we also have the view that the current situation is not all that advantageous from the standpoint of any party. Lives are being lost, a lot of money is being spent. It's a stalemate. The economy of Namibia is going no place. It is an economic burden for South Africa.

As I have said, in addition there is the question of the domestic/political calculus within South Africa. Maybe the time has come to get this one resolved one way or the other.

. . . .

Document 563

Response by the Department of State Deputy Spokesman (Romberg) to a Question Asked at the Department of State Daily Press Briefing, July 2, 1982 (Extract)[30]

Cuban Troops and Namibian Negotiations

. . . .

. . . There continue to be reports and questions from a variety of sources suggesting some change in the U.S. position on the relationship of Namibian negotiations to the question of Cuban troops in Angola. There has been no change in the U.S. Government's public or private position on this matter since the early months of this administration. The relationship between the Namibia and Angola situations is a fact, not an invention or precondition of our government or of any other government. In these highly complex negotiations involving fundamental choices for all the key parties, there can be no preconditions on any side. We continue to believe that the success of our effort to achieve internationally recognized independence for Namibia will depend in part on whether it is possible to achieve parallel progress on the issue of Cuban withdrawal from Angola. These two issues are related as a matter of logic and geography, but they are being handled as separate matters in separate channels.

. . . .

[30] Source: Office of Press Relations, Department of State. The briefing began at 12:37 p.m. The questioner referred to SWAPO's rejection of the linkage concept.

Document 564

Address by the Deputy Assistant Secretary of State for African Affairs (Wisner) Before the Yale Conference on South Africa, Buck Hill Falls, Pennsylvania, September 22, 1982[31]

Southern Africa: The Future of a Relationship

The past year and a half has been a period of almost unprecedented activity for the United States in Africa. We have been deeply engaged in a broad range of African issues—Namibia, Angola, South Africa, Chad, the Horn of Africa, and an effort to alleviate the suffering caused by drought in the Sahel. The administration has clearly pursued an "activist" policy, working to further our global and regional interests in Africa with vigor and determination.

The centerpiece of this effort has been southern Africa. The political issues there clearly demanded attention: our allies among the industrial democracies wanted progress toward a peaceful resolution of the Namibian problem; African countries insisted Namibia should be the principal focus of American attention; our own national strategic interests were directly in play; and finally, the several interlocking problems in that region suggested a "window of opportunity" for thoughtful and deliberate diplomacy.

It is particularly for this reason that I want to express the administration's appreciation to the organizers of this gathering for their initiative and for the constructive and positive approach they took to dealing with the problems of southern Africa. Bringing this group together will, I am sure, have a catalytic effect in bringing forth new ideas, reinvigorating current initiatives, and hopefully, laying to rest other less effective approaches to the problem. There is enough good will, organizational talent, and financial muscle here in this room to make a significant step toward peaceful evolutionary change in southern Africa. The will to do so is evident by the number of you who took the time to come to this conference.

Rather than look at U.S.-South African relations solely in a bilateral context, let's try first to place it in a wider focus. Globally, South Africa is a highly industrialized country, but in overall terms of trade, it is not of crucial importance to any other industrialized country, nor is any other industrialized country of crucial importance to it. There is very little which is produced by South Africa which cannot be replaced, although at a price, by substituting some other commodity from elsewhere in the world, or through conservation, or by recycling existing stocks.

It is important to recognize, at the outset, that what is important in our relationship is not some absolute dependence upon each other, but, rather, a recognition that we each have something to offer the other—if only we can bring together our common interests. Whether we can do so will not be a function of geography, strategic minerals or metals, but, rather, a compatibility of values and interests—social, political, and economic.

Let us also look at South Africa's position in its region, and at our interests in that area. South Africa is without question a hub of transportation, communications, and technologically sophisticated services. Many of its immediate neighbors are critically dependent upon them, and for the majority-ruled states of southern Africa the economic cost of going it alone without that which South Africa has to offer would probably be something close to bankruptcy.

We, too, have interests in these other states of Africa. Tens of thousands of American businesses and American citizens work and live in the independent countries of southern Africa. The U.S. petroleum sector has important projects in at least a dozen countries along the Western Coast of Africa. Nigeria is our second most important source of imported petroleum; our trade with the countries of sub-Saharan Africa, excluding South Africa, exceeded $22 billion. There are 42 independent nations there, a not insignificant political bloc in the United Nations and other international fora. We cannot afford to ignore them, or to subordinate our political need to work constructively with them, in order just to maintain a favorable relationship with only one country at the tip of that continent.

U.S. business likewise has a considerable stake in the stability of our relationship with that continent. Although many American corporations have sizeable interests in South Africa, very few are without important interests elsewhere on that continent as well. Certainly no major manufacturer of

[31] Source: Department of State files.

consumer goods or specialty industrial equipment is unaware of the market represented by sub-Saharan Africa.

Business, however, like politics, prospers only in a climate of stability, trust, and material benefit. Setting aside the matter of internal politics in sub-Saharan countries as too vast and diverse to cover on an occasion like this, let us hone in, instead, on two problems that constitute one of the most important efforts of contemporary American foreign policy.

The first of these is trying to find a solution to the Namibian problem which will bring independence to that country, eliminating a major irritant in relationships in southern Africa. I want to stress for you—as hard-headed business executives, distinguished officials, and students of that part of the world—that the U.S. motives in this are not borne of some abstract idealism—although a desire to see self-government by the consent of the governed is hardly an abstract ideal. It is, rather, motivated by the pragmatic judgment that our interests are not served by conflict between two groups of nations—both of them potential partners and allies of ours. The fighting and bloodshed, destructive in human, material, and political terms, can only serve the sinister goals of our strategic adversary. Our own national interests are best served by peace, trust, and an end to conflict between our potential trading partners and our strategic allies. We think it may be possible to work out a solution to the Namibian problem which will bring independence to that country, peace in the region, and safe and secure borders for all the countries of southern Africa—including, explicitly, South Africa and Angola. That is the focus of one facet of our diplomacy, and the next several months may tell us if we can succeed.

Namibia is, of course, only one element in our efforts in southern Africa. The clear and obvious need of that part of the world is a framework for regional security and stability which will allow, and in fact encourage, all of its nations to work together for their mutual betterment. Nothing is more destructive to the effort to find ways of improving the circumstances their peoples live in than reversion to tribalism, factional in-fighting, and cross-border military activity. The countries of that region urgently need to work for unity and national reconciliation within their borders, and cooperation and sharing of information and technical capabilities between them. We believe that if we can succeed in resolving the Namibian problem in a way that gives all of the states of the region confidence in the safety and security of their borders, we will have achieved significant progress toward conditions which favor our long-term national interests in that part of the world.

But we need to understand that Namibia is not the alpha and omega of U.S. policy interests in the region; there is a long agenda to which we need lend our efforts, including working toward a more productive relationship with Mozambique and Angola, supporting the development of a strong, stable, and pro-Western Zambia and Zimbabwe, and assisting in the stable and democratic development of Botswana, Lesotho, and Swaziland. All of the countries of the region want and need desperately to enhance their security and economic development; U.S. diplomacy has a role to play here in our own national interests, but it can only do so if it has the confidence of both sides in the southern African equation, as well as the strong and resolute backing of the American people and American business.

The second major focus of our diplomacy is to encourage trends in South Africa which will make it possible for us to have a more acceptable relationship than that which has characterized our recent past.

At the outset, it is important to say that no one can or should dictate to South Africans how their society should be structured, or how their political system should be run. At the same time, however, it is important to recognize that our own democratic values make it difficult for us to be political or economic partners with a societal structure that has many attributes fundamentally incompatible with our own values.

While there are many differences among the institutions of the industrialized democracies, including as they do the Japanese, the Western Europeans, the English-speaking dominions such as Canada, Australia, New Zealand—and include such diverse forums as our own Presidential system, the Westminster-style parliamentary system, the "socialist monarchies" of Belgium, Holland, and the Scandinavian countries—all have certain common features: prime among these is the fundamental and sacred concept of individual dignity. One man is as good as any other man, be he white, brown, yellow, or black; Anglo-Saxon, Cherokee, Quebecois, Walloon, Fleming, pied-noir, paisano, or nobility. The right of citizenship is unalterable by reason of race, creed, sex, religion, or political affiliation. Due process does not—and cannot, in a democracy—distinguish between white and black, rich or poor, native or import. And, above all, there is the absolute requisite for the electoral consent of the governed—all of the governed. Many chambers has democracy's mansion; but irrespective of the hue of the outer shell, the fundamental characteristics must be the same for all who profess to believe in it. We Americans could not consider ourselves partners of any who did not share our fundamental values. It is not a matter of legislation, it is, rather, a matter of shared national conviction, transcending party politics.

There are, fortunately, significant signs of change within South Africa which promise to make it easier for the United States to develop a more normal relationship with that country. We need to look carefully at what we might do to encourage them—in our own interest.

At this point, it is worth identifying some of the things which distinguish the current administration's approach from approaches taken in the recent past.

—We believe South Africa has now begun a process of internal evolution which, if successful, will make closer cooperation between our two countries possible.

—We believe it is preferable to cooperate with and encourage this process, rather than stand on the sidelines, declining to have contact and communication, denying ourselves the opportunity to constructively assist in that process.

—We believe there are a number of things that both the U.S. Government and American businesses and citizens can do to help, and we further believe it self-evident in our national interest to try to do so.

Our record of accomplishment in the recent past has not been impressive. Where there is no communication, there is no influence. Where there is no economic intercourse, there is no leverage. When one preaches sermons based on one's own perceptions of morality in one's own particular circumstances, one not infrequently forfeits the opportunity to gain the attention of, and influence, those who come from substantially different circumstances. Because policies based on ostracism or tongue-lashing threaten and do not encourage, they have never reformed their targets.

It is clear, however, from recent political developments inside South Africa, that a process of change is underway. We all hope that the change we are witnessing will give a greater voice in government to all the governed—rather than preserving the role of government for a narrow minority. It is not my purpose here to explain South African change, nor to offer any judgment upon it, its likely result, or whether the U.S. Government has any view about the method South Africans choose to pursue their political, social, and economic evolution. But at the same time, I believe it is important to recognize that change is taking place, and that we have a political, a strategic, an economic, and indeed, a moral obligation to encourage positive trends which are compatible with our own interests.

There will be those both within and outside South Africa who will be skeptical about the prospects for its success. Skepticism in the abstract is a positive virtue; actively seeking to undermine or refusal to support positive change means that one has consciously chosen the side of violence. South Africans, both black and white, will themselves have to determine how far and how fast they believe they can go. Neither we nor any others can do that for them. We do, however, need to look at what our own contributions can be.

At this point I'd like to tackle head-on one of the popular nostrums which has been making the rounds: the idea that the U.S. corporate community might force change by withholding investment in South Africa, and that if the business community were to decline to do so on its own, it should be pressured into such by institutional "disinvestment"—either mandated by law or by public pressure.

Nothing could be more nonsensical, nor more destructive, of our objectives. Nearly 2,000 years ago, a Roman viceroy made notorious the concept of washing one's hands of responsibility for events about to take place. Nothing in man's history before or since suggests that any good has ever come from sticking one's head in the sand, declining to shoulder the burden of one's responsibilties.

Let me illustrate the point about the effect of economic growth (the presumptive result of any investment) on social and political change. A recent special supplement on "Manpower" to the respected South African weekly, the *Financial Mail*, had this to say:

> "An all-out effort is needed by South African companies to devise new approaches and strategies to maximise their most valuable resource—people. In

coming to grips with the skills shortage, companies have few options. They can optimise the use of their existing workforce through training, or increase their skills pool through immigration, making better use of women, or advancing blacks. The first three all have limited potential. Ultimately the answer must lie in the upgrading of black skills.

"South Africa has been extremely wasteful of its human resources.

"Only 1.6% of the whites have gone no further than primary school level. But 24.7% of Asians, 59% of coloureds and a staggering 84% of blacks are in this category.

"It is reckoned that only 32,000 whites have just primary or lower level education, as against 6.36 million blacks. Those who have reached matriculation level represent 30% of white manpower, 10% of Asians, 2% of coloureds and 3.3% of blacks."

The history of mankind shows clearly that economic development is the most important single engine of social and political change. People—the human resource—is its most important fuel. The fact that the business community, including industrial and manufacturing sectors, appreciates this is the best single hope for the future.

It seems almost incredible that people who would style themselves as "liberals"—which Webster's dictionary tells us are people "favorable to progress and reform"—can possibly believe that our mutual ends are served by denying investment capital which can only be used for the long-term improvement of South Africa's human resource. It is certainly unclear how economic stagnation, unemployment, failure to use the human resource to its fullest potential, can possibly serve the goal of improving educational opportunities for South Africa's nonwhite majority. What can people who advocate cutting off all ties with a society they do not agree with, and withdrawing all economic links, hope to accomplish? How will this benefit the people they profess to wish to help?

"Disinvestment" is a negative approach to problem-solving, irrational in terms of the South African example it is applied to, and destructive of what ought to be our objective—to help encourage moderate elements within South Africa who wish to see reform which will improve prospects for that country's domestic stability, and help rebuild bridges to a world which has largely cut it off.

It seems clear to us that our own American national interests dictate taking the more positive course of action; that through constructive engagement with those elements of South African society which we believe offer the best prospects for transforming their country into one with which the remainder of the free world can deal with clear conscience, we try to assist the process of change. This will require communication, not ostracism; contacts, not avoidance; and a deliberate effort to encourage moderate, progressive elements in South African society. At heart, we Americans are both a practical and an optimistic people. Our sense of practicality gave us strength, in ways not dissimilar to the fundamental strengths of South Africa's people. We share a desire to make a difference where we can make a difference. Our optimism led us toward the conviction, a century ago, that our greatest potential would be realized through unity at a time of great internal conflict; and in this century, through a conviction that our national destiny was best served by strong and responsible participation in the family of nations. In ways it is not necessary to dwell upon here, South Africa has faced similar challenges in the past, and—like us—faces them today.

Responsibility for justifying, and, ultimately, fulfilling this optimism rests upon all our shoulders—not just those of government. Government has begun to do its part through concrete actions in pursuit of our policy of peaceful evolutionary change. Let me briefly update you on where we stand:

—The program of scholarships for black South Africans is now in high gear. The total number of scholarship recipients currently in the program is 117; a contract between AID and IIE has been awarded for the selection of up to 150 potential scholarship recipients for September 1983.

—In the area of non-apartheid in-country education activities we have successfully initiated Self-Help Projects totaling $190,000. We have joined community action level groups to help support community sponsored non-apartheid education activities. It is our intention to continue these efforts and to expand them in Fiscal Year 1983.

—A third area of activity covers the Joint Matriculation Board Exam Preparation Program. In Fiscal 1982 we committed $300,000 to this program which is designed as a tutorial program to boost the number of black students passing the Joint Matriculation Board.

—We are beginning, this coming weekend, a new program of Management Development Assistance for Black South Africans. A three-person project design team will arrive in South Africa on September 25 to begin work on what we see as a multimillion dollar effort to assist black managers, administrators, and community program leaders. It is our intention to jointly develop management training programs with U.S. corporations active in South Africa and with such black institutions as the National African Chamber of Commerce, the Black Management Forum, and the Management and Leadership Development Association and the American Chamber of Commerce. In short, we are putting U.S. Government funds directly in support of the Sullivan Principles.[32] Let me use this occasion to request the support and cooperation of U.S. firms active in South Africa as we approach you over the coming months to forge a closer partnership between the U.S. private sector and the U.S. Government.

There are many other areas where a positive contribution can be made. I have outlined for you what we are doing to back up our rhetoric in favor of peaceful evolutionary change. The American corporate community can play a most important role in this, for it is through commerce, industry, manufacturing, transportation, and communications that by far the greatest percentage of contact between the two countries occurs.

We are putting our money and our energy where our rhetorical commitments lie. We challenge all those standing on the sidelines to demonstrate how their approach is of benefit to black South Africans and to bringing about that change which we all so much wish to see in South Africa.

Businesses that commit themselves and their resources to constructive change will be understood and their contribution recognized. There need be no reason for defensiveness, but courage, determination and a willingness to invest in the future is required. It is the best, the most worthwhile, and the most responsible of actions, and has always been that which distinguished America's corporate pioneers. It is the course of action this administration has chosen, and we hope for a full partnership with business as we proceed.

Academic institutions likewise occupy a vital center. It is incumbent upon all of us to recognize that if we seek positive change, we have to work to help bring it about. We, in this administration, are working hard to achieve that objective. I know the Americans in this audience, whatever their political persuasions, share that objective. We must work together to help bring it about.

Thank you.

Document 565

Communiqué Issued by the Contact Group, New York, October 1, 1982[33]

The Contact Group Takes Stock

The Foreign Ministers of Canada, France, the United Kingdom, and the United States, and the State Secretary of the Foreign Office of the Federal Republic of Germany,[34] met in New York on 1 October to take stock of the progress made in the Namibia negotiations since their previous meeting in Luxembourg on 18 May.[35]

The Ministers reviewed the consultations which took place during July and August in New York between the Contact Group and representatives of the frontline states and SWAPO, and the concurrent consultations with South Africa. They expressed satisfaction with the results of these discussions.

---

[32] In March 1977, representatives of 11 major U.S. companies and black church leaders met with Secretary of State Cyrus Vance in Philadelphia to discuss guidelines for U.S. business operations in South Africa. The resultant guidelines, known as the Sullivan Principles, after the head of the black church delegation, Reverend Leon Sullivan, were as follows: nonsegregation in all eating, work, and comfort facilities; equal pay and fair employment practices for all employees; equal pay for comparable work; development training to prepare black employees for supervisory, administrative, technical, and clerical positions; more promotions of black employees to management and supervisory positions; and improvement in the quality of employees' nonwork environment (housing, transportation, schools, health, and recreation).

[33] Source: U.S. Mission to the United Nations Press Release USUN–73 (82), October 1, 1982.

[34] The Foreign Ministers were as follows: Canada, Allan MacEachen; France, Claude Cheysson; United Kingdom, Francis Pym; United States, George Shultz; and Federal Republic of Germany, State Secretary of the Foreign Office Berndt von Staden.

[35] See documents 560 and 561.

The Ministers welcomed the agreement of the parties to the negotiations to the constitutional principles for the Namibian Constituent Assembly. They noted that all parties had agreed that the method to be employed to elect the Constituent Assembly would be decided in accordance with the terms of UNSCR 435, and insisted that the issue should not cause delay in the implementation of UNSCR 435. They expressed appreciation of the constructive and flexible attitude of the parties, which enabled substantial progress to be made on impartiality and the size, composition, and deployment of the military component of UNTAG. They noted that on 24 September representatives of the frontline states, Nigeria, SWAPO, and the Contact Group had reported to the Secretary-General on the results of the consultations which had taken place.

The Ministers reiterated their commitment to the early implementation of UNSCR 435 in order to enable the people of Namibia to exercise their right to self-determination and to bring peace and security to the region. They paid tribute to the efforts already made by the Secretary-General and his staff and agreed that arrangements for the implementation of the plan were proceeding satisfactorily.

The Ministers agreed that a valuable opportunity now existed to achieve a settlement within the time frame envisaged which would strengthen peace and security and foster economic development in the region. They noted that the objective of achieving such a settlement was shared by all Contact Group governments.

Document 566

Transcript of a Department of State Press Briefing, New York, October 6, 1982 (Extracts)[36]

Efforts to Achieve a Settlement in Namibia

. . . .

Q. Are you suffering from paranoia about Cuba, as the Angolan Foreign Minister seems to think?[37]

A. I wouldn't call it paranoia, no. We're trying to negotiate a settlement, and it is our firm conviction that for there to be a settlement, we have to be practical, we have to be realistic, we have to recognize that there is a certain political reality in the region; and we are seeking to address that reality.

It's not a question of American paranoia; it's a question of a longstanding situation that remains unresolved—on the one hand, the continued occupation of Namibia by South Africa and on the other hand, the continuing presence in Angola, 7 years after independence, of foreign forces.

We believe there is an historic opportunity to resolve these questions in parallel, recognizing that they are distinct issues to be handled in separate channels.

. . . .

Q. Could you give a characterization of the meetings that have been held in Luanda recently by Mr. Wisner and Mr. Walters? Can you say how things are going, or are you prevented from doing so?

A. We believe that there has been substantial progress toward the framework of an agreement on all the issues that remain; but we are some distance still from a final agreement, and we are going to "give it our best shot."

We have no evidence that anybody else has a different view or wishes to break things off or to claim that there has been any kind of breakdown or impasse. So I would say that as long as that is the case, as long as people are anxious, as we are, to continue the dialogue, we will continue to do so also.

Q. Have you detected a new, and from your standpoint, more depressing tone in the bilateral talks with Angola in the last week or two?

. . . .

A. I would not characterize the tone as having shifted sharply for the worse. I

---

[36] Source: Department of State files. The briefing was conducted at the U.N. Plaza Hotel on background by a senior Department of State official beginning at 3:30 p.m.

[37] Reference is to Angolan Foreign Minister Paulo Jorge's news conference at the United Nations on October 5, in which he said, "The American administration is suffering a kind of paranoia on this question of Cubans." See *New York Times*, October 6, 1982, p. A8, and *Washington Post*, October 6, 1982, p. A18.

would simply say that we are dealing with some very difficult issues. We have some distance to go, and we have not gotten to the degree of precision and specificity that would require to get an agreement. We do have considerable elements of agreement about a framework that would enable us to settle this problem.

Q. When you say you haven't received the specificity that is required, I take it you mean that you have been unable to get anywhere on a timetable for the withdrawal of Cuban troops?

A. I'm not going to go beyond what I've said. These are diplomatic discussions and will remain that way.

. . . .

Q. Do you have any comment on the contents of the letter as published in Zimbabwe today that the President wrote to the frontline states?

A. I haven't seen the press reports that you are referring to, sir, so I don't know what was published in the Zimbabwe press today, but we have had a number of communications at the very highest levels of our government with the highest levels of various African governments. This particular document that you refer to I'm not going to confirm or deny the existence of, or the validity of, but we do communicate at the highest levels, which simply signifies that this government, the U.S. Government, attaches the very greatest importance to these negotiations and engages in them at the highest level and will continue to do that. I think that is the key point. But there was no addressing of this issue or the contents of the letter at the luncheon that just took place.

Q. I know you have been reluctant all along to draw a direct link between Cuban troops there in Angola and the Namibian settlement, but could you say this: If you could resolve the issue of troops in Angola, do you think it would take you very long to finish the Namibian problem?

A. We've made really very considerable progress on the Namibian issues, skipping the Namibian issues that concern aspects of Resolution 435. Those which remain are manageable issues there. There are intellectually identifiable solutions to all of them, and I don't anticipate that any of them will be major hurdles as soon as we can make the necessary parallel progress that we will require now on the Angola question.

Q. So, in other words, the Cuban troops there remain the stumbling block to the Namibian settlement?

A. They remain an important issue, an important issue. There are other issues, obviously, as you know on the Namibia question which are not yet resolved, and we are working on them with every effort to push them to agreement—such things as the question of which electoral system will be chosen and what is the composition of the U.N. force and so on. Those discussions are between us.

Q. Some of the African participants in the discussions are saying there had been really fundamental commitment by the South Africans that Namibia should be free. Will you be able to secure this, or rather than saying so, the South Africans' possible intention to grant Namibia independence or to agree to the implementation of the plan?

A. You know, in a negotiation, I think it is pretty obvious in any negotiation that the parties which have the most at stake will be the ones playing their cards close to their chest. Any other pattern of behavior would be remarkable. We wouldn't expect South Africa to be any different in that respect.

I would say this: We feel the South African Government has been involved in this exercise in good faith, that it does wish to see a settlement of this question. It doesn't have anything to gain from the continued open-ended development of the war. It is costly in both treasury and in lives for all sides. We don't see any evidence that the South African Government wishes the Namibian conflict to continue in the future.

Their interest in the settlement is obviously based on the terms of that settlement, and they, like any party, will seek to get the best terms they can. So I don't think it's a blank check. No, it's not a "settlement at any price" any more than it is to SWAPO.

Q. There seems to be always this problem of the Americans being optimistic about a settlement in Namibia coming early and all the other parties keep saying that there is so much to be done yet. Would you be willing to, say, take any rough time estimates of how long you think this thing is going to go?

A. It's hard to do that. I'm not sure I'm all that eager to be laying down additional timetables. We have had some targets in the past: some of them have slipped; some of them have not. I think we have made remarkable progress in terms of speed on the Phase Two issues which involve the whole conflicts raised, the U.N. force which would go into place during the transition.

Basically, in the period May to August of this year, we have resolved virtually all of those questions which, if the parties wished to, could go on for years. So from that sense, we are very clear in our own analysis that there has been significant progress that has been made.

Clearly, when parties are entering into the final stages, the really tough patches of the negotiations, it is in their interest to indicate that, no, there still is a substantial distance and, no, we have major issues to resolve and so forth. That is [the] normal negotiations part of a bargaining approach. If I were the Angolans, the South Africans, or the Tanzanians, I'd say the same thing. But I don't think privately—and this is what I have underlined—I don't think privately that any of the key parties would deny the substantial progress that has been made and that includes the Angolan Government, it includes SWAPO, it includes the South Africans, and includes the chairman of the frontline states.

Q. Are you identified as a key player in all these negotiations, on the outstanding key issues remaining?

A. I think I more or less have. There are several Namibia issues—the choice of an electoral system to be used by the Constituent Assembly. There is agreement that that choice, first of all, will be made consistent with the terms of 435; second that it will be made within the context of either straight proportional representation or pure single-member districts and that that decision must be made at the appropriate time, and that that implies that whatever may be said publicly, that both SWAPO and the frontline, on the one hand, and South Africa, on the other hand, accept that that is the way it will be done.

Secondly, the issue of the composition of the U.N. force, both the military and civilian components thereof, there has been a lot of progress on that, but there are still some units of the U.N. force which have not been identified. Discussions continue on that issue.

Finally, there are some logistical planning details for the force which are still being worked out between the Secretariat of the United Nations and the South African authorities. That's on that side of the agenda. Then, there is the issue that we are seeking to get parallel progress on, which concerns an agreement on the issue of Cuban withdrawal from Angola.

In connection with that and with the Namibia plan, there has to be progress on—there is progress on the question of a cease-fire and the precise arrangements for a cease-fire. We are working on that issue as well, so I think that's basically—

Q. Is any date for a cease-fire being tossed about?

A. As soon as possible.

Q. Could you characterize what the differences might be on the question of the cease-fire and the arrangements involved in that?

A. I don't think it really ever serves a purpose for a mediator to try and characterize the differences in the public arena even on a background basis, but I would say this: the situation is considerably more complicated than it might have appeared to be at first. It's not simply a case of saying, "There shall be peace on Day X." There has to be a procedure that involves clearly understood commitments on all sides as to how forces will become disengaged, first of all; and secondly, in which areas they will become disengaged and what the definition of "cease-fire" really is.

We are dealing here with a situation in which there are forces of the Governments of both Angola and South Africa; there are guerrillas involved; there are foreign patrons of the government involved, at least in Angola; so it's not an easy matter. But we have actually discussed and achieved, I think, considerable progress on the framework for a cease-fire, some of the broad principles of a cease-fire, the mechanisms of a cease-fire. We are now to a few issues about the cease-fire which remain to be worked out.

Q. In answer to an earlier question, you said it wasn't paranoia, but political realism that governs your concern over Cuban troops. I wonder if you could expand on that a little, even though it may seem obvious. Did you not mean that it is political realism to expect that if South Africa is to agree to Namibian independence, South Africa will want in return the departure of Cuban troops?

A. We mean that there has to be something in it in political and security terms for everybody. That is precisely your point, I'm thinking, but it's not a one-sided deal. We don't see any great desire on the part of either Angolans or Africans for the indefinite continuation in Angola of the Cuban Expeditionary Force.

Q. Do you expect there to be something in the deal for the United States? And if so, how does that tie up with your own characterization of being a mediator?

A. The United States, I think, is really straightforward. We have an interest in a prosperous and relatively secure southern Africa. What we see today is a potentially prosperous southern Africa and a rather insecure environment there, in which there is cross-border activity in both directions, in which there is some degree of polarized conflict, some degree of international involvement in fueling these conflicts.

We would like to bring that whole spiral, that whole syndrome, as best we can under a greater measure of control. It is in our interest to see a more stable and more secure southern Africa for a variety of reasons, political, strategic, economic, and so on. So that's what we have to gain by it. I don't think it's a question that's more complicated than that.

Q. But you characterized, if I understood you right, your own role, at least the U.S. role, as that of a mediator, is that correct?

A. Yes, indeed—we and our partners of the Five. Absolutely.

Q. So you're participant mediators, right?

A. Most mediators have an interest in mediating or they wouldn't do it. In that sense, yes.

Q. Well, in industrial relations, mediators can get paid for cutting the middle, and they don't have an interest other than that.

A. Well, this is an active mediation, if you want to call it that. Sure, we have an interest in the success of our mediation.

Q. Yes. I'm not questioning that. But you have an interest in what the outcome should be, not just in getting an outcome.

A. I think that's fair to say, sure. I'd be surprised if it would be otherwise.

Q. I think the impression is that the United States is more interested in getting Cuban troops out of Angola than anybody else is.

A. I don't think it's a question of characterizing who is the most interested in the issue. We are interested in getting a settlement. We don't see that there is a whole lot of prospect of getting one if you can't get progress on that issue.

Q. Progress is good enough, though? I mean an understanding that there will be a future, as he was saying yesterday, if Angola and Cuba agree on a future—the beginning of a gradual reduction. Is that good enough?

A. I'm not going to define the terms of settlement here in this forum. We are talking about something which is sufficiently credible, sufficiently tangible that it provides a basis for everyone to go forward. That's what we are seeking.

I'm not going to comment on public speeches of Paulo Jorge any more than he would want to comment on mine.

Q. Oh, he will. (Laughter)

Q. What can you say about normalization of diplomatic relations between Angola and the United States in this process?

A. Simply that we have always felt from the beginning of this administration—and in that respect, although not in every respect, we are behaving in a manner fully consistent with our predecessors, going back to President Ford—that the issue we are talking about does have a bearing on our diplomatic relations or lack of them.

If settlement occurs, if there is a regional settlement, I would expect that we would see, in that context, movement toward the normalization of our relations with Angola. It is certainly something which we have the impression is desired by virtually everyone in the region and by our allies, and we have no reason not to want it ourselves.

Q. In the normalization issue, is there a linkage or parallelism? (Laughter)

A. We're talking about all these things being possible in the same context. It's as simple as that.

Q. Can you explain this? In 1978, during the Carter administration, the Cubans were in Angola. In fact, they have been there since 1975. At the Geneva Conference in January 1978,[38] this Cuban issue was never raised. It never has been until this administration came to power. How did the issue of the Cubans suddenly materialize? At what point did this administration realize

---

[38] Presumably, this is a reference to the Pre-Implementation Conference held in Geneva, January 7–14, 1981.

that the Cubans were a serious factor in your approach to the solution of the Namibian issue?

Toward the end of the Carter administration, it was likely that a settlement was "at the end of the tunnel." At least, the South Africans weren't even complaining (?) publicly or privately about it.

A. In 1978, there was a U.N. or Western plan on Namibia which became enshrined in terms of Security Council Resolution 435.

Q. —which is the basic document there.

A. —which is the basic document and on which we are proceeding. There were 3 years of negotiations on that basis which, in the final analysis, produced zero. They produced a framework, they produced an outline of a plan, they produced a lot of things; but they did not produce implementation; they did not produce independence for Namibia. That is what we are seeking, and it is on that that we must be judged in the final analysis.

There is no doubt but that this question has agonized us and others for many, many years. We have no incentive in continuing; we have no intention of just drawing it out for an indefinite future. We're trying to get an agreement of settlement as soon as possible.

So if you're asking at what point did we discover the truth (laughter), I think we discovered it pretty early on. There is nothing new about this. What countinues to amaze us is that when people throw questions at us saying, "Gee, we thought this Cuban issue had sort of faded into the distance, that it wasn't an important issue." It's been important in our view from day one of our effort, which goes back a year and a half ago. We have said so. We haven't changed our tune at all.

We're not seeking public recriminations about it in debate, but this has been our reality. When asked, we have said so.

Q. The election point—when one decides which election system to adopt, you said, at the appropriate time, is it Phase One or Phase Three now the South Africans are suggesting—in other words, do you decide after implementation or do you decide before implementation of the plan?

A. There is an intentional ambiguity here which I am not going to define with any greater precision. Let me put it this way: The way in which it will be resolved will be acceptable to both SWAPO and South Africa—the time frame of it.

Q. A year ago you said it was the hope of the Contact Group to have a settlement in Namibia by the end of this year. Can you redefine that time frame now?

A. I think if you look at the guidance and the statements that have been made, you will find we have said for some time now that we would envisage the prospect of implementation beginning in 1982. For those who don't follow it daily—and I admire those of you who don't—(laughter) "implementation" means the implementation of U.N. Resolution 435. That in itself will take months, so starting the process in 1982 will not produce independence until 1983. It remains our view that implementation can begin in 1982.

Document 567

Statement by the Alternate Representative at the United Nations (Luce) Before the U.N. General Assembly, October 21, 1982[39]

Explanation of the U.S. Vote on Draft Resolution A/37/L.5

First, Mr. President,[40] I should like to repeat what American representatives have said so often in this chamber. We strongly oppose the South African system of apartheid; it is against our principles, and deeply repugnant to our own political and social values. America's record of action, and not just words, against the apartheid system has been quite clear and consistent. We were, for example, the first major country to institute an arms embargo against South Africa. It is thus not that we question the motives of the resolution's sponsors which makes us oppose this resolution, but rather the manner of proceeding. The United States believes the demise of apartheid can best come from peaceful reform within South Africa itself, rather than from further

---

[39] Source: U.S. Mission to the United Nations Press Release USUN 91-(82), October 21, 1982; printed also in U.N. document A/37/PV.40. For the text of draft resolution A/37/L.5, which was later adopted by the U.N. General Assembly, see *infra*.

[40] Imre Hollai (Hungary).

assaults on South African actions in the international arena.

We are most disturbed that in attempting to oppose apartheid, a system which we all consider objectionable, some members of the United Nations have proposed a measure which would do grave injury to institutions which were established to serve all nations. In seeking improperly to influence the International Monetary Fund on a member country's request to draw on fund resources, this Assembly would contribute not to an easing of the system of apartheid, but to damaging international financial institutions. In this regard, many members of this Assembly are not even members of the IMF.

Worst of all, we see this resolution as a further assault on the fabric of international organizations themselves. No one in this hall can be ignorant of the attack made on the integrity of such previously non-politicized institutions as the International Atomic Energy Agency and the International Telecommunications Union over the recent weeks.[41] Here we can now add the International Monetary Fund to the list of those organizations under attack due to short-term political goals. It is most distressing that the international organizations which do the most good—which serve the people in a most beneficial and effective way—are those most under attack these days.

The draft resolution on IMF credits to South Africa is inappropriate in several particular ways. First, it mistakes the relationship between this assembly and the IMF as a specialized agency of the United Nations. The IMF has an elected board of member countries whose role it is to make the financial decisions. For this Assembly to interfere in that process would be a serious and crippling derogation of the functions of the IMF Board of Governors. Secondly, the draft resolution appears to proceed from the incorrect premise that drawing rights for IMF members are a privilege or a concession on the part of the organization. This, of course, is untrue. IMF members are entitled to drawing rights by virtue of their membership in accordance with established statutes and procedures.

The third and most important objection to the draft resolution is the application of political rather than economic criteria to the IMF decisionmaking which is the resolution's intent. The apolitical nature of the IMF is essential to its ability effectively to fulfill its important functions in the international monetary system and, consequently, its ability to serve the economic interests of the world community—just as the apolitical nature of the IAEA, ITU, UNESCO, etc., is essential for them to perform their noble functions.

Despite conflicts of a political, social, and even military nature that have arisen among IMF members over the years, IMF members have carefully respected the fact that it is an economic institution designed to pursue broad economic objectives shared by all members. Any introduction of political considerations into decisions on IMF financing could invite similar actions in other cases, ultimately undermining the credibility and effectiveness of the Fund.

It is well known to members of this body that, as articulated by President Reagan at the Cancun summit[42] and since that time in all discussions on global negotiations, the United States is vitally interested in the preservation of the jurisdiction, functions, powers, and integrity of the specialized agencies. This draft resolution is precisely the kind of inappropriate politicization of the specialized agencies which will do irreparable damage to the international economic system if such a process were allowed to continue or even to spread. Such a debasement of the IMF would continue and spread such a shortsighted course, much to the serious detriment if not permanent damage of all the specialized financial and other international organizations whose correct functioning is so vital to so many members of this Assembly. The United States has defended the integrity of these institutions and has supported them to a degree matched by no other country, a policy posited on their functioning on economic grounds. We will, as in the past, oppose any attempt to turn them into political agents and will determine our future policies toward them accordingly.

Finally, separate from the overriding issues of the independence and effectiveness of the specialized international organizations, my government is convinced that isolating and punishing the Government of South Africa, as this draft resolution seeks

[41] Reference is to the attempts made by Arab nations in September and October 1982 to expel Israel from these institutions. Also see documents 101 and 102.

[42] Regarding the Cancun summit, held in Cancun, Mexico, from October 22 to 24, 1981, see *American Foreign Policy: Current Documents, 1981*, Chapter 5, Part F.

to do, is not the way to effect the change that we all desire for the people of that country. We believe that constructive change is taking place and we are determined to continue to encourage South Africa to hold to a firm course in that direction. The draft resolution would have exactly the opposite effect, strengthening the hand of those in South Africa who argue that no matter what policies the South Africa Government pursues, the world will only criticize and continue to isolate and destroy it.

Because the means proposed by the resolution's sponsors can in no way be said to justify the presumed ends, my delegation is quite vigorously opposed to this resolution and will vote against it.

Document 568

Resolution 37/2 Adopted by the U.N. General Assembly, October 21, 1982[43]

The U.N. General Assembly Requests IMF Not to Issue Credits to South Africa

The General Assembly,

Having learned of the application by South Africa to the International Monetary Fund for a credit of one billion special drawing rights,

Recalling its resolutions on the policies of *apartheid* of the Government of South Africa, particularly its repeated requests to the International Monetary Fund for the termination of loans and credits to South Africa,[44] and its resolution 36/172 0 of 17 December 1981 on investments in South Africa,

1. *Again requests* the International Monetary Fund to refrain from granting any credits or other assistance to South Africa;

2. *Urges* States members of the International Monetary Fund to take appropriate action towards that end;

3. *Urges* the Security Council to consider the matter as soon as possible with a view to taking appropriate action;

4. *Requests* the Secretary-General to undertake urgent consultations with the International Monetary Fund and to report to the General Assembly as soon as possible on the implementation of the present resolution.

Document 569

Transcript of a Department of State Press Briefing, November 2, 1982 (Extracts)[45]

Recent Developments in Southern Africa

Senior State Department Official. Good afternoon. Just a brief opening comment or two: We have seen a good number of comments and reports which would suggest that the negotiations concerning a settlement in southern Africa in some sense have come to a close or are in some sense stalemated. It is for that reason, among others, that I thought it would be useful—it has been some time since we have had any real contact—that we have a backgrounder.

Such reports and such speculation are not accurate. There have been a number of important developments in the negotiations over the course of the past month: Ministerial contact up in New York among members of the Contact Group, at which action plans in pursuit of this negotiating effort were discussed and agreed; numerous contacts between members of the Contact Group and African frontline states—all the parties concerned.

I and my deputies have been in regular contact with our British and French counterparts in recent weeks. All the members of the Contact Group and others in the Western community of nations are eagerly following these negotiations or making contributions to the success of them.

In addition, work continues between the U.N. Secretariat in New York and all the parties, including the South African Gov-

---

[43] Source: U.N. General Assembly Resolution 37/2. The resolution was adopted by a vote of 121 to 3 (including the United States), with 23 abstentions.

[44] See General Assembly Resolution 36/172 D. [Footnote in the source text.]

[45] Source: Department of State files. The briefing was conducted on background by a senior Department of State official beginning at 3 p.m.

ernment with a view to resolving the remaining issues on Namibia itself, that is, issues connected directly with U.N. Resolution 435, the Electoral System and the Composition of the U.N. Force, UNTAG.

To mention yet another example, there was, of course, a meeting between Secretary Shultz and the Angolan Foreign Minister in early October.[46] We envisage during the coming month further intensive consultations and discussions amongst all the parties. The Vice President's trip to Africa,[47] for example, while it has much broader objectives, will undoubtedly and inevitably get into these questions, particularly during his meetings with his Nigerian, Zambian, and Zimbabwian counterparts, but virtually on all his stops because Namibia and Angola are of great interest to all the governments that will be visited on the Vice President's trip, November 10–23, I think the dates are.

We anticipate other direct contacts with various parties during the month of November. We have every reason to believe that our allies share our assessment of the situation in these negotiations and fully share our desire for success.

I would go further and say this is a complex negotiation—we knew that from the beginning. We are into some of the tougher issues now. We have always had objectives—these are longstanding objectives. We continue to pursue the course toward the realization of those objectives. We don't have any reason to conclude that that goal cannot be reached. We have no evidence from any party that there is a better way, and we have heard from no party any suggestion that we should stop doing what we're doing. The door has not been closed by anyone, and no one has said the negotiations have come to an end. So that is the way we look at the coming period.

The dialogue continues, particularly among the parties directly concerned on the Namibia issues; but also the bilateral dialogue that we are maintaining with the Angolan Government, both directly and indirectly, will continue.

I think with that general introduction, I might just take any questions that there might be on those negotiations or on other issues.

. . . .

Q. Having said that, what is the main hangup at this point? Is it the Cuban troops in Angola?

A. We have, as you know from previous announcements we've made, we have made very substantial progress on all the Namibia issues. Phase One is complete; Phase Two is virtually complete. We are going to need comparable movement on the issues we're discussing bilaterally with the Angolans, which center around the issue of Cuban troop withdrawal. This is a very complicated issue; it's a very grave and serious issue for all parties concerned. But we wouldn't be doing this, wouldn't be continuing this, if we didn't feel that progress was being made and that it was worth continuing.

Q. On the Cuban-Angola issue, is there any progress on that as well? In other words, perhaps progress certainly on the Namibia unilateral issue, but comparable progress—any measurable progress on Cuban withdrawal?

A. I think there is a very substantial measure of understanding that has developed in the course of these negotiations with the Angolans that have been going on now for some 12 months. If we had not made progress, we wouldn't be continuing—that's the point I'm trying to make.

I'm not going to go into the details of these negotiations beyond what I've said. But I think there is a growing measure of understanding of what must happen for us to get a settlement.

Q. What is puzzling—it doesn't seem to me to take a great extended period of time for the American objectives to be comprehended by the other party, that you want a Cuban withdrawal. What does "substantial understanding" mean by Angola?

A. It's one thing to have an understanding about what will be necessary; it's something else to actually bargain a settlement that involves very difficult issues for the parties to that settlement. We are talking here about changing the realities that have existed for 6 or 7 years in that country—and not our doing it, but their doing it, because they agree to it, as the sovereign government concerned.

. . . .

Q. Are you trying to get the withdrawal of all Cuban forces from Angola; some, or a change in their function?

A. We have said that we seek and we think it will be necessary to get parallel

[46] Secretary Shultz and Angolan Foreign Minister Jorge met at the United Nations on October 5.

[47] Regarding Vice President Bush's trip to Africa, see footnote 23 to document 548.

withdrawal in Phase III. The South Africans pulled out of Namibia, as you know, and we are seeking a commitment on Cuban withdrawal; that is, military forces, combat forces, during Phase III, from Angola.

That is the answer. The only answer I can give you at this point.

Q. Commitment or actual withdrawal?

A. There has to be a commitment before we go into Phase III, which would then be implemented in Phase III.

Q. Is that the only thing—the Cubans in Angola? If that were resolved, would you expect to get the question of impartiality and election procedures, is that taken that that would be easily solved or partly solved?

A. Other matters are important issues. I don't mean to downplay them, but I think, given the spirit that all parties have shown on the Namibia question so far, that we would expect that they would fall into place.

Q. Is there a second track going between Washington and Havana on Cuban withdrawal?

A. These negotiations, from the beginning we have assumed, should be conducted with the parties who are directly concerned on the ground in southern Africa, and that's where we are seeking to negotiate them.

So I think that's the best answer I can give you. We are not negotiating Cuban withdrawal with Havana.

The Angolan Government has made it known that this is a matter that they would have to discuss with the government in Havana, that's fine.

. . . .

Q. Why is it so important that we get an arrangement for a withdrawal of Cuban troops from Angola as part of an overall settlement?

A. I think there are two answers to your question; there are two parts to the answer.

We saw during the period 1977 to 1980 a lengthy, drawn-out negotiating process under the leadership of the Western Contact Group focused on U.N. Resolution 435. That effort was extensive, exhaustive for all concerned and did not produce a successful result.

One of the reasons we believe it did not is because it attempted to isolate Namibia as though Namibia existed in a vacuum, and it did not address the broader regional questions and the broader regional environment in which Namibia lives now and will live presumably after independence.

We feel that was a critically missing ingredient just from the standpoint of common sense and of security of all parties. In addition, we felt it was unlikely—whatever may have been said—that the South African Government would find it in its interest to proceed to a settlement, if that settlement would be tantamount to political suicide domestically.

There's got to be something in a settlement for everybody if there's going to be a settlement. That's the bottom line.

Another aspect here, which I think is appropriate for me to mention, there has been a distorting element in the equation in southern Africa since 1975. Previous to that time, in much of the Third World and in Africa, specifically, there had been a fabric of mutual restraint as between the superpowers in terms of the projection of their own military forces in that area.

It is precisely that fabric of restraint which we would like to restore, not only in southern Africa but everywhere else in the world. So it's completely consistent with our broader global objectives.

. . . .

Q. Isn't there intense danger to the Luanda regime if the Cubans actually withdraw?

A. In taking the difficult decisions that are involved in this settlement, difficult for South Africa, difficult for Namibians who live in Namibia, difficult for Angolans who live in Angola, there are difficult decisions on all sides.

We don't downplay for a minute the difficulty of this decision the MPLA Government in Luanda faces.

As I said at the outset, nobody ever believed it would be easy, but we do believe it can be done and we do believe that the many problems that beset Angola today are being and can be addressed through the proposals that we have put forward. We are not asking any of the parties to walk over the edge of a cliff. We are not asking them to take a whole series of irreversible steps all up front. We are not unreasonable people, in other words.

If I could just say a word again about Phase III, which is a concept whose substance may elude some. It is an extensive period of time. There is an almost infinite variety of possibilities for arranging parallel withdrawal in Phase III. If there is a desire to settle, there is the possibility of a compromise on this issue.

Phase III, as I said, could last for months. There is a chance for each side to examine and look at the good faith and the performance of the other side. We are not asking anyone to take it on faith and to just exist without any resources of its own.

. . . .

Q. Could I just follow that up briefly? There has been some talk of the possibility of a black African force, or a Lusophone force or even with possible French participation as possibly replacing over a period the Cuban troops in Angola.

Can you enlighten us at all about those reports?

A. There have been a lot of trial balloons. We are conducting this negotiation in the first instance with the Government of Angola. Were that government to express interest in a substitute force of that kind or some other kind that involved nonaligned forces, for example, that's for them to put forward. We would certainly look at it.

. . . .

Q. I just want to ask, what happens next? Do you have a month of these bilateral negotiations, followed by what? Group negotiations? Can you kind of take it beyond a month?

A. We're seeking, obviously, to make further progress in terms of our own discussions with the Angolans about the Cuban withdrawal issue. There are other issues on the Namibia track which we're still pursuing and will continue to pursue.

As you know, it has never been our position that Angola and Cuban troop withdrawal are part of the U.N. plan—they're not. They're not part of the mandate of the Five. The Five has the mandate—the Western Five—of looking at the Namibia question and trying to resolve it in the context of 435, which we're doing.

But it is we, the United States, who are primarily involved in the discussion with the Angolans as a bilateral discussion on Cuban troop withdrawal.

Q. Is it unfair to say that there is a stalemate on the issue of Cuban withdrawal?

A. Yes, absolutely I think it's unfair. I think it's grossly inaccurate. We have a continuing discussion underway. Negotiations are continuing as we sit here. We pass messages to them. They pass messages to us directly and indirectly. They have raised questions. We're trying to answer those questions. It is a live negotiation. They have not asked us to go home. They have not told us they can't negotiate the issue. I mean, that's why I'm here, in part, is to try and get the point across that the discussions and the negotiations do continue.

The fact that there are difficult issues in the negotiations should not be a secret to anyone.

. . . .

Q. The Canadians and the French have both kind of expressed some reservations about the current track. I think Cheysson probably more explicitly than the Canadians. Can you address their concerns about it, or do you deny that there are any problems?

A. I would say that it is one thing to have a position on the historical legitimacy of relating Angola to Namibia. It is something else to make a judgment as to the prospects and the political realities of the negotiation. The French have stated a certain position during their recent travels in Africa. I don't believe they speak for anyone else in the Five when they said what they did, but it is the common assessment of all five at the highest levels that as a matter of political reality, if we're to get a Namibia settlement, we're going to need this parallel movement that we have been seeking.

I don't think any of the governments in the Five would argue with that proposition.

. . . .

Document 570

Statement Issued by the Department of State, November 3, 1982[48]

IMF Loan for South Africa

Considerable interest has been focussed on the U.S. position with respect to South Africa's request to draw on IMF resources in conjunction with a Fund-approved stabilization program. We wish to make clear that today's IMF Executive Board decision on the South African request[49] should be based solely on the economic merits of the program. The Fund is a financial institution, the effectiveness of which would be undermined if political factors entered into its judgments.

The United States has, in the appropriate political forums, forcefully expressed its abhorrence of apartheid and of violence from whatever quarter in southern Africa. The U.S. position on the South African drawing indicates no change in our opposition to apartheid nor in our opposition to the use of force to resolve political differences in the region.

Document 571

Transcript of a Press Briefing by Vice President Bush, November 9, 1982 (Extracts)[50]

The U.S. Role in the Namibia Negotiations

. . . .

THE VICE PRESIDENT. . . . The Contact Group is alive and well and united. The Contact Group Ministers met in early October in New York,[51] reestablished that commitment to seek a settlement in Namibia. The group understands our view that without an agreement on Cuban troop withdrawal from Angola, a settlement is much more difficult. There would be no settlement. And while there are problems remaining, I think it's fair to cite some progress over the past 18 months. For example, all parties are engaged in a new initiative for peace. And some might think, "Well, that's not much of an accomplishment," but when you see the complexities involved with these many countries, it is. We worked through almost all the Namibia agenda with the South Africans—SWAPO and with the frontline Africans and the United Nations. Those issues which disrupted the peace process during the last administration have been resolved and we've opened a dialogue with Angola on matters that are of great sensitivity to them and on their future. And we're discussing, as I mentioned, the Cuban troop withdrawal—a fact that, to most observers, seemed quite unlikely a year or so ago.

So, we are committed to being a catalyst for peace in the area. We know that we can't dictate a peace and we know that it's got to be an effort of many, many parties. But we are committed. And one of the things that I am determined to convey to the African leaders is the depth of our commitment. With no further adieu, I'll be glad to respond to any questions.

Q. Instead of an easy one, let me ask you if you think there can be a solution giving Namibia independence without the withdrawal of Cuban troops from Angola or are the two inextricably linked?

THE VICE PRESIDENT. It seems unlikely at this point that there would be such a solution. The main thing is to get that separation of South Africa, pull back, and I would say that it would be highly unlikely that there would be a solution without a satisfactory resolution to the Cuban troop question.

Q. What are the chances for the Cubans withdrawing?

THE VICE PRESIDENT. I probably ought to defer to Secretary Crocker because he's been so intimately involved. But as I said in my statement, all countries are talking, and I guess I should say that I think there's a good shot at that. These negotiations seem

---

48 Source: Office of Press Relations, Department of State; posted statement. The statement was posted earlier that day before the Department of State Daily Press Briefing beginning at 12:10 p.m., and was referred to in the briefing.

49 Reference is to $1 billion of the IMF sources which the Executive Board of the IMF agreed the South African Government could draw upon. See *IMF Survey*, November 15, 1982, p. 362.

50 Source: White House Press Release, November 9, 1982, Office of the Press Secretary to the President. Chester Crocker, Assistant Secretary of State for African Affairs, also participated in the briefing, which took place in the Treaty Room of the Old Executive Office Building, beginning at 4:06 p.m.

51 See document 565.

to go and then stop and go and stop and all of that, but I'd say that we are determined to keep pressing forward. And we wouldn't be doing it if we thought it was futile.

. . . .

Q. A number of African countries think the hang-up on Namibia is not the Cuban troops in Angola—it is South African imperialism into Angola.

THE VICE PRESIDENT. Well, I think that anything that—

Q. —troops that are coming in. Why not go to South Africa and tell them what is causing this problem?

THE VICE PRESIDENT. Well, our agenda's set. The South African Foreign Minister is coming here, and I think there will be some of that. But, I think, clearly if the formula that we're suggesting with, I'm sure there'll be variations before everything is finally done result in a separation so that Angola will not have that concern anymore. We will have proved to have an extraordinarily useful role in Africa, and that's what we want to do. We don't want to dictate. We want to—we're not there to try to impose settlements, but you, yourself, point to a major reason for wanting to see the approach that Mr. Crocker and others are following be successful. Yes, a couple more.

Q. Mr. Crocker, Zimbabwe settled, assuming, which is a big assumption because you've been at it for years. Namibia settled. What do you suppose will be the next big political pressure point? Or will there be one? Will that take care of things or will dissolution of South Africa perhaps be the next point? What do you expect next on the horizon?

MR. CROCKER. The immediate question that we're going to be looking at, both now and after a settlement, is to try to strengthen and build a greater security and stability in southern Africa. I think there is a misleading tendency on occasion to assume that after Namibia, then the next question is "a solution" in South Africa. That's going to be a long-term proposition. It's going to involve incremental movement, rather than a sudden solution. And, in any event, the immediate question is to try and restore and build security in a region that is, that has far too little of it—not just Namibia and Angola but throughout.

. . . .

Document 572

Statement by the Alternate Representative at the United Nations (Luce) Before the U.N. General Assembly, November 12, 1982 (Extract)[52]

The United States Opposes Isolation of South Africa

. . . .

Mr. Chairman, we have listened with interest to the statements of other delegations. We were moved by the words of our good friend and colleague, the distinguished representative of Nigeria,[53] who is Chairman of the Special Committee against Apartheid. We understand his intensely felt abhorrence of the system of apartheid and his commitment to bringing about its elimination. However, we cannot endorse his belief that South Africa's increasing isolation—political, economic, and cultural—will bring about the kind of constructive change we so urgently and vigorously seek.

In our judgment, such a course is not a prescription for change but a blueprint for disaster, a course whose human consequences would be felt not only in South Africa itself, but throughout the region. To pursue such a course would constitute an admission of defeat. It would deny hope to those in South Africa—black and white alike—who seek a peaceful way out of the nightmare of apartheid. It would condemn those whose lives we seek to improve to an unending and deepening cycle of violence and repression—a cycle of violence that would have grave consequences not only for South Africa, but for the region as a whole. It would create conditions that would make anything but a violent cataclysm impossible. Surely, this is not what the Ambassador of Nigeria intends; but it is, I fear, the logical consequence of the approach he has advocated.

---

[52] Source: U.S. Mission to the United Nations Press Release USUN 123-(82), November 12, 1982; printed also in U.N. document A/37/PV.66.

[53] Reference is to Nigerian Representative Yusuf Maitama-Sule's remarks on November 9, 1982. For text, see U.N. document A/37/PV.59.

We do not pretend that the actions we have taken or may undertake in the future will, in and of themselves, bring about full democracy in South Africa. Ultimately, the future of that country will be decided by the people of South Africa themselves. But those in South Africa who work for peaceful change need and deserve our understanding, our encouragement, and our support.

South Africans do not need to be told that the status quo is deplorable and untenable. They do not need to be told that the black population, which, it is anticipated, will double to nearly 40 million by the end of the century, will not forever endure that suffocation of its aspirations. They do not need to be told that repression at home and intimidation directed against South Africa's neighbors are no substitute for a successful effort to address South Africa's own internal problems and policies. White South Africans need no reminder that their future, and that of their children, can only be secured if they in turn are willing to accommodate the interests and aspirations of South Africa's blacks. South Africans need not be reminded that change is needed, dramatic, constructive, peaceful change. These are self-evident truths.

These self-evident truths, moreover, are present today in South Africa's perception of itself. The South African Government has announced proposals for replacing the present whites-only Parliament with a tricameral legislature, in which South Africans of Asian and mixed descent would for the first time be accorded a degree of political representation.[54] We cannot celebrate a proposal that perpetuates a racial approach to political enfranchisement, and continues to exclude the 72 percent black majority from national political life. It is nonetheless significant that these proposals reflect increasing awareness within South Africa of the need to move toward a broader sharing of power. There are other indications that a process of change has begun. How rapidly this evolution will occur cannot now be foreseen. But it is underway.

For its part, the United States is committed to supporting, by deed as well as word, a process of peaceful change away from apartheid. So long as there are people in South Africa, black and white, making a sincere and determined effort to create a system based on liberty, equality, and democracy, they will have our full encouragement and support.

We will not be party to policies that can only encourage a deepening cycle of violence and repression. We will not support policies that substitute one repressive system for another. Possibilities for peaceful change exist in South Africa. Indeed, peaceful change is underway. The opportunity still exists for reason and democratic will to prevail. We can and must make every effort to preserve for the people of South Africa—black and white—an alternative to violent confrontation on the one hand and hopeless paralysis on the other. We hope others will join us in these efforts.

Thank you, Mr. President.

Document 573

Statement Issued by the Department of State, November 16, 1982[55]

Angola Releases Three Americans in a Prisoner Exchange

We have received confirmation that a prisoner exchange has been completed today in Lusaka, Zambia, resulting in the release of the three Americans who have been held by the Angolan Government. The exchange was carried out by the International Committee of the Red Cross (ICRC) with the cooperation of South Africa, the Soviet Union, Zambia, the MPLA government of Angola, the National Union for the Total Independence of Angola (UNITA), the South African Red Cross, and the United States. The United States has been working since August 1981 to accomplish the release of the three Americans through a prisoner exchange. The complex exchange involved the release of two Soviet military personnel held by UNITA in UNITA-controlled territory in Angola; the release of the three Americans held by the Popular Movement for the Liberation of Angola (MPLA) in Luanda; and the release of a Soviet prisoner, a number of Angolan soldiers, and one Cuban held by South Africa; and the release of remains of soldiers killed in combat held by various parties. The Zambian Government cooperated in providing the venue for the exchange in Lusaka. The exchange was able to take

---

[54] South African Prime Minister Botha announced the proposals on July 30, 1982.

[55] Source: Department of State files.

place only through cooperation of all the parties involved; we are grateful to all of them. We are especially grateful to the ICRC which has acted as the intermediary and has worked with the parties to overcome innumerable obstacles. The exchange can be seen in a sense as a microcosm of the overall southern Africa negotiating effort and is an example to the parties of what can be accomplished by working together.

The families of the Americans have been notified of their release. The Americans are currently enroute to the United States to join their families. Their names are Gary Acker, Geoffrey Tyler, and Gustavo Grillo.

The administration had made obtaining the release of those Americans a priority concern. Assistant Secretary of State for African Affairs Chester A. Crocker had repeatedly raised this matter with the Angolan Government, making clear that the prisoner cases were an element in the continuing Angola–U.S. dialogue. Visits to Luanda as part of the negotiating effort included visits by a U.S. official to the prisoners to underscore our concern about them. We are, of course, pleased that the Luanda authorities have released the Americans they held and regard this as a gesture of good faith on their part. We are also pleased that UNITA from the outset of the discussions on the exchange cooperated in working out the complex arrangements which involved the transportation of the two Soviets[56] out of UNITA-controlled territory in Angola.

While the Italian Government was not involved in the exchange, we want to express our appreciation to the Italian Government for the very helpful assistance it has provided to us over the past year and previously in dealing with the cases of the American prisoners and on other consular-related matters.

---

[56] Mollaeb Kolya and Ivan Chernietsky.

Document 574

Transcript of a Press Conference by Vice President Bush, Nairobi, November 21, 1982 (Extracts)[57]

Condemnation of Apartheid but Support for Dialogue With South Africa

. . . .

Q. Mr. Vice President, none of the other Western countries in the Contact Group have publicly been in support of linkage. In fact one of them, France, has publicly attacked it. During your trip, a number of African leaders and newspapers also strongly criticized the proposed linkage. Last night we read that President Moi himself has taken strong issue. When you return to Washington will [*do*] you think what you have heard on this trip regarding linkage will have some impact on American policy in this regard and, if so, how?

THE VICE PRESIDENT. Well, of course, it will have an impact, in the sense that part of my trip has been factfinding, to find the depths of the sentiments by others. This idea that we have in which we are being supported by the Contact Group and others—and I recognize that there are some public expressions of concern—seems to be the only specific idea for how you actually accomplish an end that everybody wants. So I am not going to go into the details of all the conversations I have had with these great leaders in Africa but, yes, there is some concern about linkage. But I would also make this prediction: that if this proves to be successful there will be a great deal of saying thank heavens that the United States was able to be a catalyst. I think what the African leaders are saying; Namibian independence is an important thing and it shouldn't be contingent on something else. We are for 435, we have said so, there is nothing in our support for 435 that talks about Cuban troops. We see this as a way to accomplish the fulfillment of an independent Namibia, an Angola free of foreign

[57] Source: Press Release, November 21, 1982, Office of the Press Secretary to the Vice President. The press conference was held at Nairobi Airport prior to Bush's departure.

force and a separation between South African forces and Angola and if this can be accomplished I expect a lot of people will say well, that was well done, United States. That's our position and we are going to stay with it and we respect those who point out to us the differences. If we are successful in being a catalyst I doubt that there will be much criticism of the United States because, long range, the objectives are the same. What people don't want to do is feel that Namibian independence has to be tied to something else and we understand that. Your point about taking that back, I will take that back and make that point very clear to those in the United States who may not understand it. I think our President understands that; I believe our Secretary of State does.

Q. Have you considered, mentioned, or discussed the possibility of replacing Cuban Forces in Angola with an OAU peacekeeping force?

THE VICE PRESIDENT. Without going into detail, part of any solution would clearly have to be the security of Angola itselt. The answer to your question would be no, I have not. I can give you a definitive answer on that. I have not, but there are a lot of discussions going on with our top experts in the State Department doing the discussing in terms of security for all countries in a post settlement southern Africa.

. . . .

Q. Would the replacement of Cuban Forces by OAU peacekeeping troops be acceptable to the United States?

THE VICE PRESIDENT. I cannot answer that question. I think less [?] what is acceptable to the United States in this context is what is acceptable to the parties that are involved that is the point that is being talked about now, and that's why your question is a little ahead of where the action is. But we think that there has to be a secure Angola. We think that there has to be a Namibian accordance with the United States, and so what specific arrangements are resolved will have to be resolved in consultation with the parties involved once agreement is reached, and that's a little ahead of where we are.

. . . .

Q. As well as criticizing linkage between Cuban troops and Namibia, frontline leaders have also stated that they're critical of U.S. policy of "contructive engagement" with South Africa. What can you say are the positive effects that the U.S. policy has brought?

THE VICE PRESIDENT. Well, if you take a look inside of Africa, I think you're seeing much more fairness in employment as a result of the requirements that we place in terms of our doing business there, things of that nature. But the other thing I'd say is that we have not felt that sanctions have been particularly effective where used. We felt that sanctions are things that hurt others; others than are intended to hurt and so we also think that discussion is very, very important. Dialogue is important, and I have not heard anyone suggesting that we not continue that latter approach of dialogue and discussion in trying to put pressure. You know, there has been some feeling that I picked up, not in this country so much, that if the United States, because of our size, and perhaps power, people say if you snap your fingers, some other sovereign country is going to do something different. My experience has been that it doesn't work that way. Life isn't that way. It's just regrettably not that simple. We are opposed to apartheid; we think it's wrong, morally wrong, wrong every other way. Now then you get to the question: What do you do about it? How do you effect change? Honest people can differ on how you bring independence to Namibia and freedom so we get some argument along the lines that you mention but not so much because I think people recognize that perhaps we are in a quasi-unique position to be helpful in this constructive change.

Q. The feeling is that it is not only dialogue that South Africa is engaging with the United States but it is a friendship, and it is this friendship between the United States and South Africa that is helping apartheid.

THE VICE PRESIDENT. Well, I would argue the second point whether friendship helps apartheid. We have good relations with countries that we diametrically differ with on a lot of things so I won't start clicking them off, but it won't take a great deal of imagination here for you to name them yourselves. We believe that dialogue is very, very important, and we're going to continue to have a dialogue. The dialogue—if there's a feeling here and I'm glad you raised this question—the dialogue means approval of the status quo or if dialogue means approval—in this instance we're talking about apartheid or a society that says to an entire race you're inferior—dialogue should not be construed to mean that. Believe me, the United States is publicly and specifically committed in opposition to apartheid and we are in favor of constructive change and we will work for constructive change but I think that the worse thing that could happen, or a bad thing, put it this way, would be for the United States to withdraw or pull right back across the Atlantic Ocean and live comfortably with a nice economy and live "comfy" inside ourselves. We don't see that as a moral role, whether it be in trying to effect change in Namibia or whether it be trying to work for fair play and equity in South Africa. And so I'm one who survived 2 years as Ambassador to the United Nations and there I got used to an awful lot of rhetoric, and my answer to the—what's the word?—rhetoricians—those who put out a lot of rhetoric—is what would you do? How would you solve it? Now we're embarked on a couple of approaches and we've told our friends and we're not expecting unilateral agreement—but if we can be successful, I expect people will say, "Well done, United States of America." But whether we're successful or not, the point that I've been able to make, because of this kind of visit, a frank exchange we've had with the Vice President and with the President, is that our intentions are honorable intentions. We are working for peace; we are working for equity and we're going to continue to do that. We may not always be right and we can darn sure pick up some good suggestions as to how we can be more effective, but that's what good diplomacy is about and that's been the big benefit of this trip, an ability to take the gloves off and sit down across from each other and discuss it eyeball to eyeball, total frankness, no holding back because of diplomatic niceties. We keep doing that, we're going to solve a lot of problems around here. It's been in that spirit that I have been received by the leaders of Kenya. Thank you all very much.

Document 575

Statement by the Alternate Representative at the United Nations (Luce) Before the U.N. General Assembly, November 23, 1982[58]

Explanation of U.S. Votes on Draft Resolutions A/37/L.32 and A/37/625 (Final Resolutions, Respectively, 37/35 and 37/32)

Mr. President, the United States is vitally interested in the question of Namibia and the future of the southern African region. Specifically, we are determined that South Africa's occupation of Namibia must end, and that Namibia must be brought to internationally recognized independence under the terms of Resolution 435, both quickly and peacefully. Together with other members of the Western Contract Group and the frontline states, we have been working very hard to achieve this objective. While an extensive discussion of these efforts and the progress which has been made is best reserved for the agenda item on Namibia, since these resolutions deal principally with Namibia, it is important to register here our conviction that progress has been made toward Namibian independence, and that with the continued cooperation of the parties concerned, a successful conclusion to these ongoing negotations can be achieved.

My government's objections to these resolutions, therefore, do not reflect any lack of support for Namibian independence. Rather, our problems with them center on how and under what conditions this independence can be achieved. In fact, we believe that many of the prescriptions contained in these resolutions, along with their rhetorical excesses, will not be helpful in bringing Namibia to independence nor in encouraging the changes we all agree must take place within South Africa.

The United States will vote against draft resolution A/37/L.32. We are compelled to do so, much against our natural inclinations, by the grave deficiencies of the resolution itself. The recommendations con-

---

[58] Source: U.S. Mission to the United Nations Press Release USUN 145-(82), November 24, 1982.

tained in this resolution do not in any way materially advance the progress of decolonization. We are disturbed by operative paragraph 4 of this resolution, which recognizes the legitimacy of peoples under "colonial domination" to exercise their right to self-determination by "all the necessary means at their disposal."[59] Such a statement, it seems to us, comes perilously close to providing blanket endorsement for random and indiscriminate murder, hijacking, or the killing of diplomats. These and other such crimes are always wrong, however just the cause, however grave the provocation. Our common humanity demands that certain minimal forms of conduct be obeyed by all parties at all times.

My delegation also objects to operative paragraph 7 of this resolution, and the parallel resolution, which suggests that foreign economic or other interests in the non-self-governing territories are somehow, by their very nature, detrimental either to the interests of Namibians or to the people of other non-self-governing territories.[60] The United States categorically rejects this suggestion. My government's opposition to the recommendations contained in operative paragraph 10[61] are all well-known. The United States does not believe that the presence of military bases on non-self-governing territories necessarily interferes with the full exercise of the right to self-determination. A call for the immediate and unconditional withdrawal of all military installations from non-self-governing territories is therefore unwarranted.

Mr. President, with regard to the resolution contained in document A/37/625,[62] our first and most fundamental objection is to the continued recognition of SWAPO as the sole representative of the Namibian people and the call for U.N. agencies to provide aid to SWAPO. The people of Namibia have not yet had the opportunity to choose a representative in free and fair elections, so as yet there is no authentic representative of the Namibian people. Moreover, my government believes it is wholly inappropriate for U.N. agencies to provide aid to national liberation movements, particularly those engaged in warfare or other forms of violence, since this serves to politicize these agencies, to undermine their effectiveness, and, as we have warned in the past, to jeopardize support for them. In this connection, the United States Congress has passed legislation which specifically forbids funds provided for international organizations and programs from being made available for the United States proportionate share of any program for SWAPO.[63]

The United States has played a major role in providing assistance to the Namibian people, particularly to those who have been displaced by the conflict. For example, of the $57 million worth of assistance the World Food Program has given to Southern African refugees through 1981, the United States has provided approximately $16 million. Moreover, the United States has provided approximately one third of all the extensive aid to Namibians and other displaced persons in Southern Africa by the U.N. High Commissioner for Refugees, 18 percent of U.N. Development Program aid, 25 percent of World Health Organization aid, etc. To the extent possible, consistent with the legislation I have just mentioned and the resources available, we hope to continue our assistance to the Namibian people. However, it will henceforth be incumbent on my government, before making its voluntary contributions to U.N. agencies, to deduct its share of money for programs for SWAPO per se, though not—as

---

[59] Paragraph 4 of draft resolution A/37/L.32 was adopted without change in U.N. General Assembly Resolution 37/35. The paragraph reads as follows:

"*Affirms once again* its recognition of the legitimacy of the struggle of the peoples under colonial and alien domination to exercise their right to self-determination and independence by all the necessary means at their disposal."

[60] Paragraph 7 of draft resolution A/37/L.32 was adopted without change in U.N. General Assembly Resolution 37/35. The paragraph reads as follows:

"*Condemns* the continuing activities of foreign economic and other interests which are impeding the implementation of the Declaration with respect to colonial Territories, particularly Namibia."

[61] Paragraph 10 of draft resolution A/37/L.32 was adopted without change in U.N. General Assembly Resolution 37/35. It reads as follows:

"*Calls upon* the colonial Powers to withdraw immediately and unconditionally their military bases and installations from colonial Territories and to refrain from establishing new ones."

The final version, U.N. General Assembly Resolution 37/35, which incorporated the language of paragraphs 4, 7, and 10 without change, was adopted on November 23 by a vote of 141 to 2 (including the United States), with 8 abstentions.

[62] U.N. General Assembly Resolution 37/32 (draft resolution A/37/625) was adopted on November 23 by a vote of 128 to 4 (including the United States), with 20 abstentions.

[63] Reference may be to pending legislation, which became section 154 of P.L. 97–377, Continuing Appropriations for Fiscal Year 1983, approved on December 21, 1982. For the text of this section, see 96 Stat. 1919.

we have seen—for Namibians of any political persuasion.

Futhermore, we object to the resolution's call for Namibian membership in specialized agencies and international organizations. Membership in such bodies for non-self-governing territories is not only impractical, it also tends to politicize these organizations and hinder their efforts to achieve their proper technical and humanitarian objectives.

Finally, Mr. President, in the seventh preambular paragraph of this resolution, the United States and other Western countries are accused of "efforts to deprive the Namibian people of their hardwon victories in the liberation struggle."[64]

This is an irresponsible accusation, totally contrary to the facts of the situation. It is well known, for example, that after more than a decade of no progress whatsoever toward Namibian independence, it was the United States in 1976 which helped bring the Namibian question, along with other southern African issues, to the forefront of international diplomatic activity. After the initial efforts of the United States and its Western Contact Group partners to negotiate independence for Namibia encountered obstacles—obstacles not of our making—we relaunched Namibian negotiations with redoubled vigor. In fact, this has been one of the very highest priority diplomatic initiatives of this U.S. administration. From the President on down, we have invested an enormous amount of time, energy, and political capital in trying to achieve peaceful independence for Namibia under the terms of Resolution 435. Our officials at all levels have held innumerable consultations and negotiating sessions here, in Windhoek, in frontline and other African capitals, in Pretoria, and in European capitals. We have taken political risks and put our prestige on the line. Just this past week, our Vice President visited seven African countries, and Namibian independence was at the top of his agenda.

In short, we are working hard for a peaceful transition to internationally recognized independence for Namibia. Moreover, these efforts have made real progress and they hold considerable promise. To be accused of working against Namibian independence is a great disappointment.

Therefore, we have asked for a separate vote on this paragraph; and we hope that those who are determined, along with us, to continue the arduous search for negotiated independence for Namibia, will join us in voting against it.[65]

For all these reasons, Mr. President, my delegation will vote against the resolution. We will by no means, however, abandon our continuing efforts to bring independence to Namibia and to provide assistance to the Namibian people.

[64] Preambular paragraph 7 of draft resolution A/37/625 reads as follows:

"*Aware* that the struggle of the people of Namibia is in its most crucial stage 0 and has sharply intensified as a consequence of the stepped-up aggression of the illegal colonialist regime of Pretoria against the people of the Territory and the increased general support rendered to that regime by the United States of America and other Western States, coupled with efforts to deprive the Namibian people of their hard-won victories in the liberation struggle, and that it is therefore incumbent upon the entire international community decisively to intensify concerted action in support of the people of Namibia and their sole representative, the South West Africa People's Organization, for the attainment of their goal."

Document 576

Remarks by the Assistant Secretary of State for African Affairs (Crocker) and the South African Foreign Minister (Botha), November 26, 1982[66]

Botha's Discussions With Department of State Officials

Assistant Secretary Crocker. Ladies and gentlemen of the press, it is my honor to introduce the Foreign Minister of South Africa, the honorable Pik Botha. We do not have a press statement, and this is not a press conference, but I think he might be prepared to take a few questions. Mr. Minister.

Foreign Minister Botha. Thank you, Dr. Crocker. If there are a few questions, I'm available to endeavor to reply to them.

[65] Preambular paragraph 7 was adopted without change in the final version, U.N. General Assembly Resolution 37/32, on November 23 by a vote of 87 to 26 (including the United States), with 27 abstentions. Regarding this debate and vote, see U.N. document A/37/PV.77.

[66] Source: Department of State files. The remarks were made at the Diplomatic Entrance of the Department of State upon Foreign Minister Botha's departure.

Q. Do you have a plan for breaking the impasse with Angola over the Cuban troop issue, Mr. Minister?

FOREIGN MINISTER. I'm not aware of an impasse.

Q. How would you describe the situation?

FOREIGN MINISTER. Where?

Q. In the Namibian negotiations?

FOREIGN MINISTER. Promising, promising. I think that the American Government has a real chance—an opportunity—an internationally acceptable solution.

Q. Is a multinational peacekeeping force to replace the Cubans acceptable to South Africa as a parallel (inaudible) in the Mideast settlement at all?

FOREIGN MINISTER. I cannot give a final answer to that today. That would depend to a very large measure on the composition of such a force, but in general our understanding is, in order to lower the tensions in that part of the world that the Cuban troop withdrawal would not be substituted by any foreign forces.

Q. Does the suggestion of a foreign—multinational force—you don't see as a necessarily positive step in getting the impasse broken?

FOREIGN MINISTER. That suggestion—that proposal has not been made to me by any party.

Q.–The American Government hasn't made it to you or any other officials in South Africa?

FOREIGN MINISTER. Not thus far.

Q. What are the problems, sir, in resolving the Namibian question?

FOREIGN MINISTER. The major problem is the lack of trust, the lack of trust on the part of the Angolan Government. And they are of the opinion that the South African forces and Southwest African forces constitute a severe threat to them. The anti-SWAPO leaders inside the territory feel that the Cuban presence is not conducive and will not make a free and fair election possible. And all the moves that we are discussing, there is this problem of overcoming. There is distrust in the motives of each other. Of course, from our point of view, we do not see the necessity of foreign troops in our region at all. But quite apart from the effect which the Cuban presence would have on a free and fair election in the territory and the tension that has been generated by their presence, we feel that foreign troops are not welcome in our region—in any of the countries of southern Africa. And the South Africa Government would not be able to tolerate it—the presence of foreign troops.

Q. That includes a peacekeeping force or a multinational force, is that what you mean by that?

FOREIGN MINISTER. We are of the opinion that it is not necessary to have a peacekeeping force because we have offered nonaggressive pacts and agreements to all our neighbors—to all our neighbors.

Q. But that would include the U.N. force, which in fact you agreed to—

FOREIGN MINISTER. That is a different matter. The U.N. force would be there to observe. We agreed to that way back in 1978.[67] That is a different matter altogether.

Q. Mr. Minister, can you tell us what you discussed with the Secretary?

FOREIGN MINISTER. Well, it'd take quite a while.

Q. Tell us the good parts. (Laughter)

Q. —or the bad. (Laughter)

FOREIGN MINISTER. I had an extremely interesting and intelligent conversation with your Secretary of State. He is obviously a man with a vast knowledge of economics on top of politics and I can not go beyond—at this stage—go beyond saying that we made it clear to one another where we stand. He told me the views of the American Government on the situation in general in southern Africa, how the U.S. Government would see or wish to see future developments in the region as a whole, making it clear that the United States Government was interested in stability in the region, in economic development, in social and political stability, and explained to me what plans the United States have to improve and increase the stability in the region as a whole. I also had very interesting discussions with other members of the State Department on the latest developments in the world at large, political and economic. So, by and large, this was a very profitable meeting—a visit of myself to Washington at this stage. I'm going back with the feeling that the United States, if it could succeed in creating an economic upswing in this coun-

[67] On April 25, 1978.

try and all around the world at large, can indeed look forward to an era of prosperity in the free world which I believe is the most effective answer to Soviet penetration and the Soviet onslaught on the weak areas in the world.

Q. Do you have any sense, sir, of U.S.-South African divergence in any way on the Namibian question?

FOREIGN MINISTER. There are slight differences—

Q. What are they, sir?

FOREIGN MINISTER.—of opinion on certain methods, but by and large, I am not aware of any substantial disagreement facing either of the two governments at the present stage.

Q. Sir, did you discuss any aspects of the apartheid policies?

FOREIGN MINISTER. We did touch on the internal situation in the whole of southern Africa, but I would not wish to expand on the details of the discussion.

Q. Are there any circumstances under which South Africa would accept SWAPO government in Namibia if it went through the U.N. 435 process and SWAPO won the election, would South Africa be prepared to accept that?

FOREIGN MINISTER. I have stated so before that if there is a fair and free election, if a fair and free election takes place in the territory, then all parties and I emphasize all parties—Angola, South Africa, the frontline states, the United Nations, the Soviet Union, then everybody must accept that result. Thank you very much.

Q. Thank you.

Document 577

Transcript of a Department of State Press Briefing, November 26, 1982 (Extracts)[68]

The United States Favors Parallel Withdrawal in Southern Africa

. . . .

[SENIOR ADMINISTRATION OFFICIAL.] Concerning the Vice President's trip, which we regard as an unqualified success—the more so because of his willingness to stick to an arduous schedule with the interruption of a visit to the Brezhnev funeral in Moscow—I just would make a few observations on that.

First, despite an impression which I think has been created to some extent, his visit was not timed to or does not figure into any particular state of play on the Namibia–Angola negotiations. That trip was planned 6 months previously and had far broader objectives than to seek to engage the parties he met in an actual negotiation concerning Namibia and Angola.

The Vice President was not seeking to establish new policies, but rather to provide a detailed opportunity for face-to-face exchange, to explain our goals and policies, and to hear the views of our hosts.

The Vice President made clear a number of things on our side, including our support for African development, our desire to be as helpful as we can given the economic crisis facing so many African countries, and the fact that we are able to do more to the extent that our friends are prepared to do more to help themselves.

He emphasized our commitments in the field of human rights and justice under law. On all of his stops he made clear our readiness to bolster African regional security, whether in West Africa, in the Horn of Africa or in southern Africa. He repeated our commitment of longstanding to seek an agreement leading to Namibia's independence and explained our position on the need to address at the same time and in the same context the broader question of regional security, including and involving the presence of foreign forces in southern Africa, notably in Angola.

He made the point, in essence, that we can play and are prepared to play through our active diplomacy the role of catalyst, something which perhaps we are uniquely suited to play.

We have seen some stories about the reaction, if I can put it that way, of a number of the leaders with whom the Vice President met, which purport to indicate a rejection of American policy in southern Africa.

I assume that you know that we have not been seeking to establish in any formal

---

[68] Source: Office of Press Relations, Department of State. The briefing was conducted on background by a senior administration official beginning at 4:05 p.m.

sense a linkage of Cuban troops to Namibian independence. We're, rather, trying to get across the point that there is a practical requirement for parallel movement, however it might be described.

We do believe that it's vital to address regional security, and we do think that the Cuban issue in Angola is integral to that.

. . . .

As to the visit of Foreign Minister Pik Botha[69] itself, I'll make a few general comments before taking your questions.

This was not seen as a negotiating session. Neither we nor the South Africans had planned it to be a negotiating session on either bilateral issues or on the Namibia–Angola process. It was, rather, a chance for two men who had not previously had any chance to work together, to get acquainted, to exchange views, review the premises behind the policies of each side, so that there will be the maximum possibility for being able to work successfully together down the road. Personal contact in this regard, we feel, is very important.

From our standpoint, we found the meetings to provide a useful opportunity to reaffirm—to identify and to discuss a sustainable basis for constructive relations between our two countries. On the Namibia–Angola negotiations, yes. On the broader questions of regional security and how it might be strengthened in southern Africa, yes. And also on how we can best encourage a process which we believe to be underway of constructive change in South Africa toward a system based upon consent, and away from a system based on legally entrenched racism.

. . . .

Q. What about the multinational force idea? He seemed cool to the idea. Who was supporting it? How far has this proposal gone?

A. It is described in various media as a proposal. I wouldn't want to go beyond saying that it's not, at this point, a concrete proposition that's being put before any party. It is among the possibilities that hypothetically one might talk about.

So in that sense the Minister was simply saying that he hasn't been asked to comment upon it, apart from by the press. I mean, he hasn't had a proposition along those lines put before him by us or by anyone else.

Q. What is the American view?

A. We have an open mind. We're prepared to look at the various questions that are raised by the Angola Government as to how the Namibia transition and its own security could be addressed under the framework that we're suggesting. So we rule out nothing a priori, but I don't want to imply that there is a proposal along those lines that has any concrete status as an American proposal or a Contact Group proposal or anything else.

. . . .

Q. Are the Americans going to negotiate with the Cubans on this issue directly? Is there any consideration of that? Have they asked the Cubans whether they're willing to pull out?

A. We are negotiating this as a catalyst between the parties who are directly concerned in the region—those who live there—I mean those who live there permanently—and we don't think that it would be a confidence-building measure for anyone if we were to start implying that the solution lay elsewhere, that we were going to be involved in an act of deciding the fate of others over their heads. That's just not the approach we have taken, and we haven't been asked to take that approach by any of the parties concerned.

. . . .

Q. Can you tell us what are the hangups in this whole thing? I know that's a general question, but over the past 6 months we've been told an agreement is imminent, and then it never quite comes about. I'm just wondering if you could just detail what are the problems?

A. I don't think I have anything terribly new to add to that question. We have achieved agreement on virtually all the Namibia issues. As I've said, there are a couple of outstanding ones—at latest count, about one and a half—that relate to Resolution 435 in the Namibia process itself; and, of course, there is this other

[69] For the text of Foreign Minister Botha's remarks, see *supra*.

question of the necessity of getting a commitment on the issue of Cuban troop withdrawal.

That's to be technical about it. To be more philosophical about it, I don't think I could have put it better myself than the South African Foreign Minister put it when he said there's a problem of trust.

When we started out this exercise, the position on the one side was the Cubans might go after Namibia's independence, which is asking the people who distrust that promise to take it on faith—and that works both ways. We are the first to say that there is a gulf of trust in the region which we are seeking to overcome, and that the problem of trust or distrust exists on both sides. So I think that's the underlying question which our negotiation is designed to try and remedy.

. . . .

Q. At what point do we want the Cuban troops to withdraw and at what point do the South Africans want the Cuban troops to withdraw? Is there unanimity of agreement there at what stage we want the Cubans to withdraw from Angola?

A. I would just indicate at this point that we're in the middle of a bargaining process as honest brokers. And, again, neither side in any negotiation can expect to get the total of its desired maximum position. But it is our view that we need to get this kind of an agreement/commitment on parallel withdrawal in order for us to get a Namibian settlement, and on that there's no disagreement, and it's just a fact of life.

. . . .

Q. A simple one: You used the word "parallelism." What exactly do you have in mind there?

A. U.N. Resolution 435 begins on date "X" and that is the beginning of Phase III. Independence of Namibia comes on day "Y" and that's the end of Phase III, and the difference between those two dates will, at a minimum, be 7 to 8 months and it could well be a year or whatever, depending on how long it takes the Constituent Assembly to organize itself, to do its work, to write a constitution and so forth.

What we mean by "parallelism" is that in the context of Phase III, which provides in detail for South African troop withdrawal from Namibia, that Cubans would be withdrawn from Angola.

. . . .

Q. Two questions, away from Angola and Namibia but on South Africa. In the meetings today, I'd like to ask you about two issues and whether they came up.

One, destablization allegations in other parts of southern Africa and their effects on friends like Zambia, or Malawi by South Africa; and, two, human rights with respect to recent bannings in South Africa. Did those come up today?

A. As was indicated in the statement that was made by the South African Foreign Minister, we did discuss a range of international, regional and bilateral issues. Yes, we did discuss regional stability in southern Africa in several of the meetings that he had today in the building.

We discussed the situation as we saw it and heard their views on a number of other countries in the region, and the importance of working to bolster rather than undermine security. That means, obviously, we talked about such countries as the ones you mentioned—Mozambique, Zambia, Zimbabwe, and so forth.

We also had an exchange of views, as the Foreign Minister indicated, on developments inside South Africa itself.

. . . .

Q. How would you characterize the relationship between the United States and the other members of the Contaet Group? For instance, France was very critical last month of the U.S. mention of a Cuban withdrawal.

A. I wouldn't go beyond what we have said. There was a meeting of the Western Five Foreign Ministers a little over a month ago in which we reviewed the bidding, made clear on all sides that there was an acceptance of the reality that this was the only way to get a settlement. I think it's fair to say that we and our allies are all working, all rowing in the same direction.

We may have different public formulation, but I think we share the same assessment of the reality.

Q. Thank you.

Document 578

Prepared Statement by the Deputy Assistant Secretary of State for African Affairs (Lyman) Before Two Subcommittees of the House Foreign Affairs Committee, December 2, 1982 (Extract)[70]

Export Controls and Constructive Engagement in Southern Africa

Chairman Wolpe and Chairman Bingham, the administration welcomes this opportunity to testify before your respective committees concerning U.S. policy toward South Africa and the role that economic, trade and investment policy play in U.S.-South African relations. In the context of this hearing, I would like to begin by responding to the committees' interest in the broader approach of U.S. relations with South Africa, our policy of constructive engagement. To put the economic issues in perspective, let me then begin with an overview of administration policy.

U.S. policy objectives toward the Republic of South Africa include: fostering movement toward a system of government by consent of the governed, and away from the racial policy of apartheid both as a form of racial discrimination and national political disenfranchisement of blacks, continued access to four strategic nonfuel minerals where the United States and OECD countries are either import-or price-dependent on South Africa, assuring the strategic security of the Cape Sea routes through which pass vital U.S. oil supplies from the Middle East, and regional security in southern Africa. Peace and stability are needed so that this key region can develop and prosper, so that peaceful change can occur in South Africa, and so that the region does not slide into an escalating cycle of destructive cross-border violence exploited by our adversaries as we are pursuing these goals. Our objectives are pursued through a regional policy of constructive engagement, constructive engagement not only with South Africa, but with all the states of the region. The specific components of our regional approach include: first, internationally recognized independence for Namibia; second, internationally supported programs of economic development in all the developing countries of the region; third, a negotiated framework that will permit agreement on the issue of withdrawal of Cuban troops from Angola; fourth, détente between South Africa and the other states in the region; and fifth, peaceful, evolutionary change in South Africa itself away from apartheid and toward a system of government to be defined by South Africans themselves, but firmly rooted in the principle of government by consent of the governed.

The United States is presently leading a major diplomatic effort designed to achieve independence for the territory of Namibia based on implementation of U.N. Security Council Resolution 435.

In a separate but parallel negotiating process, the United States is seeking to resolve the related issue of the presence of Cuban forces in adjacent Angola, with the impact that their presence has in terms of southern African regional security.

The United States believes that a resolution of these conflicts is essential to build a regional climate conducive to constructive change inside South Africa away from apartheid. U.S. policy toward South Africa is thus both a bilateral policy and also an important part of our policy toward a key region, a region also vital in global terms.

President Reagan indicated that the United States views the apartheid system as repugnant to basic U.S. values. He has stated that as long as there is a sincere and honest effort to move away from apartheid in South Africa, the United States should be helpful in encouraging that process.[71] On this basis, the United States has indicated to South Africa that relations with the United States are based on the commitment of the South African Government to reform away from apartheid and on South African cooperation in moving toward an internationally recognized settlement for Namibian independence.

The United States has no blueprint for a future political system for South Africa. Nor would we have a right to attempt to impose such a plan if we had one. We do have a right to ask South Africa to respect the same

[70] *Controls on Exports to South Africa: Hearings Before the Subcommittees on International Economic Policy and Trade and on Africa of the Committee on Foreign Affairs, House of Representatives, Ninety-seventh Congress, Second Session* (Washington, 1983), pp. 172–180.

[71] See *American Foreign Policy: Current Documents, 1981,* document 592.

universal principles of human rights and human freedoms that we seek for peoples everywhere.

For all South Africans, as for people everywhere, we ask government based squarely on the freely expressed consent of the governed. South Africa's present system of government is not, although there are signs of a willingness to move toward such government.

The subcommittee has asked whether, as a result of its apartheid policy, the Department considers South Africa to be a gross violator of internationally recognized human rights. The Department's view with respect to the human rights situation in South Africa is expressed in some detail in our annual human rights report to Congress.[72] The Department would not argue that South Africa is not a violator of internationally recognized human rights. However, the Department does not advocate a formal determination that South Africa (or any other country) is a gross violator, because such determinations are barriers to dialogue that might serve to induce the human rights improvements that we seek. In situations where there is a consistent pattern of gross violations, the intent of the legislation is being carried out by refraining from security assistance and from issuance of licenses for crime control equipment. However, formal designations would largely rob the legislation of its desired effect by signaling to the designated party that the United States saw no hope for improvement.

Apartheid is by no means the only system by which contemporary governments deny citizens freedom of speech and assembly, the right to democratic participation in government, and equality under the law. Government by and with the consent of the governed remains a rare commodity in our world. The principles of freedom, equality, democracy, and the standards of human rights which so many endorse for South Africa are also utterly absent from the political practice of many other nations not similarly subject to either the scrutiny or sanctions applied to South Africa. This double standard has itself hindered constructive changes in that country by persuading some South Africans that their country will always be singled out for negative pressure and be held accountable to standards not applied uniformly elsewhere, and by persuading others that constructive change, when it does occur, will not be honestly recognized for what it is.

The United States is looking beyond mere expressions of sympathy and outrage toward practical and effective means to help end apartheid. This hearing focuses specific attention on the export of several items to South Africa, but might be said to address the general issue of what influence we have to foster change in South Africa. The real issue is whether a policy of denial is, in and of itself, going to cause such disruption in the South African economy that the South African Government will have no choice but to abandon apartheid. We believe that the change we wish to see in South Africa is more likely to take place in a relationship of mutual confidence.

The committees have asked for an explanation of how trade controls relate generally to U.S. relations with South Africa. I speak to this question and to the question of what role a regime of trade controls can play in the effective pursuit of peaceful, evolutionary change in South Africa away from apartheid.

The United States has restricted trade with South Africa since 1961 to a greater or lesser extent as a means of denial and symbolic disassociation from its racial system. A strict U.S. arms embargo was followed by a mandatory U.N. arms embargo in 1977.

The decision of the Carter administration to go beyond the mandatory arms embargo to also restrict all exports to the police and military was not similarly emulated by other nations. A call by oil exporting countries for a boycott of oil shipments to South Africa met with very mixed adherence.

Experience presents questions that may legitimately be asked with regard to the use of trade controls as a coercive instrument of foreign policy with regard to South Africa. It would seem a fair assumption to make that symbolism per se is not the only objective of trade controls implemented for foreign policy purposes. Trade controls are also expected to have a substantive impact on the situation which one is trying to affect, in this instance, South Africa's apartheid policies.

What, then, has been the effect of trade controls on internal change in South

---

72 Reference to *Country Reports on Human Rights Practices for 1981: Report Submitted to the Committee on Foreign Affairs, U.S. House of Representatives and the Committee on Foreign Relations, U.S. Senate by the Department of State* (Washington, February 1982), pp. 232–258.

Africa? There are some rather particular results. Over the course of the past 20 years, South Africa has developed the world's tenth largest arms industry and is now becoming an exporter of arms. Over the course of the past 10 years, South Africa has become a world leader in synthetic fuel production. Over the course of the past 5 years, South Africa has made giant strides toward nuclear self-sufficiency as regards the production and fabrication of low enriched uranium.

The logic of this sequence does not lead to the conclusion that all controls should be abolished. On the contrary, this administration has continued to implement a wide set of controls on trade and exports to South Africa. But we do need to question seriously the efficacy of particular controls, to look carefully at them to see whether they are indeed fulfilling their objective—in some cases whether the objective is better addressed by other policy tools. The criteria should be the impact these controls have on events in the country. The record shows that controls have encouraged greater self-sufficiency, and that they have not in themselves been sufficient to encourage a process of change.

The point of our policy is not merely to criticize or seem to criticize practices of a government. If our views are to have effect, our objective must be to devise and implement an effective and constructive means [of] policy by which the United States can encourage genuine change in South Africa.

As described earlier, the objective of constructive engagement is to create a climate of confidence in which persons can be encouraged to make difficult changes, on Namibia and on domestic change. In specific reference to export controls, we need to maintain those controls which serve as an instrument for symbolically and substantively disassociating ourselves from the apartheid regime in South Africa. At the same time, we do not believe that a regime of controls or coercive leverage by itself is a sufficient means to encourage the process of change in South Africa. In that regard, we oppose proposals for total embargoes to South Africa.

The United States has identified three areas where significant change is underway in South Africa, and which can lead to meaningful reform away from apartheid: economic growth, education, and trade union development. In order to help insure that the change which is beginning to take place moves in a peaceful direction away from apartheid, the administration has moved to support people and programs both inside and outside the government in South Africa seeking to develop a new nonracial system. As this hearing focuses on trade controls as an instrument of foreign policy, let me address the relationship between economic growth and movement away from apartheid as it affects our policy and the activities of the U.S. private sector.

The South African Government and its business community even more so recognizes that it is not possible to segregate South Africa economically into separate economies. The growth of the economy has resulted in a growing demand for skilled manpower. While South Africa's economic growth was historically based on the exploitation of unskilled black labor, the development of a modern diversified economic system requires that blacks be included on an equal wage base with whites. Economic growth, therefore, renders ineffective the apartheid political system. The United States has traditionally supported American private sector trade and investment in South Africa. While not promoting U.S. trade and investment in South Africa, we opposed disinvestment by U.S. firms from South Africa and have supported the Sullivan Principles, a voluntary code of fair employment practices.

The Reagan administration believes that U.S. firms can help to foster meaningful change away from apartheid. U.S. economic interests in South Africa are substantial. Two-way trade totaled over $5.3 billion in 1981, with the United States holding its position as South Africa's leading trading partner. U.S. direct investment in South Africa now stands at over $2.5 billion. Over 200 U.S. firms, affiliates, and subsidiaries do business in South Africa. While the United States continues to fully adhere to the arms embargo, the vast majority of U.S. exports to South Africa are unaffected by any special export controls.

I have prepared for the committee a detailed description of the legislative and administrative mechanisms of controls which are currently being administered. In the detailed description, it will be evident that the existing controls are substantial. The arms embargo remains fully in force, and remains an important symbol of disassociation from apartheid. Where changes have been made in other controls, such as those made earlier this year and discussed with this committee, they were made because they were found to be counterproductive and to be having no effect in encouraging the process of change.

. . . .

Document 579

Statement by the Alternate Representative at the United Nations (Luce) Before the U.N. General Assembly, December 9, 1982[73]

Explanation of U.S. Vote on U.N. General Assembly Resolution 37/69

Mr. President, in our statement during the debate on this agenda item,[74] we reiterated our profound and longstanding opposition to apartheid. We also explained why we believe our policy of constructive engagement is more likely to bring about positive changes in South Africa than is the policy of all-out confrontation, punishment, and isolation of South Africa, which is the philosophical basis of these resolutions. Thus, while our objective—an end to racism in South Africa—is not fundamentally different from the objective the resolutions seek to promote, the means by which we think this objective can best be achieved are so profoundly different from those the resolutions advocate, that we are obliged to vote against all of them except A/37/L.27, "United Nations Trust Fund for South Africa."

Beyond our fundamental difference in approach, there are many specific elements in the resolutions which we find unacceptable. At this time, I want to address only a few of them:

—The African National Congress is commended for intensifying armed struggle against the South African Government. Moreover, nowhere in the resolutions do we find any language urging reconciliation, negotiations, mutual understanding, and the like. It is a sad commentary on the attitudes within this body when resolutions urge war and forget peace.

How can we ignore, Mr. President, the first statement in Article I, Chapter I, of the United Nations Charter, which says that the very first purpose of this organization is:

> "To maintain international peace and security, and to that end . . . [75] to bring about by peaceful means (I repeat, by *peaceful means*), and in conformity with the principles of justice and international law, adjustment or settlement of international disputes or situations which might lead to a breach of the peace."

The "armed struggle" which these resolutions endorse is by definition not a peaceful means of solving what we all acknowledge is a morally repugnant and dangerous situation. These resolutions, therefore, are directly contrary to the U.N. Charter and to the most fundamental principle on which it is based.

—The United States is specifically denounced, in preambular paragraph 21 of Resolution A/37/L.17, entitled "Situation in South Africa,"[76] for providing "comfort and encouragement to the racist regime of South Africa." This is a deliberate distortion of our policy, implying that my government supports racism and racists. It does not; and we utterly reject such allegations. We therefore call for a separate vote on this paragraph.

—Likewise, in operative paragraph 3 of the same resolution, "major Western Powers" are accused of encouraging South African aggression against its neighbors. This is another slander. The United States has in no way supported South African aggression against anyone. Quite the contrary, in fact. We were the first major country to impose an arms embargo against South Africa, in 1962;[77] and we have been among the most stringent in enforcement of our arms embargo. As for economic and cultural sanctions, there is no reason whatsoever to suppose they would have any practical effect on South Africa's relations with its neighbors, except perhaps to heighten tensions and make armed conflict more likely.

—In the resolution on "Military and Nuclear Collaboration With South Africa,"[78]

---

[73] Source: U.S. Mission to the United Nations Press Release USUN 175–(82), December 9, 1982.

[74] See document 567.

[75] Ellipsis appears in the source text.

[76] *Infra.*

[77] The United States announced on October 19, 1962 that it forbade the sale of arms to South Africa which could be used to enforce apartheid; it announced on August 2, 1963 that it would end the sale of all arms to South Africa, effective at the end of 1963.

[78] U.N. document A/37/L.20.

the United States, Israel, and other "Western countries" are denounced for assisting South Africa "in its nuclear plans." This also is simply not true. The United States is committed to a nuclear policy intended to prevent the development or acquisition of nuclear explosive devices by any non-nuclear-weapon state. Under United States law, no nuclear materials, equipment, or sensitive nuclear technology may be exported to any non-nuclear-weapon state unless all its nuclear facilities are covered by IAEA safeguards. Moreover, South Africa is not a party to the NPT. We have long insisted that NPT adherence is also a precondition for supply of U.S. nuclear fuel for South Africa's reactors. As a practical matter, no United States licenses for export of nuclear materials or equipment to South Africa have been issued by the United States since 1975. We are actively engaged in a dialogue with South Africa designed to further the foregoing nonproliferation objectives in that country, as elsewhere around the world.

—The United States is attacked for continuing and increasing what is called "economic collaboration" with South Africa. It is nowhere even noted, however, that over 40 African countries carry on active trade with South Africa, in many cases in very substantial amounts. In 1980, South African exports to the rest of Africa grew by 50 percent over 1979, to more than 1 billion rand, and they remained over the billion rand level in 1981. South African imports from the rest of Africa increased by 10.1 percent in 1980 and another 10.3 percent in 1981. There is also active trade between South Africa and countries of COMECON—the Soviet and East European economic bloc—with South Africa importing $51 million worth of goods from COMECON countries in 1981, as compared to $38 million in 1980. Regrettably, this hypocrisy—condemning the United States for trading with South Africa while continuing to do so oneself—is not limited to African and Communist bloc countries. For example, in this year's general debate, the Foreign Minister of Sweden called for the imposition of "comprehensive mandatory sanctions against South Africa."[79] Yet, trade figures for the first half of 1981 reveal that exports to South Africa continue to rise faster than to any other country in Sweden's international trade, and that South Africa ranks as Sweden's 23d biggest customer, up from 35th in 1978. Moreover, the South African Government's Foreign Trade Organization lists Sweden as one of the country's 10 most important suppliers.

—The IMF is condemned for making a loan to South Africa,[80] and the Universal Postal Union is applauded for expelling it.[81] This effort to turn the specialized agencies into political footballs can only serve to undermine their missions of real service to all countries and peoples. Indeed, to expel a country from the *Universal* Postal Union, and I stress *Universal*, makes a mockery of the organization's very name and purpose.

—Expanded assistance for South African national liberation movements from U.N. agencies is urged, while the legitimacy of these movements' armed struggle is reaffirmed. Once again, this undermines one of the most fundamental principles of this organization—the peaceful settlement of conflicts. We have repeatedly stated our opposition to the use of any U.N. funds for the support of so-called national liberation movements, most especially those engaged in armed struggle. In this connection, it should be noted that the U.S. Congress has passed legislation this year which forbids any funds provided for international organizations and programs from being made available for the U.S. proportionate share of any programs for the PLO or SWAPO. This clearly signals that our opposition to U.N. assistance to national liberation movements is no longer merely rhetorical. In the case of the PLO and SWAPO, we have already begun to take action to withhold our share of funds from U.N. programs assisting them. If U.N. aid to ANC and PAC continues, the United States may well find it necessary to implement similar measures.

These are only some of the elements in the apartheid resolutions which we find objectionable, Mr. President, and I hope our discussion of them makes clear to this Assembly why we are voting "No." Moreover, we find it regrettable that on a matter of such widespread concern, the sponsors of the resolutions did not see fit to hold advance consultations on them outside their own group, nor to make any real effort to bring about the widest possible consensus behind these resolutions. There is, after all, a very broad international consensus

[79] Reference is to Swedish Foreign Minister Lennart Bodström's address before the U.N. General Assembly on October 15, 1982. For text, see U.N. document A/37/PV.33.

[80] See document 568.

[81] At the 17th Congress of the Universal Postal Union at Lausanne, May 22–July 4, 1974, the members voted to deny participation to South Africa.

against apartheid, which we share; and it should be possible to pass anti-apartheid resolutions by consensus.

With regard to the resolution entitled "United Nations Trust Fund for South Africa," my delegation is pleased to join consensus in favor of it. Our support, moreover, is more than rhetorical. We have given $400,000 annually to this fund. A related example of concrete support for South African blacks is our $1 million annual contribution to the U.N. education and training program for South Africa. On a bilateral basis, we have established a program which will in 1982 spend $4 million to bring 117 black South Africans, who would otherwise be disadvantaged by the apartheid education system, to the United States for university training. A similar effort is planned for 1983. Also in 1983, $2.3 million has been planned to assist South African blacks in such fields as small business management training.

In closing, Mr. President, I want to emphasize again that our negative vote on 9 of these 10 resolutions in no way diminishes our commitment to continue working, in a practical and effective way, for the elimination of apartheid and the establishment of racial justice in South Africa.

Document 580

Resolutions 37/69–A and 37/69–C, Adopted by the U.N. General Assembly, December 9, 1982[82]

"Policies of Apartheid of the Government of South Africa"

Situation in South Africa

The General Assembly,

Recalling and reaffirming its resolutions on this question, particularly resolution 36/172 of 17 December 1981,

Having considered the reports of the Special Committee against *Apartheid*,[83]

Reaffirming that *apartheid* is a crime against humanity and a threat to international peace and security,

Bearing in mind that it proclaimed 1982 International Year of Mobilization for Sanctions against South Africa,

Conscious of the responsibility of the United Nations and the international community towards the oppressed people of South Africa and their national liberation movement, as proclaimed, in particular, in General Assembly resolution 3411 C (XXX) of 28 November 1975,

Convinced that it is incumbent on the international community to provide all necessary assistance to the oppressed people of South Africa and their national liberation movement in their legitimate struggle for the establishment of a democratic society pursuant to their inalienable rights, in conformity with the principles contained in the Charter of the United Nations and the Universal Declaration of Human Rights,[84]

Commending the oppressed people of South Africa and their liberation movements, particularly the African National Congress, for intensifying the armed struggle against the racist regime,

Reaffirming that the *apartheid* regime is totally responsible for precipitating violent conflict through its policy of *apartheid* and inhuman repression,

Gravely concerned at the intensification of repression in South Africa, the growing number of deaths in detention and the

---

[82] Source: U.N. General Assembly Resolution 37/69–A, C. U.N. General Assembly Resolutions 37/69–A through J (draft resolutions A/37/L.17 through L.28), were adopted on December 9, 1982. Resolution 37/69–A, "Situation in South Africa," was adopted by a vote of 118 to 14, with 11 abstentions; Resolution 37/69–C, "Comprehensive and Mandatory Sanctions Against South Africa," was adopted by a vote of 114 to 10, with 19 abstentions.

Following are the votes on the other parts of the resolution not printed here: 37/69–B (draft A/37/L.18), 135 to 3, with 8 abstentions; 37/69–D (draft A/37/L.20), 120 to 8, with 16 abstentions; 37/69–E (draft A/37/L.21), 142 to 1, with 3 abstentions; 37/69–F (draft A/37/L.22), 113 to 18, with 10 abstentions; 37/69–G (draft A/37/L.23), 138 to 1, with 7 abstentions; 37/69–H (draft A/37/L.26), 134 to 1, with 9 abstentions; 37/69–I (draft A/37/L.27), adopted without a vote; and 37/69–J (draft A/37/L.28), 125 to 6, with 13 abstentions. The United States voted against all parts of this resolution, except 37/69–I, which was adopted without a vote.

[83] *Official Records of the General Assembly, Thirty-seventh Session Supplement No.* 22 (A/37/22); and *ibid., Supplement No. 22A* (A/37/22/Add.1-S/15383/Add.1 and A/37/22/Add.2-S/15383/Add.2). [Footnote in the source text.]

[84] General Assembly resolution 217 A (III). [Footnote in the source text.]

imposition of death sentences on freedom fighters of the African National Congress,

Reaffirming that freedom fighters of South Africa should be treated as prisoners of war in accordance with Additional Protocol I[85] to the Geneva Conventions of 12 August 1949,[86]

Commending the courageous struggle of the black workers of South Africa for their inalienable rights,

Condemning the policy of "bantustanization" designed to dispossess further the African majority of its inalienable rights and to deprive it of citizenship, as well as the continuing forced removals of black people, as an international crime,

Gravely concerned at the growing number of displaced and missing persons resulting from the criminal policies of the racist regime of South Africa,

Reaffirming that *apartheid* cannot be reformed but must be totally eliminated,

Denouncing the manoeuvres of the racist regime of South Africa to divide the oppressed people through so-called constitutional dispensations and other means, and commending the oppressed people for rejecting those manoeuvres,

Recognizing that comprehensive and mandatory sanctions by the Security Council under Chapter VII of the Charter of the United Nations are essential to avert the grave threat to international peace and security resulting from the policies and actions of the *apartheid* regime of South Africa,

Considering that political, economic, military and any other collaboration with the *apartheid* regime of South Africa encourages its persistent intransigence and defiance of the international community and its escalating acts of repression and aggression,

Reaffirming that the policies and actions of the *apartheid* regime, the strengthening of its military forces and its escalating acts of aggression, subversion and terrorism against independent African States have resulted in frequent breaches of the peace and constitute a grave threat to international peace and security,

Deploring the attitude of those Western permanent members of the Security Council that have so far prevented the Council from adopting comprehensive sanctions against that regime under Chapter VII of the Charter,

Condemning all military, nuclear and other collaboration by certain Western States and Israel with South Africa,

Gravely concerned at the pronouncements, policies and actions of the Government of the United States of America which have provided comfort and encouragement to the racist regime of South Africa,

Concerned that some Western countries and Israel continue military and nuclear co-operation with South Africa, in gross violation of the provisions of Security Council resolution 418 (1977), of 4 November 1977, and have failed to prevent corporations, institutions and individuals within their jurisdiction from carrying out such co-operation,

Gravely concerned that the racist regime of South Africa has continued to obtain military equipment and ammunition, as well as technology and know-how, to develop its armaments industry and to acquire nuclear-weapon capability,

Recognizing that any nuclear-weapon capability of the racist regime of South Africa constitutes a threat to international peace and security and a grave menace to Africa and the world,

Commending all States which have provided assistance to Angola and other front-line States in accordance with the relevant resolutions of the United Nations,

Condemning any encouragement to the *apartheid* regime in its acts of aggression, direct or indirect, as hostile to the interests of peace and freedom,

Strongly condemning the activities of those transnational corporations that continue to collaborate with the *apartheid* regime, especially in the military, nuclear, petroleum and other fields, and of those financial institutions that have continued to provide loans and credits to South Africa,

Emphasizing the conclusion of the Paris Declaration on Sanctions against South Africa that the continuing political, economic and military collaboration of certain Western States and their transnational corporations with the racist regime of South Africa encourages its persistent intransigence and defiance of the international community and constitutes a major obstacle to the elimination of the inhuman and criminal system of *apartheid* in South Africa,

---

85 A/32/144, annex I. [Footnote in the source text.]

86 United Nations, *Treaty Series*, vol. 75, Nos. 970–973. [Footnote in the source text.]

and the attainment of self-determination, freedom and national independence by the people of Namibia,[87]

Recalling and reaffirming the Declaration on South Africa contained in its resolution 34/93 0 of 12 December 1979,

Commending the efforts of trade unions, religious institutions, student organizations and anti-*apartheid* movements in their campaigns against transnational corporations and financial institutions collaborating with the racist regime of South Africa,

1. *Strongly condemns* the *apartheid* regime of South Africa for its brutal repression and indiscriminate torture and killings of workers, schoolchildren and other opponents of *apartheid,* and the imposition of death sentences on freedom fighters;

2. *Vehemently condemns* the *apartheid* regime for its repeated acts of aggression, subversion and terrorism against independent African States, designed to destabilize the whole of southern Africa;

3. *Reiterates* its firm conviction that the *apartheid* regime has been encouraged to undertake these criminal acts by the protection afforded by major Western Powers against international sanctions;

4. *Condemns* the policies of certain Western States, especially the United States of America and Israel, and of their transnational corporations and financial institutions which have increased political, economic and military collaboration with the racist regime of South Africa despite repeated appeals by the General Assembly;

5. *Reaffirms* its conviction that comprehensive and mandatory sanctions by the Security Council under Chapter VII of the Charter of the United Nations, universally applied, are the most appropriate and effective means by which the international community can assist the legitimate struggle of the oppressed people of South Africa and discharge its responsibilities for the maintenance of international peace and security;

6. *Again urges* the Security Council to determine that the situation in South Africa and in southern Africa as a whole, resulting from the policies and actions of the *apartheid* regime of South Africa, constitutes a grave and growing threat to international peace and security, and to impose comprehensive and mandatory sanctions against the regime under Chapter VII of the Charter;

7. *Demands* the immediate and unconditional withdrawal of all troops of the *apartheid* regime of South Africa from Angola and demands that South Africa respect fully the independence, sovereignty and territorial integrity of Angola and other independent African States;

8. *Further demands* that the racist regime of South Africa pay full compensation to Angola and other independent African States for the damage to life and property caused by its acts of aggression;

9. *Urges* all States that have not yet done so to adopt separate and collective measures for comprehensive sanctions against South Africa, pending action by the Security Council;

10. *Calls upon* the Government of the United Kingdom of Great Britain and Northern Ireland to take the necessary measures to stop the supply of oil from Brunei to South Africa;

11. *Requests* all intergovernmental organizations to exclude the racist regime of South Africa and to terminate all co-operation with it;

12. *Expresses serious concern* over the continued granting of credits by the International Monetary Fund to the racist regime of South Africa and requests it to terminate such credits forthwith;

13. *Requests* the International Atomic Energy Agency to refrain from extending to South Africa any facilities which may assist it in its nuclear plans and, in particular, to exclude South Africa from all its technical working groups;

14. *Again calls upon* all States and organizations to refrain from any recognition of or co-operation with the so-called "independent" bantustans;

15. *Appeals* to all States that have not yet done so to accede to the International Convention on the Suppression and Punishment of the Crime of *Apartheid;*[88]

16. *Reaffirms* the legitimacy of the struggle of the oppressed people of South Africa and their national liberation movement by all available means, including armed struggle, for the seizure of power by the people, the elimination of the *apartheid* regime and the exercise of the right of self-determination by the people of South Africa as a whole;

---

[87] A/CONF.107/8, para. 210. [Footnote in the source text.]

[88] General Assembly resolution 3068 (XXVIII), annex. [Footnote in the source text.]

17. *Demands* that the *apartheid* regime treat captured freedom fighters as prisoners of war under the Geneva Conventions of 12 August 1949[89] and Additional Protocol I thereto;[90]

18. *Again proclaims* its full support of the national liberation movement of South Africa as the authentic representative of the people of South Africa in their just struggle for liberation;

19. *Appeals* to all States to provide all necessary humanitarian, educational, financial and other necessary assistance to the oppressed people of South Africa and their national liberation movement in their legitimate struggle;

20. *Urges* the United Nations Development Programme and other agencies of the United Nations system to expand their assistance to the oppressed people of South Africa and to the South African liberation movements recognized by the Organization of African Unity, namely, the African National Congress of South Africa and the Pan Africanist Congress of Azania, in consultation with the Special Committee against *Apartheid;*

21. *Decides* to continue the authorization of adequate financial provision in the budget of the United Nations to enable those liberation movements to maintain offices in New York in order to participate effectively in the deliberations of the Special Committee and other appropriate bodies;

22. *Invites* all Governments and organizations to assist, in consultation with the national liberation movements of South Africa and Namibia, persons compelled to leave South Africa because of their objection, on the ground of conscience, to serving in the military or police forces of the *apartheid* regime;

23. *Reaffirms* the commitment of the United Nations to the total eradication of *apartheid* and the establishment of a democratic society in which all the people of South Africa as a whole, irrespective of race, colour, sex or creed, will enjoy equal and full human rights and fundamental freedoms and participate freely in the determination of their destiny.

. . . .

[89] United Nations, *Treaty Series,* vol. 75, Nos. 970–973. [Footnote in the source text.]

[90] A/32/144, annex I. [Footnote in the source text.]

Comprehensive and Mandatory Sanctions Against South Africa

The General Assembly,

Recalling its resolution 36/172 B of 17 December 1981, the Paris Declaration on Sanctions against South Africa[91] and the Programme for the International Year of Mobilization for Sanctions against South Africa,[92]

Having considered the report of the Special Committee against *Apartheid,*[93]

Considering that the policies and actions of the racist regime of South Africa, its military build-up and its nuclear plans constitute a grave threat to international peace and security,

Reaffirming its conviction that comprehensive and mandatory sanctions by the Security Council under Chapter VII of the Charter of the United Nations, universally applied, are the most appropriate and effective means by which the international community can assist the legitimate struggle of the oppressed people of South Africa and discharge its responsibilities for the maintenance of international peace and security,

Recognizing the urgent need for the termination of military, nuclear, economic and technological collaboration with the racist regime of South Africa, as well as the cessation of sports, cultural and other relations with South Africa,

Deploring the attitude of those Western permanent members of the Security Council that have so far prevented the Council from adopting comprehensive sanctions against South Africa under Chapter VII of the Charter,

Deploring also the attitude of those States, in particular the United States of America and Israel, which have continued and increased their political, economic and other collaboration with South Africa,

Gravely concerned over the activities of those transnational corporations that continue to collaborate with the *apartheid* re-

[91] A/CONF.107/8, sect. X.A. [Footnote in the source text.]

[92] *Official Records of the General Assembly, Thirty-sixth session, Supplement No. 22A* (A/36/22/Add.1 and 2), document A/36/22/Add.2, annex. [Footnote in the source text.]

[93] *Ibid., Thirty-seventh Session, Supplement No. 22* (A/37/22); and *ibid., Supplement No. 22A* (A/37/22/Add.1-S/15383/Add.1 and A/37/22/Add.2-S/15383/Add.2). [Footnote in the source text.]

gime, especially in the petroleum and other fields, and of those financial institutions that have continued to provide loans and credits to South Africa, and over the failure of the States concerned to take effective action to prevent such collaboration,

Expressing serious concern over the greatly increased investments in and loans to South Africa from the United Kingdom of Great Britain and Northern Ireland, the United States of America, the Federal Republic of Germany and Switzerland,

Commending all States which have taken effective measures, in accordance with relevant resolutions, for the elimination of *apartheid* in South Africa,

Expressing great appreciation to intergovernmental organizations and non-governmental organizations, in particular anti-*apartheid* and solidarity movements, trade unions and religious bodies, as well as cities and other local authorities, which have taken action to isolate the racist regime of South Africa and to promote support for comprehensive sanctions against that regime,

Commending the decision taken by the Universal Postal Union at its eighteenth Congress at Rio de Janeiro to expel South Africa from the Union,

Having learned of the current moves to reverse the foregoing decision taken at the eighteenth Congress of the Universal Postal Union,

Recognizing the important role of the mass media in promoting isolation of the racist regime in South Africa and comprehensive sanctions against South Africa,

Commending the activities of the Special Committee against *Apartheid,* with the assistance of the Centre against *Apartheid* of the Secretariat and the co-operation of Governments and organizations, in promoting the widest possible support for sanctions against South Africa,

1. *Requests* all Governments and organizations to continue activities in implementation of the programme for the International Year of Mobilization for Sanctions against South Africa beyond 1982;

2. *Requests* all States, especially Western States concerned and Israel to cease all collaboration with the racist regime of South Africa and to implement the relevant resolutions of the United Nations;

3. *Requests* all States concerned to take action against corporations and other interests which violate the mandatory arms embargo against South Africa or which are involved in the illicit supply to South Africa of oil from States which have imposed an embargo against South Africa;

4. *Again requests* the Security Council to consider action under Chapter VII of the Charter of the United Nations towards comprehensive and mandatory sanctions against South Africa and, in particular, to take measures:

(a) To monitor effectively and to reinforce the mandatory arms embargo against South Africa;

(b) To prohibit all co-operation with South Africa in the military and nuclear fields;

(c) To prohibit imports of any military equipment or components from South Africa;

(d) To prevent any co-operation or association with South Africa by any military alliances;

(e) To impose an effective embargo on the supply of oil and oil products to South Africa;

(f) To prohibit financial loans to and new investments in South Africa, as well as all promotion of trade with South Africa;

5. *Requests and authorizes* the Special Committee against *Apartheid* to intensify its activities for the total isolation of the racist regime of South Africa and for promoting comprehensive and mandatory sanctions against South Africa;

6. *Urges* all States members of the Universal Postal Union to resist the strong campaign being launched for the purpose of reinstating South Africa's membership in the Union;

7. *Invites* all Governments, parliaments, non-governmental organizations, anti-*apartheid* and solidarity movements, trade unions, religious bodies and other groups to intensify and concert efforts to promote comprehensive sanctions against South Africa in co-operation with the Special Committee.

Document 581

Statement Issued by the Department of State, December 14, 1982[94]

Why Tambo Got a U.S. Visa and Mphephu Did Not

Q. Why was Tambo given a visa while the President of Venda was not?

A. Mr. Tambo was invited to attend meetings of the U.N. Special Committee on Apartheid, November 3–7, at U.N. Headquarters in New York. Consistent with our obligations under the U.N. Participation Act[95] and with our responsibilities as host of the United Nations, a visa was issued to Mr. Tambo for this purpose. As you know, the ANC has been accorded observer status by the United Nations.

The so-called "President" of Venda homeland and four other officials have applied for U.S. visas on South African passports and have stated that their visit would be private. These applications are under consideration.

The United States does not recognize the so-called independent "homelands." We regard the homelands as integral parts of the Republic of South Africa and view their inhabitants as South African citizens. We are therefore only prepared to consider visa applications from individuals who characterize themselves as officials of the so-called independent homelands on the basis of their South African citizenship and documentation.

---

[94] Source: Office of Press Relations, Department of State; posted statement. The statement was posted in response to a question asked at the Department of State Daily Press Briefing of December 10.

[95] Reference is to P.L. 79–583, the United Nations Participation Act of 1945, enacted on December 20, 1945. For text, see 59 Stat. 619–621.

Document 582

Statement by the French Representative at the United Nations (Barre de Nanteuil) Before the U.N. General Assembly, December 15, 1982[96]

Efforts of the Contact Group to Bring About a Settlement in Namibia

I have the honour today to speak on behalf of the Governments of Canada, France, the Federal Republic of Germany, the United Kingdom, and the United States.

As all members of this Assembly are aware, our five governments have entered into negotiations to secure an internationally recognized settlement of the Namibian problem. A solution to this problem is long overdue. In the past few months intensive efforts have been made to overcome the remaining obstacles.

During July and August, consultations were held in New York between the Contact Group and representatives of the frontline states, Nigeria, and the South West Africa People's Organization (SWAPO), and there were concurrent consultations with South Africa. These talks enabled us to reach agreement on important aspects of the settlement proposal that were outstanding. The results of these consultations were conveyed to the Secretary-General in September at a meeting in which the Five, the frontline states, Nigeria, and SWAPO participated.

Our Foreign Ministers met in New York on 1 October and welcomed the acceptance by the parties of the constitutional principles which are to govern the Namibian Constituent Assembly. They also noted that substantial progress had been made on the question of the impartiality, and on the size, composition, and arrangements for deployment of the military component of the United Nations Transition Assistance Group (UNTAG). In this regard we should like to express our gratitude to the Secretary-General and his staff for their valuable contribution. We should also like to pay a tribute to the Secretariat for its efforts to complete preparations for the UNTAG operation.

Even with this progress, however, some issues still have to be settled. The commit-

---

[96] Source: U.N. document A/37/PV.105.

ment of the Five to a successful conclusion of this exercise remains firm, and Namibian independence remains our goal. We believe that it is in the interests of the international community, and more specifically the sovereign states of southern Africa, that this problem be resolved as soon as possible. Our governments remain convinced that only through negotiations will it be possible to achieve a lasting settlement while ensuring Namibian independence, which is what we all seek.

Neither in form and [*nor*] substance do the draft resolutions before us today[97] recognize either the seriousness of the present situation or the opportunity that now exists to find a peaceful solution. They will not bring the goal of Namibian independence any closer. Although the Five have reservations on numerous aspects of the draft resolutions, we shall abstain so as not to jeopardize our role in the negotiations. Our abstentions are purely procedural and in no way imply any position on the intrinsic merits of these draft resolutions.

Intensive consultations are continuing on the remaining unsettled issues. The Contact Group wishes once again to emphasize the importance of the cooperation of all the parties concerned in this effort if we are to succeed.

The opportunity now exists to bring about a settlement which would make it possible both to strengthen peace and security and to foster economic development in the region. We see no real alternative to these negotiations, other than the continuation of the conflicts in the area, with the ever-increasing suffering that would result for the peoples of southern Africa. We denounce violence from whatever source either to promote or to prevent change. We call on the international community for its support in the effort to achieve our common goal of peaceful negotiated settlement.

---

[97] Reference is to draft resolution A/37/24, adopted as U.N. General Assembly Resolution 37/233 on December 20. For text, see document 585.

Document 583

Statement by the Alternate Representative at the United Nations (Lichenstein) Before the U.N. Security Council, December 16, 1982 (Extract)[98]

The United States Deplores the South African Raid on Lesotho

. . . .

The Government and the people of the United States deeply deplore the South African attack into the neighboring country of Lesotho launched in the early morning hours of 9 December.[99] We deeply regret the tragic loss of innocent life that resulted from that attack. All concerned, including South Africa, must realize that violence cannot and will not solve the grave problems that confront the peoples of southern Africa.

Among the principles that animate the foreign policies of my country and govern our relations with all other nations, none is more fundamental, none more steadfastly held, than the non-use of force in conflict resolution. The only appropriate means for solving the problems of this and all other regions of the world are peaceful negotiation and conciliation.

We have made this position eminently clear to the Government of South Africa. It is at the core of the negotiations that we, in concert with many other States, African and non-African, are pursuing with regard to Namibia.

The requirement for peaceful coexistence and co-operation is nowhere more evident than in the relationship between Lesotho and South Africa. Lesotho is

---

[98] Source: U.N. document S/PV.2408, pp. 7–10.

[99] On December 9, South African commandos raided Lesotho's capital, Maseru, killing over 30 people. South Africa claimed that the victims were members of the African National Congress, including four top leaders of the movement. Lesotho said that the victims were refugees, and that it did not allow the ANC to operate in its territory. See *New York Times*, December 9, 1982, pp. A1, A16, December 10, 1982, p. A14, and December 11, 1982, p. 11; and *Washington Post*, December 10, 1982, pp. A1, A34, and December 12, 1982, p. A31.

uniquely vulnerable. It must have the assurance that its sovereignty and territorial integrity will be respected.

We have listened to the judicious statement of His Majesty King Moshoeshoe II. We welcome in particular his assurance that Lesotho is committed to the principles of co-operation and peaceful coexistence. We believe this assurance offers a firm and positive basis for establishing the necessary diplomatic channels through which Lesotho and South Africa can and must work together to allay their concerns and to solve their common problems.

Violence, from whatever quarter, must be condemned. Those who would promote or resort to violence must know that the consequence can only be more violence, an escalating cycle that presents only obstacles to solving real problems. More than most countries, South Africa surely must appreciate the consequences of further eroding international restraints against the use of violence. Whatever South Africa's concerns may have been, however legitimate they may have seemed, we cannot believe that they could not be resolved through diplomacy, or that they could in any way justify this violation of Lesotho's sovereignty and the resulting loss of innocent life.

The resolution that has been adopted by the Council[1] embodies principles to which my Government, as I have said, attaches the highest importance. It reaffirms the solemn obligation of all States to refrain from the threat or use of force against the territorial integrity and political independence of any State. It reaffirms the right of all States, including Lesotho, to receive and provide humanitarian assistance to those seeking asylum in accordance with humanitarian principles and with obligations clearly established in international conventions. It firmly reiterates the importance of seeking to resolve international problems through peaceful means.

Those are principles which my Government wholly and unequivocally endorses. They are indeed consistent with the strenuous efforts of my Government to promote practical, negotiated solutions to the problems of southern Africa, solutions that also would contribute to lasting peace and stability in the region. Thus, we voted in favour of the resolution.

[1] The reference is to Resolution 527, adopted unanimously by the Security Council on December 15. On December 14, the General Assembly adopted without a vote Resolution 37/101 (draft A/37/L.54), "Invasion of Lesotho by South Africa." The resolution condemned South Africa for the raid, commended the Government of Lesotho for opposing apartheid and giving sanctuary to refugees from apartheid, and urged the Security Council to take "immediate steps" to deter South Africa from further actions of this type.

Document 584

Remarks by President Reagan, December 18, 1982 (Extract)[2]

Perception of Progress in Namibia Negotiations

. . . .

Q. Mr. President, South Africa—how long will you pursue your policy of constructive engagement to bring about independence for Namibia, particularly in view of last week's raid into Lesotho?[3]

THE PRESIDENT. Well, we let them know our unhappiness about that. But we have made progress. And we have made progress with both factions there, and with the other frontline states in Africa. And we are going to continue and do our best to settle that peacefully.

. . . .

---

[2] Source: White House Press Release, December 18, 1982, Office of the Press Secretary to the President; printed also in *Weekly Compilation of Presidential Documents,* December 27, 1982, p. 1646. President Reagan was interviewed in the Roosevelt Room of the White House by Independent Radio Networks.

[3] See *supra.*

Document 585

Resolution A/37/233–B Adopted by the U.N. General Assembly, December 20, 1982[4]

Implementation of Security Council Resolution 435 (1978)

The General Assembly,

Reaffirming the imperative need to proceed without any further delay with the implementation of Security Council resolution 435 (1978) of 29 September 1978, which, together with Council resolution 385 (1976) of 30 January 1976, is the only basis for a peaceful settlement of the question of Namibia,

Taking note of the consultations which have been held with a view to achieving the implementation of Security Council resolution 435 (1978) and also noting that those consultations have so far failed to bring about its implementation,

Condemning the attempts to link the independence of Namibia with totally extraneous issues, in particular the withdrawal of Cuban troops from Angola, an issue which falls within the exclusive domestic jurisdiction of a sovereign Member State,

1. *Reaffirms* the direct responsibility of the United Nations for Namibia pending its achievement of genuine self-determination and national independence;

2. *Reiterates* that Security Council resolution 435 (1978), in which the Council endorsed the United Nations plan for the independence of Namibia, is the only basis for a peaceful settlement of the question of Namibia and demands its immediate and unconditional implementation without qualification or modification;

3. *Firmly rejects* the persistent attempts by the United States of America and South Africa to establish any linkage or parallelism between the independence of Namibia and any extraneous issues, in particular the withdrawal of Cuban forces from Angola, and emphasizes unequivocally that the persistence of such attempts would only retard the decolonization process in Namibia as well as constitute interference in the internal affairs of Angola;

4. *Requests* the Security Council to exercise its authority for the implementation of its resolution 435 (1978) so as to bring about the independence of Namibia without further delay.

[4] Source: U.N. General Assembly Resolution 37/233–B. The resolution was adopted by a vote of 129 to 0, with 17 abstentions (including the United States). Resolution 37/233–A, "Situation in Namibia resulting from the illegal occupation of the Territory by South Africa," was adopted by a vote of 120 to 0, with 23 abstentions (including the United States); Resolution 37/233–C, "Programme of work of the United Nations Council for Namibia," was adopted by a vote of 139 to 0, with 8 abstentions (including the United States); Resolution 37/233–D, "Dissemination of information and mobilization of international public opinion in support of Namibia," was adopted by a vote of 127 to 0, with 20 abstentions (including the United States); Resolution 37/233–E, "United Nations fund for Namibia," was adopted by a vote of 141 to 0, with 5 abstentions (including the United States). For the texts of Resolutions A/37/233–A and A/37/233–C, see *ibid.*, pp. 67–72, and 73–83.

C. Zambia and Zimbabwe

Document 586

Address by the Assistant Secretary of State for African Affairs (Crocker) Before the Conference on Zimbabwe, New York, March 26, 1982[1]

The Role of the U.S. Private Sector in Zimbabwe

Thank you for the opportunity to participate in this conference and to speak on a subject on which I feel strongly, the present and future relationship between the United States and Zimbabwe. The United States has many and varied links with Zimbabwe, the more important of which include substantial political, economic, religious, and educational ties. The high regard shown for Prime Minister Mugabe when he visited in August 1980,[2] and for President Banana

[1] Source: Department of State files; printed also in Department of State *Bulletin*, June 1982, pp. 47–49. The African American Institute and the American Bar Association Section on International Law were joint sponsors of the conference.

[2] Mugabe visited the United States on August 27, 1980. See *American Foreign Policy: Basic Documents, 1977–1980*, pp. 1231–1232.

when he came in October of last year demonstrates the overall esteem Americans have for the Zimbabwean people and for their leaders.

I am honored and pleased to be sharing this platform with Zimbabwe's distinguished Minister of Finance, Economic Planning and Development—Dr. Bernard Chidzero—who is accompanied by a delegation representing Zimbabwe's public and private sectors. I am also pleased to see so many distinguished members of the American business community here today. Your presence underscores the seriousness of this meeting.

The United States believes that Zimbabwe can become a showcase of economic growth and political moderation in southern Africa, a region of substantial strategic importance to us. That belief rests on facts, not illusions. At a time when much of neighboring Africa risks sliding into an economic abyss, Zimbabwe has the possibility of pointing by example to a brighter future whose central element is economic rationality. Endowed with rich resources, diverse and talented manpower, exceptional economic self-sufficiency, and a solid legacy of infrastructure and administrative institutions, Zimbabwe has the ingredients for a positive program of development and nation building. We are committed to assist Zimbabwe and Prime Minister Mugabe toward achieving those goals. We share fully Zimbabwe's strong belief that relations among the nations of southern Africa must be based upon the principles of mutual respect for sovereignty, independence, and territorial integrity as well as the pursuit of practical policies of political restraint and the belief in negotiated solutions to festering conflicts. Within that context, we believe that the recent extension of the preferential trade agreement between Zimbabwe and the Republic of South Africa is a concrete reflection of the region's potential for mutually beneficial coexistence in the face of basic political difference.

We are aware that Prime Minister Mugabe and his colleagues face tough choices as the leaders of their nation, choices that call for resourcefulness and determined leadership. Often in such challenging circumstances, consistent pursuit of a path of vision and of moderation requires the leaders of a nation to walk a tightrope. Our judgment is that Prime Minister Mugabe seeks to follow such a course. It is in substantial part for this reason that we have sought a good overall relationship with Zimbabwe since independence.

Lest you conclude that I plan to talk today of grand strategy or the tactics of the Namibia negotiations, let me assure you that I am aware of our agenda: investment and development. But these things do not occur—or fail to occur—in a political vacuum.

Zimbabwe is a very special country. Zimbabwe is also an important partner and friend of the United States at the center of the destiny of southern Africa. One of the roles of a friend is sometimes to speak plainly in the knowledge that the friend may then choose to heed or to disregard what is said. Among nations that clearly respect each other's sovereignty and independence, friendship can be strengthened by the good will expressed by the act of speaking plainly. What I am about to say about how we see the future of the economy of Zimbabwe falls in that category.

In an effort to encourage the post-independence government and to demonstrate our firm commitment to Zimbabwe's success as a new nation, the United States pledged $225 million over a 3 year period at the March 1981[3] Zimbabwe Conference on Reconstruction and Development. That pledge is consistent with this administration's stated objectives of constructive engagement in southern Africa and with the goal of assisting the economic development of African nations. It specifically indicates our recognition of both Zimbabwe's obvious potential and its special needs during the first 3 years of independence.

However, the modern history of economic development demonstrates that government-to-government assistance programs—important as they are—cannot by themselves assure the capital, expertise, or motivation required to achieve sustained economic growth. The worldwide economic downturn has exacerbated the problems inherent in strategies which depend primarily on public sector activity and which ignore or actively discourage individual initiative and the private sector. The need to correct the widespread imbalance between public and private economic activity is increasingly recognized in scholarly studies, analyses by international development institutions, and by the leaders of developing countries themselves.

We are fully aware that in Zimbabwe, as in other developing countries, the reputation of capitalism has suffered by associa-

[3] The pledge was announced on March 24, 1981.

tion with colonialism. But what is past need not be prologue. As Prime Minister Mugabe has stated clearly, only Zimbabwe's exceptional private sector can generate the resources needed to improve national welfare. Sadly, the experience of some African and other developing countries illustrates the tragedy of economic planning that only redistributes poverty and stifles the universal drive of people to produce and to earn.

As part of the Reagan administration's worldwide policy of support for economic development, we have embarked upon several new approaches in our assistance programs. We believe these will strengthen the role of indigenous private sectors and facilitate U.S. private investment to stimulate developing economies.

An excellent example of this approach is our aid-funded Commodity Import Program (CIP) which the Zimbabwe Government is presently considering. This program has been consciously designed to assist local business firms overcome the constraints imposed by the shortage of foreign exchange. It also gives priority to the replacement of outdated and obsolete capital equipment, particularly in the transportation, civil engineering, and manufacturing sectors. The CIP will also provide balance-of-payment support, help to stimulate economic growth rising from the private sector, and will create new jobs for Zimbabwe's rapidly expanding work force. Local currency counterpart funds generated by the program will be used by the Zimbabwe Government for mutually agreed upon activities in the fields of education, health, agriculture, and small-scale enterprise, with priority being given to reconstruction and rehabilitation of facilities in the former tribal trust lands. Used in this manner the CIP will have the dual purposes of stimulating the Zimbabwe commercial sector and of helping the Zimbabwe Government meet its development needs.

Zimbabwe, as suggested above, has a magnificent asset in a well-developed, modern infrastructure which includes a relatively well-trained labor force, food self-sufficiency and export capability, a good and improving transportation system, a sound communications network, a strong industrial base, and sophisticated financial institutions.

While this infrastructure is exceptionally well developed by regional standards, it functioned in the past basically to meet the needs of only a small segment of the population. At independence the Government of Zimbabwe made very clear its commitment to expand and share more broadly the economy's wealth and improve social and economic services as rapidly as possible. As a result, there have been increased expectations and large public spending to meet those expectations which could eventually threaten Zimbabwe's economic viability, particularly if economic growth does not keep pace.

The formidable challenge, then, for Zimbabwe is to attempt to adapt a highly productive economy in the direction of greater equity and broadened participation without succumbing to sometimes inflated expectations for immediate gratification, a process that could place excessive strain on finite resources, manpower, and infrastructure and thereby weaken the base of the economic system. Such a development could also weaken the Zimbabwe Government's own capacity to meet its peoples' needs and might risk sending the country into the position of so many other states today: low growth, loss of food self-sufficiency, and expanding budget deficits.

To meet this challenge, the path of wisdom for Zimbabwe is not to permit unique opportunities for dynamic economic growth with equity to escape, perhaps irretrievably. We hope, instead, that Zimbabwe's leaders will devise an innovative approach to economic policy free of the theoretical rigidities which could bar the achievement of the practical results that they and their people want.

The United States recognizes that in the coming decades Zimbabwe will need massive amounts of capital for social programs to redress the past imbalances. Although Zimbabwe has the capacity to generate some of this capital domestically, there will be a need for a substantial injection of external capital including private investments.

Zimbabwe's own private sector is unique because of the economy's high degree of self-sufficiency. Where the local private sector provides social as well as economic benefits—employment, training, expansion of opportunities—these should be sustained, not subject to the limitations of budget shortfalls. The private sector is an important source of new talents and ideas. With independence and the end of sanctions, foreign investor participation can play a comparable role. Because the United States is sympathetic to and supportive of the Zimbabwe Government's efforts to respond to rising expectations, we are convinced that the American private sector can be an additional major factor in helping Zimbabwe achieve sustained growth and a continued broadening of effective participation with modern economic sector [*Sic*].

Zimbabwe as a market for trade and investment is no stranger to the U.S. private sector, and the lifting of sanctions refueled considerable interest among U.S. firms for expanded and new involvement there. Expanded trade which would flow from new investment would help to strengthen ties between our two countries.

Private foreign investment, however, does not always automatically occur even when it appears natural and logical to governments that it should. By the same token, the private sector cannot assume that conditions and policies in developing countries are designed primarily to maximize opportunity for profit. It is a two-way street.

It is our view that both the Zimbabwe Government and the U.S. private sector have responsibilities, therefore, to smooth the way for investment and to make it productive. Today, however, it appears that both parties have become somewhat wary and cautious to the point that progress in attracting investments may not get properly launched and may fall short. I see the following issues as potentially discouraging to U.S. foreign investment, problems which I would signal to the Government of Zimbabwe and the foreign investors.

Lack of a clear, publicly stated government policy on the role and rules of the game for the private sector. Some companies have found particularly unsettling suggestions of eventual state control of most economic activity. The private sector might interpret as detrimental to its productive role the creation of a Minerals Marketing Board. We believe that the Zimbabwe Government's efforts to clarify its approach to the role of the private sector will be especially helpful, and that its readiness to work with the private sector toward achieving these goals through private investment will bear rich fruit.

A second factor is uncertainty over foreign exchange availability, remittances of earnings, transport facilities, expertise availability, and the effect of government deficits on the ability of the private sector to operate effectively.

Third, the business community, for purposes of its long-term planning, is following current domestic political developments in Zimbabwe as they assess whether the country's hopes for stable and orderly progress will in fact be realized.

Fourth, delays or difficulties in reaching common understanding on agreements which will promote increased private investment, the OPIC agreement as a case in point, are bound to encourage critics and discourage friends of the positive relationship which is developing between the United States and Zimbabwe.

In sum, American investors are unsure if they can enter Zimbabwe's market, make money, and remit a competitive portion of their profits. What they need, therefore, is, predictability, a clearer idea of what the ground rules are, better channels of communications, clear signals that the Government of Zimbabwe has assessed the evidence and has opted to create a climate designed to stimulate investment.

Despite these issues, it is our basic assessment that Zimbabwe offers considerable and varied opportunities for the American investor. To take advantage of these opportunities, the American business community will need to demonstrate its ability to produce and to respond to locally relevant needs. This can best be done by developing specific, creative, and versatile investment proposals which will benefit Zimbabwean society as a whole. For example:

—Agro-industrial projects that emphasize training, expanded opportunities for all Zimbabwean farmers, and growth of production, i.e., projects which help meet several of Zimbabwe's objectives even more efficiently than government programs aimed at the same sectors.

—Industrial activities that promise employment, economic advancement, and increased foreign exchange earnings for the country.

—Innovative management styles that allow for cooperation with government, the most rapid pace of development of Zimbabwean top management, and sensitivity to local conditions.

In our view, it is clear that Zimbabwe is at a major crossroad of its economic future. I want to stress the potential that can be exploited if the public and private sectors of our two countries can work energetically and cooperatively to keep Zimbabwe on the road of economic growth.

This conference can mark the beginning of a determined effort on both sides to build a climate of positive reinforcement, spurred by extra efforts on each side to create and follow through on specific promising investment opportunities.

If this opportunity is seized, we will all reflect on this conference as an historic step in a process to the greater good of Zimbabwe, the United States, and southern Africa. In my view, failure to do so would represent, on our part and on the part of Zimbabwe, that we have done much less than our best and that a great opportunity has been lost.

Document 587

Testimony by the Assistant Secretary of State for African Affairs (Crocker) Before the Senate Foreign Relations Committee, April 16, 1982 (Extract)[4]

The Basis of U.S. Commitment to Zimbabwe

. . . .

QUESTION 3. Could you comment on how the administration views recent events in Zimbabwe? In light of these developments, is the continuation of our very significant ESF program still fully justified?

A. Recent events in Zimbabwe, such as the call for a one-party state, the clampdown on press freedom, and the attempt to muzzle political opposition, are of considerable concern to us. On the other hand, however, we are encouraged by the fact that solid internal dialogue is developing within Zimbabwe society. Mr. Mugabe's recent appointment of two whites and several ZAPU party members to substantive Cabinet posts supports his strategy of reconciliation and increased communication.

The basis of our commitment to Mr. Mugabe as a force for moderation and a solid bulwark in the region remains valid. The GOZ is aware of the substantial contribution we are making toward Zimbabwe's development and has made excellent use of U.S. assistance to date.

Mr. Mugabe considers the U.S. one of Zimbabwe's most important friends. We believe that the positive approach he is taking to our efforts to work with parties in the region to reach a settlement in Namibia and to improve overall conditions of security in southern Africa reflect the warm and friendly relations that exist between our two countries and justifies continuing our present levels of economic support for Zimbabwe. Our involvement there is viewed by Zimbabweans as honorable and constructive.

. . . .

Document 588

Toast by Vice President Bush, Harare, November 16, 1982[5]

U.S. Relations With Zimbabwe

Your Excellency the Prime Minister, Mrs. Mugabe, Honorable Chief Justice, Honorable Ministers, Your Excellencies the members of the Diplomatic Corps, Your Worship the Mayor of Harare, distinguished guests, ladies and gentlemen.

Thirty-one hours ago in Moscow, I discussed my mission to Africa with the President of Pakistan, Zia Al-Huk. When I mentioned Prime Minister Mugabe, President Zia made reference to something with which informed men everywhere on Earth agree. Therefore, I want to acknowledge that I stand in the presence of a genuine statesman, the Prime Minister of Zimbabwe, Robert Mugabe. His stature in the world is well established, highly respected; and it will be more formidable in the years to come.

Mr. Prime Minister, you know very well that some greeted the birth of this new nation with grim doubts. Some wondered

---

[4] Source: *Fiscal Year 1983 Security Assistance: Hearings Before the Committee on Foreign Relations, United States Senate, Ninety-seventh Congress, Second Session* (Washington, 1982), pp. 312–313. This was the response of the Department of State to an additional question submitted for the record by Senator Kassebaum.

[5] Source: Press Release, November 16, 1982, Office of the Press Secretary to the Vice President; printed also in Department of State *Bulletin*, January 1983, pp. 42–43. The toast was given at a state dinner hosted by Zimbabwean Prime Minister Robert Mugabe.

whether a revolutionary movement could govern. Others pointed to the gulf of mistrust and hatred engendered by years of war. You faced multiple challenges:

—how to develop peacefully in a region full of polarized conflicts;

—how to retain and build upon one of Africa's strongest and most diversified free market economies while also spreading its benefits to the majority of the population;

—how to retain the confidence, skills and loyalty of white Zimbabweans while responding to the aspirations of those who fought and voted for you.

Mr. Prime Minister, it is not my job as your guest to issue a report card on your leadership and your new nation. You have faced awesome challenges, some overcome, some still on your agenda. I do want to say on behalf of the Reagan administration that we support the policy of reconciliation to which you have committed yourself—just as we support the constitutional agreements reached at Lancaster House.[6] We believe Zimbabwe represents a noble experiment in the midst of a strife-torn region. It also represents an effort to put aside the past and begin a work of healing. We have supported your country because its success is consistent with U.S. principles and U.S. interests. I will report to President Reagan that Zimbabwe continues to deserve our support, because America is committed to backing peaceful change, economic development, and the rule of law.

Mr. Prime Minister, I am proud that my country has played a part in Zimbabwe's young life. You might recall that when Zimbabwe gained independence, the United States was one of the first to open an embassy in this city. Since then, American assistance to Zimbabwe has amounted to many tens of millions; and shortly after President Reagan took office, my government pledged nearly a quarter of a billion U.S. dollars in new aid. America has not only avowed its faith in Zimbabwe, but proven it.

At this point I would be remiss if I failed to congratulate Zimbabwe on a remarkable honor—its recent election to the United Nations Security Council. Mr. Prime Minister, this election demonstrates that the larger community of nations possesses the same sturdy faith in Zimbabwe as do you and I. It also represents a recognition of Zimbabwe's importance in international affairs.

Zimbabwe has played an important role in the effort to achieve Namibian independence. Mr. Prime Minister, you have pressed for a Namibian settlement with both urgency and skill. Just as important, Zimbabwe itself provides a model on which efforts to free Namibia could succeed; compromise and dedication will once again win through.

As you know, Mr. Prime Minister, since first taking office President Reagan and his administration have labored for a Namibian settlement. We have spared no effort. We have worked with the Western Contact Group, with the frontline states, with SWAPO, and with the Government of South Africa. Assistant Secretary Crocker, present this evening, has spent more time on this than on any other African matter.

Mr. Prime Minister, we intend to serve as a disinterested and honest broker. The United States possesses neither troops nor proxies in the region. We have no colonial interests, nor do we have military ambitions. On the contrary, the sole American interests in southern Africa are the interests of all men in all places: freedom and peace. Our efforts follow distinguished precedents. American labors, directed by Secretary of State Kissinger, helped build peace between Israel and Egypt. British efforts, of course, helped lead to your own independence. So today we labor on, with Zimbabwe and other nations, to clear the region of all foreign troops so that Namibia might be free.

A top priority in our diplomacy is southern Africa, where the choices between regional strife and regional cooperation are stark. The inescapable need for peaceful change is challenged by a climate of fear, distrust, foreign intervention and cross-border violence. The United States is committed to the search for constructive change in southern Africa.

The United States wants an end to South Africa's occupation of Namibia. At the same time the United States wants an end to Angola's suffering, and to the dangerous cycle of violence in the region.

Our number one strategic objective in Africa is to help establish a framework of restraint that discourages outside intervention in African conflicts, while it encourages negotiated solutions and constructive change.

A moment ago I mentioned our journey to Moscow. No doubt you have all seen photographs of Secretary Brezhnev's funer-

---

[6] In December 1979.

al. The image that struck me most—one that I will never forget—was the magnificent, stately display of young Russian soldiers.

As I watched those young men, I could not help noting that they were the same ages as my own four sons. And I felt again what I have often felt since taking up this office: a sudden, sharp sense of the responsibility that lies on those who lead nations. Mr. Prime Minister, I know that you share that sense of responsibility. And I know that you will continue to exercise your responsibility for the good of this exciting new nation and in the interests of peace.

Ladies and gentlemen, please raise your glasses and join me in a toast to Prime Minister Robert Mugabe, and to the Republic of Zimbabwe.

Document 589

Statement and Remarks by Vice President Bush, Harare, November 18, 1982[7]

Bush Takes Leave of Zimbabwe

I have a brief statement, and then I would be glad to respond to any questions.

We're leaving Zimbabwe after a visit that's far too brief. I feel that our time has been well spent. I've had lengthy and useful talks with Prime Minister Mugabe. We've discussed the nature of the U.S. assistance program in Zimbabwe, the state of diplomatic relations, and the course that those relations should take. We discussed, as well, the major issues of this region, the quest for a peaceful settlement in Namibia; and early independence for that country represented one of our major subjects of discussion. We discussed the implications of Zimbabwe's membership in the United Nations Security Council, and I shared with the Prime Minister some of my experiences at the United Nations when I was the U.S. permanent representative at the United Nations.

President Reagan sent me to Africa to meet with our friends and learn about their efforts at national development. I am happy to tell you that I will carry back an encouraging report from Zimbabwe. In this new nation, national reconciliation is recognized as a matter of paramount urgency. In fact, it's the only possible course, and I've assured the Prime Minister of our unrelenting support for his efforts to heal the old wounds, and to lead Zimbabwe to political and economic stability. Growth with equity represents a goal which Zimbabwe has both the will and the capacity to achieve. Problems exist, certainly, but in our short time here I have seen the Zimbabweans share an earnest desire to overcome these problems together. I wish them well, and I thank them all once again for the extraordinary hospitality that we've enjoyed in our very brief stay here.

I'll be glad to respond to any questions.

Q. Mr. Vice President, I'm with Reuters. After hearing Mr. Mugabe's views on Namibia, have you any reason to rethink or reconsider the U.S. stand on the issue of the Cuban troops departure in advance of any settlement?

VICE PRESIDENT. No, we believe that we understand his views very clearly. I would refer you to him in terms of whether he understands what we are attempting to do. In the places we have gone, and discussed our role, catalytic role, there seems to be more understanding, but I think it's something that probably should be referred to him. Our position is well known, it's clear, we cannot dictate a solution. We hope we will be a catalyst for peace there.

Any others?

Sir?

Q. Is Mr. Botha right that you are out of step with the spirit of the Reagan policy in South Africa?

VICE PRESIDENT. Well, I didn't see his first statement, but I saw his second, in which he said that he had been misquoted, or there was some feeling he understood our position, and I didn't see it, so I can't comment on it. I don't know exactly what it was that he was referring to. But there is no difference between the President and me on this policy, believe me.

Q. Was the question of human rights as regards detentions and as regards possible abuse of any prisoners in Zimbabwe raised by you or any member of the delegation during the talks?

VICE PRESIDENT. Well, we had with us the Assistant Secretary of State for Human

---

[7] Source: Press Release, November 18, 1982, Office of the Press Secretary to the Vice President. Bush made these remarks at Harare airport prior to his departure.

Rights, and that matter is always discussed in a very frank and friendly way.

Q. Mr. Vice President, you refer to problems you've seen in Zimbabwe. What do you perceive the main ones to be?

Vice President. No, nice try, but I'm not going to go away highlighting differences. But in terms of problems, I think I could cite our talks with the Agricultural Minister,[8] and the Minister of Lands,[9] where they discussed some of the problems that lie ahead in the fulfillment of their objectives in terms of agriculture. I also would say the economy. My first statement or comment really alluded to comments between any differences we might have, and I would not go into that. But in terms of the problems we discussed, ones that we're trying to be helpful with, I'd say development, economic development, is the main one, and there we have been able to be of some assistance, not nearly so much as I guess we'd like, or as Zimbabwe would like. But there were some very upbeat things, along with the discussion of the problems, agriculture being foremost among them.

Q. Do I take that to mean, Mr. Vice President, that you do agree that there are problems and differences between yourselves and Zimbabwe?

Vice President. Well, I suppose there are differences between us and 163 other members of the United Nations, if that's what the latest count is. But the thing I note, as we leave, is that the similarities far outweigh the differences. But I expect there are some; I think one was mentioned right here earlier in terms of Namibia. How great the difference is that remains, I don't know. We don't expect 100 percent agreement, and we've never gotten 100 percent agreement with our allies, friends, and those opposing us.

Any others?

Well, thank you all very, very much for coming out.

---

[8] Denis R. Norman.

[9] Moven Mahachi.

Document 590

Toast by Vice President Bush, Lusaka, November 18, 1982[10]

"The United States Supports Zambia"

Mr. Secretary General, Mrs. Mulemba, Members of the Central Committee, Members of the Cabinet, Mr. Chief Justice, Mr. Speaker, distinguished guests, ladies and gentlemen.

Today Mrs. Bush will visit council house number 394 in Chilenje. It is a humble building. Several decades ago the son of a poor preacher was raised there. In those days Zambia was not ruled by its own people, but by those in a foreign capital, thousands of miles away. The preacher's son, Kenneth Kaunda, grew up to work with the people of Zambia to change that.

For 18 years now, Zambians have governed Zambia. Your political institutions demonstrate your commitment to human freedom and dignity. You practice democracy. As I moved about Lusaka today, I could not fail to notice that you are preparing for the 1983 elections. In 1983, as in past elections, this nation will acknowledge that the Government of Zambia is responsible to the Zambian people.

You believe in a sturdy and independent judiciary. Like my own country, Zambia possesses a written constitution and extensive legal codes. Zambia adheres to the rule not of individual men, but of the law.

In Zambia's 18 years of independence, your national life has grown vigorous. Two points especially strike me. First, the value you place on a free press. Just a few weeks ago, when he dedicated your new mass media complex, President Kaunda restated Zambia's commitment to an unfettered but responsible press. A free press contributes to a sense of national identity, to honesty in government, and to the impartial administration of the law. You in Zambia know that.

Second, I have been impressed by this nation's stunning success in education. Like Americans, Zambians have possessed a reverence for learning. In Zambia, those en-

[10] Source: Press Release, November 18, 1982, Office of the Press Secretary to the Vice President; printed also in Department of State *Bulletin*, January 1983, pp. 43–45. Bush offered his toast at a state luncheon at the Intercontinental Hotel.

trusted with power have realized that they need not fear educated citizens, but rather welcome an informed electorate as a source of national strength and political well-being. As President Kaunda has said, "Any nation or people which does not value trained intelligence is doomed."

Your Honor, when this nation achieved independence, it contained fewer than 100 university graduates. Today, Zambia boasts a fine national university, teacher training and technical institutions, and several thousand new graduates each year. I call that success.

Your Honor, I am proud that my country has played a part in this nation's life. You might recall that when Zambia achieved independence, the United States was one of the first to establish a resident embassy here.[11] From the first we offered not only friendship, but cultural exchanges and, still more important, technical and economic aid. The relative mix of our programs has changed over the years to meet your needs. In recent years, our economic assistance program in Zambia, one of the largest in Africa, has reflected the importance both our governments place on the growing of food. Food aid, commodity imports, and help with your planning, research, and marketing have all represented aspects of our program.

Zambia's leaders have candidly stated that the economic mess that beset us all has sharply curtailed the resources you can dedicate to this country's development. My country is willing to provide special economic assistance. At the same time, however, we believe that expanded private investment in Zambia is necessary to strengthen this country's economy. But President Reagan is cutting inflation and providing incentives that will spur private investment and lead to sustained growth. The best way Americans can help the world economy is by strengthening our own.

Your Honor, the United States supports Zambia because doing so accords with American principles and American interests. Yet our friendship represents not only shared interests, but, as all warm friendships must, common experiences. Both the United States and Zambia have gathered languages, customs, and races into one nation. Your rallying cry, "One Zambia, one nation," expresses the same sentiment as our own national motto, "E pluribus unum," out of many, one. For two centuries the United States has represented a model for other nations. Now for nearly two decades, Zambia has done the same.

Your Honor, Zambia's example possesses particular importance for southern Africa. President Kaunda has worked long and selflessly as a leader of the frontline states to bring independence to Namibia. Since first taking office in 1981, President Reagan and his administration have done the same. As I stated in Zimbabwe, we have spared no effort. We have worked with the Western Contact Group, with the frontline states, with SWAPO, and with the Government of South Africa. Assistant Secretary Crocker has spent more time on this than on any other African matter. Your Honor, as I have made clear in Senegal, Nigeria, and Zimbabwe, the United States seeks to serve as a disinterested and honest broker. We possess neither troops nor proxies in the region. We have neither colonial interests nor military ambitions. Instead, the sole American interests in Africa are the interests of all men in all places: freedom and peace. Your Honor, we follow distinguished precedents. American efforts helped build peace between Israel and Egypt. British work helped lead to Zimbabwe's independence. As we work, Your Honor, we take realism as our watchword. As President Kaunda has written, we must avoid "both cynical pessimism and facile optimism and discover some hard realisms." We will labor on until all foreign troops withdraw from southern Africa, so Namibia might be free.

Two weeks ago, I was enjoying the autumn in Washington with my family. Three days ago I stood in the chill winter wind in Moscow. As I watched a stately display of Russian soldiers, I couldn't help thinking that many of them were the same age as our four sons. Today I am in a city of flame trees and jacarandas, experiencing a beautiful African summer. Again, in Zambia I have noticed many young men the same age as our sons.

Seasons change. Languages differ. But, Your Honor, the dreams in the hearts of young men and women remain the same. They are dreams of careers pursued in freedom and prosperity. They are dreams of families raised in peace. Your Honor, through the wisdom and labors of Kenneth Kaunda and many present today, in Zambia those dreams can come true.

Ladies and gentlemen, please join me in toasting President Kaunda, the Secretary General, and the Republic of Zambia.

[11] On October 24, 1984.

D. Zaire

Document 591

Testimony by the Assistant Secretary of State for African Affairs (Crocker) Before the Senate Foreign Relations Committee, April 16, 1982 (Extract)[1]

Proposed U.S. Security Assistance to Zaire

. . . .

SENATOR KASSEBAUM. . . . Let me move on to Zaire. What are our objectives in Zaire?

MR. CROCKER. Senator, in the broadest terms we look at Zaire and we see it as one of the largest countries in Africa. It has a large population. It borders with nine countries. It is the keystone of stability in central and southern Africa.

Zaire plays an important role in terms of our southern African diplomacy which is not all that often recognized. But, of course, it is also in every sense but formal name a frontline state with very important interests at stake along the Angolan border. It is a country with which we have had friendly relations for many years. We seek to continue those relations. But above all, we seek to reinforce in every way we can both the development chances for Zaire and the territorial integrity of Zaire, which as you know has been threatened many times in the past.

So we seek to reinforce those relations of friendship, to reinforce territorial integrity, and to give the country a chance over a longer term to turn the corner toward real development, bearing in mind the many problems that it faces and its unique colonial history and the Belgian legacy, which did not leave a very strong basis for nation building and development, let us be honest about it.

[1] Source: *Fiscal Year 1983 Security Assistance: Hearings Before the Committee on Foreign Relations, United States Senate, Ninety-seventh Congress, Second Session* (Washington, 1982), pp. 294–295.

Beyond that, I would point out that while the Zaire program attracts a lot of attention in this country and a fair degree of controversy, I think what is not recognized is that on a per capita basis our assistance levels in Zaire are among the very lowest in all of Africa. We are seeking really modest increases from a very low base, given Zaire's importance and the importance of our interests there.

SENATOR KASSEBAUM. I think that is very true. I would like to ask you, though, why, according to figures that I have been given, we are doubling military assistance to Zaire. Would you explain why this is, in the light of reports—or perhaps this is the reason—of significant deterioration in the brigades now in Zaire?

MR. CROCKER. I beg your pardon? Deterioration of what?

SENATOR KASSEBAUM. Of the brigades, 21st and 31st Brigades in Zaire, that are regarded as main deterrents, I gather, to any threat of invasion.

MR. CROCKER. That is correct. Senator, we are focusing our increase on the military side. It is a doubling, as I said, from a very low level to $20 million that we are seeking. The credits are to be used primarily to maintain Zaire's logistically critical C–130 fleet and strengthen ground transport and communication equipment that are identified with the battalions you referred to, largely in Shaba Province.

We are seeking, of course, to make it possible for these key units to be more reliable, to be better equipped, to have better leadership and to have better maintenance. There have been problems, as you referred to, with the C–130 fleet as well as in the brigade that is based in Shaba. We frankly do not feel we can be credible or that we will have any impact at the level that currently exists, and we are seeking to increase that level for that reason.

If I could be more specific on the C–130 program for the moment, last June the Department of Defense sent a study team to Zaire to look at the C–130 situation. It was impressed with the fact that these aircraft are used for both essential military and for economic purposes, that there are enormously heavy demands on the small fleet of aircraft, that they are not therefore sidelined for maintenance as often as they should be.

Maintenance has been inadequate. It has been underfunded. And we are seeking to directly address that problem by developing an in-country maintenance program for that fleet.

The same basically applies to the brigades that you referred to; principally, the 21st Brigade in Shaba.

SENATOR KASSEBAUM. There are those who think that there even has been deliberate misuse of military aid in Zaire. And it apparently has been somewhat of a chronic problem in trying to maintain any improvements in military organization there. Do you see this aid leading to lasting improvement, or is there still a structural problem there and a management problem that means this money will just more or less be wasted?

MR. CROCKER. Senator, our view is that there are indeed management problems, both in the civilian and military sector, in Zaire. We do not think it is helpful to dissemble on that point.

We also think it is worth pointing out that, for example, in Zaire's contribution to the Chad peacekeeping force, Zaire was the first to step forward. It was a courageous decision. It sent paratroopers to Chad. They performed very well indeed, as has their resupply from Zaire up to Chad.

So obviously, the potential is there, and we are seeking to improve it at all times. . . .

. . . .

Document 592

Statement by Representative Howard Wolpe Before the House Foreign Affairs Committee, May 11, 1982 (Extract)[2]

Impasse With the Reagan Administration Over Limitation of Foreign Military Sales Credits to Zaire

. . . .

The administration had proposed in the case of Zaire to double the military assistance from $10.5 million, which is being extended this year, to $20 million in 1983. It also requested a $15 million economic support fund commodity import program.

The subcommittee recommends instead bill language that would limit FMS credits for fiscal year 1983 definitively to $4 million. The bill language is required in the judgment of the subcommittee because of the administration's refusal last year to uphold the House-Senate conference decision to provide $6 million in military aid for Zaire.

I wanted to say a few words about that. The committee will recall that the chairman individually and all the subcommittee chairmen collectively sent correspondence to the administration when we were notified of the administration's intent to totally ignore the agreement that had been reached in conference this past year with respect to a $6 million limitation of FMS credits to[3] Zaire.

I personally had spoken with key officials within the administration urging that they not violate the agreement reached in the conference report language.

It seems to me that this committee has worked very hard with the administration to maintain a relationship of trust and mutual confidence that in the past had not required us to earmark in a very specific way limitations on military assistance.

It has always been understood that if, indeed, an emergency situation arose, involving matters of American national security, that we as a subcommittee and the full

---

[2] Source: *Foreign Assistance Legislation for Fiscal Year 1983: Markup Before the Committee on Foreign Affairs, House of Representatives, Ninety-seventh Congress, Second Session* (Washington, 1982), Part 8, p. 182. Wolpe was chairman of the Subcommittee on Africa.

[3] On August 12, 1982, the Department of State responded to a March 9, 1982, query by Wolpe on this subject under cover of a letter from Assistant Secretary of State for Congressional Relations Powell A. Moore as follows: "The $6 million figure for FY 1981 was a recommendation, not a ceiling, and the Administration judged that the $10.5 million contained in the original request to the Congress was the minimum necessary to safeguard our interests in Zaire and to help achieve our goals there. There was considerable support for this position in both Houses of Congress. The proposed $20 million in FY 1983 security assistance is similarly responsive to the legitimate security interests of Zaire." See *Implementation of Congressionally Mandated Human Rights Provisions: Hearings Before the Subcommittees on Europe and the Middle East, on Asian and Pacific Affairs, on Human Rights and International Organizations, and on Africa of the Committee on Foreign Affairs, House of Representatives, Ninety-seventh Congress, First and Second Sessions* (Washington, 1982), Volume II, p. 336.

committee were prepared to honor and to respect the necessity for flexibility on the part of the administration.

In this circumstance there has been no such showing of new emergency before us. It is simply the administration's arrogance that allowed it to move forward in total disregard of the language that had been developed and the agreements that had been reached by the House and Senate conferees.

I think it is critical, therefore, that from this point on the Zairian military aid levels be earmarked by way of limitation in committee bill language, and that is the purpose of this amendment that is now before the committee.

. . . .

Document 593

Statement by the Deputy Assistant Secretary of State for African Affairs (Lyman) Before the House Foreign Affairs Committee, May 11, 1982 (Extract)[4]

Limitation on Aid for Zaire

Congressmen, Mr. Chairman, I am Princeton Lyman, Deputy Assistant Secretary for Africa.

The administration would oppose both the proposed section 103 (a) and (b).[5] On the FMS program, we are working with our allies to have two brigades well trained and well officered, and able to move to defend that country. If you look at the leadtime on military assistance items, the effect of the FMS limitation would mean that in 1984 no C-130's would be flying in Zaire, and that cannot be what we want and that cannot be what we want to plan ahead to.

The two units that are being trained by our allies are well disciplined and operate the way we want to see professional military units operate. We don't want to take the support out from those two units.

I would also call attention to the 103(b) proposal, which denies any ESF for Zaire. We have just seen the committee vote more economic support for Tunisia on the grounds that economic problems are critical to the country's stability and defense. The Subcommittee on Africa last year recommended more economic aid for Zaire.

In our proposals for ESF, we are trying to assist economically, particularly the private sector which has not been able to obtain foreign exchange for raw materials or supplies, and which therefore is operating well under capacity. To deny any ESF to Zaire is to prevent us from helping people who are able to work productively and who are in very difficult straits because of the overall economic situation in Zaire.

So we would hope that both provisions, 103(a) and 103(b), could be eliminated because we think they really are detrimental not only to our security interests, but also to the economic benefit of Zaire.[6]

. . . .

Document 594

Statement and Remarks by Vice President Bush, Kinshasa, November 23, 1982 (Extract)[7]

U.S. Support for Zaire

As a visitor departing Zaire and its proud capital Kinshasa, I feel truly honored and

---

[4] Source: *Foreign Assistance Legislation for Fiscal Year 1983*, Part 8, p. 186.

[5] The text of section 103 (a) read as follows: "For the fiscal year 1983, the principal amount of loans guaranteed under section 24(a) of the Arms Export Control Act for Zaire may not exceed $4,000,000, and no credits (or participations in credits) may be extended under section 23 of that Act for Zaire." Section 103 (b) read as follows: "For the fiscal year 1983, no assistance may be provided to Zaire under chapter 4 of part II of the Foreign Assistance Act of 1961." For the text of H.R. 6370, the bill to amend the Foreign Assistance Act of 1961 and the Arms Export Control Act, see *ibid*, pp. 320-352.

[6] Following Lyman's statement, the committee, by voice vote, approved a motion by Representative Wolpe agreeing to Section 103. *Ibid.*, p. 188. Following the action of the committee in cutting U.S. assistance to Zaire, AZAP, Zaire's official news agency, reported President Mobutu's decision to renounce U.S. aid. See *Washington Post*, May 14, 1982, p. A20.

[7] Source: Press Release, November 23, 1982, Office of the Press Secretary to the Vice President. Bush's comments were made prior to his departure.

privileged. Honored to have been so generously and graciously received, and privileged to have had the opportunity to carry the warm greetings of President Reagan and the American people to President Mobutu and the people of Zaire. My discussions with President Mobutu and others have been friendly, wide-ranging and fruitful.

I am deeply impressed by the great achievements made by Zaire since its independence in all fields. These achievements are particularly striking given the extraordinary difficulties which this government faced in the early years of its independence.

The United States and Zaire have had a long and close relationship. We are proud of the history of American private and governmental assistance to Zaire. During our visit here, my wife, Barbara, and I have seen positive results of our cooperative efforts by missionaries, Peace Corps volunteers, private investors and government assistance.

I am convinced of the determination of the people of Zaire to achieve the goals of social and economic development and political security.

These goals will take much work and sacrifice. It will not be easy. I can offer no simple solutions, for there are none. It will take the cooperation of many nations and international organizations for success. We recognize that Zaire cannot do this alone. But I am convinced that as Zaire makes a major effort it will find that others stand ready to assist.

Investment has an important role to play in development, and I have discussed this question with President Mobutu. I am pleased to announce that during my visit here, the United States and Zaire have agreed to begin negotiations leading to a bilateral investment treaty to encourage and set the framework for American private investment in Zaire.

My visit has also enabled me to review with President Mobutu issues of mutual concern. I have benefited from his knowledge and perspective. I will carry back with me to President Reagan the fruits of those discussions and the impression I have received of the important role of Zaire as a leading and reasonable voice on the African Continent. Our two nations have worked together on many international and regional problems, and I am convinced after my talks here, that we will continue to do so.

I am pleased to welcome a high-level delegation of Zairian leaders who will come to Washington for further discussions concerning our relations with Zaire. The visit has been set for the first week in December.

We have long had a wide-ranging and intense dialogue with the Government of Zaire on all subjects of mutual interest. To broaden this dialogue even further on the political plane, I have invited President Mobutu to send three leading political figures from the Central Committee to Washington for a special visit in 1983.

As I leave Zaire today, my wife and I will always remember the friendliness of its people, and the openness of its leaders. Relations between our two nations are, and will remain, close. I wish to thank President Mobutu and the people of Zaire for their hospitality which has made my visit to Zaire so successful and enjoyable.

Thank you very much.

Q. Thank you Mr. Vice President. You said that the United States and Zaire were going to sign a bilateral investment treaty. We would like to know if this is an isolated case or within a global framework as we see in a number of other countries?

VICE PRESIDENT. Well, this one is bilateral. It will simply be between Zaire and the United States. There are other precedents for this. We have a few other investment bilateral treaties. What it does is reflect, on our part at least—it reflects our continuing strong interest in doing more in terms of investment and trade with Zaire.

Q. But the United States has often said that they would not interfere in the decisionmaking processes of say, the IMF or the World Bank. How do you interpret the amendment by two members of the American Congress to prevent American aid to Zaire as long as we have not signed an agreement with either the World Bank or IMF?[8] Is such a measure justifiable?

VICE PRESIDENT. Well, I think that the bottom line should be a full cooperation with the IMF, give-and-take, making sure IMF understands Zaire's needs. But we do feel that it is important that Zaire be af-

---

[8] On May 28, Senators Nancy Kassebaum and Paul Tsongas introduced an amendment to Title V of the International Security Enhancement Act of 1982, S. 2608, prohibiting the appropriation of ESF aid to Zaire until the President certified that Zaire had reached agreement with the IMF. See *Legislative Activities Report of the Committee on Foreign Relations, United States Senate, Ninety-seventh Congress, January 5, 1981–December 23, 1982* (Washington, 1983), p. 105.

forded the benefits that would come from the United States Congress to want to see compliance with IMF for economies that are having a rough time. But I would not—I would—this as an intervention in the internal affairs of Zaire. Certainly that's not the intention of this administration.

We are interested in being helpful bilaterally and through these multilateral agencies in helping Zaire overcome with its enormous resources—overcome the severe financial problems that it faces.

. . . .

E. West Africa: Cameroon, Ghana, Liberia, Nigeria, and Senegal

Document 595

Statement by the Secretary of State (Haig) Before the U.S. Investment and Trade Commission to Africa, January 8, 1982 (Extracts)[1]

Visit of a Cabinet Trade Delegation to West Africa

. . . .

I do, on behalf of Secretary Baldrige and Secretary Block, welcome all of you here—Ambassadors, members of the Congress and very distinguished members of the private sector of the United States. I think we have the executive leadership of some 26 corporations here, and what this is all designed to do is to launch a great ship, if you will, a safari in reverse, leaving the jungles of Washington for the relative calm of the continent of Africa.

. . . .

I do want to highlight the fact that this is the first high-level Cabinet trade delegation traveling from abroad for this administration, and I do also want to highlight the fact that never has such a high-level group been put together for a similar mission, to my knowledge, in the history of our country. I think it demonstrates, as perhaps nothing else can, President Reagan's sensitivity for the developing world, for the commitments he made at Cancun, and for his fundamental belief that economic growth is best provided through the private sector where mutual advantages of investment and development are achieved by both sides.

It is no unusual fact that the four countries involved—Cameroon, Ivory Coast, Nigeria, and Morocco—are themselves exemplifiers of internal self-help, the initiatives and ingenuity of the peoples of their own country because they are models in a very difficult area of economic growth and development.

That probably explains the sense of hospitality that we feel for the governments concerned already as a result of their ambassadorial work here in Washington, and you Ambassadors who are going along on the trip can consider yourselves as vice presidents for marketing.

I know that we view this important trip with a great deal of optimism. It has been my view—and I've espoused it—and I know it is the President's view that the developing world is becoming increasingly important to Western industrialized societies.

I know, for example, as we look at our own trade balances that the increasing percentage is going to the developing countries, and I know also that international peace and stability can only be achieved by economic growth and the achievement of social justice worldwide.

It has been our perception and the President's perception that international peace and stability, accompanied by social and economic development and social justice, must be achieved through peaceful means. Therefore, in addition to what I call "bottom line" or productivity and profit aspects of this mission, I think you can all take a great deal of self-satisfaction that you're engaged in an even broader mission: That is one that confirms the mutuality of efforts

---

[1] Source: Department of State Press Release 14, January 11, 1982. Haig spoke at the Department of State.

[2] The delegation visited the Ivory Coast from January 9 to 12, Nigeria from January 12 to 14, Cameroon from January 14 to 16, and Morocco from January 16 to 18.

and cooperative private investment which is geared to the welfare of peoples and not bureaucracies who sometimes substitute their judgment for the individuality of liberty and freedom of our people.

So I wish you the very best. We're delighted here in the Department of State to have you here as sort of a launching pad for this very important mission, and I eagerly await the results of what I know will be an extremely successful voyage. Thank you.

. . . .

Document 596

Statement Issued by the Department of State, February 4, 1982[3]

U.S. Policy Toward the Confederation of Senegal and Gambia

Q. Would you have any objection to confederation process of the Gambia and Senegal, considering that one country has intervened militarily to restore the government of the other?[4]

A. Confederation of the Gambia and Senegal is a bilateral issue. We would note that Senegalese troops entered the Gambia under provisions of a 1967 Mutual Defense Treaty and at the invitation of the Gambian Government. In addition, confederation procedures have followed the constitutional process of each country. The President sent congratulatory messages to Presidents Diouf and Jawara when the Treaty of Confederation was signed.

[3] Source: Office of Press Relations, Department of State; posted statement. The statement was posted in response to a question asked at the Department of State Daily Press Briefing on February 3, 1982.

[4] On July 30, 1981, rebels attempted to overthrow the Government of Gambia. At the request of Gambia, Senegal suppressed the coup attempt. Senegal and Gambia signed a Unification Pact in Dakar on December 17, 1981, establishing a confederation, which was subsequently ratified by the Parliaments of both countries. The Pact entered into force on January 31, 1982.

Document 597

Testimony by the Assistant Secretary of State for African Affairs (Crocker) Before the Senate Foreign Relations Committee, April 16, 1982 (Extract)[5]

The Rationale for Proposed U.S. Assistance to Ghana

. . . .

Q. In view of the apparently deteriorating situation in Ghana since Jerry Rawlings overthrew a pro-West, democratically elected government last January, why is the administration proposing almost $20 million in foreign assistance for that country in fiscal year 1983?

A. Ghana's historic political instability is rooted in the failure of successive governments to deal effectively with major structural economic problems. Real per capita income has fallen nearly 30 percent from 1974 to 1981. It was the failure to arrest this decline that undermined the democratic government of Dr. Hilla Limann and created the raison d'etre for the coup. We are, of course, concerned when any democratically elected government is overthrown. That happened in Ghana and we cannot change what happened. It seems to me it is in our interest in the present situation to do what we can to ensure that Ghana returns to a democratic process. This, at least in part, depends on economic recovery, which would improve the prospects for the success of any future democratic government. We want to help that process.

Continued deterioration of Ghanaian conditions would provide an inviting target of opportunity for countries, such as Libya, which traditionally "fish in troubled waters" and could have a destabilizing effect on Ghana's moderate West African neighbors.

The new government's foreign policy is in flux and it is still trying to develop a

[5] Source: *Fiscal Year 1983 Security Assistance: Hearings Before the Committee on Foreign Relations, United States Senate, Ninety-seventh Congress, Second Session* (Washington, 1982), p. 313. This was the response of the Department of State to an additional question submitted for the record by Senator Kassebaum.

policy to cope with its economic crisis. The Ghanaian Government has reestablished a relationship with Libya and hopes for substantial economic aid. However, given the Libyans' poor record of fulfilling aid promises, and Ghana's proud tradition of nationalism, we expect Ghana will avoid allowing Libya to gain an undue influence over its policy. Ghanaian officials have told us they want a constructive relationship with the United States and will pursue a nonaligned policy. We are carefully watching whether Ghanaian deeds match these words and are monitoring Ghana's human rights performance which so far has avoided the excesses that followed the coup of 1979.[6] Our policy is to encourage respect for human rights.

We believe our fiscal year 1983 foreign assistance proposal will enable us to engage in a constructive dialogue with Ghana's new rulers on economic policy, at an appropriate time, and give us the flexibility to contribute—with other traditional donors and international financing institutions—to what we hope will be a bold Ghanaian economic reform effort and eventually a stable democratic system. We believe this is the best way to support moderation, human rights and political stability in Ghana.

. . . .

Document 598

Remarks by President Reagan and Cameroon President Ahidjo, July 26, 1982[7]

Meeting With President Ahidjo of Cameroon

THE PRESIDENT. It's been an honor and a pleasure to meet with President Ahmadou Ahidjo of Cameroon and to—Cameroon and to discuss the views and hopes of a major U.S. trading partner in Africa.

Our discussions today reconfirm the mutual respect our two countries have enjoyed for over 20 years. Our meeting covered a wide range of issues. Particularly useful was our discussion of southern Africa and the Middle East. I listened with interest to President Ahidjo's views on these difficult issues, and I hope he has also gained a better understanding of the role that we're trying to play.

We also had a useful discussion of the enormous economic burdens faced by Africa's developing countries and a possible role for the United States private sector in addressing these problems.

An American trade and investment mission, headed by Secretaries Baldrige and Block, visited Cameroon and several other African countries last January.[8] We continue to believe that private enterprise is the most effective means for fostering sound economic development. And I'm very pleased that Cameroon has opened its doors to American businessmen.

I hope that our two countries will enjoy increasingly close economic and trade relations in the years ahead.

Finally, our discussion gave me an opportunity to commend President Ahidjo for his outstanding leadership concerning the refugee problem. Over the past several years, Cameroon has hosted over 200,000 refugees fleeing civil wars and harsh regimes in neighboring countries. The United States has tried to help where it could, working through the United Nations High Commissioner for Refugees, to alleviate the heavy burden that this has brought to Cameroon.

We urge other nations to contribute to the international effort and give continuing support to the countries of first asylum and to the refugees themselves.

I know that the President will be meeting with a wide range of administration officials and members of the House and Senate during his Washington stay. And I'm certain that he will find them eager to expand the excellent working relations that we have with the Government of Cameroon. His discussions here are laying a foundation for enhanced cooperation and ever-closer ties of friendship between the United States and

---

6 The reference is to the overthrow of the government of General Fred W. K. Akuffo on June 4, 1979.

7 Source: White House Press Release, July 26, 1982, Office of the Press Secretary to the President; printed also in *Weekly Compilation of Presidential Documents*, August 2, 1982, pp. 957–958. The remarks were made at the departure ceremony on the South Lawn of the White House beginning at 1:08 p.m., following the meeting between Presidents Reagan and Ahidjo. President Ahidjo spoke in French and his remarks were translated by an interpreter.

8 See document 595.

Cameroon. And we're delighted to welcome him here to the United States. Mr. President. (Applause)

PRESIDENT AHIDJO. I am pleased after my last visit to the United States of America in 1967[9] to have been given this opportunity to come back once more to this great and beautiful country on the kind invitation of President Ronald Reagan with whom I have just had cordial and fruitful discussions.

With regard to our bilateral relations, the discussions were an opportunity to reaffirm the esteem that the Cameroonian and American people have for each other and to express our satisfaction with the close links of mutually advantageous cooperation existing between our two countries for over 20 years now.

With regard to the determination expressed on both sides and with the potentials of our two countries, there is no doubt that this cooperation will grow and be consolidated in the future. This is already evident in the four agreements recently signed[10] by the two governments to finance interior agricultural projects and training programs for a total amount of $12,000,200.

We also carried out a wide review of problems of common interest in Africa and the world. With regard to Africa, we expressed the need to accelerate the accession of Namibia to independence and to work toward the elimination of apartheid for the advent of majority rule in South Africa.

We also expressed the hope that the present crisis in Chad and within the Organization of African Unity will be satisfactorily solved as soon as possible. With regard to world affairs, we expressed our common determination to support in all circumstances the right of peoples to progress, peace, and self-determination. In this connection, we acknowledge the need to work in concert in a concerted manner to ensure respect for the basic principles of international relations such as nonrecourse to force, the peaceful settlement of conflicts and peaceful coexistence as well as the promotion of a more just, balanced and stable framework of cooperation between industrialized and developing countries as part of global negotiations to usher in a new international economic order.

Lastly, I wish to seize this opportunity to extend my sincere thanks to President Reagan and to the Government and the people of the United States for the warm welcome accorded us. (Applause)

Document 599

Remarks by President Reagan and Liberian Chairman Doe, August 17, 1982[11]

A Presidential Assurance of Support

THE PRESIDENT. It has been a pleasure to welcome Liberian Head of State Samuel K. Doe on his first visit to the United States.

It is especially fitting that we should be meeting this year as the United States and Liberia celebrate 120 years of diplomatic relations. Our discussions gave us an opportunity to reaffirm the special friendship and mutual respect between our two countries.

Clearly, a firm bond unites Liberians and Americans who have come together professionally and socially throughout the years. Our two governments have a long history of cooperation on bilateral and international issues.

Chairman Doe told me of his government's ambitious goals, including the return to democratic institutions and economic stabilization. We welcome his emphasis on bringing the benefits of development to every corner of Liberia. And today we discussed how the United States can assist Liberia in achieving these goals.

As I stated clearly in our discussion, the United States stands by its commitments to Liberia, and looks forward to continued, mutual cooperation. My meeting with Chairman Doe marks the beginning of his 2-week visit to the United States. And he

---

[9] Ahidjo visited the United States from October 19 to 25, 1967. See *American Foreign Policy: Current Documents, 1967*, p. 248.

[10] The agreements, which dealt with agricultural education, seed multiplication, and livestock and agricultural development, were formally signed on August 15, 1982.

[11] Source: White House Press Release, August 17, 1982, Office of the Press Secretary to the President; printed also in *Weekly Compilation of Presidential Documents*, August 23, 1982, pp. 1041–1042. The remarks were made at the departure ceremony on the South Lawn of the White House beginning at 12:59 p.m., following the meeting between President Reagan and Chairman Doe.

made me a little envious when he told me that his next stop after Washington is going to be—well, not exactly the next stop, but the next one after—is going to be Los Angeles, California.

But in addition to meeting with a wide range of administration officials and members of the Congress, he will have an opportunity to meet many Americans outside the government, and Liberians who live in the United States as well.

The personal ties among our private citizens play an important role in the special relationship between our two countries. I hope the longstanding ties between our two peoples, and between our governments, will be further strengthened in the years ahead.

And, Mr. Chairman, you are most welcome. (Applause)

CHAIRMAN DOE. Ladies and gentlemen of the press, I am extremely happy to be in the United States of America, long considered the land of the free and the home of the brave. My visit here today is in response to the kind invitation extended me by President Ronald Reagan, a man of abiding courage, strong will, and foresight.

As you know, Liberia and the United States have a long and historic friendship—we span more than 150 years. However, as Liberia's first leader to visit the United States,[12] my presence here is significant in two principle respects: firstly, to first reaffirm our traditional friendship with the United States; secondly, the portrayal to the world the United States continuing identification with and support of Liberia. In discussions with President Reagan I have explained the causes of the Liberian revolution and the economic problems which presently confront the country. I also voiced my country's hopes and aspirations for the maintenance of the free enterprise system and our adhering to democratic ideals. Together President Reagan and I discussed matters of international concern, particularly the war in Lebanon and independence for Namibia.

I also outlined the economic measures being taken by our government to achieve economic recovery and promote private sector investment. We are sure that these conditions are indispensable to the achievement of the smooth transition of the present government in 1985.

Ladies and gentlemen of the press, President Reagan assured me we can continue to count on America's understanding and support for the fulfillment of the objectives of our revolution. This is a most welcome assurance. It demonstrates the Reagan administration's commitment to maintaining the United States economic and strategic interests in Liberia. Our country serves as a mirror through which African nations can assess America's support and commitment to developing countries. It is our belief that with the kind of mutual interests we share, the United States should recognize that Liberia could serve as a mirror through which its support to developing countries could be assured.

Thank you very much. (Applause)

Document 600

Transcript of a White House Press Briefing, August 17, 1982 (Extracts)[13]

"Liberia Is Our Oldest Friend in Africa"

. . . .

SENIOR ADMINISTRATION OFFICIAL. . . . Liberia is our oldest friend in Africa. It is a relationship, a bilateral relationship, by which, overall, American-African relations are often judged.

This administration, unlike its predecessors, has taken very seriously the question of how we do get along with Liberia. And we have made a major effort, as have the Liberians, over the course of the past 18 months or so to address common problems.

I think it should be stressed that when the new government came into power in Liberia it faced an enormous array of problems, inherited problems. It faced those problems in an atmosphere of international economic downturn involving particularly poor markets, low-priced markets for the raw materials that Liberia primarily relies upon.

---

[12] Former Liberian Presidents Edwin Barclay, William V.S. Tubman, and William A. Tolbert had each visited the United States.

[13] Source: Office of the Press Secretary to the President. The briefing was on background and was conducted by senior administration officials beginning at 1:11 p.m. in the Briefing Room of the White House.

During this period of time, we have significantly expanded the level of American support for Liberia in an effort to back a government which is doing, evidently, so much to back and to help itself. Liberia has one of the finest records in Africa for adherence to and commitment to the kinds of conditions that are negotiated between individual countries and the world financial community, whether it's in the banking area or in terms of the International Monetary Fund. This is noteworthy.

Liberia has been making significant strides in the area of austerity measures designed to live within its own means and, in such circumstances, we do what we can to be supportive. So, this accounts for the level of effort that we have been making.

What also accounts for it is the reality of a sustained and determined drive by the new government in Liberia to address human rights issues and to commit itself to a program of gradual return to democratic rule, civilian rule which the government has publicly committed itself to.

So, for all these reasons, plus the reality that we, as a country, have significant interests in Liberia, we attach great importance to this visit and look forward to its continuation in the coming days.

. . . .

SENIOR ADMINISTRATION OFFICIAL. We have dealt with governments on the basis of our own interests. We do not ourselves choose governments or select the means by which they come to power. We've tried to work in a situation that was very confused and difficult at the outset in order to assist an old friend, which we've referred to as our oldest friend on the continent—a relationship going back nearly 150 years—to assist an old friend and, at the same time, to protect our own interests and put them on a longer-term footing. And we're very pleased at the progress which was made even in the early months after the coup and which has been accelerated, particularly over the past year.

And the other thing—I might refer you, also, to the latest human rights report which has been published by the Congress[14] to give you the latest views of our government concerning the present human rights situation. There have been several other—I should mention, there have been several other improvements since then that are not in that report that have to do with the general amnesty which was declared on December 23, 1981 and, secondly, the lifting of the curfew following the Head of State's return from his Asian and Arab trip in May of this year.

. . . .

Document 601

Toast by Vice President Bush, Dakar, November 11, 1982[15]

U.S. Warm and Close Relations With Senegal

It is a privilege, as the representative of a nation profound in its belief in liberty and human dignity, to begin my visit to the African Continent in a country that has so clearly and so consistently demonstrated the same beliefs. When liberty and law rule, citizens can rejoice; leaders can be well pleased with their stewardship.

Relations between the Republic of Senegal and the United States have almost certainly never been warmer or closer than they are now. Ninety-nine years ago, the United States established a consulate on the Island of Gorée;[16] in 1960 we opened our Embassy. For more than 20 years we have worked together to make sure our relationship would be mutually beneficial. Our efforts have been crowned by success—especially, I would like to think, since January, 1981. The two administrations which took office then—yours under the leadership of President Diouf[17] and ours under the leadership of President Reagan—have

---

[14] Reference is to *Country Reports on Human Rights Practices for 1981: Report Submitted to the Committee on Foreign Affairs, U.S. House of Representatives and the Committee on Foreign Relations, U.S. Senate by the Department of State* (Washington, February 1982), pp. 139–146.

[15] Source: Press Release, November 11, 1982, Office of the Press Secretary to the Vice President; printed also in Department of State *Bulletin*, January 1983, p. 35. The toast was offered at the Prime Minister's state dinner.

[16] The United States established a consulate on the island of Gorée on December 20, 1883.

[17] President Léopold Sédor Senghor resigned at midnight on December 31, 1978, and was succeeded by the then Prime Minister, Abdou Diouf.

raised our bilateral relations to a particularly privileged level. In this respect we can especially be pleased with our work.

Our increasingly close cooperation reflects many of the common ideals and aspirations of our two societies and peoples. We share a fundamental commitment to the peaceful solution of conflicts and to the rule of law. We both affirm unshakable attachment to our democratic institutions, to human rights, and to the inalienable liberty of all men and all women.

This close collaboration also reflects, I think, the personal philosophies of the leaders of our two governments. Neither President Diouf nor President Reagan believes in magic solutions to difficult problems. They have affirmed as leaders the simple propositions that progress can only be achieved through sacrifice, hard work and common sense. Your daily actions show how true the Senegalese proverb is that "man is the best cure for his own ills." As our philosopher—President Thomas Jefferson asked, "How can great results be obtained except by great efforts?" You have our pledge that the United States is committed to seek an end to the ills which assail us all, to advance justice and dignity throughout the world. Criticism is directed every day at the United States. But I ask our friends to consider this: has any great power in human history so consistently used its great power for purposes so benign?

I think not.

President Reagan's administration will make no easy promises which it cannot keep. We will not posture for the sake of easy good will. And we will not direct gratuitous criticisms at others. We have demonstrated clearly that we will honor F.H.A.A.[18] and improve on our commitments to our traditional friends in Africa and elsewhere.

I would like to thank you and your government for the welcome extended to us here. Senegal is a country that smiles on the stranger. This friendship comes ultimately from the heart of a people, and it is found in great abundance in Senegal. An American is at home where hard work and human dignity are respected. An American is at home where liberty and justice prevail. For these reasons, especially, an American is at home in Senegal.

In this spirit, ladies and gentlemen, let me ask you to join me in a toast to Presidents Abdou Diouf and Ronald Reagan and to the spirit of collaboration, to the spirit of friendship which prevails between the Senegalese and American peoples.

[18] This is apparently a typographical error. The record does not indicate to what the Vice President was referring.

Document 602

Joint Communiqué Issued by the United States and Nigeria, Lagos, November 13, 1982 (Extract)[19]

The United States and Nigeria Exchange Views

Joint communiqué issued during the official visit to the Federal Republic of Nigeria of Mr. George Bush, Vice President of the United States of America, Friday 12th to Sunday 14th November 1982. The Vice President of the United States of America, Mr. George Bush, accompanied by Mrs. Bush and a delegation of high ranking government officials, paid an official visit to the Federal Republic of Nigeria from November 12 to 14, 1982, at the invitation of his Nigerian counterpart, Dr. Alex Ifeanyichukwu Ekwueme. Vice President Bush had the honour to pay courtesy calls on His Excellency Alhaji Shehu Shagari, President of the Federal Republic of Nigeria, and on the Honorable Dr. Joseph Wayas, President of the Senate.

Official talks were held between the visiting Vice President and his host accompanied by his delegation. During these talks, which were characterized by cordiality and understanding, the two Vice Presidents exchanged information on global, political, cultural, economic, and social developments. They examined various aspects of the present state of their bilateral relations and means of further developing and strengthening them. They also exchanged views on the world situation and their respective countries' position on a number of international issues, including some now before the 37th session of the United Nations General Assembly. The two Vice Presidents agreed on a number of areas where

[19] Source: Press Release, November 13, 1982, Office of the Press Secretary to the Vice President; printed also in Department of State *Bulletin*, January 1983, pp. 40–42. The joint communiqué was read to the press by Nigerian Minister for External Affairs Chief Patrick Bolokor beginning at 12:30 p.m., following Bush's meeting with Ekwueme.

Nigeria and the United States can work together to foster world peace and prosperity. They affirmed their continued support for the United Nations and endorsed its collective efforts to achieve world peace. The two Vice Presidents welcomed the steps being taken to effect a lasting, durable and just peace in the Middle East, in conformity with Security Council resolutions.

South Africa and Namibia: As to the future of southern Africa, the two Vice Presidents agreed that it is of vital importance to work urgently for the achievement of peace and regional security in southern Africa. The two Vice Presidents reaffirmed the opposition of their governments and nations to apartheid and racial discrimination. As regards Namibia, the two sides reaffirmed their conviction of the necessity for rapid decolonisation and independence for Namibia on the basis of recognized democratic principles and the will of the majority of the people. They agreed that an internationally acceptable independence for Namibia under the terms of United Nations Security Council Resolution 435 remains an objective of highest priority for both governments. The work of the five-nation Western Contact Group and of Nigeria and the frontline African states to secure Namibian independence was again strongly endorsed and it was agreed that close consultations between the two governments, and other members of both groups would continue. Vice President Bush reviewed his government's parallel efforts to insure the timely withdrawal of all foreign forces from the area, and it was agreed that the matter should continue to be the subject of bilateral discussions between the United States and the Governments of Angola and South Africa. Vice President Ekwueme reaffirmed his government's position that the withdrawal of Cuban troops from Angola must not be a condition for movement towards Namibia's independence. Vice President Bush indicated the United States objective is parallel and consistent with the security interests of all parties.

OAU and other African issues: Vice President Bush noted his government's strong support for the Organization of African Unity, and commended the organization's efforts to secure peace and foster African development. The two Vice Presidents reaffirmed their governments' views on the need for a cease-fire and an early referendum in the Western Sahara in conformity with resolutions passed at the Organization of African Unity summit meeting in Nairobi in June 1981.[20] The two Vice Presidents expressed satisfaction at efforts to secure reconcilation and their national unity in Chad and pledged the support of their governments in assisting the Government of Chad.

Economic relations: The two leaders discussed plans for the seventh round of bilateral talks to be held under the aegis of Vice President Ekwueme in Lagos in February 1983. These talks will include cooperation in the areas of agriculture, energy, science and technology, health, trade and investment, and education. The Vice Presidents agreed that they look forward to continuing close contact on the joint economic bilaterals and that each will play host to the meetings in the future which take place in his own capital city.

Vice Presidents Ekwueme and Bush expressed satisfaction over the inaugural meeting of the Nigeria–United States business council in September 1982 as a concrete and effective measure to implement earlier bilateral discussions. They also took note of the concrete results achieved by the United States–Nigeria Joint Agricultural Consultative Committee (JACC), which has contributed significantly to increased cooperation between the United States and Nigeria in support of expanding Nigerian agricultural production, as well as to increased sale of American agricultural products. They noted that the United States Agency for International Development has signed a contract to provide for increased staff support to the Joint Agricultural Consultative Committee.

The two leaders also exchanged views on the current state of the world economy. Mr. Bush highlighted the steps being taken by the United States to reduce inflation and lower interest rates in order to set the stage for long-term real growth of the American economy. Dr. Ekwueme highlighted the measures recently taken by the Federal Government of Nigeria to adjust economic activity to expected levels of oil income.

Commercial and agriculture: The United States side expressed its determination to continue to work to increase trade with Nigeria despite the current problems in the economies of both countries using the full range of available facilities such as the Export-Import Bank, the Overseas Private Investment Corporation, the new export trad-

[20] Regarding this OAU resolution, see *American Foreign Policy: Current Documents, 1981*, document 393.

ing company legislation, and with a maximum role played by the private sector. The Nigerian side welcomed this determination and for its part confirmed the recent opening of a Nigerian trade and investment center in New York and its plans to open another one in Chicago before the end of 1982.

Note was also taken of new United States Department of Agriculture credit programs which may become available for Nigeria. These would provide direct credit blended with export credit guarantees which would effectively reduce the overall cost of credit.

Democracy and human rights: Vice President Bush expressed the strong admiration of his country and its people for Nigeria's deeply-held commitment to democracy and human rights. The deep appreciation of the United States Government was expressed for the participation of President Shangari's personal representative as a keynote speaker at the recently-held Washington Conference on Free Elections.[21]

Travel and exchanges: Both sides viewed with satisfaction the tradition of fruitful exchanges between citizens of the Federal Republic of Nigeria and the United States. Both sides reviewed the United States decision of July 15, 1982, to issue multiple entry visas valid during four years to most categories of Nigerian nonimmigrant visa applicants. Ways were discussed to reduce to the minimum extent possible the remaining procedural barriers in documenting persons for travel between the Federal Republic of Nigeria and the United States and to work toward reciprocity in visa issuance procedures.

The two Vice Presidents expressed their very deep satisfaction at the useful contacts which were made during this visit and hoped that they would form the basis of future development in their already cordial bilateral relations.

The Vice President of the United States of America, Mr. George Bush, expressed his gratitude and pleasure to his host, Dr. Alex Ekwueme for the hospitality and warm reception accorded to him and his delegation. . . .

. . . .

[21] Regarding this conference, see footnote 6 to document 130.

F. The Horn of Africa

Document 603

Letter From the Assistant Secretary of State for African Affairs (Crocker) to the Editor of the "New York Times", January 21, 1982[1]

Periled Ethiopians Can Still Stay Here

To THE EDITOR: Anthony Lewis's Jan. 4 column,[2] suggesting that the Reagan Administration was embarking on a wholesale deportation of Ethiopian refugees ("Hypocrisy Wins Again"), contains some serious inaccuracies and distortions.

In fact, the recent change in the treatment of Ethiopians by the Immigration and Naturalization Service only brings their status into line with that of most other nationalities in the United States. Up until last summer, Ethiopians were allowed to remain and work in the U.S. even if their visas had expired, under what is called "extended voluntary departure status."

This special status was adopted following the Ethiopian revolution in 1974—during the period of Ethiopia's "Red Terror," when large numbers of Ethiopians were being killed in both Government-sponsored and random violence. At that time, the State Department recommended to the Immigration and Naturalization Service that Ethiopians in the United States not be forced to return to Ethiopia while these conditions persisted.

Such voluntary departure programs have been adopted only rarely. This policy provided for humane treatment of thousands of Ethiopians in this country as a temporary response to conditions in Ethiopia at that time.

Although the human rights picture in Ethiopia is still very bleak, the level of chaos

[1] Source: *New York Times*, February 1, 1982, p. A14.

[2] Lewis charged (p. A23) that at the same time that Ambassador Jeane Kirkpatrick was denouncing the "savagery" of the Marxist regime in Ethiopia, the Immigration and Naturalization Service of the Department of Justice was notifying Ethiopian refugees in the Boston area that their voluntary departure status in the United States was being revoked owing to the stabilization of conditions in Ethiopia. Ethiopians enjoying such status were permitted employment for 1 year, renewable after review.

and violence in most of the country has declined since the period of the Red Terror and the other post-revolutionary excesses. It is now possible for Ethiopians who are not on their Government's "wanted" list to return without fear of falling victim to persecution.

Ethiopians who are bona fide refugees (i.e., those who have been admitted into the United States as refugees from processing centers overseas) are in no danger of being asked to leave. Neither are those Ethiopians who do have well-founded fear of persecution from the Government should they return.

All applications for political asylum are reviewed on a case-by-case basis; asylum is granted to those applicants who do show a well-founded fear of persecution.

Ethiopians who are here for education, medical treatment or whatever may also stay as long as their visas remain valid. Those who are affected by the suspension of extended voluntary departure status for Ethiopians are those who no longer have any legitimate reason for remaining in the United States.

CHESTER A. CROCKER

Document 604

Transcript of a White House Press Briefing, March 9, 1982[3]

Background to the U.S. Visit of Somalian President Siad Barre

SENIOR ADMINISTRATION OFFICIAL. This will be President Siad's third visit to the United States. He came here first during the Ford administration when he was President of the OAU.[4] He came last year on a private visit during which time he met with Secretary Haig and Secretary Weinberger.

He will arrive today and spend about 3 days here in Washington during which time he will meet with Secretary Haig, Secretary Weinberger, Peter McPherson of AID, President Reagan, of course; the following day, members of the Congress and heads of international organizations like the IMF and World Bank.

The visit is a good will visit. There is no specific purpose in mind. This visit has been planned for some time. This is part of the strengthening of relations between the United States and Somalia, a process which has been going on for the past 3½ years. The highlight of the strengthening of relations took place really in August of 1980 when we signed the access agreement[5] giving the United States access to Somali ports and harbors.

Our interests there are strategic, basically, humanitarian. We support the international effort to feed the refugees and provide other kinds of care for the refugees. We have very little economic interest there, although there are a number of American oil companies actively exploring for oil in Somalia. Somalia is a poor country, one of the poorest in the world. They depend on exports of live animals—sheep, goats, cattle, and camels—to the Arabian peninsula for over 80 percent of their export earnings. The bulk of the remainder of those earnings comes from bananas.

Our relations are quite good now. When we began to change our relationship after the expulsion of the Soviet military advisors in November 1977, there was an impediment to better relations, and that centered around the fact that the Somali Armed Forces remained actively in the Ogaden. However, in time they removed those troops from the Ogaden, which permitted us to enter into a military assistance relationship, essentially, FMS credits and some grant aid. That amount of that aid is, over 3 fiscal years, $60 million. The money is being used for nonlethal items, for defensive equipment—trucks, for example, radar—defensive radar equipment, and communications gear and things of that kind.

Our economic assistance program was reinstituted in 1978 and now amounts to about $15 million annually in development assistance, considerably more in humanitarian assistance, mostly P.L.–40 [*480*] Title II food to the refugees.[6] And I'll stop there for questions.

---

[3] Source: Office of the Press Secretary to the President. The briefing was conducted on background by a senior administration official beginning at 10:01 a.m. in the Briefing Room of the White House.

[4] Siad Barre was President of the OAU from June 13, 1974 to July 27, 1975.

[5] Regarding the U.S.-Somalian Access Agreement, signed on August 22, 1980, see *American Foreign Policy: Basic Documents 1977–1980*, pp. 1237–1238.

[6] Title II of P.L.–480 permits the furnishing,

Q. You mean $60 million was military and $15 million economic?

SENIOR ADMINISTRATION OFFICIAL. No. $60 million over a 3-year period is what we've dispersed for military assistance. Again, largely defensive equipment and nonlethal equipment entirely. The economic assistance program is running $15 million roughly a year for development assistance, much more for humanitarian assistance—basically P.L.–40 [*480*] Title II and also Title I.[7] Also nonlethal—or other nonfood items for refugee assistance. We also have an economic support fund which amounts to $20 million this year.

Q. Do you have a ballpark figure on the amount—over the past 3 years on the economic assistance?

SENIOR ADMINISTRATION OFFICIAL. Last year the economic assistance—and, again, the bulk of this was for refugees—was in excess of $90 million. The previous year was less than that, but still substantial.

Somalia is the third largest recipient of U.S. economic assistance in Africa. Most of that, again, in the humanitarian side.

Q. It sounds like, to the extent of the consultations while he's here, it can be more than good will.

SENIOR ADMINISTRATION OFFICIAL. We will be talking, of course, about economic assistance, about military assistance, about the situation that exists in the Horn of Africa and beyond the Horn of Africa, in the area in general. Somalia, as you may know, faces the problem of Cuban forces in Ethiopia. There is an active guerrilla war which is supported by the Libyans, by the Soviets, cross border operations into Somalia on a very frequent basis, elements who are very well armed and equipped.

Q. In Somalia there's a guerrilla war?

SENIOR ADMINISTRATION OFFICIAL. That's correct, yes. Since the signing of the tripartite agreement between South Yemen, Libya, and Ethiopia last year,[8] the activities against Somalia have increased. Libyan money, in a great way, [is] responsible for that. The Libyans have made it clear, Qaddafi has stated publicly that it is an aim of his government to overthrow the government of Mohamed Siad Barre. One of the reasons for this is because the Somalis have given us access to the facilities out there. And also because Somalia never broke with Egypt. It was one of the three Arab countries, along with Oman and Sudan, which did not break relations with Egypt and which has maintained relations with Egypt all along. Egypt is a very important friend to Somalia.

Q. What kind of use are we making of these bases, the facilities there?

SENIOR ADMINISTRATION OFFICIAL. As of right now, very little. Berbera, for example, does not have one U.S. Government official, either military or otherwise. We are beginning to make improvements to that air strip in Berbera. And we plan to let the contract to improve the port later this year. That's about the state of the business right now. In time, there will be more use made of the facility. We have occasional ship visits to either Berbera or Mogadishu.

Q. So are they trying to increase, now, their military assistance, and economic?

SENIOR ADMINISTRATION OFFICIAL. The Somalis would like to have more assistance from us, yes.

Q. How much?

SENIOR ADMINISTRATION OFFICIAL. Well, they've never put a price tag on it. They would like to have expanded assistance in all fields if they can get it. We are very sympathetic to their needs, but there are constraints on how much we can do for Somalia or any other one country.

Q. Despite the fact that almost half of the refugees of the world live right in Somalia right now?

SENIOR ADMINISTRATION OFFICIAL. Well, that's not true any longer. It was true about a year and a half ago when the flood of refugees was coming in at as much as 2,000 a day. The figure was in excess of 1,000,000. And the largest refugee population, by far, existed in Somalia. Those were people in camps. There was another estimated half a million or more outside of camps.

Q. They came from Ethiopia?

SENIOR ADMINISTRATION OFFICIAL. Yes, from Ethiopia.

---

among other things, of agricultural commodities to meet famine or other urgent relief requirements. For the basic legislation, see 68 Stat. 454, and subsequent amendments.

[7] Title I of P.L.–480 authorizes the sale of agricultural commodities to foreign countries on credit terms.

[8] The treaty between Libya, Ethiopia, and the People's Democratic Republic of Yemen (PDRY) was signed in Aden on August 19, 1981. It provided for the deployment of the armed forces of the signatories in each other's territory under certain circumstances.

Q. One million in camps, one-half million out?

SENIOR ADMINISTRATION OFFICIAL. One million plus, yes. The top figure was 1.3 million. And maybe 300,000, 500,000 out of the camps. Nobody could tell you. Putting quite a strain on Somalia's very limited resources. The refugee population today is diminished. It's in the neighborhood of 600,000 to 700,000. Nobody can tell you exactly. But that's still a very substantial refugee population. And it's going to demand a continued effort by the international community to keep these people clothed and fed. And we're hoping to make them more self-sustaining through food for work and other projects of this kind as time goes on. We want to avoid, everybody wants to avoid the Palestinian kind of situation where the refugees stay in camps for years and years and years.

Q. Are you referring to the Somalia National Liberation Front as the guerrilla group that you are talking about, and how large do you estimate their forces?

SENIOR ADMINISTRATION OFFICIAL. The Somali Democratic Salvation Front, as it is generally known (it used to be called the Somali Salvation Front), is composed of Somalis who have left the country. The nucleus of this was a group of officers who had attempted a coup in April of 1978, had failed, left the country, and started a military movement outside, based in Ethiopia. The Ethiopians, with Soviet backing, provided them with assistance and now Libya is providing them with more assistance. We don't know the exact number. But it's estimated in the neighborhood of 2,000 or so.

Q. Inside the country?

SENIOR ADMINISTRATION OFFICIAL. No, they're in Ethiopia. They come in, raid a police station or a small military unit, and then fade out again very quickly.

Q. Do you have a figure on the amount of money we're spending to improve the airstrip and harbor?

SENIOR ADMINISTRATION OFFICIAL. Yes I do. The FY'82 funds are in the neighborhood of $25 million. We have allocated a very small portion of this for the airstrip, and construction on improving that airstrip has begun using a Somali contractor. The bulk of the $25 million will go for the port, extending the quay there, adding on a quay of about 330 meters, and making other improvements in the port. We're asking the Congress for an additional $30 million, in FY'83, to complete the port project and to finish the airstrip project.

Q. Is the Ogaden war, is that, the Ogaden is calm now?

SENIOR ADMINISTRATION OFFICIAL. Relatively speaking, yes. There are occasional dust-ups but if anything, the action has shifted inside Somalia as these guerrilla groups come across the border and raid and then go back. But there's still some activity in the Ogaden by the Western Somalia Liberation Front which used to be very active but now is very—well, almost inactive but still conducts occasional raids against Ethiopian forces. Yes?

Q. What's the situation on the human rights in Somalia now? There's some organization calling itself the Somali Community of America has some pretty hard things to say about—

SENIOR ADMINISTRATION OFFICIAL. Yes, I've read the literature of these various organizations and there's some truth to it and a lot of hyperbole. There are human rights violations in Somalia. The report that's been done by the U.S. Government acknowledges that.[9] There are a number of political prisoners. But there is no evidence of gross violations of human rights—torture, murder of prisoners, that kind of thing.

Recently, the government released a number of prominent political prisoners including the former prime minister and the former commandant of the police force. Others were also released and we are informed by the Somali officials that they intend to release all of the political prisoners. And this seems to be happening in drips and drabs now. Yes?

Q. Has Somalia in any kind of formal way abandoned its claim to the Western Ogaden or the Western Somalia?

SENIOR ADMINISTRATION OFFICIAL. Yes, in a formal way, it has said that it has no territorial ambitions against any of its neighbors. However, the Somalis continue to insist on what they call "self-determination" for the people of the Ogaden and this is unacceptable to Ethiopia.

Q. How about the claims—the original claims to Djibouti in the northern section of Kenya which is—

SENIOR ADMINISTRATION OFFICIAL. Those are dead issues. The Somalis and

[9] See *Country Reports on Human Rights Practices for 1981* (Somalia), pp. 226–231.

Kenyans have improved relations. The Somalis have relinquished any claim whatever to the northeastern province—now, it used to be called the northern frontier district of Kenya. And the two countries have moved to improve their relations in the past half year. It's moving in the right direction. The Somalis have neither the military capability nor the political will to pursue any kind of claim against Kenya. They're realists and they know this would harm their relations with the United States, with other friends including the Saudis and certainly with Africa. And so it's a dead issue. But the Kenyans have a residue of suspicion against the Somalis because of the animosity between the two countries that goes back 20 or more years. Yes?

Q. Could I follow that? I just wanted to ask you if they had any position on that Eritrean War?

SENIOR ADMINISTRATION OFFICIAL. They don't take an active part in this. But their position is that the Eritreans like other oppressed peoples in Ethiopia—this is what they say, should be allowed the right of self-determination. So, they support that movement, yes.

Q. Have there been any moves to remove the clauses in the constitution calling for integration of all that—Somali which do include territories in Kenya?

SENIOR ADMINISTRATION OFFICIAL. Yes, there was a modification of that when the new constitution was promulgated about 2 years ago.

Q. And how was it modified?

SENIOR ADMINISTRATION OFFICIAL. I can't quote you the text of it but it softened it considerably. Yes?

Q. Are we seeking any changes in the access rights agreement—any increase in our access rights—anything like that?

SENIOR ADMINISTRATION OFFICIAL. No, the access agreement as it now stands is wholly satisfactory to us. It meets our needs entirely.

Q. Is there a limitation on the size of shipping that could go into the ports there? In other words, could it accommodate an aircraft carrier?

SENIOR ADMINISTRATION OFFICIAL. It cannot accommodate an aircraft carrier. A carrier would have to stand outside in both Mogadishu Harbor and Berbera. The inner harbor in Berbera is rather small. The outer harbor is big and could take a carrier. But what we need to do is to improve the inner harbor to take more shipping and perhaps larger shipping.

Q. Was the access agreement primarily for U.S. military vessels?

SENIOR ADMINISTRATION OFFICIAL. Not just vessels but for U.S. military purposes—aircraft, for example, if we want to have free flights go in there or if we ever want to stage out of there. But the navy has had the primary interest in making use of those facilities some day. Let me emphasize again that we aren't really using them much yet and they haven't really been improved all that much yet. We've been moving deliberately in achieving this.

Q. Will American personnel be stationed there?

SENIOR ADMINISTRATION OFFICIAL. There are no plans at the moment for this coming year to station any American personnel there. Construction will be done by commercial firms and it could be that there will be a need for American engineering, naval or armed forces—engineering personnel to oversee it, to come in and go out. But there's no plan to have any people stationed there in the immediate future.

Q. If I can just follow up. Once the construction is completed it will require maintenance, I would presume,

SENIOR ADMINISTRATION OFFICIAL. A maintenance, caretaker kind of force, yes. And I can't give you any exact numbers because I haven't seen them. The original plans have been modified and I can't tell you. But it would not be a large force. There's no plan to have any large force of Americans stationed at any of these facilities.

Q. So all the large carriers couldn't get to the ports there, Mogadishu and Berbera. You said that you are including the ports.

Are you going to be utilizing the facilities in Somalia for the continuous use of the rapid deployment forces like for instance in Diego Garcia in the Indian Ocean?

SENIOR ADMINISTRATION OFFICIAL. No, I don't think that is a plan for continuous major use. It's more for the potential, when we might need it, and I think more regular use by ships that are in the area, not so much a part of the rapid deployment force, but of the elements of the Seventh Fleet that are in the area or of the Com Mid-East Force.

We did use Berbera for Operation Bright Star,[10] a very limited use of the facility, logistics, basically, bringing heavy equipment in by air and by sea and having engineers, U.S. engineers, a force of about 300 men, use those for projects that helped the local community. It was simply a logistics exercise and so we have used it for Bright Star.

Q. Yes, but will this situation about increasing the access or the use of the facilities in Somalia, do you see anything could be construed as maybe concerning and creating some worries in the Gulf Cooperation Council?[11] Because the Gulf Cooperation Council was talking recently, as recently as maybe a couple of weeks ago, about establishing their own rapid deployment forces and utilizing the whole area into protecting their own self, you know, without the presence of the United States or Soviet fleets in the area. So what do you comment, please?

Senior Administration Official. I can't really say what they might say. I can only tell you that there have been no expressions of deep concern by the Gulf States over the use of Somalian facilities by American forces.

Q. Do you see Somalia as a potential for the forward headquarters for the rapid deployment forces being discussed by the Pentagon now?

Senior Administration Official. I don't know. It might be one of those areas which would be under consideration, but I don't know if Somalia would provide what they need.

Q. Forgive me if you went over this at an earlier point in the briefing, but is it correct that the weapons that we have provided to Somalia so far have been defensive, entirely defensive in nature and is there any consideration being given to changing that?

Senior Administration Official. First of all, we haven't supplied any weapons. In fact, we haven't supplied anything. We have made arrangements to begin the supply of equipment which will consist mainly of radar, vehicles, trucks, a team to come out to repair their existing radar, and some communications gear. That's what we've agreed to. And that's used up most of the $60 million. The small amount remaining is being considered for possibly some other items. But as it stands now, it's been wholly defensive and nonlethal in nature.

Q. And is there any consideration being given to changing that? I mean, might that be an issue in these talks?

Senior Administration Official. I'm not aware of any serious consideration of changing that basic policy.

Q. Could you give a breakdown of the FY'83 requests for Somalia in the military, economic and—

Senior Administration Official. The administration is asking for $30 million for military assistance to Somalia of map [*MAP*] and FMS.

We will be going ahead with development assistance at about the same level, roughly $15 million or $16 million. Title II, between $16 million and $24 million of Title II food for the refugees. Title I at about $15 million. That's concessional, though. Let's see, ESF at $20 million this year, possibly higher next year. I'm not certain on that. Those are the major components of the projected assistance.

There is assistance outside of the directly bilateral to the UNHCR. There'll be $16.8 million, I believe, to the UNHCR effort in Somalia.

In addition, Congress has passed a special—provided a special allocation of $30 million for refugees in Africa, of which $12 million is earmarked for Somalia. Much of this money will go to projects to make the refugees more self-sufficient. And we are looking to ideas from the private voluntary organizations out there for this.

Q. Are they being absorbed in Somalia, the Ethiopian refugees?

Senior Administration Official. Not yet. Many of them have come in and who have not gone into camps and have moved out into various parts of the country, and in a sense they're absorbed. But they are putting a great strain on the limited resources the country has. And mind you, these are all Somalis, with some exception. I should say maybe 30 percent or more are what they

---

[10] Operation Bright Star was a joint military exercise held in November and December 1981 involving the forces of the United States, Egypt, Sudan, Somalia, and Oman.

[11] The Gulf Cooperation Council was formed on February 4, 1981, during a meeting in Riyadh between representatives of Saudi Arabia, Kuwait, Bahrain, Oman, and the UAE. On May 26, 1981, the Charter of the Gulf Cooperation Council was signed in Abu Dhabi by representatives of Saudi Arabia, Kuwait, Bahrain, Qatar, the UAE, and Oman. The declared aim of the Council was the coordination of the members' policies in all fields. See *Middle East Journal*, Summer 1981, p. 366, and Autumn 1981, pp. 599–600.

call Galla or Oromo people who are not Somalis, but they are being accepted by the Somalis anyway.

I think this is one thing you should remember, is that the Somalis, from the very beginning, have accepted this enormous number of refugees, knowing that it was going to put strains on their resources. They have a very positive attitude about helping the refugees.

Q. Thank you.

Q. Our relations with Somalia are very similar in a way to the relations with Sudan and in the situation many parallels have been drawn. Yet it would appear the Sudan is going to receive several times as much aid over the next few years. Is there any particular reason there?

SENIOR ADMINISTRATION OFFICIAL. It's a bigger country, its needs are greater, and perhaps the perception is that its security problems are more immediate.

Q. What's your comment on the request of the FY 1983 that was submitted by Alexander Haig—submitted by Alexander Haig last week to the Congress that the amount—the figure that was requested for the—to be assistance in 1983 is less than the number and the figure of 1982, which is substantially—

SENIOR ADMINISTRATION OFFICIAL. I'm not in a position to comment. I just got back to town and I'm not aware of that. Does anybody else here want to comment on that? Sorry.

Q. How troubled is Siad Barre by Qaddafi? And in general, what does he want to talk to the President and Secretaries of State and Defense about?

SENIOR ADMINISTRATION OFFICIAL. He is troubled by Qaddafi, by the very clear pronouncements by Qaddafi that it is the aim of Libya to help overthrow the Siad government. And he's aware that Qaddafi is a very unpredictable individual. He's aware that the Libyans are training people in urban terrorism as well as in guerrilla warfare. And he's aware that the Libyans have resources that can be put to use. Certainly, this will be a part of what he wants to talk to President Reagan and Secretaries Haig and Weinberger about. I think he wants essentially to see what our response is to his concerns about these major security problems, along with the economic problems that face Somalia today.

THE PRESS. Thank you.

Document 605

Testimony by the Assistant Secretary of State for African Affairs (Crocker) Before two Subcommittees of the House Foreign Affairs Committee, March 9, 1982 (Extract)[12]

Human Rights in Somalia

. . . .

8. Amnesty International has expressed a great deal of concern over Somalia's human rights record. Amnesty recently stated that "In Somalia, any expression of criticism of the government may lead to arrest and detention without trial. Those detained are believed to be held without charge. They may, however, be charged with subversion and tried by the National Security Court where internationally accepted standards for a fair trial are not observed. If found guilty, they could face a death penalty or life imprisonment." Did you discuss Somalia's human rights record with President Siad Barre during his recent visit to Washington?

A. In January 1982 our Ambassador in Mogadishu[13] emphasized the administration's commitment to human rights and reiterated congressional interest in Somalia's political prisoners. In February, on the eve of Siad's visit to the United States, several prominent political prisoners were released. During his visit to Washington in March, we expressed our support for the release of political prisoners and urged continued progress in that regard.

. . . .

---

[12] Source: *Implementation of Congressionally Mandated Human Rights Provisions: Hearings Before the Subcommittees on Europe and the Middle East, on Asian and Pacific Affairs, on Human Rights and International Organizations, and on Africa of the Committee on Foreign Affairs, House of Representatives, Ninety-seventh Congress, First and Second Sessions* (Washington, 1982), Volume II, p. 335. The March 9 hearing was held before the Subcommittees on Human Rights and International Organizations and on Africa. The answer by Crocker was sent under the cover of a letter dated August 12 from Assistant Secretary of State for Congressional Relations Powell A. Moore to Representative Howard Wolpe, Chairman of the House Subcommittee on African Affairs, in response to written questions submitted by Wolpe during the March 9 hearings on human rights in Africa. For the text of the March 9 testimony by Crocker, see *ibid.*, pp. 225–253.

[13] Donald K. Petterson.

Document 606

Remarks by the Secretary of State (Haig) and Somalian President Siad Barre, March 11, 1982[14]

Presidents Reagan and Siad Barre Discuss Bilateral Relations

SECRETARY HAIG. Good morning, ladies and gentlemen. I want to take this opportunity to introduce our distinguished visitor the President of Somalia—President Siad Barre.

Somalia has been a very good friend of the United States. We have collaborated closely in security affairs. Somalia has been a very receptive and hospitable recipient of hundreds of thousands of refugees from the Ogaden; refugees from Soviet-supplied armaments in the region. We had very fine discussions this morning—very productive discussions with the President. And on that note, I'd like to introduce our very distinguished visitor. Mr. President.

PRESIDENT SIAD. First of all, I'm very happy to meet the press and I hope that if my English is bad, you will forgive me. I'm Somali. I'm not English.

Secondly, I have come to Washington, D.C., at the invitation of President Ronald Reagan on an official working visit. My visit is intended to make a positive contribution toward the existing friendly relations of cooperation and understanding between our two countries.

We are grateful for the warm reception and the hospitality accorded to me and my delegation. I have discussed bilateral relations and other international questions of mutual concern with the President and I found a great identity of views on these matters.

The discussion was fruitful and I'm confident that our talks will lead to the opening of a new chapter of closer cooperation between our two countries.

I wish to express my gratitude to the American people and government for the continual assistance they have extended to the development of Somalia and the humanitarian support they gave to the large refugee population inside Somalia. Thank you very much.

[14] Source: White House Press Release, March 11, 1982, Office of the Press Secretary to the President. The remarks were made at the West Driveway of the White House beginning at 12:08 p.m., following Siad Barre's meeting with Secretary Haig and President Reagan.

Document 607

Transcript of a White House Press Briefing, March 11, 1982 (Extracts)[15]

Somali Requests for U.S. Assistance

SENIOR ADMINISTRATION OFFICAL. You heard what the Secretary and the President said.[16] The meetings that we've had in the last few days have been very cordial. They focused on our mutual concerns in the area, on Somalia's needs, and our ability and our desire to respond within the constraints that we have to those needs.

Q. What do they want?

SENIOR ADMINISTRATION OFFICIAL. What do they want? Continued economic assistance. We have been providing them with assistance on a fairly high level. They're the third largest recipient of American aid in Africa on the economic side and also on military assistance.

Q. Do you have the figures in mind that you can give us?

SENIOR ADMINISTRATION OFFICIAL. Yes. Overall economic aid in the last fiscal year amounted to more than $90 million. Most of this was food and other items for the refugees. Military assistance has consisted of $20 million each fiscal year—1980, 1981, 1982—total $60 million of military assistance, which has been given for nonlethal items, including trucks, communications gear, and radar, basically.

Q. Did we agree to up the ante and give them more aid which we understand he was seeking—military and economic?

SENIOR ADMINISTRATION OFFICIAL. This is being considered.

[15] Source: Office of the Press Secretary to the President. The briefing was given on background by a senior administration official beginning at 12:25 p.m. in the Briefing Room of the White House.

[16] *Supra.*

Q. What have they asked for?

SENIOR ADMINISTRATION OFFICIAL. They have asked for as much as we might be able to provide. Nothing specific, no specific figures. It's been a general request for more help in meeting their needs.

Q. I mean, do they want weapon systems—lethal weapon systems? Do they want a different category of military aid now?

SENIOR ADMINISTRATION OFFICIAL. They have not asked for anything different from the category that we have been providing them with at this time.

Q. Did they complain about slow deliveries or absence of deliveries?

SENIOR ADMINISTRATION OFFICIAL. They used to complain about the slowness of our deliveries. We are doing our best to accelerate deliveries of the trucks, for example, and they are aware of that and we believe that we will be able to accelerate the deliveries.

. . . .

Q. To what extent did the Qaddafi intervention feature in the talks?

SENIOR ADMINISTRATION OFFICIAL. In the talks, it was discussed. The Somalis are greatly concerned about the activities of Qaddafi in the area as a whole and in Somalia itself. Qaddafi has openly said that his aim is to overthrow the government of President Siad. The Libyans are training anti-Siad forces. They are equipping them to the point now that these Libyan forces are better armed than the Somali forces that they confront.

Q. Aren't they also facing a threat from Ethiopia as well?

SENIOR ADMINISTRATION OFFICIAL. Yes—well, that's always—there's a persistent threat depending on the status of the war in the Ogaden. Right now the actual violence in the Ogaden has diminished considerably. And we don't believe that there is any threat of an imminent invasion. But with the longstanding dispute between them, with the Soviet presence, with the Cubans there, it is a potential threat that cannot be ignored.

Q. What is the U.S. position on the Qaddafi intervention so far?

SENIOR ADMINISTRATION OFFICIAL. We've made it clear that we are very concerned about it.

Q. Do you think Libya is better armed, as you say, than the Somali forces, or are they—

SENIOR ADMINISTRATION OFFICIAL. We're not talking about Libyans. We're talking about the Somali Salvation Democratic Front, who are Somali dissidents based in Ethiopia, supported by the Soviets and lately financed and armed to some extent by the Libyans. These are not—they're not a force of the size to be able to defeat the Somali army, but they are able to conduct hit-and-run raids along that long border and cause some problems for the Somali police and the Somali army in isolated incidences.

Q. Is there any Cuban intervention here?

SENIOR ADMINISTRATION OFFICIAL. There is no direct Cuban intervention actively directed against Somalia at this time.

Q. —the base of Berbera, the facilities of Berbera you discussed, was everything in order there, that—no problems? Are those—

SENIOR ADMINISTRATION OFFICIAL. There was no discussion of that today. There have been discussions during the visit, yes, and this is going ahead.

. . . .

Document 608

Senate Concurrent Resolution 110, Introduced by Senators Paul Tsongas and Nancy Kassebaum, June 24, 1982[17]

Voluntary Departure Status of Ethiopian Refugees

Whereas the United States has been a source of refuge for individuals fleeing po-

[17] Source: *Congressional Record,* June 24, 1982, pp. S7500–S7501. The concurrent resolution was also sponsored by Senators Kennedy, Moynihan, D'Amato, Levin, Dodd, Sarbanes, Inouye, and Cranston. Also on June 24, an identical resolution was introduced in the House of Representatives as House Concurrent Resolution 368 by Represent-

litical persecution, communism, and government terror and abuse;

Whereas since the 1974 overthrow of the Ethiopian Government, its military regime has become closely aligned with the Soviet Union and has engaged in gross violations of the human rights of its citizens through mass arrests, summary executions, indefinite detention, torture, disappearances, and absolute government control over speech, religion, assembly, media, and trade unions;

Whereas as a consequence of this the United States extended voluntary departure status to Ethiopians living in the United States so that they would not be required to return home to face possible interrogation, imprisonment, torture, or execution;

Whereas it is estimated that at least 15,000 Ethiopians are presently in the United States in such status;

Whereas in August 1981, the Department of State abruptly recommended termination of this extended voluntary departure program without public discussion or comment;

Whereas those Ethiopians who have lived in the United States for several years fear return to their country where they may well encounter persecution because of previous and outspoken opposition to their government's ill treatment of their countrymen and because of their residence in the United States; and

Whereas the forced return of Ethiopians would run counter to our stated national concern and commitment for other groups and individuals who have fled communism and persecution: Now, therefore, be it

Resolved by the Senate (the House of Representatives concurring), That it is the sense of Congress that—

(1) Ethiopians who have resided in the United States for a substantial period of time should not be forced to return to Ethiopia to face an uncertain future because of their opposition to political persecution and oppression,

(2) prompt resolution of this issue is important to allay the legitimate fears of those Ethiopians who might be subjected to persecution by their government if they are forced to return, and

(3) the Secretary of State should recommend to the Attorney General that extended voluntary departure status continue to be granted to all Ethiopian nationals who have continuously resided in the United States since before January 1, 1980.

---

atives Dixon and Kemp. See *ibid.*, pp. H3957–H3959.

It was reported in the *New York Times*, July 7, 1982, p. A8, that on July 6 the Department of State responded to congressional pleas and reversed its policy toward Ethiopian refugees, proposing that they be allowed to remain in the United States.

Document 609

Address by the Deputy Assistant Secretary of State for African Affairs (Bishop) Before the Sudan–U.S. Business Council, October 22, 1982[18]

U.S. Relations With Sudan

Ambassador Eissa, Sayed Bashir, Mr. Knost, distinguished guests, ladies and gentlemen: Many years ago, at one of those rare times when the government of General De Gaulle and the Government of the United States were disagreeing over NATO, U.S. Forces in Europe, and several other such issues, our Ambassador in Paris, "Chip" Bohlen, reminded his Embassy staff that, "There was a lot more to French-American relations than what the governments say to each other." That is true with virtually every country in the world, and despite the very important role the Governments of the Sudan and the United States play between our two countries, we firmly believe that private individuals and private organizations play a growing and critical role in determining the scope and quality of relations among our two peoples.

It is, therefore, gratifying to consider the important work being done by the Sudan–U.S. Business Council and of private companies in general. We wish you well at your Washington meeting. Although, like you, we wish there could be even more business between our two countries, we are pleased to note the progress made during the past 5 years. Companies such as Arkel and Chevron have expanded their activities in the Sudan while others such as Citibank and Tenneco have established important new operations in the country. Despite the many serious economic problems which exist in

---

[18] Source: Department of State files. Bishop delivered the address at the U.S. Chamber of Commerce.

the Sudan and worldwide, which I shall discuss further later, there has been a remarkable expansion of trade between the two countries. The year the Council was formed, two-way trade was below $75 million, according to our own statistics. In 1981, less than 5 years later, two-way trade had more than doubled to over $190 million. That represents substantial growth of both imports and exports. I acknowledge that the total amount of trade remains small compared to our other trading partners and even in terms of the potential that could be achieved under happier economic circumstances. Nevertheless, the Sudan is one of our most important trading partners in Africa, and the trend is clear and sustained.

We are impressed with the role the private sector is playing in the expansion of trade and the improvement in bilateral relations. The Reagan administration values highly the role of the private sector as a catalyst in development. You are directly experiencing the de facto assistance and the actual economic benefits that result from the investment and involvement of our firms. The Council has played a notably helpful role in assuring that the Government of Sudan designs domestic programs, such as the new investment law, that facilitate the role of companies. We also appreciate the Council's role in assisting the Sudanese in their own self-help efforts. We believe that self-help by the recipient countries is essential to successful development.

Our experience with the Sudan is consistent with our experience elsewhere in the sense that we are learning that in the 1980's both sides will need to recognize that development is much more complex than either of us may have been willing to admit publicly. Solutions to basic problems go beyond simple economic remedies or political labels. There will be a need for:

Sustained cooperation;

Sophisticated analysis;

Realistic planning;

Adequate stability internally and internationally;

Programs in donor countries that allow expanded trade and investment;

Programs in recipient countries that support and enhance assistance.

There is in short the need for the kind of openness, candor, detail, and mutual respect that will allow a mature and sophisticated dialogue between both countries over time. There has to be give-and-take; as long as so many serious problems exist, solutions will not be possible overnight. Moreover, it will be necessary for both governments to continue to play a large role and to support the private sector. Fortunately, I believe that these considerations have been recognized by both governments, and the kind of mature, sustained dialogue I mentioned is indeed taking place. Thus, the two governments must simultaneously maintain a broad and continuing exchange of views, information and advice while also keeping interested companies advised of political, diplomatic, and economic developments. For our part, we are happy to do so either in an institutional context such as with the Council or informally and directly with individual companies. We support and encourage the expansion of business and trade relations and stand ready to provide whatever assistance we can.

My impression is that both in Khartoum and in Washington there is close cooperation, active support, and good relations between the governments and business representatives in the context of U.S.–Sudan affairs. Certainly, it is true that Ambassador Eissa, now the dean of Arab Ambassadors in Washington,[19] has a well-earned reputation for openness and encouragement. I know that our Embassy in Khartoum takes a similar approach to fostering trade and business. The Embassy has the full backing of the Washington agencies involved with Sudan.

I am also pleased to report that bilateral relations between the United States and Sudan are excellent. We consider President Nimeiri to be one of the most thoughtful and courageous leaders in the region and the Sudan to be a good and close friend. This view has been held by Republicans and Democrats alike in both the executive branch and in Congress. Our policy of close friendship for Sudan is fully supported by the American public and their representatives.

That support is evident in the statistic covering U.S. economic and military support for the Sudan. In fiscal year 1982 total U.S. Government assistance for Sudan was on the order of $300 million, after Egypt, the largest in Africa. This represents an increase of 1,500 percent over 1979 totals. As with trade there was steady increase in

---

[19] The dean of the Arab Ambassadors in Washington was Egyptian Ambassador Ashraf A. Ghorbal.

assistance between 1978 and 1982. In part this was related to the time it took for programs first proposed in 1977 and 1978 to be implemented and for our bilateral aid program to gain momentum. It also represented a growing awareness of the urgent need for financial and military support.

It may not be possible, however, to maintain 1982 levels. This comment leads me to discuss the key issues and developments which will affect our assistance levels over the near term. We can make two assumptions with reasonable certainty: (a) Sudan will continue to require foreign economic and security assistance over the short run; and (b) the United States will play a major role in providing such assistance. We can also assume that each side looks forward to and will work toward regional peace and stability with a view toward allowing economic and social development to proceed. There are nevertheless, a number of imponderables that complicate the overall picture making it difficult, on the one hand, to know how much assistance will be needed and, on the other hand, to know how much will be available. The uncertainties posed by this dilemma will likely provide the greatest short-term strain in our bilateral relations. This, by the way, also characterizes our relations with other friends in Africa and elsewhere. There are three clusters of considerations that affect the overall situation. These are the international situation in the Middle East and Africa, the international economic situation, especially as it affects and is reflected in the United States and, finally, the economic situation in the Sudan.

In reviewing the international situation, there are trouble spots aplenty, but there are also some rays of hope. Despite the untimely assassination of President Sadat,[20] its own economic problems and regional turmoil, Egypt appears stable, and Egyptian-Sudanese relations remain very good. The anarchy in Chad seems to have been stopped and the Habre government, which both the Sudan and we support, has begun the long, hard task of reconciliation. We were encouraged by the general acceptance the Habre government[21] has obtained from its fellow Africans, especially in Kinshasa recently at the Francophone summit. The OAU is facing a difficult period over the seating of the Sahrawi Republic, but Qadhafi's prestige suffered a blow when the OAU summit failed to take place on schedule in Tripoli. South of the Sudan in Uganda and Kenya there have been problems, to be sure, but both govenrments are relatively stable and, significantly, consider the Sudan an important, friendly neighbor.

The Horn remains an area of great concern to both of our governments. As you know, we have developed close relations with Somalia in the last 5 years. We provided emergency military assistance to the Somalis last summer when Ethiopia and Somali dissidents attacked. We made clear that we would not stand idly by while Ethiopia, backed as it is by the Soviet Union and with Cuban combat troops stationed there, attacked a friendly neighbor. Nevertheless, Somalia remains controversial within Africa because of its unrenounced claims to territory beyond its present, internationally-recognized boundaries. We have made clear to the Siad Barre government that the United States Government does not support its claims to territory beyond its borders and that we cannot tolerate the use of any assistance we provide to be used for the purpose of regaining such territory.

Ethiopia, though more stable than 4 or 5 years ago, remains a nation in turmoil. As noted the Soviets and Cubans remain there. A major, though inconclusive battle took place in Eritrea earlier this year. There has been fighting along the Somali border. Ethiopia, South Yemen, and Libya formed a tripartite alliance late in 1981. We are concerned that this agreement was designed to foster Libya's aims of destabilizing friendly governments in the region.

The Middle East has also been in turmoil. Strife in Lebanon, war between Iraq and Iran, and the continued Soviet occupation of Afghanistan are troubling both to the Sudan and United States. However, here again, there are some hopeful signs. The Reagan Middle East peace proposal[22] has been welcomed by many, including most Arabs, and the United States has been encouraged by the Fez declaration.[23] In exchanges with the Arabs, including one recently with Ambassador Eissa, we note a seriousness and positiveness that certainly the United States shares and which provides hope that at last progress can be made in achieving peace in the Middle East. Similarly, negotiations on Namibian independence have, according to one African diplomat

[20] Sadat was assassinated on October 6, 1981.

[21] On June 7, the forces of Hissène Habré occupied Chad's capital, Ndjamena, and on June 19, he officially became Head of State.

[22] See document 318.

[23] See document 320.

who has participated in the negotiations, achieved "tremendous progress". Much remains to be done, but much has been accomplished as well. At the same time, the United States is implementing a strategy that will have it playing a more active role in southwest Asia, northeast Africa, and the Indian Ocean area so that we shall be better able to support our friends in the region and deter Soviet-inspired or assisted efforts to upset friendly governments and alter the strategic balance. We are implementing this policy not only to assist friends but also to preserve our own important interests.

This policy is, frankly, expensive. It is part of the Reagan administration's effort to develop our international capabilities to assure peace and our own national security. In general, there has been solid support for this initiative. However, continuing worldwide recession, coupled with inflation and high levels of unemployment in most developed countries including the United States has led to a debate within the United States over whether we can afford to proceed to give priority to national security-related expenditures while cutting back on domestic social programs, considering the overall economic situation. This debate is manifested in Congress as it considers the budget. There have been several significant budget confrontations during the Reagan administration, especially in the Democratic-controlled House of Representatives. Presently, although we are in fiscal year 1983, we do not have a budget. Rather, the government is operating under a continuing resolution which expires in December. We anticipate a major debate over several features of the administration's already stringent budget, including foreign assistance. I have noted support for the Sudan that exists in Congress; the opposition there is not to assistance for the Sudan. Rather, assistance to Sudan may be affected by the broader, domestic debate over general budget limits and priorities.

The third cluster is Sudan's own domestic economic situation. As you know, the Sudan has been trying to overcome several difficulties some of which reflect the underdeveloped state of this vast land while others are the reflections in Sudan of the same international problems I have already mentioned including inflation, high oil prices, high interest rates, limited credit and such. Unfortunately, Sudan's debt and payments situation have reached critical levels. We believe that it is essential for the Sudanese Government to come to terms with the IMF. We cannot intervene in these negotiations, although we are prepared and already have discussed the elements of a Sudan–IMF agreement informally with the IMF and Sudanese officials. We are also prepared to take the lead in organizing related support in the forms of debt relief and additional financial assistance. In short, we are prepared to play an active and positive role internationally to help the Sudan together with its other friends to develop an extensive package of assistance that will provide the breathing space needed for the Sudan to overcome its present economic difficulties. This can only be done if the Sudan first reaches an agreement with the IMF and then implements the economic measures that are specified in the agreement. These steps are necessary so that the large number of public and private creditors who wish to preserve their legitimate claims will be confident that every reasonable effort is being made by the international donor community to resolve Sudan's problems in a sound, fair manner. With an IMF agreement in place it will be easier for the donors to proceed to other measures which will be needed if Sudan is to overcome its present problems.

We believe these measures, however painful and difficult in the short run, are the most hopeful in the long run for Sudan. We recognize that the Government of Sudan has already taken many economic reform measures. Unfortunately, more are necessary, not only in terms of the performance of the Sudanese economy but also for the Sudan to maintain its credibility and international creditworthiness at a time when so many other countries also urgently need help.

In conclusion, I can state unequivocally that on the government-to-government level relations are good and that the United States Government is prepared through its bilateral programs and together with other friends and international organizations to be as helpful as positive [*possible?*] with the Sudan. We encourage our companies to explore business and investment possibilities and projects in the Sudan, perhaps in cooperation with Sudan's other friends. Recent developments in the Middle East and Africa provide some hope that tensions generally can be reduced, but we cannot deny that instability and turmoil continue to exist in the region. There are elements active in the region which are hostile both to the Sudan and the United States. Both to work for peace where possible and to deter subversion and aggression, the Sudan and the United States will work together. We shall also do our utmost to assist Sudan economically within the limits of stringent budget restrictions. For our assistance to succeed, especially if we are to help persuade others to provide extraordinary assistance to Sudan at a time of intense economic difficulties, it is essential that the Sudan do its part as well.

It will be necessary under these circumstances that we maintain the kind of mature, sustained dialogue I mentioned earlier. It is good to know that the Sudan–U.S. Business Council will be available to assist in this process.

G. Chad and Libya

Document 610

Transcript of the Department of State Daily Press Briefing, January 21, 1982 (Extract)[1]

U.S. Assistance to the OAU Peacekeeping Force in Chad

. . . .

Q. What is the U.S. attitude with regard to additional aid to the OAU peacekeeping force in Chad, either through the United Nations or bilaterally?

A. We recognize that the peacekeeping operation will need to find further sources of funding if it remains in Chad for an extended period of time, which in fact may be necessary.

We're hopeful that the OAU will find sufficient funds from a variety of donors to enable this important operation to continue until a negotiated settlement can be reached within Chad.

Q. Will the United States be willing to play its part, as has often been said, in other contexts in finding these funds or providing these funds?

A. In terms of our own funding, we've already authorized $12 million, and at present we have no plans to provide additional funds.

Q. Is it the feeling that the $12 million is enough as a U.S. contribution?

A. Again, I think that I would simply say that at present we don't have plans. I could give you a little detail, if you would want, on what's happened with that money.

As you know, the President determined on December 5, 1981, that $12 million would be made available for support of the Zairian and Nigerian contingents of the OAU peacekeeping force.

Our assistance is limited to the supplying of nonlethal military supplies and equipment and to the provision of air transportation.

We made an initial round of deliveries to Zaire for its contingent in mid-December. Supplies were flown out in four C–141 U.S. military air command aircraft.

These same aircraft transported heavy equipment for the Zairian contingent from Kinshasa to Ndjamena and airlifted the Kenyan and Zambian observers and their equipment from Nairobi to Ndjamena.

We are currently completing air shipment—I should note that this is a status report that's about a week old, so when I say "currently," I don't know exactly how that fits in—but completing air shipment of priority items for the Nigerian contingent by commercial air charter and MAC flights. These items are principally tents, boots, items to enable the Nigerian Air Force to operate in remote fields in Chad, and rafts and boating equipment for the Chari River.

. . . .

---

[1] Source: Office of Press Relations, Department of State. Alan Romberg, Department of State Acting Spokesman, conducted the briefing, which began at 12:36 p.m.

Document 611

Transcript of the Department of State Daily Press Briefing, January 29, 1982 (Extract)[2]

The United States Denies Military Personnel Are Attached to the OAU Peacekeeping Force in Chad

. . . .

Q. Alan, Libya claims that American servicemen are included in the OAU peacekeeping force in Chad. Do you have anything on that?

A. Yes, I do. This is one more example of Libyan falsification and distortion. The peacekeeping force in Chad is an OAU operation stemming from a purely OAU initiative.

The United States was pleased to support this initiative and has been providing transportation and material assistance to the force at the request of the OAU states. American military personnel have been in Chad only in connection with the delivery of this material to the OAU force. There are no American military personnel attached to the peacekeeping force or currently in Chad.

. . . .

[2] Source: Office of Press Relations, Department of State. Alan Romberg, Department of State Acting Spokesman, conducted the briefing, which began at 12:31 p.m.

Document 612

Remarks by Vice President Bush, Lagos, November 13, 1982 (Extract)[4]

Denial of Any U.S. Role in Failure of OAU Summit in Tripoli

. . . .

Q. (Unidentified reporter) I want the Vice President to clarify if America was instrumental in the failure of the last OAU summit in Libya[5] because of Qaddafi?

VICE PRESIDENT. Well, let me be very clear on Qaddafi. We don't like what Qaddafi stands for, and I'll be very honest in saying that we don't like his support of international terrorism. We are opposed to his destabilization of neighboring countries. Having said that, I will repeat, the deliberations of the Organization of African Unity are for the Organization of African Unity to determine. And we have our differences with Qaddafi, and I'm very happy to go into them for you but since we do not see him as a stabilizing influence anywhere in this continent or any place else, and anyone who avows the international use of terror for political change will have our opposition. And I speak right as strong and steady as I can make it. Having said that, the deliberations in the past at OAU and who heads it up and all of that, that is a matter for the Organization of African Unity. And that is our position.

. . . .

[4] Source: Press Release, November 13, 1982, Office of the Press Secretary to the Vice President. Bush's remarks were made prior to his departure from Nigeria.

[5] See footnote 35 to document 550.

H. East Africa: Kenya

Document 613

Toast by Vice President Bush, Nairobi, November 19, 1982[1]

Bush Voices U.S. Support for Kenya

Kenya commands not only Americans' interest, but their imaginations. For when Americans think of Africa, their thoughts often turn to Kenya. This is natural. We have seen great beauty elsewhere in Africa. But little equals, and nothing surpasses, the beauty of this land; the excitement and diversity of its culture and its accomplishments in advancing the welfare of its people.

On the first Independence Day 19 years ago,[2] Jomo Kenyatta declared that this nation would strive "to ensure that all citizens are delivered from the affliction of poverty, ignorance, and disease." Americans admire those efforts.

Since that first Uhuru Day, you have chosen political institutions which themselves demonstrate your commitment to human dignity and freedom. Kenya possesses a democratically elected parliament, a sturdy and independent judiciary, civilian control of the military, and a free press. Like America, you have a constitution that enshrines your principles. And like the American Constitution, your constitution clearly specifies the rights of individual citizens, "Every person in Kenya," and I quote, "is entitled to life, liberty, security of person and the protection of the law."

In 1978, your constitution made possible the peaceful transfer of authority to his Excellency President Moi.[3] On August first, your constitution underwent a harsher test. The United States and the world watched with anxiety.[4] But Kenya, its leaders, and peoples perservered. You have avoided the cycle of violence that, once begun, can assume a fierce life of its own. You have reflected the rule of law. This is no mean achievement.

Mr. Vice President, the United States supports Kenya because doing so accords with American principles and interest. But our relationship with Kenya is not just one of support. It is one of frienship—friendship based on common experiences. Each of us gained independence after bitter struggles. Each of us rejected authoritarian governments and instead chose democracy. And each of us has gathered people of different colors, ethnic strains, and creeds together in one nation. Kenya's national motto "Harambee"—pull together—suits the United States as well.

Mr. Vice President, I know that Kenya has suffered from the economic difficulties that beset us all. We, like you, wish we could solve our economic problems with both ease and speed. But we cannot. Hard work and sound policies are the only answers. In the United States, President Reagan is working to rebuild America's economic strength, cutting inflation, reducing the growth of government, its involvement in the economy; in short, he is working to put America back to work. He is providing incentives that will lead to greater private investment and hence to sustained growth. The best way the United States can contribute to the world economy is by strengthening its own.

Here in Kenya, you too grasp the need to cut back bureaucracy and slash regulation. You too understand the critical role of more private investment. President Moi's September 21 blueprint for economic growth represents an encouraging start. We look forward to his success.

Mr. Vice President, like all on this continent, Kenyans view events in southern Africa with deep concern. President Moi has worked selflessly to foster compromise and thereby achieve Namibian independence. From the very first, President Reagan and his administration have done the same. As I said in Zambia and Zimbabwe,[5] we have

[1] Source: Press Release, November 19, 1982, Office of the Press Secretary to the Vice President. Bush offered his toast at a luncheon hosted by Kenyan Vice President Mwai Kibaki at the Intercontinental Hotel.

[2] December 12, 1963.

[3] On October 10, 1978, Moi succeeded Kenyatta, who died on August 22, 1978.

[4] At the Department of State Daily Press Briefing on August 2, Acting Spokesman Alan Romberg said: "We consider Kenya to be a good and close friend. We continue to support President Moi in the democratically established Government of Kenya.

"We are gratified that the attempt to circumuent the constitutional process in Kenya has apparently failed." (Office of Press Relations, Department of State)

[5] See documents 588–590.

spared no effort. We have worked with the Western Contact Group, with the frontline states, with SWAPO, and with the Government of South Africa. We have committed ourselves to bringing peace to southern Africa and independence to Namibia.

As I have made clear throughout my visit to Africa, the United States seeks to serve as an impartial and honest broker. We possess neither troops nor proxies in the region. We have neither colonial interests nor military ambitions. On the contrary, the sole interest of America in southern Africa are the interests of all men in all places: freedom and peace.

Our only soldiers are soldiers of peace—over 2,000 Peace Corps volunteers throughout Africa, with almost 300 right here in Kenya and about 700 in southern Africa.

Mr. Vice President, we agree that the question of Namibia should be decided on its own merits, and that those merits are clear: Namibia must be free. But the Namibian problem, Mr. Vice President, is like a knot. To untie it, one must work from both ends at once. We shall therefore labor on, with Kenya and others, to remove all foreign troops from the region, so that Namibia might at last be free.

In several days President Moi departs for the OAU summit. He and Kenya have led the OAU through difficult times, you have worked for peace and a better Africa. We admired the way President Moi led the OAU, an institution we support strongly. This is the only way the OAU can be led; the OAU cannot be a forum for discord and violence.

The world yearns for peace. Four days ago I stood in Moscow. No doubt you've all seen photographs of Secretary Brezhnev's funeral. As I mentioned in Zimbabwe, Mr. Vice President, the image that struck me—one that I'll never forget—was the stately magnificent display by Russian soldiers. As I watched those young men, I couldn't help thinking that many of them were just the same age as our four sons. I felt then what I have often felt since taking up this office—a sudden, sharp sense of the responsibility that lies on those who lead nations.

Mr. Vice President, I know that both you and President Moi share that deep sense of responsibility. And I know that you will exercise that responsibility for the good of the people of Kenya, and in the interest of peace.

Ladies and gentlemen, please join me in a toast: To His Excellency President Daniel Arap Moi; to Vice President Kibaki; to the Republic of Kenya; and to the warmth and strength of our friendship.

Chapter 15. Latin America

A. Regional Policies

Document 614

Transcript of a Department of State Press Conference, Buenos Aires, March 10, 1982[1]

Argentina and Central America

Q. What role can Argentina play in Central America? Can Argentina and the United States, together with other countries, form some kind of peace force?

A. I think Argentina is very concerned about the situation in Central America, as indeed all of the states of the hemisphere are. I think I would not want to put words in the mouths of Argentine spokesmen but I would think that Argentina would wish to be present, to be active in whatever action is taken in Central America. I would not suggest by that there has been discussed here and there is no question now of any sort of peacekeeping force of the kind you referred to.

One of the characteristics of the present situation is that all countries of the hemisphere feel menaced by a situation which is occurring in Central America, even though it may be quite far away.

Q. Did you discuss the possibility of a meeting between (President Reagan and President Galtieri)? A. No, that was not discussed. As you know there was a contact at the highest level immediately prior to the inauguration of President Viola. And I'm sure that both countries will consider it normal that their leaders see each other quite frequently.

Q. Is there a possibility that the Central American situation will be discussed under the auspices of the OAS? Does the Rio Treaty[2] have any bearing on the matter?

A. This is something like the question asked by the representative of the *Washington Post.* I think that all of us are aware of the fact that there is the instrument of the Rio Treaty and that it could be involved.

As you know, the Rio Treaty calls for a variety of common action, including but not limited to common military action. Common political action. Economic action is also in the treaty. I think it is widely agreed that the notion of some collective action in the current situation is necessary. For example, the three democratic countries or would-be democracies, Costa Rica, Honduras, and El Salvador, have gotten together in a Central American democratic community, in order to ask for the economic and political support of other democracies. Colombia, Venezuela, and the United States have responded to that appeal so that the notion of some collective 0 action is there. But I would not wish to give you the impression that collective action of all of the American states in the framework of the Rio Treaty or of the OAS is either imminent or necessary. It's a possibility that we all should be aware of.

Q. You have said that the ideal government in Central America would be midway between Somoza and Sandino. If that possibility does not materialize, what outcome—left or right—would you prefer?

A. Well, I think the possibility does exist. You have in El Salvador a reform-minded government, which was born out of the overthrow of the Romero military government.[4] It is reformist in two senses. In the first place it has put through one of the most important land reforms that's ever been attempted in this hemisphere, I say put through because one important part of

---

[1] Source: Department of State files. The press conference was conducted by the Assistant Secretary of State for Inter-American Affairs, Thomas O. Enders, who was in Argentina for talks with the Argentine Government. Enders' brief introductory remarks in Spanish are omitted.

[2] The Inter-American Treaty of Reciprocal Assistance (Rio Treaty) entered into force for the United States on December 3, 1948; for text, see 4 Bevans 559.

[3] Regarding the Central American Democratic Community, see document 667.

[4] On October 15, 1979, an informal grouping of young and middle-grade army officers overthrew the government of General Carlos Humberto Romero.

it, that is to say the distribution of the largest estates has already been accomplished. And instead of there being 242 landowners for estates with over 500 hectares there are now 32,000. In addition to that, the most difficult part is under way, that is to say the distribution of the small properties that were held either by sharecroppers or by tenant farmers. That is only just begun; it must be completed this year.

The second element of reform is, of course, the creation of political institutions which are democratic and which engage broad participation of the population. The first step in that process is expected to take place at the end of this month in the March 28 election. But it must be followed by the establishment of a new constitution, and elections for President and Parliament. The idea is, of course, for Salvador to give itself the first legitimate government it has ever had. And there appears to be quite a bit of momentum in the electoral campaign in spite of all—I don't want to give you the impression that this is all accomplished—obviously there's going to be a long struggle. But I think that very clearly there is developing a way between the extremes of the right and the left in El Salvador and (inaudible).

Q. Cuba, the USSR, and other so-called socialist countries obviously have their own point of view on Central America. However President Reagan and Secretary Haig are now confronted by an apparently more moderate proposal put forth by France and Mexico. What is your government's attitude with respect to this proposal?

A. We very much respect and appreciate the sincerity with which the President of Mexico has put forward his most recent proposal.[5] We share his concerns about the militarization of the area, about the arms race in the area, and the continuing of violence in El Salvador and the violence of neighboring countries. Many of the proposals with regard to Nicaragua that were made by the Mexican President were also proposals that the United States made to Nicaragua itself last August and September.[6] However, there is one element which is different. For the United States the normalization of relations with Nicaragua depends essentially on Nicaragua ceasing its support for the insurgents in El Salvador. This element was not presented in the proposal of the Mexican President. We have had since the proposal further discussions with the Mexican Foreign Minister Jorge Castaneda and we expect to have more in the future, perhaps as early as this weekend. Our view is very similar to that of the Mexicans—if, in fact, there is a way to obtain a political agreement with Nicaragua, that [*then*?] we must take it. But so far, a vital element is missing. And that is the continued very substantial support of Nicaragua for insurgency in (El Salvador).

Q. Some private organizations such as Freedom House have denounced the persecution—even the threatened annihiliation—of the Miskitos Indians by the Sandinista government. Can you give us some information on this? Also, the United States will undertake to broadcast to Central America on a new radio station called Radio Marti. Can you provide details?

A. On the first question: I think it is now well known that a very large number of Miskito Indians living on the east coast of Nicaragua have been forced to leave their villages and to go to new encampments prepared by the Nicaraguan Government against their will. In the course of this forced removal, women and children and men have died. The villages themselves have been burned and a large number of refugees have been forced to cross the border into Honduras. As of the time I left Washington some 6,000 refugees had gathered in Honduras. And by now their number may be as high as 10,000. Clearly, a major repression is under way against the Miskito Indians which is a minority ethnic group which does not wish to adopt the political and cultural norms established by the Sandinist government.

As regards Radio Marti, it is a proposal that is now before the American Congress made by the United States administration.[7] It is a proposal to break the monopoly of news and political commentary that the Cuban radio holds over its own people to tell the Cuban people what is happening in their country. Cuba is a country which has had very ambitious foreign adventures in the last 20 years, in Africa and now in Central America. However, it is the Cuban people who have paid the bill. Their standard of living now is very little higher than it was 20 years ago, when the revolution oc-

---

[5] An apparent reference to the address by Mexican President José López Portillo, February 21, 1982, in Managua, Nicaragua; for extracts, see document 671.

[6] Regarding these discussions, see *Washington Post*, December 10, 1981, p. A1.

[7] Regarding Radio Marti, see document 674.

curred, and that standard of living can be maintained only by very substantial assistance from the Soviet Union. Adventures of this kind would not be possible if the Cuban people knew more clearly what their government is doing. And the proposal is to give them the means to know. This is not a proposal, let me say, to direct news to Central America.

Q. In conversations, Argentine labor leaders have repeatedly compared Poland and Argentina. They point out that both countries are controlled by the military under a state of siege, that union activities are proscribed, that there are hundreds of people in jail with no charges against them and no due process. Why, then, is Argentina treated differently by the U.S. Government from Poland? Why is one government punished and the other not?

A. It is not for the United States to express opinions about the domestic situation in this country. I would, however, make two comments; leaving the opinions of labor leaders or others to themselves. First, Poland is a country in which a foreign power—the Soviet Union—has paramount influence. The influence consists of a large number of Soviet military units stationed in the country and the presence on the borders of Poland of other units which the Soviet Union has made quite clear would be prepared to move into Poland in order to assure the maintenance of the regime which is not one that the Polish people support. I think that situation has no parallel at all in Argentina. I would like to say, however, what I said yesterday, that is to say that the United States and other countries in the world have been heartened to see Argentina moving to restore the rights of the individual and I added that the friends of Argentina, and I would include very emphatically the United States, are confident that Argentina will carry that process to its completion.

Q. You remarked yesterday when you left the foreign ministry, that there is almost complete agreement between the United States and Argentina. What is lacking to remove the qualifier "almost"? Were you more pessimistic or more optimistic after speaking with Galtieri and Alemann? You hold the opinion that the United States and Argentina—if not working directly together—must have similar position in GATT if we are to avoid the resurgence of protectionism. GATT and transnational enterprises sometimes work at cross-purposes. How can our countries work together on this?

A. Your second question: everybody and every country has the right to its own opinion on enterprises that operate across frontiers. I would only note in that regard that the international competition for investment has become very sharp indeed. The United States has become a country which imports very large amounts of foreign enterprises and capital, as well as exporting a great deal, and we are convinced that we would be much less well off than we now are without it. The very large majority of the members of the GATT appear to be convinced that the import and export of capital is necessary for the proper functioning of an international economy. But I do not wish to suggest that the United States would attempt to convince this country or any other that it would receive foreign capital or enterprise. That is entirely a decision for each government to take. As regards to conversations yesterday, they were indeed in my judgment very positive and there is no doubt at all that both countries have a great deal to benefit from economic and political cooperation.

Q. Inter-American cooperation in El Salvador is a recurrent [?] there and you spoke of possible political collaboration between democratic countries and of a democratic union in Central America. Does the U.S. Government believe in light of its previous experiences not only in Latin America but in other parts of the world that the final solution might, indeed, be military not political?

A. Yes, it is very different. We have consistently taken the view, it is our view now, that the proper goal for the policy in Central America is, indeed, a political solution; that clearly in order to reach a political solution you have to create the right kind of security in military circumstances. But for us, the social, political, and economic changes are at least as important, or more important, than military circumstances. That is why we put so much emphasis on land reform and the creation of democratic institutions and on a broad and cooperative plan of economic assistance and opportunities for the area. And talking about collective action of American states, the Caribbean Basin initiative is a typical example of what can be done because there you have a group together as initiators of the program, countries with such different political views as Mexico, Venezuela, United States, and Canada. And Argentina, as you know, has brought an important contribution to this effort. So we should be looking for forms of multilateral cooperation which can bridge the sometimes different analyses and perceptions that countries have.

Q. Argentina needs to develop export markets in order to overcome balance-of-payments problems. Can the United States help Argentina in this? Also, will the US support Argentine initiatives in antidumping of agricultural products on the world market?

A. This is one of the developing points of important common interest between Argentina and the United States. Countries that are providing subsidies for their agricultural exports on a very large scale have not only eliminated some of the traditional markets that Argentina and the United States had but are beginning to compete with us, in markets such as in the Middle East or in Japan that Argentina and the United States have traditionally served on a basis of free competition. So that we have a situation in which a heavily subsidized and therefore discriminatory competition is occurring. This is a very serious situation for both of us and we intend to cooperate very closely in overcoming it. I should add that as regards Argentina's exports I told my interlocutors here that we would like to study with them very closely ideas that they may have or that we may be able to develop, and how we can develop trade in two directions. I insist in both directions. The member of the American Cabinet who is responsible for commercial negotiations, Ambassador Brock, will be down here I think within a month for a meeting of the bilateral economic commission between the two countries, which will be an important occasion to give a new impulse to precisely this kind of search.

Q. President Reagan has announced a program of economic aid for the underdeveloped countries of Central America and the Caribbean. Some observers believe this has come 20 years too late because explosive socioeconomic problems and corrupt dictatorships have developed in that time which are now being exploited by the extreme left. What do you think?

A. I would like to agree with one part of your question and disagree with the other. I think the plan is late. I think the offer of assistance to these fragile and menanced economies is late, that we should have done it much before. But it's better to do it now than not at all. That means, of course, that we'll have to have even bigger effort and a more far-reaching effort than we would have had to have 20 years ago. I think it is wrong, however, to think that these are all repressive governments with serious social and political problems. Many of them, in fact two thirds of them, in the Caribbean Basin are democracies, and indeed the number of nondemocratic regimes can be counted with the fingers of one hand. Nicaragua, and there are others as well, that I would put in that category but most of the countries are democracies and the idea is to keep them that way.

Q. The *Washington Post* yesterday questioned U.S. nuclear policy in Latin America and in Argentina, in particular.

A. Let me say if I can that the United States has not recognized the distinction that some countries make between a peaceful nuclear device, so called, and an atomic weapon. I think we have made this position very clear on a number of occasions and I don't want to leave any doubt about it at all.

Document 615

Address by the Under Secretary of the Treasury for Monetary Affairs (Sprinkel) Before the Twenty-Third Annual Meeting of the Inter-American Development Bank, Cartagena, Colombia, March 30, 1982[8]

U.S. Policy Toward the Inter-American Development Bank

Mr. Chairman, Mr. President, fellow Governors, ladies and gentlemen, it is a great honor and a pleasure for me to be here today to represent the United States at this twenty-third annual meeting of the Inter-American Development Bank. Secretary Regan has asked me to convey his regards and best wishes for a successful meeting.

I would like to offer my thanks to the government and people of Colombia for the warm welcome and generous hospitality they have extended to me and all the members of the U.S. delegation. It has been a real pleasure to visit this beautiful and historic city of Cartagena. This year's meeting has provided me with a wonderful opportunity to meet with my colleagues from Latin America, and to learn more about the Inter-

---

[8] Source: Department of the Treasury files.

American Development Bank and the important role it plays in the hemisphere.

The role of the Bank in furthering the growth and development of Latin America and the Caribbean has been highlighted at this year's meeting by the ongoing discussions of the proposed replenishment of IDB resources. In this context, I would like to take this opportunity to describe for you today the framework within which my government will be formulating its final position regarding participation in the proposed sixth replenishment. I would hope that this will help to maintain the momentum of the negotiations, and aid others in formulating their positions, so that fruitful discussions can continue at the next session in Berlin in July.

The survival and growth of the Inter-American Development Bank since its creation more than 20 years ago adequately testifies to the importance of the institution and the mutual benefits derived by borrowers and donors alike. I do not need to remind you of the special importance of Latin America and the Caribbean to my government. President Reagan's recent address to the Organization of American States outlined a bold new initiative designed to deal with the special problems and critical needs of the countries of the Caribbean Basin.[9]

This Caribbean Basin Initiative is a multination plan to promote economic growth in the Caribbean and Central America, and was developed in cooperation with Canada, Mexico, Venezuela, and more recently, Colombia. We are now seeking congressional approval of the major elements of our contribution to the Caribbean Basin, which include first, a one-way free trade area; second, special tax incentives for investment; and third, increased financial assistance.

The IDB itself has undertaken a key role in this initiative—to coordinate the formulation of economic development plans for the countries of Central America. We would like to commend the IDB for its willingness to undertake this program. All of these efforts are strongly supported by the United States as positive measures to address immediate, specific needs which are unique to countries of this particular region.

But, the special programs I have mentioned are just that—"special." They can only be complementary to the long-term, on-going work of the Inter-American Development Bank. The best hope for sustained growth and prosperity in the region lies in the hands of the countries themselves. The multilateral development banks, in particular the IDB, can play a key role in encouraging growth and prosperity.

It was within this context of better defining the role of the multilateral development banks that we undertook just over a year ago to assess U.S. participation in the MDB's. Many of you now have read the recently completed study.[10] The central conclusions of that study are that the multilateral development banks are effective instruments for promoting a healthy and growing world economy, and that U.S. participation in the MDB's has served important U.S. economic, political, and humanitarian interests.

At the same time, the assessment recognizes that the effectiveness of the multilateral development banks can be improved by enhancing their role as financial catalysts, and as providers of sound economic policy advice, through insistence on appropriate macroeconomic and sector policies. The assessment also recognizes the considerable scope for increased financial leverage of the capital resources of all the banks, in particular the IDB, whose financial strength and degree of recognition in capital markets is consistently reflected in its Triple-A bond ratings.

We will be seeking, within the context of the proposed sixth replenishment of IDB resources, to implement many of the recommendations of the assessment. We believe these recommendations are critical to the future effectiveness and viability of the IDB; and the extent to which they are implemented will play a major role in determining the nature of U.S. participation in the institution.

We are aware of the fact that the IDB is a multilateral institution, and that the influence of any single shareholder is limited. But, I believe we can arrive at a consensus which supports our objectives, and that, together we can move forward in a deliberate and well conceived fashion. Our major goal is, after all, to make the IDB an even more effective institution; this is a goal which we all share.

Turning now to the specifics of our program, there are three basic objectives which

---

[9] For the text of President Reagan's speech on the Caribbean Basin Initiative, February 24, see document 672.

[10] Department of the Treasury, *U.S. Participation in the Multilateral Development Banks in the 1980s* (Washington, February 1982).

we are pursuing. These objectives are: greater private sector involvement; a shift in the allocation of resources towards those countries which are most in need, and which demonstrate a desire and ability to make the best use of those resources; and, while bearing in mind the need to maintain the strong financial reputation of the IDB, an increase in the financial leverage of contributions and subscriptions to the IDB, to reflect the strengthened position in international financial markets of some of the IDB's major borrowers.

With respect to the first of these objectives—greater private sector involvement—let me emphasize that our attitude toward international policy questions generally is consistent with our own internal economic policy. Internationally, as well as domestically, we are committed to the free market system. We are convinced that economic growth and productivity can be advanced most effectively, both at home and abroad, through greater reliance on private economic activity.

In terms of the IDB, we anticipate an increased emphasis on its role as a catalyst for private investment flows. Taxpayers in the donor countries should not be expected to shoulder burdens which can be accommodated by the free play of market incentives. To this end the IDB can facilitate attractive investment environments in their borrower countries by:

—encouraging free and open markets;

—reducing barriers to private capital investment flows;

—encouraging sound economic policies;

—limiting the scope of government; and

—helping those countries prepared to help themselves.

Private sector cofinancing represents a significant source of potential private sector involvement in development. The IDB has already begun to tap this source, approving twenty "complementary" loans totaling $513 million in the period 1976 through 1981. This is a commendable effort, and we fully support the IDB's plans to expand its complementary financing program.

All of the multilateral development banks must recognize that public sources of development resources will remain strictly limited over the coming years, and steps must be taken to increase the flow of private cofinancing. If cofinancing is to come close to realizing its full potential, it must be shown to be in the best interests of the three participating parties—*the borrower, the private lender*, and *the IDB*. The terms and flexibility of cofinancing instruments will have to be made more attractive to the private lenders. The borrowers will need to realize that limited IDB funds can be blended with additional resources through private cofinancing, and that such arrangements are a natural element of the evolutionary process of development assistance.

Discussion of the IDB's catalytic role brings me to our second major objective in the bank: the pursuit of well-formulated maturation and graduation policies. In the IDB in particular, where per capita incomes of borrowing member countries are relatively high, we will be encouraging an increasing reliance by its borrowers on hard window funds, thereby releasing scarce concessional funds for allocation among only the poorest countries.

We understand the substantial development needs of Latin America and the Caribbean. We are not convinced, however, that these needs can be financed *only* with concessional funds of the amount and on the terms currently provided by the Fund for Special Operations. While we are willing to consider some replenishment of resources to be provided on terms more concessional than in the IDB's capital window, these resources should be allocated only to the poorest countries of the region which cannot afford nor have adequate access to alternative sources of finance.

At the same time, in order that sufficient hard window funds can be made available to "maturing" IDB borrowers, the higher income borrowers must reduce their reliance on IDB capital, and turn increasingly to private markets in which they have already demonstrated their credit-worthiness.

I have already discussed the role of private cofinancing in providing assistance to IDB borrowers. Such cofinancing is a natural element of the maturation/graduation process which we foresee in the IDB. But, in order for this graduation/maturation policy to be successfully implemented, and in order to attract the private cofinancing which is a part of that process, the IDB must link its loans and technical assistance to appropriate microeconomic and sector policy advice, and to the pursuit by its borrowers of appropriate monetary and fiscal policies. On the microeconomic policy side, this advice should address:

—reducing impediments to market determination of prices;

—minimizing producer and consumer subsidies; and

—eliminating bureaucratic constraints to a dynamic private sector.

On the macroeconomic side, the IDB should, through its lending, support and facilitate the implementation of IMF programs where appropriate, and generally work to ensure that its projects are being carried out in an environment conducive to sustainable economic growth and development.

We are convinced that when such policies are introduced, and rigorously adhered to, the climate for both domestic and foreign private investment will significantly improve.

A third major objective we will be pursuing in the sixth replenishment is increased financial leverage of the IDB's capital resources. As the IDB prepares for another expansion of its resources, we believe it is imperative to question how great an increase is needed, given the considerable scope for further expansion of the Bank's financial leverage. The IDB is a mature financial institution with a proven track record in international credit markets. Given the obvious constraints on budgetary outlays from IDB donor countries in the eighties, and the continuing need for a significant IDB lending program, it is essential that use of IDB resources be maximized.

There are two specific areas in which we are focusing our attention: paid-in capital and usable callable capital. While I will leave the details to our representative in the replenishment negotiations, let me just make a few key points.

First, we believe there is considerable potential for expanding the Bank's lending program without requiring an unrealistic direct budgetary contribution from participating countries. Second, a key component of a successful maturation/graduation policy will be an increasing use of higher income borrowers' contributions and subscriptions as backing for IDB bonds. These countries already borrow considerable sums on their own in commercial markets, and there is no reason their paid-in and callable capital cannot be 100 percent usable by the bank in its borrowing operations. Third, as retained earnings provide for higher levels of accumulated reserves, the argument in favor of high proportions of paid-in capital becomes less convincing. Maintenance of a lending rate which fully covers all the Bank's costs and appropriate adjustments in amortization and grace periods will permit the IDB's existing paid-in capital and reserves to continue to generate further profits, thereby enhancing the equity cushion and preventing the decapitalization of the institution.

I have mentioned today the three goals which are the structural underpinnings of our approach to the proposed resource replenishment for the IDB. These goals were formulated in the context of a thorough assessment of all the multilateral development banks. We are pursuing these goals not because we believe the banks have done a bad job in the past, or because U.S. support for these institutions has weakened, but rather because we believe that the banks can do an even better job in the future, and because achievement of our goals and objectives will result in stronger, more effective institutions which can count on the support of both traditional and new donor countries.

In sum, we support continued growth in the IDB's lending program. We favor the concept of increasing reliance on nontraditional donors to help finance that lending program. Development assistance should support an evolutionary process in which funds are allocated to countries most in need, while those countries which already have access to alternative sources of finance rely less and less on development bank funds. Consistent with maintaining the financial integrity of the Bank and its financial maturity we expect the Bank to be able to better leverage subscriptions made by member governments. Development assistance should be seed money to encourage the adoption of appropriate economic policies which will result, in turn, in increased access to private markets.

The IDB itself has evolved over the previous 20 years so that it also can "mature" out of total dependence on donor country contributions to a reliance on its own ability to attract private resources. This is the future we foresee for the IDB, and we believe it is a promising one.

Document 616

Address by the Assistant Secretary of State for Inter-American Affairs (Enders) Before the Inter-American Press Association, Chicago, September 30, 1982[11]

Areas of Challenge in the Americas

It is a privilege to speak to this audience. The Inter-American Press Association and its members have contributed greatly over the years to our joint quest for a stronger and more united hemisphere. It is true that cooperation among individual governments of North and South America, Central America, and the Caribbean has sometimes been blunted by misunderstanding and miscalculation. But no one has been more conscious than this body that the countries of the hemisphere are natural friends and allies in a world that is unstable and often dangerous.

This year, the Americas face challenges and opportunities as daunting as any in the past. Our wisdom, unity, and ability to communicate are confronted by no less than three separate challenges. They are:

—The crisis in Central America;

—The potential for interstate conflict exemplified by the South Atlantic crisis; and

—The need to manage high levels of foreign debt to safeguard the potential we all have for a new sustained expansion.

Let me address each in turn.

In 1979, when Somoza fell to a vast but Marxist-led coalition, many concluded that the only question was how soon and how far Central America would be driven toward Marxism. And indeed the months that followed saw the launching of a "final offensive" in El Salvador by guerrilla forces with strong support from Nicaragua and Cuba. In Guatemala, there was a new outburst of guerrilla warfare.

Central America seemed ripe for violence. Only one country was governed democratically; elsewhere the military was in charge, in some cases mainly through repression. Yet the armies did not look very formidable. In most cases they were barracks bound, organized for administration rather than combat. Foreign disapproval had deprived them of modern equipment and training. In El Salvador a cruelly inequitable landholding system put 40% of the land in the hands of 2% of the landholders. Throughout the isthmus, economic life was unsettled by the double scourges of local uncertainty and global recession.

Today the outlook is different. In El Salvador, the guerrillas and their foreign backers have lost the initiative. They now face a Salvadoran Army that is better equipped and organized and has learned how to fight in the field. Redistribution of 20% of the country's arable land has deprived the guerrillas of an issue they hoped to exploit. And the massive turnout in the March election—in the face of insurgent threats—wrecked their claims to widespread support. Although it goes on, the guerrillas can no longer hope to win the war they began.

Honest elections with massive turnouts have also been held in Costa Rica and Honduras—with extremist parties winning almost no support. In Guatemala a new government has begun to limit human rights abuse and to improve the situation in the Indian highlands.

And though economic conditions are still often precarious, the outlook for lasting development has been significatnly improved by the Caribbean Basin initiative, through which the United States is adding its weight to the contributions of the Mexican-Venezuelan oil facility and the efforts of Canada and Colombia.

Whatever else they have settled, these developments have revealed the vitality of democracy and destroyed the myth that Central America is moving inexorably toward Marxist dictatorship.

In Nicaragua, where the myth was born, the classic shape of dictatorship is becoming ever more evident, as the regime wields its power in crude provocation of the church, in persecution of its Indian minority, in repression of press and personal freedoms. Little by little the original revolutionary coalition has disintegrated. The Sandinistas themselves have split. And as open repression and militarism have re-emerged, disenchantment and even armed resistance have also spread.

The Marxist-Leninists show no sign of drawing the conclusions of these reverses. Instead of questioning their false premises, they are reacting with more of the same—

[11] Source: *Current Policy* No. 424, September 30, 1982, Bureau of Public Affairs, Department of State.

more arms, more repression, more terrorism.

Nicaragua already has the largest armed forces in Central American history and is expanding them further. In an effort to overcome resistance by its people—and to build a base for projecting power in the area—Nicaragua has imported some 2,000 Cuban military and security advisers, and some 50–60 Soviet and East European military and security advisers. Members of the Palestine Liberation Organization's military arm have also been involved. Having already imported Soviet tanks, Nicaragua is preparing to bring in jet combat aircraft.

Meanwhile, the regionalization of terrorism goes on. Arms trafficking from Nicaragua to El Salvador is active and at high levels. Terrorist operations against Costa Rica have intensified. So blatant are Nicaraguan actions that Costa Rica—a democracy with no army—last month issued a *libro blanco* detailing official Nicaraguan terrorisms and other violations against Costa Rica. The recently concluded hostage incident in Honduras graphically exposed another aspect of efforts to spin a regional web of terror. Over 100 Honduran businessmen were seized in a vain effort to force the release of a Salvadoran guerrilla leader, Alejandro Montenegro, arrested in August while planning operations against El Salvador from Honduras.

At the same time, Cuba's capability to project power in the region has been greatly augmented. Cuba's arsenal now includes sophisticated Soviet weapons, such as MiG–23/Floggers, AN–26 transport aircraft, a Koni-class frigate, submarines, guided-missile attack boats, and hydrofoils. Ominously Cuba has expanded its airlift capability; there are even indications that Cuba intends to strengthen its amphibious capability. In this context, Cuban construction of a battalion-size military compound and a 9,000-foot runway in Grenada and the improvement of airfields in Nicaragua is additional evidence of Cuba's increased potential to sustain military operations well beyond its own shores.

As opposed to the 1960's, when Moscow generally pursued what it referred to as a "peaceful path" to change, armed violence now plays a major role in Soviet policy in Central America. The Soviet Union supports guerrilla movements directly through Communist parties and front organizations and indirectly through Cuba, Nicaragua, and Grenada. Moscow's huge annual $3 billion economic subsidies—over and above Soviet military grants—effectively underwrite Cuba's aggressive behavior and enable Castro to maintain the largest per capita military force in the hemisphere. Lately Moscow has taken a more direct role in Grenada, pledging to buy all of that island's main exports and promising an impressive array of technical assistance projects.

These actions by Nicaragua, Cuba, and the Soviet Union mean that local struggles in Central America will continue—more violent, bitter, and long lasting than they otherwise would be. But they do not mean that the Marxist-Leninists will prevail. On the contrary, it is clear that they will not prevail—provided the democracies remain clear minded about what they are aiming for and provided they maintain the effort.

I say clear minded, for it is not too soon for the democracies to begin to define the conditions in which Central America could be at peace. Some of these conditions are obvious. There can be no peace if any country in the area attempts to export revolution to another, maintaining in its territory the headquarters, logistical support, and training grounds of an insurgency directed against a neighbor—as Nicaragua does against El Salvador. Equally, there can be no peace, if any country imports large numbers of foreign military and security advisers and heavy offensive weapons—as Nicaragua is also doing.

Should we not then aim at agreement—subject to effective verification—that no country in Central America will import heavy offensive weapons and that foreign military and security advisers will be reduced to a common low level or be removed entirely?

Equally important is what happens within the states of the area. Just as it is wrong to let the Salvadoran guerrillas shoot their way to a share of power they are unwilling to compete for at the polls, so it would be wrong to exclude from political participation those who may now be ready to accept peaceful competition within emerging democratic institutions. We are encouraged by the actions of the Salvadoran Government to hold out the hand of reconciliation to its adversaries.

And unless Nicaragua permits the development of democratic or, at least, pluralistic institutions in which power is allocated by free elections, its neighbors will never trust it to keep the peace. For if there is any lesson in the politics of the 20th century, it is that governments that must face their people in free elections do not often make war on their neighbors.

It is up to Nicaraguans to determine what government Nicaragua should have. But an object of our policy should clearly be to persuade Nicaragua to put its oft-repeated commitment to pluralistic democracy into practice. We must use the dialogue that we proposed to the Nicaraguans a year ago to explore how a way can be found back from militarization to internal reconciliation and peace with neighbors.

If the democracies hold to these principles, backing those that adhere to them with economic and political and military assistance, peace will come to Central America. No one expects it to emerge full blown this fall, or next year, or maybe even the year after, but it will come—if the democracies sustain the effort.

In the past the United States has generally neglected Central America only to send in the troops when things got out of hand. U.S. troops are no solution now. What can help is a dependable U.S. commitment. The United States will help its friends in the area defend themselves from violent minorities from within—and hostile neighbors from without—and as long as it is necessary.

Central America is the land bridge between the two Americas. The advance of Marxist-Leninists there would be profoundly threatening to the hemisphere. The people of Central America have it in their power to prevent that by a combination of resistance and reform. We must go on helping them.

From Central America to the South Atlantic is a considerable distance. Yet all of us in this room were forced earlier this year to shift our focus from one to the other. Perhaps the most fundamental question arising from the Falklands/Malvinas crisis is how better in the future to prevent war in the hemisphere.

The inter-American system has a unique record of cooperative action to preserve the peace. But it was not able to do so in the South Atlantic crisis. For some, the question that came out of the South Atlantic crisis is, why didn't the system provide automatic and unanimous support for one of the belligerents? And because it didn't, shouldn't it somehow be restructured so that it would do so in the future?

For me the questions are different. Why didn't the inter-American system keep the peace? Should it be restructured so that it will be more effective? How can we avoid new wars in the future, sparked by one of the many territorial disputes with which the hemisphere is laced? I think there are already some tentative answers to these questions.

First, territorial and other disputes must not be allowed to fester. Machinery exists to anticipate disputes and permit their peaceful and definitive settlement: various inter-American arbitration and conciliation agreements, Organization of American States peacekeeping mechanisms, the International Court of Justice, even the treaty of Tlatelolco[12] which established the world's first nuclear free zone in a populated area. What appears lacking is the will to use this machinery to prevent and resolve contentious problems. The United States and other countries of the area have at one time or another been involved in calming or negotiating most of them. But this is a branch of hemispheric diplomacy that deserves fresh attention.

Second, the maintenance of a peaceful equilibrium within the hemisphere is everyone's business. The military expenditures of the countries of Latin America come to only 1.4% of gross national product (GNP)—a quarter of the average in the developing world as a whole. We all share an interest in maintaining that record and in avoiding arms races. And where competitive procurement cannot be avoided, it is vital that existing disputes not be exacerbated. My own country has acted in the last

---

[12] The Treaty for the Prohibition of Nuclear Weapons in Latin America (commonly known as the Treaty of Tlatelolco) originated in 1962 with a Brazilian proposal to establish a nuclear-weapons-free zone in Latin America. Extensive negotiations among the Latin American countries culminated in the signing of the treaty in February 1967. The treaty has entered into force for 22 Latin American and Caribbean states but is not yet in effect for Argentina, Brazil, Chile, and Cuba.

The basic treaty prohibits development or acquisition of nuclear weapons by Latin American states. Only Latin American countries are eligible to become contacting parties to the treaty, but there are two additional protocols to which nations outside Latin America can adhere. Under Protocol I, states outside the treaty zone undertake to apply the denuclearization provisions of the treaty to their territories within the zone. The United States ratified Protocol I in 1981. Protocol II obligates the nuclear weapons states to respect the Latin American nuclear-free zone i.e., not to use or threaten to use nuclear weapons against the parties to the treaty nor to contribute in any way to acts involving a violation of the treaty's basic provisions. The United States ratified Protocol II in 1971.

generation almost as if it could simply ignore this problem. U.S. arms sales as a proportion of South American purchases fell from 75% in 1960 to 20% in 1970 and to 7% in 1980. The reduction in training and in-depth contacts between the U.S. and most South American militaries has also been precipitous. Improved contacts and in some cases additional arms transfers may be needed to help avoid subregional imbalances of power and preserve the peace. Others in the hemisphere and in friendly outside countries can similarly assist.

Third, we must all prevent regional conflicts from having strategic consequences, introducing East–West tensions where they do not belong, or even changing the East–West balance. It would not be wise for any of us to permit Moscow to become a major source of military modernization. And Cuba is working hard to exploit the South Atlantic conflict to reduce its isolation within the hemisphere.

I doubt that these tasks require institutional changes. But they do require greater perceptiveness about the possible threats to peace and particularly about the ways in which American states relate to each other.

There was a time when most of us thought of the inter-American system as consisting of only two participants—Latin America and North America. It wasn't very long ago that the United States and others attempted—and failed—to organize a "new dialogue" on that basis.

Such formulas have never done justice to the richness of the hemisphere's potential and the variety of our concerns. They make even less sense now that Latin American countries have grown so much in economic weight, population, and worldwide influence, and now that the new countries of the Caribbean have joined the system. What we should strive for is a system which reflects our diversity, which lessens tensions rather than adds to them, and which preserves what until now has been one of the New World's distinctive achievements—peace among its nations.

The challenge with the widest impact is the problem of foreign debt. Debt issues affect virtually every country in this hemisphere. At stake is the ability of each of our countries to realize its potential for sustained expansion.

The hemisphere has an impressive record of high growth. Taking the average for the last 20 years, the economies of Latin America and the Caribbean have expanded at an annual rate of 5.7% in real terms. This rate has been consistently higher than that of both the developed countries and of the developing countries as a whole.

Many factors have contributed to this record. Trade—access to foreign markets including markets within the region itself—has been one of the great motors of growth. U.S. imports from Latin America and the Caribbean have grown from $4 billion in 1960 to $39 billion in 1980—which averages out to a compound growth rate of more than 12% a year for the last 20 years. This is in nominal terms and includes the price escalation on petroleum, but even so it is impressive when compared to U.S. inflation, which averaged about 5% during this period.

Imported capital has also been vital to Latin America's growth. Direct investment from the United States increased from $8.4 billion in 1960 to $38.3 billion in 1980, and direct foreign investment by other nations in Latin America now exceeds $15 billion. Borrowed capital has grown even more dramatically. The long-term foreign debt of the developing countries of the hemisphere grew from $39 billion in 1973 to some $197 billion in 1981; this is equivalent to roughly 30% of its total output.

This capital has been put to good use. Moreover, it is not inappropriate that Latin America, which has a disproportionate share of the world's growth potential, should also attract a major share of world capital flows. With their great resources, their increasingly skilled and disciplined work force, and their growing capacity to export energy and agricultural and industrial goods, there can be no doubt that the countries of the hemisphere are fundamentally credit worthy.

Each country's situation is different and must be considered as a separate case. But there are three themes in the current situation common to most.

—One is the impact of rising budget deficits on import demand. The high growth of the 1970's was obtained in part through ever higher budget deficits. In the past 10 years, the combined deficits of the developing countries of the hemisphere have more than doubled in relation to GNP, in some cases reaching the 15% or even the 20% level. The resulting high activity and inflation have fueled an enormous demand for foreign goods and services.

—The second is the worldwide recession, which has cut sharply into export earnings as the prices of basic commodities on which the economies of the hemisphere still depend have fallen, often precipitously.

—The third is the cumulative effect of the debt itself, due partly to its size, partly to sharp runup of interest rates over the past 5 years. Governments everywhere—yes, in the United States but also in Europe and, indeed, in the hemisphere as well—have been putting excessive demands on the small pool of savings we all generate. In doing so, we all have contributed to high interest rates. For example, Latin America undertook some $28 billion of net new long-term borrowings in 1981 from world markets, much of it from the United States. For comparison, the total net savings generated by the U.S. economy during 1981 was $147.4 billion.

I think the adjustments that we all must undertake are clear. All of us, including the United States, have to pare down the growth of public spending and raise public receipts. All of us, including the United States, have to hold down the growth of money supply to prevent inflationary increases in demand. The United States is undertaking its own adjustment policies—witness President Reagan's efforts to lower budget deficits and control money supply—and has empathy for others whose problems are worse and whose economies are less flexible. If we do, the pressure on savings and external balances will abate, and, as the industrial countries emerge from recession, both the pool of savings and their import demand will grow and the short-term problem will gradually dissolve.

In the meanwhile, an exceptional effort of cooperation, mutual understanding, and mutual adjustment must be undertaken to make sure that access to capital markets is not needlessly interrupted while basic adjustment measures are taken. This is basically a question between borrowing governments and the markets themselves. But in some exceptional cases, other governments can play a role. Thus, in August the United States and Mexico cooperated to mobilize $4.5 billion in financing in order to allow time for talks with the International Monetary Fund and preparation of a stabilization plan to proceed. The United States also encouraged and welcomed the decision of Argentina and Britain to remove their mutual financial sanctions and thus free up resources of great utility to both countries.

One final remark. In the short term, as unemployment grows and as the required adjustments look ever more painful, the one path which tempts all, including some in the United States, is the escapism of protection. In that direction lies assured disaster. An open trading system is and must remain one of our highest foreign policy priorities. The upcoming ministerial of the General Agreement on Tariffs and Trade may be one of the more important in decades precisely because the pressures are building in all of our countries to pursue the illusory goal of trying to save jobs by not competing.

I have outlined three broad areas of challenge and the guidelines we are using to confront each of them. I believe we are making progress. In the past year:

—The United States and Mexico have started to achieve a relationship that reflects their exceptional importance to each other. Now comes the harshest test, as the economic slowdown in both countries threatens to aggravate all our joint accounts: trade, finance, immigration. We must be steadfast.

—We have committed ourselves to help countries of the Caribbean Basin protect themselves against outside intervention, strengthen or develop democratic institutions, and overcome economic disasters. That effort will succeed if it is sustained.

—We are beginning to respond to new realities in South America. We were rebuilding close bilateral relationships with each country after a decade of drift, when the shadow of the South Atlantic crisis fell across our efforts. We are now relaunching those efforts, joining others to maintain the networks of constructive relationships essential to peace and to sustained economic development.

There are great strengths in the Americas: a common heritage which rejects outside interference; enormous human and natural resources for growth; and, not least, a pervasive and resilient belief in the democratic ideal. If we act consistently, and with a clear head, on our strengths rather than exacerbate our weaknesses—and if we insist that outsiders respect our efforts—this hemisphere will yet be a model for the rest of the world.

Document 617

Transcript of a White House Press Briefing, October 25, 1982[13]

The President's Trip to Latin America

MR. ALLIN. We'll have the printed announcement here in just a minute. My colleague will read it to you, what he has. This is a background briefing attributable to a senior administration official.

SENIOR ADMINISTRATION OFFICIAL. Thanks, Mort.

The announcement says at the invitation of the Presidents of Brazil, Colombia, and Costa Rica, the President will make a working visit to Latin America, November 30 to December 4. Have you got it there? You've got it there.

Q. Is that all? Is that the official—

SENIOR ADMINISTRATION OFFICIAL. He will leave Washington on November 30—I'm continuing on it. On December 1 and 2, he will be in Brazil as the guest of President Figueiredo. On December 3 he will be in Colombia as a guest of President Betancur. On December 4 he will be in Costa Rica as the guest of President Monge returning to Washington that evening. Got the announcement.

Q. How about first names on Betancur and Monge and how do you spell Monge?

SENIOR ADMINISTRATION OFFICIAL. M-o-n-g-e, Luis Alberto.

Q. Luis?

SENIOR ADMINISTRATION OFFICIAL. L-u-i-s Alberto.

Q. Luis is not on background, I mean—

SENIOR ADMINISTRATION OFFICIAL. No, no.

Q. Okay, here's the key question. Why Brazil?

SENIOR ADMINISTRATION OFFICIAL. Hang on just a minute. Let me get—have you got it all there? All right. Let me—

Q. —spells his name, with a c-u-r?

Q. What about Betancur?

SENIOR ADMINISTRATION OFFICIAL. Belisiario.

Q. Thanks.

Q. Spell it, please.

SENIOR ADMINISTRATION OFFICIAL. B-e-l-i-s-i-a-r-i-o.

Q. —a-r—

SENIOR ADMINISTRATION OFFICIAL.—a-r-i-o. Belisiario.

Now, could I say a word on background about the visit—the visits, the trip. This is a trip, as you can see, that takes in three countries in Latin America with quite different perspectives. Brazil, of course, if you look on the map is enormous, Portuguese-speaking; Colombia, a Spanish-speaking democracy just been through election; Costa Rica, representative of the Central American countries.

This is a visit to discuss matters of mutual interest including economic recovery in the hemisphere, the future of the inter-American system in the wake of the South Atlantic crisis, on-going security threats in the hemisphere, and the promotion of democracy.

As you know, the President has put particular emphasis on hemispheric relations since he announced for the Presidency nearly 3 years ago. He started out with a concept of the special character of relations within North America, the North American Accord. He devoted particular attention to the cultivation and development of Mexican-American affairs, including a great deal of personal attention. He developed the Caribbean Basin Initiative and you've seen here a large number of leaders from the area—President Lopez-Portillo was the President's first visitor.[14] And, indeed, they saw each other before he was inaugurated. Since that time, we have had President Duarte of El Salvador, President Herrera Campins of Venezuela.[15] We have had President Suazo Cordova of Honduras and President Monge of Costa Rica.[16] President

---

[13] Source: Office of the Press Secretary to the President. A senior administration official conducted the briefing, which began at 6:30 p.m., on background in the White House Briefing Room.

[14] Regarding President López Portillo's visit to Washington and Camp David, June 8–9, 1981, see *American Foreign Policy: Current Documents, 1981*, documents 689 and 690.

[15] Regarding President Duarte's visit, see *ibid.*, document 701. For information on President Herrera Campins' visit, see *ibid.*, documents 738 and 739.

[16] Regarding the visit of President Suazo, see *Weekly Compilation of Presidential Documents*, July 19, 1982, pp. 903–904. For information on President Monge's visit, see document 688.

de la Espriella of Panama was just here.[17] President Belaunde of Peru is coming here on November 8th to the 12th.

And you had the President—if you look back over the speech he gave to the Organization of American States launching the Caribbean Basin Initiative[18]—he expressed his own vision about relations in the Americas. And he spoke of the "unlimited potential of these two great land masses"—were the words he used, and of U.S. participation in a community that he saw as belonging as much to others in the hemisphere as to us—words that I recall his dictating himself in the course of doing that speech.

The last time that American Presidents visited this area—maybe I could give you some of that. President Carter was in Brazil in 1978. But before that, you have to go a long ways back to President Eisenhower in 1960, President Truman in 1947. President Roosevelt made two stops there in 1943 and 1936.

President Kennedy visited Columbia in 1961. It is the most recent trip. President Roosevelt was there in 1934.

As for Costa Rica—President Johnson visited it in 1968. That was the last visit. I think the last visit of an American President to Central America—President Kennedy was there in 1963.

Q. President Carter went to Panama.

Senior Administration Official. Yes; the Central Americans usually refer to Central America as not including Panama, as the Panamanians do. But you could do it either way. You are quite right. Carter did go to Panama.

Q. What is the timing on this? Why this? Why now? Why then, I mean?

Q. Where is Mexico? Is Mexico Central America?

Senior Administration Official. Mexico—he has just been down to the border to see—

Q. He was in Mexico for 19.5 minutes—Mr. Reagan—Tijuana.

Senior Administration Official. He has just been down to see the President-elect.[19] Obviously, the President-elect would not have invited him down to Mexico City.

Q. Isn't the Mexican Inauguration December 1st?

Senior Administration Official. Yes; it is.

Q. Well, does this not conflict with that? Or would not some of these leaders be in Mexico?

Senior Administration Official. The Mexican Inauguration is not going to—they are inviting representatives of foreign governments. And they explicitly noted that they would welcome the Ambassadors resident in Mexico City. I believe they expect to have an austere Inaugural, without foreign visitors of rank.

Q. Could you discuss the reasons for his visit to each of these countries? Can you develop, also, the relations—could you talk about the development of relations between Brazil and the United States since President Carter's rather cold reception in San Diego?

Senior Administration Official. I think it would be fair to say that our relationship between Brazil and the United States, which had been as close as any that we have had in the world in the post-Second World War period, deteriorated gradually until it reached its lowest point in 1977 in a controversy over human rights and nuclear nonproliferation. Brazil at that time cancelled our bilateral security assistance relationship which had been one of the centerpieces of our relationship. Since that time, particularly in the last 2 years, there has been a significant improvement in our relationship. You recall that earlier this year in the midst of the Falklands crisis President Figueriedo came to the United States and we had some very cordial talks here, at which time he suggested that the President come back. We think of our relationship with Brazil as something that indeed does bear close cultivation. The two countries have much in common. You know, they are both continental countries. They are both free enterprise countries. They are both strongly anti-Communist countries. They have quite different geographic and developmental positions, but within that framework, meaning that our foreign policies look on a number of issues quite differently, we have some very fundamental interests together, including very fundamental mutual economic interests.

Q. Before you go into the other two countries, sir, could you develop that? What

[17] Regarding the visit of President de la Espriella, see document 698.

[18] For the text of this speech, February 24, see document 672.

[19] Regarding President Reagan's meeting with Mexican President-Elect de la Madrid, see document 700.

has happened since 1978 on the U.S. attitude toward alleged human rights abuses in Brazil and also on the nuclear nonproliferation.

Senior Administration Official. Well, the human rights—allegations of human rights abuses in Brazil have largely dropped off and as far as we can tell human rights abuses in Brazil are almost unknown, if not unknown. Brazil has meanwhile taken on a process of what it calls abertura, which means opening of Portuguese—a political opening, an important stage of which will occur very shortly. November 15th Brazil is holding direct elections for Governor, for the lower house of their Parliament, and for one-third of the members of the upper house, which is a major step toward the restoration of parliamentary democracy in Brazil.

Q. What decision—

Senior Administration Official. Excuse me, could I just add one more thing to that is that Vice President Bush was down in Brazil last year and worked out an agreement with the Brazilians whereby one of the outstanding nuclear issues that we had with them could be set aside concerning the fuel supply of an American produced reactor in Brazil. And the tone and the frequency of our exchanges has improved very markedly in the last 2 years.

Q. What happened in the case of that reactor? How did that get resolved? What was it that resolved it?

Senior Administration Official. The United States agreed that this fuel load could be bought elsewhere rather than the United States and so the question of the exact safeguard regime to be applied to that supply if coming from the United States was made moot. (Laughter)

Q. Why is this trip taking place?

Senior Administration Official. Let me just—so you will understand it. It is a conflict of law. The American law says that at any time U.S. materials—nuclear materials—are exported, that the recipient country should apply a certain regime of safeguards to all of its nuclear facilities whether or not they are related to the transaction. Brazilian law and the law of a number of other countries says that they would be bound by their bilateral agreements with the United States—their bilateral agreement with the United States which was signed before our nuclear nonproliferation act—specifies that safeguards are required only on the facilities to which the materials are going. So there is a conflict between their bilateral agreement with the United States and the U.S. law passed subsequently. That is the issue, and it doesn't seem quite so obvious.

Q. Can you explain why this trip is being made at this particular time, November 30th to December 4th?—because we understand that it had been planned for later. So is there some important reason why it was pushed into the remainder of the year?

Senior Administration Official. No. I think your understanding is incorrect that it had been planned for later. This is something the President has wanted to do for some time. And the trip now seems to us particularly appropriate, given the nature of the four items which I mentioned, the importance of them in inter-American affairs: economic recovery, post-Falkland situation, the ongoing security problems as well as this long struggle to promote democracy. The latter two are longer-range matters; the first two are quite immediate.

Q. Is this correct, or incorrect that this trip, in fact, was scheduled at first as a trip by Secretary Shultz as a preliminary?

Senior Administration Official. There was discussion of that as a possibility, but it was not so scheduled.

Q. Is there any concern among—within the White House about the President not being here to see the appropriations bills through the lame duck session, or is some thought being given to delaying the lame duck session or something?

Senior Administration Official. I don't know what the exact dates of it are, but I'm sure that he will be able to handle it.

Q. November 29th—so he'll be gone for those—he'll be gone for the start of it?

Senior Administration Official. If that's when it starts—

Q. Will there be any discussion of the deficit—billons of dollars in loans that Brazil has made which they might default?

Senior Administration Official. He'll be gone the 30th—began the 29th—

Q. So there's no concern?

Senior Administration Official. Not that I know of. He'll be able to handle it.

Senior Administration Official. I don't want to give you the impression that this is a specific—I mean, not that level of specificity of this—an action trip with a given—with regard to a given economic problem. But clearly the question of high debts, continued access to capital markets, adjustment for debt services—one of the major economic problems in the hemisphere. And I'm sure it will be discussed during this trip.

Q. Were other countries considered for—

SENIOR ADMINISTRATION OFFICIAL. These were the ones that we worked on from the start.

Q. Did you have invitations from any other countries?

SENIOR ADMINISTRATION OFFICIAL. Yes.

Q. Argentina?

SENIOR ADMINISTRATION OFFICIAL. No, the—I'm sorry. This is not [an] invitation. We have a number of outstanding invitations from a number of countries, but—quite a number more, but they were not considered at this time.

Q. Those two issues that you said that are not longer-range, do you see some urgency in terms of having to discuss them—that is, economic recovery and all of this—of course, this adjustment for debt service, and also the political situation of inter-American relations? Is there urgency—

SENIOR ADMINISTRATION OFFICIAL. We think those are very much—very prominent questions at the moment, the beginning of an economic recovery in the United States, ongoing economic problems in the area. The post-Falklands situation is clearly important. There's been a great deal of debate in the inter-American system about what—how the system should emerge.

I would point out to you also, though, with regard to the question of democracy that there is now—has been for several years—a long trend toward—slow trend toward return to democratic institutions in Latin American that you can find in South America. Brazil is certainly a case in point. Argentina is beginning to head in that direction, as Bolivia has just done so; and in Central America, which is quite striking as you look at the evolution in the last several years.

Q. Will there be anything on the steel dumping of cheap steel? They do a lot of steel making, you know.

SENIOR ADMINISTRATION OFFICIAL. They do a lot of iron and steel making, but that is—but we've had some discussions on that. That's not a major issue in U.S.-Brazilian relations.

Q. Why is this trip going to take place shortly after what you mention as, you know, an important event in terms of political life in Brazilian elections? Why is it going to take place shortly after the Brazilian elections?[20]

SENIOR ADMINISTRATION OFFICIAL. This was a convenient time for the President to travel. It would, of course, not have been appropriate to go immediately before the elections. In most countries you don't do that. This was the earliest available time after the elections to do so.

Q. Then you're—you deny the Brazilian press saying that Reagan called the Brazilian President and said he wanted to come before the elections and they said, no, it would be better if you come after?

SENIOR ADMINISTRATION OFFICIAL. There wasn't any discussion of the President going before the elections.

Q. Did President Reagan call the Brazilian President last Wednesday?

SENIOR ADMINISTRATION OFFICIAL. This was not done by a President via President call.

Q. There was no Presidential call to—

SENIOR ADMINISTRATION OFFICIAL. No.

SENIOR ADMINISTRATION OFFICIAL. I think I might say in regard to Rich's question, the President will obviously be in touch with—in close consultation with the congressional leadership prior to the session and, as always, must exert both domestic and foreign responsibilities and will be able to do that from wherever he is.

THE PRESS. Thank you.

---

[20] The Brazilian elections were held November 15, 1982.

Document 618

Address by the Secretary of State (Shultz) Before the General Assembly of the Organization of American States, November 17, 1982[21]

Reflections Among Neighbors

Mr. Chairman,[22] distinguished Foreign Ministers and Heads of Delegation, Mr. Secretary General,[23] Mr. Assistant Secretary General[24] distinguished delegates, observers and guests, ladies and gentlemen: It's a pleasure to join you.

I'm here more to listen than to talk. Moreover, though I have visited nearly all of the countries represented in our organization—some of them many times—this is the first time I have participated in a meeting of the OAS.

Last February, in the speech before the OAS Permanent Council in which he announced the Caribbean Basin Initiative, President Reagan emphasized the major themes of his administration's Latin American policy: democracy, self-determination, economic development, and collective security. "These two great land masses North and South," he said, "can show the world that our many nations can live in peace, each with its own customs and language and culture but sharing a love for freedom and a determination to resist outside ideologies that would take us back to colonialism." Less than 2 weeks from now the President will begin a visit to Latin America that is a personal expression of this vision of a cooperative effort aimed at full development of the enormous human and economic potential concentrated in this hemisphere.

I come today before this General Assembly convinced that the inter-American system is vital to peace and security for the nations of this hemisphere. We have over the years formulated a juridical base for keeping the peace, for resolving disputes and even for the sovereignty of our nations. Independence, sovereignty, nonintervention are themes that run through our Charter, the record of our meetings and our inter-American experience. We have advanced these ideas further than other collective bodies and we have been well served by them.

I don't propose even to try to cover every issue before this Assembly, but rather to concentrate on a few of my main reflections as I join this discussion among neighbors and friends.

One set of reflections is about the nature of the inter-American system itself—of which this unique organization is the formal expression, and the OAS Charter and Rio Treaty the formal guarantees—but which also consists of a great network of bilateral and multilateral relationships among the American states.

Geography makes us neighbors. History, religion, and the shared experience of the frontier make us friends. There is far more that unites us in this hemisphere than can ever divide us. That in itself is enough to explain why each of us participates in the system. But it is probably not what has made the system durable and valuable.

The striking thing to me, thinking over what has occurred in our lifetimes, is the success the American states have had in preventing war. True enough, there was the Chaco War in the thirties,[25] then conflicts between Costa Rica and Nicaragua, Ecuador and Peru, and El Salvador and Honduras; most recently, the tragic South Atlantic crisis we tried so hard to prevent. Also, there have been violent insurgencies, often manipulated from outside.

But for all the territorial disputes that divide us, for all the internal struggles that threaten us, these are the only instances of war between states in a half century in which every other part of the world has been convulsed in war. In a climate of general security we each have been able to avoid the levels of military expenditures that countries in other less fortunate regions could not dispense with. The developing countries of the Americas have been able to limit defense spending to 1.4 percent of GNP, a quarter of what the developing world as a whole spends on military preparations. And although our global responsibilities impose a heavy burden of military expenditures, the United States does not and need not fortify borders with its neighbors.

---

[21] Source: Department of State Press Release 350, November 17, 1982; also printed in Department of State *Bulletin*, December 1982, pp. 64–67.

[22] Rodrigo Lloreda Caicedo, Foreign Minister of Colombia.

[23] Alejandro Orfila of Argentina.

[24] Ambassador Val T. McComie of Barbados.

[25] The Chaco War between Paraguay and Bolivia lasted from 1933 to 1938.

One reason why the inter-American system has proved so durable and valuable must be that in most cases it has kept the peace. Since 1948, the OAS has been called upon formally or informally on no less than 50 separate occasions involving the settlement of disputes. From the Cuban missile crisis to local border conflicts, the inter-American system has contributed, often decisively, to keeping the peace.

But will it in the future? We know that war came to the South Atlantic despite our efforts. We know that turbulence in Central America, where local conflicts have been exploited from the outside, can threaten the peace. And despite a variety of agreements and even treaties, we are well aware that it has been a long time since one of the territorial disputes among us has been definitively settled.

Once actually confronted with crisis, I have no doubt that we will all react with good intentions, urging negotiations, offering good offices. But recent experience suggests that could be too late. Good intentions matter, but they are not enough.

Take Central America as an example. Everyone seems to be talking peace. Yet most states in this area are challenged by insurgency. They are threatened by economic and political strife. They have brought in foreign military advisers, in one country in very large numbers.

Clearly, no strategy for peace can succeed if those who take up arms against their fellow citizens and neighbors go unopposed. That principle applies in Central America as well as elsewhere. Peace is impossible without security. Our security assistance programs, for El Salvador and for our other threatened friends, stem from that basic consideration. Neither democracy, nor human rights, nor socioeconomic equity are possible in a climate of insecurity, where hostile neighbors or violent internal minorities make war on society.

But if peace requires strength, strength in turn infuses an obligation to make peace. Fortunately, not all of the conditions for war are present in Central America. Most states still lack the major offensive weapons that would be needed for an attack on their neighbors. That may give us our opening. Why shouldn't we encourage the governments of Central America to agree, all of them, on a basis of reciprocity and strict verification, not to import major offensive weapons?

Clearly that's only part of the solution, but it would be a start. There will be danger to peace as long as foreign troops or military advisers are present. Why not go for agreement among Central American countries, again on a basis of reciprocity and verification, to reduce their numbers to some low agreed level, or to zero?

The same treatment—reciprocity and verification—could be applied to practical mutual undertakings to end any and all support for violent activity on the territory of others.

As you think about it, other steps would be necessary as well. Internal conflicts threaten to spill over borders, so each state should be encouraged to create processes by which internal adversaries can be reconciled, human rights respected, and political competition substituted for violent confrontation.

Reconciliation leads to that fundamental value, democracy. We all know that in the end there is no enduring stability and legitimacy without it. We also know that democracies are far less likely to go to war than governments whose leaders need not obtain the consent of the people. In Central America the democratic transformation of all the states in the area is not only a desirable step that each may set for itself; it may well be a precondition for a durable peace.

A number of countries, meeting in San Jose recently, went through a similar thought-process, trying to identify the conditions for peace in the area.[26] If the countries of Central America could all agree on these conditions, the next step would be to begin to discuss how they could be implemented. My point is simple. If you can identify the fundamental elements of a problem, you have some chance of solving it. If you can't, no amount of negotiations or good offices will help.

And of course, should one Central American country attack another, the Rio Treaty is there to protect the victim and restore peace. If it is clear in advance that it will be invoked, the Treaty will have a deterrent effect—as it has had in so many circumstances since it was signed.

Of course, the Central American situation is not the only threat to hemispheric peace. The South Atlantic war of this spring has reminded us of how many boundary and territorial disputes remain unsettled in our region, and of the potential cost of leaving these unaddressed.

---

[26] Regarding this meeting, see document 699.

The United States, while traditionally neutral on the particular claims asserted in regional territorial and boundary disputes, is *not* neutral on the overriding principle of peaceful dispute settlement. This implies an obligation on *both* parties to a dispute to seek effective means of peaceful resolution, either by negotiations, perhaps with OAS assistance, or by recourse to the various means of judicial, arbitral, conciliation, and other third-party devices available under multilateral and regional agreements or ad hoc. International law provides a variety of means; the will to use these means has been too often lacking. The OAS pioneered the development of international mechanisms for such purposes throughout this century; it must now show leadership in promoting their use.

This is advice that the United States itself follows: we are currently in litigation with Canada, in a special chamber of the International Court of Justice, over the delineation of our important maritime boundary in the Gulf of Maine.[27]

Earlier this month we were pleased to support a balanced resolution on the Falklands/Malvinas question in the United Nations.[28] We could support in this body a similar resolution. We hope that both actions will prove effective in promoting a peaceful solution to this dispute.

Finally, let me take one more case. Nuclear explosives. We are undertaking a new effort to persuade the Soviet Union that its security and that of the United States can be protected and enhanced by reducing the numbers of nuclear weapons. While that effort proceeds, there is a strategy open to us to avoid the introduction or creation of nuclear arms in those countries of the hemisphere which have so far been free of them. This is the strategy conceived and launched at Tlatelolco in 1967 to protect against the use or threat of nuclear weapons, and which led to a treaty already in effect for 22 Latin American and Caribbean countries. One of the most potentially serious sources of tension and war could be eliminated if the nuclear weapons free zone of the Tlatelolco Treaty were to be ratified by all eligible states.

In sum, the inter-American system has helped produce a great achievement: a general if not total freedom from war. Preserving that achievement is a major challenge for the future.

---

27 Regarding this litigation, see document 298.

28 For the text of this resolution, see document 661.

My second group of reflections concerns the management of our economies.

We are all members of the world economy, and not dependent on the inter-American system for the management of our economies in the same way we are for the preservation of peace. Yet what each of us does—in the management or mismanagement of our domestic economies—can greatly affect others in the hemisphere—positively or negatively.

For the developing countries of the hemisphere, this last generation has been a period of soaring growth. The motors of that growth—savings and investment—have been largely fueled from within. For example, gross savings are now about 22 percent of GNP, among the highest in the world. But external factors—substantial expansion of markets in the United States for hemispheric exports, the opening up of trade within South America, within Central America, and within the Caribbean, the development of new markets in Europe and Japan, major increases in private investment, in borrowings from multilateral development banks, and above all in commercial bank loans—have contributed much too. U.S. imports from Latin America and the Caribbean have grown from $4 billion in 1960 to $39 billion in 1980—which averages out to a compound growth rate of more than 12 percent a year for the last 20 years. This is in nominal terms and includes the price escalation on petroleum, but even so it is impressive when compared to U.S. inflation, which averaged about 5 percent during this period.

The mix between internal and external factors has varied from country to country. In some cases favorable external conditions have compensated for domestic rigidities; in others, unfavorable external developments have undermined otherwise sound development plans. One point is evident: size has not been a determinant of success. You don't have to be large to succeed.

Until recently, the balance was positive: we were all enjoying the fruits of growth, the developing countries of the hemisphere at the phenomenal rate of nearly 6 percent a year in real terms for 20 years. Put another way, the economic size of Latin America has *tripled* in absolute terms since 1960. And although much of the conventional wisdom emphasizes diversification of trade, Western Hemisphere countries still matter enormously to each other. In 1980, trade within the hemisphere as a whole—including Canada—came to $155 billion, 42 percent of the hemisphere's total trade with the world. Latin America taken as a whole is the United States biggest customer.

Now we are all in a period of adjustment, including the United States. Many of us, including the United States, must compress our budget deficits and control our money supply if we are to master inflation and create the conditions for renewed growth. This is a process that begins at home, where we must each accept primary responsibility for correcting the excesses of the recent past. But falling world trade volume, interest rates that though falling are still high, the threat of protectionism, the backlash of one country's cutback on another's trade, and the ripple effects of one country's financial difficulties on another—all complicate our individual adjustment.

Nothing would be more devastating than a wave of import protectionism now. Yet such a wave threatens to burst in a number of countries, including my own. As is often the case, the way to avoid going backward is to go forward. Our best collective tactic, it seems to me, is to build in new worldwide defenses through the GATT: joint standstill in protectionist measures and a commitment to broaden and deepen the GATT in North–South trade and trade in services. That is the task of the GATT ministerial that convenes next week. It is a task to which each and every one of us must contribute, for the inevitable alternative to keeping the world trading system mutually open is the kind of disaster that engulfed the world in the 1930's.

It would be equally devastating if debtors and creditors were to fail to find those mutual accommodations that will permit borrowing countries to have sustained access to the financial markets. Just as borrowers must cut their current account deficits, raise domestic interest rates, and keep exchange rates realistic, so lenders should in some cases be ready to restructure or in exceptional cases, reschedule. Borrowers must look realistically to their responsibilities. And lenders should recognize that stabilization programs will be more likely to succeed if accompanied by net flows of new money.

The International Monetary Fund can play an essential role in this process by providing new money on a selective basis while helping countries to define stabilization programs. And in some cases individual countries can appropriately facilitate the adjustment by providing short term credit to allow time to negotiate a Fund agreement, as in the case of the credit arranged for Mexico in August.[29]

This is a long chain of actions that must be taken in a mutually supportive way. It starts at home. It requires sacrifices. It involves both private entities and governments. And it will require a high order of mutual confidence to succeed. But we must succeed. It is quite clear that the penalties for failure could be enormous.

Beyond the adjustment, of course, will come the recovery. The U.S. economy is now poised for just that. As always it will succeed only if there is new investment and new savings. But it is not too early to begin thinking through the requirements for sustained growth in the hemisphere. Having a disproportionate share of the world's growth potential, this hemisphere should provide a substantial impulse to the renewed momentum for global expansion.

That brings me to my third set of reflections, on what you might call the balance of our interdependence. No one doubts that we depend vitally on each other, for our prosperity, for our security, for peace. We can celebrate it—or we can deplore it—but it is a fact. This year's crises—in finance, in the South Atlantic, in Central America—have underscored it.

But it is also natural that we should each be concerned about the balance of mutual accommodation. Some of the most difficult and important questions in international relations revolve around relations among neighbors. If we have to adjust our economies, who should adjust more or most? If we must compromise to keep the peace, who should go the longest way? And how do you measure it?

I think we all agree that matters such as these must not be decided simply by might or size, but by principle and concept. I do not mean by that that we should attempt to write a book of codes anticipating every situation and dictating pre-agreed rules of the game. But we should always be prepared to examine together the justice and consistency of our actions, so that a balance acceptable to all can emerge.

One important way of extending the range of long-term options—at least for some of the most vulnerable states—is the Caribbean Basin Initiative. President Reagan's trade and investment proposals will be up for decision in the Congress later this

---

[29] Regarding fhe financial agreements between the United States and Mexico, see document 695.

month. These trade and investment incentives exemplify the creative mutual adjustments needed to spur growth. They will help to unleash in behalf of long-term growth the drive of the private sector as an engine of development financing, technical innovation, and productive employment. The stimulus they will provide will go far to ensuring the productivity of the emergency assistance already being disbursed.

The breadth and originality of the Caribbean Basin Initiative have led to some interesting side effects. One is that we have decided to increase special funds to the OAS to provide training opportunities for Caribbean Basin countries. Another is the realization that most of the peoples of the hemisphere now live in countries that have attained relatively advanced levels of development. These so-called "middle-income" countries properly receive less traditional public assistance than do poorer countries—yet they are also, precisely because of their relative development, countries that are ready for new kinds of partnership to accelerate balanced development. The issue here, it seems to me, is less one of money rather than of dynamism, creativity, and entrepreneurship. But it is an issue very much worth keeping in mind as we seek ways to develop greater balance within the hemisphere.

Finally, let me conclude with a word about democracy in the hemisphere. Our record is uneven. For some countries—Colombia, Costa Rica, Mexico, Venezuela, Barbados, Jamaica, Trinidad, indeed most of the Caribbean—democratic institutions have functioned without interruption for a generation and more. Other countries have faced instability despite long democratic periods. A few have experienced only interludes of democratic governance.

But what is most striking is that democracy is everywhere the hemisphere's recurring ideal and practical standard. In fact, our collective commitment is so strong that sometimes I think even the criticism of our failings is intensified by it. Certainly, the Inter-American Human Rights Commission has no equal in any other region of the world.

Am I not right in thinking that our practice of democracy is making progress? In the last few years, Ecuador, Honduras, and Peru have all fully reaffirmed their democratic traditions. The Dominican Republic has sustained its newer tradition. Brazil's *abertura*, so strikingly underscored by Monday's elections,[30] has been underway for a decade. And today, Argentina's and Uruguay's commitment to a return to democratic politics, Bolivia's new elected government, the democratic transformation in El Salvador—all offer genuine hope for the future.

I know that much remains to be accomplished, that sharp swings have taken place in the past, that gains already made have not in all cases been fully consolidated. But more than two-thirds of our membership—21—now have governments chosen through open, competitive elections. And more will soon join that list.

One of the principal reasons for President Reagan's trip to several countries of Latin America beginning the end of this month is in fact to underscore this democratic momentum, to bolster it—and to emphasize our own firm commitment to that process.

If this trend holds, it will be the greatest achievement of the Americas. I can think of no more urgent business for this organization than to find ways in which the gains for democracy already made can be protected and additional gains made. For democracy strengthens both the peace and the ability to cooperate.

Thank you.

Document 619

Remarks by President Reagan at a Press Briefing, December 4, 1982 (Extracts)[31]

"I Think We Really Established Some Friendships"

Q. —you have been partying all night. Don't you have—(inaudible)?

THE PRESIDENT. No, I just brought a birthday cake and then I brought a farewell

---

30 November 15, 1982.

31 Source: *Weekly Compilation of Presidential Documents*, December 20, 1982, pp. 1613–1616. These remarks were made during a question-and-answer session with reporters aboard *Air Force One* while returning to Washington from San Pedro Sula, Honduras. Only those remarks related to the trip are printed.

cake for our military man who is leaving after 26 years—the man who handles all the baggage.

Q. You don't look tired.

Q. You don't look tired at all.

THE PRESIDENT. You should have been used to that after the campaign. (Laughter) No, I am not tired.

Q. So you enjoyed the trip?

THE PRESIDENT. Yes, I think it was a real fruitful one.

Q. Do you think you accomplished anything?

THE PRESIDENT. Yes, I do. I think that we established some very good relations there.

Q. Do you think that the six Presidents that you visited with got to know you a lot better at close distance rather than long distance?

THE PRESIDENT. Yes, even though I had met a couple of them before when they had come up here—no, I think we really established some friendships—mutual friendships. I feel very close to them and I think they do to me.

Q. Do you think President Rios Montt announced that on—

THE PRESIDENT. What?

Q. Is President Rios Montt's announcement about—announcing the election laws in March of 1983, setting in pattern the eventual election of a democratic government? Is that enough to justify the resumption of military aid to Guatemala?

THE PRESIDENT. We have got a whole lot of material which he very frankly brought for us to study. I frankly think that they have been getting a bad deal. You know, he was elected President in 1974 and was never allowed to take office. So when this particular coup came, the officers who conducted the coup came to him and put him into the office he had been elected to. But he is totally dedicated to democracy in Guatemala. They have some very real problems that we, as I say, are going to—they brought and they made quite a presentation and brought a lot of information and material to us. And frankly I am inclined to believe that they have been getting a bum rap.[32]

Q. Are you leaning toward resuming the aid there on what he told you in your talks?

THE PRESIDENT. This is going to depend, of course, on all this information that has been provided to us, but I would think so.

Q. Mr. President, do you think you sent a clear signal to Nicaragua, to the Sandinista government by talking with all the Presidents around Nicaragua? And what would that signal be?

THE PRESIDENT. The main thing was that—we were not particularly trying to aim a signal to them. We were trying to do what I said clear back in the campaign that I wanted to do. And that is to get all these countries in the Americas, in this hemisphere to recognize what a force for good in the world we could be if we did have an accord. And so we will do more of this, and with others. We had to start someplace.

Q. Why did we fly around Nicaragua today, instead of just taking the shorter route over the country?

THE PRESIDENT. I do not know. I imagine, probably, because there was some concern about going into their airspace. I do not know. I have not asked anyone. I looked at the map there in my own room. And it seemed to me that a fairly direct route did take us over water on the Pacific side, and then to turn into land and Honduras—it did not seem to me that it was too much out of the way.

. . . .

Q. Did you have any favorite president out of all those you met on this 5-day—

THE PRESIDENT. Oh, I wouldn't answer that question. (Laughter)

Q. We want to fix this good—

THE PRESIDENT. I must say, I felt very good about all of them and I thought that we established quite a relationship.

Q. How are you going to get your horse back?[33]

Q. We thought we smelled an odor back there—(Laughter)—

Q. Does he have to be in quarantine?

THE PRESIDENT. I assume there's some rules about that, yes.

[32] For the President's remarks following his meeting with Guatemalan President Jose Efrain Rios Montt, see *ibid.*, December 13, 1982, pp. 1577–1578.

[33] A reference to a present from Brazilian President João Baptista de Oliveira Figueiredo.

Q. You're going to have so many horses, you're going to have to buy a new ranch. (Laughter)

THE PRESIDENT. This one is only on loan.

Q. On loan. Is he going to fly back—(inaudible)—going to come back by train—

THE PRESIDENT. By train? (Laughter)

Q. South America?

THE PRESIDENT. No, you'd be surprised how much of that kind of transportation there is now because of racing. They ship horses all around the world to Europe over and back over to Europe and from South America—the tracks down there—up here.

So, I suppose it's just a case of finding out sometime when there's a shipment going. It's a great horse. (Laughter)

Q. (Inaudible)—are you able to ride him now or is he still—

THE PRESIDENT. Oh, yes, that's the one I'm riding since Little Man left us—

Q. El Alamein?

THE PRESIDENT. Yes, he's a good ride. He is.

Q. Now that he's broken in.

THE PRESIDENT. Yes. Well, no, he was always all right when you were on him. He was most dangerous when he was on the ground. And I don't know whether that's the way they train them or something so that, you know, they'll feel more macho when they get on or not. But—no, and even now, you know, I always feed him carrots after a ride. And you have to be more careful with him than any other or he'll eat you off to the elbow. (Laughter). Gets the carrot and starts on fingers.

Q. Well, you should have more carrot and less stick. (Laughter) (Inaudible)

THE PRESIDENT. More carrot and less what?

Q. Stick. (Laughter)

Q. More carrot and less stick.

Q. Has this changed your views any about Latin America? Do your policies—see any perspective differently after this trip?

THE PRESIDENT. Well, I learned a lot because that's what I want to do is—I didn't go down there with any plan for the Americas or anything. I went down to find out from them their views. And you'd be surprised, yes, because, you know, they're all individual countries. I think one of the greatest mistakes in the world that we've made has been in thinking—lumping—thinking Latin America. You don't talk that way about Europe. You recognize the difference between various countries. And the same thing is true here.

So I went down to say to them what my dream was about this accord and then say, "Now, how can we make it work?"

Q. Were they surprised at that attitude? Did they think that was a change in attitude?

THE PRESIDENT. I think so. No one actually specifically said it. But I think they did.

Q. In Colombia, where things may have been a little shakier than other places, was there a surprised President there in that approach?

THE PRESIDENT. I think we established a very close friendship there, in spite of the toast.[34] (Laughter)

Q. (Inaudible)

THE PRESIDENT. That what?

Q. (Inaudible)

THE PRESIDENT. Oh?

Q. Seems like a long day, but this morning, the protesting—(inaudible)—a whole speech.

THE PRESIDENT. Again?

Q. (Inaudible)—

Q. I mean, he stayed in the—(inaudible). You know that when the guards sort of moved toward him, all the people waved him away.

THE PRESIDENT. I know. Well, it's—

Q. It's a real—evidently it's a democracy.

THE PRESIDENT. Yes, yes.

Q. Mr. President, is your dream likely to take any more tangible form now that you've talked about it with these heads of state? Is there anything that you've got in mind about furthering that idea?

THE PRESIDENT. I think it's a thing that has to grow and develop through the Organization of American States, through get-

---

[34] For the text of Colombian President Belisario Betancur's remarks, see Foreign Broadcast Information Service, *Daily Report: Latin America*, December 6, 1982, pp. F1–F3.

ting more bilateral actions. I just—I think we've—It's been a very worthwhile trip.

Q. Mr. President, what sort of message were you trying to send to Nicaragua with the—(inaudible)—the latter part of your trip—(inaudible)—one Central American country that you did not visit and you did not talk with leaders. Is there some message that you were trying to send to them with this trip?

THE PRESIDENT. No, not really. No, this is—and, as you know, we've tried to communicate with Nicaragua. We've tried to convince them there could be another way to go.

Q. You know—just one last question—the *New York Times* said that you have heard from the new Soviet President and he is interested in these, you know, working out something, negotiations on the things he proposed on the expanded hot line, etc. Is that true?

THE PRESIDENT. You know, the idea that has been kind of indicated is that we didn't have any communications. We've been in constant communication with the Soviet Union and—yes, we haven't had time to deal with that. But I understand that his reply has come expressing an interest in those things that—

Q. They are receptive then?

THE PRESIDENT. Yes.

THE PRESS. Thank you.

THE PRESIDENT. And I know how you really want to be accurate. It was a bridged loan, not a "breached loan." (Laughter)

Document 620

Transcript of a Department of State Press Briefing, December 6, 1982[35]

Support for Democracy in Latin America

SENIOR STATE DEPARTMENT OFFICIAL. This was a trip in which the President wanted to do three things. He wanted to underscore his own support for the democratic developments in this area.

George Shultz and I were adding up the numbers, just as a kind of intellectual exercise, at the end of the trip, and George asked, "What percentage of the population in Latin America now lives under some form of democratic regime", and we came out with something on the order of 90 percent, given changes that are now occurring in Brazil.

Obviously these are all kinds of different democratic systems, but there is an unmistakable trend, and one purpose of the trip which came through, I think very strongly, in each of the President's statements, as well as in his private talks was to express support and encouragement for that.

Secondly, we had a whole range of bilateral economic issues to deal with and some multilateral ones.

The President wanted to underscore that it was important to manage our economic relations with this part of the world, and, indeed, I think it is fair to say that whereas in earlier times, the dependency, often then a theme in Latin America, ran one way, from Latin America to the United States. I think it would be accurate to say now that our own sense of our interdependency with this area of depending very much on their economic performance, whether it is in maintaining their records as debtors that pay, or in the way in which they handle their trade and investment affairs, is very substantial as a major trading, financial and investment partner.

In that regard, you saw us find a way through a difficult export incentive problem in Brazil—their use of export incentives, which has been decreasing.[36] Now that they are under particular pressure on their balance of payments, they want to continue them. We want to keep them headed toward phasing these out. We were able to reach a compromise on that issue when we were there.

You also saw us, of course, provide a loan, and I just underscore that it is a loan. It was negotiated and arranged beforehand to Brazil in order to enable them to get from this point to the agreement with the IMF on a stabilization loan after a stabilization program has been established. That is a bridging exercise for 90 days, but I think it

[35] Source: Department of State files. The briefing, which began at 11:20 a.m., was conducted on background by a senior Department of State official.

[36] Regarding the discussions with Brazil, see document 708.

is symbolic of the interest that we both share in keeping the system working and keeping access of a major country like Brazil to the international financial institutions while it makes the necessary adjustment.

In Brazil, we also—and I think this is going to be important—and agreed on a series of one-time reviews and analyses and recommendations on our relationship, touching not only the economic/financial area, but also the controversial nuclear, the promising space and technology, and a new item on our agenda, the possibility of cooperation in the industrial field on military projects.

Brazil and the United States have had a series of difficult bilateral issues with each other over the last 10 years: countervailing duties is one major one; human rights was, no longer is, another; differences on nuclear policy are a third. But underlying that has also been the question of how to readjust and redefine relationships between these two very big countries in such a way so that the Brazilian sense of independence can be fully satisfied at the same time that the kind of cooperation that is really necessary between these two very big and powerful countries is achieved.

It has been hard to get right. We are not sure that—I don't want to promise too much out of this—I am not sure that we have got it right now, but we have got a new opportunity to try to define the balance on this and get the two countries headed back toward a relationship of a mutually supportive type that we have had before and should have in the future.

In the case of Colombia, we have a government which has a strong election mandate behind it, but some very serious internal problems.[37]

You saw that the Colombian Government is attempting to deal with its long-term insurgency problem by offering an amnesty. That amnesty has been rejected by some of its opponents, particularly the M-19 Urban Group, and we think that it is unlikely to be very successful with the rural group, but it is an important experiment in dealing with opposition movements, and we have wished the Colombians well on it.

They raised with us, publicly and privately, a number of larger issues: The Inter-American Development Bank negotiations, which are currently deadlocked over the amount that should be given to the four big countries. They are not, interestingly enough, deadlocked over the amount that should be made avilable to a country like Colombia.

But we think it will be worked out and will be successful in proposing a major expansion of this instrument in the course of the future.

We talked here about sugar, as we did in a number of other places, which is a matter of concern, and a range of trade problems, including subsidy, countervailing deed problems, and narcotics.

We also talked at length about Central America and about views which are to some degree at variance on how to deal with Central America, and in many ways they are also the same; that is to say that Colombia shares our view that ultimately there must be a democratic solution in each of the countries in Central Ameria, and that this must be our firm goal.

In the case of the four Central American countries, if I could say a brief word about issues dealt with in each of those cases. The meeting with Alvaro Magaña, the Provisional President of El Salvador, dealt very much with the question of human rights in that country, with our President making very clear our concern that progress that has been made in the past should be maintained and pressed forward.[38]

Magaña noted that he is establishing a Human Rights Commission in order to provide an alternative means for dealing with human rights complaints, and also to collect information on human rights, which will be composed of a member for the Salvadoran administration, a military member, but include also a prominent labor leader, a priest, as well as four independent lawyers.

Obviously, how well that does depends on what, how vigorously it acts, so we ought to wait for results, but this is a step forward.

The President also expressed his concern about bringing to justice the murderers of American citizens in El Salvador in very firm terms.

Some of that discussion was dedicated to the economic situation in Central America and in El Salvador, with the President of El Salvador stating very vigorously his concern about the development of the economy there.

---

[37] Regarding the President's visit in Colombia, see document 711.

[38] Regarding the President's meeting with Salvadoran President Alvaro Magaña, see document 703.

He said that the situation has improved enough from a security point of view so that entrepreneurs are ready to invest again in this country. But it is a very import-dependent economy, as all the economies of Central America are, and they have got a balance of payments constraint on it. Is there some way in which you can release that balance-of-payments constraint, so that the investment can get on and people can buy the kind of process, intermediate process goods that are necessary?

In the case of Monge, a similar focus in our private meetings on democracy and the advancement of the economy there.[39] He expressed an interest in developing his northern provinces which are being infiltrated by Nicaragua, and we told him that indeed we would be able to help with an agricultural loan, we thought, and we would look for some more funds that would provide some offsetting advantages to low income persons in Costa Rica, as they go through their really quite successful stabilization plan.

In Honduras, sugar and money were very much a theme of the Honduran President there, too. As with Magaña and Monge, he hopes very much from the Caribbean Basin initiative, and we do have a mock-up schedule for it in Ways and Means on Thursday.

He would like very much to see a change in U.S. sugar policy as indeed would our other interlocutors in the trip.

In the case of Rios Montt, he gave us a general outline of his policy.[40] He said that in particular he was emphasizing winding up the death squads, and he thought he had done so, that had been active notably around the cities; prosecuting the anti-insurgents campaign more vigorously in the countryside in two ways—one by a larger number of men; and, two [?], there are about 25,000 people now in the Guatemalan Army, and they are achieving some notable successes against the insurgencies—and, two, in a rural self-defense program in Guatemala, in the countryside, in which villages are being, for the first time, given some means of armament to defend themselves, and are doing so against increasing insurgent attacks on villages.

He emphasized anticorruption, and said that he was trying to clean up what he regarded as a century of corrupt practices, and he said that for the first time in this country, which is 60 or 70 percent Indian, we have Indian representatives in our Council of State; 33 percent. He thinks it should go to two-thirds to represent their element of the population. He hopes that this will be a major element in the constitution which he is looking forward to drafting.

He told us that the Constitutional Assembly law, electoral law, would be edicted on March 23, along with the law and the constitutional political parties, but he believed that—and he said this again in subsequent meetings with the President—that he would hold elections, constitutional elections, in the course of 1983.

The President had expressed interest in moving on toward democracy as rapidly as possible and encouraged him on the Constitutional Assembly elections.

Rios Montt said that he would like, above all, economic help. He also needed some military help. The President did not promise to grant the sales of a variety of commercial items, military items, which is the current issue under discussion. We are not discussing—anybody is discussing military assistance. The question is, can Guatemala buy commercial items. The President did not make a commitment on that, and that issue, contrary to some of the reports you have seen, remains undecided, and I can't tell you when it will be decided.

Similarly, just to clear up that one, once again, that the President did not intend to make a Salvadoran certification in the remarks that he made after meeting with Alvaro Magaña. That is a complex process which we will be handling in the course of the next month.

Overall, I think a couple of remarks I would like to make about the trip itself and how it felt, the President obviously got on very well with the people he was dealing with. He not only had extremely cordial sets of meetings with Figueiredo and Monge whom he knows well already, in what could have been the more difficult stop in the trip, in Colombia, he obviously got on immediately very well with Betancur, and they had both a very personal and a very animated discussion on all of these issues on the background in the course of what turned out to be a long personal meeting between the two, is really what happened in Bogota.

The President clearly was enjoying himself. He said repeatedly that he was there to

---

[39] Luis Alberto Monge, President of Costa Rica.

[40] For remarks by the President concerning his meeting with Guatemalan President Jose Efrain Rios Montt, see *Weekly Compilation of Presidential Documents*, December 20, 1982, pp. 1613–1616.

listen and he did listen and to learn and he did learn. He wanted to, coming back on the plane, tell some of that to people in the United States, and I think wanted to stress the diversity and individuality of the countries. He was there. He used the language—"You'd be surprised how different they are", I think, the people in the press, and found himself quoted this morning as saying that he was surprised.

No, I don't think so, and I think the basic purpose that the President had in this trip, was to mark a priority to the hemisphere, something that he himself has been pursuing since he first met with López Portillo and then went to Canada and then this Caribbean Basin Initiative and now this trip. I think, and I think he thinks, this was accomplished. We really do want to mark that priority and to see whether we can't make these relationships work better than they have been, and more effectively.

I don't think you meant for me to talk that length of time, but I haven't quite used all the time you have, so—

Q. In some of your remarks about the question of selling—he didn't refer to them but we know—helicopter spare parts to Guatemala, the thing, your statements about whether the President did mean that he was talking about a certification in these remarks he apparently made on the plane on the way, about differences. This appears to be kind of what we sometimes call a rolling back from a lot of the things that were reported rather prominently on the trip.

What is the purpose of putting the stress on these clarifications?

A. I assume that you want to get this thing as it was and is, and so I wanted to note, as I did, in a backgrounder down in San Jose, immediately after he saw Alvaro Magaña that in fact he was not certifying, and it should not be so interpreted as in fact it was, and that in his remarks on Rios Montt, after they met, that he was not saying that he had decided that military assistance in any form should be sent, that is not the question, or that indeed commercial sales should be made. Those decisions have not been made.

And, frankly, as to the other remark, I think we just misinterpreted it.

Q. But he did say that he was inclined to do so; when asked about whether he would resume sales to Guatemala, he said, "Yes, I am."

A. Yes, that is quite right, but that is not a decision, and the President did not mean that, as I say, with authority as being a decision.

Q. Do you think that Guatemala received a bum rap, as President Reagan suggested?

A. I think what has not come through clearly is how much the situation has changed in the last 9 months. There is no question at all about the fact that the Lucas regimes, and earlier regimes, in Guatemala, were, one, repressive; and, two, corrupt; three, followed a basically anti-Indian policy, and that has been one of the—and, that, four, there were major human rights violations in the countryside and in the cities. We think that there were some 2,000 members of death squads operating in the neighborhood of Guatemala City.

We think there have been significant changes since that time. When the President said that this is clearly a matter of great personal integrity, he meant it, and I think it is demonstrable. He is a person who was elected, we believe, President of Guatemala in 1974. He went to Europe and came back, worked as a school teacher. Nobody can challenge, I think, his personal probity. He has made tremendous efforts to clean up the corruption in the military system—I think with some success. He has wound up those death squads that operated in the capital area, in particular.

These advances on taking account of the Indian population in several ways, one, giving them some means to defend themselves, and, secondly, bringing them into the government, are really quite remarkable steps forward.

He has started—I think it would be fair to say he is only saying he is making the first step down the road toward a constitutional government, and we would really like to see that go further. More than that is, we asked ourselves, "If somebody does this kind of stuff, and then there is no support forthcoming from outside, then maybe it is an open invitation for the enemies that he has, particularly on the right, in Guatemala to knock him off."

So that is why we have been giving consideration to taking a step further. One step has already been made, you know, in this in that Congress decided in the fall to give $10 million worth of economic assistance to Guatemala in the Caribbean Basin Initiative supplemental.

Now, it is true that human rights abuses continue, notably in the countryside. It is true that there are human rights abuses which are attributable to government forces or government-affiliated forces. It is also true that there are large numbers of human rights violations that are attributable to the insurgents operating as, in effect, the insurgents tried to cut the link that may be developing between the government and the Indian populations of the highlands.

One of the things that the insurgents are doing now, that they didn't do a year ago, is to attack villages. So, yes, I think it adds up to a bum rap, because it is the old question of, you know, sort of the better being the enemy of the good. People say, "Why haven't you ended all of these human rights abuses totally", and so anybody who tries to move ahead then is somehow not worthy of our support.

I think that is the kind of thing he is trying to get at.

Q. Can I follow up just very quickly? Is it likely that the President will approve some form of military aid to Guatemala, and will he recommend that?

A. Once again, we are not talking about military aid, we are talking about commercial sales. That is the issue that we have been looking at, and which we have been consulting on with the Congress.

I can't tell you what or when the President will decide. I think it is not knowable at this point.

Q. On those remarks with respect to Guatemala, two organizations, America's Watch, and National Council of Churches, have sent delegations down there in the last 2 months, and they have reported on the situation in the countryside, and many of their remarks contradict directly what Rios Montt has said and, to some degree, with what you have said.[41]

Were those reports brought to the attention of the President prior to the meeting with Rios Montt, and did he bring them up during his meeting? And, secondly, is the State Department still taking the position that there was not enough fraud in the elections last year in Guatemala to rule out the actual outcome, or to make fraudulent the actual outcome?

A. On the first question, the President knew of the existence of the reports, and he knew what their tenor was. He had not read them prior to his talks.

With regard to the elections last year in Guatemala, we still do not know of fraud on a scale that would have changed the outcome.

I'm sorry, you had one in between.

Q. No, that was basically it.

Q. Did you say that he knew of the tenor of the reports? I didn't catch that.

A. He knew of the reports, that the reports had been made, and what their basic thrust was.

I'm sorry, he did not take the reports up with Rios Montt. He raised the theme of human rights violations as one of the concerns that the United States has, but not in terms of the reports, however.

Q. In Honduras, there is a tremendous amount of discontent within the government as well as without, on the amounts of money being spent on military assistance to the Honduran Government, and less being spent on human needs around the country. Was this discussed at all?

A. No. It was in other terms, that the Government of Honduras would like to have its military assistance on a grant basis. It did not ask for more. It asked for it not to be in the form of loans, thinking that they could not, in their present economic situation as a poor country, the poorest in the area, sustain those costs.

However, as you know, Honduras is a major recipient of economic assistance, and it receives approximately three times economic assistance as it does military. And there was no suggestion by our interlocutors there that they wanted to change that. If they want more economic, we would certainly welcome that, but they did not complain about the balance. And I think your premise is really not an accurate one, if I understood what you are saying, that there was a lot of concern in the Honduras Government about this. Frankly, I am unaware of that. It was not raised.

Q. Just to clarify a point that has been troublesome lately.

Does the State Department consider that it has any sort of an understanding with Congress, or with any specific committees or subcommittees of Congress, about reaching some kind of general consensus before proceeding on these commercial sales to Guatemala?

---

[41] An apparent reference to the highly critical report, *Human Rights in Guatemala: No Neutrals Allowed,* issued November 23, 1982, by Americas Watch.

A. Let me clear that one up and tell you how it came up.

A year ago, the question was raised by members of the House Foreign Affairs Committee of attaching to an aid authorization bill an amendment which would have prohibited any economic or military assistance to Guatemala. I had a series of discussions at that time with Chairman Mike Barnes of the House Foreign Affairs Subcommittee on Inter-American Affairs on that subject, in which I urged him not to do that as closing off possible ways to help if in fact there were an evolution in the political and human rights situation.

Mike Barnes and I reached an agreement, which I think is still not fully understood by all members of the committee, but which they have a different recollection of. I wrote it down at the time, and I am about to provide to the committee my own note on it.

What I said was, "Look, if we reprogram any economic or military assistance, money, budget money, U.S. budget money, we have to go to the Foreign Operations Subcommittee of the House and the same committee on the Senate side, and then give them an opportunity to comment on that.["]

We don't give them formally a veto under our congressional practice, but in point of fact if they raise objections then obviously this is a very serious matter which is taken into consideration. In fact, I think almost always if there are objections, then the reprogramming doesn't go forward.

I said, "Let us undertake"—I did undertake to do the same thing with regard to the House Foreign Affairs Committee on any reprogramming of military and economic assistance for Guatemala. I regard myself as bound by that agreement. That agreement does not concern commercial sales, because there is no reprogramming involved. But I think that we are still committed, and indeed have had very substantial consultations—Steve Bosworth was up before the two Houses on Tuesday doing just that.

Q. Have you talked with Barnes, because his understanding of this on the public record seems to be somewhat different than yours.

A. That is why I am going to send him my note. He did not write it down at the time, and it would have been very helpful if he did. I did send him my note. I am going to do it again, and to Zablocki.

Q. Just as a technical thing, we have to phrase this as "A senior official said that Assistant Secretary Enders did this—?

A. Yes, I have no problem with that. I think that I should put my own note of this. I think it makes the distinction very clear on the record by sending it up to Zablocki and Barnes, which I am going to do. Sorry.

Q. First, about Guatemala, it seems that the U.S. administration is ready to back Guatemala's loans by IMF, the World Bank, Inter-American Development Bank. That was a change of policy—

A. That is correct, on the basis of the improvements that have occurred.

Q. And it is something you are going to do. Have you started already?

A. Yes.

Q. How much are the loans altogether? It was in the order of $130 million?

A. I don't know what is outstanding and in the pipeline and under consideration. I can't tell you that. We will have to have somebody get that.

Q. My second question is that, of course, the Inter-American Development Bank was the subject of talks in Colombia. We all know what Betancur was saying, and you said that you hope they wanted to work out an agreement for a major expansion of resources. How much?

A. Well, negotiations are not through. I just wanted, for your information, to note what the problem is.

There are two categories of countries—there are several, actually—but there are two major distinctions. One is the big, highly advanced countries—Mexico, Venezuela, Brazil, and Argentina—and they have a so-called Category A, and then all the other countries have different provisions, and there are limits to the amount that Category A can get, and the whole purpose is to get it to the less developed countries.

During the last few years, Venezuela has not been taking down its Category A funds. Venezuela would now, in spite of the fact that it has a high income and substantial reserves, would now like to do so again. And the chief problem is, how do you fit Venezuela into a more or less fixed part without producing a demand, notably on the U.S. Congress, that would not be sufficient—I mean would be unacceptable to our political opinion?

So, it is a very difficult issue, a tough negotiating issue, but all of the proposals that are now being discussed would result in a substantial, real expansion, over and above the rate of inflation—well over and above the rate of inflation—for the activities for the Bank as a whole.

So that is not challenged by the United States. It is just exactly this individual problem of how you deal with Venezuela that nobody has found a good solution to yet.

Q. Yes, but there are the problems of negotiations. It seems that the United States wants to reduce their contribution to the soft loan window of the Inter-American Development Bank from $175 million to $75 million a year.

A. We are certainly going to—we are very probably going to reduce our contribution to the soft loan window, thinking that the number of countries to which it really applies is now largely in the Caribbean Basin, the poorest countries, the bottom of the line in many cases. But that is not a major issue in the negotiations. I mean, the negotiations are not hung up on that. They are hung up on the so-called Category A countries.

Q. And the replenishment fund, I mean, the amount of replenishment, is not an issue?

A. The two are related, you see, because if in fact you put Venezuela back in, then you have a very substantially larger figure for the total amount that comes out at the end. That is the biggest problem of all. There are some other problems, but that is what it is hung up on at the moment. I think this is going to be worked out, though. We are reasonably confident that this negotiation is going to succeed.

Q. A moment ago you said the President's remarks were interpreted, misinterpreted. Were you referring to his remarks on certification? I wasn't quite sure what you were referring to.

A. I was referring to his remarks about, which he made on the plane, saying that you, the American people, would be surprised at about how diverse the countries were, which were interpreted as saying that he was surprised.

Q. I thought you were referring to his remarks in reply to a question in El Salvador.

A. On the other two issues about whether we had certified or not, I wanted to be quite clear that his act was not, and that he had not decided on Guatemala.

Q. Then I want to recall his quote on that. He was asked if he was, if he did intend to certify, and he said—"On the basis of what I know now, yes, of course", which seemed to most of us down there to be a pretty firm statement.

A. Not so intended as a certification.

Q. Not intended to be. And did you know why he spoke in such firm words? I know you had a briefing there, but most of us were filing his words while you were briefing, unfortunately, and we couldn't get to hear what you were saying.

A. We had a word on this afterwards as to what his intention was. He wishes to be encouraging. He thinks there has been progress. He was not making a final judgment. That is the distinction, I think, that we really want to add here.

Q. In Brazil and Colombia, the leaders seemed in their toast to be encouraging defusion of tension in Central America, and made favorable reference to Mexico and Venezuela and their ideas.

As a result of this trip and your having listened to those leaders and others, is there a possibility now that the United States will encourage direct negotiations between Honduras and Nicaragua and will itself undertake a more comprehensive negotiation with Nicaragua?

A. As you know, the Hondurans and Nicaraguans are in contact with each other at several levels. Both military commanders will meet periodically, and also they met at Foreign Minister level when the Honduran Foreign Minister went to Nicaragua a couple weeks ago and saw Daniel Ortega. So that part of the picture is of course contacts go on, and we, as you will recall, reacted in an encouraging sense to the Mexican initiative. We thought that it should be part of a larger approach, a regional approach overall. We continue to think that that is the case, because you can't sort of take one issue out and say that this is the problem, let's deal with it.

There are a whole bunch of interrelated issues, but we definitely would be encouraging that. By the way, we did not really have much discussion with the Brazilians on Central America, and they did not make privately any recommendations of the kind that you suggest, nor did, by the way, the Colombians.

Q. Not privately.

A. No.

Q. And the prospect of U.S.-Nicaraguan negotiations that are more comprehensive level?

A. I don't think the issue is the level. The issue is the substance. The Nicaraguans will tell you that the issue is the level, but they don't want to deal with our Ambassador on this subject. They want to have a meeting in another country with a higher level representative. But the question is, what are the negotiations about, and part of the process that you see underway is to identify what the goals are, and that is what the San Jose Declaration is all about.[42]

Now, you may have noted that George Shultz said in his OAS speech[43]—maybe you didn't note it. It wasn't major, it wasn't highlighted there, but let me point it out to you.

He said, talking about the San Jose approach, that it is really important to know where you are going, what your goals are, and let's find out how many countries agree with those goals, and if they do agree with them, we can get on with the next stage, which would be how to implement them, how to get to them.

We still don't know whether Nicaragua agrees with them, and we would like to know further about, in the case of Guatemala, whether Guatemala agrees with them enough so that it will really move down a timetable for democratic elections.

So there are some major questions on two of those countries. But that is our next focus, that is, do you accept the objectives. If you do, let's see what we can do about it.

Q. Anything about time estimates on those consultations, on San Jose?

A. They have been underway now. Their Foreign Minister has made a number of trips in that regard. We think there will be another meeting of Foreign Ministers sometime early in the next year to take stock. They expect to have a meeting of a number of countries at a nonofficial level in a so-called forum for peace and democracy, in which they want to get all the peace plans together and have a look at them, and make a report then to the Foreign Ministers, and we will see what the next stage after that is. But let's find out exactly what the goals have to be. So, I think level is sort of, in a sense, a red herring at this point. The question is, what is the substance.

Q. Thank you, very much.

[42] For the text of the Final Act of the San Jose meeting, see document 699.

[43] For the text of Shultz's speech, see document 618.

B. The War in the South Atlantic

Document 621

Statement Read by the President's Deputy Press Secretary (Speakes), April 2, 1982[1]

U.S. Efforts To Obtain a Cessation of Hostilities and Argentine Withdrawal From the Falkland Islands

Our situation report indicates the Argentine Government now claims to have occupied the Falkland Islands and such others as the South Georgias and South Shetlands. The British Government acknowledges that an invasion has taken place, but we have no information other than conflicting reports on fighting or casualties.

We have made clear to the Government of Argentina that we deplore use of force to resolve this dispute. We have called on Argentina to cease, immediately, hostilities, and to withdraw its military forces from the Falkland Islands.

We are continuing to work bilaterally—and in multilateral forums such as the United Nations—to obtain a cessation of hostilities and a withdrawal.

Because of our concern over the tensions between Argentina and the United King-

[1] Source: *Weekly Compilation of Presidential Documents*, April 5, 1982, p. 422. This statement was read at the White House press briefing held at 12:41 p.m., during which Speakes stated that on April 1 at 8:21 p.m. President Reagan "placed a call to the President of Argentina. They spoke with the assistance of interpreters for 50 minutes, concluding at 9:14. The President appealed to the President of Argentina to avoid the use of force and seek a peaceful solution." (White House Press Briefing, April 2, 1982, p. 5)

dom, the United States Government welcomes and strongly supports the statement by the President of the U.N. Security Council, made yesterday on behalf of the Council.[2] We fully endorse the Council's call for the exercise of utmost restraint at this time, the avoidance of the use or threat of force in the region, and for the continuation of the search for a diplomatic solution.

Document 622

Statement by the Alternate Representative at the United Nations (Lichenstein) Before the U.N. Security Council, April 3, 1982[3]

U.S. Support for Peaceful Settlement of the Dispute Over the Falkland Islands

My delegation joins you, Mr. President, in extending a warm welcome to our friends the Foreign Ministers of Argentina and Panama.[4]

When the Council met Thursday evening[5] to hear an urgent appeal from the Permanent Representative of the United Kingdom concerning the situation in the South Atlantic, we and other members of the Council joined in expressing our concern and in calling for both governments to exercise restraint and to continue the search for a diplomatic solution.

Unfortunately, despite appeals by the Secretary-General[6] and by my President as well, the situation has now deteriorated. As we have stated on many occasions in this Council and repeat once again with respect to the action by Argentina, we feel that the use of force to solve problems is deeply regrettable and will not produce a just and lasting settlement of the dispute.

We therefore intend to vote in favor of the draft resolution.[7] The United States Government is especially interested in finding a solution to this dispute since both governments involved are close friends and valued friends. My government stands ready to support any constructive approach to the solution of this problem and urges a return to negotiations as soon as possible. We have, of course, made clear to both sides that we are ready to help in any capacity to bring the parties together at an early date and to contribute to a peaceful settlement of this dispute.

Document 623

Resolution 502 (1982), Adopted by the U.N. Security Council, April 3, 1982[8]

Demand for a Cease-Fire, Argentine Withdrawal, and a Diplomatic Solution

The Security Council,

Recalling the statement made by the President of the Security Council at the 2345th meeting of the Security Council on 1 April 1982 (S/14944) calling on the Governments of Argentina and the United Kingdom of Great Britain and Northern Ireland to refrain from the use or threat of force in the region of the Falkland Islands (Islas Malvinas),

Deeply disturbed at reports of an invasion on 2 April 1982 by armed forces of Argentina,

Determining that there exists a breach of the peace in the region of the Falkland Islands (Islas Malvinas),

1. *Demands* an immediate cessation of hostilities;

2. *Demands* an immediate withdrawal of all Argentine forces from the Falkland Islands (Islas Malvinas);

---

[2] Reference is to the statement issued by the President of the U.N. Security Council, Kamanda wa Kamanda (Zaire), on April 1, 1982. For text, see U.N. document S/14944.

[3] Source: U.N. document S/PV.2350.

[4] Reference is to Nicanor Costa Méndez and Jorge E. Illueca, respectively.

[5] April 1, 1982.

[6] For the text of the statement of April 1, 1982, by U.N. Secretary-General Javier Pérez de Cuéllar, see *UN Chronicle*, May 1982, p. 6.

[7] *Infra.*

[8] Source: U.N. Security Council Resolution 502 (1982). This resolution, sponsored by the United Kingdom, was adopted by a vote of 10 (including the United States) to 1, with 4 abstentions. Following adoption of this resolution, the Council agreed to a request by Panama not to vote on its draft resolution (U.N. document S/14950) which called on the United Kingdom "to cease its hostile conduct, refrain from any threat or use of force and cooperate with the Argentine Republic in the decolonization of the Malvinas Islands, the South Georgias, and the South Sandwich Islands."

3. *Calls* on the Governments of Argentina and the United Kingdom to seek a diplomatic solution to their differences and to respect fully the purposes and principles of the Charter of the United Nations.

Document 624

Transcript of the Department of State Daily Press Briefing, April 5, 1982 (Extract)[9]

British Use of the U.S. Base on Ascension Island

. . . .

Q. Has there been any British request for refueling or resupply facilities on the part of the United States?

A. I noted some press reports regarding British use of the facility on Ascension Island. Our view on this is that Ascension Island is a British possession. The United Kingdom has the legal right to land military aircraft there after notifying the U.S. Air Force Commander at the airfield. The U.S. Government is obligated, under a 1962 agreement governing its use of the airfield,[10] to cooperate in the United Kingdom use of logistic, administrative, or operating facilities; and therefore, such use of the airfield does not, in any way, constitute U.S. involvement in the United Kingdom-Argentine dispute.

. . . .

---

[9] Source: Office of Press Relations, Department of State. Dean Fischer, Department of State Spokesman, conducted the briefing which began at 12:28 p.m.

[10] Reference is to the Agreement Relating to the Use of the Airfield at Widewake on Ascension Island by Aircraft of the Royal Air Force, effected by notes exchanged at Washington, August 29, 1962; for text, see 13 UST 1917.

Document 625

Statement Issued by the White House, April 7, 1982[11]

Secretary of State Haig's Consultations With the Governments of the United Kingdom and Argentina

This morning the President met with his national security advisors to review the situation in the South Atlantic. After the meeting the President is departing for Jamaica where he will meet with Prime Minister Seaga to further the close working dialogue opened during the Prime Minister's visit last year. He then continues on to Barbados where he will meet with leaders of Eastern Caribbean countries to discuss regional issues of mutual concern.

In keeping with the initiatives the President has taken with both Prime Minister Thatcher and President Galtieri and his offer of assistance,[12] the President has directed Secretary of State Haig to continue consultations with the Governments of the United Kingdom and Argentina in the interest of assisting both parties in the search for a peaceful resolution of the dispute in the South Atlantic.

The President directed Secretary Haig to proceed to London and Buenos Aires at the invitation of both governments.[13]

---

[11] Source: *Weekly Compilation of Presidential Documents*, April 12, 1982, pp. 452–453.

[12] It was reported that in his telephone conversation with President Reagan on April 1, 1982, "President Galtieri emphatically rejected President Reagan's offer to send Vice President Bush immediately to Buenos Aires to assist in a solution." (*Falkland Islands Review: Report of a Committee of Privy Counsellors*, p. 71)

[13] Secretary Haig visited London, April 8–9; Buenos Aires, April 9–11; London, April 12–13; and returned to Washington, April 13; thereafter, he visited Buenos Aires, April 15–19, and Caracas, April 19, and returned to Washington, April 19, 1982.

Document 626

Joint Statement by the Governments of the Ten States Members of the European Community, Brussels, April 10, 1982[14]

Embargo of Military Exports to Argentina and Suspension of Imports to Argentina

The Ten have discussed the serious situation arising from the invasion of the Falkland Islands by Argentina.

The Ten recall that, by their statement of 2 April, they condemned the flagrant violation of international law constituted by the armed action of Argentina.[15]

The Ten remain deeply concerned by the continuation of this crisis which endangers international peace and security. They therefore attach the greatest importance to the effective and immediate implementation of Security Council resolution 502 in all its aspects,[16] namely, the cessation of hostilities, the immediate withdrawal of all Argentine forces from the Islands and the search, by the Governments of Argentina and the United Kingdom, for a diplomatic solution.

To these ends, and in a spirit of solidarity among the countries members of the Community, the Ten decide to take a series of measures with respect to Argentina which it is important to carry out as soon as possible.

In this connexion, the Governments of the Ten have already decided to apply a total embargo on the exports of arms and military equipment to Argentina.[17]

They will also take the necessary measures to prohibit all imports of Argentine origin into the Community.[18]

As these measures are of an economic nature, they will be taken in accordance with the relevant provisions of the treaties of the Community.

As the situation arising from the invasion of the Falkland Islands by the Argentine armed forces is a matter of serious concern for the international community as a whole, the Ten call upon other Governments to associate themselves with their decisions in order to ensure, within the shortest possible time, the full implementation of Security Council resolution 502.

Document 627

Resolution 359 (490/82), Adopted by the OAS Permanent Council, April 13, 1982[19]

The Situation Obtaining Between Argentina and the United Kingdom in Relation to the Malvinas (Falkland) Islands

WHEREAS:

The dispute between the Republic of Argentina and the United Kingdom of

---

[14] Source: U.N. document S/14976, April 14, 1982. This text was annexed to a letter of April 13, 1982, from Edmonde Dever, Permanent Representative of Belgium at the United Nations, to Kamanda wa Kamanda, President of the U.N. Security Council. The members of the European Community are Belgium, Denmark, France, the Federal Republic of Germany, Greece, Ireland, Italy, Luxembourg, the Netherlands, and the United Kingdom.

[15] For the text of the joint statement of April 2, 1982, by the Foreign Ministers of the ten states members of the European Community, see U.N. document S/14949.

[16] For text of U.N. Security Council Resolution 502 (1982), see document 622.

[17] The Ten had agreed on April 9, 1982, to ban arms deliveries to Argentina. In unilateral actions, France, the Federal Republic of Germany, Italy, the Netherlands, and the United Kingdom had previously banned such arms sales.

[18] Council Regulation (EEC) No. 877/82 of April 16, 1982, suspended imports from Argentina for 1 month; Council Regulation (EEC) No. 1176/82 of May 18, 1982, extended the suspension until May 24; and Council Regulation (EEC) No. 1254/82 of May 24, 1982, extended it indefinitely. For texts of these EEC regulations, see *Official Journal of the European Communities*, vol. 25, No. L 102, April 16, 1982, No. L 136, May 18, 1982, and L 146, May 25, 1982, respectively. On May 17, 1982, Denmark stated its intention to extend the import ban through domestic legislation rather than Community regulation; Ireland and Italy dropped the import ban on May 17, but they agreed not to allow Argentina to use their countries to circumvent the import ban by the other member states; and they maintained the arms embargo. On April 14, 1982, Argentina had banned imports from those countries which suspended imports from Argentina.

[19] Source: OAS document OEA/Ser.G CP/RES.359 (490/82). This resolution, sponsored by Colombia, Costa Rica, and Ecuador, was adopted by consensus.

Great Britain and Northern Ireland in relation to the Malvinas (Falkland) Islands is endangering the peace of the hemisphere, and

The fundamental principles and purposes established in the Charter of the Organization of American States[20] include those of strengthening the peace and security of the continent, preventing possible causes of difficulties and ensuring the peaceful settlement of disputes,

THE PERMANENT COUNCIL OF THE ORGANIZATION OF AMERICAN STATES, RESOLVES:

1. To express its profound concern over the serious situation that the Republic of Argentina and the United Kingdom of Great Britain and Northern Ireland now face.

2. To express its fervent hope that a rapid, peaceful solution can be found to the disagreement between the two nations within the context of the rules of international law.

3. To offer its friendly cooperation in the peace efforts already under way, in the hope of contributing in this way to a peaceful settlement of the dispute that will avert once and for all the danger of war between countries that deserve the respect of the international community.

Document 628

Statement by the Representative at the Organization of American States (Middendorf) Before the OAS Permanent Council, April 20, 1982[21]

"It Seems . . . Inappropriate To Seek Consideration of This Matter Within the Rio Treaty"

Thank you, Mr. Chairman. Mr. Chairman, the United States Delegation is deeply disturbed by the implications of the proposed action that we are called upon to discuss here today. In brief, we question whether such a proposal is either necessary or appropriate and whether, therefore, it may contribute to a peaceful settlement.

We would have thought it unnecessary to come before the OAS today. Nevertheless, if a majority of the members believes the time has come to build upon our work of last week in the Permanent Council, there is more than ample basis for us to do so under the OAS Charter. As we all agreed last week in the resolution put forth by the distinguished representatives of Colombia, Ecuador, and Costa Rica,[22] and approved by this body by consensus, the proper role for our Organization in this difficult situation is to be available to assist the ongoing efforts to reach a peaceful solution and to maintain our availability as a valuable source of support in these efforts. Articles 59 and 60 of the OAS Charter provide an entirely appropriate vehicle for this entire Organization to serve that role. Article 24 of the Charter expressly contemplates precisely the sort of mechanisms such as good offices, mediation, conciliation, and investigation that may be needed in this case; and by contrast, convocation under the Rio Treaty,[23] as is proposed today, seems to us inappropriate for the present context.

At a time when Secretary Haig is engaged in an ongoing effort to promote a peaceful settlement within the framework of U.N. Resolution 502, which we are anxious not to prejudice, it seems to my government particularly inappropriate to seek consideration of this matter within the Rio Treaty. Despite its utility for peacekeeping purposes, the Rio Treaty is generally viewed as an instrument for developing and implementing collective security measures. While, of course, there has been no suggestion whatsoever that we consider adopting such measures, the mere fact of our meeting under the Rio Treaty rubric will inevitably cast the activities of this group in an unhelpful confrontational light. So, it occurs to us, that we could avoid such an unfortunate cast to our deliberations and achieve our purposes equally well, Mr. Chairman, if not better, by meeting under the OAS Charter, and accordingly it is the

---

[20] For the Charter of the Organization of American States, signed at Bogotá, April 30, 1948, entered into force for the United States, December 13, 1951, see 2 UST 2394; and for its amendment of February 27, 1967, see 21 UST 607.

[21] Source: OAS document OEA/Ser.G CP/ACTA 493/82 corr. 1, pp. 29–30; printed also in Department of State *Bulletin*, June 1982, pp. 84–85.

[22] *Supra.*

[23] For text of the Inter-American Treaty of Reciprocal Assistance (Rio Treaty), signed at Rio de Janeiro, September 2, 1947, entered into force for the United States, December 3, 1948, see 4 Bevans 559.

intention of my delegation to abstain on the proposed resolution under consideration.[24] Thank you, Mr. Chairman.

Document 629

Resolution 360 (493/82), Adopted by the OAS Permanent Council, April 20, 1982[25]

Convocation of the Twentieth Meeting of Consultation of Ministers of Foreign Affairs of the Rio Treaty

WHEREAS:

In its note dated April 19, 1982,[26] the Government of Argentina requested convocation of the Organ of Consultation, pursuant to Article 6 of the Inter-American Treaty of Reciprocal Assistance,[27] to consider the measures that it would be advisable to take for the maintenance of the peace and security of the hemisphere, and

The Permanent Council of the Organization of American States has heard the statement by the Permanent Representative of Argentina[28] denouncing a grave situation that threatens the peace and security of the hemisphere and that affects the sovereignty and territorial integrity of his country, and describing the measures that the Argentine Government has adopted in exercise of the right of legitimate self-defense,

THE PERMANENT COUNCIL OF THE ORGANIZATION OF AMERICAN STATES RESOLVES:

1. To convene the Organ of Consultation under the provisions of the Inter-American Treaty of Reciprocal Assistance, and in accordance with Article 70 of the Rules of Procedure of this Permanent Council,[29] to consider the grave situation that has arisen in the South Atlantic.

2. To decide that the Organ of Consultation shall meet at the headquarters of the General Secretariat of the Organization on April 26, 1982, at 10 a.m.

3. To constitute itself and to act provisionally as Organ of Consultation, pursuant to Article 12 of the Inter-American Treaty of Reciprocal Assistance.

Document 630

Statement by the Secretary of State (Haig) Before the Twentieth Meeting of Consultation of Ministers of Foreign Affairs of the Rio Treaty, April 26, 1982[30]

Inappropriateness of Collective Security Under the Rio Treaty in the Falkland Islands Dispute

Mr. President, distinguished colleagues, special delegates, ladies and gentlemen:

We meet here in the Hall of the Americas at a time when we are reminded of the Western Hemisphere's tradition of democracy, its record of achievement, and its devotion to peace. The Organization of American States is the living testimony that our cooperation can be a force for interna-

---

[24] *Infra.*

[25] Source: OAS document OEA/Ser.G CP/RES. 360 (493/82) corr. 1. This resolution, sponsored by Argentina, was adopted by a vote of 18 to 0, with 3 abstentions (including the United States).

[26] For text of the note from Raúl A. Quijano, Permanent Representative of Argentina to the Organization of American States, to Francisco Bustillo, Uruguayan Chairman of the OAS Permanent Council, see OAS document OEA/Ser.F/II.20 Doc. 6/82.

[27] Reference is to the Rio Treaty, regarding which see footnote 23 above.

[28] For text of the statement of April 20, 1982, by Ambassador Quijano, see OAS document OEA/Ser.G CP/ACTA 493/82 corr.1, pp. 4–13.

[29] Article 70 of the Permanent Council's Rules of Procedure provides that the Permanent Council shall decide by the vote of an absolute majority of the states that have ratified the Inter-American Treaty of Reciprocal Assistance whether the Meeting of Consultation should be held. For text, see OAS Permanent Council, *Rules of Procedure of the Permanent Council* (OEA/Ser.G CP/doc.1112/80, October 1, 1980 (Washington: OAS General Secretariat, 1980)), p. 19.

[30] Source: OAS document OEA/Ser.F/II.20 Doc. 20/82, pp. 21–23; also printed in Department of State *Bulletin*, June 1982, pp. 85–86. Secretary Haig spoke at the first session of the General Committee of the Twentieth Meeting of Consultation of Ministers of Foreign Affairs of the Rio Treaty which convened in the Hall of the Americas at the OAS General Secretariat in Washington at 4:05 p.m.

tional progress. Clearly, a vigorous inter-American system is of fundamental importance to the future of this hemisphere.

These facts must be uppermost in our minds as we consider how best to advance toward a peaceful solution to the South Atlantic controversy. All of us know that we are dealing today with an enormously difficult and sensitive problem. Both the Republic of Argentina and the United Kingdom assert that their rights to the Islands have been denied. Argentina is motivated by a deep national commitment to establish possession of the Islands. It is frustrated by years of what it considers to be fruitless negotiation. Britain emphasizes its long-standing possession of the Islands and asserts that the wishes of the inhabitants must be respected in any lasting settlement.

To understand these competing claims and the emotions on both sides does not mean to pass judgment on their validity. But this organization—and the world community—long ago made the judgment that force should not be used to solve international disputes. We shall all suffer if this fundamental principle of both the international order and hemispheric order, which the Rio Treaty was designed to protect, is ignored. I think all of us are aware of how many members of the OAS are involved in a dispute over territory with one or more of their neighbors.

In the current conflict, the surest guide to a peaceful settlement is to be found in United Nations Security Council Resolution 502. It requires an immediate cessation of hostilities, an immediate withdrawal of Argentine forces on the Islands, and that the resolution of the problem be sought through diplomacy. These three points form the indispensable basis for a solution: They form an integrated whole. They have been accepted by both parties or at least have not been rejected by either of them.

In support of Resolution 502, the United States has offered its assistance to both Britain and Argentina. We have acted in the spirit of friendship with both countries. Heartened by the confidence of both governments, for the past 3 weeks I have pursued the possibilities of averting wider conflict and a framework for a peaceful settlement, here in Washington, in Buenos Aires, and in London. These discussions have been long and difficult. They could not have been otherwise in the context of this anguishing controversy. President Reagan believes that the United States has perhaps a unique ability to assist the parties. Under his direction, I have made myself available to both, accepting their invitations to sound out their views and suggesting avenues to approach a framework of peace.

Throughout this arduous period, we have been aware that the stakes for the international community, the Americas, and the two countries are very great. Continued military action will exact a heavy price. The enemies of the West could find fresh opportunities to seek that position of influence on the mainland of the Americas they have so long sought.

It is quite clear that the crisis has reached a critical point. New military action has taken place. Unless a settlement can be found in the next few days, more intensive fighting is likely to occur.

The conflict over the Islands affects us all. As we consider what we can do to help the situation, let us recall these points:

First, there has been a use of force by an American state already followed by a U.N. Security Council resolution which clearly sets forth the basis for a peaceful solution. While we should take advantage of the peaceful settlement procedures available to us in this forum, it would be neither appropriate nor effective to treat this dispute within the collective security framework implied by the Rio Treaty.

Second, any resolution considered for adoption by the foreign ministers should be examined against the criteria of whether it contributes to the peace process, whether it impairs the peace efforts already endorsed by the Organization of American States and whether it strengthens the ability of this organization to contribute in the future to easing crises.

Our participation in the inter-American system pledges us to strengthen the peace and security of the hemisphere. In the search for a solution that both parties can accept with honor and responsibility, the United States remains at the disposition of the parties. At this critical hour, we are redoubling our peace efforts. With your help, we may succeed. Thank you, Mr. Chairman.

Document 631

Memorandum of Agreement, Proposed by the United States to Argentina and the United Kingdom, April 27, 1982[31]

Proposal for an Interim Settlement and Negotiation of the Falkland Islands Dispute

PREAMBLE:

On the basis of United Nations Security Council Resolution 502, and the will of the Argentine Republic and of the United Kingdom to resolve the controversy which has arisen between them, renouncing the use of force, both Governments agree on the following steps, which form an integrated whole:

PARAGRAPH 1

1. Effective on the signature of this Agreement by both Governments, there shall be an immediate cessation of hostilities.

PARAGRAPH 2

2. Beginning at 0000 hours local time of the day after the day on which this Agreement is signed, and pending a definitive settlement, the Republic of Argentina and the United Kingdom shall not introduce or deploy forces into the zones (hereinafter, "zones"), defined by circles of 150 nautical miles' radius from the following coordinate points (hereinafter, "coordinate points"):

A) Lat. 51°40′ S
Long. 59°30′ W
B) Lat. 54°20′ S
Long. 36°40′ W
C) Lat. 57°40′ S
Long. 26°30′ W

2.1. Within 24 hours of the date of this Agreement, the United Kingdom will suspend enforcement of its "zone of exclusion" and Argentina will suspend operations in the same area.

2.2. Within 24 hours of the date of this Agreement, Argentina and the United Kingdom will commence the withdrawal of their forces in accordance with the following details:

2.2.1. Within seven days from the date of this Agreement, Argentina and the United Kingdom shall each have withdrawn one-half of their military and security forces present in the zones on the date of this Agreement, including related equipment and armaments. Within the same time period, the United Kingdom naval task force will stand off at a distance equivalent to seven days' sailing time (at 12 knots) from any of the coordinate points, and Argentine forces that have been withdrawn shall be placed in a condition such that they could not be reinserted with their equipment and armament in less than seven days.

2.2.2. Within fifteen days from the date of this Agreement, Argentina shall remove all of its remaining forces from the zones and redeploy them to their usual operating areas or normal duties. Within the same period, the United Kingdom shall likewise remove all of its remaining forces from the zones and shall redeploy such forces and the naval task force and submarines to their usual operating areas or normal duties.

2.3. In accordance with its letter of acceptance of even date, the United States shall verify compliance with the provisions of this paragraph, and the two Governments agree to cooperate fully with the United States in facilitating this verification.

PARAGRAPH 3

3. From the date of this Agreement, the two Governments will initiate the necessary procedures to terminate simultaneously, and without delay, the economic and financial measures adopted in connection with the current controversy, including restrictions relating to travel, transportation, communications, and transfers of funds between the two countries. The United King-

---

[31] Source: OAS document OEA/Ser.F/II.20 Doc. 74/82, May 28, 1982; also printed in Department of State *Bulletin*, October 1982, pp. 85–86. The copy printed here was transmitted by letter (undated) from Ambassador J. William Middendorf II, Delegate to the Twentieth Meeting of Consultation of Ministers of Foreign Affairs of the Rio Treaty, to Estanislao Valdés Otero, Uruguayan President of the Twentieth Meeting of Consultation, for circulation among the delegations accredited to that meeting.

According to a clarification attached to the transcript of the Department of State Daily Press Briefing of April 28, 1982, identical proposals were sent to London and Buenos Aires simultaneously overnight between Monday and Tuesday, April 26–27, 1982. This represented some minor adjustments of the draft proposals given to British Foreign Secretary Pym when he departed Washington on April 23, 1982. (Office of Press Relations, Department of State)

dom at the same time shall request the European Community and third countries that have adopted similar measures to terminate them.

PARAGRAPH 4

4. The United Kingdom and Argentina shall each appoint, and the United States has indicated its agreement to appoint, a representative to constitute a Special Interim Authority (hereinafter "the Authority") which shall verify compliance with the obligations in this Agreement (with the exception of paragraph 2), and undertake such other responsibilities as are assigned to it under this Agreement or the separate Protocol regarding the Authority signed this date. Each representative may be supported by a staff of not more than ten persons on the islands.

PARAGRAPH 5

5.1 Pending a definitive settlement, all decisions, laws and regulations hereafter adopted by the local administration on the islands shall be submitted to and expeditiously ratified by the Authority, except in the event that the Authority deems such decisions, laws or regulations to be inconsistent with the purposes and provisions of this Agreement or its implementation. The traditional local administration shall continue, except that the Executive and Legislative Councils shall be enlarged to include:

(A) two representatives appointed by the Argentine Government to serve in the Executive Council; and

(B) representatives in each Council of the Argentine population whose period of residence on the islands is equal to that required of others entitled to representation, in proportion to their population, subject to there being at least one such representative in each Council. Such representatives of the resident Argentine population shall be nominated by the Authority.

The flags of each of the constituent members of the Authority shall be flown at its headquarters.

5.2 Pending a definitive settlement, neither Government shall take any action that would be inconsistent with the purposes and provisions of this Agreement or its implementation.

PARAGRAPH 6

6.1 Pending a definitive settlement, travel, transportation, movement of persons and, as may be related thereto, residence and ownership and disposition of property, communications and commerce between the mainland and the islands shall, on a non-discriminatory basis, be promoted and facilitated. The Authority shall propose to the two Governments for adoption appropriate measures on such matters. Such proposals shall simultaneously be transmitted to the Executive and Legislative Councils for their views. The two Governments undertake to respond promptly to such proposals. The Authority shall monitor the implementation of all such proposals adopted.

6.2 The provisions of paragraph 6.1 shall in no way prejudice the rights and guarantees which have heretofore been enjoyed by the inhabitants on the islands, in particular rights relating to freedom of opinion, religion, expression, teaching, movement, property, employment, family, customs, and cultural ties with countries of origin.

PARAGRAPH 7

7. December 31, 1982 will conclude the interim period during which the two Governments shall complete negotiations on removal of the islands from the list of Non-Self-Governing Territories under Chapter XI of the United Nation's Charter[32] and on mutually agreed conditions for their definitive status, including due regard for the rights of the inhabitants and for the principle of territorial integrity, in accordance with the purposes and principles of the United Nations Charter, and in light of the relevant Resolutions of the United Nations General Assembly. The negotiations hereabove referred to shall begin within fifteen days of the signature of the present Agreement.

PARAGRAPH 8

8. In order to assist them in bringing their negotiations to a mutually satisfactory

---

[32] For text of the U.N. Charter, signed at San Francisco, June 26, 1945, entered into force for the United States, October 24, 1945, see 3 Bevans 1153. For the list of Non-Self-Governing Territories under Chapter XI of the U.N. Charter, see U.N. document A/37/23 (Part I), October 8, 1982, "Report of the Special Committee on the Situation With Regard to the Implementation of the Declaration on the Granting of Independence to Colonial Countries and Peoples" (covering its work during 1982), Chapter I, paragraph 58, pp. 24–25.

settlement by the date stipulated in the preceding paragraph, the Authority shall, after consultation with the Executive Council, make specific proposals and recommendations as early as practicable to the two Governments, including proposals and recommendations on:

8.1 The manner of taking into account the wishes and interests of the islanders, insofar as islands with a settled population are concerned, based on the results of a sounding of the opinion of the inhabitants, with respect to such issues relating to the negotiations, and conducted in such manner, as the Authority may determine;

8.2 Issues relating to the development of the resources of the islands, including opportunities for joint cooperation and the role of the Falkland Islands Company; and

8.3 Such other matters as the two Governments may request, including possible arrangements for compensation of islanders, or matters on which the Authority may wish to comment in light of its experience in discharging its responsibilities under this Agreement.

8.4 The Governments have agreed on the procedure in sub-paragraph 8.1 without prejudice to their respective positions on the legal weight to be accorded such opinion in reaching a definitive settlement.

PARAGRAPH 9

9. Should the Governments nonetheless be unable to conclude the negotiations by December 31, 1982, the United States has indicated that, on the request of both Governments, it would be prepared at such time to seek to resolve the dispute within six months of the date of the request by making specific proposals for a settlement and by directly conducting negotiations between the Governments on the basis of procedures that it shall formulate. The two Governments agree to respond within one month to any formal proposals or recommendations submitted to them by the United States.

PARAGRAPH 10

10. This Agreement shall enter into force on the date of signature.

Document 632

Resolution I, Adopted by the Twentieth Meeting of Consultation of Ministers of Foreign Affairs of the Rio Treaty, April 28, 1982[33]

Appeal for Peaceful Settlement of the Conflict Over the Malvinas (Falkland) Islands

THE TWENTIETH MEETING OF CONSULTATION OF MINISTERS OF FOREIGN AFFAIRS, CONSIDERING:

The principles of inter-American solidarity and cooperation and the need to find a peaceful solution to any situation that endangers the peace of the Americas;

That a dangerous confrontation has arisen between the United Kingdom of Great Britain and Northern Ireland and the Argentine Republic, which was aggravated today by the events that have arisen from the presence of the British navy in the South Atlantic, within the security region referred to in Article 4 of the Rio Treaty;

That the primary purpose of the Inter-American Treaty of Reciprocal Assistance is the maintenance of the peace and security of the hemisphere, which, in the case that has arisen, requires ensuring the peaceful settlement of the dispute;

That to facilitate peaceful settlement of the dispute, it is urgent that hostilities cease, since they disturb the peace of the hemisphere and may reach unforeseeable proportions;

That it is an unchanging principle of the inter-American system that peace be preserved and that all the American states unanimously reject the intervention of

[33] Source: OAS document OEA/Ser.F/II.20 Doc. 28/82 rev. 3. This resolution, drafted by a working group headed by Bolivian Foreign Minister Gonzalo Romero Alvarez García, was adopted by a vote of 17 to 0, with 4 abstentions (including the United States). The second plenary session convened in the Hall of the Americas at the OAS General Secretariat in Washington at 11:30 a.m. Earlier on April 28, 1982, in the General Committee, Herbert B. Thompson, U.S. Alternate Representative to the OAS, said that the United States had abstained because it could not express its views on the resolution during Secretary Haig's peace efforts. (OAS document OEA/Ser.F/II.20 Doc. 27/82, p. 21)

extra-continental or continental armed forces in any of the nations of the hemisphere;

That Argentina's rights of sovereignty over the Malvinas (Falkland) Islands, as stated in some important resolutions passed by various international forums, including the Declaration of the Inter-American Juridical Committee on January 16, 1976,[34] which states: "That the Republic of Argentina has an undeniable right of sovereignty over the Malvinas Islands," must be borne in mind, and

That the peace efforts being made with the consent of the parties must be emphasized, and that inter-American solidarity contributes to that objective, and

HAVING SEEN:

Resolution 502 (1982) of the United Nations Security Council, all of whose terms must be fulfilled; Resolution 359 of April 13, 1982, adopted by the Permanent Council of the Organization of American States,[35] and the Declaration adopted unanimously by the Ministers of Foreign Affairs at the opening session of the Twentieth Meeting of Consultation (Doc. 14/82),[36] and in conformity with the Inter-American Treaty of Reciprocal Assistance,

RESOLVES:

1. To urge the Government of the United Kingdom of Great Britain and Northern Ireland immediately to cease the hostilities it is carrying on within the security region defined by Article 4 of the Inter-American Treaty of Reciprocal Assistance, and also to refrain from any act that may affect inter-American peace and security.

2. To urge the Government of the Republic of Argentina likewise to refrain from taking any action that may exacerbate the situation.

3. To urge those governments immediately to call a truce that will make it possible to resume and proceed normally with the negotiation aimed at a peaceful settlement of the conflict, taking into account the rights of sovereignty of the Republic of Argentina over the Malvinas (Falkland) Islands and the interests of the islanders.

4. To express the willingness of the Organ of Consultation to lend support, through whatever means it considers advisable, to the new initiatives being advanced at the regional or world level, with the consent of the parties, which are directed toward the just and peaceful settlement of the problem.

5. To take note of the information received about the important negotiations of the Secretary of State of the United States of America and to express its wishes that they will be an effective contribution to the peaceful settlement of the conflict.

6. To deplore the adoption by members of the European Economic Community and other states of coercive measures of an economic and political nature, which are prejudicial to the Argentine nation and to urge them to lift those measures, indicating that they constitute a serious precedent, inasmuch as they are not covered by Resolution 502 (1982) of the United Nations Security Council and are incompatible with the Charters of the United Nations and of the OAS and the General Agreement on Tariffs and Trade (GATT).[37]

7. To instruct the President of the Twentieth Meeting of Consultation to take immediate steps to transmit the appeal contained in operative paragraphs 1, 2 and 3 of this resolution to the Governments of the United Kingdom of Great Britain and Northern Ireland and of the Republic of Argentina, and also to inform them, on behalf of the foreign ministers of the Americas, that he is fully confident that this appeal will be received for the sake of peace in the region and in the world.

8. To instruct the President of the Twentieth Meeting of Consultation immediately to present this resolution formally to the Chairman of the United Nations Security Council, so that he may bring it to the attention of the members of the Council.[38]

---

[34] For text of the Declaration of the Inter-American Juridical Committee of January 16, 1976, see OAS Inter-American Juridical Committee, Rio de Janeiro, *Work Accomplished by the Inter-American Juridical Committee During Its Regular Meeting Held From January 12 to February 13, 1976* (OEA/Ser.Q/IV.12 CJI-27 (Washington: OAS General Secretariat, 1976)), pp. 19–22.

[35] For text, see document 627.

[36] The Declaration adopted on April 26, 1982, reads as follows:

"The Twentieth Meeting of Consultation of Ministers of Foreign Affairs, taking into account Resolution 359 of the Permanent Council and the serious situation that has brought about this meeting, urges that peace be maintained in the hemisphere and that law prevail as a basis for international relations." (OAS document OEA/Ser.F/II.20 Doc. 14/82)

[37] For text of the General Agreement on Tariffs and Trade, concluded at Geneva, October 30, 1947, entered into force for the United States, January 1, 1948, see 4 Bevans 639.

[38] For text of the letter of April 28, 1982, from

9. To keep the Twentieth Meeting of Consultation open, especially to oversee faithful compliance with this resolution, and to take such additional measures as are deemed necessary to restore and preserve peace and settle the conflict by peaceful means.

Document 633

Letter From the Argentine Foreign Minister (Costa Méndez) to the Secretary of State (Haig), April 29, 1982[39]

Argentine Reservations Regarding the Memorandum of Agreement Proposed by the United States

DEAR MR. SECRETARY OF STATE: We have carefully reviewed the document you sent us[40] and have compared it with our previous proposals and with the viewpoints we have maintained in our various meetings. From that review, significant differences have emerged, some of which give rise to difficulties that it is essential to overcome.

As my Government has already stated to you, the objective the Argentine Government has set is recognition of its sovereignty over the Malvinas Islands. This central element of our discussions is the ultimate justification of the actions taken by my country, and as I have had occasion to tell you many times, constitutes for us an unrenounceable goal.

Along with the question of sovereignty, the current crisis gives rise immediately to the need to establish a provisional regime for administration of the islands, as an essential step in the process of separating the two military forces and as a reasonable pause in the face of the logical impossibility of formalizing their final fate at this time.

The conversations we have held have been based primarily on these two questions—recognition of sovereignty and a provisional administrative regime. Solution of the remaining problems will be simpler if there is agreement on the two points that I have just mentioned.

The one certain thing is that the two are intimately connected to each other. To the extent that the provisions relating to the recognition of our sovereignty are imprecise, for us it is necessary—if we do not want to return to the frustrating situation that prevailed before April 2—to establish mechanisms that give us broader powers in administration of the islands.

On the other side of the coin, if it were clear that Argentina's sovereignty would be recognized in the end, then we could be more flexible regarding the matter of temporary administration.

The document sent by the Secretary of State falls short of Argentine demands and does not satisfy its minimal aspirations for either of the two points. To the contrary, unfavorable changes have been made to both. The number of Argentine representatives involved in administration of the islands has been decreased, and the opportunity of expanding my country's control in the event that negotiations on the basic issue go on endlessly without a solution has been barred. Thus we are faced with the real possibility of establishing a predominantly British administration with no fixed expiration date.

As concerns the matter of sovereignty, the concept of territorial integrity has been stripped of all meaning. Further, the new element of a virtual referendum to determine the "wishes" of the inhabitants has been introduced in open opposition to United Nations Resolution 2065[41] and the

---

the President of the Twentieth Meeting of Consultation of Ministers of Foreign Affairs, Estanislao Valdés Otero, to the President of the U.N. Security Council, Kamanda wa Kamanda, see U.N. document S/15008.

[39] Source: OAS document OEA/Ser.F/II.20 Doc. 78/82, May 28, 1982, pp. 2–3; also printed in Department of State *Bulletin*, October 1982, pp. 86–87. The copy printed here was attached to a note of May 28, 1982, from Costa Méndez to the President of the Twentieth Meeting of Consultation of Ministers of Foreign Affairs of the Rio Treaty, Estanislao Valdés Otero, Foreign Minister of Uruguay. For that note, see document 646.

[40] Reference is to the U.S. proposal of April 27, 1982; for text, see document 631.

[41] U.N. General Assembly Resolution 2065 (XX) of December 16, 1965, invited Argentina and the United Kingdom to negotiate a peaceful solution to their dispute over the sovereignty of the Islands, "Bearing in mind the provisions and objectives of the Charter of the United Nations and of General Assembly resolution 1514 (XV) and the interests of the population of the Falkland Islands (Malvinas)." For text, see United Nations General Assembly, Official Records: Twentieth Session, Supplement No. 14 (A/6014), *Resolutions Adopted by the General Assembly During Its Twentieth Session, 21 September–22 December 1965* (New York), p. 57.

unwavering position sustained by Argentina.

The Secretary knows that we cannot accept these changes. In my opinion, other formulas must be found. For this effort, we will always be at the disposal of the Secretary. These formulas should provide for the balance that I referred to above in order to weigh properly the data relating to the matter of sovereignty against the provisions regulating temporary administration of the islands. These provisions should have a fixed term and include gradually larger Argentine participation or, in lieu of this, the provisions should be made precise enough to offer security for recognition of Argentina's rights within a specific period.

If Argentina's position were encompassed, agreement would be facilitated enormously and the final text of the document would not pose any insurmountable problems.

Thank you once again for your arduous and difficult negotiations.

Accept, Mr. Secretary, the renewed assurances of my highest consideration.

NICANOR COSTA MÉNDEZ

Document 634

Statement by the Secretary of State (Haig), April 30, 1982[42]

Economic Sanctions Against Argentina and Offer of Matériel Support to the United Kingdom

The South Atlantic crisis is about to enter a new and dangerous phase, in which large-scale military action is likely. I would like to bring you up to date on what we have done, why, and what we must do now.

We have made a determined effort to restore peace through implementation of U.N. Security Council Resolution 502. That resolution calls for an end to hostilities, the withdrawal of Argentine forces from the Islands; and a diplomatic settlement of the fundamental dispute.

The United States made this extraordinary effort because the stakes in human lives and international order required it. From the outset, the United States has been guided by the basic principle of the rule of law and the peaceful settlement of disputes. The collapse of that principle could only bring chaos and suffering.

We also made this effort because the crisis raised the vital issues of hemispheric solidarity at a time when the Communist adversaries seek positions of influence on the mainland of the Americas, and latent territorial disputes in much of the hemisphere called for unity and the resolute defense of principle. We acted as well because the United States has the confidence of the parties. The United Kingdom is our closest ally, and Prime Minister Thatcher's government looked to us to pursue a peaceful solution. We have also recently developed a better relationship with Argentina as part of our success in revitalizing the community of American states. President Galtieri also requested our involvement.

Under the direction of President Reagan, I participated in many days of intense discussions with the parties in the search of a framework for implementing U.N. Security Council Resolution 502. Our initial aim was to clarify the position of the parties and to offer suggestions on how those positions might be reconciled. We took no position on the merits of either the British or Argentine claims to the Islands. As the prospects for more intense hostilities arose, we put forth an American proposal.[43] It represented our best estimate of what the two parties could reasonably be expected to accept, and was based squarely on our own principles and concern for the rule of law.

We regard this as a fair and a sound proposal. It involves a cessation of hostilities, withdrawal of both Argentine and British forces, termination of sanctions, establishment of a United States-United Kingdom-Argentine interim authority to maintain the agreement, continuation of the traditional local administration with Argentine participation, procedures for encouraging cooperation in the development of the Islands, and a framework for negotiations on a final settlement, taking into account the interests of both sides and the wishes of the inhabitants.

---

[42] Source: Department of State Press Release 150, April 30, 1982; printed also in Department of State *Bulletin*, June 1982, pp. 87–88. Dean Fischer, Department of State Spokesman, introduced the Secretary of State at 11:30 a.m.

[43] For text, see document 631.

We had reason to hope that the United Kingdom would consider a settlement along the lines of our proposal, but Argentina informed us yesterday that it could not accept it.[44] Argentina's position remains that it must receive an assurance now of eventual sovereignty or an immediate de facto role in governing the Islands which would lead to sovereignty.

For its part, the British Government has continued to affirm the need to respect the views of the inhabitants in any settlement.

The United States has thus far refrained from adopting measures in response to the seizure of the Islands that could have interfered with our ability to work with both sides in the search for peace.

The British Government has shown complete understanding for this position. Now, however, in light of Argentina's failure to accept a compromise, we must take concrete steps to underscore that the United States cannot and will not condone the use of unlawful force to resolve disputes.

The President has therefore ordered the suspension of all military exports to Argentina, the withholding of certification of Argentine eligibility for military sales,[45] the suspension of new Export-Import Bank credits and guarantees, and the suspension of Commodity Credit Corporation guarantees.

The President has also directed that the United States will respond positively for requests to matériel support for British forces. There will, of course, be no direct U.S. military involvement.

American policy will continue to be guided by our concerns for the rule of law and our desire to facilitate an early and fair settlement. The United States remains ready to assist the parties in finding that settlement. A strictly military outcome cannot endure over time. In the end, there will have to be a negotiated outcome acceptable to the interested parties. Otherwise, we will all face unending hostility and insecurity in the South Atlantic.

[44] For the text of the letter from Argentine Foreign Minister Costa Méndez to Secretary Haig of April 29, 1982, see *supra*.

[45] Reference is to the Presidential certification required by section 725b of the International Security and Development Act of 1981, P.L. 97–113, approved December 29, 1981; for text, see *American Foreign Policy: Current Documents, 1981*, document 720.

Document 635

Transcript of a Department of State Press Conference, April 30, 1982[46]

The Falkland Islands Situation

Senior State Department Official. I thought it might be helpful to refresh your memories a little bit so you have some historic background before we go to your questions. First, with respect to the question of the Falklands/Malvinas issue, there have been some 17 years of negotiations between the United Kingdom and Argentina on this subject. It's been based on a 150-year historic claim by Argentina for sovereignty over what they refer to as the Malvinas, and an equally strongly held view by Great Britain that the Islands were sovereign British territory, having been discovered originally by Cook.

The most recent negotiation occurred this past February in New York. During that time, as I've been able to ascertain, the British side continued to hold to its position which is essentially one based on the self-determination of the islanders, and the Argentine side continued to insist on the transfer of sovereignty, which they claimed was not negotiable and was a fact.

It was clear from discussions in Buenos Aires that these meetings in February left a very high level of frustration among the already frustrated Argentine negotiators, some of whom had been involved during the whold span of this negotiation of 17 years.

The first inkling the United States had of difficulty was on March 28, not involving the Falklands, but rather a dispute between the Argentines who had a work force on the Island of South Georgia and British authorities there, and a request from the British Government to the United States to intervene in their behalf to peacefully resolve a dispute that had been going on for a matter of days.

On March 30, the United States had a first, very minor, indication of unusual force readiness on the part of the Argentines. On March 31, Ambassador Henderson[47] visited

[46] Source: Department of State files. The press conference, which began at 2:30 p.m., was conducted on background by a senior Department of State official.

[47] Sir Nicholas Henderson, British Ambassador to the United States.

the Department, spoke to me personally, and laid out a full panorama of steps underway by Argentine forces which suggested to the United Kingdom that military action was about to take place in the Falklands.

Based on that intelligence and our corroboration of it, on April 1 we instructed our Ambassador to not only contact the Foreign Office in Buenos Aires, but President Galtieri, and to express and register our strongest concern. The result of that was a flat turndown by the Argentine Government. I also, that same day, discussed the issue with the Argentine Ambassador[48] here in Washington, and did not receive a satisfactory reply. On the evening of April 1, President Reagan called President Galtieri, and after 2 hours of delay, raised the issue with him on the telephone. President Galtieri stated it was too late, and there was nothing that could be done about the military operations which were then underway.

The actual invasion occurred chronologically on April 2. On April 3, the United Nations met in emergency session, and U.N. Resolution 502, supported by the United States very actively, was approved, on that same date, London announced its decision to take action under the U.N. Article 51;[49] and troop movements, fleet movements, et cetera, began to develop.

Basically, I think it's important to recognize that in the context of the development of this crisis, it was somewhat of a surprise not just to the United States, but perhaps more importantly to Great Britain. But from the very outset, this government viewed the Argentine invasion as an extremely serious issue. We also recognized that we had a unique role in this issue that we had to play. That was reflected first in our fundamental support of U.N. Resolution 502, which called first for the cessation of hostilities; second, the withdrawal of Argentine forces; and third, a political solution.

The reason we recognized that we had a unique role to play was, first, that we have good relationships with both governments, but perhaps most importantly because both governments, at the highest level, requested our immediate and active intervention—both governments. The reason we felt we did not have the luxury to refuse these requests were multiple—the first and most profound of which we touched upon in this morning's statement,[50] and that is that a basic premise of President Reagan's foreign policy—as it has been in the past in all American foreign policies, but especially acute now after the years of violent change that we have witnessed—that we must be advocates, and strong advocates, of peaceful change in the rule of law. The consequences of such violations that go ignored and untended we have seen by a proliferation of such activity dating back from the Vietnam period, running through Africa, the Middle East, Southeast Asia, and this hemisphere.

The second imperative for American involvement was the historic special relationship with Great Britain and the interrelationship of that relationship with the NATO alliance. Above all, we were extremely sensitive to the essential need of avoiding the repetition of the scars of Suez.

In the context of the alliance itself, you will note that the European nations, the Economic Community, rallied promptly behind Great Britain in the institution of sanctions. And in the wake of the political difficulties within the alliance associated with Afghanistan and Poland and the existing economic and strategic difficulties that exist within the alliance family today, we felt it vitally important that we not be presumed to let nature be taking its course, and not to become actively involved.

There was the additional question of our overall hemispheric relationships and policies. It was clear that were this matter to be left untended or to drift immediately into the OAS, it would have been a very destabilizing issue, which would have resolved itself along Spanish-speaking/English-speaking lines; and hemispheric unity could have been fractured in the early hours of the crisis. The diplomatic activity instituted by the United States tended to ameliorate and moderate these highly charged issues. In the same context, had it been left to drift within the United Nations after U.N. Resolution 502, it could have taken on historic North–South overtones—imperialism and colonialism versus the developing world. And so that required American activity.

Beyond that, it is clear that we were sensitive to the East–West overtones and the likelihood that the Soviet Union might

[48] Esteban A. Takacs.

[49] British Prime Minister Thatcher stated before Parliament on April 3, 1982, that a large task force would begin to sail for the Falklands on April 5; for the text of her statement, see Great Britain, *Parliamentary Debates* (Commons), 6th series, 21 (1982) 633–638. Article 51 of the U.N. Charter provided for the right of self-defense.

[50] *Supra.*

use the opportunity to "fish in troubled waters." Indeed, on the first day of my visit to Buenos Aires, after a year and a half of absence, the Cuban Ambassador and a planeload of high Cuban officials suddenly reappeared in Buenos Aires with offers of unflinching support.

Throughout our efforts to resolve this issue peacefully, there have been two profound divergencies of view between Great Britain, on the one hand, and Argentina on the other. Great Britain has felt, with considerable intensity, that the issue of the wishes of the inhabitants of the Islands must be given a high precedence in the determination of the future of the Islands themselves. And as I mentioned this morning, throughout our discussions with the Argentine Government, they insisted on one of two alternatives—either an a priori acceptance of ultimate sovereignty for Argentina or the creation of de facto governing arrangements on the Islands which would lead inevitably to such an outcome.

Despite the hours of discussion and effort in which differences were narrowed and grounds for possible compromise were surfaced, when I left Buenos Aires the last time,[51] as I arrived at the airport, I received, despite the framework that we had put together the night before, a renewed demand for a guarantee of transfer of sovereignty to Argentina.

The discussions, as we conducted them, revolved around, first, the conditions for the withdrawal of forces on both sides; interim arrangements for the governing of the Islands; and a framework for negotiations to determine future outcome. In the light of the new Argentine demand—and as I say, on occasions, we had arrived at one point that looked promising, only to find that 24 hours later, it would be totally withdrawn and a new set of demands; and this was the repeated pattern of our talks in Buenos Aires—that based on that situation, the United States tried to devise as best it could a fair and just solution dealing with the three areas I spoke to and in more detail than in our formal statement this morning.

This arrangement would have required concession on the part of both Great Britain and Argentina. And as I say, in my discussions with Foreign Minister Pym here in Washington last week[52] and subsequent communications, we had reason to hope that despite the difficulties—and there were many for Great Britain—that they would be willing to accept such a framework and such a proposal.[53] On the other hand, the response from Argentina was a negative one,[54] and a reiteration that they must either have a confirmation of ultimate sovereignty in the terms of the agreement itself and as the outcome of the negotiations or de facto arrangements on the Islands immediately, which would lead to such an outcome. So in hindsight and in any objective assessment, one would have to say that the United Kingdom has been reasonable and forthcoming throughout the discussions, and that Argentina has been less so.

It is the basic American position, of course, that we cannot be or be perceived to be participating in an arrangement which would reward aggression, although we do feel that the past history of this thing would not make us rigid adherents to the status quo ante either.

That is where the situation rested, and that's what caused the President to decide to authorize the actions that were announced this morning. Clearly, this is not the end. Ultimately, a negotiated settlement must and, I am confident, will be found. It means a phase is over and a new phase will begin, and it may be that some military action will be the next benchmark for more intense reconsideration in both capitals of the situation. It may be, as well, that other formulas—and we discussed countless other formulas—will appear and will provide a vehicle for the parties to finesse what have become hard points of honor with both.

Now, I welcome your questions.

Q. The measures that were announced this morning seem to be moderate, not affecting the mainstream of either Argentine investments or trade with the United States.

In that light, can they be seen as a prelude to further steps if this situation should continue?

A. Clearly, there are many additional steps which the United States could take and is prepared to take if circumstances require it.

I think it is important to recognize that it may well be that the United States at some

[51] April 19, 1982.

[52] Secretary Haig met with British Foreign Secretary Pym in Washington, April 22–23, 1982.

[53] For the U.S. proposal of April 27, 1982, see document 631.

[54] For the Argentine response of April 29, 1982, see document 633.

future time in another phase could continue to play a constructive role.

It is also important to remember that there are a number of other considerations that must be taken into account as one assesses the options open to the United States at this time.

Our signals are essentially political because in practical terms the full panoply of American economic or trade or financial leverage would not be instrumental in changing the situation.

What is important is the political signal that has been sent, and that's a signal which lays responsibility on the Government of Argentina for the failure in this phase. It is the confirmation that the United States will now change what has been a more balanced posture with respect to the crisis—although I must tell you again that despite some of the press speculation you've seen, the United Kingdom, the Prime Minister, and Foreign Minister are well aware of the posture that we have taken, the reasons we have taken it, and they support that and have supported it from the outset.

But we have now clearly been placed in a position where it is necessary for the international community to recognize why the crisis continues at this hour.

Q. It was mentioned in the statement today that the President is willing to respond positively to any requests for matériel or support from Britain.

Does that include military resupply, or could you define it better for us?

A. I think it's best to answer it in the context of a number of ongoing historic relationships we have had with British forces across a broad spectrum, and it must also be reviewed in the context of obligations we have in certain areas such as the Ascension Islands, which of course are being utilized by the British, which are owned by the British, and for which American presence there and utilization there of those facilities involve reciprocal obligations.

I think I want to make very, very clear that there's no prospect of any kind, as we stated in this morning's statement, of direct American military involvement in this situation at this time. None at all.

There have been certain levels of assistance provided, but the British Government has been very moderate in its requests. I can't say what the level will be in the days ahead, until we recieve the request; then we'll consider them case by case. But I think the President's inclination is to recieve them favorably unless they represent some fundamental violation of our longstanding relationship.

Q. Could you give us some estimate of the play of forces right now? What ships might likely be ready to open fire, how soon shooting might break out, and if anybody outside of these two combatants are in the way, specifically the Soviet Union?

A. I don't want to go into too much detail here. Clearly, it's a dangerous thing for a third party to do as forces are beginning to approach one another in a very dangerous way. I think public discussion of the issue would be both inappropriate and possibly dangerous for one or the other of the parties, and I can't do that.

I can say this: that the proximity of forces is such now that should one side or the other violate the two sanitized areas that both have applied now in that 200-mile circle around the Islands, either by air or surface or subsurface, engagement and the likelihood of a clash is high.

Q. I wonder if you could comment on the Soviet role to date so far? You mentioned that the Cubans have sent an Ambassador and a number of officials to Argentina. There have been reports that the Soviet Union has given the Argentines intelligence data such as the position of the British fleet.

You, yourself, have warned several times about possible roles for the Soviets here. Would you expand on that?

A. We are naturally extremely sensitive to this. We are aware that the Soviets have been in touch with the Argentine Government, but I would not be justified in suggesting that there are any near-term, verified indicators of a dramatic or direct Soviet involvement at this point.

There have been a number of rumors that perhaps the Soviets have offered intelligence support to Argentina. I've seen them as you have. I've also been assured by the Argentine Government that they would not accept such proffers. That might change in the in the period adhead.

Q. It appears that there is a kind of an orchestration between ourselves and the British in applying pressure to Argentina. Mr. Pym is now coming, I believe, here and then to the United Nations in New York. It looks like the British are willing to hold off until they see the effects of what the U.S. Govenrment has done today.

I think my question basically is, can you explain any of that, and can you tell us what comes next?

A. First, let me assure you that such is not the case. I saw a report—a misinformed report, I think a day or two ago—to the effect that British forces had held up their activity for a certain period at our request to permit the negotiations to proceed.

This is not true. It is totally lacking in any basis in fact. We have not requested anything of that kind from the British Government. We do not believe that it would be appropriate to do so.

We have fully engaged ourselves in a process designed to get a peaceful solution, but we do not feel that it is our role to influence the conduct of the forces of either side, and I don't think we would be successful if we tried.

Q. The other part of the question is really, was Mr. Pym coming here or going to the United Nations? Are you going up to the United Nations, and is the matter going to be sent to them next or what is the next step?

A. I think it remains to be seen. We have been avid supporters of U.N. Resolution 502. That has been the basic framework and the premise under which American diplomatic activity has been launched and conducted.

There are several venues open to the parties, certainly to Argentina. One is the OAS. They've been there this week. They could reopen their activity there. The other is the United Nations. As you know, Foreign Minister Costa Mendez is there today. You note that he stated today publicly that Argentina would accept all the provisions of U.N. Resolution 502.[55] That's the most definitive statement of that kind that I have noted, although they have suggested the same to me informally but usually with the caveats associated with what the political solution would provide for—transfer of sovereignty.

I make the point very strenuously that it is this government's position that a negotiated settlement of this issue remains an outcome which we must continue to strive for.

Q. Have you suggested that any of our citizens leave Argentina? Are any of our citizens who are there in trouble?

A. We put out a travel advisory yesterday to American citizens, and at the outset of this crisis we had alerted American official personnel of the situation. I think enough said.

Q. Could you tell us whether, in your judgment, the Argentine junta right now is sufficiently cohesive to make the kind of major diplomatic decisions that have to be made to head off war?

A. I think that remains to be seen, and it doesn't serve any purpose for me—even in a background session—to indulge in observations which could have an impact on the demeanor and the flexibility of that government to deal with this difficult question. Maybe that's a good question for history.

Q. Was it your analysis of Mr. Costa Mendez's statement earlier that that represented in fact no change in their policy and thus really didn't affect things one way or the other?

A. Do you mean the adherence to 502?

Q. Yes.

A. I think it's too early to say. I would suggest that neither side wants conflict. Argentina certainly does not want conflict. They are going to seek ways to delay the prospect of conflict. One cannot fault them for that, and one must look at their activities in that context.

Q. I would like to return to the Soviets for a moment. Have you or any Department officials talked with the Soviets about the Falkland Islands crisis, specifically the role the two countries are playing in it?

And, secondly, do you envision any scenario in which the United States and the Soviet Union could come in direct conflict or confrontation over this issue?

A. I don't think it serves any purpose to speculate about that, nor does it serve any purpose to air diplomatic communications that may or may not have taken place, especially at this stage of the situation.

Q. How do you construe Mr. Costa Mendez's statement today that he had not rejected your most recent proposal?

A. I think the answer to that question is one of subjective bias. There was a very, very clear turndown of the proposals in the written reply that we have received, but I am not upset by such a comment.

---

[55] Argentine Foreign Minister Costa Méndez made the statement under reference in a brief meeting with reporters at the United Nations shortly after Secretary Haig announced U.S. sanctions against Argentina on April 30, 1982, according to a Reuter Newswire report of the same date.

Q. You spoke before about one of the earlier considerations being the need to maintain hemispheric unity, and now you've obviously, in effect, broken with Argentina, and I wonder what you think is going to happen now to hemispheric unity.

A. First, I don't want to suggest the United States has broken with Argentina. I do want to suggest that we had arrived at a point in time when [it] was necessary for the American public and the international community to know precisely why we were where we are, so close to potential conflict.

I do not anticipate that this will be well received in all Latin American capitals. However, all of our hemispheric friends must also recognize that many of them have similar territorial disputes with one neighbor or one power or another, and that the United States adherence to a rule of law and peaceful change and diplomatic solutions to these controversies is an espousal of a principle from which they themselves benefit.

We would hope that they would share with us our concern about the importance of that principle.

Q. Do you think if Argentina would in fact seriously accept Resolution 502, as Costa Mendez seems to have implied today, that could still head off war?

A. There are any number of formulas. Of course, with Resolution 502 you must look at the essence of the question. First, it calls for a cessation of hostilities. That would have the practical consequence of achieving the objective.

Second, the withdrawal of Argentine forces from the Islands. That's a very important step, and it is not one that the Argentines have refused to consider. Where the hangup comes is "a political solution will be found." If that political solution involves a willingness to sit down and negotiate without precondition or to have it adjudicated by other parties without preconditions, then 502 does indeed, as did our proposal, provide a framework for a peaceful solution.

Thank you very much.

Document 636

Note From the Argentine Foreign Minister (Costa Méndez) to the Secretary of State (Haig), May 2, 1982[56]

Argentine Protest Against U.S. Sanctions

EXCELLENCY: I have the honor of addressing Your Excellency to refer to the statement that you made on April 30,[57] speaking on your Government's behalf, in connection with the conflict between my country and Great Britain in the South Atlantic region. Your statement contains assertions and announces measures that my Government cannot let pass without making the pertinent corrections.

The gesture on the part of the United States Government is not only very unfriendly but also surprising. In fact, only a few hours before, the United States was acting as a friend to the parties, assisting them in the search for a just and honorable negotiated arrangement. Now, alleging that its efforts have failed, it takes upon itself the unilateral defense of one of the parties and imposes unacceptable sanctions against us, for the ostensible purpose of breaking our determination, of using force to impose upon us solutions that conform to the very particular views that the United States Government maintains on the matter.

Your Excellency blames Argentina for the failure of the negotiations, emphasizing its inability to reach a compromise. Nothing is said of the intransigence of the British or of the aggressive posture they have adopted. You disregard the fact that at the time of your statement, a powerful British air and naval force was completing its preparations to attack my country. Quite to the contrary, the Secretary of State finds it just to aid in the aggression by providing the British forces with the material assistance they require, which is a very odd way of cooperating to keep the conflict from becoming worse.

---

[56] Source: OAS document OEA/Ser.F/II.20 Doc. 40/82, May 4, 1982. The text printed here was quoted in a note from Argentine Special Delegate Raúl A. Quijano to the President of the Twentieth Meeting of Consultation of Ministers of Foreign Affairs of the Rio Treaty, Estinslao Valdés Otero, on May 4, 1982, with a request that it be distributed as an official document of that meeting.

[57] For the text of Secretary Haig's statement of April 30, 1982, see document 634.

I can do no less than reject the statements made by the Secretary of State and the attitude that follows from them. My Government can prove that it has gone much further than the Government of the United Kingdom in its willingness to compromise and negotiate. It has made significant concessions and has demonstrated flexibility on all points. However, clearly it cannot allow negotiations to end in our capitulation or in the renunciation of our most fundamental rights.

Argentina did not reject the proposals set forth by the Government of the United States. In our talks, the Secretary of State acknowledged that we were not being required to accept the proposals as a whole and that we could make our observations. This we did just hours before the Secretary of State made his statement. We expressed our willingness to talk and our desire to find formulas for settlement.

The attitude on the part of the United States comes at a time when the ministers of foreign affairs of this hemisphere, meeting under the terms of the Inter-American Treaty of Reciprocal Assistance, are supporting Argentina's statements and calling for an end to the fighting. It is strange, then, that the Secretary of State should invoke hemispheric solidarity as one of the underlying considerations for his conduct, when in fact the attitude that he adopts reflects an open disregard for it.

Your Excellency cannot fail to see that the position taken by your Government will have a significant impact on relations between our two countries. The Argentine people will never understand or forget that at one of the most critical moments in their history, in contrast to the solidarity that they received from all corners of the hemisphere, the United States preferred to take the side of an extra-hemispheric power, thereby abetting it in its aggressive designs. I do not believe I would be exceeding my powers by adding that the stance by the United States will seriously damage its ties with the other nations of the Americas.

In view of the foregoing and on behalf of my Government, I lodge a most formal protest over the terms of the declaration of April 30, which I consider to be unfriendly and incompatible with the friendly relations that our countries have maintained until now.

Accept, Excellency, the assurances of my highest consideration.

NICANOR COSTA MÉNDEZ

Document 637

Peruvian-U.S. Proposal, May 5, 1982[58]

Draft Interim Agreement on the Falkland/Malvinas Islands

1. An immediate ceasefire, concurrent with:

2. Mutual withdrawal and non-reintroduction of forces, according to a schedule to be established by the Contact Group.

3. The immediate introduction of a Contact Group composed of Brazil, Peru, The Federal Republic of Germany and the United States into the Falkland Islands, on a temporary basis pending agreement on a definitive settlement. The Contact Group will assume responsibility for:

(A) Verification of the withdrawal;

(B) Ensuring that no actions are taken in the Islands, by the local administration, which would contravene this interim agreement; and

(C) Ensuring that all other provision of the agreement are respected.

4. Britain and Argentina acknowledge the existence of differing and conflicting

---

[58] Source: Department of State *Bulletin*, October 1982, p. 87. This proposal resulted from an initiative of President Fernando Belaúnde Terry of Peru with U.S. cooperation.

In a statement before the House of Commons on May 7, 1982, British Foreign Secretary Francis Pym said that the United Kingdom had signified its acceptance of an interim agreement on May 6, 1982; he stated the terms of the agreement under discussion: (1) mutual withdrawal; (2) cease-fire; (3) small group of countries to supervise withdrawal, undertake interim administration in consultation with the islanders' elected representatives, and help with negotiations on the status of the islands, "without prejudice to our principles or to the wishes of the islanders;" and (4) suspension of exclusion zones and lifting of economic sanctions. Pym claimed that Argentina had impeded such an agreement by insisting on transfer of sovereignty over the islands to Argentina as a precondition of negotiations on a final settlement and by asking for a cease-fire without a clear link to Argentine withdrawl. (*Parliamentary Debates* (Commons), 6th series, 23 (1982) 395–403) Argentina declined to consider the Peruvian-U.S. proposal, but asked instead for the good offices of U.N. Secretary-General Pérez de Cuéllar; see *infra*.

views regarding the status of the Falkland Islands.

5. The two Governments acknowledge that the aspirations and interests of the Islanders will be included in the definitive settlement of the status of the Islands.

6. The Contact Group will have responsibility for ensuring that the two Governments reach a definitive agreement prior to April 30, 1983.

Document 638

Note From the Argentine Special Delegate to the Twentieth Meeting of Consultation of Ministers of Foreign Affairs of the Rio Treaty (Quijano) to the President of the Twentieth Meeting of Consultation (Valdes Otero), Washington, May 7, 1982[59]

Argentine Acceptance of U.N. Intervention for a Peaceful Solution of the Conflict Over the Malvinas, South Georgia, and Sandwich Islands

EXCELLENCY: I have the honor to address Your Excellency to inform you of the text of the communiqué issued on May 5, 1982 by the Permanent Mission of the Argentine Republic to the United Nations, which states the following:

> "1. The Argentine Government reaffirms that it is willing to negotiate a peaceful solution to the conflict over the Malvinas, South Georgia and Sandwich Islands.
>
> "2. The first step toward a solution must be an immediate cease-fire.
>
> "3. Argentina accepts the intervention of the United Nations at this time, through the Secretary General or the Security Council, or the combined action of both, as it considers this the most appropriate way.[60]
>
> "4. In keeping with this position, the Argentine Government answered the Secretary General of the United Nations on May 5, 1982 and has accepted its intervention."

I request that this note be distributed on an urgent basis as an official document of the Twentieth Meeting of Consultation of Ministers of Foreign Affairs.

Accept, Excellency, the renewed assurances of my highest consideration.

RAÚL A. QUIJANO

Document 639

Statement Read by the President's Deputy Press Secretary (Speakes), May 21, 1982[61]

"We Will Meet Our Commitments to Great Britain"

The President and this administration have been intensely involved in the search for peace since the beginning of the dispute in the South Atlantic.

Our deep concern over the threat of conflict has been evident to the international community. We have made bilateral and multilateral efforts in support of that effort. We continue today to be in contact with those at the United Nations and elsewhere who are also striving for a peaceful solution under U.N. Security Council Resolution 502 and the U.N. Charter.

Let me emphasize there will be no involvement whatsoever of U.S. military personnel in the conflict in the South Atlantic.

---

[59] Source: OAS document OEA/Ser.F/II.20 Doc. 46/82. The source text bears the reference number VS No. 20 (2.1.41)/82.

[60] The President of the U.N. Security Council, Ambassador Ling Qing (China), in a statement of May 5, 1982, on behalf of all members of the Security Council, expressed "deep concern" at the deterioration of the situation in the South Atlantic region, and conveyed the "strong support" of the Council members for the efforts of the U.N. Secretary-General in his contacts with the two parties. For text, see U.N. document S/15047.

[61] Source: Office of the Press Secretary to the President; printed also in *Weekly Compilation of Presidential Documents*, May 24, 1982, p. 678. This statement was read at the press briefing which began at 12:03 p.m. in the White House Briefing Room.

As the President and Secretary Haig have said we will meet our commitments to Great Britain. Any responses made to requests for assistance will be carefully evaluated on a case-by-case basis. We will, however, not address reports of specific requests for assistance or how we respond.

Our position throughout this dispute has been to do whatever we can to advance the chances for a peaceful resolution and that remains our stance. Every step, every action of the President and the United States Government shall be taken with one thought in mind: a peaceful solution. We stand ready to assist in any way we can.

Document 640

Statement by the U.N. Secretary-General (Pérez de Cuéllar) Before the U.N. Security Council, May 21, 1982[62]

Breakdown of U.N. Efforts To End the Crisis

Mr. President, I felt it my duty to inform you yesterday evening that my efforts to facilitate an agreement between the Republic of Argentina and the United Kingdom in respect of the Falkland Islands (Islas Malvinas), initiated in pursuance of my responsibilities as Secretary-General, did not offer the present prospect of bringing an end to the crisis.[63] The armed conflict persists and threatens to grow worse. In these grave circumstances, I wish to give the Council an account of the actions I have taken in pursuit of the objectives of Security Council Resolution 502 (1982).

Following the adoption of that resolution, I continued my contacts with the parties and with the President of the Security Council concerning the situation. The views which I expressed were based on the Charter and on Resolution 502 (1982), the implementation of which I repeatedly urged. I also made arrangements for contingency planning within the Secretariat so that the United Nations could be in a position to implement effectively any responsibilities which might be entrusted to it.

As long as the efforts of the Government of the United States to facilitate a peaceful solution of the dispute in the context of the Council's resolution were underway, I voiced the hope that they would succeed; and I expressed the view that nothing should be done to interfere with that delicate process. At the same time, I affirmed my readiness to do all I could to be of assistance in achieving a peaceful solution.

In separate meetings on 19 April with the Permanent Representatives of Argentina and of the United Kingdom and also with the Permanent Representative of the United States,[64] I outlined the assistance that the United Nations could render, if requested, in pursuance of any understanding or agreement that the parties might reach consistent with Resolution 502 (1982). I stated that for example, a small presence of United Nations civilian and military observers could be used to supervise any agreed withdrawal of armed forces and civilian personnel, as well as any interim administrative arrangements. A United Nations "umbrella" for such arrangements could also be provided, as could a United Nations temporary administration. I indicated that any arrangements of this kind would require the prior authorization of the Security Council, that, as a practical matter, they would presuppose the consent of the parties and that such arrangements were mentioned without prejudice to the possibility of other types of action that the Security Council might decide upon. An informal note was given to the Permanent Representatives summarizing these ideas. Meanwhile, in connexion with these ideas, detailed plans were developed as part of the contingency planning I have mentioned which could be made available to the parties at the appropriate time, on the understanding that implementation would require a decision of the Security Council.

On 30 April I met at United Nations Headquarters with Mr. Nicanor Costa Mendez, Minister for Foreign Affairs and Worship of the Republic of Argentina. Later that day I received a letter from Mr. Alexander Haig, Secretary of State of the United States of America, which provided information on the American proposal which had been presented to the parties and a state-

---

62 Source: U.N. document S/PV.2350 (interpretation from Spanish).

63 Reference presumably is to the letter of May 20, 1982, from U.N. Secretary-General Pérez de Cuéllar to the President of the U.N. Security Council, Ambassador Ling Qing; for text, see U.N. document S/51099.

64 Reference is to Eduardo A. Roca, Sir Anthony D. Parsons, and Jeane J. Kirkpatrick, respectively.

ment of the position taken by the United States in the light of the existing situation.

In separate meetings on 2 May with the Secretary of State for Foreign and Commonwealth Affairs of the United Kingdom, Mr. Francis Pym, and with the Permanent Representative of Argentina, I handed over an aide-mémoire in which I expressed my deep concern over the grave situation and emphasized my conviction that the United Nations had a most serious responsibility under the Charter urgently to restore peace and to promote a just and lasting settlement. I stated that the implementation of Resolution 502 (1982) was imperative.

In my aide-mémoire, I suggested that the two governments agree to take simultaneously the following steps, which were conceived as provisional measures, without prejudice to the rights, claims or position of the parties concerned. I proposed specifically that at a specified time, "T":

(a) The Argentine Government begin withdrawal of its troops from the Falkland Islands (Islas Malvinas) and the United Kingdom Government redeploy its naval forces and begin their withdrawal from the area of the Falkland Islands (Islas Malvinas), both governments to complete their withdrawal by an agreed date;

(b) Both governments commence negotiations to seek a diplomatic solution to their differences by an agreed target date;

(c) Both governments rescind their respective announcements of blockades and exclusion zones and cease all hostile acts against each other;

(d) Both governments terminate all economic sanctions;

(e) Transitional arrangements begin to come into effect under which the above steps would be supervised and interim administrative requirements met.

Reiterating my readiness to be of assistance, I recalled my conversations with the Permanent Representatives of the two parties on 19 April 1982 and I stated that practical arrangements for a United Nations role in a settlement could be completed expeditiously, subject to the consent of the parties and the decision of the Security Council.

On 5 and 6 May I received responses from the Government of Argentina and from the Government of the united Kingdom, respectively. Both accepted the approach contained in the aide-mémoire as providing a basis or framework for an agreement that would bring the armed conflict to a halt and make possible a peaceful settlement. At the same time, the responses raised a number of points on which agreement was needed.

On 7 May the Under-Secretary for Foreign Affairs of Argentina, Mr. Enrique Ros, arrived in New York to represent Argentina in the exchanges. Since that date I have had some 30 separate meetings with the two sides with the purpose of assisting them in reaching an agreement along the lines suggested in my aide-mémoire of 2 May 1982. The intention was to develop the ideas spelled out in my aide-mémoire with a view to defining point by point the elements of a mutually acceptable text.

In my judgment, essential agreement was obtained, toward the end of last week, on the following points:

1. The agreement sought would be interim in nature and would be without prejudice to the rights, claims or positions of the parties concerned.

2. The agreement would cover: (a) a cease-fire; (b) the mutual withdrawal of forces; (c) the termination of exclusion zones and of economic measures instituted in connexion with the conflict; (d) the interim administration of the territory; and (e) negotiations on a peaceful settlement of their dispute.

3. The initiation of these various parts of an agreement would be simultaneous.

4. Withdrawal of forces would be phased and would be under the supervision of United Nations observers.

5. The interim administration of the territory would be under the authority of the United Nations. The United Nations flag would be flown. Argentina and the United Kingdom would establish small liaison offices, on which their respective flags could be flown.

6. The parties would enter into negotiations in good faith under the auspices of the Secretary-General of the United Nations for the peaceful settlement of their dispute and would seek, with a sense of urgency, the completion of these negotiations by 31 December 1982, taking into account the Charter of the United Nations and the relevant resolutions of the General Assembly. These negotiations would be initiated without prejudice to the rights, claims or position of the parties and without prejudging the out-

come. The negotiations would be held in New York or its vicinity.

The crucial differences that remained concerned the following points, on which various options were being considered, at my suggestion:

1. Certain aspects of the interim administration of the territory;

2. Provisions for the extension of the time-frame for completion of negotiations and the related duration of the interim administration;

3. Certain aspects of mutual withdrawal of forces;

4. The geographic area to be covered by the terms of the interim agreement.

On 17 May the British Permanent Representative delivered to me the draft of an interim agreement on the Falkland Islands (Islas Malvinas)[65] dispute which I transmitted to the Argentine Under-Secretary for Foreign Affairs on the same day. During the night of 18–19 May I received the text of an Argentine draft of such an interim agreement,[66] which I promptly made available to the British side.

On studying these texts it was apparent that they did not reflect the progress which had, in my view, been achieved in the previous exchanges and that the differences on the four points unfortunately remained.

On 19 May I spoke by telephone with President Galtieri and Prime Minister Thatcher to express my concern and suggest certain specific ideas which might assist the parties at this critical stage. Both agreed to give them consideration. I subsequently presented to the two sides on the same day a further aide-mémoire listing, as I have just done for the Council, the points on which I felt essential agreement had been reached and the four crucial questions which remained unresolved. I pointed out that the extent of agreement was, in my opinion, substantial and important—so much so that, if it were incorporated in the text of an interim agreement, the requirements of Security Council Resolution 502 (1982) would be met. I expressed my deep concern, however, that unless the remaining points were resolved in the very immediate future, all that had been accomplished would be lost and the prospects for the early restoration of peace frustrated.

In the desire to be of assistance to the parties in the urgent requirement of overcoming these differences, I also included suggestions and formulations in my aide-mémoire of 19 May which might satisfactorily meet their preoccupations on the four important issues still unresolved, without prejudice to the rights, claims, or position of either.

It remains my belief that an agreement along the lines developed in the exchanges over the past 2 weeks, incorporating the approaches suggested in my aide mémoire of 19 May, could restore peace in the South Atlantic and open the way for an enduring solution of the longstanding dispute between two Member States. By yesterday evening, however, the necessary accommodations had not been made. I concluded that, in the light of the Security Council's responsibilities under the Charter for the preservation of peace, I must urgently inform you, Mr. President, of my appraisal of the situation. I did so at 9 o'clock last night.

I should like to express appreciation for the important support that the Security Council has given to my efforts and for the understanding shown by the Council members as the exchanges with the parties have been under way. I would reiterate my personal commitment to be of assistance in every way toward the lasting resolution of this problem.

The prospect that faces us is one of destruction, continuing conflict and, above all, the loss of many, many young lives. Efforts must continue to find the means of avoiding this and restoring peace. There is no other course.

Document 641

Statement Issued by the British Government, May 21, 1982[67]

Falkland Islands: Negotiations for a Peaceful Settlement

1. It is now almost seven weeks since Argentina invaded the Falkland Islands.

---

[65] For text of the British draft of an interim agreement, see the Annex, *infra*.

[66] For text of the Argentine draft of an interim agreement, see document 645.

[67] Source: Department of State *Bulletin*, October 1982, pp. 87–90. A slightly different version of this document issued by the British Foreign and Commonwealth Office was laid before the British Parliament by the British Government on May 20, 1982, a day begore the date given in the source text; see *New York Times*, May 21, 1982, p. A8.

This unlawful use of force in unprovoked aggression threatened not only to destroy the democratic way of life freely chosen by the Falkland Islanders but also the basis on which international order rests. The invasion was also a singular act of bad faith: it took place when Britain and Argentina were engaged in negotiations in accordance with requests from the United Nations.

2. On 1 April the President of the United Nations Security Council had formally appealed to Argentina not to invade the Falkland Islands. Yet on 2 April Argentina invaded. On 3 April the United Nations Security Council passed its mandatory Resolution 502, demanding a cessation of hostilities and an immediate withdrawal of all Argentine forces from the Islands. The same day, Argentina took South Georgia. In the ensuing weeks she has shown no sign of complying with the Security Council Resolution: on the contrary, she has continued a massive build up of the occupying forces on the Falkland Islands. There could hardly be a clearer demonstration of disregard for international law and for the United Nations itself.

3. Britain need have done nothing more than rest on the mandatory Resolution of the Security Council. Indeed, Britain's inherent right of self-defense under Article 51 of the United Nations Charter would have justified the Government in adopting a purely military policy for ending the crisis. But, in pursuit of a peaceful settlement, Britain adopted a policy, frequently explained by the Government in Parliament, of building up pressure on Argentina.

Military pressure was exerted by the rapid assembly and despatch of the British Naval Task Force. Diplomatic pressure, first expressed in Security Council Resolution 502, was built up by the clear statements of condemnation of Argentine aggression which were made by many countries across the world. It was widely recognised that aggression could not be allowed to stand, since otherwise international peace and order would be dangerously prejudiced in many regions. The members of the European Community, Australia, New Zealand, Canada and Norway joined Britain in rapidly imposing economic measures against Argentina.

4. Britian dedicated her maximum diplomatic efforts to the search for a negotiated solution, and the Government kept Parliament as fully informed as the confidentiality of difficult negotiations would allow. Efforts for an interim agreement to end the crisis were first undertaken by the United States Secretary of State, Mr. Alexander Haig. His ideas for an interim agreement were discussed repeatedly with Argentina and Britain. The Government expressed their willingness to consider Mr. Haig's final proposals, although they presented certain real difficulties. Argentina rejected them. The next stage of negotiations was based on proposals originally advanced by President Belaunde of Peru and modified in consultations between him and the United States Secretary of State.[68] As the Foreign and Commonwealth Secretary informed Parliament on 7 May,[69] Britain was willing to accept the final version of these proposals for an interim agreement. But Argentina rejected it.

5. Since then, the Secretary-General of the United Nations, Senor Perez de Cuellar, has been conducting negotiations with Britain, represented by our Permanent Representative at the United Nations, Sir Anthony Parsons, and Argentina, represented by the Deputy Foreign Minister, Senor Ros. In these negotiations, as in earlier ones, Britain made repeated efforts to establish whether Argentina was willing to be sufficiently flexible to make a reasonable interim agreement possible. But it became increasingly clear that Argentina was not seeking an agreement but was playing for time in the negotiation in the hope of holding on to the fruits of aggression, with all that this would imply for the international rule of law. There was an important meeting of British Ministers, attended by Sir Anthony Parsons and the British Ambassador in Washington, Sir Nicholas Henderson on Sunday 16 May. On the following day. Sir Anthony Parsons returned to New York and handed to the United Nations Secretary-General two documents:

A draft interim agreement between Britian and Argentina which set out the British position in full.[70]

A letter to the Secretary-General[71] making clear the British position that the Falkland Islands dependencies were not covered by the draft interim agreement.

6. Sir Anthony Parsons made clear to the Secretary-General that the draft agree-

---

[68] For text of the Peruvian–U.S. proposal of May 5, 1982, see document 637.

[69] Regarding British Foreign Secretary Pym's statement before the House of Commons on May 7, 1982, see footnote 58 above.

[70] For text, see annex, below.

[71] For text, see *New York Times*, May 21, 1982, p. A8.

ment represented the furthest that Britain could go in the negotiations. He requested that the Secretary-General should give the draft to the Argentine Deputy Foreign Minister. The Secretary-General did this, and asked for a response within two days. Argentina's first response to the Secretary-General, late on 18 May, was equivocal and contained points known to be unacceptable to the United Kingdom. Early on 19 May, Sir Anthony Parsons pointed this out to the Secretary-General and requested that Argentina's final position should be conveyed within the two day period orginally set for a reply to the British draft agreement.

7. Argentina's response,[72] which HMG received late on 19 May, represented a hardening of the Argentine position and amounted to a rejection of the British proposals.

8. The Government's approach in all the negotiations has been based on important principles, which ministers have set out repeatedly in Parliament:

A. International Law: Argentina's unlawful aggression must end and Security Council Resolution 502 must be implemented. Aggression must not be rewarded, or small countries across the world would feel threatened by neighbours with territorial ambitions.

B. Freedom: The Falkland Islanders are used to enjoying free institutions. The executive and legislative councils were established with their agreement and functioned with their participation. Britain insisted that any interim administration in the Falkland Islands must involve democratically elected representatives of the Islanders, so as to enable the latter to continue to participate in the administration of their affairs and to ensure that they could express freely their wishes about the future of the Islands, in accordance with the principle of self-determination.

C. Sovereignty: Britain has no doubt of her sovereignty over the Falkland Islands, having administered them peacefully since 1833. Nevertheless, successive British Governments have been willing, without prejudice, to include the question of sovereignty in negotiations with Argentina about the future of the Falkland Islands. In the recent negotiations, the Government have been willing that an interim agreement should provide for new negotiations about the future of the Islands, which likewise could discuss sovereignty in good faith, so long as there was no prejudgement as to the outcome of negotiations. Although Argentina seemed, at one point in the United Nations Secretary-General's negotiations, to be accepting a formula about not prejudging the outcome of future negotiations, she continued to insist on other provisions running counter to this, thus casting grave doubt on the seriousness of this acceptance. This doubt was reinforced by repeated public statements by Argentine leaders.

9. Britain upheld these principles in the draft agreement which we presented on 17 May to the United Nations Secretary-General:

The agreement provided for complete Argentine withdrawal from the Falkland Islands within 14 days, thus terminating the aggression and upholding international law.

It provided that the legislative and executive councils representing the Falkland Islanders would continue in existence and be consulted by the UN interim administrator, thus maintaining the democratic structure of the administration.

It provided explicitly that the outcome of negotiations about the future of the Islands was not prejudged, thus safeguarding the British position on sovereignty. Britain, in participating in those negotiations, would have been guided by the wishes of the Islanders.

10. In the Secretary-General's negotiations, Britain has insisted that the Falkland Islands dependencies should not be covered by an interim agreement to end the crisis. South Georgia and the South Sandwich Islands are geographically distant from the Falkland Islands themselves. They have no settled population. The British title to them, of which the Government have no doubt, does not derive from the Falkland Islands, and these territories have been treated as dependencies of the Falkland Islands only for reasons of administrative convenience.

11. Throughout the negotiations, Britain has been firm on the essential principles but willing to negotiate on matters where these principles were not breached. In particular:

A. In return for Argentine withdrawal from the Falkland Islands, Britain was willing (Article 2(3)) [see following annex][73] to withdraw her task force to a distance of 150 nautical miles. She was also willing to have

[72] For text, see document 645.

[73] Bracketed note appears in the source text.

international verification (Article 6(4)) of the mutual withdrawal, in which the United Nations might have made use of surveillance aircraft from third countries.

B. Britain was willing that the exclusion zones (Article 3) declared by herself and Argentina, and the economic measures (Article 5) introduced during the present crisis, should be lifted from the moment of ceasefire, although these actions would give more comfort to Argentina than to Britain.

C. Britain was prepared to accept the appointment of a UN Administrator (Article 6(3)) to administer the government of the Falkland Islands. Britain wanted him to discharge his functions in consultation with the representative institutions in the Islands—the legislative and executive councils—which have been developed in accordance with the terms of Article 73 of the UN Charter. (This makes clear that the interests of the inhabitants of non-self-governing territories are paramount and refers to the need to take due account of the political aspirations of the peoples.) It is inconceivable that Britain, or any other democratic country, could accept that her people should be deprived of their democratic rights. Britain was nevertheless willing to accept that one representative from the Argentine population of the Islands (some 30 people out of 1800) should be added to each of the councils.

Additionally, Britain was willing to accept the presence of up to 3 Argentine observers on the Islands in the interim period.

D. Britain was willing (Article 7) to agree to re-establishment of communications, travel, transport, postage, etc., between the Falkland Islands and the Argentine mainland, on the basis existing before the invasion.

E. Britain was willing to enter into negotiations (Article 8) under the auspices of the UN Secretary-General for a peaceful settlement of the dispute with Argentina about the Falkland Islands and to seek the completion of these negotiations by the target date of 31 December 1982. Our position was that no outcome to the negotiations should be either excluded or predetermined.

12. Argentina's final position in the negotiations speaks for itself. In particular:

A. Argentina insisted that South Georgia and the South Sandwich Islands be covered by the interim agreement. One effect of this would be that British forces would have to withdraw from the British territory of South Georgia.

B. Argentina wanted thirty days for the completion of the withdrawal of forces. She wanted all forces to return to their normal bases and areas of operation, thus requiring British forces to be enormously further away than Argentine ones.

C. Argentina wanted the administration of the Islands to be exclusively the responsibilty of the United Nations. There would have been Argentine and British observers. The administration would have been free to appoint advisers from the population of the Islands, in equal numbers from the Argentine population and from the population of British orgin. The flags of Britain and Argentina would have flown together with that of the United Nations.

D. Argentina wanted free access for her nationals to the Islands, with respect inter alia to residence, work and property. Argentina also opposed a provision in the British draft agreement (end of Article 6(3)) about the UN Administrator exercising his powers in conformity with the laws and practices traditionally observed in the Islands. It was evident that Argentina hoped to change the nature of Falklands society and its demographic make-up in the interim period, and thus prejudge the future.

E. Argentina proposed a formula about negotiations on the future of the Islands which stated that they should be "initiated" without prejudice to the rights and claims and positions of the two parties. Argentina would not accept an additional phrase stating also that the outcome would not be prejudged. Argentine leaders continued in public to say that Argentina insisted on having sovereignty. In the negotiations Argentina also resisted a provision in the British draft (beginning of Article 9) which would have ensured that the interim arrangements should stay in place until a definitive agreement about the future of the Islands could be implemented. Argentina's evident aim in resisting this was that, if no definitive agreement had been reached by the target date of 31 December 1982, the interim administration would cease to exist and a vacuum be created which Argentina could hope to fill.

13. The present crisis was brought about by Argentina's unlawful act of aggression. In their subsequent attitude the Argentine Government showed that they had no respect either for democratic principles or for the rule of law. Britain stands firmly for both.

ANNEX—FALKLAND ISLANDS: DRAFT INTERIM AGREEMENT

The Government of the Republic of Argentina and the Government of the United Kingdom of Great Britian and Northern Ireland, responding to Security Council Resolution 502 (1982) adopted on 3 April 1982 under Article 40 of the Charter of the United Nations.

Having entered into negotiations through the good offices of the Secretary-General of the United Nations for an interim agreement concerning the Falkland Islands (Islas Malvinas), hereinafter referred to as "The Islands,"

Having in mind the obligations with regard to non-self-governing territories set out in Article 73 of the Charter of the United Nations, the text of which is annexed hereto.[74]

Have agreed on the following:

ARTICLE 1

1. No provision of this Interim Agreement shall in any way prejudice the rights, claims and positions of either party in the ultimate peaceful settlement of their dispute over the Islands.

2. No acts or activities taking place whilst this Interim Agreement is in force shall constitute a basis for asserting, supporting or denying a claim to territorial sovereignty over the Islands or create any rights of sovereignty over them.

ARTICLE 2

1. With effect from a specified time, 24 hours after signature of this Agreement (hereinafter referred to as Time "T"), each party undertakes to cease and thereafter to refrain from all firing and other hostile actions.

2. Argentina undertakes:

(A) To commence withdrawal of its armed forces from the Islands with effect from Time "T;"

(B) To withdraw half of its armed forces to at least 150 nautical miles away from any point in the Islands by Time "T" plus seven days; and

(C) To complete its withdrawal to at least 150 nautical miles away by Time "T" plus fourteen days.

3. The United Kingdom undertakes:

(A) To commence withdrawal of its armed forces from the Islands with effect from Time "T";

(B) To withdraw half of its armed forces to at least 150 nautical miles away from any point in the Islands by Time "T" plus seven days; and

(C) To complete its withdrawal to at least 150 nautical miles away by Time "T" plus fourteen days.

ARTICLE 3

With effect from Time "T", each party undertakes to lift the exclusion zones, warnings and similar measures which have been imposed.

ARTICLE 4

On the completion of the steps for withdrawal specified in Article 2, each party undertakes to refrain from reintroducing any armed forces into the Islands or within 150 nautical miles thereof.

ARTICLE 5

Each party undertakes to lift with effect from Time "T" the economic measures it has taken against the other and to seek the lifting of similar measures taken by third parties.

ARTICLE 6

1. Immediately after the signature of the present Agreement, Argentina and the United Kingdom shall jointly sponsor a draft resolution in the United Nations under the terms of which the Security Council would take note of the present Agreement, acknowledge the role conferred upon the Secretary-General of the United Nations therein, and authorise him to carry out the tasks entrusted to him therein.

2. Immediately after the adoption of the resolution referred to in paragraph 1 of this Article, a United Nations administrator, being a person acceptable to Argentina and the United Kingdom, shall be appointed by the Secretary-General and will be the officer administering the government of the Islands.

---

[74] Not printed with the source text.

3. The United Nations administrator shall have the authority under the direction of the Secretary-General to ensure the continuing administration of the government of the Islands. He shall discharge his functions in consultation with the representative institutions in the Islands which have been developed in accordance with the terms of Article 73 of the Charter of the United Nations, with the exception that one representative from the Argentina population normally resident on the Islands shall be appointed by the administrator to each of the two institutions. The administrator shall exercise his powers in accordance with the terms of this Agreement and in conformity with the laws and practices traditionally obtaining in the Islands.

4. The United Nations administrator shall verify the withdrawal of all armed forces from the Islands, and shall devise an effective method of ensuring their nonreintroduction.

5. The United Nations administrator shall have such staff as may be agreed by Argentina and the United Kingdom to be necessary for the performance of his functions under this Agreement.

6. Each party may have no more than three observers in the Islands.

ARTICLE 7

Except as may be otherwise agreed between them, the parties shall, during the currency of this Agreement, reactivate the Exchange of Notes of 5 August 1971, together with the Joint Statement on Communications between the Islands and the Argentine mainland referred to therein.[75] The parties shall accordingly take appropriate steps to establish a special consultative committee to carry out the functions entrusted to the Special Consultative Committee referred to in the Joint Statement.

ARTICLE 8

The parties undertake to enter into negotiations in good faith under the auspices of the Secretary-General of the United Nations for the peaceful settlement of their dispute and to seek, with a sense of urgency, the completion of these negotiations by 31 December 1982. These negotiations shall be initiated without prejudice to the rights, claims or positions of the parties and without prejudgement of the outcome.

ARTICLE 9

This Interim Agreement shall enter into force on signature and shall remain in force until a definitive agreement about the future of the Islands has been reached and implemented by the parties. The Secretary-General will immediately communicate its text to the Security Council and register it in accordance with Article 102 of the Charter of the United Nations.

Document 642

Note From the Argentine Special Delegate to the Twentieth Meeting of Consultation of Ministers of Foreign Affairs of the Rio Treaty (Quijano) to the President of the Twentieth Meeting of Consultation (Valdes Otero), May 21, 1982[76]

Argentine Position in Peace Negotiations Conducted by the U.N. Secretary-General

EXCELLENCY: I have the honor to address Your Excellency to inform you that, in addition to my note VS No. 33 of May 21, 1982,[77] the following explanation of the position taken by my government in the recent peace negotiations conducted by the Secretary-General of the United Nations is felt to be pertinent.

The Argentine Government immediately and with high hopes accepted the negotiations begun by the Secretary-General of the United Nations aimed at finding, on an urgent basis, a way to an alternative acceptable to the parties in dispute, avoiding expansion of the crisis caused by the United Kingdom with loss of life and great suffering.

---

[75] For the texts of the Argentine-British Joint Statement, initialed at Buenos Aires on July 1, 1971, and the British note of August 5, 1971, to the Argentine Government, see Great Britain, *Parliamentary Debates* (Commons), 5th series, 823 (1971) 14–17.

[76] Source: OAS document OEA/Ser.F/II.20 Doc. 62/82, May 22, 1982.

[77] For text, see OAS document OEA/Ser.F/II.20 Doc. 61/28. For text of a similar note, see document 645.

As a repeated demonstration of its historical position vis-à-vis the United Nations, the Argentine Government from the outset had full confidence in the role the Organization, and especially the Secretary-General, could play in these serious circumstances to preserve international peace and security and to remove all vestiges of colonialism in the world.

From the beginning of the Secretary-General's negotiations, the Argentine Delegation respected the need for maintaining a high degree of confidentiality in order to allow a free exchange of ideas aimed at reaching beneficial results, and to respect the efforts that the Secretary-General had initiated.

The statements made by the Argentine Delegation during the course of negotiations were aimed only at clarifying the elements in the negotiation that were becoming public knowledge and at providing a good-faith interpretation of the facts in strict accordance with the truth.

Nevertheless, as has been pointed out in the letters addressed to the Chairman of the Security Council and to Your Excellency, the negotiations carried out under the auspices of the Secretary-General took place while the United Kingdom was continuing its unceasing acts of aggression in the South Atlantic region, attacking not only military objectives, but also civilian facilities on the Malvinas Islands and unarmed transport vessels assigned to providing food, medicines, and fuel for the islanders. All of this shows the British duplicity of professing to be exercising acts of self-defense and of being committed to ensuring the protection of the islanders, and of purporting to negotiate while the military aggression went on.

The Argentine Republic agreed to negotiate despite the aggression and also accepted from the outset the approach and methodology suggested by the Secretary-General, and accordingly avoided initiatives aimed at delaying, interrupting or suspending his negotiations.

The approach and methodology suggested by the Secretary-General were not respected by the British Government. This was clearly demonstrated when the Delegation of the United Kingdom, upon requesting suspension of the negotiations, invoked the need to engage in consultation and broke in with a written proposal[78] that constituted a complete draft of a treaty that the Argentine Republic was to accept within hours, with only the possibility of making purely formal rather than substantive amendments, and disregarding entirely the compromises Argentina had made in an effort to reach an agreement.

The British proposal was submitted at a time considered crucial by the Secretary-General, and when Mr. Pérez de Cuellar was optimistically performing his task of quickly bringing the parties' positions together. It is therefore obvious that the British position was intended to hamper the work and frustrate exercise of the Secretary General's good offices with a proposal that was absolutely immutable and the the British knew beforehand was unacceptable.

In view of the circumstances described, which meant an unfair and arbitrary interruption in the procedure previously accepted by both parties, and which disregarded a week's process of negotiation, the Argentine Republic then submitted a reasonable proposal,[79] reiterating that it was an expression of Argentine willingness to continue negotiating in the working framework suggested by the Secretary-General.

The Argentine proposal did not answer nor was it aimed at answering the proposed British treaty, but rather sought to outline the flexible and balanced position of our country, and the Secretary-General was so informed.

At this point, it is pertinent to make the following comments on the proposal of the Argentine Republic that I transmitted to Your Excellency in the note mentioned in the beginning of the present communication:

The preamble takes account of Security Council Resolution 502 (1982), the United Nations Charter, and pertinent resolutions of the United Nations General Assembly. It accepts the assistance of the Secretary-General in accordance with the provisions of Article 40 of the United Nations Charter, to achieve a negotiated settlement with regard to the Malvinas, Georgias del Sur, and Sandwich del Sur Islands. That is, with regard to the present crisis and the sovereignty dispute over the Malvinas, Georgias del Sur and Sandwich del Sur Islands, the Republic of Argentina has accepted, in utter good faith and with the strictest respect for the law, the action taken

[78] For text of the British draft of an interim agreement, see annex, *supra*.

[79] For text of the Argentine proposal, see document 645.

by the Security Council and the work done by mandate of the General Assembly during 17 years of unsuccessful negotiations.

The Malvinas, Georgias del Sur, and Sandwich del Sur Islands are the geographical ambit of the sovereignty dispute over the three island groups, and this has been expressly accepted by the Government of the United Kingdom in legal instruments negotiated by the two parties, of which the United Nations was fully informed in identical, simultaneous communications. It is important to recall that both Governments adopted the joint communiqué released in Buenos Aires and London on July 26, 1977, recognizing that the upcoming negotiations would be over the three archipelagos in question (document A/32/110), bearing in mind the provisions of paragraph 5 of Resolution 31/49 of the United Nations General Assembly.[80]

Moreover, the British Government, in referring to Article 73 of the United Nations Charter, is clearly setting a precondition to negotiations for settlement of the dispute, and expressly violating the spirit and letter of Resolution 2065 (XX)[81] and others approved by the United Nations General Assembly on the Malvinas Islands question.

In relation to the first of the aspects essential to a settlement of the present crisis, that is, the withdrawal of military forces from the South Atlantic, Argentina proposed proceeding on a broad and flexible basis which, based on the good faith of the parties, would obviate any factor that could exert pressure on or disturb the substantive negotiations. It is in just this sense that the United Nations was supposed to play a part in supervising and verifying the withdrawal of the military forces on both sides, which process would have been governed throughout by that to which the two Governments had agreed, and by the relevant precedents. The United Kingdom, however, wanted to keep its fleet only 150 nautical miles off the Islands and the continental coast upon completion of the mutual withdrawal of military forces, and would accept no provision concerning its subsequent action and ultimate purpose. It doubtlessly wanted to create an impression that Argentina was withdrawing its forces under pressure and the threat of the British vessels. This cannot be countenanced by a Sovereign State and, moreover, offers no guarantee that the British Government would not create some incident to justify a colonial restoration by force.

In regard to the interim administration that should have been established during the brief time that negotiation between Argentina and the United Kingdom would take, the Argentine Government proposed, under moderate, balanced and objective guidelines, and without prejudging the positions of the parties, an administration exercised exclusively by the United Nations, to which local advisory services would be added to safeguard adequately the interests of the islanders in accordance with the relevant resolutions of the General Assembly.

What is more, Argentina undertook to maintain all services provided to the islanders since 1971, and in so doing assured to the inhabitants of the Islands a series of benefits and air and sea communications with the mainland and thence with the rest of the world.

The United Kingdom, on the other hand, proposed that, with the sole exception of the United Nations Administrator, the colonial institutions be reinstated, and demanded that this Administrator perform his functions in consultation with the colonial institutions in the face of the fact that the inhabitants are a minuscule group of about 800 families living under the colonial regime represented by the monopolistic Islands Company.

There can be no doubt that the British demands were directed expressly at the maintenance of the status quo prior to 2 April 1982 and were thereby intended to affect the entire process of substantive negotiations in prospect.

Argentina proposed that those negotiations be started at once in order to settle the issue of sovereignty over the three archipelagos—the Malvinas, the Georgias del Sur and the Sandwich del Sur groups, on an urgent basis and not later than 30 June 1983 under the auspices of the Secretary-General of the United Nations.

What is more, in its eagerness to reach a peaceful, fair and negotiated settlement quickly, the Argentine Government proposed that the Secretary-General be assisted in the negotiations by a contact group consisting of Representatives of four United Nations Member States.

The confidence of Argentina in the institutions of the United Nations went be-

---

80 For text of U.N. General Assembly Resolution 31/49 of December 1, 1976, see *Yearbook of the United Nations, 1976* (New York, 1979), p. 747.

81 Regarding U.N. General Assembly Resolution 2065 (XX) of December 16, 1965, see footnote 41 to document 633.

yond the strict framework of the negotiations that would go forward under the auspices of the Secretary-General. My Government's proposal provided that, in the event that no final settlement of the dispute had been reached, the Secretary-General would present a Report to the General Assembly, the sovereign and democratic Organ of the Organization, so that it might lay down guidelines for a settlement of the dispute.

To the contrary, the United Kingdom, according to Article 8 of its draft treaty, assumed no obligation whatever for bringing the negotiations for a final settlement of the issue to a conclusion within an adequate and fair period of time.

With its long experience of suffering the British technique of putting off negotiations indefinitely, Argentina thus risked a repetition of the long process of frustrations which it has had to deal with ever since Great Britain deprived it of part of its territory in order to impose a colonial regime there.

Moreover, the British proposal created an undefined situation in which, the duration of the interim United Nations administration being made dependent on agreement between the parties, the United Kingdom would be able to prolong that administration indefinitely by rejecting any negotiated solution. In other words, the United Nations would keep its obligation to administer in accordance with British will. The decision to prolong the interim administration, in the event of failure of the negotiations once the deadline is passed, cannot depend on one of the parties, but must be the responsibility of the United Nations General Assembly.

Throughout this whole negotiation process conducted by the Secretary-General, Argentina has really acted in all good faith, and with discretion and moderation, and with the firm purpose of reaching a just and lasting settlement to a crisis which affects its territorial integrity and its dignity as a nation.

The Argentine Government is persuaded that the international community, most of whose members have acknowledged Argentina's rights of sovereignty over the Malvinas, Georgias del Sur, and Sandwich del Sur Islands, will concur in this just position because history does not turn back, and restoration of colonialism by force is no longer countenanced by either the conscience or the morality of civilized nations.

I am requesting Your Excellency to have this note distributed urgently as an official document of the Twentieth Meeting of Consultation of Ministers of Foreign Affairs.

Accept, Excellency, the renewed assurances of my highest consideration.

RAÚL A. QUIJANO

Document 643

Statement by the Representative at the United Nations (Kirkpatrick) Before the U.N. Security Council, May 22, 1982[82]

Call for "an All-Out Effort to Settle This Tragic Conflict"

Mr. President, I should like to begin by expressing the appreciation of my government for your judicious and skillful leadership of the affairs of this Council in this deeply troubled time, as we seek a solution to the tragic conflict underway in the South Atlantic.

We desire to express in this public arena our gratitude to the Secretary-General for his tireless and determined efforts to find a peaceful resolution to the conflict between the United Kingdom and Argentina. The Secretary-General knows, as we should like the world as well to know, that he enjoyed the active support and cooperation of the United States in his search for a peaceful resolution of the conflict.

This conflict poses a particularly acute problem for persons and nations who love peace and also for this international body whose very raison d'etre is to promote and ensure the peaceful settlement of disputes.

The United States stands behind the principle that the use of force to settle disputes should not be allowed anywhere, and especially in this hemisphere where a significant number of territorial disputes remain to be solved diplomatically. For the United States, the Falkland crisis has been and still is a particularly agonizing, tragic event. As the whole world knows, we have a

[82] Source: U.S. Mission to the United Nations Press Release USUN-37(82), May 22, 1982.

longstanding alliance and, beyond that, the closest relations of friendship with Great Britain, the country from which our political institutions, law, and language derive. But we have not forgotten for a moment our close geographical, economic, and political relations with our Latin neighbors. We do not only care about this hemisphere, we are part of this hemisphere, and we share many of the aspirations, goals, and dreams of all nations of the Americas. Our own culture and society are deeply influenced by a growing Hispanic population. We can never turn our backs on, or be insensitive to, hemispheric goals and aspirations that we ourselves have promoted and defended.

That is why the United States tried so hard to avoid the conflict on the Falklands, why we are hoping so intensely to reduce and isolate it, and why we are eager and ready to back any realistic diplomatic initiative which will put a just end to it. And we especially mean to stay in close touch with our Latin neighbors while efforts are made to solve this tragic conflict, in order to restore peace with honor so that once again we can concentrate our efforts on the resolution of our problems. The quicker we put this tragic conflict behind us, the quicker we can begin building our future. And there, as always, Latin America will find how deeply the United States is committed to the cause of peace and prosperity in our hemisphere.

Mr. President, as the fighting intensifies and the cost in lives mounts in the South Atlantic, I think we all share a sense of anguish that it has not yet been possible to prevent this tragic conflict.

We have all come to appreciate how deep the roots of the conflict are. Britain, in peaceful possession of the Falkland Islands for 150 years, has been passionately devoted to the proposition that the rights of the inhabitants should be respected in any future disposition of the Islands. No one can say that this attitude, coming from a country that has granted independence to more than 40 countries in a generation and a half, is a simple reflex to retain possession.

Yet we know too how deep is the Argentine commitment to recover islands they believe were taken from them by illegal force. This is not some sudden passion, but a long-sustained national concern that also stretches back 150 years, heightened by the sense of frustration at what Argentina feels were nearly 20 years of fruitless negotiation.

From the start it has been widely recognized that the conflict engages basic principles without which a peaceful international order cannot stand. Unless the principle is respected that force must not be used to settle disputes, the entire international community will be exposed to chaos and suffering. And unless the right of self-defense is granted, only those countries that use force first will have the protection of law.

The Security Council was profoundly right to reassert those principles in Resolution 502, which forms the indispensable framework in which a peaceful solution has been sought and will ultimately be found. It is of fundamental importance that both Argentina and Britain have accepted Resolution 502 in its entirety.

For the United States, the conflict has a special poignancy. We do not take—have never taken—any position on the underlying claims. Britain is a country to which we are bound by unique ties of friendship, values, and alliance. And Argentina is also an old friend, a country of immigrants and settlers like our own, a country with which we share the enormous human and national potential of the New World experience.

That a conflict of such dimensions should take place, and that it should occur here, in the Western Hemisphere—whose countries have long shared a particular commitment to each other, to their mutual welfare and to peace—causes us the deepest concern. This conflict, however urgent, cannot be permitted to obscure the common engagement of all American states to the rule of law and to the well-being of this hemisphere.

So it was natural that the United States should make a particular effort to help Argentina and Britain find a solution.

That effort began before April 2nd, when we offered to the two sides our good offices to help find a solution to the South Georgia incident.

After April 2nd, both President Galtieri and Prime Minister Thatcher asked the United States to see whether it could be of assistance. At President Reagan's direction, Secretary of State Haig undertook two rounds of intense discussions in both capitals. Finally, on April 27th, as prospects for more intense hostilities arose, we put forward a proposal.[83] It represented our best estimate of what the two parties could reasonably be expected to accept. It was

---

[83] For text of the U.S. proposal of April 27, 1982, see document 631.

founded squarely on Resolution 502 by providing for a cessation of hostilities, withdrawal of forces, and a political settlement of the dispute.

The British Government indicated that it would seriously consider our proposal, although it presented certain real difficulties for it. However, the proposal was not acceptable to Argentina.

Immediately afterward, President Belaunde of Peru, after consultation with Secretary Haig, took the initiative to put forward a much simplified peace plan,[84] also drawing on the fundamental elements of Resolution 502.

On May 5th a draft text was forwarded by Peru to Buenos Aires; we forwarded the same text to London.

Britain made clear that it could seriously consider the proposal. Argentina chose not to consider it, asking instead that the Secretary-General use his good offices as, of course, it was its full privilege to do.

Mr. President, the tragic conflict before us also has special poignancy for the United Nations. It is precisely the kind of problem this organization was created to resolve. The Charter commits us

> " . . . [85] to bring about by peaceful means, and in conformity with the principles of justice and international law, adjustment or settlement of international disputes or situations which might lead to a breach of the peace.
>
> "To develop friendly relations among nations based on respect for the principle of equal rights and self-determination of peoples, and to take other appropriate measures to strengthen universal peace.
>
> "To achieve international cooperation in solving international problems . . . .
>
> "To be a centre for harmonizing the actions of nations in the attainment of these common ends."

The United Nations record in dealing with this conflict is commendable. The Security Council responded rapidly to the Argentine seizure of the Islands. The fact that both parties accepted Resolution 502 proves that it was a constructive response.

The Secretary-General's determined and imaginative efforts were, of course, fervently welcomed by all of us. Again the elements of settlement seemed to be present or nearly present. Again peace eluded us. I believe the institutions of the United Nations have functioned in this crisis in the manner foreseen by its founders and its Charter. We can be proud of it; proud, especially, of the Secretary-General.

We have already heard his account of his search for a formula that could resolve the conflict.[86] I think all of us have been deeply impressed by the skill and sensitivity, by the judgment and fairness that the Secretary-General brought to this task. That his effort has not so far succeeded does not mean that it has not realized important gains, notably in the establishment of a mutually acceptable concept of negotiations. The United States will wholeheartedly support any initiative that can help Argentina and Britain make peace with honor.

Despite all our efforts, the problem is not solved. Young men die in icy waters, on freezing beaches.

The dispute that appeared to many to be simple has nonetheless proved extraordinarily difficult to resolve. But we must not abandon the effort. Resolution 502, with its concept of linked and simultaneous cessation of hostilities, withdrawal of forces, and negotiations, must remain the framework of the search for peace. The problem is too important—for the rule of law, for the future of the Americas, for many of us friends of Britain and Argentina—not to make an all-out effort to settle this tragic conflict, so costly in every way.

Document 644

Resolution 505 (1982), Adopted by the U.N. Security Council, May 26, 1982[87]

Renewal of the U.N. Secretary-General's Good Offices

The Security Council,

Reaffirming its resolution 502 (1982) of 3 April 1982,

---

[84] For text of the Peru–U.S. proposal of May 5, 1982, see document 637.

[85] Ellipses appear in the source text.

[86] For text of the statement by U.N. Secretary-General Pérez de Cuéllar before the Security Council on May 21, 1982, see document 640.

[87] Source: U.N. Security Council Resolution

Noting with the deepest concern that the situation in the region of the Falkland Islands (Islas Malvinas) has seriously deteriorated,

Having heard the statement made by the Secretary-General to the Security Council at its 2360th meeting on 21 May 1982, as well as the statements in the debate of the representatives of Argentina and of the United Kingdom of Great Britain and Northern Ireland,

Concerned to achieve as a matter of the greatest urgency a cessation of hostilities and an end to the present conflict between the armed forces of Argentina and of the United Kingdom of Great Britain and Northern Ireland,

1. *Expresses* appreciation to the Secretary-General for the efforts which he has already made to bring about an agreement between the parties, to ensure the implementation of Security Council Resolution 502 (1982), and thereby to restore peace to the region;

2. *Requests* the Secretary-General, on the basis of the present resolution, to undertake a renewed mission of good offices bearing in mind Security Council Resolution 502 (1982) and the approach outlined in his statement of 21 May 1982;

3. *Urges* the parties to the conflict to cooperate fully with the Secretary-General in his mission with a view to ending the present hostilities in and around the Falkland Islands (Islas Malvinas);

4. *Requests* the Secretary-General to enter into contact immediately with the parties with a view to negotiating mutually acceptable terms for a cease-fire, including, if necessary, arrangements for the dispatch of United Nations observers to monitor compliance with the terms of the cease-fire;

5. *Requests* the Secretary-General to submit an interim report to the Security Council as soon as possible and, in any case, not later than seven days after the adoption of the present resolution.[88]

---

505 (1982); also printed in Department of State *Bulletin*, July 1982, p. 87. This resolution, introduced by Uganda on behalf of the cosponsors, Guyana, Ireland, Jordan, Togo, and Zaire, was adopted unanimously. For Ambassador Kirkpatrick's explanation of the U.S. vote in the U.N. Security Council on May 26, 1982, see *ibid.*

[88] For U.N. Secretary-General Pérez de Cuéllar's interim report of June 2, 1982, see document 651.

Document 645

Note From the Argentine Embassy to the Department of State, May 26, 1982[89]

Argentine Proposal Submitted During Negotiations at the United Nations

The Embassy of the Argentine Republic presents its compliments to the Department of State and has the honor to inform, with regard to the proposal of the United Nations Secretary-General referred to the conflict over the Islas Malvinas and its dependencies, the position of the Government of the Argentine Republic was clearly stated in the Proposed Agreement submitted in the course of the negotiations held at the United Nations, which text reads as follows:

"The Government of the Argentine Republic and the Government of the United Kingdom of Great Britain and Northern Ireland, hereinafter referred to as 'the Parties',

"In response to the provisions of Security Council Resolution 502 (1982) of April 3, 1982, and taking into account the Charter of the United Nations, Resolution 1514 (XV)[90] 2065 and other Resolutions of the General Assembly on the question of the Malvinas (Falkland) Islands, have accepted, in accordance with Article 40 of the Charter of the United Nations, the assistance of the Secretary-General of the United Nations and have engaged in negotiations and arrived at the following provisional agreement relating to the Malvinas, South Georgia and South Sandwich Islands, hereinafter referred to as 'The Islands' for the purposes of this agreement.

---

[89] Source: Department of State *Bulletin*, October 1982, p. 90. The text of the Argentine proposal was also transmitted earlier by letter of May 21, 1982, from Raúl Quijano, Special Delegate, to Estanislao Valdés Otero, President of the Twentieth Meeting of Consultation of Ministers of Foreign Affairs of the Rio Treaty. (OAS document OEA/Ser.F/II.20 Doc. 61/82) For Ambassador Quijano's explanation of the Argentine position, see his letter of May 21, 1982, to Foreign Minister Valdés, document 642.

[90] For text of U.N. General Assembly Resolution 1514 (XV) of December 14, 1960, see *American Foreign Policy: Current Documents, 1960* (Washington, 1964), pp. 110–111.

"I. 1. The geographical scope of the area within which the withdrawal of troops is to be carried out shall comprise the Malvinas, South Georgia and South Sandwich Islands.

"2. The withdrawal of the forces of both parties shall be gradual and simultaneous. Within a maximum period of thirty days, all armed forces shall be in their normal bases and areas of operation.

"II. With effect from the signature of this agreement, each party shall cease to apply the economic measures which it has adopted against the other and the United Kingdom shall call for the same action by those countries or groups of countries which, at its request, adopted similar measures.

"III. 1. Supervision of the withdrawal of the forces of both countries shall be carried out by specialized personnel of the United Nations, whose composition shall be agreed with the parties.

"2. The interim Administration of the Islands while the negotiations for final settlement of the dispute are in progress shall conform to the following provisions:

"A) The Administration shall be exclusively the responsibility of the United Nations with an appropriate presence of observers of the parties.

"B) The said Administration shall perform all functions (executive, legislative, judicial and security) through officials of different nationality from that of the parties.

"C) Notwithstanding the provisions of 2(A) and (B), and in order not to cause unnecessary changes in the way of life of the population during the period of the interim Administration by the United Nations, local judicial functions may be exercised in accordance with the legislation in force on April 1, 1982 to the full extent compatible with this agreement. Similarly, the United Nations interim Administration may appoint as advisers persons who are members of the population of British origin and Argentines resident in the Islands, in equal numbers.

"D) The flag of the parties shall fly together with that of the United Nations

"E) During the period of interim Administration, communications shall be kept open, without discriminatory restrictions of any kind for the parties, including freedom of movement and equality of access with respect to residence, work and property.

"F) Freedom of communication shall also include the maintenance of freedom of transit for the state airline (Lade) and for merchant ships and scientific vessels, in addition, telephone, telegraph and telex communications, Argentine television transmissions and the state petroleum (YPF) and gas services shall continue to operate freely.

"IV. The customs, traditions and way of life of the inhabitants of the Islands, and their social and cultural links with their countries of origin, shall be respected and safeguarded.

"V. 1. The parties undertake to enter immediately into negotiations in good faith under the auspices of the Secretary-General of the United Nations for the peaceful and final settlement of the dispute and, with a sense of urgency, to complete these negotiations by December 31, 1982, with a single option to extend until June 30, 1983, in order to comply with the Charter of the United Nations, Resolutions 1514 (XV), 2065 (XX) and other relevant resolutions of the General Assembly on the question of the Malvinas Islands. These negotiations shall be initiated without prejudice to the rights and claims or positions of the two parties and in recognition of the fact that they have divergent positions on the question of the Malvinas, South Georgia and South Sandwich Islands.

"2. The negotiations shall be held in New York.

"3. The Secretary-General of the United Nations may be assisted in the negotiations by a contract group composed of representatives of four States members of the United Nations. To that end, each party shall nominate two States and shall have the right to a single veto of one of the States nominated by the other.

"4. The Secretary-General of the United Nations shall keep the Security Council assiduously informed of the progress of the negotiations.

"VI. If the period specified in point V(1) above expires without the attainment of a final agreement, the Secretary-General shall draw up a report addressed to the General Assembly of the United

Nations, in order that the latter may determine, as appropriate and with greater urgency, the lines to which the said final agreement should conform in order to achieve a speedy settlement of the question."

The Argentine Government, in the light of the position stated in the aforementioned proposed agreement, which reflects the reasonableness which has continuously inspired its negotiating behaviour, deeply regrets that the peace efforts carried out the U.N. Secretary-General, in which pursuance and final success the Argentine Republic trusted, have been frustrated as a result of the unilateral decision of the British Government announced on May 20th.[91]

The real possibilities of reaching a peaceful settlement to the conflict and of avoiding, with the responsibility that the situation demanded, further bloodshed and an imminent breaking of peace and security in the hemisphere, finally proved to be disregarded by the intransigence and stubbornness with which the Government of the United Kingdom has tried to make the use of force prevail over reason and peace.

The Government of the Argentine Republic, therefore, formally holds the Government of the United Kingdom of Great Britain and Northern Ireland responsible for the serious consequences which in the future may stem from its denial to exhaust the available means towards a peaceful settlement, and expressly reserves its rights to a legitimate defense recognized by the United Nations Charter.

The Embassy of the Argentine Republic avails itself of this opportunity to renew to the Department of State the assurances of its highest consideration.

---

[91] Reference is to the debate on the Falkland Islands with British Prime Minister Thatcher before the House of Commons on May 20, 1982; for text, see Great Britain, *Parliamentary Debates* (Commons), 6th series, 24 (1982) 477–483.

Document 646

Statement by the Secretary of State (Haig) Before the Twentieth Meeting of Consultation of Ministers of Foreign Affairs of the Rio Treaty, May 27, 1982[92]

Inapplicability of Collective Security Under the Rio Treaty Because of Argentine First Use of Force in the Falkland Islands

Mr. Chairman, distinguished colleagues and ambassadors, Mr. Secretary General, Mr. Assistant Secretary General, ladies and gentlemen:

As the fighting intensifies and the cost in lives mounts in the South Atlantic, I think we all share a sense of anguish that it has not been possible to prevent this terrible conflict. It touches traditions and sympathies that run deep in our past and our national experiences. It is a loss and failure of our generation.

We grieve over the heartbreak and the bereavement that the conflict brings to so many families in Argentina and in Great Britain. We too share the emotions and pain of those families. Is there a country among us that has not counted itself a friend of both countries?

Our hemipshere, and the Western society of nations would be far poorer without their notable contributions to our common civilization. When friends fight, it is truly tragic.

It is from Great Britain that the United States drew the inspiration for many of its most cherished institutions. Most of us stood at the side of Great Britian in two world wars in this century. Great Britain is a vital partner in the alliance with Europe

---

[92] Source: OAS document OEA/Ser.F/II.20 Doc. 67/82, pp. 28–35; also printed in Department of State *Bulletin*, July 1982, pp. 87–90. Very minor textual and syntactical changes have been made on the copy printed here following comparison with an as-delivered text in the Department of State files. Secretary Haig spoke before the fourth session of the General Committee of the Twentieth Meeting of Consultation of Ministers of Foreign Affairs of the Rio Treaty which convened in the Hall of the Americas at the OAS General Secretariat in Washington at 4:35 p.m.

which is the first line of defense for Western civilization against the dangers of Soviet aggression.

Argentina is an American Republic, one of us. It is a nation, like the United States, founded on the republican ideal that all men are created equal. Like my country it is a nation of immigrants and settlers whose own culture and civilization have long had the respect of my countrymen and of the world.

President Reagan moved early in his administration to make clear the high value we place on our relations with the Government of Argentina and the high esteem in which we hold the Argentine people.

But it is not only our friendship and our ties with the two countries that are at stake.

This festering dispute has suddenly become a violent conflict that poses dangers to the very institutions and principles which bring us here and that have made this hemisphere, in many ways, the envy of the world.

The war puts the inter-American system under stress. Some say that this is an "anti-colonial war," because the islands were formally administered as a British Colony. Some say that since this is a war that pits an American republic against an outside power, the Rio Treaty requires that all its members come to the assistance of the American Republic.

Others say that it is impossible to speak of colonialism when a people is not subjugated to another, and when, as we all know, there was no such subjugation on the island. Others say there is no way in which the inter-American system—which protects regional order based on law and the peaceful settlement of disputes—can be interpreted as sanctioning the first use of armed force to settle a dispute.

With full respect for the views of others, the United States position is clear: Since the first use of force did not come from outside the hemisphere, this is not a case of extra-continental aggression against which we are all committed to rally.

As we deal with this crisis, let us agree that there is far more to unite the nations of this hemisphere than to divide them. We must—we simply must—keep the future in mind. If we are to learn anything from the grim events of recent weeks, it is that conflict might have been averted if there had been better communication and confidence among American states. We should take as our guide the work of the generations of statesmen who gave us an inter-American system that is both as visionary as it is practical. Their legacy is statecraft that is calm, that is reasoned, and that is, above all, just.

The very presence in this hall of so many distinguished statesmen indicates that we do agree—all of us—that the inter-American system is important. It has served us well. For two generations and more this hemisphere has been the region in the world most free of the scourges of war. The inter-American system and the Rio Treaty have constrained and almost eliminated armed conflict beteeen states of the Americas. The countries of Latin America spend less of their national resources for arms than any other area in the world. They have suffered less from Communist infiltration or aggression than any other part of the developing world. None of that would have been possible without the inter-American system of security.

The post-World War II achievements of the OAS, now in its 92nd year as the world's oldest regional international body, are largely responsible for our collective record as the world's haven from war. The contributions of the OAS to regional peace and harmony are almost too numerous to mention. Let me cite a few:

This organization helped restore peace along the borders between Nicaragua and Costa Rica on four separate occasions: 1948, 1955, 1959, and 1978.

Similar OAS efforts helped contribute to calming disputes, as between Ecuador and Peru in 1955, and again in 1980; or Honduras and Nicaragua in 1957; or to diminishing tensions, as between Bolivia and Chile in 1962, and between Haiti and the Dominican Republic in 1963.

In 1971 the OAS successfully urged Ecuador and the United States to avoid widening their differences over international fishing boundary rights. As one Ecuadorean writer noted at that moment, this OAS action proved that "the inter-American system functions and that its most powerful member did not vacillate one instant in recognizing the equality of its weaker associated partner."

By taking an early and steadfast stand against the violations of diplomatic staffs and premises, the Organization played a vital humanitarian role, in 1980, in ending terrorist takeovers. One of these situations was a diplomatic mission (Colombia), and the other an OAS office (El Salvador).

During the 1962 Cuban missile crisis, the legal position of the OAS had a major psychological and practical effect on the Soviet Union.

In another serious instance the OAS imposed sanctions on a member state when it was proved that the intentions of that regime (Trujillo, in the Dominican Republic) were aimed at assassination of the president of another OAS country (Romulo Betancourt of Venezuela).

When riots broke out in the Panama Canal Zone in 1964, and I was there that evening at Tuckerman Airport, an OAS team assisted in stopping bloodshed; the Organization's principled solidarity eventually helped bilateral negotiations to resolve what Woodrow Wilson called the greatest problem dividing the United States and Latin America from each other.

In the Dominican Republic in 1965, after the outbreak of civil war, the Organization acted decisively to restore peace, setting the stage for an impressive democratic evolution.

When fighting between Honduras and El Salvador broke out in 1969, OAS action helped put a quick stop to the bloodshed and to the fighting. Within 48 hours the OAS arranged a cease-fire, with contending forces withdrawing to status quo ante bellum.

For me the inter-American system is one of the unique forces that has helped the New World realize its very special and privileged destiny: A hemisphere with almost unlimited human and material potential, yet with the means to prevent or control the conflicts that have prevented other continents from realizing their potential.

The South Atlantic conflict could put into danger the principles and institutions that we have constructed so laboriously and which have served us so well. We must protect the integrity of our institutions so that they can serve us as well in future crises—which could affect any of us—as well as they have served us in the past.

We now face a conflict that involves us all, but to which the Rio Treaty does not well apply. It is a dispute over competing claims of sovereignty, each with profound historical and emotional sources.

We know how deep is the Argentine commitment to recover the islands Argentines believe were taken from them by illegal force. This is not some sudden passion, but a longstanding national concern that reaches back 150 years, and is heightened by the sense of frustration over what Argentina feels were nearly 20 years of fruitless negotiation.

We know, too, how deeply Britain, in peaceful possession of the disputed territory for 150 years, has been devoted to the proposition that the rights and the views of the inhabitants should be considered in any future disposition of the islands. No one can say that Britain's attitude is simply a colonial reflex to retain possession of distant islands. In the last 20 years no less than nine members of this Organization of American States have received their independence in peace and good will from Great Britain.

For its part, the United States has not taken—and will not take—any position on the substance of the dispute. We are completely neutral on the question of who has sovereignty. Indeed, 35 years ago, at the 1947 signing of the Final Act of the Rio Conference which created the Rio Treaty, the United States Delegation made this clear at the same time it set forth our position that the Treaty is without effect upon outstanding territorial disputes between American and European states.

Faced now with a conflict for which the inter-American system was not designed, American Republics have turned instinctively to that fundamental principle of world order, the encouragement of the peaceful settlement of disputes.

That is precisely what the United States did from the outset of this crisis.

Our effort began even before April 2, when we offered to the two sides our good offices to help find a solution to the South Georgia incident. Argentina declined.

Then, when it became apparent that Argentina was preparing to land troops on the Islands, President Reagan called President Galtieri to urge him not to go ahead. We told President Galtieri in the most friendly but in the most serious terms what the consequences would be. I can hardly take any satisfaction today to know that our predictions have proved correct.

After April 2 both President Galtieri and Prime Minister Thatcher asked the United States to see whether it could be of assistance. At President Reagan's direction, I undertook two rounds of intense discussions in each capital.

The first meeting of the Organ of Consultation also promoted peaceful negotiation. Meeting in this very hall, we, the Foreign Ministers of the Americas, urged that peace be maintained and that law prevail as the foundation of our international relations.

Immediately afterward, President Belaunde of Peru took the initiative to put forward a peace plan, drawing also on the fundamental elements of the United Nations Resolution 502. We worked in close consultation with him at that time.

Let me now report to you some of the specific elements involved in our efforts to resolve this dispute, which has proved so extraordinarily difficult to resolve. On April 27, as prospects for more intense hostilities arose, the United States put forth a proposal of its own. It represented our best estimate of what the two parties could reasonably be expected to accept. It was founded squarely on Resolution 502.

That proposal called for negotiations on the removal of the Islands from the list of non-self-governing territories. It specified that the definitive status of the islands must be mutually agreed, with due regard for the rights of the inhabitants and for the principle of territorial integrity. And it referred both to the purposes and principles of the Charter, and to the relevant resolution of the General Assembly.

I hope, gentlemen, that you will consider the nature of that proposal very carefully today, and what it truly signifies.

These negotiations were to be completed by the end of the year. Pending that, an interim authority, composed of Argentina, Britain, and the United States, was to oversee the traditional local administration to be sure that no decision was taken contrary to the agreement itself. Argentine residents of the Islands were to participate in the councils for this purpose and in proportion to their numbers. During the interim period travel, transportation, and movement of persons between the Islands and the mainland were to be promoted and facilitated without prejudice to the rights and guarantees of the inhabitants.

The proposed interim authority of three countries was then to make proposals on how to take into account the wishes and interests of the inhabitants, and on what the role of the Falkland Islands Company should be.

Should the negotiations not succeed in the time afforded, the United States was to be asked to engage in a formal mediation/conciliation effort in order to resolve the dispute in 6 months.

The British Government indicated that it would give the most serious consideration to acceptance of our proposal, although it presented certain real difficulties for it. However, Minister Costa Mendez informed me that the proposal was not acceptable to Argentina.

On May 5 a simplified text was forwarded by Peru to Buenos Aires at the initiative of President Belaunde.[93] It called for:

—A cease-fire;

—Concurrent withdrawal and nonintroduction of forces;

—Administration of the Islands by a contact group pending definitive settlement, in consultation with the elected representatives of the Islands;

—Acknowledgement of conflicting claims;

—Acknowledgement of the aspirations and interests of the islanders would be included in the final settlement;

—Undertaking by the contact group to ensure that the two parties reached a definitive agreement by April 30, 1983.

Britain made clear that it could seriously consider accepting the proposal. Argentina declined to consider it, asking instead for the Secretary-General to use his good offices, as, of course, it was its full privilege to do.

To promote negotiations is also what the Security Council and the United Nations Secretary-General have done.

We are heartened that the two parties—and the Security Council as a whole—have now been able to agree to give a new mandate to the Secretary-General to find a basis for peace.

What has been the approach of the international community as a whole must remain the policy of this body.

We must strive to resolve the conflict, not seek to widen it.

We must work to use the rule of law and the principle of nonuse of force to settle the conflict, not seek to challenge these vital principles.

---

[93] For the Peruvian-U.S. proposal of May 5, 1982, see document 637.

We must search for ways in which we can all join in helping to bring about peace, not ask the Rio Treaty mechanism to adjudicate a conflict for which it was never conceived.

It is right and proper that signatories to the Rio Treaty should convoke a meeting of Foreign Ministers when they perceive a threat to peace in the hemisphere. It is this right which has served us so well in preserving peace in the hemisphere. In times of danger we need the collective wisdom of all members of this body. This is of critical importance to the smallest among us who cannot afford large standing armies to defend their independence. It is this principle of collective security on which rests that other principle—nonintervention—which is vital to our relations.

We here have a special responsibility to ensure the peace of the hemisphere, as signatories of the Inter-American Treaty of Reciprocal Assistance, of the Charter of the Organization of American States, of the Charter of the United Nations, and as nations of the Western Hemisphere. We should take no action and make no decisions which increase tensions without enhancing the prospects for a negotiated settlement of the struggle in the South Atlantic.

Resolution 502 embodies the principles which must govern our search for peace. We must have the strength and the vision to seek a solution, described well to us by President Figueiredo,[94] in which there is neither a victor nor a vanquished.

The Secretary-General of the United Nations has now been given a new mandate to search for peace. The most important thing we could do here would be to give our unanimous collective support to those efforts. We should reassert the validity of Resolution 502 as the indispensable framework in which a peaceful solution has been sought, and I am confident will ultimately be found. And we should call on both parties to reach a peaceful negotiated solution.

As the Secretary-General of the United Nations proceeds, I would hope he would give particular attention to the ideas put forward by the President of Peru 10 days ago,[95] as well as those advanced by the Government of Brazil on May 24.[96] Although they may require completion and adjustment, these proposals contain much that is equitable and fair; they merit our careful attention.

For our part the United States has remained in touch with both parties throughout the crisis. We have tried in countless ways to help Argentina and Britain to find a peaceful solution. We are actively engaged in working with the Secretary-General in support of his most recent mandate for peace.

This conflict has by now proven that the young men of Argentina and Great Britain can fight with skill, courage, and determination. They have the courage to die for the dignity of their nations. They have the strength and valor to endure in desperate struggle in a desperate climate.

Now the time has come for older heads to accept the risks of compromise and the hazards of conciliation to bring the suffering and the dying to an end. Wisdom as well as struggle is a test of valor. The dignity of a nation is honored not only with sacrifices but with peace. The South Atlantic has reverberated with the fury of war. It must now be calmed by the wisdom and the courage of peace. Thank you, Sir. [Applause]

---

[94] President João Baptista de Oliveira Figueiredo of Brazil used the phrase "neither victors nor defeated" at a meeting with President Reagan in the White House on May 12, 1982. Following the meeting a senior Reagan administration official told reporters that "the two Presidents . . . hope for a very early solution to the problem in which there would be neither victors nor defeated on either side but the honorable and just requirements of both sides could be met." (Transcript of a Background Briefing by a senior administration official on President Figueiredo's visit, May 12, 1982, Office of the Press Secretary to the President)

[95] Reference presumably is to a proposal of May 20, 1982, by President Fernando Belaúnde Terry of Peru; see Foreign Broadcast Information Service, *Daily Report: Latin America*, May 24, 1982, p. J1.

[96] Reference presumably is to a letter of May 24, 1982, from Brazilian Foreign Minister Ramiro Elysio Saraiva Guerreiro to the President of the U.N. Security Council, Ambassador Ling Qing of China; for text, see U.N. document S/15108.

Document 647

Note From the Argentine Foreign Minister (Costa Méndez) to the President of the Twentieth Meeting of Consultation of Ministers of Foreign Affairs of the Rio Treaty (Valdés Otero), May 28, 1982[97]

"At No Time Did [Argentina] Term Unacceptable the Proposals of the United States"

MR. PRESIDENT: I have the honor to address Your Excellency with respect to the document of this Meeting of Consultation bearing the title "Texts of the Proposals for Agreement Made by the Government of the United States to the Governments of Argentina and of the United Kingdom of Great Britain and Northern Ireland" (doc.74/82),[98] to present a copy of the letter that, in my capacity as Minister of Foreign Affairs and Worship of the Argentine Republic, I sent on April 29, 1982, to Secretary of State Alexander Haig, Jr., informing him of the Argentine Government's views on the proposals for agreement made by the Government of the United States.[99]

In making known this reply, the Argentine Government wishes to state, as the attached letter shows, that at no time did it term unacceptable the proposals of the United States Secretary of State. Instead its objection was directed primarily at certain specific points, including some changes that had been made in the document compared to previous drafts, and it suggested that other formulas be sought. It added that if "Argentina's position were encompassed, agreement would be facilitated enormously and the final text of the document would not pose any insurmountable problems."

The Argentine Government wishes this important point to be made clear, in view of the statements that have been made in the sessions of the General Committee of this Meeting of Consultation, which were ratified by circulation of the document cited.

I request that this note with its attachment be distributed immediately as an official document of the Twentieth Meeting of Consultation of Ministers of Foreign Affairs.

Accept, Excellency, the renewed assurances of my highest consideration.

NICANOR COSTA MÉNDEZ

[97] Source: OAS document OEA/Ser.F/II.20 Doc. 78/82, May 28, 1982, p. 1; also printed in Department of State *Bulletin*, October 1982, p. 86. Argentine Foreign Minister Costa Méndez was in Washington for the Twentieth Meeting of Consultation of Ministers of Foreign Affairs of the Rio Treaty which convened on April 26, 1982.

[98] For text, see document 631.

[99] For text, see document 633.

Document 648

Statement by the U.S. Delegate (Middendorf) Before the Twentieth Meeting of Consultation of Ministers of Foreign Affairs of the Rio Treaty, May 29, 1982[1]

"The Resolution Before Us . . . Ignores What the Legal Effects of the First Use of Force Would Be"

Mr. President, distinguished foreign ministers and ambassadors, special delegates, Mr. Secretary General, Mr. Assistant Secretary General. I would like to thank the Chairman of the Working Group, the distinguished Foreign Minister of Bolivia, and I would like to thank the distinguished Chairman, the Foreign Minister of Uruguay, and all who worked so hard in the sincere work that has taken place here over the last 2 days. Mr. President, I would like to explain my delegation's abstention on the resolution before us.[2] However, before doing so, I would like to thank the distinguished Delegation of Colombia for its initiative in proposing a very positive and useful draft resolution. It contained a number of important advantages. With very

[1] Source: OAS document OEA/Ser.F/II.20 Doc. 81/82 corr. 1, pp. 13–14; printed also in Department of State *Bulletin*, July 1982, p. 90. Middendorf spoke before the sixth session of the General Committee of the Twentieth Meeting of Consultation of the Rio Treaty which convened at 1:30 a.m. in the Hall of the Americas at the OAS General Secretariat in Washington.

[2] For text of the resolution, see *infra*.

minor changes we were prepared to support it and regret that we were not afforded an opportunity to do so.

When we began our deliberations the day before yesterday, Secretary of State Haig in his address to this distinguished assembly made clear our commitment to the inter-American system.[3] He suggested that we search for ways in which we all could join to bring peace. Here, for the last 2 days, my delegation has worked and cooperated in that effort. Regrettably my delegation does not feel that the resolution which this assembly has asked to approve serves that purpose. We believe the resolution before us to be one-sided. It charges some; it ignores the actions of others. It ignores what the legal effects of the first use of force would be; further, there is no recognition that there must be compliance by both parties with all the elements of United Nations Security Council Resolution 502 to govern the search for peace in which we are engaged. We are pleased, however, that the resolution carefully avoids language which would seek to force observation of its parts by the signatory states.

With respect to that section of the present resolution which calls upon the United States, we have listened very attentively to our colleagues here in this forum. The United States will lift the measures announced with regard to Argentina immediately upon the provisions of the Security Council Resolution 502 having been implemented. And finally, we wish to assure all here that we will continue vigorously to pursue, in cooperation with others in this hemisphere, a search for a formula which will lead to an early, equitable, and peaceful settlement.

My delegation hopes that the two parties will find peace. We remain heartened that they have agreed in giving the Secretary-General of the United Nations his new mandate for peace, and we firmly support that effort.

The United States firmly believes, as Secretary Haig so wisely said, that there is far more to unite nations of this hemisphere than to divide us. We believe that all in this distinguished assembly, with whom we have worked so closely in the past and with whom we will work closely in the days and years to come, share our determination to preserve that which we already have so as to achieve our future potential, and my delegation remains committed to that very parctical and real ideal. Thank you, Mr. President.

[3] For the text of Secretary Haig's statement on May 27, 1982, see document 646.

Document 649

Resolution II, Adopted by the Twentieth Meeting of Consultation of Ministers of Foreign Affairs of the Rio Treaty, May 29, 1982[4]

Request for the Rio Treaty States to Give Argentina "the Support That Each Judges Appropriate"

WHEREAS:

Resolution I of the Twentieth Meeting of Consultation of Ministers of Foreign Affairs, adopted on April 28, 1982, decided "to keep the Twentieth Meeting of Consultation open, especially to oversee faithful compliance with this resolution, and to take such additional measures as are deemed necessary to restore and preserve peace and settle the conflict by peaceful means";[5]

That resolution urged the Government of the United Kingdom "immediately to cease the hostilities it is carrying on within the security region defined by Article 4 of the Inter-American Treaty of Reciprocal Assistance, and also to refrain from any act that may affect inter-American peace and security," and urged the Government of the Republic of Argentina "to refrain from taking any action that may exacerbate the situation";

The same resolution urged the Governments of the United Kingdom and the Ar-

[4] Source: OAS document OEA/Ser.F/II.20 Doc. 80/82 rev. 2; also printed in Department of State *Bulletin*, July 1982, pp. 90–91. This resolution, sponsored by Argentina, Colombia, and Costa Rica, and revised by the Working Group headed by Bolivian Foreign Minister Romero Alvarez Garcia, was adopted by a vote of 17 to 0, with 4 abstentions (including the United States), at the fourth plenary session which convened in the Hall of the Americas at the OAS General Secretariat in Washington at 3:40 a.m.

[5] For the text of Resolution I of the Twentieth Meeting of Consultation of Ministers of Foreign Affairs of the Rio Treaty of April 28, 1982, see document 632.

gentine Republic "to call a truce that will make it possible to resume and proceed normally with the negotiation aimed at a peaceful settlement of the conflict, taking into account the rights of sovereignty of the Republic of Argentina over the Malvinas Islands and the interests of the islanders";

While the Government of the Argentine Republic informed the Organ of Consultation of its full adherence to Resolution I and acted consistently therewith, the British forces proceeded to carry out serious and repeated armed attacks against the Argentine Republic in the zone of the Malvinas Islands, within the security region defined by Article 4 of the Inter-American Treaty of Reciprocal Assistance, which means that the United Kingdom has ignored the appeal made to it by the Twentieth Meeting of Consultation;

Following the adoption of Resolution I, the Government of the United States of America decided to apply coercive measures against the Argentine Republic and is giving its support, including material support, to the United Kingdom, which contravenes the spirit and the letter of Resolution I;

As a culmination of its repeated armed attacks, beginning on May 21, 1982, the British forces launched a broad-scale military attack against the Argentine Republic in the area of the Malvinas Islands which affects the peace and security of the hemisphere;

The deplorable situation raised by the application of political and economic coercive measures that are not based on present international law and are harmful to the Argentine people, carried out by the European Economic Community—with the exception of Ireland and Italy—and by other industrialized states, is continuing; and

The purpose of the Inter-American Treaty of Reciprocal Assistance is to "assure peace, through adequate means, to provide for effective reciprocal assistance to meet armed attacks against any American State, and in order to deal with threats of aggression against any of them,"

THE TWENTIETH MEETING OF CONSULTATION OF FOREIGN AFFAIRS, RESOLVES:

1. To condemn most vigorously the unjustified and disproportionate armed attack perpetrated by the United Kingdom, and its decision, which affects the security of the entire American hemisphere, of arbitrarily declaring an extensive area of up to 12 miles from the American coasts as a zone of hostilities, which is aggravated by the circumstance that when these actions were taken all possibilities of negotiation seeking a peaceful settlement of the conflict had not been exhausted.

2. To reiterate its firm demand upon the United Kingdom that it cease immediately its acts of war against the Argentine Republic and order the immediate withdrawal of all its armed forces detailed there and the return of its task force to its usual stations.

3. To deplore the fact that the attitude of the United Kingdom has helped to frustrate the negotiations for a peaceful settlement that were conducted by Mr. Javier Pérez de Cuéllar, the Secretary-General of the United Nations.

4. To express its conviction that it is essential to reach with the greatest urgency a peaceful and honorable settlement of the conflict, under the auspices of the United Nations, and in that connection, to recognize the praiseworthy efforts and good offices of Mr. Javier Pérez de Cuéllar, the Secretary-General of the United Nations, and to lend its full support to the task entrusted to him by the Security Council.

5. To urge the Government of the United States of America to order the immediate lifting of the coercive measures applied against the Argentine Republic and to refrain from providing material assistance to the United Kingdom, in observance of the principle of hemispheric solidarity recognized in the Inter-American Treaty of Reciprocal Assistance.

6. To urge the members of the European Economic Community, and the other states that have taken them, to lift immediately the coercive economic or political measures taken against the Argentine Republic.

7. To request the states parties of the Rio Treaty to give the Argentine Republic the support that each judges appropriate to assist it in this serious situation, and to refrain from any act that might jeopardize that objective.

If necessary, such support may be adopted with adequate coordination.

8. To reaffirm the basic constitutional principles of the Charter of the Organization of American States and of the Inter-American Treaty of Reciprocal Assistance, in particular those that refer to peaceful settlement of disputes.

9. To keep the Organ of Consultation available to assist the parties in conflict with their peace-making efforts in any way it may support the mission entrusted to the United Nations Secretary-General by the Security Council, and to instruct the President of the Meeting of Consultation to keep in continuous contact with the Secretary General of the United Nations.

10. To keep the Twentieth Meeting of Consultation open to see to it that the provisions of this resolution are faithfully and immediately carried out and to take, if necessary, any additional measures that may be agreed upon to preserve inter-American solidarity and cooperation.

Document 650

Declaration Adopted by the Twentieth Meeting of Consultation of Ministers of Foreign Affairs of the Rio Treaty, May 29, 1982[6]

Call for Assistance by the American Republics for Argentina to Overcome the Harmful Effects of the British Blockade and International Sanctions

THE TWENTIETH MEETING OF CONSULTATION OF MINISTERS OF FOREIGN AFFAIRS, DECLARES:

That the blockade of the Argentine coastline and the proclamation of the so-called "exclusion areas" imposed by the United Kingdom of Great Britain and Northern Ireland for sailing in waters of the American Hemisphere and in its security zone, as set out in the Inter-American Treaty of Reciprocal Assistance, violate the principles or rules of international law on the freedom of the seas. Therefore, it requests the United Kingdom to revoke those unlawful proclamations and to cease immediately the actions by which it intends to enforce them.

That the coercive measures against the Argentine Republic imposed by certain countries constitute a violation of the principles of international law set forth in the charters of the United Nations and Organization of American States. Therefore it urges the countries that have adopted such measures to cease application of them and asks all the American republics, particularly the countries that are parties to the Inter-American Treaty of Reciprocal Assistance, to provide Argentina any assistance they may be capable of providing to offset the harmful effects of this unlawful coercion.

[6] Source: OAS document OEA/Ser.F/II.20 Doc. 77/82 rev. 2. This declaration, presented by Bolivia and Ecuador, was adopted by a vote of 17 to 0, with 4 abstentions (including the United States). There was no explanation of the U.S. abstention in the vote on the declaration.

Document 651

Interim Report by the U.N. Secretary-General (Pérez de Cuéllar), Submitted to the U.N. Security Council, June 2, 1982[7]

Failure to Negotiate a Cease-Fire

1. The present interim report is submitted in pursuance of resolution 505 (1982), which the Security Council adopted at its 2368th meeting on 26 May 1982. In resolution 505 (1982), the Council requested the Secretary-General to undertake a renewed mission of good offices, bearing in mind Security Council resolution 502 (1982) and the approach outlined in his statement of 21 May 1982; to enter into contact immediately with the parties, with a view to negotiating mutually acceptable terms for a cease-fire; and to submit an interim report to the Council as soon as possible and, in any case, not later than seven days after the adoption of the resolution.

2. In the afternoon of 26 May, I met separately with the parties and requested that each provide within 24 hours a statement of the terms it considered acceptable for a cease-fire. It was my hope, as I explained to the parties, that, on the basis of their replies, terms could be developed which would be mutually acceptable. I indicated that arrangements for the dispatch of United Nations observers to monitor compliance with the terms of a cease-fire, as mentioned in resolution 505 (1982), could be made on short notice, with the approval of the Security Council.

[7] Source: U.N. document S/15151.

3. On 27 May, I received a message from the British Secretary of State for Foreign and Commonwealth Affairs, providing an indication of the terms acceptable to the United Kingdom for a cease-fire. On the same day, I received a first response from the Argentine Government, which was supplemented on 28 May by a communication on the terms for a cease-fire acceptable to Argentina.

4. I have had extensive exchanges with the parties, including conversations by telephone with the Minister for Foreign Affairs and Worship of Argentina. During these exchanges, which continued until this morning, I explored various approaches in seeking the degree of agreement necessary for a cease-fire.

5. It is my considered judgement that the positions of the two parties do not offer the possibility of developing at this time terms for a cease-fire which would be mutually acceptable. In accordance with the mandate given to me by resolution 505 (1982), I shall, nevertheless, maintain close contact with the parties in the event that an opportunity can be found in which the exercise of my good offices can contribute to bringing this tragic crisis to an end.

Document 652

Revised Draft U.N. Security Council Resolution, Vetoed by the United Kingdom and the United States, June 4, 1982[8]

Request for a Cease-Fire and Simultaneous Implementation of Resolutions 502 (1982) and 505 (1982)

The Security Council,

Reaffirming its resolutions 502 (1982) and 505 (1982) and the need for implementation of all parts thereof,

1. *Requests* the parties to the dispute to cease-fire immediately in the region of the Falkland Islands (Islas Malvinas) and to initiate, simultaneously with the cease-fire, the implementation of resolutions 502 (1982) and 505 (1982) in their entirety;

2. *Authorizes* the Secretary-General to use such means as he may deem necessary to verify compliance with this resolution;

3. *Requests* the Secretary-General to submit an interim report to the Security Council within 72 hours and to keep the Council informed concerning the implementation of this resolution.

Document 653

Statement by the Representative at the United Nations (Kirkpatrick) Before the U.N. Security Council, June 4, 1982[9]

"Were it Possible to Change Our Vote We Should Like to Change It From a Veto . . . to an Abstention"

The decision taken by this Council today is, I think we all understand, a terribly important one: it marks one more failure in a series of failed efforts to mediate a conflict that is more than 200 years old—one more failed attempt to substitute reason for force, negotiation for violence, words for bombs and bullets.

Today's decision, then, marks one more step in a process of escalation whose end is not yet in sight. Phase one of this most recent conflict ended with the Argentine occupation of the Falklands. Phase two may well end with British reoccupation of the Falklands. Where will phase three end?

Affirmed in the vote of the majority today is the will to negotiation and to peace. Affirmed in the veto of my Government—to which I will return in a moment—is the principle that force should not be allowed to triumph.

One of my sons handed me this morning a poem of another man who disapproves of

[8] Source: U.N. document S/15156/Rev.2. This resolution, sponsored by Panama and Spain, failed of adoption by a vote of 9 in favor to 2 against (the United Kingdom and the United States), with 4 abstentions. For the explanation of the vote by the U.S. Representative, Jeane J. Kirkpatrick, on June 4, 1982, see *infra*. The U.N. Security Council meeting began at 4 p.m.

[9] Source: U.N. document S/PV.2373. For Secretary Haig's explanation of the U.S. vote, see the press briefing of June 5, 1982, *infra*.

Argentina's forceful act against the Malvinas Islands. In some lines in a poem called "An English Poem" the great Argentine writer Borges wrote:

> "I offer you my ancestors, my dead men, the ghosts that living men have honoured in marble, my father's father killed on the frontier of Buenos Aires, two bullets through his lungs, bearded and dead, wrapped by his soldiers in the hide of a cow; my mother's grandfather, just 24, heading a charge of 300 into Peru—now ghosts on vanished horses."

The friends of Argentina, of the Americas and of world peace hope that Argentina will have few such offerings from this war and from the postwar period. We hope—all of us here, I believe—that cooperation can be restored, friendships mended, urgent tasks recommenced, of building in the New World a truly new world.

My government has worked hard for mediation and settlement of this dispute. We have been rent by the clash of values, loyalties and friends. That clash continued down through the registration of the vote on this issue. I am told that it is impossible for a government to change a vote once it is cast, but I have been requested by my government to record the fact that were it possible to change our vote we should like to change it from a veto—a "no", that is—to an abstention.

Document 654

Transcript of a Press Briefing by the Secretary of State (Haig), Versailles, June 5, 1982 (Extracts)[10]

Explanation of the Change in U.S. Voting Instructions in the U.N. Security Council

. . . .

Q. Can you tell us about what happened in terms of our vote at the United Nations and why didn't you wake up the President?

. . . .

SECRETARY HAIG. We had a resolution which emanated from Spain and Panama that has been in the hopper up in New York for, I think, about 48 hours.[11] The original version of it was a version that we would veto. It has been subject to some softening and evolution over the last 24 hours. I am speaking up to last night. When I got back from the foreign ministers' dinner last night I had a call from Washington advising me that the instructions I had left with them at 6 p.m. that we would veto should be reconsidered in the light of our experts' assessment of the situation. I took that assessment and I informed them to inform U.S.–UN to abstain. Now as sometimes happens when you are 2,000 miles away, the vote was cast when, I think 3 minutes later, the instruction arrived, and it was explained by the U.S.–UN Ambassador,[12] and I think you are aware of that. That is the case. It is just that simple.

Q. What made you change your—

SECRETARY HAIG. I made the decision and it is very appropriate that I should make the decision on an issue like that.

Now I want to just point out to you that the choice was veto or abstention. I looked very, very carefully at the language of the resolution, which was very close to something that would have been acceptable. But lacking in specificity with respect to the obligation for the withdrawal of forces—there was no time certain. Remember, we had a little discussion on that I think yesterday afternoon in Paris, or whenever we met last—the day before.[13] And with that lacking, I felt it did not justify a veto if it could be corrected and if there was a mind to at

---

10 Source: White House Press Release, June 5, 1982, Office of the Press Secretary to the President. Secretary Haig accompanied President Reagan to Versailles for the economic summit of industrialized nations, held from June 4 to 6, 1982. The press briefing began at 8:03 p.m.

11 For the text of the revised draft U.N. Security Council resolution vetoed by the United Kingdom and the United States on June 4, 1982, see document 652.

12 For Ambassador Kirkpatrick's statement before the U.N. Security Council on June 4, 1982, see *supra*.

13 In reply to a question asked at a press briefing in Paris on June 4, 1982, following a meeting between President Reagan and British Prime Minister Thatcher, Haig said: "I think both leaders are aware of the desirability to keep bloodshed to a minimum. . . . This depends fundamentally on the willingness of the Argentines to withdraw and to set a schedule—a fixed date certain for such withdrawal, and then for the commanders on the ground to work out the detail." (Department of State Press Release 191, June 16, 1982)

the United Nations, but there was not so we abstained. And that is a responsibility that I bear and it is not a major nuance of difference whether it was a veto or an abstention. Neither one was a vote for. There are shades of difference every time we have a UN vote.

Q. Mr. Secretary, the Argentines have refused to implement 502 for 8 weeks. What made you think they might be prepared to implement it now? Yesterday—

SECRETARY HAIG. Well, I didn't vote yes for it. The United States didn't vote yes. The United States abstained because this resolution was very close to something that would be acceptable as distinct from something that was totally unacceptable. And I think you know what our interests are. They are to have the fighting stop at the earliest possible date.

. . . .

Q. —why didn't you call Mrs. Kirkpatrick directly? Why go through Washington for all these explanations? It seems—(laughter)—that 3 minutes would have been saved—

SECRETARY HAIG. Have you ever—have you ever been involved in the State Department or the Pentagon or the Department of the Army, dear?

Q. I'm referring about the communications between—

SECRETARY HAIG. You don't talk to the company commander when you have a corps and a division in between. You are always sure that everyone is singing from the same sheet of music.

Q. Well, did you talk to the Commander-in-Chief, Mr. Secretary? How about that?

. . . .

SECRETARY HAIG. It is a decision that normally fits totally within my category of responsibility. The President was told after the fact of the event, and that's—what? Am I going to get the President up at 1 in the morning or 12:30 a.m.?

. . . .

Q. He had—the last time nobody woke him, there was a problem, you'll recall.

SECRETARY HAIG. Ahhh. (Laughter) Somewhat different. Somewhat—a nuanced vote is—take the United Nations. My God, the man would be up 24 hours a day with Haig on the other end and I'd be up, too.

. . . .

Q. Why did you make the change?

SECRETARY HAIG. Well, because, as I said, the resolution itself had come very far away toward being acceptable, very far away as a result of a lot of hard work by a lot of reasonable, concerned people in New York.

Q. What was it specifically, Mr. Secretary?

SECRETARY HAIG. Pardon?

Q. What specifically took it far away from what was acceptable?

SECRETARY HAIG. Well, there were two—two problems, essentially. One is: I think the British Government was concerned that the linkage between the cease-fire and the withdrawal was not as firm as they wanted it. Frankly, I felt it was very firm because it was very explicit about supporting UN Resolution 502 and 502 calls precisely for a cease-fire and a withdrawal as well as a political solution.

The second part did bother me and that was the fact there was no date certain for withdrawal and while the supervisory authority of the Secretary-General was very clear with respect to the cease-fire and potential violations of the cease-fire, it was less clear with respect to the withdrawal. And, therefore, if there were confusions and there frequently are in such a complex situation, it might have collapsed into something even more tragic than we're faced with today.

So, we said abstain—not good enough.

Q. What gave you the confidence about 502 when it's been defined for 8 weeks? Why did you think Argentina would pay more respect to 502 now than 8 weeks ago when it was proposed?

SECRETARY HAIG. They commit themselves to 802—502 and they make a time certain. That's what this has been about. I hope you're not suggesting that if there was a change of mind in Argentina that we should ignore that and then continue to march.

Q. But they've ignored 502 for so long, why would they accept it now?

SECRETARY HAIG. They're in a somewhat different position now.

Q. Mr. Secretary, when your instructions arrived too late, were you involved in the decision to announce your instructions anyway?

SECRETARY HAIG. No, I was not.

Q. Mrs. Kirkpatrick was—

SECRETARY HAIG. But it's a very—you know, I understand it. It's a very logical thing. It's not a big problem.

. . . .

Q. Do you mean to say that on yesterday afternoon you hadn't seen a text, that you only saw one later? Or that you decided that—

SECRETARY HAIG. I had a discussion at 6 p.m. yesterday afternoon on the text before our experts had analyzed it. I had the report of our experts last night at the time that I made the decision. All were unanimously in favor of an abstention.

. . . .

Document 655

Editorial Note

Brigadier General M. B. Menendez, Commander of Argentine Forces in the Falkland Islands, and Major General J. J. Moore, Commander of British Land Forces in the Falkland Islands, signed an Instrument of Surrender on June 14, 1982, effective 23:59 Greenwich mean time (20:59 local time) that day. The surrender included those Argentine forces deployed in and around Port Stanley, those others on East Falkland, West Falkland, and all the outlying islands. For the text of the Instrument of Surrender, see U.N. document S/15231.

Document 656

Letter From the Argentine Chargé at the United Nations (Listre) to the President of the U.N. Security Council (De la Barre de Nanteuil), June 18, 1982[14]

Argentine Observance of a de Facto Cease-Fire

On express instructions from my Government, I have the honour to bring the following to the attention of the Security Council with regard to the question of the Malvinas, South Georgia and South Sandwich Islands:

After vetoing the draft resolution ordering the cease-fire, which was voted by the majority of the Council on 4 June 1982, the United Kingdom of Great Britain and Northern Ireland has continued its armed aggression against my country and has completed the military occupation of Puerto Argentino, the capital of the Malvinas, on 14 June. The self-defence exercised by Argentina in order to safeguard its territorial integrity could not prevail against the military superiority of the aggressor.

Consequently, the Commander of the Argentine forces defending the Malvinas had to surrender the personnel under his command in order to avoid greater loss of human life.

Throughout the developments which led to this situation the United Kingdom of Great Britain and Northern Ireland ignored the demand for an immediate cease-fire contained in Security Council resolution 502 (1982) of 3 April 1982 and also the exhortation of the Council contained in paragraph 3 of that resolution to the Governments concerned to seek a peaceful solution of the dispute by means of negotiations.

As is well known, the United Kingdom vetoed the draft resolution of 4 June, submitted by Panama and Spain, thus making clear its refusal to carry out the cease-fire and to accept resolution 505 (1982), although it had been adopted unanimously and, obviously, with its own affirmative vote.

Argentina cannot and will not accept the situation of force which Great Britain has thus sought to impose. Today, it is clearer

---

[14] Source: U.N. document S/15234.

than ever that the United Kingdom's aim is to ensure by any means the continuation of a situation of colonial domination in the South Atlantic, in open violation of the Charter of the United Nations.

The Argentine Republic is now addressing the Security Council again to make clear, as it has done on previous occasions, its full readiness to carry out resolutions 502 (1982) and 505 (1982). My country hopes likewise that the Council will continue its efforts to secure the full compliance of the United Kingdom with these resolutions.

The United Kingdom is maintaining its troops on the Islands, its fleet in the South Atlantic, the naval and air blockade against Argentina and also the economic aggression carried out with the participation of other industrialized countries.

In addition, the United Kingdom has now extended its military operations to the South Sandwich Islands, as the Argentine Mission informed the Security Council in note No. 171 of 17 June circulated in Security Council document S/15230, by attacking the scientific station "Corbeta Uruguay" which the Argentine Republic has maintained in those Islands for a number of years.

In view of the present circumstances, there is a *de facto* cessation of hostilities which Argentina is now observing. However, this cessation of hostilities will be precarious as long as the British policy of continuing the military occupation, the blockade and the economic aggression continues.

The total cessation of hostilities will be achieved only when the United Kingdom agrees to lift the naval and air blockade and the economic sanctions referred to above and when it withdraws the military forces occupying the Islands and the naval task force and the nuclear submarines which it has deployed in the area.

The Argentine Republic points out, once again, that only negotiations within the framework of the United Nations and in conformity with the pertinent resolutions—negotiations in which Argentina has always been ready to participate—can lead to a final settlement of the dispute, thus eliminating a situation of illegal colonial domination, which is sustained by force and which in itself constitutes a permanent threat to peace.

I request that this note be circulated as a Security Council document.

ARNOLDO M. LISTRE

Document 657

Statement by President Reagan, July 12, 1982[15]

Termination of Economic Sanctions Against Argentina

I have ordered termination of economic sanctions against Argentina, effective today, July 12. These sanctions, which were imposed April 30, include withholding of new Export-Import Bank credits, insurance and guarantees, and new Commodity Credit Corporation guarantees. I have made this decision after a thorough review of the situation in the South Atlantic following the cessation of hostilities.[16] It is important now for all parties involved in the recent conflict to put the past behind us, and to work for friendship and cooperation. The United States, for its part, will do all it can to strengthen its historic ties among nations of this hemisphere.

---

[15] Source: *Weekly Compilation of Presidential Documents,* July 19, 1982, pp. 893–894. This statement was distributed by Larry Speakes, Deputy Press Secretary to the President, at the press briefing in the Briefing Room of the White House at 10:17 a.m.

[16] British and Argentine notes of July 9 and 11, 1982, respectively, recognized the de facto cessation of hostilities since June 14, and arranged for the return of the remaining 593 Argentine prisoners of war.

Document 658

Prepared Statement by the Assistant Secretary of State for Inter-American Affairs (Enders) Before a Subcommittee of the House Foreign Affairs Committee, August 5, 1982[17]

The Origins and Consequences of the Falklands/Malvinas Conflict

Mr. Chairman: I was delighted to receive your invitation to review with this Committee the impact of the Falklands/Malvinas Islands conflict on the Inter-American System and specifically on U.S. relations with Latin America.

The clash between Argentina and the United Kingdom erupted suddenly, then as quickly disappeared from the headlines. It left in its wake some haunting questions—about how to prevent war in the hemisphere, about the future of Inter-American cooperation, even about regional stability and progress.

This is not the first time that these islands have vividly illustrated the risk of massive repercussions from modest origins. These "few spots of earth which, in the desert of the ocean, had almost escaped notice" once brought "the whole system of European empire" to the point of convulsion. The remark is from *Thoughts on the Late Transactions Respecting Falkland's Islands*, written by Samuel Johnson in 1771.

This prepared statement addresses the disturbing consequences of the 1982 Falklands/Malvinas crisis beginning in Part 6. Parts 2–5 record something of the origins and course of the conflict itself.

The territory immediately at issue consists of 2 main islands and some 200 smaller ones located in the South Atlantic 480 miles northeast of Cape Horn. The islands cover a total area of 4,700 square miles. Their terrain is alternately boggy and hilly, the environment wind-swept and virtually treeless. Samuel Johnson described it as "a bleak and barren spot in the Magellanick Ocean of which no use could be made". But Johnson never went there to see for himself. A U.S. Foreign Service officer who did so more than two centuries later in the course of her consular duties reported that "work is hard but life is simple and not uncomfortable." According to the 1980 census, the population was 1,813—down from the 1931 peak of 2,392. The predominant economic activity is the production of fine wool.

It is their relationship to the outside world rather than their marginal profitability that has made these islands a source of seemingly endless contention. Even their name reflects disagreement: though in English they are known as the Falklands, in the Spanish-speaking world they are invariably known as the Malvinas. There is even controversy over which European first sighted the islands in the 16th century.

But the central dispute has always been over sovereignty. In 1770, England, France, and Spain almost went to war over small outposts embodying competing claims to exclusive dominion on the islands. That crisis was resolved pragmatically when Spain restored to England the settlement of Port Egmont on Saunders Island off West Falkland, founded orginally by English settlers in 1766, then seized by Spain. In turn, Spain kept Port Louis, which had originally been founded by France in 1764 on East Falkland. Both Spain and England maintained their broader sovereignty claims.

In 1774, apparently for reasons of economy, England withdrew from Port Egmont, leaving behind a leaden plaque declaring that "Falkland's Island" was the "sole right and property" of King George III. From 1774 to 1811 the islands were administered without challenge by a succession of Spanish governors under the authority of the Viceroyalty of La Plata in Buenos Aires.

In 1820, Argentina formally claimed sovereignty over the then uninhabited islands as the successor to Spain. In one of the many ironies of this history, the Frigate *Heroina* sent to enforce Argentina's control was commanded by David Jewett, one of the many British subjects who fought in the Wars of Liberation in the service of the Argentine Republic. In 1826, Argentina established a new capital at the protected harbor of Stanley on East Falkland. In 1833, after a series of incidents over fishing rights, one of which had led to action by the

---

[17] Source: *Latin America and the United States After the Falklands/Malvinas Crisis: Hearings Before the Subcommittee on Inter-American Affairs of the Committee on Foreign Affairs, House of Representatives, Ninety-seventh Congress, Second Session* (Washington, 1982), pp. 114–126. The subcommittee met at 2:15 p.m., Representative Michael D. Barnes, chairman of the subcommittee, presiding.

USS *Lexington* against Argentine authorities, the corvette HMS *Clio* reasserted Britain's claim.

For nearly a century and a half—until an Argentine naval force invaded Port Stanley last April 2—Britain administered the islands, first as a Crown Colony, then as a self-governing dependency. The royally chartered Falklands Islands Company undertook the first large-scale settlement of the islands, and provided ships that made four or five round trips a year to Britain exchanging the islands' wool and hides for everything from chocolates to building materials.

Argentina's commitment to recover territories Argentines believe were illegally wrested from them by force is documented in countless pamphlets, articles, and books, some of them distributed widely in Latin America. For the past 40 years or so, the claim to the "Malvinas" has been an important component of Argentine nationalism, endorsed by prominent civilian and military leaders across the political spectrum.

Immediately after World War II, Argentina moved its claims beyond the bilateral exchanges that had marked its efforts to recover the islands in the nineteenth and early twentieth century. At inter-American conferences in Rio in 1947, Bogota in 1948, Washington in 1953, and Caracas in 1954, Argentine delegations introduced resolutions pressing Argentina's claims within a general framework of decolonization. In the arctic summer of 1947–48, an Argentine task force of two cruisers and six destroyers conducted maneuvers off the islands, but left when Britain dispatched warships in response.

Argentine diplomacy registered a significant gain in 1964. Since 1946, the United Nations had treated the United Kingdom as the Administering Authority under Chapter XI of the U.N. Charter. United Nations General Assembly Resolution 2065(XX) called upon Argentina and the United Kingdom to initiate talks with a view to resolving their conflicting sovereignty claims peacefully. Confidential bilateral talks began in 1966. With numerous ups and downs and occasional interruptions, Argentine-U.K. negotiations continued for 16 years. Agreements were reached providing for Argentine facilitation of air travel and communications, postal and medical services, education and oil supply. The two sides remained far apart, however, on the basic issue of sovereignty and such related issues as land ownership and residence by Argentines. The last pre-crisis round of talks took place in New York in February 1982, ending barely 6 weeks before Argentina attempted to settle the matter by force.

It has been said that Britain's approach reflected a stubborn colonialist reflex. The fact that over the last generation no fewer than nine members of the Organization of American States have received their independence in peace and good will from Great Britain suggests that the situation was rather more complex. The resident islanders, hardy individuals predominantly of Scottish and Welsh extraction, proved to be satisfied with British rule and adamantly united in opposing Argentine claims. Throughout the negotiations, Britain stood by the proposition that the rights and views of the inhabitants must be respected in any future disposition of the islands.

The standoff became rooted in principle as well as nationality: Britain arguing for self-determination, Argentina for territorial integrity.

The United States has at no time taken a legal position on the merits of the competing sovereignty claims. In the nineteenth century, U.S. officials made clear that—because the British claims antedated 1823—the United States did not consider the reassertion of British control a violation of the Monroe Doctrine. The United States, however, refused to become embroiled in the sovereignty issue, and took no position on Argentine and British sovereignty claims.

Thirty-five years ago, at the signing of the Final Act of the 1947 Rio Conference which created the Rio Treaty, the United States delegation, headed by Secretary of State George C. Marshall, made clear our view that the Rio Treaty is without effect upon outstanding territorial disputes between American and European states—and explicitly refused to endorse Argentina's claim.

U.S. neutrality on the question of sovereignty has been confirmed repeatedly since then—at the Organization of American States and the United Nations as well as during the recent fighting. I reassert it again today, before this body: The United States takes no position on the merits of the competing claims to sovereignty, nor on the legal theories on which the parties rely.

For the record, I would like to add that although we of course have an interest in peace there as elsewhere, the United States has no direct interest in the islands. Because some comments abroad have suggested otherwise, I state explicitly that the United States has never had, and does not now have, any interest in establishing a military base of any kind on these islands. The only occasion on which any U.S. military presence has ever been contemplated was in April–May 1982 as a contribution to a peaceful resolution had one been agreed to between Argentina and the United Kingdom.

Argentina's surprise military occupation of the islands beginning April 2 provoked dismay and apprehension throughout the international community. The next day, April 3, the United Nations Security Council adopted Resolution 502, demanding immediate cessation of hostilities and withdrawal of Argentine troops, and calling on Argentina and the United Kingdom to resolve their differences diplomatically. Invoking the right of self-defense under Article 51 of the U.N. Charter, the United Kingdom dispatched a war fleet toward the islands.

The looming military confrontation put the inter-American system under great stress. Some said that because war would pit an American republic against an outside power, the Rio Treaty required that all its members come to the assistance of the American republic.

Others said that the inter-American system—which protects regional order based on law and the peaceful settlement of disputes—could in no way be interpreted to support the resort to force to settle a dispute.

The United States' position was that because the unlawful resort to force did not come from outside the hemisphere, this was not a case of extra-continental aggression against which we were—and are—all committed to rally.

These different responses to a conflict for which the inter-American System was not designed led to heated exchanges among foreign ministers at the meeting of the Rio Treaty Organ of Consultation that began April 26. Two days later, the Organ adopted by a vote of 17–0–4 (the United States abstaining) a resolution that urged an immediate truce, recognition of the "rights of sovereignty of the Republic of Argentina over the Malvinas (Falkland) Islands and the interests of the islanders," and called for "negotiation aimed at a peaceful settlement of the conflict."

Negotiation of a peaceful settlement of the conflict had in fact been the central objective of the United States response to the crisis.

U.S. efforts to encourage a negotiated settlement began even before the initial use of force. In late March, we offered to the two sides our good offices to help find a peaceful solution to an incident on South Georgia Island on March 19 when an Argentine salvage team was threatened with expulsion for operating without British permission. On April 1, learning that Argentine military action appeared imminent, President Reagan called President Galtieri to urge that Argentina desist from the use of force.

After Argentina forcibly occupied the islands, both President Galtieri and Prime Minister Thatcher encouraged the United States to see whether it could be of assistance in finding a solution. At President Reagan's direction Secretary Haig undertook two rounds of intense discussions in each capital.

On April 27, as prospects for more intense hostilities increased, the United States put forward a proposal of its own. It represented our best estimate of what the two parties could reasonably be expected to accept. It was founded squarely on U.N. Security Council Resolution 502, which both sides asserted they accepted.

The U.S. proposal called for negotiations to remove the islands from the list of Non-Self-Governing Territories under Chapter XI of the U.N. Charter. It specified that the definitive status of the islands must be mutually agreed, with due regard for the rights of the inhabitants and for the principle of territorial integrity. And it referred both to the purposes and principles of the U.N. Charter, and to the relevant resolutions of the U.N. General Assembly.

Those negotiations were to be completed by the end of the year. Pending their conclusion, an interim authority composed of Argentina, Britain, and the United States was to oversee the traditional local administration, to be sure that no decision was taken contrary to the agreement. Argentine residents of the islands were to participate in local councils for this purpose. During the interim period travel, transportation and movement of persons between the islands and the mainland were to be promoted and facilitated without prejudice to the rights and guarantees of the inhabitants.

The proposed interim authority of three countries was to make proposals to facilitate the negotiations, including recommendations on how to take into account the wishes and interests of the inhabitants, and on what the role of the Falkland Islands Company should be.

Should the negotiations not have been completed by year's end, the United States was to be asked to engage in a formal mediation/conciliation effort in order to resolve the dispute within 6 months.

The British Government indicated that our proposal presented certain real difficulties but that it would seriously consider it. However, the proposal was not acceptable to the Argentine Government, which continued to insist that any solution must have a predetermined outcome.

On April 30, in light of Argentina's continued unwillingness to compromise, we took concrete measures to underscore that the United States could not and would not condone the unlawful use of force to resolve disputes. The President ordered limited economic and military measures affecting Argentina, and directed that we would respond positively to requests for matériel support for British forces, but without any direct U.S. military involvement. Secretary Haig's statement announcing these measures emphasized our belief that no strictly military outcome could endure, that a negotiated settlement would be necessary in the end, and that the United States remained ready to assist the parties in finding that settlement.

On May 5, President Belaunde of Peru took the initiative to put forward a new peace plan, drawing also on the fundamental elements of Resolution 502. We worked closely with him. The simplified text forwarded by Peru to Buenos Aires and London called for: an immediate cease-fire; concurrent withdrawal and non-reintroduction of forces; administration of the islands by a contact group pending definitive settlement, in consultation with the elected representatives of the islanders; acknowledgement of conflicting claims; acknowledgement in the final settlement of the aspirations and interests of the islanders; and an undertaking by the contact group to ensure that the two parties reached a definitive agreement by April 30, 1983.

Britain made clear that it could seriously consider the proposal. Argentina asked instead for the U.N. Secretary-General to use his good offices as, of course, it was its full privilege to do.

By this time, however, the military tempo was rapidly overtaking the negotiators. On May 2, two torpedoes from a British submarine sank the *General Belgrano*, Argentina's only cruiser. On May 4, a sea-skimming missile from an Argentine jet devastated the HMS *Sheffield*, a modern British destroyer. Despite intense new efforts by the U.N. Secretary-General, the war we had worked so hard to avoid had come in earnest.

By June 14, when the Union Jack was again raised over Port Stanley, what Horace Walpole had in 1770 called "a morsel of rock that lies somewhere at the very bottom of America" had become the improbable scenario of bitter fighting. More than a thousand men and women were dead. Billions of dollars had been expended. Emotions had surfaced in both countries that promise to make this issue and others even harder to resolve in the future.

I said at the outset that the South Atlantic war faces us with several haunting questions.

Perhaps the most fundamental is how better to prevent war in the future in this hemisphere.

Many of us feared as soon as Argentina acted April 2 that the fighting would escalate. Argentina, it is true, did not cause casualties in its takeover. But that did little to diminish the shock. Any use of force invites further use of force. The shock in this case was increased because the two countries were both linked in friendship to us and to each other. It grew when brave men on both sides began to risk and lose their lives. But perhaps the deepest shock came because war between states had been virtually unknown in the Americas in our time.

In the world as a whole, some 4 million persons have lost their lives in armed action between states since the Second World War. Including the toll in the South Atlantic, fewer than 4,000 of them have died in the Western Hemisphere. The countries of Latin America spend less of their national resources for arms than any other area in the world. Their military expenditures come to only 1.4 percent of GNP—a quarter of the average in the Third World as a whole.

The South Atlantic war—the fact of major fighting and the clear advantages demonstrated by modern weapons—means that military institutions, throughout the hemisphere but especially in South America, have powerful new claims to resources. Because Latin America's military institutions and arsenals are relatively modest in size, demands for advanced weapons systems and for the expertise to maintain and employ them are likely to increase. Governments will also look for self-sufficiency in defense industries, for bigger stocks of weapons.

Budgetary limitations will of course constrain purchases, but we would be mistaken to expect arms modernization to be deferred as a result of the South Atlantic conflict. On the contrary. The duration and intensity of the fighting called into question the assumption that the Inter-American System guarantees that interstate conflicts in this hemisphere would be limited to a few days of actual fighting.

A new emphasis on military preparedness in a region long plagued by territorial disputes and military involvement in politics would undeniably challenge every member of the Inter-American System.

The hemisphere is laced with territorial questionmarks. The prevalence of territorial tensions (e.g., among Argentina–Chile–Peru–Bolivia–Ecuador, Colombia–Venezuela–Guyana, Nicaragua–Colombia, Guatemala–Belize) puts a premium on the peaceful settlement of disputes. To take just one example, tensions between Guatemala and Belize (the only place in the hemisphere other than the Falklands where the United Kingdom stations combat troops) will continue to fester if unresolved.

The challenge to regional peacekeeping is far from hopeless, however. The U.S. response to the crisis may serve to deter others from resorting to force. Moreover, the Inter-American System equips the New World with the means to prevent or control the conflicts that have kept other continents from realizing their potential.

Machinery exists to anticipate disputes and permit their peaceful and definitive settlement: various inter-American arbitration and conciliation agreements, OAS peacekeeping mechanisms, the International Court of Justice, even the Treaty of Tlatelolco,[18] which established the world's first nuclear free zone in a populated area. What appears lacking is the will to use this machinery to prevent and resolve contentious problems. The United States and other countries of the area have at one time or another been involved in calming or negotiating most of them. But this is a branch of hemispheric diplomacy that deserves fresh attention.

The interest of American states is clearly to avoid arms races. Even where competitive procurement cannot be avoided altogether, they will want to see that existing disputes are not needlessly exacerbated. U.S. arms sales as a proportion of South American purchases fell from 75 percent in 1960 to 25 percent in 1970, and 7 percent in 1980. The reduction in training and in-depth contacts between the United States and most South American militaries has been equally precipitous.

These patterns raise a question worth pondering in the wake of the Falklands/Malvinas episode. Can the United States maintain a degree of military access and communication with the states of South America so as to help maintain the regional balance of power with such limited personnel, doctrinal, and matériel relationships?

A related challenge is to prevent regional conflicts from having strategic consequences, changing the East–West balance. This is a real problem, for history shows the Soviet Union and its proxies are ready and eager to take advantage of instability. Should Moscow be willing to provide arms at bargain prices as it did to Peru in the 1970's, economic constraints on Latin American purchases of military equipment from traditional Western sources could give the Soviets a unique opportunity to forge closer links with established governments in South America. Cuba (and Nicaragua) rushed forward to exploit the Falklands crisis. In Argentina some talked of playing the Cuban card. We do not believe Argentina will turn to the country that harbors in its capital the extremely violent Argentine terrorist organization—the Montoneros. But Cuba will be working hard to use the crisis to lessen its current isolation within the hemisphere.

A second legacy of the conflict is the need to overcome resentments of the United States that were triggered by the crisis.

Although the immediate emotional strains of the crisis are already receding, the perception of the United States as a reliable ally to Latin American nations in times of crisis will take time to restore.

The commitment of the United States to the hemisphere and its institutions has been called into question. I have already noted the importance we attach to the OAS, that we have taken no position on the question of sovereignty, and that in our view no Rio

---

[18] For text of the Treaty for the Prohibition of Nuclear Weapons in Latin America (Treaty of Tlatelolco) of February 14, 1967, see 22 UST 762.

Treaty action could apply to this particular contingency. Nonetheless, U.S. support for what on May 29 the second meeting of the Rio Treaty Organ of Consultation condemned as an "unjustified and disproportionate" U.K. military response was taken by some to mean that the U.S. commitment to the Inter-American System was superficial at best.

The fact that the conflict remained localized and ended relatively rapidly helped mitigate damage to U.S. interests. Nonetheless, our bilateral relationships with certain countries have unquestionably been affected adversely. The most severe impact is obviously on relations with Argentina. But Venezuela, Panama, and Peru were also highly critical of our support for the United Kingdom's military response, and will be watching closely the future evolution of the sovereignty issue. In contrast, U.S. relations with most other South American countries, Mexico and the Caribbean Basin appear less affected.

The lasting effects of this mood, which varies from country to country, will depend on how the post-crisis situation evolves and what posture we adopt. Reactions may change as the position taken by the United States is better understood. But the widespread view that the United States does not take Latin America seriously could increase North–South and nonaligned rhetoric and inhibit cooperation in support of U.S. interests. The argument that the United States and United Kingdom acted as industrialized powers cooperating to keep a developing country "in its place" makes us once again a target for anti-colonialist and anti-imperialist emotions that will make it harder for us to accomplish our objectives.

It would be wrong to conclude from such reactions that the United States should not have acted as it did. There can be no position for the United States other than to oppose the unlawful use of force to settle disputes.

The first lesson for U.S. policy is that this is a time for steadiness of purpose rather than for grandiose gestures, statements, or proposals. During the coming months, it will be especially important that we meet our commitments, protect our interests and respond to those of our neighbors in a meaningful and resourceful manner.

The Caribbean Basin Initiative[19] is vitally important in this regard. Many Basin countries now wonder whether our contribution to the CBI will ever materialize. If Congress were not to act, the concerns these countries now express about their future and our commitment to them would deepen, widening opportunities for Soviet and Cuban adventurism. It is now up to the United States to deliver.

We must maintain our commitment in Central America, where democratic processes are vulnerable, and where fragile government institutions face a major challenge from Cuban supported guerrilla movements. Our political, economic, and security assistance is essential to help them meet this challenge and make progress toward democracy, economic development, and the effective protection of human rights.

While we must continue to seek innovative solutions to the problems of our immediate neighborhood, we must understand what is happening in South America is also important to us. This was evident in the midst of the Falklands conflict—for example, in the visit of President Figueiredo to Washington.[20] The conflict between Argentina and the United Kingdom was a major topic of discussion. The exchange made clear that the positions of the United States and Brazil differed, but that our basic interests and objectives were similar. For several years now, we have simply not given South America the attention its place in the world and our interests warrant.

This brings me to a third challenge, the conundrum of our relations with Argentina. Despite our many similarities, U.S.-Argentine relations have seldom been close.

The President's vision of regionwide cooperation had led us to make efforts to improve ties to South America, including Argentina. In the case of Argentina, however, those efforts had not yet borne fruit by the time of the crisis. We must continue to seek a dialogue that can develop the bilateral and multilateral framework for more fully cooperative relations.

During the South Atlantic crisis, our ties with Argentina proved too weak to promote effective cooperation in support of common interests. Repeated efforts were made by us

[19] For documentation on the Caribbean Basin Initiative, see Chapter 15, Part C.

[20] General João Baptista de Oliveira Figueiredo, President of Brazil, visited Washington, May 11–13, 1982, for meetings with President Reagan and Secretary of State Haig on May 12 and with the Permanent Council of the Organization of American States on May 13; for documentation, see *Weekly Compilation of Presidential Documents,* May 17, 1982, pp. 628–632.

and by others—before the Argentine landing on the islands, again when the British fleet was approaching, and again when the U.S. and Peruvian and U.N. peace plans were advanced in turn—to explain to Argentine leaders what would happen if they did what they proposed to do. Although our predictions consistently proved accurate, they were not believed. Communication failed utterly.

Our objectives with Argentina today include encouraging economic recovery, peaceful resolution of the dispute between the United Kingdom and Argentina, and, of course, political comity. Yet our ties to the government in Buenos Aires are now more limited than previously. How long this will last depends on several factors. But the fundamental point is that we all share a compelling interest in an Argentina that is true to hemispheric traditions and free of foreign Communist influence. We do not want the Soviets to be their only alternative. Neither do they. We all should be prepared to help Argentina maintain conditions in which its people can realize their free world vocation.

So we must begin, in orderly fashion, to build the solid, realistic relationship so evidently lacking until now.

Finally, the South Atlantic crisis has highlighted economic problems in South America and throughout the hemisphere.

Even before the crisis, many of the region's countries were feeling the effects of the world recession on their development. The problems vary. Virtually all depend heavily on international trade and on access to international financial markets. Some have contracted substantial debt. The South Atlantic crisis could crystallize doubts about stability and creditworthiness on a regionwide level, particularly if arms procurement were to divert resources from development priorities.

The major lesson here is the need for cooperation in economic management—not merely with Argentina, but with Brazil, Venezuela, and Mexico.

Many of the problems now associated with the South Atlantic crisis have been developing for some time. The growing assertiveness and needs of major developing countries are not new. Let us hope that the crisis will strengthen our ability to work more realistically together.

Before the crisis erupted in the South Atlantic, we had already begun to develop more sustained hemispheric relationships.

—We had started to achieve with Mexico a relationship that reflects its exceptional importance to the United States and its role in world affairs. Now comes the harshest test of that new relationship, as the economic slowdown in both countries threatens to aggravate all our joint accounts: trade, finance, immigration. We must be steadfast.

—We had committed ourselves to help countries of the Caribbean Basin protect themselves against outside intervention, strengthen or develop democratic institutions, and overcome economic disasters. Now we must deliver.

—We were beginning to respond to new realities in South America, rebuilding close bilateral relations with each country after a decade of drift, when the shadow of the South Atlantic crisis fell across our efforts. Now we must relaunch those efforts, joining others to maintain the network of constructive relationships that is essential to peace.

What this crisis may ultimately mean for the United States is not that our recent decisions were wrong—they were right—but that the accummulation from our past decisions reveals a flaw in our outlook. We have pursued an a la carte approach, ignoring our friends when it suited us, yet demanding their help or agreement when it served our interest. We took too much for granted, and invested too little. When we needed close and effective dialogue on April 2, we didn't have it.

When a fight in distant islands reverberates around the world, the fundamental lesson is not how little we need each other but how closely connected we are. Our task is to make interdependence work, not against us, but for us. This requires long term commitments that will enhance our ability to influence events and protect our interests.

Document 659

Testimony by the Assistant Secretary of State for Inter-American Affairs (Enders) Before a Subcommittee of the House Foreign Affairs Committee, August 5, 1982 (Extracts)[21]

Lessons for U.S. Policy From the Falklands/Malvinas Crisis

MR. ENDERS. It is a very important topic. I have prepared testimony which covers the background of the conflict as well as the aftermath, and the questions posed in the aftermath.[22]

If I could, I would like to submit that. I would like also to submit along with it a statement that we have prepared on the actions taken by the United States during the period of April and May of this year to assist the parties to reach a peaceful solution to their dispute, including the various proposals put forward.[23]

MR. BARNES. Without objection, we will include both of those prepared statements in the record.

MR. ENDERS. The clash between Argentina and the United Kingdom came up very suddenly, and it subsided very suddenly, but I think it does leave behind it some important questions.

I am struck, looking back, that this is not the first time that the islands have illustrated the risk of massive repercussions from the quiet, modest origins. These "few spots of earth which, in the desert of the ocean, had almost escaped notice" once brought "the whole system of European empire" to the point of convulsion. That remark is from "Thoughts on the Late Transactions Respecting Falkland's Islands," which was written by Samuel Johnson in 1771. This has happened before.

As you look out from the crisis, I think one should pose oneself four questions. Most fundamental would appear to be how better in the future can war in the hemisphere be prevented.

War between states in the hemisphere has in fact been virtually unknown in the hemisphere in our time. The military expenditures of the countries of Latin America come to only 1.4 percent of GNP, which is a quarter of the average in the Third World as a whole. The inter-American system has a unique record of cooperative action to preserve the peace. Before the Falklands/Malvinas war, there was the war between Honduras and El Salvador, you will recall the "soccer war."

There were border clashes involving Nicaragua and Costa Rica. There have been border actions involving Peru and Ecuador, but that is all that has occurred in our lifetime, and although those actions themselves are regrettable, it is a remarkable record compared with other parts of the world.

Yet when we needed close and effective dialog in this case to prevent war, we didn't have it, either before or after April 2. In fact, Argentina's initial moves were not detected until late March. We tried, the United States tried repeatedly and failed repeatedly during the crisis to communicate to Argentina the consequences of the actions that they proposed to take.

If you look to the consequences, to the conclusions people will draw from that, I think it is clear that the fact that the South Atlantic proved possible at all means that military institutions throughout the hemisphere, but especially in South America, will have powerful, new claims on resources. Budgetary limitations will, of course, strain purchases, but we would be mistaken to expect weapons modernization to be deferred as a result of the Falklands/Malvinas conflict.

On the contrary, the duration and intensity of the fighting was a direct challenge to the assumption that the inter-American system guarantees that interstate conflicts in this hemisphere would be limited to a few days of actual fighting. People are going to look to their self-sufficiency in weapons and in technology, and they are going to look to more modern technology.

A new emphasis on military preparedness in a region long plagued by territorial disputes and military involvement in politics would undeniably challenge every member of the inter-American system.

The hemisphere is laced with territorial disputes that will continue to fester if unresolved. The United States and other countries of the area have at one time or

---

[21] Source: *Latin America and the United States After the Falklands/Malvinas Crisis*, pp. 109–113, 152–154.

[22] For text of Enders' prepared statement, see *supra*.

[23] For text of the statement under reference, see *infra*.

another been involved in calming or negotiating most of them. But this is a branch of hemispheric diplomacy that deserves fresh and vigorous attention.

The interest of American States is clearly to avoid arms races. Even where competitive procurement cannot be avoided altogether, they will want to see that existing disputes are not needlessly exacerbated. U.S. arms sales as a proportion of South American purchases fell from 75 percent in 1960 to 25 percent in 1970, to 7 percent in 1980. The reduction in training and in-depth contacts between the United States and most South American militaries has been equally precipitous.

These patterns raise a question worth pondering in the wake of the Falklands/Malvinas episode. Can the United States help avoid subregional imbalances of power without greater military access and communication than we have today? I believe the answer is no, and that some additional U.S. arms transfers within the stated policies will be needed to help preserve the peace.

A related challenge is to prevent regional conflicts from having strategic consequences, changing the East–West balance. It would be costly for all of us in this hemisphere should Moscow gain access to the southern cone, perhaps as a source of military modernization. And Cuba is working hard to exploit the crisis to lessen its isolation within the hemisphere.

A second problem that we should ask ourselves is how to overcome resentments directed against the United States that were triggered by the crisis.

I say "triggered" because the reactions in one or two countries were so uniform as to suggest the concerns they conveyed were at least in some cases already there. I think it is ironical that the sharpest reactions came from two friendly democracies, Venezuela and Peru. Reaction, on the other hand, in the biggest countries and elsewhere was much more muted.

We are just now emerging from the immediate emotional aftermath of the crisis, but the perception of the United States as a reliable ally to Latin American nations in times of crisis will take time to restore.

It would be wrong to conclude from such reactions that the United States should not have acted as it did. There can be no position for the United States other than to oppose the unlawful use of force to settle disputes.

The first lesson for U.S. policy is that this is a time for steadiness of purpose rather than for grandiose gestures or renewed statements of good intentions or proposals or commissions. During the coming months, it will be especially important that we meet our commitments, protect our interests and respond to those of our neighbors in a meaningful and resourceful manner. That means above all vigor in our bilateral diplomacy.

The Caribbean Basin initiative is also vitally important in this regard. Our national credibility is at stake.

But if we must continue to seek innovative solutions to the problems of our immediate neighborhood, we must now understand that what is happening in South America is also important to us. For several years or indeed perhaps for more than a decade now, we have simply not given South America the attention its place in the world and our interests warrant.

This brings me to the conundrum of our relations with Argentina. Despite our many similarities, United States-Argentine relations have seldom been close.

The President's vision of regionwide cooperation had led us to make efforts to improve ties to South America, including Argentina. Yet during the South Atlantic crisis, our ties with Argentina proved too weak to promote effective cooperation in support of common interests. And some effects of the crisis could make our relations even more conflictual.

So we must begin, in orderly fashion, to build the solid, realistic relationship so evidently lacking until now. We all share a compelling interest in an Argentina that is true to hemispheric traditions and free of foreign Communist influence. We do not want the Soviets to be their only alternative. Neither do they. We all should be prepared to help Argentina maintain conditions in which its people can realize their free world vocation.

With regard to the Falklands/Malvinas dispute itself, we hope the two parties will find a process by which they can reach a peaceful solution of their dispute in accordance with the principles of the United Nations Charter.

Finally, the South Atlantic crisis has highlighted economic problems in South America and throughout the hemisphere.

Even before the crisis, many of the region's countries were feeling the effects of the world recession on their development. A side effect could be to crystallize foreign doubts about stability and creditworthiness on a regionwide level, particularly if arms procurement were to divert resources from development priorities.

The basic lesson here is the need for cooperation in economic management—not merely with Argentina, but with Brazil, Venezuela, and Mexico.

Before the crisis erupted in the South Atlantic, we had already begun to develop more sustained hemispheric relationships:

We had started to achieve with Mexico a relationship that reflects its exceptional importance to the United States and its exceptional importance in world affairs. Now comes the harshest test of that new relationship, as the economic slowdown in both countries threatens to aggravate all our joint accounts: Trade, finance, immigration.

We had committed ourselves to help countries of the Caribbean Basin protect themselves against outside intervention, strengthen or develop democratic institutions, and overcome economic disasters. We must deliver.

We were beginning to respond to new realities in South America, rebuilding close bilateral relations with each country after a decade of drift when the shadow of the South Atlantic crisis fell across our efforts. We must relaunch those efforts, joining others to maintain the networks of constructive relationships essential to peace.

What this crisis may ultimately mean for the United States is not that our recent decisions were wrong—I believe that they are manifestly right—but that the accumulation from our past decisions reveals a flaw in our outlook. We have taken too much for granted, and invested too little.

When a fight in distant islands can cause reverberations around the world, the fundamental lesson is not how little we need each other but how closely connected we are. Our task is quite clear, to make interdependence work, not against us, but for us.

Thank you very much, Mr. Chairman.

. . . .

Mr. Barnes. Thank you, Mr. Secretary.

You seem to be posing almost a paradox in your testimony, at a couple of points in your prepared testimony, as I look at it.

You didn't go into this quite as specifically in your comments this afternoon, but at one point you say that the interest of the United States is to avoid arms races in Latin America, and then you seem to be going on to say that one way we can have increased influence in the region is to increase our own arms sales and our military training in the region.

Maybe I am misreading you, but if I am not, what you seem to be saying is the only way to avoid arms races is to get into participating in those arms races.

Can you tell me what you are really trying to say or is that what you are really trying to say?

Mr. Enders. What I am trying to say is that in a part of the world in which military establishments are indeed very influential in national policies—that of course applies very distinctly to the Southern Cone, where the question of maintaining the peace is now posed in a more acute form than we thought it was earlier—that influence with those military establishments is in fact important.

The United States has, over much of our lifetime, maintained very close contacts with the military throughout this region. Most of them have been to our schools. They had imported our weapons. We had kept in very close contact with them.

This close contact, this import of weapons, this interchange between our military establishment and theirs, did not result in arms races, as I think in fact the historic figures, very low figures on military spending in the region indicate. We certainly would not want to behave in such a way so as to set off such an arms race, but I think we should be responsive within our existing authorities to their interest in renewing the personal ties on the one hand and, on the other hand, in our purchasing larger amounts of weapons.

What is a specific case in point on this? I think the specific case in point goes back more than 10 years ago when two U.S. administrations attempted to prevent the introduction of jet aircraft into Latin America. One of the reasons the ties were eroded so much over this period was that in the course of that effort, I think a very sincere and well-meaning effort, but a failed effort, jet aircraft were indeed introduced into Latin America. They were not ours.

In one case they were the Soviet Union's. The arms spending of the area did not rise significantly relative to gross national product, but U.S. influence in this important sphere did diminish very sharply. We thought we were preventing an arms race at that time. All we were doing in effect was diminishing our own ability to deal with the real needs of the area.

You started out, Mr. Chairman, by saying that we should listen to the degree we can and be responsive. I think we should listen in this area also.

MR. BARNES. In this same regard, you said in your testimony this afternoon that we should all be prepared to help Argentina maintain conditions in which its people can realize their free world vocation, following up a statement that we don't want the Soviets to be their only alternative, and neither do they.

I think everyone on the committee would agree with that objective. The question I would pose is how do we go about achieving that goal? The information that I get indicates that the administration is seriously contemplating an early certification which would again permit arms sales to Argentina. Is this something that you think is an appropriate approach, given the recent history of Argentina's use of its military? Does it really help us accomplish the objectives that we have there, and aren't there other steps that we can take vis-à-vis Argentina that would be more constructive in terms of improving our relations?

MR. ENDERS. I think there is no decision on certification, and I would not expect early certification, to respond to that part of your comment, Mr. Chairman.

With regard to the steps that could be taken to improve our relationship, to make it more solid, I think perhaps the most important steps are in the economic sphere. Argentina is undergoing a severe economic crisis now, the question of how its debt is to be managed, and this is a basically creditworthy country, with a basically sound foreign balance, but having some very severe internal economic problems.

That question probably should be very high on our agenda. The decision to remove economic sanctions responds to that.

I would not wish to suggest that building a long-term relationship with Argentina is only a question of military ties and arms.

I would hope you would agree that the certification question, the original decision by the Humphrey–Kennedy legislation to withhold arms purchases to Argentina which was based on human rights violations in Argentina,[24] once it has been demonstrated, as we are now authorized to do, that those human rights violations are no longer substantial, are no longer important, and indeed the most serious ones have disappeared entirely, then this certification should make it possible to lift the embargo.[25]

That does not mean the United States would sell large amounts of equipment to Argentina, because the normal rules, licensing requirements would remain in effect.

MR. BARNES. Let me respond to that. I think you are right, that Congress did specifically take a step to modify the legislation, so as to permit that action. But the Congress retains a strong interest in this whole issue, perhaps stronger than it was when we acted last year on the certification requirement.

There is more focus on Argentina now than there was 1 year ago, and in that respect I would hope that when you make the certification—and you indicated you are not planning to make it anytime soon—that will give the Congress an opportunity to review it.

In the past, as you know, there have been some instances in which this kind of action was taken when the Congress was either on recess or about to go on recess, and it made it difficult for the Congress to fulfill its responsibilities in reviewing these decisions. Can you give us an assurance that when and if you reach this decision, it will be handled in a way that will be consistent with the ability of this committee to review the decision?

MR. ENDERS. We would certainly wish to consult with this committee and with the other interested committees in the Congress, Mr. Chairman, in advance.

---

[24] The Kennedy–Humphrey amendment, which was added as Section 620B to the Foreign Assistance Act of 1961 by Section 11 of the International Security Assistance Act of 1977 (P.L. 95–92), enacted August 4, 1977, prohibited all military sales and assistance to Argentina. For text of the section, see 91 Stat. 619.

[25] Section 725 of the International Security and Development Cooperation Act of 1981 (P.L. 97–113), enacted December 29, 1981, repealed Section 620B of the Foreign Assistance Act of 1961, and it authorized military sales and assistance to Argentina provided that the President certified that Argentina had made significant progress in human rights and that such sales and assistance were in the U.S. national interests. For the text of Section 725 of P.L. 97–113, see *American Foreign Policy: Current Documents, 1981*, document 720.

Document 660

Paper Submitted by the Assistant Secretary of State for Inter-American Affairs (Enders) to a Subcommittee of the House Foreign Affairs Committee, August 5, 1982[26]

U.S. Efforts to Reach a Peaceful Solution of the Falklands Crisis During the Period of April to May 1982

Legal Aspects of Falklands/Malvinas Crisis Negotiations

This paper addresses three aspects of the negotiations which occurred during April and May of 1982 to avert the war in the South Atlantic: the United States posture on the underlying dispute over sovereignty of the Islands; the content of the three most intensive settlement efforts, focusing on the two in which the United States was most closely involved; and the consideration given to use of the International Court of Justice.

U.S. Position on Claims to the Islands

Throughout the more than 200-year history of this dispute, the United States has maintained a legal neutrality on the competing United Kingdom and Argentine claims to the Falklands/Malvinas, urging that their dispute be resolved through peaceful means in accordance with international law. In the post-World War II era, the United States has abstained on United Nations or Organization of American States resolutions that implied a position on the merits.

United States neutrality is also reflected in the United States position on the nonapplicability of the Monroe Doctrine. Because the dispute over the Islands predated the Monroe Doctrine, and because the United States took no position on the dispute over sovereignty, the State Department long ago expressed the view that the reinsertion of a British presence on the Islands in 1833 was not a new attempt at colonization, and that the Doctrine is thus inapplicable.

In addition to declining to take a position on the merits, the United States has not taken a position on the underlying legal theories on which the parties rely. Specifically, the United States has taken no view on the relative weight to be given to Britain's position on self-determination for the Islanders, and Argentina's emphasis on the principle of territorial integrity with the mainland. The application of the principle of self-determination to the Falklands has raised a number of legal questions in view of the size and origin of the population, the existence of other legal principles which may be applicable given the history and nature of the dispute, and, in particular, the interpretation placed by Argentina on the principle of territorial integrity contained in United Nations General Assembly decolonization resolutions such as Resolution 1514 (XV).

This United States position of neutrality was maintained throughout, and facilitated our attempts to mediate, the crisis.

While remaining neutral on the merits of the dispute, the United States has acknowledged the fact of longstanding United Kingdom administration of the Islands. The United States has accordingly dealt with the United Kingdom on matters related to the Islands and has on occasion acquiesced in United Kingdom accession to bilateral agreements and international conventions on behalf of them. The United States position in such instances has been consistent with acknowledgment of the United Kingdom's de facto responsibility for the Islands' foreign relations as the administering authority in peaceful possession. This pragmatic policy of dealing with the administrator in de facto control is also that of the United Nations, which has accepted from the United Kingdom, as the administering authority, annual reports under Chapter XI of the United Nations Charter regarding Non-Self-Governing Territories.

April–May 1982 Negotiations

There were three intensive efforts after the Argentine occupation of the Islands to avert the coming military confrontation; each resulted in textual elaborations of the positions of both sides on acceptable outcomes on the range of issues involved in a package to promote a peaceful settlement. All of these efforts addressed four common elements:

[26] Source: *Latin America and the United States After the Falklands/Malvinas Crisis*, pp. 127–134. Enders submitted this paper to the Subcommittee on Inter-American Affairs of the House Foreign Affairs Committee when he testified. For his testimony of August 5, 1982, see *supra*.

—a cease-fire, linked to a mutual withdrawal of forces within a short period, and a commitment on non-reintroduction of forces, subject to third-party verification (this element was consistent with United Nations Security Council Resolution 502, operative paragraphs 1 and 2 of which called for an immediate cessation of hostilities and withdrawal of Argentine forces from the Islands);

—interim administrative arrangements for the Islands, based on some form of third-party supervision of local government, including provision for Argentine access to the Islands during this period;

—the composition and definition of the functions of the third-party mechanism to assist the parties in implementation of an agreement; and

—a framework for negotiations to reach a definitive settlement, including a deadline or target date, and the role in such negotiations for third-party assistance.

Each side, of course, approached these common elements from a different perspective, which in some cases shifted as the diplomatic and military situation changed over time. The United Kingdom was willing to consider variations on the form of administration of the Islands, subject to certain basic guarantees in respect of local rights and institutions. It was prepared to accept third-party assistance in implementation of an agreement, subject to inclusion of some role for the United States. United Kingdom insistence on a cease-fire coupled with immediate withdrawal of Argentine forces from the Islands remained firm, consistent with its legal position based on Article 51 of the United Nations Charter relating to self-defense, and United Nations Security Council Resolution 502. The United Kingdom also insisted that nothing in an agreement prejudice the final outcome of the negotiations. This insistence focused in particular on the drafting of a formula on future negotiations that was neutral on the issue of sovereignty, and on provisions to control Argentine intercourse with the Islands at prewar levels, consistent with a 1971 agreement between the two countries.

Argentina, in turn, sought either effective interim control of the Islands' administration, including freedom of access to the Islands, or assurance that the formula on a definitive settlement would automatically result in confirmation of Argentine sovereignty over the Islands at some fixed future time. While accepting the concept of a cease-fire linked to mutual withdrawal of forces, Argentina sought an immediate United Kingdom withdrawal of its units to home bases; the United Kingdom viewed such a formula for the withdrawal period as imbalanced (since Argentine forces would remain within close range of the Islands) and as removing a necessary deterrent to Argentine violation of the terms of an agreement. Argentina sought drafting of the negotiation mandate to emphasize decolonization and the principle of territorial integrity with the mainland, and resisted references to a right of self-determination on the part of the Islanders which were desired by the United Kingdom. Argentina, in light of the long history of prior talks with the United Kingdom, took the position that the mandate had to be placed under a firm and short deadline date.

Both sides shared an evaluation that provisions on interim arrangements and the framework for reaching a definitive settlement were interlinked elements of the negotiation, each prepared to be flexible in one area for gains in the other.

The three principal initiatives are discussed below, and the resulting texts are attached.[27]

United States Proposal of April 27. The first effort, that of Secretary Haig, culminated in a fairly detailed set of proposals to the two parties on April 27. It was based on the three strenuous weeks of consultations he had held in London, Buenos Aires and Washington, and our best perception of what might ultimately prove acceptable to each side. Its approach, and many of its elements, reappeared in subsequent proposals to and by the two parties.

The United States draft memorandum of agreement provided for an integral cease-fire and withdrawal linkage. The formula for providing for balanced withdrawals proved troublesome in each of the three negotiations, given the vastly different geographic perspectives of each side. The United States proposal resolved the problem by a formula based on parity in reinsertion time, rather than on conventional but more difficult geographic withdrawal distances. These commitments, and that of non-reintroduction of forces into the Islands and defined surrounding areas, were to be verified by the United States.

The proposal called for immediate steps to terminate simultaneously the various economic and financial measures each party

[27] For these texts, see *ibid.*, pp. 135–151.

had adopted, and for the United Kingdom to request termination of similar measures taken by its allies.

Local self-government on the Islands was to be restored. The office of Governor was to remain vacant, and its powers exercised by the next-ranking official, appointed by the United Kingdom. The local Executive and Legislative Councils were to be retained, but augmented by representation of the small local Argentine resident population by means of at least one representative in each Council, and by inclusion of two Argentine Government representatives in the upper, Executive Council. A Special Interim Authority was to be created, composed of a representative of each side and of the United States. The flags of each constituent country were to be flown at its headquarters. The Authority was to have supervision over Island administration, exercised by means of a veto power in the event the Authority, by majority vote, deemed an act of the local government to be inconsistent with the agreement. In all other cases, the Authority was called upon to ratify expeditiously all local decisions, laws and regulations.

The proposal called for decolonization of the Islands as the negotiation objective. This was framed in terms of removing the Islands from the list of Non-Self-Governing Territories under Chapter XI of the United Nations Charter. The potential means were not limited, but the conditions for their definitive status had to be mutually agreed. The negotiation mandate maintained neutrality on the competing legal positions of the two sides, noting that of each by shorthand references to due regard for the rights of the inhabitants and the principle of territorial integrity. Reference was made to relevant United Nations General Assembly resolutions (which would include general decolonization resolutions and specific resolutions on the subject of the Falklands/Malvinas).

Foreshadowing the contact group concept utilized in later proposals, the United States formulation provided a role for the Special Interim Authority to catalyze the negotiations with recommendations to the two sides, in particular on the sensitive issues of how to take into account the wishes of the Islanders and the role of the Falkland Islands Company. If the negotiations did not prosper by the deadline date (December 31, 1982), a second phase of negotiations, under a new 6-month target date, was to occur in which the United States would act as a mediator/conciliator to press for an agreement.

With respect to contacts with the mainland, the draft agreement stated a principle of promotion and facilitation of nondiscriminatory travel, commercial communications, and other links. The proposal provided for recommendation by the Authority to the two Governments of specific measures on such matters, and for securing the views of the local Councils on the recommendations. These provisions were balanced by an obligation to respect the traditional rights and guarantees of the Islanders.

The United Kingdom, which had not yet landed on the Falklands/Malvinas or suffered any serious combat losses, found the proposal difficult, but was willing to give it "serious consideration." This was the only time the United Kingdom considered a proposal to cover the South Georgia and South Sandwich Dependencies as well as the Falklands/Malvinas (sensitivity to the implications of use of the English and Spanish names for the Islands resulted in the United States proposal defining the island groups by coordinates).

Despite many attractive features for the Argentines, the Argentine Foreign Minister replied on April 29 that the Government of Argentina could not accept the formulation since it gave them neither effective interim control nor assurances of obtaining sovereignty as a result of the negotiation process.

Peru–United States Proposal. At the initiative of the President of Peru, and with our cooperation, another effort was launched, culminating on May 5 with a more skeletal proposal, limited in geographic scope to the Falklands/Malvinas. A cease-fire and withdrawal of forces were inseparably linked, but all implementing detail was to be deferred for decision by a Contact Group composed of representatives of Brazil, Peru, the Federal Republic of Germany, and the United States.

The Contact Group was to verify the military provisions of an agreement. It would assume administration of the government of the Islands in consultation with the elected representatives of the Islanders, and ensure that no actions were taken inconsistent with the agreement. All details on implementation of administration—financial questions, applicable law, administrative, legal and appointive links to Britain, the role of the Councils, the exercise of powers of the office of Governor—were to be deferred for later decision by the Contact Group. The result conceivably might have paralleled the United States proposal once elaborated, but the door was open to other variations of third-party administration and the role to be played thereunder by the existing local institutions.

The existence of the parties' differing legal positions was noted; the proposal also included an acknowledgment that the "aspirations and interests" of the Islanders were to be "included" in a definitive settlement.

Finally, the Contact Group assumed a responsibility to attempt to ensure that the two governments reached a negotiated agreement on the future of the Islands by April 30, 1983. Again, the detail of modalities for the negotiation, and the role and procedures of the Contact Group in facilitating a result, were deferred for later decision. The negotiation formula was neutral, but included a deadline date as Argentina desired.

The United Kingdom indicated that it was willing to give this proposal serious consideration; Argentina, after the initiation of talks under the auspices of the United Nations Secretary-General, preferred to shift the focus of negotiations to New York.

United Nations Negotiations. With continued change in the military situation and, from the United Kingdom's perspective, in the wake of failure to secure agreement on the basis of substantial concessions reflected in the United States and Peruvian proposals, the positions of both sides hardened in a number of respects as evidenced by the texts each side publicly released at the breakdown of these talks in late May.

Both sides accepted the concept of a United Nations administration with generally defined authority. This formulation reflected a substantial concession by the United Kingdom on maintenance of administrative links to Britain in favor of local self-rule under United Nations supervision. Again, critical details would have had to be defined in implementing agreements or by United Nations Security Council resolution. United Nations verification of military disengagement provisions was also accepted by both sides in principle, as well as the auspices of the United Nations Secretary-General to conduct the negotiations.

The publicly-released positions permitted identification of very limited other common ground. The United Kingdom sought to subject a United Nations administration to local law and practices, "in consultation with" the Islands' representative institutions, which Argentina resisted. Argentina sought immediate, expanded access to the Islands, which the United Kingdom would not accept for fear that the population and character of the Islands might be unilaterally altered during the interim period. Argentina desired a firm deadline for negotiation to be followed, if necessary, by reference of the dispute to the United Nations General Assembly for decision; the United Kingdom rejected recourse to the General Assembly, and continued to consider a rigid timetable unrealistic. On these and other points (e.g., extent of geographical coverage; military withdrawal details; self-determination references), the two sides ended far apart.

The Secretary-General made last-minute proposals to the two sides before the talks unraveled. Prime Minister Thatcher, as events overtook these suggestions, simply noted that Argentina could not possibly have accepted them. We are unaware of any formal Argentine response. To our knowledge, the content of these suggestions was not publicly released.

Subsequent Developments. The United Kingdom and Argentine texts tabled at the conclusion of the Secretary-General's first round of negotiations remain the final textual elaboration of their views on settlement issues. There followed efforts in the Security Council to negotiate a resolution that would substitute for an agreement, notably involving a useful Brazilian draft text. None was the subject of intensive substantive negotiation. These efforts culminated in the Security Council's adoption, on May 26, of Resolution 505, which asked the Secretary-General to renew his good offices to secure a cease-fire; and in the United Kingdom–United States veto, on June 4, of a Spanish/Panamanian draft resolution that sought a cease-fire and implementation of the previous Security Council resolutions, under verification of the Secretary-General, but with inadequate detail on withdrawal procedures and other elements to serve as a mutually agreeable vehicle for settlement of the conflict.

Possible Role for the International Court of Justice.

The focus of United Nations General Assembly resolutions on the subject, the efforts of both countries over 16 years, and of the peacemaking efforts in the spring, was on a negotiated settlement of the dispute.

The United States Government is committed to the use of the International Court of Justice to resolve legal disputes, consistent with Article 36(3) of the United Nations Charter. The submission to a Chamber of the Court of our differences with Canada over delimitation of a maritime boundary in the Gulf of Maine is a concrete example. The dispute on sovereignty over the Falklands/Malvinas is an issue which the Court could appropriately decide. United States negotiators this spring raised this matter with both sides. Neither has ever indicated a willingness to have recourse to the Court over the Falklands/Malvinas. The case does not fall within the compulsory jurisdiction of the Court, and the agreement of both parties is thus necessary to submit the case for binding decision.

The United Kingdom on two occasions since World War II sought to submit to the Court the related dispute on sovereignty over the South Georgia and South Sandwich Island Dependencies, but Argentina did not agree to do so.

The United States continues to believe that a peaceful solution to this longstanding controversy is required, consistent with the United Nations Charter obligations of both parties, and it may be that possible use of the Court will be reconsidered among the other possible settlement options, including renewed negotiations, that would be consistent with Article 33 of the Charter.

Document 661

Resolution 37/9, Adopted by the U.N. General Assembly, November 4, 1982[28]

Request for Negotiation of the Dispute Over the Sovereignty of the Falkland Islands (Malvinas)

The General Assembly,

Having considered the question of the Falkland Islands (Malvinas),

Aware that the maintenance of colonial situations is incompatible with the United Nations ideal of universal peace,

Recalling its resolutions 1514 (XV) of 14 December 1960, 2065 (XX) of 16 December 1965, 3160 (XXVIII) of 14 December 1973[29] and 31/49 of 1 December 1976,

Recalling also Security Council resolutions 502 (1982) of 3 April 1982 and 505 (1982) of 26 May 1982,

Taking into account the existence of a *de facto* cessation of hostilities in the South Atlantic and the expressed intention of the parties not to renew them,

Reaffirming the need for the parties to take due account of the interests of the population of the Falkland Islands (Malvinas) in accordance with the provisions of General Assembly resolutions 2065 (XX) and 3160 (XXVIII),

Reaffirming also the principles of the Charter of the United Nations on the non-use of force or the threat of force in international relations and the peaceful settlement of international disputes,

1. *Requests* the Governments of Argentina and the United Kingdom of Great Britain and Northern Ireland to resume negotiations in order to find as soon as possible a peaceful solution to the sovereignty dispute relating to the question of the Falkland Islands (Malvinas);

2. *Requests* the Secretary-General, on the basis of the present resolution, to undertake a renewed mission of good offices in order to assist the parties in complying with the request made in paragraph 1 above and to take the necessary measures to that end;

3. *Requests* the Secretary-General to submit a report to the General Assembly at its thirty-eighth session on the progress made in the implementation of the present resolution;

4. *Decides* to include in the provisional agenda of its thirty-eighth session the item entitled "Question of the Falkland Islands (Malvinas)".

---

[28] Source: U.N. General Assembly Resolution 37/9. This resolution, sponsored by 20 Latin American states, was adopted by a vote of 90 (including the United States) to 12 (including the United Kingdom), with 52 abstentions. For the explanation of the U.S. vote by Kenneth L. Adelman, Deputy Representative to the United Nations, before the U.N. Security Council on November 4, 1982, see *infra*.

[29] For text of U.N. General Assembly Resolution 3160 (XXVIII) of December 14, 1973, see *Yearbook of the United Nations, 1973* (New York, 1976), pp. 713–714.

Document 662

Statement by the Deputy Representative at the United Nations (Adelman) Before the U.N. General Assembly, November 4, 1982[30]

Support for Renewal of Negotiations on the Question of the Falkland Islands (Malvinas)

Mr. President, the United States has always supported a negotiated settlement between the United Kingdom and Argentina in their tragic conflict over the Falkland Islands (Islas Malvinas). At the outset of the conflict, my government made sustained efforts to bring the two parties to the negotiating table. We said at that time, "the United States stands behind the principle that the use of force to settle disputes should not be allowed anywhere, and especially in this hemisphere where a significant number of territorial disputes remain to be solved diplomatically. For the United States, the Falkland crisis has been and still is a particularly agonizing, tragic event. As the whole world knows, we have a long-standing alliance and, beyond that, the closest relations of friendship with Great Britain, the country from which our political institutions, law and language derive. But we have not forgotten for a moment our close geographical, economic and political relations with our Latin neighbors. We do not only care about this hemisphere, we are part of this hemisphere, and we share many of the aspirations, goals and dreams of all nations of the Americas . . . "[31]

That is why the United States tried so hard to avoid the conflict on the Falklands, why we hoped so intensely to reduce and isolate it, and why we support any realistic diplomatic initiative which will put a just end to it. The search for a negotiated settlement to this conflict led the United States to support Security Council Resolutions 502 and 505. The essential elements of those resolutions remain the framework of the search for peace. The same vital need for a negotiated solution that would put this conflict once and for all behind us underlies our vote today.

This resolution before us, in its revised and final form, expressly reaffirms the principles of the United Nations Charter concerning non-use of force in international relations. We welcome its references to cessation of hostilities and to the intention of the parties not to renew them. The cost, in blood and treasure, to both Argentina and the United Kingdom dictates that force must never again be used in this dispute. We assume, therefore, in supporting this resolution a shared responsibility for preventing the use of force in the future.

The United States would not have voted for any resolution which prejudged the question of sovereignty or the outcome of negotiations. We have never taken a position on the question of sovereignty and we do not now do so. We conclude, however, that the resolution before us does not legally prejudice the position of either Argentina or the United Kingdom and, in fact, opens the way toward negotiations in good faith without any preordained result.

Finally, in calling on the parties to negotiate, let us not forget, Mr. President, that these islands are and have been for generations the home of a small, but resolute, population of island people. The United States assumes that negotiations undertaken by the United Kingdom and Argentina must necessarily take into account the aspirations of the Falkland Islanders.

In supporting this resolution, the United States affirms that this dispute, like all others, should be settled by discussion and never by force and that the fate of peoples should never be settled without due account being taken of their views, values, interests, and rights.

Let these principles and those of the United Nations Charter itself governing peaceful resolution of disputes serve as a basis for negotiation to close this unhappy chapter and move forward again toward peace, understanding and development in this hemisphere.

---

[30] U.S. Mission to the United Nations Press Release USUN–112(82).

[31] The quotation is from the statement by Ambassador Kirkpatrick before the U.N. Security Council on May 22, 1982; for text, see document 643. Ellipsis appears in the source text.

Document 663

Statement by the Representative at the Organization of American States (Middendorf) Before the General Committee of the OAS General Assembly, November 18, 1982[32]

Support for a Peaceful Solution "Without Any Preordained Result and Taking Into Account the Aspirations and Interests of the Islanders"

The United States is pleased to be able to support this resolution[33] as we were to support a similar resolution in the United Nations earlier this month.[34] Both resolutions are balanced and we believe that both hold promise for contributing importantly to a fundamental principle of our inter-American system; the maintenance of peace and the peaceful settlement of disputes that threaten international security. Armed conflict among nations is inevitably tragic, both for the parties involved and for the international community at large. For the United States, the conflict of the South Atlantic was especially tragic, for it involved one of our closest allies and a friend and brother nation of our own hemisphere. This may help explain the extraordinary efforts my country took to help the two sides find a path of peace in the South Atlantic.

The United States always has supported a peaceful settlement between Argentina and the United Kingdom in the Falkland/Malvinas dispute. Our sustained efforts during the conflict to bring both parties to the negotiating table offer irrefutable evidence of United States interest in peace, and the well-being of this hemisphere. That interest continues undiminished in this dispute as in other territorial disputes. The United States supported wholeheartedly the search for peace in the United Nations Security Council Resolutions 502 and 505 and, of course, most recently in company with many of our hemispheric colleagues in the United Nations General Assembly Resolution 37/9.

With respect to the description of the agenda item here,[35] the United States would have preferred adoption of the United Nations practice of referring to the Falklands/Malvinas in alternate, or the approach of the draft resolution itself which refers to the situation in the South Atlantic. Our voting for the resolution under this description of the agenda item is, of course, without prejudice to our well known position on neutrality on the merits of the dispute.

The resolution of this General Assembly supports United States [*Nations*] General Assembly Resolution 37/9 which reaffirms the purpose and principles of the UN Charter, and the OAS Charter, concerning the non-use of force in international relations.

With regard to the first preambular paragraph, we believe that it properly recalls the grave losses that have occurred from the conflict in the South Atlantic, and that, while the present circumstances in that area do not threaten the peace, dangers may always be posed whenever there is a failure to peacefully and definitively resolve a territorial dispute. This is a theme Secretary of State Shultz addressed in this forum on Wednesday.[36]

Moreover, the resolution before us, as was the case with the General Assembly Resolution 37/9, is evenhanded. It does not legally prejudice the position of either party to the dispute. By supporting the UN resolution it makes welcome references to cessation of hostilities and to the intention of the parties not to renew them. Thus it underscores the view of all of us that the only means permissible for resolving this dispute are peaceful means and helps to open the way toward finding a peaceful solution, in good faith, without any preordained result, and taking into account the aspirations and interest of the Islanders. It is for this reason that the United States voted to support this resolution, Mr. President. Thank you very much.

---

[32] Source: Annex III to OAS document OEA/Ser.P AG/ACTA 176/82, pp. 87–88. Middendorf spoke before the 4th session of the General Committee of the 12th regular session of the OAS General Assembly which convened in the Hall of the Americas in the OAS General Secretariat in Washington at 7 p.m.

[33] For text, see *infra*.

[34] For text, see document 661.

[35] The topic entitled "The Question of the Malvinas Islands" was included in the agenda of the 12th regular session of the OAS General Assembly at the request of Argentina. For the Argentine explanatory memorandum transmitted on September 17, 1982, see OAS document OEA/Ser.P AG/doc.1495/82 add. 1.

[36] For the text of Secretary Shultz's address before the OAS General Assembly on November 17, 1982, see document 618.

Document 664

Resolution 595 (XII-0/82), Adopted by the OAS General Assembly, November 20, 1982[37]

Support for Negotiation of the Sovereignty Dispute in the South Atlantic Area

The General Assembly,

Having seen:

That the serious events that occurred in 1982 in the South Atlantic area, within the security region defined in Article 4 of the Inter-American Treaty of Reciprocal Assistance, have given rise to a situation that affected and still seriously affects the peace and security of the American hemisphere;

That the Permanent Council of the Organization of American States and the Twentieth Meeting of Consultation of Ministers of Foreign Affairs considered these events thoroughly, and also urged the parties to the dispute in the South Atlantic to seek a peaceful solution; and

Considering:

That at the request of twenty American States, the Thirty-seventh General Assembly of the United Nations recently adopted Resolution 37/9 of November 4, 1982, with regard to this sovereignty dispute, and

That the aforementioned resolution of the United Nations also urges a peaceful solution to the dispute,

Resolves:

1. To express its support of Resolution 37/9 of November 4, 1982, of the Thirty-seventh General Assembly of the United Nations, in which the governments of Argentina and the United Kingdom are requested to resume negotiations aimed at seeking a peaceful solution to the sovereignty dispute as soon as possible, and the Secretary-General is requested to use his good offices to assist the parties in carrying out the aforementioned resolution.

2. To exhort the parties to the dispute to carry out that resolution.

3. To transmit this resolution to the President of the General Assembly and to the Secretary-General of the United Nations, so that note may be taken of the opinion of the American states regarding a situation that affects the peace and security of the hemisphere.

[37] Source: OAS General Assembly, Twelfth Regular Session, Washington, D.C., November 15–21, 1982: *Proceedings* (Washington: OAS General Secretariat, 1982), vol. I (OEA/Ser.P/XII.0.2), p. 27. This resolution, presented by 20 member states, was adopted by a vote of 20 (including the United States) to 0, with 7 abstentions, by the General Committee on November 18, 1982, and approved by the 8th plenary session of the 12th General Assembly which convened in the Hall of the Americas at the OAS General Secretariat at 11:30 a.m. on November 20. For the explanation of the U.S. vote by Ambassador Middendorf before the General Committee on November 18, 1982, see *supra*.

C. Mexico, Central America, the Caribbean

Document 665

Memorandum From President Reagan to the Secretary of State (Haig), January 28, 1982[1]

Determination to Authorize Continued Assistance for El Salvador

Presidential Determination
No. 82–4

Subject: Determination to Authorize Continued Assistance for El Salvador

Pursuant to Sections 728(b), (d) and (e) of the International Security and Development Cooperation Act of 1981,[2] I hereby:

(1) determine that the Government of El Salvador is making a concerted and signifi-

[1] Source: *Presidential Certification on El Salvador: Hearings Before the Subcommittee on Inter-American Affairs of the Committee on Foreign Affairs, House of Representatives, Ninety-seventh Congress, Second Session* (Washington, 1982), vol. I, pp. 2–3.

[2] P.L. 97–113, enacted December 29, 1981; for text, see 95 Stat. 1519.

cant effort to comply with internationally recognized human rights;

(2) determine that the Government of El Salvador is achieving substantial control over all elements of its own armed forces, so as to bring to an end the indiscriminate torture and murder of Salvadoran citizens;

(3) determine that the Government of El Salvador is making continued progress in implementing essential economic and political reforms, including the land reform program;

(4) determine that the Government of El Salvador is committed to the holding of free elections at an early date and to that end has demonstrated its good faith efforts to begin discussions with all major factions in El Salvador which have declared their willingness to find and implement an equitable political solution to the conflict;

(5) determine that the Government of El Salvador has made good faith efforts to investigate the murders of the six United States citizens in El Salvador in December 1980 and January 1981[3] and bring to trial those responsible;

(6) authorize the obligation of funds in fiscal years 1982 and 1983 for assistance for El Salvador under chapter 2 or 5 of part II of the Foreign Assistance Act of 1961,[4] the issuance of letters of offer and the extension of credits and guarantees for El Salvador under the Arms Export Control Act,[5] and the assignment of members of the Armed Forces to El Salvador to carry out functions under either of these Acts.

This determination together with the justification therefor shall be reported to the Congress immediately.[6]

This determination shall be published in the *Federal Register*.

RONALD REAGAN

[3] The reference is to Ursuline Sister Dorothy Kazel, Maryknoll Sisters Ita Ford and Maura Clarke, and lay missionary Jean Donovan, murdered in El Salvador on December 2, 1980; and to Mark Pearlman and Michael Hammer, land reform advisers murdered in El Salvador on January 3, 1981.

[4] P.L. 87–195, enacted September 4, 1961; for text, see 75 Stat. 424.

[5] P.L. 90–629, enacted October 29, 1968; for text, see 82 Stat. 1320; as amended by P.L. 94–329, enacted June 30, 1976; for the text, see 90 Stat. 729.

[6] See the report, *infra*.

Document 666

Report to the Congress by the Reagan Administration, Undated[7]

Justification for Presidential Determination to Authorize Continued Security Assistance for El Salvador

Section 728 of the International Security and Development Cooperation Act of 1981, PL 97–113, states that a wide range of security assistance may be provided and certain military personnel assigned to El Salvador only if the President makes a specific certification. The following constitutes the justification for this certification, pursuant to Sections 728(b), (d) and (e).

The issues on which periodic certification are [*is*] required have been important elements of the Salvadoran Government's policies since the overthrow of President Humberto Romero in October 1979. Romero was the last in a line of military officers who had ruled El Salvador for nearly 50 years. On October 15, 1979, a group of military officers who sought to introduce economic and political reforms overthrew Romero and created a civilian-military coalition called the Revolutionary Governing Junta. The original junta lasted 3 months. Its military members then reached an agreement with the Christian Democratic Party to form a new government. Despite several changes in its composition, this second junta has remained in power and is committed to sweeping economic and political changes aimed at reducing the causes of the present division and strife. The junta has instituted a series of reforms which are being implemented despite the violent opposition of groups on the extreme right and of Marxist guerrillas and terrorists, supported from Cuba and Nicaragua, who favor armed revolution. Each of the specific issues are addressed below:

Compliance With Internationally-Recognized Human Rights. A full report on the troubled human rights situation in El Salvador for

[7] Source: *Presidential Certification on El Salvador*, vol, I, pp. 4–9. The report accompanied a memorandum from President Reagan to Secretary of State Haig, dated January 28, 1982, *supra*.

1981 will be sent to Congress at the end of this month.[8] El Salvador is now in a state of active civil strife involving the government and armed groups of the left and right. As in similar circumstances in history, such civil strife has produced violations of human rights by elements on each side, because of partisan animosities, acts of retaliation, the settling of personal scores, and the disruption of the judicial system. These are long-term problems, and their correction is difficult over the short term.

Along with the general disintegration of institutions in El Salvador after the October 1979 coup, the judicial system had nearly collapsed by January 1981. Conditions of internal strife make it possible for terrorists to intimidate judges, witnesses, and government officials, blocking or slowing the process of investigation and judgment. Investigative efforts are impeded by the chaos caused by guerrilla and terrorist activities and movement of people out of the country and within it. These conditions greatly complicate the Salvadoran Government's efforts to bring an end to human rights abuses.

Despite coup threats from the extreme right, intensified guerrilla warfare from the extreme left, and terrorism from both sides, the Salvadoran Government has made significant progress in moving El Salvador toward a democratic process for resolving conflicts. It is also implementing important socioeconomic reforms designed to reduce the causes of the present terrorism and violence. Junta President Jose Napoleon Duarte's commitment to eliminating human rights abuses is a matter of public record. He himself has been the victim of abuses in the past. He was deprived of his electoral victory as President in 1972, arrested, beaten and exiled. Members of his Christian Democratic Party have been, and continue to be, victims of violence from both the extreme left and the extreme right. More than 20 Christian Democratic mayors were murdered during 1981.

The Salvadoran Government, since the overthrow of General Romero, has taken explicit actions to end human rights abuses. The paramilitary organization "ORDEN" has been outlawed, although some of its former members may still be active. A military code of conduct was adopted in October 1980 explicitly prohibiting any actions by military personnel injurious to human rights. While the Salvadoran conflict, like most civil conflicts, has been characterized by many examples of savagery on all sides, the military high command has instructed the officer corps to ensure that all soldiers adhere to the code of conduct. A number of officers sympathetic to the violent right have been removed from command positions or reassigned to positions less sensitive to the domestic situation. Nevertheless, ultra-rightist ad hoc groups still operate without official sanction. Their apparent loose organization and the intermittent nature of their activities, coupled with the apparent complicity of some individual members of the security forces, makes identification of possible perpetrators very difficult.

In sum, despite formidable obstacles, the Salvadoran Government is making a concerted and significant effort to comply with internationally recognized human rights.

Control Over All Elements of its Own Armed Forces. This is a key issue in attempting to ensure a democratic future for El Salvador. Traditionally, the National Guard and the Treasury Police were often used to serve the private interests of their officers and of powerful landowners and businessmen. It is a characteristic feature of many societies, including El Salvador's, that personal ties often are stronger than legal obligations to standing regulations or orders from top government officials. These relationships are extremely difficult to eliminate totally, making the establishment of full central authority over subordinate officials a slow process. Despite the obstacles, the government is gradually consolidating its control. Elections to set in motion a democratic process, whereby the people can choose their own leaders, will be a major step in strengthening the legitimacy of the central authorities.

Through the removal of officers, institution of a code of conduct, and command emphasis on civilian-military relations and halting abuses, the government has taken concrete steps to bring all elements of its armed forces under control. These efforts are beginning to have a positive effect. The level of violence—and particularly the number of deaths—is difficult to quantify, but statistics compiled by our Embassy in San Salvador indicate a declining level of violence over the past year and a decrease in alleged abuses by security forces. There has been a definite trend in this regard.

---

[8] An apparent reference to *Country Reports on Human Rights Practices for 1981: Report Submitted to the Committee on Foreign Affairs, House of Representatives, and the Committee on Foreign Relations, U.S. Senate, by the Department of State, Ninety-seventh Congress, Second Session,* Joint Committee Print (Washington, 1982), pp. 424–434.

Despite the government's intentions to do so, all abuses will not end in the immediate future. The guerrillas continue to justify terror and violence as acceptable tactics in their efforts to disrupt the society and overthrow the government. Moreover, guerrilla bands routinely operate accompanied by family members and other noncombatants, making it difficult to avoid noncombatant casualties when these groups are found and engaged by the military.

One of the principal missions of our military trainers in El Salvador is to increase the professionalism of the armed forces and improve the system of military discipline and command and control, thus reducing the abuses suffered in the past by the civilian population at the hands of the armed forces. To the extent that members of the armed forces see themselves first as military professionals, they are less likely to take action on behalf of partisan political causes or private interests. Discipline in the army and sensitivity to the problem of military abuse of civilians have improved and should improve further through professional training programs, such as those we are instituting for Salvadoran officers and infantrymen in the United States.

Economic and Political Reforms. When the Christian Democrats joined the Revolutionary Governing Junta they did so to open the political process in El Salvador and carry out socioeconomic reforms. One of the cornerstones of the reform program is land reform. This program has been particularly targeted by extremists of the right and left. Through assassinations of agrarian reform officials and intimidation of peasants, the extreme right seeks to defeat the implementation of the law, while the extreme left is attempting to derail a program that has seriously undercut its popular support. One part of that program, the distribution of landed estates over 1,235 acres to farmers who work on them, has been carried out and compensation to former owners is being made. A monthly report on beneficiaries, titles granted and compensation paid is now periodically provided to Congressman Long. A second part of the program is designed to transfer ownership of small farms to all tenants and sharecroppers. The titling process got off to a slow start. The process has accelerated since mid-year and provisional titles are now being issued at the rate of 4,000 per month. The Salvadoran Campesinos Union (UCS), in response to the government's request, has prepared a report detailing problems with the program which remain to be addressed in the months ahead. There is a legislative prohibition against U.S. assistance being used in planning for expropriation or in paying compensation to former landowners.

Other reforms already achieved include the establishment of marketing authorities for the country's major exports, coffee and sugar, and of government majority participation in the banking system. These ambitious changes are being carried out under wartime conditions, which makes implementation all the more difficult.

Free Elections. Free elections are the cornerstone of the Salvadoran Government's policy. President Duarte, other members of the junta, and Defense Secretary Jose Garcia, have made clear privately and publicly their commitment to free and fair constituent assembly elections in March 1982 and presidential elections in 1983. Planning for the constituent assembly elections scheduled to take place on March 28, 1982, is well underway. A central electoral council to conduct the elections has been established and is functioning. The elections council drew up a draft election law in May 1981 and invited all parties that renounce violence to participate in the electoral process. The new electoral law was promulgated by the junta in December after thorough discussion among the political parties. Seven parties, ranging from the nonviolent left to the far right, are participating in the process. The Salvadoran Government has sounded out dozens of democratic countries on the possibility of their sending electoral observers, and formal invitations were sent out at year's end.

The government has explicitly left open the door for others, including the opposition political-guerrilla coalition, the FMLN–FDR, to participate. Two leftist parties associated with the FMLN–FDR, the social democratic MNR and the Communist UDN, were designated by the government as legally constituted political parties with the need only to comply with a simple procedure to be inscribed on the ballot. President Duarte publicly invited all political parties and groups who renounce violence and wish to participate in the elections to join in a dialogue on the electoral ground rules. The government has offered amnesty to guerrillas and removed the legal state of siege for political parties, which will permit all to campaign freely. In response, the FMLN–FDR has denounced the elections and rejected the government's standing invitation to join in a discussion of electoral issues. Instead, the FMLN–FDR has maintained that any elections must be preceded by negotiations between the government and all elements of the FMLN–FDR resulting in a restructuring of the government and the military. Moreover, the guerrillas have prepared and are implementing an accelerated campaign of sabotage and terrorism to intimidate and to disrupt the elections, as evidenced by the attack on Ilopango Airport on January 27.

Efforts to Investigate the Murders of U.S. Citizens (required under Section 728 (e)). The investigations of the murders of the four American churchwomen and the two land reform advisors have been underway over the past year. All key Salvadoran officials fully recognize how important it is to resolve these matters and have stated publicly and privately that the investigations of these crimes will continue until those responsible are brought to justice.

In the churchwomen case, six members of the National Guard have been under detention since May 1981. On October 27, the Government of El Salvador formally requested additional FBI assistance with this investigation (and the land reform advisors case) and in early December an FBI representative saw leading members of the government most concerned with the issue. (In the early part of the investigation, the FBI had done fingerprint and ballistics analysis at the request of the Salvadorans.) To reinvigorate the investigation, the present investigating commission, composed of high-level officials, established a new working group in early December 1981 to collate prior reports, review and analyze them, interview all witnesses as well as the six National Guardsmen detained on suspicion of participation, and determine what technical assistance the FBI can provide. The working group has been hard at work throughout the past 2 months. It has uncovered additional evidence which gives hope of substantial new progress.

The Salvadoran Government has also been pursuing in good faith the investigation of the murders of the two American agrarian reform advisors at the Sheraton Hotel in San Salvador. Two suspects have been identified. In April 1981, the Salvadoran Government arrested one of the two suspects and requested the extradition of his suspected accomplice from the United States. On December 19 a Salvadoran judge signed an order suspending all judicial action in the case. The Salvadoran Attorney General has appealed this judicial action. The appeal has stayed the lower court's judicial order pending the appellate review. Meanwhile, one of the suspects has been released in San Salvador and is reportedly now in a neighboring country. The other suspect is free on bail in Miami pending resolution in U.S. courts of his extradition case. The new Salvadoran working group established to reinvestigate both this case and the churchwomen's murder case will shortly be pursuing, with our technical assistance, several new avenues of investigation which we hope will lead to additional evidence.

On these bases, it is concluded that the Government of El Salvador has made a concerted, significant, and good faith effort to deal with the complex political, social, and human rights problems it is confronting and that progress is being made. It should be noted that it is only 1 year since the general guerrilla offensive and outside assistance to the guerrillas from Nicaragua, Cuba, and other Communist and radical states forced the United States to reassess its policy towards El Salvador. Since that time our concern for the elements of this certification have become a factor of increased significance in our bilateral relationship with El Salvador. There can be no doubt that much more must be done in these areas, but significant initial steps have been taken in this short timeframe. Progress is apparent and we have every reason to believe it will continue.

It is therefore concluded that the considerations set forth in Section 728(d) and (e) of the International Security and Development Cooperation Act of 1981 are satisfied.

Document 667

Declaration by Representatives of Costa Rica, El Salvador, Honduras, Colombia, Venezuela, and the United States, Tegucigalpa, January 29, 1982[9]

Declaration of Tegucigalpa

The Foreign Ministers of the countries comprising the Central American Democratic Community, Costa Rica, El Salvador, and Honduras, meeting in Tegucigalpa, Honduras, with the Foreign Ministers of Colombia, Venezuela, and the Assistant

[9] Source: Department of State files; English translated text of Spanish original.

Secretary of State for Inter-American Affairs of the United States on the occasion of the inauguration of the new Government of Honduras, declare:

First—That the Foreign Ministers of Venezuela and Colombia and the Assistant Secretary of State for Inter-American Affairs of the United States met at the invitation of the Foreign Ministers of the nations comprising the Central American Democratic Community, in order to be informed about the community, the principles upon which it is based, the purposes which guide it and the fundamental objectives it seeks to achieve.[10]

Second—That the Foreign Ministers of the countries comprising the Central American Democratic Community, following a briefing on their reasons for joining together, set forth the following basic purposes:

1) The creation of a climate of security based upon confidence and stability.

2) The promotion of democratic values and the consolidation of representative democracy as a means of solving the problems facing their societies.

3) The reaffirmation of the unrestricted respect for, and defense of human rights, condemnation of terrorism and subversion, and reiteration of political solidarity with the nations comprising the community, especially in any situation in which any one of its members might be the victim of any form of aggression, threat, or any form of international pressure, in which case this solidarity would be based upon the principles and norms of inter-American legal instruments.

4) At the same time, the countries comprising the Central American Democratic Community propose individual and collective efforts to eradicate the fundamental causes of underdevelopment and exploitation; to individually and collectively make harmonious use of their natural resources, and to coordinate the activities of governments in the promotion, stimulation and development of the private sector, through production and investment.

5) The Central American Democratic Community invites democratic nations and those nations with greater economic resources such as Colombia, the United States, and Venezuela, to cooperate in the adoption, in the near term, of those actions and measures necessary to accomplish the community's purpose and objectives.

Third—The Foreign Ministers of Colombia and Venezuela and the Assistant Secretary of State for Inter-American Affairs of the United States express their satisfaction at the combined efforts proposed by the signatories of the Central American Democratic Community in favor of the strengthening and defense of democracy and the achievement of economic and social development; reiterate their support and their intention to cooperate in the fulfillment of principles and objectives of institutionalizing liberty, democracy, and development, upon the firm and true foundations of peace and regional security. At the same time, they express their desire to maintain a system of permanent consultation and information at the Foreign Minister level, in order to improve relations and perfect mechanisms which will make possible the completion of cooperative programs.

Fourth—The Foreign Ministers of Colombia, Costa Rica, El Salvador, Honduras, and Venezuela and the Assistant Secretary of State for Inter-American Affairs of the United States express the firm resolve of their respective governments to defend the freedom of their people and the sovereignty of their states, ratifying their absolute adherence to the principles and purposes of the OAS and UN charters and their intention to call upon the mechanisms offered by the inter-American system to defend their national integrity against any form of armed aggression.

Fifth—The Foreign Ministers of El Salvador, Colombia, Costa Rica, Honduras, and Venezuela and the Assistant Secretary of State for Inter-American Affairs of the United States declare:

A) Their unswerving conviction that the full development potential of the peoples of America can be fulfilled only through democratic and representative government in which the civil and political rights of citizens enjoy the same importance and protection as economic and social rights.

B) The renewal of their support for the resolution supporting the electoral process in El Salvador approved by the General Assembly of the Organization of American States adopted the 7th of December of 1981 in Castries, St. Lucia.[11]

---

[10] Regarding the formation of the Central American Democratic Community, see *New York Times*, February 4, 1982, p. A12.

[11] For the text of this resolution, see Department of State *Bulletin*, January 1982, p. 7.

C) Their desire that Central America be a region of peace, and to that end they condemn any kind of interference in the internal affairs of Central American nations.

D) Their rejection of an arms race in Central America which subtracts resources from the development of nations.

E) The clear necessity of offering the region economic regeneration, as recognized by the Nassau declaration of the 13th [*11th*?] of July of 1981[12] and by the resolution creating the Central American Democratic Community adopted the 19th of January of 1982 in San Jose.

F) Call upon the nations of the hemisphere who share the principles inspiring the community to lend their cooperation in solving the problems in the area by supporting the Central American Democratic Community.

Sixth—Finally, the Foreign Ministers of El Salvador, Colombia, Costa Rica, Honduras, and Venezuela and the Assistant Secretary of State for Inter-American Affairs of the United States propose to meet in the near future to consider the state of democracy in Central America and the measures which may be taken in its defense in the face of any kind of totalitarian aggression.

Seventh—The Foreign Ministers of Colombia, Costa Rica, El Salvador, Venezuela, and the Assistant Secretary of State for Inter-American Affairs of the United States express their deep satisfaction with the way in which the democratic process in Honduras has been culminated today under the exemplary leadership of former President General Policarpo Paz Garcia and with the full support of the Honduran Armed Forces, constituting a magnificent example of application and realization of the principles and ideals of the Central American Democratic Community. At the same time, they express their sincere best wishes to His Excellency the President, Doctor Roberto Suazo Cordova, in the performance of his governmental duties and their gratitude to the Government of Honduras for his generous hospitality and the many courtesies received during their stay in that country.

---

[12] For the text of the joint communiqué issued July 11, 1981, see *ibid.*, September 1981, p. 68.

Document 668

Prepared Statement by the Assistant Secretary of State for Inter-American Affairs (Enders) Before a Subcommittee of the House Appropriations Committee, February 1, 1982[13]

"The Decisive Battle for Central America Is Underway in El Salvador"

The President is expected shortly to sign a determination under Section 506(A) of the Foreign Assistance Act of 1961, as amended,[14] allocating up to $55 million in emergency security assistance to El Salvador. This assistance will be in the form of U.S. military matériel, services and training.

Why was this action taken?

First, because there is an unforeseen emergency requiring immediate security assistance.

After the failure of their much-heralded "final offensive" in January 1981, insurgent cadres appear to have rethought their strategy, concluding that the FMLN/FDR did not have the broad popular support necessary to achieve victory by frontal attack on the government and armed forces. They abandoned the strategy of building popular support and instead turned to attacking the economy in a "guerra prolongada" or war of attrition. The new strategy calls for hit-and-run attacks against small military units and lightly-defended economic targets, such as bridges, electrical transmission

---

[13] Source: *Foreign Assistance and Related Programs Appropriations for 1983: Hearings Before a Subcommittee of the Committee on Appropriations, House of Representatives, Ninety-seventh Congress, Second Session* (Washington, 1982), Part I, pp. 33–36. Enders testified before the Subcommittee on Foreign Operations.

[14] This section of the International Security Assistance Act of 1979 provides that the President, if he determines and reports to the Congress that an "unforeseen emergency exists which requires immediate military assistance to a foreign country or international organization" and the "emergency needs cannot be met under the authority of the Arms Export Control Act or any other law," may direct the drawdown of Department of Defense supplies, services, or military training in an amount not to exceed $10 million in any fiscal year. (P.L. 96–92; 93 Stat. 702) The $10 million figure was increased each year, reaching $75 million in the International Security and Development Cooperation Act of 1981. (P.L. 97–113; 95 Stat. 1526)

lines, and dams. The intention is to damage severely an economy that was already in crisis and to undermine the morale of the government and popular confidence in it. Since then, attacks on El Salvador's economic infrastructure have caused almost $50 million damage to electrical and communications systems, bridges and rail lines, bringing increased hardship to the Salvadoran people.

We watched this tactic develop, concluding by year-end that it was endangering not the Salvadoran Armed Forces, but people's livelihood. An economic emergency was resulting.

Meanwhile, Nicaragua was being transformed into an ever more efficient platform for supporting insurgency in El Salvador. We have watched as the FMLN headquarters unit was developed on Nicaraguan soil, clandestine logistics routes perfected, guerrilla training camps set up. The number of Cuban military and security advisors in Nicaragua doubled during 1981 to between 1,800 and 2,000. Munitions and weapons resupply to the insurgents in El Salvador is again approaching levels reached before the "final offensive." Nicaragua also brought in modern tanks and is preparing for the introduction of supersonic aircraft, thus acquiring an offensive capability. Nicaragua has become a twofold threat to its neighbors: as the supportsystem for insurrection, and because of the development of its offensive capacity.

Another factor is the FMLN/FDR's use of force and intimidation to disrupt the election campaign that began last week and will conclude March 28 with voting for a Constituent Assembly. This will be El Salvador's first step toward the establishment of a fully legitimate government—one elected by the people. After nearly 50 years of military rule, this is a bold but vulnerable move. The guerrilla FMLN is determined to sabotage and block the establishment of an elected government.

Finally, we faced an emergency of an even more urgent character. In the early morning of January 27, a guerrilla attack on the Ilopango Air Base outside San Salvador severely damaged a large part of the Salvadoran Air Force—including a number of the Huey helicopters we provided to El Salvador early last year at the direction of Presidents Carter and Reagan. The Hueys are El Salvador's only transport helicopters, and they are critically important to the mobility and rapid response capability of the Salvadoran Army—even more so in the wake of bridge and rail sabotage. The guerrilla success on January 27 will undoubtedly be followed by additional high-visibility raids on key military and civilian targets. Unless the helicopters are replaced quickly, the Salvadoran Armed Forces will be unable to respond effectively.

The magnitude of the military and economic challenge from the guerrillas could not be foreseen at the time the administration's revised FY'82 security assistance request was submitted to the Congress in early 1981. As a result, we have had to commit all of the $25 million in Foreign Military Sales credits and MAP grants made available by the Congress in the 1982 appropriation. Most of this assistance, $15 million, is financing the training in the United States of some 500 Salvadoran officer candidates and the 1,000 members of a second quick reaction battalion. Additional junior officers are essential to a modest expansion of the army; enlisted volunteers are plentiful, trained officers are not. Over the longer term, this training will improve Salvadoran military capability and command and control. It was not designed to meet, and will not meet, the short-term threat so graphically illustrated by the Ilopango attack. But having fully committed available funds, we have no means of replacing the equipment lost in that attack or of supplying the weapons and ground vehicles and communications gear urgently needed now to meet the mounting guerrilla effort to sabotage the elections. To withhold 506(A) assistance at this point would be to abandon El Salvador.

Second, because the decisive battle for Central America is underway in El Salvador.

Cuba is systematically expanding its capacity to project military power beyond its own shores. The arrival this year of a second squadron of MiG–23/Floggers and the 63,000 tons of war supplies imported from the Soviet Union in 1981 have added substantially to an air, land, and sea arsenal that was already the area's most powerful.

Nicaragua is being exploited as a base for the export of subversion and armed intervention throughout Central America.

If, after Nicaragua, El Salvador is captured by a violent minority, who in Central America would not live in fear? How long would it be before major strategic U.S. interests—the canal, sea lanes, oil supplies—were at risk?

For most of its life as a nation, our country has faced no threat from its neighbors. But, unless we act decisively now, the future could well bring more Cubas: totalitarian regimes so linked to the Soviet Union that they become factors in the military balance, and so incompetent economically that their citziens' only hope becomes that of one day migrating to the United States.

Third, because if we do not sustain the struggle now, we shall fall back into that terrible vicious circle, in which in Central America the only alternative to right-wing dictatorship is left-wing dictatorship.

General Romero's traditionalist military government was overturned 2 years ago by a military-civilian coalition committed to reform—land reform and the transformation of El Salvador into a democracy. We supported the reforms then, we support them now. And real progress has been made—for all the civil strife, even though there is a long way to go, above all in bringing violence under control.

Let me say a word more about violence before closing. Violence has always been high in El Salvador, but it became epidemic after the extreme left obtained outside support for armed warfare. The issue of violence and counterviolence has been and is at the center of our dealings with the Salvadoran Government. Some of it has been brought under control. Charges against the murderers of our countrywomen are about to be brought—at last our best estimates show a steady decline in noncombatant deaths over the past year, a thousand officers and men from the security forces have been transferred, punished, or retired, the extremist organization ORDEN abolished.

But it is not necessary to believe every alleged massacre story—in particular reports by the insurgent radio station of the killing of more than 900 people in Morazan appear highly exaggerated—to know that massive problems remain. This morning's report of the killing of 17 alleged guerrillas in San Salvador is a case in point. We do not know whether this was a guerrilla organization or not, whether arms were seized or not, but we are not ready to buy the notion that a firefight occurred and deeply deplore the excessive violence used against those involved. And of course, violence by the guerrillas—who boast of the casualties they inflict—goes on.

Our intention is to keep up the pressure, to get the problem of violence under as much control as it can be in circumstances of civil strife, in order to promote the full scope of our interests in the region, interests we believe are widely shared in this country:

—Defense of our national security interests against the Soviet/Cuban challenge;

—Promotion of democratic, open societies in our immediate neighborhood.

Document 669

Statement by the Assistant Secretary of State for Inter-American Affairs (Enders) Before a Subcommittee of the House Foreign Affairs Committee, February 2, 1982[15]

"The Control of Violence Is at the Center of Our Relationship With the Salvadoran Government"

MR. ENDERS. Thank you very much, Mr. Chairman.[16] It is a pleasure to be back. I do welcome the opportunity to come and discuss with the committee the certification that the President has made under law, and I welcome very much your opening remark that we should attempt to achieve a bipartisan approach to this very difficult problem that we all must face in Central America, a problem we cannot turn our backs on, however much we might wish to do so at times.

And let me say that on behalf of the administration that it is fully committed to the goals which were set out in the Foreign Assistance Act with regard to El Salvador. We understand the act to say yes, there is a challenge to our national security, and that is why economic and security assistance are authorized. But it says at the same time, we must use our assistance to help El Salvador control the violence in that country, make land reform work, develop a democratic process, and bring the murderers of our countrymen and countrywomen to justice. The certification that was made by the Pres-

---

15 Source: *Presidential Certification on El Salvador*, vol. I, pp. 24–29. For the text of Enders' prepared statement, see *ibid.*, pp. 30–36. The Senate also held hearings on certification; see *Certification Concerning Military Aid to El Salvador: Hearings Before the Committee on Foreign Relations, United States Senate, Ninety-seventh Congress, Second Session* (Washington, 1982).

16 Representative Michael D. Barnes. For Barnes' opening remarks, see *Presidential Certification on El Salvador*, vol. I, pp. 10–11.

ident last week shows that there has indeed been substantial progress toward each of the goals laid out in law.

Let me start if I could with the human rights issues. The law requires us to certify that El Salvador is making a concerted and significant effort to comply with internationally recognized human rights and is achieving substantial control over all elements of its armed forces. It does not say that human rights problems must be eliminated. It does demand progress.

There is no question that the human rights situation in El Salvador is deeply troubled, as is detailed in our annual report which has just been submitted to the Congress. The explosion of violence and counterviolence following the extreme left's receipt of outside support for guerrilla warfare has accentuated already high historic levels of violence, strained the system of justice to the breaking point, and eroded normal social constraints against violence. Countless violations of human rights have arisen from partisan animosities of both left and right, personal vendettas, retaliations, provocations, intimidation, and sheer brutality. The breakdown in this society has been profound and will take years to heal.

Accurate information—I think we all have found out that is very hard to establish. The responsibility for the overwhelming number of deaths is never legally determined nor usually accounted for by clear or coherent evidence. Seventy percent of the political murders known to our Embassy were committed by unknown assailants. And there is much special pleading going on also in this. For example, many of you have read about something called the Legal Aid Office of the Archbishopric—Socorro Judico is its Spanish name; it is often cited in the international media. It strangely lists no victims of guerrilla and terrorist violence. Apparently they do not commit violence. In January the Apostolic Delegate Rivera y Damas deprived this legal aid office of any right to speak on behalf of the Archbishopric. That was a statement which was approved by the other bishops of El Salvador.

There is another organization, the Central American University, that collects statistics, too. Its bias may be apparent from the fact that it does include a category of persons killed by what I believe Congressman Bonker[17] referred to as paramilitary organizations. And they are called in Spanish ajusticiados, referring to persons that have received justice at the hands of their executioners.

Finally, I should say that the organization that calls itself the Human Rights Commission, which occasionally issues statistics from outside the country, just did recently on the incident in Mozote, has become itself a propaganda vehicle for the insurgency. It has no independent information-gathering capability.

The most difficult of all to assess are the repeated allegations of massacres. The ambiguity lies in the fact that there are indeed incidents in which the noncombatants have suffered terribly at the hands of the guerrillas, rightist vigilantes, government forces, or some or all of them, but at the same time the insurgency has repeatedly fabricated or inflated alleged mass murders as a means of propaganda.

Last year in a widely publicized case, the massacre of 1,000 people in a cave was related by Radio Venceremos. Actually this charge had just been repeated by a Belgian priest broadcasting for the radio. It was picked up in the media in convincing detail until geologists determined that there was no large cave in that region, and the atrocity could not have occurred.

There was another incident in April when 600 people were alleged to have been killed crossing the border from El Salvador into Honduras at the Rio Lempa. We asked the United Nations High Commissioner for Refugees representatives if they could have a look, and they did and they found that there was no evidence of the outrage occurring.

On the other hand, as you yourself indicated in your opening statement, there are terrible incidents that occur. In my belief, one did occur 2 nights ago. The 19 people that died in San Salvador, I do not know whether there were weapons found there, whether these people were members of guerrilla organizations, but I find it hard to accept that there was a firefight, that this was a military action as has been alleged. And I deeply deplore as this Government does the excessive violence of the Salvadoran forces in this incident.

We sent two Embassy officers down to investigate the reports that you referred to, Mr. Chairman, of the massacre in Mozote in the Morazan Province. It is clear from the report that they gave that there has been a confrontation between the guerrillas occu-

---

17 For Representative Bonker's statement, see *ibid.*, pp. 12–15.

pying Mozote and attacking Government forces last December. There is no evidence to confirm that Government forces systematically massacred civilians in the operations zone, or that the number of civilians remotely approached the 733 or 926 victims cited in the press. I note they asked how many people there were in that canton, and were told probably not more than 300 in December, and there are many survivors including refugees now.

So we have to be very careful about trying to adduce evidence to the certification. We try, our Embassy tries to investigate every report we receive, and we use every opportunity to impress on the El Salvador Government and army that we are serious about practicing human rights and that they must be, too.

The results are slow in coming. I would agree with you on that. But they are coming. Since October 1979, the Salvadoran authorities have done much more than repeatedly emphasize to officers and men the need to protect human rights. They have broken the traditional links between large landowners and the security forces by outlawing the paramilitary organization ORDEN. They have promulgated a military code of conduct that highlights the need to protect human rights. They have transferred, retired, cashiered, or punished 1,000 officers and men for various abuses of authority, and they have gradually reasserted their control over scattered local security force personnel by strengthening the authority of the high command.

In consequence, the level of noncombatant violence, to judge by our best estimates and by the trends that appear in the two other agencies that I cited, the figures that they have, appear to have declined by more than half over the last year.

Mr. Chairman, let me focus on this because I think it is a matter of some importance here. The American Civil Liberties Union report, which I have read with deep interest, was published in or contained information which was up through or up to September 1981. It did not have available to it the figures that our own Embassy has been very carefully compiling since September 1980, and it did not have the advantage of the short-term trends rather than the broad general treatment that that report or those reports which are issued weekly can provide.

I would say that the same is true of the Amnesty International report,[18] which actually is without historical reference. It does not compare the earlier years, so that you cannot tell whether the crucial issue that has been posed by the certification process, the issue of whether there has been progress, can be judged, because I assume what is meant by progress in this instance is progress from the time of American involvement in El Salvador, progress recently, and sustained progress.

The figures show it. We have September, October, November, December figures for 1980 which show something on the order of 800, 779, 575, 665 political murders. That is for 1980. We have the same figures for this year which show September, 171, October, 161, November, 302. It shows December, 200. Our returns are showing markedly different numbers on the same methodology.

Let me be clear this is not a complete report. Nobody has a complete report. The Embassy says that maybe it is within 30 percent of the total, but I cannot say for certain that that is the case. But nonetheless, it is a coherent attempt to answer the question that you have raised, are we getting something more than merely exhortations or sweet words, are we getting some results. This is the indication that I submit to you that we are.

Let me make clear, Mr. Chairman, the control of violence is at the center of our relationship with the Salvadoran Government. We mean to see it reduced to the minimum level consistent with existing civil strife.

You mentioned the reforms. The law asks us to certify that El Salvador is making continuing progress in implementing essential economic and political reforms, including the land reform. I think you know that progress in land reform has been substantial in the sense that estates that are larger than 1,235 acres have been distributed to farmers who work on them, and compensation to former owners is being made.

The second part of the program transferred ownership of small farms to tenants and sharecroppers. I think this is politically and socially the most important part, but it has been the toughest part of the process. You said that you did not think that titling was going ahead. Actually it has accelerated. Titles are being issued at the rate of 4,000 a month, and a total of 22,000 have been issued.

You referred to the document that was issued by the campesinos' organization, the

[18] For a summary of the Amnesty International report, see *ibid.*, pp. 209–212.

Union Comunal Salvadorena, at the request of President Duarte. We did detail many problems of a security nature, desire to get on with the titling even faster than they have with the program, because we have been involved in trying to promote both, but when this request to accelerate the program was used by many in an effort to discredit, the UCS went out of its way to emphasize that the Government was responsive to its concerns, and that the union expected to participate massively in the election in consequence of this in its letter of January 25, more than a month after the report you cite:

"As for the Agrarian Document that was presented in an updated form to President Duarte by UCS in December 1981, dealing with the implementation of Decree 207, we note that many of the suggestions have been taken into account by the Government. . . .[19] This document was presented without any intention of giving ammunition to the enemies of the Land Reform Process.

"From December 1, 1981, the system of liaison between the Armed Forces and the UCS began to function and now we can rely on a high ranking responsible person who has a direct connection with the Ministry of Defense. . . . the political consciousness of the Salvadoran campesinos has changed substantially, influenced by the agrarian changes that have taken place lately. . . . we understand that the vote is a weapon of democracy and this time the elections will mean for us a definitive bond cementing our land tenure."

Anyone who wants to know what elections mean in a troubled society ought to think twice about that.

The law asks that we certify that the Government is committed to the holding of free elections at any early date. We think this is the case, Mr. Chairman. Preparations for constituent assembly elections on March 28, 1982, are well advanced. A new electoral law was drawn up after thorough discussion among the participating political parties. Eight parties ranging from the nonviolent left to the far right are now participating in the election. Momentum is growing. An independent labor group of campesinos and trade unions and the businessmen's association have appealed for the public to vote. The Council of Bishops, including the Apostolic Administrator of the Catholic Church, had this to say:

"We see in the elections . . . a possible beginning of a solution to the current crisis. . . . Through this Constituent Assembly election, we will pass from a de facto government to a constitutional government, which is of fundamental importance for the development of the country's life. . . . It would be ideal for all citizens to participate in the elections. That is why we regret that some of our brothers are rejecting them."

The law also asks us to certify in complex language that, to this end; that is, to the end of early free elections, the Government has demonstrated its good-faith efforts to begin discussions with all major political factions in El Salvador which have declared their willingness to find and implement an equitable solution to the conflict, with such solution to involve commitment first to renouncement of further military or paramilitary activity, and second, to the electoral process with internationally recognized observers.

Now, it is clear, Mr. Chairman, that the FDR/FMLN is not committed to the current electoral process. Guerrillas have burned down-town halls, threatened to kill anybody found with voting ink on his finger, and assassinated or intimidated local officials and candidates.

Nor—I think this is important—is the FDR/FMLN committed to elections in the future. An apparently authoritative December statement by the two organizations says only that there should be a plebiscite to ratify the Government after the guerrillas have gained a share of power.

This plebiscite would take place only after 6 months have passed and would not offer voters a choice between competing slates. In other words, with some cosmetics, this is the Nicaraguan model.

President Duarte, in contrast, has invited all political parties and groups to renounce violence and participate in the elections after an advanced dialog on the ground rules. Communists and social democratic parties were both formally recognized and invited to participate. Nonetheless, the FDR/FMLN refused even to discuss electoral ground rules.

You may recall Apostolic Delegate Rivera y Damas, who gave personal support to the election process, said that not to believe in elections or see in them a solu-

[19] Ellipses in quoted paragraphs appear in the source text.

tion gives no right to resort to blackmail and fraud on one hand or sabotage on the other. I believe voters have the right to express what they feel.

Mr. Chairman, I appreciate the opportunity to have discussed in detail the issues which I think are at the heart of the certification process.

I would recall, in summarizing the remaining part of my statement, that the Foreign Assistance Act expresses, as well as humanitarian and political values, the need to defend our national security interests and that those interests are incontestably being challenged in Central America in ways that we cannot ignore.

I would add to that that if we are not able or willing to sustain the struggle, to press on with the Salvadoran Government toward political and social reforms and the control of violence, that we will fall back into that terribly vicious circle that we have tried, all of us, to avoid in which in Central America the only alternative to a rightwing dictatorship is a leftwing dictatorship.

General Romero's traditionalist military government was overturned 2 years ago by a military civilian coalition committed to reform, the land reforms we have been talking about and transformation of El Salvador into a democracy. We supported the reforms then. We support them now.

Some may be proposing that we now cut off aid to El Salvador. I do not see, Mr. Chairman, how that could advance the goals embodied in the Foreign Assistance Act, whether they are security, democracy, or human rights.

I think it is pretty clear that the hope for democracy would be extinguished. We have only to look at Nicaragua. The Soviet Union and Cuba would have a new opening to expand their access to the American mainland, and the American mainland in Central America would become a factor in the East–West struggle.

I must say, I wonder how, given the experience that we have seen in Nicaragua with suppression of the Miskito Indians on the east coast and 5,000 political prisoners and repeated closings of *La Prensa*, and the independent radio stations, and the pressure on the church, I wonder how it would promote human rights to repeat the experiment in El Salvador.

Our intention is to keep the pressure on, to keep the pressure on our friends, to keep the pressure on the Government, and the army in order to promote the full scope of our interests in El Salvador.

We think that there is a wide agreement in this country that we should pursue two basic interests in El Salvador in the area: On the one hand, the defense of our national security interests against the challenge of the Soviet Union and Cuba; on the other hand, the promotion of more democratic and more humane societies in our immediate neighborhood.

Thank you, Mr. Chairman.

Document 670

Transcript of a Press Conference by President Reagan, February 18, 1982 (Extracts)[20]

U.S. Options in Central America

. . . .

Q. Thank you. Mr. President, the Secretary of State has said that the United States will do whatever is necessary to head off guerrilla victory in El Salvador. And that the mood of the American people should not necessarily determine our course there. Do you agree with that statement and under what conditions would you send combat troops to El Salvador?

The President. Once again, Jim, we get into an area, there are all kinds of options, economic, political, security and so forth, can be used in situations of this kind. And as I've said so often, I just don't believe that you discuss those options or what you may or may not do in advance of doing any of those things, except that I will say, lest there be some misunderstanding, there are no plans to send American combat troops into action anyplace in the world.

Q. I'd just like to follow that up. Can you just envision any circumstances under which we would be sending U.S. combat troops to El Salvador?

---

[20] Source: White House Press Release, February 18, 1982, Office of the Press Secretary to the President; also printed in *Weekly Compilation of Presidential Documents*, February 22, 1982, pp. 189–194.

THE PRESIDENT. Well, maybe if they dropped a bomb on the White House I might get mad.

. . . .

Q. Mr. President, have you approved of covert activity to destabilize the present Government of Nicaragua?

THE PRESIDENT. No, we're supporting them. Oh, wait a minute, wait a minute. I'm sorry. I was thinking El Salvador, because of the previous—when you said that—Nicaragua.

Here again, this is something upon which the national security interest—I will not comment. But let me say something about all of Central America right now, and questions on that subject. Next week I will be addressing the Organization of American States on that entire subject, and therefore, I will save any answers to any questions on that subject.

Q. If I could follow up—do you approve—or do you care to state what the policy is as far as having American covert operations to destabilize any existing government without specific reference to Nicaragua?

THE PRESIDENT. Yes. I'm going to say this is like discussing the options. No comment on this. Yes, George.

Q. Mr. President, although you have no plan to send combat troops to El Salvador, plans that could be developed quickly, I'd like to hear some expression of your commitment, if there is one, not to use American combat forces in El Salvador? And just how far will your administration go to keep the Duarte government in power?

THE PRESIDENT. George, your question again gets to that thing that I have always said I think has been wrong in the past when our government has done it—and I will not do it—and that is to put down specific do's or don't's with regard to some situation that deals with not only security matters but even such things as trying to influence a situation such as the one in Poland. I think that to do so is just giving away things that reduce your leverage. Judy.

. . . .

Q. Thank you, Mr. President. I'm sorry, but I'd like to go back to Latin America and El Salvador for a minute. In the 1960's, the CIA came up with a secret plan to get us involved in Vietnam in a surreptitious, covert manner. Is it possible that you can tell us that there is no secret plan now devised by the CIA or any other agency in government to surreptitiously involve Americans in similar activities in Latin America? And can you also assure the American people that we will not go in there secretly without you and this government giving us some pre-warning?

THE PRESIDENT. Lesley, you know there's a law by which things of this kind have to be cleared with congressional committees before anything is done. But again, if I may point to something. I'm not in total agreement with the premise about Vietnam. If I recall correctly, when France gave up Indochina as a colony, the leading nations of the world met in Geneva with regard to helping those colonies become independent nations. And since North and South Vietnam had been, previous to colonization, two separate countries, provisions were made that these two countries could by a vote of all their people together decide whether they wanted to be one country or not. And there wasn't anything surreptitious about it, that when Ho Chi Minh refused to participate in such an election, and there was provision that people of both countries could cross the border and live in the other country if they wanted to and when they began leaving by the thousands and thousands from North Vietnam to live in South Vietnam, Ho Chi Minh closed the border and again violated that part of the agreement. And openly, our country sent military advisors there to help a country which had been a colony have such things as a national security force, an army, you might say, or a military to defend itself. And they were doing this, I recall, correctly, also, in civilian clothes, no weapons, until they began being blown up where they lived and walking down the street by people riding by on bicycles and throwing pipe bombs at them and then they were permitted to carry side arms or wear uniforms, but it was totally a program until John F. Kennedy, when these attacks and forays became so great that John F. Kennedy authorized the sending in of a division of Marines. And that was the first move toward combat troops in Vietnam.

So I don't think there's any parallel there between covert activities or anything—

Q. Will you tell me that there will not be [a] secret plan, that you will not tell the American people about?

THE PRESIDENT. I can't answer your question for the same reason that I couldn't answer George's. I just can't answer on that.

. . . .

Q. Does the United States have solid evidence of increased movement in arms from Russia, through Cuba, to Nicaragua and other places in Central America? If so, what will you do about it?

THE PRESIDENT. We are convinced by the evidence that the arms that are flowing into Nicaragua are coming by way of Cuba, and their connection with the Soviet Government—they have shipped in a greater tonnage of arms this last year than they have at any time since the Cuban Missile Crisis. And we know that the Nicaraguan army is of tremendous size beyond anything that they might need for possible defense. But again I will not go beyond that because, again, next week—and Bill, I didn't call you by name because I thought that you both might have the same name, and then I would be in trouble.

Q. I would like to follow up that question. The understanding that was reached in 1962 between President Kennedy and Khrushchev that ended the Cuban Missile Crisis provided that the Russians would not in the future introduce offensive weapons into Cuba.[21] Some of the weapons recently introduced, like MIG's, may classify as offensive weapons. Do you believe that the Soviets in Cuba are abiding by the understanding not to bring in offensive weapons?

THE PRESIDENT. Again, you are talking on a subject that is under review and discussion right now in our administration and I would rather not answer that question now.

. . . .

[21] See the statement read by President Kennedy at a news conference, November 20, 1962, *American Foreign Policy: Current Documents, 1962*, (Washington, 1966), pp. 461–463.

Document 671

Address by Mexican President López Portillo, Managua, February 21, 1982[22]

"Let Us All Give Each Other a Last Chance"

Nicaraguan brothers, I have the privilege of being with you, among you, as I was 2 years ago, summoned by the name of Sandino, because of what this time of struggle and sacrifice meant to what is now seen as the path and model of liberation. With the people of Mexico, I deeply regret that this day was stained with the sacrifice of Nicaraguan blood. Please accept the condolences of the Mexican people and the firm message: Terrorism will not intimidate us and threats will not restrain us. [applause]

When I learned of the decision of the Nicaraguan Government and the FSLN National Directorate to confer upon me the order of Gen. Augusto Cesar Sandino in the grade of Battle of San Jacinto, which now does honor to my chest, as the representative of the Mexican people, I felt deeply honored by that decision, and most sincerely moved because it is an insignia that symbolizes the ideals of our peoples. I receive this decoration with great humility and I interpret it as a tribute to Mexican-Nicaraguan solidarity. Through me, Nicaraguan brothers, please receive the fraternal and sincere thanks of the Mexican people for such a high distinction.

We reiterate here what we have said publicly and in private to one party and the other: Central American and even Caribbean revolutions are above all the struggles of poor and oppressed people to live better and with more freedom. To describe them as something else and act as if they were otherwise is counterproductive. This in the end brings about that which one sought to avoid. Hope should not be cancelled and people and their rights should not be hemmed in. [applause]

Mexico's posture with regard to the Sandinist revolution is based on this assessment. Our support for the struggle of the Nicaraguan people against the Somozist tyranny was not a last-minute affair. Our support for the Junta of National Recon-

[22] Source: Foreign Broadcast Information Service, *Daily Report: Latin America*, February 22, 1982, pp. P6–P8. The source text indicates that it consists of excerpts from his speech.

struction and the FSLN during the equally difficult struggle to reconstruct a country that was destroyed and to consolidate a young state, was extended from the very beginning, and I believe that I can confirm that it has been unfailing. Today, now that time has passed, I can say loudly and with pride, and I am sure with the agreement of all Mexicans; our solidarity with the Nicaraguan revolution is a source of pride to Mexico. [applause]

For the aforementioned reasons, and because I fully share the authentic and supportive sympathy that struggles like this one have always generated in Mexican sensibilities; this support has become a true cornerstone of our foreign policy. It is not and will not be afflicted with the vicissitudes of repentance or disillusion and it will certainly not yield to terror or threats. [applause]

Neither foreign pressure and provocations nor the natural internal impatience and demands have altered the Nicaraguan leaders' commitment to their people. They have made no changes in the position that they have outlined to the international community on many occasions. I pay tribute here to such constancy and honesty in political conduct and to their firm determination to avoid bloodying the postrevolution. [applause]

To my Sandinist friends I say: Continue on your path, which is the one chosen by the people. Mexico has been and will always be at your side. [applause] Always at your side. It has been there in times of joy and it is there now in times of difficulty, in times when the horizon is darkened by the clouds of foreign threat, not only to Nicaragua, but also to the entire region.

An intervention in Central America and the Caribbean would represent a gigantic historic error, in addition to constituting a return to phases that sought to give rights by force. It would provoke a continental upheaval and the resurgence of a deep anti-U.S. feeling in the best men of all Latin America. I can assure—[interrupted by applause] I can assure my good friends in the United States that what is occurring here in Nicaragua, what is happening in El Salvador, and the wind that is blowing throughout the entire region does not represent an intolerable danger to the basic interests and the national security of the United States. However, they do imply a risk of historic condemnation if there is a violent curtailment of the rights that the U.S. people undoubtedly demand for themselves; self-determination with independence, dignity, and the exercise of sovereignty. [applause]

I am happy to have heard from Commander Ortega the five points that the junta has proposed and that have been publicly and openly accepted here by the Nicaraguan people. [applause] The fact that I also dare to say this publicly in front of these people means only that it is time for reason to prevail. The fact that we all agree to seek peace requires that we all adhere to peaceful reasoning. That is why I dare to outline my proposal to the people here, to the region, and to the United States.

It is not an overall peace for the region, since as such it could hardly be successful. It is a matter of proposing—through channels that are separate, if close and possibly convergent over the medium term—means for negotiation, for the exchange of concessions and formalization of these concessions that could lead to a climate of détente, peace, democracy, stability, and development.

This option necessarily implies two premises. Each interested party must make real concessions, and second, no one should be obliged to renounce his basic principles or his vital interests.

There are three thorny points in the region's conflict: Nicaragua, El Salvador and, if one wishes to look at things directly, the relationship between Cuba and the United States. [applause] I believe that if these last two countries were to follow the path opened by the talks between the U.S. Secretary of State and the Vice President of the Cuban Councils of State and Ministers, there would be real possibilities for dialogue to be converted into negotiations.[23]

The present détente in southern Africa allows for predicting certain real possibilities in this regard. I do not wish to go into detail at this point; however, we emphatically accept the possibility that Mexico may play a more active role in this regard. We have some useful ideas which we think are effective on the subject. They are based essentially on the complex, but not unresolvable system of mutual concessions by each party.

With every consideration, I dare to refer to El Salvador. It is obvious that the aggravation of the war, of violence, and of tragedy have reached extreme levels. Mex-

---

[23] Regarding these talks between Secretary Haig and Cuban Vice President Rodriguez, see *New York Times*, January 28, 1982, p. A4.

ico, which for some time has advocated a political and negotiated solution to the Salvadoran conflict, sees with great concern the increasingly limited possibility that negotiation will put an end to the bloodbath suffered by those people, who are subject to the risks of unbearable victories or intolerable intervention. Between elections without negotiation and negotiation without elections, there is undoubtedly a solution consisting of a commitment to a constituent assembly. I do not wish to go into this in detail at this time. I will say only that this solution could be one formula submitted to all the interested parties for discussion. Similarly, I believe that the main U.S. concerns regarding the possible consequences of a negotiated resolution of the Salvadoran crisis should be resolved. Mexico and other countries that are friends and even allies of the United States could be in a position to provide guarantees in this regard.

Finally, and I wish to be more specific in this case, I propose here a number of steps and ideas that fortunately coincide with those that have been expressed about Nicaragua's situation in the region. There are three basic points for a possible relaxation of tensions in the area.

First the U.S. Government must rule out all threat or use of force against Nicaragua. It is dangerous, unworthy and unnecessary. [applause] Invoking the close relationship between Mexico and its neighbor to the north, I reiterate from here my direct and respectful call to President Reagan, who fortunately has already made statements in this regard; no armed intervention in Central America and certainly not in Nicaragua. [applause]

Second, I say this with reflection and with the greatest consideration to these threatened people. It is possible and indispensable to begin a process of balanced reduction of military troops in the area. If the bands of Somozist guardsmen who are operating along the border between Honduras and Nicaragua are disarmed and if the training of similar groups within the United States is brought to an end, thus eliminating a real threat to this country's safety, one could believe that the Nicaraguan Government will simultaneously give up both the purchase of weapons and airplanes and the use of its scarce resources to maintain military troops on a scale that worries bordering and nearby countries. This is what I consider to be the truth, with all respect, Nicaraguans. [applause]

The third and last point is: I believe that it is feasible and desirable to draft a system of nonaggression pacts between Nicaragua and the United States, on the one hand, and between Nicaragua and its neighbors on the other. Such instruments would formalize previously reached agreements and, to the extent that they were not directed against any particular party, they would contribute significantly to the establishment of a lasting peace in the region.

I have no doubts that if this system of pacts became a reality, the main points of dispute in relations between Nicaragua and the United States could be resolved by negotiations immediately afterward.

These points constitute the public part of Mexico's proposal. They constitute a number of serious and realistic measures, free of demagoguery and of national or personal ambition. They are based on a simple, but decisive idea: If each party accepts that his neighbor should and can live however he wishes, the difference of interests and approaches are surmountable through negotiation.

On the foreign front, Mexico does not defend one or another ideology. It defends principles. It defends the supreme right of peoples to self-determination and to respect for the sovereignty of each country. In the name of these principles, in the name of responsibility that my position implies and in the name of the imperative need for peace, I make a call from Managua to peoples and their rulers: The consequences of failure are unthinkable. I appeal to men of good will. Let us all give each other a last chance. We will make good use of it. Thank you very much. [applause]

Document 672

Address by President Reagan Before the Permanent Council of the Organization of American States, February 24, 1982[24]

Caribbean Basin Initiative

Mr. Chairman, distinguished permanent representatives, Mr. Secretary General,[25]

---

[24] Source: *Weekly Compilation of Presidential Documents,* March 1, 1982, pp. 217–223. The President spoke at 12:37 p.m. in the Hall of the Americas at the Organization of American States in Washington. He was introduced by Ambassador Victor C. McIntyre of Trinidad and Tobago, Chairman of the Permanent Council. The address was broadcast live over the Voice of America system.

[25] Alejandro Orfila of Argentina.

distinguished members of the diplomatic corps, ladies and gentlemen: It's a great honor for me to stand before you today. The principles which the Organization of American States embodies—democracy, self-determination, economic development, and collective security—are at the heart of U.S. foreign policy. The United States of America is a proud member of this organization. What happens anywhere in the Americas affects us in this country. In that very real sense, we share a common destiny.

We, the peoples of the Americas, have much more in common than geographical proximity. For over 400 years our peoples have shared the dangers and dreams of building a new world. From colonialism to nationhood, our common quest has been for freedom.

Most of our forebears came to this hemisphere seeking a better life for themselves. They came in search of opportunity and, yes, in search of God. Virtually all descendants of the land and immigrants alike have had to fight for independence. Having gained it, they've had to fight to retain it. There were times when we even fought each other.

Gradually, however, the nations of this hemisphere developed a set of common principles and institutions that provided the basis for mutual protection. Some 20 years ago, John F. Kennedy caught the essence of our unique mission when he said it was up to the New World "to demonstrate that man's unsatisfied aspiration for economic progress and social justice can best be achieved by free men working within a framework of democratic institutions."[26]

In the commitment to freedom and independence, the peoples of this hemisphere are one. In this profound sense, we are all Americans. Our principles are rooted in self-government and nonintervention. We believe in the rule of law. We know that a nation cannot be liberated by depriving its people of liberty. We know that a state cannot be free when its independence is subordinated to a foreign power. And we know that a government cannot be democratic if it refuses to take the test of a free election.

We have not always lived up to these ideals. All of us at one time or another in our history have been politically weak, economically backward, socially unjust, or unable to solve our problems through peaceful means. My own country, too, has suffered internal strife, including a tragic civil war. We have known economic misery, and once tolerated racial and social injustice. And, yes, at times we have behaved arrogantly and impatiently toward our neighbors. These experiences have left their scars, but they also help us today to identify with the struggle for political and economic development in the other countries of this hemisphere.

Out of the crucible of our common past, the Americas have emerged as more equal and more understanding partners. Our hemisphere has an unlimited potential for economic development and human fulfillment. We have a combined population of more than 600 million people; our continents and our islands boast vast reservoirs of food and raw materials; and the markets of the Americas have already produced the highest standard of living among the advanced as well as the developing countries of the world. The example that we could offer to the world would not only discourage foes; it would project like a beacon of hope to all of the oppressed and impoverished nations of the world. We are the New World, a world of sovereign and independent states that today stand shoulder to shoulder with a common respect for one another and a greater tolerance of one another's shortcomings.

Some 2 years ago, when I announced as a candidate for the Presidency, I spoke of an ambition I had to bring about an accord with our two neighbors here on the North American continent. Now, I was not suggesting a common market or any kind of formal arrangement. "Accord" was the only word that seemed to fit what I had in mind.

I was aware that the United States has long enjoyed friendly relations with Mexico and Canada, that our borders have no fortifications. Yet it seemed to me that there was a potential for a closer relationship than had yet been achieved. Three great nations share the North American continent with all its human and natural resources. Have we done all we can to create a relationship in which each country can realize its potential to the fullest?

Now, I know in the past the United States has proposed policies that we declared would be mutually beneficial not only for

---

26 The reference is to President Kennedy's address at a White House reception for Members of Congress and the Diplomatic Corps of the Latin American Republics, March 13, 1961; see *Public Papers of the Presidents of the United States: John F. Kennedy, 1961* (Washington, 1962), pp. 170–175. The passage quoted by President Reagan appears on p. 171.

North America but also for the nations of the Caribbean and Central and South America. But there was often a problem. No matter how good our intentions were, our very size may have made it seem that we were exercising a kind of paternalism. At the time I suggested a new North American accord, I said I wanted to approach our neighbors not as someone with yet another plan, but as a friend seeking their ideas, their suggestions as to how we could become better neighbors.

I met with President López Portillo in Mexico before my inauguration and with Prime Minister Trudeau in Canada shortly after I had taken office. We have all met several times since—in the United States, in Mexico and Canada—and I believe that we have established a relationship better than any our three countries have ever known before.

Today I would like to talk about our other neighbors—neighbors by the sea—some two dozen countries of the Caribbean and Central America. These countries are not unfamiliar names from some isolated corner of the world far from home. They're very close to home. The country of El Salvador, for example, is nearer to Texas than Texas is to Massachusetts. The Caribbean region is a vital strategic and commercial artery for the United States. Nearly half of our trade, two-thirds of our imported oil, and over half of our imported strategic minerals pass through the Panama Canal or the Gulf of Mexico. Make no mistake: The well-being and security of our neighbors in this region are in our own vital interest.

Economic health is one of the keys to a secure future for our Caribbean Basin and to the neighbors there. I'm happy to say that Mexico, Canada, and Venezuela have joined in this search for ways to help these countries realize their economic potential.

Each of our four nations has its own unique position and approach. Mexico and Venezuela are helping to offset energy costs to Caribbean Basin countries by means of an oil facility that is already in operation. Canada is doubling its already significant economic assistance. We all seek to ensure that the people of this area have the right to preserve their own national identities, to improve their economic lot, and to develop their political institutions to suit their own unique social and historical needs. The Central American and Caribbean countries differ widely in culture, personality, and needs. Like America itself, the Caribbean Basin is an extraordinary mosaic of Hispanics, Africans, Asians, and Europeans, as well as native Americans.

At the moment, however, these countries are under economic siege. In 1977, 1 barrel of oil was worth 5 pounds of coffee or 155 pounds of sugar. Well, to buy that same barrel of oil today, these small countries must provide 5 times as much coffee—nearly 26 pounds—or almost twice as much sugar—283 pounds. This economic disaster is consuming our neighbors' money, reserves, and credit, forcing thousands of people to leave for other countries, for the United States, often illegally, and shaking even the most established democracies. And economic disaster has provided a fresh opening to the enemies of freedom, national independence, and peaceful development.

We've taken the time to consult closely with other governments in the region, both sponsors and beneficiaries, to ask them what they need and what they think will work. And we've labored long to develop an economic program that integrates trade, aid, and investment—a program that represents a long-term commitment to the countries of the Caribbean and Central America to make use of the magic of the marketplace, the market of the Americas, to earn their own way toward self-sustaining growth.

At the Cancun summit last October,[27] I presented a fresh view of a development which stressed more than aid and government intervention. As I pointed out then, nearly all of the countries that have succeeded in their development over the past 30 years have done so on the strength of market-oriented policies and vigorous participation in the international economy. Aid must be complemented by trade and investment.

The program I'm proposing today puts these principles into practice. It is an integrated program that helps our neighbors help themselves, a program that will create conditions under which creativity and private entrepreneurship and self-help can flourish. Aid is an important part of this program, because many of our neighbors need it to put themselves in a starting position from which they can begin to earn their own way. But this aid will encourage private-sector activities, not displace them.

The centerpiece of the program that I am sending to the Congress is free trade for

---

[27] The reference is to the meeting of leaders of developed and developing countries at Cancun, Mexico, October 22–23, 1981; for documentation, see *American Foreign Policy: Current Documents, 1981*, Chapter 5, Part F.

Caribbean Basin products exported to the United States. Currently some 87 percent of Caribbean exports already enter U.S. markets duty free under the Generalized System of Preferences. These exports, however, cover only the limited range of existing products—not the wide variety of potential products these talented and industrious peoples are capable of producing under the free-trade arrangement that I am proposing.

Exports from the area will receive duty-free treatment for 12 years. Thus, new investors will be able to enter the market knowing that their products will receive duty-free treatment for at least the payoff lifetime of their investments. Before granting duty-free treatment, we will discuss with each country its own self-help measures.

The only exception to the free trade concept will be textile and apparel products, because these products are covered now by other international agreements. However, we will make sure that our immediate neighbors have more liberal quota arrangements.

This economic proposal is as unprecedented as today's crisis in the Caribbean. Never before has the United States offered a preferential trading arrangement to any region. This commitment makes unmistakably clear our determination to help our neighbors grow strong.

The impact of this free trade approach will develop slowly. The economies that we seek to help are small. Even as they grow, all the protections now available to U.S. industry, agriculture, and labor against disruptive imports will remain. And growth in the Caribbean will benefit everyone with American exports finding new markets.

Secondly, to further attract investment, I will ask the Congress to provide significant tax incentives for investment in the Caribbean Basin. We also stand ready to negotiate bilateral investment treaties with interested Basin countries.

Third, I'm asking for a supplemental fiscal year 1982 appropriation of $350 million to assist those countries which are particularly hard hit economically. Much of this aid will be concentrated on the private sector. These steps will help foster the spirit of enterprise necessary to take advantage of the trade and investment portions of the program.

Fourth, we will offer technical assistance and training to assist the private sector in the Basin countries to benefit from the opportunities of this program. This will include investment promotion, export marketing, and technology transfer efforts, as well as programs to facilitate adjustments to greater competition and production in agriculture and industry. I intend to seek the active participation of the business community in this joint undertaking. The Peace Corps already has 861 volunteers in Caribbean Basin countries and will give special emphasis to recruiting volunteers with skills in developing local enterprise.

Fifth, we will work closely with Mexico, Canada, and Venezuela, all of whom have already begun substantial and innovative programs of their own, to encourage stronger international efforts to coordinate our own development measures with their vital contributions, and with those of other potential donors like Colombia. We will also encourage our European, Japanese, and other Asian allies, as well as multilateral development institutions, to increase their assistance in the region.

Sixth, given our special valued relationship with Puerto Rico and the United States Virgin Islands, we will propose special measures to ensure that they also will benefit and prosper from this program. With their strong traditions of democracy and free enterprise, they can play leading roles in the development of the area.

This program has been carefully prepared. It represents a farsighted act by our own people at a time of considerable economic difficulty at home. I wouldn't propose it if I were not convinced that it is vital to the security interests of this Nation and of this hemisphere. The energy, the time, and the treasure we dedicate to assisting the development of our neighbors now can help to prevent the much larger expenditures of treasure as well as human lives which would flow from their collapse.

One early sign is positive. After a decade of falling income and exceptionally high unemployment, Jamaica's new leadership is reducing bureaucracy, dismantling unworkable controls, and attracting new investment. Continued outside assistance will be needed to tide Jamaica over until market forces generate large increases in output and employment—but Jamaica is making freedom work.

I've spoken up to now mainly of the economic and social challenges to development. But there are also other dangers. A new kind of colonialism stalks the world today and threatens our independence. It is brutal and totalitarian. It is not of our hemisphere, but it threatens our hemisphere and has established footholds on American soil for the expansion of its colonialist ambitions.

The events of the last several years dramatize two different futures which are possible for the Caribbean area: either the establishment or restoration of moderate, constitutional governments with economic growth and improved living standards, or further expansion of political violence from the extreme left and the extreme right, resulting in the imposition of dictatorships and, inevitably, more economic decline and human suffering.

The positive opportunity is illustrated by the two-thirds of the nations in the area which have democratic governments. The dark future is foreshadowed by the poverty and repression of Castro's Cuba, the tightening grip of the totalitarian left in Grenada and Nicaragua, and the expansion of Soviet-backed, Cuban-managed support for violent revolution in Central America.

The record is clear. Nowhere in its whole sordid history have the promises of communism been redeemed. Everywhere it has exploited and aggravated temporary economic suffering to seize power and then to institutionalize economic deprivation and suppress human rights. Right now, 6 million people worldwide are refugees from Communist systems. Already, more than a million Cubans alone have fled Communist tyranny.

Our economic and social program cannot work if our neighbors cannot pursue their own economic and political future in peace, but must divert their resources, instead, to fight imported terrorism and armed attack. Economic progress cannot be made while guerrillas systematically burn, bomb, and destroy bridges, farms, and power and transportation systems—all with the deliberate intention of worsening economic and social problems in hopes of radicalizing already suffering people.

Our Caribbean neighbors' peaceful attempts to develop are feared by the foes of freedom, because their success will make the radical message a hollow one. Cuba and its Soviet backers know this. Since 1978 Havana has trained, armed, and directed extremists in guerrilla warfare and economic sabotage as part of a campaign to exploit troubles in Central America and the Caribbean. Their goal is to establish Cuban-style, Marxist-Leninist dictatorships.

Last year, Cuba received 66,000 tons of war supplies from the Soviet Union—more than in any year since the 1962 missile crisis. Last month, the arrival of additional high performance MIG–23 Floggers gave Cuba an arsenal of more than 200 Soviet warplanes—far more than the military aircraft inventories of all other Caribbean Basin countries combined.

For almost 2 years, Nicaragua has served as a platform for covert military action. Through Nicaragua, arms are being smuggled to guerrillas in El Salvador and Guatemala. The Nicaraguan Government even admits the forced relocation of about 8,500 Miskito Indians. And we have clear evidence that since late 1981, many Indian communities have been burned to the ground and men, women, and children killed.

The Nicaraguan junta cabled written assurances to the OAS in 1979 that it intended to respect human rights and hold free elections. Two years later, these commitments can be measured by the postponement of elections until 1985, by repression against free trade unions, against the media, minorities, and in defiance of all international civility, by the continued export of arms and subversion to neighboring countries.

Two years ago, in contrast, the Government of El Salvador began an unprecedented land reform. It has repeatedly urged the guerrillas to renounce violence, to join in the democratic process, an election in which the people of El Salvador could determine the government they prefer. Our own country and other American nations through the OAS have urged such a course. The guerrillas have refused. More than that, they now threaten violence and death to those who participate in such an election.

Can anything make more clear the nature of those who pretend to be supporters of so-called wars of liberation?

A determined propaganda campaign has sought to mislead many in Europe and certainly many in the United States as to the true nature of the conflict in El Salvador. Very simply, guerrillas, armed and supported by and through Cuba, are attempting to impose a Marxist-Leninist dictatorship on the people of El Salvador as part of a larger imperialistic plan. If we do not act promptly and decisively in defense of freedom, new Cubas will arise from the ruins of today's conflicts. We will face more totalitarian regimes tied militarily to the Soviet Union—more regimes exporting subversion, more regimes so incompetent yet so totalitarian that their citizens' only hope becomes that of one day migrating to other American nations, as in recent years they have come to the United States.

I believe free and peaceful development of our hemisphere requires us to help governments confronted with aggression from outside their borders to defend themselves. For this reason, I will ask the Congress to provide increased security assistance to help friendly countries hold off those who would destroy their chances for economic and social progress and political democracy. Since 1947 the Rio Treaty has established reciprocal defense responsibilities linked to our common democratic ideals. Meeting these responsibilities is all the more important when an outside power supports terrorism and insurgency to destory any possibility of freedom and democracy. Let our friends and our adversaries understand that we will do whatever is prudent and necessary to ensure the peace and security of the Caribbean area.

In the face of outside threats, security for the countries of the Caribbean and Central American area is not an end in itself, but a means to an end. It is a means toward building representative and responsive institutions, toward strengthening pluralism and free private institutions—churches, free trade unions, and an independent press. It is a means to nurturing the basic human rights freedom's foes would stamp out. In the Caribbean we above all seek to protect those values and principles that shape the proud heritage of this hemisphere.

I have already expressed our support for the coming election in El Salvador. We also strongly support the Central American Democratic Community formed this January by Costa Rica, Honduras, and El Salvador. The United States will work closely with other concerned democracies inside and outside the area to preserve and enhance our common democratic values.

We will not, however, follow Cuba's lead in attempting to resolve human problems by brute force. Our economic assistance, including the additions that are part of the program I've just outlined, is more than five times the amount of our security assistance. The thrust of our aid is to help our neighbors realize freedom, justice, and economic progress.

We seek to exclude no one. Some, however, have turned from their American neighbors and their heritage. Let them return to the traditions and common values of this hemisphere, and we all will welcome them. The choice is theirs.

As I have talked these problems over with friends and fellow citizens here in the United States, I'm often asked, "Well, why bother? Why should the problems of Central America or the Caribbean concern us? Why should we try to help?" Well, I tell them we must help, because the people of the Caribbean and Central America are in a fundamental sense fellow Americans. Freedom is our common destiny. And freedom cannot survive if our neighbors live in misery and oppression. In short, we must do it because we're doing it for each other.

Our neighbors' call for help is addressed to the us all here in this country—to the administration, to the Congress, to millions of Americans from Miami to Chicago, from New York to Los Angeles. This is not Washington's problem; it is the problem of all the people of this great land and of all the other Americas—the great and soverign republics of North America, the Caribbean Basin, and South America. The Western Hemisphere does not belong to any one of us; we belong to the Western Hemisphere. We are brothers historically as well as geographically.

Now, I'm aware that the United States has pursued good neighbor policies in the past. These policies did some good, but they're inadequate for today. I believe that my country is now ready to go beyond being a good neighbor to being a true friend and brother in a community that belongs as much to others as to us. That, not guns, is the ultimate key to peace and security for us all.

We have to ask ourselves why has it taken so long for us to realize the God-given opportunity that is ours. These two great land masses north and south, so rich in virtually everything we need—together our more than 600 million people can develop what is undeveloped, can eliminate want and poverty, can show the world that our many nations can live in peace, each with its own customs and language and culture, but sharing a love for freedom and a determination to resist outside ideologies that would take us back to colonialism.

We return to a common vision. Nearly a century ago a great citizen of the Caribbean and the Americas, José Martí, warned that, "Mankind is composed of two sorts of men, those who love and create and those who hate and destroy." Today more than ever the compassionate, creative peoples of the Americas have an opportunity to stand together, to overcome injustice, hatred, and oppression, and to build a better life for all the Americas.

I have always believed that this hemisphere was a special place with a special destiny. I believe we are destined to be the beacon of hope for all mankind. With God's help, we can make it so. We can create a peaceful, free, and prospering hemisphere based on our shared ideals and reaching from pole to pole of what we proudly call the New World.

Thank you.

Document 673

Testimony by the Secretary of State (Haig) Before the House Foreign Affairs Committee, March 2, 1982 (Extracts)[28]

"We Are Going to Succeed and Not Flounder As We Did in Vietnam"

[SECRETARY HAIG.] . . . Now let me turn to another area of great concern to us, the Caribbean Basin, where we face two distinct but related challenges: first, the economic and social upheavals that mark the development process; second, the threat to democracy and individual rights from the forces of totalitarianism in Cuba and elsewhere, supported by the Soviet Union.

Last week, the President spoke at length on our new Caribbean Basin initiative.[29] This program is a first step toward meeting these challenges. As the President explained, the United States will work with Mexico, Canada, and Venezuela to assist countries facing severe economic problems. The American part of the package includes trading opportunities, investment incentives, and increased financial assistance.

Beyond the economic challenge, the countries of the Caribbean are also confronted by a growing threat from Cuba and its new-found ally, Nicaragua. In recent years, Cuba has embarked on a systematic campaign to destabilize legitimate governments in Jamaica, Colombia, Honduras, El Salvador, and elsewhere. At the same time, Cuba has systematically expanded its ability to project its military power beyond its own shores. The Soviets shipped more military supplies to Cuba last year than at any time since 1962. Most notably, Cuba recently acquired a second squadron of Mig–23/Floggers.

In Nicaragua, Soviet, East European, and Cuban military advisers are building Central America's largest military establishment with Soviet-supplied arms. Disturbing accounts of the Government's campaign against the Miskito Indians are reaching the outside world. Meanwhile, the clandestine infiltration of arms and munitions from Nicaragua into El Salvador is again approaching the high levels recorded just before last year's "final offensive."

The United States has tried to communicate with Cuba and Nicaragua. We have offered a way out of confrontation. We have sought explanations for the massive military buildups that consume the scarce resources of development. But our efforts have thus far been rebuffed.

The threat to democracy from opponents of peaceful change is particularly acute in El Salvador. The Duarte government is committed to political reform, free elections, and economic development. Its opponents, supported by Nicaragua and Cuba, are determined to win by force what they could not achieve by the ballot. In the face of such threats to the democratic process, the United States has firmly stated its commitment to free elections.

The U.S. position has been embraced by the Organization of American States. At the meeting of the OAS in St. Lucia last December, 11 of 29 OAS nations voted in favor of the Salvadoran program for elections—only 3 voted against.[30] Indeed, a collective response to the danger is emerging within Central America. The Governments of Costa Rica, Honduras, and El Salvador, which recently formed the Central American Democratic Community, have now been joined by Venezuela, Colombia, and the United States to help carry through the democratic transformation of El Salvador.[31]

---

[28] Source: *East-West Relations—U.S. Security Assistance: Hearing Before the Committee on Foreign Affairs, House of Representatives, Ninety-seventh Congress, Second Session* (Washington, 1982), pp. 4–5, 17–21, 24–27, 33–40. Only those portions of the hearing dealing with Central America are printed.

[29] See the address, *supra*.

[30] For the text of the resolution adopted at St. Lucia, see Department of State *Bulletin*, January 1982, p. 7.

[31] Reference is to the Declaration of Tegucigalpa, January 29, 1982; for text, see document 667.

We must not be misled by the myth that the Duarte government has refused to negotiate an end to the trouble in El Salvador with the guerrillas. President Duarte has offered to negotiate on the electoral process, so that elections can proceed peacefully and the people of El Salvador can choose their own leaders without fear. The United States support this call.

I note that the Council of Bishops of El Salvador supports the electoral process, too, and has echoed the Government's call for all groups to desist from using violence to block the elections.

. . . .

MR. LAGOMARSINO. Thank you, Mr. Chairman.[32]

Mr. Secretary, on page 11 of your statement you say that you note that the Council of Bishops of El Salvador supports the electoral process there. As a matter of fact, the bishops have at least twice adopted such resolutions, once as recently as 2 weeks ago.

Last week in a hearing in this very room, three union leaders representing, it was said, some 500,000 campesinos, field workers, stated that they were supporting the process, too, and that they were going to vote and that their followers were going to vote, even though they knew that they had been threatened by the guerrillas that anyone with a violet-dyed little finger was going to stand a chance of being shot.

And that organization, the largest campesino organization in the country, has also endorsed the election process. I think that is very significant, because they are the ones who this is supposed to be all about and they are indicating that they want to go the electoral way.

The administration, as you have noted, has proposed a new Caribbean Basin initiative. I notice that, although the President did not mention it directly in his speech, that in the backup material there was an item referring to the role of OPIC, the insurance agency. I would urge on you that OPIC be made to play a large part in this proceeding because they have already been, as you well know, heavily engaged in the Caribbean, in Haiti, and Jamaica. I would hope more publicity would be given to their role so that business would contact them and would become aware of the services that they can provide in that area.

They are very important, because many smaller businesses, I think, can play a very active and very important role, especially in some of the smaller nations. And they do of course require that kind of insurance.

Would you share with the committee your views as to why the American people should care about the problems and prospects of the troubled area next door in Central America?

SECRETARY HAIG. Well, sir, I think much has been done to suggest there are strong parallels between the American approach today to Salvador and that to South Vietnam some years ago. I think this is a terrible distortion of reality and one which overlooks a number of fundamental differences.

First and foremost is the difference with respect to the strategic importance of Central America as a region and the member republics of the region to the United States. Today that region is our fourth largest trading partner. One-half of our oil moves through the waters of the Caribbean and the Canal. Roughly one-half of our overall global trade moves through that same region.

As a Nation, we have been plagued recently to the tune of one and a half million undocumented entries, illegal entries into the United States this last year alone—that is the year 1980, excuse me.

All of this underlies the strategic importance of the Central American region from the standpoint of military capability. At time of conflict, it would control the flow of our logistics support to our half a million Americans who are positioned forward in Europe to maintain the defense of those assets, not alone the importance of maintaining our ability to defend Western Europe at large.

So this is a vitally important region and it is a region today that is plagued by two extremely urgent dangers. The one is socieconomic, resulting from the inflated cost of energy to those governments, sometimes twentyfold, and the simultaneous decline in the remuneration for their one-or two-product economies. It has had a devastating socioeconomic impact.

And second is the willingness of the Soviet Union and Cuba to manipulate these human tragedies in the interest of spreading totalitarian Marxist-Leninist ideology, to do so with training, arms, and equipment. And you know, I often said about Southeast Asia, if America and the execu-

[32] Representative Clement J. Zablocki.

tive branch in its consultation with the Congress at the time had included a very careful assessment on whether the outcome in Southeast Asia was in the vital interest of the American people, had they concluded affirmatively, I believe they would have taken actions which were commensurate with that judgment. Had they concluded negatively, then we would never have become involved in the first instance.

Now, let me tell you, I come down on the side in such an assessment with Central America that the outcome of the situation there is of vital interest to the American people and must be so dealt with. Now, that means not necessarily some of the horrendous brow-furrowings that I notice developing on the committee, but a very sophisticated long-range approach, an approach that involves multilateralism, that avoids the danger of the risk of big brotherism from the colossus of the north.

Now, we are in the process of doing that in a style dealing in a multilateral way, an approach dealing with the socioeconomic needs of the region as well as the security needs of the region. And the order of magnitude is 5 to 1 in favor of economic development.

Now, this is an area of vital interest to the American people, and as I said recently, I know the American people will support what is prudent and necessary, providing they think we mean what we say and that we are going to succeed and not flounder as we did in Vietnam.

Mr. Lagomarsino. Thank you.

Chairman Zablocki. Mr. Fascell.

. . . .

Mr. Fascell. Mr. Secretary, I support the concepts of the Caribbean Basin initiative, because I'm convinced we do have to make a long-term commitment to those countries which are nearest to us for all of the economic, political, security reasons, all of the reasons that we know about so well. And I gather that we are to take from the presentation of this initiative that that is this administration's posture, that this is the beginning of a long-term commitment to the Caribbean Basin.

Secretary Haig. There is no question about it, and I think even the one-way free trade commitment is for some 11 years.

Mr. Fascell. Well, I am not ready to say that that is long enough or too short. But I just wanted to be sure that we are speaking the same language regarding the U.S. commitment to the Caribbean Basin. This add-on of additional economic and military assistance is to be viewed in that light. This is not a quick fix.

Secretary Haig. No, it is not a quick fix, except from the standpoint, Mr. Fascell, that we need a front loaded and quick application to get this overall program moving. The real long-term benefits come in the trade and investment area. But the reason we had to front load the $350 million is to get these economies into a position where they could even begin to buy the raw materials that they need to get the development process going, as an example.

Mr. Fascell. It has been alleged that most of this is budgetary support. Is that a correct allegation?

Secretary Haig. Budgetary support? I think in general, yes. That is what we are after. We are trying to get them viable in a terribly difficult situation—and we are just on the verge of being too late. We have got to move this thing quickly.

Mr. Fascell. Is there anything dramatic or more dramatic that we can expect with respect to the Salvador situation than we are now apprised of?

Secretary Haig. Well, I am not so sure that I can answer that question. I expect that the tensions and surprises between now and the election are going to grow, because Nicaragua, for example, is terrified at the prospect of a successful election in Salvador, and their efforts in support of the guerrillas have grown tremendously in recent weeks. Their officials have spoken to their concern about a successful election in Salvador and what that means in Nicaragua, which has postponed any election and any consideration of an election until 1985.

Mr. Fascell. The so-called right-wing candidate in El Salvador is publicly campaigning, is he not?

Secretary Haig. Yes.

Mr. Fascell. And as far as the guerrilla groups are concerned, they are still boycotting the electoral process, is that correct?

Secretary Haig. I think that is the current assessment and I do not anticipate it would change.

Mr. Fascell. What is our assessment of the efforts to totally disrupt the election to be held in March?

Secretary Haig. Well, as I say, I think these efforts will grow. There are some indications also, however, that it is putting a great burden on the guerrilla structure, because they have to take different kinds of tactics. They have to get into municipal areas. They have hit some of the election locations. They have got records. They are intimidating and blackmailing potential voters.

And I think it is going to have an effect, which again will give those that are looking for other solutions an excuse to say the election is not meaningful. The election as a process is meaningful and it is important that we continue to support it. And I am hopeful that it will be conducted with credible outcomes.

Mr. Fascell. I can see how people might argue as to how an election should be held. But I cannot see how people could argue that an election should be held.

What is the status of international observers at this election?

Secretary Haig. Well, we have had a rather encouraging response to the observer request from Salvador, which we have supported. Great Britain has agreed to send observers; 18 of the OAS countries have voted favorably to send observers, and not a single OAS participating nation vetoed such a proposal. Some did abstain.

Mr. Fascell. Thank you, Mr. Secretary.

. . . .

Mr. Hamilton. Let me come to another question.

One of your statements in an interview recently said that the El Salvadoran resistance movement was controlled from outside. I don't know if I quote you exactly, but that is approximately right. Now, what do you mean by that? Do you mean by that that resistance movement is controlled by the Soviets or the Cubans? It is [*Is it*] controlled by the Nicaraguans? Is it controlled by El Salvadorans located outside of El Salvador? That statement can be interpreted a number of ways, and it is an important one, at least in my attempt to understand the situation and what you mean by that.

Secretary Haig. What I mean is that the operations of the guerrilla forces inside Salvador are controlled from external command and control.

Mr. Hamilton. Now, is that external control—

Secretary Haig. Mr. Hamilton, I am not going to go into any great detail other than to inform you that the Intelligence Committee has been briefed and detailed this past week and the evidence is overwhelming and irrefutable. The trouble with it is when it is aired publicly, it puts sources in jeopardy, which I do not think would be a responsible thing for me to do.

Mr. Hamilton. Well, the trouble is when it is left as it is, it is very ambiguous and the ambiguity occurs because you can interpret that to mean that it is controlled by the Cubans or by Nicaraguans or it is controlled by El Salvadorans, and that makes a big differnce.

Secretary Haig. It is not controlled by El Salvadorans.

Mr. Hamilton. It is not controlled by them?

Secretary Haig. No.

Mr. Hamilton. So the command and control is controlled by foreigners, then, in the El Salvadoran instance?

Secretary Haig. That is correct. And of course, when you build a temple of the Soviet Union versus Cuba versus the Sandinista, clearly there are differences. You cannot just put a template and say each is totally equated to the other. On the other hand, there is a consistent pattern of a heavy Soviet involvement in the activities of Cuba worldwide, and conversely there are also, I am sure, things that Cuba does that irritates the Soviet Union from time to time because they are a sovereign nation, although they get a good bulk of their GNP from Soviet sufferance.

Now, the same thing is evolving in Nicaragua but probably in a more nascent state. Nicaragua is not a rubber stamp of Cuba but it is becoming one increasingly, and with every passing day the pervasive Cuban influence in Nicaragua is a source of growing concern not only to the United States but, even more importantly, to the neighboring states bordering Nicaragua who are beginning to feel, as is El Salvador, this activity. Costa Rica, for example.

Mr. Hamilton. Thank you very much, Mr. Secretary.

Chairman Zablocki. Mr. Goodling.

Mr. Goodling. Mr. Secretary, I have one comment that I would prefer that you do not respond to because I have two questions I want to ask you during the time that I have. My comment is that I hope that the Caribbean package will come to us in such a manner that I can do a little picking and choosing, or if not, that we can arrange it up here so that I might do that because I think that the whole economic package is something that, had it been applied 20 years ago, we probably wouldn't be faced with the problems that we now face.

I want to support that. I have no problems with security assistance to the struggling democracies in the area. I am reminded of a story of four elderly women playing bridge, talking most of the time, one trying to impress them about her furs. The second wanted to indicate that she had the best grandchildren. The third thought she would get into the topic of sex but was interrupted by the fourth, who said what was was, let's drop it at that. [Laughter]

And I just want to make sure that when we talk, then, about security assistance to countries other than those struggling democracies, that we truly know what was, was, and what is, is, so that we don't end up just providing the opportunity for more people to die in that particular region.

That wás the statement.

. . . .

MR. GOODLING. And one last question. I am sure you are aware that later today we are going to consider House Concurrent Resolution 226, that is, the Yatron resolution concerning efforts to establish a safe environment for elections in El Salvador. Would you care to comment on that particular resolution, how you see it, whether you think it is wise? Do you have any concerns or thoughts about it?

SECRETARY HAIG. Well, I think anyone welcomes suggestions, responsible suggestions for how to deal with this problem. We have had the position, taken the position of supporting President Duarte in his approach, and that approach is an aproach which does not, as some of the misinformed propaganda would suggest, reject negotiations. Not at all.

As a matter of fact, from the beginning he has called for negotiations. But one of the aspects that he has insisted on, and I think subjectively understandably, is a termination of the violence as a precondition for a sound electoral process. I would say there is a nuance of difference between that and the resolution you are talking about in that area that I would hope could be improved.

MR. GOODLING. Thank you, Mr. Secretary.

. . . .

MR. SOLARZ. Thank you very much, Mr. Chairman.

MR. SECRETARY, a few weeks ago President Portillo made what many of us thought was a very constructive and forthcoming speech in Managua in which he offered to use the good offices of Mexico in an effort to resolve the differences between our own country and Nicaragua and between our own country and Cuba, as well as to find a way to achieve a peaceful resolution of the conflict in El Salvador.[33]

As far as I could determine, both Nicaragua and Cuba have responded affirmatively to his offer, but I do not believe our own Government has yet been heard from. I would appreciate it if you could let us know what our response has been to President Portillo's offer.

SECRETARY HAIG. Well, as I pointed out in reference to the resolution which will be considered today, I think we welcome any constructive proposal that would offer hope for resolving the problem in El Salvador and Nicaragua and the hemisphere at large that is responsible, that is built on realistic and sound premises.

Now President Lopez Portillo's offer seemed to me to lack one fundamental ingredient, and it is an ingredient, incidentally, which I raised with the Nicaraguan Foreign Minister in fairly lengthy discussions and which have been discussed with the Government of Cuba.

In the smaller sense, the Nicaraguan-Salvadoran sense, it is that the parties who wish to responsibly negotiate a solution to the tensions must commit themselves to a termination of the illegal activities which are the cause of the tensions, and unfortunately that is not directly dealt with in President's Lopez Portillo's proposal. But we will continue to discuss this with our Mexican friends, as a matter of fact, in the not-too-distant future.

MR. SOLARZ. Are we prepared to have Mexico serve as an intermediary between ourselves and the Nicaraguans or the Cubans?

SECRETARY HAIG. I don't reject it and I don't accept it, though we are perfectly capable of conducting such discussions ourselves. But if good offices would help to bridge a problem, why we don't walk away from that either.

MR. SOLARZ. Mr. Secretary, as you will undoubtedly recall, in the spring of 1979,

[33] See document 671.

the Salisbury government, headed by Ian Smith, in then-Rhodesia, arranged for the so-called internal settlement elections in which the patriotic front refused to participate on the grounds that they felt they could not get a fair shake in elections supervised and organized by the security forces in that country.

Following the elections in the spring of that year, which by the way we supported, the British took an initiative which undertook to bring the war in Zimbabwe to an end through direct negotiations between the patriotic front and the Salisbury government. These negotiations ultimately succeeded in finding a formula for bringing the war to an end.

Do you think that we could support, following the elections in El Salvador, a comparable effort to achieve a negotiated resolution of the conflict in El Salvador in which the Government of El Salvador and representatives of the forces fighting them in the field would attempt to sit down, possibly with the help of intermediaries, to see if a way can be found to resolve their differences and bring the fighting to an end?

And if it worked in Zimbabwe, why couldn't such an approach work in El Salvador?

SECRETARY HAIG. Well, there are, of course, very important differences, and I am sure you recognize that.

I think the problem is to be sure, in whatever we do, Mr. Solarz, and the last chapter of Zimbabwe has not been written, that whatever we do we contribute to the self-determination and the free expression and the popular choice of the people of El Salvador.

And if we remain faithful to that principle, which is the ultimate of the democratic principles and values that you and I both espouse, then we are not going to be active participants in the distribution of power which results in an abuse of the interest of the people, and that has been the problem on this negotiation wicket. You know it as well as I do.

Now that does not mean that we are not prepared to consider and view positively any formula, any arrangement, which does not do violence to that principle.

MR. SOLARZ. Mr. Secretary, you have said in your testimony a little bit earlier that the preservation of a friendly government in El Salvador is a vital American interest. Does this mean that if the situation in El Salvador should develop in such a fashion that a military victory on the part of the guerrillas appears imminent that you would favor the introduction of American combat forces into El Salvador in order to prevent that eventuality from taking place?

SECRETARY HAIG. No, not at all. You know, you talk about dialectic fencing. I do not know of any official of the executive branch, Mr. Solarz, who has suggested for a moment that consideration is being given to the direct involvement of American forces in El Salvador.

However, without exception people keep asking and, let me tell you, there are no such plans under consideration. There have been none, and even were the worst outcome that you outlined to happen—and you distorted a little bit what I said about the vital interest—I would not be one who would suggest for a moment that if the people of El Salvador, on their own, without external coercion, without external subversion, without external command and control, decided on whatever political system, whatever political system, that is their business.

And so long as they do not use that system to upset the norms of acceptable international behavior and threaten their neighbors, that is their choice, and we have to support it.

Now I hope I have answered your question.

MR. SOLARZ. Well, you really have not, but since my time has expired, I am afraid I have no recourse at this time, but perhaps we can pursue this at some further point.

CHAIRMAN ZABLOCKI. Mr. Leach.

MR. LEACH. Well, I would like to amplify a bit on some of Steve's comments and to return briefly to the El Salvador issue.

I would like, as a Member of Congress and as a Republican, to stress one issue above all, and that is that in the last month there has been a quantum change in the American public perception of our involvement in El Salvador and the presence of military advisers. The existence of advisers jeopardizes bipartisan support for the President's foreign policy. It jeopardizes support for the party of the President in this fall's elections, and it jeopardizes support for the Presidency itself on a whole spectrum of issues, economic as well as security oriented.

And on this basis, as well as on the basis that many neutral observers believe that our approximately 50 advisers have served a counterproductive purpose, I cannot think of a more propitious time for their withdrawal.

I also cannot think of a more propitious time to welcome, in a very serious way, the initiative of third parties such as the Mexican President to serve as neutral intermediaries. Our Government risks a great deal if we, too, lightly spurn the initiative of Mr. Lopez-Portillo, especially on grounds as you have just outlined earlier, that we would demand preconditions for negotiations. Preconditions strike me as being nothing less than ridiculous at this point in our dealings in that part of the world.

Finally, I think it should be very clear that the U.S. Government today is walking or treading a very dangerous line with regard to respect for the law as it applies under the War Powers Resolution.[34] As you know, a year ago, the Department made it very clear that the War Powers Resolution did not apply because our advisers were not in imminent danger of being involved in conflict. But things have changed in the last year, and I would just ask two questions.

What prospect is there for withdrawal of our advisers? Second, what prospect is there of serious consideration of the initiative offered by Mr. Lopez-Portillo and, third, if there is no serious prospect of that type of negotiation and that type of withdrawal, I think the administration should be very prepared for the Congress to insist upon very strict compliance with the War Powers Resolution.

Secretary Haig. Mr. Leach, I suppose you have not taken your time with this preamble that I would like to ask you in what way you see the War Powers Resolution violated. I think that is important and you have not made that clear.

Mr. Leach. Well, perhaps I could read the War Powers Resolution—several citations from it. "The President is called upon to consult with Congress before the introduction of U.S. Armed Forces into hostilities or situations where imminent involvement in hostilities is clearly indicated by the circumstances." It looks to me as if hostilities exist. It looks to me as if, given the phenomenal new activism of the guerrilla operations, that the U.S. forces could easily be subjected to some sort of terrorist acts.

Also, if we look at the activism of recent events, it would seem that perhaps the situation has changed to the extent that the administration should consult with Congress under the provisions of this resolution.

Secretary Haig. Well, I would say that at this juncture none of the legal authorities with whom I stay in constant touch would share that judgment. It does not deprive you of your entitlement to make your speech, but I think 50 American advisers in a country that is being plagued with external intervention is not an unreasonable measure, especially when one looks at the ground rules under which they have been operating and continue to operate and, I must add, most successfully.

As you know, we have shifted the burden of incountry activity increasingly to external training and we have Salvadoran forces in our installations today in large numbers receiving the kind of training which we believe is in the interest of the American people and responsible government to provide.

Mr. Leach. Let me ask in return, do you really think that 50 people are making much difference for all the risks and liabilities that are attendant with them? We now have identified so closely with the El Salvadoran Government that we are partially considered in the eyes of the world to have intervened in a colonialist fashion. We have identified to the point of being pointed out as complicitous of human rights violations.

Is that risk worth taking for what 50 people can do?

Secretary Haig. I think it is more important to know what is right and not what the rest of the world may think, although it is important that we try to influence their judgment constructively and do what is right, Mr. Leach. And I hope that that will be your advocacy as well.

Now you can differ with me or with the executive branch on determining what is right, and that is your privilege and your responsibility, but I have an equal responsibility, and that is to tell you that I do not share the judgment you have premised your question with.

Mr. Leach. So you do not see an early withdrawal of our advisers?

Secretary Haig. Not at all.

Mr. Leach. Well, I am saddened.

Chairman Zablocki. The Chair wishes to advise that there is a rollcall in process and we probably have time for only one or

---

34 House Joint Resolution 542 of November 7, 1973 (P.L. 93–148, 87 Stat. 555).

two more questions. I really apologize to the members, particularly the lower bench, who have not had an opportunity to ask questions. Perhaps we could have the Secretary back at some future date to continue the meeting.

SECRETARY HAIG. Of course, Mr. Chairman. I welcome the opportunity to meet with the members, and even if some would like to in the next week or two meet informally, those who have not had an opportunity to ask questions, I am happy to do that.

CHAIRMAN ZABLOCKI. Well, we will continue with the questions and try to arrange another date and begin where we stopped.

SECRETARY HAIG. I feel rather disappointed myself, looking at the remaining agenda. [Laughter]

CHAIRMAN ZABLOCKI. Mr. Secretary, we call upon Mr. Studds.

MR. STUDDS. Let me see if I can lay upon you what you refer to as three inquisitorial burdens, or what I would have called questions. I would like to get at—

SECRETARY HAIG. You see, that's why you never get quoted in your staff meetings. [Laughter]

MR. STUDDS. You have to be very careful about these things. I would like to get at, if I can, your perception of what is going on in El Salvador, perhaps by way of calling on Mr. Solarz' attempts to do so and Mr. Leach's as well.

You in your testimony today have referred to the foreign components of command and control with respect to rebel military operations in El Salvador. Mr. Hamilton and others, I think, were trying to get how broadly important you think that is with respect to events as a whole within El Salvador.

I want to know how you perceive the opposition in that nation to its current Government. In other words, if there were no Cuba and if there were no Soviet Union, would there still be a revolution in El Salvador?

SECRETARY HAIG. Well, I think, Mr. Studds, there has been one revolution in the sense that over an extended period—and this is not uncommon throughout a number of Latin American republics—and I think you know as well as I that there have been a continuing dynamic evolution of political events and affairs, but if we take, for example, the early 1970's in El Salvador, where President Duarte along at that time with the current Social Democratic leader, Ungo, were elected successfully and again the pluralistic desires of the people were cast aside and junta arrangement—a military government—was imposed.

Subsequently, Mr. Ungo came in what we call a temporary compromise, which is moving, I think, constructively in the direction of pluralism. Now the question is, did they or are we going to continue to favor that pluralistic outcome?

MR. STUDDS. That was not the question.

SECRETARY HAIG. Or are we going to espouse policies which would introduce totalitarianism?

MR. STUDDS. That was not my question. That is your question. My question is if there were no Cuba and no Soviet Union on the face of the Earth today, in your judgment would there still be a revolution in El Salvador nonetheless?

SECRETARY HAIG. My answer to that question was there has been that kind of a revolution and I think the results of that would increasingly succeed. In other words, that there would be free elections. There would be a presidential election subsequently, and there would be a democratic government in El Salvador.

The disruption of that process comes from Cuba and the Soviet Union. Does that answer your question?

MR. STUDDS. No, it does not. I might have come to another question that it would have been an answer to, but that does not.

President Lopez-Portillo said in his speech that the Central American and Caribbean revolutions are, above all, "the struggles of poor and oppressed people to live better. To say they are something else and to act as if they were is counterproductive. You finish up achieving what you wanted to avoid." That is a quote from the President of Mexico and it was to that assessment that I really wanted your reaction.

SECRETARY HAIG. Well, I really avoid like the plague making public assessments of the heads of state of friendly governments. I have known Lopez-Portillo for some time. I consider him both a constructive force in the hemisphere and a good friend of the United States and, therefore, I am not going to engage in nitpicking him with extracted quotes.

MR. STUDDS. I did not ask you to nitpick.

Let me try one other thing.

SECRETARY HAIG. I might have been driven in that direction, Mr. Studds, quite possibly.

MR. STUDDS. Mr. Solarz referred to your words, I believe you said, of the situation in El Salvador and Nicaragua is of vital interest to the United States. Mr. Leach and others pursued that as well.

I want to know just how vital you think it is. You referred to the lessons of history and you also at one point mentioned Vietnam and I will, because of time, refrain from expressing my fear about this particular President of the United States drawing any lessons from the history that he seems to recall of Vietnam.

But let me ask you to what extent, if any—

SECRETARY HAIG. Were you there, Mr. Studds, in Vietnam?

MR. STUDDS. No. I was here trying to get us out of there.

SECRETARY HAIG. Where were you at the time, just for my own personal interest.

MR. STUDDS. Where was I when?

SECRETARY HAIG. During the Vietnam conflict.

MR. STUDDS. Which particular part of it?

SECRETARY HAIG. Start to finish.

MR. STUDDS. That, unfortunately, is how I got myself in my current mess. I ran for this institution because I thought it was a tragic error.

SECRETARY HAIG. I recall that, yes, all right.

MR. STUDDS. I am hopefully not about to see the same error repeated. The question is this: To what extent, if any, do you perceive the national security of this country—of our country—imperiled by the events in Central America?

SECRETARY HAIG. Well, Mr. Studds, we are not talking about prestige. That is not the question of vital interest.

I think we are talking about the strategic significance of a region and that is what I referred to in the earlier question. That region, in unfriendly hands or in the hands of governments that were influenced by Marxist-Leninist direction from Moscow through Cuba, would be a very serious threat to the American people.

But, you know, if you look worldwide at the refugee movement over the past 5 or 6 years, where have the host of refugees come from? They have come from Communist Marxist-Leninist repression and I hope you have given careful thought to the impact of totalitarian regimes in this hemisphere and especially in Central America, where today we have an unprecedented flow of immigration.

Now I think that is something American people understand and especially American legislators with local constituencies for whom they must answer questions.

MR. STUDDS. Well, I will try to think about that if you promise to think about what my question was. You almost made me forget it.

SECRETARY HAIG. Well, if I could do that, then I have been very clever today.

MR. STUDDS. The question had to do with national security and not prestige and not illegal immigrants.

SECRETARY HAIG. No, that is a vital aspect of national security, clearly. I am talking about the geostrategic location, the trade routes, the control.

MR. STUDDS. Mr. Leach's point, if I understood it, is that if you believe that the security of the Nation is threatened by the events in Nicaragua and El Salvador, then obviously, as the President of this Nation or the Secretary of State of this Nation, there is virtually no limit to the steps that one will take in order to protect what is perceived to be a threat to our national security.

SECRETARY HAIG. Well, I don't know that I would like to put it in the terms of there being virtually no limits to steps that would be taken. I would suggest that it would be more appropriate to portray the imperatives that are associated with vital interest in terms of what are the most prudent and most likely to succeed steps that can be realistically taken.

CHAIRMAN ZABLOCKI. The Chair will have to close this meeting, Mr. Secretary. The Secretary has exceeded his time by 15 minutes and we have a rollcall. I am tempted to close this meeting as some of the TV dramas close.

The continuation of the second serial of this hearing will be scheduled at the earliest possible date and hold your breath until that date. The committee stands adjourned, subject to the call of the Chair.

Document 674

Statement by the Assistant Secretary of State for Inter-American Affairs (Enders) Before the House Committee on Foreign Affairs, March 3, 1982[35]

Radio Marti

Thank you very much, Mr. Chairman.[36]

It is a pleasure to be back before the committee in support of this important bill.

Perhaps in presenting the proposal, Mr. Chairman, I could start with Cuban society itself. Cuba is not a country like other countries. There have been improvements in social and health services over the last 20 years, but they are perhaps much less impressive than might have been expected in a country like that.

The economy, which is organized in a familiar Soviet command model, has registered a general failure. Despite growing Soviet assistance in sales of oil at low prices and purchases of sugar at high prices—and it is worth noting that the whole Soviet aid effort is the equivalent of about one-quarter of the GNP of Cuba—per capita income has been stagnant and steadily falling relative to much of Latin America. Yet Cuba projects power in the world. The Soviet Union is subsidizing it with about $3 billion in economic aid, and last year alone gave it some 66,000 tons of military equipment and war supplies.

With this kind of assistance Cuba's Armed Forces are stronger than any other in the Western Hemisphere other than the United States. It has 40,000 soldiers in Africa, dominates 2 countries there, does in Africa for the Soviet Union what the Gurkha mercenaries did for 19th century England. In Central America, Cuba is attempting to unite the left and is committed to the violent overthrow of established governments, and it maintains no less than 1,800 to 2,000 military and security personnel in Nicaragua.

In other words, Mr. Chairman, what we have here is a would-be foreign policy giant allied to an economic pygmy whose peoples have had to sacrifice all hope for a rising standard of living to foreign advantages.

Most countries cannot overcommit to state interests in a manner of this sort because the people force them to address the people's concerns. But Cubans lack the means to hold their government accountable.

The proposal that we discuss today—Radio Marti—is intended to supply what the Cuban public is missing: Reliable news about Cuban life, features, sports, and entertainment that are alternatives to those offered by a government that rules not for the people but for itself.

This is not a proposal to tell the Cuban people about the United States. The Voice of America, whose charter is international news and American features and culture, already does that. It can be heard in Spanish. So also can Florida radio stations broadcasting in Spanish to Cuban-Americans. These stations can tell Cubans much about us, but they are not a good source of information about what is going on in Cuba itself.

Nor is this a project to incite Cubans to revolt against their own society. There is provocation enough in the redistributed poverty, in the depressing austerity, in the unemployment and underemployment of educated Cubans, in the rigid regimentation and in Castro's speeches that only further sacrifice life ahead. But it would be immoral and irresponsible to attempt to set a people against a government that monopolizes the means of coercion.

This radio is a proposal to give Cubans the means they now lack to know what kind of society has been imposed on them, to have a source of news and entertainment that is not manipulated by the state, to find out what is really happening in their country, why so many have gone off to foreign military duty, not always to return, and what the state does with the wealth of the Cuban people.

The radio, like Radio Free Europe and Radio Liberty before it, is intended gradual-

---

[35] Source: *Radio Broadcasting to Cuba (Radio Marti): Hearings and Markup Before the Committee in Foreign Affairs, House of Representatives, Ninety-seventh Congress, Second Session* (Washington, 1982), pp. 1–5. For the Senate hearing on Radio Marti, see *Departments of State, Justice, and Commerce, the Judiciary, and Related Agencies Appropriations for Fiscal Year 1983: Hearings Before a Subcommittee of the Committee on Appropriations, United States Senate, Ninety-seventh Congress, Second Session* (Washington, 1982), Part 2, pp. 707–741. The House passed a bill (H.R. 5427) providing funding for Radio Marti on August 10, 1982. The Senate reported (S. Rept. 97–544) the House version of the bill with amendments on September 15. Debate on the proposal did not begin until December 6, and the bill never came to a vote due to a filibuster; see the discussion in *Congress and Foreign Policy 1982*, Committee on Foreign Affairs, U.S. House of Representatives, Committee Print (Washington, 1983), pp. 92–94.

[36] Representative Clement J. Zablocki.

ly to earn its audience through its special sensitivity to needs the state ignores. It will speak to young people of the sports and music they love. It will speak to adults of the great Cuban and Hispanic-American heritage they admire, which so often the state denatures. And it will give news on whose probity listeners can rely.

We know that in Eastern Europe it took years to earn an audience. Little by little that audience expanded. Radio Free Europe now has perhaps 70 percent of the Polish radio audience. Can there be any real doubt that the changes of the last decade would have occurred without that trustworthy, humane outside contact?

Our proposal is thus to begin a sustained effort over many years to help the Cubans know more about their country and thus to hold the government accountable in ways that it is not possible now to do.

People say to us would it not be better to negotiate with the Cubans; or it is not like us to engage in propaganda; or then Cuban countermeasures will hurt us too much.

Well, we have tried to talk with Cuba in the past, and it would be wrong to rule out trying it again. But I have to say that the record is daunting.

In 1977 we started talking seriously to the Cubans, saying we wanted to create conditions in which the legacy of the past—the embargo, political tension—could be overcome. We suggested a gradual withdrawal of the more than 20,000 Cuban troops from Angola. After all, we said, the civil war was over. The need for foreign intervention was difficult to argue. But while we talked, Cuba went into Ethiopia.

Conversations continued. In mid-1978 Cuba launched upon an aggressive strategy in Central America, uniting the left parties first of Nicaragua, then of El Salvador, then of Guatemala, committing them to the destruction of established governments. Talks went on. In 1980, while we were still talking, Castro turned the desire of many of his countrymen to flee Cuba into a hostile act against the United States—the Mariel boatlift.

Mr. Chairman, it is not wrong to talk to adversaries. Often it is only prudent. But what counts is not the medium but the message in this case. Talks cannot be a complete Cuban policy any more than diplomatic exchanges are a complete Soviet or Polish policy. Diplomacy enables us to talk to the government. We must also talk to the people.

Others ask should we be associated with propaganda? No; we should not be associated with propaganda. We will not succeed in attracting an audience in Cuba if we offer them propaganda. If there are false reports on the radio, the listeners will react. If false reports continue, they will turn off. Only by respecting its audience can a project like this succeed.

So it must be the creature of no political tendency, of no action group, of no vested interest. We have acquired experience in Radio Free Europe and Radio Liberty of how to do that, even though, as we all know, the beginnings were indeed difficult.

Cuba has threatened to retaliate against Radio Marti by interference against U.S. broadcasters, but Cuba was already causing serious interference in the 1960's and has been interfering more and more in recent years.

In 1979, when the United States was trying hard to improve relations with Cuba, Havana announced plans for several new radio transmitters, including two 500-kilowatt stations. That is 10 times the power of the largest U.S. station. These transmitters, including two very large units believed ready for use now or soon, could cause extensive interference in the United States. Should such interference become deliberate and promiscuous, the United States would have to consider appropriate action, possibly including "fast-track" regulatory procedures so that affected stations can increase power or change frequencies when targeted.

The Congress may wish to consider some form of compensation for stations affected by additional aggressive interference should all else fail.

I recognize that it is difficult to contemplate increased expenditures in a year of budgetary cutbacks. The $10 million in startup costs for Radio Marti are expected to come from reprograming of already budgeted funds and not represent an increase in fiscal year 1982 appropriations. Subsequent years should cost somewhat less. Experts believe this is a lean budget. We believe it is a relatively low cost, low risk way to reach the Cuban people.

To assist the administration in formulating its plan for broadcasting to Cuba, a Presidential Commission was established last September. The members of the Commission were appointed in mid-January. They include F. Clifton White, who is here today and I understand will testify before you tomorrow, is the Chairman, as well as former Senator from Florida, Richard Stone, and Jorge L. Mas, among others.

As a result of its first two meetings, the Commission has strongly endorsed the concept of radio broadcasting to Cuba, as well as much of the preparatory work already undertaken by various agencies of this administration.

Specifically, the Commission has recommended that broadcasting to Cuba be undertaken by an independent, nonprofit entity, Radio Broadcasting to Cuba, Inc., which will operate Radio Marti in much the same way that RFE/RL, Inc., now operates Radio Free Europe and Radio Liberty.

Radio Broadcasting to Cuba, Inc., has already been incorporated as a preliminary step. Proposed legislation introduced before this committee authorizes support for it under the oversight of the Secretary of State pending the designation of an appropriate oversight agency, presumably the Board for International Broadcasting.

The Commission recommends that Radio Marti be operated by RBC, Inc., as a medium-wave AM 50-kilowatt station in accordance with domestic and international regulations.

The Presidential Commission at yesterday's public session heard statements from various broadcasting associations. I understand they will testify separately before this committee.

Mr. Chairman, Radio Marti is designed to respond to a basic human need: The need to have access to information on events and policies that effect the lives of individuals. Freedom of information is what we are talking about here, a fundamental freedom recognized by every responsible individual and government in the world.

This right has been consistently denied to the Cuban people since Castro came to power in 1959. Radio Marti will help fill this longstanding information gap.

To those of us who have lived in a Communist state, it will be quite easy to know just how much Radio Marti can affect the lives of Cubans. For those of us who have not lived in a Communist state, it is an opportunity to offer hope and the means to make informed judgments on the actions of their own governments. For a people bottled up in a system of oppression they did not seek and cannot remove, that can be precious.

Thank you very much, Mr. Chairman.

Document 675

Transcript of a Press Briefing by the Secretary of State (Haig), New York, March 6, 1982[37]

U.S.-Mexican Discussions on the Situation in Central America

SECRETARY HAIG. First, I want to just briefly review the character of the discussions I've had with Foreign Secretary Castañeda of Mexico, and then submit myself to your questions.

I want to emphasize that this is the first occasion that I've had to discuss with Secretary Castañeda the recent proposals of President Lopez Portillo on the Central American crisis and the proposals that he made recently in a speech at Managua.

I used the occasion to thank Secretary Castañeda for Mexico's warm support for President Reagan's Caribbean Basin initiative, support that was prompt and forthcoming following the President's recent speech.

We used the occasion to have a wide tour de horizon of global and regional questions and, most importantly of course, the situation in Central America.

During the meeting I had an opportunity to hear firsthand and in detail from the Secretary Mexico's peace plan for the Central American region.

We talked about current U.S. relations with Nicaragua, with Cuba, in light of President Lopez Portillo's proposals, and I reiterated the necessity for both to stop arming insurgents in the hemisphere.

As you know, one area of concern we had with our understanding of President Lopez Portillo's proposals was their failure to grapple very directly with the issue of Nicaraguan involvement in El Salvador. We had an opportunity to discuss this at length and

---

[37] Source: Department of State Press Release 87, March 8, 1982; also printed in Department of State *Bulletin*, May 1982, pp. 68–71. Secretary Haig was in New York to meet with Mexican Foreign Minister Jorge Castaēda de la Rosa. The press briefing was held at the U.N. Plaza Hotel beginning at 3:20 p.m.

to review possible modifications to the Mexican approach.

I visualize in the period ahead these discussions will continue. For example, I will meet again next weekend here in New York with Secretary Castañeda.

I, of course, expressed our hope that the Mexican Government will support the elections in El Salvador later this month.

We discussed in some detail next week's meeting of the Nassau Four who are associated with the Caribbean Basin initiative.[38] After many meetings with Mr. Castañeda, starting with the very earliest period of President Reagan's administration—and, incidentally, I want to emphasize that I spoke to the President in California this morning just before this meeting, received his guidance on the position that we would take with respect to the Mexican proposals, and they were, of course, reflected in my discussions.

As is always the case, I have developed a very close and I think frank and constructive relationship with Mr. Castañeda as has President Reagan with President Lopez Portillo. We very much appreciate the relationship that has been established between our two governments even though on some issues we differ, not the least of which is one I just discussed with respect to interventionism.

I do feel that our meeting resulted in a greater convergence of view on this very difficult subject, and I look forward to continuing these discussions in the period ahead with the view towards finding a solution to this very dangerous—and increasingly so—problem.

I think I've said enough now. I welcome your questions.

Q. Commander Wheelock, a member of the Council of the State of Nicaragua is in town, and he reiterated in Washington two days ago his willingness to meet with the State Department to go over the peace plan and their problems.

Can you respond to that offer?

Secretary Haig. I think it's too early to say. I do want to emphasize that we made some proposals as early as last August to the Government of Nicaragua with the view toward arriving at a negotiated settlement to the difficulties in the region.[39]

Some of the aspects of that proposal were contained in President Lopez Portillo's Managua speech. The area that concerned us the most was the one that did not address in specific terms Nicaraguan involvement in El Salvador which we feel is an essential and primary aspect of a negotiated solution.

After those initial discussions by Mr. Enders in Managua in August, we communicated some further details to the Government of Nicaragua. Unfortunately, the response we received was neither encouraging nor forthcoming.

Dependent on how the talks go with our Mexican friends, and perhaps next weekend and in the period following that, we'll see where they lead.

Q. Mr. Secretary, a couple of questions, please. If the Mexicans work in some phraseology that would accommodate what you regard as critical—the cessation of the flow of arms to the El Salvadoran guerrillas through Nicaragua—would the United States then be prepared to pick up the Mexican proposal of looking for a negotiated solution? That would be the first question.

And the second one: Does your very presence here, Mr. Secretary, and your meeting with the Foreign Minister of Mexico indicate a desire at this point on the part of the Administration to try to find a way out of the El Salvador crisis through a negotiated solution?

Secretary Haig. First, let me suggest to you that it has been the policy of the United States Government from the outset of this situation to attempt to find solutions which would be the product of peaceful negotiations. Let there be no doubt about that. That has been the underlying premise of everything the President has done.

With respect to the details you asked about in the Lopez Portillo plan, I think it's too early to say beyond the general observation that the exchanges we had here this afternoon were encouraging and brought that process forward. In other words, they were positive. But there are still many uncertainties that have to be refined, and I don't think the place to refine them is in the public venue.

Q. Mr. Secretary, Mr. Guiterrez, the Nicaraguan who is now in the Mexican Embassy in El Salvador, is he or is he not an agent who was assisting the rebels?

Secretary Haig. I think there's been a number of statements made, and I un-

---

[38] A reference to the forthcoming meeting with the Foreign Ministers of Canada, Mexico, Venezuela, and Colombia; see *ibid.*, pp. 64–68.

[39] Regarding the 1981 discussions, see *Washington Post*, December 10, 1981, p. A1.

derstand one made at 1 o'clock today by the Salvadoran President, President Duarte, on this subject, and I'd just as soon let those statements stand and run their course.

Q. Did you discuss with Mr. Castañeda the status of this person who you pointed out as being evidence—

SECRETARY HAIG. We had an exchange of views on it, and, as I say, a great deal has been said locally. Since the local authorities—those on the ground, whatever their point of view—seem to be the most knowledgeable, I would leave it right there.

Q. Mr. Secretary, you said before Congress, though, that he was an agent, he was aiding the rebels. Is that true or not?

SECRETARY HAIG. I said we had the report that there was a Nicaraguan involved in the insurgency in Salvador, and that he had been captured. And that is true.

Q. Is that report false, though, now?

SECRETARY HAIG. No. I believe it is true.

Q. Did you know, Mr. Secretary, at the time on Thursday that this gentleman—the Nicaraguan or the student, rebel, or whatever—that he had already escaped, or had that not yet been brought to your attention?

SECRETARY HAIG. I think the circumstances—and whether you would describe it as escape or whatever—I will leave to those who were on the ground, eyewitnesses. I think there was some further information put out on that today, and I'm sure there will be in the days ahead.

Q. The fact that the Mexican Government is currently harboring this man, as you have pointed out as the Nicaraguan infiltrator, certainly we can take that as evidence that we and the Mexican Government are very far apart on any sort of agreement with regard to this issue, aren't we?

SECRETARY HAIG. With regard to what issue?

Q. With regard to how to solve the crisis in El Salvador if you take as evidence the fact that you can't even seem to agree with the Mexicans on who this man is or what he is.

SECRETARY HAIG. Wait a minute. That's your interpretation of the situation; it is not mine. As I say, this is a question for the Salvadoran authorities—who are involved in the capture of this fellow and the Mexican authorities who have given him refuge—to clarify in the hours and weeks ahead, and I'm sure they will.

Do not always assume that events of that kind represent full cognizance by the authorities involved on either side. Just let the facts shake out.

Q. Mr. Secretary, Senator Byrd had a press conference today and called for advance congressional approval before any troops were sent to El Salvador.

What's the administration's view on that resolution that he is going to propose on Monday?

SECRETARY HAIG. I wasn't aware of it. I think we have a War Powers Act which is a very, very impressive and rather complete set of constraints on the executive branch with respect to the deployment of U.S. combat forces anywhere in the world.

But I do not find it particularly relevant because, as I have said and as the President has said repeatedly, there are no plans, I know of no one in the executive branch who's made such proposals, that would involve the direct intervention of American forces in this hemisphere.

Q. Mr. Secretary, as I understand what the Mexicans are saying, their number one priority is for more talking between the United States and Cuba which they feel is basic to the settlement of the problem in the region.

There was one meeting of yourself and a Cuban official in Mexico City.[40] Are you willing to take the discussions between the United States and Cuba further, either using Mexico as an intermediary or without an intermediary?

SECRETARY HAIG. Mr. Oberdorfer, I think it's clear from the fact that the President initiated the talks that took place between the Vice President and myself in Mexico City, that his policy, as it has been in the Polish crisis as well, is to maintain communication and contact. Indeed, in times of crisis and increased tension, such communication becomes more, rather than less, important. I don't see any change in that policy of President Reagan in the weeks and months ahead.

I haven't answered your question, and I'm not going to. I don't mean to be cute, Don. I just think the way and how communications will be conducted are matters which are best left without a lot of public hoopla.

Q. There are a number of Congressmen and other officials in the United States that

[40] On the talks between Haig and Cuban Vice President Carlos Rafael Rodriguez, see *New York Times*, January 28, 1982, p. A4.

have said that your charge of Nicaraguan and Cuban involvement in El Salvador is cover for the continued aid of the Reagan Administration for the junta.

Can you offer any shred of evidence of the Nicaraguan arms shipments and Cuban involvement?

SECRETARY HAIG. I think I again would refer you to the very knowledgeable statements—and they were bipartisan statements—made by the representatives of the Senate and the House Intelligence Committees who were briefed this past week on this subject—in the case of the Senate, it was Senator Goldwater, and I think in the case of the House, Representative Bolen [*Boland*] a Democrat—that this evidence was substantial and persuasive.

Q. Can you tell us what it is?

SECRETARY HAIG. What would you do with it?

Q. Sir, you told the House Appropriations Subcommittee the other day you were releasing some information soon to back up the U.S. accusations regarding Cuban involvement and Nicaraguan involvement. Is that still coming? Will that be made public soon?

SECRETARY HAIG. We're preparing a briefing now, and I looked at the dry run of it yesterday and felt that it needed some improvement. I hope it will be delivered by Wednesday of next week, possibly as early as Tuesday—maybe even Monday.

I want to see it again. I want to be sure that Mr. Casey and the Director of DIA are very comfortable that we are not subjecting sources that must be preserved to undue risk, and I think you know this is the responsible position that we must take. It not only involves the future viability of our ability to acquire necessary intelligence, but in some instances it can involve the lives of participants.

Q. Mr. Secretary, one of the things the Salvadorans have said, and you've referred us to them now, is that there are camps located in Mexico where training is going on for rebels in El Salvador. Is that true?

SECRETARY HAIG. I'm not going to add any more to that situation other than to point out that the Salvadoran Government has a viewpoint and evidence to support it, and I'm sure the Mexican Government has its own point of view and let's let that speak for itself.

Q. Well, for sure you've referred it—

SECRETARY HAIG. I'm not going to intervene in it, other than to tell you, as I did, that there was such an event and that there's a great deal to substantiate the validity—

Q. Could you at least—

SECRETARY HAIG. I have no question. I'm not self-conscious about what I said on it, and I'm not apologetic for it. I believe it is absolutely correct.

Q. There are figures—

SECRETARY HAIG. No. I made no reference to subject, and I'm not going to.

Q. You did or did not?

SECRETARY HAIG. I did not, and I will not.

Q. Mr. Secretary, could I take you back to an earlier question, please? At the outset this administration gave a very cool response to the Mexican President's proposal. Now you seem to be going about it much more seriously.

What is it that has represented or produced this change in attitude on the part of the administration? Or is it that the administration finds itself in such a fix in El Salvador that the Mexican proposal may be indeed a sought-after way out of the crisis?

SECRETARY HAIG. Not at all. In the first place, I don't accept the premises with which you introduced your question which are subjective judgments on you part and not factual, if you mind my being as obnoxious as you were with your question.

Let me say that from the outset we have been in very close touch with the Mexican Government on the situation in El Salvador and the very worrisome trends in Nicaragua.

I do not describe our response as cool. I don't give a value judgment to our response in terms of qualitative judgments. We did point out that we felt the proposals as we understood them were inadequate, especially with respect to the issue I just touched upon.

We continue to believe that. That is why it was important and valuable to discuss these proposals firsthand as we did today. In that process I think both sides learned something, as is always the case when well-meaning people, attempting to solve problems rather than create them, sit down and talk in a cordial, constructive atmosphere. And that was the result of today's discussion.

Q. If you could strike a closer meeting of the minds on this proposal—say after next weekend's talks with the Foreign Minister—does the Mexican proposal's central offer of a negotiated solution between the two sides—

SECRETARY HAIG. It's too early to say. But let me assure you that President Reagan's intention is to explore every avenue that could lead to a successful and appropriate peaceful resolution to the situation in Central America. To do otherwise would be irresponsible, and that includes exploring the Mexican initiative in depth and continuing on exploring the initiatives which we have been considering for an extended period of time.

We haven't reached the point in those assessments that I can answer your question with the definity that you would prefer.

Q. Mr. Secretary, Secretary Enders has said that the United States opposes direct negotiations between the Duarte government and the leftist opposition. Is that still U.S. policy?

SECRETARY HAIG. It has never been U.S. policy to oppose negotiations between the Government of El Salvador and the guerrilla leaders. What we have opposed is negotiations which, a priori, would have the objective, without an expression of the will of the people of El Salvador, to split up political power.

We have urged negotiations which would permit the guerrilla leadership to join in the electoral process—self-determination of the people of El Salvador—and that happens to be precisely the view of President Duarte. He has added a condition that such negotiations cannot be conducted while bloodshed and terrorism continue, and I think that is a very acceptable, prudent and understandable condition.

Q. Mr. Secretary, you said previously that you hoped that the Mexican Government would support elections in Salvador. Is that realistic, considering last year's French-Mexican communiqué on Salvador rejecting elections as a viable solution and recognizing the opposition as a representative force in El Salvador?[41]

SECRETARY HAIG. I'm not sure I understand what you're saying.

Q. Whether it is realistic for you to hope that Mexico will support elections in El Salvador after the joint French-Mexican communiqué of last year criticizing elections or describing elections as not being a viable solution.

SECRETARY HAIG. I think it's one thing to have an attitude with respect to the potential benefits of a process and another to support the process itself. I think the governments of the hemisphere—a large number of them, especially those in the local area—rejected the French-Mexican proposal. We did too; we were not comfortable with it.

But that time has passed and we are at another point in time in a dynamic situation, and my expression of hope that they will support the election is simply what it says.

Q. Mr. Secretary, did anything else happen as a result of your talks today? Presumably you take their proposal back to Washington and Foreign Minister Castañeda the same.

But do the Mexicans go to any of the other parties involved with American thoughts or proposals, or is it intra-governmental at this point?

SECRETARY HAIG. We're now dealing bilaterally with the Mexican Government in an exchange of views on ideas they have to bring progress. We have been conducting our own discussions, as I pointed out earlier, and it's too early to say where we will go from here.

Q. Mr. Secretary, the Mexican Government fundamentally disagrees on one specific point—United States aid to El Salvador. I understand the Mexican Government has come out strongly opposed to any more U.S. military aid.

Are you accepting this from the Foreign Minister?

SECRETARY HAIG. We have discussed the full range of issues associated with the Nicaraguan question, the Salvadoran question, and the Cuban question. I don't think it serves any purpose for me to lay out in detail how both of us come to these various problems, other than to say that we had a very constructive and I think valuable exchange.

Q. What was the Foreign Minister's reaction to what I presume would have been your proposal to broaden the Mexican proposal to include a call for a ban on arms being transshipped through Nicaragua to the rebels?

SECRETARY HAIG. I would prefer to let my statement stand, which suggested that

---

41 Regarding this communiqué, see *ibid.*, August 29, 1981, p. 1.

we had a constructive discussion and modifications and add-ons and different approaches were discussed that might offer some hope for progress.

Q. Mr. Secretary, in President Lopez Portillo's proposal, one of the main points suggests that Nicaragua and the United States should sign a pact of nonaggression.

Did you discuss that with Mr. Castañeda?

SECRETARY HAIG. We discussed the full range of President Lopez Portillo's speech in Managua—every one of the details—and that was one of the details, yes. Everything that was in that speech was discussed.

Q. Do you have a comment to that?

SECRETARY HAIG. Not yet. All of these things that would go forward that might constitute a viable negotiating proposal are interrelated, and any one of them draws its character from those alongside of it. I have said that the sine qua non, if you will, of potential normalization of relations between the United States and Nicaragua involves the cessation of their intervention in neighboring states.

Thank you very much.

THE PRESS. Thank you, Mr. Secretary.

Document 676

Transcript of an Interview With the Director of Central Intelligence (Casey), March 8, 1982 (Extract)[42]

The Soviet Threat in Central America and the Caribbean

Q. Mr. Casey, there's a great deal of concern that this country might be dragged into a Vietnam-like quagmire in El Salvador. In your view, is that fear warranted?

A. No. I don't think El Salvador or what we're likely to do there bears any comparison to Vietnam. In the first place, El Salvador is on our doorstep. And we're not just talking about El Salvador; we're talking about Central America—Costa Rica, Honduras and Guatemala. The insurgency is beamed at all those countries. Furthermore, this is part of a worldwide problem.

Q. Worldwide in what sense?

A. Around the middle of the'70s, the Soviets assessed the impact of Vietnam on American public opinion and decided we probably would be restricted in our ability to respond to low-level insurgency operations. In the last seven years, starting with the dispatch of sophisticated weapons to join up with Cuban troops in Angola, they have developed a very innovative and brilliant mix of tactics: Political, diplomatic, destabilization, subversion, terrorist and support of insurgencies. And they have applied this around the world.

Over this past year alone, you've had insurgencies in North Yemen, Chad, Morocco, Kampuchea, El Salvador, Guatemala. You have incipient insurgencies in many African countries. The Soviets work in some concert with Cuba, Libya and North Korea. They work with Angola against Namibia and Zaire; with Ethiopia against Somalia, and with Libya and Ethiopia against the Sudan.

Q. How are the Soviets involved?

A. What happens in these insurgencies is that the Soviets go in and exploit the underlying social and economic discontents, which are plentiful. That gives them a base. They feed it with trained men and with arms. That drives away investment. The insurgents sabotage economic targets, and so economic discontent grows. And as the discontent grows, more people go over to the insurgents' side.

It's almost a no-lose proposition for the Soviets. They can stay in the background. They sell their arms and get up to 20 percent of their hard currency from Libya and other countries that can pay for the arms. It's something we have very great difficulty coping with.

Q. What is Cuba's role in all this?

A. Here's a country of 10 million, with 50,000 people around the world—military and civilian. Besides the Cuban troops in Angola and Ethiopia, there are 12,000 technical trainees in East Germany and Czechoslovakia and 5,000 to 6,000 students in the Soviet Union. They have 50 people here, 60 people there—in Africa, in the Middle East and in Latin America.

They can do this because of the demographics that led them to get rid of 120,000

---

[42] Source: *U.S. News and World Report*, March 8, 1982, pp. 23–24. Only the portion of the interview dealing with Central America and the Caribbean is printed.

people in the Mariel sealift. There has been a 50 percent jump in the 15-to-19 age group in the Cuban population. That's quite a latent force that Castro has no work for at home and can use for mischief abroad. He said in a speech just a few months ago that he would like to send 10,000 young Cubans to Siberia to chop down trees for construction projects in Cuba.

Q. Do you have evidence that matériel is being supplied by Cuba to the guerrillas in El Salvador on a significant scale?

A. Oh, yes. Without it the guerrillas wouldn't be able to sustain an insurgency.

Q. And Nicaragua? What part does it play?

A. This whole El Salvador insurgency is run out of Managua by professionals experienced in directing guerrilla wars. You've got to appreciate that Managua has become an international center. There are Cubans, Soviets, Bulgarians, East Germans, North Koreans, North Vietnamese, representatives of the PLO. North Koreans are giving some weapons they manufacture. The PLO provides weapons they've picked up around their part of the world. There are American weapons that the Vietnamese brought in in substantial quantities—mostly small arms that were left behind in Vietnam.

Q. How large are these foreign groups operating in Managua?

A. In the case of the Cubans, 6,000 are in the country, of whom 4,000 are in civil work and maybe 1,800 or 2,000 are in military and security work. The East Germans and Soviets each have somewhere between 50 and 100. The Bulgarians, the North Koreans and the Vietnamese are fewer. They all have their little function: The East Germans work on the security system; Cubans work on the general strategy, and the Soviets work, for the most part, on the large weapons that have come in. The North Koreans and Vietnamese are good at caching arms and digging tunnels and things like that.

Q. Why is the administration apparently so concerned about the arrival in Cuba of crates presumably containing a squadron of MiG-23s—a plane that already is operating there?

A. Well, Cuba has the biggest air force in the hemisphere next to ours. The new planes are just part of a buildup. But I don't know that we are that concerned. Jimmy Carter made it an issue when MiG-23s arrived in Havana, and he didn't do anything about it.[43] I think this President has been rather careful not to make it an issue—although I wouldn't say we're unconcerned.

Q. Does what is happening now in Cuba violate the 1962 Kennedy–Khrushchev agreement ending the missile crisis?

A. Oh, sure it does because the'62 agreement said the Soviets would send no offensive weapons, and it also said there would be no export of revolution from Cuba. The agreement has been violated for 20 years.

Q. So the aircraft coming to Cuba now are attack planes—

A. They're attack airplanes, yes.

Q. Are they nuclear capable?

A. They can be made nuclear capable. There's an export version which is not nuclear capable. We haven't seen these planes yet. They're not out of the crate. The probability is they're the export version, but it just takes a little bit of wiring and a little bit of work and some pilot training to make them nuclear capable.

On the other hand, the Soviets have better ways to hit us with nuclear bombs. It's more likely these planes are for the purpose of building Cuba up militarily, modernizing their Army, probably paying them for their work in Africa—to keep their forces in Angola and Ethiopia. Their Army probably feels happy if it gets modern equipment, and they probably wangled these planes out of the Soviets.

Q. Could these MiGs be destined ultimately for Nicaragua?

A. We think that Nicaragua is lengthening its runways at three airports for the purpose of being able to take this kind of fighter. It probably hasn't been determined whether the planes will go from Cuba to Nicaragua or whether additional planes will go directly from the Soviet Union.

Q. Is there a point at which the United States says to the Soviet Union and Cuba, "This far and no further"?

A. That's the $64 question. I don't think the American public generally perceives the threat in as serious a light as we may perceive it at this stage. I think we'll come to

---

[43] See the remarks by President Carter at a news conference, November 30, 1978, *Public Papers of the Presidents of the United States: Jimmy Carter, 1978* (Washington, 1979), pp. 2100–2101.

our senses and face up to it. But you've got a problem not only of American public opinion but of Latin American public opinion. It's the gringo problem: They don't want us down there.

When we go down there, we play into the hands of the Marxists to a degree; we give them a rallying point. The President has made it clear that there is no intention of sending troops there. Exactly what to do to help these countries defend themselves is a very difficult, complex political, diplomatic, military decision. You can't make it without public understanding and public support.

Q. Is there any sign that Latin American opinion is changing and becoming more supportive of the United States?

A. A year ago no Latin American country was greatly concerned about what was happening in El Salvador. Yet when Mexico and France spoke out in support of the El Salvador insurgents several months ago, 12 Latin American countries dissented. That shows growing concern. At the OAS meeting in St. Lucia a couple of months ago, there was a 22-to-3 vote in support of orderly elections in El Salvador. The three dissenters were Nicaragua, Mexico and Grenada. Just two or three weeks ago, Costa Rica, El Salvador and Honduras got together and called upon Venezuela, Colombia and the United States to help protect them against Nicaragua.

Increasingly, the Colombians and the Venezuelans are getting concerned. The Mexicans should be concerned because they could be the next target. I read now that they've got at least the beginnings of a quick-reaction force. So maybe they're coming around. Also, there is dissidence in Nicaragua. A lot of Nicaraguans think that the Sandinistas are betraying the revolution. They resent having the country taken over and run by Cubans.

So we can hope that developments in Central America will breed a reaction. You say "Halt" to all this when you're not saying it alone, when you're not perceived to be behaving in Central America the way the Soviets behave in Poland and when you have enough Latin American participation so that you're helping them instead of doing the whole thing for them.

Q. Concretely, what threat do these developments in Central America pose for the U.S.?

A. Well, just look at what is happening down there. Nicaragua, a country of 2½ million people, has an Army twice the size of El Salvador's, which has twice the population and is fighting for its life. Nicaragua is sitting there with a big Army that's getting bigger, with Soviet tanks and airfields being extended and pilots being prepared for Soviet supersonic planes. When and if that happens—I think it will happen in six months—Nicaragua will have military dominance over the rest of Central America, with a population 7 times theirs.

If Cuba, with 10 million people, and Nicaragua, with 2½ million people, take over the rest of Central America and build up the armies on the scale of their own, you would have a very large army down there on our doorstep. Mexico is sitting there with a military force of about 150,000 today and never thought of having anything more.

Q. Are the persistent reports true that government troops are responsible for most of the massacres of civilians in El Salvador?

A. Nobody knows where all these casualties come from. This is civil war. Sometimes they come from the government, and sometimes they come from the guerrillas. We are satisfied that the government is sensitive to the importance of disciplining its forces and is making a genuine effort to do so. But that's going to be very slow and not entirely satisfactory to our public opinion. El Salvador has a violent society, and the law is kind of slow. A man can't be convicted of murder without a witness under their law. And those who sit in judgment risk their lives because the society is violent. So judges have a tendency to duck the responsibility.

But the widely propagated notion that all the massacres of civilians are perpetrated by the government and not by the guerrillas is clearly false. In the final analysis, you have to make up your mind whether you would prefer a Marxist-Leninist dictatorship to a society that is capable of reform.

. . . .

Document 677

Testimony by the Under Secretary of Defense for Policy (Iklé) Before a Subcommittee of the Senate Judiciary Committee, March 11, 1982 (Extracts)[44]

The Role of Cuba in International Terrorism and Subversion

SECRETARY IKLE. I do, sir.

I am pleased, Mr. Chairman,[45] that you invited me to appear before your committee. You have asked me to discuss, among other things, the role of Castro's Cuba in promoting violence, terrorism, and armed opposition movements. The purpose of such Cuban intervention in other countries is to undermine governments that seek economic and social progress within a democratic framework, or to extend the global reach of the Soviet military establishment, or both.

With its population of less than 10 million and a land area of about 44,000 square miles, Cuba is involved globally, providing military and technical advisers and assistance thousands of miles away, as this chart which we have here will show you, in Libya, Iraq, South Yemen, Angola, Ethiopia, the Congo, Mozambique, and Vietnam, among others. Castro currently has about 60,000 Cubans serving overseas, including 35,000 military and 25,000 civilian technicians. Cuba has about 20,000 troops in Angola alone, and about 12,000 troops in Ethiopia.

. . . .

Given these farflung interventions, Cuba's military capability is obviously far in excess of any defensive needs. Its army of 225,000 includes 9 active and 18 reserve divisions. In addition, there are hundreds of thousands of reserves, militia, and other paramilitary forces. Cuba has 650 tanks, over 200 Mig fighters in its air force, including a recently arrived second squadron of Mig–23's. Cuba's navy includes 50 torpedo and missile attack boats, 2 attack submarines, and a frigate.

Overall, 2.3 percent of Cuba's population is in the regular armed forces, and about 1 of every 20 Cubans participates in some kind of security mission. By comparison, Mexico, with seven times Cuba's population, maintains regular defense forces half the size of Cuba's and involving less than two-tenths of 1 percent of its population. We in the United States have less than 1 percent of our people in the regular Armed Forces.

How does Cuba sustain such large forces on a faltering economy? It relies, as it has for twenty years, on the Soviet Union to keep it afloat. In 1981 the Soviets provided $3 billion in economic assistance, and at least $500 million in military assistance. The U.S.S.R. sent three times more military equipment to Cuba in 1981 than in 1980 and more than in any year since 1962. The U.S.S.R. shipped about 66,000 metric tons into Cuba in 1981. The next chart will show you the trends in this assistance. See the rising curve there in Soviet military assistance and deliveries to Latin America. It speaks for itself, Mr. Chairman.

. . . .

SENATOR DENTON. Could we let the press and the audience just see that for a minute, Dr. Ikle?

. . . .

SENATOR DENTON. I notice one interesting thing, Dr. Ikle, and that is the drop of those supplies after the Cuban missile crisis when a Democratic President looked the crocodile in the eye and that dip took place—John F. Kennedy.

SECRETARY IKLE. That is when the pressure was on for this supply to be curtailed.

SENATOR DENTON. How his brother can now be, along with a Republican, calling for a freeze when they have a 6-to-1 nuclear advantage is incredible to me.

SECRETARY IKLE. Now, why, Mr. Chairman, is the Soviet Union willing to expend such resources on Cuba? Because the Soviets realize the importance of their position in Cuba as a threat to the Atlantic Alliance; they realize it more fully than do many Americans and more fully than most Eu-

---

[44] Source: *The Role of Cuba in International Terrorism and Subversion: Hearings Before the Subcommittee on Security and Terrorism of the Committee on the Judiciary, United States Senate, Ninety-seventh Congress, Second Session* (Washington, 1982), pp. 85, 87–90, 93–98. The omitted pages are the charts referred to in the text which are not printed.

[45] Senator Jeremiah Denton.

ropeans. Moscow knows that in time of war half of NATO's supplies would come through our gulf ports. They are aware that 44 percent of all foreign tonnage, and 45 percent of the crude oil for the United States, pass through the Caribbean. They understand the importance of the Panama Canal and the South Atlantic sealanes of communication that carry about two-thirds of west Europe's petroleum and nearly half of our imports.

But perhaps more importantly the Soviets seek to change our southern borders from the peaceful conditions of the past by building potentially hostile forces in Central America and the Caribbean. They may expect that we will have to divert our attention and forces from other interests elsewhere. It is high time, Mr. Chairman, that our allies overseas begin to recognize this strategy.

Take Grenada; a highly visible ongoing Cuban project is the construction of their airport capable of accommodating advanced jet aircraft and a naval facility. In December 1981, Grenadian Minister of National Mobilization, Selwyn Strachan, publicly boasted that Cuba will eventually use the new airport in his country to supply troops in Angola. And ominously he added that because of its strategic location, the airport may also be used by the Soviet Union.

SENATOR DENTON. Would you repeat that sentence, the relationship between the airport in Grenada to supplies in Angola?

SECRETARY IKLE. This was the Minister of National Mobilization, Selwyn Strachan, who boasted that Cuba will eventually use the new airport that is being built in Grenada with Cuban and Soviet help to supply troops—yes, to supply troops to Angola, to move out to Angola from Cuba. And then he added that because of its strategic location, it may also be used by the Soviet Union to come into the Caribbean presumably.

SENATOR DENTON. It could be used by the Soviet Union to come into the—

SECRETARY IKLE. Caribbean area.

SENATOR DENTON. The Caribbean area.

SECRETARY IKLE. Or the Cubans to move out via Grenada to Africa.

SENATOR DENTON. It could also be used to bring into the Latin American area a military air force presence which would be a very interesting factor in the balance.

SECRETARY IKLE. That is right.

Now, by relying on Cuban mercenaries as surrogates, the Soviets are able to carry out their interventionist policies without risking the hostile reaction, or at least the same hostile reaction, from the American people and the Third World that a direct involvement of Soviet troops and personnel would engender. That is the advantage from their point of view.

Latin America provides an excellent microcosm of how the Soviet-Cuba partners cooperate in tandem. As U.S. advisers with Latin American countries were cut back from—and listen to these numbers—from 516 in 1970 to 70 in 1981.

SENATOR DENTON. That's on the chart, and would you say again—the abscissa and ordinate—what are those?

SECRETARY IKLE. The number of military advisers in Latin American countries, and you see the decline—the blue column there declining steadily from 1970, 516, to 70 in 1981. These are the advisers we have for the area to the south of the United States.

SENATOR DENTON. Would you mind letting the press see that, for whatever use they care to make of it?

. . . .

SECRETARY IKLE. The gray ones on top are the Cuban and U.S.S.R. advisers that have moved into the area, while we moved out. And you might show it to the press.

So 1981, as this chart shows, Soviets and Cubans had 50 times as many military advisers in Latin America as the United States—Mr. Chairman, 50 times. Moreover, from 1962 to 1981, the Soviets provided more than twice as much security assistance to Latin America as did the United States, roughly $4 billion for the U.S.S.R. compared with $1.5 billion for the United States. Again, you see here the blue line, the U.S. security assistance to Latin America declining, particularly after 1975, and the red line rising, the Soviet assistance to Latin America.

. . . .

SENATOR DENTON. With respect to your chart showing the Latin American advisers and to place in perspective the comparison with Afghanistan, in which the Soviet Union has division upon division, to our involvement in Nicaragua, how many advisers do we have in Nicaragua?

SECRETARY IKLE. In El Salvador?

SENATOR DENTON. I think they compared it to—

SECRETARY IKLE. El Salvador, I'm sure. In Nicaragua, of course, we just have the Embassy personnel.

SENATOR DENTON. They compared it to U.S. interference in Nicaragua, sir.

SECRETARY IKLE. Oh, right, but they would not call those advisers. But, in any event, the people cannot tell the difference between 50 and 90,000 maybe. We have 53 advisers, up to a maximum of 53 advisers in El Salvador, and there are over 80,000 Soviet forces in Afghanistan.

So we need not wonder that totalitarianism is making inroads; it is receiving far more support than democratic pluralism. Not only 50 times as many military advisers, but a far higher level of military assistance.

Mr. Chairman, the Castro regime is linked to the Soviet Union not only through its tools but also through its methods. Castro has not only been armed with all this weaponry by his Soviet masters, he has also been inspired and tutored in the methods of totalitarianism by experts in Moscow. I would like to illustrate this for three issues that are of central concern to your committee.

First, the use of terrorism to spread totalitarian control has been practiced in strikingly similar fashion by the Soviet Union and by Fidel Castro.

Second, the use of deception, particularly deception to mislead Western media, has been developed to a fine art by both Castro and the Soviets.

Third, there is the destruction of the chances for democratic elections by the entrapment of Western democracies into alleged negotiations which become a process for the totalitarians to seize the monopoly of power.

Let me add some more details to describe each of these three practices.

First, on terrorism. A great deal of the current debate has been about the question of Soviet control over various terrorist groups. This is, of course, a question of some importance. However, it is by no means the only important issue in determining Western policy toward terrorist groups. In the first place, terrorism is an assault on the most basic human rights, an attack on civil society. In the second place, terrorism is usually associated with a political program. It is a device for seizing power and maintaining it, foreclosing for the indefinite future any substantial expansion of elementary political liberties. Third, even if terrorist "armies" are not directed from Moscow, their acts may lead to the expansion of Soviet influence and control, and indeed, in some cases, they aim precisely at destablizing a government, allied or otherwise associated with the United States, at detaching it from the open Western world and forcing it into the closed Soviet orbit.

SENATOR DENTON. In previous hearings of the subcommittee, we have established our awareness of the fact that the evidence does not indicate that the Soviet Union by any means exercises complete and detailed control over terrorism globally. She has just made a gross bet on the side of terrorism, black or red, left or right, as being to their net advantage.

But in some areas of the world, such as Latin America, they have relatively direct control over the degree, kind, and direction of terrorism. This is the case with the Moscow–Havana link where a Soviet general exercises control over the intelligence service of Cuba, the DGI.

SECRETARY IKLE. Right, this assessment is correct.

SENATOR DENTON. We have also brought out, sir, that since the Tricontinental Conference in 1966, there exists a marked commonality among terrorist groups, a commonality that extends even to textbooks, such as the "Mini-Manual for Urban Guerrillas" which can be found in Czechoslovakia, in the Sudan, in Libya, in New York City, as well as in Nicaragua, El Salvador, and elsewhere. It is a coordinated effort, blatantly similar in terms of tactics, direction, and technique, a technique which, as I said before, is boringly evident to anyone who takes more than a casual look at it. Yet, this is not known in the United States. In fact, when the name Carlos was brought up with respect to the Qadhafi threat against the President and other officials, the members of the Foreign Relations Committee who were present did not know who Carlos was. To me, this is incredible but understandable in that what has been revealed in this subcommittee as fact has not been reported to the American public.

SECRETARY IKLE. Adding to what you just said, Mr. Chairman, let me introduce a particular example of Soviet-controlled terrorism which has received little attention. One of the most dangerous and most neglected of all the terrorist movements, the Armenian Secret Army for the Liberation of Armenia (ASALA). It has formally announced that its strategy is to gain control of the eastern third of Turkey, our ally, to "free" it so called from the Turkish Government and to unite it with the Soviet Union. This is an area of the world which is, of course, critically important for the eastern Mediterranean and for the southern region of NATO. It is also critical for Egypt and Israel and the rest of the Middle East.

It does not matter very much whether the Armenian Secret Army is directly commanded by Moscow. It is an efficient and brutal executor of the murder of innocent civilians. It has intimidated governments allied with Turkey and law-abiding Armenian communities as well. If it were to be successful in its aims, it would lead directly to the expansion of the Soviet Union.

Perhaps more than any other terrorist movement, it illustrates the irrelevance of some of the issues that have preoccupied the debate in the West on terrorism. Whether the Armenian terrorist movement is acting on its own, or under Moscow's direction, if it succeeds, it will come down to the same thing. Here lies a lesson for our current concerns in Central America.

Let me turn now to the related question of deception. Marxist guerrillas in Latin America have been largely recruited from the upper and middle classes and the student population. They use deception to make it hard for domestic or foreign intelligence agencies and—an important point—even harder for the press to identify and track them. The guerrillas disguise themselves often as peasants, and sometimes as government soldiers. Government uniforms serve as cover for an assault on the government, or as cover for terror against the population in their campaign to destabilize the country and to have the government forces blamed for the terror. It serves to confuse domestic and foreign opinion. And the terrorists disguised as peasants can lead even a carefully controlled government counterattack to be misdirected at the real peasants, or appear to be misdirected to the media observers when it hits guerrillas in peasant costume.

So Marxist guerrillas, using terror to inspire counter terror and to disrupt civil society, create a Catch-22 situation for any regime attempting to improve civil rights and specifically to introduce elections. The guerrillas say that fair elections are impossible in a situation of great civil disorder, while they do everything they can to create such disorder.

Guerrilla disguises do not include only their dress, but also their words. Rebel leaders argue for negotiations and political solutions instead of an election. The phrase political solution should be understood as a code word for a coalition, sometimes encouraged by friendly as well as hostile outside powers, in which the rebel leaders will dedicate themselves ruthlessly to eliminate all other members of the coalition, and in particular those who favor progress toward a representative government and civil rights. The so-called broad-based coalition will then narrow to the rebel leaders themselves. This is the process, of course, that has been happening in Nicaragua.

SENATOR DENTON. And it is the process by which they approached the so-called unconditional negotiations in Vietnam.

SECRETARY IKLE. Right. Guerrilla leaders in Latin America sometimes sound like democrats when they protest oppression of freedoms in current traditional authoritarian societies or even in democracies. This should not confuse us, Mr. Chairman. Castro, for example, has been entirely frank in identifying democracy as an anachronism. Speaking in Chile at the time of Allende when he visited down there, Fidel Castro said that anachronisms such as elections and freedom of the press are doomed by history. They—and I am quoting Castro—"exist as long as the people do not have enough strength to change them."

Now, this leads to my third point, Mr. Chairman, the substitution of alleged negotiations for genuine elections so as to eliminate the possibility of free elections ever thereafter. This was the method chosen to cover up the Stalinization of Eastern Europe, and this is the method now being peddled in this country—including, Mr. Chairman, here on Capitol Hill—to cover up the Stalinization of Central America.

Far too often have the governments of the great democracies used their influence to press moderate leaders into coalitions with Marxists where they were unlikely to survive since the Marxists were intent on seizing the monopoly of power. Sometimes we seem to have trusted Marxist assurances that liberty would be introduced in due time, as Harry Hopkins relied on Stalin's assurances about freedom in Poland. Sometimes, eager to get Soviet cooperation on other matters, we used a coalition as a face-saving way of abandoning support for democracy. So, at the close of World War II, American and British leaders gradually pressed the Polish Government in exile in London, which included socialists and a wide range of political views, to enter the Soviet-controlled Lublin government with the result we see persisting four decades later. Something similar happened in each of the six East European countries.

In Romania, for example, the Allied Powers meeting in December 1945, agreed that the Government should not be broadened to include members of the opposition, but the opposition leaders that counted were excluded at the insistence of the Soviet Union. The two opposition parties were represented by two carefully selected nobodies. The coalition government then proceeded to exclude them by giving them no ministerial portfolios, and then by excluding them from cabinet meetings. The United States and the United Kingdom protested to no avail. An election was eventually held under general conditions of intimidation, with the inevitable outcome. Then a mass trial of 91 dissidents modeled on the Moscow trials.

When Somoza was replaced in Nicaragua by the Sandinistas, the OAS was promised there would be elections. Now these elections have been indefinitely postponed and the repression of opposition groups and of freedom in Nicaragua is going on with full force.

Constraints on civil rights, poverty, and inequities, all too frequently exist in developing societies. They are not, however, the cause of Marxist attempts to overthrow the government. And when the Marxist guerrillas succeed, they do not improve civil rights—they worsen them. Nor do they improve the economic situation, as we well know. Cuba had one of the highest per capita incomes in Latin America—indeed, it was No. 3 in the hemisphere before Castro came in; I think it is now No. 12. Castro's economic policies have been an unmitigated disaster. And in Eastern Europe the economic failure of the Communist economic bloc is plainly visible today.

We know that Cuban subversive activities are not confined solely to El Salvador. Cuba has coordinated clandestine support organizations in Honduras, Costa Rica, and Guatemala. Cuban subversive activities have surfaced in virtually every Caribbean basin country. Even Mexico, which thinks it has good relations with Cuba.

In South America, Cuba provides advice, safe havens, communications training, and some financial support to many clandestine organizations that employ violence, including Colombia's M–19, Uruguay's Tupamaros, Argentina's Montoneros, and Chile's MIR.

I think you know, Mr. Chairman, the Cubans became involved with known arms smugglers in supplying the Nicaraguan revolutionaries prior to the ouster of Somoza in July of 1979. They found that connection mutually profitable and expanded their ties to include known drug smugglers who had the contacts and the equipment necessary to facilitate arms shipments. One of the Colombian drug dealers was involved on behalf of Havana in a clandestine shipment of arms to the Colombian M–19 in an operation that involved hijacking a Colombian cargo plane. Cuba provided the funds used by the dealer to purchase the arms and transport them to Colombia. In return, Cuba facilitated the drug dealer's marihuana traffic to Florida. Just recently, this drug dealer was arrested in Mexico after he had arrived there with $700,000 which the Cubans had given him to purchase arms for the Colombian M–19.

And the Cuban connection with the PLO is well-documented. In recent years there have been dozens of contacts between Cuba and PLO leaders. In fact, on November 17, 1981, PLO leader Yasir Arafat sent a message to Castro reaffirming his support for Cuba.

Before concluding, let me try to dispose of a fallacy about our relations with Castro that is fairly common in Europe, and even has its defenders here. It is sometimes argued that Fidel Castro became a pawn of Moscow out of necessity, that he has been hostile to the United States simply in reaction to our hostility toward his regime. Implicit in this line of thinking is that if we would only be nice to him and try to understand him, he would moderate his behavior. We have a test of this theory. The previous administration conducted a test.

They made significant efforts to improve U.S. relations with the Castro government. The previous administration opened an interest section in Havana and permitted the Cuban Government to do the same in Washington. It relaxed travel restrictions on Cuban diplomats and lifted the restrictions on vessels which had called at Cuban ports, formerly restricted from calling on U.S. ports. The Carter administration also encouraged increased cultural exchanges, lifted the ban on travel by U.S. citizens to Cuba, and permitted the resumption of charter flights between Cuba and the United States.

It is worth recalling the response of Fidel Castro to those friendly overtures. During the Carter administration Castro increased the number of Cuban military personnel in Angola by more than 40 percent, from about 14,000 to 20,000. He introduced the Cuban presence in Ethiopia, reaching a high of 17,000 men in 1978. He initiated a massive effort to subvert non-Communist regimes in Latin America. These actions hardly support the contention that a more conciliatory approach by the United States to United States-Cuban relations will make Castro our friend.

Mr. Chairman, some of your distinguished colleagues in both Houses seem to be suggesting that we should deny help to the Government of El Salvador, a government that is now trying to hold genuine elections and to build and protect a democratic order. Some suggest that instead of elections there should be negotiations, a compromise with those who are ideologically opposed to the very idea of elections.

I wonder if those who offer such counsel know what sort of precedent they are suggesting. They are saying, are they not, that President Truman made a mistake in supporting the Government of Greece against Communist terrorists, and that we should have had negotiations to bring the totalitarians into power in Greece, like in the rest of Eastern Europe. They are saying, are they not, that it was a mistake for Presidents Truman, Eisenhower, Kennedy, Johnson, Nixon, Ford, and Carter to support Israel against the terrorist onslaught, and that instead we should have negotiations with the PLO.

This is the large issue of principles, Mr. Chairman, that is at stake.

Thank you, Mr. Chairman.

. . . .

Document 678

Testimony by the Assistant Secretary of State for Inter-American Affairs (Enders) Before a Subcommittee of the Senate Judiciary Committee, March 12, 1982[46]

"One of the Most Difficult Problems in Foreign Policy"

SENATOR DENTON. As the chairman of the subcommittee, I have been learning a great deal. I had no idea that the Soviet-Cuban activity to promote world revolution was as all pervasive and as active as it is. Your statement today adds to my education.

Having visited Panama recently and having gotten a briefing from the unified commander in that area and having attended a reception which was attended by diplomats from all over Latin America, I have added to my understanding of these issues. What you say today makes me even more alarmed about what is going on and about the vast difference between what is actually taking place in Central America and what our public perceives and understands about that situation.

In Panama, it was estimated by the business community, by left-wing political functionaries and aspirants for government positions, that the Soviets are subsidizing at least 1,000 Panamanian students at their university in Moscow.

In previous hearings, we have brought out that the KGB normally and without any attempt at disguise runs the DGI, the Cuban intelligence agency.

You have put in perspective the amount of aid that Cuba is getting from the Soviets—did you say $3 billion a year?

MR. ENDERS. Yes; $3 billion a year.

SENATOR DENTON. One-third of Cuba's gross national product?

MR. ENDERS. One-quarter, sir, is what we estimate.

SENATOR DENTON. When we combine that with the report yesterday from Dr. Ikle of how that translates into advisers, military

---

[46] Source: *The Role of Cuba in International Terrorism and Subversion*, pp. 148–152, 155–161. For Enders' statement, see *ibid.*, pp. 142–148. The ellipsis is a statement by Senator John P. East.

equipment, and so forth, it is mind boggling to me the difference between that which is really going on and that which is perceived.[47]

One thing all of these diplomats from South America emphasized to me was the U.S. failure to follow through on commitments such as in Vietnam. Diem is a good example, whose assassination we effectively acquiesced in.

Chou [*Thieu*] and his government is another example. After we did win a military victory there and got a four-point agreement, by virtue of pressures which were unremitting both from the media and from Congress, we managed not to follow through on our commitment to him. We permitted the North Vietnamese divisions to crush South Vietnam and to take over their country with the resulting economic and sociological consequences.

The South Americans are not unaware of what happened to Diem and the Shah of Iran. In the case of Iran, the prophet, the great bearded Ayatollah, who in Paris was portrayed as the savior of the situation, has not improved the situation in Iran, has not improved U.S. interests in Iran. The South Americans are well aware of this unrealistic and disturbing element of U.S. foreign policy.

Mr. Ambassador, with reference to the four major Guatemalan guerrilla groups that met in Managua, you mentioned having copies of the actual secret agreements made during that meeting.[48] Could you furnish the subcommittee—

MR. ENDERS. With pleasure.

SENATOR DENTON. Without objection, these documents will be entered into the record. I did mention that there has not been terrorism in the United States like that which has occurred in other nations. But for your information, Mr. Ambassador, in our second to last hearing we had two policemen, special agents, from the Miami area who testified concerning Cuban Government involvement in drug traffic into the United States.[49] They also testified that they knew of 240 U.S.S.R.-manufactured grenades in the Miami area alone. When you think what a man with a pistol and one or two shots can do in a hotel in Washington, D.C., and start thinking about the thousands of Cuban agents that are in the Miami area alone, one can see the potential for terrorism and the potential for destruction in the United States. Thank God it has begun to become more widely understood.

Have you seen any evidence, sir, that guerrilla training of insurgents targeted against Central America has occurred in Mexican territory and, if so, would you describe the nature of such training and the nature of such evidence?

MR. ENDERS. Mr. Chairman, could I first comment a bit on your first remarks about the problem of the leftwing and the rightwing dictatorial or violent regimes. Obviously, one of the most difficult problems in foreign policy—I think we have all been impressed by the fact that Nicaragua has swung from a repressive rightwing regime to a repressive leftwing regime and seems, in spite of all of the efforts of the United States and a number of other countries to, say, present economic assistance and political connections—after all, Nicaragua has received, over the last 2 years, $600 or $700 million of economic assistance from the free world countries, including a $125 million cumulative from the United States. But it has marched steadily toward a one-party state without any remission. I think a great many Americans see this as a dilemma for our foreign policy.

I would say this, that when you have in front committed to a rightwing or strong military ruler, such as the Shah, and you then urge him on toward reform, it is quite possible that sometimes you weaken rather than strengthen him and it would be arguable this is what happened in Vietnam or arguable that this is what happened in Iran.

SENATOR DENTON. Weaken in what way, by pushing him too fast or by just the conspicuousness of our apparent help?

MR. ENDERS. Very often our effort to get such a ruler to embrace our values, our political values, makes him—undermines the basis on which he holds power. But that, I say, is when a commitment has been made. But when you have a country that wants to change itself—and this is the case of El Salvador—wants to change itself by reforming, to get out of the dilemma of the extreme right or extreme left, you move away from an old-line military regime, then you have a different situation. I say El Salvador is different because the old-line military regime, not unlike that of Somoza, not

---

[47] See *supra*.

[48] The secret agreements, along with additional responses to subcommittee questions, appear as exhibit C in the appendix to this hearing. [Footnote in the source text. For the texts, see *The Role of Cuba in International Terrorism and Subversion*, pp. 249–265.]

[49] For text of this hearing, see *ibid.*, pp. 23–77.

unlike that of Guatemala, came in determined to implement a land reform on a very broad scale and political reforms and to create democratic institutions. We got behind those reforms under the last administration and under this one. We did not impose them. We did not organize the reforms for them. We did not tell them they should do it. But we got behind them giving them economic and military aid because the revolution speared reforms and the immediate reaction from the violent left was to go into and act as insurgents.

In another case, Mr. Chairman, Central America, Guatemala, where the polarization is much greater, we have refrained from active and substantial support to the Guatemalan Government. We know that that Government is being challenged by a Marxist-Leninist organization. It is organized and supported in Cuba. We know that civil strife has been going on in that country for 25 years and that this is the third wave of it, third and very dangerous wave.

On the other hand, we have told the Guatemalan Government repeatedly that we do not see how they can ultimately stabilize the situation if it appears in their own country that everybody that is not actively for them is potentially regarded as an enemy by them and that the situation polarizes and those who wish to develop an alternative in the center are not permitted to move forward. We take the Guatemalan situation very seriously. But we have not committed the government in the way we have in El Salvador.

So I think it is important in thinking about the dilemma that you speak of, Mr. Chairman, to see where we are going before we commit a great country like the United States because we should carry through on commitments once they are made; therefore, we have to be particularly careful before in fact we engage ourselves.

Senator Denton. I by no means meant to imply that the Shah of Iran and Duarte were comparable. Duarte is far from a rightwing leader, which is another mystery to me, as to the way he is being portrayed. He has been trying to institute reforms. He is far left in his orientation from what we would choose to have, I would imagine. He is certainly not considered a rightwinger down there and the way he is portrayed in the American press astounds me. I just meant that the consistency of Americans following through on commitments to back certain rulers trying to deal with difficult circumstances, such as rampant terrorism, is a dismaying situation.

Mr. Enders. Well, I think the Cuban revolutionaries and the Soviet revolutionaries behind them want to put us in that dilemma and they want to have us in the position in which it is either—we either stick with Somoza or we have to take the Sandinistas. We should not permit ourselves to be locked into that choice. I think the fundamental objective of our policy in the region should be precisely to give ourselves the alternative choice of some social and political change.

Senator Denton. Would the Department's position be to see that the relatively young nations of Central and South America, with their revolutions coming in the late 19th century and early 20th century still going on, to see that they provide for the land and social reforms necessary to permit a sense of public confidence or assurance that their government is doing the best they can. Is that not generally the wish of the United States?

Mr. Enders. Yes, it is, Mr. Chairman. But I think we have to be aware that the countries are very different. There were three countries with traditional military style rightwing authoritarian governments: Guatemala, Nicaragua, and in the past, El Salvador. But Costa Rica is very different. You know, it overthrew such a military government 30 years ago and has had 30 years of model democracy. Honduras had a military government for the last 12 years. But in an election with 80-percent turnout, pretty good figure from an American point of view, 80-percent turnout, they elected a moderate center democratic regime. The small country of Belize, just now independent, is a democracy. Panama is a country of mixed institutions but not a repressive country. So each country has different problems. There was a particularly harsh land problem in El Salvador, partly because it is the most heavily populated country in the area and the man-to-land ratio is very unfavorable and partly also because so much of the land was in the hands of a relatively small number of people, creating an explosive social situation. Similar but not so severe conditions existed in Nicaragua. Thus, each of them have to be taken differently.

But you have, on the one hand, while trying to deal with economic and social problems of those countries as they mature, the problem of outside interference that has got to be dealt with too. Not only Cuba engaging in uniting the left and organizing the threats against the government, as you and I have both described, but also what you might call the ripple effect in Central America. When the challenge was being mounted against Somoza in Nicaragua, the Cuban consulate in San Jose, the capital of the neighboring state of Costa Rica, was used as the commander in control post and it was from there that the orders, the communications, and the logistics were organized.

Now that the struggle is going on in El Salvador, it is in Managua, the capital of Nicaragua, that the commander and control apparatus is present and the logistics is organized and the training is organized.

As you mentioned earlier, we have given the evidence which we have for this, which we regard as irrefutable, to the two intelligence committees, and the chairmen of the two intelligence committees have testified to its convincing character.

SENATOR DENTON. I will turn this over to Senator East but before I do, I did not mean to characterize the governments as all rightwing, all in need of that much push by us to reform. What I meant to draw out is that the United States is not simply in favor of a bunch of rich autocratic dictators staying in place so that we can capitalize on trade with them at the expense of the poor peasants. We are, in general, inclined toward the same view as the liberals are with respect to that area and we must recognize that there are countries down there doing almost superhuman—making almost superhuman achievements in that direction.

The big point I was trying to make, that this outside supply of military equipment, terrorist propaganda, technique, wherewithal, must be cut off.

. . . .

MR. ENDERS. Let me make several remarks.[50] First, in the United States we have always been a government of values, of human and political values, as well as a government of interests. We have both in the world. I do not think that the concern for democracy and human rights is a concern which should be identified with one American administration only. Indeed, I think that it was the Congress that took the lead very vigorously at the start of the 1970's in promoting human rights policies and this Government, this administration, has recognized human rights policy as a permanent interest, the phrase used, of the United States. I think that is really common ground for all of us. I agree with you.

SENATOR EAST. Excuse me. How would we, for instance, describe our desire to continue to improve relations with Communist China?

MR. ENDERS. Perhaps I could go on.

SENATOR EAST. Go ahead.

MR. ENDERS. The second thing I would say about that is, I would agree with you here, is that it is nonsensical to over value our influence abroad, to believe that our views on what kind of political institutions one should have, our particular social arrangements, are the model to which everybody else must comply. Sometimes in the past, Americans have had that kind of assurance. I would agree with you that it is wrong to have that.

That said, I would say—and the third remark I would make, that with regard to Latin America, that the idea of democracy is a very strong one in the Americas. That two-thirds of the countries in the area are democracies in some form and almost all of those that are not feel they must recognize democracy as the ideal. Exceptions, of course, are Cuba which does not feel that it must recognize that as the ideal and we feel now Nicaragua, becoming every day a more repressive state.

But others, even when they are not democracies, feel they must recognize that the rule of law and democratic institutions are an ideal and people want to return to that.

The fourth thing I would say is that we agree very much that we should not attempt to use our relationship as somehow a kind of pressure point on human rights issues. There is a kind of internal inconsistency here. Somehow you say that you know, that if you are interested in changing human rights patterns in a given country, if you do not—if you are not present, if they have no stake in the relationship with you, there are no common goals, no sense of commitment one to the other, that it is very hard to achieve the kind of improvement that as one goal of our policy we have been seeking in human rights.

So, in contrast to some of the tactics applied earlier, we have, in fact, cultivated

---

[50] Enders was responding to a statement by Senator East on human rights and U.S. foreign policy, not printed; for the text of this statement, see *ibid.*, pp. 152–155.

the relationships we have throughout the continent and I did not mean to suggest earlier that we are not cultivating our relationship, diplomatic and political relationship with the Guatemalan Government or other governments in the hemisphere, that we are trying to keep them at arms length. Only by doing so, it seems to us, that countries will feel that they have a commitment to the United States, that there are common goals and when we make observations, as we have in a number of countries, that human rights issues, do we have some chance of having people react that there is some reason why we should pay attention to what the United States has to say.

In other words, we have attempted to create relationships of solidarity in which these problems can be addressed rather than antagonistic ones.

I would share very much your view that the United States does not have the influence, does not have the power, does not have the authority to dictate and should not attempt to dictate to other countries what their practices will be. But it is a permanent value of this country and, therefore, we do pursue it in relationships with many of the countries in which problems exist.

Now I would, finally, agree with you very strongly that, and I would like to talk about my area only, that human rights violations by leftwing governments must be as vigorously exposed by the international community and human rights organizations as those by rightwing governments. That has not always been the case in the past and it is one of the reasons why we have felt it necessary to go to such efforts on the Miskito Indians. The chairman mentioned that at the start of the session, because it was not becoming clear that in fact a massive repression was underway against an ethnic group in Nicaragua, an ethnic group that could not threaten Managua.

Of course, all the Miskito Indians were not going to take over the country. They wanted to be left alone and also to be free to not agree with the government in Nicaragua, the Sandinistas, to do what they wanted to do. Twelve thousand refugees crossed the border into Honduras, as a result of the repression.

So, yes, the human rights violations on all sides must be known.

SENATOR EAST. Then I would simply make this point: I can appreciate your area is Central America and Latin America and you are not going to be expected to speak for the rest of the world in terms of the administration's policy. But it strikes me the administration today, as well as the Carter administration, runs into some very, very difficult problems with the so-called human rights test. I think, as a composite of a whole lot of other things to consider it is useful, but to make it the litmus test of a viable relationship between our country and other countries, I would submit, as a matter of political reality in the world, is hopelessly unworkable. Again, I do not see it being applied in the Middle East as regards Saudi Arabia and Jordan. I do not see it being applied in the Far East, as regards Communist China.

It seems to be applied very fully and selectively in a very high profile in your area of Latin America and Central America and I am not sure, Mr. Secretary, to our disadvantage in that we are asking for the impossible. We are asking for the unworkable, that which has never been, and, unknowingly, unwittingly, it works clearly to the advantage of the very thing you say we have to be concerned with in terms of the security of this country, which this subcommittee is concerned with, namely, the Soviet-Cuban connection in Central America and in Latin America.

Then I will end on this note; not to place all of the blame, if blame is the right word, on this administration—I think they are part of the policy that evolved out of the previous administration, to some extent, somewhat a captive of it.

But I notice the Mexican Government continues to build its relationship with Cuba or with the Sandinistas and I do not see it is insisting on human rights—granted, you are not representing the Mexican Government. But suppose they were working with Mexico to achieve those ends that we see that the Mexican Government is seeking to attain, utilizing that standard. They utilize it with respect to the governments they see to the right. As for those to the left, Portillo embraced Castro.

Candidly, it strikes me that it is very selectively applied and always to those governments perceived as being right of center. I think, if the human rights concept is not to bring itself into a position of a totally laughable concept, it will have to be universally applied and to Communist China, for example.

I submit, once you start to do it, it will be as clear as a bell that it is totally unrealistic. The realities of international relations cannot be reduced to a slogan such as human rights and elevated into the first principle of foreign policy.

I think in the real world of international relations, it will come to our undoing and I think to some extent it has contributed to the undoing, in Latin America.

MR. ENDERS. Senator, I meant to say we were a government both of value and interests. After your last remarks, I would say we were a government of interests as well as values too. We must have both together and I think we must have both together for the reason that there is in fact great political strength in the development of democratic values and human rights but that cannot be the only concern of our foreign policy. One of the things that in the past might have happened in Latin America, we have had an a la carte approach. We deal with countries in the area on the basis of one item that we are particularly interested in and then we ignore all of the rest of the concerns, including a lot of their concerns.

We ought to have policies with countries that address them as countries, as well as address some single category of relationship and I would agree that you must put them all together and, above all, you should have the cultivation of a relationship over a long period of time as an important goal and that applies to something on both sides about what can be done in relationship with a country.

SENATOR DENTON. Thank you. I certainly understand the importance of the principle that this country has interests in the sense of vital national interests, selfish interests, which are of great importance, which we try to apply in international affairs. I think that is the best possible heading that could be placed upon such important anomalies as our dealing with Red China because in the long term our policies are all contributing toward that which is pragmatically conducive to the preservation of our own freedom in this Nation and to the longer range threat to freedom possible throughout the world. I believe occasionally we have to make arrangements which, on the face of it, and taken in isolation, appear to be counter to human rights, such as whatever interests we might have with Red China at this time.

But, over the long term, for one pragmatic reason or another, it seems we serve both ends but it is often not obvious. I hope that is not totally cryptic.

MR. ENDERS. I understand very well.

SENATOR DENTON. Turning to my earlier question, which you adroitly avoided, regarding terrorist activity in Central America—terrorists operating in Central America being trained in Mexico, I realize that we have a very sensitive set of relations around the world, including those with Mexico. To the degree that there may be any terrorist activity or any terrorist training in Mexico, I would ascribe it to Mexico's leadership's feeling the necessity to walk a tightrope, similar to that which Torrijos was walking. So I do not ask you that question with an intent to bruise our relations or to assign guilt to Mexico, but we do have the situation in which they are asking for sort of unconditional negotiations with the rebels in El Salvador. In addition, we have our Secretary of State saying, well, he can go along with the serious discussion about that but it does—from the Mexican point of view, it does omit one of the important policy requisites of ours, namely, that the external aid from the Moscow–Havana thing be cut off.

I would be interested in any comment you would care to make with regard to what you know about terrorist activity, terrorist training in Mexico because it looks like a double-tongued position we are taking.

MR. ENDERS. Well, I would not wish to suggest, Mr. Chairman, that there are any activities which are being fostered or supervised by the Mexican Government. I take it that your question did not refer to that.

SENATOR DENTON. Not necessarily, no, sir.

MR. ENDERS. But it is a fairly open society and that we have in fact had reports that this open society and fairly open territory have been used in the past for the passage of arms certainly to some of the revolutionary movements in Central America, in neighboring Guatemala. But also some further south, too. So, indeed, there are such reports, Mr. Chairman.

SENATOR DENTON. As an experienced Foreign Service officer, how would you estimate the impact of the success of terrorist technique which Marighella outlined?[51] Suppose the terrorists were to be successful in El Salvador? What would be your assessment of its impact regarding Latin America?

MR. ENDERS. Well, two things: I think, first of all, the pressure on the neighbors would be enormous and immediate. You

[51] The reference is to a book by Brazilian Communist Carlos Marighella entitled *Mini-Manual for Urban Guerillas.*

know, Costa Rica has no army. So if you have got two states associated with Cuba in the central part of Central America, you would find that it would not be long before you would get a progressive, I am sure it would be called, social-political change in Costa Rica, although the great majority of the—practically everybody in Costa Rica would be against that.

It is not very far, as we know, to Panama with its canal. It is not very far to cross Honduras which has suffered from a severe economic problem, as has Costa Rica. It is not very far across there to Guatemala where there is a major insurgency underway. So there would be no obstacle for that insurgency almost immediately and, of course, Guatemala is on the southern border of Mexico and shares its—its people share many of the languages and ethnic traits of the people in southern Mexico.

So you have a—I spoke earlier of a ripple effect. You would have a ripple effect of some real power underway.

I think the second thing that would be said would be that the United States has shown the will or the power to influence events to outcomes which are compatible with United States interests and they would draw the conclusion from that that the way in which they regarded the United States and their willingness to identify with and work with the United States. I think that they would then begin to recalculate their own interests.

SENATOR DENTON. The testimony yesterday from Dr. Ikle indicated that the time schedule of these shifts in military power as well as, say, the psychological effect of the installation in El Salvador of the Nicaraguan-type government—you said the military situation there seems to be on the verge of great changes; in other words, the balance of power in that area, even with respect to the U.S. capacities to deal with it we effectively have a 1½-ocean navy for a 3-ocean commitment. If you have the Caribbean and the Gulf, we have a 1½ navy for a 4-ocean commitment. Such things as Soviet Mig's utilizing runways now under preparation and so forth, I believe, from a military point of view, would represent another factor of great importance other than the psychological effect which you just mentioned.

MR. ENDERS. Yes. You know, we have never had to be worried about a major threat on our borders, either north or south. This has been a uniquely favorable geographic position which of course is not shared by the Soviet Union. It has to be worried about its southern border and indeed it has 1 million men on the Chinese border. The United States already must be concerned about the buildup in Cuba. We are well aware of the fact that if in fact there were a crisis in Europe, that the resupply of Europe would have to be largely through the Gulf and the Caribbean area and that there is the possibility that it could be challenged or threatened by Cuba and that the diversion of resources would be required for that, substantial resources.

If, in fact, we were to face the same kind of buildup in Central America, the impact on our military situation would be yet graver.

SENATOR DENTON. I believe that in one of the hearings I attended in the Senate Armed Services Committee last week, Admiral Hayward testified that 40 to 50 percent of the seaborne traffic necessary to reallocate, redistribute the military climate of our forces, 40 to 50 percent of that would have to flow through the Panama Canal were there to be such a European development. With the change in military balance, which seems pending within the next matter of a few months, I am amazed at the context in which this whole matter is being placed for the American public's consumption by those who are the sole transporters of perspective.

You have said that the Department of State has evidence that the Cuban Government has engaged in drug smuggling activities in the United States, citing the case of Jaime Guillot Lara, a Colombian now in jail in Mexico, who claims to have funneled arms and money to Colombian leftist groups in shipping arms shipments to the United States. You described that in your opening statement.

Can you talk more about the evidence apart from the Jaime Guillot Lara case? There have been press reports that Guillot received $700,000 from Raoul Castro himself. Does the Department of State have any evidence as to who gave Guillot arms or anything else you can state with regard to this?

MR. ENDERS. Mr. Chairman, we do not have further information to put in the public record. However, we would be happy to work with members of the subcommittee on a classified basis.

SENATOR DENTON. We shall submit other questions in that vein and look forward to receiving the responses.[52]

---

52 Ambassador Enders' answers to subcommit-

I referred in my opening remarks to a *New York Times* article about Cuba's school for exporting communism.[53] The article referred to the Isle of Youth, formerly the Isle of Pines. As you know, it is a small island 30 miles off the southwest coast of Cuba.

According to the article, since 1977, some 26,000 children from Cuba, Africa, and Central America have been brought to this island, this Cuban island, for controversial work and study programs that are a mixture of study and Communist indoctrination. There have been reports for several years that not all of the children on the island, especially those from Africa, are there voluntarily.

General Simon stated that many children are abused and sent to the island without the knowledge or consent of their parents.

Do you have any information to be furnished concerning this island and the allegations that some of these children were abducted? Yesterday, I inserted a copy of this article into the record and we did receive an affirmative response from Dr. Ikle saying these were not just rumors. These were facts.

Do you have anything to add to that?

MR. ENDERS. Well, I think it is probably quite true, and as far as we can tell, in a number of cases has been true, that young people have been taken to the island without the consent of their parents. Whether they have in fact been taken there without their own consent is less easy to determine. But we have heard reports of that. But I am on much surer grounds on the former from what I know, Mr. Chairman, than on the latter.

SENATOR DENTON. The ages of those children range from 9 years old up. We will be having hearings beginning March 22, which will be revelatory regarding some of the Communist activities in Africa and how "humane" some of these activities are.

In view of your schedule, Mr. Ambassador, we will submit the rest of our questions to you for the record. We thank you very much for your most informed and enlightened testimony.

Would you please furnish the subcommittee with copies of the documents you mentioned in your statement concerning insurgency in Honduras and captured documents and declarations which demonstrate the true motive and origins of the guerrillas there. You mentioned a school book from a 1-year training program held in Cuba in 1980. We would very much appreciate inclusion in our record of those documents and reports.

MR. ENDERS. We will.

SENATOR EAST. I too would like to thank the Secretary for coming. We appreciate your patience and being very helpful.

MR. ENDERS. Thank you, Senators.

---

tee questions appear as exhibit B in the appendix to this hearing. [Footnote in the source text. For the Department of State response to these questions, see *The Role of Cuba in International Terrorism and Subversion*, pp. 221–248.]

[53] For Denton's opening remarks, see *ibid.*, pp. 139–142. The article referred to, "Cuba's School for Exporting Marxism," by Jo Thomas, appeared in the *New York Times Magazine*, October 4, 1981; also reprinted in *The Role of Cuba in International Terrorism and Subversion*, pp. 126–131.

Document 679

Transcript of a Department of State Press Briefing, March 13, 1982 (Extracts)[54]

U.S. Policy in Central America

. . . .

What I am trying to make clear about Salvador is what I said on the Hill the other day. This is a global problem. In some respects, that is why it is not a repeat of Vietnam. We treated Vietnam not as a global problem, in general, but rather as a regional struggle, or an in-country struggle, for hearts and minds, and that was a distortion of the earlier period of America's strategic thinking that emerged in the early sixties where, you recall, we used to talk about the spectrum of deterrence.

We had nuclear deterrence, because we had superiority. We had conventional deterrence, and somehow we had to deal with the problem of counterinsurgency. You remember the special forces and all the resources and so-called hearts and minds struggle that emerged during that period.

[54] Office of Press Relations, Department of State. The briefing, which began at 9:48 a.m., was conducted on background by a senior Department of State official.

It tended to drive us into viewing the struggle in Southeast Asia in a very narrow band of what I call geopolitical leverage, that we could somehow fight that and defeat it on the ground in a complementary or a corresponding response to the hearts and minds question.

It was a terribly misleading and specious approach.

The problem was global there. The problem is global in Salvador.

Now, it is quite natural with all of the national attention, your attention, and the focuses on, "Are we doing enough to save El Salvador with a limited amount of economic aid and even more limited amount of military aid", that, of course, if you apply that litmus test, serious doubts have to emerge.

Why do they have to emerge? Well, first, everyone that applies the analysis says that it is an open-ended receptacle for Cuban arms and Nicaraguan support, and the only thing left for the United States is to do what we did in Vietnam, up the ante of creeping escalation and increasing involvement.

Let me tell you, the President's policy is to avoid precisely that and to deal with this issue as a global problem. That means that we have to harness, and we have been, the full panoply of political, economic and security assets of the United States to deal with this problem in Moscow, in Havana, in the regional context, the OAS, and in Salvador itself.

In the Salvadoran aspect, it is only a small, admittedly high profile, very visible picture, but it is not our approach.

And I urge you not to be overly mesmerized by a myopic preoccupation with that problem.

In that context, from the outset, we have been actively engaged in the full panoply of the assets I spoke to. That is where you get to the problem here at home, which, admittedly, concerns me a great deal.

You can't talk about all of the work that is underway, the discussions, the directions in policy. So, there is this fixation.

If you take one narrow end of the—to use that bad word again—the spectrum of American assets to deal with the problem and focus on it, and then start delineating constraints on your ability to deal in that area, such as the kinds of resolutions that are developing on the Hill by well-meaning guys, who have developed the kinds of fears that we have just talked about, for understandable reasons, then you skew the whole panoply of executive assets that are available to apply to the management of the outcome.

That, I think, is dangerous, because it risks distortions and anomalies which then perhaps have to create new ones to compensate for them. That is not good, either—that is not good, either.

So, I just say that I have given you that little theological dissertation to whet your appetites and you can ask additional questions, if you want, but I really do want to reemphasize again that we are not changing our policy. It has been the same from the very beginning, and it is to avoid a Vietnam model, not to pursue one.

I think we must have learned something from Vietnam. If we didn't learn the lesson that it was a global problem, that we mismanaged badly by local preoccupation, then we didn't learn anything.

Q. Well, sir, some of the preoccupation in El Salvador focuses on people being killed there, and whether this country might become more heavily involved there if we agree to send American troops.

Aren't those legitimate issues for public concern, public debate?

A. Of course they are, but they are not—you see there is a constant drift to that. No one—and I think if you go back in the record, you will find no one has threatened to use military force in El Salvador. The President has said there were no plans. I have said there were no plans. That is a simple fact of life. I don't know of any responsible official in the administration who has suggested the use of forces. But to go out public every day and have to reiterate that does constitute a jeopardy to the panoply of the application of American national power to bring about a peaceful settlement on terms which protect America's vital interests.

The more people ask the question, despite the fact that it has been answered repeatedly, why the more skewed the conduct of the full panoply of your assets becomes.

I have said that no prudent leader is going to draw fences around the options that are available to him. If he does, he then affects the calculus of the parties with which he is dealing, and it can affect him in a profound way.

Q. But isn't the fixation on the possible use of troops to some extent caused by the failure on the administration's side to point out what the alternatives are? I think that some segments of the public look at the situation on the ground they are worsening and see the possibility that d'Aubuisson and the right wing might have power as a result of the elections, a polarization down there, face the fact that we might—quote/unquote—lose El Salvador, and then this administration be confronted with a very dramatic either/or situation, either some kind of massive involvement to prevent the loss of El Salvador.

A. No. There you are, again. I understand the logic—.

Q. That is what I am trying to say. What are the alternatives?

A. The alternative is to recognize that this is a global problem and is going to be solved in global terms, or we will ultimately and could ultimately be faced with a decision as to whether we give up Central America and all that implies, or not. But, you know, again, I want to just emphasize that everything you deal with is a consequence of historic forces, an evolution of realities.

I noticed somebody saying, well, you know, this administration doesn't know what it is doing or where it is going.

I am rather hard-pressed to accept that from critics who presided over the loss of Angola, the loss of Ethiopia, the loss of Southern Yemen, the loss of Iran, the loss of Afghanistan, the re-introduction of Cuban-sponsored insurgency in this hemisphere starting in a major way in about 1978. These are the problems that we were faced with in January.

Now, the question is, are we going to drive carefully and in the same evolutionary way and try to deal with it in an affective manner.

Q. But let me follow up, doesn't the embrace of a global solution, or treating this as a global problem, change to some extent the direction of American policy?

It sounds to me—and correct me if I am wrong—that you are saying that we have to talk to the Russians about this, we have to talk to the Cubans about this.

A. Of course. As we did in the case of Vietnam, but always in a somewhat different way.

Q. Doesn't that take us down more the negotiating track than the track of putting all our eggs in the election basket?

A. No. It takes you down a multiplicity of tracks. It means that there are discussions that must be held. There are steps that must be taken in the political, the economic and in the security areas, which tend to influence calculi in Moscow, in Havana, in Nicaragua, and in the regional context.

It is a very complex mosaic of interrelated actions which must be consistent, credible, and hopefully will ultimately bring about a successful outcome.

Now, I am not pessimistic unless we castrate ourselves.

. . . .

Q. Are you suggesting that you can persuade the Soviets, given the description you say exists, to back off the supply of things to the Cubans, and to persuade the Cubans themselves to back off from their Communist efforts?

A. I am suggesting that you don't have the luxury of dealing with this problem in any other way. There is no other way to deal with it effectively other than in more traumatic ways that some people fear, but not in El Salvador.

Q. Can you give us some specific examples of how—you say you are dealing with Moscow and Havana—how, specifically, have you been?

A. No, I can't make a public disclosure of these things. They are all interrelated. There are other regional problems which are of interest to the Soviet Union as well, including those that are disadvantageous to them. You can apply diplomatic and political leverage.

But you have the same problem. That analysis that I gave you of the Soviet Union, you could translate into Havana where a similar set of systematic failures have become pervasive.

Against all that, you have to apply a calculus of what the Marxist-Leninist leadership has been historically. Above all, do not assume some naive expectations. These are tough guys. Castro is a tough guy. They do not necessarily succumb to Western rationalizations, as clear as they may be to us.

They are very culturally conscious of power. And when you get to the Soviet Union today, you look at their larder of assets to deal globally, and it is almost exclusively an unprecedented military capability.

These are the dangers.

Q. Could I go to your premise, because I think the premise that you have pointed out is the thing that a lot of the argument, public argument, has been about over the past several months, and that is that El Salvador is fundamentally a global problem.

You have asserted that it is commanded and controlled from the outside; that it is supported by the outside; whereas the critics have relied on much more of an historical Salvador and Central America context flowing out of history of the social forces and the groups within the country.

A. Yes.

Q. Could you give us a little more of your thinking behind the conclusion that this is fundamentally a global problem?

A. In making that observation . . . you always risk the distortion that you don't believe it is also an in-country problem of some magnitude.

There is in Central America, as has been stated, an historic change. It has lagged in time, the emergence of more modern democratic attitudes.

We know that. Costa Rica is a very good exception. Venezuela, which had its revolution, is another good exception, but if you can look at the others, then you find the old ways—the military dictatorships or oligarchy arrangements, which had a few overtones in El Salvador, with the families down there.

It doesn't mean that we don't have a requirement to deal with that. My God, it is essential. But it is that that is being exploited by the external command and control, and which in strategic terms, not in value terms, and again I don't want to relegate value terms to something less important to the United States than the strategic aspect. Both have to be dealt with, and both must be kept in context. But in strategic terms, if this external interventionism continues to spread, if it achieves momentum before the reforms that you are seeking in the socioeconomic and political area can take root, and it is going to take a decade or more. And we haven't got the resources to go in and just eliminate these human problems.

We have got to deal with it in both terms. I would suggest, however, if we could get an exclusion of intervention, continue to apply political and economic assets in a multilateral framework so it doesn't get the label of "big brotherism", which is anathema in the region, and which is what we have tried to avoid in the Caribbean Basin Initiative, then we have great reason for hope that modernization will continue, that social justice will be achieved, to the degree that it ever is totally achieved in any system, and that democracy and democratic principles will increasingly make headway.

You can't afford to focus on one and forget the other, because one external intervention of the magnitude of what we are witnessing in Nicaragua and Salvador, if left untended despite our best hopes in the progress you make, you are going to have an extreme outcome.

Q. If I might follow that point, you have said some fairly interesting things lately which seem to draw a line between Cuba and Central America and the northern tier of South America.

Do you still think that, given the approach you are setting out here, taking Nicaragua specifically, it is still salvageable in terms of your strategic interests?

A. Of course.

Q. How interested are you in the Mexican proposals[55] with that in mind?

A. Let's talk about the Mexican proposal.

I have seen the observations that we are either cool to it or rejected it or now we have suddenly been driven to be happy with it.

None of those observations are accurate.

First, in August, we went to Nicaragua. Tom Enders went down and laid out a series of proposals that involved mutual guarantees, limits on Nicaraguan armaments, and a sine qua non that a negotiating approach was an agreement by the Sandinistas to terminate their assistance to the movement in El Salvador and to leave their neighbors alone—get a commitment to do so.

Frankly, they rejected that. We discussed that. I have been in constant communication with Castañeda and with López Portillo. I discussed it when I was in Mexico City.

They went down there and they built on what had been rejected by the Nicaraguans in the U.S. proposal, that includes specific things like nonaggression pacts with

[55] See Secretary Haig's press briefing, *supra.*

neighbors and possible peacekeeping forces, and, again, it was an almost myopic preoccupation with the Nicaraguan-Salvadoran case, if you get what I am driving at.

That doesn't mean Mexico doesn't understand the global character of this thing either. If you will go back and look at the speech of [*that*] López Portillo made last week,[56] the beginning of the week, he poll-parroted exactly what I have said. You have got to look at Cuba and you have got to look at the Soviet Union in this mix, and you have got to deal with all of them.

The judgments we have to make, with respect to the Mexican proposal, which unfortunately lacked the definitive in the sine qua non area. Their proposal, if you read it carefully, at least as we interpreted it here, did not touch upon in specific terms the guarantee to keep the hell out of the affairs of neighboring states.

Without that, it only becomes a delaying negotiating tactic to permit the activity to continue, or at least we have to be concerned, as Americans, that that might be the outcome, and we cannot permit that.

I have made that clear to the Mexicans. They understand it. They do not reject it. But we are in a constant communication on the thing, and I will be discussing it again this weekend with Castañeda—tomorrow, Sunday, as a matter of fact.

We have to make a judgment, how is the best way to deal with that. We are every bit as capable as the Mexicans of dealing with the Nicaraguans. We certainly are with the Cubans and with the Soviets. In fact, we are better able to.

It doesn't mean that we don't welcome ancillary communication and ancillary suggestion, and so we would not reject out of hand, and indeed we welcome intelligent suggestions that would bring this thing to a peaceful solution, which will not put in jeopardy the vital interest that we are concerned about, either in the value terms or in the strategic interests of the United States.

That is the answer to your question. It is too early to say, but it isn't a question of whether we are being forced into the arms of the Mexican proposal. Hell, we have been engaged in that from the beginning. It isn't a case of whether we have decided that their framework is better. As of now, we think it lacks the essential ingredient which is necessary, but they are busy trying to deal with that.

Q. What about the analysis that things may continue to turn sour in El Salvador, that the right wing could do very well in the election, if not win it, and that the Mexican proposal may ultimately provide the Americans with a fig leaf to get out from under a mess?

A. Again, that is the Vietnam syndrome all over again, a negotiated settlement, hearts and minds, establish a balance of forces internally.

None of that is relevant. None of it is relevant, unless you have dealt with the global aspect of it. Is Cuba going to continue an insurgency offensive in Central America, which is not exclusively focused on El Salvador, or the militarization of Nicaragua, but involves Colombia, and Honduras, Guatemala, Costa Rica, and perhaps tomorrow, Mexico.

These are all part of the same problem. There is no graceful declaring yourself a winner and pulling out, like we tried to do in Vietnam. That is a little harsh on the Vietnam solution. The problem with Vietnam was that we negotiated a settlement, but we didn't have the national will to enforce the sanctions that must underline any international agreement. That was the problem.

Had we been willing to do that, you would probably still have a viable South Vietnam today.

Q. Could you address the options you think you might have in the event of a right wing victory in the election?

A. I wouldn't want to see too many predictions that that would be the outcome. I don't delude myself that the right wing candidate enjoys both charisma and a great deal of popular support at home. I think you all must understand that that support is founded on the fact that he said he is going to solve the problem. He is going to clean house and he is going to get bloodshed and terrorism off the back of the people. That is a very appealing practice.

Q. What do the people think about that?

A. When you are a victim of this thing, you don't become necessarily a banner-carrier for esoteric values. It is very easy for us to do that here in a comfortable position, but when your children and families are affected—

Q. The Christian Democrats think they will be the principal victims of those activities.

[56] See document 671.

A. There is some concern, sure. But it is too early to say how that thing will come out. I don't mean to suggest to you that we will be happy with a right wing victory. That would complicate everything here tremendously. It goes without saying. But I am not so sure that the Salvadorans do not understand that.

But to the degree that we engage in rhetorical irresponsibility here at home with respect to support for a democratic process, as weak as far as it is under Duarte, to that degree, you affect the subjective attitudes of an electorate, whose lives are on the line.

Q. By saying it could only be solved in the global framework, are you not laying yourself open to the line of thinking that you have become so discouraged by the situation on the ground that you have found it necessary to shift the focus?

A. Not at all. We never shifted the focus. We started this way. That is the point I made at the outset. That has never been. Do you think, for a moment, the provision of 52 or 53 American advisers and the level of military assistance were designed to achieve a military victory? In Salvador? Not at all.

You have got to hold in reasonable balance the forces for a pluralistic outcome, a democratic outcome, given what you can within the limits available to you, that can be supported by our assets and our own assessment of what makes the difference. The difference is not going to be there.

Q. Well, if you are going to go into a global showdown in El Salvador—

A. That is not what anybody is saying at all. That is exactly where you are wrong. It is not a global showdown.

Q. What is it?

A. It is the application, it is the conduct of affairs, historically. It has never been different. The same thing in Poland. It is not a global showdown. It is a recognition that the Soviet Union has certain interests and certain vulnerabilities, and that we have political, economic and security assets with which to deal with them in such a way that they conclude in their own calculation that the advantages of moderation and a shift in direction outweigh the advantages that a continuation of interventionism that they launched in an unusual way starting in about 1976.

You are a historian. You have lived in this town. You know these things. Why do you have to put it in a question of a global showdown? We are not talking about a global showdown. We are in a global showdown. We were from the day that we started out with the Soviet Union. In that context, we have diverging interests.

In some instances, we have converging interests. Certainly the levels of armaments expenditure is one. Nuclear growth is another. Economic interface is a third. Stability in a decent dialogue is a fourth.

Q. If you are dealing with them, if you are trying to give them a message, let's say, about El Salvador, if you put pressure on them in Country X in South Asia, how do you make sure that they get the message that your action in Country X is designed to discourage them from subverting governments in Latin America?

A. There is another aspect to that question that probably should remain unsaid. Again, if you look at the historic evolution of Marxist-Leninism, you have a Russian empire in trouble. The Soviet ideology has always grasped the self-proclaimed right through wars of national liberation to support a legitimate quest for social justice to spread revolution.

Now, that was a very comfortable position at the end of the second war in ideological terms, and it provided a very nice framework which was contradictory and confusing to many in the West, to justify what they were doing.

They really were more rhetorical than they were actual until we saw the offensives in Africa, the Middle East, and Southeast Asia, but that is probably not a lack of will; it was a lack of both resources and capability to project their power, as well as a greater degree of vigor in the West in dealing with it.

Now, the picture has changed from the Soviets' objective point of view. How has it changed? Well, the Soviets suddenly found themselves in Afghanistan being bogged down, where they are the protectors of the status quo and a new revolutionary movement is threatening them.

We have a liberation movement in Poland.

Ask yourselves the question, as you debate a Soviet official, if we were to apply the yardsticks you insist you have a right to apply in a global sense in the developing world to areas within your traditional sphere of influence, or even in areas of strategic importance to you that are not in that sphere, what would be your position?

What I am saying is, Soviet vulnerabilities have changed.

Now, I don't mean to suggest anything, because . . . your next question would be, "You mean you are going to start subverting Poland?" The answer is no. But it must be a recognized vulnerability in Moscow. It must be.

Q. What sense do you have in your debates with the Soviet officials, if you bring these things up, that they will have an effect, that this will work, and that this will create a situation that we want?

A. There are never any guarantees. It is not something overnight. It is something that we must be careful with, because of the sensitivity, and hopefully with an unrestricted panoply of Western assets with which to deal. . . .

. . . .

Q. I understand, but don't you run the risk of—and how would you face the risk—of reaching a bottom line situation in Central America, while you were still debating these pressure tactics? In other words, the situation keeps deteriorating there, and then you could be forced into a situation on the ground.

A. No. In the first place, I think, at this juncture, I will stick my neck out and say there will be an election in Salvador. The situation has not deteriorated to the degree that intense public focus might suggest. I mean by that that it is good. It wasn't good a year ago, but, my God, when we came in in January, there was a serious doubt whether the whole thing was about to collapse.

There is a strong consensus in Salvador, a popular consensus that Duarte, the election, that the guerrillas, that the guerrillas are bad, they are oppressive of the people, but that they want a successful election. And where does that come from? It comes from the church, it comes from the peasant organizations, it comes from the trade union organizations, the business community. It is there. And you go down there and you know it is there.

. . . .

Q. You think, then, that Nicaragua is salvageable (inaudible)?

A. I think Nicaragua today is salvageable. It is clear from private polls taken by the private sector, not the Sandinistas, that the Sandinista's level of support in Nicaragua is about 25 percent, that the large bulk of the Nicaraguan people are very uncomfortable by what is going on.

There is a still remaining viable private sector, there is a strong church that is independent. There is a trade union movement, which is independent, and wants to remain that way. There is a press, in which, admittedly, by playing with broken fingernails on a marble wall, continues to function, and wants to function, and that is adjusting its own demeanor downward in the sense of freedom, but that is in order to preserve their integrity for tomorrow.

That final chapter has not been written, but all of the trends are extremely worrisome, and that is why we have an obligation to highlight what is going on. It would be irresponsible in the extreme to turn our back to what is happening in Nicaragua. That is not just a question of convincing the American people to support our repressive policies in Salvador. That is a problem of profound moral issues. We have to do it. Because, God knows, in 6 months or a year or 2 years, there is a microcosm of Havana in Nicaragua, you would be then demanding why in God's name did you let this happen? Why didn't you tell us? We have to.

Q. Have you asked—I want to come back for just a minute to this exclusion of armaments statement—have you asked either the Soviets or the Cubans through your own channels to stop sending arms into the area? Have you received any kind of a response?

A. Without saying yes to you, of course, among a whole number of other things that we deal with.

Q. Have you received anything encouraging?

A. I can't tell you. I am not discouraged. I think we have to continue, and we don't have the luxury not to.

Q. And yet—I understand your analysis of the Soviet Union's position and how it has changed—but the Cubans, on the other hand, who are probably the more proximate problem here, have been under sanctions, political and economic sanctions for many, many years now, and yet, as you yourself point out, there is support for these kinds of activities throughout the hemisphere that has increased.

Now, what is there in that situation?

A. Why has it increased? That is the first thing to ask yourself, as an historian.

Q. All right, why has it increased?

A. I would suggest to you it increased after Vietnam when they saw the emerging American policy consequences of Vietnam, when they felt they could move in an unprecedented way, and they started to do it.

Now, what about Moscow, and that has certain differences. But when you talk about sanctions, first, those economic sanctions have had a devastating impact on Cuba. Anyone who visits Cuba today just opens his eyes and you see the consequences of it. So it is not meaningless. But they work out a very comfortable economic modus for them. That was the Soviet Union. They don't have a balance-of-payments problem. They get their energy for subsidized sugar that the Soviets pay for, plus $9 million a day of Soviet support.

Now, that is becoming increasingly difficult, especially for those forces [that] are deployed to Africa, 40,000 to 50,000. That costs money. And who is paying the bills? The Soviet Union. Castro knows that he is going to be judged by history ultimately as to what he did for his people, and he hasn't done very much. He is not a dumbhead, we know that. He is not a dumbhead. He is gutsy and toughminded, and has been extremely skilled in dealing with up-hill/down-hill Western and American pressures. And he has responded to it.

If you go back and look at the missile crisis period, when the first Cuban offensive occurred in this hemisphere, we then had more assets and we had a greater national will to deal with such threats in the Kennedy years, before the involvement in Southeast Asia. We had a full panoply program then. I know, because I worked it. I worked for Cy Vance when he was the executive agent in the interdepartment committee that Jack Kennedy set up and sort of put under the wing of Bobby Kennedy. We had a whole host of programs, as many as a thousand items which we reported on weekly to Jack Kennedy. It involved education, it involved aid programs, it involved counterinsurgency training, it involved police equipment in Central America. It was a full panoply. And Castro drew the conclusion about that time that this was just a loser for him, so he pulled his horns back. He didn't terminate it. He didn't abandon his revolution or his credentials, but he didn't start up again at the level we have seen back in'76, or'78, excuse me.

Q. Excuse me, this is about the nicest thing I have ever heard you say about Fidel Castro—

A. What do you mean?

Q. As to his skill.

A. I have also referred to him from time-to-time as the armpit—(Laughter)

Q. Maybe this is just the ones I remember. But what you are saying suggests to me that there may be some carrots that the United States could apply to Cuba.

A. Of course.

Q. And we have heard—at least I remember hearing more about the kinds of sticks we might have had available to use on Cuba.

A. When you have been engaged in a 6-year self-delusion that carrots solve the problems of the world, in dialectic fashion, you have got to make it very clear that there are other things as well, and there are sticks. And the perception that America had to face in 1981 was that we were devoid of the will to even consider sticks.

That is what I call the reapplication of balance in the American foreign policy.

Now, there are some that might subjectively consider that a partisan question. It is not a partisan question, because it started in the period of Gerry Ford, and the American people put in someone who articulated an even further expression of that approach.

If you look at any speech I give, I talked about the balance in the technical conduct of American foreign policy. On the one hand, we cannot afford to overlook the preoccupation with the realpolitik, because that affects America's sense of right.

I said, on the other hand, we cannot conduct ourselves with a compulsive quest for ephemeral piety while we ignore realpolitik, because that offends America's sense of reality. And that is what happened in the post-Vietnam period. We swung to pieties.

The truth is somewhere in between, and a sound foreign policy is consistently that. It is consistently bipartisan. It is one of the tragedies of the upcoming congressional election—the hypering of the Salvadoran issue. No American foreign policy will be successful unless it is bipartisan. The issue should be debated not on partisan terms but philosophic terms.

Q. Have we offered Cuba an improvement in relations in exchange for moderation?

A. What?

Q. Have we offered Cuba an improvement in relations in exchange for moderation on their part?

A. It is very damaging to discuss publicly what we have or what we haven't done. But, please, assume that everybody that is in the executive branch is not a gibbering chimpanzee. (Laughter)

Q. Sir, can you give us any guidance on reports of a covert destabilization campaign against Nicaragua, any intelligence at all, on reports that the United States is engaging in a covert destabilization campaign against Nicaragua? Can you give us any guidance on that at all?

A. The guidance I give you is that the President's policy on that subject is clear. It has not changed. Those who have been adding little homilies to the airwaves are not in the national security structure, and are wrong, and are not reflecting the President's view.

. . . .

Document 680

Transcript of a Press Conference by the Secretary of State (Haig), New York, March 15, 1982[57]

U.S. Policy in Central America

SECRETARY HAIG. . . . There have been a number of articles written and press attention and since the discussions on Salvador and Nicaragua have been rather intense, I thought it would be in your interest to put the current state of play in sharper focus and to be sure that focus is clear in the days and weeks ahead. We've of course, had a very busy and very useful day and a half here, and I do think it's important if we all work from the very same base of facts as the events in the week ahead unfold.

It has been reported that there exists a basis for discussion or negotiation with Nicaragua. I certainly hope so. What does exist at this point, however, are proposals. President Lopez Portillo has made proposals. So have the Nicaraguans made proposals and the United States has made proposals.

Let me spend a moment on the United States proposals. These are proposals which Assistant Secretary Tom Enders here in attendence made last August in Managua and which I reiterated to the Nicaraguan Foreign Minister at the OAS assembly in Saint Lucia in December.

They contain five points.

The first point is an offer of bilateral nonaggression. If you will—a commitment through mutual high-level reassertion of our Rio treaty engagements.

The second point—a United States political commitment on the activities of Nicaraguan exiles in this country. That involves, of course, the application of the longstanding United States neutrality act.

Thirdly, a regional undertaking not to import heavy offensive weapons and to reduce the number of foreign military and security advisers to a reasonably low level. This would be a commitment by all of the countries in Central America.

Fourthly, a proposal to the United States Congress for renewed United States aid.

And fifthly, for the Nicaraguans to get out of El Salvador—to wind up the command and control, the logistics, including weapons, ammunition, and training camps.

Now, I discussed these specific proposals with Foreign Secretary Castañeda. Mexico had already drawn on them in making its own proposals in Managua two weeks ago. I told him that these proposals could be the basis for a settlement with Nicaragua. That, of course, does not mean that we should not or are not willing to look at other ideas. But there is a sine qua non, as we have stated repeatedly—that is that the Sandinistas have to get out of El Salvador.

Now with respect to the interest in both Nicaragua and Cuba, Mexico can play an important role in facilitating contacts. Secretary Castañeda already did that in November when I met with Cuban Vice President Rodriguez in Mexico City. I am hopeful that Mexico will continue and go on playing that kind of a role. It's most helpful. Of course, any such meetings will have to be strictly bilateral and the United States will present and receive proposals on its own behalf.

As I pointed out yesterday[58] and as I pointed out in my testimony early last

---

[57] Source: Department of State Press Release 100, March 17, 1982. The press conference was held in the U.N. Plaza Hotel beginning at 12 noon.

[58] Reference is to Secretary Haig's press conference, March 14, 1982. (Department of State Press Release 99, March 17, 1982)

week[59] and as an unnamed spokesman pointed out this Saturday morning[60] to a group of Washington State Department Press people, the El Salvador problem has a major global and regional as well as a local aspect. That is a fact of theological and practical reality.

Certainly the conflict has to be dealt with on the ground—political and militarily—in El Salvador itself. There's never been a question of that. But the neighboring state, Nicaragua, is also deeply involved and part of this solution, therefore, lies in Nicaragua and the regional powers. Venezuela, Mexico can also help in this regard.

Beyond that Cuba is a big part of the problem because it was Cuba that unified the left-wing parties in El Salvador and did so in Havana with Castro's personal involvement, trained their men, provided initial armament, arranged for other arms supply and is now involved in command and control in Managua—Cubans.

And the Soviet Union is also involved, and deeply so, because that's where the resources and arms come from for Cuba and other recipient guerrilla movements—that's where the Communist radical net is run from without which the insurgents themselves could not exist.

So, and I repeat again, Salvador is at once a global, a regional and a local problem. In solving it, we have to act in all three areas. That does not mean, I repeat, that does not mean, nor did it ever mean that the Soviets or the Cubans, for that matter, must be invited to the negotiating table. Not at all. Or even that you set up any form of negotiations with respect to those two nations. It does mean that you use the range of your influence in each area in working toward a solution and I repeat again, a myopic fixation in El Salvador alone will not solve the problem.

Now, I hope we have put this, these issue, in somewhat sharper context and therefore I welcome your questions and whatever explorations.

Q. Mr. Secretary, has this Cuban presence and the command and control in Managua been presented to the congressional intelligence committee as part of the evidence over the last couple of weeks?

SECRETARY HAIG. That's clearly a facet of the information that has been provided. Although the specific focus has been on the Nicaraguan involvement, an ancillary aspect is the very heavy role that Cuba is playing in that involvement.

Q. Is this new evidence or has this evidence existed for some time?

SECRETARY HAIG. This is evidence that has been available for an extended period, but which mounts daily in its both credibility, volume and specificity.

Q. Mr. Secretary, does this mean a de facto rejection of the peace proposal of President Lopez Portillo?

SECRETARY HAIG. Not at all. It represents what we described it as representing. We have made some proposals, the Mexican Government has bridged off of those proposals and broadened them somewhat, and perhaps even changed the characterization of some of them in substantive terms. We are exchanging views, and we'll continue, and, as I have pointed out, I think we enlarged the understanding both on our side and on the Mexican side over this weekend as a result of the talks we've had.

Q. Mr. Secretary, on this myopic fascination with El Salvador, who do you think is really responsible? I remember you raised it almost immediately after you assumed the post of Secretary of State. I know you sent Mr. Bushnell—who I guess has gone to other areas now—

SECRETARY HAIG. Not really.

Q. He chided us once about our overemphasizing El Salvador.

SECRETARY HAIG. No, no. Please do not be subjective, Sandy. I think there's a natural tendency to do this, and I think a Secretary of State has the obligation to do his best to put the issue in perspective. Now why is there a tendency to do it? That's very clear. People are being killed in El Salvador. That's where the action is, and it is very natural that there would be an intense focus on that situation.

But it is also the responsibility of public officials to do their very best to keep the entire problem in clear focus, and that's my obligation, among others.

Q. Mr. Secretary, a two-part question: Do you regard the unexpected testimony of

---

59 Presumably a reference to Haig's testimony before the Senate Appropriations Committee, March 10, 1982; see *Foreign Assistance and Related Programs Appropriations, Fiscal Year 1983: Hearings Before a Subcommittee of the Committee on Appropriations, United States Senate, Ninety-seventh Congress, Second Session* (Washington, 1983), Part 1, pp. 56–88.

60 See the press briefing, *supra*.

the young Nicaraguan at the press conference as a major setback in the effort to sell American policy?

Secretary Haig. It isn't an effort to sell American policy. The press, for a prolonged period before we started a week ago to bring forth the facts, were demanding the facts, and I think with justification.

We have been attempting to respond to that pressure, not only from the media but from the United States Congress who, after all, have to provide the resources for the implementation of our policy.

This young fellow, I suppose, was an embarrassment, but again I would ask you to ask yourselves a question, he was a Nicaraguan and whether he was what he said he was initially and repeatedly or whether he was what he said he was during his press interview is less significant than the fact that he is a Nicaraguan who was fighting in Salvador and whose credibility is clearly open to question.

Q. Did anyone goof in presenting this man, do you think?

Secretary Haig. I don't think anybody goofs if they try to bring forth the facts as we know them. That, after all, is what you people have a right and have been insisting on and have a right to insist on. Just because somebody sang a sour note—one individual—certainly doesn't constitute a major problem if it is objectively witnessed.

Q. But it is a minor embarrassment?

Secretary Haig. No question about it. I think I'm the one on Friday that when I went into the press room said, "I'm sorry I'm late, I've been wiping the egg off my face."

Q. Mr. Secretary, you mentioned that the El Salvador issue is global and regional. And you did say that neither Nicaragua nor Cuba would be invited to the negotiating table.

How can you resolve a global and regional problem if you do not invite them to negotiate?

Secretary Haig. No. That is not what I said. What I said was that the fact that it is a global and regional problem does not necessarily mean that we have initiated negotiations in the very clear context of those terms for the El Salvador problem.

The Cuban involvement in the hemisphere is wide and extensive, and it is not confined to El Salvador. You know that.

Q. Yes. But how can you—

Secretary Haig. The Soviet involvement is also extensive in the hemisphere through the provision of arms, support for so-called wars of liberation.

Our dealings with Cuba and our dealings with the Soviet Union involve, and will involve, bilateral discussions in which this and a host of other interrelated issues will clearly be the focus of attention.

It does not mean, as some have suggested, that suddenly we are bringing the Soviet Union into negotiation on matters of great importance and significance to the hemisphere.

Q. Mr. Secretary, in your considerable dialogue with the Soviet Union on Cuba and Latin American relations, are you going to press for the withdrawal of the MiGs that are being deployed to Nicaragua?

Secretary Haig. Am I going to—I'm sorry, I missed the—

Q. Are you going to make a pressure for the withdrawal of the MiGs? They're supposed to have a nuclear capability and are they being deployed in Nicaragua?

Secretary Haig. We have made it very clear that we would consider the introduction of MiG aircraft into Nicaragua as a grave development. We've made that clear to the Government of Nicaragua and, as a matter of fact, the Foreign Minister of Nicaragua in St. Lucia assured me that there were no such plans to make such introduction.

That, of course, runs rather contrary to the daily assessments we make with respect to the improvement of the airfields—four of them—in Nicaragua which have been proceeding at a startling rate and the evidence of which was shown to our Washington press corps last week through overhead photography.[61] The reality that there are a number of Nicaraguan students being trained for high performance aircraft in Eastern Europe, which of course, would suggest that means in the fighter category—a MiG model.

Q. Mr. Secretary, could I come back to your Nicaraguan discussion? Did you get the impression through talking to the Mexican Foreign Secretary that there was any

[61] A reference to the briefing on Central America by John Hughes and Admiral Bobby Ray Inman, Deputy Director of Central Intelligence, at the Department of State, March 9, 1982.

give in the Nicaraguan position on either withdrawing or reducing their help to the Salvadoran insurgents? Because he seemed rather optimistic, and after talking to you, that with the given proposals on the table he could make some headway.

And, secondly, on that same question, do you plan any time soon to have any direct talks other than perhaps through the Embassy with the Nicaraguans?

And, thirdly, where do you stand with the Cubans? The Mexican Foreign Secretary made a major point about his proposals and his discussions with you on possible normalization. He said talks that could lead to normalization with Cuba.

Is there anything at all gelling on that? Do you plan any period of talks with the Cubans?

SECRETARY HAIG. These are all very important questions. With respect to the question of Minister Castañeda's attitude, a sense of optimism if you will, that the sine qua non, as I described it, of the U.S. position is achievable, I think, but I can't speak for him, represents a subjective judgment on his part because the logic and the right of that issue stands on its own two feet.

I would not want to go beyond that in a way that would suggest that he had already received such a commitment from the Nicaraguan Government, because I don't know that to be the fact, and I suspect to the contrary.

With respect to future talks with the Nicaraguans, I would prefer to leave that ambiguous in the sense of not laying out specific plans or proposals or venues or courses of actions or personalities; but rather to suggest to you that we have a multiplicity of ways with which to maintain contact, not the least of which is the presence of our Embassy in Managua and the recent arrival of our Ambassador, Ambassador Quainton, in Managua.

That should not be interpreted as an answer to your question, but merely to point out that there is no paucity of our ability to communicate in a number of ways.

With respect to Cuba, there again I don't think it serves a useful purpose to lay out the specific ways in which communications will be conducted. As you know, the President announced at a press conference that I had met with the Cuban Vice President. All I can suggest to you at this moment is that talks will continue.

Q. Mr. Secretary, the proposal by the Mexicans is in the area, includes negotiations and talks after the Salvadoran election? He confirmed that yesterday, the Foreign Minister of Mexico. after the elections.

Doesn't this undermine the strong position of countries like your country and Venezuela that all the election—putting most emphasis on the election? Or is it because you are thinking of the possibility of a right-wing victory in El Salvador?

SECRETARY HAIG. Let me assure you that the position we have taken on this issue has nothing to do with the outcome of the elections in Salvador. That's an internal problem for the people of Salvador to solve, and that's what an election is all about.

What we have insisted on and which we continue to believe is that this election this month is a very important benchmark in the evolution of the pluralization of the Salvadoran society and democratic process.

I think Ambassador Hinton discussed that on national television this morning, and that has occured, but has occurred with the objective of a democratic rather than a totalitarian outcome. And so it is not in our interest to conduct our own affairs and our involvement in this situation in such a way that we put in jeopardy that very important process that will take place this month.

Q. Mr. Secretary, can we ask a housekeeping question?

Q. You seem to be unhappy with the fact that Fidel Castro unified the left in El Salvador. You are also unhappy—

SECRETARY HAIG. I didn't make a value judgment. I just stated fact.

Q. All right. You also didn't like the fact that the military garrison being built in Nicaragua has Cuban design, Russian design. Now you want to set limits for the number of advisers in Nicaragua and advisers in El Salvador, but who sets the limits for the United States?

SECRETARY HAIG. I think you didn't listen to me very clearly, and that must suggest a preconceived notion between your ears.

I said that this would be a multilateral approach involving all the nations of the region, and I merely put it forward as an approach, one that we consider would make important contributions to peace and stability in the region. And, of course, the United States would be obligated in conformance with the agreements arrived at to control its level.

Now that doesn't answer the nettling part of your question which would be impossible for me to answer, given your perspective and mine.

Q. Mr. Secretary, just a housekeeping question. How many times have you talked with Judge Clark in the past 36 hours?

SECRETARY HAIG. Oh, heaven's sake.

Q. The reason I am asking the question is a high State Department official had a background briefing on Saturday. You had an extensive news conference yesterday. You have an extensive one today. And it kind of looks like there's a white paper being issued today.

SECRETARY HAIG. Not at all. I would never describe it as a white paper. I would describe it as an effort—and a justified effort—to put in sharper focus the current state of play in Central America and the American approach to it.

I don't know what you mean by—what that has to do with communications with Bill Clark. I speak to Bill Clark every day, any number of times in a day, and that's as it should be.

Q. Well, the President got off the helicopter yesterday—

SECRETARY HAIG. Ah, that's what—I think the President addressed that on the aircraft this morning and I would refer you to his comments on that, rather than try to interpret for him.

You will find a wire service report on that when you leave this meeting.

Q. Mr. Secretary, is the bottom line here that you're not as optimistic as the Foreign Minister of Mexico who said there is a basis for agreement now?

SECRETARY HAIG. No. The bottom line is that it's important that we have a sharper focus on the state of play. I suppose everyone views these things differently, dependent on their own perspectives of the complexity and magnitude of the problem and their subjective interest in the outcome.

We are trying to give to the press a very clear picture of where we stand, and do not interpret it as a value judgment, excessive optimism or excessive pessimism, or huge gaps of approach between the Mexicans and the United States. They have been very helpful in this process, we've been conducting a steady dialogue with them, and the results of that dialogue have been very constructive.

Q. So there is progress being made, whether or not there's—

SECRETARY HAIG. I think it's too early to say. Whether there's real progress being made depends on whether you consider the review of proposals which would seek a peaceful solution as progress. I happen to think it is progress, and I think the American people who [*would*] view that as progress.

Q. Precisely what do you mean by command and control? You speak of Nicaraguan command and control in El Salvador, Cuban command and control. Do you mean directive command and control, or do you mean that they are part of the command?

In other words, what we're seeking for is the degree of independence as a military force of the El Salvadoran guerrillas.

SECRETARY HAIG. I would refer to it as a substantial role in directing the operations in Salvador.

Q. The Cubans?

SECRETARY HAIG. The Nicaraguans.

Q. With the Cubans?

SECRETARY HAIG. With the Cubans in full participation.

Q. Mr. Secretary, the only condition or the only reason the U.S. does not normalize relations with Nicaragua is because of the help to El Salvador?

SECRETARY HAIG. That's a very, very important aspect of the current tensions between Washington and Managua, without question. But we would be equally concerned, and we are, by any manifestation of Nicaraguan activity in other neighboring states such as Costa Rica.

Q. Mr. Secretary, if we could just drop into focus just a touch more, because that's what you said you wanted to come here to do—Tom Enders went down to Nicaragua with a series of proposals which you outlined. The Nicaraguans said no. Foreign Minister Castañeda came here yesterday, outlining basically the same proposals, or suggesting the same proposals.

He said he's taking them back and he sounded optimistic.

Can you sharpen the focus?

SECRETARY HAIG. I thought I had sharpened it rather well—that we put some proposals out, and I gave you the five specific areas which we put forward. You know that President Lopez Portillo gave a speech in Managua, I think two weeks ago now, in which those proposals were largely included—different language and different packaging, if you will—but it was also broadened—those proposals were broadened, and, as a matter of fact, the Cuban question was introduced.

Q. And one (inaudible)—

SECRETARY HAIG. And the key part of it—and we reacted at the time, with total consistence, that the sine qua non that I touched upon was not in the proposal in a way that we could be assured or even understand it. Subsequently, that comment, together with some other comments—and I reiterated over this weekend the five points of the American position to Secretary Castañeda—and he made a public statement which was touched upon, I think by Bernie because it wasn't lost on Bernie, that he was optimistic that that sine qua non was achievable, but not in an exclusive or single way but rather as a part of some other assurances that would have to be included.

Well, that's normal, and I don't think anybody should be taken aback by that.

Thank you.

Document 681

Message to the Congress by President Reagan, March 17, 1982[62]

Transmittal of the Proposed Caribbean Basin Economic Recovery Legislation

On February 24, before the Organization of American States, I outlined a major new program for economic cooperation for the Caribbean Basin. Today I am transmitting this plan to the Congress for its action.

The economic, political and security challenges in the Caribbean Basin are formidable. Our neighbors need time to develop representative and responsive institutions, which are the guarantors of the democracy and justice that freedom's foes seek to stamp out. They also need the opportunity to achieve economic progress and improve their standard of living. Finally, they need the means to defend themselves against attempts by externally-supported minorities to impose an alien, hostile and unworkable system upon them by force. The alternative is further expansion of political violence from the extreme left and the extreme right, resulting in the imposition of dictatorships and—inevitably—more economic decline, and more human suffering and dislocation.

Today, I seek from the Congress the means to address the economic aspect of the challenge in the Caribbean Basin—the underlying economic crisis which provides the opportunities which extremist and violent minorities exploit.

The crisis facing most of the Basin countries is real and acute. Deteriorating trade opportunities, worldwide recession, mounting debt burdens, growing unemployment and deep-seated structural problems are having a catastrophic impact throughout the region. This economic disaster is consuming our neighbors' money reserves and credit, forcing thousands of people to emigrate, and shaking even the most established democracies.

This is not a crisis we can afford to ignore. The people of the Caribbean Basin are our neighbors. Their well-being and security are in our own vital interest. Events occurring in the Caribbean Basin can affect our lives in profound and dramatic ways. The migrants in our midst are a vivid reminder of the closeness of this problem to all of us.

The program I am presenting to Congress today is integrated and designed to improve the lives of the peoples of the Caribbean Basin by enabling them to earn their own way to a better future. It builds on the principles of integrating aid, self-help and participation in trade and investment which I emphasized at the Cancun Summit last October. It is a different kind of assistance program for developing countries, based on principles and practices which are uniquely American and which we know have worked in the past. It will help revitalize the economies of this strategically critical region by attacking the underlying causes of economic stagnation. Most significantly, it helps expand economic opportunities for the people of the Caribbean Basin to make possible the achievement of a lasting political and social tranquillity based on freedom and justice.

I want to emphasize that this program is not an end in itself. What we seek in the

---

62 Source: *Weekly Compilation of Presidential Documents,*March 22;1982, pp. 323–327.

final analysis is to help the people in the Basin build for themselves a better life, not just economically but across the full spectrum of human needs and aspirations. History, and particularly the history of this Hemisphere, has shown that a pluralistic society with strong, free private institutions—churches, free trade unions, businesses, professional and other voluntary associations, and an independent press—is our best hope in moving toward that ultimate goal.

Our development program takes this into account; it will encourage progress in the beneficiary countries toward reasonable workplace conditions and opportunities for workers to associate freely and bargain collectively.

The United States has been developing this program in close consultation with the countries of the region and with other donor countries. Last July, we joined with Canada, Mexico and Venezuela to launch a multilateral action program for the region.[63] It was agreed that each country would develop its own program but within a multilateral consultative framework. Mexico and Venezuela are operating an oil facility for the Caribbean Basin. Canada is more than doubling its aid. The program I am presenting today is our contribution.

We have worked carefully with both government officials and the private sector in the Basin countries to assess their needs and their own priorities. We have also consulted with other potential donors, including Colombia, as well as multilateral development institutions. This program is part of an overall coordinated effort by countries within and outside the region. Its structure will ensure not only that our own actions will be effective, but that their impact will be multiplied by the efforts of many others.

The program is based on integrated and mutually-reinforcing measures in the fields of trade, investment and financial assistance:

—Its centerpiece is the offer of one-way free trade. I am requesting authority to eliminate duties on all imports from the Basin except textiles and apparel items subject to textile agreements. The only other limitation will be for sugar; as long as a sugar price support program is in effect, duty-free imports of sugar will be permitted only up to specified ceilings. Safeguards will be available to U.S. industries seriously injured by increased Basin imports. Rules of origin will be liberal to encourage investment but will require a minimum amount of local content (25 percent). I will designate beneficiary countries taking into account such factors as the countries' self-help policies.

—I am proposing an extension of the 10 percent tax credit that now applies only to domestic investment to new equity investments in qualifying Caribbean Basin countries. A country would qualify for the benefit for a period of five years by entering into a bilateral executive agreement with the U.S. to exchange information for tax administration purposes.

—I am requesting a supplemental appropriation for the FY 1982 foreign assistance program in the amount of $350 million in emergency economic assistance. This assistance will help make possible financing of critical imports for the private sector in Basin countries experiencing a severe credit crunch. I expect to allocate the emergency supplemental in the region as follows:

El Salvador: $128 million. El Salvador's economy is in desperate straits. The insurgents have used every tactic of terrorism to try to destroy it. El Salvador desperately needs as much assistance to stimulate production and employment as we can prudently provide while also helping other countries of the region.

Costa Rica: $70 million. Costa Rica has a long tradition of democracy which is now being tested by the turmoil of its economy. Once Costa Rica has embarked on a recovery plan, it will need significant assistance to succeed in restoring investor confidence and credit to its hard-hit private sector.

Honduras: $35 million. The poorest country in the Central American region, Honduras faces severe balance of payments constraints, spawned primarily from falling prices of major exports and rising import costs.

Jamaica: $50 million. Jamaica's recovery is under way but continued success is still heavily dependent on further quick-disbursing assistance to overcome a shortage of foreign exchange for raw materials and spare parts.

Dominican Republic: $40 million. The Dominican Republic is attempting to adjust to

[63] A reference to the Conference of Ministers on Caribbean Basin Development held in Nassau, Bahamas, from July 11 to 12, 1981. Secretary of State Haig and the Foreign Ministers of Canada, Mexico, and Venezuela attended. See *American Foreign Policy: Current Documents, 1981*, documents 692 and 693.

drastically-reduced economic activity brought on primarily by falling prices of its major export crop (sugar) and heavy dependence on imported oil. Critical economic reforms must take place in a difficult political climate as elections grow near. Once the free trade provisions go into effect, the Dominican Republic will also receive as a result of the duty-free quota for its sugar exports immediate benefits going beyond the $40 million indicated here.

Eastern Caribbean: $10 million. Economic stagnation has dried up investment and strangled development in these island ministates where unemployment is a particular problem, especially among youths.

Belize: $10 million. Newly-independent Belize faces a perilous economic situation brought on by falling sugar prices and stagnant growth. Belize needs short-term assistance as a bridge to the development of its own considerable natural resources.

Haiti: $5 million. Illegal immigration from Haiti is spurred by stagnant economic activity and a credit-starved private sector in a country already desperately poor.

Latin American Regional/American Institute for [Free] Labor Development (AIFLD): $2 million. Free labor movements, assisted by our small AIFLD programs, can be the underpinning of a healthy private sector and its ability to expand and grow, leading the region to stable social and economic progress.

In a separate action I am also requesting action on the economic assistance program for FY 1983. This includes $664 million in economic assistance for the Caribbean Basin. This program will be directed largely into longer-term programs aimed at removing basic impediments to growth. Although not a part of the legislation which I am transmitting today, the FY 1983 aid request is an integral part of our overall program for the Caribbean Basin. We cannot think of this program as a one-time injection of U.S. interest and effort. If it is to succeed it must be a sustained commitment over a number of years. I strongly urge the Congress to approve this request in full.

In addition to these legislative requests, I am directing the following actions, which are within the discretion of the Executive Branch:

—We will extend more favorable treatment to Caribbean Basin textile and apparel exports within the context of our overall textile policy.

—We will seek to negotiate bilateral investment treaties with interested countries.

—We will work with multilateral development banks and the private sector to develop insurance facilities to supplement OPIC's political risk insurance coverage for U.S. investors.

—The U.S. Export-Import Bank will expand protection, where its lending criteria allow, for short-term credit from U.S. banks, as well as local commercial banks, to Caribbean Basin private sectors for critical imports.

—With the governments and private sectors of interested countries, we will develop private sector strategies for each country. These strategies will coordinate and focus development efforts of local business, U.S. firms, private voluntary organizations, the U.S. Government, and Puerto Rico and the Virgin Islands. The strategies will seek new investment and employment opportunities and will also seek to remove impediments to growth including lack of marketing skills, trained manpower, poor regional transport, and inadequate infrastructure.

Puerto Rico and the U.S. Virgin Islands have a longstanding special relationship with the United States. Their development must be enhanced by our policy toward the rest of the region. We have consulted closely with Puerto Rico and the Virgin Islands about the Caribbean Basin Initiative and the legislation I am requesting today will reflect Puerto Rican and Virgin Island interests in many important ways.

—The Accelerated Cost Recovery System (ACRS) and the Investment Tax Credit (ITC) will be extended to property used by companies operating in Puerto Rico and the U.S. Virgin Islands. Similar benefits will be available to other U.S. possessions.

—Excise taxes on all imported rum will be transferred to Puerto Rico and the Virgin Islands.

—Inputs into Caribbean Basin production from Puerto Rico and the U.S. Virgin Islands will be considered domestic inputs from Caribbean Basin countries for purposes of the rules of origin.

—Industries in Puerto Rico and the Virgin Islands will have access to the same safeguards provisions as mainland industries.

In addition, we will support proposed legislation which will permit products from the Virgin Islands whose foreign content does not exceed 70 percent to receive duty-free treatment. At present the maximum foreign content permitted is 50 percent.

To further the intergrated agricultural development of the Caribbean Basin, we will make greater use of the agricultural and forestry research, extension and training facilities of the Federal Government and those of Puerto Rico and the United States Virgin Islands, especially the tropical agricultural research facility at Mayaguez, Puerto Rico.

All these elements in the Caribbean Basin program are inextricably linked together, and to the fundamental objective of helping our neighbors help themselves. A key principle of the program is to encourage a more productive, competitive and dynamic private sector, and thereby provide the jobs, goods and services which the people of the Basin need for a better life for themselves and their children. All the elements of this program are designed to help establish the conditions under which a free and competitive private sector can flourish.

Most countries in the Basin already recognize that they must reform many of their economic policies and structures in profound and sometimes painful ways in order to take advantage of the new economic opportunities of this program. We—the United States and other outside donors—can offer assistance and support, but only the people in the Basin themselves can make this program work.

Some of the benefits of this program will take considerable time to mature; others are designed to have an immediate effect. But the challenge is already upon us; the time to begin is now. I urge the Congress to act with maximum speed.

I also urge the Congress to consider very carefully any changes in this program. The actions in trade, aid and investment are interrelated. Each supports the other, so that together they comprise a real spur toward the entrepreneurial dynamism which the area so badly needs. A significant weakening in any of them could undermine the whole program.

In the Caribbean Basin, we seek above all to support those values and principles that shape the proud heritage of this Nation and this Hemisphere. With the help of this Congress, we shall see these values not only survive but triumph in a Caribbean Basin which is a community of peace, freedom and prosperity.

Document 682

Statement by the U.S. Official Observer Delegation to the El Salvador Constituent Assembly Elections, March 29, 1982[64]

The Election in El Salvador

The official United States delegation to the March 28, 1982 El Salvador Constituent Assembly elections, having personally visited a number of polling areas around the country, believes these elections were fair and free.

One of our members, Dr. Howard Penniman, an elections expert who has participated in some 45 difficult elections, observes that yesterday's election was one of the most massive expressions of popular will he has ever seen.

The tremendous turnout, perhaps over one million, underscores the sense of commitment of the people.

Over and over again we heard the people say, "We are voting for peace and an end of the violence. We believe this election can be a new beginning for this country."

It is difficult to express the patience and purpose with which the Salvadoran people turned out to vote, enduring long hours in line to cast their ballots and, in some instances, attempts by the insurgents to scare them off. The election clearly is a repudiation of the guerrillas' claim that they represent the will of the Salvadoran people.

In general the election process itself was orderly and peaceful. The voting proce-

---

[64] Source: *Report of the U.S. Official Observer Mission to the El Salvador Constituent Assembly Elections of March 28, 1982*, A Report to the Committee on Foreign Relations, United States Senate by Senator Nancy L. Kassebaum, Ninety-seventh Congress, Second Session, Committee Print (Washington, 1982), pp. 5–6. The U.S. Official Observer Delegation was headed by Senator Nancy Landon Kassebaum and included: Congressmen John Murtha and Robert Livingston; Father Theodore Hesburgh, President of the University of Notre Dame; Dr. Clark Kerr, President Emeritus of the University of California, Berkeley; Dr. Howard Penniman, American Enterprise Institute; Dr. Richard Scammon, Elections Research Center; and Deputy Assistant Secretary of State for Inter-American Affairs Everett E. Briggs. The delegation departed Andrews Air Force Base on March 26, 1982, and spent 4 days in El Salvador.

dures adhered to rules established by the Central Elections Commission. There were poll watchers from at least two parties at each table we visited, and the election officials worked seriously at their responsibilities, both in processing the voters and later in counting the ballots. We did see some minor technical problems during the day, but we saw no indication of fraud. We believe they had no influence on the outcome of the elections.

Because of the threats of violence during the voting, the Central Elections Commission made the decision to concentrate the polling places in some 300 sites. This did cause some confusion. By the early hours of the morning, there were long lines all over the country. For example, in Santa Tecla, a suburb of San Salvador, we estimate that some 10,000 people were standing in line to vote at 9 a.m. We were concerned that not all would have a chance to vote. But by the end of the day, election officials assure us that most of the voters were attended to. The Salvadoran people have said in overwhelming numbers that they want peace and an end to the violence.

We hope that the sense of commitment and cooperation that the voters demonstrated yesterday at the polls will be reflected in the efforts of the leadership of the Constituent Assembly that they have elected. The people have asked for a new beginning and they most definitely deserve it.

Document 683

Statement by the Secretary of State (Haig) at the Department of State Daily Press Briefing, March 29, 1982[65]

The Elections in El Salvador

I'm pleased to see you in your true glory in this room.

I would like to make a formal statement on the outcome of the elections in Salvador yesterday. I want first and foremost to express my admiration for the people of El Salvador. Ordinary Salvadoran men and women, in unprecedented numbers, yesterday displayed awesome courage and civic responsibility. The Salvadoran people's stunning personal commitment to the power of the democratic vision is an unanswerable repudiation of the advocates of force and violence.

Secondly, I would like to note that yesterday's results are a military defeat for the guerrillas quite as much as a political repudiation. Despite their clear intention to disrupt the elections, the guerrilla forces were unable to shake either the people or the security forces at their moment of greatest vulnerability. Moreover, the behavior of the armed forces proved that although in El Salvador, soldiers by law cannot vote, their professionalism this weekend served the cause of democracy.

We should be aware, of course, that despite their undeniable repudiation by the people of El Salvador, the guerrillas still have the external support to continue their campaign of terror at levels that would be impossible if they depended on their own people.

Finally, these elections are a major achievement in the development of democracy in El Salvador. We are confident that the Constituent Assembly, given the extraordinary mandate it has received from the Salvadoran people, will find ways to hold out a hand of conciliation to those adversaries who are prepared to take part peacefully in the democratic process now so encouragingly under way in El Salvador.

Formidable tasks still lie ahead. The Salvadoran people have dramatically demonstrated their desire for peace and for democracy. We and free peoples everywhere must be proud of the victory we have all won. We owe it to ourselves, as well as to the people of El Salvador, to continue to support these courageous people as they advance the political reform process, to strengthen the land reform program, and to curb indiscriminate violence caused by extremists from both the left and the right. We believe yesterday's success greatly advances these long-term objectives.

Thank you.

---

[65] Source: Office of Press Relations, Department of State. The briefing began at 12:24 p.m. Secretary Haig left the briefing after reading his statement.

Document 684

Draft U.N. Security Council Resolution on Central America, April 1, 1982[66]

Appeal to All Member States to Refrain From the Direct, Indirect, Overt or Covert Use of Force Against Any Country of Central America and the Caribbean

The Security Council,

Having heard the statement by the Coordinator of the Governing Junta of National Reconstruction of Nicaragua, Commandant of the Revolution Daniel Ortega Saavedra, the statement by the Permanent Representative of the United States and other statements made before the Council,

Gravely concerned at the deterioration of the situation in Central America and the Caribbean,

Taking into account Article 2, paragraph 4, of the Charter of the United Nations and other relevant provisions of the Charter concerning the pacific settlement of disputes,

Considering that the present crisis in the region of Central America and the Caribbean affects international peace and security and that all Member States have an interest in the solution of the crisis by peaceful means,

Recalling resolution 2131 (XX) on the inadmissibility of intervention in the domestic affairs of States and the protection of their independence and sovereignty, adopted by the General Assembly on 21 December 1965, and resolution 2160 (XXI) on strict observance of the prohibition of the threat or use of force in international relations, and of the right of peoples to self-determination, adopted by the General Assembly on 30 November 1966,

1. *Reminds* all Member States of their obligation to respect the principles of the Charter, and in particular those relating to:

(a) Non-intervention and non-interference in the domestic affairs of States;

(b) Self-determination of peoples;

(c) Non-use of force or threat of force;

(d) The territorial integrity and political independence of States;

(e) Pacific settlement of disputes;

2. *Reminds* all Member States that resolution 2131 (XX) condemns the use or threat of force in relations between States as acts contrary to the purposes and principles of the Charter of the United Nations;

3. *Appeals* to all Member States to refrain from the direct, indirect, overt or covert use of force against any country of Central America and the Caribbean;

4. *Appeals* to all parties concerned to have recourse to dialogue and negotiation, as contemplated in the Charter of the United Nations, and calls upon all Member States to lend their support to the search for a peaceful solution to the problems of Central America and the Caribbean;

5. *Requests* the Secretary-General to keep the Security Council informed concerning the development of the situation in Central America and the Caribbean.

Document 685

Statement by the Deputy Representative at the U.N. Security Council (Lichenstein), April 2, 1982[67]

"We Have Unfortunately Not Been Able to Find That Common Ground"

The United States had hoped to be able to join in a consensus resolution of this body, had hoped that it would be possible still to find common ground, still to make

---

[66] Source: U.N. document S/14941 (1982). In response to a request by Nicaragua (U.N. document S/14913 (1982)), the Security Council held eight meetings on March 25, 26, 29, 30, 31, and April 2, 1982, on the situation in Central America. Panama and Guyana submitted the draft resolution. On April 2, 1982, the Security Council failed to adopt the draft resolution due to the negative vote of one of its permanent members, the United States. The vote on the draft resolution was 12 to 1, with 2 abstentions (United Kingdom and Zaire).

[67] Source: U.N. document S/PV.2347. All brackets and parenthetical notes are in the source text.

what we would regard and what we would have hoped our 14 colleagues would regard as a constructive contribution to the de-escalation of a situation of tension within Central and South America. We have unfortunately not been able to find that common ground.

We do not feel that the draft resolution,[68] against which I have just voted, was in any way supportive of our own institution, the Security Council, or of the United Nations, or, indeed, of the experienced and well-established inter-American system for the resolution and conciliation of disputes amongst member States.

As Ambassador Kirkpatrick said in her statement in this chamber today,[69] part of the problem with this draft resolution has indeed been the definition of "the problem." From the point of view and perspective of the United States, the door to negotiation and conciliation—bilateral, regional and multilateral—is now open and has always been open. From the perspective of the United States, the allegations of Commandante Ortega were without foundation, are today without foundation and have always been without foundation. I reiterate again tonight that that door to negotiation and conciliation remains open.

The defect—I should say the further defect—of the draft resolution against which I voted is that it failed to identify certain key elements of the true and genuine and urgent problem of Central and South America, a problem created in major part by the intervention of the Sandinista Junta in the affairs of its neighbours—intervention and adventurism sustained and supported and encouraged by other Powers both within this hemisphere and outside this hemisphere.

> "With reference to this draft resolution, we believe that its Selective invocation and application of universal principles does not strengthen either the principles or the organizations dedicated to their realization and implementation. It breeds cynicism. It harms the United Nations. [It undermines the inter-American system.] It mocks the search for peace." (*Supra, p. 8*)

I have just quoted from remarks made earlier today by Ambassador Kirkpatrick.

I quote further:

> "The Government of Nicaragua espouses and practises a very particular conception of non-intervention, a very particular conception of non-alignment: the kind that, in the end, saps the meaning and the power of both." (*Supra*, p. 12)

I quote further:

> "We desire to live at peace with all our neighbours. We shall continue our efforts to develop a constructive relationship with the Government of Nicaragua. Secretary of State Alexander Haig has made clear that we are prepared to work . . . . on the basis of mutual respect to that end.
>
> "Various proposals have been offered for conciliation among the nations of the region and the hemisphere. The United States, interested in the constructive resolution of tension and conflict,"—

and I might add, in common with the views, intentions and affirmations expressed in this chamber by many representatives of other American republics—

> "remains ready to do its part to ensure peace in the region and to enhance the prospects for democracy and development for all [of the] people [of this hemisphere]." (*Supra*, p. 18)

[68] *Supra.*

[69] For Ambassador Kirkpatrick's statement, see U.N. document S/PV.2347.

Document 686

Transcript of a Department of State Press Briefing, April 8, 1982 [70]

U.S. Proposals to Nicaragua

State Department Official. Good morning. Let me introduce the briefing if I might. As you know, it is *on background*—for your guidance only. The subject is Nicaragua.

Your briefer has a scheduling problem, which means that he won't be here terribly long, but he does have some opening remarks that he wants to make, and then will be happy to take your questions.

[70] Source: Office of Press Relations, Department of State. The briefing, which began at 11 a.m., was conducted on background by a senior Department of State official.

Senior State Department Official. I propose to make this a fairly short backgrounder. It comes at a stage when, as all of you know, we're in the process of an ongoing dialogue with Nicaragua. And because it is ongoing, there is quite a lot that I will not be prepared to discuss.

What I propose to do, briefly, is to summarize the elements of a number of proposals which were conveyed yesterday by Ambassador Quainton, our Ambassador in Managua, to the Nicaraguan Government. This dialogue has had obvious diplomatic and public relations sides over the recent months. As you are aware, a similar effort was made last August by Ambassador Enders, and again in December when the Secretary spoke to the Foreign Minister of Nicaragua in Saint Lucia.[71] But in the absence of any clear understanding of the issues at stake, there was a certain amount of confusion as to what U.S. policy has been, and I propose in outlining the elements of the current proposals to avoid any similar misunderstanding. I don't want to get ahead, though, of the normal diplomatic conversations on the issue. I might say that a reason for this presentation is in the news which is coming out of Managua today regarding Anthony Quainton's call yesterday.

This is a summary of the proposals, of which there are eight. It is an expansion, if you will, of the five Enders proposals. The first is the cessation of Nicaragua's support for insurgencies in neighboring countries. We are emphasizing that we must have results on this before any results can be achieved on other aspects of the proposal, what has been called our sine qua non.

The second point is a statement dealing with Nicaraguan exile activities in the United States. This would, in effect, be a political declaration to address Nicaragua's concerns. The third is a U.S.-Nicaraguan statement on friendly relations, a joint statement pledging noninterference in each other's affairs or in the affairs of others in the region.

The fourth is a proposal for arms and military force limitations. This will be a regional ban on the importation of heavy offensive weapons. We have also proposed that foreign military advisers in the region be reduced to low reasonable levels, and that military security forces be cut to levels commensurate with security needs.

The fifth is a proposal on international verification, and this derives from the very interesting Honduran proposal. The Nicaraguans, in the context of a regional arrangement, would make their airports, military installations, ports, borders, and sensitive zones accessible to visits by representatives of the OAS or other regional organizations.

The sixth would be a proposal on economic cooperation. This will be in the context of an overall agreement. It would involve Nicaragua's participation in our part of the CBI, including the United States trade and investment initiatives. We would be willing to propose to our Congress—all other things being equal—the reestablishment of direct economic assistance. We would propose this to our Congress.

The seventh item is a proposal on human and cultural exchanges and what we call "confidence building." And finally, the eighth, we notice that the FSLN recently stated to COPPAL a commitment—reiteration of its earlier commitment—to the principles of political pluralism, a mixed economy, and nonalignment. This, as well as the earlier FSLN commitment to the OAS concerning the holding of free elections would be important determinants of the political context of our future relations.

With that, I will stop and field your questions.

Q. Is this the beginning of the negotiations that were talked about when Haig and Castaneda met, or is this a prelude? Are there still expected to be higher level talks soon?

A. I don't think we can prejudge where this is going to go. A problem for us all along has been to engage with the Nicaraguans in discussions, negotiations—call them what you will; it doesn't really matter. There was a nonresponse, if you will, to Mr. Enders. We very much appreciated the Mexican efforts to use their influence on the Nicaraguans so that the Nicaraguans would show responsiveness. In that sense what has now happened—and we hope will lead to something else—reflects the help, the assistance which the Mexicans have been willing to give.

Whether or not out of these initial discussions will come more formal negotiations, obviously, some of these points involve countries other than just the United States and Nicaragua. If we're talking about, for example, the international verification, that's not simply a bilateral matter.

---

[71] See *American Foreign Policy: Current Documents, 1981*, document 712.

If we're talking about arms and military force limitations, that's not simply a bilateral matter—in fact, it doesn't involve us that much directly—and so on. So I can't prejudge at this time whether or not this will lead to more formal discussions, broader discussions, or involve more people. We hope it's a beginning, a beginning with which we had felt somewhat frustrated in the past we hadn't actually gotten underway.

Q. Could you be a little more explicit about why you think this has a better chance than the previous two efforts? What is it that the Mexicans have done? What is it that the Nicaraguans have done in response to that?

A. I wouldn't characterize it as having a better chance. In other words, I don't want to leave you with the idea that we are extraordinarily optimistic at this point. But what we are trying to do very persistently, as long as there is an opportunity, a possibility, of being able to exchange views with Nicaragua, and seeking to get a response from them to our proposals—asking them for their own proposals or their comments on ours—is to get the process underway, the process on which we have made repeated efforts; and this is the latest effort on our part to get the thing going.

In the future [*past*?], the Mexicans have shown sensitivity—I think this was clear in President Lopez Portillo's speech in Managua—to most of our concerns, including the enormous military buildup in Nicaragua. To the extent that the Mexicans, who do have a positive influence with Managua, can contribute to getting the Nicaraguans seriously to consider these issues which are of such importance to us and to Nicaragua's neighbors, all to the good. We have been very grateful to Mexico for taking that supportive position.

Q. Could I follow that just with one question? Do you have anything explicit from the Nicaraguans indicating that they will give you a response, serious or otherwise?

A. Let me put it this way. The Nicaraguans were interested; they took very careful notes. I don't want to go into much detail here, but let me limit myself by saying they asked us, for instance, what channels we would want to use in the future, that sort of thing, and initially, at least, Ambassador Quainton and his interlocutors had a good meeting.

Q. Are there more requirements, from the U.S. point of view, in the eight-point package than there were in either the Enders or the Haig approach?

A. Aside from the sine qua non, the major difference is that we have actually sharpened these a little bit. The U.S.-Nicaraguan statement on friendly relations, a joint statement pledging noninterference, that's a more precise formulation than we sought before. The purpose of such a statement would be to respond to the Nicaraguan stated fears of U.S. invasion.

The arms limitation, the force limitations and advisers, that's a little more precise, more specific, than our previous formulation. The verification is also something new. We have gone further this time in talking about the resumption of economic ties than we did before. The last ones were more general. We were seeking to get some kind of a response, and we didn't. We've been a little bit more specific this time.

I have just given you the outlines, obviously. I'm not prepared to give you all the details, but these are the outlines.

Q. I don't understand your last point. Are you asking for a specific Nicaraguan commitment to hold elections as part of this package?

A. The last package did not address the environment in Nicaragua. The subject was discussed, obviously, and has been discussed between us and them on various occasions. This time what we are saying to the Nicaraguans is that all of this will be easier, and those things which we are prepared to do which are positive towards you in, say, the economic, social, and so on side of things, will be greatly facilitated if you keep your commitments already on the record, both to the OAS and subsequently to COPPAL, if you keep these commitments active and actually carry them out.

I don't want to say, because this is a set of proposals, whether these are issues on which we have to have a reply or what the reply should be. The one starting point for a meaningful exchange is the cessation of arms to El Salvador.

Q. The last point, does this mean you are saying, if you will cease hostilities, we are prepared to do various other things of a positive nature which is out there. But the way you stated it, could you clarify this? The last point seems to be—the Lord giveth; the Lord taketh away—kind of thing, namely, that, even if you do cease hostilities, but if we don't like your internal situation, we can still call everything off. Is that what you're trying to say or not?

A. No, I'm not trying to say either. And I don't really think I want to say much more about this because this is a set of proposals, and we want the other side to be very clear about, as I say, where we're coming from.

Q. You said the Ambassador was asked what channel he wanted to use in the future. How did he reply?

A. I think the channel is not the important thing; the important thing is to have an exchange going.

Q. May I come back to this last point, please, because I don't know just what you mean, but the way it's been laid out here, it sounds like that in addition to laying down a sine qua non condition, that they must stop interfering in the affairs of other countries. You're also stating that they must pursue a specific code of conduct in their internal affairs if they are going to get any place with U.S. aid or assistance. If you're not specific about this, it leaves a very gaping question.

A. It shouldn't. I'll state it exactly. Let me read it again. The FSLN statement to COPPAL reiterating a commitment to the principles of political pluralism, a mixed economy, and nonalignment, as well as the earlier FSLN commitment to the OAS concerning the holding of free elections will be important determinants of the political context of our future relations.

I'm not prepared to interpret further what that means. I think it speaks for itself.

Q. Could you amplify Point 2? Is that purely a U.S. bilateral reference to the Neutrality Act?[72] How do you propose to handle it?

A. Let me say this. Our neutrality laws and other legislation forbid the training activity of exiled groups operating in the United States who are attempting to overthrow a government with which we have relations.

A statement concerning this would be a political statement, because obviously the administration's policy already is to keep an eye on groups which we suspect may be up to "monkey business." What we're offering here is something to allay one of the main fears that the Nicaraguans have: We would make a political statement—it's a political statement—to leave it absolutely clear, with no doubt in anybody's mind as to where this government stands with respect to what might be going on. This has been something which has been of great concern to the Nicaraguans, and what this represents is an effort on our part to meet some of the requirements that the Nicaraguans have expressed to us over time.

Q. Do we do more than that? Do we guarantee that we will move in and stop these exiles from training in Florida and places like that?

A. The neutrality laws are as I've described them, and there are things the U.S. Government can do and things it cannot do. What the U.S. Government can do in this case would be to express our policy with respect to something which could happen. If it did happen, it would be a question for the law that exists to deal with them. I can't go beyond that.

Q. How would you deal with free-lance or third-party exiles whom the Nicaraguans believe us to be financing? Rightly or wrongly, as a result of press stories that have appeared here, there has been talk about Somozistas in Honduras, or Argentinian groups, and so on. Are you taking a "hands off" position on that, that that's their problem?

A. I think that's covered on the international verification—at least, that's the purpose of that particular paragraph—international verification, which in effect is [that] the Honduran peace plan would address the activities in the countries and how they impact on each other. That's obviously, a very important element of this whole package.

Q. On the subject of foreign advisers, would that be limited to military advisers, political advisers, and would it include the 3,000 or so teachers they are sending from Cuba?

A. I'm not prepared right now to be specific on that.

Q. What do you consider an adviser?

A. At this point, I don't want to be more specific [on] that.

Q. A follow-up on that, on the question of advisers, we're calling our people in El Salvador trainers. Are U.S. trainers, military trainers included in that category?

A. We're talking about Nicaragua primarily, and our concern, obviously, is directed not at 35 or 36, or whatever it may be at any given moment, people who are training. We're talking about actual military advisers. What we're focusing on—these are

[72] For the relevant sections of U.S. neutrality laws, see 18 U.S.C. 951–970.

our proposals; these are not anybody else's proposals. I'm not going to give somebody else proposals to give to me—that's up to them to do. But what we're talking about is what concerns us. What concerns us are the 2,000 military advisers, plus other national advisers. In Nicaragua, there are Soviet military advisers; there are military advisers from Eastern Europe; Yassar Arafat claims that he has military advisers there. I'm talking about the military advisers who are of concern to us.

I've got about 3 more minutes, and I've got to take off, so let's see how many I can do.

Q. I wanted to ask about the verification. Would this verification also—would Honduran airports, the Honduran side of the border be accessible to OAS observers under this proposal?

A. I think everything is negotiable. That's up to the parties themselves, obviously; but this is a starting point.

Q. The Nicaraguans have said that yesterday's meeting was a positive step, but they also added that they would like to proceed on the basis of negotiations pursuant to Commander Ortega's statement at the United Nations and Lopez Portillo's statement in Managua. Do you see any problem with that formulation of their response to your proposals?

A. I think I answered you earlier when I referred to the Mexican role and the possibility of broadened discussions. For the present, we have made some proposals which are fairly specific, and we hope that this time there will be counter proposals.

Now, proposals can be of two kinds—actually, they can probably be of more than two kinds. But, immediately what comes to mind is, you can have substantive proposals, and you can have procedural proposals. The important thing is to have an exchange going. And that is what we are trying to stimulate, and have been trying to stimulate now for months and months and months.

One more question.

Q. Who did the Ambassador meet with yesterday? And also is there a deadline for any counter-proposals set by the United States?

A. I'm not prepared to answer the first one. As to the second one, the obvious answer would be no, but this has been going on a long time; and the sooner we get back into a position of normalizing our relationship with Nicaragua, the happier we will be. Obviously—I assume it's obvious—we have felt a sense of frustration in the nonresponse from Nicaragua. We hope that this time there will be a response. I would prefer to leave it to them to say who it was they were talking with.

I've got to go.

Q. Do you expect to go forward after the 15th?

A. (No answer)

Document 687

Statement by the Principal Deputy Assistant Secretary of State for Inter-American Affairs (Bosworth) Before a Subcommittee of the House Foreign Affairs Committee, June 15, 1982[73]

U.S. Relations With Grenada

Thank you very much, Mr. Chairman.[74] It is a pleasure to be here this afternoon to meet with the subcommittee and members of the full committee to discuss U.S. relations with Grenada.

I would like, Mr. Chairman, to treat the subject of our relations with Grenada within the broader context of U.S. relations with the countries of the eastern Caribbean subregion. This is a region which has become increasingly important to the United States.

During the past 16 years, six countries of the eastern Caribbean have peacefully achieved their independence from Great Britain. With the exception of Grenada, all now have freely elected, democratic governments characterized by their respect for individual rights and the rule of law.

The President's announcement of the Caribbean Basin program in February, and his emphasis upon the eastern Caribbean in particular, was tangible evidence of this

---

[73] Source: *United States Policy Toward Grenada: Hearing Before the Subcommittee on Inter-American Affairs of the Committee on Foreign Affairs, House of Representatives, Ninety-seventh Congress, Second Session* (Washington, 1982), pp. 27—31; for Bosworth's prepared statement, see *ibid.*, pp. 31–41.

[74] Representative Michael D. Barnes.

region's importance not only to the United States but to other major countries of the area.

Working with Mexico, Venezuela, Colombia, and Canada, the United States has proposed a major and integrated program of trade, investment, and assistance to promote the economic development and social well-being of these island nations, as well as the other countries of the Caribbean Basin. To underscore the importance we attach to this region, President Reagan visited Barbados in April[75] and personally met with elected leaders of many of these new nations.

The democractic governments of this region are seeking to improve the welfare of their peoples within a commitment to freedom, democracy, and respect for human rights. This commitment stands in some contrast to the situation in Grenada.

Maurice Bishop's "New Jewel Movement"[76] overthrew the constitutional government of Prime Minister Eric Gairy in March 1979. The new government initially promised early elections and improved observance of human rights. Its actual performance, however, has been quite different.

It has postponed elections indefinitely and has taken a number of actions which have seriously eroded the human rights of the Grenadian people. Basic freedoms and due process of law have been effectively denied in Grenada. At the same time, Grenada's People's Revolutionary Government, the PRG, has adopted a military foreign policy harshly critical of the United States and has openly alined itself with Cuba and the Soviet Union.

The New Jewel Movement's coup d'etat marked the first nonconstitutional change of government in the Commonwealth Caribbean.

I would like at this point, Mr. Chairman, to review very briefly the performances we have observed of Mr. Bishop's government in a number of key areas.

First, with regard to democracy. At the celebration of the third anniversary of his coup in March, Prime Minister Bishop again said publicly that Westminster-style democracy is dead in Grenada. PRG leaders ridicule the system favored by all other Commonwealth Caribbean countries as democracy for 5 seconds when votes are cast every 5 years.

In Grenada, political pluralism and the legal organization of freely competing political parties have been replaced by a people's democracy of grassroots parish assemblies, controlled by the New Jewel Movement, which serves as an instrument of, rather than as a check on, the PRG itself.

In the area of human rights, the situation has shown continued deterioration since the PRG came to power. No independent press is allowed to operate. There is no freedom of assembly, no due process of law.

Over 100 political prisoners remain under detention and many have never been formally charged with any crime. The Department of State's 1981 human rights report to the Congress[77] gives details on this situation and merits careful reading.

Grenada's economy is in trouble. Like those of its neighbors, it has been seriously affected by the worldwide recession and depressed prices for its export crops. While employing increasingly authoritarian measures to consolidate internal political control, the PRG has permitted the continued existence of private sector economic activity. But private investment is at a standstill in part because most of Grenada's scarce foreign exchange is devoted to public projects, like the Cuban-constructed Point Salines International Airport.

The country relies heavily on foreign assistance, much of it from Cuba and other radical Soviet bloc countries, for the modest rate of current economic growth it has attained. Tourism, traditionally the most dynamic industry, has been declining much more than in other Caribbean countries. The PRG's anticapitalist, anti-American rhetoric has hardly helped to encourage foreign investment or tourism.

With regard to foreign policy, the PRG, unlike its neighbors, maintain close relations with Cuba, Soviet bloc countries, and radical Arab States, which are among its primary sources of aid. The oversized airport project is being built principally with Cuban assistance.

In turn, Grenada has adopted foreign policy positions closely linked to those of Cuba and the Soviet Union, and it has

[75] For documentation on President Reagan's visit to Jamaica, April 7–8, 1982, and Barbados, April 8–11, see *Weekly Compilation of Presidential Documents*, April 19, 1982, pp. 457–465.

[76] JEWEL is the acronym for Joint Endeavor for Welfare, Education, and Liberation.

[77] *Country Reports on Human Rights Practices for 1981*, pp. 435–444.

strongly criticized U.S. policies like the Caribbean Basin initiative. Grenada, for example, voted with Cuba and the Soviet Union in the United Nations on both Afghanistan and Kampuchea.

In stark contrast to its commonwealth Caribbean neighbors, the PRG has followed the Cuban lead on the South Atlantic crisis, deriding British colonialism. We expect Grenada will repay its debt to Cuba with more than verbal support and votes by providing Cuba access to the Point Salines Airport for transit flights to Africa and other military uses.

Grenada's neighbors have watched carefully as the PRG has become a center for solidarity meetings and established close ties to small, radical movements from elsewhere in the Caribbean. Grenada to some degree acts as a bridge for Cuba to radical or, as some would prefer to say, progressive groups in the eastern Caribbean.

Cuba has provided training to Grenada's vastly expanded security forces and has stationed small numbers of military advisers on the island. Cuba and the Soviet Union have provided arms, transportation, and communications equipment to the Grenadian security forces.

At the same time, Cuba's role in the construction of the Point Salines Airport—a field which will be capable of handling advanced military aircraft—adds a new and serious dimension to our security concerns. It is difficult, if not impossible, to identify any economic justification for the enormous investment being undertaken in the construction of this airfield.

Relations between the United States and the PRG are seriously strained and have been so for some time. As I have indicated, the United States has significant differences with the Government of Grenada on fundamental issues.

For its part, since it took power, the PRG has viewed the United States with hostility and suspicion. Relations were strained under the previous administration. With no change in the attitude or policies of the PRG, they remain cool and are conducted at a level appropriate to the PRG's conduct.

Despite the PRG's professed interest in a high level dialog, we have seen no credible evidence that it is seriously interested in improving relations. On the contrary, PRG anti-American statements seem designed precisely to foster a climate of confrontation with the United States.

For example, Prime Minister Bishop has called President Reagan a "fascist" and has been quoted in the press as describing the Caribbean Basin initiative as "chicken feed" and "an insult" which is "only aimed at achieving military interests."

Moreover, Grenada has charged on numerous occasions and without a shred of evidence that the United States is preparing an invasion of Grenada, and that various U.S. military and naval exercises in the region are part of those preparations.

U.S. direct interests in Grenada are not significant. We maintain diplomatic relations but not at the ambassadorial level. Private sector linkages are minimal, primarily some tourism activity and a medical school, which has some 600 U.S. students.

Nevertheless, we would be seriously concerned should Grenada become a base for subversion in the eastern Caribbean. In particular, we would be concerned if Grenada were to permit Cuba military access to the Point Salines Airport when it is completed. We have made these concerns known to the PRG.

At the same time, Mr. Chairman, we are strengthening our relations with the democratic nations of the eastern Caribbean and we are working with them to address their economic problems. Most face critical problems such as unemployment rates of over 30 percent, severe shortages of skilled workers and managers, dependence on a single crop and a single market, low agricultural productivity, and small domestic markets.

The United States is working to address these problems with assistance in such areas as skills training, agricultural diversification and marketing, and infrastructural improvements which would permit goods to be produced and moved to markets.

Our total proposed assistance to the eastern Carribbean region in fiscal year 1982 is $54 million plus the $10 million supplemental proposed under the Caribbean Basin initiative.

The President had the opportunity to listen firsthand to the concerns of the eastern Caribbean leaders in April and to describe his proposals for the Caribbean Basin initiative.

We are also increasing our cooperation in the area of security. Most eastern Caribbean countries maintain no armed forces. With only modest constabulary forces for defense, these countries are potentially vulnerable to takeovers by armed groups on the left like Maurice Bishop's New Jewel Movement, or by criminal elements, such as the group that tried to stage a coup in Dominica last December.

These countries need our help, and enactment of the Caribbean Basin program would provide quick-disbursing assistance to address their most immediate infrastructure and development needs. At the same time, it would offer trade and investment benefits to achieve self-sustaining growth, which will strengthen democratic institutions.

The United States desires mutually beneficial relations with all the countries of the region, and Grenada is no exception. Our interest in improved relations with Grenada, however, can only be realized if there are some changes on the part of the PRG, changes that would show that Grenada wants good relations and is prepared to take concrete steps to that end.

For example, if Grenada is serious about having a normal relationship with the United States, it should halt its unrelenting stream of anti-American propaganda and false statements about U.S. policies and actions.

Grenada should move to restore constitutional democracy, including prompt, free, and fair elections, as was promised on numerous occasions by the New Jewel Movement in the early days after the coup. There should be a return to the high standard of human rights observance that is typical of the Caribbean commonwealth islands.

Finally, Grenada should practice genuine nonalinement rather than continuing its present role as a surrogate of Cuba. These changes or even significant progress toward them would indicate a serious interest on Grenada's part in building good relations with the United States and playing a responsible role in the region. We would respond to them positively.

Thank you, Mr. Chairman, I would be pleased to respond to any questions or comments that you or other members of the subcommittee might have.

Document 688

Transcript of a White House Press Briefing, June 22, 1982[78]

Visit of Costa Rican President Monge

Senior Administration Official. You heard the two Presidents describe the main themes they cover.[79] President Monge of Costa Rica, through a very tight bond between the success—future success of Costa Rican democracy and a democracy in the area and its—the ability of that country to solve its economic and social problems—he came here with very vigorous support for the President's Caribbean Basin Initiative; as he put it, in all three parts; that is to say, not only the immediate one-time economic assistance, but above all the trade measures, the important proposal for diminishing and removing tariffs in the area, and the incentives to investment.

And he came also to plead the case for other countries in the area. He said that—he told the President that he had been in touch with the AFL-CIO to explain to them why he supported this, why he thought it was so fundamental for the area.

As you know, Mr. Monge is a long-time labor leader. He was an organizer in the 1940's, and he's been the Secretary General of the Inter-American Labor Organization as well as heading the Social Democratic Party in Costa Rica and has many friends in the American labor movement.

He told the President, also, that he'd been up on the Hill and that he talked to the chairmen of committees on the House side and would on the Senate side urging their quick action on the Caribbean Basin Initiative.

The President reiterated to Mr. Monge that—his very strong support for the Caribbean Basin Initiative, which he described as fundamental to the future of the area.

They had a long exchange on the subject of the developments in Nicaragua and the

---

[78] Source: Office of the Press Secretary to the President. This was a background briefing conducted by a senior administration official in the Briefing Room of the White House beginning at 12:20 p.m.

[79] For the remarks made by Presidents Reagan and Monge after their meeting on June 22, see *Weekly Compilation of Presidential Documents,* June 28, 1982, pp. 826–827.

threat from Cuba and Nicaragua to the area. President Monge characterized Nicaragua as a state that was becoming a totalitarian dictatorship with strong support from Cuba. He noted that not all of his colleagues in the socialist movement in Western Europe had come yet to that conclusion. The President asked him why, and he said, well, you know, they—it's a little difficult when you've been wrong, perhaps, to admit immediately how wrong you are. He himself said that although Costa Rica and his own party had very vigorously supported the Sandinistas, the Nicaraguan revolutionaries when they came to power, that they had become disillusioned; thought it was a militaristic and expansionistic government. And he himself very much hoped—he was attempting to persuade all other socialists, and notably the European socialists, of this—he noted that, in fact, a number of particularly those from Southern Europe have themselves come to this conclusion.

President Monge described the situation of the democracies—you heard him allude to that out in front—in the area as being caught in a pincher between, on the one hand, very severe economic and social problems and, on the other hand, a strong drive from Cuba and Nicaragua and from Marxists-Leninists throughout the area. He believed that working closely with the United States and with other countries in the area, particularly the affairs of the Caribbean Basin Initiative, that these can be overcome.

There was a brief exchange on the subject of the Falkland Island–Malvinas crisis with President Monge indicating that he understood very well how the United States must conduct a global policy concerned with preventing the destruction of freedom or the expansion of Communist forces throughout the world, how Europe and Britain play an important role in that strategy, and how important it is that that strategy succeed not only for the United States and Europeans but also for Latin America as a whole. These, I think, were the highlights.

Questions?

Q. The last time I was there, the country was virtually bankrupt, and desperately needed some concessions from the IMF. Can you update us on where they are now?

Senior Administration Official. Yes; the country is bankrupt. It is not able to pay on its very large debt, which is about $2.7 billion. For a country of about 2½ million people, that is a very substantial debt. The debt was run up by previous administrations but also the result of the collapse of coffee prices.

His government is negotiating with the IMF for a stabilization plan under which new credit can be provided and an orderly payment of the existing debt undertaken. The IMF has put conditions for that. Those conditions are a very substantial reduction of the balance of payments gap and of the domestic budget deficit. And this new government has already taken very courageous steps in increasing the cost of electricity, of gasoline, of almost all basic commodities in that country and raising taxes in order to diminish that deficit.

The negotiations are still in course. We hope that they will succeed toward the end of the summer.

Q. —be able to reduce any of the social services that make Costa Rica—

Senior Administration Official. Yes; he has already made some steps in that direction.

Q. What kind?

Senior Administration Official. Well, for example, the availability of some subsidies for rent has been diminished, and they are now—after having raised the prices of basic commodities—they are now looking at all of their social services to see whether there are those that cannot be cut off, or must not be cut off now under present circumstances.

Q. What is the scope of U.S. aid now? And did the President have any increase in mind when he said outside he personally committed his administration's support?

Senior Administration Official. Well, we have this year $18 million in food aid, $13 million in development assistance, and $50 million in ESF—Economic Support Funds.

Q. Fifty or 15?

Senior Administration Official. I beg your pardon. I misspoke on both occasions. It is $20 million in Economic Support Funds for a total of $51 million. And in addition to that, a major portion of the emergency appropriation which we have proposed to Congress under the Caribbean Basin Initiative would be for Costa Rica. The total proposed to Congress is $350 million, as some of you know. And the amount that would go to Costa Rica of that would be $70 million. That is to say that, if in fact the Congress accepts this program, the U.S. aid effort in this country would be $121 million this year.

Q. They also are exporters of textiles and sugar, and both of those are somewhat limited by the terms of the CBI. Any relief there?

SENIOR ADMINISTRATION OFFICIAL. No; I do not think so, but in the view of President Monge, his country is, sort of, tailor-made for the Caribbean Basin Initiative, particularly on the trade side. Why? Because they have a relatively skilled workforce. They are at the point of beginning to diversify away from traditional, staple industries like sugar and coffee into light manufactures and also into market agriculture of fruits and vegetables. And this is precisely the kind of situation that the Caribbean Basin Initiative is intended to encourage and a situation in which the Costa Ricans could in fact, probably, begin to earn their way in a rather short time.

Q. President Monge appealed for, in his words, solidarity and assistance outside and overcoming economic problems. Has he asked for increases in these aid levels?

SENIOR ADMINISTRATION OFFICIAL. No; he has asked that the Caribbean Basin Initiative as a whole be passed, which would contain these elements.

Q. Has President Monge asked for help from the United States to ease the measures from the IMF.

SENIOR ADMINISTRATION OFFICIAL. No; there was a brief discussion of the International Monetary Fund, negotiations between Costa Rica and the Fund, and it was on an informational basis only—in other words, Mr. Monge informed the President where they stood.

Q. In the case of aggression from the Sandinista junta, is the United States ready to help Costa Rica?

SENIOR ADMINISTRATION OFFICIAL. Well, you saw the President underscore his commitment to the inter-American system and the United States is bound under the Rio Treaty to come to the assistance of countries that are threatened or attacked—that are subject to aggression. The United States takes that commitment very seriously and would, indeed, in the case of aggression in the Americas, the United States would indeed be prepared to join others in carrying out its obligations.

Q. That was applied in the Argentine case too?

SENIOR ADMINISTRATION OFFICIAL. I don't think anybody ever thought that the Rio Treaty, which does in fact say explicitly that the Treaty will protect American states against the aggression of outside countries—that the treaty was ever intended to provide protection to a country that made the first use of force, that itself initiated the conflict.

Q. Just how imminent does this Marxist-Leninist threat you spoke of to the Monge government—are they in any imminent danger of being toppled?

SENIOR ADMINISTRATION OFFICIAL. No, no. Mr. Monge was not at all—Mr. Monge was talking less of his internal situation—although there have been some subversive activities in his country—than he was of the presence of what he termed a Marxist-Leninist government in Central America—the Nicaraguan Government and the threat it posed to its neighbors.

Q. To which Central American countries is there an imminent or a near-term threat?

SENIOR ADMINISTRATION OFFICIAL. Well, the Nicaraguan Government is deeply involved in supporting the insurgents in El Salvador, and has in fact run close border operations into Honduras, and I think clearly Mr. Monge was raising concerns about what the attitude of the Nicaraguan Government would be towards his own country. Although it was not mentioned in the discussion, I think both Presidents are acutely aware of the fact that the Nicaraguan Government has, although itself is running only a small country, has built up the largest army in Central American history.

Q. Before his inauguration he was interested in an international force operating only on the Costa Rican side—frontier—since Nicaragua wouldn't consent. Where does that stand now?

SENIOR ADMINISTRATION OFFICIAL. As you know, we are going to have some more discussions on that. We have not come to that yet, . . . but I expect it will come up in the course of the conversations.

THE PRESS. Thank you.

Document 689

Report Prepared in the Department of State, July 27, 1982 (Extract)[80]

The Situation in El Salvador

Executive Summary

Severe civil strife has continued in El Salvador in the period covered by this report. The newly-elected Government of National Unity continues to be engaged in a struggle with a guerrilla movement which is, with outside support, attempting to seize power by force. The on-going violence continues to result in reports of violations of basic human rights committed by leftist guerrillas, right-wing terrorists and members of the government security forces. We continue to be concerned over the human rights situation and the course of the reform program in El Salvador. Nevertheless, there are tangible signs of progress by the Government of National Unity, and we believe a firm base has been established for further progress in the months ahead.

The development of democratic order in El Salvador is likely to be, over the long term, the best guarantee of human rights improvement. In this regard, the most important development in El Salvador in recent months has been the initiation of a democratic political process based on free elections. One-and-one-half million Salvadorans (over 80% of the eligible electorate) voted in the March 28, 1982 elections. These elections, closely monitored by large numbers of international observers and journalists, selected a 60-member Constituent Assembly, charged with forming an interim government and writing a new constitution.

As the Assembly continues its work leading up to elections for a permanent government after adoption of the constitution, the popular accountability inherent in the democratic process will channel the widespread desire of the Salvadoran people for a return to law and order into pressure on all political elements for action in this area.

The new government has already undertaken substantial steps to ensure continued progress in human rights areas:

—The Minister of Defense has ordered that all violations of citizens' rights be stopped immediately and directed punishment of military offenders.

—Over the past six months 109 members of the Salvadoran Armed Forces were disciplined for various offenses, including 56 cases submitted to judicial action. In addition, 20 members of the civil defense forces were disciplined in the ongoing effort to prevent abuses by the paramilitary forces.

—Despite continued resistance in some quarters, demonstrable progress has been made in the land reform program, including the issuance of over 10,000 Phase III (Land-to-the-Tiller) provisional titles in the last 6 months—4,865 issuances since the elections.

—The Government and the Armed Forces have undertaken an effort to restore those farmers illegally evicted from their land following the confusion over the Constituent Assembly's modification of Decree 207. Some 2,000 families have been returned to their farms by the Armed Forces since June 1.

—The Salvadoran Government has begun proceedings under Salvadoran law to bring to justice those accused of the December 1980 killings of four American churchwomen.

The report which follows is designed to provide the Congress with the most comprehensive and objective analysis possible under the certification requirement. We believe the report shows tangible signs of progress in each of the areas covered under the certification requirement.

Summary

The most important development in El Salvador during the certification period was progress in the development of representative government. The Salvadoran people elected a Constituent Assembly, which has designated an interim coalition Government of National Unity, is functioning as an interim legislative body, and will draft a new constitution and set the ground rules and the date for presidential elections.

The Constituent Assembly elections, held March 28, were hotly contested by six

---

[80] Source: *Presidential Certification on El Salvador: Hearings and Markup Before the Committee on Foreign Affairs and its Subcommittee on Inter-American Affairs, House of Representatives, Ninety-seventh Congress, Second Session* (Washington, 1982), vol. II, pp. 465–469; for the complete report, see *ibid.*, pp. 465–513. The report was prepared with respect to the subjects covered in Section 728(d) of the International Security and Development Act of 1981, P.L. 97–113; for text of this section, see 95 Stat. 1556.

parties, supervised by an independent Central Elections Commission (CCE) and monitored by more than 200 international observers. President Duarte and the president of the CCE invited all parties to participate, including those on the far left associated with the guerrillas, but the latter refused to take part or negotiate how they could have participated with security guarantees. The turnout of one and a half million voters exceeded all expectations and constituted a severe setback for the guerrillas, who had called for a boycott and attempted to disrupt the voting by force of arms.

During this certification period, the land reform program advanced, was subject to some challenges, and was relaunched. The net result is that Phase I of the agrarian reform has been consolidated further; and demonstrable progress was also made on Phase III. Ambiguous legislation passed by the Constituent Assembly in May gave rise to the widespread belief, in and outside of El Salvador, that Phase III was being suspended and the entire reform process was in jeopardy. One effect of this misconception was a surge in illegal evictions in the countryside.

Faced with this situation, the Government of National Unity, as one of its first official acts, began a campaign personally directed by President Magana to put the land reform programs back on track. Supported by the military, the President acted to ensure that all reform activities go forward, to distribute the first permanent land titles to Phase III beneficiaries, to pay the first compensation to affected owners, to direct high-level military and government participation in issuance of provisional titles throughout the country, and to issue military orders to support the agrarian reform and to assist in reinstallation of illegally evicted beneficiaries. Perhaps most importantly, the government appointed a strong president of FINATA, the government agency which administers Phase III.

Our conclusion is that despite continuing problems and strong challenges, there has been demonstrable progress in implementing essential economic and political reforms, including land reform, in El Salvador during the certification period: Five permanent titles were issued to cooperatives and 48 owners were compensated, but of major importance was the fact that 178,530 Phase I beneficiaries were, as a result of government-supported technical assistance and agricultural credit programs, able to begin their third crop year. For most, that alone represents three consecutive years of progress. Since January 1, 11,238 Phase III titles, including 4,865 since the March 28 election, were issued, together with the first 251 permanent titles. The first former owners of lands redistributed under Decree 207 were paid $614,219, and 7,017 essential field inspections were carried out.

Democratic elections will, of course, give the Salvadoran people a regular opportunity to gauge the performance of their elected leaders and the political parties on the reforms.

Although the monthly total of deaths attributed to political violence declined somewhat (according to available statistics), human rights violations and terrorism continued to be a major problem during the certification period.

There continue to be reports of human rights abuses on the part of various branches of the Salvadoran security forces. There have been, however, significant efforts by the Salvadoran leadership to correct the problem. Since October 15, 1979, at least 1,000 members of the Salvadoran security forces have been disciplined for abuses of authority. Ministry of Defense records show that during this certification period, 109 members of the Salvadoran Armed Forces were disciplined for various offenses, of which 56 cases have been submitted for judicial action. In addition, at least 20 members of the civil defense forces were disciplined in a special effort to crack down on abuses committed by paramilitary forces.

On March 10, 1982, Minister of Defense Garcia issued an instruction to all military personnel stating that all illegal actions and violations of the rights of citizens must cease and ordering the punishment of those failing to heed this order. But continued training is necessary for building upon the progress already achieved in raising the level of discipline and professionalism.

Although serious problems remain, we conclude that the Government of El Salvador is making a concerted and significant effort to comply with internationally recognized human rights. Given the orders issued by the Armed Forces concerning human rights abuses and the codes of conduct promulgated to achieve this objective, and in light of the substantial efforts to improve the disciplinary system, we conclude that the Government of El Salvador is achieving substantial control over all elements of its own armed forces. Moreover, the establishment of responsible democratic institutions is a major step toward channeling popular desires for peace, law, and order into public accountability for the government's performance in these areas of concern. In addition, democratic institutions provide a peaceful channel for resolving conflict and disagreements.

Substantial progress has been made in the murder case involving four American churchwomen. In February, the investigatory working group turned its final report over to the National Guard. The National Guard found sufficient evidence in the report to dismiss six guardsmen and turn them over to a civilian court. The presiding judge, in turn, examined the evidence and determined that it was sufficient to justify charging five of the former guardsmen with aggravated homicide. They were remanded to prison pending the resolution of their trial. The trial judge has initiated and largely completed the judicial inquiry required under Salvadoran law. We expect the date of the trial to be set this fall.

The Government of El Salvador has moved to reinvigorate the investigation into the murder of the two American land reform advisors and their Salvadoran colleague by forming in April a new investigative working group to uncover additional evidence. To date all efforts have failed to provide any clues as to the whereabouts of John J. Sullivan, an American freelance journalist who disappeared in San Salvador in December 1980. The investigation of Mr. Sullivan's disappearance has received the attention of the highest levels of the Salvadoran Government.

End Summary

. . . .

Document 690

Statement by the Assistant Secretary of State for Inter-American Affairs (Enders) Before the House Foreign Affairs Committee, July 29, 1982[81]

"For All the Problems There Are Real Gains Being Made in That Unhappy Country"

MR. ENDERS. Thank you very much, Mr. Chairman.[82]

I have prepared the usual prepared statement. If I could submit it to you for the record and make oral remarks I would appreciate it.

CHAIRMAN ZABLOCKI. Without objection it is so ordered.

MR. ENDERS. It is about 3 years, Mr. Chairman, since the United States has been deeply engaged in El Salvador. You remember that we backed a reforming group of army officers who came to power in October 1979. There have been two Congresses since that time, two U.S. administrations. We have spent much money and I think even more psychic energy on El Salvador since that time.

Perhaps before I go to the last 6 months I could summarize what has been achieved in that period. I think it is important to set the framework in which we are talking.

Up until 1979 El Salvador was ruled by a military government that periodically arranged for its own reelection. In 1982 El Salvador has a government that emerged from an election in which nearly all adult El Salvadorans participated.

You asked about land reform. In 1979 most of El Salvador's best land belonged to a few hundred wealthy families. In fact, 40 percent of all of El Salvador's farmland belonged to less than 2 percent of the

---

[81] Source: *Presidential Certification on El Salvador*, vol. II, pp. 14–19; for Enders' prepared statement, see *ibid.*, pp. 20–34. The Senate also held a hearing on the certification; see *Presidential Certifications on Conditions in El Salvador: Hearing Before the Committee on Foreign Relations, United States Senate, Ninety-seventh Congress, Second Session* (Washington, 1982).

[82] Representative Clement J. Zablocki; for Chairman Zablocki's opening remarks, see *Presidential Certification on El Salvador*, vol. II, pp. 11–12.

families on the land. Today half of that 40 percent, or 20 percent, of all land in El Salvador has been redistributed to 60,000 poor farmworkers and their families.

In 1979 El Salvador's violent left seemed to have history on its side. Today despite Cuban and Nicaragua backing, a much ballyhooed final offensive and a broad attack on the elections, guerrilla progress has been arrested and the slow process of overcoming their armed violence has begun.

I think the most striking measure of progress is the transformation of the military of that country from an institution dedicated to the status quo, backing the oligarchy, to one that spearheads land reform and supports constitutional democracy.

Mr. Chairman, El Salvador is strategically important to the United States. Should it fall to Cuban and Nicaraguan-supported armed minority, would there be any country in Central America that would be secure? Surely it would not be Costa Rica which has no army. Not Honduras which would be caught between the Marxist-Leninist countries, nor Guatemala already challenged by an insurgency. It might not be long before Panama and Southern Mexico were at risk.

El Salvador I think is also important to us politically. If we abandon a country that reforms its land-holding system and transforms itself into a democracy, who in the future will choose reform or democracy when it is challenged by guerrilleros supported from outside?

El Salvador is also important to us because of its proximity. There are a lot of Salvadorans living in our country already, perhaps 10 percent of their population. Should El Salvador and Central America fall to insurgency far more of their people will come here.

The law which you cited, Mr. Chairman, sets conditions for military assistance to El Salvador. The administration believes that progress toward the goals which are set in the law is indeed essential to the success of American policy in El Salvador.

We believe that the facts amply justify the certification required by law. In one area, creation of democratic institutions, the gains are very substantial. In other words, human rights and aspects of the land reform, progress is marred, but we believe is real.

Let me start with the elections. I would like to start with them because they are the key to so much else. Over time governments that must answer to the people are far less likely to cause or tolerate abuses of human rights. We believe that if democracy can be made to work, all our goals can ultimately be met.

All of us saw on television, the long, long lines of Salvadorans waiting to vote, in some cases under the threat or fact of violence. One of our election observers, Father Ted Hesburgh of Notre Dame, found thousands of people walking in from rebel-held areas back in the hills near the Honduras borders. "They had all been menaced by the guerrillas," he wrote in his diary, "but they were still voting and this again was a victory for the people."[83]

There were 200 foreign observers, 800 media representatives and millions of television spectators saw what happened. No significant fraud was reported or charged by either the losing or the winning party.

Yet there are some people who say that these results weren't valid because the extreme left didn't participate. But the extreme left didn't participate despite efforts by then President Duarte, supported by the United States, to convince them to do so.

That, Congressman Barnes,[84] was what they were required to do under our certification conditions. There were required to the end of free elections to make contact with the parties that believed in elections. But instead of participating in the elections these parties and groups of the extreme left attacked the elections, threatening individual voters with maiming and death.

Some have said that the extreme left didn't participate in the elections because its candidates feared for their lives. In fact they were trying to make the voters fear for their lives.

I don't think anybody can minimize the difficulties that the new Salvadoran democracy faces. Its government is a coalition. All the skills of compromise and comity that we have gradually learned in this country are still to be learned down there. Democratic processes must start in the middle of economic collapse and ongoing strife, yet they are starting.

Returning to human rights, all available evidence suggests that the most serious violations of human rights, deaths attributa-

---

[83] See *Report of the U.S. Official Observer Mission*, pp. 12–14.

[84] For Representative Barnes' remarks, see *Presidential Certification on El Salvador*, vol. II, pp. 12–14.

ble to political violence, are on a slow downward trend. A complete tabulation of monthly totals from five different sources is contained in the certification and in my prepared statement.

All of these statistics are defective—I agree with Congressman Barnes—probably those of the dissident organizations more than others. They do not make their data available for verification. Whatever their methodology, they show a common downward trend. They all show less killing.

Some who are concerned with human rights have expressed perplexity at this encouraging trend. They argue that political deaths are down because most people who are a threat have been killed, or that the killers are concealing their work more skillfully.

There may be something much less sinister at work here. The government has been working hard to control both official violence and the guerrillas. Moreover the genius of democracy is to provide alternatives to violence to reconciling opposing political interests and political patience.

The reporting organizations show particularly low totals since the elections. I want to underscore this point because there continue to be allegations that political violence has increased since the new government took office. We can't support that conclusion by any evidence.

I do not mean to suggest that today's level of killing, however much reduced from yesterday's, is acceptable. It is certainly not. Nor are other aspects of the human rights picture wholly satisfactory.

For the last 3 years, the judicial system has been virtually paralyzed. Persons suspected of political crimes have rarely been arrested. Persons arrested have almost never been convicted. Salvadorans, fearing for their lives, cannot rely on their system of justice to function.

In the last 6 months, there have been some improvements. Arrests have been made more quickly and surely than before in political crimes or crimes alleged to involve powerful or well-situated persons. Yet trials and convictions still do not occur. They must now begin again.

The recent appointment of widely respected persons to the Supreme Court is an important first step.

Allegations of disappearance and torture continue. The U.S. Embassy investigates every case it hears of, to the best of its ability.

I might add here for Chairman Barnes that we do not and in most cases do not expect to give any details on information we receive for two reasons, Mr. Barnes. One is that we are concerned about the safety of our sources.

Another is that we are concerned about the safety of the persons allegedly subject to torture or mistreatment. Unless those persons on both sides are well out of jeopardy we are unlikely to be able to give in any public session information of the detailed kind that you have requested.

There have also been many fewer allegations of massacres during this reporting period than last. This may be in part because many earlier reports proved to be fabricated or exaggerated. Whatever the reason, fewer large-scale incidents have come to our attention.

El Salvador is in the grip of civil strife. The guerrillas claim the right to kill in the name of a higher good. So do death squads on the right. But little by little the violence appears to be receding.

I have made remarks in my prepared statement on the question of the control of all elements of the armed forces, but I would like if I could, Mr. Chairman, to put a particular emphasis on land reform and perhaps I could move directly to that.

This is the question that has aroused the greatest controversy in El Salvador and in the United States in the last 6 months.

Immediately after the elections, there was a concerted attempt to derail land reform. In the name of perfecting flaws in reform legislation—and there were some very real flaws; for example, it was prohibited to rent agricultural land, a self-destructive provision in a country whose economy was already devastated by sabotage—the Constituent Assembly and some members of the new government sent out a massive political signal to the country that the reforms had been suspended. Evictions of peasants surged. New titling applications stopped.

Then came the counterattack. Issuance of provisional titles resumed, altogether 4,865 such titles have been given out since March 28, compared to a total of 127,215 before then. But perhaps the most decisive development on this point is that since the elections the first definitive titles have been given out; the first compensation paid to small plot owners.

This is particularly important. I was talking to beneficiaries in the countryside. They asked consistently, "When are we going to get our final titles? How can we be sure we can build a house on the land we are on without a final title?"

They were assured they could do that. But they were uncertain and wavery. Final titles are absolutely vital.

We believe that some 2,000 evictees have been restored to the land they rented, less than those turned out, but the effort is continuing with strong support from the military. And evictions have apparently fallen sharply in July.

It is important to be clear on what has and hasn't happened.

The most sweeping part of the reform program—phase I under which 328 large estates were converted into 287 working cooperatives consisting of more than 30,000 of their former workers—continues to function normally.

Phase II—under which 1,700 medium-sized estates were to be taken over, among them the country's best coffee farms—was deferred from the very start as beyond the country's administrative and financial capability. Neither the Carter nor the Reagan administrations backed it, rightly in my view. In contrast to the very large farms, many of the phase II farms were owner-operated and quite efficient.

It is on the land-to-the-tiller program—phase III—that the controversy has centered. What is the future of phase III? That depends on three factors which to some degree can be influenced by the Salvadoran Government and by our Government, and to some degree are independent of us both.

The first factor is the security situation. It can make or break the program. If I could I would like to have you look at the chart. This chart shows, Mr. Chairman, the area in which the largest numbers of provisional titles under the land-to-the-tiller program has been given. This area here which is in the west of the country of El Salvador, you find in terms of numbers of applications, percentages of the estimated maximum, you find, taking a department like this, as many as 80 percent of the estimated maximum number of beneficiaries have received provisional titles.

Over here the numbers fall down quite sharply. The highest in this central part and eastern part is 27 and it goes down as low as 3 percent in one department. Yet this is the area in which you find the insurgency activity, here and here and here on the border and here insurgency activity in this part of the country is very low.

What I am saying is that there is a direct relationship between what happens in the war and what happens in the reform program. It is not surprising that that would be the case.

The second factor that is important in estimating the future of this program is owner resistance. Most of the owners are small-or medium-sized landholders. It may not be widely known here, but their average holding is 24 hectares. That is to say only about three times the maximum that one of their tenants can claim.

They are not absentees generally. Indeed they often have influential positions in local government or commerce or security forces. Although the pattern varies, many owners have used intimidation, legal means, or violence to prevent or reverse the transfer of land.

There is a lot the Salvadoran Government and Army can do about this. They can act promptly to restore evictees to the land and they are doing that now. They can push the process of issuing both provisional and definitive titles vigorously. And they can begin to compensate owners. One powerful reason that owners resist is that practically none of them have been paid for their lands; and definitive titling is conditioned on compensation payment.

Compensation is one way we can help. The House Foreign Affairs Committee earmarked the local currency proceeds of $20 million of the supplemental appropriations for the Caribbean Basin Initiative to land reform compensation. This is a welcome action to remedy a weak point in the reform program.

I want to say the success of this phase III land reform depends also on campesino participation. He has to take the initiative and go to the department headquarters and start the process going. There are a lot of explanations why this has not been occurring on the scale expected by the original proposers of the reform, inertia or fear of retaliation and so forth.

It is up to the Government to encourage, protect, and provide for a specific plan under which this could be achieved.

Mr. Chairman, I appreciate your tolerance of this long statement. I would like to make one final comment.

I think all of us are aware of the limitations of the certification process. We are asked to make an up or down judgment. Reality is of course a mass of positives and negatives. It requires us to threaten to cut off military assistance to achieve the goals of our policy when we know that an actual cutoff would defeat the goals of those policies. For who doubts that if the United States ceases to provide security assistance to El Salvador there will be no more elections. There will be no more land reform. In the ensuing chaos the killing will not diminish, it will soar.

Clearly there are enough contradictions in the process that has been designed to prevent us from being self-righteous about it.

With that said the administration and I believe the Government of El Salvador have attempted to use certification as a means to achieve the required progress. What I am reporting today is that for all the problems there are real gains being made in that unhappy country.

Thank you, Mr. Chairman.

Document 691

Prepared Statement by the Principal Deputy Assistant Secretary of State for Inter-American Affairs (Bosworth) Before a Subcommittee of the House Banking, Finance and Urban Affairs Committee, August 5, 1982[85]

The Situation in Guatemala

Thank you, Mr. Chairman,[86] for inviting us to appear before your committee today to continue our dialogue on Guatemala. I would like to begin by reviewing briefly overall U.S. policy and objectives in Central America. Our goal is the evolution of stable democratic societies, free to concentrate on their economic and social development, and secure from external threat. To achieve that goal we have:

—supported developing democratic processes and elections in El Salvador, Costa Rica, and Honduras;

—developed a program of comprehensive economic cooperation through the Caribbean Basin Initiative and ongoing foreign assistance loans and grants; and

—provided security assistance to some countries to help them defend themselves against externally supported subversion and terrorism.

Our goal in Guatemala is the same as in the other countries of the area. In fact, as the largest and most populous country of Central America, Guatemala has a crucial, even pivotal, role in the region. It has considerable resources, but it also has serious economic and social problems and faces an active, Cuban backed guerrilla movement.

Our efforts to establish the type of relationship with Guatemala in which we could assist in meeting these problems were largely blocked by the policies pursued by the previous Guatemalan Government. The deplorable human rights situation in Guatemala and the lack of a credible framework for progress meant that we were able to support only a few loans promoting basic human needs. In brief, we could not work with a regime whose actions were as abhorrent as they were counterproductive, and our bilateral relationship was effectively frozen.

This pattern was broken on March 23. A group of young officers brought to power a new government determined to eliminate official repression and corruption, to improve conditions for all of Guatemala's peoples, to combat the insurgency, and to return the country to democratic rule. Since March 23 a number of important steps have been taken:

—The government has reduced political violence, particularly in urban areas, where its command and control is strongest. Political violence in rural areas continues and may even be increasing, but its use as a political tactic appears to be a guerrilla strategy, not a government doctrine. Eyewitness reports of women among the

---

[85] Source: *Inter-American Development Bank Loan to Guatemala: Hearing Before the Subcommittee on International Development Institutions and Finance of the Committee on Banking, Finance and Urban Affairs, House of Representatives, Ninety-seventh Congress, Second Session* (Washington, 1982), pp. 9–17. The purpose of the hearing was to examine whether or not Guatemala should be considered by the United States as eligible for normal access to the multilateral development banks. Section 701 of the International Financial Institutions Act (P.L. 95–118) required that the U.S. representative at multilateral development banks oppose any aid for a country which has a government that is a gross and consistent violator of internationally respected human rights, except for aid designed to meet basic needs; for the text, see 91 Stat. 1069.

[86] Representative Jerry M. Patterson.

attackers, Embassy interviews with massacre survivors, the use of weapons not in the army inventory, and most importantly, the increasing tendency of rural villagers to seek the army's protection all suggest that the guerrillas are responsible in major part for the rising levels of violence in rural areas.

—No specific charges of government torture have been brought to our attention. In contrast to the past, the new government has publicly acknowledged, though in some cases belatedly, detentions. In the two prominent instances involving Dr. Juan Jose Hurtado and 16 students detained in June, the government released Dr. Hurtado into the custody of the Guatemalan Red Cross and a representative of the Catholic Church; the students were released into their parents' custody. This kind of action is unprecedented in recent Guatemalan history.

—An amnesty program carried out in June saw almost 2,000 people step forward to accept it.

—Exiled religious workers have been invited back into the country and a constructive dialogue opened up with the church. For example, Bishop Gerardi, the former president of the Episcopal Conference, has returned to Guatemala from Costa Rica, where he was living for his own safety. In another instance, a nun deported by Honduras for distributing literature supporting Salvadoran guerrillas was quietly released to church authorities by the Guatemalan Government.

—In direct contrast to the previous government's exclusive emphasis on military action against the guerrillas, this government is committed to rural development. Even as overall government expenditures are being reduced, programs to develop the social infrastructure of the highlands are being expanded. Just 2 weeks ago the government announced a $5 million program to provide minimum shelter in support of a food for work program to people displaced through political strife.

—Invitations have been extended to Amnesty International, the Inter-American Commission on Human Rights, and the United Nations Human Rights Commission to visit Guatemala to make their own evaluations of the situation. In late July, the Guatemalan Foreign Minister received visiting West German Social Democrat Guenter Herterich. The Lucas government had refused all such contacts.

—Lastly, the government offered to negotiate unconditionally with the guerrilla forces, a proposal which the guerrillas rejected without serious exploration.

The guerrilla cadres have responded to the new Government and its policies with increased violence. They are clearly responsible for the massacre of innocent men, women, and children in Sanquiya, Chichicastenago, in May and in the region of the Ixil triangle in June. The guerrillas appear to have begun a concerted campaign to intimidate Indian villagers from participating in the Community Defense Forces, a popular program responding to the traditional efforts of these close-knit villages to protect themselves from outsiders. The guerrillas constitute a formidable threat to any Guatemalan government. Full-time, trained, armed guerrillas may number as many as 3,500. This cadre of permanent military units is supplemented by approximately 10,000 irregular "local defense" guerrillas. A support infrastructure of some 30,000–60,000 sympathizers constitutes a third level.

Violence and terrorism compound the economic problems presently confronting the new government. In the economy's modern sector, 1982 production is running 10% below 1981. Traditional agriculture and handicrafts, vital to the people of the highlands, are being seriously disrupted. Liquid foreign exchange reserves are virtually exhausted. Through May of this year, foreign exchange available for imports necessary for industrial production as well as agricultural supplies and consumer goods was 42% below the 1981 level for the same period. Although Guatemala is a petroleum producer, actual current production is only 10–15% of the country's petroleum consumption.

We welcomed from the start the new directions announced by the Rios Montt government, and we have encouraged the new government to make constructive changes. However, we decided to wait for signs of tangible progress on areas of concern to the United States before changing our own policies.

The government's announcement of the state of seige at the beginning of last month gave us particular cause for concern, even though many countries have or have had similar measures. Now that the state of seige has been in effect for more than a month, the actual implementation appears much less severe than the rhetoric that accompanied its inception implied. There have been no summary trials and executions.

We have now concluded that the record of the past 4 months, while not perfect, demonstrates that the new government has a commitment to positive change and new opportunity in Guatemala.

We have therefore decided to move forward carefully to reinforce the positive developments in Guatemala. Further progress is clearly needed, and we believe U.S. policy can help by recognizing the constructive change which has already taken place and encouraging additional progress. By acting now, we can send the message to all Guatemalan sectors that with improvements in human rights performance the United States is prepared to cooperate in ways meaningful to Guatemala's needs.

We believe our approach should be measured. We are proposing no dramatic new initiatives. We are, however, accelerating disbursements in our AID pipeline and reallocating development assistance funds from projects cancelled in other countries. We have been responsive to Guatemala's request for help to feed and shelter the thousands of people displaced by the fighting in the rural areas. We hope to provide further assistance of this kind.

We welcome the House Foreign Affairs Committee's decision to allot a portion of the available funds in the Caribbean Basin Initiative to Guatemala to help meet its critical balance-of-payments problems. On July 18 President Rios Montt took note of this Congressional action, welcomed it as recognition of an improvement in human rights, and said that Guatemala should work even harder to improve the human rights situation. This is precisely the message we need to confirm to help obtain further progress.

Guatemala is well-placed to take advantage of the trade and investment incentives under the Caribbean Basin Initiative. At the same time, we believe we should be prepared to support access by Guatemala to the multilateral development banks to assist in financing sound, well-conceived economic and social development projects.

Our actions cannot be limited to economic and development assistance alone—that would be unrealistic considering the threat posed by the insurgents. We hope that the full House and Senate will support the action of the House Foreign Affairs Committee in approving $250,000 in IMET for FY'83. To fail to do so would ignore the security situation of Guatemala and abrogate our responsibility to help improve the human rights situation in all sectors of Guatemalan society. Depending on developments in Guatemala we would be prepared to consider authorizing some military sales and additional security assistance to help meet that country's essential security needs. We will, of course, continue to consult closely with the Congress in all aspects of U.S. policy toward Guatemala.

Mr. Chairman, we cannot ignore the importance of Guatemala to the stability of Central America and our own vital national interests in that region. After several years of escalating violence, an opportunity now exists for the United States to use its influence to encourage the development of a new and more humane society for all Guatemalans—if we act. It would be neither fair nor wise to turn our back on a country which holds so much potential for the future of its people and the region. Inaction would seriously jeopardize continued human rights improvements, economic advancement, and political stability.

I will be pleased to respond to your questions and comments.

Document 692

Report Prepared in the Department of State, Undated[87]

Amendment to the July 27, 1982, Presidential Certification on El Salvador

Summary

Substantial progress has been made in the murder case involving four American

---

[87] Source: *Presidential Certification on El Salvador*, vol. II, pp. 515–517. Secretary Shultz transmitted this report to Congress with a covering memorandum dated August 10, 1982; for text of the memorandum, see *ibid.*, p. 514. This report was required as a result of congressional action earlier in the summer of 1982. On June 23, 1982, the House passed H.J. Res. 494 by a vote of 399 to 1. This resolution reinstated the requirement for certification that the Government of El Salvador was making good faith efforts to investigate the murders of U.S. citizens in El Salvador, and to bring to justice those responsible for the murders. The Senate passed H.J. Res. 494 on July 27, 1982, by a roll call vote of 95 to 2, with one member responding "present."

churchwomen. In February, the investigatory working group turned its final report over to the National Guard. The National Guard found sufficient evidence in the report to dismiss six guardsmen and turn them over to a civilian court. The presiding judge, in turn, examined the evidence and determined that it was sufficient to justify charging five of the former guardsmen with aggravated homicide. They were remanded to prison pending the resolution of their trial. The trial judge has initiated and largely completed the judicial inquiry required under Salvadoran law. We expect the date of the trail to be set this fall.

The Government of El Salvador has moved to reinvigorate the investigation into the murder of the two American land reform advisors and their Salvadoran colleague by forming in April a new investigative working group to uncover additional evidence. To date all efforts have failed to provide any clues as to the whereabouts of John J. Sullivan, an American freelance journalist who disappeared in San Salvador in December 1980. The investigation of Mr. Sullivan's disappearance has received the attention of the highest levels of the Salvadoran Government.

INVESTIGATION OF THE MURDERS AND DISAPPEARANCE OF U.S. CITIZENS

There have been a number of developments in the investigation of those responsible for the murders of four American churchwomen in El Salvador in December 1980. In late 1981 and early 1982, the Salvadoran investigative team, with FBI technical assistance including a polygraph test, achieved a major breakthrough in the investigation. As a result, five suspects were dismissed from the National Guard and placed under arrest on February 8, 1982. A sixth man who had previously left the National Guard was arrested at the same time. On February 10, jurisdiction over the six men was transferred to civilian Judge Bernardo Rauda Murcia. The National Guard delivered to the court its report on the investigation of the case, as well as physical evidence obtained during the investigation. On February 13, Judge Rauda charged five of the six men with aggravated homicide and released the sixth, who was found not to have been involved in the murders. Judge Rauda then began the required judicial investigation. Pursuant to El Salvador's Napoleonic Code system, the Judge must hear testimony and evidence, study the same, and order additional testimony and examination as he deems necessary. Following this judicial investigation, the Judge decides whether to order the case to trial. Judge Rauda is still in the judicial investigation stage of the process. Even so, he has stated publicly that he expects to order the case to trial.

The Salvadoran Government has also moved to reinvigorate the investigation of the murders of two American land reform advisors, Mark Pearlman and Michael Hammer, and their Salvadoran colleague, Rodolfo Viera, at the Sheraton Hotel in San Salvador in January 1981. In 1981 two individuals, Hans Adolpho Krist and Ricardo Sol Meza, were charged with the murders by the Salvadoran Government; Sol Meza was imprisoned in El Salvador and Hans Krist was located in Miami. The Government of El Salvador, on the basis of supporting documentation, requested the extradition of Krist pursuant to the U.S.–El Salvador treaty of 1911. The United States Government thereupon initiated an extradition proceeding against him in the federal district court in Miami. In October 1981, a Salvadoran judge suspended further judicial action against the two accused on the grounds that insufficient evidence has been developed to implicate them in the murders. The Salvadoran Attorney General appealed this order, but the suspension was upheld by the Court of Criminal Appeals on April 13, 1982. As a result of the affirmance of the suspension, the U.S. District Court for the Southern District of Florida on June 23 dismissed the pending extradition request against the accused in Miami (Krist) and released him from custody. The other accused (Sol Meza) had been freed from custody in El Salvador at the time of the October 1981 suspension order.

In April 1982, an investigative working group was established by the Salvadoran Government in an attempt to uncover sufficient additional evidence relating to the murders to warrant reopening the case in accordance with Salvadoran law. It held its first formal meeting on May 20, with all members present, including a National Guard officer assigned to head the group. After completing a study of files, the working group began interviewing potential witnesses in June. The FBI is prepared to provide appropriate technical assistance, including polygraph examinations at the appropriate time. It is our hope that these efforts will produce significant new evidence that will make it possible to bring to justice those responsible for these reprehensible crimes. Preliminary results are encouraging.

John J. Sullivan of Bergen, New Jersey, is a freelance journalist who disappeared while on an assignment in El Salvador. He was last seen on December 28, 1980, at the Sheraton Hotel in El Salvador. He apparently left the hotel shortly after his arrival from the United States. Immediately after his absence was reported to the Embassy, he became the object of a thorough search by Embassy officers who also alerted Salvadoran police authorities. The Salvadoran Government made Mr. Sullivan the object of a countrywide alert. Mr. Sullivan's disappearance has received and continues to receive the attention of the highest levels of the Salvadoran Government. President Duarte's interest in the case continued during his term of office, and he communicated his personal concern to all elements of the Salvadoran Government. This same willingness to assist was shared by, among others, Defense Minister Garcia, who directed military investigators to pursue leads provided by the Embassy. At the working level Salvadoran officials have aided Embassy officers in cross-checking information received from a variety of sources. For example, senior judges have personally assisted officers in researching the closed records which contain descriptions of unidentified corpses.

Notwithstanding the lack of success to date, the Embassy and the Department of State continue to pursue all leads that could possibly provide an answer to the mystery of Mr. Sullivan's disappearance. United States Government concern over this case has been reemphasized at the highest levels of the Salvadoran Government, and the Department is satisfied that it has been accorded the cooperation of the Salvadoran authorities in this matter and that such cooperation will continue.

We conclude therefore that the Government of El Salvador has made good faith efforts since the first certification was made to investigate the murders of the six United States citizens in El Salvador in December 1980 and January 1981 and to bring to justice those responsible for those murders, and has taken all reasonable steps to investigate the disappearance of journalist John Sullivan in El Salvador in January 1981.

Document 693

Address by the Assistant Secretary of State for Inter-American Affairs (Enders) Before the Commonwealth Club, San Francisco, August 20, 1982[88]

Building the Peace in Central America

The obstacles to peace in Central America stand more clearly exposed with every new crisis. Central America has deep political divisions, among nations as well as within them. It suffers severe economic troubles, with the world recession devastating economies already weakened by high oil prices and internal inefficiencies. And it is fragmented by social tensions, with population growth straining public services and popular aspirations outrunning the historically possible.

But the tangle of violence that has taken so many lives traces directly to the clash of two polar approaches to these problems. One is the way of the violent right—to ignore socioeconomic problems and, when that proves impossible, to shoot the messengers of despair. The other is the way of the violent left—to magnify injustices and provoke confrontations so as to rationalize shooting their way to power.

The persistence with which extremist minorities seek to resolve the region's problems by the use of violence dominates the outside world's perception of Central America. Yet the real story of Central America's last 3 years is that first the right and now the left have steadily lost ground to those who believe democracy and the rule of law—not violence—are the only feasible path to progress.

Let me take a minute to outline that story. For it provides a key to the real opportunities now emerging to end the violence and build the peace. We used to think of Central America as a collection of petty dictatorships. And so—if you except Costa Rica's vigorous democracy and allow for the coarseness of the stereotype—it often was. That does not mean that there was not economic growth and social change. Often, indeed, vigorous economic development and social change collided with unchanging, unresponsive, and sometimes repressive political institutions.

---

[88] Source: *Current Policy* No. 414, August 20, 1982, Bureau of Public Affairs, Department of State.

The old order cracked with the flight of Somoza in July 1979. For more than 40 years, the Somozas ruled Nicaragua. But little by little the regime lost support—of the church, of the press, and of businessmen and professionals, many of whose sons and daughters took to the hills or the streets—and in the end it was making war on its own people.

A few months later, the repressive government of General Romero in El Salvador, the latest in a string of military governments that had run that country since the 1930's, was overthrown by a group of young officers pledged to create democratic institutions and reform the cruelly unequal landholding system.

It is one of history's less happy patterns that extremism breeds extremism. Instead of seeing the weakening of traditional dictatorships as an opportunity to organize democracy, the fall of Somoza and the troubles of other established governments whetted the appetites of radicals with motivations ranging from the utopian to the cynical. In Nicaragua, a hard core of Marxist-Leninist ideologues began to consolidate a monopoly of force with Cuban assistance, building the largest military establishment in Central American history.

Convinced their own power would be safe only if similar governments were installed elsewhere in Central America, Nicaragua's new *caudillos* joined with Cuba to train and supply violent leftists in El Salvador attempting to seize power by exploiting the turbulence unleashed by the breakdown of traditional order and the new government's reform efforts.

Central America's violent left burst on stage claiming to have history on its side. The claim reflected two practical advantages. One was psychological. The combination of ignorance and revulsion with which the outside world views Central America enabled men and women trained mainly in the arts of terror to portray themselves as liberators. The other was military. Government forces were certainly authoritarian, but they were also weak, garrison bound, and internationally isolated. As of 1979, the armies of Nicaragua, El Salvador, and Guatemala were all cut off from U.S. training, sales, or even purchases; then, as now, Costa Rica had no army. In contrast, guerrilla forces could draw upon local alienation, extensive support from Cuba—in training, arms, and propaganda—and the help of terrorists from South America and even the Middle East.

Ironically, these advantages backfired. Overconfidence in both their popular appeal and their outside arms supplies led the Salvadoran guerrillas to militarize their strategy. In early 1981, they launched a "final offensive" that failed disastrously. In March 1982 they tried to prevent elections and instead provoked a massive turnout of voters in repudiation of what the guerrillas stood for. Although many of them fight on, El Salvador's guerrillas stand revealed as a destructive minority rejected by Salvadoran society.

Similar misjudgments have also warped the Sandinista regime in Nicaragua. Little by little the Sandinistas have pushed aside those whose sacrifices helped bring down Somoza—the free press, the church, political parties, unions, the private sector. Some 2,000 Cuban and Eastern-bloc military and security advisers have merged with the regime's leadership. With disenchantment spreading even among Sandinista heroes like Eden Pastora, "Commandante Cero," there is now open repression against religious leaders and ethnic minorities—the very groups whose protection is the essence of pluralism. History is beginning to repeat itself. Elections have been postponed, demonstrations are increasingly frequent, and some groups have even taken up arms. The new Nicaraguan regime is turning into a new dictatorship based once again on a privileged and militarized caste. Like the Somoza regime before it, Nicaragua's government is beginning to make war on its own people.

But if the violent left is not sweeping the isthmus, the beneficiaries have not been its traditional rival, the violent right. When the military government of El Salvador was overthrown nearly 3 years ago, the new reforming junta was challenged not only by the extreme left's guerrillas but also by the extreme right acting through death squads and some elements of the security forces. The result was an explosion of violence. Eighteen months ago anywhere from 600 to 2,000 civilians were losing their lives each month, depending on whose figures you accept. The country was sick with political violence.

That sickness has not yet been cured. But its virulence has been checked. In the last few months, noncombatant deaths have averaged 300 to 500 a month—again, depending on whom you believe—and appear to be declining steadily. This is still a horrible toll in a country of 5 million people, but 300 to 1,500 fewer deaths a month is undeniably a positive trend.

Why is political violence declining in El Salvador? It has partly been a matter of the consolidation of the new reforming government, which has gradually contained guerrilla violence and increased its authority over security forces, gradually creating a climate in which violence is less and less expedient, even if it is still not adequately deterred and controlled and punished.

But I think there is something even more important at work here. Nascent democratic institutions are providing an alternative to violence as a means of political expression. In the March election, six parties ranging from extreme right to center left competed in a campaign that was not violence free but which was not meaningfully influenced by the use of force. The new Salvadoran democracy is doing what it is supposed to do—bringing a broad spectrum of forces and factions into a functioning political system.

At the same time, a broad land reform has for the first time given *campesinos* a personal stake in society. Twenty percent of all farmland has been redistributed from some 2,000 owners, many of them absentees, to 60,000 poor farmworkers and their families.

Perhaps the most striking measure of progress is the transformation of the military from an institution dedicated to the status quo to one that spearheads land reform and supports constitutional democracy.

The shift toward democracy is not limited to El Salvador. In November 1981 a massive turnout voted in a new democratic government in Honduras after many years of military rule. This February, a similar turnout reaffirmed Costa Rican democracy and voted the Social Democratic opposition into government. Not incidentally, in democratic Costa Rica and Honduras, as in El Salvador, the extreme left received practically no popular support in the elections.

Meanwhile in Guatemala a coup overthrew a repressive government that was fighting organized guerrillas with increasingly indiscriminate violence. The new government—although still military—has greatly reduced official abuses, is discussing Constituent Assembly elections, and has replaced the old hostility and suspicion toward rural villagers with efforts to give them the means to develop and defend their communities.

In a word, alternatives have appeared to the violent extremes of Central America's past.

The United States has played a key role in nurturing these alternatives. Belatedly and at first fitfully, but with a steadiness all the more striking for the fact that we have kept our basic course under two quite different U.S. administrations, we have thrown our weight behind the well-being and security of our neighbors.

The great bulk of our effort has been economic and political. No less than 85% of all aid authorized by or requested of the Congress for fiscal years 1981 to 1983 is economic. To enable the countries of the area to earn their own way in the future, the President has proposed an innovative program of tariff concessions and tax incentives, the Caribbean Basin Initiative, which Congress is now considering. Its passage would provide a vital impulse to confidence and peace in the region.

Equally important has been our political commitment. Agrarian reform was a Salvadoran idea, but it could not have gotten off the ground in 1980 if we had not backed it. And it might have died this spring if we had not persisted in our support. The elections in Honduras and El Salvador were also developed locally, but they easily could have derailed had we not backed them so strongly. Nor are human rights an import from the United States. The great majority of Central Americans long for an end to lawlessness. But we do believe that the constancy of our interest has helped them make progress toward controlling human rights abuses.

At the same time, we have not ignored legitimate needs for security assistance. Faced with the guerrilla offensive in El Salvador and realizing that a Communist network was funneling weapons and ammunition in support of that offensive, President Carter authorized military sales to El Salvador. President Reagan has continued to provide military assistance. The amounts have been and remain much less than our economic aid and the items unsophisticated.

We have no wish or intention to prolong or spread the conflict—quite the opposite. But we could not and we will not stand idly by and watch, in El Salvador or elsewhere, internationally recognized governments—undertaking reforms we support—having to throw untrained recruits short of ammunition into battle against Cuban-trained guerrillas supplied and coordinated from abroad.

By the same token, we are giving limited military assistance to Honduras, which has become a new Cuban and Nicaraguan target for terror and armed intimidation. Even Costa Rica, a country without an army, has come to us to discuss security assistance. Its people, too, fear the threat of an aggressive Nicaragua with mushrooming armed might and dedicated to the export of violent revolution.

If much has been accomplished, much remains to be done. In El Salvador, the democratic transformation must be completed: presidential elections held, the system of justice reestablished, the land reform defended, the violence and destruction ended, and the still dangerous guerrillas convinced that they cannot shoot their way to power and that they will have to compete for it at the polls.

In Guatemala, the democratic transformation must be begun, the abuses of Indians and others in the countryside ended, and the *campesinos* enabled to develop in peace.

In Honduras and Costa Rica and El Salvador and Guatemala, weak, bankrupt, or near-bankrupt economies must be refloated, and helped to attract new investment and trade.

In Nicaragua, a way back must be found from ever greater concentration of power and militarization—and from ever greater repression of its own citizens and ever greater danger to its neighbors.

Of all these problems, it is Nicaragua that is the most worrisome. It was the new Sandinista government that regionalized the conflict in Central America by backing the violence in El Salvador. Sandinista leader Daniel Ortega once told me that the FMLN, the Salvadoran guerrilla coalition, is "*nuestro escudo*"—"Nicaragua's shield." And Sandinista support has not lessened. The FMLN's headquarters are in Nicaragua. It receives sustained logistic support from Nicaragua, above all by airdrop and sea delivery but also by land. Its training camps are in Nicaragua.

And now Nicaragua is expanding the violence to Costa Rica and Honduras. As more and more Nicaraguans have voted with their feet—13,000 Miskito and Sumo Indians and thousands of ex-Sandinistas have followed anti-Sandinistas into neighboring havens—Managua has begun to pressure and threaten its neighbors. In downtown San Jose, Nicaraguan intelligence officers operating out of the Nicaraguan Embassy organize terrorism, including bombing an airline office, while Nicaraguan troops cross into Costa Rican territory and harass small farm owners and Nicaraguan planes violate Costa Rican airspace. In Tegucigalpa, the Sandinista-backed Salvadoran FMLN recently blacked out the capital by dynamiting the electrical system, while Nicaragua threatens Honduras overtly, mobilizing its army and militia and redeploying troops along the Honduran frontier.

What can be done to sustain and develop the alternatives to the irresponsible spread of violence? Clearly, so long as violent minorities from within—or hostile neighbors from without—assert the right to use force, there can be no alternative to military preparedness and the maintenance of security. The United States will help its friends in the area to defend themselves from both threats, as long as it is necessary.

But this response alone is not enough. We must also seek out and explore every opportunity for reconciliation and peace. His Holiness, Pope John Paul II, recently emphasized this moral imperative in separate letters to the bishops of Nicaragua and El Salvador. In both, he called for reconciliation and unity. The letter to Nicaragua was censored by the Sandinistas, who first officially prevented its publication, then reversed themselves. In his letter to El Salvador, after noting the "new institutional perspectives recently opened" by the elections, the Pope said that "an indispensable condition for accommodation [is][89] the ceasing of all hostilities and the renunciation of the use of arms."

This is not an impossible dream. Steps are available to give substance to the Pope's vision. The opportunities for reconciliation are most evident in El Salvador. Out of that country's travail have come a constituent assembly, a provisional coalition government, and a commitment to continued democratization. Some of the forces previously enamored of violent solutions—mainly from the far right—have begun to abide by the law and participate in the political process. Others—mainly from the far left—have yet to find a way to withdraw from their commitment to violence.

The new government in El Salvador has seen the opportunity. On August 3, at President Magana's initiative, the leaders of the political parties joined with the President to adopt a united action plan to end divisions within El Salvador.[90] One of the plan's key

---

[89] Bracketed note appears in the source text.

[90] For the text of this plan, see *Presidential Certification on Progress in El Salvador: Hearing Before the Committee on Foreign Relations, United States Senate, Ninety-eighth Congress, First Session* (Washington, 1983), pp. 53–57.

elements is the creation of a new Commission for Peace. The commission is to comprise institutions, groups, and respected individuals charged specifically with evaluating the requirements for peace and proposing solutions. Together with similar new commissions on human rights and on the political process, the Commission for Peace is an important further step toward national reconciliation.

These are all very positive signs. The important thing is to do them seriously. Amnesty must offer genuine security with the participation of the church and international organizations. And dialogue must involve listening as well as talking, giving an opportunity to adversaries to explain how they could participate in the new democratic institutions. The United States very much hopes the new government will act with speed and imagination in this vital area.

Building the peace on a regional basis is even more complex. Order among nations requires order within nations as well as arrangements that respect their territorial integrity and national identity. The regionalization of tensions derives from crises in all these areas.

Here too, bases for progress exist. The issues are too numerous to be subject to simple sweeping solutions. But many individual proposals and possibilities exist to deal with particular pieces of the problem.

Honduras has put forward a proposal for peace with Nicaragua calling for an end to border incursions, a freeze on imports of heavy weapons, and comprehensive verification. These proposals have been endorsed by its partners in the Central American Democratic Community—Costa Rica and El Salvador.

The United States has also made proposals. Beginning nearly a year ago and more intensively since April, we have attempted to engage Nicaragua in a dialogue. We have tried to respond to Nicaragua's concerns, while meeting those of Nicaragua's neighbors, and our own.

The Sandinistas tell us that they fear an invasion by the United States. So we have offered to enter into a formal nonaggression agreement. The Sandinistas tell us that ex-Somocistas are training in the United States to invade Nicaragua. We have assured them that we are enforcing our Neutrality Act, which makes it a federal crime to launch an attack, or to conspire to attack, another country from the United States.

The Sandinistas tell us we are regionalizing the conflict, preparing Honduras, El Salvador, and Costa Rica as bases for action against them. So we have suggested that each country in Central America agree to put a reasonable, low limit on the numbers of foreign military and security advisers it has, and we have suggested that each country pledge not to import any additional heavy offensive weapons. Both commitments, of course, would have to be subject to international verification.

Nicaragua would also have to meet the concerns that its neighbors and we share. We asked that Nicaragua cease its involvement in the conflict in El Salvador. The Sandinistas say that they are not aware of any such involvement, but are willing to end it if we just give them the information we have. In our most recent exchanges we suggested that removing the combined guerrilla headquarters from Nicaragua would be a good place to start and offered to help the Sandinistas locate it. For example, the point from which guerrilla operations in El Salvador are being directed was recently in a Managua suburb. We are confident that although it moves around a great deal within Nicaragua it can be found. Nicaragua has yet to respond.

Similarly, Nicaragua must cease its terrorist and other aggressive actions against Honduras and Costa Rica.

We have raised a second issue, which also deeply concerns Nicaragua's neighbors. This is the trend in the organization and use of state power in Nicaragua. It is, of course, for Nicaragua to decide what kind of government it has. No one challenges that. We don't. Its neighbors don't.

But we believe we are all entitled to ask what assurance can any of us have that promises of noninterference will be kept if the Nicaraguan state remains the preserve of a small Cuban-advised elite of Marxist-Leninists, disposing of growing military power and hostile to all forms of social life but those they dominate? And we are also entitled to ask what is to become of internationally recognized human rights under these conditions? Such questions are not a defense, secret or otherwise, for a return to a discredited Somocismo. They could be answered in the fulfillment of the Sandinistas' own original commitments to democracy and regional peace.

These are some of the ideas we have advanced, not in any prescriptive sense but to start a dialogue to generate a response, to try to create a climate. There is no one way to guarantee peace in Central America. But our collective experiences suggest action is necessary on each of four fronts.

Within each state there should be a process of reconciliation in which adversaries can substitute political competition for armed competition. This implies, as indicated by His Holiness the Pope, a renunciation of violence and incorporation within the civic process. Given the deep divisions in each country, this requires that democratic, or at least pluralistic, institutions be respected or established and broad participation in them encouraged.

Between states there should be an end to the export of subversion. This means the removal, subject to comprehensive verification, of the headquarters, logistical support, and training camps of guerrilla movements installed outside the country of their origin.

There should be an end to heavy arms buildups that threaten neighbors and disrupt the traditional regional military equilibrium. The easiest way would seem to be a commitment by all countries in the area not to bring in specified weapons, such as more tanks or combat aircraft—also subject, of course, to verification.

Finally, there should be limits to foreign involvement, particularly in matters affecting security, to help the region forge its own peaceful equilibrium on its own terms. Each country should put a common ceiling on the number of outside military and security advisers and troops, subject to reciprocity and full verification. Why not make it zero?

A number of democratic countries—the United States, Honduras, Costa Rica, and others—have all attempted a dialogue with Nicaragua this past year. We have little to show for it. But we should not abandon this idea. Rather, perhaps the democratic countries should come together and see whether they cannot formulate a common approach. The potential cornerstones of peace are there. The question is how to put them together.

In the past the United States has generally neglected Central America—only to send in the troops when things got out of hand. U.S. troops are no solution now. What can help is sustained U.S. commitment—not only in helping to overcome violence and not only in helping restore and develop economies but in the development of democratic institutions. For everything we know about the 20th century tells us that governments that must face the people in elections do not long abuse their human rights. Nor do they often threaten their neighbors.

I will grant you that that is a tall order. But in a region important to us because of its strategic position, because of its proximity, because of our human ties with it, nothing less will do. We cannot walk away.

Document 694

Letter From Mexican President López Portillo and Venezuelan President Herrera to President Reagan, Mexico City and Caracus, September 7, 1982[91]

Peace and Stability in Central America

MR. PRESIDENT AND FRIEND: Concerned by events which seriously threaten the peace between Nicaragua and Honduras, even more Central America, we have written to the Presidents of said countries concerning the need to abstain from carrying out any act that could aggravate the situation and with the idea of sponsoring a constructive dialog that will permit the necessary rapprochement and cooperation between the parties.

Recently your administration through the words pronounced by Ambassador Thomas O. Enders, Under Secretary of State for Inter-American Affairs, at the Commonwealth Club of San Francisco, August 20, 1982,[92] expressed its concern over peace in Central America on pointing out:

> "Each new crisis makes it possible to see more clearly the obstacles that oppose a peace in Central America.
>
> "Central America is the scene of deep political divisions both between the distinct nations and within the heart of each one of them. It is the victim of great economic disruptions; its economic systems, already weakened both by the elevated prices of petroleum and by internal

---

[91] Source: *Honduras and U.S. Policy: An Emerging Dilemma: Hearing Before the Subcommittee on Inter-American Affairs of the Committee on Foreign Affairs, House of Representatives, Ninety-seventh Congress, Second Session* (Washington, 1982), pp. 97–98. The source text was translated from Spanish by the Congressional Research Service, Library of Congress. The two Presidents sent similar, though not identical, letters to Roberto Suazo Cordova, President of Honduras, and Daniel Ortega Saavedra, Coordinator of the Government of National Reconstruction of Nicaragua; see *ibid.*, 99–102.

[92] *Supra.*

insufficiencies, have been devastated by the world recession. To this one must add the fragmentation caused by social tensions, excessive demands imposed on public services by the demographic growth and the popular aspirations that exceed their historical possibilities."

We see with equal concern the deterioration of the Central American situation with the danger of a generalized conflict extending to all of the region. The situation between Honduras and Nicaragua is grave and has come to have attempts at armed confrontation.

The cooperation program of San Jose has brought out the particular interest of our countries in peace and stability in the area, in the recovery from their economic problems and in the attainment of their political stability. Mexico and Venezuela, tied to the region geographically, cannot be detached from the problems that may occur there. With full solidarity and absolute respect for nonintervention in the inter-American matters of the countries of the area, our countries feel that they should, in the most fraternal way, express points of view that could contribute to the solution of the problems and in that way preserve the continent as a peace reserve.

We share with the United States the objective of reaching international peace, as well as internal stability and the overcoming of economic difficulties in an atmosphere of freedom and development.

Although it is true that we share those objectives, at times we have differed in the treatments and methods that should be employed to reach them.

Encouraged by these purposes we take the liberty of proposing to you the advantages of jointly exploring the ways that are still open in order to curb the current and troublesome escalation, the increase in tensions and the dangerous general expectations with respect to their outcome.

At the same time that we have urged the Nicaraguan Government to adopt measures aimed at preventing military confrontations on the border with Honduras, we also feel it appropriate for the support, organization and positioning of Somocist ex-guardsmen to cease.

We express our conviction that in that way it is possible to advance and therefore we congratulate them at the same time that we sincerely invite them to reinforce the dialogue in such a way that would allow a true negotiation capable of overcoming the difficulties.

At the same time we propose to you the need to advance effectively in the reaching of a global agreement that would facilitate a true peace between Honduras and Nicaragua, which will be reflected positively in the world framework of tensions and confrontations.

In this connection, it is appropriate to remember the peace initiatives in Central America with respect to the possibility of an arms limitation with international controls in the region.

In the declaration of San Jose of Costa Rica, May 8, 1982,[93] on the occasion of the Inaugural Ceremony of the President of Costa Rica, Luis Alberto Monge, six heads of state of the region concerned over the armaments race in the area expressed the need to "adjust the military troops and war equipment to the levels strictly necessary for the defense of national sovereignty, territorial integrity and the maintenance of public order, subject to the requirements universally accepted in all democratic societies governed by law."

We hope, Mr. President, that these ideas have a positive reception and serve as the basis for the peace and stability of the area.

JOSE LOPEZ PORTILLO

LUIS HERRERA CAMPINS

Document 695

Letter From President Reagan to the Speaker of the House of Representatives (O'Neill), September 8, 1982[94]

Credit Facilities to the Bank of Mexico

DEAR MR. SPEAKER: In accordance with the provisions of Section 10 of the Gold Re-

[93] Regarding the Declaration of San Jose, May 8, 1982, see Foreign Broadcast Information Service, *Daily Report: Latin America*, May 10, 1982, pp. P-1–P-2.

[94] Source: White House Press Release, September 8, 1982, Office of the Press Secretary to the President; printed also in *Weekly Compilation of Presidential Documents*, September 13, 1982, pp. 1102–1103. An identical letter was sent to the President of the Senate, George Bush.

serve Act of 1934, as amended (31 U.S.C. 822a), I determined on August 24, 1982, that the United States, through the Exchange Stabilization Fund of the Department of the Treasury ("ESF"), should stand ready to provide to the Bank of Mexico ("Bank") credit with a possible maturity of longer than 6 months but not to exceed 1 year.

According to the terms of the proposed agreement with the Bank, the ESF will provide credit facilities to the Bank in an amount of $600 million for a term of 3 months, with a possibility of three 3-month renewals, to expire no later than August 23, 1983. The Bank's obligations under the agreement will be unconditionally guaranteed by the Government of Mexico.

The ESF agreement is part of a multilateral effort involving other major countries, acting through the Bank for International Settlements ("BIS"), the ESF and the Federal Reserve System to provide short-term facilities amounting to $1.85 billion to the Bank. Under the agreement between the Bank and the BIS, the ESF and the Federal Reserve System will share with the BIS in the proceeds of drawings by Mexico from the International Monetary Fund (IMF) and in certain other arrangements to assure repayment of this multilateral financing. The Mexican Government has undertaken to arrange a major program of economic adjustment in cooperation with the IMF, which will serve as the basis for IMF balance of payments financing for Mexico during the next 3 years. The multilateral arrangement, of which the ESF agreement is an integral part, is designed to provide immediate support for Mexico's external position while the IMF arrangement is being negotiated and other sources of financing are being arranged by Mexico.

Mexico at present faces extreme balance-of-payments problems of a magnitude and character which, if not addressed through the measures outlined above, could lead to substantial disruption of international money, financial, and exchange markets. The provision of financing by the ESF is a key component of a multilateral effort, centered on an economic adjustment program to be agreed between the IMF and Mexico, to strengthen Mexico's economic and financial position. Because of Mexico's extreme financial difficulties and the time that may be required before Mexico's economic adjustment measures begin to take effect, it may take more than 6 months before Mexico is able fully to repay credit advanced by the ESF. The mobilization of resources by other participants in this multilateral financing arrangement effort also recognizes this possibility. I have therefore determined that these facts present unique and exigent circumstances and that the ESF must be prepared to extend credit to Mexico for a term greater than 6 months but not to exceed 1 year.

Sincerely,

RONALD REAGAN

Document 696

Letter From President Reagan to Mexican President López Portillo, Undated[95]

Bringing Peace to Central America

DEAR PRESIDENT: Thank you for your letter of September 7,[96] which I read with great interest, and which is very constructive.

We and others share your concern over the dangerous situation which engulfs Central America today. Now, more than ever before, is the time for those who believe in democracy, respect human rights, and do not interfere in the internal affairs of other nations to speak out in support of these principles. I believe that any meaningful attempt to address the problems of Central America must be within a regional context that achieves:

A. Democratic pluralism within each nation that includes free and fair elections in which all those who wish to do so may participate freely.

B. An end to support for terrorist and insurgent groups in other countries of the region.

C. A fully verifiable regional agreement banning the importation of heavy weapons.

D. A fully verifiable regional agreement limiting foreign security and military advisors.

---

[95] Source: *Honduras and U.S. Policy: An Emerging Dilemma*, p. 103. The letter was presumably sent in September 1982. President Reagan sent an almost identical letter to the President of Venezuela, which is *ibid.* For the Honduran and Nicaraguan replies to the Mexican-Venezuelan initiative, see *ibid.*, pp. 104–108.

[96] See document 694.

These principles have been strongly and repeatedly endorsed by the democratic nations of the region; the declaration of San Jose, issued at the time of the inauguration of President Monge, and the comprehensive peace proposal put forward by the Government of Honduras are only two recent examples of such support. We also have tried to embody these principles in the proposals which we have put forward to the Government of Nicaragua over the past many months. I am pleased to see your own strong statement of these principles in the letter you have graciously sent me. It is our firm belief that only through the diligent pursuit of these principles can a lasting peace be achieved in Central America.

In this regard, many of the democratic countries of the region plan to send their foreign ministers to meet in San Jose in early October.[97] This meeting will afford a full opportunity for the democratic nations of the region to review the current situation and determine how best to initiate the difficult process of bringing peace to the region. Those nations' representatives will surely review all the existing proposals for peace in Central America with particular emphasis on the observations contained in your letter.

I think it was the great Mexican patriot Benito Juarez who said, "Peace is respect for other people's rights." Unfortunately, this is a lesson that not all governments have yet learned. As long as nations continue to interfere in the affairs of their neighbors and to promote destabilization and terrorism, there can be no peace in Central America. Fortunately, however, democracy is alive and strong in the region, and, as your letter amply testified, there is a will on the part of the democratic nations to pursue all avenues available to achieve a just peace.

I applaud your effort and pledge our full support to our shared objective of bringing peace to Central America. I am sure that the democratic countries of the region will welcome it.

Sincerely,

RONALD REAGAN

---

[97] Regarding the October 1982 meeting in San Jose, see document 699.

Document 697

Statement by the Principal Deputy Assistant Secretary of State for Inter-American Affairs (Bosworth) Before a Subcommittee of the House Foreign Affairs Committee, September 21, 1982[98]

The Situation in Honduras

MR. BOSWORTH. Thank you, Mr. Chairman,[99] very much. It is my pleasure to be here this afternoon to discuss with you the current situation in Honduras and U.S. policy toward that country.

I have submitted, Mr. Chairman, for the record, a rather extensive and detailed prepared statement on those subjects and I would intend, with your permission, to simply summarize that statement very briefly now in oral fashion and then proceed to attempt to respond to any questions or comments that you and your colleagues might have.

MR. BARNES. That is fine. We will include your entire prepared statement in the record.

MR. BOSWORTH. Thank you very much, Mr. Chairman.

Mr. Chairman, as one examines the current situation in Central America and particularly in Honduras, I think in the case of that country, one is struck by two essential features. One is that Honduras has made what is by any measurement remarkable progress in the past 18 months, or somewhat longer, in the establishment of civilian democratic institutions.

A new democratically elected civilian government took office on January 27 of this year, ending a long string of military government in that country.

I would stress, Mr. Chairman, that that democratic process is one which had received and continues to receive very strong and unequivocal support from the United States, a support which started, I might add, under the previous administration and which has continued under the current administration.

---

[98] Source: *Honduras and U.S. Policy: An Emerging Dilemma*, pp. 2–5; for Bosworth's prepared statement, see *ibid.*, pp. 6–13. Bosworth appeared before the Subcommittee on Inter-American Affairs.

[99] Representative Michael D. Barnes.

I think, then, that is one of the fundamental features that one must bear in mind when looking at Honduras.

The second feature which I think is also fundamental, but, however, is not encouraging—it is rather threatening and of considerable concern—is the threat which now exists to the Government of Honduras and to Honduran sovereignty and territorial integrity as a result of the activites of the Nicaraguans and the Salvadoran guerrillas, the FMLN, who have been operating in and through Honduras a considerable period of time.

Honduras thus is faced with a rather painful dilemma, Mr. Chairman, and that is whether it should accept passively this abuse of the territory which in the first instance, of course, calls into question Government control over that territory; and in the second instance, may well pose some rather fundamental threats to Honduran security itself, or whether it should attempt to defend itself against threats with all the risks that carries with it.

And that is, in fact, the dilemma which the Government of Honduras faces now.

Mr. Chairman, I think it is important in the particular case of this country, to examine very briefly its economy. It is, of course, the poorest country on a per capita income basis in Central America.

It has suffered over the past few years the same problems that all of the countries of the region have suffered, problems of declining export earnings and declining prices for its major export commodities, rising energy costs, most of which is imported.

As a result, one finds that the Honduran economy is stagnant, it is not growing and, in fact, has suffered a decline in real income in the past couple of years.

We have attempted on behalf of the United States, Mr. Chairman, to respond to that economic problem with a considerable increase in our economic assistance resources.

In fiscal year 1982, for example, we had earlier budgeted and programmed for Honduras a total of slightly over $43 million in economic assistance.

That will now, of course, be supplemented by some $35 million in economic support fund assistance, which will be provided to Honduras under the Caribbean Basin Initiative.

Over the longer term, I would simply add parenthetically that it is our belief that the trade and investment initiatives of the Caribbean Basin Initiative will bring considerable benefit and economic opportunity to Honduras and over the prospect of working its way out of this stagnant economic situation.

Honduras is also a country which is characterized by the presence of a large number of refugees. This refugee influx began, of course, some time ago, and which increased during the civil war in Nicaragua and, at the present time, we would estimate there are some 30,000 refugees living in Honduras.

Approximately half of those are Salvadoran, a few are Guatemalan, and the remainder is Nicaraguan. It is the latter which are growing rapidly.

The majority consists of Nicaraguan Indians who have come into Honduras from along the Nicaraguan coastal area.

As I mentioned in some detail in the prepared statement, Mr. Chairman, we have noted over the past several months a very considerable increase in the internal security and external security threat to Honduras.

There has been a rise of terrorism, terrorism which we believe is quite clearly attributable to the Salvadoran guerrilla movement and in some instances appears to be attributable to actions undertaken by Nicaragua, itself, directly.

The most recent example of these terrorist incidents is, of course, the very tragic event which is still underway, the holding of a large number of businessmen and two ministers as hostage in San Pedro Sula.

I think, Mr. Chairman, the nature of the terrorist demands in this particular case are somewhat revealing, in that their demands are not related to social, economic, or political conditions within Honduras itself. Rather, they are related to the question of Honduran attempts to make it more difficult for Salvadoran and other terrorists to operate through their territory, and it would thus appear these are externally stimulated and externally organized terrorist activities.

They are not, as I said, terrorist activities which appear to have an agenda of Honduran issues.

Honduras, itself, Mr. Chairman, finds itself and feels itself very much under a rising threat, political and military, from Nicaragua.

The statement which I have submitted for the record details to some degree the nature of their comparative military establishments, and I think makes it quite clear that far from being in a threatening position, Honduras is, itself, in a threatened position.

We have attempted, Mr. Chairman, in a very modest way to respond to the Honduran perception and our perception of an increased security threat to that country, and, as you mentioned in your opening statement, we have increased in a modest fashion our security assistance resources for that country.

I would stress that those resources are devoted primarily to training, communications, and internal transport. They are devoted, in fact, to the provision of very low technology types of equipment and assistance to the Honduran Army and Air Force. The Honduran Armed Forces are badly in need of such assistance.

Honduras, itself, Mr. Chairman—in closing, if I might—has taken a very strong lead within the region in attempting to pursue vigorously all possible diplomatic and political solutions to the problem of rising tensions in the region, and, on March 23 of this year, it advanced in the Organization of American States and elsewhere, a very comprehensive six-point plan to reduce tensions in the region.[1]

That plan is outlined in considerable detail in the statement, and I will try to summarize it here. I would only say this is a plan which has received a very positive response from some of the other governments in the region, not including particularly Nicaragua, and has received a general endorsement from the United States.

It is, in fact, quite consistent with some of the proposals which we have been making to the Government of Nicaragua in our own efforts to sustain a bilateral dialog with that regime.

You mentioned as well, in your opening statement, Mr. Chairman,[2] the letter which was recently sent by the Presidents of Venezuela and Mexico to the Governments of Honduras, Nicaragua, and the United States.[3] I would only say that we are studying that letter very carefully.

We treat it and will treat it with utmost seriousness. We recognize that both Venezuela and Mexico are countries with deep interests in the region and are countries with whom we have had for a very long period of time a very useful dialog in attempting to pursue all possible ways toward the reduction of tensions in the region.

So I would simply offer assurances that we do treat these proposals recently received from those two governments with great seriousness and are in the process of preparing to respond.

I think I will end my opening remarks there, Mr. Chairman, and make myself available for any questions or comments you or your colleagues might have.

Thank you.

Document 698

Transcript of a White House Press Briefing, October 1, 1982[4]

Visit of Panamanian President de la Espriella

SENIOR ADMINISTRATION OFFICIAL. Let me first say a word about the schedule of the visit overall. The President has been up here, the President of Panama has been up here for several days. He has had an opportunity to, in addition to meeting with the President now—they met together in a very small group for 15 minutes and then with a larger group in the Cabinet Room for another 15 minutes.

In addition to that, he's met Acting Secretary Kenneth Dam; Secretary Weinberger; met with two groups on the Hill, one with Senators Baker, Laxalt, and Hollings, and this morning with a group from the House; met with labor leaders here; received a medal and given a speech before the America Society in New York; and is talking at the National Press Club this afternoon.

---

[1] The Honduran peace proposal was presented before the Protocolary Meeting of the Permanent Council of the Organization of American States, held in Washington, March 23, 1982, by Edgardo Paz Barnica, Foreign Minister of Honduras; for text, see OAS document CP/ACTA 486/82, March 23, 1982.

[2] For Barnes' opening remarks, see *Honduras and U.S. Policy*, pp. 1–2.

[3] For the text of the letter to President Reagan, see document 694. The letters to Honduras and Nicaragua are in *Honduras and U.S. Policy*, pp. 99–102.

[4] Source: Office of the Press Secretary to the President. This was a background briefing conducted by a senior administration official in the Briefing Room of the White House beginning at 12:10 p.m.

In addition to that, he'll be meeting with the World Bank and the multilateral banks and a variety of private investors.

This has been an unusually warm atmosphere, I think. The new Espriella administration which took office 60 days ago has marked some new directions in Panamanian foreign policy. It moved very quickly to disassociate itself from talk of creating in the aftermath of the Falklands/Malvinas crisis a separate Latin American institution which had been suggested by some, including, discussed at some length by some of the predecessors of this Government. It gave very strong and helpful support to the United States on the Puerto Rico issue in the United States [*Nations*].

At this meeting here today, the President said that he wanted, he was looking forward to a warm working relationship with the—President Reagan, with the Panamanian administration. He said that a healthy economy in Panama would be of benefit to both our countries and that was one of the purposes of the Caribbean Basin Initiative and that it would be very important to put the emphasis on private investment.

He pointed out that he was concerned about Nicaragua and Cuba and the destructive role they were playing in the area, and he pledged to work together with Panama on the Canal issues.

President de la Espriella responded by saying that his Government is very strongly supportive of the Caribbean Basin Initiative, which he thinks is essential to the future development of the area. He pointed out that—he and his associates pointed out that there have been 3 good years, which he termed the most successful in history in the operation of the Canal. And indeed, we say that that corresponds very much to our own view. Revenues have been at an all-time high, the tonnage passing through the Canal has been at all-time high. I'd be glad to give those who are interested information on this. And revenues have been able to cover increased capital expenditures and the operating expenditures entirely. It has been a success story.

With regard to the dangers in the area, President de la Espriella said that he also was very concerned about them, that he thought that the important thing was to develop democracy in all the countries of the area, and noted that Panama is headed toward democratic elections in 1984, and that this is vital, as he sees it, to the future of his country.

He added that the President should consider that he was among friends in Panama, and expressed his admiration for President Reagan personally and this administration.

In the course of the agreement, there were two important agreements that were signed. One is a bilateral investment treaty which assures national treatment for the investors of both countries in the other country.

Q. Initialed?

SENIOR ADMINISTRATION OFFICIAL. Initialed. It, very importantly, includes a procedure for the settlement of investment disputes, if necessary, through a course to third party arbitration.

In addition to that, an agreement was signed or initialed, again, setting up a study on alternatives to the present canal. This is the first step toward determining the best way to meet the maritime transportation needs of the next century. The question is, of course, do we enlarge the existing canal? Do we build a third set of locks? Is a sea level canal to be built or what?

Thirdly, and also importantly, Acting Secretary Dam and the Panamanian Foreign Minister agreed to request the Panamanian Canal Board to study two important issues that must be decided in the operation of the canal. One, concerning the wage structure of the canal. There are, in fact, two wage structures in place and that is causing friction and concern. And the second is the possibility of additional investment in this canal to bring it to its, what is regarded as its theoretical maximum capacity before the end of the century.

Overall, I think this is a meeting which was characterized by a very warm and supportive tone on both sides. Now, I'll see if I can answer your questions.

Q. Did the President apologize for having opposed for so long the turning over of the canal to Panama?

SENIOR ADMINISTRATION OFFICIAL. No. The President—

Q. Did he say anything about it at all?

SENIOR ADMINISTRATION OFFICIAL. The President said, as I mentioned earlier, pledged to work together with the Panamanians effectively on canal issues. As you may know, the President has earlier said that, on a number of occasions, pledged himself to implement fully the Panama Canal Treaty[5] as the law of the land.

---

[5] For information on the Panama Canal Treaty signed in 1977 and ratified in 1978, see *American Foreign Policy: Basic Documents, 1977–1980*, pp. 1379–1424.

Q. Well, when you said that the canal has been a great success story, is there any sense in the administration that, perhaps, the President's position was wrong after all?

SENIOR ADMINISTRATION OFFICIAL. We've played the cards from where they lay before and have worked as hard as we could with the, under the President's instructions, with the new management to make it a success.

As you know, it is a United States—the United States remains in the leading role in the Panama Canal company at the present time, but cooperation with the Panamanian officials has proceeded very effectively. So this is a long transition. The transition has been operating well.

Q. But since it's been taken—I mean, the responsibility is being shared more and they have such a success story, doesn't it prove that the President was wrong?

SENIOR ADMINISTRATION OFFICIAL. No, I don't think that that issue is—

Q. Oh, say yes. (Laughter)

Q. The President didn't think he was?

Q. Perhaps changed his mind about the treaties since he opposed them and the—

SENIOR ADMINISTRATION OFFICIAL. That was not discussed.

Q. Pardon me?

SENIOR ADMINISTRATION OFFICIAL. That was not discussed. It was a forward-looking meeting. It was not a meeting looking back.

Q. Well, even if it was not discussed, is it the view of the administration that this has proved to be the correct course?

SENIOR ADMINISTRATION OFFICIAL. The view of the administration is that we have a treaty that we should apply as effectively as we can and we've been doing just that.

Q. He also said about the canal since then—you say deal with the cards he's got—if there are any violations the United States should go back and seize the canal. Of the treaty.

SENIOR ADMINISTRATION OFFICIAL. Any violations?

Q. Of the treaty. And now you present a picture of a very warm, amicable agreement to work out difficulties and look ahead.

SENIOR ADMINISTRATION OFFICIAL. I'm sorry?

Q. Doesn't this—could you say there's no looking back? It doesn't make his past comments obviously contrived political rhetoric? There's no change here? Are you saying there's no change here?

SENIOR ADMINISTRATION OFFICIAL. The President, when he came to office was confronted by a treaty that had been passed by the Senate and signed by the previous administration and he did not say that he supported it or thought it was the best way to go, but he did pledge himself to implement it, and that is what we are doing. I don't think that it need be carried beyond that.

Q. Sir, do you still know of or believe that it is the—that this is still not believed that this is the best way to go? Given his druthers—

SENIOR ADMINISTRATION OFFICIAL. That was not discussed.

Q. Did he agree with your estimate that it's a success story now?

SENIOR ADMINISTRATION OFFICIAL. Well, that was presented on both sides by those that are directly concerned with the administration of the canal. I don't think that even the President's concerns about the treaty and those of the—in the debate in the United States—were so much concerns directly about the implementation of the treaty, but about larger issues.

Q. Did the President warn the Cubans before they—before the Panamanians came here—that if they continue their activities in Central America the United States will probably take back the canal? Was that discussed? Was that done at the United States request? That is what the papers have reported.

SENIOR ADMINISTRATION OFFICIAL. A group of Cubans invited themselves we understand recently to go down to Panama and to talk with Panamanian officials. There is—I can't say that—I can't speak for them, obviously, but as far as we are concerned that was an entirely independent action on the Cubans' part.

Q. Did you ask the Panamanians to make that point known, that you—that the United States would take back the canal if Cuba didn't settle down?

SENIOR ADMINISTRATION OFFICIAL. No.

Q. Was the issue of an American base on Panama discussed?

SENIOR ADMINISTRATION OFFICIAL. Not at the meetings at the White House.

Q. Was it discussed—

Q. The State Department?

SENIOR ADMINISTRATION OFFICIAL. Yes, there was a review of that at the Defense Department and at the State Department and in other meetings. There are no issues that are of particular importance at the moment. The relationship seems to be going smoothly.

Q. But are there any plans for another military installation in Panama or just the ones that already are there?

SENIOR ADMINISTRATION OFFICIAL. The ones that are already there.

Q. How important is it politically to the United States to have Panama's backing for the American position in Central America?

SENIOR ADMINISTRATION OFFICIAL. I think we will find—you may have noticed here an emerging pattern of countries that have been expressing themselves more and more openly on, one, the need to keep the democratic transformation going in the area and, two, their concerns about the developments in Nicaragua and the continued pressures from Cuba. You had here not very long ago a representative of Costa Rica, a long-time democracy, a neutral country without an army, saying very much the same thing.

Q. Is Panama expected to join the CDC [*CADC*]—that democratic community or something?

SENIOR ADMINISTRATION OFFICIAL. I don't know. I think there have been some contacts between them but I don't think they are conclusive.

Q. Were there discussions on building up Panamanian Armed Forces to improve their security?

SENIOR ADMINISTRATION OFFICIAL. No. We have a—I mean not beyond the existing military cooperation agreements that we have which provide for a small security assistance program and military training—IMET it is so called.

Q. Could you give us some detail on the discussions about El Salvador, and particularly whether the Panamanian President was pleased or displeased with the way the situation has been evolving there since the election?

SENIOR ADMINISTRATION OFFICIAL. We did not have a detailed discussion of El Salvador with him, although we believe that in fact given his emphasis on democracy and creating democratic institutions that he would share our view, that there has been indeed progress.

THE PRESS. Thank you.

Document 699

Final Act of the Meeting of Foreign Ministers of Countries Interested in the Promotion of Democracy in Central America and the Caribbean, San José, October 4, 1982 (Extract)[6]

Declaration on Democracy in Central America

The representatives of the Governments of the Republics of Belize, Colombia, El Salvador, the United States of America, Honduras, Jamaica, and Costa Rica, and the observer representative of the Government of the Dominican Republic, convinced that direct dialogue among democratic countries is the appropriate way to review the situation in their states and, therefore, to search for solutions to common problems, met in San Jose, on October 4, 1982, . . .

. . . .

The opening session was held in San Jose at 9:30 a.m. and was attended by the President of the Republic of Costa Rica, Luis Alberto Monge, who delivered the inaugural address.

In order to have a moderator for the discussions, the meeting of Ministers unani-

---

[6] Source: Department of State *Bulletin*, December 1982, pp. 69–70. The meeting was attended by the Prime Minister of Belize, who concurrently held the Foreign Minister portfolio, and the Foreign Ministers of Colombia, El Salvador, Honduras, Jamaica, and Costa Rica. Assistant Secretary for Inter-American Affairs Enders attended as a special representative of the Secretary of State. Panama and the Dominican Republic designated special observers. The Panamanian observer did not sign the final act. The omitted portion is a list of those in attendance. On October 5, 1982, at the Department of State Daily Press Briefing, Acting Spokesman Romberg stated, in reference to the declaration, "The Government of the United States believes that this initiative of these regional democracies marks an important step forward in the promotion of representative democracy and the resolution of regional tensions within a peaceful framework. We hope other governments in the region will seriously address the concepts set forth in the final act of the conference. They provide a blueprint for peace in the region."

mously elected Mr. Fernando Volio Jimenez, Minister of Foreign Affairs and Worship of Costa Rica, as Chairman.

The participants agreed on the following points as the final result of their deliberations:

1. They expressed their conviction that it is the ineludible task of governments that have been legitimized by the will of the people, expressed at the polls, to defend, promote, and develop a democratic, representative, pluralistic, and participatory system, and that the time has come to define the conditions that will permit the reestablishment of a lasting and stable peace in Central America;

2. They recognized the challenges facing the democratic institutions of our countries, and the unavoidable duty to face them firmly;

3. They likewise recognized that it is necessary and desirable to establish organizations to help maintain and improve democratic institutions;

4. They noted that democratic institutions, in addition to serving as a means of expressing the sovereignty of the people, should contribute to the strengthening of peace and solidarity among peoples and the promotion of economic development, freedom, and social justice;

5. They reaffirmed the fundamental importance of respect for international law and treaties as the basis of regional cooperation and security;

6. They stated that the maintenance of peace and democratic institutions requires respect for the fundamental values of human dignity emanating from the Supreme Being, and the elimination of existing conditions of social injustice;

7. They stressed the need for the prevention and solution of conflicts between states to be channeled through the mechanisms for peaceful settlement recognized by international law, and emphasized that it is the duty of governments to use such mechanisms to if necessary, to create special mechanisms to achieve that end;

8. They noted that the current world economic crisis produces phenomena such as disproportionate foreign indebtedness, a deterioration of the international financial system, and an increasing imbalance in the terms of trade among states;

9. They considered that such phenomena result in unemployment, inflationary trends, serious financial problems, and political, economic, and social conflicts which are exploited by totalitarianism for the purpose of destabilizing the democratic way of life and government;

10. They noted the objective enunciated this year by the Chiefs of State and Government on the occasion of the inauguration of the President of Honduras, Dr. Roberto Suazo Cordova, on January 27; of the President of Costa Rica, Mr. Luis Alberto Monge, on May 8; of the President of Colombia, Dr. Belisario Betancur, on August 7; of the President of the Dominican Republic, Dr. Salvador Jorge Blanco, on August 16; and in the Joint Communiqués of the Presidents of Costa Rica and El Salvador of June 17, of the Presidents of Honduras and El Salvador, of June 10, and of the Presidents of Costa Rica and Panama, of September 26, of this same year, and that such objectives point to the adoption of measures for the achievement of peace, democracy, security, development, freedom, and social justice.

THEY THEREFORE DECLARE:

I: Their faith in and support for the principles of representative, pluralistic, and participatory democracy which, when properly understood, constitute a way of life, of thinking, and of acting which can accommodate within its scope different social and economic systems and structures having a common denominator, which is respect for life, for the security of the individual, for freedom of thought, and for freedom of the press, as well as the right to work and to receive proper remuneration, the right to fair living conditions, to the free exercise of suffrage, and of other human, civil, political, economic, social, and cultural rights.

II. Their concern about the serious deterioration of the conditions of the present international economic order and international financial system, which gives rise to a process of destabilization, anguish, and fear, affecting, in particular, those countries that have a democratic system of government. In this regard, they appeal to the industrialized democratic countries to step up their cooperation with the democratic countries of the area by implementing bold and effective initiatives to strengthen the recovery and economic and social development efforts of the various interested countries in the area. As part of this cooperation, the initiative of the President of the United States of America with regard to the Caribbean Basin is especially urgent and should be encouraged and fully implemented as soon as possible. Likewise, those present recognize the economic cooperation and assistance efforts undertaken by the Governments of the Nassau Group: Canada, Colombia, Mexico, the United States, and Venezuela.

They support current efforts towards subregional economic integration, including the Central American Common Market and the Caribbean Community and point out the urgency of updating and improving those integration processes which are now in trouble in order to place them in an appropriate political, economic, juridical, and institutional framework.

III. Their conviction that, in order to promote regional peace and stability, it is necessary to support domestic political understandings that will lead to the establishment of democratic, pluralistic, and participatory systems; to the establishment of mechanisms for a continuing multilateral dialogue; to absolute respect for delimited and demarcated borders, in accordance with existing treaties, compliance with which is the proper way to prevent border disputes and incidents, observing, whenever applicable, traditional lines of jurisdiction; to respect for the independence and territorial integrity of states; to the rejection of threats or the use of force tò settle conflicts; to a halt to the arms race; and to the elimination, on the basis of full and effective reciprocity, of the external factors which hamper the consolidation of a stable and lasting peace.

In order to attain these objectives, it is essential that every country within and without the region take the following actions:

a) Create and maintain truly democratic government institutions, based on the will of the people as expressed in free and regular elections, and founded on the principle that government is responsible to the people governed;

b) Respect human rights, especially the right to life and to personal integrity, and the fundamental freedoms, such as freedom of speech, freedom of assembly, and religious freedom, as well as the right to organize political parties, labor unions, and other groups and associations;

c) Promote national reconciliation where there have been deep divisions in society through the broadening of opportunities for participation within the framework of democratic processes and institutions;

d) Respect the principle of non-intervention in the internal affairs of states, and the right of peoples to self-determination;

e) Prevent the use of their territories for the support, supply, training, or command of terrorist or subversive elements in other states, end all traffic in arms and supplies, and refrain from providing any direct or indirect assistance to terrorist, subversive, or other activities aimed at the violent overthrow of the governments of other states;

f) Limit arms and the size of military and security forces to the levels that are strictly necessary for the maintenance of public order and national defense;

g) Provide for international surveillance and supervision of all ports of entry, borders, and other strategic areas under reciprocal and fully verifiable arrangements;

h) On the basis of full and effective reciprocity, withdraw all foreign military and security advisers and forces from the Central American area, and ban the importation of heavy weapons of manifest offensive capability through guaranteed means of verification.

The preceding actions represent the essential framework that must be established in each State in order to promote regional peace and stability.

The signing countries call on all the peoples and governments of the region to embrace and implement these principles and conditions as the basis for the improvement of democracy and the building of a lasting peace.

They note with satisfaction the efforts being made in that direction, and deem that the achievement of these objectives may be reached more fully through the reestablishment of the rule of law and the organization of election processes that will guarantee full participation of the people, without any discrimination whatsoever.

THEY RESOLVE

IV. To create a democratic organization to provide development assistance and advisory services for elections, the purpose of which organization will be to maintain the electoral system and to develop, strengthen, and stimulate its utilization in the inter-American area, providing advice to countries that request it about its practice and implementation. The organization will operate either autonomously, sponsored by the countries represented in the meeting and by other interested countries, or as a section or branch of the Inter-American Institute of Human Rights, since suffrage is an essential part of the theory and practice of human rights.

To request the Minister of Foreign Affairs and Worship of Costa Rica, Mr. Fernando Volio Fernandez, to prepare an appropriate document, containing the comments of the participants in this meeting and of the representatives of other democratic countries and to circulate it among them and implement it as soon as possible.

V. Lastly, they agree to participate in a Forum for Peace and Democracy, the purpose of which will be to contribute to the implementation of the actions and the attainment of the objectives contained in this document, and, within the framework of this declaration, to study the regional crisis and analyze the various peace proposals or initiatives aimed at solving it. The Forum may be broadened by the inclusion of the collaboration of other democratic States.

The Forum may entrust specific tasks to representatives of given participating countries, who will report on the results; and will transmit the final act of this meeting, so that comments and opinions deemed advisable, may be presented to the Forum.

The representatives requested the Minister of Foreign Affairs and Worship of Costa Rica, on behalf of the participating governments, to transmit this declaration to the governments of the region and other interested governments, and to obtain their views on the principles and conditions for peace that it contains.

They agreed to convene a new meeting as soon as possible, in order to evaluate the development of the objectives of the declaration.

VII. The Plenary Session in this meeting of Foreign Ministers noted with pleasure the presence of Panama and the Dominican Republic as observers.

The representatives expressed their appreciation to the Government of the Republic of Costa Rica for the courtesies it extended to them, which made possible the successful completion of their deliberations.

Signed at San Jose, Republic of Costa Rica, on October 4, 1982.

Document 700

Transcript of a White House Press Briefing, October 6, 1982[7]

Meeting With Mexican President-Elect de la Madrid

Senior Administration Official. Meetings between Presidents of Mexico and the United States have taken place regularly since the Taft administration here and in the postwar period, occasionally in the interwar period, we had meetings between Presidents-elect of Mexico and those of the United States.

And, as you know, President Reagan met with President Lopez Portillo prior to his inauguration on the border also. And this meeting that is occurring now is the exact analog of that.

The schedule that Mort referred to calls for two meetings between President Reagan and President-elect de la Madrid in the Hotel Coronado in San Diego. It's going to be followed by a luncheon.

The President will have his senior advisors with him. He'll also have—on the Mexican side, we have basically a group of officials closely associated with de la Madrid in the campaign there, many of them concerned with foreign affairs, as well, of course, as their Ambassador to the United States.

Now, President Reagan has given a very high priority to creating a relationship of confidence and cooperation with Mexico. It's hard to think of two countries that are more interdependent than our two. And he moved very early in his border meeting and subsequently Lopez Portillo was the first foreign visitor here. He came to Camp David.[8] You'll recall subsequent meetings.

---

[7] Source: Office of the Press Secretary to the President. The briefing, which was held in the Briefing Room of the White House beginning at 11:24 a.m., was conducted on background by a senior administration official. Miguel de la Madrid Hurtado won the July 1982 Presidential election in Mexico. He took office on December 1, 1982.

[8] Regarding López Portillo's visit to Washington and Camp David, June 8–9, 1981, see *American Foreign Policy: Current Documents, 1981*, documents 689 and 690. The two Presidents also attended the International Meeting on Cooperation and Development in Cancun, Mexico, October 22–23, 1981; for documentation on that meeting, see *ibid.*, Chapter 5, Part F.

We've had an exceptional schedule of consultations in meetings between high-level officials on both sides.

We believe that some real progress has been made in the course of the last 18 months in the Mexican-United States relationship. This is reflected I think in the statements by leaders on both sides with Mexican President Lopez Portillo talking about the respect and dignity with which Mexico is treated and regarded in the United States. We have had many consultations, but some important differences on foreign policy matters, particularly with regard to Central America. In our bilateral relationship, there have been significant steps forward.

We have seen the energy relationship between the two countries, which was a matter of considerable suspicion in the mid and latter part of the 1970's, gradually move forward into one of cooperation.

We have not solved some of the trading problems that exist between Mexico and the United States, but we have certainly kept them from festering and important negotiations are underway at the present moment on them.

We have found that we could indeed consult in advance in a friendly and supportive atmosphere on the very difficult question of immigration. The United States did so prior to introducing its legislation which is now in the last stages of congressional action. I don't want to say that we have asked for or obtained a Mexican approval of that immigration legislation, but Mexico has been very explicit, as I noted President-elect de la Madrid was the other day in recognizing the United States right to legislate in this field and hoping the United States would make sure the human rights of Mexican workers in this country are protected and enhanced. And, indeed, that is an important part of the legislation which is now under consideration in the Congress. And, of course, when the Mexican financial crisis broke this summer, the United States and Mexico reached a series of very important agreements which were subsequently enlarged to include other countries. I think they're familiar to you, but let me recall them—a $1.85 billion multinational support package was negotiated, half of it contributed by the United States; a $1 billion advance payment on oil purchases for the strategic petroleum reserve was negotiated, as well as a $1 billion commodity credit corporation line of credit.[9]

The purpose of these agreements was to provide short-term financing for Mexico while it is giving it time to develop a stabilization plan and to carry forward negotiations with the International Monetary Fund which are now underway.

We are, of course, not a party to those negotiations with the International Monetary Fund. Overall, we think that the outlook is good for the continuation and development of the kind of relationship that we and the Mexican President have been seeking. We note that President-elect de la Madrid just a couple of days ago on October 3d had to say that, himself, given existing good will, he said in an interview, willingness to treat each other with dignity and cordiality, mutually beneficial agreements can be reached as, indeed, some already have. And he said further that he thought that the areas of conflict between our two nations receive more publicity than our areas of cooperation.

This meeting is not a meeting to get into operational matters, to attempt to determine policy, to negotiate or reach agreements on any subject. It is a meeting very much like the one that occurred 18 months ago for the two men to get to know each other, to talk about their philosophy of government, problems, and the possibilities they see in the future for each country both internally and externally. Let me stop there and see what you have in the way of questions.

Q. Are any Treasury officials going in the American party and will there be anything worked out in terms of a clearinghouse between the peso and the dollar or any actual moves in that direction?

Senior Administration Official. No, as I say, this is—no specialized officials are going on either side. The Mexican President-elect is just that, a President-elect. He is not there to negotiate or act for his government on operational matters. The officials that are going along on this side are—in addition to senior White House advisers—foreign affairs officials. And I note that those that are accompanying the President-elect on their side are people who come from the party—the PRI, in large measure—but are in large measure concerned with foreign affairs.

Q. Will you elaborate your remark that the energy relationship has improved?

Senior Administration Official. You may recall the frictions that the energy relationship gave rise to in the 1970's—a

[9] Regarding the financial agreements, see document 695.

Mexican concern about becoming overdependent on the United States market, a feeling that on the part of Mexico that possibly it would be subject to U.S. pressures to increase its production of energy beyond what it would wish to do; and, indeed, I would say a hypersensitivity to the question overall. I think it's noteworthy that in May of this year the United States and Mexico—I am sorry, May of 1981—the United States and Mexico were able to move very fast for a first agreement to purchase for our strategic petroleum reserve organization 50,000 barrels per day of Mexican oil for stockpile—an agreement which I think is suggestive of the new emerging relationship. And a similar agreement with an advance payment was reached in August, as you know.

Q. You are not saying that the financial situation that is so desperate now is not going to come up?

SENIOR ADMINISTRATION OFFICIAL. No, I would expect that the Mexican President would give his analysis of his country's situation in the financial and economic area just as our President would of ours and that they would indeed talk about it. I want to distinguish that very clearly though from the suggestion that there are going to be any negotiations or any operational matters or indeed any attempt to set policy in that area.

Q. Well, is there any chance that the U.S. side could come prepared to talk about policy options for the future after de la Madrid takes office?

SENIOR ADMINISTRATION OFFICIAL. I think that that is putting it in a too operational sense. This is not a meeting with an agenda. It is not a meeting which is designed to lay out matters that would then be decided subsequently. It is not that kind of meeting at all. The President's first meeting with Lopez Portillo was not that kind either.

Q. But what if the two Presidents could decide that they might want to do something later on?

SENIOR ADMINISTRATION OFFICIAL. Well, as I say, I think that neither anticipate that it will be that kind of a meeting.

Q. Will the President of the United States respond with his analysis of the situation? For instance, some view that nationalizations and the extent of government involvement in the economy that the IMF is concerned about?

SENIOR ADMINISTRATION OFFICIAL. I would be very surprised if the U.S. President were to express views about what Mexico or indeed any other country wants—steps it wishes to take in its internal policies.

Q. What will they talk about? (Laughter)

SENIOR ADMINISTRATION OFFICIAL. I think they will talk about the economic situation in both countries. Both have been in a recession. The United States is coming out. Mexico is going into a period of stagnation. I am sure that they will talk about Central America. I think that they will talk about the operation of the world financial and economic system overall. My guess is that they will indeed talk about the major issues that are the ongoing issues in the relationship—that is to say trade, immigration, fisheries, border questions. But they will talk about them—if they do—in terms of a very general outlook. And I am trying to make the distinction here between a policy or operational option-choosing approach and a general outlook.

Q. Can you tell us how de la Madrid differs from Lopez Portillo politically, to the right, to the left? Where is he in there? Just what are the—how is he—

SENIOR ADMINISTRATION OFFICIAL. I think that is a question which you should address to Mexican officials—

Q. Well, we must have some idea. I mean, you are speaking on background. Could you just tell us—

SENIOR ADMINISTRATION OFFICIAL.—and ask them to define themselves.

Q. Sir, we have heard that the former Mexican Ambassador, Dr. Margain, who was formally secretariat of de la Hacienda—the equivalent of our Secretary of the Treasury—

SENIOR ADMINISTRATION OFFICIAL. Right.

Q. —that he is now in the Senate of Mexico. Now I have heard from reliable sources that he ran for the Senate because Dr. de la Madrid wished him to do so. Do you know if he will accompany the President-elect?

SENIOR ADMINISTRATION OFFICIAL. He is not on the list that we have for people accompanying the President-elect.

Q. What is the immigration—

Q. Since Mexico is now the largest exporter of oil to the United States—

SENIOR ADMINISTRATION OFFICIAL. That is right.

Q. —outstripping Saudi Arabia by about 2-to-1, do you think that President Reagan and the administration wanting to keep those Mexican oil supplies going will preclude the President's options in the Middle East?

SENIOR ADMINISTRATION OFFICIAL. Over the last year Mexico has indeed very substantially increased its exports to this country. To some minor degree, as I mentioned earlier, that was the result of the strategic petroleum reserve agreement, but that is only really quite minor since the total now is almost 20 times greater than that. It has been through the commercial activities of the Mexican oil companies and their American counterparts. And Mexico has consistently priced its oil and provided other terms in this period so that it could maintain and increase its share in the U.S. market, and it's a relationship that we welcome. But it is a commercial relationship.

Q. What is the border situation—immigration?

Q. And the link with the current legislation, please, sir.

SENIOR ADMINISTRATION OFFICIAL. Well, the situation with regard to immigration on the border is that the transitive undocumented persons from Mexico to the United States, of course, continues. It is a matter to which the Simpson–Mazzoli bill is directed in a number of ways.[10] Let me recall to you briefly the major things that the Simpson–Mazzoli bill will do.

It would, on the one hand, impose sanctions on employers in the United States that employ persons that do not have the right to work in the United States. It would at the same time create an amnesty for persons who had been in the United States as undocumented workers for more than a certain period of time, and it would create new ability to police effectively our safety and fair wage laws as they apply or could apply to workers that have been undocumented in the past. So it's a mix of things. In addition to that, it would increase by 20,000 the annual immigration quota for Mexico and Canada.

Q. Which is what?

SENIOR ADMINISTRATION OFFICIAL. Twenty thousand.

Q. No. It was increased by 20,000.

SENIOR ADMINISTRATION OFFICIAL. Yes.

Q. In Mexico?

SENIOR ADMINISTRATION OFFICIAL. And Canada, yes.

Q. What is the count for the—

SENIOR ADMINISTRATION OFFICIAL. It's 20.

Q. Oh, I see.

Q. How many—

Q. I want to get back to my question of before. Is it the administration's view that the increase in Mexican oil exports to the United States improves the President's flexibility and options in the Middle East? And if so, are there going to be attempts to continue that—keeping that flow at a high level?

SENIOR ADMINISTRATION OFFICIAL. Let me take the question on the other side—is that our dependence on Middle East oil has, in fact, decreased sharply from the latter part of the 1970's, and it is a major and significant change in the international energy picture and in the international strategic picture. It does clearly give more options to the United States, less vulnerability than was true of the period of the 1970's. I would wish to say that this is something that the United States welcomes, to have a better balance of its supply relationships. Obviously, that's an object of policy overall. But it is the market that has produced this.

Q. Is the administration considering any increase or addition to the aid that we have already provided to Mexico in its economic crisis? And if so, what kinds of things are you considering?

SENIOR ADMINISTRATION OFFICIAL. As I say, the packages worked out in August were packages which were designed to create time for a stabilization plan development and negotiations with the IMF. Those are going on now. And so this is not a subject which we expect to be dealt with at the meeting or which is currently under consideration.

Q. It's not under consideration now?

SENIOR ADMINISTRATION OFFICIAL. No. Those packages stand and they are designed to give—they were designed to give

---

[10] Immigration reform legislation was introduced in the Congress on March 17, 1982, by Senator Alan K. Simpson and Representative Romano L. Mazzoli, chairmen of the Senate and House subcommittees on immigration and refugees, respectively. The Senate version (S.2222, S. Rept. 97–485) passed the Senate on August 17, 1982. The House version (HR 7357, H. Rept. 97–890, Parts I and II) died when the House was unable to complete action on the measure before adjournment, December 18, 1982.

a time for working out of these longer-term matters and negotiations.

Q. If the President-elect should ask for some further aid from the United States, what kinds of things—

SENIOR ADMINISTRATION OFFICIAL. You're getting into very hypothetical questions now. I—

Q. Well, let's leave the first part off. What kinds of things could the administration do for Mexico further?

SENIOR ADMINISTRATION OFFICIAL. As I say, there's no—that's not a current policy issue, and I have no reason to expect that it will become one.

Q. What's the timetable on this stabilization plan? How much breathing time is there?

SENIOR ADMINISTRATION OFFICIAL. The packages that were developed in August are essentially 3-month packages. I don't know whether the precise timing is all that significant because they were clearly rather large sums of money, which were designed to provide a margin in between, and negotiations with the fund discussions are actively underway at the present time.

Q. How would you characterize the effects of the Mexican financial crisis on border businesses? How would you describe them?

SENIOR ADMINISTRATION OFFICIAL. The situation in the course of the last year has been one in which much of the time the Mexican peso has been judged by the market to be over valued. And that has meant that there was a very strong advantage for Mexicans to come to make purchases in the United States, a particular advantage. And a very substantial trade of that kind developed. The abrupt change in the value of the peso and the controls that have been put on have, obviously, eliminated much of that business.

Q. What has been the impact on American businesses along the border?

SENIOR ADMINISTRATION OFFICIAL. Oh, I think it has been one, first, of very substantial expansion early in the year, and very substantial contraction now.

Q. How many undocumented—

Q. You made a big point of saying that the United States is not involved in these IMF negotiations. Could you at least comment, in a general way, on the reports that the United States does favor certain steps to be taken by Mexico to—

SENIOR ADMINISTRATION OFFICIAL. No; I do not want to comment on that.

Q. Does the United States believe that—

SENIOR ADMINISTRATION OFFICIAL. We are not involved in the discussions with the IMF.

Q. Does the United States believe the de la Madrid government will be more receptive to the U.S. position on the Caribbean Basin?

SENIOR ADMINISTRATION OFFICIAL. We have had a series of agreements and disagreements on the Caribbean Basin as a whole. As you know, we are joined together in the Caribbean Basin Initiative. Mexico is part of it, along with Venezuela, Colombia, and Canada, and the United States. And we have agreed on the essentiality of addressing that. Mexico is providing assistance in oil purchases, and, in spite of its financial crisis, is continuing to do that. And recently that was reaffirmed.

I think it would be entirely wrong to speculate at all on positions that the President-elect would take. I am sure he will be defining those, but, largely, after he takes office in the same manner an American President-elect would.

Q. So you are saying that it is unlikely the President will get any indication of how de la Madrid may approach the Caribbean Basin Initiative or problems in Central America?

SENIOR ADMINISTRATION OFFICIAL. I am not saying that. I am saying that I am not speculating on that.

Q. Are they likely just to survey what the situation is, and leave it at that as opposed to—

SENIOR ADMINISTRATION OFFICIAL. I am sure that they will look at the area. I am sure they will talk about Central America and the economic and political and security problems in the area. I am sure they will.

SENIOR ADMINISTRATION OFFICIAL. Let us take two more questions.

Q. Can you tell us if Lopez Portillo's [and] de la Madrid's policies with regard to Central America are roughly the same?

SENIOR ADMINISTRATION OFFICIAL. I am not aware that the President-elect of Mexico has defined a—

Q. He did run for President, right? I am assuming he put out some position on it, right?

Senior Administration Official. He ran for President. And his own statements to the—I think that—I am not at all certain that Central America played a very substantial role in the campaign. But I am sure that there are statements from him on that. Mexico—let me say, overall, that Mexican foreign policy has a very broad continuity to it from administration to administration. And I am sure that that will be a factor in whatever policy he defines. But I think it is not for us now to start trying to say what his policy is before he has defined it, and then compare it with earlier ones.

Q. But he has not defined a position on Central America?

Senior Administration Official. He has—to the degree I can recall the statements during the campaign, they were statements which were very supportive of the basic Mexican position on the area. Let me put it the other way around. The campaign did not signal differences in this area.

Q. You said the traffic of illegal immigrants has continued since the deepening of the economic crisis. Has it worsened? And, if so, by how much?

Senior Administration Official. It is very hard to get a fix on that. There were some indications of a larger number in August, fragmentary indications. We are not absolutely certain whether they continue or not at the present time. There probably are—there appear to be somewhat larger numbers. But it is not—it is very hard to tell, because you are dealing only with those that are apprehended.

Q. How about the Tijuana–San Diego border? Is there any rough estimate of how many people do come in?

Senior Administration Official. In that particular part of the border?

Q. Yes.

Senior Administration Official. There may be, but I do not know what it is.

Q. What is the current attitude toward them coming in?

Senior Administration Official. I think I have here, if I might cite to you, a quote from de la Madrid on that, or at least a statement in his October 3d interview with John Houston.[11] He did say that Mexico does not have the economic ability at the present time to provide sufficient employment for all of its own people, and that the United States does require laborers for work that its own citizens do not—

Q. Could you go back to, "And the United States—"

Senior Administration Official. All right, this is a paraphrase.

Q. Yes, I understand.

Senior Administration Official. The United States does require laborers for work that its own citizens do not wish to undertake—said that there is a structural imbalance in the Mexican economic system which provokes migration. And it's this imbalance within the Mexican economy which must be addressed according to Mr. de la Madrid and not its result, the illegal migration problem.

With respect to the illegal migration problem, two countries must make sure that the human dignity and rights of these workers are respected. The United States has the right to establish its own immigration policy. President-elect de la Madrid expressed his hope for a humanitarian policy. This is a quote, "So that the Mexican workers can be treated in the same manner and with the same equality as U.S. workers."

And, indeed, that is one of the objectives of the Simpson–Mazzoli bill.

Q. What is Mexico's—what's Mexico's unemployment rate?

Senior Administration Official. It's very hard to tell because the underemployment is such a major phenomenon in Mexico. But it's an entirely—I mean, there's no way you can compare their situation with the United States with slightly less than 10 percent. The figures simply do not come out on the same basis. On that basis—on an underemployment would be a very high figure indeed.

Q. Secretary Shultz will be there on—

Senior Administration Official. Yes, he will.

Q. And what are they doing in Tijuana? Just placing a reef [*wreath*]—is that the—

Senior Administration Official. That's correct.

Q. The reef [*wreath*] where?

Senior Administration Official. Benito Juarez Monument.

The Press. Thank you.

---

[11] The interview has not been further identified.

Document 701

Address by the Ambassador to El Salvador (Hinton) Before the American Chamber of Commerce in San Salvador, El Salvador, October 29, 1982[12]

The System of Justice in El Salvador

It is an honor and a pleasure to be speaking once again at the American Chamber of Commerce. Fifteen months ago, I spoke to you in my initial address in El Salvador about U.S. policy and its compatability with the goals so eloquently expressed in the armed forces proclamation of October 15, 1979.

Today I want to stress the constancy of American policy, to assess briefly progress made and set-backs borne these last 15 months, and then to address a critical issue which in my opinion requires a solution if the democratic process in El Salvador is not to be frustrated.

The aims of our policy remain exactly as I outlined them to you on July 31, 1981:

—To help a friendly neighbor defend itself against an armed insurrection aided and manipulated by Cuba;

—To help resolve the structural problems which beset this country;

—To help the people to decide their own destiny through the electoral process; and

—To stimulate political reconciliation in El Salvador.

In these past 15 months, El Salvador and Salvadorans have come a long way. Although much remains to be done, the democratic process is working. March 28, 1982, is a day that will live forever in all of our memories.[13]

Fifteen months ago in discussing the war and paying deserved tribute to your armed forces, I urged on you the need for unity in the face of the common enemy. Since I spoke, the armed forces, in defending our common heritage against Marxist subversives supported by Nicaragua, Cuba, and others of similar totalitarian persuasion, have incurred over 4,000 additional casualties. The price is a heavy one, but El Salvador's Army is slowly but surely winning the war.

This war effort is now supported by a government of national unity. Four political parties share a common commitment to the objectives of President Magana's administration. As spelled out in the Apeneca pact, these objectives are peace, democratization, human rights, economic recuperation, consolidation of the reforms, confidence and security, and the improvement of El Salvador's image abroad. The United States is proud to be cooperating with and assisting a government dedicated to achievement of such aims.

Much is required for success. The democratic reform process so stunningly progressing here, despite civil conflict, depends not only on political tolerance, freedom of expression, economic recovery, commitment to social justice, and resolute military defense but also on civic commitment to make the rule of law a living reality. It is not enough that El Salvador's Constitution and laws protect individual rights, that El Salvador subscribes to a long list of international human rights conventions. The reality must change to more closely match the ideal.

Reflecting today on my experiences in El Salvador, I would no doubt be well advised to talk of other things—perhaps to talk of the economy, of the private sector's determined efforts to keep working despite everything, including the sad practice of some Salvadorans blowing up the economic infrastructure and other Salvadorans keeping desperately needed capital outside the country; of what I consider to be, in war economy conditions, sound governmental policy; and of American economic assistance—over $230 million this year. Or perhaps I should analyze basic issues posed by enormous population pressure and rapid population growth. Another subject, for another day, might be reflections on educational requirements to prepare citizens for their critical role in a functioning democracy.

But, for better or worse, today I want to talk of a subject so many of you, because of indifference or shame or fear or for what other reason I know not, leave in eloquent silence.

Neither internal confidence nor external support can long survive here in the ab-

[12] Source: Department of State *Bulletin*, December 1982, pp. 68–69. The source text is the text as prepared for delivery.

[13] The reference is to the El Salvador Constituent Assembly elections of that date.

sence of an effective system of criminal justice. Until all are protected by the law, until all are subject to the law, El Salvador will lack a fundamental prerequisite for a healthy society and, I might add, for a healthy economy.

In the first 2 weeks of this month, at least 68 humans beings were murdered in El Salvador under circumstances which are familiar to everyone here. Every day we receive new reports of disappearances under tragic circumstances. American citizens in El Salvador have been among the murdered, among the disappeared. Is it any wonder that much of the world is predisposed to believe the worst of a system which almost never brings to justice either those who perpetrate these acts or those who order them? The "Mafia" must be stopped. Your survival depends on it. The guerrillas of this Mafia, every bit as much as the guerrillas of Morazan and Chalatenango, are destroying El Salvador.

The battle has been joined. Both the civilian and military authorities of the Government of El Salvador have spoken out unequivocally against the abuses of basic human rights. They have backed up their words with action. They have begun the process of bringing to justice those who commit crimes under whatever banner—no matter who they might be.

In spite of the fact that determined efforts have cut the number of deaths attributable to political violence to a third or less of what it was a few years ago, by no stretch of the imagination can current levels be considered acceptable by any civilized person.

Extremists of left and right continue to murder wantonly, apparently basing their despicable actions on rumor, ideological persuasion, heresay, and personal animosity. Common criminals are having a field day. There is no doubt that El Salvador's political agony provides cover for common thugs. Everyone here knows that kidnapping for criminal gain has been carried out under the guise of political action. The problem exists at every step of the criminal justice process. Who among you is not intimidated by it?

Who dares to speak out when you witness a person being dragged off by "heavily armed men in civilian clothes" in the middle of the night? Who will bear witness to murder? Where are sufficiently trained detectives to investigate the wave of crimes committed daily?

Are there anywhere near enough properly trained and rewarded prosecutors to deal with the violence in the society as to make successful prosecution virtually impossible for any but a self-confessed criminal? Are judges sufficiently protected and isolated so as to assure verdicts based neither on bribery nor on fear? Can the prison system absorb and control those who should be convicted?

These are questions with which all civilized societies must deal, but it is sad to see a society in which the answers are so painfully and consistently inadequate.

If you are not convinced that I am talking about a fundamental and critical problem, consider these facts. Since 1979 perhaps as many as 30,000 Salvadorans have been killed illegally; that is, not in battle. Less than 1,500 cases of "crimes against the person"—that is, homicide, assault, and battery—have been prosecuted before your courts. Most striking of all, there have been less than 200 convictions for these crimes.

This is El Salvador's problem. El Salvador must solve it. The United States can do some things to help. We, for instance, can and do insist on our legitimate right to assure that justice is done in the case of murdered American citizens. We hope that successful prosecution of these crimes will open the door for similar success in crimes involving Salvadoran citizens. That is why I believe that the successful prosecution of these cases is just as essential for the future of the Salvadoran criminal justice system as it is for the continuance of U.S. assistance.

To further this cause, we can provide the technical assistance of the Federal Bureau of Investigation (FBI) in using modern investigation techniques. We stand ready to provide assistance to the Government and courts of El Salvador in the reform of the criminal justice system. Personally, however, I believe needed assistance could better come from other Latin countries where a modernized Napoleonic Code applies. But all will come to naught unless the will exists in this country to make it happen, unless the will exists to punish those who are responsible, regardless of their station in life.

Finally, as the representative of the United States in El Salvador, I can try to communicate as clearly and honestly as I can the sentiments of the American people, the Congress, and the administration on this subject. The message is simple: El Salvador must have substantial progress on bringing the murders of our citizens, including those who ordered the murders, to justice; in advancing human rights; and controlling the abuses of some elements of the security forces. If not, the United States, despite our other interests and our commitment to the struggle against communism, could be forced to deny assistance to El Salvador.

Beyond all of this, a more effective justice system is essential to ending the war. Your government has announced that it is trying to develop a mechanism whereby those guerrillas can lay down their arms and return to the democratic fold. This is a supremely difficult task. Years of destruction and killing are not forgotten overnight.

We in the United States know this. The bitterness of our Civil War, which left over 350,000 dead and almost that many wounded, continued for the better part of a century—even with unconditional amnesty and full political participation for virtually every rebel.

Nevertheless the fighting here will end someday. And when it does, those who lay down their arms must be able to do so with the knowledge that they will be fairly treated in accordance with the laws and procedures established by the elected representatives of the Salvadoran people.

In closing I would like to commend to you some words spoken by a man at the head of a nation wracked by armed rebellion; a man who, in spite of his loathing for armed force, used armed force to suppress that rebellion; a man who eventually died at the hands of a political assassin.

> "With malice toward none, with charity for all, with firmness in the right . . . let us strive on to finish the work we are in, to bind up the nation's wounds, to care for him who shall have borne the battle and for his widow and his orphan, to do all which may achieve and cherish a just and lasting peace among ourselves and with all nations."[14]

---

[14] The reference is to President Abraham Lincoln's second inaugural address, March 4, 1865.

Document 702

Address by the Representative at the Organization of American States (Middendorf) Before the Committee for 806 and 807, November 8, 1982[15]

Programs Underway for the Caribbean Basin Initiative

I have deeply appreciated the work which this committee has done on behalf of maintaining an open market in the United States for Latin America and for other developing countries. This is a difficult time in which to be a free trader. There is always a great temptation to restrain imports in an effort to protect American jobs and American production. That temptation is particularly strong in times of economic difficulties. But that temptation, as we all know, is a terrible illusion, which ends by costing the U.S. economy far more in terms of jobs, productivity, and international competitiveness than we gain.

I am also grateful for the support which this committee has given to the President's Caribbean Basin initiative. Like open market policies in general, the trade and investment proposals in the Caribbean Basin initiative appear to many critics to involve considerable costs. We have tried to make clear to the Congress and to the public that the long-term benefits of strong and dynamic economies in the Caribbean Basin are far greater to the U.S. economy than any short-term costs. I believe that that message is becoming clearer and better understood, and I am optimistic that the Congress will take the action necessary this month or early in December to pass the two remaining portions of the initiative—namely the one-way free trade area and the investment incentive.

For my main theme tonight, however, I would like to turn to a somewhat more heartening subject than the challenge of fighting protectionism. I would like to talk about a part of the Caribbean Basin initia-

---

[15] Source: *Current Policy* No. 442, November 8, 1982, Bureau of Public Affairs, Department of State; also printed in Department of State *Bulletin*, February 1983, pp. 79–83. The address was given in Washington. Provisions 806 and 807 in the U.S. tariff schedule provide that goods assembled abroad from U.S.-made components pay duty only on the value of the assembly and not on the U.S. components.

tive which has received very little public attention but which nevertheless is functioning effectively already. Most discussions of the initiative focus only on the legislation which we have presented to the Congress. But there is a range of activities already underway in this administration that began under authority in existing legislation. I would like to briefly discuss these programs with you. None of these programs is of dramatic or startling scope. None of them will turn the economies of the region around single-handedly. However, taken as a whole there is already a significant impact derived from the initiative in supporting the efforts of the Caribbean Basin countries themselves.

This portion of the initiative under prior legislation involves activities by every interested agency of the U.S. Government. It derives from a strong commitment by the President and his individual Cabinet officials to devote as many resources as possible to strengthening each agency's programs in the Caribbean Basin region. Given the extraordinarily difficult budgetary constraints that all government agencies face these days, the scope of the programs which I am about to describe would not have been possible without the personal commitments of top Cabinet-level officials within this administration.

The first sector that I would like to discuss is agriculture. Agriculture still forms the basis of most of this region's economies, but output has been growing slowly recently and per capita food production in many countries has been declining. A high proportion of land is idle or badly used. Services to the agricultural sector are deficient. In general agriculture is viewed by many as an unpromising and backward occupation. There is thus a great need not only for expansion of production but also a thoroughgoing modernization. Despite the very significant programs which we have had in the region for years through the U.S. AID program, much remains to be done. A revitalization of the agricultural sector is crucial to meet the food needs of the region's growing population, as well as to increase export earnings.

To an important extent, many of these problems can be traced to inappropriate government policies that provided inadequate incentives to producers. I will address this policy issue later. Technical assistance is also crucial to improved performance, and the U.S. Department of Agriculture (USDA) has put together a substantial program in this area.

First, USDA is promoting an increased regional understanding of U.S. agricultural health and sanitary regulations. This includes providing technical assistance for inspection procedures, for the operation of fumigation facilities, and for training in enforcing health and sanitary regulations.

Second, USDA is offering technical assistance to the Caribbean Basin countries to better gear their agricultural production to the standards of the world market. This involves assistance on how to achieve acceptable quality standards, procedures for proper labeling and testing, and techniques for minimizing losses during distribution and storage.

Third, USDA is strengthening agricultural research and technology transfer through institutions within the Caribbean Basin area and at existing facilities in the United States. Particularly important in this regard is the enhancement of the Mayaguez Institute for Tropical Agriculture in Puerto Rico.

Fourth, USDA has begun to play an important role in facilitating the involvement of U.S. agribusiness in the Caribbean Basin countries. A recently established Agribusiness Promotion Council will advise USDA on particular programs to insure that projects are appropriately designed for the individual conditions of the Caribbean Basin countries.

Fifth, USDA will assist governments on the management and conservation of forest, soil, and water resources.

Sixth, USDA is ready to provide technical assistance to Caribbean Basin governments or private institutions to develop or improve crop credit insurance schemes. This will help to stimulate farmers to use more modern technology and increase productivity.

Seventh, USDA is establishing an agricultural information center for U.S. business. This would provide a single source for U.S. traders and investors, as well as for Caribbean Basin exporters to obtain necessary market information and opportunities for agricultural investment.

Another very interesting effort in the agricultural field is being made by the Peace Corps. Peace Corps volunteers are sometimes uniquely placed to see what people with fancier titles or offices might miss. The Peace Corps is modifying some of its programs and training to help volunteers analyze both the opportunities and the problems regarding the modernization and expansion of small-scale agricultural business. The Peace Corps has already begun to train some volunteers to perform prefeasibility studies and help develop business and marketing plans primarily in, but not limited to, agribusiness.

Interestingly, the Peace Corps training initiatives pick up another of President Reagan's themes—private sector involvement. The training of volunteers to assist in developing better business planning is also underway through private groups and increased cooperation with the Agency for International Development (AID) and other governmental organizations.

Let me turn now to the industrial area. Industrial modernization has been one of the top priorities of countries in this region for years. The share of manufacturing in gross domestic product is still low—under 20 percent in most countries. All of these countries offer small internal markets, and most firms in the region are small and inexperienced in—perhaps fearful of—operating in larger foreign markets. There is a significant lack of such crucial management skills as marketing, quality control, and financial management. And yet the region also has very significant assets. Most countries, especially in the English-speaking Caribbean, have a high level of social services with a generally well-educated healthy labor force.

The basic infrastructure in most countries is at least adequate, although there are significant maintenance problems and considerable need for improvement. Above all, most of these countries have leadership which realizes the need for providing an appropriate policy environment and incentives to the private sector. It certainly is a clear policy priority to encourage industrial growth as indispensable to absorb the high levels of unemployment in the region and to generate production for exports to turn the balance-of-payments crisis around. New investments both by local business and by foreign investors is clearly recognized as a critical need to regenerate and expand the productive base in these countries.

The Department of Commerce in March opened its Caribbean Basin Business Information Center to provide comprehensive economic information to U.S. business representatives interested in dealing in the Caribbean Basin. The response of the U.S. business community has been dramatic; literally thousands of companies have asked for guidance on trade and investment opportunities. Commerce experts are prepared to brief U.S. business on the policies and practices of Caribbean Basin countries and provide practical advice to resolve specific problems facing U.S. business representatives. The center has developed a wide network of contacts in the Caribbean Basin in both the government and private sectors and is thus well placed to arrange appropriate contacts for individual U.S. investors and business representatives. Commerce also serves as a clearinghouse for referring companies to other specialized U.S. Government programs focusing on business development in the Caribbean Basin. The center also works with local Department of Commerce district offices throughout the United States in arranging seminars on business opportunities in the Caribbean Basin area. The first of these regional seminars will be held November 12 in New Orleans. It will include a comprehensive group of U.S. Government experts and representatives from Caribbean Basin companies. The center thus offers a single location for comprehensive and efficient services to U.S. business representatives to find out how to sell their products in the Caribbean Basin, how to invest in that area, and how to buy from the region.

Related to the Department of Commerce's work in improving the information flow to U.S. business is the wider governmental effort to help countries in the area improve their investment climate. Several agencies of the U.S. Government, led by the Office of the U.S. Trade Representative, have developed a worldwide program of bilateral investment treaties. I see this as an important and highly visible way to improve the investment climate in developing countries. The countries of the Caribbean Basin have expressed particularly keen interest in the program, and we have recently concluded an agreement with Panama. This treaty is designed to provide a clear set of rights and obligations of the host government, of the foreign investor, and of the U.S. Government. The U.S. Government has developed a prototype or model treaty containing the following key elements:

—Provisions concerning entry and duration of investment;

—Treatment for established U.S. investors which is no less favorable than that given domestic investors and other foreign investors;

—Prompt, adequate, and effective compensation in the event of nationalization;

—Unrestricted repatriation and other transfers of assets; and

—Dispute settlement provisions.

I find it particularly interesting that several European governments have already in place a set of similar arrangements and are interested in expanding this network. We may, therefore, be on the threshold of a major clarification of the way in which foreign investors are expected to operate. The treaty program insures that the concerns of all parties are fully taken into account. I, therefore, believe that the investment regime which results from the treaty program will be a lasting one.

To date we have signed two agreements with Egypt and Panama. So we have a lot of work ahead of us before my hopes for this program are fully realized. However, the advantages that flow from improved and stable investment climates are increasingly recognized by developing countries. There is growing interest in this program, and we are ready to discuss it with any interested country.

One of the key agencies in supporting U.S. private activities in developing countries has been the Overseas Private Investment Corporation (OPIC). OPIC is very significantly increasing its activities in the Caribbean Basin. Its programs offer insurance to U.S. investors operating in developing countries to cover political risks—expropriation, war, and inconvertibility. This is the core of OPIC's activities and an important incentive for investment in the region. In fiscal years (FY) 1981 and 1982, 47 new projects in the Caribbean Basin were insured by OPIC for a total of $361 million of new project investment.

A smaller but increasingly important function of OPIC has been finance, including direct loans to small and medium-sized joint ventures. In FY 1981 and 1982, OPIC supported 18 projects in the Caribbean Basin for a total of $149 million of new project financing. In FY 1982, OPIC also supported 16 investment feasibility studies in eight Caribbean Basin countries.

Together these OPIC programs represent more than a doubling of what OPIC was doing in FY 1980. And I expect that these activities will continue to increase in the coming years.

OPIC has also been particularly active in organizing investment missions to this region. The missions which OPIC led to Jamaica and Haiti in late 1981 were highly successful. Another mission is planned for the eastern Caribbean area this month, in addition to followup visits to Jamaica and Haiti. A particularly innovative and exciting program is the investment "telemission." Two weeks ago OPIC and AID cosponsored such a mission for the Caribbean area. The mission brought together, by use of satellite television links, business and government representatives from several cities of the United States with their counterparts in the English-speaking Caribbean, Haiti, and the Dominican Republic. The resulting lively discussion of investment and trade opportunities and problems promises to result in some interesting and significant new investment flows.

Finally, OPIC is making a major effort to reach out into the business community rather than just respond to inquiries coming into its office. OPIC has instituted a number of procedures to improve the information flow to U.S. businesses about its programs and the opportunities in the Caribbean Basin.

The Export-Import Bank is also active in this region. The top management of the Export-Import Bank (Eximbank) has enthusiastically supported the Caribbean Basin initiative and strengthened the focus of the bank onto this region. In FY 1981, $555 million in credits, insurance, and guarantees were committed by Eximbank to Caribbean Basin purchasers of U.S. goods and services. The bank hopes to improve this performance significantly over the next few years, keeping in mind of course its statutory constraint of operating only where there is reasonable prospect of repayment. The bank also is expanding its guaranty facilities for short-term credits to local commercial banks in credit-worthy markets.

Let me now turn to an area in which work is underway, but in which we have not yet developed a specific program. This is the area of transportation. Virtually everyone concerned with the problems of the Caribbean Basin agrees that improved accessibility for people and goods is an extremely important element. We have found this to be a particularly difficult area in which to devise solutions to the problems we know exist. To oversimplify the problem somewhat, it appears that this is one of those vicious circles. Costs are high in the Caribbean Basin area partly because traffic volumes are relatively small and routes are fragmented, while the high-cost transport system discourages the development of more efficient operations and greater volume. How to break this vicious circle is still a major unresolved question, and it is a prominent item on our future agenda.

As a first step, we are trying to define more precisely what the problems and constraints are. In a meeting arranged by Caribbean/Central American Action with shippers early this year, we came to the conclusion that—contrary to some of our own expectations—capacity is not a problem, even assuming significant growth in trade over the next few years. The problems in this low-volume/high-tariff situation appear to be in the structure of routes, in the operation of port facilities, and possibly in marketing. We are planning a similar diagnostic meeting with the airlines, and we are in contact with other institutions which have been working on this issue, including, interestingly enough, CARICOM (the Caribbean Common Market) and the European Community. We are also analyzing comments on transportation problems which AID officers and others in the field have reported.

AID has long had important programs in the basin area. But the overall approach of our economic assistance policy toward the region has changed in three very significant ways.

First, the Caribbean Basin has clearly become a higher priority in our global economic assistance program, and the level of our program to the region has just about doubled since FY 1980. In that year (FY 1980), our programs to the Caribbean Basin added up to $324 million. In FY 1982, our regular programs amounted to $475 million, to which we added $350 million in the special supplemental for a total of $825 million. For FY 1983 we are requesting about $665 million for the region, and we are anticipating future programs for FY 1984 and beyond at roughly that order of magnitude, although I must caution that final decisions on those budgets have not yet been taken.

Second, AID is paying much greater attention to economic policy issues in its assistance programs. AID is upgrading its economic analysis capabilities and is working to maintain a close dialogue with Basin governments on key policy issues and to assist them in implementing reforms. Because of their impact on private sector activity, government policies in such areas as agricultural pricing and exchange rates are extremely important to overall economic performance.

Third, a very significant change has been an increased emphasis on private sector support. This is a broad-based change, but I would like to cite several specific and innovative programs as illustrative of our overall efforts. Costa Rica's Agro-Industrial and Export Bank—called BANEX for short—is one striking example. AID's $10 million loan commitment last year was a crucial factor in bringing this institution about. It is new and quite small but surprisingly successful already. It provides an integrated program of credit, export management assistance, and export-oriented banking services for producers and traders of nontraditional Costa Rican exports.

Two things about this project are particularly significant in my mind. First, this is a privately owned bank in Costa Rica's state-owned banking system—conceived, implemented, and managed by the Costa Rican private sector. It has shown a degree of innovation, risk taking, and sound management which is an important example to the whole Costa Rican economy—and perhaps to the region as a whole—about what the private sector can accomplish even in very difficult economic circumstances. Secondly, the institution is dedicated not just to supporting existing exporters but to developing new nontraditional export lines—that means searching out potential export products, finding markets, establishing distribution channels, and insuring product quality standards and reliable delivery systems. This comprehensive approach to the problem of export promotion is another way in which this institution is an example to the rest of the Costa Rican and regional economy.

So as not to take up too much of your time, let me tick off a few other innovative AID projects which are underway or in the planning stages and which are specifically directed at the private sector:

—A loan to establish the Caribbean Agricultural Trading Company, an inter-island marketing project which will stimulate increased trade and agricultural production in the eastern Caribbean;

—A loan to establish a new, privately owned development finance company in Haiti;

—A loan to Jamaica to provide investment funds for equity and debt financing for medium-size agroindustrial and manufacturing enterprises;

—Grants to establish a Caribbean Basin information network as well as to support an emerging twin-chamber program whereby U.S. Chambers of Commerce are linked to business associations in the basin countries for the purpose of stimulating trade and investment opportunities;

—A loan to establish a regional development bank in the eastern Caribbean; and

—Joint OPIC–AID support for a marketing campaign and investment missions to increase the awareness of the U.S. business community about investment opportunities in the Caribbean.

Let me say just a few words about the role of Puerto Rico and the U.S. Virgin Islands within the Caribbean Basin initiative. We all recognize that Puerto Rico and the U.S. Virgin Islands are important components of the U.S. presence in the Caribbean area. Clearly we need to insure that the economic development of the U.S. possessions is enhanced by U.S. policy toward the Caribbean region, and we welcome the contribution that these possessions are making to implementation of the Caribbean Basin initiative.

The U.S. Government has been in close consultation with the Governments of Puerto Rico and the U.S. Virgin Islands about the Caribbean Basin initiative and their role in it. Suggestions made by these governments have been taken into account in designing Caribbean Basin initiative proposals and legislation.

Puerto Rico and the U.S. Virgin Islands will play a major role in technical assistance, private sector development, and transportation within the Caribbean region. In fact, we see these areas as a focal point for assistance to the whole region. Several ways in which this can occur are as follows:

—Strengthening the Tropical Agricultural Research Center in Mayaguez, Puerto Rico;

—Funding for an Eastern Caribbean Center for Educational, Cultural, Technical, and Scientific Interchange at the College of the Virgin Islands;

—Use of Puerto Rican and U.S. Virgin Islands facilities, personnel, and firms in technical assistance programs and development projects; and

—Expansion of airports in the U.S. Virgin Islands and other measures to encourage the development of Puerto Rico and the Virgin Islands as a transportation hub for the Caribbean region.

Finally, I am pleased to note that Puerto Rico is already active in promoting closer links with other Caribbean Basin countries. Particularly noteworthy are the broad-ranging programs of technical cooperation with Jamaica and with St. Lucia.

Let me conclude by describing to you a general interagency effort, led by AID, to devise an overall strategy in support of the private sector for each of the Caribbean Basin countries. The object of the exercise is to develop concrete plans to promote a more dynamic and productive private sector. Our efforts are primarily within the U.S. Government, but we are consulting closely with the U.S. private sector and with representatives of interested governments and private sectors of the Caribbean Basin region.

The general approach is first to assess which areas in each country offer the greatest potential for augmenting production for local consumption and for exports and, secondly, to identify constraints in moving toward this goal. We assume that major constraints in most cases will be such intangibles as management experience and marketing knowhow, particularly in the export sector. But there are likely to be also some very specific problems in the areas of financing and infrastructure. Finally, we also will want to identify specific disincentives, including those derived from governmental policies.

Out of this assessment of potential and constraints, we plan to devise a long-term strategy to promote a productive private sector. This would involve actions by the local business community, by local governments, by U.S. Government agencies, and by the U.S. private sector. Some of the devices that might be useful in our joint efforts would be:

—Efficient investment promotion offices and missions;

—Seminars, training, and other human resources development;

—Improved marketing networks;

—Trading companies; and

—Technology transfer programs.

What I have tried to show is that there is already underway within the U.S. Government a large, although quiet, effort to help the people of the Caribbean Basin turn their countries into dynamic and productive economies offering tangible hope for prosperity and political stability. Much remains to be done. And there are probably new issues and new areas that are still out there waiting to challenge us. But the effort has begun even while we are still seeking congressional approval for the major trade and investment incentives embodied in the legislation.

Obviously our success is dependent on you, the private sector. We can help provide information, encourage more rational economic policies by the Caribbean Basin governments, and provide some incentives and assistance through our various U.S. Government programs and through the trade and investment programs which are awaiting congressional action. But all of this is just support for what you, the private sector, can do.

There is a growing wave of interest within the U.S. private sector in the Caribbean Basin region. Some of the most impressive people of the U.S. business community have devoted large amounts of their high-value time to supporting the initiative and to helping turn the economies of the Caribbean Basin around. I need only mention the establishment of such institutions as the U.S. Business Committee on Jamaica, Caribbean/Central American Action, and the CBI Coalition. Existing organizations such as the Council of the Americas, the U.S. Chamber of Commerce, and the Association of Chambers of Commerce in Latin America have also been generous in their support. And I want to emphasize my gratitude for the efforts that this committee has made in support of expanding trade and investment with the Caribbean Basin and other developing regions of the world.

I ask you to intensify those efforts. I think the opportunities are there and will increase. The payoff—in terms of promoting the U.S. national interest, as well as the individual interest of private business—will be substantial.

Document 703

Transcript of a White House Press Briefing, San José, December 3, 1982[16]

Meeting With Salvadoran President Magaña

MR. SPEAKES. Let me have your attention please. We are about to begin the background on the meeting with the President of El Salvador. It will be on background, attributed to a senior American official, and following this briefing we will have the joint communiqué, which is a page and a half, single-spaced. It will be available for you at the conclusion of the briefing.

Also one other announcement. There is a good possibility that we will be able to go back to our original schedule for tomorrow using helicopters. If that takes place you will get a notice under your door later tonight. Otherwise plan to follow the revised schedule.

SENIOR ADMINISTRATION OFFICIAL. Good evening. The President and President Magaña of El Salvador met together for about 45 minutes tonight; Secretary Shultz, their Foreign Minister Fidel Chavez Mena also present.

President Reagan expressed strong support for the efforts being made by the Salvadoran Government to introduce democratic institutions, continued land reforms, and human rights abuses. He also expressed support for the ongoing effort at containing the insurgency. The Salvadoran President gave a detailed description of the human rights situation in his country and the efforts that have been made to bring human rights abuses under control—progress that has been made. He also gave an account of the military situation currently, including the action which is taking place, the government offensive in the eastern province of La Union, and he dwelled at some length on the difficult economic situation that had been brought about by worldwide recession and also by the effects of the insurgency, indicating that there were a number of entrepreneurs and factories that were ready to start production again but that the lack of foreign exchange made it very difficult to do so in many cases because much of Salvadoran industry is dependent upon imported materials to process.

The President stated his interest in seeing that the—those responsible for the murders of United States citizens in El Salvador—churchwomen and the two American land reform workers—those responsible for those murders be brought to justice promptly and effectively.

The two leaders also discussed the general situation in Central America, the effect of continued substantial arms deliveries to the insurgents in El Salvador from Nicaragua being an important—indeed decisive factor in the continuation of the insurgency. It was a very warm meeting and we will have for you in Spanish and in English a short

---

16 Source: Office of the Press Secretary to the President. This was a background briefing conducted by senior administration officials in the Hotel Irazu beginning at 8:55 p.m. President Reagan was in Costa Rica as part of his trip to Latin America, November 30 to December 4, 1982. For a Department of State press briefing on this trip, December 6, 1982, see document 620.

communiqué of about a page and a half which is issued by the two Presidents following their talk.

Questions.

Q. Are we going to renew our military aid? I mean, was the President satisfied with the statements on human rights?

SENIOR ADMINISTRATION OFFICIAL. The question is, are we going to renew our military aid? Was the President satisfied on human rights? The questions involved in certification were discussed in detail, however no conclusion was reached on them. The certification itself, as you know, is due in January. The United States has an ongoing program of military assistance. In order to continue it, it must certify every 180 days on four subjects which I think are familiar to many of you. Those subjects were discussed but no conclusion was reached.

Q. Well, the President certainly seemed to indicate that he was favorably inclined. He said that based on everything he has heard, they would certainly be satisfied—certified.

SENIOR ADMINISTRATION OFFICIAL. The President, as I say, expressed strong support for the Salvadoran efforts to introduce democratic institutions and carry on the reforms, bringing human rights abuses under control. This was not a certification excercise per se.

Q. When the President indicated his interest in having the murderers of American citizens brought to justice, did the President of El Salvador indicate that any progress had been made in those cases?

SENIOR ADMINISTRATION OFFICIAL. The question was, did the President of El Salvador indicate that any progress had been made in bringing to justice the murderers of American citizens in El Salvador? President Magaña referred to the start of the trial of those accused of murdering the four American churchwomen as evidence of progress, the fact that two guardsmen are to be tried also for the murder of the two American land reform workers.

He did note, however, that in the case of Lieutenant Lopez Siprian, believed, alleged to be the intellectual author of the murder of the AIFLD workers, that the Salvadorian court had set that aside and, indeed, dismissed the case against him, an action which occurred yesterday.

The President told us that there were, in fact, other remedies that could be looked at under Salvadorian law. He made, however, no final prediction as to how this case could be handled, other than that it would be continued.

Q. You say that the President promised to bring to justice promptly and effectively those who have done wrong things. Do you recall how long ago it was that the four churchwomen were murdered?

SENIOR ADMINISTRATION OFFICIAL. The four churchwomen were murdered on December 2 of 1980. The investigation which finally broke the case was done outside the normal legal system and it concluded in February of 1982 as a result of a special three-man commission named by the armed forces.

Since that time, the entire basis of evidence, all the testimony of the witnesses, has been redone, as required under Salvadoran law, by the prosecuting judge and the case prepared and is now being tried.

Q. Aside from the money we already know about, in response to President Magaña's appeal for help in foreign exchange to his factories that are just waiting to begin production, did we make any new promises of bridging loans, perhaps, something in the way of new aid?

SENIOR ADMINISTRATION OFFICIAL. No. The need was outlined, but no remedies were proposed at the meeting.

Q. If I may, did President Reagan suggest that he would take a look at this request or this need?

SENIOR ADMINISTRATION OFFICIAL. One of the issues which the economy of El Salvador faces is the fact that the Common Market, Central American Common Market, which groups a number of countries in this area and which has proved to be quite successful in promoting trade and industry, is not functioning.[17] Its clearing mechanism has not been working for the last year and a half as a result of the disruptions caused by the Salvadorian war, by the actions of Nicaragua and a number of other factors.

One of the questions raised was how could this Common Market be—going

---

17 On December 13, 1960, representatives of El Salvador, Guatemala, Honduras, and Nicaragua signed a general treaty on Central American economic integration in Managua, Nicaragua. The treaty entered into force, June 3, 1961. Costa Rica subsequently adhered to the agreement. For documentation, see *American Foreign Policy: Current Documents, 1961*, pp. 268–278.

again. Nobody has a clear answer to that. But I think it's an indication of one direction in which we'll all have to look.

Q. Could I ask you whether President Magana requested economic aid—

SENIOR ADMINISTRATION OFFICIAL. No. No, no.

Q. —or military aid you describe.

SENIOR ADMINISTRATION OFFICIAL. He described the economic situation as very serious, all the more serious because, in fact, there were the means to get the economy started again if we could find some release of the foreign exchange constraint.

Q. Most of us haven't seen the pool report of the President's remarks yet. Would you amplify a little bit more about what his thinking is on the recertification? Is he, in other words, prepared under current evidence to go ahead with this? And if so, does that—I mean, is that what he said or is that what he meant? Does that mean that unless things deteriorate further he will seek recertification? Or is he genuinely awaiting more evidence and is undecided?

SENIOR ADMINISTRATION OFFICIAL. The question was is the President saying that he is satisfied with the evidence that has been presented to him on certification and he's prepared to recommend or will be prepared to recommend that in January or is he stopping short of making that statement?

Let me say again the President is making in this meeting no attempt to decide the question of certification. That is an elaborate process involving the collection of evidence and the weighing of it, which is beginning now again, and which must be presented in mid-January. The President was not saying that he is accomplishing that now. He was expressing, though, very strong support for the goals of the policy that we have been pursuing in El Salvador; that is to say, the creation of the democratic institutions in the reforms in that country, and for the effort that the Salvadoran Government is making to carry those out. Those, by the way, are the goals that are implicit and, in some cases, explicit in the whole certification process.

Maybe we can get one of these that are back here first.

Q. Do you see any significance, sir, in the fact that the President of the Constituent Assembly, Mr. D'Aubuisson was not present in these meetings tonight?

SENIOR ADMINISTRATION OFFICIAL. The question was: Is there any significance in the fact that the President of the Salvadoran Constituent Assembly, Roberto D'Aubuisson, was not present in the meetings tonight? I'm not aware that they normally travel as a leadership group, and I would not attribute any particular significance to that.

Q. Could I follow that up, sir? Could I follow that up?

SENIOR ADMINISTRATION OFFICIAL. Yes, go ahead.

Q. —ask if the current power struggle between D'Abuisson and more moderate conservatives in the military who are linked to President Magaña—if that struggle was discussed between the two Presidents tonight?

SENIOR ADMINISTRATION OFFICIAL. The question was: Was the current power struggle between moderate elements in the military and Roberto D'Aubuisson discussed tonight between the two Presidents? And I would say that questions of internal Salvadoran politics of this kind were not discussed.

Q. On October 29th, Ambassador Hinton did a speech in El Salvador, said everything except aid was going to be cut off unless there was dramatic progress made in four areas?[18] Did the fact that the nuns' killers—or the five accused of killing them have been bound over for trial, sufficient progress since October 29th made the United States Government change not only its rhetoric but its view of certification?

SENIOR ADMINISTRATION OFFICIAL. The question was: Deane Hinton in a speech a month ago all but threatened to see that United States aid to El Salvador would be cut off unless there were progress on murders of American citizens and human rights abuses. Is the fact that the five National Guardsmen are being—have been indicted and are being tried for the murder of the four American churchwomen sufficient to get the United States to continue its assistance?

As you know—I think you know—there are four criteria that have been in the law from the start on certification, which is to say the control of human rights abuses, getting all elements of the armed forces under control, continuing the land reform and carrying out democratic elections. And to that have been added requirements that

---

18 For the text of Hinton's address, see document 701.

progress be made on the murders of the American citizens, so that the question of the indictment trial of the alleged murderers of the American churchwomen is only one element which has to be taken into consideration in making a certification.

Q. Has President Magaña provided any new evidence of Nicaragua's participation in the insurgency in El Salvador?

SENIOR ADMINISTRATION OFFICIAL. The question is: Did President Magaña provide new evidence of the involvement of Nicaragua in the insurgency? Answer: He said, indeed, that he had evidence. We did not discuss it then because we also have evidence to the same end, that substantial flows of logistic support from Nicaragua have continued in recent months and, indeed, throughout this year. We think we have substantial evidence on this now, and so the assertion of President Magaña, on the basis of his evidence, did not surprise us at all. We did not discuss it in detail. Yes.

Q. Did the two discuss any need to raise the level of military advisors and to increase the amount of U.S. military aid to El Salvador?

SENIOR ADMINISTRATION OFFICIAL. The question: Did the two discuss the need to raise the number of military advisors or the amount of military aid to the country? Answer: No, they did not. The number of United States training personnel in El Salvador—where is my colleague?

SENIOR ADMINISTRATION OFFICIAL. Under 55.

SENIOR ADMINISTRATION OFFICIAL. What is it this week?

SENIOR ADMINISTRATION OFFICIAL. It's about 50 for this week.

SENIOR ADMINISTRATION OFFICIAL. About 50. It's bounced up and down in the course of the last year. No discussion of increasing that or of increased military assistance.

Q. Was there any discussion of the prospects to end the war in El Salvador?

SENIOR ADMINISTRATION OFFICIAL. There was substantial discussion about the creating of the peace commission as a means of providing a basis for an amnesty and for the reintegration of dissidents into the political system of El Salvador. And, indeed, that was an important topic of discussion.

Q. And what—I am sorry. Could I have a chance to follow up?

SENIOR ADMINISTRATION OFFICIAL. Please.

Q. What were the conclusions which were reached then?

SENIOR ADMINISTRATION OFFICIAL. The conclusions that were reached were that this is, indeed, an important and necessary step forward that the Salvadoran Government has announced in principle, and intends to implement in the near future.

Q. Who are the members of the Peace Commission?

SENIOR ADMINISTRATION OFFICIAL. The members of the Peace Commission have not been named. Those of the Human Rights Commission have—Church, Army, and three independents, along with one representative of the UPD—the Labor Party, the labor association. Similarly, when the Peace Commission is named, it is expected that it will contain a similar spectrum of Salvadoran society, perhaps not exactly the same.

Q. You said that President Magaña gave a description of the military situation inside El Salvador. Can you tell us what he said about it—how serious it was?

SENIOR ADMINISTRATION OFFICIAL. He said that the government forces were on the offensive, that they had been out to Chalatenango on the Honduran border in the last 3 weeks, and had cleared the province quite efectively. They were now over in La Union, and had had several good days. He expected this action to continue on the part of the Salvadoran Army. It was an upbeat description of the military action.

SENIOR ADMINISTRATION OFFICIAL. The last question here from this gentleman, please.

Q. —of what these two leaders are saying to each other about the violence, how can we be sure of the credibility of what the Salvadoran Government tells us given what they first said about the last shooting of the Americans and then the later autopsy showing powder burns about them?

SENIOR ADMINISTRATION OFFICIAL. The question is what are the two leaders really saying to each other? How can we be sure of what the Salvadoran Government is saying given the last experience concerning the shooting of an American citizen in which a report given originally was changed or proved to be incomplete or inaccurate as a result of an autopsy?

President Magaña, I think, has been one of the leaders in developing the Human

Rights Commission concept, because he thinks that it is essential to have an alternative source of information, and above all a place where people can go who have been threatened or have been the victims, or whose friends and relatives have been the victims of human rights abuses to obtain redress. The purpose is to get an instrument which is out of the direct line of command of the government which nonetheless can act by persuasion on the rest of Salvadoran society.

As you know, the United States Embassy, headed by Ambassador Hinton who is here, spends a great deal of time trying to document the human rights situation in El Salvador, and seeking to use its influence to obtain redresses in the cases that it can and that it identifies.

So we feel that we do not have to take the word of any Salvadoran on this issue. We attempt to inform ourselves. But that should not be read as, in any way, impugning our faith in the judgment of President Magaña, who I think is sincerely, deeply committed to diminishing human rights abuses in that country.

Mr. Speakes. Sorry, we cannot take any more. We have now been informed that the green schedule, which is the original with the helicopters on it, is operative. We will slip a note under the door.

The communiqué is available in the rear, I believe. Also, the advance text of tomorrow's speech will be available at 10:30 a.m. in the Press Office.

The Press. Thank you.

Document 704

Statement by the Assistant Secretary of State for Inter-American Affairs (Enders) Before Two Subcommittees of the House Foreign Affairs Committee, December 14, 1982 (Extract)[19]

Dealing With the Reality of Cuba

Mr. Enders. Thank you very much, Congressman Bingham.

Let me begin by associating myself from the other end of the street with what Congressman Barnes had to say.[20] We worked together on a very large number of issues, international energy, trade, and foreign assistance over the years, nuclear questions, and I have been privileged to know you well, sir, and have found that all of this has been very constructive and very helpful.

I, too, am sorry to see that you are leaving this body, and look forward to staying in touch.

Mr. Bingham. Thank you very much.

Mr. Enders. Mr. Chairman, you asked in your invitation for an assessment of Cuba's role in the world and our relationship to it.

There is nothing quite like it.

Cuba is at once a would-be foreign policy giant ceaselessly projecting political-military influence overseas, and it is an economic dwarf that for years has showed itself incapable of providing for the material progress of its people.

More than 70,000 Cubans, both civilians and members of the armed forces, are abroad on various internationalist missions, most of them military, in the Caribbean, Central America, to Southeastern and Central Africa, to both sides of the Red Sea, and even Asia; and over the last 2 years, Cuba has been engaged in an arms buildup which has been unprecedented since 1962. In each of the 2 years, we expect that some [where] between 60,000 and 70,000 tons of armaments will have been imported into Cuba.

Cuban domestic policy has registered, I think, what can be characterized as a general failure.

Organized in the familiar Soviet command model, the economy receives growing Soviet assistance in grants, subsidies for oil, and purchase of sugar at high prices. Yet although Cuban aid alone from the Soviet Union is now equivalent to more than a quarter of Cuban GNP, per-capita income in Cuba has been stagnant and is falling steadily relative to the rest of Latin America. Even the much acclaimed initial improvements in social and health services have lost luster with the passage of time.

Infant mortality and life expectancy already met high standards in 1959; under Castro, they have improved less than in many other developing countries. For al-

---

[19] Source: *Issues in United States-Cuban Relations: Hearings Before the Subcommittees on International Economic Policy and Trade and the Subcommittee on Inter-American Affairs of the Committee on Foreign Affairs, House of Representatives, Ninety-seventh Congress, Second Session* (Washington, 1983), pp. 2–7; for Enders' prepared statement, see *ibid.*, pp. 8–20.

[20] Not printed; for text, see *ibid.*, p. 2. 0

most a quarter of a century, and this is important, social mobility has been capped by the permanence of a self-perpetuating elite more rigid than any traditional oligarchy, the same people in the same places.

This configuration of domestic stagnation and foreign ambition is the legacy of a generation of struggle to export the revolution. For its first 10 years in power the new Communist government in Havana tried to replicate its revolution elsewhere in Latin America.

Virtually every country was affected. In Venezuela, Colombia, Guatemala, Peru, and Bolivia, guerrilla forces actually flourished briefly. One by one, however, these Cuban-assisted insurrections were defeated, and following the death of Che Guevara on a Bolivian hillside in 1967, Cuba stopped trying in Latin America—for a while.

Instead, it concentrated on Africa, where weaker, less legitimate governments offered better opportunities. Cuba had maintained extensive contacts and some military missions in Africa since the early 1960's. By the mid-1970's, Cuban troops were fighting in Angola to assure the supremacy of the MPLA over its rivals. The stage had been set for the appearance of Cuban troops under Soviet command in Ethiopia.

In 1978, Cuba turned once again to Latin America. Central America, where high economic growth had not been matched by political change and where repressive, narrowly-based military governments clung to power, seemed ripe for revolution.

Cuba's intervention helped tip the scale against the Somoza government in Nicaragua. El Salvador, Guatemala, Honduras, and Colombia were targeted as follow-ons. In each case Cuba attempted to weld together disparate local revolutionary factions into a unity, provided training in Cuba and supplied—or arranged for the supply of—arms to attack the existing government.

Over the last 3 years, traces on individual weapons and analysis of other guerrilla materiel and documents have revealed a pattern that, to use the words of the September 22, 1982 staff report[21] by the Subcommittee on Oversight and Evaluation of the House Permanent Select Committee on Intelligence "showed Cuba, with Nicaraguan participation, to be heavily involved in the coordination, control, and movement" of a substantial amount of arms and other supplies obtained from Communist countries.

Throughout most of this period our response has been to help the intended victims of the export of revolution to defend themselves. In the 1960's, this policy was entirely successful. The more recent campaign in Latin America opened with a success for Cuba—the triumph of Sandinistas in Managua. But, provided we remain willing to help threatened countries in Central America, there will be no more.

At the same time, we have sought to complicate the already difficult task of running a command economy in Cuba by withholding the trade and credit of Cuba's natural market, the United States. It is not clear whether socialist Cuba ever had much growth potential. Our embargo has made sure that the cost to the U.S.S.R. of preventing per-capita income from falling has increased steadily.

Finally, we have kept Cuba at arm's-length, and have thus denied it the legitimacy—and consequently access to other governments in the hemisphere—normal relations with us would confer.

These have been the basic elements of our policy generally, and they are now. But a major effort was made in 1975–80, under two administrations, to develop an alternative. During these years, we attempted to moderate Cuba's behavior by talks aimed at progressive normalization of our relations. The theory was that an isolated Cuba had no stake in the international community, and thus had no reason to exercise restraint.

This bipartisan effort failed. Not only did it not induce Cuba to moderate its behavior, arguably it resulted in or at least was followed by even bolder, more aggressive action by Castro.

Let me review the record, if I could, in a little bit of detail. In 1975, we made our first secret contacts, suggesting the exploration of ways to remove tension and hostility. Late in that year, the Cubans sent troops into Angola.

In 1977, we again started talking seriously to the Cubans, this time much more ambitiously, saying we wanted to create conditions in which the legacy of the past—the embargo and the political tension—

---

[21] *U.S. Intelligence Performance in Central America: Achievements and Selected Instances of Concern,* Staff Report, Subcommittee on Oversight and Evaluation, Permanent Select Committee on Intelligence, Ninety-seventh Congress, Second Session, Committee Print (Washington, 1982).

could be overcome. In very high-level, secret talks, our negotiators explored a series of steps with the eventual goal of removal of the embargo and full diplomatic relations, in return for curbs on Cuban activities regarding Puerto Rico and a gradual withdrawal of the more than 20,000 Cuban troops from Angola. After all, the civil war was over. While we talked, Cuba went into Ethiopia.

Conversations continued. In mid-1978, Cuba launched upon a new aggressive strategy in Central America, uniting violent factions first in Nicaragua, then El Salvador, then Guatemala, committing them to the destruction of their established governments.

Talks went on. In 1980, Castro turned the desire of many of his countrymen to flee Cuba into a hostile act against the United States—the Mariel boatlift.

This record suggests that Cuba believes that a process of negotiation with the United States is in its interest. During those years, Cuban representatives repeatedly argued that the United States must take no action to help governments in Central America because that would undercut the negotiation process. In other words, the process was intended to restrain us, but it did not restrain them.

And the process could be, and indeed was used to maintain Cuban access to other countries in the hemisphere. After all, Havana argued to Latin American governments, the United States is talking to us; you should cut your own deal with us now while you can.

Cuba's desire to recreate the process, if not the results, of negotiations was evident again this spring when a campaign of signals was launched involving private U.S. citizens who were told Cuba was anxious to discuss settlements in Central America as well as other differences between the United States and Cuba.[22]

I have been asked, why didn't the United States respond to these signals? Couldn't it have been an opportunity to seek a new direction in Cuban-American affairs?

The answer is this: We had indeed taken the initiative to sound out Cuba's interests and intentions at very high level, first in November 1981 and again in March 1982. In each case we were told, yes, Cuba wants to talk with the United States. But in each case we were told that what could be talked about was the bilateral agenda—migration, tourism, intelligence overflights, the embargo, diplomatic relations, Guantanamo.

Puerto Rico and the Third Country agenda—Cuba's aggressive actions in Central America and Africa—were not negotiable. We must, we were told, learn to accept social change, but Cuba could not compromise on its commitment to fraternal national liberation organizations. In other words, Cuba would receive concessions, not give them.

It is noteworthy that Cuba did not choose to carry on these discussions through existing channels, but used as the medium persons outside government who had no knowledge of previous or current exchanges when it launched its campaign of signals in behalf of negotiations a month later. We concluded that, once again, Castro did not wish to talk seriously, but did wish to strike an apparently conciliatory posture.

If you are interested in pursuing this question of the campaign of signals and how it was organized, we do have some classified information which we would be happy to make available to you on what was done and how that was done, if you and other members of the committee wish to see it.

It is quite interesting.

I would not exclude testing the Cubans again at some point on the possibilities of discussions. But the record—and the current posture—give little encouragement.

There are those who say we should go beyond past negotiating approaches, with the explicit or implicit trade of normalization with the United States in return for Cuban restraint in Third Countries. We should drop Third Country demands, these experts say, and normalize our bilateral relations.

The magnetism of American society and economy would then, in the long run, prove irresistible. We should do away with economic measures that limit bilateral trade and financial transactions, renew diplomatic relations, and welcome Cuba back to the Organization of American States—assuming that Cuba were willing to return, and that other states would accept its return.

On the record, at least, Castro would welcome any opportunity to take advantage of relaxed economic relations with the Unit-

---

22 See the article by Anthony Lewis in *New York Times,* May 6, 1982, p. A27.

ed States. And he might be more cooperative on some bilateral issues, at least at the outset.

But history also makes unmistakably clear that Castro would not tolerate any loosening of state control inside Cuba, and that he would continue and perhaps even intensify the activities which threaten to undermine our national security and that of our friends. And that is precisely the problem with this approach: It would address neither the basic inequities of the Cuban system nor the fundamental orientation of Cuban foreign policy, which is to encourage armed revolution elsewhere along the lines which it took in Cuba.

Others, more ambitious still, want to try to wean Cuba away from the Soviet Union. Even assuming that Castro were of a mind to alter his allegiance to the U.S.S.R.—something Castro, himself, has always denied vehemently, most recently on December 11—the price would be more than we could pay. The Soviet Union's annual economic assistance now approaches the equivalent of $4 billion.

We might have a little difficulty up here in persuading the Congress to replace even a part of that remarkable largesse. Moreover, there is little prospect that Castro, himself, would forsake Soviet military assistance, which enables Cuba to play its chosen role as a nerve center, training ground, and arsenal for revolution in the Third World.

In effect, Soviet military and economic assistance permits the Cuban leaders to go on indulging their taste for war and revolution long after they would otherwise have had to come to terms with their own failures.

If negotiation, unilateral normalization, and weaning away won't work, what remains? What remains is shoring up threatened friends, complicating economic management, withholding legitimacy. This administration has steadfastly helped our friends defend themselves from Cuban interference, and has tightened our economic countermeasures, particularly those designed to deny Cuba the hard currency that Castro uses to help pay for armed violence and terrorism.

And we must not forget the people of Cuba. The most eloquent testimony to their continued resistance is the flight of more than 10 percent of Cuba's population since Castro came to power. This is all the more noteworthy when you think so many of the Marielitos that came to this country were, in fact, kids, very young people who came from all parts of society, and were looking for simple liberty.

Not even the effort by the Cuban Government to tarnish the image of those fleeing Cuba by forcibly expelling common criminals and the mentally ill during the 1980 Mariel boatlift can diminish the heroism and tenacity of the Cuban people. Over two decades of communism have not eradicated the traditional Cuban love of liberty and tolerance for diversity, which is part of the hemisphere's common Western heritage.

We intend to underscore our deep commitment to the Cuban people by responding to their own wish to know the truth by increasing the dissemination of regular, objective, factual news about Cuba. We hope Radio Marti will begin its broadcasts next year.[23] As Jose Marti said, "Witnessing a crime in silence is equivalent to committing it." Nothing illustrates Castro's genuine fear of domestic opinion more than the hysterical denunciations by Cuban authorities of plans for Radio Marti.

Looking over this record, in the end two qualities seem to be needed in dealing with Cuba: Vigilance and patience. Vigilance, because this is an extraordinarily aggressive state, and now a heavily armed one. Patience, because it cannot last forever.

While Castro has been probing Latin America and Africa for new revolutionary opportunities, other developing countries have outperformed Cuba economically and socially. But the worst is still to come. The big growth impulse over the past generation has been the expanding Soviet subsidy. No one believes that a stagnant U.S.S.R. will be willing or able to increase the subsidy in the future as rapidly as in the past.

So, Cuba will fall further and further behind, become less and less relevant to other countries, more and more marginal to the new world. At some point—for all the oppression they suffer—the Cuban people will find a way to repudiate a leadership that thinks that all they need is the glory earned by internationalists oppressing other peoples—and not their own well-being and freedom.

Mr. Chairman, you asked a number of specific questions. I hope sufficiently succinct answers to each of them are in the

---

[23] See document 674.

tables or in an annex to the written testimony.

Could I also introduce Advisor to the Assistant Secretary for Consular Affairs, Ms. B. J. Harper, who is appearing with me this afternoon?

Thank you.

Document 705

Amendment to the Continuing Appropriations for Fiscal Year 1983, December 21, 1982[24]

The Boland Amendment

Sec. 793. None of the funds provided in this Act may be used by the Central Intelligence Agency or the Department of Defense to furnish military equipment, military training or advice, or other support for military activities, to any group or individual, not part of a country's armed forces, for the purpose of overthrowing the Government of Nicaragua or provoking a military exchange between Nicaragua and Honduras.

---

[24] Source: Section 793 of P.L. 97–377 (96 Stat. 1865). Representative Boland, Chairman of the House Permanent Select Committee on Intelligence, offered this amendment as a substitute for an amendment offered by Representative Harkin on December 8, 1982. Harkin's amendment stated:

"None of the funds provided in this Act may be used by the Central Intelligence Agency or the Department of Defense to furnish military equipment, military training or advice, or other support for military activities, to any group or individual, not part of a country's armed forces, for the purpose of assisting that group or individual in carrying out military activities in or against Nicaragua. (*Congressional Record,* 97th Congress, 2d Session (December 8, 1982), p. H9148.)

The House approved the Boland substitute amendment on December 8, 1982, by a margin of 411 to 0. Although the Senate failed to approve a similar amendment proposed by Senator Moynihan, the prohibition passed by the House was retained in conference as section 793 of the continuing resolution providing continuing appropriations for fiscal year 1983. For a fuller discussion of the Boland amendment, see *Congress and Foreign Policy 1982,* Committee on Foreign Affairs, U.S. House of Representatives, Committee Print (Washington, 1983), pp. 87–88.

D. South America

Brazil

Document 706

Statement by the Assistant Secretary of State for Inter-American Affairs (Enders) Before a Subcommittee of the House Foreign Affairs Committee, July 14, 1982[1]

U.S.-Brazilian Relations

As you mentioned, Mr. Chairman,[2] Brazil is a very great country. It is larger in area than the continental United States. It has a great coastline and almost 8,000 miles of unsecured inland borders which touch every South American country except Ecuador and Chile.

I think it is a tribute to the genius of Brazil and the ability of Brazilian diplomacy that in contrast to many of the other states of Latin America, those borders are entirely uncontested between Brazil and its neighbors.

Brazil has a GNP of a quarter of a trillion dollars which makes it, by our count, the eighth largest market economy. It has developed a sophisticated industrial sector which produces a large share of capital goods as well as most of the country's consumer goods.

It has some $23 billion worth of exports, making it a great exporting country. It is interesting to note that Brazil, like the United States, exports about 10 percent of its gross national product and is quite dependent on international trade. Industrialized products make up just about half of its exports.

Brazil is also one of the great agricultural exporters of the world, and is rapidly gaining in terms of the share of the world agricultural trade that it supplies.

All of these statistics are impressive, but we should remember, Mr. Chairman, about

---

[1] Source: *United States-Brazilian Relations: Hearing Before the Subcommittee on Inter-American Affairs of the Committee on Foreign Affairs, House of Representatives, Ninety-seventh Congress, Second Session* (Washington, 1982), pp. 2–7; for Enders' prepared statement, see *ibid.,* pp. 7–22.

[2] Representative Michael D. Barnes.

half of Brazil's national territory remains underdeveloped. It is also true that in the north and northeast, there are areas in which social and economic indices rival those of some of the poorest countries in the world.

Like a lot of other oil importing developing countries, Brazil faces some very substantial economic difficulties in the short term. It is now spending about half its export earnings on oil and the remainder for debt service.

At the end of 1980, there was a serious balance of payments crisis developing which led Brazil to adopt a very stringent monetary and fiscal restraint program which included a program of import demand management.

Inflation, which had been running at very high levels, dropped steadily in the second half of the last year, and extensive export incentives produced a trade surplus of more than $1 billion by the year's end.

However, these forward steps were brought at the cost of a deep recession and by the year's end, the gross domestic product of Brazil registered -2 or -3 percent for the year, the first downward turn of any magnitude in the Brazilian economy in a generation.

That domestic recession now appears to be abating somewhat, and I think that Brazil has shown what a developing country can do when it has to put its economic house in order quickly.

It has done this with great subtleness and flexibility, but I think it is true that the generally poor state of the world economy makes it difficult for Brazil to develop its export-producing capacity for both industrial products and commodities. Undoubtedly, the current difficulties will continue for some time.

Overall, however, I think that everybody who has looked at the way the Brazilians handle their economy, and its great strength and suppleness are convinced that substantial growth will resume in that country relatively soon, and that long, steady upward march that the Brazilians have been noted for will go on.

Now, in political terms, Brazil is just emerging from a period of about 20 years of relatively closed, highly centralized politics. A program of democratic evolution, which they call the Abertura, is gradually moving Brazil toward greater decentralization and more citizen participation in the political process.

Under the Figueiredo administration, the country will hold direct gubernatorial and congressional elections in November. I think all of us can view this evolving effort at democracy with great respect and admiration.

If you look at Brazil's foreign policy, in recent years it has sought to diversify international relationships and to develop new foreign markets.

Brazil has developed economic and trading relationships on a truly global scale, and has earned Brazil respect and influence throughout Europe, Africa, and in the Middle East as well as in this hemisphere.

Brazil's foreign policy prominently features Brazil's status as a developing country, but while expanding its global reach, Brazil maintains a clear identification with Latin America. Over the past 10 years, Brazilian ties with other countries of South America have improved steadily and we expect Brazil will continue to place high priority on the development of continental relations.

Now, the relationship between Brazil and the United States has gone through several phases since our very close cooperation during the Second World War. In the mid-seventies, our relationship was under very substantial stress, but since then, it has improved steadily.

Today, our ties are again sound and characterized by basic shared values, mutual respect and increasing political and economic interaction. This was well-reflected in the visit of President Figueiredo.[3] His exchange of views with President Reagan on global, regional, and bilateral issues was very extensive, very open, and I think exceptionally constructive.

Our basic convergence on major issues was reaffirmed but even where there was disagreement there was understanding and respect.

Both countries are committed to a stable and just international environment with open markets and free economic competition. We both have a vested interest in a peaceful hemisphere free from outside interference.

The South Atlantic crisis which you mentioned, Mr. Chairman, was a major topic of discussion during the visit of President

[3] Regarding President Figueiredo's visit to the United States, see footnote 20 to document 658.

Figueiredo and the exchange made quite clear that while our respective positions are different, our objectives were very similar.

Unlike the United States, Brazil recognizes Argentina's sovereignty over the disputed islands, but like the United States, Brazil does not and did not support the use of force to validate it.

Like the United States, Brazil was and is concerned that the South Atlantic conflict not result in instability or polarization in the hemisphere.

Brazil supported Secretary Haig's efforts to find a peaceful solution to the conflict, and gave its full support to subsequent efforts of the Secretary General, and indeed, advanced specific proposals of its own to promote a negotiated solution within a U.N. framework.

There was very close consultation between the two Presidents and the two governments during the entire period of the crisis.

Now that the fighting is over, we expect that Brazil will use its influence to promote a permanent solution that takes into consideration the interests of all of the parties and contributes to the stability of the hemisphere. That is our objective as well.

Now, in saying that we have a convergence of views on many issues, I do not mean to suggest that there are not differences. There are. It is important to understand that both governments are making a serious effort to resolve or contain them.

For example, a conflict in our respective nuclear legislation and policies has prevented the satisfactory implementation of our nuclear supply relationship under a bilateral nuclear agreement signed in 1972.[4]

Since the agreement was signed in 1972, the Congress passed legislation, the Nuclear Non-Proliferation Act of 1978,[5] which put more stringent conditions on nuclear cooperation and in particular on the kinds of and extent of safeguards that should be obtained from recipient counties in U.S. nuclear cooperation arrangements.

The Brazilian Government has taken the view that the safeguard requirements in the original agreement—that is to say that all material and technology supplied by the United States should be subject to internationally recognized safeguards—are adequate in themselves, and so there has been a difference of view which resulted from differing legislation.

During Vice President Bush's visit to Brazil in October,[6] we were able to find a mutually acceptable means to set this problem aside for later solution. I think it is quite clear, Mr. Chairman, that in this area substantial adjustment between the two countries' policies must be sought if a way to developing nuclear cooperation is to be opened.

There are also divergencies on a number of global political issues, but in most of these cases, the objectives of the United States and of Brazil are similar, even if our perspectives and approaches differ.

In Southern Africa, for example, our objectives are fully compatible, but we view differently some of the points of the overall problem. I think we both are committed to a stable Southern Africa free from outside pressure or influence and we have been in touch with each other on how to achieve that.

Brazil is, as you know, not a member of the Namibian contact group, but has followed that diplomacy very closely.

We now have a very substantial amount of direct investment in Brazil, approximately $8 billion, and American banks hold at least $16 billion of Brazil's roughly $62 billion foreign debt.

Now, that is directly. If you count what goes through London banks, the amount is even higher. We are Brazil's single most important customer in trade, purchasing approximately 18 percent of Brazil's exports. Manufactured goods and iron and steel are the principal Brazilian products sold to the United States.

Brazil, in turn, is an important market for us, and they buy about 19 percent of their imports from us. Altogether, in dollar terms, there is about $8 billion in turnover.

A lot of our day-to-day issues concern trade. Brazil has a critical need to increase trade surpluses and accordingly, provides protection for some of its producers and sometimes seeks to stimulate exports through subsidies.

Such practices stimulate bilateral friction.

[4] For the text of the 1972 U.S.–Brazil agreement on cooperation for civil uses of atomic energy, see 23 UST 2477.

[5] P.L. 95–242; 92 Stat. 120.

[6] Regarding Bush's trip to Latin America, October 11–17, 1981, see Department of State *Bulletin*, January 1982, pp. 12–15.

The other side of the coin is that some of our practices, for example, our use of quotas to protect our own domestic sugar producers and the levying of U.S. tariffs on ethanol imports affect products important to Brazil.

Brazilians believe our sugar quota will cost their exports no less than $400 million in 1982. We believe this figure is much too high, but don't doubt that there will be a cost.

I think you are familiar with the discussions over graduation, switching from developing to developed country rules in international trade and finance.

That is also a difference between us. In our "Generalized System of Preferences," we have graduated some Brazilian products that appear to have reached a world standard of competitiveness in addition to those that meet the absolute competitive need test.

The World Bank also has a graduation policy which we accept and which Brazil continues to question. I think in the case of the international financial institutions where we are talking about a possible graduation toward the end of the decade, the difference may be more in perceptions.

Any graduation would be, in fact, a transitional arrangement that would take a number of years and would involve relatively slow changes in status. I think often when people in Brazil talk about graduation and the international financial institutions, they envisage sort of dropping off the edge at some future point.

That is not the World Bank's idea, and it is certainly not the policy the United States is supporting.

On the security, or military, side of our relationship, I think we can say that it is in most cases adequate to the current needs of both countries. We do have an annual joint security review at the staff level.

We have a fairly constant two-way flow of high-level military officials and except for this year, our Navies participate jointly in exercises within the UNITAS framework.

One thing that is lacking that I would like to point to specifically, Mr. Chairman, is mutual exposure among our junior-and middle-level officers.

Brazilian and United States military services formerly enjoyed a broad training relationship in which officers of each country were exposed to the other's doctrines, systems, and operational techniques.

These interchanges gradually generated a confidence, an understanding, a respect between the two services that was precious to both of us.

Today, training exchanges are effectively blocked by the Symington and Glenn amendments[7] to the Foreign Assistance Act, which prohibits us from funding military education for a country that receives nuclear enrichment or reprocessing equipment, materials, or technology.

Unless we are prepared to allow our institutions and the future generations of military leaders of both countries to forego these advantages, we will need to find a way around that particular restriction.

Brazil's dependence on the United States for military supplies is a thing of the past. Today Brazil has emerged as an important arms producer and exporter in its own right, and turns to Europe for those high technology systems and equipment it is not yet ready to produce itself.

It is not likely that Brazil will turn back to the United States for major military purchases except possibly as a supplier of specific technologies for production in Brazil under licensing arrangements.

The United States has arrangements of this kind with a number of close allies. Perhaps it would be worth considering whether they would not be appropriate with Brazil.

Let me say in closing, Mr. Chairman, that Brazil and the United States are among the few countries that conduct a worldwide foreign policy. It is inevitable, given our different stages of economic development, geographic location, and perceived global role, that those policies should in some cases be inconsistent with each other.

Neither country can be expected to challenge the integrity of its worldwide policies

---

[7] The Glenn amendment, enacted on June 30, 1976, as part of the International Security Assistance and Arms Export Control Act of 1976 (P.L. 94–329), added Section 669 to the Foreign Assistance Act of 1961. Section 669 was amended and restated in the International Security Assistance Act of 1977, enacted on August 3, 1977 (P.L. 95–92). A few additional changes to this section were made in the International Security Act of 1978. (P.L. 95–384, 92 Stat. 735) The amendment deals with nuclear enrichment transfers. The Symington amendment, enacted as part of the International Security Assistance Act of 1977, added Section 670 to the Foreign Assistance Act of 1961. The amendment dealt with nuclear reprocessing transfers and nuclear detonations. For the text of this section, see 91 Stat. 620.

and substitute for them either Brazil-specific or United States-specific policies.

Having said that, it may well be that some of the policies—well, let me speak for the United States—that some of our policies have effects not intended when applied to Brazil. No other country is really like Brazil. It has an economic potential as great as that of the United States.

Yet, many parts are in the early stage of development. It is Western in values, strongly anti-Communist, vigorously free enterprise, yet reasonably independent in its stance toward the world.

Our goal should be, I think, to develop economic, military, and political relations with Brazil which are characterized by the richness and mutual confidence of the sort that we have in relationships with the handful of other great friendly nations in the world.

We should review our policies, I believe. Not to challenge the principles in them which are generally essential to the well-being of this country, but to see whether there is a way in which those policies can be applied so as to contribute to the development of a much richer and closer relationship.

Thank you very much.

Document 707

Transcript of a Press Briefing by the Secretary of the Treasury (Regan), October 5, 1982 (Extracts)[8]

Brazil's Economic Problems

. . . .

Q. As you know, Mr. Secretary, Brazil has been adjusting its economy for quite some time now, but apparently it's not working. Do you believe Brazil will have to go to the IMF and that Brazil will continue to have the support of the private international banks?

SECRETARY REGAN. Well, I won't try to forecast what the Brazilians will do vis-à-vis IMF. I do know this, from conversations with the finance minister, and having read the President's speech to the United Nations recently,[9] that they're very cognizant of their problem. Brazil hopes to be differentiated from other Latin countries who are currently having economic difficulties, and pointing out that they can make it if they do get this differentiated treatment from the world's bankers.

We have been talking to the banks about this. They naturally—particularly the regional banks—are finding that it's been very difficult in these recent periods to put out new money or additional money to some of the Latin nations because of the worldwide adverse publicity and what that does to their stockholders and people in the marketplace looking at their bank.

So I think from that point of view it's going to be a difficult problem for everybody. But we are working closely with the Brazilian Financial Ministry in order to try to help them in these problems over the next few months.

Q. (Inaudible.) You mentioned that the Treasury is working with the private banks in New York and other parts to help the Mexicans.[10] Are you talking to the private banks about the Brazilian case also?

SECRETARY REGAN. Oh, yes. We have had discussions with the private bankers about Brazil. But again, you've got to remember, the United States is different than most nations. We don't try to insist or put our will as a government on what our banks will do. They are private, they have freedom of choice. They can disregard our advice, or they can follow our advice. But we are in discussions with them.

Q. What's their reaction initially?

SECRETARY REGAN. Well, they're very glad to get what information we have. I think in a lot of cases, in spite of everything that everybody tries to say and people think they are saying a lot, there still isn't enough information about the actual situation. And I think the more information, the more light that can be shed on the problem, the better off they will be from the private sector point of view.

. . . .

---

8 Source: U.S. Information Agency files. The briefing, sponsored by the U.S. Information Agency, was held in Washington.

9 For the text of President Figueiredo's address before the U.N. General Assembly on September 27, see U.N. document A/37/PV.5.

10 See document 695.

Q. . . . In his speech at the United Nations last week, the Brazilian President offered a diagnosis and suggested remedies for the international crisis that in many respects are in complete opposition with what you have said in Toronto[11] and Secretary Shultz related last week in—at the United Nations.[12]

According to some Brazilian officials involved in this speech, one of the things the President was saying among other things was, if it comes—if Brazil has to go to a rescheduling, the country will not accept to limit the deal to the IMF shopping list.

I would like to know your reaction to this speech and how do you interpret it.

SECRETARY REGAN. Well, I think that when it comes to acceptance or nonacceptance of an IMF program, this is purely voluntary. But on the other hand, if you don't accept the program, you don't get the money.

So you have to—this is a point at which the IMF and the nation negotiate just what sort of terms. The IMF does not want to have a country undercut its own social structure in order to accomplish something in the economic or the financial area. But on the other hand, it does insist that loans cannot be made without some conditionality. And the degree of the conditionality, I think, is what is at discussion here.

We have never said that they ought to have a real tough program for Brazil, nor have we said we should have a real soft program for Brazil. All we're suggesting is that if Brazil needs to refinance through the IMF, then it has to accept some conditions of the IMF in order to accomplish that.

Q. . . . What about his speech, the Presidential speech?

SECRETARY REGAN. What do you mean, what about it?

Q. . . . How do you react to the general propositions made by President Figueiredo—

SECRETARY REGAN. Well, I think he made a lot of good points in his speech. Some I disagreed with, but the majority, I could see what he was driving at. After all, Brazil has been changing its complex more toward a manufacturing nation than an agricultural nation, yet in the process of change right now, all of its agricultural products are down in price. Whether it's coffee or soy beans or rubber or what have you, all of these commodities at the same time are off. This is indeed unfortunate.

But I think that Brazil can make it. But it's going to require some belt-tightening at this point.

. . . .

Document 708

Transcript of a Press Briefing by the Secretary of the Treasury (Regan), Brasilia, December 1, 1982 (Extracts)[13]

U.S. Policy and Brazil's Economic Problems

SECRETARY REGAN. I would like to start off by trying to explain something that Secretary Shultz, I understand, said I would explain, which is the nature of this bridging loan that has been made to Brazil.

As President Reagan indicated earlier, the United States has provided short-term liquidity support to Brazil totalling $1.23 billion. All of these funds are very short-term and they are repayable within ninety days. This is direct government-to-government financing designed to provide additional short-term liquidity while Brazil implements economic policies adopted at the October meeting of Brazil's National Monetary Council. We have full assurance of repayment by Brazil and have every confidence in Brazil's ability to cope with a difficult world economic situation. Brazil has agreed to repay us as it receives funds from two sources on which it can draw—the International Monetary Fund's compensatory financing facility and its reserve position in the IMF, also known as the reserve traunch.

This source of funds should not—should not—be confused with the IMF program

---

[11] The reference is to the IMF–World Bank meetings held in Toronto, September 6–9; see document 66.

[12] For the text of Secretary Shultz's address before the U.N. General Assembly, September 30, see document 8.

[13] Source: White House Press Release, December 1, 1982, Office of the Press Secretary to the President. Secretary Regan conducted the briefing at the Hotel Nacional beginning at 6:40 p.m.

which Brazil has just announced that they will apply for, which is the extended fund facility. Now for those who may be interested, I will be happy to discuss the differences between these sources of funds after I finish my statement.

These arrangements have been under discussion between the United States and Brazil since late October, but were just completed within the last few days prior to our leaving for Brazil. Recent short-term bank lending to Brazil by United States and other banks is completely independent of our government-to-government arrangement. And I would add that lending by private banks reflects their confidence in Brazil's economic soundness and a recognition of the commitment of the Brazilian Government and its people to undertake needed economic adjustments.

And now I will take questions.

Q. Will you give us the interest rate and explain to me whether money actually changes hands or whether there is a guarantee of paper?

SECRETARY REGAN. The question is, what is the lending rate if any and does any money actually change hands. The answer to this is, yes, money actually does change hands. Brazil needs foreign exchange on a temporary basis. Brazil has money due to it or that it can draw on in the IMF. In between those times there is a short-fall. What we have done is to loan them from our Exchange Stabilization Fund, which is administered by Treasury, this $1.23 billion. The normal rate of interest for that as called for by law is the short-term Treasury finance costs—in other words our 90-day costs of financing for the Federal Government.

Q. Could you give us a number or a range?

SECRETARY REGAN. A number? Treasury bills currently, 90-day bills are somewhere in the, what, 8 to 8.25 range and they have gone as high as 9 in recent weeks and as low as 7.75.

Q. Would Brazil have defaulted on its loan unless we had gone through with this short-term financing?

SECRETARY REGAN. That is a matter of speculation. I don't know whether they would have or not.

Q. Then what precipitated our move?

SECRETARY REGAN. Nothing precipitated the move. It was not a precipitous move. This is something—this credit arrangement and swapping through the Exchange Stabilization Fund is not something new to the United States. We have been doing this for 20 years—that this Exchange Stabilization Fund has been on the books. We have done this with Great Britain, for example, with Italy, with Mexico this summer, and now Brazil. There is nothing new or precipitous about the actions of the Treasury in doing such a thing.

Q. Mr. Secretary, we are a little bit confused because we were told—I think we were told on *Air Force One*, we were told by briefers last week that there was no new aid during this—or no announcements. Can you explain how it came about that this was announced today?

SECRETARY REGAN. . . . First of all, this is not aid. This is not aid. This is a loan—a short-term financing arrangement—a banking arrangement, if you will, in which interest is charged and there is collateral. So, it's far from aid.

Secondly, as far as the announcement is concerned, ordinarily, in banking circles, one doesn't make announcements of this type. This is a —I won't say an everyday occurrence, but it's not unique. And in monetary movements because there are markets out there that fluctuate on rumors and other things, you ordinarily, as a government, don't talk about such arrangements or discussions. But, nonetheless, reporters have raised questions with us about that. Now, what I did this morning, I waited until we got down here and this morning got together with the Finance Minister and the Planning Minister and asked them specifically, could we release this news since there was so much interest in it. They agreed that we should and we released it.

. . . . . .

Q. What is your assessment as to how important this loan is? Is it critical to Brazil in its present financial difficulties? Could they have made it without it? How do you assess that?

SECRETARY REGAN. . . . I don't know that I could speculate too much on this because there are other sources of money—perhaps they could have stretched out—perhaps they couldn't. But this helped Brazil in—over these next few days and—few weeks until such time as they can actually make their longer-term arrangements with the IMF which is the EFF funding that I referred to in my opening remarks.

So, let's say that it was a nice thing for us to do. It was helpful to Brazil and it furthered the relationships between both countries. . . .

Q. Following up on that. What sort of signal do you hope this sends to other lenders—other countries, private and public? Do you and the President hope this will be a sign for others to help Brazil out and to help out other countries who are willing to take austerity steps?

SECRETARY REGAN. . . . Obviously, this is a sign to banks, private lenders, that the United States and Brazil are standing together in this time that Brazil needs help. Everyone knows that Brazil is having problems. Brazil is a great nation—has a great long-term future. Temporarily, it is in some type of straits. There is a provision in the IMF rules that allows Brazil to draw on the IMF. We're helping them move on—I think that will be seen as a favorable sign by most commercial banks. . . .

Q. The United States is known to be on record of wanting to graduate Brazil out of the World Bank whereas Brazil is holding that she would still continue to draw loans from the World Bank. Have you reached compromise on that question?

SECRETARY REGAN. The question is, it's known that the United States has favored graduating Brazil, among other countries, I might add, out of the soft-loan window in the World Bank and even from some of the hard-loan windows of the World Bank in order to put it into the world market. Brazil is resisting this. We have not as yet discussed that topic. We've discussed many topics, but I can honestly tell you at this point, we have not gotten around to that one. We probably will be discussing it with them. . . .

Q. Sir, is there in addition to this loan another American import, in order to give Brazil another loan through the BIS?

SECRETARY REGAN. The question is is there another loan through the BIS or through any other arrangement by the United States on a loan to Brazil.

Not that I know of at this time. . . .

Q. This loan—that is said, this temporary loan—is due in 90 days. And you also said that it should be eventually repaid. The liquidity that Brazil will now have by—you will be compensated by the Extended Facility from the IMF. Do you then expect that the agreement for the Extended Facility will be over in 90 days—that Brazil will be able to do this in 90 days?

SECRETARY REGAN. Well, don't confuse two things—that it's not necessarily contingent that a nation has to have an Extended Facility—an extended fund financing through the IMF before it gets a CFF loan or is allowed to draw on its reserve traunch. Now, that may sound like a bunch of doubletalk to you, but that's the way we in finance normally talk.

Let me explain what I'm talking about here. After 35 years, it becomes part of a habit. As far as what you're inferring here—that Brazil should have its extended fund financing—that's what they announced over the weekend. That's where the IMF sends a team into the nation. There's a team in, for example, Mexico now. There's a team now that has come to Brazil. They will go over what they think should be done with the Brazilian economy in order to qualify for an IMF loan. That's the longer term loan that Brazil is seeking. That does not depend on what is happening in the short term.

The CFF, the Compensatory Financing Facility—try that one three times and fast—what that's designed to do is to help with exports. When your exports fall precipitously—any nation for any reason, most usually its price—if the price of a particular commodity falls and the exporting country, as a result is short on exchange, that's what this financing facility is for, to make up that difference on a short-term basis, shorter than the long-term loan, the EFF loan. So, you have CFF and EFF—EFF being long term, CFF depending on exports and being short term. So, I hope I've explained the two. All the traunch. [?] That's the double dip, that's the second dip that you get in taking down money that is due to you in the IMF. Every member nation in the IMF can draw at certain times on funds that it has put up at the IMF—can take it back, if you will.

Brazil is allowed to take another traunch back. The amount depends upon the percentage that you have above the fund.

Q. Brazil has a liquidity problem at this moment.

SECRETARY REGAN. Yes.

Q. The United States is advancing a bridging loan to solve that momentary liquidity problem. Brazil in the next weeks will be receiving their compensatory financing and its—Right?

SECRETARY REGAN. Right.

Q. Its reserve position. Now, we will have to pay back the Treasury within 90 days.

SECRETARY REGAN. That's right.

Q. So, if, at that point, it does not receive its Extended Facility, you will again have a liquidity problem. Correct?

SECRETARY REGAN. Not necessarily. It will depend on what happens to (a) the Brazilian economy and (b) the world economy in that 90-day period and how much the commercial banks put up for Brazil. So, there are many things that hinge on this. So, one doesn't necessarily follow the other.

Q. It will depend also if by then Brazil will have concluded its agreement for an Extended Facility with the IMF?

SECRETARY REGAN. I don't quite follow that one.

Q. If within 90 days, Brazil would have concluded—

SECRETARY REGAN. That's entirely possible that within 90 days Brazil will conclude. But I leave that to you to talk to Brazil about. They are talking to the IMF team. I am not.

. . . .

Q. Mr. Secretary, Brazilians have been unhappy about what they perceive as an American unwillingness to increase its investments in agencies like the World Bank and the Interamerican Development Bank, both of which have replacements coming out—which they think that they will need and companies [countries?] like them will need in the coming 5 or 6 years.

My question is has the American position changed at all because of this trip?

SECRETARY REGAN. No. The American position has not. I just got through explaining this to the Cabinet Ministers of Brazil. We in the Reagan administration have certain things that we would like to do with these multilateral agencies—IMF, World Bank, IDA, IBD [*IDB*?], and the rest. But the administration proposes and Congress disposes.

The Congress has been reluctant in view of our budget deficits, in view of the stringencies that we are putting on the domestic economy and on domestic lending and on domestic programs, to be more generous in the foreign field. So, as a result, we are trying to win the Congress over to our point of view.

We carefully explained this—that what is going on, the realities of the situation. We will be as generous as we possibly can in making further replenishments to all of these institutions.

Q. Mr. Secretary, it is obvious that the crises have reached the point where you have to take extraordinary measures to rescue countries. You have been trying to convince the banks not to freeze their operations with Brazil, especially the small and regional banks. Do you think that you will be more successful in the next weeks?

SECRETARY REGAN. Let us get this straight. The Treasury has not been trying to convince banks of this. The Treasury has not been talking directly to banks—large, small, U.S., foreign, or what have you. We are not leaning on them in any way to do whatever it is that might be right under these circumstances.

I do think that in our public statements and so on, general statements, that we are trying to differentiate Brazil from some other nations that have been having financial problems—Brazil being a large nation, the fifth or sixth largest nation in the world, 128 million people, a very robust economy as you can see and a growing economy—has a temporary problem. And this is not brought on by anything that the Brazilians necessarily did. It has been brought on by disinflation in the world by conditions in other countries and the result.

So, as a result, we have tried to differentiate as far as our institutions are concerned the Brazilian problem from others.

. . . .

SECRETARY REGAN. There is a question on the floor here if you do not mind. It has to do with the sugar quota. This is not necessarily my field. But I will try to explain it as I understand it. And, if you need a followup, I would suggest Ambassador Brock.

From our point of view, what happened on this sugar proclamation[14]—this was something that was done last week. It did not necessarily have Brazil in view. There are many sugar producers who are exporters to the United States among our very close friends. As a result of some technical

---

14 A reference to Presidential Proclamation 5002 of November 30, 1982, which modified quotas on certain sugars, syrups, and molasses; for text, see *Weekly Compilation of Presidential Documents*, December 6, 1982, pp. 1548–1549.

changes that were permitted, we allowed some more sugar into the country that will benefit exporters and reprocessors of sugar. This will help American consumers. It certainly will help these foreign nations. So the United States went ahead with this proclamation.

Now, the overall question—the much larger question of sugar and what to do about it in the world—that is something that probably will come up with one of these working groups that were set up by the President today to go through a very serious discussion with the Brazilians. Time, necessarily, would not permit the detailed discussion of that—that we should have with them on this subject.

Q. Mr. Secretary, could you please differentiate—since you brought it up—the difference between the external debt problems of Mexico, Argentina, and Brazil—and why this is a special case?

. . . .

Q. Thank you. Mr. Secretary, Brazil has maintained that the U.S. sugar quotas cost Brazil—could cost Brazil up to $400 million this year in exports. Have you any idea how much this new technicality will alleviate that?

SECRETARY REGAN. No, I don't have the foggiest notion, very frankly. Does anyone have that—

SENIOR OFFICIAL. Modest.

SECRETARY REGAN. "Modest" is the adjective used.

Q. What about that question on differentiating—

SECRETARY REGAN. Different—what about it?

Q. Could you differentiate between—could you, sir, differentiate between the external debt problems, since they are listed as sort of a troika, of Mexico, Argentina, and Brazil?

SECRETARY REGAN. Well, how much time do I have? (Laughter) I'm serious about this. This is not something you can say, "A is good, B is bad, and C is in between."

Q. I'm not asking—

SECRETARY REGAN. That's a very difficult differentiation. You have three major Latin nations here—one a major exporter of oil, another that engaged in some type of conflict, and as a result, had assets frozen. (Laughter)

Q. —hard times?

SECRETARY REGAN. Beg your pardon?

Q. —the shooting war, Colonel.

SECRETARY REGAN. Well, to us Marines, there are types of wars. (Laughter)

And the third is a nation that's a large exporter that is a growing nation, that's been caught up in the world disinflation period. And the price of at least four or five of its major commodities is at the bottom. Now, that nation—Brazil—obviously will export more as time goes on.

The Mexican problem—the new President who was inaugurated today is going to deal with that, and he has a very elaborate statement as to how he intends to go through a period of austerity in Mexico in order to accomplish that. But Mexico will not be exporting the same type of commodities and in a different fashion than Brazil.

The Argentine is a separate problem entirely from these two because of the peculiar problems of the freezing of the assets, what that did to their credibility in the world and how they have to pick up from there. So there are three distinct problems among these nations.

Q. If I could followup a little bit on that—you mentioned that this bridging loan—that this bridging loan is one that was—the type of which was extended to Mexico earlier. Are you trying to say that the crisis—financial crisis in Brazil is on the scale of Mexico's? And, two, are there any other bridging loans that were considered?

SECRETARY REGAN. Well, as far as bridging loans are concerned, again, this is a temporary expedient that's used until such time as the nation can get the money from the IMF. Mexico had that same type of problem. Are they problems of the same magnitude? I don't think so. I think one is more serious than the other.

Q. Which one?

SECRETARY REGAN. Mexico.

. . . .

Chile

Document 709

Statement Issued by the Department of State, March 12, 1982[1]

U.S. Vote on U.N. Resolution on Chile

Q. Why did the United States vote with Argentina, Brazil, Pakistan, Philippines, and Uruguay to oppose lifting the state of emergency in Chile? Was this not a first?

A. The U.S. Government voted against the resolution on Chile sponsored by Denmark, Mexico, and the Netherlands during the 38th session of the U.N. Human Rights Commission.[2] The resolution called for an end to the state of emergency in Chile, extended the mandate of the Special Rapporteur for another year, and condemned Chile for alleged violations of human rights. The U.S. Government took its position after carefully evaluating the situation in Chile in the context of the U.N. Human Rights Commission resolutions about other areas of the world. Admittedly, there are still human rights problems in Chile.

Nevertheless, the United States has opposed the adoption of this resolution because it is a prime example of the complaint which we have consistently leveled against many HRC actions in that it demonstrates the double standard by which various regimes in the Communist and non-Communist worlds are judged. With very few other nations, Chile is singled out for special treatment. We do not believe that the circumstances in Chile, when compared with the situation in many other countries in the world, justify continuation of such special treatment.

In this regard, the United States also proposed an amendment under which Chile would be considered under the general agenda item covering human rights violations in any part of the world instead of a separate agenda item. Although defeated, supporters of the amendment included the United States, Argentina, Australia, Brazil, Canada, Fiji, the Federal Republic of Germany, Japan, Jordan, Pakistan, Panama, Philippines, and Uruguay. China, Costa Rica, India, Italy, Peru, the United Kingdom, and Zaire abstained.

The 37th session of the Human Rights Commission passed a similar resolution on Chile by a vote of 22–4–17, in which the United States was joined in opposition by Brazil, Uruguay, and Argentina. During the 36th session of the U.N. General Assembly, the United States also voted "no" on a like resolution on Chile (83–20–36) on which the United States was joined by all of the Latin nations except for Peru, Ecuador, and Dominican Republic, who abstained, and Venezuela, who voted in favor.[3]

Document 710

Statement by the Representative at the United Nations (Gershman) in the Third Committee of the U.N. General Assembly, December 10, 1982[4]

Human Rights in Chile

The Government of the United States will vote for the amendment proposed by the delegate of the United Kingdom[5] because it is a step—albeit a very small step—toward some balance in an approach of the situation on human rights in Chile. But we

[1] Source: Office of Press Relations, Department of State; posted statement. The statement was posted in response to a question asked at the Department of State Daily Press Briefing on March 11, 1982.

[2] Resolution 1982/25 was adopted at the 56th meeting of the U.N. Commission on Human Rights on March 10, 1982, by a roll-call vote of 28 to 6 (Argentina, Brazil, Pakistan, Philippines, the United States, and Uruguay), with 8 abstentions (China, Costa Rica, Fiji, Japan, Jordan, Panama, Peru, and Zaire).

[3] For the statement by Carl Gershman before the third committee of the U.N. General Assembly, December 3, 1981, explaining U.S. opposition to what became Resolution 36/157, adopted by the U.N. General Assembly on December 16, 1981, see *American Foreign Policy: Current Documents, 1981*, document 728.

[4] U.S. Mission to the United Nations Press Release USUN 182-(82), December 10, 1982. Gershman delivered the statement in explanation of the U.S. vote on draft resolution A/C.3/37/L.53, which concerned human rights in Chile. For text of the draft resolution, see U.N. document A/37/745, pp. 46–48.

[5] The U.K. amendment proposed eliminating the recommendation that the mandate of the Special Rapporteur on Chile be extended; see the Report of the Third Committee, December 14, 1982, U.N. document A/37/745. The U.K. amendment was adopted by a roll-call vote of 46 to 42, with 42 abstentions.

will vote against the resolution as a whole contained in document L.53. We do so for the same reasons expressed by our representative at the last session of the Commission on Human Rights in March.[6] The United States does not believe that the circumstances in Chile, when compared with the situation existing prior to 1977 or by comparison with many other countries in the world, justify continuation of the Special Rapporteur or this unbalanced resolution. In our view, the overall human rights situation in Chile has improved in comparison with the post-coup period of 1973–1977, though the pace has slowed since 1980.

There have been no confirmed disappearances since October 1977. The use of torture, once considered to be a systematic and widespread practice among security forces, has significantly diminished since 1976, although there continue to be reports of torture and mistreatment of prisoners by security officials. There have been no cases of indefinite detention without charges since 1976. Furthermore, in October 1982 the Government of Chile announced the formation of a special commission to review cases of exiles to facilitate the return of many to Chile.

The acting President of the Chilean Human Rights Commission stated that the decision to establish the Commission was highly positive and gives hope of an eventual dialogue aimed at a reconciliation of all Chileans. We share that hope.

There have been several other indications of positive change:

—The number of political prisoners has been reduced to less than 150, and the Chilean Government allows regular access to them by the International Committee of the Red Cross.

—The judiciary has gained greater independence and in recent years has examined and reviewed all arrests and charges of a political nature.

—In recent years, Chile has confronted terrorist situations, including assassinations and bombings, aimed at provoking violent political change without overreaction by security forces.

The resolution before us does not recognize these signs of progress in Chile. Instead, it proposes for Chile standards and terms which most nations do not meet and constitutes another example of application to the non-Communist nations of Latin America of standards not observed elsewhere. Such unbalanced treatment of selected Latin American nations does not advance the cause of human rights, but undermines respect for judgments on human rights by this body.

The resolution urges, for example, that the Chilean authorities reestablish free trade union rights, and we fully support that goal. But how many members of the United Nations respect the right of free association and permit the existence of free trade unions? Not a few of those who will vote today to establish free trade unions in Chile categorically outlaw them at home. Some, I regret to say, have consigned workers seeking to organize to jail or psychiatric prisons.

Mr. Chairman, according to the documented report of Freedom House,[7] a highly respected human rights organization that monitors respect for human rights throughout the world, Chile is freer than 54 countries including two sponsors of the resolution before us. The degree of freedom is equivalent to that in 13 other countries, including another sponsor of the resolution. While it is not feasible to appoint a special rapporteur for each of these 67 countries, the implication here of a double standard on human rights reflects no credit on the United Nations.

We do not believe that the resolution before us is balanced with respect to the situation in Chile. Nor do we believe that it has been presented in the context of a fair, balanced, and constructive approach to human rights violations worldwide. My delegation will, therefore, vote against this resolution.[8]

Thank you, Mr. Chairman.

---

[6] Concerning the U.S. position in March, see *supra*.

[7] An apparent reference to *Freedom At Issue*, 64 (January–February 1982).

[8] The amended resolution was passed as U.N. General Assembly Resolution 37/183 by a vote of 85–17 (United States)–14 on December 17, 1982.

Colombia

Document 711

Transcript of a Press Briefing by the Secretary of State (Shultz), Enroute to Colombia, December 3, 1982 (Extract)[1]

The United States and Colombia

SECRETARY SHULTZ. We are coming to Colombia because this is an important country to the United States and the interests of the United States.

There are an underlying set of things that make that so. First of all, Colombia is a country with a democratic government and a tradition of democracy. This is a value that we share and that we think is of tremendous importance everywhere but particularly we are seeking to emphasize this point throughout our hemisphere. So that is a first point.

Second, we are concerned for peace in our hemisphere. Our hemisphere over the decades has been the most peaceful in the world and we seek to keep it that way.

We know that there is turmoil in Central America right now, which, with Colombia is—surrounds the Caribbean Basin. And we are doing everything we can to support the democratic countries to help them in their ability to counter the threats to their stability. And we believe that Colombia, as a Caribbean country, has a similar interest. So we want to discuss that interest, of course.

Third, we have a great interest in and stake in the economic development of this area. Colombia is one of the donor countries, along with ourselves, in the Caribbean Basin Initiative. We think that economic development is a key to stability. And it is a key, obviously, to a better life for people in the region. That is what the Caribbean Basin Initiative is all about. So we want to discuss the issues involved.

One of the aspects of the Caribbean Basin Initiative involves trade. And, in fact, the approach of this initiative is one that has a certain amount of aid involved in it. And there is flowing to the Caribbean Basin on the order of $1 billion a year, all things taken together now in all forms of aid. But there is a certain element of that in it. But, even more, we are seeking to emphasize the importance of trade and investment in this whole process.

I know that Colombia, as we are, as everybody is, we are all concerned about the importance of economic expansion and about the threats to protection of markets that accompany poor economic conditions. We have been fighting that battle and I feel sure that we will hear a lot about the dangers of protectionism when we are here. We agree on that. So we want to discuss that subject and what strategies we may mutually pursue toward it.

So these are things that represent values in common that we have that are, you might say, part of the reality of why it is that over a period of years the relationship between Colombia and the United States have been good ones.

And we also share a problem, on different ends of it, that is very important to us and I think to Colombia, namely, the problem of drugs and the flow from Colombia to the United States of a large amount of drugs. And there are all sorts of elements to it. One can say they would not come to the United States if people in the United States didn't buy them, so that is part of the problem. There is the—all of the things having to do with interdiction of this flow, and then of course there is the origination point. So this is a problem that we have and which we will want to discuss along with the issues of democracy, peace, trade, both in the Caribbean area generally and with respect to Colombia. And I might say we have a pretty healthy amount of trade between the United States and Colombia.

Q. Mr. Secretary, are there—so Colombia and the United States have slightly different views about the nature of the violence in Central America? When Colombia signed on with the Costa Rican conference in October[2] some say that that was under the previous—that initiative was made by the previous President.[3] This new President[4] is less of a known quantity to the

[1] Source: Department of State Press Release 363, December 6, 1982; printed also in Department of State *Bulletin*, January 1983, pp. 15–17. Secretary Shultz conducted the briefing aboard *Air Force One*.

[2] The reference is to the meeting of foreign ministers in San Jose, Costa Rica, on October 4, 1982; see document 699.

[3] Julio Cesar Turbay Ayala, President of Colombia, 1978–1982.

[4] Belisario Betancur.

United States in that he may have some differences in views. Is that one of the things you want to explore?

SECRETARY SHULTZ. He may very well have some different views, and it may very well be that as this visit unfolds it will have more rough spots in it than we would like. On the other hand we have these points in common. We have problems to talk about and the way to deal with important problems in an area that is of significance to you is to go there and talk about them. So that is—

Q. (Inaudible)—I mean what—we have the feeling on this ride to Colombia that something has shaped up that is almost confrontational. Are we off base on that?

SECRETARY SHULTZ. I suppose that depends upon your definition of confrontational, but there may be some differences of view. That remains to be seen. At any rate the way in which we will approach it is to state our views and to discuss them and to lay the groundwork for a strong relationship between our countries.

Q. What is the main difference? I mean what has cropped up? Is it Central America and the turbulence or is it trade and protectionism?

SECRETARY SHULTZ. We are not there yet, and I am not sure just what there may be.

Q. Are you worried that you are going to have a relatively hostile toast or a somewhat negative toast by the Colombian President? Have you gotten some indication?

SECRETARY SHULTZ. There are indications that we try to get from our Ambassador working there and they are provided with thinking that we have and we are trying to compose this visit, and have for some time, so that it will be a constructive one. And all that I am saying here is that constructive does not necessarily mean that everything goes in apple-pie order, but rather that you bring things to the surface whatever they are and grapple with them. And I don't want to make a statement about what may be the most difficult issues for us to discuss.

Q. What about the big demonstrations that are spreading there? What is the cause of those?

SECRETARY SHULTZ. I don't want to speculate on problems within their country.

Q. (Inaudible.)

SECRETARY SHULTZ. There has been an explosion—where was that,—

UNIDENTIFIED SPEAKER.—yesterday—

SECRETARY SHULTZ. Yesterday. Mormon's—

UNIDENTIFIED SPEAKER.—Temple. Remember this is a country with a lot of terrorism in it, too, and terrorism which is continued—indeed, intensified over the last couple of months. I think it is under control in terms of the government. But I don't think you should necessarily take every incident in the context of the visit.

Q. Mr. Secretary, Betancur has said, number one, that the United States considers Latin America its backyard patio. Number two, that it does not have a real Latin American policy. There are all kinds of reports that it is feeling warmer toward Cuba than since it cut off relations and that it is feeling warmer toward Nicaragua and is thinking about joining the nonallied nations. Clearly, this shows a lot of differences in U.S. policies. How does the administration feel about that? How are you going to try to rectify that? Do you want to bring Colombia back into the U.S. fold? What are your objectives on that?

SECRETARY SHULTZ. I don't think it is a question of the U.S. fold. It is a question of putting forward to them what are their thoughts about how our inter-American system can be improved—The inter-American system is something we all have a big stake in—of discussing these and other issues with them so that they understand our thinking, we understand theirs. So that is what we are planning to do.

Q. Will it be with the premise that it is moving closer to Cuba and Nicaragua and are against—sort of contrary to our policy at the moment?

SECRETARY SHULTZ. Well, I am not making any particular premises. They have made a number of statements of the kind that you have quoted and they have moved in the direction of the nonaligned movement and so on. So those are things that—some of those things we will have some things to say about.

Q. We will say something about that?

SECRETARY SHULTZ. Well, we will discuss these issues with them. But, of course, they are a sovereign country as we are. And they will decide for themselves, of course, what they want to do. But we will be here to discuss all of these issues with them.

Q. What about their policy in seeking amnesty for—or offering amnesty to at least one of the insurgent groups? Does the United States look with favor on that sort of thing, or do we feel that these insurgents are part of the overall pattern that you and the President have outlined in the past as plaguing Central America.

SECRETARY SHULTZ. Well, as Ambassador Enders brought out, they have been plagued with terrorism in Colombia for quite some period of time. Their effort to do something about it through the offer of amnesty seems like a constructive thing to do. And it is something they are managing. And I wish them the best of success with it. If you look at the—at the material in the San Jose Conference report which Colombia signed, you see that the democratic nations that went there called upon all of the countries of the region to seek pluralism, to try to bring discordant elements in their society into the democratic process, in the legitimate governmental process, and this, it seems to me, you can take as an expression of that on the part of Colombia.

Q. Do we have any sign that President Betancur is still on board on that conference? I mean, have they sent any signals suggesting that they now have some misgivings about joining it?

SECRETARY SHULTZ. Not that I know of.

Q. Explicit in this invitation, did we ask Colombia—I mean did we sort of invite ourselves, basically, or did we want to go to Colombia or what I'm trying to say is it sounds like we're not so welcomed?

SECRETARY SHULTZ. Oh, I think we're welcomed enough. We raised the question with the Colombian Government and they responded and we had some difficulties with precisely what the arrangements should be—just working out the mechanics of it. But I don't think anything beyond that.

Q. What are we going to do about drugs, specifically? I mean is there a great difference of opinion in trying to stop it or are they—do they object to us intruding into their own country's affairs? What are we asking them to do with drugs?

SECRETARY SHULTZ. There are various ways in trying to contend with the production of drugs and some of them are more comprehensive than others and we'll want to talk about these and explore the attitude of the new government to them.

I don't want to say, well, there's one, two, three, four, and five and we're going to push for four. But rather to say there are—there is a general subject here and we'll want to explore it.

Q. Is there any difference of view, do you think, in this area—

SECRETARY SHULTZ. This remains to be seen how much difference of view there is.

Q. You don't know how they feel about this problem?

SECRETARY SHULTZ. We know that they share our concern about the whole drug scene and it's a question of what means people are willing to use and how effective you evaluate those means to be.

Q. Don't drugs contribute substantially to their economy?

SECRETARY SHULTZ. Yes and no. That is, there is an amount of money that is paid for the drugs, obviously, but that goes to—also helps to support an element in the society that is often not very constructive, to put it mildly—just as the drug trade in the United States has connected with it an element in our society that we don't particularly admire.

. . . .

INDEX

EDITOR'S NOTE: The references in this index are to document numbers, not page numbers.